W9-BJF-358

TEACHER WRAPAROUND EDITION

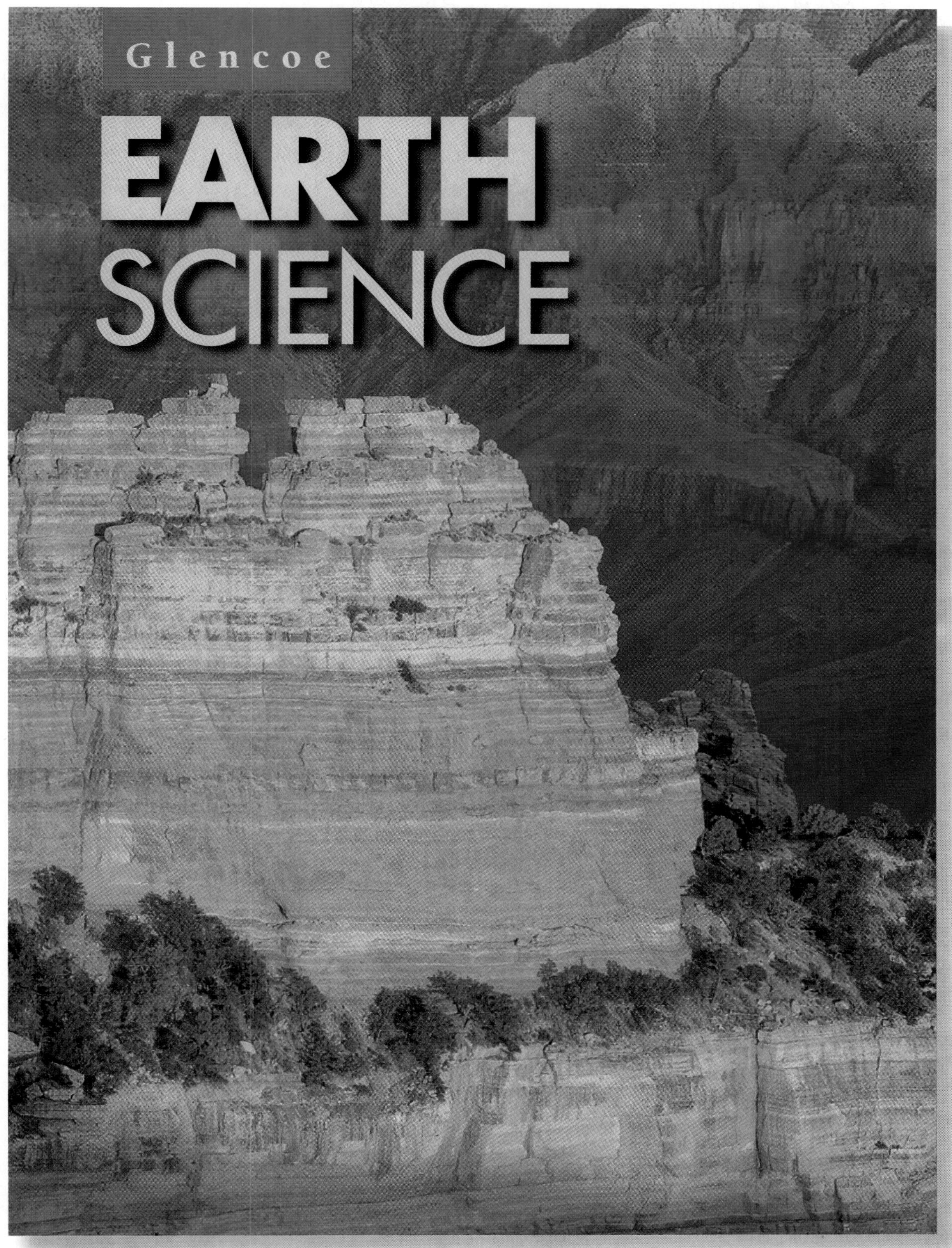

GLENCOE
McGraw-Hill
New York, New York Columbus, Ohio Mission Hills, California Peoria, Illinois

GLENCOE Earth Science

Student Edition
Teacher Wraparound Edition
Laboratory Manual: SE
Laboratory Manual: TE
Study Guide: SE
Study Guide: TE
Teaching Transparency Package
Section Focus Transparency Package
Science Integration Transparency Package
Assessment
Performance Assessment
Computer Test Bank
MindJogger Videoquiz
English/Spanish Audiocassettes
Interactive Videodisc Program

Glencoe/McGraw-Hill
A Division of The ***McGraw-Hill*** *Companies*

Send all inquiries to:

Glencoe/McGraw-Hill
936 Eastwind Drive
Westerville, OH 43081
ISBN 0-02-827809-7

Printed in the United States of America
1 2 3 4 5 6 7 8 9 VH 01 00 99 98 97 96

Teacher Guide

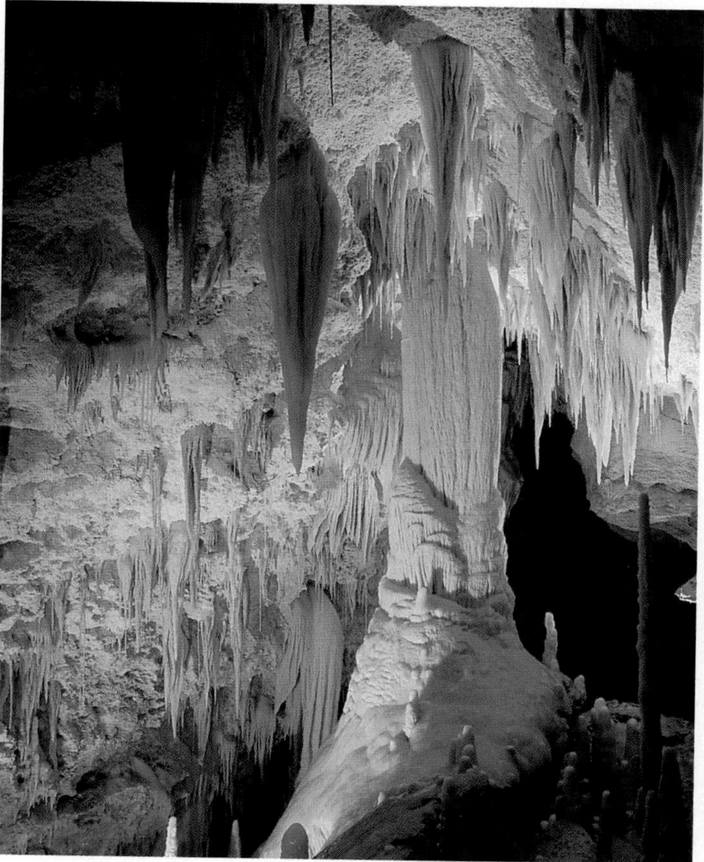

Table of Contents

Student Edition

Table of Contents

Table of Contents

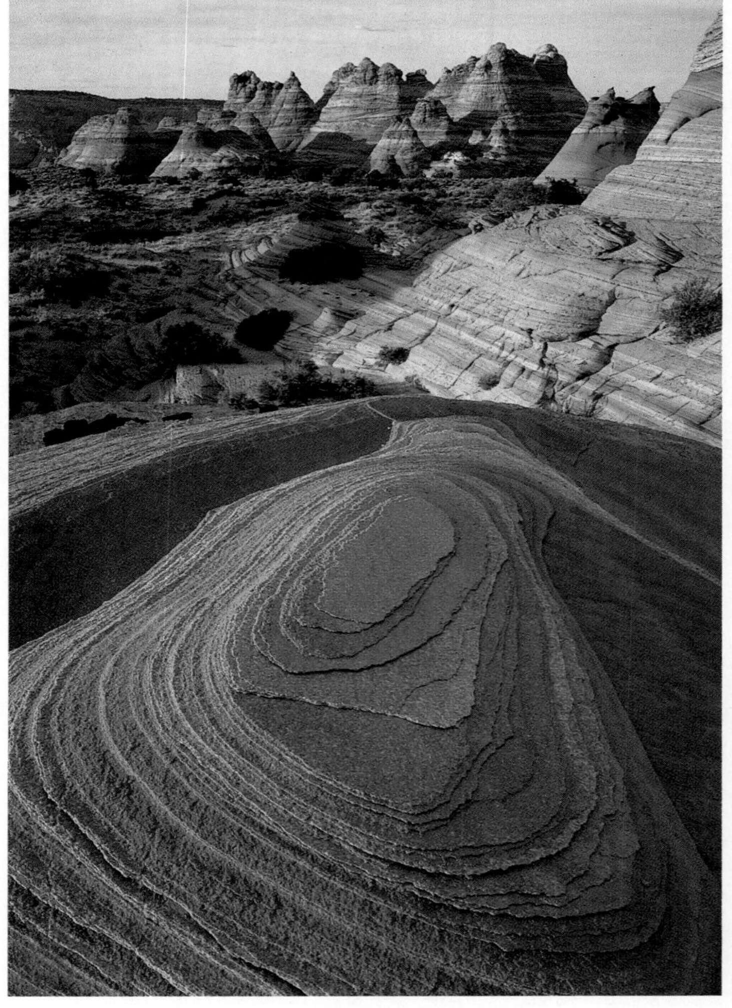

Introducing the Author Team

RALPH M. FEATHER, JR. teaches geology, astronomy, Earth science, and integrated science, and serves as Science Department Chair at the Derry Area School District in Derry, PA. He holds a B.S. in geology and an M.Ed. in geoscience from the Indiana University of Pennsylvania, and is currently working on his Ph.D. at the University of Pittsburgh. Mr. Feather has more than 25 years of teaching experience in secondary science and has supervised student teachers for more than 20 years. He is a past recipient of the Outstanding Earth Science Teacher Award from the National Association of Geology Teachers. In 1991, Mr. Feather received the Presidential Award for Excellence in Science and Mathematics Teaching. Mr. Feather also received the 1991 award for Excellence in Earth Science Teaching from the Geological Society of America. He is a member of the Geological Society of America, the National Science Teachers Association, the National Association for Research in Science Teaching, the National Association of Geology Teachers, the National Earth Science Teacher's Association, and the Planetary Society.

SUSAN SNYDER teaches Earth science and serves as Science Department Chair at Jones Middle School, Upper Arlington School District, Columbus, Ohio. She has served on the Boards of Directors for state and national science organizations. Ms. Snyder received a B.S. in comprehensive science from Miami University, Oxford, Ohio, and an M.S. in Entomology from the University of Hawaii. She has more than 23 years of teaching experience. Ms. Snyder, in addition to receiving Exemplary Earth Science and Career Awareness in Science Teaching Team awards from NSTA, has received Outstanding Teacher awards from the National Association of Geology Teachers, the National Marine Educators Association, and the Geological Society of America. She has been a state recipient of the Presidential Award for Excellence in Science and Math Teaching from NSTA, the Ohio Teacher of the Year, and one of four finalists for the National Teacher of the Year.

Responding to Changes in Science Education

The need for new directions in science education

By today's projections, seven out of every ten American jobs will be related to science, mathematics, or electronics by the year 2000. And according to the experts, if students haven't grasped the fundamentals—they probably won't go further in science and may not have a future in a global job market. Studies also reveal that students are avoiding taking "advanced" science classes.

The time for action is now!

In the past decade, educators, public policy makers, corporate America, and parents have recognized the need for reform in science education. These groups have united in a call to action to solve this national problem. As a result, three important projects have published reports to point the way for America:

- **Project on National Science Standards ...** by the National Research Council.
- **Benchmarks for Science Literacy ...** by the American Association for the Advancement of Science.
- **Scope, Sequence, and Coordination of Secondary School Science ...** by the National Science Teachers Association (NSTA).

Together, these reports spell out unified guiding principles for new directions in U.S. science education. *Glencoe Earth Science* is based on these guiding principles:

- developing scientific, technological, and mathematical literacy in all students.
- educating students to use scientific principles and processes appropriately in making personal decisions.
- helping students to experience the richness and excitement of knowing about and understanding the natural world.
- teaching students how to engage intelligently in public discourse and debate about matters of scientific and technological concern.

GLENCOE EARTH SCIENCE answers the challenge!

At Glencoe Publishing, we believe that *Glencoe Earth Science* will help you bring science reform to the front lines—the classrooms of America. But more importantly, we believe it will help students succeed in science so that they will want to continue learning about science through high school and into adulthood.

In response to the goals of science curriculum reform, *Glencoe Earth Science* promotes:

- solid, accurate content,
- a thematic orientation,
- hands-on activities that promote a constructivist approach through more student-planned activities,
- frequent practice of science process skills,
- integration of science concepts across the curriculum,
- numerous opportunities for performance assessment, and
- decision making and problem solving.

GLENCOE EARTH SCIENCE is loaded with activities.

You'll choose from dozens of activities in the ***Student Edition.*** These activities are easy to set up and manage and will allow you to teach using a hands-on, inquiry-based approach to learning.

MiniLABs and **Activities** involve students in learning and applying scientific methods to practice thinking skills and construct science concepts. They provide an engaging, diverse, active program. MiniLABs require a minimum of equipment, and students may take responsibility for organization and execution.

Activities develop and reinforce or restructure concepts as well as develop the ability to use process skills. Activity formats are structured to guide students to make their own discoveries. Students collect real evidence and are encouraged through open-ended questions to reflect and reformulate their ideas based on this evidence.

In each chapter there is one open-ended Activity called **Design Your Own Experiment** that gives students a broad topic to explore and guides them with leading questions to the point where they can determine the direction of the investigation themselves. Students are asked to brainstorm hypotheses, make a decision to investigate one that can be tested, plan procedures, and in the end, think about why their hypotheses were supported or not.

GLENCOE EARTH SCIENCE integrates science and math.

Mathematics is a tool that all students, regardless of their career goals will use throughout their lives. *Glencoe Earth Science* provides opportunities to hone mathematics skills while learning about the natural world. **Using Math, Practice Problems, MiniLABs,** and **Activities** offer numerous options for practicing math, including making and using tables and graphs, measuring in SI, and calculating. **Across the Curriculum** strategies in the *Teacher Wraparound Edition* provide additional connections between science and mathematics.

GLENCOE EARTH SCIENCE integrates the sciences for understanding.

No subject exists in isolation. At appropriate points in *Glencoe Earth Science,* attention is called to other sciences in the *Student Edition,* the *Teacher Wraparound Edition,* and in the *Teacher Classroom Resources.*

Connect to... margin features relate basic questions in physics, chemistry, Earth science, and life science to one another. Suggested answers to these questions are contained in the *Teacher Wraparound Edition.* Opportunities for **Integration** of science topics are highlighted throughout the *Student Edition.* Further explanation of how to weave the **Integration** topic into your lesson is provided in the *Teacher Wraparound Edition.* Look for this logo for ideas on how to make the sciences connect for your students. *Science Integration Activities* are full-page activities in the *Teacher Classroom Resources* that relate physics, chemistry, Earth science, and life science to each other. *Science Integration Transparencies* also relate the sciences to one another using full-color illustrations that can be projected with the overhead. These opportunities for integrating the sciences will help your students discover the science behind things they see every day.

It's time for new directions in science education.

The need for new directions in science education has been established by the experts. America's students must prepare themselves for the high-tech jobs of the future. We at Glencoe believe that *Glencoe Earth Science* answers this challenge. We believe *Glencoe Earth Science* will assist you better in preparing your students for a lifetime of science learning.

Themes & Scope & Sequence

Our society is becoming more aware of the interrelationship of the disciplines of science. It is also necessary to recognize the precarious nature of the stability of some systems and the ease with which this stability can be disturbed so that the system changes. For most people, then, the ideas that unify the sciences and make connections between them are the most important.

Themes provide a construct for unifying the sciences. Woven throughout *Glencoe Earth Science,* themes integrate facts and concepts. Like story lines, themes provide "big ideas" that link the science disciplines. Themes are an important part of any teaching strategy because they help students see the importance of truly understanding concepts rather than simply memorizing isolated facts. While there are many possible themes around which to unify science, we have chosen four: Energy, Systems and Interactions, Scale and Structure, and Stability and Change.

Energy

Energy is a central concept of the physical sciences that pervades the biological and Earth sciences. In physical terms, energy is the ability of an object to change itself or its surroundings—the capacity to do work. In chemical terms, it forms the basis of reactions between compounds. In biological terms, it gives living systems the ability to maintain themselves, to grow, and to reproduce. Energy sources are crucial in the interactions among science, technology, and society.

Systems and Interactions

A system can be incredibly tiny, such as an atom's nucleus and electrons; extremely complex, such as an ecosystem; or unbelievably large, as the stars in a galaxy. By defining the boundaries of the system, one can study the interactions among its parts. The interactions may be a force of attraction between the positively charged nucleus and negatively charged electron. In an ecosystem, on the other hand, the interactions may be between the predator and its prey, or among the plants and animals.

Scale and Structure

Used as a theme, "structure" emphasizes the relationship among different structures. "Scale" defines the focus of the relationship. As the focus is shifted from a system to its components, the properties of the structure may remain constant. In other systems, an ecosystem for example, which includes a change in scale from interactions between prey and predator to the interactions among systems inside an animal, the structure changes drastically. In *Glencoe Earth Science,* the authors have tried to stress how we know what we know and why we believe it to be so. Thus, explanations remain on the macroscopic level until students have the background needed to understand how the microscopic structure operates.

Stability and Change

A system that is stable is constant. Often the stability is the result of a system being in equilibrium. If a system is not stable, it undergoes change. Changes in an unstable system may be characterized as trends (position of falling objects), cycles (the motion of planets around the sun), or irregular changes (radioactive decay).

Theme Development

These four major themes are developed within the student material and discussed throughout the ***Teacher Wraparound Edition.*** Each chapter of *Glencoe Earth Science* incorporates at least one of these themes. These themes are interwoven throughout each level and are developed as appropriate to the topic presented.

The ***Teacher Wraparound Edition*** includes a **Theme Connection** section for each unit opener. This section provides a framework for integrating concepts discussed in the unit opener. Each chapter opener includes a **Theme Connection** section to explain the chapter's themes and to point out the major chapter concepts supporting those themes. Throughout the chapters, **Theme Connections** show specifically how a topic in the ***Student Edition*** relates to the themes.

Theme connections stressed in each chapter of *Glencoe Earth Science* are indicated in the chart on page 11T.

GLENCOE EARTH SCIENCE Chapters	Themes: Scale and Structure	Energy	Stability and Change	Systems and Interactions
1 The Nature of Science				✔
2 Matter and Its Changes	✔			
3 Minerals	✔			
4 Rocks			✔	
5 Views of Earth	✔			
6 Weathering and Soil		✔		
7 Erosional Forces		✔		
8 Water Erosion and Deposition				✔
9 Earthquakes		✔		
10 Volcanoes		✔		
11 Plate Tectonics		✔		
12 Clues to Earth's Past			✔	
13 Geologic Time			✔	
14 Atmosphere		✔		
15 Weather			✔	
16 Climate			✔	
17 Ocean Motion		✔		
18 Oceanography	✔			
19 Our Impact on Land				✔
20 Our Impact on Air and Water				✔
21 Exploring Space		✔		
22 The Sun-Earth-Moon System				✔
23 The Solar System	✔			
24 Stars and Galaxies	✔			

Resources for Different Needs

Hands-On Activities

In addition to the wide array of instructional options provided in the student and teacher editions, *Glencoe Earth Science* also offers an extensive list of support materials and program resources. Some of these materials offer alternative ways of enriching or extending your science program, others provide tools for reinforcing and evaluating student learning, while still others will help you directly in delivering instruction. You won't have time to use them all, but the ones you use will help you save the time you have.

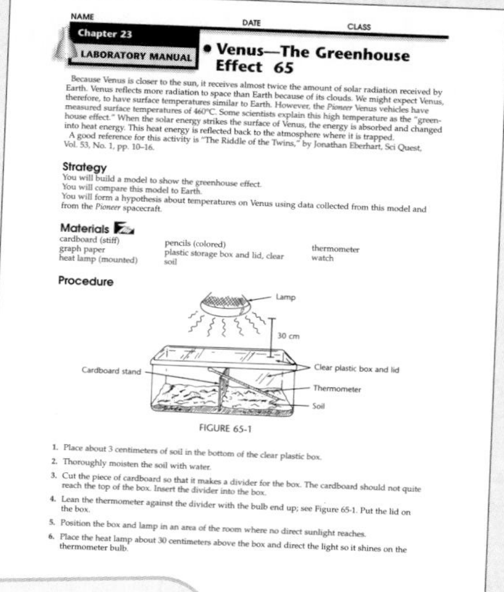

NAME DATE CLASS

Chapter 23 LABORATORY MANUAL

Venus—The Greenhouse Effect 65

Because Venus is closer to the sun, it receives almost twice the amount of solar radiation received by Earth. Venus reflects more radiation to space than Earth because of its clouds. We might expect Venus, therefore, to have surface temperatures similar to Earth. However, the *Pioneer* Venus vehicles have measured surface temperatures of 460°C. Some scientists explain this high temperature as the "greenhouse effect." When the solar energy strikes the surface of Venus, the energy is absorbed and changed into heat energy. This heat energy is reflected back to the atmosphere where it is trapped.

A good reference for this activity is "The Riddle of the Twins," by Jonathan Eberhart, Sci Quest, Vol. 53, No. 1, pp. 10–16.

Strategy

You will build a model to show the greenhouse effect.
You will compare this model to Earth.
You will form a hypothesis about temperatures on Venus using data collected from this model and from the *Pioneer* spacecraft.

Materials

cardboard (stiff)
graph paper
heat lamp (mounted)
pencils (colored)
plastic storage box and lid, clear
soil
thermometer
watch

Procedure

FIGURE 65-1

1. Place about 3 centimeters of soil in the bottom of the clear plastic box.
2. Thoroughly moisten the soil with water.
3. Cut the piece of cardboard so that it makes a divider for the box. The cardboard should not quite reach the top of the box. Insert the divider into the box.
4. Lean the thermometer against the divider with the bulb end up; see Figure 65-1. Put the lid on the box.
5. Position the box and lamp in an area of the room where no direct sunlight reaches.
6. Place the heat lamp about 30 centimeters above the box and direct the light so it shines on the thermometer bulb.

163

If you want more hands-on options, the *Lab Manual* offers you one or more additional labs per chapter. Each lab is complete with setup diagrams, data tables, and space for student responses.

Reinforce basic lab and safety skills, including graphing and measurement, with activities from the *Lab and Safety Skills* book.

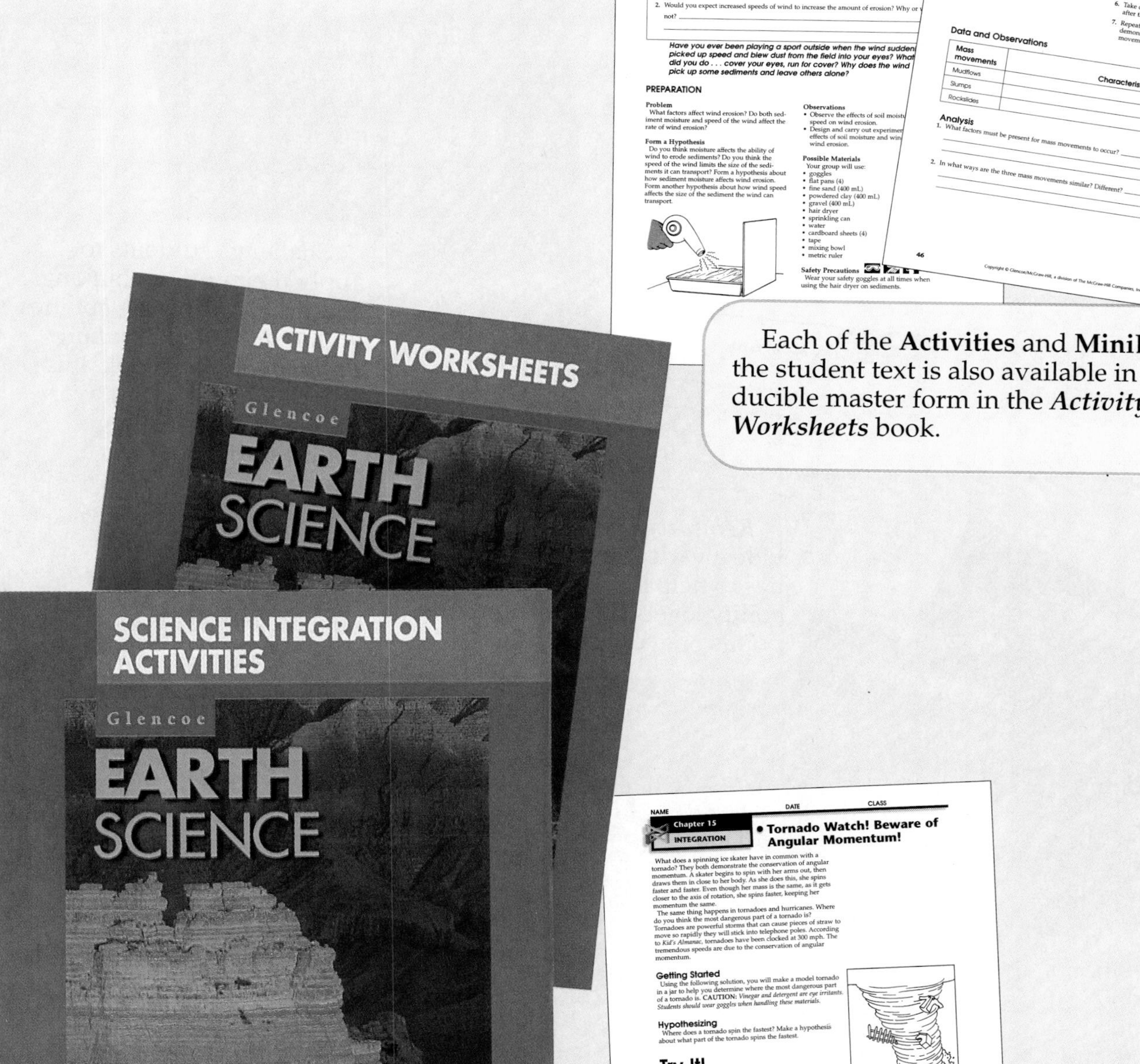

Each of the **Activities** and **MiniLABs** in the student text is also available in reproducible master form in the *Activity Worksheets* book.

Science Integration Activities are laboratory activities that relate Earth and life science to specific physical science chapters.

Reinforcement and Enrichment

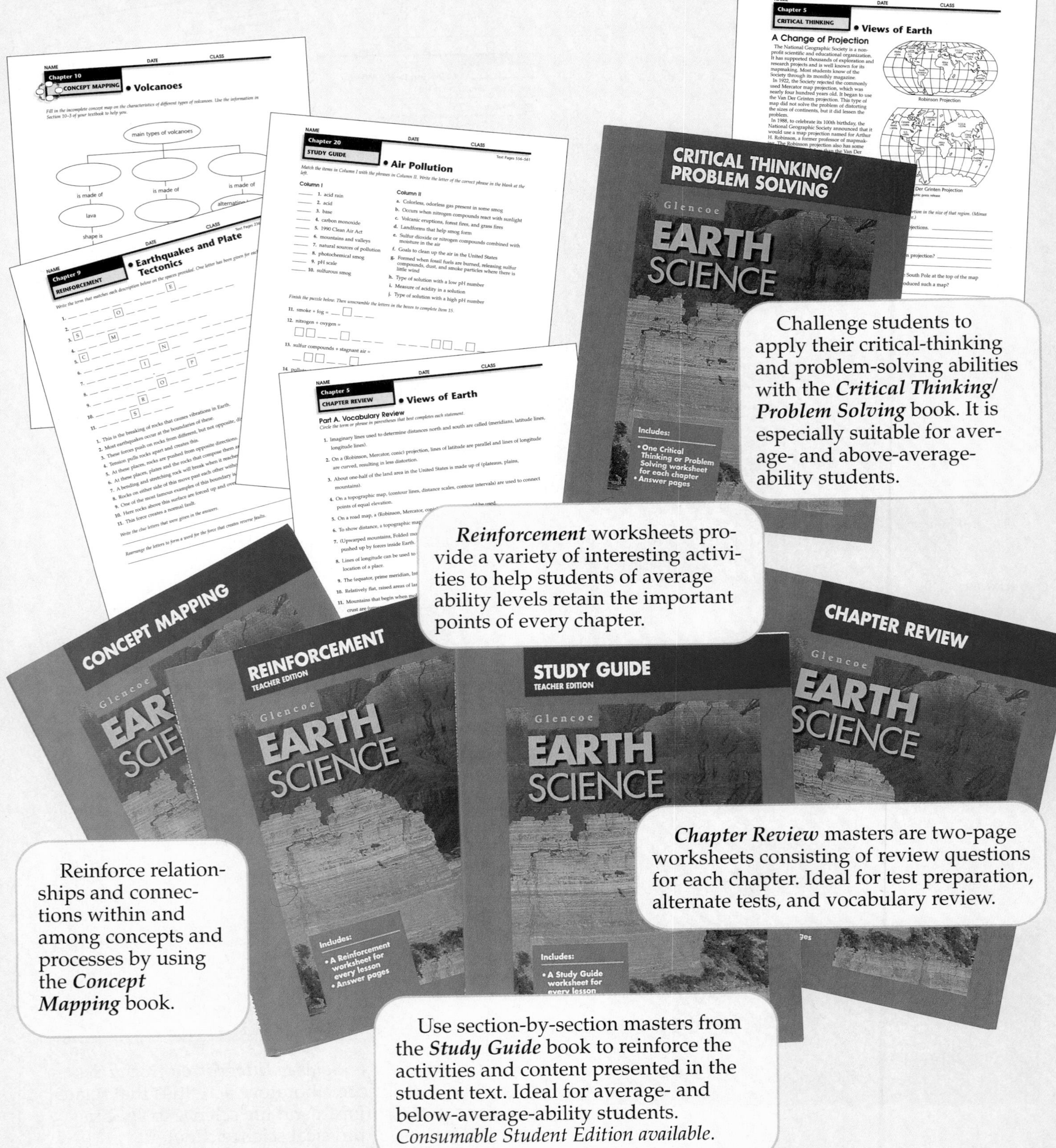

Challenge students to apply their critical-thinking and problem-solving abilities with the *Critical Thinking/ Problem Solving* book. It is especially suitable for average- and above-average-ability students.

Reinforcement worksheets provide a variety of interesting activities to help students of average ability levels retain the important points of every chapter.

Chapter Review masters are two-page worksheets consisting of review questions for each chapter. Ideal for test preparation, alternate tests, and vocabulary review.

Reinforce relationships and connections within and among concepts and processes by using the *Concept Mapping* book.

Use section-by-section masters from the *Study Guide* book to reinforce the activities and content presented in the student text. Ideal for average- and below-average-ability students. *Consumable Student Edition available.*

Enrichment worksheets challenge your students of above average ability to design, interpret, and research scientific topics based on the text in each lesson.

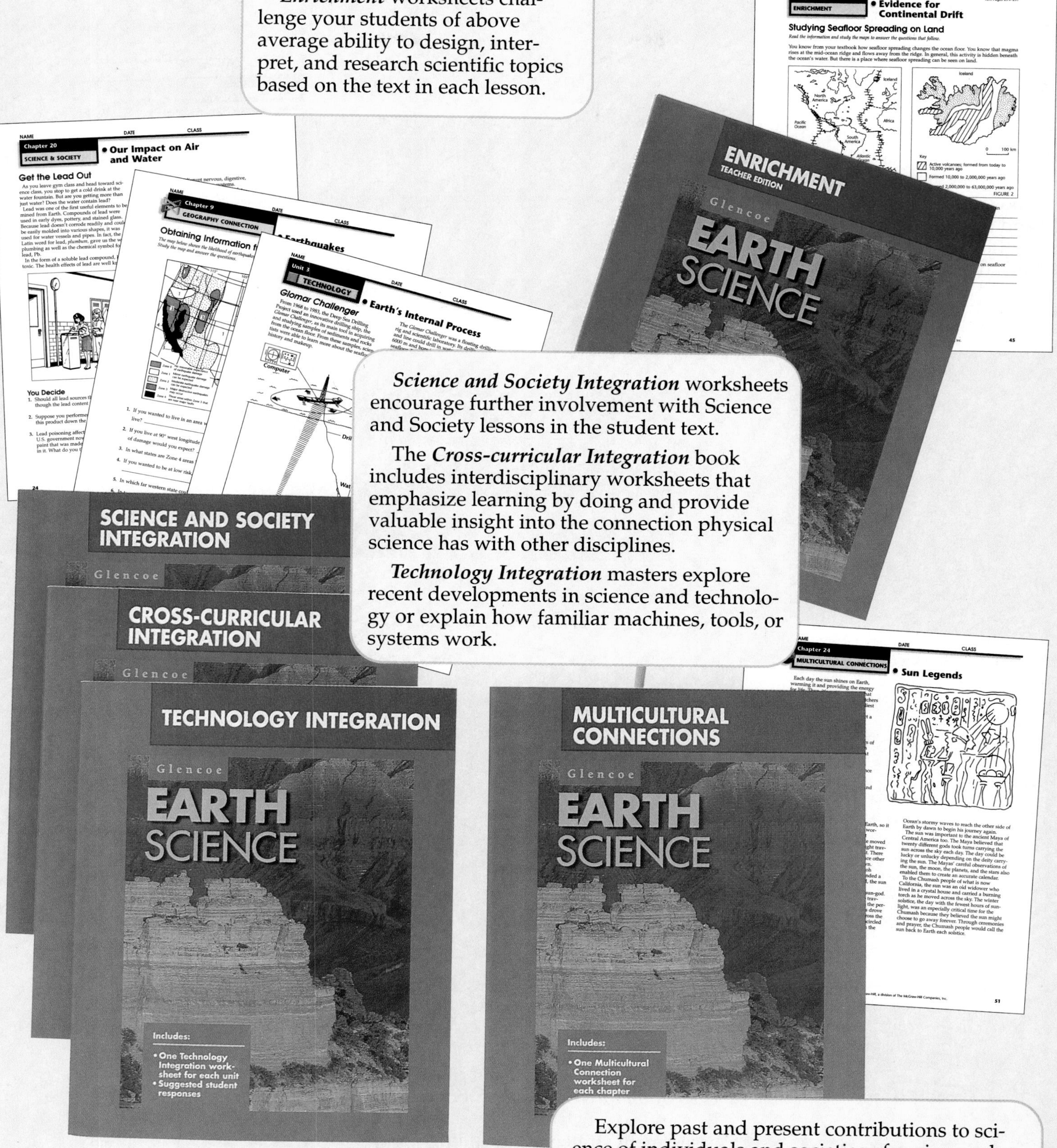

Science and Society Integration worksheets encourage further involvement with Science and Society lessons in the student text.

The ***Cross-curricular Integration*** book includes interdisciplinary worksheets that emphasize learning by doing and provide valuable insight into the connection physical science has with other disciplines.

Technology Integration masters explore recent developments in science and technology or explain how familiar machines, tools, or systems work.

Explore past and present contributions to science of individuals and societies of various cultural backgrounds through the readings and activities in the ***Multicultural Connections*** book.

Assessment

Assess student learning and performance through a variety of questioning strategies and formats in the *Assessment* book. Test items cover activity procedures and analysis as well as science concepts within the four pages of reproducible masters available for each chapter.

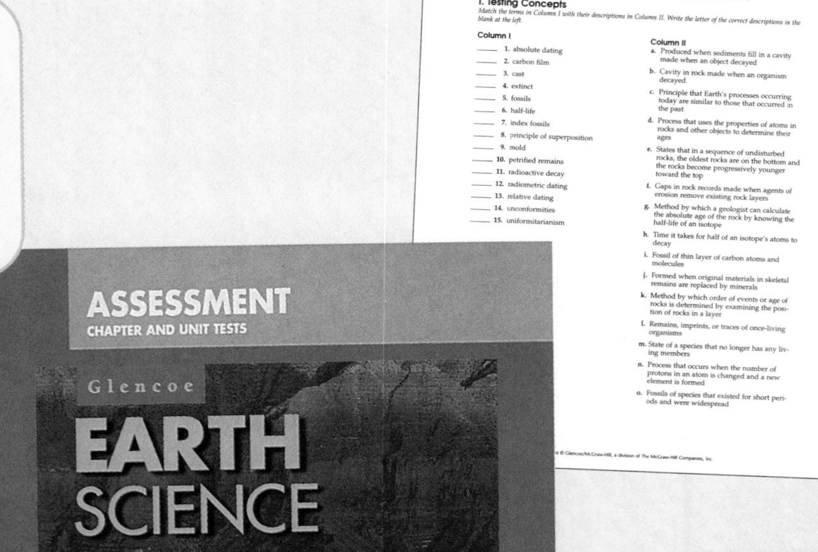

NAME DATE CLASS

Chapter 12

CHAPTER TEST • **Clues to Earth's Past**

I. Testing Concepts

Match the terms in Column I with their descriptions in Column II. Write the letter of the correct descriptions in the blank at the left.

Column I

_____ 1. absolute dating
_____ 2. carbon film
_____ 3. cast
_____ 4. extinct
_____ 5. fossils
_____ 6. half-life
_____ 7. index fossils
_____ 8. principle of superposition
_____ 9. mold
_____ 10. petrified remains
_____ 11. radioactive decay
_____ 12. radiometric dating
_____ 13. relative dating
_____ 14. unconformities
_____ 15. uniformitarianism

Column II

a. Produced when sediments fill in a cavity made when an object decayed
b. Cavity in rock made when an organism decayed
c. Principle that Earth's processes occurring today are similar to those that occurred in the past
d. Process that uses the properties of atoms in rocks and other objects to determine their ages
e. States that in a sequence of undisturbed rocks, the oldest rocks are on the bottom and the rocks become progressively younger toward the top
f. Gaps in rock records made when agents of erosion remove existing rock layers
g. Method by which a geologist can calculate the absolute age of the rock by knowing the half-life of an isotope
h. Time it takes for half of an isotope's atoms to decay
i. Fossil of thin layer of carbon atoms and molecules
j. Formed when original materials in skeletal remains are replaced by minerals
k. Method by which order of events or age of rocks is determined by examining the position of rocks in a layer
l. Remains, imprints, or traces of once-living organisms
m. State of a species that no longer has any living members
n. Process that occurs when the number of protons in an atom is changed and a new element is formed
o. Fossils of species that existed for short periods and were widespread

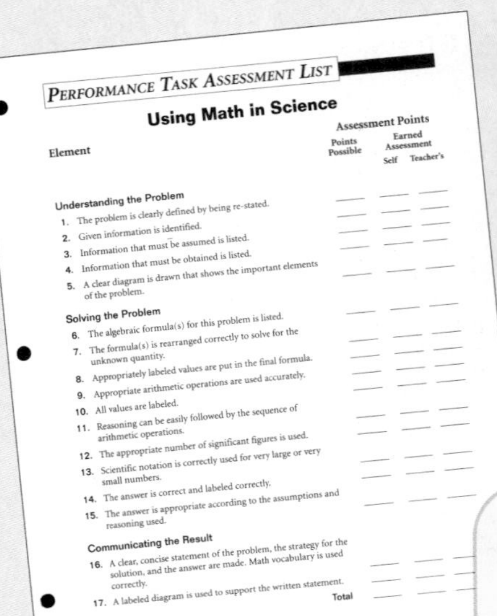

PERFORMANCE TASK ASSESSMENT LIST

Using Math in Science

Element	Points Possible	Earned Assessment: Self	Earned Assessment: Teacher's
Understanding the Problem			
1. The problem is clearly defined by being re-stated.	____	____	____
2. Given information is identified.	____	____	____
3. Information that must be assumed is listed.	____	____	____
4. Information that must be obtained is listed.	____	____	____
5. A clear diagram is drawn that shows the important elements of the problem.	____	____	____
Solving the Problem			
6. The algebraic formula(s) for this problem is listed.	____	____	____
7. The formula(s) is rearranged correctly to solve for the unknown quantity.	____	____	____
8. Appropriately labeled values are put in the final formula.	____	____	____
9. Appropriate arithmetic operations are used accurately.	____	____	____
10. All values are labeled.	____	____	____
11. Reasoning can be easily followed by the sequence of arithmetic operations.	____	____	____
12. The appropriate number of significant figures is used.	____	____	____
13. Scientific notation is correctly used for very large or very small numbers.	____	____	____
14. The answer is correct and labeled correctly.	____	____	____
15. The answer is appropriate according to the assumptions and reasoning used.	____	____	____
Communicating the Result			
16. A clear, concise statement of the problem, the strategy for the solution, and the answer are made. Math vocabulary is used correctly.	____	____	____
17. A labeled diagram is used to support the written statement.	____	____	____
Total	____	____	____

Performance Assessment in the Science Classroom provides classroom assessment lists and scoring rubrics for a variety of assessment strategies, including group assessment, oral presentations, modeling, and writing in science.

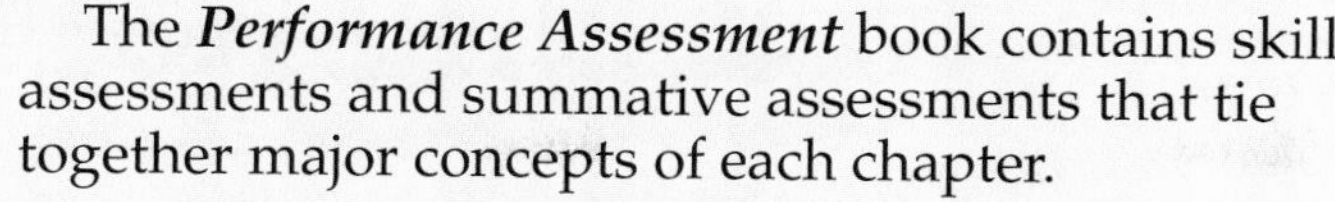

The *Performance Assessment* book contains skill assessments and summative assessments that tie together major concepts of each chapter.

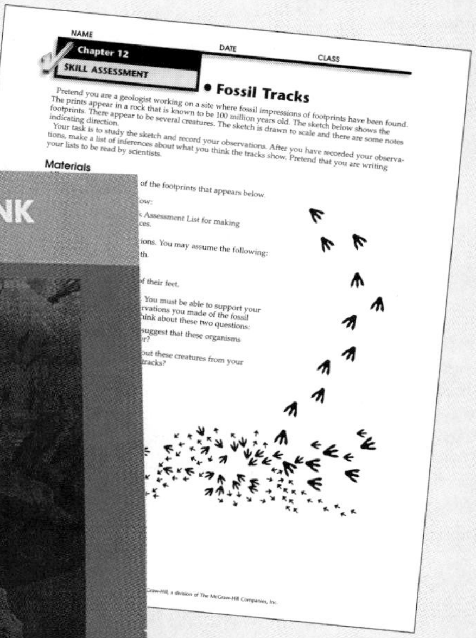

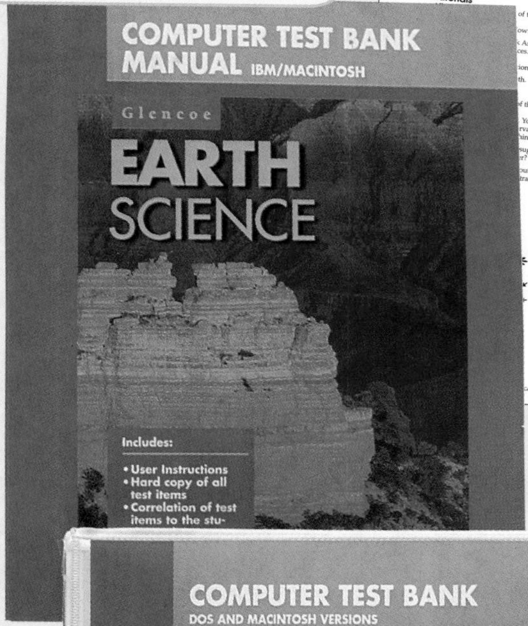

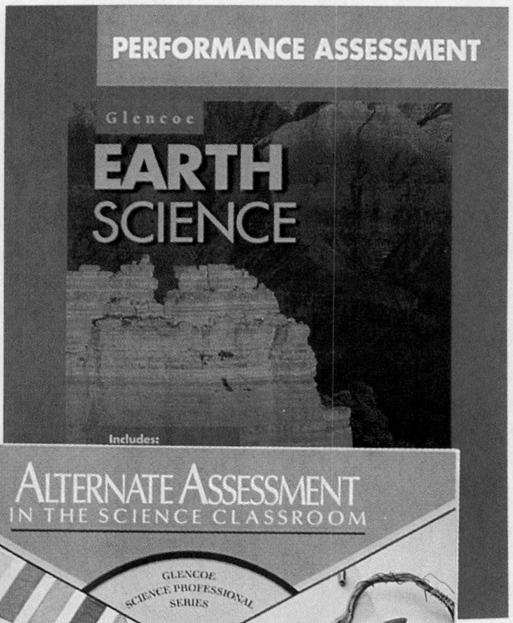

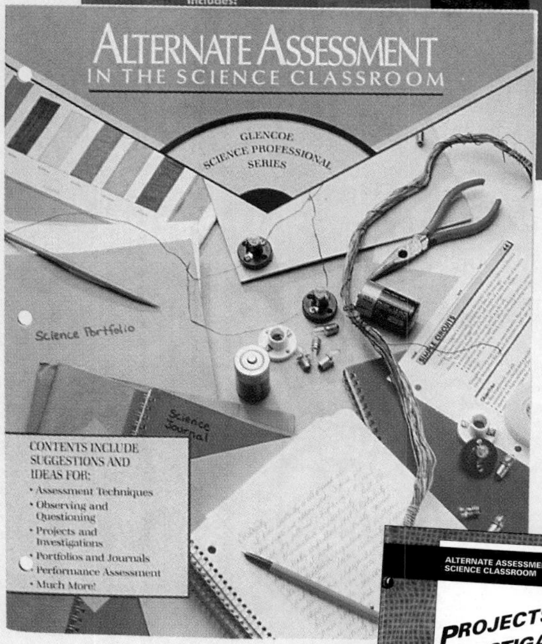

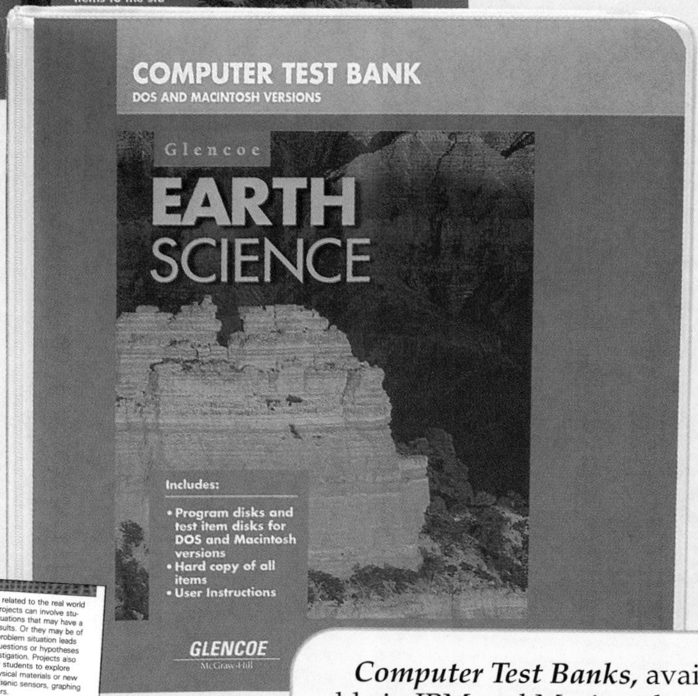

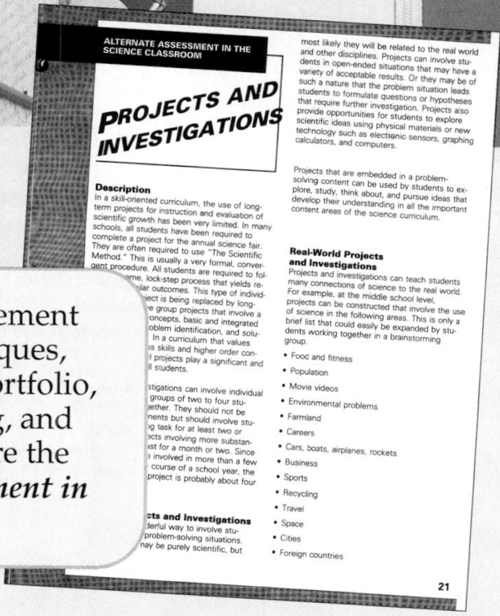
ALTERNATE ASSESSMENT IN THE SCIENCE CLASSROOM

PROJECTS AND INVESTIGATIONS

Description
In a skill-oriented curriculum, the use of long-term projects for instruction and evaluation of scientific growth has been very limited. In many schools, all students have been required to complete a project for the annual science fair. They are often required to use "The Scientific Method." This is usually a very formal, convergent procedure.

most likely they will be related to the real world and other disciplines. Projects can involve students in open-ended situations that may have a variety of acceptable results. Or they may be of such a nature that the problem situation leads students to formulate questions or hypotheses that require further investigation. Projects also provide opportunities for students to explore scientific ideas using physical materials or new technology such as electronic sensors, graphing calculators, and computers.

Projects that are embedded in a problem-solving content can be used by students to explore, study, think about, and pursue ideas that develop their understanding in all the important content areas of the science curriculum.

Real-World Projects and Investigations
Projects and investigations can teach students many connections of science to the real world. For example, at the middle school level, projects can be constructed that involve the use of science in the following areas. This is only a brief list that could easily be expanded by students working together in a brainstorming group.

- Food and fitness
- Population
- Movie videos
- Environmental problems
- Farmland
- Careers
- Cars, boats, airplanes, rockets
- Business
- Sports
- Recycling
- Travel
- Space
- Cities
- Foreign countries

21

Computer Test Banks, available in IBM and Macintosh versions, provide the ultimate flexibility in designing and creating your own test instruments. Select test items from two different levels of difficulty, or write and edit your own.

How and when to implement various assessment techniques, including performance, portfolio, observing and questioning, and student self-assessment, are the focus of ***Alternate Assessment in the Science Classroom.***

Teaching Resources

Chapter-by-chapter *Lesson Plans* will help you organize your lessons more efficiently.

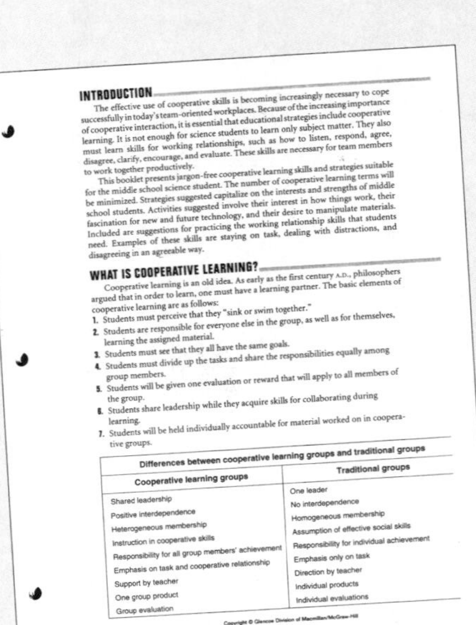

INTRODUCTION

The effective use of cooperative skills is becoming increasingly necessary to cope successfully in today's team-oriented workplaces. Because of the increasing importance of cooperative interaction, it is essential that educational strategies include cooperative learning. It is not enough for science students to learn only subject matter. They also must learn skills for working relationships, such as how to listen, respond, agree, disagree, clarify, encourage, and evaluate. These skills are necessary for team members to work together productively.

This booklet presents jargon-free cooperative learning skills and strategies suitable for the middle school science student. The number of cooperative learning terms will be minimized. Strategies suggested capitalize on the interests and strengths of middle school students. Activities suggested involve their interest in how things work, their fascination for new and future technology, and their desire to manipulate materials. Included are suggestions for practicing the working relationship skills that students need. Examples of these skills are staying on task, dealing with distractions, and disagreeing in an agreeable way.

WHAT IS COOPERATIVE LEARNING?

Cooperative learning is an old idea. As early as the first century A.D., philosophers argued that in order to learn, one must have a learning partner. The basic elements of cooperative learning are as follows:

1. Students must perceive that they "sink or swim together."
2. Students are responsible for everyone else in the group, as well as for themselves, learning the assigned material.
3. Students must see that they all have the same goals.
4. Students must divide up the tasks and share the responsibilities equally among group members.
5. Students will be given one evaluation or reward that will apply to all members of the group.
6. Students share leadership while they acquire skills for collaborating during learning.
7. Students will be held individually accountable for material worked on in cooperative groups.

Differences between cooperative learning groups and traditional groups

Cooperative learning groups	Traditional groups
Shared leadership	One leader
Positive interdependence	No interdependence
Heterogeneous membership	Homogeneous membership
Instruction in cooperative skills	Assumption of effective social skills
Responsibility for all group members' achievement	Responsibility for individual achievement
Emphasis on task and cooperative relationship	Emphasis only on task
Support by teacher	Direction by teacher
One group product	Individual products
Group evaluation	Individual evaluations

Cooperative Learning in the Science Classroom contains background information, strategies, and practical tips for using cooperative learning techniques whenever you do activities from *Glencoe Earth Science.*

Enhance your presentation of science concepts with the color transparency packages. The ***Teaching Transparency Package*** includes two full-color transparencies per chapter and a **Study Guide** booklet with reproducible student worksheets and blackline reproductions for each of the program's full-color transparencies. The ***Section Focus Transparency Package*** includes one full-color transparency for each section of the student text and a **Study Guide** booklet with reproducible student worksheets. The ***Science Integration Transparency Package*** includes one full-color transparency per chapter and a **Study Guide** booklet with student worksheets.

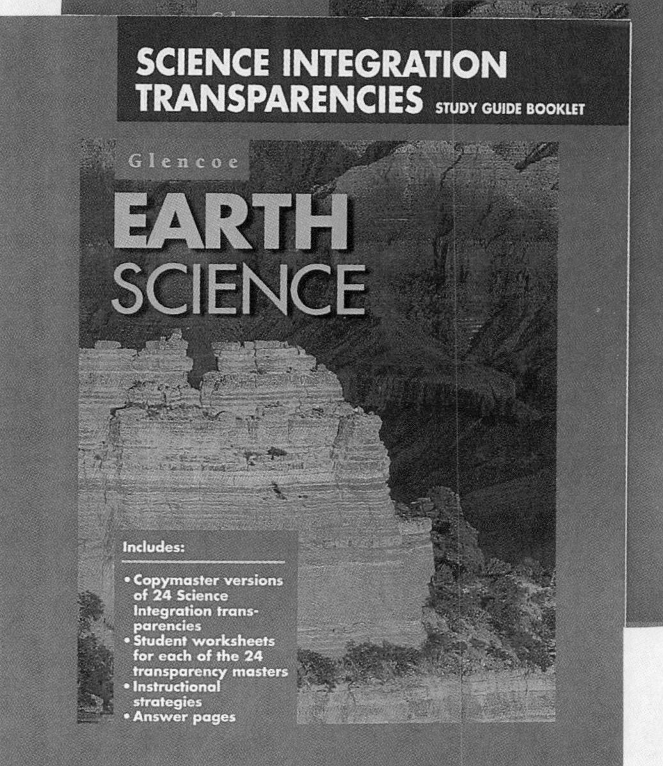

Help your Spanish-speaking students get more out of your science lessons by reproducing pages from the ***Spanish Resources*** book. In addition to a complete English-Spanish glossary, the book contains translations of all objectives, key terms, activities, and main ideas for each chapter of the student text.

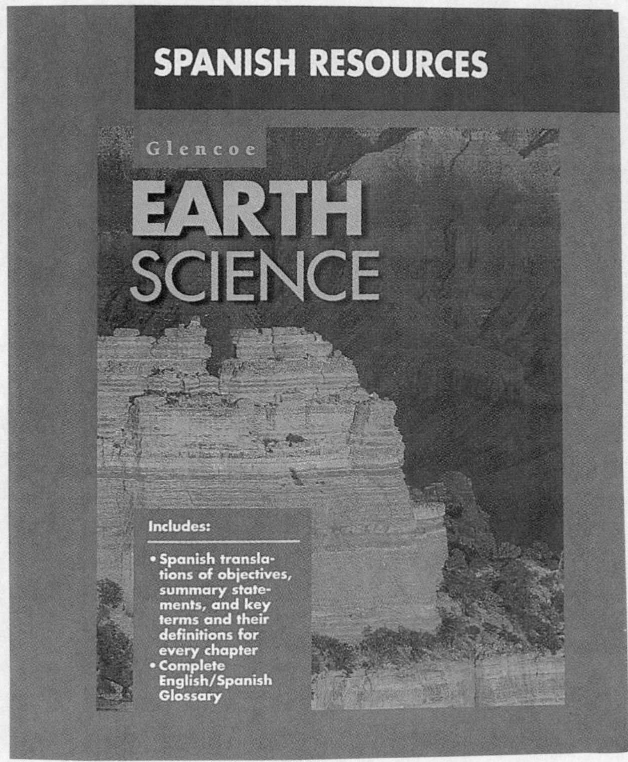

The Technology Connection

Glencoe Earth Science offers a wide selection of video and audio products to stimulate and challenge your students.

Interactive videos that provide a fun way for your students to review chapter concepts make up the ***MindJogger Videoquiz*** series.

The ***Glencoe Interactive Videodisc Program*** includes interactive lessons that illustrate and reinforce major physical science concepts.

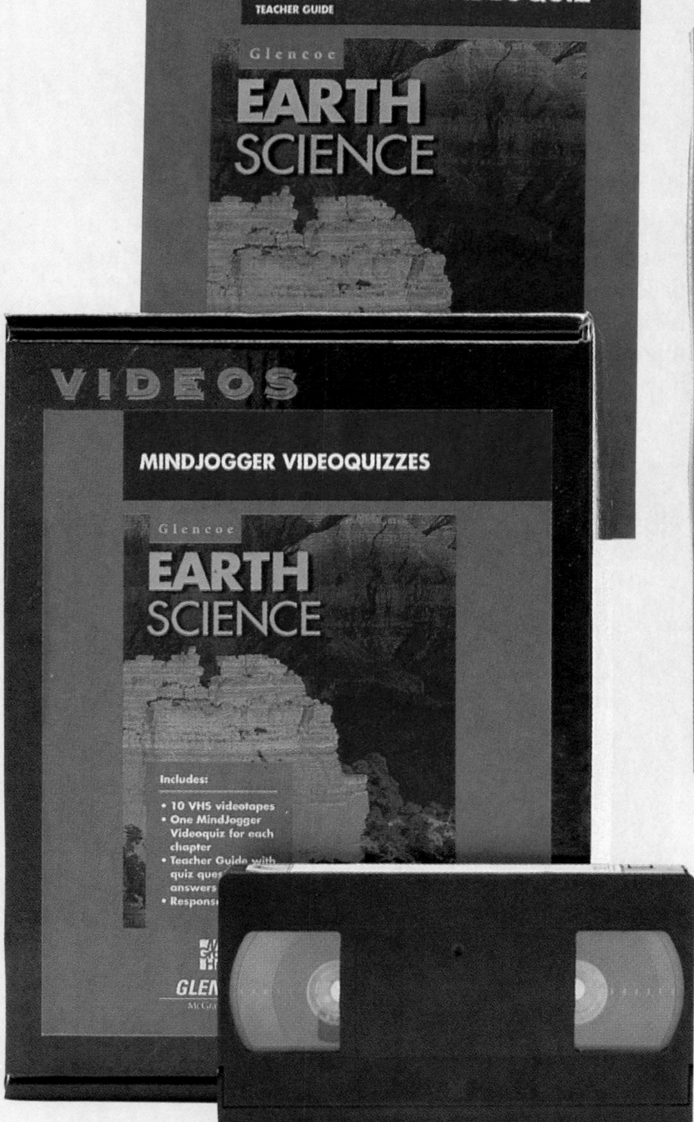

The ***English/Spanish Audiocassettes*** summarize the content of the Student Edition in both English and Spanish.

The *Secret of Life* videotapes produced by WGBH in Boston can demonstrate the myriad ways in which our expanding knowledge of DNA and heredity have affected all areas of biology and created many ethical dilemmas.

Lab Partner Software provides spreadsheet and graphing tools to record and display data from lab activities.

The ***Infinite Voyage*** (videotapes and videodiscs) is 20 programs from the award-winning PBS series, covering physical sciences, biology, ecology and environmental education, archaeology, and ancient history. An ***Instructor's Guide*** accompanies each videotape.

Program Resources

Glencoe is proud to offer quality educational technology from the ***National Geographic Society.*** These interactive learning tools remove the walls from your classroom and transport your students to the far corners of the world. Award-winning titles from National Geographic give students exciting, easy-to-use resources. With the click of a mouse, students can explore the world—and all that's in it—through video, photographs, sound, and text. Also available from Glencoe is the ***Science and Technology Videodisc Series (STVS),*** based on the Mr. Wizard television program. Both National Geographic Society and STVS products have been correlated to each chapter of ***Glencoe Earth Science.***

NATIONAL GEOGRAPHIC SOCIETY

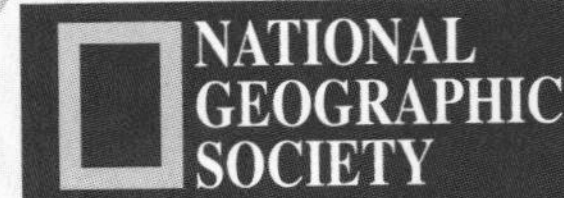

- STV (Single-Topic Videodiscs)
  - Atmosphere
  - Water
  - Human Body Volumes 1, 2, & 3
  - Plants
  - The Cell
  - Rain Forest
  - Solar System
  - Restless Earth
  - Biodiversity

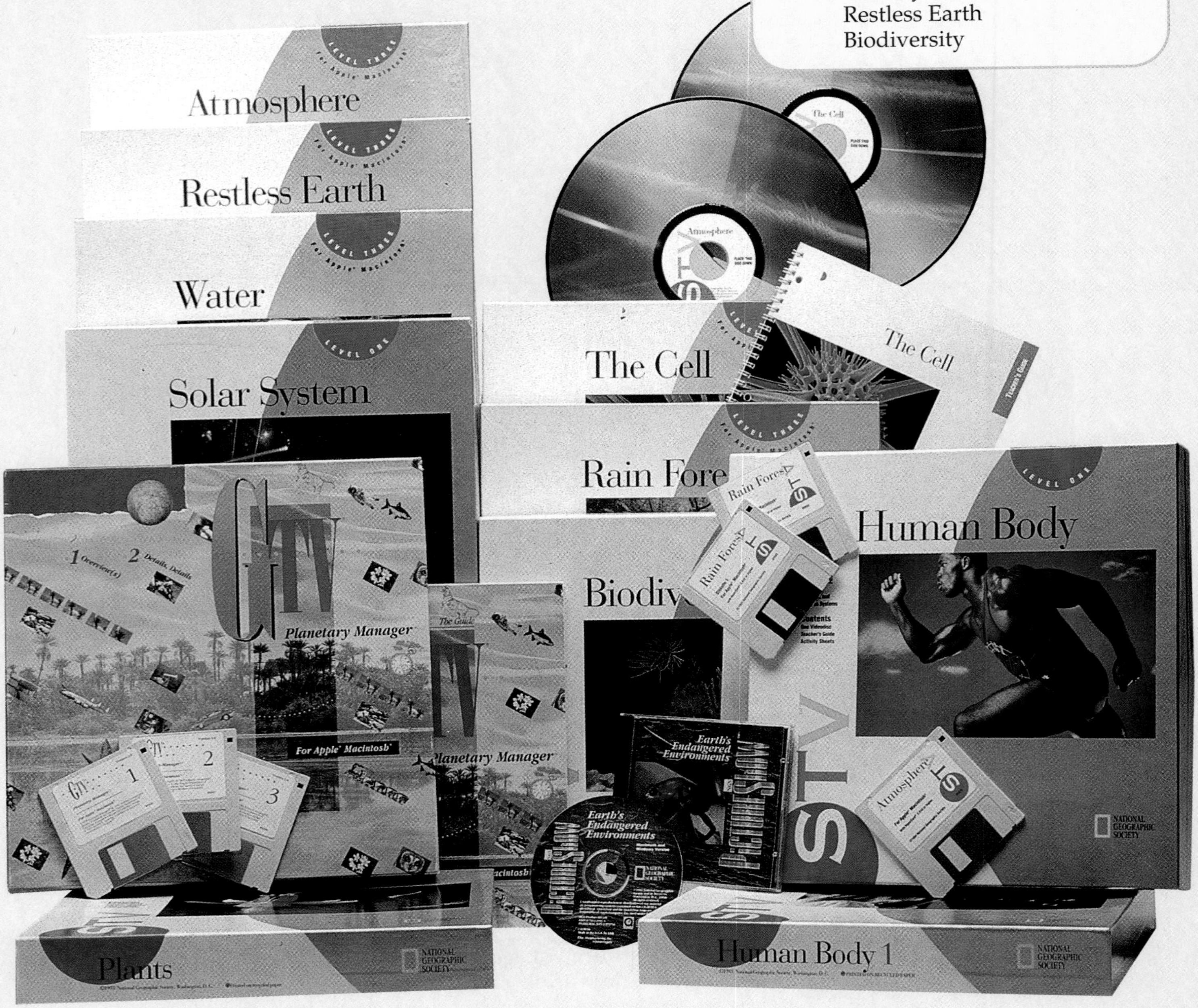

National Geographic Society

- GTV (Group-Topic Videodiscs)
  - Planetary Manager

The *Science and Technology Videodisc Series* is a seven-disc series that contains more than 280 full-motion video reports. Reports cover a broad spectrum of topics relating to current research in various science fields, innovations in technology, and science and society issues. In addition to reinforcing science concepts, the videoreports are ideal for illustrating science methods, laboratory techniques, and careers in science.

National Geographic Society
Newton's Apple (Videodisc)
- Physical Sciences
- Life Sciences

National Geographic Society
CD-ROM
- NGS Picture Show

Constructivism

Strategies suggested in *Glencoe Earth Science* support a constructivist approach to science education. The role of the teacher is to provide an atmosphere in which students design and direct activities. To develop the idea that science investigation is not made up of closed-end questions, the teacher should ask guiding questions and be prepared to help his or her students draw meaningful conclusions when their results do not match predictions. Through the numerous activities, cooperative learning opportunities, and a variety of critical thinking exercises in *Glencoe Earth Science,* you can feel comfortable taking a constructivist approach to science in your classroom.

Activities

A constructivist approach to science is rooted in an activities-based plan. Students must be provided with sensorimotor experiences as a base for developing abstract ideas. *Glencoe Earth Science* utilizes a variety of learning-by-doing opportunities. **MiniLABs** allow students to consider questions about the concepts to come, make observations, and share prior knowledge. **MiniLABs** require a minimum of equipment, and students may take responsibility for organization and execution.

Design Your Own Activities develop and reinforce or restructure concepts as well as develop the ability to use process skills. **Design Your Own Activity** formats guide students to make their own discoveries. Students collect real evidence and are encouraged through open-ended questions to reflect and reformulate their ideas based on this evidence.

Cooperative Learning

Cooperative learning adds the element of social interaction to science learning. Group learning allows students to verbalize ideas, and encourages the reflection that leads to active construction of concepts. It allows students to recognize the inconsistencies in their own perspectives and the strengths of others'. By presenting the idea that there is no one, "ready-made" answer, all students may gain the courage to try to find a viable solution. **Cooperative Learning** strategies appear in the ***Teacher Wraparound Edition*** margins whenever appropriate.

And More...

Flex Your Brain—a self-directed, critical-thinking matrix is introduced in Chapter 1, "The Nature of Science." This activity, referenced wherever appropriate in the **Teacher Wraparound Edition** margins, assists students in identifying what they already know about a subject, then in developing independent strategies to investigate further.

Students are encouraged to discover the pleasure of solving a problem through a variety of features. The **Science and Society** features in each chapter invite students to confront real-life problems. **Explore the Issue** or **Explore the Technology** questions encourage students to reflect on issues related to technology and society. The **Skill Handbook** gives specific examples to guide students through the steps of developing thinking and process skills. **Developing Skills** and **Thinking Critically** sections of the **Chapter Review** allow the teacher to assess and reward successful thinking skills.

Developing and Applying

Thinking Skills

Science is not just a collection of facts for students to memorize. Rather, it is a process of applying those observations and intuitions to situations and problems, formulating hypotheses, and drawing conclusions. This interaction of the thinking process with the content of science is the core of science and should be the focus of science study. Students, much like scientists, will plan and conduct research or experiments based on observations, evaluate their findings, and draw conclusions to explain their results. This process then begins again, using the new information for further investigation.

Basic Process Skills

Observing

The most basic process is observing. Through observation—seeing, hearing, touching, smelling, tasting—the student begins to acquire information about an object or event. Observation allows a student to gather information regarding size, shape, texture, or quantity of an object or event.

Classifying

One of the simplest ways to organize information gathered through observation is by classifying. Classifying involves the sorting of objects according to similarities or differences.

Using Numbers

Numbers are used to quantify information, including variables and measurements. Quantified information is useful for making comparisons and classifying data or objects.

Communicating

Communicating information is an important part of science. Once all the information is gathered, it is necessary to organize the observations so that the findings can be considered and shared by others. Information can be presented in tables, charts, a variety of graphs, or models.

Measuring

Measuring is a way of quantifying information in order to classify or order it by magnitude, such as area, length, volume, or mass. Measuring can involve the use of instruments and the necessary skills to manipulate them.

Inferring

Inferences are logical conclusions based on observations and are made after careful evaluation of all the available facts or data. Inferences are a means of explaining or interpreting observations and are based on making judgments. Therefore, inferences can be invalid.

Predicting

Predicting involves suggesting future events based on observations and inferences about current events. Reliable predictions are based on making accurate observations and measurements and interpreting them accurately.

Using Space/Time Relationships

This process skill involves describing the spatial relationships of objects and how those relationships change with time. For example, a student may be required to describe the motion, direction, symmetry, or shape of an object or objects.

Sequencing

Sequencing involves arranging objects or events in a particular order and may imply a hierarchy or a chronology. Developing a sequence involves the skill of identifying relationships among objects or events. A sequence may be in the form of a numbered list or a series of objects or ideas with directional arrows.

Comparing and Contrasting

Comparing is a way of identifying similarities among objects or events, while contrasting identifies their differences. Comparing and contrasting provides a way of describing and evaluating what is known about something.

Recognizing Cause and Effect

Recognizing cause and effect involves observing actions or events and making logical inferences about why they occur. Recognizing cause and effect can lead to further investigation to isolate a specific cause of a particular event.

Interpreting Scientific Illustrations

Illustrations provide examples that clarify difficult concepts or give additional information about the topic being studied. Interpreting illustrations involves processing visual information into a conceptual construct.

Integrated Process Skills

Interpreting Data

Interpreting data involves synthesizing information (collected data) to make generalizations about the problem under study and apply those generalizations to new problems. Interpreting data may therefore involve many of the other process skills, such as predicting, inferring, classifying, and using numbers.

Defining Operationally

Forming operational definitions involves stating the meaning of something in terms of its function. Operational definitions are formed through observation.

Experimenting

Experimenting involves gathering data to test a hypothesis. For data to be reliable, the experiment must be conducted under controlled conditions with a limited number of variables.

Controlling Variables

Controlling variables requires understanding and regulating all the possible variables that might affect the outcome of an experiment. Failure to control variables can lead to unreliable results.

Formulating Hypotheses

Formulating a hypothesis involves making observations followed by some kind of inference as to what those observations mean. The hypothesis is then tested via experimentation to determine its validity.

Formulating Models

A model is a way to concretely represent abstract ideas or relationships. Models can also be used to predict the outcome of future events or relationships. Models may be expressed physically, verbally, or mentally.

Concept Mapping

Concept Maps are visual representations or graphic organizers of relationships among concepts. Concept mapping may involve sequencing temporal events in which a final outcome is observed (events chain), or in which the last event relates back to the beginning of the sequence (cycle map). Hierarchies can be represented by network tree concept maps. Central and supporting ideas that are nonhierarchical can be represented by spider concept maps.

Making and Using Tables

Making tables involves understanding cause and effect and relationships among ideas and representing those relationships in a tabular format.

Making and Using Graphs

Making graphs involves interpreting data and representing that data in a visual format.

Interaction of content and process

Glencoe Earth Science encourages the interaction between science content and thinking processes. We've known for a long time that hands-on activities are a way of providing a bridge between science content and student comprehension. *Glencoe Earth Science* encourages the interaction between content and thinking processes by offering literally hundreds of hands-on activities that are easy to set up and do. In the student text, the **MiniLABs** require students to make observations and collect and record a variety of data. Full-page **Activities** connect hands-on experiences to the content information.

At the end of each chapter, students use thinking processes as they complete **Developing Skills, Thinking Critically,** and **Performance Assessment** questions.

Skill Handbook

The **Skill Handbook** provides the student with another opportunity to practice the thinking processes relevant to the material they are studying. The **Skill Handbook** also provides examples of the processes that students may refer to as they do the **Skillbuilders, Activities,** and **MiniLABs.**

Thinking Skills in the *Teacher Wraparound Edition*

These processes are also featured throughout the *Teacher Wraparound Edition.* In the margins are suggestions for students to write in a journal. Keeping a journal encourages students to communicate their ideas, a key process in science.

Flex Your Brain is a self-directed activity designed to assist students in developing thinking processes as they investigate content areas. Suggestions for using this decision-making matrix are in the margins of the *Teacher Wraparound Edition* whenever appropriate for the topic. Further discussion of **Flex Your Brain** can be found in the *Activity Worksheets* booklet of the *Teacher Classroom Resources.*

Thinking Skills Map

On page 28T, you will find a Thinking Skills Map that indicates how frequently thinking skills are encouraged and developed in *Glencoe Earth Science.*

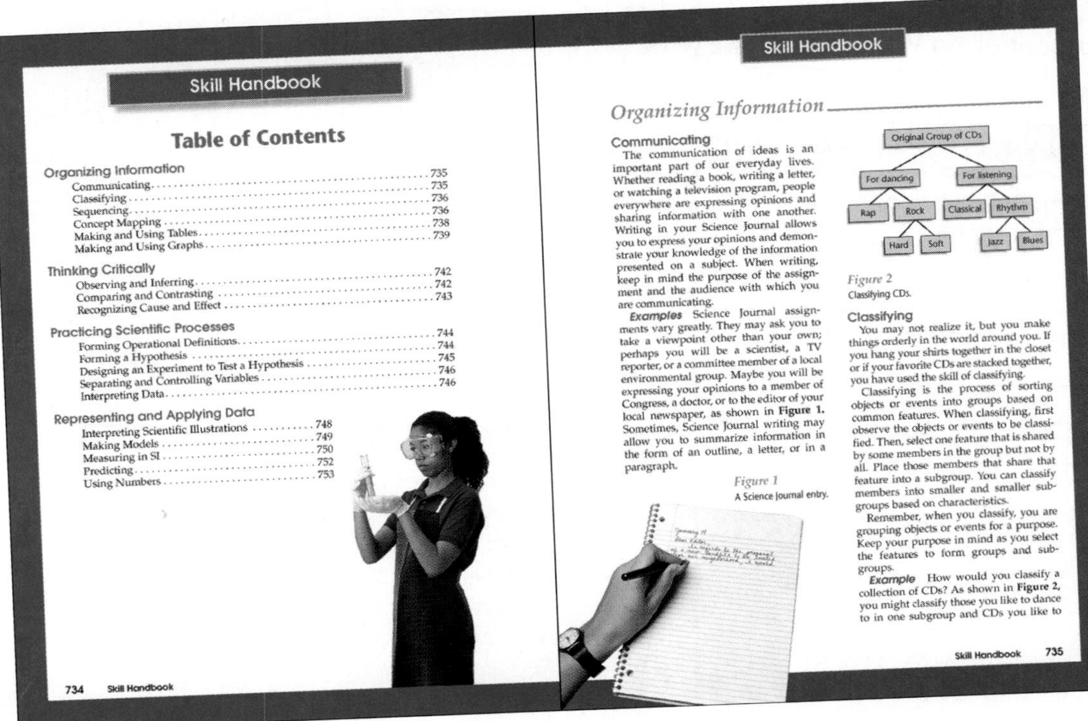

Skill Handbook

Table of Contents

734 Skill Handbook

Skill Handbook

Organizing Information

Communicating

The communication of ideas is an important part of our everyday lives. Whether reading a book, writing a letter, or watching a television program, people everywhere are expressing opinions and sharing information with one another. Writing in your Science Journal allows you to express your opinions and demonstrate your knowledge of the information presented on a subject. When writing, keep in mind the purpose of the assignment and the audience with which you are communicating.

Examples Science Journal assignments vary greatly. They may ask you to take a viewpoint other than your own; perhaps you will be a scientist, a TV reporter, or a committee member of a local environmental group. Maybe you will be expressing your opinions to a member of Congress, a doctor, or to the editor of your local newspaper, as shown in **Figure 1.** Sometimes, Science Journal writing may allow you to summarize information in the form of an outline, a letter, or in a paragraph.

Figure 1
A Science Journal entry.

Figure 2
Classifying CDs.

Classifying

You may not realize it, but you make things orderly in the world around you. If you hang your shirts together in the closet or if your favorite CDs are stacked together, you have used the skill of classifying.

Classifying is the process of sorting objects or events into groups based on common features. When classifying, first observe the objects or events to be classified. Then, select one feature that is shared by some members in the group but not by all. Place those members that share that feature into a subgroup. You can classify members into smaller and smaller subgroups based on characteristics.

Remember, when you classify, you are grouping objects or events for a purpose. Keep your purpose in mind as you select the features to form groups and subgroups.

Example How would you classify a collection of CDs? As shown in **Figure 2,** you might classify those you like to dance to in one subgroup and CDs you like to

Skill Handbook 735

Developing Thinking Skills

Thinking Skills

Thinking Skills	Chapters 1	2	3	4	5	6	7	8	9	10	11	12	13	14	15	16	17	18	19	20	21	22	23	24
ORGANIZING INFORMATION																								
Communicating	✓	✓	✓	✓	✓	✓	✓	✓	✓	✓	✓	✓	✓	✓	✓	✓	✓	✓	✓	✓	✓	✓		✓
Classifying		✓	✓	✓		✓		✓		✓							✓	✓		✓				
Sequencing			✓	✓			✓			✓	✓	✓	✓								✓	✓	✓	✓
Concept Mapping	✓	✓	✓	✓	✓	✓	✓	✓	✓	✓	✓	✓	✓	✓	✓	✓	✓	✓	✓	✓	✓	✓	✓	✓
Making and Using Tables	✓	✓	✓	✓		✓	✓	✓	✓		✓	✓	✓	✓	✓	✓		✓	✓	✓		✓	✓	
Making and Using Graphs			✓						✓			✓	✓	✓		✓		✓	✓	✓		✓		
THINKING CRITICALLY																								
Observing and Inferring		✓	✓	✓	✓	✓	✓	✓	✓	✓	✓	✓	✓	✓	✓	✓	✓	✓	✓	✓	✓	✓	✓	✓
Comparing and Contrasting	✓	✓	✓		✓	✓	✓	✓	✓	✓	✓			✓	✓	✓		✓	✓	✓	✓	✓	✓	✓
Recognizing Cause and Effect			✓			✓	✓	✓			✓		✓	✓	✓	✓	✓	✓	✓	✓	✓	✓	✓	✓
Forming Operational Definitions	✓	✓	✓	✓	✓	✓	✓		✓				✓		✓	✓		✓			✓	✓	✓	✓
PRACTICING SCIENTIFIC PROCESSES																								
Forming a Hypothesis		✓	✓	✓	✓	✓	✓	✓	✓	✓	✓	✓	✓	✓	✓	✓	✓	✓	✓	✓		✓	✓	✓
Designing an Experiment to Test a Hypothesis	✓	✓	✓		✓	✓	✓	✓	✓		✓	✓		✓	✓	✓	✓	✓	✓	✓	✓	✓		✓
Separating and Controlling Variables		✓	✓	✓		✓	✓	✓	✓					✓	✓	✓	✓	✓			✓	✓	✓	✓
Interpreting Data	✓	✓	✓	✓	✓	✓	✓	✓	✓	✓	✓	✓	✓	✓	✓	✓	✓	✓	✓	✓	✓	✓	✓	✓
REPRESENTING AND APPLYING DATA																								
Interpreting Scientific Illustrations				✓	✓							✓			✓			✓		✓			✓	✓
Making Models					✓		✓	✓		✓	✓	✓	✓	✓	✓	✓	✓	✓	✓		✓	✓	✓	✓
Measuring in SI	✓	✓			✓	✓	✓		✓	✓	✓		✓	✓	✓	✓	✓	✓	✓		✓	✓	✓	✓
Predicting										✓	✓				✓		✓				✓		✓	
Using Numbers	✓	✓	✓		✓	✓	✓		✓		✓	✓	✓	✓	✓	✓		✓	✓	✓			✓	✓

Flex Your Brain

A key element in the coverage of problem-solving and critical-thinking skills in *Glencoe Earth Science* is a critical-thinking matrix called **Flex Your Brain.**

Flex Your Brain provides students with an opportunity to explore a topic in an organized, self-checking way, and then identify how they arrived at their responses during each step of their investigation. The activity incorporates many of the skills of critical thinking. It helps students to consider their own thinking and learn about thinking from their peers.

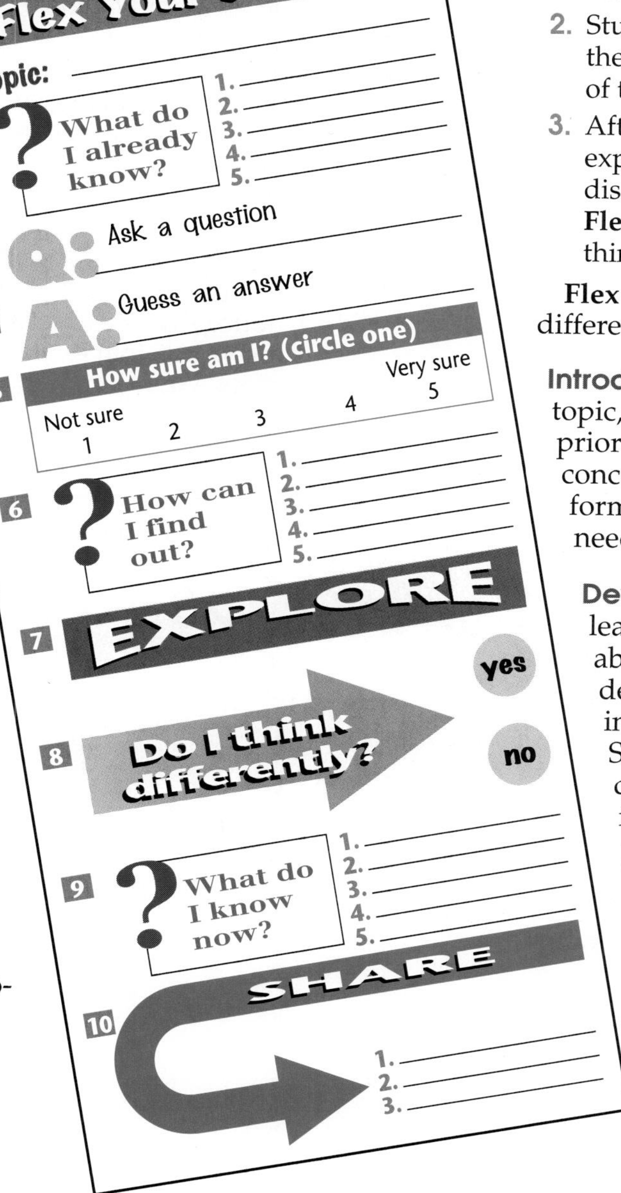

Where is Flex Your Brain found?

Chapter 1, "The Nature of Science," is an introduction to the topics of critical thinking and problem solving. **Flex Your Brain** accompanies the text section in the introductory chapter. A worksheet for **Flex Your Brain** appears on page 5 of the *Activity Worksheets* book of the *Teacher Resources.* This version provides spaces for students to write in their responses.

In the *Teacher Wraparound Edition,* suggested topics are given in each chapter for the use of *Flex Your Brain.* You can photocopy the worksheet master from the *Teacher Resources.*

Using Flex Your Brain

Flex Your Brain can be used as a whole-class activity or in cooperative groups, but is primarily designed to be used by individual students within the class. There are three basic steps.

1. Teachers assign a class topic to be investigated using **Flex Your Brain.**
2. Students use **Flex Your Brain** to guide them in their individual explorations of the topic.
3. After students have completed their explorations, teachers guide them in a discussion of their experiences with **Flex Your Brain,** bridging content and thinking processes.

Flex Your Brain can be used at many different points in the lesson plan.

Introduction: Ideal for introducing a topic, **Flex Your Brain** elicits students' prior knowledge and identifies misconceptions, enabling the teacher to formulate plans specific to student needs.

Development: Flex Your Brain leads students to find out more about a topic on their own, and develops their research skills while increasing their knowledge. Students actually pose their own questions to explore, making their investigations relevant to their personal interests and concerns.

Review and Extension: Flex Your Brain allows teachers to check student understanding while allowing students to explore aspects of the topic that go beyond the material presented in class.

Concept Maps

In science, concept maps make abstract information concrete and useful, improve retention of information, and show students that thought has shape.

Concept maps are visual representations or graphic organizers of relationships among particular concepts. Concept maps can be generated by individual students, small groups, or an entire class. *Glencoe Earth Science* develops and reinforces four types of concept maps—the **network tree, events chain, cycle concept map,** and **spider concept map**—that are most applicable to studying science. Examples of the four types and their applications are shown on this page and page 31T. Students can learn how to construct each of these types of concept maps by referring to the **Skill Handbook.**

Building Concept Mapping Skills

The **Developing Skills** section of the **Chapter Review** provides opportunities for practicing concept mapping. A variety of concept mapping approaches is used in almost every chapter. Students may be directed to make a specific type of concept map and be provided the terms to use. At other times, students may be given only general guidelines. For example, concept terms to be used may be provided and students required to select the appropriate model to apply, or vice versa. Finally, students may be asked to provide both the terms and type of concept map to explain relationships among concepts. When students are given this flexibility, it is important for you to recognize that, while sample answers are provided, student responses may vary. Look for the conceptual strength of student responses, not absolute accuracy. You'll notice that most network tree maps provide connecting words that explain the relationships between concepts. We recommend that you not require all students to supply these words, but many students may be challenged by this aspect.

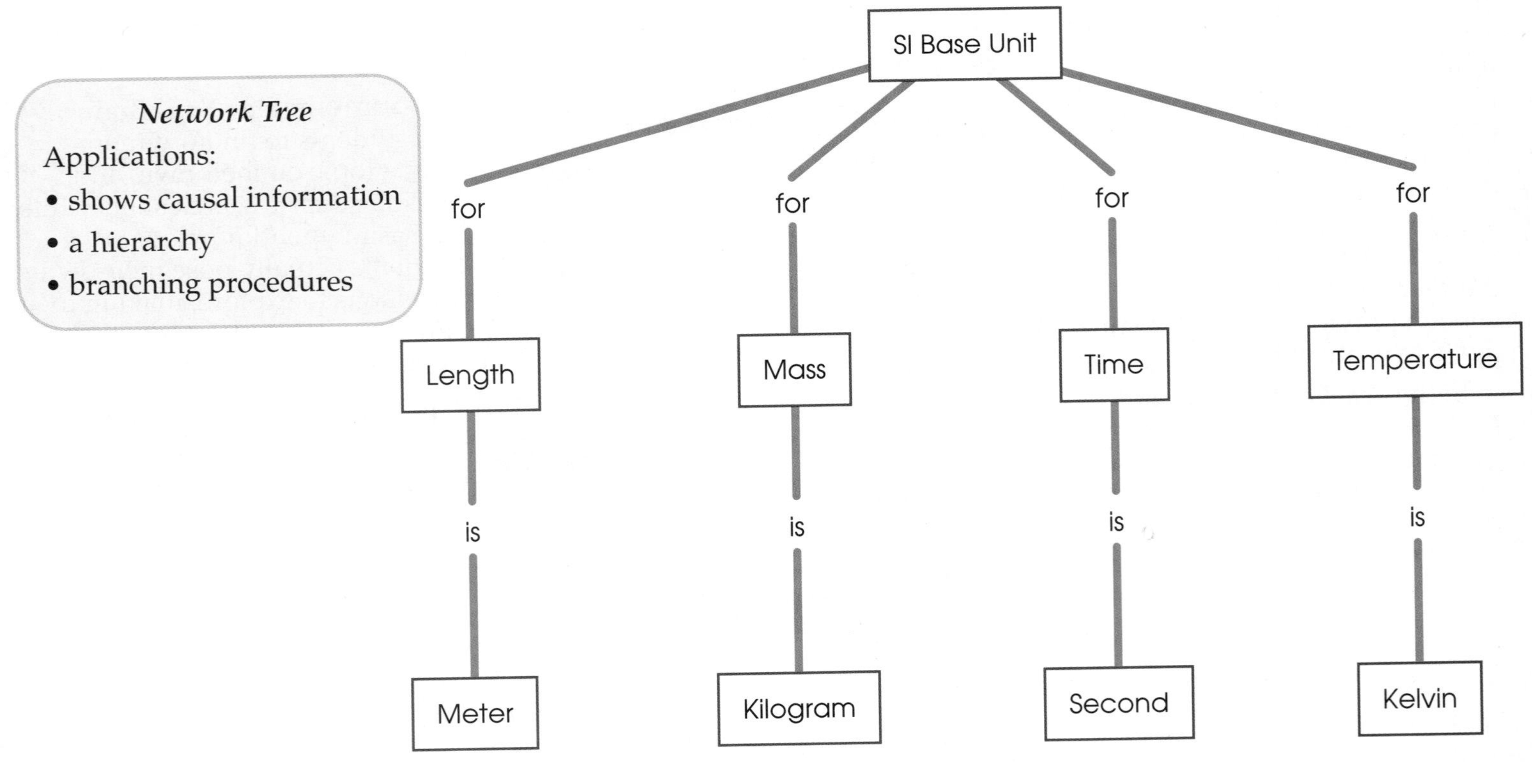

Concept Mapping Booklet

The *Concept Mapping* book of the *Teacher Classroom Resources,* too, provides a developmental approach for students to practice concept mapping.

As a teaching strategy, generating concept maps can be used to preview a chapter's content by visually relating the concepts to be learned and allowing the students to read with purpose. Using concept maps for previewing is especially useful when there are many new key science terms for students to learn. As a review strategy, constructing concept maps reinforces main ideas and clarifies their relationships. Construction of concept maps using cooperative learning strategies as described in this Teacher Guide will allow students to practice both interpersonal and process skills.

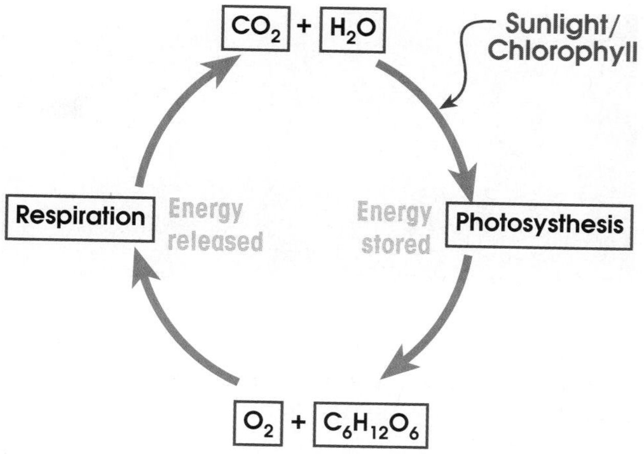

Cycle Concept Map

Application:

- shows how a series of events interact to produce a set of results again and again

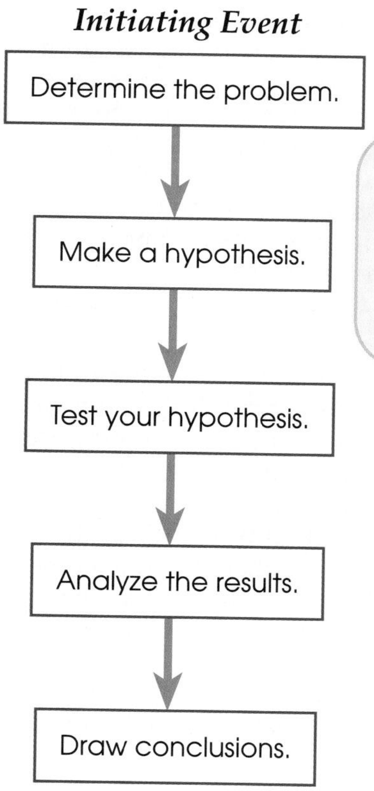

Initiating Event

Events Chain

Applications:

- describes the stages of a process
- the steps in a linear procedure
- a sequence of events

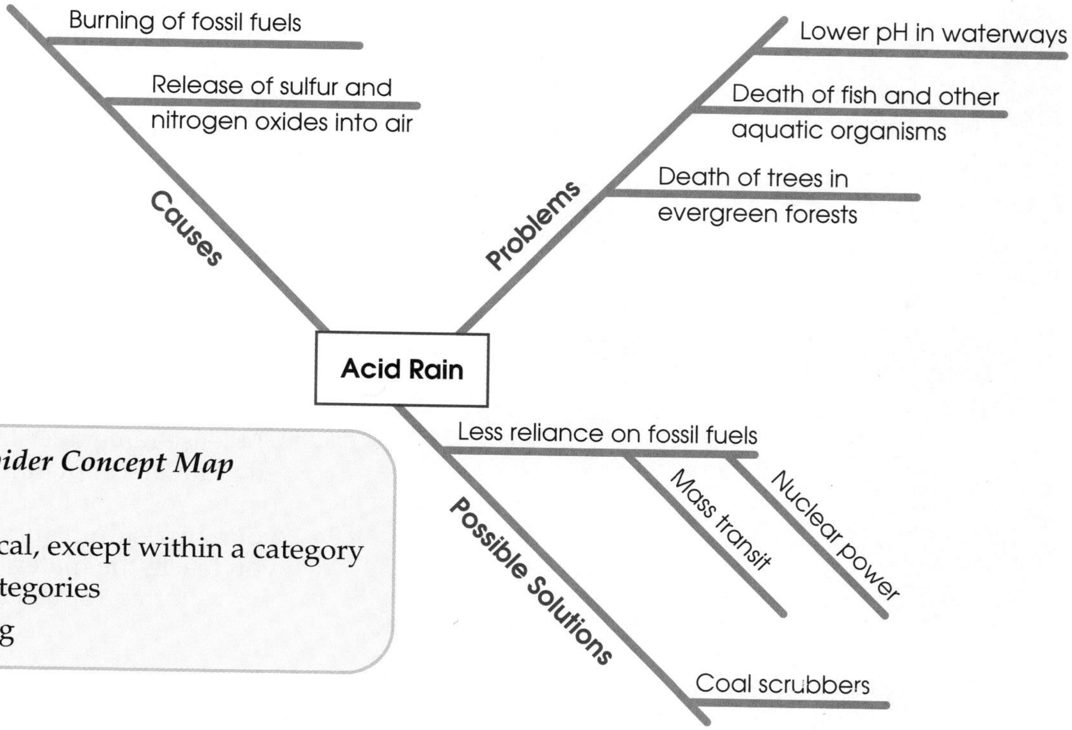

Spider Concept Map

Applications:

- nonhierarchical, except within a category
- unparallel categories
- brainstorming

Planning Your Course

Glencoe Earth Science provides flexibility in the selection of topics and content that allows teachers to adapt the text to the needs of individual students and classes. In this regard, the teacher is in the best position to decide what topics to present, the pace at which to cover the content, and what material to give the most emphasis. To assist the teacher in planning the course, a planning guide has been provided.

Glencoe Earth Science may be used in a full-year, two-semester course that is comprised of 180 periods of approximately 45 minutes each. This type of schedule is represented in the table under the heading of Single-Class Scheduling. As an alternative, the table also outlines a plan for block scheduling, which is described in the next section.

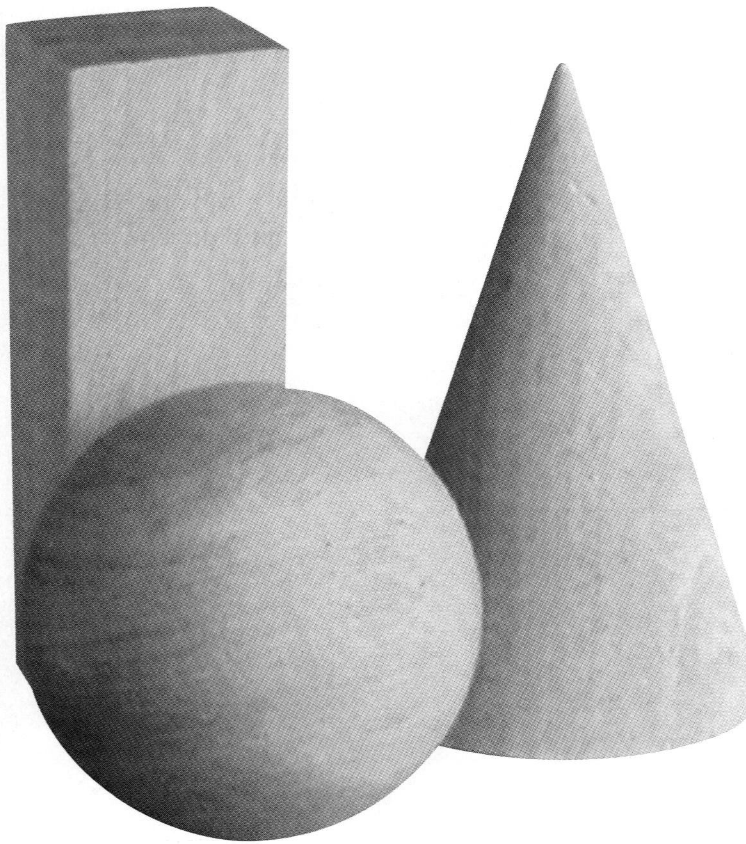

Block Scheduling

To build flexibility into the curriculum, many schools are introducing a block scheduling approach. Block scheduling often involves covering the same information in fewer days with longer class periods. Thus, a course that lasts an entire year may take only one semester under a block scheduling approach. This type of approach allows curriculum supervisors and teachers to tailor the curriculum to meet students' needs while achieving local and/or state curriculum goals. Long, concentrated periods of study can facilitate the learning of complex material. Furthermore, students may be able to take a wider variety of coursework under a block scheduling plan than under a traditional full-year plan, thus enriching their high-school experience and giving them a broader foundation for college-level work.

If you follow a block schedule, you may want to consider either combining lessons or eliminating certain topics and spending more time on the topics you do cover. *Glencoe Earth Science* provides the flexibility that allows you to tailor the program to your needs. *Glencoe Earth Science* also provides a wide variety of support materials that will help you and your students whether you follow a block schedule or full-year schedule. A block schedule may enable you to complete some of the longer **Activities** in one class period. Have students fill out the accompanying ***Activity Worksheets*** from the ***Teacher Classroom Resources*** as they complete the activities. The ***Teacher Classroom Resources*** provide a wealth of materials that provide classroom management support.

In the table shown here, it is assumed that for block scheduling the course will be taught for one semester and include 90 periods of approximately 90 minutes each.

Please remember that the planning guide is provided as an aid in planning the best course for your students. You should use the planning guide in relation to your curriculum and the ability levels of the classes you teach, the materials available for activities, and the time allotted for teaching.

Planning Guide for GLENCOE EARTH SCIENCE Unit	Chapter/Section	Scheduling Single-Class (180 days)	Block (90 days)
UNIT 1	Earth Materials	31	17
1	THE NATURE OF SCIENCE	7	4
1-1	What is Earth science?	1	$\frac{1}{2}$
1-2	Science and Society: Applying Science	1	$\frac{1}{2}$
1-3	Solving Problems	2	$1\frac{1}{2}$
1-4	Measurement and Safety	2	1
	Chapter Review	1	$\frac{1}{2}$
2	MATTER AND ITS CHANGES	8	4
2-1	Atoms	2	1
2-2	Combinations of Atoms	2	1
2-3	Matter	2	1
2-4	Science and Society: Energy from Atoms	1	$\frac{1}{2}$
	Chapter Review	1	$\frac{1}{2}$
3	MINERALS	7	4
3-1	Minerals	2	1
3-2	Mineral Identification	2	$1\frac{1}{2}$
3-3	Uses of Minerals	1	$\frac{1}{2}$
3-4	Science and Society: Uses of Titanium	1	$\frac{1}{2}$
	Chapter Review	1	$\frac{1}{2}$
4	ROCKS	9	5
4-1	The Rock Cycle	2	$1\frac{1}{2}$
4-2	Igneous Rocks	1	$\frac{1}{2}$
4-3	Metamorphic Rocks	2	1
4-4	Sedimentary Rocks	2	1
4-5	Science and Society: Burning Waste Coal	1	$\frac{1}{2}$
	Chapter Review	1	$\frac{1}{2}$

Planning Guide for GLENCOE EARTH SCIENCE Unit	Chapter/Section	Scheduling Single-Class (180 days)	Block (90 days)
UNIT 2	The Changing Surface of Earth	28	11
5	VIEWS OF EARTH	7	
5-1	Landforms	2	
5-2	Viewpoints	1	
5-3	Maps	2	
5-4	Science and Society: Mapping Our Planet	1	
	Chapter Review	1	
6	WEATHERING AND SOIL	6	3
6-1	Weathering	2	1
6-2	Soil	2	1
6-3	Science and Society: Land Use and Soil Loss	1	$\frac{1}{2}$
	Chapter Review	1	$\frac{1}{2}$
7	EROSIONAL FORCES	7	4
7-1	Gravity	1	$\frac{1}{2}$
7-2	Science and Society: Developing Land Prone to Erosion	2	1
7-3	Glaciers	1	$\frac{1}{2}$
7-4	Wind	2	$1\frac{1}{2}$
	Chapter Review	1	$\frac{1}{2}$
8	WATER EROSION AND DEPOSITION	8	4
8-1	Surface Water	1	$\frac{1}{2}$
8-2	Groundwater	3	$1\frac{1}{2}$
8-3	Science and Society: Water Wars	1	$\frac{1}{2}$
8-4	Ocean Shoreline	2	1
	Chapter Review	1	$\frac{1}{2}$

Planning Guide

Unit	Chapter/Section		Single-Class (180 days)	Block (90 days)
Planning Guide for GLENCOE EARTH SCIENCE			**Scheduling**	
Unit 3	Earth's Internal Processes		24	13
9	Earthquakes		7	4
	9-1	Forces Inside Earth	2	$1\frac{1}{2}$
	9-2	Earthquake Information	2	1
	9-3	Destruction by Earthquakes	1	$\frac{1}{2}$
	9-4	Science and Society: Living on a Fault	1	$\frac{1}{2}$
	Chapter Review		1	$\frac{1}{2}$
10	Volcanoes		8	4
	10-1	Volcanoes and Earth's Moving Plates	2	1
	10-2	Science and Society: Energy from Earth	1	$\frac{1}{2}$
	10-3	Eruptions and Forms of Volcanoes	2	1
	10-4	Igneous Rock Features	2	1
	Chapter Review		1	$\frac{1}{2}$
11	Plate Tectonics		9	5
	11-1	Continental Drift	2	1
	11-2	Seafloor Spreading	2	1
	11-3	Theory of Plate Tectonics	3	2
	11-4	Science and Society: Before Pangaea, Rodinia	1	$\frac{1}{2}$
	Chapter Review		1	$\frac{1}{2}$
Unit 4	Change and Earth's History		16	8
12	Clues to Earth's Past		8	4
	12-1	Fossils	1	$\frac{1}{2}$
	12-2	Science and Society: Extinction of Dinosaurs	2	1
	12-3	Relative Ages of Rocks	2	1
	12-4	Absolute Ages of Rocks	2	1
	Chapter Review		1	$\frac{1}{2}$

Unit	Chapter/Section		Single-Class (180 days)	Block (90 days)
Planning Guide for GLENCOE EARTH SCIENCE			**Scheduling**	
13	Geologic Time		8	4
	13-1	Evolution and Geologic Time	2	1
	13-2	Science and Society: Present-Day Rapid Extinctions	2	1
	13-3	Early Earth History	1	$\frac{1}{2}$
	13-4	Middle and Recent Earth History	2	1
	Chapter Review		1	$\frac{1}{2}$
Unit 5	Earth's Air and Water		36	21
14	Atmosphere		8	4
	14-1	Earth's Atmosphere	2	1
	14-2	Science and Society: The Ozone Layer	1	$\frac{1}{2}$
	14-3	Energy from the Sun	2	1
	14-4	Movement of Air	2	1
	Chapter Review		1	$\frac{1}{2}$
15	Weather		7	4
	15-1	What is weather?	2	1
	15-2	Weather Patterns	2	$1\frac{1}{2}$
	15-3	Forecasting Weather	1	$\frac{1}{2}$
	15-4	Science and Society: Changing the Weather	1	$\frac{1}{2}$
	Chapter Review		1	$\frac{1}{2}$
16	Climate		7	5
	16-1	What is climate?	1	1
	16-2	Climate Types	2	$1\frac{1}{2}$
	16-3	Climatic Changes	2	$1\frac{1}{2}$
	16-4	Science and Society: How can global warming be slowed?	1	$\frac{1}{2}$
	Chapter Review		1	$\frac{1}{2}$

Unit	Chapter/Section	Single-Class (180 days)	Block (90 days)
17	**Ocean Motion**	**7**	**4**
	17-1 Ocean Water	2	1
	17-2 Ocean Currents	1	1
	17-3 Ocean Waves and Tides	2	1
	17-4 Science and Society: Tapping Tidal Energy	1	½
	Chapter Review	1	½
18	**Oceanography**	**7**	**4**
	18-1 The Seafloor	2	1½
	18-2 Life in the Ocean	2	1
	18-3 Science and Society: Pollution and Marine Life	2	1
	Chapter Review	1	½
Unit 6	**You and the Environment**	**13**	**7**
19	**Our Impact on Land**	**6**	**3**
	19-1 Population Impact on the Environment	2	1
	19-2 Using the Land	2	1
	19-3 Science and Society: Should recycling be required?	1	½
	Chapter Review	1	½
20	**Our Impact on Air and Water**	**7**	**4**
	20-1 Air Pollution	2	1½
	20-2 Science and Society: Acid Rain	2	½
	20-3 Water Pollution	2	1½
	Chapter Review	1	½

Unit	Chapter/Section	Single-Class (180 days)	Block (90 days)
Unit 7	**Astronomy**	**32**	**13**
21	**Exploring Space**	**7**	
	21-1 Radiation from Space	2	
	21-2 Science and Society: Light Pollution	1	
	21-3 Artificial Satellites and Space Probes	2	
	21-4 The Space Shuttle and the Future	1	
	Chapter Review	1	
22	**The Sun-Earth-Moon System**	**6**	**3**
	22-1 Planet Earth	2	1
	22-2 Earth's Moon	1	½
	22-3 Science and Society: Exploration of the Moon	2	1
	Chapter Review	1	½
23	**The Solar System**	**9**	**5**
	23-1 The Solar System	1	½
	23-2 The Inner Planets	2	1½
	23-3 Science and Society: Mission to Mars	1	½
	23-4 The Outer Planets	2	1½
	23-5 Other Objects in the Solar System	2	½
	Chapter Review	1	½
24	**Stars and Galaxies**	**10**	**5**
	24-1 Stars	2	1
	24-2 The Sun	1	½
	24-3 Evolution of Stars	3	2
	24-4 Galaxies and the Expanding Universe	2	1
	24-5 Science and Society: The Search for Extraterrestrial Life	1	–
	Chapter Review	1	½

Technology in the Classroom

Using the Internet in the Classroom

The Internet is the world's largest computer network. To access the Internet, you need a computer with communication software, a modem, and a phone line. A modem is a device that enables computer data to travel to another computer via phone lines. Many computers come equipped with an internal modem. To access the Internet, you also must have an account with an Internet service provider. Some cities provide free accounts, but commercial access can be inexpensive.

After you have access to the Internet, you can use it to enhance your teaching in a variety of ways. You will be able to obtain a countless variety of lessons, activities, project ideas, and labs on any topic you choose. Simply make your selection, print, and hand out to your students. If you have students with special needs or wish to incorporate cultural diversity into an existing lesson, you can find help on the Internet.

In addition to providing science lessons, the Internet can provide the most up-to-date information on any topic you may wish to research. In addition, you may access an untold number of graphics of all kinds, videos, animation sequences, and software. With the electronic mail—E-mail—capabilities of the Internet, you may exchange ideas with teachers worldwide, consult with scientists, and order products.

Students also benefit from education on the Internet. Because the Internet is used in education, business, and in leisure, students who become familiar with it will be better prepared for the future. Use of the Internet in the classroom is also a powerful motivator for all students, no matter what their needs are.

Using E-mail, students can compare and contrast lab data with students in the next town, or on the other side of the world. E-mail enables students to consult with scientists about long-term projects and get homework help from peers. Students work harder to express themselves correctly when they send messages to scientists or to people in other countries via E-mail.

As students use the Internet for information retrieval to enhance their lab reports and other classroom activities, they develop good search and retrieval strategies. These strategies require careful analysis, evaluation, and application. An added benefit is that when students use the Internet, they are judged only on what they say and how they say it. Because differences in personal appearance, gender, culture, ability, and disability are not a part of Internet communication, students learn to value expertise in a culturally diverse setting.

Students will not only be able to access a wealth of information on the Internet, they will also be able to publish their own products. Labs that they have designed and conducted themselves can be published on the Internet for other student and teacher Internet users.

© The World Wide Web

To make publishing and accessing information easier, you and your students can use a section of the Internet called the World Wide Web. If you think of the Internet as a supermarket, the Web could be one of the sections in the supermarket. To access the World Wide Web, you must install software called a web browser in your computer. Once you are on the Web, you can access materials that resemble those of a library, a movie theater, an art gallery, a museum, or a shopping mall. You may browse through books, magazines, and scientific periodicals. You may view pictures, maps, paintings, and movies with CD-quality sound, or play interactive educational games. You might order classroom supplies, equipment, or books from home pages of scientific supply companies. A home page is the first page you see when you enter a Web site. Your students may want to create their own classroom home page on the Web. Classes around the country have created home pages that explain their topics of study, supply data from experiments, and publish various science activities and projects. Other schools may access these home pages to compare data or to get ideas for their own projects.

A word of caution: there is no censorship on the Internet, unless you use software or subscribe to a server that censors material inappropriate to the classroom. Without such devices, students can easily find material that you or their parents find objectionable. You will need to supervise and monitor student use of the Internet carefully. However, you will find it well worth the effort when your students become efficient users of the Internet.

Education

Tech-Prep

What Is Tech Prep?

Tech prep is a rigorous and focused program of study that aims to create a work force in the United States that is technically literate. It is designed to prepare students enrolled in a general curriculum for the demands of further education or for employment by providing them with essential academic and technical foundations, along with problem-solving, group-process, and lifelong-learning skills. These goals can be achieved by integrating vocational study with higher-level academic study.

What Are the Characteristics of the Tech Prep Curriculum?

In 1990, Congress passed the Carl D. Perkins Vocational and Applied Technology Act to set aside funds for the development and administration of Tech Prep programs. The criteria outlined in Title III of the Perkins Act specify that tech prep programs take place during the last two years of high school, followed by two years of post-secondary occupational education, and that this education culminate in a certificate or associate degree. The Secretary's Commission on Achieving Necessary Skills (SCANS), an arm of the United States Department of Labor, published a report in June 1991 that outlined several competencies that characterize successful workers. The Tech Prep curriculum seeks to address these competencies, which include the

- ability to use resources productively.
- ability to use interpersonal skills effectively, including fostering teamwork, teaching others, serving customers, leading, negotiating, and working well with individuals from culturally diverse backgrounds.
- ability to acquire, evaluate, interpret, and communicate data and information.
- ability to understand social, organizational, and technological systems.
- ability to apply technology to specific tasks.

How Does Tech Prep Relate to the Middle School Curriculum?

Tech prep provides an alternative to the college-prep course of study that leads to a career goal. Because of this, tech prep is available to all students whether they are taking a college prep, vocational, or general course of study. The middle school years provide an opportunity to identify those students who might benefit from a tech-prep curriculum once they reach high school. They also provide an opportunity to introduce unfamiliar students to technological applications leading to career opportunities, or to provide practice for students who already have some knowledge of how technology is used. Young children are fascinated by the technology that surrounds them, and they are especially quick to learn how to use and apply it. Take advantage of their enthusiasm by preparing them for a possible tech-prep education when they are in middle school.

How Does *GLENCOE EARTH SCIENCE* Address Tech Prep Issues?

Glencoe Earth Science helps you develop scientific and technological literacy in your students through a variety of performance-based activities that emphasize problem solving, critical thinking skills, and teamwork. In the *Student Edition*, **Problem Solving, Using Technology,** and **Design Your Own Experiment** provide opportunities for practical applications of concepts. **Using Computers** and **Using Math** features give additional practice in computer and math applications. **Unit Projects** provide ideas for activities that can be used as extended projects or for science fairs.

Collecting weather data using computers

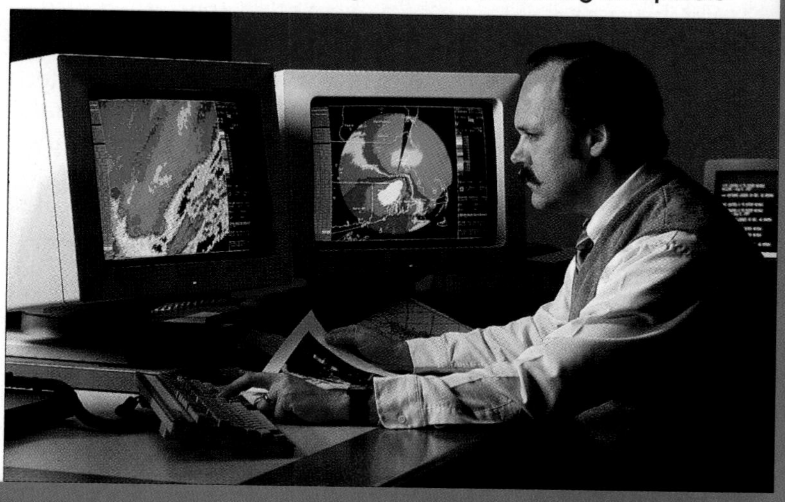

Cultural Diversity

American classrooms reflect the rich and diverse cultural heritage of the American people. Students come from different ethnic backgrounds and different cultural experiences into a common classroom that must assist all of them in learning. The diversity itself is an important focus of the learning experience.

Diversity can be repressed, creating a hostile environment; ignored, creating an indifferent environment; or appreciated, creating a receptive and productive environment. Responding to diversity and approaching it as a part of every curriculum is challenging to a teacher, experienced or not. The goal of science is understanding. The goal of multicultural education is to promote the understanding of how people from different cultures approach and solve the basic problems all humans have in living and learning.

Cultural Diversity in Science

Every culture has utilized science to explore fundamental questions, meet challenges, and address human needs. The growth of knowledge in science has advanced along culturally diverse roots. No single culture has a monopoly on the development of scientific knowledge. The history of science is rich with the contributions and accomplishments of men and women from diverse cultural backgrounds. A brief look at some of the milestones in science reveals this diversity. Cultural groups on all continents have devised methods for measuring time and space. For example, the Mayan civilization, which flourished in what is now southern Mexico, Guatemala, and Belize, developed sophisticated and accurate mathematical systems and calendars. Lewis Latimer, an African-American draftsman and inventor, contributed to the development of the electric light bulb and drew the plans that resulted in the 1876 patent of the telephone. Today, individuals from diverse cultural and ethnic backgrounds continue to make significant contributions to science. The **People and Science** feature in the ***Student Edition*** of *Glencoe Earth Science* highlights some of these individuals and their contributions.

The scientific enterprise is a human enterprise that utilizes science processes (observing and inferring, classifying, and so on) to discover, explore, and explain the environment. Consequently, students must experience and understand that all people, regardless of the cultural orientation, have made major contributions to science. ***Glencoe Earth Science*** addresses this issue. In addition to the individuals highlighted in the ***Student Edition,*** the **Cultural Diversity** sections of the ***Teacher Wraparound Edition*** provide information about people and groups who have traditionally been misrepresented or omitted. The intent is to build awareness and appreciation for the global community in which we all live.

Goals of Multicultural Education

The ***Glencoe Earth Science Teacher Classroom Resources*** include a ***Multicultural Connections*** booklet that offers additional opportunities to integrate multicultural materials into the curriculum. By providing these opportunities, ***Glencoe Earth Science*** is helping to meet four major goals of multicultural education:

1. promoting the strength and value of cultural diversity
2. promoting human rights and respect for those who are different from oneself
3. promoting social justice and equal opportunity for all people
4. promoting equity in the distribution of power among groups

These goals are accomplished when students see others like themselves in positive settings in their textbooks. They also are accomplished when students realize that major contributions in science are the result of the work of hundreds of individuals from diverse backgrounds. ***Glencoe Earth Science*** has been designed to enable you, the science teacher, to achieve these goals.

Books that provide additional information on multicultural education are

Atwater, Mary, et al. *Multicultural Education: Inclusion of All.* Athens, Georgia: University of Georgia Press, 1994.

Banks, James A. (with Cherry A. McGee Banks). *Multicultural Education: Issues and Perspectives.* Boston: Allyn and Bacon, 1989.

Selin, Helaine. *Science Across Cultures: An Annotated Bibliography of Books on Non-Western Science, Technology, and Medicine.* New York: Garland, 1992.

Meeting Individual Needs

Each student brings his or her own unique set of abilities, perceptions, and needs into the classroom. It is important that the teacher try to make the classroom environment as receptive to these differences as possible and to ensure a good learning environment for all students.

It is important to recognize that individual learning styles are different and that learning style does not reflect a student's ability level. While some students learn primarily through visual or auditory senses, others are kinesthetic learners and do best if they have hands-on exploratory interaction with materials. Some students work best alone and others learn best in a group environment. While some students seek to understand the "big picture" in order to deal with specifics, others need to understand the details first in order to put the whole concept together.

In an effort to provide all students with a positive science experience, this text offers a variety of ways for students to interact with materials so that they can utilize their preferred method of learning the concepts. The variety of approaches allows students to become familiar with other learning approaches, as well.

Ability Levels

The activities are broken down into three levels to accommodate all student ability levels. ***Glencoe Earth Science Teacher Wraparound Edition*** designates the activities as follows:

L1 activities are basic activities designed to be within the ability range of all students. These activities reinforce the concepts presented.

L2 activities are application activities designed for students who have mastered the concepts presented. These activities give students an opportunity for practical application of the concepts presented.

L3 activities are challenging activities designed for the students who are able to go beyond the basic concepts presented. These activities allow students to expand their perspectives on the basic concepts presented.

The chart on pages 40T-41T gives tips you may find useful in structuring the learning environment in your classroom to meet students' special needs. In addition, **Inclusion Strategies** that address special needs are provided in the bottom margins of the *Teacher Wraparound Edition.*

Limited English Proficiency

In providing for the student with limited English proficiency, the focus needs to be on overcoming a language barrier. Once again, it is important not to confuse ability in speaking/reading English with academic ability or "intelligence." In general, the best method for dealing with LEP, variations in learning styles, and ability levels is to provide all students with a variety of ways to learn, apply, and be assessed on the concepts. Look for this symbol LEP in the teacher margin for specific strategies for students with limited English proficiency.

Learning Styles

We at Glencoe believe it is our responsibility to provide you with a program that allows you to apply diverse instructional strategies to a population of students with diverse learning styles. Several learning styles are emphasized in the ***Teacher Wraparound Edition:*** Kinesthetic, Visual-Spatial, Logical-Mathematical, Interpersonal, Intrapersonal, Linguistic, and Auditory-Musical. A student with a kinesthetic style learns from touch, movement, and manipulating objects. Visual-spatial learners respond to images and illustrations. Using numbers and reasoning are characteristics of the logical-mathematical learner. A student with an interpersonal style has confidence in social settings, while a student with an intrapersonal style may prefer to learn on his or her own. Linguistic learning involves the use and understanding of words. Finally, auditory-musical learning involves listening to the spoken word and to tones and rhythms.

Any student may display any or all of these styles depending on the learning situation. The ***Student Edition*** and ***Teacher Wraparound Edition*** provide a number of strategies for encouraging students with diverse learning styles. These include **Using Math, Activities, MiniLABs,** and **Science Journal** features. The ***Teacher Wraparound Edition*** contains **Visual Learning, Science Journal,** as well as a number of other strategies. Look for this logo LS that identifies strategies for different learning styles.

Meeting Individual Needs

	Description	Sources of Help/Information
Learning Disabled	All learning-disabled students have an academic problem in one or more areas, such as academic learning, language, perception, social-emotional adjustment, memory, or attention.	*Journal of Learning Disabilities* *Learning Disability Quarterly*
Behaviorally Disordered	Children with behavior disorders deviate from standards or expectations of behavior and impair the functioning of others and themselves. These children may also be gifted or learning-disabled.	*Exceptional Children* *Journal of Special Education*
Physically Challenged	Children who are physically disabled fall into two categories—those with orthopedic impairments and those with other health impairments. Orthopedically impaired children have the use of one or more limbs severely restricted, so the use of wheelchairs, crutches, or braces may be necessary. Children with other health impairments may require the use of respirators or other medical equipment.	Batshaw, M.L. and M.Y. Perset. *Children with Handicaps: A Medical Primer.* Baltimore: Paul H. Brooks, 1981. Hale, G. (Ed.). *The Source Book for the Disabled.* New York: Holt, Rinehart & Winston, 1982. *Teaching Exceptional Children*
Visually Impaired	Children who are visually disabled have partial or total loss of sight. Individuals with visual impairments are not significantly different from their sighted peers in ability range or personality. However, blindness may affect cognitive, motor, and social development, especially if early intervention is lacking.	*Journal of Visual Impairment and Blindness* *Education of Visually Handicapped* American Foundation for the Blind
Hearing Impaired	Children who are hearing impaired have partial or total loss of hearing. Individuals with hearing impairments are not significantly different from their hearing peers in ability range or personality. However, the chronic condition of deafness may affect cognitive, motor, and social development if early intervention is lacking. Speech development also is often affected.	*American Annals of the Deaf* *Journal of Speech and Hearing Research* *Sign Language Studies*
Limited English Proficiency	Multicultural and/or bilingual children often speak English as a second language or not at all. The customs and behavior of people in the majority culture may be confusing for some of these students. Cultural values may inhibit some of these students from full participation.	*Teaching English as a Second Language Reporter* R.L. Jones (Ed.). *Mainstreaming and the Minority Child.* Reston, VA: Council for Exceptional Children, 1976.
Gifted	Although no formal definition exists, these students can be described as having above-average ability, task commitment, and creativity. Gifted students rank in the top five percent of their class. They usually finish work more quickly than other students, and are capable of divergent thinking.	*Journal for the Education of the Gifted* *Gifted Child Quarterly* *Gifted Creative/Talented*

Tips for Instruction

With careful planning, the needs of all students can be met in the science classroom.

1. Provide support and structure; clearly specify rules, assignments, and duties.
2. Practice skills frequently. Use games and drills to help maintain student interest.
3. Allow students to record answers on tape and allow extra time to complete tests and assignments.
4. Provide outlines or tape lecture material.
5. Pair students with peer helpers, and provide class time for pair interaction.

1. Provide a clearly structured environment with regard to scheduling, rules, room arrangement, and safety.
2. Clearly outline objectives and how you will help students obtain objectives.
3. Reinforce appropriate behavior and model it for students.
4. Do not expect immediate success. Instead, work for long-term improvement.
5. Balance individual needs with group requirements.

1. Openly discuss with the student any uncertainties you have about when to offer aid.
2. Ask parents or therapists and students what special devices or procedures are needed, and if any special safety precautions need to be taken.
3. Allow physically disabled students to do everything their peers do, including participating in field trips, special events, and projects.
4. Help nondisabled students and adults understand physically disabled students.

1. Help the student become independent. Modify assignments as needed.
2. Teach classmates how to serve as guides.
3. Limit unnecessary noise in the classroom.
4. Provide tactile models whenever possible.
5. Describe people and events as they occur in the classroom.
6. Provide taped lectures and reading assignments.
7. Team the student with a sighted peer for laboratory work.

The *Student Edition* and *Teacher Wraparound Edition* contain a variety of strategies for addressing the individual learning styles of students:

- Both structured and open-ended **Activities**
- Hands-on **MiniLABS**
- **Enrichment** activities
- **Visual Learning** strategies
- **Across the Curriculum** strategies

The following Glencoe products also can help you tailor your instruction to meet the individual needs of your students:

- **Study Guide**
- **Teaching Transparencies**
- **Section Focus Transparencies**
- **Concept Mapping**
- **MindJogger Videoquiz**
- **English/Spanish Audiocassettes**
- **Critical Thinking/Problem Solving**
- **Cooperative Learning Resource Guide**
- Various multimedia products, including **Interactive Videodisc Program, The Secret of Life Series, The Infinite Voyage Series, Science and Technology Videodisc Series, National Geographic Society Series**

1. Seat students where they can see your lip movements easily, and avoid visual distractions.
2. Avoid standing with your back to the window or light source.
3. Using an overhead projector allows you to maintain eye contact while writing.
4. Seat students where they can see speakers.
5. Write all assignments on the board, or hand out written instructions.
6. If the student has a manual interpreter, allow both student and interpreter to select the most favorable seating arrangements.

1. Remember, students' ability to speak English does not reflect their academic ability.
2. Try to incorporate the student's cultural experience into your instruction. The help of a bilingual aide may be effective.
3. Include information about different cultures in your curriculum to help build students' self-image. Avoid cultural stereotypes.
4. Encourage students to share their cultures in the classroom.

1. Make arrangements for students to take selected subjects early and to work on independent projects.
2. Let students express themselves in art forms such as drawing, creative writing, or acting.
3. Make public services available through a catalog of resources, such as agencies providing free and inexpensive materials, community services and programs, and people in the community with specific expertise.
4. Ask "what if" questions to develop high-level thinking skills. Establish an environment safe for risk taking.
5. Emphasize concepts, theories, ideas, relationships, and generalizations.

Assessment

What criteria do you use to assess your students as they progress through a course? Do you rely on formal tests and quizzes? To assess students' achievement in science, you need to measure not only their knowledge of the subject matter, but also their ability to handle apparatus; to organize, predict, record, and interpret data; to design experiments; and to communicate orally and in writing. *Glencoe Earth Science* has been designed to provide you with a variety of assessment tools, both formal and informal, to help you develop a clearer picture of your students' progress.

Performance Assessment

Performance assessments are becoming more common in today's schools. Science curricula are being revised to prepare students to cope with change and with futures that will depend on their abilities to think, learn, and solve problems. Although learning fundamental concepts will always be important in the science curriculum, the concepts alone are no longer sufficient in a student's scientific education.

Defining Performance Assessment

Performance assessment is based on judging the quality of a student's response to a performance task. A performance task is constructed to require the use of important concepts with supporting information, work habits important to science, and one or more of the elements of scientific literacy. The performance task attempts to put the student in a "real-world" context so that the class learning can be put to authentic uses.

Performance Assessment Is Also a Learning Activity

Performance assessment is designed to improve the student. While a traditional test is designed to take a snapshot of what the student knows, the performance task involves the student in work that actually makes the learning more meaningful and builds on the student's knowledge and skills. As a student is engaged in a performance task with performance assessment lists and examples of excellent work, both learning and assessment are occurring.

Performance Task Assessment Lists

Performance task assessment lists break the assessment criteria into several well-defined categories. Possible points for each category are assigned by the teacher. Both the teacher and the student assess the work and assign the number of points earned. The teacher is scoring not only the quality of the product, but also the quality of the student's self-assessment.

Besides using the performance task assessment list to help guide his or her work and then to self-assess it, the student needs to study examples of excellent work. These examples could come from published sources, or they could be students' work. These examples include the same type of product for different topics, but they would all be rated excellent using the assessment list for that product type.

Performance Assessment in *GLENCOE EARTH SCIENCE*

Many performance task assessment lists can be found in Glencoe's ***Performance Assessment in the Science Classroom.*** These lists were developed for the summative and skill performance tasks in the ***Performance Assessment*** book that accompanies the ***Glencoe Earth Science*** program. The ***Performance Assessment*** book contains a mix of skill assessments and summative assessments that tie together major concepts of each chapter. The lists can be used to support **MiniLABs, Activities,** and the **Performance Assessment** problems in the **Chapter Review.** Glencoe's ***Alternate Assessment in the Science Classroom*** provides additional background and examples of performance assessment. Activity sheets in the ***Activity Worksheets*** book provide yet another vehicle for formal assessment of student products. The **MindJogger Videoquiz** series offers interactive videos that provide a fun way for your students to review chapter concepts. You can extend the use of the videoquizzes by implementing them in a testing situation. Questions are at three difficulty levels: basic, intermediate, and advanced.

Assessment and Grading

Assessment is giving the learner feedback on the individual elements of his or her performance or product. Therefore, assessment provides specific information on strengths and weaknesses, and allows the student to set targets for improvement. Grading is an act to evaluate the overall quality of the performance or product according to some norms of quality. From the performance task assessment list, the student can see the quality of the pieces. The points on an assessment list can be summed and an overall grade awarded. The grade alone is not very helpful to the student, but it does describe overall quality of the performance or product. The information from both the assessment list and the grade should be reported to the student, parents, and other audiences.

Assessing Student Work with Rubrics

A rubric is a set of descriptions of the quality of a process and/or a product. The set of descriptions includes a continuum of quality from excellent to poor. Rubrics for various types of assessment products are in the Glencoe Professional Development Series booklet: ***Performance Assessment in the Science Classroom.***

When to Use the Performance Task Assessment List and When to Use the Rubric

Performance task assessment lists are used for all or most performance tasks. If a grade is also necessary, it can be derived from the total points earned on the assessment list. Rubrics are used much less often. Their best use is to help students periodically assess the overall quality of their work. After making a series of products, the student is asked how he or she is doing overall on one of these types of products. With reference to the standards of quality set for that product at that grade level, the student can decide where on the continuum of quality his or her work fits. The student is asked to assign a rubric score and explain why the score was chosen. Because the student has used a performance task assessment list to examine the elements of each of the products, he or she can justify the rubric score. Experience with performance task assessment lists comes before use of a rubric.

Group Performance Assessment

Recent research has shown that a cooperative learning environment improves student learning outcomes for students of all ability levels. ***Glencoe Earth Science*** provides many opportunities for cooperative learning and, as a result, many opportunities to observe group work processes and products. ***Glencoe Earth Science: Cooperative Learning Resource Guide*** provides strategies and resources for implementing and evaluating group activities. In cooperative group assessment, all members of the group contribute to the work process and the products it produces. For example, if a mixed-ability, four-member laboratory work group conducts an activity, you can use a rating scale or checklist to assess the quality of both group interaction and work skills. An example, along with information about evaluating cooperative work, is provided in the booklet ***Alternate Assessment in the Science Classroom.***

The Science Journal

A science journal is intended to help the student organize his or her thinking. It is not a lecture or laboratory notebook. It is a place for students to make their thinking explicit in drawings and writing. It is the place to explore what makes science fun and what makes it hard.

Portfolios: Putting It All Together

The portfolio should help the student see the "big picture" of how he or she is performing in gaining knowledge and skills and how effective his or her work habits are. The portfolio is a way for students to see how the individual performance tasks done during the year fit into a pattern that reveals the overall quality of their learning. The process of assembling the portfolio should be both integrative (of process and content) and reflective. The performance portfolio is not a complete collection of all worksheets and other assignments for a grading period. At its best, the portfolio should include integrated performance products that show growth in concept attainment and skill development.

The Portfolio: Criteria for Success

To be successful, a science portfolio should

1. improve the student's performance in science.
2. promote the student's skills of self-assessment and goal setting.
3. promote a sense of ownership and pride of accomplishment in the student.
4. be a reasonable amount of work for the teacher.
5. be highly valued by the teacher receiving the portfolio the next year.
6. be useful in parent conferences.

The Portfolio: Its Contents

Evidence of the student's growth in the following five categories should be included.

1. Range of thinking and creativity
2. Use of scientific method
3. Inventions and models
4. Connections between science and other subjects
5. Readings in science

For each of the five categories, students should make indexes that describe what they have selected for their portfolios and why. From their portfolio selections, have students pick items that show the quality of their work habits. Finally, have each student write a letter to next year's science teacher introducing him- or herself to the teacher and explaining how the work in this section shows what the student can do.

Opportunities for using Science Journals and Portfolios

Glencoe Earth Science presents a wealth of opportunities for performance portfolio development. Each chapter in the student text contains enrichment activities and connections with life, society, and literature. Each of the student activities results in a product. A mixture of these products can be used to document student growth during the grading period. Descriptions, examples, and assessment criteria for portfolios are discussed in ***Alternate Assessment in the Science Classroom.*** Glencoe's ***Performance Assessment in the Science Classroom*** contains even more information on using science journals and making portfolios. Performance task assessment lists and rubrics for both journals and portfolios are found there.

Content Assessment

While new and exciting performance skill assessments are emerging, paper-and-pencil tests are still a mainstay of student evaluation. Students must learn to conceptualize, process, and prepare for traditional content assessments. Presently and in the foreseeable future, students will be required to pass pencil-and-paper tests to exit high school and to enter college, trade schools, and other training programs.

Glencoe Earth Science contains numerous strategies and formative checkpoints for evaluating student progress toward mastery of science concepts. Throughout the chapters in the student text, **Section Wrap-up** questions and application tasks are presented. This spaced review process helps build learning bridges that allow all students to confidently progress from one lesson to the next.

For formal review that precedes the written content assessment, *Glencoe Earth Science* presents a three-page **Chapter Review** at the end of each chapter. By evaluating the student responses to this extensive review, you can determine whether any substantial reteaching is needed.

For the formal content assessment, a two-page review and a four-page chapter test are provided for each chapter in the ***Review and Assessment*** book. Using the review in a whole-class session, you can correct any misperceptions and provide closure for the text. If your individual assessment plan requires a test that differs from the chapter test in the resource package, customized tests can be easily produced using the ***Computer Test Bank.***

Cooperative Learning

What Is Cooperative Learning?

In cooperative learning, students work together in small groups to learn academic material and interpersonal skills. Group members each learn that they are responsible for accomplishing an assigned group task as well as for learning the material. Cooperative learning fosters academic, personal, and social success for all students.

Recent research shows that cooperative learning results in

- development of positive attitudes toward science and toward school.
- lower drop-out rates for at-risk students.
- building respect for others regardless of race, ethnic origin, or sex.
- increased sensitivity to and tolerance of diverse perspectives.

Establishing a Cooperative Classroom

Cooperative groups in the high school usually contain from two to five students. Heterogeneous groups that represent a mixture of abilities, genders, and ethnicity expose students to ideas different from their own and help them learn to work with different people.

Initially, cooperative learning groups should work together for only a day or two. After the students are more experienced, they can work with a group for longer periods of time. It is important to keep groups together long enough for each group to experience success and to change groups often enough that students have the opportunity to work with a variety of students.

Students must understand that they are responsible for group members learning the material. Before beginning, discuss the basic rules for effective cooperative learning: (1) listen while others are speaking, (2) respect other people and their ideas, (3) stay on tasks, and (4) be responsible for your own actions.

The *Teacher Wraparound Edition* uses the code **COOP LEARN** at the end of activities and teaching ideas where cooperative learning strategies are useful. For additional help, refer again to these pages of background information on cooperative learning.

Using Cooperative Learning Strategies

The ***Cooperative Learning Resource Guide*** of the ***Teacher Classroom Resources*** provides help for selecting cooperative learning strategies, as well as methods for troubleshooting and evaluation.

During cooperative learning activities, monitor the functioning of groups. Praise group cooperation and good use of interpersonal skills. When students are having trouble with the task, clarify the assignment, reteach, or provide background as needed. Answer questions only when no students in the group can.

Evaluating Cooperative Learning

At the close of the lesson, have groups share their products or summarize the assignment. You can evaluate group performance during a lesson by frequently asking questions to group members picked at random or having each group take a quiz together. You might have all students write papers and then choose one at random to grade. Assess individual learning by your traditional methods.

Managing Activities

In the Science Classroom

Glencoe Earth Science engages students in a variety of experiences to provide all students with an opportunity to learn by doing. The many hands-on activities throughout *Glencoe Earth Science* require simple, common materials, making them easy to set up and manage in the classroom.

MiniLAB

MiniLABs are intended to be short and occur many times throughout the text. The integration of these activities with the core material provides for thorough development and reinforcement of concepts.

Design Your Own Experiment

What makes science exciting to students is working in the lab, observing natural phenomena, and tackling concrete problems that challenge them to find their own answers. *Glencoe Earth Science* provides more than the same "cookbook" activities you've seen hundreds of times before. Students work cooperatively to develop their own experimental designs in **Design Your Own Experiments.** They discover firsthand that developing procedures for studying a problem is not as hard as they thought it might be. Watch your students grow in confidence and ability as they progress through the self-directed **Design Your Own Experiments.**

Preparing Students for Open-Ended Lab Experiences

To prepare students for the **Design Your Own Experiments,** you should follow the guidelines in the ***Teacher Wraparound Edition,*** especially in the sections titled Possible Procedures and Teaching Strategies. In these sections, you will be given information about what demonstrations to do and what questions to ask students so that they will be able to design their experiment. Your introduction to a **Design Your Own Experiment** will be very different from traditional activity introductions in that it will be designed to focus students on the problem and stimulate their thinking without giving them directions for how to set up their experiment. Different groups of students will develop alternative hypotheses and alternative procedures. Check their procedures before they begin. In contrast to some "cookbook" activities, there may not be just one right answer. Finally, students should be encouraged to use questions that come up during the activity in designing a new experiment.

If you feel that your students are not prepared to begin designing experiments, you may want to practice some paper-and-pencil lab designs using the following format: Select a simple scenario and ask students to design an experiment that will test a hypothesis they make about the problem presented in the reading. Give them a set of questions that will lead them to an appropriate experimental design.

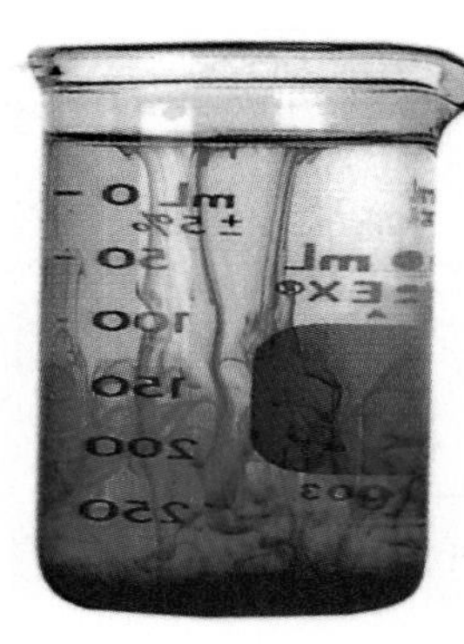

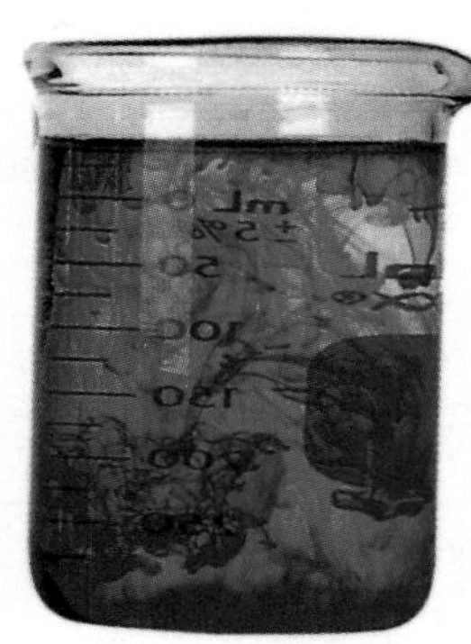

Laboratory Safety

Safety is of prime importance in every classroom. However, the need for safety is even greater when science is taught. The activities in ***Glencoe Earth Science*** are designed to minimize dangers in the laboratory. Even so, there are no guarantees against accidents. Careful planning and preparation as well as being aware of hazards can keep accidents to a minimum. Numerous books and pamphlets are available on laboratory safety with detailed instructions on preventing accidents. In addition, the ***Glencoe Earth Science*** program provides safety guidelines in several forms. The ***Lab and Safety Skills*** booklet contains detailed guidelines, in addition to masters you can use to test students' lab and safety skills. The ***Student Edition*** and ***Teacher Wraparound Edition*** provide safety precautions and symbols designed to alert students to possible dangers. Know the rules of safety and what common violations occur. Know the **Safety Symbols** used in this book. Know where emergency equipment is stored and how to use it. Practice good laboratory housekeeping and management to ensure the safety of your students.

Disposal Alert This symbol appears when care must be taken to dispose of materials properly.	**Animal Safety** This symbol appears whenever live animals are studied and the safety of the animals and the students must be ensured.
Biological Hazard This symbol appears when there is danger involving bacteria, fungi, or protists.	**Radioactive Safety** This symbol appears when radioactive materials are used.
Open Flame Alert This symbol appears when use of an open flame could cause a fire or an explosion.	**Clothing Protection Safety** This symbol appears when substances used could stain or burn clothing.
Thermal Safety This symbol appears as a reminder to use caution when handling hot objects.	**Fire Safety** This symbol appears when care should be taken around open flames.
Sharp Object Safety This symbol appears when a danger of cuts or punctures caused by the use of sharp objects exists.	**Explosion Safety** This symbol appears when the misuse of chemicals could cause an explosion.
Fume Safety This symbol appears when chemicals or chemical reactions could cause dangerous fumes.	**Eye Safety** This symbol appears when a danger to the eyes exists. Safety goggles should be worn when this symbol appears.
Electrical Safety This symbol appears when care should be taken using electrical equipment.	**Poison Safety** This symbol appears when poisonous substances are used.
Plant Safety This symbol appears when poisonous plants or plants with thorns are handled.	**Chemical Safety** This symbol appears when chemicals used can cause burns or are poisonous if absorbed through the skin.

Preparation of Solutions

It is most important to use safe laboratory techniques when handling all chemicals. Many substances may appear harmless but are, in fact, toxic, corrosive, or very reactive. Always check with the manufacturer or with Flinn Scientific, Inc., (312) 879-6900. Chemicals should never be ingested. Be sure to use proper techniques to smell solutions or other agents. Always wear safety goggles and an apron. The following general cautions should be used.

1. Poisonous/corrosive liquid and/or vapor. Use in the fume hood. Examples: ***acetic acid, hydrochloric acid, ammonia hydroxide, nitric acid.***
2. Poisonous and corrosive to eyes, lungs, and skin. Examples: ***acids, limewater, iron(III) chloride, bases, silver nitrate, iodine, potassium permanganate.***
3. Poisonous if swallowed, inhaled, or absorbed through the skin. Examples: ***glacial acetic acid, copper compounds, barium chloride, lead compounds, chromium compounds, lithium compounds, cobalt(II) chloride, silver compounds.***
4. Always add acids to water, never the reverse.
5. When sulfuric acid or sodium hydroxide is added to water, a large amount of thermal energy is released. Sodium metal reacts violently with water. Use extra care when handling any of these substances.

Unless otherwise specified, solutions are prepared by adding the solid to a small amount of distilled water and then diluting with water to the volume listed. For example, to make a 0.1M solution of aluminum sulfate, dissolve 34.2 g of $Al_2(SO_4)_3$ in a small amount of distilled water and dilute to a liter with water. If you use a hydrate that is different from the one specified in a particular preparation, you will need to adjust the amount of the hydrate to obtain the required concentration.

Chemical Storage & Disposal

General Guidelines

Be sure to store all chemicals properly. The following are guidelines commonly used. Your school, city, county, or state may have additional requirements for handling chemicals. It is the responsibility of each teacher to become informed as to what rules or guidelines are in effect in his or her area.

1. Separate chemicals by reaction type. Strong acids should be stored together. Likewise, strong bases should be stored together and should be separated from acids. Oxidants should be stored away from easily oxidized materials, and so on.
2. Be sure all chemicals are stored in labeled containers indicating contents, concentration, source, date purchased (or prepared), any precautions for handling and storage, and expiration date.
3. Dispose of any outdated or waste chemicals properly according to accepted disposal procedures.
4. Do not store chemicals above eye level.
5. Wood shelving is preferable to metal. All shelving should be firmly attached to the wall and should have antiroll edges.
6. Store only those chemicals that you plan to use.
7. Hazardous chemicals require special storage containers and conditions. Be sure to know what those chemicals are and the accepted practices for your area. Some substances must even be stored outside the building.
8. When working with chemicals or preparing solutions, observe the same general safety precautions that you would expect from students. These include wearing an apron and goggles. Wear gloves and use the fume hood when necessary. Students will want to do as you do whether they admit it or not.
9. If you are a new teacher in a particular laboratory, it is your responsibility to survey the chemicals stored there and to be sure they are stored properly or disposed of. Consult the rules and laws in your area concerning what chemicals can be kept in your classroom. For disposal, consult up-to-date disposal information from the state and federal governments.

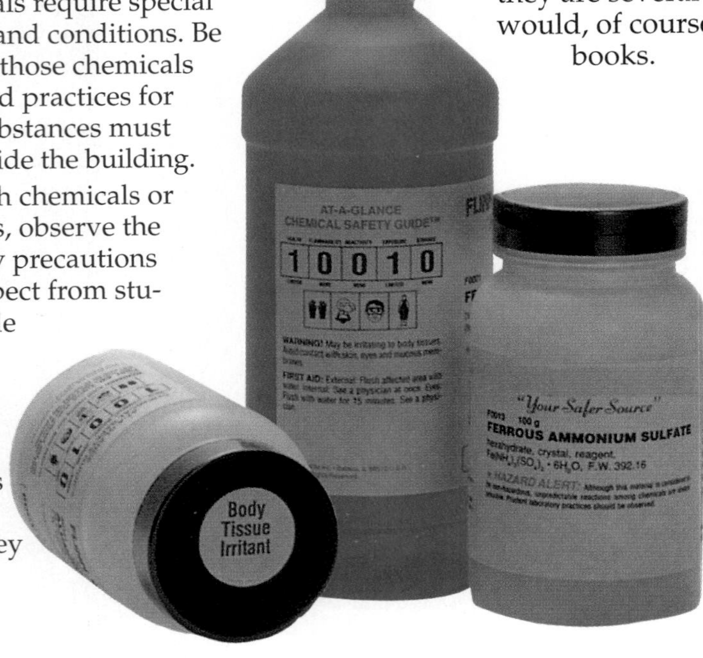

Disposal of Chemicals

Local, state, and federal laws regulate the proper disposal of chemicals. These laws should be consulted before chemical disposal is attempted. Although most substances encountered in high school biology can be flushed down the drain with plenty of water, it is not safe to assume that this is always true. It is recommended that teachers who use chemicals consult the following books from the National Research Council:

Prudent Practices for Handling Hazardous Chemicals in Laboratories. Washington, DC: National Academy Press, 1981.

Prudent Practices for Disposal of Chemicals from Laboratories. Washington, DC: National Academy Press, 1983.

These books are useful and still in print, although they are several years old. Current laws in your area would, of course, supersede the information in these books.

Disclaimer

Glencoe Publishing Company makes no claims to the completeness of this discussion of laboratory safety and chemical storage. The material presented is not all-inclusive, nor does it address all of the hazards associated with handling, storage, and disposal of chemicals, or with laboratory management.

Activity Materials

Get the materials you need quickly and easily!

Glencoe and Science Kit, Inc. have teamed up to make materials selection for *Glencoe Earth Science* easier with an activity materials folder. This folder contains two convenient ways to order materials and equipment for the program: the **Activity Plan Checklist** and the **Activity Materials List** master.

Call Science Kit at 1-800-828-7777 to get your folder.

Materials Support Provided By:
Science Kit® & Boreal®Laboratories
Your Classroom Resource
777 East Park Drive
Tonawanda, NY 14150-6784
800-828-7777 Fax 716-874-9572

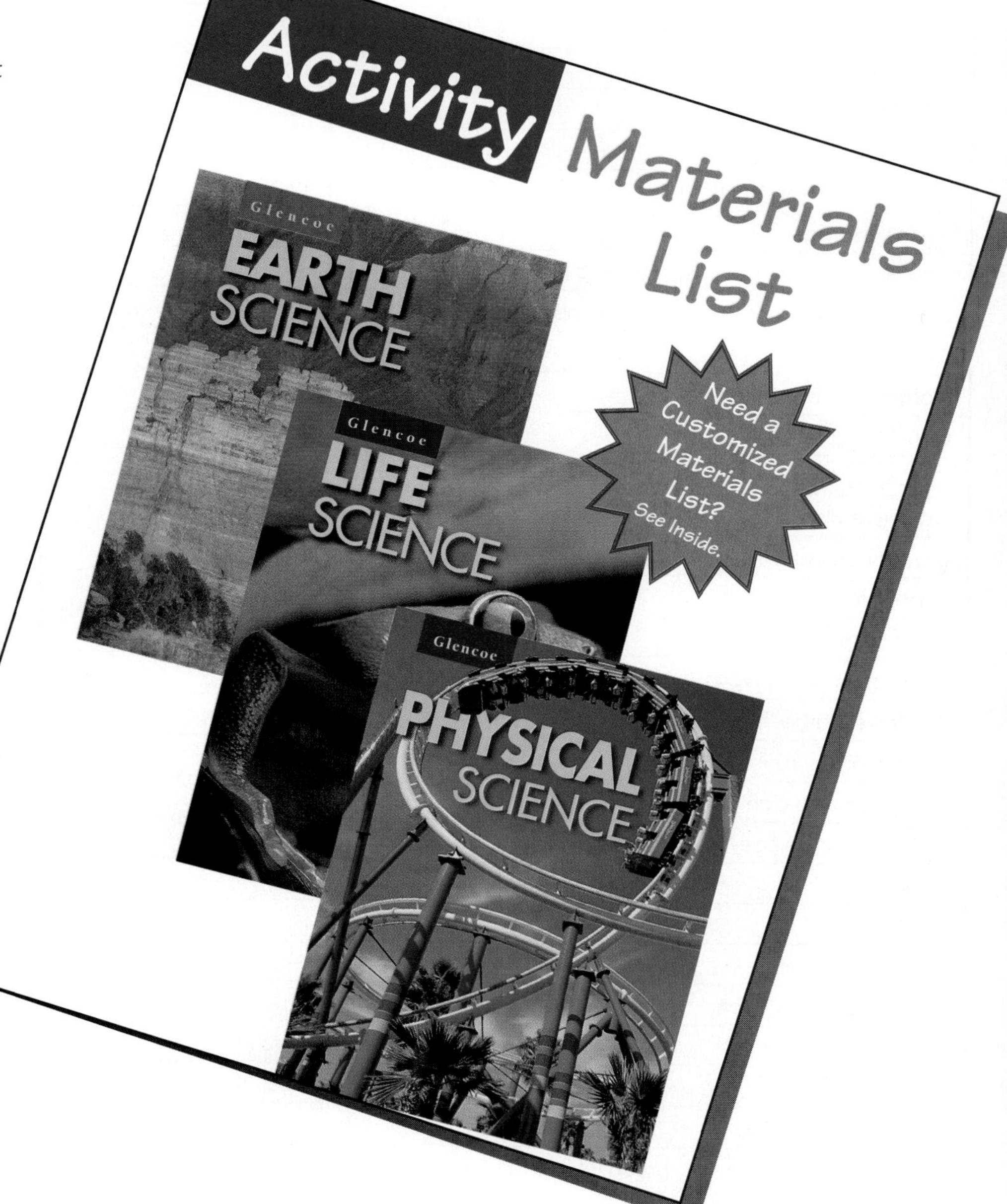

Non-Consumables

Item	Activity	MiniLAB	Explore
Apron	16-1, 18-2		
Aquarium, (2) identical, 1 with lid	16-2		
Balance	1-1, 2-1, 2-2, 3-2, 17-1	397, 541	
Ball, deflated		397	
Beaker(s), 100-mL	2-2		
Beaker(s), 250-mL	5-1, 6-1, 6-2, 15-1, 19-1	206, 216	
Beaker(s), 250-mL, glass		412	
Beaker(s), 500-mL	17-1		
Beaker(s), 500-mL (2)			477
Bottle(s), clear, plastic 2-L (2)			421
Bottle(s), clear, plastic 2-L, with cap	19-2		503
Bowl, mixing	7-2		
Box(es), clear, plastic (2)	14-2		
Box(es), shoe with lid (1)	12-2		
Box(es), storage, clear plastic		492, 493	
Box(es), storage, clear plastic with lid (1)	5-1	486	
Calcite, transparent, rectangular samples		69	
Calculator		378, 656	
Camera, instant (with film)	21-2		
Can, large coffee	16-1		
Can, shiny metal		425	
Casserole dish, clear		310	
Clay, modeling	2-2	296	235, 265
Clipboard	24-2		
Cloth bags, heavy	21-2	87	
Clothespin, spring-type			671
Container, large, to collect rain or snow			557
Container, 16-ounce, plastic			31
Cooking pot or pan	20-1		
Copper, small pieces	3-2	40	
Cork, small	2-2, 8-1	492	
Coverslip		513	
Cup, small, plastic			61
Dissecting probe or pin		284	
Dropper	18-2	572	201, 503, 513
Fan, electric, 3-speed	17-2		
Fasteners, brass (100)	12-2		
Filters, gelatin or Plexiglas®, green, red, and blue			583

Item	Activity	MiniLAB	Explore
Flashlight(s) (1)	21-1	453	
Flashlight(s), identical (3)			583
Flask, 1000-mL, with 1-hole rubber stopper	17-1		
"Fossils" such as feathers, shells, plastic plants and animals, bones		296	325
Freezer		49	
Garbage bag, small (~13-L)		541	
Glass, small		486	
Glass, small, filled with water	21-1		
Glass tubing bent at right angle	17-1		
Globe	2-1, 9-1, 22-2	453, 613	
Globe or atlas			451
Globe or world map		378	119
Goggles, safety	3-1, 3-2, 4-1, 4-2, 6-1, 6-2, 7-2, 12-2, 13-2, 16-1, 17-1, 18-2, 20-1, 24-1		265, 391
Graduated cylinder, 100-mL	1-1, 2-1, 3-2, 6-1, 6-2	49, 216	265
Graduated cylinder, 250-mL	2-2		
Gypsum, transparent, rectangular pieces		69	
Hair dryer	7-2		
Halite, transparent, rectangular pieces		69	
Hammer, rock		87	
Hand lens	3-1, 3-2, 4-1, 4-2, 6-2, 15-2	284, 464	
Hand pump with pressure gauge		397	
Hot plate	3-1, 6-1, 17-1, 20-1	310	391
Iron nail, small	3-2		
Jar(s), baby food, with lids (4)		572	
Jar(s), tall widemouthed (1)		430	
Lamp, gooseneck with 75-watt bulb	22-1		
Light source	17-2		
Light source, overhead with reflector	7-1, 14-2		
Light source, without a shade or reflector	22-2		613
Magnet(s)	8-2		
Magnet(s), bar	11-1		
Magnetic compasses, small (2)	11-1		
Magnifying glass	21-1		
Magnifying glass or stereomicroscope		190	
Marbles		606	
Marbles and lead weights, nuts and bolts			639
Marker, permanent	20-1		31, 671
Marker, transparency, fine-point	5-1, 5-2, 11-1	695	

Non-Consumables

Item	Activity	MiniLAB	Explore
Mathematical compass		656, 695	
Measuring cup			31
Metal block, small	2-2		
Meterstick(s)	2-1, 8-1, 13-2, 23-2, 24-1	615, 695	
Metric measuring tape		378, 613	
Metric ruler	5-1, 5-2, 6-1, 7-1, 7-2, 9-1, 11-1, 11-2, 13-2, 14-2, 17-2, 23-1, 24-1	206, 464, 656, 681, 695	355, 531, 639, 671
Microscope		513	555
Microscope or magnifying glass		64, 157	
Microscope slide, glass	3-2	513	555
Mineral samples	3-2		
Mirrors, concave, convex, and plain (1 of each)	21-1		
Model landform, plastic	5-1		
Mohs' scale of hardness	3-2		
Mortar and pestle		87	
Motor oil, used	18-2		
Muscovite, thin "books"		69	
Pails, plastic (2)	8-1		
Pan(s), cake			639
Pan(s), flat (4)	7-2		
Pan(s), flat, shallow (1)	17-1, 18-2	87, 151	61
Pan(s), large, rectangular (1)		206	
Pan(s), shallow (2)	3-1		
Paper, green construction			355
Paper clips, small (100)	12-2		
Paper clips, or dried beans	19-1		
Pen, blue		675	
Pen, marking	4-2		
Pennies (100)	12-2		
Phonograph record, LP		606	
Pipe cleaners (100)	12-2		
Pipet			477
Playing cards (1 deck)	13-1		
Polystyrene ball	22-2		
Projector, overhead	5-2		
Protractor	22-1	281	
Psychrometer	16-1		
Quartz, small piece	2-2		

Item	Activity	MiniLAB	Explore
Refrigerator	20-1		
Remote-controlled car	21-2		
Ring stand	14-2		
Ring stand, with clamp	17-2		
Rock specimen(s), igneous (9)	4-1		
Rock specimen(s), large (~ 30 cm in diameter)	21-2		
Rock specimen(s), metamorphic and their corresponding parent rocks (8 rocks total)		99	
Rock specimen(s), sedimentary, unknown	4-2		
Rock specimen(s), several igneous, sedimentary, and metamorphic		87	85, 147
Rock specimen(s), small	1-1, 2-1, 2-2		
Rubber band(s)	6-2, 14-1, 19-2	256	
Rubber tubing	8-1, 17-1		
Sand from volcanic beaches		284	
Scissors	6-2, 13-2, 14-1, 17-1, 23-2, 24-2	606	293, 355
Scissors or razor knife	5-2		
Screen, portable	21-2		
Sediment samples		102	
Self-sealing bag, small plastic		430	
Shoe box lid, large			171
Shoes (tennis, baseball, golf, hiking boots, etc.) with a variety of different soles			5
Sponge	2-2		
Spoon, aluminum or silver	21-1		
Spoon, plastic	17-1	492	
Spray bottle		176	
Sprinkling can	7-2		
Steel file	3-2		147
Stereomicroscope	8-2, 20-1	284	
Stick or dowel	2-1		
Stirrer		281	61
Stopwatch or clock with second hand	6-2, 8-1, 17-2, 19-1, 21-2, 22-1		355
Stove			31
Streak plate	3-2		
Stream table	7-1		
Stream table or large pan	8-1		
String	2-1, 9-1		671
String, ~ 1 m in length		65	
Teapot			31

Non-Consumables

Item	Activity	MiniLAB	Explore
Teaspoon		486	265
Telescope, refracting (small)	24-2		
Test-tube(s), large (1)	3-1		
Test-tube rack	3-1		
Thermal mitt	3-1, 6-1, 14-2, 17-1, 20-1, 22-1	310	391
Thermometer, Celsius	19-2, 22-1	425	
Thermometer, Celsius, (2) identical	2-1, 15-1		
Thermometer, Celsius, (3) identical	16-2		
Thermometer, Celsius, (4) identical	14-2, 16-1		
Thumbtacks	6-2		
Thumbtacks or pins	23-1		
Towel, cloth, small	17-1		
Towel, cloth, white			555
Transparency	5-1, 5-2		
Tripod, small	24-2		
Turntable		606	
Tweezers		284	355
Tweezers or dissecting probe		102	
Volcanic debris (pumice, obsidian, ash, scoria, and basalt)		284	
Water meter at home	20-2		
Weight, heavy		87	
Wind sock or paper strip	16-1		
Wood, cross section showing growth rings		464	
Wood block(s), building type		256	
Wood block(s), large	7-1		
Wood block(s), small	2-2, 8-1		
World map		127	293
World map, showing latitude and longitude lines	10-1		
Yarn, green, orange, and blue			355

Consumables

Item	Activity	MiniLAB	Explore
Adding machine tape	13-2, 23-2		
Baking soda			265
Balloon, large round	14-1		671
Can, small coffee	14-1		
Can, small metal with cap			391
Candle	21-1		
Cardboard, 5 cm × 5 cm piece	3-1		
Cardboard, 21.5 cm × 28 cm piece	23-1		
Cardboard, 50 cm × 60 cm piece	21-1		
Cardboard, corrugated sheets or foam board	5-2		
Cardboard, large sheet	15-1, 17-1, 18-2, 24-2		
Cardboard, large sheets (4)	7-2		
Cardboard milk carton, small			325
Chalk		681	
Chalk, identical pieces (6)	6-1		
Chalk, or water-soluble marker	9-1		
Cheesecloth, 10 cm × 10 cm squares	6-2		
Clay, powdered, 400 mL	7-2		
Coffee can lids, plastic, or margarine tub lids (4)	20-1		
Coffee can lids, plastic, small (3)	6-2		
Cotton balls	18-2		
Cups, large polystyrene or plastic (3)	6-2		
Feathers	18-2		
Flour, white			639
Food coloring		310, 412, 486	477
Garbage (food scraps, yard wastes, small piece of plastic, small metal item, foam cup, paper or newsprint)	19-2		
Gauze, 2-cm square	15-1		
Gelatin, dry, different colors			639
Gelatin, plain, small box	20-1		
Glue, white, all-purpose	5-2	87	
Gravel	6-2, 18-2	176, 216	171
Gravel, 400 mL	7-2		
Ice, block containing sand, clay, and gravel	7-1		
Ice, crushed	17-1	425, 430	477
Ice, cubes		40, 412	
Newspaper			265
Paper, sheet(s) of, black construction	22-1		

Consumables

Item	Activity	MiniLAB	Explore
Paper, sheet(s) of, construction	14-1	606	
Paper, sheet(s) of, graph	9-1, 12-2, 18-1, 19-2	287	
Paper, sheet(s) of, graph, metric	1-1		
Paper, sheet(s) of, plain white	5-2, 6-2, 11-1, 16-1, 17-2	102, 122, 284, 675	147, 531, 583
Paper, sheet(s) of, plain white, large	24-2	656, 695	
Paper, sheet(s) of, tracing	10-1		293
Paper plates, large		281	
Paper towel roll, empty	21-1	593	
Paper towels	4-2, 18-2	425	265
Pencil(s)	5-2, 6-2, 13-2, 23-1, 23-2, 24-1	206, 656	531
Pencils, colored	12-2, 13-2, 14-2		
Petroleum jelly			325
pH ion paper and pH chart			557
Plaster of paris		281	325
Plastic wrap	19-2		
Salt, table	3-1, 17-1	40, 64, 486	61
Sand	6-2, 7-1, 8-1	40, 176, 216	171
Sand, beach, 3 different types	8-2		
Sand, fine, 400 mL	7-2		
Sand or cereal		281	
Soap, dishwashing	18-2	572	421
Soil sample(s)	6-2	157, 206	
Soil sample(s), clay-rich	6-2		
Soil sample(s), dark-colored	14-2		
Soil sample(s), dry	19-2		201
Sponge	18-2		
Steel wool (without soap)		151	
Straw, drinking	14-1		
String	18-2, 23-1, 23-2		
String, cotton	3-1, 15-1		
String, 125-cm long		681	
Sugar, granulated	3-1	40	
Tape, duct			421
Tape, masking	5-1, 7-2, 11-1, 14-2, 15-1, 21-1, 22-1, 24-1	49, 492, 606	
Tape, transparent	14-1		
Toothpicks	3-1, 18-2		
Vinegar, white	6-1		265

Item	Activity	MiniLAB	Explore
Water, hot		412, 430	
Water, muddy		40	
Water, ocean or fresh, containing plankton		513	
Water, pond		572	
Water, room temperature		425	
Water, stream		572	
Water, tap	1-1, 2-1, 2-2, 3-2, 4-2, 6-1, 6-2, 7-2, 8-1, 14-2, 15-1, 17-1, 17-2, 18-2, 20-1	40, 49, 87, 151, 176, 216, 281, 310, 486, 492, 572	31, 201, 325, 391, 421, 503
Water, tap, tinted with food coloring	5-1		
Water, warm tap			61, 477
Water, well		572	
Waxed paper		87	201

Chemical Supplies

Item	Activity	MiniLAB	Explore
Glycerin	17-1		
Hydrochloric acid, 5%, with dropper	3-2, 4-2		
Salt water	3-1	40	
Sugar solution	3-1		

Student Bibliography

General Science Content

Binkerhoff, Richard F. *One-Minute Readings: Issues in Science, Technology, and Society.* Menlo Park, CA: Addison-Wesley, 1992.

Cash, Terry. *175 More Science Experiments to Amuse and Amaze Your Friends: Experiments! Tricks! Things to Make!* New York: Random House, 1991.

Churchill, E. Richard. *Amazing Science Experiments with Everyday Materials.* New York: Sterling Publishing Co., Inc., 1991.

Lewis, James. *Hocus Pocus Stir and Cook, The Kitchen Science-Magic Book.* New York: Meadowbrook Press, Division of Simon and Shuster, Inc., 1991.

Mandell, Muriel. *Simple Science Experiments with Everyday Materials.* New York: Sterling Publishing Co., Inc., 1989.

Roberts, Royston. *Serendipity: Accidental Discoveries in Science.* New York: John Wiley and Sons, Inc., 1989.

Strongin, Herb. *Science on a Shoestring.* Menlo Park, CA: Addison-Wesley Publishing Co., 1985.

Physics

Aronson, Billy. "Water Ride Designers Are Making Waves," *3-2-1 Contact,* Aug. 1991, pp. 14-16.

Hajda, Joey and Lisa B. Hajda. "Sparking Interest in Electricity," *Science Scope,* Nov./Dec. 1994, pp. 36-39.

Hardy, John W. "Adaptive Optics," *Scientific American,* June 1994, pp. 60-65.

Heiligman, Deborah. "There's a Lot More to Color Than Meets the Eye," *3-2-1 Contact,* Nov. 1991, pp. 16-20.

Lipkin, R. "Metal Dendrites Sprout in Microgravity," *Science News,* Dec. 1994, p. 375.

McGrath, Susan. *Fun with Physics.* Washington, DC: National Geographic Society, 1986.

Raskin, Jef. "Foiled by the Coanda Effect," *Quantum,* Sept./Oct. 1994, pp. 5-11.

Terres, John K. *How Birds Fly.* Mechanicsburg, PA: Stackpole Books, 1994.

Ward, Allen. *Experimenting with Batteries, Bulbs, and Wires.* New York: Chelsea House, 1991.

Chemistry

Barber, Jacqueline. *Chemical Reactions.* Washington, DC: Lawrence Hall of Science, NSTA, 1986.

Barber, Jacqueline. *Of Cabbage and Chemistry.* Washington, DC: Lawrence Hall of Science, NSTA, 1989.

Benrey, Ronald. *Alternative Energy Sources: Experiments You Can Do...from Edison.* Washington, DC: Thomas Alva Edison Foundation, Edison Electric Institute, 1988.

Cornell, John. *Experiments with Mixtures.* New York: Wiley, John and Sons, Inc., 1990.

Zubrewski, Bernie. *Messing Around with Baking Chemistry: A Children's Museum Activity Book.* Boston, MA: Little Brown and Co., 1981.

Biology

Ashworth, William. *The Encyclopedia of Environmental Studies.* New York: Facts on File, 1991.

Bombaugh, Ruth. *Science Fair Success.* Hillside, NJ: Enslow Publishers, 1990.

Dewey, Jennifer Owings. *A Day and Night in the Desert.* Boston, MA: Little, Brown, 1991.

Leslie, Clare Walker. *Nature All Year Long.* New York: Greenwillow, 1990.

Markmann, Erika. *Grow It! An Indoor/Outdoor Gardening Guide for Kids.* New York: Random House, 1991.

McGrath, Susan. *The Amazing Things Animals Do.* Washington DC: National Geographic Society, 1989.

Nilsson, Lennant. *The Body Victorious.* New York: Delacorte Press, 1987.

Palca, Joe. "The Promise of a Cure," *Discover,* June 1994, pp. 76-86.

Stevenson, L. Harold. *The Facts on File Dictionary of Environmental Science.* New York: Facts on File, 1991.

Thorn-Miller, B. and John Catena. *The Living Ocean: Understanding and Protecting Marine Diversity.* Washington, DC: Island Press, 1991.

Earth Science

Ardley, Neil. *The Science Book of Air.* New York: Gulliver Books, Harcourt, Brace, Jovanovich, Publishers, 1991.

Ardley, Neil. *The Science Book of Water.* New York: Gulliver Books, Harcourt, Brace, Jovanovich, Publishers, 1991.

Barrow, Lloyd H. *Adventures with Rocks and Minerals: Geology Experiments for Young People.* Hillsdale, NJ: Enslow, 1991.

Booth, Basil. *Volcanoes and Earthquakes.* Englewood Cliffs, NJ: Silver Burdett Press, 1991.

Javna, John. *50 Simple Things Kids Can Do to Save the Earth.* Kansas City: The Earth Works Group, Andrews and McMeel, a Universal Press Syndicate Co., 1990.

VanCleave, Janice. *Earth Science for Every Kid.* New York: John Wiley and Sons, Inc., 1991.

Wood, Robert W. *Science for Kids: 39 Easy Geology Activities.* Blue Ridge Summit, PA: Tab Books, 1992.

Teacher Bibliography

Curriculum

Aldridge, William G. "Scope, Sequence, and Coordination: A New Synthesis for Improving Science Education," *Journal of Science Education and Technology.*

Banks, James A. "Multicultural Education: For Freedom's Sake," *Educational Leadership,* Dec. 1991/Jan. 1992, pp. 32-35.

Beane, James A. "Middle School, The Natural Home of the Integrated Curriculum," *Educational Leadership,* Oct. 1991, pp. 9-13.

Chemistry of Life: 1988 Curriculum Module. Princeton, NJ: Woodrow Wilson National Fellowship Foundation, 1988.

Driver, R. *The Children's Learning in Science Project, Monographs on Preconceptions in Science.* Leeds, England: Center for Studies in Science and Mathematics Education, University of Leeds, 1984-1989.

Hazen, Robert M. and James Trefil. *Science Matters: Achieving Scientific Literacy.* New York: Doubleday, 1991.

Philips, William. "Earth Science Misconceptions," *The Science Teacher,* Oct. 1991, pp. 21-23.

Piaget, J. *To Understand Is to Invent: The Future of Education.* New York: Grossman Publishers, 1973.

Rutherford, E. James and Andrew Ahlgren. *Science for All Americans.* New York: Oxford University Press, 1990.

Teaching Methods

Altshular, Kenneth. "The Interdisciplinary Classroom," *The Physics Teacher,* Oct. 1991, pp. 428-429.

Hart, Diane. *Authentic Assessment: A Handbook for Educators.* Menlo Park, CA: Addison-Wesley, 1994.

Humphreys, David. *Demonstrating Chemistry.* Hamilton, Ontario: McMaster University, 1983.

Johnson, David W. and Roger T. Johnson. *Cooperative Learning: Warm-Ups, Grouping Strategies, and Group Activities.* Edina, MN: Interaction Book Company, 1985.

Johnson, David W., Roger T. Johnson, and Edythe Johnson Holubec. *Circles of Learning.* Edina, MN: Interaction Book Company, 1990.

Johnson, David W., Roger T. Johnson, and Edythe Johnson Holubec. *Cooperation in the Classroom.* Edina, MN: Interaction Book Company, 1991.

Kahle, Jane Butler. "Why Girls Don't Know," *What Research Says to the Science Teacher—The Process of Knowing,* Vol. 6, 1990, pp. 55-67.

Novak, Joseph. "Clarify with Concept Maps," *The Science Teacher,* Oct. 1991, pp. 44-49.

Penick, John. "Where's the Science?" *The Science Teacher,* May 1991, pp. 27-29.

Content Area Books

Physics

Arons, A.B. *A Guide to Introductory Physics Teaching.* New York: John Wiley and Sons, 1990.

Carpenter, D. Rae, Jr. and Richard B. Minnix. *The Dick and Rae Physics Demo Notebook.* Lexington, VA: DICK and RAE Inc., 1993.

Seeds, M.A. *Horizons: Exploring the Universe.* Belmont, CA: Wadsworth, 1995.

Urone, Paul Peter. *Physics with Health Science Applications.* New York: Harper and Row Publishers, 1986.

Walpole, Brenda. *175 Science Experiments to Amuse and Amaze Your Friends.* New York: Random House, 1988.

Chemistry

Element of the Week. Batavia, IL: Flinn Scientific, Inc., 1990.

Ground to Grits: Scientific Concepts in Nutrition/Agriculture. Columbia, SC: South Carolina Department of Education, 1982.

Joesten, Melvin. *World of Chemistry.* Philadelphia, PA: Saunders College Publishing, 1991.

Mitchell, Sharon and Frederick Juergens. *Laboratory Solutions for the Science Classroom.* Batavia, IL: Flinn Scientific, Inc., 1991.

Solomon, Sally. "Qualitative Analysis of Eleven Household Compounds," *Journal of Chemical Education,* April 1991, pp. 328-329.

Biology

Benenson, Abram, ed. *Control of Communicable Diseases in Man.* Washington, DC: American Public Health Association, 1990.

Enger, Eldon and Bradley Smith. *Environmental Science: A Study of Interrelationships.* Dubuque, IA: W.C. Brown Publishing, 1991.

Grimes, Deanna. *Infectious Diseases.* Mosby Yearbook, Clinical Nursing Series. St. Louis: Mosby, 1991.

Hancock, Judith M. *Variety of Life: A Biology Teacher's Sourcebook.* Portland, OR: J. Weston Walch, 1987.

Middleton, James I. "Student-Generated Analogies in Biology," *American Biology Teacher,* Jan. 1991, pp. 42-46.

Earth Science

Lasca, Norman P. "Build Me a River," *Earth,* Jan. 1991, pp. 59-65.

Sae, Andy S. W. "Dynamic Demos," *The Science Teacher,* Oct. 1991, pp. 23-25.

Supplier Addresses

Audio-Visual Suppliers

Ambrose Video Publishing, Inc.
Exclusive Distributor of Time-Life Videos
28 West 44th Street, Suite 2100
New York, NY 10036
(800) 526-4663

Barr Media Group
12801 Schabarum Avenue
Irwindale, CA 91706
(800) 234-7878

Center for the Humanities
Box 1000
90 S. Bedford Road
Communications Park
Mount Kisco, NY 10549
(800) 431-1242

Clearvue, Inc.
6465 N. Avondale Avenue
Chicago, IL 60631
(800) 253-2788

Coronet/MTI Film and Video
4350 Equity Drive
Columbus, OH 43228
(800) 777-2400

Education Development Center
55 Chapel Street
Newton, MA 02158
(800) 225-4276

Educational Activities, Inc.
P.O. Box 392
Freeport, NY 11520
(800) 645-3739

Encyclopaedia Britannica Educational Corp.
310 South Michigan Avenue
Chicago, IL 60604
(800) 323-1229

Films, Inc.
5547 North Ravenswood Ave.
Chicago, IL 60640
(800) 343-4312

Handel Film Corp.
8787 Shoreham Drive
Los Angeles, CA 90069
(800) 395-8990

Hawkhill Associates
125 East Gilman Street
P.O. Box 1029
Madison, WI 53701
(800) 422-4295

International Film Bureau
332 S. Michigan Ave., Ste. 450
Chicago, IL 60604-4382
(800) 432-2241

JCE Software
Department of Chemistry
University of Wisconsin-Madison
1101 University Avenue
Madison, WI 53706
(608) 263-2837

Mindscape, Inc.
Educational Division
88 Rowland Way
Novato, CA 94945
(800) 866-5967

National Geographic Society
Educational Services
1145 17th Street, N.W.
Washington, DC 20036-4688
(800) 647-5463

Optical Data Corp.
30 Technology Drive
Warren, NJ 07059
(800) 248-8478

Pyramid Films
P.O. Box 1048
Santa Monica, CA 90406
(800) 421-2304

TVOntario
1140 Kildare Farm Road
Suite 308
Cary, NC 27511
(800) 331-9566

Videodiscovery
1700 Westlake Ave. N., Ste. 600
Seattle, WA 98109-3012
(800) 548-3472

Ward's Natural Science Intl., Inc.
Source of CHEM Study Films
P.O. Box 92912
Rochester, NY 14692
(800) 962-2660

University Rental Services

Indiana University
Instructional Support Services
Bloomington, IN 47405-5901
(800) 552-8620

Kent State University
Audio-Visual Services
330 University Library
Kent, OH 44242
(800) 338-5718

SUNY College at Buffalo
Butler Library Media Services
Bonita J. Percival
1300 Elmwood Avenue
Buffalo, NY 14222-1095
(716) 878-6682

Washington State University
Instructional Support Services
Pullman, WA 99164-5604
(509) 335-7336

Software Suppliers

Agency for Instructional Technology (AIT)
Box A
Bloomington, IN 47402-0120
(800) 457-4509

American Chemical Society
1155 16th Street NW
Washington, DC 20036
(800) 227-5558

Bergwall Productions, Inc.
540 Baltimore Pike
P.O. Box 2400
Chadds Ford, PA 19317
(800) 645-3565

Carolina Biological Supply Co.
2700 York Road
Burlington, NC 27215
(800) 334-5551

Cross Educational Software
P.O. Box 1536
508 E. Kentucky Avenue
Ruston, LA 71270
(800) 768-1969

Educational Images, Ltd.
P.O. Box 3456, West Side
Elmira, NY 14905
(800) 527-4264

Educational Materials and Equipment Co. (EME)
P.O. Box 2805
Danbury, CT 06813-2805
(800) 848-2050

Focus Media, Inc.
63 Commercial Avenue
Garden City, NY 11530
(516) 248-1888

IBM Educational Systems
Department PC
4111 Northside Parkway
Atlanta, GA 30327
(800) 426-9920

J and S Software
P.O. Box 1276
Port Washington, NY 11050
(800) 767-8696

Merlan Scientific, Ltd.
247 Armstrong Avenue
Georgetown, Ontario,
Canada L7G 4X6
(800) 387-2474

Minnesota Educational Computing Corp. (MECC)
6160 Summit Drive
Minneapolis, MN 55430
(800) 685-6322

Project Seraphim
Department of Chemistry
University of Wisconsin-Madison
1101 University Avenue
Madison, WI 53706
(608) 263-2837

Queue, Inc.
338 Commerce Drive
Fairfield, CT 06432
(800) 232-2224

Sunburst Communications
39 Washington Avenue
Pleasantville, NY 10570
(800) 431-1934

Glencoe

EARTH SCIENCE

McGraw-Hill

New York, New York   Columbus, Ohio   Mission Hills, California   Peoria, Illinois

A GLENCOE PROGRAM

Glencoe Earth Science

Student Edition
Teacher Wraparound Edition
Study Guide SE and TE
Reinforcement SE and TE
Enrichment SE and TE
Concept Mapping
Critical Thinking/Problem Solving
Activity Worksheets
Chapter Review
Chapter Review Software
Lab Manual SE and TE
Science Integration Activities
Cross-Curricular Integration
Science and Society Integration

Transparency Packages:
- Teaching Transparencies
- Section Focus Transparencies
- Science Integration Transparencies

The Glencoe Science Professional Development Series
- Performance Assessment in the Science Classroom
- Lab and Safety Skills in the Science Classroom
- Cooperative Learning in the Science Classroom
- Alternate Assessment in the Science Classroom
- Exploring Environmental Issues

Technology Integration
Multicultural Connections
Performance Assessment
Assessment
Lesson Plans
Spanish Resources
MindJogger Videoquizzes and Teacher Guide
English/Spanish Audiocassettes
CD-ROM Multimedia System
Interactive Videodisc Program
Computer Testbank—DOS and Macintosh Versions

Cover Photograph: The sunset on the Grand Canyon in Arizona was photographed by Jack Dykinga.

Glencoe/McGraw-Hill
A Division of The **McGraw-Hill** *Companies*

Send all inquiries to:
Glencoe/McGraw-Hill
936 Eastwind Drive
Westerville, OH 43081

ISBN 0-02-827808-9
Printed in the United States of America
1 2 3 4 5 6 7 8 9 RRDW/LP 02 01 00 99 98 97 96

Authors

Ralph Feather, Jr. is a teacher of geology, astronomy, Earth science, and integrated science, and serves as Science Department Chair in the Derry Area School District in Derry, Pennsylvania. Mr. Feather has 25 years of teaching experience in secondary science. He holds a B.S. in Geology and an M.Ed. in Geoscience from Indiana University of Pennsylvania. Mr. Feather is currently completing a Ph.D. in "Writing Across the Curriculum to Learn Science" at the University of Pittsburgh. Mr. Feather received the 1991 Presidential Award for Excellence in Science Teaching and the 1991 Geological Society of America Award for Excellence in Earth Science Teaching. He is a member of the National Association for Research in Science Teaching, Geological Society of America, National Association of Geology Teachers, National Earth Science Teacher's Association, and the Planetary Society. Mr. Feather is coauthor of *Science Interactions, Merrill Earth Science,* and *Science Connections* from Glencoe Publishing Company.

Susan Leach Snyder is a teacher of Earth science and serves as Science Department Chair at Jones Middle School, Upper Arlington School District, Columbus, Ohio. Ms. Snyder received a B.S. in Comprehensive Science from Miami University, Oxford, Ohio, and an M.S. in Entomology from the University of Hawaii. She has 23 years of teaching experience. Ms. Snyder, in addition to receiving Exemplary Earth Science and Career Awareness in Science Teaching Team awards from NSTA, has received Outstanding Teacher awards from the National Association of Geology Teachers, the National Marine Educators Association, and the Geological Society of America. She has been a state recipient of the Presidential Award for Excellence in Science and Math Teaching from NSTA, the Ohio Teacher of the Year, and one of four finalists for the National Teacher of the year. Ms. Snyder is a coauthor of *Science Interactions* and *Merrill Earth Science* from Glencoe Publishing Company.

Contributing Writers

Linda Barr
Freelance Writer
Westerville, Ohio

Dan Blaustein
Science Teacher and Author
Evanston, Illinois

Pam Bliss
Freelance Science Writer
Grayslake, Illinois

Mary Dylewski
Freelance Science Writer
Houston, Texas

Nancy Ross-Flanigan
Syndicated Science Reporter
Detroit, Michigan

Helen Frensch
Freelance Writer
Santa Barbara, California

Steve Glazer
Freelance Writer
Champaign, Illinois

Rebecca Johnson
Freelance Science Writer and Author
Sioux Falls, South Dakota

Devi Mathieu
Freelance Science Writer
Sebastopol, California

Patricia West
Freelance Writer
Oakland, California

Consultants

Earth Science

Michael Bikerman, Ph.D
Associate Professor of Geology
University of Pittsburgh
Pittsburgh, Pennsylvania

Anthony E. D'Agostino
President
T D Geoscience
Midland, Texas

Richard Duschl
Professor of Science Education
Vanderbilt University
Nashville, Tennessee

Jay Stanley Hobgood, Ph.D.
Associate Professor of Geography
The Ohio State University
Columbus, Ohio

Larry A. Lebofsky, Ph.D.
Senior Research Scientist
Luna & Planetary Laboratory
University of Arizona
Tucson, Arizona

John Misock
Director of Consumer Health Services
Wyoming Department of Agriculture
Cheyenne, Wyoming

Multicultural

Karen Muir, Ph.D.
Lead Instructor
Department of Social and Behavioral Sciences
Columbus State Community College
Columbus, OH

James B. Phipps, Ph.D.
Instructor
Grays Harbor College
Aberdeen, Washington

Safety

Robert Joseph Tatz, Ph.D.
Instructional Lab Supervisor
The Ohio State University
Columbus, Ohio

Reviewers

Beth A. Beckwith
Kenwood Trail Junior High School
Lakeville, Minnesota

David Burch
Eastern Green County Schools
Bloomfield, Indiana

Sister Carmela Anne
Gesu School
Philadelphia, Pennsylvania

Betty Crowder
Rochester Community School
Rochester, Michigan

Susan Engledow
Clay Junior High School
Carmel, Indiana

Dr. Timothy Folkomer
Penn Wood East Junior High School
Yeadon, Pennsylvania

John A. Fradiska, Jr.
Thomas Johnson Middle School
Frederick, Maryland

Michael Goodrich
Lake Oswego High School
Lake Oswego, Oregon

Patricia Kenzig
St. John Bosco
Parma Heights, Ohio

Martha McIlveene
LaFayette Middle School
LaFayette, Georgia

Kathleen McMichael
Escambia High School
Pensacola, Florida

Arren L. Ostroff
Reynolds Junior High School
Lancaster, Pennsylvania

David Rhoads
Junction City High School
Junction City, Kansas

John Rooke
Pittsford Central School
Pittsford, New York

Richard Wisemiller
Clearwater Discovery School
Clearwater, Florida

Contents

UNIT 1

Earth Materials 2

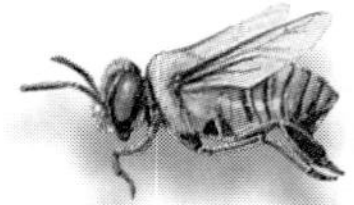

Contents

UNIT 2 The Changing Surface of Earth 116

Contents

Contents

UNIT 3

Earth's Internal Processes 232

Contents

Contents

Contents

Contents

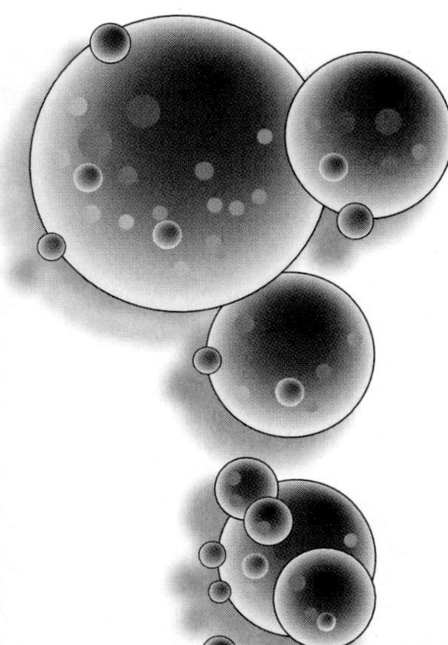

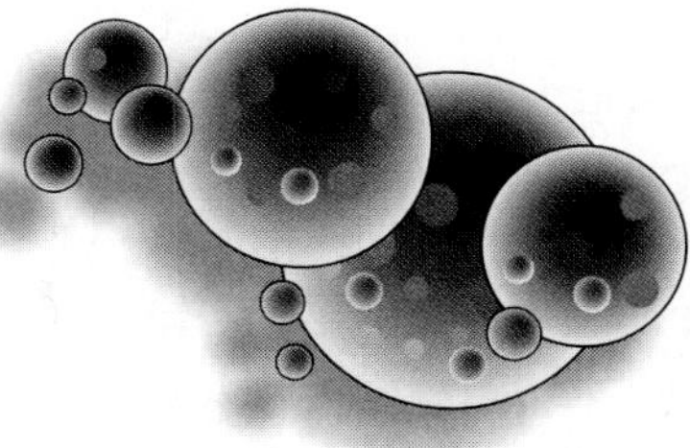

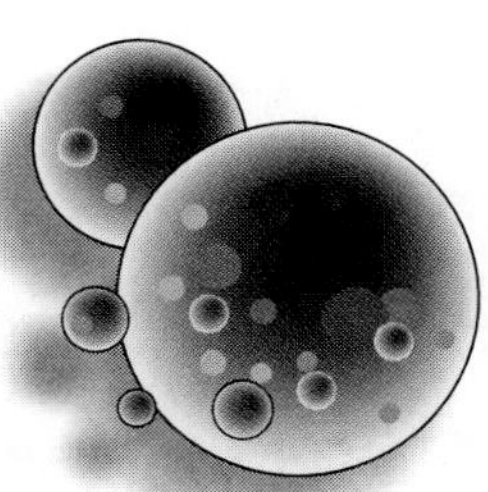

Contents

UNIT 7 Astronomy 580

Contents

Appendices

Activities

Activities

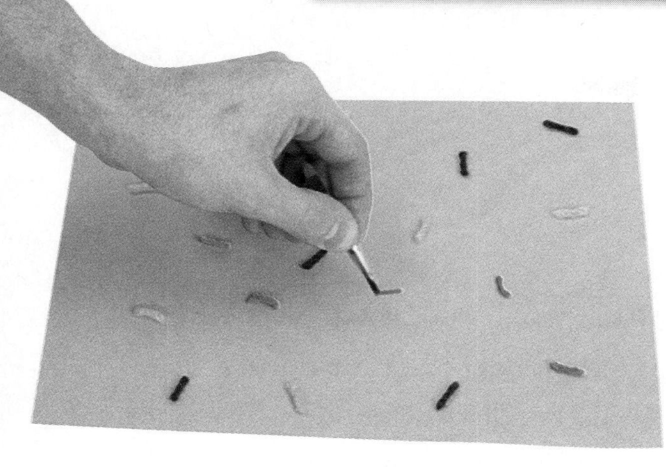

Explore Activities

MiniLABS

MiniLABS

Problem Solving

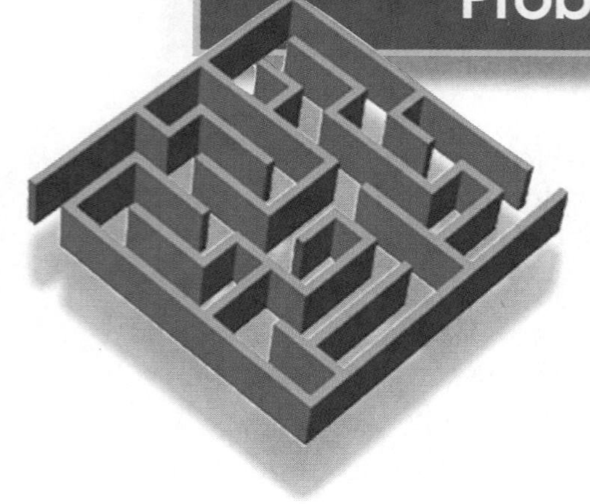

Using Technology

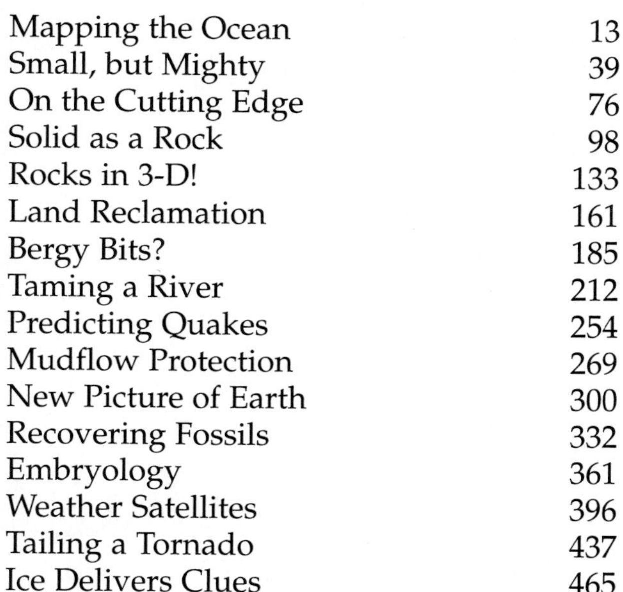

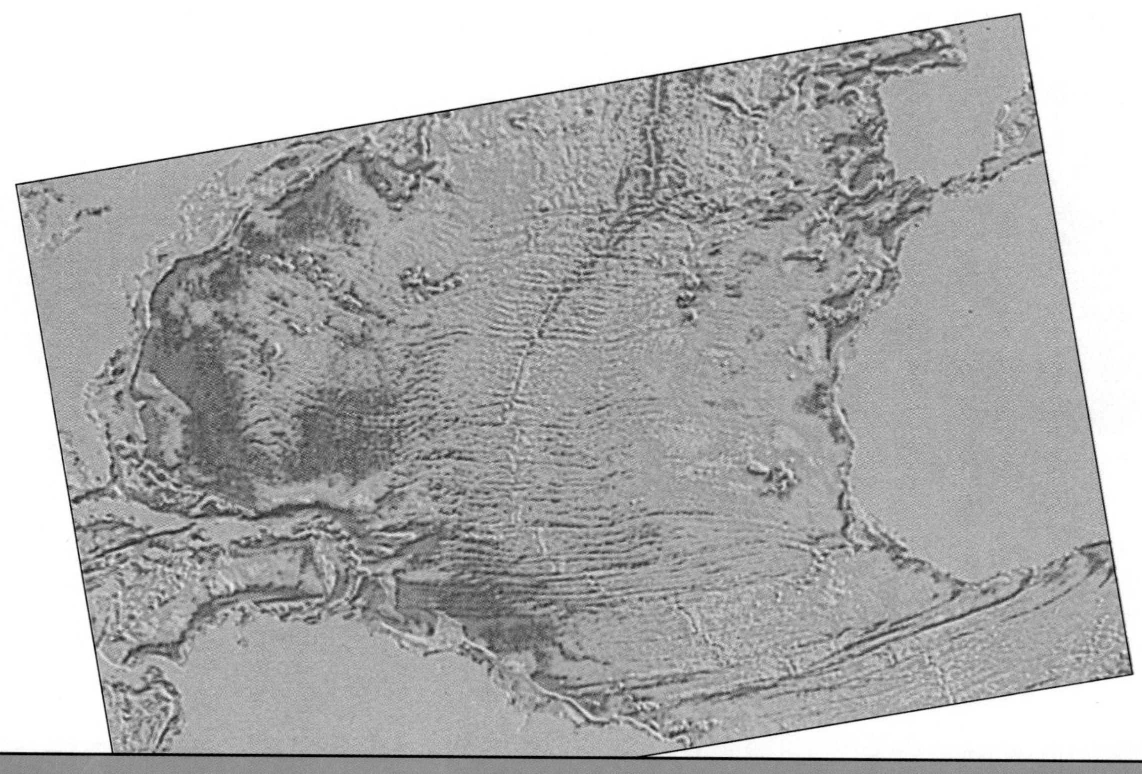

Skill Builders

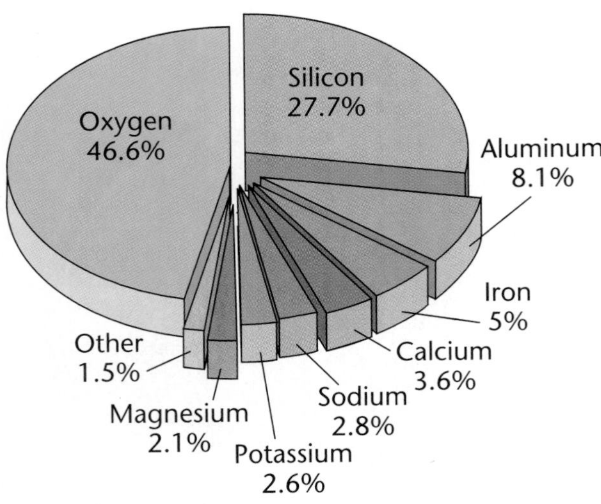

GRAPHICS

Element	Atomic No.	Mass No.
Fluorine	9	19
Lithium	3	7
Carbon	6	12
Nitrogen	7	14
Beryllium	4	9
Boron	5	11
Oxygen	8	16
Neon	10	20

ORGANIZING INFORMATION

THINKING CRITICALLY

DESIGNING AN EXPERIMENT

People and Science

Science Connections

Science and Art

Science and History

Science Connections

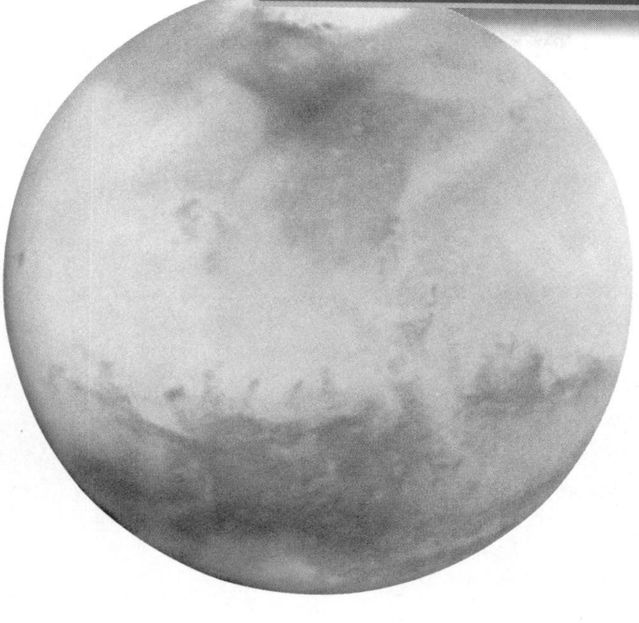

Science and Literature

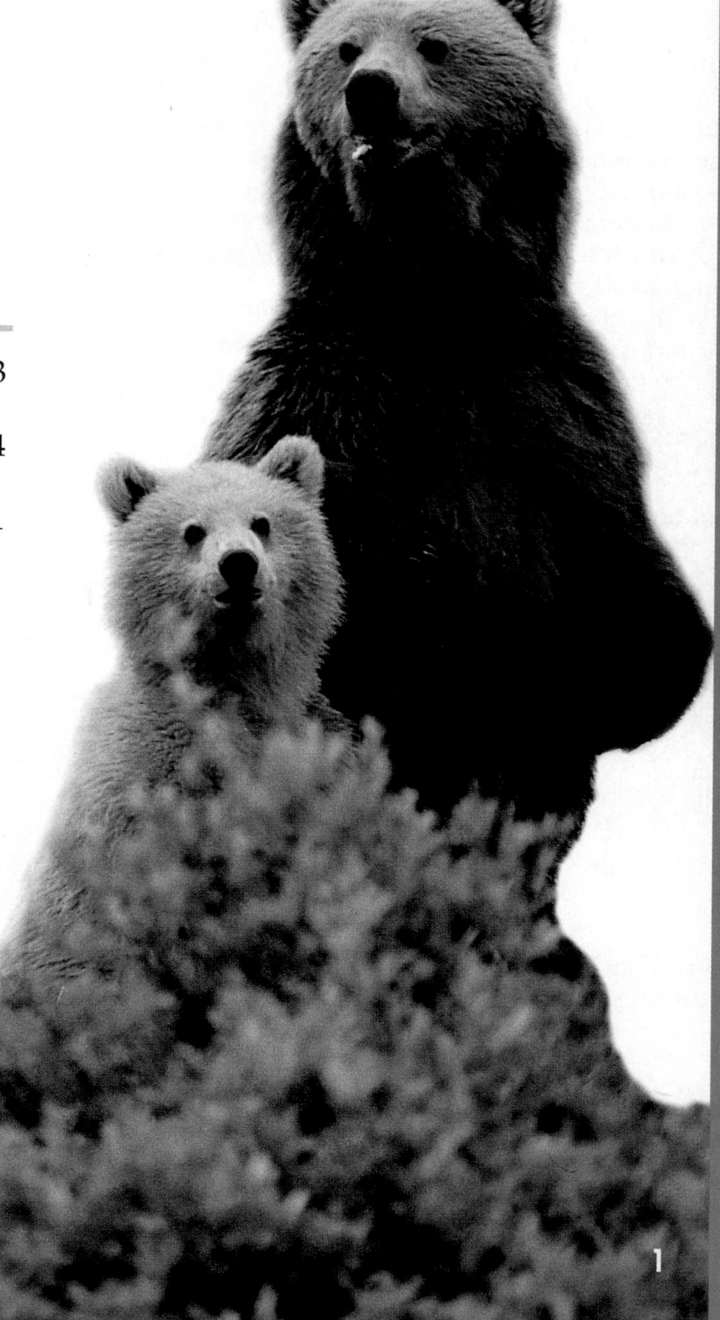

UNIT 1

Earth Materials

In Unit 1, students are introduced to the branches of science involved in Earth science. Students apply science to the solving of problems and work with methods used in scientific measurement. Through lab activities, students are introduced to Earth materials. The organization of the unit leads students through the elements of basic science, introduces them to atomic structure, and then builds on this information by presenting them with the structure, formation, identification, and uses of minerals and rocks. The differences between atoms and molecules are described. Minerals are defined, and mixtures of minerals are identified as rocks. The rock cycle and the three major classifications of rocks are described.

CONTENTS

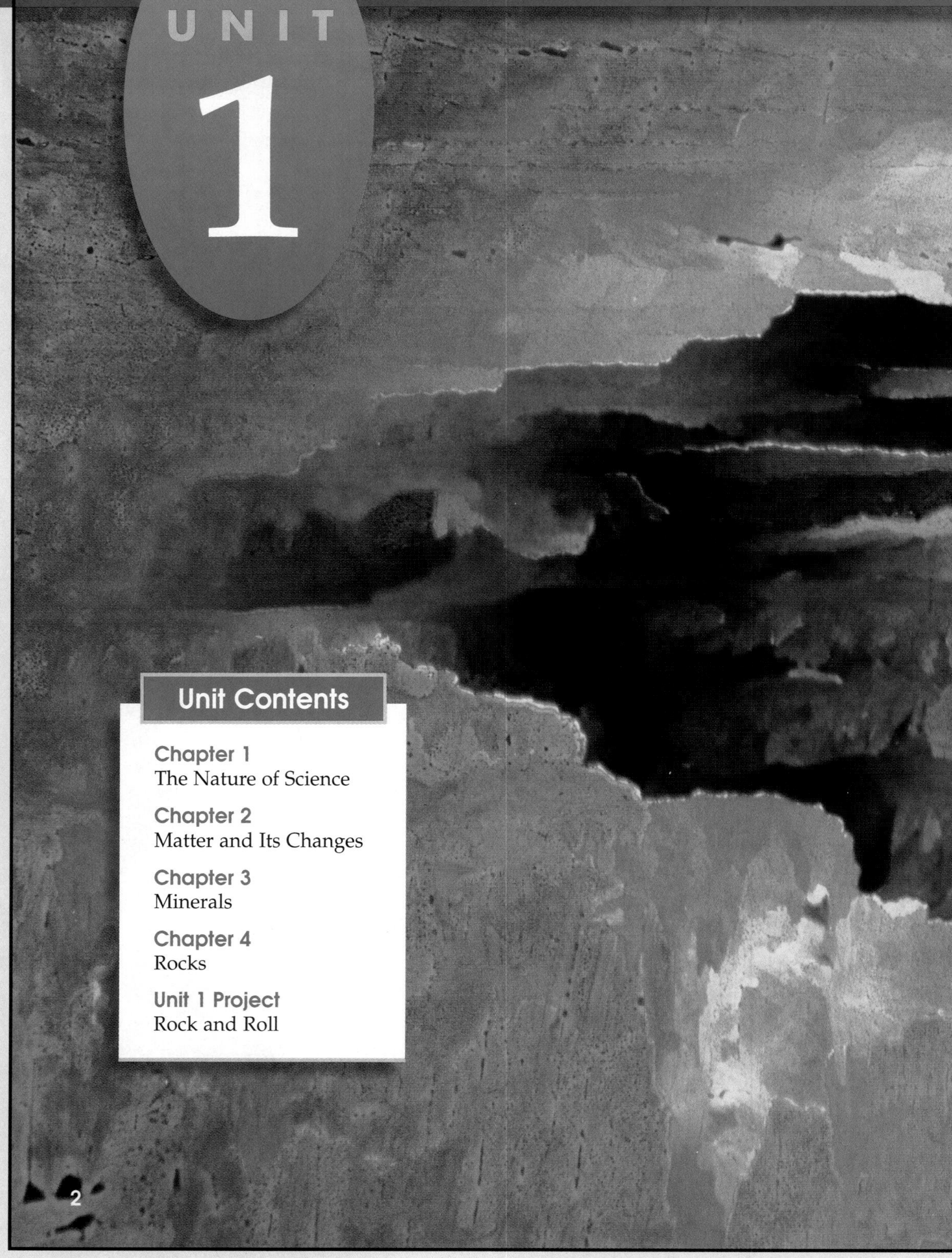

Science at Home

Minerals in the Home Have students brainstorm and compile lists of objects in the home that are made of common minerals. Have them list the mineral from which each object is made. L1 LEP COOP LEARN

Earth Materials

What's Happening Here?

Earth science is the study of planet Earth and its place in space. Think about that. Where would you begin to study Earth? Would you break apart a mineral and magnify it a thousand times, like the sulfur crystals shown here, to unlock the secrets of its structure? Or would you gaze at the skies to learn more about our planet? Earth scientists do both. They study Earth close up and from a distance, using technology such as microscopes and space satellite cameras. In this unit, you will learn more about Earth science and the materials, such as minerals, that make up Earth.

Science Journal

In your Science Journal, write a paragraph explaining how the microscope and the space satellite both contribute to the study of Earth science.

Theme Connection

Scale and Structure/Stability and Change Models are used to describe the internal structure of minerals and how this internal structure is responsible for a mineral's properties. The stability of rocks on Earth and the interaction of processes that cause rocks to change via the rock cycle reinforce the theme of stability and change.

Cultural Diversity

Gems and Gemstones Have students research the importance of gems and gemstones to several cultures around the world. Have them include societies with monarchies as well as elected governments. Students may also research how ancient cultures in a particular location regarded gems and gemstones and compare the historical perspective with the present-day view. L1

INTRODUCING THE UNIT

What's Happening Here?

Ask students to tell you about the different scales shown in the photos. Point out to students that in this unit, they will study Earth as a planet and, on a much smaller scale, Earth materials. They will study the structure of atoms and how this structure affects how atoms react to form molecules that make up minerals and rocks.

Background

Thin sections of crystals, as shown here for sulfur, are made by grinding a mineral crystal extremely thin. The section must be thin enough for light to pass through it. Sulfur belongs to the native elements class of minerals. As shown, thin sections of this mineral are pale yellow to yellowish gray. The native element sulfur may react with other elements to form sulfate minerals such as gypsum and anhydrite.

Previewing the Chapters

- Have students compile a brief list of materials they use at home that would be classified as compounds or mixtures. Use preconceptions of students to demonstrate the differences between compounds and mixtures.
- Students should be encouraged to search through Chapter 3 for photographs that demonstrate important identifying characteristics of minerals.

Tying to Previous Knowledge

Ask students to bring in and share with the class any rock or mineral collections they might have. After studying the minerals and rocks collected by students, ask the class why they think the specific samples were collected.

Chapter Organizer

Section	Objectives	Activities/Features
Chapter Opener		Explore Activity: What is the best shoe design for rock climbing? p. 5
1-1 **What is Earth science?** (1 session, ½ block)*	1. **Differentiate** among the following Earth sciences: geology, meteorology, astronomy, and oceanography. 2. **Identify** the topics you'll be studying this year in Earth science.	Connect to Life Science, p. 7 MiniLAB: How many Earth sciences are there? p. 8 Skill Builder: Concept Mapping, p. 9 Science Journal, p. 9
1-2 **Science and Society Technology: Applying Science** (1 session, ½ block)*	1. **List** ways technology helps you. 2. **Discuss** ways that the use of technology can be harmful.	Science Journal, p. 10 Explore the Technology, p. 11
1-3 **Solving Problems** (2 sessions, 1½ blocks)*	1. **Describe** some problem-solving strategies. 2. **List** steps commonly used in the scientific method. 3. **Distinguish** among hypotheses, theories, and laws.	Using Technology: Mapping the Ocean, p. 13 Using Math, p. 14 Problem Solving: Experimenting, p. 16 Connect to Life Science, p. 17 Skill Builder: Comparing and Contrasting, p. 18 Using Computers: Word Processing, p. 18
1-4 **Measurement and Safety** (2 sessions, 1 block)*	1. **List** the SI units for the following measurements: length, mass, weight, area, volume, density, and temperature. 2. **Differentiate** between the terms *mass* and *weight* and the terms *area* and *volume.* 3. **State** three lab safety rules.	Using Math, p. 20 Using Math, p. 21 Activity 1-1: Rock Density, pp. 22-23 MiniLAB: How do you convert Fahrenheit temperatures to Celsius? p. 24 Skill Builder: Measuring in SI, p. 25 Using Math, p. 25 Science & History, p. 26 Science Journal, p. 26

* A complete Planning Guide that includes block scheduling is provided on pages 32T-35T.

Activity Materials

Explore	Activities	MiniLABs
page 5 shoes (tennis, baseball, golf, hiking boots, etc.) with a variety of different soles	pages 22-23 100-mL graduated cylinder, beaker, tap water, small rock, metric graph paper, balance	page 24 Fahrenheit and Celsius thermometers

Chapter 1 The Nature of Science

Teacher Classroom Resources

Reproducible Masters	Transparencies
Study Guide, p. 5 **Reinforcement**, p. 5 **Enrichment**, p. 5 **Activity Worksheets**, p. 9 **Technology Integration**, pp. 5-6	**Section Focus Transparency 1,** Getting down to Earth
Study Guide, p. 6 **Reinforcement**, p. 6 **Enrichment**, p. 6 **Science and Society Integration,** p. 5	**Section Focus Transparency 2,** Effects of Technology
Study Guide, p. 7 **Reinforcement**, p. 7 **Enrichment**, p. 7 **Lab Manual 1,** Problem Solving and Scientific Method **Lab Manual 2,** The Law of Probability **Concept Mapping**, p. 7 **Critical Thinking/Problem Solving,** p. 7	**Section Focus Transparency 3,** What's the Problem? **Teaching Transparency 1,** FLEX Your Brain
Study Guide, p. 8 **Reinforcement**, p. 8 **Enrichment**, p. 8 **Activity Worksheets,** pp. 7-8, 10 **Lab Manual 3,** Measuring Using SI Units **Lab Manual 4,** Mass and Weight **Science Integration Activity 1,** Mealworm Olympics **Cross-Curricular Integration,** p. 5 **Multicultural Connections,** pp. 5-6	**Section Focus Transparency 4,** Don't Be a Mad Scientist **Teaching Transparency 2,** SI/Metric to English Conversions **Science Integration Transparency 1,** Weight and Mass

Teaching Resources

Glencoe Earth Science Interactive Videodisc
Earth Science CD-ROM
Spanish Resources
English/Spanish Audiocassettes
Cooperative Learning Resource Guide
Lab Partner
Lab and Safety Skills
Lesson Plans

Assessment Resources

Chapter Review, pp. 5-6
Assessment, pp. 5-8
Performance Assessment in the Science Classroom (PASC)
MindJogger Videoquiz
Alternate Assessment in the Science Classroom
Performance Assessment
Chapter Review Software
Computer Test Bank

Key to Teaching Strategies

The following designations will help you decide which activities are appropriate for your students.

L1 Level 1 activities should be within the ability range of all students.

L2 Level 2 activities should be within the ability range of the average to above-average student.

L3 Level 3 activities are designed for the ability range of above-average students.

LEP LEP activities should be within the ability range of Limited English Proficiency students.

LS These activities are designed to address different learning styles.

COOP LEARN Cooperative Learning activities are designed for small group work.

P These strategies represent student products that can be placed into a best-work portfolio.

GLENCOE TECHNOLOGY

The following multimedia resources are available from Glencoe.

The Infinite Voyage Series
Miracles by Design
Living with Disaster
Science and Technology Videodisc Series (STVS)
Physics
New Skid Control
Video Astronomy
Bipedal Robot
Ecology
Evaluating Artificial Reefs
Lake Erie Discovery
National Geographic Society Series
STV: Restless Earth
STV: Atmosphere
Earth Science CD-ROM

Teacher Classroom Resources

This is a representation of key blackline masters available in the Teacher Classroom Resources.

Teaching Aids

Section Focus Transparencies

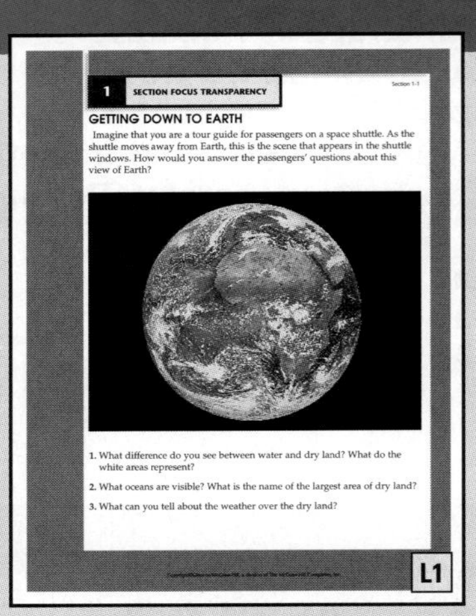

1 SECTION FOCUS TRANSPARENCY

GETTING DOWN TO EARTH

Imagine that you are a tour guide for passengers on a space shuttle. As the shuttle moves away from Earth, this is the scene that appears in the shuttle windows. How would you answer the passengers' questions about this view of Earth?

1. What difference do you see between water and dry land? What do the white areas represent?
2. What oceans are visible? What is the name of the largest area of dry land?
3. What can you tell about the weather over the dry land?

L1

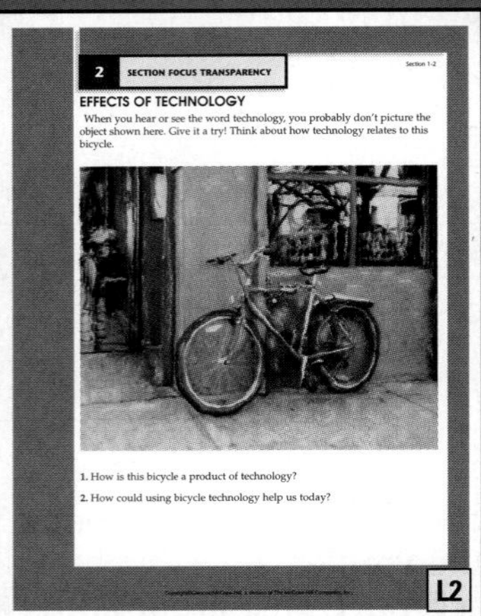

2 SECTION FOCUS TRANSPARENCY

EFFECTS OF TECHNOLOGY

When you hear or see the word technology, you probably don't picture the object shown here. Give it a try! Think about how technology relates to this bicycle.

1. How is this bicycle a product of technology?
2. How could using bicycle technology help us today?

L2

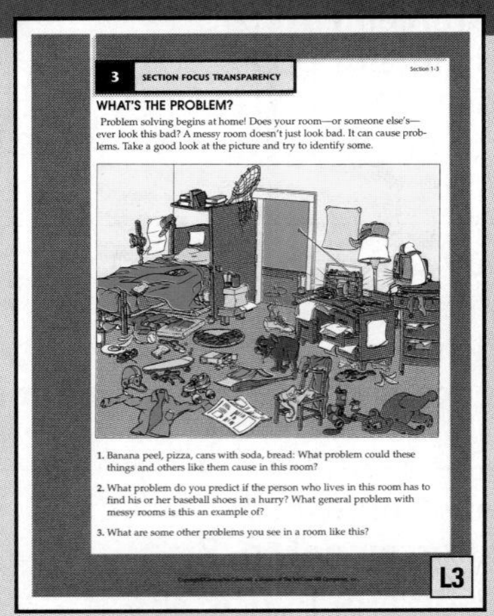

3 SECTION FOCUS TRANSPARENCY

WHAT'S THE PROBLEM?

Problem solving begins at home! Does your room—or someone else's—ever look this bad? A messy room doesn't just look bad. It can cause problems. Take a good look at the picture and try to identify some.

1. Banana peel, pizza, cans with soda, bread: What problem could these things and others like them cause in this room?
2. What problem do you predict if the person who lives in this room has to find his or her baseball shoes in a hurry? What general problem with messy rooms is this an example of?
3. What are some other problems you see in a room like this?

L3

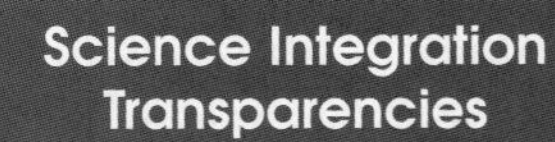

Science Integration Transparencies

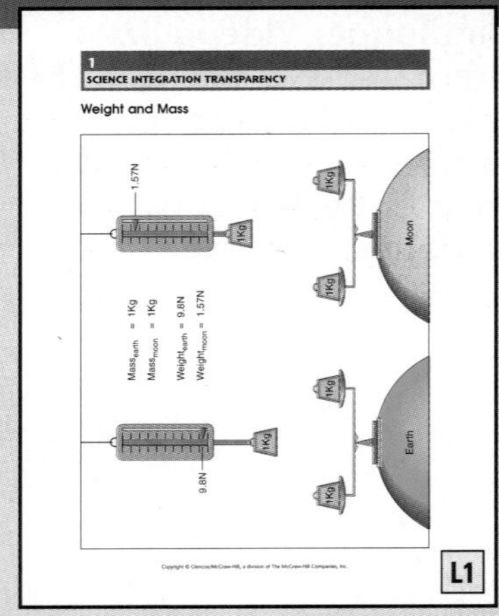

1 SCIENCE INTEGRATION TRANSPARENCY

Weight and Mass

L1

Teaching Transparencies

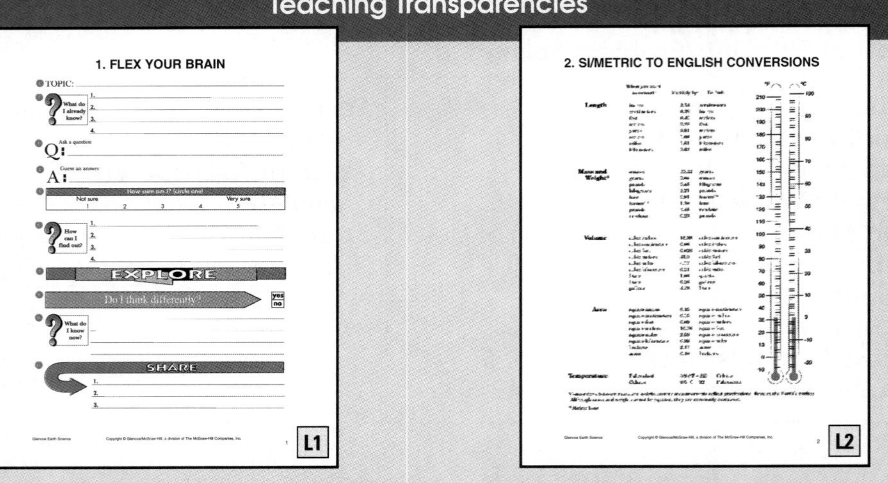

1. FLEX YOUR BRAIN

L1

2. SI/METRIC TO ENGLISH CONVERSIONS

L2

Meeting Different Ability Levels

Study Guide

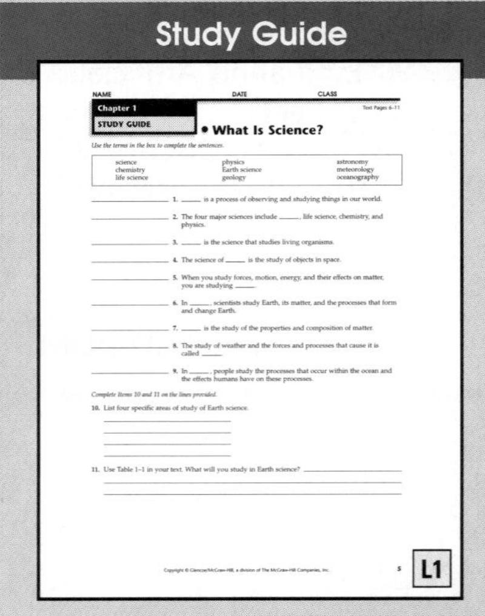

NAME DATE CLASS

Chapter 1 STUDY GUIDE • What Is Science? Text Pages 6–11

Use the terms in the box to complete the sentences.

science	physics	astronomy
chemistry	Earth science	meteorology
life science	geology	oceanography

1. _____ is a process of observing and studying things in our world.
2. The four major sciences include _____, life science, chemistry, and physics.
3. _____ is the science that studies living organisms.
4. The science of _____ is the study of objects in space.
5. When you study forces, motion, energy, and their effects on matter, you are studying _____.
6. In _____, scientists study Earth, its matter, and the processes that form and change Earth.
7. _____ is the study of the properties and composition of matter.
8. The study of weather and the forces and processes that cause it is called _____.
9. In _____, people study the processes that occur within the ocean and the effects humans have on these processes.

Complete Items 10 and 11 on the lines provided.

10. List four specific areas of study of Earth science.
11. Use Table 1-1 in your text. What will you study in Earth science?

 5

L1

Reinforcement

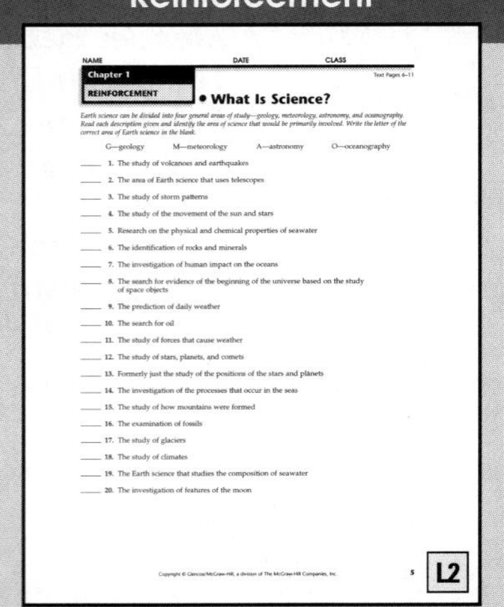

NAME DATE CLASS

Chapter 1 REINFORCEMENT • What Is Science? Text Pages 6–11

Earth science can be divided into four general areas of study—geology, meteorology, astronomy, and oceanography. Read each description given and identify the area of science that would be primarily involved. Write the letter of the correct area of Earth science in the blank.

G—geology M—meteorology A—astronomy O—oceanography

1. The study of volcanoes and earthquakes
2. The area of Earth science that uses telescopes
3. The study of storm patterns
4. The study of the movement of the sun and stars
5. Research on the physical and chemical properties of seawater
6. The identification of rocks and minerals
7. The investigation of human impact on the oceans
8. The search for evidence of the beginning of the universe based on the study of space objects
9. The prediction of daily weather
10. The search for oil
11. The study of forces that cause weather
12. The study of stars, planets, and comets
13. Formerly just the study of the positions of the stars and planets
14. The investigation of the processes that occur in the seas
15. The study of how mountains were formed
16. The examination of fossils
17. The study of glaciers
18. The study of climates
19. The Earth science that studies the composition of seawater
20. The investigation of features of the moon

 5

L2

Enrichment Worksheets

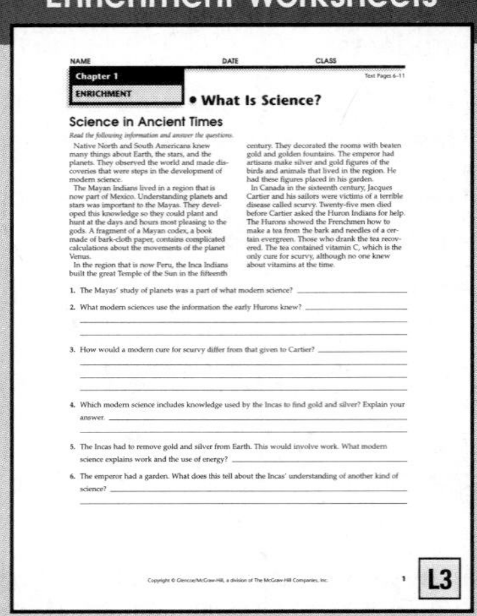

NAME DATE CLASS

Chapter 1 ENRICHMENT • What Is Science? Text Pages 6–11

Science in Ancient Times

Read the following information and answer the questions.

Native North and South Americans knew many things about Earth, the stars, and the planets. They observed the world and made discoveries that were steps in the development of modern science.

The Mayan Indians lived in a region that is now part of Mexico. Understanding planets and stars was important to the Mayas. They developed this knowledge so they could plant and hunt at the days and hours most pleasing to the gods. A fragment of a Mayan codex, a book made of bark-cloth paper, contains complicated calculations about the movements of the planet Venus.

In the region that is now Peru, the Inca Indians built the great Temple of the Sun in the fifteenth century. They decorated the rooms with beaten gold and golden fountains. The emperor had artisans make silver and gold figures of the birds and animals that lived in the region. He had these figures placed in his garden.

In Canada in the sixteenth century, Jacques Cartier and his sailors were victims of a terrible disease called scurvy. Twenty-five men died before Cartier asked the Huron Indians for help. The Hurons showed the Frenchmen how to make a tea from the bark and needles of a certain evergreen. Those who drank the tea recovered. The tea contained vitamin C, which is the only cure for scurvy, although no one knew about vitamins at the time.

1. The Mayas' study of planets was a part of what modern science?
2. What modern sciences use the information the early Hurons knew?
3. How would a modern cure for scurvy differ from that given to Cartier?
4. Which modern science includes knowledge used by the Incas to find gold and silver? Explain your answer.
5. The Incas had to remove gold and silver from Earth. This would involve work. What modern science explains work and the use of energy?
6. The emperor had a garden. What does this tell about the Incas' understanding of another kind of science?

 1

L3

Chapter 1 The Nature of Science

Hands-On Activities

Science Integration Activity

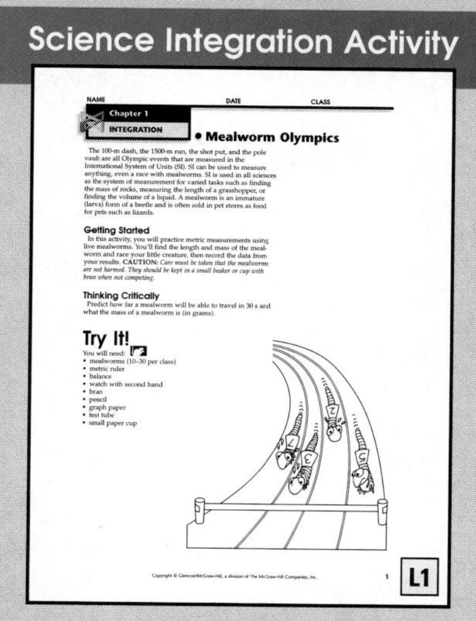
Chapter 1 INTEGRATION
Mealworm Olympics
Getting Started
Thinking Critically
Try It!
L1

Lab Manual

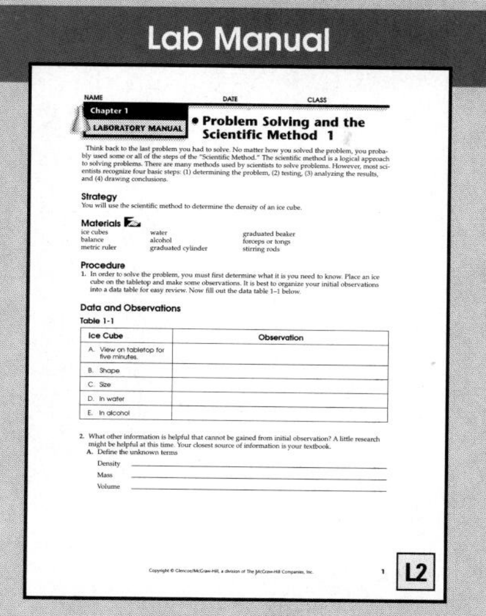
Chapter 1 LABORATORY MANUAL
Problem Solving and the Scientific Method 1
Strategy
Materials
Procedure
Data and Observations
L2

Assessment

Performance Assessment

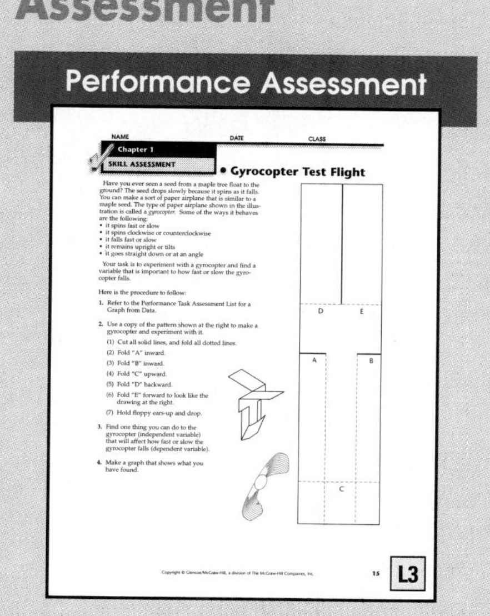
Chapter 1 SKILL ASSESSMENT
Gyrocopter Test Flight
L3

Enrichment and Application

Critical Thinking/ Problem Solving

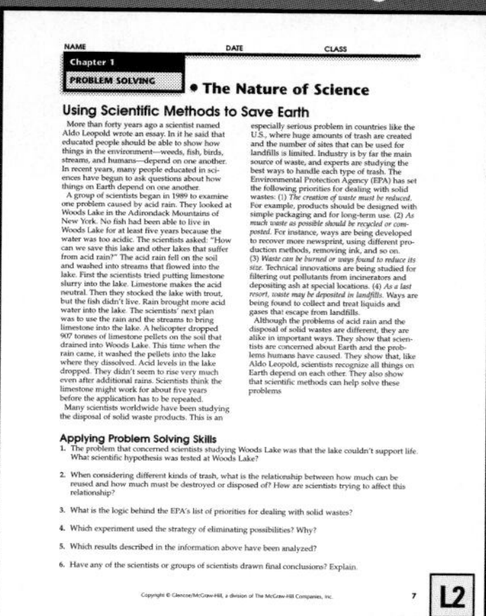
Chapter 1 PROBLEM SOLVING
The Nature of Science
Using Scientific Methods to Save Earth
Applying Problem Solving Skills
L2

Cross-Curricular Integration

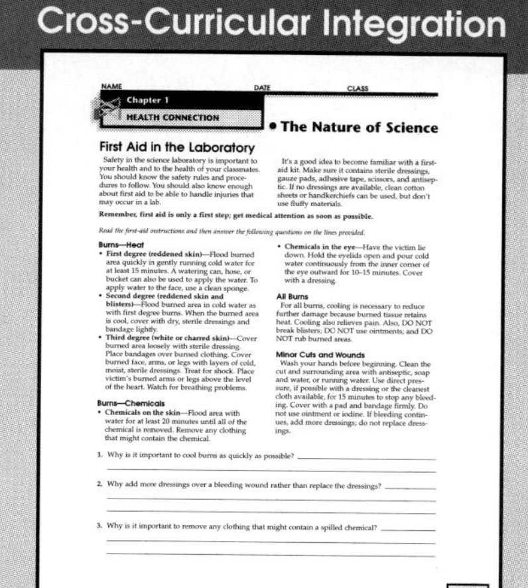
Chapter 1 HEALTH CONNECTION
The Nature of Science
First Aid in the Laboratory
L1

Science and Society Integration

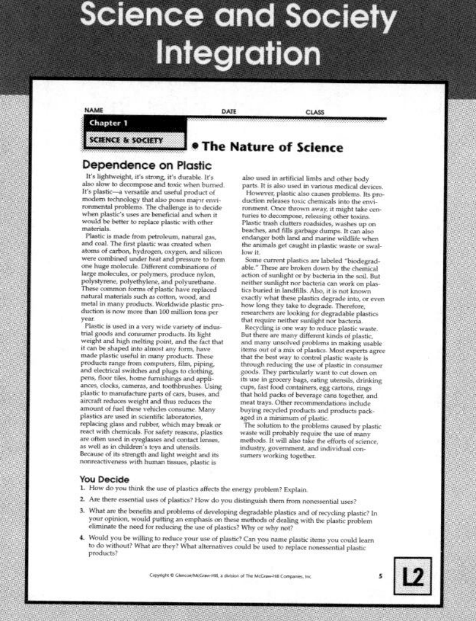
Chapter 1 SCIENCE & SOCIETY
The Nature of Science
Dependence on Plastic
You Decide
L2

Technology Integration

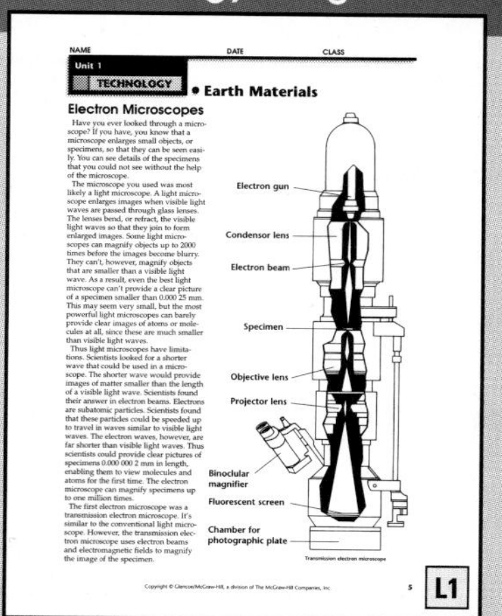
Unit 1 TECHNOLOGY
Earth Materials
Electron Microscopes

L1

Multicultural Connections

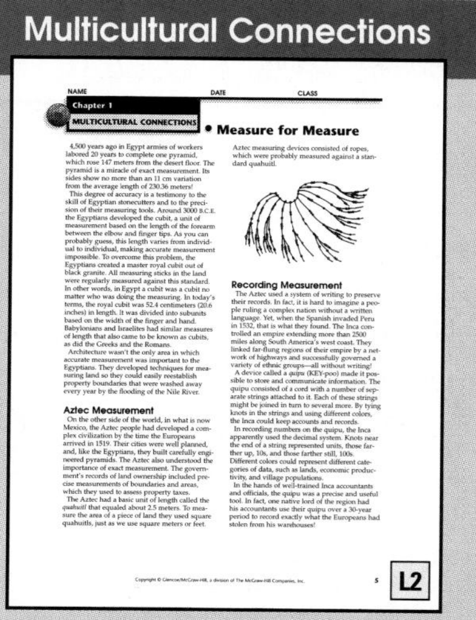
Chapter 1 MULTICULTURAL CONNECTIONS
Measure for Measure
Aztec Measurement
Recording Measurement
L2

Concept Mapping

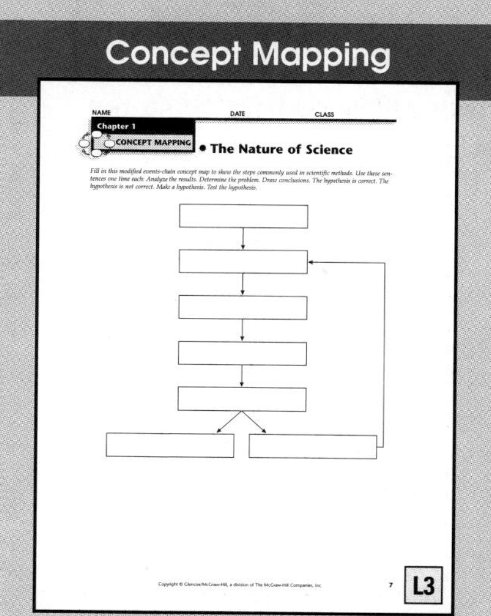
Chapter 1 CONCEPT MAPPING
The Nature of Science
L3

Chapter 1

The Nature of Science

CHAPTER OVERVIEW

Section 1-1 This section defines science, differentiates among chemistry, physics, life science, and earth science; and defines the four specific areas of Earth science.

Section 1-2 Science and Society The relationship between science and technology is discussed. Advantages and disadvantages of technology are examined.

Section 1-3 Problem-solving strategies, steps in scientific method, and the evolution of theories from hypotheses are presented.

Section 1-4 The International System of Units (SI) is introduced. Safety procedures to be used during activities are listed.

Chapter Vocabulary

science
Earth Science
geology
meteorology
astronomy
oceanography
technology
scientific method
hypothesis
variable
control
theory
law
International System of Units (SI)
mass
weight
gravity

Theme Connection

Systems and Interactions Systems and interactions is the theme of this chapter. Science is a system of knowledge based on observations. Science is generally divided into four areas, but the topics overlap. Earth science is generally divided into four areas, and these topics also overlap. The interaction of science and technology is the focus of Section 1-2.

Previewing the Chapter

4

Learning Styles

Look for the following logo for strategies that emphasize different learning modalities. LS

Visual-Spatial	Activity, pp. 7, 20; Reteach, p. 8; Visual Learning, p. 19; Science and History, p. 26
Interpersonal	Across the Curriculum, p. 13
Intrapersonal	Explore, p. 5; MiniLAB, p. 8
Logical-Mathematical	Across the Curriculum, p. 21; Activity 1-1, pp. 22-23; MiniLAB, p. 24
Linguistic	Science and History, p. 26
Auditory-Musical	Activity, p. 14

Chapter 1

The Nature of Science

The climber in this photo is using the results of many scientific experiments to safely enjoy the thrill of rock climbing. Experiments have led to the development of strong, stretchable ropes that can protect a climber in the event of a fall. The gear used to attach the rope to the rock is the result of years of experimenting with light, strong metal alloys. The rubber on the climber's shoes has been found to be the best compound for providing traction and durability on rock.

EXPLORE ACTIVITY

What is the best shoe design for rock climbing?

1. Make a list of the characteristics you would expect a good shoe to have for rock climbing.
2. Observe the soles of various kinds of shoes. Examine hiking boots, tennis shoes, soccer cleats, baseball cleats, and other shoes.
3. Based on the characteristics you chose, predict which shoes would be the best for climbing steep rocks, or design a rock-climbing shoe that has the best features of several shoes.

Observe: In your Science Journal, discuss some ways you could test the traction of different shoes on rock. Carry out some of these experiments.

Previewing Science Skills

- In the **Skill Builders**, you will **map concepts, compare and contrast**, and **measure in SI**.
- In the **Activity**, you will **design an experiment, hypothesize**, and **analyze data**.
- In the **MiniLABS**, you will investigate specific areas of study in Earth science, and learn about SI conversions.

EXPLORE ACTIVITY

Purpose

LS **Intrapersonal** Students will observe different shoes and predict which shoes are best for climbing steep rocks. L1

Preparation

Have students bring extra shoes from home to class. Also, have them bring pictures of different kinds of shoes they see in magazines and newspaper ads. Ask the students to concentrate on finding pictures that show the soles of the shoes.

Materials

shoes and pictures of shoes

Observe

The most obvious way to test the shoes would be for students wearing the shoes to climb rocks; however, since the shoes are not the same size, different people would have to do the testing. This could affect the results. Therefore, students should try to devise a way of testing the traction without wearing the shoes. They might put their hands into the shoes, push onto a rock wall with the shoe, and try to slide it down the wall. Or they may put a weight in the shoe and place it on a flat rock. By tilting the rock, students can compare the angle at which each shoe slips.

Assessment

Process Have students use modeling clay to design the shape of the sole of the shoe they predict would be best for climbing rocks. Use the Performance Task Assessment List for Model in **PASC,** p. 51. P

Assessment Planner

Portfolio

Refer to page 27 for suggested items that students might select for their portfolios.

Performance Assessment

See page 27 for additional Performance Assessment options.
Skill Builders, pp. 9, 18, 25
MiniLABs, pp. 8, 24
Activity 1-1, pp. 22-23

Content Assessment

Section Wrap-ups pp. 9, 11, 18, 25
Chapter Review, pp. 27-29
Mini Quizzes, pp. 9, 18, 25

Group Assessment

Opportunities for group assessment occur with Cooperative Learning Strategies and Flex Your Brain Activities.

Section 1•1

Prepare

Section Background

A scientist's attitude about science is critical to his or her career. Scientists must be willing to allow others to question and challenge their ideas. Scientists must have a tolerance for the ideas and opinions of others.

Preplanning

To prepare for the MiniLAB, obtain a selection of books that students can use to investigate various fields of Earth science.

1 Motivate

Bellringer

Before presenting the lesson, display **Section Focus Transparency 1** on the overhead projector. Assign the accompanying **Focus Activity** worksheet. L1 LEP

Tying to Previous Knowledge

Lead a discussion that will help students realize that they have been practicing science all their lives. Lead them to conclude that observations, inferences, and drawing conclusions are all skills important to scientists.

GLENCOE TECHNOLOGY

CD-ROM

Earth Science CD-ROM

Have students perform the interactive exploration for Chapter 1 to reinforce important chapter concepts and thinking processes.

1•1 What Is Earth Science?

Science Words

- science
- Earth science
- geology
- meteorology
- astronomy
- oceanography

Objectives

- Differentiate among the following Earth sciences: geology, meteorology, astronomy, and oceanography.
- Identify the topics you'll be studying this year in Earth science.

Science

Science is all around you. It is such a common part of your life that you probably take it for granted. Have you ever wondered why there are seasons, why volcanoes erupt, or whether life exists on other planets? Do you wonder how people find the answers to these and other questions?

They use science. Science means "having knowledge." **Science** is a process of observing and studying things in our world. Many of these observations can't be explained easily and therefore present problems. Science involves trying to solve these problems. Science is a process that enables you to understand your world. Every time you try to find out how and why things look and act the way they do, you are a scientist. For example, if you wonder and try to figure out why some sunsets are more colorful than others, you are doing science. **Figure 1-1** shows just a few of the many worlds you can explore using science.

Collecting Scientific Knowledge

Scientific knowledge has accumulated since people first began observing the world around them. At first, people had only their senses to rely on for their observations. Early astronomers studied the night sky with just their eyes because they didn't

Figure 1-1

Earth science includes the study of climate, volcanoes, space, and much more.

Program Resources

Reproducible Masters

Study Guide, p. 5 L1
Reinforcement, p. 5 L1
Enrichment, p. 5 L3
Activity Worksheets, pp. 5, 9 L1
Technology Integration, pp. 5-6

Transparencies

Section Focus Transparency 1 L1

PHYSICS
Basic concepts of physics are involved in the motions of Earth and the moon and in the formation of stars.

Figure 1-2
The major sciences

CHEMISTRY
You'll learn basic concepts of matter when you study rocks and minerals.

LIFE SCIENCE
Organisms have an important role in Earth's history and the environment.

EARTH SCIENCE
Physics, chemistry, and life science are involved in exploring Earth and its place in space.

have telescopes yet. They acquired knowledge slowly. Today, we have instruments such as microscopes that magnify small objects, satellites that take photographs of Earth and other planets, telescopes that probe the depths of space, and computers that store and analyze information. Today we are learning more information, we are learning it faster, and there are more new inventions and discoveries than ever before.

The Major Sciences

Science can be applied to just about anything, and hundreds of special subject areas fall within the broad scope of "science." But basically, science can be divided into four general areas: chemistry, physics, life science, and Earth science. These general topics do overlap. For example, in Earth science, chemistry, physics, and life science are studied as they relate to Earth. In **Figure 1-2** you can see what these different sciences are about and how they are connected to each other.

CONNECT TO
LIFE SCIENCE

When geologists study fossils, they learn a lot about what life was like in the past. Limestone is a rock that often contains fossils of marine organisms. ***Research*** in the library to find out the names of some organisms that you might find as fossils in limestone.

2 Teach

Discussion

Using the four general categories of chemistry, physics, life science, and Earth science, ask students to name as many different kinds of scientists as possible. Students should realize that many of the disciplines overlap.

CONNECT TO
LIFE SCIENCE

Answer Examples might include corals, bryozoans, starfish, fish, brachiopods, sponges, trilobites, mollusks, sea urchins, and crinoids.

Activity

LS **Visual-Spatial** Have students prepare a bulletin board display of current topics in science. Discuss several of these with students. L1

- Ask the school librarian to arrange a session during which the use of science books, reference books, and magazines is explained.

 Use **Technology Integration,** pp. 5-6, as you teach this lesson.

GLENCOE TECHNOLOGY

Videodisc

The Infinite Voyage: Miracles by Design

Chapter 4
Biodegradable Plastic: The Miracle Material?

Chapter 6
New Ceramics: New Uses

Theme Connection

Systems and Interactions Oceanography is one of the topics students will study in Earth science. In their study, they will learn about the properties and composition of seawater, the plants and animals in the ocean, and the motion of waves. Ask: **Besides Earth science, which other major sciences will you be learning about when you study oceanography?** *chemistry, life science, and physics*

Community Connection

Career Day Invite a scientist to talk about his or her career.

MiniLAB

Purpose

LS **Intrapersonal** Students will classify Earth science disciplines and describe what a scientist working in each of these fields studies. L1

Analysis

hydrology: study of fresh water; volcanology: volcanoes; mineralogy: minerals; paleontology: fossils; stratigraphy: layers of sedimentary rocks; seismology: earthquakes; petrology: rocks; geomorphology: surface features; geochemistry: properties of Earth materials; crystallography: atomic structure of minerals

Assessment

Process Have students list topics that would be studied in each of the four elements of oceanography: chemistry, biology, physics, and geology. Use the Performance Task Assessment List for Making and Using a Classification System in **PASC**, p. 49. P

Activity Worksheets, pp. 5, 9

3 Assess

Check for Understanding

Have students answer questions 1 and 2 in the Section Wrap-up.

Reteach

LS **Visual-Spatial** Show students pictures of objects in nature, such as the sun, clouds, rocks, sea life, planets, fossils, and so on. Have students identify the Earth science(s) associated with each.

MiniLAB

How many Earth sciences are there?

Although the four major areas of Earth science are geology, meteorology, astronomy, and oceanography, each of these is composed of subtopic areas of its own.

Procedure

1. Look at the list of specific areas of study below.
2. Identify in which of the four major areas of Earth science they belong.

Analysis

What would a scientist working in each of these fields study?

hydrology	seismology
volcanology	petrology
mineralogy	geomorphology
paleontology	geochemistry
stratigraphy	crystallography

Earth Science

Earth science is the study of Earth and space. It is the study of such things as the transfer of energy in Earth's atmosphere; the evolution of land forms; patterns of change that cause weather; the scale and structure of stars; and the interactions that occur among the water, atmosphere, and land.

Just as science can be divided into the four general areas of Earth science, chemistry, physics, and life science, Earth science in this book is divided into four specific areas of study.

Geology

Geology is the study of Earth, its matter, and the processes that form and change Earth. Some of the things you'll explore are volcanoes, earthquakes, maps, fossils, mountains, and land use. Geologists search for oil, study volcanoes, identify rocks and minerals, study fossils and glaciers, and determine how mountains form.

Meteorology

Meteorology is the study of weather and the forces and processes that cause it. You'll learn about storm patterns, climates, and what factors cause our daily weather. A meteorologist is a scientist who studies weather patterns in order to predict daily weather.

Astronomy

Astronomy is the study of objects in space, including stars, planets, and comets. Before telescopes, like the radiotelescope shown in **Figure 1-3,** were invented, this branch of Earth

Figure 1-3
Radiotelescopes are used to collect information from beyond our solar system.

Inclusion Strategies

Gifted Have students choose one of the four major areas of specialization in Earth science to research. Have them list the tools, equipment, and/or instruments used by scientists in this field. L3

science mainly dealt with descriptions of the positions of the stars and planets. Using powerful telescopes, we can observe amazing sights, like that in **Figure 1-4.** Today, astronomers who study space objects seek evidence about the beginning of the universe. The study of astronomy helps scientists understand Earth's origin.

Figure 1-4

Using powerful new telescopes, we can extend our observations deeper into space.

Oceanography

Oceanography is the study of Earth's oceans. Oceanographers conduct research on the physical and chemical properties of ocean water. Oceanographers also study the processes that occur within oceans and the effects humans have on these processes.

As you study these topics, imagine how all this information was collected over the years. People just like you had questions about what they observed, and they used science to find the answers. In section 1-3, you'll learn ways that you too can find answers to questions and solutions to problems.

Section Wrap-up

Review

1. Compare and contrast meteorology and oceanography.
2. List three topics you'll study this year in Earth science.
3. **Think Critically:** The following paragraph summarizes one idea of how the dinosaurs may have died. Explain how this paragraph relates to Earth science.

   Evidence suggests that a large object from outer space may have crashed into Earth's crust. Dust from this collision blocked out the sun's light. Earth became colder, killing some plants and animals.

Skill Builder

Concept Mapping

Make a network tree concept map that shows which of the following topics are studied in a particular topic of Earth science. Use the following terms: *Earth science, geology, waves, currents, astronomy, oceanography, stars, volcanoes, planets, meteorology, fossils, weather, climate.* If you need help, refer to Concept Mapping in the **Skill Handbook.**

Science Journal

Look at the table of contents in this book and name ten careers in Earth science. Make a list of these careers in your Science Journal. Check the career resources in the library or guidance office for help.

4 Close

•MINI•QUIZ•

Use the Mini Quiz to check students' recall of chapter content.

1. **_____ is a process that enables you to understand your world.** *Science*
2. **_____ is the study of Earth.** *Geology*
3. **The study of weather and the forces and processes that cause it is _____ .** *meteorology*

Section Wrap-up

Review

1. Both are topics in Earth science. Meteorology is the study of Earth's atmosphere. Oceanography is the study of Earth's oceans.
2. Answers will vary, but may include: earthquakes, maps, storm patterns, stars, planets, and chemical properties of ocean water.
3. **Think Critically** Geology deals with factors that form and change Earth's crust. Plants and animals, including marine ones, were affected by the impacts. Astronomy is the study of space objects, including the sun. Weather and climate are topics of meteorology.

Skill Builder

Possible solution:

Earth Science
Includes these four general areas of science
Geology — Includes the study of — Fossils, Volcanoes
Astronomy — Includes the study of — Stars, Planets
Meteorology — Includes the study of — Weather, Climate
Oceanography — Includes the study of — Waves, Currents

P

Assessment

Content Use this Skill Builder to assess students' abilities to make a network tree concept map. Ask students to extend their concept map to include other topics that would be studied in Earth science. Use the Performance Task Assessment List for Concept Map in **PASC,** p. 89. P

Science Journal

Answers will vary. In addition to those resources listed for students, information on Earth science careers can be obtained from the American Geological Institute, the United States Geological Survey (USGS), or colleges and universities.

SCIENCE & SOCIETY

Section 1•2

Prepare

Section Background

It is estimated that human knowledge doubles every few years due to technological breakthroughs.

1 Motivate

Bellringer

Before presenting the lesson, display **Section Focus Transparency 2** on the overhead projector. Assign the accompanying **Focus Activity** worksheet. L1 LEP

Tying to Previous Knowledge

Ask students what our knowledge of space would be like if we did not have telescopes, computers, and other instruments. Students will say that we would know only what we can see. Explain that it is because of technology (the use of scientific discoveries) that we have these instruments with which to study our universe.

2 Teach

Science Journal

Accept all reasonable journal entries. Students should include what the modern device does and as much as they can about how it works. This later explanation will vary with the knowledge of the student.

SCIENCE & SOCIETY

TECHNOLOGY:

1•2 Applying Science

Science Words

technology

Objectives

- List ways technology helps you.
- Discuss ways that the use of technology can be harmful.

Technology and You

The study of science doesn't just add to our understanding of our natural surroundings, it also allows us to make discoveries that help us. **Technology** is the use of scientific discoveries. Everywhere you look, you can see ways that science and technology have shaped your world.

Technology has produced such diverse and important things as robots that check underwater oil rigs for leaks and manufacture products, as shown in **Figure 1-5,** new fibers to make air-supported roofs such as those used in some sports arenas, and calculators and computers that process information.

Technology Is Transferable

The interesting thing about technology is that it is transferable. That means that it can be applied to new situations. For example, all of the types of technology that are mentioned above were developed for use in outer space. Scientists developed robotic parts, new fibers, and microminiaturized instruments for spacecraft and satellites. After these materials were developed, many were modified for use here on Earth. Technology that was developed by the military, like radar and sonar, have applications in astronomy, meteorology, geology, and oceanography today.

Science Journal

Pretend you can travel back in time to the year 1800. Consider all of the advancements that have been made in science since that time. In your Science Journal, write a dialogue between you and someone living at that time as you try to explain what a modern device such as a television set, microwave oven, computer, or car is like.

Figure 1-5

Robots are commonly used in many industries. They are also used to explore other planets.

Program Resources

Reproducible Masters

Study Guide, p. 6 L1
Reinforcement, p. 6 L1
Enrichment, p. 6 L3
Science and Society Integration, p. 5

Transparencies

Section Focus Transparency 2 L1

The Effects of Technology

Let's further examine technology that helps us. Computers do everything from helping us predict weather to monitoring earthquakes. Robotics and computers enable us to make underwater submersibles to study the ocean floor and search for life in space. We use satellites to monitor pollution problems, locate hurricanes, and even track endangered species.

We have the technology to clear forests and build cities, slow down erosion along rivers, and even make it rain in some regions. Humans can change our surroundings on a large scale to meet our needs. We have even developed the technology to spend time in space, as in **Figure 1-6.**

Technology Can Cause Problems

Not all of the changes created by technology are good. For example, many types of technology create water, soil, and air pollution. Technology can cause other problems too. When forests are cleared to build cities, soil erosion increases, and weather patterns change. Although technology sometimes creates new jobs for people, some jobs are lost. In some cases, skills that people have become obsolete. In other instances, robots and computers can be used more cheaply than people.

Figure 1-6

Technology has enabled humans to travel beyond Earth.

Section Wrap-up

Review

1. How can technology be helpful?
2. How can technology cause problems?

Explore the Technology

The Panama Canal allows ships to travel between the Atlantic and Pacific Oceans without having to pass around South America. Because the level of the Atlantic is higher than the Pacific's, the canal was built with a system of locks to prevent flooding of lowlands in Panama. The locks also prevent species of organisms from traveling from one ocean to the other. We have the technological know-how to construct a wider and deeper canal that would permit larger modern ships to get through. It would be built without locks. What should be considered before building the new canal?

SCIENCE & SOCIETY

3 Assess

Check for Understanding

Have students answer questions 1 and 2 in the Section Wrap-up.

Reteach

Have student groups make two lists, one describing the benefits and the other the problems of technology.

Extension

For students who have mastered this section, use the **Reinforcement** and **Enrichment** masters.

4 Close

Have students describe what their world would be like if technology did not exist. Students will likely describe a world similar to that of the early humans.

Section Wrap-up

Review

1. Technology helps us study and monitor our environment and change our surroundings to meet our needs.
2. It can create problems such as pollution, soil erosion, weather pattern change, and loss of habitat for other organisms.

Explore the Technology

An advantage is that large ships could travel easily between the Atlantic and Pacific oceans. A disadvantage is that without locks, organisms could also travel easily from one ocean to another. This could disrupt the normal environment by allowing competition among species that would not normally interact.

Inclusion Strategies

Gifted Ask students to make a time line of all the technological advances they can find that have occurred since 1940. Have students work in small groups to illustrate their work and show changes in the design, price, and so on for some inventions. L3

Integrating the Sciences

Physical Science Early studies in light led to the development of cameras. Studies in mechanics led to the development of robotics. Both technologies have been applied in the design of robotic submersibles, where television cameras act as eyes and robotic claws as hands.

Section 1•3

Prepare

Section Background

- Strategies are skills or procedures used in problem solving. Strategies can be used singly or in combination to solve a problem.
- Most scientists do not see themselves as following a stepwise procedure to solve a problem. Scientists may get new ideas, form new hypotheses, and think of new experiments before previous ones are finished and the data analyzed. However, upon analysis, the scientific process basically follows the course presented in this section.
- In a scientific experiment, factors that don't change are the constants. The factor being tested is the independent variable. The factor that changes as a result of changing the independent variable is called the dependent variable.

1 Motivate

Bellringer

Before presenting the lesson, display **Section Focus Transparency 3** on the overhead projector. Assign the accompanying **Focus Activity** worksheet. L1 LEP

Tying to Previous Knowledge

Students have had to solve a variety of problems throughout their lives. This section will help students see that many strategies are used to solve a variety of scientific and nonscientific problems.

1•3 Solving Problems

Science Words

scientific method
hypothesis
variable
control
theory
law

Objectives

- Describe some problem-solving strategies.
- List steps commonly used in the scientific method.
- Distinguish among hypotheses, theories, and laws.

Problem-Solving Strategies

Soccer practice, dinner, homework, chores, watching your favorite television program . . . how will you squeeze them all in tonight? Is this a problem you are facing? There are many methods you can use to find solutions to problems. These are called strategies. Let's look at one strategy you can use to solve the problem of how to squeeze so many activities into one evening.

One Approach

To solve any problem, you need to have a strategy. Identifying the problem is the first step of any strategy. Next, you need to collect information about the problem. You need to know the basic facts of when soccer practice begins and ends, how much homework you have, what chores need to be done, and when the TV program is on. After you have determined these things, you might try writing out a time schedule. First, write in the activities that have fixed times. Then, fill in each of the other activities. You may have to try different arrangements before you find the solution that you think is the best.

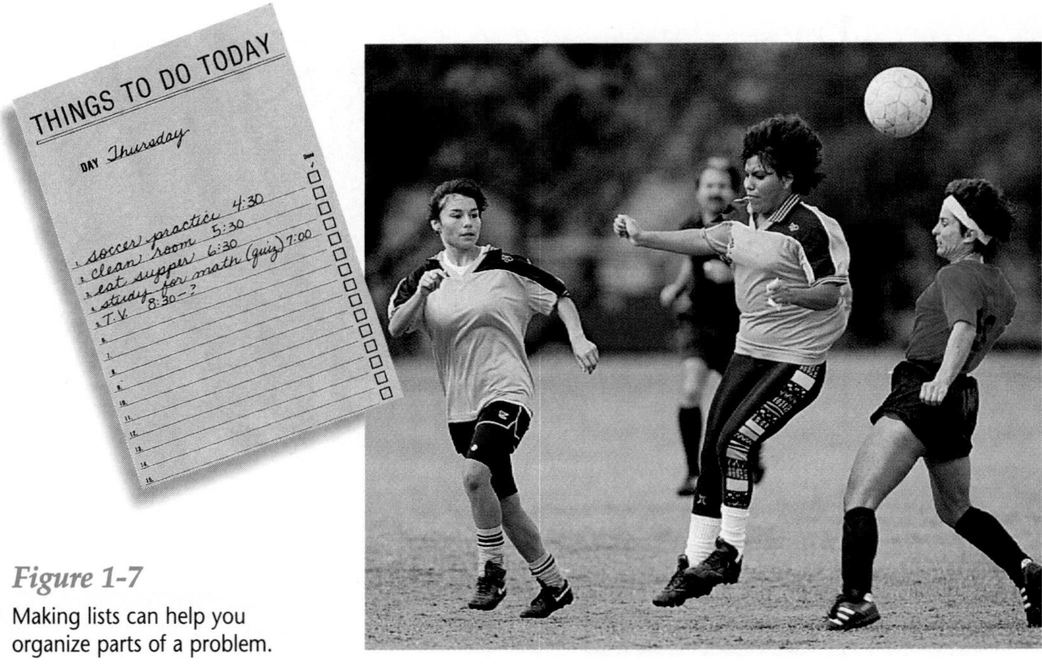

Figure 1-7
Making lists can help you organize parts of a problem.

Program Resources

Reproducible Masters

Study Guide, p. 7 L1
Reinforcement, p. 7 L1
Enrichment, p. 7 L3
Concept Mapping, p. 7
Critical Thinking/Problem Solving, p. 7
Lab Manual 1, 2

Transparencies

Section Focus Transparency 3 L1
Teaching Transparency 1

Other Strategies

There are other ways to solve problems. You might try the strategy of eliminating possibilities. You could do this by trying options until you find the one that works. This method is also known as trial and error.

Sometimes, patterns can help you make predictions about a problem. Organizing data in a table or drawing will help you recognize patterns. For example, suppose three of your friends became sick because of something they ate. You could use a table of what each had recently eaten to look for patterns. Similar food items would be good candidates for causing their illness.

Another strategy is to solve a simpler, related problem, or to make a model, drawing, or graph to help you visualize the problem. If your first strategy does not work, keep trying different strategies.

USING TECHNOLOGY

Mapping the Ocean

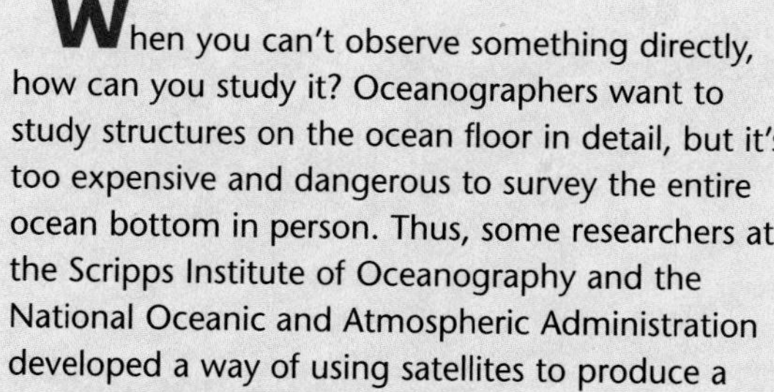

When you can't observe something directly, how can you study it? Oceanographers want to study structures on the ocean floor in detail, but it's too expensive and dangerous to survey the entire ocean bottom in person. Thus, some researchers at the Scripps Institute of Oceanography and the National Oceanic and Atmospheric Administration developed a way of using satellites to produce a detailed image of the global seafloor.

A Bumpy Ocean Surface

The images are possible thanks to technology that allows satellites high above Earth to measure the height of the ocean surface to within a centimeter. This gives scientists a detailed map of the shape of the ocean surface, with broad bumps and dips. The dips and bumps are caused by the gravitational attraction between the water and seafloor features. A 2000-meter undersea volcano, for example, produces a bump on the ocean surface that is about 2 meters high. By analyzing the map of the ocean surface, scientists were able to infer the shape of the seafloor.

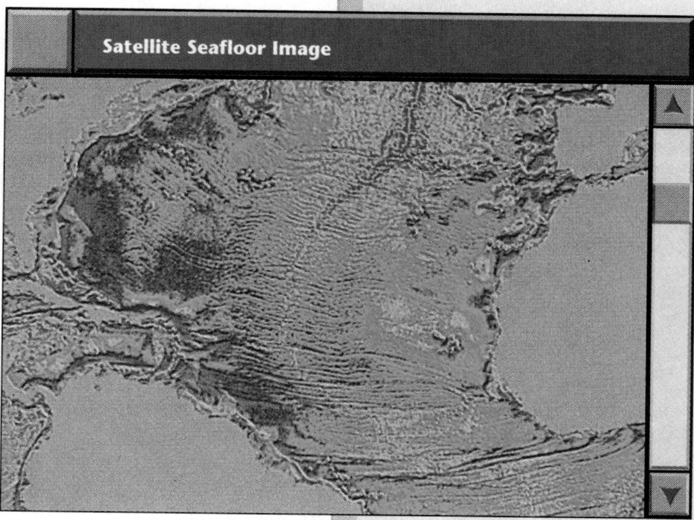

Think Critically: What do you think might be some limitations of this method of mapping?

2 Teach

Revealing Preconceptions

Emphasize that there is no set way to solve a problem. Any logical plan can be implemented. In fact, there are often several ways to solve the same problem.

USING TECHNOLOGY

Ask students how computers might make this sort of technology possible. Satellites can determine the shape of the ocean surface by transmitting electromagnetic waves toward the ocean surface. These waves reflect off of the water and back to the satellite. By timing precisely how long it takes for the electromagnetic waves to travel round-trip, computers can calculate how far away the water is from the satellite. Computers help sort the huge amounts of data and turn it into a usable map.

Think Critically

Although the satellite map provides a good overall map of the global seafloor, scientists must rely on acoustic echo-sounding techniques to investigate an area of the seafloor in detail. The latest such equipment can provide views of the seafloor with about 100 times greater detail than the satellite map.

Across the Curriculum

Social Studies Have groups of students brainstorm to compile a list of social problems such as world hunger or war. Then have them suggest problem-solving strategies that might be used to solve each one. L1 LS

Use these program resources as you teach this lesson.

Concept Mapping, p. 7

Critical Thinking/Problem Solving, p. 7

Enrichment

Have students interview their parents to see how they use problem solving in their lives.

Activity

LS **Auditory-Musical** Prior to beginning class, place the following objects into six different shoe boxes: a penny, a paper clip, a sponge, a spool, a roll of tape, and a shoe. Tape the boxes shut. During class, list the objects on the chalkboard. Have pairs of students try to figure out which object is in each box. After all partners have observed all boxes, ask students to explain the problem-solving strategies they used during this activity. COOP LEARN L1

USING MATH

computing, geometry, exponents, measuring

GLENCOE TECHNOLOGY

Videodisc

The Infinite Voyage: Living with Disaster

Introduction

Chapter 1

Microbursts: How the Airline Industry Copes

Chapter 5

Earthquakes: A Turbulence Beneath the Earth

Chapter 10

Adapting to the Nature of Volcanoes: Sakurajima

Figure 1-8

This mudslide caused serious damage.

Critical Thinking

Imagine yourself mowing the lawn. Suddenly, you come to the edge of a slope, and you discover a large hole where the soil has sunk several feet. The hole wasn't there last week when you mowed the grass. What caused the hole? Where did all the soil go? **Figure 1-8** shows a similar case in which more than just part of a lawn sank down a slope.

After thinking a bit, you remember that there was a severe thunderstorm a few days ago. Perhaps the rain had something to do with the formation of the hole. Maybe the water running down the slope carried away the soil. You may not be aware of it, but you are using critical-thinking skills.

Critical-Thinking Skills

Critical thinking is a process that uses certain skills to solve problems. For example, you *identified the problem* by mentally comparing the slope with how it was the last time you saw it. You *separated important information from unimportant information* when you considered factors that may have affected the slope during the past week. Important factors you may have noted include that it happened only along the slope in the yard, and not on its flatter parts. You also remembered the unusually heavy rain a few days ago. Unimportant factors include the wind that affected all parts of the yard equally, or the sunshine that the entire yard was exposed to. Then you went one step further and analyzed your conclusion that heavy rain could carry away soil on a slope. By performing these three critical thinking skills, you may have solved the problem.

List several mathematical concepts that you might use as you study Earth Science.

Improving Your Critical Thinking Skills

This book uses an activity called "Flex Your Brain" to help you think about and examine your thinking. "Flex Your Brain" is a way to keep your thinking on track when you are investigating a topic. It takes you through steps of exploration from what you already know and believe, to new conclusions and awareness. Then, it encourages you to review and talk about the steps you took.

"Flex Your Brain" and other features of this book will help you improve your critical-thinking skills. You will get your first chance to "Flex Your Brain" on the next page.

Cultural Diversity

Computers and Goddesses For over 1000 years, rice farmers on the island of Bali decided when to plant and irrigate their crops based on advice from Dewi Danu, the water goddess. Farm cooperatives called *subaks* were linked through a network of temples, and water use was controlled by the high priests. A new system, implemented in 1978, built dams and canals for irrigation, and provided pesticides and fertilizers. The farmers kept their fields in continuous production. However, the chemicals killed the fish and eels living in the canals, threatening an important protein source in the farmers' diet. The pests became resistant to the chemicals, and the rice crops suffered greatly. An anthropologist and an ecologist made a computer model showing that the ancient system had conserved water, preserved the soil, and controlled pests. The

You start with what you know about a topic and move on to new conclusions and new awareness. You end by reviewing and discussing the steps you took.

Flex Your Brain

1 **Topic:** ______________________

2 **What do I already know?**
1. ______
2. ______
3. ______
4. ______
5. ______

3 **Q:** Ask a question ______________________

4 **A:** Guess an answer ______________________

5 **How sure am I? (circle one)**

Not sure — Very sure
1 2 3 4 5

6 **How can I find out?**
1. ______
2. ______
3. ______
4. ______
5. ______

7 **EXPLORE**

8 **Do I think differently?** yes / no

9 **What do I know now?**
1. ______
2. ______
3. ______
4. ______
5. ______

10 **SHARE**
1. ______
2. ______
3. ______

1 Fill in the topic.

2 Jot down what you already know about the topic.

3 Using what you already know (step 2), form a question about the topic. Are you unsure about one of the items you listed? Do you want to know more? Do you want to know what, how, or why? Write down your question.

4 Guess an answer to your question. In the next few steps, you will be exploring the reasonableness of your answer. Write down your guess.

5 Circle the number in the box that matches how sure you are of your answer in step 4. This is your chance to rate your confidence in what you've done so far and, later, to see how your level of sureness affects your thinking.

6 How can you find out more about your topic? You might want to read a book, ask an expert, or do an experiment. Write down ways you can find out more.

7 Make a plan to explore your answer. Use the resources you listed in step 6. Then, carry out your plan.

8 Now that you've explored, go back to your answer in step 4. Would you answer differently?

9 Considering what you learned in your exploration, answer your question again, adding new things you've learned. You may completely change your answer.

10 It's important to be able to talk about thinking. Choose three people to tell about how you arrived at your response in every step. For example, don't just read what you wrote down in step 2. Try to share how you thought of those things.

Cultural Diversity (con't)

soil had been able to yield the same amounts of the same crop every year for centuries. Ask students to explain why computers are good for modeling and studying environmental problems. They may say that computers can be used to analyze a lot of data in a short period of time.

FLEX Your Brain

Use the Flex Your Brain activity to have students explore SEASONS. P

Activity Worksheets, p. 5

Activity

To acquaint students with this strategy, divide the class into small groups and have them explore a topic using the Flex Your Brain worksheet. Students should have some familiarity with the topic chosen. Possible topics might include cacti, volcanoes, robots, or topics from a list the class brainstorms. See steps on the student page for a more detailed description of the Flex Your Brain process. A reproducible version of the Flex Your Brain activity with space for students to write in their responses can be found on page 5 in the **Activity Worksheets** booklet in the **Teacher Classroom Resources.**

Use **Teaching Transparency 1** as you teach this lesson.

GLENCOE TECHNOLOGY

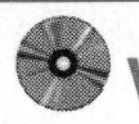

Videodisc

STVS: Physics

Disc 1, Side 1

New Skid Control (Ch. 4)

Video Astronomy (Ch. 19)

Disc 1, Side 2

Bipedal Robot (Ch. 2)

Problem Solving

Solve the Problem

1. A possible hypothesis is that darker-colored fabrics will absorb more heat than lighter-colored fabrics.
2. The hypothesis was tested by placing thermometers inside equally-sized pockets of similar material of different colors. The pockets were exposed to the same intensity of sunlight for the same amount of time. The differences between the beginning temperature and ending temperature were recorded for each sample. Because the only difference between the samples during the experiment was the fabric color, analyzing the change of temperature inside each pocket will either support or not support the hypothesis.

Think Critically

Whether the hypothesis was supported depends on what the hypothesis was. If students predicted that the darker-colored fabrics would absorb more heat, then the hypothesis was supported.

GLENCOE TECHNOLOGY

Videodisc

STVS: Ecology

Disc 6, Side 1

Evaluating Artificial Reefs (Ch. 11)

Disc 6, Side 2

Lake Erie Recovery (Ch. 22)

Problem Solving

Experimenting

Suppose it is your job to pick out new uniforms for your school band. Other students have expressed their concern about how hot uniforms are during football games and parades. You suspect that some colors of uniforms will be warmer than others, so you decide to design an experiment to determine which color absorbs the least amount of heat.

First, obtain fabric samples of each color. Then, cut the samples to the same size and fold them into pockets. Place a thermometer inside each pocket and place them in the sun. After recording the beginning temperature of each sample, and the temperature at the end of ten minutes, analyze your data.

Solve the Problem

1. What is your hypothesis in this experiment?
2. How did you test your hypothesis?

Think Critically:

Suppose the results of your experiment are as follows. Was your hypothesis supported? Explain.

Color	Beginning Temperature	Temperature After 10 Minutes
Red	24°C	26°C
Black	24°C	28°C
Blue	24°C	27°C
White	24°C	25°C
Green	24°C	27°C

Using Scientific Methods

If you want to stop soil from washing away on a slope in your yard, what can you do? Scientists use a series of planned steps, called a **scientific method,** to solve problems. A basic scientific method is listed in **Table 1-1.** It's important to note that scientists don't always follow these exact steps or do the steps in this order. However, most scientists follow some type of step-by-step method. How can a scientific method be used to solve the slope problem?

Steps in a Scientific Method

You've already done the first step by identifying the problem. The next step is to gather facts that you think may have a bearing on the problem. Then make a hypothesis about how you might stop the soil from washing away. A **hypothesis** is a prediction about a problem that can be tested. You might hypothesize that a wall built at the base of the slope will act as a barrier to the soil. Now you're ready to test your hypothesis.

Table 1-1

A Scientific Method
1. Determine the problem.
2. Make a hypothesis.
3. Test your hypothesis.
4. Analyze the results.
5. Draw conclusions.

You might build a wall at the base of the slope and use a hose to wet the soil. If the soil washes away, your hypothesis was not supported and therefore needs to be revised. You could conclude that building a wall like you did does not work to prevent the soil from washing away. You might make a new hypothesis and start the problem-solving process over again.

Variables and Control

An experiment should test only one variable at a time. A **variable** is a changeable factor in an experiment. Building the wall was the variable you tested. Other variables you might decide to test one at a time are planting different types of vegetation on the slope, planting more vegetation on the slope, as in **Figure 1-9,** replacing the soil with another type, or changing the angle of the slope.

A **control** is a standard for comparison. The slope before the wall was built was the control in your experiment. By comparing the control with the other trials, you could tell whether the wall stopped the problem.

CONNECT TO

LIFE SCIENCE

You have learned that oceanographers use sound to study things they cannot see. Biologists use ultrasound, sound above the range that humans can hear, to study cells and tissues they can't see. Suppose you are a biologist testing the effects of ultrasound on cells. ***Identify*** the control in this experiment.

Figure 1-9 Planting trees and other plants on a slope is one way to reduce erosion.

CONNECT TO

LIFE SCIENCE

Answer The control is cells that are not exposed to ultrasound.

Inquiry Question

Why should you test only one variable at a time? *If more than one variable is tested at a time, you don't know what is causing the end result. By testing one variable at a time, you can better determine the cause-effect relationship.*

3 Assess

Check for Understanding

FLEX Your Brain

Use the Flex Your Brain activity to have students explore SCIENTIFIC METHODS. P

Activity Worksheets, p. 5

Reteach

Have students identify the hypothesis, variable, and control for an experiment titled "How does the speed of wind affect the height of waves on the ocean?" One hypothesis might be that heavy wind results in high waves. The variable is the speed of the wind. The control is the wave heights when wind conditions are calm.

Extension

For students who have mastered this section, use the **Reinforcement** and **Enrichment** masters.

4 Close

• MINI • QUIZ •

Use the Mini Quiz to check students' recall of chapter content.

1. **In an experiment, the _____ is the proposed answer to the problem being tested.** *hypothesis*
2. **In an experiment, the _____ is the changeable factor.** *variable*
3. **In an experiment, the _____ is a standard of comparison.** *control*

Section Wrap-up

Review

1. Identify the problem; collect information; make lists to help organize information; use trial and error; solve a simpler problem; make a model or drawing or graph; separate important information from unimportant information; analyze your conclusion; use the scientific method.
2. (1) determine the problem, (2) make a hypothesis, (3) test your hypothesis, (4) analyze the results, (5) draw conclusions
3. **Think Critically** It is a hypothesis.

Using Computers

A possible hypothesis is, "When sand is added to clay, the soil erodes more slowly than when the soil is entirely clay." To test the hypothesis, two boxes of soil, one entirely clay and the other a mix of clay and sand, could be made. Under one end of each box, a 2 cm wooden block could be placed. Water could be siphoned from a bucket onto each slope for equal amounts of time and with the same pressure. The amount of erosion could be observed. P

Figure 1-10
Hypotheses are tested many times before they are accepted as theories.

Theories and Laws

Scientists are constantly testing hypotheses. When new data gathered over a long period of time support a hypothesis, scientists become convinced that the hypothesis is correct. They use such hypotheses to form theories. An explanation backed by results obtained from repeated tests or experiments is a **theory.**

A scientific **law** is a rule of nature that describes the behavior of something in nature. Generally, laws predict or describe what will happen in a given situation but don't explain why. An example of a law is Newton's first law of motion. It states that an object continues in motion, or at rest, until it's acted upon by an outside force. You can use scientific methods to help you solve problems. Whether your problem is deciding what route you should follow home or wondering why a rock looks the way it does, a step-by-step method will lead you toward a reasonable solution.

Section Wrap-up

Review

1. What are some strategies you can use to solve problems?
2. What are the steps in a scientific method?
3. **Think Critically:** Imagine that you feel the school building shake, and you think an earthquake was the cause. Is that a hypothesis or a theory?

Skill Builder

Comparing and Contrasting

Compare and contrast a scientific variable with a control. If you need help, refer to Comparing and Contrasting in the **Skill Handbook.**

Using Computers

Word Processing Use your word processing skills to design an experiment to test how changing the type of soil on a slope affects soil loss. Be sure to include your hypothesis and explain how you would test it.

Skill Builder

Both are necessary in order to conduct a scientific experiment. A variable is a changeable factor in an experiment. A control is a standard for comparison.

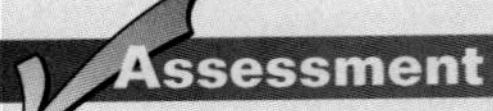

Assessment

Content Use this Skill Builder to assess students' abilities to compare and contrast a theory and a law. Use the Performance Task Assessment List for Writing in Science in **PASC,** p. 87. P

Measurement and Safety

1•4

Measurement

How could you measure the size of the floor of a cave without a ruler or measuring tape? You might count your steps across the cave floor. You could then say that the cave is 25 steps by 30 steps. But this step measurement wouldn't mean the same thing to your friends because their steps would be different from yours. Because of this problem, there are standard units used for measurement.

Today, the measuring system used by most people around the world is the **International System of Units (SI).** SI is a modern version of the metric system. SI is based on a decimal system that uses the number 10 as the base unit.

Length

The standard unit in SI for length is the meter. It's about the length of a guitar. A decimeter is one-tenth of a meter. A centimeter is one one-hundredth of a meter. And a millimeter is one one-thousandth of a meter. A common unit for longer distances is the kilometer. A kilometer is 1000 times greater than a meter. Refer to Appendixes A and B for further explanation of SI and English/SI conversions.

Science Words

International System of Units (SI)
mass
weight
gravity

Objectives

- List the SI units for the following measurements: length, mass, weight, area, volume, density, and temperature.
- Differentiate between the terms *mass* and *weight* and the terms *area* and *volume.*
- State three lab safety rules.

Figure 1-11
Under the glass lies the official kilogram mass used by the United States. *What standards of measurement do you use?*

19

Section 1•4

Prepare

Section Background

The density of water is 1 g/mL. The densities of other substances are sometimes compared to the density of water. This comparison is called specific gravity.

Preplanning

- To prepare for Activity 1-1, obtain a graduated cylinder, rock, graph paper, metric ruler, and balance for each student group.
- To prepare for the MiniLAB, obtain a calculator for each student group.

1 Motivate

Bellringer

Before presenting the lesson, display **Section Focus Transparency 4** on the overhead projector. Assign the accompanying **Focus Activity** worksheet. L1 LEP

Tying to Previous Knowledge

Ask: **How big is big? How heavy is heavy? How hot is hot? How slow is slow?** *Students should realize that it is difficult to describe size, weight, temperature, and speed unless you can make comparisons. Students should realize that systems of units are needed.*

Program Resources

 **Reproducible Masters**

Study Guide, p. 8 L1
Reinforcement, p. 8 L1
Enrichment, p. 8 L3
Cross-Curricular Integration, p. 5
Activity Worksheets, pp. 5, 7-8, 10 L1
Science Integration Activities, pp. 1-2
Lab Manual 3, 4
Multicultural Connections, pp. 5-6

 **Transparencies**

Section Focus Transparency 4 L1
Science Integration Transparency 1
Teaching Transparency 2

Visual Learning

Figure 1-11 What standards of measure do you use? *Examples may include a ruler, a bathroom scale, a measuring cup, in addition to classroom laboratory supplies such as the masses on a balance, and a graduated cylinder.* LS LEP

2 Teach

Demonstration

Demonstrate how a balance, spring scale, and graduated cylinder are used. Make sure students understand that a balance measures mass, a spring scale measures weight, and a graduated cylinder measures liquid volume.

Activity

LS Visual-Spatial Show students two identical jars. Fill one with jelly beans, the other with pennies. Ask: **Which jar has the greater volume?** *Prove that both jars have the same volume by emptying them and filling each with water. Both hold the same amount.* Refill the jars with the jelly beans and pennies, then ask: **Which jar has more mass? Which weighs more?** *Students will probably say that the jar of pennies has more mass and weighs more.*

USING MATH

5 newtons

INTEGRATION Physics

Mass is both a measure of the amount of matter in an object and a measure of the resistance of a body to change in motion. *Weight* takes into account the mass of an object and the gravitational force on that mass. Students often confuse the terms *weight* and *mass*. Explain that the mass of an object affects its weight but the weight of an object does not affect its mass.

Use these program resources as you teach this lesson.

Cross-Curricular Integration, p. 5

Science Integration Activities, pp. 1-2

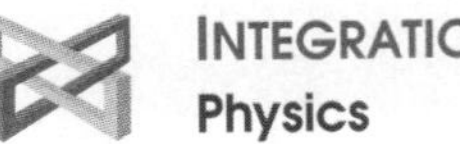

INTEGRATION Physics

Mass

Mass is a measure of the amount of matter in an object. Mass depends on the number and kinds of atoms that make up an object. Mass does not change with gravitational force. The mass of an object is determined by comparing it with known masses using a balance.

The standard unit of measure for mass is a kilogram. The mass of one bagel is about 57 grams. One gram equals 1000 milligrams, so what would be the mass of one bagel in milligrams? It would be 57 000 milligrams.

Weight

Weight is a measure of gravitational force on a mass. **Gravity** is an attractive force that exists between all objects. If you could weigh yourself on the moon, you would weigh one-sixth the amount you weigh on Earth. This is because the moon's gravitational force is one-sixth that of Earth's.

The standard unit for weight is a newton, named after Sir Isaac Newton, who was the first person to describe gravity. A medium-sized apple weighs about 1 newton.

USING MATH

If an object weighs 30 newtons on Earth, how much would it weigh on the moon?

Area

Some measurements, such as area, require a combination of SI units. Area is the amount of surface included within a set of boundaries. Let's say you want to know the area of a field. First, you'd measure its length and width with a meterstick, and then you'd multiply these two measurements to find the area. In SI, area is expressed in units such as square centimeters (cm^2).

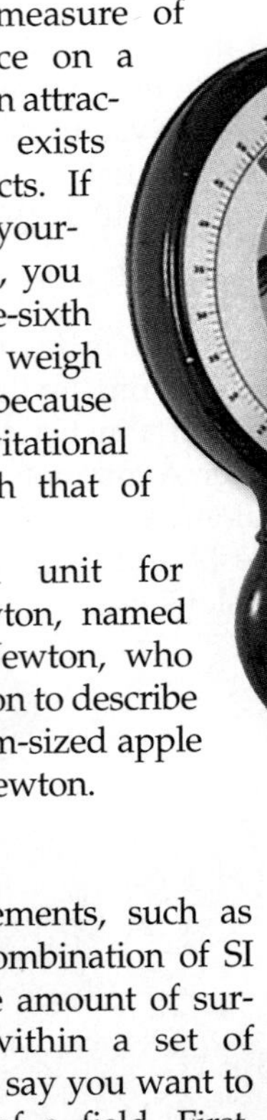

Figure 1-12
When you weigh yourself, you are measuring the force of gravity.

Volume

Volume is a measure of how much space an object occupies, so if you wanted to know the volume of an aquarium, such as the one in **Figure 1-13,** you'd need to know its length, width, and depth. Then you'd multiply these three measurements to find the volume. The cubic meter (m^3) is the basic unit of volume in SI for solids, but liquid volumes are often measured in liters (L) and milliliters (mL). Liquid volume measurements are made using graduated cylinders and beakers. Because one milliliter of a liquid will just fill a container with a 1 cm^3 volume, milliliters can be expressed as cubic centimeters. For example, an aquarium full of water is 11 356 mL or 11 356 cm^3.

Figure 1-13

The volume of this aquarium can be found by multiplying its length, width, and height.

USING MATH

A wood block has dimensions of 2 cm, 1.5 cm, and 3 cm. What is its volume in cubic centimeters?

Density

Density is a measure of the amount of matter that occupies a particular space. It's determined by dividing the mass of an object by its volume.

$$\textbf{density} = \frac{\textbf{mass}}{\textbf{volume}} \qquad D = \frac{m}{v}$$

An SI unit that is often used to express density is grams per cubic centimeter (g/cm^3). How might you express the density of a liquid? We often use grams per milliliter (g/mL).

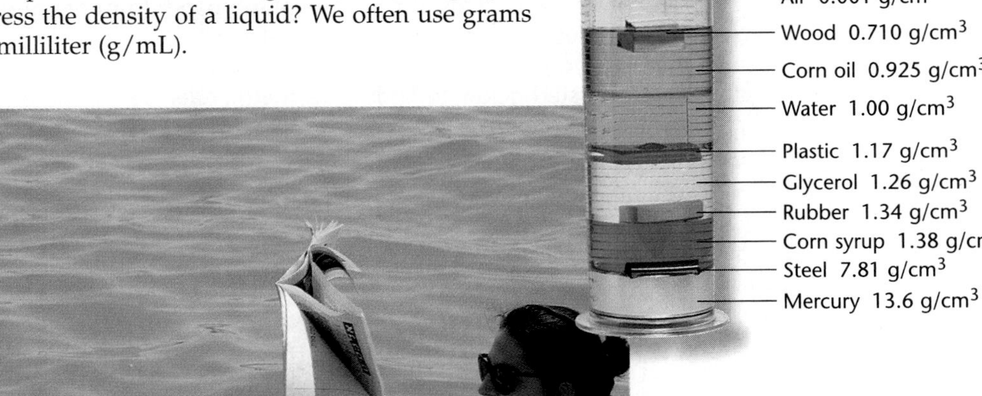

Figure 1-14

Materials of lower density float on other materials of greater density. This woman can easily float in the more dense Dead Sea.

Use these program resouces as you teach this lesson.

Teaching Transparency 2

Science Integration Transparency 1

Across the Curriculum

Mathematics Have students write the formulas for and explain how to find the area, volume, and density of solid objects. L1 LS

Inquiry Questions

- **Define the following words: milliliter, micrometer, kilogram.** *milliliter—one one-thousandth of a liter; micrometer—0.000 001 of a meter; kilogram—1000 times greater than a gram*
- **Convert these units: 1 km = _____ mm; 3 cm = _____ mm; 250 mm = _____ cm.** *1 000 000; 30; 25*

USING MATH

9 cubic centimeters

NATIONAL GEOGRAPHIC SOCIETY

Videodisc

STV: Restless Earth

Andes; South America

52201

Sandstone towers; Algeria

52219

Glacial lake; Canada

52253

STV: Atmosphere

Smog; Chicago, Illinois

38685

Storm clouds; Seattle, Washington

38724

Earth as seen from orbiting satellite

38702

Activity 1-1

PREPARATION

Purpose

LS **Logical-Mathematical** Students will calculate the density of a rock using two different methods. L1 COOP LEARN

Process Skills

designing an experiment, communicating, measuring in SI, using numbers, interpreting data, making and using tables, comparing and contrasting, forming operational definitions

Time

1 hour

Materials

Flat rocks such as shale or slate are the easiest to work with in this experiment.

Alternative Materials If the rocks are too large to fit into the graduated cylinders, have students use beakers or overflow cans to determine the volume of their rocks.

Possible Hypotheses

One way to determine the volume is to use the graph paper and metric ruler. The other way is to measure water displacement in the graduated cylinder. Mass is measured with the balance. Density is calculated by dividing mass by volume.

Activity Worksheets, pp. 5, 7-8

PLAN THE EXPERIMENT

Possible Procedures

- One way to figure density is to place the rock on the graph paper and draw around it. Remove the rock and count the boxes within the traced area. This represents the area of the base of the rock. (Each box will represent one square mm or cm.) Next, use the metric ruler to measure the height of the rock. Multiply

Activity 1-1

Design Your Own Experiment
Rock Density

You've learned that density is the relationship of the mass of an object to its volume. It's pretty easy to find the density of liquids and regularly shaped solids, but how could you find the density of a rock? It's a solid, but it doesn't have a regular geometric shape. How could you find its volume? One way is to measure the displacement of water. When an object is placed in water, it pushes away the water that used to occupy that space. Using this method, the volume of a solid object can be determined.

PREPARATION

Problem

What are two methods you could use to determine the density of a rock?

Form a Hypothesis

Based on what you know about the formula for density, write a hypothesis that explains two methods you could use with the materials listed below to find the density of a rock.

Objectives

- Design an experiment to use two different methods to find the density of a rock.
- Analyze the data that you collect.

Possible Materials 

- graduated cylinder or beaker
- water
- rock
- graph paper (mm or cm grid)
- balance
- goggles
- metric ruler

Inclusion Strategies

Physically Challenged Have students who have difficulty doing the testing be in charge of formulating the hypothesis and checking the plan to make sure the steps are in logical order.

PLAN THE EXPERIMENT

1. As a group, agree upon and write out your hypothesis statement.
2. As a group, list the steps you need to take to test your hypothesis. Be specific, describing exactly what you will do at each step.
3. Make a list of the materials that you will need to complete each portion of your experiment.
4. Design a data table in your Science Journal so that it will be ready to use as your group collects data.

Check the Plan

1. Read over your entire experiment to make sure that all steps are in logical order.
2. Do you have to run any tests more than one time?
3. *Make sure your teacher approves your plan before you begin.*

DO THE EXPERIMENT

1. Carry out the experiment as planned.
2. While the experiment is going on, write down any observations that you make and complete the data table in your Science Journal.

Analyze and Apply

1. How did you **measure** the volume of the rock in each of your two methods?
2. How did you **measure** the mass of the rock?
3. **Compare** the density figures you got using your two different methods.
4. Which method do you think was the more accurate of the methods you tried? Why?
5. **Compare** your methods with those used by other groups.
6. Of all the methods that people in your class tried, which do you think is the best method to use to **measure** the density of irregularly shaped solids? Why?

Suppose you want to determine the density of a very large rock, one that is too big to fit into a beaker. What would you do?

the area of the base times the height. This will equal the volume of the rock. Use the balance to determine the mass. Divide mass by volume to find density.

- A second way is to partially fill a graduated cylinder with water. Record the volume of the water. Place the rock into the water and record the new volume. Find the volume of the rock by subtracting the beginning volume from the ending volume. Use the balance to determine the mass. Divide mass by volume to find density.

Teaching Strategies

When students are counting the boxes on the graph paper, suggest that they count all complete boxes in their tracing first. Then, add in the partial boxes to find the total surface area.

DO THE EXPERIMENT

Expected Outcome

Using the graph paper-metric ruler approach to finding density is a difficult and inaccurate method.

Analyze and Apply

1. See possible procedures above.
2. See possible procedures above.
3. Answers will vary.
4. The displacement method; irregular shapes like rocks are hard to measure directly.
5. Methods will likely be similar.
6. Using displacement to find volume and a balance to find mass are the best methods. By dividing mass by volume, density is calculated. This method results in fewer errors in measurement.

Go Further

Fill a bucket to the top with water. Carefully place the rock into the bucket. Catch and measure the overflow to find the rock's volume. Use a balance to measure its mass. Divide mass by volume to find density.

Assessment

Performance Have students swap rocks with another group. Have each group find the density of its new rock using the displacement method. Have the two groups compare their results for the same rocks. Use the Performance Task Assessment List for Carrying Out a Strategy and Collecting Data in **PASC**, p. 25. P

MiniLAB

Purpose

LS **Logical-Mathematical** Students will convert Fahrenheit temperatures to Celsius. L1

Teaching Strategies

Have students examine Fahrenheit and Celsius thermometers.

Analysis

1. 85°F = 29°C
2. –40°C = –40°F

Assessment

Performance To further assess students' understanding of how to convert Fahrenheit and Celsius temperatures, have them convert the following temperatures: 0°C (32°F), 100°C (212°F), 98.6°F (37°C). Use the Performance Task Assessment List for Using Math in Science in **PASC**, p. 29. P

Activity Worksheets, pp. 5, 10

3 Assess

Check for Understanding

FLEX Your Brain

Use the Flex Your Brain activity to have students explore SI.

Activity Worksheets, p. 5

Reteach

Have students take measurements from food labels and practice converting them to smaller and larger SI units.

Extension

For students who have mastered this section, use the **Reinforcement** and **Enrichment** masters.

MiniLAB

How do you convert Fahrenheit temperatures to Celsius?

Temperatures are often reported for public weather information in the non-SI units of the Fahrenheit scale, rather than the Celsius scale.

Procedure

1. To convert from °F to °C, subtract 32 from the Fahrenheit temperature and divide by 1.8.
2. To convert from °C to °F, multiply the Celsius temperature by 1.8 and add 32.

Analysis

1. Convert 85°F to °C.
2. Convert -40°C to °F.

Temperature

Temperature is a measure of how hot or cold something is. As you probably know, temperature is measured with a thermometer. What you probably didn't know is that the SI unit for temperature is a kelvin. On the Kelvin scale, absolute zero is 0, the coldest temperature.

The symbol for kelvin is K. Instead of using kelvin thermometers, many scientists use Celsius thermometers. The symbol for a Celsius degree is °C. The Celsius temperature scale is based on the freezing and boiling points of water. The freezing point of pure water is 0°C, and the boiling point is 100°C. A comfortable room temperature is 21°C, and the average human body temperature is about 37°C. You can use these temperatures as reference points when you measure other Celsius temperatures. Now, suppose you wanted to change Celsius temperatures to SI. You'd simply add 273.16 to the degrees Celsius to find the number of kelvins.

Figure 1-15

Temperature affects our daily activities.

degrees Celsius + 273.16 = kelvin

Making accurate measurements in SI is an important part of any experiment. If you don't make accurate measurements, your results and conclusions are invalid.

Figure 1-16

Thermal gloves, goggles, an apron, and safe technique help to protect this student while she heats a solution in a flask.

Safety

Some of the laboratory activities in this book that you'll complete will require you to handle potentially hazardous materials. When performing these activities, safe practices and methods must be used. Scientific equipment and chemicals need to be handled safely and properly, as **Figure 1-16** shows. The safety rules that follow will help you protect yourself and others from injury and will make you aware of possible hazards.

Cultural Diversity

International Numbers Have students research several systems of units, including SI, Native American, Chinese, and Greek. Have them compare and contrast the different systems. L2

Inclusion Strategies

Gifted Have interested students research the history of the metric system and how it evolved into SI. L3

Safety Rules

1. Before beginning any lab, understand the safety symbols shown in Appendix D.
2. Wear goggles and a safety apron whenever an investigation involves heating, pouring, or using chemicals.
3. Always slant test tubes away from yourself and others when heating them. Keep all materials away from open flames. Tie back long hair and loose clothing.
4. Never eat or drink in the lab, and never use laboratory glassware as food or drink containers. Never inhale chemicals, and don't taste any substance or draw any material into a tube with your mouth.
5. Know what to do in case of fire. Also, know the location and proper use of the fire extinguisher, safety shower, fire blanket, first aid kit, and fire alarm.
6. Report any accident or injury to your teacher.
7. When cleaning up, dispose of chemicals and other materials as directed by your teacher, and always wash your hands thoroughly after working in the lab.

Figure 1-17
Laboratories should have proper safety equipment available.

Section Wrap-up

Review

1. Explain the differences between mass and weight and between area and volume.
2. When should you use safety goggles? Refer to Appendix D.
3. **Think Critically:** Which SI units would you use to measure the amount of saltwater in an aquarium, the mass of a rock, the density of a rock?

Skill Builder
Measuring in SI

Use your knowledge of SI units to answer the following questions. If you need help, refer to Measuring in SI in the **Skill Handbook.**

1. How many milligrams are in one gram?
2. How many meters are in a kilometer?
3. How many centimeters are in a meter?

USING MATH

If 30 milliliters of fresh water have a mass of 30 grams, what is the density of water? If 100 milliliters of seawater have a mass of 125 grams, what is the density of the seawater?

4 Close

•MINI•QUIZ•

Use the Mini Quiz to check students' recall of chapter content.

1. **One kilometer equals ______ meters.** *1000*
2. **______ is a measure of the amount of matter in an object.** *Mass*
3. **The measure of the force of gravity on an object is the object's ________ .** *weight*
4. **What is the temperature scale used by most scientists?** *Celsius*

Section Wrap-up

Review

1. Mass is the amount of matter in an object. Weight is a measure of the force of gravity on an object's mass. Area is the amount of surface included within a set of boundaries, and volume is a measure of how much space an object occupies.
2. Safety goggles should be worn when heating, pouring, using chemicals, or whenever danger to the eyes exists.
3. **Think Critically** Volume of an aquarium: milliliters, cubic centimeters, or liters; mass of a rock: grams or kilograms; density of a rock: grams/cubic centimeter or kilograms/cubic meter

USING MATH

water = 1 gram/milliliter
saltwater = 1.25 grams/milliliter

Skill Builder

1. 1000
2. 1000
3. 100

Assessment

Oral Use this Skill Builder to assess students' abilities to measure in SI by having them describe the SI units that would be most nearly equivalent to inches and ounces. Use the Performance Task Assessment List for Using Math in Science in **PASC**, p. 29. P

Sources

- *The Man Who Walked Through Time,* by John Fletcher, Vintage Books, New York, 1989.
- *A Natural History Guide—Grand Canyon National Park,* by Jeremy Schmidt, Houghton Mifflin Company, Boston, 1993.
- *The Encyclopedia of Native America,* by Trudy Griffin-Pierce, Michael Friedman Publishing Group, Inc., New York, 1995.

Background

- Limestones, sandstones, and shales are sedimentary rocks that generally form in water. Some sedimentary rocks are aeolian (formed by the wind). Some igneous rocks are formed when a volcano, which is a crack in Earth's crust, spews lava and other debris onto Earth's surface. Other igneous rocks form deep beneath the crust in Earth's upper mantle. Metamorphic rocks like gneiss and schist form when heat and pressure change pre-existing rocks.
- Several unconformities, or gaps in the rock record, are present in the rocks of the Grand Canyon. An unconformity represents a period of erosion, nondeposition, or deformation. The contact between the tilted rocks of the Grand Canyon Series and the overlying, horizontal sedimentary rocks is an angular unconformity.

Teaching Strategies

- Discuss the title of this feature with students. Help them to conclude that by observing processes occurring on the Earth today, geologists are able to infer what may have happened in Earth's past.

Science & History

Science Journal

Locate a road cut or some other rock outcrop or interesting geological feature. Observe the feature, then use what you know about rocks and Earth processes to describe and illustrate the history of the feature.

The Present Is the Key to the Past

Standing on the rim of the Grand Canyon is an incredible experience. There aren't many places where you can look down into a 1.6 km-deep gouge in Earth's crust. The Grand Canyon isn't just a tourist attraction, though. It's also a unique opportunity to observe a large chunk of Earth's geological history. The thick, colorful layers of rocks that can be observed along the canyon walls hold clues to the processes that formed and changed them.

Once Upon a Time, Over a Billion Years Ago . . .

At the very bottom of this awesome gorge lie the oldest rocks, which formed over 1.7 billion years ago. Some of these rocks formed when ancient volcanoes in northern Arizona erupted, while others formed when magma cooled deep within Earth.

Later, quiet seas covered much of the canyon area. When the seas retreated, the minerals and other bits of debris in the water formed layers of sandstones, limestones, and shales. Forces within Earth tilted and folded these layers. Then, over hundreds of millions of years, more layers of shales, limestones, and sandstones formed over this area. The youngest rocks in the canyon are about 225 million years old.

Geologists have proposed many ideas as to how the Grand Canyon formed. Some thought a single, catastrophic event formed the gorge, while others hypothesized that it was a remnant of a once-molten planet. The most accepted hypothesis, however, is that the Colorado River slowly carved the canyon during the past 15 to 20 million years.

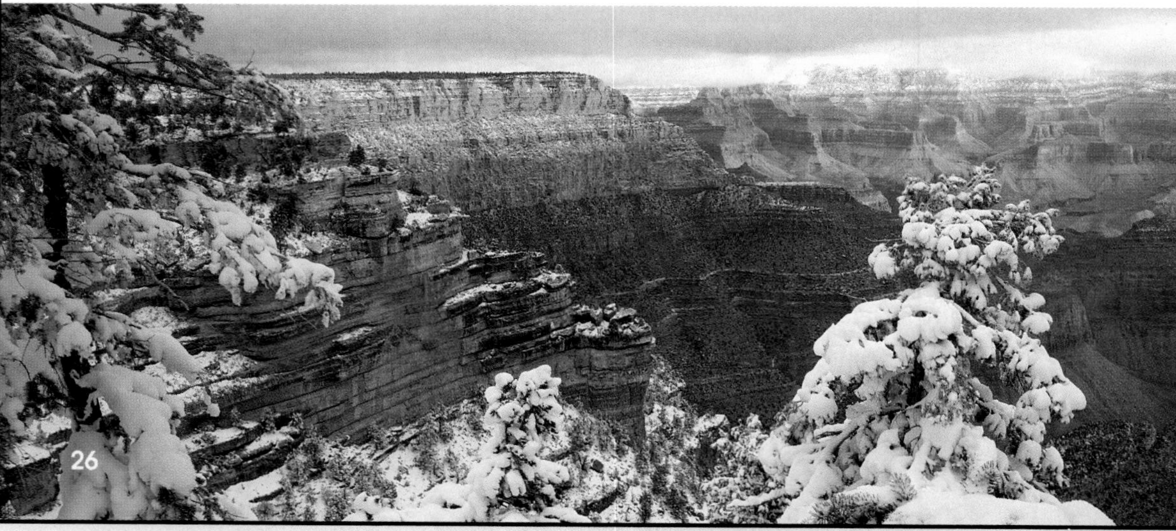

26

LS **Linguistic** Have students use the references listed to find out more about the terms used to name the rock formations of the Grand Canyon. Some of the terms are descriptive, i.e., the Redwall Limestone. Other terms are taken from various Native American groups that once lived or still live in the area. For example, the term *Kaibab* is a Native American one that means "mountain lying on its side." L1

- Allow students who have visited the canyon to describe their experiences and impressions of this natural wonder.

LS **Visual-Spatial** Obtain a topographic map of the Grand Canyon area. Have students examine the map to discover that the nearly 300-mile long canyon (measured along the river) is a series of gorges, cliffs, mesas, buttes, and other topographic features.

Chapter 1

Review

Summary

1-1: What Is Earth Science?

1. Geology is the study of Earth and the processes that form and change it. Meteorology is the study of weather and the forces that cause it. Astronomy is the study of objects in space. Oceanography is the study of Earth's oceans.

1-2: Science and Society: Applying Science

1. Technology has made possible various things you use every day, such as calculators and computers.
2. Technology not only contributes to but also helps solve problems such as pollution and erosion.

1-3: Solving Problems

1. Problem-solving strategies include identifying the problem; collecting data about the problem; eliminating possibilities; using trial and error; solving a simpler, related problem; and making a model or drawing.
2. Commonly used steps in scientific methods include determining the problem, making a hypothesis, testing, analyzing results, and drawing conclusions.
3. A hypothesis is a prediction about a problem that can be tested. Hypotheses may be used to form theories, which are explanations backed by results obtained from repeated tests or experiments. A law is a rule of nature.

1-4: Measurement and Safety

1. In SI, the unit for length is the meter; mass, the kilogram; weight, the newton; area, square centimeters; volume, cubic meters; and density, grams per cubic centimeter.
2. Mass is the amount of matter in an object. Weight is the measure of the force of gravity on an object. Area is the amount of surface in a set of boundaries. Volume is a measure of how much space an object occupies.
3. Lab safety includes understanding how to do the activity, using caution while working with flames, never eating or drinking in the lab, using care with all substances, and reporting any accidents to your teacher.

Key Science Words

a. astronomy	i. mass
b. control	j. meteorology
c. geology	k. oceanography
d. gravity	l. science
e. Earth science	m. scientific method
f. hypothesis	n. technology
g. International System of Units (SI)	o. theory
h. law	p. variable
	q. weight

Reviewing Vocabulary

Match each phrase with the correct term from the list of Key Science Words.

1. having knowledge by observing and studying things around you
2. the study of objects in space
3. the use of scientific discoveries
4. a prediction that can be tested
5. a factor in an experiment that changes
6. a scientific rule of nature

Chapter 1 Review

Summary

Have students read the summary statements to review the major concepts of the chapter.

Reviewing Vocabulary

1. l	**6.** h
2. a	**7.** g
3. n	**8.** i
4. f	**9.** q
5. p	**10.** j

Assessment

Portfolio Encourage students to place in their portfolios one or two items of what they consider to be their best work. Examples include:

- Skill Builder, p. 9
- Flex Your Brain, p. 15
- Using Computers, p. 18 P

Performance Additional performance assessments may be found in **Performance Assessment** and **Science Integration Activities.** Performance Task Assessment Lists and rubrics for evaluating these activities can be found in Glencoe's **Performance Assessment in the Science Classroom.**

GLENCOE TECHNOLOGY

MindJogger Videoquiz

Chapter 1 Have students work in groups as they play the Videoquiz game to review key chapter concepts.

Checking Concepts

1. a
2. b
3. b
4. c
5. a
6. c
7. c
8. a
9. c
10. d

Understanding Concepts

11. A volcano erupts with much force, throwing material into the air. Thus, a knowledge of forces, motion, and energy is needed to study volcanoes. Knowing the composition of the material ejected might also help the scientist.

12. Some types of technology cause pollution, erosion, and weather changes.

13. A hypothesis is an educated guess as to the answer to a problem. A theory is an explanation of a problem that is backed by results obtained from repeated testing.

14. Both are measures. Mass measures the amount of matter in an object. It is measured using a balance. Weight is a measure of the force of gravity and is determined using a spring scale.

15. Volume of a solid is the length times the width times the height. Area is length times width. By measuring the third dimension, height, the volume of the box could be calculated.

Thinking Critically

16. Susan will need to understand geological, physical, and chemical processes in order to understand how organisms interact with their environment.

17. Answers will vary, but students might list writing implements, calculators, electricity, and computers.

Chapter 1 Review

7. a modern version of the metric system
8. the amount of matter in an object
9. a measure of gravitational force
10. the study of weather conditions

Checking Concepts

Choose the word or phrase that completes the sentence or answers the question.

1. The word *science* means to _______.
   a. have knowledge c. study
   b. observe d. solve
2. _______ is the study of organisms.
   a. Chemistry c. Geology
   b. Life Science d. Physics
3. Oceanographers study Earth's _______.
   a. place in space c. weather
   b. oceans d. glaciers
4. ______ involves the study of stars.
   a. Chemistry c. Astronomy
   b. Physics d. Geology
5. The volume of a box is best measured in _______.
   a. cubic centimeters c. newtons
   b. grams d. centimeters
6. A _______ is a standard used for comparison in an experiment.
   a. variable c. control
   b. theory d. law
7. The volume of a beaker of water is best measured in _______.
   a. meters c. milliliters
   b. centimeters d. degrees Celsius
8. A balance is used to measure _______.
   a. mass c. volume
   b. weight d. density
9. ______ is measured with a thermometer.
   a. Length c. Temperature
   b. Area d. Volume
10. Which of these is *not* a lab safety rule?
    a. Slant tests tubes away from people when heating them.
    b. Know where the fire extinguisher is.
    c. Wash your hands after working in the lab.
    d. Taste substances to identify them.

Understanding Concepts

Answer the following questions in your Science Journal using complete sentences.

11. Why would a scientist studying a volcano also need some knowledge of physics and chemistry?
12. How have advances in technology affected our planet?
13. How does a theory differ from a hypothesis?
14. Compare and contrast mass and weight.
15. How could you determine the volume of a cardboard box given that its area is 100 m^2?

Thinking Critically

16. Susan has decided to become an oceanographer. In addition to taking life science courses, she must take geology, physics, and chemistry courses. Explain why.
17. Describe how you use technology to do your homework.
18. Suppose you had two plants—a cactus and a palm. You planted them both in potting soil and watered them daily. After a week, the cactus was dead. What problem-solving strategies could you use to find out why the cactus died?
19. Are the steps of a scientific method always followed in the order given on page 16? Explain.
20. The moon's gravitational force is one-sixth that of our planet. How would your mass differ on the moon?

18. Answers will vary, but may include collecting information about the requirements of both plants to survive, and then eliminating possibilities.

19. Although this sequence is probably the most logical, often experiments lead to new hypotheses or the discovery of new data, which require that further testing be done on the same problem. The steps are not always followed in that order.

20. It wouldn't. Mass is a measure of the amount of matter in an object. You would have the same mass no matter where you were.

Developing Skills

21. Concept Mapping See student page.

22. Using Variables, Constants, and Controls One possible solution is to boil a small quantity of water in a pot on the

Chapter 1 Review

Developing Skills

If you need help, refer to the **Skill Handbook.**

21. **Concept Mapping:** Make a concept map using the following terms and phrases: *newton, cubic meter, length, mass, volume, kilogram.*

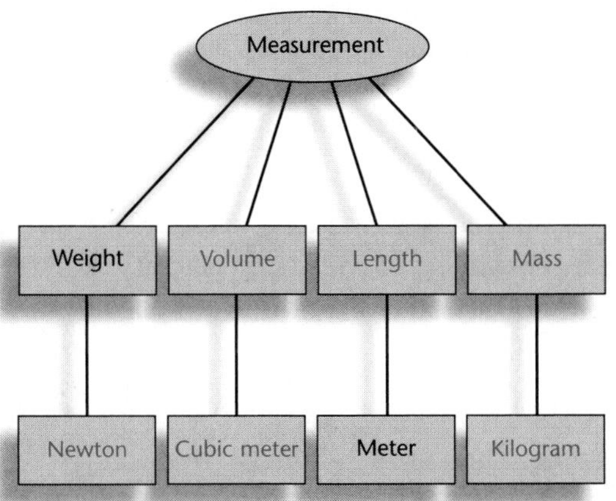

22. **Using Variables, Constants, and Controls:** Suppose you wanted to know whether crystals grow better in cold or warm water. How would you set up a simple experiment to test this?
23. **Comparing and Contrasting:** Contrast science and technology.
24. **Sequencing:** Ann wants to see how much rain falls in her city during March. Sequence the following steps in the most logical order that she needs to follow to solve her problem.
    a. Collect rain.
    b. Make a rain gauge.
    c. Measure the amount of rainfall each day.
    d. Research how much rain usually falls during March in her city.
    e. Hypothesize how much rain will fall.
    f. Graph her results.
25. **Measuring in SI:** Describe how you would calculate the volume of air inside a balloon like the one in the photograph.

Performance Assessment

1. **Carrying Out a Strategy and Collecting Data:** Perform an activity to study what happens to air as it is heated. Partially fill a balloon with air. Then tape the balloon to a ring stand with a heating lamp above it. Record the temperature near the balloon, the size of the balloon, and the time at set intervals. Use SI units. Record your data in a table.
2. **Designing an Experiment:** Design an experiment to determine the effects of water on small plants. Use three identical plants. Record the amount of water used and plant growth using SI units.
3. **Forming a Hypothesis:** Find a rock that is about the size of your fist, and determine its density. Hypothesize whether the size of a rock affects its density. Test your hypothesis by using a hammer to split the rock into pieces. Determine the density of one of the pieces. Was your hypothesis supported? Explain.

stove. Slowly add sugar to the water until the sugar no longer dissolves. Let the solution cool to room temperature. Next, stir the solution and pour equal amounts of it into two jars of equal size. Cover each jar with a lid or foil to prevent evaporation. Place one jar in the refrigerator and the other over a heat register.

23. **Comparing and Contrasting** Science is a process of observing and studying things in order to understand the world. Technology applies what is learned through science to improve our style of life.
24. **Sequencing** Answers may vary slightly, but the most logical sequence is probably d, e, b, a, c, and f.
25. **Measuring in SI** One possible solution is to place a large bucket onto a tray and fill the bucket to the top with water. Next, tie a piece of string to a rock. Carefully place the rock and string into the bucket. Measure the volume of the water that overflows into the tray with a graduated cylinder. Remove the rock and string from the bucket. Tie the free end of the string to a balloon. The string should be short enough that when the balloon and attached rock are placed in the bucket, the balloon is submerged. Refill the bucket to the top with water. Place the balloon into the bucket and measure the amount of water that overflows. By subtracting the amount of overflow in the first procedure from the amount of overflow in the second procedure, the balloon's volume can be determined.

Performance Assessment

1. The molecules of air inside the balloon move apart, causing the balloon to inflate. Use the Performance Task Assessment List for Carrying Out a Strategy and Collecting Data in **PASC,** p. 25. P
2. The designs should describe the constants: identical plants, pots, amount and type of soil, measuring technique, and frequency of watering. The variable is the amount of water given to each plant on each designated day. Use the Performance Task Assessment List for Designing an Experiment in **PASC,** p. 23. P
3. The density will not change because the mass-to-volume ratio does not change. Use the Performance Task Assessment List for Formulating a Hypothesis in **PASC,** p. 21. P

Chapter Organizer

Section	Objectives	Activities/Features
Chapter Opener		Explore Activity: Change water from a liquid to a gaseous state. p. 31
2-1 **Atoms** (2 sessions, 1 block)*	1. **Identify** matter as anything that has mass and takes up space. 2. **Describe** the internal structure of an atom. 3. **Explain** why isotopes of the same element have the same atomic number but different mass numbers.	Connect to Life Science, p. 36 Skill Builder: Comparing and Contrasting, p. 37 Using Math, p. 37
2-2 **Combinations of Atoms** (2 sessions, 1 block)*	1. **Describe** several ways atoms combine to form compounds. 2. **Compare** and **contrast** compounds and mixtures.	Using Technology: Small, but Mighty, p. 39 MiniLAB: What are some different forms of matter? p. 40 Problem Solving: A Full Cup of Tea, p. 41 Connect to Chemistry, p. 42 Science Journal, p. 42 Skill Builder: Concept Mapping, p. 42 Activity 2-1: Scales of Measurement, p. 43
2-3 **Matter** (2 sessions, 1 block)*	1. **Distinguish** between chemical and physical properties. 2. **Contrast** the four states of matter.	Using Math, p. 45 People and Science: Dr. Samuel B. Mukasa, Isotope Geochemist, p. 48 MiniLAB: What happens when water freezes? p. 49 Science Journal, p. 50 Using Math, p. 50 Skill Builder: Making and Using Tables, p. 51 Using Computers: Graphing, p. 51 Activity 2-2: Determining Density, pp. 52-53
2-4 **Science and Society Issue: Energy from Atoms** (1 session, ½ block)*	1. **Describe** how nuclear energy is made. 2. **Explain** advantages and disadvantages of the Yucca Mountain nuclear waste storage site.	Explore the Issue, p. 56

* A complete Planning Guide that includes block scheduling is provided on pages 32T-35T.

Activity Materials

Explore	Activities	MiniLABs
page 31 measuring cup, tap water, plastic container to hold the water, permanent marker, teapot, stove	page 43 balance, 100-mL graduated cylinder, 2 metersticks, 3 thermometers, rock sample, glove, stick or dowel, string, tap water pages 52-53 balance, piece of quartz, 100-mL beaker, piece of modeling clay, 250-mL graduated cylinder, small wood block, tap water, small metal block, sponge, small cork, small rock	page 40 muddy water, ice cubes, water, sand, sugar, salt water, salt, small pieces of copper page 49 100-mL graduated cylinder or small beaker, tap water, masking tape, freezer

Chapter 2 Matter and Its Changes

Teacher Classroom Resources

Reproducible Masters	Transparencies
Study Guide, p. 9 **Reinforcement,** p. 9 **Enrichment,** p. 9 **Lab Manual 7,** Electrical Charges **Critical Thinking/Problem Solving,** p. 8 **Cross-Curricular Integration,** p. 6	**Section Focus Transparency 5,** A Closer Look **Teaching Transparency 3,** Structure of Atoms
Study Guide, p. 10 **Reinforcement,** p. 10 **Enrichment,** p. 10 **Activity Worksheets,** pp. 11-12, 15 **Lab Manual 5,** Mixtures and Compounds **Lab Manual 6,** Ions **Science Integration Activity 2,** Presto Change-O **Concept Mapping,** p. 9	**Section Focus Transparency 6,** Great Combinations
Study Guide, p. 11 **Reinforcement,** p. 11 **Enrichment,** p. 11 **Activity Worksheets,** pp. 13-14, 16 **Lab Manual 8,** Density and Buoyancy **Lab Manual 9,** States of Matter **Multicultural Connections,** pp. 7-8	**Section Focus Transparency 7,** What's the Matter with This Picture? **Science Integration Transparency 2,** Relative Kinetic Energy **Teaching Transparency 4,** The Periodic Table
Study Guide, p. 12 **Reinforcement,** p. 12 **Enrichment,** p. 12 **Science and Society Integration,** p. 6	**Section Focus Transparency 8,** Powerful Issues

Teaching Resources

Glencoe Earth Science Interactive Videodisc
Earth Science CD-ROM
Spanish Resources
English/Spanish Audiocassettes
Cooperative Learning Resource Guide
Lab Partner
Lab and Safety Skills
Lesson Plans

Assessment Resources

Chapter Review, pp. 7-8
Assessment, pp. 9-12
Performance Assessment in the Science Classroom (PASC)
MindJogger Videoquiz
Alternate Assessment in the Science Classroom
Performance Assessment
Chapter Review Software
Computer Test Bank

Key to Teaching Strategies

The following designations will help you decide which activities are appropriate for your students.

L1 Level 1 activities should be within the ability range of all students.

L2 Level 2 activities should be within the ability range of the average to above-average student.

L3 Level 3 activities are designed for the ability range of above-average students.

LEP LEP activities should be within the ability range of Limited English Proficiency students.

LS These activities are designed to address different learning styles.

COOP LEARN Cooperative Learning activities are designed for small group work.

P These strategies represent student products that can be placed into a best-work portfolio.

GLENCOE TECHNOLOGY

The following multimedia resources are available from Glencoe.

The Infinite Voyage Series
Unseen Worlds
Miracles by Design
Science and Technology Videodisc Series (STVS)
Chemistry
Images of Atoms
Earth Science CD-ROM

Teacher Classroom Resources

This is a representation of key blackline masters available in the Teacher Classroom Resources.

Teaching Aids

Section Focus Transparencies

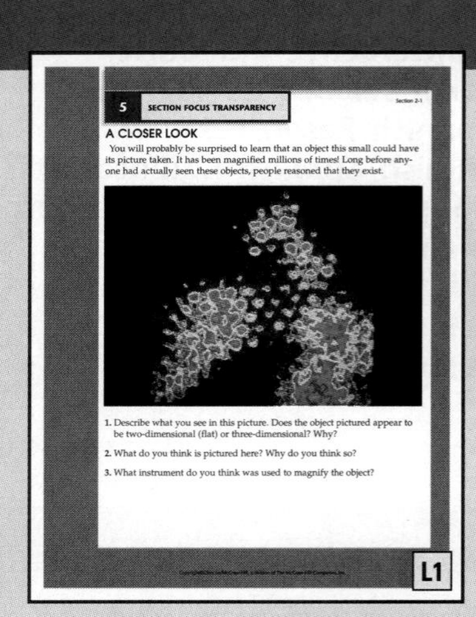

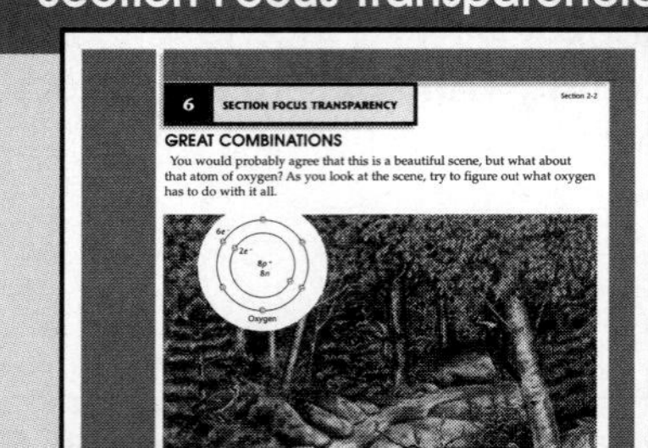

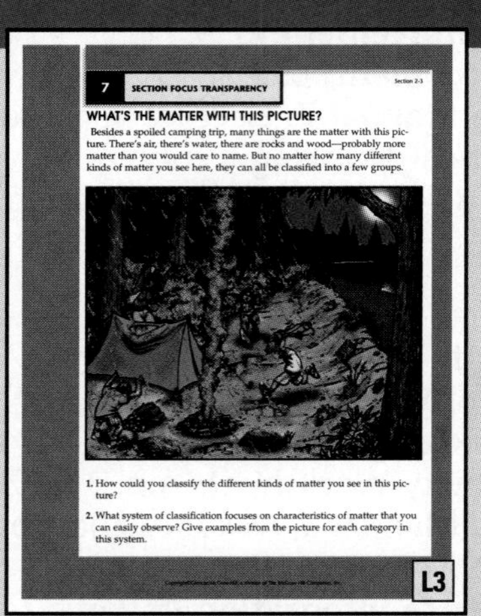

Science Integration Transparencies

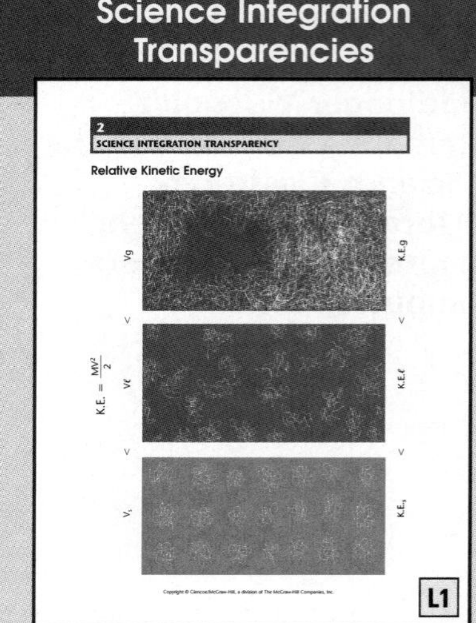

Teaching Transparencies

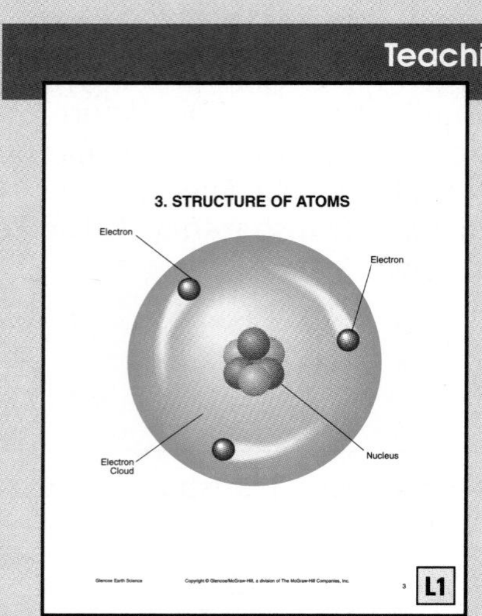

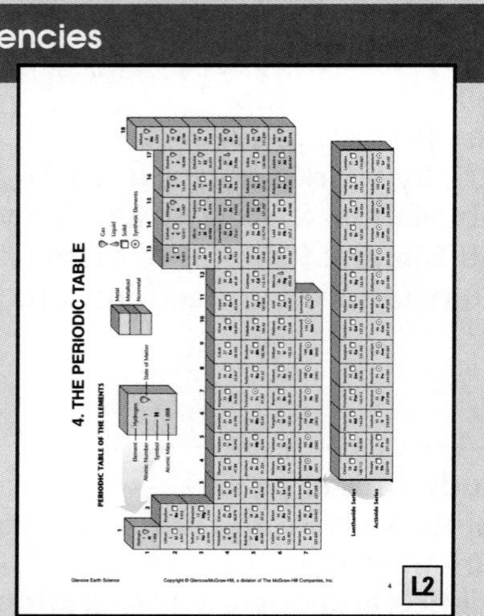

Meeting Different Ability Levels

Study Guide

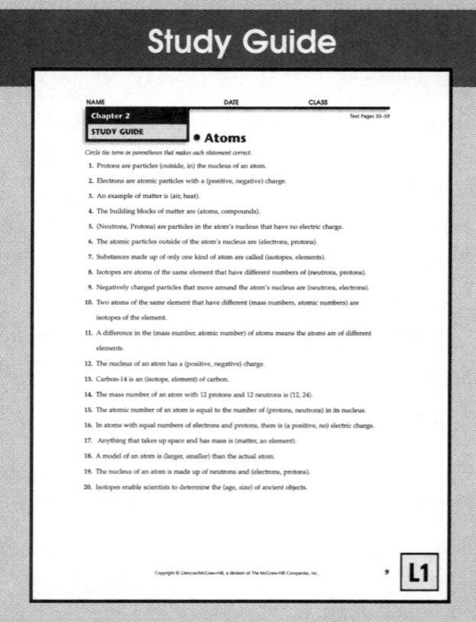

Reinforcement

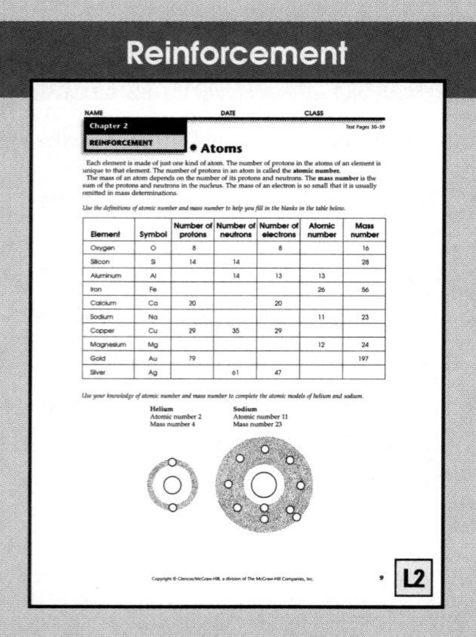

Enrichment Worksheets

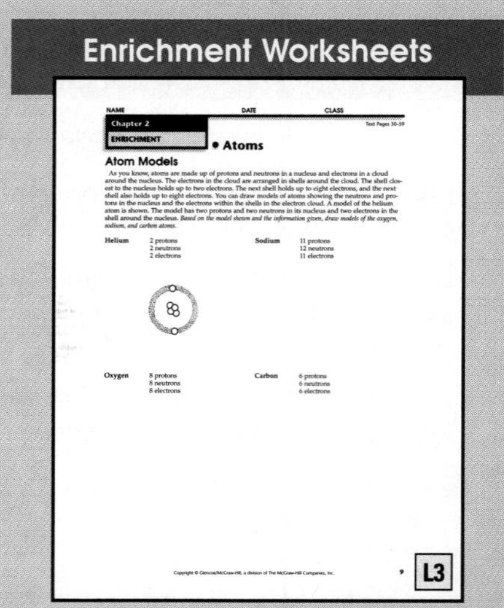

Chapter 2 Matter and Its Changes

Hands-On Activities

Science Integration Activity

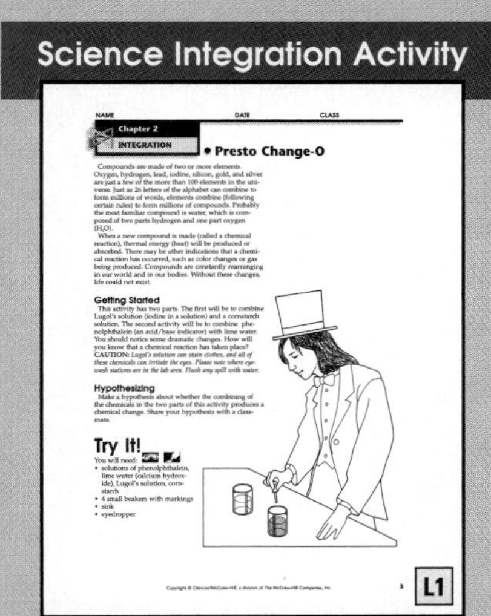

Lab Manual

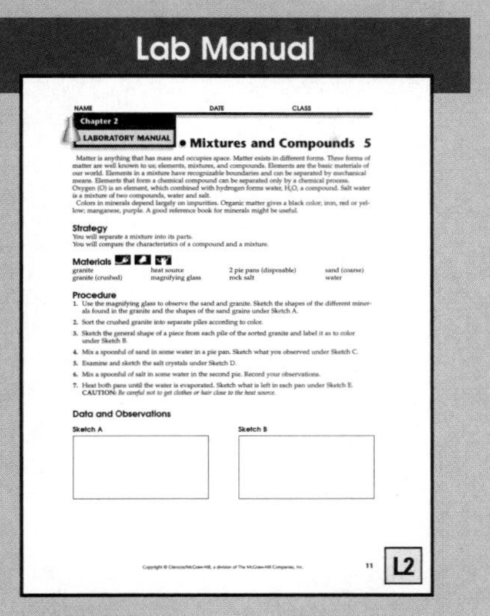

Assessment

Performance Assessment

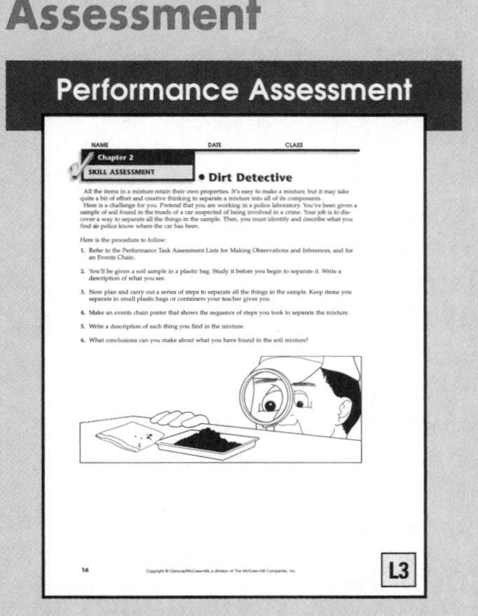

Enrichment and Application

Critical Thinking/ Problem Solving

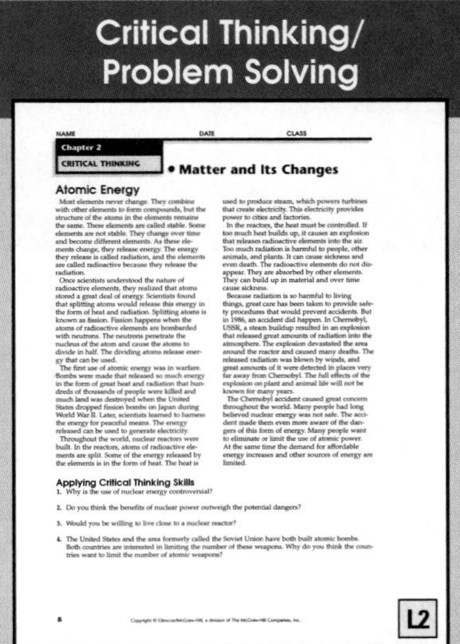

Cross-Curricular Integration

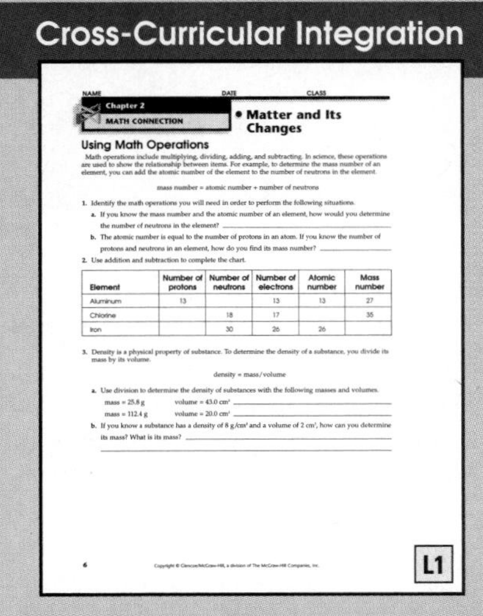

Science and Society Integration

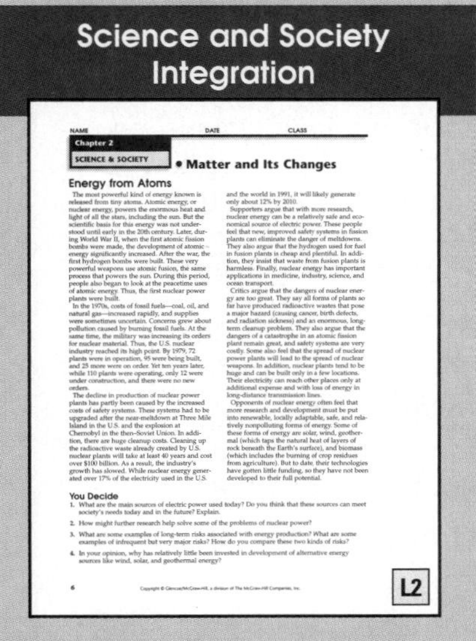

Multicultural Connections

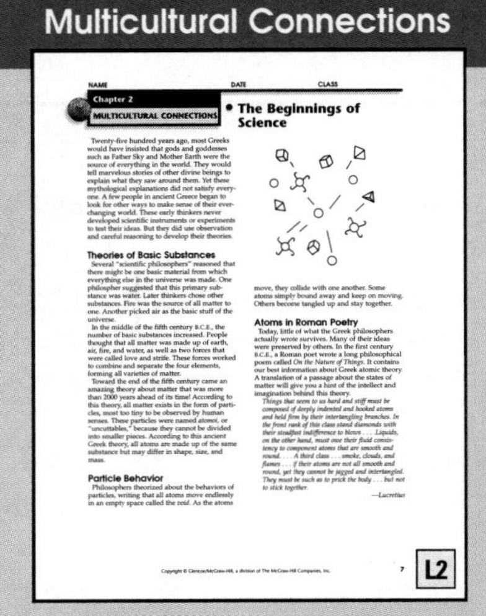

Concept Mapping

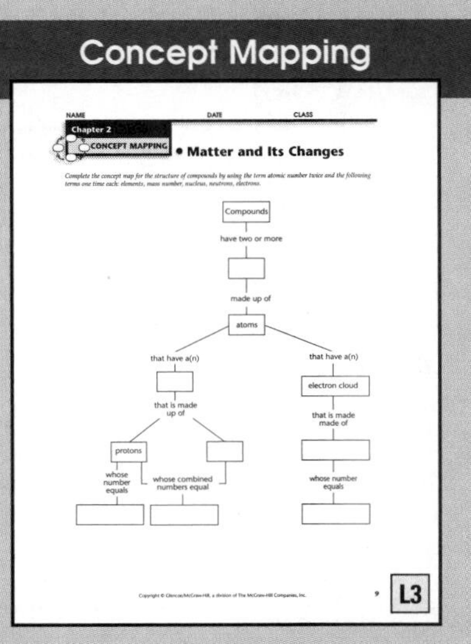

Chapter 2

Matter and Its Changes

CHAPTER OVERVIEW

Section 2-1 Atoms are described in this section. Also, the structural relationship between atoms and elements is explored.

Section 2-2 This section describes how atoms combine to form molecules and compounds. Physical and chemical changes of compounds and mixtures are discussed.

Section 2-3 Physical properties of matter are presented. The states of matter are compared. Students also discover that when matter changes state, energy is gained or lost by atoms or molecules.

Section 2-4 **Science and Society** Issues involved with the storage of nuclear waste produced by nuclear fission are presented in this section.

Chapter Vocabulary

matter, atom, element, proton, neutron, electron, mass number, atomic number, isotope, molecule, compound, chemical property, ion, mixture, solution, physical property, density, nuclear energy, fission, nuclear waste

Theme Connection

Scale and Structure Large-scale models are used to show atomic and molecular structure. The properties of matter are determined by the structure of its atoms and molecules. Nuclear energy is produced by changes in the structure of atoms.

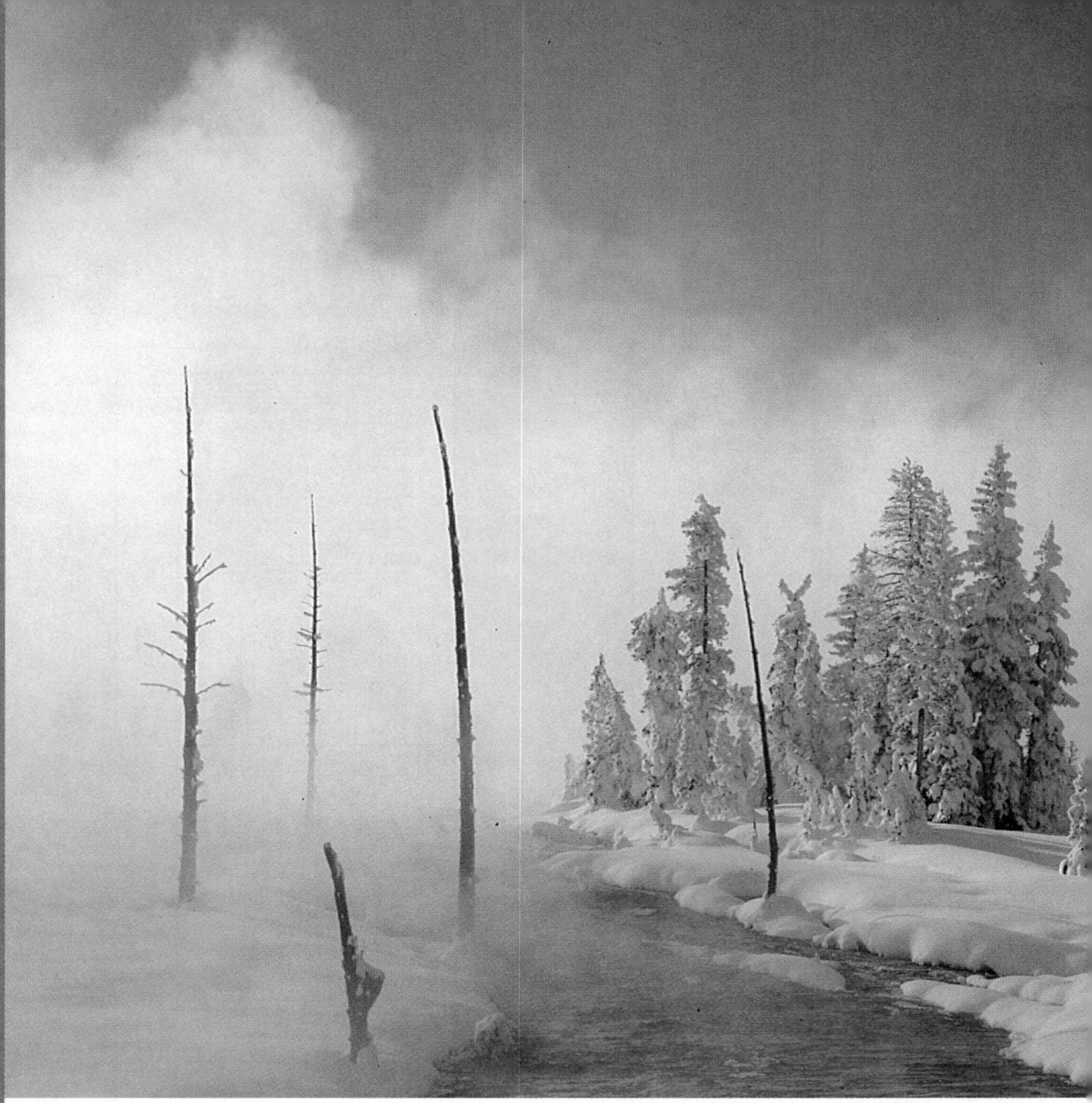

Previewing the Chapter

30

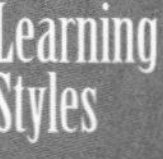

Look for the following logo for strategies that emphasize different learning modalities. LS

Kinesthetic	MiniLAB, p. 40; Activity 2-1, p. 43
Visual-Spatial	Explore, p. 31; Demonstration, pp. 33, 35, 39, 46, 47; Visual Learning, pp. 33, 35-38, 45, 46, 49, 50, 55
Interpersonal	Brainstorming, pp. 34, 44; Reteach, p. 36; MiniLAB, p. 49; Activity 2-2, pp. 52-53
Linguistic	Science Journal, pp. 33, 50, 55; Integrating the Sciences, pp. 36, 41; Cultural Diversity, p. 40; Visual Learning, p. 34

Chapter 2

Matter and Its Changes

You've probably walked by various bodies of water from time to time. You may have seen mist rising from a lake on a cool autumn morning or noticed ice forming on the lake's surface in the winter. If so, you have observed water as a solid, a liquid, and a gas.

EXPLORE ACTIVITY

Change water from a liquid to a gaseous state.

1. Pour one cup of water into a glass container.
2. Mark the level of water in the container with a permanent marker.
3. Empty the container into a teapot.
4. With the help of an adult, heat the water in the teapot until it boils.
5. Carefully pour the water in the teapot into the measuring container.

Observe: What did you see coming out of the teapot? What do you notice about the amount of water that remains? In your Science Journal, explain what you think has happened to the water.

Previewing Science Skills

- In the **Skill Builders**, you will **outline, map concepts,** and **make and use tables.**
- In the **Activities**, you will **observe** and **collect and organize data.**
- In the **MiniLABs**, you will **classify, observe,** and **infer.**

Assessment Planner

Portfolio
Refer to page 57 for suggested items that students might select for their portfolios.

Performance Assessment
See page 57 for additional Performance Assessment options.
Skill Builders, pp. 37, 42, 51
MiniLABs, pp. 40, 49
Activities 2-1, p. 43; 2-2, pp. 52-53

Content Assessment
Section Wrap-ups, pp. 37, 42, 51, 56
Chapter Review, pp. 57-59
Mini Quizzes, pp. 37, 42, 51

Group Assessment
Opportunities for group assessment occur with Cooperative Learning Strategies and Flex Your Brain Activities.

EXPLORE ACTIVITY

Purpose

LS **Visual-Spatial** Use the Explore Activity to introduce students to the different states of matter. Inform students that water is found in its solid, liquid, and gaseous state on Earth's surface, making it a unique planet. L1 LEP COOP LEARN

Preparation

Prior to the activity, obtain a one-cup measuring device and a glass container.

Materials

teapot, glass container, one-cup measure

Teaching Strategies

Students must use permanent markers for marking the glass cup. Caution students to heat the teapot with the help of an adult.

Observe

Students should indicate that they saw steam coming out of the teapot as the water was heated to a boil. In their Science Journals, students should indicate that some of the water was changed to the gaseous state when the water boiled. This water escaped from the teapot as steam. The amount of liquid water that remained, therefore, was less than the amount they started with.

Assessment

Oral Ask students to discuss their results within groups and to have one representative of each group explain to the class what conclusions the group has drawn. Use the Performance Task Assessment List for Group Work in **PASC**, p. 97. P

Prepare

Section Background

- Of the 109 known elements, only 90 occur in nature. Elements that do not occur in nature are those with atomic numbers from 93 to 109, as well as technetium, atomic number 43, and promethium, atomic number 61.
- The maximum number of electrons in an energy level within the electron cloud at any given time can be determined using the formula $2n^2$, where n represents the number of the energy level. For example, the first energy level can hold $(2)(1^2)$, or 2 electrons. The fourth energy level can hold $(2)(4^2)$, or 32 electrons.

Preplanning

- If possible, obtain a large periodic table and display it on the wall in the room.
- Obtain a set of colorful, interlocking, plastic building blocks.
- Polystyrene balls of various sizes and colors and toothpicks are needed to make models of different atoms.

1 Motivate

Bellringer

Before presenting the lesson, display **Section Focus Transparency 5** on the overhead projector. Assign the accompanying **Focus Activity** worksheet. L1 LEP

Tying to Previous Knowledge

Students should recall that most soft drink cans are made from the lightweight element aluminum.

2•1 Atoms

Science Words

matter
atom
element
proton
neutron
electron
mass number
atomic number
isotope

Objectives

- Identify matter as anything that has mass and takes up space.
- Describe the internal structure of an atom.
- Explain why isotopes of the same element have the same atomic number but different mass numbers.

The Building Blocks of Matter

What do this book, the air you breathe, and the food you eat all have in common? The book, the air, and the food are all matter. **Matter** is anything that takes up space and has mass.

Look at **Figure 2-1.** You can't always see matter as clearly as you see the sun. For example, you can't see air. But matter, in its various forms, is all around you. Air is a colorless gas, water is a transparent liquid, and rocks are colorful solids. Why do the characteristics of one form of matter differ from the characteristics of another? Because matter is made up of **atoms.** The structure of those atoms determines the characteristics of the matter you observe.

Atoms

All matter is composed of "building blocks." The structure of these building blocks determines the structure of the matter you observe. Think about when you were younger and

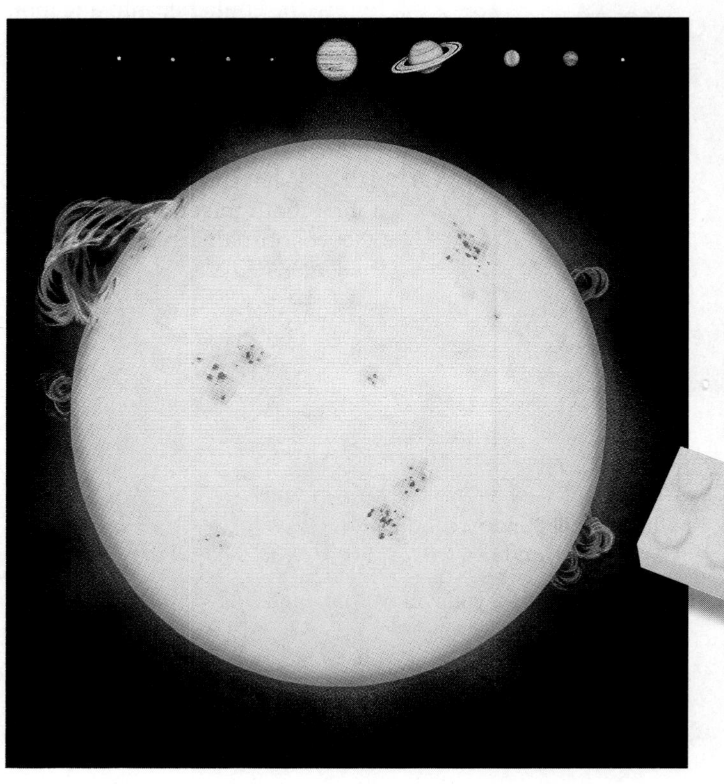

Figure 2-1
More than 99 percent of the matter in our solar system is contained in the sun. *How do we define matter?*

Program Resources

Reproducible Masters
Study Guide, p. 9 L1
Reinforcement, p. 9 L1
Enrichment, p. 9 L3
Cross-Curricular Integration, p. 6
Critical Thinking/Problem Solving, p. 8
Lab Manual 7

Transparencies
Section Focus Transparency 5 L1
Teaching Transparency 3

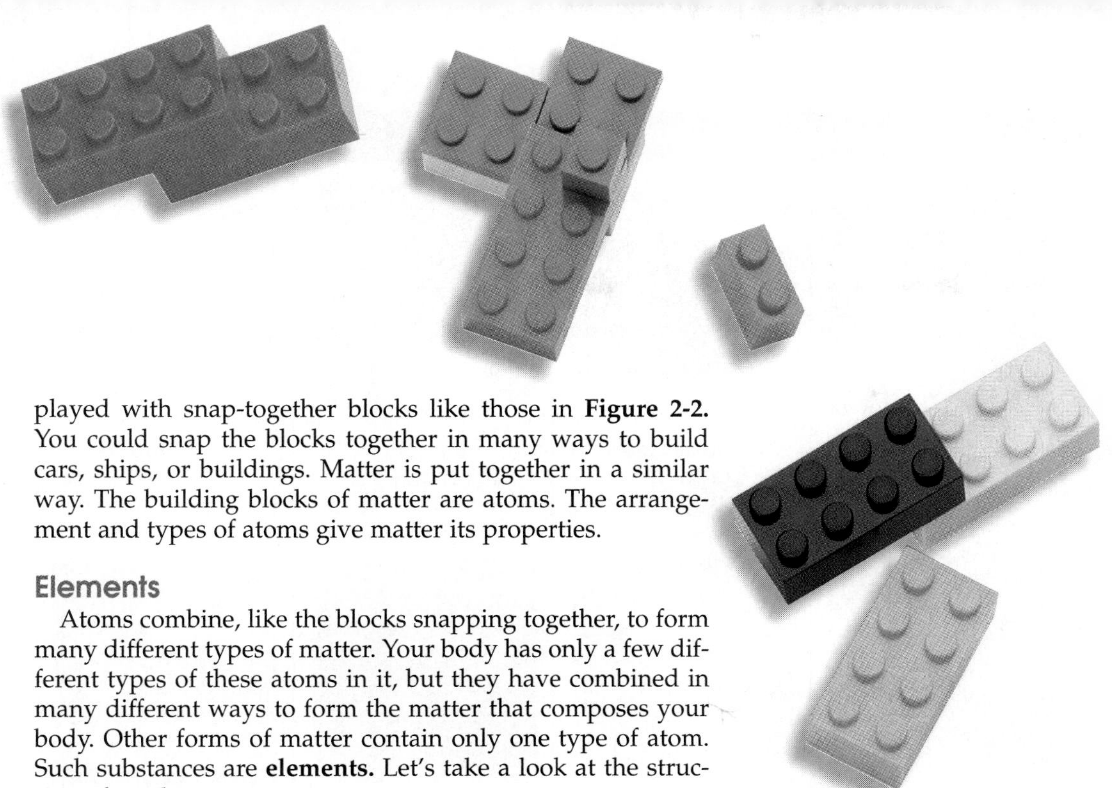

played with snap-together blocks like those in **Figure 2-2.** You could snap the blocks together in many ways to build cars, ships, or buildings. Matter is put together in a similar way. The building blocks of matter are atoms. The arrangement and types of atoms give matter its properties.

Elements

Atoms combine, like the blocks snapping together, to form many different types of matter. Your body has only a few different types of these atoms in it, but they have combined in many different ways to form the matter that composes your body. Other forms of matter contain only one type of atom. Such substances are **elements.** Let's take a look at the structure of an element.

Suppose you have a copper wire. What kind of atoms are in the wire? Because copper is an element, it's made up of only copper atoms. Look at **Table 2-1.** It shows some minerals containing elements and their uses. Appendix F of your book is a table of the known elements called the periodic table.

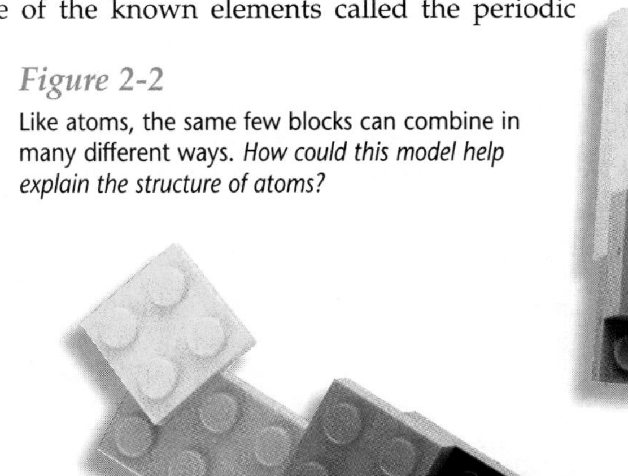

Figure 2-2

Like atoms, the same few blocks can combine in many different ways. *How could this model help explain the structure of atoms?*

2 Teach

Revealing Preconceptions

Some students may not realize that substances they cannot see are also matter. Show that air is matter by blowing up a balloon. Then have students use a balance to demonstrate that the balloon filled with air has more mass than the empty balloon.

Demonstration

LS **Visual-Spatial** Use interlocking plastic blocks to demonstrate how atoms are the building blocks of matter.

Visual Learning

Figure 2-1 How do we define matter? *Matter is anything that takes up space and has mass.*

Figure 2-2 How could this model help explain the structure of atoms? *Atoms combine, like blocks snapping together, to form many different types of matter. The structure of the atoms gives matter its properties.* LEP LS

GLENCOE TECHNOLOGY

Videodisc

The Infinite Voyage: Unseen Worlds

Chapter 9

Studying the Basic Building Blocks: The Atom

CD-ROM

Earth Science CD-ROM

Have students perform the interactive exploration for Chapter 2 to reinforce important chapter concepts and thinking processes.

Science Journal

Electrical Wire Have students research why electrical wire is often made of copper. Have them write a report about the use of copper as electrical wire in their Science Journals. If some students discover that aluminum is also used in electrical wire, ask them to find out why different substances are used and include this explanation in their Science Journals. L1 LS

Community Connection

Basic Business Have students visit businesses that are located near the school. They should look for substances used in the businesses that are composed of only one element. Students could bring in samples of the items they discover. Some examples might include aluminum cans, copper and aluminum wire, gold chains and rings, silver tea sets, and graphite (carbon) lubricants. L1

FLEX Your Brain

Use the Flex Your Brain activity to have students explore THE STRUCTURE OF ATOMS.

Activity Worksheets, p. 5

Brainstorming

LS **Interpersonal** Have student groups use the periodic table in Appendix E to come up with a list of about ten elements they think would be found in Earth's rocks. Then tell students that oxygen is the most common element found in Earth's rocks. Have the groups write brief paragraphs explaining how oxygen, a gas, can be a major component of a solid. Students' answers can be used to discuss how the properties of elements change when they become part of a compound, which will be covered in the next section. L1 COOP LEARN

Visual Learning

Table 2-1 Discuss the terms *iron ore* and *bauxite ore.* Make sure students realize that most minerals have to be extracted from the rock in which they occur. A mineral is an ore if it exists in a large enough amount that it can be mined at a profit. The term *ore* is usually used to refer to metallic minerals and the deposits containing them. For example, *iron ore* is a common term, whereas *fluorite ore* is not. LEP LS

Use **Critical Thinking/ Problem Solving,** p. 8, as you teach this lesson.

Table 2-1

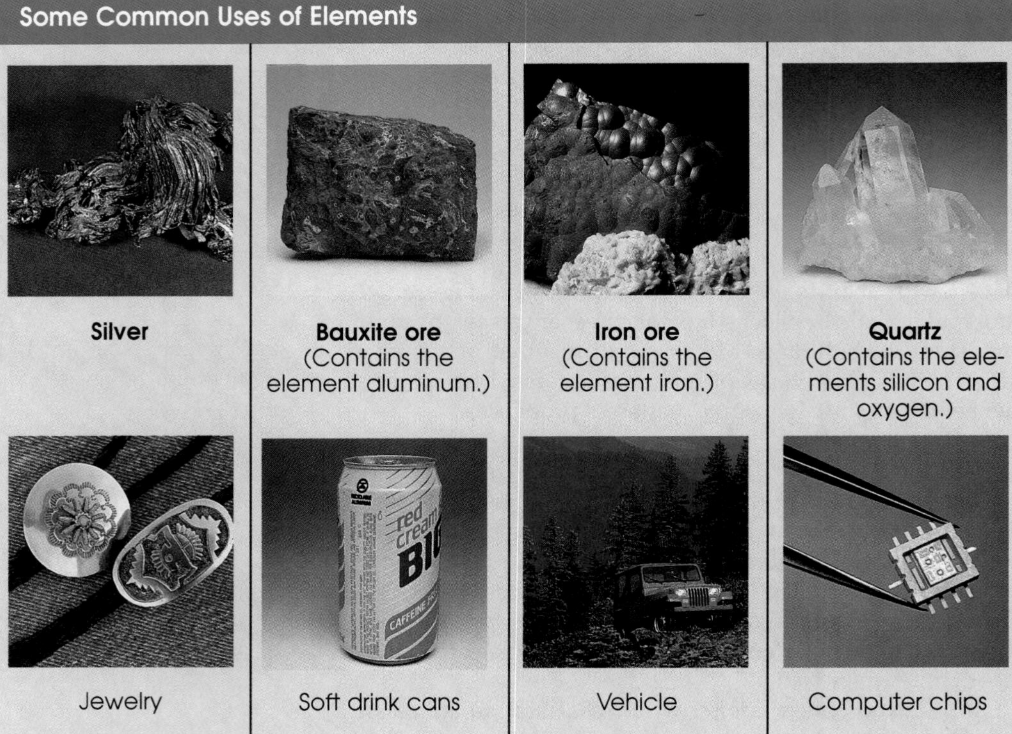

Some Common Uses of Elements			
Silver	**Bauxite ore** (Contains the element aluminum.)	**Iron ore** (Contains the element iron.)	**Quartz** (Contains the elements silicon and oxygen.)
Jewelry	Soft drink cans	Vehicle	Computer chips

Models of the Structure of Atoms

You already know that atoms are very small. Atoms are far too small to be seen, even with a microscope. How can you study something this small? How can you determine the internal structure of an atom?

When substances are too large or too small to handle or directly observe, models are often used to take their place. Have you ever worked with a model airplane like the one shown in **Figure 2-3A?** If so, your model was a smal version of a large object. In the case of atoms, the opposite is true. A large model is made of a very small object. We construct drawings, sculptures, and mental pictures of the internal structure of atoms. These models are based on information we've gathered by observing the ways atoms react when in contact with other atoms or with light.

Theme Connection

Scale and Structure In order to study atoms, models are used. Atoms are too small to be seen, but models of a much larger scale enable you to study the internal structure of atoms. The use of large-scale models to study the internal structure of atoms reinforces the theme of scale and structure.

Integrating the Sciences

Physical Science Each energy level within the electron cloud is divided into orbitals. Each orbital can hold up to two electrons of opposite spin.

Protons and Neutrons

Let's construct a mental model of the internal structure of an atom. Three basic particles make up an atom—protons, neutrons, and electrons. Protons and neutrons are located in the center of an atom and make up its nucleus. **Protons** are particles that have a positive electrical charge. **Neutrons** are particles that have no electrical charge. The nucleus, therefore, has a positive charge because there is no negative charge to counter the positive charge from the protons. This positive electrical charge of the nucleus is balanced by the electrons that surround the nucleus.

Electrons

Electrons are negatively charged particles that move around the nucleus. There is one electron for each proton. The hive in **Figure 2-3B** represents the nucleus of the atom. The bees flying around the hive in all directions are like the electrons circling the nucleus. You can't determine exactly where each bee is, but each is usually close to the hive. **Figure 2-3C** shows electrons existing as a negatively charged electron cloud. This cloud completely surrounds the nucleus of the atom. Electrons can be anywhere within the cloud, but evidence suggests that they are located near the nucleus most of the time. They are very much like a swarm of bees flying around its hive.

Figure 2-3

Models help us learn about materials that are too large to handle or too small to directly observe.

B Bees swarm around their hive but seldom stray far from home. *How is a beehive like a nucleus?*

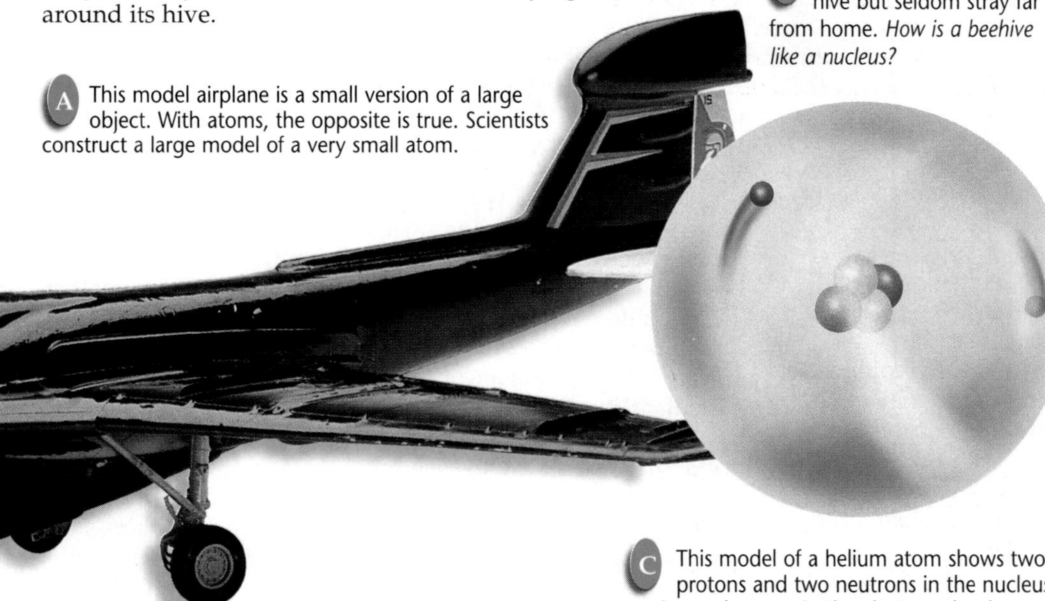

A This model airplane is a small version of a large object. With atoms, the opposite is true. Scientists construct a large model of a very small atom.

C This model of a helium atom shows two protons and two neutrons in the nucleus, and two electrons in the electron cloud.

Inquiry Question

After students have read pages 34 and 35, ask the following questions. **If a uranium atom contains 92 protons and 142 neutrons, what is the atomic mass?** *92 + 142 = 234* **A neutral atom of oxygen-17 has eight protons and nine neutrons. How many electrons does the atom have?** *eight*

Demonstration

 **Visual-Spatial** Use different-colored polystyrene balls and toothpicks to demonstrate the structures of hydrogen, helium, and oxygen nuclei. Use one color for protons and another for neutrons. Then ask: **Where are the electrons of each atom?** *They are orbiting the nucleus much as bees buzz around a hive.* LEP

GLENCOE TECHNOLOGY

Videodisc

The Infinite Voyage: Unseen Worlds

Chapter 10

The Scanning Tunneling Microscope: Observing Atomic Particles

STVS: Chemistry

Disc 2, Side 1

Images of Atoms (Ch. 4)

Visual Learning

Figure 2-3 How is a bee hive like a nucleus? *The hive represents the nucleus of the atom. The bees flying around the hive are like the electrons circling the nucleus.* LEP LS

Inclusion Strategies

Learning Disabled Let students familiar with atomic structure help other students construct simple models of an atom. Have students work in small groups using styrofoam balls and wire. Use peer teaching. Students having difficulty could place symbols on the styrofoam balls. They should use (+) for protons and (-) for electrons.

Student Text Question

If carbon has six protons, how many neutrons does it have? *six neutrons*

CONNECT TO

LIFE SCIENCE

Answer Isotopes can assist doctors in diagnosing disease. The movement of tagged blood can be evaluated for abnormalities. Problems of the circulatory system are frequently detected in this way.

Visual Learning

Figure 2-4 What is the mass number and atomic number of carbon-14? *Its mass number is 14 and its atomic number is 6.* LEP LS

3 Assess

Check for Understanding

FLEX Your Brain

Use the Flex Your Brain activity to have students explore ISOTOPES.

Activity Worksheets, p. 5

Reteach

LS **Interpersonal** Have students use different-colored polystyrene balls to construct the hydrogen-1 and hydrogen-2 isotopes. LEP

Extension

For students who have mastered this section, use the **Reinforcement** and **Enrichment** masters.

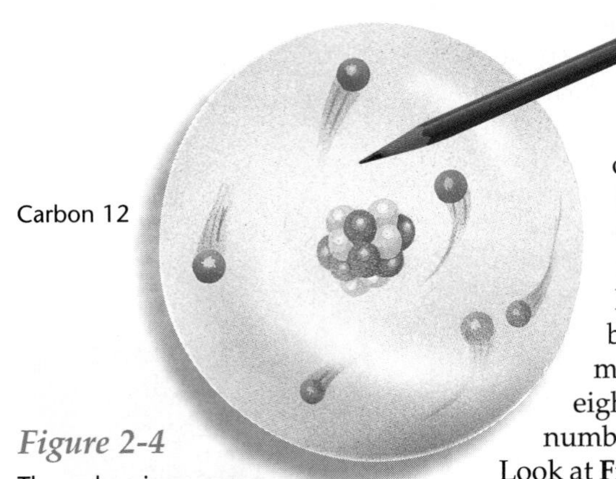

Figure 2-4

The carbon in your pencil lead is mostly carbon-12. Its mass number is 12 and its atomic number is 6. *What is the mass number and atomic number of carbon-14?*

Mass Numbers and Atomic Numbers

Just as an atom has a characteristic number of protons, neutrons, and electrons, it also has a characteristic mass. The **mass number** of an atom is equal to the number of protons and neutrons making up its nucleus. Just as you have more mass when you are carrying many books, an atom has more mass if it contains more particles. Thus, oxygen, which contains eight protons and eight neutrons, has a mass number of 16. Carbon has a mass number of 12. Look at **Figure 2-4.** If carbon has six protons, how many neutrons does it have?

Electrons aren't counted when we compute an atom's mass number. This is because electrons aren't massive enough to be included in the calculations.

Atomic Number

Another property of an atom that's convenient to know is its atomic number. An atom's **atomic number** equals the number of protons in its nucleus. This number also equals the number of electrons contained in its electron cloud. All atoms of a specific element have the same atomic number. For example, all atoms of iron have an atomic number of 26. How many protons does an atom of iron contain? Whether it's in the metal of a car fender or in the nails in a bookcase, an iron atom has 26 protons.

CONNECT TO

LIFE SCIENCE

Some isotopes of elements are radioactive. Physicians can introduce these isotopes into a patient's circulatory system. The low-level radiation they emit allows them to be tracked as they move throughout the patient's body. ***Explain*** how this would be helpful in diagnosing a disease.

Isotopes

If the number of protons in an atom is changed, a new element is formed. The number of neutrons can be changed, however, without changing the element. All that happens is that the atom's mass changes. Atoms of the same element that have different numbers of neutrons in their nuclei are called **isotopes. Table 2-2** lists isotopes of some common elements. Note that the number of protons remains the same for each element, but the number of neutrons changes.

Some isotopes are used for medical purposes. Others provide us with a way to determine the age of ancient objects. Geologists use these isotopes to date fossils and layers of rock. Archaeologists use them to determine the age of artifacts, such as the mummified body shown in **Figure 2-5.** You will be learning more about isotopes and some of their uses in Chapter 12.

Integrating the Sciences

Chemistry Appendix F shows the periodic table. Vertical columns of elements in the periodic table are families or groups. Elements within a family or group have similar properties and the same number of electrons in the outermost orbital, and can replace one another in a compound. Horizontal rows of elements are called periods.

Archaeology Have students research how archaeologists use isotopes with short half-lives to determine the ages of artifacts such as clothing, wood, bones, and structures. Refer students to Chapter 13 for a discussion of half-lives and absolute dating methods. L2 LS

Table 2-2

Isotopes			
Isotope	**Number of Protons**	**Number of Neutrons**	**Number of Electrons**
Hydrogen-1	1	0	1
Hydrogen-2	1	1	1
Hydrogen-3	1	2	1
Carbon-12	6	6	6
Carbon-14	6	8	6
Uranium-234	92	142	92
Uranium-235	92	143	92
Uranium-238	92	146	92

Figure 2-5

Some isotopes help archaeologists determine the age of clothing, wood, bones, and other structures. *How does this help us understand ancient civilizations?*

Our model of an atom allows us to predict how a particular element will react when it's in contact with another element. As you continue to investigate matter in this chapter, you will explore how atoms of different elements combine to form the matter around you.

Section Wrap-up

Review

1. How does the air you breathe fit the definition of matter?
2. Explain why the overall electrical charge of an atom is neutral.
3. **Think Critically:** Oxygen-16 and oxygen-17 are two different isotopes of oxygen. The numbers 16 and 17 represent their mass numbers. How many protons and neutrons are in each isotope?

Skill Builder

Comparing and Contrasting

Review the material in Section 2-1. How do atoms and elements differ? How are they the same? If you need help, refer to Comparing and Constrasting in the **Skill Handbook**.

USING MATH

The mass number of nitrogen is 14. Find its atomic number in the table shown in Appendix F. Then determine the number of neutrons in its nucleus.

Visual Learning

Figure 2-5 How does this help us understand ancient civilizations? *Archaeologists use isotopes to help date ancient artifacts. Once they know the approximate age of the artifacts, they can reconstruct the cultural and physical environment of ancient civilizations using data linked to that particular era.* LEP IS

4 Close

•MINI•QUIZ•

Use the Mini Quiz to check students' recall of chapter content.

1. **What form of matter contains only one type of atom?** *elements*
2. **Which particle in the nucleus of an atom is positively charged?** *proton*
3. **Where are electrons found?** *in the electron cloud*
4. **Atoms of the same element that have different numbers of neutrons are ______ .** *isotopes*

Section Wrap-up

Review

1. Air has mass and takes up space.
2. The number of positively charged protons in the nucleus equals the number of negatively charged electrons in the electron cloud.
3. **Think Critically** Oxygen-16 has eight protons and eight neutrons; oxygen-17 has eight protons and nine neutrons.

USING MATH

Answer 7, 7

Skill Builder

Answers will vary slightly, but students should indicate that atoms, the building blocks of all matter, are composed of three kinds of particles. Atoms are the basic units that compose all matter. An element is matter made of only one type of atom.

Assessment

Content Assess students' abilities to identify key concepts by having them compare and contrast key concepts in a section of the textbook. Use the Performance Task Assessment List for Writing in Science in **PASC,** p. 87. P

Section 2•2

Prepare

Section Background

- Unlike mixtures, compounds form when one substance chemically reacts with another.
- Atoms tend to be stable when they have eight electrons in the outer shell of the electron cloud.
- Solid solutions are called alloys.

Preplanning

- To prepare for the MiniLAB, obtain small amounts of sand, sugar, or salt.
- To prepare for Activity 2-1, obtain the materials listed on page 43.

1 Motivate

Bellringer

Before presenting the lesson, display **Section Focus Transparency 6** on the overhead projector. Assign the accompanying **Focus Activity** worksheet. L1 LEP

Tying to Previous Knowledge

Remind students that electrons are located outside the nucleus in the electron cloud. Ask students which electrons, those closer to the nucleus or those farther from the nucleus, would most likely react to form compounds.

Visual Learning

Figure 2-6 How can the same elements, made from the same type of atoms, help make two materials that are so different? *The materials are different because the elements combine chemically to form new compounds.* LEP IS

2•2 Combinations of Atoms

Science Words

molecule
compound
chemical property
ion
mixture
solution

Objectives

- Describe several ways atoms combine to form compounds.
- Compare and contrast compounds and mixtures.

How Atoms Combine

Suppose you've just eaten a snack such as an apple or an orange. It's unlikely that you were concerned about the elements in the snack. Yet anything you eat and anything you touch has some combination of the same few elements in it. The sugar in the apple or orange contains the elements carbon, oxygen, and hydrogen. Some of the air around you contains carbon dioxide, a combination of carbon and oxygen.

In **Figure 2-6,** both the oranges in the tree and the carbon dioxide in the air contain oxygen. Yet in one case oxygen is in a colorless, gaseous form. In the other case it's part of a structure that's hard and colorful. They are different because the atoms of elements combine chemically to form new substances called compounds. When they do, the properties of the individual elements change. Let's see how this happens.

Figure 2-6

The air surrounding this tree contains some of the same elements as the fruit hanging from its branches. *How can the same elements, made from the same type of atoms, help make two materials that are so different?*

Molecules and Compounds

One way that atoms combine is by sharing the electrons in the outer-most portion of their electron clouds. The combined atoms form a **molecule.** For example, two atoms of hydrogen can share electrons with one atom of oxygen to form one molecule of water. Water is a compound composed of molecules. A **compound** is a type of matter that has properties different from the properties of each of the elements in it.

The properties of hydrogen and oxygen are changed when they combine to form water. Under normal conditions on Earth, you will find the elements oxygen and hydrogen only as gases.

Program Resources

Reproducible Masters

Study Guide, p. 10 L1
Reinforcement, p. 10 L1
Enrichment, p. 10 L3
Activity Worksheets, pp. 11-12, 15 L1
Science Integration Activities, pp. 3-4
Concept Mapping, p. 9
Lab Manual 5, 6

Transparencies

Section Focus Transparency 6 L1

Figure 2-7

A molecule of water has chemical properties that are different from those of hydrogen and oxygen atoms.

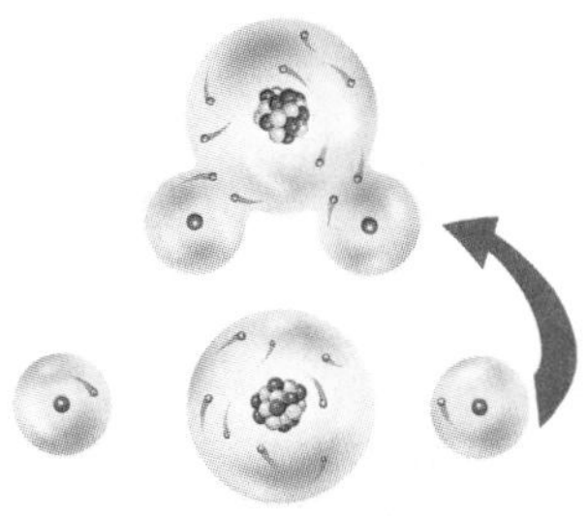

When hydrogen and oxygen combine to form a compound, the new substance has chemical properties that are different from those of the elements in it, as shown in **Figure 2-7.**

Chemical Properties

Chemical properties describe how one substance changes when it reacts with other substances. For example, the chemical properties of iron cause it to change to rust when it reacts with water and oxygen.

USING TECHNOLOGY

Small, but Mighty

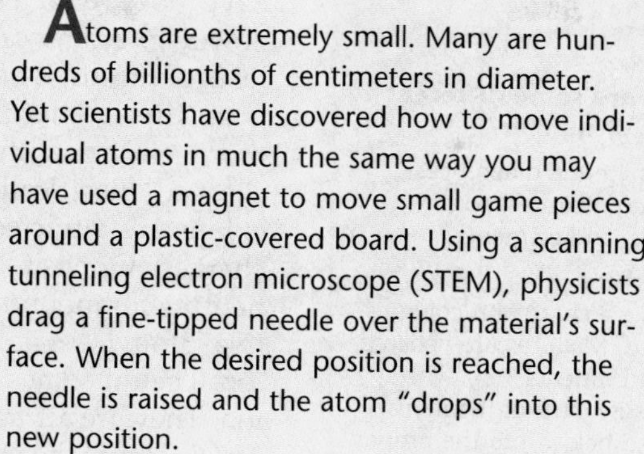

Atoms are extremely small. Many are hundreds of billionths of centimeters in diameter. Yet scientists have discovered how to move individual atoms in much the same way you may have used a magnet to move small game pieces around a plastic-covered board. Using a scanning tunneling electron microscope (STEM), physicists drag a fine-tipped needle over the material's surface. When the desired position is reached, the needle is raised and the atom "drops" into this new position.

One at a Time

This discovery may lead to the building of molecules one atom at a time. New drugs that would cure or eliminate certain illnesses could be constructed using this method. Even smaller electrical circuits could be made for everything from watches to computers. The illustration shows xenon atoms arranged to spell out "IBM."

Xenon Atoms Arranged by STEM

Think Critically: How could STEMs be used to permanently store information and what would be the potential impact of this use?

2 Teach

Demonstration

LS Visual-Spatial Soak some steel wool in vinegar to remove the soap or any other coating on the wool. Thoroughly rinse the steel wool and place it in a shallow open dish. Place the dish on the windowsill and have students observe what happens to it over the next few days. LEP

USING TECHNOLOGY

For more information, see "Manipulating Atoms," *Popular Science,* July 1990, p. 30.

Think Critically

The atoms can be arranged into almost any pattern. For example, the illustration shows atoms that have been manually placed to spell out "IBM." The illustration has been magnified more than 2 million times. The atoms are about 8 billionths of a centimeter apart. Data could be stored at densities more than one million times greater than can be stored today using conventional data-storage methods.

GLENCOE TECHNOLOGY

Videodisc

The Infinite Voyage: Miracles by Design

Chapter 2

Improving Steel: Examining Chemical Makeup

Use **Concept Mapping,** p. 9, as you teach this lesson.

Inclusion Strategies

Gifted Have students brainstorm to compile a list of the many mixtures of people and their diverse characteristics. Responses might include musical groups, people in a classroom, other school groups, city residents, people in the workplace, club members, and so on. Ask each student to pick one of these mixtures and write a story using these people as the characters. L3

Behaviorally Disordered In one area of the classroom, open a bottle of vinegar, perfume, or clove oil without identifying the substance to the students. Have students raise their hands when they detect the odor. Students should be able to describe the direction of the flow of molecules of the gas fumes from the bottle through the air. Ask several days in advance if any students are allergic to perfume.

INTEGRATION Chemistry

Present-day physicists believe an atom has no definite shape and that electrons can be anywhere in an atom's electron cloud.

MiniLAB

Purpose

LS **Kinesthetic** Students will determine the differences between mixtures, compound, and elements. L1

COOP LEARN

Teaching Strategies

Once students have completed the list, have them make a solution from two or more of the items on their list. This can be done by mixing salt or sugar into a beaker of water. Ask them how they could separate the materials in solution.

Mixtures	Compounds	Elements
air	water	gold
muddy water	ice	oxygen
salt water	sugar	hydrogen
sand	salt	copper

Analysis

1. A solution can be made when one item is dissolved in another.
2. Compounds are chemical combinations of two or more elements that cannot be separated physically.

Assessment

Oral To further assess students' understanding of different forms of matter, have them classify various materials around the room. Use the Performance Task Assessment List for Making Observations and Inferences in **PASC**, p. 17. P

Activity Worksheets, pp. 5, 15

INTEGRATION Chemistry

MiniLAB

What are some different forms of matter?

Determine the differences between mixtures, compounds, and elements.

Procedure

1. Make a chart with columns titled, Mixtures, Compounds, and Elements.
2. Classify each of the items listed below into the proper column on your chart.
3. Experiment to make a solution using two or more of the items listed: air, sand, gold, hydrogen, muddy water, sugar, ice, saltwater, water, salt, oxygen, copper.

Analysis

1. How does a solution differ from other mixtures?
2. How does an element differ from a compound?

Ions

You know that atoms combine by sharing electrons from the outer portion of their electron cloud. But atoms also combine because they've become positively or negatively charged.

As you discovered earlier, atoms are usually neutral—they have no overall electric charge. Under certain conditions, however, atoms can lose or gain electrons. When an atom loses electrons, it has more protons than electrons so the atom is positively charged. When an atom gains electrons, it has more electrons than protons so the atom is negatively charged. Electrically charged atoms are called **ions.**

Ions are attracted to each other when they have opposite charges. Oppositely charged ions join to form electrically neutral compounds. Table salt forms in this way. A sodium (Na) atom loses an electron and becomes a positively charged ion. Then it comes close to a negatively charged chlorine (Cl) ion. They are attracted to each other and form the compound NaCl. This is the compound that you use on your french fries or popcorn.

Mixtures

Your backpack probably looks similar to the one shown in **Figure 2-8.** If you look inside, you will see an example of a **mixture.** Many different objects are mixed together, but each retains its own properties. Your math book isn't any different whether it's beside your ruler or beside your history book.

Figure 2-8

Your backpack contains a variety of objects that together, form a mixture.

Cultural Diversity

Ocher Ocher is an iron oxide compound that occurs naturally. Archaeological evidence and observations of contemporary, nonindustrial societies show that ocher is used in a wide variety of ways, including for treating wounds, for tanning hides, and as a pigment for art and body decoration. Ocher was used in the prehistoric production of rock paintings at Lascaux and other locations. It is still used today for coloration in artwork. One source of ocher, the iron ore hematite, which produces a bright red coloration, appears to have been mined in Swaziland, Africa, as early as 44 000 years ago. Have interested students research historic and present-day cultures that use body coloration to determine the material used and the reasons for body decoration. L2 LS

Solutions

Salt water is an example of a kind of mixture called a solution. When one substance of a mixture is dissolved in another substance, a **solution** is formed. In the case of salt water, the properties of the salt molecules aren't changed just because they're mixed in with the water. The salt molecules are separated from each other by other molecules within the water. Therefore, the salt has dissolved in the water. Another property of a solution is that it is the same throughout. One part of a solution is the same as all other parts. To make the salt water a solution, we stir it. Stirring the solution spreads the salt molecules evenly throughout.

Separating Components of Mixtures and Compounds

The components of a mixture can be separated by physical means. You can sit at your desk and pick out the separate items in your backpack. You can let the water evaporate and the salt will remain. But is it possible to separate the components of a compound in a similar way?

Suppose you take sugar and try to separate its carbon atoms from its hydrogen and oxygen atoms. How can you do it? It's much more difficult than separating the components of a mixture. The only way is to separate the carbon, hydrogen, and oxygen atoms of each sugar molecule. This is an example of a chemical change. A chemical change converts one substance into one or more new substances with different chemical properties.

Problem Solving

A Full Cup of Tea

You come home from school on a cold, rainy day. You normally drink milk after school, but, given the weather, today you decide to have a cup of hot tea. You brew the tea and pour yourself a generous cup. "Too generous," you note with a frown, for you have filled the cup to its rim. "How will I be able to add sugar to my tea?" Very carefully, you place first one and then two teaspoons of sugar in the cup. You expect it to overflow, but it doesn't.

Solve the Problem:

1. **Why didn't the tea overflow?**
2. **What happened to the two teaspoons of sugar as you gently stirred the cup of tea?**

Think Critically:

Try the same thing, but this time allow the cup of tea to cool down and then try to place two teaspoons of sugar in the totally full cup.

1. Did you observe the same results?
2. Was it as easy to dissolve the sugar into the cold tea?
3. How can you explain any differences you might have observed?

Problem Solving

Solve the Problem

1. Sugar entered the spaces between the water molecules.
2. As the tea is stirred, more sugar is exposed to the water, allowing more of the sugar to dissolve and fill the spaces between the water molecules.

Thinking Critically

1. no
2. no
3. Water molecules are closer together in cold tea than in warm tea. Therefore, less of the sugar can fit between the water molecules, making it more difficult to dissolve all of the sugar.

3 Assess

Check for Understanding

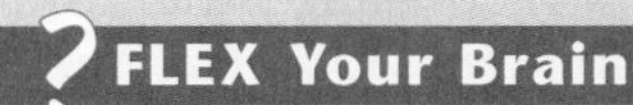

FLEX Your Brain

Use the Flex Your Brain activity to have students explore OCEAN WATER AS A MIXTURE. P

Activity Worksheets, p. 5

Reteach

Demonstrate how the properties of substances change when they combine to form a compound. Do the same to show how the components of a mixture retain their properties.

Extension

For students who have mastered this section, use the **Reinforcement** and **Enrichment** masters.

Integrating the Sciences

Environmental Science Have students research the damage done to the environment by certain common compounds such as chlorofluorocarbons (CFCs), which are used as refrigerants. CFCs are responsible for damaging Earth's ozone layer. L2 LS P

Community Connection

Ionic Bonds Invite a pharmacist or chemist working for a local company to class. Ask them to discuss and show examples of the two most common types of bonds found in compounds. In covalent bonds, the outermost electrons are shared by the atoms in the compound. In compounds with ionic bonds, ions are held together by the strong attraction of the opposite charges.

CONNECT TO

CHEMISTRY

Answer Since the salt dissolved in water can be tasted, its chemical properties have not changed. Physical properties such as crystal size have changed.

4 Close

• MINI • QUIZ •

1. **Electrically charged atoms are _______ .** *ions*
2. **A(n) _______ forms when substances combine but retain their own properties.** *mixture*
3. **What type of change converts one substance into one or more new substances?** *chemical change*

Section Wrap-up

Review

1. Atoms can share electrons to form molecules. They can also lose or gain electrons to form ions. Ions attract each other and combine to form molecules.
2. The chemical properties of the sugar and tea have not changed. Evaporation alone will separate the sugar from the tea.
3. Think Critically Boiling salt water or allowing it to evaporate will separate the salt and water.

Science Journal

Answers will vary, but students should mention that the hydrogen atoms are located toward one side of the water molecule. The end with the hydrogen atoms would be slightly positive, while the opposite end would be slightly negative.

Figure 2-9
The ocean is a mixture of many different forms of matter. Ocean water is a solution.

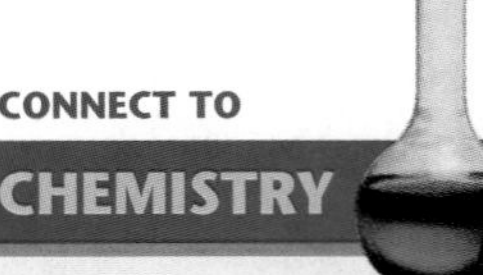

CONNECT TO

CHEMISTRY

When one substance dissolves in another, some of the properties of the dissolving substance change. When salt dissolves in water, ***decide*** if its chemical or physical properties change.

Exploring Matter

Sweetened tea, air, salt water, and the contents of your backpack are all examples of mixtures. The plants and coral shown in **Figure 2-9** are also a mixture. In each case, the materials within the mixture retain their individual properties. The materials themselves are made of compounds. The atoms of these compounds lost their individual chemical properties when they combined. As you continue to explore matter, use the mental models you've developed for atoms, elements, molecules, compounds, and mixtures.

Section Wrap-up

Review

1. How do atoms or ions combine to form molecules?
2. Why is sweetened tea considered a mixture rather than a compound?
3. Think Critically: How can you determine if salt water is a solution or a compound?

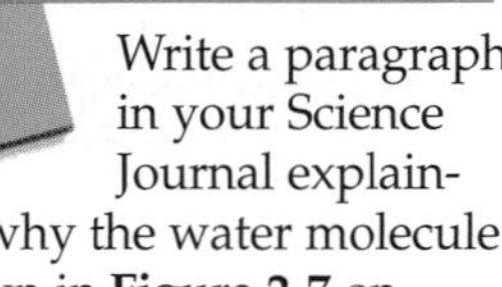

Science Journal

Write a paragraph in your Science Journal explaining why the water molecule shown in **Figure 2-7** on page 39 tends to be positively charged on one side and negatively charged on the other. In other words, explain why it is referred to as a polar molecule.

Skill Builder
Concept Mapping

Make an events chain map using the terms *mixtures, atoms, molecules, compounds, electrons, protons,* and *neutrons.* If you need help, refer to Concept Mapping in the **Skill Handbook**.

Skill Builder

Atoms are the building blocks of matter.
→ **Electrons, protons,** and **neutrons** make up **atoms.**
→ **Atoms** make up **molecules.**
→ **Molecules** make up **compounds** and **mixtures.**

Assessment

Content Assess students' understanding of the structure of matter by having them construct a concept map using listed terms. Use the Performance Task Assessment List for Concept Map in **PASC,** p. 89. P

Activity 2-1 Scales of Measurement

How would you describe some of the objects in your classroom? Perhaps the bulletin board is the size of the top half of a door. This description is not very useful. Wouldn't it be better to measure the actual size of the bulletin board? Measuring physical properties in a laboratory experiment will help you make better observations.

Problem

How are physical properties of objects measured in SI?

Materials

- balance (beam)
- graduated cylinder (100 mL or larger)
- metersticks (2)
- thermometers (3)
- stick or dowel
- rock sample
- string
- globe
- water

Procedure

1. Begin at any station and determine the measurement requested. Record your observations in a data table and list sources of error.
   a. Use a balance to determine the mass, to the nearest 0.1 g, of the rock sample.
   b. Use a graduated cylinder to determine the volume, to the nearest 0.5 mL, of the water.
   c. Use 3 thermometers to measure the average temperature, to the nearest 0.5°C, at a certain location in the room.
   d. Use a meterstick to measure the length, to the nearest 0.1 cm, of the stick or dowel.
   e. Use a meterstick and string to measure the circumference of the globe. Be accurate to the nearest 0.1 cm.
2. Proceed to the other four stations as directed by your teacher.

Analyze

1. **Compare** your measurements with those who used the same objects. Review the values provided by your teacher. How do the values you obtained compare with those provided by your teacher and those of other students?
2. **Calculate** your percentage of error in each case. Use this formula.

$$\frac{\text{your value} - \text{teacher's value}}{\text{teacher's value}} \times 100 = \%\text{ of error}$$

Conclude and Apply

3. **Decide** what percentage of error will be acceptable. Generally, being within 5% to 7% of the correct value is considered good. If your values exceed 10% error, what could you do to improve your results and reduce error? What was the most common source of error?

Data and Observations

Sample data

Station	Sample	Value of Measurement	Causes of Error
a	rock	Mass = 168 g	See
b	water	Volume = 54 mL	teacher
c	____ (location)	Average temp. = 70 °C	margin
d	dowel	Length = 77 cm	notes.
e	globe	Circumference = 99 cm	

Activity 2-1

Purpose

LS **Kinesthetic** Demonstrate safety, accuracy, and precision in using simple laboratory equipment to determine some of the physical properties of sample objects. L1

COOP LEARN

Process Skills

measuring in SI, communicating, using numbers, interpreting data, and forming operational definitions

Time

40 minutes

Safety Precautions

Caution students to handle equipment and materials with care.

Activity Worksheets, pp. 5, 11-12

Teaching Strategies

- Set up stations in advance for each of the five tasks.
- Obtain rock samples ranging in mass from 110 to 399 grams.
- Using a graduated cylinder half-full of water, remind students how to read a meniscus.

Troubleshooting Each sample should be identified with a letter or number to avoid later confusion.

- Before providing students with the correct values, show them how to determine percentage of error.

Answers to Questions

1. Answers will vary depending on the samples used and students' results.
2. Answers will vary depending on the samples used and students' results.
3. Any value under 10% error should be accepted. Taking several measurements of the same property should decrease error. Common errors include: **balance:** not preset at 0 g, pan not clear of other materials, sliding value indicator not set in slot, balance not level, incorrect reading of scale; **graduated cylinder:** incorrect reading of water level; **thermometers:** inaccurate or broken, misreading of temperature scale; **meterstick:** not starting measurement at 0 cm, inordinate stretching of string, string not exactly placed around circumference, misreading of scale. Depending on the actual errors, a discussion of this question should lead to an understanding of the pitfalls to avoid in order to increase the accuracy of values.

Assessment

Oral To further assess students' understanding of the physical properties of objects, have them measure various objects in the classroom. Use the Performance Task Assessment List for Using Math in Science in PASC, p. 29. P

Section 2•3

Prepare

Section Background

- The main difference between molecules in each state of matter involves the amount of energy contained in the molecules. As energy is added to a solid, it will change to a liquid. More energy will cause the liquid to change to a gas, and still more energy will change the gas to a plasma. Changing a gas to a plasma, however, takes a great deal of energy.
- As a substance changes to a state of matter with a higher energy level, energy is absorbed and stored. As a substance changes to a state of matter with a lower energy level, the stored energy is released.

Preplanning

- To prepare for the MiniLAB, obtain access to a freezer.
- To prepare for Activity 2-2, obtain the materials listed on page 52.

1 Motivate

Bellringer

Before presenting the lesson, display **Section Focus Transparency 7** on the overhead projector. Assign the accompanying **Focus Activity** worksheet. L1 LEP

Brainstorming

LS **Interpersonal** Place several items on a table in the front of the classroom. Use items with a wide variety of physical properties. Have student groups discuss and list as many physical properties of the items as possible.

2•3 Matter

Science Words

physical property
density

Objectives

- Distinguish between chemical and physical properties.
- Contrast the four states of matter.

Physical Properties of Matter

So far in this chapter, you've been investigating chemical properties of matter—the properties that describe how one substance changes into another substance. But you can observe other properties of matter. The properties that you can observe without changing a substance into a new substance are **physical properties.**

What are some physical properties of your clothing? If you say your jeans are blue, soft, and about 80 cm long like the ones in **Figure 2-10,** you've described some of their physical properties. You can observe these without changing the material in your jeans into a new substance.

Density

One physical property that you will use to describe matter is density. **Density** is a measure of the mass of an object divided by its volume. Generally, this measurement is given

Figure 2-10
Blue, soft, room for two legs—these are the physical properties of a pair of blue jeans. *In your Science Journal, list the physical properties of five items in the classroom.*

Program Resources

Reproducible Masters
Study Guide, p. 11 L1
Reinforcement, p. 11 L1
Enrichment, p. 11 L3
Activity Worksheets, pp. 13-14, 16 L1
Lab Manual 8, 9

Transparencies
Section Focus Transparency 7 L1
Teaching Transparency 4
Science Integration Transparency 2

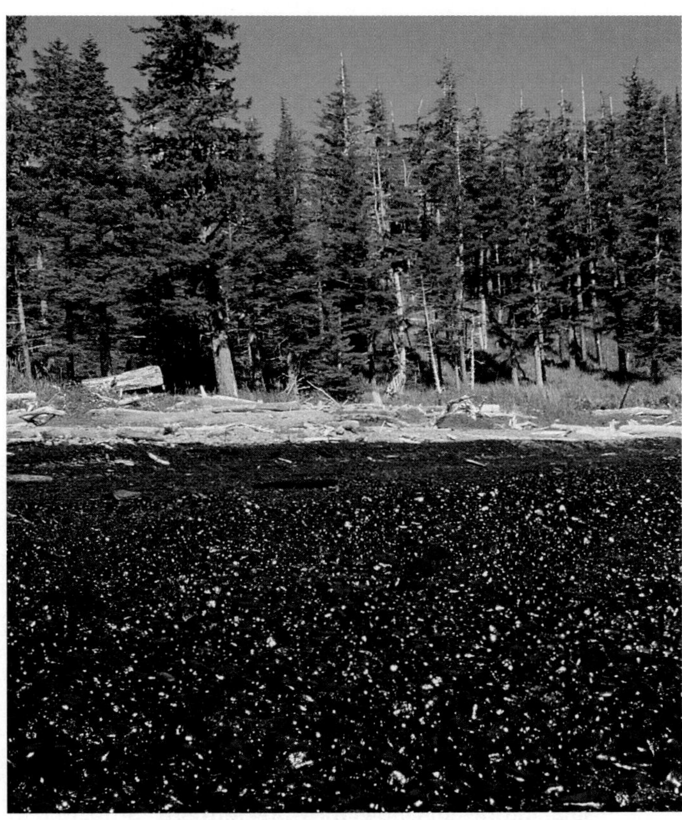

Figure 2-11

One physical property of oil is its density. *How does the density of oil compare with the density of water?*

in grams per cubic centimeter (g/cm^3). For example, the average density of liquid water is 1 g/cm^3. So 1 cm^3 of water has a mass of 1 g.

Suppose you have a small cube and need to find its density. First, measure its mass and volume. Suppose its volume is 2 cm^3 and its mass is 8 g. Use the formula $D = \frac{M}{V}$.

$$D = \frac{M}{V}$$

$$D = \frac{8\ g}{2\ cm^3}$$

$$D = \frac{4\ g}{cm^3} \quad \text{or} \quad 4\ g/cm^3$$

An object that's more dense than water will sink, whereas one that's less dense will float. You've heard about the oil spills off the coast of the United States. Why does this oil, shown in **Figure 2-11,** float on the surface of the water and wash up on the beaches?

USING MATH

You can find the volume of a rectangular solid by multiplying its length, width, and height. A pine board has dimensions of 4.05 cm, 8.85 cm, and 164 cm. Determine the volume and density of the board if its mass is 2580 g.

2 Teach

Student Text Question

Why does this oil, shown in Figure 2-11, float on the surface of the water and wash up on the beaches? *Oil floats on water because it is less dense than water.*

Visual Learning

Figure 2-10 **In your Science Journal, list the physical properties of five items in the classroom.** *Answers will vary. Some examples include, desk: wooden, hard, metal, gray; blackboard: black, flat, hard, dusty.*

Figure 2-11 **How does the density of oil compare with the density of water?** *Oil is less dense than water.* LEP IS

USING MATH

Answer 5878.17 cm^3, 2.28 g/cm^3

GLENCOE TECHNOLOGY

Videodisc

The Infinite Voyage: Miracles by Design

Chapter 6

New Ceramics: New Uses

Chapter 7

Ceramic Superconductors: Rapid Transportation

Chapter 8

Ceramic Superconductors: Effects on the Computer

Integrating the Sciences

Physical Science Density is a physical property of a substance. Ask students, **What will happen if three liquids of differing densities, such as water, maple syrup, and vegetable oil, are placed into one container?** *The densest liquid of the three will sink to the bottom of the container while the liquid with the least density will float on top of the other two.*

Community Connection

Different Densities Ask a representative from the water company or sewage treatment plant to visit the class. Ask them to describe how their job involves working with liquids of different densities. You could ask them to discuss how water purification or sewage treatment is affected if large quantities of oil or gasoline leak into the water supply or sewage.

Demonstration

LS Visual-Spatial Have students observe as you pour syrup and milk into two separate containers. Ask students to contrast the rates at which the two liquids flow. Lead a discussion as to why the two liquids flow so differently. Help students conclude that one of the reasons the rates of flow differ is that the attraction among the molecules of the syrup is greater than that among the milk molecules. LEP

Discussion

Ask students to compare and contrast the processes of evaporation and boiling. Both involve a change of state from a liquid to a gas. Evaporation occurs at the liquid's surface; boiling occurs throughout the liquid.

Visual Learning

Figure 2-12C What happened to the gas in this hot air balloon? *The molecules of gas move apart until they're evenly spaced throughout the balloon, which is why the balloon expands.* LEP LS

Use Labs 8 and 9 in the **Lab Manual** as you teach this lesson.

States of Matter

Think back to breakfast this morning. You may have had solid toast, liquid milk or juice, and of course you breathed air, which is a gas. If you have seen a lightning bolt during a summer storm, you have seen matter in its plasma state. On Earth matter occurs in four physical states. These four states are solid, liquid, gas, and plasma. What causes the differences among these four states of matter?

Figure 2-12

The attraction between atoms or molecules and their rate of movement determines whether matter occurs in a solid, liquid, gas, or plasma state.

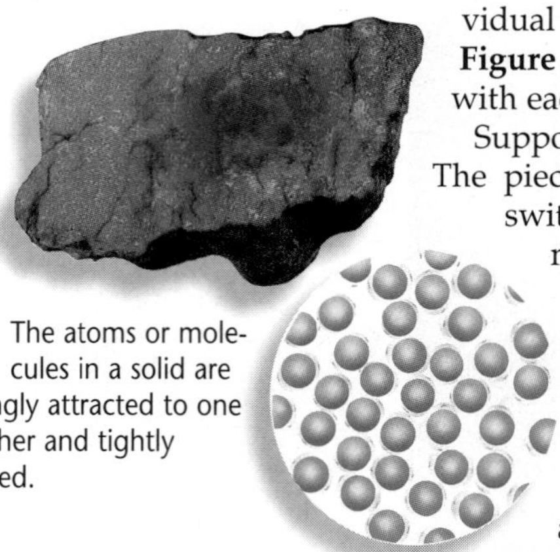

A The atoms or molecules in a solid are strongly attracted to one another and tightly packed.

Solids

The reason some matter is solid is that its atoms or molecules are in a fixed position relative to each other. The individual atoms or molecules of the turquoise shown in **Figure 2-12A** may vibrate, but they don't switch positions with each other. You can make a mental model of this.

Suppose you have a puzzle with its many pieces in place. The pieces are packed so tightly that no one piece can switch positions with another piece. But the pieces can move a little. For example, you can twist the whole puzzle a few millimeters without breaking it apart. If it's on a table, you can shake the table and the puzzle's individual pieces will vibrate. But the pieces of the puzzle are held together even though they move.

The puzzle pieces in our model represent atoms or molecules of a substance in a solid state. Such atoms or molecules are strongly attracted to each other and resist being separated.

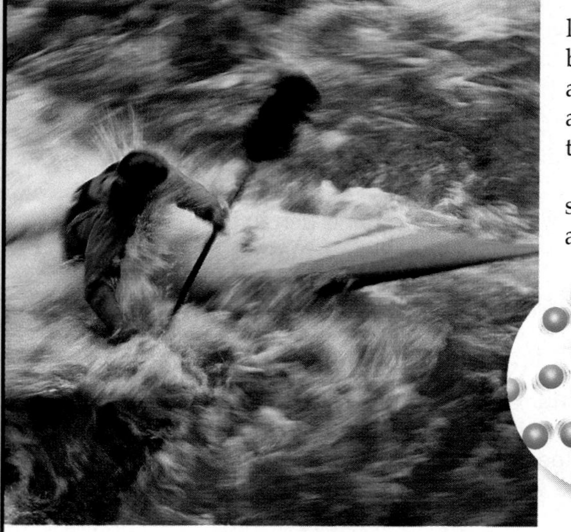

Liquids

Look at Figure **2-12B.** Atoms or molecules in a liquid are also strongly attracted to each other, but they aren't as strongly attracted as they are in a solid. Atoms or molecules remain close to one another in a liquid but are free to change positions with each other. This allows liquids to flow.

When you sit down to breakfast, you may have several liquids at the table. You may have milk in a glass and syrup on your pancakes. Both are

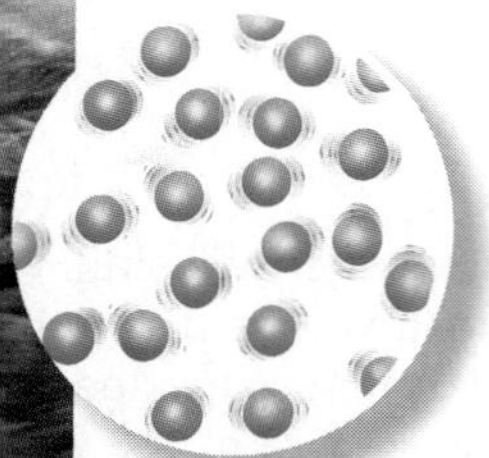

B The atoms or molecules in a liquid are attracted to each other, but not as strongly as those of a solid. They are free to move over and around each other.

Theme Connection

Scale and Structure The fact that matter changes state reinforces the theme of scale and structure. As thermal energy is added to a substance, molecules move farther away from each other, their mutual attractive forces weaken, and the internal structure of the substance changes. Eventually molecules are far enough away that they can move over and around each other. If enough thermal energy is added, very little attractive force remains between the molecules and they freely move in all directions.

substances in the liquid state, even though one flows more freely than the other.

A liquid flows as it takes the shape of the container it's placed in, but it resists changes in volume. You can pour orange juice into a short, wide glass and it will match the shape of the glass. You can then pour the same juice into a tall, skinny glass and it will flow until it matches the shape of its new container. It does so because its molecules move over and around each other.

Gases

Gases behave the way they do because their atoms or mole-cules have very little attractive force on each other. This causes them to move freely and independently. Air fresheners work because of this property. If an air freshener is placed in a corner, it isn't long before molecules from the air freshener have spread throughout the room. Gases fill the entire container they are placed in, which is why the hot air balloon shown in **Figure 2-12C** expands. The atoms or molecules move apart until they're evenly spaced throughout the balloon.

C The atoms or molecules of a gas are not strongly attracted to each other. *What happened to the gas in this hot air balloon?*

Plasma

What's the most common state of matter? So far we've investigated matter in the solid, liquid, and gaseous states. But most of the matter in the universe is in the plasma state. Matter in this state is composed of ions and electrons. Many of the electrons normally in the electron cloud have escaped and are outside of the ion's electron cloud.

Stars are composed of matter in the plasma state. Plasma also exists in the magnetic field near Jupiter. On Earth, plasma is found in lightning bolts, as shown in **Figure 2-12D.**

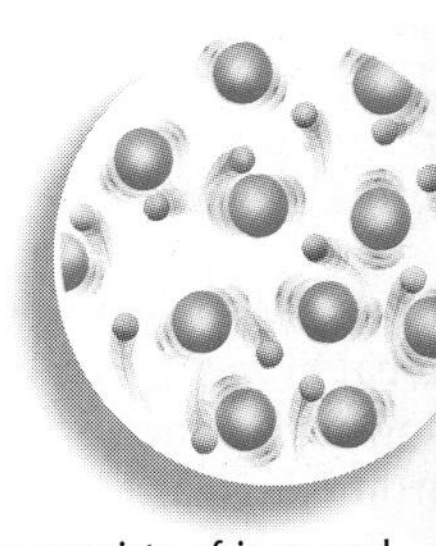

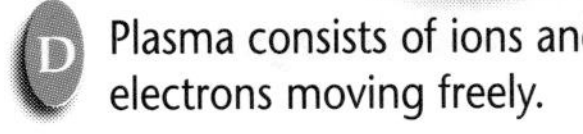

D Plasma consists of ions and electrons moving freely.

Revealing Preconceptions

Some students may not realize that matter can change from a solid to a gas without going through the liquid phase. This process is called sublimation.

Demonstration

LS **Visual-Spatial** Obtain a piece of dry ice (carbon dioxide in a frozen, solid state). Place the dry ice on a plate in view of students. The dry ice will quickly change into carbon dioxide gas via sublimation. Students should note that it doesn't pass through a liquid state. **CAUTION:** *Do not touch the dry ice. Always use a thermal mitt and tongs to manipulate the ice.* LEP

Discussion

Discuss the fact that energy is needed to change the state of a material. The amount of energy needed to change a solid to a liquid is the heat of fusion for that material. For example, the heat of fusion for water is 334 kJ/kg. It takes 334 kJ (kilojoules) of energy to melt 1 kg of ice.

Use **Science Integration Transparency 2** as you teach this lesson.

Inclusion Strategies

Gifted Have students perform the following activity to explore energy absorption as water changes state. Put 100 mL of water and 5 ice cubes in a 600-mL beaker. Record the temperature of the water. Then, slowly heat the beaker and water, recording the temperature at one-minute intervals. Note when the ice melts and when the water begins to boil. Measure and record the temperature as the water boils for 5 minutes. Graph the temperature of the water versus time. Ask: **What was the maximum temperature reached when ice was still in the water?** *0°C* **What was the maximum temperature reached?** *100°C* **What do the horizontal portions of your graph represent?** *changes of state* L3

People and Science

Dr. Samuel B. Mukasa, Isotope Geochemist

On the Job

Q **Dr. Mukasa, please explain how you use isotopes in your work.**

A Isotopes can be used for tracing the sources of magma (molten rock beneath Earth's surface) and mineral deposits from very deep in Earth. Dating rocks also helps in putting Earth's history together—figuring out when the continents broke up and when mountains formed. Isotopes can be used to date when rocks actually formed.

Q **Do you ever work with scientists in other fields?**

A Yes, I do. To give you an example, in studying the breakup of the western edge of the old supercontinent Gondwanaland into Antarctica and New Zealand, there are several things you can look for in the rocks. Rocks involved in the breakup zone get very deformed—almost like a car wreck in which two cars slam into each other. The mangled up rocks have patterns of structures in them that are wonderful telltale signs about exactly what the process of breakup was. I work with structural geologists who can interpret these patterns.

Personal Insights

Q **Have you had an interest in geology since you were young?**

A I grew up in East Africa, and for weekend activities, we used to climb volcanoes. Realizing that Earth was alive and that volcanoes were erupting, I began to wonder, "Why is this happening here and not over there?"

Career Connection

Find the address for the Geological Society of America (ask for help from your school librarian or at the reference desk of your local library). Write for the brochure, "Future Employment Opportunities in the Geological Sciences." When you receive the brochure, go through it, and make a list of promising careers.

- **Oceanographer**
- **Geologist**

People and Science

Background

- According to the theory of continental drift, the continents once were united in a single landmass known as Pangaea. Pangaea separated into the two supercontinents Laurasia and Gondwanaland, which eventually broke up into the continents we recognize today.
- Part of Mukasa's work focuses on the area in western Antarctica where New Zealand broke away from Gondwanaland. When Earth's crust broke up, magma oozed out and formed rock. By studying rocks that formed at the time of the breakup, researchers can tell exactly when the breakup took place. The chemical composition of the rocks also reveals where within Earth the magma came from.

Teaching Strategies

Ask students to consider whether studying Earth's history has any practical value. In leading a discussion of their opinions, point out that the processes that shaped Earth in the past still are going on, and that Earth's geologic history holds clues to past climate changes.

Career Connection

In the past, many geologists and geochemists worked for mining and oil companies, but there are fewer jobs in those industries today. Now, more opportunities lie in environmental remediation—fixing damage to the environment caused by strip mining and improper disposal of toxic and hazardous wastes—and in detecting clues to Earth's past climate changes by analyzing sediments from the ocean floor and cores of ice preserved in the ice caps. To prepare for careers in these areas, students need high school and college courses in math, environmental science, geology, and chemistry. Knowledge of computer modeling also is useful.

For More Information

Students could contact local environmental remediation companies and landfills to find out whether they employ geochemists, and if so, for what purposes. They might also check with the state geological survey to find out whether isotopic dating has played any part in studies of the region's geologic history.

Changing the State of Matter

Matter is changed from a liquid to a solid at its freezing point and from a liquid to a gas at its boiling point. You're probably familiar with the freezing and boiling points of water. Water changes from a liquid to a solid at its freezing point of 0°C. It boils at 100°C. Water is the only substance that occurs naturally on Earth as a solid, liquid, and gas.

Other substances don't naturally exist in these three states on Earth. Their boiling and freezing points are above or below the temperatures we experience. Temperatures and conditions needed for matter to exist as plasma are even less common on Earth.

The attraction between atoms or molecules and their rate of movement are two factors that determine the state of matter. When you melt ice you increase the rate of movement of its molecules. They are then able to move apart. Adding thermal energy to the ice causes this change. As **Figure 2-13** shows, solid metal can be converted into liquid when thermal energy is added.

Changes in state can also occur because of increases or decreases in pressure. You can demonstrate this by applying pressure to an ice cube. It will change to liquid water even though no thermal energy was added.

What happens when water freezes?

Procedure

1. Pour water into a graduated cylinder or small beaker so that it is about half-filled.
2. Mark the level of the water with a small piece of masking tape.
3. Place the uncovered container of water in the freezer until all of the water turns to ice.

Analysis

1. How does the level of the ice in the container compare with the original level of the water?
2. What happened to the physical properties of the water when it changed to ice?

Figure 2-13

A solid metal can be converted to liquid by adding thermal energy to its molecules. *What is happening to the molecules during this conversion?*

Visual Learning

Figure 2-13 What is happening to the molecules during this conversion? *Their rate of movement is increasing. Also, the attraction between the molecules has lessened.* LEP LS

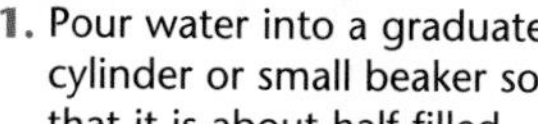

Purpose

LS **Interpersonal** Students will observe the effects of freezing water. L1

COOP LEARN

Materials

graduated cylinders or small beakers, water, freezer, masking tape

Teaching Strategies

As long as the container is uncovered, it will not break when the water expands as it freezes.

Analysis

1. The level of the ice is higher than the level of the liquid water.
2. Water expands as it freezes but does not change mass. Therefore, ice is less dense than liquid water.

Assessment

Oral To further assess students' understanding of what happens when water freezes, ask them to explain why people can go ice fishing. Use the Performance Task Assessment List for Making Observations and Inferences in **PASC**, p. 17. P

Activity Worksheets, pp. 5, 16

Cultural Diversity

A Nutty Meal The acorn was the most important staple food of Californian Native Americans. A corn mush or soup was the main daily food for most. Ground acorns were used to make breads, and acorn nuts to produce coffee and tea. Acorns gathered by Native Americans helped the Pilgrims survive their first winter in 1620.

All acorns contain tannin, a substance that is very bitter, but different kinds of acorns contain different amounts. Humans cannot digest large quantities of tannin, so it must be removed before the acorns are eaten. Tannin is readily soluble in water, so this is done through leaching. Native Americans either buried the acorns in the mud of a swamp for a year, or let shelled acorns mold in baskets that were then buried in freshwater sand. The acorns were edible when they turned black.

Science Journal

LS Linguistic Lists should include reasonable examples of each state, such as water, air, books, beads, food, coins, ice, etc.

USING MATH

Answer Proper. Since ice floats, its density is less than 1, and proper fractions represent numbers less than 1.

Visual Learning

Figure 2-14 What effect would this have on the fish? *Fish could not survive the winter, because lakes would freeze solid from the bottom up.*  LEP LS

3 Assess

Check for Understanding

FLEX Your Brain

Use the Flex Your Brain activity to have students explore DIFFERENT STATES OF MATTER.

Activity Worksheets, p. 5

Reteach

Demonstrate how water changes state. Place an ice cube in a pan on your desk. As the ice cube warms, it will change to liquid water. Then show students how ice will change to a liquid when pressure is applied by pressing down on the ice with a massive object.

Extension

For students who have mastered this section, use the **Reinforcement** and **Enrichment** masters.

Science Journal

In your Science Journal, list and classify common solids, liquids, and gases that you use every day.

USING MATH

Twenty cc of water has a mass of 20 g. Its density can be represented by the fraction $^{20}/_{20}$. Suppose you freeze the water. Is the density of the ice represented by a proper fraction or an improper fraction? Explain you reasoning.

Changes in Physical Properties

Chemical properties of matter don't change when the matter changes state. But some of its physical properties change. For example, the density of water changes as it changes state. In which state is water the most dense? You may be tempted to say "when it's a solid," but think about this. Although most materials are more dense in their solid state than in their liquid state, ice will float in liquid water; therefore, ice is less dense than liquid water. This is because water molecules move farther apart and the water expands as it freezes.

Some physical properties of substances don't change when they change state. For example, water is colorless and transparent in each of its states.

Classifying Matter

Chemical and physical properties allow us to identify and classify matter. One way to classify matter is by its state. Matter in one state can often be changed to another state by adding or removing thermal energy. Look at **Figure 2-15.** Changes in thermal energy may explain why there is no liquid water on the planet Mars, yet photographs of its surface show what appear to be ancient stream beds. Scientists

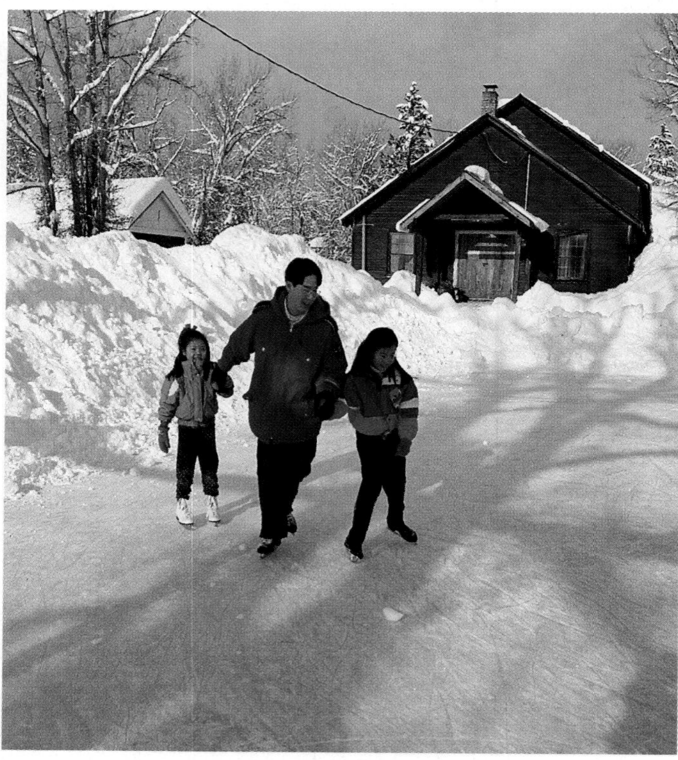

Figure 2-14

If ice were more dense than water, lakes would freeze solid from the bottom up. *What affect would this have on the fish?*

Inclusion Strategies

Gifted Have students explain why the boiling point of water differs from one location to another. The temperature at which a liquid boils depends on atmospheric pressure. Atmospheric pressure differs with elevation; boiling points of liquids also vary with elevation. The boiling point of water at sea level is 100°C; in Denver, CO, at 1600 m above sea level, it is 95°C. L3

Across the Curriculum

History James Prescott Joule investigated the kinetic theory, involving the interaction of matter and energy due to particle motion. Because of his father's illness, he entered the family brewing business. Joule used income from the brewery to support his scientific investigations on the kinetic theory and thermodynamics, the flow of energy in systems. Have student volunteers research Joule and his work. L3

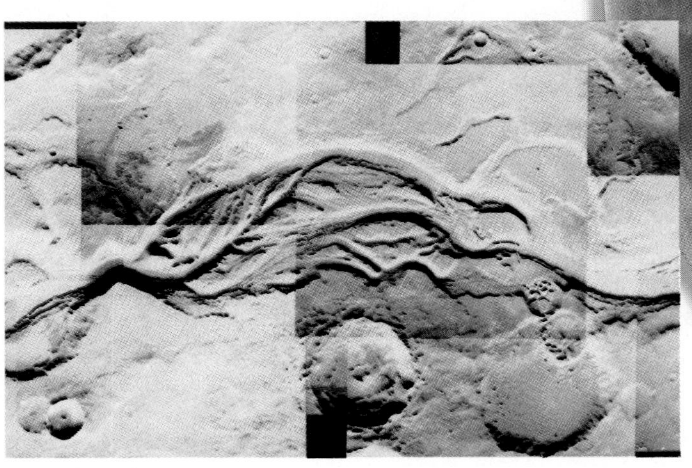

believe that the liquid water froze to form polar ice caps. Some of the water may have soaked into the ground and frozen. When matter changes state in this way, it retains its chemical properties while some of its physical properties change.

Figure 2-15
This valley on the planet Mars was possibly carved by water.

Section Wrap-up

Review

1. Compare and contrast the movement of water molecules when water is in a solid, liquid, and gaseous state.
2. The planet Mars, as shown in **Figure 2-15,** has what appear to be ancient stream beds, yet there's no liquid water on Mars. Explain what may have happened to Mars' liquid water.
3. **Think Critically:** Suppose you blow up a balloon and then place it in a freezer. Later, you find that the balloon has shrunk and has liquid in it. Explain what has happened.

Using Computers

Graphing Research the melting and boiling points in degrees Celsius of several compounds, including water. Use your computer to make a line graph showing the temperatures at which these several compounds change state from solid to liquid to gas.

Skill Builder

Making and Using Tables

Jonathon had a glass of milk, an orange, celery sticks, and a peanut butter and jelly sandwich for lunch. Make a table listing the state of matter of each item of his lunch. Also list at least one physical property of each item. If you need help, refer to Making and Using Tables in the **Skill Handbook.**

4 Close

•MINI•QUIZ•

1. **A property you can observe without changing a substance into a new substance is a(n) _____ property.** *physical*
2. **The relationship between the mass of an object and its volume is _____ .** *density*
3. **The four states of matter are _____ .** *solid, liquid, gas, and plasma*

Section Wrap-up

Review

1. Molecules vibrate but are prevented from moving over and around each other in ice (solid). In liquid water, the molecules move past each other. In water vapor (gas), the molecules move freely and rapidly.
2. The low atmospheric pressure on Mars may have caused some of the liquid water to evaporate. Some of the liquid water froze to form polar ice caps. Some water may have soaked into the ground and frozen.
3. **Think Critically** The temperature of the air was lowered. The molecules of air moved closer together, reducing the size of the balloon. Molecules of water vapor in the air condensed to form liquid water.

Using Computers

Answers will vary. Students should include 0°C for the change from solid ice to liquid water, and 100°C for the change from liquid water to gas. Accept any graphs that indicate the melting and boiling points of several compounds.

Skill Builder

Students' tables will vary. One possible solution is shown.

Item	State	Physical Properties
milk	liquid	white, cold
sandwich	solid	made of bread, peanut butter, and jelly
orange	solid, liquid	orange, round
celery	solid	green, stringy

Assessment

Performance Assess students' understanding of states of matter by having them make a table about their breakfast. Use the Performance Task Assessment List for Data Table in **PASC,** p. 37. P

Activity 2-2

PREPARATION

Purpose

LS **Interpersonal** Design and carry out an experiment to measure the volume and mass of various objects and to determine their densities. L1 LEP COOP LEARN

Process Skills

measuring in SI, using numbers, interpreting data, inferring, communicating, making and using tables, comparing and contrasting, forming operational definitions, forming a hypothesis, designing an experiment, separating and controlling variables

Time

One class period will be required for students to devise a method of measuring the volume of the objects and to complete the measurements. Another class period will be needed for students to calculate the density of the objects and to discuss the procedure and outcome.

Materials

Alternate Materials A sample of any nonsoluble mineral may be substituted for the quartz.

Possible Hypotheses

- The volume of an object can be determined by submerging it in water and measuring the volume of the water displaced.
- The volume of an object can be determined by measuring its length, width, and height.
- The density of an object is determined by dividing its mass by its volume.

Activity Worksheets, pp. 5, 13-14

Activity 2-2

Design Your Own Experiment
Determining Density

What has a greater density—a rock or a sponge? Does cork have a greater density than clay? There are two factors that contribute to the density of an object. Think back to the equation you learned earlier in this chapter.

PREPARATION

Problem

What processes can be used to determine the densities of several objects?

Form a Hypothesis

State a hypothesis about what process you can use to measure and compare the densities of several materials.

Objectives

- List some ways that the density of an object can be measured.
- Design your own experiment that compares the densities of several materials.

Possible Materials

- pan balance
- beaker (100 mL)
- graduated cylinder (250 mL)
- water
- sponge
- piece of quartz
- piece of clay
- small wood block
- small metal block
- small cork
- rock
- ruler

Safety Precautions

Be wary of sharp edges on some of the materials and take care not to break the beaker or graduated cylinder.

52

Theme Connection

Scale and Structure Determining the density of substances reinforces the theme of scale and structure. Objects that have higher mass than other objects of the same volume may have a more compact structure. Molecules in the more massive object may also be composed of more massive atoms. In either case, the overall structure of the object has an effect on its density.

PLAN THE EXPERIMENT

1. As a group, agree upon and write out the hypothesis statement.
2. As a group, list the steps that you need to take to test your hypothesis. Be specific, describing exactly what you will do at each step. List your materials.
3. Using the equation that density = mass/volume, as a group, devise a method of determining the mass and volume of each material to be tested.
4. Design a data table in your Science Journal so that it is ready to use as your group collects data.

Check the Plan

1. Read over your entire experiment to make sure that all steps are in a logical order.
2. Should you run the process more than once for any of the materials?
3. Identify any constants, variables, and controls of the experiment.
4. *Make sure your teacher approves your plan before you proceed.*

DO THE EXPERIMENT

1. Carry out the experiment as planned.
2. While the experiment is going on, write down any observations that you make and complete the data table in your Science Journal.

Analyze and Apply

1. Do you **observe** anything about the way more-dense objects feel compared with less-dense objects of the same size?
2. What happens when a cork is placed in water?
3. Based on this, would you **hypothesize** that a cork is more dense, the same density, or less dense than water?
4. Without measuring the density of an object that floats, **conclude** how you know that it has a density of less than 1.0 g/cm^3.

Go Further

How would the data you collected about the density of the clay be affected if you were to break the clay into two smaller pieces and repeat the experiment? Try it and see if there is any effect on the data.

PLAN THE EXPERIMENT

Possible Procedures

- Most students will realize that the volume and mass of each object must be determined in order to calculate the density. However, students may have difficulty devising a method for measuring volume.
- Measuring the volume of water displaced by an object will provide the volume of the object.
- The volume of objects with straight sides can be obtained by measuring the width, length, and height.
- The mass of an object can be obtained by using the pan balance.

Teaching Strategies

Tying to Previous Knowledge Some students will recall or realize that the density of some materials can be compared by attempting to float one material within another.

Troubleshooting The clay must be oil-based and not water-soluble. Since the wood block may absorb water, it should not be left in water for any extended length of time.

DO THE EXPERIMENT

Expected Outcome

Students should be able to measure the volume and mass of each object and calculate their densities within 10% error.

Analyze and Apply

1. Students should notice that denser objects feel heavier than less dense objects of the same size. Objects like this are said to have greater heft.
2. Cork floats when placed in water.
3. Students should hypothesize that cork is less dense than water.
4. Water has a density of 1 gm/cm^3. Any object that floats in water must have a density less than 1 gm/cm^3.

Go Further

The density of the clay is not affected by the size of the piece as long as the same sample of clay is used.

Assessment

Performance To further assess students' understanding of density and measuring physical properties, have them repeat the above experiment using different samples of the same materials they originally tested. Have them list possible causes of any differences observed. Use the Performance Task Assessment List for Carrying Out a Strategy and Collecting Data in **PASC**, p. 25. P

Prepare

Section Background

The United States Department of Energy's Office of Civilian Radioactive Waste is currently studying the Yucca Mountain site in order to determine whether the site is safe for storage of nuclear waste. The study will continue through the year 2001.

1 Motivate

Bellringer

Before presenting the lesson, display **Section Focus Transparency 8** on the overhead projector. Assign the accompanying **Focus Activity** worksheet. L1 LEP

Tying to Previous Knowledge

Have students recall that neutrons are located inside the nuclei of atoms. When neutrons are fired at uranium-235 atoms, the U-235 nuclei split and release more neutrons and energy.

2 Teach

Brainstorming

Ask students to imagine a small room full of mousetraps that are each set to spring when hit. A Ping-Pong ball sits in each trap and will shoot through the air if the mousetrap snaps. Ask students to describe what would happen if a single Ping-Pong ball were thrown into the room. This discussion should be used to present how a chain reaction happens in a nuclear power plant.

ISSUE:

2•4 Energy from Atoms

Science Words

nuclear energy
fission
nuclear waste

Objectives

- Describe how nuclear energy is made.
- Explain advantages and disadvantages of the Yucca Mountain nuclear waste storage site.

Nuclear Energy

Most electricity in the United States is generated in power plants that use fossil fuels. However, there are alternate sources of energy. **Nuclear energy** is an alternate energy source produced from atomic reactions. When the nucleus of a heavy element is split, lighter elements are formed and energy is released.

Fission

Fission is the splitting of nuclei of atoms in heavy elements such as uranium. The most commonly used fuel in fission power plants is the uranium-235 isotope. It occurs in ore in some sandstone in the Rocky Mountains. After the ore is mined, the uranium is concentrated and then placed in long metal pipes called fuel rods. The fuel rods sit in a pool of cooling water within a large chamber called a nuclear reactor, shown in **Figure 2-16.** Neutrons are fired into the fuel, which begins a chain reaction that in turn releases heat. This heat is used to boil water to make steam. The steam drives a turbine, which turns a generator, producing electricity.

Figure 2-16

Most of the high-level radioactive waste in the United States comes from spent fuel rods used in nuclear power plants.

Program Resources

Reproducible Masters

Study Guide, p. 12 L1
Reinforcement, p. 12 L1
Enrichment, p. 12 L3
Science and Society Integration, p. 6

Transparencies

Section Focus Transparency 8 L1

2 Points of View

Storing Nuclear Waste in Yucca Mountain

One major problem with nuclear energy is the waste material that is produced. **Nuclear waste** from power plants is highly radioactive. Some of this waste will remain radioactive for more than ten-thousand years. Nuclear waste must be safely stored in order to keep it from entering the environment. Yucca Mountain in Nevada has been chosen as a possible storage site for this nuclear waste. Geologists working for the U.S. Department of Energy have concerns about three major hazards: volcanoes, earthquakes, and groundwater. They believe the Yucca Mountain area, shown in **Figure 2-17,** is a good site because the area is remote, very little rain falls, the water table is far below the proposed storage facility, and the land is already owned by the U.S. government. They also believe that any earthquakes that may occur in the area will affect only surface buildings, not the deeply buried storage area.

Figure 2-17

The U.S. Department of Energy's Office of Civilian Radioactive Waste is currently studying the Yucca Mountain site in order to determine whether the site is safe for storage of nuclear waste. The study will continue through the year 2001 and cost approximately $5 billion.

Visual Learning

Figure 2-18 Why is it so important for scientists to determine the cause of this deposit of limestone? *If the veins of calcite were deposited by upwelling groundwater, nuclear waste could leak out into the environment.* LEP 

GLENCOE TECHNOLOGY

Videodisc

The Infinite Voyage: Unseen Worlds

Chapter 11

The Fermi Lab Accelerator: Splitting the Atom

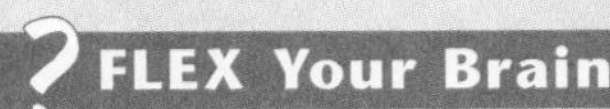

3 Assess

Check for Understanding

FLEX Your Brain

Use the Flex Your Brain activity to have students explore NUCLEAR WASTE STORAGE.

Activity Worksheets, p. 5

Reteach

Have students research how nuclear waste is stored.

Extension

For students who have mastered this section, use the **Reinforcement** and **Enrichment** masters.

Across the Curriculum

Medicine Nuclear radiation therapy is very successful in the treatment of some cancers. For diagnostic purposes, radioactive isotopes can be injected into the body and instruments can monitor their movement throughout the body. Have interested students research the production and medical uses of radioactive isotopes. L3

Science Journal

 **Linguistic** Have students free write in their Science Journals about characteristics that a good nuclear waste storage site should possess. When finished, place students into pairs and have them write a formal position paper about characteristics that every nuclear waste storage site should possess. L2 COOP LEARN

4 Close

Discuss why many people wouldn't choose to live next to a nuclear waste storage site.

Section Wrap-up

Review

1. Nuclear waste from power plants.
2. Answers will vary but may include: in favor, the area is remote; opposed, earthquakes could cause movement along faults running through the storage facility.

Explore the Issue

Answers will vary, but students should support their opinions with valid arguments based on known facts.

Figure 2-18

Geologists believe that the cream-colored veins of calcite in this deposit were formed either by rainwater percolating down from the surface or by groundwater rising upward from below. *Why is it so important for scientists to determine the cause of this deposit of limestone?*

Search for Other Locations

Not everyone agrees that Yucca Mountain is a safe location for storage of nuclear waste. As shown in **Figure 2-18,** a distinctive deposit of limestone has formed at one location, Trench 14. Geologists for the Department of Energy believe the deposit formed as very small amounts of rainwater percolated downward toward the water table. Geologists working for the state of Nevada believe the Trench 14 limestone was formed by an upwelling of groundwater. This could lead to a release of toxic waste into the environment. Critics of the site are also concerned about the many earthquake faults that exist in the area. They are concerned that an earthquake could cause movement along faults running through the storage facility. This, they believe, could disrupt waste containers and produce cracks through which contaminated groundwater might flow into the environment. Even without an earthquake, critics are concerned about the water. Rainwater could percolate downward or groundwater could rise up. Either way, corrosion of the containers could be accelerated, exposing nuclear waste.

Section Wrap-up

Review

1. What is the source of most of the nuclear waste that needs to be stored in a safe location?
2. List one form of evidence in favor of and one opposed to the use of Yucca Mountain as a nuclear waste storage site.

Explore the Issue

Should the Department of Energy abandon the study of the Yucca Mountain nuclear storage site? If yes, what other arrangements might be made in order to cope with the nuclear waste? If no, how would you alleviate the concerns voiced about the dangers of volcanoes, earthquakes, and groundwater contamination at the Yucca Mountain site?

Chapter 2 Review

Summary

2-1: Atoms

1. Matter is everything that has mass and takes up space. Atoms are the building blocks of matter.
2. Protons and neutrons make up the nucleus of an atom. Protons have a positive charge whereas neutrons have no charge. Electrons surround the nucleus, forming an electron cloud. Electrons are negatively charged.
3. Isotopes are atoms of the same element. Isotopes have the same atomic number, but differ in their number of neutrons.

2-2: Combinations of Atoms

1. A compound is a substance made of two or more elements. The properties of a compound differ from the chemical and physical properties of the elements of which it is composed.
2. Atoms join to form molecules—the building blocks of compounds. A mixture is a substance in which each of the components retains its own properties.

2-3: Matter

1. Physical properties can be observed and measured without causing a chemical change in a substance. Chemical properties can be observed only when one substance reacts with another substance.
2. Atoms or molecules in a solid are in fixed positions relative to one another. In a liquid, the atoms or molecules are close together but are freer to change positions. Atoms or molecules in a gas have very little attractive force on one another. Plasma is composed of ions and electrons.

2-4: Science and Society: Energy from Atoms

1. Nuclear energy is produced from atomic reactions.
2. Use of the Yucca Mountain nuclear waste storage site has both supporters and critics.

Key Science Words

a. atom
b. atomic number
c. chemical property
d. compound
e. density
f. electron
g element
h. fission
i. ion
j. isotope
k. mass number
l. matter
m. mixture
n. molecule
o. neutron
p. nuclear energy
q. nuclear waste
r. physical property
s. proton
t. solution

Reviewing Vocabulary

Match each phrase with the correct term from the list of Key Science Words.

1. building block of matter
2. particle with no electric charge
3. splitting of nuclei of atoms in heavy elements
4. anything that takes up space and has mass
5. a solution is one type
6. moves around the nucleus of an atom
7. composed of only one type of atom
8. mass divided by volume
9. two or more atoms combine to form this building block of compounds
10. atom of the same element but with different number of neutrons

Chapter 2

Review

Summary

Have students read the summary statements to review the major concepts of the chapter.

Reviewing Vocabulary

1. a	**6.** f
2. o	**7.** g
3. h	**8.** e
4. l	**9.** n
5. m	**10.** j

Assessment

Portfolio Encourage students to place in their portfolios one or two items of what they consider to be their best work. Examples include:

- MiniLAB, classification chart, p. 40
- FLEX Your Brain, p. 41
- Integrating the Sciences, p. 41
- Activity 2-2, pp. 52-53 P

Performance Additional performance assessments may be found in **Performance Assessment** and **Science Integration Activities.** Performance Task Assessment Lists and rubrics for evaluating these activities can be found in Glencoe's **Performance Assessment in the Science Classroom.**

GLENCOE TECHNOLOGY

MindJogger Videoquiz

Chapter 2 Have students work in groups as they play the Videoquiz game to review key chapter concepts.

Chapter 2 Review

Checking Concepts

1. c
2. b
3. a
4. a
5. b
6. c
7. d
8. b
9. c
10. a

Understanding Concepts

11. All are atomic particles. Protons have a positive charge; electrons a negative charge; and neutrons have no charge. Protons and neutrons make up the nucleus of an atom, whereas electrons move around the nucleus in an electron cloud.

12. density = mass ÷ volume; since 1 mL = 1 cm^3
23 g ÷ 25 cm^3
= 0.92 g/cm^3

13. Materials that combine to form molecules go through chemical changes, and the chemical and physical properties of each material change. In mixtures of materials, the materials retain their chemical properties, although some of their physical properties may change.

14. The number of protons in the nucleus of the atom is equal to the number of electrons in the electron cloud.

15. Fission. As heavy atoms split through the process of fission, lighter atoms form and energy is released.

Chapter 2 Review

Checking Concepts

Choose the word or phrase that completes the sentence.

1. _______ contain only one type of atom.
a. Plasmas c. Elements
b. Mixtures d. Solids

2. A(n) _______ has a positive charge.
a. electron c. neutron
b. proton d. plasma

3. In an atom, the _______ form a cloud around the nucleus.
a. electrons c. neutrons
b. protons d. positively charged particles

4. Carbon has a mass number of 12. Thus, it has _______ protons and _______ neutrons.
a. 6, 6 c. 6, 12
b. 12, 12 d. 12, 6

5. On Earth, molecular oxygen is usually a _______.
a. solid c. liquid
b. gas d. plasma

6. An isotope of carbon is _______.
a. boron-12 c. carbon-14
b. nitrogen-12 d. hydrogen-2

7. Electrically charged atoms are _______.
a. molecules c. isotopes
b. solutions d. ions

8. The color of your clothes is a(n) _______.
a. chemical property
b. physical property
c. isotope property
d. molecular property

9. A rock with a volume of 4.0 cm^3 and a density of 3.0 g/cm^3 has a mass of _______.
a. 0.75 g c. 12.0 g
b. 3.0 g d. 4.0 g

10. Water changes state at _______.
a. 0°C and 100°C c. 0°C and 32°C
b. 32°C and 100°C d. 32°C and 212°C

Understanding Concepts

Answer the following questions in your Science Journal using complete sentences.

11. Compare and contrast protons, electrons, and neutrons.

12. What is the density of 25 mL of cooking oil if its mass is 23 grams?

13. How do compounds and mixtures differ?

14. If an atom has no charge, what is true about its protons and electrons?

15. What process releases energy from an atom? Explain.

Thinking Critically

16. Would isotopes of the same element have the same number of electrons? Explain.

17. Two chlorine ions are both negatively charged. Will they combine to form a molecule? Why or why not?

18. You pour cooking oil into a glass of water. You briefly stir the materials in the glass. Does your glass contain a mixture? Does it contain a solution?

19. When oxygen combines with iron in the presence of water, rust is formed. Is this a chemical or physical property of iron?

20. Why is nuclear waste considered so dangerous?

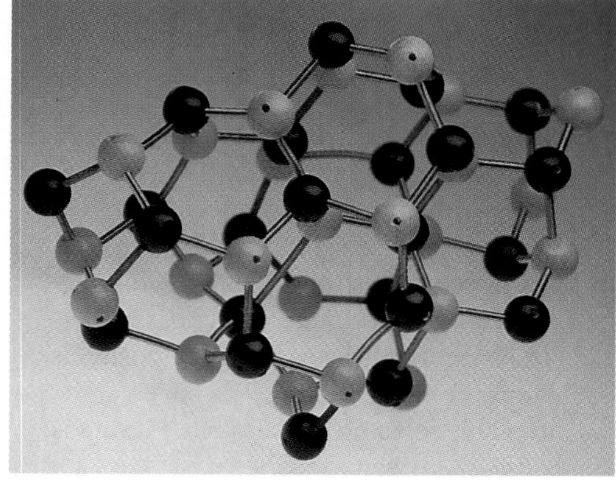

Think Critically

16. Yes, isotopes differ in the number of neutrons.

17. They will not combine; like charges repel. However, chlorine atoms do combine to form chlorine gas. The two chlorine atoms share a pair of electrons.

18. Yes, the oil and water is a mixture. It is not a solution, however, because neither the water nor the oil is evenly spread throughout the other.

19. Chemical.

20. Nuclear waste is radioactive and very harmful to living tissue. The radioactivity lasts for many years and must be stored where it will not enter the environment.

Developing Skills

21. Classifying Iron, aluminum, and gold are elements; carbon dioxide, water, and sugar are compounds.

22. Making and Using Graphs: (See graph at right, bottom of p. 59.)
The mass number increases as the atomic number increases.

Developing Skills

If you need help, refer to the **Skill Handbook.**

21. Classifying: Use Appendix F to classify the following substances as elements or compounds: iron, aluminum, carbon dioxide, gold, water, and sugar.

Element	Atomic No.	Mass No.
Fluorine	9	19
Lithium	3	7
Carbon	6	12
Nitrogen	7	14
Beryllium	4	9
Boron	5	11
Oxygen	8	16
Neon	10	20

22. Making and Using Graphs: Use the data above to make a line graph of increasing mass number and atomic number of each element. What is the relationship between mass number and atomic number?

23. Hypothesizing: You put a bottle full of water in the freezer to cool it quickly. You forgot about it, though, and found a broken glass when you went to get it. What hypothesis can you make about water as it changes from a liquid to a solid?

24. Observing and Inferring: Your brother is drinking a dark-colored liquid from a clear glass. As you watch from across the room, you think to yourself that the cola is probably refreshing. Is thinking that the liquid is cola an observation or an inference?

25. Concept Mapping: Finish the network tree below to illustrate the three main parts of an atom.

Performance Assessment

1. **Model:** Use different-sized and different-colored foam balls and wooden sticks to make models of the atomic structure of the first ten elements in the periodic table.
2. **Making and Using a Classification System:** Classify all the items in your refrigerator according to physical state. Then list at least two chemical and two physical properties of each item. Observe or test the properties you list.
3. **Model:** Research how the model of an atom has evolved with time. Construct models of the early theories of the atom.

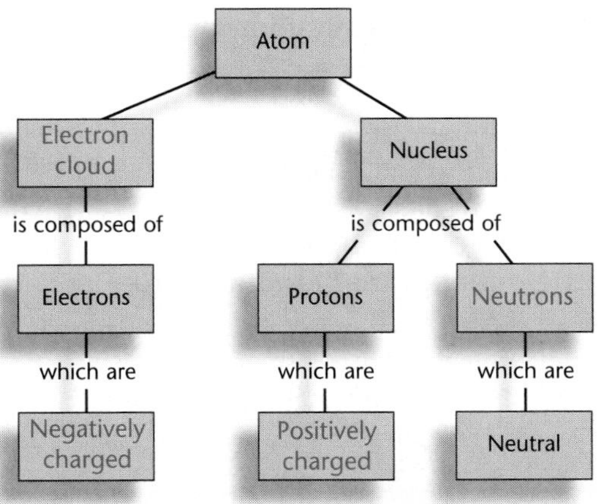

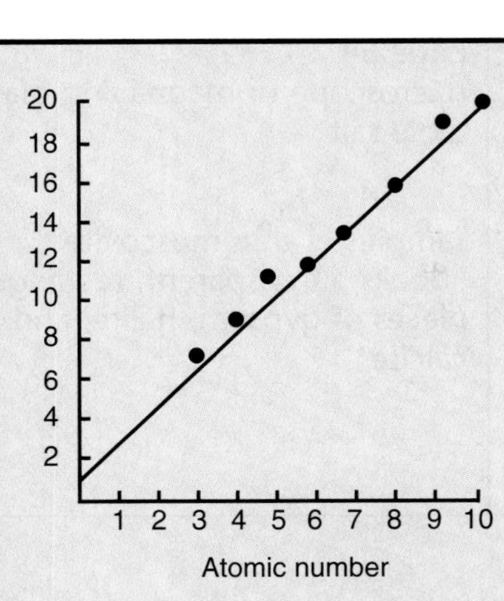

23. Hypothesizing Water expands as it freezes.

24. Observing and Inferring It is an inference because the liquid might be tea or perhaps grape juice.

25. Concept Mapping See student page.

Performance Assessment

1. Students' models will vary, but they should use different-colored foam balls for protons and neutrons (in the nucleus) and electrons (in the electron cloud). Use the Performance Task Assessment List for Model in **PASC,** p. 51. P
2. Answers will vary, but might include the following: Soft drink; slightly acidic, contains sugar, will chemically react and provide energy; brown and cold. Student reports will vary depending on the procedures individual students use. Use the Performance Task Assessment List for Making and Using a Classification System in **PASC,** p. 49. P
3. Students may use the models provided in this chapter and other models provided in physics and chemistry books. Students should show the different models that have been studied, using a timeline. Some examples they may use include the Bohr model and the quantum model. To help students begin with this project, you may wish to share Integrating the Sciences on p. 4, TWE with them. Use the Performance Task Assessment List for Model in **PASC,** p. 51. P

Chapter Organizer

Section	Objectives	Activities/Features
Chapter Opener		Explore Activity: Make a saltwater solution. p. 61
3-1 **Minerals** (2 sessions, 1 block)*	1. **List** five characteristics all minerals share. 2. **Give examples** of two ways that minerals form.	Using Math, p. 63 MiniLAB: What do salt crystals look like up close? p. 64 Activity 3-1: Crystal Formation, p. 65 Skill Builder: Classifying, p. 66 Using Computers: Spreadsheet, p. 66
3-2 **Mineral Identification** (2 sessions, 1½ blocks)*	1. **List** the physical properties used to identify minerals. 2. **Describe** how physical properties such as hardness and streak are used to identify minerals.	MiniLAB: How can special properties be used to i dentify a mineral? p. 69 Problem Solving: Sometimes It's Gold, Sometimes It's Not, p. 70 Connect to Chemistry, p. 71 Skill Builder: Making and Using Graphs, p. 71 Science Journal, p. 71 Activity 3-2: Mineral Identification, pp. 72-73
3-3 **Uses of Minerals** (1 session, ½ block)*	1. **Discuss** characteristics gems have that make them different from and more valuable than other minerals. 2. **List** the conditions necessary for a mineral to be classified as an ore.	Using Technology: On the Cutting Edge, p. 76 Connect to Physics, p. 77 Using Math, p. 77 Skill Builder: Concept Mapping, p. 77
3-4 **Science and Society Technology: Uses of Titanium** (1 session, ½ block)*	1. **List** the properties of titanium that make it so useful in biomedicine, sporting equipment, and other applications. 2. **Identify** the minerals that are mined for titanium.	Explore the Technology, p. 79 Science & Art, p. 80 Science Journal, p. 80

* A complete Planning Guide that includes block scheduling is provided on pages 32T-35T.

Activity Materials

Explore	Activities	MiniLABs
page 61 small plastic cup; warm tap water; table salt; stirrer; flat, shallow pan	page 65 salt solution, sugar solution, large test tube, toothpick, cotton string, hand lens, 2 shallow pans, test-tube rack, cardboard, table salt, granulated sugar, hot plate, thermal mitt, safety goggles pages 72-73 mineral samples, hand lenses, balance, 100-mL graduated cylinder, tap water, piece of copper, glass slide, small iron nail, steel file, streak plate, 5% hydrochloric acid with dropper, safety goggles, Mohs scale of hardness, this textbook	page 64 microscope or magnifying glass, table salt page 69 samples of thin muscovite "books;" transparent, rectangular pieces of gypsum, halite, and calcite

Teacher Classroom Resources

Reproducible Masters	Transparencies	Teaching Resources
Study Guide, p. 13 **Reinforcement**, p. 13 **Enrichment**, p. 13 **Activity Worksheets**, pp. 17-18, 21 **Lab Manual 10**, Crystal Formation **Lab Manual 11**, Mineral and Optical Crystallography **Science Integration Activity 3**, Crystal Garden **Concept Mapping**, p. 11 **Critical Thinking/Problem Solving**, p. 9 **Cross-Curricular Integration**, p. 7	**Section Focus Transparency 9**, Repeating Patterns **Science Integration Transparency 3**, Ionic Crystals **Teaching Transparency 5**, Crystal Systems	**Glencoe Earth Science Interactive Videodisc** **Earth Science CD-ROM** **Spanish Resources** **English/Spanish Audiocassettes** **Cooperative Learning Resource Guide** **Lab Partner** **Lab and Safety Skills** **Lesson Plans**
Study Guide, p. 14 **Reinforcement**, p. 14 **Enrichment**, p. 14 **Activity Worksheets**, pp. 19-20, 22	**Section Focus Transparency 10**, What's the Difference? **Teaching Transparency 6**, Mohs Scale	**Assessment Resources**
Study Guide, p. 15 **Reinforcement**, p. 15 **Enrichment**, p. 15 **Lab Manual 12**, Mineral Resources **Lab Manual 13**, Removal of Waste Rock **Multicultural Connections**, pp. 9-10	**Section Focus Transparency 11**, Precious or Not?	**Chapter Review**, pp. 9-10 **Assessment**, pp. 13-16 **Performance Assessment in the Science Classroom (PASC)** **MindJogger Videoquiz** **Alternate Assessment in the Science Classroom** **Performance Assessment** **Chapter Review Software** **Computer Test Bank**
Study Guide, p. 16 **Reinforcement**, p. 16 **Enrichment**, p. 16 **Science and Society Integration**, p. 7	**Section Focus Transparency 12**, What Would You Use?	

Key to Teaching Strategies

The following designations will help you decide which activities are appropriate for your students.

L1 Level 1 activities should be within the ability range of all students.

L2 Level 2 activities should be within the ability range of the average to above-average student.

L3 Level 3 activities are designed for the ability range of above-average students.

LEP LEP activities should be within the ability range of Limited English Proficiency students.

LS These activities are designed to address different learning styles.

COOP LEARN Cooperative Learning activities are designed for small group work.

P These strategies represent student products that can be placed into a best-work portfolio.

GLENCOE TECHNOLOGY

The following multimedia resources are available from Glencoe.

The Infinite Voyage Series
The Future of the Past
National Geographic Society Series
GTV: Planetary Manager
Earth Science CD-ROM

Teacher Classroom Resources

This is a representation of key blackline masters available in the Teacher Classroom Resources.

Teaching Aids

Section Focus Transparencies

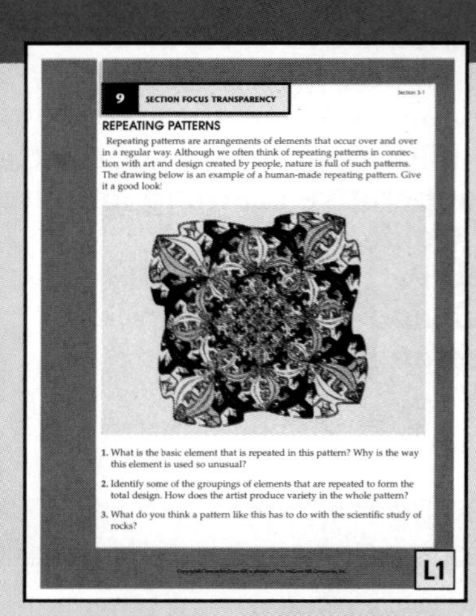

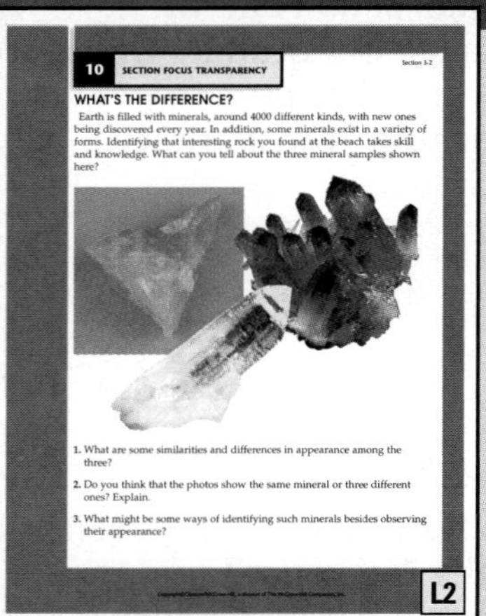

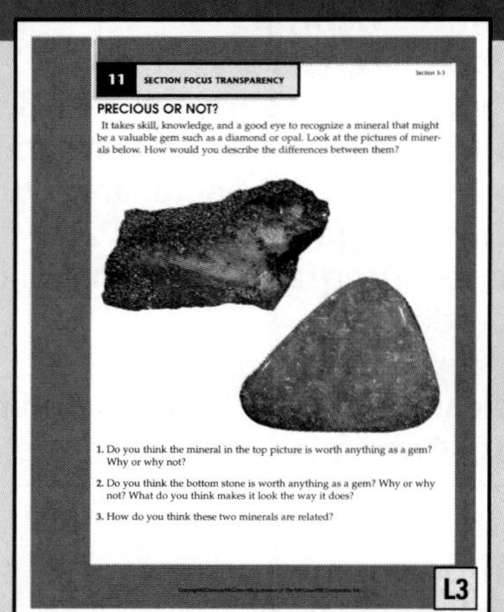

Science Integration Transparencies

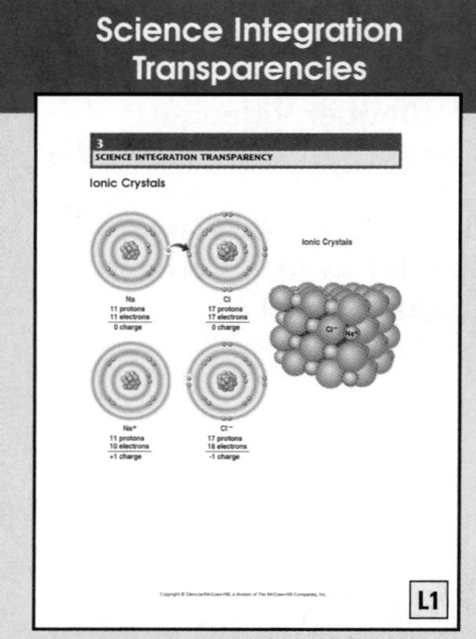

Teaching Transparencies

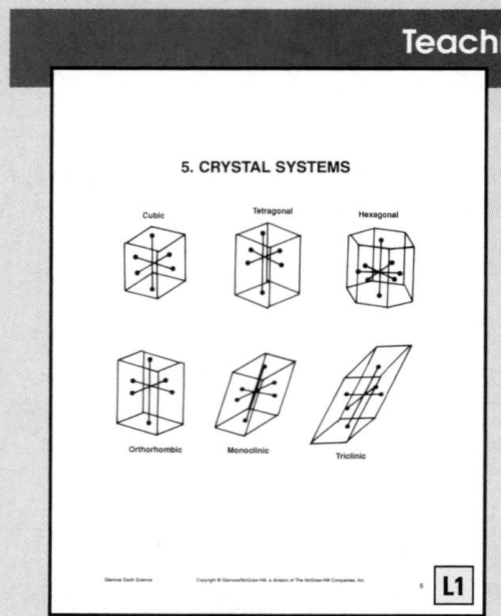

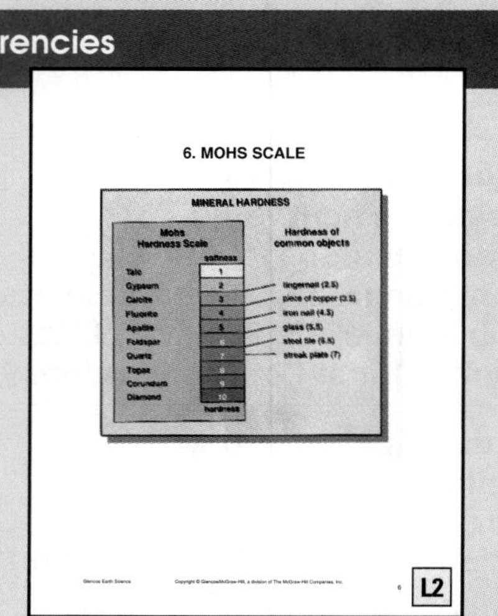

Meeting Different Ability Levels

Study Guide

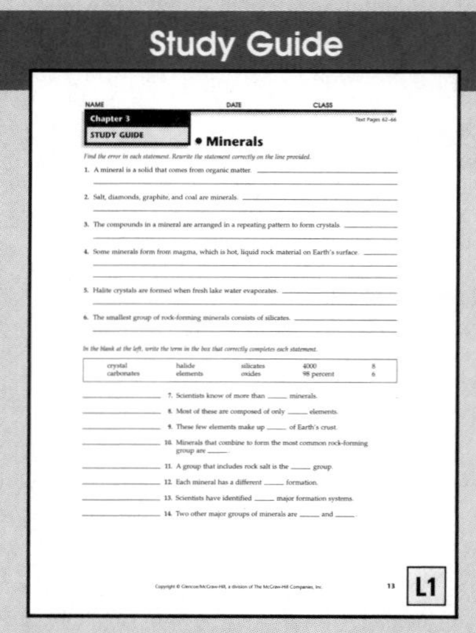

Reinforcement

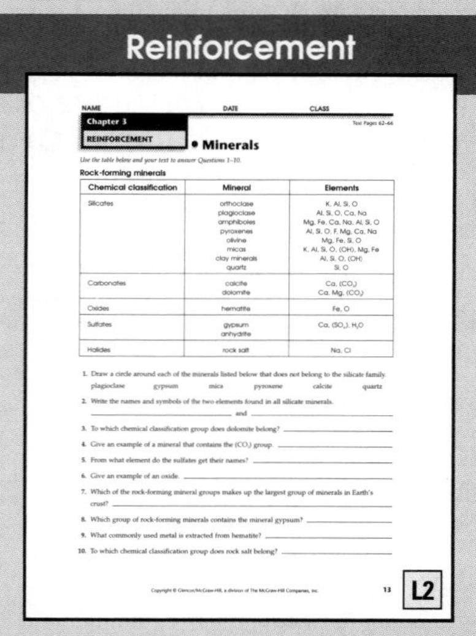

Enrichment Worksheets

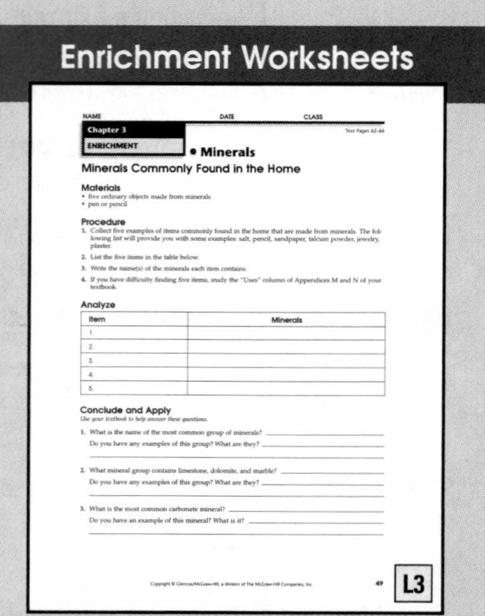

Hands-On Activities

Science Integration Activity

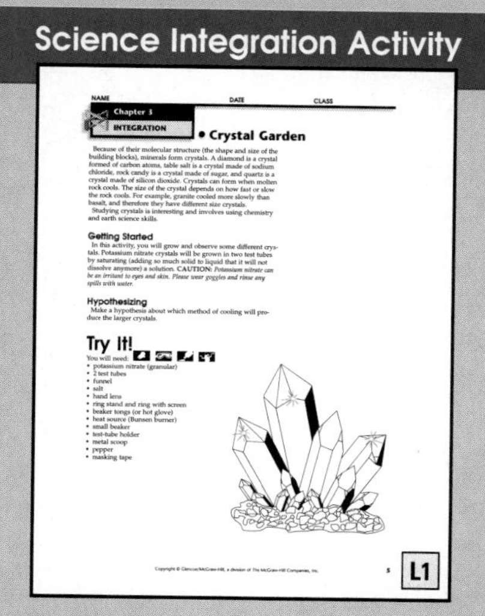

Lab Manual

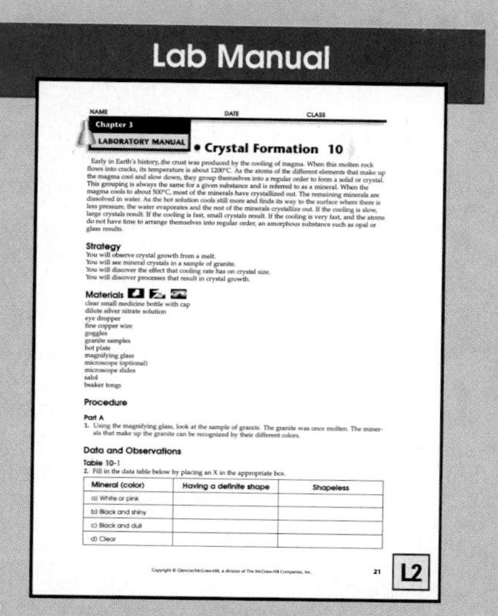

Assessment

Performance Assessment

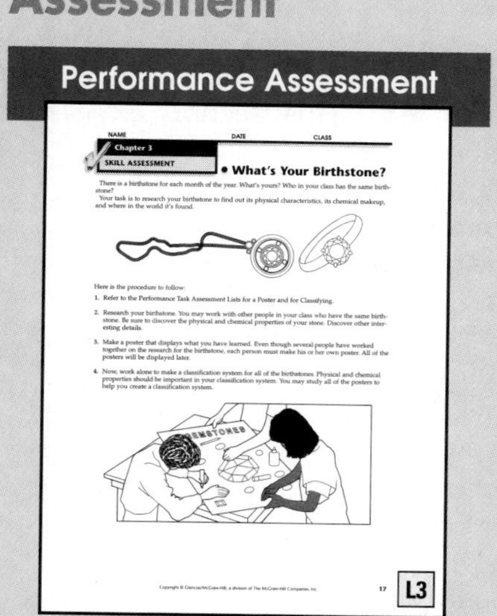

Enrichment and Application

Critical Thinking/ Problem Solving

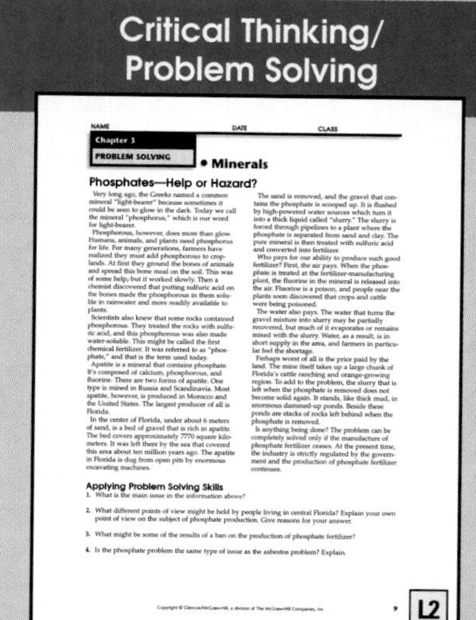

Cross-Curricular Integration

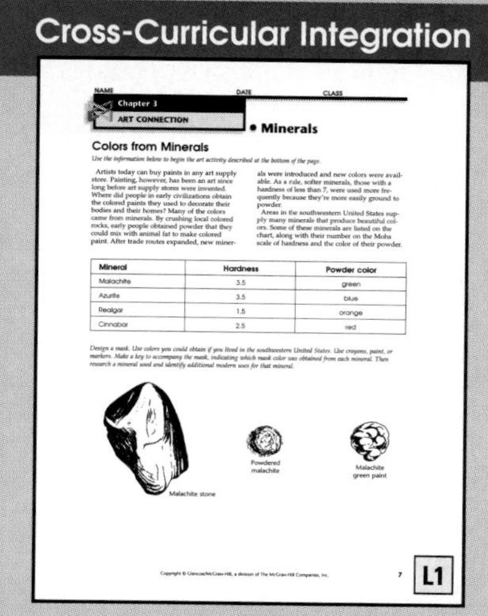

Science and Society Integration

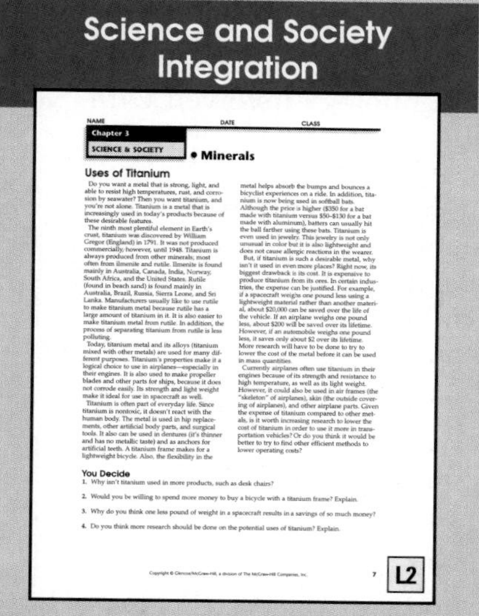

Multicultural Connections

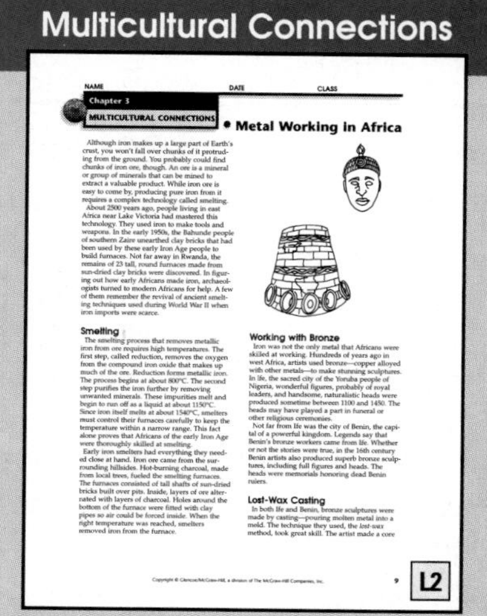

Concept Mapping

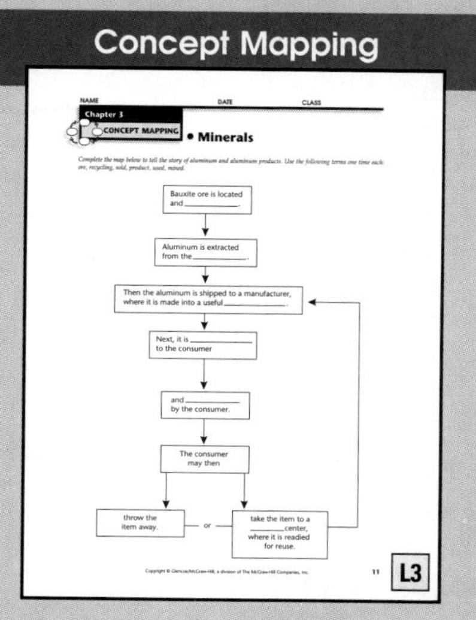

Chapter 3

Minerals

CHAPTER OVERVIEW

Section 3-1 This section explains the five characteristics shared by all minerals. Classification of minerals into six crystal systems based on the internal structure of minerals is explained. The ways in which minerals form and how they can be grouped are also described.

Section 3-2 This section describes how physical properties of a mineral are used to identify it.

Section 3-3 The characteristics that make a mineral a gem are explained, as are conditions needed in order for minerals to be classified as ores.

Section 3-4 **Science and Society** Students are introduced to the technology involved with using titanium in biomedicine, sporting equipment, and other applications. The properties of titanium that make it so useful in these applications are reviewed.

Chapter Vocabulary

mineral	streak
crystal	cleavage
magma	fracture
silicate	gem
hardness	ore
luster	titanium

Theme Connection

Scale and Structure The structure of minerals is presented on an atomic scale when discussing the atomic arrangement inside mineral crystals. This atomic arrangement and other characteristics that define minerals should be emphasized in all lessons. Emphasizing the relationship between the internal structure of a mineral and its properties and uses will help to clarify the uniqueness of these solids that make up Earth's rocks.

Previewing the Chapter

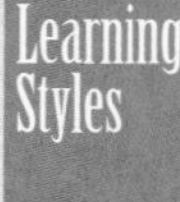

Learning Styles

Look for the following logo for strategies that emphasize different learning modalities. LS

Kinesthetic	Inclusion Strategies, p. 63; Close, p. 79; Science & Art, p. 80
Visual-Spatial	Explore, p. 61; Revealing Preconceptions, p. 63; Visual Learning, pp. 63, 68, 70, 75, 77, 78; Reteach, pp. 64, 70; Activity 3-1, p. 65; Demonstration, pp. 68, 75; MiniLAB, p. 69
Interpersonal	MiniLAB, p. 64; Activity, p. 68; Activity 3-2, pp. 72-73
Linguistic	Science Journal, pp. 64, 76; Across the Curriculum, p. 76; Science & Art, p. 80

Chapter 3

Minerals

Minerals are used for many things. They are used in jewelry, pencil lead, powders, and in bicycle frames. Table salt, for example, is the mineral halite. The salt flat shown at left is composed of the evaporate minerals halite and gypsum. Evaporate minerals form when water evaporates, leaving salt and other substances behind.

EXPLORE ACTIVITY

Make a saltwater solution.

1. Fill a cup or beaker about half full of warm tap water.
2. Add about a teaspoon of table salt to the water.
3. Stir the water until all the salt has dissolved. Continue to add salt and stir until no more salt will dissolve.
4. Gently pour the water into a pan, and place the pan on a shelf where it will not be disturbed.
5. Check on the pan twice each day for two or three days.

Observe: Keep a log in your Science Journal describing what has happened to the saltwater solution at the end of three days.

Previewing Science Skills

- In the **Skill Builders**, you will **classify**, **graph**, and **map concepts**.
- In the **Activities**, you will **observe**, **collect**, and **organize data**.
- In the **MiniLABs**, you will **experiment** and **compare**.

EXPLORE ACTIVITY

Purpose

LS **Visual-Spatial** Use the Explore Activity to introduce students to one method of mineral formation. Inform students that they will be learning more about minerals as they read the chapter. L1 LEP COOP LEARN

Preparation

Several days before you begin this chapter, have students bring in flat pans. Obtain several packages of table salt, NaCl.

Materials

one beaker, one flat pan, and salt for every two students

Teaching Strategies

Test the water to be used in the activity to be sure it is warm, but not hot enough to cause burns. Explain that warm water rather than cold water is used to speed up the rate at which the salt dissolves. Have students hypothesize how their stirring affects the dissolving process.

Observe

Students should observe crystals forming around the edge and on the bottom of the flat pan. As the water evaporates, salt comes out of solution and forms into cubic crystals.

Assessment

Performance Have students study the crystals that formed in the flat pan under a microscope. Ask them to draw the shape of the crystals in their Science Journal. Use the Performance Task Assessment List for Scientific Drawing in **PASC,** p. 55. P

Assessment Planner

Portfolio
Refer to page 81 for suggested items that students might select for their portfolios.

Performance Assessment
See page 81 for additional Performance Assessment options.
Skill Builders, pp. 66, 71, 77
MiniLABs, pp. 64, 69
Activities 3-1, p. 65; 3-2, pp. 72-73

Content Assessment
Section Wrap-ups, pp. 66, 71, 77, 79
Chapter Review, pp. 81-83
Mini Quizzes, pp. 66, 71, 77

Group Assessment
Opportunities for group assessment occur with Cooperative Learning Strategies and Flex Your Brain Activities.

Section 3•1

Prepare

Section Background

The chemical composition of a specific mineral is not always exactly the same. In some minerals, an atom with a similar size and the same charge can substitute for other atoms. In olivine, $(Mg,Fe)_2SiO_4$, for example, iron can be totally replaced by magnesium without changing the olivine to another mineral. Some forms of olivine contain iron and magnesium.

Preplanning

- Obtain table salt for the MiniLAB.
- To prepare for Activity 3-1, obtain the materials listed on page 65.
- Obtain a piece of granite from a scientific supply company or a local tombstone maker.

1 Motivate

Bellringer

Before presenting the lesson, display **Section Focus Transparency 9** on the overhead projector. Assign the accompanying **Focus Activity** worksheet. L1 LEP

Tying to Previous Knowledge

Have students recall from Chapter 2 that atoms are the building blocks of matter and that atoms combine to form molecules and compounds. The structure of a mineral is determined by the repeating pattern of atoms and molecules in the mineral.

3•1 Minerals

Science Words

mineral
crystal
magma
silicate

Objectives

- List five characteristics all minerals share.
- Give examples of two ways that minerals form.

What is a mineral?

Have you ever used minerals? **Figure 3-1** shows a few of the ways we use minerals every day. A **mineral** is a naturally occurring, inorganic solid with a definite structure and composition. Although 4000 different minerals are found on Earth, they all share five characteristics.

Inorganic and Naturally Occurring Minerals

First, all minerals are formed by natural processes. Rock salt, diamonds, and graphite are minerals because they formed naturally. You'll investigate more about these processes later in this lesson.

Second, minerals are inorganic. They aren't alive, never were alive, and are not made by life processes. Coal is made of carbon from living things. Although geologists do not classify coal as a mineral, some people do. Miners, for example, generally classify anything taken from the ground that has commercial value as a "mineral resource."

Crystalline Solids

The third characteristic that minerals share is that they are all solids. Remember that all solids have a definite volume and shape. A gas such as air and a liquid such as water aren't minerals because neither has definite shape.

Fourth, every mineral is an element or compound with a chemical composition unique to that mineral. For example, rock salt's composition gives it a distinctive flavor.

Finally, the atoms in a mineral are arranged in a pattern that is repeated over and over again. Graphite's arrangement of atoms makes it feel soft and slippery. Opal, on the other hand, is classified as a "mineraloid" because its atoms are not arranged in a definite structure.

Figure 3-1

Shown here are just a few examples of how we use minerals. *In your Science Journal, list the five characteristics that all minerals share.*

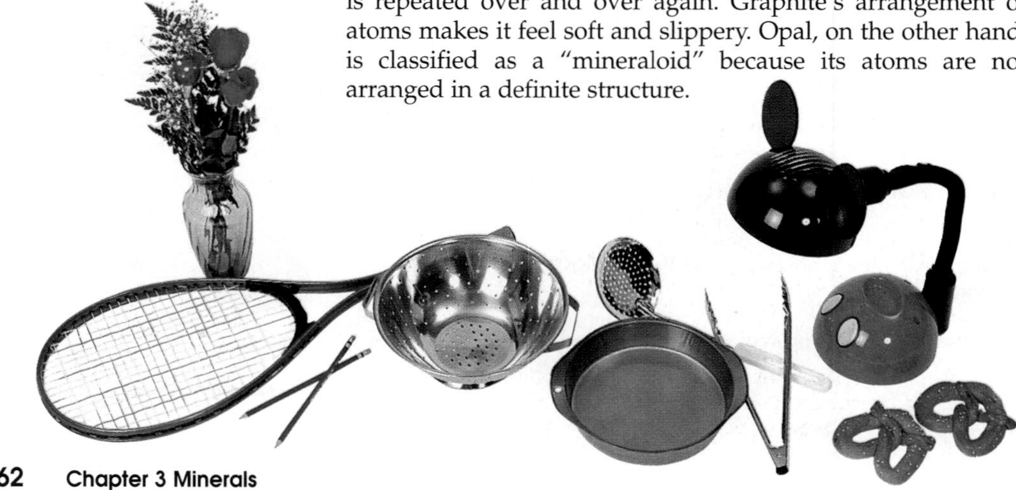

Program Resources

Reproducible Masters
Study Guide, p. 13 L1
Reinforcement, p. 13 L1
Enrichment, p. 13 L3
Cross-Curricular Integration, p. 7
Activity Worksheets, pp. 17-18, 21 L1
Science Integration Activities, pp. 5-6
Critical Thinking/Problem Solving, p. 9
Concept Mapping, p. 11
Lab Manual 10, 11

Transparencies
Section Focus Transparency 9 L1
Science Integration Transparency 3
Teaching Transparency 5

Figure 3-2

Some mineral specimens, such as smoky quartz, have flat surfaces and sharp edges, showing crystal structure on the outside (A). Even if a mineral such as rose quartz doesn't show its crystal structure on the outside, its atoms are still arranged in a crystal structure (B).

The Structure of Minerals

Did you know that each little grain of salt in a salt shaker is a cube? The atoms contained in each grain of salt are grouped in such a way that they form a cube. These cubes are crystals. A **crystal** is a solid in which the atoms are arranged in repeating patterns. **Table 3-1** shows examples of the six major crystal systems.

Crystals

Not all mineral crystals have smooth surfaces and sharp edges like the quartz crystal in **Figure 3-2A.** The quartz in **Figure 3-2B** has atoms arranged in repeating patterns, but you can't see the crystal structure on the outside of the mineral. This is because the quartz in **Figure 3-2B** developed in a tight space, while the quartz in **Figure 3-2A** developed freely in an open space. The hexagonal crystal structure of this quartz is obvious. See **Figure 3-3** for an example of a cubic crystal system.

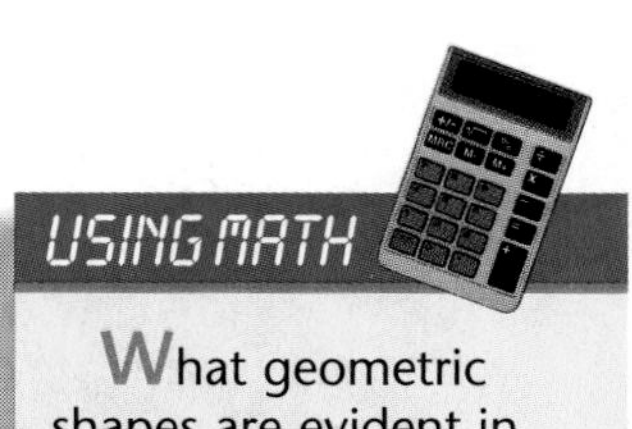

USING MATH

What geometric shapes are evident in the crystal systems shown below?

Table 3-1

Crystal Systems

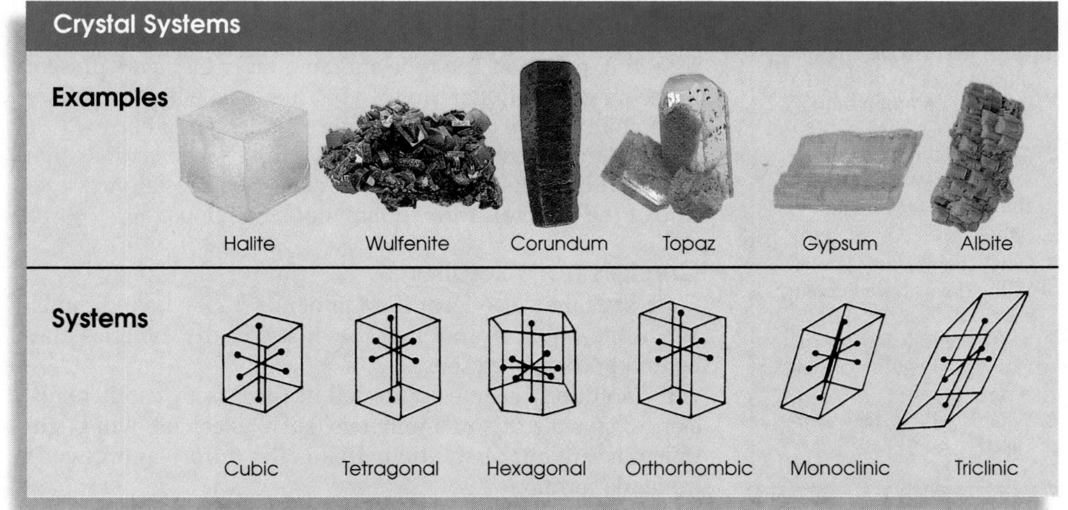

2 Teach

FLEX Your Brain

Use the Flex Your Brain activity to have students explore CHARACTERISTICS SHARED BY ALL MINERALS.

Activity Worksheets, p. 5

Revealing Preconceptions

LS **Visual-Spatial** Students may think that all minerals are as beautiful as cut diamonds and other gems. Show students a piece of jewelry containing a gemstone. Also obtain some sheets of mica. Have students contrast the minerals.

Visual Learning

Figure 3-1 In your Science Journal, list five characteristics that all minerals share. *Minerals are naturally occurring, inorganic solids with unique compositions and distinct internal structures.* LEP LS

USING MATH

square, rectangle, hexagon, triangle

GLENCOE TECHNOLOGY

CD-ROM

Earth Science CD-ROM

Have students perform the interactive exploration for Chapter 3 to reinforce important chapter concepts and thinking processes.

Use **Concept Mapping,** p. 11, as you teach this lesson.

Inclusion Strategies

Learning Disabled Have students glue several sugar cubes together to form a large cube. After the glue has dried, instruct students to place the cube into a glass of water. When the sugar has dissolved, remove the glue skeleton and let it dry. Have them experiment with other geometric designs to form other "crystal" shapes. LS

MiniLAB

Purpose

LS **Interpersonal** Students will observe physical properties of isometric (cubic) crystals of table salt. L1

Materials

microscope or magnifying glass, table salt

Analysis

1. All the salt grains are cubes.
2. Other minerals of the isometric system include copper, diamond, fluorite, galena, gold, pyrite, and silver.
3. Halite belongs to the isometric crystal system.

Assessment

Oral To further assess students' understanding of different crystal systems, have them classify samples of crystals that you provide. Use the Performance Task Assessment List for Making Observations and Inferences in **PASC**, p. 17. P

Activity Worksheets, pp. 5, 21

3 Assess

Check for Understanding

FLEX Your Brain

Use the Flex Your Brain activity to have students explore CRYSTAL FORMATION.

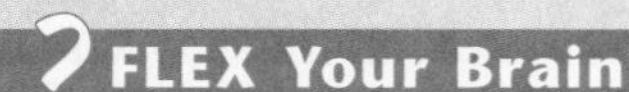

Activity Worksheets, p. 5

Reteach

LS **Visual-Spatial** Hold up several items in front of the class. Ask students whether or not each item is a mineral.

Figure 3-3

Atoms of the mineral galena arrange themselves in a cubic crystal system.

MiniLAB

What do salt crystals look like up close?

Procedure

1. Use a microscope or a magnifying glass to observe grains of common table salt.
2. Compare the shape of the salt crystals with those shown in **Table 3-1.**

Analysis

1. What characteristics do all of the grains have in common?
2. Try to identify another mineral with the same crystal system as salt.
3. What is this crystal system called?

How Minerals Form

There are three ways that minerals form. One way is from the cooling of hot melted rock material, called **magma.** As magma cools, its atoms lose energy, move closer together, and begin to combine into compounds. Molecules of the different compounds that are forming begin to arrange themselves into repeating patterns. The type and amount of elements present in the magma help determine what minerals will form. Many different minerals can form from a single magma body.

When molten rock material cools rapidly, the crystals that form can be quite small. In such cases, the crystalline structure of the minerals formed may not be obvious.

Crystals from Solution

Crystals may also form from minerals dissolved in liquids. When the liquid evaporates, the atoms in the minerals stay behind and form crystals.

If a solution becomes saturated or filled with another substance, crystals of some minerals, such as calcite, will begin precipitating out of solution. This is the third way in which minerals form.

Theme Connection

Scale and Structure Comparing the cubic structure of salt crystals with the structure of other crystals shown in **Table 3-1** reinforces the theme of scale and structure. The internal atomic structure of each crystal can be compared by drawing large-scale line drawings as shown.

Science Journal

Describing Minerals In their Science Journals, have students write a description of seven objects around the room. Encourage them to select any items that they wish. Instruct them that the description must provide evidence that distinguishes the objects as minerals or not. L1 LS

Activity 3-1

Crystal Formation

So far in this chapter, you've learned about mineral crystals and how they form. You've even observed crystals of table salt form when your saltwater solution evaporated in the Explore Activity. In this activity, you'll have a chance to observe this process further and to learn about another method of mineral formation.

Problem

How do minerals form from solution?

Materials   

- salt solution
- sugar solution
- large test tube
- toothpick
- cotton string
- hand lens
- shallow pans (2)
- test-tube rack
- cardboard
- table salt
- granulated sugar
- hot plate
- thermal mitt

Procedure

1. Gently mix separate solutions of salt in water and sugar in water. Keep stirring the solutions as you add salt or sugar to the water. Stop mixing when no more salt or sugar will dissolve into the solution.
2. Pour the sugar solution into one of the shallow pans. Use the hot plate to gently heat the solution.
3. Place the test tube in the test-tube rack. Using a thermal mitt to protect your hand, pour some of the hot sugar solution into the test tube. **CAUTION:** *The liquid is hot. Do not touch the test tube without protecting your hands.*
4. Tie the thread to one end of the toothpick. Place the toothpick across the opening of the test tube so the thread is in the sugar solution.
5. Cover the test tube with a piece of cardboard and place the rack containing the test tube in a location where it will not be disturbed.
6. Pour a thin layer of the salt solution into the second shallow pan.
7. Place the pan in a location where it will not be disturbed.
8. Leave both the test tube and the shallow pan undisturbed for at least one week.
9. At the end of one week, examine each solution and see whether crystals have formed. Use a hand lens to observe the crystals.

Analyze

1. **Compare** and **contrast** the crystals that formed from the salt and sugar solutions with each other. How do they compare with samples of table salt and sugar?
2. What happened to the salt water in the shallow pan?
3. Did this same process occur in the test tube? **Explain.**

Conclude and Apply

4. What caused the formation of crystals in the test tube? What caused the formation of crystals in the shallow pan?
5. Sugar is harvested from plants. Is sugar a mineral? **Explain.**
6. **Relate** the formation of crystals in this activity to mineral crystal formation.

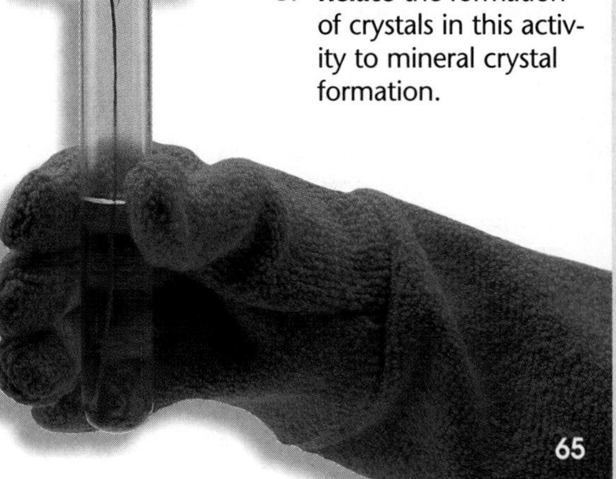

65

3. No, the liquid in the test tube cooled, and sugar crystals precipitated from a saturated solution.
4. As the sugar solution cooled, the water was not able to hold all the sugar, and crystals formed. As the water evaporated from the salt solution, the water became saturated and crystals formed.
5. No, sugar is an organic compound.
6. Crystals can form by precipitation from a solution or by evaporation of a liquid. Mineral crystals can also form in either of these two ways, as well as from cooling liquid rock material.

Assessment

Content To further assess students' understanding of crystal formation, have them work in groups of four. Encourage them to create a story that explains what they think happens to the atoms of the material to allow it to gradually form into crystals. Use the Performance Task Assessment List for Writing in Science in **PASC**, p. 87. P

Activity 3-1

Purpose

LS **Visual-Spatial** Interpret data and perform an experiment in which students will demonstrate and describe two methods of growing crystals. L1 LEP COOP LEARN

Process Skills

observing and inferring, communicating, interpreting data, experimenting, classifying, sequencing, comparing and contrasting, recognizing cause and effect, forming operational definitions

Time

20 minutes on two different days

Safety Precautions

Caution students not to handle test tubes without protecting their hands. Also, caution students not to touch the hot plate and to wear safety goggles during the entire experiment.

Activity Worksheets, pp. 5, 17-18

Teaching Strategies

Troubleshooting The beakers need to remain undisturbed for at least a week if you wish to have large crystals grow. When solutions are cooled suddenly, only small crystals will form. The more gradually the solution is cooled, the larger the crystals tend to grow.

- You may wish to add seed crystals on the thread to help the precipitation of sugar.
- Stereomicroscopes are excellent to use for the observation of the crystals in Step 9.

Answers to Questions

1. Crystals of salt will be cubic; sugar crystals will be orthorhombic. Sample crystals have the same structure but are probably smaller.
2. The water evaporated.

INTEGRATION Chemistry

Chemical formulas for many common rock-forming minerals are similar. All silicate rock-forming minerals contain silicon and oxygen.

4 Close

•MINI•QUIZ•

1. **What is a mineral?** *a naturally occurring, inorganic solid, with a definite structure and composition*
2. **A _____ is a solid in which the atoms are arranged in repeating patterns.** *crystal*
3. **Minerals can form when hot, melted rock material, called _____ , cools.** *magma*

Section Wrap-up

Review

1. A mineral must be naturally occurring, inorganic, a solid, and have a definite structure and limited composition.
2. Minerals can solidify from a magma, precipitate out of solution, or form as a solution evaporates.
3. **Think Critically** Silicon and oxygen; these two elements are common and when they combine, they form a stable structure capable of enduring weathering processes.

Using Computers

Students may use a wide variety of applications to design their graphs, including a bar graph, a shaded-block graph, or a pie graph. Answers should match percentages given in **Figure 3-4.**

INTEGRATION Chemistry

Mineral Compositions and Groups

Some 90 elements occur naturally in Earth's crust. Ninety-eight percent of the crust is made up of only eight of these elements, as shown in **Figure 3-4**. Of the 4000 known minerals, only a few dozen are common, and these are composed of the eight common elements of Earth's crust. Most of these common rock-forming minerals are silicates, but other groups are also included. Feldspar and quartz, both silicates, and calcite, a carbonate, are examples of rock-forming minerals.

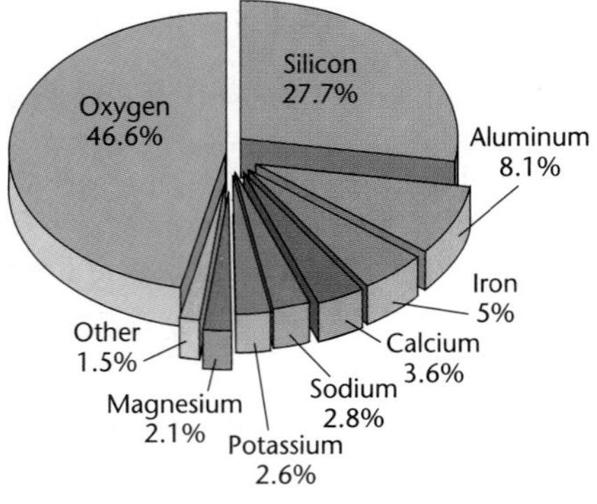

Figure 3-4

Most of Earth's crust is composed of these elements.

Silicates

Silicates are minerals that contain silicon and oxygen and usually one or more other elements. Silicon and oxygen are the two most abundant elements in Earth's crust. Other minerals are classified according to their composition. Major groups of minerals include the carbonates, oxides, sulfides, sulfates, halides, hydroxides, phosphates, and native elements.

You now know a lot more about common rock salt than you did before reading this section. You know that its real name is halite and that it is a mineral. You also know that halite has a cubic crystal shape that is formed when salt water evaporates.

Section Wrap-up

Review

1. What five conditions must a substance meet to be a mineral?
2. Describe two ways that minerals can form.
3. **Think Critically:** What two elements are found within all silicate minerals? In your Science Journal, explain why silicates are so common in Earth's crust.

Skill Builder

Classifying

Classify each of these minerals into the correct mineral group. Evaluate their chemical formulas using Appendix E. If you need help, refer to Classifying in the **Skill Handbook.**

siderite ($FeCO_3$)	barite ($BaSO_4$)
talc ($Mg_3Si_4O_{10}(OH)_2$)	enstatite ($MgSiO_3$)
silver (Ag)	sylvite (KCl)

Using Computers

Spreadsheet Refer to **Figure 3-4** above. Use your computer to make a graph of your own design that shows the relative percentages of the eight most common elements in Earth's crust.

Skill Builder

Siderite and malachite are carbonates. Barite is a sulfide. Talc and enstatite are silicates. Cinnabar is a sulfide. Silver is a native metal, and sylvite is a halide.

Assessment

Oral Call on students to assess their abilities to classify the listed minerals based on composition. Use the Performance Task Assessment List for Making Observations and Inferences in **PASC,** p. 17. P

Mineral Identification

3•2

Physical Properties

How can you tell the difference between one of your classmates and another? You can tell the difference between them without even thinking about it because you observe things about them that make them different. The color of a classmate's hair or the shape of his or her face helps you tell him or her from the rest of your class. Hair color and face shape are two properties unique to individuals.

Appearance

Individual minerals also have unique properties. These properties help us tell the difference between minerals. Look at **Figure 3-5.** Color and appearance are just two of the clues that are used to identify minerals.

But these clues alone aren't enough to tell most minerals apart. The minerals pyrite and gold are both gold in color and can appear to be the same. But gold is worth a lot of money, whereas pyrite has little value. You need to look at other properties of minerals to tell them apart.

Science Words

hardness
luster
streak
cleavage
fracture

Objectives

- List the physical properties used to identify minerals.
- Describe how physical properties such as hardness and streak are used to identify minerals.

Figure 3-5
Like people, minerals have many different characteristics.

Program Resources

Reproducible Masters

Study Guide, p. 14 L1
Reinforcement, p. 14 L1
Enrichment, p. 14 L3
Activity Worksheets, pp. 19-20, 22 L1

 **Transparencies**

Section Focus Transparency 10 L1
Teaching Transparency 6

Section 3•2

Prepare

Section Background

- Minerals softer than unglazed porcelain tile will leave a streak on the tile, whereas minerals harder than the tile will scratch it.
- Relatively large samples of muscovite or biotite are called "books" because the individual sheets of mica can be separated along one cleavage plane, similar to the pages in a book.
- The hardness of a mineral is related to crystal structure and to the type of atomic bond in the mineral.

Preplanning

- To prepare for Activity 3-2 and the MiniLAB, obtain a complete set of mineral samples for each student or group of students.
- Collect the other materials needed for Activity 3-2 and put them into kits for each student or group of students.

1 Motivate

Bellringer

Before presenting the lesson, display **Section Focus Transparency 10** on the overhead projector. Assign the accompanying **Focus Activity** worksheet. L1 LEP

Tying to Previous Knowledge

Have students recall physical properties from Chapter 2. Remind students that physical properties can be observed without changing a substance into a new substance. Show students two or three different minerals and have them list several physical properties of each.

2 Teach

Demonstration

LS Visual-Spatial Explain that certain minerals have unique physical properties. Obtain some sulfur and explain that its bright yellow color is unique. Drop dilute hydrochloric acid on calcite to show the fizzing reaction. **CAUTION:** *Be sure you and all students wear goggles.* Demonstrate the magnetic property of magnetite. LEP

Activity

LS Interpersonal Form groups to have students test the properties of hardness and streak of five mineral samples, including quartz, talc, calcite, galena, and pyrite. L1 COOP LEARN

Visual Learning

Figure 3-6 Talc can be scratched with your fingernail. Why is this true? *Because talc has a hardness of only 1 on the Mohs hardness scale.* LEP LS

GTV: Planetary Manager
Industry

47573

Use **Teaching Transparency 6** as you teach this lesson.

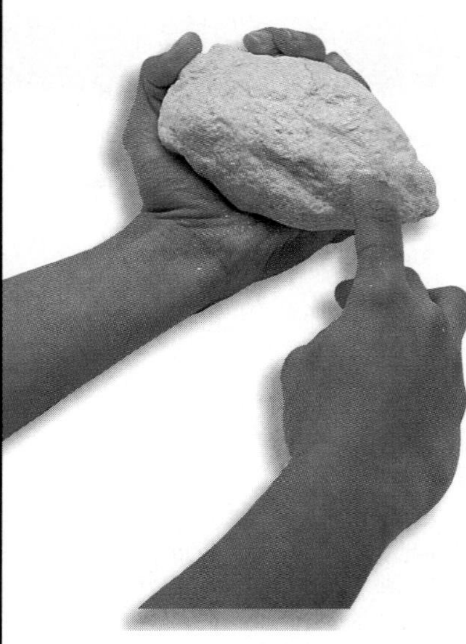

Figure 3-6
Talc can be scratched with your fingernail. *Why is this true?*

Hardness

A measure of how easily a mineral can be scratched is its **hardness.** The mineral talc, shown in **Figure 3-6,** is so soft you can scratch it loose with your fingernail. You might be familiar with talcum powder made from this mineral. Diamonds, on the other hand, are the hardest mineral. Some diamonds are used as cutting tools. A diamond can be scratched only by another diamond.

In order to compare the hardnesses of minerals, a list of common minerals and their hardnesses was developed. The German scientist Friedrich Mohs developed the Mohs scale of hardness, as seen in **Table 3-2.** The scale lists the hardnesses of ten minerals, with 1 being the softest and 10 the hardest.

Here's how the scale works. Let's say you have a clear or whitish-colored mineral that you know is either calcite or quartz. You scratch it on your fingernail and then on a bright, shiny piece of copper. You find that the mineral scratches your fingernail but doesn't scratch the copper. Because the hardness of your fingernail is 2.5 and that of a piece of copper is 3.5, you can determine the unknown mineral's hardness to be about 3. Because quartz has a hardness of 7, your mystery mineral must be calcite.

Table 3-2

Mineral Hardness

Mohs Hardness Scale

	softest	**Hardness of Common Objects**
Talc	1	
Gypsum	2	fingernail (2.5)
Calcite	3	piece of copper (3.5)
Fluorite	4	iron nail (4.5)
Apatite	5	glass (5.5)
Feldspar	6	steel file (6.5)
Quartz	7	streak plate (7)
Topaz	8	
Corundum	9	
Diamond	10	
	hardest	

Across the Curriculum

Auto Mechanics Some motor oil has a dark gray color to it. This is caused by graphite. Have students find out why graphite is added to motor oil. Because of its softness, graphite can be used to lubricate the moving parts of a motor. Graphite can also be used to lubricate moving parts in door-operating and locking mechanisms. Graphite powder is squeezed into the door mechanism.

Luster

Luster describes how light is reflected from a mineral's surface. Luster is defined as either metallic or nonmetallic. Minerals with a metallic luster, like the galena shown in **Figure 3-7,** always shine like metal. Metallic luster can be compared to the shine of a fancy metal belt buckle or the shiny chrome trim on some cars.

When a mineral does not shine like metal, its luster is nonmetallic. Examples of terms for nonmetallic luster include dull, pearly, and silky.

Figure 3-7

Galena has a metallic luster, which means that it shines like metal.

Color

The color of a mineral can also be a clue to its identity. A mineral whose color helps in its identification is sulfur. Sulfur has a distinctive yellow color. However, just remember that, as you learned with gold and pyrite, color alone usually isn't enough to identify a mineral.

Streak

Streak is the color of the mineral when it is broken up and powdered. When a mineral is rubbed across a piece of unglazed porcelain tile, as in **Figure 3-8,** a streak is left behind. This streak is the powdered mineral. Gold and pyrite can be identified with the streak test. Gold has a yellow streak and pyrite has a greenish black or brown-black streak.

The streak test works only for minerals that are softer than the streak plate. Very soft minerals will leave a streak even on paper. The last time you used a pencil to write on paper, you used the streak of the mineral graphite. Graphite is used in pencil lead because it is soft enough to leave a streak on paper.

Figure 3-8

Color is not always useful for mineral identification. Hematite, for example, can be dark red, gray, or silvery in color. Its streak, however, is always dark red-brown.

MiniLAB

How can special properties be used to identify a mineral?

Observe the differences in print viewed through clear minerals.

Procedure

1. Obtain samples of the following clear minerals: gypsum, muscovite mica, halite, and calcite.
2. Place each over the print on this page and observe the letters.

Analysis

1. What happens to light as it passes through these minerals?
2. What mineral can be identified by the print's double image? What special property is used to identify this mineral?

MiniLAB

Purpose

LS **Visual-Spatial** Students will observe how special properties can be used to identify minerals. L1 LEP

Materials

transparent samples of calcite (Iceland spar), muscovite, gypsum, halite, and quartz; magnifying glass

Teaching Strategies

Safety Precautions Caution students to handle the magnifying glass with care.

Analysis

1. As the light passes through each of the minerals, its path is bent.
2. Calcite. Calcite bends light in two directions as it passes through the mineral. Double refraction is the special property used to identify transparent calcite (Iceland spar).

Assessment

Oral To further assess students' understanding of this phenomenon, ask them to describe the double image of a dot through different planes of the transparent calcite. Tell them to spin the calcite around and describe what happens to the dot. Use the Performance Task Assessment List for Making Observations and Inferences in **PASC,** p. 17. P

Activity Worksheets, pp. 5, 22

Cultural Diversity

Quartz The mineral quartz has been recognized for its hardness and utility since prehistoric times. Quartz tools have been found at sites such as Zhoukoudien, China, that are more than 350 000 years old. But quartz has also been esteemed by many cultures for its beauty. The Japanese and Chinese carved clear rock quartz into art objects and spheres, as did the Greeks. Large transparent crystals are found in the Malagasy Republic, Japan, Burma, and Brazil. Quartz occurs in many colors and has been used for ornamentation. Purple amethyst comes from Mexico and Brazil. Cairngorm, a brown quartz, was named after the Cairngorm Mountains of Scotland. It can also be found in Switzerland, Japan, and Colorado.

Use **Section Focus Transparency 10** as you teach this lesson.

Problem Solving

Solve the Problem

1. Gold has a yellow streak.
2. Gold, with a hardness of 2.5–3, will probably not scratch copper, which has a hardness of 3.
3. No, she probably has found pyrite. Pyrite has a greenish-black streak and a hardness of 6.5.

Think Critically

1. bright yellow color, metallic luster
2. specific gravity (heft), fracture

Visual Learning

Figure 3-9 If you broke quartz, would it look the same? Explain. *No, quartz has fracture and breaks with rough, jagged edges.* LEP IS

3 Assess

Check for Understanding

FLEX Your Brain

Use the Flex Your Brain activity to have students explore MINERAL IDENTIFICATION.

Activity Worksheets, p. 5

Reteach

IS **Visual-Spatial** Obtain a sample of magnetite. Have students determine that magnetite has a metallic luster, a hardness greater than glass, a black color, a black streak, fracture, and is magnetic.

Extension

For students who have mastered this section, use the **Reinforcement** and **Enrichment** masters.

Problem Solving

Sometimes It's Gold, Sometimes It's Not

On a recent family vacation, Maria visited several areas of California. Because she had worked in a jewelry store that summer, she decided to explore Sutter's Mill, the place where gold was discovered in 1849. Maria saw some bright yellow metallic objects glistening in the clear water of a fast-moving stream. She reached into the water and withdrew what appeared to be four or five nuggets of gold.

Relying on her experience in the jewelry store, Maria excitedly tested the nuggets. She found that the gold nuggets left a greenish black powder when rubbed across a piece of white porcelain. The nuggets scratched a piece of copper she found in her room.

Solve the Problem:

1. **What color streak does gold have?**
2. **Is gold hard enough to scratch copper?**
3. **Did Maria strike it rich?**

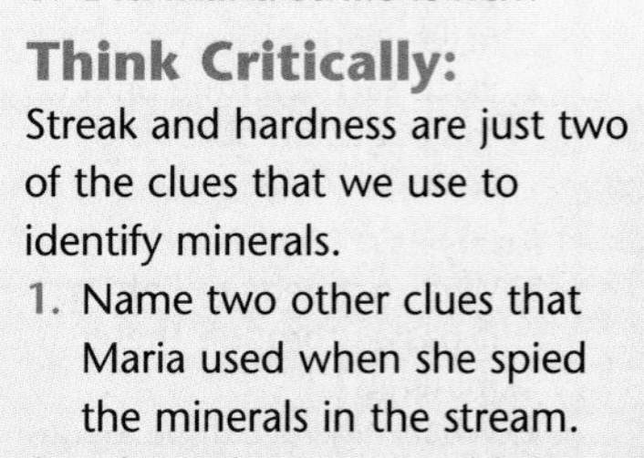

Think Critically:

Streak and hardness are just two of the clues that we use to identify minerals.

1. Name two other clues that Maria used when she spied the minerals in the stream.
2. What other tests could she have performed to determine whether her sample was gold?

Figure 3-9
Weak bonds within the structure of mica allow it to be broken along smooth, flat cleavage planes. *If you broke quartz, would it look the same? Explain.*

Cleavage and Fracture

The way a mineral breaks is another clue to its identity. Minerals that break along smooth, flat surfaces have **cleavage.** Cleavage, like hardness, is determined by the arrangement of the mineral's atoms. Mica is a mineral that has perfect cleavage. You can see in **Figure 3-9** how it breaks along smooth, flat surfaces. If you were to take a layer cake and separate its layers, you would show that the cake has cleavage. But not all minerals have cleavage. Minerals that break with rough or jagged edges have **fracture.** Quartz is a mineral with fracture. If you were to grab a chunk out of the side of that cake, it would be like breaking a mineral with fracture.

Integrating the Sciences

Chemistry Demonstrate the property of cleavage by separating a layer cake between layers. Explain that cleavage of a mineral occurs along planes where the chemical bonds are weaker. This can be related to the weak bond icing has for the layer of cake above and the one below. Then explain how a mineral fractures by grabbing a chunk out of the side of the cake. This can be related to the chemical bonds within a mineral being about the same in all directions. Because of this, the breakage is irregular.

Other Properties

Some minerals have unique properties. Magnetite, as you can guess by its name, is attracted to magnets. Lodestone, a form of magnetite, will pick up iron filings like a magnet. Light bends in two directions when it passes through some calcite specimens, causing you to see a double image, as in **Figure 3-10.** Calcite can also be identified because it fizzes when hydrochloric acid is put on it.

You can see that you sometimes need more information than just color and appearance to identify most minerals. You might also need to test its streak, its hardness, its luster, and its cleavage or fracture. You can be just as good at identifying minerals as you are at recognizing your friends in class.

CONNECT TO

CHEMISTRY

Why does calcite fizz when hydrochloric acid (HCl) is dropped onto it? ***Determine*** what chemical reaction occurs.

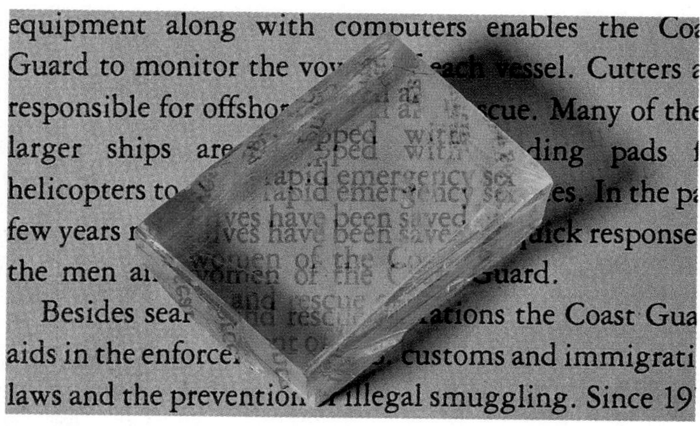

Figure 3-10

Iceland spar, a clear specimen of calcite, can be identified by its unique ability to bend light in two directions, causing a double image.

Section Wrap-up

Review

1. What's the difference between a mineral that has cleavage and one that has fracture?
2. How can an unglazed porcelain tile be used to identify a mineral?
3. **Think Critically:** What hardness does a mineral have if it is scratched by glass but scratches an iron nail?

Skill Builder

Making and Using Graphs

Make a bar graph of the hardnesses of the common objects used for comparison with the minerals in the Mohs scale of hardness. If you need help, refer to Making and Using Graphs in the **Skill Handbook.**

Science Journal

In your Science Journal, make a list of five minerals. Next to the name of each mineral, list at least two physical properties that can be used to identify the mineral.

CONNECT TO

CHEMISTRY

Answer The chemical formula of calcite is $CaCO_3$. HCl reacts with calcite to release CO_2 in the form of a bubbling gas. $CaCl_2$ also forms.

$$CaCO_3 + 2HCl \rightarrow H_2O + CO_2 + CaCl_2$$

4 Close

•MINI•QUIZ•

1. **What is the hardest known mineral?** *diamond*
2. **The way light is reflected from a mineral is called _____ .** *luster*
3. **The color of a powdered mineral is the mineral's _____ .** *streak*
4. **When a mineral breaks along smooth, flat planes, the mineral is said to have _____ .** *cleavage*

Section Wrap-up

Review

1. A mineral with cleavage breaks along smooth, flat planes. A mineral that fractures breaks with rough or jagged edges.
2. A mineral softer than an unglazed porcelain tile will leave a powdered streak on the tile. The streak color can identify the mineral.
3. **Think Critically** between 4.5 and 5.5

Science Journal

Answers may include: sulfur, yellow color and smell; quartz, hardness and luster; galena, dark gray streak and heft; calcite, fizzes with HCl and cleavage; pyrite, dark green-gray streak and hardness.

Skill Builder

Hardness (0–10) bar graph: Finger-nail, Copper penny, Iron nail, Glass, Steel file, Streak plate

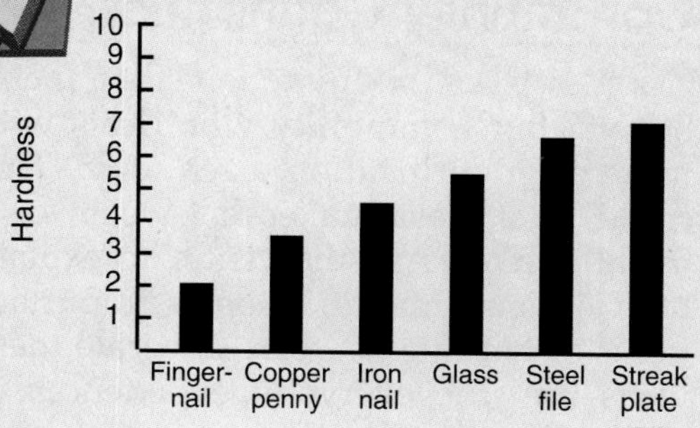

P

Assessment

Performance Assess students' graphing abilities by comparing their graphs with the one illustrated. Use the Performance Task Assessment List for Graph from Data in **PASC,** p. 39. P

Activity 3-2

PREPARATION

Purpose

LS **Interpersonal** Design and carry out an investigation to identify unknown mineral samples. L1 COOP LEARN

Process Skills

communicating, classifying, making and using tables, comparing and contrasting, forming a hypothesis, interpreting data, using numbers, observing and inferring, separating and controlling variables, designing an experiment

Time

60-80 minutes

Materials

Obtain several sets of mineral samples. Label the minerals and use a key so you can distinguish them.

Safety Precautions

Remind students about the safe use of acids. Students should wear goggles and aprons. HCl may cause burns. If spillage occurs, rinse with water. Also caution students to handle glass slides and other materials with sharp edges carefully.

Possible Hypotheses

1. Hardness would be the first property used to identify an unknown mineral.
2. Streak would be the first property used to identify an unknown mineral.
3. Luster would be the first property used to identify an unknown mineral.
4. A combination of properties works best to identify unknown minerals. First you study their general appearance. This then will direct you to other properties.

Activity Worksheets, pp. 5, 19-20

Activity 3-2

Design Your Own Experiment

Mineral Identification

Some properties of minerals make them easy to identify, while others are not much help at all. Some minerals can be identified by one property. Others require the testing of several properties for identification.

PREPARATION

Problem

Which property would you try first to identify an unknown mineral?

Form a Hypothesis

State a hypothesis about which property you think will be most useful in identifying minerals.

Objectives

- Determine which properties of a mineral you will use for identification purposes.
- Design an experiment that uses these properties to help in identifying minerals.

Possible Materials

- mineral samples
- hand lens
- pan balance
- graduated cylinder
- water
- piece of copper
- glass slide
- small iron nail
- steel file
- streak plate
- 5 percent hydrochloric acid (HCl) with dropper
- goggles
- Mohs scale of hardness
- Appendices M and N

Safety Precautions

Review the safe use of acids. Wear goggles and an apron. Be careful when handling materials with sharp edges.

CAUTION: *HCl may cause burns. If spillage occurs, rinse with water.*

Inclusion Strategies

Gifted After students complete Section 3-2 and Activity 3-2, have them play a game based on 20 Questions. One student can think of a mineral while others try to narrow the choice by asking five yes or no questions related to luster, hardness, cleavage or fracture, and so on. This activity encourages the students to use good questioning strategies and classification and memory skills. L3

Community Connection

Mineral Identification Invite to class a member of your community who deals with mineral identification each day. This could be a glass maker, a jeweler, or a metal worker. Ask the visitor to explain how mineral identification is important in his or her line of work. Integrate these ideas into the everyday experiences of your students.

PLAN THE EXPERIMENT

1. As a group, agree upon and write your hypothesis statement.
2. As a group, list the steps that you will need to test your hypothesis. Be specific, describing exactly what you will do at each step.
3. Make a list of the materials that you will need to complete your experiment.
4. Make a list of the various properties of minerals that you will test.
5. Make a list of any special properties you expect to observe or test.

Check the Plan

1. Read over your entire experiment to make sure that all steps are in a logical order.
2. Should you test any of the properties more than once for any of the minerals?
3. Will you summarize data in a graph, table, or chart?
4. How will you determine whether certain properties indicate a specific mineral?
5. *Make sure your teacher approves your plan and that you have included any changes suggested in the plan.*

DO THE EXPERIMENT

1. Carry out the experiment as planned.
2. While conducting the experiment, write down any observations that you or other members of your group make and summarize your data in your Science Journal.

Analyze and Apply

1. Which property was most useful in identifying your samples? Which property was least useful?
2. **Compare** the properties that worked best for you with those that worked best for other students.
3. **Discuss** reasons why one property is useful and others are not.

Go Further

If all you had were a piece of paper, a steel knife, and a glass bottle, could you distinguish between calcite and quartz? What other test would help you identify calcite?

Go Further

Students should realize that calcite and quartz can be easily distinguished based on hardness. Quartz will scratch all of the items in the backpack; calcite will scratch none of them. Adding HCl to the sample would cause calcite to fizz, but not quartz.

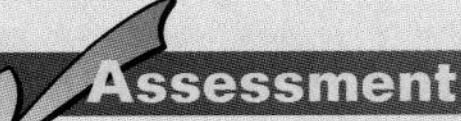

Assessment

Performance To further assess mineral identification, ask students to bring mineral samples from home or supply students with additional mineral samples and have them repeat this activity to identify the additional samples. Use the Performance Task Assessment List for Carrying Out a Strategy and Collecting Data in **PASC**, p. 25. P

PLAN THE EXPERIMENT

Possible Procedures

- Students may begin by scratching each mineral using the Mohs scale of hardness or the Field scale of hardness.
- Students may obtain a streak color for each mineral and use this property to attempt mineral identification.
- Students may begin by separating minerals according to luster.
- Students may first lay out all minerals, study their appearance and heft (specific gravity), and decide which property would be most helpful in identifying each mineral.

DO THE EXPERIMENT

Expected Outcome

Students will discover that whichever property they choose, it will probably not be enough to identify all minerals. Usually, they will discover that using a combination of properties is best when identifying unknown mineral samples.

Analyze and Apply

1. Although answers will vary, hardness and streak will generally be the properties most commonly cited as most useful. Color is usually the least helpful property.
2. Comparisons among groups will vary, but should lead to discussions about different ways to test minerals.
3. Discussion among groups will vary, but color will most likely prove to be unreliable. Hardness and streak are very useful because these properties tend to be the same for all samples of the same mineral.

Section 3•3

Prepare

Section Background

- The value of diamonds varies depending on whether or not they are tinted. The most common diamonds of gem quality have yellow or brown tints and are less valuable than diamonds with no tints. Diamonds with blue or pink tints are more valuable than those with no tints.
- Ores located deep in Earth's crust are removed by underground mining. Ores near Earth's surface are removed by open-pit mining.

1 Motivate

Bellringer

Before presenting the lesson, display **Section Focus Transparency 11** on the overhead projector. Assign the accompanying **Focus Activity** worksheet. L1 LEP

Tying to Previous Knowledge

Have students recall the last time they saw jewelry in the window of a jewelry store or at a department store. Have students describe the jewelry. Most will say it was shiny, or colorful, or looked brilliant under the lights of the store.

GTV: Planetary Manager

Industry

47572

3•3 Uses of Minerals

Science Words

gem
ore

Objectives

- Discuss characteristics gems have that make them different from and more valuable than other minerals.
- List the conditions necessary for a mineral to be classified as an ore.

Gems

What makes one mineral more useful or valuable to us than another? Why are diamonds and rubies considered to be valuable? The next time you go shopping, look in the window of a jewelry store. Chances are you will see rings, bracelets, and maybe even a watch with diamonds or other gems on them. What properties do gems possess that make them valuable?

Properties of Gems

Gems or gemstones like the ones in **Figure 3-11** are highly prized minerals because they are rare and beautiful. Many gems are cut and polished and used for jewelry. They are brighter and more colorful than common samples of the same mineral.

The difference between a gem and the common form of the same mineral can be slight. Amethyst, a gem form of quartz, contains just traces of manganese in its structure. This manganese gives amethyst a desirable purple color. And sometimes, a gem has a crystal structure that allows it to be cut and polished to a higher quality than that of a non-gem mineral.

Figure 3-11

It is easy to see why gems are prized—for their beauty and rarity. Shown here are watermelon tourmaline, turquoise, polished amethyst, and unpolished amethyst. Shown above are a ruby and an opal.

Program Resources

Reproducible Masters

Study Guide, p. 15 L1
Reinforcement, p. 15 L1
Enrichment, p. 15 L3
Lab Manual 12, 13
Multicultural Connections, pp. 9-10

Transparencies

Section Focus Transparency 11 L1

Figure 3-12
Ore must be processed and refined into more useful materials. *When is a mineral considered an ore?*

Ores

If you look around your room at home, you will find many things made from mineral resources. See how many you can name. Is there anything in your room with iron in it? If so, the iron may have come from the mineral hematite. The aluminum in soft-drink cans comes from the mineral bauxite.

Bauxite and hematite are minerals that can also be called ores. A mineral is an **ore** if it contains a useful substance that can be mined at a profit. Aluminum can be refined from bauxite, as shown in Figure **3-12,** and made into the useful products shown in **Figure 3-13.** These products are worth more money than the cost of the mining, so bauxite is an ore.

Figure 3-13
Bauxite ore is used to make aluminum products.

2 Teach

Demonstration

LS **Visual-Spatial** Demonstrate a smelting process used for separating metals from an ore by mixing some black copper oxide and some powdered charcoal in the bottom of a test tube. A tablespoon of each will be enough. Carefully heat the mixture for a few minutes. Pour the hot mixture into a beaker of water. The copper will settle to the bottom, and the waste will float on the water.

Discussion

Briefly explain the 1849 California gold rush to students. Then ask: **Why were the miners able to pan the water to recover the gold?** *Because of its high specific gravity, gold will sink to the bottom of the pan.*

Visual Learning

Figure 3-12 When is a mineral considered an ore? *A mineral is an ore if it contains a useful substance that can be mined at a profit.* **LEP** 

GLENCOE TECHNOLOGY

Videodisc

The Infinite Voyage: The Future of the Past

Chapter 4

The Statue of Liberty Restoration Project

Chapter 7

Restoring the Parthenon

Community Connection

Beauty of Gems Invite a local jeweler or lapidary, a person who cuts and polishes minerals, to come to class to discuss methods used to bring out the beauty of gems. Amethyst is a variety of quartz often used as a gemstone. Have a jeweler display some amethyst jewelry for the class. Have the jeweler ask students what they think is the most precious gem. Many students will be surprised to learn that rubies and emeralds are considered more valuable than diamonds because of their relative rareness. Have the lapidary explain what a diamond looks like when it is first found and what makes it so brilliant when used in jewelry. Diamond disperses light more than most other minerals, thus making it so brilliant.

USING TECHNOLOGY

For more information about the uses of synthetic diamonds alone or as edged or coated surfaces, have students research this in a chemistry textbook.

Think Critically

These diamonds aren't minerals because they are made by people. The plastic coating must be reapplied from time to time. A diamond coating would be harder and not wear off.

3 Assess

Check for Understanding

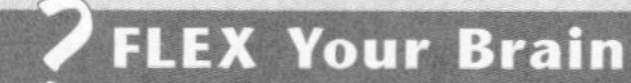

Use the Flex Your Brain activity to have students explore USES FOR GEMS.

Activity Worksheets, p. 5

Reteach

Have students read advertisements to discover what gems are commonly used in jewelry. Ask them to also find out what minerals the gems are set in.

Extension

For students who have mastered this section, use the **Reinforcement** and **Enrichment** masters.

USING TECHNOLOGY

On the Cutting Edge

You probably knew that diamonds were used in jewelry, but did you know that diamonds are used on drill bits and other instruments? Diamond-tipped drill bits can cut through hard substances such as steel and rock. Diamonds are used on the bits because they are the hardest mineral.

Scientists have developed a way to put a thin coating of diamonds on objects such as the record needle shown in this photo. They use methane gas and microwaves to make the diamonds. A methane molecule consists of a carbon atom surrounded by four hydrogen atoms. Microwaves are used to strip the hydrogen atoms away from the molecule. Then the carbon atoms link together on the surface of the object being coated, forming tiny rows of diamonds. This process can be used to make diamond-edged surgical scalpels, razor blades, dental drills, diamond-tipped record needles, and diamond-coated computer parts.

Think Critically:

The diamonds scientists make using methane gas and microwaves aren't true minerals. Why not?

Diamond-Tipped Record Needle

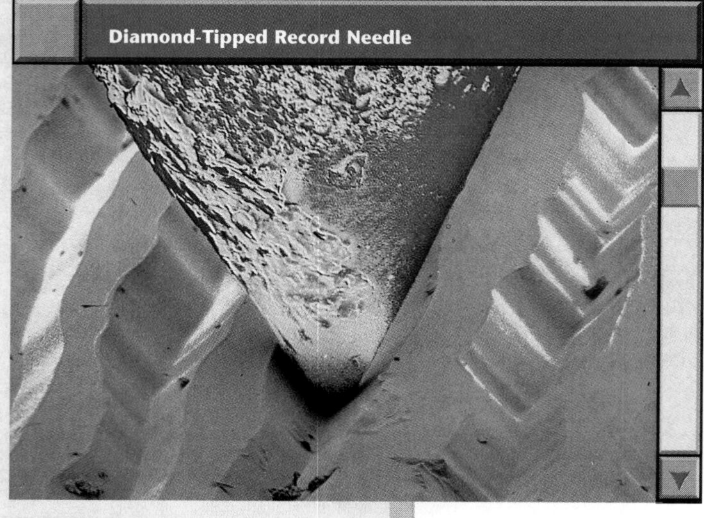

Waste Rock Removal

Many ores are obtained from large open-pit mines like the one shown in **Figure 3-14.** When the ore is mined, it contains unwanted material along with the valuable material. The waste rock or material must be removed before the ore can be used. Removing the waste rock can be expensive, and in some cases, harmful to the environment. If the cost of removing the waste rock gets higher than the value of the desired material, the mineral will no longer be classified as an ore.

Think back to the last soft drink you had in an aluminum can. What do you think would happen if people stopped using aluminum cans? This would cause the demand for aluminum to go down. Some bauxite mines would close down because they would no longer be able to make money. The value of a mineral can change if the supply of or the demand for that mineral changes.

CONNECT TO PHYSICS

Answer The average density, and therefore specific gravity, of gold ore could be higher than that of a pyrite ore because the density, and therefore specific gravity, of gold is greater than the density, and therefore specific gravity, of pyrite.

Across the Curriculum

Geography and World Cultures Have students research and record areas of the world that supply large amounts of the world's diamonds, gold, rock salt, bauxite, iron, and other mineral resources. Have students write a brief paragraph explaining the importance of these mineral resources to each area's economy. L1 LS P

Science Journal

Fake Diamonds Tell students that someone has placed an ad in the newspaper that reads: "Real gems for sale! We'll prove these are genuine diamonds by cutting glass with them before your very eyes!" In their Science Journals, have students describe why cutting glass wouldn't prove the stones were precious diamonds. Many minerals other than diamonds can cut glass. L1 LS

Figure 3-14

Many ores are obtained from large open-pit mines. *What would happen to this mine if the demand for its ore decreased? What would happen if the demand increased?*

You'd be surprised to find out all of the things that come from ores. Iron, used in everything from frying pans to ships, is obtained from its ore, hematite. Zinc is obtained from sphalerite. Copper, used in coins and electrical wires, among other things, is obtained from chalcopyrite. Some other ores of copper, malachite, and azurite are gemstones. As you can see, gems and ores are important mineral resources.

CONNECT TO

PHYSICS

Decide how the physical property of density could be used to determine whether a possible ore contains gold or pyrite ("fool's gold").

Section Wrap-up

Review

1. Compare and contrast gem-quality amethyst with regular quartz.
2. **Think Critically:** Why couldn't a company stay in business if the mineral it was mining were no longer an ore?

USING MATH

Investigate and show how early prospectors used density to determine whether they had found gold or pyrite.

Skill Builder

Concept Mapping

Make an events chain showing why bauxite can be an ore. Use the following terms and phrases: *gives aluminum, ore, mined at profit, bauxite.* If you need help, refer to Concept Mapping in the **Skill Handbook.**

Visual Learning

Figure 3-14 What would happen to this mine if the demand for its ore decreased? What would happen if the demand increased? *If the demand decreased, the mine might close down because it would no longer be able to make a profit. If the demand increased, production would increase as well.* LEP LS

4 Close

• MINI • QUIZ •

Use the Mini Quiz to check students' recall of chapter content.

1. **Minerals that are highly prized because of their rareness and beauty are called _____ .** *gems*
2. **Minerals that contain useful substances that can be mined at a profit are _____ .** *ores*

Section Wrap-up

Review

1. Amethyst is a variety of quartz that contains impurities that color it. Pure quartz is colorless.
2. **Think Critically** If the mineral could not be mined at a profit, it would no longer be an ore. A small company would sustain losses.

USING MATH

Gold has a greater density than pyrite, and will sink.

Skill Builder

Possible Solution:

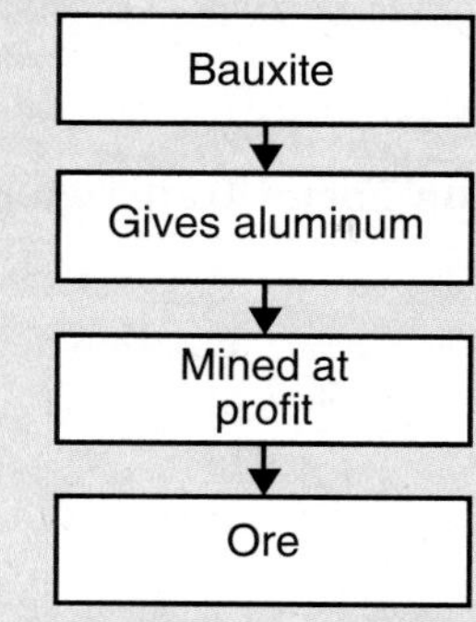

Assessment

Content Use this Skill Builder to assess students' abilities to create a concept map. Ask students to explain how bauxite is an ore of aluminum. Use the Performance Task Assessment List for Concept Map in **PASC,** p. 89. P

Prepare

Section Background

- Titanium ores are very common in Earth's crust. However, the ore deposits are widely dispersed rather than concentrated in large deposits. Because of this, only a few countries produce commercial quantities of titanium.
- Titanium is nontoxic and does not activate the body's immune system to reject the artificial implant. In fact, artificial bone made of titanium can be made in a way that natural bone will grow over and around it.

1 Motivate

Bellringer

Before presenting the lesson, display **Section Focus Transparency 12** on the overhead projector. Assign the accompanying **Focus Activity** worksheet. L1 LEP

Tying to Previous Knowledge

Remind students that in order for a deposit of a mineral containing titanium to be considered an ore, the titanium must be mined and produced at a profit.

2 Teach

Visual Learning

Figure 3-15C What other quality of titanium makes it useful in the production of artificial body parts? *Titanium is nontoxic, so the body's immune system does not reject it.* LEP LS

TECHNOLOGY:

3•4 Uses of Titanium

Science Words

titanium

Objectives

- List the properties of titanium that make it so useful in biomedicine, sporting equipment, and other applications.
- Identify the minerals that are mined for titanium.

Titanium

You might know someone who uses golf clubs with titanium shafts or a racing bicycle containing titanium. Perhaps you know someone who has needed a hip replacement made from titanium. **Titanium** is a durable, lightweight metal derived from minerals such as ilmenite or rutile.

Properties of Titanium

Titanium is used in automobile body parts, such as connecting rods, valves, and suspension springs. It is also used in the production of aircraft. The properties of titanium that make it so valuable to the automobile and aircraft industries are its durability and light weight. These same properties make titanium valuable in the production of sports equipment, such as tennis rackets. In fact, wheelchairs used by people who want to race or play basketball are often made from titanium. The light weight and durable nature of titanium, as well as the fact that it is a nontoxic metal, also make it useful in the production of hip replacements and other artificial body parts. **Figure 3-15** illustrates several uses for titanium.

Figure 3-15

Titanium's durability and light weight make it useful in a variety of applications.

A Wheelchairs used for racing and playing basketball often have parts made from titanium.

78

Program Resources

Reproducible Masters

Study Guide, p. 16 L1
Reinforcement, p. 16 L1
Enrichment, p. 16 L3
Science and Society Integration, p. 7

Transparencies

Section Focus Transparency 12

B Titanium is used in the pivots on airplane wings, allowing the wings to move forward and back for maximum lift and speed.

Ilmenite and Rutile

Two minerals that are classified as ores of the element titanium are ilmenite and rutile. There are two separate methods presently used by manufacturers to obtain the element titanium from each of its ores. One method is to dissolve ilmenite in sulfuric acid, thereby producing titanium dioxide and iron sulfate. In the other method, rutile, which contains a higher concentration of titanium, is combined with chlorine at high temperatures. This process produces titanium tetrachloride ($TiCl_4$), often called "tickle." The second method is growing in use because the iron sulfate produced by the first method is harmful to the environment.

Section Wrap-up

Review

1. What properties of titanium make it so useful in sports equipment and biomedical research?
2. Which two minerals are ores of titanium?

Explore the Technology

Manufacturers are more likely to produce titanium tetrachloride by combining the mineral rutile with chlorine at high temperatures. Why is this true?

C Titanium is strong enough to be used for total hip replacements. *What other quality of titanium makes it useful in the production of artificial body parts?*

SCIENCE & SOCIETY

3 Assess

Check for Understanding

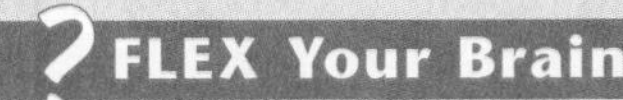

Use the Flex Your Brain activity to have students explore WAYS TO OBTAIN TITANIUM FROM ITS ORE.

Activity Worksheets, p. 5

Reteach

Have students research what sports equipment at nearby malls or sports equipment stores is made from material containing titanium. Ask them to explain why titanium was used to make the equipment.

Extension

For students who have mastered this section, use the **Reinforcement** and **Enrichment** masters.

4 Close

LS **Kinesthetic** Provide the class with two pieces of the same sports equipment, one made of material containing titanium, the other not. Have students compare their weight and durability.

Section Wrap-up

Review

1. Titanium is lightweight and durable.
2. ilmenite and rutile

Explore the Technology

The reaction between ilmenite and sulfuric acid produces iron sulfate, which is harmful to the environment.

Across the Curriculum

Biomedicine and Sports Have students study the article about the use of titanium in human body implants and sports equipment. Encourage them to research the use of titanium in other products. Ask students to reaffirm the reasons titanium is used in these products. L2

Biography

- Jamyang Singe, a Tibetan painter who lives and teaches in the United States, maintains the tradition of using hand-mixed paints in the creation of Tibetan tankas. A tanka (TAHN-kuh) is a painting of Tibetan Buddhist religious subjects. The painting shown in the text is a detail from a large tanka by one of Singe's students.

Background

- In addition to pigments, paints also contain adhesives that cause the paint to stick to the surface, and binders that protect the pigment particles from exposure to air and help make the paint spreadable.
- Traditional mineral paints for tanka paintings are formulated by mixing powders with water and glue made from the hides of water buffaloes. First, a few drops of water are mixed with the glue and heated until the glue dissolves. Drops of this mixture are added to the powdered pigment until the desired consistency is obtained, then it is brushed onto the canvas. If too much glue is used, the paint takes on a yellowish tint and is likely to crack. If too little glue is used, the dried paint will fall off the canvas.
- Artists must use protective gear, such as masks and gloves, when grinding minerals that contain toxins. Art supplies intended for use by children and untrained adults are deliberately compounded to avoid the use of toxic materials.

Science & ART

This yak, painted by A. Kahn, is outlined in gold paint. The yak's tongue, nose, and eyes are tinted with cinnabar.

Minerals as Paint Pigments

Ultramarine, burnt sienna, vermilion, crimson, azure, ochre, cerulean blue—these exotic-sounding names describe colors artists use in their paintings and drawings. The substances that give color to paints, crayons, and pastel chalks are called pigments. Today, most artists' pigments are made artificially, using synthetic dyes from petroleum or using chemical processes that create desired combinations of minerals. But many pigments were originally made by digging minerals from the ground and grinding them into fine powders.

Some traditional artists prefer the more subtle colors produced by ground minerals and still use ancient methods to make their own paints. Many of the minerals that are used as pigments contain poisonous substances, such as lead, arsenic, copper, and mercury, and must be handled with skill and care.

White pigments are made from compounds containing calcium, zinc, titanium, or lead.

Red colors can be made from a cinnabar, a mineral containing mercury and sulfur. Depending on how the powder is ground, it can produce colors ranging from pale pink to bright vermilion or deep maroon. Tiny particles of mercury give cinnabar pigments a silvery sparkle.

Shades of green, yellow-green, and blue-green are made from copper-containing minerals such as malachite and azurite.

The rich, dark blue known as ultramarine is made from lapis lazuli, a mineral containing silicon, sulfur, and sodium. Lapis pigments sometimes include spangles of iron pyrite, also called fool's gold.

Yellow comes from many sources. Ochre is a yellow clay that contains iron. When heated in an oven, it turns brick red. Sienna is a dark yellow clay that contains iron and manganese. It turns brown—becoming burnt sienna—when roasted in an oven. Other yellow minerals include arsenic combined with sulfur and lead combined with antimony.

Gold, silver, and a few other metals can be made into shimmering paints. Gold that has been painted onto a canvas can be rubbed or burnished with stone to make it gleam.

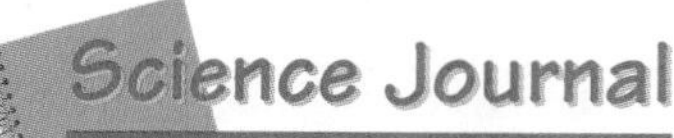

Science Journal

Research how artists make their own paints. In your Science Journal, write a paragraph describing the process.

Teaching Strategies

LS Kinesthetic Many artists' colors are still made from minerals, though they are created by chemical means rather than by grinding stone. Provide students with pastel chalks, water colors, or tempera paints and invite them to create a painting or a color palette that demonstrates the colors of various minerals. L1

LS Linguistic Encourage students to use dictionaries, encyclopedias, and other reference materials to investigate the composition of pigments used in oil paints, water colors, tempera paints, and so on. Terms students might want to find out about include cadmium, cobalt, orpiment, umber, turquoise, and Prussian blue. L1

Sources

Ralph Mayer, *The Artist's Handbook of Materials and Techniques.* 3rd edition. New York: Viking, 1970.

Chapter 3

Review

Summary

3-1: Minerals

1. All minerals are formed by natural processes and are inorganic solids with unique compositions and distinct internal structures.
2. Minerals have crystal structures in one of six major crystal systems.
3. Minerals can form when magma cools, when liquids containing dissolved minerals evaporate, or when particles precipitate from solution.

3-2: Mineral Identification

1. Hardness is a measure of how easily a mineral can be scratched. Luster describes how light is reflected from a mineral's surface. Color is a property that sometimes can be used to identify a mineral.
2. Streak is the color of the powder left by a mineral on an unglazed porcelain tile. Minerals that break along smooth, flat surfaces have cleavage. Minerals that break with rough or jagged surfaces have fracture.

3-3: Uses of Minerals

1. Gems are minerals that are more rare and beautiful than common minerals.
2. An ore is a mineral or group of minerals that can be mined at a profit.

3-4: Science and Society: Uses of Titanium

1. Titanium is a durable, lightweight metal derived from minerals such as ilmenite and rutile.
2. The properties of titanium make it ideal for use in sports equipment and as hip replacements, among other things.
3. Two methods exist for manufacturers to obtain titanium from its ores ilmenite and rutile.

Key Science Words

a. cleavage
b. crystal
c. fracture
d. gem
e. hardness
f. luster
g. magma
h. mineral
i. ore
j. silicate
k. streak
l. titanium

Reviewing Vocabulary

Match each phrase with the correct term from the list of Key Science Words.

1. naturally occurring solid
2. hot, melted rock material
3. mineral containing silicon, oxygen, and usually one or more other elements
4. how light is reflected from a mineral
5. a mineral obtained from ilmenite or rutile
6. valuable, rare mineral
7. a mineral mined at a profit
8. breakage along smooth, flat planes
9. solid with a repeating arrangement of atoms
10. the color of a mineral's powder

Chapter 3

Review

Summary

Have students read the summary statements to review the major concepts of the chapter.

Reviewing Vocabulary

1. h	**6.** d
2. g	**7.** i
3. j	**8.** a
4. f	**9.** b
5. l	**10.** k

Assessment

Portfolio Encourage students to place in their portfolios one or two items of what they consider to be their best work. Examples include:

- Skill Builder, p. 71
- Activity 3-2 results, analysis, and application, pp. 72-73
- Across the Curriculum, p. 76 P

Performance Additional performance assessments may be found in **Performance Assessment** and **Science Integration Activities.** Performance Task Assessment Lists and rubrics for evaluating these activities can be found in Glencoe's **Performance Assessment in the Science Classroom.**

MindJogger Videoquiz

Chapter 3 Have students work in groups as they play the Videoquiz game to review key chapter concepts.

Chapter 3 Review

Checking Concepts

1. d
2. c
3. a
4. c
5. b
6. d
7. b
8. c
9. c
10. d

Understanding Concepts

11. One method of obtaining titanium from its ore produces titanium dioxide and iron sulfate. The iron sulfate is harmful to the environment.

12. Air isn't a mineral because it isn't a solid and its components aren't arranged in a repeating pattern.

13. Both are terms used to describe how a mineral breaks. Cleavage refers to breakage along smooth, flat surfaces. Mica cleaves. Fracture describes minerals that break with rough or jagged edges, such as quartz.

14. The properties that make titanium useful are its durability and light weight.

15. Eight

Thinking Critically

16. On Earth, water can exist as a solid, a liquid, and/or a gas. Water is a mineral only when it is a solid that has formed naturally.

17. There are six sides to each cubic crystal.

18. No, sugar, although it is a solid formed in nature with a definite composition and internal structure, is not a mineral because it is an organic compound.

19. No, a diamond is harder than a streak plate and will scratch the plate.

20. Using common objects and the minerals on the Mohs scale of hardness allows you to determine the relative hardness of any mineral.

Chapter 3 Review

Checking Concepts

Choose the word or phrase that completes the sentence.

1. Minerals _______ .
   a. can be liquids
   b. have no crystal structure
   c. are organic
   d. are inorganic
2. All silicates contain _______ .
   a. magnesium
   b. silicon and aluminum
   c. silicon and oxygen
   d. oxygen and carbon
3. _______ is hot, melted rock material.
   a. Magma
   b. Quartz
   c. Salt water
   d. A mineral
4. Quartz is a(n) _______ .
   a. oxide
   b. carbonate
   c. silicate
   d. sulfide
5. _______ is a measure of how easily a mineral can be scratched.
   a. Luster
   b. Hardness
   c. Cleavage
   d. Fracture
6. The color of a powdered mineral on an unglazed porcelain tile is its _______ .
   a. luster
   b. density
   c. hardness
   d. streak
7. Quartz breaks with _______ .
   a. cleavage
   b. fracture
   c. luster
   d. smooth surfaces
8. _______ can be used in hip replacements.
   a. Iron
   b. Carbon
   c. Titanium
   d. Steel
9. The largest group of minerals is the ______ .
   a. oxides
   b. halides
   c. silicates
   d. sulfides
10. Halite forms _______ crystals.
    a. triclinic
    b. hexagonal
    c. monoclinic
    d. cubic

Understanding Concepts

Answer the following questions in your Science Journal using complete sentences.

11. Describe the environmental concerns involved with obtaining titanium.
12. Explain why air is not a mineral.
13. Compare and contrast the properties of cleavage and fracture. Give an example of a mineral that cleaves and one that fractures.
14. Why is titanium useful in sports equipment?
15. How many sides to a crystal are there for minerals belonging to the hexagonal crystal group?

Thinking Critically

16. Water is a nonliving substance formed by natural processes on Earth. It has a unique composition. Sometimes water is a mineral and other times it is not. Explain.
17. How many sides are there to a perfect salt crystal, such as the one shown below?
18. Suppose you let a sugar solution evaporate, leaving sugar crystals behind. Are these crystals minerals? Explain.
19. Will diamond leave a streak on a streak plate? Explain.
20. Explain how you would use **Table 3-2** on p. 68 to determine the hardness of any mineral.

Developing Skills

If you need help, refer to the **Skill Handbook.**

21. **Observing and Inferring:** Suppose you found a white, nonmetallic mineral that was harder than calcite. You identify the sample as quartz. What are your observations? What is your inference?
22. **Interpreting Data:** Suppose you were given these properties of a mineral: pink color, nonmetallic, softer than topaz and quartz, scratches apatite, harder than fluorite, has cleavage, and is scratched by a steel file. What is it?
23. **Outlining:** Make an outline of how at least seven physical properties can be used to identify unknown materials.
24. **Measuring in SI:** The volume of water in a graduated cylinder is 107.5 mL. A specimen of quartz, tied to a piece of string, is immersed into the water. The new water level reads 186 mL. What is the volume of the piece of quartz?
25. **Concept Mapping:** Make a network tree concept map showing six crystal systems and examples from each group. Use the following words and phrases: *orthorhombic, hexagonal, cubic, tetragonal, monoclinic, triclinic, topaz, corundum, halite, wulfenite, gypsum, and albite.*

Performance Assessment

1. **Carrying Out a Strategy and Collecting Data:** Collect samples of objects that you think are minerals. Following procedures learned in Activity 3-2, identify each mineral. Use a mineral identification book for help in listing some uses of the minerals you identify.
2. **Model:** Go to the library to research the six major mineral crystal systems. Use cardboard to make models of each major crystal shape for each system.
3. **Lab Report:** In Activity 3-1, you observed two ways in which crystals can form. Perform the experiment again, but this time add only one half as much salt and sugar to the separate solutions you are making. Write a lab report that describes your results and compares the results with those you obtained in the original experiment.

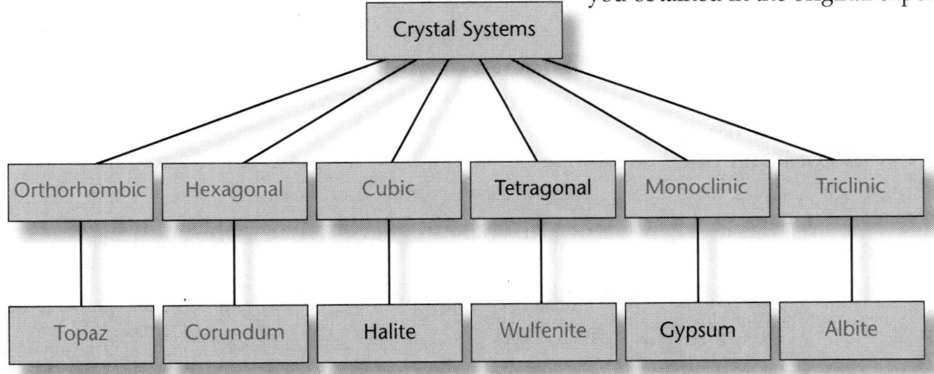

Chapter 3 Review

Developing Skills

21. **Observing and Inferring** The observations include the color, luster, and hardness of the mineral. The inference is that the mineral is quartz.
22. **Interpreting Data** feldspar
23. **Outlining** Answers will vary but should include at least the boldfaced terms in Section 3-2.
24. **Measuring in SI** 186 mL – 107.5 mL = 78.5 mL, 78.5 cm^3
25. **Concept Mapping** See student page.

Performance Assessment

1. Answers will vary, but procedures used by students should closely resemble work done on Activity 3-2. Students may include samples of wood or synthetic objects from home. Help them understand why these objects are not considered minerals. Use the Performance Task Assessment List for Making Observations and Inferences in **PASC,** p. 17. P
2. Students can use **Table 3-1** to construct models of the six major crystal systems. Use the Performance Task Assessment List for Model in **PASC,** p. 51. P
3. Answers will vary. Since there was not a saturated solution, smaller crystals or no crystals will form. It may take longer for crystals to precipitate out. Use the Performance Task Assessment List for Lab Report in **PASC,** p. 47. P

Assessment Resources

 **Reproducible Masters**

Chapter Review, pp. 9-10
Assessment, pp. 13-16
Performance Assessment, p. 17

Glencoe Technology

Chapter Review Software
Computer Test Bank
MindJogger Videoquiz

Chapter Organizer

Section	Objectives	Activities/Features
Chapter Opener		Explore Activity: Determine what rocks are made from. p. 85
4-1 **The Rock Cycle** (2 sessions, 1½ blocks)*	1. **Differentiate** between a rock and a mineral. 2. **Describe** the rock cycle and the changes that a rock may undergo.	MiniLAB: How do rocks change during the rock cycle? p. 87 Connect to Chemistry, p. 88 Skill Builder: Concept Mapping, p. 88 Science Journal, p. 88 Science & Art, p. 89 Science Journal, p. 89
4-2 **Igneous Rocks** (1 sessions, ½ block)*	1. **Recognize** magma and lava as the materials that cool to form igneous rocks. 2. **Contrast** the formation of intrusive and extrusive igneous rocks. 3. **Contrast** granitic and basaltic igneous rocks.	Connect to Life Science, p. 91 Science Journal, p. 92 Activity 4-1: Igneous Rocks, pp. 94-95 Skill Builder: Interpreting Scientific Illustrations, p. 96 Using Math, p. 96
4-3 **Metamorphic Rocks** (2 sessions, 1 block)*	1. **Describe** conditions that cause metamorphic rocks to form. 2. **Classify** metamorphic rocks as foliated or nonfoliated.	Using Technology: Solid as a Rock, p. 98 MiniLAB: How do metamorphic rocks form? p. 99 Skill Builder: Sequencing, p. 100 Using Computers: Graphing, p. 100
4-4 **Sedimentary Rocks** (2 sessions, 1 block)*	1. **Explain** how sedimentary rocks form from sediments. 2. **Classify** sedimentary rocks as detrital, chemical, or organic in origin.	MiniLAB: What are rocks made of? p. 102 Connect to Chemistry, p. 104 Using Math, p. 105 Problem Solving: The Geology of Buildings, p. 106 Skill Builder: Interpreting Data, p. 107 Using Math, p. 107
4-5 **Science and Society Technology: Burning Waste Coal** (1 session, ½ block)*	1. **Realize** that new technologies are enabling companies of today to solve problems caused by mining operations of the past. 2. **Describe** the process of cogeneration, and show how it is beneficial.	Explore the Technology, p. 109 Activity 4-2: Sedimentary Rocks, p. 110

* A complete Planning Guide that includes block scheduling is provided on pages 32T-35T.

Activity Materials

Explore	Activities	MiniLABs
page 85 several rock samples (igneous, metamorphic, and sedimentary)	pages 94-95 igneous rock samples, safety goggles, hand lens page 110 unknown sedimentary rock samples, marking pen, 5% hydrochloric acid, dropper, safety goggles, hand lens, paper towels, tap water	page 87 several different rock samples, rock hammer and heavy cloth bags in which to crush the rocks, mortar and pestle, small flat pan, tap water, all-purpose white glue, waxed paper, heavy weight page 99 8 rocks—4 metamorphic ones and their corresponding parent rocks page 102 sediment samples, sheet of white paper, tweezers or dissecting probe

Teacher Classroom Resources

Reproducible Masters	Transparencies
Study Guide, p. 17 **Reinforcement,** p. 17 **Enrichment,** p. 17 **Activity Worksheets,** p. 27 **Critical Thinking/Problem Solving,** p. 10 **Cross-Curricular Integration,** p. 8	**Section Focus Transparency 13,** Steady as a Rock? **Science Integration Transparency 4,** Cooling Rate and Crystal Size **Teaching Transparency 7,** The Rock Cycle
Study Guide, p. 18 **Reinforcement,** p. 18 **Enrichment,** p. 18 **Activity Worksheets,** pp. 23-24 **Lab Manual 14,** Gas Production in Magma **Concept Mapping,** p. 13	**Section Focus Transparency 14,** Changing Rock
Study Guide, p. 19 **Reinforcement,** p. 19 **Enrichment,** p. 19 **Activity Worksheets,** p. 28 **Lab Manual 15,** Metamorphic Processes	**Section Focus Transparency 15,** Mountain View
Study Guide, p. 20 **Reinforcement,** p. 20 **Enrichment,** p. 20 **Activity Worksheets,** p. 29 **Lab Manual 16,** Concretions **Science Integration Activity 4,** Zoo Mix-up **Multicultural Connections,** pp. 11-12	**Section Focus Transparency 16,** It's Sedimentary! **Teaching Transparency 8,** Sedimentary Rock
Study Guide, p. 21 **Reinforcement,** p. 21 **Enrichment,** p. 21 **Activity Worksheets,** pp. 25-26 **Science and Society Integration,** p. 8	**Section Focus Transparency 17,** Waste? —Not!

Teaching Resources

Glencoe Earth Science Interactive Videodisc
Earth Science CD-ROM
Spanish Resources
English/Spanish Audiocassettes
Cooperative Learning Resource Guide
Lab Partner
Lab and Safety Skills
Lesson Plans

Assessment Resources

Chapter Review, pp. 11-12
Assessment, pp. 17-20
Performance Assessment in the Science Classroom (PASC)
MindJogger Videoquiz
Alternate Assessment in the Science Classroom
Performance Assessment
Chapter Review Software
Computer Test Bank

Key to Teaching Strategies

The following designations will help you decide which activities are appropriate for your students.

L1 Level 1 activities should be within the ability range of all students.

L2 Level 2 activities should be within the ability range of the average to above-average student.

L3 Level 3 activities are designed for the ability range of above-average students.

LEP LEP activities should be within the ability range of Limited English Proficiency students.

LS These activities are designed to address different learning styles.

COOP LEARN Cooperative Learning activities are designed for small group work.

P These strategies represent student products that can be placed into a best-work portfolio.

GLENCOE TECHNOLOGY

The following multimedia resources are available from Glencoe.

Science and Technology Videodisc Series (STVS)
Earth & Space
Fibers from Rocks

National Geographic Society Series
STV: Restless Earth
STV: Water
GTV: Planetary Manager
Glencoe Earth Science Interactive Videodisc
The Rock Cycle
Earth Science CD-ROM

Teacher Classroom Resources

This is a representation of key blackline masters available in the Teacher Classroom Resources.

Teaching Aids

Section Focus Transparencies

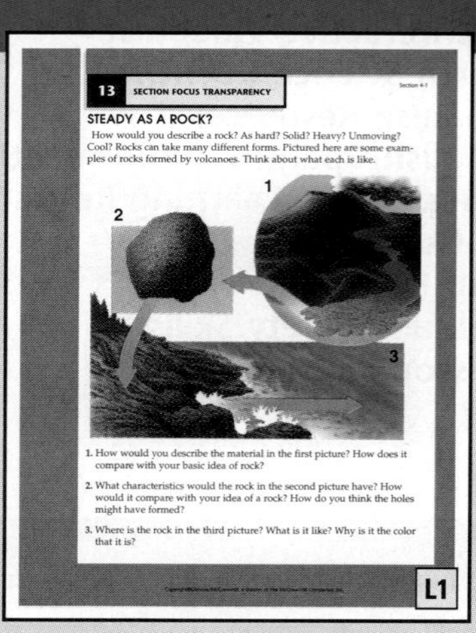

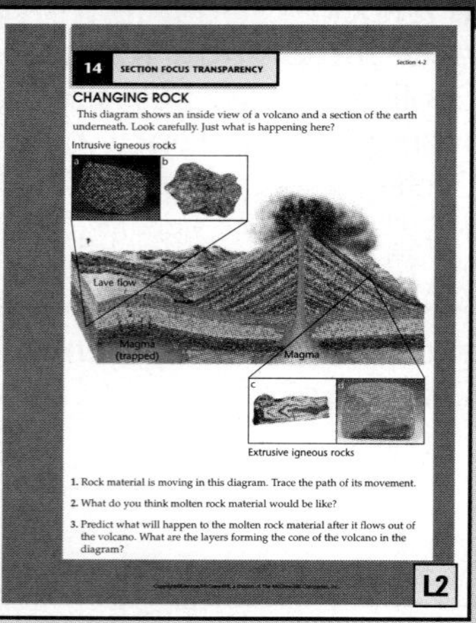

Science Integration Transparencies

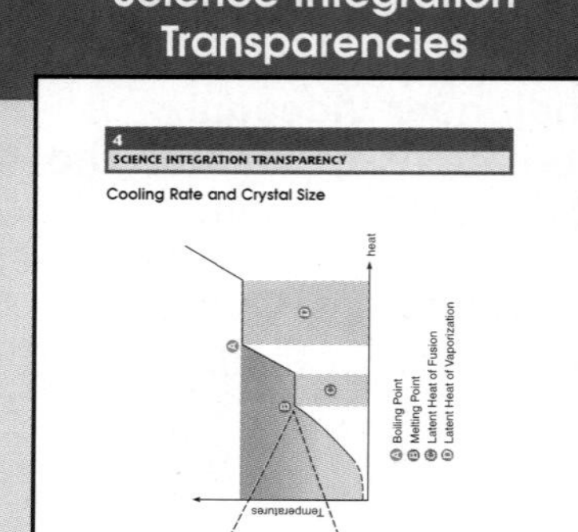

Teaching Transparencies

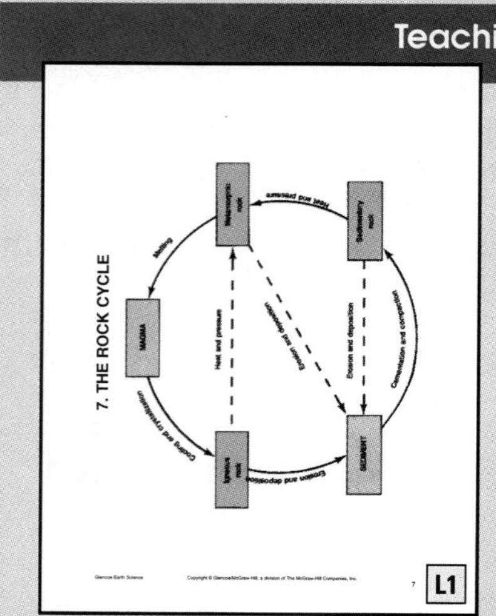

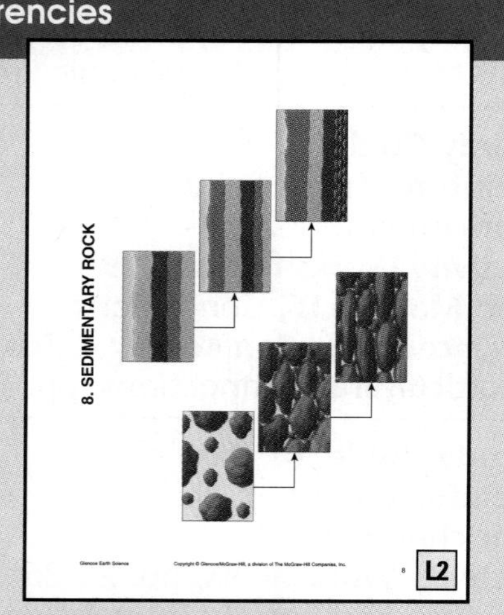

Meeting Different Ability Levels

Study Guide

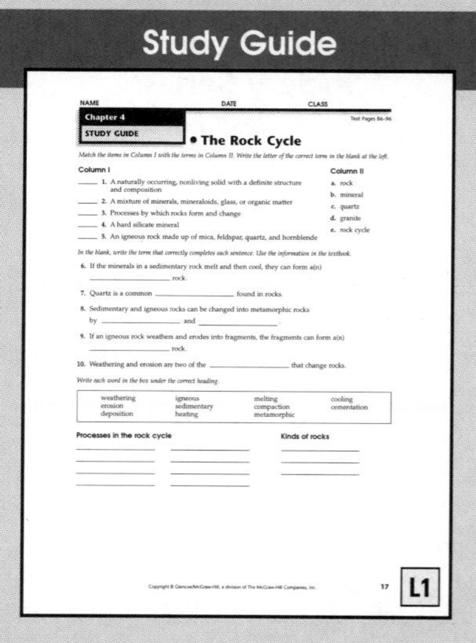

Reinforcement

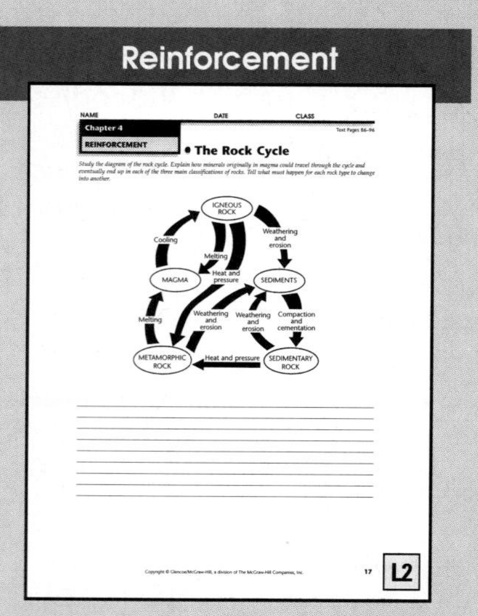

Enrichment Worksheets

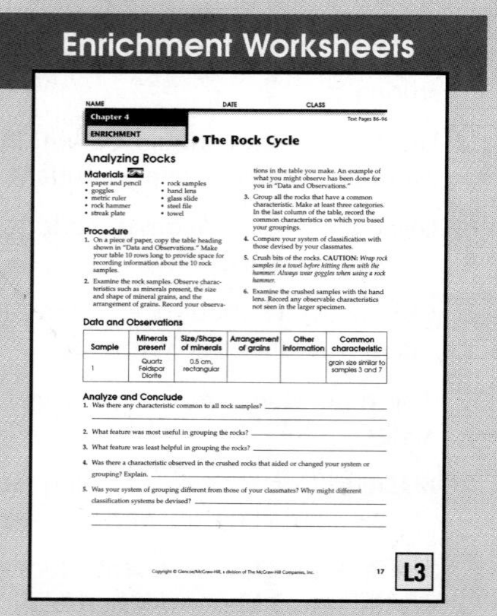

Hands-On Activities

Science Integration Activity

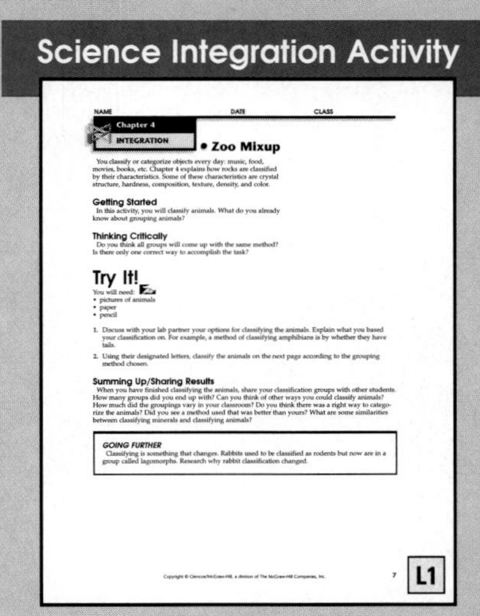

Lab Manual

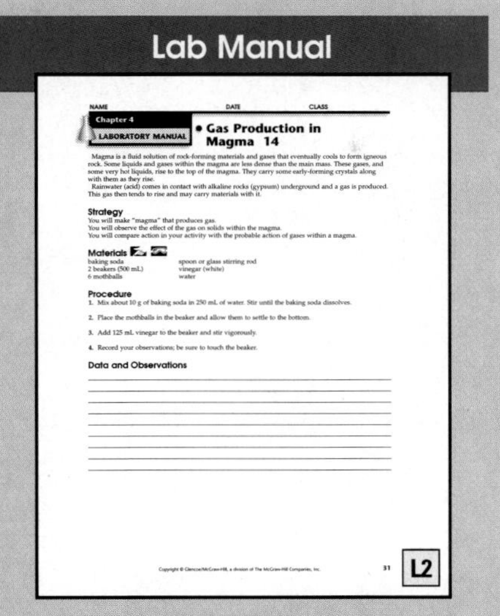

Assessment

Performance Assessment

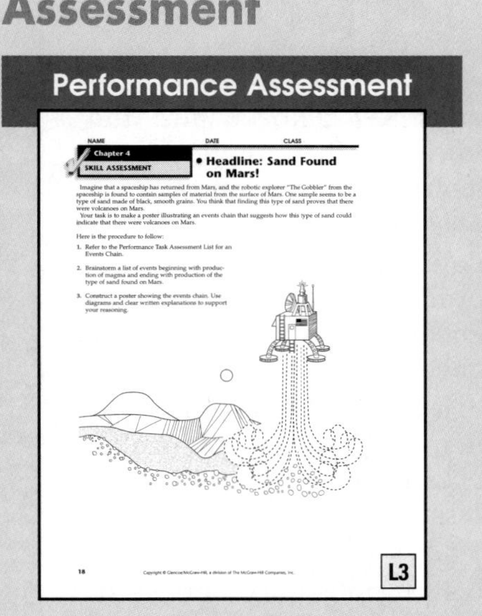

Enrichment and Application

Critical Thinking/ Problem Solving

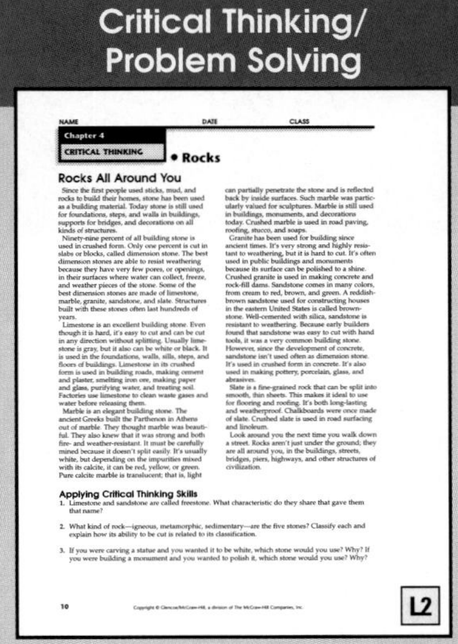

Cross-Curricular Integration

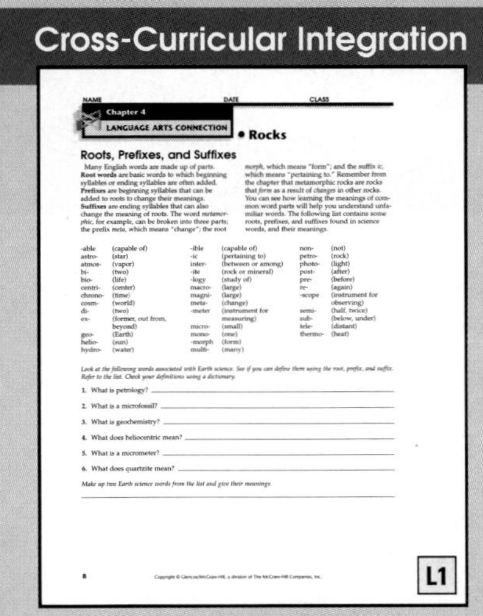

Science and Society Integration

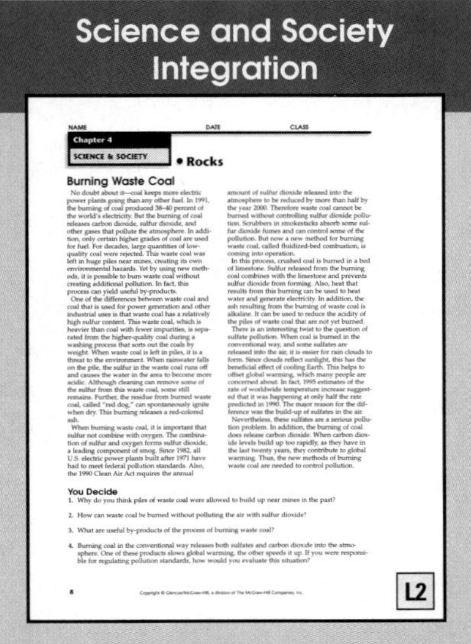

Multicultural Connections

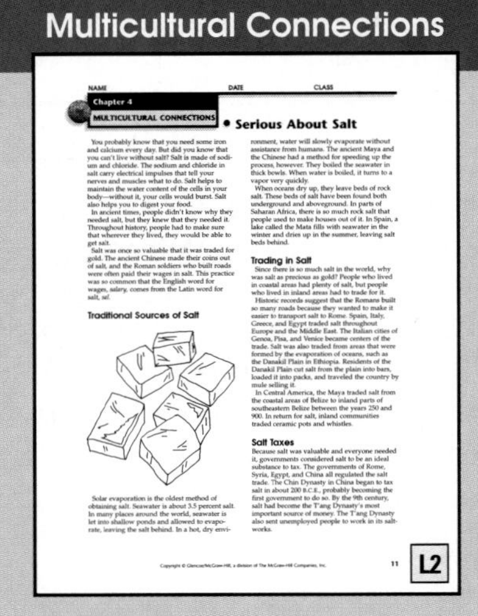

Concept Mapping

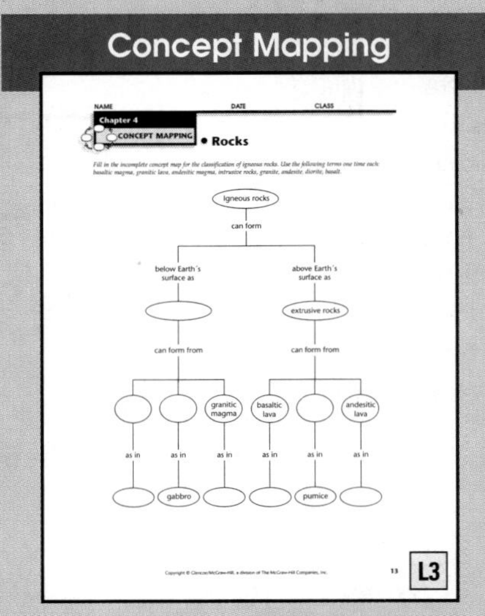

Chapter 4

Rocks

CHAPTER OVERVIEW

Section 4-1 Rocks and the processes they undergo are described in this section.

Section 4-2 This section explains how igneous rocks form and contrasts intrusive igneous rocks with extrusive igneous rocks.

Section 4-3 This section explains how metamorphic rocks form and how they are classified.

Section 4-4 How sedimentary rocks form is the emphasis of this section. The processes of compaction and cementation are described.

Section 4-5 **Science and Society** This section introduces students to a technological improvement on the handling of waste coal.

Chapter Vocabulary

rock	foliated
rock cycle	nonfoliated
igneous rock	sedimentary rock
lava	sediment
intrusive	compaction
extrusive	cementation
basaltic	waste coal
granitic	cogeneration
metamorphic rock	

Theme Connection

Stability and Change/Systems and Interactions The theme of stability and change is presented as students learn that rocks undergo changes through a process known as the rock cycle. The theme of systems and interactions is presented as students learn that the interaction of processes causes the changes in rocks.

Previewing the Chapter

Section 4-1 The Rock Cycle
- ► What is a rock?
- ► The Rock Cycle

Section 4-2 Igneous Rocks
- ► Origin of Igneous Rocks
- ► Classification of Igneous Rocks

Section 4-3 Metamorphic Rocks
- ► Origin of Metamorphic Rocks
- ► Classification of Metamorphic Rocks

Section 4-4 Sedimentary Rocks
- ► Origin of Sedimentary Rocks
- ► Classification of Sedimentary Rocks
- ► Another Look at the Rock Cycle

Section 4-5 Science and Society: Technology: Burning Waste Coal

84

Look for the following logo for strategies that emphasize different learning modalities. LS

Kinesthetic	Science & Art, p. 89; Reteach, p. 93; MiniLAB, p. 102
Visual-Spatial	Explore, p. 85; Visual Learning, pp. 86, 91, 92, 97, 98, 103, 105, 106, 108; Science & Art, p. 89; Demonstration, pp. 98, 105; MiniLAB, p. 99; Activity, p. 103
Interpersonal	MiniLAB, p. 87; Activities 4-1, pp. 94-95; 4-2, p. 110
Logical-Mathematical	Integrating the Sciences, p. 98
Linguistic	Science & Art, p. 89; Across the Curriculum, pp. 91, 93; Science Journal, pp. 92, 103, 105

Chapter 4

Rocks

This boulder stands like a sentinel in the desert sun of Arizona. Though it looks large and imposing, it is made of tiny particles of sand and other materials tightly pressed together. Other rocks are formed from molten lava ejected from volcanoes or from the remains of once-living plants and animals. If you examine rocks close up, you can sometimes tell what they are made of.

EXPLORE ACTIVITY

Determine what rocks are made from.

Rocks are all around you. You may have collected samples of rock or tried skipping a stone across a lake. You probably have noticed that not all of them look the same. Can you describe what rocks are made of?

1. Collect three or four different fragments of rocks from around your home.
2. Draw a picture of the details in each rock.
3. Look for different types of material within the same rock; review the term mixture from Chapter 2.

Observe: What do you notice about each rock? Are your rocks mixtures? If so, what are they mixtures of? Write your observations in your Science Journal.

Previewing Science Skills

- In the **Skill Builders**, you will **map concepts, interpret scientific illustrations, sequence events,** and **interpret data.**
- In the **Activities**, you will **classify, analyze,** and **draw conclusions.**
- In the **MiniLABs**, you will **classify, observe,** and **infer.**

Assessment Planner

Portfolio
Refer to page 111 for suggested items that students might select for their portfolios.

Performance Assessment
See page 111 for additional Performance Assessment options.
Skill Builders, pp. 88, 96, 100, 107
MiniLABs, pp. 87, 99, 102
Activities 4-1, pp. 94-95; 4-2, p. 110

Content Assessment
Section Wrap-ups, pp. 88, 96, 100, 107, 109
Chapter Review, pp. 111-113
Mini Quizzes, pp. 88, 96, 100, 107

Group Assessment
Opportunities for group assessment occur with Cooperative Learning Strategies and Flex Your Brain Activities.

EXPLORE ACTIVITY

Purpose

LS **Visual-Spatial** Use the Explore Activity to introduce students to the compositions of different rocks. L1 LEP COOP LEARN

Preparation

Have each student bring in several rocks from home.

Materials

one magnifying glass for each group of students, rocks brought in by students

Teaching Strategies

- Have students work in groups of four. Individual student roles should include a reader, a materials handler, a recorder, and a reporter.
- Have students identify different minerals in each rock.
- Allow students time to discuss the size and shape of each rock.
- Call on the reporters of each group to answer the in-text questions.

Observe

Answers will vary. Yes, rocks are classified as mixtures. They are mixtures of minerals, mineraloids, glass, or organic matter.

Assessment

Performance Have groups exchange rocks with other groups and redo the Explore Activity. Ask each group to discuss any differences they note in the rocks of other groups. Use the Performance Task Assessment List for Making Observations and Inferences in **PASC,** p. 17. P

Section 4•1

Prepare

Section Background

There is no set path that a rock undergoes to become another rock. A rock from any of the three groups of rocks can be changed into a rock belonging to another group, or it can be changed into a rock belonging to its original group.

Preplanning

To prepare for the MiniLAB, obtain small rock samples that can be crushed into a powder. Also obtain some white glue and waxed paper.

1 Motivate

Bellringer

Before presenting the lesson, display **Section Focus Transparency 13** on the overhead projector. Assign the accompanying **Focus Activity** worksheet. L1 LEP

Visual Learning

Figure 4-2 How are rocks different from minerals? *Rocks are mixtures of minerals, mineraloids, glass, or organic matter. Minerals are inorganic elements or compounds with atoms arranged in a definite structure.* LEP LS

GLENCOE TECHNOLOGY

CD-ROM

Earth Science CD-ROM

Have students perform the interactive exploration for Chapter 4 to reinforce important chapter concepts and thinking processes.

4•1 The Rock Cycle

Science Words

rock
rock cycle

Objectives

- Differentiate between a rock and a mineral.
- Describe the rock cycle and the changes that a rock may undergo.

What is a rock?

Imagine that you're on your way home from a friend's house when you notice an unusual rock in a driveway. You pick it up, wondering why it looks different from most of the other rocks there. The other rocks are flat and dull, but this one is rounded and has shiny crystals in it. You decide to stick the interesting rock in your pocket and ask your Earth science teacher about it tomorrow.

What exactly should you ask your teacher? You might begin by asking, "What is a rock?" and "Why are rocks so different from one another?"

Figure 4-1

Granite is a mixture of feldspar (A), quartz (B), mica (C), hornblende (D), and other minerals.

Program Resources

Reproducible Masters

Study Guide, p. 17 L1
Reinforcement, p. 17 L1
Enrichment, p. 17 L3
Cross-Curricular Integration, p. 8
Activity Worksheets, pp. 5, 27 L1
Critical Thinking/Problem Solving, p. 10

Transparencies

Section Focus Transparency 13 L1
Teaching Transparency 7
Science Integration Transparency 4

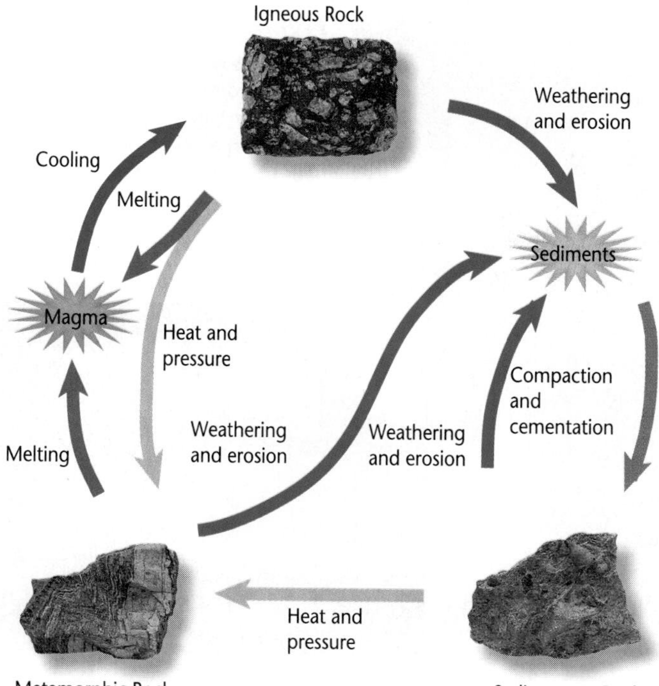

Figure 4-2
This model of the rock cycle shows how rocks are constantly changed from one form to another. *How are rocks different from minerals?*

Forming Rocks

A **rock** is a mixture of minerals, mineraloids, glass, or organic matter. You learned about the mineral quartz in the last chapter. You know that it's a common mineral found in rocks. Other common rock-forming minerals include feldspar, hornblende, and mica. **Figure 4-1** shows all these minerals mixed together to form the rock granite.

But how do these minerals mix together? And once they've formed a rock, do they stay in that same rock forever? Let's find out.

The Rock Cycle

Figure 4-2 is a model of the **rock cycle,** showing the three types of rock and how they are formed. You'll learn more about sedimentary, igneous, and metamorphic rocks later in this chapter. For now, look at the rock cycle and notice that rocks are changed by processes such as weathering, erosion, compaction, cementation, melting, and cooling. For example, a sedimentary rock can be changed by heat and pressure to form a metamorphic rock. The metamorphic rock can then melt and later cool to form an igneous rock. The igneous rock may then weather and erode and the fragments from it might form another sedimentary rock. Heat and pressure can also change igneous rocks into metamorphic rocks.

MiniLAB

How do rocks change during the rock cycle?

Procedure

1. Have your teacher crush several different samples of rock into a fine powder.
2. Place the powder into a flat pan.
3. Mix a solution of water and white glue.
4. Pour the solution into the pan and mix thoroughly with the powder.
5. Place a layer of waxed paper over the mixture, then place a heavy weight on top of the waxed paper.

Analysis

1. After several days, remove the weight and examine the mixture.
2. How is the process used to make the mixture similar to one portion of the rock cycle?
3. Describe other processes that might be used to model other parts of the rock cycle.

Inclusion Strategies

Physically Challenged Place students into groups of three. Appoint one student to be the handler in each group, one to be the recorder, and one to be the reporter. The reporter should be any student who is considered physically challenged. This student can be responsible for reporting the data observed and recorded by his or her group. Place large samples of basalt, granite, gneiss, slate, shale, sandstone, and limestone on a table in front of the class. Ask student groups to study the samples and to describe them. Have students determine whether the samples they brought from home for the Explore Activity are similar to the rocks on display.

2 Teach

MiniLAB

Purpose

LS **Interpersonal** Students will observe the formation of sedimentary rocks. L1 COOP LEARN

Materials

small rock samples for crushing into powder, white glue, waxed paper, heavy weights

Analysis

1. Small pieces of rock are mixed through the glue solution. Solid pieces of rock are suspended in the glue solution. The mixture is a colloid.
2. The rocks are crushed into sediment that is held together by the glue solution and compacted by the heavy weight, just as sediment in nature is glued together by groundwater solutions and compacted by overlying sediment.
3. Answers will vary.

Assessment

Oral As students perform the activity and answer Analysis question 3, ask them to relate each procedure to steps in the rock cycle. Use the Performance Task Assessment List for Model in **PASC**, p. 51. P

Activity Worksheets, pp. 5, 27

CONNECT TO CHEMISTRY

See page 88.

Answer As thermal energy increases, atoms and molecules can move around and past each other, changing the material to a liquid state.

3 Assess

Check for Understanding

FLEX Your Brain

Use the Flex Your Brain activity to have students explore the ROCK CYCLE.

Activity Worksheets, p. 5

Reteach

Demonstrate that rocks are mixtures by showing a sample of granite.

Extension

For students who have mastered this section, use the **Reinforcement** and **Enrichment** masters.

4 Close

•MINI•QUIZ•

1. **A mixture of one or more minerals, mineraloids, glass, or organic matter is a(n) _____ .** *rock*
2. **Granite is a mixture of _____ .** *quartz, feldspar, hornblende, and mica*

Section Wrap-up

Review

1. minerals, mineraloids, glass, or organic matter
2. how rocks change to become other rocks
3. Think Critically Magma is melted material. Sediments are eroded rock fragments. Sedimentary rock is formed from rock fragments.

Science Journal

As magma cools, thermal energy is lost. The atoms begin arranging into repeating patterns.

Figure 4-3

Geologists working in the field gather information about the rock cycle. Later, they analyze the data in a laboratory, perhaps using a computer.

CONNECT TO

CHEMISTRY

As heat increases inside Earth, materials contained in rocks begin to melt. ***Decide*** what is happening to the atoms and molecules to cause this change of state.

In Chapters 5 and 6, you will explore weathering, erosion, deposition, and other processes involved in the rock cycle. The rock cycle shows how all of these processes interact to form and change the rocks around you. Like the geologists in **Figure 4-3,** let's now investigate how igneous, metamorphic, and sedimentary rocks fit into the rock cycle.

Section Wrap-up

Review

1. What materials mix together to form a rock?
2. What is the rock cycle?
3. Think Critically: Look at the model of the rock cycle. How would you define *magma* based on **Figure 4-2?** How would you define *sediments* and *sedimentary rock?*

Skill Builder

Concept Mapping

Make a concept map that explains how igneous rocks can become sedimentary, then metamorphic, and finally, other igneous rocks. If you need help, refer to Concept Mapping in the **Skill Handbook.**

Science Journal

As magma cools, it solidifies. In your Science Journal, write a description that explains what happens to the atoms and molecules to cause this change of state.

Skill Builder

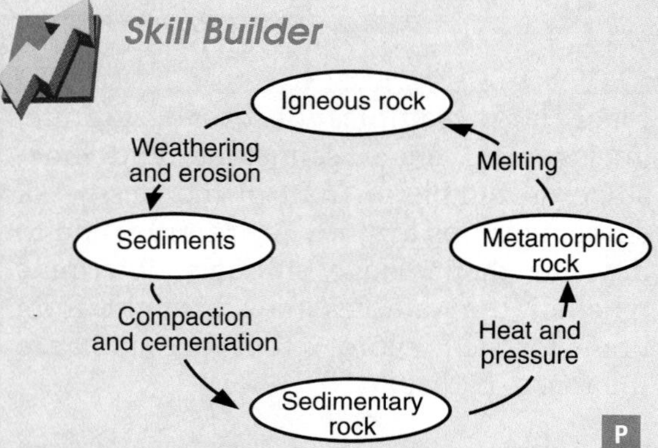

Assessment

Content Use the Skill Builder to assess students' abilities to construct concept maps and their understanding of the rock cycle. Use the Performance Task Assessment List for Concept Map in **PASC,** p. 89. P

Science & ART

Set in Stone

Since humans first appeared on Earth, they have relied on rocks in many ways. Stone Age people used rocks as tools and weapons. Medieval sculptors carved intricate designs into the limestone and sandstone façades of numerous buildings. Today, masons engrave names, dates, and spiritual sayings onto granite cemetery markers. Read on to learn about a unique way in which glacial rocks were once used by the Inuit of the northern Hudson Bay area.

Cairns

If you have ever been hiking in the wilderness, you may have stumbled upon small piles of rocks left by previous hikers. These rock piles are known as cairns. Cairns are often erected to serve as landmarks. They can aid even the most experienced hikers in finding their way, especially in landscapes with few natural landmarks.

Inukshuit

Now, imagine yourself hiking through glaciated lands of the Arctic—without a compass. Surrounded by lakes, snow, and unchanging horizons, how could you navigate? You might rely on cairns erected thousands of years ago by various Inuit groups. These cairns are called inukshuit (singular, inukshuk), which means "something acting in the capacity of man."

An inukshuk is a humanlike stone figure ranging from about one to four meters in height. The figures were used to aid travelers crossing the frozen tundra. For instance, the inukshuk shown on this page alerted travelers that there was only one path leading into and out of the valley in which the cairn stands.

Stone Scarecrows

Probably one of the most important uses of these stone figures was in the hunt for caribou, which provided food and fur for the Inuit. Hunters would mimic the sounds of wolves to frighten the caribou, setting the herd in motion between the long lines of inukshuit. Thinking the stone sentinels were actually people, the caribou would stay between the cairns. Hunters would hide among the inukshuit to ensure that the herd continued to move forward. Once the animals reached the top of a hill or the end of a valley, other hunters used bows and arrows to kill their prey.

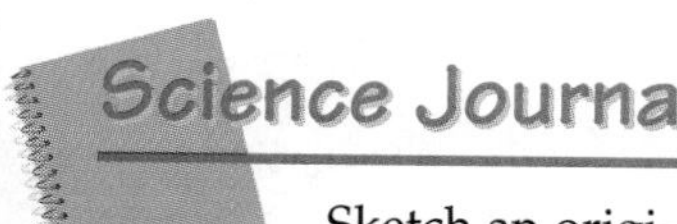

Science Journal

Sketch an original inukshuk that might be used by a modern traveler navigating between two known points in your area—for example, between your school and a nearby building. Have one or two other students figure out the symbolism in your drawing.

Science & Art

Sources

- *People of the Deer,* by Farley Mowat, Bantam Books, Inc., New York.
- "Sentinels of Stone," by Fred Bruemmer, *National History Magazine,* Jan. 1995, pp. 56-62.

Background

- Inuit presently inhabit the northeastern tip of Siberia, the coastal regions of Alaska, the islands in the Bering Sea, northern Canada and its many islands, and the eastern and western coastal areas of Greenland.
- Glaciated landscapes like those of the Arctic are difficult to navigate without instrumentation due to the lack of discernible landmarks. Inukshuit are still used today; in fact, most Inuit are familiar with the cairns in their territories and use them to navigate the sheer-cliffed headlands and mazes of islands in the glacial terrain.
- The writings of Farley Mowat are thought to have brought to light the plight of the Inuit. In fact, many people think that the author's work was the basis for initiating much of the legislation aimed at protecting and preserving the Inuit cultures.

Teaching Strategies

LS **Visual-Spatial** Before students read this feature, draw some common street signs—yield, merge, lane ends, slippery when wet, and so on—on large index cards. Flash each card and ask students to identify the sign and explain what each means. Tie this activity into the use of inukshuit as travelers' aids.

LS **Kinesthetic** Have students use small pebbles and glue to construct three-dimensional miniature models of their inukshuit. Have each student write a brief description of his or her sculpture and display this next to the model.

LS **Linguistic** Read aloud the first few pages of the chapter "Stone Men and Dead Men" from Mowat's book, *People of the Deer.* Discuss the significance of the inukshuit (Inukok) from the writer's point of view.

Section 4•2

Prepare

Section Background

- The size and arrangement of mineral grains determine igneous rock textures. Rocks with phaneritic textures are coarse-grained, and individual grains can be seen with the unaided eye. Rocks with aphanitic textures are fine-grained, and individual minerals are not visible with the unaided eye. Rocks with porphyritic textures contain large minerals surrounded by smaller minerals. In rocks with glassy textures, no mineral crystals are visible.
- As magma cools, different minerals will crystallize at different temperatures. This relationship is known as Bowen's reaction series.

Preplanning

To prepare for Activity 4-1, obtain small igneous rock samples and hand lenses. Samples should be boxed and labeled.

1 Motivate

Bellringer

Before presenting the lesson, display **Section Focus Transparency 14** on the overhead projector. Assign the accompanying **Focus Activity** worksheet. L1 LEP

Brainstorming

Have students explain why igneous rocks are considered the parents of all rocks. Students should conclude that igneous rocks were the first to form as Earth cooled, billions of years ago.

4•2 Igneous Rocks

Science Words

igneous rock
lava
intrusive
extrusive
basaltic
granitic

Objectives

- Recognize magma and lava as the materials that cool to form igneous rocks.
- Contrast the formation of intrusive and extrusive igneous rocks.
- Contrast granitic and basaltic igneous rocks.

Origin of Igneous Rocks

In June of 1991, Mount Pinatubo in the Philippines erupted. Perhaps you've heard of other recent volcanic eruptions. When most volcanoes erupt, they eject a thick, gooey flow of molten material. This material is similar to fudge candy before it has cooled. You know that if you allow the fudge to cool, it

Figure 4-4

Magma trapped below Earth's surface is insulated by the rocks surrounding it. This holds in the heat and causes the magma to cool slowly. The atoms have time to arrange into large crystals called mineral grains.

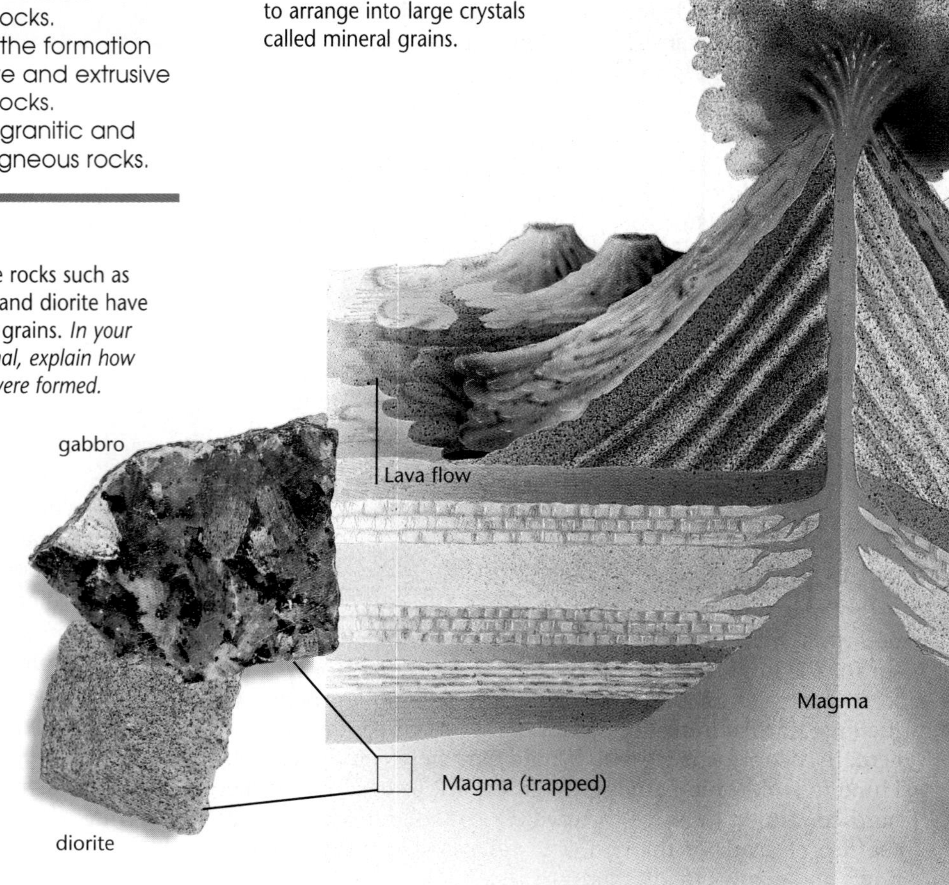

A Intrusive rocks such as gabbro and diorite have large crystal grains. *In your Science Journal, explain how these rocks were formed.*

Program Resources

Reproducible Masters

Study Guide, p. 18 L1
Reinforcement, p. 18 L1
Enrichment, p. 18 L3
Activity Worksheets, pp. 5, 23-24 L1
Lab Manual 14
Concept Mapping, p. 13

Transparencies

Section Focus Transparency 14 L1

becomes hard and you have to cut it with a knife. When molten material from a volcano or from deep inside Earth cools, it forms **igneous rocks** such as the ones in **Figure 4-4.** But why do volcanoes erupt, and where does the molten material come from?

Magma

Temperatures reach about 1400°C at depths between 60 to 200 km below Earth's surface. The rocks at this depth are under great pressure from overlying rocks. Radioactive elements in the rocks generate thermal energy, heating the rocks. In certain locations on Earth, the temperature and pressure are just right to melt the rocks and form magma.

The magma is less dense than the surrounding solid rock, so it is forced upward toward Earth's surface. Magma that eventually reaches Earth's surface flows from volcanoes as **lava.**

CONNECT TO

LIFE SCIENCE

The material ejected by an erupting volcano affects living things. ***Research*** and ***discuss*** how the lives of the people of the Philippines changed by the eruption of Mt. Pinatubo.

B Extrusive rocks such as rhyolite and obsidian form from fast-cooling lava. Magma is forced upward toward Earth's surface, where it cools to form extrusive igneous rocks.

2 Teach

Visual Learning

Figure 4-4A In your Science Journal, explain how these rocks were formed. *They were formed by magma trapped below Earth's surface. Insulated by the rocks surrounding it, the magma cooled slowly.* LEP LS

CONNECT TO

LIFE SCIENCE

Answer Accept all reasonable responses. Answers may include a reference to layers of ash from the volcano and its effects on the health of the people and the economy of the country.

GLENCOE TECHNOLOGY

Videodisc

Glencoe Earth Science Interactive Videodisc

Side 1, Lesson 1

Igneous Processes

2252-2483

2485-2793

Use **Concept Mapping,** p. 13, as you teach this lesson.

Across the Curriculum

Language Arts Have students use dictionaries to compare the origins of the words *intrusive* and *extrusive* with the origins of *interior, inside, exterior,* and *exit.* L1 LS

Integrating the Sciences

Chemistry Tell students that pumice floats on water because of its low density, which is caused by gases that were trapped in the lava as it cooled. Tell them that scoria also has this type of texture, but scoria does not float. Ask students to explain why this is true. *Scoria forms from basaltic lava, which contains heavier atoms than those of the lava from which pumice forms.*

Teacher F.Y.I.

Some igneous rocks are formed when particles ejected by volcanic eruptions become consolidated. Rocks with this type of texture are called pyroclastic rocks. Volcanic tuff is an igneous rock with pyroclastic texture.

Inquiry Questions

- **Why does lava cool more quickly than magma?** *The lava is exposed to cooler temperatures than the magma is.*
- **Why are extrusive igneous rocks fine-grained?** *The rapid cooling of the lava does not allow time for atoms to form large mineral grains.*
- **Igneous rocks such as andesite and diorite contain minerals found in both basaltic and granitic rocks. What does this tell you about the melted material from which the andesite and diorite formed?** *The composition of the melted material lies between the basaltic end and the granitic end of the spectrum.*

Science Journal

LS Linguistic Students' mineral lists should include quartz, orthoclase feldspar, and muscovite for granitic rocks; hornblende, augite, and plagioclase feldspar for andesitic rocks; and plagioclase feldspar, augite, and olivine for basaltic rocks.

Visual Learning

Figure 4-5 Did the lava that formed these rocks cool quickly or slowly? Explain your answer. *You can tell that the lava cooled quickly because no visible mineral grains formed. The atoms did not have time to arrange into large crystals.* LEP LS

Figure 4-5
Pumice (A), obsidian (B), and scoria (C) are actually glass, but are classified as extrusive igneous rocks. *Did the lava that formed these rocks cool quickly or slowly? Explain your answer.*

Intrusive Rocks

Magma is made up of atoms of melted minerals. When it cools, the atoms rearrange themselves into new crystals called mineral grains. Rocks form as these mineral grains grow together. Rocks that form below Earth's surface are **intrusive** igneous rocks. Generally, intrusive igneous rocks have large mineral grains. Intrusive rocks are found at Earth's surface when the kilometers of rock and soil that once covered them have been removed, or when forces in Earth have pushed them up. You will be investigating these forces in later chapters.

Science Journal

In your Science Journal, make a list of minerals you would expect to find in granitic, andesitic, and basaltic rocks.

Extrusive Rocks

Extrusive igneous rocks are formed when lava cools on Earth's surface. When lava flows on Earth's surface, it is exposed to air and moisture. Lava cools quickly under these conditions. The quick rate of cooling keeps large mineral grains from growing. The atoms don't have time to arrange into large crystals. Extrusive igneous rocks have a fine-grained texture.

Figure 4-5 shows pumice, obsidian, and scoria. These objects cooled so quickly that no visible mineral grains formed. Most of the atoms in these objects are not arranged into neat crystal patterns. Obsidian, scoria, and pumice are actually glass but are classified as extrusive igneous rocks.

In the case of pumice and scoria, air and other gases become trapped in the gooey molten material as it cools. Many of these gases eventually escape, but holes are left behind where the rock formed around the pockets of gas.

Integrating the Sciences

Chemistry Show students a rock with a porphyritic texture. Such rocks have a groundmass of relatively small crystals in which large crystals are embedded. Ask them to hypothesize how such a rock might form. *Since minerals within a body of magma don't all crystallize at the same time (or temperature), some mineral crystals become fairly large before others even begin to form. If the magma is suddenly erupted to the surface, where it will cool rapidly, other small crystals will solidify. The result is a rock of porphyritic texture.*

Classification of Igneous Rocks

You've learned that igneous rocks are called intrusive or extrusive depending on where they formed. A way to further classify these rocks is by magma type. As shown in **Table 4-1,** an igneous rock can form from basaltic, granitic, or andesitic magma.

INTEGRATION Chemistry

Table 4-1

Common Igneous Rocks

Type of Magma or Lava	Intrusive	Extrusive
Basaltic	Gabbro	Basalt
		Scoria
Andesitic	Diorite	Andesite
Granitic	Granite	Rhyolite
		Pumice
		Obsidian

Basaltic Rocks

Basaltic igneous rocks are dense, heavy, dark-colored rocks that form from basaltic magma. Basaltic magma is rich in iron and magnesium. Basaltic lava flows from the volcanoes in Hawaii as shown in **Figure 4-6.** How does this explain the black beach sand common in Hawaii?

Granitic and Andesitic Rocks

Granitic igneous rocks are light-colored rocks of a lower density than basaltic rocks. Granitic magma is thick and stiff and contains a lot of silicon and oxygen. Granitic magma can build up a great deal of pressure, which is released during violent volcanic eruptions.

Andesitic rocks have mineral compositions between those of granitic and basaltic rocks. Many volcanoes in the Pacific Ocean are andesitic.

Figure 4-6

Basalt is the most common extrusive rock. Sediments from weathered and eroded basalt form the black-sand beaches of the Hawaiian Islands.

INTEGRATION Chemistry

The composition of magma determines the type of minerals that can form and determines the temperature at which the magma flows. Basaltic magma high in iron and magnesium tends to remain solid at much higher temperatures than granitic, silica-rich magma does. The higher temperatures of basaltic magma enable it to flow very quickly.

Use Lab 14 in the **Lab Manual** as you teach this lesson.

3 Assess

Check for Understanding

FLEX Your Brain

Use the Flex Your Brain activity to have students explore IGNEOUS ROCKS.

Activity Worksheets, p. 5

Reteach

LS **Kinesthetic** Have students compare the masses of similar-sized samples of granitic and basaltic rocks. While one student closes his or her eyes, have the second student place the appropriate rocks in the first student's hands. Encourage students to hypothesize which rocks are basaltic and which are granitic based on the heft of the rock. Ask students to explain why one rock sample feels so much heavier than the other. COOP LEARN LEP

Extension

For students who have mastered this section, use the **Reinforcement** and **Enrichment** masters.

Across the Curriculum

Language Arts The word *igneous* comes from the Latin word *ignis,* which means "fire." Ask students to find out where the words *metamorphic* and *sedimentary* come from. Ask them to use a dictionary that shows the roots of these words. If necessary, review the meaning of the term *root word.* L1 LS

Activity 4-1

PREPARATION

Purpose

LS **Interpersonal** Design and carry out an investigation to classify igneous rocks by their characteristics. L1 COOP LEARN

Process Skills

communicating, making and using tables, forming operational definitions, forming a hypothesis, observing and inferring, separating and controlling variables, classifying, and interpreting data

Time

one class period to plan and begin the experiment; one-half class period to complete the experiment and summarize results

Materials

igneous rock samples (9), hand lens, **Table 4-1**

Possible Hypotheses

Igneous rocks can be classified by several of their characteristics. They can be classified by general color (light or dark) based on their composition. They can also be classified by their cooling rate (large visible crystals—slow cooling rate; small crystals—fast cooling rate).

Activity Worksheets, pp. 5, 23-24

PLAN THE EXPERIMENT

Possible Procedures

1. Separate rock samples into different-colored piles.
2. Classify according to color.
3. Separate rock samples into piles based on individual crystal size.
4. Classify rock samples based on the size of individual crystals.

Activity 4-1

Design Your Own Experiment
Igneous Rocks

One way that rocks can form is from melted rock material or magma. Some rocks formed in this way cool quickly from lava at or near Earth's surface. Others cool slowly from magma deep inside Earth. Can igneous rocks be classified and studied based on how they cool? Is the color of the rocks associated with mineral content, and can this property also be used to help classify igneous rocks?

PREPARATION

Problem

How can we classify igneous rocks?

Form a Hypothesis

Based on observations made of rocks supplied with this exercise, state a hypothesis about how their characteristics can be used to classify them.

Objectives

- Observe differences in rocks that have formed quickly compared with those that have formed slowly. Also, observe any differences in the rocks' color.
- Design an experiment that tests whether a variable such as crystal size is observable and whether it indicates how the rock may have formed.

Possible Materials

- igneous rock samples (9)
- hand lens
- Table 4-1

Inclusion Strategies

Gifted Upon completion of this activity, have students relate each of the characteristics noted in the hypothesis to Bowen's reaction series. Ask students to be specific about why certain characteristics are explained by Bowen's reaction series, especially as it relates to partial crystallization of different minerals. Have them determine which minerals crystallize from magma first and what the compositions of these minerals are. Ask them to relate rock composition to where the rocks are likely to have cooled, deep underground or at Earth's surface. L3

PLAN THE EXPERIMENT

1. As a group, agree upon and write your hypothesis statement.
2. As a group, list the steps that you need to take to test your hypothesis. Be specific, describing exactly what you will do at each step.
3. Make a list of the materials that you will need to complete your experiment.
4. Design a data table with two columns in your Science Journal. The first column should be labeled *Color,* the second column *Texture.*

Check the Plan

1. Read over your entire experiment to make sure that all steps are in a logical order.
2. Identify any constants and the variables of the experiment.
3. Have you allowed for a control? How will the control be treated?
4. Do you have to run any tests more than once?
5. Will the data be summarized in a graph?
6. *Make sure your teacher approves your plan and that you have included any changes suggested in the plan.*

DO THE EXPERIMENT

1. Carry out the experiment as planned.
2. While the experiment is going on, write down any observations that you make and complete the data table in your Science Journal.

Analyze and Apply

1. Dark-colored igneous rocks are classified as basaltic, light-colored ones as granitic, and intermediate-colored ones as andesitic. Based on this, how would your rocks be classified?
2. Would you **classify** obsidian as basaltic or granitic? Look closely at one edge before you make up your mind.
3. **Decide** what minerals might cause the varying colors found in your rocks.
4. Igneous rocks that form slowly have large crystals. Those that form quickly have small crystals. Did yours form quickly or slowly?

Go Further

What process could form a rock that has large crystals surrounded by small crystals? Place some pumice and some scoria in two separate containers of water. Explain the cause of what you observe.

4. Numbers 1, 2, 5, 6, 7, and 9 probably formed quickly at or near Earth's surface. Numbers 3, 4, and 8 probably formed slowly, deep under Earth's surface.

Go Further

The rock began forming deep underground and was then ejected onto Earth's surface where its crystals finished forming. This type of rock is a porphyry. The pumice floats because of trapped gases. Although scoria also has trapped gases, its iron and magnesium content causes it to sink.

Assessment

Performance Give students five different samples of igneous rocks that they have not previously seen. Ask students to classify the unknown rocks, using the procedures from this activity. Use the Performance Task Assessment List for Making Observations and Inferences in **PASC**, p. 17. P

Teaching Strategies

Tying to Previous Knowledge Recall that intrusive igneous rocks have large crystals and extrusive igneous rocks have very small crystals or no crystals at all. Also recall that basaltic igneous rocks tend to be dark in color and granitic igneous rocks tend to be light in color.

Troubleshooting Rock samples should be identified by a number taped onto the rock or box. Label them as follows: 1—obsidian; 2—basalt; 3—granite; 4—diorite; 5—pumice; 6—rhyolite; 7—andesite; 8—gabbro; 9—scoria. However, do not make rock names available to students immediately.

- The texture of samples 5 and 9 appears to be permeable and filled with small pores. This type of texture is *vesicular.*

DO THE EXPERIMENT

Expected Outcome

Students should realize that igneous rocks can be and are classified by color and crystal size, which correspond to composition and cooling rate.

Analyze and Apply

1. Students should classify numbers 2, 8, and 9 as basaltic; 1, 3, 5, and 6 as granitic; and 4 and 7 as andesitic.
2. Students may first classify obsidian as basaltic. Upon close inspection, students should notice the light gray color at the edges of the sample.
3. Elements in quartz, feldspar, and muscovite probably cause the light color. Dark colors are probably caused by iron and magnesium in hornblende, augite, and biotite.

4 Close

•MINI•QUIZ•

Use the Mini Quiz to check students' recall of chapter content.

1. **When melted material from a volcano or deep inside Earth cools and hardens, it forms ______.** *igneous rocks*
2. **______ igneous rocks form deep inside Earth and contain large mineral grains.** *Intrusive*
3. **Light-colored igneous rocks are classified as _____.** *granitic rocks*

Section Wrap-up

Review

1. The magma or lava is rich in iron and magnesium; thus, iron- and magnesium-rich minerals form. These minerals are dark-colored and are denser than silica-rich minerals.
2. Intrusive rocks contain large mineral grains and are said to be coarse-grained. Extrusive rocks are made of small grains and thus are fine-grained.
3. **Think Critically** Granite and rhyolite are both igneous rocks composed of the same minerals. Both are classified as light-colored, granitic rocks. Granite has larger mineral grains than rhyolite because it forms deep underground.

USING MATH

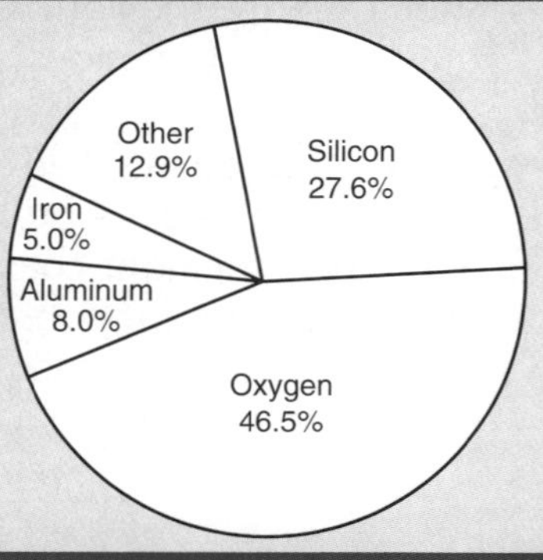

Figure 4-7
In the Phillipines, the eruption of Mt. Pinatubo caused tons of volcanic ash to settle over the land.

The classification of an igneous rock tells you a lot about its origin, formation, and composition. Basalt is an extrusive, basaltic igneous rock. This means that it formed on Earth's surface, where cooling was fast, giving the rock a fine-grained texture. Basalt has a high concentration of iron and magnesium because it formed from basaltic magma.

Igneous rocks are the most abundant type of rock on Earth. In this chapter, you have learned how igneous rocks are formed from the magma of volcanoes. In Chapter 10, you will learn more about volcanoes, and their effects on people. **Figure 4-7** shows one way erupting volcanoes impact people's lives and property.

Section Wrap-up

Review

1. Why do some types of magma and lava form igneous rocks that are dark colored and dense?
2. How do intrusive and extrusive igneous rocks differ?
3. **Think Critically:** How are granite and rhyolite similar? How are they different?

Skill Builder

Interpreting Scientific Illustrations

Suppose you are given a photograph of two igneous rocks. You are told one is an intrusive rock and one is extrusive. By looking only at the photographs, how could you know which is which? If you need help, refer to Interpreting Scientific Illustrations in the **Skill Handbook.**

USING MATH

Four elements make up more than 85% of all the rocks in the world.

Oxygen—46.5%
Silicon—27.6%
Aluminum—8.0%
Iron—5.0%

Make a circle graph of these data.

Skill Builder

Texture is used to differentiate igneous rocks. Intrusive rocks are made of relatively large mineral grains, whereas extrusive rocks are fine-grained.

Assessment

Oral Assess students' abilities to interpret scientific illustrations by questioning them about how they classified the rocks in the illustration. Use the Performance Task Assessment List for Making Observations and Inferences in **PASC,** p. 17. P

Metamorphic Rocks 4•3

Origin of Metamorphic Rocks

You wake up, go into the kitchen, and pack a lunch for school. You place a sandwich and a cream-filled cake in the bag. As you leave for school, you decide to throw in an apple. At lunchtime, you open your lunch bag and notice things have changed. Your cream-filled cake doesn't look good anymore. The apple was resting on the cake all morning. The heat in your locker and the pressure from the apple have changed the form of your lunch. Rocks like those in **Figure 4-8** can also be affected by temperature changes and pressure.

Metamorphic Rocks

Rocks that have changed due to temperature and pressure increases or that undergo changes in composition are **metamorphic rocks.** Metamorphic rocks can be formed from changes in igneous, sedimentary, or other metamorphic rocks. What occurs in Earth to change these rocks?

Science Words

metamorphic rock
foliated
nonfoliated

Objectives

- Describe conditions that cause metamorphic rocks to form.
- Classify metamorphic rocks as foliated or nonfoliated.

Figure 4-8

The mineral grains in granite (A) are flattened and aligned when pressure is applied to them. Gneiss (B) is formed. *What other conditions can cause metamorphic rocks to form?*

Section 4•3

Prepare

Section Background

Generally, the overall chemical compositions of metamorphic rocks are very similar to the compositions of the rocks from which they formed. New minerals form only when pressures and temperatures are extreme.

Preplanning

To prepare for the MiniLAB, obtain boxed sets of minerals and rocks. Common rock-forming minerals and samples from each of the three types of rocks should be included. The samples should be labeled.

1 Motivate

Bellringer

Before presenting the lesson, display **Section Focus Transparency 15** on the overhead projector. Assign the accompanying **Focus Activity** worksheet. L1 LEP

Tying to Previous Knowledge

Show students pieces of pink quartzite and pink marble. Have students test the physical properties of quartz and calcite to determine which specimen is quartzite and which is marble.

Program Resources

Reproducible Masters

Study Guide, p. 19 L1
Reinforcement, p. 19 L1
Enrichment, p. 19 L3
Activity Worksheets, pp. 5, 28 L1
Lab Manual 15

Transparencies

Section Focus Transparency 15 L1

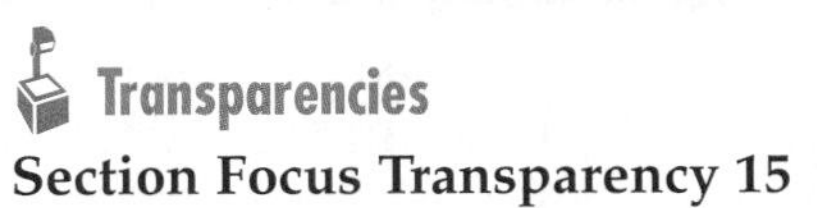

Visual Learning

Figure 4-8 What other conditions can cause metamorphic rocks to form? *Changes in temperature or changes in rock composition also cause metamorphic rocks to form.* LEP LS

2 Teach

USING TECHNOLOGY

Inform students that Granirex is available as a flexible veneer that can be heated and bent, making it a versatile building material.

Think Critically

Granirex is made from crushed granite that is glued together. The mineral grains aren't interconnected in this human-made material.

Demonstration

LS **Visual-Spatial** Use a toaster set on medium to demonstrate how metamorphic changes can be caused by heat generated from nearby magma bodies. Have a volunteer slice the toast and compare the color and texture of the outer surface of bread with the untoasted center. LEP

Visual Learning

Figure 4-9 In your Science Journal, explain why slate is useful as patio and stepping stones, and as roofing shingles. *Slate is colorful and can be broken into thin, flat plates. Water cannot penetrate slate.* LEP LS

USING TECHNOLOGY

Solid as a Rock

Rocks are used as building materials because of their durability and appearance. Large slabs of rock, however, are expensive and difficult to work with. Their weight alone requires special handling and strong support.

What if a way were found to reduce the weight, yet keep the strength of rock? A company in Italy has made a material that looks like granite, wears like granite, and in fact, is about 95 percent granite. Granirex is a human-made material made of crushed granite that's glued together. This material weighs much less than granite and ranges in thickness from less than 0.5 cm to almost 1 cm. Granirex can be used on countertops, as floors, to make furniture, and to cover walls. It comes in a variety of colors. In addition to this, Granirex costs about 50 percent less than granite.

Think Critically:

Granite is made of interlocking mineral crystals that have grown together. How does Granirex differ from this?

98 Chapter 4 Rocks

Heat and Pressure

Rocks beneath Earth's surface are under great pressure from overlying rock layers. Once the heat and pressure reach a certain point, the rocks melt and magma forms. But what happens if the heat isn't high enough or the pressure isn't the amount needed to cause melting?

In areas where melting doesn't occur, some mineral grains are flattened like the cake in your lunch bag. Sometimes, minerals exchange atoms with surrounding minerals and new or bigger minerals form.

In Section 4-1, you saw that an igneous rock can be transformed into a metamorphic rock. For example, the igneous rock granite can be changed into the metamorphic rock gneiss (NISE).

Depending upon the amount of pressure applied, one type of rock can change into several different metamorphic rocks. Shale, for example, will change into slate. As more and more pressure

GLENCOE TECHNOLOGY

Videodisc

Glencoe Earth Science Interactive Videodisc

Side 1, Lesson 1

Metamorphic Processes

5385-6351

Integrating the Sciences

Physics Obtain samples of slate and schist. Using **Figure 4-8**, have students determine where pressure was applied to change each rock. *Pressure would have been applied perpendicular to the alignment of mineral grains.* L1 LS

Community Connection

Rock Uses Ask students to canvas the area near their homes to look for instances of metamorphic rocks being used. Examples include marble in statues and slate as roof tile. L1

Figure 4-9

The different minerals in shale result in the many different colors of slate. *In your Science Journal, explain why slate is useful as patio and stepping stones, and roofing shingles.*

is applied, the slate can change into phyllite, then schist, and eventually gneiss. Schist can also form when basalt is metamorphosed.

Classification of Metamorphic Rocks

You've learned that metamorphic rocks can be formed from changes in igneous, sedimentary, or other metamorphic rocks. Heat and pressure trigger the changes. The resulting rocks can be classified according to their texture.

Foliated Rocks

When mineral grains flatten and line up in parallel bands, the metamorphic rock has a **foliated** texture. Two examples of foliated rocks are slate and gneiss. Slate forms from the sedimentary rock shale. The minerals in shale are arranged into layers when they're exposed to heat and pressure. As **Figure 4-9** shows, slate is easily separated along these foliation layers. The minerals in slate are so tightly compacted that water can't pass between them.

Gneiss, another foliated rock, forms when granite and other rocks are changed. Quartz, feldspar, mica, and other minerals in granite aren't changed much, but they are rearranged into alternating bands.

Nonfoliated Rocks

In some metamorphic rocks, no banding occurs. The mineral grains change, grow, and rearrange, but they don't form bands. This process produces a **nonfoliated** texture.

MiniLAB

How do metamorphic rocks form?

Procedure

1. From your teacher, obtain samples for four metamorphic rocks and four nonmetamorphic rocks; be sure each of the metamorphic rocks formed from one of the nonmetamorphic rocks.
2. Observe each of the rocks.
3. In your Science Journal, make a list of the characteristics of each.

Analysis

1. Compare your observations of the characteristics of the metamorphic rocks with your observations of the nonmetamorphic rocks.
2. Which of the nonmetamorphic rocks was the "parent" of each of the metamorphic rocks?

MiniLAB

Purpose

LS **Visual-Spatial** Students will determine which rocks changed to form certain samples of metamorphic rocks. L1 COOP LEARN

Materials

samples of gneiss, granite, marble, limestone, quartzite, sandstone, slate, and shale; and hand lenses

Teaching Strategies

Arrange rocks into two groups: metamorphic, which includes gneiss, marble, quartzite, and slate; and nonmetamorphic, which includes granite, limestone, sandstone, and shale.

Analysis

1. no written answer
2. One possible answer is that granite is the parent rock of gneiss; limestone of marble; sandstone of quartzite; and shale of slate.

Assessment

Performance To further assess students' understanding of metamorphic rock origins, repeat the activity with four different samples, one of which is not a parent rock. Use the Performance Task Assessment List for Making Observations and Inferences in **PASC**, p. 17. P

Activity Worksheets, pp. 5, 28

Across the Curriculum

Gemology Use the Flex Your Brain activity to have students explore THE FORMATION OF ZIRCON. Zircon is a mineral often used as a gemstone. It develops in igneous and metamorphic rocks. Gem-quality zircon is produced by heat-treating naturally occurring zircon. Colors are often produced by heat treatments. Yellow, orange, and red zircon gems are called *hyacinth.* Colorless or gray gems are called *jargoon.* Zircon is a source of zirconium. Other minerals of metamorphic origin to explore include corundum (sapphire and ruby) and tremolite (jade). L1

3 Assess

Check for Understanding

FLEX Your Brain

Use the Flex Your Brain activity to have students explore the FORMATION OF METAMORPHIC ROCKS.

Reteach

Have students sketch foliated and nonfoliated metamorphic rocks. Call on individual students to describe what their sketches show.

Extension

For students who have mastered this section, use the **Reinforcement** and **Enrichment** masters.

4 Close

•MINI•QUIZ•

Use the Mini Quiz to check students' recall of chapter content.

1. **_______ rocks are rocks that have changed due to temperature and pressure increases.** *Metamorphic*
2. **The igneous rock granite can be changed into the metamorphic rock _______.** *gneiss*

Section Wrap-up

Review

1. The temperature and pressure that cause metamorphism are lower than those needed to form igneous rocks.
2. Metamorphic rocks are classified by texture. Foliated rocks are banded; nonfoliated rocks are not.
3. **Think Critically** Marble has a shiny luster. It contains colorful minerals. It is easy to shape.

Using Computers

Student computer illustrations should resemble **Figure 4-8**.

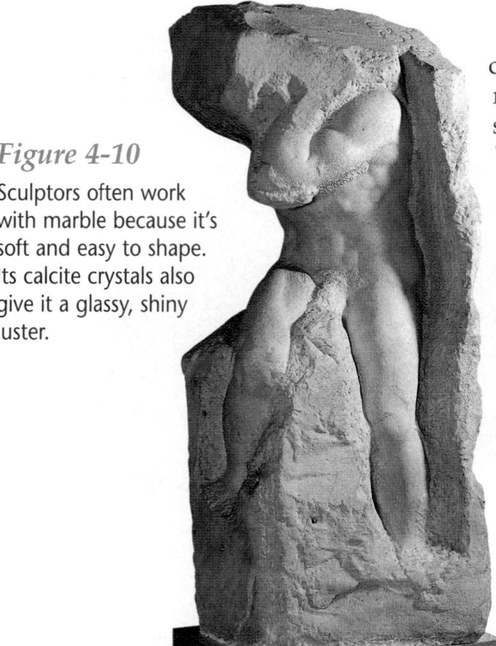

Figure 4-10

Sculptors often work with marble because it's soft and easy to shape. Its calcite crystals also give it a glassy, shiny luster.

Sandstone is a sedimentary rock that's often composed mostly of quartz minerals. When its mineral grains are changed by heat and pressure, the nonfoliated rock quartzite is formed. The only change that occurs is in the size of the mineral grains.

Another nonfoliated metamorphic rock is marble. Marble forms from the sedimentary rock limestone, which is composed of calcite. Look at **Figure 4-10.** The calcite crystals give marble the glassy, shiny luster that makes it a popular material for sculpturing. Usually, marble contains several other minerals besides calcite. For example, hornblende and serpentine give marble a greenish tone, whereas hematite makes it red.

So far, we've traveled through only a portion of the rock cycle. We still haven't observed how sedimentary rocks are formed and how igneous and metamorphic rocks evolve from them. The next section will complete our investigation of the rock cycle.

Section Wrap-up

Review

1. How is the formation of igneous rock different from that of metamorphic rock?
2. How are metamorphic rocks classified? What are the characteristics of rocks in each of these classifications?
3. **Think Critically:** Marble is used to make sculptures. What properties of marble make it useful for this purpose?

Skill Builder

Sequencing

Put the following events in a sequence that could explain how a metamorphic rock might form from an igneous rock. (HINT: Start with *igneous rock forms.*) Use each event just once. If you need help, refer to Sequencing in the **Skill Handbook.**

Events: *sedimentary rock forms, weathering occurs, heat and pressure are applied, igneous rock forms, metamorphic rock forms, erosion occurs, sediments are formed, deposition occurs*

Using Computers

Graphing With **Figure 4-8** as a model, use the graphic mode on a computer to illustrate how applied pressure causes alignment of mineral grains. Be sure to indicate from which direction pressure was applied.

Skill Builder

Igneous rock forms. Weathering occurs. Sediments are formed. Erosion occurs. Deposition occurs. Sedimentary rock forms. Heat and pressure are applied. Metamorphic rock forms.

Assessment

Content Assess students' abilities to sequence events by having them perform this Skill Builder exercise. Use the Performance Task Assessment List for Events Chain in **PASC,** p. 91. P

Sedimentary Rocks 4•4

Origin of Sedimentary Rocks

Most of the rocks below Earth's surface are igneous rocks. Igneous rocks are the most common rocks on Earth. But chances are, you've seen more sedimentary rocks than igneous rocks. Seventy-five percent of the rocks at Earth's surface are sedimentary rocks.

Science Words

sedimentary rock
sediment
compaction
cementation

Objectives

- Explain how sedimentary rocks form from sediments.
- Classify sedimentary rocks as detrital, chemical, or organic in origin.

Sedimentary Rocks

Sedimentary rocks form when sediments become pressed or cemented together or when sediments precipitate out of solution. **Sediments** are loose materials such as rock fragments, mineral grains, and bits of plant and animal remains that have been moved by wind or water. Minerals that are dissolved in water are also sediments. But where do sediments come from? If you look at the model of the rock cycle, you will see that they come from already-existing rocks that are weathered and eroded.

Weathering is the process that breaks rocks into smaller pieces. **Table 4-2** shows how these pieces are classified by size. Sediments are moved by water, wind, ice, or gravity. The movement of weathered material is called erosion.

Table 4-2

Sediment Sizes

	Clay	Silt	Sand	Gravel
Size Range	<0.004 mm	0.004-0.06	0.06-2 mm	>2 mm
Examples of rock formed from	Shale	Siltstone	Sandstone	Conglomerate

Program Resources

Reproducible Masters

Study Guide, p. 20 L1
Reinforcement, p. 20 L1
Enrichment, p. 20 L3
Activity Worksheets, pp. 5, 29 L1
Science Integration Activities, pp. 7-8
Lab Manual 16
Multicultural Connections, p. 11

Transparencies

Section Focus Transparency 16 L1
Teaching Transparency 8

Section 4•4

Prepare

Section Background

- Sediment carried by water and other agents of erosion is sorted by size. As the agent loses energy, larger pieces are deposited. Finer sediments are transported further.
- Generally, sedimentary rocks are the only rocks that contain fossils. The high temperatures and pressures involved in forming igneous and metamorphic rocks destroy any fossils present in parent rocks.

Preplanning

To prepare for the MiniLAB and the proposed demonstrations, obtain different-sized sediments, including sand, silt, clay, and rounded and angular gravel.

1 Motivate

Bellringer

Before presenting the lesson, display **Section Focus Transparency 16** on the overhead projector. Assign the accompanying **Focus Activity** worksheet. L1 LEP

Tying to Previous Knowledge

Have students recall the physical properties of quartz from Chapter 3. Lead a discussion that will help students conclude that the hardness of quartz makes it resistant to weathering. Point out that most of the sand-sized grains found in many sandstones are quartz.

2 Teach

MiniLAB

Purpose

LS **Kinesthetic** Students will determine what type of rocks most likely form from different types of sediment. L1 COOP LEARN

Materials

mixtures of different-sized and -shaped sediments such as sand grains, gravel, and silt- or clay-sized grains; tweezers or dissecting probe

Teaching Strategies

If a powerful binocular scope is available, students will be able to observe that silt-sized particles are angular.

Analysis

1. no written answer
2. Students should describe their sediments by size and angularity.
3. sandstone from sand, conglomerate from gravel, shale from silt or clay

Assessment

Content To further assess students' understanding of sedimentary rocks, have students compare their sediment piles with samples of minerals they learned about in Chapter 3. Use the Performance Task Assessment List for Carrying Out a Strategy and Collecting Data in **PASC**, p. 25. P

Activity Worksheets, pp. 5, 29

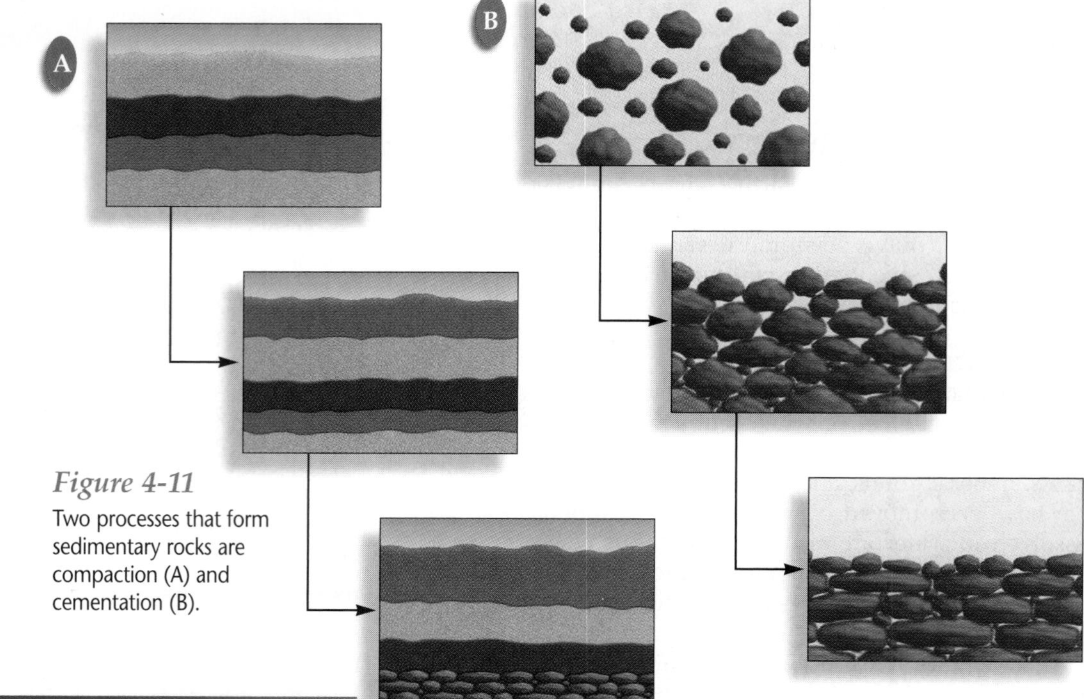

Figure 4-11
Two processes that form sedimentary rocks are compaction (A) and cementation (B).

MiniLAB

What are rocks made of?

Procedure

1. Spread different samples of sediment on a sheet of paper.
2. Use tweezers or a dissecting probe to separate the sediments.
3. Classify the sediments based on size—large, medium, or small.
4. Separate each of these three piles into two more piles based on shape—rounded or angular.

Analyze

1. Compare the different piles of sediments.
2. Describe each pile.
3. What rock is probably made from each type of sediment that you have?

Compaction

Erosion moves sediments to a new location, where they are then deposited. Here, layer upon layer of sediment builds up. Pressure from the upper layers pushes down on the lower layers. If the sediments are small, they can stick together and form solid rock. This process, shown in **Figure 4-11,** is called **compaction.**

You've compacted sediments if you've ever made mud pies. Mud is made of small, clay-sized sediments. They easily stick together under the pressure applied by your hands.

Cementation

If sediments are large, like sand and pebbles, pressure alone can't make them stick together. Large sediments have to be cemented together. **Cementation** occurs in the following way. Water soaks through soil and rock. As it moves, it dissolves minerals in the rock such as calcite, hematite, and limonite. These minerals are natural cements. The solution of water and dissolved minerals moves through open spaces between sediments. The natural cements are deposited around the pieces of sediment, and they stick together. A group of sediments cemented together in this way forms a sedimentary rock.

Inclusion Strategies

Learning Disabled Have students cut two cardboard milk cartons to a height of 10 cm each. Instruct them to punch several holes in the sides and bottom of one carton, then fill it one-third full of washed pebbles. Have them prepare a mixture of two parts white glue to one part water, then hold the perforated carton above the other carton and pour the mixture over the pebbles, collecting the liquid that runs through for reuse. Next, students should pour the mixture several more times to cover all pebbles, and let the carton stand in a warm place for 24 hours. Have students strip away the carton and describe their sedimentary "rocks."

Sedimentary Rock Layers

Sedimentary rocks often form as layers, like those shown in **Figure 4-12.** The older layers are on the bottom because they were deposited first. Then, more sediments pile up and they, too, become compacted and cemented together to form another layer of rock.

Sedimentary rock layers are a lot like the papers in your locker. The oldest papers are on the bottom, and the ones you get back today will be deposited on top of them. However, if you disturb the papers by searching through them for a pencil at the bottom of the pile, the older ones may come to the top. Sometimes, layers of rock are disturbed by forces within Earth. The layers are overturned, and the oldest are no longer on the bottom.

Classification of Sedimentary Rocks

Sedimentary rocks can be composed of just about anything. Sediments come from weathered and eroded igneous, metamorphic, and sedimentary rocks. Sediments also come from the remains of plants and animals. The composition of a sedimentary rock depends upon the composition of the rocks and living things its sediments came from.

Like igneous and metamorphic rocks, sedimentary rocks are classified by their composition and by the way they formed. Sedimentary rocks are usually classified as detrital, chemical, or organic.

Detrital Sedimentary Rocks

The word *detrital* comes from the Latin word *detritus,* which means "to wear away." Detrital sedimentary rocks are made from the broken fragments of other rocks. These sediments are compacted and cemented together.

Figure 4-12

These sedimentary rock layers formed from the compaction and cementation of many layers of sediments. *In your Science Journal, compare and contrast compaction and cementation.*

Activity

LS **Visual-Spatial** Place students into groups of three. Supply each group with containers of clay, fine sand, coarse sand, and rounded and angular gravel. Make samples of shale, siltstone, sandstone, conglomerate, and sedimentary breccia available to each group. Have students use a hand lens to match sediment type with the appropriate rock sample. One student in each group should prepare a report of the conclusions drawn by the group.

Visual Learning

Figure 4-12 In your Science Journal, compare and contrast compaction and cementation. *Compaction and cementation are the two processes that form sedimentary rocks. In compaction, pressure from upper layers of sediment causes small sediments to stick together. In cementation, natural cements are deposited around pieces of large sediment.* LEP LS

Inquiry Question

What generalization can you draw about detrital sedimentary rocks? *All detrital sedimentary rocks are composed of sediments such as plants, animals, and/or minerals and rocks that are joined by compaction and cementation.*

Science Journal

Pet Rock Place a "pet rock," Conrad Conglomerate, in front of the class. Have students examine the rock and write a brief geologic history in their Science Journals that explains how the conglomerate formed. Then have students hypothesize what might happen to Conrad if he is exposed to Earth's processes. Remind students to use their knowledge of the rock cycle. L1 LS

GLENCOE TECHNOLOGY

 **Videodisc**

Glencoe Earth Science Interactive Videodisc

Side 1, Lesson 1

Sedimentary Processes

7577-8157

Discussion

Ask students the following questions. **How do sedimentary cements form?** *Certain minerals are dissolved in water. When the solution moves through sediments, the minerals can be deposited around the sediments, causing the pieces to stick together to form rocks.* **What are sediments?** *fragments of rocks, minerals, plants, and animals*

Teacher F.Y.I.

Agents capable of transporting the gravel found in conglomerates and breccias include water, glaciers, and gravity. The rounded gravel of conglomerates form from grinding and abrasion. Therefore, the depositional environments for conglomerates include stream channels and alluvial fans. The angular fragments of breccias were not subjected to turbulent long-distance transport prior to deposition. Depositional environments of breccias include talus slopes and glacial moraines.

Inquiry Questions

- **What are the three groups of sedimentary rocks?** *detrital, chemical, and organic*
- **What is the difference between conglomerates and breccias?** *Sediments that compose conglomerates are well-rounded. If the sediments are angular, the rock is a breccia.*

CONNECT TO

CHEMISTRY

Answer Groundwater becomes acidic. The acid reacts with the calcite in limestone, dissolving it and leaving a cavern in the layers of limestone.

Use **Science Integration Activities,** pp. 7-8, as you teach this lesson.

CONNECT TO

CHEMISTRY

You may know of large caves or caverns that have formed underground in limestone deposits. ***Decide*** what causes these caverns to form.

Clastic Texture

Detrital sedimentary rocks are often referred to as clastic rocks because of their texture. The word *clastic* comes from the Greek word *klastos,* meaning "broken." Detrital sedimentary rocks have a clastic texture, but as you will see, so do some organic rocks.

Shape and Size of Sediments

Detrital rocks are named according to the shape and size of the sediments. For example, conglomerate and breccia both form from large sediments. If the sediments have been well rounded, the rock is called conglomerate. If the sediments are not rounded and have sharp angles, the rock is called breccia.

The gravel-sized sediments in both conglomerate and breccia may consist of any type of rock or mineral. Often, they are chunks of the minerals quartz or feldspar. They can also be pieces of rocks such as gneiss, granite, or limestone. The cement holding them all together is usually quartz or calcite.

Have you ever looked at the concrete in sidewalks and driveways? Look at **Figure 4-13.** Concrete is made of gravel and sand grains that have been cemented together. The structure is similar to that of naturally occurring conglomerate, but is it considered a rock?

Figure 4-14 shows the sedimentary rock sandstone. Sandstone is formed from smaller particles than conglomerates and breccias. Its sand-sized sediments are usually grains of the minerals quartz and feldspar, but can be just about any mineral. These sand grains can be compacted together if clay particles are also present, or they can be cemented.

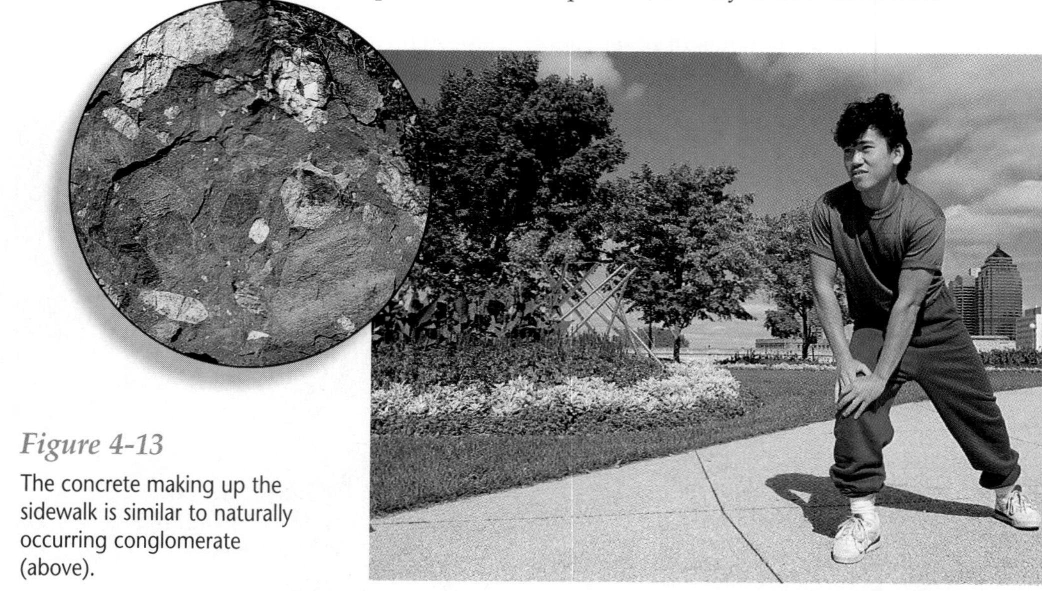

Figure 4-13

The concrete making up the sidewalk is similar to naturally occurring conglomerate (above).

Cultural Diversity

Rock Art Humans have used rocks for many things: shelter, weapons, and tools, for example. But rocks have also provided a wonderful space for artistic and linguistic expression. Artistic pictures on rock have been found dating back 30 000 years or more. Human figures are rare, but other animal figures are common. Many scenes show hunts or other aspects of daily life. The pictures are engraved or painted on walls. Many are found in chambers that have resonant qualities. Because of this, some scientists suggest that the pictures might have been part of religious rituals. Eventually, some of the symbols were used as pictographs or early writing systems. Native Americans created petroglyphs or rock drawings that can still be seen in many areas of the American Southwest.

Shale is a detrital sedimentary rock that requires no cementation to hold its particles together. Its sediments are clay-sized particles. Clay-sized sediments are compacted together by pressure from overlying layers.

Chemical Sedimentary Rocks

Chemical sedimentary rocks form when minerals are precipitated from a solution or are left behind when a solution evaporates. Think back to our discussion of minerals in Chapter 3. We found that salt is deposited in the bottom of a glass when saltwater solution evaporates. In a similar way, minerals collect when seas or lakes evaporate. The deposits of minerals that precipitate out of solution, or remain after evaporation, form rocks.

Limestone

The mineral calcite is carried in solution in ocean water. When calcite comes out of solution and its many crystals grow together, limestone is formed. Limestone may also contain other minerals and sediments, but it's at least 50 percent calcite. Limestone is usually deposited on sea or ocean floors. Large areas of the United States are underlain by limestone because oceans once covered much of the country for millions of years.

Rock Salt

When lakes and seas evaporate, they often deposit the mineral halite. Halite, mixed with a few other minerals, forms rock salt. Rock-salt deposits range in thickness from a few meters to more than 400 m. People mine these deposits because rock salt is an important resource. It's used in the manufacturing of glass, paper, soap, and dairy products. The halite in rock salt is used as table salt.

USING MATH

It took 300 million years for a layer of plant matter about 0.9 to 2.1 m thick to produce a bed of bituminous coal 0.3 m thick. At this rate, estimate the depth of plant matter that produced a bed of coal 0.6 m thick.

Figure 4-14

This rock formed from sand deposited in layers by desert winds. *Why does this sandstone look so much like desert sand dunes?*

Revealing Preconceptions

Ask students where oil and natural gas are found. Many students probably think that oil and natural gas exist underground in cavelike chambers. Point out that oil and natural gas often exist in openings among the sediments in sandstone or in limestones.

Demonstration

LS **Visual-Spatial** Have students gather around a large table or desk. Place samples of calcite, limestone, and marble on the table for students to observe. Ask a volunteer to explain how the samples are alike and how they differ. Place a few drops of dilute HCl acid on each sample. Students will observe that all samples fizz. Ask the following questions based on the demonstration. **Why do all three samples react to acid?** *Calcite reacts to HCl. Limestone and marble contain calcite.* **How do the two rocks differ?** *Limestone forms when calcite precipitates from seawater or when seashells are cemented together. The sedimentary rock limestone can be changed to marble if the limestone is subjected to increases in temperature and pressure.*

Visual Learning

Figure 4-14 Why does this sandstone look so much like desert sand dunes? *Because the rock formed from sand deposited in layers by the wind.* LEP LS

Science Journal

Describing Sedimentary Rocks Place samples of shale, sandstone, and conglomerate on a table in front of the students. Ask them to free-write about any similarities or differences they see among the rock samples. After they complete the free-writing exercise, have students write a brief formal paragraph describing how sediment sizes vary among a shale, a sandstone, and a conglomerate. L1 LS

USING MATH

Answer 1.8 to 2.4 m

Use **Teaching Transparency 8** as you teach this lesson.

Problem Solving

Solve the Problem

1. The different rocks were used to enhance the beauty of the buildings as well as for their shape and resistance to weathering.
2. The layered rocks were chosen because they can be broken into smooth, flat surfaces.

Think Critically

1. limestone, sandstone, granite, and slate
2. concrete, bricks, and tiles

Visual Learning

Figure 4-15 What is chalk made of? *Chalk is made of the shells of animals such as mussels, corals, and snails.* LEP LS

3 Assess

Check for Understanding

FLEX Your Brain

Use the Flex Your Brain activity to have students explore DETRITAL, CHEMICAL, or ORGANIC SEDIMENTARY ROCKS.

Activity Worksheets, p. 5

Reteach

Pass samples of shale, sandstone, and conglomerate around the room. Then place the rocks on a cement slab behind a safety screen. Crush the rocks with a hammer. Have the students examine the sediments. **CAUTION:** *Wear safety goggles.*

Problem Solving

The Geology of Buildings

While on a field trip in the city, Peter and his classmates observed rocks used as building materials. In the city square, Peter noticed flowers arranged in a rock terrace. The rocks were light colored and contained many small fossils.

Next, the class entered an historical district. Peter saw a building made from light-pink rocks with small crystals of quartz. Continuing down the street, he observed another building with columns. This one was constructed of a light-colored rock containing large mineral grains. Further down, he saw a wooden building with a roof made of dark, layered tiles.

Solve the Problem

1. **Why were so many different rocks used in the buildings?**
2. **What property of rocks was shown by the dark, layered tiles?**

Think Critically:

You have learned much in this chapter about the different properties of minerals and rocks.

1. Based on this knowledge, name the four different types of rock that Peter observed.
2. What rocklike materials do people make and use for buildings and other structures?

Organic Sedimentary Rocks

When rocks form from the remains of once-living things, they are organic sedimentary rocks. One of the most common organic sedimentary rocks is fossil-rich limestone. Like chemical limestone, fossil-rich limestone is made of the mineral calcite. But fossil-rich limestone also contains remains of once-living ocean animals instead of just calcite that has separated from ocean water.

Useful Sedimentary Rocks

Animals such as mussels, corals, and snails make their shells from the mineral calcite. When they die, their shells accumulate on the ocean floor. These calcite shells are compacted and cemented together and fossil-rich limestone is formed. If the shell fragments are relatively large, the rock is called coquina (koh KEE nuh). If the shells are microscopic, the rock is called chalk. Look at **Figure 4-15.** When your teachers use naturally occurring chalk to write with, they're actually crushing and smearing the calcite shells of once-living ocean animals.

Another useful sedimentary rock is coal. Coal forms when pieces of dead plants are buried under other sediments in swamps. These plant materials are chemically changed by microorganisms. The resulting sediments are compacted over millions of years to form coal. In Chapter 18, you will learn how we use coal as a source of energy.

Figure 4-15
The White Cliffs of Dover, England, are composed mostly of chalk. *What is chalk made of?*

Another Look at the Rock Cycle

You have seen that the rock cycle has no beginning and no end. Rocks are continually changing from one form to another. Sediments come from rocks and other objects that have been broken apart. Even the magma that forms igneous rocks comes from the melting of rocks that already exist.

All of the rocks that you've learned about in this chapter formed through the processes of the rock cycle. And all of the rocks around you, including those used to build houses and monuments, are part of the rock cycle. They are all changing. The rock cycle is a continuous, dynamic process.

Section Wrap-up

Review

1. Where do sediments come from?
2. List chemical sedimentary rocks that are essential to your health or used to make life more convenient. How is each used?
3. **Think Critically:** Use the rock cycle to explain how pieces of granite and slate could be found in the same piece of conglomerate.

USING MATH

Sediment sizes are presented in Table 4-2. How many times larger than clay are the largest grains of silt and sand?

Skill Builder
Interpreting Data

You are told that a detrital sedimentary rock is composed of sediments of the following sizes: gravel, sand, and silt. The larger sediments are surrounded by the smaller sediments, which are cemented together by quartz. What is the name of this rock? If you need help, refer to Interpreting Data in the **Skill Handbook.**

Extension

For students who have mastered this section, use the **Reinforcement** and **Enrichment** masters.

4 Close

• MINI • QUIZ •

Use the Mini Quiz to check students' recall of chapter content.

1. **Water that soaks into Earth's crust is called _____ .** *groundwater*
2. **_____ rocks are sedimentary rocks that form from minerals dissolved in solution.** *Chemical sedimentary*
3. **Rock salt is an example of a(n) _____ sedimentary rock.** *chemical*

Section Wrap-up

Review

1. rocks, minerals, and plant and animal remains
2. Answers may include halite—table salt; sylvite—potassium in fertilizer; and gypsum—plaster of paris and wallboards.
3. **Think Critically** If granite and slate were both exposed to weathering at Earth's surface, fragments of both rocks could have become sediments that eventually were cemented and compacted to form a conglomerate.

USING MATH

The largest grains of silt are about 15 times larger than grains of clay and the largest grains of sand are about 500 times larger than grains of clay.

Skill Builder

The observation that the rock contains sediments of greatly varying sizes indicates that it's a conglomerate. The observation that larger particles (the gravel) are held together by silica cement and compacted small sediments (sand and silt) indicates that the rock is detrital with a clastic texture.

Assessment

Content Use this Skill Builder to assess students' ability to interpret data. Show students several detrital rocks and ask them to identify them. Use the Performance Task Assessment List for Making Observations and Inferences in **PASC,** p. 17. P

Prepare

Section Background

Burning waste coal provides energy for the generation of electricity and reduces pollution in the environment.

Preplanning

To prepare for Activity 4-2, obtain boxed sets of minerals and rocks. Common rock-forming minerals and samples from each of the three types of rocks should be included.

1 Motivate

Bellringer

Before presenting the lesson, display **Section Focus Transparency 17** on the overhead projector. Assign the accompanying **Focus Activity** worksheet. L1 LEP

Tying to Previous Knowledge

Ask students to recall what they know about coal. Most students will know that coal is black, can leave a residue on the hands, and can be burned for energy.

2 Teach

Visual Learning

Figure 4-16 Explain the process by which this coal can be burned without polluting the air. *The coal is pulverized and mixed with limestone. The limestone removes more than 90 percent of the coal's sulfur dioxide content.* LEP LS

SCIENCE & SOCIETY

TECHNOLOGY:

4•5 Burning Waste Coal

Science Words

waste coal
cogeneration

Objectives

- Realize that new technologies are enabling companies of today to solve problems caused by mining operations of the past.
- Describe the process of cogeneration, and show how it is beneficial.

Cogeneration from Waste Coal

Recall from Section 4-4 that coal is an organic sedimentary rock. It has been and still is economically important to the technological advancement of the United States. It supplies fuel for electricity. Although mines of today are technologically advanced and the companies involved work within regulations to minimize the effects of mining on the environment, this has not always been so. The effects of old mining can be seen in many places in the United States. In some areas of the country, large piles of **waste coal,** like that shown in **Figure 4-16,** lie near coal mines that have been abandoned for years.

Burning Waste Coal

Waste coal is a by-product of coal mining. It is poor-quality coal that could not be used at the time it was mined and was usually piled up on one side of the mine. The piles of waste coal not only are unsightly, but because of high sulfur content, they also can generate acid runoff when rainwater flows through them.

With processes available today, this coal can be burned without creating air pollution. The coal is trucked to a burning facility where it is pulverized and mixed with pulverized limestone. The limestone removes more than 90 percent of sulfur dioxide emissions. This surpasses current government-mandated levels. Compliance with pollution-control laws is regulated by monitoring air-quality levels.

Figure 4-16
Waste coal piles can still be found in many areas of the country. *Explain the process by which this coal can be burned without polluting the air.*

Once the coal-limestone mixture has been burned, the residue ash is trucked back to its original pile. Mixing with limestone has changed the acidic waste coal to alkaline ash. It creates no acid mine drainage and works to alleviate the acidic problems caused by the pile of waste coal. The ash has a high affinity for water, and when it is hydrated, it changes to a low-grade cement. The resulting concrete mound is buried and covered by layers of topsoil. The topsoil

Program Resources

Reproducible Masters

Study Guide, p. 21 L1
Reinforcement, p. 21 L1
Enrichment, p. 21 L3
Science and Society Integration, p. 8
Activity Worksheets, pp. 5, 25-26 L1

Transparencies

Section Focus Transparency 17 L1

is seeded to establish vegetation. The lay of the land has been returned to what it was, and the mound can be used as a location for a park or playground.

Cogeneration

Some companies use waste coal to produce and export electricity. In addition to the electricity produced by burning waste coal, low-pressure steam from the process can be exported to meet community heating needs.

When power is generated in a power plant such as the one shown in **Figure 4-17,** both electrical and thermal energy are produced. The electrical power is used, but often the remaining power is lost as wasted thermal energy. In the process of **cogeneration,** both the electrical and thermal energy are used by the plant producing it.

Figure 4-17
Burning waste coal generates both thermal and electrical energy.

Section Wrap-up

Review

1. Even though the ash produced by the burning of waste coal is returned to the waste site, why is this process considered good for the environment?
2. How does the process of cogeneration benefit not only the company using it, but others in the community as well?

Explore the Technology

Although the technology involved in burning waste coal and disposing of the ash is relatively new, there already are several other possible uses for the idea. Coal seams in surface mines vary in quality. Some have a greater potential for acid mine drainage. In order to work these surface mines, the ash from burning waste coal could be used in the mine to alleviate the acidity.

SCIENCE & SOCIETY

3 Assess

Check for Understanding

FLEX Your Brain

Use the Flex Your Brain activity to have students explore COGENERATION.

Activity Worksheets, p. 5

Reteach

Burning waste coal will help prolong the time that fossil fuels can provide us with power. Ask students to describe what they think life will be like on Earth once all fossil fuel reserves are exhausted. Have them include the effects on transportation, jobs, and the economy.

Extension

For students who have mastered this section, use the **Reinforcement** and **Enrichment** masters.

4 Close

While students study **Figure 4-16**, ask them to explain why returning waste coal to the original site is good for the environment.

Section Wrap-up

Review

1. The ash is not acidic. It works to alleviate the acidic problems caused by the pile of waste coal.
2. Electricity and heat energy produced by the plant during operation is sent to other locations where it is needed. The company provides energy for the community.

Explore the Technology

By using the waste coal to alleviate the problem of acidity from overlying rock layers, larger amounts of the energy resource can be mined with minimum effect on the environment. Areas that were once totally unworkable can become useful because of this technology.

Activity 4-2

Sedimentary Rocks

Sedimentary rocks are formed by the compaction and cementation of sediment. Because sediment is found in all shapes and sizes, do you think these characteristics could be used to classify detrital sedimentary rocks? Sedimentary rocks can also be classified as chemical or organic.

Problem

How are rock characteristics used to classify rocks as detrital, chemical, or organic?

Materials

- unknown sedimentary rock samples
- marking pen
- 5 percent hydrochloric acid (HCl)
- dropper
- goggles
- hand lens
- paper towels
- water

Procedure

1. In your Science Journal, make a Data and Observations chart similar to the one shown below.
2. Determine the types of sediments in each sample. Using **Table 4-2**, classify the sediments in the detrital rocks as gravel, sand, silt, or clay.
3. Put a few drops of HCl on each rock sample. Bubbling on a rock indicates the presence of carbonate minerals.

CAUTION: *HCl is an acid and can cause burns. Wear goggles. Rinse spills with water. Wash hands afterwards.*

4. Look for fossils and describe them if any are present.
5. Determine whether each sample has a clastic or nonclastic texture.
6. Classify your samples as detrital, chemical, or organic. Identify each rock sample.

Analyze

1. Why did you test the rocks with hydrochloric acid? What minerals react with hydrochloric acid?
2. What is needed in order for sedimentary rocks to form from fragments?
3. The mineral halite forms by evaporation. Would you classify halite as a detrital, a chemical, or an organic rock?

Conclude and Apply

4. **Determine** how sedimentary rocks with a clastic texture differ from rocks with a nonclastic texture.
5. **Explain** how you can classify sedimentary rocks.

Data and Observations

Sample data

Sample	Observations	Minerals or Fossils Present	Sediment Size	Detrital, Chemical, or Organic	Rock Name
A	fizzes in HCl	calcite, fossils	usually silt	organic	limestone
B		quartz, feldspar, hematite	sand	detrital	sandstone
C		kaolinite, feldspar	clay	detrital	shale
D		pebbles composed of any mineral or rock	sand and pebble	detrital	conglomerate
E	tastes salty	halite	varies	chemical	rock salt

Activity 4-2

Purpose

Interpersonal Observe, identify, and classify sedimentary rocks. L1 COOP LEARN

Process Skills

observing and inferring, communicating, classifying, forming operational definitions, and interpreting qualitative data

Time

50 minutes

Safety Precautions

Be sure students are wearing goggles and aprons when using hydrochloric acid.

Activity Worksheets, pp. 5, 25-26

Teaching Strategies

Divide sedimentary rock samples into kits of known and unknown rocks. Sample kits should be the same for each laboratory group.

Troubleshooting If the activity is going to be done more than once, check that rock kits did not get mixed up.

Answers to Questions

1. to determine whether calcite was present—calcite effervesces in the presence of HCl; carbonates
2. fragments and a cementing agent
3. Because evaporites form by chemical processes, halite is classified as a chemical rock.
4. Rocks with a clastic texture are composed of pieces of other rocks, minerals, and/or shells. Rocks of a nonclastic texture are not composed of pieces of other rocks but are formed by chemical or organic means.
5. Sedimentary rocks are classified as detrital, chemical, or organic. Detrital rocks can be classified according to particle size and shape. Chemical rocks are classified by the process that formed them and by composition. Organic rocks are classified by the organic process that formed them.

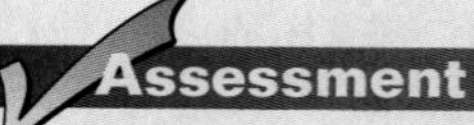

Assessment

Performance Provide students with large samples of unidentified rocks. Ask them to determine whether the rocks are sedimentary, and, if so, whether they are detrital, chemical, or organic. Use the Performance Task Assessment List for Carrying Out a Strategy and Collecting Data in **PASC**, p. 25. P

Chapter 4
Review

Summary

4-1: The Rock Cycle
1. A rock is a mixture of one or more minerals, mineraloids, glass, or organic matter.
2. The rock cycle includes all processes by which rocks form.

4-2: Igneous Rocks
1. Magma is molten material that hardens to form igneous rocks.
2. Intrusive igneous rocks form when magma cools below Earth's surface. Extrusive igneous rocks form when lava cools at Earth's surface.
3. Basaltic rocks are dense, heavy, dark-colored rocks. Granitic rocks are light colored and less dense than basalts. Andesitic rocks are intermediate between basaltics and granitics.

4-3: Metamorphic Rocks
1. Increases in heat and pressure can cause metamorphic rocks to form.
2. Slate and gneiss are classified as foliated, or banded, metamorphic rocks. When banding is not visible, as in quartzite, metamorphic rocks are classified as nonfoliated.

4-4: Sedimentary Rocks
1. Sedimentary rocks form when fragments of rocks, minerals, and/or organic materials are compacted and cemented together.
2. Detrital sedimentary rocks form when fragments of other rocks are compacted and/or cemented together. Chemical sedimentary rocks precipitate out of solution or are left behind by evaporation. Organic sedimentary rocks are made mostly of once-living organisms.

4-5: Science and Society: Burning Waste Coal
1. Pulverized waste coal is mixed with pulverized limestone and burned. The ash produced is alkaline and can be used to alleviate mine acid drainage.
2. Cogeneration occurs when both electrical and thermal energy produced by a power plant are used.

Key Science Words

a. basaltic
b. cementation
c. cogeneration
d. compaction
e. extrusive
f. foliated
g. granitic
h. igneous rock
i. intrusive
j. lava
k. metamorphic rock
l. nonfoliated
m. rock
n. rock cycle
o. sediment
p. sedimentary rock
q. waste coal

Reviewing Vocabulary

Match each phrase with the correct term from the list of Key Science Words.

1. mixture of one or more minerals, mineraloids, glass, or organic matter
2. processes that form and change rocks
3. molten material at Earth's surface
4. igneous rocks that form when lava cools
5. a rock formed by heat and pressure
6. quartzite has this kind of texture
7. fragments of rocks, minerals, plants, and animals
8. sediments are pressed together
9. sediments become glued together
10. poor-quality coal piled up near old mines

Chapter 4

Review

Summary

Have students read the summary statements to review the major concepts of the chapter.

Reviewing Vocabulary

1. m	**6.** l
2. n	**7.** p
3. j	**8.** d
4. e	**9.** b
5. k	**10.** q

Assessment

Portfolio Encourage students to place in their portfolios one or two items of what they consider to be their best work. Examples include:
- Skill Builder, p. 88
- Activity 4-1 analysis and application, p. 95
- MiniLAB analysis, p. 99 P

Performance Additional performance assessments may be found in **Performance Assessment** and **Science Integration Activities.** Performance Task Assessment Lists and rubrics for evaluating these activities can be found in Glencoe's **Performance Assessment in the Science Classroom.**

GLENCOE TECHNOLOGY

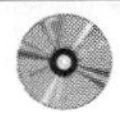 **Videodisc**

Glencoe Earth Science
Interactive Videodisc
Use videodisc lesson 1, *The Rock Cycle*, to review the principles presented in this chapter.

 **MindJogger Videoquiz**

Chapter 4 Have students work in groups as they play the Videoquiz game to review key chapter concepts.

Chapter 4 Review

Checking Concepts

1. d	**6.** b
2. d	**7.** c
3. a	**8.** c
4. d	**9.** d
5. a	**10.** a

Understanding Concepts

11. Because rocks are constantly changing due to Earth processes.

12. Both are molten materials that cool and harden to form igneous rocks. Both form from the melting of existing rock.

13. All are sedimentary rocks that form at or near Earth's surface. Detrital rocks are made of fragments of rocks and minerals. Chemical rocks form either from solution or by evaporation. Organic rocks contain an abundance of organic matter.

14. The piles of waste coal are unsightly, and because of their high sulfur content, they can generate acid runoff when rainwater flows through them.

15. Both the electrical and thermal energy produced by the plant are used.

Thinking Critically

16. Granite is an intrusive rock that forms deep within Earth. The magma from which it forms is not exposed to air.

17. Marble is a metamorphic rock. The processes that form it often destroy any organic remains.

18. Coquina is formed by an organic process. It is made of broken shells that are cemented together. Its texture is clastic.

19. The texture of all detrital sedimentary rocks is clastic.

20. They contain silica-rich minerals that are light in color. Examples include quartz, feldspar, and muscovite.

Developing Skills

21. Concept Mapping Metamorphic: foliated and nonfoliated; gneiss and quartzite. Sedimentary: detrital, organic, and chemical; sandstone, chalk, and halite. Intrusive: granitic, andesitic, and basaltic; granite, diorite, and gabbro. Extrusive: granitic, andesitic, and basaltic; rhyolite, basalt, and andisite.

22. Comparing and Contrasting Both are molten materials that form deep within Earth due to high pressure and temperatures. Basaltic magma is dense and rich in iron and magnesium. Granitic magma is thick and stiff and contains a lot of silicon and oxygen.

23. Hypothesizing The sequence has been disturbed since it was deposited because younger rocks overlie older rocks in most rock sequences.

Chapter 4 Review

Checking Concepts

Choose the word or phrase that completes the sentence or answers the question.

1. Magma reaches Earth's surface because it is _______ than the surrounding rocks.
a. more dense c. cooler
b. more massive d. less dense

2. Igneous rocks form from _______ .
a. sediments c. gravel
b. mud d. magma

3. _______ rocks have large mineral grains.
a. Intrusive c. Obsidian
b. Extrusive d. Basaltic

4. During metamorphism of shale into slate, minerals _______.
a. partly melt c. grow larger
b. become new minerals d. align into layers

5. Gneiss is a(n) _______ rock.
a. foliated c. intrusive
b. nonfoliated d. extrusive

6. ________ is a rock made of large, angular pieces of sediments.
a. Conglomerate c. Limestone
b. Breccia d. Chalk

7. Conglomerates form in much the same way as shales, sandstones, and _______.
a. limestones c. breccias
b. evaporites d. precipitates

8. _______ occurs when a power plant uses both the electrical and thermal power produced by the plant.
a. Wasted thermal energy
b. Inefficiency
c. Cogeneration
d. Loss of power

9. _______ forms when water carries sulfur from coal in solution.
a. An open pit c. A surface mine
b. Soil d. Acidic water

10. Which of these is not an organic rock?
a. shale c. chalk
b. coal d. coquina

Understanding Concepts

Answer the following questions in your Science Journal using complete sentences.

11. Explain why the rock cycle has no beginning and no end.

12. Compare magma and lava.

13. Compare and contrast detrital rocks with organic and chemical rocks.

14. Explain why waste coal can be harmful to the environment.

15. Explain the process of cogeneration.

Thinking Critically

16. Granite, pumice, and scoria are igneous rocks. Why doesn't granite have air holes like the other two?

17. Why are only a few fossils found in marble?

18. Explain why coquina is classified as an organic rock with a clastic texture.

19. What is true about the texture of all detrital sedimentary rocks?

20. Why are granitic igneous rocks light in color?

Developing Skills

If you need help, refer to the **Skill Handbook.**

21. **Concept Mapping:** Copy and complete the concept map shown below. Add rectangles and connecting lines so you can include examples of each classification of rock.

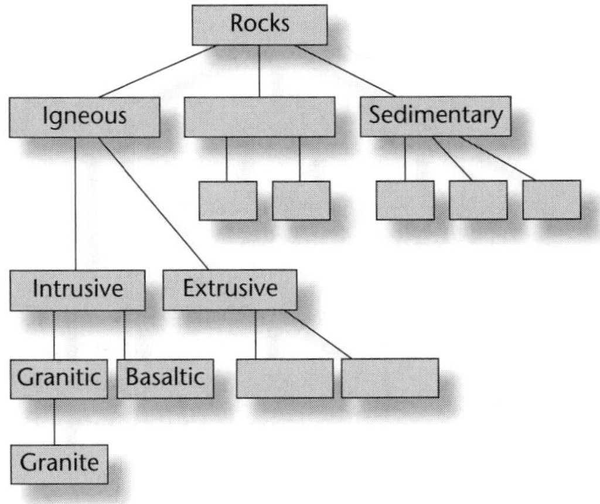

22. **Comparing and Contrasting:** Compare and contrast basaltic and granitic magmas.
23. **Hypothesizing:** A geologist found a sequence of rocks in which 200-million-year-old shales were lying on top of 100-million year-old sandstones. Hypothesize how this could happen.
24. **Measuring in SI:** The rock shown on the opposite page is a limestone that contains fossils. Find the average length of the fossils.
25. **Recognizing Cause and Effect:** Explain the cause and effects of pressure and temperature on shale.

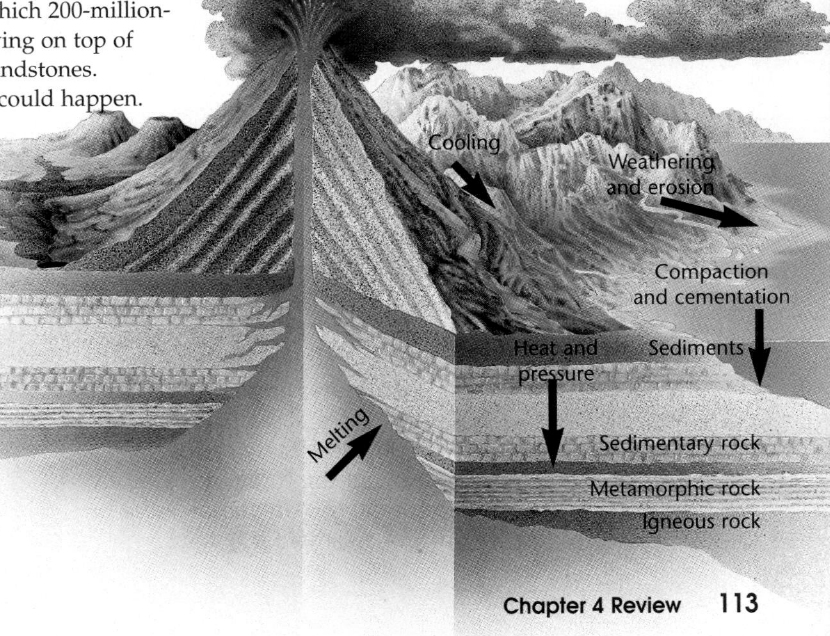

Performance Assessment

1. **Formulating a Hypothesis:** Based on what you learned in Activity 4-1, what would you expect to see if an intrusive igneous rock that contained even more iron and magnesium than basaltic rocks were placed on the table in front of you? Describe what you would expect to see as far as crystal size and color of the rock.
2. **Making and Using a Classification System:** In Activities 4-1 and 4-2, you learned how to classify igneous rocks and sedimentary rocks. Devise and carry out an activity to classify metamorphic rocks.
3. **Model:** Using skills from the MiniLAB on page 87, use sand, gravel, mud, clay, and a salt solution to make at least three metamorphic and three sedimentary "rocks." Label your rocks and explain how each forms in nature.

Chapter 4 Review

24. Measuring in SI Answers will vary but should be approximately 1.5 cm.

25. Recognizing Cause and Effect Pressure and temperature increases caused by overlying rocks can cause the minerals in shale to rearrange. Over time, the effects of the temperature and pressure will produce a slate.

Performance Assessment

1. Intrusive igneous rocks would have large crystals that are easily seen in the sample. The general color of the rocks would be very dark, even darker than basaltic rocks, because they would contain a higher concentration of iron and magnesium than basaltic rocks do. Some students may indicate that the rock would have a greenish color because of the high concentration of the mineral olivine. Use the Performance Task Assessment List for Formulating a Hypothesis in **PASC,** p. 21. P
2. Students may classify metamorphic rocks based on their appearance. Whether a metamorphic rock is banded (foliated) or not is determined by how it forms. Foliated rocks occur because of mineral-grain rearrangement. Nonfoliated rocks form when mineral grains are recrystallized. Expect students to classify slate, phyllite, schist, and gneiss as foliated, and quartzite and marble as nonfoliated. Use the Performance Task Assessment List for Making and Using a Classification System in **PASC,** p. 49. P
3. Student approaches to this activity will vary widely. Observe student activity and make suggestions where appropriate. Use the Performance Task Assessment List for Model in **PASC,** p. 51. P

Objectives

LS **Logical-Mathematical** Students will collect, organize, and display a collection of minerals and rocks. L1

Summary

In this project, students will realize the value of common Earth materials. By collecting and organizing their own collection of minerals and rocks found in Earth's crust, they will appreciate the wide diversity found in Earth materials. Students will collect mineral and rock samples from around their neighborhood and from as far away as they can. The collection will be separated into mineral and rock samples and presented in a display designed by the student.

Time Required

Students should begin this project as they begin studying Unit 2 and should continue working on it throughout the unit. Preparation for this project can be used as a motivation for Unit 2. One-half of one class period should be used to introduce students to the task of collecting their samples. As students perform the Activities in Unit 2, they will gain knowledge on how to classify and organize their samples. Once they have learned this concept, one class period should be used for students to classify their collected minerals and rocks. Students should expect to spend several hours outside of class researching information about their samples and constructing their displays. One class period should be set aside for students to present their completed displays to the class.

UNIT PROJECT 1

Rock and Roll

You take a walk along a well-traveled path and find a shiny, black rock in the path. You reach down and pick it up. It's interesting, but what will you do with it? You might wonder if it's worth anything.

Earth's surface is covered with treasures. Some are valuable, but the value of others only becomes apparent when they're viewed as part of a collection of Earth's rocks and minerals.

In this project you'll collect and organize samples of minerals and rocks from around your school, home, and neighborhood. You could also send requests to people you might know around the country. Make it part of your project to collect rocks and minerals from as many different places as you can.

Procedures

1. As you collect samples, think of a way to separate them into groups. You might separate your samples based on where they originated.
2. Determine if you're dealing with single minerals or rocks containing a mixture of minerals. Your collection of rocks and minerals should have two basic subdivisions. One should classify samples based on their mineral content. The other should classify rocks into one of the three major types (igneous, metamorphic, or sedimentary). Further subdivide your rock samples according to the classification system you learned in Chapter 4. If you find that most of your samples are of one type, think of ways to increase the number of samples of other types. Your goal is to build a well-rounded, complete rock and mineral collection.
3. Make a wood or cardboard box in which you can display each of

Preparation

- Establish cooperative groups of three students each. Encourage students to make one collection for the cooperative group. Students could devise a method to use so that individual samples are identified.
- Several days before beginning Chapter 3, show students some rock samples you have collected from around the school grounds. Point out how different each sample is and ask students to brainstorm as to what may be causing the noted differences.

your samples. Think of a way to protect your samples so they can be displayed for other students to enjoy. When you make/display your box, allow room near each sample to display information obtained during research in the library.

4. Create labels for each of your samples that include answers to the following questions. If necessary, go to the library and research the answers.
   - Where was each sample found?
   - What type of geologic feature is associated with the location of each sample? For example, the rocks may be igneous rocks from a lava flow.
   - What is the composition of each sample? Identify the primary mineral contained in each mineral sample and the more prominent minerals found in each of your rock samples.
   - Once you determine the mineral content of each sample, find out how people use them.
   - To which crystal systems do your mineral samples and the minerals in your rocks belong?
5. Based on the information you've collected, write a short description of each sample in your collection. Include information about each of your samples that describes its origin, composition, and use. Describe everyday uses that people have for the rocks and minerals you've collected.

Going Further

Each year new and rare minerals are discovered. Many of these minerals are found only in one or two locations. Even so, they are classified by their crystal structure. Based on the research you did on the crystal systems involved in your samples, classify each of your samples by its crystal structure. Near where you've mounted each sample, draw a diagram of the crystal system to which each one belongs.

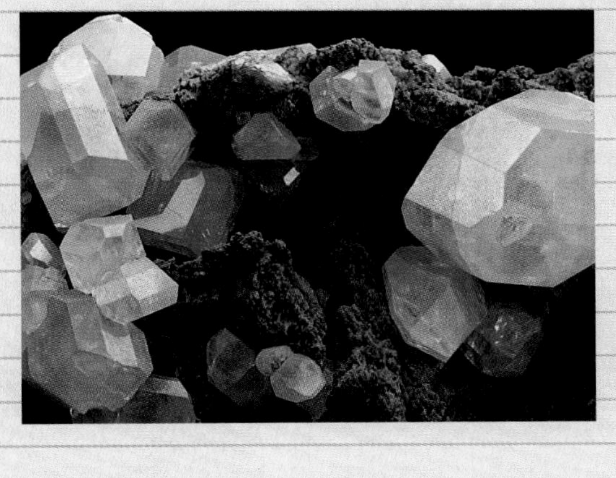

Teaching Strategies

- This project integrates the study of minerals and rocks with chemistry. The chemical composition of each sample collected by the students is one of the factors that causes the differences noted between samples.
- Before dividing the class into cooperative groups, ask students to discuss any rock or mineral collections they might have with other members of the class.
- Help students realize that procedures learned while doing the Activities in Unit 2 can be used when organizing their own collected samples.
- If students have trouble deciding on what kind of display they should construct for their samples, place examples of mineral and rock collections around the classroom so students can walk around to view them. Encourage students to come up with new, original ideas to use in their displays.

Go Further

Explain to students that minerals are classified into different crystal systems based on the internal arrangements of atoms within the mineral. Crystals of different systems vary in the lengths of and angles separating axes drawn outward from the crystal center. For example, in the cubic crystal system, there are three axes of equal length that intersect at right angles. Refer students to Table 3-1 on page 63 or obtain models of the different crystal systems and demonstrate how the location and angle of separation between axes determines the crystal system. Ask students to explain why the minerals that are located in their rock samples do not display the crystal shapes shown in Table 3-1.

References

Berry, L.G. & Brian Mason. *Mineralogy*, 2nd ed. New York: W.H. Freeman and Co., 1983.

Klein, Cornelis & Cornelius S. Hurlbut, Jr. *Manual of Mineralogy*, 20th ed. New York: John Wiley & Sons, Inc., 1985.

UNIT 2

The Changing Surface of Earth

In Unit 2, students will discover how features on Earth's surface form. They will begin by studying different kinds of landforms. Then, they will examine the processes and agents that create these surface features as they learn about weathering and erosion.

CONTENTS

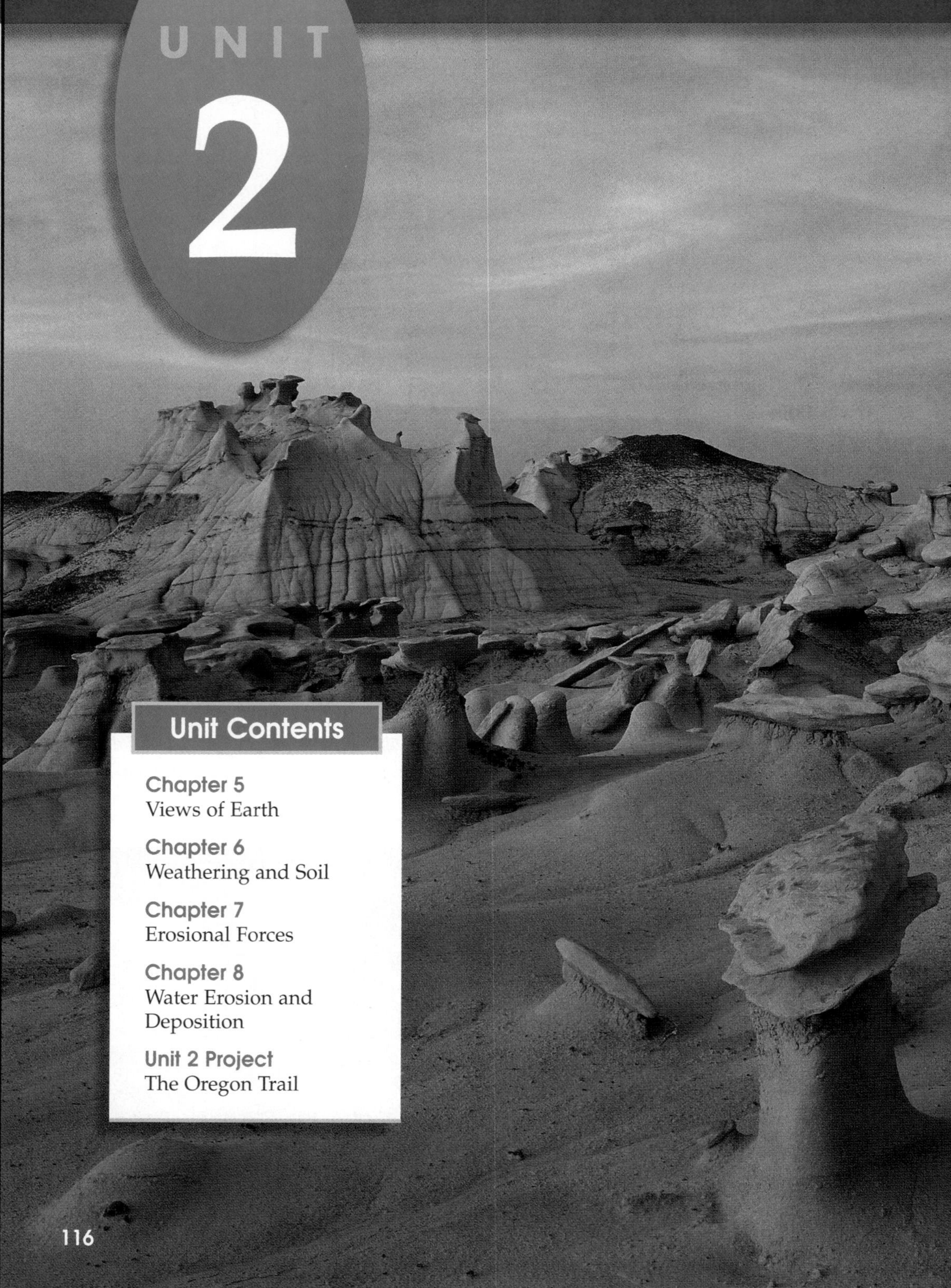

Science at Home

Erosion Solutions Have students select areas near their homes that show soil erosion problems. Have them model different methods to minimize erosion of these areas.

The Changing Surface of Earth

What's Happening Here?

Earth's surface is constantly changing. Some processes of change alter entire landscapes. Wind, for example, can blow sediments that slowly wear away at Earth's surface, leaving behind beautiful pillars of sculpted rock spread across a vast landscape. Huge boulders of hard rock may balance delicately upon thin shafts of worn, softer rock. Some processes may alter Earth's surface at a microscopic level. Gypsum flowers may form beneath Earth's surface in caves as minerals build up molecules at a time. As you study this unit, you'll learn about the many processes that change the shape of our world.

Science Journal

Investigate the shape of Earth's surface where you live. How do you think the surface may have changed over time? In your Science Journal, write about what it may be like to go far back in time to the exact same spot. What would Earth's surface look like? What might it look like far in the future?

INTRODUCING THE UNIT

What's Happening Here?

Have students examine the photographs and read the text. Ask them to make a connection between the sculptured landscape and the gypsum flowers. Point out to students that in this unit, they will learn about the processes and agents that change Earth's surface.

Background

Weathering and erosion are the processes that change Earth. Agents of erosion include gravity, glaciers, and wind, but the most important agent is water. The landform shown here was created when water weathered and eroded softer materials. Gypsum flowers are created when water chemically alters minerals in a cave.

Previewing the Chapters

- Have the students identify photographs in the chapters that show examples of erosion caused by gravity, ice, wind, and water.
- Have students participate in a scavenger hunt through the unit, looking for photographs of the four types of mountains, soil evolution, glacier deposition, and the stages of stream development.

Tying to Previous Knowledge

Have students recall what they learned about the properties of rocks in Chapter 4. Because landforms are made of various sizes and kinds of rocks, have students hypothesize why some landforms are more easily weathered than others and why different parts of the same landform weather at different rates.

Theme Connection

Stability and Change Inform students that landforms are constantly changing. Have them research to find out how local landforms have changed throughout time. L2

Cultural Diversity

Living on the River Have students research and write a report on how various cultures utilize river systems. Many cultures have developed civilizations around rivers. Other cultures view rivers as an important part of religion. L2

Chapter Organizer

Section	Objectives	Activities/Features
Chapter Opener		Explore Activity: Use a globe or world map. p. 119
5-1 **Landforms** (2 sessions)*	1. **Differentiate** between plains and plateaus. 2. **Compare** and **contrast** folded, upwarped, fault-block, and volcanic mountains.	Using Math, p. 121 MiniLAB: What would a profile of the major landforms of this country look like? p. 122 Science Journal, p. 123 Connect to Chemistry, p. 125 Skill Builder: Concept Mapping, p. 125 Using Computers: Spreadsheet, p. 125
5-2 **Viewpoints** (1 session)*	1. **Differentiate** between latitude and longitude. 2. **Describe** how latitude and longitude are used to identify locations. 3. **Calculate** the time and date in different time zones.	MiniLAB: How are latitude and longitude used to locate places on a map? p. 127 Connect to Life Science, p. 128 Skill Builder: Interpreting Scientific Illustrations, p. 129 Using Math, p. 129
5-3 **Maps** (2 sessions)*	1. **Differentiate** among Mercator, Robinson, and conic projections. 2. **Describe** how contour lines and contour intervals are used to illustrate elevation on a topographic map. 3. **Explain** why topographic maps have scales.	Using Technology: Rocks in 3-D! p. 133 Problem Solving: Using a Topographic Map, p. 135 Skill Builder: Measuring in SI, p. 136 Science Journal, p. 136 Activity 5-1: Making a Topographic Map, p. 137
5-4 **Science and Society Technology: Mapping Our Planet** (1 session)*	1. **Describe** how Landsat satellites collect information about Earth's surface. 2. **Compare** the data-collecting technique of the Topex-Poseidon satellite with sonar.	Explore the Technology, p. 139 Using Math, p. 139 Activity 5-2: Modeling Earth, pp. 140-141 Science & History: The Art of Mapmaking, p. 142 Science Journal, p. 142

* A complete Planning Guide that includes block scheduling is provided on pages 32T-35T.

Activity Materials

Explore	Activities	MiniLABs
page 119 globe or world map	page 137 plastic model landform; water tinted with food coloring; transparency; clear, plastic storage box with lid; 250-mL beaker; metric ruler; tape; transparency marker pages 140-141 fine-point transparency marker, blank transparency, overhead projector, sheet of white paper, pencil, corrugated cardboard sheets or foam board sheets, scissors or razor knife, glue, metric ruler	page 122 sheet of unlined paper, pencil page 127 world map

Teacher Classroom Resources

Reproducible Masters	Transparencies
Study Guide, p. 22 **Reinforcement**, p. 22 **Enrichment**, p. 22 **Activity Worksheets**, p. 34 **Science Integration Activity 5**, Being a Root Is Dirty Work **Concept Mapping**, p. 15	**Section Focus Transparency 18**, Ups and Downs **Teaching Transparency 9**, U.S. Physiographic Regions
Study Guide, p. 23 **Reinforcement**, p. 23 **Enrichment**, p. 23 **Activity Worksheets**, p. 35 **Lab Manual 17**, Determining Latitude **Lab Manual 18**, Time Zones	**Section Focus Transparency 19**, Some Other Time **Teaching Transparency 10**, Latitude/Longitude
Study Guide, p. 24 **Reinforcement**, p. 24 **Enrichment**, p. 24 **Activity Worksheets**, pp. 30-31 **Lab Manual 19**, Comparing Maps **Lab Manual 20**, Using a Clinometer **Critical Thinking/Problem Solving**, p. 11 **Cross-Curricular Integration**, p. 9 **Science and Society Integration**, p. 9 **Multicultural Connections**, pp. 13-14	**Section Focus Transparency 20**, It All Depends
Study Guide, p. 25 **Reinforcement**, p. 25 **Enrichment**, p. 25 **Activity Worksheets**, pp. 32-33	**Section Focus Transparency 21**, State-of-the-Art Mapping **Science Integration Transparency 4**, Using Sound to Make Maps

Teaching Resources

Glencoe Earth Science Interactive Videodisc
Earth Science CD-ROM
Spanish Resources
English/Spanish Audiocassettes
Cooperative Learning Resource Guide
Lab Partner
Lab and Safety Skills
Lesson Plans

Assessment Resources

Chapter Review, pp. 13-14
Assessment, pp. 32-35
Performance Assessment in the Science Classroom (PASC)
MindJogger Videoquiz
Alternate Assessment in the Science Classroom
Performance Assessment
Chapter Review Software
Computer Test Bank

Key to Teaching Strategies

The following designations will help you decide which activities are appropriate for your students.

L1 Level 1 activities should be within the ability range of all students.

L2 Level 2 activities should be within the ability range of the average to above-average student.

L3 Level 3 activities are designed for the ability range of above-average students.

LEP LEP activities should be within the ability range of Limited English Proficiency students.

LS These activities are designed to address different learning styles.

COOP LEARN Cooperative Learning activities are designed for small group work.

P These strategies represent student products that can be placed into a best-work portfolio.

GLENCOE TECHNOLOGY

The following multimedia resources are available from Glencoe.

Science and Technology Videodisc Series (STVS)
Earth & Space
Studying the Pacific Ocean
Exploring Lake Superior's Bottom
Mapping with a Rifle
Map Science
Charting Air Space

National Geographic Society Series
STV: Restless Earth

Earth Science CD-ROM

Teacher Classroom Resources

This is a representation of key blackline masters available in the Teacher Classroom Resources.

Teaching Aids

Section Focus Transparencies

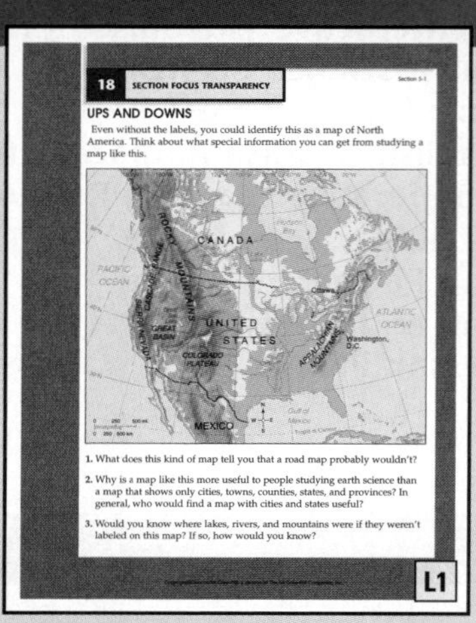

18 SECTION FOCUS TRANSPARENCY

UPS AND DOWNS

Even without the labels, you could identify this as a map of North America. Think about what special information you can get from studying a map like this.

1. What does this kind of map tell you that a road map probably wouldn't?
2. Why is a map like this more useful to people studying earth science than a map that shows only cities, towns, counties, states, and provinces? In general, who would find a map with cities and states useful?
3. Would you know where lakes, rivers, and mountains were if they weren't labeled on this map? If so, how would you know?

L1

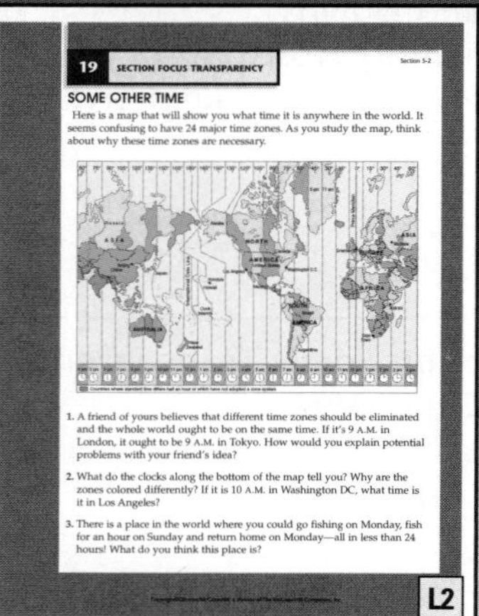

19 SECTION FOCUS TRANSPARENCY

SOME OTHER TIME

Here is a map that will show you what time it is anywhere in the world. It seems confusing to have 24 major time zones. As you study the map, think about why these time zones are necessary.

1. A friend of yours believes that different time zones should be eliminated and the whole world ought to be on the same time. If it's 9 A.M. in London, it ought to be 9 A.M. in Tokyo. How would you explain potential problems with your friend's idea?
2. What do the clocks along the bottom of the map tell you? Why are the zones colored differently? If it is 10 A.M. in Washington DC, what time is it in Los Angeles?
3. There is a place in the world where you could go fishing on Monday, fish for an hour on Sunday and return home on Monday—all in less than 24 hours! What do you think this place is?

L2

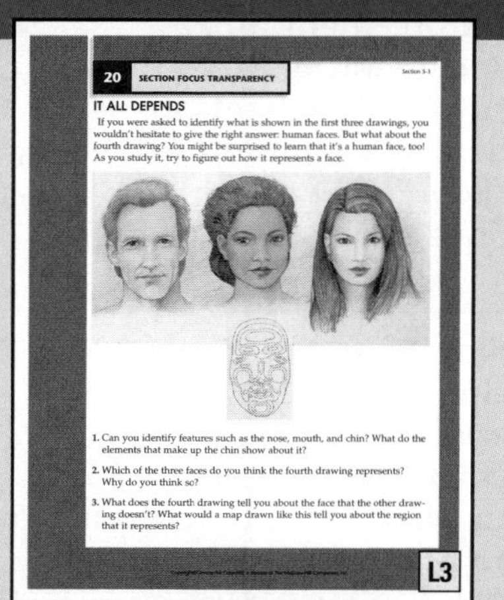

20 SECTION FOCUS TRANSPARENCY

IT ALL DEPENDS

If you were asked to identify what is shown in the first three drawings, you wouldn't hesitate to give the right answer: human faces. But what about the fourth drawing? You might be surprised to learn that it's a human face, too! As you study it, try to figure out how it represents a face.

1. Can you identify features such as the nose, mouth, and chin? What do the elements that make up the chin show about it?
2. Which of the three faces do you think the fourth drawing represents? Why do you think so?
3. What does the fourth drawing tell you about the face that the other drawing doesn't? What would a map drawn like this tell you about the region that it represents?

L3

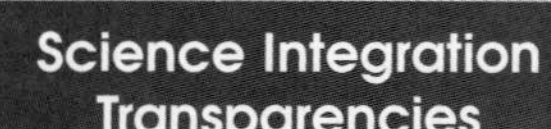

Science Integration Transparencies

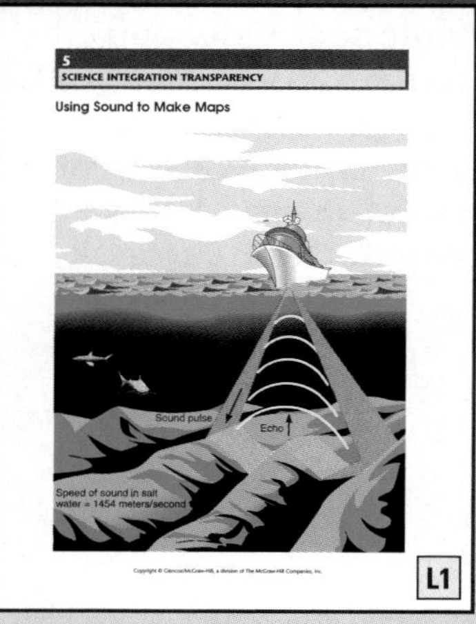

5 SCIENCE INTEGRATION TRANSPARENCY

Using Sound to Make Maps

L1

Teaching Transparencies

9. U.S. PHYSIOGRAPHIC REGIONS

L1

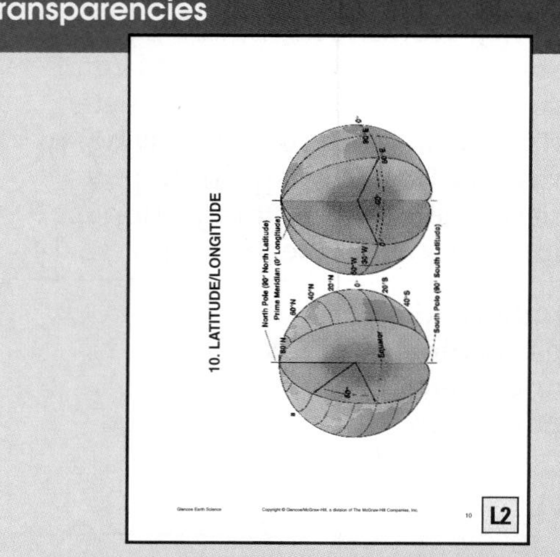

10. LATITUDE/LONGITUDE

L2

Meeting Different Ability Levels

Study Guide

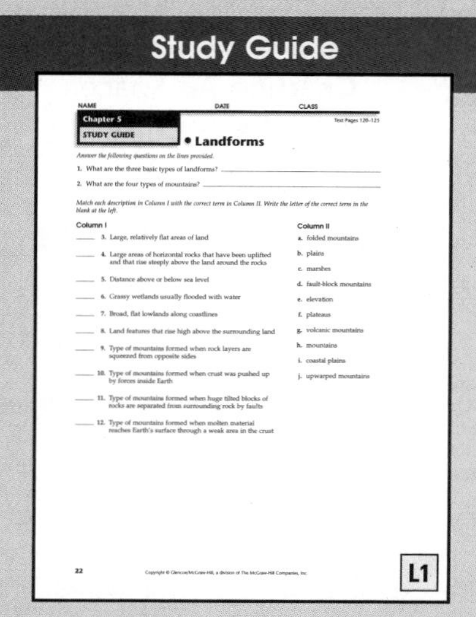

NAME DATE CLASS

Chapter 5 STUDY GUIDE

• Landforms

Answer the following questions on the lines provided.

1. What are the three basic types of landforms?
2. What are the four types of mountains?

Match each description in Column I with the correct term in Column II. Write the letter of the correct term in the blank at the left.

Column I	Column II
3. Large, relatively flat areas of land	a. folded mountains
4. Large areas of horizontal rocks that have been uplifted and that rise steeply above the land around the rocks	b. plains
5. Distance above or below sea level	c. marshes
6. Grassy wetlands usually flooded with water	d. fault-block mountains
7. Broad, flat lowlands along coastlines	e. elevation
8. Land features that rise high above the surrounding land	f. plateaus
9. Type of mountains formed when rock layers are squeezed from opposite sides	g. volcanic mountains
10. Type of mountains formed when crust was pushed up by forces inside Earth	h. mountains
11. Type of mountains formed when huge tilted blocks of rocks are separated from surrounding rock by faults	i. coastal plains
12. Type of mountains formed when molten material reaches Earth's surface through a weak area in the crust	j. upwarped mountains

L1

Reinforcement

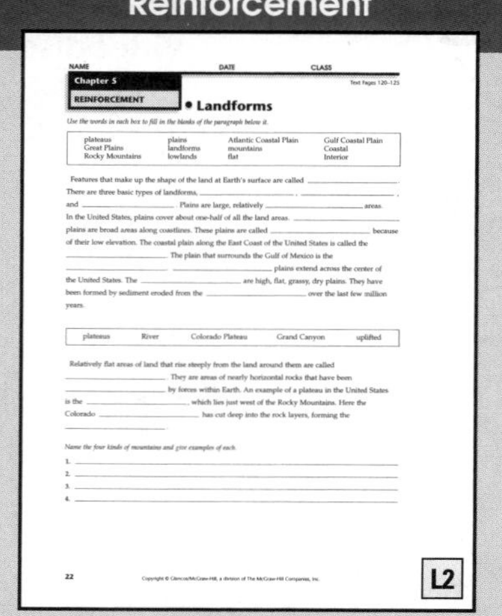

NAME DATE CLASS

Chapter 5 REINFORCEMENT

• Landforms

Use the words in each box to fill in the blanks of the paragraph below it.

plateaus, plains, Atlantic Coastal Plain, Gulf Coastal Plain, Great Plains, landforms, mountains, Coastal, Rocky Mountains, lowlands, flat, Interior

plateaus, River, Colorado Plateau, Grand Canyon, uplifted

Name the four kinds of mountains and give examples of each.

L2

Enrichment Worksheets

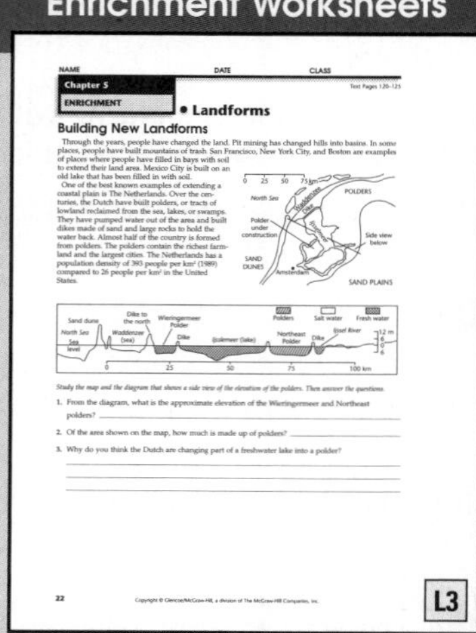

NAME DATE CLASS

Chapter 5 ENRICHMENT

• Landforms

Building New Landforms

Study the map and the diagram that shows a side view of the elevation of the polders. Then answer the questions.

1. From the diagram, what is the approximate elevation of the Wieringermeer and Northeast polders?
2. Of the area shown on the map, how much is made up of polders?
3. Why do you think the Dutch are changing part of a freshwater lake into a polder?

L3

Hands-On Activities

Science Integration Activity

Chapter 5 INTEGRATION • Being a Root Is Dirty Work!

L1

Lab Manual

Chapter 5 LABORATORY MANUAL • Determining Latitude 17

L2

Assessment

Performance Assessment

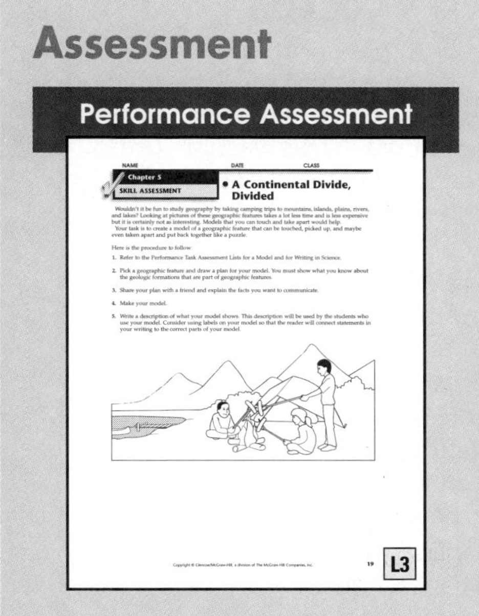
Chapter 5 SKILL ASSESSMENT • A Continental Divide, Divided

L3

Enrichment and Application

Critical Thinking/ Problem Solving

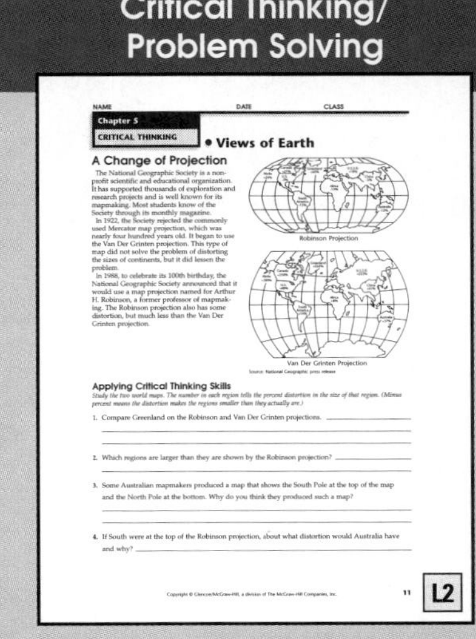
Chapter 5 CRITICAL THINKING • Views of Earth

A Change of Projection

L2

Cross-Curricular Integration

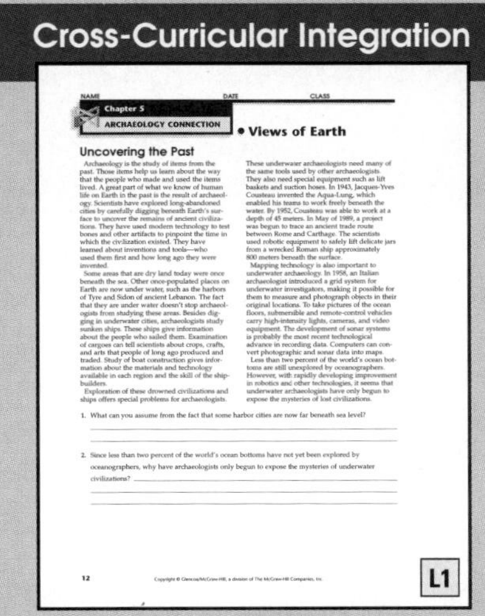
Chapter 5 ARCHAEOLOGY CONNECTION • Views of Earth

Uncovering the Past

L1

Science and Society Integration

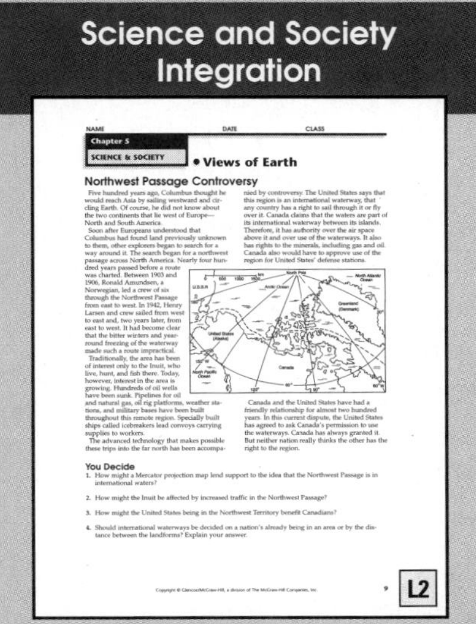
Chapter 5 SCIENCE & SOCIETY • Views of Earth

Northwest Passage Controversy

L2

Multicultural Connections

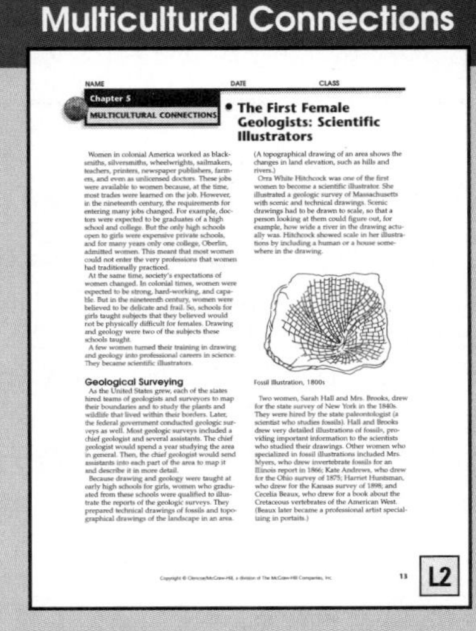
Chapter 5 MULTICULTURAL CONNECTIONS • The First Female Geologists: Scientific Illustrators

L2

Concept Mapping

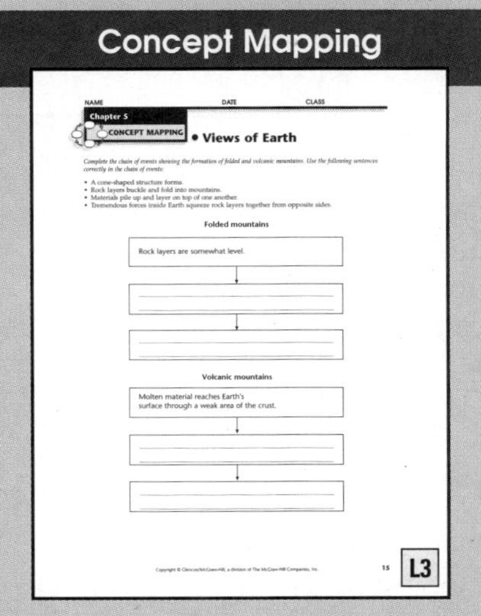
Chapter 5 CONCEPT MAPPING • Views of Earth

L3

Chapter 5

Views of Earth

CHAPTER OVERVIEW

Section 5-1 This section presents the structural differences among plains, plateaus, and mountains.

Section 5-2 Concepts discussed in this section include latitude and longitude.

Section 5-3 Mercator, Robinson, and conic projections are defined and discussed. Students are introduced to topographic maps.

Section 5-4 **Science and Society** This section explains how remote sensing is used to make maps of Earth.

Chapter Vocabulary

plain
plateau
folded mountain
upwarped mountain
fault-block mountain
volcanic mountain
equator
latitude
prime meridian
longitude
International Date Line
Mercator projection
Robinson projection
conic projection
topographic map
contour line
contour interval
map legend
map scale
Landsat Satellite
Topex-Poseidon Satellite
sonar

Theme Connection

Scale and Structure The structural differences among major landforms are the focus of Section 5-1. In Sections 5-2 and 5-3, students focus on understanding the scale and structure of maps. Section 5-4 explains how remote sensing is used to study some Earth structures.

Previewing the Chapter

118

Learning Styles

Look for the following logo for strategies that emphasize different learning modalities. LS

Kinesthetic	Activity 5-1, p. 137; Activity 5-2, pp. 140-141
Visual-Spatial	Explore, p. 119; Activity, pp. 121, 123, 133; Visual Learning, pp. 121, 122, 124, 127, 128, 131, 132, 134, 139; MiniLAB, p. 122; Across the Curriculum, pp. 124, 131; Reteach, p. 135
Interpersonal	Activity, pp. 126, 135; Science & History, p. 142
Logical-Mathematical	MiniLAB, p. 127

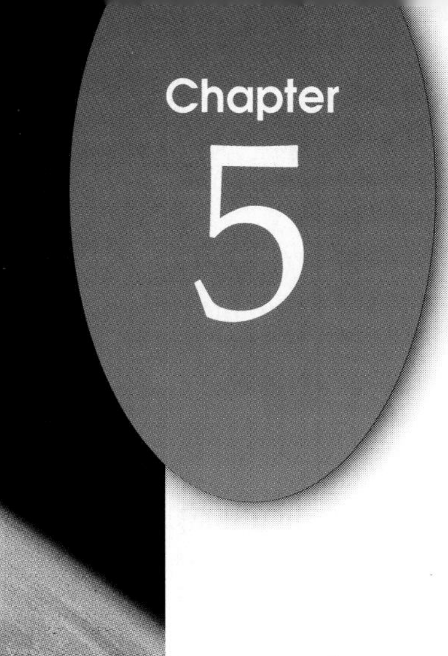

Views of Earth

Did you know that we are able to use cameras attached to satellites to take pictures of Earth from space? This method of studying our planet is a form of a technology called remote sensing. Photographs taken from these cameras show us many details of Earth's surface. Look at the picture again. Can you pick out the rivers and flat areas in this photograph? How can you recognize the higher elevations?

EXPLORE ACTIVITY

Use a globe or world map.

1. Find the Andes Mountains on the globe or map.
2. Locate the Amazon, the Ganges, and the Mississippi rivers.
3. Locate the Indian Ocean, the Sea of Japan, and the Baltic Sea.
4. Now, find the continents of Australia, South America, and North America.
5. Locate your own country.

Observe: Choose one country on the globe or map and describe its major physical features in your Science Journal.

Previewing Science Skills

- In the **Skill Builders**, you will **map concepts, interpret scientific illustrations,** and **measure in SI.**
- In the **Activities**, you will **observe, measure, use numbers,** and **interpret data.**
- In the **MiniLABs**, you will **interpret scientific illustrations** and **make a model.**

EXPLORE ACTIVITY

Purpose

LS **Visual-Spatial** Use the Explore Activity to review basic geography with students. Inform them that they will be learning more about landforms and maps as they read the chapter. L1 COOP LEARN

Preparation

Obtain enough globes or world maps for each group of three students.

Materials

one globe or world map for every three students

Teaching Strategies

- If time allows, have students locate places that are currently in the news.
- Have students locate their homes in at least four different ways. For example, "My home is east of city Y, west of city X, south of Canada, and north of the equator" might be one response.

Observe

Answers will vary according to the country chosen and the view of Earth that is used.

Assessment

Content Ask students to describe in writing how mountains and rivers are indicated on the globe or world map that they used. Use the Performance Task Assessment List for Making Observations and Inferences in **PASC,** p. 17. P

Assessment Planner

Portfolio

Refer to page 143 for suggested items that students might select for their portfolios.

Performance Assessment

See page 143 for additional Performance Assessment options.
Skill Builders, pp. 125, 129, 136
MiniLABs, pp. 122, 127
Activities 5-1, p. 137; 5-2, pp. 140-141

Content Assessment

Section Wrap-ups, pp. 125, 129, 136, 139
Chapter Review, pp. 143-145
Mini Quizzes, pp. 125, 129, 136, 139

Group Assessment

Opportunities for group assessment occur with Cooperative Learning Strategies and Flex Your Brain Activities.

Section 5•1

Prepare

Section Background

- Plateaus are one of the effects of mountain building. The Colorado Plateau of Arizona, New Mexico, Utah, and Colorado is associated with the Rocky Mountains. The Allegheny and Cumberland Plateaus of Pennsylvania, Kentucky, and Tennessee are associated with mountain-building processes that formed the Appalachians.
- In this text, mountains are classified according to their most dominant characteristics. It should be noted that folding, faulting, upwarping, and igneous and metamorphic activity are processes involved in building mountains.

Preplanning

Make sure there are enough metric rulers for the MiniLAB.

1 Motivate

Bellringer

Before presenting the lesson, display **Section Focus Transparency 18** on the overhead projector. Assign the accompanying **Focus Activity** worksheet. L1 LEP

Tying to Previous Knowledge

Have students recall visiting or seeing pictures of other areas of the world. In this section, students will learn about different kinds of landforms.

5•1 Landforms

Science Words

plain
plateau
folded mountain
upwarped mountain
fault-block mountain
volcanic mountain

Objectives

- Differentiate between plains and plateaus.
- Compare and contrast folded, upwarped, fault-block, and volcanic mountains.

Plains

There are a lot of interesting landforms around the world. A landform is a feature that makes up the shape of the land at Earth's surface. **Figure 5-1** shows the three basic types of landforms: plains, plateaus, and mountains.

We all know what mountains are. In our minds, we can see tall peaks reaching towards the sky. But what do you think of when you hear the word *plains?* You might think of endless flat fields of wheat or grass. That would be accurate, because many plains are used to grow crops. We call these large, relatively flat areas **plains.** Plains found near the ocean are called coastal plains. Flat, grassy areas used to grow crops or for grazing are called interior plains. Together, these two types of plains make up one-half of all the land in the United States.

Coastal Plains

Coastal plains are broad areas along the ocean's shore. They are often called lowlands because of their low elevations. Elevation refers to distance above or below sea level. As you might guess, sea level has zero elevation. The Atlantic Coastal Plain is a good example of this type of landform. It stretches along the East Coast of the United States. This area is characterized by low rolling hills, swamps, and marshes. A marsh is grassy wetland, usually flooded with water.

Figure 5-1

Three basic types of landforms are plains, plateaus, and mountains.

Program Resources

Reproducible Masters

Study Guide, p. 22 L1
Reinforcement, p. 22 L1
Enrichment, p. 22 L3
Activity Worksheets, pp. 5, 34 L1
Science Integration Activities, pp. 9-10
Concept Mapping, p. 15

Transparencies

Section Focus Transparency 18 L1
Teaching Transparency 9

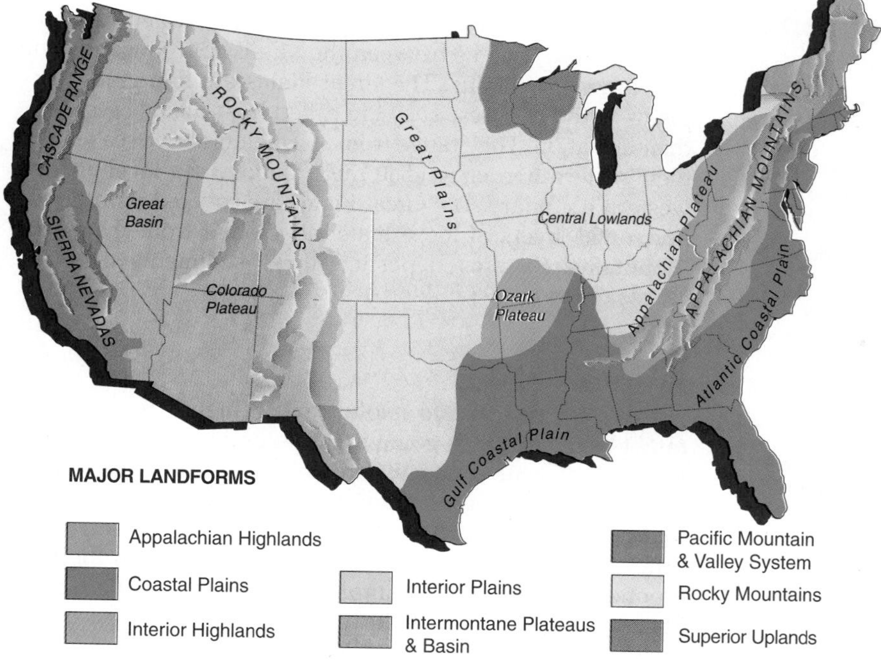

Figure 5-2

The United States is made up of eight major landforms. *In your Science Journal, describe the region that you live in.*

If you hiked along the Atlantic Coastal Plain, you would realize it isn't perfectly flat. Many low hills and valleys have been carved by rivers. What do you suppose caused the Atlantic Coastal Plain to form? It actually began forming under water about 70 million years ago from sediments composed of marine organisms that fell to the ancient ocean floor. When sea level dropped, the plain was exposed.

Another example of this landform is the Gulf Coastal Plain. It includes the lowlands in the southern United States that surround the Gulf of Mexico. Much of this plain was formed from sediments deposited by the Mississippi River as it entered the Gulf of Mexico.

USING MATH

The elevation of Denver, Colorado, is about 1624.5 meters above sea level. The elevation of New Orleans, Louisiana, is 1626 meters lower than Denver's. Find the elevation of New Orleans.

Interior Plains

A large portion of the center of the United States is called the interior plains. The interior plains of the United States are shown in **Figure 5-2.** They extend from the Appalachian Mountains in the east to the Rocky Mountains in the west, to the Gulf Coastal Plain in the south. They include the rolling hills of the Great Lakes area and the Central Lowlands around the Missouri and Mississippi rivers.

2 Teach

Activity

LS **Visual-Spatial** Display a relief map of North America. Have students compare and contrast the different landforms. L1 LEP

Inquiry Question

What created many of the low hills and valleys on the Atlantic Coastal Plain? *rivers*

Visual Learning

Figure 5-2 In your Science Journal, describe the region that you live in. *Answers will vary. However, students should use terms associated with one of the eight major landforms listed in* ***Figure 5-2.*** LEP LS

USING MATH

1.5 meters below sea level or –1.5 meters

GLENCOE TECHNOLOGY

CD-ROM

Earth Science CD-ROM

Have students perform the interactive exploration for Chapter 5 to reinforce important chapter concepts and thinking processes.

Cultural Diversity

Landforms and Life Landforms play an important part in the culture of the people living near them. For instance, Mount Everest and its mountain neighbors near Nepal are sacred to the Sherpas. The Sleeping Bear Dunes in Michigan are part of a Chippewa legend. According to the story, a mother bear and her two cubs were forced to swim across Lake Michigan to escape a forest fire. The mother made it to shore, climbed a tall dune, and looked for her cubs. She is still there today, a dark sand dune atop a plateau, and her cubs have become the North and South Manitou Islands. Indigenous Australians view landforms in a special way. In their religion, certain rock formations are considered to be ancient spirits who have turned themselves into stone. A high, stony escarpment is thought to represent the edge of the world.

Use **Concept Mapping,** p. 15, as you teach this lesson.

MiniLAB

Purpose

LS **Visual-Spatial** Students will make a profile of some major landforms in the United States. L1 LEP

Materials

Figure 5-2, metric ruler

Teaching Strategies

Use an overhead projector, a transparency of **Figure 5-2,** a clear transparency to represent the students' papers, and a marking pen to show how the profile should be made.

Analysis

1. If the profile is made through the center of the U.S., the beginning of the profile will be steep, to represent mountains. This is followed by a high, flat profile representing plateaus, a low, flat profile depicting plains, another high, flat profile showing plateaus, a high, steep profile representing mountains, and a low, flat profile illustrating plains.
2. The profile going north to south will vary according to the route that is taken, but it will not show as much variation in altitude as will the west-east route.

Assessment

Performance To further assess students' understanding of making a profile, have students repeat the process by making a profile of another route across the U.S. Have students compare their two profiles. Use the Performance Task Assessment List for Model in **PASC**, p. 51. P

Activity Worksheets, pp. 5, 34

MiniLAB

What would a profile of the major landforms of this country look like?

Make a profile, or side view, of the United States.

Procedure

1. Place the bottom edge of a piece of paper across the middle of **Figure 5-2,** extending from the west coast to the east coast.
2. Mark where different landforms are located along this edge.
3. Use Appendix H and the descriptions of the landforms in Section 5-1 to help you draw the profile.

Analysis

1. Describe how your profile changed shape as you moved from west to east.
2. Describe how the shape of your profile would be different if you moved from north to south.

A large portion of the interior plains is referred to as the Great Plains. They lie between the Mississippi lowlands and the Rocky Mountains. The Great Plains are flat, grassy, dry plains with few trees. They are called high plains because of their elevation. They range from 350 meters above sea level at their eastern border to 1500 meters above sea level at their western boundary. The Great Plains are covered with nearly horizontal layers of loose materials eroded from the Rocky Mountains. Streams deposited these sediments over the course of the last 28 million years.

Plateaus

If you would like to explore some higher regions, you might be interested in going to the second basic type of landform—a plateau. **Plateaus** are relatively flat raised areas of land. They are areas made up of nearly horizontal rocks that have been uplifted by forces within Earth. Plateaus are different from plains in that they rise steeply from the land around them. A good example of a plateau in the United States is the Colorado Plateau, which lies just west of the Rocky Mountains. As **Figure 5-3** shows, the Colorado River has cut deeply into the rock layers of the plateau, forming the Grand Canyon. Because the Colorado Plateau is located in a very dry region, only a few permanent rivers have developed on its surface. If you hiked around on this plateau, you would see a desert landscape.

Figure 5-3 Rivers cut deep into the Colorado Plateau. *How are plateaus different from plains?*

Across the Curriculum

Social Studies Have students determine why more than half of the world's human population lives on plains. Students should discover that plains are often fertile farmlands. L1 P

Visual Learning

Figure 5-3 How are plateaus different from plains? Plateaus are flat like plains, but they rise steeply from the land around them. LEP LS

Figure 5-4
Folded mountains form when rock layers are squeezed from opposite sides.

Mountains

Plains and plateaus are relatively flat. If you want to tackle a steep rock face, you must go to the third basic type of landform—a mountain. Mountains rise high above the surrounding land, often providing a spectacular view from the top. The world's highest mountain peak is Mount Everest, in the Himalayan Mountains. It is more than 8800 meters above sea level. By contrast, mountain peaks in the United States reach just over 6000 meters. Mountains vary greatly in size and in how they are formed. The four main types of mountains are folded, upwarped, fault-block, and volcanic.

Folded Mountains

The first mountains we will investigate are folded mountains. If you ever travel through a road cut in the Appalachian Mountains, you'll see rock layers that are folded like the ones in **Figure 5-4.** Folded rock layers look like a rug that has been pushed up against a wall. What do you think caused this to happen?

Tremendous forces inside Earth force rock layers together. When rock layers are squeezed from opposite sides, they buckle and fold into **folded mountains.** You'll learn more about the forces that create mountains in Chapters 9, 10, and 11.

The Appalachian Mountains are folded mountains that formed in this way 300 to 250 million years ago. They are the oldest mountains in North America and also one of the longest ranges, stretching from Quebec, Canada, south to Alabama. At one time, the Appalachians were higher than the Rocky Mountains, but weathering and erosion have worn them down to less than 2000 meters above sea level.

Science Journal

The Himalayan Mountains are still growing taller. In your Science Journal, describe why you think this is happening. Then, find out if you were right. Record your findings.

Community Connection

Planning Projects Have several students interview a city or county engineer to find out why he or she needs to know about local landforms when planning new roads and other projects. Have the students share this information with their classmates. L1 P

Science Journal

Students should discover that the Himalayas are being pushed up as India converges with Asia. Students will learn more about convergent plate boundaries in Chapter 11.

Inquiry Question

- **Why aren't the Appalachian Mountains as high as the Rocky Mountains?** *They are much older, and weathering and erosion have worn them down.*

Activity

- Help students locate the Himalayan, Appalachian, and Rocky Mountains on a world map.
- Obtain photos of the three basic kinds of landforms. Have students classify each landscape as a plain, plateau, or mountainous region. *National Geographic* is a good source of landscape photography. L1 LEP LS

Videodisc

STV: Restless Earth

Dome mountains; Appalachians, Georgia

52236

Fault-block mountain; Teton Range, Wyoming

52235

Folded mountains; Swiss Alps

52234

Visual Learning

Figure 5-6 What types of peaks are characteristic of fault-block mountains? *sharp, jagged peaks* LEP IS

CONNECT TO
CHEMISTRY

Answer Mauna Loa has gentle slopes. It therefore would not contain materials high in water and silica.

Use **Science Integration Activities,** pp. 9-10, as you teach this lesson.

3 Assess

Check for Understanding

Have students contrast the processes that formed the Appalachians with those that formed the Black Hills. Students should realize that the difference involves the direction of force—lateral forces formed the Appalachians, while vertical forces were responsible for the formation of the Black Hills.

Reteach

- Use wooden blocks or rectangular sponges cut at various angles to demonstrate the formation of fault-block mountains.
- Demonstrate the formation of folded mountains by laying a piece of paper on a flat surface. Have a student place his or her hand on one end. Have another student put his or her hand on the other end. Have the students slide the ends of the paper toward the center.

Extension

For students who have mastered this section, use the **Reinforcement** and **Enrichment** masters.

Figure 5-5

Upwarped mountains form when crust is pushed up by forces inside Earth.

Upwarped Mountains

The southern Rocky Mountains in Colorado and New Mexico, the Black Hills in South Dakota, and the Adirondak Mountains in New York are **upwarped mountains.** These mountains were formed when crust was pushed up by forces inside Earth. Over time, the sedimentary rock on top of the crust eroded, leaving behind the igneous and metamorphic rock underneath. These igneous and metamorphic rocks then eroded to form sharp peaks and ridges, as shown in **Figure 5-5.**

Fault-Block Mountains

The Grand Teton Mountains of Wyoming and the Sierra Nevada Mountains in California formed in yet another way. **Fault-block mountains** are made of huge tilted blocks of rocks that are separated from surrounding rock by faults. A fault is a large crack in rocks along which there is movement. As **Figure 5-6** shows, when these mountains formed, one block was tilted and pushed up. The other block was pushed down. If you decide to go to the Tetons or to the Sierra Nevadas, you'll see the sharp, jagged peaks that are characteristic of fault-block mountains.

Figure 5-6

Fault-block mountains are created when faults occur. Some rock blocks move up, while others move down. *What types of peaks are characteristic of these mountains?*

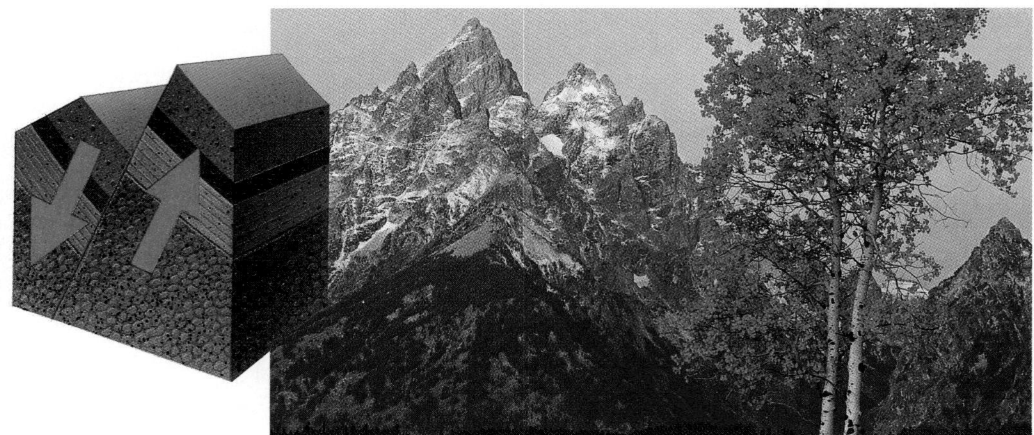

Across the Curriculum

Geography Use a world map to show students where major volcanic mountain chains are located. LEP IS

Figure 5-7
Volcanic mountains form when molten material oozes from Earth's crust and forms a cone-shaped structure.

Volcanic Mountains

Mount St. Helens in Washington and Mauna Loa in Hawaii are two of many volcanic mountains in the United States. **Volcanic mountains** like the one shown in **Figure 5-7** begin when molten material reaches the surface through a weak area of the crust. The materials pile up, one layer on top of another, until a cone-shaped structure forms. The Hawaiian Islands are just the peaks of huge volcanoes that stick out above the water.

Plains, plateaus, and mountains offer a wide variety of landforms to explore. They range from low coastal plains and high desert plateaus to mountain ranges thousands of meters high.

CONNECT TO CHEMISTRY

The composition of erupting materials helps determine a volcano's shape. High amounts of water and silica create violently erupting volcanoes with steep sides. Find a picture of Mauna Loa and ***observe*** its shape. Do its eruptions usually contain high amounts of water and silica?

Section Wrap-up

Review

1. Describe the eight major landforms in the United States.
2. What causes some mountains to be folded and others to be upwarped?
3. **Think Critically:** If you wanted to know whether a particular mountain was formed by a fault, what would you look for?

Using Computers

Spreadsheet Design a spreadsheet that compares the origin and features of folded, upwarped, fault-block, and volcanic mountains.

Skill Builder
Concept Mapping

Make an events chain concept map to explain how upwarped mountains form. If you need help, refer to Concept Mapping in the **Skill Handbook**.

4 Close

•MINI•QUIZ•

1. A _____ is a feature that makes up the shape of the land at Earth's surface. *landform*
2. _______ plains are lowlands along coastlines. *Coastal*
3. The Great Lakes area is part of the ______ plains. *interior*

Section Wrap-up

Review

1. Appalachian highlands, coastal plains, interior highlands, interior plains, intermontane plateaus and basin, Pacific mountain and valley system, Rocky Mountains, and Superior uplands.
2. Folded mountains form when rock layers are squeezed from opposite sides. Upwarped mountains form when crust is thrust upward by pressure inside Earth.
3. **Think Critically** Look for huge tilted blocks of rock that are separated from surrounding rocks by large cracks.

Using Computers

Mountain Type	Origin	Features
Folded	rock layers squeezed from sides	folded rock layers
Up-warped	crust pushed up from below	sharp peaks and ridges of igneous and metamorphic rock
Fault-Block	rocks move along fault	huge tilted blocks of rocks separated by faults
Volcanic	molten material reaches the surface	cone-shaped mountain

Skill Builder

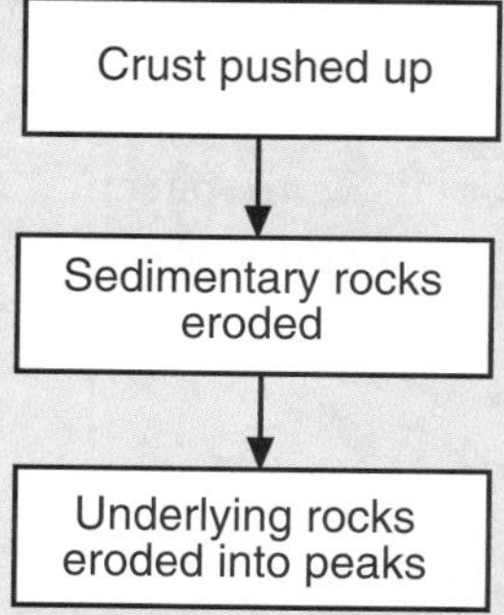

Assessment

Oral Use this Skill Builder to assess students' abilities to make an events chain concept map. Ask students where the formation of sedimentary rocks would fit into this events chain. Use the Performance Task Assessment List for Events Chain in **PASC,** p. 91. P

Section 5•2

Prepare

Section Background

Latitude is defined as the angle formed between the zenith line of any given point on Earth's surface and the plane of Earth's equator.

Preplanning

To prepare for the MiniLAB, obtain enough world maps for each student or group of students.

1 Motivate

Bellringer

Before presenting the lesson, display **Section Focus Transparency 19** on the overhead projector. Assign the accompanying **Focus Activity** worksheet. L1 LEP

Activity

LS **Interpersonal** Have pairs of students use globes to describe the location of an interesting place that they have visited or read about. L1

STV: Restless Earth
Continents today

52179

5•2 Viewpoints

Science Words

equator
latitude
prime meridian
longitude
International Date Line

Objectives

- Differentiate between latitude and longitude.
- Describe how latitude and longitude are used to identify locations.
- Calculate the time and date in different time zones.

Latitude and Longitude

If you are going to explore landforms, you might want to learn how to find locations on Earth. If you wanted to go to the Hawaiian Islands, how would you describe their location? You might say that they are located in the Pacific Ocean. That's correct, but there is a more precise way to locate places on Earth. You could use lines of latitude and longitude. These lines form an imaginary grid system that enables points on Earth to be located exactly.

Latitude

First, look at **Figure 5-8.** The **equator** is an imaginary line that circles Earth exactly halfway between the North and South Poles. The equator separates Earth into two equal halves, called the northern hemisphere and the southern

Figure 5-8

The degree value used for latitude is the measurement of the imaginary angle created between the equator, the center of Earth, and that location (A). Likewise, longitude is the measurement of the angle created between the prime meridian, the center of Earth, and that location (B).

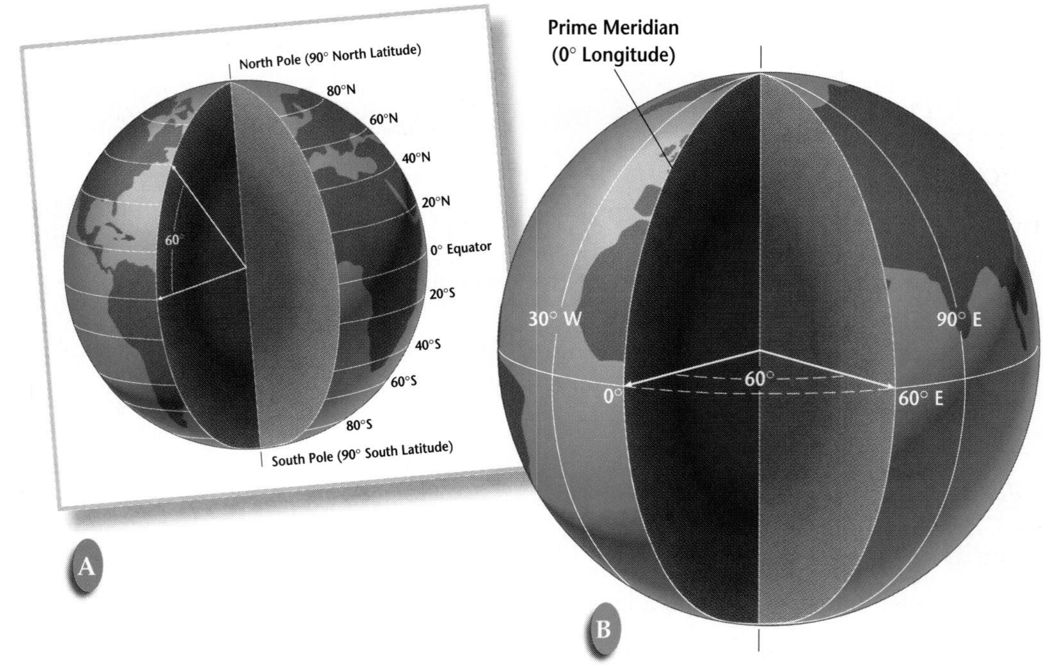

Program Resources

Reproducible Masters

Study Guide, p. 23 L1
Reinforcement, p. 23 L1
Enrichment, p. 23 L3
Activity Worksheets, pp. 5, 35 L1
Lab Manual 17, 18

Transparencies

Section Focus Transparency 19 L1
Teaching Transparency 10

hemisphere. The lines running parallel to the equator are called lines of latitude, or parallels. **Latitude** refers to distance in degrees either north or south of the equator. Just as other parallel lines do not intersect, lines of latitude do not intersect.

The equator is numbered 0° latitude. The poles are each numbered 90°. Therefore, latitude is measured from 0° at the equator to 90° at the poles. Locations north of the equator are referred to by degrees north latitude. Locations south of the equator are referred to by degrees south latitude. For example, Minneapolis, Minnesota, is located at 45° north latitude.

Longitude

Latitude lines are used for locations north and south of the equator, but what about locations in east and west directions? These vertical lines, seen in **Figure 5-8,** have two names—meridians and lines of longitude. Just as the equator is used as a reference point for north/south grid lines, there's a reference point for east/west grid lines. This reference point is the **prime meridian.** This imaginary line represents 0° longitude. In 1884, astronomers decided the prime meridian should go through the Greenwich (GREN itch) Observatory near London. **Longitude** refers to distances in degrees east or west of the prime meridian. Points west of the prime meridian have west longitude measured from 0° to 180°, while points east of the prime meridian have east longitude, also measured from 0° to 180°.

The prime meridian does not circle Earth as the equator does. Rather, it runs from the North Pole through Greenwich, England, to the South Pole. The line of longitude on the opposite side of Earth from the prime meridian where east lines of longitude meet west lines of longitude is the 180° meridian. This line is also known as the International Date Line.

Using latitude and longitude, you can locate Hawaii more accurately, as illustrated in **Figure 5-9.** Hawaii is located at 20° north latitude and about 155° west longitude, or 20°N, 155°W. Note that latitude comes first when we discuss the coordinates (latitude and longitude) of a particular location. Read on to see how longitude lines are used to tell time on Earth.

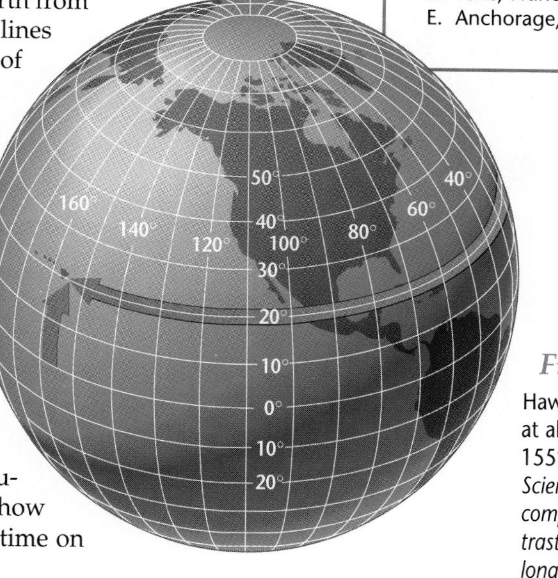

Figure 5-9

Hawaii is located at about 20°N, 155°W. *In your Science Journal, compare and contrast latitude and longitude.*

MiniLAB

How are latitude and longitude used to locate places on a map?

Procedure

1. Find the equator and prime meridian on a world map.
2. Move your finger to latitudes north of the equator, then south of the equator. Move your finger to longitudes west of the prime meridian, then east of the prime meridian.

Analysis

1. Identify the cities that have the following coordinates:
   A. 56°N; 38°E
   B. 34°S; 18°E
   C. 23°N; 82°W
   D. 13°N; 101°E
   E. 38°N; 9°W
2. Determine the latitude and longitude of the following cities:
   A. London, England
   B. Melbourne, Australia
   C. Buenos Aires, Argentina
   D. Paris, France
   E. Anchorage, Alaska

MiniLAB

Purpose

LS **Logical-Mathematical** Students will locate cities using longitude and latitude. L1

Materials

world map or globe, pencil, and paper

Teaching Strategies

Have students complete this activity in pairs. Have them compare their answers with those obtained by other groups.

Analysis

1. A. Moscow, Russia
   B. Cape Town, South Africa
   C. Havana, Cuba
   D. Bangkok, Thailand
   E. Lisbon, Portugal
2. A. 51°N, 1°W
   B. 38°S, 145°E
   C. 36°S, 62°W
   D. 49°N, 2°E
   E. 61°N, 150°W

Assessment

Performance To further assess students' understanding of latitude and longitude, have them use a map to determine the longitude and latitude of their hometown. Use the Performance Task Assessment List for Making Observations and Inferences in **PASC,** p. 17. P

Activity Worksheets, pp. 5, 35

Visual Learning

Figure 5-9 In your Science Journal, compare and contrast latitude and longitude. *Both are lines on a map and part of a grid system for referencing locations. Latitude refers to distances north and south of the equator. Longitude refers to distances east and west of the prime meridian.* LEP LS

2 Teach

CONNECT TO

LIFE SCIENCE

Answer It is caused by a decrease in the number of hours of sunlight.

Visual Learning

Figure 5-10 What time would it be in Los Angeles when the students in Atlanta returned home at 3 P.M.? *noon*

LEP LS

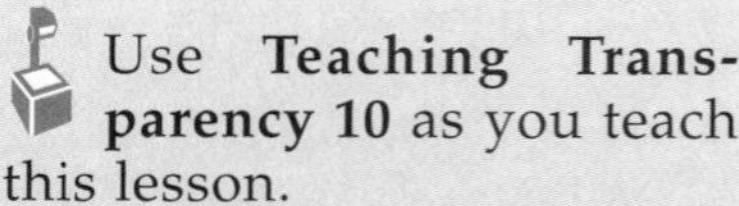

Use **Teaching Transparency 10** as you teach this lesson.

3 Assess

Check for Understanding

FLEX Your Brain

Use the Flex Your Brain activity to have students explore LATITUDE.

Activity Worksheets, p. 5

Reteach

To help students with the concept of time zones, obtain a globe that has an indicator showing time zones.

Extension

For students who have mastered this section, use the **Reinforcement** and **Enrichment** masters.

CONNECT TO

LIFE SCIENCE

Many organisms use biological clocks to "tell time." The timing mechanisms are triggered by changes in the environment and changes within the organism. ***Infer*** what environmental change causes trees to become dormant in the fall.

Earth Time

What time is it right now? That depends on where you are on Earth. We keep track of time by measuring Earth's movement in relation to the sun. Earth rotates one full turn every 24 hours. When one half of Earth is facing the sun, the other half is facing away from it. For the half facing the sunlight, it is daytime. For the half in darkness, it is nighttime. And because Earth is constantly spinning, time is always changing.

Time Zones

How can you know what time it is at any particular location on Earth? Earth is divided into time zones. Because Earth takes 24 hours to rotate once, it is divided into 24 time zones, each one hour different. Each time zone is 15 degrees wide. There are six different time zones in the United States. Because Earth is rotating, the sun rises earlier in Atlanta, Georgia, than it does in Los Angeles, California. In Atlanta at 7:00 A.M. you would be on your way to school, like the students in **Figure 5-10A.** But in Los Angeles, it's 4:00 A.M. and you would be asleep, like the student in **Figure 5-10B.** If you lived in Los Angeles, and were in your first or second period class, a student in Atlanta would be at lunch.

As you can see in **Figure 5-11,** the time zones do not strictly follow lines of longitude. Time zone boundaries have been adjusted in local areas. For example, if a city were split by a time

Figure 5-10

Earth is divided into 24 time zones, each one hour different. There are six time zones in the United States.

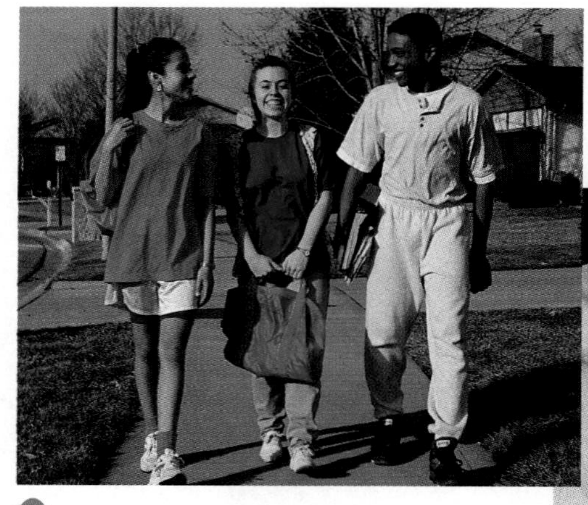

A Atlanta, Georgia, lies in the Eastern time zone. Students there would be on their way to school at 7:00 A.M. in the morning.

B But a student in Los Angeles, California, which lies in the Pacific time zone, would still be fast asleep. *What time would it be in Los Angeles when the students in Atlanta returned home at 3:00 P.M.?*

zone boundary, great confusion would result. In such a situation, the time zone boundary is moved to outside of the city.

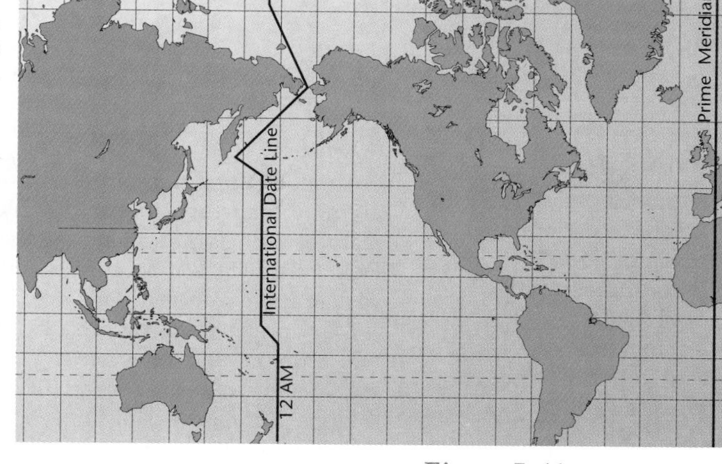

Figure 5-11

Time zones are roughly determined by lines of longitude.

Calendar Dates

We all know that a day ends and the next day begins at 12 midnight. If it is 11:59 P.M. Tuesday, two minutes later it is 12:01 A.M. Wednesday. Every time zone experiences this transition from one day to the next. The calendar advances to the next day in each time zone at midnight.

You gain or lose time each time you travel through a time zone until at some point you gain or lose a whole day. The **International Date Line** is the 180 degree meridian that is the transition line for calendar days. If you were traveling west across the International Date Line, you would advance your calendar one day. If you were traveling east you would move your calendar back one day.

Section Wrap-up

Review

1. How do lines of latitude and longitude help us find locations on Earth?
2. What are the longitude and latitude of New Orleans?
3. **Think Critically:** How could you leave home on Monday to go sailing, sail for an hour on Sunday, and return home on Monday?

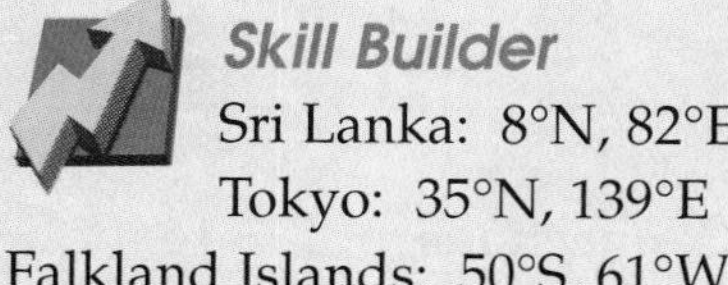

Skill Builder

Interpreting Scientific Illustrations

Use Appendix G to find the approximate longitude and latitude of the following locations: Sri Lanka; Tokyo, Japan; and the Falkland Islands. If you need help, refer to Interpreting Scientific Illustrations in the **Skill Handbook.**

USING MATH

If you left London on the Concord jet airplane at 8 A.M., London time, you would arrive in New York at 6 A.M., New York time. You would have crossed five time zones during your flight. How long did the trip take?

4 Close

• MINI • QUIZ •

Use the Mini Quiz to check students' recall of chapter content.

1. **Lines of _____ are used to locate places north and south of the equator.** *latitude*
2. **Lines of _____ are used to locate points east and west of the prime meridian.** *longitude*
3. **The 180° meridian is also called the _____ .** *International Date Line*

Section Wrap-up

Review

1. Lines of latitude and longitude give us a precise way to locate places on Earth.
2. 90° west longitude, 30° north latitude
3. **Think Critically** If you lived just west of the International Date Line, you could sail in waters just east of the International Date Line, and return home back across the date line at night.

USING MATH

It would be 4:00 A.M. in New York when the flight leaves London. If it arrives in New York at 6:00, it would be a two-hour flight.

Skill Builder

Sri Lanka: 8°N, 82°E
Tokyo: 35°N, 139°E
Falkland Islands: 50°S, 61°W

Assessment

Content Use this Skill Builder to assess students' abilities to interpret scientific illustrations. Ask students to name the continent located between 116° and 153° east longitude and 11° and 39° south latitude. *Australia is the answer.* Use the Performance Task Assessment List for Making Observations and Inferences in **PASC,** p. 17. P

Section 5•3

Prepare

Section Background

- The major publisher of topographic maps in the U.S. is the United States Geological Survey (USGS). Other map publishers include the Department of Defense, the Department of Agriculture, and the Forest Service.
- Standard maps produced by the USGS are called quadrangles. Quadrangle maps are bounded by parallels and meridians. The maps are named for obvious features within the area shown on the map. No two quadrangles of the same series in the same state can have the same name.

Preplanning

To prepare for Activity 5-1, obtain the following items for each group of students: plastic model landform, transparency, clear plastic storage box with lid, a beaker, a metric ruler, tape, and transparency marker.

1 Motivate

Bellringer

Before presenting the lesson, display **Section Focus Transparency 20** on the overhead projector. Assign the accompanying **Focus Activity** worksheet. L1 LEP

Tying to Previous Knowledge

Have a map of your city available for students to examine. Although the students may be familiar with the city, they may never have used a city map to get around. Use the map to locate familiar places—your school, a mall, and so on.

5•3 Maps

Science Words

Mercator projection
Robinson projection
conic projection
topographic map
contour line
contour interval
map legend
map scale

Objectives

- Differentiate among Mercator, Robinson, and conic projections.
- Describe how contour lines and contour intervals are used to illustrate elevation on a topographic map.
- Explain why topographic maps have scales.

Map Projections

Think of the different types of maps you have seen. There are road maps, weather maps, and maps that show physical features such as mountains and valleys. They are all models of Earth's surface. But because Earth's surface is curved, it is not easy to represent on a flat piece of paper.

Maps are made using projections. A map projection is made when points and lines on a globe's surface are transferred onto paper. There are several different ways to make map projections. But all types of projections have some sort of distortion in either the shapes of land masses or their areas.

Mercator Projection

One type of map is a Mercator projection. A **Mercator projection** has correct shapes of continents, but their areas are distorted. Lines of longitude are projected onto the map parallel to each other. As you learned earlier, only latitude lines are parallel. Longitude lines meet at the poles. When longitude lines are projected as parallel, areas near the poles are

Figure 5-12

Because Earth's surface is curved, all types of map projections distort either the shapes of land masses or their areas.

A — A Mercator projection exaggerates the areas near the poles.

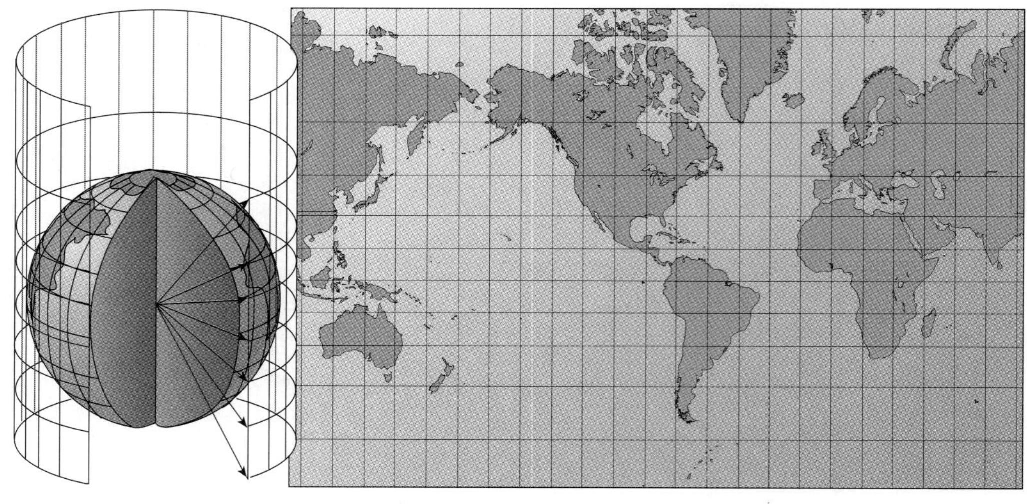

Program Resources

Reproducible Masters
Study Guide, p. 24 L1
Reinforcement, p. 24 L1
Enrichment, p. 24 L3
Cross-Curricular Integration, p. 9
Science and Society Integration, p.9
Activity Worksheets, pp. 5, 30-31 L1
Critical Thinking/Problem Solving, p. 11
Lab Manual 19, 20
Multicultural Connections, pp. 13-14

Transparencies
Section Focus Transparency 20 L1

exaggerated. Look at Greenland in the Mercator projection in **Figure 5-12A.** It appears to be larger than South America. Greenland is actually much smaller than South America. Mercator projections are mainly used on ships and airplanes.

Robinson Projection

A map that has accurate continent shapes and shows accurate land areas is the **Robinson projection.** As in **Figure 5-12B,** lines of latitude remain parallel, and lines of longitude are curved as they would be on a globe. This results in less distortion near the poles.

Conic Projection

A third type of projection is a conic projection. You use this type of projection, shown in **Figure 5-12C,** whenever you look at a road map or a weather map. **Conic projections** are used to produce maps of small areas. They are made by projecting points and lines from a globe onto a cone.

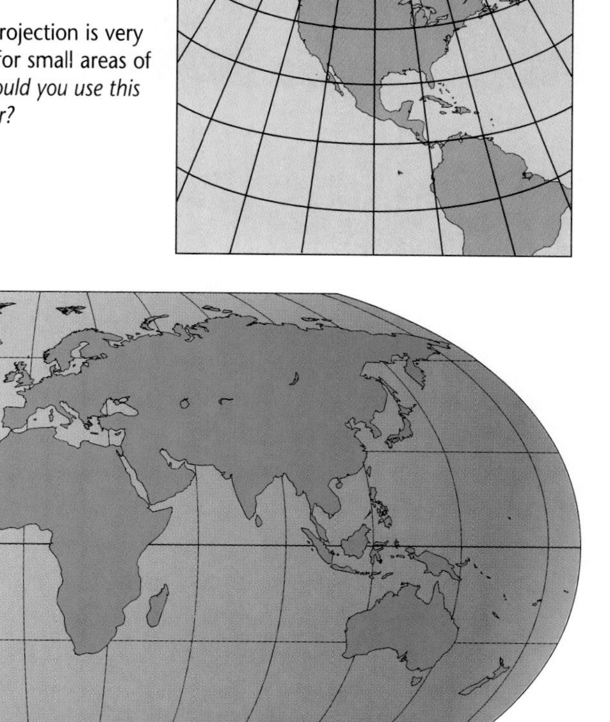

C A conic projection is very accurate for small areas of Earth. *What could you use this type of map for?*

B A Robinson projection shows less distortion near the poles than a Mercator projection.

2 Teach

Inquiry Question

How are map projections made? *Points and lines on a globe's surface are transferred onto paper.*

Discussion

Have students contrast the three types of projections.

Concept Development

Use a photo of Earth from space to discuss why, due to Earth's size, globes and maps must be used to represent physical and cultural features of the planet's surface.

Visual Learning

Figure 5-12C What could you use this type of map for? *A conic projection is used for road maps and weather maps.* LEP

GLENCOE TECHNOLOGY

Videodisc

STVS: Earth & Space

Disc 3, Side 2

Map Science (Ch. 21)

Charting Air Space (Ch. 22)

Mapping with a Rifle (Ch. 20)

Use **Critical Thinking/Problem Solving,** p. 11, as you teach this lesson.

Across the Curriculum

Vocational Have some blueprints of houses and other structures available for students to examine. Have students compare and contrast maps and blueprints. L1 LS

Inclusion Strategies

Gifted Have students research other types of map projections besides Mercator, Robinson, and conic maps. Have them report their results in a table. L3

Teacher F.Y.I.

Most USGS quadrangles use the English System of units rather than SI. Therefore, contour intervals are given in feet above or below sea level instead of in meters on most topographic maps.

Visual Learning

Figure 5-13C What do contour intervals tell us about elevation? *Contour intervals tell us the difference between two side-by-side contour lines.*

Inquiry Question

List several natural and cultural features you would find on topographic maps. *mountains, hills, plains, lakes, rivers, roads, dams, and houses*

GLENCOE TECHNOLOGY

Videodisc

STVS: Earth & Space

Disc 3, Side 2

Studying the Pacific Ocean (Ch. 14)

Exploring Lake Superior's Bottom (Ch. 15)

Use these program resources as you teach this lesson.

Cross-Curricular Integration, p. 9

Multicultural Connections, pp. 13-14

Figure 5-13

This sequence shows how a topographic map of a landform is made.

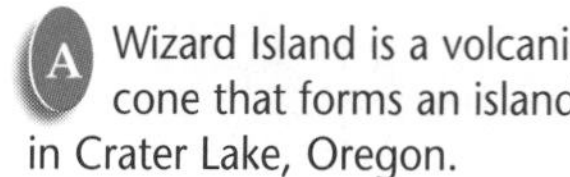

A Wizard Island is a volcanic cone that forms an island in Crater Lake, Oregon.

Topographic Maps

If you wanted to go hiking, a conic map projection would get you to the mountain. Next, you would need a detailed map showing the hills and valleys of that specific area. A **topographic map** shows the changes in elevation of Earth's surface. With this map, you could tell how steep the mountain trail is. It would also show natural features such as mountains, hills, plains, lakes, and rivers, and cultural features such as roads, cities, dams, and other structures built by people.

Contour Lines

Before starting your hike up the mountain, you would look at the contour lines on your topographic map to see the trail's changes in elevation. A **contour line** is a line on a map that connects points of equal elevation. Elevation refers to the distance of a location above or below sea level. The difference in elevation between two side-by-side contour lines is called the **contour interval.** If the contour interval was 10 meters, then when you walked between those two lines on the trail, you would have climbed or descended 10 meters.

B Different points of elevation are projected onto paper.

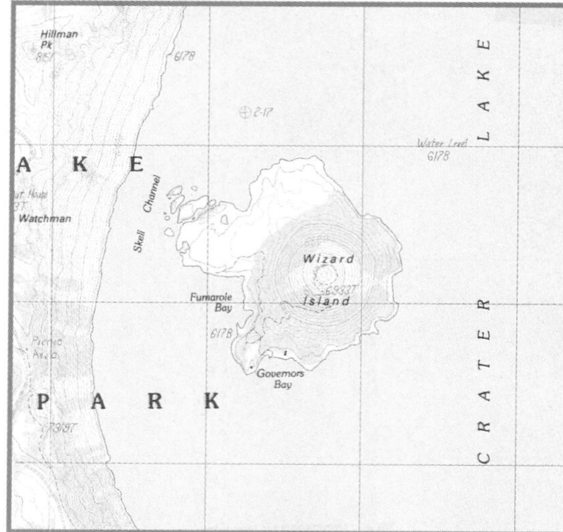

C The points of elevation are connected to form a topographic map of the island. *What do contour intervals tell us about elevation?*

As **Figure 5-13** shows, the size of the contour interval can vary. For mountains, the contour lines might be very close and the contour interval might be as great as 100 meters. This would tell you that the land is very steep because there is a large change in elevation between lines. However, if there isn't a great change in elevation and the contour lines are far apart, your map might have a contour interval of 5 meters.

Index Contours

Some contour lines, called index contours, are marked with their elevation. If the contour interval is 5 meters, you can tell the elevation of other lines around the index contour by adding or subtracting 5 meters from the elevation indicated on the index contour.

USING TECHNOLOGY

Rocks in 3-D!

You have learned that topographic maps are two-dimensional models of Earth. On such maps, contour lines connect points of equal elevation. Topographic maps are used to study features on Earth's surface.

To unravel Earth's complex structure, however, geologists also need to know what the rock beds "look like" in three dimensions. With computers, topographic maps are digitized to get the "top layer" of data for the 3-D maps. Digitizing is a process by which points are located on a coordinate grid.

Digging Deeper

Geologists then use data from wells drilled into the crust to obtain information about other layers of rocks beneath the surface. The computer analyzes all the data and generates a three-dimensional map that shows what the rocks of an area look like. The map shown in the photograph illustrates how the drainage basin of an ancient river system was changed when forces at Earth's surface and forces within Earth acted on the river in Montana.

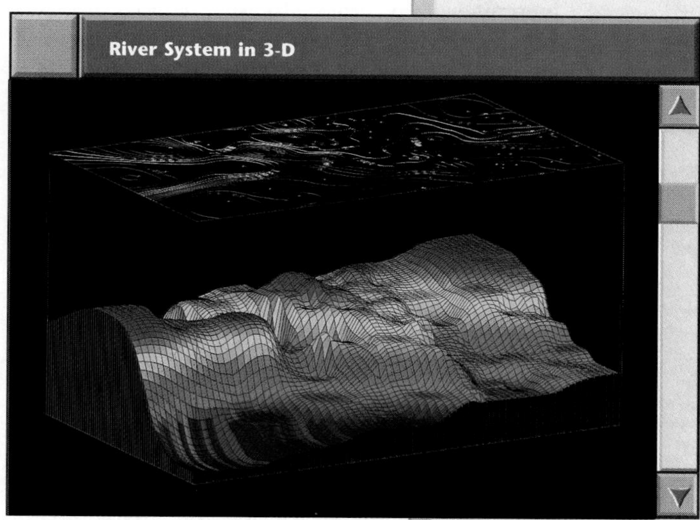
River System in 3-D

Think Critically:

List one advantage a 3-D map has over a 2-D map.

USING TECHNOLOGY

- Show students a photo of an outcrop. Have them use clay to construct a 3-D model of the rocks. Then have students hypothesize what the rock beds look like in the third dimension.
- For more information, see "Geologic Models in Three Dimensions" by Nick Van Driel, *Geotimes,* September 1989, pp. 12-13.

Think Critically

Answers may vary, but students should realize that 3-D maps allow geologists to "see" subsurface structures.

Activity

LS **Visual-Spatial** If possible, obtain a topographic map of your region for students to examine. L1

Inquiry Questions

- **What is the contour interval on a map if two side-by-side contour lines are labeled as 200 meters and 300 meters?** *The contour interval is 100 meters.*
- **How can you distinguish between an index contour and a regular contour line?** *An index contour is marked with its elevation. A regular contour line is not labeled.*
- **Why wouldn't a 5-meter contour interval be used on a topographic map of a mountainous region?** *The map would not be readable because the lines would be too close together.*

Use **Science and Society Integration,** p. 9, as you teach this lesson.

Problem Solving

Solve the Problem

1. Cedar Mountain
2. The hiker going to Orr Mountain had the steepest climb. The contour lines are closer together.
3. Answers will vary but should include road, stream or river, water tank, railroad, creek, and highway.

Think Critically

1. The hiker going to Cedar Well probably reached his or her destination first because he or she traveled over gentle or flat slopes. Since a straight-line path is probably not the quickest way to the top of either Orr Mountain or Cedar Mountain because of steep slopes, forests, streams, and lack of direct trails, use of available trails would probably save time. The hiker heading for the top of Orr Mountain would be most likely to reach the top second, using available trails.
2. Once at the top, the two hikers would have unobstructed views of the other summit. But, because of the distances, each would need strong binoculars to see the other.

Visual Learning

Figure 5-14 In your Science Journal, explain why this is the case. *Contour lines form Vs when they cross streams because streams flow in depressions that are beneath the elevation of the surrounding land surface.* LEP IS

Figure 5-14

Contour lines form Vs whenever they cross streams. *In your Science Journal, explain why this is the case.*

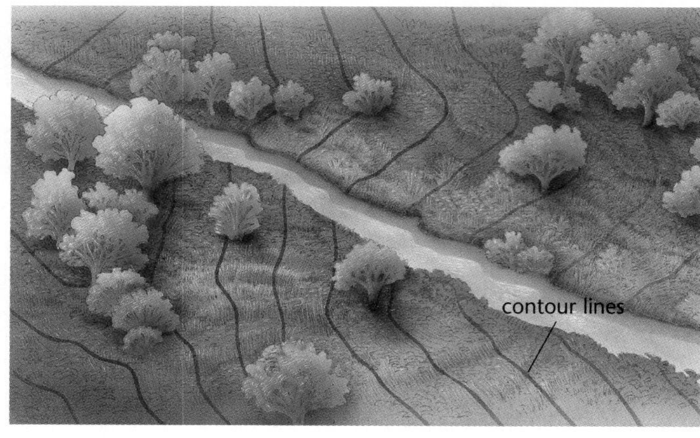

Here are some rules to remember when examining contour lines.

1. **Contour lines close around hills and basins or depressions.** To decide whether you're looking at a hill or basin, you can read the elevation numbers or look for hachures. Hachures are short lines at right angles to the contour line that are used to show depressions. These lines point toward lower elevations.
2. **Contour lines never cross.** If they did, it would mean that the spot where they cross would have two different elevations.
3. **Contour lines form Vs that point upstream whenever they cross streams.** This is because streams flow in depressions that are beneath the elevation of the surrounding land surface. Look at **Figure 5-14.** When the contour lines follow the depression, they appear as Vs pointing upstream on the map.

Figure 5-15

Here are some typical symbols used on topographic maps.

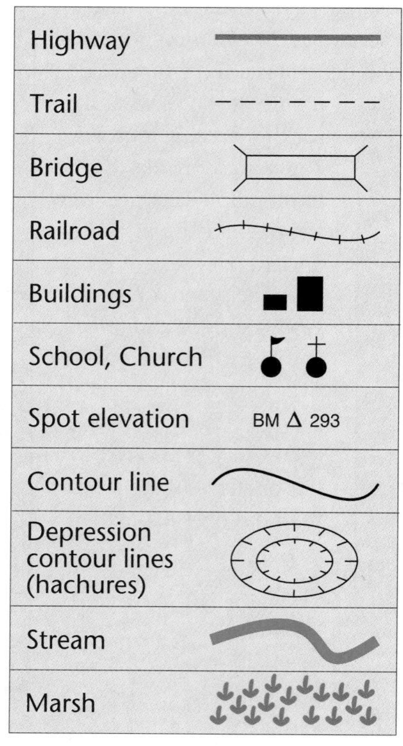

Map Legend and Scale

Another thing you would want to know before you set out on your hike is, "How far is it to the top of the mountain?" Because maps are small models of Earth's surface, distances and sizes of things on a map are proportional to the real thing on Earth. This is accomplished using "scale" distances.

Map Legend

Topographic maps and most other maps have a legend. A **map legend** explains what the symbols used on the map mean. Some frequently used symbols for topographic maps are shown in **Figure 5-15** and Appendix H.

Map Scale

The **map scale** is the relationship between the distances on the map and actual distances on Earth's surface. Scale is often represented as a ratio. For example, a topographic map of the Grand Canyon may have a scale that reads "1:80 000." This means that one unit on the map represents 80 000 units on land. If the unit you wanted to use was a centimeter, then one cm on the map would equal 80 000 cm on land. The unit of distance may be in feet or millimeters or any other measure of distance. However, the units of measure on each side of the ratio must always be the same. A map scale may also be in the form of a small bar graph that is divided into a number of units. The units are the scaled-down equivalent distances to real distances on Earth.

Problem Solving

Using a Topographic Map

The map below is a topographic map of an area in California. One sunny day, three hikers started from the point marked with the + in the center of the map. One hiker tackled the peak of Cedar Mountain, another the peak of Orr Mountain, while the third headed for Cedar Well.

All three traveled at the same rate on flat or gentle slopes. Their climb slowed as the ground grew steeper.

Solve the Problem:

1. **Which peak is the highest?**
2. **Which hiker had the steepest climb? Explain using contour lines.**
3. **Name three items found in a map legend that the hiker heading for Orr Mountain crossed before reaching his or her goal.**

Think Critically:

1. If each hiker could choose any route to his or her destination, which one do you think reached his or her goal first? Explain.
2. Once at the top, could the hiker on Cedar Mountain see the hiker on Orr Mountain? Why or why not?

Activity

IS Interpersonal Have pairs of students sketch maps of the neighborhood around the school. When maps are completed, have partners exchange with other partners. Allow students to compare and contrast at least three or four maps. After examining the maps, students should realize the need for a uniform system of representing features at Earth's surface and the importance of accurate observations and measurements. L1 **COOP LEARN**

Inquiry Question

Why is the marsh topographic symbol sometimes found with contour lines with hachures? *Water gathers in low spots, indicated on a topographic map by hachures. A marsh is a watery lowland.*

3 Assess

Check for Understanding

FLEX Your Brain

Use the Flex Your Brain activity to have students explore TOPOGRAPHIC MAPS. P

Activity Worksheets, p. 5

Reteach

IS Visual-Spatial Have students use the map in the Problem Solving activity to identify roads, streams, contour lines, index contours, woodlands, and the map scale.

Extension

For students who have mastered this section, use the **Reinforcement** and **Enrichment** masters.

4 Close

•MINI•QUIZ•

Use the Mini Quiz to check students' recall of chapter content.

1. **A _____ map shows the changes in elevation of Earth's surface.** *topographic*
2. **A _____ is a line on a map that connects points of equal elevation.** *contour line*
3. **Short lines at right angles to contour lines that are used to show depressions are called _____ .** *hachures*
4. **Contour lines form Vs that point _____ whenever they cross streams.** *upstream*
5. **A map's _____ explains what symbols used on the map mean.** *legend*

Section Wrap-up

Review

1. In a Mercator projection, lines of longitude are parallel to one another. Thus, a Mercator map distorts regions near the poles, making them appear much larger than they really are.
2. One spot cannot have two different elevations.
3. **Think Critically** They are 8 km apart. The change in elevation is at least 150 m.

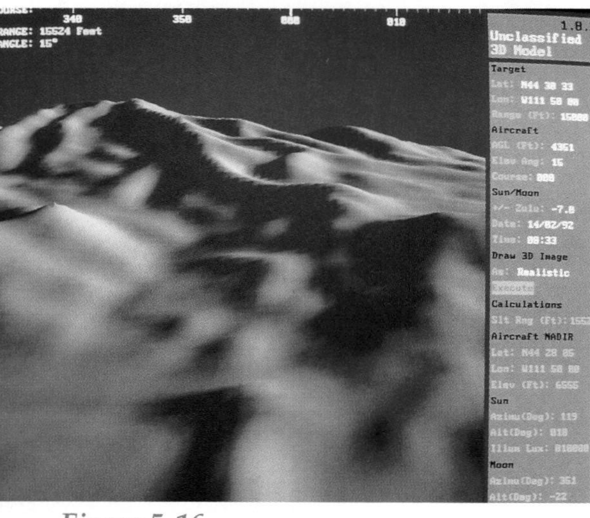

Figure 5-16

Computers have revolutionized the way cartographers make maps.

Uses of Maps

As you have learned, there are many different ways to view Earth. The map you choose to use will depend upon your need. For instance, if you wanted to determine New Zealand's location relative to Canada, you would probably examine a Mercator projection. In your search, you would use lines of latitude and longitude, and map scale. If you wanted to travel across the country, you would rely on a conic projection. And if you wanted to scale the highest peak in your county, you would take along a topographic map.

As **Figure 5-16** shows, mapmaking or cartography has experienced a technological revolution in the past few decades. Remote sensing and computers have changed the way maps are made. Read more about the history of cartography in this chapter's Science & History feature.

Section Wrap-up

Review

1. Why does Greenland appear to be larger on a Mercator projection than it does on a Robinson projection?
2. Why can't contour lines ever cross?
3. **Think Critically:** Suppose you have a topographic map with a contour interval of 50 m. According to the map scale, 1 cm on the map equals 1 km. The distance between points A and B on the map is 8 cm. Four contour lines lie between them. How far apart are the points and what is the change in elevation?

Science Journal

Draw a map in your Science Journal that your friends could use to get from school to your home. Include symbols and a map scale.

Skill Builder

Measuring in SI

Use the topographic map in Problem Solving to practice measuring in SI.

1. How far is it from Cedar Well to Orr Mountain?
2. How big is Antelope Sink at its widest place?

If you need help, refer to Measuring in SI in the **Skill Handbook.**

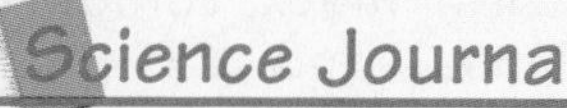

Science Journal

Maps will vary but should include symbols, a legend, and a scale.

Skill Builder

1. approximately 8 km
2. about 0.3 km

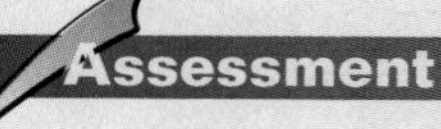

Assessment

Performance Use this Skill Builder to assess students' abilities to measure in SI. Ask students to draw a line labeled X-Y on the topographic map in Problem Solving. Have them measure the line. Use the Performance Task Assessment List for Using Math in Science in **PASC,** p. 29. P

Making a Topographic Map

Have you ever wondered how topographic maps are made? Today, radar and remote sensing devices aboard satellites collect data, and computers and graphic systems make the maps. In the past, surveyors and aerial photographers collected data. Then maps were hand drawn by cartographers, or mapmakers. In this activity, you can try your hand at cartography.

Problem

How is a topographic map made?

Materials

- plastic model landform
- water tinted with food coloring
- transparency
- clear plastic storage box with lid
- beaker
- metric ruler
- tape
- transparency marker

Procedure

1. Using the ruler and the transparency marker, make marks up the side of the storage box 2 cm apart.
2. Secure the transparency to the outside of the box lid with tape.
3. Place the plastic model in the box. The bottom of the box will be zero elevation.
4. Using the beaker, pour water into the box to a height of 2 cm. Place the lid on the box.
5. Use the transparency marker to trace the top of the water line on the transparency.
6. Using the scale 2 cm = 10 m, mark the elevation on the line.
7. Remove the lid and add water until a depth of 4 cm is reached.
8. Map this level on the storage box lid and record the elevation.
9. Repeat the process of adding water and tracing until you have the hill mapped.
10. Transfer the tracing of the hill onto a white sheet of paper.

Analyze

1. What is the contour interval of this topographic map?
2. How does the distance between contour lines on the map show the steepness of slope on the landform model?
3. **Determine** the total elevation of the hill.
4. How was elevation represented on your map?

Conclude and Apply

5. How are elevations shown on topographic maps?
6. Must all topographic maps have a 0-m elevation contour line? **Explain.**
7. **Compare** the contour interval of an area of high relief with one of low relief on a topographic map.

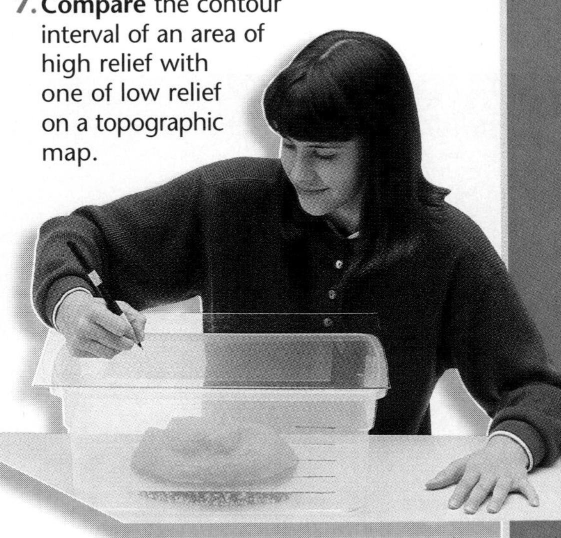

Activity 5-1

Purpose

LS **Kinesthetic** Students will make a topographic map from a landform model. L1

Process Skills

measuring in SI, making models, interpreting data, comparing and contrasting

Time

45 minutes

Activity Worksheets, pp. 5, 30-31

Teaching Strategies

Alternate Materials If plastic model landforms are unavailable, use clay. Water-soluble flow pens are good replacements for transparency pens.

Troubleshooting For acceptable results, students must be directly over the model when tracing the contour lines. Best results are obtained when one eye is closed. If students do not trace from the same position each time, a difference in tracing angle can cause the traced lines to touch or even cross.

- Some students may need extra help in understanding the scale to be used.
- A few drops of food coloring added to the water make it easier to detect the model/water contact when tracing.
- Use beakers or cups to remove some of the water when the activity is over, before attempting to move the full box to the sink to pour out the water.

Answers to Questions

1. 10 m
2. The closer together the contour lines are on the map, the steeper the slopes on the model. Increased distances between contour lines indicate flat areas of the model.
3. The elevation of students' hills will vary, but they should always equal the height of the model in centimeters times 500.
4. Elevation is indicated by the lines drawn on the transparencies. These lines are called contour lines.
5. by contour lines
6. No, the 0-m contour line is only on maps with elevations at sea level.
7. Generally, the greater the relief of an area, the larger the contour interval. Relatively flat areas of low relief are represented by smaller contour intervals.

Assessment

Performance To further assess students' understanding of making topographic maps from landform models, have them repeat the activity using a second landform model shape. Have them compare and contrast their two completed topographic maps. Use the Performance Task Assessment List for Model in **PASC**, p. 51. P

Prepare

Section Background

Sonar *(SOund Navigation And Ranging)*, was first used in World War I to detect submarines using echoes that bounced off their hulls.

Preplanning

To prepare for Activity 5-2, have students bring cardboard from home.

1 Motivate

Bellringer

Before presenting the lesson, display **Section Focus Transparency 21** on the overhead projector. Assign the accompanying **Focus Activity** worksheet. L1 LEP

2 Teach

INTEGRATION
Physics

A sound wave travels in water much faster than it does in air because the water molecules are closer together. The velocity of sound at 0° C in dry air is about 332 m/s. In water, it is 1454 m/s.

3 Assess

Check for Understanding

Have a volunteer explain why Sea Beam maps can be so detailed. They should respond that the depth readings overlap to provide much data.

5•4 TECHNOLOGY: Mapping Our Planet

Science Words

Landsat Satellite
Topex-Poseidon Satellite
sonar

Objectives

- Describe how Landsat Satellites collect information about Earth's surface.
- Compare the data-collecting technique of the Topex-Poseidon Satellite with sonar.

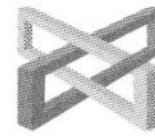

INTEGRATION
Physics

Remote Sensing from Space

As you learned in Activity 5-1, today we rely on remote sensing and radar to collect much of the data used for making maps.

Landsat Satellites

Landsat Satellites detect different wavelengths of energy reflected or emitted from Earth's surface. Each Landsat has a mirror that moves to scan Earth's surface. On this mirror are rows of detectors that measure the intensity of the energy they receive from Earth. This information is transmitted to Earth as a series of 0s and 1s. The result is a digital image. Digital images are computer images that show each of the different wavelengths of energy as different colors. These images show landforms in great detail.

Topex-Poseidon Satellite

The **Topex-Poseidon Satellite** (Topex stands for topographic experiment) uses radar to compute the distance to the ocean's surface. Radar waves are high-frequency radio signals that are sent from the satellite to the ocean. As **Figure 5-17** illustrates, a receiving device then picks up the returning echo as it bounces off the water. The distance to the water's surface is calculated using the speed of radar and the time it takes for the radar to be reflected back. Since there is more gravitational force between ocean water and massive structures on the ocean floor, water forms bulges over mountains and depressions over valleys. With this information, computers draw ocean-bottom maps that show features as small as 13 km.

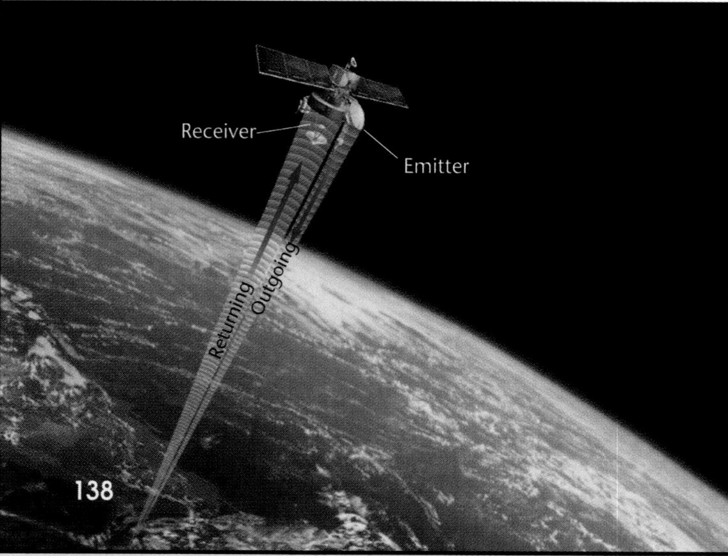

Figure 5-17
Using high-frequency radio waves, the Topex-Poseidon Satellite can map small features on the ocean floor.

138

Program Resources

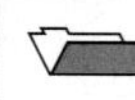
Reproducible Masters
Study Guide, p. 25 L1
Reinforcement, p. 25 L1
Enrichment, p. 25 L3
Activity Worksheets, pp. 5, 32-33 L1

Transparencies
Section Focus Transparency 21 L1
Science Integration Transparency 5

Remote Sensing Under Water

Sonar refers to the use of sound waves to detect ocean-bottom structures. First, a sound wave is sent from a ship towards the ocean floor. A receiving device then picks up the returning echo when it bounces off the bottom. The distance to the bottom is calculated by a computer on the ship using the speed of sound in water and the time it takes for the sound to be reflected.

Sea Beam

Using a new technology called Sea Beam, scientists are making very detailed, accurate maps of the ocean floor. A ship with Sea Beam, like the one shown in **Figure 5-18,** has more than a dozen sonar devices, each aimed at different parts of the seafloor. As the ship goes back and forth across the seafloor, readings of depth overlap. Computers take this information and make a detailed, continuous map of the ocean floor.

These new Sea Beam maps are very useful. For example, fishing companies can use them to locate underwater canyons where certain fish might be found. Oceanographers use them to study the ocean.

Originally, all Sea Beam maps were classified as secret. Because they were so accurate, government officials didn't want other countries to have detailed maps of the ocean floor around the United States. They feared that hostile submarines could use the maps to navigate our coastal areas. Now, most of the Sea Beam maps have been released to the public.

Figure 5-18

Sea Beam can also make detailed maps of the ocean floor. *What are some uses for these maps?*

Section Wrap-up

Review

1. How do Landsat Satellites collect information about Earth's surface?
2. In your Science Journal, explain the similarities between the data-collecting methods of Topex-Poseidon and sonar.

Explore the Technology

Landsat satellite information is used for more than just making maps. The digital images are used to locate soil erosion problems, monitor desert and forest growth, explore for minerals, study ocean currents, measure pollution, determine population density, and even track migrating animals. Explain how Landsat information can be used to plan the growth of cities.

USING MATH

Sound travels through water at 1454 meters per second. If a ship sends a sonar signal to the ocean floor and it reflects back to the ship in 2.25 seconds, how deep is the ocean at this point?

SCIENCE & SOCIETY

Reteach

Tell students to close one eye, hold one index finger 15 cm from their noses, and observe the finger. Next, tell them to stay in the same position, open the eye that was closed, close the other eye, and look at the finger again. Ask them how their two views are different. Have them relate what they observed to how Sea Beam works.

Extension

For students who have mastered this section, use the **Reinforcement** and **Enrichment** masters.

4 Close

•MINI•QUIZ•

1. **There is more ______ force between ocean water and mountains than between ocean water and depressions on the ocean floor.** *gravitational*
2. **The distance to the bottom of the ocean is calculated by knowing the ______ of sound in water and the time it takes sound to be reflected.** *speed*

Section Wrap-up

Review

1. Landsats use rows of detectors or mirrors to detect wavelengths of energy reflected or emitted from Earth's surface.
2. Both bounce energy off of the surfaces they are studying. By measuring the time it takes for an echo to be received, the distance to the object can be determined.

Visual Learning

Figure 5-18 What are some uses for these maps? *Sea Beam maps can be used by fishing companies to locate underwater canyons where certain fish might be, or by oceanographers to study the ocean.* LEP LS

Explore the Technology

Cities can be planned so that they do the least destruction to the environment and so that natural resources can be used to the greatest advantage.

USING MATH

Answer 1454 m × 2.25 seconds = 3271.5 m

PREPARATION

Purpose

LS **Kinesthetic** Students will show the relationship between topographic maps and landforms by making a 3-D model from a topographic map. L1 LEP COOP LEARN

Process Skills

communicating, forming operational definitions, forming a hypothesis, using numbers, designing an experiment, interpreting scientific illustrations, making models, observing and inferring

Time

45 minutes

Materials

Have students save cardboard at home and bring it to school for this activity.

Safety Precautions

Caution students working near the overhead-projector light that it can get very hot. If students are using razor knives in place of scissors, instruct them in the proper use of this tool.

Possible Hypothesis

Students might hypothesize that they can make the model by stacking pieces of cardboard or foam board to show elevation differences. They might use the transparency marker and transparency to trace over the topographic map. The transparency placed onto an overhead projector could be focused onto a piece of paper taped to the wall. By cutting out the contour lines on this paper, a pattern for each level of the model could be made.

Activity Worksheets, pp. 5, 32-33

Activity 5-2

Design Your Own Experiment
Modeling Earth

Have you ever built a model plane, train, or car? Modeling is more than just fun. Models are used to help engineers and designers build actual planes, trains, and cars. A topographic map is a two-dimensional model—on flat paper. How can you build a three-dimensional model of a landform?

PREPARATION

Problem

How can a 3-D model be made of an area shown on a topographic map?

Form a Hypothesis

Based on the drawing below, state a hypothesis about how you can make a large model of Blackberry Hill, such that its base is as long as a piece of notebook paper.

Objectives

- Design and make a 3-D model that shows the relationship between topographic maps and landforms.
- Interpret data from your model.

Possible Materials

- transparency marker (fine point)
- blank transparency
- overhead projector
- sheet of white paper
- pencil
- tape
- corrugated cardboard sheets or foam-board sheets
- scissors or razor knife
- glue
- metric ruler

Safety Precautions

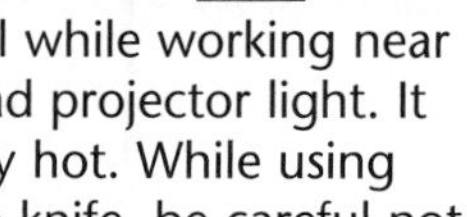

Be careful while working near the overhead projector light. It can get very hot. While using scissors or a knife, be careful not to cut yourself or the desk top.

PLAN THE EXPERIMENT

Possible Procedures

One possible procedure is that the transparency marker is used to copy lines of Blackberry Hill onto the transparency. A piece of paper is taped to the wall. Then, the overhead projector is used to project the contour lines from the transparency onto the paper. The distance from the overhead to the paper is adjusted so that all of the contour lines fit onto the paper. By using scissors, students cut along the contour lines of the paper to make their patterns. A sheet of cardboard or foam board is cut to the original size of the paper as a base for the model. The paper patterns are placed onto additional sheets and the sheets are cut to their correct shapes. By stacking the sheets in the correct order and gluing them together, an accurate model is made.

PLAN THE EXPERIMENT

1. With your partner, design a way that you can make an enlarged copy of the topographic features of Blackberry Hill using a transparency marker, overhead projector, pencil, sheet of white paper, and tape. Write down the steps you will take.
2. Explain how you can use the contour lines on your white paper as patterns for making the different layers of your model.
3. Describe a way to make your 3-D model using stacked sheets of cardboard or foam board.

Check the Plan

1. Read over your entire plan to make sure that all steps are in a logical order.
2. *Make sure your teacher approves your plan before you proceed.*

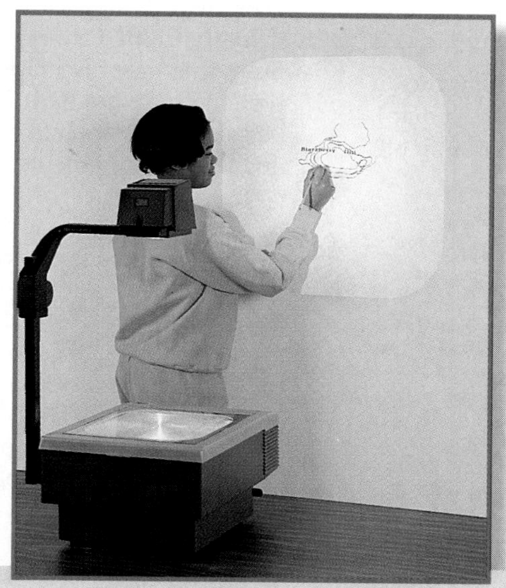

DO THE EXPERIMENT

1. Build your model as planned.
2. While the activity is going on, write down any observations that you make in your Science Journal.

Analyze and Apply

1. **Compare** your model with other students'. How are they similar? How are they different?
2. **Determine** the horizontal scale of your model.
3. **Infer** what the height of each piece of board in your model represents.
4. **Describe** the most difficult part of making your model.
5. **Describe** the easiest part.

Go Further

Design a way to make your scale model have gentle slopes instead of the step effect you have with your board model.

Teaching Strategies

Troubleshooting Have students include four contour lines in their model.

- Some students will not know how to cut out the pattern. They should begin by cutting along the outside contour line and tracing it onto cardboard before cutting along the second contour line. Each contour line pattern should be traced before a new cut is made into the paper.

DO THE EXPERIMENT

Expected Outcome

The model will look like a hill. It will have a base and four additional levels.

Analyze and Apply

1. Models will be similar in shape. There may be slight differences in the height of the models because the thickness of the cardboard or foam board may vary.
2. The horizontal scale will vary slightly from model to model but should be approximately 1 cm = 43 m. Students will find this by measuring their paper in cm. The length of a standard piece of notebook paper is 27.7 cm. Using the scale on the topographic map, the hill is approximately 1.2 km, or 1200 m, in its longest dimension. By dividing 1200 by 27.7, the scale 1 cm = 43 m is found.
3. The height of each piece of board represents the contour interval, 10 m.
4. Answers will vary.
5. Answers will vary.

Go Further

Answers will vary. One idea is to fill in the steps with modeling clay. Then smooth the clay up the slope.

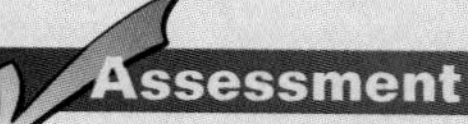

Assessment

Performance To further assess students' understanding of making a 3-D landform model from a topographic map, have them make a model using the topographic map they made in Activity 5-1. Have them compare their completed model with the plastic model they used in Activity 5-1. Use the Performance Task Assessment List for Model in **PASC**, p. 51. P

Sources

- Bricker, Charles, and R.V. Tooley. *Landmarks of Mapmaking.* Ware, England: Dorset Press, 1989.
- Malkower, Joel, ed. *The Map Catalog: Every Kind of Map and Chart on Earth and Even Some Above It.* New York: Vintage Books, 1986.

Background

- Aerial photography has the advantage of taking a long view of Earth's surface, so that a large number of objects can be shown arranged in their proper positions. Spy satellites are extremely adept at aerial photography. They can photograph objects less than 30 cm across from a distance of 160 km.
- Aerial photographs can be placed in a wild photogrammetric machine to obtain accurate measurements of objects photographed. Pairs of overlapping air photographs are set up in the machine in accordance with the control data already obtained. This allows a technician to recreate the position and orientation in space at the two moments of exposure of film. It is then possible to obtain a three-dimensional model of the ground. A cartographer uses the model to obtain distances and positions of features photographed.

Science & History

The Art of Mapmaking

As early as 2300 B.C., the Babylonians drew maps of individual plots of land. Their maps served as the basis for mapmaking in Europe in the Middle Ages. Later, the Babylonians constructed simple maps of the world. One Babylonian map carved in stone about 500 B.C. showed seven circles containing the names of countries and cities. A pair of lines in the center probably represented the Euphrates River.

Science Journal

How have you used a map lately? In your Science Journal, write an essay about how a map helped you in a difficult situation.

The Beginning of Modern Mapmaking

In the 13th century, mapmaking changed dramatically. From that time on, maps began to be based more on observation and measurement. The best mapmakers charted the seas, because mariners had compasses and other devices to make angular measurements.

The earliest mapmakers were usually artists. They often decorated their maps with artistic details. Notice those on the map of the western hemisphere shown here. This map was made in the 1600s. How does it differ from present-day maps? How is it similar?

Present and Future Maps

Although present-day mapmakers or cartographers owe a great deal to those of the past, aerial photography has changed the way maps are made today. Photogrammetry, the ability to take measurements from photographs, has eliminated the need for a cartographer to visit a site that is being mapped. Maps can now be made from aerial photographs.

Today's cartographers use computer technology to make and update maps. When they enter data on a computer, the computer draws the map. Digital map data can be used in a number of ways. In the latest automobiles, map data will soon eliminate the need to pull out maps on a motor trip. Computer programs will inform drivers where they are and how to reach their destination.

Teaching Strategies

- Discuss the importance of mapmaking in the history of the United States. In 1777, George Washington appointed a geographer and surveyor to make maps of the country. Thomas Jefferson and his congressional Committee on Public Land proposed a large-scale surveying and mapping program in 1784. After Jefferson became president, he created what came to be known as the Army Corps of Engineers to carry out this work.
- Ask students what important event during the Jefferson administration required the work of mapmakers. *(The Louisiana Purchase added over 2 million km^2 to the area of the United States. All this new land had to be mapped.)*

Activity

LS **Interpersonal** Have students work in groups to research the mapmaking work of the Army Corps of Engineers. Ask them to list the most important uses for which maps prepared by the corps have been employed.

L1 COOP LEARN

Chapter 5 Review

Summary

5-1: Landforms

1. Plains are large, flat areas that cover much of the United States. Plateaus are high, relatively flat areas next to mountains.
2. There are four types of mountains: folded, upwarped, fault-block, and volcanic.

5-2: Viewpoints

1. Latitude refers to the distance in degrees north or south of the equator. Longitude refers to distance in degrees east or west of the prime meridian.
2. Earth is divided into 24 time zones, each one hour ahead or behind the adjacent zone.

5-3: Maps

1. Because Earth is curved, map projections are distorted. The main types of projections are Mercator, Robinson, and conic.
2. A contour line on a topographic map connects points of equal elevation. The difference in elevation between contour lines is the contour interval.
3. A scale is used to show the relationship between map distances and the actual distances on Earth's surface.

5-4: Science and Society: Mapping Our Planet

1. Landsat Satellites detect energy reflected from Earth's surface, while the Topex-Poseidon Satellite uses radar to gather information for maps.
2. Sonar uses sound waves bounced off the ocean floor to detect ocean-bottom features.

Key Science Words

a. conic projection
b. contour interval
c. contour line
d. equator
e. fault-block mountain
f. folded mountain
g. International Date Line
h. Landsat Satellite
i. latitude
j. longitude
k. map legend
l. map scale
m. Mercator projection
n. plain
o. plateau
p. prime meridian
q. Robinson projection
r. sonar
s. Topex-Poseidon Satellite
t. topographic map
u. upwarped mountain
v. volcanic mountain

Reviewing Vocabulary

Match each phrase with the correct term from the list of Key Science Words.

1. high, flat area next to mountains
2. mountain formed when Earth's crust is squeezed from opposite sides
3. imaginary line parallel to the equator
4. 0° longitude
5. projection used mainly for navigation
6. map that shows changes in elevation
7. line connecting points of equal elevation
8. change in elevation between adjacent contour lines
9. instrument that uses sound waves to detect features
10. instrument that uses radar to study ocean-bottom structures

GLENCOE TECHNOLOGY

MindJogger Videoquiz

Chapter 5 Have students work in groups as they play the Videoquiz game to review key chapter concepts.

Chapter 5 Review

Summary

Have students read the summary statements to review the major concepts of the chapter.

Reviewing Vocabulary

1. o
2. f
3. i
4. p
5. m
6. t
7. c
8. b
9. r
10. s

Assessment

Portfolio Encourage students to place in their portfolios one or two items of what they consider to be their best work. Examples include:

- Across the Curriculum, p. 122
- Community Connection, p. 123
- FLEX Your Brain, p. 135 P

Performance Additional performance assessments may be found in **Performance Assessment** and **Science Integration Activities.** Performance Task Assessment Lists and rubrics for evaluating these activities can be found in Glencoe's **Performance Assessment in the Science Classroom.**

Chapter 5 Review

Checking Concepts

1. b
2. d
3. b
4. a
5. c
6. d
7. b
8. b
9. c
10. b

Understanding Concepts

11. Both are relatively flat areas. The Atlantic Coastal Plain stretches along the East Coast of the U.S., has low elevation, and contains swamps and marshes. The Great Plains are in the interior of the U.S., are high in elevation, and are relatively dry.

12. Both rise high above the surrounding land. Folded mountains form when forces within Earth cause rock layers to buckle and fold. Volcanic mountains form when molten materials cool off, solidify, and pile up.

13. Mercator projections distort landmasses near the poles. Because it is near the South Pole, Antarctica would appear to be larger than it actually is.

14. There is little relief on the Great Plains. Thus, because the area is so flat, a topographic map of the Great Plains would have a small contour interval.

15. Ships using Sea Beam sonar have more than a dozen data-collecting devices as opposed to just one device on conventional ships. Thus, Sea Beam systems can gather more data. Also, because Sea Beam readings overlap, more complete maps can be made.

Thinking Critically

16. The map of the Atlantic Coastal Plain would show little change in elevation. The contour interval would be small. The map of the Rockies would show many closed contours, indicating mountain peaks. The contour interval would be very large due to the rugged topography.

17. Tuesday

18. 160°

19. Contour lines connect points of equal elevation. A particular point on Earth's surface cannot be at two different elevations. Therefore, the lines can't overlap.

20. One unit on the map equals 50 000 of the same unit on Earth's surface.

Developing Skills

21. Measuring in SI The area covered is approximately 144 km^2.

22. Comparing and Contrasting Mercator projections exaggerate the areas near the poles. They are used mainly for navigation. Robinson projections have accurate continent shapes and less distortion near the poles. Conic projections are used to produce maps of small areas. They are used for road maps or weather maps.

Chapter 5 Review

Checking Concepts

Choose the word or phrase that completes the sentence.

1. _______ make up about 50 percent of all land areas in the United States.
   a. Plateaus
   b. Plains
   c. Mountains
   d. Volcanoes
2. The North Pole is located at _______ degrees north latitude.
   a. 0
   b. 180
   c. 50
   d. 90
3. The Hawaiian Islands are________ mountains.
   a. fault-block
   b. volcanic
   c. upwarped
   d. folded
4. Lines parallel to the equator are _______.
   a. lines of latitude
   b. prime meridians
   c. lines of longitude
   d. contour lines
5. Earth can be divided into 24 time zones that are _______ degrees apart.
   a. 10
   b. 34
   c. 15
   d. 25
6. _______ projections are very distorted at the poles.
   a. Conic
   b. Topographic
   c. Robinson
   d. Mercator
7. A _______ map shows changes in elevation at Earth's surface.
   a. conic
   b. topographic
   c. Robinson
   d. Mercator
8. _______ is measured with respect to sea level.
   a. Contour interval
   b. Elevation
   c. Conic projection
   d. Sonar
9. _______ are used to show depressions.
   a. Vs
   b. Scales
   c. Hachures
   d. Legends
10. The Grand Canyon is part of the_______.
    a. Great Plains
    b. Colorado Plateau
    c. Rocky Mountains
    d. Appalachian Mountains

Understanding Concepts

Answer the following questions in your Science Journal using complete sentences.

11. Compare and contrast the Atlantic Coastal Plain and the Great Plains. Be sure to discuss how they were formed.
12. Compare and contrast volcanic and folded mountains. Draw a diagram of each type of mountain.
13. Maps are made by projecting points and lines on a globe's surface onto paper. Why would Antarctica appear to be larger on a Mercator map than it actually is?
14. Would a topographic map of the Great Plains have a large or small contour interval? Explain.
15. How does the information gathered by ships using Sea Beam sonar differ from that collected with standard methods that use one sonar device?

Thinking Critically

16. How would a topographic map of the Atlantic Coastal Plain differ from a topographic map of the Rocky Mountains?
17. If you left Korea early Wednesday morning and flew to Hawaii, on what day of the week would you arrive?
18. If you were flying directly south from the North Pole and reached 70° north latitude, how many more degrees of latitude would be left to pass over before reaching the South Pole?
19. Why can't two contour lines overlap?
20. What does a map scale of 1:50 000 mean?

Developing Skills

If you need help, refer to the **Skill Handbook.**

21. **Measuring in SI:** What is the area in square kilometers of the topographic map in the Problem Solving feature in Section 5-3?
22. **Comparing and Contrasting:** Compare and contrast Mercator, Robinson, and conic map projections.

23. **Concept Mapping:** Make a network tree concept map that explains how topographic maps are used. Use the following terms: *topographic maps, mountains, rivers, natural features, contour lines, changes in elevation, equal elevation, hills, plains.*

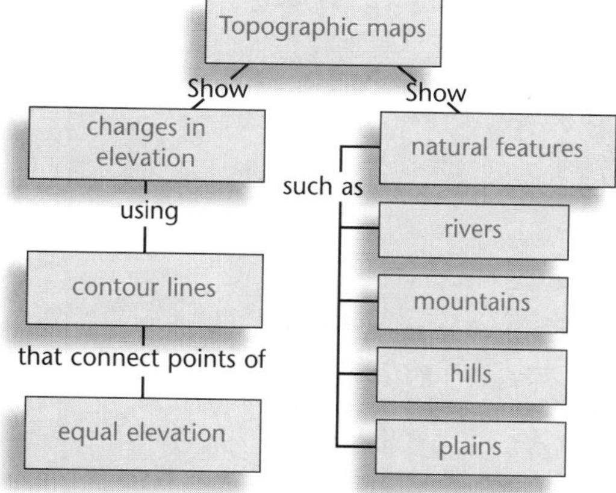

24. **Sequencing:** Arrange these cities in order from the city with the earliest time to that with the latest time on a given day: Anchorage, AK; San Francisco, CA; Bangor, ME; Columbus, OH; Houston, TX.
25. **Interpreting Data:** If a map has a scale of 1 cm = 80 000 cm, how far on the map would two cities be if they were 3 km apart on Earth's surface?

Performance Assessment

1. **Checking Lab Skills:** In the MiniLAB on page 122, you learned how to make a profile. Make a profile of the model you made of Blackberry Hill in Activity 5-2.
2. **Model:** Make a 3-D model of a canyon using the same materials as those listed in Activity 5-2. To begin, draw a topographic map of a canyon on a sheet of note paper. Have at least four contour lines on your map.
3. **Problem Solving:** Use modeling clay to construct a physiographic map to scale of the United States. Be sure to include all of the landforms shown in **Figure 5-2.**

Assessment Resources

Reproducible Masters

Chapter Review, pp. 13-14
Assessment, pp. 32-35
Performance Assessment, p. 19

Glencoe Technology

Chapter Review Software
Computer Test Bank
MindJogger Videoquiz

Chapter 5 Review

23. **Concept Mapping** See student page for a possible solution.
24. **Sequencing** Anchorage, San Francisco, Houston; Bangor and Columbus have the same time.
25. **Interpreting Data** 300 000 cm ÷ 80 000 cm = 3.75 cm

Performance Assessment

1. Students will look at their models from different angles; therefore, profiles will vary somewhat. All profiles will show that the line slopes up from the baseline, levels out, and then slopes down to the baseline. Use the Performance Task Assessment List for Model in **PASC,** p. 51. P
2. The student-created topographic map is the pattern for the model. The base of the model is a sheet of cardboard the size of the piece of notebook paper. This sheet represents the deepest part of the sinkhole. To make the next layer up from the bottom, students will need to cut out the center contour line on their pattern, throw away this piece of the pattern, copy the remaining pattern onto a piece of cardboard, cut the cardboard to match the pattern, and glue the cardboard to the cardboard base. Use the Performance Task Assessment List for Model in **PASC,** p. 51. P
3. Students should use cardboard to make the bases for their maps. Use the Performance Task Assessment List for Model in **PASC,** p. 51. P

Chapter Organizer

Section	Objectives	Activities/Features
Chapter Opener		**Explore Activity:** Compare different rates of weathering. p. 147
6-1 **Weathering** (2 sessions, 1 block)*	1. **Contrast** mechanical weathering and chemical weathering. 2. **Explain** the effects of climate on weathering.	**Problem Solving:** Gabriella Saves the Freezer, p. 150 **Connect to Chemistry,** p. 151 **Activity 6-1:** Weathering Chalk, pp. 152-153 **MiniLAB:** How does rust form? p. 154 **Skill Builder:** Recognizing Cause and Effect, p. 155 **Using Computers:** Spreadsheet, p. 155
6-2 **Soil** (2 sessions, 1 block)*	1. **Explain** how soil evolves from rock. 2. **Describe** soil by comparing the A, B, and C soil horizons. 3. **Discuss** how environmental conditions affect the evolution of soils.	**Connect to Life Science,** p. 157 **MiniLAB:** What is soil made of? p. 158 **Connect to Life Science,** p. 159 **Activity 6-2:** Soil Characteristics, p. 160 **Using Technology:** Land Reclamation, p. 161 **Skill Builder:** Concept Mapping, p. 163 **Science Journal,** p. 163
6-3 **Science and Society Issue: Land Use and Soil Loss** (1 session, ½ block)*	1. **Describe** the importance of soil and activities that lead to its loss. 2. **Explain** how soil loss can be minimized.	**Explore the Issue,** p. 165 **Using Math,** p. 165 **People and Science:** Susan Colclazer, Naturalist, p. 166

* A complete Planning Guide that includes block scheduling is provided on pages 32T-35T.

Activity Materials

Explore	Activities	MiniLABs
page 147 several rock samples (igneous, metamorphic, and sedimentary), sheet of white paper, metal file	pages 152-153 6 identical pieces of chalk, 2 small beakers, metric ruler, tap water, white vinegar, hot plate, 100-mL graduated cylinder, safety goggles, thermal mitt page 160 soil samples, 3 plastic coffee-can lids, sand, cheesecloth squares, clay-rich soil, rubber bands, gravel, hand lens, three 250-mL beakers, tap water, thumbtack, sheet of white paper, 3 large polystyrene or plastic cups, stopwatch or clock with second hand, 100-mL graduated cylinder, scissors	page 154 steel wool, shallow pan, tap water page 158 soil samples, magnifying glass or microscope

Chapter 6 Weathering and Soil

Teacher Classroom Resources

Reproducible Masters	Transparencies
Study Guide, p. 26 **Reinforcement,** p. 26 **Enrichment,** p. 26 **Activity Worksheets,** pp. 36-37, 40 **Lab Manual 21,** Chemical Weathering **Concept Mapping,** p. 17	**Section Focus Transparency 22,** Weathering Heights **Science Integration Transparency 6,** Physical Change or Chemical Change? **Teaching Transparency 11,** Water Cycle
Study Guide, p. 27 **Reinforcement,** p. 27 **Enrichment,** p. 27 **Activity Worksheets,** pp. 38-39, 41 **Lab Manual 22,** Soil Infiltration by Groundwater **Science Integration Activity 6,** A Wormy Situation **Critical Thinking/Problem Solving,** p. 12 **Cross-Curricular Integration,** p. 10	**Section Focus Transparency 23,** Down and Dirty **Teaching Transparency 12,** Soil Evolution
Study Guide, p. 28 **Reinforcement,** p. 28 **Enrichment,** p. 28 **Science and Society Integration,** p. 10 **Multicultural Connections,** pp. 15-16	**Section Focus Transparency 24,** Losing Ground

Teaching Resources

Glencoe Earth Science Interactive Videodisc
Earth Science CD-ROM
Spanish Resources
English/Spanish Audiocassettes
Cooperative Learning Resource Guide
Lab Partner
Lab and Safety Skills
Lesson Plans

Assessment Resources

Chapter Review, pp. 15-16
Assessment, pp. 36-39
Performance Assessment in the Science Classroom (PASC)
MindJogger Videoquiz
Alternate Assessment in the Science Classroom
Performance Assessment
Chapter Review Software
Computer Test Bank

Key to Teaching Strategies

The following designations will help you decide which activities are appropriate for your students.

L1 Level 1 activities should be within the ability range of all students.

L2 Level 2 activities should be within the ability range of the average to above-average student.

L3 Level 3 activities are designed for the ability range of above-average students.

LEP LEP activities should be within the ability range of Limited English Proficiency students.

LS These activities are designed to address different learning styles.

COOP LEARN Cooperative Learning activities are designed for small group work.

P These strategies represent student products that can be placed into a best-work portfolio.

GLENCOE TECHNOLOGY

The following multimedia resources are available from Glencoe.

National Geographic Society Series
GTV: Planetary Manager

Glencoe Earth Science Interactive Videodisc
The Rock Cycle
Mysteries of the Cave
Earth Science CD-ROM

Teacher Classroom Resources

This is a representation of key blackline masters available in the Teacher Classroom Resources.

Teaching Aids

Section Focus Transparencies

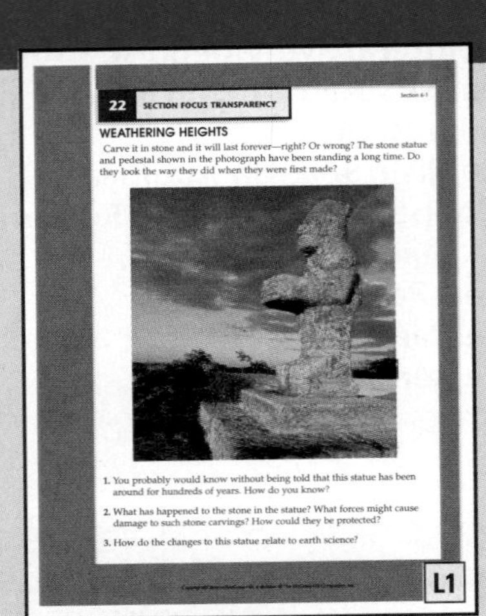
22 SECTION FOCUS TRANSPARENCY

WEATHERING HEIGHTS

Carve it in stone and it will last forever—right? Or wrong? The stone statue and pedestal shown in the photograph have been standing a long time. Do they look the way they did when they were first made?

1. You probably would know without being told that this statue has been around for hundreds of years. How do you know?
2. What has happened to the stone in the statue? What forces might cause damage to such stone carvings? How could they be protected?
3. How do the changes to this statue relate to earth science?

L1

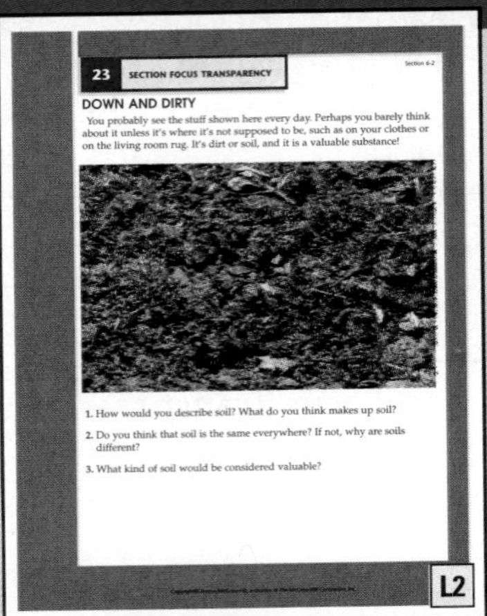
23 SECTION FOCUS TRANSPARENCY

DOWN AND DIRTY

You probably see the stuff shown here every day. Perhaps you barely think about it unless it's where it's not supposed to be, such as on your clothes or on the living room rug. It's dirt or soil, and it is a valuable substance!

1. How would you describe soil? What do you think makes up soil?
2. Do you think that soil is the same everywhere? If not, why are soils different?
3. What kind of soil would be considered valuable?

L2

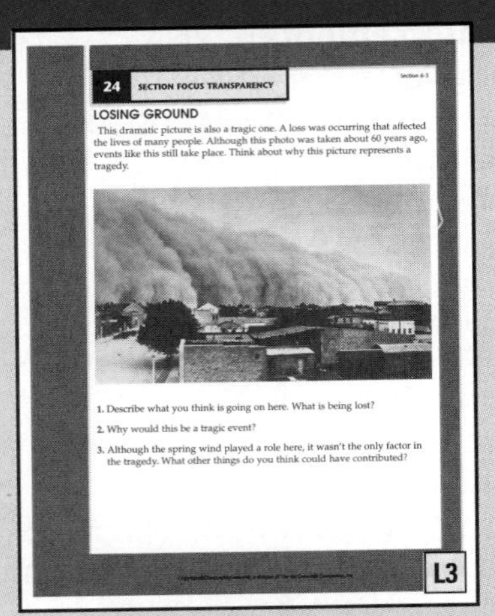
24 SECTION FOCUS TRANSPARENCY

LOSING GROUND

This dramatic picture is also a tragic one. A loss was occurring that affected the lives of many people. Although this photo was taken about 60 years ago, events like this still take place. Think about why this picture represents a tragedy.

1. Describe what you think is going on here. What is being lost?
2. Why would this be a tragic event?
3. Although the spring wind played a role here, it wasn't the only factor in the tragedy. What other things do you think could have contributed?

L3

Science Integration Transparencies

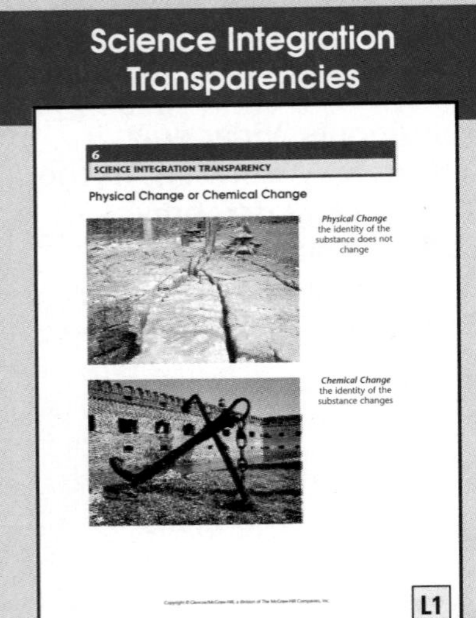
6 SCIENCE INTEGRATION TRANSPARENCY

Physical Change or Chemical Change

Physical Change the identity of the substance does not change

Chemical Change the identity of the substance changes

L1

Teaching Transparencies

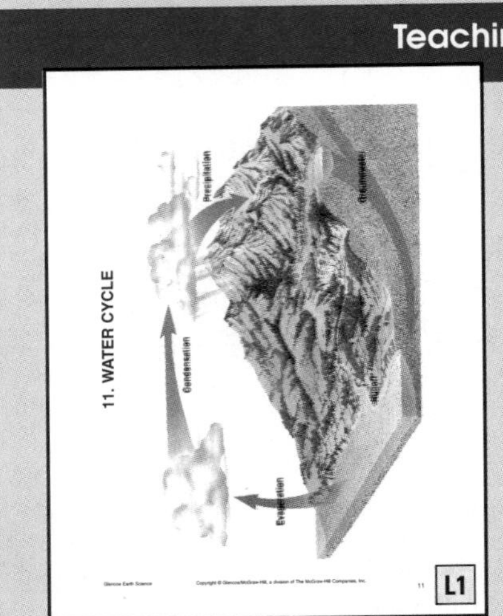

L1

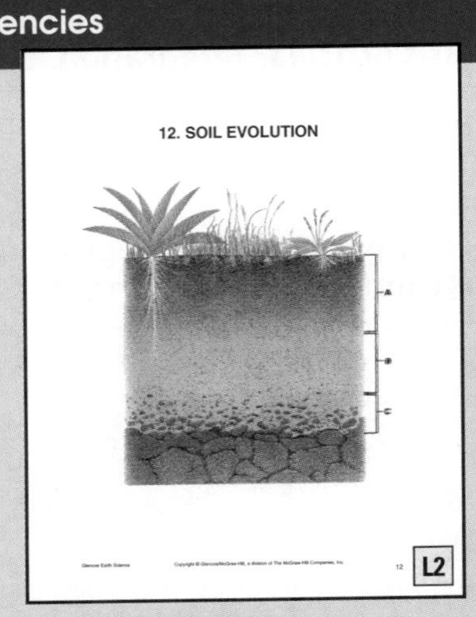

L2

Meeting Different Ability Levels

Study Guide

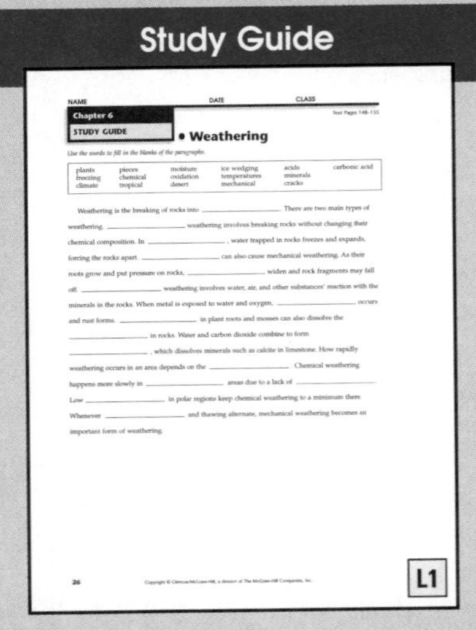
Chapter 6 STUDY GUIDE • Weathering

L1

Reinforcement

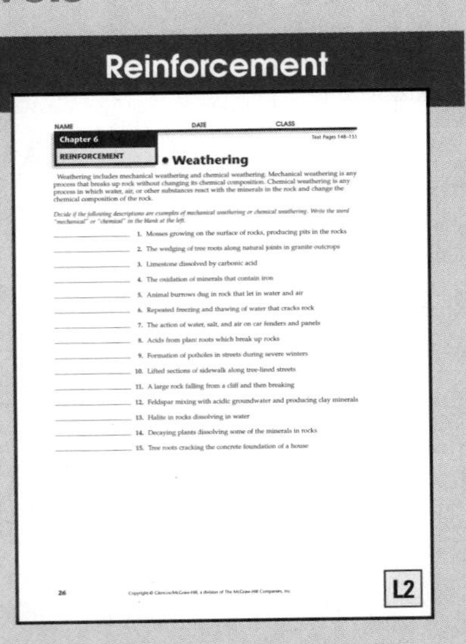
Chapter 6 REINFORCEMENT • Weathering

L2

Enrichment Worksheets

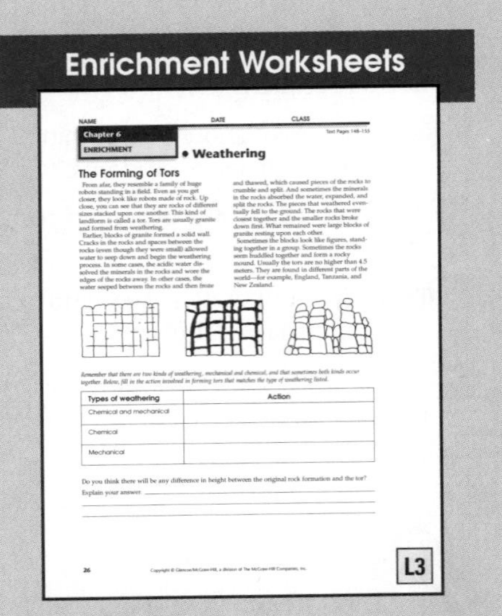
Chapter 6 ENRICHMENT • Weathering

The Forming of Tors

Types of weathering	Action
Chemical and mechanical	
Chemical	
Mechanical	

L3

Hands-On Activities

Science Integration Activity

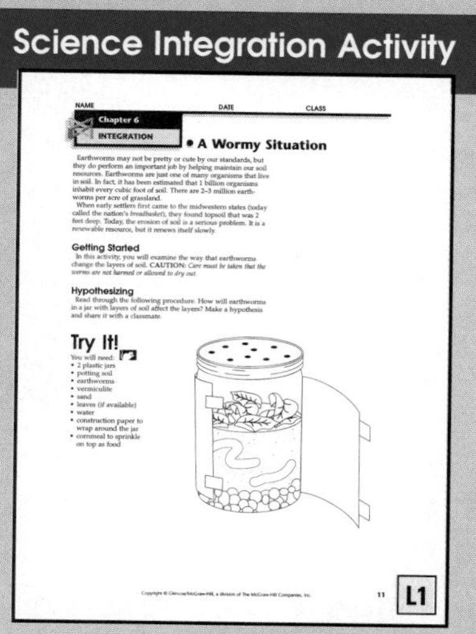
NAME DATE CLASS
Chapter 6
INTEGRATION
• A Wormy Situation
Getting Started
Hypothesizing
Try It!
L1

Lab Manual

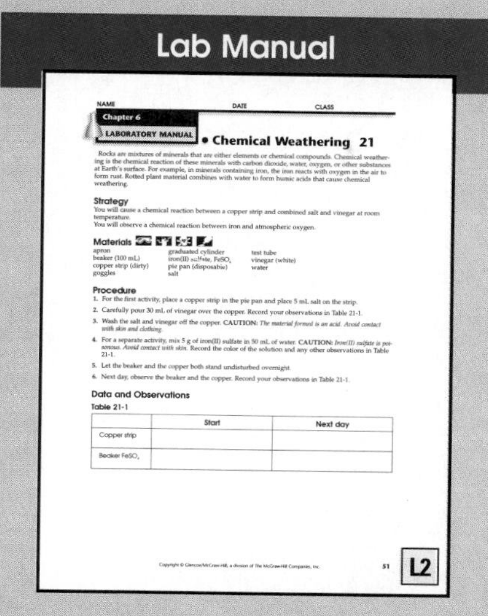
NAME DATE CLASS
Chapter 6
LABORATORY MANUAL
• Chemical Weathering 21
Strategy
Materials
Procedure
Data and Observations
Table 21-1

	Start	Next day
Copper strip		
Beaker $FeSO_4$		

L2

Assessment

Performance Assessment

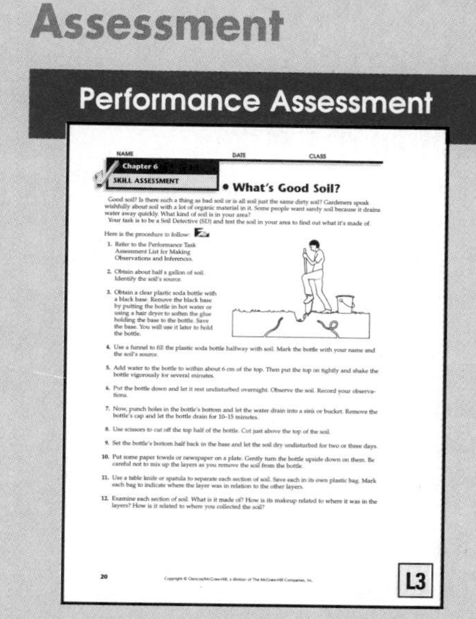
NAME DATE CLASS
Chapter 6
SKILL ASSESSMENT
• What's Good Soil?
L3

Enrichment and Application

Critical Thinking/ Problem Solving

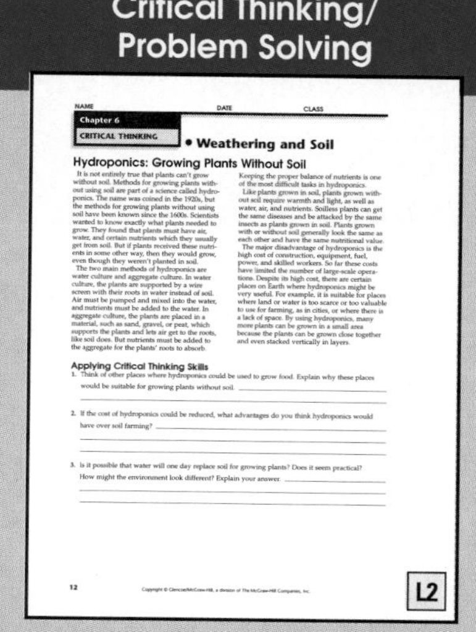
NAME DATE CLASS
Chapter 6
CRITICAL THINKING
• Weathering and Soil
Hydroponics: Growing Plants Without Soil
Applying Critical Thinking Skills
L2

Cross-Curricular Integration

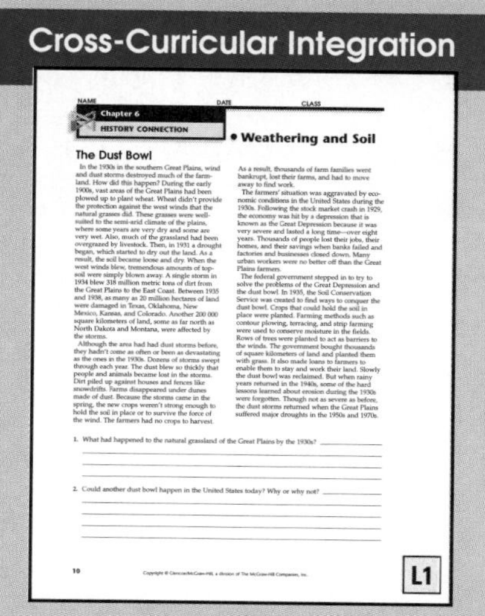
NAME DATE CLASS
Chapter 6
HISTORY CONNECTION
• Weathering and Soil
The Dust Bowl
L1

Science and Society Integration

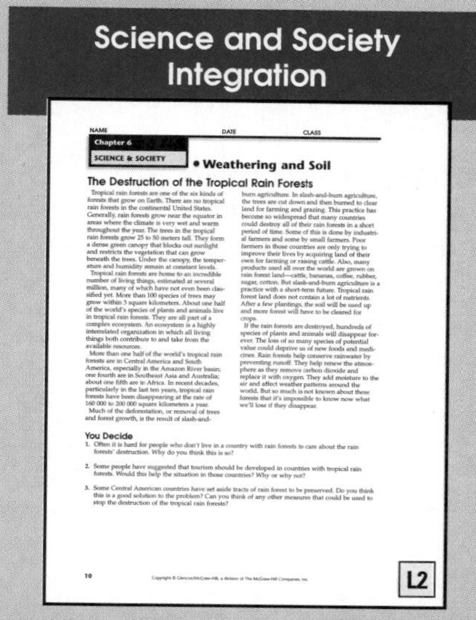
NAME DATE CLASS
Chapter 6
SCIENCE & SOCIETY
• Weathering and Soil
The Destruction of the Tropical Rain Forests
You Decide
L2

Multicultural Connections

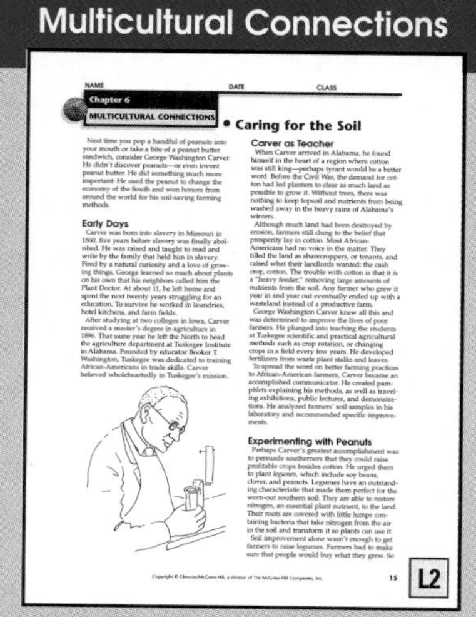
NAME DATE CLASS
Chapter 6
MULTICULTURAL CONNECTIONS
• Caring for the Soil
Carver as Teacher
Early Days
Experimenting with Peanuts
L2

Concept Mapping

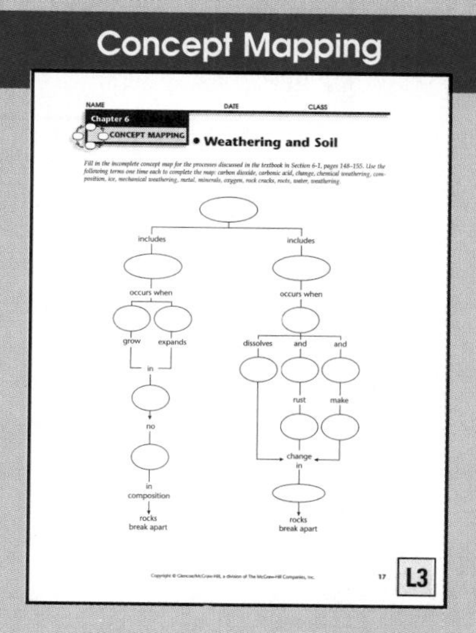
NAME DATE CLASS
Chapter 6
CONCEPT MAPPING
• Weathering and Soil

L3

Chapter 6

Weathering and Soil

CHAPTER OVERVIEW

Section 6-1 This section discusses mechanical and chemical weathering.

Section 6-2 The evolution of soil from weathered rock is introduced.

Section 6-3 **Science and Society** Human activities that cause soil loss are discussed.

Chapter Vocabulary

weathering	climate
mechanical weathering	soil
	humus
ice wedging	soil profile
chemical weathering	horizon
	leaching
oxidation	desertification

Theme Connection

Energy/Stability and Change The energy theme is developed through the discussion of ways that mechanical weathering results from different forces. Stability and change is developed in discussion of how soils evolve from weathered sediments and organic matter.

Previewing the Chapter

Look for the following logo for strategies that emphasize different learning modalities. LS

Kinesthetic	Explore, p. 147; Activity 6-2, p. 160
Visual-Spatial	Inclusion Strategies, p. 149; Science Journal, p. 150; Visual Learning, pp. 150, 151, 154, 158, 159, 164; MiniLAB, p. 154
Interpersonal	Activity 6-1, pp. 152-153; Using Computers, p. 155; MiniLAB, p. 158; Reteach, pp. 162, 165
Linguistic	Science Journal, p. 163

Chapter 6

Weathering and Soil

The mysterious statues shown here are on Easter Island in the South Pacific Ocean. Probably long before anyone can unravel their meaning, nature will wear them away by the process of weathering. Weathering pits and roughens the stone of monuments and rocks in nature.

All stone and rock weathers over time. Grains of sediment fall out. Cracks develop on the surface and deep inside. Weathering causes the stone of monuments to crumble away gradually. Weathering also causes rocks in nature to fracture, buckle, and crumble into soil and sediment.

EXPLORE ACTIVITY

Compare different rates of weathering.  

1. Obtain several kinds of rocks.
2. Over white paper, rub one rock against a metal file.
3. Repeat this process with each kind of rock.
4. Compare the amount of broken-off particles from each rock.

Observe: Which rock breaks apart most easily? In your Science Journal, describe each rock based upon your observations.

Previewing Science Skills

- In the **Skill Builders**, you will **recognize cause and effect** and **map concepts**.
- In the **Activities**, you will **hypothesize, observe, infer, interpret data**, and **measure**.
- In the **MiniLABs**, you will **observe** and **compare and contrast**.

Assessment Planner

Portfolio
Refer to page 167 for suggested items that students might select for their portfolios.

Performance Assessment
See page 167 for additional Performance Assessment options.
Skill Builders, pp. 155, 163
MiniLABs, pp. 154, 158
Activities 6-1, pp. 152-153; 6-2, p. 160

Content Assessment
Section Wrap-ups, pp. 155, 163, 165
Chapter Review, pp. 167-169
Mini Quizzes, pp. 155, 163

Group Assessment
Opportunities for group assessment occur with Cooperative Learning Strategies and Flex Your Brain Activities.

EXPLORE ACTIVITY

Purpose

LS **Kinesthetic** Use the Explore Activity to introduce mechanical weathering. Inform students that they will learn more about how rocks weather and soils evolve. L1 LEP

Preparation

Gather several samples of rocks including sandstones, shales, granites, and basalts.

Materials

Each student will need samples of rocks and a metal file.

Teaching Strategies

Have students use different amounts of force as they rub the file against the rocks. Then ask: **How does the amount of force applied to the rocks affect the size and amount of particles that fall from each rock?** Students will observe that greater force produces more and bigger particles.

Observe

Students should observe that some rocks break into particles more easily than others.

Assessment

Process Have students look at the rock particles with a hand lens or microscope. Then have them complete a table that compares the small particles with the rocks. Similarities may include color and texture. Differences might include size and shape. Also, perhaps only certain minerals from the rock were broken off. Use the Performance Task Assessment List for Data Table in **PASC,** p. 37. P

Section 6•1

Prepare

Section Background

- The smaller the object, the greater its surface area per unit of volume. Mechanical weathering exposes more surface area of a rock to chemical weathering by breaking large masses of rock into smaller units.
- In igneous rocks, the first minerals to crystallize from magma or lava weather the fastest. Quartz, which is the last mineral to form, is very resistant to weathering.
- The sedimentary rocks, shale and limestone, weather rapidly in humid environments.

Preplanning

- To prepare for Activity 6-1, obtain 6 pieces of chalk, 2 small beakers, a metric ruler, white vinegar, a hot plate, a graduated cylinder, and safety goggles for each group.
- To prepare for the MiniLAB, obtain steel wool and shallow pans.

1 Motivate

Bellringer

Before presenting the lesson, display **Section Focus Transparency 22** on the overhead projector. Assign the accompanying **Focus Activity** worksheet. L1 LEP

Tying to Previous Knowledge

Have students recall from Chapter 3 that minerals have different hardnesses. Have students determine which minerals listed on the Mohs scale of hardness would be the most resistant to mechanical weathering.

6•1 Weathering

Science Words

weathering
mechanical weathering
ice wedging
chemical weathering
oxidation
climate

Objectives

- Contrast mechanical weathering and chemical weathering.
- Explain the effects of climate on weathering.

Evidence of Weathering

The next time you take a walk or a drive, notice the sand and grit along the sidewalk and curb and the layer of gritty dirt lying at the bottom of road cuts. Much of the gritty sediment you see comes from small particles that break loose from concrete curbs and from rocks exposed to the natural elements. These sediments are evidence of weathering.

Conditions and processes in the environment cause the weathering of rock and concrete. In Chapter 4, the rock cycle showed how sedimentary rocks form. But did you know that sediments can also form soil? Both soil formation and the development of sedimentary rocks are dependent on the process of weathering.

Weathering is the process that breaks down rocks into smaller and smaller fragments. Over millions of years, the process of weathering helped change Earth's surface. **Figure 6-1** illustrates how weathering wears down mountains to hills. Weathering blurs the writing on tombstones and slowly breaks down statues. Weathering can also cause potholes in streets. The two types of weathering are mechanical and chemical. Although mechanical and chemical weathering are discussed separately, the two processes work together to break down rock.

Figure 6-1
Over long periods of time, weathering helps change sharp, jagged mountains into smooth, rolling mountains and hills.

Program Resources

Reproducible Masters

Study Guide, p. 26 L1
Reinforcement, p. 26 L1
Enrichment, p. 26 L3
Activity Worksheets, pp. 5, 36-37, 40 L1
Concept Mapping, p. 17
Lab Manual 21

 **Transparencies**

Section Focus Transparency 22 L1
Teaching Transparency 11
Science Integration Transparency 6

Figure 6-2

Tree roots can break up sidewalks.

A As trees grow, their roots spread throughout the soil.

B As roots grow under a sidewalk, they expand and force the concrete to crack.

C Over time, the sidewalk buckles and breaks apart.

Mechanical Weathering

Mechanical weathering breaks apart rocks without changing their chemical composition. Each fragment and particle weathered away by a mechanical process retains the same characteristics as the original rock. Mechanical weathering can be caused by growing plants, expanding ice, growing crystals, lightning, and expansion and contraction with heating and cooling. These physical processes create enough force to break rocks into smaller pieces.

Plants

Plant roots grow into cracks of rocks where they find water and nutrients. As roots grow, they wedge rocks apart. If you've skated on a sidewalk and tripped over a crack near a tree, you have experienced the results of mechanical weathering. The sidewalk near the tree in **Figure 6-2** shows signs of weathering. How could cracks in rocks occur in the same way?

Animals burrowing in soil contribute to weathering. They carry materials to the surface, where more weathering takes place.

2 Teach

Inquiry Question

Ask students to **Explain how small weathering changes lead to big changes in the surface of Earth.** *The small changes occur over a long period of time—millions of years. Eventually these small changes become large changes.*

GLENCOE TECHNOLOGY

Videodisc

Glencoe Earth Science Interactive Videodisc

Side 1, Lesson 1

Weathering

8162-8531

8533-10328

CD-ROM

Earth Science CD-ROM

Have students perform the interactive exploration for Chapter 6 to reinforce important chapter concepts and thinking processes.

NATIONAL GEOGRAPHIC SOCIETY

Videodisc

GTV: Planetary Manager

Landscape

48117

48119

Community Connection

Remodeling Buildings Have students answer the question: **Why do people sandblast building exteriors made of stones or brick?** *Sandblasting "weathers away" the dirty outer surfaces of the rock, exposing a clean surface.*

Inclusion Strategies

Learning Disabled Have students collect pictures of objects that are being weathered. Photographs might include cracks in rocks, sidewalks, buildings, and so on. LS

Problem Solving

Solve the Problem

1. The glass could have broken.
2. Water in the lemonade expands when it freezes, pushing out on the glass container.
3. The volume increases.

Think Critically

1. When water in cracks of rocks freezes, it expands, forcing the rocks to break apart.
2. This will occur in temperate climates where there is freezing and thawing. Mechanical weathering by water is slow in dry areas and in warm areas where ice doesn't form.

Visual Learning

Figures 6-2 and 6-3 Each figure shows how weathering occurs. Have students explain how both roots of plants and ice wedging combine to break up sidewalks. *As roots push through the concrete, they create space for water to invade. As the invading water freezes and pushes outward, it create more space for roots to grow.* LEP IS

Use Lab 21 in the **Lab Manual** as you teach this lesson.

Use **Teaching Transparency 11** as you teach this lesson.

Problem Solving

Gabriella Saves the Freezer

On a hot day, Gabriella baby-sat six-year-old Tanya and her baby brother. While Gabriella tended the baby, Tanya made lemonade. Tanya filled a glass jar with lemonade concentrate and water, put a lid on it, and stuck the glass jar in the freezer to cool quickly. Then she forgot about it. When Gabriella brought the baby into the kitchen, she discovered the glass bottle of lemonade and removed it from the freezer before a messy accident could occur.

Solve the Problem:

1. **What could have happened to the glass bottle of lemonade in the freezer?**
2. **Why?**
3. **How does the volume of water change when it freezes?**

Think Critically:

1. How does this same process weather rocks?
2. In what parts of the world would this kind of weathering occur? In what parts of the world would this mechanical weathering process not occur?

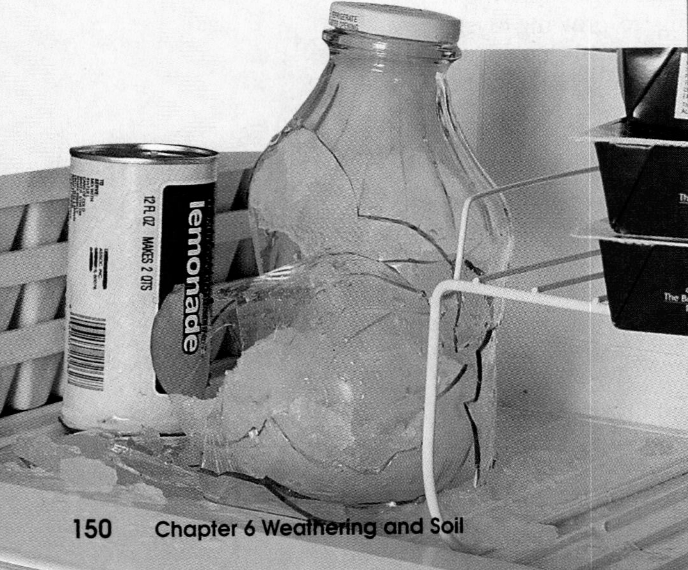

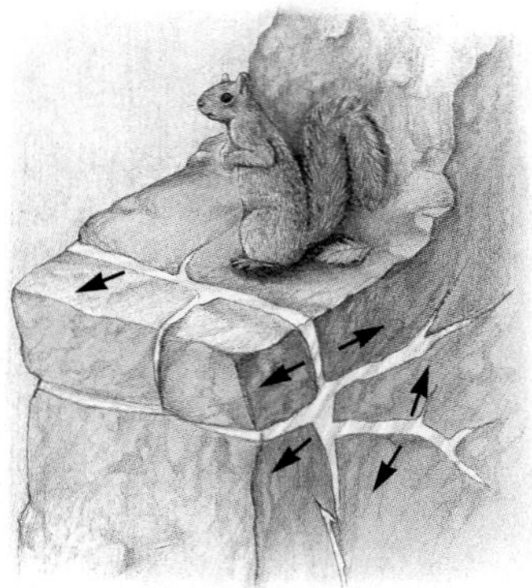

Figure 6-3

When water freezes in cracks of rocks, it expands. Pressure builds and breaks the rock apart. When the ice thaws and the water refreezes, this process reoccurs.

Ice Wedging

The mechanical weathering process known as **ice wedging** is illustrated in **Figure 6-3.** Ice wedging can wear down rocks rapidly. At night, in cold areas, low temperatures freeze water. During the day, warmer temperatures thaw the ice. Ice wedging is particularly noticeable in the mountains, where it contributes to the wearing down of sharp mountain peaks to rounded hills, a process pictured in **Figure 6-1.** This cycle of freezing and thawing not only breaks up rocks but also breaks up roads and highways. When water gets into cracks in road pavement and freezes, it forces the pavement apart. This can lead to the formation of potholes in roads. Weathering by both roots and ice wedging can rapidly reduce rocks to rubble. Breaking up rocks through mechanical weathering exposes a greater surface area to chemical weathering. This illustrates how mechanical and chemical weathering work together to break down rock.

Science Journal

IS **Visual-Spatial** Have students draw a series of pictures that show how a mountain changes shape over time because of weathering. L1

Figure 6-4

This limestone cave is a product of chemical weathering. *How did water help form this cave?*

Chemical Weathering

The second type of weathering occurs when water, air, and other substances react with the minerals in rocks. This type of weathering is called **chemical weathering** because the chemical composition of the rock changes. Let's see how chemical weathering happens.

Water

Water is an important agent of chemical weathering. When the hydrogen and oxygen atoms in water react with the chemicals in some rocks, new compounds form. The resulting composition is much different from that of the original rock.

Acids

Naturally formed acids can weather rocks chemically. When water mixes with carbon dioxide from the air, a weak acid, carbonic acid, forms. Carbonic acid is the same weak acid formed when soft drinks are carbonated. Carbonic acid reacts with minerals such as calcite, the main mineral in limestone. The product of this reaction then dissolves and can be carried away. Over thousands of years, carbonic acid has weathered enough limestone to create caves, such as the one shown in **Figure 6-4.**

When carbonic acid comes in contact with granite rock, chemical weathering occurs. Over a long time, the mineral feldspar in the granite is broken down into silica, a potassium salt, and the clay mineral kaolinite. Kaolinite clay makes up a high percentage of the material in some soils. Clay is an end-product of weathering.

Some roots and decaying plants give off acids that can dissolve minerals in rock. Removing these minerals weakens the rock. Eventually the rock will break into smaller pieces. The next time you find a moss-covered rock, peel back the moss and look at the small pits underneath. Acids from plant roots caused the pits.

INTEGRATION Chemistry

CONNECT TO CHEMISTRY

The chemical formula for calcite, a common rock-forming mineral, is $CaCO_3$. Use the Periodic Table, Appendix F on page 712, to ***identify*** the chemicals in this formula.

Visual Learning

Figure 6-4 How did water help form this cave? *Acidic groundwater flowed through the rock and chemically weathered the limestone.*

 LEP  LS

INTEGRATION Chemistry

Chemical reactions occur when substances react to produce new substances that have different properties from the original substances. The substances that you start with are the reactants. The new substances formed by the reaction are the products.

CONNECT TO CHEMISTRY

Ca is calcium, C is carbon, and O is oxygen.

3 Assess

Check for Understanding

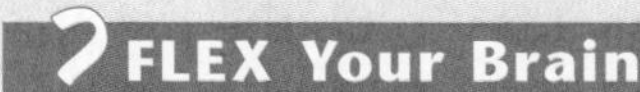

FLEX Your Brain

Use the Flex Your Brain activity to have students explore OXIDATION.

Activity Worksheets, p. 5

Reteach

Ask students, **How could you tell which of two tombstones, both made of limestone, is older without looking at the dates?** *It is often more difficult to read the engravings on an older tombstone because chemical weathering has caused more damage to the older stone.*

Extension

For students who have mastered this section, use the **Reinforcement** and **Enrichment** masters.

Activity 6-1

PREPARATION

Purpose

Interpersonal Students will design and carry out an experiment to study variables that affect chemical weathering. Be certain to differentiate between chemical weathering of chalk by an acid and the settling of chalk flakes into the water. L1 COOP LEARN

Process Skills

communicating, forming a hypothesis, designing an experiment, separating and controlling variables, observing and inferring, recognizing cause and effect, interpreting data, making and using tables, using numbers

Time

45 minutes to do the preparation and to plan the experiment, 45 minutes to do the experiment and answer the Analyze and Apply questions

Materials

Sticks of chalk can be purchased from most teachers' stores and office supply stores.

Safety Precautions

Caution students to wear safety goggles and to be careful when using the hot plate and heated vinegar.

Possible Hypotheses

Students may think that chalk will dissolve in both water and vinegar or that only the vinegar will weather the chalk. Students may assume that the small particles will react faster and the heat will speed up the process.

Activity Worksheets, pp. 5, 36-37

Activity 6-1

Design Your Own Experiment
Weathering Chalk

Chalk is a type of limestone made of the shells of tiny animals. When you write your name on the chalkboard or draw a picture on the driveway with a piece of chalk, what happens to the chalk? It is mechanically weathered. This experiment will help you understand how chalk can be chemically weathered.

PREPARATION

Problem

How can chalk be chemically weathered? What variables affect the rate of chemical weathering?

Form a Hypothesis

In this experiment, you will test three variables that can affect the rate of chemical weathering. Write hypotheses about how surface area, acidity, and heat affect the rate of chemical weathering of chalk.

For example, if you place a piece of chalk in water and another in acid (vinegar), what do you think will happen? If you break a piece of chalk and drop the pieces in acid, how will the rate of weathering affect the pieces compared with a whole piece of chalk? If you heat the acid, how will that affect the rate of weathering?

Objectives

- To design experiments to compare the effect of acidity, surface area, and heat on the rate of chemical weathering of chalk.
- To understand some of the factors that affect chemical weathering.

Possible Materials

- 6 equal pieces of chalk
- 2 small beakers
- metric ruler
- water
- white vinegar
- hot plate
- graduated cylinder
- safety goggles

Safety Precautions

Wear safety goggles when pouring acids. Be careful when using a hot plate and heated solutions.

152

Theme Connection

Stability and Change Stability and change are demonstrated by testing the variables in this experiment.

PLAN THE EXPERIMENT

1. Develop hypotheses about the effects of acidity, surface area, and heat on chemical weathering.
2. Devise a way to test your first hypothesis. List the steps needed to test the hypothesis.
3. Repeat this for your other two hypotheses.
4. Design data tables in your Science Journal. Use one for acidity, one for surface area, and one for heat.

Check the Plan

1. Read over your plan to make certain that the steps are in a logical order.
2. Identify what remains constant in your experiment and what varies. Each test should have only one variable.
3. Have you allowed for a control in each experiment?
4. Summarize your data in a graph. Decide from reading the Skill Handbook which type of graph to use.
5. *Make sure your teacher approves your plan before you start the experiment.*

DO THE EXPERIMENT

1. Carry out the three experiments as planned.
2. While the experiments are going on, write your observations and complete the data tables in your Science Journal.

Analyze and Apply

1. **Analyze** your graph to find out which substance—water or acid—weathered the chalk more quickly. Was your hypothesis supported?
2. **Infer** from your data obtained in the surface-area experiment whether the amount of surface area makes a difference in the rate of chemical weathering. Explain why this occurs.
3. **Conclude** from the last experiment how heat affects the rate of chemical weathering. What does this imply about weathering in the tropics?

Go Further

Based on your results, predict where chemical weathering will be greater, in a cold climate or a warm climate.

PLAN THE EXPERIMENT

Possible Procedures

To test the effect of an acidic solution, place a piece of chalk in a beaker of water and another piece of equal size in a beaker of vinegar. To test the variable of size on chemical weathering, place a whole piece of chalk in a beaker and break an equal-sized piece of chalk into a second beaker. Pour vinegar into the beakers. To test the effect of temperature on chemical weathering, place one stick of chalk in vinegar at room temperature and another in heated vinegar.

Teaching Strategies

Troubleshooting Students may need to review the term *surface area.* Students may not realize that a smaller particle has a greater surface area for its volume than does a larger particle.

DO THE EXPERIMENT

Expected Outcome

Water has no visible effect on chalk. There is no chemical reaction. Chalk bubbles and reacts with vinegar. Small pieces of chalk react faster. Heated vinegar causes a faster reaction.

Analyze and Apply

1. Chalk weathers more quickly in vinegar. Answers about the hypothesis will vary.
2. The greater the surface area, the faster the weathering. More surface area means more contact with the vinegar.
3. Warm temperatures increase the rate of chemical weathering. In the tropics, chemical weathering occurs more often than mechanical weathering.

Go Further

Chemical weathering is greater in warm climates. Limestone is used as a building stone and as an additive in concrete and cement. Chemical weathering causes these building materials to crumble.

Assessment

Content Have students write song lyrics about variables that affect chemical weathering. Use the Performance Task Assessment List for Writer's Guide to Fiction in **PASC**, p. 83. P

Visual Learning

Figure 6-5 What caused these rocks to be a reddish color? *They are red because the iron in the rocks has oxidized.*

Figure 6-6 The type of rock also influences how fast a surface weathers. Why? *Some rocks are harder and thus more resistant to weathering than others. Some types of rock react to chemicals in the air, while others do not.* LEP LS

MiniLAB

Purpose

LS **Visual-Spatial** Students will learn about chemical weathering by observing how rust forms. L1 LEP

Materials

steel wool, shallow glass pan, water

Teaching Strategies

Safety Precautions Warn students to be careful when handling steel wool. Sharp points can pierce the skin.

Analysis

1. Rust forms.
2. The steel wool oxidizes in the presence of the water.
3. The chemical composition of the steel wool is changed just as the iron in rocks is weathered.

Assessment

Performance Have students design experiments to see how exposure time to an acid affects the chemical weathering of various metals (i.e., steel wool, a steel nail, a copper penny). Use the Performance Task Assessment List for Designing an Experiment in **PASC**, p. 23. P

Activity Worksheets, pp. 5, 40

Oxygen

Oxygen helps cause chemical weathering. You've seen rusty cars and swing sets. Rust is caused by oxidation. **Oxidation** occurs when a material such as iron is exposed to oxygen and water. When rocks containing iron are exposed to water and the oxygen in the air, the iron in the rock "rusts" and turns reddish, as seen in **Figure 6-5.**

MiniLAB

How does rust form?

Find out what happens when you leave steel wool in water.

Procedure

1. Place some steel wool in a glass dish with 1 cm of water.
2. Observe for several days.

Analysis

1. What changes occurred?
2. What caused the changes?
3. How are these changes related to weathering?

Effects of Climate on Weathering

Mechanical and chemical weathering occur everywhere. However, climate affects the rate and type of weathering. **Climate** is the pattern of weather that occurs in a particular area over many years. In cold climates where freezing and thawing are frequent, mechanical weathering breaks down rocks rapidly through the process of ice wedging.

Chemical weathering is more rapid in warm, wet climates. Thus, chemical weathering occurs rapidly in tropical areas such as the Amazon River region of South America. Lack of moisture in deserts and low temperatures in polar regions keep chemical weathering at a minimum in those climates. How weathering affects rock depends on the type of rock, as illustrated in **Figure 6-6.**

Mechanical and chemical weathering work together. For example, when rocks break apart because of mechanical weathering, exposing more surface area, this increases the rate of chemical weathering. This was shown in Activity 6-1.

Figure 6-5

These rocks have been chemically weathered. *What caused them to be a reddish color?*

Across the Curriculum

History Explain to students that the Statue of Liberty has to be repaired periodically because of damage caused by weathering. Ask students, **What could be done to help slow down this damage?** *The statue could be coated with a protective material that will prevent chemicals in the air from reacting with its metal. The chemicals in the smog in New York City could be eliminated.* P

Cultural Diversity

Road Construction Roads are constructed from a variety of materials. Have students research some of the paving materials being used around the world and hypothesize which are most resistant to weathering. Remind students that climatic differences around the world affect weathering processes. L2

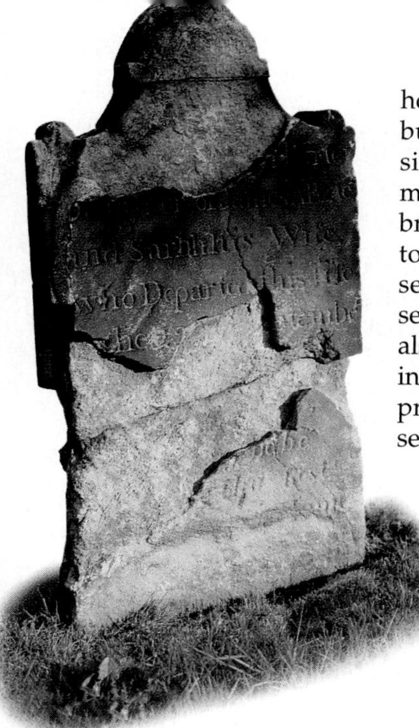

Now you can understand how weathering affects roads, buildings, streets, cemeteries, sidewalks, rocks, caves, and mountains. When weathering breaks down rocks, it contributes to the rock cycle by making sediment that can form into sedimentary rocks. Weathering also begins the process of breaking down rock into soil. This process is discussed in the next section.

Figure 6-6

These old tombstones are about the same age, but they have weathered differently. The type of rock also influences how fast a surface weathers. *Why?*

Section Wrap-up

Review

1. What is the difference between mechanical and chemical weathering?
2. How is mechanical weathering affected by climate?
3. **Think Critically:** How can water be a factor in both mechanical and chemical weathering?

Using Computers

Spreadsheet Make a spreadsheet that (1) identifies examples of weathering that you see around your neighborhood and school and (2) classifies each example as the result of mechanical weathering, chemical weathering, or both.

Skill Builder

Recognizing Cause and Effect

Identify the cause and effect in each of these examples of weathering. If you need help, refer to Recognizing Cause and Effect in the **Skill Handbook.**

1. Acid rain has turned a bronze statue green.
2. Tree roots are exposed in cracks in your sidewalk.
3. A piece of limestone has a honeycomb appearance.

4 Close

•MINI•QUIZ•

Use the Mini Quiz to check students' recall of chapter content.

1. **Ice wedging is a type of ______ weathering.** *mechanical*
2. **______ weathering occurs when the mineral composition of the rock is changed.** *Chemical*
3. **______ occurs when a metal is exposed to oxygen and water.** *Oxidation*

Section Wrap-up

Review

1. Mechanical weathering breaks a rock into smaller pieces without changing its composition. Chemical weathering changes a rock's composition.
2. In temperate climates, the freezing and thawing of water increases mechanical weathering.
3. **Think Critically** Ice causes ice wedging. Acidic groundwater reacts with minerals to weather rocks chemically.

Using Computers

LS **Interpersonal** One way of designing a spreadsheet is to list Weathering Examples in the first column. A second column might be labeled Mechanical Weathering, and a third column might be labeled Chemical Weathering. Students may use a symbol in a column that applies to each weathering example. P

Skill Builder

1. Acid rain is the cause. The effect is discoloration.
2. The tree roots may have caused the cracks. Or, the cracks may have formed due to other types of weathering, thus exposing the roots.
3. Movement of acid groundwater over the limestone caused chemical weathering. The effect of the chemical weathering is honeycombing.

Assessment

Oral Use this Skill Builder to assess students' abilities to recognize cause and effect. Ask students to discuss an additional cause/effect relationship in weathering. Use the Performance Task Assessment List for Making Observations and Inferences in **PASC,** p. 17. P

Section 6•2

Prepare

Section Background

- Residual soils are soils that form by the gradual weathering of bedrock and are not moved. These soils are especially thick on gentle slopes.
- Some soils are not related to the underlying bedrock. These soils were eroded from the areas where they formed and were deposited in new locations. Soil horizons in these transported soils are usually poorly defined or absent.

Preplanning

- To prepare for the MiniLAB, have digging tools, buckets, and hand lenses or microscopes available.
- To prepare for Activity 6-2, have available the materials listed on page 160.

1 Motivate

Bellringer

Before presenting the lesson, display **Section Focus Transparency 23** on the overhead projector. Assign the accompanying **Focus Activity** worksheet. L1 LEP

Field Trip

Take students to an area near the school where they can examine an exposed soil profile. Badly eroded gullies, road cuts, and steep slopes are good places to observe soil horizons.

6•2 Soil

Science Words

soil
humus
soil profile
horizon
leaching

Objectives

- Explain how soil evolves from rock.
- Describe soil by comparing the A, B, and C soil horizons.
- Discuss how environmental conditions affect the evolution of soils.

Formation of Soil

How often have you been told, "Take off those dirty shoes before you come into this house"? Ever since you were a child, you've had experience with what many people call dirt, which is actually soil. Soil is found in lots of places: empty lots, farm fields, gardens, and forests.

What is soil and where does it come from? The surface of Earth is covered by a layer of rock and mineral fragments produced by weathering. As you learned in Section 6-1, weathering gradually breaks rocks into smaller and smaller fragments. But these fragments are not soil until plants and animals live in them. Plants and animals add organic matter, such as leaves, twigs, and dead worms and insects to the rock fragments. Soil begins to evolve. **Soil** is a mixture of weathered rock, organic matter, mineral fragments, water, and air. **Figure 6-7** illustrates the process of soil-making. Soil is a material capable of supporting vegetation. Climate, types of rock, slope, amount of moisture, and length of time rock has

Figure 6-7

Soil is constantly evolving from rock.

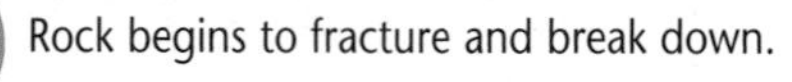

A Rock begins to fracture and break down.

B As rock weathers into smaller fragments, plants begin to grow in the weathered rock.

Program Resources

Reproducible Masters

Study Guide, p. 27 L1
Reinforcement, p. 27 L1
Enrichment, p. 27 L3
Cross-Curricular Integration, p. 10
Activity Worksheets, pp. 5, 38-39, 41 L1
Science Integration Activity, pp. 11-12
Critical Thinking/Problem Solving, p. 12
Lab Manual 22

Transparencies

Section Focus Transparency 23 L1
Teaching Transparency 12

been weathering influence the formation of soil.

Soil can be considered a complex ecosystem. Soil may contain small rodents, insects, worms, algae, fungi, bacteria, and decaying organic matter. When soil is developing, organic material, such as plants, decays. This material decays until the original form of the matter has disappeared. The material turns into dark-colored matter called **humus.** Humus serves as a source of nutrients for plants, providing nitrogen, phosphorous, potassium, and sulfur. Humus also promotes good soil structure and helps soil retain water. As worms, insects, and rodents burrow throughout the soil, they mix the humus with the fragments of rock. In good-quality surface soil, about half of the volume is humus and half is broken-down rock.

Soil can take thousands of years to form and can range in thickness from 60 m in some areas to just a few centimeters in others. A fertile soil is one that supplies nutrients for plant growth. Soils that develop near rivers often are fertile. Other soils, such as those that develop on steep slopes, may be nutrient-poor and have low fertility.

Soils have small spaces in them. These spaces fill with air or water. In swampy areas, water may fill these spaces year-round. In other areas, soil may fill up with water after rains or during floods.

CONNECT TO

LIFE SCIENCE

In tropical areas with heavy rainfall, rain washes all the elements from the soil. High temperatures and bacteria destroy the humus. The soil becomes so empty of nutrients that plants cannot grow there. ***Infer*** from this whether it would be easy to farm in these areas.

C Worms, insects, bacteria, and fungi living among the plant roots add organic matter to the soil.

D When plants and animals in the soil die, they break down, or decay, and form dark humus.

2 Teach

Teacher F.Y.I.

In one gram of soil, there can be hundreds of millions of organisms.

Inquiry Question

Explain why topsoil is fertile. *Humus is full of nutrients.*

Revealing Preconceptions

Students might think that all soil profiles are equally well developed. Explain that sometimes soil profiles do not show distinct A, B, and C horizons because of disturbances that have occurred or because the soils are too young.

Videodisc

GTV: Planetary Manager

Agriculture

47653

47654

48103

Use **Teaching Transparency 12** as you teach this lesson.

Theme Connection

Stability and Change Ask students, **What important soil component would be missing if plants and animals did not decay?** *humus*

Visual Learning

Figure 6-8 **How do you know that this meadow has a well-developed A horizon?** *The presence of grasses, trees, and flowers indicates enough topsoil to support growing plants.* LEP LS

MiniLAB

Purpose

LS **Interpersonal** Students will examine and compare soil samples that they have collected. L1 COOP LEARN

Materials

soil samples, sheet of white paper, plastic bags or envelopes to store samples, microscope or hand lens, light source

Teaching Strategies

Have students identify sources of organic materials.

Analysis

1. Students will find sediments and organic matter, such as feathers, leaves, bark, and insect parts.
2. Students might compare texture, color, and the type and amount of organic matter.

Assessment

Performance To further assess students' understanding of soil, have them separate soil components into different piles: rock fragments, sand, clay, topsoil, humus, and organisms. Use the Performance Task Assessment List for Making Observations and Inferences in PASC, p. 17. P

Activity Worksheets, pp. 5, 41

MiniLAB

What is soil made of?

Examine a sample of soil closely to compare it with other students' samples.

Procedure

1. Collect a sample of soil.
2. Observe it closely with a magnifying glass or a microscope.

Analysis

1. Describe the different particles found in your sample. Did you find any remains of once-living organisms?
2. Compare and contrast your sample with those other students have collected. How are the sample the same? How are they different?

Soil Profile

You may have seen layers of soil if you've ever dug a deep hole or driven by a steep slope such as a road cut where the soil and rock are exposed. You might have noticed that plants grow in the top layer of soil. The top layer of soil is darker than the soil layers below it. These different layers of soil make up what is called a **soil profile.** Each layer in the soil profile is called a **horizon.** There are generally three horizons. They are labeled A, B, and C, as in the diagram in **Figure 6-8.** The photo in **Figure 6-9** shows soil horizons in an eroded hillside. Look for examples of soil horizons in road cuts and along steep slopes.

Figure 6-8

Under this meadow is soil with a specific profile.

A The soil profile of this meadow has at least three horizons.

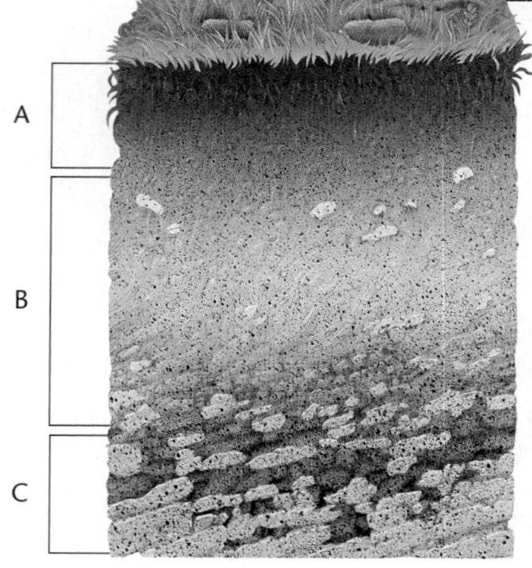

B The horizons in the soil profile of this meadow show different degrees of soil evolution. The A horizon contains humus and small grains of rock. It has changed the most from the underlying rock layer. The B horizon contains minerals leached from the A horizon and little or no humus. The C horizon contains minerals leached from the B horizon and partly weathered rock. *How do you know that this meadow has a well-developed A horizon?*

Inclusion Strategies

Gifted Have students find out how soils are classified. Then have students research the different types of soils in your state.

- Have students research and construct a compost pile that can be compared with the surrounding soil and analyzed throughout the year. Students can transfer the compost to a garden plot in the spring. Interested students should contact the state Department of Natural Resources for information on what should be included in the compost pile. Students could also enlist the services of the Industrial Technology Department to help construct a storage bin. Garden stores can also be helpful. L3

Horizon A

The A horizon is the top layer of soil. It's also known as topsoil. Topsoil has more humus and smaller rock and mineral particles than the other, less evolved layers in a soil profile. If you dig up a scoop of topsoil and look at it closely, you will see soil, dark in color and containing grains of rock and minerals, decayed leaves, roots of plants, and insects and worms. The A horizon is the most fully evolved soil layer in a soil profile. This means that the A horizon has changed the most from weathered rock.

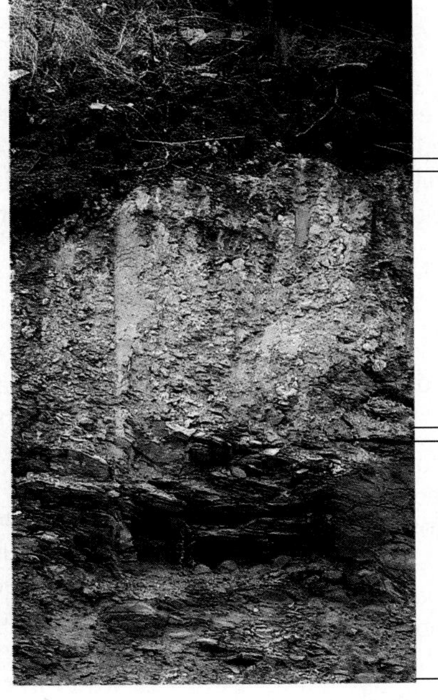

Figure 6-9

Each soil horizon represents a different stage of evolution of this soil.

Horizon B

The layer below the A horizon is the B horizon. This layer is less evolved. It is lighter in color than the A horizon because it has less humus. Some plant roots reach into this horizon, which usually contains elements washed down from the A horizon by the process of leaching. **Leaching** is the removal of soil materials dissolved in water. Water runs down through the soil horizons, leaching out soil materials and depositing them in the layers below. The process of leaching resembles making coffee in a drip coffee-maker. In a coffee-maker, water drips into ground coffee. In the soil, water seeps into the A horizon. In a coffee-maker, the water absorbs the flavor and color from the coffee and flows down into a coffeepot. In the soil, the water reacts with humus to form an acid. This acid dissolves some of the elements from the minerals in the A horizon and carries them into the B horizon. Some leaching also occurs in the B horizon and moves into the C horizon.

Horizon C

The C horizon is below the B horizon. It is the bottom layer in a soil profile. Some materials in this layer were leached from the B horizon. The C horizon also contains partly weathered rock that is beginning the long, slow process of evolving into soil. What would you find if you dug all the way to the bottom of the C horizon? As you might have guessed, there would be solid rock. This is the parent rock that gave rise to the soil horizons above it.

CONNECT TO

LIFE SCIENCE

Fungi and bacteria are decomposers, found mainly in horizon A. Decomposers break down the complex organic material in animals and plants into smaller molecules, creating humus. ***Infer*** from this what our world would be like without decomposers.

Inquiry Questions

- **Why are sediments in the A horizon smaller than those in the B and C horizons?** *They have been exposed to more agents of weathering.*
- **Why is the top layer of certain soil profiles darker in color than the horizons below?** *The top layer in such soils contains humus.*
- **How can chemicals such as fertilizers and herbicides dumped onto topsoil pollute groundwater?** *The chemicals are leached and eventually enter the groundwater supply.*

CONNECT TO

LIFE SCIENCE

Leaves, bark, and animal parts would litter the planet's surface. The organic materials could not recycle into new materials such as humus.

Videodisc

GTV: Planetary Manager

Soil

47797

47798

48113

48116

Use Lab 22 in the **Lab Manual** as you teach this lesson.

Visual Learning

Figure 6-9 Have a volunteer compare and contrast the A and B horizons in a soil profile. LEP LS

Integrating the Sciences

Life Science Have students research why some plants grow better in humus-rich soils. Students might want to actually plant three identical plants in various soils and display how growth is affected by soil type. L2

Activity 6-2

Purpose

LS **Kinesthetic** Students will compare and contrast different soils. L1 LEP

Process Skills

observing and inferring, comparing and contrasting, forming operational definitions, classifying, communicating, separating and controlling variables, and interpreting data

Time

two class periods

Activity Worksheets, pp. 5, 38-39

Teaching Strategies

Alternate Materials Binocular microscopes will show more of the details of the soil than will hand lenses.

Troubleshooting Have a bucket of fresh soil for students to use in this activity.

- Be sure students punch the same number of holes in each cup. Emphasize that these holes are a control device. Different numbers of holes would introduce another variable into the experiment.
- Before they start, have students check to be sure that the cheesecloth is securely fastened to the bottom of the cups.

Activity 6-2 Soil Characteristics

There are thousands of different kinds of soils around the world. Around your area, you've probably noticed that there are a number of different soils. Collect samples of soil to compare from around your neighborhood and from designated areas of your school grounds.

Problem

What are the characteristics of soils?

Materials

- soil sample
- sand
- gravel
- clay
- water
- watch
- paper
- scissors
- thumbtack
- cheesecloth squares
- graduated cylinder
- plastic coffee can lids (3)
- rubber bands
- 250-mL beakers (3)
- large polystyrene or plastic cups (3)
- hand lens

Procedure

1. Spread your soil sample on a sheet of paper.
2. Describe the color of the soil, and examine the soil with a hand lens. Describe the different particles.
3. Rub a small amount of soil between your fingers. Describe how it feels. Also press the soil sample together. Does it stick together? Wet the sample and try this again. Record all your observations.
4. Test the soil for permeability (the ability of water to move through a substance). Label the three cups A, B, and C. Using a thumbtack, punch an equal number of holes in and around the bottom of each cup.
5. Cover the area of holes with a square of cheesecloth. Secure the cloth on each cup with a rubber band.
6. To hold the cups over the beakers, cut the three coffee-can lids so that the cups will just fit inside the hole (see photo). Place a cup and lid over each beaker.
7. Half-fill cup A with dry sand and cup B with clay. Half-fill cup C with a mixture of equal parts of sand, gravel, and clay.
8. Use the graduated cylinder to pour 100 mL of water into each cup. Record the time when the water is first poured into each cup and when the water first drips from each cup.
9. Allow the water to drip for 25 minutes, then measure and record the amount of water in each beaker.

Analyze

1. **Describe** your soil sample in as much detail as possible.
2. Which substance tested in steps 4-9 is most permeable? Least permeable?

Conclude and Apply

3. How does the addition of gravel and sand affect the permeability of clay?
4. **Describe** three characteristics of soil. Which characteristics affect permeability?
5. Use your observations to **explain** which soil sample would be best for growing plants.

Answers to Questions

1. Answers will vary by soil samples used. Characteristics should include color, types and percentages of particles, organisms, texture, and drainage.
2. The sand, gravel, and clay mixture is probably the most permeable, although if the sand is very coarse it may be more permeable. Clay is least permeable.
3. It increases the permeability.
4. Characteristics include color, types and percentages of particles, types and amounts of organisms, texture, and permeability. Types of particles and percentage of different soils affect permeability.
5. Answers will vary but should be explained.

Assessment

Performance To further assess students' understanding of soil characteristics, have them design and perform an experiment to find out how the permeability of the soil sample is affected when different quantities of gravel, sand, and clay are mixed into the sample. Use the Performance Task Assessment List for Designing an Experiment in **PASC,** p. 23. P

Types of Soil

The texture of soil depends on the proportion of sand, silt, and clay. In Activity 6-2, you discovered that the texture of soil affects how water runs through it. That is not all you'll discover from examining soil profiles.

If you examine a soil profile in one place, it will not look exactly like a soil profile from another location. The two profiles will look different in a number of ways, as you would see if you examined samples of soil from different locations, such as from a desert, a prairie, and a temperate area. Deserts are dry. Prairies are semidry. The temperate zone profile represents a soil from an area with a moderate amount of rain and moderate temperatures.

The thickness of the soil horizons and the soil composition of the profiles depend on a number of conditions. One condition that strongly affects soil profiles and composition is climate. Examples of three

USING TECHNOLOGY

Land Reclamation

In the United States, sand and gravel, as well as over 60 percent of coal, are obtained by surface mining. In surface mining, huge machines remove the earth above a coal seam and dump it. In the past, the dumped material remained where it was; the mined area remained as desolate as a moon landscape.

Reclamation

The 1977 Federal Strip Mine Law requires that topsoil, the A horizon, now be replaced on surface-mined land. Today, when dozers remove topsoil, it is stockpiled. The material between the topsoil and the coal is blasted to fragments. Then the fragments are transported to a hollow or small valley, sorted, and regraded into land with a minimum slope.

Successful reclamation depends on getting a good topsoil on the land as quickly as possible. Machines carry the stockpiled topsoil to the valley and cover the fragmented rock. Replacing topsoil allows new vegetation to grow rapidly and helps prevent erosion, dirt running into streams, and desolate hillsides. Reclamation experts have used organic waste such as composted sewage and garbage, bark mulch, and other wastes to fertilize the topsoil of reclaimed areas. Some reclaimed surface-mined land is more productive than it was before mining.

Mine Reclamation

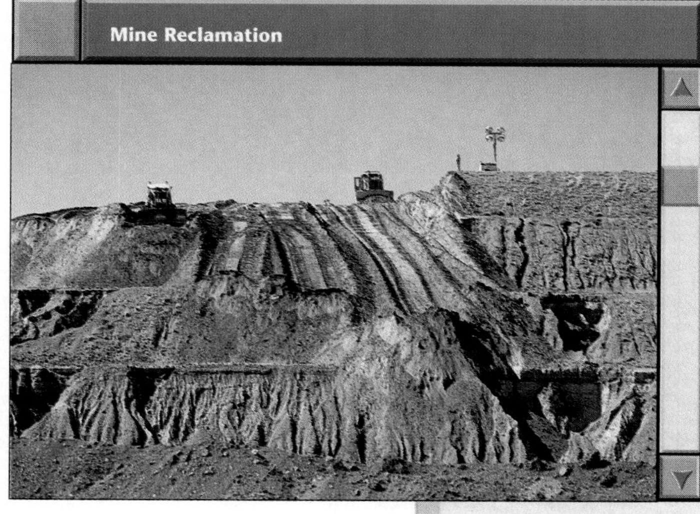

Think Critically: Compare the soil profile of unreclaimed mined land with the soil profile of unmined land. How are they different?

Inquiry Question

Why do you think some soils are only a few centimeters thick? *Wind and water erode soils from some regions and deposit them elsewhere. Soil thickness is also affected by the slope of the land. Soils won't form on steep slopes because weathered rock will slide down the slopes. In some areas, weathering is very slow because there is little moisture; therefore, soils in dry areas evolve very slowly.*

USING TECHNOLOGY

Explain that underground mining is more expensive and dangerous than strip or surface mining. Although surface mining disrupts the soil, underground mining also brings out slag and pumps out acidic water that cause environmental problems.

Think Critically

In reclaimed land, the A profile is put back on top. But beneath that, the B and C profiles are mixed.

NATIONAL GEOGRAPHIC SOCIETY

Videodisc

GTV: Planetary Manager

Soil

48168

48212

Community Connection

Local Soil Have a farmer, soil analyst, or agricultural consultant come to class and talk about local soils. Have the person discuss how different soils affect crop or garden yields.

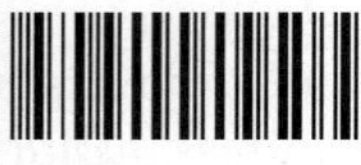

GTV: Planetary Manager
Agriculture

47525

3 Assess

Check for Understanding

FLEX Your Brain

Use the Flex Your Brain activity to have students explore SOIL PROFILES.

Activity Worksheets, p. 5

Reteach

LS **Interpersonal** Prior to Activity 6-2, number and label four buckets as follows: (1) Large gravel pieces, (2) Pea-sized gravel, (3) Topsoil containing humus, and (4) Light-colored sand and clay. Fill each bucket with the appropriate sediment(s). Give each group of students a clear plastic tube or graduated cylinder to use. Ask students to use these sediments and their tube to make a soil profile with four horizons, arranged in order. The arrangement of sediments should be, from bottom to top: the large gravel pieces, which represent the bedrock; the pea-sized gravel, which represents the C horizon; the sand and clay, which make up the B horizon; and the topsoil, which is the A horizon. **COOP LEARN**

Extension

For students who have mastered this section, use the **Reinforcement** and **Enrichment** masters.

soil profiles from different climates are shown in **Figure 6-10.**

Chemical weathering is slower in areas where there is little rainfall. Soils in dry climates contain little organic material. The soil horizons in dryer areas are thinner than soil horizons in wetter climates. The amount of precipitation affects how much leaching of minerals has occurred in the soil. Soils that have been leached are light in color. Some can be almost white.

Another condition that affects soil development is time. Time changes the characteristics of soil. If the weathering of the rock has been going on for a short time, the parent rock of the soil determines the soil characteristics. As the weathering continues for a longer time, the soil resembles the parent rock less and less.

Slope also affects soil profiles. On steep slopes, soil horizons are often poorly developed. In bottomlands, where there is a lot of water, soils are often very thick, dark, and full of organic material. A south-facing slope receives more solar radiation and consequently has a different soil development from a north-facing slope. The amount of humus in the soil also affects soil profiles. In the United States, there are nine groups of soils recognized as well as many subgroups. The map in **Figure 6-11** shows the nine main soil groups.

Figure 6-10

Prairie soils are brown and fertile with thick grass roots that fill the deep A horizon. Temperate soils are loose, brown soils with less-developed A horizons than prairie soils. Desert soils are coarse, light-colored, and contain a lot of minerals. Of the three soil types shown here, desert soils have the least-developed A horizon.

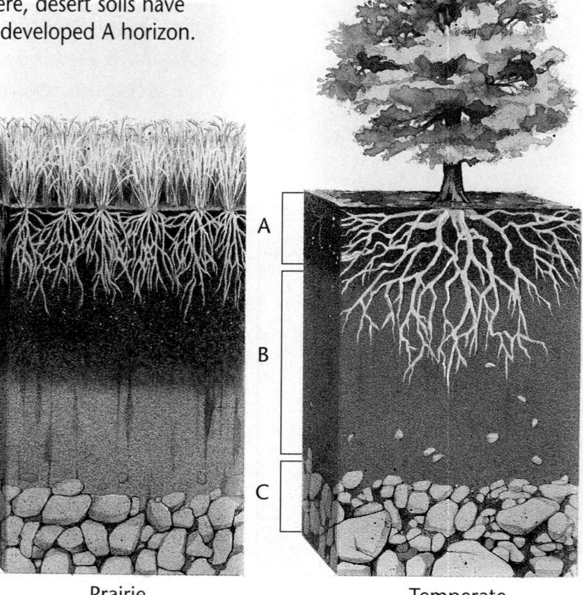

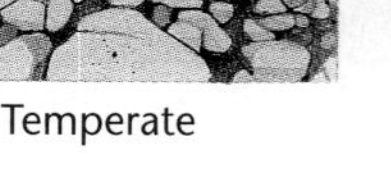

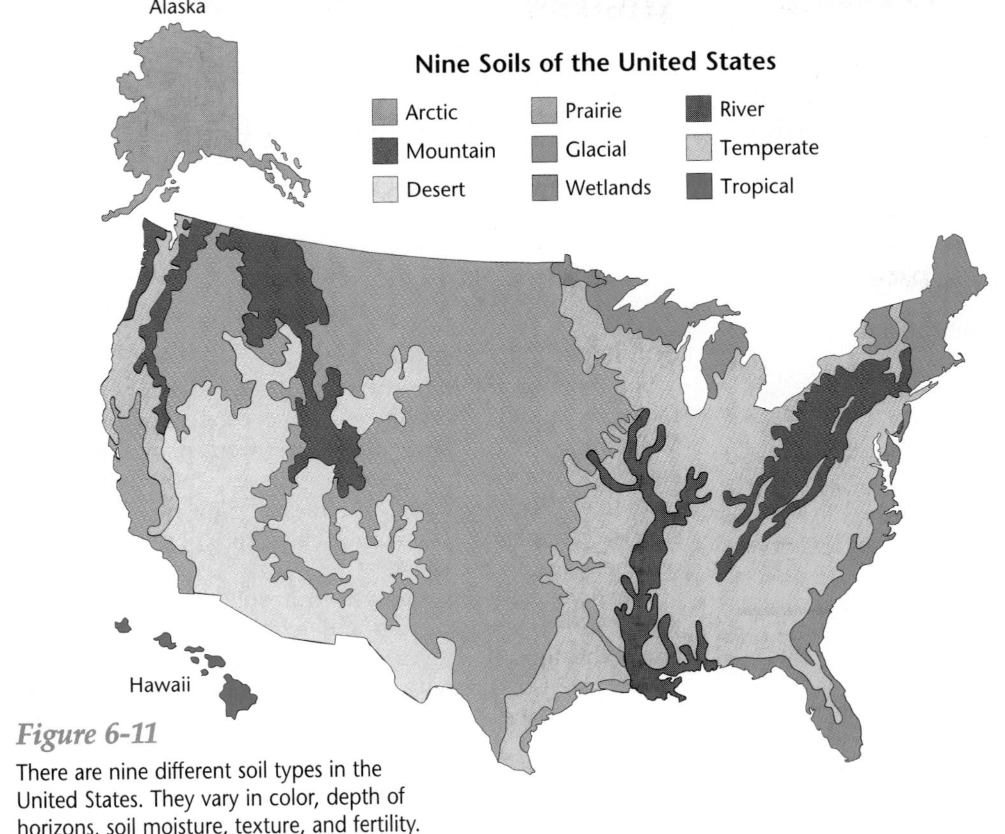

Figure 6-11

There are nine different soil types in the United States. They vary in color, depth of horizons, soil moisture, texture, and fertility.

Section Wrap-up

Review

1. How do organisms help soils develop?
2. Why do soil profiles contain layers or horizons?
3. Why does horizon B contain minerals from horizon A?
4. **Think Critically:** Why is the soil profile in a rain forest different from one in a desert?

Skill Builder
Concept Mapping

Make an events chain map that explains how soil evolves. Use the following terms and phrases: *soil is formed, humus develops, rock is weathered, plants grow, worms and insects move in, humus mixes with weathered rock.* If you need help, refer to Concept Mapping in the **Skill Handbook.**

Science Journal

Research how farmers can improve the quality of soil by planting legumes. Write a summary of what you learn in your Science Journal.

4 Close

•MINI•QUIZ•

Use the Mini Quiz to check students' recall of chapter content.

1. **_____ is the dark-colored organic matter made of decaying organisms.** *Humus*
2. **Each layer in a soil profile is called a _____ .** *horizon*
3. **The _____ soil horizon is the least evolved.** C

Section Wrap-up

Review

1. Organisms add organic materials to the soil, create humus, mix humus with fragments of rock, and churn the soil, allowing air between soil particles.
2. As soil evolves, layers form. The least-evolved layer is the bottom or C horizon. As this gradually changes, a B horizon develops on top. Finally, an A horizon forms above that.
3. Minerals in the A horizon dissolve in acidic water and flow down into the B horizon.
4. **Think Critically** Because the thicknesses and compositions of their horizons differ. Conditions that affect the profiles include climate, type of bedrock, slope, and the absence or presence of vegetation and organisms.

Skill Builder

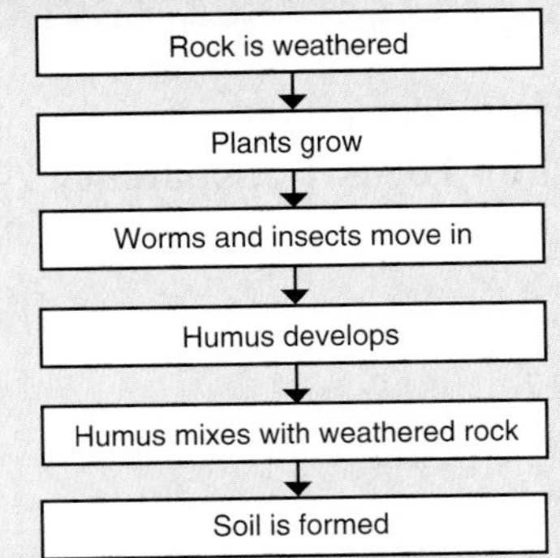

Assessment

Performance Have students make an events chain concept map to show how materials in the A horizon are leached into the B horizon. Use the Performance Task Assessment List for Events Chain in **PASC,** p. 91. P

Science Journal

LS **Linguistic** Nitrogen-fixing bacteria living on the roots of legumes enrich the soil by changing atmospheric nitrogen into a form of nitrogen that plants can use.

SCIENCE & SOCIETY

Section 6•3

Prepare

Section Background

Plowing disrupts soil. Topsoil is constantly lost, but farmers have tried to improve farming techniques to save soil.

1 Motivate

Bellringer

Before presenting the lesson, display **Section Focus Transparency 24** on the overhead projector. Assign the accompanying **Focus Activity** worksheet. L1 LEP

Tying to Previous Knowledge

Students should know that farmers and gardeners often use fertilizers on soil. Have students explain why fertilizers are used.

2 Teach

Visual Learning

Figure 6-13 How does this conserve soil? *No-till farming does not disrupt the soil. Therefore, it is harder for wind and water to erode the soil.* LEP LS

USING MATH

$18\ km^2 \times 24\ hr \times 365\ days =$
$157\ 680\ km^2/y \times 175y =$
$27\ 594\ 000\ km^2$

6•3 ISSUE: Land Use and Soil Loss

Science Words

desertification

Objectives

- Describe the importance of soil and activities that lead to its loss.
- Explain how soil loss can be minimized.

Agriculture

Soil Is an Important Resource

Soil is important. Many of the things we take for granted—food, paper, and cotton—have a direct connection to the soil. Vegetables, grains, and cotton come from plants, livestock such as cattle and pigs feed on grasses, and paper comes from trees. Plants, grasses, and trees all grow in soil. Without soil, we cannot grow food or raise livestock or produce paper or other products we need.

When vegetation is removed from soil, the soil is exposed to the direct action of rain and wind. Rain and wind can erode the topsoil and carry it away, destroying the soil's structure. Also, without plants, soil development slows and sometimes stops because humus is no longer being produced.

2 Points of View

Plowing Disrupts the Soil

Every year the population of Earth increases by 93 million people. More people need more food. Farmers plow more fields to raise more food for the increasing population. This increases pressure on our soil resources.

Soils have not always been managed effectively. Plowing soil is the mechanical turning and loosening of the soil to improve it for crops. Plowing soil removes the plant cover that holds soil particles in place, leaving soils open to wind and water erosion. Sometimes, as shown in Figure 6-12, the wind blows soil from a plowed field. Soil erosion in many places occurs at a much faster rate than the natural processes of weathering can replace it.

Soil loss is particularly severe in the tropics. Tropical rains running down steep slopes quickly erode soil. Each year, thousands of square kilometers of tropical rain forest are cleared for farming and grazing. Soils in tropical rain forests appear rich in nutrients but are almost sterile below the first few centimeters. When the rain forest is removed, the soil is useful to farmers for only a few years before the nutrients are gone. The soil then becomes

Figure 6-12

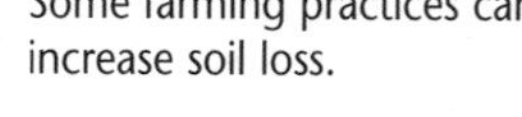

Some farming practices can increase soil loss.

Program Resources

Reproducible Masters

Study Guide, p. 28 L1
Reinforcement, p. 28 L1
Enrichment, p. 28 L3
Science & Society Integration, p. 10
Multicultural Connections, pp. 15-16

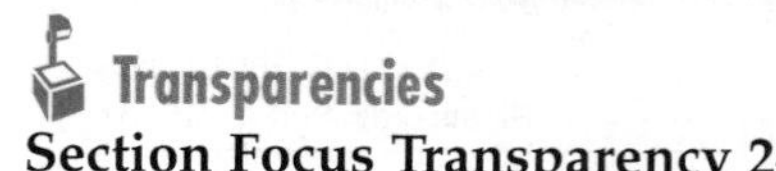

Transparencies

Section Focus Transparency 24

infertile. Farmers clear new land, repeating the process and increasing the damage to the soil.

Near the deserts of the world, sheep and cattle eat every bit of grass. When natural vegetation is removed from land that receives little rain, plants don't grow back. This leads to a loss of soil through wind erosion. Groundwater evaporates. The dry, unprotected surface can be blown away. The desert spreads. Desert formation, called **desertification,** is currently happening on every continent.

Figure 6-13

In no-till farming, the soil is not plowed before planting. *How does this conserve soil?*

Farmers Work to Minimize Soil Loss

All over the world, farmers take steps to minimize soil erosion. They plant shelter belts of trees to break the force of the wind and cover bare soils with decaying plants to hold soil particles in place. In dry areas, instead of plowing under the natural vegetation to plant crops, farmers graze animals on the vegetation. Proper grazing management can retain plants and reduce soil erosion.

Steep slopes, prone to erosion, can be taken out of cultivation or terraced. In the tropics, planting trees to block the force of rain falling on open ground reduces erosion. On gentle slopes, plowing along the natural contours of the land or planting crops in strips helps reduce water erosion. In strip cropping, a crop that covers the ground is alternated with a crop such as corn that leaves a considerable amount of land exposed. In recent years, many farmers have begun the practice of no-till farming. Normally, farmers till or plow their fields three or more times a year. In no-till farming, seen in **Figure 6-13,** plant stalks are left in the field. At the next planting, farmers seed crops without destroying these stalks and without plowing the soil. No-till farming provides cover for the soil all year round and reduces erosion.

USING MATH

About 18 square km of rain forests disappear each hour. At this rate, all rain forests in the world will be gone in about 175 years. How many square kilometers of rain forests exist on Earth currently?

Section Wrap-up

Review

1. Why is more and more land plowed?
2. What farming practices minimize soil loss?

Explore the Issue

Studies show that for every 3.5 cm of topsoil lost, crop yields drop by about 6 percent. How can we protect soil and still provide the necessities of life?

SCIENCE & SOCIETY

3 Assess

Check for Understanding

Have students answer questions 1 and 2 in the Section Wrap-up.

Reteach

LS **Interpersonal** Form groups to sketch the school yard, noting the locations of all buildings, parking lots, sidewalks, and so on. Ask each group to estimate the amount of land being used for human activities and describe how these activities affect the soil. COOP LEARN

Extension

For students who have mastered this section, use the **Reinforcement** and **Enrichment** masters.

4 Close

Have students explain how various human activities result in soil loss.

Section Wrap-up

Review

1. The population of Earth increases. Poor soil management leads to soil infertility and soil erosion.
2. Answers may include terracing, no-till farming, grazing instead of plowing, contour plowing, strip cropping, and planting shelter belts.

Explore the Issue

Ideas will vary but may include planting more vegetation, artificially adding humus to soil, taking care that land is not overgrazed, rotating crops, and better understanding of conservation techniques.

Community Connection

Farming Practices Have students research how contour plowing, strip cropping, and terracing maintain soil fertility and reduce erosion. L1

Soil Farms Have students research how soil farms could be used to create soils naturally and artificially. L2

Across the Curriculum

Geography Have students find evidence that desertification is occurring in Africa, China, and the United States. L2

People and Science

Background

- Bryce Canyon, in south-central Utah, is not a single canyon, but a network of canyons and ravines that run for about 32 km along the eastern side of the Paunsaugunt Plateau. In the park area, the plateau's topmost layers of limestones, sandstones, and siltstones have been weathered into fantastic pinnacles, spires, and columns.
- Rain, freeze-thaw cycles, and gravity all have contributed to shaping the formations in Bryce Canyon National Park.

Teaching Strategies

Show students an assortment of photographs taken in Bryce Canyon National Park, and lead a discussion of the weathering processes that have shaped the formations.

Career Connection

Career Path A limited number of science-related jobs, both full-time and seasonal, are available through the National Park Service. In addition to naturalists, the park service hires professional biologists, geologists, and specialists in many other branches of science. For most positions, a strong background in biology, geology, or natural resources is necessary. Volunteer opportunities also are available in local, state, and national parks.

For More Information

Students can write for brochures on career and volunteer opportunities. Request the "Careers: Seasonal" or "Volunteers" brochures from Department of the Interior, National Park Service, P.O. Box 37127 (Room 1013), Washington, DC 20013-7127. Up to three brochures on specific parks also may be ordered.

People and Science

Susan Colclazer, Naturalist
Bryce Canyon National Park

On the Job

Personal Insights

Q What would we see if we visited Bryce Canyon National Park?

A As you come to the park, you make a tremendous transition, driving by grass and sagebrush, then entering the towering Ponderosa pine forest at the park boundary. As you reach an overlook parking area, suddenly everything seems to drop away in front of you. With just a short walk, you see canyons filled with incredibly-shaped, colored rock formations we call hoodoos. If you look across the valley and up, you see a set of pink cliffs that look just like the ones beneath your feet. Then you start thinking about what might have happened to create this place.

Q Are the interesting colors of the canyon's rock formations due to oxidation?

A Yes. Iron, maganese, and magnesium oxides give the shades of yellow, blue, purple, pink, and orange. The white is from limestone, which makes up most of the top rock layers in the park. Different weather and angles of light hitting the rocks make the colors almost seem to change right in front of you.

Q When we think of the effects of weathering on rock, we tend to think about very long-term changes. Have you witnessed any changes in the time you've worked in the park?

A During storms, you might actually see a large chunk of the rim wash away. I have seen trails relocated because a rock slide completely buried them. One night, about half of the spire on a formation called the Sentinel broke off. People who've been around the area longer than I have can tell you about many formations that are now just piles of rubble.

Career Connection

Geologists aren't the only scientists who are interested in Bryce Canyon. Archeologists, sociologists, and botanists have made studies there. Make a list of things the following scientists might study in the canyon, and tell how their findings would add to the overall picture of the canyon's history.

- Archaeologist
- Botanist

References

- Cvancara, Alan M. *A Field Manual for the Amateur Geologist.* Upper Saddle River, NJ, Prentice-Hall, 1985.
- Matthews, Rupert O. *The Atlas of Natural Wonders.* New York, Facts on File Publications, 1988.
- National Geographic Society. *Our Continent: A Natural History of North America.* Washington, DC, National Geographic Society, 1976.
- Sullivan, Walter. *Landprints.* New York, Times Books, 1984.

Chapter 6

Review

Summary

6-1: Weathering

1. Mechanical weathering breaks apart rocks without changing their chemical composition. Ice and plant roots can cause mechanical weathering. Chemical weathering changes the composition of the rock. Chemical weathering can be caused by acidic water and oxygen.
2. Climate affects the rate and type of weathering.

6-2: Soil

1. Soil develops when rock is weathered and organic matter is added.
2. In a soil profile, the A horizon, or topsoil, is dark in color and contains weathered rock and organic matter. The B horizon has little or no humus and usually contains materials leached from the A horizon. The C horizon contains partly weathered rock and some materials leached from the B horizon.
3. Soil characteristics depend on the climate of the area, the type of parent rock, the slope of the land, the amount of humus in the soil, and the length of time the soil has been evolving.

6-3: Science and Society: Land Use and Soil Loss

1. Soil is important for food. Soil development stops when vegetation is removed from soil.
2. The increasing population on Earth leads to development of the land to provide food. More development can lead to soil erosion, but farmers try to stop this with soil conservation methods.

Key Science Words

a. chemical weathering
b. climate
c. desertification
d. horizon
e. humus
f. ice wedging
g. leaching
h. mechanical weathering
i. oxidation
j. soil
k. soil profile
l. weathering

Reviewing Vocabulary

Match each phrase with the correct term from the list of Key Science Words.

1. breaking down rocks without changing the chemical composition
2. weathering in which the composition of the rock is changed
3. mixture of weathered rock and organic matter
4. decayed organic matter
5. the A, B, and C layers of soil
6. each layer in a soil profile
7. a process that carries dissolved materials downward in soil
8. desert formation
9. rock is forced apart by ice
10. chemical weathering process due to exposure to water and oxygen

Chapter 6

Review

Summary

Have students read the summary statements to review the major concepts of the chapter.

Reviewing Vocabulary

1. h	**6.** d
2. a	**7.** g
3. j	**8.** c
4. e	**9.** f
5. k	**10.** i

Assessment

Portfolio Encourage students to place in their portfolios one or two items of what they consider to be their best work. Examples include:

- Activity 6-1 results and answers, p. 153
- Across the Curriculum, p. 154
- Using Computers, p. 155 P

Performance Additional performance assessments may be found in **Performance Assessment** and **Science Integration Activities.** Performance Task Assessment Lists and rubrics for evaluating these activities can be found in Glencoe's **Performance Assessment in the Science Classroom.**

GLENCOE TECHNOLOGY

Videodisc

Glencoe Earth Science

Interactive Videodisc

Use videodisc lesson 2, *Mysteries of the Cave,* to review the principles of weathering.

MindJogger Videoquiz

Chapter 6 Have students work in groups as they play the Videoquiz game to review key chapter concepts.

Chapter 6 Review

Checking Concepts

1. d
2. c
3. a
4. a
5. d
6. c
7. a
8. b
9. a
10. d

Understanding Concepts

11. By eliminating overgrazing, planting trees as wind blocks, and practicing no-till farming and other techniques.
12. Rock is exposed to air and water and weathering processes. All of these factors can cause rocks to weather physically and chemically. When humus is added over time, these changes result in the formation of soil.
13. A burrowing worm churns the soil, causing mechanical weathering. Substances released by the worm can cause chemical weathering and can add humus.
14. The B horizon is not exposed to air and as much water as the A horizon is. The B horizon is closer to the parent rock.
15. Removing trees causes soil nutrients to be lost. Also, without roots to hold the soil in place, water and wind carry it away.

Thinking Critically

16. Due to the lack of moisture, mechanical weathering would be more effective in a desert than chemical weathering.
17. As water freezes and thaws in cracks in the pavement, the pavement is forced apart, creating gaps and potholes on streets and roads.
18. Soil is important because without it we cannot grow food or wood products or graze animals.

Chapter 6 Review

Checking Concepts

Choose the word or phrase that completes the sentence.

1. Acids that are produced by plants can cause _______.
   a. desertification
   b. overgrazing
   c. mechanical weathering
   d. chemical weathering
2. Freezing and thawing weathers rocks because water _______ as it freezes.
   a. contracts c. expands
   b. gets more dense d. percolates
3. _______ occurs when roots force rock apart.
   a. Mechanical weathering
   b. Leaching
   c. Ice wedging
   d. Chemical weathering
4. _______ causes rust to form.
   a. Oxygen c. Feldspar
   b. Carbon dioxide d. Paint
5. Poor farming practices in areas that receive little rain can result in _______.
   a. ice wedging c. leaching
   b. oxidation d. desertification
6. Chemical weathering is most rapid in _______regions.
   a. cold, dry c. warm, moist
   b. cold, moist d. warm, dry
7. _______ is a mixture of weathered rock and organic matter.
   a. Soil c. Carbon dioxide
   b. Limestone d. Clay
8. Decayed organic matter is called _______ .
   a. leaching c. soil
   b. humus d. sediment
9. Humus is found almost exclusively in the _______ .
   a. A horizon c. C horizon
   b. B horizon d. D horizon
10. No-till farming helps prevent _______ .
    a. Leaching c. Overgrazing
    b. Crop rotation d. Soil erosion

Understanding Concepts

Answer the following questions in your Science Journal using complete sentences.

11. How have farmers tried to stop soil loss from their land?
12. Explain how soil evolves from rock.
13. How can a worm help soil develop?
14. Explain why the B horizon is less weathered than the A horizon.
15. Explain how the clearing of forests, as in the photo below, contributes to soil loss.

Thinking Critically

16. Which type of weathering, mechanical or chemical, would you expect to be more effective in a desert region? Explain.
17. How does ice wedging damage roads and streets in cold climates?
18. Why is soil so important?
19. Why is it difficult to replace lost topsoil?
20. Explain how chemical weathering can form a cavern.

19. Topsoil in the A horizon develops over a long period of time. It is hard to speed up this natural process.
20. Acidic groundwater flowing through underground rocks can dissolve the rocks. Over time, the dissolution can create a large cavity, or cavern.

Developing Skills

21. **Sequencing** Student sequencing charts will vary, but they should include weathering of rock and leaching.
22. **Concept Mapping:** Possible solution: see Student Edition.
23. **Using Variables, Constants, and Controls** The control was the pan containing the soil without grass. The constants were the same amount and kind of soil, identical pans and wooden wedges, same amount of water, and the same rate of pouring it. The variable was the grass on top of the soil in the second pan.

Developing Skills

For help, refer to the **Skill Handbook.**

21. **Sequencing:** Do a sequence chart of soil development.
22. **Concept Mapping:** Complete the events chain concept map that shows two ways in which acids can cause chemical weathering.

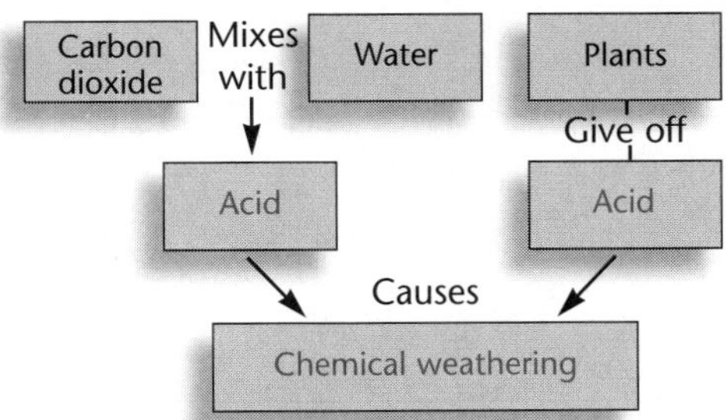

23. **Using Variables, Constants, and Controls:** Juan Carlos wanted to know if planting grass on a slope would prevent soil from being washed away. To find out, he put the same amount and kind of soil in two identical pans. In one of the pans, he planted grass. To create equal slopes for his test, he placed identical wooden wedges under one end of each pan. He was careful to pour the same amount of water at the same rate over the soil in the two pans. What is Juan's control? What factors in his activity are constants? What is the variable he is testing?
24. **Recognizing Cause and Effect:** In Juan Carlos's activity, he found that in the pan containing soil and grass, the least amount of soil washed away. What are the cause and the effect in his observation?
25. **Classifying:** Classify the following events as either chemical or mechanical weathering: rocks that contain iron rust; freezing and thawing of water cause cracks to form in the street; acids from mosses leave small pits in rocks; roots of trees break rocks apart; and water seeping through cracks in limestone dissolves away some of the rock.

Performance Assessment

1. **Design an Experiment:** In Activity 6-1, you observed how an acid (vinegar) causes chemical weathering of a rock (chalk). Now design an experiment to find out how the concentration (or strength) of an acid affects the rate of chemical weathering. State your hypothesis clearly and eliminate all variables except the one you want to test. Perform your experiment.
2. **Design a Model:** Demonstrate how leaching occurs in soil. Review the procedures of Activity 6-2 on page 160 before you begin. The following list of materials is suggested: a soil sample, red powdered tempera paint, plastic coffee-can lid, cheesecloth, rubber band, 250-ml beaker, thumbtack, large plastic cup, graduated cylinder, and water.
3. **Poster:** Plant three identical plants in three different types of soils. Keep everything constant in your experiment except the type of soil. Over a period of weeks, observe and measure plant growth. Then make a poster display to share your results with your classmates. The poster should show how the soil type affected plant growth.

Assessment Resources

Reproducible Masters

Chapter Review, pp. 15-16

Assessment, pp. 36-39

Performance Assessment, p. 20

Glencoe Technology

Chapter Review Software

Computer Test Bank

MindJogger Videoquiz

24. Recognizing Cause and Effect The grass was the cause. The effect was the amount of soil that washed away.

25. Classifying *Chemical Weathering:* rocks that contain iron rust, acids from mosses leave small pits in rocks, acid groundwater seeping through cracks in limestone dissolves away some of the rock. *Mechanical Weathering:* freezing and thawing of water cause cracks to form in the street, roots of trees break rocks apart.

Performance Assessment

1. A possible experimental design could be to dilute vinegar with water to create various vinegar concentrations. A hypothesis might be that the more concentrated the acid, the more quickly the weathering will occur. Constants would include the amount of liquid, size of the beaker, size of the chalk, time, and temperature. Use the Performance Task Assessment List for Designing an Experiment in **PASC,** p. 23. P
2. The paint will represent the material that is leached. Use the Performance Task Assessment List for Model in **PASC,** p. 51. P
3. Constants in this experiment are the type and age of the plants, amount of soil, size of pot, amount of water, exposure to light, and the device and technique used to measure the plants. The variable is the soil type. Use the Performance Task Assessment List for Poster in **PASC,** p. 73. P

Chapter Organizer

Section	Objectives	Activities/Features
Chapter Opener		Explore Activity: Find out how sediments move from one location to another. p. 171
7-1 **Gravity** (1 session, ½ block)*	1. **Define** *erosion* and *deposition*. 2. **Compare** and **contrast** slumps, creep, rockslides, and mudflows.	Using Math, p. 173 MiniLAB: What causes mass movements? p. 176 Skill Builder: Concept Mapping, p. 177 Using Computers, p. 177
7-2 **Science and Society Issue: Developing Land Prone to Erosion** (2 sessions, 1 block)*	1. **Describe** ways that erosion can be reduced in some high-risk areas. 2. **Explain** why problems develop when people live on land prone to excessive erosion.	Explore the Issue, p. 179
7-3 **Glaciers** (1 session, ½ block)*	1. **Describe** the movement of glaciers. 2. **Explain** glacial erosion. 3. **Compare** and **contrast** till and outwash.	Using Math, p. 180 Connect to Chemistry, p. 184 Using Technology: Bergy Bits? p. 185 Activity 7-1: Glacial Grooving, p. 186 Skill Builder: Sequencing, p. 187 Science Journal, p. 187
7-4 **Wind** (1 session, ½ block)*	1. **Explain** how wind causes deflation and abrasion. 2. **Discuss** how loess and dunes form.	MiniLAB: How do plant roots help hold soil in place? p. 190 Problem Solving: Fighting Deflation, p. 191 Activity 7-2: Blowing in the Wind, pp. 192-193 Connect to Life Science, p. 194 Skill Builder: Sequencing, p. 195 Using Math, p. 195 Science & Art, p. 196 Science Journal, p. 196

* A complete Planning Guide that includes block scheduling is provided on pages 32T-35T.

Activity Materials

Explore	Activities	MiniLABs
page 171 sand, gravel, large shoe-box lid	page 186 stream table with sand; ice block embedded with sand, clay, and gravel; wood block; metric ruler; overhead light source with reflector pages 192-193 safety goggles, 4 flat pans, 400 mL fine sand, 400 mL powdered clay, 400 mL gravel, handheld hair dryer, sprinkling can, tap water, 4 sheets of lightweight cardboard, tape, mixing bowl, metric ruler	page 176 sand, gravel, water in spray bottle page 190 grass sod, magnifying glass or stereoscopic microscope

Teacher Classroom Resources

Reproducible Masters	Transparencies	Teaching Resources
Study Guide, p. 29 **Reinforcement,** p. 29 **Enrichment,** p. 29 **Activity Worksheets,** p. 46 **Lab Manual 23,** Mass Movements **Critical Thinking/Problem Solving,** p. 13 **Multicultural Connections,** pp. 17-18	**Section Focus Transparency 25,** Slide? Slump? Creep? **Teaching Transparency 13,** Mass Movements	**Glencoe Earth Science Interactive Videodisc** **Earth Science CD-ROM** **Spanish Resources** **English/Spanish Audiocassettes** **Cooperative Learning Resource Guide** **Lab Partner** **Lab and Safety Skills** **Lesson Plans**
Study Guide, p. 30 **Reinforcement,** p. 30 **Enrichment,** p. 30 **Science and Society Integration,** p. 11	**Section Focus Transparency 26,** Ocean View, Slide Included	
Study Guide, p. 31 **Reinforcement,** p. 31 **Enrichment,** p. 31 **Activity Worksheets,** pp. 42-43 **Lab Manual 24,** Model Glacier **Science Integration Activity 7,** Melting Glaciers and Ice Cubes	**Section Focus Transparency 27,** Monster Movers **Science Integration Activity 7,** Friction Opposes Motion **Teaching Transparency 14,** Glacial Erosional Features	**Assessment Resources** **Chapter Review,** pp. 17-18 **Assessment,** pp. 40-43 **Performance Assessment in the Science Classroom (PASC)** **MindJogger Videoquiz** **Alternate Assessment in the Science Classroom** **Performance Assessment** **Chapter Review Software** **Computer Test Bank**
Study Guide, p. 32 **Reinforcement,** p. 32 **Enrichment,** p. 32 **Activity Worksheets,** pp. 44-45, 47 **Concept Mapping,** p. 19 **Cross-Curricular Integration,** p. 11	**Section Focus Transparency 28,** Not Just a Breath of Fresh Air	

Key to Teaching Strategies

The following designations will help you decide which activities are appropriate for your students.

L1 Level 1 activities should be within the ability range of all students.

L2 Level 2 activities should be within the ability range of the average to above-average student.

L3 Level 3 activities are designed for the ability range of above-average students.

LEP LEP activities should be within the ability range of Limited English Proficiency students.

LS These activities are designed to address different learning styles.

COOP LEARN Cooperative Learning activities are designed for small group work.

P These strategies represent student products that can be placed into a best-work portfolio.

GLENCOE TECHNOLOGY

The following multimedia resources are available from Glencoe.

Science and Technology Videodisc Series (STVS)

Chemistry
- Snowflakes
- Sand Blasting with Dry Ice

Earth & Space
- Wind Profiler
- Wind Engineering

Ecology
- Soil Crusts in the Desert

National Geographic Society Series

STV: Restless Earth

STV: Water

GTV: Planetary Manager

Earth Science CD-ROM

Teacher Classroom Resources

This is a representation of key blackline masters available in the Teacher Classroom Resources.

Teaching Aids

Section Focus Transparencies

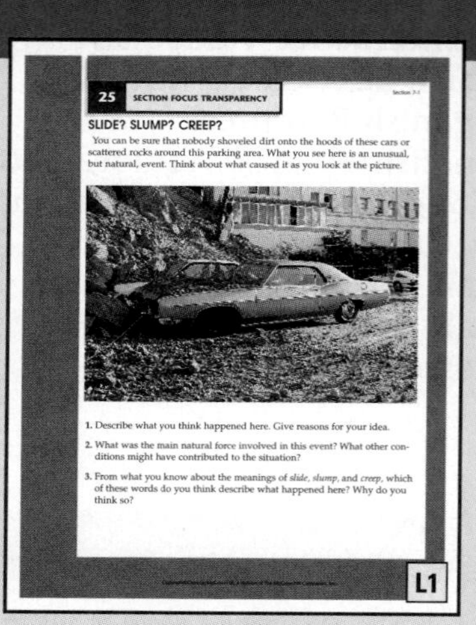

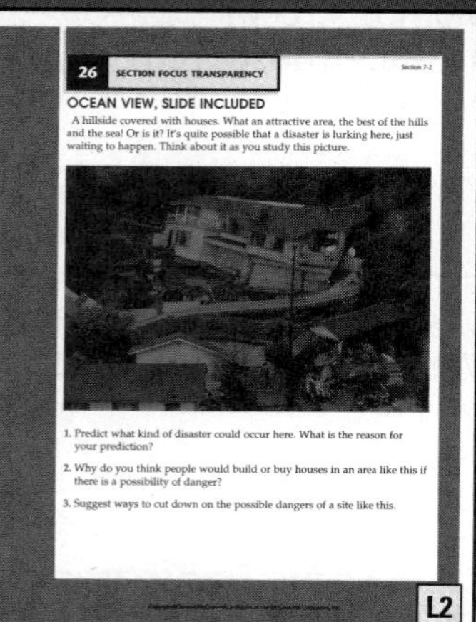

Science Integration Transparencies

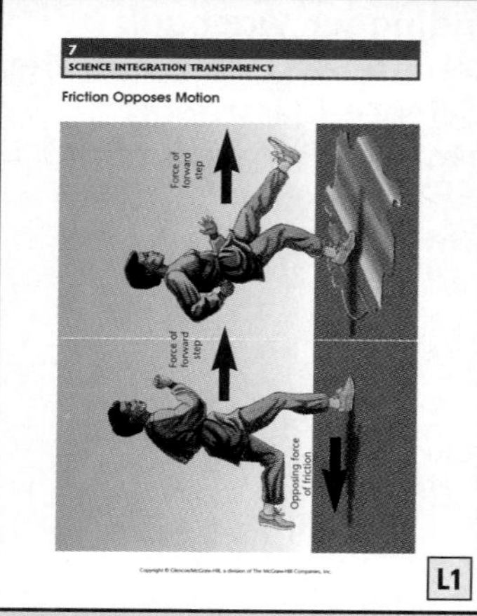

Teaching Transparencies

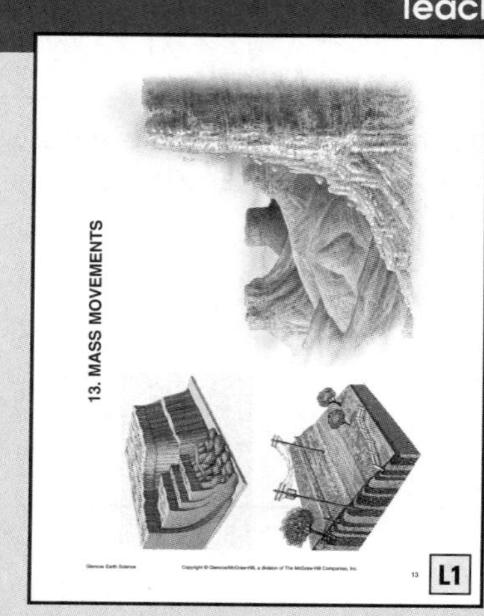
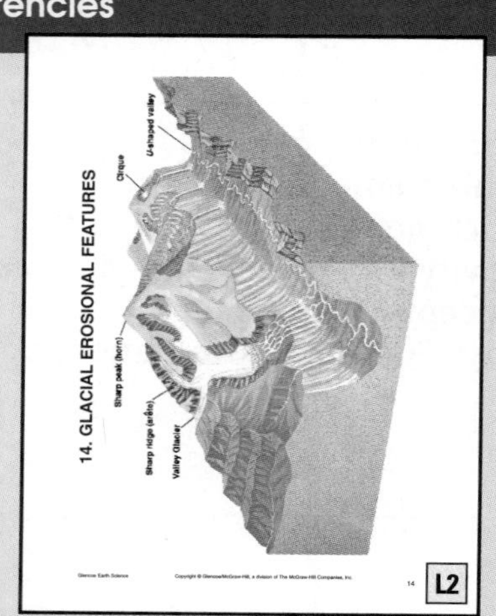

Meeting Different Ability Levels

Study Guide

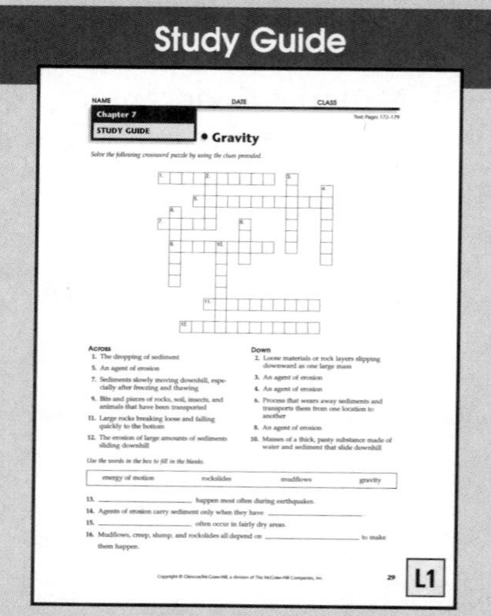

Reinforcement

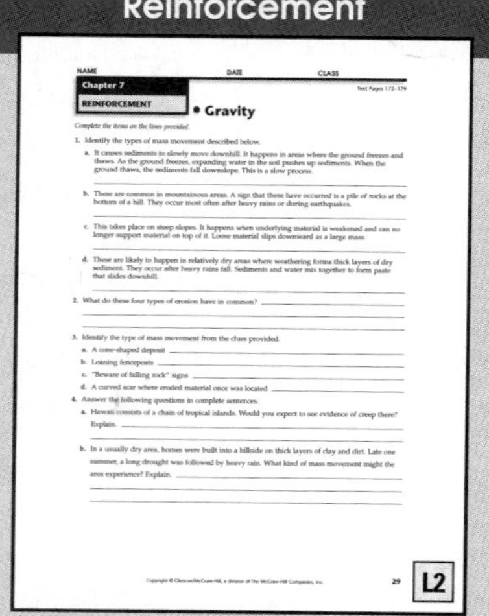

Enrichment Worksheets

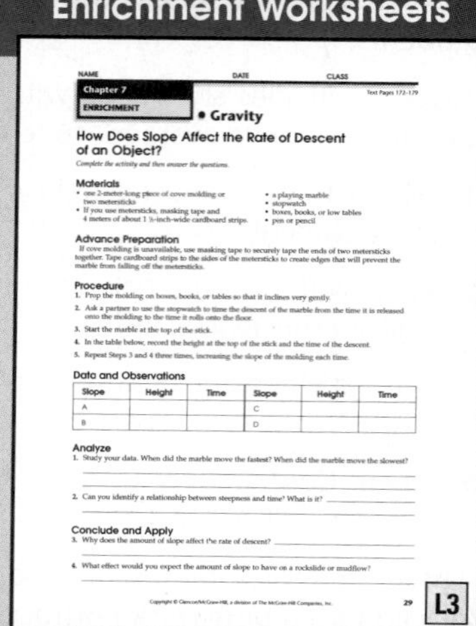

Hands-On Activities

Science Integration Activity

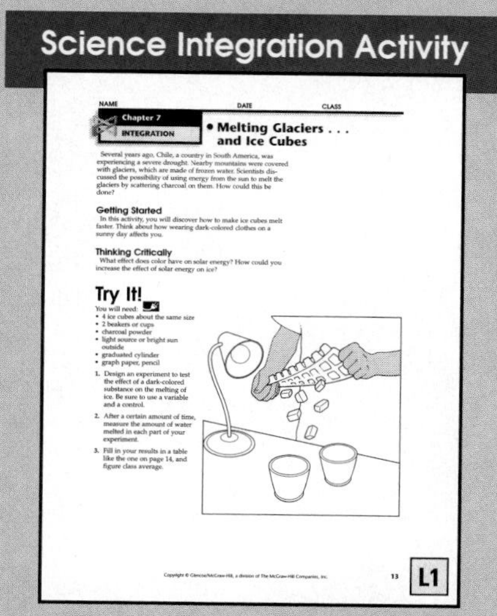
Chapter 7 INTEGRATION
Melting Glaciers . . . and Ice Cubes
L1

Lab Manual

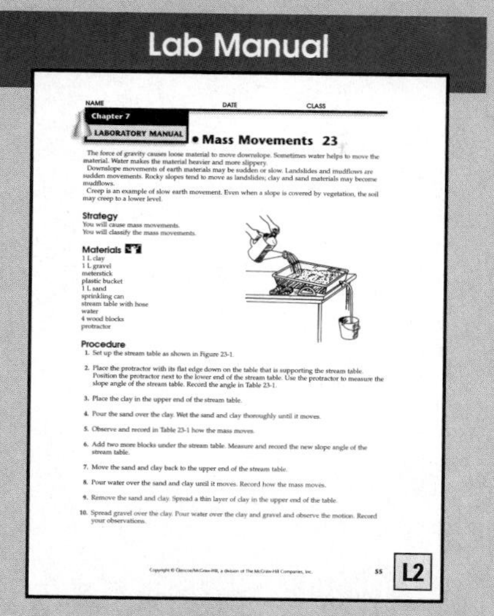
Chapter 7 LABORATORY MANUAL
Mass Movements 23
L2

Assessment

Performance Assessment

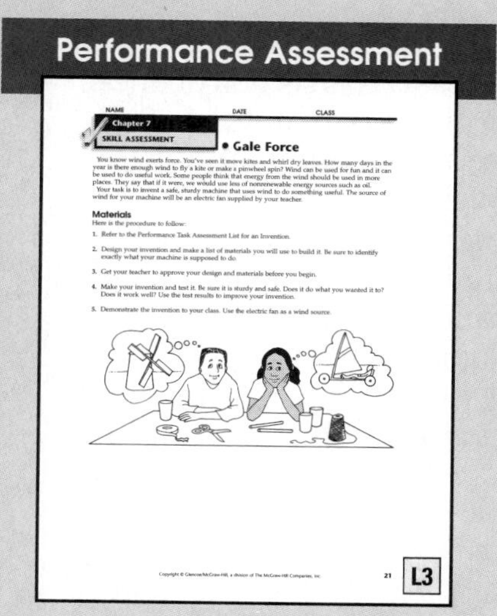
Chapter 7 SKILL ASSESSMENT
Gale Force
L3

Enrichment and Application

Critical Thinking/ Problem Solving

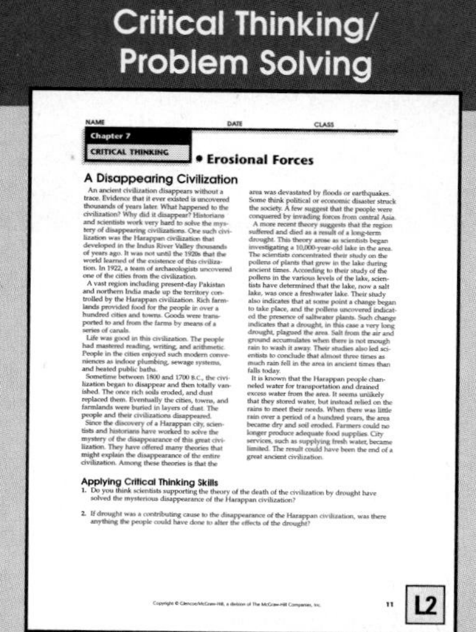
Chapter 7 CRITICAL THINKING
Erosional Forces
A Disappearing Civilization
L2

Cross-Curricular Integration

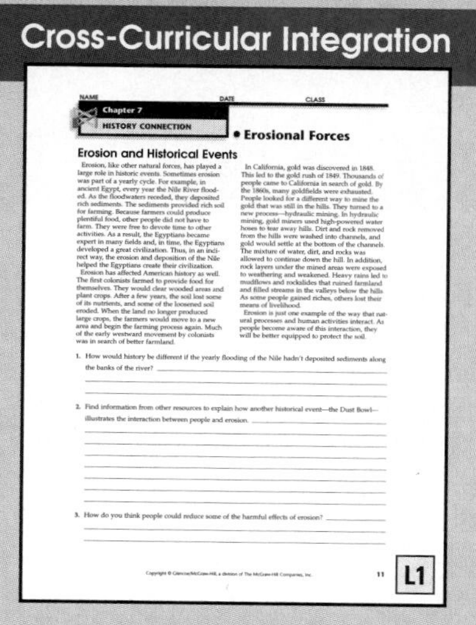
Chapter 7 HISTORY CONNECTION
Erosional Forces
Erosion and Historical Events
L1

Science and Society Integration

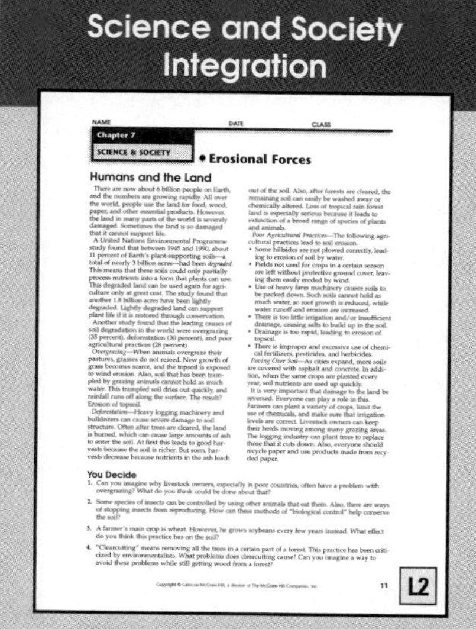
Chapter 7 SCIENCE & SOCIETY
Erosional Forces
Humans and the Land
L2

Multicultural Connections

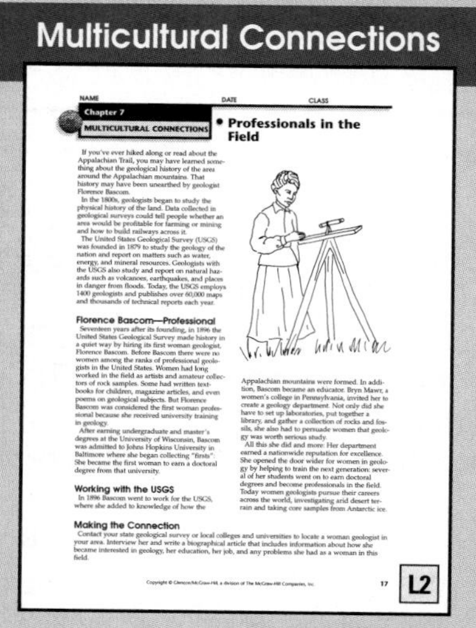
Chapter 7 MULTICULTURAL CONNECTIONS
Professionals in the Field
L2

Concept Mapping

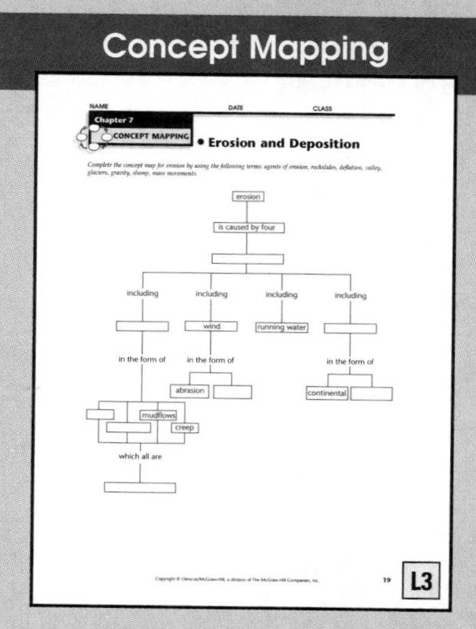
Chapter 7 CONCEPT MAPPING
Erosion and Deposition
L3

Chapter 7

Erosional Forces

CHAPTER OVERVIEW

Section 7-1 This section defines erosion and deposition and describes different mass movement.

Section 7-2 Science and Society Students will examine the problems associated with developing land prone to erosion.

Section 7-3 This section discusses how water in the form of ice—glaciers—is an agent of erosion and deposition.

Section 7-4 This section presents wind as an agent of erosion and deposition.

Chapter Vocabulary

erosion
deposition
mass movement
slump
creep
glacier
plucking
till
moraine
deflation
abrasion
loess

Theme Connection

Energy/Stability and Change Gravity, glaciers, and wind provide energy to change Earth's landforms.

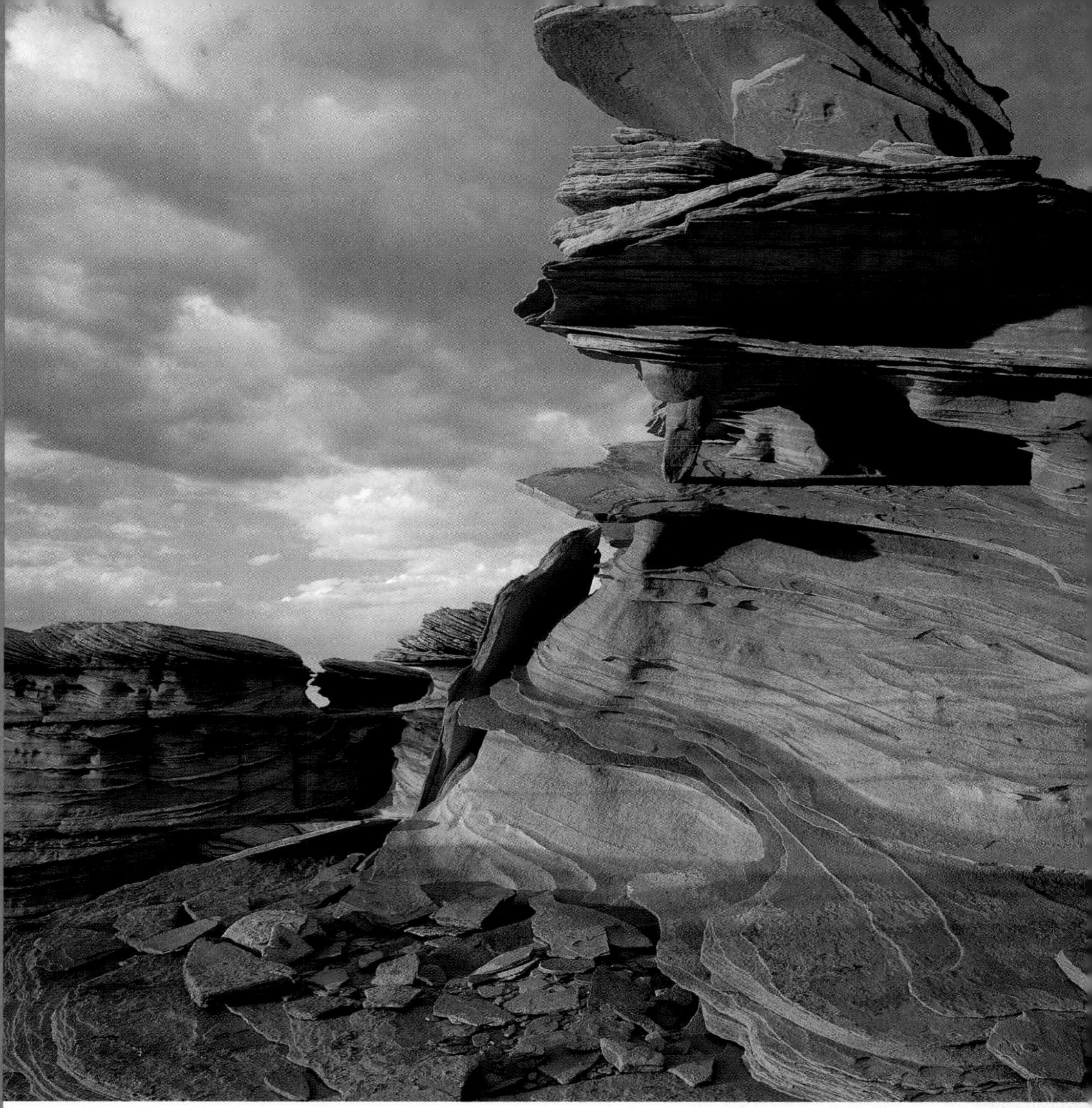

Previewing the Chapter

Section 7-1 Gravity
- Erosion and Deposition
- Erosion and Deposition by Gravity

Section 7-2 Science and Society: Issue: Developing Land Prone to Erosion

Section 7-3 Glaciers
- Continental and Valley Glaciers
- Glacial Erosion
- Glacial Deposition

Section 7-4 Wind
- Wind Erosion
- Reducing Wind Erosion
- Deposition by Wind

170

Learning Styles

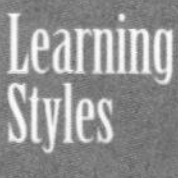

Look for the following logo for strategies that emphasize different learning modalities. LS

Kinesthetic	Explore, p. 171; Integrating the Sciences, p. 179; MiniLAB, p. 190
Visual-Spatial	Visual Learning, pp. 173-176, 178, 184, 189, 191; MiniLAB, p. 176; Demonstration, p. 181; Reteach, p. 185; Activity 7-1, p. 186
Interpersonal	Reteach, p. 178; Cultural Diversity, p. 190; Activity 7-2, pp. 192-193
Linguistic	Across the Curriculum, p. 174; Reteach, p. 175; Theme Connection, p. 176; Science Journal, p. 187; Science & Art, p. 196

Chapter 7

Erosional Forces

In Chapter Six, you learned about weathering of Earth's surface. Weathering breaks down rocks into smaller particles. Then forces of nature move these particles and deposit them elsewhere. One of these forces, wind, blew sand particles that eroded this natural rock sculpture in Vermillion Cliffs Wilderness in Utah. Erosional forces constantly change the surface of Earth, making changes in our landscape.

EXPLORE ACTIVITY

Find out how sediments move from one location to another.

1. Place a small pile of sand and gravel in one end of a large shoe box lid.
2. Move the pile to the other end of the lid without touching the particles with your hands.
3. Try to move the sand in a number of different ways.

Observe: How many methods did you use? How did your methods compare with forces of nature that move sediments? Explain your ideas in your Science Journal.

Previewing Science Skills

- In the **Skill Builders**, you will **map concepts, compare and contrast**, and **sequence**.
- In the **Activities**, you will **design experiments, observe, infer**, and **analyze**.
- In the **MiniLABs**, you will **design experiments, observe**, and **infer**.

EXPLORE ACTIVITY

Purpose

LS **Kinesthetic** Use the Explore Activity to introduce different ways to move sediments. Inform students that this chapter will discuss more about agents of erosion and deposition. L1 LEP

Preparation

Obtain sand and gravel for students to use.

Materials

sand, gravel, shoe box lids, and safety goggles

Teaching Strategies

- Have all students wear safety goggles at all times during this activity.
- Ideas for moving the sediments might include flushing them with water, blowing on them, tilting the shoebox lid, or taking a piece of paper and pushing them along.

Observe

Comparisons are as follows:

- flushing with water: rainfall and stream movement
- blowing: wind
- tilting the surface: creating a steep slope
- pushing: the bulldozing effect of glaciers

Assessment

Content Have students imagine that they are grains of sand in the Explore Activity. Have them create a short story about their experiences when a human blows into the box lid. Use the Performance Task Assessment List for Writer's Guide to Fiction in **PASC**, p. 83. P

Assessment Planner

Portfolio

Refer to page 197 for suggested items that students might select for their portfolios.

Performance Assessment

See page 197 for additional Performance Assessment options.
Skill Builders, pp. 177, 187, 195
MiniLABs, pp. 176, 190
Activities 7-1, p. 186; 7-2, pp. 192-193

Content Assessment

Section Wrap-ups, pp. 177, 179, 187, 195
Chapter Review, pp. 197-199
Mini Quizzes, pp. 177, 187, 195

Group Assessment

Opportunities for group assessment occur with Cooperative Learning Strategies and Flex Your Brain Activities.

Section 7•1

Prepare

Section Background

- Landscapes undergo constant change as materials are moved from one location to another.
- All geological processes require energy—energy of wind, water, gravity, and vulcanism.

Preplanning

To prepare for the MiniLAB, obtain large pans with sand and gravel for each group of students.

1 Motivate

Bellringer

Before presenting the lesson, display **Section Focus Transparency 25** on the overhead projector. Assign the accompanying **Focus Activity** worksheet. L1 LEP

Tying to Previous Knowledge

Have students recall from Chapter 1 that gravity is the force that attracts everything toward Earth. Elicit that this same force causes loose material to move down a slope.

NATIONAL GEOGRAPHIC SOCIETY

Videodisc

STV: Restless Earth

Landslide

52225

Mudflow dams; Japan

52229

7•1 Gravity

Science Words

erosion
deposition
mass movement
slump
creep

Objectives

- Define erosion and deposition.
- Compare and contrast slumps, creep, rockslides, and mudflows.

Erosion and Deposition

Have you ever been by a river just after a heavy rain and seen the water look as muddy as the water in **Figure 7-1?** Rivers look muddy when there is a lot of dirt and soil in them. Some of the dirt comes from along the river bank, but the rest was carried to the river from much more distant sources.

Muddy water is a product of erosion. The process of **erosion** wears away surface materials and moves them from one location to another. The major agents of erosion are gravity, glaciers, wind, and water. The first three will be discussed in this chapter. Running water and wave erosion will be discussed in Chapter 8. Another kind of erosion is shown in **Figure 7-2.**

As you investigate the agents of erosion, you will notice that they have several things in common. Gravity, glaciers, wind, and water all wear away materials and carry them off. But these agents erode materials only when they have enough energy of motion to do work. For example, air can't erode sediments when the air is still. But once air begins moving and develops into wind, it can carry dust, soil, and even rock along with it.

Figure 7-1

The muddy look of some rivers comes from the load of sediment carried by the water.

Program Resources

Reproducible Masters

Study Guide, p. 29 L1
Reinforcement, p. 29 L1
Enrichment, p. 29 L3
Activity Worksheets, pp. 5, 46 L1
Critical Thinking/Problem Solving, p. 13
Multicultural Connections, pp. 17-18
Lab Manual 23

Transparencies

Section Focus Transparency 25 L1
Teaching Transparency 13

Another thing that the agents of erosion have in common is that they all drop their load of sediments when their energy of motion decreases. This dropping of sediments is called **deposition.** Deposition is the final stage of an erosional process. Sediments and rocks are deposited. The surface of Earth is changed. But next year or a million years from now, those sediments may be eroded again.

Erosion and Deposition by Gravity

Gravity is the force of attraction that exists between all objects. Because Earth has great mass, other objects are attracted to Earth. This makes gravity a force of erosion and deposition. Gravity causes loose materials to move down a slope. When gravity alone causes materials to move downslope, this type of erosion is called **mass movement.** Some mass movements are very slow; you hardly notice that they're happening. Others, however, happen very quickly. Let's examine some types of mass movements.

USING MATH

If a rock falls from the edge of a cliff and touches nothing to slow it down, gravity causes it to accelerate (go faster) as it falls. The formula $v = gt$ can be used to find the speed, v, after t seconds. In the formula, g is the acceleration due to gravity, 9.8 m/s^2. Calculate the speed of a falling rock after two seconds of free-fall.

Figure 7-2

This hill has been eroded. *What was the agent of erosion?*

2 Teach

USING MATH

At two seconds the speed would be 9.8 $m/s^2 \times 2$ or 19.6 m/s^2.

Inquiry Question

What are two characteristics that all agents of erosion have in common? *They carry sediments only when they have enough energy of motion. They drop their load of sediments as the energy of motion decreases.*

Visual Learning

Figure 7-2 What was the agent of erosion? *The agent of erosion was human activity with trail cycles and four-wheelers.* LEP LS

NATIONAL GEOGRAPHIC SOCIETY

Videodisc

GTV: Planetary Manager

Landscape

47491

47869

NATIONAL GEOGRAPHIC SOCIETY

CD-ROM

Earth Science CD-ROM

Have students perform the interactive exploration for Chapter 7 to reinforce important chapter concepts and thinking processes.

Inclusion Strategies

Gifted Have students develop a crossword puzzle using the new science words presented in this chapter. They can use definitions from the chapter for clues. In addition, ask students to design an experiment to simulate one type of erosion discussed in the chapter. L3

Integrating the Sciences

Physical Science Mass movements overcome friction when they move. Have students research "friction" and describe how it affects sediments on a slope. *Friction is the force that resists motion between two touching surfaces. On a slope, this force tends to hold sediments in place.*

Enrichment

Have interested students discover the relationship between slope and occurrences of slump. Slump often occurs when slopes have been oversteepened. The material near the top of a slope is held in place by the materials nearer the base of the slope. Slopes are commonly oversteepened when construction workers remove materials near the base of a slope. When this basal material is removed, the slope becomes unstable. Gravity pulls the mass downward. Slopes can also be made unstable (oversteepened) when overburden from a construction project is piled up. The overload causes stress on underlying layers. When the underlying layers are too weak to anchor the overlying materials, slumps result. L2

Visual Learning

Figure 7-3 Ask students why slumps occur frequently after earthquakes or heavy, prolonged rains. LEP LS

NATIONAL GEOGRAPHIC SOCIETY

Videodisc

GTV: Planetary Manager

Landscape

48105

48119

Figure 7-3

Slumps occur when material slips downslope as one large mass.

Slump

A **slump** is a mass movement that happens when loose materials or rock layers slip down a slope. In a slump, strong rock or sediment lies over weaker materials. The underlying material weakens and can no longer support the rock and sediment above. The soil and rock slip downslope in one large mass. Sometimes a slump happens when water penetrates the upper layer on a slope, but cannot flow through the lower layers. Water and mud build up. The upper layer of sediments slips along the mud and slides downslope. A curved scar is left where the slumped materials originally rested, as shown in **Figure 7-3.** Slumps happen most frequently after earthquakes or heavy, prolonged rains.

Figure 7-4

Perhaps you can find evidence of soil creep around your home or school. Look for tilted retaining walls and fences and even sod that has stretched apart.

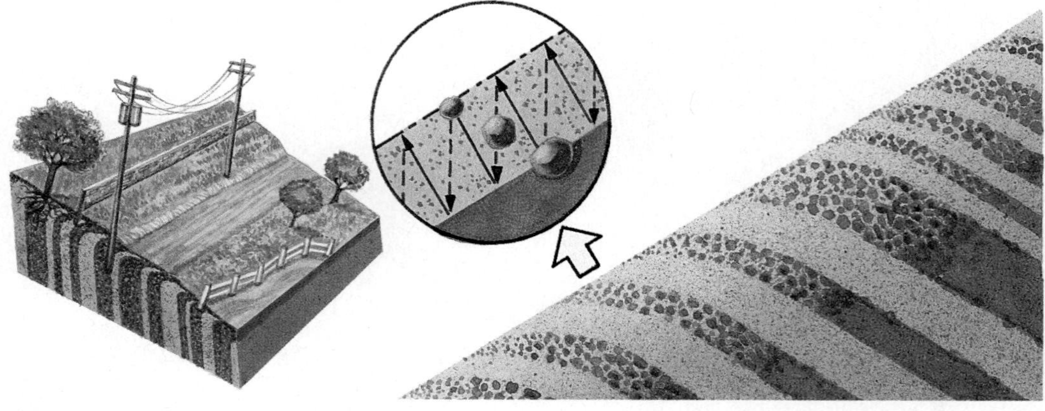

A Several years of creeping downslope can cause objects such as utility poles and fenceposts to lean.

B Below the surface, as the ground freezes, expanding ice in the soil pushes up fine-grained sediment particles. Then, when the soil thaws, the sediment falls downslope, often less than a millimeter at a time.

Across the Curriculum

Language Arts Have students use dictionaries to look up the meaning of *slump*. Ask volunteers to read aloud the definitions that describe a person's physical appearance and the condition of economic activity. Then ask students what all meanings of the word have in common. They should be able to conclude that in every case, *slump* describes a decline or collapse of something. L1 LS

Use **Multicultural Connections,** pp. 17-18, as you teach this lesson.

Creep

On your next drive, look along the roadway for slopes where trees, utility poles, and fenceposts lean downhill. Leaning poles indicate another mass movement called creep. **Creep** gets its name from the way sediments slowly inch their way down a hill. As **Figure 7-4** illustrates, creep is common in areas of freezing and thawing.

Rockslides

"Falling Rock" signs warn of another type of mass movement called a rockslide. Rockslides happen when large blocks of rock break loose from a steep slope and start tumbling. As they fall, these rocks crash into other rocks and knock them loose. More and more rocks break loose and tumble to the bottom. Rockslides are very fast and can be very destructive in populated mountain areas like the Alps. They commonly occur in mountainous areas or where there are steep cliffs, as portrayed in **Figure 7-5.** Rockslides happen most often after heavy rains or during earthquakes, but they can happen on any rocky slope at any time without warning.

Figure 7-5

Piles of broken rock at the bottom of a cliff tell you that rockslides have occurred and are likely to happen again.

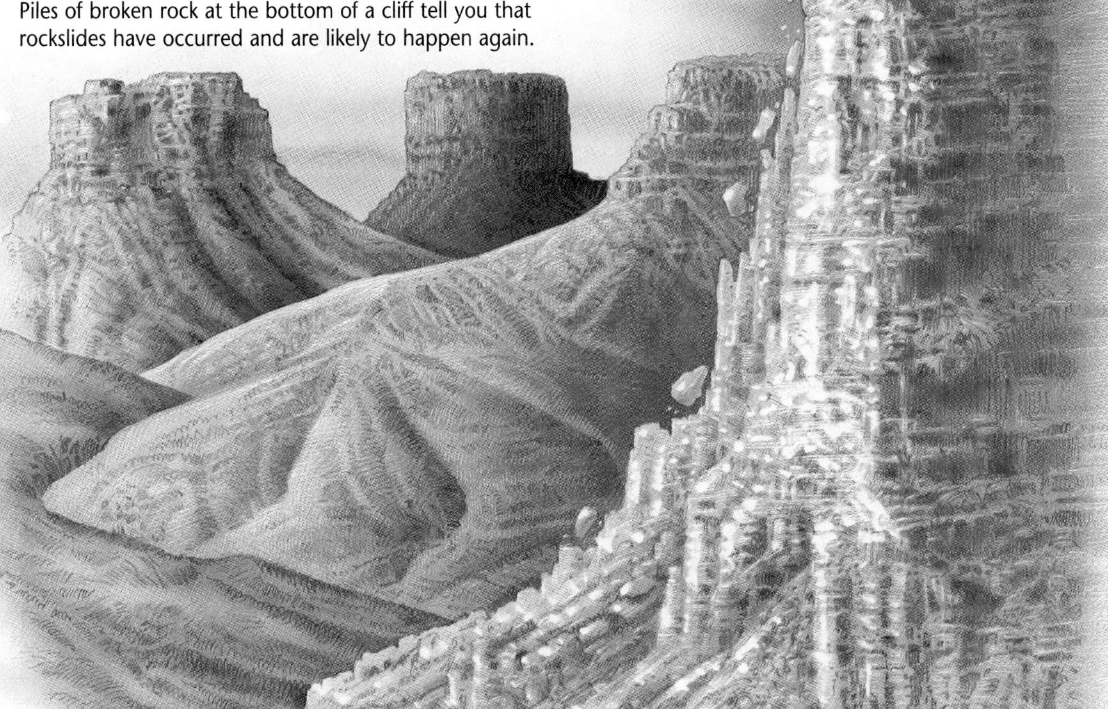

Visual Learning

Figure 7-5 Have students use the figure on this page to explain how mass movements result in less steep slopes. Have them compare the slope of the cliff prior to weathering and erosion to its slope after materials have been removed near the top. Ask students to use this figure to explain what talus slopes are and how they form. *Talus slopes are piles of loose material that often form at the bases of very steep rock outcrops. They are composed of the materials that were weathered and eroded from the outcrop.* LEP LS

Inquiry Questions

- **What do slump and creep have in common?** *Both are mass movements; both occur on slopes.*
- **Does creep occur in our area?** *Answers will depend upon your climate and the topography of your area.*

3 Assess

Check for Understanding

FLEX Your Brain

Use the Flex Your Brain activity to have students explore SLOPE.

Activity Worksheets, p. 5

Reteach

LS **Linguistic** Have students write poems about the four kinds of mass movements. Then have them share the poems with their classmates.

Extension

For students who have mastered this section, use the **Reinforcement** and **Enrichment** masters.

Theme Connection

Stability and Change Have students explore the connection between weathering and erosion relating to rockslides. Weathering fragments a rock cliff. Chemical and mechanical weathering breaks the rocks into small, unconsolidated pieces. Materials on a slope (or cliff) do not fall unless they are unconsolidated. The erosional agent of gravity causes the pieces to fall.

Community Connection

Construction Invite an engineer to speak about the importance of knowing about mass movements, weathering, and erosion when considering building sites for roads, dams, and buildings.

MiniLAB

Purpose

LS **Visual-Spatial** Students will model mass movements. L1 COOP LEARN

Materials

large pan, sand, gravel, water

Analysis

1. Mass movements need steep slopes, although creep occurs on less steep slopes. All types occur more often when sediments are saturated with water.
2. All result in the slope becoming less steep and sediments being eroded from the slope and deposited at lower elevations. Mudflows and rockslides occur very quickly.

Assessment

Performance To further assess students' understanding of mass movements, have them take before and after photos to show the effects of these movements and mount them along with explanations on a poster. Use the Performance Task Assessment List for Poster in PASC, p. 73. P

Activity Worksheets, pp. 5, 46

MiniLAB

What causes mass movements?

Procedure

1. Put moist sand and gravel in a pan. Use these sediments to model land forms showing how mass movements of sediments occur.
2. Set up situations to model mudflows, slumps, and rockslides.

Analysis

1. What factors must be present for mass movements to occur?
2. In what ways are the three mass movements similar? Different?

The fall of a single, large rock down a steep slope can cause serious damage to structures at the bottom. Rock falls like the one in **Figure 7-6** frequently occur in mountainous areas. During the winter, freezing and thawing of ice in the cracks of the rock cause pieces of the rock to fracture. In the spring, the pieces of rock eventually break loose and fall down the mountainside.

Mudflows

Imagine traveling along a mountain road during a rain storm. Suddenly a wall of mud, the consistency of chocolate pudding, slides down a slope and threatens to cover your car. You've been caught in a mudflow, a thick mixture of sediments and water flowing down a slope. The mudflow in **Figure 7-7** caused a lot of destruction.

Mudflows usually occur in relatively dry areas where weathering accumulates thick layers of dry sediments. When heavy rains fall in these areas, water mixes with sediments and forms a thick, pasty substance. Gravity causes this mass to slide downhill. When a mudflow finally reaches the bottom of a slope, it loses its energy of motion and deposits all the sediments and debris it has been carrying. These deposits usually form a mass that spreads out in a cone shape.

Figure 7-6

In the Alps, a rock fell from the cliff above and struck this new apartment the day before the residents were supposed to move in.

176

Visual Learning

Figure 7-6 Why did this happen? *This occurred because the apartment was built at the bottom of a slope where rock falls occur.*

Figure 7-7 How do mudflows differ from other mass movements? *Mudflows come from small sediments saturated with water.* LEP LS

Theme Connection

Stability and Change Have students research to find out how rockslides, mudflows, avalanches, creep, and slump can be prevented. LEP LS

Use Lab 23 in the **Lab Manual** as you teach this lesson.

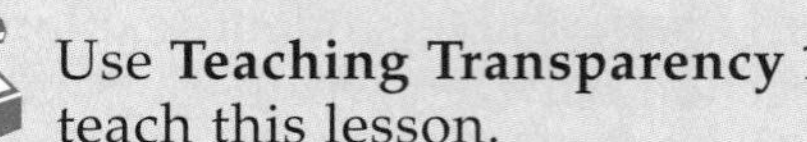

Use **Teaching Transparency 13** as you teach this lesson.

Figure 7-7

A mudflow has enough energy to move almost anything in its path. Notice the cone shape of the mudflow. *How do mudflows differ from slumps, creep, and rockslides?*

Mudflows, rockslides, creep, and slump are similar in some ways. They're all more likely to happen on steep slopes. They all depend on gravity to make them happen. And, regardless of the type of mass movement, it will occur more often after a heavy rain because the water adds mass and lubricates the area where different layers of sediment meet.

Can you think of one more way these mass movements are alike? All mass movements erode sediments from the top of a slope and deposit them farther downslope. The result is that mass movements constantly change the shape of a slope so that it becomes less steep.

Section Wrap-up

Review

1. Define erosion and name the agents that cause it.
2. How does erosion change the surface of Earth?
3. What characteristics do all types of mass movements have in common?
4. **Think Critically:** When people build houses and roads, they often pile up dirt or cut into the sides of hills. Predict how these activities affect sediments on a slope.

Using Computers

Spreadsheet Using a spreadsheet, make a diagram comparing the four different types of mass movements. Compare at least four factors that affect mass movements of Earth's surface.

Skill Builder
Concept Mapping

Make a concept map about mass movements using these terms: *gravity, slump, creep, rockslides, mudflows, curved scar, leaning trees and poles, rock piles, and cone-shaped masses.* If you need help, refer to Concept Mapping in the **Skill Handbook.**

4 Close

• MINI • QUIZ •

1. **What are four examples of mass movements?** *slump, creep, rockslides, mudflow*
2. **How do climatic conditions affect mass movements?** *All mass movements occur more often after a heavy rain because water adds mass to the sediments and makes them slippery.*
3. **How do mass movements affect the angle of a slope?** *Mass movements make a slope less steep.*

Section Wrap-up

Review

1. Erosion wears away surface materials and moves them from one location to another. Agents include gravity, glaciers, wind, and water.
2. The surface changes shape when sediments are transported from one location to another.
3. All happen on steep slopes; depend on gravity; occur more often after heavy rain; and result in the production of less steep slopes.
4. **Think Critically** Piling up dirt and cutting into the hills create steep slopes. Steep slopes are unstable and prone to erosion.

Using Computers

A sample spreadsheet is shown at left.

Type of Mass Movement	Sediment Size	Speed	Evidence
Slump	varies; small clay molecules	intermediate	curved scar
Creep	varies; often small	slow	leaning posts
Rockslide	large	fast	rock piles
Mudflow	small	fast	cone-shaped deposit

Skill Builder

The concept map starts with gravity and, as seen on spreadsheet, goes from mass movement to results of the mass movement. P

Assessment

Content Use this Skill Builder to assess students' abilities to interpret illustrations. Have them identify each photo in section as slow, fast, or very fast mass movement. Use the Performance Task Assessment List for Making Observations and Inferences in **PASC,** p. 17. P

Prepare

Section Background

For centuries in Peru, the Philippines, Japan, and China, vast numbers of people have lived and produced crops on terraces.

1 Motivate

Bellringer

Before presenting the lesson, display **Section Focus Transparency 26** on the overhead projector. Assign the accompanying **Focus Activity** worksheet. L1 LEP

2 Teach

Visual Learning

Figure 7-8 How do terraces prevent erosion? *They slow water's energy and motion.* LEP LS

3 Assess

Check for Understanding

Have students answer questions 1 and 2 in the Section Wrap-up.

Reteach

LS **Interpersonal** Have students draw pictures showing what might have been done to help protect the house shown in **Figure 7-9** from falling down the slope.

SCIENCE & SOCIETY

7•2 ISSUE: Developing Land Prone to Erosion

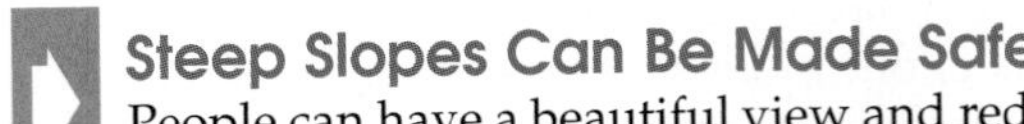

Objectives

- Describe ways that erosion can be reduced in some high-risk areas.
- Explain why problems develop when people live on land prone to excessive erosion.

Living on the Edge

Some people like to live in houses and apartments on the sides of hills and mountains. Realtors say that people want to live in these places for the good view. But when you consider gravity as an agent of erosion, do you think steep slopes are safe places to live?

2 Points of View

Steep Slopes Can Be Made Safe

People can have a beautiful view and reduce erosion on steep slopes. Planting vegetation is one of the best ways to reduce erosion. Plant roots hold soil in place. Plants also absorb large amounts of water. A person living on a steep slope might also build terraces or retaining walls to reduce erosion.

Figure 7-8
Terracing is a way to prevent erosion on slopes. In Madagascar, terraces have existed for a long time. *How do terraces prevent erosion?*

Terraces are broad, step-like cuts made into the side of a slope, as shown in **Figure 7-8.** When water flows into a terrace, it slows down and loses its energy. Terracing slows soil erosion. Retaining walls made of concrete or railroad ties can also reduce erosion by keeping soil and rocks from sliding downhill. However, preventing mass movements on a slope is more difficult because rain or earthquakes can cause the upper layers of rock to slip over the lower layers.

Program Resources

Reproducible Masters

Study Guide, p. 30 L1
Reinforcement, p. 30 L1
Enrichment, p. 30 L3
Science and Society Integration, p. 11

Transparencies

Section Focus Transparency 26 L1

Building on Steep Slopes Is Dangerous

When people build homes on steep slopes, they must constantly battle erosion that occurs naturally. Sometimes when they build, people make a slope steeper or remove vegetation. This speeds up the erosion process and creates additional problems. Some steep slopes are prone to slump because of weak sediment layers underneath. Not even planting bushes and trees could save the houses in **Figure 7-9.**

Figure 7-9

Building on steep slopes can have severe consequences.

People who live in areas with erosion problems spend a lot of time and money trying to preserve their land. Sometimes they're successful in slowing down erosion, but they can never eliminate it and the danger of mass movement. Eventually gravity wins and cliffs cave in. Sediments constantly move from place to place, changing the shape of the land forever.

Section Wrap-up

Review

1. How can erosion be reduced on steep slopes?
2. How does building on slopes increase erosion?

Explore the Issue

Imagine that you live on a cliff overlooking a river. You love your house and the beautiful view. Unfortunately, the river below floods frequently. The river is undercutting the cliff where you live. Several times the city has evacuated your family. Finally, the mayor informs your family that you must move. She cites the danger of living on the cliff and the cost of evacuating you each time. Is this fair? Should communities be allowed to control where people live? How does your home site affect taxes and insurance rates in the community? Construct a play in which students present both sides of this issue.

SCIENCE & SOCIETY

Extension

For students who have mastered this section, use the **Reinforcement** and **Enrichment** masters.

4 Close

Explain why people can slow down erosion, but not eliminate it. Students should conclude that planting vegetation, terracing, and using walls slows erosion. There is no way to stop it completely.

Section Wrap-up

Review

1. People can plant vegetation and construct terraces and retaining walls to reduce erosion.
2. When people build on slopes, they often make the slopes steeper. Sometimes they remove the vegetation that provides stability to the slope. Also, the weight of a structure at the top of a slope puts stress on the supporting rocks.

Explore the Issue

Some students may feel that people should decide for themselves where to live. Other students will argue that the community should impose limitations when community safety and money are involved. Answers will vary about taxes and insurance rates. But insurance rates go up if insurance companies must constantly pay for damage. Help students turn their arguments into a dramatic dialogue for a play.

Integrating the Sciences

Life Science Have students design and carry out an experiment to demonstrate how plant roots help hold soil and prevent erosion on slopes. Accept all reasonable designs. Students may notice that plants with fibrous roots spreading near the surface do a better job of holding the soil in place than plants with long taproots. L2 COOP LEARN LS P

Section 7•3

Prepare

Section Background

- Glaciers move along horizontally when the mass of the ice exerts enough pressure to cause the bottom molecules to flow.
- The most recent ice age began during the Pleistocene epoch. During this epoch, there were seven ice advances followed by intervals of warmer climate called interglacial periods. Scientists call the present time an interglacial period.
- Valley glaciers tend to create a rugged topography, whereas continental glaciers smooth the landscape by eroding high spots and filling low places.
- Glacial deposits in the United States are found from the northern border of the United States to the Ohio and Missouri Rivers and in the mountains of the west.

Preplanning

To prepare for Activity 7-1, obtain the materials listed on page 186.

1 Motivate

Bellringer

Before presenting the lesson, display **Section Focus Transparency 27** on the overhead projector. Assign the accompanying **Focus Activity** worksheet. L1 LEP

Tying to Previous Knowledge

In Chapter 2, students learned that water exists in three states—gas, liquid, and solid. A glacier is a solid, but the pressure of the overlying ice partially melts the bottom layers.

7•3 Glaciers

Science Words

glacier
plucking
till
moraine

Objectives

- Describe the movement of glaciers.
- Explain glacial erosion.
- Compare and contrast till and outwash.

USING MATH

Most glaciers move extremely slowly, sometimes as slowly as 25 centimeters per day. On average, how many meters will a slow glacier move in 1 year?

Continental and Valley Glaciers

Does it snow where you live? In some areas of the world, it is so cold that snow remains on the ground year-round. When snow doesn't melt, it begins piling up. As it accumulates, the weight of the snow becomes great enough to compress its bottom layers into ice. Eventually the snow can pile so high that the ice on the bottom partially melts and becomes putty-like. The whole mass begins to slide on this putty-like layer, and it moves downhill. This moving mass of ice and snow is a **glacier.**

Glaciers are agents of erosion. As glaciers pass over land, they erode it, changing its features. Glaciers then carry eroded material along and eventually deposit it somewhere else. Glacial erosion and deposition change large areas of Earth. There are two types of glaciers: continental glaciers and valley glaciers.

Continental Glaciers

Continental glaciers are huge masses of ice and snow. As you see in **Figure 7-10,** in the past, continental glaciers covered up to 28 percent of Earth. Scientists call the periods when glaciers covered much of the land *ice ages.* The most recent ice age began over a period of 2 to 3 million years ago. Then, about

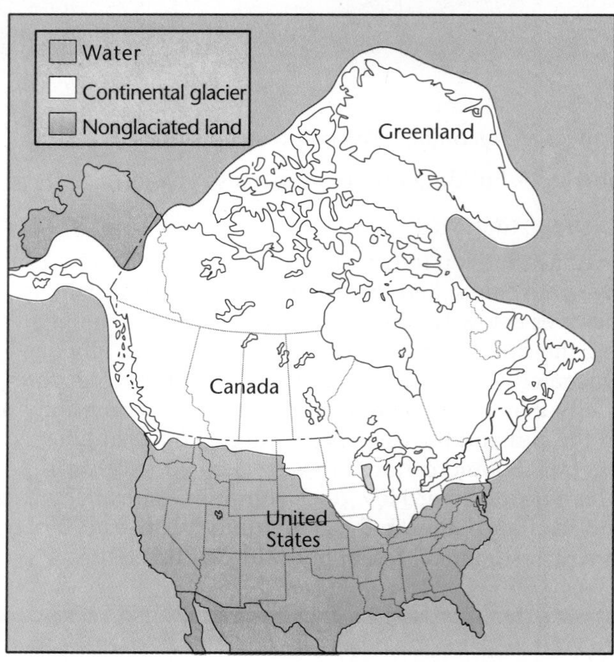

Figure 7-10
This map shows the extent of continental glaciation in North America about 20 000 years ago. *Was your area glaciated?*

Program Resources

Reproducible Masters
Study Guide, p. 31 L1
Reinforcement, p. 31 L1
Enrichment, p. 31 L3
Activity Worksheets, pp. 5, 42-43 L1
Science Integration Activities, pp. 13-14
Lab Manual 24

Transparencies
Section Focus Transparency 27 L1
Teaching Transparency 14

Figure 7-11

Continental glaciers and valley glaciers are both agents of erosion.

A Today, a continental glacier covers Antarctica.

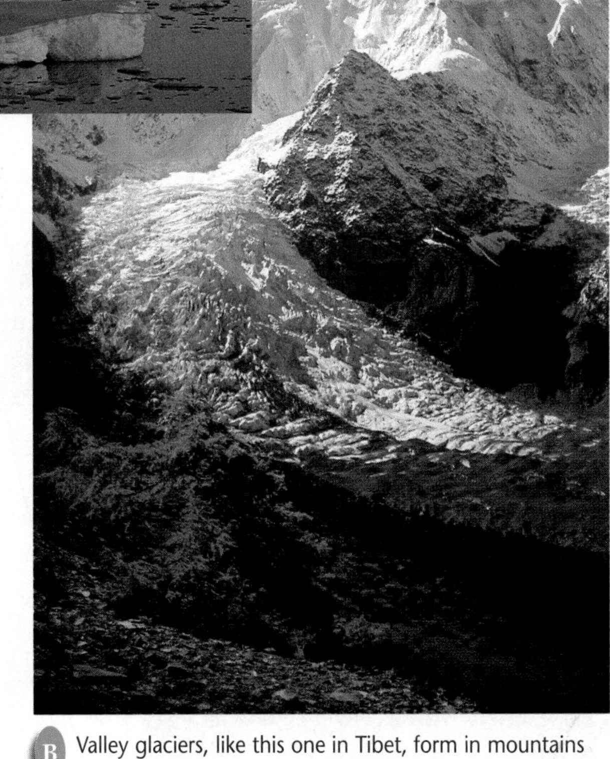

B Valley glaciers, like this one in Tibet, form in mountains whose peaks lie above the snowline, where snow lasts all year.

20 000 years ago, the ice sheets began to melt. Today, glaciers like the one in **Figure 7-11A** cover only 10 percent of Earth, mostly near the poles in Antarctica and Greenland. Continental glaciers are such thick sheets of ice that they can almost bury mountain ranges on the land they cover. Glaciers make it impossible to see most of the land features in Antarctica. During the time when much of North America was covered by ice, the average air temperature on Earth was about 5°C lower than it is today.

Valley Glaciers

Valley glaciers occur even in today's warmer climate. In the high mountains where the average temperature is low enough to prevent snow from melting during the summer, valley glaciers grow and creep along. **Figure 7-11B** shows a valley glacier in Tibet.

How is it possible that something as fragile as snow or ice can become an agent of erosion that can push aside trees, drag along rocks, and erode the surface of Earth?

2 Teach

Demonstration

LS **Visual-Spatial** Demonstrate how a solid, like ice, can flow by mixing cornstarch with water until the mixture looks like a solid. Have a volunteer pick up a handful and tilt his or her hand to deposit the mixture in a cup. Observe that the mixture flows like a liquid. When the mixture reaches the bottom of the cup, it again resembles a solid. Relate the plastic-like cornstarch solution to the base of a glacier. LEP

Revealing Preconceptions

Ask students how many degrees the average surface temperature of Earth would have to drop to bring on another ice age. They will likely guess many degrees. Actually, the answer is about 2°C in the tropics, 6 to 8°C in the midlatitudes, and 10°C in the higher latitudes.

Student Text Question

How is it possible that something as fragile as snow or ice can become an agent of erosion that can push aside trees, drag along rocks, and erode the surface of Earth? *Rocks and sediments loosened by ice are carried along by the glacier. These rocks and sediments erode the land over which the glacier moves. A glacier often moves slowly but with great force.* LEP

USING MATH

365 days × 25 cm =
9125 ÷ 100 $\frac{cm}{m}$ = 91 m

Use Lab 24 in the **Lab Manual** as you teach this lesson.

Use **Teaching Transparency 14** as you teach this lesson.

Across the Curriculum

History Inform students that during the last ice advance, people traveled from Asia to North America across the Bering land bridge. After students locate the Bering Strait on a map, discuss that during the last ice advance, much of Earth's water was in glaciers, and sea level was much lower. A strip of land connected Asia and North America. Today, this area is below sea level.

Enrichment

- Have students examine the map of the bottom of the ocean on pages 504-505. Have them identify the position of the continental shelves. Inform students that when the last ice age was at its peak, sea level was 137 meters lower than it is today. Many of the structures on the continental shelf would have been at or above sea level. This should lead to a discussion of the effects of glaciation. L1
- Have students use the map to predict where the shoreline of North America might be if all of the ice in Greenland and Antarctica melted. Have them draw diagrams that show that future shoreline. The sketches should show much of the present-day east and Gulf coasts underwater. Also have students research the fate of the Maldive Islands if sea level rises. L2

Content Background

Explain to students that core samples of ocean sediments are used to study Earth's ancient climate. Shells of small sea organisms found in these sediments are used to determine the temperature of the water in which they lived. Thus, scientists can tell how much ice existed on Earth during different geologic periods.

Inquiry Question

Explain how layers of ice can be distinguished in glaciers. *The layers form when annual snow deposits are followed by dry seasons during which dust is deposited.*

Glacial Erosion

As they move over land, glaciers are like bulldozers, pushing loose materials out of their path. **Figure 7-12A** shows this. Eroded sediments get pushed in front of a glacier, carried underneath it, and piled up along its sides. Glaciers also weather and erode rock and soil that isn't loose. When glacial ice melts, water flows into cracks in rocks. Later, the water refreezes in these cracks, expands, and fractures the rock into pieces. (**Figure 6-3** on page 150 illustrates this ice wedging process.) These rock pieces are then lifted out by the glacial ice sheet. This process, called **plucking,** results in boulders, gravel, and sand being added to the bottom and sides of a glacier.

As a glacier moves forward, plucked rock fragments and sand at its base scrape the soil and bedrock, eroding even more material than ice alone could. When bedrock is gouged deeply by dragged rock fragments, marks such as those in **Figure 7-12B** are left behind. These marks, called grooves, are deep, long, parallel scars on rocks. Less-deep marks are called striations (stri AY shuns). These marks indicate the direction the glacier moved.

Figure 7-12

The diagram and photos show landforms characteristic of glacial erosion.

A No agent of erosion is more powerful than an advancing glacier.

B When glaciers melt, striations or grooves may be found on the rocks beneath. These glacial grooves on Kelley's Island, Ohio, are 10 m wide and 5 m deep.

182

Evidence of Valley Glaciers

If you visit the mountains, you can see if valley glaciers ever existed there. You might look for striations, then search for evidence of plucking. Glacial plucking often occurs near the top of a mountain where a glacier is in contact with a wall of rock. Valley glaciers erode bowl-shaped basins, called cirques, in the sides of the mountains. A cirque (SURK) is shown in **Figure 7-12C.** If two or more glaciers erode a mountain summit from several directions, a ridge, called an arête (ah RET), or sharpened peak, called a horn, forms. These and other features are shown in **Figure 7-12.** The photo in **Figure 7-12D** shows a mountain horn.

Valley glaciers flow down mountain slopes and along valleys, eroding as they go. Valleys that have been eroded by glaciers have a different shape from those eroded by streams. Stream-eroded valleys are normally V-shaped. Glacially eroded valleys are U-shaped because a glacier plucks and scrapes soil and rock from the sides as well as from the bottom. **Figure 7-14,** on page 187, compares a U-shaped valley with a V-shaped valley.

D A horn is a mountain pinnacle formed by glacial action in three or more cirques.

C This cirque, a bowl-shaped depression, was formed by erosion at the head of a valley glacier.

Inquiry Questions

- **What is a cirque and how does it form?** *A cirque is a bowl-shaped basin that is created in the side of a mountain where glacial plucking has occurred. Often a cirque forms where a glacier begins.*
- **How does plucking occur?** *Glacial snow and ice melt and flow down into cracks in rocks. When the water refreezes in these cracks, it expands and breaks the rock into pieces.*
- **What are grooves?** *long parallel scars scraped into rocks by glaciers*
- **What causes a mountain horn?** *A mountain horn forms on mountain peaks that have been glaciated. Three or more cirques have scoured out the rock and left fairly sharp ridges between the cirques.*

 **Videodisc**

STV: Restless Earth

Glacier; Alaska

52251

Glacial valley; New Zealand

52252

Boulders deposited by glacier

52254

STV: Water

Iceberg and penguins; Bransfield Strait, Antarctica

52533

Discussion

Have students discuss why valley glaciation leaves different topographic features than continental glaciation. The discussion should include the fact that valley glaciers create a more rugged topography. Continental glaciers tend to smooth the landscape by removing high spots and filling in low places.

CONNECT TO
CHEMISTRY

Answer Ice is less dense because as water freezes, the molecules move apart, taking up more space.

GLENCOE TECHNOLOGY

Videodisc

STVS: Chemistry
Disc 2, Side 1
Snowflakes (Ch. 3)

Sand Blasting with Dry Ice (Ch. 8)

Enrichment

- Have students research and summarize the origin of the Great Lakes and the Matterhorn in Switzerland. L2
- Have students describe changes that might occur in daily living when the next ice age begins. L1

CONNECT TO
CHEMISTRY

Icebergs float because ice is less dense than water. Density relates mass to volume. The formula for finding density is $D = M/V$. When water freezes, the crystal arrangement changes and makes ice, a solid, less dense than water, a liquid. The density decreases. Using the formula, ***infer*** what happens to the volume.

Glacial Deposition

When glaciers begin to melt, they no longer have enough energy to carry much sediment. The sediment drops or is deposited on the land.

Till

When the glacier slows down, a jumble of boulders, sand, clay and silt drop from its base. This mixture of different-sized sediments is called **till.** As shown in **Figure 7-13**, till deposits can cover huge areas of land. During the last ice age, continental glaciers in the northern United States dropped enough till to completely fill valleys and make these areas appear flat. Till areas include the wide swath of wheat land running northwestward from Iowa to northern Montana, some farmland in parts of Ohio, Indiana and Illinois, and the rocky pastures of New England.

Till is also deposited in front of a glacier when it stops moving forward. Unlike the till that drops from a glacier's base, this second type of deposit doesn't cover a very wide area. Because it's made of the rocks and soil that the glacier has been pushing along, it looks like a big ridge of material left behind by a bulldozer. Such a ridge is called a **moraine.** Other moraines are deposited along the sides of glaciers and sometimes in the middle. A moraine is shown in **Figure 7-13.**

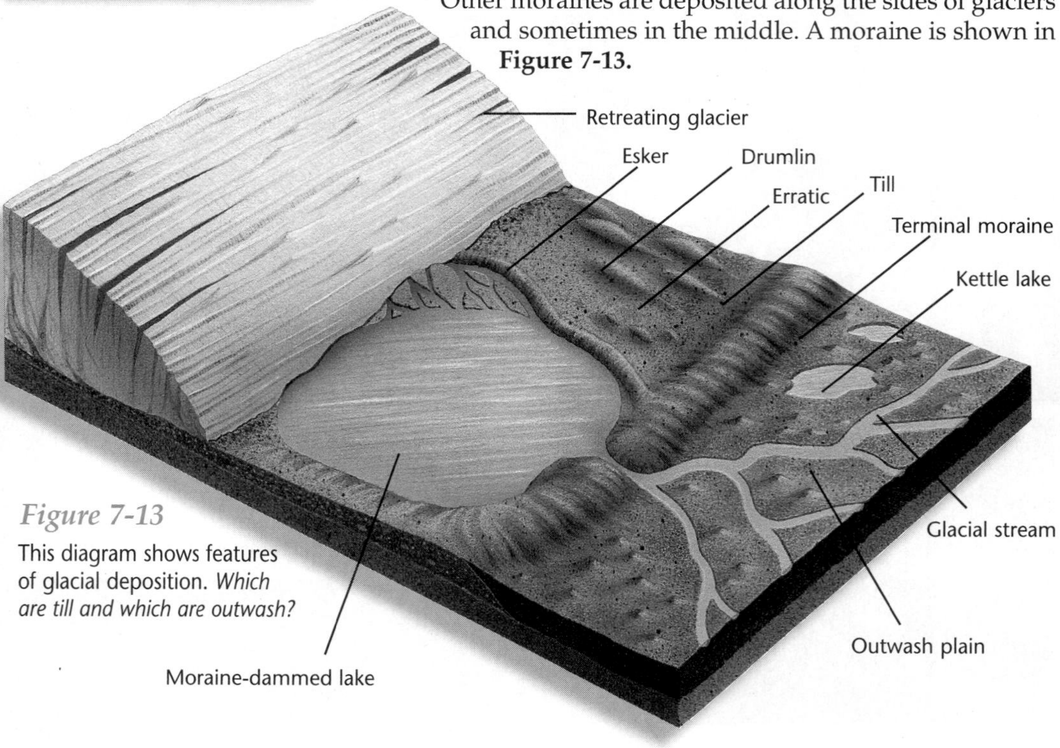

Figure 7-13
This diagram shows features of glacial deposition. *Which are till and which are outwash?*

Visual Learning

Figure 7-13 Which are till and which are outwash? *Moraines and erratics are till deposits. Eskers, outwash plains, and layered sediment are from outwash.* LEP LS

Outwash

When melting exceeds snow accumulation, the glacier retreats or starts to melt. Material deposited by the meltwater from a glacier is called *outwash*. Outwash is shown in **Figure 7-13.** The meltwater carries sediments and deposits them in layers much as a river does. Heavier sediments drop first so the bigger pieces of rock are deposited closer to the glacier. The outwash from a glacier can also form into a fan-shaped deposit when the stream of meltwater drops sand and gravel in front of the glacier.

Another type of outwash deposit looks like a long winding ridge. This deposit forms beneath a melting glacier when meltwater forms a river within the ice. This river carries sand and gravel and deposits them within its channel. When the glacier melts, a winding ridge of sand and gravel, called an esker, is left behind. An esker is shown in **Figure 7-13.** Meltwater also forms *outwash plains* of deposited materials in front of a retreating glacier.

USING TECHNOLOGY

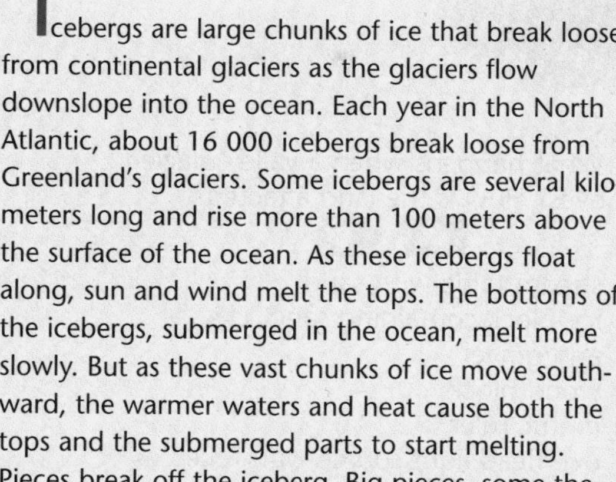

Bergy Bits?

Icebergs are large chunks of ice that break loose from continental glaciers as the glaciers flow downslope into the ocean. Each year in the North Atlantic, about 16 000 icebergs break loose from Greenland's glaciers. Some icebergs are several kilometers long and rise more than 100 meters above the surface of the ocean. As these icebergs float along, sun and wind melt the tops. The bottoms of the icebergs, submerged in the ocean, melt more slowly. But as these vast chunks of ice move southward, the warmer waters and heat cause both the tops and the submerged parts to start melting. Pieces break off the iceberg. Big pieces, some the size of an average house, are called bergy bits.

More than 85 percent of Earth's fresh water is locked up in glacial ice. Scientists estimate that an iceberg about 270 square kilometers would provide over 7 billion cubic meters of fresh water! A tug could tow this iceberg at a rate of about 32 kilometers per day. This may be the only way to bring drinking water to areas of the world that need fresh water, but at this slow rate of towing, not much ice would be left.

A Bergy Bit

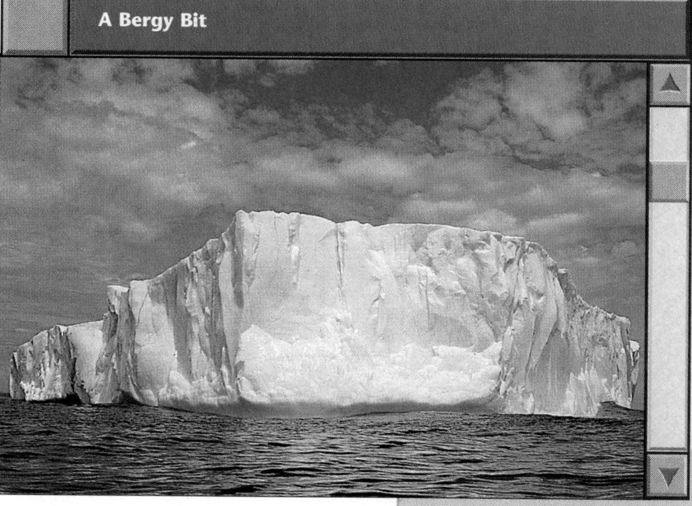

Think Critically:

What areas of the world would benefit most from using icebergs as a source of fresh water? How would towing icebergs affect the environment?

USING TECHNOLOGY

Have students brainstorm a list of potential problems with towing icebergs. One logistical concern is melting, which could be reduced by insulating icebergs during travel.

Think Critically

- Places should be close to oceans and might include Saudi Arabia, western Australia, the Sahara Desert, the Yuma Desert of California, and the Atacama Desert of Chile.
- As the ice melts, it will cool the surface of the ocean. This could have adverse effects on some species and change the microclimate of the area.

3 Assess

Check for Understanding

FLEX Your Brain

Use the Flex Your Brain activity to have students explore GLACIATION.

Activity Worksheets, p. 5

Reteach

LS **Visual-Spatial** To show students how glacial plucking occurs, submerge a brick in water for one full day. Then, place the water-soaked brick in a freezer overnight. Show the frozen brick to students. They will observe that part of the brick has crumbled. LEP

Extension

For students who have mastered this section, use the **Reinforcement** and **Enrichment** masters.

Across the Curriculum

Geography Inform students that the Alps, Sierra Nevadas, Rockies, and Himalayas were all greatly eroded by glaciers during the last ice advance. Have students locate these mountain ranges on a map and describe some of the glacial features they are likely to find in each locale. L1

Community Connection

Field Trip If you are in an area where glacial features can be seen, plan a field trip to study these features.

Activity 7-1

Purpose

LS **Visual-Spatial** Students will observe how valley glaciers affect a surface. L1 LEP COOP LEARN

Process Skills

communicating, interpreting data, making models, making and using tables, comparing and contrasting, recognizing cause and effect, forming operational definitions, measuring in SI

Time

50-60 minutes

Safety Precautions

Caution students to not burn themselves on the overhead light.

Activity Worksheets, pp. 5, 42-43

Materials

You need to prepare freezer trays of ice, gravel, and clay a day before the students perform this activity.

Teaching Strategies

Troubleshooting Have students adjust the overhead light to provide enough heat to melt the ice.

Answers to Questions

1. The channel will be *U*-shaped to the point where the glacier stopped. From that point on, the valley will be *V*-shaped. A row of small hills of till marks the end position of the glacier.
2. The larger outwash sediments are deposited closest to the glacial front. Smaller sediments are carried farther from the glacial front. Placement of the sediment shows direction.
3. Valley glaciers have a "bulldozing" effect that produces *U*-shaped valleys with steep sides and relatively flat bottoms.

Activity 7-1 Glacial Grooving

Throughout the world's mountainous regions there are 200 000 valley glaciers moving in response to local freezing and thawing conditions, as well as gravity.

Problem

What happens when a valley glacier moves? How is the land affected?

Materials  

- stream table with sand
- ice block containing sand, clay, and gravel
- wood block
- metric ruler
- overhead light source with reflector

Procedure

1. Set up the stream table as shown. Place the wood block under one end of the table to give it a slope.
2. Cut a narrow channel, like a river, through the sand. Measure and record its width and depth. Draw a sketch that includes these measurements.
3. Position the overhead light source to shine on the channel as shown.

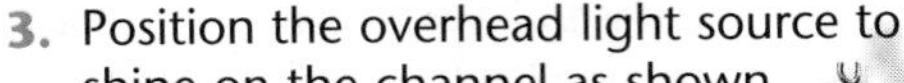

4. Force the ice block into the river channel at the upper end of the stream table.
5. Gently push the "glacier" along the river channel until it's halfway between the top and bottom of the stream table and is positioned directly under the light.
6. Turn on the light and allow the ice to melt. Observe and record what happens. Does the meltwater change the original channel?
7. Measure and record the width and depth of the glacial channel. Draw a sketch of the channel and include these measurements.

Analyze

1. **Explain** how you can determine the direction a glacier traveled from the location of deposits.

Conclude and Apply

2. Explain how you can **determine** the direction of glacial movement from sediments deposited by meltwater.
3. How do valley glaciers affect the surface over which they move?

Data and Observations

Sample Data

Sample Data	Width	Depth	Observations
Original channel	6 cm	3 cm	stream channel looked V-shaped
Glacier channel	8 cm	4 cm	U-shaped channel
Meltwater channel	6 cm	3.5 cm	V-shaped channel

186

Assessment

Performance To further assess students' understanding of glacial erosion, have them design an experiment to test the effects of one of the following variables: slope, pressure applied to the ice block, mass of the ice block, amount of sediments in the ice block, or the width of the original channel. Use the Performance Task Assessment List for Designing an Experiment in **PASC**, p. 23. P

Figure 7-14
A U-shaped valley formed by a glacier, as shown in photo A, looks much different from a valley cut by a river, shown in photo B. The U-shaped valley is in Gates of the Arctic National Park in Alaska. The V-shaped valley was cut by the Yellowstone River.

Glaciers from the last ice age changed the surface of Earth. Glaciers eroded mountain tops and scoured out valleys like the one in **Figure 7-14A.** In Chapter 8 you'll learn about water-eroded valleys like the one in **Figure 7-14B**. Glaciers also deposited sediments over vast areas of North America and Europe. Today, glaciers in the polar regions and in mountains continue to change the surface features of Earth.

Section Wrap-up

Review

1. How does a glacier cause erosion? What processes come into play?
2. Explain how till and outwash are different.
3. **Think Critically:** Suppose that in a field in Indiana, you find a large rock that matches rocks normally found in Canada. Give one explanation of how it got there.

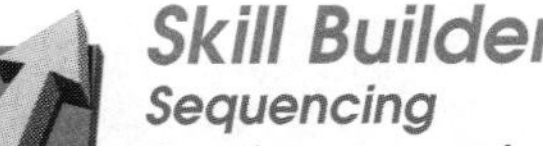

Skill Builder
Sequencing
Put the stages of glacial development and erosion into a correct sequence. If you need help, refer to Sequencing in the **Skill Handbook.**

Science Journal

An *erratic* is a rock fragment deposited by a glacier. Erratic comes from the Latin word *errare* "to wander." Research how glaciers erode and deposit erratics. In your Science Journal, write a poem about the "life" of an erratic.

4 Close

•MINI•QUIZ•

1. ______ causes sediments to be added to the sides and bottom of a glacier. *Plucking*
2. Large striations are called ______. *glacial grooves*
3. Cirques are created by ______ glaciers. *valley*

Section Wrap-up

Review

1. Glaciers erode by scraping, scouring, pushing big blocks, and plucking. In the processes of erosion, plucking and weathering come into play.
2. Till is a mixture of boulders, sand, and silt deposited directly from glacial ice. Outwash sediment is deposited by glacial meltwater and is sorted by size. Large sediments are closer to the glacier; smaller ones are farther away. Outwash has layers.
3. **Think Critically** A glacier may have plucked the boulder out of bedrock in Canada and carried it south until its energy of motion could carry it no farther. It was deposited. The boulder is an erratic.

Skill Builder

Sequences can vary, but should include points on how a glacier develops by a surplus of snow in cold temperatures, how it erodes by plucking and abrading, and how it deposits material.

Assessment

Content Use this Skill Builder to assess students' abilities to classify. Have students classify glacial deposits by types of glaciation, erosion, landforms, and deposits. Use the Performance Task Assessment List for Science Journal in **PASC,** p. 103. P

Science Journal

LS **Linguistic** Glaciers pick up and carry along erratics. Erratics dragged along the base of a glacier may scour bedrock, carving striations or grooves. Once a glacier begins to melt, it drops its load. Erratics are left behind as the glacier retreats. Students' poems should include some of these points. P

Section 7•4

Prepare

Section Background

- Sand-sized particles bounce along the ground in a series of intermittent leaps of varying lengths, depending on grain size, mass, and wind velocity. If a sand-sized particle strikes other sand grains, it displaces them, and they strike and displace more particles horizontally. Abrasion by the wind depends on the availability of suspended particles that act as scouring tools.
- Sand dune migration occurs when wind blows sand up the windward side of a sand dune and drops it over the leeward side. When sand piles too high, a sheetlike mass of sand slips down the leeward side of the dune.

Preplanning

- To prepare for Activity 7-2, obtain the listed materials.
- To prepare for the MiniLAB, obtain sod, newspapers, trowels, magnifying glasses or stereomicroscopes.

1 Motivate

Bellringer

Before presenting the lesson, display **Section Focus Transparency 28** on the overhead projector. Assign the accompanying **Focus Activity** worksheet. L1 LEP

Tying to Previous Knowledge

Have students recall seeing dust carried by the wind. Ask students how wind speed affects the amount and kind of material that the wind can transport.

7•4 Wind

Science Words

deflation
abrasion
loess

Objectives

- Explain how wind causes deflation and abrasion.
- Discuss how loess and dunes form.

Wind Erosion

When air moves, it can pick up loose material and transport it to other places. Air differs from other erosional forces in that it cannot pick up heavy sediments. But because wind is not confined to a river channel or a glacial valley, wind can transport and deposit sediments over large areas. Sometimes wind carries dust from fields or volcanoes high into the atmosphere and deposits the dust far away.

Deflation and Abrasion

Wind erodes Earth's surface by deflation and abrasion. When wind erodes by **deflation**, it blows across loose sediment, removing small particles such as clay, silt, and sand, leaving coarse material behind. When these wind-blown sediments strike rock, they erode by **abrasion.** Both deflation and abrasion happen to all land surfaces but occur mostly in deserts, beaches, and plowed fields. In these areas, few plants anchor the sediments. When winds blow over them, there is nothing to hold them down. **Figure 7-15** illustrates deflation.

Wind erosion by abrasion is similar to the action of a crew of restoration workers sandblasting a building. These workers use machines that spray a mixture of sand and water against a building. The blast of sand wears away dirt from stone, concrete, or brick walls. It also polishes the building walls by breaking away small pieces and leaving an even, smooth finish.

Figure 7-15

Deflation produces airborne sediments and leaves behind what is called desert pavement.

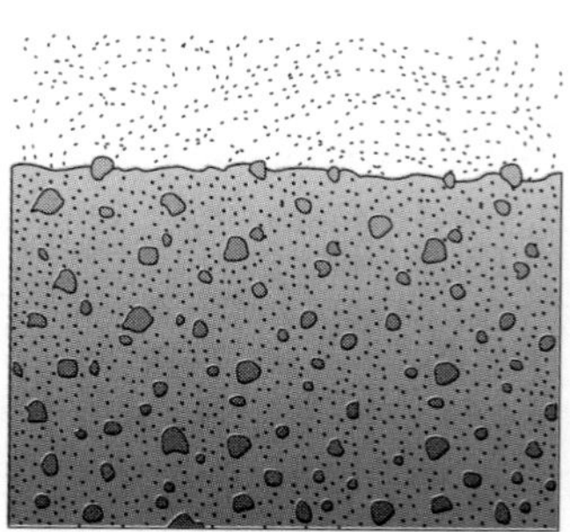

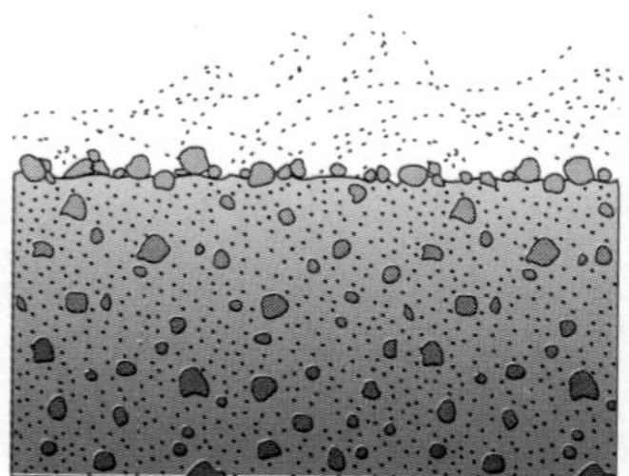

A As deflation begins, wind blows away silt and sand.

B Deflation continues to remove finer particles. Deflation lowers the surface.

C After the finer particles are blown away, larger pebbles and rocks form a pavement that prevents further deflation.

Program Resources

Reproducible Masters

Study Guide, p. 32 L1
Reinforcement, p. 32 L1
Enrichment, p. 32 L3
Cross-Curricular Integration, p. 11
Activity Worksheets, pp. 5, 44-45, 47 L1
Concept Mapping, pp. 19-20

Transparencies

Section Focus Transparency 28 L1

Figure 7-16

Photo A shows how Egypt's desert winds have abraded the Sphinx. Photo B shows a worker using abrasion to clean and smooth a limestone waterfall.

Wind acts like a sandblasting machine rolling and blowing sand grains along. These sand grains strike rocks and break off small fragments. The rocks become pitted or worn down. **Figure 7-16** shows a comparison of machine and wind abrasion.

Sand Storms

Even when the wind blows strongly, it seldom bounces sand grains higher than one-half meter from the ground. Sand grains are too heavy for wind to lift high in the air. However, sandstorms do occur. When the wind blows with great force in the sandy parts of deserts, sand grains bounce along and collide with other sand grains, causing more and more grains to rise into the air. These wind-blown sand grains form a low cloud, just above the ground. Most sandstorms occur in deserts and sometimes on beaches and in dry riverbeds.

Figure 7-17

During the 1930s, the southern part of the Great Plains of the United States was known as the Dust Bowl because dust storms swept the soil away. Dust storms still occur around the world in places such as Mongolia, in western India, in the Sahel region of Africa, and in the United States.

Dust Storms

When soil is moist, it stays packed on the ground. But when it has not rained for a long while, the soil dries out and can be eroded by wind. Because soil particles weigh less than sand, wind can pick them up and blow them high into the atmosphere. But because silt and clay particles are flat, the wind must blow faster to lift these fine particles of soil than to lift grains of sand. But once the wind does lift them, it can hold these particles and carry them long distances. In the 1930s, silt and dust picked up in Kansas fell in New England and in the North Atlantic Ocean.

Dust storms play an important part in soil erosion. Where the land is dry, dust storms can cover hundreds of miles. The storms blow topsoil from open fields, overgrazed areas, and places where vegetation has disappeared. A dust storm is shown in **Figure 7-17.**

Visual Learning

Figure 7-15 Have students define *desert pavement. Desert pavement is wind-polished, densely packed pebbles left behind after the wind removes smaller particles. Desert pavement protects underlying materials from further deflation.* LEP LS

2 Teach

Activity

Have students search the school grounds for sediments that have been transported. They may find grit on curbs, dust on leaves, and fine sediments on the windowsills. Have students discuss the sources of the sediments and how the sediments were transported. L1

Inquiry Questions

Have a volunteer compare and contrast deflation and abrasion. Ask students: **How can you tell if rocks have been abraded?** *They are pitted and have shiny surfaces due to abrasion by sand grains.*

GLENCOE TECHNOLOGY

Videodisc

STVS: Earth & Space

Disc 3, Side 1

Wind Profiler (Ch. 20)

Wind Engineering (Ch. 21)

Videodisc

STV: Restless Earth

Sandstone towers; Algeria

52219

Terraced mountainside; Nepal

52257

Caravan and dunes; Sahara

52255

INTEGRATION
Life Science

- A plant's root system may equal or exceed its shoot system. In some plants, the total weight of the root system is much greater than the shoot system.
- On each root are root hairs. These contribute to the large surface area that roots have for holding soil.

MiniLAB

Purpose

LS **Kinesthetic** Students will observe how roots help hold soil in place and reduce erosion. L1 LEP

Materials

pieces of sod, old newspaper, trowels, magnifying glass or stereomicroscope

Teaching Strategies

Have students work on old newspaper to help with the cleanup process.

Analysis

1. A good drawing of a root will show root hairs.
2. Grass roots have a lot of surface area for holding onto soil particles. Also, they twist and turn around the soil particles.

Assessment

Oral Inform students that the part of the carrot we eat is really a root. Have students explain why grass roots are better for preventing erosion than carrot roots. Use the Performance Task Assessment List for Making Observations and Inferences in **PASC**, p. 17. P

Activity Worksheets, pp. 5, 47

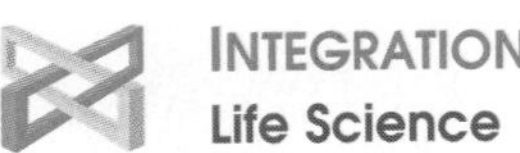

INTEGRATION
Life Science

MiniLAB

How do plant roots help hold soil in place?

Procedure

1. Obtain a piece of grass sod.
2. Carefully remove the soil from the sod roots by hand. Examine the roots with a magnifying glass or stereoscopic microscope.

Analysis

1. Draw several roots in your Science Journal.
2. What characteristics of grass roots help hold soil in place and thus help reduce erosion?

Reducing Wind Erosion

As you've learned, wind erosion is most common where plants do not exist to protect the soil. One of the best ways to slow or stop wind erosion is to plant vegetation.

Windbreaks

People in many countries plant vegetation to reduce wind erosion. For centuries, farmers have purposely planted trees along their fields to act as windbreaks to prevent soil erosion. As the wind hits the trees, its energy of motion is reduced. The wind no longer has the energy to lift particles.

In a study, a thin belt of cottonwood trees reduced the effect of a 25-kilometer-an-hour wind to about 66 percent of its normal speed. Tree belts reduce wind erosion and also trap snow and hold it on land, adding to the moisture of the soil.

Roots

Along many steep slopes, sea coasts, and deserts, people plant vegetation to hold the soil grains in place, thus reducing wind erosion. The best vegetation to plant to stop wind erosion has a fibrous root system as grasses do. Grass roots are shallow, slender, and have many fibers. They twist and turn between particles in the soil and hold the soil in place.

Planting vegetation is a good way to reduce the effects of deflation and abrasion. But if the wind is strong and the soil is dry, nothing can stop it completely. **Figure 7-18** shows a project to stop wind erosion.

Figure 7-18

This marram grass was planted to stabilize sand dunes in Cornwall, England. *How does grass slow erosion?*

Cultural Diversity

Desertification In many areas of the world, deserts are spreading because of drought and because people remove native vegetation. To prevent desert spreading, Niger is trying to control the migration of sand dunes. Have students use **Figure 7-18** to help them find out what people in other parts of the world have done to slow the erosion of sand dunes. LS

Figure 7-19

These loess cliffs formed along the Yellow River in China.

Deposition by Wind

Sediments blown away by wind are eventually deposited. These windblown deposits develop into several types of landforms.

Loess

Some large deposits of windblown sediments are found by the Yellow River in China, shown in **Figure 7-19,** and near the Mississippi River. These wind deposits of fine-grained sediments are known as **loess** (LES). Strong winds that deflated glacial outwash areas carried the sediments and deposited them. The sediments settled on hilltops and in valleys. Once there, the particles were packed together, creating a thick, buff-colored deposit lacking layers.

Loess is as fine as talcum powder. Many farmlands of the midwestern United States are on the fertile soils that have evolved from loess deposits. Loess is also found in China, where the sand and silt blow in from the Gobi and Ordos deserts.

Problem Solving

Fighting Deflation

If you travel in a desert, you might see large rocks piled several feet high at the bases of utility poles, fence posts, and houses. In places where this hasn't been done, deflation can occur at the bottoms of structures. In fact, some poles might lean. Windblown sediments cause fine scratch marks on unprotected structures.

In some places, sand may have blown across the highway. In areas where there are fences lining the highway, there is very little sand on the road.

Solve the Problem

1. **Infer from the information above why people pile rocks against the bases of poles, posts, and houses in desert regions.**
2. **Explain how fences help control the natural deposition of sand on desert highways.**

Think Critically:

If you lived in the desert, what are some ways that you could reduce wind erosion around your home?

Problem Solving

Solve the Problem

1. They protect the bottoms of the poles, posts, and houses from deflation.
2. Fences cause sand to collect and form dunes before it reaches highways.

Think Critically

Stacking rocks around structures will reduce abrasion and deflation; using fences and planting vegetation around the yard will reduce deflation.

Visual Learning

Figure 7-18 How does grass slow erosion? *The extensive root system of grasses holds soil in place.*

Figure 7-19 What are these cliffs made of? *wind-blown silt* LEP LS

Videodisc

GTV: Planetary Manager

Dust in the Wind

Show 2.6, Side 2

31907-38777

STV: Water

Desert community; Coachella Valley, California

52597

GLENCOE TECHNOLOGY

Videodisc

STVS: Ecology

Disc 6, Side 1

Soil Crusts in the Desert

(Ch. 4)

Across the Curriculum

Geography On a map, have students locate China, the Gobi and Ordos deserts, and the Yellow River. Then have them determine the direction of the wind that forms the loess deposits in China. L1

Activity 7-2

PREPARATION

Purpose

Interpersonal Students will observe how soil moisture and wind velocity affect wind erosion. L1 LEP COOP LEARN

Process Skills

designing an experiment, separating and controlling variables, observing and inferring, interpreting data, recognizing cause and effect, communicating, forming a hypothesis, making models, using numbers

Time

45 minutes for planning the experiment, 45 minutes for doing the experiment

Materials

Students can bring hair dryers and sprinkling cans from home. Deep baking pans or paint trays will help contain the sediment.

Safety Precautions

- Caution students to wear safety goggles when anyone is blowing sediments.
- Do not use glass pans.

Possible Hypotheses

Students may suspect that moisture will add weight to the sediments and also cause sediments to stick to one another. They might deduce, therefore, that moisture will cause a decrease in erosion. They will probably hypothesize that the greater the velocity of the wind, the larger the sediments it can transport.

Activity Worksheets, pp. 5, 44-45

Activity 7-2

Design Your Own Experiment
Blowing in the Wind

Have you ever played a sport outside and suddenly had the wind blow dust into your eyes? What did you do? Turn your back? Cover your eyes? How does wind pick up sediment? Why does wind pick up some sediments and leave others on the ground?

PREPARATION

Problem

What factors affect wind erosion? Do both sediment moisture and speed of wind affect the rate of wind erosion?

Form a Hypothesis

How does the amount of moisture in the sediment affect the ability of wind to erode the sediments? Does the speed of the wind limit the size of sediments it can transport? Form a hypothesis about how sediment moisture affects wind erosion. Form another hypothesis about how wind speed affects the size of the sediment the wind can transport.

Objectives

- Observe the effects of soil moisture and wind speed on wind erosion.
- Design and carry out experiments that test the effects of soil moisture and wind speed on wind erosion.

Possible Materials

- goggles
- flat pans (4)
- fine sand (400 mL)
- powdered clay (400 mL)
- gravel (400 mL)
- hair dryer
- sprinkling can
- water
- cardboard sheets (4)
- tape
- mixing bowl
- metric ruler

Safety Precautions  

Wear your safety goggles at all times when using the hair dryer on sediments.

Inclusion Strategies

Visually Impaired Place students who have difficulty doing the experiment in charge of formulating and evaluating the hypotheses.

PLAN THE EXPERIMENT

1. As a group, agree upon and write out your hypothesis statements and work on the experiment.
2. List the steps needed to test your first hypothesis. Plan specific steps and vary only one factor at a time. Then, list the steps needed to test your second hypothesis. Test only one factor at a time.
3. Mix the sediments in the pans. Plan how you will fold cardboard sheets and attach them to the pans to keep sediments from flying everywhere.
4. Design data tables in your Science Journal. Use them as your group collects data.

Check the Plan

1. Read over your plan to make certain that all steps are in logical order.
2. Identify the constants and the variables of the experiments.
3. Do you have to run any test more than one time?
4. Will the data be summarized in graphs?
5. *Make sure your teacher approves your plan before you proceed.*

DO THE EXPERIMENT

1. Carry out the experiments as planned.
2. During the experiments, write observations that you make and complete the data tables in your Science Journal.

Analyze and Apply

1. **Compare** your results with those of other groups.
2. What relationship is there between the sediment moisture and the amount of sediment eroded?
3. **Graph** the relationship that exists between the speed of the wind and the size of the sediments it transports.
4. How does the energy of motion explain the results of your experiment?

Go Further

Repeat your second experiment. This time, instead of mixing sediments together, test the sediments separately. How did this change your results?

PLAN THE EXPERIMENT

Possible Procedures

- One way to test the effect of moisture on wind erosion is to mix equal amounts of sediments, divide them, and place one half in each pan. Tape a sheet of folded cardboard to one end of each pan. Sprinkle water onto the soil in one pan. Put on safety glasses. Set the hair dryer at medium and blow the sediments toward the cardboard in each pan from the same angle and distance for two minutes.
- To test the effect of wind velocity on wind erosion, begin as described above, only do not sprinkle one pan with water. Instead, both pans should contain dry sediments. Put on safety glasses and blow one pan for two minutes on a low setting. Blow the other pan from the same angle and distance for two minutes on a high setting.

Teaching Strategies

Troubleshooting Caution students that the angle and distance of the hair dryers from the pans must be the same.

DO THE EXPERIMENT

Expected Outcome

Students observe that soil moisture slows down wind erosion. The greater the wind speed, the greater the size and amount of sediment transported.

Go Further

Students may see that when the sediments are tested separately, the smaller sediments are more easily eroded because the larger sediments are not there to act as obstacles to the wind.

Analyze and Apply

1. Students should have similar results.
2. Students should observe that moist sediments are not easily eroded.
3. They should see by graphing that the greater the speed of the wind, the larger the sediments it can move.
4. Erosion depends on energy of motion. When energy gives out, materials are deposited.

Assessment

Performance To further assess students' understanding of wind erosion, have them design an experiment that will allow them to collect enough data to graph the effects of moisture on the amount of the sediment that will erode. Use the Performance Task Assessment List for Designing an Experiment in **PASC**, p. 23. P

CONNECT TO

LIFE SCIENCE

Answer Grasses would be the better to plant.

Inquiry Question

Tell students that along some beaches, people lay old Christmas trees in the sand to keep the sand from eroding. Large dunes develop in these areas. Ask students why this happens. *The trees act as barriers to the wind and trap the sand grains, which eventually form dunes.*

Enrichment

Have students find out why off-highway vehicles are so damaging to desert soils. One reference is *National Geographic Magazine,* January 1987, pp. 42-76. L1

3 Assess

Check for Understanding

FLEX Your Brain

Use the Flex Your Brain activity to have students explore SAND DUNES.

Activity Worksheets, p. 5

Reteach

Have students work in groups to determine the effect of clumps of grass on the development of sand dunes. Each team will need the following items: safety goggles, a flat pan filled with sand, a hair dryer, and clumps of grass.

Extension

For students who have mastered this section, use the **Reinforcement** and **Enrichment** masters.

CONNECT TO

LIFE SCIENCE

Red clover has a tap root system consisting of one main root that grows directly downward. Grasses have a fibrous root system. ***Infer*** which type of plant would be the best to plant along coastal sand dunes to prevent wind erosion.

Dunes

What happens when wind blows sediments against an obstacle such as a rock or a clump of vegetation? The sediments settle behind the obstacle. More and more sediments build up and eventually a dune is formed. A dune is a mound of sand drifted by the wind. **Figure 7-20** shows sand dunes.

Sand dunes constantly move as wind erodes them and deposits the sand elsewhere. On Cape Cod, Massachusetts and along the Gulf of California, the coast of Oregon, and the eastern shore of Lake Michigan, you can see beach sand dunes. Sand dunes accumulate where there are sand and prevailing winds or sea breezes that blow daily.

To visualize how a dune forms, think of the sand at the back of a beach. That sand is dry because the ocean and lake waves do not reach these areas. The wind blows this dry sand farther inland until an obstruction such as a rock slows the wind. The wind sweeps around or over the rock. Like a river, air drops its load of sediment when its energy of motion slows. Sand starts to accumualte behind the rock. As the sand continues to accumulate, the mound of sand becomes an even greater obstacle and traps even more sand. If the wind blows long enough, the mound of sand will become a sand dune.

Sand will continue to accumulate and build a dune until the sand runs out or the obstruction is removed. Some sand dunes may grow to 50 to 180 meters high, but most are much lower.

Figure 7-20

Dunes are the most common wind deposits. Sand dunes form in deserts and beaches where sand is abundant. They are constantly changing and moving as wind erodes them.

Dune Migration

A sand dune has two sides. The side facing the wind has a gentler slope. The side away from the wind is steeper. Examining the shape of a dune tells you the direction the wind usually blows from.

Unless sand dunes are planted with grasses, most dunes don't stay still. They migrate or move away from the direction of the wind. This migration process is shown in **Figure 7-21.** Some dunes are known as traveling dunes because they move across desert areas as they lose sand on one side and accumulate it on the other.

When dunes and loess form, the landscape is changed. Wind, like gravity, running water, and glaciers, shapes the land as it erodes sediments. But the new landforms created by these agents of erosion are themselves being eroded. Erosion and deposition are part of a cycle of change that constantly shapes and reshapes the land.

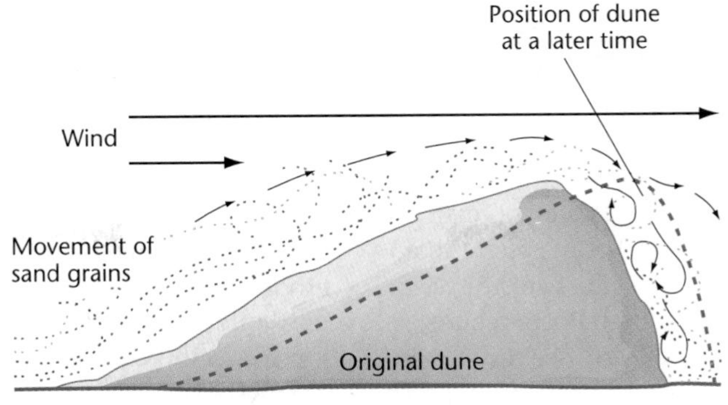

Figure 7-21

As wind blows the sand, the grains jump, roll, and slide up the gentler slope of the dune, accumulate at the top, then slide down the steeper slope on the side away from the wind.

Section Wrap-up

Review

1. Compare and contrast abrasion and deflation. How do they affect the surface of Earth?
2. Explain the differences between dust storms and sandstorms. How does this affect the deposition of sand and dust?
3. **Think Critically:** You notice that snow is piling up behind a fence outside your apartment building. Why?

Skill Builder

Sequencing

Sequence the following events that describe how a sand dune forms. If you need help, refer to Sequencing in the **Skill Handbook.**

a. Grains collect to form a mound.

b. Wind blows sand grains until they hit an obstacle.

c. Wind blows over an area and causes deflation.

d. Vegetation grows on the dune.

USING MATH

Between 1972 and 1992, the area of the Sahara Desert in Africa increased by nearly 700 square kilometers in Mali and the Sudan. Much of this desertification was due to drought and the removal of vegetation. Calculate the average number of square kilometers the desert increased each year between 1972 and 1992.

4 Close

•MINI•QUIZ•

Use the Mini Quiz to check students' recall of chapter content.

1. **The wind erosion called ______ leaves behind large pebbles and boulders.** *deflation*
2. **______ is similar to sandblasting a building.** *Abrasion*
3. **______ is a fine-grained wind deposit.** *Loess*

Section Wrap-up

Review

1. Deflation occurs when wind picks up and transports small sediments, leaving behind heavier sediments such as pebbles and boulders. Abrasion is a natural form of sandblasting. Blowing sand grains strike and break off small fragments of rock. Both abrasion and deflation erode and change surface features.
2. Sandstorms remain close to the ground. Sand grains travel along the ground and don't go far at one time, as seen in dune migration. In dust storms, wind picks up dust and carries it great distances. Loess can be deposited far from its origin.
3. **Think Critically** When the wind strikes the fence, it loses some of its energy of motion and can carry some snow no farther.

USING MATH

700/20 = 35 square kilometers per year

Skill Builder

The most logical sequence of events is c, b, a, and d.

Assessment

Content Assess students' abilities to sequence by having them list the steps involved in the creation of loess deposits. Use the Performance Task Assessment List for Events Chain in **PASC,** p. 91. P

Credit

Dust Storm Disaster

Words and Music by Woody Guthrie

TRO—©—Copyright 1960 (Renewed) 1963 (Renewed) Ludlow Music, Inc., New York, New York

Used by Permission

Biography

Woody Guthrie Woody Guthrie was perhaps the most significant folk musician of modern times. His music has influenced folk singers and writers from Pete Seegar, with whom he performed, to Bob Dylan. Guthrie was born in Oklahoma in 1912. From his late teens on, he spent much of his life traveling the nation, often staying with and performing for hobos and migrant workers. His songs depict the plight of the underdog and the beauty of the landscape. He died of Huntington's chorea in 1967 after spending his final years in a hospital. Many of Guthrie's experiences are told in his autobiography, *Bound for Glory.*

Heitor Villa-Lobos Another composer who used local themes was Heitor Villa-Lobos, born in 1897 in Brazil. At that time, Brazilian music was based on traditional European styles. Villa-Lobos was among those who brought diverse native South American nature themes into his country's music. A prolific composer, he wrote approximately 2000 compositions before his death in 1959.

Teaching Strategies

- Discuss how over-farming and over-grazing land can leave soil exposed and vulnerable to erosion.
- Have students speculate on how overexposed land can be harmed by rain as well as by drought.

Science & ART

Science Journal

Have you ever been caught in a dust storm? Or in some other storm where you couldn't see more than a foot or two ahead of you? In your Science Journal, write a description of the experience. Tell how you found your way without being able to see well.

The Music of Erosion

In the 1930s, the soil in large parts of Texas, Oklahoma, Colorado, Kansas, and New Mexico was blowing away. Overgrazing and overfarming had stripped vast expanses of the land of protective grass. Drought had dried the soil. Wind eroded the land. It blew away soil one day then deposited a new pile of dust a few days later. This dry region became known as the Dust Bowl.

Woody Guthrie wrote and sang folk songs about the hardships of the Dust Bowl. His song "The Great Dust Storm" describes a region where, according to Guthrie, "the dust flows and the farmer owes."

The storm took place at sundown
It lasted through the night.
When we looked out next morning
We saw a terrible sight.

We saw outside our window
Where wheatfields they had grown,
Was now a rippling ocean
Of dust the wind had blown.

It covered up our fences,
It covered up our barns,
It covered up our tractors
In this wild and dusty storm.©

Guthrie's songs tell of hardship and pain. But they also tell of courage and humor. "Dust Can't Kill Me" is a song about a man who refuses to be destroyed even after the dust storms take everything he has. In "Dust Pneumonia Blues," he sings about a man's trip to Texas. His girlfriend isn't used to water anymore, so she faints in the rain. The man has to throw a bucket of dirt in her face to revive her.

LS Linguistic Have students research how the problems of the dust bowl were remedied and how a reoccurrence in the late 1940s and early 1950s was avoided. L2

- Ask students to think of popular songs that depict erosional forces in action.
- Discuss how erosional forces can be beneficial as well as deterimental to farming, such as the Egyptians' dependance on annual flooding of the Nile. Ask whether they can think of any land in the U.S. that may have benefited from deposition of fertile soil.

Chapter 7

Review

Summary

7-1: Gravity

1. Erosion is the process that wears down and transports sediments. Deposition occurs when an agent of erosion loses its energy of motion and can no longer carry its load.
2. Slump, creep, rockslides, and mudflows are all mass movements related to gravity.

7-2: Science and Society: Developing Land Prone to Erosion

1. Vegetation, terraces, and retaining walls can reduce erosion on slopes.
2. Building on steep slopes and removing vegetation from slopes increase erosion.

7-3: Glaciers

1. Glaciers are powerful agents of erosion.
2. Plucking adds rock and soil to a glacier's sides and bottom as water freezes and thaws and breaks off pieces of surrounding rocks.
3. Striations and grooves are gouged out in bedrock by rock fragments being transported by a glacier.
4. Till is a jumble of sediments deposited directly from glacial ice and snow. Outwash is glacial debris deposited by meltwater of the glacier.

7-4: Wind

1. Deflation occurs when wind erodes only fine-grained sediments, while course sediments like pebbles and boulders are left behind. The pitting and polishing of rocks and sediments by windblown sediments is called abrasion.
2. Deposits of fine-grained particles that are tightly packed form loess. Dunes begin to form when windblown sediments pile up behind an obstacle.

Key Science Words

a. abrasion
b. creep
c. deflation
d. deposition
e. erosion
f. glacier
g. loess
h. mass movement
i. moraine
j. plucking
k. slump
l. till

Reviewing Vocabulary

Match each phrase with the correct term from the list of Key Science Words.

1. process of wearing down and transporting weathered sediments
2. slow movement of sediments downhill because of freezing and thawing
3. downward movement of rock and soil under influence of gravity
4. mass movement in which materials move as one large mass
5. erosion caused by freezing and thawing of glacial ice
6. wind erosion that leaves coarse sediments behind
7. mixture of rocks and sediments deposited in ridges by glacial snow and ice
8. a thick mass of ice and snow that flows over land
9. erosion caused by natural sandblasting
10. thick, densely packed deposits of dust

Chapter 7

Review

Summary

Have students read the summary statements to review the major concepts of the chapter.

Reviewing Vocabulary

1. e
2. b
3. h
4. k
5. j
6. c
7. i
8. f
9. a
10. g

Assessment

Portfolio Encourage students to place in their portfolios one or two items of what they consider to be their best work. Examples include:

- Skill Builder Concept Map, p. 177
- Integrating the Sciences, p. 179
- Science Journal, p. 187 P

Performance Additional performance assessments may be found in **Performance Assessment** and **Science Integration Activities.** Performance Task Assessment Lists and rubrics for evaluating these activities can be found in Glencoe's **Performance Assessment in the Science Classroom.**

GLENCOE TECHNOLOGY

MindJogger Videoquiz

Chapter 7 Have students work in groups as they play the Videoquiz game to review key chapter concepts.

Checking Concepts

1. b	**6.** c
2. c	**7.** d
3. d	**8.** a
4. b	**9.** a
5. b	**10.** c

Understanding Concepts

11. Slumping occurs on a steep slope when underlying sediments are weakened. Gravity causes the overlying sediments to slip downward as a large mass. Slumping results in a curved scar in the slope.

12. Till is dropped from the front and base of a glacier. It's a mixture of different-sized sediments. Outwash is deposited by meltwater. The larger sediments are deposited closer to the edge of the melting glacier than are the smaller sediments.

13. Weathering breaks rocks into smaller fragments. Erosion wears away surfaces and moves fragments to a new location. Both processes have an effect on changing the shape of land forms.

14. The greater the moisture, the greater the mass movement.

15. People use terracing, retaining walls, and vegetation.

Thinking Critically

16. Striations are made by glacial debris embedded in the bottom or sides of the ice. The debris gouges the bedrock as the glacier moves, thus recording the movement of the glacier. Striations are generally parallel to glacial movement.

17. A fine mesh wire will prevent only larger particles such as pebbles and boulders from eroding. Smaller sediments like sand, silt, and dust will blow through the mesh.

18. Planting vegetation or erecting fences can reduce or even prevent dune migration.

19. The mass of the overlying snow and ice compresses the underlying layers. This pressure can cause the ice to partially melt. The melting then causes movement not only at the glacier's bottom, but also within the glacier.

20. Warmer weather at lower elevations could cause the front end to melt and to appear to retreat. Colder temperatures at higher elevations would allow the snow and ice to accumulate and cause the glacial tail end to advance.

Developing Skills

21. Making and Using Tables See next page.

Chapter 7 Review

Checking Concepts

Choose the word or phrase that completes the sentence or answers the question.

1. Which of the following is the slowest type of mass movement?
   a. abrasion c. slump
   b. creep d. mudflow
2. The best vegetation to plant to reduce erosion has a _______.
   a. tap root system
   b. striated root system
   c. fibrous root system
   d. sheet root system
3. Where a valley glacier started, a(n) _______ is created.
   a. esker c. till
   b. moraine d. cirque
4. Glacial erosion _______.
   a. happens in warm places
   b. leaves behind landforms such as arêtes and grooves
   c. happened only in the past
   d. happens only in the present
5. A mass of snow and ice in motion is a(n) _______.
   a. loess deposit c. outwash
   b. glacier d. abrasion
6. Glacier-created valleys are _______.
   a. V-shaped c. U-shaped
   b. L-shaped d. S-shaped
7. An example of a structure created by deposition is a(n) _______.
   a. cirque c. striation
   b. abrasion d. dune
8. One characteristic that all agents of erosion have in common is _______.
   a. they carry sediments when they have enough energy of motion
   b. they are most likely to erode when sediments are moist
   c. they create deposits called dunes
   d. they erode large sediments before they erode small ones
9. Wind erosion in which pebbles and boulders are left behind is called _______.
   a. deflation c. abrasion
   b. loess d. sandblasting
10. A(n)_______ is a bowl-shaped erosional feature formed by glacial plucking.
    a. striation c. cirque
    b. esker d. moraine

Understanding Concepts

Answer the following questions in your Science Journal using complete sentences.

11. Discuss the causes and effects of slumping.
12. How does the deposition of till differ from the deposition of outwash?
13. Compare and contrast weathering and erosion.
14. How does the amount of soil moisture affect mass movement?
15. Discuss ways people can reduce erosion on slopes.

Thinking Critically

16. How can striations give information about the direction a glacier moved?
17. How effective would a retaining wall made of fine wire mesh be against erosion?
18. Sand dunes often migrate. What can be done to prevent the migration of beach dunes?
19. Scientists have found evidence of movement of ice within a glacier. Explain how this may occur. (HINT: Recall how putty-like ice forms at the base of a glacier.)
20. The front end of a valley glacier is at a lower elevation than the tail end. How does this explain melting at its front end while snow is still accumulating at its tail end?

Developing Skills

If you need help, refer to the **Skill Handbook.**

21. **Making Tables:** Make a table to contrast continental and valley glaciers.
22. **Designing an Experiment:** Explain how to test the effect of glacial thickness on a glacier's ability to erode.
23. **Sequencing:** Copy and complete the events chain to show how a sand dune forms. Use the terms *sand rolls, migrating, wind blows, sand accumulates, dune, dry sand, obstruction traps,* and *stabilized.*

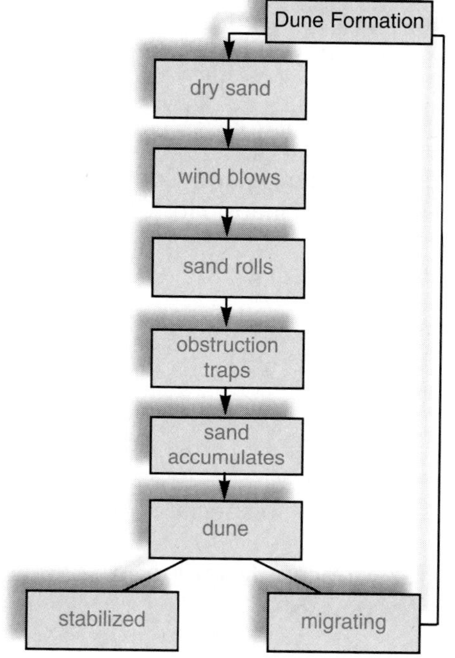

24. **Hypothesizing:** Hypothesize why the materials of loess deposits were transported farther than those of sand dune deposits.
25. **Interpreting Scientific Illustrations:** Look at the map of Ohio on the right. In which part of Ohio would you find erosion and deposition caused by glaciers of the last ice age? How would you expect the terrain to differ throughout the state?

Performance Assessment

1. **Design an Experiment:** In the MiniLAB on page 176, you made models of landforms of different mass movements. Based on what you learned, design an experiment to see how the amount of moisture added to sediments affects slump erosion. Design your experiment to keep all variables constant except the amount of moisture in the sediment. Try your experiment.
2. **Design a Study:** In Activity 7-2, on pages 192 and 193, you learned how sediment moisture and the speed of the wind affect erosion. Based on your observations, design and carry out an experiment to see how vegetation or small fences placed in the sediments affect wind erosion. Use the results to help your class reduce erosion around your school and home. If you live in a snowy area, use these ideas to help control blowing snow.
3. **Poster:** Make a poster of magazine photos showing glacial features in North America. Include photos and descriptions of glacial features not covered in this chapter. Add a map showing where each feature is located.

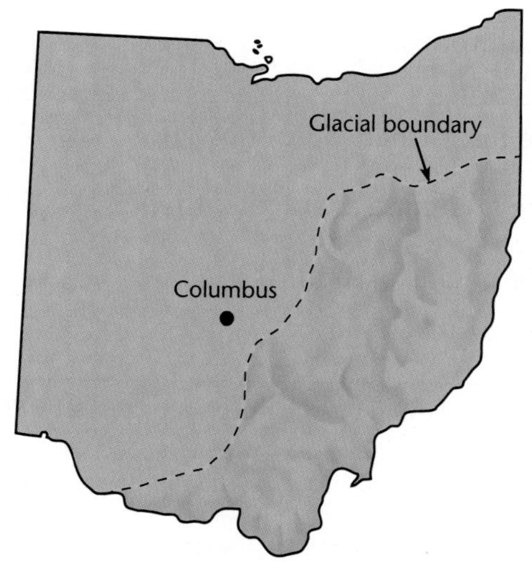

22. **Designing an Experiment** Two ice blocks, one thicker than the other, could be guided with the same amount of force over a pan containing sand.
23. **Sequencing** See student page.
24. **Hypothesizing** Loess is made of very small sediments that wind can carry farther.
25. **Interpreting Scientific Illustrations** Glacial deposits and erosional features are found north of the glacial boundary line. The terrain of the glaciated region is much smoother and flatter than that of the nonglaciated area. The glaciated area contains gently rolling hills and depositional features such as eskers and terminal moraines. Till covers large areas. The nonglaciated area has much greater relief and steep stream valleys.

Performance Assessment

1. Student designs will vary. Students should keep all variables except moisture constant in their tests. Use the Performance Task Assessment List for Designing an Experiment in **PASC,** p. 23. P
2. Student designs will vary. Vegetation and small fences act as windbreaks, reducing the amount of erosion. Students may report that small dunes of sediments developed in their pans. Use the Performance Task Assessment List for Designing an Experiment in **PASC,** p. 23. P
3. The posters will vary. Use the Performance Task Assessment List for Poster in **PASC,** p. 73. P

21.

	Continental Glacier	Valley Glacier
Erosional Features	striations, flat landscape	U-shaped valley, cirques, striations, sharp peaks
Depositional Features	glacial erratics, till, outwash, moraines, flat landscape	glacial erratics, till, outwash, moraines

Chapter Organizer

Section	Objectives	Activities/Features
Chapter Opener		Explore Activity: Things That Affect Water Erosion, p. 201
8-1 **Surface Water** (1 session, ½ block)*	1. **Explain** what causes runoff. 2. **Compare** rill, sheet, gully, and stream erosion. 3. **Discuss** the three different stages of stream development. 4. **Describe** how alluvial fans and deltas form.	Connect to Physics, p. 204 MiniLAB: Where does most erosion occur in a stream? p. 206 Problem Solving: Washed Out, p. 207 Activity 8-1: Stream Speed, pp. 210-211 Using Technology: Taming a River, p. 212 Skill Builder: Comparing and Contrasting, p. 213 Using Computers: Spreadsheet, p. 213
8-2 **Groundwater** (3 sessions, 1½ blocks)*	1. **Describe** the groundwater system. 2. **Explain** the effect that soil and rock permeability have on groundwater movement. 3. **Describe** ways that groundwater erodes and deposits sediments.	Using Math, p. 215 MiniLAB: How can you measure pore space? p. 216 Connect to Chemistry, p. 217 Science Journal, p. 218 Skill Builder: Comparing and Contrasting, p. 218 Science & History: Huang Ho, China's Sorrow, p. 219 Science Journal, p. 219
8-3 **Science and Society Issue: Water Wars** (1 session, ½ block)*	1. **Give examples** of ways people use water. 2. **Explain** why some communities must rely on water diversion for their water supply. 3. **Identify** a problem caused by water diversion.	Science Journal, p. 221 Explore the Issue, p. 221
8-4 **Ocean Shoreline** (2 sessions, 1 block)*	1. **Describe** forces that cause shoreline erosion. 2. **Compare** and **contrast** different types of shorelines. 3. **List** some origins of sand.	Activity 8-2: What's so special about sand? p. 225 Skill Builder: Concept Mapping, p. 226 Using Math, p. 226

* A complete Planning Guide that includes block scheduling is provided on pages 32T-35T.

Activity Materials

Explore	Activities	MiniLABs
page 201 waxed paper, dry soil samples, tap water, dropper	pages 210-211 large rectangular pan or stream table, sand to fill the pan or stream table, 2 plastic pails, rubber tubing, meterstick, small cork, water, clock or stopwatch with second hand, 2 wooden blocks page 225 3 samples of different beach sands, stereomicroscope, magnet	page 206 large rectangular pan, soil samples, ruler, pencil, tap water, 250-mL beaker page 216 100 mL sand, 100 mL gravel, two 250-mL beakers, 100-mL graduated cylinder, tap water

Chapter 8 Water Erosion and Deposition

Teacher Classroom Resources

Reproducible Masters	Transparencies
Study Guide, p. 33 **Reinforcement,** p. 33 **Enrichment,** p. 33 **Activity Worksheets,** pp. 48-49, 52 **Lab Manual 25,** Transporting Soil Materials by Runoff **Science Integration Activity 8,** Super Solvent **Multicultural Connections,** pp. 19-20	**Section Focus Transparency 29,** Rolling with the River **Teaching Transparency 15,** Streams
Study Guide, p. 34 **Reinforcement,** p. 34 **Enrichment,** p. 34 **Activity Worksheets,** p. 53 **Lab Manual 26,** Capillary Action **Lab Manual 27,** Carbon Dioxide and Limestone **Concept Mapping,** p. 21 **Critical Thinking/Problem Solving,** p. 14	**Section Focus Transparency 30,** Under the Surface **Science Integration Transparency 8,** Sticky Water
Study Guide, p. 35 **Reinforcement,** p. 35 **Enrichment,** p. 35 **Science and Society Integration,** p. 12 **Technology Integration,** pp. 7-8	**Section Focus Transparency 31,** Mystery at Sea
Study Guide, p. 36 **Reinforcement,** p. 36 **Enrichment,** p. 36 **Activity Worksheets,** pp. 50-51 **Lab Manual 28,** Waves, Currents, and Coastal Features **Cross-Curricular Integration,** p. 12	**Section Focus Transparency 32,** At the Sea Show **Teaching Transparency 16,** Beach Landforms

Teaching Resources

Glencoe Earth Science Interactive Videodisc
Earth Science CD-ROM
Spanish Resources
English/Spanish Audiocassettes
Cooperative Learning Resource Guide
Lab Partner
Lab and Safety Skills
Lesson Plans

Assessment Resources

Chapter Review, pp. 19-20
Assessment, pp. 44-47
Performance Assessment in the Science Classroom (PASC)
MindJogger Videoquiz
Alternate Assessment in the Science Classroom
Performance Assessment
Chapter Review Software
Computer Test Bank

Key to Teaching Strategies

The following designations will help you decide which activities are appropriate for your students.

L1 Level 1 activities should be within the ability range of all students.

L2 Level 2 activities should be within the ability range of the average to above-average student.

L3 Level 3 activities are designed for the ability range of above-average students.

LEP LEP activities should be within the ability range of Limited English Proficiency students.

LS These activities are designed to address different learning styles.

COOP LEARN Cooperative Learning activities are designed for small group work.

P These strategies represent student products that can be placed into a best-work portfolio.

GLENCOE TECHNOLOGY

The following multimedia resources are available from Glencoe.

The Infinite Voyage Series
Living with Disaster

Science and Technology Videodisc Series (STVS)
Physics
Cutting with Water
Chemistry
Geothermal Wells

National Geographic Society Series
STV: Restless Earth
GTV: Planetary Manager

Glencoe Earth Science Interactive Videodisc
Mysteries of the Cave

Earth Science CD-ROM

Teacher Classroom Resources

This is a representation of key blackline masters available in the Teacher Classroom Resources.

Teaching Aids

Section Focus Transparencies

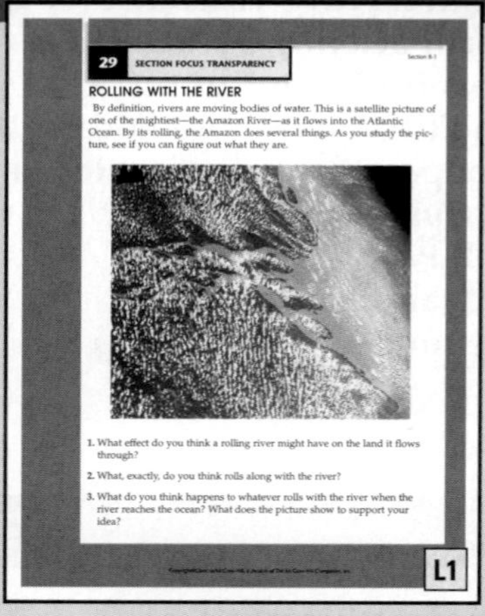

29 SECTION FOCUS TRANSPARENCY Section 8-1

ROLLING WITH THE RIVER

By definition, rivers are moving bodies of water. This is a satellite picture of one of the mightiest—the Amazon River—as it flows into the Atlantic Ocean. By its rolling, the Amazon does several things. As you study the picture, see if you can figure out what they are.

1. What effect do you think a rolling river might have on the land it flows through?
2. What, exactly, do you think rolls along with the river?
3. What do you think happens to whatever rolls with the river when the river reaches the ocean? What does the picture show to support your idea?

L1

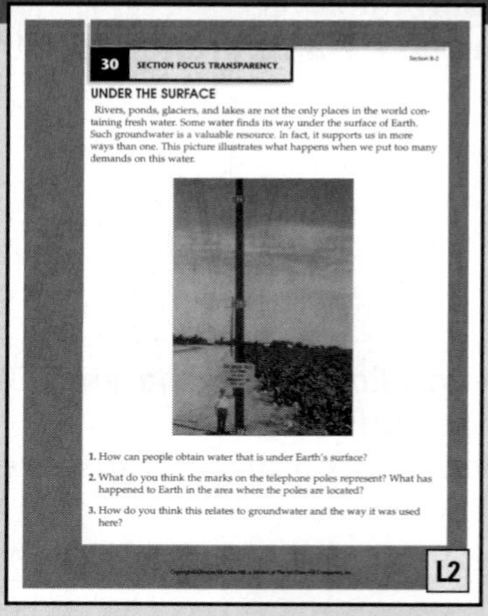

30 SECTION FOCUS TRANSPARENCY Section 8-2

UNDER THE SURFACE

Rivers, ponds, glaciers, and lakes are not the only places in the world containing fresh water. Some water finds its way under the surface of Earth. Such groundwater is a valuable resource. In fact, it supports us in more ways than one. This picture illustrates what happens when we put too many demands on this water.

1. How can people obtain water that is under Earth's surface?
2. What do you think the marks on the telephone poles represent? What has happened to Earth in the area where the poles are located?
3. How do you think this relates to groundwater and the way it was used here?

L2

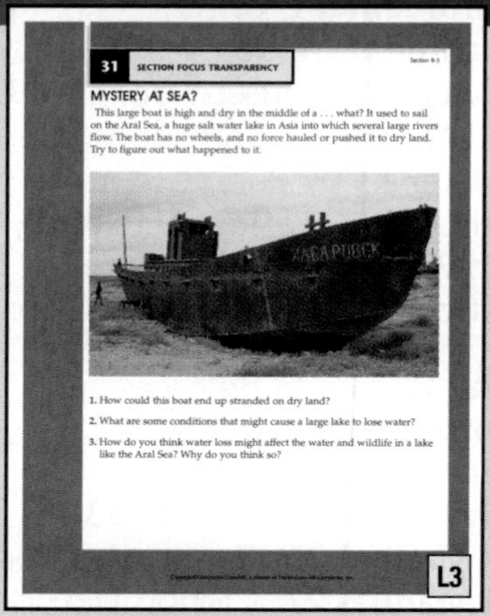

31 SECTION FOCUS TRANSPARENCY Section 8-3

MYSTERY AT SEA?

This large boat is high and dry in the middle of a . . . what? It used to sail on the Aral Sea, a huge salt water lake in Asia into which several large rivers flow. The boat has no wheels, and no force hauled or pushed it to dry land. Try to figure out what happened to it.

1. How could this boat end up stranded on dry land?
2. What are some conditions that might cause a large lake to lose water?
3. How do you think water loss might affect the water and wildlife in a lake like the Aral Sea? Why do you think so?

L3

Science Integration Transparencies

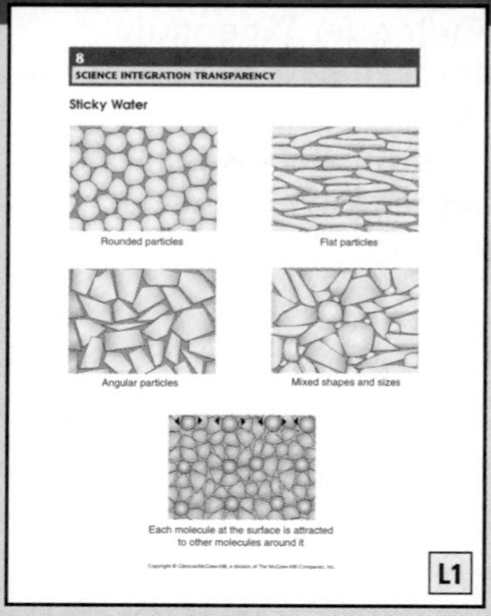

8 SCIENCE INTEGRATION TRANSPARENCY

Sticky Water

Rounded particles

Flat particles

Angular particles

Mixed shapes and sizes

Each molecule at the surface is attracted to other molecules around it

L1

Teaching Transparencies

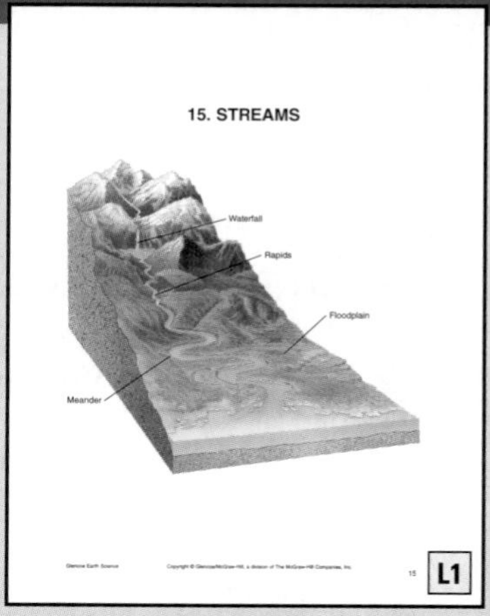

15. STREAMS

Waterfall

Rapids

Floodplain

Meander

L1

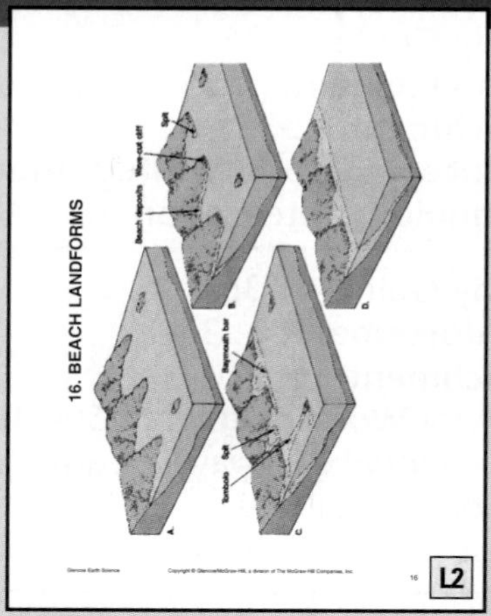

16. BEACH LANDFORMS

L2

Meeting Different Ability Levels

Study Guide

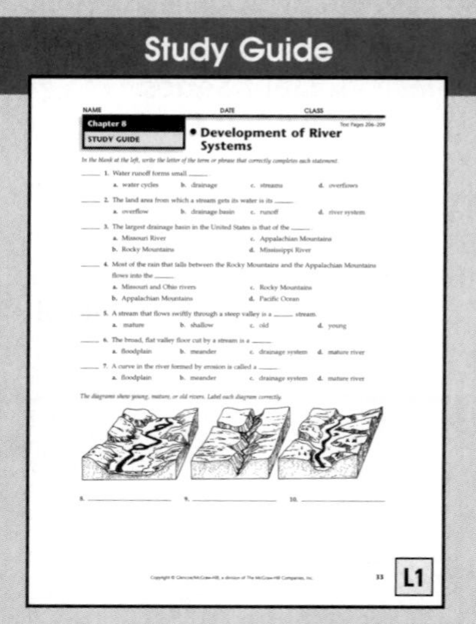

NAME DATE CLASS

Chapter 8 STUDY GUIDE • Development of River Systems Text Pages 206–209

In the blank at the left, write the letter of the term or phrase that correctly completes each statement.

_____ 1. Water runoff forms small _____.
a. water cycles b. drainage c. streams d. overflows

_____ 2. The land area from which a stream gets its water is its _____.
a. overflow b. drainage basin c. runoff d. river system

_____ 3. The largest drainage basin in the United States is that of the _____.
a. Missouri River c. Appalachian Mountains
b. Rocky Mountains d. Mississippi River

_____ 4. Most of the rain that falls between the Rocky Mountains and the Appalachian Mountains flows into the _____.
a. Missouri and Ohio rivers c. Rocky Mountains
b. Appalachian Mountains d. Pacific Ocean

_____ 5. A stream that flows swiftly through a steep valley is a _____ stream.
a. mature b. shallow c. old d. young

_____ 6. The broad, flat valley floor cut by a stream is a _____.
a. floodplain b. meander c. drainage system d. mature river

_____ 7. A curve in the river formed by erosion is called a _____.
a. floodplain b. meander c. drainage system d. mature river

The diagrams show young, mature, or old rivers. Label each diagram correctly.

8. _____ 9. _____ 10. _____

Copyright © Glencoe/McGraw-Hill, a division of The McGraw-Hill Companies, Inc. 33

L1

Reinforcement

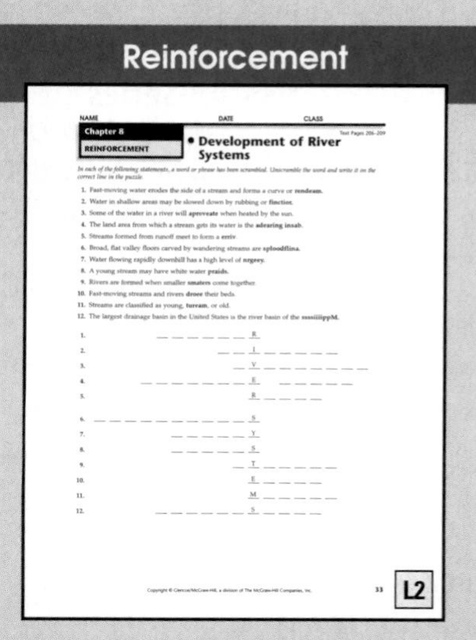

NAME DATE CLASS

Chapter 8 REINFORCEMENT • Development of River Systems Text Pages 206–209

In each of the following statements, a word or phrase has been scrambled. Unscramble the word and write it on the correct line in the puzzle.

1. Fast-moving water erodes the side of a stream and forms a curve or **rendeam.**
2. Water in shallow areas may be slowed down by rubbing or **finction.**
3. Some of the water in a river will **aproveate** when heated by the sun.
4. The land area from which a stream gets its water is the **adearing insab.**
5. Streams formed from runoff meet to form a **erriv.**
6. Broad, flat valley floors carved by wandering streams are **sploodflina.**
7. Water flowing rapidly downhill has a high level of **nrgeey.**
8. A young stream may have white water **praids.**
9. Rivers are formed when smaller **smaters** come together.
10. Fast-moving streams and rivers **droee** their beds.
11. Streams are classified as young, **tuream**, or old.
12. The largest drainage basin in the United States is the river basin of the **ssasiiiippM.**

1. _ _ _ _ _ _ R
2. _ _ I _ _ _ _ _
3. _ V _ _ _ _ _ _ _
4. _ _ _ _ _ _ _ E _ _ _ _ _
5. R _ _ _ _
6. _ _ _ _ _ _ _ _ _ _ S
7. _ _ _ _ _ Y
8. _ _ _ _ _ S
9. _ T _ _ _ _ _
10. E _ _ _ _
11. M _ _ _ _ _
12. _ _ _ _ _ _ S _ _ _ _

Copyright © Glencoe/McGraw-Hill, a division of The McGraw-Hill Companies, Inc. 33

L2

Enrichment Worksheets

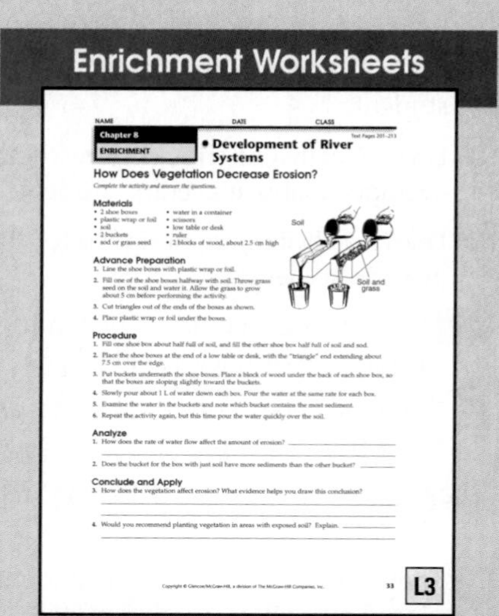

NAME DATE CLASS

Chapter 8 ENRICHMENT • Development of River Systems Text Pages 201–213

How Does Vegetation Decrease Erosion?

Complete the activity and answer the questions.

Materials
- 2 shoe boxes
- plastic wrap or foil
- soil
- 2 buckets
- sod or grass seed
- water in a container
- scissors
- low table or desk
- ruler
- 2 blocks of wood, about 2.5 cm high

Advance Preparation
1. Line the shoe boxes with plastic wrap or foil.
2. Fill one of the shoe boxes halfway with soil. Throw grass seed on the soil and water it. Allow the grass to grow about 5 cm before performing the activity.
3. Cut triangles out of the ends of the boxes as shown.
4. Place plastic wrap or foil under the boxes.

Procedure
1. Fill one shoe box about half full of soil, and fill the other shoe box half full of soil and sod.
2. Place the shoe boxes at the end of a low table or desk, with the "triangle" end extending about 7.5 cm over the edge.
3. Put buckets underneath the shoe boxes. Place a block of wood under the back of each shoe box, so that the boxes are sloping slightly toward the buckets.
4. Slowly pour about 1 L of water down each box. Pour the water at the same rate for each box.
5. Examine the water in the buckets and note which bucket contains the most sediment.
6. Repeat the activity again, but this time pour the water quickly over the soil.

Analyze
1. How does the rate of water flow affect the amount of erosion? _____
2. Does the bucket for the box with just soil have more sediments than the other bucket? _____

Conclude and Apply
3. How does the vegetation affect erosion? What evidence helps you draw this conclusion? _____
4. Would you recommend planting vegetation in areas with exposed soil? Explain. _____

Copyright © Glencoe/McGraw-Hill, a division of The McGraw-Hill Companies, Inc. 33

L3

Chapter 8 Water Erosion and Deposition

Hands-On Activities

Science Integration Activity

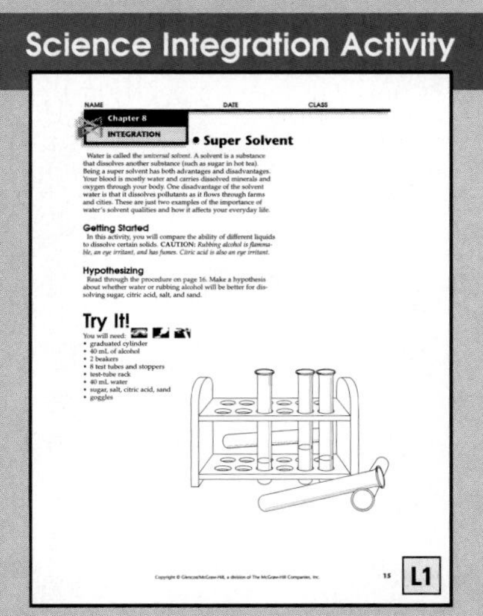

Lab Manual

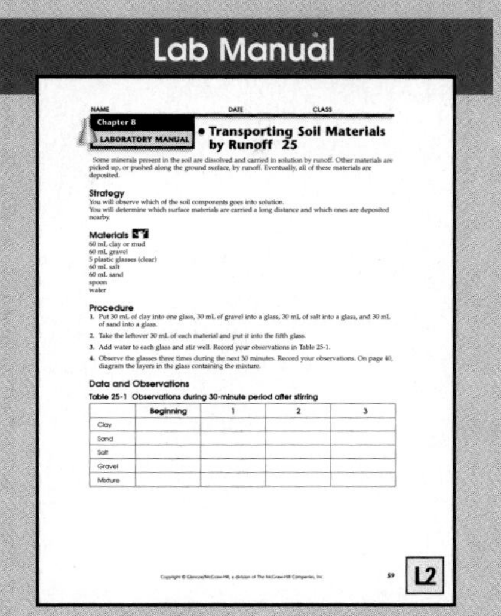

Assessment

Performance Assessment

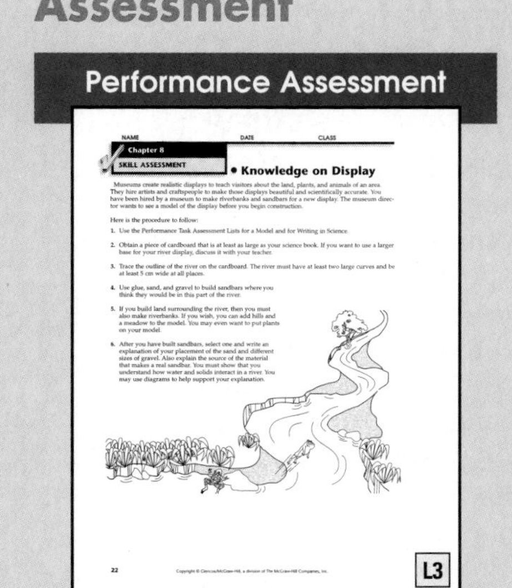

Enrichment and Application

Critical Thinking/ Problem Solving

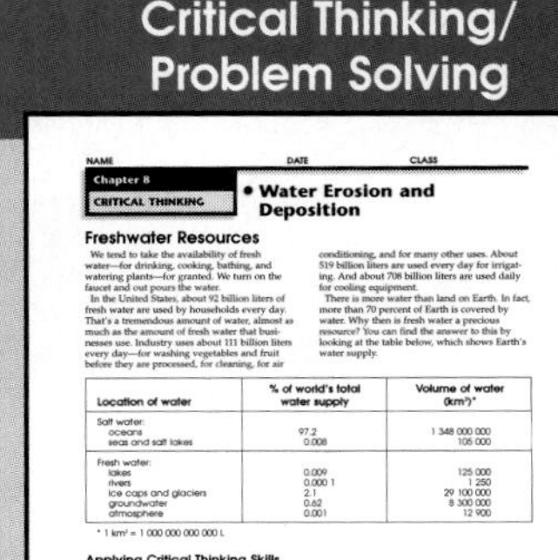

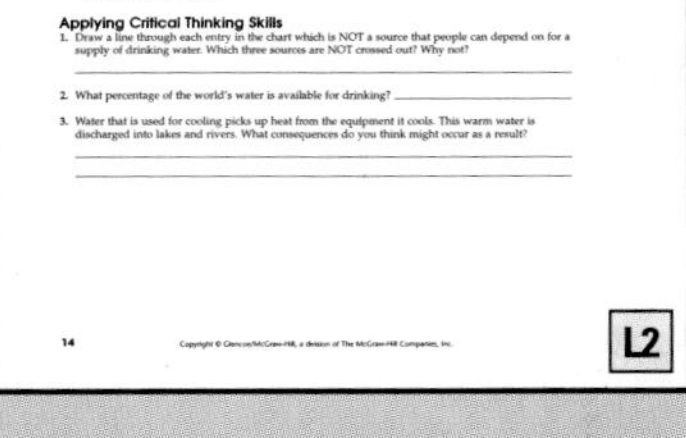

Cross-Curricular Integration

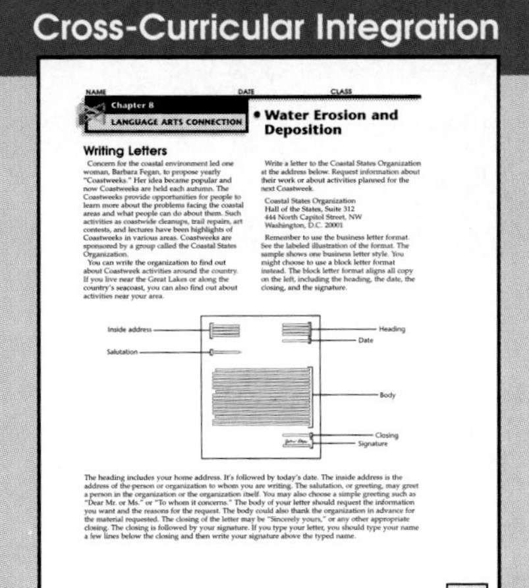

Science and Society Integration

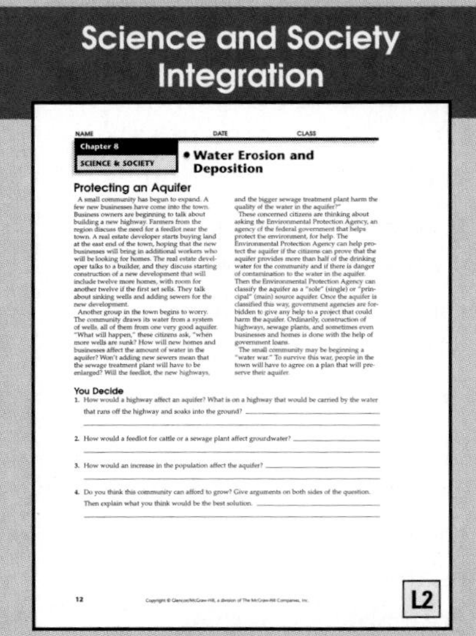

Technology Integration

Multicultural Connections

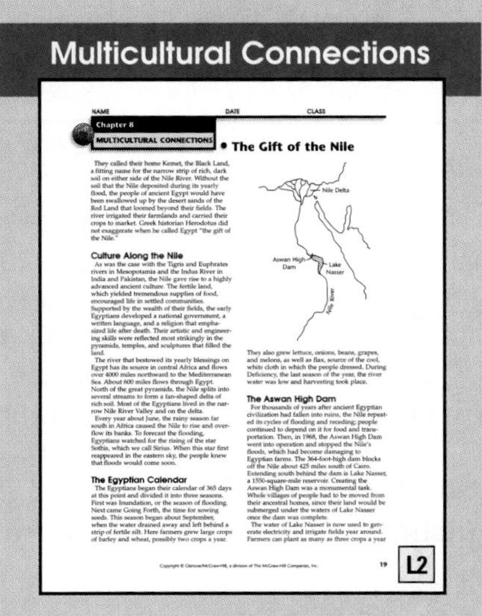

Concept Mapping

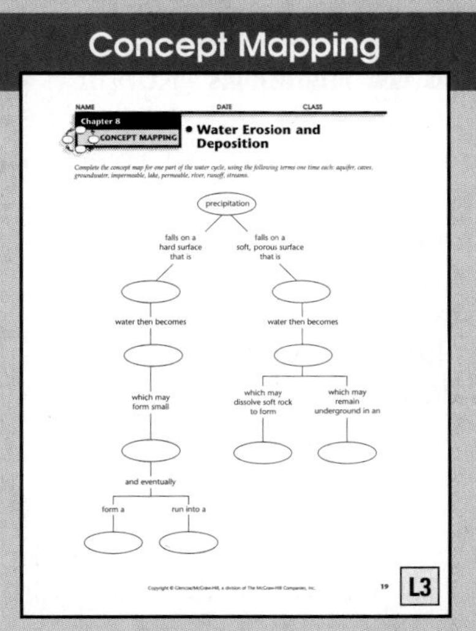

Chapter 8

Water Erosion and Deposition

CHAPTER OVERVIEW

Section 8-1 This section discusses surface water as an important agent of erosion and deposition.

Section 8-2 This section defines groundwater and explains how it flows through and changes soil and rocks.

Section 8-3 Science and Society The problem of a limited water supply in some regions is discussed. Conflicts exist between conserving natural resources and diverting water for human use.

Section 8-4 This section examines erosion and deposition along shorelines.

Chapter Vocabulary

runoff	zone of saturation
rill erosion	water table
gully erosion	artesian well
sheet erosion	spring
drainage basin	hot spring
meander	geyser
floodplain	cave
alluvial fan	longshore current
delta	beach
groundwater	barrier island
permeable	
impermeable	
aquifer	

Theme Connection

Systems and Interactions Runoff goes to streams, and streams join to eventually form river systems. Water flowing through pores in rocks forms the groundwater system. Ocean water interacts with shorelines to create erosional and depositional features.

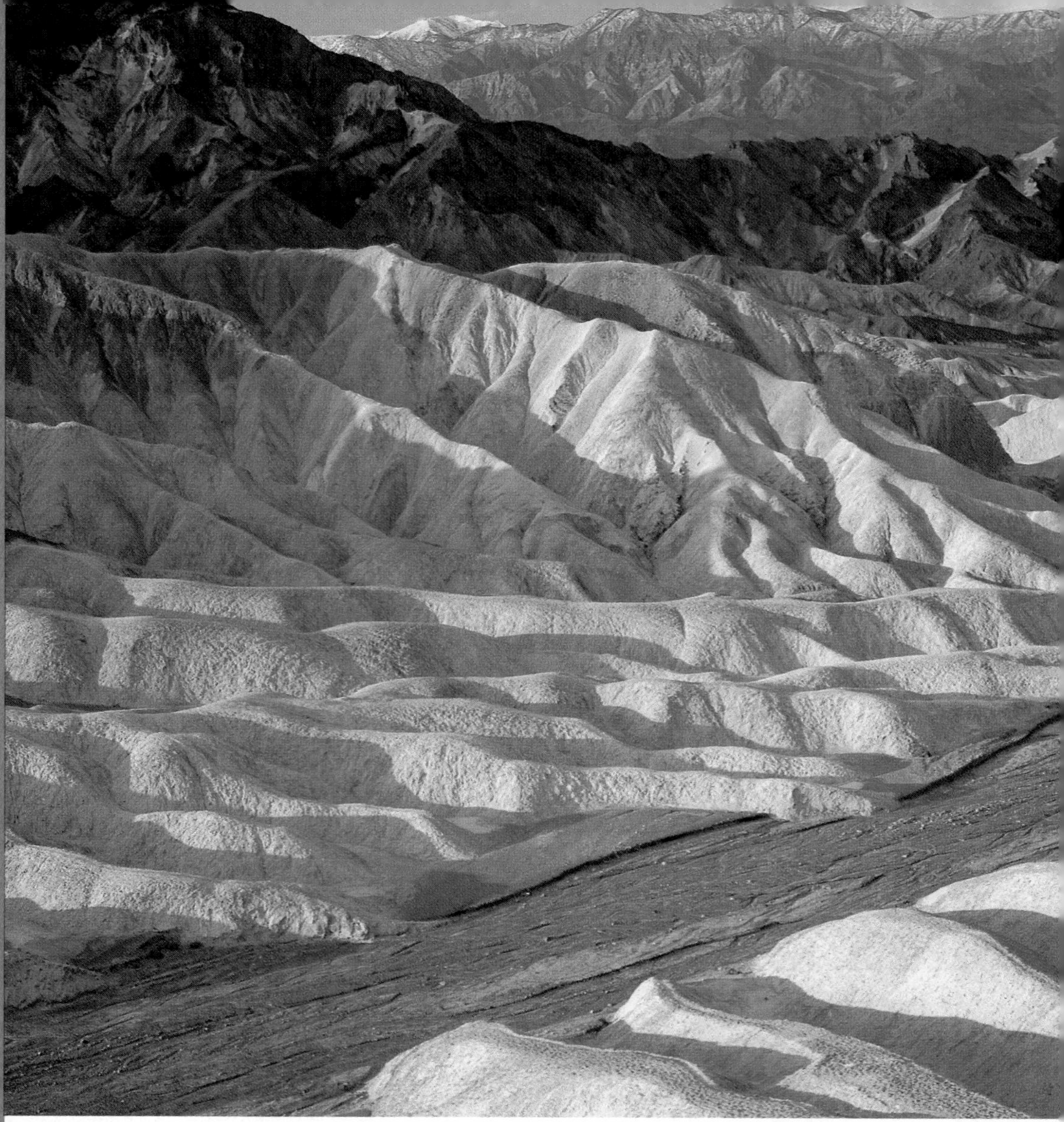

Previewing the Chapter

Look for the following logo for strategies that emphasize different learning modalities. 

Kinesthetic	Explore, p. 201
Visual-Spatial	Visual Learning, pp. 205, 207-209, 213, 217, 223, 224; MiniLAB, p. 206; Reteach, pp. 212, 217; Activity 8-2, p. 225; Science & History, p. 219
Interpersonal	Enrichment, p. 204; Activity 8-1, pp. 210-211; Science & History, p. 219; Reteach, p. 221
Logical-Mathematical	MiniLAB, p. 216
Linguistic	Science Journal, pp. 217, 220, 223

Chapter 8

Water Erosion and Deposition

Do you know what caused the patterns in this landscape? Water! It erodes more sediments than any other agent of erosion. It's easy to see why—moving water has great energy of motion. Sometimes rainwater just soaks into sediments, other times it moves down the slope because of gravity's pull. What factors do you think determine whether rain soaks into the ground or runs off and erodes the surface?

EXPLORE ACTIVITY

Things That Affect Water Erosion

1. Place a piece of waxed paper on your desktop.
2. Make a mound of dry soil on top of the paper.
3. Slowly drip water from an eyedropper onto your mound and observe what happens.
4. Drip the water more quickly and continue to observe what happens.
5. Repeat the 4 previous steps, but this time change the slope of your mound. Start again with dry soil.

Observe: In your Science Journal, record how the time over which rain falls and the slope of the land affect how much erosion takes place.

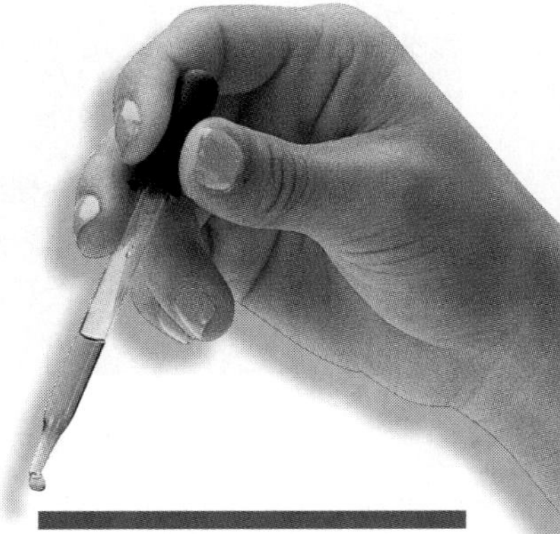

Previewing Science Skills

- In the **Skill Builders**, you will **compare and contrast**, and **map concepts.**
- In the **Activities**, you will **hypothesize, design an experiment, observe, classify,** and **interpret data.**
- In the **MiniLABs,** you will **make a model, observe and infer,** and **record observations.**

Assessment Planner

Portfolio
Refer to page 227 for suggested items that students might select for their portfolios.

Performance Assessment
See page 227 for additional Performance Assessment options.
Skill Builders, pp. 213, 218, 226
MiniLABs, pp. 206, 216
Activities 8-1, pp. 210-211; 8-2, p. 225

Content Assessment
Section Wrap-ups, pp. 213, 218, 221, 226
Chapter Review, pp. 227-229
Mini Quizzes, pp. 213, 218, 226

Group Assessment
Opportunities for group assessment occur with Cooperative Learning Strategies and Flex Your Brain Activities.

EXPLORE ACTIVITY

Purpose

LS **Kinesthetic** Use the Explore Activity to help students discover how both the time span over which rain falls and the slope of the land affect erosion. L1 COOP LEARN

Preparation

Before doing this activity, be sure the soil that students will be using is dry. To dry it, place the soil on a cookie sheet and bake it on a low oven setting.

Materials

dry soil, waxed paper, paper towels, and an eyedropper for each student group

Teaching Strategies

In step 3, have students slowly drip their drops onto the same place on their mound, one on top of another. In step 4, have them select another place on their mound with the same grade as they used in step 3 to quickly drip their drops on top of one another.

Observe

Students will state that when the time span over which rain falls is short, there is more erosion. On a steeper slope, there is more erosion.

Assessment

Performance Have students design an experiment to see how the kind of sediment that a slope is made of affects its erosion. Use the Performance Task Assessment List for Designing an Experiment in **PASC,** p. 23. P

Section 8•1

Prepare

Section Background

- A drainage basin is separated from other basins by high ground called a divide. As a river system evolves, rills and gullies erode the divide. With time, the divide becomes more and more narrow.
- Major drainage patterns include dendritic drainage, which resembles a tree; rectangular drainage, which forms when bedrock is fractured; trellis drainage, which results from an area's being covered with hard and soft bedrock; and radial drainage, which forms when a central structure is a part of the landscape.

Preplanning

- To prepare for the MiniLAB, obtain large pans and soil.
- To prepare for Activity 8-1, obtain the materials listed on page 210.

1 Motivate

Bellringer

Before presenting the lesson, display **Section Focus Transparency 29** on the overhead projector. Assign the accompanying **Focus Activity** worksheet. L1 LEP

Tying to Previous Knowledge

Have students recall from Chapter 6 the importance of water in weathering sediments. In this section, they will learn that once weathered, sediments also can be eroded by water.

8•1 Surface Water

Science Words

- runoff
- rill erosion
- gully erosion
- sheet erosion
- drainage basin
- meander
- floodplain
- alluvial fan
- delta

Objectives

- Explain what causes runoff.
- Compare rill, sheet, gully, and stream erosion.
- Discuss the three different stages of stream development.
- Describe how alluvial fans and deltas form.

Runoff

Water that doesn't soak into the ground or evaporate flows across Earth's surface and is called **runoff.** If you've ever spilled milk while pouring it, you've experienced something similar to runoff. You can picture it in your mind. You start pouring a glass of milk, but it overflows, spilling all over the table. Then, before you can grab a towel to clean up the mess, the milk runs off the table and onto the floor. This is similar to what happens to rainwater that doesn't soak into the ground or evaporate. It runs along the ground and eventually enters streams, lakes, or the ocean.

Factors Affecting Runoff

But what factors determine whether rain soaks into the ground or runs off? The amount of rain and the time span over which it falls are two factors that affect the amount of runoff. Light rain falling over several hours will probably have time to soak into the ground. Heavy rain falling in less than an hour or so will run off because it doesn't have time to soak in.

Another factor that affects the amount of runoff is the slope of the land. Gentle slopes and flat areas hold water in place, giving it a chance to evaporate or sink into the ground. On steep slopes, however, gravity causes the water to run off before either of these things can happen.

A

B

Figure 8-1

In areas with gentle slopes and abundant vegetation, as in A, there is little runoff and erosion. In areas such as B, the lack of vegetation has lead to severe soil erosion.

Program Resources

Reproducible Masters

Study Guide, p. 33 L1
Reinforcement, p. 33 L1
Enrichment, p. 33 L3
Activity Worksheets, pp. 48-49, 52 L1
Science Integration Activities, pp. 15-16
Lab Manual 25
Multicultural Connections, pp. 19-20

Transparencies

Section Focus Transparency 29 L1
Teaching Transparency 15

As you can see in **Figure 8-1,** the amount of vegetation, such as grass, also affects the amount of runoff. Just like milk running off the table, water will tend to run off smooth surfaces that have little or no vegetation. Plants and their roots act like sponges to soak up and hold water. By slowing down runoff, plants and roots help prevent the erosion of soil.

Figure 8-2

During floods, the high volume of fast-moving water erodes large amounts of soil.

The Effects of Gravity

INTEGRATION
Physics

Gravity is the attracting force all objects have for one another. The greater the mass of an object, the greater its force of gravity. Because Earth has a much greater mass than any of the objects on it, Earth's gravitational force pulls objects toward its center of mass. Water falling down a slope is evidence of gravity. As objects drop to Earth's surface, they pick up speed. This happens because gravity is a constant accelerating force. On Earth, for example, a falling object moves 9.8 meters per second faster than it did during the previous second. Thus, when water falls down a slope, it picks up speed. Its energy of motion is much greater, and, as shown in **Figure 8-2,** it erodes more quickly than slower-moving water.

Use Lab 25 in the **Lab Manual** as you teach this lesson.

2 Teach

Inquiry Questions

- After students have read the information about runoff, pose the questions. **What happens to water that doesn't soak into the ground or evaporate?** *It becomes runoff.* **What factors affect runoff?** *amount of rain, time span over which rain falls, slope of land, amount of vegetation*
- **Predict what happens to the amount of runoff from an area when an asphalt parking lot is built on top of the soil.** *Runoff increases because the asphalt prevents water from soaking into the ground.*

INTEGRATION Physics

All objects near Earth's surface fall at the same rate of acceleration. As they fall, they encounter air resistance. The amount of air resistance depends on the size, shape, and speed of the falling object. The air resistance increases as the speed of the falling object increases. When the air resistance (the upward force) equals the downward force of gravity, the object no longer accelerates. Its velocity is constant.

GLENCOE TECHNOLOGY

CD-ROM

Earth Science CD-ROM

Have students perform the interactive exploration for Chapter 8 to reinforce important chapter concepts and thinking processes.

Inquiry Question

Have students explain how rill erosion could evolve into gully erosion. *If a stream flows along the same path for a substantial amount of time, the channel becomes wider and deeper.*

Enrichment

- Have students research what happens to local runoff. L3
- Have students experiment with growing a variety of plants on a constant slope. The purpose of their experiments is to see which plants are best in reducing runoff and soil erosion. Have them write a report on their results to place in their portfolios. L3 P

LS **Interpersonal** Have student groups see how different surfaces affect runoff. Each team will need a paint tray half filled with soil, a piece of cardboard, a clump of grass, and a beaker of water. Have students design and execute an experiment using the cardboard to simulate a paved street and the clump of grass to simulate a grassy field. L1
COOP LEARN

STV: Restless Earth

Colorado River, Grand Canyon; Arizona

52244

Kawerong Delta; Papua New Guinea

52247

Murray River; Australia

52246

CONNECT TO **PHYSICS**

Energy is the ability to cause change or to do work. There are two types of energy, potential energy and kinetic energy. Potential energy is stored energy. Kinetic energy is energy in motion. ***Infer*** which type of energy the water eroding the stream channel below is demonstrating.

Water Erosion

Suppose you and several friends walk the same way to school each day through a field or empty lot, always walking in the same footsteps as you did the day before. By now, you've worn a path through the field. Water also wears a path as it travels down a slope.

Rill and Gully Erosion

You may have seen a scar or small channel on the side of a slope that was left behind by running water. This is evidence of rill erosion. **Rill erosion** begins when a small stream forms during a heavy rain. As this stream flows along, it has enough energy to carry away plants and soil. There's a scar left on the slope where the water eroded the plants and soil. If a stream frequently flows in the same path, rill erosion may evolve into gully erosion.

In **gully erosion,** a rill channel becomes broader and deeper. Large amounts of soil are removed to form a gully as shown in **Figure 8-3**.

Figure 8-3

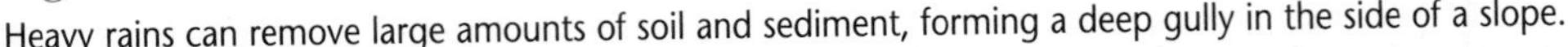
Heavy rains can remove large amounts of soil and sediment, forming a deep gully in the side of a slope.

Sheet Erosion

Water often erodes without being in a stream channel. For example, when it rains over a fairly flat area, the rainwater accumulates until it eventually begins moving down a gentle slope. **Sheet erosion** happens when rainwater flows into lower elevations, carrying sediments with it, as shown in **Figure 8-4.** In these lower elevations, the water loses some of its energy of motion and it drains into the soil or slowly evaporates.

Figure 8-4

The runoff that causes sheet erosion eventually loses its energy of motion. The sediments left behind cover the soil like a sheet.

Stream Erosion

Sometimes water continues to flow along a depression it has created. It then becomes a stream like the one shown in **Figure 8-5.** As the water in a stream moves along, it constantly picks up sediments from the bottom and sides of its channel. Water picks up and carries some of the lightweight sediments, while large, heavy particles just roll along the bottom of the stream channel. All of these different-sized materials scrape against the bottom and sides of the channel, where they continue to knock loose more sediments. Because of this, a stream continually cuts a deeper and wider channel.

Figure 8-5

This is a cross section of a typical stream channel. *How will the shape of this channel change over time?*

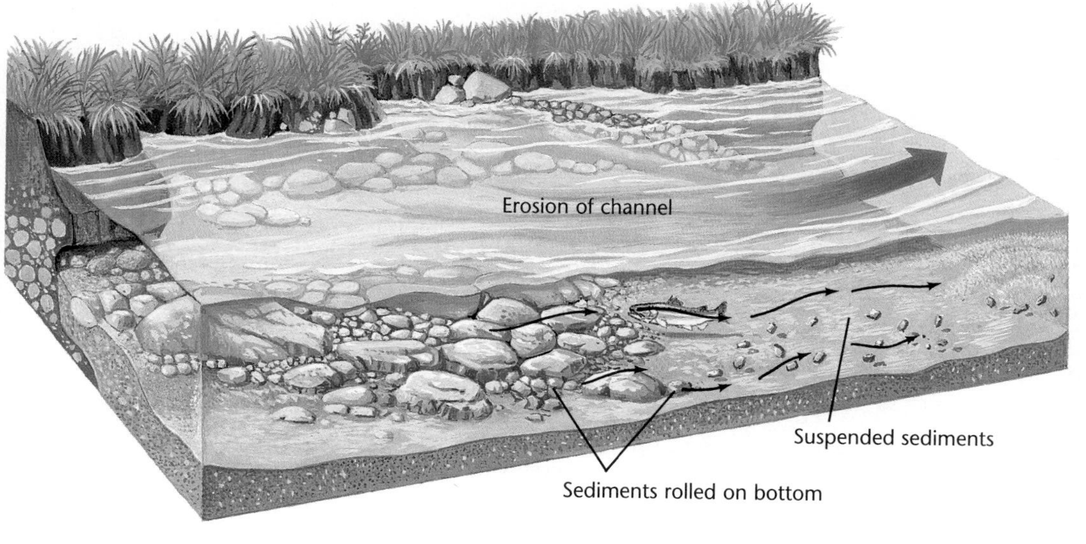

CONNECT TO

PHYSICS

Answer Water flowing downstream is an example of kinetic energy.

Activity

Take students outside to look for evidence of water erosion around the school grounds. Some things they might find include small channel scars on the sides of slopes or low, flat areas where fine sediments have been deposited.

Discussion

Have students contrast the runoff from paved streets and grassy fields during both a thunderstorm and a gentle rain.

Visual Learning

Figure 8-5 How will the shape of this channel change over time? *It will get wider and deeper.* LEP 

GLENCOE TECHNOLOGY

 **Videodisc**

STVS: Physics

Disc 1, Side 2

Cutting with Water (Ch. 9)

Community Connection

Construction Sites Arrange for a local contractor or a city engineer to visit the class. Ask the person to explain how construction areas are evaluated in terms of runoff and drainage. The students may be able to visit a construction site to see the work firsthand. This would be a good opportunity to discuss career options in this area.

MiniLAB

Purpose

Visual-Spatial Students will observe stream erosion. L1 LEP COOP LEARN

Materials

large pan, soil, pencil

Teaching Strategies

Explain to students that they should observe the erosion that occurs on the inside and the outside of the stream channel as it turns.

Analysis

1. It erodes the most sediments along the outside of the curves.
2. In a curving stream, the rate of erosion along the sides of the stream is greater on the outside of curves than on the inside of curves.

Assessment

Performance To further assess students' understanding of where most erosion occurs, before using the water, have them place markers such as golf tees on the inside and outside of the curves in their channel. Have them measure the distance from each marker to the center of the streambed. At the end of the experiment, have students measure marker distances again. Use the Performance Task Assessment List for Carrying Out a Strategy and Collecting Data in **PASC**, p. 25. P

Activity Worksheets, pp. 5, 52

MiniLAB

Where does most erosion occur in a stream?

Procedure

1. Fill a large pan with soil.
2. Use the edge of a ruler or a pencil to level the soil, and use your hands to gently pack it down.
3. With your finger or a pencil, make a stream channel in the soil. Put several bends or turns in the channel so that the water will not be able to flow along a straight path.
4. Lay a pencil under one end of the pan so that you create a gradual slope.
5. Slowly pour water from a beaker into the channel from the higher end of the pan.

Analysis

1. Describe where the stream erodes the most sediments.
2. Describe how the path of a stream of running water affects the rate at which erosion takes place.

River System Development

Is there a stream in your neighborhood or town? Maybe you've been fishing or swimming in that stream. Each day, thousands of liters of water flow through your neighborhood or town in that stream. Where does all the water come from?

River Systems

The stream in your neighborhood is really a part of a river system. The water in the stream came from rills, gullies, and smaller streams located upstream. Just as the tree in **Figure 8-6** is a system containing twigs, branches, and a trunk, a river system also has many parts. Water runs off of the ground and enters small streams. Where small streams join, a larger stream forms. Finally, these larger streams merge, forming a larger body of water called a *river.*

Figure 8-6

River systems can be compared with the structure of a tree.

A: A large portion of the streams and rivers in the United States are part of the Mississippi River drainage basin. *What river represents the "trunk" of the river system?*

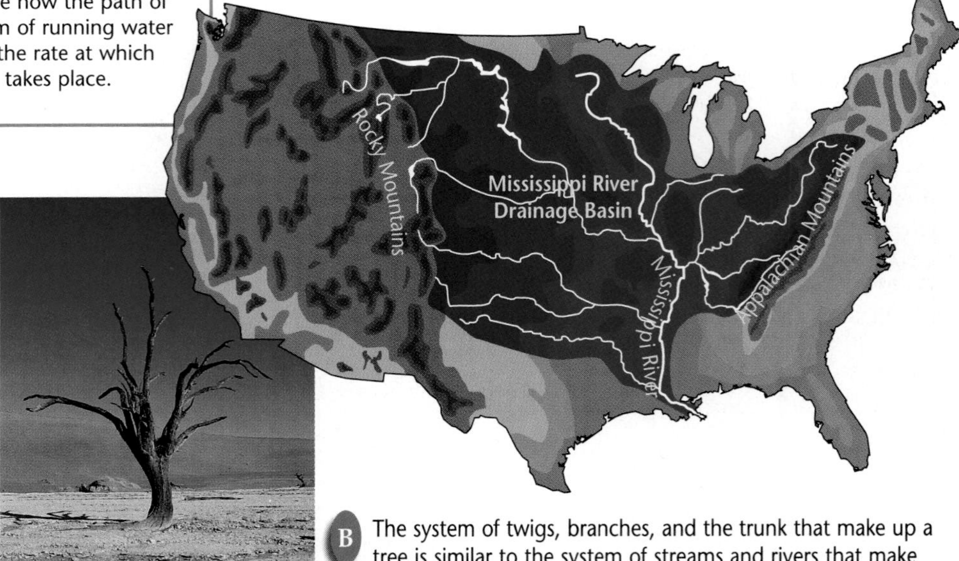

B: The system of twigs, branches, and the trunk that make up a tree is similar to the system of streams and rivers that make up a river system.

Use **Teaching Transparency 15** as you teach this lesson.

Drainage Basins

The land area from which a stream gets its water is called a **drainage basin.** A drainage basin can be compared to a bathtub. Water that collects in a bathtub flows toward the drain. Likewise, all of the water in a river system eventually flows to one location—the main river. The largest drainage basin in the United States is the Mississippi River drainage basin.

Stages of Stream Development

There are many different types of streams. Some are narrow and swift–moving, and others are very wide and slow–moving. Streams differ because they are in different stages of development. These stages depend on the slope of the ground over which the stream flows. Streams are classified as young, mature, or old. **Figure 8-7,** on the next two pages, describes how each of the stages comes together to form a drainage basin.

The stages of development aren't always related to the age of a river. The New River in West Virginia, for example, is one of the oldest rivers in North America. However, it has a steep valley and cascades through raging rapids.

Problem Solving

Washed Out

Suppose you are really looking forward to Friday, when your class plans to have a picnic at the park next to the river. You live in an area of the state near where two smaller rivers meet to form the larger river next to the park. Weather reports tell you that northern areas of the state have had heavy rain, and more is expected over the next few days. It's been really cloudy where you live, but so far it hasn't rained.

Friday comes. There's a fine mist in the air, but it still hasn't rained in your town. It's early in the morning, but you decide to go to the park early to help set up. You pedal your bike to the park. Much to your surprise, the picnic area next to the river is underwater and the picnic must be canceled.

Think Critically:

How can the park be flooded if it didn't rain in your area?

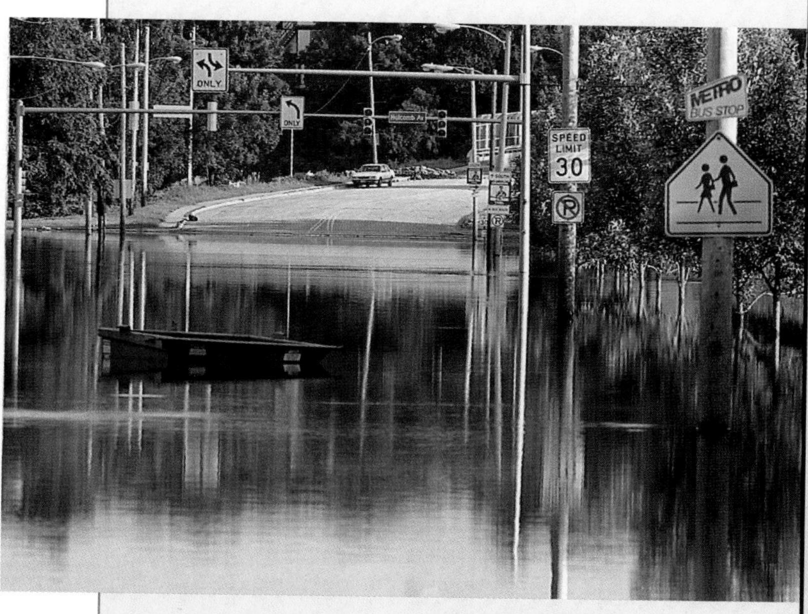

Student Text Questions

See p. 206

- **Is there a stream in your neighborhood or town?** *Answers will vary depending on location. Have a map of your area available for students to examine.*
- **But just where does that water come from?** *Answers will vary. Have students refer to a map and look at areas upstream.*

Visual Learning

Figure 8-6A What river represents the "trunk" of the river system? *the Mississippi River* Have students trace the pattern of this drainage system from its source to its mouth. They should use Appendix H on page 716 to name several of the major tributaries of the Mississippi. Have students discuss why the main river follows the path it does. LEP IS

Problem Solving

Think Critically

The river flooded due to runoff from the land in the upstream areas of the state. The river next to the park was a part of the same drainage system as the streams farther north. Locations downstream from heavy rainfall are subject to flooding.

Community Connection

Local Erosion Have students photograph places where water erosion has occurred in the community. L1

Visual Learning

Figure 8-7A Would you expect to see the water moving rapidly or slowly in a young stream? *rapidly*

Figure 8-7B Would you expect to see many large rapids or waterfalls along a mature stream? *No, most mature streams flow over less steep land than where rapids and waterfalls are located.* LEP LS

Discussion

Ask students how the erosional energy of a stream changes as it matures. Stress that as a stream matures, its erosional energy is no longer concentrated along its bottom. Streams begin meandering because the velocity of the water varies throughout the width of the channel. On the side of the stream where the current is strongest, erosion is greatest.

Inquiry Question

Explain why most whitewater rafting is done in young rivers. *These rivers flow downhill with enough energy to form rapids. Older rivers cannot provide the thrilling rides that young rivers can.*

Videodisc

GTV: Planetary Manager

Water, Water Everywhere

Show 2.7, Side 2

38779-41076

Figure 8-7

Streams of all stages of development can be found in most major river systems.

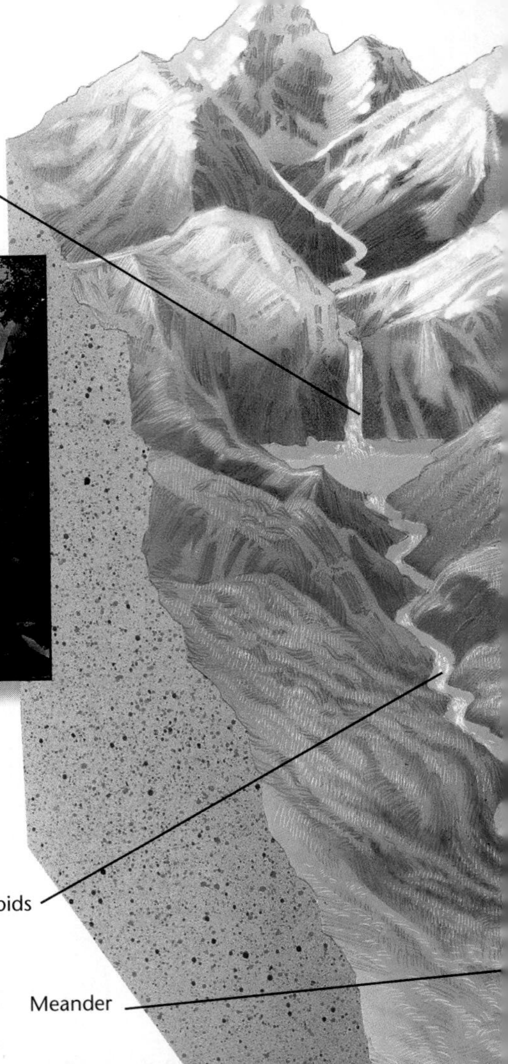

Waterfall

Rapids

Meander

A Young streams are found in mountainous or hilly regions and flow down steep slopes. *Would you expect to see the water moving rapidly or slowly in a young stream?*

Young Streams

A stream that flows swiftly through a steep valley and has steep sides is a young stream. A young stream may have whitewater rapids and waterfalls. Because the water is flowing rapidly downhill, it has a high level of energy and erodes the stream bottom more than its sides.

Mature Streams

The next stage in the development of a stream is the mature stage. A mature stream flows less swiftly through its valley. Most of the rocks in the stream bed that cause waterfalls and rapids have been eroded away.

The erosional energy of a mature stream is no longer concentrated on its bottom. Now, the stream starts to erode more along its sides, developing curves. These curves form because the speed of the water varies throughout the width of the channel.

Water in shallow areas of a stream is slowed down by the friction created by the bottom of the river. In deep areas, less of the water comes in contact with the bottom. This means that deep water has less friction with the bottom of the stream and therefore flows faster. This faster-moving water erodes the side of the stream where the current is strongest, forming curves. A curve that forms in this way is called a **meander. Figure 8-7C** shows what a meandering stream looks like from the air.

B A curving stream that flows down a gradual slope is a mature stream. *Would you expect to see many large rapids or waterfalls along a mature stream? Explain.*

Integrating the Sciences

Physical Science Take students to a local stream. Have them determine the velocity both at the middle and at the edge of the stream by measuring 10 m along the bank and timing how long it takes a fishing bob to float the 10 m. Velocity equals distance divided by time. Tell students erosion is greatest where the velocity is greatest. Have them determine where in the stream erosion is greatest. L1 COOP LEARN

Use **Multicultural Connections,** pp. 19-20, as you teach this lesson.

The broad, flat valley floor carved by a meandering stream is called a **floodplain.** When a stream floods, it will often cover a part of or the whole floodplain.

Old Streams

The last stage in the development of a stream is the old stage. An old stream flows slowly through a broad, flat floodplain that it has carved. The lower Mississippi River is in the old stage.

Major river systems usually contain streams in all stages of development. At the outer edges of a river system, you find whitewater streams moving swiftly down mountains and hills. At the bottom of mountains and hills, you find streams that are starting to meander and are in the mature stage of development. These streams meet at the trunk of the drainage basin to form a major river.

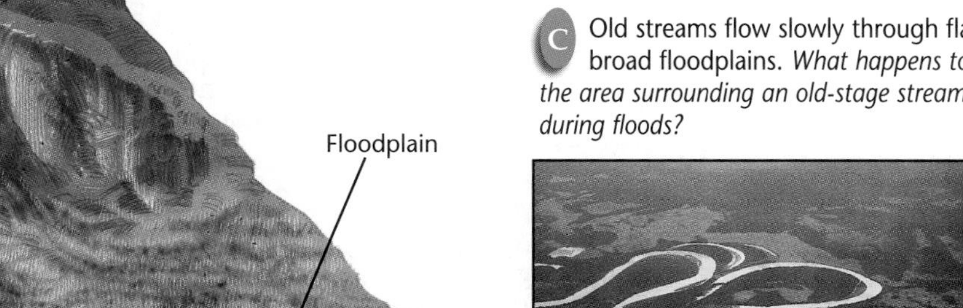

C Old streams flow slowly through flat, broad floodplains. *What happens to the area surrounding an old-stage stream during floods?*

Visual Learning

Figure 8-6A Have students look again at this figure and answer the question: **Where are the youngest parts of the drainage system? Where is the older part?** *The young rivers are at the outer edges of the system in the mountains and hills. The oldest part of the system is the Mississippi River itself.*

Figure 8-7C What happens to the area surrounding an old-stage stream during a flood? *It is covered with water.* Have a volunteer compare and contrast young and mature streams. LEP LS

Enrichment

Have students research the erosional effects of the Colorado or Mississippi Rivers. L2 P

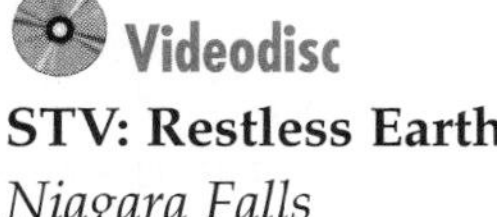

Videodisc

STV: Restless Earth

Niagara Falls

52243

River carrying sediment

52245

Sandbar; Georgia

52248

Across the Curriculum

History Have students do some research to find out how, because the Rio Grande meanders, the border between the United States and Mexico, which is formed by the river, has changed over time. Mexico has had to cede some land to the United States. L2

Activity 8-1

PREPARATION

Purpose

LS **Interpersonal** To observe both the effect of slope on the speed of a stream and the effect of stream speed on streambed erosion. L1

COOP LEARN

Process Skills

designing an experiment, forming a hypothesis, communicating, making a model, observing and inferring, recognizing cause and effect, making and using tables, separating and controlling variables, interpreting data

Time

45 minutes to plan the experiment, 45 minutes to do the experiment

Materials

Pans should be as large as possible. If stream tables are available, they may be used for large groups of students.

Possible Hypotheses

Students might hypothesize that the steeper the slope of a stream, the greater the stream's speed. They might hypothesize that the greater the speed of a stream, the greater the erosion.

Activity Worksheets, pp. 5, 48-49

PLAN THE EXPERIMENT

Possible Procedures

- Students might level the sand in their pan with a pencil and use a pencil to make a stream channel in the sand. They might place one wooden block under one end of the pan. A bucket could be placed below the low end of the pan to catch overflow. Students might use a meterstick to measure the length

Activity 8-1

Design Your Own Experiment

Stream Speed

Have you ever wondered what it would be like to make a raft and use it to float on a river? Do you think that guiding a raft would be easy? Probably not. You'd be at the mercy of the current. The greater the speed of the river, the stronger the current.

PREPARATION

Problem

What factors affect a stream's speed? How does the speed of a stream affect the water's ability to erode?

Form a Hypothesis

Think about streams you have observed, then consider various factors that may affect how fast a stream flows. Do you think the slope of a stream affects its speed? Do you think the speed of a stream affects the amount of erosion that takes place? Form a hypothesis about how the slope of a stream affects the speed of a stream. Form another hypothesis about how the speed of a stream affects erosion.

Objectives

- Design and carry out an experiment to show the relationship between the slope of a stream bed and a stream's speed.
- Design and carry out an experiment to show the relationship between the speed of a stream and a stream's ability to erode.
- Observe the effects of slope of a stream on speed of the stream.
- Observe the effects of speed of a stream on erosion.

Possible Materials

- a large pan or stream table
- sand to fill the pan or stream table
- plastic pails (2)
- rubber tubing
- meterstick
- small cork
- water
- stopwatch
- wooden blocks

210

Inclusion Strategies

Physically Challenged Have students who have difficulty performing the experiment be in charge of formulating and evaluating the hypotheses.

PLAN THE EXPERIMENT

1. As a group, agree upon and write out the hypotheses statements.
2. As a group, list the steps that you need to take to test your hypotheses. Include in your plan how you will (a) make your stream channel, (b) adjust the height of the slope, (c) measure the length of the stream channel, (d) use tubing and one of the pails to begin the water flowing down the stream, (e) catch the overflow water at the other end of the stream table or pan with your other pail, (f) determine the time it takes the cork to flow down the stream channel, and (g) observe the amount of erosion that takes place.
3. You will need a data table. Design one in your Science Journal so that it is ready to use as your group collects data.

Check the Plan

1. Read over your entire plan to make sure that all steps are in logical order.
2. Identify any constants and the variables of the experiment.
3. Have you allowed for a control in your experiment?
4. Do you have to run any tests more than one time?
5. Will the data be summarized in graphs? Decide which type of graph to use.
6. *Make sure your teacher approves your plan and that you have included any changes suggested in the plan.*

DO THE EXPERIMENT

1. Carry out the experiment as planned.
2. While the experiment is going on, write down any observations that you make and complete the data tables in your Science Journal.

Analyze and Apply

1. **Calculate** the speed of your streams using the formula: speed = $\frac{\text{distance}}{\text{time}}$.
2. Were sediments carried along with the water to the end of your stream channels?
3. Did the slope affect the speed of the streams in your experiment?
4. Did the streams with the greatest or least slopes erode the most sediments?

Go Further

Repeat your experiment, but this time see if you can devise a way to collect and measure the amount of erosion that takes place on different slopes.

of the stream channel. One student could siphon the water from one pail into the high end of the stream channel while a second student places a cork into the water at the top of the channel. A third student could use a stopwatch to time the cork's trip from the top of the stream channel to the bottom. By dividing the length of the streambed by the cork's travel time, students can determine the speed of the stream. Students could observe the amount of erosion by examining the sediments that have collected at the low end of the pan and in the overflow bucket. Students could repeat the experiment several times and average their results.

- Students could repeat the experiment using two blocks stacked on top of one another to make a steeper slope.

Teaching Strategies

Troubleshooting Demonstrate to students how to use the rubber tubing to siphon water from one of the pails into their streambed.

DO THE EXPERIMENT

Expected Outcome

Students will observe that both stream speed and erosion increase when the slope is greater.

Analyze and Apply

1. Answers will vary, but the stream with the greater slope will have a greater speed.
2. yes
3. Yes, the greater the slope, the greater the speed of the stream.
4. The stream with the greatest slope did.

Go Further

Students might scoop up the sediments that have collected in the low end of the pan and those in the overflow bucket. After evaporating the water, only sediments will remain. By using a balance, students could measure the mass of the eroded sediments.

Assessment

Performance To further assess students' understanding of streams, have student teams design a way to test the effect of stream shape on the speed of a stream. Use the Performance Task Assessment List for Designing an Experiment in **PASC**, p. 23. P

USING TECHNOLOGY

- Approximately 12% of the population of the United States lives on land that periodically floods.
- On a floodplain where there are no levees, floodwaters spread over a wide area where the soil can absorb some of the water.

Think Critically

Levees built upstream prevented the water from spreading out from the river banks; therefore, the water that remained was funneled to places downstream at great speed. Fast-moving water erodes more sediments than slow-moving water.

3 Assess

Check for Understanding

FLEX Your Brain

Use the Flex Your Brain activity to have students explore DRAINAGE BASINS.

Activity Worksheets, p. 5

Reteach

Visual-Spatial Have students examine rivers shown on maps or in photographs. Ask students to classify these rivers as being young, mature, or old rivers. LEP

Extension

For students who have mastered this section, use the **Reinforcement** and **Enrichment** masters.

USING TECHNOLOGY

Taming a River

A river that overflows its banks can bring disaster. Such was the case in the Mississippi River flood of 1993 when parts of nine Midwestern states were under water.

For many years, people living along the Mississippi River have relied on levees and dams to keep out floodwaters. Levees are earthen barriers built along rivers. Dams are structures that block the flow of water, causing it to build up behind the dam into a reservoir lake.

Both levees and dams can prevent damage to cities and farms when the flooding is not too extreme. But during the flood of 1993, the levees and dams couldn't keep out the water. In fact, the funneling effect caused by the levees caused the floodwaters to move faster and deeper than they would have if the levees had not been there.

Think Critically:

Describe in your Science Journal how levees that were built upstream contributed to increased erosion problems downstream.

Mississippi River Levee Breaking

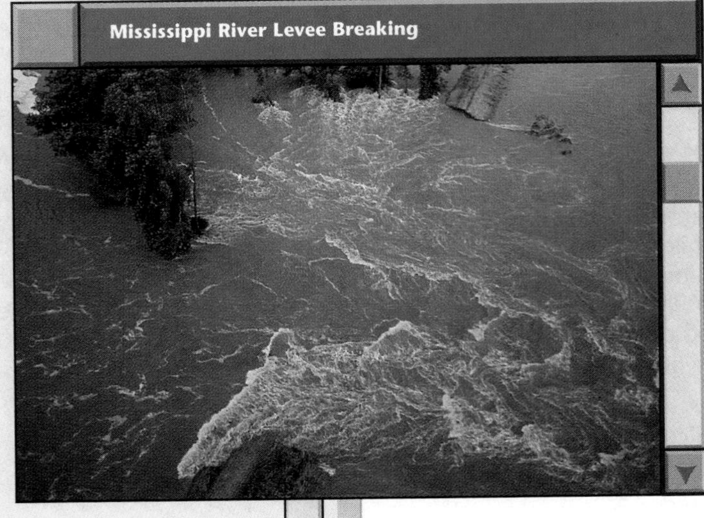

Deposition by Surface Water

As water moves throughout a river system, what do you suppose happens as it loses some of its energy of motion? The water can no longer carry some of its sediments, and they are deposited.

Some stream sediments aren't carried very far at all before they are deposited. In fact, many sediments are deposited within the stream channel itself. Other stream sediments travel great distances before they are deposited. Sediments picked up when rill and gully erosion occur are examples. Water usually has a lot of energy of motion as it moves down a steep slope. When the water begins flowing on a level surface, it slows down, loses energy of motion, and drops its sediments.

Across the Curriculum

Language Have students find out how deltas got their name. They will learn that both the Greek capital letter delta (Δ) and the deposit have a triangular shape. L1

Geography Have students use Appendix H to explain how sediments on a hillside in Memphis, Tennessee, might end up in the Mississippi Delta. Students should conclude that sediments eroded from the hillside by rill and gully erosion are carried to a local stream, which eventually feeds into the Mississippi River. When the river enters the Gulf of Mexico, it loses its energy of motion and deposits the sediments. L1

Figure 8-8

Alluvial fans commonly occur at the base of steep mountain slopes. *How does the amount and type of vegetation effect the alluvial fan?*

One type of deposit that results, an **alluvial fan,** is shaped like a triangle as shown in **Figure 8-8.** If the sediments are not deposited until the water empties into an ocean, gulf, or lake, the deposit is known as a **delta.**

Let's use the Mississippi River as an example to tie all of this section together. Runoff causes rill and gully erosion as it picks up sediments and carries them into the larger streams that flow into the Mississippi River. The Mississippi is quite large and has a lot of energy. It can erode many sediments. As it flows, it cuts into its banks and picks up more sediments. In other places, where the land is flat, the river deposits some of its sediments in its own channel.

Eventually, the Mississippi River reaches the Gulf of Mexico. There it flows into the gulf, loses most of its energy of motion, and dumps its sediments in a large deposit on the Louisiana coast. This deposit, shown in **Figure 8-9,** is the Mississippi Delta.

Figure 8-9

This satellite image of the Mississippi Delta shows how sediments accumulate when the Mississippi River empties into the Gulf of Mexico.

Section Wrap-up

Review

1. How does the slope of an area affect its runoff?
2. Describe the three stages of stream development.
3. **Think Critically:** How is a stream's rate of flow related to the amount of erosion it causes and the size of the sediments it deposits?

Skill Builder

Comparing and Contrasting

Compare and contrast alluvial fans and deltas. If you need help, refer to Comparing and Contrasting in the **Skill Handbook.**

Using Computers

Spreadsheet Design a table using spreadsheet software to compare and contrast sheet, rill, gully, and stream erosion.

Skill Builder

Both form when water flows onto a level surface, loses velocity, and deposits sediments. Alluvial fans are common at the bases of mountains. Deltas form where water empties into an ocean, gulf, or lake.

Assessment

Process Have students use their answers to the Skill Builder to draw pictures of alluvial fans and deltas. Use the Performance Task Assessment List for Scientific Drawing in **PASC,** p. 55. P

Visual Learning

Figure 8-8 How does the amount and type of vegetation affect the alluvial fan? *Vegetation traps sediments. Vegetation that is low to the ground will have more effect than vegetation that has more vertical growth.* LEP LS

4 Close

•MINI•QUIZ•

1. **A(n) ______ consists of small and large merging streams.** *river system*
2. **The land area where a stream gets its water is a(n) ______ .** *drainage basin*
3. **Curves in mature streams are called _____ .** *meanders*

Section Wrap-up

Review

1. The greater the slope, the greater the runoff.
2. A youthful stream has a high level of energy and erodes the stream bottom more than its sides. A mature stream flows less swiftly, and erosion is concentrated along the sides of the stream. In an old stream, water meanders slowly through a broad, flat floodplain.
3. **Think Critically** The greater the stream's rate of flow, the greater the amount of erosion and the larger the sediment size it deposits.

Using Computers

Possible answers should include information on the sediments transported, slope steepness, and evidence for each type of erosion. P

Section 8•2

Prepare

Section Background

Most natural water contains carbonic acid because rainwater dissolves carbon dioxide from the air and from decaying plants. When groundwater comes in contact with limestone, the carbonic acid reacts with calcite in the rocks to form soluble calcium bicarbonate.

Preplanning

To prepare for the MiniLAB, obtain sand, gravel, beakers, and graduated cylinders.

1 Motivate

Bellringer

Before presenting the lesson, display **Section Focus Transparency 30** on the overhead projector. Assign the accompanying **Focus Activity** worksheet. L1 LEP

Tying to Previous Knowledge

Have students recall from Chapter 6 that water in soil leaches substances to lower horizons. Ask students where the water comes from to do this. It soaks into the soil from the surface.

8•2 Groundwater

Science Words

- groundwater
- permeable
- impermeable
- aquifer
- zone of saturation
- water table
- artesian well
- spring
- hot spring
- geyser
- cave

Objectives

- Describe the groundwater system.
- Explain the effect that soil and rock permeability have on groundwater movement.
- Describe ways that groundwater erodes and deposits sediments.

Groundwater System Development

What would have happened if the spilled milk in Section 8-1 had run off the table onto a carpeted floor? It would have quickly soaked into the carpet. Water that falls on Earth can also soak into the ground.

But what happens to the water then? Water that soaks into the ground becomes a part of a system, just as water that stays above ground becomes a part of a river system. You already know that soil is made up of many small rock fragments and that there is weathered rock beneath the soil. Between these fragments and pieces of weathered rock are spaces called pores, as shown in **Figure 8-10.** Water that soaks into the ground collects in these pores and becomes part of what is called **groundwater.**

Figure 8-10
Some soils and rocks have connected pores through which water can move.

Program Resources

Reproducible Masters
Study Guide, p. 34 L1
Reinforcement, p. 34 L1
Enrichment, p. 34 L3
Activity Worksheets, p. 53 L1
Concept Mapping, p. 21
Critical Thinking/Problem Solving, p. 14
Lab Manual 26, 27

Transparencies
Section Focus Transparency 30 L1
Science Integration Transparency 8

Permeability

A groundwater system is similar to a river system. However, instead of having channels that connect different parts of the drainage basin, the groundwater system has connecting pores. Soil and rock are **permeable** if water can pass through them. Sandstone is an example of a permeable rock.

Soil or rock that has many large connected pores is highly permeable. Water can pass through it easily. Soil or rock that has few or small pores is less permeable because water can't easily pass through. Some material, such as clay, has very small pores or no pores at all. This material is **impermeable,** which means that water cannot pass through it.

USING MATH

In an experiment, you find that 100 mL of gravel (Total Volume) can hold 31 mL (Volume of Pore Spaces, VPS) of water. Calculate the percentage of pore space (porosity) using the following formula.

$$\frac{\text{VPS}}{\text{Total Volume}} \times 100 = \text{\% Porosity}$$

Groundwater Movement

How deep into Earth's crust do you suppose groundwater can go? Groundwater will keep going to lower elevations until it reaches a layer of impermeable rock. When this happens, the impermeable rock acts like a barrier and the water can't move down any deeper. As a result, water begins filling up the pores in the rocks above the impermeable layer. A layer of permeable rock that transmits water freely is an **aquifer.** The area where all of the pores in the rock are filled with water is the **zone of saturation.** The upper surface of this zone is the **water table,** as seen in **Figure 8-11.**

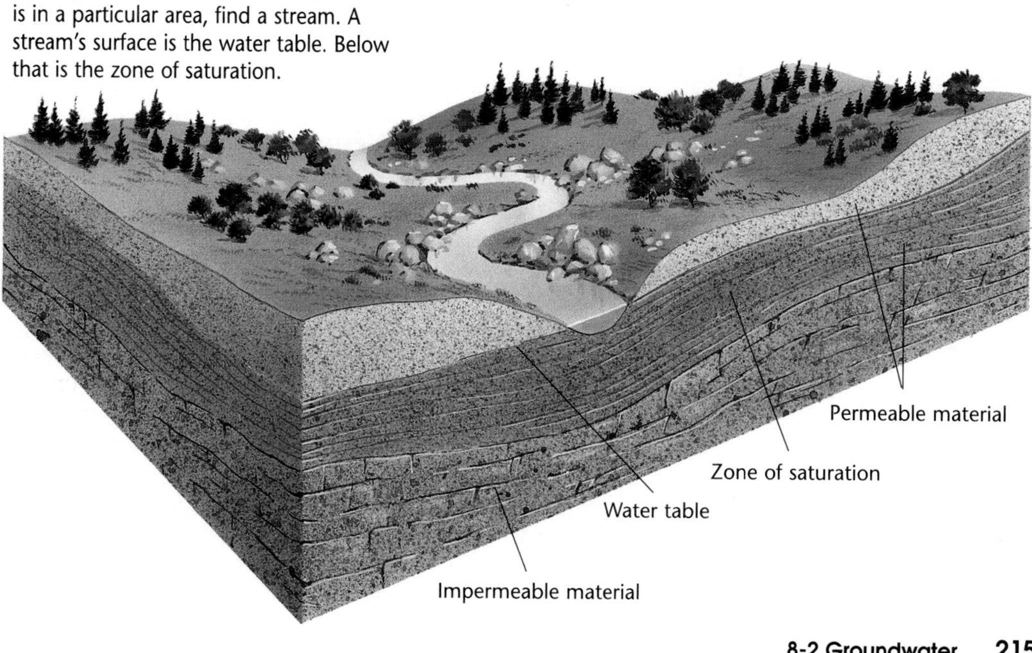

Figure 8-11

If you want to know where the water table is in a particular area, find a stream. A stream's surface is the water table. Below that is the zone of saturation.

2 Teach

USING MATH

The answer is 31% porosity. Challenge students to use this formula with different variables.

Inquiry Questions

- **Since groundwater has no channels, how is water transferred to different locations within a groundwater system?** *It travels through interconnecting pores.*
- **What causes the speed of groundwater to vary from place to place?** *The permeability of the rocks affects the speed.*

GLENCOE TECHNOLOGY

Videodisc

STVS: Chemistry

Disc 2, Side 2

Geothermal Wells (Ch. 17)

NATIONAL GEOGRAPHIC SOCIETY

Videodisc

STV: Restless Earth

Carlsbad Cavern; New Mexico

52241

Geyser; Wyoming

52194

Use Lab 26 in the **Lab Manual** as you teach this lesson.

Theme Connection

Systems and Interactions Ask students to discuss how pollutants from landfills, agriculture, and industry might affect the groundwater quality. Pesticides, solvents, septic tank cleaners, and other toxic wastes get into soil and permeable rocks from runoff. Some of these pollutants become dissolved in groundwater. Pollutants in groundwater can cause harm to all organisms that use the water.

MiniLAB

Purpose

LS **Logical-Mathematical** Students measure pore space. L1

Materials

two 250-mL beakers, 100 mL sand, 100 mL gravel, graduated cylinder, water

Teaching Strategies

- The sand and the gravel mixtures should be of relatively uniform grain size and perfectly dry for best results.
- Ask students to predict which material will allow more water to be poured in before reaching capacity.

Analysis

1. They will be about equal in the total amount of pore space. Although the individual pore spaces are larger among gravel grains, there are fewer of them when compared to the smaller but more numerous pore spaces among the sand grains. Results averaged from the whole class should show that it takes about the same amount of water to fill both materials.
2. It would not change. The individual spaces would be smaller, but there would be more of them.

Assessment

Content To further assess students' understanding of pore space, have them draw a magnified image of the pore space and sediments in their two beakers. Use the Performance Task Assessment List for Scientific Drawing in **PASC**, p. 55. P

Activity Worksheets, pp. 5, 53

Figure 8-12

The pressure of water in a sloping aquifer keeps an artesian well flowing. *What limits how high an artesian well could be placed in an aquifer?*

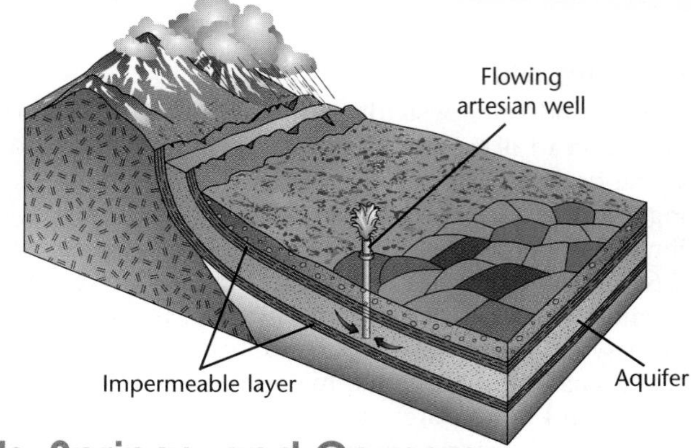

MiniLAB

How can you measure pore space?

Procedure

1. Put 100 mL of sand in one beaker and 100 mL of gravel in another beaker.
2. Fill a graduated cylinder with 100 mL of water.
3. Pour the water slowly into the beaker with the sand and stop when the water just covers the top of the sand.
4. Record the volume of the water used.
5. Repeat the procedure with the gravel.

Analysis

1. Which substance has more pore space—sand or gravel? How do you know?
2. If you repeated your experiment, but first crushed your gravel into smaller pieces, how would the pore space change?

Wells, Springs, and Geysers

What's so important about the zone of saturation and the water table? Many people get drinking water from groundwater in the zone of saturation. Water wells are drilled down into the zone of saturation.

Wells

Water flows into a well, and a pump brings it to the surface. A well must go down at least past the top of the water table to reach water. Sometimes during dry seasons, a well can go dry because the water table drops. Having too many wells in one area can also cause the water table to drop. This happens because more water is taken out of the ground than can be replaced by rain.

There is a type of well that doesn't need a pump to bring water to the surface. An **artesian well** is a well in which water under pressure rises to the surface. Artesian wells are less common than other wells because of the unique conditions they require, as shown in **Figure 8-12.**

An artesian well requires a sloping aquifer located between two impermeable layers. Water will enter at the high part of the sloping aquifer. Water in the higher part of the aquifer puts pressure on the water in the lower part. If a well is drilled into the lower part of the aquifer, the pressurized water will flow to the surface. Sometimes there is enough pressure to force the water into the air, forming a fountain.

Springs

In some places, the water table meets Earth's surface. When this happens, water flows out and forms a **spring.** Springs are found on hillsides or in any other place where the water table is exposed at the surface. Springs can be used as a source of fresh water.

The water from most springs is cold. But in some places, groundwater is heated and comes to the surface as a **hot spring.** The groundwater is heated by rocks that come in contact with molten material under Earth's surface.

Geysers

One of the places where groundwater is heated is in Yellowstone National Park in Wyoming. In Yellowstone, there are hot springs and geysers. A **geyser,** like the one in **Figure 8-13A,** is a hot spring that erupts periodically, shooting water and steam into the air. Groundwater is heated to very high temperatures, causing it to expand underground. This expansion forces some of the water out of the ground, taking the pressure off of the remaining water. The remaining water boils quickly, with much of it turning to steam. The steam shoots out of the opening like steam out of a teakettle, forcing the remaining water out with it. Yellowstone's famous geyser, Old Faithful, in the photo in **Figure 8-13B,** shoots about 40 000 liters of water and steam into the air once each hour.

CONNECT TO CHEMISTRY

Although limestone is commonly said to *dissolve* in groundwater, that doesn't accurately describe what happens. Weakly acidic groundwater reacts with limestone. This reaction produces compounds that dissolve more easily in water than limestone does. ***Infer*** what effect acid rain might have on a statue made of limestone.

Groundwater Erosion and Deposition

Just as water is the most powerful agent of erosion on Earth's surface, it can also have a great effect underground. As mentioned in Chapter 6, when water mixes with carbon dioxide in the air, it forms a weak acid. One type of rock that is easily dissolved by this acid is limestone. As acidic groundwater moves through natural cracks in limestone, it dissolves the rock. Gradually, the cracks in the limestone are enlarged until an underground opening called a **cave** is formed.

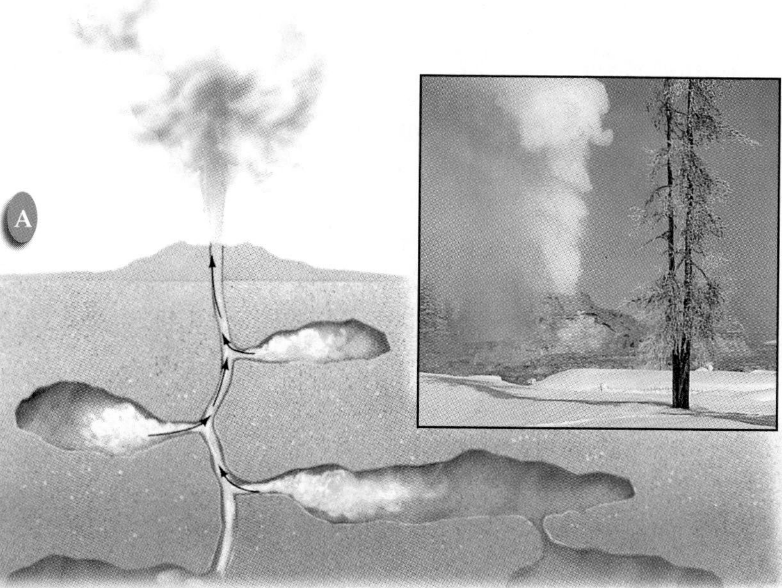

Figure 8-13

After a geyser erupts (A), water runs back into underground openings where it is heated and erupts again. Yellowstone's famous geyser, Old Faithful (B), erupts once each hour.

CONNECT TO CHEMISTRY

Answer The acid in acid rain reacts chemically with the substances in the limestone statue. Then, water dissolves these substances. The statue shows signs of chemical weathering.

Visual Learning

Figure 8-12 What limits how high an artesian well could be placed in an aquifer? *The amount of water in the aquifer above the well has to have great enough pressure to force water out the well opening.* LEP LS

3 Assess

Check for Understanding

FLEX Your Brain

Use the Flex Your Brain activity to have students explore GROUNDWATER.

Activity Worksheets, p. 5

Reteach

LS **Visual-Spatial** Half-fill a beaker with limestone chips. Pour carbonated water over the chips and have students observe what happens. Help them conclude that the carbonated water represents groundwater and weathers the limestone.

Extension

For students who have mastered this section, use the **Reinforcement** and **Enrichment** masters.

Inclusion Strategies

Gifted Have groups of students make models that show how the position of the water table affects the formation of a well, geyser, hillside spring, stream, lake, hot spring, and artesian well. L3

Science Journal

Yellowstone Have students write short reports on Old Faithful and other features in Yellowstone National Park. L1 LS

4 Close

• MINI • QUIZ •

Use the Mini Quiz to check students' recall of chapter content.

1. **Water that collects in pores in soils and rocks is _____ .** *groundwater*
2. **Soils and rocks are _____ if water cannot pass through them.** *impermeable*
3. **A permeable rock that transmits water freely is a(n) _____ .** *aquifer*
4. **The area where all pores in a rock body are completely filled with water is the _____ .** *zone of saturation*

Section Wrap-up

Review

1. It soaks into the ground and collects among pores.
2. The more permeable a soil or rock is, the faster groundwater can flow through it.
3. They form when cracks in rock are enlarged as the surrounding rock dissolves.
4. Think Critically Yes, groundwater erodes sediments as it travels through the pores in rock and soil.

Science Journal

- Students will find out that geothermal energy is energy that comes from the internal heat of Earth. Sources of the energy include volcanoes, magma bodies, and certain tectonic boundaries.
- Limitations include restricted geographic areas, problems with salt and thermal pollution, and cost, among others.

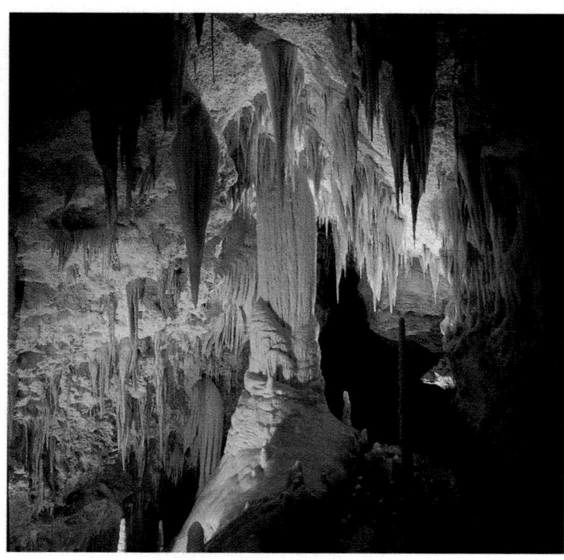

Figure 8-14

Water containing dissolved calcium ions forms interesting features in caves. Look at the features in the cave shown above and try to infer how they formed.

Cave Formation

You've probably seen a picture of the inside of a cave, or perhaps you've visited one. Groundwater not only dissolves limestone to make caves, but it also can make spectacular deposits on the insides of caves, as shown in **Figure 8-14.**

Water often drips slowly from cracks in the cave walls and ceilings. This water contains calcium ions dissolved from the limestone. If this water evaporates while hanging from the roof of a cave, a deposit of calcite is left behind. Stalactites form when this process happens over and over. Where drops of water fall to the floor of the cave, a stalagmite forms.

Sinkholes

If underground rock is dissolved near the surface, a sinkhole may form. A sinkhole is a depression that forms when the roof of a cave collapses.

In summary, when rain falls and becomes groundwater, it might dissolve a cave, erupt from a geyser, or be pumped from a well to be used at your house.

Section Wrap-up

Science Journal

Read an article about geothermal energy and draw a diagram in your Science Journal explaining how it works. Also list the limitations of this energy source.

Review

1. How does water enter the groundwater system?
2. How does the permeability of soil and rocks affect the flow of groundwater?
3. Explain how caves form.
4. **Think Critically:** Would you expect water in wells, geysers, and hot springs to contain eroded materials? Why or why not?

Skill Builder

Comparing and Contrasting

Compare and contrast wells, geysers, and hot springs. If you need help, refer to Comparing and Contrasting in the **Skill Handbook.**

Skill Builder

All bring water to Earth's surface. In a well, water must be pumped to the surface. In geysers and hot springs, the water is hot. A geyser is a hot spring that periodically erupts.

Assessment

Performance Have students prepare a table that presents their conclusions. Use the Performance Task Assessment List for Data Table in **PASC,** p. 37. P

Huang Ho, China's Sorrow

Any study of erosion by rivers will be somehow incomplete if you don't learn about the Huang Ho, or Yellow River, of China. This river got its name from the soft yellow earth it carries. It empties 1 billion tons of this sediment into the sea every year. Its deposit creates an average of 25 km^2 of newly formed land at the river's mouth annually.

Science Journal

If you were placed in charge of flood control in your area, what measures would you propose? In your Science Journal, write your proposal.

History of Flooding

In the past 4000 years, the Huang Ho has flooded 1500 times. It is responsible for killing more people than any other river in the world with its floods. The first recorded flooding of this river occurred in 2297 B.C. By 602 B.C. the Chinese had begun to build dikes, which are walls or banks erected along a river for flood protection.

In 1887, heavy rains fell in Honan Province. The Huang Ho burst through 21-m high dikes. About a million people died in this flood. Another million may have died in the famine that followed. The worst flood of the Huang Ho in terms of the people killed occurred more recently, in 1931. About 3.7 million died in that flood. A flood of a different sort occurred in 1938. That's when the Chinese general Chiang Kai-shek had his troops destroy the river's dikes in order to slow down the Japanese army. The general achieved his purpose, but the flood killed more than 500 000 people and left 13 million homeless.

For thousands of years, floods caused major changes of the river's course, keeping it from returning to its original position after a flood. The lower Huang Ho has changed the most, flowing northeastward to the Po Gulf after one flood and southeastward into the main body of the Yellow Sea after another.

Respite from Floods

Since 1949 there have been no breaks in the dikes that would cause serious floods. This is due in great part to a special program that enlists people to collect data comparing the level of the river bed to the height of the dikes in every area along the river. If the river bed has risen, the people set to work raising the level of the dikes to hold back the waters. They also build reservoirs on the floodplains to control the river's flow, as shown in **Figure 8-15.** Still, the river bed continues to rise at the rate of 1.8 m per year in some areas.

Figure 8-15

A new flood control dam on the Huang Ho River.

Cultural Diversity

More Precious Than Oil Turkey is interested in constructing a "peace pipeline" running from the Ceysan and Seyhan Rivers across thousands of miles of desert. This project would provide drinking water to more than 15 million people in Syria, Jordan, Saudi Arabia, and the Gulf states. One pipeline would run 1700 miles from Turkey to Saudi Arabia. The other would run 2400 miles ending at Oman.

The two rivers dump 39 million cubic meters (10.3 billion gallons) of water into the Mediterranean Sea each day. Many of the countries involved are concerned at having Turkey control the water supply for the entire area, but Turkish officials say they would not deny water, even to an enemy. Turkish hospitality requires that the first thing one offers a visitor is something to drink.

Sources

- Brush, Lucien M., M. Gordon Wolman, and Huang Bing-Wei, eds. *Taming the Yellow River: Silt and Floods.* Boston: Kluwer Academic Press, 1989.
- Fradin, Dennis Brindell. *Disaster! Floods.* Chicago: Children's Press, 1982, pp. 34-36.

Background

- The Huang Ho is 4672 km long, making it the second-longest river in China. It is about 900 km longer than the Mississippi. It rises in the mountains of Tsinghai Province and flows to the Huanghai, or Yellow Sea, off the northeast coast of China.

Science Journal

Answers may include having sand bags available to make portable dikes, planning evacuation procedures, and monitoring weather and other conditions upstream.

Teaching Strategies

LS **Visual-Spatial** Have students locate the drainage basin of the Huang Ho on a map of China. *Students will locate an area in the Tsinghai Province surrounding the lakes that are the source of the river.*

- The river flows through a channel that has risen higher than the floodplain on either side. *The rise of the channel has been caused partly by soil carried in the river.*

LS **Interpersonal** Encourage students to work in groups to produce a model riverbed. Ask them to show what happens when the riverbed rises above the floodplain. **COOP LEARN**

Prepare

Section Background

According to the Water Council, by the year 2000, there will be an inadequate supply of water in 17 of the nation's 106 water regions.

1 Motivate

Bellringer

Before presenting the lesson, display **Section Focus Transparency 31** on the overhead projector. Assign the accompanying **Focus Activity** worksheet. L1 LEP

Tying to Previous Knowledge

Have students recall that many people live in areas prone to flooding. Explain that one way to reduce flooding is to build dams. Dams also make available large quantities of water to communities.

2 Teach

Science Journal

LS **Linguistic** Students should realize that direct uses include drinking, baths, washing, watering lawns, and recreation. Indirect uses include water used in food production (growing vegetables and livestock) and in manufacturing.

Student Text Question

Where does your town's water come from? *Students may need to do research to find the answer to this question.*

8•3 ISSUE: Water Wars

Objectives

- Give examples of ways people use water.
- Explain why some communities must rely on water diversion for their water supply.
- Identify a problem caused by water diversion.

Water as a Resource

How much water do you use each day? An average person in the United States uses about 397 liters every day. That's enough to fill 1118 soft-drink cans!

Just imagine how much water an entire community uses each day for fire hydrants, street cleaning, and water fountains like the one shown in **Figure 8-16.** Where does your town's water come from? While some towns have easily accessible aquifers, large rivers, reservoirs, or lakes nearby, others must use pipelines to transport water from distant locations. The city of Los Angeles, California gets its water from several sources. Among these sources are streams more than 400 km north of Los Angeles in the Sierra Nevada mountains.

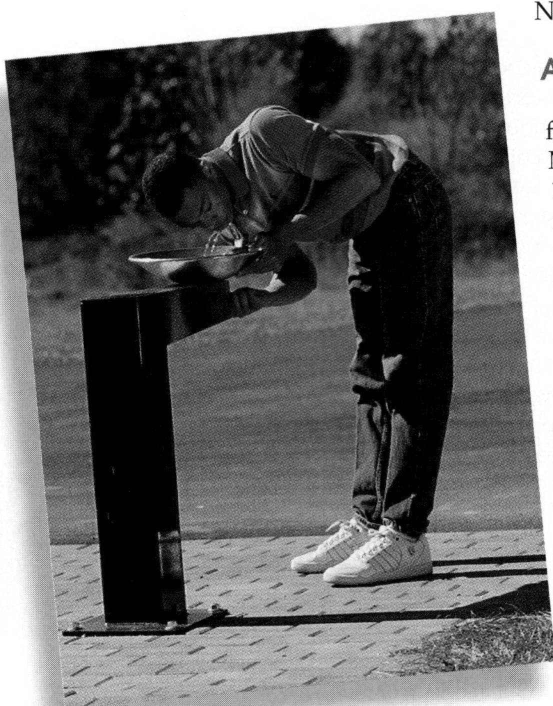

Figure 8-16
The availability of water is not something to be taken for granted.

A Bitter Battle

The streams that Los Angeles has diverted for its water needs feed into the unique Mono Lake. Since the diversion began in 1941, the lake's level has dropped 13.5 meters and its volume has been cut in half. People began to worry that Mono Lake might dry up. If this happened, not only would a beautiful lake be lost, but an entire ecosystem would be extinguished as well. Thus began a battle between the city of Los Angeles and a host of geologists and ecologists.

In 1994, after hearing arguments from both scientists and Los Angeles city officials, the California Water Resources Control Board decided that Los Angeles must allow the lake level to rise 5 meters above the 1994 water level. While this reduces the amount of water Los Angeles can divert from Mono Lake, it doesn't cut it off completely.

Program Resources

Reproducible Masters

Study Guide, p. 35 L1
Reinforcement, p. 35 L1
Enrichment, p. 35 L3
Science and Society Integration, p. 12
Technology Integration, pp. 7-8

Transparencies

Section Focus Transparency 31

2 Points of View

Conserve the Natural Resource

One of the concerns about lowering Mono Lake's water levels is the increased mineral and salt concentrations, shown in **Figure 8-17.** With less fresh water flowing into the lake, it became nearly twice as salty. Many ecologists hypothesized that the increased salt concentrations threatened the populations of brine shrimp and alkali flies, which are an important food source for many migratory birds that move through the area. Aside from possibly losing their food, migratory waterfowl lost much of their shoreline habitat.

Figure 8-17
These structures, called tufa towers, are formed by mineral-rich springs. As Mono Lake's water level dropped, many of these structures were revealed.

Water Needed by People

Prior to the board's decision, the water diverted from Mono Lake provided about 17 percent of the water used by Los Angeles. Now the city can no longer depend on diverting water from the Mono Basin to meet that need. Water conservation measures, already common to Southern California, are now even more important to the city. It also means that the city must look for other water sources, an expensive proposition.

As Earth's population continues to increase, greater demands are placed on Earth's freshwater supply. With the increased demand, there will likely be more conflicts between conserving natural resources and the need for water for agriculture, industry, and recreation. Where will we get the fresh water we will need?

Science Journal

You drink only a small part of the water you use. Much more goes into each shower or bath you take. In your Science Journal, write about other ways you use water directly or indirectly.

Section Wrap-up

Review

1. What are four ways that you use water each day?
2. What is a problem caused by water diversion?

Explore the Issue

The human population in the southwestern United States is increasing rapidly. As a result, there is a greater demand for water in a dry climate. To solve this problem, some have proposed building a giant canal to divert water from the Great Lakes. Infer what some of the problems might be if the canal is built.

SCIENCE & SOCIETY

3 Assess

Check for Understanding

Have students answer questions 1 and 2 in the Section Wrap-up.

Reteach

LS **Interpersonal** Divide the class into two groups. One group will represent people from a city who want to divert water from a distant lake to supply the city with water. The other group represents people who live near the lake and environmentalists. Have students role-play various people: city officials, farmers, industrial leaders, homeowners, wildlife managers, and so on. COOP LEARN

Extension

For students who have mastered this section, use the **Reinforcement** and **Enrichment** masters.

4 Close

Ask students to explain the advantage and disadvantage of water diversion.

Section Wrap-up

Review

1. consuming foods and beverages that contain water, flushing toilets, taking baths and showers, using products manufactured with it, eating foods that come from irrigated fields, relying on it to treat wastewater
2. Diverting water can cause environmental problems. Wildlife that depend on the water may suffer if the water is diverted from their natural habitat.

Inclusion Strategies

Gifted Have students discuss water-shortage problems and propose possible solutions. L3

Explore the Issue

Some students will say that the canal should be built because people in the southwest need the water. Also, the Great Lakes contain a tremendous amount of water. The states that surround the lakes would probably do fine without some of the water. Others will feel that it would be unfair to divert the water since this could hurt these states economically and harm the environment.

Section 8•4

Prepare

Section Background

- The movement of material along a shoreline is directly related to the wind velocity.
- Textural terms used to describe sediments are based on size, not composition. Below is a chart of sediment sizes.

Sediment Type	Diameter (mm)
sand	0.07 - 2
granule	2 - 4
pebble	4 - 64
cobble	64 - 256

- The Atlantic and Gulf Coasts of North America are noted for their extensive barrier island beaches. Atlantic City, New Jersey, and Galveston, Texas, are built on barrier islands.

Preplanning

To prepare for Activity 8-2, obtain the following for each group: three different types of beach sand, a stereomicroscope, and a magnet.

1 Motivate

Bellringer

Before presenting the lesson, display **Section Focus Transparency 32** on the overhead projector. Assign the accompanying **Focus Activity** worksheet. L1 LEP

Tying to Previous Knowledge

Many students have visited shorelines. Others who have not had this opportunity have probably seen them on television. Have students recall the shoreline structures they have seen.

8•4 Ocean Shoreline

Science Words

longshore current
beach
barrier island

Objectives

- Describe forces that cause shoreline erosion.
- Compare and contrast different types of shorelines.
- List some origins of sand.

The Shore

Picture yourself sitting on a beautiful white sand beach. Palm trees sway in the breeze above your head, and small children play in the quiet waves lapping at the water's edge. It's hard to imagine a place more peaceful than this shore. Now picture yourself sitting along another shore. You're on a high cliff, overlooking waves crashing onto huge boulders below. Both of these settings are shorelines. This is where land meets the ocean.

The two shorelines we just described are very different. Why are they so different? Both are subjected to the same forces. Both experience the same surface waves, tides, and currents. These cause both shorelines to constantly change. Sometimes you can see these changes from hour to hour. We'll look at why these shorelines are different, but first, let's learn about the forces that carve shores.

Shoreline Forces

Along all shorelines, like the one in **Figure 8-18A,** surface waves constantly move sediments back and forth. The waves shape shorelines by eroding and redepositing sediments. The tides also shape shorelines. Every day tides raise and lower the place on the shoreline where surface waves erode and deposit sediments.

Figure 8-18

A Waves, tides, and currents cause shorelines to constantly change.

B Waves approaching the shoreline at an angle create a longshore current. When the water built up by waves returns to sea, a rip current forms. *Why is it wise to avoid rip currents when swimming at a beach?*

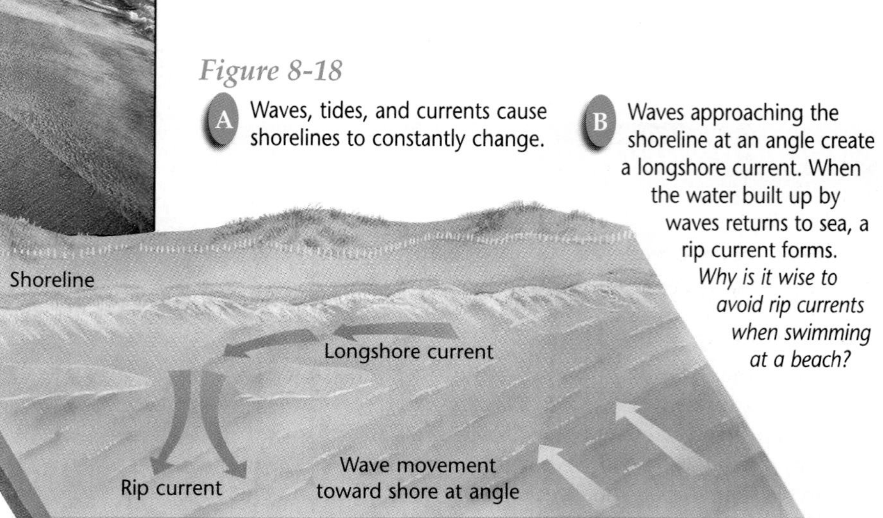

Program Resources

Reproducible Masters

Study Guide, p. 36 L1
Reinforcement, p. 36 L1
Enrichment, p. 36 L3
Activity Worksheets, pp. 50-51
Cross-Curricular Integration, p. 12
Lab Manual 28

Transparencies

Section Focus Transparency 32 L1
Teaching Transparency 16

Waves usually collide with a shore at slight angles. This creates a **longshore current** of water that runs parallel to the shore, as shown in **Figure 8-18B.** Longshore currents carry many metric tons of loose sediments and act like rivers of sand in the ocean. What do you suppose happens if a longshore current isn't carrying all of the sand it has the energy to carry? It will use this extra energy to erode more shoreline sediments.

You've seen the forces that affect all shorelines. Now we'll look at the differences that make one shore a flat, sandy beach and another shore a steep, rocky cliff.

Figure 8-19

Along a rocky shoreline, the force of pounding waves breaks rock fragments loose and grinds them into smaller and smaller sediments.

Rocky Shorelines

Along rocky shorelines like the one in **Figure 8-19,** rocks and cliffs are the most common features. Waves scour the rocks to form hollows or notches. Over time, these enlarge and become caves. Rock fragments broken from the cliffs are ground up by the endless motion of waves. These fragments act like the sand on sandpaper.

Softer rocks are eroded away before harder rocks, leaving islands of harder rocks. This takes many years, but remember that the ocean never sleeps. In a single day, about 14 000 waves will crash onto any shore.

The rock fragments produced by eroding waves are sediments. When rocky shorelines are being eroded away, where do you think the sediments go? Waves carry them away and deposit them where water is quieter. If you want to relax on a nice wide, sandy beach, you probably won't go to a rocky shoreline.

2 Teach

Activity

If possible, take students to an ocean coastline to observe the effects of the longshore current.

Visual Learning

Figure 8-18 Why is it wise to avoid rip currents when swimming at a beach? *Rip currents pull swimmers away from shore. People sometimes drown when caught in these currents.* LEP LS

GLENCOE TECHNOLOGY

 **Videodisc**

The Infinite Voyage: Living with Disaster

Chapter 4

Save the Beaches: Soil Erosion from Barrier-Reef Islands

 **Videodisc**

STV: Restless Earth

Crashing waves: Oregon

52249

Shoreline; Point Reyes, California

52175

 Use Lab 28 in the **Lab Manual** as you teach this lesson.

Use **Teaching Transparency 16** as you teach this lesson.

Science Journal

Rocky Shores Have students write poems in their journals describing the shoreline shown in **Figure 8-19**. Poems should describe a steep shoreline with heavy surf. L1 LS

Visual Learning

Figure 8-21 To help students understand the dynamic nature of a beach area, show films featuring beach environments. LEP IS

Enrichment

Have students research the successfulness of building jetties, floating objects offshore, or burying large plastic tubes of sand on beaches to prevent erosion. L2

3 Assess

Check for Understanding

FLEX Your Brain

Use the Flex Your Brain activity to have students explore SHORELINES.

Activity Worksheets, p. 5

Reteach

Obtain photographs or slides of various kinds of coastlines. Have students describe what caused the coastline features shown in each photograph. LEP

Extension

For students who have mastered this section, use the **Reinforcement** and **Enrichment** masters.

Figure 8-20

Sand varies in size, color, and composition. This sand contains shell fragments and tiny grains of quartz.

Sandy Beaches

Smooth, gently sloping shorelines are quite different from steep, rocky shorelines. Beaches are the main feature here. **Beaches** are deposits of sediment that run parallel to the shore. They extend inland as far as the tides and waves are able to deposit sediment.

Beaches are made of different materials like the sand shown in **Figure 8-20.** Some are made of rock fragments from the shoreline, and others consist of seashell fragments. These fragments range from pebbles large enough to fill your hand to fine sand. Sand grains are 0.07 mm to 2 mm in diameter. Why do many beaches have sand-sized particles? This is because waves break rocks and seashells down to sand-sized particles. The constant wave motion bumps sand grains together and, in the process, rounds their corners.

What kinds of materials do you think make up most beach sands? Most are made of resistant minerals such as quartz. However, sand in some places is composed of other things. For example, Hawaii's black sands are made of basalt, and green sands are made of the mineral olivine. Jamaica's white sands are made of coral and shell fragments.

Sand Erosion and Deposition

Sand constantly is carried down beaches by longshore currents to form features such as those seen in **Figure 8-21.** Sand is also moved by storms and the wind. Thus, beaches are fragile, temporary features that are easily damaged by storms and human activities such as construction.

Figure 8-21

Longshore currents move sediment along shorelines, changing beaches and creating baymouth bars and spits, like those in this aerial photograph of Martha's Vineyard, Massachusetts.

Integrating the Sciences

Physics Inform students that because sands have different compositions, their densities are also different. Ask students, **How would the density of a sand grain affect its movement on a beach? Would you expect sand grains to be sorted by density on a beach?** *The grains that are more dense are not transported as far by currents as less dense grains. Sands on a beach are sorted by density.*

Community Connection

Economics Many coastal cities depend on tourism to help the local economy. When beaches disappear because of erosion, tourists do not visit. For this reason, many cities have spent a lot of money to preserve their beaches. Have students research the costs involved in dredging and building sea walls. L3

What's so special about sand?

You know that sand is made of many different kinds of grains, but did you realize that the slope of a beach is actually related to the size of its grains? The coarser the grain size, the steeper the beach. Did you know that many sands are mined because they have economic value?

Problem

What characteristics can be used to classify beach sands?

Materials

- 3 samples of different beach sands
- stereomicroscope
- magnet

Procedure

1. Design a data table in which to record your data when you compare the three sand samples. You will need five columns in your table. One column will be for the samples, and the others for the characteristics you will be examining. If you need help in designing your table, refer to the Skill Handbook.
2. Use the diagram below to determine the average roundness of each sample.

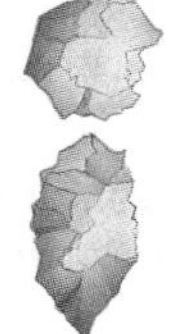
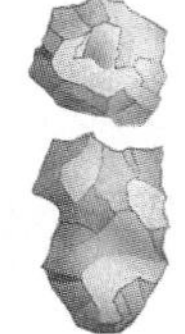
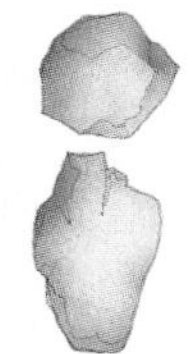

Angular Sub-angular Sub-rounded Rounded

3. Identify the grain size of your samples by using the sand gauge on this page. To determine the grain size, place sand grains in the middle of the circle of the sand gauge. Use the upper half of the circle for dark-colored particles, and the bottom half of the circle for light-colored particles.
4. Decide on two other characteristics to examine that will help you classify your samples.

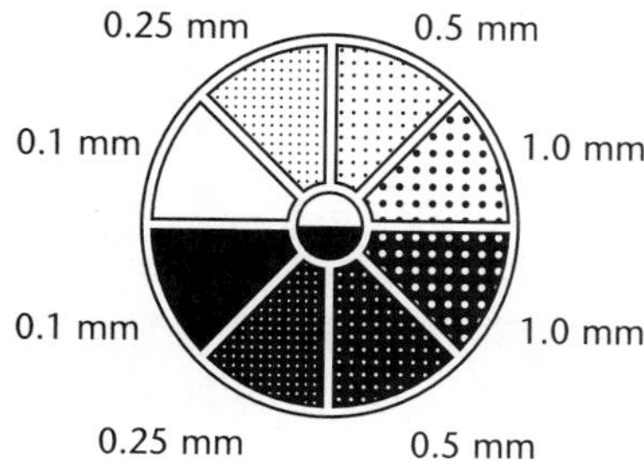

Sand Gauge

Analyze

1. Were the grains of a particular sample generally the same size? Explain.
2. Which of these sand samples do you think came from the steepest beach?
3. Were the grains in your three samples generally the same shape?

Conclude and Apply

4. What are some characteristics of beach sand?
5. Why are there differences in the characteristics of different sand samples?

Activity 8-2

Purpose

LS **Visual-Spatial** Students will classify sand based on structure and composition. L1 LEP

Process Skills

classifying, observing and inferring, comparing and contrasting, interpreting data, making and using tables

Time

45 minutes

Activity Worksheets, pp. 5, 49, 50, 51

Teaching Strategies

Alternate Materials If stereomicroscopes are not available, monocular microscopes with top illumination will work. Hand lenses may be preferable, however.

Troubleshooting Samples of beach sands may also be obtained from scientific supply distributors.

- Advise students to be careful not to mix the sand samples. They will need to examine only a small quantity of sand.

Answers to Questions

1. Usually, the grains will have been sorted by size.
2. The sample with the largest grains probably came from the steepest beach.
3. Samples from different beaches may have different shapes, but grains from the same sample should be about the same shape if they are made of only one type of material. However, if the sand is a mixture of materials, the shapes will be varied.
4. Characteristics include color, texture, roundness, grain size, luster, whether grains are attracted to a magnet, composition, and density.
5. The length of time exposed to weathering, the parent material, and erosion by wind and/or water determine the characteristics of sand in a given location.

Assessment

Performance Have students refer to Chapters 3 and 4 to infer the composition of the sand samples. Colorless, white, or transparent sands are usually quartz; green sands are olivine; black grains with high luster are obsidian; red sands are garnets; grains attracted to a magnet are magnetite; and white sands that "bubble" in acid contain carbonate minerals. Carbonate sands may have originated from limestone or seashells. Use the Performance Task Assessment List for Making Observations and Inferences in **PASC**, p. 17. P

4 Close

• MINI • QUIZ •

Use the Mini Quiz to check students' recall of chapter content.

1. **_____ raise and lower the place on the shoreline where surface waves erode and deposit sediment every day.** *Tides*
2. **_____ currents are "rivers of sand" along an ocean shoreline.** *Longshore*
3. **Rocks, cliffs, and caves are common features along _____ shorelines.** *rocky*
4. **The most common mineral found in beach sand is _____ .** *quartz*

Section Wrap-up

Review

1. waves, tides, and currents
2. Most features of steep shorelines are formed as a result of the erosion of soft materials. The more resistant rocks are left behind to form cliffs and caves. Most features of gently sloping shorelines are created by deposition. Beaches are common along these shorelines.
3. **Think Critically** Waves and currents continually change a shoreline. On steep coasts, rock fragments are carried away by waves and deposited elsewhere. Also, many beaches are made of fragments that are too large to be classified as sand.

USING MATH

In the lifetime of a 13-year-old student, 13 × 365 × 14 000 = 66 430 000 waves have crashed onto a shore.

Barrier Islands

Barrier islands are sand deposits that parallel the shore but are separated from the mainland, as shown in **Figure 8-22.** These islands start as underwater sand ridges formed by breaking waves. Hurricanes and storms add sediment to them, raising some to sea level. Once a barrier island is exposed, the wind blows the loose sand into dunes, keeping the island above sea level. As with all seashore features, barrier islands are temporary, lasting from a few years to a few centuries.

Figure 8-22

There are many barrier islands along North America's Atlantic Coast and the Gulf of Mexico. The size and shape of these islands constantly change due to wave action.

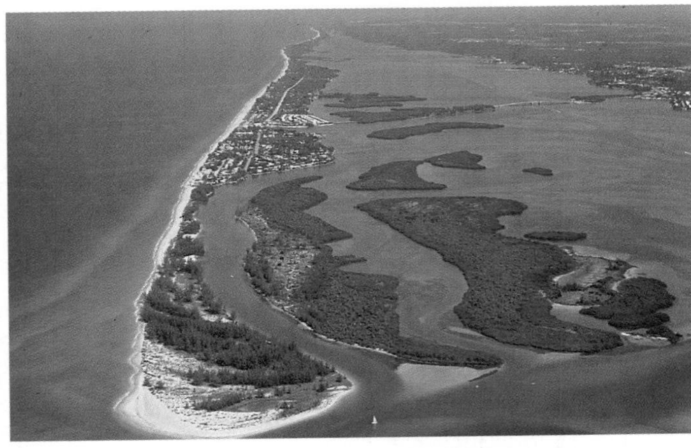

Section Wrap-up

Review

1. What are the forces that cause shoreline erosion?
2. Contrast the features you'd find along a steep, rocky shoreline with the features you'd find along a gently sloping shoreline.
3. **Think Critically:** Why is there no sand on many of the world's shorelines?

Skill Builder
Concept Mapping

Make a cycle concept map that discusses how the sand from a barrier island that is currently in place can become a new barrier island 100 years from now. Use these terms: *barrier island, breaking waves, wind, longshore currents,* and *new barrier island.* If you need help, refer to Concept Mapping in the **Skill Handbook.**

USING MATH

If in a single day, about 14 000 waves crash onto a shore, how many waves crash onto a shore in one year? Calculate how many have crashed onto a shore since you were born.

Skill Builder

Possible solution:

barrier island → breaking waves → wind → longshore current → new barrier island → barrier island

Assessment

Performance Use this Skill Builder to assess students' abilities to make concept maps. Ask students to make a concept map that shows how an arch of rock may form along a steep shoreline. Use the Performance Task Assessment List for Concept Map in **PASC,** p. 89. P

Chapter 8

Review

Summary

8-1: Surface Water

1. The amount of runoff in an area depends on the amount of rain that falls, the time period over which it falls, the slope of the land, and the amount of vegetation.
2. Rill, gully, and sheet erosion are all types of surface water erosion due to runoff.
3. Water in a stream picks up sediments from the bottom and sides of its channel.
4. Young streams flow swiftly through steep-sided valleys and erode the bottoms of their channels more than the sides. Mature streams erode the sides of their channels and form meanders. A stream in the old stage has less energy than a young stream because it moves very slowly.
5. Alluvial fans and deltas are triangular deposits that form when water loses energy of motion.

8-2: Groundwater

1. Water that soaks into the ground becomes part of the groundwater system.
2. Springs, artesian wells, hot springs, and geysers are all a part of the groundwater system.
3. Groundwater erosion results in the formation of caves and sinkholes. Groundwater deposition results in the formation of cave formations like stalactites and stalagmites.

8-3: Science and Society: Water Wars

1. People use water by drinking it, bathing, and in manufacturing and irrigation.
2. Some communities must divert water from other locations. With water diversion comes environmental problems.

8-4: Ocean Shoreline

1. Shorelines are subjected to waves, tides, and currents.
2. Rocks and cliffs are common along rocky shorelines.
3. Sandy beaches form along gently sloping shorelines. Sand forms when rocks, coral, and seashells are broken into small particles by wave action.

Key Science Words

a. alluvial fan
b. aquifer
c. artesian well
d. barrier island
e. beach
f. cave
g. delta
h. drainage basin
i. floodplain
j. geyser
k. groundwater
l. gully erosion
m. hot spring
n. impermeable
o. longshore current
p. meander
q. permeable
r. rill erosion
s. runoff
t. sheet erosion
u. spring
v. water table
w. zone of saturation

Chapter 8

Review

Summary

Have students read the summary statements to review the major concepts of the chapter.

Reviewing Vocabulary

1. s
2. o
3. p
4. b
5. w
6. j
7. g
8. e
9. k
10. f

Assessment

Portfolio Encourage students to place in their portfolios one or two items of what they consider to be their best work. Examples include:

- Enrichment, pp. 204, 209
- MiniLAB, pp. 206, 216
- Using Computers, p. 213 P

Performance Additional performance assessments may be found in **Performance Assessment** and **Science Integration Activities.** Performance Task Assessment Lists and rubrics for evaluating these activities can be found in Glencoe's **Performance Assessment in the Science Classroom.**

GLENCOE TECHNOLOGY

Videodisc

Glencoe Earth Science

Interactive Videodisc

Use the videodisc lesson 2, *Mysteries of the Cave,* to review the processes of groundwater erosion and deposition.

MindJogger Videoquiz

Chapter 8 Have students work in groups as they play the Videoquiz game to review key chapter concepts.

Chapter 8 Review

Checking Concepts

1. a	**6.** a
2. b	**7.** b
3. a	**8.** d
4. c	**9.** b
5. d	**10.** d

Understanding Concepts

11. More runoff would be produced from the lot. Grasses in the field would minimize runoff.

12. All the valleys are alike in that they are eroded by the river. The valleys differ, though, in that young river valleys have steep sides, whereas mature and old valleys are broad and flat.

13. Erosion and deposition by waves, tides, and currents cause the shoreline to change constantly.

Thinking Critically

14. The Mississippi River is in the old stage of development and thus has meanders, which begin to form in a river's mature stage.

15. The energy of the moving water, which is related to a river's stage of development, determines whether a stream erodes its bottom or its sides. Young streams erode downward; old streams erode their sides.

16. Water from your well could be diverted to the other wells, which could pose water-shortage problems or a decrease in water pressure for you.

17. A remnant like a stack would be found along steep, rocky shorelines. Storm waves erode away softer rocks, leaving stacks.

Chapter 8 Review

Reviewing Vocabulary

Match each phrase with the correct term from the list of Key Science Words.

1. water that flows over Earth's surface
2. water that flows parallel to the shore
3. a curve in a stream channel
4. a body of permeable rock through which water can flow freely
5. the area where all the pores in the rock are filled with water
6. hot springs that erupt
7. a triangular deposit that forms when a river enters a gulf or lake
8. any kind of sediment that is deposited parallel to a shore
9. water that soaks into the ground
10. a large underground opening formed when limestone dissolves

Checking Concepts

Choose the word or phrase that completes the sentence or answers the question.

1. An example of a structure created by deposition is a(n) _______.
   a. beach c. cave
   b. rill d. geyser
2. A deposit that forms when a mountain river runs out onto a plain is called _______.
   a. subsidence c. infiltration
   b. an alluvial fan d. water diversion
3. A layer of rock that water flows through is _______.
   a. an aquifer c. a water table
   b. a pore d. impermeable
4. The network formed by a river and all the smaller streams that contribute to it is a _______.
   a. groundwater system
   b. zone of saturation
   c. river system
   d. water table
5. Soils through which fluids can easily flow are _______.
   a. impermeable c. saturated
   b. meanders d. permeable
6. Streams in mountains tend to be in the _______ stage of development.
   a. young c. old
   b. mature d. meandering
7. A(n) _______ forms when the water table is exposed at the surface.
   a. meander c. aquifer
   b. spring d. stalactite
8. Heated groundwater that reaches Earth's surface is a(n) _______.
   a. water table c. aquifer
   b. cave d. hot spring
9. Beaches are most common along _______.
   a. rocky shorelines c. aquifers
   b. flat shorelines d. young streams
10. Water rises in an artesian well because of _______.
    a. a pump c. heat
    b. erosion d. pressure

Understanding Concepts

Answer the following questions in your Science Journal using complete sentences.

11. Would you expect more runoff from a parking lot or a grassy field with the same slope? Explain.
12. Compare and contrast the valleys of young, mature, and old streams.
13. Explain why shorelines are constantly changing.

18. Sands vary according to the type of parent material and the time they have been exposed to weathering by wind and water.

Developing skills

19. Making a Concept Map See student page.

20. Interpreting Data The La Plata erodes more because it has more energy of motion. Its flow is about four times greater.

21. Hypothesizing Silt is smaller than sand. As water loses energy of motion, it will drop off larger sediments (sand) first.

Thinking Critically

14. Explain why the Mississippi River has meanders.
15. What determines whether a stream, like the one shown on the right, erodes its bottom or its sides?
16. Why would you be concerned if developers of a new housing project started drilling wells near your well?
17. A stack is an island of rock along certain shorelines. Along what kind of shoreline would you find stacks? Explain.
18. Explain why beach sands collected from different locations will differ in composition, color, and texture.

Developing Skills

If you need help, refer to the **Skill Handbook.**

19. **Concept Mapping:** Complete the concept map below using the following terms: developed meanders, gentle curves, gentle gradient, old, rapids, steep gradient, wide floodplain, young

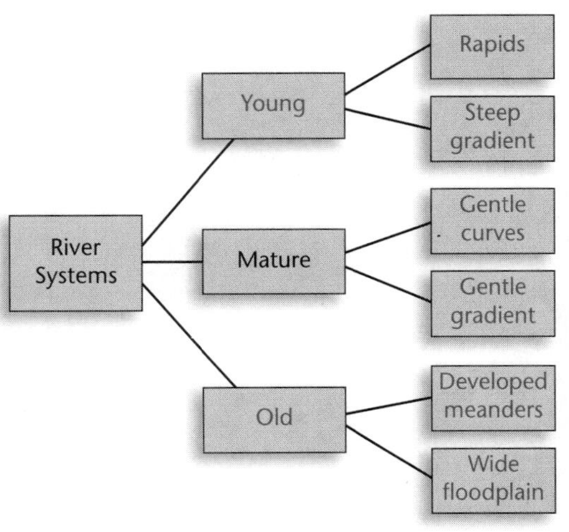

20. **Interpreting Data:** If the Brahmaputra River flows at a rate of 19 800 m^3/sec and the La Plata River flows at 79 300 m^3/sec, infer which river erodes more sediments.
21. **Hypothesizing:** Hypothesize why most of the silt in the Mississippi Delta is found farther out to sea than the sand-sized particles.
22. **Outlining:** Make an outline that explains the three stages of stream development.
23. **Using Variables, Constants, and Controls:** Explain how you could test the effect of slope on the amount of runoff produced.

Performance Assessment

1. **Designing an Experiment:** Design a way to compare the speeds of a mature meandering stream and a young straight stream.
2. **Making Observations and Inferences:** Experiment to find out the pore space of 100 mL of clay. Repeat your experiment to measure the pore space when you mix 50 mL of gravel with 50 mL of clay. Repeat once more with 50 mL of clay mixed with 50 mL of sand.
3. **Display:** Use a shoebox and clay to make a model of a limestone cave. Include stalactites, stalagmites, columns, and a sinkhole.

Assessment Resources

Reproducible Masters

Chapter Review, pp. 19-20
Assessment, pp. 44-47
Performance Assessment, p. 22

Glencoe Technology

Chapter Review Software
Computer Test Bank
MindJogger Videoquiz

Chapter 8 Review

22. **Outlining** Answers will vary, but students' outlines should include details of the three stages of development of a stream.
23. **Using Variables, Constants, and Controls** Answers may vary, but a simple way would be to use two cake pans filled with sand, two wooden blocks (one taller than the other), water, and a watch. The blocks could be placed under the pans so one pan is sloped much more than the other. The same amount of water would be poured at the top end of both pans at the same rate of speed. The amount of water reaching the bottom of the pans is the runoff.

Performance Assessment

1. Designs will vary, but students should include procedures for how they will design the two streambeds and measure the velocity. Use the Performance Task Assessment List for Designing an Experiment in **PASC,** p. 23. P
2. Students may use similar procedures to those used in the second MiniLAB in this chapter. Students will find that clay is impermeable. The particles are so close together that there is no pore space. When students mix the clay with gravel and sand, there will be an increase in pore space. Use the Performance Task Assessment List for Making Observations and Inferences in **PASC,** p. 17. P
3. Student models should include the cave structures that are listed. Use the Performance Task Assessment List for Display in **PASC,** p. 63. P

Objectives

Visual-Spatial Students will research the Oregon Trail and make a board game that simulates what a trip from Missouri to Oregon would have been like in the 1800s. L1 COOP LEARN

Summary

In this project, students will study the location of the Oregon Trail and learn about the landforms along the trail. Also, they will research the hardships that the pioneers traveling the trail would have encountered. They will design their board game as a map with spaces along the trail where events happen.

Time Required

This project is designed to be worked on throughout Unit 3. At least two class periods are needed to allow groups to research the Oregon Trail and to find out what life was like in the 1800s. Allow two to three class periods for students to make the board and cards, and to write the directions to their games. At least one class period will be needed for playing a game and responding to the questions asked in the *Go Further* section.

Preparation

- Establish cooperative groups of 2 or 3 students.
- Collect sources of information on the Oregon Trail and life in the 1800s. Also have atlases available for students to use.
- Ask students to bring poster board and markers for making the boards and cards.

UNIT PROJECT 2

The Oregon Trail

Thousands of people traveled the Oregon Trail from 1841 to the 1870s. It was a long and dangerous journey from Independence, Missouri, where the trail began, to destinations throughout Oregon. The pioneers traveled in wagons pulled by oxen over high mountains, prairies, deserts, plateaus, and rivers. If everything went smoothly along the trail, it took five months to complete the journey. But for many, the trip took much longer, and some never completed the journey at all.

The Oregon Trail in the 1800s

Research the path of the Oregon Trail. What landforms did it cross? Where were settlements along the trail? Find out why people wanted to travel over 2000 miles of wilderness to get to the Pacific Northwest. How much would it have cost a person to make the trip? What types of diseases were common in those days? What other health problems existed? What materials would they have to take with them? How did they get water? What hardships would have existed while they were crossing prairies, mountains, deserts, rivers, and plateaus? What weather problems would they have had to face?

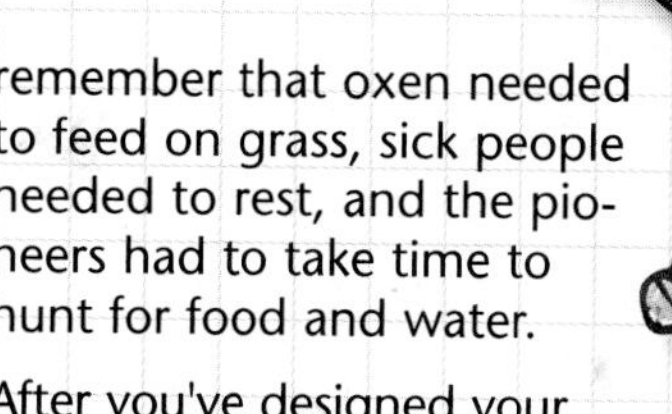

Procedures

1. Use the information in this unit and your research on the Oregon Trail to make a colorful map board game of the trail. Have spaces along the trail where players can move. Be sure to draw all important landforms and settlements along the trail.
2. Design game pieces and a way for players to move along the trail.
3. You may decide to use a spinner, dice, or another way to determine the spaces to move.
4. Label some spaces with problems people might have encountered, like "Quicksand in the river, lose your turn" or "Mudslide covers the trail, go back two spaces."
5. Design cards that players draw at various places along the trail. Cards might say, "You must hunt for food, lose one turn" or "You discover shortcut, jump ahead 3 spaces." In making your labels for the spaces and cards, consider how weather and landforms affected travel. Also, remember that oxen needed to feed on grass, sick people needed to rest, and the pioneers had to take time to hunt for food and water.
6. After you've designed your game, write directions for playing the game and describe the goal(s) of the game.

Going Further

After all members of your class have completed their board games, swap your game with another team, and play their game. After you've finished, describe similarities and differences in the games. Based on what you've learned, would you have enjoyed being in a wagon train on the Oregon Trail in the 1800s?

Teaching Strategies

- Before students begin their research, ask them how they think landforms and weather have influenced history. To stimulate discussion, ask them how early pioneers would cross mountain ranges, rivers, and deserts.
- Ask students why people would want to travel to distant places before the time of interstate highways and automobiles.
- As students are designing their boards and cards, tell them to use descriptions of weathering, erosion, and landforms as found in Chapters 5-8. Examples might include sandstorms, gully erosion, avalanches, high mountains, and others.
- Some spaces on the board should include severe weather conditions that would occur along a particular part of the trail. For example, snow, and even blizzards, could occur in the mountains; and drought, in a desert.
- Student games should include legends and a scale.

Go Further

Responses to the question about similarities and differences of the board games will vary. In response to the second question, many students will likely share that the many hardships along the Oregon Trail would have been so unpleasant that they would not have wanted to make the trip.

References

Fisher, Leonard Everett. *The Oregon Trail.* New York: Holiday House, 1990.

Parkman, Francis. *The Oregon Trail; Sketches of Prairie and Rocky-Mountain Life.* New York: Dodd, Mead, 1964.

Montgomery, Elizabeth R. *When Pioneers Pushed West to Oregon.* Champaign, Illinois: Garrard Publishing Co., 1970.

Stein, R. Conrad. *The Story of the Oregon Trail.* Chicago: Childrens Press, 1984.

UNIT 3

Earth's Internal Processes

In Unit 3, students are introduced to the relationships among earthquakes, volcanoes, and plate tectonics and how forces within Earth are tied to these relationships. Movement of hot rock material inside Earth's mantle causes plates—sections of Earth's crust—to move. This movement causes vibrations (earthquakes) and allows molten material to reach Earth's surface through volcanoes.

CONTENTS

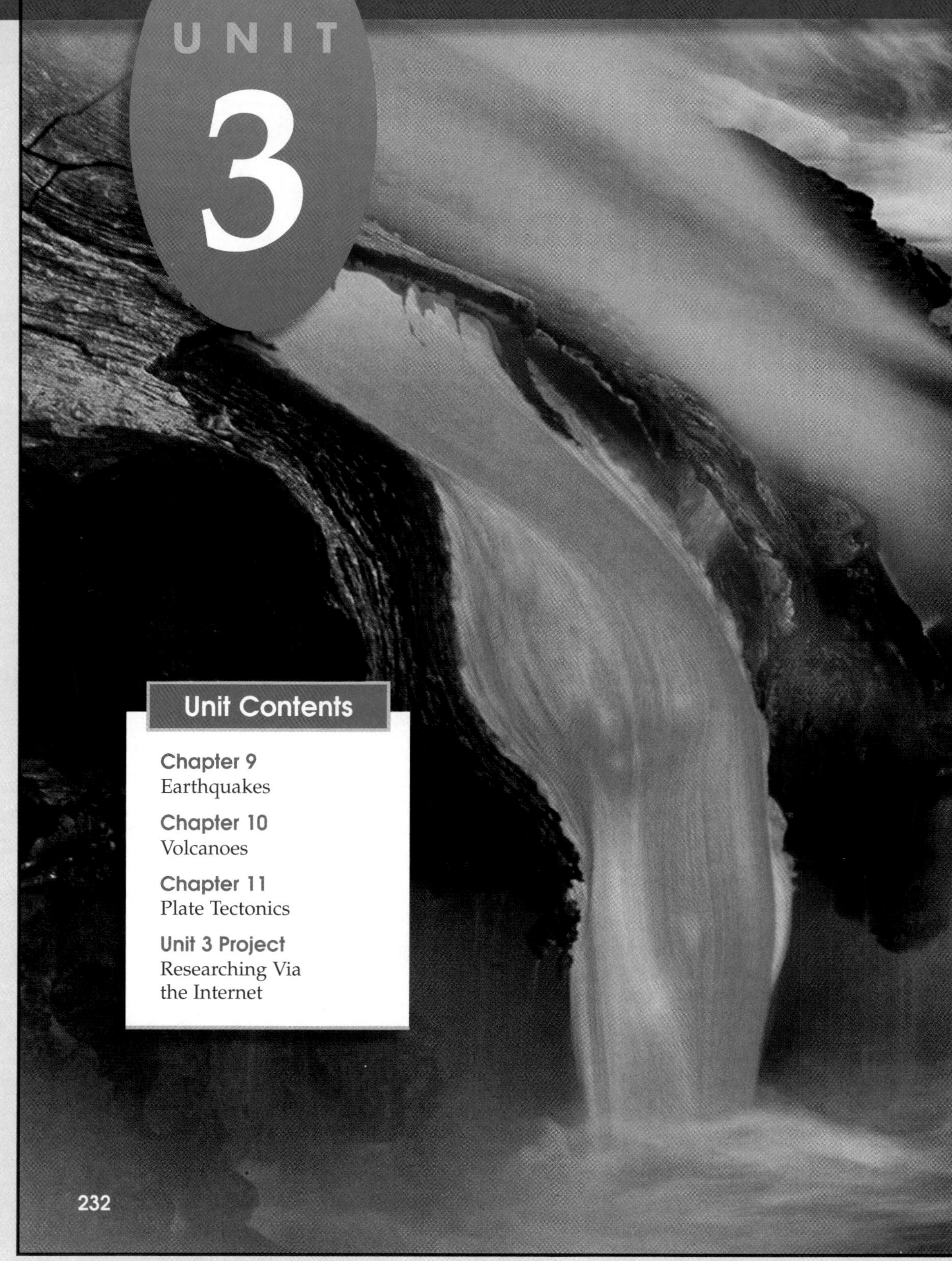

Science at Home

A World in Motion Have groups of students monitor newspapers, news magazines, and television news for stories about volcanic eruptions around the world. Encourage students to look for any relationship between earthquakes and volcanoes.

L1 COOP LEARN

Earth's Internal Processes

What's Happening Here?

Deep under the surface of Earth's crust, constant changes are taking place. Continents are shifting at an infinitesimal rate. Intense heat and pressure are melting solid rock into magma. On the surface of the planet, we go about our lives oblivious to the forces at work beneath the crust—until a spectacular event, such as the volcanic eruption shown here, reminds us of the magnitude of Earth's internal processes. Read on to learn more about volcanoes, earthquakes, and plate tectonics, and how these processes impact life on the surface of the planet.

Science Journal

A volcanic eruption is a major news event. Imagine that you are a reporter sent to cover a volcanic eruption in the Philippines. In your Science Journal, make a list of the questions you would use to interview people who witnessed the event.

Theme Connection

Energy Earthquakes are often rated on how much energy they release. An earthquake of magnitude 7 on the Richter scale releases about 32 times more energy than an earthquake of magnitude 6. Ask students how much more energy is released by a magnitude 7 quake than by a magnitude 5 quake.

Cultural Diversity

Volcanoes and Earthquakes Have students collect photos and articles about volcanoes and earthquakes from around the world. Have students make collages of the photos and discuss the cultural effects each volcano or earthquake might have had on the people living in the area. Encourage students to study why people continue to live near large, explosive volcanoes like Mount Vesuvius in Italy. L1

INTRODUCING THE UNIT

What's Happening Here?

Ask students to tell you how the photograph of the car engulfed by cooled lava relates to the larger photograph of lava flowing into the sea. Point out to students that in this unit, they will learn how forces inside Earth release great amounts of energy that can have devastating effects on Earth's surface.

Background

The lava of Kilauea is low in silica content. The low concentration of silica causes the lava to flow slowly. The lava is hot and often flows into the ocean before cooling. Although it can be destructive to villages, people and many animals can usually walk away from the slow-moving lava.

Previewing the Chapters

- Some students may be surprised that earthquakes and volcanoes are related. To preview the unit and reveal student preconceptions, have students compare and contrast **Figure 9-2** and **Figure 10-3.**
- Ask students to preview Chapter 11 to discover evidence for continental drift.

Tying to Previous Knowledge

- Ask students to recall television stories or magazine articles that demonstrated the damage done by earthquakes. Have students speculate on how they think most lives are lost during an earthquake.
- Have students list the areas of the United States most susceptible to volcanic activity.
- Ask students to use a globe of Earth to hypothesize how the continents may have once fit together.

Chapter Organizer

Section	Objectives	Activities/Features
Chapter Opener		Explore Activity: Show how forces inside Earth cause rocks to deform. p. 235
9-1 **Forces Inside Earth** (2 sessions, 1½ blocks)*	1. **Explain** how earthquakes result from the buildup of stress in Earth's crust. 2. **Contrast** normal, reverse, and strike-slip faults.	Connect to Physics, p. 238 Skill Builder: Concept Mapping, p. 240 Using Computers: Graphics, p. 240
9-2 **Earthquake Information** (2 sessions, 1 block)*	1. **Compare** and **contrast** primary, secondary, and surface waves. 2. **Explain** how an earthquake epicenter is located using seismic wave information. 3. **Describe** how seismic wave studies indicate the structure of Earth's interior.	Activity 9-1: Earthquake Depths, pp. 242-243 Science Journal, p. 244 Using Math, p. 245 MiniLAB: Can the travel time of seismic waves be used to find the distance to an earthquake? p. 246 Activity 9-2: Epicenter Location, p. 248 Problem Solving: What's in there? p. 249 Skill Builder: Making and Using Graphs, p. 251 Science Journal, p. 251
9-3 **Destruction by Earthquakes** (1 session, ½ block)*	1. **Define** *magnitude* and the *Richter scale.* 2. **List** ways to make your classroom and home more earthquake-safe.	Using Math, p. 253 Using Technology: Predicting Quakes, p. 254 MiniLAB: How can structures be made earthquake-safe? p. 256 Skill Builder: Making and Using Tables, p. 257 Using Math, p. 257
9-4 **Science and Society Technology: Living on a Fault** (1 session, ½ block)*	1. **Recognize** that most loss of life in an earthquake is caused by the destruction of human-made structures. 2. **Consider** who should pay for making structures seismic-safe.	Explore the Technology, p. 259 Science & History: Guatemala City, p. 260

* A complete Planning Guide that includes block scheduling is provided on pages 32T-35T.

Activity Materials

Explore	Activities	MiniLABs
page 235 3 small slabs of modeling clay	pages 242-243 graph paper page 248 **Figure 9-7**, metric ruler, chalk or water-soluble marker, string, globe	page 246 **Figure 9-7** page 256 wooden building blocks, rubber bands

Chapter 9 Earthquakes

Teacher Classroom Resources

Reproducible Masters	Transparencies
Study Guide, p. 37 **Reinforcement**, p. 37 **Enrichment**, p. 37 **Concept Mapping**, p. 23 **Critical Thinking/Problem Solving**, p. 15	**Section Focus Transparency 33**, Whose Fault Is It? **Science Integration Transparency 9**, Two Kinds of Waves **Teaching Transparency 17**, Types of Faults
Study Guide, p. 38 **Reinforcement**, p. 38 **Enrichment**, p. 38 **Activity Worksheets**, pp. 54-55, 56-57, 58 **Lab Manual 29**, Earthquakes **Lab Manual 30**, Locating an Earthquake **Science Integration Activity 9**, Do the Wave! **Cross-Curricular Integration**, p. 13	**Section Focus Transparency 34**, Getting Out of Line **Teaching Transparency 18**, Propagation of Earthquake Waves
Study Guide, p. 39 **Reinforcement**, p. 39 **Enrichment**, p. 39 **Activity Worksheets**, p. 59 **Multicultural Connections**, pp. 21-22	**Section Focus Transparency 35**, Scale of Destruction
Study Guide, p. 40 **Reinforcement**, p. 40 **Enrichment**, p. 40 **Science and Society Integration**, p. 13	**Section Focus Transparency 36**, Quake Safe

Teaching Resources

Glencoe Earth Science Interactive Videodisc
Earth Science CD-ROM
Spanish Resources
English/Spanish Audiocassettes
Cooperative Learning Resource Guide
Lab Partner
Lab and Safety Skills
Lesson Plans

Assessment Resources

Chapter Review, pp. 21-22
Assessment, pp. 59-62
Performance Assessment in the Science Classroom (PASC)
MindJogger Videoquiz
Alternate Assessment in the Science Classroom
Performance Assessment
Chapter Review Software
Computer Test Bank

Key to Teaching Strategies

The following designations will help you decide which activities are appropriate for your students.

L1 Level 1 activities should be within the ability range of all students.

L2 Level 2 activities should be within the ability range of the average to above-average student.

L3 Level 3 activities are designed for the ability range of above-average students.

LEP LEP activities should be within the ability range of Limited English Proficiency students.

LS These activities are designed to address different learning styles.

COOP LEARN Cooperative Learning activities are designed for small group work.

P These strategies represent student products that can be placed into a best-work portfolio.

GLENCOE TECHNOLOGY

The following multimedia resources are available from Glencoe.

The Infinite Voyage Series
Living with Disaster
Science and Technology Videodisc Series (STVS)
Earth & Space
Seismic Simulator

National Geographic Society Series
STV: Restless Earth
Earth Science CD-ROM

Teacher Classroom Resources

This is a representation of key blackline masters available in the Teacher Classroom Resources.

Teaching Aids

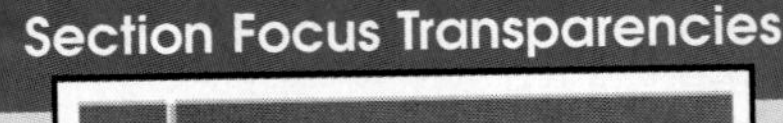

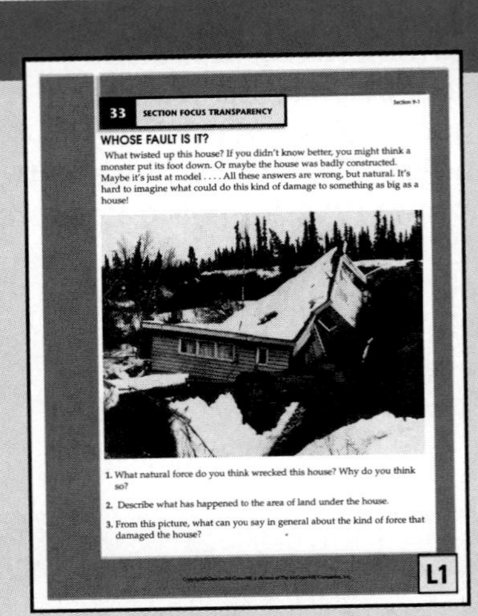
33 SECTION FOCUS TRANSPARENCY Section 9-1

WHOSE FAULT IS IT?

What twisted up this house? If you didn't know better, you might think a monster put its foot down. Or maybe the house was badly constructed. Maybe it's just at model . . . . All these answers are wrong, but natural. It's hard to imagine what could do this kind of damage to something as big as a house!

1. What natural force do you think wrecked this house? Why do you think so?
2. Describe what has happened to the area of land under the house.
3. From this picture, what can you say in general about the kind of force that damaged the house?

L1

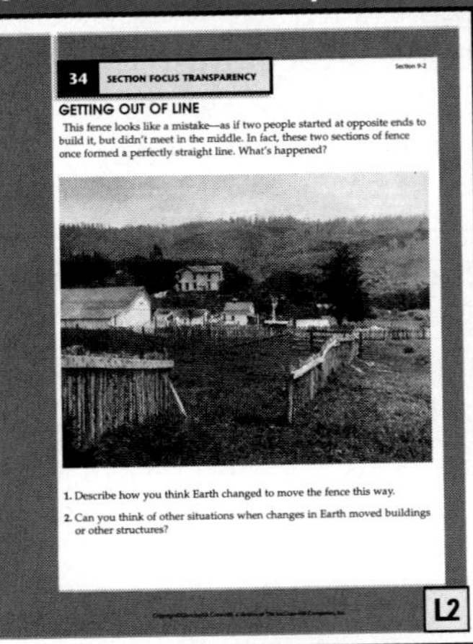
34 SECTION FOCUS TRANSPARENCY Section 9-2

GETTING OUT OF LINE

This fence looks like a mistake—as if two people started at opposite ends to build it, but didn't meet in the middle. In fact, these two sections of fence once formed a perfectly straight line. What's happened?

1. Describe how you think Earth changed to move the fence this way.
2. Can you think of other situations when changes in Earth moved buildings or other structures?

L2

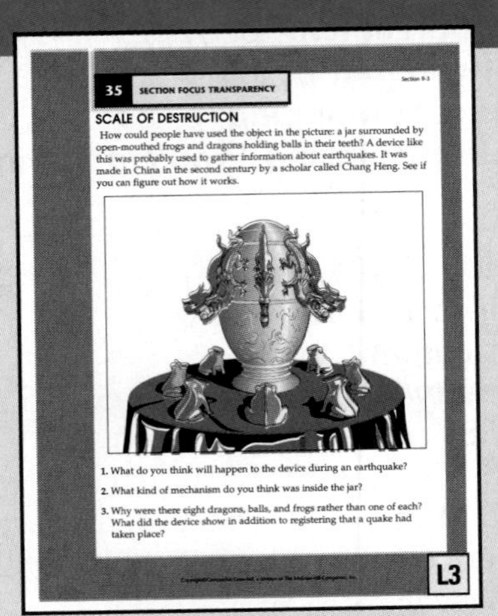
35 SECTION FOCUS TRANSPARENCY Section 9-3

SCALE OF DESTRUCTION

How could people have used the object in the picture: a jar surrounded by open-mouthed frogs and dragons holding balls in their teeth? A device like this was probably used to gather information about earthquakes. It was made in China in the second century by a scholar called Chang Heng. See if you can figure out how it works.

1. What do you think will happen to the device during an earthquake?
2. What kind of mechanism do you think was inside the jar?
3. Why were there eight dragons, balls, and frogs rather than one of each? What did the device show in addition to registering that a quake had taken place?

L3

Science Integration Transparencies

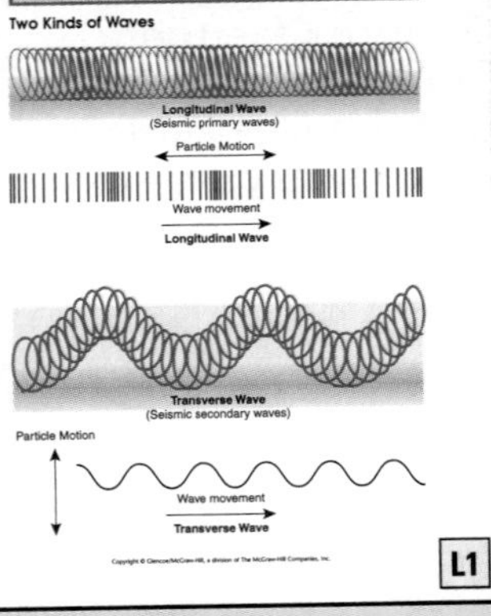
9 SCIENCE INTEGRATION TRANSPARENCY

Two Kinds of Waves

L1

Teaching Transparencies

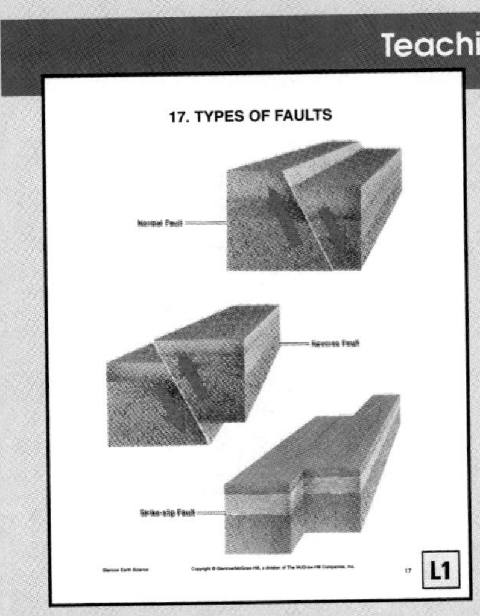
17. TYPES OF FAULTS

L1

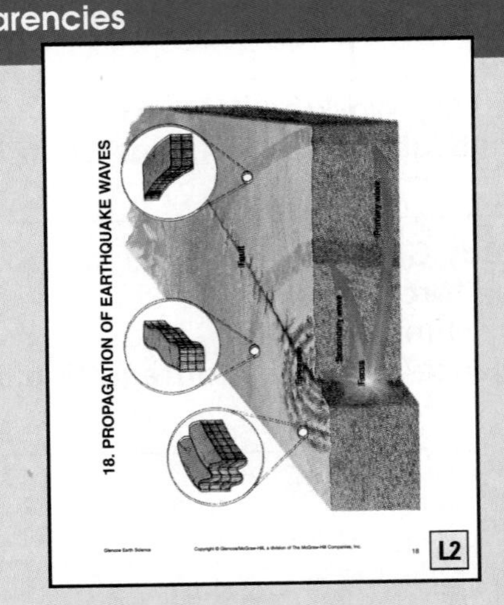
18. PROPAGATION OF EARTHQUAKE WAVES

L2

Meeting Different Ability Levels

Study Guide

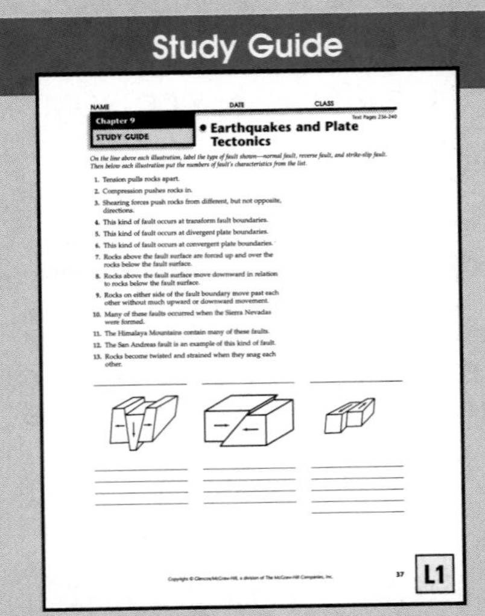
Chapter 9 STUDY GUIDE

Earthquakes and Plate Tectonics

L1

Reinforcement

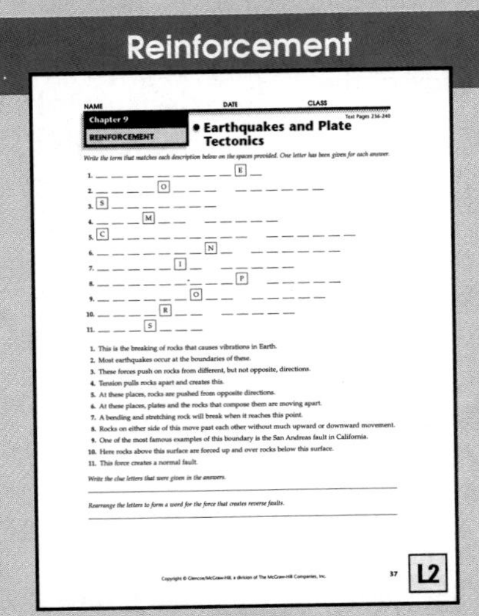
Chapter 9 REINFORCEMENT

Earthquakes and Plate Tectonics

L2

Enrichment Worksheets

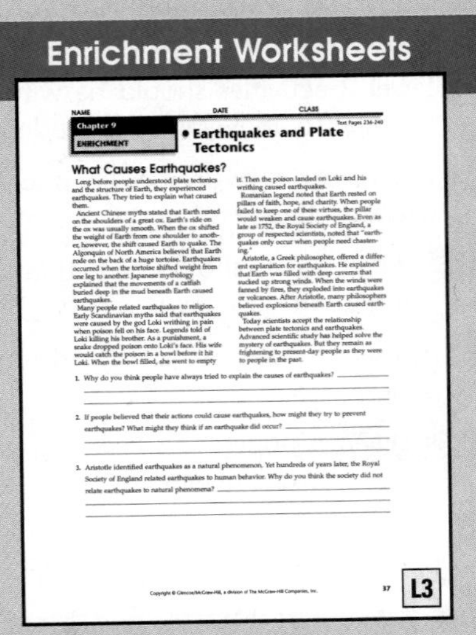
Chapter 9 ENRICHMENT

Earthquakes and Plate Tectonics

What Causes Earthquakes?

L3

Hands-On Activities

Science Integration Activity

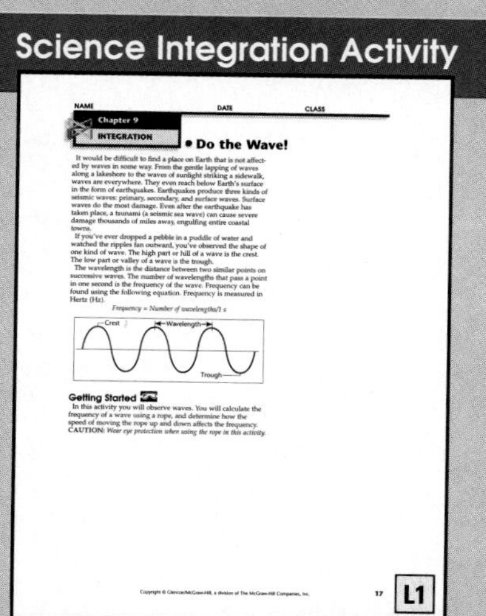
Chapter 9 INTEGRATION • Do the Wave!

Getting Started

L1

Lab Manual

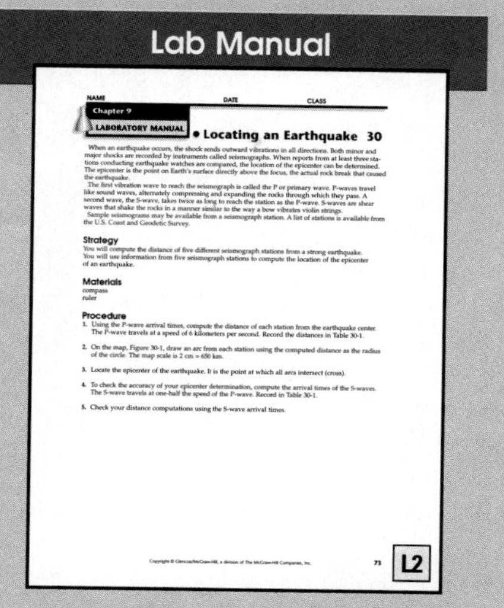
Chapter 9 LABORATORY MANUAL • Locating an Earthquake 30

Strategy

Materials

Procedure

L2

Assessment

Performance Assessment

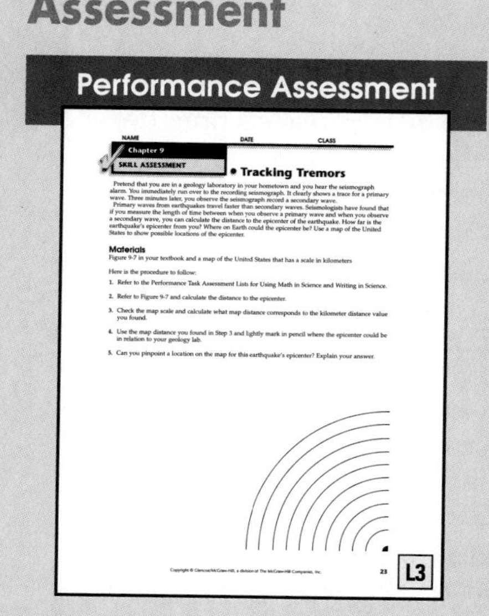
Chapter 9 SKILL ASSESSMENT • Tracking Tremors

Materials

L3

Enrichment and Application

Critical Thinking/ Problem Solving

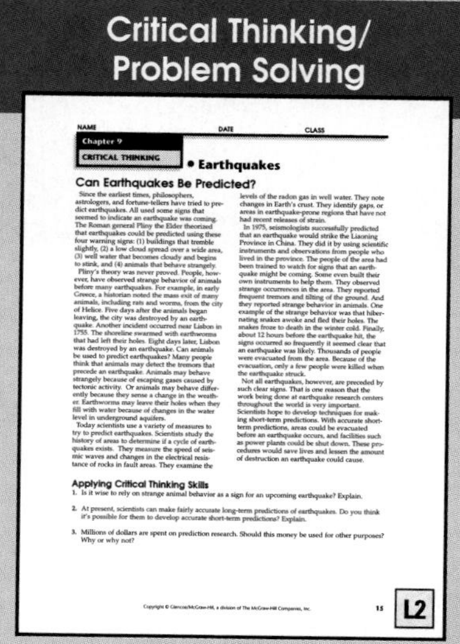
Chapter 9 CRITICAL THINKING • Earthquakes

Can Earthquakes Be Predicted?

Applying Critical Thinking Skills

L2

Cross-Curricular Integration

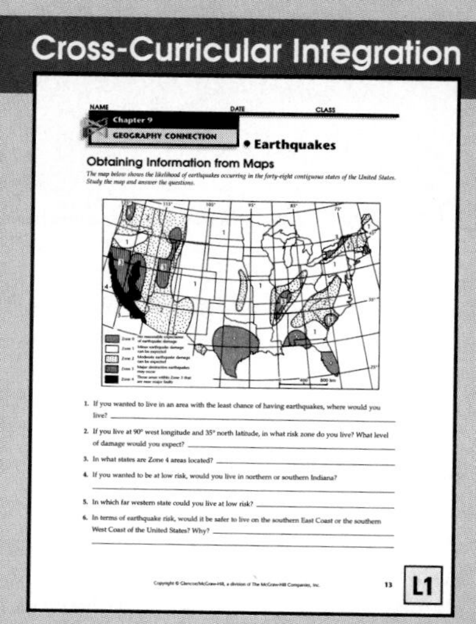
Chapter 9 GEOGRAPHY CONNECTION • Earthquakes

Obtaining Information from Maps

L1

Science and Society Integration

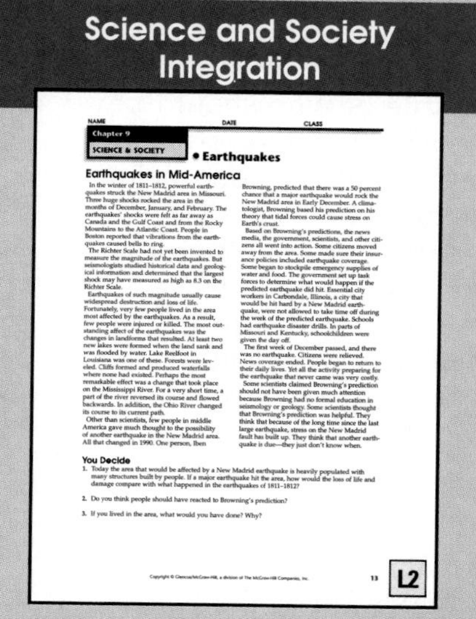
Chapter 9 SCIENCE & SOCIETY • Earthquakes

Earthquakes in Mid-America

You Decide

L2

Multicultural Connections

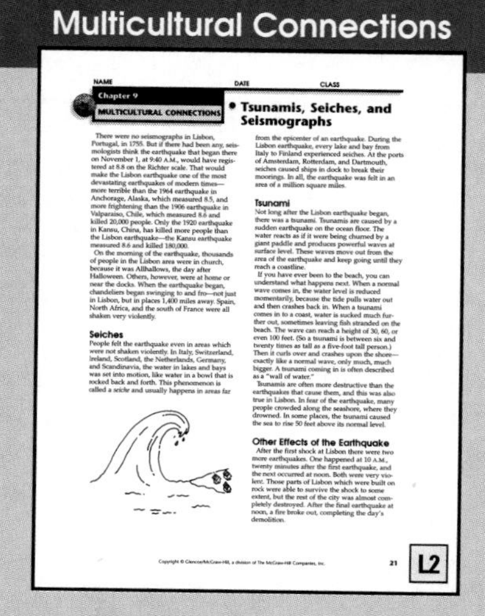
Chapter 9 MULTICULTURAL CONNECTIONS • Tsunamis, Seiches, and Seismographs

Seiches

Tsunami

Other Effects of the Earthquake

L2

Concept Mapping

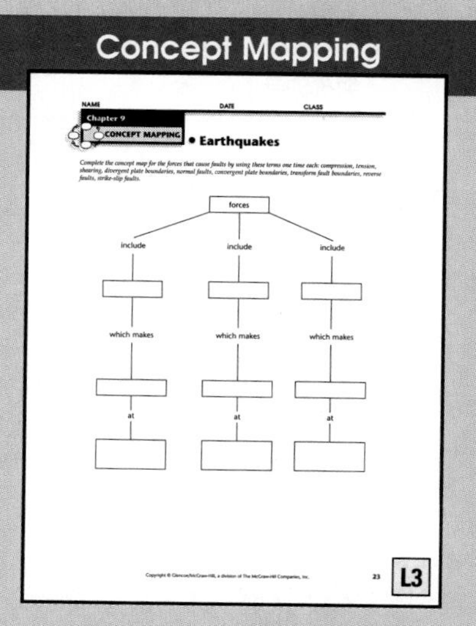
Chapter 9 CONCEPT MAPPING • Earthquakes

L3

Chapter 9

Earthquakes

CHAPTER OVERVIEW

Section 9-1 This section describes the causes of earthquakes. Three types of faults are also defined.

Section 9-2 Information that can be obtained from earthquakes is presented. Seismic waves and how they are used to locate an earthquake are discussed. A model of Earth's interior obtained from seismic data is also presented.

Section 9-3 The destruction caused by earthquakes, and methods of measuring earthquake magnitude and destruction are discussed. Earthquake safety also is introduced.

Section 9-4 **Science and Society** Students are presented with the issue of who should pay for earthquake preparation. They are asked to consider whether only people living in earthquake-prone areas should deal with the problem of preparation or whether others should help.

Chapter Vocabulary

fault	surface wave
earthquake	inner core
normal fault	outer core
reverse fault	mantle
strike-slip fault	crust
seismic wave	Moho discontinuity
focus	seismologist
primary wave	seismograph
secondary wave	magnitude
epicenter	tsunamis

Theme Connection

Energy Energy is the theme of this chapter. Forces inside Earth generate energy. This energy released during an earthquake as seismic waves should be emphasized as you teach each section.

Previewing the Chapter

234

Look for the following logo for strategies that emphasize different learning modalities. LS

Kinesthetic	Explore, p. 235; Activity, p. 237; Making a Model, p. 249
Visual-Spatial	Demonstration, p. 238; Theme Connection, p. 249; Across the Curriculum, p. 250
Interpersonal	Activity, p. 237; Brainstorming, p. 244; MiniLAB, p. 256
Logical-Mathematical	Across the Curriculum, pp. 238, 250; Activities 9-1, pp. 242-243; 9-2, p. 248; MiniLAB, p. 246; Using Math, p. 253; Integrating the Sciences, p. 254
Linguistic	Science Journal, pp. 239, 247, 256; Across the Curriculum, p. 246

Chapter 9

Earthquakes

You may have seen pictures such as the one shown here of the 1995 Hanshin-Awaji (Kobe), Japan earthquake. Have you ever thought about what caused this earthquake, or wondered if it could happen where you live? As you read this chapter, you will explore how movement and forces inside Earth produce earthquakes.

EXPLORE ACTIVITY

Show how forces inside Earth cause rocks to deform.

1. Place three pieces of clay flat on a table.
2. Place your hands on opposite ends of one of the pieces of clay.
3. Begin pushing your hands together, compressing the clay.
4. Now hold another piece of clay in your hands.
5. Begin to apply tension by gradually pulling the clay apart.
6. Holding the third piece of clay flat on the table, begin pushing so that one hand slides past the other hand.

Observe: What happens to the clay layer when your hands compress it from directly opposite directions? What happens to the clay layer when you gradually pull it apart? What happens to the clay when you push on it so that your hands eventually slide past each other? Draw a picture of each of the three clay pieces in your Science Journal.

Previewing Science Skills

- In the **Skill Builders**, you will **compare and contrast, map concepts, make and use graphs**, and **make and use tables.**
- In the **Activities**, you will **measure, construct and interpret graphs, analyze data**, and **draw conclusions.**
- In the **MiniLABs**, you will **interpret graphs, analyze data**, and **evaluate hypotheses.**

EXPLORE ACTIVITY

Purpose

LS **Kinesthetic** Use the Explore Activity to introduce students to forces that cause rocks to deform. Inform students that they will be learning how these forces can cause earthquakes. L1 LEP COOP LEARN

Preparation

Obtain several kilograms of modeling clay in various colors.

Materials

two 10 cm × 5 cm × 1 cm slabs of clay for each group of four students

Teaching Strategies

- You may wish to have students work with the clay on waxed paper.
- Advise students to gradually apply compression and tension to the slabs of clay.

Observe

Students will notice that clay folds when compressed. Tension will cause the clay to stretch, thin, and eventually break. Shear forces will cause the clay to fold and eventually to break. Student illustrations should show the above concepts.

Assessment

Content Ask students to relate what they have observed to structures they may be familiar with on Earth's surface. Use the Performance Task Assessment List for Making Observations and Inferences in **PASC,** p. 17. P

Assessment Planner

Portfolio
Refer to page 261 for suggested items that students might select for their portfolios.

Performance Assessment
See page 261 for additional Performance Assessment options.
Skill Builders, pp. 240, 251, 257
MiniLABs, pp. 246, 256
Activities 9-1, pp. 242-243; 9-2, p. 248

Content Assessment
Section Wrap-ups, pp. 240, 251, 257, 259
Chapter Review, pp. 261-263
Mini Quizzes, pp. 240, 250, 257

Group Assessment
Opportunities for group assessment occur with Cooperative Learning Strategies and Flex Your Brain Activities.

Section 9•1

Prepare

Section Background

- Compressional forces are applied to rocks at convergent plate boundaries. Tensional forces are applied where plates diverge. Shear forces are applied when plates slide past each other.
- Compressional and shear forces cause rocks to fold. But if these forces are great or are applied suddenly, breaks can occur. Tensional forces tend to cause fractures.

1 Motivate

Bellringer

Before presenting the lesson, display **Section Focus Transparency 33** on the overhead projector. Assign the accompanying **Focus Activity** worksheet. L1 LEP

Tying to Previous Knowledge

Help students recall recent earthquakes and discuss where they were located. Discuss any faults that students may be familiar with that occur in the vicinity of recent earthquakes.

GLENCOE TECHNOLOGY

CD-ROM

Earth Science CD-ROM

Have students perform the interactive exploration for Chapter 9 to reinforce important chapter concepts and thinking processes.

9•1 Forces Inside Earth

Science Words

fault
earthquake
normal fault
reverse fault
strike-slip fault

Objectives

- Explain how earthquakes result from the buildup of stress in Earth's crust.
- Contrast normal, reverse, and strike-slip faults.

Causes of Earthquakes

Think about the last time you used a rubber band to hold a roll of papers together. You knew you could stretch the rubber band only so far before it would break. Rubber bands bend and stretch when force is applied to them. Because they are elastic, they return to their original shape once the force is released. Plastic or play putty, as shown in **Figure 9-1,** acts in much the same way. With a certain amount of applied stress, plastic will undergo elastic deformation, but then it returns to normal. With additional stress, the plastic will undergo plastic deformation. Once it bends, it remains in the deformed shape.

Passing the Elastic Limit Causes Faulting

There is a limit to how far a rubber band will stretch or plastic will deform. Once this elastic limit is passed, the rubber band or plastic breaks. Rocks act in much the same way. Up to a point, applied stresses cause rocks to bend and stretch, undergoing elastic or plastic deformation. Once their elastic limit is passed, the rocks remain bent and may break. Rocks break and move along surfaces called **faults.** The rocks on either side of a fault move in different directions.

What produces the forces that cause faults to form? Obviously, something must be causing the rocks to move; otherwise, the rocks would just rest quietly without any stress

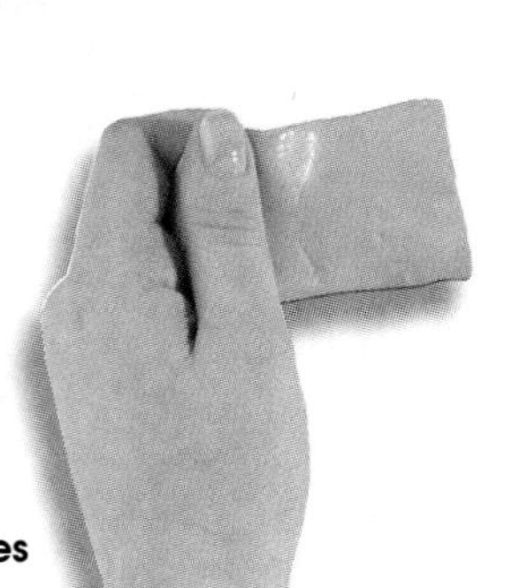

Figure 9-1

Play putty can be used to demonstrate applied stresses and the elastic limit.

Program Resources

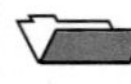

Reproducible Masters

Study Guide, p. 37 L1
Reinforcement, p. 37 L1
Enrichment, p. 37 L3
Concept Mapping, p. 23
Critical Thinking/Problem Solving, p. 15

Transparencies

Section Focus Transparency 33 L1
Science Integration Transparency 9
Teaching Transparency 17

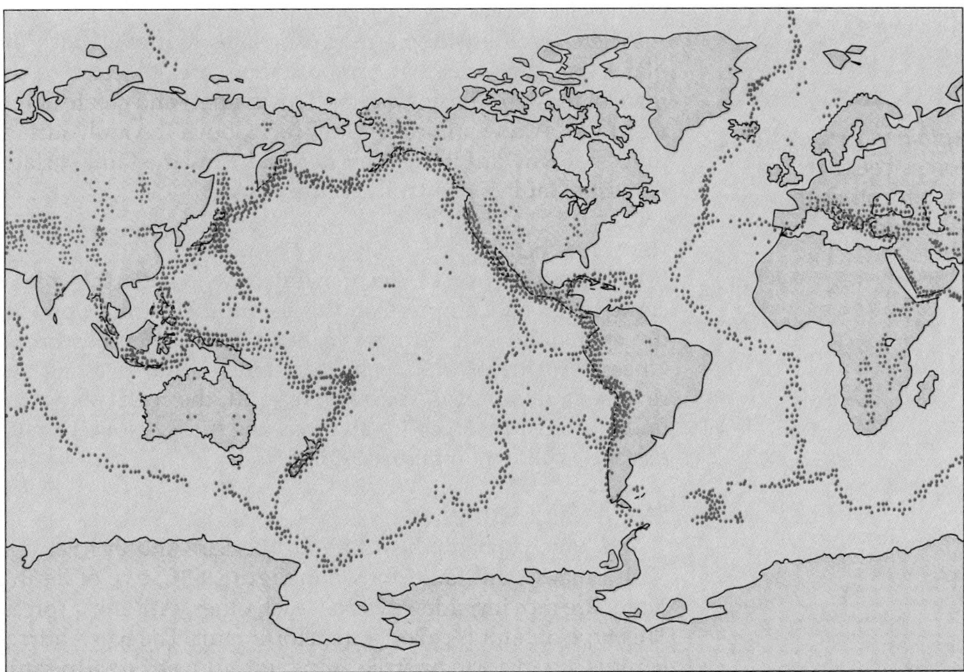

Figure 9-2

The dots represent the epicenters of the major quakes over a ten-year period. Eighty percent of earthquakes occur along the edges of the area known as the Pacific Plate. *Based on what you know of the area, why is this earthquake-prone area called the Pacific Ring of Fire?*

building up in them. However, Earth's crust is in constant motion because of forces inside Earth. These forces cause sections of Earth's crust to move, putting stress on rocks. To relieve this stress, the rocks tend to bend, compress, and stretch like plastic or rubber bands. But if the force is great enough, the rocks break. This breaking produces vibrations, called **earthquakes.**

Types of Faults

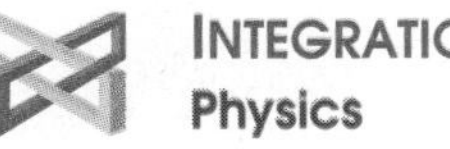

Rocks experience several types of forces where sections or plates of the Earth's crust and upper mantle meet, as shown in **Figure 9-2.** In the Explore Activity at the beginning of this chapter, you experimented with three forces—compression, tension, and shear. Compression is a force or stress that squeezes and compresses, while tension is the stress that causes stretching and elongation. Shear is the force that causes slippage and the rocks on either side of the fault to move past each other. Let's take a look at these three forces and the types of faults they create.

Visual Learning

Figure 9-2 Refer to the illustration of Earth's plates, the Pacific Plate in particular. **Based on what you know of this area, why is this earthquake-prone area called the Pacific Ring of Fire?** *Many volcanoes are located at the edge of the Pacific Plate.* LEP LS

2 Teach

Discussion

Obtain photographs or articles featuring recent earthquakes, such as the 1995 earthquake in Kobe, Japan; the 1993 Indian earthquake; the 1989 Loma Prieta, CA, earthquake; or the 1985 Mexico City earthquake to share with students. *Time, Newsweek,* or *National Geographic* are excellent sources for this type of information. Lead a discussion as to why earthquakes are able to cause such destruction.

Activity

LS **Interpersonal** Form groups of four students. Have one student serve as recorder. Have each of the other students apply compression, tension, and shear forces to bars of taffy. Have the recorder draw what happens to each bar of taffy. Have students relate this to what happens to rocks when forces are applied. Ask students what might happen if the force were applied suddenly. Encourage each team to try this. L1 COOP LEARN

LS **Kinesthetic** The point at which a rock no longer bends but rather breaks due to applied forces is the rock's elastic limit. Different materials have different elastic limits. Have students bend the materials listed to see what happens once the elastic limit is reached on a piece of cardboard, a plastic drinking straw, a wooden tongue depressor, a thin steel wire, some silicon putty, and a very thin sheet of slate or shale. Have students wear goggles during this activity. L1 LEP

INTEGRATION Physics

Three forces inside Earth—compression, tension, and shear—cause various structures to form in rocks. Normal faults are usually caused by tension, folds and reverse faults usually form due to compression, and shear forces produce strike-slip faults.

Demonstration

LS **Visual-Spatial** Contrast the three types of faults by preparing a large, triple-decker peanut butter and jelly sandwich. Cut off the crusts so the individual layers can be seen. Construct a "fault" at about a 30° angle by cutting through the sandwich. Move the separate halves of the sandwich to demonstrate normal, reverse, and strike-slip faults. Draw a low-angle reverse fault (10°) on the board and ask students to hypothesize why this type of fault is also called a thrust fault. LEP

CONNECT TO **PHYSICS**

Answer Shearing forces push on rocks from different but not opposite directions. Forces of this type do not cause rocks to collide but to slide past each other.

NATIONAL GEOGRAPHIC SOCIETY

Videodisc

STV: Restless Earth

Faulting (Art)

52204

CONNECT TO **PHYSICS**

E*xplain* why shearing forces cause strike-slip faults rather than reverse faults.

Normal Faults

Where forces inside Earth cause plates to move apart, the plates and the rocks that compose them are subjected to the force of tension. Tension can pull rocks apart and create a **normal fault.** Along a normal fault, rock above the fault surface moves downward in relation to rock below the fault surface. A normal fault is shown in **Figure 9-3A.**

Reverse Faults

Compression forces are generated where Earth's plates come together. Compression pushes on rocks from opposite directions and causes them to bend and sometimes break. Once they break, the rocks continue to move along the reverse fault surface. At a **reverse fault,** the rocks above the fault surface are forced up and over the rocks below the fault surface as shown in **Figure 9-3B.**

Strike-Slip Faults

You have probably heard about the San Andreas Fault in California. At this fault, shown in **Figure 9-3C,** two of Earth's plates are moving sideways past each other with shear forces. This type of fault is called a transform fault. The San Andreas Fault is a transform or strike-slip fault. At a **strike-slip fault,** rocks on either side of the fault surface are moving past each

Figure 9-3

As you learned in the Explore Activity, rock layers are affected differently by tension, compression, and shear forces. *With which type of force(s) would Earth's crust be stretched and thinned? With which type(s) would Earth's crust be folded and thickened?*

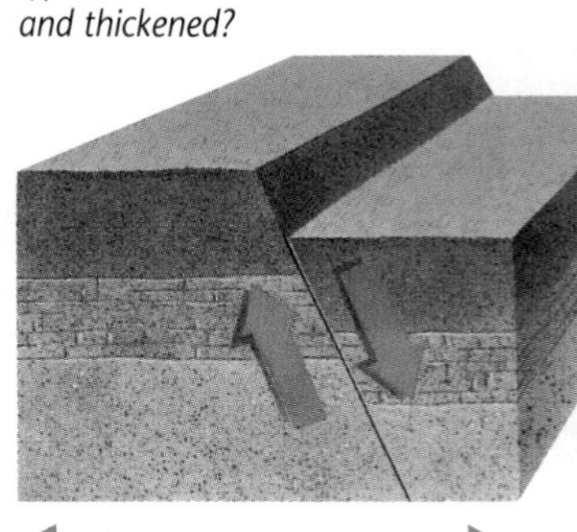

A When rock moves along a fracture caused by tension forces, the break is called a normal fault. Rock above the fault moves downward in relation to the rock below the fault surface. Normal faults can form mountains such as the Sierra Nevadas, which border California on the east.

Integrating the Sciences

Physics Ask students the following questions about forces inside Earth. **What happens to rocks when compression is gradually applied?** *Gradual pushing from opposite directions tends to make rocks bend or fold.* **What will happen if compression is applied very quickly to rocks?** *Rocks will bend until their elastic limits are reached. Once this occurs, the rocks will remain bent and may break.*

Across the Curriculum

Mathematics The Sierra Nevadas formed over a period of 10 million years. Mt. Whitney is one of the many peaks in the range that stand 4000 m above sea level. Have students compute an average annual rate of uplift. L1 LS

other without much upward or downward movement. Compare the faults in **Figure 9-3.** How do they differ?

As the rocks move past each other at a strike-slip fault, their irregular surfaces snag each other, and the rocks are twisted and strained. Not only are they deformed, but also, the snagging of the irregular surface hinders the movement of the plates. As forces keep driving the plates to move, the stress builds up and the rocks reach their elastic limit. When the rocks are stressed past their elastic limit, they break and an earthquake results.

B When compression forces break rock, the rock above the fault surface moves upward in relation to the rock below the fault surface. The mountains shown are in Rocky Mountain National Park, Colorado.

C Shear forces push on rock in opposite but not directly opposite horizontal directions. There is very little vertical movement along a strike-slip fault. When they are strong enough, these forces split rock and create strike-slip faults. Movement along faults like the San Andreas Fault shown here, is usually short and sudden, but can be slow and steady.

Visual Learning

Figure 9-3 With which type of force(s) would Earth's crust be stretched and thinned? With which type(s) would Earth's crust be folded and thickened? *Tension. Compression.* LEP LS

3 Assess

Check for Understanding

FLEX Your Brain

Use the Flex Your Brain activity to have students explore EARTHQUAKES. Students should discover that earthquakes can be caused not only by movement along plate boundaries but also by movement of magma during volcanic activity. Some students may also investigate *Earth tides.* Earth tides are the cyclic rising and falling of the surface of the solid earth. They are similar to ocean tides in that they are also the result of the gravitational attraction of the sun and moon. This fluctuation of the solid earth (of up to 20 centimeters) is often suspected to be a cause of some earthquakes.

Activity Worksheets, p. 5

Reteach

Have students use their hands or textbooks to demonstrate the movement that occurs along each of the three kinds of faults.

Extension

For students who have mastered this section, use the **Reinforcement** and **Enrichment** masters.

Integrating the Sciences

Physics After reviewing the three forces inside Earth, ask students why folds in Earth's rocks are more likely with compression than with tension. *Compression will gradually cause rock layers to bend like a sheet of paper that is pushed together. Tension will cause a thinning of Earth's crust and cracking just as paper will tear when pulled in opposite directions.*

Science Journal

Landers Quake After researching the 1992 Landers, CA, earthquake, have students write a summary in their Science Journals explaining why this earthquake is so important to the study of faults and earthquakes. *The Landers, CA, quake may have triggered other earthquakes and may indicate that a new fault is being born in the desert.* L1 LS

4 Close

•MINI•QUIZ•

Use the Mini Quiz to check students' recall of chapter content.

1. **Which type of force causes a normal fault?** *tension*
2. **Rocks above the fault surface are forced up and over the rocks below the fault surface in a ______ fault.** *reverse*
3. **The ______ Fault is a strike-slip fault.** *San Andreas*

Section Wrap-up

Review

1. Forces are applied from different, but not directly opposite, directions.
2. The compression forces can cause rocks to break. One block is forced over another, forming a reverse fault.
3. The forces that cause the faults are different. Normal faults are caused by tension. Reverse faults are due to compression. Tension allows the rocks above the fault to slide downward as the rocks are pulled apart. Compression forces one block of rocks up and over another.
4. **Think Critically** Most earthquakes occur near plate boundaries. If earthquakes have occurred in an area in the past, they will probably occur again, but it cannot be predicted when.

Using Computers

Student models should show appropriate motion of Earth for each of the fault types (normal, reverse, and strike-slip).

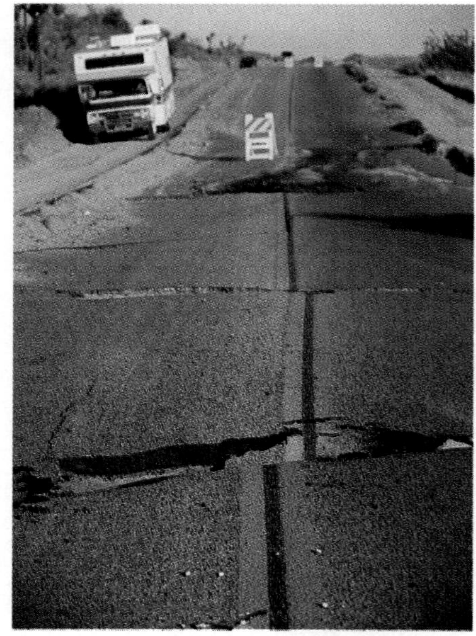

Earthquakes can be dramatic events. Some of them have devastating effects, while others go almost unnoticed. Regardless of their magnitudes, most earthquakes are the result of the plates moving over, under, and around each other. If these plates simply slid smoothly past each other, the tension, compression, and shear forces would not build up stress. But in actuality, rocks do experience these forces and stresses build up in them, causing small amounts of deformation, as seen in **Figure 9-4.** When rocks break because of the stress, energy is released along the fault surfaces and we observe the effects in the form of earthquakes.

Figure 9-4

Geologists use surface evidence like these cracks when searching for dangerous hidden fractures or faults.

Section Wrap-up

Review

1. Why is a shearing force usually generated at strike-slip fault boundaries?
2. The Appalachian Mountains formed when two of Earth's plates collided. Explain why reverse faults are the most common in these mountains.
3. The surfaces of normal faults and reverse faults look very similar. How do forces cause rocks above the fault surface to slide down at a normal fault and up at a reverse fault?
4. **Think Critically:** Why is it easier to predict *where* an earthquake will occur than it is to predict *when* it will occur?

Using Computers

Graphics Use the graphics capabilities of a computer to make simple working models of the three types of faults: normal, reverse, and strike-slip.

Skill Builder

Concept Mapping

Make a cycle concept map that shows why many earthquakes occur along the San Andreas Fault. Use the following terms and phrases: *rocks, stress, bend and stretch, elastic limit reached, earthquakes.* If you need help, refer to Concept Mapping in the **Skill Handbook.**

Skill Builder

One possible solution:

stress causes bending and stretching of rocks → the elastic limit is reached → earthquake results → causes stress → stress causes bending and stretching of rocks

Assessment

Performance Use this Skill Builder to assess students' abilities to make a cycle concept map. Have students brainstorm on the best way to construct the concept map. Use the Performance Task Assessment List for Concept Map in **PASC,** p. 89. P

Earthquake Information

9•2

Types of Seismic Waves

Have you ever seen a coiled-spring toy? When children play with a coiled-spring toy, they send energy waves through it. **Seismic waves,** generated by an earthquake, are similar to the waves of the toy. Where are seismic waves formed? How do they move through Earth and how can we use the information that they carry? Let's investigate how scientists have answered these questions.

Earthquake Focus

As you have learned, when rocks move along a fault surface, energy is released and damage occurs, as seen in **Figure 9-5.** The point in Earth's interior where this energy release occurs is the **focus** of the earthquake. Seismic waves are produced and travel outward from the earthquake focus.

Science Words

seismic wave
focus
primary wave
secondary wave
epicenter
surface wave
inner core
outer core
mantle
crust
Moho discontinuity

Objectives

- Compare and contrast primary, secondary, and surface waves.
- Explain how an earthquake epicenter is located using seismic wave information.
- Describe how seismic wave studies indicate the structure of Earth's interior.

Figure 9-5

As shown in this photograph of buildings damaged during the 1989 Loma Prieta, California earthquake, surface waves cause most earthquake damage. This earthquake was caused by the Pacific Plate slipping past the North American Plate by only 2 m. *Why would surface waves generate so much damage?*

Section 9•2

Prepare

Section Background

- Primary waves are referred to as P-waves, secondary waves as S-waves, and surface waves as L-waves.
- Shallow-focus earthquakes occur where sections (plates) of Earth's crust are diverging and near the edges of plates that are converging. Intermediate- and deep-focus earthquakes occur where one plate subducts under another.

Preplanning

- To prepare for Activity 9-1, obtain sheets of graph paper.
- To prepare for Activity 9-2, obtain string, metric rulers, and several globes of Earth.

1 Motivate

Bellringer

Before presenting the lesson, display **Section Focus Transparency 34** on the overhead projector. Assign the accompanying **Focus Activity** worksheet. L1 LEP

Tying to Previous Knowledge

Have students recall the use of the words *primary* and *secondary* in other subjects. Based on what they know about the use of these words, ask them to hypothesize as to which type of seismic wave, primary or secondary, travels through Earth faster.

Visual Learning

Figure 9-5 Why would surface waves generate so much damage? *As surface waves pass, rigid structures like buildings and bridges fail.* LEP IS

Program Resources

Reproducible Masters

Study Guide, p. 38 L1
Reinforcement, p. 38 L1
Enrichment, p. 38 L3
Cross-Curricular Integration, p. 13
Activity Worksheets, pp. 5, 54-55, 56-57, 58 L1
Science Integration Activities, pp. 17-18
Lab Manual 29, 30

Transparencies

Section Focus Transparency 34 L1
Teaching Transparency 18

Activity 9-1

PREPARATION

Purpose

LS **Logical-Mathematical** Students will design and carry out an investigation to illustrate any relationship between the depth of earthquake foci and epicenter location or the movement of Earth's plates. L1 COOP LEARN

Process Skills

observing and inferring, communicating, using numbers, interpreting data, hypothesizing, making and using tables, making and using graphs, comparing and contrasting, designing an experiment, separating and controlling variables

Time

45 minutes

Materials

graph paper, pencil

Possible Hypotheses

As sections of Earth's crust move around, they can collide at some locations and move apart at others. When they collide, stress is built up near Earth's surface. If one section slides under another, stress in rocks is built up deep down inside Earth. Stress is also built up near Earth's surface when sections of the crust split and move apart.

Activity Worksheets, pp. 5, 54-55

PLAN THE EXPERIMENT

Possible Procedures

1. Produce a graph of earthquake foci similar to the one below.

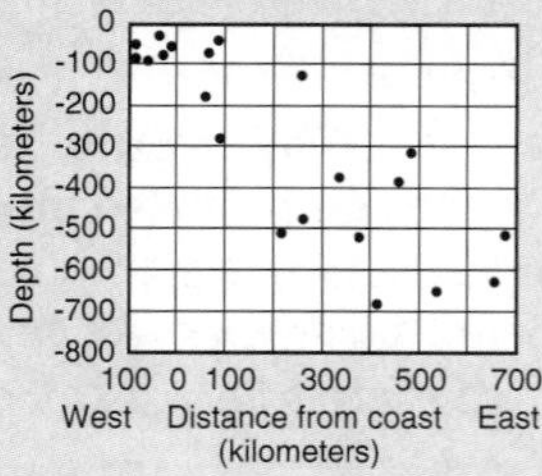

2. State any relationship noted between earthquake foci and epicenters.
3. Relate plotted data with concepts dealing with the movement of sections of Earth's crust.

Teaching Strategies

Troubleshooting Draw a blank version of the graph in Possible Procedure 1 (see left). Indicate to students the location of the coast of the continent on the graph.

Inclusion Strategies

Visually Impaired Ask some of your students to prepare copies of the maps and charts being used in this activity in a manner useful to those who are visually impaired. Heavy ink could be used to outline the locations under study, and earthquake foci could be identified by raised bumps on the maps. Students who are able could produce maps and charts using braille.

Activity 9-1

Design Your Own Experiment
Earthquake Depths

You learned earlier in this chapter that Earth's crust is broken into sections called plates. Movement of these plates generates stress within rocks that must be released. When this release of stress is sudden and rocks break, an earthquake occurs.

PREPARATION

Problem

Can a study of the foci of earthquakes tell us anything about how stress builds up in rocks and how it may be released?

Form a Hypothesis

State a hypothesis about how the movement of plates at Earth's crust could cause stress within rocks to build up and where rocks will break to relieve this stress.

Objectives

- Observe any connection between earthquake-focus depth and epicenter (the point on Earth's surface directly above the focus) location using the data provided on the next page.
- Describe any observed relationship between earthquake-focus depth and the movement of plates at Earth's surface.

Possible Materials

- graph paper
- pencil

PLAN THE EXPERIMENT

1. As a group, agree upon and write out your hypothesis statement.
2. As a group, list the steps that you need to take to test your hypothesis. Be very specific, describing exactly what you will do at each step.
3. Make a list of the materials that you will need to complete your experiment.
4. Determine how best to plot the data and observations on graph paper.

Check the Plan

1. Read over your entire experiment to make sure that all steps are in a logical order.
2. Will you summarize data in a table, or some other form of organization?
3. *Make sure your teacher approves your plan and that you have included any changes suggested in the plan.*

DO THE EXPERIMENT

1. Carry out the experiment as planned.
2. While conducting the experiment, write down any observations that you or other members of your group make and complete any data tables used in your Science Journal.

Analyze and Apply

1. Describe any observed relationship between the location of earthquake epicenters and the depth of earthquake focuses.
2. Based on the graph you have completed, **hypothesize** what is happening to the plates at Earth's surface in the vicinity of the plotted earthquake focuses.
3. In your opinion, what process is causing the earthquakes plotted on your graph paper?

Go Further

Based on the data you have plotted from the data table to the left, is the continent located east or west of the edge of the section of Earth's crust? Explain what you based your answer on. Hypothesize why none of the plotted earthquakes occurs below 700 km. Based on what you have observed and plotted, do all earthquakes occur at the same depth? Is there a relationship between earthquake depth and the movement of sections of Earth's crust?

Data and Observations

Quake	Focus Depth	Distance of Epicenter from Coast (km)
A	- 55 km	0
B	- 295 km	100 east
C	- 390 km	455 east
D	- 60 km	75 east
E	- 130 km	255 east
F	- 195 km	65 east
G	- 695 km	400 east
H	- 20 km	40 west
I	- 505 km	695 east
J	- 520 km	390 east
K	- 385 km	335 east
L	- 45 km	95 east
M	- 305 km	495 east
N	- 480 km	285 east
O	- 665 km	545 east
P	- 85 km	90 west
Q	- 525 km	205 east
R	- 85 km	25 west
S	- 445 km	595 east
T	- 635 km	665 east
U	- 55 km	95 west
V	- 70 km	100 west

shown in this activity indicate that one plate is sliding under another. The depth of earthquake foci can be used to indicate how sections of Earth's crust move.

Assessment

Oral Ask students to explain why earthquake foci occur deeper and deeper the farther the epicenter is located from the shore. Use the Performance Task Assessment List for Analyzing the Data in **PASC,** p. 27. P

DO THE EXPERIMENT

Expected Outcome

Students should realize that earthquake foci occur deeper farther inland from the shore. They should realize that this is because one section of Earth's crust is subducted under another section, causing stress deeper and deeper inside Earth.

Analyze and Apply

1. The earthquakes near the coast are shallow-focus quakes. Moving inland, the earthquake foci become progressively deeper.
2. The two plates of Earth's crust are colliding. Stress is built-up generating earthquakes.
3. One section of Earth's crust (the ocean section) is sliding under another (the continent section). As the one plate slides under the other, stress builds up, causing earthquakes to occur deeper and deeper inside Earth.

Go Further

- The section of Earth's crust being subducted from the west appears to be the more dense material found under the oceans; the continent must be located east of the coastline.
- The tremendous pressure and temperatures at this depth and below reduce the rigidity of solids. Generally, earthquakes occur because of the fracturing of solids. At the depth 700 km, the rock material is somewhat plasticlike and stress is absorbed without fracturing.
- There is a relationship between earthquake depth and the movement of sections of Earth's crust. The plots of earthquake foci

2 Teach

Science Journal

Answers will vary. Since surface waves cause one part of a building to move up while another part moves down, buildings could be placed on material that would absorb most of the up-and-down motion, similar to shock absorbers for cars. Encourage students to include drawings and insist that ideas be based on scientific fact.

Brainstorming

LS **Interpersonal** Form cooperative groups and ask the following questions. **What is an earthquake focus?** *the point in Earth's interior where energy is released from rocks* **How do primary, secondary, and surface waves differ?** *Primary waves travel the fastest and cause particles to move back and forth in the same direction as that of wave propagation. Secondary waves are slower than primary waves and cause particles to move at right angles to the direction of the waves. Surface waves are formed at Earth's surface and cause an elliptical motion, with some side-to-side motion of particles.* L1 COOP LEARN

Teacher F.Y.I.

Primary waves travel at about 6.0 km/s through granite crust. Secondary waves travel at about 3.5 km/s through the same material, while surface waves travel at about 2.0 km/s.

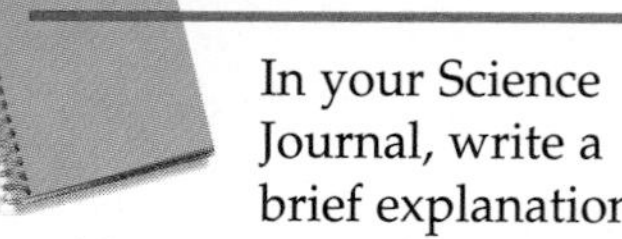

Science Journal

In your Science Journal, write a brief explanation of how you might build a building so that it would be able to withstand surface waves caused by an earthquake.

Seismic Waves

Waves that move through Earth by causing particles in rocks to move back and forth in the same direction the wave is moving are called **primary waves.** If you squeeze one end of a coiled-spring toy and then release it, you cause it to compress and then stretch as the primary wave travels through it. Particles in rocks also compress together and stretch apart, transmitting primary waves through the rock.

Now, if you and a friend stretch the coiled-spring toy between you, and then move one end up and down, a different type of wave will pass through the toy. The spring will move up and down as the wave moves along it. **Secondary waves** move through Earth by causing particles in rocks to move at right angles to the direction of the wave.

The point on Earth's surface directly above an earthquake's focus is the **epicenter** (see **Figure 9-6**). Energy that reaches the surface of Earth generates waves that travel outward from the epicenter. These waves, called **surface waves,** move by

Figure 9-6

Primary and secondary waves travel outward from the focus. Surface waves move outward from the epicenter.

A Sudden movement along a fault releases energy that causes an earthquake. The point beneath Earth's surface where the movement occurs is the focus of the earthquake.

B Primary waves and secondary waves originate at the focus and travel outward in all directions. Primary waves travel about twice as fast as secondary waves.

Fault

D Surface waves

Epicenter

C

A Focus

Theme Connection

Energy Movement of rocks deep inside Earth releases stress that has built up. The release of stress generates energy that is transmitted through Earth by seismic body waves. Generation of primary and secondary waves at the earthquake focus reaffirms energy as the theme for this chapter.

Use **Teaching Transparency 18** as you teach this lesson.

giving particles an elliptical motion, as well as a back-and-forth swaying motion.

Surface waves cause most of the destruction during an earthquake. Because most buildings are very rigid, they begin to fall apart when surface waves pass. The waves cause one part of the building to move up while another part moves down.

USING MATH

Primary waves travel at about 6 km/s through granitic crust. The distance from Phoenix, Arizona to Los Angeles, California is about 600 km. How long would it take primary waves to travel between these two cities?

Locating an Epicenter

Primary, secondary, and surface waves don't travel through Earth at the same speed. Primary waves are the fastest; surface waves are the slowest. Can you think of a way this information could be used to determine how far away an earthquake epicenter is? Think of the last time you and two friends rode your bikes to the store. You were fastest so you arrived first. In fact, the longer you rode, the farther ahead of your friends you became. Scientists use the different speeds of seismic waves to determine the distance to the earthquake epicenter.

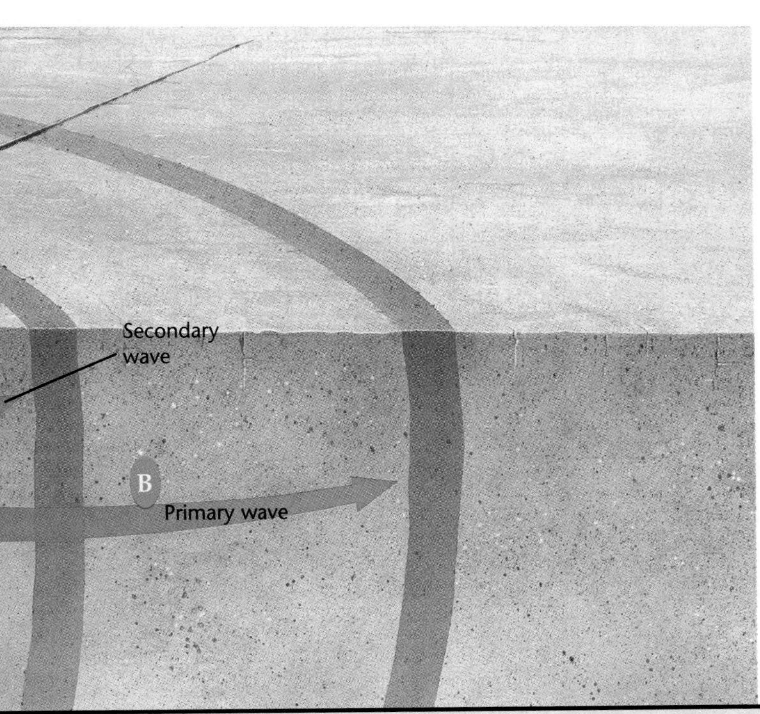

C The place on Earth's surface directly above the earthquake focus is called the epicenter. When primary and secondary waves reach the epicenter, they generate the slowest kind of seismic waves, surface waves. If you've ever floated on an inner tube in a wave pool you have experienced waves similar to surface waves.

D Surface waves travel outward from the epicenter along Earth's surface in much the same way that ripples travel outward from a stone thrown into a pond.

USING MATH

about 100 seconds

Revealing Preconceptions

Many students think that all earthquakes begin at Earth's surface. Explain that earthquakes originate at the point where rocks break. This can occur near Earth's surface or deep inside Earth's crust or asthenosphere.

Teacher F.Y.I.

Primary waves generated at the focus of an earthquake travel outward through Earth's interior. Sometimes these waves enter Earth's atmosphere and cause the loud noises associated with earthquakes.

GLENCOE TECHNOLOGY

 **Videodisc**

The Infinite Voyage: Living with Disaster

Chapter 5

Earthquakes: A Turbulence Beneath the Earth

Chapter 6

Prediciting Earthquakes: The Parkfield Experiment

STVS: Earth & Space

Disc 3, Side 2

Seismic Simulator (Ch. 9)

Inclusion Strategies

Hearing Impaired Obtain a coiled-spring toy and demonstrate each of the three types of seismic waves that have been discussed in class. Demonstrate primary waves by pushing the spring forward and then pulling it back. Demonstrate secondary waves by moving the spring from side to side. One type of surface wave can be demonstrated by causing the spring to move in an elliptical path while also moving the spring from side to side. Ask students to state which type of wave they think would cause more damage.

MiniLAB

Purpose

[LS] **Logical-Mathematical** Students will realize that varying arrival times of seismic waves can be used to determine distance to an earthquake epicenter. [L1]

Materials

Figure 9-6 on pages 244-245

Teaching Strategies

Troubleshooting Use Figure 9-6 to show students that epicenter distance can be determined if the arrival times of primary and secondary waves are plotted on a travel time graph.

Analysis

1. The difference in arrival times is a direct but not constant relationship. The difference in times increases with distance to the earthquake epicenter.
2. Student distances will vary but should fit in with interpretations found in question 1.

Distance (km)	Difference in arrival times
1500	2 min, 45 s
2250	3 min, 40 s
2750	4 min, 20 s
3000	4 min, 30 s
4000	5 min, 35 s
7000	8 min, 24 s
9000	9 min, 40 s

Assessment

Performance Have students determine distances to earthquakes whose primary and secondary wave arrival times are separated by 5 minutes and 7 minutes. Use the Performance Task Assessment List for Using Math in Science in **PASC**, p. 29. [P]

Activity Worksheets, pp. 5, 58

MiniLAB

Can the travel time of seismic waves be used to find the distance to an earthquake?

Procedure

1. Use the graph in **Figure 9-7** to determine the difference in arrival times for primary and secondary waves at the distances listed in the data table below. Two examples are provided for you.
2. Repeat step 1 for at least two other distances of your choice.

Analysis

1. Interpret what happens to the difference in arrival times as the distance from the earthquake increases.
2. Do the distances you chose fit with what you interpreted in question 1?

Distance (km)	Difference in Arrival Time
1500	2 min; 45 s
2250	
2750	
3000	
4000	5 min; 35 s
7000	
9000	

Seismograph Stations

Based on the different speeds of seismic waves, primary waves arrive first at seismograph stations, secondary waves second as seen in **Figure 9-7,** and surface waves last. This enables scientists to determine the distance to an earthquake epicenter. The farther apart the waves, the farther away the epicenter is. When epicenters are far from the seismograph station, the primary wave has more time to put distance between it and the secondary and surface waves.

Epicenter Location

If seismic wave information is obtained at three seismograph stations, the location of the epicenter can be determined, as shown in **Figure 9-8.** To locate an epicenter,

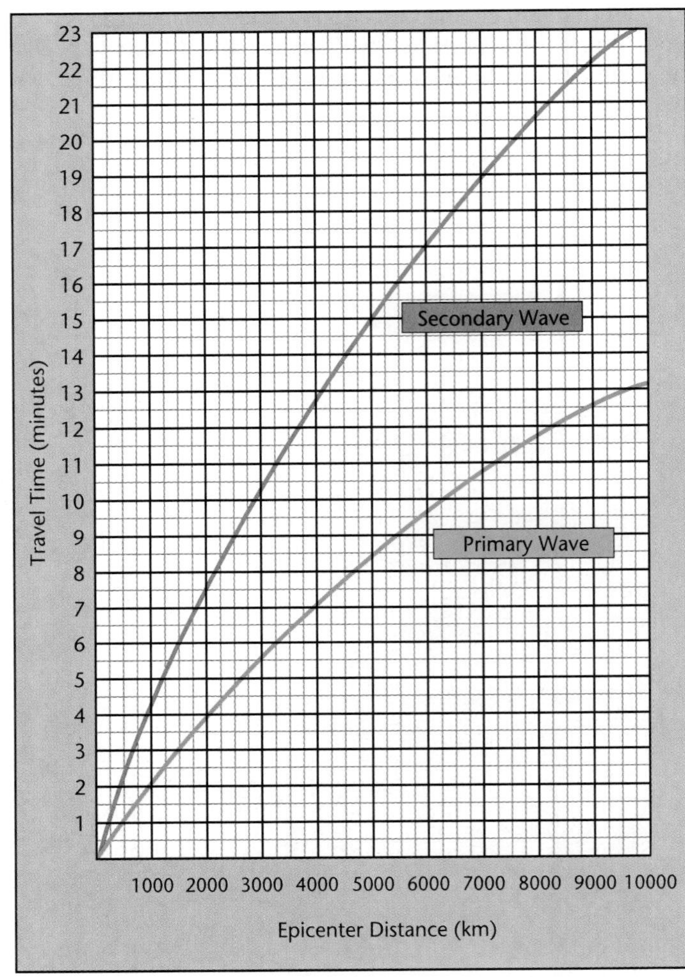

Figure 9-7

This graph shows the distance that primary and secondary waves travel over time. By measuring the difference in arrival times, a seismologist can determine the distance to the epicenter.

Across the Curriculum

Language Arts Have students research the origin of the word *seismic*. It comes from the Greek term *seismos,* meaning "shake." [L1] [LS]

Language Arts Ask students to explain why primary, secondary, and surface waves are so named. *Primary waves travel fastest and arrive at seismograph stations first. Secondary waves arrive second. Surface waves are the slowest and move along Earth's surface.* [L1] [LS]

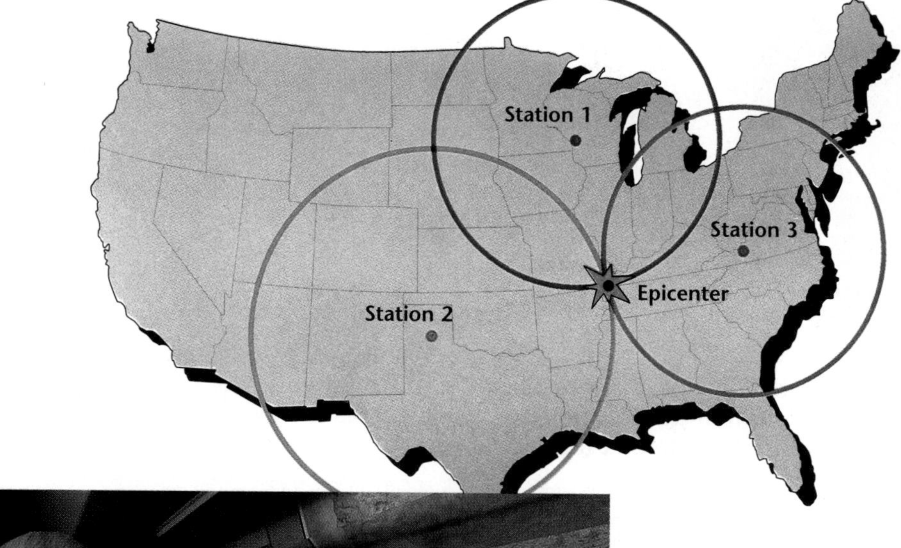

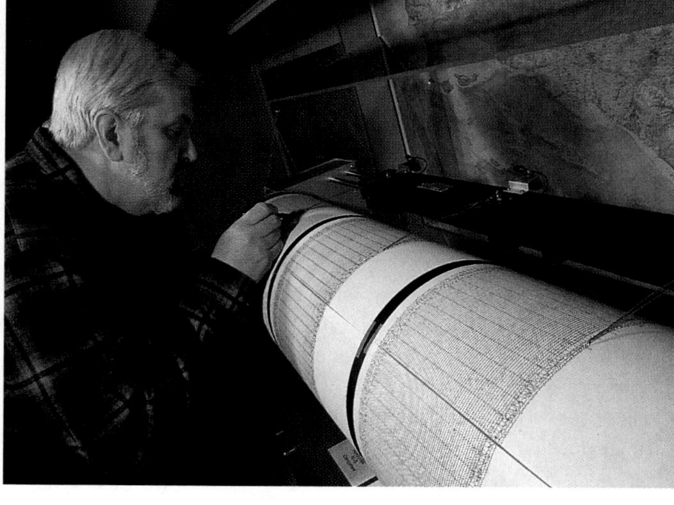

Figure 9-8

The radius of each circle is equal to the distance from the epicenter to each seismograph station. The intersection of the three circles is the location of the epicenter. *Why is one seismograph station not enough?*

scientists draw circles around each station on a map. The radius of each circle equals that station's distance from the earthquake epicenter. The point where all three circles intersect is the location of the earthquake epicenter.

Using Seismic Waves to Map Earth's Interior

Scientists have found that at certain depths within Earth, the speed and path of seismic waves change. These changes mark the boundaries of the layers in Earth with different densities, as shown in **Figure 9-10** on page 250. The Problem Solving exercise you will do later in this section demonstrates how scientists have learned about Earth's interior without ever having been there.

Visual Learning

Figure 9-8 Why is one seismograph station not enough? *Epicenter is located at intersection of circles (radius equals distance to epicenter) from three seismographs.* LEP LS

Inquiry Questions

- **Why are surface waves the most destructive seismic waves?** *Surface waves propel particles in ellipses and from side to side. Rigid structures crumble when some particles move up while other particles in the structure move down.*
- **How can seismic waves be used to measure the distance to an earthquake epicenter?** *Because seismic waves move at different speeds, the difference in their arrival times can be used to measure the distance they've traveled from the earthquake.*
- **What do changes in the speed and direction of seismic waves indicate about Earth's interior?** *Different layers have different densities.*

 **Videodisc**

STV: Restless Earth

Fault Line; Iceland

52222

Seismograph

52304

Science Journal

Epicenter Location Have students write short paragraphs in their Science Journals that explain why at least three seismograph stations are needed to locate an earthquake epicenter. Have them explain the connection between earthquake epicenters and earthquake foci. They might also explain where the various types of seismic waves originate. L1 LS

Activity 9-2

Purpose

LS **Logical-Mathematical** Interpret data on an earthquake wave travel time graph to determine the locations of earthquake epicenters. L1

Process Skills

using numbers, interpreting data, defining operationally, making and using tables, making and using graphs, comparing and contrasting

Time

50-60 minutes

Answers to Questions

1. The difference in arrival time between P- and S-waves increases as the distance of the seismic station from the earthquake increases. This time interval can be used to calculate the distance between the seismograph and the earthquake.
2. A: Mexico City, Mexico; B: San Francisco, CA
3. It takes a minimum of three seismograph stations to locate the epicenter of an earthquake.
4. Use a globe to demonstrate that these seismograph stations are between about 105° and 140° from the epicenters, and are, therefore, in the shadow zone.
5. Epicenters are located using the difference between P- and S-wave arrival times from at least three seismograph stations.

Assessment

Performance Ask students to explain why data from two seismograph stations are not enough to locate an earthquake epicenter. Use the Performance Task Assessment List for Writing in Science in **PASC**, p. 87. P

Activity 9-2 Epicenter Location

Try this activity to see how to plot the distance of several seismograph stations from the epicenters of two earthquakes and how to use that data to interpret where the earthquake epicenters were located.

Problem

Can plotting the distance of several seismograph stations from two earthquake epicenters be used to interpret the locations of the two epicenters?

Materials

- **Figure 9-7**
- metric ruler
- chalk
- string
- globe
- paper

Procedure

1. Determine the difference in arrival time between the primary and secondary waves at each station for each quake from the data table below.
2. Once you determine the arrival times of seismic waves for each seismograph station, use the graph in **Figure 9-7** to determine the distance in kilometers of each seismograph from the epicenter of each earthquake. Record these data in a data table provided by your teacher. The difference in arrival times in Paris for earthquake B is 10.0 minutes. On the graph, the primary and secondary waves are separated along the vertical axis by 10.0 minutes at 9750 km.
3. Using the string, measure the circumference of the globe. Determine a scale of centimeters of string to kilometers on Earth's surface. (Earth's circumference = 40 000 km.)
4. For each earthquake, A and B, place one end of the string at each seismic station location. Use the chalk to draw a circle with a radius equal to the distance to the earthquake's epicenter.
5. Identify the epicenter for each quake.

Analyze

1. How is the distance of a seismograph from the earthquake related to the arrival time of the waves?
2. What is the location of each earthquake epicenter?
3. How many stations were needed to accurately locate each epicenter?

Conclude and Apply

4. **Predict** why some seismographs didn't receive secondary waves from some quakes.
5. **Discuss** how epicenters are located.

Data and Observations

Location of Seismograph	Wave	Wave Arrival Times Earthquake A	Earthquake B
(1) New York	P	2:24:05 P.M.	1:19:00 P.M.
	S	2:28:55 P.M.	1:24:40 P.M.
(2) Seattle	P	2:24:40 P.M.	1:14:37 P.M.
	S	2:30:00 P.M.	1:16:52 P.M.
(3) Rio de Janeiro	P	2:29:00 P.M.	—
	S	2:38:05 P.M.	—
(4) Paris	P	2:30:15 P.M.	1:24:05 P.M.
	S	2:40:15 P.M.	1:34:05 P.M.
(5) Tokyo	P	—	1:23:30 P.M.
	S	—	1:33:05 P.M.

Location of Seismograph	Wave	Wave Arrival Times Earthquake A	Earthquake B
(1) New York	P	2:24:05 PM	1:19:00 PM
	S	2:28:55 PM	1:24:40 PM
(2) Seattle	P	2:24:40 PM	1:14:37 PM
	S	2:30:00 PM	1:16:52 PM
(3) Rio de Janeiro	P	2:29:00 PM	——
	S	2:38:05 PM	——
(4) Paris	P	2:30:15 PM	1:24:05 PM
	S	2:40:15 PM	1:34:05 PM
(5) Tokyo	P	——	1:23:30 PM
	S	——	1:33:05 PM

Calculated distance to epicenter (km) from each seismograph location

Quake	(1)	(2)	(3)	(4)	(5)
A	3750	4250	8000	9750	—
B	4500	1250	—	9750	8500

Activity Worksheets, pp. 5, 56-57

Structure of Earth

Seismic wave studies have enabled scientists to construct a model of Earth's interior, as shown in **Figure 9-9.** At the very center of Earth is a solid, very dense **inner core** composed mostly of iron and nickel. Above the solid inner core lies the liquid **outer core,** also composed of iron and nickel. Earth's **mantle** is the largest layer, lying directly above the outer core. It is made mostly of silicon, oxygen, magnesium, and iron. Earth's outermost layer is the **crust.** It is separated from the mantle by the Moho discontinuity.

Moho Discontinuity

Seismic waves speed up when they reach the bottom of the crust. This boundary between the crust and the mantle is called the **Moho discontinuity.** The boundary was discovered by the Yugoslavian scientist Andrija Mohorovičić, who inferred that seismic waves speed up because they're passing into a denser layer of the lithosphere. The lithosphere is made up of the rigid crust and upper mantle.

What's in there?

Your teacher has placed five closed and sealed boxes in front of the class. The sizes of the boxes vary but none is larger than 30 cm × 18 cm × 12 cm. Your teacher has challenged you to complete problem-solving exercises in order to earn points to be awarded. In order to earn the full amount of points available, you must list at least three facts about the contents of each box. You are permitted to do anything you need to do except open the boxes and look directly at the enclosed objects. The other exception is that you cannot damage any of the boxes in any way that might in turn damage the contents of the boxes.

Solve the Problem:

1. **Determine what tests you can conduct on each box that will reveal facts about the box's contents.**
2. **You may wish to work with another student in case more than one person is required to perform any of your chosen tests.**
3. **In your Science Journal, list any data you collect as well as your inferences concerning the contents of each box.**

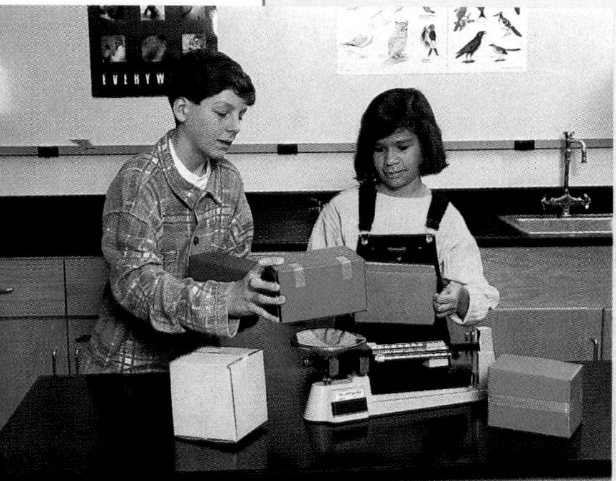

Think Critically:

How many facts did you and your partner correctly discover about the contents of each box? How is the challenge presented by your teacher related to earthquakes and mapping Earth's interior?

Making a Model

LS **Kinesthetic** Have students use information on pages 250-251 to make a model about Earth's structure. They may wish to use modeling clay or other materials. Encourage students to be as creative as possible. Ask them to explain how scientists have obtained the data necessary to make their models. L1

Solve the Problem

1. Tests that students use will vary. Some possible tests include heft, smell, and sound.
2. Encourage students to work with others.
3. Student data and inferences will vary, but should always be based on discernible characteristics.

Think Critically

The number of facts learned correctly by each team of students will vary based on the contents of each box and the students themselves. This challenge is very similar to that of scientists who study Earth's interior. They must make many inferences about Earth's structure without seeing it firsthand. They use the behavior of seismic waves as clues to Earth's structure.

Theme Connection

Energy Use the following demonstration to reaffirm energy as the theme for this chapter. Place a large, flat pan of water in front of the class. Ask a volunteer to drop a small rock into the water. Have the other students observe the waves that are generated. Explain that the wave movement in the water is similar to the movement of certain types of earthquake waves at Earth's surface. The generation of seismic waves, just as the generation of water waves in this demonstration, is caused by energy. Energy that produces seismic waves is generated by the release of stress in rock layers. LEP LS

3 Assess

Check for Understanding

FLEX Your Brain

Use the Flex Your Brain activity to have students explore EPICENTER LOCATION.

Activity Worksheets, p. 5

Reteach

Use a world map, a ruler, a drawing compass, and the data for earthquake "A" on page 248, TWE to demonstrate how an epicenter is located.

Extension

For students who have mastered this section, use the **Reinforcement** and **Enrichment** masters.

4 Close

•MINI•QUIZ•

Use the Mini Quiz to check students' recall of chapter content.

1. **Secondary seismic waves cause rock particles to move ______ to the direction of the wave.** *at right angles*
2. **The point on Earth's surface directly above an earthquake focus is the ______.** *epicenter*
3. **______ waves are the first seismic waves to arrive at a seismograph station.** *Primary*
4. **Earth's ______ is the cause of the shadow zone between 105° and 140°.** *outer core*

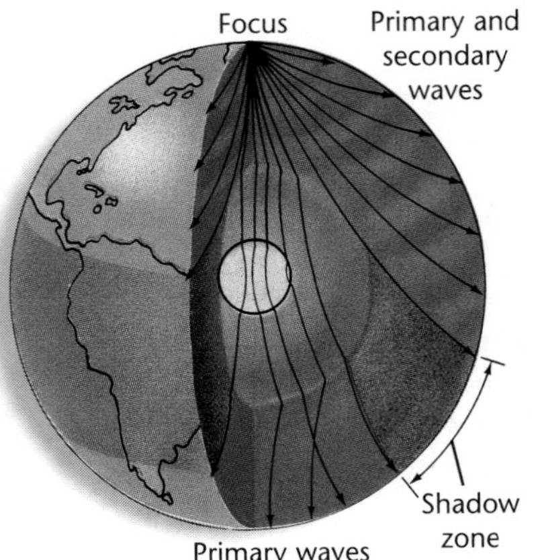

Figure 9-9

Primary waves bend when they contact the outer core, and secondary waves are stopped completely. Primary waves also bend and speed up when they enter the inner core. In fact, as shown, seismic waves gradually bend and change speed as the density of rock changes.

Primary and secondary waves slow down when they hit the plasticlike asthenosphere, part of the upper mantle, and then speed up again as they're transmitted through the solid lower mantle. In this way, the mantle is subdivided into an upper and lower layer.

There's an area on Earth, between 105° and 140° from the focus, where no waves are detected. This area is called the shadow zone. Secondary waves aren't transmitted through liquid, so they're stopped completely when they hit the liquid outer core. Primary waves are slowed and deflected but not stopped by the liquid outer core. The deflection of the primary waves and the stopping of the secondary waves create the shadow zone, as shown in **Figure 9-9.** These primary waves again speed up as they travel through the solid inner core.

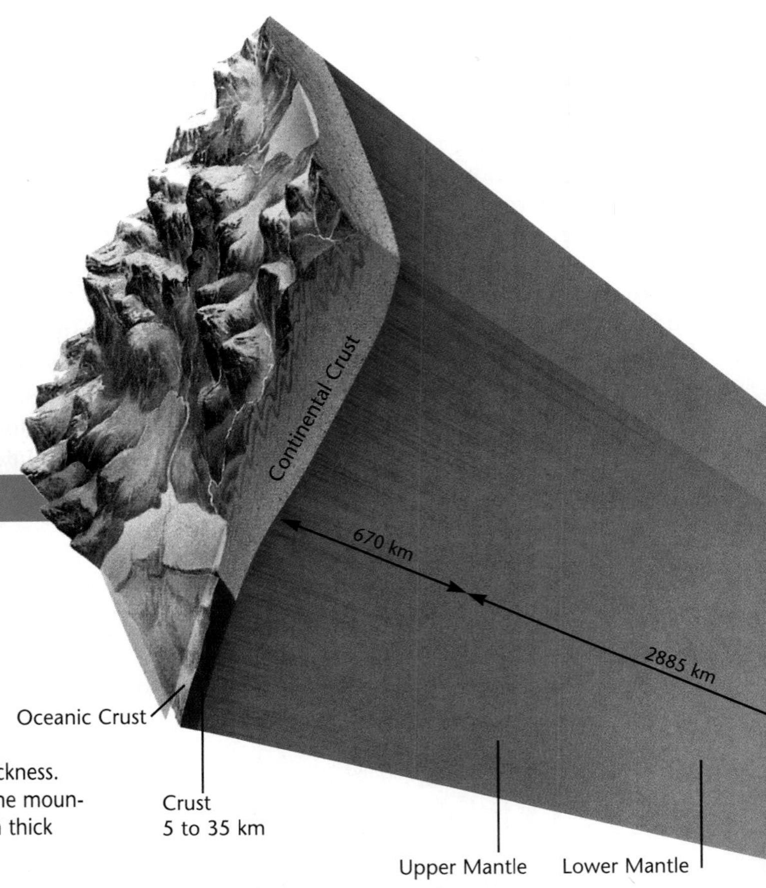

Figure 9-10

This wedge shows the layers inside Earth from the inner core. The inner core, outer core, and mantle are shown at the correct scale, but the crust is shown much thicker than it actually is.

A The crust of Earth varies in thickness. It is greater than 60 km in some mountainous regions, and less than 5 km thick under the oceans.

B Rock material in the upper mantle is described as plasticlike. It has characteristics of a solid, but also flows like a liquid when under pressure. Some kinds of taffy have this plasticlike characteristic. The taffy can be pulled apart slowly, but if you hit it on the edge of a table, it will break.

Across the Curriculum

Geography Have students draw a cross section of Earth that shows the location of an earthquake focus and epicenter. Students are to show on their cross sections where the shadow zone for the mapped earthquake would be. Students are to include proper landmasses and islands and are to identify specific locations on Earth that would be located within the earthquake's shadow zone. L2 LS

Use Lab 30 in the **Lab Manual** as you teach this lesson.

Section Wrap-up

Review

1. Which type of seismic wave does the most damage to property? Explain why.
2. Why is a seismic record from three locations needed to determine the position of an epicenter?
3. **Think Critically:** Suppose an earthquake occurs at the San Andreas Fault. What area on Earth would experience no secondary waves? Would China experience primary and secondary waves? Explain your answers.

Skill Builder

Making and Using Graphs

Use the data table below to make a graph of some travel times of earthquake waves. Which line represents primary waves? Which line represents secondary waves? If you need help, refer to Making and Using Graphs in the **Skill Handbook.**

Distance from Earthquake (km)	1500	2000	5000	5500	8600	10 000
Time (minutes)	5.0	2.5	14.0	7.0	11.0	23.5

Science Journal

When sound is produced, waves move through the air by pressing molecules together and then spreading them apart. In your Science Journal, research sound waves and describe seismic wave types to which they are similar.

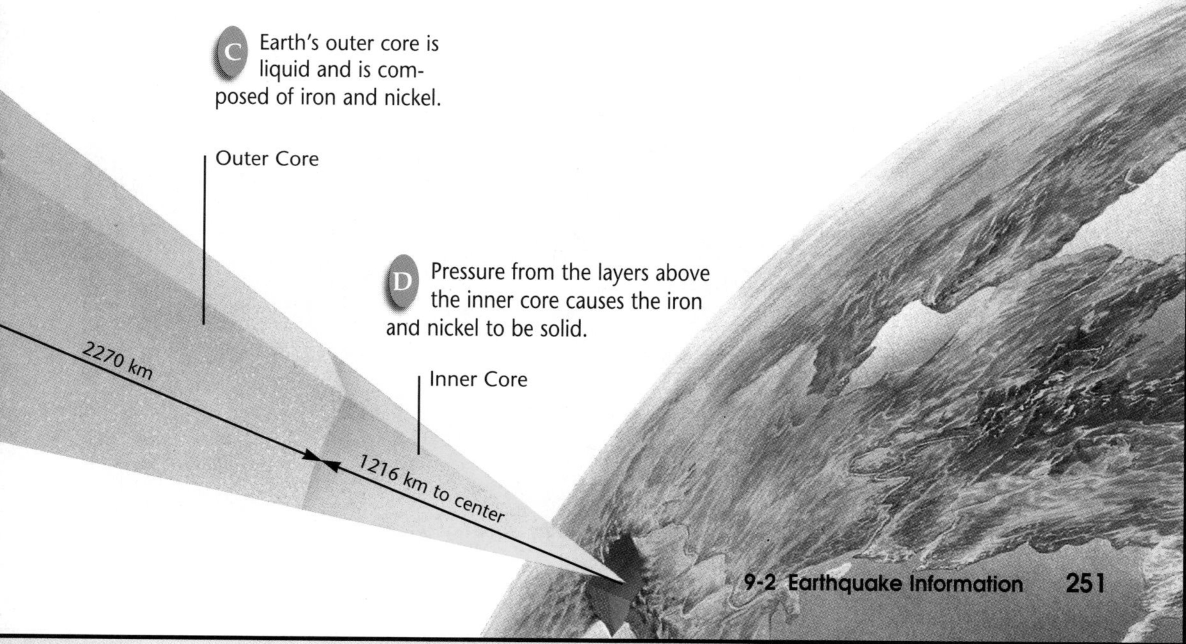

termining which points should be connected to form a curve, have them first analyze the data table to determine which data pairs correspond to P-waves and which correspond to S-waves. Start out by comparing the arrival times of waves at 1500 km and 2000 km. Clearly, two different waves are needed to account for the indicated arrival times. The P-wave was able to travel 2000 km in less time than it took for the S-wave to travel only 1500 km.

Assessment

Performance Use this Skill Builder to assess students' abilities to make and use graphs. Ask students to determine some travel times for earthquake waves at a distance of 3000 km, 4000 km, and 6000 km. Use the Performance Task Assessment List for Graph from Data in **PASC,** p. 39. P

Section Wrap-up

Review

1. Surface waves; as surface waves pass, buildings and other structures try to move in an elliptical manner, with some back-and-forth sway. This type of movement will cause solid material to crack and crumble.
2. The circles drawn from two stations will intersect in two places, giving two possible epicenter locations. Data from a third station are needed to pinpoint which of those two possible points is the epicenter location.
3. **Think Critically** No secondary waves would be recorded more than 105° from the epicenter. China would likely experience primary waves because it is outside of the shadow zone. Most secondary waves would not reach China because they would have to travel through the liquid outer core. However, some parts of China may receive some secondary waves that were deflected at the core boundary.

Science Journal

Primary seismic waves move by compressing and then stretching apart rock particles. This is the same way in which sound waves move through a material. Some of the noise associated with an earthquake may be caused by primary waves that enter the atmosphere.

Skill Builder

The P-wave is represented by the points (2000, 2.5), (5500, 7.0), and (8600, 11.0). The other points represent the slower S-wave. If students have difficulty de-

Section 9•3

Prepare

Section Background

- The extent of the damage caused by an earthquake depends on distance to the epicenter, bedrock of the area, local soil types, and the number and type of structures subjected to the quake, among other factors.
- During the 1985 earthquake, the soft, unconsolidated sediments underlying Mexico City amplified the earthquake vibrations.

Preplanning

To prepare for the MiniLAB, obtain a set of building blocks and several large rubber bands for each group of students.

1 Motivate

Bellringer

Before presenting the lesson, display **Section Focus Transparency 35** on the overhead projector. Assign the accompanying **Focus Activity** worksheet. L1 LEP

Tying to Previous Knowledge

Help students recall photographs of the destruction caused by earthquakes they may have seen in newspapers, in magazines, or on television.

Visual Learning

Figure 9-11 What happens during the earthquake that causes so much damage to highway overpasses? *Surface waves cause ground under overpass supports to move. The rigid supports collapse.* LEP LS

9•3 Destruction by Earthquakes

Science Words

seismologist
seismograph
magnitude
tsunamis

Objectives

- Define magnitude and the Richter Scale.
- List ways to make your classroom and home more earthquake-safe.

Measuring Earthquakes

On January 17, 1995, a major earthquake occurred in Kobe, Japan, causing about $100 billion of property damage and 5378 deaths. On January 17, 1994, a major earthquake occurred in Northridge, California, causing billions of dollars of property damage, as seen in **Figure 9-11,** and 61 deaths. At least 30 000 people died in the September 1993 earthquake that struck India. On October 17, 1989, an earthquake shocked the San Francisco Bay area. The quake killed 62 people and damaged billions of dollars of property. In 1988, more than 28 000 people died when an earthquake struck Armenia. What determines the amount of damage done by an earthquake, and what can you do to protect yourself from the effects? With so many lives lost and such potential destruction, as shown in **Table 9-1**, it is important for scientists to learn as much as possible about earthquakes to try and minimize their damage.

Seismology

Scientists who study earthquakes and seismic waves are **seismologists.** They use an instrument called a **seismograph** to record primary, secondary, and surface waves from earthquakes all over the world.

One type of seismograph has a drum holding a sheet of paper on a fixed frame. A pendulum with an attached pen is suspended from the frame. When seismic waves occur at the station, the drum vibrates but the pendulum remains at rest. The pen on the pendulum traces a record of the vibrations on a sheet

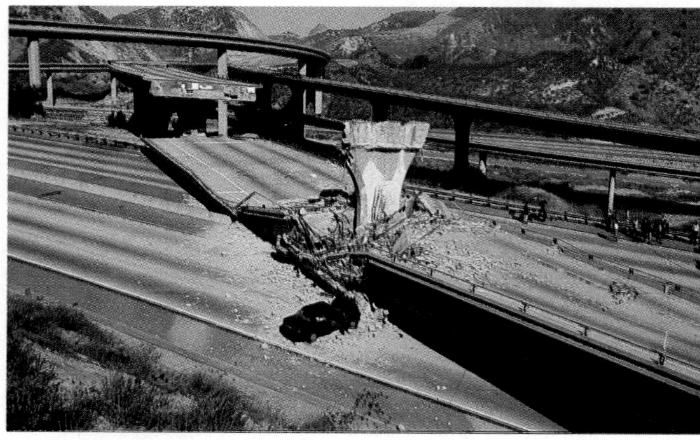

Figure 9-11
Several major highways were damaged in the January 17, 1994 earthquake in Northridge, California. *What happens during an earthquake that causes so much damage to highway overpasses?*

Program Resources

 **Reproducible Masters**

Study Guide, p. 39 L1
Reinforcement, p. 39 L1
Enrichment, p. 39 L3
Activity Worksheets, pp. 5, 59 L1
Multicultural Connections, pp. 21-22

Transparencies

Section Focus Transparency 35 L1

of paper. The height of the lines traced on the paper is a measure of the energy released, or **magnitude** of the earthquake.

Earthquake Magnitude

Not all seismographs measure vibrations in the same way. Because the Richter scale measures only local intensity on a specific type of seismograph, seismologists refer to magnitude in several other ways as well.

The Richter magnitude is based on seismic waves that travel through Earth. It deals mainly with the strength of the break, not with the length or breadth of the fault. The Richter scale describes how much energy is released by the earthquake. You

USING MATH

Calculate the difference in energy released between an earthquake of Richter magnitude 7.5 and one of magnitude 5.5.

Strong Earthquakes

Year	Location	Richter Value	Deaths
1556	Shensi, China	?	830 000
1737	Calcutta, India	?	300 000
1755	Lisbon, Portugal	8.8	70 000
1811-12	New Madrid, MO	8.3	few
1886	Charleston, SC	?	60
1906	San Francisco, CA	8.3	1500
1920	Kansu Province, China	8.5	180 000
1923	Tokyo, Japan	8.3	143 000
1939	Concepción, Chile	8.3	30 000
1960	Southern Chile	8.6	5 700
1964	Prince William Sound, AK	8.5	131
1970	Peru	7.8	66 800
1975	Laoning Province, China	7.5	few
1976	Tangshan, China	7.6	240 000
1985	Mexico City, Mexico	8.1	9 500
1988	Armenia	6.9	28 000
1989	Loma Prieta, CA	7.1	62
1990	Iran	7.7	50 000
1990	Luzon, Philippines	7.8	1621
1993	Guam	8.1	none
1993	Marharashtra, India	6.4	30 000
1994	Northridge, CA	6.7	61
1995	Kobe, Japan	6.9	5378

Table 9-1

2 Teach

USING MATH

LS Logical-Mathematical About 32 times more energy is released by an earthquake one magnitude greater than another.

$7.5 - 5.5 = 2$ magnitude difference

$32^2 = 1024$

For a difference in magnitude of 2, there is a 1024 times difference in energy released.

Using an Analogy

Tape a stiff sheet of paper to the side of a closed shoe box. Have a volunteer slowly draw a straight line from the top of the sheet to the bottom. Then, have the volunteer attempt the same feat as another student bounces a small rubber ball on the top of the box. Use this crude analogy to explain how a seismograph works.

Student Text Question

What determines the amount of damage done by an earthquake, and what can you do to protect yourself from the effects? *The amount of damage depends on the magnitude of the earthquake, the type of structures in the stricken area, population density, and the type of substrate in the area hit by the quake. Refer students to page 256 regarding earthquake safety.*

Inclusion Strategies

Learning Disabled Have students conduct research to find out about major earthquakes that have occurred during recorded history. Have them construct timelines of these earthquakes from the earliest to the most recent. The magnitude of each earthquake should be included. Have students hypothesize why certain areas have more earthquakes than others.

Videodisc

STV: Restless Earth

Preparing for Earthquakes

Unit 5, Side 2

Methods of Prediction

10743-14270

USING TECHNOLOGY

For more information, refer to "Parkfield Quakes Skip a Beat," by Richard A. Kerr, *Science,* February 19, 1993, pp. 1102-1122. Also refer to "Earth Revealed, 9: Earthquakes," video program from Annenberg/CPB, 1-800-LEARNER.

Think Critically

Seismographs, the instrument used by seismologists to record movements as they happen. They don't foretell when movements may occur. It's not known exactly when enough stress has built up to cause a specific earthquake to occur. Seismologists use the record of past earthquakes to predict a window of time during which an earthquake can be expected. P

Teacher F.Y.I.

- The Modified Mercalli Scale is used to measure the intensity or amount of damage done by an earthquake. A rating of I to II is a low-intensity quake, while an earthquake measuring XII designates total destruction of the stricken area.
- Three of the strongest earthquakes in the United States occurred along the New Madrid Fault system centered in Missouri.

Videodisc

STV: Restless Earth

Preparing for Earthquakes

Unit 5, Side 2

A Historical Pattern

14380-18374

USING TECHNOLOGY

Predicting Quakes

The year 1992 came and passed without the predicted earthquake of magnitude 6.0 or more occurring along the San Andreas Fault near Parkfield, California. Based on the fact that moderate earthquakes had occurred an average of once every 22 years since 1857, seismologists had predicted that another would occur sometime between 1988 and 1992. Instruments such as lasers, creepmeters, survey alignment instruments, and other instruments were installed in the area as part of the Parkfield Earthquake Prediction Experiment. In the creepmeters, a wire is stretched across the fault to record even minute movements.

Parkfield Quakes

Allan Lindh of the USGS believes that a magnitude-6 earthquake is bound to hit Parkfield "any old day now." One scientist, Robert Nadeau of the University of California, Berkeley, predicts that 13 earthquakes of about magnitude 1 should strike Parkfield by the end of 1996. Scientists are using the interval between jolts in a specific place as a means of determining a window of time in which earthquakes should occur. It is hoped that this research will help scientists predict larger earthquakes.

Parkfield, California

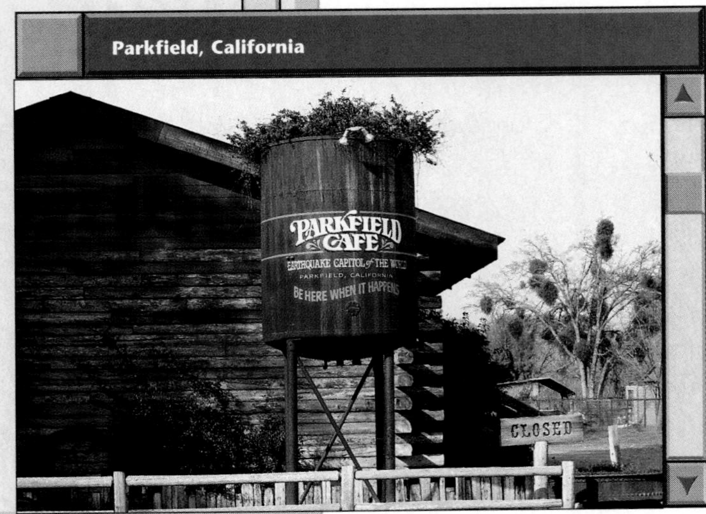

Think Critically:

Prediction of earthquakes deals with windows of time during which earthquakes should occur at a specific location. Why can't seismologists be more specific about the predicted date on which an earthquake should occur?

may have heard TV newscasters describe each 1.0 increase on the Richter scale as releasing 10 times more energy. However, about 32 times as much energy is released for every increase of 1.0 on the scale. For example, a magnitude-8.5 earthquake releases about 32 times as much energy as a magnitude-7.5 earthquake. **Table 9-2** shows how often various magnitude earthquakes are expected to occur.

Another magnitude used by seismologists is based on Earth movement or surface waves. Seismologists also use a magnitude called the moment magnitude. It is derived by multiplying the length of the fault rupture by the amount of rock movement and then again by the rock stiffness. The moment magnitude is related to the strength and size of fault movement. The magnitude usually first reported is Richter scale magnitude modified for modern equipment. After further study, the moment magnitude can be determined.

Integrating the Sciences

Life Science Have students study Table 9-1 and hypothesize why some strong earthquakes caused so much loss of life while others caused very little. L1 LS

COOP LEARN

Community Connection

Earthquake Safety Have students visit the local library to research the history of their local community concerning earthquakes that may have occurred. Invite local officials in charge of community safety to visit class and discuss any special preparations the community has concerning earthquake safety. L1

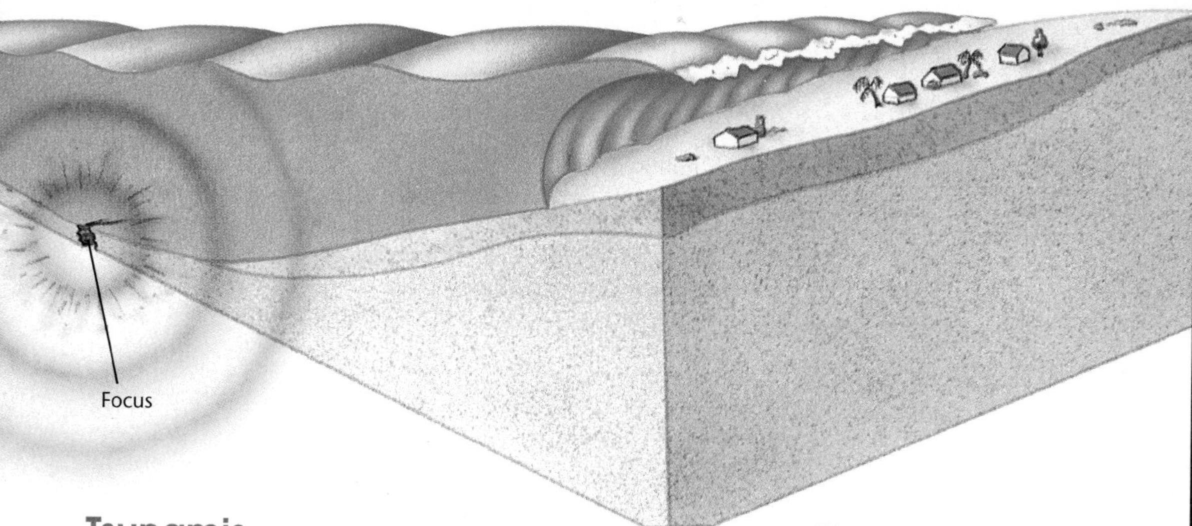

Tsunamis

Most earthquake damage happens when surface waves cause buildings, bridges, and roads to collapse. People living near the seashore, however, have another concern. An earthquake under the sea causes abrupt movement of the ocean floor. The movement pushes against the water, generating a powerful wave that travels to the surface, as shown in **Figure 9-12.** After reaching the surface, the wave can travel thousands of kilometers in all directions.

Far from shore, an earthquake-generated wave is so long that a large ship may ride over it without anyone noticing. But when one of these waves breaks on a shore, it forms a towering crest that can reach 30 m high. Ocean waves generated by earthquakes are called seismic sea waves, or **tsunamis** (soo NAHM eez).

Figure 9-12

A tsunami begins over the earthquake focus. *What might happen to towns located near the shore?*

Table 9-2

Earthquake Occurrences

Richter Magnitude	Number Expected per Year
1.0 to 3.9	> 949 000
4.0 to 4.9	6 200
5.0 to 5.9	800
6.0 to 6.9	226
7.0 to 7.9	18
8.0 to 8.9	< 2

Inquiry Question

- **Suppose an earthquake with a magnitude of 3.4 releases 9×10^{13} ergs of energy. How much energy would be released by a quake measuring 4.4?** *$32 \times 9 \times 10^{13}$ ergs $= 2.9 \times 10^{15}$ ergs*

Teacher F.Y.I.

- The Tsunami Warning System was developed by the United States in 1948 after a tsunami hit the Aleutian and Hawaiian Islands two years earlier. After a 1964 Alaskan wave took 103 lives, an improved Regional TWS was developed. Now GOES (Geostationary Operational Environmental Satellite) is able to issue warnings in as little as 2 minutes.
- More than one million earthquakes occur every year. Most are not directly observable by humans. However, on the average, 20 earthquakes strong enough to be felt occur each day in California.

Visual Learning

Figure 9-12 What might happen to towns located near the shore? *If an offshore earthquake occurs, towns near the shore could be destroyed by tsunamis.* LEP 

Cultural Diversity

Tsunami! One of the earliest recorded tsunamis struck 1400 km off the Chilean coast in 1562. In 1674, one wave reaching 100 m in height struck Indonesia. Tsunamis can produce strange results. In 1868 a Civil War sidewheeler, USS Wateree, in a Chilean port, was deposited, intact and unharmed, one-half kilometer inland, while 20 000 people on shore lost their lives. Thera, one of the Cyclades Islands, may be the remnant of a volcano that erupted, causing tsunamis that ended Minoan civilization on Crete. It has been compared to the explosion of Krakatoa in 1883, in which the resulting wave killed 30 000 people in Java. In the last 20 years, 2.8 million lives have been lost to tsunamis. One in three tsunamis originate off the Chilean coast due to the movement of the Nazca plate.

Videodisc

STV: Restless Earth

Preparing for Earthquakes

Unit 5, Side 2

Training for Disaster

18404-24134

MiniLAB

Purpose

LS **Interpersonal** Students will use seismic-safe methods of building. L1

COOP LEARN

Materials

blocks, rubber bands

Analysis

1. Structures with rubber bands around them are more likely to withstand the earthquake.
2. Concrete cement pillars could be wrapped with steel supports. The support would decrease the chances of the pillars' breaking during an earthquake.

Assessment

Performance Have students build a model seismic-safe highway. Use the Performance Task Assessment List for Model in **PASC**, p. 51. P

Activity Worksheets, pp. 5, 59

3 Assess

Check for Understanding

FLEX Your Brain

Use the Flex Your Brain activity to have students explore EARTHQUAKE PREDICTION.

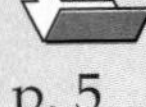

Activity Worksheets, p. 5

Reteach

Show pictures of the destruction from the 1906 earthquake in San Francisco. Ask students to speculate what caused the almost total destruction of the city. Fires were a major factor.

MiniLAB

How can structures be made earthquake-safe?

Procedure

1. Obtain a set of building blocks from your teacher.
2. On a tabletop, build one structure out of the blocks by simply placing one block on top of another.
3. Build a second structure by wrapping sections of three blocks together with rubber bands. Then wrap larger rubber bands around the entire completed structure.
4. Set the second structure on the tabletop and pound on the side of the table with a steady rhythm.

Analysis

1. Which of your two structures was better able to withstand the "earthquake" caused by pounding on the table?
2. How might the idea of wrapping the blocks with rubber bands be used in construction of supports for elevated highways?

Earthquake Safety

You've seen the destruction that earthquakes can cause. However, there are ways to minimize the damage and loss of life.

One of the first steps in earthquake safety is to study the earthquake history of a region, such as the one illustrated in **Figure 9-14.** If you live in an area that's had earthquakes in the past, you can expect them to occur there in the future. As you know, most earthquakes happen along plate boundaries. **Figure 9-2** shows where severe earthquakes have happened. Being prepared is an important step in earthquake safety.

Quake-Proofing Your Home

Make your home as earthquake-safe as possible, like the one shown in **Figure 9-13.** Take heavy objects down from high shelves and place them on lower shelves. To reduce the chance of fire from broken gas lines, see that hot-water heaters and gas appliances are held securely in place. During an earthquake, keep away from windows and avoid anything that could fall on you. Watch for fallen power lines and possible fire hazards. Stay clear of rubble that could contain sharp edges.

Figure 9-13

You can make your home more earthquake-safe by doing some very simple things, such as moving heavy objects from high shelves.

Across the Curriculum

Life Science In 1993, an 8.1 earthquake struck the island of Guam. There were no deaths and the amount of damage was much less than expected. Ask students to explain what conditions may have contributed to this. *Buildings on Guam are constructed to withstand high winds from storms. This would make buildings more seismic-safe than would otherwise be expected.*

Science Journal

Alaskan Earthquakes Have students write brief descriptions in their Science Journals of the damage done when tsunamis came ashore along the Pacific coast following the Alaskan earthquake of 1964. L1 LS

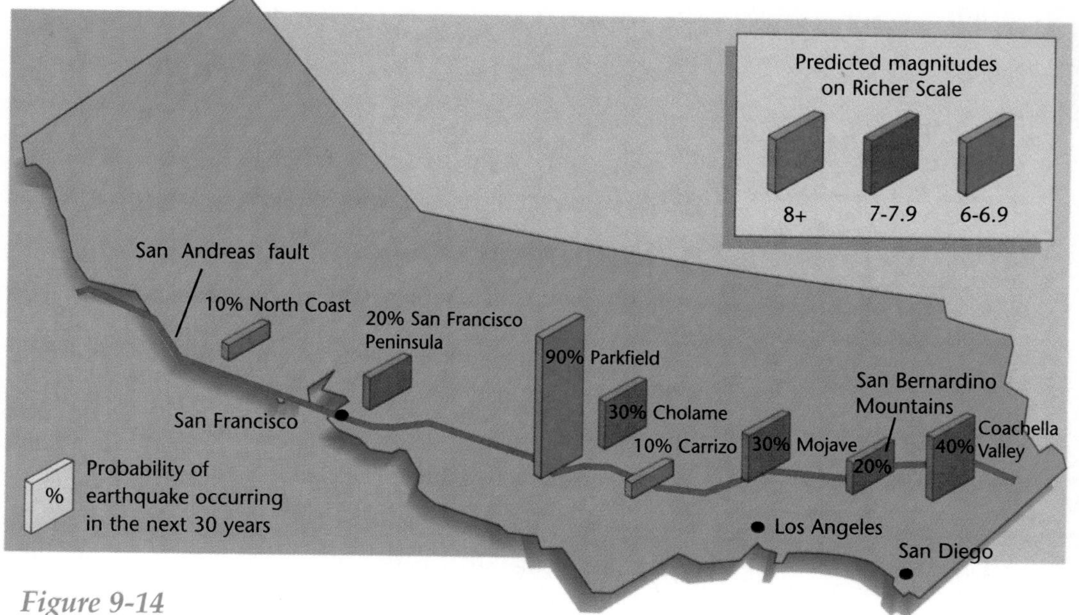

Figure 9-14

The bars on the graphic show the probabilities that an earthquake of the specified magnitude will strike these areas within the next 30 years. California residents are preparing for the major earthquakes predicted there. *What other areas besides California should be concerned about the probability of an earthquake?*

Section Wrap-up

Review

1. What can you do to prepare for an earthquake?
2. Research how animal behavior has been studied to predict earthquakes. What changes may be occurring in the environment to cause animals to act differently?
3. **Think Critically:** Explain why a seismograph wouldn't work if the pen vibrated along with the rest of the machine.

USING MATH

How much more energy would be released by an earthquake with a Richter magnitude of 8.9 than the earthquake that hit Kobe, Japan? (Refer to **Table 9-1.**)

Skill Builder

Making and Using Tables

Use **Table 9-1** to determine which quake listed had the highest magnitude. Hypothesize why the 1975 China quake resulted in fewer deaths than the 1976 quake. If you need help, refer to Making and Using Tables in the **Skill Handbook.**

Visual Learning

Figure 9-14 What other areas besides California should be concerned about earthquake probability? *Will vary, but mainly in areas near plate boundaries.* LEP LS

4 Close

•MINI•QUIZ•

1. **A(n) ______ is an instrument that records primary, secondary, and surface waves from earthquakes.** *seismograph*
2. **The energy released by an earthquake is its ______.** *magnitude*
3. **Sea waves caused by earthquakes are ______.** *tsunamis*

Section Wrap-up

Review

1. Do not place heavy objects on high shelves, and check to see that the water heater and gas appliances are well secured.
2. Some scientists suggest that animals may be detecting changes in local magnetic fields, small tremors, gasses released from the ground, or high-frequency sounds.
3. **Think Critically** In order to record vibrations, some point within the seismograph must remain at rest. Most seismographs consist of a fixed frame that is attached to Earth. A pen records the seismic waves onto paper on a vibrating drum.

USING MATH

$8.1 - 6.9 = 2.0$

$32^2 = 1024$

An 8.9 earthquake releases about 1000 times more energy than a 6.9 earthquake.

Skill Builder

The 1755 Portugal quake; the 1975 China earthquake was predicted and people were warned to be outside. The 1976 China earthquake occurred without warning.

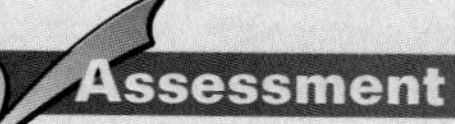

Assessment

Performance Use this Skill Builder to assess students' abilities to make and use tables. Ask students to use Table 9-1 to answer the listed questions and other questions of your design. Use the Performance Task Assessment List for Data Table in **PASC,** p. 37. P

Prepare

Section Background

The two main strategies for building earthquake resistant structures are shock-absorption and reinforcement. The goal is to prevent structures from collapsing and minimize falling debris.

1 Motivate

Bellringer

Before presenting the lesson, display **Section Focus Transparency 36** on the overhead projector. Assign the accompanying **Focus Activity** worksheet. L1 LEP

2 Teach

Student Text Question

Why were so many more lives lost in Armenia and Iran than in Loma Prieta, California? *Many buildings in Armenia and Iran weren't seismic-safe and fell on people during the earthquakes.*

3 Assess

Check for Understanding

FLEX Your Brain

Use the Flex Your Brain activity to have students explore HOMEOWNER'S OR RENTER'S EARTHQUAKE INSURANCE.

Activity Worksheets, p. 5

TECHNOLOGY: 9•4 Living on a Fault

Objectives

- Recognize that most loss of life in an earthquake is caused by the destruction of human-made structures.
- Consider who should pay for making structures seismic-safe.

Who should pay for earthquake preparation?

Throughout this chapter, you have seen pictures of the aftermath of earthquakes. What kind of damage did you see? Buildings, bridges, and highways were cracked and broken. Some were totally destroyed.

Most loss of life in an earthquake occurs when people are trapped in and on these crumbling structures. What can be done to reduce loss of life? Who should be responsible for the cost of making structures seismic-safe?

Seismic-Safe Structures

Seismic-safe structures are resistant to vibrations that occur during an earthquake. **Figures 9-15** and **9-16** show how buildings and highways can be built to resist earthquake damage.

Will making structures seismic-safe reduce the loss of life in an earthquake? Look again at **Table 9-1.** Notice that earthquakes in Armenia (December 1988), in Loma Prieta (October 1989), and in Iran (June 1990) were all close in magnitude. However, the loss of life in each of these earthquakes was quite different. Why were so many more lives lost in Armenia and Iran than in Loma Prieta?

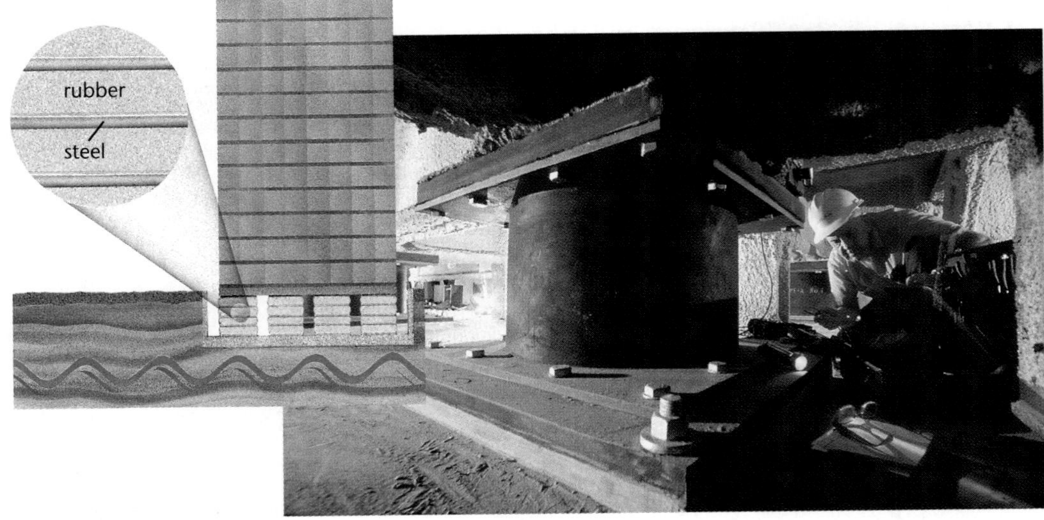

Figure 9-15
The rubber portions of this building's moorings absorb most of the wave motion of an earthquake. The building itself only sways gently. *What purpose does the rubber serve?*

Program Resources

Reproducible Masters
Study Guide, p. 40 L1
Reinforcement, p. 40 L1
Enrichment, p. 40 L3
Science and Society Integration, p. 13

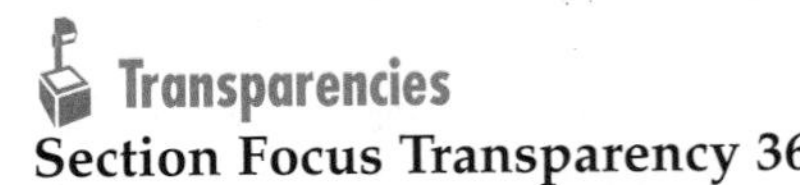

Transparencies
Section Focus Transparency 36

People in Earthquake-Prone Areas Should Prepare

Loma Prieta and countries like Japan are very susceptible to earthquakes. People living in California and Japan have been getting ready for big earthquakes for many years. Since 1971, stricter building codes have been enforced and older buildings have been reinforced. In other parts of the world, such seismic-safe structures are rare or don't exist at all.

Today in California, some new buildings are anchored to flexible, circular moorings made of steel plates filled with alternating layers of rubber and steel. **Figure 9-15** shows how they work. Tests have shown that buildings supported with these moorings should be able to withstand an earthquake measuring up to 8.3 on the Richter scale without major damage.

Sharing Seismic-Safe Technology

Highways and buildings in earthquake-prone areas can be made seismic safe. Lives and property can be saved by replacing underground water and gas pipes with ones that will bend, but not break, during an earthquake. However, seismic-safe structures are expensive and many communities in earthquake-prone areas simply can't afford them. In these areas, seismic-safe structures can be constructed only if people outside of the region are willing to help.

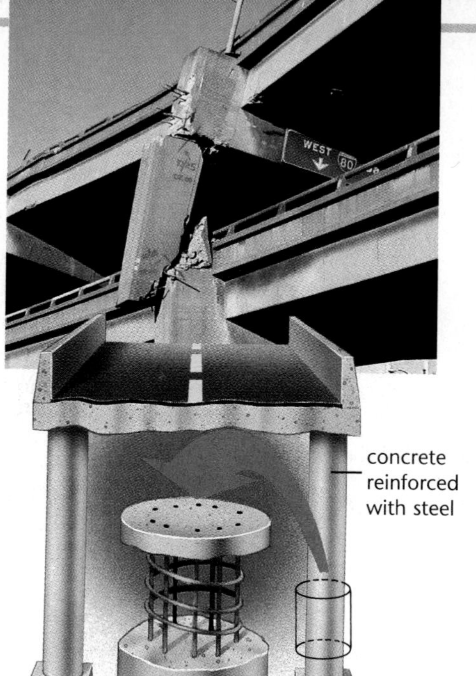

Figure 9-16

Seismic-safe highways are supported by vertical steel rods wrapped with reinforcing rods encased in concrete. The highway that collapsed in the Loma Prieta earthquake was not built this way.

Section Wrap-up

Review

1. What conditions can cause greater loss of life from one earthquake than from another of the same magnitude?
2. Why did supports for the upper deck of Highway 880 break during the 1989 Loma Prieta earthquake?

Explore the Technology

Should governments worldwide accept the responsibility of sharing the expense of providing seismic-safe structures to all earthquake-prone areas? If yes, where would funding come from, especially in countries that do not have earthquake-prone areas? If no, how can the safety of the people in earthquake-prone areas be assured?

CONNECT TO

PHYSICS

How are shock absorbers on a car similar to the circular moorings described on this page? How do they absorb shock?

SCIENCE & SOCIETY

Reteach

Show students pictures of buildings and structures that have experienced earthquakes. Have pairs of students try to determine which buildings were probably seismic-safe. COOP LEARN

Extension

For students who have mastered this section, use the **Reinforcement** and **Enrichment** masters.

4 Close

Have pairs of students draw posters that show one aspect of earthquake safety. Can show what to do in preparation for a possible earthquake, what to do during an earthquake, or after an earthquake.

Section Wrap-up

Review

1. Population density, building codes, types of buildings, time earthquake occurs, duration of quake.
2. The supports surpassed their elastic limit and broke. There were no reinforcements to hold them together.

Explore the Technology

If students answer yes, they may think that funding can be provided by the government department of housing or from insurance companies which then spread the cost to others. If they answer no, students must answer the concern for how safety can be ensured for people in earthquake-prone areas.

Visual Learning

Figure 9-15 What purpose does the rubber serve? *It acts as a shock-absorber.* LEP IS

CONNECT TO

PHYSICS

Answer Similar shape, with coils of metal. Springs are compressed to absorb stresses.

Sources

- "Earthquakes and Planning in the 17th and 18th Centuries," *Journal of Architectural Education,* vol. 33, no. 4, Summer 1980.
- *The Architecture of Antigua, Guatemala,* Verle Lincoln Annis, University of San Carlos of Guatemala, 1968.
- *This Shaking Earth,* John Gribbin, New York: G.P. Putnam's Sons, 1978.

Science Journal

Results will vary depending on earthquake chosen. Should include information on damage and loss of life, and eyewitness accounts.

Teaching Strategies

- Have students research the 1976 Guatemala City earthquake to discover its intensity on the Richter scale and what type of fault line exists there. *7.5, strike-slip*
- Discuss how cities might be planned in earthquake-prone, technology-poor areas to minimize deaths and injuries in an earthquake. *Possibilities include location of city (on flat land or hillside, rocky or muddy land, etc.); maximum building heights; minimum street widths; use of open areas, etc.*
- Have students theorize how a new location only a few miles away might be safer during an earthquake. Ask if they can think of any examples of safer and less safe sites from their own experience.
- Discuss the building codes developed in Lisbon after a disastrous earthquake in 1755 and how they would make for safer buildings. For information on this, see the article from the *Journal of Architectural Education,* listed in the Resources section.

Science & History

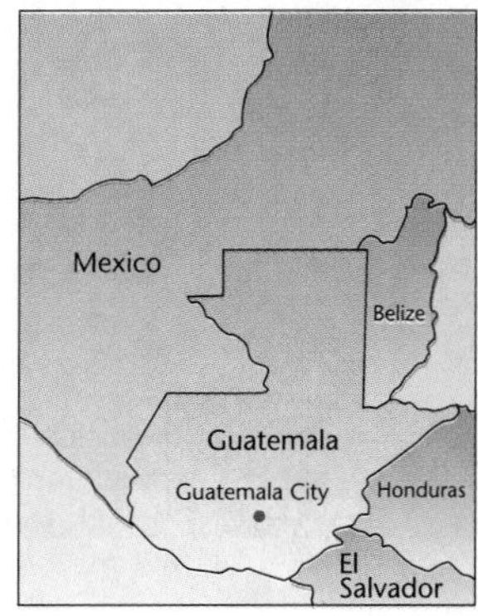

Figure 9-17
Map showing location of Guatemala City.

Guatemala City

Every so often you may read of a city being destroyed by an earthquake. It has happened more than once to Guatemala City. But in a way, Guatemala City was also created by earthquakes.

It was an earthquake in 1773 that caused Guatemala City to be founded. That quake leveled Santiago, the capital city of what was then a Spanish colony. Santiago barely survived seven major earthquakes from its founding in 1573 through 1773. The 1773 quake finally convinced the Spanish governor that the city had to be moved to a safer location. Guatemala City was built in 1776 as Santiago's replacement.

Even as Guatemala City grew, the old city of Santiago refused to die. Many residents would not leave, despite the earthquake dangers. They stuck to their homes even when the Spanish government forced all stores to close. Today it remains as the city of Antigua Guatemala, a major tourist site.

Although Guatemala City was the official capital of the area, another city became the unofficial capital. That was Quezaltenango, where a large number of the country's leading families lived. Once again an earthquake changed things, destroying Quezaltenango in 1902. Guatemala City became the new home of many of the county's most influential families and finally, the undisputed capital.

For much of its history, Guatemala City has had to contend with the constant threat of quakes without modern building technology. The builders relied on the construction techniques of the early settlers. Low buildings with massive walls were common—as were frequent repairs. Taller steel and concrete buildings didn't appear until after a series of earthquakes in late 1917 and early 1918. Even then, the new type of construction was confined to the newest sections of the city.

But low buildings and massive walls can do only so much to prevent tragedy. When the 1976 earthquake hit, 58 000 buildings were destroyed in Guatemala City. About 23 000 people died and another 80 000 people were injured, and more than a million people were left homeless. It was a terrible way to mark the city's 200th anniversary.

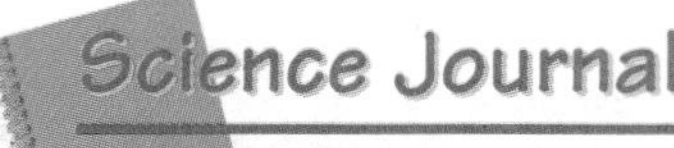

Science Journal

Research one of the historical earthquakes shown on **Table 9-1,** and the changes that resulted from it, in your Science Journal.

Chapter 9 Review

Summary

9-1: Forces Inside Earth

1. Plate movements put stress on rocks. To a point, the rocks bend and stretch. But if the force is great enough, rocks will break and produce earthquakes.
2. Normal faults form when rocks undergo tension. Compressional forces produce reverse faults. Strike-slip faults result from shearing forces.

9-2: Earthquake Information

1. Primary waves compress and stretch rock particles as the waves move. Secondary waves move by, causing particles in rocks to move at right angles to the direction of the waves. Surface waves move by, giving rock particles an elliptical and side-to-side motion.
2. Scientists can locate earthquake epicenters by measuring seismic wave speeds.
3. By observing the speeds and paths of seismic waves, scientists are able to determine the boundaries among Earth's layers.

9-3: Destruction by Earthquakes

1. The magnitude of an earthquake is a measure of the energy released by the quake. The Richter scale describes how much energy is released by an earthquake.
2. Removing objects from high shelves and securing hot-water heaters and gas appliances help prevent earthquake damage.

9-4: Science and Society: Living on a Fault

1. Most lives lost during a quake are due to the destruction of human-made structures.
2. Money for seismic-safe structures might come from people who live in the earthquake-prone area or from people in other parts of the country or the world.

Key Science Words

a. crust
b. earthquake
c. epicenter
d. fault
e. focus
f. inner core
g. magnitude
h. mantle
i. Moho discontinuity
j. normal fault
k. outer core
l. primary wave
m. reverse fault
n. secondary wave
o. seismic wave
p. seismograph
q. seismologist
r. strike-slip fault
s. surface wave
t. tsunamis

Reviewing Vocabulary

Match each phrase with the correct term from the list of Key Science Words.

1. a fault formed due to tension on rocks
2. fault due to shearing forces
3. point where earthquake energy is released
4. point on Earth's surface directly above the origin of an earthquake
5. wave that produces the most surface damage
6. layer of Earth directly below the crust
7. instrument that records seismic waves
8. measure of energy released by an earthquake
9. seismic sea wave
10. scientist who studies earthquakes

Chapter 9

Review

Summary

Have students read the summary statements to review the major concepts of the chapter.

Reviewing Vocabulary

1. j	**6.** h
2. r	**7.** p
3. e	**8.** g
4. c	**9.** t
5. s	**10.** q

Assessment

Portfolio Encourage students to place in their portfolios one or two items of what they consider to be their best work. Examples include:

- Activity 9-1 experiment design and analysis, pp. 242-243
- MiniLAB analysis, p. 246
- Using Technology, p. 254 P

Performance Additional performance assessments may be found in **Performance Assessment** and **Science Integration Activities.** Performance Task Assessment Lists and rubrics for evaluating these activities can be found in Glencoe's **Performance Assessment in the Science Classroom.**

GLENCOE TECHNOLOGY

MindJogger Videoquiz

Chapter 9 Have students work in groups as they play the Videoquiz game to review key chapter concepts.

Chapter 9 Review

Checking Concepts

Choose the word or phrase that completes the sentence.

1. Earthquakes occur when the _______ of rocks is passed.
   a. tension c. elastic limit
   b. compression d. strength
2. A _______ fault forms when the rock above the fault surface moves down relative to the rock below the fault surface.
   a. normal c. reverse
   b. strike-slip d. shearing
3. Seismic waves move outward from the _______.
   a. epicenter c. Moho discontinuity
   b. focus d. tsunami
4. _______ waves stretch and compress rocks.
   a. Surface c. Secondary
   b. Primary d. Shear
5. _______ waves are the slowest.
   a. Surface c. Secondary
   b. Primary d. Pressure
6. At least _______ seismograph stations are needed to locate the epicenter of an earthquake.
   a. two c. four
   b. three d. five
7. Primary waves _______ when they go through solids.
   a. slow down c. stay the same
   b. speed up d. stop
8. The _______ of a seismograph remains still.
   a. sheet of paper c. drum
   b. fixed frame d. pendulum
9. An earthquake of magnitude 7.5 has _______ energy than a quake of 6.5.
   a. 32 times more c. twice as much
   b. 32 times less d. about half as much
10. Most lives lost during an earthquake are due to _______.
   a. tsunamis c. collapse of buildings
   b. primary waves d. broken gas lines

Understanding Concepts

Answer the following questions in your Science Journal using complete sentences.

11. Compare and contrast normal faults with reverse faults.
12. How are primary and secondary waves alike? How are they different?
13. Explain how seismic records were used to determine that Earth's outer core is liquid.
14. What is the relationship between earthquakes with magnitudes on the Richter scale of 1.0 and 3.0?
15. In 1906, an earthquake with a magnitude of 8.6 struck San Francisco, as seen below. Most of the damage done was due to fire. Hypothesize why this occurred.

Thinking Critically

16. What kind of faults would you expect to be most common along the Mid-Atlantic Ridge? Explain.
17. Where is earthquake damage greater—nearer the focus or nearer the epicenter? Explain.
18. Explain why the pendulum of a seismograph remains at rest.
19. Tsunamis are often called tidal waves. Explain why this is incorrect.
20. Which would probably be more stable during an earthquake—a single-story wood-frame house or a brick building? Explain.

Chapter 9 Review

Checking Concepts

1. c
2. a
3. b
4. b
5. a
6. b
7. b
8. d
9. a
10. c

Understanding Concepts

11. Normal faults are due to tension; the rock above the fault surface moves down relative to the rock below the surface. A reverse fault is due to compressional forces in which rocks above the fault surface move up over rocks below the fault surface.
12. Both are released during an earthquake and both change speeds as they travel through Earth. Unlike primary waves, however, secondary waves do not travel through liquids. Also, rock particles vibrate parallel to the direction of travel of primary waves. They vibrate perpendicular to the direction of travel of secondary waves.
13. Secondary waves cannot travel through liquids and are never observed opposite a quake's focus. Primary waves slow down when they reach the outer core. Thus, scientists concluded that the outer core was liquid.
14. An earthquake with a magnitude of 3.0 releases about 1000 times as much energy as a quake with a magnitude of 1.0.
15. Fewer seismic-safe structures were in place than today. Also, more people used gas as a source of energy. Toppling buildings caused numerous gas lines to break, which led to fires.

Thinking Critically

16. The Mid-Atlantic Ridge is a spreading center or divergent boundary. Tension along the ridge causes normal faults to form.
17. Earthquake damage is greatest near the epicenter because surface waves, which cause most of the destruction of an earthquake, are released at the epicenter. The focus is deep in Earth's crust; little damage occurs near it.
18. The pendulum of a seismograph hangs from a fixed frame. Thus, the pendulum acts as a point of reference.
19. Tsunamis are caused by earthquakes that displace the ocean floor. Tides, on the other hand, are caused by the gravitational pull among the sun, the moon, and Earth.
20. The single-story wood frame house would be more stable because the wood is able to "give" more than the masonry building when surface waves travel through it.

Developing Skills

If you need help, refer to the **Skill Handbook.**

21. Concept Mapping: Complete the concept map on the right showing what faults result from the three forces. Use the following terms: *tension, compression, shear, normal faults, reverse faults,* and *strike-slip faults.*

22. Using Variables, Constants, and Controls: Leah investigated how waves are reflected from curved and flat surfaces using water, a dropper, and flexible cardboard. She filled two flat pans half-full of water andpro-duced ripples with water from the dropper. One pan held the flat cardboard; the other the curved piece. What are her variables? What should she keep constant?

23. Communicating: You are a science reporter assigned to interview the mayor about the earthquake safety of city buildings. Make a list of questions about earthquake safety that you will ask the mayor.

24. Measuring in SI: Use an atlas and metric ruler to answer the following question. Primary waves travel at about 6 km/s in continental crust. How long would it take a primary wave to travel from San Francisco, CA to Reno, NV?

25. Interpreting Scientific Illustrations: The illustration below is a typical record of earthquake waves made on a seismograph. How many minutes passed between the arrival of the first primary wave and the first secondary wave?

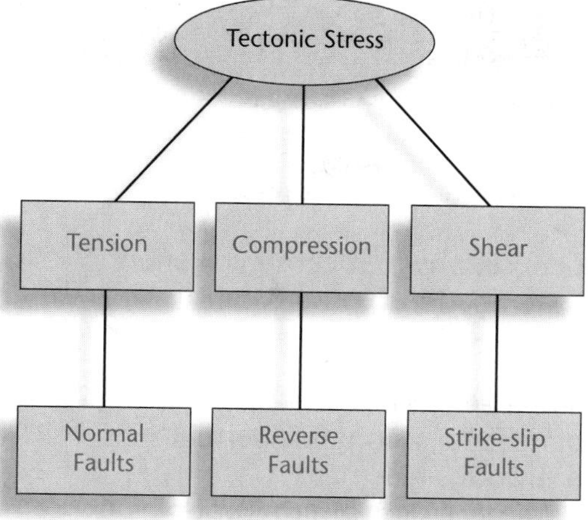

Performance Assessment

1. Formulating a Hypothesis: In Activity 9-1, you learned how earthquake depths can be related to the theory of plate tectonics. You learned that subduction of one plate under another at a convergent boundary will produce earthquakes with shallow-, intermediate-, and deep-foci. Use the concepts you have learned to hypothesize whether earthquake focuses at divergent plate boundaries would be deep, shallow, or intermediate.

2. Science Fair Display: Make a display showing why data from two seismograph stations are not enough to determine the location of an earthquake epicenter.

3. Model: Construct a working model of a tiltmeter. Demonstrate how it might predict that an earthquake is about to occur.

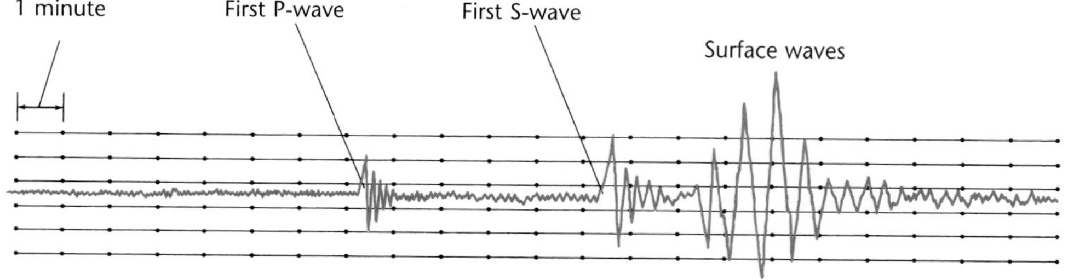

Developing Skills

21. Concept Mapping See SE page 263 for possible solution.

22. Using Variables, Constants, and Controls The only variable should be the shape of the cardboard. All other parameters should remain constant.

23. Communicating Will vary, should include questions about building codes and emergency preparedness.

24. Measuring in SI The distance between San Francisco and Reno is about 300 km. Thus, 300 km ÷ 6 km/s = 50 seconds.

25. Interpreting Scientific Illustrations about 5 minutes

Performance Assessment

1. Earthquake foci at divergent plate boundaries would be shallow because the tectonic activity at divergent plate boundaries occurs at or near Earth's surface. Earth's surface is rifted open by convection currents and molten rock material is then forced out. Use the Performance Task Assessment List for Formulating a Hypothesis in **PASC,** p. 21. P

2. Data from two seismograph stations would enable you to determine two possible locations for the earthquake epicenter. Data from a third station would be needed to determine which of the two locations is the epicenter. Use the Performance Task Assessment List for Science Fair Display in **PASC,** p. 53. P

3. Student models should demonstrate changes in tilt that might be caused by changes in ground level due to an earthquake. Use the Performance Task Assessment List for Making Observations and Inferences in **PASC,** p. 17. P

Chapter Organizer

Section	Objectives	Activities/Features
Chapter Opener		Explore Activity: Make a model volcano. p. 265
10-1 **Volcanoes and Earth's Moving Plates** (2 sessions, 1 block)*	1. **Describe** how volcanoes can affect people. 2. **Describe** conditions that cause volcanoes. 3. **Describe** the relationship between volcanoes and Earth's moving plates.	Using Math, p. 267 Using Technology: Mudflow Protection, p. 269 Activity 10-1: Locating Active Volcanoes, pp. 270-271 Skill Builder: Concept Mapping, p. 273 Science Journal, p. 273
10-2 **Science and Society Technology: Energy from Earth** (1 session, ½ block)*	1. **List** the benefits of using geothermal energy to produce electricity. 2. **Describe** the process of using hot dry rock to produce electricity. 3. **Compare** and **contrast** geothermal energy from magma bodies with geothermal energy from hot dry rock.	Explore the Technology, p. 275
10-3 **Eruptions and Forms of Volcanoes** (2 sessions, 1 block)*	1. **Relate** the explosiveness of a volcanic eruption to the silica and water vapor content of its lava. 2. **Describe** three forms of volcanoes.	Connect to Life Science, p. 277 Problem Solving: Comparing Volcanic Rocks, p. 280 MiniLAB: How can you model different types of volcanic cones? p. 281 Skill Builder: Sequencing, p. 282 Science Journal, p. 282
10-4 **Igneous Rock Features** (2 sessions, 1 block)*	1. **Give examples** of intrusive igneous features and how they form. 2. **Explain** how a volcanic neck and a caldera form.	MiniLAB: Volcanoes eject many different types of material. p. 284 Connect to Physics, p. 285 Skill Builder: Comparing and Contrasting, p. 286 Using Computers: Graphics, p. 286 Activity 10-2: Identifying Types of Volcanoes, p. 287 Science & Art: One Hundred Views of Mount Fuji, p. 288 Science Journal, p. 288

* A complete Planning Guide that includes block scheduling is provided on pages 32T-35T.

Activity Materials

Explore	Activities	MiniLABs
page 265 modeling clay, teaspoon, baking soda, safety goggles, 100-mL graduated cylinder, white vinegar, newspaper, paper towels	pages 270-271 **Appendix G**, tracing paper, **Figures 9-1** and **10-3** page 287 **Table 10-1**, graph paper	page 281 granulated substance such as sand or cereal, 2 large paper plates, plaster of paris, tap water, stirring rod, protractor page 284 volcanic debris including pumice, obsidian, ash, scoria, and basalt; beach sand from volcanic areas; sheets of white paper to contain samples; pin or dissecting probe; magnifying lens; tweezers; stereoscopic microscope

Teacher Classroom Resources

Reproducible Masters	Transparencies	Teaching Resources
Study Guide, p. 41 **Reinforcement,** p. 41 **Enrichment,** p. 41 **Activity Worksheets,** pp. 60-61 **Multicultural Connections,** pp. 23-24	**Section Focus Transparency 37,** Deep Within the Earth . . . **Teaching Transparency 19,** Active Volcanoes and Hot Spots	**Glencoe Earth Science Interactive Videodisc** **Earth Science CD-ROM** **Spanish Resources** **English/Spanish Audiocassettes** **Cooperative Learning Resource Guide** **Lab Partner** **Lab and Safety Skills** **Lesson Plans**
Study Guide, p. 42 **Reinforcement,** p. 42 **Enrichment,** p. 42 **Science and Society Integration,** p. 14	**Section Focus Transparency 38,** Hot Rocks! **Science Integration Transparency 10,** Generating Electricity from Steam	
Study Guide, p. 43 **Reinforcement,** p. 43 **Enrichment,** p. 43 **Activity Worksheets,** p. 64 **Lab Manual 32,** Volcanic Preservation **Science Integration Activity 10,** It's Just a Phase! **Concept Mapping,** p. 25 **Critical Thinking/Problem Solving,** p. 16 **Cross-Curricular Integration,** p. 14	**Section Focus Transparency 39,** There She Blows!	**Assessment Resources** **Chapter Review,** pp. 23-24 **Assessment,** pp. 63-66 **Performance Assessment in the Science Classroom (PASC)** **MindJogger Videoquiz** **Alternate Assessment in the Science Classroom** **Performance Assessment** **Chapter Review Software** **Computer Test Bank**
Study Guide, p. 44 **Reinforcement,** p. 44 **Enrichment,** p. 44 **Activity Worksheets,** pp. 62-63, 65 **Lab Manual 31,** Effect of Magma on Surrounding Rock	**Section Focus Transparency 40,** Melted Rocks, Solid Rocks **Teaching Transparency 20,** Volcanic Landforms	

Key to Teaching Strategies

The following designations will help you decide which activities are appropriate for your students.

L1 Level 1 activities should be within the ability range of all students.

L2 Level 2 activities should be within the ability range of the average to above-average student.

L3 Level 3 activities are designed for the ability range of above-average students.

LEP LEP activities should be within the ability range of Limited English Proficiency students.

LS These activities are designed to address different learning styles.

COOP LEARN Cooperative Learning activities are designed for small group work.

P These strategies represent student products that can be placed into a best-work portfolio.

GLENCOE TECHNOLOGY

The following multimedia resources are available from Glencoe.

The Infinite Voyage Series
Living with Disaster
To the Edge of the Earth

Science and Technology Videodisc Series (STVS)
Earth & Space
Miniature Volcanoes
Indian Pompeii
Chemistry
Geothermal Wells

National Geographic Society Series
STV: Restless Earth
GTV: Planetary Manager

Glencoe Earth Science Interactive Videodisc
The Rock Cycle
Volcanoes: Erupting Mountains

Earth Science CD-ROM

Teacher Classroom Resources

This is a representation of key blackline masters available in the Teacher Classroom Resources.

Teaching Aids

Section Focus Transparencies

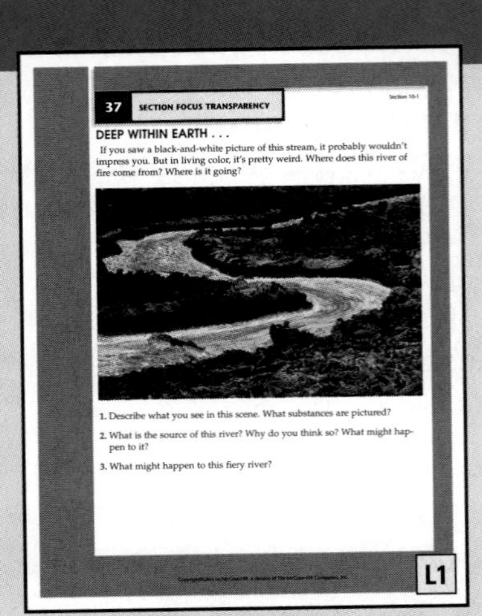

37 SECTION FOCUS TRANSPARENCY

DEEP WITHIN EARTH . . .

If you saw a black-and-white picture of this stream, it probably wouldn't impress you. But in living color, it's pretty weird. Where does this river of fire come from? Where is it going?

1. Describe what you see in this scene. What substances are pictured?
2. What is the source of this river? Why do you think so? What might happen to it?
3. What might happen to this fiery river?

L1

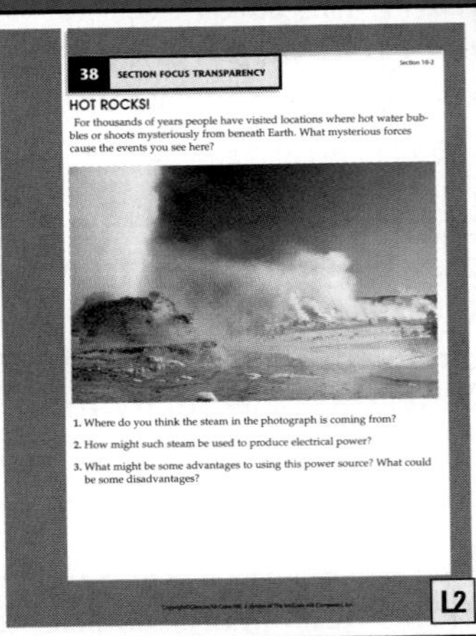

38 SECTION FOCUS TRANSPARENCY

HOT ROCKS!

For thousands of years people have visited locations where hot water bubbles or shoots mysteriously from beneath Earth. What mysterious forces cause the events you see here?

1. Where do you think the steam in the photograph is coming from?
2. How might such steam be used to produce electrical power?
3. What might be some advantages to using this power source? What could be some disadvantages?

L2

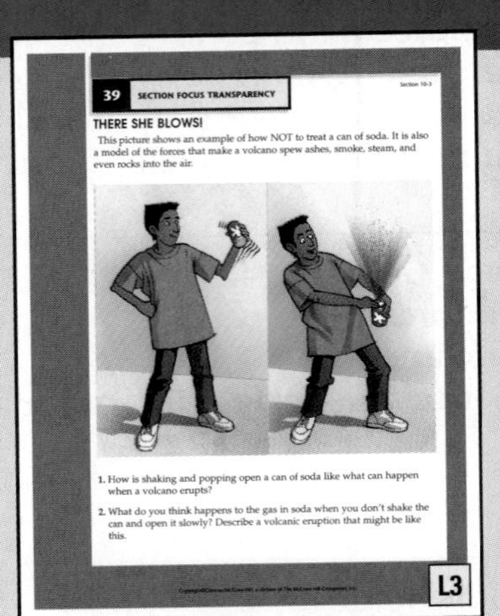

39 SECTION FOCUS TRANSPARENCY

THERE SHE BLOWS!

This picture shows an example of how NOT to treat a can of soda. It is also a model of the forces that make a volcano spew ashes, smoke, steam, and even rocks into the air.

1. How is shaking and popping open a can of soda like what can happen when a volcano erupts?
2. What do you think happens to the gas in soda when you don't shake the can and open it slowly? Describe a volcanic eruption that might be like this.

L3

Science Integration Transparencies

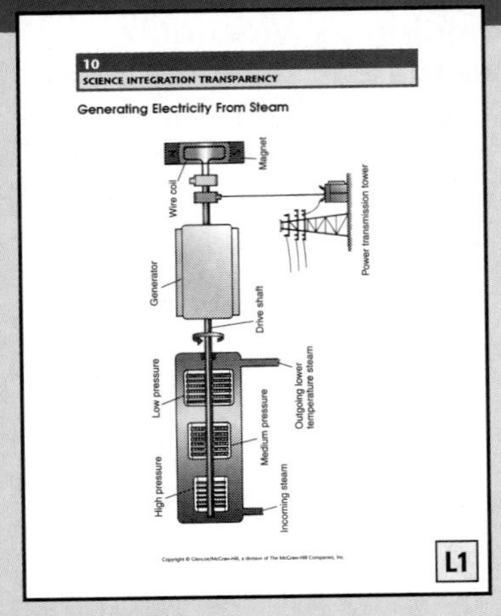

10 SCIENCE INTEGRATION TRANSPARENCY

Generating Electricity From Steam

L1

Teaching Transparencies

19. ACTIVE VOLCANOES AND HOT SPOTS

Hot Spots
Active Volcanoes
Ocean Ridges

L1

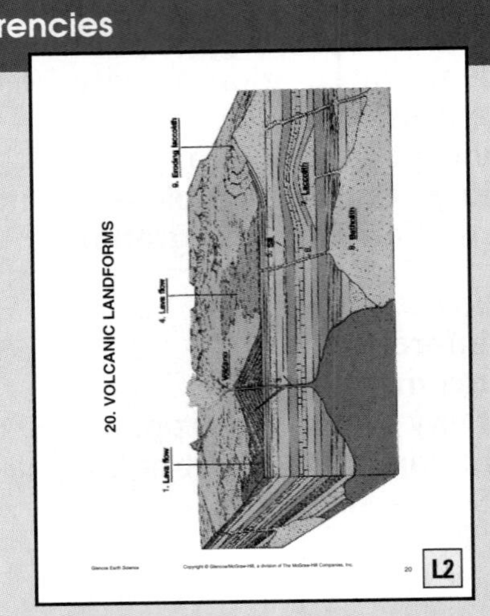

20. VOLCANIC LANDFORMS

L2

Meeting Different Ability Levels

Study Guide

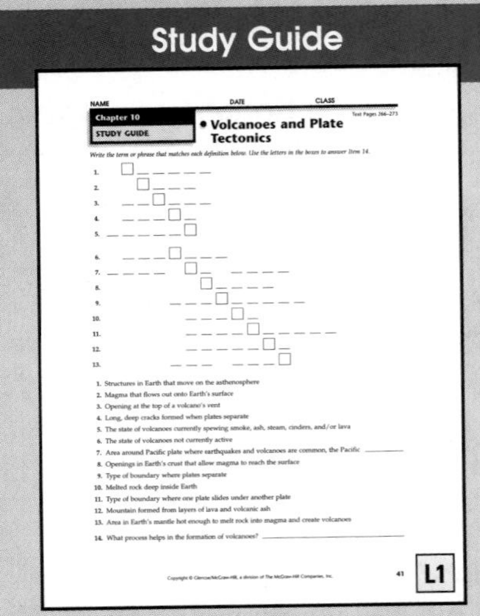

Chapter 10 STUDY GUIDE

• Volcanoes and Plate Tectonics

1. Structures in Earth that move on the asthenosphere
2. Magma that flows out onto Earth's surface
3. Opening at the top of a volcano's vent
4. Long, deep cracks formed when plates separate
5. The state of volcanoes currently spewing smoke, ash, steam, cinders, and/or lava
6. The state of volcanoes not currently active
7. Area around Pacific plate where earthquakes and volcanoes are common, the Pacific
8. Openings in Earth's crust that allow magma to reach the surface
9. Type of boundary where plates separate
10. Melted rock deep inside Earth
11. Type of boundary where one plate slides under another plate
12. Mountains formed from layers of lava and volcanic ash
13. Area in Earth's mantle hot enough to melt rock into magma and create volcanoes
14. What process helps in the formation of volcanoes?

L1

Reinforcement

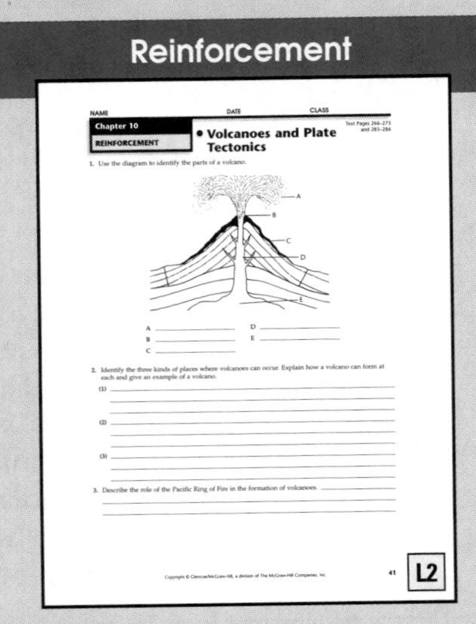

Chapter 10 REINFORCEMENT

• Volcanoes and Plate Tectonics

1. Use the diagram to identify the parts of a volcano.
2. Identify the three kinds of places where volcanoes can occur. Explain how a volcano can form at each and give an example of a volcano.
3. Describe the role of the Pacific Ring of Fire in the formation of volcanoes.

L2

Enrichment Worksheets

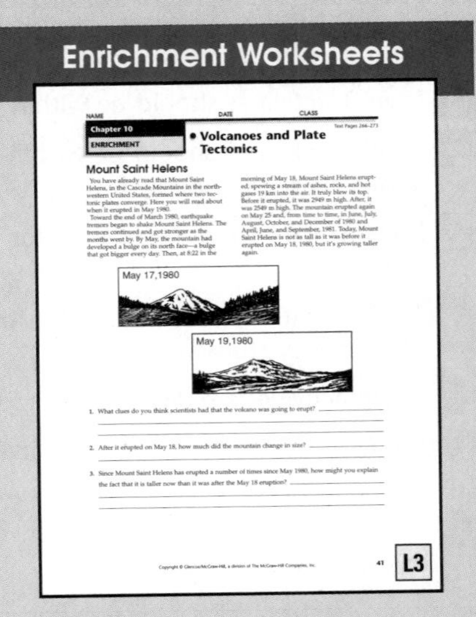

Chapter 10 ENRICHMENT

• Volcanoes and Plate Tectonics

Mount Saint Helens

May 17,1980

May 19,1980

1. What clues do you think scientists had that the volcano was going to erupt?
2. After it erupted on May 18, how much did the mountain change in size?
3. Since Mount Saint Helens has erupted a number of times since May 1980, how might you explain the fact that it is taller now than it was after the May 18 eruption?

L3

Hands-On Activities

Science Integration Activity

Chapter 10 INTEGRATION • It's Just a Phase!

L1

Lab Manual

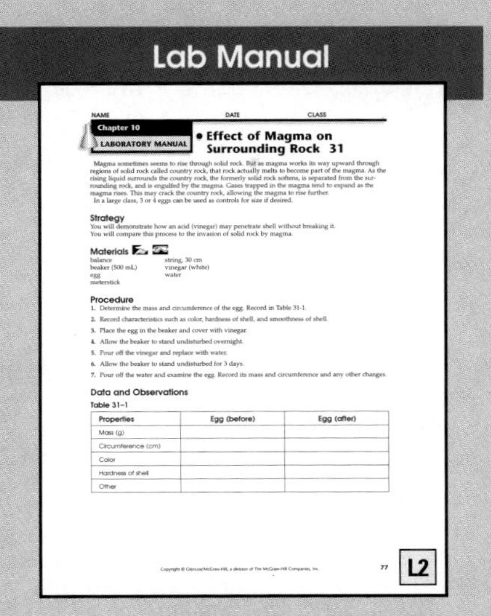
Chapter 10 LABORATORY MANUAL • Effect of Magma on Surrounding Rock 31

L2

Assessment

Performance Assessment

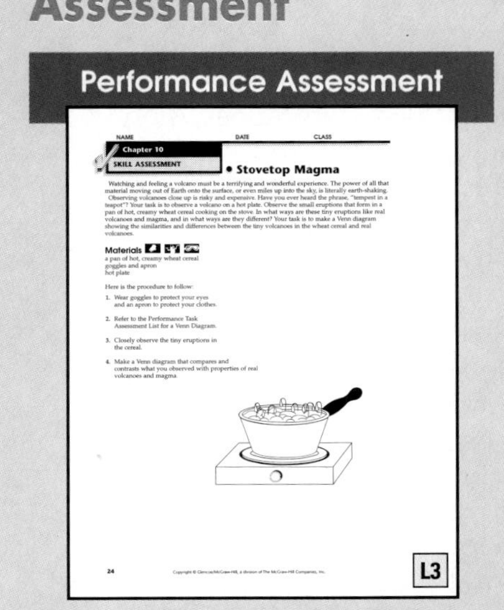
Chapter 10 SKILL ASSESSMENT • Stovetop Magma

L3

Enrichment and Application

Critical Thinking/ Problem Solving

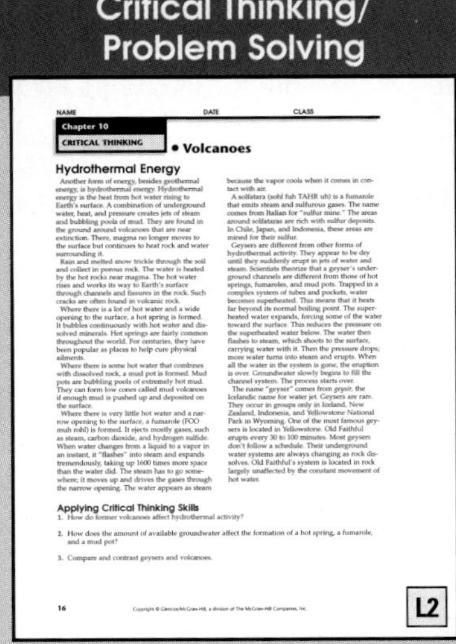
Chapter 10 CRITICAL THINKING • Volcanoes

L2

Cross-Curricular Integration

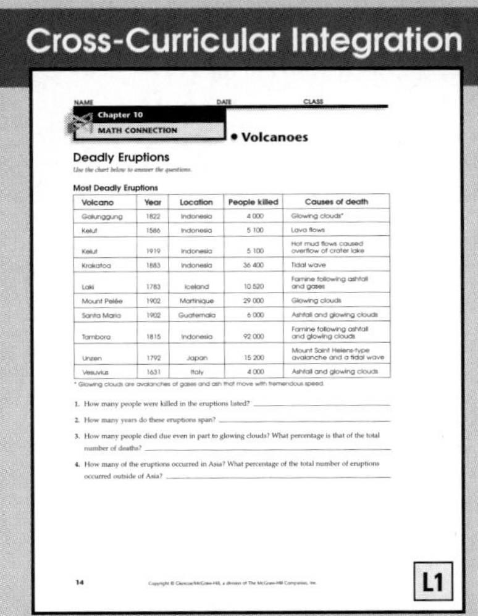
Chapter 10 MATH CONNECTION • Volcanoes

L1

Science and Society Integration

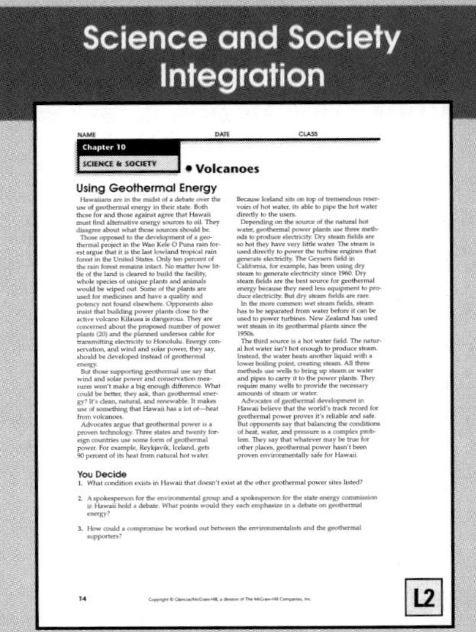
Chapter 10 SCIENCE & SOCIETY • Volcanoes

L2

Multicultural Connections

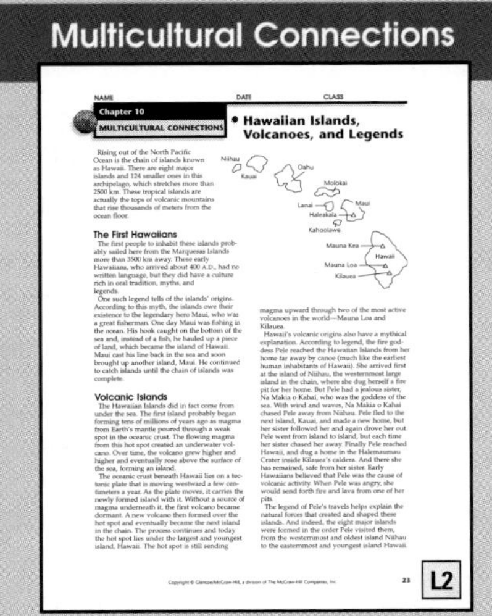
Chapter 10 MULTICULTURAL CONNECTIONS • Hawaiian Islands, Volcanoes, and Legends

L2

Concept Mapping

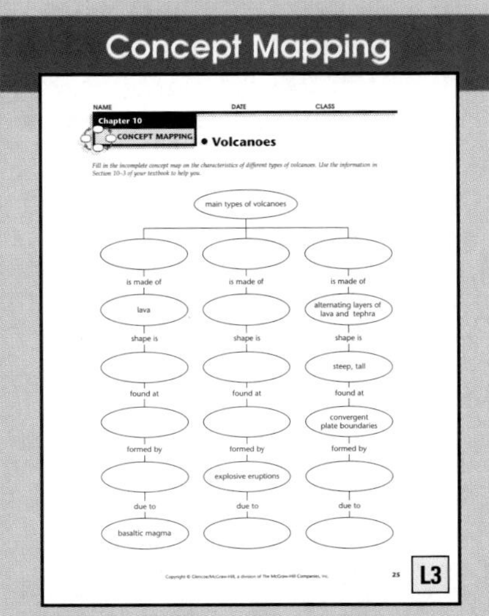
Chapter 10 CONCEPT MAPPING • Volcanoes

L3

Chapter 10

Volcanoes

CHAPTER OVERVIEW

Section 10-1 Volcanoes, how they form, and how they can affect people are discussed. The link between volcanism and Earth's moving plates is presented.

Section 10-2 Science and Society Methods used to generate electricity from geothermal energy are discussed. The technology of hot dry rock (HDR) used in geothermal energy is presented. Geothermal energy from magma is also described.

Section 10-3 The relationship between lava composition and the explosiveness of a volcano is presented. Three forms of volcanoes are described.

Section 10-4 This section compares and contrasts the mode of formation and other characteristics of several intrusive rock features.

Chapter Vocabulary

volcano	shield volcano
vent	tephra
crater	cinder cone
Pacific Ring of Fire	composite volcano
hot spot	batholith
geothermal energy	dike
	sill
hot dry rock (HDR)	volcanic neck
	caldera

Theme Connection

Energy/Stability and Change The energy involved in the formation of magma—its movement upward through the mantle, and finally its flow onto the surface as lava—should be focal points of the chapter. Stability and change is a secondary theme for this chapter, when the evolution of volcanoes is presented.

Previewing the Chapter

264

Look for the following logo for strategies that emphasize different learning modalities. LS

Kinesthetic	Explore, p. 265; Activity, p. 279
Visual-Spatial	Visual Learning, pp. 267, 268, 272, 274, 277, 280, 283, 285; Demonstration, p. 269; Across the Curriculum, p. 272; Reteach, p. 272; Science & Art, p. 288
Interpersonal	MiniLAB, pp. 281, 284; Activity 10-2, p. 287
Logical-Mathematical	Activity 10-1, pp. 270-271
Linguistic	Across the Curriculum, p. 267; Science Journal, p. 277

Volcanoes

The explosive eruption of Mount Pinatubo in the Philippines in 1991 ejected tons of volcanic ash into the atmosphere. Volcanoes can be spectacular and dangerous. Massive ejections of volcanic ash into Earth's atmosphere can cause drastic changes in the environment. On a smaller scale, volcanic eruptions affect humans in many ways. Can you list harmful and also beneficial effects that volcanoes have?

EXPLORE ACTIVITY

Make a model volcano. 

Volcanoes erupt in many different ways. What happens inside a volcano to cause an eruption?

1. Use clay to make a small model volcano with a crater at the top.
2. Place a small amount of baking soda (less than ¼ teaspoon) and a drop of red food coloring in the crater.
3. After putting on safety goggles to protect your eyes, add approximately 20 mL of vinegar to the baking soda in the crater.

Observe: What happens to the baking soda and food coloring when the vinegar is added? Infer how your model eruption is similar to an actual eruption, and how it is different.

Previewing Science Skills

- In the **Skill Builders**, you will **map concepts, sequence events,** and **compare and contrast.**
- In the **Activities**, you will **hypothesize, measure, observe, predict, classify, infer,** and **interpret data.**
- In the **MiniLABs**, you will **formulate models, observe,** and **compare and contrast.**

EXPLORE ACTIVITY

Purpose

LS **Kinesthetic** Use the Explore Activity to introduce students to a study of volcanic eruptions. L1 LEP COOP LEARN

Preparation

Obtain enough modeling clay, baking soda, red food coloring, vinegar, and safety goggles for each group.

Teaching Strategies

Safety Precautions All students should wear their safety goggles during the activity.

- Caution students to use only a small amount of baking soda.

Troubleshooting

- Have each group place a small metal cup in the crater of the model volcano to hold the baking soda and vinegar.
- Cover work areas with plastic.

Observe

Gases and other materials flow out of the volcano as it erupts. This is similar to how trapped gases can cause a real volcano to erupt. The difference is that in a real volcano, the force that causes the eruption comes from deep in Earth's crust. It is not caused by a reaction of surface materials.

Assessment

Process Have students express in writing how the model volcano and the real volcano compare. Use the Performance Task Assessment List for Writing in Science in **PASC,** p. 87. P

Assessment Planner

Portfolio

Refer to page 289 for suggested items that students might select for their portfolios.

Performance Assessment

See page 289 for additional Performance Assessment options.
Skill Builders, pp. 273, 282, 286
MiniLABs, pp. 281, 284
Activities 10-1, pp. 270-271; 10-2, p. 287

Content Assessment

Section Wrap-ups, pp. 273, 275, 282, 286
Chapter Review, pp. 289-291
Mini Quizzes, pp. 273, 282, 286

Group Assessment

Opportunities for group assessment occur with Cooperative Learning Strategies and Flex Your Brain Activities.

Section 10•1

Prepare

Section Background

Lava from volcanoes in Hawaii and Iceland is basaltic. Mount Saint Helens is made of granitic lava, which contains large quantities of silica and water.

Preplanning

To prepare for Activity 10-1, obtain a poster-sized world map and map pins or markers.

1 Motivate

Bellringer

Before presenting the lesson, display **Section Focus Transparency 37** on the overhead projector. Assign the accompanying **Focus Activity** worksheet. L1 LEP

Tying to Previous Knowledge

Have students recall how earthquakes occur where plates of Earth's surface move apart or come together. Ask them to speculate on how moving magma might affect the movement of plates on Earth.

GLENCOE TECHNOLOGY

CD-ROM

Earth Science CD-ROM

Have students perform the interactive exploration for Chapter 10 to reinforce important chapter concepts and thinking processes.

10•1 Volcanoes and Earth's Moving Plates

Science Words

- **volcano**
- **vent**
- **crater**
- **Pacific Ring of Fire**
- **hot spot**

Objectives

- Describe how volcanoes can affect people.
- Describe conditions that cause volcanoes.
- Describe the relationship between volcanoes and Earth's moving plates.

Volcanoes and You

A **volcano** is a vent in Earth's surface that often forms a mountain when layers of lava and volcanic ash erupt and build up. Most of Earth's volcanoes are dormant, which means that they are not currently active, but more than 600 are active. Active volcanoes sometimes spew smoke, steam, ash, cinders, and flows of lava.

In 1980, Mount Saint Helens in Washington State erupted. It was one of the largest recent volcanic eruptions in North America. Geologists warned people to leave the area surrounding the mountain. Most people left, but a few stayed. A total of 63 people were killed as a result of the eruption. Heat from the eruption melted snow, which also caused flooding in the area.

Eruption of the Century

In June, 1991, Mount Pinatubo erupted in the Philippines, killing nearly 900 people. The eruption is considered the largest of any volcano this century. As much as 27 million metric tons

Figure 10-1

Kilauea in Hawaii has been continually erupting since January 3, 1983, becoming the most active volcano on Earth. Living with volcanoes as active as Kilauea can create serious problems for homeowners. Losses have reached $61 million as 181 homes have been destroyed.

Program Resources

Reproducible Masters

Study Guide, p. 41 L1
Reinforcement, p. 41 L1
Enrichment, p. 41 L3
Activity Worksheets, pp. 5, 60-61 L1
Multicultural Connections, pp. 23-24

Transparencies

Section Focus Transparency 37 L1
Teaching Transparency 19

of sulfur dioxide and ash were thrown into Earth's upper atmosphere. It's possible that this material was the cause of the lowered global temperatures and record ozone losses that were observed as recently as 1993.

Just prior to the eruption of Mount Pinatubo, Mount Unzen in Japan erupted. Forty-one people lost their lives, including several volcanologists who were studying the erupting volcano and producing an educational program.

Figure 10-2

Volcanic ash covered several buildings in Iceland during an eruption in 1973. *With the obvious danger, why do people insist on living near volcanoes?*

Most Active Volcano

For centuries, the Kilauea volcano in Hawaii has been erupting, but not explosively. Most of the town of Kalapana Gardens was destroyed in May 1990. No one was hurt because the lava moved slowly. The most recent series of eruptions from Kilauea, as seen in **Figure 10-1**, began in January 1993. Kilauea is the world's most active volcano.

USING MATH

Approximately 7000 flows of quickly moving, hot gas and volcanic debris called pyroclastic flows have occurred on Mount Unzen from 1991 through 1994. On average, how many pyroclastic flows can be expected to occur on Mount Unzen each month?

What causes volcanoes?

What happens inside Earth to create volcanoes? Why are some areas of Earth more likely to have volcanoes than others?

You learned in Chapter 4 that magma forms deep inside Earth. Heat and pressure cause rock to melt and form magma. Some deep rocks already are molten. Others are hot enough that a small rise in temperature or drop in pressure can melt them to form magma.

2 Teach

Teacher F.Y.I.

Pyroclastic flows and surges have been responsible for most deaths and injuries caused by volcanic eruptions in the 20th century. A pyroclastic flow and surge caused almost all of the 29 000 deaths during Mount Pelée's eruption on the island of Martinique in 1902.

USING MATH

If 7000 flows have occurred in four years, or 48 months, the number that can be expected each month would equal 7000 ÷ 48 = 146. Expect 146 pyroclastic flows each month on the flanks of Mount Unzen in Japan.

Visual Learning

Figure 10-2 With the obvious danger, why do people insist on living near volcanoes? *Answers will vary; possible answers include fertile soil for farming or access to harbors.* LEP LS

GLENCOE TECHNOLOGY

 **Videodisc**

The Infinite Voyage: Living with Disaster

Chapter 8

Nevado del Ruiz: A Volcanic Disaster

Chapter 9

The Nature of Volcanoes: Nevado del Ruiz

Chapter 10

Adapting to the Nature of Volcanoes: Sakurajima

Integrating the Sciences

Chemistry Eruptions of Kilauea are less explosive than those of many other volcanoes'. Have students determine what is true about the chemical composition of lava from Kilauea that makes it different from many other volcanoes and causes less explosive eruptions. *Lava from Kilauea is basaltic—a hot, fast-flowing lava that does not trap gases.*

Across the Curriculum

Language Arts Have students read a book about famous eruptions such as the 1902 eruption of Mount Pelée and read how it affected the people there. Ask volunteers to share what they learn with their classmates. L2 LS

Visual Learning

Figure 10-3 **What process might be occurring at these boundaries that causes rock material to melt and be forced upward to form volcanoes?** *Hot, less dense magma is rising along the boundaries forming the volcanoes.* LEP LS

Video Presentation

- Show the video "Volcanoes," which is a part of the NOVA television program. The film is available from Ambrose Video, 381 Park Avenue South, New York, NY 10016.
- Show the video "Volcanism," *Earth Revealed,* The Annenberg/CPB Collection, 1-800-LEARNER.

Revealing Preconceptions

Some students may think only people living near a volcano are affected when the volcano erupts. Inform them that ash from Mount Saint Helens fell on much of the United States in 1980. Winds are able to carry volcanic debris thousands of kilometers. Gases and ash from Mount Pinatubo remained in the upper atmosphere for years after the eruption.

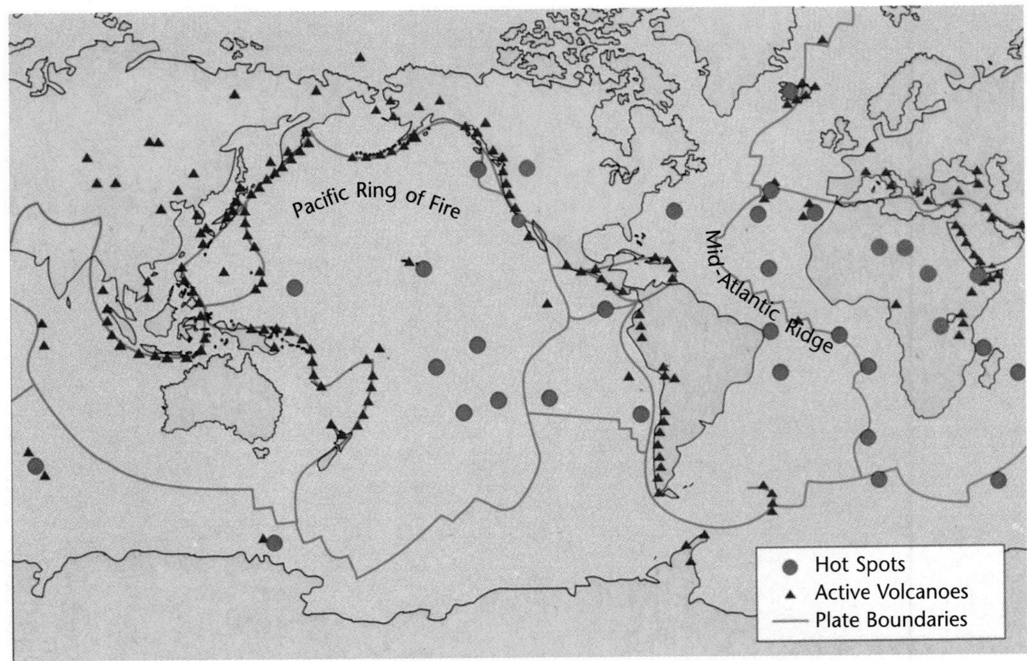

Figure 10-3

The diagram above shows active volcanoes and hot spots around the world. All of the earthquakes and volcanoes in the Pacific Ring of Fire can be attributed to tectonic movement where the Pacific Plate meets other plates. *What process might be occurring at these boundaries that causes rock material to melt and be forced upward to form volcanoes?*

Magma Forced Upward

Magma is less dense than the rock around it, so it is very slowly forced upward toward Earth's surface. You can see this process if you turn a bottle of cold syrup upside down. Watch the dense syrup force the less-dense air bubbles slowly upward to the top.

After many thousands or even millions of years, magma reaches Earth's surface and flows out through an opening called a **vent.** As lava flows out, it cools quickly and becomes solid, forming layers of igneous rock around the vent. The steep walled depression around a volcano's vent is the **crater.**

Where do volcanoes occur?

Volcanoes form in three kinds of places that are directly related to the movement of Earth's plates. Volcanoes occur where plates are moving apart, where plates are moving together, and at locations called hot spots. There are many examples of volcanoes around the world at these three different types of locations. Let's explore Iceland, Mount Saint Helens, and Hawaii.

Divergent Boundaries

Iceland is a large island in the North Atlantic Ocean. It is near the Arctic Circle and has some glaciers. But, as seen in

Community Connection

Volcanoes and You Encourage students to visit the office of the city planner or a similar local government official to ask questions about how volcanic activity might affect your geographic location. Once students obtain as much information as possible, invite the city planner or other official to visit the class to present information about local volcanic activity.

Use **Teaching Transparency 19** as you teach this lesson.

Use **Multicultural Connections,** pp. 23-24, as you teach this lesson.

Figure 10-2, on page 267, it also has volcanoes. Iceland has volcanic activity because it sits on top of the Mid-Atlantic Ridge.

The Mid-Atlantic Ridge is a divergent plate boundary, an area where Earth's plates are moving apart. Where plates separate, they form long, deep cracks called rifts. Magma flows from rifts as lava and is quickly cooled by the seawater. As more lava flows, it builds up from the seafloor. Sometimes the volcanoes and rift eruptions rise above sea level, forming islands such as Iceland.

Convergent Boundaries

Mount Saint Helens is one of several volcanoes that make up the Cascade Mountain Range of Oregon and Washington in the northwestern United States. Mount Saint Helens and the other volcanic peaks in the Cascade Range formed because of a convergent plate boundary. Earth's plates move together at convergent plate boundaries.

USING TECHNOLOGY

Mudflow Protection

On November 13, 1985, Colombia's Nevado del Ruiz volcano erupted. On that day, nearly 23 000 people lost their lives, not from the exploding mountain or from lava flows, but from mud flows. Mud flows are another hazard of volcanoes. Many volcanic peaks have a high enough elevation that they are covered with snow fields and glaciers. The heat from volcanic activity melts this snow and ice during an eruption. This can mean disaster for people living below such a volcano. The melted snow mixes with ash from the eruption and soil from the mountain and flows rapidly downhill, as it did in Colombia.

The Japanese have developed mud-flow control technology to protect populated areas below active volcanoes. Their technology is designed to slow the mud as it flows down valleys. They have installed concrete and steel damlike structures in valleys where mud flows have occurred before.

Think Critically: In addition to these structures, the Japanese have developed other methods designed to provide protection from volcanic eruptions. For example, television cameras are used as earthquake sensors to help them detect eruptions. What will mud-flow control enable villagers to do in case of eruptions? Why would earthquake sensors be used to detect volcanic eruptions?

Mudflow Dams, Japan

Demonstration

LS **Visual-Spatial** Attach an air pump to a balloon neck and then place the balloon under a large piece of denim. As you gradually inflate the balloon, explain that the bulge in the cloth represents lava that causes doming on the cloth "volcano." Ask students what will happen if you continue to inflate the balloon. Students should conclude that as the "lava dome" continues to increase in size, there's a good probability that the "volcano" will erupt. Inform them that bulging and earthquakes are often precursors to eruptions, as was the case prior to the 1980 Mount Saint Helens eruption. LEP

USING TECHNOLOGY

For more information, see "Eruption in Colombia" by Bart McDowell, *National Geographic Magazine*, May 1986, pp. 641-653.

Think Critically

Mudflow control will provide villagers with time to evacuate the area. Underground movements of huge bodies of magma and vast amounts of gases cause the earthquakes that accompany volcanic eruptions. Using the sensors could perhaps give people time to evacuate the area, if needed.

Videodisc

STV: Restless Earth

Mudflow dams; Japan

52229

Cultural Diversity

The Aleut The name *Alaska* comes from the Aleut language and means "mainland." The Aleut, like the Eskimo, are probably descendants of Asian migrants who crossed the Bering Strait about 3000 years ago. The Aleut live on the western part of the Alaskan peninsula and the Aleutian Islands, a chain of about 70 small islands of volcanic origin. Traditionally, the Aleut made their living by hunting and trapping animals such as caribou, seals, otters, whales, walruses, fish, birds, and mollusks. Kayaks, one- to two-person boats, were used to travel and hunt alone. Larger, open boats were used for group hunting of larger prey such as whales. In the past, most Aleut lived near freshwater areas protected from attack by neighboring groups. Related families lived together in villages. A chief ruled several villages, passing the title on to his heirs.

Activity 10-1

PREPARATION

Purpose

LS **Logical-Mathematical** Design and carry out an investigation in which data interpretation will show the relationships among locations of active volcanoes, earthquakes, hot spots, and boundaries of Earth's plates. L1 COOP LEARN

Process Skills

communicating, interpreting data, observing, hypothesizing, and measuring in SI

Time

50 minutes

Materials Use a large, poster-sized world map, suitable for students to use for marking. If the map is mounted on cardboard, students can stick map pins into it.

Safety Precautions

If the map is mounted for pinning, caution students to handle map pins with care.

Possible Hypotheses

1. A positive correlation is expected between the locations of active volcanoes and the locations of earthquake epicenters. It is likely that a study of this correlation will also include a study of Earth's moving plates.
2. The locations of active volcanoes will be in the same general location as earthquake epicenters.

Activity Worksheets, pp. 5, 60-61

Activity 10-1

Design Your Own Experiment

Locating Active Volcanoes

Volcanoes form when hot, melted rock material is forced upward to Earth's surface. As the melted rock moves inside Earth, vibrations occur, which are felt as earthquakes. In this activity, you will design an experiment to see whether the locations of active volcanoes are correlated to the locations of recent earthquakes.

PREPARATION

Problem

Is there a correlation between the locations of active volcanoes and the locations of earthquake epicenters?

Form a Hypothesis

State a hypothesis about whether you expect to see a correlation between the locations of active volcanoes and the locations of earthquake epicenters.

Objectives

- Plot the locations of several active volcanoes.
- Describe any correlation you see between locations of volcanoes and locations of earthquake epicenters.

Possible Materials

- Appendix G
- tracing paper
- **Figure 9-2,** page 237
- **Figure 10-3,** page 268

270

PLAN THE EXPERIMENT

Possible Procedures

1. Obtain a world map showing latitude and longitude lines.
2. Either plot directly on the map or on a tracing of the map.
3. Plot each active volcano according to its latitude and longitude.
4. Obtain a map with earthquake epicenters plotted on it.
5. Transfer earthquake epicenter locations to your map of active volcano locations.
6. Interpret any correlation that is shown.
7. Compare your map of active volcano and earthquake epicenter locations with the locations of boundaries of Earth's moving plates.
8. Interpret any correlation of active volcano and earthquake epicenter locations with Earth's moving plate boundaries.

PLAN THE EXPERIMENT

1. As a group, agree upon and write out your hypothesis statement.
2. As a group, list the steps that are needed to test your hypothesis. Be specific, describing exactly what you will do at each step.
3. Determine how best to plot the provided volcano latitude and longitude data on a tracing of Earth's surface.
4. Make a list of any special conditions or facts you expect to observe or test.

Check the Plan

1. Read over your experiment to make sure that all steps are in a logical order.
2. Determine the manner in which you will summarize data and state conclusions about any correlations you discover.
3. How will you determine whether certain facts or conditions will indicate a correlation of volcano locations with locations of earthquake epicenters?
4. *Make sure your teacher approves your plan and that you have included any changes suggested in the plan.*

DO THE EXPERIMENT

Data and Observations

Volcano	Latitude	Longitude
#1	64° N	19° W
#2	28° N	34° E
#3	43° S	172° E
#4	35° N	136° E
#5	18° S	68° W
#6	25° S	114° W
#7	20° N	155° W
#8	54° N	167° W
#9	16° N	122° E
#10	28° N	17° W
#11	15° N	43° E
#12	6° N	75° W
#13	64° S	158° E
#14	38° S	78° E
#15	21° S	56° E
#16	38° N	26° E
#17	7° S	13° W
#18	2° S	102° E
#19	38° N	30° W
#20	54° N	159° E

1. Carry out the experiment as planned.
2. While conducting the experiment, write down any observations that you make in your Science Journal.
3. Compare the plot of volcanoes you have constructed with **Figures 9-2** and **10-3** on pages 237 and 268.

Analyze and Apply

1. **Describe** any patterns of distribution that active volcanoes form on Earth.
2. **Describe** any patterns of distribution of earthquake epicenters shown in **Figure 9-2** on page 237.
3. **Compare and contrast** any patterns that you observe with the locations of Earth's plates and hot spots.

Go Further

Write a hypothesis to explain any patterns you observed for locations of volcanoes, earthquake epicenters, Earth's moving plate boundaries, and hot spots. Propose ways in which geologists might test your hypothesis.

Go Further

- Students should see the relationship of active volcanoes and earthquake epicenters around the Pacific Ocean. They should notice that earthquakes and active volcanoes also occur in the vicinity of Earth's moving plate boundaries and hot spots.
- Accept all proposals for testing student hypotheses, and discuss those that sound reasonable as well as those that do not.

Assessment

Performance Tell students that a large number of extinct volcanoes have been located in the midst of one of Earth's large moving ocean plates. Ask them to explain what might have caused the volcanoes. Use the Performance Task Assessment List for Making Observations and Inferences in **PASC**, p. 17. P

Teaching Strategies

Tying to Previous Knowledge Review from Chapter 5 how to determine locations using lines of latitude and longitude.

Troubleshooting Have available copies in the same scale, of maps showing active volcano locations, earthquake epicenter locations, and boundaries of Earth's moving plates.

DO THE EXPERIMENT

Expected Outcome

Students should see a positive correlation between active volcano location and the locations of earthquake epicenters. They should also hypothesize about a relationship to Earth's moving plates.

Analyze and Apply

1. Because only 20 of the approximately 600 active volcanoes are plotted, some students may not be able to detect a pattern. They may note that more volcanoes appear to be associated with the Pacific Ocean.
2. Students should note that most epicenters are located around the Pacific Ocean. Other locations fall into patterns in the mid-Atlantic Ocean, in southern Europe, in the Middle East, and north of India.
3. Students should indicate that active volcanoes, earthquake epicenters, and boundaries of Earth's moving plates occur in the same general areas. Students should also indicate that some volcanoes occur in the vicinity of known hot spots.

Student Text Question

Mount Saint Helens is just one volcano in the Pacific Ring of Fire. What are the names of some others? *Mount Rainier, Mount Hood, Mount Jefferson, Crater Lake, and Mount Shasta are just a few.*

Visual Learning

Figure 10-4 Based on the position and latitude of the Hawaiian Emperor Seamounts, has the Pacific Plate always moved in the same direction? *No, a large bend in the chain indicates a direction change in the movement of the Pacific Plate.* LEP LS

3 Assess

Check for Understanding

FLEX Your Brain

Use the Flex Your Brain activity to have students explore HOW VOLCANOES FORM. P

Activity Worksheets, p. 5

Reteach

LS **Visual-Spatial** Draw a cross section of an area where one of Earth's moving plates is sliding under another. Explain how material from one plate melts due to changes in pressure and temperature as it is subducted. The melted material is less dense than the surrounding material and thus is forced toward Earth's surface to form volcanoes. LEP

Extension

For students who have mastered this section, use the **Reinforcement** and **Enrichment** masters.

Figure 10-4

The Hawaiian Islands have formed as the Pacific Plate moves over a hot spot. Continued movement of the Pacific Plate formed Oahu, Molokai, Maui, and Hawaii over a period of about five million years. Compare parts A and B of this figure. *Based on the position and attitude of the Hawaiian Emperor Seamounts, has the Pacific Plate always moved in the same direction? Explain.*

Here, the Juan de Fuca Plate is converging with and sliding under the North American Plate. Magma is created in the subduction zone when the plate being pushed down under the North American Plate gets deep enough and hot enough to partially melt. The magma is then forced upward to the surface, forming the volcanoes of the Cascades.

Such volcanoes have formed all around the Pacific Plate where it collides with other plates. This area around the Pacific Plate where earthquakes and volcanoes are common is called the **Pacific Ring of Fire,** as seen in **Figure 10-3** on page 268. Mount Saint Helens is just one volcano in the Pacific Ring of Fire. What are the names of some others?

Hot Spots

Like Iceland, the Hawaiian Island are volcanic islands. But unlike Iceland, they haven't formed at a plate boundary. The Hawaiian Islands are in the middle of the Pacific Plate, far from its edges. What process could be forming them?

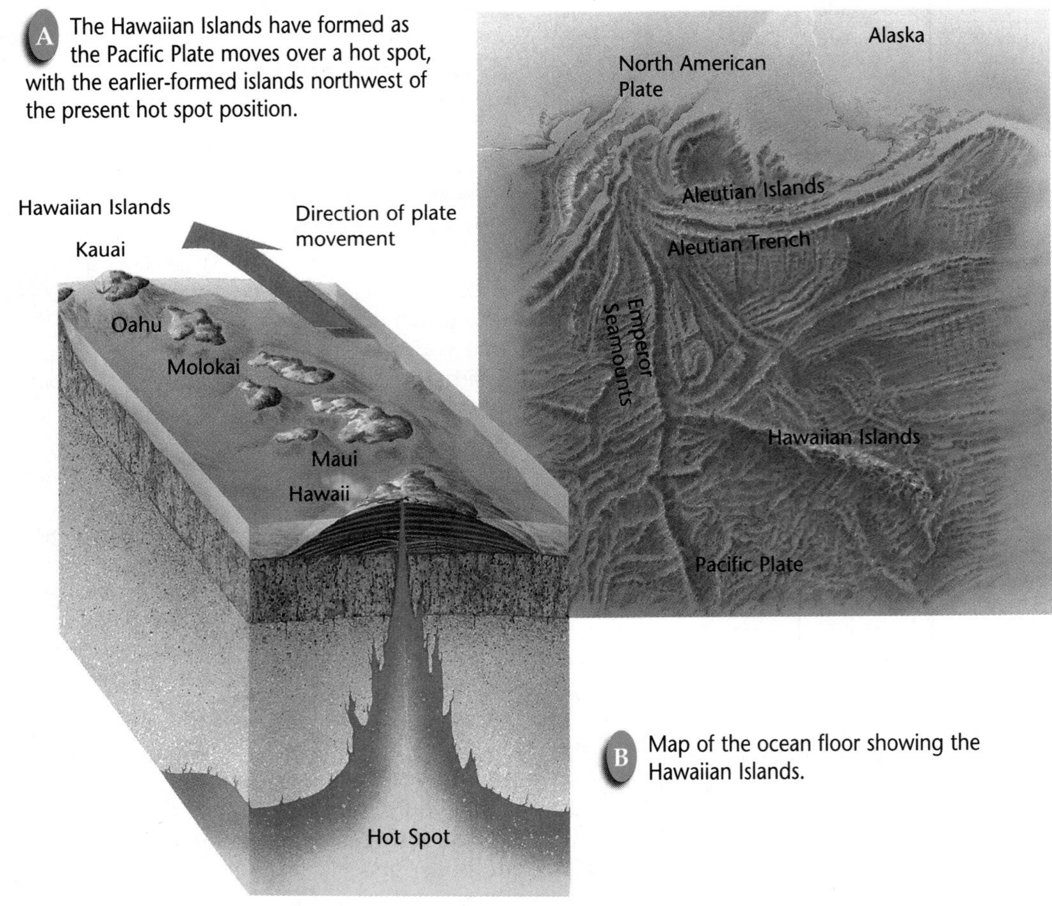

A The Hawaiian Islands have formed as the Pacific Plate moves over a hot spot, with the earlier-formed islands northwest of the present hot spot position.

B Map of the ocean floor showing the Hawaiian Islands.

Across the Curriculum

Geography Display a map of the world on a bulletin board in the classroom. Have each student in the class locate one active volcano on the map. Then, have each student place a pin with the name of the volcano at the proper position on the map. Have the class as a whole note any patterns. Ask students to list countries that have a greater number of active volcanoes than most. L1 LS

Geologists believe that some areas in the mantle are hotter than other areas. Some geologists believe that hot spot magma originates at the mantle-outer core boundary. These **hot spots** melt rock, which is then forced upward toward the crust as magma. The Hawaiian Islands sit on top of a hot spot under the Pacific Plate. Magma from deep in Earth's mantle has melted through the crust to form several volcanoes. Those that rise above the water form the Hawaiian Islands, as shown in **Figure 10-5.**

As you can see in **Figure 10-4,** the Hawaiian Islands are all in a line. This is because the Pacific Plate is moving over the stationary hot spot. The island of Kauai is the oldest Hawaiian island and was once located where the big island of Hawaii is today. As the plate moved, Kauai moved away from the hot spot and became dormant. Continued movement of the Pacific Plate formed Oahu, Molokai, Maui, and Hawaii over a period of about five million years.

Loihi (Submarine volcano)

Figure 10-5

Computer image showing the island of Hawaii and Loihi, a submarine volcano. If Loihi reaches the surface, it will form a new island.

Section Wrap-up

Review

1. How are volcanoes related to Earth's moving plates?
2. As rock material melts, it becomes less dense. Explain what's happening to the atoms and molecules to cause this.
3. **Think Critically:** If the Pacific Plate stopped moving, what would happen to the island of Hawaii?

Skill Builder

Concept Mapping

Make a concept map that shows how the Hawaiian Islands formed over a hot spot. Use the following terms and phrases: *volcano forms, plate moves, volcano becomes dormant, new volcano forms.* If you need help, refer to Concept Mapping in the **Skill Handbook.**

Science Journal

Scientists were able to predict approximately when Mount Pinatubo in the Philippines would erupt. They based their predictions on changes in Earth's crust, shallow earthquakes, and changes in gaseous output. Research this and other recent eruptions and, in your Science Journal, write a report on what equipment volcanologists use to predict volcanic eruptions.

4 Close

•MINI•QUIZ•

1. **What is the world's most active volcano?** *Kilauea*
2. **What is a crater?** *the opening at the top of a volcano's vent*
3. **What is the Pacific Ring of Fire?** *a belt around the Pacific Plate along which earthquakes and volcanoes are common*

Section Wrap-up

Review

1. Volcanoes form when lava flows onto Earth's surface where plates are moving apart; one moving plate subducts under another and the magma eventually reaches Earth's surface, or plates move over hot spots in Earth's mantle.
2. As matter changes state from a crystalline solid to a liquid, the atoms and molecules lose their tight-fitting pattern. They move over and around each other. More volume is required to contain the loosely arranged molecules. Thus, the material is less dense.
3. **Think Critically** As long as the hot spot provided new magma, the island would grow larger and larger.

Science Journal

Answers will vary. Students' replies should include instruments such as tiltmeters, creepmeters, lasers, seismographs, and instruments to measure gaseous content.

Skill Builder

Possible solution:

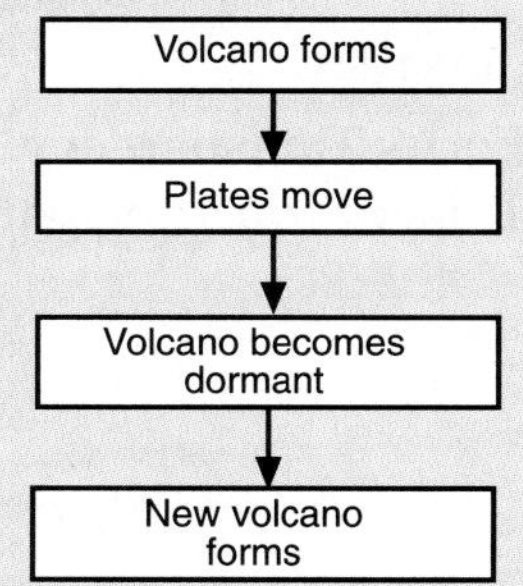

Assessment

Performance Assess students' abilities to make a concept map by having them share their maps with the class. Use the Performance Task Assessment List for Concept Map in **PASC,** p. 89. P

Prepare

Section Background

The Geysers, the first commercial geothermal energy power plant in the United States, is located 144 km north of San Francisco and was built in 1960. By 1986, The Geysers was generating enough electricity to satisfy the needs of San Francisco and Oakland.

1 Motivate

Bellringer

Before presenting the lesson, display **Section Focus Transparency 38** on the overhead projector. Assign the accompanying **Focus Activity** worksheet. L1 LEP

Tying to Previous Knowledge

Have students recall the geyser called Old Faithful. Heat under Earth's surface periodically heats groundwater until steam builds up and the pressure of the steam causes the geyser to erupt. Tapping this heat supply is what geothermal heat is all about.

2 Teach

Visual Learning

Figure 10-7 Which type of geothermal energy, natural geothermal or HDR, produces less carbon-dioxide emissions? *HDR* LEP IS

TECHNOLOGY:

10•2 Energy from Earth

Science Words

geothermal energy
hot dry rock (HDR)

Objectives

- List the benefits of using geothermal energy to produce electricity.
- Describe the process of using hot dry rock to produce electricity.
- Compare and contrast geothermal energy from magma bodies with geothermal energy from hot dry rock.

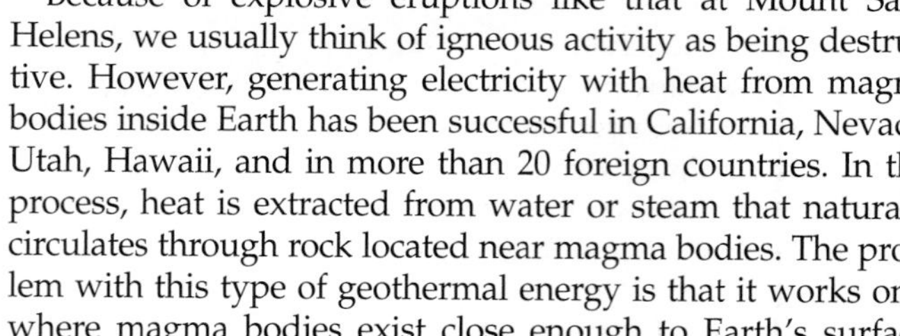

Electricity from Geothermal Energy

Because of explosive eruptions like that at Mount Saint Helens, we usually think of igneous activity as being destructive. However, generating electricity with heat from magma bodies inside Earth has been successful in California, Nevada, Utah, Hawaii, and in more than 20 foreign countries. In this process, heat is extracted from water or steam that naturally circulates through rock located near magma bodies. The problem with this type of geothermal energy is that it works only where magma bodies exist close enough to Earth's surface. This occurs only at certain locations around the planet. A new technology that generates electricity from hot dry rock and does not rely on pre-existing natural reservoirs of hot water may eventually decrease human dependence on fossil fuels.

Geothermal Energy from Magma

Magma bodies inside Earth hold tremendous amounts of thermal energy. This **geothermal energy** can be used to generate electricity. The heat from magma can be used to heat water and produce steam in a power plant. The steam is pressurized and then spins turbines that run generators to make electricity.

The United States currently leads the world in the use of geothermal energy. In the four states mentioned above, 70 hydrothermal plants have a capacity to generate 2800 megawatts of electricity. Unless a way is found to enable geothermal energy to be used worldwide, it cannot come close to matching the convenience of energy from fossil fuels. If geothermal energy can be used in place of resources such as fossil fuels, several benefits could be realized. These benefits include reductions in the threat of oil spills on coastlines, mine waste, radioactive waste, and pollutants from burning fossil fuels. Also, geothermal plants presently being used are very reliable.

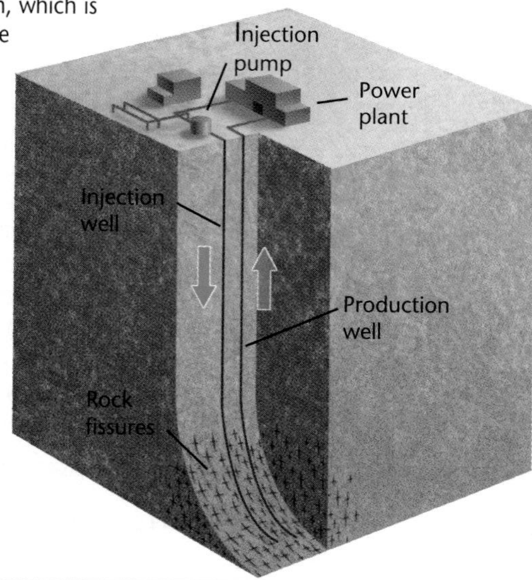

Figure 10-6

A new technology, called hot dry rock (HDR), could greatly increase the use of geothermal energy. Heat from hot rock material is used to heat water and make steam, which is used to generate electricity.

Program Resources

Reproducible Masters

Study Guide, p. 42 L1
Reinforcement, p. 42 L1
Enrichment, p. 42 L3
Science and Society Integration, p. 14

Transparencies

Section Focus Transparency 38 L1
Science Integration Transparency 10

Geothermal Energy from Hot Dry Rock (HDR)

Geothermal energy can also be derived from Earth without relying on the presence of magma. This new technology, called **hot dry rock (HDR),** involves pumping water into hot dry rock that has been fractured, as seen in **Figure 10-6.** The water is pumped down one well, circulated through fractures made in the rock, then forced up a second well. The water returning to Earth's surface is hot water. As with geothermal energy from magma bodies, the hot water is used to produce steam. The steam is pressurized and used to spin turbines, which in turn run generators to make electricity.

HDR is more available as a resource than heat from magma. This is because temperature increases with depth into Earth and hot dry rock occurs almost everywhere. However, if the hot dry rock is very deep, the cost of drilling forces the overall cost of this energy source upwards. In contrast, harm to the environment caused by geothermal energy is much lower than for other resources such as fossil fuels, as shown in **Figure 10-7.** Does the lower amount of harm to the environment outweigh the much higher cost of HDR? Presently, HDR is too expensive even though it is a much cleaner energy source. But this could change in the future.

In addition to the problem of drilling, HDR requires that the rock have fissures or cracks in it in order for the water to pass through and be heated. If the cracks don't already exist, they must be created. If pollution problems become so severe that a cleaner energy source must be used no matter the cost, or if improved drilling methods bring the cost of HDR down, it could prove to be an extremely valuable resource.

Carbon Dioxide Emissions for Different Fuel Sources

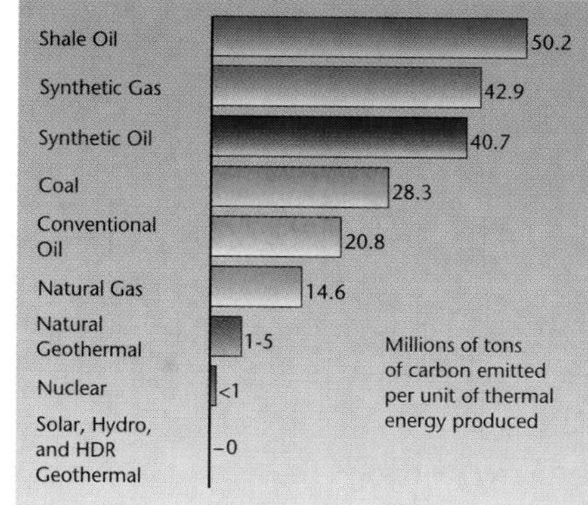

Figure 10-7

Compared with other energy sources, geothermal energy produces very little environmental pollution. *Which type of geothermal energy, natural geothermal or HDR, produces less carbon-dioxide emissions?*

Section Wrap-up

Review

1. List two things that make geothermal energy beneficial.
2. Describe how hot dry rock is used to generate electricity.

Explore the Technology

HDR sounds like a great way to provide electricity without harming the environment. But there are concerns. HDR systems require water, and the water that is heated and brought to the surface may contain toxic chemicals. Still, if the problems can be handled, HDR may be a useful alternative energy source.

SCIENCE & SOCIETY

3 Assess

Check for Understanding

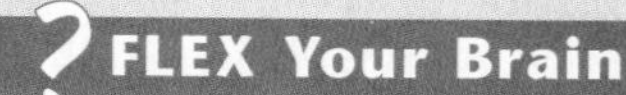

FLEX Your Brain

Use the Flex Your Brain activity to have students explore HOT DRY ROCKS (HDR).

Activity Worksheets, p. 5

Reteach

Have two students stand at the board. One of them is responsible for geothermal energy from HDR and the other for geothermal energy from magma. Have students in the class brainstorm about ways in which the two methods are similar and ways in which they are different. Have the students at the board write down any concepts the class discusses.

Extension

For students who have mastered this section, use the **Reinforcement** and **Enrichment** masters.

4 Close

Activity

Invite a person from your local power company to visit the class and discuss possible uses for HDR in your area.

Section Wrap-up

Review

1. Advantages include reductions in oil spill threats and mine waste.
2. Water is pumped down into hot dry rocks, where it is heated and then brought to the surface, where it is used to produce steam. The steam is pressurized and used to spin turbines, which in turn run generators to make electricity.

Explore the Technology

Have students work in groups of two and discuss the problems listed. Ask students to propose methods to cope with the problems discussed. Accept all answers but insist that students use common sense and logic when proposing their solutions.

Section 10•3

Prepare

Section Background

- Composite volcanoes are also known as stratovolcanoes because of the stratified layers of tephra and lava that make up their flanks.
- Pahoehoe is a basaltic lava that forms a smooth or ropy-looking surface. Basaltic lava that flows with rough, jagged, sharp edges is called *aa.*
- Volcanic ash is any extruded material 2.0 mm or less in diameter. Volcanic bombs are ejected fragments larger than 64 mm.

Preplanning

To prepare for the MiniLAB, obtain cereal, sand, plaster of paris, protractors, and paper plates for each pair of students.

1 Motivate

Bellringer

Before presenting the lesson, display **Section Focus Transparency 39** on the overhead projector. Assign the accompanying **Focus Activity** worksheet. L1 LEP

Tying to Previous Knowledge

Most students have probably opened a warm carbonated beverage only to have it gush from its container. Compare this to volcanic eruptions. Gases in the beverage, along with the relatively warm temperature, cause the liquid to be forced from the container. In a similar way, water vapor and other gases determine the force of a volcanic eruption.

10•3 Eruptions and Forms of Volcanoes

Science Words

shield volcano
tephra
cinder cone
composite volcano

Objectives

- Relate the explosiveness of a volcanic eruption to the silica and water vapor content of its lava.
- Describe three forms of volcanoes.

Types of Eruptions

Some volcanic eruptions are explosive and violent, like those from Mount Pinatubo and Mount Saint Helens. But in others, the lava quietly flows from a vent, as in the Kilauea volcano eruptions. What causes this difference?

There are two important factors that determine whether an eruption will be explosive or quiet. One is the amount of water vapor and other gases that are trapped in the magma. The other factor is whether the magma is basaltic or granitic, as you learned about in Chapter 4. Let's look first at the gas content of the magma.

Trapped Gases

Have you ever shaken a soft drink container and then quickly opened it? The pressure from the gas in the drink builds up and is released suddenly when you open the can, spraying the drink. In the same way, gases such as water vapor and carbon dioxide are trapped in magma by the pressure of the surrounding magma. As the magma nears the surface, the pressure is reduced. This allows the gas to escape from the magma. Gas escapes easily from some magma during quiet eruptions. Gas that gets trapped under high pressure eventually escapes, causing explosive eruptions such as that seen in the photographs of Mount Saint Helens in **Figure 10-8.**

Approximate time: 8:32 A.M.

Approximate time: 38 seconds

Figure 10-8
A calm day in Washington was suddenly interrupted when Mount Saint Helens erupted at 8:32 A.M. on May 18, 1980, as shown in this sequence of photographs. *Why was the eruption so violent compared with eruptions of volcanoes like Kilauea?*

Program Resources

Reproducible Masters
Study Guide, p. 43 L1
Reinforcement, p. 43 L1
Enrichment, p. 43 L3
Cross-Curricular Integration, p. 14
Activity Worksheets, pp. 5, 64 L1
Science Integration Activities, pp. 19-20
Concept Mapping, p. 25
Critical Thinking/Problem Solving, p. 16
Lab Manual 32

Transparencies
Section Focus Transparency 39 L1

Magma Composition

The second major factor that affects the type of eruption is the composition of the magma. Basaltic magma contains less silica, is very fluid, and produces quiet, nonexplosive eruptions such as those at Kilauea. This type of lava pours from volcanic vents and runs down the sides of the volcano. These quiet eruptions form volcanoes over hot spots such as Hawaii. They also flow from rift zones such as those in Iceland. Because the magma is very fluid when it is forced upward in a vent, trapped gases can escape easily in a nonexplosive manner. Sometimes gas causes lava fountains during quiet eruptions, as illustrated in **Figure 10-10** on page 279.

Granitic magma, on the other hand, produces explosive, violent eruptions such as those at Mount Saint Helens. It often forms in the subduction zones where Earth's plates are converging. Granitic magma, as you learned in Chapter 4, is very thick and contains a lot of silica. Because it is thick, it gets trapped in vents, causing pressure to build up beneath it. When an explosive eruption occurs, the gases expand rapidly, often carrying pieces of lava in the explosion.

CONNECT TO

LIFE SCIENCE

Opposition to geothermal energy in Hawaii concerns environmental damage. Find out how severe the damage is expected to be. ***Describe*** how the changes in the rain forest could affect animal habitats.

Approximate time: 42 seconds

Approximate time: 53 seconds

2 Teach

INTEGRATION
Chemistry

One factor that determines how a volcano erupts is the composition of the magma. Basaltic magma is liquid at higher temperatures than granitic magma. This makes it flow more easily and allows gases to escape. This leads to nonexplosive eruptions.

CONNECT TO

LIFE SCIENCE

Answer Depending on which source students use, they will report that damage to the tropical rain forest will be limited to clearing the area for the power plant and roads, or that any damage will have far-reaching effects to surrounding areas. Cleared areas could affect movement and the search for food by animals that live in the rain forest.

Visual Learning

Figure 10-8 Why was the eruption so violent compared with eruptions of volcanoes like Kilauea? *Magma found in Mount Saint Helens contains more trapped gases and water and is of granitic composition.* LEP LS

Science Journal

Magma Composition Have students refer back to Chapters 3 and 4 concerning the chemical composition of minerals and igneous rocks. Students learned that as magma cools, different minerals will crystallize at different temperatures. Ask students to use what they have learned about mineral crystallization and to research Bowen's reaction series in order to write a one-page report in their Science Journals about why some magmas are hotter than others. *The temperature at which a magma melts is determined in part by the chemical composition of the magma. The hotter a magma, the more easily it flows.* L2 LS

Brainstorming

After students have read pages 276 and 277, have them brainstorm in order to answer the following question: **What determines the explosiveness of a volcanic eruption?** *the amount of gases trapped in the magma, the chemical composition of the magma, and the water content of the magma*

Inquiry Questions

- **Why does granitic lava erupt so explosively?** *Granitic lava contains a lot of silica, which tends to trap water vapor and other gases. Pressure builds, and when it is finally released, an explosive eruption occurs.*
- **Where does granitic magma accumulate most of its water?** *At subduction zones, wet oceanic crust and sediments are carried down into the mantle. This water then becomes trapped in the magma that forms.*

STV: Restless Earth

Mount St. Helens; Washington State

52192

Mount St. Helens; Washington State, 1980

52196

Mount St. Helens; Washington State, 1977

52226

Mount St. Helens; Washington State, 1980

52227

Magma Water Content

Another factor that causes granitic magma to erupt explosively is its high water content. The magma at subduction zones contains a great deal of water vapor. This is because of the wet oceanic crust that is carried into the subduction zone. The trapped water vapor in the thick magma causes explosive eruptions. Some magmas have an andesitic composition (between granitic and basaltic). Because of their higher silica content, they also produce eruptions more violent than those from basaltic magmas.

Forms of Volcanoes

A volcano's form depends on whether it is the result of a quiet or an explosive eruption and the type of lava it is made of—basaltic, granitic, or an intermediate composition. Volcanoes are of three basic forms—shield volcanoes, cinder cone volcanoes, or composite volcanoes, as seen in **Figure 10-9.**

Figure 10-9

The form of volcano that is produced is determined by the nature of its eruption.

A When hot, thin lava flows from one or more vents without violent eruptions, it builds into a gentle slope when it cools. This creates a shield volcano such as Mauna Ulu in Hawaii.

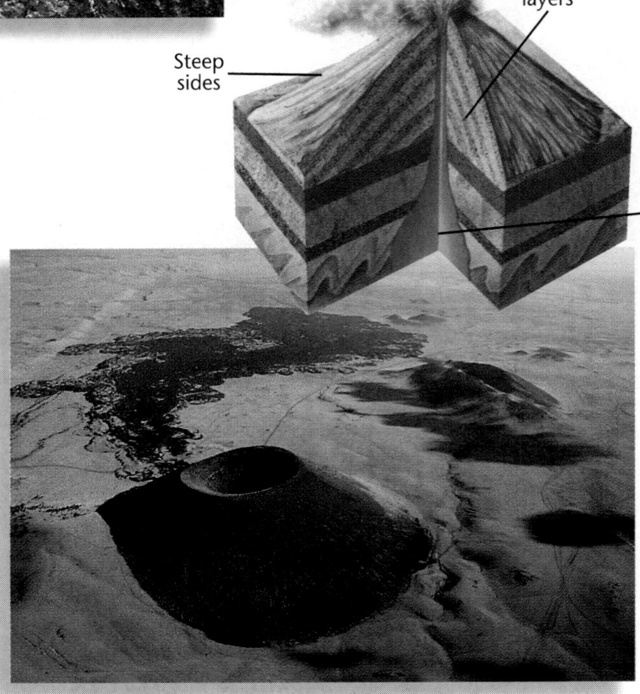

B Explosive eruptions throw lava high into the air. The lava cools and hardens into tephra. When tephra falls to the ground, it forms a steep-sided, loosely consolidated cinder cone volcano. Pictured here is a cinder cone in Arizona.

Across the Curriculum

Geography Ask students to hypothesize why some people live so close to volcanoes knowing that eruptions can be dangerous. *Students' responses might include economic reasons, the scenery, and the rarity of explosions.*

Economics Have a volunteer who listed economic reasons as one reason people live so close to dangerous volcanoes explain what some of the economic reasons might be. *One idea students may describe involves the richness of volcanic soil for growing vineyards and other crops.*

Shield Volcano

Quiet eruptions spread out basaltic lava in flat layers. The buildup of these layers forms a broad volcano with gently sloping sides called a **shield volcano.** Examples of shield volcanoes are the Hawaiian Islands.

Cinder Cone Volcano

Explosive eruptions throw lava high into the air. The lava cools and hardens into different sizes of volcanic material called **tephra.** Tephra varies in size from volcanic ash—the smallest—to cinders, to larger rocks called bombs. When tephra falls to the ground, it forms a steep-sided, loosely consolidated **cinder cone** volcano.

Figure 10-10

Usually the hot, thin lava flows of Kilauea are nonviolent eruptions. *What could be causing the lava fountain shown above?*

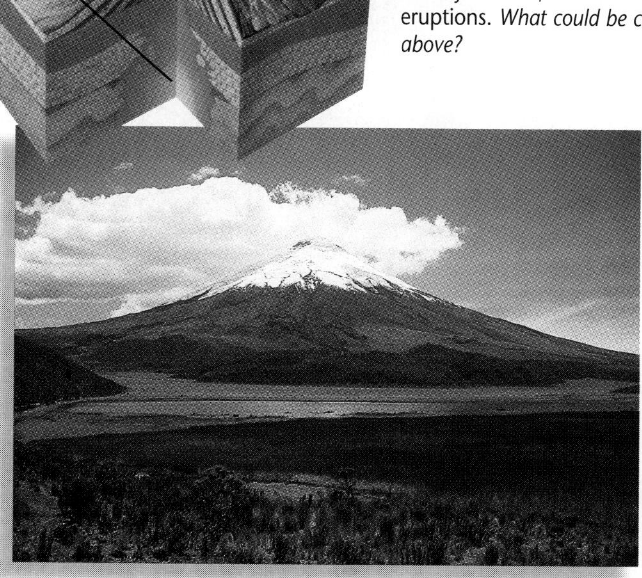

Whenever volcanic eruptions vary between violent and quieter times, tephra layers alternate with lava layers. A volcano built by this layering of tephra and lava has a composite form, such as Cotopaxi in Ecuador shown here or Mount Saint Helens.

Activity

Kinesthetic Have groups of students use sand, gravel, small rocks, and modeling clay to construct realistic models of the three major forms of volcanoes. L1 LEP COOP LEARN

Teacher F.Y.I.

Mauna Loa in Hawaii is the largest active volcano on Earth. This shield volcano rises more than 9 km above the ocean floor.

Inquiry Question

Just as with volcano Nevado del Ruiz, massive mudflows occurred following the May 1980 eruption of Mount Saint Helens. What do you think caused the mudflows around Mount Saint Helens? *Snowfields and glaciers had developed at high elevations. When Mount Saint Helens erupted, this snow and ice melted and mixed with sediments to form massive mudflows.*

Revealing Preconceptions

Most students think that volcanic eruptions occur only at the top of the mountain in the previously formed crater. Inform students that the initial eruption of Mount Saint Helens in 1980 occurred on the flank of the mountain as well as at the top. Tremendous amounts of debris were forced laterally from the volcano, knocking down thousands of 60-m-high trees.

Use these program resources as you teach this lesson.

Critical Thinking/Problem Solving, p. 16

Concept Mapping, p. 25

Inclusion Strategies

Gifted Have each student write a story about a volcanic eruption as told from the point of view of a human observer, or someone caught in the vicinity of the erupting volcano. The stories should include descriptions of the eruption in detail, from the early stages of development to the aftermath. Encourage creativity but insist on scientific accuracy. L3

Visual Learning

Figure 10-10 What could be causing the lava fountains shown in this figure? *gases and water vapor trapped in lava* LEP LS

Problem Solving

Solve the Problem

1. extrusive
2. The dark-colored rock probably contains iron and magnesium; the light-colored rock probably contains more silicon and oxygen.

Think Critically

Yes, place both rocks in a container of water to see if one of them floats. Trapped gases can reduce the density of the rock, thus allowing it to float. If one floats and the other sinks, the one that sinks would be denser and probably contain minerals higher in iron and magnesium. Silica-rich pumice floats because of trapped gases.

3 Assess

Check for Understanding

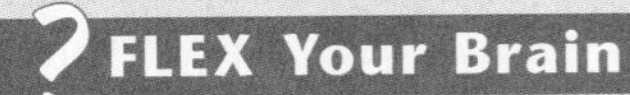

Use the Flex Your Brain activity to have students explore FORMS OF VOLCANOES.

Activity Worksheets, p. 5

Comparing Volcanic Rocks

During your study of volcanoes and the material that is ejected from volcanoes, you are given two different igneous rocks. One is dark-colored, the other is light-colored. Your task is to determine how the rocks formed and what elements they likely contain.

The two rocks are very fine-grained and full of holes. The holes were caused by escaping gases during the cooling of these rocks. You learned in Chapter 4 that the color of volcanic rocks can indicate what minerals each rock contains. Dark-colored rocks tend to contain minerals high in iron and magnesium, whereas light-colored rocks tend to have a higher concentration of silica-rich minerals.

Solve the Problem:

1. **Based on the size of grains in the rocks, do you think the igneous rocks are intrusive or extrusive?**
2. **Based on the overall color of the rocks, what elements do you think they are likely to contain?**

Think Critically:

Because both rocks are full of holes formed by gases as the rock cooled, it is possible that gases are also trapped inside both rocks. If you are correct in your assumption about the element content of each rock, is there a method to further test element content and possible presence of trapped gas inside the rocks? Explain.

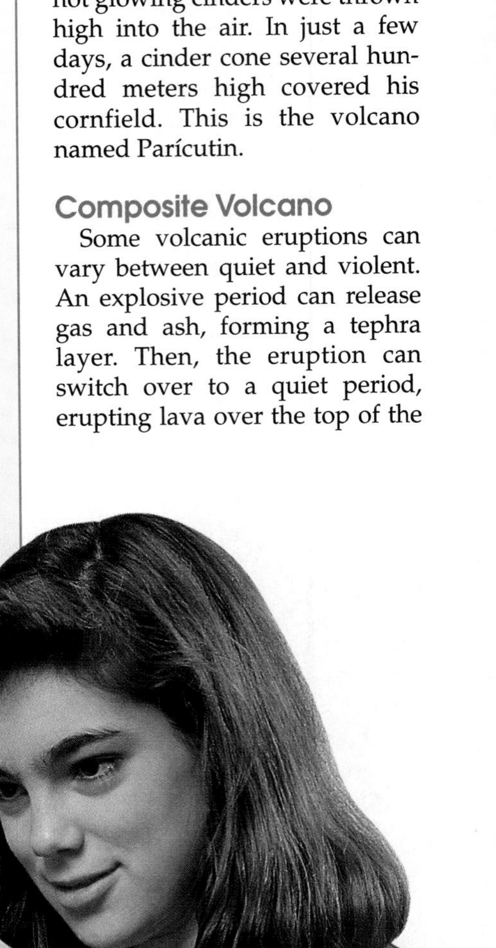

A Mexican farmer learned about cinder cones one morning when he went to his cornfield. He noticed that a hole in his cornfield that had been there for as long as he could remember was emitting smoke that smelled like sulfur. Throughout the night, hot glowing cinders were thrown high into the air. In just a few days, a cinder cone several hundred meters high covered his cornfield. This is the volcano named Parícutin.

Composite Volcano

Some volcanic eruptions can vary between quiet and violent. An explosive period can release gas and ash, forming a tephra layer. Then, the eruption can switch over to a quiet period, erupting lava over the top of the

Across the Curriculum

History Have students find out about the eruptions of Mount Vesuvius in Italy—in particular, the eruption of 79 A.D. and how it affected Pompeii and Herculaneum. Students' reports should include what has been learned about life in Pompeii since excavation of the city began in the 1800s. L2

Inclusion Strategies

Hearing Impaired/Learning Disabled Have students work in small groups to make clay models of shield volcanoes, cinder cone volcanoes, and composite volcanoes. Both lava and tephra should be represented.

Figure 10-11
Mount Pinatubo in the Philippines erupted violently in 1991.

tephra layer. When this cycle of lava and tephra is repeated over and over in alternating layers, a **composite volcano** is formed. Composite volcanoes are found mostly where Earth's plates converge and form subduction zones. Mount Saint Helens is an example.

As you can see, there are many factors that affect volcanic eruptions and the form of a volcano, as seen in **Table 10-1.** Mount Saint Helens was formed as the Juan de Fuca Plate was subducted under the North American Plate. The basaltic ocean floor was melted. As it was forced upward, the basaltic magma mixed with surrounding rock material and became more silica-rich. Successive eruptions of lava and tephra produced the composite volcano that towers above the surrounding landscape. Magma inside the volcano solidified, blocking the opening to the surface. Pressure continued to build until in May of 1980, Mount Saint Helens released the pressure in a series of explosive eruptions, as seen in **Figure 10-8** on pages 276 and 277.

The same forces that caused the Mount Saint Helens volcanic activity also caused the 1991 eruptions of Mount Unzen and Mount Pinatubo, as seen in **Figure 10-11.** These volcanoes violently erupted after lying dormant for 200 and over 600 years, respectively. The islands of Japan and the Philippines are volcanic island arcs, formed as the Pacific and the Philippine Plates converged with the Eurasian Plate.

MiniLAB

How can you model different types of volcanic cones?

Procedure

1. Pour a granulated substance such as sand onto one spot on a paper plate, forming a model of a cinder cone volcano.
2. Mix a batch of plaster of paris and pour it onto one spot on another paper plate, forming a model of a shield volcano.
3. Use a protractor to measure the slope angles of the sides of the volcanoes. Allow the model of the shield volcano to dry before measuring its slope angle.

Analysis

1. Which of your volcano models has steeper sides?
2. What form of volcano is represented by the model with steeper sides?
3. Infer why this is so.

MiniLAB

Purpose

LS **Interpersonal** Students will formulate models of cinder cone and shield volcanoes. L1 LEP COOP LEARN

Materials

granulated material (dry cereal or sand), plaster of paris (thick, cooked, hot cereal could also be used), paper plates, protractors

Teaching Strategies

Safety Precautions Handle hot cereal carefully during preparation.

Troubleshooting Review how to measure angles with a protractor, if necessary.

Analysis

1. the one made of granulated material
2. cinder cone volcano
3. The cinder cone volcano is steeper because it is made of material formed during explosive eruptions. Lava that forms shield volcanoes is ejected with much less force. Thus, shield volcanoes have gently sloping flanks.

Assessment

Content To further assess students' understanding of volcano shapes, have them draw a cutaway diagram of each type in their Science Journals. Use the Performance Task Assessment List for Scientific Drawing in **PASC**, p. 55. P

Activity Worksheets, pp. 5, 64

Integrating the Sciences

Physics Have students look over **Figure 10-8** on pages 276 and 277. Ask them to explain what provided the force that caused the tremendous release of gas and ash from Mount Saint Helens. *The granitic magma inside the volcano is rich in silica that tends to trap gases. When an earthquake caused the north slope of Mount Saint Helens to break loose, pressure was released and the gases escaped in a sudden explosion.*

Extension

For students who have mastered this section, use the **Reinforcement** and **Enrichment** masters.

Reteach

Have students make tables listing the type of lava, the shape, the type of eruption, and an example of each of the three kinds of volcanoes.

4 Close

• MINI • QUIZ •

1. ______ magma is thick and contains a lot of silica. *Granitic*
2. The three forms of volcanoes are ______ . *shield, cinder cone, and composite volcanoes*
3. Volcanic material ejected high into the air during explosive volcanic eruptions is ______ . *tephra*

Section Wrap-up

Review

1. Water vapor and other gases contained in the magma and the composition of the magma determine whether eruptions are quiet or explosive.
2. Granitic magmas are silica-rich. A high silica content makes magma thick. The more silica, the thicker the magma.
3. **Think Critically** The lava from Krakatoa was probably granitic because of the explosive nature of the eruption. It also may have been andesitic, containing a large amount of water vapor.

Science Journal

Answers will vary. People had to wear masks to protect themselves from the ash. Almost 900 people were killed and the lives of more than 1 million more were disrupted. When typhoons hit shortly after the eruption, rivers of rain-soaked ash destroyed bridges, power lines, and more than 110 000 homes. Almost two years after the eruption, 20 000 people were still living in tent cities. P

Table 10-1

Twelve Selected Eruptions in History

Volcano and Location	Year	Type	Eruptive Force	Magma Content: Silica	Magma Content: H_2O	Ability of Magma to Flow	Products of Eruption
Etna, Sicily	1669	composite	moderate	high	low	medium	lava, ash
Tambora, Indonesia	1815	cinder	high	high	high	low	cinders, gas
Krakatoa, Indonesia	1883	cinder	high	high	high	low	cinders, gas
Pelée, Martinique	1902	cinder	high	high	high	low	gas, ash
Vesuvius, Italy	1906	composite	moderate	high	low	medium	lava, ash
Mauna Loa, Hawaii	1933	shield	low	low	low	high	lava
Parícutin, Mexico	1943	cinder	moderate	high	low	medium	ash, cinders
Surtsey, Iceland	1963	shield	moderate	low	low	high	lava, ash
Saint Helens, WA	1980	composite	high	high	high	low	gas, ash
Kilauea Iki, Hawaii	1989	shield	low	low	low	high	lava
Pinatubo, Philippines	1991	composite	high	high	high	low	gas, ash
Galeras, Colombia	1993	cinder	high	high	high	low	gas, ash

Section Wrap-up

Review

1. Some volcanic eruptions are quiet and others are violent. What causes this difference?
2. Why are granitic magmas thicker than basaltic magmas?
3. **Think Critically:** In 1883, Krakatoa in Indonesia erupted. Which kind of lava did Krakatoa erupt—basaltic, granitic, or intermediate? How do you know?

Skill Builder
Sequencing

Arrange the following events of the history of Mount Saint Helens in correct order in your Science Journal: erupts in 1980, composite volcano formed, subduction zone formed, silica-rich magma forced upward, pressure builds, magma in volcano solidifies. If you need help, refer to Sequencing in the **Skill Handbook.**

Science Journal

In your Science Journal, write a brief description of conditions in the Philippines just after Mount Pinatubo erupted. Include an account of how people have coped with the devastation following the eruption.

Skill Builder

1. subduction zone formed
2. silica-rich magma forced upward
3. composite volcano formed
4. pressure builds
5. erupts in 1980
6. magma in volcano solidifies

Assessment

Performance Assess students' abilities to sequence events by having them sequence events that would have occurred as Mount Pinatubo erupted. Use the Performance Task Assessment List for Events Chain in **PASC,** p. 91. P

Igneous Rock Features

10•4

Intrusive Features

We can observe volcanic eruptions because they are examples of igneous activity on the surface of Earth. But there is far more igneous activity underground because most magma never reaches the surface to form volcanoes. As you learned in Chapter 4, magma that cools underground forms intrusive igneous rock. What forms do intrusive igneous rocks take on? You can look at some of these features in **Figure 10-12.**

Batholiths

The largest intrusive igneous rock bodies are **batholiths.** They can be many hundreds of kilometers wide and long and several kilometers thick. Batholiths form when magma cools underground before reaching the surface. However, not all of them are hidden in Earth. Some batholiths have been exposed at Earth's surface by erosion. The granite domes of Yosemite National Park, as seen in **Figure 10-13A,** are exposed parts of a huge batholith that extends across much of the length of California.

Science Words

batholith
dike
sill
volcanic neck
caldera

Objectives

- Give examples of intrusive igneous features and how they form.
- Explain how a volcanic neck and a caldera form.

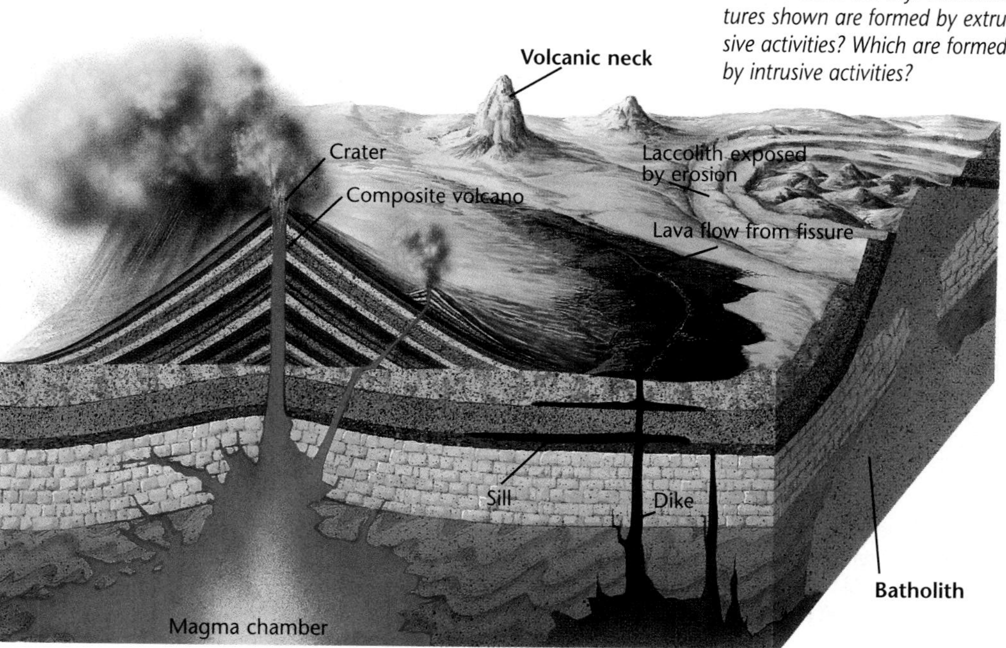

Figure 10-12

This diagram shows intrusive and other features associated with volcanic activity. *Which features shown are formed by extrusive activities? Which are formed by intrusive activities?*

Section 10•4

Prepare

Section Background

Crater Lake, Oregon, formed about 7000 years ago when a volcano spewed 40 to 50 cubic kilometers of volcanic material into the air. With the magma chamber then partly emptied, 1500 m of the original 3600-m cone collapsed. Rainwater has filled the caldera to form a lake.

Preplanning

Obtain different types of volcanic ejecta from a scientific supply company for the MiniLAB.

1 Motivate

Bellringer

Before presenting the lesson, display **Section Focus Transparency 40** on the overhead projector. Assign the accompanying **Focus Activity** worksheet. L1 LEP

Tying to Previous Knowledge

Have students recall that when one of Earth's moving plates slides under another, some of the rock material melts and is forced upward toward Earth's surface. Some of this rising magma cooled to form intrusive igneous rock structures.

Program Resources

Reproducible Masters

Study Guide, p. 44 L1
Reinforcement, p. 44 L1
Enrichment, p. 44 L3
Activity Worksheets, pp. 5, 62-63, 65 L1
Lab Manual 31

Transparencies

Section Focus Transparency 40 L1
Teaching Transparency 20

Visual Learning

Figure 10-12 Which features shown are formed by extrusive activities? Which are formed by intrusive activities? *Extrusive: crater, composite volcano, lava flow. Intrusive: dike, sill, batholith, volcanic neck, and laccolith.* LEP IS

2 Teach

MiniLAB

Purpose

LS **Interpersonal** Students will observe characteristics of different types of material ejected from volcanoes. L1 LEP COOP LEARN

Materials

volcanic material, especially volcanic ash, scoria, obsidian, and/or volcanic beach sand; pin or dissecting probe; microscope

Teaching Strategies

Safety Precautions Volcanic material is extremely abrasive. Students should wash their hands thoroughly after completing this activity.

Analysis

1. Volcanic material is glassy. Volcanic ash appears sharp and jagged. Volcanic beach sand resembles tiny beads of glass. Scoria has a frothy texture, full of holes. Obsidian is smooth and glassy.
2. Volcanic products commonly exhibit many properties of glass.

Assessment

Performance To further assess students' understanding of volcanic materials, ask them which ones they think contained trapped gases while cooling. Most students will easily recognize that the large pores in pumice and scoria were gas-filled chambers. Use the Performance Task Assessment List for Making Observations and Inferences in **PASC**, p. 17. P

Activity Worksheets, pp. 5, 65

MiniLAB

What types of materials are ejected by volcanoes?

Procedure

1. Obtain some samples of products of volcanic eruptions.
2. Use a pin or dissecting probe to scratch away particles of volcanic rock.
3. Use a magnifying lens and tweezers to separate the products into different piles.
4. Rub the different-sized particles, volcanic ash, and beach sand from volcanic areas slowly between your fingers.

Analysis

Place the volcanic material under an illuminated microscope and take note of the physical properties of each type of material. 1. Describe what you see and feel. 2. What physical properties of these materials might be used to identify them as having a volcanic origin?

Dikes and Sills

Magma sometimes squeezes into cracks in rock below the surface. This is like squeezing toothpaste into the spaces between your teeth. Magma that is squeezed into a generally vertical crack that cuts across rock layers and hardens is called a **dike.** Magma that is squeezed into a horizontal crack between rock layers and hardens is called a **sill.** Both features are shown in **Figures 10-13C** and **10-13D.** Dikes and sills run from a few meters to hundreds of meters long. Some magma that forms a sill may continue to push the rock layers upward. This forms a dome of rock called a laccolith.

Other Features

When a volcano stops erupting, the magma hardens inside the vent. Erosion begins to wear away the volcano. The cone is much softer than the solid igneous rock in the vent. Thus, the cone erodes away first, leaving behind the solid igneous core as a **volcanic neck.** Ship Rock, New Mexico, is a volcanic neck, as seen in **Figure 10-13B.** It is just one of many volcanic necks in the southwestern United States.

Figure 10-13

Intrusive igneous bodies can form in many different sizes and shapes. Some of the most common are batholiths, dikes, sills, and volcanic necks. *What characteristics of dikes and sills probably caused them to be named as they are?*

A Most of the bare rock visible in Yosemite National Park is a batholith that has been exposed by erosion.

Across the Curriculum

History The faces on Mount Rushmore have been carved from an intrusive igneous rock body that has been exposed at Earth's surface. Have students report on the historical significance of each of the people carved on Mount Rushmore. Also ask them to find out why only the heads were carved. *Metamorphic rocks located in the cliff face prevented full body statues from being carved.* L2

Use **Teaching Transparency 20** as you teach this lesson.

Use Lab 31 in the **Lab Manual** as you teach this lesson.

Sometimes after an eruption, the top of a volcano may collapse down into the partially emptied magma chamber. This produces a very large opening called a **caldera,** as shown in **Figure 10-14.** You studied the topography of a caldera in Chapter 5. Crater Lake in Oregon is a caldera that is now a lake.

CONNECT TO

PHYSICS

You have learned that large bodies of magma underground are gradually forced upward toward Earth's surface. ***Determine*** what forces inside Earth are responsible for forcing the magma upward.

B Ship Rock in New Mexico is a volcanic neck.

C The horizontal sill shown here is located in Yellowstone National Park. It formed when magma squeezed between rock layers.

D The vertical dike shown here is located in Israel. It formed when magma was squeezed into a vertical crack in the surrounding rock layers.

Visual Learning

Figure 10-13 What characteristics of dikes and sills probably caused them to be named as they are? *their shape and how they intrude the surrounding rock* LEP LS

CONNECT TO

PHYSICS

Answer As magma forms, it becomes less dense than surrounding rocks. The denser rocks surrounding the magma push on it, forcing it to rise. The less dense magma is forced upward through cracks in the overlying rock.

3 Assess

Check for Understanding

FLEX Your Brain

Use the Flex Your Brain activity to have students explore INTRUSIVE IGNEOUS ROCK BODIES.

Activity Worksheets, p. 5

Reteach

Make and use flash cards of the intrusive rock features.

Extension

For students who have mastered this section, use the **Reinforcement** and **Enrichment** masters.

Community Connection

Igneous Rock Bodies Have students research the type of rocks found near your area. If any of them are igneous, bring in samples and ask students to determine whether the rock formation is intrusive or extrusive. If no igneous rock body exists in your area, ask a local geologist to visit class and discuss the location of the nearest igneous rock body. L2

Enrichment

- Have students do research to find out when and how the Sierra Nevada batholith formed and what the size of the complex is thought to be. L2
- Have students find out how the volcanic neck and related dikes at Ship Rock, New Mexico, formed. L2

4 Close

•MINI•QUIZ•

1. **The largest intrusive igneous rock bodies are _____.** *batholiths*
2. **Magma that squeezes into horizontal cracks between rock layers forms a(n) _____.** *sill*
3. **A(n) _____ forms when the top of a volcano collapses.** *caldera*

Section Wrap-up

Review

1. A caldera forms when the top of a volcano collapses into the partially emptied magma chamber. A crater is the opening.
2. A volcanic neck forms as magma hardens in the vent of the volcano. As a volcano is eroded, the neck remains.
3. The magma chamber is partially emptied due to the eruption. Gravity then pulls downward on the top of the volcano.
4. **Think Critically** The features formed when magma cooled underground. Erosion later exposed the dome.

Using Computers

Student answers will vary but should include the major intrusive igneous rock bodies illustrated and described in **Figure 10-12.**

Figure 10-14
Crater Lake formed when the top of the volcano collapsed, forming a caldera, as shown in the sequence above.

You have learned in this chapter about one way that Earth's surface is continually built up and how it is worn down. The surface is built up by volcanoes. Also, igneous rock is formed when magma hardens below ground. Eventually, the processes of erosion wear down the rock, exposing batholiths and forming volcanic necks.

Section Wrap-up

Review

1. What's the difference between a caldera and a crater?
2. What is a volcanic neck and how does it form?
3. Explain how calderas form.
4. **Think Critically:** Why are the dome features of Yosemite National Park actually intrusive volcanic features when they are exposed at the surface in the park?

Using Computers

Graphics Use the graphics capabilities of your computer to produce an illustration of igneous rock features based on **Figure 10-12.**

Skill Builder

Comparing and Contrasting

Compare and contrast dikes, sills, batholiths, and laccoliths. If you need help, refer to Comparing and Contrasting in the **Skill Handbook.**

Skill Builder

All are intrusive igneous features. Dikes and sills are tabular. Laccoliths are domed. Dikes and sills are smaller than batholiths and laccoliths.

Assessment

Process Use this Skill Builder to assess students' abilities to compare and contrast. Ask students to explain in writing the difference between a sill and a dike. Use the Performance Task Assessment List for Writing in Science in **PASC,** p. 87. P

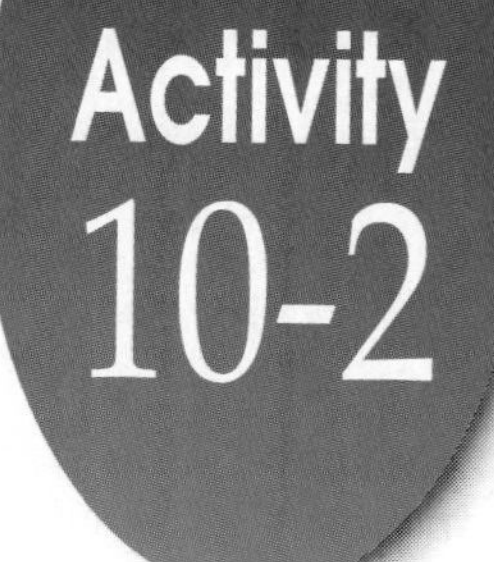

Identifying Types of Volcanoes

You have learned that certain properties of magma are related to the type of eruption and the form of the volcano that will develop. Try this activity to see how to make and use a table that relates the properties of magma to the form of volcano that develops.

Problem

Are the silica and water content of a volcano related to the form of volcano that develops?

Materials

- **Table 10-1** on page 282
- paper
- pencil

Procedure

1. Copy the graph shown at right.
2. Using the information from **Table 10-1**, plot the magma content data for each of the volcanoes listed by writing the name of the basic type of volcano in the appropriate spot on the graph. The data for the 1669 eruption of Mount Etna has already been plotted for you on the diagram.
3. When the plotting of all 12 volcanoes has been completed, analyze the patterns of volcanic types on the diagram to answer the questions.

Analyze

1. What relationship appears to exist between the ability of the magma to flow and the eruptive force of the volcano?
2. Which would be more liquid in its properties, a magma that flows easily or one that flows with difficulty?
3. What relationship appears to exist between the silica or water content of the magma and the nature of the material ejected from the volcano during the eruptions?

Conclude and Apply

4. How is the ability of the magma to flow related to its silica and water content?
5. **Infer** which of the two variables (silica or water content) appears to have the greater effect on the eruptive force of the volcano.
6. **Describe** the relationship that appears to exist between the silica and water content of the magma and the type of volcano that is produced.

Data and Observations Sample Data

Silica content of magma	Water content of magma: low	Water content of magma: high
high	Composite composite cinder	cinder cinder cinder cinder composite composite
low	shield shield shield	

Activity 10-2

Purpose

LS **Interpersonal** Relate the physical and chemical properties of magma to the nature of the volcanic eruptions and the volcanic form. L1

COOP LEARN

Process Skills

classifying, inferring, communicating, interpreting data, and hypothesizing

Time

30-40 minutes

Activity Worksheets, pp. 5, 62-63

Teaching Strategies

Troubleshooting Enlarge the figure to be used in this activity and distribute copies onto which students are to plot the data given.

Answers to Questions

1. the greater the ability of the magma to flow, the lower the eruptive force of the volcano, and vice versa
2. a magma that flows easily
3. Volcanoes with magma that is low in silica and water tend to produce lavas that are more fluid. Magma and lava high in silica and water tend to produce cinders, ash, and superheated gases.
4. The ability of a magma or lava to flow is greater when the silica and water contents are low.
5. The silica content seems to have a greater effect than does the water content.
6. Shield volcanoes result from magma with relatively low amounts of silica and water. The lavas from cinder cone volcanoes have relatively high amounts of silica and water. Composite volcanoes appear to eject materials with a range of chemical properties.

Assessment

Content To further assess students' understanding of volcano type identification, see Performance Assessment question 3 on page 291. Use the Performance Task Assessment List for Data Table in **PASC**, p. 37. P

Science & ART

One-Hundred Views of Mount Fuji

Why would an artist draw one hundred pictures of an inactive volcano? Japanese artist Katsushika Hokusai never seemed to tire of drawing Mount Fuji, the highest mountain in Japan. Sometimes he made the mountain fill the picture. One time, it served as the backdrop for a slender crane perched amid low, snow-frosted bushes. One drawing showed Mount Fuji through a thicket of bamboo. In still another, the mountain was a dim outline, barely visible through a summer shower.

Many of Hokusai's ink drawings of Mount Fuji were made into woodcuts by gluing the drawing to a block of hardwood. Then a carver whittled away the wood between the lines, leaving the design Hokusai had drawn. After ink was applied to the raised design, the block was used to make prints.

Born in 1760 in what is now Tokyo, Hokusai signed his drawings and paintings with many different names, choosing a new name at least every ten years. He also moved often, living in more than 90 places during his 89 years of life. This restlessness extended to his art. Hokusai experimented with a wide range of subjects, from drawings of Japanese actors, to book illustrations, to his exquisite landscapes. Only Mount Fuji seemed to hold his attention.

The artist worked from early morning until after dark, creating thousands of prints during his lifetime. His most famous work is *Thirty-Six Views of Mount Fuji,* actually a collection of 46 color prints published from 1826 to 1833. Hokusai followed this in 1834 and 1835 with *One-Hundred Views of Mount Fuji,* drawings in black, white, and gray.

Fuji last erupted in 1707, and its symmetrical, snow-capped volcanic crater is recognizable in every drawing in both of Hokusai's collections. Each time he drew the mountain, though, he changed his perspective and the composition of the picture. Hokusai did not feel confined to what he could see and sometimes inserted people into his drawings. Several scenes show Mount Fuji as viewed from merchants' shops.

Mount Fuji is considered sacred and a symbol of Japan. Thousands climb it every year. Perhaps Hokusai's many woodcuts gave Japanese who lived far from the mountain an opportunity to feel closer to this sacred spot. The drawings definitely earned Hokusai a reputation as a master artist and a major influence on both Japanese and Western art.

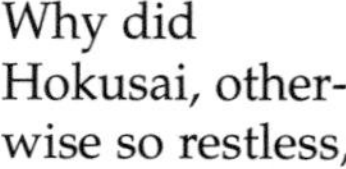

Science Journal

Why did Hokusai, otherwise so restless, draw one mountain over and over again? Write in your Science Journal why you think Mount Fuji had so much power over this artist.

Sources

- Hillier, J. *Hokusai: Paintings, Drawings and Woodcuts.* New York: Phaidon Publishers, 1955.
- *Encyclopaedia Britannica,* "Hokusai." Vol. 5, 1985, pp. 978-979.

Biography

Katsushika Hokusai (1760-1849) showed an interest in drawing when he was only five, yet he produced most of his lasting works after the age of 60. Although Hokusai married twice and had children, he was an unsociable hermit. He spent his days drawing, indifferent to people around him and even to the needs of his own body. Yet Hokusai appealed for more time to draw. He said, "From about the age of 50 I produced a number of designs, yet of all I drew prior to the age of 70 there is nothing of any great note. At the age of 73 I finally apprehended something of the true quality of birds, animals, insects, fishes, and of the vital nature of grasses and trees. Therefore, at 80 I shall have made some progress, at 90 I shall have penetrated even further the deeper meaning of things, at 100 I shall have become truly marvelous, and at 110, each dot, each line shall surely possess a life of its own." Hokusai died at age 89, but not unnoticed. Many Japanese artists copied his style. Some changed their professional names to identify with him, calling themselves Hokkei, Hokuba, and Hokuju. Hokusai also influenced the work of artists outside Japan, such as James Whistler, Vincent van Gogh, Edgar Degas, Paul Gauguin, and Henri de Toulouse-Lautrec.

Other Works by Hokusai

"The Poems of China and Japan Mirrored to Life," "Views of Famous Bridges," "Snow, Moon, and Flowers," "One Hundred Poems Explained by the Nurse."

Teaching Strategies

LS **Visual-Spatial** Ask students to paint or draw ten different views of the same object. They can add details that do not exist, as Hokusai did, as long as they include the object. Afterward, discuss the challenges that students faced in depicting one object so many times. Have students explain the advantages of transforming a drawing into a woodcut. (Many prints can be made, all "originals.") L1

- Ask students to describe what they know about the physical composition of Mount Fuji. *It's a composite volcano with steep sides made from layers of silica-rich lava and ash. It's in the Pacific Ring of Fire.*

Chapter 10

Review

Summary

10-1: Volcanoes and Earth's Moving Plates

1. Volcanoes can be dangerous to people, causing deaths and destroying property.
2. Rocks in the mantle melt to form magma, which is forced upward toward Earth's surface. When the magma flows through vents, it's called lava and forms volcanoes.
3. Volcanoes along rift zones form when magma flows onto the seafloor. The lava builds up from the seafloor to form an island. Volcanoes over hot spots form when the magma breaks through the crust. Volcanoes also form when an ocean plate is subducted under another plate. Here, the subducted plate melts to form magma.

10-2: Science and Society: Energy from Earth

1. Geothermal energy can reduce our dependence on oil and reduce air pollution.
2. A new technology, hot dry rock (HDR) is being developed to use Earth's internal heat to generate energy. Heat from hot rock is used to heat water and make steam, which is used to generate electricity.

10-3: Eruptions and Forms of Volcanoes

1. Basaltic lavas are thin and flow easily, producing quiet eruptions. Silica-rich lavas are thick and stiff, and thus produce very violent eruptions. Water vapor in magma adds to its explosiveness.
2. Shield volcanoes are mountains made of basaltic lava and have gently sloping sides. Cinder cones are steep-sided and are made of tephra. Composite volcanoes, made of silica-rich lava and tephra, are steep-sided.

10-4: Igneous Rock Features

1. Batholiths, dikes, sills, and laccoliths form when magma solidifies underground.
2. A caldera forms when the top of a volcano collapses, forming a very large depression.

Key Science Words

a. batholith
b. caldera
c. cinder cone
d. composite volcano
e. crater
f. dike
g. geothermal energy
h. hot dry rock (HDR)
i. hot spot
j. Pacific Ring of Fire
k. shield volcano
l. sill
m. tephra
n. vent
o. volcanic neck
p. volcano

Reviewing Vocabulary

Match each phrase with the correct term from the list of Key Science Words.

1. mountain made of lava and/or volcanic ash
2. large depression formed by the collapse of a volcano
3. solid magma core of a volcano
4. volcano with gently sloping sides
5. ash and cinders thrown from a volcano
6. steep-sided volcano of lava and tephra
7. largest igneous intrusion
8. an opening through which lava flows
9. an igneous intrusion formed between rock layers
10. energy that comes from magma or HDR

Chapter 10

Review

Summary

Have students read the summary statements to review the major concepts of the chapter.

Reviewing Vocabulary

1. p
2. b
3. o
4. k
5. m
6. d
7. a
8. n
9. l
10. g

Assessment

Portfolio Encourage students to place in their portfolios one or two items of what they consider to be their best work. Examples include:

- Activity 10-1, pp. 270-271
- Flex Your Brain, p. 272
- Science Journal, p. 282 P

Performance Additional performance assessments may be found in **Performance Assessment** and **Science Integration Activities.** Performance Task Assessment Lists and rubrics for evaluating these activities can be found in Glencoe's **Performance Assessment in the Science Classroom.**

GLENCOE TECHNOLOGY

MindJogger Videoquiz

Chapter 10 Have students work in groups as they play the Videoquiz game to review key chapter concepts.

Chapter 10 Review

Checking Concepts

1. c	**6.** a
2. b	**7.** b
3. a	**8.** b
4. c	**9.** d
5. c	**10.** b

Understanding Concepts

11. Volcanoes differ in size and shape mainly due to the composition of the lava that forms them. Volcanoes also differ depending upon where they form.

12. Lava flowing from rift zones is basaltic. The basaltic lava flows from fissures and can build up to form shield volcanoes. Volcanoes that form along areas where one of Earth's plates slides under another are composite volcanoes made of layers of silica-rich lava and tephra.

13. Answers will vary slightly. A typical response might be: Lava flows onto Earth's surface through the vent of a volcano. The opening at the top of a volcano's vent is the crater. A caldera forms when the top of a volcano collapses into the partially emptied magma chamber.

14. mudflows

15. As the Pacific Plate moves over a hot spot in Earth's mantle, old volcanoes become dormant and then extinct, while new ones form.

Thinking Critically

16. Students should recall from Chapter 7 that glaciers form at high elevations and high latitudes. Iceland is at a relatively high latitude. The Mid-Atlantic Ridge, on the other hand, is a feature on the ocean bottom related to Earth's moving plates. Because glaciers and volcanoes are caused by different processes, there is no reason why they can't coexist.

17. Basaltic lava, unlike silica-rich lava, is very fluid. Because it flows easily, relatively mild eruptions are produced by basaltic-lava volcanoes.

18. Volcanoes along rift zones and subduction zones form when Earth's plates move apart or collide, respectively. The enormous forces produced by plate movements can produce earthquakes.

19. Students should be able to infer that the volcano, like those in the Cascades, formed as the result of subduction. Displaying a map of North and South America might be helpful in answering this question. Referring students to a map showing the boundaries of Earth's plates would also be useful.

20. Areas with volcanic activity such as Italy, Mexico, New Zealand, and Japan, to name a few, are able to make use of geothermal energy. Most any area could

Chapter 10 Review

Checking Concepts

Choose the word or phrase that completes the sentence.

1. Composite volcanoes form near locations where Earth's plates are _______.
a. diverging
b. sticking and slipping
c. converging
d. sliding past each other

2. Hawaii is made of volcanoes due to _______.
a. plates moving apart
b. a hot spot
c. plates moving together
d. rift zones

3. Lavas ______ produce violent volcanic eruptions.
a. rich in silica
b. that are fluid
c. made of basalt
d. rich in iron

4. Magma that is rich in iron produces ______ eruptions.
a. thick
b. caldera
c. quiet
d. explosive

5. A _______ is made of tephra.
a. shield volcano
b. caldera
c. cinder cone
d. composite volcano

6. Kilauea is a _______.
a. shield volcano
b. composite volcano
c. cinder cone
d. rift zone

7. Magma that squeezes into a vertical crack in rock layers and then hardens is a _______.
a. sill
b. dike
c. volcanic neck
d. batholith

8. A _______ is a dome-shaped igneous intrusive body.
a. dike
b. laccolith
c. sill
d. batholith

9. HDR geothermal energy comes from _______.
a. fossil fuels
b. electricity
c. the sun
d. hot dry rock

10. Geothermal energy _______.
a. relies on heat from the sun
b. reduces need for fossil fuels
c. increases air pollution
d. isn't possible in the United States

Understanding Concepts

Answer the following questions in your Science Journal using complete sentences.

11. Why do volcanoes differ in size and shape?

12. Contrast volcanoes that form where Earth's plates diverge with those that form where one of Earth's plates slides under another.

13. Explain how these terms are related: vent, caldera, and crater.

14. What conditions about the 1985 eruption of Columbia's Nevado del Ruiz caused most of the nearly 23 000 deaths?

15. Why does the State of Hawaii have many volcanic islands instead of just one large island?

Thinking Critically

16. Explain how glaciers and volcanoes can exist on Iceland.

17. What kind of eruption is produced when basaltic lava flows from a volcano? Explain.

18. How are volcanoes related to earthquakes?

19. A mountain called Misti is a volcano in Peru. Peru is on the western border of South America. How might this volcano have formed?

20. In addition to Iceland and Hawaii, where else on Earth do you think people could use geothermal energy? What if HDR became economical?

Developing Skills

If you need help, refer to the **Skill Handbook.**

21. Concept Mapping: Make a network tree concept map that compares quiet eruptions with explosive eruptions. Use the following words and phrases: *high silica, flows easily, granitic, explosive, cinder cone, Parícutin, shield, low silica,* and *basaltic.*

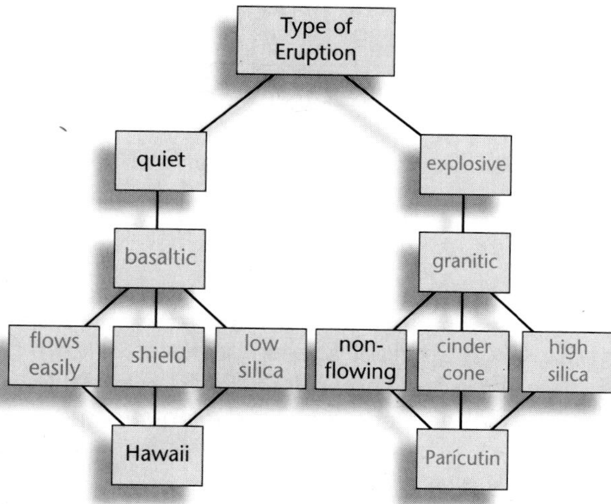

22. Observing and Inferring: A volcano violently erupted in Indonesia in 1883. What can you infer about the magma's composition? If people saw the eruption, what were they able to observe about the flow of the lava?

23. Comparing and Contrasting: Compare and contrast batholiths and laccoliths.

24. Classifying: Mount Fuji's steep sides are made of layers of silica-rich lava and ash. Classify Mount Fuji.

25. Measuring in SI: The base of the volcano Mauna Loa is about 5000 m below sea level. The total height of the volcano is 9560 m. What percentage of the volcano is above sea level? Below sea level?

Performance Assessment

1. **Model:** Build a cut-away model of a geothermal-energy power plant that shows how water might be pumped into hot dry rock, changed to steam, and then returned to the surface to run a turbine.
2. **Asking Questions:** In Activity 10-1, you learned that the locations of active volcanoes are related to earthquakes, boundaries of Earth's moving plates, and hot spots. Based on what you have learned, what could be said about an area in the midst of a continent that shows evidence of a large number of ancient, extinct volcanoes?
3. **Data Table:** In Activity 10-2, you identified types of volcanoes and plotted them on a table based on the composition of the magma that was forced out of them. Based on what you have learned, research the 1991 eruption of Mount Unzen in Japan and the 1982 eruption of El Chichón in Mexico and plot them on your table.

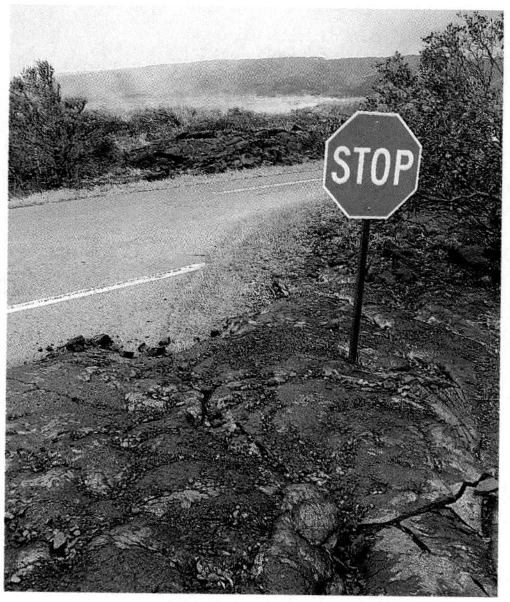

use the hot dry rock technology.

Developing Skills

21. Concept Mapping See student page.

22. Observing and Inferring The eruption was violent; thus, the amounts of silica and water vapor were high. Such lava is stiff and thick, and if people did observe the flow, they would have seen it flow slowly.

23. Comparing and Contrasting Both are intrusive igneous rock structures that form when magma cools deep within Earth. Batholiths are much larger, though, than laccoliths. Laccoliths are domed.

24. Classifying Mount Fuji is a composite volcano.

25. Measuring in SI Of the total height, 4560 m is above sea level. Thus, about 48% is above sea level and 52% is below sea level.

Performance Assessment

1. Encourage students to be creative. They could use the illustration in **Figure 10-6** on page 274. Refer students to "Tapping the Fire Down Below" by David Tenebaum in the January 1995 issue of *Technology Review*, pp. 38-47. Use the Performance Task Assessment List for Model in **PASC,** p. 51. P
2. If evidence is found that shows an area underwent a great deal of volcanic activity in the past, this could indicate that the area was once located on a plate boundary. If this is true, the area could once more become active if the plate boundary started moving again. Use the Performance Task Assessment List for Asking Questions in **PASC,** p. 19. P
3. The eruptions of Mount Unzen and El Chichón are similar to the eruptions of Mount Pinatubo and Mount Saint Helens. This would indicate that material thrown out in both eruptions was high in silica and water content. Both volcanoes would be classified as composite volcanoes. Use the Performance Task Assessment List for Data Table in **PASC,** p. 37. P

Chapter Organizer

Section	Objectives	Activities/Features
Chapter Opener		Explore Activity: Do the following activity to see how clues on adjoining pieces of a cut-up photograph can be used to re-form the image. p. 293
11-1 **Continental Drift** (2 sessions, 1 block)*	1. **Explain** the theory of continental drift. 2. **Discuss** four pieces of evidence for the theory of continental drift.	MiniLAB: Can clues such as fossils, types of life, and rock structures be used to determine whether continents now separated were once joined? p. 296 Skill Builder: Comparing and Contrasting, p. 297 Science Journal, p. 297
11-2 **Seafloor Spreading** (2 sessions, 1 block)*	1. **Describe** seafloor spreading. 2. **Relate** how age and magnetic clues confirm seafloor spreading.	Using Technology: New Picture of Earth, p. 300 Connect to Chemistry, p. 301 Skill Builder: Concept Mapping, p. 301 Using Math, p. 301 Activity 11-1: Seafloor Spreading, pp. 302-303
11-3 **Theory of Plate Tectonics** (3 sessions, 2 blocks)*	1. **Compare** and **contrast** divergent, convergent, and transform plate boundaries. 2. **Describe** how convection current might be the cause of plate tectonics. 3. **Describe** the effects of plate tectonics found at each type of boundary.	Activity 11-2: Seafloor Spreading Rates, p. 306 Problem Solving: The Fit Isn't Perfect, p. 307 MiniLAB: How do convection currents form? p. 310 Connect to Physics, p. 313 Skill Builder: Recognizing Cause and Effect, p. 313 Science Journal, p. 313
11-4 **Science and Society Technology: Before Pangaea, Rodinia** (1 session, ½ block)*	1. **Describe** evidence in support of the separation of the North American Plate from the Antarctic Plate. 2. **Track** the North American Plate after separation from the Antarctic Plate and before the formation of Pangaea.	Explore the Technology, p. 315 People and Science: Vicki Hansen, Associate Professor of Geological Science, p. 316

* A complete Planning Guide that includes block scheduling is provided on pages 32T-35T.

Activity Materials		
Explore	**Activities**	**MiniLABs**
page 293 photographs from magazines, scissors	pages 302-303 metric ruler, paper, 2 small magnetic compasses, tape, bar magnets, pen or marker page 306 metric ruler	page 296 3 different colors of modeling clay; small objects to represent fossils such as shells, feathers, plastic plants and animals, and bones page 310 thermal mitt, clear casserole dish, tap water, hot plate, food coloring

Teacher Classroom Resources

Reproducible Masters	Transparencies
Study Guide, p. 45 **Reinforcement**, p. 45 **Enrichment**, p. 45 **Activity Worksheets**, p. 70 **Lab Manual 33,** Continental Drift **Critical Thinking/Problem Solving**, p. 17 **Cross-Curricular Integration,** p. 15	**Section Focus Transparency 41,** Catch My Drift?
Study Guide, p. 46 **Reinforcement**, p. 46 **Enrichment**, p. 46 **Activity Worksheets**, pp. 66-67 **Science Integration Activity 11,** May the Magnetic Force Be with You! **Technology Integration**, pp. 9-10	**Section Focus Transparency 42,** What a Spread! **Science Integration Transparency 11,** Magnetizing Matter
Study Guide, p. 47 **Reinforcement**, p. 47 **Enrichment**, p. 47 **Activity Worksheets**, pp. 68-69, 71 **Concept Mapping**, p. 27 **Multicultural Connections**, pp. 25-26	**Section Focus Transparency 43,** Boundary Interactions **Teaching Transparency 21,** Earth's Layers **Teaching Transparency 22,** Convergence
Study Guide, p. 48 **Reinforcement**, p. 48 **Enrichment**, p. 48 **Science and Society Integration**, p. 15	**Section Focus Transparency 44,** Tropical Antarctica

Teaching Resources

Glencoe Earth Science Interactive Videodisc
Earth Science CD-ROM
Spanish Resources
English/Spanish Audiocassettes
Cooperative Learning Resource Guide
Lab Partner
Lab and Safety Skills
Lesson Plans

Assessment Resources

Chapter Review, pp. 25-26
Assessment, pp. 67-70
Performance Assessment in the Science Classroom (PASC)
MindJogger Videoquiz
Alternate Assessment in the Science Classroom
Performance Assessment
Chapter Review Software
Computer Test Bank

Key to Teaching Strategies

The following designations will help you decide which activities are appropriate for your students.

L1 Level 1 activities should be within the ability range of all students.

L2 Level 2 activities should be within the ability range of the average to above-average student.

L3 Level 3 activities are designed for the ability range of above-average students.

LEP LEP activities should be within the ability range of Limited English Proficiency students.

LS These activities are designed to address different learning styles.

COOP LEARN Cooperative Learning activities are designed for small group work.

P These strategies represent student products that can be placed into a best-work portfolio.

GLENCOE TECHNOLOGY

The following multimedia resources are available from Glencoe.

Science and Technology Videodisc Series (STVS)
Earth & Space
Moving Continents
National Geographic Society Series
STV: Restless Earth
Glencoe Earth Science Interactive Videodisc
Volcanoes: Erupting Mountains
Earth Science CD-ROM

Teacher Classroom Resources

This is a representation of key blackline masters available in the Teacher Classroom Resources.

Teaching Aids

Section Focus Transparencies

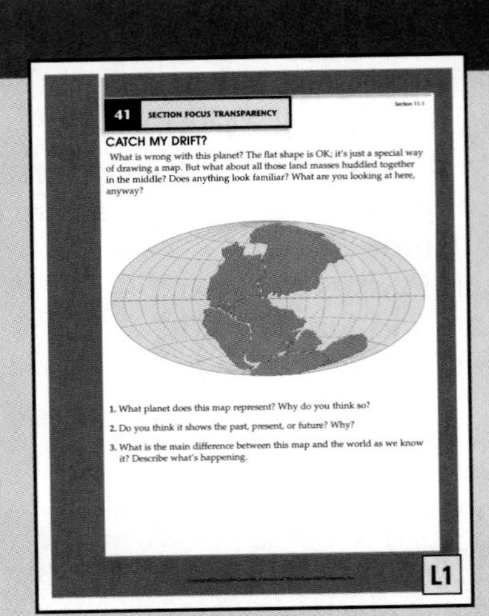

41 SECTION FOCUS TRANSPARENCY — Section 11-1

CATCH MY DRIFT?

What is wrong with this planet? The flat shape is OK; it's just a special way of drawing a map. But what about all those land masses huddled together in the middle? Does anything look familiar? What are you looking at here, anyway?

1. What planet does this map represent? Why do you think so?
2. Do you think it shows the past, present, or future? Why?
3. What is the main difference between this map and the world as we know it? Describe what's happening.

L1

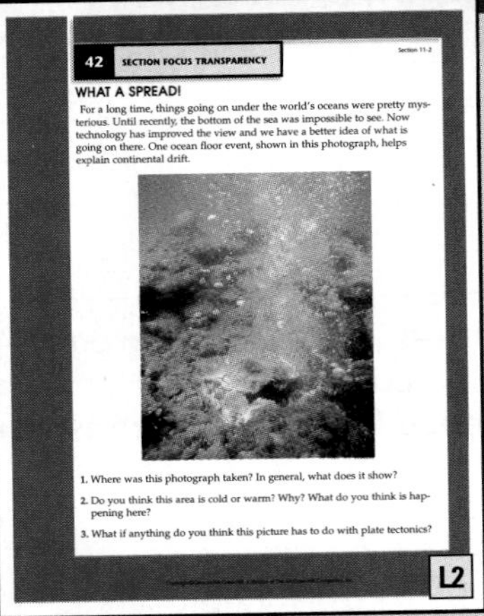

42 SECTION FOCUS TRANSPARENCY — Section 11-2

WHAT A SPREAD!

For a long time, things going on under the world's oceans were pretty mysterious. Until recently, the bottom of the sea was impossible to see. Now technology has improved the view and we have a better idea of what is going on there. One ocean floor event, shown in this photograph, helps explain continental drift.

1. Where was this photograph taken? In general, what does it show?
2. Do you think this area is cold or warm? Why? What do you think is happening here?
3. What if anything do you think this picture has to do with plate tectonics?

L2

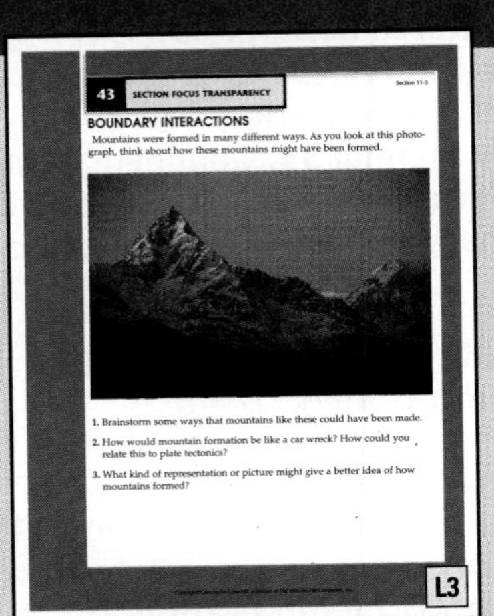

43 SECTION FOCUS TRANSPARENCY — Section 11-3

BOUNDARY INTERACTIONS

Mountains were formed in many different ways. As you look at this photograph, think about how these mountains might have been formed.

1. Brainstorm some ways that mountains like these could have been made.
2. How would mountain formation be like a car wreck? How could you relate this to plate tectonics?
3. What kind of representation or picture might give a better idea of how mountains formed?

L3

Science Integration Transparencies

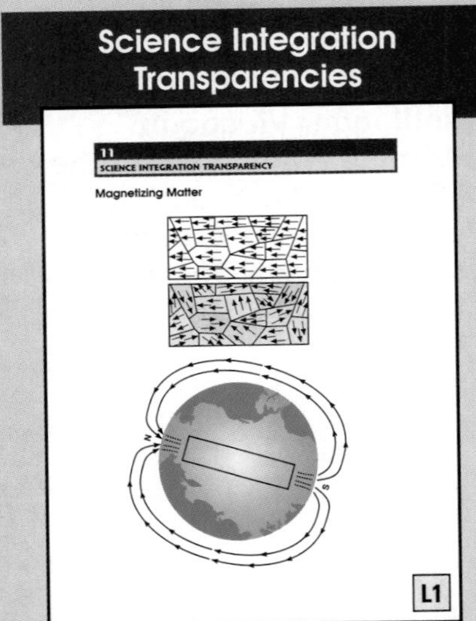

11 SCIENCE INTEGRATION TRANSPARENCY

Magnetizing Matter

L1

Teaching Transparencies

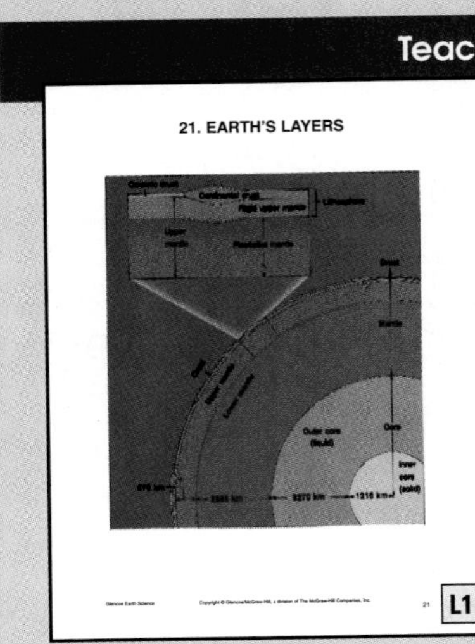

21. EARTH'S LAYERS

L1

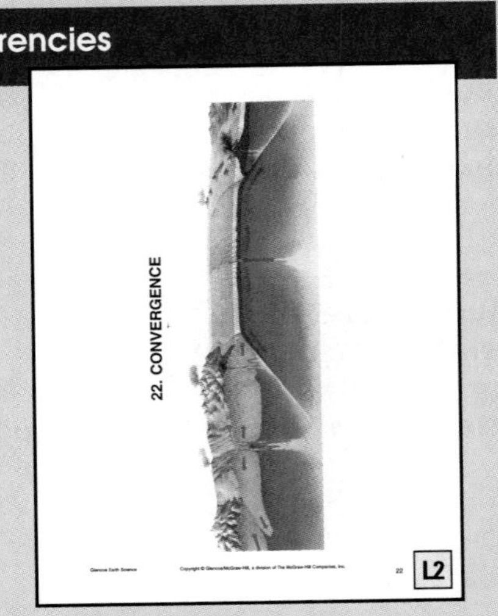

22. CONVERGENCE

L2

Meeting Different Ability Levels

Study Guide

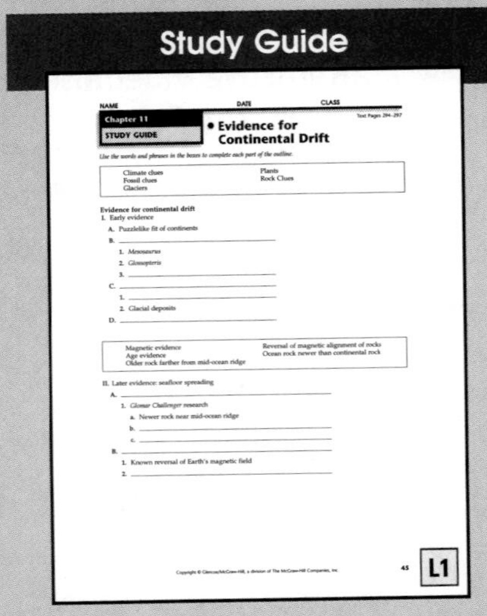

NAME DATE CLASS

Chapter 11 STUDY GUIDE • **Evidence for Continental Drift** — Text Pages 294–297

Use the words and phrases in the boxes to complete each part of the outline.

Climate clues, Fossil clues, Glaciers, Plants, Rock Clues

Evidence for continental drift

I. Early evidence
- A. Puzzlelike fit of continents
- B. ____
  1. *Mesosaurus*
  2. *Glossopteris*
  3. ____
- C. ____
  1. ____
  2. Glacial deposits
- D. ____

Magnetic evidence, Age evidence, Older rock farther from mid-ocean ridge, Reversal of magnetic alignment of rocks, Ocean rock newer than continental rock

II. Later evidence: seafloor spreading
- A. ____
  1. *Glomar Challenger* research
     - a. Newer rock near mid-ocean ridge
     - b. ____
     - c. ____
- B. ____
  1. Known reversal of Earth's magnetic field
  2. ____

Copyright © Glencoe/McGraw-Hill, a division of The McGraw-Hill Companies, Inc. 45

L1

Reinforcement

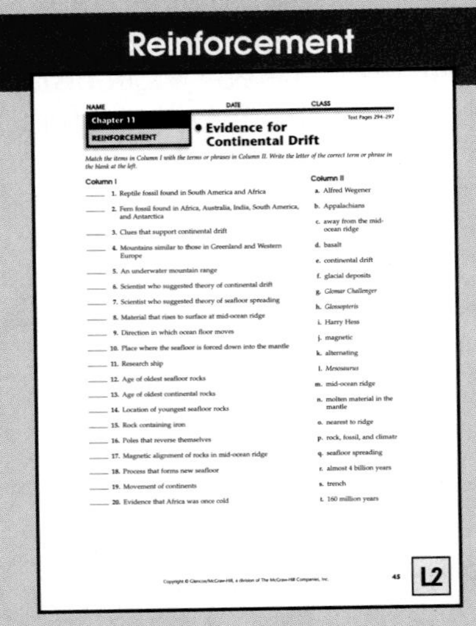

NAME DATE CLASS

Chapter 11 REINFORCEMENT • **Evidence for Continental Drift** — Text Pages 294–297

Match the items in Column I with the terms or phrases in Column II. Write the letter of the correct term or phrase in the blank at the left.

Column I	Column II
____ 1. Reptile fossil found in South America and Africa	a. Alfred Wegener
____ 2. Fern fossil found in Africa, Australia, India, South America, and Antarctica	b. Appalachians
____ 3. Clues that support continental drift	c. away from the mid-ocean ridge
____ 4. Mountains similar to those in Greenland and Western Europe	d. basalt
____ 5. An underwater mountain range	e. continental drift
____ 6. Scientist who suggested theory of continental drift	f. glacial deposits
____ 7. Scientist who suggested theory of seafloor spreading	g. *Glomar Challenger*
____ 8. Material that rises to surface at mid-ocean ridge	h. Glossopteris
____ 9. Direction in which ocean floor moves	i. Harry Hess
____ 10. Place where the seafloor is forced down into the mantle	j. magnetic
____ 11. Research ship	k. alternating
____ 12. Age of oldest seafloor rocks	l. *Mesosaurus*
____ 13. Age of oldest continental rocks	m. mid-ocean ridge
____ 14. Location of youngest seafloor rocks	n. molten material in the mantle
____ 15. Rock containing iron	o. nearest to ridge
____ 16. Poles that reverse themselves	p. rock, fossil, and climate
____ 17. Magnetic alignment of rocks in mid-ocean ridge	q. seafloor spreading
____ 18. Process that forms new seafloor	r. almost 4 billion years
____ 19. Movement of continents	s. trench
____ 20. Evidence that Africa was once cold	t. 160 million years

Copyright © Glencoe/McGraw-Hill, a division of The McGraw-Hill Companies, Inc. 45

L2

Enrichment Worksheets

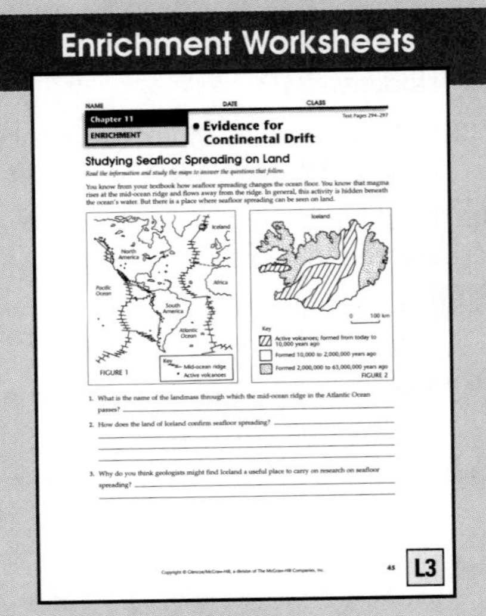

NAME DATE CLASS

Chapter 11 ENRICHMENT • **Evidence for Continental Drift** — Text Pages 294–297

Studying Seafloor Spreading on Land

Read the information and study the maps to answer the questions that follow.

You know from your textbook how seafloor spreading changes the ocean floor. You know that magma rises at the mid-ocean ridge and flows away from the ridge. In general, this activity is hidden beneath the ocean's water. But there is a place where seafloor spreading can be seen on land.

1. What is the name of the landmass through which the mid-ocean ridge in the Atlantic Ocean passes? ____
2. How does the land of Iceland confirm seafloor spreading? ____
3. Why do you think geologists might find Iceland a useful place to carry on research on seafloor spreading? ____

Copyright © Glencoe/McGraw-Hill, a division of The McGraw-Hill Companies, Inc. 45

L3

Hands-On Activities

Science Integration Activity

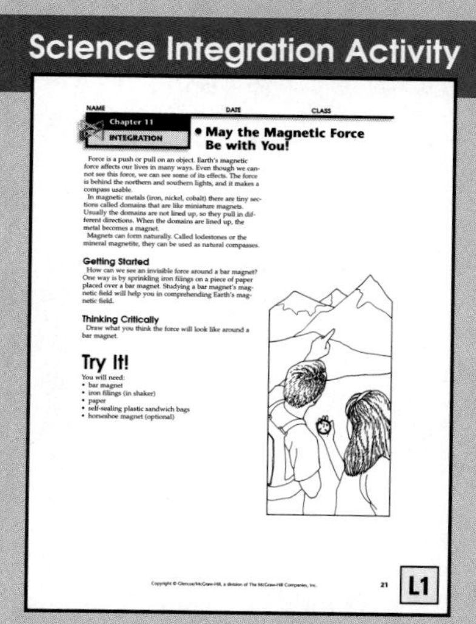

Chapter 11 INTEGRATION

May the Magnetic Force Be with You!

Getting Started

Thinking Critically

Try It!

L1

Lab Manual

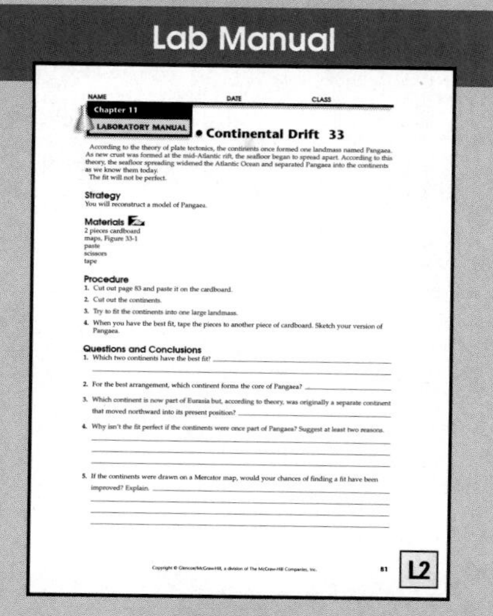

Chapter 11 LABORATORY MANUAL

Continental Drift 33

Strategy

Materials

Procedure

Questions and Conclusions

L2

Assessment

Performance Assessment

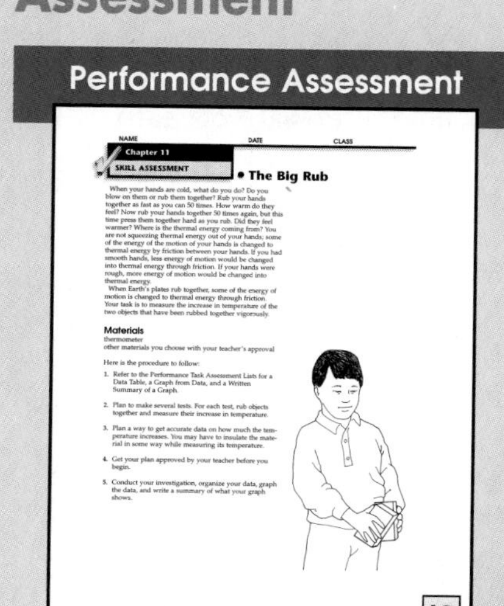

Chapter 11 SKILL ASSESSMENT

The Big Rub

Materials

L3

Enrichment and Application

Critical Thinking/ Problem Solving

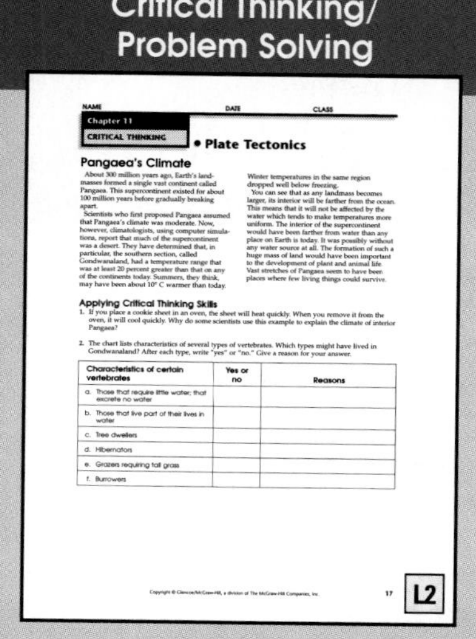

Chapter 11 CRITICAL THINKING

Plate Tectonics

Pangaea's Climate

Applying Critical Thinking Skills

L2

Cross-Curricular Integration

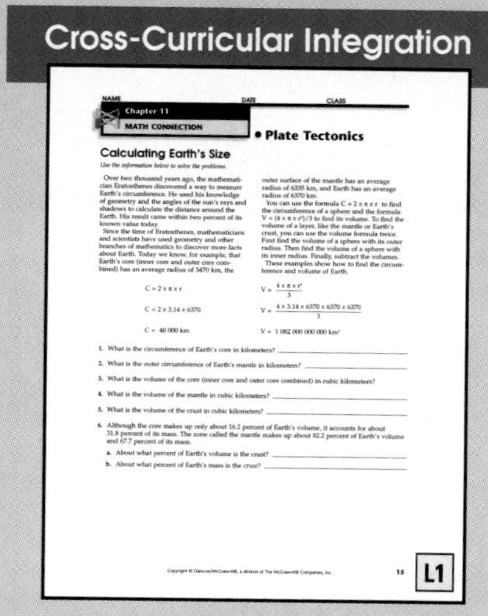

Chapter 11 MATH CONNECTION

Plate Tectonics

Calculating Earth's Size

L1

Science and Society Integration

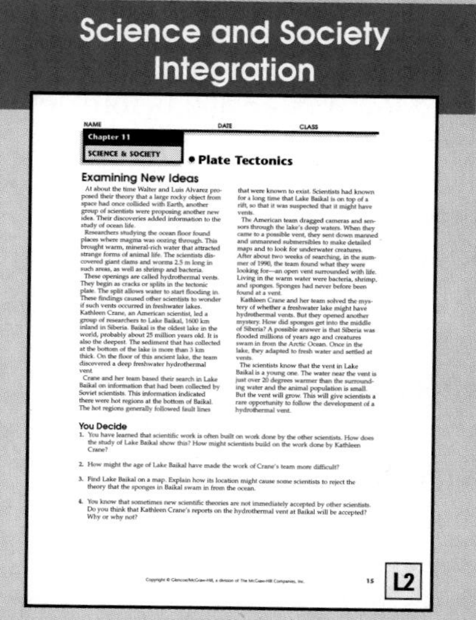

Chapter 11 SCIENCE & SOCIETY

Plate Tectonics

Examining New Ideas

You Decide

L2

Technology Integration

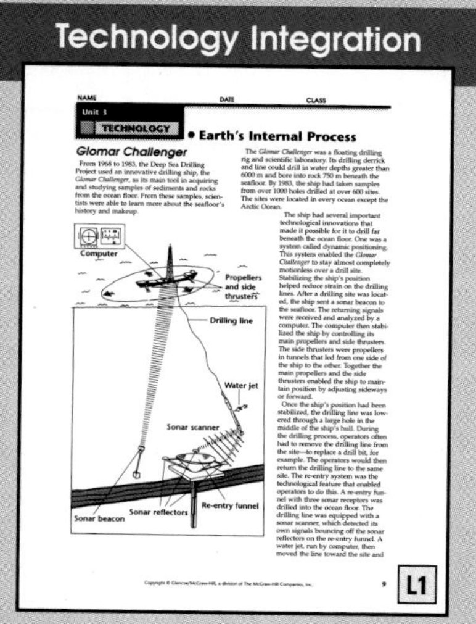

Unit 1 TECHNOLOGY

Earth's Internal Process

Glomar Challenger

L1

Multicultural Connections

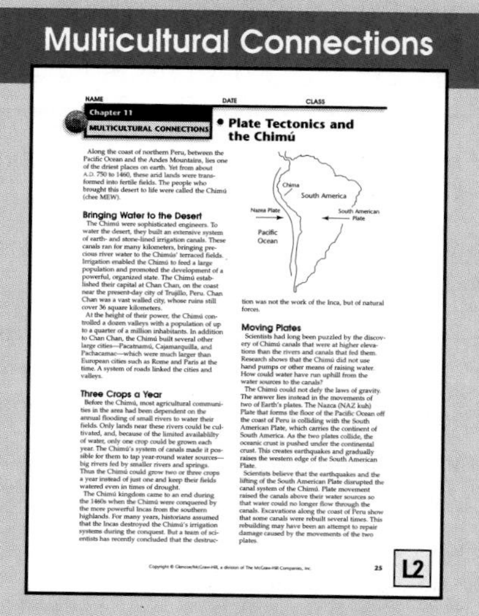

Chapter 11 MULTICULTURAL CONNECTIONS

Plate Tectonics and the Chimú

Bringing Water to the Desert

Three Crops a Year

Moving Plates

L2

Concept Mapping

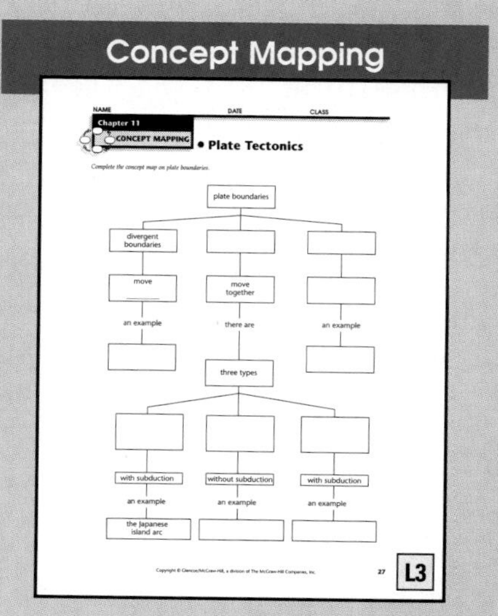

Chapter 11 CONCEPT MAPPING

Plate Tectonics

L3

Chapter 11

Plate Tectonics

CHAPTER OVERVIEW

Section 11-1 Fossil, climate, and rock clues that support continental drift and the existence of Pangaea are presented.

Section 11-2 An explanation of seafloor spreading is provided and, along with age evidence, is presented as more support for continental drift.

Section 11-3 Plate tectonics is explained in terms of divergent, convergent, and transform plate boundaries. Causes and effects of plate tectonics are presented.

Section 11-4 **Science and Society** Computer animation, as well as fossil and rock clues, are described in support of the idea that a supercontinent named Rodinia existed before Pangaea.

Chapter Vocabulary

continental drift
Pangaea
seafloor spreading
magnetometer
plate tectonics
plate
lithosphere
asthenosphere
divergent boundary
convergent boundary
subduction zone
transform fault
convection current

Theme Connection

Energy The transfer of energy in Earth's interior sets up massive convection currents in the mantle. These convection cells are thought to be the driving force that causes the movements of Earth's plates.

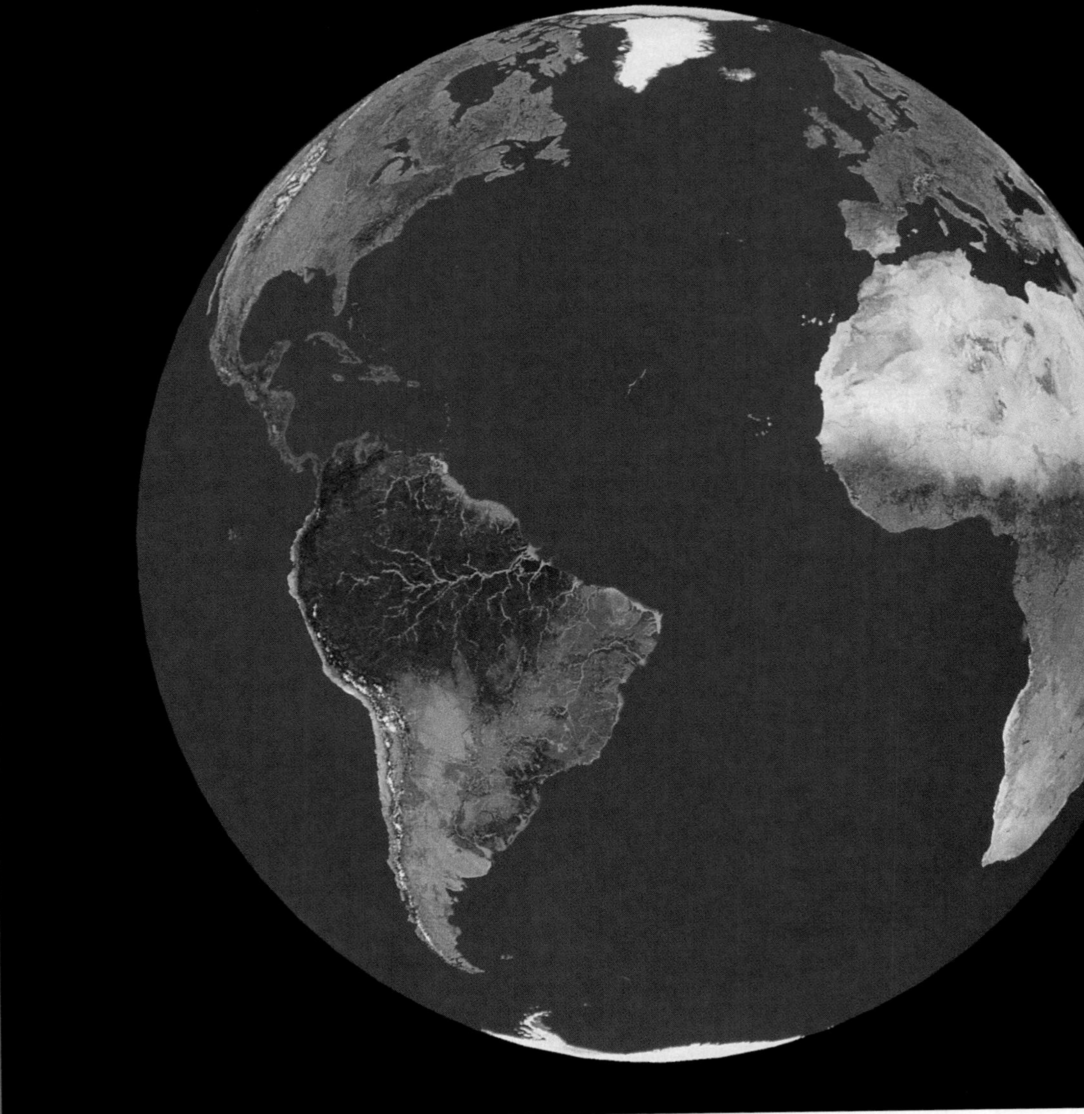

Previewing the Chapter

Learning Styles

Look for the following logo for strategies that emphasize different learning modalities. LS

Kinesthetic	Explore, p. 293; MiniLAB, p. 296
Visual-Spatial	Visual Learning, pp. 295, 296, 299, 300, 305, 308, 311, 312, 315; Demonstration, p. 299; Activity, p. 305; MiniLAB, p. 310; People and Science, p. 316
Interpersonal	Reteach, p. 300; Activity 11-1, pp. 302-303; Activity, p. 311
Logical-Mathematical	Activity 11-2, p. 306
Linguistic	Across the Curriculum, p. 302

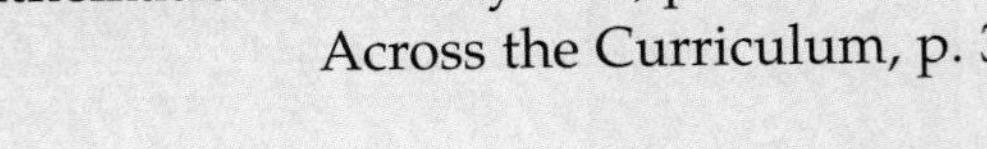

LS

Chapter 11

Plate Tectonics

This photograph of Earth is unique because the clouds have been removed using a computer. You can see the shapes of the continents just like on a map. Look very closely at the general shapes of the continents. Do you see any relationship between continents? If this photograph of Earth were cut into pieces, could you fit the pieces back together? What clues might you use?

EXPLORE ACTIVITY

Do the following activity to see how clues on adjoining pieces of a cut-up photograph can be used to re-form the image.

1. Working with a partner, obtain photographs of interest to you from an old magazine. Do not look at each other's photographs.
2. You and your partner are each to cut one picture into small pieces.
3. Exchange pictures with your partner.
4. Using clues on surrounding pieces, re-form the image of the photograph your partner has cut into small pieces.

Observe: What characteristics of the cut-up photograph did you use to re-form the image? Can you think of other examples in which characteristics of objects are used to match them up with other objects?

ing Science Skills

ill Builders, you will outline, map concepts, ognize cause and effect.

ctivities, you will analyze and interpret ake a model, observe, and infer.

iniLABs, you will experiment, compare ntrast, observe and infer, othesize.

Assessment Planner

age 317 for suggested items that night select for their portfolios.

nce Assessment

317 for additional Performance nt options.
lers, pp. 297, 301, 313
, pp. 296, 310
11-1, pp. 302-303; 11-2, p. 306

Content Assessment

Section Wrap-ups, pp. 297, 301, 313, 315
Chapter Review, pp. 317-319
Mini Quizzes, pp. 297, 301, 313, 315

Group Assessment

Opportunities for group assessment occur with Cooperative Learning Strategies and Flex Your Brain Activities.

EXPLORE ACTIVITY

Purpose

LS **Kinesthetic** Use the Explore Activity to introduce students to continental drift. Briefly explain that the concept of continental drift states that Earth's continents have changed positions over time. L1 LEP COOP LEARN

Preparation

Several days before you begin this chapter, obtain scissors for each student in the class.

Materials

scissors, thin white paper

Teaching Strategies

- Have students compare their results with other students' results. Discuss differences and similarities.

Troubleshooting Explain that it is not necessary that the cut-up photograph outlines fit together perfectly, because students are trying to match only the general shapes.

Safety Precautions Caution students to handle scissors with care.

Observe

Some photographs are easier to fit together than others. In general, the shapes of the photograph pieces enable students to guess how pieces may once have fit together.

Assessment

Process Ask students to explain in their Science Journals what characteristics of some photographs made them easier to fit together than others. Use the Performance Task Assessment List for Writing in Science in **PASC,** p. 87. P

Section 11•1

Prepare

Section Background

- About 200 million years ago, Pangaea covered about 40% of Earth's surface, while a large ocean, Panthalassa, covered the rest of the planet. Pangaea broke up to form Laurasia and Gondwanaland, which were separated by the Tethys Sea.
- Fossils of *Lystrosaurus*, a small reptile that lived about 200 million years ago, have been found in South Africa, Antarctica, and India.
- Certain species of green turtles swim from South America to Ascension Island in the mid-Atlantic to lay their eggs. The turtles may have started this trip when continents were much closer. As the seafloor spread, the instinctive trip became longer.

Preplanning

To prepare for the MiniLAB, obtain modeling clay of different colors, bones, and objects such as plastic plants and animals to be used as "fossils."

1 Motivate

Bellringer

Before presenting the lesson, display **Section Focus Transparency 41** on the overhead projector. Assign the accompanying **Focus Activity** worksheet. L1 LEP

Tying to Previous Knowledge

Have students recall how magma forms. Have students discuss how rising magma affects the overlying crust.

11•1 Continental Drift

Science Words

continental drift
Pangaea

Objectives

- Explain the theory of continental drift.
- Discuss four pieces of evidence for the theory of continental drift.

Evidence for Continental Drift

When you look at a map of Earth's surface, one thing is very obvious. In **Figures 11-1** and **11-2** you see that the edges of some continents look as if they would fit together like a puzzle. In the early 1800s, as accurate maps of Earth's surface were first being developed, other people also noticed this fact.

Pangaea

Alfred Wegener thought that the fit of the continents wasn't just a coincidence. He believed that all the continents were joined together at some point in the past, and in a 1912 lecture, he proposed the idea of continental drift. The theory of **continental drift** states that continents have moved horizontally to their current locations. Wegener believed that all continents were once connected as one large landmass that broke apart about 200 million years ago. When the continents broke apart, they drifted to their present positions. He called this large landmass **Pangaea** (pan JEE uh), which means "all land."

Figure 11-1

Glossopteris, Mesosaurus, and other organisms shown in this illustration lived in many areas of Pangaea. Their fossils are now found on separate continents.

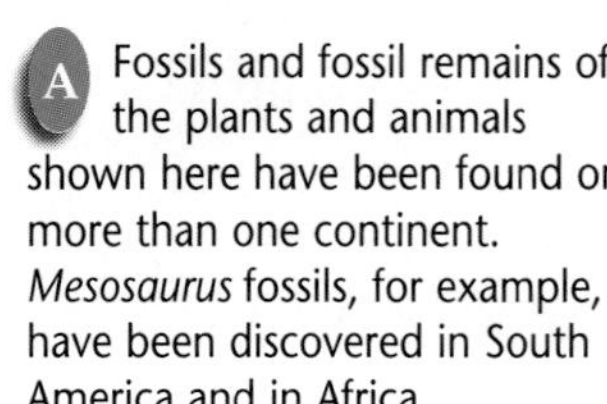

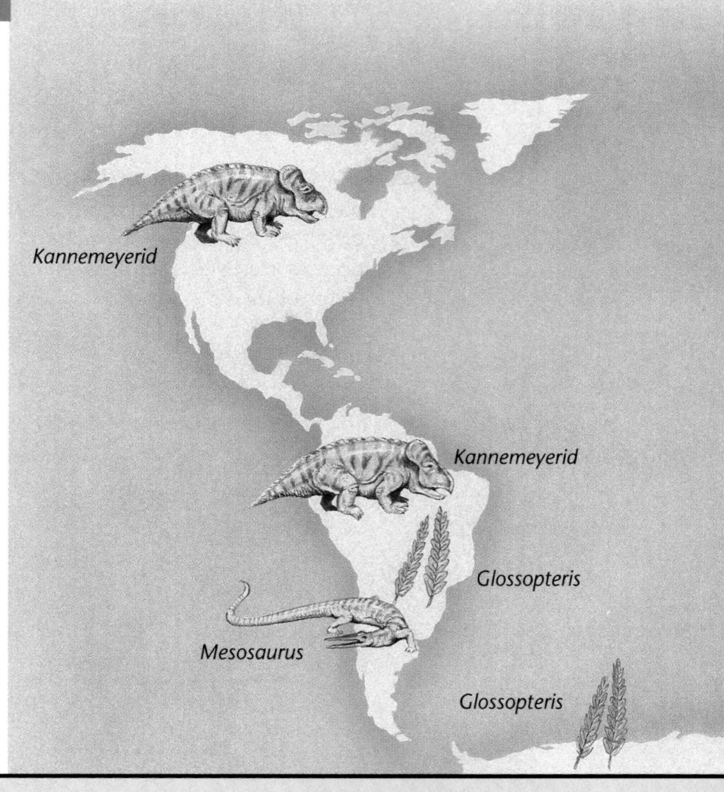

A Fossils and fossil remains of the plants and animals shown here have been found on more than one continent. *Mesosaurus* fossils, for example, have been discovered in South America and in Africa.

Program Resources

Reproducible Masters

Study Guide, p. 45 L1
Reinforcement, p. 45 L1
Enrichment, p. 45 L3
Activity Worksheets, pp. 5, 70 L1
Critical Thinking/Problem Solving, p. 17
Cross-Curricular Integration, p. 15
Lab Manual 33

Transparencies

Section Focus Transparency 41 L1

Since Wegener's death in 1930, his basic theory, that the continents moved, has been accepted. The evidence Wegener had to support his theory wasn't enough to convince many people during his lifetime. However, Wegener's early evidence has since been joined by other important proofs. Let's explore both Wegener's clues and some newer ones.

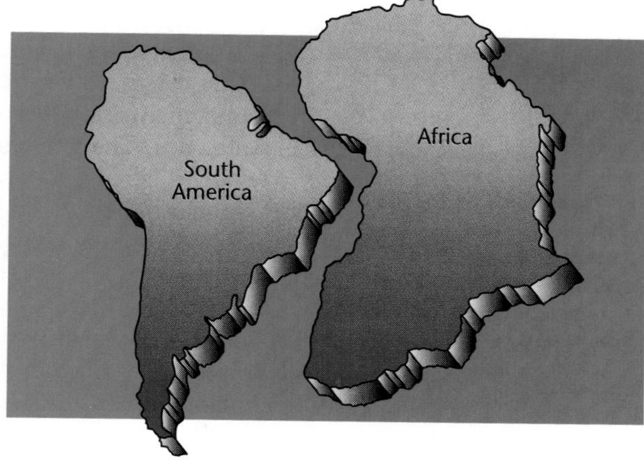

Figure 11-2

The eastern coastline of South America and the western coastline of Africa look like they would fit together as puzzle pieces.

Fossil Clues

Besides the puzzlelike fit of the continents, other clues were found from fossils. Fossils of the reptile *Mesosaurus* have been found in South America and Africa, as shown in **Figure 11-1.** This swimming reptile lived in fresh water and on land. How could fossils of the *Mesosaurus* be found so far apart? It's very unlikely that it could have swum between the continents. Wegener thought this reptile lived on both continents when the continents were connected.

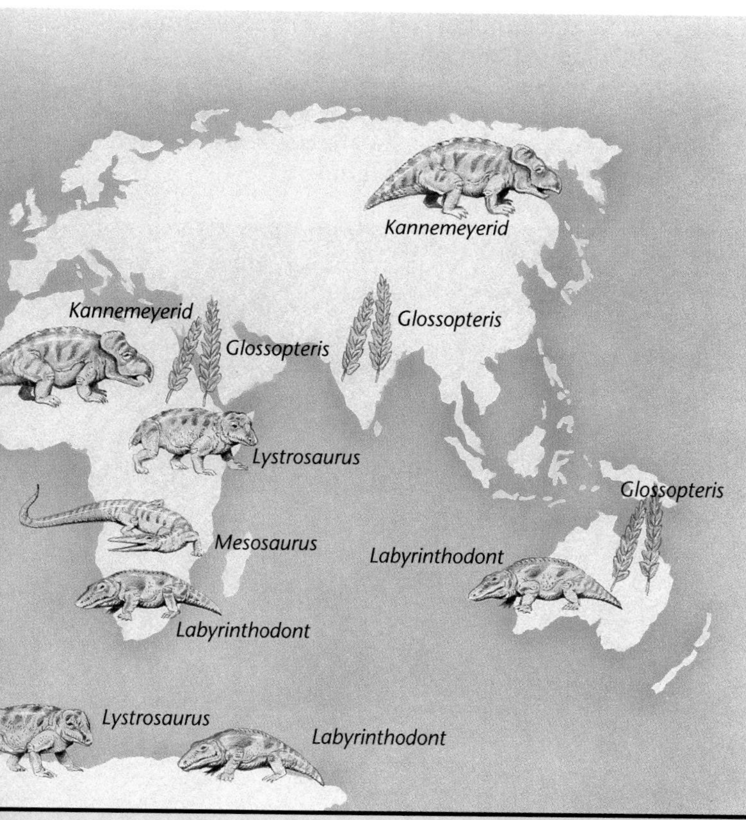

B *How does the study of* Glossopteris, Mesosaurus, Kannemeyerid, Labyrinthodont, *and other fossils support Wegener's hypothesis of continental drift?*

2 Teach

Teacher F.Y.I.

Wegener's idea of continental drift was rejected mainly because he suggested that the continents plowed through oceanic crust. Sir Harold Jeffries had shown that oceanic crust was too rigid for this to occur, regardless of the mechanism.

GLENCOE TECHNOLOGY

CD-ROM

Earth Science CD-ROM

Have students perform the interactive exploration for Chapter 11 to reinforce important chapter concepts and thinking processes.

3 Assess

Check for Understanding

Use the Flex Your Brain activity to have students explore CONTINENTAL DRIFT.

Activity Worksheets, p. 5

Reteach

Have students brainstorm why some of the photographs used in the Explore Activity were easier to reconstruct.

Extension

For students who have mastered this section, use the **Reinforcement** and **Enrichment** masters.

Across the Curriculum

History Have students research the life and scientific work of Alfred Wegener. Encourage students to read about his work in Greenland and how that research led him to formulate his idea of continental drift.

Visual Learning

Figure 11-2 How does the study of *Glossopteris, Mesosaurus, Kannemeyerid, Labyrinthodont,* and other fossils support Wegener's hypothesis of continental drift? *These animals and plants could not have swum across oceans, so continents must have been close together for them to occur on different continents.* LEP LS

MiniLAB

Purpose

LS **Kinesthetic** Students will reaffirm that geologic clues can be used to show how continents now separated were once together. L1 LEP

Materials

modeling clay of various colors, objects to use as "fossils"

Teaching Strategies

Troubleshooting Prepare "fossils," "continents," and smaller "landmasses" prior to class. Position "landmasses" around the room prior to students entering.

Analysis

1. Answers will vary, but students should be able to reconstruct at least some of the original clay landmass.
2. similar mountain forms, similar "fossils," and similarly colored clay
3. Answers will vary, but students may set those continents aside until more of the original landmass is reconstructed.

Assessment

Oral Have students explain in their Journals what characteristics they used to reconstruct the original "landmass." Then, call on them to read their answers in class. Use the Performance Task Assessment List for Writing in Science in PASC, p. 87. P

Activity Worksheets, pp. 5, 70

MiniLAB

Can clues such as fossils, types of life, and rock structures be used to determine whether continents now separated were once joined?

Procedure

1. Build a three-layer landmass using clay.
2. Mold the clay into mountain ranges.
3. Place similar "fossils" into the clay at various locations around the landmass.
4. Form five continents from the one landmass. Also, form two smaller landmasses out of different clay with different mountain ranges and fossils.
5. Place the five continents and two smaller landmasses around the room.
6. Students who did not make or place the landmasses will locate the drifted continents and construct a drawing that shows how they were once positioned.

Analysis

1. Were students able to reconstruct all or part of the original clay landmass?
2. What clues, if any, were useful in reconstructing the original landmass?
3. How did students deal with continents that initially didn't seem to fit?

Another fossil that helps support the theory of continental drift is *Glossopteris*. In **Figure 11-3** you see this fossil fern, which was found in Africa, Australia, India, South America, and later in Antarctica. The presence of this fern in so many areas with widely different modern climates, as you see in **Figure 11-1,** led Wegener to believe that all of these areas were once connected and had a similar climate.

Climate Clues

Fossils of warm-weather plants were found on the island of Spitzbergen in the Arctic Ocean. Wegener believed that Spitzbergen drifted from the tropic regions. He also used glacial clues to support his theory. Glacial deposits and grooved bedrock found in southern areas of South America, Africa, India, and Australia indicated that these continents were once covered with glaciers. How could you explain why glacial deposits were found in these areas where no glaciers exist today? Wegener thought that these continents were all connected and covered with ice near Earth's South Pole at one time.

Rock Clues

If the continents were connected at one time, then rocks that make up the continents should be the same. Similar rock structures *are* found on different continents. Parts of the Appalachian Mountains of the eastern United States are similar to those found in Greenland and western Europe. If you were to travel to South America and western Africa, you would find rock structures that are very similar. These clues, found in rocks, support the idea that the continents were connected when these rock structures formed.

Figure 11-3
This fossil fern, *Glossopteris*, grew in a warm tropical climate.

Visual Learning

Figure 11-4 Based on what is presented in the diagrams and assuming that the rate of movement will stay the same, what will happen to the Atlantic Ocean during the next 100 million years? *It will widen.* LEP LS

Science Journal

Continental Movement New evidence suggests that mountains in southwest South America match up with the older Appalachians. Have students speculate on how the model of Pangaea might change if this proves true. *Accept all reasonable ideas. Before colliding with Africa, North America may have been positioned to the west of South America. Refer students to Section 11-4 on page 314.* L2

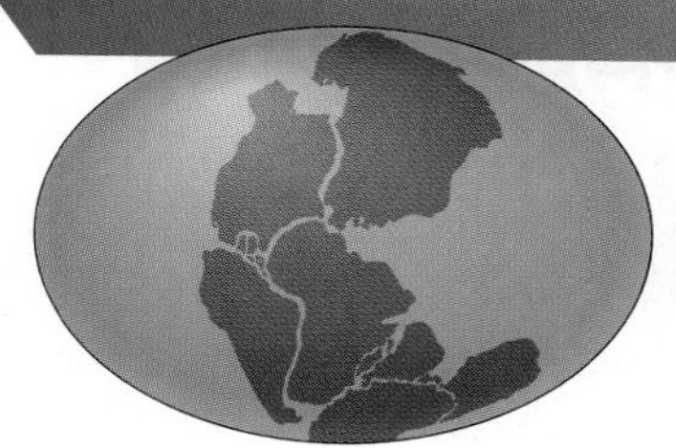

250 million years ago

180 million years ago

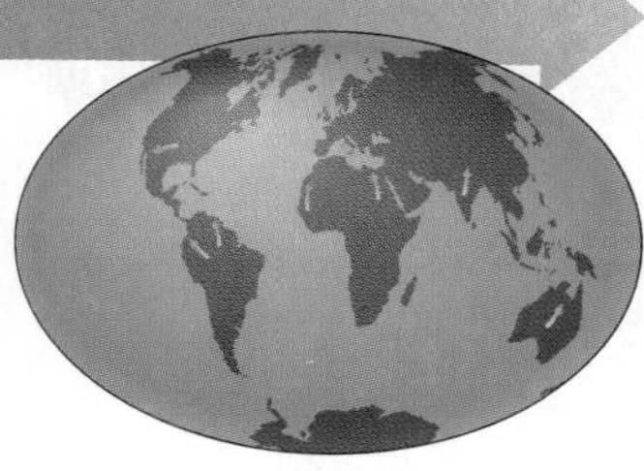

Present

How could continents drift?

Although Wegener provided evidence to support his theory of continental drift he couldn't explain, how, when, or why these changes in the position of the continents, shown in **Figure 11-4,** had taken place. Because other scientists at that time could not provide these explanations either, Wegener's idea of continental drift was rejected. The idea was so different that most people closed their minds to it.

Rock, fossil, and climate clues were the main points of evidence for the continental drift theory. Later, after Wegener's death, more clues were found and new ideas related to continental drift were discovered. One of these new ideas, seafloor spreading, helped provide an explanation of how the continents could move.

Figure 11-4
These computer models show the probable course that continents have taken. On the far left is their position 250 million years ago, in the middle is their position 180 million years ago, and at right is their current position. *Based on what is presented in the diagrams and assuming that the rate of movement will stay the same, what will happen to the Atlantic Ocean during the next 100 million years?*

Section Wrap-up

Review

1. State one reason why Wegener's ideas about continental drift were not accepted.
2. How did Wegener use climate clues to support his hypothesis about continental drift?
3. **Think Critically:** Why would you expect to see similar rocks and rock structures on two landmasses that were connected at one time?

Skill Builder
Comparing and Contrasting

Compare and contrast the location of fossils of the tropical plant *Glossopteris,* as shown in **Figure 11-3,** with the climate that exists at each location today. If you need help, refer to Comparing and Contrasting in the **Skill Handbook.**

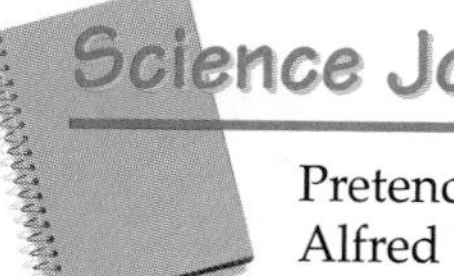

Science Journal

Pretend you are Alfred Wegener in the year 1912. In your Science Journal, write a letter to another scientist explaining your idea about continental drift. Try to convince this scientist that your theory is correct.

4 Close

•MINI•QUIZ•

1. ______ refers to the idea that continents have moved apart over time. *Continental drift*
2. ______ is the name given by Wegener to the large landmass that broke apart to form the continents. *Pangaea*
3. The discovery of ______, a freshwater reptile found both in South America and Africa, provided support for continental drift. *Mesosaurus*

Section Wrap-up

Review

1. Wegener could not explain how, when, or why the continents drifted.
2. He felt that fossils of warm-weather plants found on islands in the Arctic Ocean, as well as glacial deposits and grooved bedrock found in South America, Africa, India, and Australia, supported the idea of continental drift.
3. **Think Critically** When the landmass separated, each part would have retained similar rocks and rock structures.

Science Journal

Inform students that scientists at the lecture presented by Wegener were indignant about the idea. Philip Lake stated that Wegener was not seeking the truth and was blind to other arguments. Professor R. T. Chamberlin claimed Wegener's ideas ranged from unlikely to ludicrous.

Skill Builder

Glossopteris fossils are found on all continents in the southern hemisphere. The climates of each continent are different. Several of these continents are not tropical, yet *Glossopteris* was a tropical plant.

Assessment

Oral Ask students to explain how the location of *Glossopteris* fossils provides support for continental drift. *All locations where the fossils have been found may once have been connected and probably had a similar climate.* Use the Performance Task Assessment List for Making Observations and Inferences in **PASC,** p. 17. P

Section 11•2

Prepare

Section Background

- As the ocean floor slowly separates, new rocks form at a mid-ocean ridge. The spreading process moves older rocks on either side of the ridge farther apart.
- Paleomagnetism is the study of the magnetic properties of ancient rocks.

Preplanning

To prepare for Activity 11-1, obtain two small magnetic compasses, two bar magnets, and a metric ruler for each group of students.

1 Motivate

Bellringer

Before presenting the lesson, display **Section Focus Transparency 42** on the overhead projector. Assign the accompanying **Focus Activity** worksheet. L1 LEP

Tying to Previous Knowledge

Help students recall how lava moves whenever it erupts at Earth's surface through fissures. Remind them that lava flows outward in both directions, similar to the movement of Earth's crust on either side of a mid-ocean ridge.

11•2 Seafloor Spreading

Science Words

seafloor spreading
magnetometer

Objectives

- Describe seafloor spreading.
- Relate how age and magnetic clues confirm seafloor spreading.

Clues on the Ocean Floor

Up until the early 1950s, little was known about the ocean floors. Scientists didn't have the technology needed to explore the deep oceans. But the invention of echo-sounding devices allowed the construction of accurate maps of the ocean floor. Soon, scientists discovered a complex ocean floor that had mountains and valleys just like continents have above water. They also found a system of ridges and valleys extending through the center of the Atlantic and in other oceans around the world. The mid-ocean ridges form an underwater mountain range that extends through the center of much of Earth's oceans. This discovery raised the curiosity of many scientists. What formed these mid-ocean ridges?

Figure 11-5

As the seafloor spreads apart at a mid-ocean ridge, new seafloor is created. The older seafloor moves away from the ridge in both directions. *If seafloor spreading is happening, what evidence should you expect to find by studying rocks taken from the seafloor?*

Age of ocean floor in millions of years

150-200	100-150	50-100	0-50	50-100	100-150	150-200

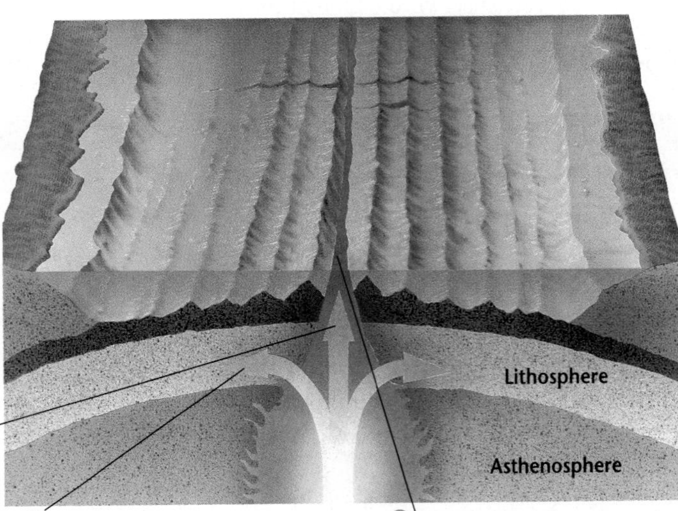

A Hot, less-dense, partially molten rock material from deep inside Earth is forced by gravity upward from the cooler, denser surrounding rock.

B The hot, less-dense rock material is forced upward into the plasticlike portion of the upper mantle. As it approaches the more rigid upper mantle and crust, it is deflected in opposite directions.

C Plates of Earth's crust and rigid upper mantle are forced apart and carried along with the moving hot rock material in the asthenosphere. A rift forms into which molten rock from the upper mantle is forced until it finally flows out onto Earth's surface as lava.

Program Resources

Reproducible Masters

Study Guide, p. 46 L1
Reinforcement, p. 46 L1
Enrichment, p. 46 L3
Activity Worksheets, pp. 5, 66-67 L1
Science Integration Activities, pp. 21-22
Technology Integration, pp. 9-10

Transparencies

Section Focus Transparency 42 L1
Science Integration Transparency 11

Figure 11-6
The research ship *Glomar Challenger* helped in the exploration of the world's oceans and the seafloor.

The Seafloor Moves

In the early 1960s, Princeton University scientist Harry Hess suggested an explanation. His now-famous and accepted theory is known as **seafloor spreading.** Hess proposed that hot, less-dense material in the mantle is forced upward to the surface at a mid-ocean ridge. Then it turns and flows sideways, carrying the seafloor away from the ridge in both directions, as seen in **Figure 11-5.** As the seafloor spreads apart, magma located a few kilometers below the ridge moves upward and flows from the cracks. It solidifies and forms new seafloor. The seafloor that is carried away from the ridge cools, contracts, and becomes more dense than the plasticlike asthenosphere below it. The seafloor begins to sink downward, forming trenches. The theory of seafloor spreading was later shown to be correct by the two following pieces of evidence.

Age Evidence

In 1968, scientists aboard the research ship *Glomar Challenger* began gathering information about the rocks in the seafloor. The *Challenger,* as shown in **Figure 11-6,** was equipped with a drilling rig that allowed scientists to drill into the seafloor to obtain rock samples. The scientists began drilling to study the age of rocks in the seafloor and made a remarkable discovery. They found no rocks older than 180 million years. In contrast, some continental rocks are almost four billion years old. Why were these seafloor rocks so young?

Scientists also found that the youngest rocks were located at the mid-ocean ridges. The age of the rocks became increasingly older farther from the ridges on both sides. The evidence for seafloor spreading was getting stronger.

2 Teach

Visual Learning

Figure 11-5 If seafloor spreading is happening, what evidence should you expect to find by studying rocks taken from the seafloor? *Rocks get older away from the mid-ocean ridge.* LEP LS P

Demonstration

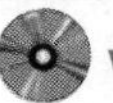 **Visual-Spatial** If possible, obtain a tectonic globe that enables you to demonstrate continental movement as you teach this section and Section 11-3. LEP

Student Text Question

Why were these seafloor rocks so young? *They had formed relatively recently.*

GLENCOE TECHNOLOGY

STVS: Earth & Space
Disc 3, Side 2
Moving Continents (Ch. 8)

NATIONAL GEOGRAPHIC SOCIETY

 **Videodisc**

STV: Restless Earth
Introduction
Unit 1, Side 1
Prologue

00001-05012
Plate Tectonics

10403-14511

 Use **Science Integration Tranparency 11** as you teach this lesson.

Theme Connection

Energy Moving hot rock inside Earth's mantle provides energy for seafloor spreading. The energy in rising hot rock causes Earth's surface to bulge and split. As the hot rock turns and moves sideways, it carries plates of Earth's lithosphere away from each other. The energy involved in this process reaffirms the theme for this chapter.

USING TECHNOLOGY

Volcanic and earthquake activity in the western United States and in Iceland seems to be related to rising hot rock material. Earthquake activity around New Madrid, Missouri, may be connected to the sinking rock masses located under the United States.

Think Critically

The cool matter under the center of North America explains the lack of volcanic activity and variety of earthquakes. The volcanic activity on Iceland occurs because of rising, hot rock at a spreading (diverging) plate boundary.

3 Assess

Check for Understanding

FLEX Your Brain

Use the Flex Your Brain activity to have students explore SEAFLOOR SPREADING.

Activity Worksheets, p. 5

Reteach

LS Interpersonal Have pairs of students construct three-dimensional models of rifting at a mid-ocean ridge. **LEP** **COOP LEARN**

INTEGRATION Physics

The study of reversals of Earth's magnetic field over time has led to the discovery of magnetic evidence in support of moving plates in Earth's lithosphere.

USING TECHNOLOGY

New Picture of Earth

What does the interior of Earth look like? Since the early 1900s, scientists have been using earthquakes to create models of the structure of Earth's interior. When an earthquake occurs, it generates seismic waves that travel through Earth.

Seismic Tomography

Using a new technique called seismic tomography, scientists have made a new model of Earth's interior. In seismic tomography, a computer combines data from earthquakes all around the world. The models from the computer show hot, rising masses of rock (red) and cool, sinking masses of rock (blue). Cool rock material beneath Manchuria seems to be sliding under a warm mass beneath Japan. A large spike of cold rock is located under the crust of much of North America. A large collection of hot rock material is located directly under Iceland.

Think Critically:

Consider the spike of cold rock located under North America and the hot rock material under Iceland. Explain how these features could be related to earthquakes and/or volcanoes. How might the data obtained with seismic tomography help support the theories concerning plate movement at Earth's surface?

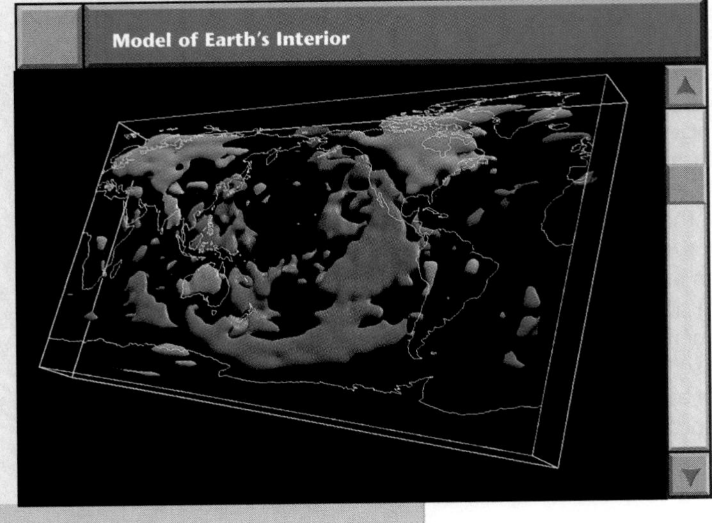

Magnetic Clues

The final bit of evidence in support of the theory of seafloor spreading came from magnetic clues found in the iron-bearing basalt rock from the ocean floor.

Scientists know that Earth's magnetic field has reversed itself several times in the past, as illustrated in **Figure 11-7.** Iron minerals in rocks such as basalt align themselves according to the magnetic field orientation at the time that they form. If Earth's magnetic field is reversed, new iron minerals being formed would reflect that magnetic reversal.

Scientists found that rocks on the ocean floor showed many magnetic reversals. They used a **magnetometer,** a sensitive instrument that records magnetic data. The magnetic alignment of the rocks reverses back and forth in strips parallel to the mid-ocean ridge.

This discovery provided strong support that seafloor spreading was indeed happening. The magnetic reversals showed that new

Visual Learning

Figure 11-7 Why is this considered evidence for seafloor spreading? *The magnetic polarity patterns in the oceans show that new rock is forming at the mid-ocean ridges.* **LEP** **LS**

CONNECT TO CHEMISTRY

Answer The *Curie point* is the temperature at which the magnetic properties of a magnetic substance change. Iron minerals lose their magnetism when heated to the Curie point.

rock was being formed at the mid-ocean ridges.

The ideas of Alfred Wegener and Harry Hess changed the way people think about Earth's crust. Fossil, rock, and climate evidence supporting the theory of continental drift is too strong to be discounted. Seafloor spreading proves that ocean floors change too. You'll see in Section 11-3 how these two ideas are closely related.

Normal polarity

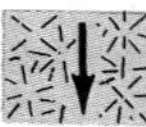
Reversed polarity

Figure 11-7

Changes in magnetic polarity of the rock on both sides of mid-ocean ridges reflect the past reversals of Earth's magnetic poles. *Why is this considered evidence for seafloor spreading?*

CONNECT TO CHEMISTRY

Find out what the Curie point is and ***describe*** in your Science Journal what happens to iron minerals when they are heated to the Curie point.

Section Wrap-up

Review

1. How does the magnetic alignment of iron minerals help support the theory of seafloor spreading?
2. What eventually happens to seafloor that is carried away from a mid-ocean ridge?
3. **Think Critically:** How is seafloor spreading different from continental drift?

Skill Builder
Concept Mapping

Make a concept map that discusses the evidence for continental drift using the following terms and phrases: *continental edges, same fossils, climate, rock structures, on different continents, mountains with similar features, continental ice sheets,* and *puzzle pieces.* If you need help, refer to Concept Mapping in the **Skill Handbook.**

USING MATH

On average, North America is moving 1.25 cm per year away from the Mid-Atlantic Ridge. Using this rate, determine how far apart the continents of North America and Africa will be after 200 million years.

4 Close

•MINI•QUIZ•

Use the Mini Quiz to check students' recall of chapter content.

1. **A(n) ______ is an underwater mountain range.** *mid-ocean ridge*
2. **What happens to hot, less-dense material at a mid-ocean ridge?** *It is forced upward toward Earth's surface.*
3. **How old are the oldest ocean-floor rocks found by scientists aboard *Glomar Challenger*?** *about 160 million years old*

Section Wrap-up

Review

1. Iron minerals in ocean-floor rocks align with the magnetic field present when the rocks formed. Alternating magnetic bands parallel to mid-ocean ridges have been found and thus support the idea of seafloor spreading.
2. It cools, contracts, and becomes denser than the asthenosphere below. It begins to sink downward at trenches.
3. **Think Critically** Seafloor spreading states that continents move with the seafloor. Continental drift proposed that the continents plowed through the seafloor.

USING MATH

If the North American Plate is moving 1.25 cm per year away from the Mid-Atlantic Ridge, North America and Africa separate by 2.5 cm more each year. After 200 million years, they will be separated by 500 000 000 cm or 5000 km. P

Skill Builder

Possible Solution:

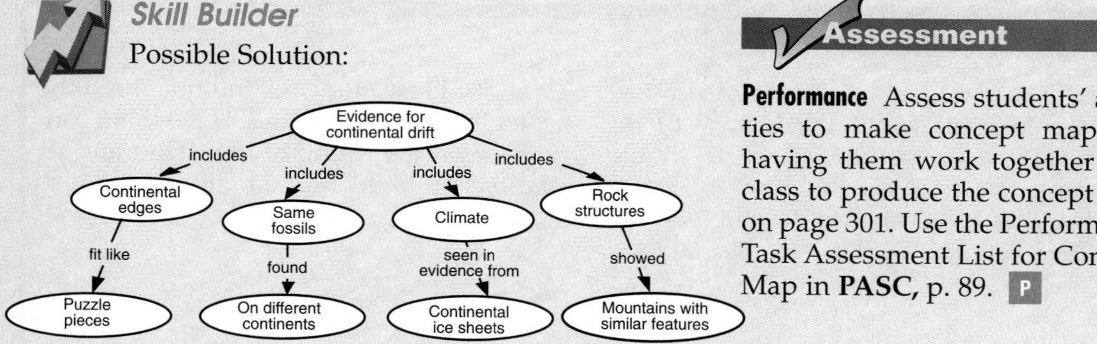

Assessment

Performance Assess students' abilities to make concept maps by having them work together as a class to produce the concept map on page 301. Use the Performance Task Assessment List for Concept Map in **PASC**, p. 89. P

Activity 11-1

PREPARATION

Purpose

LS **Interpersonal** Design and carry out an experiment to model seafloor spreading and magnetic reversals. L1

COOP LEARN

Process Skills

communicating, sequencing, comparing and contrasting, forming a hypothesis, designing an experiment, measuring in SI, observing and inferring, interpreting data, inferring, recognizing and using spatial relationships, formulating models

Time

48 minutes

Possible Hypotheses

A model showing how Earth's reversing magnetic fields support the theory of seafloor spreading can be developed using bar magnets and small magnetic compasses.

Activity Worksheets, pp. 5, 66-67

PLAN THE EXPERIMENT

Possible Procedures

1. Cut a strip of paper between 40 and 60 cm in length.
2. Fold the paper strip and place it between two close desks as shown in the illustration.
3. Place the magnets as shown in the illustration.
4. Place two compasses next to each other on either side of the space between the desks.
5. Draw a line along each side of the space between the desks to represent the edges of the ocean ridge.
6. Beside the line, draw arrows showing the direction the compass needles are pointing.

Activity 11-1

Design Your Own Experiment
Seafloor Spreading

Magnetic data support the theory of seafloor spreading. When magnetic iron minerals, such as magnetite, are heated to the Curie point (about 580°C) in a magma body, they lose their magnetism. When these iron minerals once again cool off, they become magnetized in the direction of Earth's magnetic field at that time. In this activity, develop a model showing how magnetic clues indicate that the seafloor is spreading apart.

PREPARATION

Problem

Develop a model showing how magnetic clues indicate that the seafloor is spreading apart.

Form a Hypothesis

State a hypothesis about how a model can show how magnetic clues are used to indicate that the seafloor is spreading apart.

Objectives

- Make a model of how magnetic clues are used to indicate seafloor spreading.
- Describe how the Curie point is involved in a study of magnetic clues on the seafloor.

Possible Materials

- metric ruler
- paper
- small magnetic compasses (2)
- tape
- bar magnets
- pen or marker

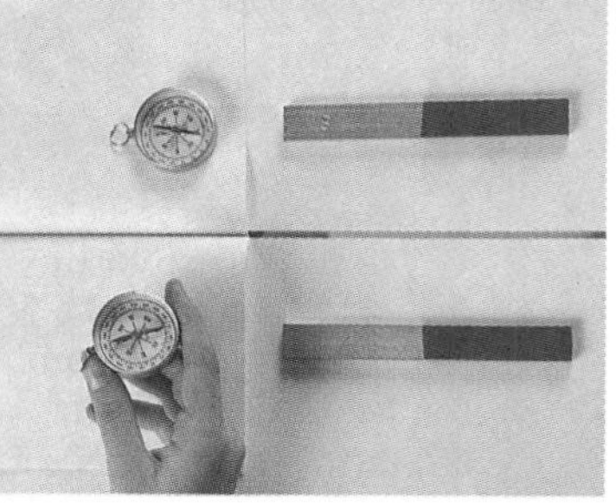

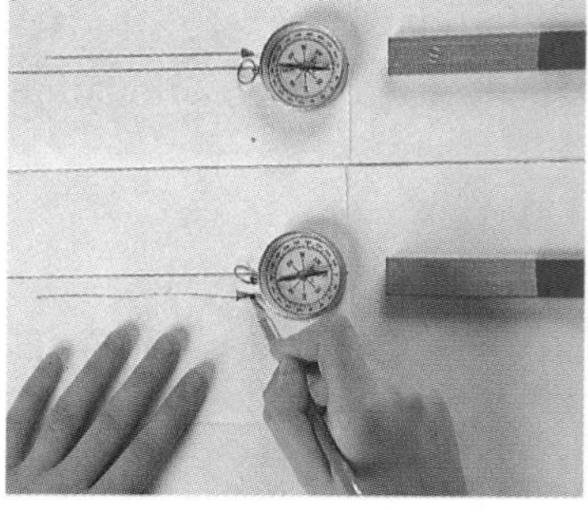

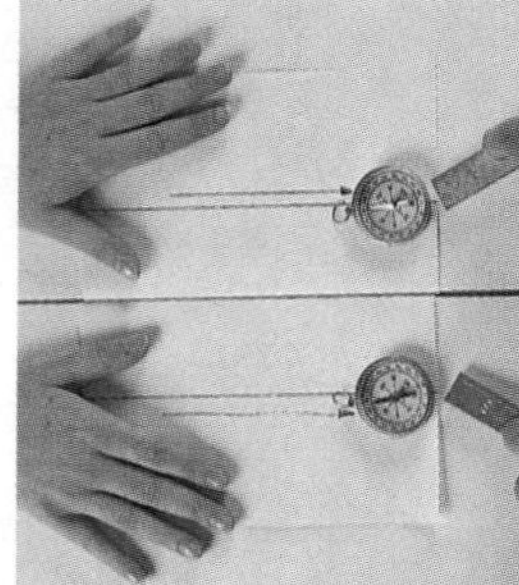

Across the Curriculum

History Have students write reports in their Science Journals about the history of the study of the ocean floor. Reports should compare and contrast the work of Harry Hess and of crews aboard the ships *Glomar Challenger* and *JOIDES Resolution.* L2 LS

Geography Have students find out about the geologic history of Iceland. Have them concentrate on the rifting of the island and its relationship to the Mid-Atlantic Ridge. L2

PLAN THE EXPERIMENT

1. As a group, agree upon and write out your hypothesis statement.
2. As a group, list the steps needed to test your hypothesis. Be very specific, describing exactly what your group will do at each step.
3. Make a list of the materials that your group will need to make your model and complete your experiment.
4. Determine how to make your model of seafloor spreading.
5. Determine how your model will demonstrate magnetic clues from the ocean floor.

Check the Plan

1. Read over your entire experiment to make sure that all steps are in a logical order.
2. Using the illustration provided as an example, determine whether the plan for your model will be able to demonstrate seafloor spreading.
3. Will you use the small magnetic compasses to demonstrate how magnetic clues, including alternating directions of magnetic north, indicate seafloor spreading?
4. How will you use the paper to demonstrate seafloor spreading?
5. *Make sure your teacher approves your plan before you proceed.*

DO THE EXPERIMENT

1. Carry out the experiment as planned and construct your model.
2. While constructing your model, write down in your Science Journal any observations that you or other members of your group make.
3. Demonstrate how your model uses magnetic clues, such as those caused by alternating directions of magnetic north, to support the theory of seafloor spreading.

Analyze and Apply

1. When you have developed your model, **compare** your ideas with those of other groups of students in your class.
2. You may wish to **modify** your model to incorporate ideas that other teams are successfully using.
3. Where are the "oldest" marks on the strip of paper?
4. On the seafloor, is the youngest rock near or far from the mid-ocean ridges?

Go Further

Does your model support the concept of seafloor spreading? Explain the role of the bar magnets in your model. What do they represent? Explain how flipping the model's bar magnets is a model of the behavior of Earth's magnetic field.

7. Manipulate the model to show how alternating magnetic alignment (magnetic reversals) in rocks supports seafloor spreading.

Teaching Strategies

Tying to Previous Knowledge Help students recall that plates in Earth's lithosphere move. Evidence of movement can be found in the magnetic orientation of rocks on both sides of the mid-ocean ridges. As new rocks continually form at mid-ocean ridges, an ongoing record of Earth's magnetic field is preserved. Older rocks are further from the ridge.

DO THE EXPERIMENT

Expected Outcome

If students develop trouble during the model manipulation, suggest that each time the strip of paper is moved outward, four steps must be completed: (1) the new edges of the ridge must be traced with straight lines; (2) the compasses must be placed back at the edges of the ridge; (3) the magnet must be turned 180°; and (4) new arrows showing how the compasses point must be drawn.

Analyze and Apply

1. Comparisons should provide opportunities for discussion.
2. Encourage students to modify and improve on their designs.
3. The oldest marks on the strip of paper are by its edges.
4. On the seafloor, the youngest rock is nearest the mid-ocean ridges, where new seafloor is almost constantly produced.

Go Further

- No, the model merely provides a way to demonstrate evidence in support of seafloor spreading.
- The bar magnets represent Earth's magnetic field.
- Throughout geologic time, Earth's magnetic field has reversed. Flipping the bar magnets mimics this behavior.

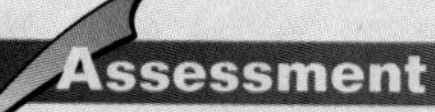

Assessment

Performance To further assess students' abilities to model concepts in plate tectonics, give them hypothetical continents and bits of evidence. Have students reconstruct a hypothetical Pangaea from the evidence you present. Use the Performance Task Assessment List for Model in **PASC**, p. 51. P

Section 11•3

Prepare

Section Background

- The Rio Grande Rift, which runs from Colorado through New Mexico and into Texas, is concealed under sediment and basalt. The rift is widening due to surrounding plate movements.
- Rocks in Alaska's Wrangell Mountains were formed on the floor of the Pacific Ocean, 9600 km away from their present location. These rocks and others in Alaska are thought to have been "scraped off" oceanic plates as the plates were subducted into the asthenosphere.
- The Red Sea formed due to divergence along a triple junction, which includes the Great Rift Valley in Africa and the Gulf of Aden.

Preplanning

- To prepare for the MiniLAB, obtain a clear casserole dish and food coloring for each group of students.
- To prepare for Activity 11-2, obtain several metric rulers.

1 Motivate

Bellringer

Before presenting the lesson, display **Section Focus Transparency 43** on the overhead projector. Assign the accompanying **Focus Activity** worksheet. L1 LEP

Tying to Previous Knowledge

Have students recall some of the recent earthquakes around the world. Plot the locations of the quakes on a map. Then, use the map to show that most earthquakes occur in specific areas.

11•3 Theory of Plate Tectonics

Science Words

plate tectonics
plate
lithosphere
asthenosphere
divergent boundary
convergent boundary
subduction zone
transform fault
convection current

Objectives

- Compare and contrast divergent, convergent, and transform plate boundaries.
- Describe how convection currents might be the cause of plate tectonics.
- Describe the effects of plate tectonics found at each type of boundary.

Plate Tectonics

With the discovery of seafloor spreading, scientists began to understand what was happening to Earth's crust and upper mantle. The idea of seafloor spreading showed that more than just continents were moving, as Wegener had thought. It was now evident to scientists that sections of the seafloor and continents move around in relation to one another.

Plate Movements

By 1968, scientists had developed a new theory that combined the main ideas of continental drift and seafloor spreading. The theory of **plate tectonics** states that Earth's crust and upper mantle are broken into sections. These sections, called **plates,** move around on the mantle. The plates can be thought of as rafts that float and move around on the mantle.

Composition of Earth's Plates

Plates are composed of the crust and a part of the upper mantle, as seen in **Figure 11-8.** These two parts together are called the **lithosphere** (LITH uh sfihr). This rigid layer is about 100 km thick and is less dense than material underneath. The plasticlike layer below the lithosphere is called the **asthenosphere** (as THEN uh sfihr). The less-dense plates of the lithosphere "float" and move around on the denser asthenosphere. The interaction of the plates on the asthenosphere is similar to

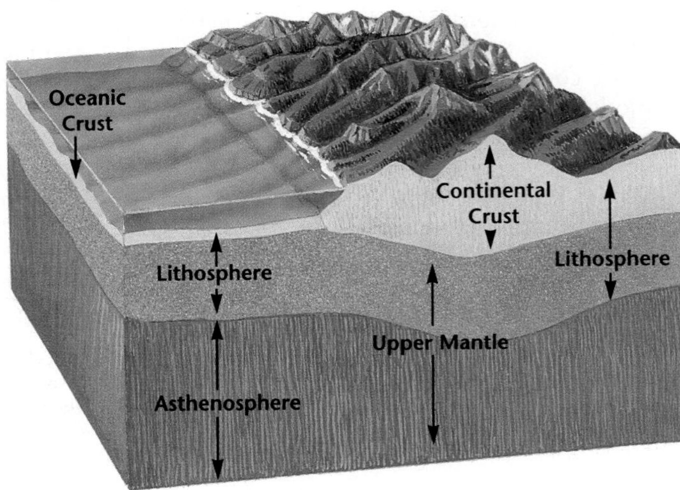

Figure 11-8
Plates of the lithosphere are carried along by convection currents within Earth's asthenosphere.

Program Resources

Reproducible Masters
Study Guide, p. 47 L1
Reinforcement, p. 47 L1
Enrichment, p. 47 L3
Activity Worksheets, pp. 5, 68-69, 71 L1
Concept Mapping, p. 27
Multicultural Connections, pp. 25-26

Transparencies
Section Focus Transparency 43 L1
Teaching Transparencies 21 and **22**

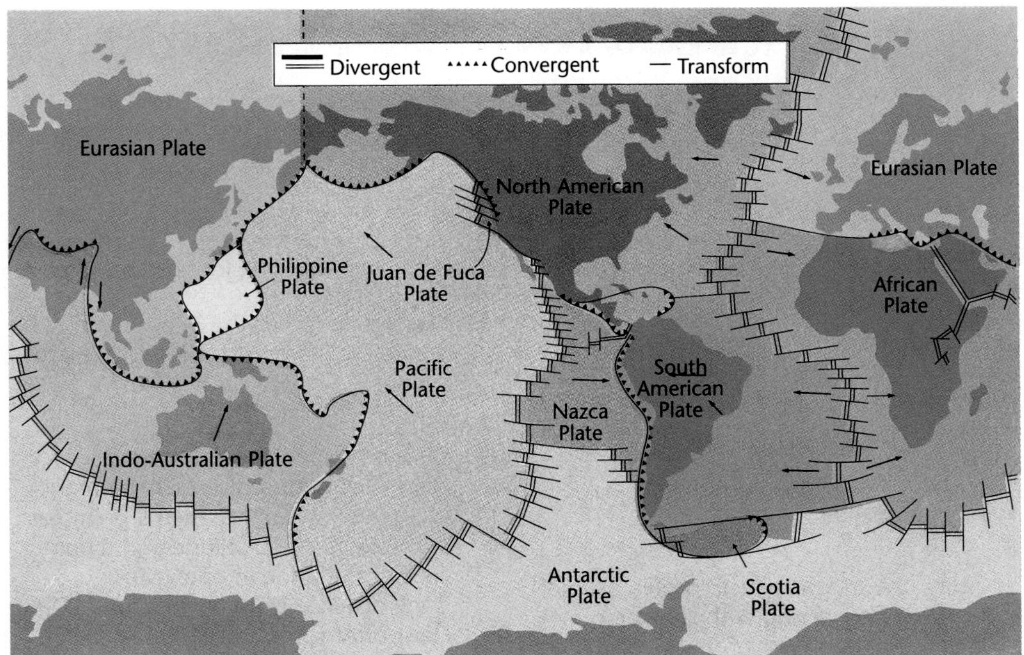

Figure 11-9

This diagram shows the major plates of the lithosphere, their direction of movement, and the type of boundary between them. *Based on what is shown in this figure, what is happening to the Nazca Plate where it meets the South American Plate?*

that of large, flat stones when they are placed in clay. By applying force, you can push the stones through the clay.

Plate Boundaries

What happens when plates move? They can interact in three ways. They can move toward each other and collide, they can pull apart, or they can simply move past one another. When the plates interact, the result of their movement is seen at the plate boundaries, as in **Figure 11-9.** Movement along any plate boundary requires that adjustments be made at the other boundaries. What is happening to the Atlantic Ocean between the North American and African plates? Compare this with what is happening along the western margin of South America.

Divergent Boundaries

The boundary between two plates that are moving apart from one another is called a **divergent boundary.** You learned about divergent boundaries when you read about seafloor spreading. In the Atlantic Ocean, the North American Plate is moving away from the Eurasian and the African plates, as seen in **Figure 11-9.** That divergent boundary is called the Mid-Atlantic Ridge. The Great Rift Valley in eastern Africa is another example of a divergent plate boundary. Here, a valley has formed where two continental plates are separating.

Across the Curriculum

Language Arts Inform students that many scientists other than Alfred Wegener and Harry Hess contributed ideas that led to plate tectonics. Some of them include A.L. Du Toit, S.K. Runcorn, Bruce Heezen, Arthur Holmes, J. Tuzo Wilson, Jack Oliver, Lynn R. Sykes, Fred Vine, D.H. Matthews, L.W. Morley, Robert Dietz, Allan Cox, Richard Doell, and Brent Dalrymple. Ask the librarian from your community library to visit class and bring books on plate tectonics in which students could read about contributions made by these scientists.

2 Teach

Teacher F.Y.I.

The rate at which Earth's plates move is about the same as the rate at which your fingernails grow.

Visual Learning

Figure 11-9 Based on what is shown, what is happening to the Nazca Plate where it meets the South American Plate? *It is descending beneath the South American Plate in a subduction zone.* LEP LS

Activity

LS **Visual-Spatial** Show students a topographic map of the ocean floor, which is available from the National Geographic Society. Have students determine locations on the map where subduction is probably occurring. Have them also locate divergent plate boundaries.

Inquiry Questions

After students have read about divergent and convergent boundaries, pose these questions. **What is a divergent boundary?** *a boundary where two plates move apart from each other* **Name two divergent boundaries.** *the Mid-Atlantic Ridge and the Great Rift Valley* **What happens when an oceanic plate collides with a continental plate?** *The denser oceanic plate sinks under the continental plate.* L1 COOP LEARN

Purpose

LS **Logical-Mathematical** Interpret rock polarity data to determine the rate of seafloor spreading. L1 COOP LEARN

Process Skills
communicating, sequencing, making and using tables, predicting, observing and inferring, measuring in SI, using numbers, interpreting data

Time
50-60 minutes

Activity Worksheets, pp. 5, 68-69

Troubleshooting In Step 6, make sure students use the normal polarity average for distance.

- The rate of spreading shown by the data is about 2.5 cm/yr. Divergence at some mid-ocean ridges is occurring at rates of up to 6.0 cm/yr.

Answers to Questions

1. Rocks nearest the ridge are younger than rocks farther from the ridge.
2. The peaks and valleys on the graph correspond to the pattern of reversing arrows on the strip of paper constructed in Activity 11-1.
3. The line should be about 2.5 cm long. This is determined by adding the rates of movement on each side of the mid-ocean ridge.
4. About 300 million years ago, assuming a relatively constant rate of spreading.
5. When this position in Africa was located near the Mid-Atlantic Ridge, South America, North America, and Europe were also located near the Mid-Atlantic Ridge. All four continents would have been close to each other. These data support the idea of Pangaea.

Activity 11-2 Seafloor Spreading Rates

So far, you've learned a lot about seafloor spreading, magnetic reversals, and plate tectonics. How can you use your knowledge to reconstruct Pangaea? Try this activity to see how you can determine where a continent may have been located in the past.

Problem

Can magnetic clues, such as magnetic field reversals on Earth, be used to help reconstruct Pangaea?

Materials

- metric ruler
- pencil

Procedure

1. Study the magnetic field profile below. You will be working with six major peaks east and west of the Mid-Atlantic Ridge for both normal and reversed polarity.
2. Place the ruler through the first peak west of the main rift. Determine and record the distance in kilometers to the Mid-Atlantic Ridge.
3. Repeat step 2 for each of the six major peaks east and west of the main rift, for both normal and reversed polarity.
4. Find the average distance from peak to ridge for each pair of corresponding peaks on either side of the ridge. Record these values.
5. Use the normal polarity readings to find the age of the rocks at each average distance.
6. Using normal polarity readings, calculate the rate of movement in cm/year. Use the formula *distance = rate × time* to calculate the rate. You must convert kilometers to centimeters.

Analyze

1. Compare the age of the igneous rock found near the mid-ocean ridge with that of the igneous rock found farther away from the ridge.
2. In what way does the information shown on the graph relate to the procedure in Activity 11-1?

Conclude and Apply

3. On your paper, **draw** a line that represents the amount of total movement that would occur between a point east of the Mid-Atlantic Ridge and a point west of the ridge in one year.
4. If the distance from a point on the coast of Africa to the Mid-Atlantic Ridge is approximately 2400 km, **calculate** how long ago that point in Africa was at or near the mid-ocean ridge.
5. Using the data you have recorded, **determine** the position of Africa in relation to other continents when the point in Africa mentioned in step 4 was at or near the mid-ocean ridge.

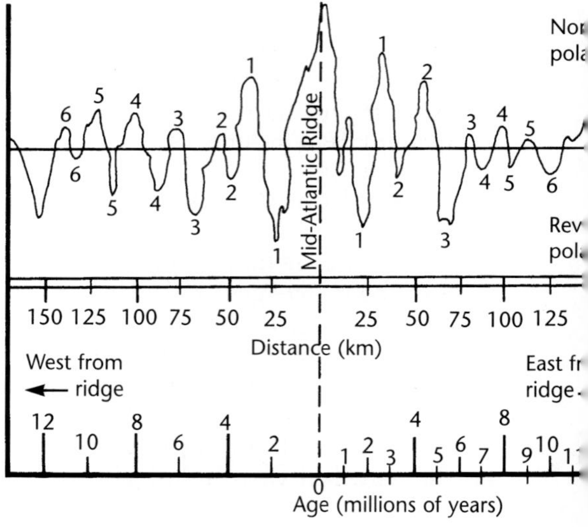

Assessment

Performance To further assess students' understanding of seafloor spreading, have them measure the distance between a point on the eastern coast of the United States and the mid-ocean ridge. Have students determine how long ago that point was near the mid-ocean ridge. Use the Performance Task Assessment List for Using Math in Science in **PASC**, p. 29. P

Sample Data

Peak	1	2	3	4	5	6
Distance west normal polarity	40	60	75	100	120	140
Distance east normal polarity	36	60	80	100	118	145
Average distance	38	60	78	100	119	142
Distance west reversed polarity	25	50	65	88	113	130
Distance east reversed polarity	23	45	70	88	105	125
Average distance	24	48	68	88	109	128
Age from scale (millions of years)	3.5	4.5	6.7	8.0	9.0	10.5
Rate of movement (cm/year)	1.1	1.2	1.2	1.3	1.3	1.4

Convergent Boundaries

If new crust is being added at one location, why doesn't Earth's crust keep getting thicker? As new crust is added in one place, it disappears at another. The disappearance of crust can occur when seafloor cools, becomes denser, and sinks, or where two plates collide at a **convergent boundary.**

There are three types of convergent boundaries. When an ocean-floor plate collides with a less-dense continental plate, the denser ocean plate sinks under the continental plate. The area where an oceanic plate descends into the upper mantle is called a **subduction zone.** Volcanoes occur above subduction zones.

Figure 11-10 on page 308 shows how this type of convergent boundary creates a deep-sea trench where one plate is subducting under the other. High temperatures and pressures cause the subducted plate to melt as it descends under the other plate. The newly formed magma is forced upward along these plate boundaries, forming volcanic mountains. The Andes Mountains of South America contain many volcanoes. They were formed at the convergent boundary of the Nazca and the South American plates.

The Fit Isn't Perfect

Recall the Explore Activity you performed at the beginning of this chapter. While you were trying to fit pieces of a cut-up photograph together, what clues did you use?

Take an old map of the world and cut out each of the continents. Lay them out on a tabletop and try to fit them together, using techniques you used in the Explore Activity. You will find that the pieces of your Earth puzzle, the continents, do not fit together very well. Yet several of the areas on some continents fit together extremely well.

Solve the Problem:

If you have ever worked on a puzzle, you have probably used scientific methods to solve the puzzle. With each piece, you look at its general shape and specific hints on its surface that help you find where the piece fits into the puzzle. In this activity, you will find out how continents can be thought of as pieces of a much larger puzzle. And, how their shapes can be used to show how they are related.

1. **Take out another old map, one that shows the continental shelves as well as the continents.**
2. **Cut the continents out of the second map including the continental shelves.**

Think Critically:

When the continents are pieced together with the continental shelves attached, almost all of them fit together well. Why did this slight change of including the continental shelves solve the problem dealing with how the continents fit together? What is true about the continental shelves that indicates they should be included with maps of the continents?

Problem Solving

Solve the Problem

Include the continental shelves with the continents in the cutout pieces. This should help the continents fit together much better.

Think Critically

The continental shelves are part of the continents. The present-day coastlines are the result of the modern sea level and do not represent a plate boundary.

Demonstration

Obtain a piece of flexible foam padding about 8 cm thick. Cut the foam in half to form two "plates." Apply compressional force to demonstrate the folding that occurs when two continental plates converge. Also demonstrate the process of subduction that occurs when an oceanic plate and a continental plate converge. LEP

 Videodisc

STV: Restless Earth

Rifting, Great Rift Valley; Africa

52299

Folded rock and monastery; Himalaya

52263

San Andreas Fault; California

52169

Across the Curriculum

Language Arts Have students use dictionaries to define the terms *diverge* and *converge.* Once they have found the definitions of these terms, ask the following questions. **Why is the Mid-Atlantic Ridge classified as a divergent plate boundary?** *The seafloor is spreading apart at the Mid-Atlantic Ridge.* **What kinds of landforms result from the collision of two plates?** *Volcanic mountains form when oceanic and continental plates converge. Volcanic island arcs form where two oceanic plates converge. Folded mountain ranges develop when two continental plates converge.*

Visual Learning

Figure 11-10 After students study **Figure 11-10**, select three volunteers to illustrate the different types of convergent boundaries on the chalkboard, on the overhead projector, or on poster paper. Ask other students to do the same with divergent plate boundaries. LEP LS

Videodisc

STV: Restless Earth

Geologist measuring plate movement

52171

Scientist studying movement along fissure

52297

GLENCOE TECHNOLOGY

Videodisc

Glencoe Earth Science Interactive Videodisc

Side 1, Lesson 4

Crustal Plates and Volcanoes

43091-46345

Subduction Zones

50389-51913

Ocean-Ocean Collisions

The second type of convergent boundary occurs when two ocean plates collide, or when seafloor that has become denser due to cooling begins to sink. Whether caused by two ocean plates colliding or by the sinking of denser seafloor, one plate bends and slides under the other, forming a subduction zone as shown in **Figure 11-10C.** A deep-sea trench is formed, and the new magma that is produced rises to form an island arc of volcanoes. The islands of Japan are volcanic island arcs formed when two oceanic plates collided.

The third type of convergent boundary occurs when two continental plates collide. Because both of these plates are less dense than the material in the asthenosphere, usually no subduction occurs. The two plates just collide and crumple up,

Figure 11-10

As Earth's plates pull apart at some boundaries, they collide at others, forming mountains and volcanoes.

(A) As one continental plate converges with another, subduction stops and mountains are formed.

(B) Where continental lithospheric plates are pulled apart at divergent boundaries, a rift valley forms. If the rift valley separates further, it may flood and become an ocean.

(C) As an oceanic plate converges with a less-dense continental plate, the continental plate is forced upward and the oceanic plate slides under it at a subduction zone. As the oceanic plate slides into the subduction zone, it starts to melt. The melted rock is less dense than surrounding rock and is forced upward, forming volcanoes.

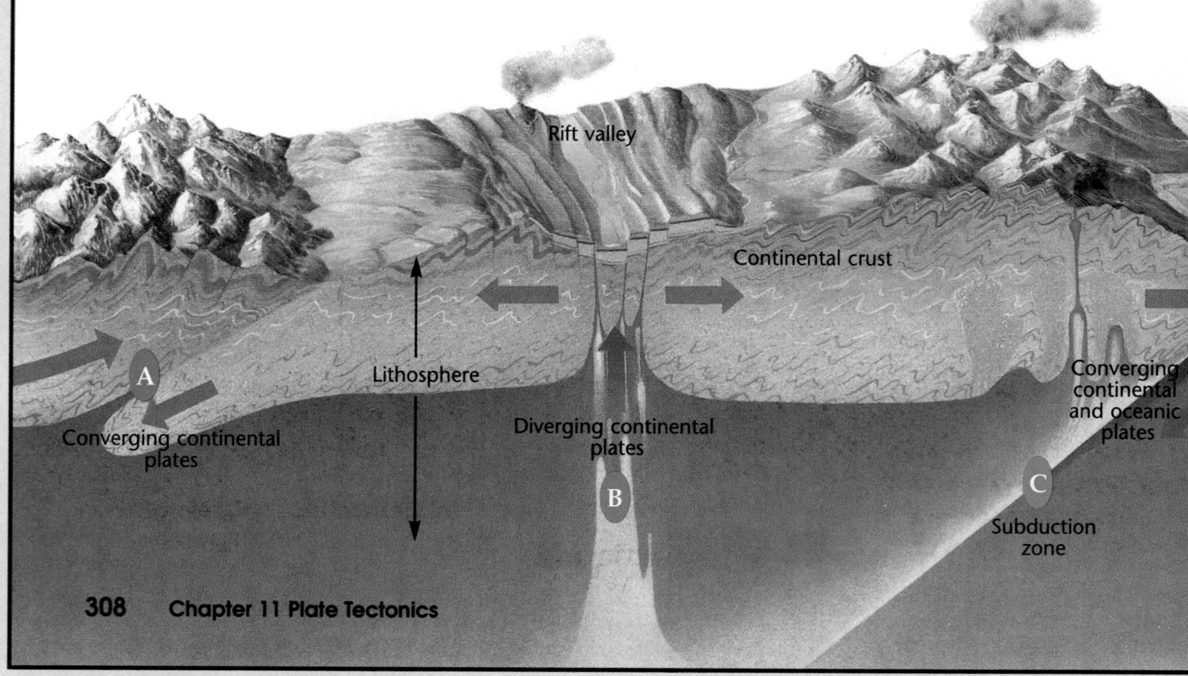

Cultural Diversity

Masai The Great Rift Valley extends through eastern Africa, creating a canyon more than 80 km wide. Along this rift valley, seminomadic pastoralists, the Masai, make their living. The focus of Masai life is cattle. Meat is not a normal part of the diet, as the Masai do not hunt. They believe it a sacrilege to break the earth, so they do not farm. They live from the produce of their herds, moving from one grazing land to another. Four to eight families and cattle live within a *kraal,* a circular area enclosed by a thornbush fence. The main organizing factor for Masai society is age sets. For example, each Masai male moves, with his age set, through a series of grades (including warrior grades) each lasting about 15 years. As one ages, one eventually becomes an elder who can make decisions for the tribe.

forming mountain ranges. Earthquakes are common at these convergent boundaries. The Himalayan Mountains in Asia were formed when the Indo-Australian Plate crashed into the Eurasian Plate.

Transform Fault Boundaries

The third type of plate boundary occurs at a **transform fault.** Transform faults occur when two plates slide past one another and are moving either in opposite directions or in the same direction at different rates. As one plate slides past another, earthquakes occur. The Pacific Plate is sliding past the North American Plate, forming the famous San Andreas Fault, as seen in **Figure 11-11** on the next page. The San Andreas Fault is a transform-fault plate boundary. It has been the site of many earthquakes.

D A mid-ocean ridge forms whenever diverging plates continue to separate after being flooded. As the rising magma cools, it forms new ocean crust.

E A subduction zone forms whenever two oceanic plates collide or one oceanic plate that has become denser due to cooling begins to sink under another. Volcanic island arcs form above the subduction zone, as the descending plate reaches depths where melting occurs.

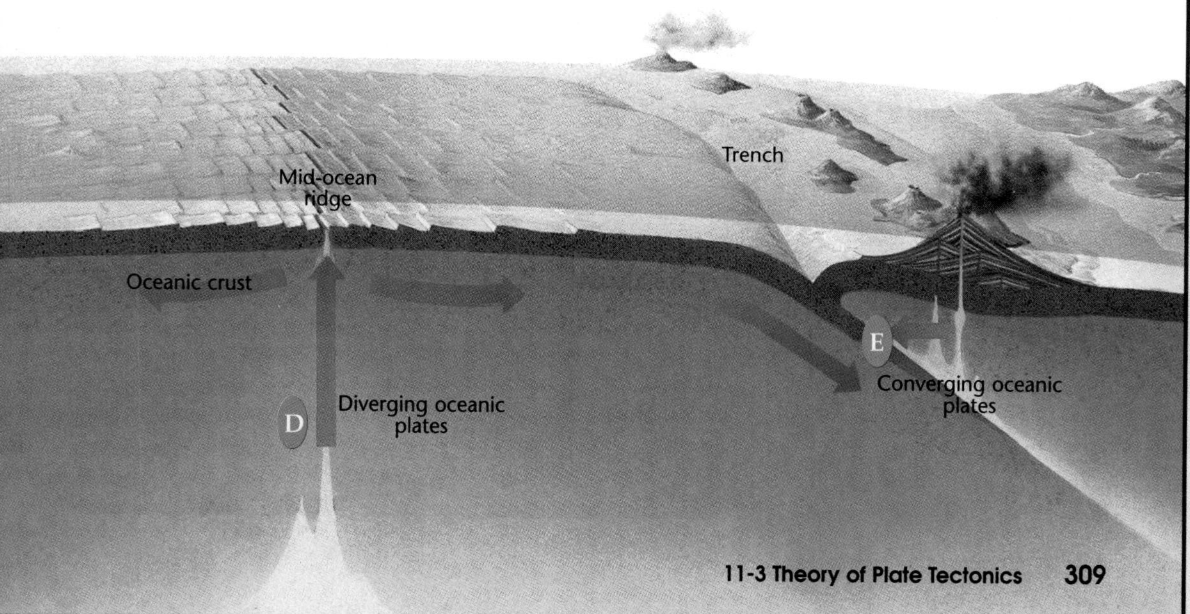

Teacher F.Y.I.

- Creepmeters, lasers, and geostationary satellites are used to measure plate movement.
- The Pacific and North American Plates, sliding past each other along the San Andreas Fault, each move an average of about 5 cm per year.

Revealing Preconceptions

Ask students to stand perfectly still. Then ask them whether or not they are moving. Explain that Earth movements such as rotation, revolution, and plate movements are not felt by humans. Have students find out the velocities at which each of the processes mentioned occurs.

STV: Restless Earth

Pangaea, 225 million years ago

52176

Pangaea, 125 million years ago

52177

Pangaea, 65 million years ago

52178

Integrating the Sciences

Physics Thermal energy is transferred from one place to another by three methods. One of these, *convection,* is thought to provide the energy needed to power the movement of Earth's plates. Ask students to research energy transfer by convection currents and then have them answer the following. **Describe the driving mechanism of Earth's plates.** *Hot, plasticlike material in the asthenosphere is forced upward toward the lithosphere. When the hot material reaches the lithosphere, it moves laterally and carries Earth's plates. As the material cools, it sinks. These huge convection currents in the mantle are the driving force of plate tectonics.* L2

MiniLAB

Purpose

LS **Visual-Spatial** Students will observe convection currents and infer what causes them to form. L1

LEP COOP LEARN

Materials

food coloring; water; thermal mitts; clear, colorless glass container; hot plate

Teaching Strategies

Safety Precautions Have students wear thermal mitts to protect their hands.

Troubleshooting If students experience difficulty observing convection currents, instruct them to drop the food coloring into the water soon after turning on the hot plate.

Analysis

1. Answers will vary.
2. Transfer of energy and the resulting density differences cause convection currents.
3. One possible solution is to begin heating the water only on one side.

Assessment

Oral To further assess students' understanding of convection currents, have them observe a heated pan of noodle soup. Ask students to explain what is happening. Use the Performance Task Assessment List for Making Observations and Inferences in **PASC**, p. 17. P

Activity Worksheets, pp. 5, 71

MiniLAB

How do convection currents form?

Procedure 

1. Fill a clear, colorless casserole dish with water to 5 cm from the top.
2. Center the dish on a hot plate and heat. **CAUTION:** *Wear thermal mitts to protect your hands.*
3. Add a few drops of food coloring to the water directly above the hot plate.
4. Observe what occurs in the water.
5. In your Science Journal, describe what you observe. If possible, make an illustration of what you observe.

Analysis

1. Determine whether any currents form in the water.
2. If so, infer what causes the currents to form.
3. If not, determine how to change the experiment in order to cause currents to form.
4. After receiving permission from your teacher, try to redesign the experiment and check to see if currents form.

Causes of Plate Tectonics

There have been many new discoveries about Earth's crust since Wegener's day. But one question still remains. What causes the plates to move and the seafloor to spread? Scientists now think they have a pretty good idea. They think that plates are moved by the same basic process that is used to heat some buildings.

Convection Currents

In a forced air heating system, air is warmed in the furnace and a blower forces it into each room of the building. The air is forced upward from the register and releases its heat to surrounding air. The cooler air, which is more dense, sinks to the floor of the room. It returns to the furnace, through the cold air return, to be reheated. This entire cycle of heating, rising, cooling, and sinking is called a **convection current.** This same process occurring in the mantle is thought to be the force behind plate tectonics.

Scientists believe that differences in density cause hot, plasticlike rock in the asthenosphere to be forced upward toward the surface. When this plasticlike rock reaches Earth's lithosphere, it moves horizontally and carries plates of the lithosphere with it, as described earlier. As it cools, the plasticlike rock becomes denser. It then sinks into the mantle, taking overlying crust with it.

These huge convection cells provide the energy to move plates in the lithosphere, as shown in **Figure 11-12.** They are also the cause of many of Earth's surface features.

Figure 11-11

The San Andreas Fault forms a transform-fault boundary where the Pacific Plate is sliding past the North American Plate.

A This photograph shows an aerial view of the San Andreas Fault.

Theme Connection

Energy Convection currents transfer energy from one location to another. Energy from inside Earth is transferred to other locations within Earth by this process. The concept of convection currents being the mechanism to power plate tectonics reaffirms the theme of *energy* for this chapter.

 Use **Teaching Transparencies 21** and **22** as you teach this lesson.

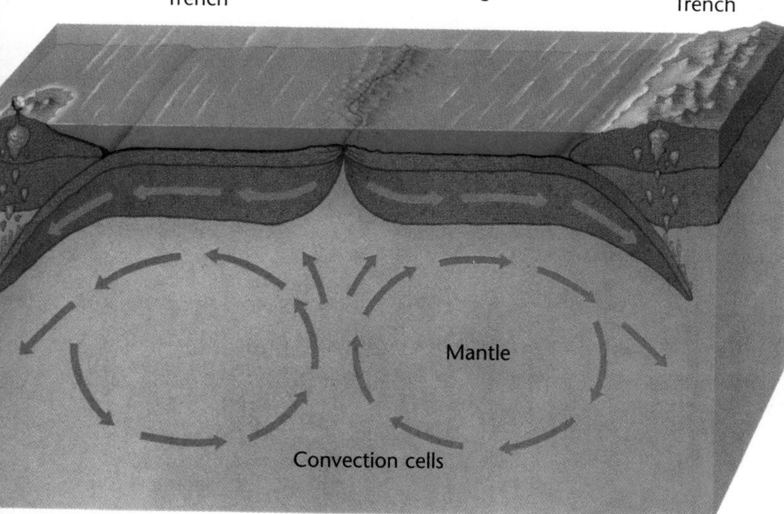

Figure 11-12

Pictured is one theory of how convection currents (see arrows) are the driving force of plate tectonics. In this theory, convection is limited to the upper mantle only. In another theory, convection currents occur throughout the mantle. In yet another, convection is confined to hot plumes being forced upward from near the core.

Effects of Plate Tectonics

Many of the landforms caused by plate tectonics are shown and described in **Figure 11-10** on pages 308-309. As you can see, many different landforms are caused by plate tectonics. However, the main effects of plate tectonics are volcanoes and earthquakes. Earth is a dynamic planet with convection currents inside that power the movement of plates. As the plates move, they interact. The interaction of plates produces forces that build mountains, rift ocean basins, and cause volcanoes and earthquakes.

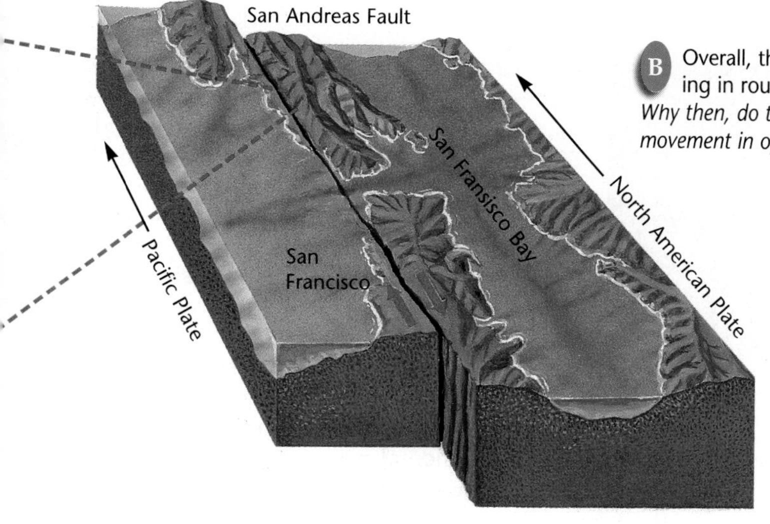

B Overall, the two plates are moving in roughly the same direction. *Why then, do the red arrows show movement in opposite directions?*

Activity

LS **Interpersonal** Form four groups and assign each group one of the following topics to master and present to the class: convergent boundaries, divergent boundaries, transform fault boundaries, and the driving mechanism of plate tectonics. L1 COOP LEARN

Visual Learning

Figure 11-11 San Andreas Fault — Why do the red arrows show movement in opposite directions? *The western side (Pacific Plate) of the fault is moving faster than the eastern side (North American Plate).* LEP LS

Inquiry Question

Earthquakes are associated with some plate boundaries. Why do you think this is so? *Much force is involved with plate movements. As plates collide or slide past one another, pressure is released as earthquakes.*

Videodisc

STV: Restless Earth

Translation in California

Unit 4, Side 2

San Andreas Fault

00001-01776

San Francisco

01885-03955

Life on the Fault Line

03974-08400

Inclusion Strategies

Learning Disabled Have students place a piece of long, plastic tubing into the neck of a strong balloon and secure the tube so no air can escape from the balloon. Have them place the balloon at the bottom of an aquarium tank, with the tubing extending over the top. Add a layer of moist sand and then a layer of dry sand, each about 2 mm deep. Alternate layers several times. Have a student blow up the balloon slowly until the sand begins to crack to simulate an earthquake.

Gifted Gifted students may take this simulation one step further. Have those students build a model city on the top of the sand. A student can videotape the "earthquake" and students can prepare a documentary showing how the quake affected the "city." L3

Visual Learning

Figure 11-13 **What type of force occurs when Earth's crust is pulled in opposite directions?** *tension* LEP LS

CONNECT TO

PHYSICS

Answer

Convergent boundary forces applied: → ←
Divergent boundary forces applied: ← →
Transform fault boundary forces applied: ↑↓

3 Assess

Check for Understanding

FLEX Your Brain

Use the Flex Your Brain activity to help students explore PLATE TECTONICS.

Activity Worksheets, p. 5

Reteach

Using a supermarket conveyor belt as an analogy, explain how Earth's plates move.

Extension

For students who have mastered this section, use the **Reinforcement** and **Enrichment** masters.

Figure 11-13

Fault-block mountains can form when Earth's crust is stretched by tectonic forces. *What type of force occurs when Earth's crust is pulled in opposite directions?*

Fault-block mountains

Collapse of crust

Faults and Rift Valleys

Tension forces associated with diverging plates tend to stretch Earth's crust, causing fault blocks to tilt or slide down and form fault-block mountains, as shown in **Figure 11-13.** Generally, the faults that form from tension are normal faults. Once the divergence causes a separation, rift valleys can form. Examples of rift valleys are the Great Rift Valley in Africa, shown in **Figure 11-14,** and the valleys that occur in the middle of mid-ocean ridges, which are mountains that form on either side of rift valleys. Examples include the Mid-Atlantic Ridge and the East Pacific Rise.

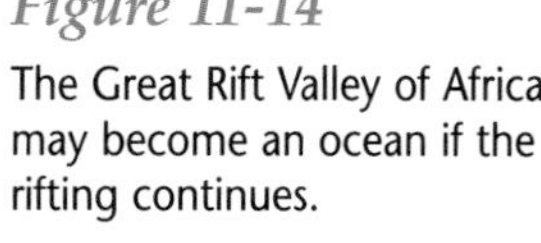

Figure 11-14

The Great Rift Valley of Africa may become an ocean if the rifting continues.

Mountains, Arcs, and Volcanoes

Compression forces produce several effects that can take place when plates converge. If the converging plates are both continental, the forces generated cause massive folding of rock layers into mountain ranges such as the Himalayan Mountains or the greatly eroded Appalachian Mountains, shown in **Figure 11-15.** Reverse faults may also occur if the forces are great enough. If the two converging plates are oceanic plates, one plate slides under the other and island arcs and volcanoes form. If an oceanic plate converges on a continental plate, the oceanic plate slides under the continental plate, melting occurs, and volcanoes form. Entire mountain ranges can form at this type of convergent boundary.

Integrating the Sciences

Meteorology/Oceanography Inform students that convection currents play a role in circulation and the transfer of energy in other Earth systems. Convection currents transfer energy within the atmosphere. Density currents within Earth's oceans are also caused by convection currents. Have students study books on meteorology and oceanography to find other examples of convection currents. L2

Strike-Slip Faults

If one plate is sliding past another, the forces are not directly opposite. The plates stick and then slide along massive strike-slip faults. One such example is the San Andreas Fault. When plates move suddenly, vibrations are generated inside Earth that are felt as an earthquake. Plate tectonics explains how activity inside Earth can affect Earth's crust differently in different locations. We have seen how plates have moved since Pangaea separated. What was Earth like before that?

CONNECT TO PHYSICS

In what directions are forces applied at convergent, divergent, and transform fault boundaries? ***Demonstrate*** these forces using wooden blocks or your hands.

Figure 11-15

Satellite photo of Valley and Ridge Province in the Appalachian Mountains.

Section Wrap-up

Review

1. What happens to plates at a transform fault boundary?
2. What occurs at plate boundaries associated with seafloor spreading?
3. Think Critically: Using **Figure 11-9** and Appendix G, determine what natural disasters might be likely to occur in Iceland.

Skill Builder

Recognizing Cause and Effect

What causes a divergent boundary to form? What is the effect of collision on the edges of continental plates? Answer these questions, then write a cause-and-effect statement explaining the relationship between convection currents and plate movement. If you need help, refer to Recognizing Cause and Effect in the **Skill Handbook.**

Science Journal

Research the 1992 Landers, California earthquake. In your Science Journal write a brief summary explaining why this earthquake is so important to the study of plate tectonics and plate boundaries.

4 Close

•MINI•QUIZ•

Use the Mini Quiz to check students' recall of chapter content.

1. **Boundaries along which plates are moving apart are ______ boundaries.** *divergent*
2. **A(n) ______ forms when an oceanic plate collides with a continental plate.** *subduction zone*
3. **Subduction usually doesn't occur when two ______ plates converge.** *continental*
4. **A(n) ______ ______ is a plate boundary where two plates slide past each other.** *transform fault*
5. **________ ________ are thought to provide the energy to move Earth's plates.** *Convection currents*

Section Wrap-up

Review

1. Plates slide past one another.
2. Plates of the lithosphere diverge.
3. Think Critically Iceland is a portion of the Mid-Atlantic Ridge, which is a site of volcanic activity and earthquakes associated with their activity.

Science Journal

The largest earthquake to hit California in 40 years may have triggered other earthquakes and may indicate that a new fault is being born in the desert. The plate boundary between the Pacific Plate and the North American Plate may be shifting eastward.

Skill Builder

Differences in density force hot rock material upward, causing a diverging boundary. When continental plates collide, the pressure causes the edges to buckle and fold, forming mountains. Convection currents in the mantle transfer energy, which causes the overlying plates to move.

Assessment

Performance Assess students' abilities to recognize cause-and-effect relationships by having students write a cause-and-effect statement explaining seafloor spreading and volcanic activity in the middle of oceans. Use the Performance Task Assessment List for Writing in Science in **PASC,** p. 87. P

Prepare

Section Background

In science, theories are constantly changing. When research provides information that does not fit with accepted theories, they must change or new theories must be devised. The concept of Rodinia is one such example.

1 Motivate

Bellringer

Before presenting the lesson, display **Section Focus Transparency 44** on the overhead projector. Assign the accompanying **Focus Activity** worksheet. L1 LEP

Tying to Previous Knowledge

Help students recall movements of the continents that are thought to have occurred since the breakup of Pangaea.

2 Teach

Teacher F.Y.I.

Clues from volcanic rocks and early Paleozoic fossils located in the Appalachian Mountains, the Famatinian Mountains in Argentina, and the Mozambique Mountains in Africa provide evidence that the Atlantic Ocean has opened more than once.

TECHNOLOGY: Before Pangaea, Rodinia

Objectives

- Describe evidence in support of the separation of the North American Plate from the Antarctic Plate.
- Track the North American Plate after separation from the Antarctic Plate and before the formation of Pangaea.

Antarctic Collisions

Scientists studying rock types and structures in Antarctica use computer models to show how this new evidence supports formation of a supercontinent long before Pangaea. Evidence presented in the computer model indicates that this landmass, named Rodinia, formed more than 750 million years ago.

Fossil Clues

As Rodinia broke apart, a rift valley formed in an area now occupied by the Pensacola Mountains in Antarctica. The rift deepened and rivers poured in water containing sediment. Shallow seas formed over the area of the rift. The presence of sandstone and fossils of the warm-water animal *Archaeocyatha* found in rocks dating back to the Cambrian Period suggest a separation of East Antarctica, as shown in **Figure 11-16,** from another continental landmass, probably the North American Plate, about 540 million years ago.

Quartz sandstones found in the area are full of worm burrows known as *Skolithus*. These trace fossils of ancient filter-feeders are very similar to fossils found in western North America. This supports the theory that the North American Plate was joined to the Antarctic Plate about 540 million years ago.

Figure 11-16
The Transantarctic Mountains, shown here, mark a very old plate boundary between East Antarctica and another continental plate.

Magnetic, Mountain, and Margin Clues

Whenever paleomagnetic evidence from North American and African rocks dated before the Mesozoic Era is entered into the computer model, movement of these two continents is different from that measured since Pangaea broke up. When data from volcanic rocks and early Paleozoic fossils located in the Appalachian Mountains and in mountains of Argentina and Africa are entered into the computer model, the model illustrates that the Atlantic Ocean has opened more than once and that movement of these landmasses has changed.

Program Resources

Reproducible Masters

Study Guide, p. 48 L1
Reinforcement, p. 48 L1
Enrichment, p. 48 L3
Science and Society Integration, p. 15

Transparencies

Section Focus Transparency 44 L1

The computer model now indicates that Rodinia split apart about 750 million years ago. The continental plates then moved around and came back together as Pangaea about 260 million years ago. Pangaea then split apart and the continental plates began moving to their present positions.

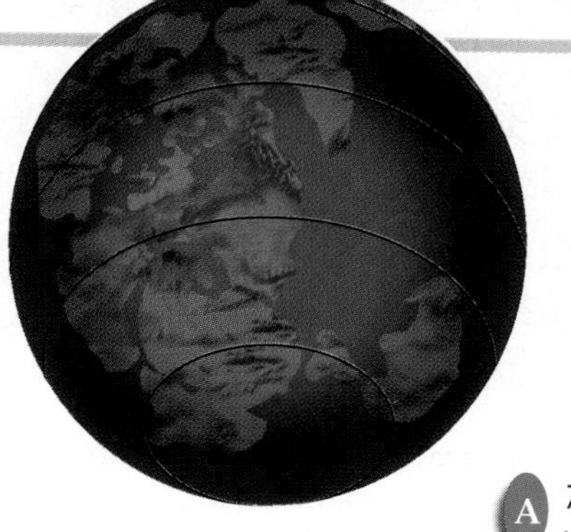

A 750 million years ago

North America on the Move

Simulations on the computer model indicate that the North American Plate broke away from East Antarctica and then moved up the western side of the South American Plate, as shown in **Figure 11-17.** During this journey the eastern side of the North American Plate evidently collided with the western side of the South American Plate several times before finally colliding with Africa in the formation of Pangaea. Each time a collision occurred, some rock containing fossils of one continent would be left on the other continent. Also, mountain ranges may have formed in this way, providing the evidence used in present-day computer simulations.

B 550 million years ago

Figure 11-17

Evidence indicates that a supercontinent, called Rodinia, existed long before Pangaea. *Why is it likely that rocks and rock formations in eastern North America are similar to rocks and rock formations found in western South America?*

Section Wrap-up

Review

1. What two continental plates were probably joined, forming the Transantarctic Mountains?
2. List two pieces of evidence supporting the theory that a supercontinent formed long before Pangaea.

Explore the Technology

A great deal of data were needed before these new ideas about an earlier supercontinent could be presented. In fact, research is still going on concerning the interpretation of the collected data. The use of computer simulations of continental movement help make this study easier to understand. Based on what you have learned and what you know about computer simulations, how do you think this process is accomplished?

SCIENCE & SOCIETY

3 Assess

Check for Understanding

FLEX Your Brain

Use the Flex Your Brain activity to help students explore ROCK CLUES IN SUPPORT OF RODINIA.

Activity Worksheets, p. 5

Reteach

Have students use the information provided on pages 314 and 315 while drawing an illustration of what Rodinia may have looked like.

Extension

For students who have mastered this section, use the **Reinforcement** and **Enrichment** masters.

4 Close

•MINI•QUIZ•

1. **_______ is the name given to the landmass that may have formed before Pangaea.** *Rodinia*
2. **Which fossil provides support for the idea that the North American Plate was joined to the Antarctic Plate about 540 million years ago?** *Skolithus*
3. **_______ evidence is evidence from the ancient magnetic properties of rocks.** *Paleomagnetic*

Visual Learning

Figure 11-17 Why is it likely that rocks and rock formations in eastern North America are similar to rocks and rock formations found in western South America? *In this interpretation, eastern North America and western South America were once joined together.* LEP IS

2. presence of quartz sandstones and warm-water fossils

Explore the Technology

Have students research other ways that computer simulation is used to study Earth.

Section Wrap-up

Review

1. the Antarctic and North American plates

People and Science

Background

- Hansen's work is part of NASA's *Magellan* project. Researchers on the project study four types of data: high-resolution black-and-white radar pictures; altimetry, or topographic data; emissivity data, which show how different surfaces reflect radar signals; and gravity data, which provide clues to processes going on inside the planet.
- Venus was chosen for study because of its similarity to Earth in size, age, and density. The *Magellan* data show that in spite of those similarities, the two planets are quite different. For example, Venus has no asthenosphere. On Earth, the asthenosphere allows the lithosphere to slide on top of the mantle.

Teaching Strategies

LS **Visual-Spatial** Show students photos of Earth and Venus taken from space. Ask them to consider what conclusions they might draw about the processes that shaped Earth if they could study the planet only from a distance. Discuss how they might develop and test models.

Career Connection

Career Path A strong background in math and all areas of science is recommended. Courses that encourage problem solving are especially valuable. So are extracurricular activities—from hiking and bird-watching to computer modeling and browsing the World Wide Web—that give students an opportunity to explore their environment and puzzle over how things work.

People and Science

VICKI HANSEN, *Associate Professor of Geological Science*

On the Job

Q What are you trying to learn about plate tectonics on Earth?

A I'm very interested in what happens at convergent boundaries, at depths deeper than where earthquakes occur (10 to 15 km). I want to know how things move in these environments deep inside Earth.

Q How can you study something that takes place so deep in Earth?

A You look at old mountain belts that preserve the deep parts of convergent boundaries. When you look at the rocks in these belts, they have beautiful patterns, because they flowed like putty when they were deep inside Earth. The patterns in those rocks are used to figure out how that part of the crust was flowing.

Q Explain how your studies of Venus led you to reject one theory and come up with another one.

A Some people proposed that deep troughs on Venus are subduction zones, as on Earth. However, the deep troughs are circular, and their shapes and fracture patterns are more easily explained by a theory in which these features are blisters in the crust, formed by hot plumes from deep inside, bubbling up. As we look at more data, this theory holds up better than a subduction theory.

Personal Insights

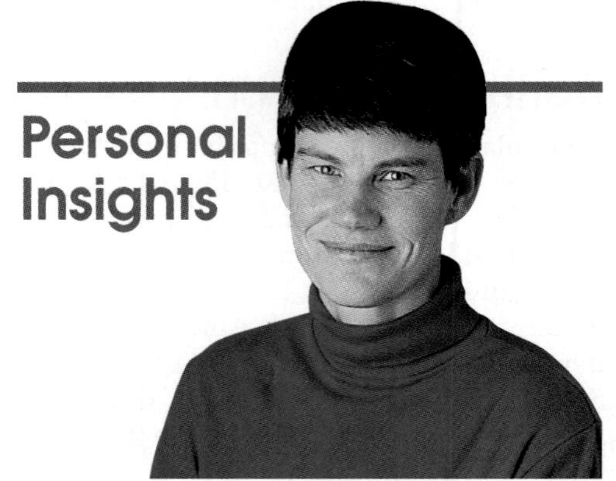

Q Your work has taken some unexpected turns. What has that taught you?

A I never expected to be studying Venus. But that allowed me to come to it with a fresh, childlike view. I think that's a very valuable thing to bring to science. A scientist is interested in puzzles, and you can't predict what shape those puzzles are going to come in. I hope in the next 10 years, I'll be working on something else I couldn't have predicted.

Career Connection

The U.S. Geological Survey has maps of Venus based on data from NASA's *Pioneer* and *Magellan* Venus orbiters. Look at one of these maps and compare the features of Venus and Earth.

Write questions about Earth you'd like the following scientists to answer:

- **Structural Geologist**
- **Seismologist**

For More Information

- *Magellan* information and images can be obtained through SPACELINK, an electronic information system especially for teachers who want to use NASA materials in their classes. Contact spacelink.msfc.nasa.gov.
- The U.S. Geological Survey has maps of Venus based on data from NASA's *Pioneer* Venus orbiter and the *Soviet Venera 15/16* missions, and is producing new maps based on *Magellan* data. Order from:

  U.S. Geological Survey
  Mail Stop 306
  Branch of Distribution
  Denver Federal Center
  P.O. Box 25286
  Denver, CO 80225
- For more information on USGS maps, contact:

  Earth Science Information Center
  U.S. Geological Survey
  507 National Center
  Reston, VA 22092

Chapter 11 Review

Summary

11-1: Continental Drift

1. The theory of continental drift states that continents have moved to their present positions on Earth.
2. The puzzlelike fit of the continents, fossils, climatic evidence, and similar rock structures support Wegener's idea of continental drift.

11-2: Seafloor Spreading

1. Seafloor spreading is the spreading apart of the seafloor at the mid-ocean ridges.
2. Seafloor spreading has been proven by magnetic evidence in rocks and in the age of rocks on the ocean floor.

11-3: Theory of Plate Tectonics

1. Plates move away from each other at divergent boundaries. Plates collide at convergent boundaries. At a transform fault, two plates move horizontally past each other.
2. Hot, plasticlike material from the mantle is forced upward to the lithosphere, moves horizontally, cools, and then sinks back into the mantle. The movement of this material sets up convection currents, the driving force of plate tectonics.
3. Convergent boundaries are the location of most mountain belts, volcanoes, and earthquakes. Mid-ocean ridges and rift zones occur at divergent boundaries. Major earthquakes occur at transform fault boundaries.

11-4: Science and Society: Before Pangaea, Rodinia

1. Fossil evidence in the Transantarctic Mountains and paleomagnetic data support this interpretation.
2. It is thought that the North American Plate broke away from an ancient supercontinent called Rodinia, moved around the other continental plates, and collided with them again to form Pangaea.

Key Science Words

a. asthenosphere
b. continental drift
c. convection current
d. convergent boundary
e. divergent boundary
f. lithosphere
g. magnetometer
h. Pangaea
i. plate tectonics
j. plates
k. seafloor spreading
l. subduction zone
m. transform fault

Reviewing Vocabulary

Match each phrase with the correct term from the list of Key Science Words.

1. instrument for studying Earth's magnetic field
2. plasticlike layer below the lithosphere
3. idea that continents moved to their current positions on Earth by plowing through the ocean floor
4. large landmass made of all continents
5. force behind plate tectonics
6. process that forms new seafloor
7. large sections of Earth's crust and upper mantle
8. boundary where plates move apart from each other
9. boundary at which plates collide
10. place where plates slide past one another

GLENCOE TECHNOLOGY

Videodisc

Glencoe Earth Science
Interactive Videodisc
Use the videodisc lesson 4, *Volcanoes: Erupting Mountains,* to review the effects of crustal movement.

MindJogger Videoquiz

Chapter 11 Have students work in groups as they play the Videoquiz game to review key chapter concepts.

Chapter 11

Review

Summary

Have students read the summary statements to review the major concepts of the chapter.

Reviewing Vocabulary

1. g	**6.** k
2. a	**7.** j
3. b	**8.** e
4. h	**9.** d
5. c	**10.** m

Assessment

Portfolio Encourage students to place in their portfolios one or two items of what they consider to be their best work. Examples include:

- Visual Learning, p. 299
- Activity 11-1 experiment design and analysis, pp. 302-303
- MiniLAB analysis, p. 310 P

Performance Additional performance assessments may be found in **Performance Assessment** and **Science Integration Activities.** Performance Task Assessment Lists and rubrics for evaluating these activities can be found in Glencoe's **Performance Assessment in the Science Classroom.**

Chapter 11 Review

Checking Concepts

Choose the word or phrase that completes the sentence.

1. Earth's asthenosphere is found in the _______.
   a. crust c. outer core
   b. mantle d. inner core
2. The San Andreas Fault is a _______.
   a. divergent boundary
   b. subduction zone
   c. convergent boundary
   d. transform fault boundary
3. The theory of _______ states that continents moved to their present positions.
   a. subduction
   b. seafloor spreading
   c. continental drift
   d. erosion
4. During the formation of Rodinia, East Antarctica is thought to have collided with the _______ Plate.
   a. South American c. Indo-Australian
   b. African d. North American
5. Evidence from _______ indicates that many continents were near Earth's South Pole.
   a. glaciers
   b. mid-ocean ridges
   c. volcanoes
   d. plates
6. _______ of iron in rocks supports the theory of seafloor spreading.
   a. Plate movement
   b. Subduction
   c. Magnetic alignment
   d. Weathering
7. The Great Rift Valley is a _______ boundary.
   a. convergent c. transform fault
   b. divergent d. lithosphere
8. The theory of _______ states that plates move around on the asthenosphere.
   a. continental drift
   b. seafloor spreading
   c. subduction
   d. plate tectonics
9. A _______ forms when a plate slides under another plate.
   a. transform fault
   b. divergent boundary
   c. subduction zone
   d. mid-ocean ridge
10. When two oceanic plates collide, _______ form.
    a. folded mountains
    b. island arcs
    c. transform faults
    d. mid-ocean ridges

Understanding Concepts

Answer the following questions in your Science Journal using complete sentences.

11. Compare and contrast continental drift and plate tectonics.
12. Why was the theory of continental drift initially not accepted by many scientists?
13. Explain the relationship between a mid-ocean ridge and seafloor spreading.
14. Compare and contrast divergent, convergent, and transform fault boundaries.
15. Explain how island arcs form.

Thinking Critically

16. Why are there few volcanoes in the Himalayas, but many earthquakes?
17. Glacial deposits often form at high latitudes near the poles. Explain why glacial deposits have been found in Africa.
18. How is magnetism used to support the theory of seafloor spreading?
19. Explain why volcanoes do not form along the San Andreas Fault.
20. Why wouldn't the fossil of an ocean fish found on two different continents be good evidence of continental drift?

Chapter 11 Review

Checking Concepts

1. b	**6.** c
2. d	**7.** b
3. c	**8.** d
4. d	**9.** c
5. a	**10.** b

Understanding Concepts

11. Both propose that the present-day continents have moved over time into their current positions. However, continental drift could not provide a mechanism for these movements. The theory of plate tectonics was derived using data from continental drift and seafloor magnetic studies.

12. Continental drift was met with opposition by certain scientists because the idea was new. Also, because Wegener could not explain how such massive bodies of rock could move, his idea was not taken seriously during his lifetime.

13. A mid-ocean ridge, which is an underground mountain chain, is the point where convection pushes the old seafloor apart, allowing magma to rise. As the magma cools, new seafloor is formed. This process of ocean floor formation is called seafloor spreading.

14. All are places where two plates, which are thick slabs of Earth's crust and upper mantle, interact. Divergent boundaries occur where plates move apart from each other. Convergent boundaries form where two plates collide. A transform fault is a boundary in which plates move horizontally past one another.

15. Island arcs form along some convergent plate boundaries. When two oceanic plates collide, magma forms as one plate subducts and melts. The magma rises and forms an island arc of volcanoes.

Thinking Critically

16. Unlike most continent-continent collisions, subduction is occurring as the Indian plate is colliding with the Eurasian plate to form the Himalayas. Because two continental plates are colliding, and the angle of subduction is shallow, there is essentially no volcanism in these mountains.

17. Africa was once located near the South Pole when all the continents were joined as a single landmass.

18. Alternating magnetic bands are symmetrical with respect to a mid-ocean ridge.

19. The San Andreas Fault is a transform fault boundary. There is no subduction along such plate boundaries; thus, there is no volcanism.

Developing Skills

If you need help, refer to the **Skill Handbook.**

21. **Hypothesizing:** Mount St. Helens in the Cascade Mountain Range is a volcano. Use **Figure 11-9** and Appendix F to hypothesize how it may have formed.
22. **Outlining:** Outline the major points in Section 11-1.
23. **Measuring in SI:** Movement along the African Rift Valley is about 2.1 cm per year. If plates continue to move apart at this rate, how large will the rift be (in meters) in 1000 years? In 15 500 years?
24. **Comparing and Contrasting:** Compare and contrast the formation of the Andes Mountains and the Himalayas, as shown below.
25. **Concept Mapping:** Make an events chain concept map that describes seafloor spreading.

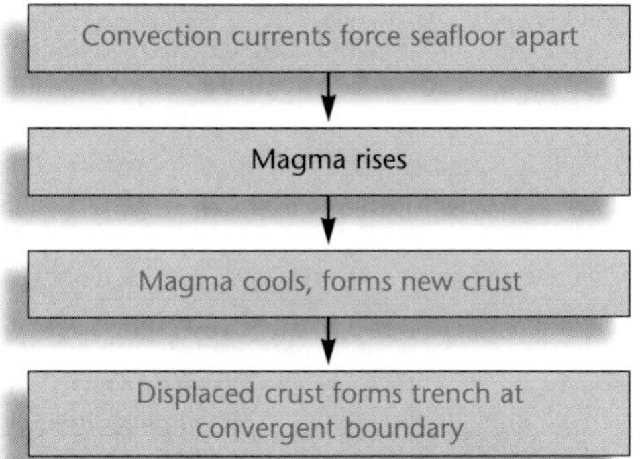

Performance Assessment

1. **Asking Questions:** In Activity 11-1, you constructed a model that supported the theory of seafloor spreading. Based on the model you constructed, what additional information about the seafloor would be helpful to add support to the ideas presented in your model?
2. **Making Observations and Inferences:** In the MiniLAB on page 310, you observed convection currents produced in water as it was heated. Try the experiment again placing pieces of wood, small pieces of rubber bands, or sequins into the water. Do their movements support your observations and inferences from the MiniLAB?
3. **Model:** Use plywood and a map of the world to construct a working model of plate tectonics. Use a sheet of plywood as a base and attach movable wood continents. When the model is complete, the continents should move from Pangaea to their present positions.

319

20. Fossils of terrestrial organisms are used to support continental drift. Fish are found in oceans, and oceans surround all of the continents; therefore, most fossil fish aren't good evidence of continental drift.

Developing Skills

21. Hypothesizing The volcanoes in the Cascade Range formed when two plates collided at a convergent boundary. The plates were either both oceanic or one was oceanic and the other continental. Volcanoes do not form at the third type of converging boundary—continent-continent.

22. Outlining Students' outlines should include all the evidence that supported Wegener's continental drift plus a brief description of seafloor spreading.

23. Measuring in SI 21 m, 325.5 m

24. Comparing and Contrasting Both formed as the result of converging plates. However, the Andes formed as an oceanic plate descended beneath a continental plate. The Himalayas formed as two continental plates collided.

25. Concept Mapping See student page.

Performance Assessment

1. Student answers will vary. Students should indicate that measuring the age of rock units at equal distances from the mid-ocean ridges should provide support for seafloor spreading. Also, students might realize that scientists are now able to observe geologic processes as they occur at the mid-ocean ridge. Evidence of recent magma extrusion would offer support as well. Use the Performance Task Assessment List for Asking Questions in **PASC,** p. 19. P

2. If light enough materials are used, they should be carried in the water and circulate around within the convection currents. Students should acknowledge that this observation would support their observations and inferences from the MiniLAB. Use the Performance Task Assessment List for Making Observations and Inferences in **PASC,** p. 17. P

3. Suggest that students tie the plywood continents together with string or wire so they can be moved back and forth. Use the Performance Task Assessment List for Model in **PASC,** p. 51. P

UNIT PROJECT 3

Researching Via the Internet

How do you use resources to find out more about a topic in which you are interested? In the past, you might have gone to the library and used a card catalog or periodical listing to find books, magazine and newspaper articles that were related to your topic. Now, at most libraries, you can find these same book and article listings on a computer. Many libraries have put their holdings in one large database to make research less time consuming and more successful.

Within the last few years, a new and more powerful source for information retrieval has become widely available. This source of information is called the Internet. If you have a computer or have access to a school computer, you can do research on the Internet without ever leaving your chair.

What is the Internet?

The internet is made up of millions of computers all around the world that are linked to each other. The information available in these computers is varied and vast. You can find information on almost any imaginable topic. Using electronic mail, or e-mail, you can speak directly to an expert in a particular field or to a person in another country. Some computers store articles or entire books about particular subjects. Others contain thousands of photographs and illustrations.

Getting Started

To use the Internet you must have a way to access it. Many schools have direct access to the Internet or have a connection through a local college or university. A phone line can also give you access by way of a commercial server. Each server differs slightly in the way it works. Time, practice, and perhaps some cooperative work with a few friends will help you locate the information you need.

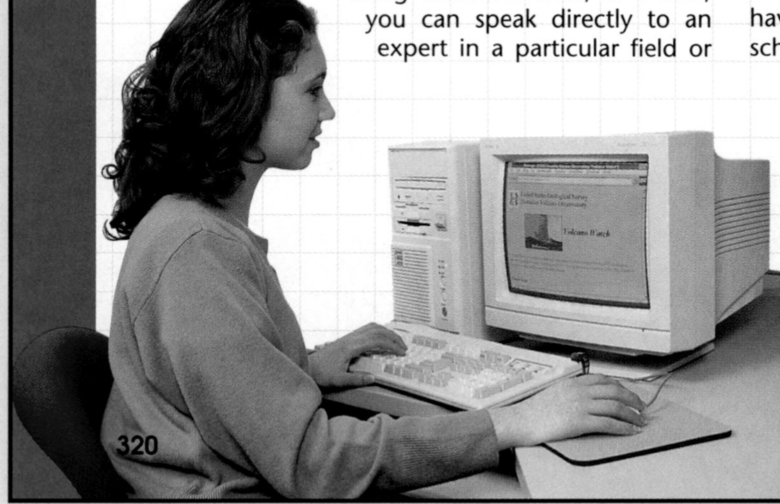

Objectives

LS **Intrapersonal** Students will search for, gather, and analyze information from the Internet about earthquakes or volcanoes. They will make presentations to the class using the information they obtained in their searches. L1

Summary

The Internet is a collection of data bases stored in hundreds of thousands of computers that are loosely linked together. Accessing the Internet requires a computer, modem, and a subscription with one of the commercial servers. Using the Internet, students can access scientists and universities, as well as private corporations throughout the world. After deciding on a topic about which they would like to learn more, students will collect data and prepare a report that contains text and graphics, and perhaps sound and photography.

Time Required

One-half class period will be needed to discuss the requirements of the project and to decide if students will work independently or with a partner. Each student will need approximately 3 hours on-line at the computer and an additional 3 to 5 hours to prepare a report. Allow an additional 2 to 3 days for student presentations.

Preparation

- If students will be using a computer lab or computers in the library, arrange access with the person in charge.
- Prepare a letter to parents telling them that students will be using Internet resources.
- Make a list of URLs (Internet addresses) that students can use as a starting point. Since URLs change often, it is especially important that you check the addresses before you provide them to students.
- If you are not familiar with the Internet, ask another faculty member for background help.

Reference books on using the Internet will be helpful as will consulting with persons already proficient at research using the Internet.

Beginning Your Search

For this project you will use the Internet to find out more about earthquakes or volcanoes. Decide on a topic you wish to research and report on to the rest of your class. You may choose to investigate a particular earthquake or volcano, or a more general topic such as seismographs or volcano prediction. Make sure your teacher approves your research topic before beginning. Pick a topic that isn't too broad or too narrow.

Internet Yellow Pages

An Internet yellow pages contains the Internet addresses for locating information on any imaginable topic. However, because no one is in charge of the Internet, an Internet address may be available for a time, and then the people managing the address may decide to remove it.

Internet Search Tips

One important method for finding information is a search tool. A search tool allows you to type in a key word or words. The tool then searches thousands of sites on the Internet for those that contain your key words. After a few seconds, the search tool returns many addresses for other links related to your topic. The gopher is one type of search tool. There are thousands of gopher servers available on the Internet.

Making Your Presentation

After you've completed your search for information and gathered all of your data, you should be ready to prepare a presentation for your class. Your presentation should be put together using a multimedia computer program. Your presentation should consist of at least five different screens with text, graphics, and perhaps sound and photo. Design each screen so this it is appealing to the audience. Your report should include information from at least five sites on the Internet. Identify your sites and explain to the class how you got to them.

A word of caution. Not everything on the Internet is valid. Much of the information has not been edited, reviewed, or even verified as true. If you have questions about anything you find, ask a parent, teacher, or other adult to help you determine if it is useful or not.

Teaching Strategies

- Remind students to take notes while they are online, just as they would for any other research project. URLs are important for navigating back to an area of interest.
- If students work in pairs, it is best to have a student who does not have Internet access at home work with one who does.
- Remind students that community libraries and university libraries provide Internet access. There may be a fee for logging onto the Internet.
- Explain that search engines may provide useful starting points. The Web Crawler is one example.
- Provide students with a rubric that explains what portion of their grade will be determined by each part of their Internet project.

Go Further

Once students have begun to use the Internet, they can use it as a vehicle to answer many different questions and complete other classroom exercises. You may wish to assign another problem that challenges them even further.

References

The following books—all 1995 copyrights—are available from Ventana Press, P.O. Box 13964, Research Triangle Park, North Carolina 27709-3964:

- *HTML Publishing on the Internet for Mac*
- *Internet Roadside Attractions*
- *Walking the World Wide Web*

UNIT 4

Change and Earth's History

In Unit 4, students are introduced to the record of Earth's past. Earth's evolutionary history and the development of the geologic time scale are presented. A major concept developed in this unit is the measurement of geologic time units by changes in or extinctions of life-forms or changes on Earth. For example, possible causes for the extinction of dinosaurs are examined in Chapter 12, and present-day rapid extinctions are discussed in Chapter 13.

CONTENTS

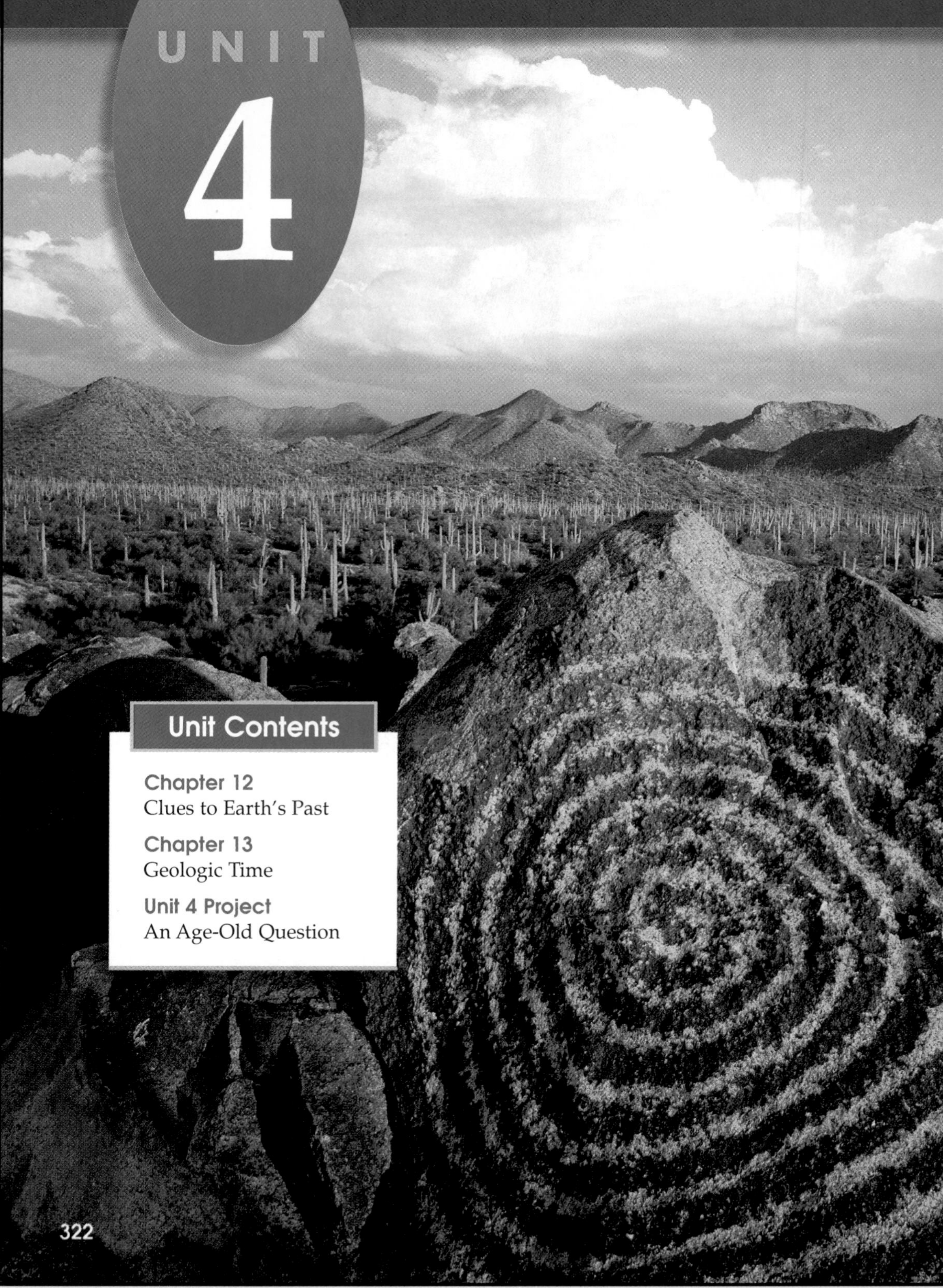

Science at Home

Fossil Collecting Have students study rock exposures near their homes for evidence of fossils, or have students study rocks they collected while on trips. Students may also bring in fossils they have collected or that others have collected for them from other locations. Have students share their fossils with the class. L1

Change and Earth's History

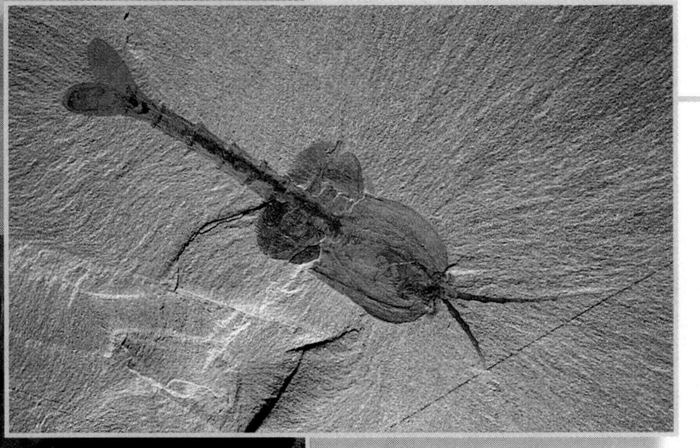

What's Happening Here?

The spiral shown here is a petroglyph or rock drawing. Thousands of years ago, humans etched these figures into stones, thus taking the first steps toward creating a written language. Though this may seem like a long time ago, those years represent less than one percent of Earth's history.

What was happening on Earth during the other 99 percent of time? Oceans covered much of the planet, glaciers formed then receded, and the continents broke apart. Some 600 million years ago, fossils of the first marine animals, such as the arthropod shown in the smaller photo, made an abrupt appearance in the fossil record. In this unit, you will explore this mysterious occurrence and other changes that took place during Earth's vast geological history.

Science Journal

In the library, research the geologic eras that make up Earth's history. In your Science Journal, describe some of the major events that occurred during each period.

Theme Connection

Stability and Change Evolution of life-forms throughout geologic time is the focus of this unit. Ask students what scientists from the future might think if they found that many different life-forms became extinct at the same time that human civilization first developed.

Cultural Diversity

Present-Day Near Extinctions Have students research why buffalo almost became extinct when the western United States was settled by pioneers. Native Americans harvested the buffalo at a rate that allowed the population to replenish itself. How did the two cultures differ? How might this difference have led to the near extinction of the buffalo?

INTRODUCING THE UNIT

What's Happening Here?

Ask students to tell you how the photograph of *Waptia fieldensis* relates to the petroglyph shown in the larger photo. *Waptia fieldensis* is one of the earliest life-forms for which we have a fossil record. Discuss with students the time that elapsed between this organism's existence and the appearance of humans as evidenced by the petroglyph shown in the larger photo.

Background

Waptia fieldensis is a fossil from the Burgess Shale. The Burgess Shale is the name given to a rock unit formed 530 million years ago. It holds fossils from many organisms that lived in an ancient sea. The Burgess Shale is found in the Canadian Rockies about 8000 feet above sea level. More life-forms lived in this sea than are found throughout Earth's present-day oceans.

Previewing the Chapters

- Have pairs of students study the figures in Section 12-1 for examples of how fossils form. Have them devise a simple demonstration that shows one of these processes.
- Direct students to **Figure 13-4.** Ask them to explain why one moth has a survival advantage over the other moth in the left-hand photo. Is the same moth at an advantage or a disadvantage in the photo on the right?

Tying to Previous Knowledge

Ask students if they have ever dug a hole in their yard and found leaves, bones, or other items buried in the soil. Have students relate this to the processes that cause fossil formation.

Chapter Organizer

Section	Objectives	Activities/Features
Chapter Opener		Explore Activity: Make a model of a fossil to see one way they might form. p. 325
12-1 Fossils (1 session, ½ block)*	1. **List** the conditions necessary for fossils to form. 2. **Describe** processes of fossil formation. 3. **Explain** how fossil correlation is used to determine rock ages.	Using Math, p. 326 MiniLAB: What type of fossils might be preserved from our time? p. 327 Connect to Life Science, p. 331 Using Technology: Recovering Fossils, p. 332 Skill Builder: Concept Mapping, p. 333 Science Journal, p. 333
12-2 Science and Society Issue: Extinction of Dinosaurs (2 sessions, 1 block)*	1. **Discuss** the meteorite-impact hypothesis of dinosaur extinction. 2. **Describe** several hypotheses about why dinosaurs became extinct.	Connect to Chemistry, p. 336 Explore the Issue, p. 336
12-3 Relative Ages of Rocks (2 sessions, 1 block)*	1. **Describe** several methods used to date rock layers relative to other rock layers. 2. **Interpret** gaps in the rock record. 3. **Give an example** of how rock layers may be correlated with other rock layers.	Problem Solving: Rock Correlation, p. 341 Skill Builder: Interpreting Data, p. 342 Using Computers: Spreadsheet, p. 342 Activity 12-1: Relative Age Dating of Geologic Features, p. 343
12-4 Absolute Ages of Rocks (2 sessions, 1 block)*	1. **Identify** how absolute dating differs from relative dating. 2. **Describe** how the half-lives of isotopes are used to determine a rock's age.	MiniLAB: What are the dates of some events in Earth's history? p. 345 Using Math, p. 347 Skill Builder: Making and Using Tables, p. 347 Science Journal, p. 347 Activity 12-2: Radioactive Decay, pp. 348-349 People and Science: Enriqueta Barrera, Geochemist, p. 350

* A complete Planning Guide that includes block scheduling is provided on pages 32T-35T.

Activity Materials

Explore	Activities	MiniLABs
page 325 small, cardboard milk carton; plaster of paris; water; leaf; shell; bone; petroleum jelly	page 343 No special materials are needed. pages 348-349 shoe box with lid, 100 brass fasteners, 100 paper clips, 100 pennies, 100 pipe cleaners, graph paper, colored pencils	page 327 No special materials are needed. page 345 No special materials are needed.

Chapter 12 Clues to Earth's Past

Teacher Classroom Resources

Reproducible Masters	Transparencies	Teaching Resources
Study Guide, p. 49 **Reinforcement,** p. 49 **Enrichment,** p. 49 **Activity Worksheets,** p. 76 **Lab Manual 35,** Carbon Impressions **Science Integration Activity 12,** Keep on Trackin'! **Concept Mapping,** p. 29 **Critical Thinking/Problem Solving,** p. 18 **Cross-Curricular Integration,** p. 16 **Technology Integration,** pp. 11-12	**Section Focus Transparency 45,** Rock or Wood? **Teaching Transparency 23,** Index Fossils	**Glencoe Earth Science Interactive Videodisc** **Earth Science CD-ROM** **Spanish Resources** **English/Spanish Audiocassettes** **Cooperative Learning Resource Guide** **Lab Partner** **Lab and Safety Skills** **Lesson Plans**
Study Guide, p. 50 **Reinforcement,** p. 50 **Enrichment,** p. 50 **Science and Society Integration,** p. 16	**Section Focus Transparency 46,** What Dun It?	**Assessment Resources**
Study Guide, p. 51 **Reinforcement,** p. 51 **Enrichment,** p. 51 **Activity Worksheets,** pp. 72-73 **Lab Manual 34,** Principle of Superposition	**Section Focus Transparency 47,** Relatively Speaking . . . **Teaching Transparency 24,** Layers of Rock	**Chapter Review,** pp. 27-28 **Assessment,** pp. 80-83 **Performance Assessment in the Science Classroom (PASC)** **MindJogger Videoquiz** **Alternate Assessment in the Science Classroom** **Performance Assessment** **Chapter Review Software** **Computer Test Bank**
Study Guide, p. 52 **Reinforcement,** p. 52 **Enrichment,** p. 52 **Activity Worksheets,** pp. 74-75, 77 **Multicultural Connections,** pp. 27-28	**Section Focus Transparency 48,** How Old Is It? **Science Integration Transparency 12,** Dating the Earth	

Key to Teaching Strategies

The following designations will help you decide which activities are appropriate for your students.

L1 Level 1 activities should be within the ability range of all students.

L2 Level 2 activities should be within the ability range of the average to above-average student.

L3 Level 3 activities are designed for the ability range of above-average students.

LEP LEP activities should be within the ability range of Limited English Proficiency students.

LS These activities are designed to address different learning styles.

COOP LEARN Cooperative Learning activities are designed for small group work.

P These strategies represent student products that can be placed into a best-work portfolio.

GLENCOE TECHNOLOGY

The following multimedia resources are available from Glencoe.

The Infinite Voyage Series
The Great Dinosaur Hunt

Science and Technology Videodisc Series (STVS)
Chemistry
Carbon-14 Dating

Glencoe Earth Science Interactive Videodisc
Dinosaurs: Footprints in the Rock

Earth Science CD-ROM

Teacher Classroom Resources

This is a representation of key blackline masters available in the Teacher Classroom Resources.

Teaching Aids

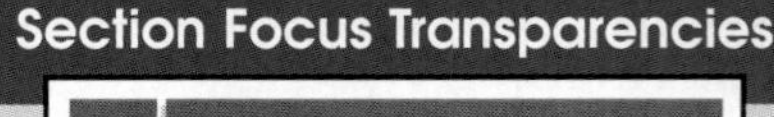
Section Focus Transparencies

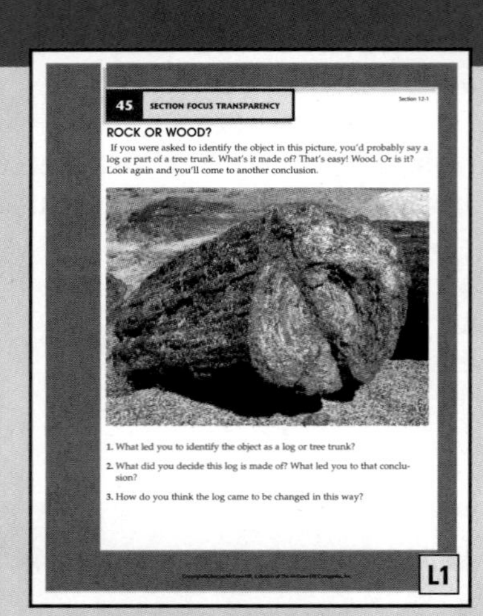
45 SECTION FOCUS TRANSPARENCY

ROCK OR WOOD?

If you were asked to identify the object in this picture, you'd probably say a log or part of a tree trunk. What's it made of? That's easy! Wood. Or is it? Look again and you'll come to another conclusion.

1. What led you to identify the object as a log or tree trunk?
2. What did you decide this log is made of? What led you to that conclusion?
3. How do you think the log came to be changed in this way?

L1

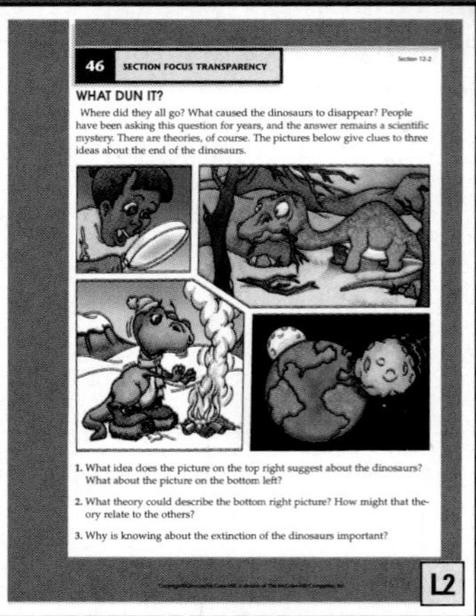
46 SECTION FOCUS TRANSPARENCY

WHAT DUN IT?

Where did they all go? What caused the dinosaurs to disappear? People have been asking this question for years, and the answer remains a scientific mystery. There are theories, of course. The pictures below give clues to three ideas about the end of the dinosaurs.

1. What idea does the picture on the top right suggest about the dinosaurs? What about the picture on the bottom left?
2. What theory could describe the bottom right picture? How might that theory relate to the others?
3. Why is knowing about the extinction of the dinosaurs important?

L2

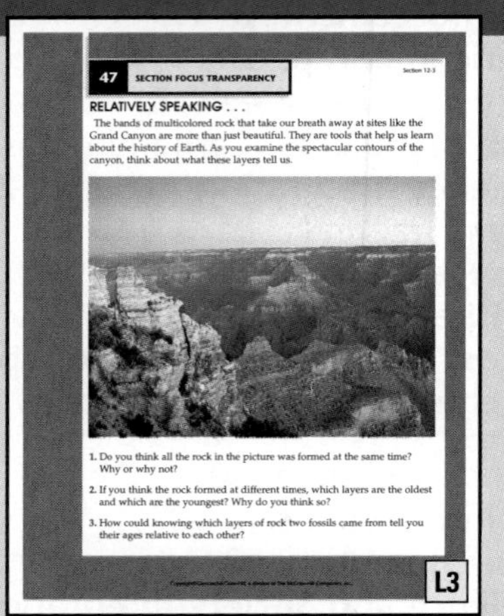
47 SECTION FOCUS TRANSPARENCY

RELATIVELY SPEAKING . . .

The bands of multicolored rock that take our breath away at sites like the Grand Canyon are more than just beautiful. They are tools that help us learn about the history of Earth. As you examine the spectacular contours of the canyon, think about what these layers tell us.

1. Do you think all the rock in the picture was formed at the same time? Why or why not?
2. If you think the rock formed at different times, which layers are the oldest and which are the youngest? Why do you think so?
3. How could knowing which layers of rock two fossils came from tell you their ages relative to each other?

L3

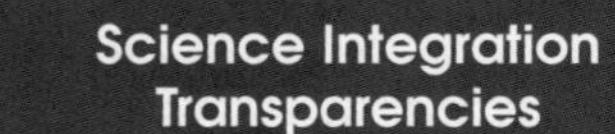
Science Integration Transparencies

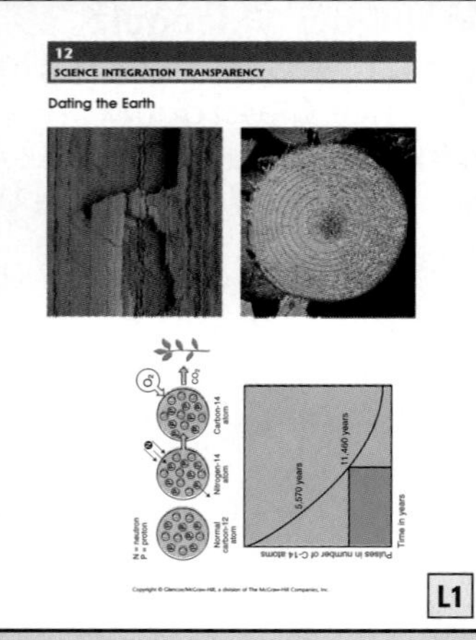
12 SCIENCE INTEGRATION TRANSPARENCY

Dating the Earth

L1

Teaching Transparencies

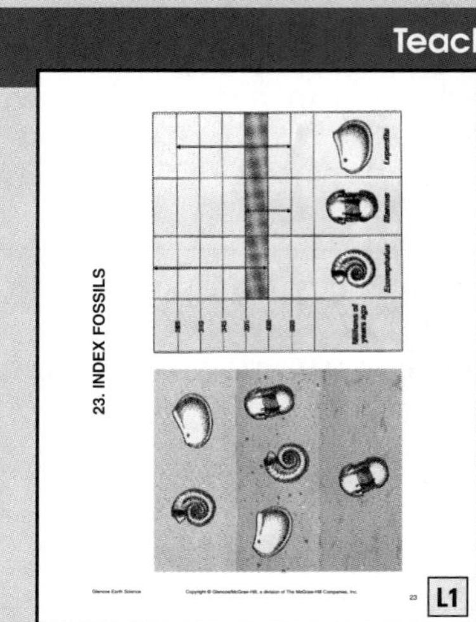

L1

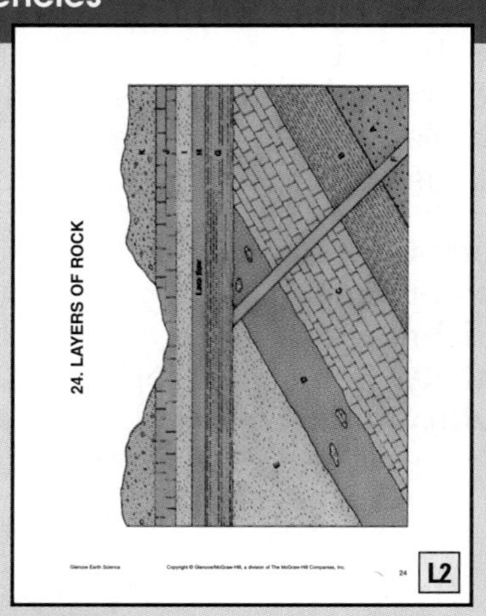

L2

Meeting Different Ability Levels

Study Guide

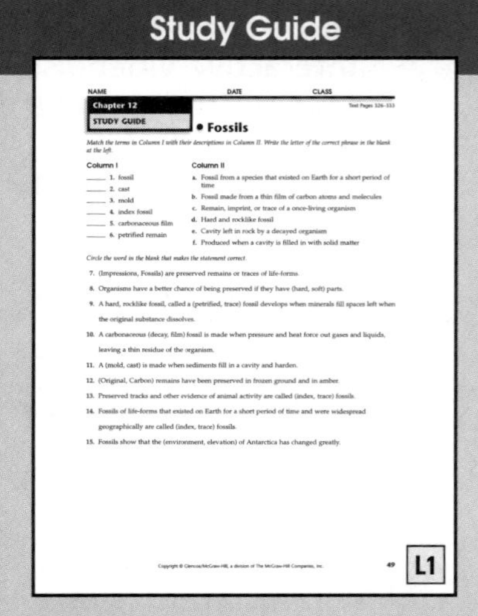
Chapter 12 STUDY GUIDE

• Fossils

L1

Reinforcement

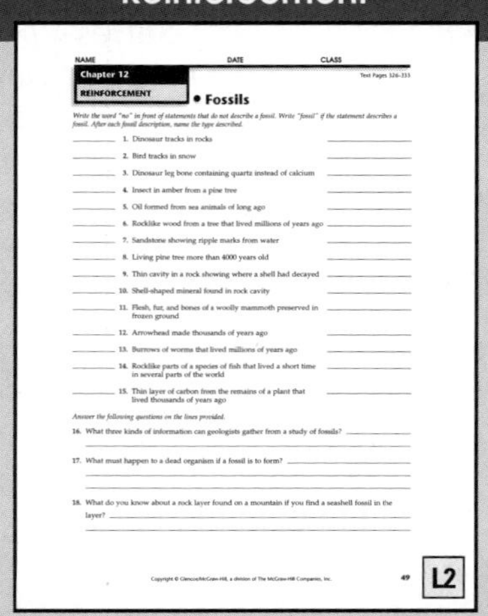
Chapter 12 REINFORCEMENT

• Fossils

L2

Enrichment Worksheets

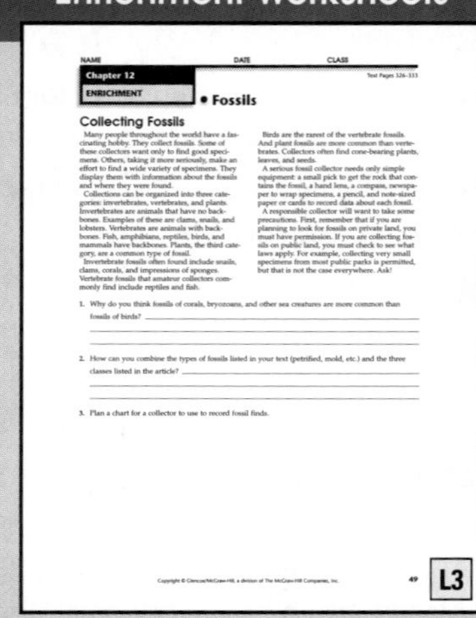
Chapter 12 ENRICHMENT

• Fossils

Collecting Fossils

L3

Hands-On Activities

Science Integration Activity

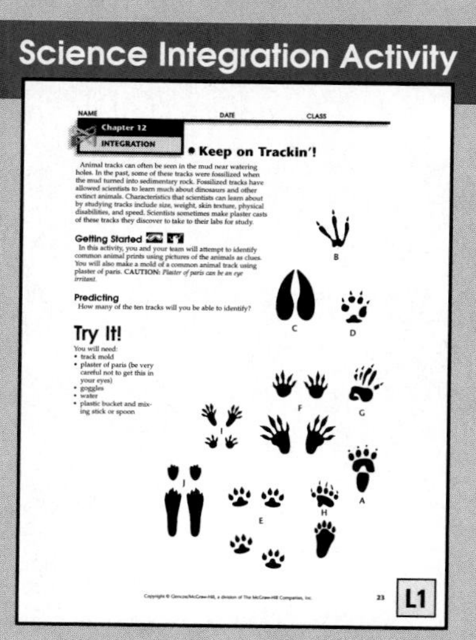
Chapter 12 INTEGRATION

Keep on Trackin'!

Getting Started

Predicting

Try It!

L1

Lab Manual

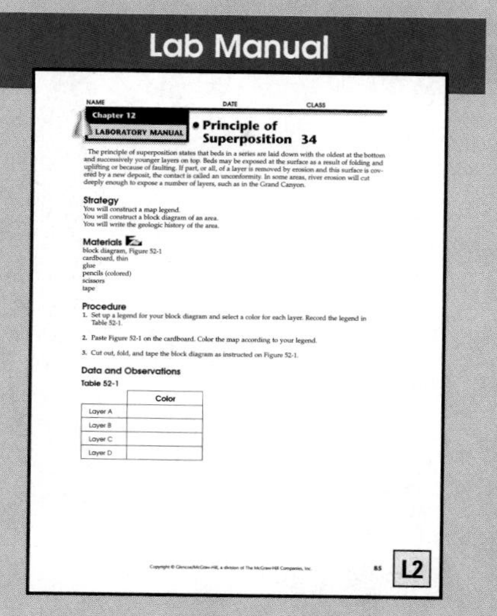
Chapter 12 LABORATORY MANUAL

Principle of Superposition 34

Strategy

Materials

Procedure

Data and Observations

Table 52-1

	Color
Layer A	
Layer B	
Layer C	
Layer D	

L2

Assessment

Performance Assessment

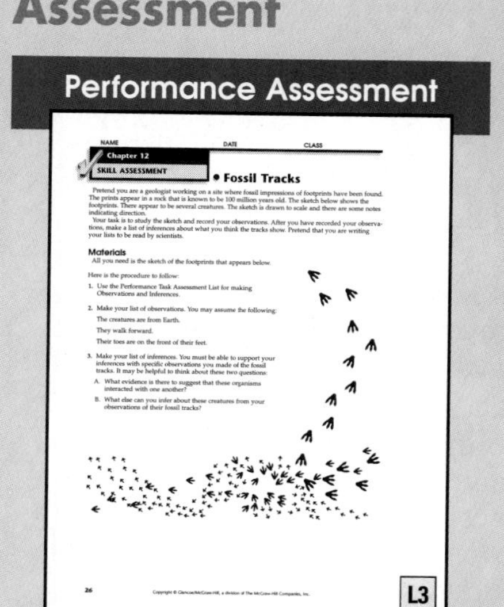
Chapter 12 SKILL ASSESSMENT

Fossil Tracks

Materials

L3

Enrichment and Application

Critical Thinking/ Problem Solving

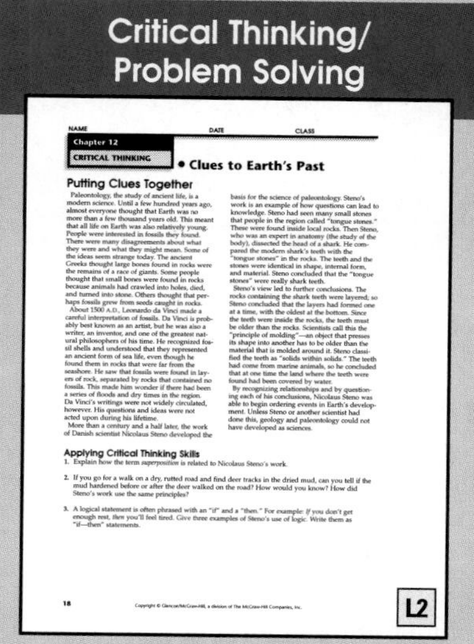
Chapter 12 CRITICAL THINKING

Clues to Earth's Past

Putting Clues Together

Applying Critical Thinking Skills

L2

Cross-Curricular Integration

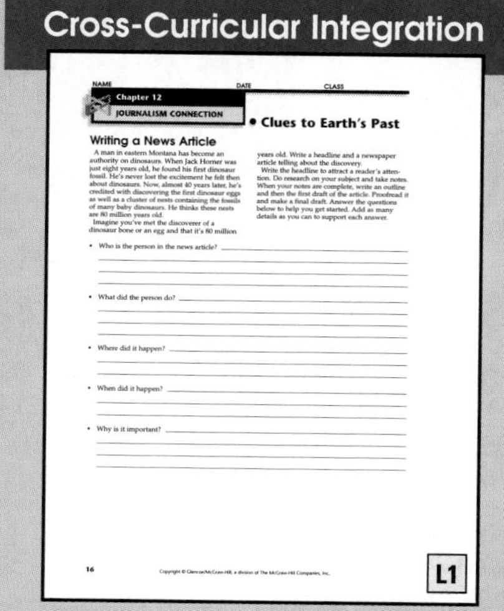
Chapter 12 JOURNALISM CONNECTION

Clues to Earth's Past

Writing a News Article

L1

Science and Society Integration

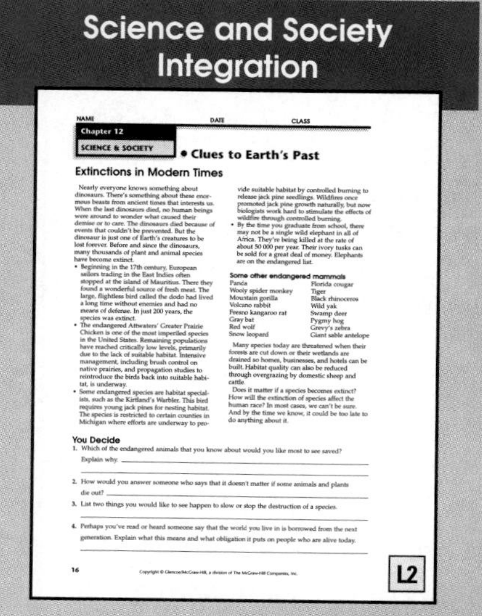
Chapter 12 SCIENCE & SOCIETY

Clues to Earth's Past

Extinctions in Modern Times

You Decide

L2

Multicultural Connections

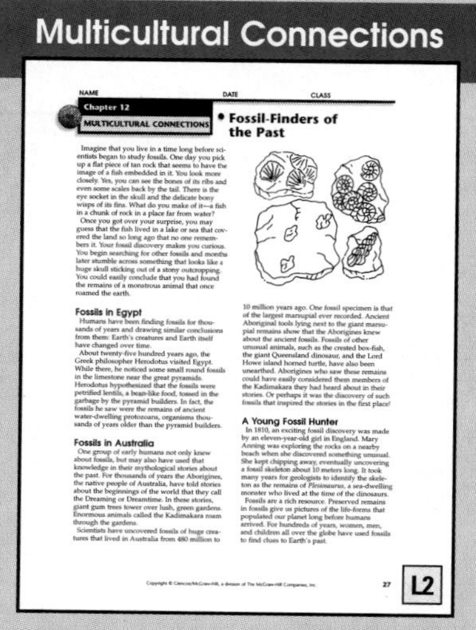
Chapter 12 MULTICULTURAL CONNECTIONS

Fossil-Finders of the Past

Fossils in Egypt

Fossils in Australia

A Young Fossil Hunter

L2

Concept Mapping

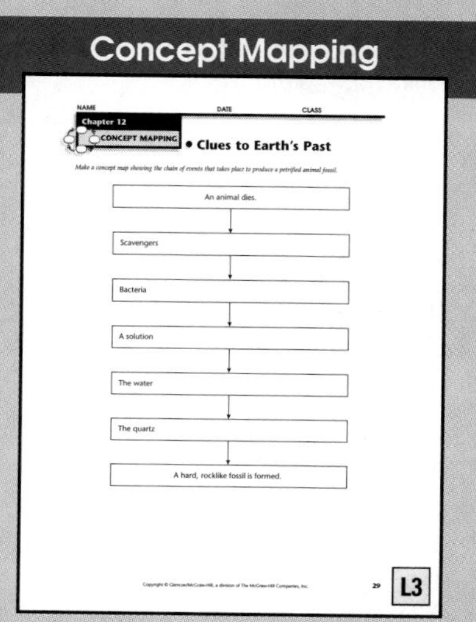
Chapter 12 CONCEPT MAPPING

Clues to Earth's Past

An animal dies.

Scavengers

Bacteria

A solution

The water

The quartz

A hard, rocklike fossil is formed.

L3

Chapter 12

Clues to Earth's Past

CHAPTER OVERVIEW

Section 12-1 This section describes fossils and the conditions needed for them to form. Use of fossils as indicators of age and ancient environments concludes the section.

Section 12-2 Science and Society Conflicting theories about how dinosaurs became extinct are explored. The Explore the Issue feature asks students to indicate whether they believe the impact theory or one of the alternative theories. Students are asked to list evidence that helped them make the decision.

Section 12-3 This section explains how relative ages of rocks are determined. Methods used to correlate rocks are also described.

Section 12-4 Section 12-4 contrasts absolute and relative dating. Radioactive decay is also described.

Chapter Vocabulary

- fossils
- petrified remains
- carbonaceous film
- mold
- cast
- index fossils
- extinct
- principle of superposition
- relative dating
- unconformity
- absolute dating
- radioactive decay
- half-life
- radiometric dating
- uniformitarianism

Theme Connection

Stability and Change The evolution of life-forms throughout geologic time as shown by the fossil record should be a major focus of the chapter. The changes in life-forms on Earth can be used to obtain relative ages of rocks and date geologic events.

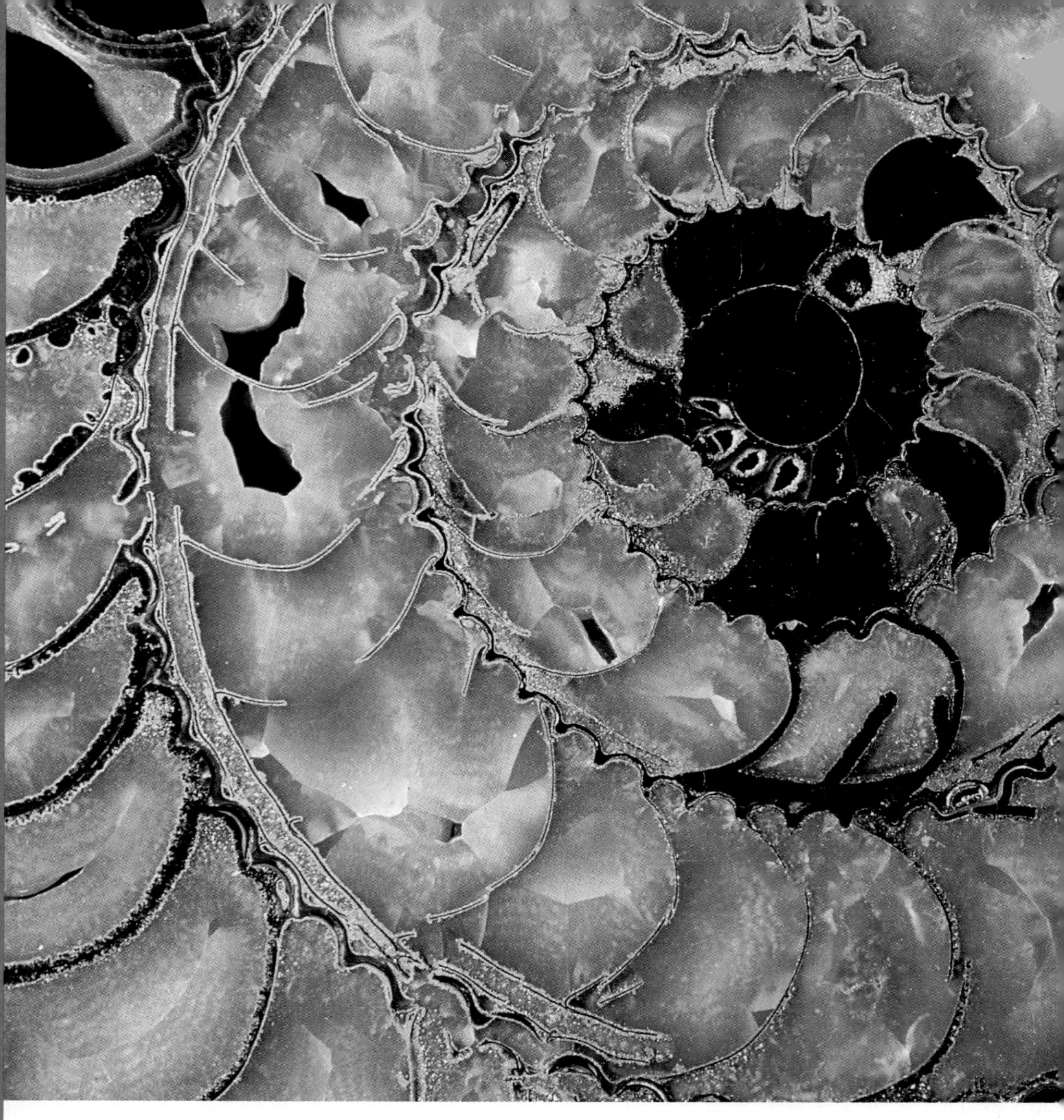

Previewing the Chapter

Learning Styles

Look for the following logo for strategies that emphasize different learning modalities.

Kinesthetic	Explore, p. 325
Visual-Spatial	Visual Learning, pp. 328, 329, 331, 339, 340, 342, 344, 346; Demonstration, pp. 338, 339
Interpersonal	MiniLAB, p. 327; Discussion, p. 328; Making a Model, p. 330; Reteach, p. 332; Activity, p. 335; Integration, p. 344; Activity 12-2, pp. 348-349; Theme Connection, p. 341
Logical-Mathematical	Activity 12-1, p. 343; MiniLAB, p. 345; Integrating the Sciences, p. 345
Linguistic	Science Journal, pp. 327, 335; Inclusion Strategies, p. 327

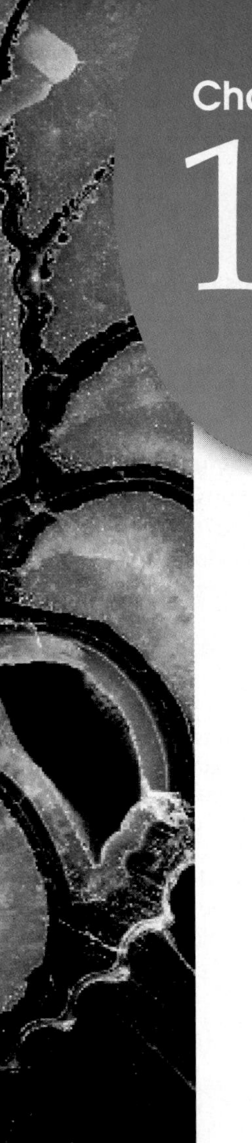

Chapter 12

Clues to Earth's Past

Pictured here is a fossil ammonite. This marine invertebrate animal lived during the Cretaceous Period. Finding particular fossils indicates the age of the rock in which they are found. What else do you think we could learn from fossils? How do they form? What evidence of their past life do we have?

EXPLORE ACTIVITY

Make a model of a fossil to see one way they might form. 

1. Cut the top off of a small milk carton and add enough plaster of paris to fill it halfway.
2. Mix enough water with the plaster so that it's smooth and thick.
3. Coat a leaf, shell, or bone with a thin layer of petroleum jelly.
4. Press it into the plaster.
5. Allow the plaster to dry at least 24 hours and then remove the leaf, shell, or bone.

Observe: In your Science Journal, discuss how the imprints compare with the original object. Can you determine, from the imprints alone, what object made them? How do you think imprints of once-living organisms are made?

Previewing Science Skills

- In the **Skill Builders**, you will **map concepts, interpret data,** and **make and use tables.**
- In the **Activities**, you will **interpret data, analyze,** and **conclude.**
- In the **MiniLABs**, you will **observe and infer.**

Assessment Planner

Portfolio
Refer to page 351 for suggested items that students might select for their portfolios.

Performance Assessment
See page 351 for additional Performance Assessment options.
Skill Builders, pp. 333, 342, 347
MiniLABs, pp. 327, 345
Activities 12-1, p. 343; 12-2, pp. 348-349

Content Assessment
Section Wrap-ups, pp. 333, 336, 342, 347
Chapter Review, pp. 351-353
Mini Quizzes, pp. 333, 336, 342, 347

Group Assessment
Opportunities for group assessment occur with Cooperative Learning Strategies and Flex Your Brain Activities.

EXPLORE ACTIVITY

Purpose

LS **Kinesthetic** Use the Explore Activity to introduce students to one method of fossil formation. Inform students they will be learning more about fossils and how they form. L1

Preparation

Have students bring in small, clean, empty milk cartons; and leaves, shells, or clean meat bones. Obtain a package of plaster of paris and a container of petroleum jelly.

Materials

one small milk carton for each student; enough plaster of paris to fill each carton half-full; water; petroleum jelly; and leaves, shells, or bones

Observe

Student descriptions will vary, depending on how well they performed the activity. However, they should note that the "fossil" they make resembles the original object. For some "fossils," students will be able to determine what object made them, but for others, they may need additional information.

Assessment

Performance Have students redo the Explore Activity using a very soft object, such as jello or grape jelly. Ask students whether it was as easy to produce a "fossil" of a soft object. Ask them how this is important to the study of the conditions necessary to form fossils. Use the Performance Task Assessment List for Carrying Out a Strategy and Collecting Data in **PASC**, p. 25. P

Section 12•1

Prepare

Section Background

- Scientists think that certain reptiles swallowed stones to aid in digestion. When the organism died and decayed, the polished stones, called gastroliths, were left behind. Gastroliths and fossilized fecal materials, or coprolites, are trace fossils.
- Facies fossils are the remains of organisms that were restricted to a stratigraphic facies or were adapted to living in a restricted environment. Facies fossils enable paleontologists to reconstruct models depicting ancient climates.

Preplanning

Obtain fossils described in this section for students to observe.

1 Motivate

Bellringer

Before presenting the lesson, display **Section Focus Transparency 45** on the overhead projector. Assign the accompanying **Focus Activity** worksheet. L1 LEP

USING MATH

Student Text Question

What evidence do we have of past life on Earth? *Fossils are evidence of past life.*

12•1 Fossils

Science Words

fossil
petrified remains
carbonaceous film
mold
cast
index fossil

Objectives

- List the conditions necessary for fossils to form.
- Describe processes of fossil formation.
- Explain how fossil correlation is used to determine rock ages.

Traces from Our Past

The dense forest reverberates as an *Allosaurus* charges forward in pursuit of an evening meal. On the other side of the swamp, a herd of apatosaurs moves slowly and cautiously onward. The adults surround the young to protect them from predators. Soon, night will fall on this prehistoric day, 160 million years ago.

Does this scene sound familiar to you? It's likely that you've read about dinosaurs and other past inhabitants of Earth before. But how do you know they really existed? What evidence do we have of past life on Earth? Scientists reconstruct what an animal looked like from its fossil remains, as in **Figure 12-1.**

Figure 12-1

Scientists and artists can reconstruct what dinosaurs looked like using fossil remains (A). The fossils being reconstructed are a *Velociraptor* attacking a *Protoceratops* (B). The fossils were actually found in this position by paleontologists.

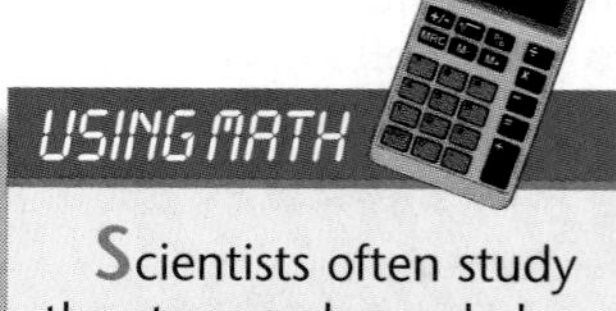

USING MATH

Scientists often study the step angle made by animal footprints.

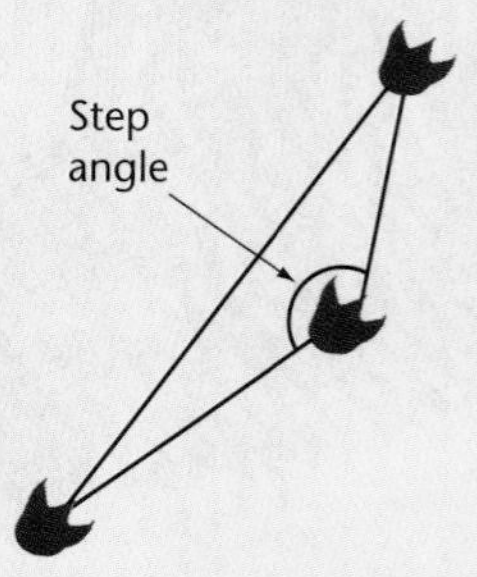

Design a way to find your step angle.

Program Resources

Reproducible Masters

Study Guide, p. 49 L1
Reinforcement, p. 49 L1
Enrichment, p. 49 L3
Cross-Curricular Integration, p. 16
Lab Manual 35
Activity Worksheets, p. 76 L1
Science Integration Activities, pp. 23-24
Concept Mapping, p. 29
Critical Thinking/Problem Solving, p. 18
Technology Integration, pp. 11-12

Transparencies

Section Focus Transparency 45 L1
Teaching Transparency 23

Figure 12-2
Rare preservation of a fossil organism without hard parts. This is a fossil leaf.

Fossil Formation

In the Explore Activity on page 325, you made imprints of parts of organisms. The imprints are records, or evidence, of life. Evidence such as the remains, imprints, or traces of once-living organisms preserved in rocks are **fossils.** By studying fossils, geologists help solve mysteries of Earth's past. Fossils have helped geologists and biologists determine approximately when life began, when plants and animals first lived on land, and when certain types of organisms, such as the dinosaurs, disappeared. Fossils tell us not only *when* and *where* organisms once lived, but also *how* they lived.

Usually the remains of dead plants and animals are quickly destroyed. Scavengers eat the dead organisms, or fungi and microorganisms cause them to decay. If you've ever left a banana on the shelf too long, you've seen this process begin. Compounds in the banana cause it to become soft and moist, and microorganisms move in and cause it to decay quickly. What keeps some plants and animals from decaying so they become fossils?

Necessary Conditions

First of all, to become a fossil, the body of a dead organism must be protected from scavengers and microorganisms. One way this can occur is when the body is buried quickly by sediments. If a fish dies and sinks to the bottom of a pond, sediments carried into the pond by a stream will rapidly cover the fish. As a result, no animals or microorganisms can get to it. However, quick burial alone isn't enough to make a fossil.

Organisms have a better chance of being preserved if they have hard parts such as bones, shells, or teeth. As you may know, these hard parts are less likely to be eaten by other organisms, they decay more slowly, and they are less likely to weather away. Unlike the leaf shown in **Figure 12-2,** most fossils that have been found are composed of the hard parts of organisms. Fossils are usually found in sedimentary rocks. The heat and pressure involved in forming igneous and metamorphic rocks often destroy fossil material.

MiniLAB

What type of fossils might be preserved from our time?

Procedure

1. Take a brief walk outside and observe the area near your school.
2. Look around and notice what type of litter has been discarded on the school grounds. Note whether there is a paved road near your school. Note anything else that is human-made.

Analysis

1. Predict what human-made or natural objects from our time might be preserved far into the future.
2. Explain what conditions would need to exist for these objects to be preserved as fossils.

MiniLAB

Purpose

LS **Interpersonal** Students will think about what conditions would be necessary for objects from our time to become fossils. L1
COOP LEARN

Teaching Strategies

- Introduce this activity by asking students how we know about conditions that existed long ago on Earth's surface.
- Form problem-solving teams with four or five students per group. Ask for a consensus list from each group. Then write each group's list of five "fossils" on the chalkboard. Have the class, on a consensus basis, infer which five are most likely to be preserved as fossils.

Analysis

1. There are no right or wrong answers for this activity. This kind of group activity is designed to make students think about conditions necessary for fossils to form.
2. To be preserved, it is best if the object has hard parts and is buried quickly. As long as these conditions are considered, the MiniLAB is a success.

Assessment

Oral To further assess students' understanding of fossil preservation, have them explain why shark teeth are often found as fossils but impressions of jellyfish are rarely found. Use the Performance Task Assessment List for Making Observations and Inferences in **PASC,** p. 17. P

Activity Worksheets, pp. 5, 76

Inclusion Strategies

Gifted Have students imagine they are fossils. Have them write their autobiographies and describe what they have seen and experienced. The stories should also include how the organism became a fossil. Encourage creativity but insist on scientific accuracy. L3 LS

Science Journal

Traces of the Past Encourage students to research what types of information can be learned about extinct animals from studying gastroliths and coprolites left by the organisms. Have students write a brief report of what they discover in their Science Journals. L2 LS

2 Teach

Visual Learning

Figure 12-3 Why have the fossils retained the shape of the original plant? *During the petrification process, original matter in an object is replaced by quartz and other minerals carried in solution. This preserves the original shape of the plant.* LEP LS

Discussion

LS **Interpersonal** Form cooperative groups. Each group is to be responsible for one of the five types of fossils discussed in this section. Once finished, each group is to direct the discussion on the type of fossils they were responsible for. L1 COOP LEARN

Inquiry Questions

- **How does a carbonaceous film form?** *As an organism decays, gases and liquids are squeezed from its body by overlying sediments. Heat also drives off the gases and liquids. The carbon atoms and molecules that remain form a fossil of the organism.*
- **How do molds and casts differ?** *When an organism dies, it may become buried in sediment. As the sediments harden to form rocks, the organism slowly decays. When the organic material is completely gone, an impression or mold is left in the rock. If sediments later fill the cavity and then harden, a cast of the organism is formed.*

GLENCOE TECHNOLOGY

CD-ROM

Earth Science CD-ROM

Have students perform the interactive exploration for Chapter 12 to reinforce important chapter concepts and thinking processes.

Figure 12-3

Much of the original matter in these petrified plant remains has been replaced by quartz and other minerals. *Why have the fossils retained the shape of the original plant?*

Petrified Remains

You have some idea of what *Tyrannosaurus rex* looked like because you've seen illustrations of this dinosaur. Perhaps you've seen skeletal remains of other dinosaurs towering above you in museums. Artists who draw *Tyrannosaurus rex* and other dinosaurs base their illustrations on fossil bones. These bones are usually petrified.

Petrified remains are hard and rocklike. Some or all of the original materials in the remains have been replaced by minerals. For example, a solution of water and dissolved quartz may flow through the bones of a dead organism. The water dissolves the calcium in the bone and deposits quartz in its place. Quartz is harder than calcium, so the petrified bone is rocklike.

We learn about past life-forms from bones, wood, and other remains that become petrified, like those in **Figure 12-3.** But there are many other types of fossils to consider.

Figure 12-4

This is a fossil that has been preserved as a carbonaceous film. This organism, called *eurypterid,* lived hundreds of millions of years ago and was a major predator in the seas.

Carbonaceous Films

The tissues of most organisms are made of compounds that contain carbon. Sometimes, the only fossil remains of a dead plant or animal is this carbon. As you know, fossils usually form when a dead organism is buried in sediments. As more and more sediments pile up, the organism is subjected to pressure and heat. These conditions force gases and liquids from the body. A thin film of carbon residue is left, forming an outline of the original organism, resulting in a type of fossil called a **carbonaceous film.** The process of chemically changing organic material is called carbonization, and is shown in **Figure 12-4.**

Across the Curriculum

Geography Have students research where petrified fossils have been found in the United States. Ask one student to locate the areas found by his or her classmates on a map of the United States. Students should determine how far away the closest find was. Ask students what is meant by the name *Petrified Forest.* L2

Use **Teaching Transparency 23** as you teach this lesson.

In swamps and deltas, large volumes of plant matter accumulate. Over millions of years, these deposits become completely carbonized, forming the sedimentary rock coal. Coal is more important as a source of fuel than as a fossil because the structure of the original plant is often lost when the coal forms.

Molds and Casts

Think again about the impressions in plaster of paris you made earlier. In nature, such impressions are made when seashells or other hard parts of organisms fall into soft sediments such as mud. The object and sediments are then buried by more sediments. Compaction and cementation turn the sediments into rock. Pores in the rock let water and air reach the shell or hard part and it then decays, leaving behind a cavity in the rock called a **mold.** Later, other sediments may fill in the cavity, harden into rock, and produce a **cast** of the original object, as shown in **Figure 12-5.**

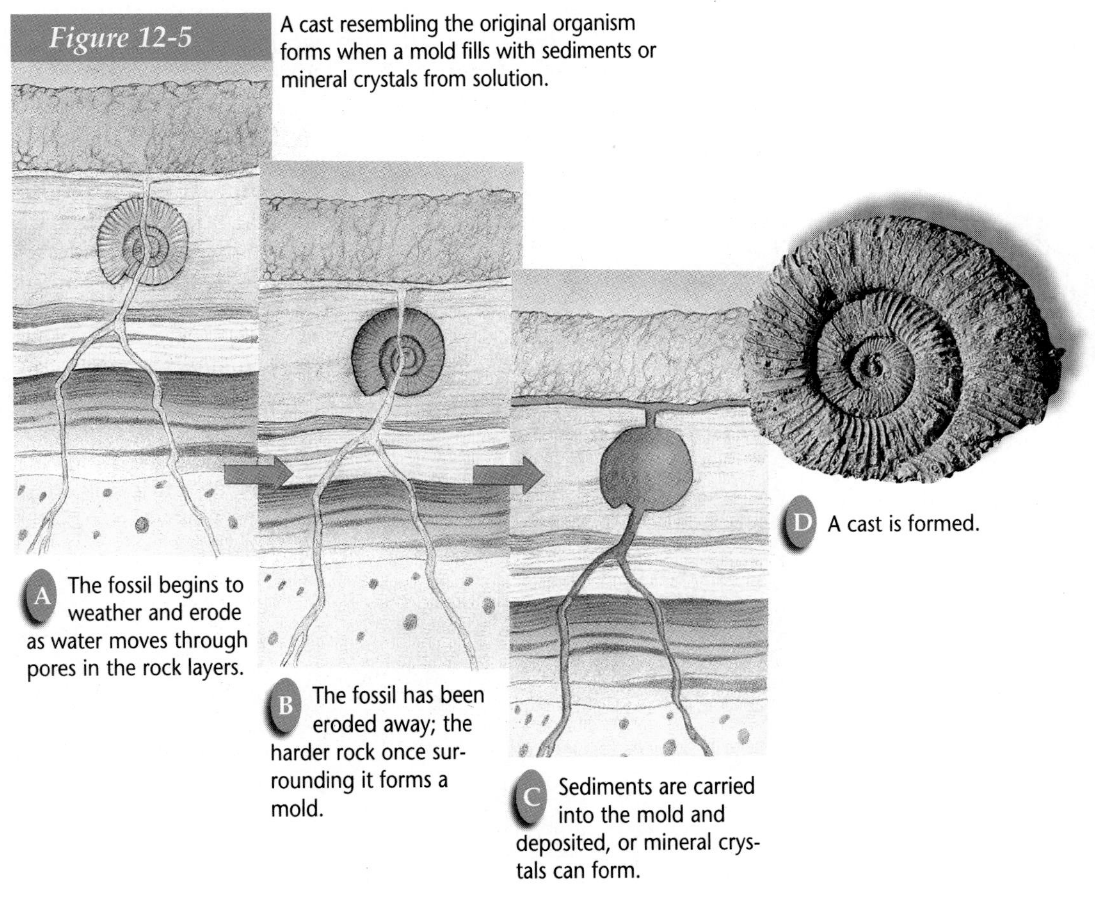

Figure 12-5 A cast resembling the original organism forms when a mold fills with sediments or mineral crystals from solution.

Revealing Preconceptions

Some students might think that fossils form only from ancient life. Ask them what happens to organisms that die and settle to the bottom of a lake or ocean. Explain that these remains are buried quickly by sediments. Once buried, they begin the process of fossilization. In time, they will become fossils.

Enrichment

Ask students to bring in fossils they might have collected or received from others. Have the class determine the type of fossil and, if possible, the organism that produced each. L1

Visual Learning

Figure 12-5 Based on Figure 12-5, which of your fossils is a mold and which is a cast? *Answers will vary, but mold should be the hollow or depression. Cast will be the bump.* LEP LS

GLENCOE TECHNOLOGY

Videodisc

The Infinite Voyage: The Great Dinosaur Hunt

Introduction

Chapter 1

Where the Great Hunt Began

Across the Curriculum

Art Determine whether any students in your class work with ceramics as a hobby. If so, have these students construct an analogy between the molds used in making ceramic statues and those formed in nature. Students may wish to use a statue to demonstrate why the internal structure of an organism is not preserved when casts are formed. L1

Inquiry Questions

- **How does amber protect a trapped insect's body from decay?** *If the amber completely covers the insect's body, it will prevent bacteria, air, and water from reacting with the insect.*
- **Why do you think the skin and hair of some woolly mammoths have been found intact?** *These animals lived during the last ice age. When they became trapped within the ice, the low temperatures kept bacteria from developing and reproducing.*

Discussion

Use the following questions to initiate a discussion about trace fossils. **How do trace fossils differ from other types of fossils?** *Trace fossils are not formed from body parts. They are evidence of an organism's activity.* **What information about early life-forms can be obtained from the depth and separation of tracks left in sediment?** *The approximate size and mass of the organism that left them can be determined.* **What could you conclude about an organism if you found small, fossilized tracks that were far apart?** *Small tracks indicate a small organism. Therefore, if tracks are far apart, the organism was probably able to move swiftly or run.*

Making a Model

LS **Interpersonal** Encourage pairs of students to produce a model of a fossil that depicts one of the five methods of formation described on pages 327-330. L1 COOP LEARN

Figure 12-6

This 40-million-year-old grasshopper was trapped in the sticky resin produced by a plant. Over time, the resin crystallized into amber, preserving the insect inside.

Original Remains

Sometimes the actual organism or parts of the organism are found. **Figure 12-6** shows an insect trapped in amber, a crystallized form of the sticky resin produced by some trees. The amber protects the insect's body from decay and petrification. Other organisms, such as woolly mammoths, have been found preserved in frozen ground. In 1991, the completely intact body of a man who lived 5300 years ago was found frozen in glacial ice in the southern Alps. It is the oldest intact human body ever discovered. Original remains have also been found in tar seeps such as the La Brea tar pit in California.

Trace Fossils

Fossilized tracks and other evidence of animal activity are called *trace fossils.* Perhaps your parents made your handprint or footprint in plaster of paris when you were born. If so, it's a record that tells something about you. From it, we can guess your approximate size and maybe your weight at that age. Animals walking on Earth long ago have left similar tracks, such as those in **Figure 12-7.** In some cases, tracks can tell us more about how an organism lived than any other type of fossil.

For example, from a set of tracks at Davenport Ranch, Texas, we have learned something about the social life of *Apatosaurus,* one of the largest known dinosaurs. The largest tracks of the herd are on the outer edges and the smallest are on the inside. This suggests that the adult apatosaurs surrounded the young as they traveled—probably to protect them from enemies. In fact, a nearby set of allosaur tracks indicates that one was stalking the herd.

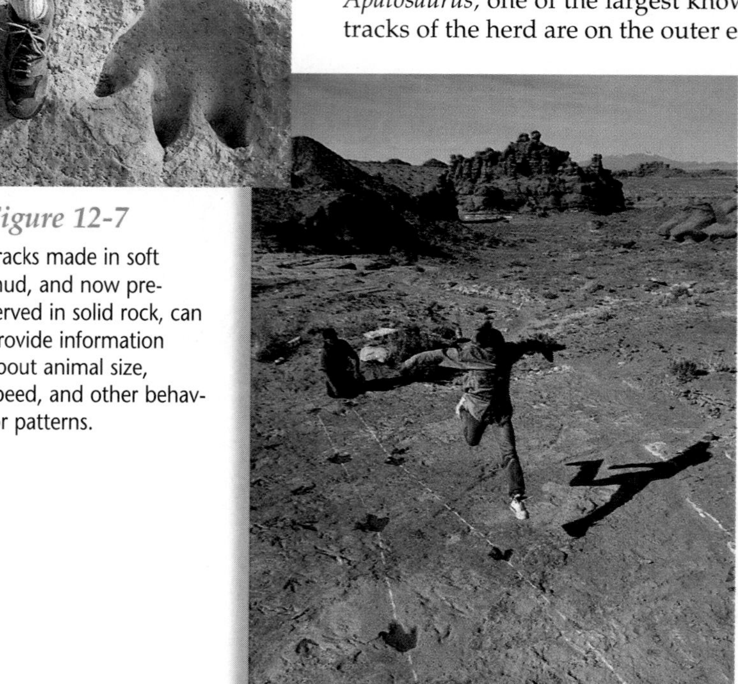

Figure 12-7

Tracks made in soft mud, and now preserved in solid rock, can provide information about animal size, speed, and other behavior patterns.

Other trace fossils include worm holes and burrows made by marine animals. These, too, tell us something about the lifestyle of these animals. As you can see, a combination of fossils can tell us a great deal about the individuals that inhabited Earth before us.

Theme Connection

Stability and Change The fact that fossils retain the shape and texture of the object they formed, and the fact that the fossil record shows that some life-forms change over time reinforce the theme of stability and change.

Community Connection

Fossil Collecting Invite a local collector of fossils to class to share his or her hobby with the class. The person might display some of his or her collection, tell about how the fossils were found and extracted from rock, and discuss from how wide an area the fossils were collected.

Figure 12-8

The sequence of sedimentary rock (A) and the fossils each contains can be used to date the rocks. The chart (B) shows when each organism inhabited Earth. *Why is it possible to say that the middle layer of rock had to be deposited between 438 and 408 million years ago?*

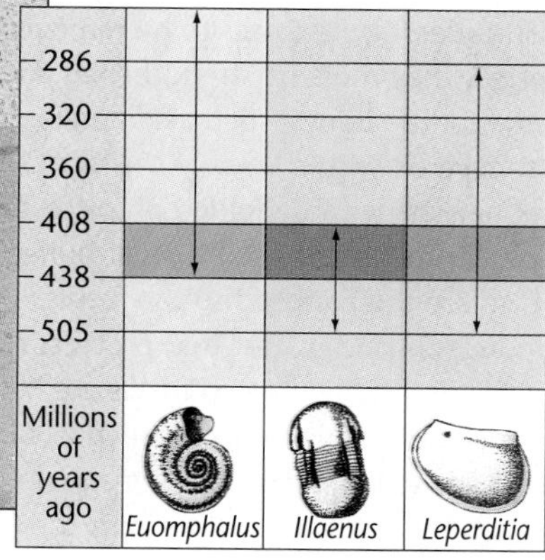

A Illustration of a sequence of rocks and the fossils they contain.

B Fossil Range Chart

Index Fossils

One thing we've learned by studying fossils is that organisms are constantly changing, or evolving. Evidence indicates that species inhabit Earth for a certain period of time before they evolve into new species or they die out completely. Some species of organisms inhabit Earth for very long periods of time without changing much. Other species remain unchanged for only a short time. It is these organisms that produce index fossils.

Index fossils are from species that existed on Earth for relatively short periods of time, were abundant, and were widespread geographically. Scientists use index fossils to determine the age of rock layers. Because few fossils meet all the requirements to be an index fossil, groups of fossils are generally used to date rocks. This is how the rock layer in **Figure 12-8** was dated.

CONNECT TO

LIFE SCIENCE

You have learned that original remains of animals can be found in tar seeps. ***Hypothesize*** why so many animals became trapped in tar seeps.

CONNECT TO

LIFE SCIENCE

Answer Water will, at times, lie on top of tar seeps, and animals become trapped while drinking the water. Other animals become trapped when they attack trapped animals.

Inquiry Question

Why are index fossils useful to Earth scientists? *Because the organisms that formed them existed for short periods of time, the fossils are very good indicators of the ages of the rocks in which they are found.*

Visual Learning

Figure 12-8 Why is it possible to say that the middle layer of rock had to be deposited between 438 and 408 million years ago? *The three fossils have ranges that overlap between 438 and 408 million years. The age of the layer cannot be dated more accurately than that.* LEP LS

Enrichment

Have an interested student research and report on the "Tollund Man." The Tollund Man is the preserved body of a human found in Tollund Fen, Denmark. His remains were spectacularly well preserved in the shallow, oxygen-starved water of the fen. Tollund Man was found with his leather cap still in place on his head. All of his facial hairs and the pores and wrinkles of his skin are easily visible. One of the things that makes this find particularly interesting is that Tollund Man has a rope noose around his neck. Scientists have inferred that he was hanged and then thrown into the fen approximately 2000 years ago. L3 P

Cultural Diversity

The Copper Man of the Alps On September 19, 1991, a German couple hiking in the Alps came across a 5000-year-old traveler, naturally mummified in a small depression covered by glacial ice. The Iceman is now known to be one of the oldest and best-preserved mummified humans. Grains on his clothing suggest that he came from lowland South Tirol. He wore finely stitched skin clothing, a woven grass cape, and boots. A deerskin quiver holds 2 arrows tipped with flint, and 12 unfinished ones. He carried two antibiotic fungi, a backpack, a half-finished longbow, high-quality flint, and a flint dagger. One of his most intriguing possessions was an ax, originally thought to be bronze but now known to be copper. It is flanged in a style not found anywhere nearby until nearly 800 years later.

USING TECHNOLOGY

Explain that the processing of fossils at museums varies, depending on how the fossils will be displayed. Students are probably most familiar with free mounts. Steel skeletons are often used to support the large bones of mastodons, dinosaurs, mammoths, and other large animals.

Think Critically

The bones have been buried for millions of years. Exposing them to air, light, and microorganisms makes them fragile.

3 Assess

Check for Understanding

FLEX Your Brain

Use the Flex Your Brain activity to have students explore FOSSILS.

Activity Worksheets, p. 5

Reteach

LS Interpersonal Divide students into groups of four. Assign the roles of reader, materials handler, "fossil" maker, and recorder. Have students determine which of the following types of sediments would best preserve fossils by pressing shells or bones into mixtures of sand and water; clay and water; and gravel and water. The recorder should report which mixture of sediments allowed the best imprint to be formed. L1 COOP LEARN

Extension

For students who have mastered this section, use the **Reinforcement** and **Enrichment** masters.

USING TECHNOLOGY

Recovering Fossils

When scientists locate an area thought to have fossils, large equipment or explosives are used to remove overlying rocks and soil. Smaller tools are then used as the excavation nears the fossils. In the final phases of recovery, tiny picks and brushes are used to remove soil from the fossils.

Preparing Fossils

In order for the fossils to be removed or transported, they must be strengthened and protected. Large, brittle bones, such as dinosaur remains, are first covered with a layer of shellac. Then, strips of wet newspaper are molded onto the fossils. Finally, a plaster mixture is used to coat burlap straps, which are then applied to the fossils. This final step produces a kind of cast that protects and supports the fossils. The reinforced fossils are now ready to be transported. Some fossils such as dinosaur bones often are so large that heavy machinery, and even helicopters, are used to transport the fossils. They then go to museums or universities, where they will undergo final preparations before being exhibited.

Think Critically: Why are remains such as dinosaur bones so fragile?

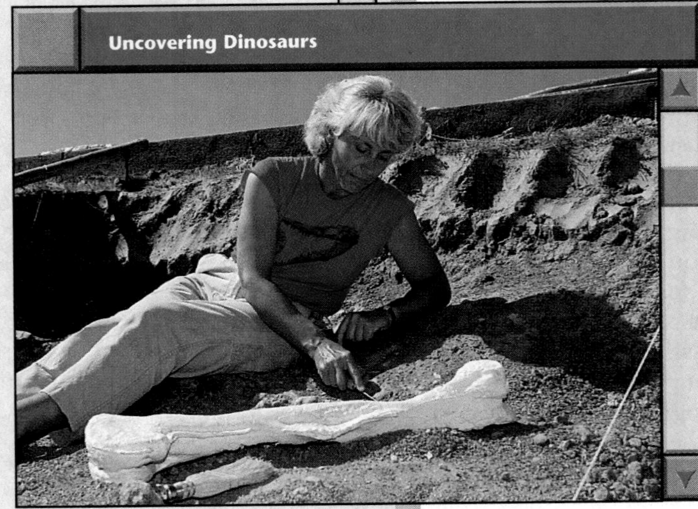

Fossils and Ancient Environments

Fossils can also be used to determine what the environment of an area was like long ago. For example, rocks in Antarctica contain fossils of tropical plants. The environment of Antarctica today certainly isn't tropical, but we know that it was at the time these fossilized plants were living.

How would you explain the presence of fossilized brachiopods, animals that lived in shallow seas, in the rocks of the midwest United States? A brachiopod fossil is shown in **Figure 12-9D.** The central portion of North America was covered by a shallow sea when the brachiopods were living, as shown in **Figure 12-9.**

Fossils tell us not only about past life on Earth, but also about the history of the rock layers that contain them. Fossils can provide information about environment, climate, and animal behavior, as well as dating the rocks.

Integrating the Sciences

Life Science Explain that life-forms have changed over time because of changes in the environment in which they lived. Some life-forms have become extinct because of severe changes in the environment, to which the organisms could not adapt.

- **How are certain fossils indicators of ancient environments?** *Some organisms are restricted to a specific environment. The rocks in which fossils of such organisms are found allow scientists to determine the environment that existed when the organisms were alive.*
- **If you found fossilized trilobites in bedrock near your school, what could you state about the ancient environment of the area?** *The area must have been covered by a shallow sea at some time in the past, because trilobites were marine animals.*

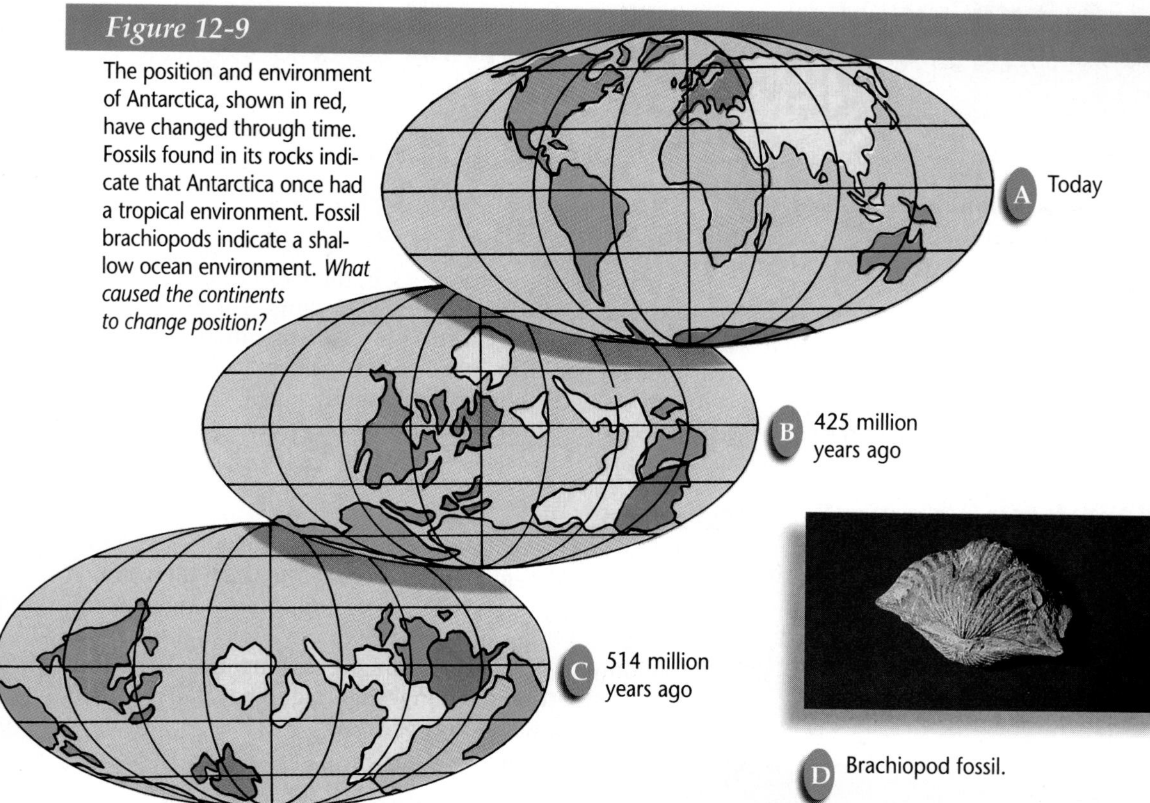

Figure 12-9

The position and environment of Antarctica, shown in red, have changed through time. Fossils found in its rocks indicate that Antarctica once had a tropical environment. Fossil brachiopods indicate a shallow ocean environment. *What caused the continents to change position?*

Section Wrap-up

Review

1. What conditions are needed for most fossils to form?
2. Describe how a mold and cast fossil might form.
3. **Think Critically:** What can be said about the ages of two widely separated layers of rock that contain the same type of fossil?

Skill Builder

Concept Mapping

Make a concept map that compares and contrasts petrified remains and original remains. Use the following terms and phrases: *types of fossils, original remains, evidence of former life, petrified remains, materials replaced by minerals,* and *actual parts of organisms.* If you need help, refer to Concept Mapping in the **Skill Handbook.**

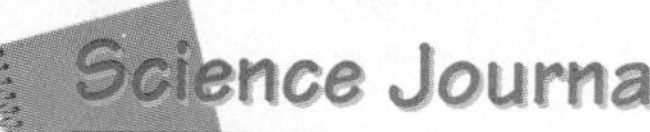

Science Journal

Collect samples of fossils or visit a museum that has fossils on display. In your Science Journal, make an illustration of each fossil. Write a brief description, noting key facts about each. Also, write about how each fossil might have been formed.

4 Close

•MINI•QUIZ•

1. ______ are remains or traces of once-living organisms preserved in Earth's rocks. *Fossils*
2. When minerals replace the original material of an organism, the fossil that forms is a(n) ______. *petrified remain*
3. A(n) ______ forms when a thin film of carbon is left behind after gases and liquids are removed from an organism. *carbonaceous film*
4. Sediment that fills a cavity and hardens forms a(n) ______ of the original organism. *cast*
5. ______ fossils are tracks and other evidence of animal activity. *Trace*

Section Wrap-up

Review

1. quick burial and the presence of hard parts
2. An object buried in sediment later decays, leaving a cavity called a mold. Later, sediments may fill the cavity, harden, and produce a cast.
3. **Think Critically** Both layers of rock formed during the period of time that the fossil-producing organism lived; the two layers of rock may be similar in age if the organism existed for only a short period of Earth's history.

Science Journal

Answers will vary, depending on which fossils students use. Students should indicate that to be preserved, fossils need to be buried quickly and should be made of hard parts.

Skill Builder

Possible solution:

Types of fossils — Petrified remains — are composed of — materials replaced by minerals — which are — evidence of former life

Types of fossils — Original remains — are composed of — actual parts of organisms — which are — evidence of former life

Assessment

Performance Assess students' abilities to make concept maps by having them construct maps and then share them with other students. Encourage students to share their ideas and to modify their own maps. Use the Performance Task Assessment List for Concept Map in **PASC,** p. 89. P

SCIENCE & SOCIETY

Section 12•2

Prepare

Section Background

Several hypotheses have been proposed to explain the extinction of dinosaurs. One hypothesis proposes that a disease of epidemic proportion swept Earth, causing the extinction. Small mammals may have been able to rob dinosaur nests of their eggs, resulting in fewer dinosaurs. Gradually changing climates also may have led to the extinction of the dinosaurs.

1 Motivate

Bellringer

Before presenting the lesson, display **Section Focus Transparency 46** on the overhead projector. Assign the accompanying **Focus Activity** worksheet. L1 LEP

Tying to Previous Knowledge

Have students recall from Chapter 11 that a large landmass called Pangaea once existed on Earth. Explain that as Pangaea separated, changes in global climate occurred. Climatic changes are considered to be one possible cause of dinosaur extinctions.

SCIENCE & SOCIETY

12•2 ISSUE:

Extinction of Dinosaurs

Science Words

extinct

Objectives

- Discuss the meteorite-impact hypothesis of dinosaur extinction.
- Describe several hypotheses about why dinosaurs became extinct.

What killed the dinosaurs?

In layers of sedimentary rock in the western United States rest the remains of thousands of dinosaurs. The bones tell us that dinosaurs were fast, agile, intelligent animals who ruled the land longer than any other organism before or since. Why are they no longer a dominant life-form on Earth? What happened to the dinosaurs, and what can we learn from their disappearance?

Extinction

The last species of dinosaurs became extinct about 66 million years ago. When a species becomes **extinct,** there are no longer any living members of its kind. Before their extinction, species of dinosaurs had dominated the land for about 160 million years. The dinosaurs are no longer on Earth, but we learn from them by investigating what caused their extinction, as shown in **Figure 12-10.**

Figure 12-10

Evidence in the rock record indicates that a large meteorite may have struck Earth at about the same time the dinosaurs became extinct. The crater to the left is in New Zealand, and shows the force with which meteors can hit Earth.

Program Resources

Reproducible Masters

Study Guide, p. 50 L1
Reinforcement, p. 50 L1
Enrichment, p. 50 L3
Science and Society Integration, p. 16

Transparencies

Section Focus Transparency 46 L1

2 Points of View

Meteorite Hypothesis

One of the many hypotheses about dinosaur extinction is that a large meteorite collided with Earth. The collision threw dust and debris into Earth's upper atmosphere. The collision also may have caused large forest fires that would have added smoke to the atmosphere.

If enough dust and smoke were released into Earth's upper atmosphere, the sun could have been completely blocked out. If the sun's energy remained blocked off for a long time, plants couldn't have carried on photosynthesis and would have died. With no food, plant-eating dinosaurs also would have died. With no plant-eating dinosaurs to prey on, meat-eating dinosaurs would have starved as well.

Figure 12-11
Volcanic eruptions such as this eject large amounts of ash, gas, and debris into the atmosphere.

Scientists have found evidence of an impact in a layer of clay in a column of sedimentary rock that was deposited at about the same time the dinosaurs became extinct. The layer contains small deformed grains of quartz very much like those found near meteorite craters elsewhere on Earth. But more importantly, the clay layer is rich in the element iridium. Iridium is rare on Earth's surface, but it is found in greater amounts in meteorites. The iridium in the clay layer may have come from the meteorite when it broke apart on impact.

Alternative Hypothesis

Some scientists disagree with the meteorite hypothesis and are looking for other explanations for dinosaur extinction. Perhaps the iridium-rich clay layer can be explained by large amounts of volcanic activity. The volcanic activity could have caused large amounts of dust to enter Earth's atmosphere, as shown in **Figure 12-11.** The rock record indicates that global temperatures started to decrease about 66 million years ago. Perhaps with colder temperatures, the dinosaurs could not adapt and eventually died.

Science Journal

Dinosaurs are alive? Some scientists do not believe that all dinosaurs became extinct about 66 million years ago. These scientists believe that some dinosaurs evolved into species that are still alive today. The species these scientists are discussing are birds, or, as some call them, *avian dinosaurs.* In fact, one source lists the smallest dinosaur as the bee hummingbird. Have students write in their Science Journals about the idea that today's birds evolved from dinosaurs that lived over 66 million years ago. Some sources of information include *Discovering Dinosaurs in the American Museum of Natural History* (1995) by M. A. Norell, E. S. Gaffney, and L. Dingus, from Nevraumont Publishing Inc., New York; *The Ultimate Dinosaur Book* (1993) by D. Lambert, Dorling Kindersley, New York; and *Dinosaur!* (1991) by D. Norman, Prentice Hall, New York. L3 LS

2 Teach

Activity

LS **Interpersonal** Ask student groups to hypothesize what might happen to life on Earth today if light from the sun were unable to reach Earth for several years. Students should realize that much of the plant life on Earth would die. Photosynthesizing organisms are the base of all food chains. Plants also produce oxygen. Their demise would affect the survival of most life-forms. L1 COOP LEARN

Discussion

Assign each group member a different hypothesis on dinosaur extinction. Have students research their assigned topics and present their findings.

3 Assess

Check for Understanding

FLEX Your Brain

Use the Flex Your Brain activity to have students explore CAUSES OF ANIMAL AND PLANT EXTINCTIONS.

Activity Worksheets, p. 5

Reteach

Show students photographs of volcanic eruptions. Ask students what might happen to Earth's atmosphere if many volcanoes erupted at the same time.

Extension

For students who have mastered this section, use the **Reinforcement** and **Enrichment** masters.

CONNECT TO

CHEMISTRY

Answer The isotopes of some elements decay at a known, fixed rate. By knowing this rate and measuring the amount of decay that has occurred, scientists can calculate the age of a material. This is radiometric dating. Students will learn more about this concept in Section 12-4 of this chapter.

4 Close

•MINI•QUIZ•

Use the Mini Quiz to check students' recall of chapter content.

1. **The last species of dinosaurs became extinct about _____ years ago.** *66 million*
2. **Louis and Walter Alvarez found a layer of clay containing _____ and _____ that supported a meteorite-impact hypothesis.** *iridium, deformed quartz grains*
3. **High concentrations of iridium in sedimentary layers can be explained by _____ activity as well as by a meteorite impact.** *volcanic*
4. **The rock record indicates that global temperatures _____ about 66 million years ago.** *decreased*

Figure 12-12

Dinosaurs dominated Earth for 160 million years. But like us, they were dependent on their environment, and when it changed too drastically, they became extinct.

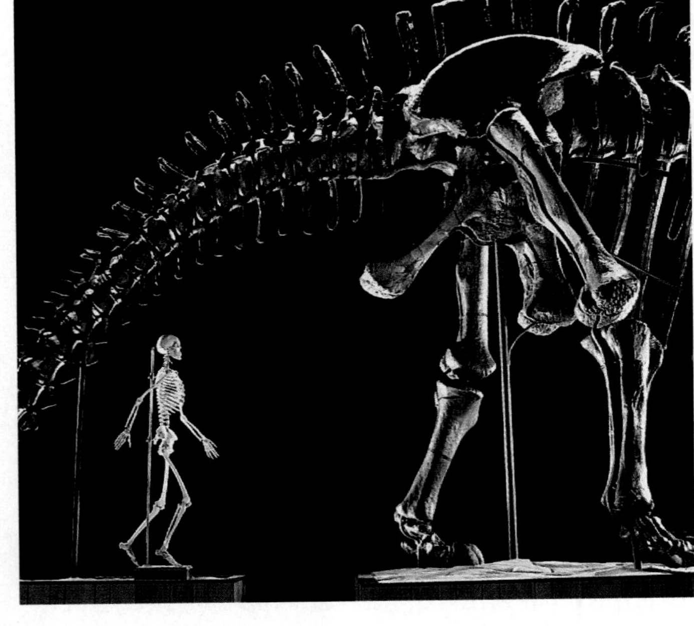

CONNECT TO

CHEMISTRY

Radiometric dating of tektites found near a buried crater on Mexico's Yucatan Peninsula indicates that the crater formed about 66 million years ago. If this age is correct, the meteorite impact may have been related to dinosaur extinction. ***Analyze*** what radiometric dating is and how it can be used to determine the tektites' age.

Another hypothesis suggests that there was nothing unusual about the extinction of dinosaurs and that they disappeared gradually because of slow changes in their environment. Perhaps these changes were brought about by shifts in the position of the continents caused by plate tectonics.

It's difficult to know for sure what caused Earth's environment to change 66 million years ago. But one thing that we have learned from the dinosaurs is that all organisms are dependent on their environments, as illustrated in **Figure 12-12.**

Section Wrap-up

Review

1. Discuss two theories that explain how iridium could have gotten into the clay layer deposited about 66 million years ago.
2. Explain how the inability of plants to photosynthesize would be harmful to the dinosaurs.

Explore the Issue

Often, the simplest explanation of an event is the most accurate. Based on this, how would you look at the issue of what caused dinosaur extinction? Which theory seems most likely to be correct? Explain your choice.

SCIENCE & SOCIETY

Section Wrap-up

Review

1. The iridium may have been deposited as the meteorite broke apart on impact. Extensive volcanic activity could have brought the element to Earth's surface.
2. If plants were not able to carry on photosynthesis, they would stop producing food. Plants would begin to die off. Dinosaurs that relied on plants for food would begin to starve. Meat-eating dinosaurs that ate the plant-eating dinosaurs would also begin to die off.

Explore the Issue

Student answers will vary. Expect several of your students to choose increased volcanic activity as the cause because of the ongoing volcanic activity on Earth today. Some students will select the meteorite impact idea because of the evidence that Earth has been hit by large meteorites in the past and that the moon has many meteorite craters on it. Accept all answers but insist that students support their answers with scientific evidence.

Relative Ages of Rocks

12•3

Science Words

principle of superposition
relative dating
unconformitiy

Objectives

- Describe several methods used to date rock layers relative to other rock layers.
- Interpret gaps in the rock record.
- Give an example of how rock layers may be correlated with other rock layers.

The Principle of Superposition

It's a hot summer day in July and you're getting ready to meet your friends at the local park. You put on your helmet and pads and grab your skateboard. But the bearings in one of the wheels are worn, and the wheel isn't spinning freely. You remember reading an article in a skateboarding magazine about how to replace wheels, and you decide to look it up. In your room is a stack of magazines from the past year, as seen in **Figure 12-13.** You know that the article came out in the January edition, so it must be near the bottom of the pile. As you dig downward, you find magazines from March, then February. January must be next.

How did you know that the January issue of the magazine would be on the bottom? To find the older edition under newer ones, you applied the principle of superposition.

Youngest Rocks on Top

The **principle of superposition** states that in an undisturbed layer of rock, the oldest rocks are on the bottom and the rocks become progressively younger toward the top. Why is this the case, and is it always true?

As you know, sediments are often deposited in horizontal beds, forming layers of sedimentary rock. The first layer to form is usually on the bottom. Each additional layer forms on top of the previous one. Unless forces, such as those generated by tectonic activity, overturn the layers, the oldest rocks are found at the bottom. When layers have been overturned, geologists use other clues in the rock layers to determine their original positions.

Figure 12-13

The pile of magazines illustrates the principle of superposition, which states that the oldest rock layer (or magazine) is on the bottom.

Program Resources

Reproducible Masters

Study Guide, p. 51 L1
Reinforcement, p. 51 L1
Enrichment, p. 51 L3
Activity Worksheets, pp. 72-73 L1
Lab Manual 34

Transparencies

Section Focus Transparency 47 L1
Teaching Transparency 24

Section 12•3

Prepare

Section Background

- The principle of faunal succession states that fossil organisms occur in rocks in a definite and determinable order. Thus, rocks formed during a particular interval of geologic time can be recognized by their fossils.
- A geologic column is a composite diagram that shows the rocks of an area in the sequence in which they occur.
- Correlation of geologic columns from many locations enables geologists to construct geologic maps. Geologic maps show the relative age, distribution, and structural features of surface rocks.

Preplanning

To prepare for Activity 12-1, sketch large illustrations of the diagrams.

1 Motivate

Bellringer

Before presenting the lesson, display **Section Focus Transparency 47** on the overhead projector. Assign the accompanying **Focus Activity** worksheet. L1 LEP

Tying to Previous Knowledge

Students experience "superposition" in their everyday lives. Have students relate how sequences of sedimentary rocks are similar to the bricks in a brick house or building. A bricklayer must place the first layer of bricks before he or she can lay another layer on top. The bricks at the base of a building are "older" than those above it.

2 Teach

Demonstration

 **Visual-Spatial** Without explaining your actions to the students, place layer upon layer of five different colored clays on top of your desk. Use a knife to carefully cut a "fault" through all the layers. Now place a sixth layer on top of the faulted ones. Ask students to determine the relative ages of the layers and the fault.

GLENCOE TECHNOLOGY

Videodisc

Glencoe Earth Science Interactive Videodisc
Side 2, Lesson 5
Stratification

5101-5417

5419-5964

5966-6359

6361-6795

Figure 12-14
Illustration and photograph of a large-scale fold in sedimentary rocks showing the exposed rock layers. The oldest layers are folded up and exposed in the center.

Relative Dating

Suppose you now want to look for another issue of a magazine. You're not sure exactly how old it is; all you know is that it arrived after the January issue. You can find it in the stack by using relative dating.

Relative dating is used in geology to determine the order of events and the relative age of rocks by examining the position of rocks in a sequence. For example, if layers of sedimentary rock are offset by a fault, you know that the layers had to be there first before a fault could cut through them. The relative age of the rocks is older than the relative age of the fault.

Relative dating doesn't tell you anything about the exact age of rock layers. You don't know if a layer is 100 million or 10 000 years old, only that it's younger than the layers below it and older than the fault cutting through it.

Other Clues Help

Relative dating works well if rocks haven't been folded or overturned by tectonic processes. For example, look at **Figure 12-14.** Which layer is the oldest? In cases where rock layers

Figure 12-15

An angular unconformity results when horizontal layers overlie tilted layers.

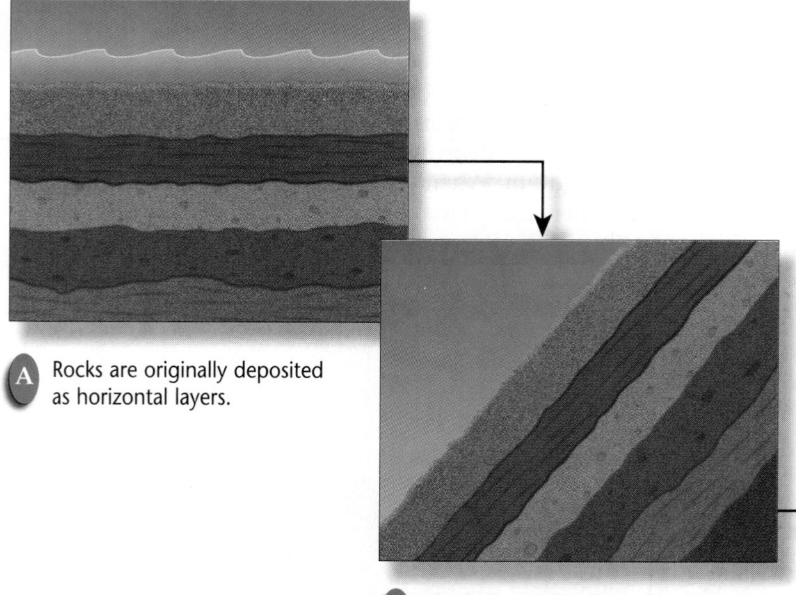

A. Rocks are originally deposited as horizontal layers.

B. The horizontal rock layers are tilted as they are deformed by tectonic forces.

Community Connection

Visiting Geologist Invite a geologist from your area to visit class. Ask him or her to discuss how rock layers are oriented in your area. Perhaps the geologist could bring core samples to show the orientation of rock layers below Earth's surface. If there is a nearby outcrop of rock layers, take students on a trip to see it.

Use **Study Guide,** p. 51, as you teach this lesson.

Use Lab 34 in the **Lab Manual** as you teach this lesson.

 Use **Teaching Transparency 24** as you teach this lesson.

have been disturbed, you may have to look for fossils and other clues to date the rocks. If you find a fossil in the top layer that's older than a fossil in a lower layer, you can hypothesize that layers have been overturned or faulted.

Unconformities

As you have seen, a layer of rock is a record of past events. But most rock records are incomplete—there are layers missing. These gaps in rock layers are called **unconformities.**

Unconformities develop when agents of erosion remove existing rock layers. They also form when a period of time passes without any new deposition occurring to form new layers of rock.

Angular Unconformities

Figure 12-15 illustrates one way an unconformity can form. Horizontal layers of sedimentary rock are tilted and uplifted, so that agents of erosion and weathering wear them down. Eventually, younger sediment layers are deposited horizontally on top of the eroded and tilted layers. Such an unconformity is called an angular unconformity.

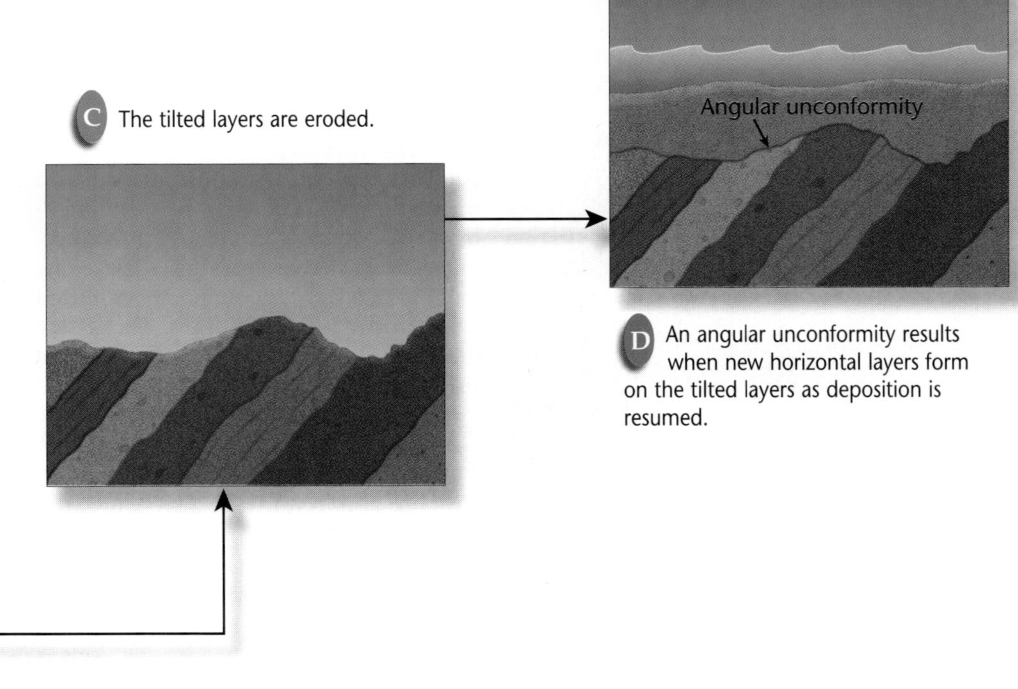

C The tilted layers are eroded.

D An angular unconformity results when new horizontal layers form on the tilted layers as deposition is resumed.

Demonstration

LS **Visual-Spatial** Use a set of books from an encyclopedia to demonstrate unconformities. Construct an angular unconformity by stacking volumes 1, 2, 3, and 4 in numerical order, with volume 1 on the bottom. Tilt the books at an angle and then horizontally place volumes 7 and 8 on top of the tilted books. Demonstrate a disconformity by stacking volumes 1, 2, 3, and 4 in numerical order, with volume 1 on the bottom. Add volumes 7, 8, and 9 to the stack. Explain that the missing volumes in each case create the unconformity. LEP

Discussion

Initiate a discussion of unconformities with students by asking the following questions:

- **What does an unconformity tell you about the geology of the area?** *At some time in the past, erosion removed some rock and/or time passed without any rock formation.*
- **How does an angular unconformity form?** *Horizontal rock layers are uplifted, tilted, and eroded. The surface between these rocks and younger horizontal rocks is an angular unconformity.*
- **How might a disconformity form?** *Horizontal rock layers are uplifted and eroded. Younger rocks are deposited on this erosional surface to form a disconformity.*

Theme Connection

Stability and Change Undisturbed rock layers remain horizontal until forces cause uplift. Once forces are applied, folding and faulting of rock layers can occur. The theme of stability and change is reinforced by the realization that the stability of horizontal layers is disrupted by forces inside Earth. This causes a change in the rock layers, which can lead to the formation of unconformities.

Visual Learning

Figure 12-15 Why is Figure 12-15D considered an angular unconformity? *The rocks below the erosional surface are at an angle to the rocks above the erosional surface.* LEP LS

Visual Learning

Figure 12-16 How could you determine how much time and/or rock is missing? *Find a section that is complete, containing the same section of rock, and correlate rock units and/or fossils.* LEP IS

Problem Solving

Solve the Problem

1. Schist and gneiss are at the base of each column.
2. At least three unconformities occur in the Westwater column; at least two are shown in the Green River column. Unconformities exist between sandstone (16) and underlying rock (sandstone [15] or shale [14]), between sandstone (8) and shale (5), and between shale (3) and schist or gneiss.
3. The rock layers numbered the same exist at both locations and can be considered extensions of the same rock layers.

Think Critically

Deposition of rocks in the Green River area was interrupted by periods of erosion and/or nondeposition, as shown by the unconformities. There are several hypotheses that could explain why rocks are missing from the Westwater column. The rocks could have been deposited and later eroded. Or, the beds may never have been deposited in the area. P

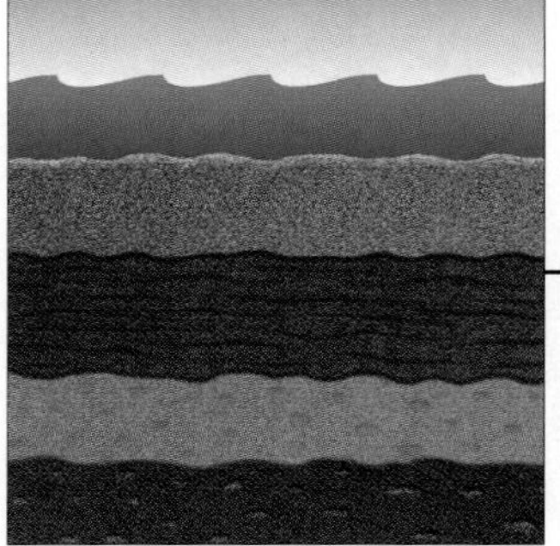

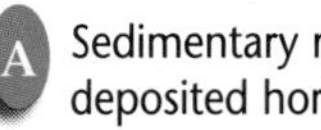

A Sedimentary rock layers are deposited horizontally.

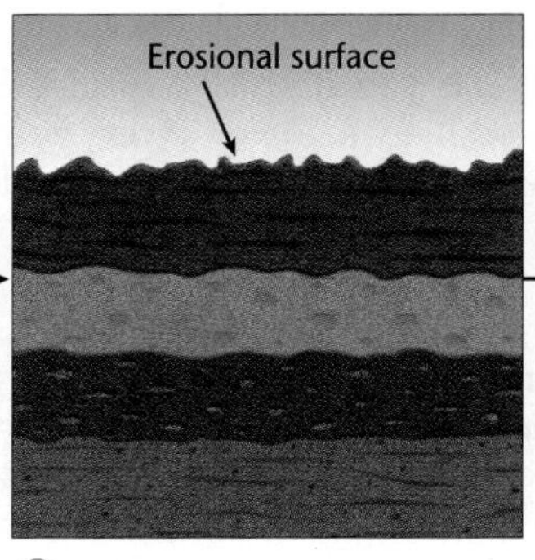

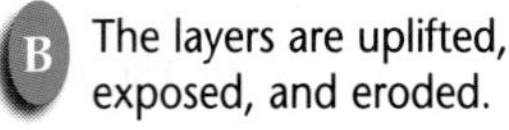

B The layers are uplifted, exposed, and eroded.

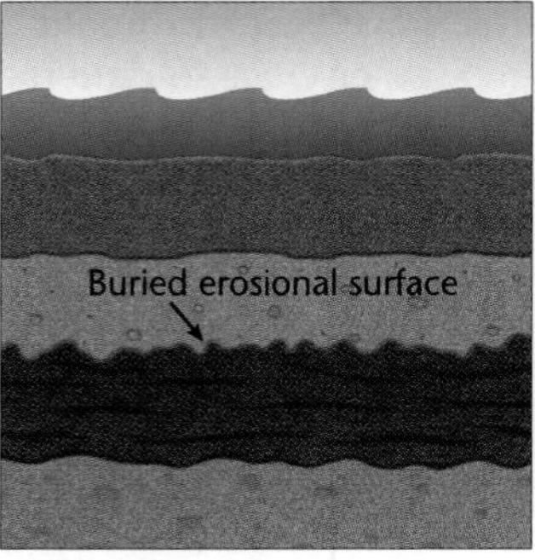

C When deposition resumes, younger horizontal sediments are deposited on the buried erosional surface.

Figure 12-16

The buried erosional surface in the far right illustration is a disconformity. *How could you determine how much time and/or rock is missing?*

Disconformity

Suppose you're looking at a sequence of sedimentary rocks. They look complete, but actually, there are layers missing. If you look closely you may find an old erosional surface. This records a time when the rocks were exposed and eroded. Later, younger rocks formed above the erosional surface when sediment deposition began again. Even though all the layers are horizontal, there's still a gap in the record. This type of unconformity, called a disconformity, is illustrated in **Figure 12-16.**

Figure 12-17

These rock layers, exposed in the Grand Canyon, can be correlated across large areas of the western U.S.

Nonconformity

Another type of unconformity, called a nonconformity, occurs when sedimentary rock layers form above metamorphic or intrusive igneous rocks. The metamorphic or igneous rock is uplifted and eroded. Sedimentary rocks are then deposited on top of this erosional surface.

Correlating Rock Layers

Suppose you're studying a layer of sandstone in Bryce Canyon in Utah. Later, when you visit Canyonlands National Park, you notice that a layer of sandstone there looks just like the sandstone in Bryce Canyon, 250 kilometers away. Above the sandstone in the Canyonlands is a layer of limestone and then another sandstone layer. You return to Bryce Canyon and find the same sequence—sandstone, limestone, and sandstone. What do you conclude?

Across the Curriculum

Geography Obtain state geologic maps of Colorado, Utah, Arizona, and New Mexico. Have students examine the maps and note that when they are arranged geographically, many of the rocks extend across state boundaries. Have students research the geologic history of this area during the Mesozoic and Cenozoic Eras. L2

Integrating the Sciences

Physics Unconformities form when rock layers are uplifted, tilted, and eroded. Ask students to explain what causes the forces necessary to produce unconformities. *Forces involved in the process of plate tectonics cause rock layers to be folded, tilted, or faulted. These forces include shear, compression, and tension. Forces caused by the agents of erosion wear away exposed rock surfaces.*

It's likely that you're actually looking at the same rocks at the two locations. These rocks are parts of huge deposits that covered this whole area of the western U.S. as seen in **Figure 12-17.** The sandstone and limestone you found at the two parks are the exposed surfaces of the same rock layers.

Evidence Used for Correlation

Geologists match up, or correlate layers of rocks over great distances, as seen in **Figure 12-18.** It's not always easy to say that a rock layer exposed in one area is the same as a rock layer exposed in another area. Sometimes it's possible to simply walk along the layer for kilometers and prove that it's a continuous unit. In other cases, such as at the Canyonlands area and Bryce Canyon, the rock layers are exposed only where rivers have cut down through overlying layers of rock and sediment. How can you prove that the limestone sandwiched between the two layers of sandstone in Canyonlands is the same limestone as at Bryce Canyon? One way is to use fossil evidence. If the same types of fossils are found in both outcrops of limestone, it's a good indication that the limestone at each location is the same age, and therefore, one continuous deposit.

Rock Correlation

Keiko and Masao spent part of their summer vacation on a field trip through Colorado and Utah. They observed many rock outcrops and recorded what they saw in journals. The geologic column on the left was drawn by Keiko from observations made in Green River, Utah. The column on the right was made by Masao from the data he collected in Westwater, Colorado. Help them reconstruct the geologic history of the area by answering the following questions.

Solve the Problem:

1. **What type of rock is found at the base of each column?**
2. **How many unconformities, and what types, can you recognize in each column?**
3. **How are the rock types similar in the two locations?**

Think Critically:

Explain the geologic history of the Green River area in terms of erosion and deposition. Why are some formations missing from the Westwater column?

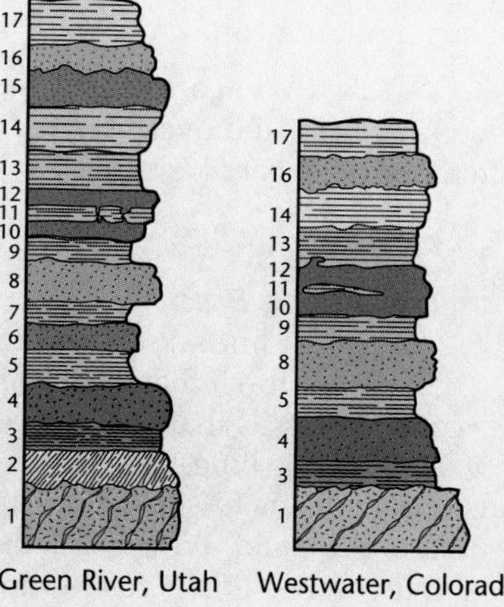

Green River, Utah   Westwater, Colorado

GLENCOE TECHNOLOGY

Videodisc

STVS: Chemistry

Disc 2, Side 2

Carbon-14 Dating (Ch. 4)

3 Assess

Check for Understanding

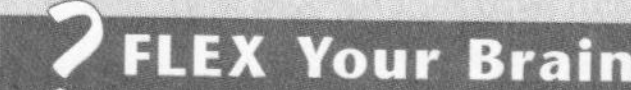

Use the Flex Your Brain activity to have students explore CORRELATION OF ROCK LAYERS.

Activity Worksheets, p. 5

Reteach

Use an overhead projector and a transparency to reconstruct the geologic columns in the Problem Solving activity. Start at the bottom of each column and explain the geologic processes involved as you move upward through the rock layers.

Extension

For students who have mastered this section, use the **Reinforcement** and **Enrichment** masters.

Integrating the Sciences

Chemistry Ask students why so few fossils are found in igneous and metamorphic rocks. Heat, changes of state, and the forces involved with increased pressure would destroy fossils as rock changes by metamorphism. Melting of rock material would also melt any organic material that occurs before igneous rocks form.

Theme Connection

Stability and Change The following activity reinforces stability in that undisturbed rock layers can be correlated across large distances. Copy three related but simple geologic columns from an introductory college-level geology book. Have students work in pairs to correlate the rocks across the three columns. L1 COOP LEARN IS

Visual Learning

Figure 12-18 What layers are present at both canyons? *Navajo SS, Carmel Fm, Entrada SS, Curtis Fm* LEP IS

4 Close

•MINI•QUIZ•

1. **What is the principle of superposition?** *In an undisturbed rock sequence, the oldest rocks are at the bottom of the sequence.*
2. **_____ is a technique that determines the ages of rocks as compared with one another.** *Relative dating*
3. **An unconformity between tilted and horizontal rock is a(n) _____.** *angular unconformity*
4. **A gap between horizontal rock layers is a(n) _____.** *disconformity*

Section Wrap-up

Review

1. Older papers would be closer to the bottom of the locker than more recent papers. Applying the principle of superposition might help in finding the papers.
2. An angular unconformity is a physical boundary in which tilted rocks are overlain by horizontal rocks. In a disconformity, all the rocks are relatively horizontal.
3. **Think Critically** The igneous intrusion is younger than the sedimentary rocks being domed upward. Sedimentary layers are almost always deposited horizontally. The layers would not be deposited in a domed, or arched, formation.

Figure 12-18

The many rock layers, or formations, in Canyonlands and Bryce Canyon have been dated and named. Some formations have been correlated between the two canyons. *Which layers are present at both canyons?* (NOTE: Fm = formation, Ss = sandstone, Gp = group.)

Are there other ways to correlate layers of rock? Sometimes relative dating isn't enough, and other dating methods must be used. In Section 12-4, you'll see how the actual age of rocks can be determined and how geologists have used this information to determine the age of Earth.

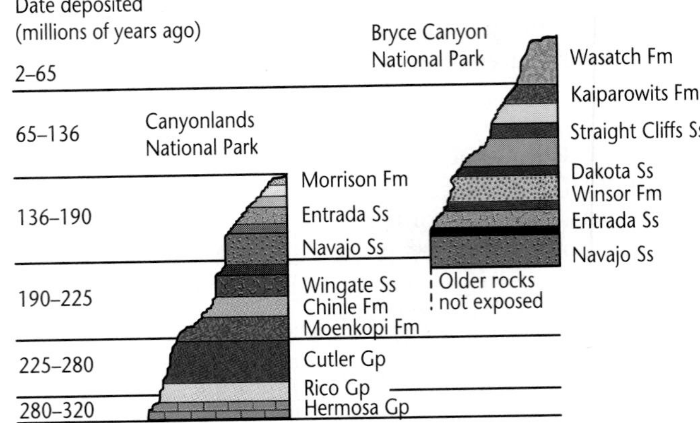

Section Wrap-up

Review

1. Suppose you haven't cleaned out your locker all year. Where would you expect to find papers from the beginning of the year? What principle in geology would you use to find these old papers?
2. Why is it more difficult to recognize a disconformity than an angular unconformity?
3. **Think Critically:** What are the relative ages of an igneous intrusion and overlying sedimentary rock layers that dome upward? Explain.

Using Computers

Spreadsheet Use the information about unconformities on pages 339 and 340 to prepare a spreadsheet listing the types of unconformities, their differences, and their similarities.

Skill Builder
Interpreting Data

A geologist finds a series of rocks. The sandstone contains a fossil that is 400 million years old. The shale contains fossils that are between 500 and 550 million years old. The limestone, which lies under the sandstone, contains fossils that are between 400 and 500 million years old. Which rock bed is oldest? Explain. If you need help, refer to Interpreting Data in the **Skill Handbook.**

Using Computers

Types of Unconformities	Differences	Similarities
Angular Unconformity	horizontal layers over tilted layers	All represent gaps in the rock record
Disconformity	horizontal layers over older horizontal layers with layers missing and erosional surface visible	All indicate times of erosion and/or no deposition
Nonconformity	Sedimentary rock layers over eroded metamorphic or igneous rock layers.	

Skill Builder

The shale is the oldest; the sandstone is the youngest.

Assessment

Performance Assess students' abilities to interpret data by illustrating this Skill Builder on the chalkboard and having them interpret relative ages. Use the Performance Task Assessment List for Analyzing the Data in **PASC**, p. 27. P

Activity 12-1 Relative Age Dating of Geologic Features

Which of your two friends is older? To answer this question, you'd need to know the relative ages of the two. You wouldn't need to know the exact age of either of your friends, just who was born first. The same is sometimes true for rock layers. Geologists can also learn a lot about rock layers without knowing their exact ages.

Problem

Can the relative ages of rocks be determined by studying the rock layers and structures?

Procedure

1. Study Figures A and B. The legend will help you interpret the figures.
2. Determine the relative ages of the rock layers, unconformities, igneous dikes, and fault in each figure.

Analyze

Figure A

1. Were any layers of rock deposited after the igneous dike formed? Explain.
2. What type of unconformity is shown? Is it possible that there were originally more layers of rock than are shown here? Explain.
3. What type of fault is shown?
4. Is it possible to determine whether the igneous dike formed before or after the fault occurred? Explain.

Figure B

5. What type of fault is shown?
6. Is the igneous dike on the left older or younger than the unconformity nearest the surface? Explain.
7. Are the two igneous dikes shown the same age? How do you know?
8. Which two layers of rock may have been much thicker at one time than they are now?

Conclude and Apply

9. Make a sketch of Figure A. On it, **identify** the relative age of each rock layer, igneous dike, fault, and unconformity. For example, the shale layer is the oldest, so mark it with a *1*. Mark the next-oldest feature with a *2,* and so on.
10. Repeat the procedure in question 9 for Figure B.

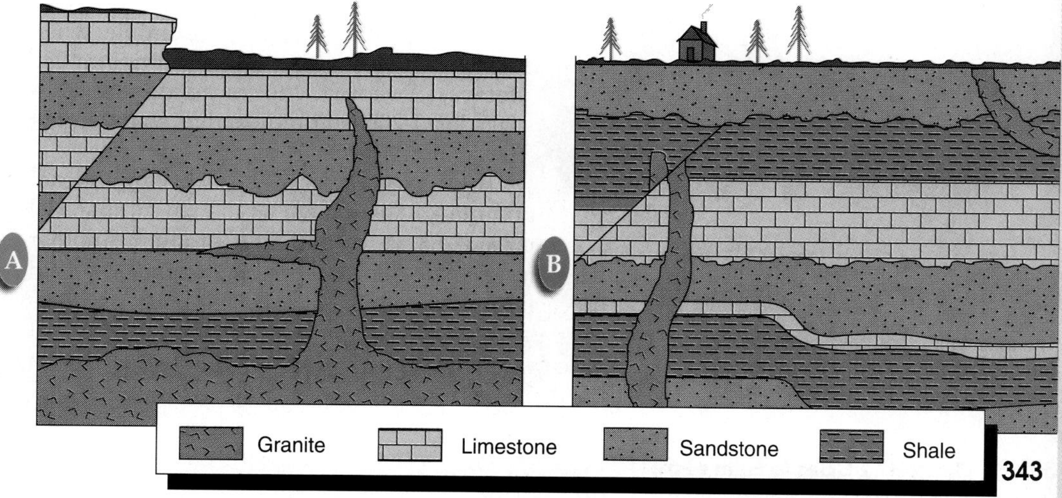

343

Activity 12-1

Purpose

LS Logical-Mathematical Determine the relative order of events by interpreting geologic cross sections. L1

Process Skills

inferring, interpreting data, formulating models, recognizing and using spatial relationships, sequencing, interpreting scientific illustrations

Time

40-45 minutes

Activity Worksheets, pp. 5, 72-73

Teaching Strategies

- Have each group examine the two cross sections closely and make a number of inferences based on the clues provided and their knowledge of superposition, unconformities, faulting, and igneous intrusions. Have each group reach consensus on each of the questions for both cross sections.

Answers to Questions

1. No, since the dike intrudes every layer, it must be the youngest feature.
2. a disconformity; yes, other rock could have existed and been eroded
3. a reverse fault
4. Since the shale is older than the overlying layers that have been offset by the fault, it was deposited *before* faulting.
5. a normal fault
6. Since the dike is offset by the fault but the unconformity is not, the dike is older.
7. Since the dike on the right intrudes the sandstone and the dike that has been offset by the fault is older than the sandstone, the two dikes formed at different times.
8. The sandstone and shale exhibit disconformities at their upper surfaces. These may indicate erosion.
9. 1) shale, 2) sandstone, 3) limestone, 4) disconformity, 5) sandstone, 6) limestone, 7) fault, 8) igneous intrusion; note that another possible solution is 7) igneous intrusion, 8) fault
10. 1) sandstone, 2) shale, 3) limestone, 4) sandstone, 5) disconformity, 6) limestone, 7) shale, 8) igneous intrusion (left), 9) fault, 10) disconformity, 11) sandstone, 12) igneous intrusion (right)

Assessment

Performance Based on what was learned concerning relative ages of rock layers, draw a block diagram similiar to those in Activity 12-1. Include sedimentary, igneous, and metamorphic rocks. Exchange diagrams with another student and interpret his or her diagram. Use the Performance Task Assessment List for Scientific Drawing in **PASC**, p. 55. P

Section 12•4

Prepare

Preplanning

- To prepare for Activity 12-2, have students bring in shoe boxes with lids. For each group, obtain 100 paper clips, 100 pennies, and 100 brass fasteners.
- To prepare for the MiniLAB, have rolls of adding machine paper and a meterstick available.

1 Motivate

Bellringer

Before presenting the lesson, display **Section Focus Transparency 48** on the overhead projector. Assign the accompanying **Focus Activity** worksheet. L1 LEP

Tying to Previous Knowledge

Have students recall from Chapter 2 that atoms of the same element with different numbers of neutrons are called isotopes. Radioactive isotopes are used in absolute dating.

INTEGRATION
Physics

LS **Interpersonal** Have pairs of students compute the age of a rock sample that contains 1/64 of the original carbon-14 isotope. *The sample is about 34 380 years old.* L1 COOP LEARN

Visual Learning

Figure 12-20 **Is any energy released during this process? If so, what?** *Yes, an alpha particle and a beta particle.* LEP LS

12•4 Absolute Ages of Rocks

Science Words

absolute dating
radioactive decay
half-life
radiometric dating
uniformitarianism

Objectives

- Identify how absolute dating differs from relative dating.
- Describe how the half-lives of isotopes are used to determine a rock's age.

INTEGRATION
Physics

Absolute Dating

As you continue to shuffle through your stack of magazines looking for articles about wheels and bearings, you decide you need to restack them into a neat pile. By now, they're a jumble and no longer in order of their relative ages, as shown in **Figure 12-19.** How can you stack them so the oldest are on the bottom and the newest on top? Fortunately, magazines have their dates printed on their covers. Thus, stacking magazines in order is a simple process. Unfortunately for geologists, rocks don't have their ages stamped on them. Or do they?

Absolute dating is a method used by geologists to determine the age, in years, of a rock or other object. Absolute dating is a process that uses the properties of atoms in rocks and other objects to determine their ages.

Radioactive Decay

In Chapter 2, you learned that an element can have atoms with different numbers of neutrons in their nuclei. Some of these isotopes undergo a process called radioactive decay. When an atom of some isotopes decays, one of its neutrons breaks down into a proton and an electron. The electron leaves the atom as a beta particle. The nucleus loses a neutron, but gains a proton. Other isotopes give off two protons and two neutrons in the form of an alpha particle as seen in **Figure 12-20.** As you know, when the number of protons in an atom is changed, as it is in **radioactive decay,** a new element is formed. For example, when an atom of the radioactive isotope uranium-238 decays, it eventually forms an atom of lead-206. Lead-206 isn't radioactive, so it will not decay any further.

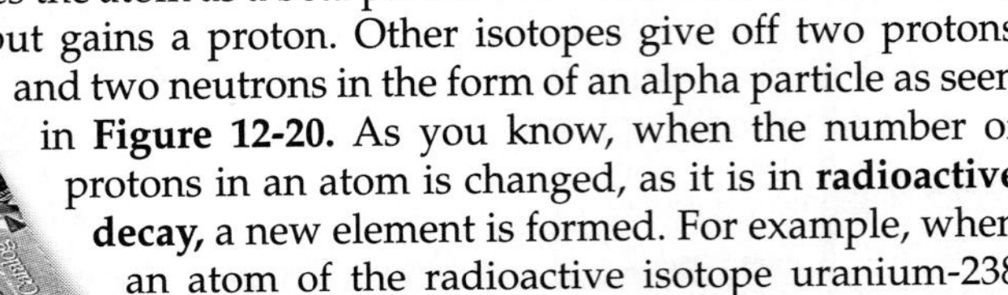

Figure 12-19
The magazines that have been shuffled through no longer illustrate the principle of superposition.

In the case of uranium decaying to lead, uranium-238 is known as the parent material and lead-206 as the daughter product. Another example of a parent material is carbon-14, which decays to its daughter, nitrogen-14. Each radioactive parent material has a certain rate at which it decays to its daughter product. This rate is known as its half-life.

Program Resources

Reproducible Masters

Study Guide, p. 52 L1
Reinforcement, p. 52 L1
Enrichment, p. 52 L3
Activity Worksheets, pp. 74-75, 77 L1
Multicultural Connections, pp. 27-28

Transparencies

Section Focus Transparency 48 L1
Science Integration Transparency 12

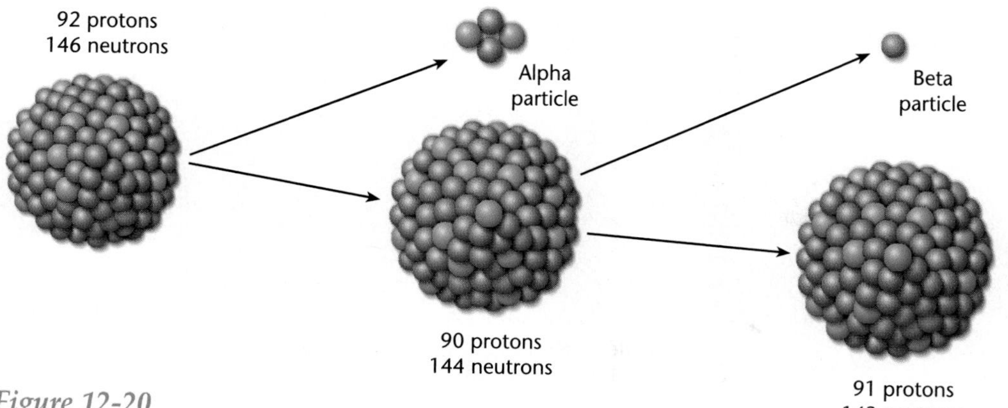

Figure 12-20

Uranium-238 decays by emitting alpha particles (two protons and two neutrons) and beta particles (one electron). A beta particle is produced when a neutron decays and becomes a proton. *Is any energy released during this process? If so, what?*

Half-Life

The **half-life** of an isotope is the time it takes for half of the atoms in the isotope to decay. For example, the half-life of carbon-14 is 5730 years. So it will take 5730 years for half of the carbon-14 atoms in an object to decay to nitrogen-14. You might guess that in another 5730 years, all of the remaining carbon-14 atoms will have decayed to nitrogen-14. However, this is not the case. Only half of the atoms of carbon-14 remaining after the first 5730 years will decay during the second 5730 years. So, after two half-lives, one-fourth of the original carbon-14 atoms still remain. Half of them will decay during another 5730 years. After three half-lives, one-eighth of the original carbon-14 atoms still remain. After many half-lives, such a small amount of the parent material remains that it may not be measurable.

Radiometric Dating

To a geologist, the decay of radioactive isotopes is like a clock ticking away, keeping track of time that's passed since rocks have formed. As time passes, the concentration of parent material in a rock decreases as the concentration of daughter product increases, as seen in **Figure 12-21** on the next page. By measuring the amounts of parent and daughter materials in a rock and by knowing the half-life of the parent, a geologist can calculate the absolute age of the rock. This process is called **radiometric dating.**

MiniLAB

What are the dates of some events in Earth's history?

Procedure

1. Sequence these events in Earth's history in relative order: Earth forms, first many-celled organisms, first land plants, first mammals, dinosaurs become extinct, first amphibians, first human ancestors, oldest known fossils.
2. Make a time line using these dates: 4.6 billion years, 3.5 billion years, 1.0 billion years, 630 million years, 408 million years, 225 million years, 66 million years, and 5 million years ago.
3. Match each event with the absolute date on your time line.

Analysis

1. Check your time line with your teacher.
2. Did you correctly list the events in relative order?
3. How does the age of Earth compare with the presence of humans on the time line?

Integrating the Sciences

Chemistry The half-life of potassium-40 is 1.3 billion years. An igneous rock is found with 25% potassium-40 and 75% daughter products. **Ask students to calculate the absolute age of this rock.** *The absolute age of the rock is 2.6 billion years (two half-lives).* L1 LS

2 Teach

MiniLAB

Purpose

LS **Logical-Mathematical** Students will determine relative and absolute dates of events in Earth's history. L1

Materials

adding machine tape, meterstick, pencil

Teaching Strategies

- Suggest a scale of 1 millimeter for each 1 million years. This will require a 4.6-meter (or longer) piece of adding machine tape.
- If a different scale is used, have students calculate the length of tape before starting.

Activity Worksheets, pp. 5, 77

Analysis

1. Opportunity for self-assessment
2.

Event	Yrs Before Present
Earth forms	4.6 B
oldest known fossils	3.5 B
1st many-celled organisms	1.0 B
1st many-celled animals	630 M
1st plants on land	480 M
1st amphibians	408 M
1st mammals	225 M
dinosaurs extinct	66 M
1st human ancestors	5 M

3. Presence of humans amounts to about 1% of Earth's age.

Assessment

Performance To further assess students' understanding of relative and absolute dating, have them determine the relative and absolute ages of students in the classroom. Use the Performance Task Assessment List for Using Math in Science in PASC, p. 29. P

Visual Learning

Figure 12-22 What other events could leave charcoal behind and provide radiocarbon dates? *Bones, wood, and any organic remains containing carbon.* LEP LS

3 Assess

Check for Understanding

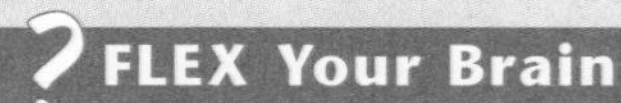

Use the Flex Your Brain activity to have students explore ABSOLUTE DATING.

Activity Worksheets, p. 5

Reteach

Ask students to imagine that a sheet of paper represents the amount of parent radioactive isotope in a rock. State that the half-life of the parent isotope is 20 seconds. After 20 seconds, tear the sheet of paper in half. Set one half of the sheet of paper aside, and explain that it represents the daughter isotope. Every 20 seconds, repeat the process with the paper that remains. Ask students to describe what has happened to the amount of parent isotope. Lead students to conclude that at some point, all of the parent isotope will decay.

Extension

For students who have mastered this section, use the **Reinforcement** and **Enrichment** masters.

USING MATH

After five half-lives, 1/32 of the original isotope remains. Five times 1600 equals 8000 years.

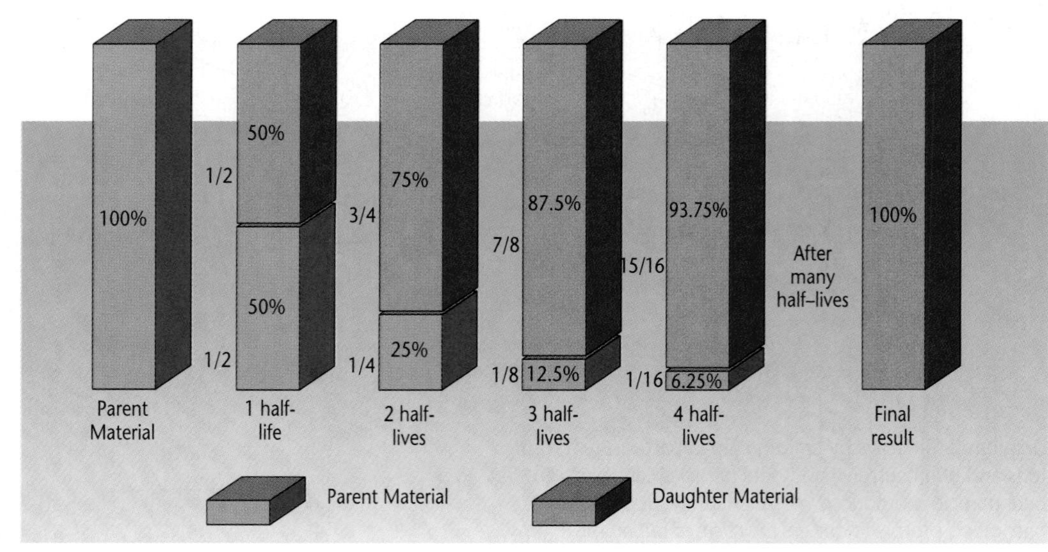

Figure 12-21

After each half-life, one-half the amount of parent material remains. Eventually, such a small amount of the parent material is left that it all decays to daughter material.

A scientist must decide which parent and daughter materials to measure when dating a rock or fossil. If the object to be dated is very old, then an isotope with a long half-life must be used. For example, if a fossil is 1 billion years old, there would be no carbon-14 left to measure. However, the half-life of uranium-238 is 4.5 billion years. Enough of the parent and daughter would still be present to measure.

Radiocarbon Dating

Carbon-14 is useful for dating fossils, bones, and wood up to 50 000 years old. Organisms take in carbon from the environment to build tissues in their bodies. When the organism dies, some of the carbon-14 decays and escapes as nitrogen-14 gas. The amount of carbon-14 remaining can be measured to determine the age of the fossil or when humans used a fire site, as in **Figure 12-22**.

Other than for carbon-14 dating, rocks that can be radiometrically dated are mostly igneous and some recrystallized metamorphic rocks. Sedimentary rocks cannot be dated by this method

Figure 12-22

Human activity can also be dated with carbon-14. Things like this campfire or other types of charcoal can be dated. *What other events could leave charcoal behind and provide radiocarbon dates?*

Integrating the Sciences

Chemistry Integrate chemistry into this lesson by asking the following questions and performing the activity given at left, above.

- **Why is radiometric dating often more useful to geologists than relative dating?** *Radiometric dating enables geologists to determine the exact ages of rocks. Relative dating produces a sequence of geologic events based on the relationships among the events.*
- **How do geologists use radioactive decay to determine the absolute age of a rock?** *The rate of decay, called the half-life, is the time it takes for half of the parent isotope to decay into the daughter isotope. The rate of decay together with the amounts of parent and daughter isotopes remaining in a rock are used to determine its absolute age.*

because the absolute age of only the sediment grains in the rock can be determined, not the rock itself. Radiometric dating has been used to date the oldest rocks found on Earth. These rocks are 3.96 billion years old. Scientists have estimated the age of Earth at 4.6 billion years.

Uniformitarianism

Before radiometric dating was available, many people had estimated the age of Earth to be only a few thousand years old. But in the 1700s, Scottish scientist James Hutton estimated that Earth was much older. He used the principle of **uniformitarianism.** This principle states that Earth processes occurring today are similar to those that occurred in the past. He observed that the processes that changed the rocks and land around him were very slow, and he inferred that they had been just as slow throughout Earth's history. Hutton hypothesized that it took much longer than a few thousand years to form the layers of rock around him and to erode mountains that once towered kilometers high. John Playfair advanced Hutton's theories, but an English geologist, Sir Charles Lyell, is given the most credit for advancing uniformitarianism.

USING MATH

The half-life of radium-226 is 1600 years. How old is an object in which 1/32 of the original radium-226 is present?

Section Wrap-up

Review

1. You discover three rock layers that have not been overturned. The absolute age of the middle layer is 120 million years. What can you say about the ages of the layers above and below it?
2. How old would a fossil be if it had only one-eighth of its original carbon-14 content remaining?
3. **Think Critically:** Suppose you radiometrically date an igneous dike running through only the bottom two layers in question 1. The dike is cut off by the upper rock layer. The dike is 70 million years old. What can you say about the absolute age of the upper layer?

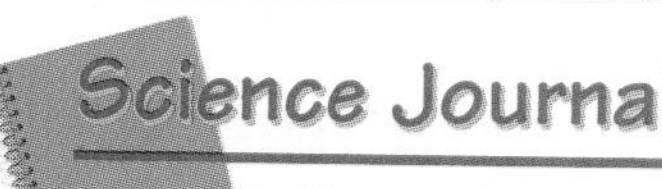

Science Journal

Research John Playfair and Sir Charles Lyell in a geology book. In your Science Journal, write about their contributions to uniformitarianism.

Skill Builder

Making and Using Tables

Make a table that shows the amounts of parent and daughter materials left of a radioactive element after four half-lives if the original parent material had a mass of 100 g. If you need help, refer to Making and Using Tables in the **Skill Handbook**.

4 Close

•MINI•QUIZ•

1. **Which method of dating determines the age of a rock in years?** *absolute dating*
2. **What is the daughter element of uranium-238?** *lead-206*
3. **What is the time it takes for half of a radioactive isotope to decay?** *half-life*

Section Wrap-up

Review

1. The top layer is less than 120 million years old; the bottom layer is more than 120 million years old. However, you can't say anything about their absolute ages.
2. After three half-lives, 1/8 of the original C-14 would remain. Thus, the fossil would be 17 190 years old.
3. **Think Critically** The upper layer is younger than 70 million years. At one time, the dike may have extended above the present middle layer into an upper layer that is no longer there. A disconformity may exist between the present middle and upper layers. The disconformity would represent a buried erosional surface that truncated part of the dike. The present upper layer may have been deposited on top of the erosional surface.

Skill Builder

Half-Life	Parent	Daughter
0	100 g	0 g
1	50 g	50 g
2	25 g	75 g
3	12.5 g	87.5 g
4	6.25 g	93.75 g

Assessment

Performance Assess students' abilities to make and use tables and graphs by having them plot the data in their table. Half-lives should go on the horizontal axis, while the percentage of parent or daughter material should appear on the vertical axis. Use the Performance Task Assessment List for Graph from Data in **PASC,** p. 39. P

Science Journal

John Playfair advanced Hutton's theories, but Sir Charles Lyell is given the most credit for advancing uniformitarianism. One reason was that Lyell's written works were easier to read. Encourage students to go into more detail.

Activity 12-2

PREPARATION

Purpose

LS **Interpersonal** Design a model and carry out an experiment that uses the model of radioactive half-lives in absolute age determination. L1 COOP LEARN

Process Skills

communicating, forming a hypothesis, designing an experiment, using numbers, interpreting data, formulating models, observing and inferring, making and using tables, making and using graphs, and collecting and organizing data

Time

one class period to formulate the model, carry out the experiment, and summarize results

Possible Hypotheses

- Pennies placed face up in a shoe box can be used to model radioactive decay. Each time the box is shaken, pennies that are face down are removed and replaced with paper clips. The face-up pennies model the parent isotope, whereas the paper clips model the daughter products. Each shake equals one half-life.
- Brass fasteners placed randomly in a shoe box can be used to model radioactive decay. With each shake of the box (half-life), remove fasteners that point toward an "X" marked on the box. Replace "decayed" fasteners with paper clips. The original brass fasteners model the parent isotope; the paper clips model the daughter products.

Activity Worksheets, pp. 5, 74-75

Activity 12-2

Design Your Own Experiment
Radioactive Decay

Radioactive isotopes decay into their daughter elements in a certain amount of time. The rate of decay varies for each individual isotope. This rate can be used to determine the age of rocks that contain the isotopes under study. In this activity, you will develop a model that demonstrates how the half-life of certain radioactive isotopes can be used to determine absolute ages.

PREPARATION

Problem

What materials can be used to model age determination using radioactive half-lives?

Form a Hypothesis

State a hypothesis about what materials can be used in a model of radioactive decay and how they will be used to model radioactive half-lives.

Objectives

- Determine what materials can best be used to model radioactive half-lives.
- Design an experiment that models absolute age determination using the half-lives of radioactive isotopes.

Possible Materials

- shoe box with lid
- brass fasteners (100)
- paper clips (100)
- graph paper
- pennies (100)
- colored pencils (2)
- pipe cleaners (100)

Safety Precautions

Hold the lid of the box on tight to avoid having objects fly out of the box.

348

PLAN THE EXPERIMENT

Possible Procedures

- Students are to place the parent isotope in the box, allow one half-life (one shake of the box) to pass, observe changes, replace changed parent isotope with daughter products, and determine how much parent isotope "decays" to daughter product during each half-life.

Inclusion Strategies

Visually Impaired Provide alternate materials that students can use to safely determine a change after each shake of the box. Suggestions include bent straws or the pipe cleaners originally listed as materials. Also, visually impaired students could be responsible for demonstrating the half-lives (shakes of the shoe box).

PLAN THE EXPERIMENT

1. As a group, agree upon and write out the hypothesis statement.
2. As a group, list the steps that you need to take to test your hypothesis. Be very specific, describing exactly what you will do at each step.
3. Make a list of the materials that you will need to complete your experiment.
4. Make a list of the various materials you will use to model radioactive decay.
5. Describe how the different materials you choose will be used in your model to demonstrate radioactive half-lives.

Check the Plan

1. Read over your entire experiment to make sure that all steps are in a logical order.
2. Should you use more than one type of material in your model?
3. Will you summarize data in a graph, table, or some other form of organization?
4. Will you use more than one graph or table or a combination of several?
5. How will you determine whether your model demonstrates absolute age determination from radioactive isotope half-lives?
6. *Make sure your teacher approves your plan and that you have included any changes suggested in the plan.*

DO THE EXPERIMENT

1. Carry out the experiment as planned.
2. While conducting the experiment, write down any observations that you or other members of your group make and complete any data tables or graphs in your Science Journal.

Analyze and Apply

1. What do the different materials you decided to use represent in your model of radioactive decay?
2. **Describe** how each of the processes or objects used in your model fits into the process of radioactive decay.
3. **Determine** what were the half-lives of the various parent materials used in your model of radioactive decay.

Go Further

Suppose you could perform the process from your model only once every 100 years. How might this affect the half-lives of the parent materials you selected?

- Once partners have obtained and used their individual data, combine the average data from all partners. Have students construct graphs for data obtained from the entire class.

Teaching Strategies

Tying to Previous Knowledge Help students recall that the half-life of a radioactive isotope is a measure of time that is definite and determinable.

Troubleshooting You may need to suggest shaking the shoe box as a model of half-life.

- To remove all fasteners, students may need to shake the box more than 15 times.
- Note that by beginning with 100 objects for the first shake, the number of objects remaining *will* be the percentage of original objects remaining.

DO THE EXPERIMENT

Expected Outcome

Students should be able to determine which materials to use as models of parent and daughter isotopes. Students should be able to determine the ratio of parent material remaining to daughter product produced during each half-life.

Analyze and Apply

1. The coins, fasteners, and pipe cleaners represent radioactive parent isotopes. The paper clips represent stable daughter products.
2. In addition to the materials identified, the box represents the rock in which radioactive decay occurs, and each shake represents a time interval.
3. Answers will vary. The number of shakes it takes to have half of each set of objects replaced is one half-life.

Go Further

Answers will vary with each pair. Using the class average might enable students to get more consistent data. Based on the model, it would take two half-lives, or two shakes, for the coins and seven shakes for the fasteners.

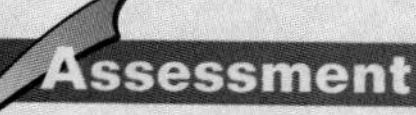

Assessment

Performance To further assess students' understanding of radioactive decay, have them repeat this activity using another material to represent the parent radioactive isotope. They may also wish to use a different material as the daughter product. Use the Performance Task Assessment List for Carrying Out a Strategy and Collecting Data in **PASC**, p. 25. P

Background

- Sediments from the Brazos River are especially valuable because they give a more detailed and accurate picture of what happened during the K/T transition than do other sites with sediments from the same time period. This is because the Brazos River sediments were deposited in a shallow sea, not in deep water. It takes longer for layers of sediment to accumulate in deep water, because they form mainly from the skeletons of dead marine animals. In shallow seas, clay and other materials from land contribute to sedimentary layers.
- The Brazos River site also is of interest because of its proximity to the crater in the Yucatan peninsula, where some scientists believe the meteorite crash occurred.

Teaching Strategies

One of the difficulties in work such as Barrera's is being sure that samples taken from different sedimentary layers actually represent different times in Earth's history. It is possible for materials to be "reworked"—that is, eroded out of older sediments and incorporated into more recent layers. Using a model of sedimentary layers, demonstrate to students how this could happen.

Career Connection

Career Path Courses in chemistry, biology, statistics, computer science, and mathematics are recommended. Most geologists share a love of nature and the outdoors. Taking a field geology course or just going on field trips with a local nature or environmental organization will increase students' understanding of Earth's processes and environments.

People and Science

ENRIQUETA BARRERA, *Geochemist*

On the Job

Q How does your work shed light on Earth's past?

A I'm studying a period about 70 to 72 million years ago. Most people say the change in the biota and oceans at this time was one of the most dramatic changes in Earth's history. These changes may have influenced how organisms have evolved. I have found evidence for a tremendous change in the circulation of the oceans.

Q Some of your work has challenged the theory that a meteorite collision 66 million years ago caused a sudden, drastic change in the environment that led to widespread extinction of plants and animals. Please tell us what you found.

A I worked with another scientist to analyze layers of sediment deposited millions of years ago under a shallow sea in Texas, and in the deep ocean near Antarctica. My job was to analyze carbon and oxygen isotope ratios in fossils. We found evidence that some extinctions may have been caused by a gradual environmental change over a period of thousands of years, rather than by sudden, dramatic change.

Personal Insights

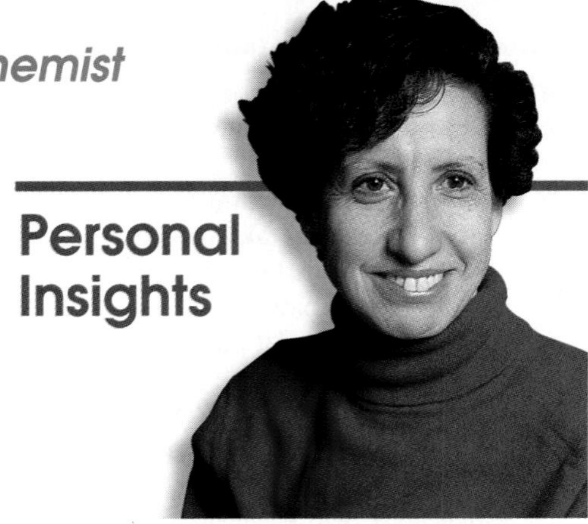

Q What has been your biggest challenge as a scientist?

A There are many challenges. It takes years of hard work to become established in a field of research. Scientific research has a rigorous methodology that involves careful observations and analysis to formulate hypotheses. As we practice science, we are constantly revising our ideas and learning about our field. This process is very exciting. As an American woman of Latin heritage, it has been a little difficult to become established in my profession, partly because there are significantly fewer women than men in this field. It takes perseverance, but I love what I do—I am really excited about this profession!

Career Connection

Visit a natural history museum or university geology department. Talk to curators or professors and find out what kind of work they do.

Write a job description for what kind of work you would like to do in this field and where you could work as a:

- **Paleontologist**
- **Geochemist**

For More Information

The following articles offer further information on topics related to Barrera's work:

- Alper, Joseph. "Earth's Near-Death Experience." *Earth,* January 1994, pp. 42-51. Discussion of Permian extinctions.
- Campbell, Wayne. "The Death of the Dinosaurs: A Canadian Scientist Finds the Smoking Gun." *Globe and Mail* (Toronto, Canada), November 7, 1992, p. D8. Evidence for asteroid impact hypothesis.
- Stanley, Steven M. "Extinctions—Or, Which Way Did They Go?" *Earth,* January 1991, pp. 18-27. Overview of mass extinctions in Earth's history.

Chapter 12

Review

Summary

12-1: Fossils

1. In order for fossils to form, hard parts of the dead organisms must be covered quickly.
2. Some fossils form when original materials that made up the organisms are replaced with minerals. Other fossils form when remains are subjected to heat and pressure, leaving only a carbonaceous film behind. Some fossils are merely the tracks or traces left by former organisms.
3. Generally, a rock layer can be no older than the age of the fossils embedded in it.

12-2: Science and Society: Extinction of Dinosaurs

1. The meteorite-impact theory of dinosaur extinction states that a large object from space collided with Earth and caused vast climate changes. Dinosaurs weren't able to adapt and eventually became extinct.
2. Another theory suggests that volcanic activity led to the extinction of the dinosaurs.

12-3: Relative Ages of Rocks

1. The principle of superposition states that older rocks lie underneath younger rocks in areas where the rocks haven't been disturbed. Faults are always younger than the rocks they cross-cut.
2. Unconformities, or gaps in the rock record, are due to erosion, nondeposition, or both.
3. Fossils and rock types are often helpful when correlating similar rock bodies.

12-4: Absolute Ages of Rocks

1. Relative dating of rocks, unlike absolute dating, doesn't provide an exact age for the rocks.
2. The half-life of a radioactive isotope is the time it takes for half of the atoms in the isotope to decay. Because half-lives are constant, absolute ages of rocks containing radioactive elements can be determined.

Key Science Words

a. absolute dating
b. carbonaceous film
c. cast
d. extinct
e. fossil
f. half-life
g. index fossil
h. principle of superposition
i. mold
j. petrified remains
k. radioactive decay
l. radiometric dating
m. relative dating
n. unconformity
o. uniformitarianism

Reviewing Vocabulary

Match each phrase with the correct term from the list of Key Science Words.

1. thin film of carbon preserved as a fossil
2. rocklike fossils made of minerals
3. fossil of species that existed for a short time and was abundant and widespread
4. states that older rocks lie under younger rocks
5. states that natural processes occur today as they did in the past
6. gap in the rock record
7. evidence of once-living organisms
8. neutrons break down during this process
9. the time it takes for half of the atoms of a radioactive isotope to decay
10. this process measures the amounts of parent and daughter materials to determine age

Chapter 12 Review

Summary

Have students read the summary statements to review the major concepts of the chapter.

Reviewing Vocabulary

1. b **6.** n
2. j **7.** e
3. g **8.** k
4. h **9.** f
5. o **10.** l

Assessment

Portfolio Encourage students to place in their portfolios one or two items of what they consider to be their best work. Examples include:

- MiniLAB Analysis, p. 327
- Enrichment, p. 331
- Problem Solving, p. 340 P

Performance Additional performance assessments may be found in **Performance Assessment** and **Science Integration Activities.** Performance Task Assessment Lists and rubrics for evaluating these activities can be found in Glencoe's **Performance Assessment in the Science Classroom.**

GLENCOE TECHNOLOGY

Videodisc

Glencoe Earth Science
Interactive Videodisc
Use videodisc lesson 5, *Dinosaurs: Footprints in the Rock*, to review the principles of relative dating.

MindJogger Videoquiz

Chapter 12 Have students work in groups as they play the Videoquiz game to review key chapter concepts.

Chapter 12 Review

Checking Concepts

1. b
2. c
3. c
4. d
5. d
6. d
7. c
8. d
9. d
10. d

Understanding Concepts

11. Absolute dates are the actual number of years that have passed. Relative dates are comparisons of events relative to a given event.
12. Hutton and others observed that geologic processes were generally very slow. These scientists were able then to conclude that if such processes were similar to those in the past, Earth must be millions—not thousands—of years old.
13. Iridium is not common on Earth. It is more common in meteorites, however. If a meteorite struck Earth while the dinosaurs lived, the impact could have changed climate conditions enough that dinosaur species weren't able to adapt and eventually became extinct. Large amounts of volcanic activity could also account for higher amounts of iridium and changed climates.
14. After one half-life, the parent-to-daughter ratio is 4/8 to 4/8. After two half-lives, the ratio is 2/8 to 6/8. After three half-lives, it is 1/8 to 7/8.
15. Animals were traveling in herds, with the young in the middle of the herd for protection.

Thinking Critically

16. The fossil record is incomplete because erosion and decay can destroy evidence of life if it's not buried quickly and protected from oxygen and moisture. Deeply buried remains are frequently destroyed by metamorphism.
17. Since the lava contains radioactive elements, an absolute age for the flow can be determined. This age can then be used to determine relative ages for the rocks above and below the flow.
18. Mammals may have raided dinosaur nests for food. Destroying large numbers of dinosaur eggs may have contributed to their extinction.
19. It's likely that any layer of shale containing volcanic dust is part of the same shale deposit. The dust-rich shale can act as a marker.
20. The half-life of carbon-14 is too short. All of the original carbon-14 in a fossil that's 2 million years old would have decayed and escaped as nitrogen gas. There would be no carbon-14 left to measure.

Chapter 12 Review

Checking Concepts

Choose the word or phrase that completes the sentence.

1. Remains of organisms in rocks are ______.
   a. half-lives c. unconformities
   b. fossils d. extinctions
2. Fossils may form when dead organisms are ______.
   a. buried slowly
   b. exposed to microorganisms
   c. made of hard parts
   d. composed of soft parts
3. ______ are cavities left in rocks when a shell or bone decays.
   a. Casts c. Molds
   b. Petrified remains d. Carbon films
4. Dinosaurs lived ______ years ago.
   a. 1000 c. 5 million
   b. 10 000 d. more than 66 million
5. Another way to state the principle of ______ is to say "the present is the key to the past."
   a. superposition c. radioactivity
   b. succession d. uniformitarianism
6. A fault can be used to find the ______ age of a group of rocks.
   a. absolute c. index
   b. radiometric d. relative
7. An unconformity between horizontal rock layers is a(n) ______.
   a. angular unconformity c. disconformity
   b. fault d. nonconformity
8. During ______, new elements are formed.
   a. superposition c. evolution
   b. uniformitarianism d. radioactive decay
9. In one type of radioactive decay, a(n) ______ breaks down, releasing an electron.
   a. alpha particle c. beta particle
   b. proton d. neutron
10. Radiometric dating indicates that Earth is ______ years old.
    a. 2000 c. 3.5 billion
    b. 5000 d. 4.6 billion

Understanding Concepts

Answer the following questions in your Science Journal using complete sentences.

11. How do relative and absolute ages differ?
12. Why did James Hutton and others infer that Earth had to be much older than a few thousand years?
13. Explain why a clay layer rich in iridium might explain why the dinosaurs became extinct.
14. How many half-lives have passed in a rock containing 1/8 of the original radioactive material and 7/8 of the daughter product?
15. If large tracks of an animal are found surrounding smaller tracks of the same animal, what might this indicate?

Thinking Critically

16. We don't have a complete fossil record of life on Earth. Give some reasons why.
17. Suppose a lava flow were found between two sedimentary rock layers. How could the lava flow be used to date the rocks? (HINT: Most lava contains radioactive isotopes.)
18. Mammals began to evolve on Earth before the dinosaurs became extinct. Suggest a hypothesis explaining how the mammals may have caused the dinosaurs to become extinct.
19. Suppose you're correlating rock layers in the western United States. You find a layer of shale that contains volcanic dust deposits. How can this layer help you in your correlation over a large area?
20. Why is carbon-14 not suitable for dating fossils formed about 2 million years ago?

Developing Skills

If you need help, refer to the **Skill Handbook.**

21. **Concept Mapping:** Make a concept map listing the following possible steps in the process of making a cast of a fossil: organism dies, burial, protection from scavengers and bacteria, replacement by minerals, fossil erodes away, mineral crystals form from solution.
22. **Observing and Inferring:** Suppose you found a rock containing brachiopods. What can you infer about the environment in which the rock formed?
23. **Recognizing Cause and Effect:** Explain why some woolly mammoths have been found intact in frozen ground.
24. **Classifying:** Suppose you were given a set of ten fossils to classify. Make a table to classify each specimen according to type.
25. **Outlining:** Make an outline of Section 12-1 that discusses the ways in which fossils form.

Performance Assessment

1. **Making Observations and Inferences:** In Activity 12-1, you learned how to determine relative ages. Based on what you learned concerning relative ages of rocks, determine the probable relative ages of the rock layers shown below.
2. **Using a Classification System:** Start your own fossil collection. Label each find as to type, approximate age, and the place where it was found. Most state geological surveys can provide you with reference material on local fossils.
3. **Model:** Use various types of material to make molds and casts of clam shells and other animal or plant hard parts. Determine which type of material would preserve fossils best. Infer how this would relate to fossil formation in nature. Materials you might use include clay, sand, fine dust, and gravel.

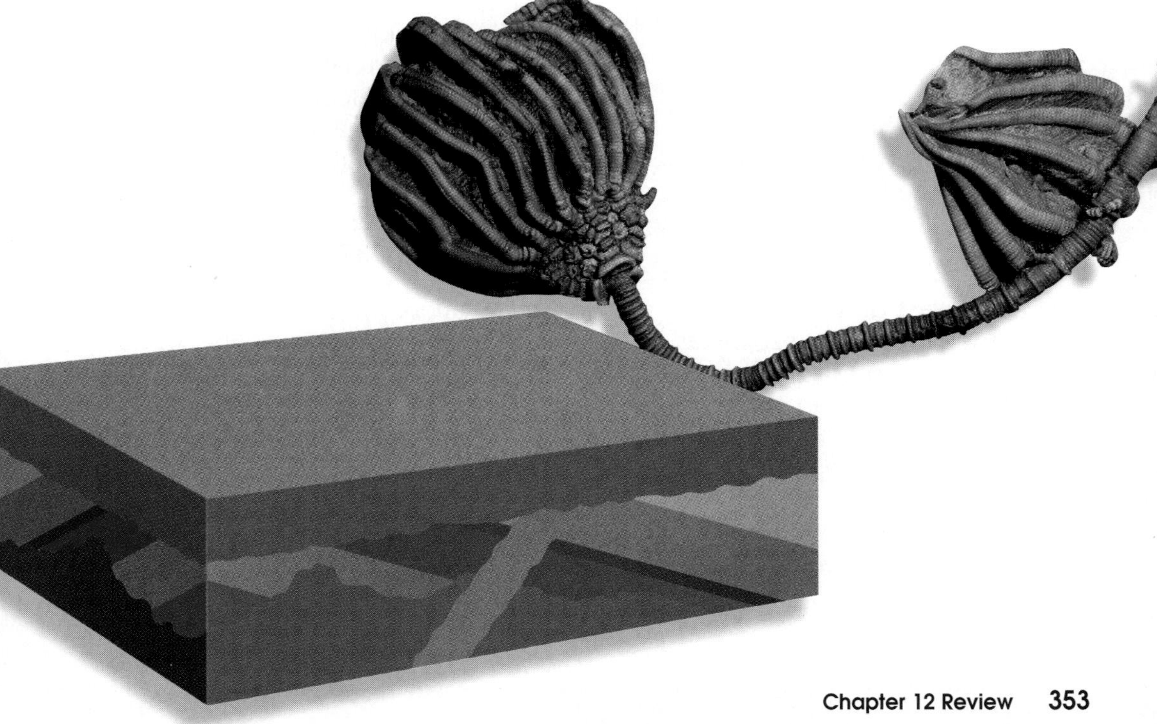

Chapter 12 Review

Developing Skills

21. **Concept Mapping** Possible solution:

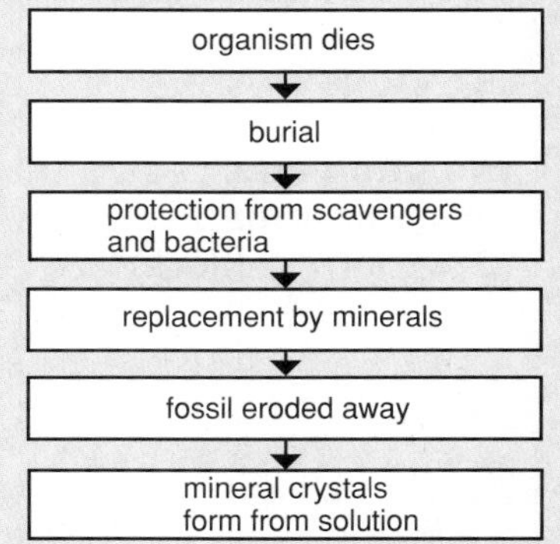

22. **Observing and Inferring** Brachiopods are marine animals. Thus, the rock formed in an ocean.
23. **Recognizing Cause and Effect** The cold temperatures caused the body functions to stop, helping to preserve the entire animal.
24. **Classifying** One way to classify them is by the process that formed them. Examples of this could include petrification, mold and cast, preservation in amber, and carbonization. Other classification schemes are possible.
25. **Outlining** Answers will vary, but the objectives listed on SE page 326 should be among the points included in students' outlines.

Performance Assessment

1. Possible answer: deposit sedimentary rocks (lower layers), tilting, intrusion of large igneous mass, intrude dike, erosion, deposition of top sedimentary layer. Use the Performance Task Assessment List for Making Observations and Inferences in **PASC,** p. 17. P
2. Classifications done by students will vary, but insist that students base their classification on observed features and scientific principles. Use the Performance Task Assessment List for Making and Using a Classification System in **PASC,** p. 49. P
3. Answers will vary. Students should infer that clay will preserve imprints, molds, and casts better than sand or gravel. Fossils of organisms that settled and were buried in clay or fine dust have a better chance of being preserved. Use the Performance Task Assessment List for Model in **PASC,** p. 51. P

Chapter Organizer

Section	Objectives	Activities/Features
Chapter Opener		Explore Activity: Make a model environment. p. 355
13-1 **Evolution and Geologic Time** (2 sessions, 1 block)*	1. **Explain** how geologic time is divided into units. 2. **Relate** organic evolution to divisions on the geologic time scale. 3. **Describe** how plate tectonics affects organic evolution.	Connect to Life Science, p. 357 Using Technology: Embryology, p. 361 Skill Builder: Recognizing Cause and Effect, p. 363 Science Journal, p. 363
13-2 **Science and Society Issue: Present-Day Rapid Extinctions** (2 sessions, 1 block)*	1. **Recognize** how humans have contributed to extinctions. 2. **Predict** what might happen to the diversity of life on Earth if land is developed without protection of natural habitats. 3. **Hypothesize** what can be done to stop or slow down the rate of species extinction.	Explore the Issue, p. 365
13-3 **Early Earth History** (1 session, ½ block)*	1. **Identify** dominant life-forms in Precambrian time and the Paleozoic Era. 2. **Draw conclusions** about how organisms adapted to changing environments in Precambrian time and the Paleozoic Era. 3. **Describe** changes in Earth and its life-forms at the end of the Paleozoic Era.	Connect to Chemistry, p. 367 Activity 13-1: Evolution Within a Species, p. 368 MiniLAB: Fossil Correlation, p. 369 Problem Solving: Paleozoic Puzzle, p. 370 Skill Builder: Making and Using Tables, p. 372 Using Computers: Database, p. 372 Science & Literature: Dreamtime Down Under, p. 373 Science Journal, p. 373
13-4 **Middle and Recent Earth History** (2 sessions, 1 block)*	1. **Compare** and **contrast** dominant life-forms in the Mesozoic and Cenozoic Eras. 2. **Explain** how changes caused by plate tectonics affected the evolution of life during the Mesozoic Era. 3. **Identify** when humans first appeared on Earth.	MiniLAB: Seafloor Spreading, p. 378 Activity 13-2: Geologic Time Line, pp. 380-381 Skill Builder: Sequencing, p. 382 Using Math, p. 382

* A complete Planning Guide that includes block scheduling is provided on pages 32T-35T.

Activity Materials

Explore	Activities	MiniLABs
page 355 green, orange, and blue yarn; scissors; metric ruler; sheet of green construction paper; tweezers; stopwatch or clock with second hand	page 368 deck of playing cards pages 380-381 adding-machine tape, meterstick or metric ruler, colored pencils, scissors, safety goggles	page 369 No special materials are needed. page 378 globe or world map, metric measuring tape, calculator

Chapter 13 Geologic Time

Teacher Classroom Resources

Reproducible Masters	Transparencies
Study Guide, p. 53 **Reinforcement**, p. 53 **Enrichment**, p. 53 **Lab Manual 36**, Geologic Time **Lab Manual 37**, Differences in a Species **Science Integration Activity 13**, It's Tough to Be a Predator! **Cross-Curricular Integration**, p. 17 **Multicultural Connections**, pp. 29-30	**Section Focus Transparency 49**, Changing Beaks **Teaching Transparency 25**, Geologic Time Scale **Teaching Transparency 26**, Paleogeographic Map
Study Guide, p. 54 **Reinforcement**, p. 54 **Enrichment**, p. 54 **Science and Society Integration**, p. 17	**Section Focus Transparency 50**, The Way of the Dinosaurs?
Study Guide, p. 55 **Reinforcement**, p. 55 **Enrichment**, p. 55 **Activity Worksheets**, pp. 78-79, 82	**Section Focus Transparency 51**, Water to Land
Study Guide, p. 56 **Reinforcement**, p. 56 **Enrichment**, p. 56 **Activity Worksheets**, pp. 80-81, 83 **Concept Mapping**, p. 31 **Critical Thinking/Problem Solving**, p. 19	**Section Focus Transparency 52**, How Long Have We Been Here? **Science Integration Transparency 13**, Plant Evolution

Teaching Resources

Glencoe Earth Science Interactive Videodisc
Earth Science CD-ROM
Spanish Resources
English/Spanish Audiocassettes
Cooperative Learning Resource Guide
Lab Partner
Lab and Safety Skills
Lesson Plans

Assessment Resources

Chapter Review, pp. 29-30
Assessment, pp. 84-87
Performance Assessment in the Science Classroom (PASC)
MindJogger Videoquiz
Alternate Assessment in the Science Classroom
Performance Assessment
Chapter Review Software
Computer Test Bank

Key to Teaching Strategies

The following designations will help you decide which activities are appropriate for your students.

L1 Level 1 activities should be within the ability range of all students.

L2 Level 2 activities should be within the ability range of the average to above-average student.

L3 Level 3 activities are designed for the ability range of above-average students.

LEP LEP activities should be within the ability range of Limited English Proficiency students.

LS These activities are designed to address different learning styles.

COOP LEARN Cooperative Learning activities are designed for small group work.

P These strategies represent student products that can be placed into a best-work portfolio.

GLENCOE TECHNOLOGY

The following multimedia resources are available from Glencoe.

The Secret of Life
It's in the Genes: Evolution
The Infinite Voyage Series
To the Edge of the Earth
The Great Dinosaur Hunt
National Geographic Society Series
STV: Restless Earth
Earth Science CD-ROM

Teacher Classroom Resources

This is a representation of key blackline masters available in the Teacher Classroom Resources.

Teaching Aids

Section Focus Transparencies

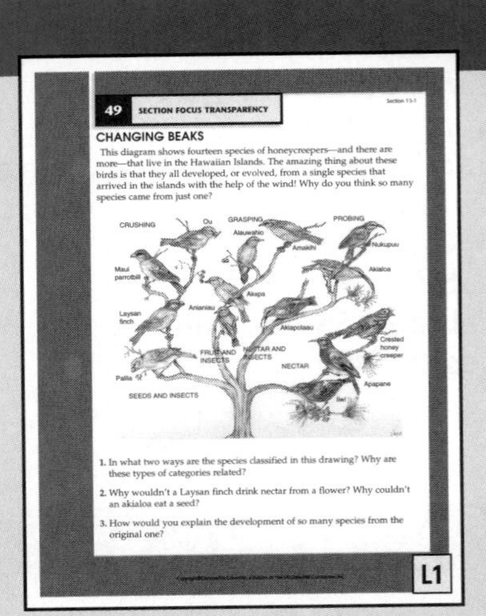

49 SECTION FOCUS TRANSPARENCY — Section 13-1

CHANGING BEAKS

This diagram shows fourteen species of honeycreepers—and there are more—that live in the Hawaiian Islands. The amazing thing about these birds is that they all developed, or evolved, from a single species that arrived in the islands with the help of the wind! Why do you think so many species came from just one?

1. In what two ways are the species classified in this drawing? Why are these types of categories related?
2. Why wouldn't a Laysan finch drink nectar from a flower? Why couldn't an akialoa eat a seed?
3. How would you explain the development of so many species from the original one?

L1

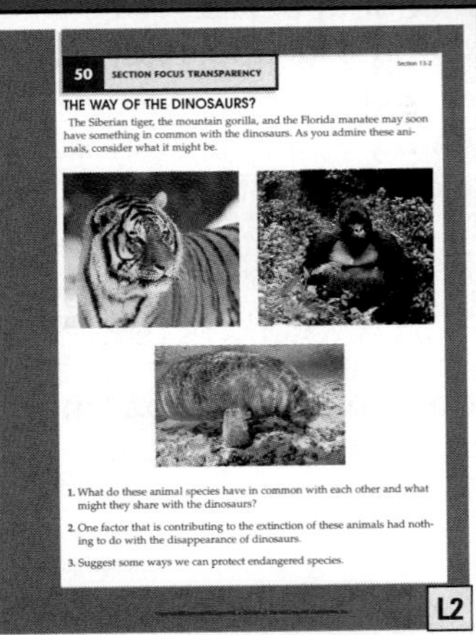

50 SECTION FOCUS TRANSPARENCY — Section 13-2

THE WAY OF THE DINOSAURS?

The Siberian tiger, the mountain gorilla, and the Florida manatee may soon have something in common with the dinosaurs. As you admire these animals, consider what it might be.

1. What do these animal species have in common with each other and what might they share with the dinosaurs?
2. One factor that is contributing to the extinction of these animals had nothing to do with the disappearance of dinosaurs.
3. Suggest some ways we can protect endangered species.

L2

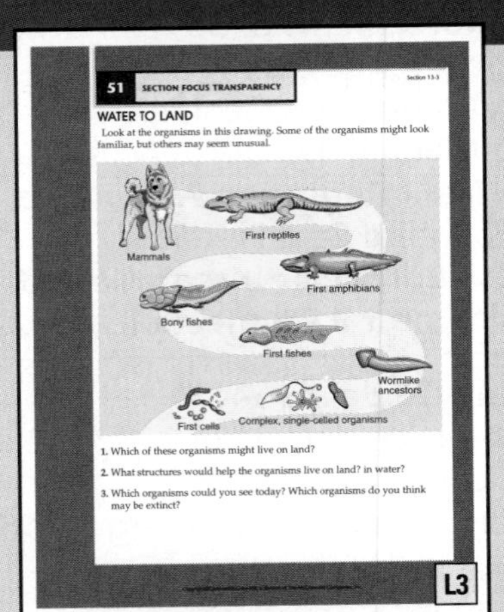

51 SECTION FOCUS TRANSPARENCY — Section 13-3

WATER TO LAND

Look at the organisms in this drawing. Some of the organisms might look familiar, but others may seem unusual.

1. Which of these organisms might live on land?
2. What structures would help the organisms live on land? in water?
3. Which organisms could you see today? Which organisms do you think may be extinct?

L3

Science Integration Transparencies

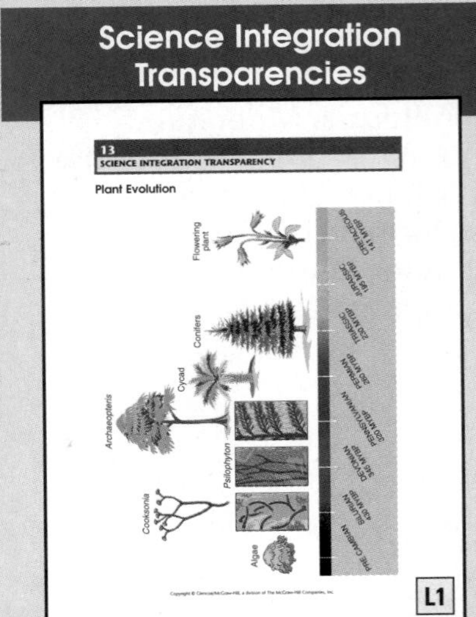

13 SCIENCE INTEGRATION TRANSPARENCY

Plant Evolution

L1

Teaching Transparencies

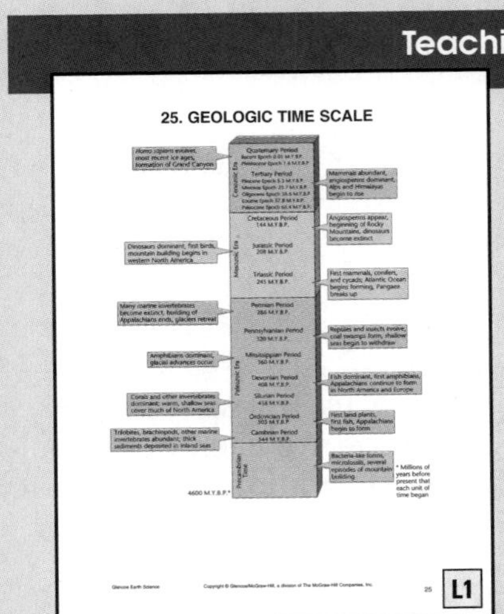

25. GEOLOGIC TIME SCALE

L1

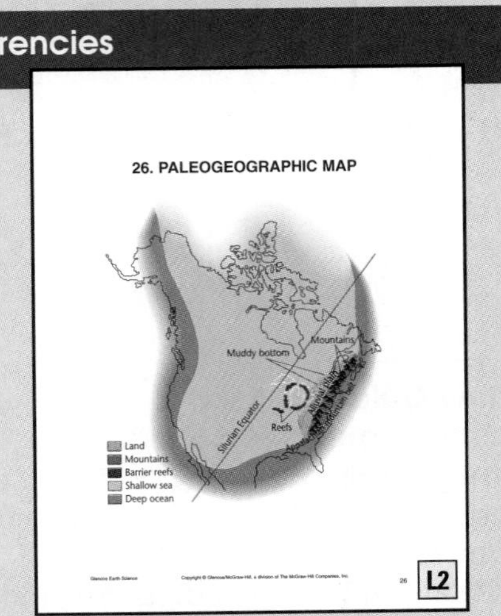

26. PALEOGEOGRAPHIC MAP

L2

Meeting Different Ability Levels

Study Guide

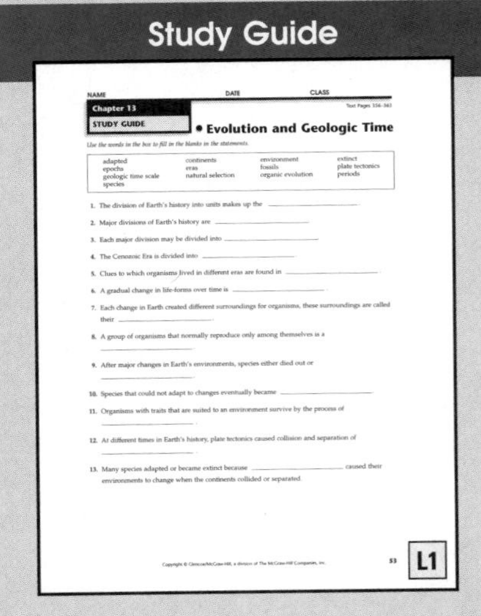

NAME DATE CLASS

Chapter 13 — STUDY GUIDE — Text Pages 356–363

• Evolution and Geologic Time

Use the words in the box to fill in the blanks in the statements.

adapted	continents	environment	extinct
epochs	eras	fossils	plate tectonics
geologic time scale	natural selection	organic evolution	periods
species			

1. The division of Earth's history into units makes up the ____________.
2. Major divisions of Earth's history are ____________.
3. Each major division may be divided into ____________.
4. The Cenozoic Era is divided into ____________.
5. Clues to which organisms lived in different eras are found in ____________.
6. A gradual change in life-forms over time is ____________.
7. Each change in Earth created different surroundings for organisms, these surroundings are called their ____________.
8. A group of organisms that normally reproduce only among themselves is a ____________.
9. After major changes in Earth's environments, species either died out or ____________.
10. Species that could not adapt to changes eventually became ____________.
11. Organisms with traits that are suited to an environment survive by the process of ____________.
12. At different times in Earth's history, plate tectonics caused collision and separation of ____________.
13. Many species adapted or became extinct because ____________ caused their environments to change when the continents collided or separated.

 53

L1

Reinforcement

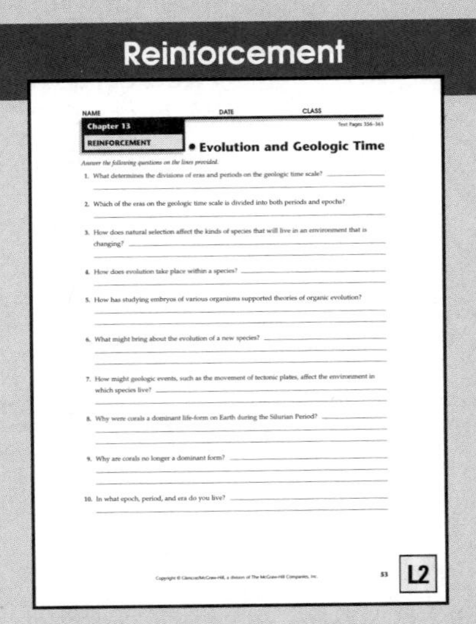

NAME DATE CLASS

Chapter 13 — REINFORCEMENT — Text Pages 356–363

• Evolution and Geologic Time

Answer the following questions on the lines provided.

1. What determines the divisions of eras and periods on the geologic time scale?
2. Which of the eras on the geologic time scale is divided into both periods and epochs?
3. How does natural selection affect the kinds of species that will live in an environment that is changing?
4. How does evolution take place within a species?
5. How has studying embryos of various organisms supported theories of organic evolution?
6. What might bring about the evolution of a new species?
7. How might geologic events, such as the movement of tectonic plates, affect the environment in which species live?
8. Why were corals a dominant life-form on Earth during the Silurian Period?
9. Why are corals no longer a dominant form?
10. In what epoch, period, and era do you live?

 53

L2

Enrichment Worksheets

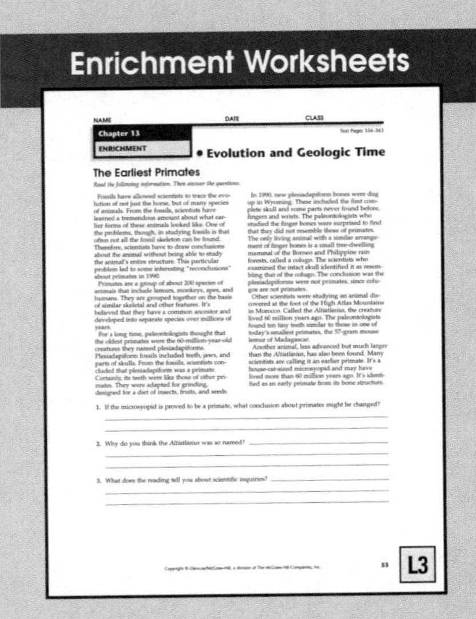

NAME DATE CLASS

Chapter 13 — ENRICHMENT — Text Pages 356–363

• Evolution and Geologic Time

The Earliest Primates

Read the following information. Then answer the questions.

Fossils have allowed scientists to trace the evolution of not just the horse, but of many species of animals. From the fossils, scientists have learned a tremendous amount about what earlier forms of these animals looked like. One of the problems, though, in studying fossils is that often not all the fossil skeleton can be found. Therefore, scientists have to draw conclusions about the animal without being able to study the animal's entire structure. This particular problem led to some interesting "reconclusions" about primates in 1990.

Primates are a group of about 200 species of animals that include lemurs, monkeys, apes, and humans. They are grouped together on the basis of similar skeletal and other features. It's believed that they have a common ancestor and developed into separate species over millions of years.

For a long time, paleontologists thought that the oldest primates were the 60-million-year-old creatures they named plesiadapiforms. Plesiadapiform fossils included teeth, jaws, and parts of skulls. From the fossils, scientists concluded that plesiadapiform was a primate. Certainly, its teeth were like those of other primates. They were adapted for grinding, designed for a diet of insects, fruits, and seeds.

In 1990, new plesiadapiform bones were dug up in Wyoming. These included the first complete skull and some parts never found before, fingers and wrists. The paleontologists who studied the finger bones were surprised to find that they did not resemble those of primates. The only living animal with a similar arrangement of finger bones is a small tree-dwelling mammal of the Borneo and Philippine rain forests, called a colugo. The scientists who examined the intact skull identified it as resembling that of the colugo. The conclusion was the plesiadapiforms were not primates, since colugos are not primates.

Other scientists were studying an animal discovered at the foot of the High Atlas Mountains in Morocco. Called the *Altiatlasius*, the creature lived 60 million years ago. The paleontologists found ten tiny teeth similar to those in one of today's smallest primates, the 57-gram mouse lemur of Madagascar.

Another animal, less advanced but much larger than the *Altiatlasius*, has also been found. Many scientists are calling it an earlier primate. It's a house-cat-sized microsyopid and may have lived more than 60 million years ago. It's identified as an early primate from its bone structure.

1. If the microsyopid is proved to be a primate, what conclusion about primates might be changed?
2. Why do you think the *Altiatlasius* was so named?
3. What does the reading tell you about scientific inquiries?

 53

L3

Hands-On Activities

Science Integration Activity

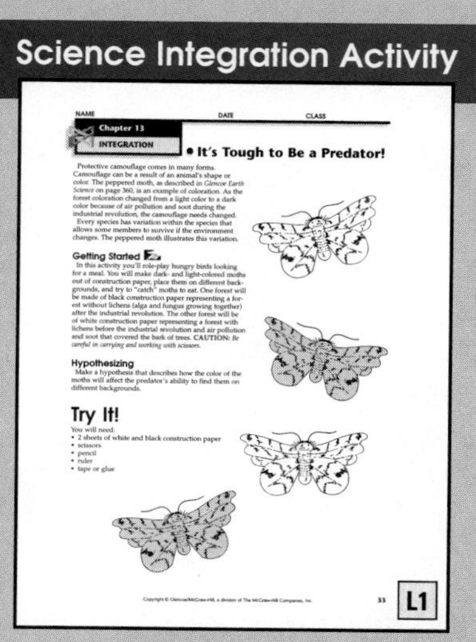

Lab Manual

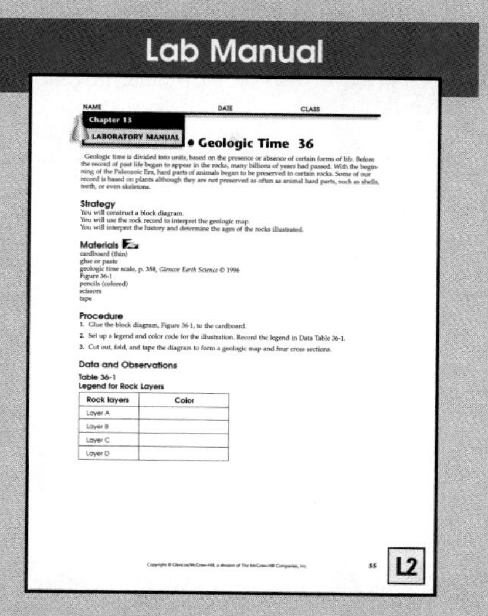

Assessment

Performance Assessment

Enrichment and Application

Critical Thinking/ Problem Solving

Cross-Curricular Integration

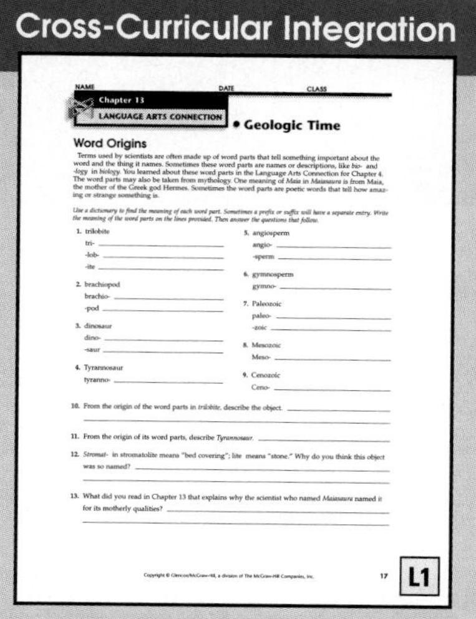

Science and Society Integration

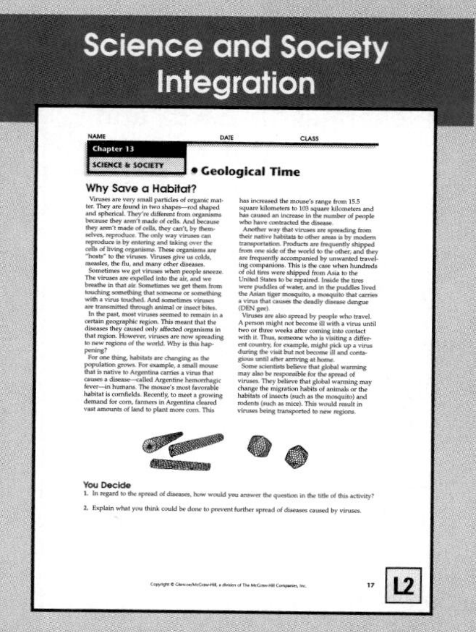

Multicultural Connections

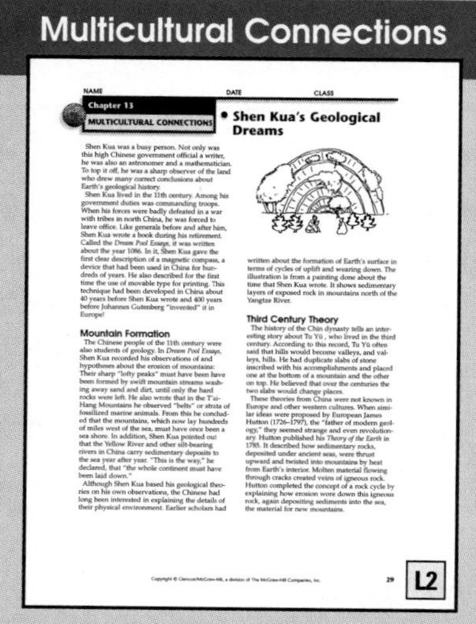

Concept Mapping

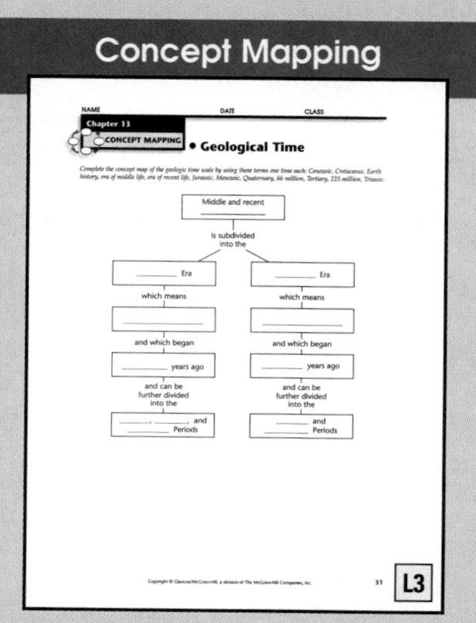

Chapter 13

Geologic Time

CHAPTER OVERVIEW

Section 13-1 This section presents the division of Earth's history into the geologic time scale. Organic evolution within a species and speciation are also introduced.

Section 13-2 Science and Society The effect humans have on the rate of extinctions is explored. Students are presented with both sides of the issue of land development with and without protection of natural habitats.

Section 13-3 Earth history during Precambrian time and the Paleozoic Era is described in this section. Changes in Earth and its life-forms in each of the two ages are presented.

Section 13-4 This section describes changes in Earth and its life-forms during the Mesozoic and Cenozoic Eras.

Chapter Vocabulary

geologic time scale	endangered habitat
era	Precambrian time
period	cyanobacteria
epoch	Paleozoic Era
organic evolution	amphibian
species	reptile
natural selection	Mesozoic Era
	Cenozoic Era

Theme Connection

Stability and Change Stability and change is the main theme emphasized in this chapter. Organic evolution (changes in life-forms), as it is used in dividing Earth's history into the geologic time scale, should be a major focus of all sections in this chapter.

Previewing the Chapter

Learning Styles

Look for the following logo for strategies that emphasize different learning modalities. LS

Kinesthetic	Explore, p. 355
Visual-Spatial	Visual Learning, pp. 357, 359, 360, 367, 371, 375, 376; Activity, p. 359; Concept Mapping, p. 359; Reteach, p. 362; MiniLAB, p. 369
Interpersonal	Activity, pp. 357, 358; Inquiry Question, p. 367; Activity 13-1, p. 368; Reteach, p. 371
Logical-Mathematical	Across the Curriculum, p. 358; Making Charts and Graphs, p. 360; MiniLAB, p. 378; Activity 13-2, pp. 380-381
Linguistic	Science Journal, pp. 359, 371, 377; Enrichment, p. 376

Geologic Time

As new fossils are discovered, our ideas about how dinosaurs lived, like these *velociraptors,* change. Dinosaurs appear to have been much more intelligent and active than we previously thought. In the following activity, use a model to find out how traits might determine whether individuals can compete and survive in an environment; then learn how traits of actual organisms have affected their success or failure.

EXPLORE ACTIVITY

Make a model environment.

1. Cut green, orange, and blue yarn into 3-cm lengths. You should have 15 pieces of each color.
2. Put them on a sheet of green construction paper.
3. Have your partner use a pair of tweezers to pick up as many pieces as he or she can in 15 seconds.

Observe: In your Science Journal, discuss whether one color was chosen more easily over another. Now suppose the construction paper represents grass, each piece of yarn represents an insect, and the tweezers represent a bird preying on the insects. Can you recognize the cause and effect as to which color of yarn your partner picks up or which color of insect would have a better chance to survive?

Previewing Science Skills

- In the **Skill Builders**, you will recognize **cause and effect**, **make and use tables**, and **sequence** events.
- In the **Activities**, you will **measure in SI**, **hypothesize**, **formulate models**, **use numbers**, and **make inferences**.
- In the **MiniLABs**, you will **measure in SI**, **use numbers**.

EXPLORE ACTIVITY

Purpose

LS **Kinesthetic** Use the Explore Activity to introduce students to the concept of natural selection. Inform students that they will be learning more about evolution and changes in Earth through time. L1

Materials

15 pieces each of green, orange, and blue yarn cut into 3-cm lengths; a sheet of green construction paper; stopwatch; scissors; and tweezers for each group

Teaching Strategies

Try to match the color of the green yarn to the color of the green construction paper.

Safety Precautions

Caution students to handle the scissors and tweezers with care.

Observe

Answers will vary but students should observe that orange and blue yarn is picked up more often and faster than green yarn. The green yarn, which represents the green insects, is picked up the least. Therefore, the green insects would have a better chance of survival because their color blends with the green background representing grass.

Assessment

Oral Have students watch other groups within the class perform the experiment. Ask them to discuss any details that help in establishing cause and effect. Use the Performance Task Assessment List for Making Observations and Inferences in **PASC,** p. 17. P

Assessment Planner

Portfolio

Refer to page 383 for suggested items that students might select for their portfolios.

Performance Assessment

See page 383 for additional Performance Assessment options.
Skill Builders, pp. 363, 372, 382
MiniLABs, pp. 369, 378
Activities 13-1, p. 368; 13-2, pp. 380-381

Content Assessment

Section Wrap-ups, pp. 363, 365, 372, 382
Chapter Review, pp. 383-385
Mini Quizzes, pp. 363, 372, 382

Group Assessment

Opportunities for group assessment occur with Cooperative Learning Strategies and Flex Your Brain Activities.

Section 13•1

Prepare

Section Background

- In 1799, William Smith, an English surveyor and geologic hobbyist, noted while working on a canal project that rock layers in any local section could be distinguished readily from those above and below by the sorts of fossils they contained. Smith's discovery proved to be a turning point in the development of a geologic time scale.
- Geologic history is based on the study of sedimentary rocks and their fossils. Although the geologic time scale was originally based on relative dating, absolute dating methods have enabled geologists to determine absolute dates of many rocks and some geologic events.

1 Motivate

Bellringer

Before presenting the lesson, display **Section Focus Transparency 49** on the overhead projector. Assign the accompanying **Focus Activity** worksheet. L1 LEP

Tying to Previous Knowledge

Many students are familiar with horses as large, grazing, hoofed animals that can carry humans on their backs. Ask students to picture a horse no larger than a dog, with several toes on its feet. Explain that fossil evidence indicates that present-day horses have evolved from much smaller, multi-toed ancestors.

13•1 Evolution and Geologic Time

Science Words

- geologic time scale
- era
- period
- epoch
- organic evolution
- species
- natural selection

Objectives

- Explain how geologic time is divided into units.
- Relate organic evolution to divisions on the geologic time scale.
- Describe how plate tectonics affects organic evolution.

Geologic Time

It's a rainy day in the prairie lands of the central United States. A herd of horses is moving toward a stream where they can find fresh drinking water. Their large, powerful muscles easily carry them across several kilometers of open grassland.

The horses are suited for this environment. Their hoofed feet allow them to run at great speeds to protect themselves from predators. The males use their speed and power to compete with other males for territory and mates. The horses' teeth allow them to grind up grass.

These characteristics allow horses to survive in the environment they live in. These same characteristics are what you would use to describe the horse—a large, powerful, hoofed animal with teeth made for grinding up grasses and grains.

Early Horses

Suppose you found a fossil animal that was the size of a dog. The animal had four toes on each of its front feet and three toes on each of its hind feet. Its teeth were sharp—suited for eating shrubs and bushes, but not for grinding grass. Would you classify this as a fossil of a horse? It may be just that.

At one time in Earth's history, as seen in **Figure 13-1,** horses were small. They had several toes and no hoofs, and they had teeth much different from the teeth of today's horses. Before that time, there were no animals we would classify as horses.

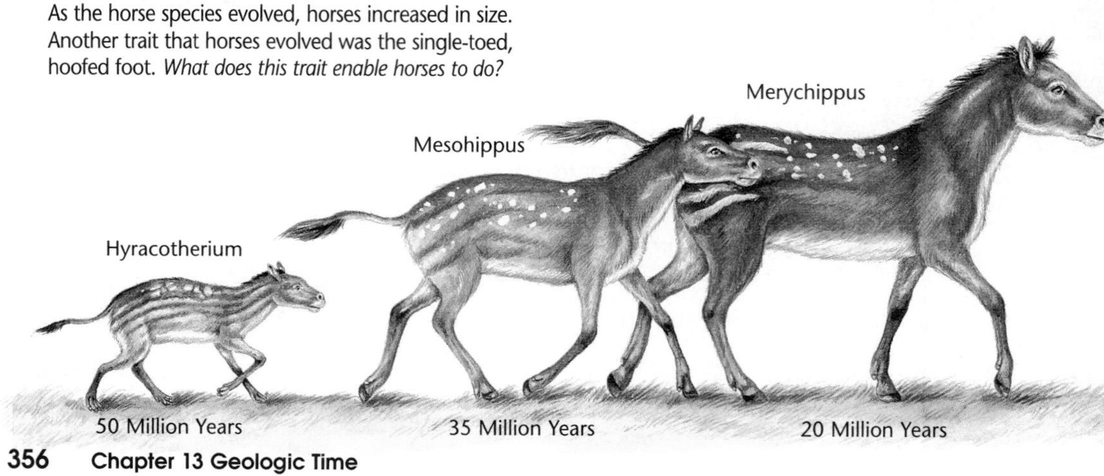

Figure 13-1

As the horse species evolved, horses increased in size. Another trait that horses evolved was the single-toed, hoofed foot. *What does this trait enable horses to do?*

Program Resources

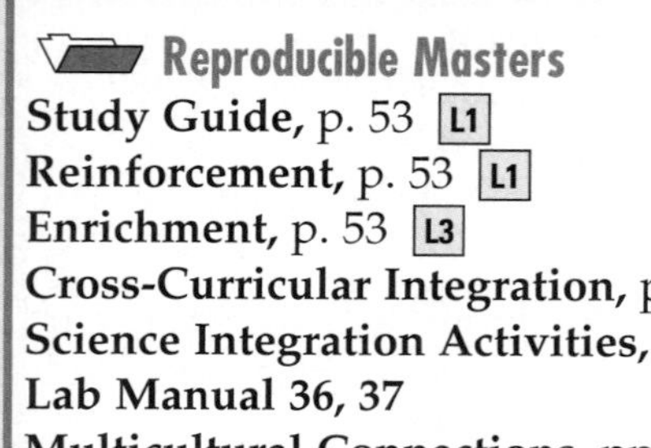

Reproducible Masters

Study Guide, p. 53 L1
Reinforcement, p. 53 L1
Enrichment, p. 53 L3
Cross-Curricular Integration, p. 17
Science Integration Activities, pp. 25-26
Lab Manual 36, 37
Multicultural Connections, pp. 29-30

Transparencies

Section Focus Transparency 49 L1
Teaching Transparency 25, 26

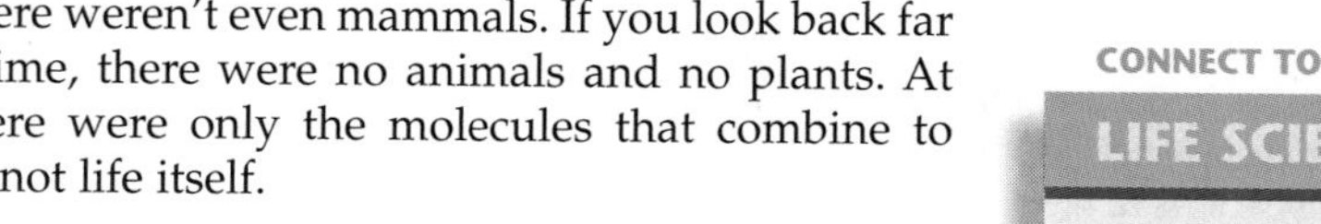

Before that, there weren't even mammals. If you look back far enough into time, there were no animals and no plants. At one point, there were only the molecules that combine to make life, but not life itself.

The Geologic Time Scale

The appearance and disappearance of types of organisms throughout Earth's history give us markers in time. We can divide Earth's history into smaller units based on the types of life-forms living during certain periods. The division of Earth's history into smaller units makes up the **geologic time scale.** Some of the divisions in the geologic time scale are also based on geologic changes occurring at the time.

The geologic time scale is a record of Earth's history, starting with Earth's formation about 4.6 billion years ago. Each period of time is named. When fossils and rock layers are dated, scientists can assign them to a specific place on the geologic time scale.

Subdivisions of Geologic Time

There are three types of subdivisions of geologic time—eras, periods, and epochs. **Eras** are major subdivisions of the geologic time scale based on differences in life-forms. As you can see in **Figure 13-2** on the next page, the Mesozoic Era began about 245 million years ago. Its end is marked by the extinction of the dinosaurs and many other organisms about 66 million years ago.

Eras are subdivided into **periods.** Periods are based on the types of life existing at the time and on geologic events, such as mountain building and plate movements.

CONNECT TO

LIFE SCIENCE

Research evolutionary changes that have occurred in horses throughout geologic time. In your Science Journal, ***write*** a report in which you ***describe*** how these changes are thought to be connected to changes in the environments in which horses have lived.

2 Teach

CONNECT TO

LIFE SCIENCE

Answer Answers will vary but should include how changing environment from brushy fields to open grasslands led to adaptations in horses that enabled them to run faster and to eat grasses instead of brush.

Visual Learning

Figure 13-1 What does this trait enable horses to do? *run fast* LEP LS

Activity

LS **Interpersonal** Have student groups discuss events that have occurred during the school year. Have them list events from the latest to earliest. Ask students to describe the number of events and the details they can remember from early in the year and compare these to events later in the year. Students should notice that events that have occurred recently are remembered in greater detail. Relate this to the fact that the record of geologic events in recent periods is much more detailed than the record of events from periods long ago. L1 COOP LEARN

Across the Curriculum

Geography Inform students that periods on the geologic time scale are often named for geographic regions where the rocks of that age were first studied. Ask them to determine where rocks of the Pennsylvanian and Mississippian periods were first studied. Rocks of the Pennsylvanian Period are found exposed in Pennsylvania. Rocks of the Mississippian Period are exposed along the Mississippi River. Ask students to determine which period on the geologic time scale represents rocks first studied in the Jura Mountains between France and Switzerland. L1

GLENCOE TECHNOLOGY

CD-ROM

Earth Science CD-ROM

Have students perform the interactive exploration for Chapter 13 to reinforce important chapter concepts and thinking processes.

Activity

LS **Interpersonal** Provide groups of students with geologic maps of your area. Ask students to determine the age of rocks located near the school or their homes. Bring in samples of rock from a local exposure and have students determine what type of rock it is. Inform them of where you obtained the rocks and have them locate the area on their maps. L1 **COOP LEARN**

LS **Interpersonal** Have groups of students list the three most recent eras. Have them identify which organisms evolved, existed, and/or became extinct in each era. Call on a student from each group to present a summary of the information listed by the group. L1 **COOP LEARN**

Revealing Preconceptions

Many students will think that scientists have obtained a complete record of Earth's past from fossils contained in the rocks. Explain that very little is known about the first 4 billion years because much of the fossil record has been destroyed. Explain that gaps in the fossil record exist in more recent rocks because of erosion.

GLENCOE TECHNOLOGY

Videotape

The Secret of Life

Use the videotape *It's in the Genes: Evolution* to present the genetic mechanism by which organic evolution occurs.

Figure 13-2

The geologic time scale is divided into subunits based on geologic events and the appearance and disappearance of types of organisms.

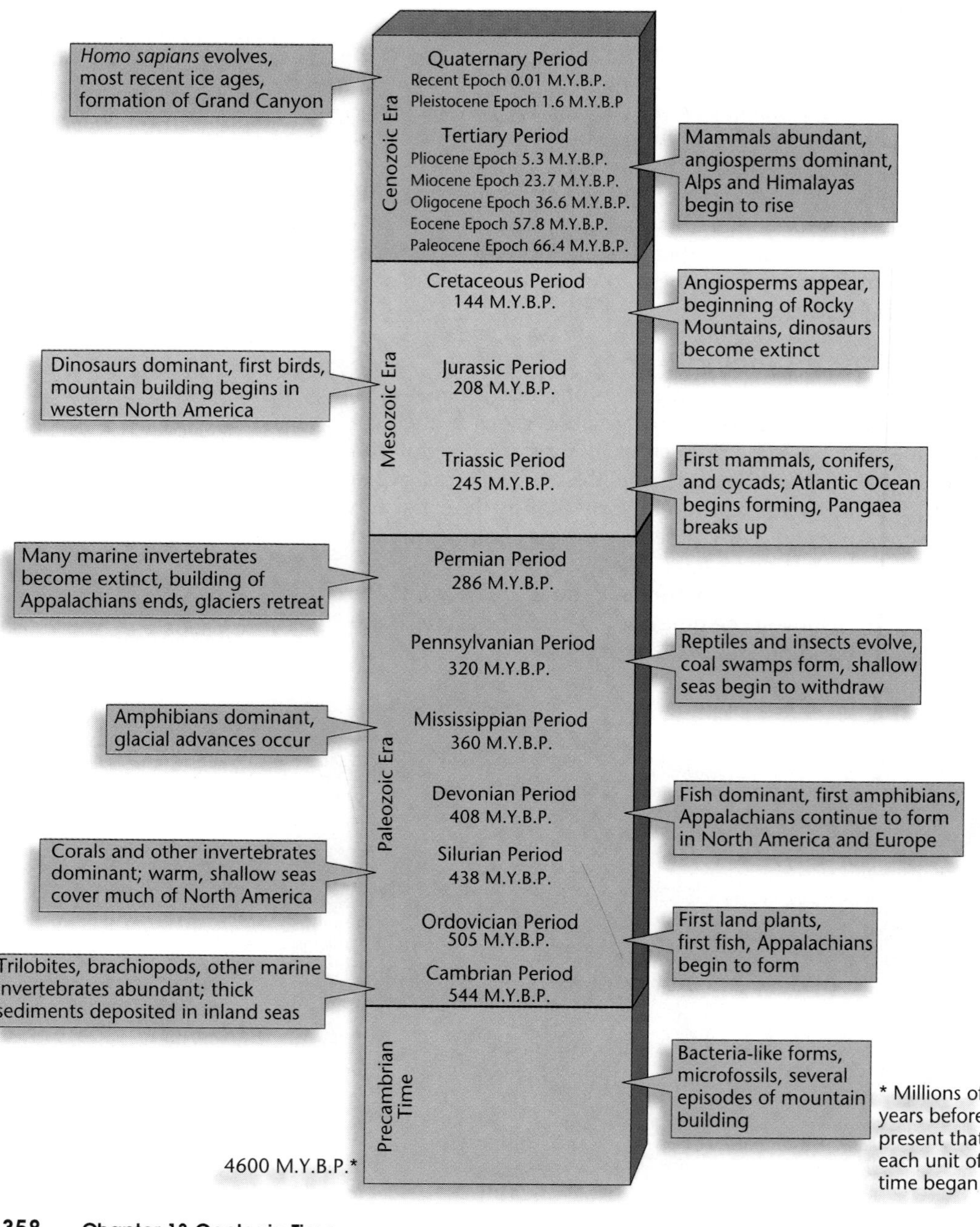

Across the Curriculum

Mathematics Have students construct a circle graph representing geologic time. Students should convert the time in each era into a percentage of the total time since Earth's formation, 4.6 billion years ago. Precambrian time represents about 87.6 percent of Earth's history. This equals about 316° of the circle graph. The Paleozoic Era comprises about 7 percent of Earth's history, or 25° on the circle graph. The Mesozoic Era comprises about 4 percent, or 14°, of the graph. The remaining 5° represents the Cenozoic Era, or 1.4 percent of Earth's history. Suggest that students use different colors to emphasize the different eras on their circle graphs. Students' circle graphs should resemble the one shown on page 385 of the Chapter Review. L1 LS

Periods may be divided into smaller units of time called **epochs. Figure 13-2** shows that only the Cenozoic Era is subdivided further into epochs. Why is this so? The fossil record and the record of geologic events is more complete in these more recent rock layers. As a result, geologists have more markers with which to divide the time scale.

Organic Evolution

INTEGRATION
Life Science

Based on the fossil record, organisms appear to have followed an ordered series of changes. This change in life-forms through time is known as **organic evolution.** Most theories describing the processes of organic evolution state that changes in the environment dictate who survives, and this in turn can result in changes in species of organisms.

Species

A **species** has often been defined as a group of organisms that normally reproduce only among themselves. For example, dogs are a species of animal because they mate and reproduce only with other dogs. As shown in **Figure 13-3,** there are some cases where organisms of different species can breed and produce offspring. These offspring, however, are unable to reproduce.

Natural Selection Within a Species

Suppose a bird species exists on an island. A few of the individuals have very hard beaks, but most have soft beaks. There are two food sources for the birds; one is soft and the

Figure 13-3

In some cases, animals of different species can breed and produce offspring. A lion (A) and a tiger (B) can produce a tigon (C). *However, because two different species are interbred, what is true of the offspring?*

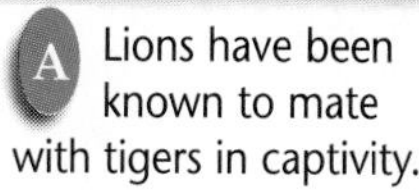

A Lions have been known to mate with tigers in captivity.

B Tigers in the wild do not live in the same regions as lions.

C The resulting offspring is called a tigon, liger, or tiglon.

Activity

Visual-Spatial Give students a geologic time scale and have them identify the eras by coloring their headings in with a colored pencil. Have students identify periods and epochs by coloring their headings in with two different colored pencils. L1 LEP

Concept Mapping

Visual-Spatial Have students make a network tree concept map of the geologic time scale. Students' maps should show the hierarchy among the divisions of time. L1 LEP

FLEX Your Brain

Use the Flex Your Brain activity to have students explore ORGANIC EVOLUTION.

Activity Worksheets, p. 5

Visual Learning

Figure 13-3 However, because two different species are interbred, what is true of the offspring? *They are sterile.* LEP LS

GLENCOE TECHNOLOGY

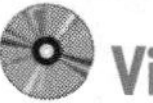

Videodisc

The Infinite Voyage: To the Edge of the Earth
Chapter 4
Exploring the Galapagos Islands

Inclusion Strategies

Gifted Have students interview a grandparent or other senior citizen. They should ask what major changes in the world the senior has observed. Changes could be in inventions, transportation, communication, the environment, health, and political and philosophical issues. Students should develop a time line of some of these major events in this person's "era." L3

Science Journal

Evolution Have students do some research in a historical geology book or biology text. In their Science Journals, have them define the terms *gradualism* and *punctuated equilibrium.* Encourage students to relate each of these terms to the study of evolution. L1 LS

INTEGRATION Life Science

The example presented is similar to what Charles Darwin discovered during the cruise *H.M.S. Beagle*. The *Beagle* traveled in the South Pacific Ocean from 1831 through 1833. Darwin believed that the adaptations of the different species of finches on the Galápagos Islands were caused by natural selection. An ongoing research study of these finches is providing evidence that indicates that natural selection is still going on in the Galápagos Islands. Refer to *The Beak of the Finch* by Jonathan Weiner, Vintage Books, New York, 1994.

Visual Learning

Figure 13-4 How might this natural selection affect future evolution? *Light-colored moths may become extinct.* LEP LS

Making Charts and Graphs

LS **Logical-Mathematical** Have students study the chart "The Victims and Survivors," from the article "Extinctions," by Rick Gore in *National Geographic,* June 1989, pp. 662-699. Have pairs of students make circle charts that show the percentage of extinctions that occurred at the end of the Ordovician Period (70 percent of all species), the Devonian Period (70 percent of all invertebrate species), the Permian Period (over 90 percent of all species), and the Cretaceous Period (all dinosaurs and about 70 percent of all other animal species). The extinction event at the end of the Permian Period is regarded as the greatest. L1 COOP LEARN

other has a hard shell around it. Now suppose the climate changes, causing the soft food to become scarce. Which of the birds will be better suited, or more fit, to survive? The birds with the harder beaks will be better able to break the hard shell on the more common food. Some of the soft-beaked birds may die from lack of food. The hard-beaked birds have a better chance of surviving and reproducing. Their offspring will inherit the trait of having a hard beak. Gradually, the number of hard-beaked birds will become greater, and the number of soft-beaked birds will decrease. The species may evolve so that nearly all of its members have hard beaks.

Natural Selection

Because the selection of the hard-beaked birds was a natural process, this process is called natural selection. Charles Darwin, a naturalist who sailed around the world from 1831 to 1836 to study wildlife, published the theory of evolution by natural selection. He proposed that **natural selection** is the process by which organisms with traits that are suited to a certain environment have a better chance of surviving and reproducing than organisms whose traits are not suited to it.

Notice in the example of the birds that individual soft-beaked birds didn't change into hard-beaked birds. A new trait becomes dominant in a species only if some members already possess that trait. If no bird in the species had possessed a hard beak, evolution into a hard-beaked species could not have occurred. The birds may have been able to survive if they could find other food to eat or adapt to other food sources, or they may have died out completely. **Figure 13-4** shows another example of natural selection.

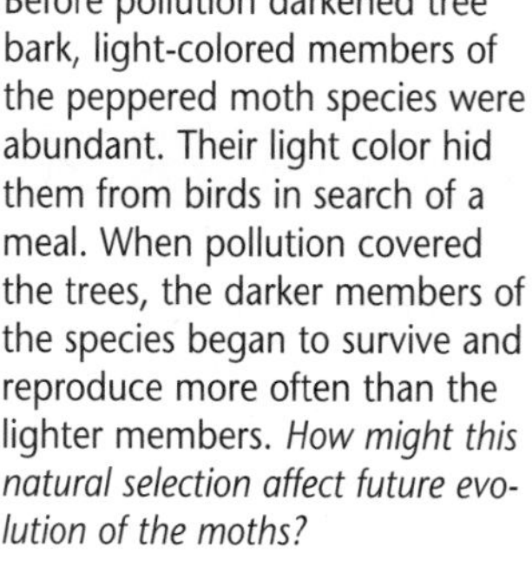

Figure 13-4

Before pollution darkened tree bark, light-colored members of the peppered moth species were abundant. Their light color hid them from birds in search of a meal. When pollution covered the trees, the darker members of the species began to survive and reproduce more often than the lighter members. *How might this natural selection affect future evolution of the moths?*

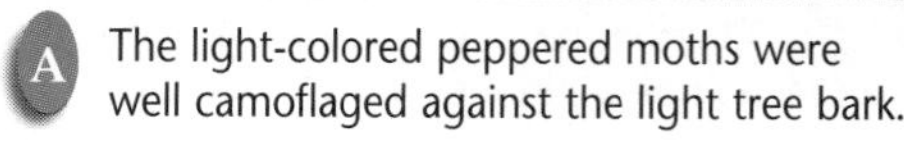

A The light-colored peppered moths were well camoflaged against the light tree bark.

B Against the pollution-darkened tree bark the light-colored moths stand out. They are then easier for birds to capture and eat.

Theme Connection

Stability and Change The natural selection of hard-beaked birds reinforces the theme of stability and change. The stability of the birds with hard beaks enables them to eat the hard-shelled food and to survive when other birds could not. The species changes because the individuals better adapted for the hard-shelled food have a better chance to produce offspring.

Use **Teaching Transparencies 25** and **26** as you teach this lesson.

Use Labs 36 and 37 in the **Lab Manual** as you teach this lesson.

Use **Study Guide,** p. 53, as you teach this lesson.

The Evolution of New Species

Natural selection explains not only how characteristics develop within a species, but also how new species arise. For example, if the soft-beaked birds in our example would have moved to a different part of the island where soft food was more available, they may have survived. The soft-beaked birds would continue to reproduce apart from the hard-beaked birds on a different part of the island. Over time, the soft-beaked birds would develop characteristics that were different from those of the hard-beaked birds, as seen in **Figure 13-5.** At some point, the birds might not be able to breed with each other. They would have evolved into two different species.

Changing Environments

Think again of the horses discussed at the beginning of this section. Why did they change over time? You have learned that fossil evidence shows that early

USING TECHNOLOGY

Embryology

Evidence for evolution has come from studying the embryos of organisms of different species. In early stages, it's difficult to tell the difference between the embryos of a reptile and a mammal just by looking at them (below). The embryos of each of these animals have tails and gill pouches during periods in their development.

Development

Embryos of these widely different organisms display similar features because similar genes are at work during their early development. As the separate organisms continue to develop, genes that have changed during the process of evolution are at work. These genes cause the wide diversity seen in the mature organisms.

By studying the similarities among the embryos of different species, we have discovered clues about which species may be closely related. Those species with similar embryo development may have shared a common ancestor in geologic history.

Early Embryos

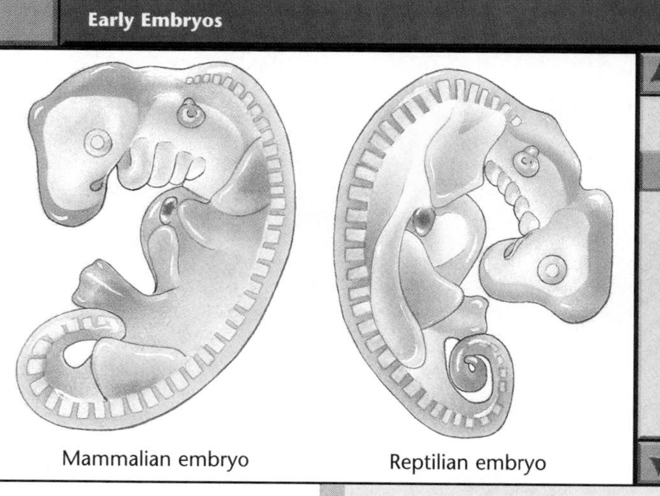

Think Critically: Mammals didn't evolve from dinosaurs, yet a mammalian embryo may have several features and developmental patterns in common with a dinosaur embryo. Explain why this might be the case.

USING TECHNOLOGY

For more information on evolution and the evidence for the theory of natural selection, see *The Beak of the Finch* by Jonathan Weiner, Vintage Books, New York, 1994 and *Hen's Teeth and Horse's Toes* by Stephen J. Gould, George J. McLeod, LTD., Toronto, Canada, 1983.

Think Critically

Mammals and dinosaurs share a common ancestor. Thus, early embryo development would be controlled by similar genes.

Enrichment

Have students research the work of early geologists in the construction of the geologic time scale. Scientists that students should research are James Hutton (1726-1797), William "Strata" Smith (1769-1838), and Charles Lyell (1797-1875). L2

Inquiry Questions

- **How do certain traits develop within a species of animal?** *If a certain trait makes an individual organism better able to survive in a particular environment, that trait will likely be passed on to offspring. Animals without the favorable trait are less likely to survive long enough to have offspring. As time passes, more and more offspring with the favorable trait survive.*
- **In the process of natural selection, do individual organisms develop new traits that make them better able to survive? Explain.** *No, individuals do not evolve new traits. If no organisms within a species possess a particular trait, the species will not be able to evolve into a species with that trait.*

Cultural Diversity

Evolving Viruses The flu is an example of a virus that evolves in order to survive. Every major flu epidemic has come from South China, where ducks, pigs, and humans are brought into daily contact. An avian flu transfers to pigs, as does a human flu variety. The viruses exchange pieces of genetic code to create a "new" flu strain. This then transfers back to humans. When it reinfects humans, it is different enough that antibodies created against the first form do not stop the new virus form. That is why flu shots protect only against last year's flu, and not the current year's variety. One variant produced a flu epidemic in 1918-1919 that killed 20 million people worldwide. Healthy individuals could die within 48 hours of feeling ill.

3 Assess

Check for Understanding

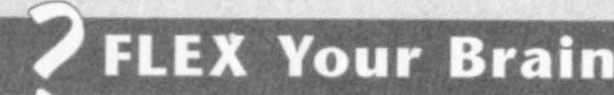

Use the Flex Your Brain activity to have students explore SPECIATION AND TECTONIC ACTIVITY.

Activity Worksheets, p. 5

Reteach

Visual-Spatial Demonstrate how life-forms change through geologic time by showing pictures or models of the development of the horse through time. Use pictures or models of the leg structure and point out how the multi-toed early horse changed over time. Indicate how the middle toe of each foot became larger and larger until now it has become a single toe. Demonstrate how the overall size of the horse has changed from the size of a dog to its present size. Relate these changes to adaptations to the changing environment.

Extension

For students who have mastered this section, use the **Reinforcement** and **Enrichment** masters.

Science Journal

Darwin believed the finches with beak traits best suited to the various environments would have a better chance of surviving and producing offspring. He believed that variations in the type of food available caused the adaptations seen in the varying shapes and sizes of the beaks. P

horses were small, multi-toed animals adapted to grazing on shrubs and bushes. As environments on Earth changed from brushy fields to open grasslands, the horse species became bigger and developed hooves and complex molars. Over millions of years, horses became adapted to open grasslands by the process of natural selection. As the environment changed, the horse species adapted and survived.

Many species that lived on Earth during its long history apparently couldn't adapt to changing environments. Such species became extinct. What processes on Earth could cause environments to change so much that species must adapt or become extinct?

The Effect of Plate Tectonics on Earth History

Plate tectonics is one process that causes changing environments on Earth. As plates on Earth's surface moved over time, continents collided with and separated from each other many times. Collisions caused mountain building and the draining of seas. Separations caused deeper seas to develop between continents. This rearranging of land and sea still causes changes in climates. How might these changes affect organisms?

If species adapt to the changes, or evolve, they survive. If a species doesn't have individuals with characteristics needed for survival in the changing environment, the species becomes extinct, as seen in **Figure 13-6.**

Figure 13-5

Ten of the many species of finches on Isle Santa Cruz in the Galápagos archipelago are shown. All of these evolved from one ancestral species. Small groups of the ancestral species became isolated when they began to specialize in the types of food they ate and the areas in which they lived. These groups eventually evolved into different species.

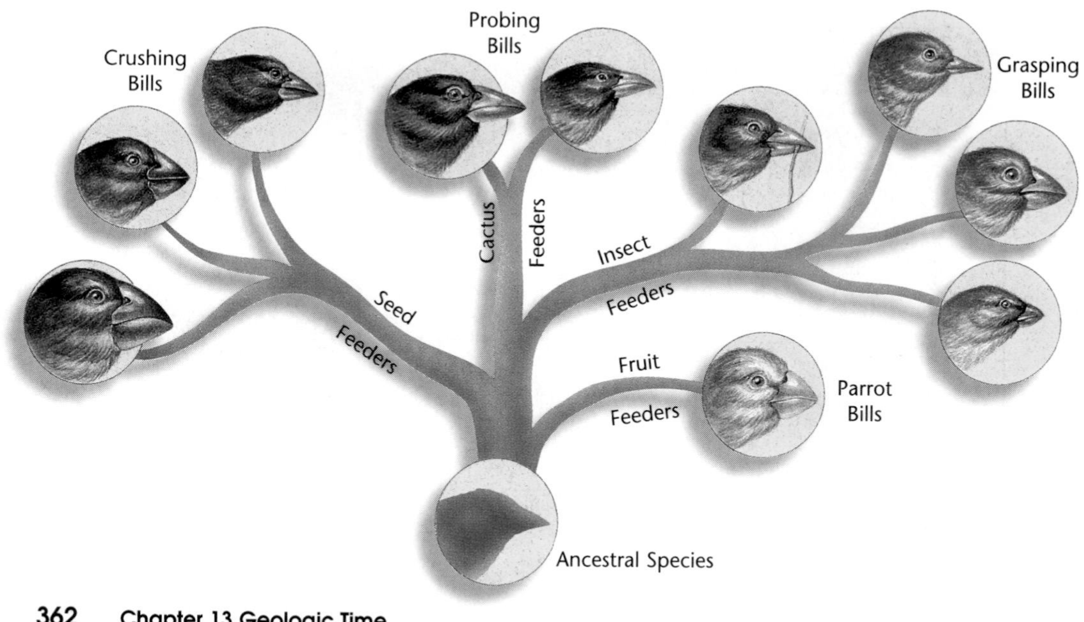

Integrating the Sciences

Life Science As plates move across Earth's surface, continents collide and separate many times. As continents collide, mountains are built up that can separate species that normally live together. Also, environments change as oceans deepen and become shallow and as land masses move. The environmental changes result in the evolution of new species and the evolution of traits within species.

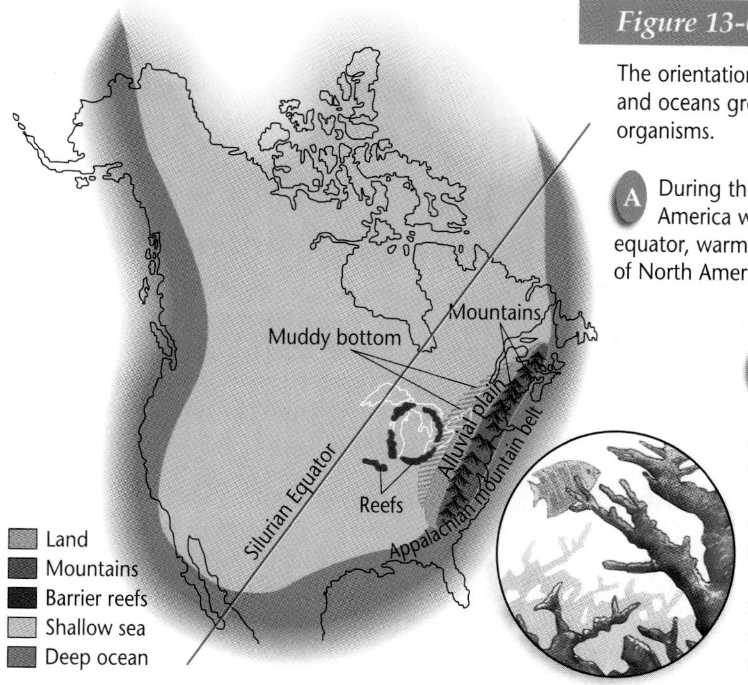

Figure 13-6

The orientation and position of continents and oceans greatly affects climate and organisms.

A During the Silurian Period when North America was positioned along the equator, warm, shallow seas covered much of North America.

B Corals, which are sea animals, were a dominant life-form in the Silurian Period. But as plate tectonic processes changed Earth's surface, climates also changed. Many species of coral did not adapt to the cooler climate. Thus, corals became less abundant, and some species became extinct. This example shows modern corals.

Section Wrap-up

Review

1. Relate organic evolution to the geologic time scale.
2. How might plate tectonics affect organic evolution?
3. **Think Critically:** Today, the moth species shown in **Figure 13-4** has many light-colored individuals. How can this be attributed to recent anti-pollution laws?

Skill Builder

Recognizing Cause and Effect

Answer the questions below. If you need help, refer to Recognizing Cause and Effect in the **Skill Handbook.**

1. Is natural selection a cause or effect of organic evolution?
2. How could the evolution of a trait within one species affect the evolution of a trait within another species? Give an example.

Science Journal

Write a paragraph in your Science Journal that explains Darwin's interpretation of the various beak types on the different species of Galápagos finches. Include illustrations to show the differences.

4 Close

•MINI•QUIZ•

1. **The geologic time scale is divided into units of time based on ______ and ______ .** *the types of life-forms existing during certain times, the geologic changes that have occurred*
2. **What is the gradual change in life-forms through time known as?** *organic evolution*
3. **A(n) ______ is a group of organisms that normally reproduce only among themselves.** *species*
4. **______ is the process by which organisms with traits that are suited to a certain environment have a better chance of survival.** *Natural selection*

Section Wrap-up

Review

1. Changes in or massive extinctions of life-forms are used to divide geologic time into units.
2. As landmasses move across Earth, climates change dramatically. Through natural selection, only individuals suited to the changes survive and reproduce. They pass their traits to their offspring. Over many generations, the species has evolved so that it can survive in the changed environment.
3. **Think Critically** Anti-pollution laws have resulted in less smog and, therefore, less dark-colored residue on the local trees. The light-colored moths are well camouflaged against the lighter bark. They are suited to survive and reproduce, passing on their light color to their offspring.

Skill Builder

1. a cause
2. Species are interdependent. Changes within the organisms of an ecosystem affect all aspects of that ecosystem. For example, if a species evolves so that it is no longer available as the primary food source for another species, the predator species must evolve so that it can prey on other sources, or it will become extinct.

Assessment

Performance Assess students' abilities to recognize cause and effect by having them hypothesize why giraffes have such long necks. Use the Performance Task Assessment List for Formulating a Hypothesis in **PASC**, p. 21. P

SCIENCE & SOCIETY

Section 13•2

Prepare

Section Background

Some scientists believe up to 20 000 species are becoming extinct each year. A large percentage of these species occur in tropical rain forests.

1 Motivate

Bellringer

Before presenting the lesson, display **Section Focus Transparency 50** on the overhead projector. Assign the accompanying **Focus Activity** worksheet. L1 LEP

Tying to Previous Knowledge

Help students recall the characteristics of the tropical rain forest biome from their study of life science. Tropical rain forests are found in low-lying regions near the equator.

2 Teach

Discussion

- Discuss the fact that 80 percent of all deforestation of Amazonian rain forests has occurred since 1980.
- Have students discuss the significance of the fact that one-quarter of all pharmaceuticals are derived from rain forest plants. Students should realize that the destruction of a habitat so rich in species has serious philosophical and economic ramifications.

SCIENCE & SOCIETY

ISSUE:

13•2 Present-Day Rapid Extinctions

Science Words

endangered
habitat

Objectives

- Recognize how humans have contributed to extinctions.
- Predict what might happen to the diversity of life on Earth if land is developed without protection of natural habitats.
- Hypothesize what can be done to stop or slow down the rate of species extinction.

Human Effects on Extinction Rates

You've learned that extinctions have occurred throughout Earth's history. They were caused by changes in environments or competition with other species for resources. Some of these extinctions may have been caused by the appearance of early humans. However, present-day humans are causing extinctions at a much greater rate.

How do humans promote extinctions?

When humans kill organisms faster than they can reproduce, the number of members in those species decreases. Such species can become endangered, as in the case of the mountain gorillas in Africa. (See **Figure 13-7**). A species becomes **endangered** when only a small number of its members are living. If the number of members of a species continues to dwindle, the species can become extinct. A species becomes extinct when no more of its members are living.

Humans promote extinctions by overhunting, through carelessness, and by making changes in the environment. Often, we take over the natural habitats of other species, leaving them with no food or space in which to live. A **habitat** is the place where organisms live, grow, and interact with each other and with the environment. Many species on Earth live in only one particular type of habitat. If that habitat is suddenly destroyed, the species does not have time to adapt, so all members of the species die.

Figure 13-7

These African mountain gorillas of Rwanda have become endangered because of habitat lost to human settlements.

2 Points of View

Development Without Habitat Protection

You may have heard about problems caused by the cutting or burning of tropical rain forests, shown in **Figure 13-8.** During the past decade, people have cleared much of these forests for farming, logging, and other industries. In doing so, they have destroyed many habitats.

Program Resources

Reproducible Masters

Study Guide, p. 54 L1
Reinforcement, p. 54 L1
Enrichment, p. 54 L3
Science and Society Integration, p. 17 L1

Transparencies

Section Focus Transparency 50

The tropical rain forest habitat covers only about seven percent of Earth's surface, but it contains 50 to 80 percent of Earth's species. Think of what would happen to these species if the tropical rain forests were destroyed.

Development with Habitat Protection

Trees and other plants in a tropical rain forest derive many of their nutrients from a continuous supply of rapidly rotting organic matter. Whenever large areas of the tropical rain forests are destroyed, plants tend not to grow back because the soil in these areas is very poorly developed. Once the plants have been destroyed, there is nothing left to supply nutrients.

Governments could restrict construction to allow both development and preservation. Projects for various industries could be planned in ways that preserve habitats or disturb them as little as possible. When land is cleared, some could be left in its natural state.

Figure 13-8
When forests are cleared, animal and plant habitat is lost. Many species may become extinct if too much forest is destroyed.

Section Wrap-up

Review

1. List three ways humans promote extinctions.
2. How does developing land for construction and farming reduce the diversity of life on Earth?
3. **Think Critically:** How might humans work to slow the rate of present-day extinctions?

Explore the Issue

Should governments of developing countries require their people to preserve portions of their land in its natural state, thereby reducing the amount of land that can be developed for farming and logging? If so, how would you answer landowners who claim that they can grow enough food for their families and livestock to live on only if they develop all of their land? If not, then how can the rate of extinction of animals and plants that are so vital to our survival be reduced?

SCIENCE & SOCIETY

3 Assess

Check for Understanding

FLEX Your Brain

Use the Flex Your Brain activity to have students explore ENDANGERED SPECIES.

Activity Worksheets, p. 5

Reteach

Show pictures of deforestation in South America and Asia. Explain that destruction of rain forests is permanent. Also explain that soil in a tropical rain forest supports farming for only a few years before new areas must be cleared.

Extension

For students who have mastered this section, use the **Reinforcement** and **Enrichment** masters.

4 Close

Ask how the loss of rain forests might affect global environments. *Rain forest plants provide atmospheric oxygen and remove atmospheric carbon dioxide. Increased levels of carbon dioxide could lead to global warming.*

Section Wrap-up

Review

1. overhunting, carelessness, changing environments
2. Developing land can destroy habitats. When the habitat is destroyed, the organisms die off.
3. **Think Critically** Answers will vary, but might include government restrictions on development.

Explore the Issue

Answers will vary. If yes, students must provide a way for the farmers to feed their entire families by farming only a portion of their land. Perhaps the World Bank could pay people to preserve parts of the natural habitat. If no, students must provide a way to cut down on the rate of extinctions of animals and plants. Governments could ask for voluntary restraint on the part of the people living on developable land. Governments of more developed countries that rely on the benefits of these natural habitats could pay people who voluntarily use restraint when developing their land.

Section 13•3

Prepare

Section Background

Trilobites are a common fossil from the Cambrian Period. They were probably not active swimmers, but crawled along the bottom scavenging for food. Trilobites were widespread and diverse, which makes them index fossils for the Paleozoic Era.

Preplanning

- To prepare for Activity 13-1, obtain one deck of regular playing cards for each group of three students.
- For the MiniLAB, prepare an illustration of a sedimentary sequence containing fossils.

1 Motivate

Bellringer

Before presenting the lesson, display **Section Focus Transparency 51** on the overhead projector. Assign the accompanying **Focus Activity** worksheet. L1 LEP

Tying to Previous Knowledge

Help students recall the chemical composition and physical properties of ozone discussed in Chapter 14. Remind students that ozone is made of three oxygen atoms (O_3) bonded together. When discussing the production of molecular oxygen (O_2) by cyanobacteria, relate the fact that ozone is produced when energy (such as that supplied by the sun or by lightning) is added to molecular oxygen (O_2).

13•3 Early Earth History

Science Words

Precambrian time
cyanobacteria
Paleozoic Era
amphibian
reptile

Objectives

- Identify dominant life-forms in Precambrian time and the Paleozoic Era.
- Draw conclusions about how organisms adapted to changing environments in Precambrian time and the Paleozoic Era.
- Describe changes in Earth and its life-forms at the end of the Paleozoic Era.

Precambrian Time

Look again at **Figure 13-2. Precambrian** (pree KAM bree un) **time** represents the longest geologic time unit of Earth's history. This time lasted from 4.6 billion to about 544 million years ago. Although the Precambrian was the longest unit of geologic time, relatively little is known about Earth and the organisms that lived during this time, as shown in **Figure 13-9.** Why is the fossil record from Precambrian time so sparse?

Precambrian rocks have been deeply buried and changed by heat and pressure. They have also been eroded more than younger rocks. These changes affect not only the rocks, but the fossil record as well. Most fossils can't withstand the metamorphic and erosional processes that most Precambrian rocks have experienced.

Figure 13-9

Scientists look for evidence of what Earth looked like during Precambrian time and what life-forms were present.

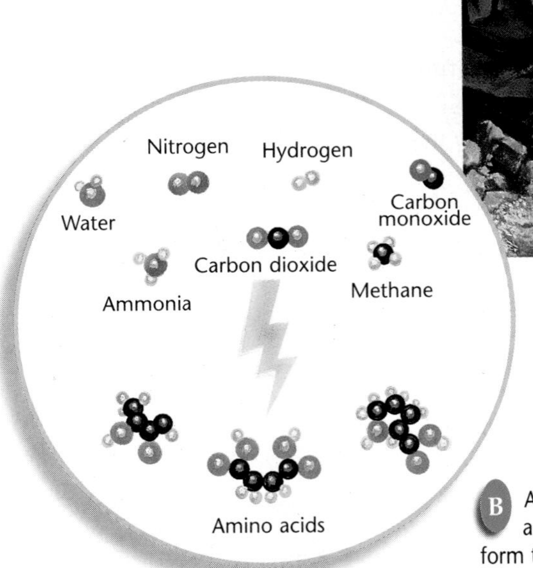

A Lightning or the sun may have provided the energy necessary to build amino acids out of the simple compounds in Earth's Precambrian atmosphere.

B Amino acids are the "building blocks of life." These amino acids reacted with each other and combined to form the compounds from which life may have evolved.

Program Resources

Reproducible Masters
Study Guide, p. 55 L1
Reinforcement, p. 55 L1
Enrichment, p. 55 L3
Activity Worksheets, pp. 78-79, 82 L1

Transparencies
Section Focus Transparency 51 L1

Figure 13-10

In some conditions, cyanobacteria produce mound-shaped layers of calcium carbonate called stromatolites. Stromatolites were common about 2.8 billion years ago and are still being formed today. *What does this imply about the lifeform cyanobacteria?*

A Stromatolites have changed very little throughout geologic time. These modern ones in Australia look very much like ancient stromatolites.

B Cross section of an individual stromatolite head.

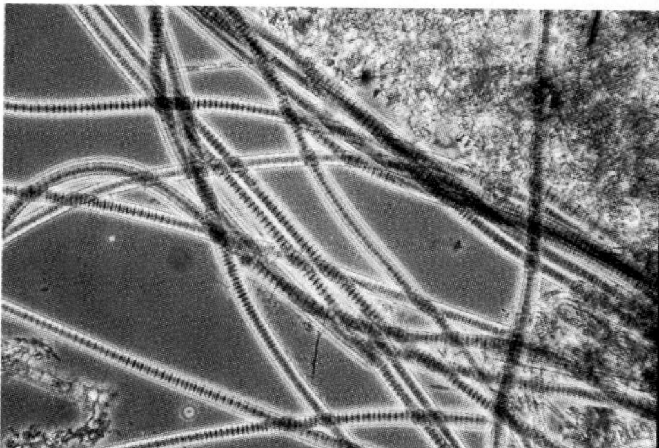

C Microscopic view of a cyanobacterium.

Early Life

It wasn't until fossilized cyanobacteria forming layered mats, called stromatolites, were found that scientists could begin to unravel Earth's complex history. **Cyanobacteria,** shown in **Figure 13-10,** are blue-green bacteria thought to be one of the earliest forms of life on Earth. Cyanobacteria first appeared on Earth about 3.5 billion years ago. As these organisms evolved, they contributed to changes in Earth's atmosphere. During the few billion years following the appearance of cyanobacteria, oxygen became a major gas in Earth's atmosphere. The ozone layer in the stratosphere also began to develop, shielding Earth from ultraviolet rays. These major changes in the air allowed species of single-celled organisms to evolve into more complex organisms.

Animals without backbones, called invertebrates, developed near the end of Precambrian time. Imprints of jellyfish and marine worms have been found in late Precambrian rocks. However, because these early invertebrates were soft-bodied, they weren't easily preserved as fossils. This is another reason the Precambrian fossil record is so sparse.

The Paleozoic Era

In Chapter 12, you discovered that fossils are more likely to form if organisms have hard parts. When organisms developed hard parts, the **Paleozoic** (pay lee uh ZOH ihk) **Era** began. Fossils were then more easily preserved.

CONNECT TO

CHEMISTRY

Cyanobacteria are thought to have been one of the mechanisms by which Earth's early atmosphere became richer in oxygen. ***Research*** the composition of Earth's early atmosphere and where these gases originated.

2 Teach

Inquiry Question

LS **Interpersonal** Have students in groups of four answer the following question: **Why was the development of single-celled cyanobacteria so important to the evolution of more complex organisms?** *As they evolved, cyanobacteria helped change Earth's atmosphere. They exchanged oxygen for other atmospheric gases. The amount of oxygen in the atmosphere increased, allowing an ozone layer to develop. The layer shielded Earth's surface from harmful ultraviolet radiation from the sun. Complex life-forms were able to evolve in the changed environment.* COOP LEARN

CONNECT TO

CHEMISTRY

Answer Gases in Earth's original atmosphere may have been in the original material that formed Earth. The gases were emitted during volcanic eruptions, or derived from comet impacts. This early atmosphere was probably composed of water vapor, carbon dioxide, and nitrogen.

Revealing Preconceptions

Ask students to hypothesize when sharks appeared on Earth. Many students will consider sharks to be modern-day animals, since they are still around. Explain that it is thought sharks evolved during the Devonian Period about 408 million years ago.

Inclusion Strategies

Visually Impaired Use plastic, plaster, or clay models of important fossils of animals and plants that lived during the Paleozoic Period. Choose models that exhibit small details of the fossils. Being able to handle the fossils will help students picture their shapes, sizes, and details. Detailed and complete examples of an actual fossil may also be used for this purpose.

Integrating the Sciences

Life Science Have students research the role cyanobacteria played in transforming Earth's early atmosphere into one containing free molecular oxygen (O_2). Encourage them to write a report about what they find out in their Science Journals. Ask them to hypothesize how life might be different if cyanobacteria had not transformed Earth's atmosphere. L2

Visual Learning

Figure 13-10 What does this imply about the lifeform cyanobacteria? *They are very well adapted to their particular environment.* LEP LS

Activity 13-1 Evolution Within a Species

Use a model in this activity to observe how adaptation within a species might cause the evolution of a particular trait, leading to the development of a new species.

Problem

How might adaptation within a species cause the evolution of a particular trait?

Materials

- Deck of playing cards

Procedure

1. Remove all of the kings, queens, jacks, and aces from a deck of playing cards.
2. Each remaining card represents an individual in a population of animals called "varimals." The number on each card represents the height of the individual. For example, the 5 of diamonds is a varimal that's 5 units tall.
3. Calculate the average height of the population of varimals represented by your cards.
4. Suppose varimals eat grass, shrubs, and leaves from trees. A drought causes many of these plants to die. All that's left are a few tall trees. Only varimals at least 6 units tall can reach the leaves on these trees.
5. All the varimals under 6 units leave the area to seek food elsewhere or die from starvation. Discard all of the cards with a number value less than 6. Calculate the new average height of the population of varimals.
6. Shuffle the deck of remaining cards.
7. Draw two cards at a time. Each pair represents a pair of varimals that will mate and produce offspring.
8. The offspring of each pair reaches a height equal to the average height of his or her parents. Calculate and record the height of each offspring.
9. Repeat by discarding all parents and offspring under 8 units tall. Now calculate the new average height of varimals. Include both the parents and offspring in your calculation.

Analyze

1. How did the average height of the population change over time?
2. If you hadn't discarded the shortest varimals, would the average height of the population have changed as much? **Explain.**
3. What trait was selected for?

Conclude and Apply

4. Why didn't every member of the original population reproduce?
5. If there had been no varimals over 6 units tall in step 5, what would have happened to the population?
6. If there had been no variation in height in the population before the droughts occurred, would the species have been able to evolve into a taller species than it started as?
7. How does this activity **demonstrate** that traits evolve in species?

Activity 13-1

Purpose

Interpersonal Formulate a model showing the role of natural selection in creating variations within a species. L1 COOP LEARN

Process Skills

formulating models, using numbers, interpreting data, forming operational definitions, recognizing cause and effect, and communicating

Time

30 minutes

Activity Worksheets, pp. 5, 78, 79

Teaching Strategies

- Remove the cards that will not be used in this activity prior to class time. This will eliminate Step 1 of the Procedure and reduce the time needed to perform the activity.
- Inform students that the natural selection process modeled in this activity is not unlike that which is thought to have led to the present-day giraffe.

Answers to Questions

1. The average height increased over time.
2. No. The average would remain at about 6.
3. height; specifically, the ability to reach food above the ground
4. Some of the original varimals weren't able to obtain enough food to survive and, therefore, weren't able to reproduce.
5. This particular population of varimals would have become extinct.
6. Probably not. If all of the individuals would have been the same height, no group of individuals would have an advantage in reaching the high food. In that case, any evolution of the varimal population would have likely occurred from some variation of a trait other than height.
7. By creating the variation of a trait within the varimal population, in this case height, the model demonstrates how the species was able to evolve into one capable of reaching food high above the ground. This process, by which individuals with more favorable traits are able to survive and produce offspring with these same traits, is known as natural selection.

Assessment

Oral To further assess students' understanding of evolution, ask them whether any individual varimal increased in height because of natural selection. Encourage students to explain their answers. *No, individuals do not evolve inheritable adaptations.* Use the Performance Task Assessment List for Making Observations and Inferences in **PASC**, p. 17. P

Era of Ancient Life

The Paleozoic Era, or era of ancient life, began about 544 million years ago. Warm, shallow seas covered much of Earth's surface during early Paleozoic time. Because of this, most of the life-forms were marine, meaning they lived in the ocean. Trilobites (TRI luh bites) were very common. Brachiopods (BRAY kee uh pahdz) and crinoids (KRI noyds), which still exist today, were also very common. Although these animals may not be familiar to you, one type of animal you are familiar with—the fish—also evolved during this era.

The Paleozoic Era is broken into seven periods. The start of the Ordovician Period is marked by the beginning of the Appalachian Mountain building process. This was probably caused by the collision of the Eurasian or African continental plate with the North American Plate.

The first vertebrates, animals with backbones, developed during the Ordovician Period. Plant life moved from the oceans onto land during the Silurian Period. Fish became dominant in the Devonian Period, as seen in **Figure 13-11.** By this time plant life had developed on land, and animals began to move onto land as well.

Figure 13-11

This giant fish, *Dunkleosteus*, lived in Ohio during the Devonian Period. It grew to over 9 m long.

MiniLAB

Fossil Correlation

In the activity, you will demonstrate how fossils are used to date rock layers. Suppose you find a sequence of sedimentary rocks containing fossils.

Procedure

1. Number the layers 1 through 3, bottom to top.
2. Identify the fossils in each layer. Suppose the bottom layer, layer 1, contains fossils B and A. Layer 2 contains fossils A, B, and C. Layer 3 contains only fossil C.
3. Determine the geologic periods each of the fossils lived. For example, fossil A lived from the Cambrian through the Devonian Periods. Fossil C lived from the Devonian through the Permian Periods, and so on.
4. Construct and interpret scientific illustrations to help you determine the ages of each rock layer.

Analysis

1. Which layer or layers were you able to date to a specific period?
2. Why isn't it possible to determine during which specific period the other layers formed?
3. What is the age or possible age of each layer?

MiniLAB

Purpose

LS **Visual-Spatial** Students will use fossils to determine the age of rock layers. L1

Teaching Strategies

- Sketch the geologic column described. Label the layers 1 through 3 and indicate which fossils are in each layer.
- Have students construct a chart like the one shown.
- For each rock layer, list the periods during which it could have formed.

	A	B	C
Perm.			↑
Penn.		↑	│
Miss.		│	│
Dev.	↑	│	│
Sil.	│	│	
Ord.	│	│	
Cam.	│		

Analysis

1. Only layer that can be dated to one period is Layer 2, since it contains both fossils A and C, from the Devonian.
2. Absence of a specific fossil does not necessarily mean that it did not exist; it may not have been found.
3. Layer 1 could be Ordovician, Silurian, or Devonian. Layer 2 is Devonian. Layer 3 could have formed anytime from the Devonian through the Permian.

Assessment

Performance Tell students that a rock layer containing fossils B and C has been found directly above a rock layer containing fossil A. Have them hypothesize when the rock may have formed. Use the Performance Task Assessment List for Formulating a Hypothesis in **PASC**, p. 21. P

Integrating the Sciences

Life Science To help students realize how each science is integrated with and dependent on other sciences, use the following questions to initiate a discussion on the history of life on Earth. **Why were most life-forms during the Paleozoic Era marine life-forms?** *Warm, shallow seas covered much of Earth's surface.* **Why are brachiopod fossils considered good indicators of ancient marine environments?** *They were very common during the Paleozoic Era, when shallow seas covered much of Earth's surface, and are still found today in sea environments.* **What might have caused the mass extinctions that occurred at the end of the Paleozoic Era?** *The environment changed, perhaps as a result of plate tectonics, because at this time all continental plates were coming together.*

Problem Solving

Solve the Problem

1. Yes, if both rock formations formed during the time that the species of *Mucrospirifer* existed.
2. During what time frame is it thought that *Mucrospirifer* existed? For example, if the particular species of *Mucrospirifer* existed for 1 million years, one formation may have been deposited at the beginning of that one-million-year period and the other formation near its end.

Think Critically

Both rock formations formed during the time that the species of *Mucrospirifer* existed.

Inquiry Questions

- **What developments enabled animal life to move from the sea onto land?** *Plant life developed on land; hard-shelled eggs of reptile developed.*
- **Why do scientists think lungfish and amphibians evolved from the same ancestor?** *Lungfish can breathe air as they travel across land from one body of water to the next.*

Enrichment

Have students research the Pennsylvanian Period's coal swamps, where much of the coal used today was formed. Show students samples of peat, lignite (palm coal), bituminous coal, and anthracite coal. Describe the process that must occur for plant remains to change into coal. Refer students to Chapter 12 for a description of this process. L2

Problem Solving

Paleozoic Puzzle

Suppose that there are many different and interesting fossils displayed around your classroom. Many of the fossil samples have been collected by other students and by your teacher. Your teacher tells you that she has studied the outcrops of rocks in the city where she attended college. It was at this time that she began her excellent collection of fossils from that area which are displayed in your room. Her favorite fossil was a particular species of brachiopod known as *Mucrospirifer*. She identified this fossil from pictures and descriptions from books on Paleozoic fossils she used while attending college.

When your teacher went on a fossil collecting trip last summer, she found what seemed to be the same type of *Mucrospirifer* fossil in a rock formation hundreds of kilometers from where she attended college.

Solve the Problem:

1. **Is it possible that both of the fossils found by your teacher are *Mucrospirifer*?**
2. **What one fact should your teacher know about *Mucrospirifer* before using her fossils to attempt dating the rock layers in which they were found?**

Think Critically: Once your teacher has determined that both samples she found were *Mucrospirifer*, what could she conclude about the rock layers near her college and those she studied on her more recent fossil collection trip?

Mucrospirifer
50 mm

Life on Land

One type of fish evolved a lung that enabled it to survive out of water. This fish had fins that allowed it to move across land. The fact that lungfish could move across land and breathe air has led scientists to theorize that lungfish were ancestors of amphibians (am FIHB ee unz). **Amphibians** live on land and breathe air, but they must return to water to reproduce. Their eggs must be kept moist in water. They first appeared during the Devonian Period and became the dominant form of vertebrate life on land by the Mississippian Period.

Over time, one species of amphibian evolved an egg with a membrane that protected it from drying out. Because of this, the species no longer needed to return to water to reproduce. By the Pennsylvanian Period, some species of amphibians had evolved into reptiles. **Reptiles** do not need to return to water to reproduce as shown in **Figure 13-13** on page 372. Reptiles have skin with hard scales that prevent loss of body fluids. This adaptation enables them to survive farther from water. They can survive in relatively dry climates, whereas amphibians cannot.

Community Connection

Fossil Collecting Take students on a field trip to an exposure of rock near your school or community. Show them how to carefully look for fossils. Bring any samples that are found back to the classroom and have students attempt to identify them using a fossil collecting book. If fossils are found and any of them can be identified, inform students as to the age of the rocks from which the fossils came.

Fossil Expert Invite a local fossil collector or museum curator into class to share his or her collection with the students and to present a demonstration of techniques used when searching for fossils. Ask him or her to identify from where near their community that some of the fossils can be collected.

Figure 13-12

Many of the coal deposits mined today in the United States began forming during the Pennsylvanian Period. Inland seas were cut off from the oceans. Swamps similar to those found in the Florida Everglades formed.

A This illustration reconstructs what a Pennsylvanian Period coal forest might have looked like 300 million years ago.

B As the vegetation is buried, it is compressed by the weight of the overlying sediment to form coal.

C Huge equipment is used in many modern coal mining operations.

End of an Era

Mass extinctions of many land and sea animals occurred, signalling the end of the Paleozoic Era. The cause of these extinctions may have been changes in the environment caused by plate tectonics. Near the end of the Permian Period, all continental plates came together to form the single landmass Pangaea and major glaciers formed.

Visual Learning

Figure 13-12 **Based on Figure 13-12A, how would you describe the environment that existed in the area near Pennsylvania when the vegetation that would eventually change to coal was buried?** *A low-lying swamp with dense vegetation.*

Figure 13-13 **What characteristic of reptile eggs prevents the developing embryos from drying out?** *A protective membrane.* LEP IS

3 Assess

Check for Understanding

FLEX Your Brain

Use the Flex Your Brain activity to have students explore PALEOZOIC LIFE.

Activity Worksheets, p. 5

Reteach

IS **Interpersonal** Have pairs of students list the characteristics of amphibians that make them different from fish and the characteristics of reptiles that make them different from amphibians. Have partners test each other on the differences and search through magazine articles for photographs of amphibians and reptiles. COOP LEARN

Extension

For students who have mastered this section, use the **Reinforcement** and **Enrichment** masters.

Integrating the Sciences

Life Science Inform students that coal begins to form when swamp plants die and partially decay. Plants are made up of molecules that contain atoms of carbon, hydrogen, and oxygen. Decay occurs when bacteria break apart these molecules, releasing oxygen and hydrogen gases and leaving carbon and impurities like sulfur behind. When coal is burned, it is the carbon that releases the heat.

Science Journal

Coal Formation Ask students to continue reviewing the production of coal by researching coal formation and writing a short report in their Science Journals explaining the stages that occur before coal is formed. L1 IS

4 Close

•MINI•QUIZ•

1. Earth's complex history began to unravel once scientists found fossilized _____. *cyanobacteria*
2. Once fish developed lungs, it is thought they evolved into _____. *amphibians*
3. When some species of amphibians evolved eggs with a membrane that protected them from drying out, they no longer needed to return to water to reproduce. These amphibians evolved into _____. *reptiles*

Section Wrap-up

Review

1. Mountains built up as continents collided, and seas drained away, creating deserts.
2. Environments changed, and many life-forms could not adapt quickly enough. When Pangaea formed, life-forms that had been separate were now together. They now competed for food. This could have led to the extinction of some organisms.
3. **Think Critically** The evolution of organisms with hard parts marked the beginning of a new era in Earth's history.

Using Computers

Illustrations and descriptions will vary. Accept any general statements that describe students' illustrations. Trilobites, brachiopods, and crinoids are all marine invertebrate animals.

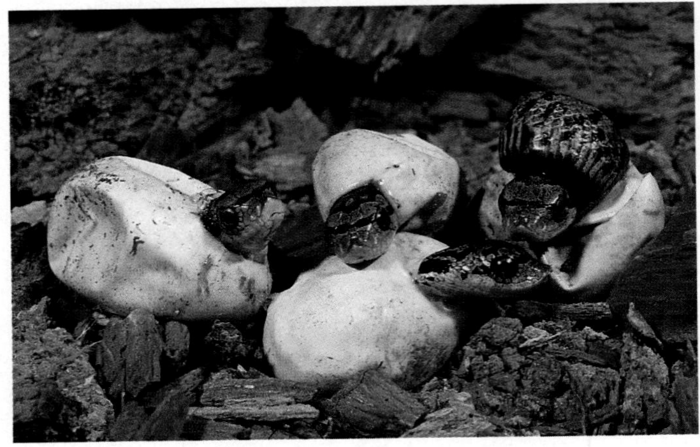

Figure 13-13

Unlike frogs, salamanders, and other amphibians, reptiles can lay their eggs on land. This allows them to survive in relatively dry environments. *What characteristic of reptile eggs prevents the developing embryos from drying out?*

The slow, gradual collision of continental plates caused mountain building. Mountain building processes caused seas to drain away, and interior deserts spread over much of the United States and parts of Europe. Climates changed from mild and warm to cold and dry. Many species, especially marine organisms, weren't able to adapt to these and other changes and became extinct.

Section Wrap-up

Review

1. What geologic events occurred at the end of the Paleozoic Era?
2. How might geologic events at the end of the Paleozoic Era have caused the mass extinctions that occurred?
3. **Think Critically:** What major change in life-forms occurred to separate Precambrian time from the Paleozoic Era?

Skill Builder

Making and Using Tables

Use **Figure 13-2** to answer these questions about the Paleozoic Era. If you need help, refer to Making and Using Tables in the **Skill Handbook.**

1. When did the Paleozoic Era begin? When did it end?
2. How long did the Silurian Period last?
3. When did the Appalachian Mountains start to form?
4. When did the first insects appear on Earth?

Using Computers

Database Research trilobites, brachiopods, and crinoids in a historical geology book or computer database. Write a paragraph in your Science Journal describing each of these organisms and its habitat. Include hand-drawn illustrations and compare them with the illustrations in the computer database on historical geology.

Skill Builder

1. 545 million years ago; 245 million years ago
2. 30 million years
3. during the Ordovician Period—between 505 million and 438 million years ago
4. during the Pennsylvanian Period—between 320 million and 286 million years ago

Assessment

Oral Assess students' abilities to make and use tables by asking them the following question: "During which era did dinosaurs exist on Earth?" Use the Performance Task Assessment List for Data Table in **PASC,** p. 37. P

Science & Literature

Dreamtime Down Under

In the traditional oral stories of the Aborigines of Australia, they have their own explanation of how our world was formed. They say the world as we know it began when Dreamtime began, long ago, before anyone can remember. Then everything was one. At first Earth was cold and dark, and the spirit Ancestors slept underground.

When the Ancestors awoke, they moved to Earth's surface and created the sun for warmth and light. Some Ancestors took the shapes of people; others became animals, plants, rain, clouds, or stars. As the Ancestors moved over Earth, they sang. Their movements and their singing shaped the land, creating hills, rivers, and other land features.

Leaving a Path

As they walked, the Ancestors left Dreaming Tracks that the Aborigines treasure and protect today. When the Ancestors tired, they returned underground. The bodies of some Ancestors remain on Earth's surface as rock outcroppings, trees, islands, and other features.

Ancient Aborigines drew maps in the sand to show where the Ancestors came out, walked, and returned underground. These sand drawings with their traditional dot patterns form the basis of Aboriginal art, like the bark painting shown above.

Dreaming the Big Bang

Some compare the Dreamtime forces that shaped Earth to the big bang theory: huge fields of energy interacting and forming planets. Much later, more energy—more Dreaming—caused the movement of Earth's crust and eventually created today's continents, including Australia.

Aborigines believe that the Ancestors still live in the land. Dreamtime continues with no foreseeable end. Today, Aborigines are struggling to maintain their ancient traditions while living in modern Australia.

Science Journal

In your Science Journal, write a poem that expresses your own view of our relationship to nature and to the land.

Teaching Strategies

- Discuss how modern dating techniques might be used to test the Aborigines' belief that certain land features and tracks were left by the Ancestors. (You might also discuss whether the Aborigines would be convinced by these modern techniques.)
- Explore ways that the changing shapes of the continents might have affected the Aborigines' flesh-and-blood ancestors.
- Ask students to relate the plight of today's Aborigines to that of Native Americans.

Sources

- Holder, Robyn. *Aborigines of Australia.* Vero Beach, FL: Rourke, 1987.
- Lawlor, Robert. *Voices of the First Day: Awakening in the Aboriginal Dreamtime.* Rochester, VT: Inner Traditions, 1991.
- Nile, Richard. *Australian Aborigines.* Austin, TX: Steck-Vaughn, 1993.

Background

In the late eighteenth century, the Aborigines' peaceful relationship with their land was threatened by the arrival of British ships. These ships were ferrying prisoners from overcrowded British prisons to colonies to be established in Australia. At first, the Aborigines thought the pale invaders were ghosts—spirits of the Ancestors marking the beginning of a new Dreamtime. But British settlers and prisoners soon took over large areas of the Aborigines' land. The Aborigines protested the loss of their land, but thousands fell victim to British guns. Many more were killed by the smallpox and tuberculosis that had been imported by the British. Aborigines, once 100 percent of Australia's population, now constitute only 1.5 percent of it. Today, Aborigines are struggling to maintain their ancient traditions and ways, while living in a modern Australian society. Many of their sacred areas have been destroyed by the spread of cities and towns. Only recently have they been able to gain some respect for their ancient culture and for their position as the first inhabitants of Australia.

Science Journal

Encourage creativity in this poem.

Section 13•4

Prepare

Section Background

- The Triassic Period, the earliest period in the Mesozoic Era, is named for three related units of rock first studied in Germany. The Jurassic Period is named after the Jura Mountains between France and Switzerland, where this age rock was first studied. The most recent period of the Mesozoic Era, the Cretaceous Period, is named for the Latin word for chalk, *creta*. The white chalk cliffs of Dover, England, are of this age.
- Humans and their direct ancestors make up a group of animals called hominids. The earliest definite hominids were of the genus *Australopithecus*. Australopithecines had many distinctly human characteristics. They were bipedal and had rounded jaws. Australopithecines lived in the open grasslands of what is now eastern and southern Africa.
- Australopithecines were smaller than modern humans. Standing less than 1.5 m tall, they weighed about 20 kg. Their brains were half the size of present-day humans' brains. Fossil evidence indicates these early ancestors of ours used tools made of bone.

Preplanning

- To prepare for Activity 13-2, obtain adding machine tape, metersticks, and scissors.
- Obtain a globe of Earth for the MiniLAB.

13•4 Middle and Recent Earth History

Science Words

Mesozoic Era
Cenozoic Era

Objectives

- Compare and contrast dominant life-forms in the Mesozoic and Cenozoic Eras.
- Explain how changes caused by plate tectonics affected the evolution of life during the Mesozoic Era.
- Identify when humans first appeared on Earth.

The Mesozoic Era

Some of the most fascinating life-forms ever to live on Earth evolved during the Mesozoic Era. One group of organisms you're familiar with—the dinosaurs—appeared during this geologic era.

The Breakup of Pangaea

The **Mesozoic** (mez uh ZOH ihk) **Era,** or era of middle life, began about 245 million years ago. At the beginning of the Mesozoic Era, all continents were joined as a single landmass. Recall from Chapter 11 that this landmass was called Pangaea, as shown in **Figure 13-14.** Pangaea separated into two large landmasses during the Triassic Period. The northern mass was *Laurasia*, and *Gondwana* was in the south. As the Mesozoic Era continued, *Laurasia* and *Gondwana* broke up and formed the present-day continents.

Species that survived the mass extinctions of the Paleozoic Era adapted to new environments. Recall that the hard scales of a reptile's skin help to retain body fluids. This trait, along with the hard shell of their eggs, enabled them to readily adapt to the drier climate of the Mesozoic Era. They became the dominant animal life-form in the Jurassic Period. Some of the reptiles evolved into archosaurs, the common ancestor of crocodiles, dinosaurs, and birds.

Figure 13-14
The supercontinent Pangaea formed at the end of the Paleozoic Era. It began to break up in the Jurassic Period.

Program Resources

Reproducible Masters

Study Guide, p. 56 L1
Reinforcement, p. 56 L1
Enrichment, p. 56 L3
Activity Worksheets, pp. 80-81, 83 L1
Concept Mapping, pp. 31-32
Critical Thinking/Problem Solving, p. 19

Transparencies

Section Focus Transparency 52 L1
Science Integration Transparency 13

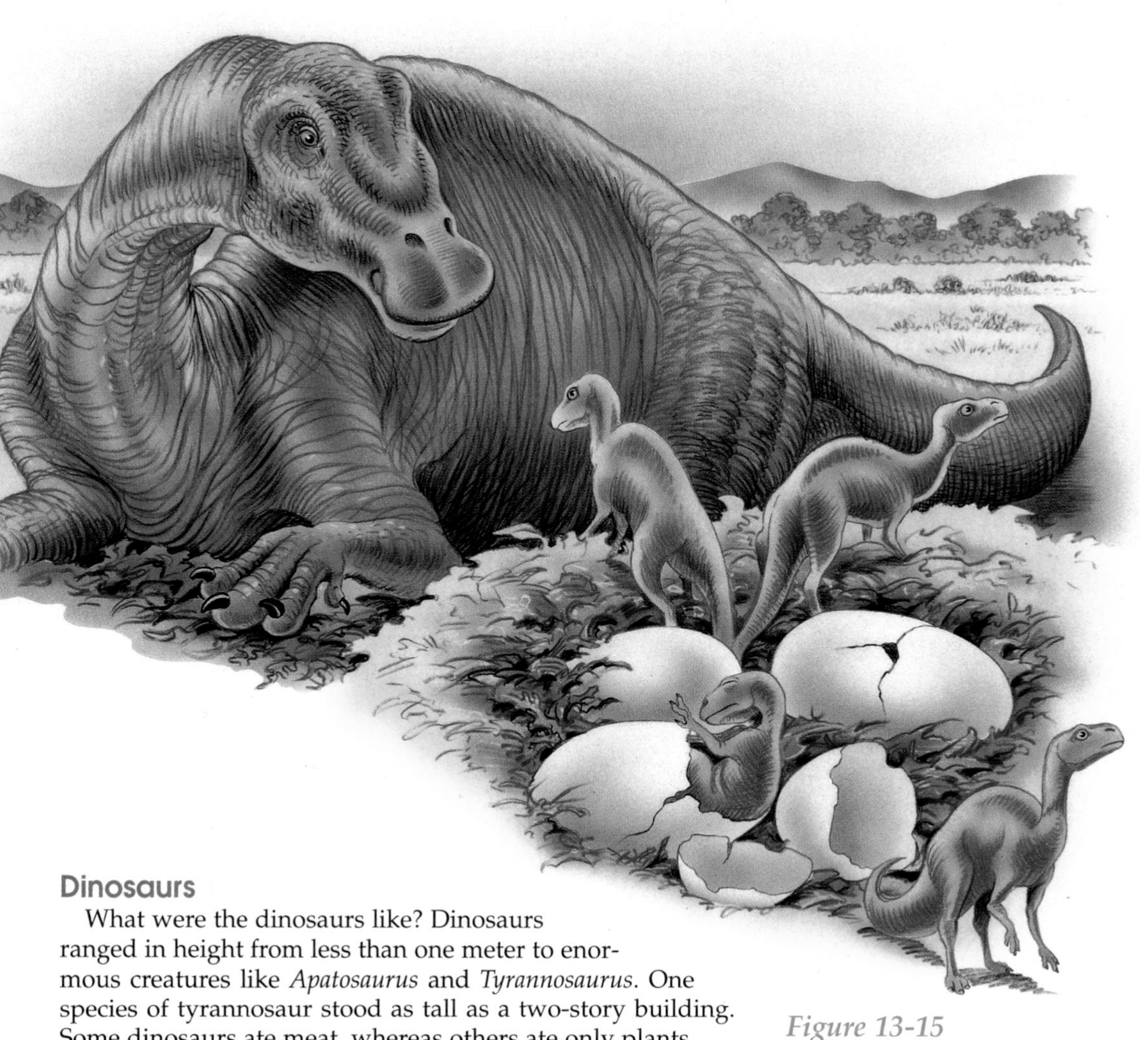

Dinosaurs

What were the dinosaurs like? Dinosaurs ranged in height from less than one meter to enormous creatures like *Apatosaurus* and *Tyrannosaurus*. One species of tyrannosaur stood as tall as a two-story building. Some dinosaurs ate meat, whereas others ate only plants.

The first small dinosaurs appeared during the Triassic Period. Larger species appeared during the Jurassic and Cretaceous Periods. Throughout the Mesozoic Era, new species of dinosaurs evolved as other species became extinct.

Recent studies indicate that dinosaurs may not have been cold-blooded, as are present-day reptiles. Tracks left in the mud by reptiles are usually close together. This indicates that reptiles generally move very slowly. Some dinosaur tracks that have been found indicate that they were much faster than most of the cold-blooded reptiles. This faster speed would be expected of warm-blooded animals, which need speed to be successful in hunting. *Gallimimus* was four meters long and could reach speeds of 80 km/h, as fast as a modern race horse.

Figure 13-15

Fossil evidence suggests that some dinosaurs, such as *Maiasaura,* may have nurtured their young. Fossil nests contain newly hatched and juvenile young. *What type of evidence might support this idea?*

1 Motivate

Bellringer

Before presenting the lesson, display **Section Focus Transparency 52** on the overhead projector. Assign the accompanying **Focus Activity** worksheet. L1 LEP

Tying to Previous Knowledge

Help students recall one hypothesis of the extinction of dinosaurs presented in Chapter 12.

2 Teach

FLEX Your Brain

Use the Flex Your Brain activity to have students explore *APATOSAURUS.* Students may be familiar with the term *Brontosaurus.* This term is no longer used to refer to these large dinosaurs. Apatosaurs were among the largest dinosaurs, with masses up to 36 metric tons. They had long necks and tails supported by massive bodies.

Activity Worksheets, p. 5

Visual Learning

Figure 13-15 What type of evidence might support this idea? *Fossils of both newly hatched and juvenile young in the nests.* LEP LS

Use **Science Integration Transparency 13** as you teach this lesson.

Use **Critical Thinking/Problem Solving,** p. 19, as you teach this lesson.

Inclusion Strategies

Learning Disabled and Behaviorally Disordered Have pairs of students identify characteristics of meat- and plant-eating dinosaurs. Supply students with drawings or models of six different dinosaurs. Have them determine whether the dinosaurs were meat- or plant-eaters. Have students describe what characteristics were useful for their analysis. COOP LEARN

Figure 13-16

Fossils of *Archaeopteryx* that are about 150 million years old show both birdlike features and dinosaurlike features. *What bird-like and dinosaur-like features can you recognize?*

A A detailed imprint of a fossil feather that is believed to be from *Archaeopteryx.*

B Considered the world's most priceless fossil, *Archaeopteryx* was found in a limestone quarry in Germany in 1861.

C A reconstruction of what *Archaeopteryx* may have looked like.

Good Mother Dinosaurs

The fossil record indicates that some dinosaurs nurtured their young and traveled in herds with adults surrounding their young. One such dinosaur is *Maiasaura,* shown in **Figure 13-15** on page 375. This dinosaur built nests in which it laid its eggs and raised its offspring. Nests have been found in clusters, indicating that more than one family of dinosaurs built in the same area. Some fossils of hatchlings have been found very close to the adult animal. This has led some scientists to hypothesize that some dinosaurs nurtured their young. In fact, *Maiasaura* hatchlings may have stayed in the nest while they grew in length from about 35 cm to more than one m.

Other evidence that leads scientists to think that dinosaurs may have been warm-blooded has to do with their bone structure. Cross sections of the bones of cold-blooded animals exhibit rings similar to growth rings in trees. The bones of some dinosaurs don't show this ring structure. Instead, they are similar to bones found in birds and mammals. These observations indicate that dinosaurs may have been warm-blooded, fast-moving, nurturing animals somewhat like present-day mammals and birds. They might have been quite different from present-day reptiles.

Visual Learning

Figure 13-16 What bird-like and dinosaur-like features can you recognize? *Bird-like: feathered wings; dinosaur-like: teeth and claws.* LEP LS

Revealing Preconceptions

Ask students if humans were alive when dinosaurs lived on Earth. Some students will think they were because of seeing cartoons and movies on television. Explain that human ancestors appeared about 5 million years ago, long after dinosaurs became extinct about 66 million years ago.

Enrichment

LS **Linguistic** Have pairs of students read an article of their choice from *Natural History,* June 1995. Have students discuss the key concepts of each article and then work together to write a summary of the main ideas of their particular article. L1 COOP LEARN

GLENCOE TECHNOLOGY

 **Videodisc**

The Infinite Voyage: The Great Dinosaur Hunt

Introduction

Chapter 1

Where the Great Hunt Began

Chapter 2

The Evolution of Extinction

Integrating the Sciences

Life Science It's important to note that plants co-evolve with the other organisms in their environment. Plants aren't "passive bystanders" in the process of natural selection. Plants select thorns, tough bark, and poisons to thwart predators. For more information, direct students to *The Dinosaur Heresies,* by Robert T. Bakker, William Morrow and Company, Inc., New York, 1986.

Community Connection

Kids and Dinosaurs Take your class to a local elementary school with children in the 3rd and 4th grades. Have students from your class present some of the information they have learned about dinosaurs to the younger children. Encourage discussion groups where the younger children can express their beliefs about dinosaurs.

Birds

The first birds appeared during the Jurassic Period of the Mesozoic Era, as seen in **Figure 13-16.** The animal *Archaeopteryx* had wings and feathers like a bird but teeth and claws like a meat-eating dinosaur. *Archaeopteryx* may not have been a direct ancestor of today's birds. But modern birds and *Archaeopteryx* probably share a common ancestor. Scientists think that birds evolved from dinosaurs. Some scientists even think that birds are dinosaurs, evolved from the advanced theropod called Troodon, shown in **Figure 13-17.** Theropods form a group of meat-eating dinosaurs that walked mainly on their hind legs.

Mammals

Mammals first appeared in the Triassic Period. Mammals are warm-blooded vertebrates that have hair or fur covering their bodies. The females produce milk to feed their young. These traits have enabled mammals to survive in many changing environments.

Figure 13-17

A highly evolved dinosaur called *Troodon* had a birdlike stance, much like a modern ostrich.

Inquiry Questions

- **What evidence supports the hypothesis that birds evolved from dinosaurs?** *Archaeopteryx had wings and feathers like a bird, but teeth and claws like a meat-eating dinosaur. Present-day birds and extinct dinosaurs share other characteristics as well.*
- **Why were mammals able to survive in many different environments?** *Females produce milk to feed the young. They were warm-blooded and had hair or fur to insulate them from extreme cold and warm temperatures.*
- **Why did angiosperms survive while other types of plants didn't?** *The hard coating on their seeds protected the seeds from harsh environments. This enabled them to adapt to varied environments.*

Teacher F.Y.I.

- Endotherms have a constant body temperature and are often said to be "warm-blooded."
- By some estimates more than three-fourths of all species on Earth died off at the end of the Mesozoic Era.

Videodisc

STV: Restless Earth

Pangaea, 225 million years ago

52176

Pangaea, 125 million years ago

52177

Science Journal

Dinosaurs Free-style Give students 15 minutes to "free write" anything they can concerning dinosaurs. After the 15 minutes, form teams of three students each. Encourage students in each group to share their results. By sharing their thoughts and questions, they will be able to write a formal report on what their group knows or still wants to know about dinosaurs. L1

LS COOP LEARN

MiniLAB

Purpose

LS Logical-Mathematical Students will use the rate of seafloor spreading to calculate the age of the Atlantic Ocean. L1 COOP LEARN

Materials

globe or world map, metric ruler, string (for measuring on the curved globe)

Teaching Strategies

This spreading rate is an average for a number of points along the Mid-Atlantic Ridge.

Analysis

1. Values used to obtain the average value for the age of the Atlantic Ocean will vary.
2. Student answers will vary, depending on the points on each continent they choose for their measurements. Separations of 6000 to 7000 kilometers would take from 160 to 200 million years to achieve. As an example, at 3.5 cm/y rate of spread, two points 7000 km apart would have started separating about 200 million years ago (700 000 000 cm ÷ 3.5 cm/y = 200 000 000 y).

Assessment

Content To further assess students' understanding of the formation of the Atlantic Ocean, have them hypothesize how environments might change near the East African Rift Valley, where separation may eventually form a new sea. Use the Performance Task Assessment List for Formulating a Hypothesis in **PASC**, p. 21. P

MiniLAB

Sea-floor Spreading

Geologists have measured the rate of sea-floor spreading at the Mid-Atlantic Ridge at approximately 3.5 to 4.0 cm per year. This rate can be used to determine the age of the Atlantic Ocean.

Procedure

1. On a globe or world map, measure the distance in kilometers between a point near the east coast of South America and a corresponding point on the west coast of Africa.
2. Assuming that the rate of motion listed above has been relatively constant, calculate how many years it took to create the present Atlantic Ocean if the continents were once joined.
3. Measure in SI several times and take the average of your results.
4. Check your predictions with the information provided in **Figure 13-2.**

Analysis

1. Did the values used to obtain your average value vary much?
2. How close did your average value come to the accepted estimate for the beginning of the breakup of Pangaea?

Figure 13-18

Angiosperms and pollinating insects co-evolved. The sweet nectar produced by many flowers attracts insects in search of food. The pollen of the flower sticks to the insect, which carries it to another flower. Some angiosperms wouldn't be able to reproduce without a particular species of insect.

Gymnosperms

During the Cretaceous Period, seas expanded inland and species of plants, animals, and other organisms continued to adapt to new environments. Gymnosperms (JIHM nuh spurmz), which first appeared in the Paleozoic Era, continued to adapt to their changing environment. Gymnosperms are called naked-seed plants because they have no fruit covering their seeds. Pines, sequoias, and firs are gymnosperms.

Angiosperms

A new type of plant, called angiosperms (ANjee uh spurmz), evolved from existing plants. Angiosperms, or flowering plants, produce seeds with hard, outer coverings. Common angiosperms were magnolias and willows.

Many angiosperms survived while other organisms did not because their seeds had hard coatings that protected them and allowed them to develop in varied environments. Angiosperms are so adaptive that they remain the dominant land plant today, as shown in **Figure 13-18.** Present-day angiosperms that evolved during the Mesozoic Era include maple and oak trees.

The end of the Mesozoic Era was a time when landmasses were breaking up and seas were draining from the land. There was also increased volcanic activity. Many life-forms, including the dinosaurs, became extinct. These extinctions were caused by changing environments. What caused the environments to change is still being actively investigated by scientists.

Theme Connection

Stability and Change Stability and change is reaffirmed as a theme in this chapter by the manner in which mammals evolved so differently, yet so alike in many ways, on widely separated landmasses. Have students compare and contrast marsupial wolves, rabbits, squirrels, and bears that evolved in Australia to their placental counterparts which evolved in similar environments in Europe and America. Students should note similarities (stability) in natural selection despite differences between (changes) placental and marsupial evolution caused by the isolation of the life-forms. L1

The Cenozoic Era

The **Cenozoic** (sen uh ZOH ihk) **Era**, or era of recent life, began about 66 million years ago when dinosaurs and many other life-forms became extinct. Many of the mountain ranges throughout North and South America began to form at this time.

During the Cenozoic Era, the climate became cooler and ice ages occurred. The Cenozoic Era is subdivided into two periods. The present-day period is the Quaternary. It began after the last ice age. Many changes in Earth, its climate, and its life-forms, shown in **Figure 13-19,** occurred in the Cenozoic Era.

Pangaea broke up during the Mesozoic Era, and continents continued to move toward their present positions.

Times of Mountain Building

The Alps formed as the African Plate collided with the Eurasian Plate. The Himalaya Mountains started to form when the Indian Plate collided with the Eurasian Plate.

As the number of flowering plants increased, their pollen and fruit provided food for the many insects and small, plant-eating mammals. The plant-eating mammals provided food for meat-eating mammals.

Figure 13-19

Many now-extinct animals lived in North America before and during the ice ages in the Pleistocene Epoch.

Content Background

- Discuss the path of possible human evolution. Relate that there is much controversy among anthropologists as to how many species of *Australopithecus* existed, but many agree that there were at least four. It's not known which gave rise to our genus, *Homo.*
- Have students note that *Homo habilis* may have evolved from *Australopithecus afarensis. Homo habilis* gave rise to *Home erectus* before becoming extinct about 1.5 million years ago. *Homo erectus* was the direct ancestor of our species, *Homo sapiens.*
- The Pleistocene Epoch is often referred to as the glacial epoch because of the ice ages that occurred during this time in Earth's history.

3 Assess

Check for Understanding

FLEX Your Brain

Use the Flex Your Brain activity to have students explore CENOZOIC LIFE.

Activity Worksheets, p. 5

Reteach

Obtain a book on early humans that shows paintings or drawings of humans on a hunting trip for the wooly mammoth and other Pleistocene mammals. Explain how over-hunting can lead to extinction. Relate this to the near extinction of the American buffalo by over-hunting in the early West.

Extension

For students who have mastered this section, use the **Reinforcement** and **Enrichment** masters.

Inclusion Strategies

Visually Impaired In order to include all students in discussions of life-forms that exist today and have existed throughout the Mesozoic and Cenozoic Periods, begin the discussion with detailed descriptions of certain dinosaurs and mammals like the wooly mammoth.

Activity 13-2

PREPARATION

Purpose

LS Logical-Mathematical Design and carry out an experiment to show how geologic time on Earth can be subdivided. L1 COOP LEARN

Process Skills

communicating, making and using tables, forming operational definitions, making models, making and using graphs, measuring in SI, using numbers, hypothesizing, sequencing, collecting and organizing data

Time

One class period to research and begin time lines. One-half class period to summarize results.

Materials

Have several rolls of adding machine tape available. Have a table available that provides the age of certain important events that have occurred in Earth's past.

Alternate Materials Rolls of brown paper towels could be used in place of the adding machine tape, especially if students want to draw sample habitats on the roll.

Safety Precautions

Caution students to handle scissors with care.

Possible Hypotheses

Great geological events, changes in the environment, and extinctions or drastic changes in life-forms can be used to subdivide geologic time.

Activity Worksheets, pp. 5, 80-81

Activity 13-2

Design Your Own Experiment

Geologic Time Line

In Chapter 12, you learned how geologists date rocks, fossils, and geologic events. Using these dates, geologists have determined that Earth is 4.6 billion years old. Geologists have also used these dates to subdivide Earth's history into different units of time. Just as you can subdivide your past into shorter periods of time by dating major events, such as your first day of school, you can subdivide Earth's history by dating major events in its past.

PREPARATION

Problem

What kind of model can be used to show the subdivisions of Earth's past?

Form a Hypothesis

Based on information provided in **Figure 13-2** and the information presented in Sections 13-3 and 13-4, state a hypothesis about what type of model you can develop to show the subdivisions of Earth's history.

Objectives

- Observe how the age of rocks, fossils, and geologic events are used to subdivide geologic time on the geologic time scale.
- Design an experiment in which a model is constructed that represents the subdivisions of geologic time.

Possible Materials

- adding machine tape
- meterstick or metric ruler
- set of colored pencils
- pencil
- scissors

Safety Precautions

Take care not to cut yourself while using the scissors.

Data and Observations

EARTH HISTORY EVENTS

Event	Years B.P.
1. oldest known rocks	3 900 million
2. oldest microfossils	3 600 million
3. early sponges	550 million
4. beginning of the Cambrian Period (Paleozoic Era)–animals evolve hard parts	545 million
5. first vertebrates (fish)	510 million
6. beginning of the Ordovician	505 million
7. beginning of Silurian Period	438 million
8. first land plants	435 million
9. beginning of Devonian Period	408 million
10. first amphibians	367 million
11. beginning of Mississippian Period	360 million
12. Appalachian Mountains rise	330 million
13. beginning of Pennsylvanian Period	320 million
14. first reptiles	315 million
15. beginning of Permian Period	286 million
16. extinction of trilobites–largest mass extinction in Earth's history	246 million
17. beginning of Triassic Period (Mesozoic Era)	245 million
18. first dinosaurs and mammals	225 million
19. beginning of Jurassic Period	208 million
20. first birds	150 million
21. beginning of Cretaceous Period	144 million
22. Rocky Mountains begin to rise	80 million
23. extinction of the dinosaurs	66 million
24. beginning of Paleocene Epoch (Cenozoic Era)	55 million

PLAN THE EXPERIMENT

1. As a group, agree upon and write out the hypothesis statement.
2. As a group, list the steps that you need to take to test your hypothesis. Be very specific, describing exactly what you will need to do at each step.
3. Make a list of the materials that you will need to complete your experiment.
4. Determine how you will construct your model of geologic time using the materials listed on the opposite page.
5. Determine a scale to use for your model of the subdivisions of geologic time.

Check the Plan

1. Read over your entire experiment to make sure that all steps are in a logical order.
2. Draw a small version of the model you plan to construct.
3. Will you summarize data in a graph, table, or some other form of organization?
4. *Make sure your teacher approves your plan and that you have included any changes suggested in the plan.*

DO THE EXPERIMENT

1. Carry out the experiment as planned.
2. Construct your model of the subdivisions of geologic time.
3. While conducting the experiment and constructing your model, write down any observations that you or other members of your group make in your Science Journal.
4. When collecting the data, be sure to include dates that are important to you as well as dates of geologic events.
5. For additional information to use on your model, use references such as geology books, history books, and encyclopedias.

Analyze and Apply

1. Which events were the most difficult to plot?
2. **Compare** events from your personal past or the existence of humans on Earth with the duration of geologic time.
3. Use a geologic time scale to determine the dates when each major division of geologic time started and ended. **Sequence** these ages on your model of geologic time.
4. **Estimate** what percent of geologic time occurred during Precambrian time?
5. During which era were you able to find the most in-depth information about geologic events for your model?

Go Further

Form a hypothesis as to why more is known about geologic events during the era for which you were able to find the most information.

25. first horses	50 million
26. first elephants	5 million
27. early human ancestors	1.5 million
28. beginning of the most recent ice age	1 million
29. first modern humans	500 000
30. continental ice retreats from North America	10 000
31. Eratosthenes calculates Earth's circumference	2 100
32. Pompeii destroyed	1 900
33. Columbus lands in America	500
34. U.S. Civil War	135
35. astronauts land on the moon	25
36. today	0

Assessment

Content Have students stretch their time scales out flat. Ask the individuals of each group how key events are displayed. Use the Performance Task Assessment List for Oral Presentation in **PASC**, p. 71. P

Go Further

Acceptable answers would include reference to the availability of more information on younger rock.

PLAN THE EXPERIMENT

Possible Procedures

1. Students will determine a way to show all of geologic time on one sheet of paper.
2. Determine scale of time to distance on the roll of paper.
3. Mark on the paper the time of specific geologic events or extinctions.

Teaching Strategies

Troubleshooting Students may have difficulty in developing a scale that works. It must be long enough to enable them to have some distance between events.

DO THE EXPERIMENT

Expected Outcome

Students should complete a long strip of paper on which key geologic events or life-form extinctions are illustrated. Students come to realize how little geologic time has passed since humans have appeared.

Analyze and Apply

1. Events in the last few million years were difficult to plot because only several millimeters of tape could be used.
2. Events from the students' past would be plotted at the point on the tape marked "today." The existence of humans accounts for about 0.03% of geologic time.
3. Answers represent the dates from Figure 13-2, p. 358.
4. Approximately 88% of geologic time is represented by Precambrian time.
5. The Cenozoic Era provides the most information about geologic events.

4 Close

• MINI • QUIZ •

1. **Which dinosaur has proven to have been a very good mother to her offspring?** *Maiasaura*
2. **During which era were dinosaurs the dominant life-form?** *Mesozoic Era*
3. **The _______ Era began about 66 million years ago.** *Cenozoic*

Section Wrap-up

Review

1. Cenozoic Era, Quaternary Period, Pleistocene Epoch
2. More abundant. When the dinosaurs became extinct, it reduced competition for food. The pollen and fruit of angiosperms provided abundent food.
3. The hard coating on the seeds protected them.
4. **Think Critically** This recent time in Earth's history has a more complete fossil record and more markers to subdivide geologic time.

USING MATH

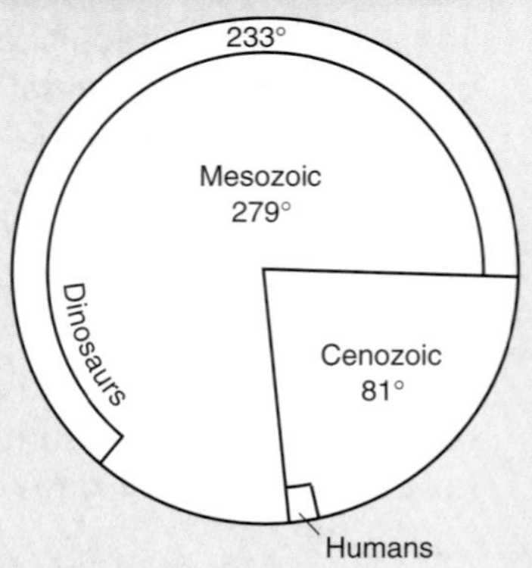

Dinosaurs were dominant for 46 million years, whereas humans have only been dominant for 10 000 years. Dinosaurs existed for 159 million years.

Figure 13-20

Kangaroos are marsupials that live in Australia and carry their young (joey) in a pouch.

Further Evolution of Mammals

Mammals evolved into larger life-forms. Recall how horses have evolved from small, multi-toed animals into the much larger, hoofed animals of today. Not all mammals remained on land. Ancestors of the present-day whales and dolphins evolved to make their lives in the sea.

As Australia and South America separated from Antarctica in the continuing break-up of Pangaea, many life-forms became isolated. They evolved separately from life-forms in other parts of the world. Evidence of this can be seen today with the dominance of marsupials in Australia. Marsupials are mammals that carry their young in a pouch, as seen in **Figure 13-20.**

Our species, *Homo sapiens*, probably appeared about 500 000 years ago, but became a dominant animal only about 10 000 years ago. As the climate remained cool and dry, many larger mammals became extinct. Some scientists think the appearance of humans may have led to the extinction of other mammals. As their numbers grew, humans competed for food that other animals relied upon. Also, fossil records indicate that early humans were hunters.

Section Wrap-up

Review

1. In which era, period, and epoch did *Homo sapiens* first appear?
2. Did mammals become more or less abundant after the extinction of the dinosaurs? Explain why.
3. How did the development of hard seeds enable angiosperms to survive in a wide variety of climates?
4. **Think Critically:** Why are the periods of only the Cenozoic Era divided into epochs?

Skill Builder

Sequencing

Arrange these organisms in sequence according to when they first appeared on Earth: *mammals, reptiles, dinosaurs, fish, angiosperms, birds, insects, amphibians, first land plants,* and *bacteria.* If you need help, refer to Sequencing in the **Skill Handbook.**

USING MATH

Make a graph comparing the periods of time that make up the Mesozoic and Cenozoic Eras. Express how long dinosaurs were dominant compared with the time humans have been dominant.

Skill Builder

Students should use Figure 13-2 on page 358 to answer this question. The sequence is bacteria, fish, land plants, amphibians, reptiles, insects, mammals, dinosaurs, birds, angiosperms.

Assessment

Performance Assess students' abilities at sequencing by having them list the evolutionary stages of horses in a sequence from earliest to the present. Use the Performance Task Assessment List for Events Chain in **PASC,** p. 91. P

Chapter 13 Review

Summary

13-1: Evolution and Geologic Time

1. Geologic time is divided into eras, periods, and epochs.
2. Divisions within the geologic time scale are based on major evolutionary changes in organisms and on geologic events such as mountain building and plate movements.
3. Plate movements cause changes in Earth's climate that affect organic evolution.

13-2: Science and Society: Present-Day Rapid Extinctions

1. Humans cause extinctions primarily by eliminating natural habitats of organisms.
2. As land is developed by humans, the diversity of life on Earth is reduced.
3. Careful planning, concern for all organisms, and strict laws can help prevent extinctions.

13-3: Early Earth History

1. Cyanobacteria were an early form of life that evolved during Precambrian Time. Trilobites, brachiopods, fish, and corals were abundant during the Paleozoic Era.
2. By the process of natural selection, bacteria evolved into higher life-forms, which evolved into many marine invertebrates during the early Paleozoic Era. Plants and animals began to move onto land once a protective ozone layer had been established.
3. During the Paleozoic Era, glaciers advanced, and seas withdrew from the continents. Many marine invertebrates became extinct.

13-4: Middle and Recent Earth History

1. Reptiles and gymnosperms were dominant land life-forms in the Mesozoic Era. Mammals and angiosperms began to dominate the land in the Cenozoic Era.
2. Plate tectonic changes in the Mesozoic Era caused climates to dry and seas to expand. These changes affected life on land and in the sea.
3. *Homo sapiens* evolved during the Pleistocene Epoch.

Key Science Words

a. amphibian
b. Cenozoic Era
c. cyanobacteria
d. endangered
e. epoch
f. era
g. geologic time scale
h. habitat
i. Mesozoic Era
j. natural selection
k. organic evolution
l. Paleozoic Era
m. period
n. Precambrian time
o. reptile
p. species

Reviewing Vocabulary

Match each phrase with the correct term from the list of Key Science Words.

1. change in the hereditary features of a species over a long period of time
2. record of events in Earth history
3. longest major division of geologic time
4. geologic time with poorest fossil record
5. process by which the best-suited individuals survive in their environment
6. evolved from the same ancestors as amphibians
7. group of individuals that normally breed only among themselves
8. the geologic era in which we live
9. a species in which only a relatively small number of members exists
10. a place where organisms live and grow

Chapter 13

Review

Summary

Have students read the summary statements to review the major concepts of the chapter.

Reviewing Vocabulary

1. k
2. g
3. f
4. n
5. j
6. o
7. p
8. b
9. d
10. h

Assessment

Portfolio Encourage students to place in their portfolios one or two items of what they consider to be their best work. Examples include:

- Science Journal, p. 362
- Activity 13-1 analysis and conclusions, p. 368
- MiniLAB analysis, p. 369 P

Performance Additional performance assessments may be found in **Performance Assessment** and **Science Integration Activities.** Performance Task Assessment Lists and rubrics for evaluating these activities can be found in Glencoe's **Performance Assessment in the Science Classroom.**

GLENCOE TECHNOLOGY

MindJogger Videoquiz

Chapter 13 Have students work in groups as they play the Videoquiz game to review key chapter concepts.

Checking Concepts

1. d
2. d
3. a
4. d
5. b
6. b
7. a
8. c
9. b
10. b

Understanding Concepts

11. Natural selection is a theory of how some traits evolve in species and how new species develop. Natural selection is a process that results in evolution. When organisms are selected for naturally, they survive, reproduce, and pass on inheritable traits to their offspring. The species evolves as certain traits become more prevalent within the population.

12. Warm, shallow seas existed during most of the early Paleozoic Era. Most of the life-forms lived in these seas. As plants and animals evolved, they moved landward during the middle of the era. During this time, vertebrates dominated the land. Changes in climate probably caused many of the extinctions that happened at the close of the era.

13. changes in climate related to plate movements, meteorite impacts, volcanism, glacial activity, competition with new species, human activities

14. During the Paleozoic Era, most of the organisms were invertebrates. Life-forms became more complex through time. Mammals became dominant during the early Cenozoic.

15. Both organisms lay eggs that hatch outside of the body. Amphibian eggs must be kept moist in water, whereas reptile eggs have a membrane that protects them from drying out.

Chapter 13 Review

Checking Concepts

Choose the word or phrase that completes the sentence.

1. The era in which you live began about _______ million years ago.
   a. 650 c. 1.6
   b. 245 d. 66
2. The process by which better suited organisms survive and reproduce is _______.
   a. endangerment c. gymnosperm
   b. extinction d. natural selection
3. The next smaller division of geologic time after the era is a(n) _______.
   a. period c. epoch
   b. stage d. eon
4. The beginning of the _______ Period was marked by the most recent ice age.
   a. Pennsylvanian c. Tertiary
   b. Triassic d. Quaternary
5. One of the earliest forms of life on Earth was the _______.
   a. gymnosperm c. angiosperm
   b. cyanobacterium d. dinosaur
6. Amphibians evolved from the same ancestors as _______.
   a. reptiles c. angiosperms
   b. lung fish d. gymnosperms
7. Dinosaurs lived during the _______ Era.
   a. Mesozoic c. Miocene
   b. Paleozoic d. Cenozoic
8. _______ have seeds without protective coverings.
   a. Angiosperms c. Gymnosperms
   b. Flowering plants d. Magnolias
9. _______ evolved to become the dominant land plant during the Cenozoic Era.
   a. Gymnosperms c. Ginkgos
   b. Angiosperms d. Algae
10. A key factor in preserving many species is _______.
    a. poaching c. construction
    b. law enforcement d. changing habitats

Understanding Concepts

Answer the following questions in your Science Journal using complete sentences.

11. How is natural selection related to evolution?
12. Briefly describe the major geologic and biological changes that took place during the Paleozoic Era.
13. Describe several causes for extinctions throughout geologic time.
14. Contrast the animal life of the Paleozoic Era with that of the early Cenozoic Era.
15. Compare and contrast reptile eggs and amphibian eggs.

Thinking Critically

16. Why couldn't plants move onto land prior to the establishment of an ozone layer?
17. Why are trilobites classified as index fossils?
18. What is the most significant difference between Precambrian and Paleozoic life-forms?
19. How might the extinction of an edible species of plant from a tropical rain forest affect animals that live in the forest?
20. In the early 1800s, a naturalist proposed that the giraffe species has a long neck as a result of years of stretching their necks to reach leaves in tall trees. Explain why this isn't true.

Thinking Critically

16. Too much harmful ultraviolet radiation from the sun reached Earth's surface prior to the establishment of the ozone layer. UV light causes harmful mutations in the cells of plants.

17. Trilobites were widespread and existed for only a limited segment of geologic time before becoming extinct. Thus, they can be used to date the rocks in which they are contained accurately.

18. Organisms of the Precambrian lacked the hard parts that evolved at the beginning of the Paleozoic.

19. Plants are at the base of most food chains. They make their own food via photosynthesis and are themselves food for primary consumers. The primary consumers, in turn, are food for secondary consumers. If the edible plant becomes extinct, extinctions of primary and secondary consumers may occur.

Developing Skills

If you need help, refer to the **Skill Handbook.**

21. **Observing and Inferring:** Use the outlines of the present-day continents to make a sketch of the Mesozoic supercontinent Pangaea.
22. **Hypothesizing:** Why did trilobites become extinct at the end of the Paleozoic Era?
23. **Interpreting Data:** Fernando found what he thought was a piece of coral in a chunk of coal. Was he right? Explain.
24. **Interpreting Scientific Illustrations:** The circle graph below represents geologic time. Determine which era of geologic time is represented by each portion of the graph.

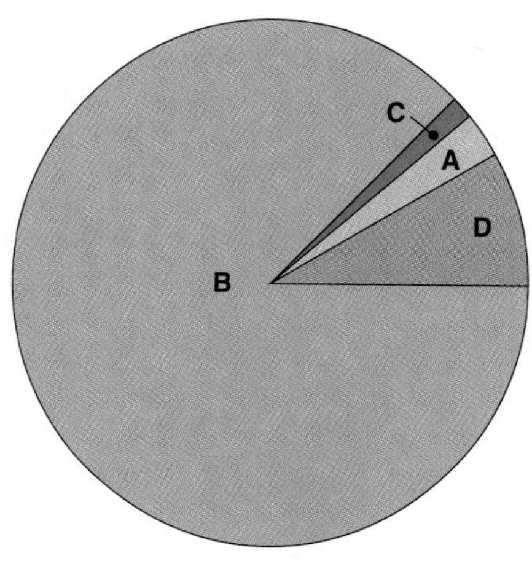

25. **Interpreting Scientific Illustrations:** The Cenozoic Era has lasted 66 million years. What percentage of Earth's 4.6 billion year history is that? How many degrees on the pie graph represent the Cenozoic Era?

Performance Assessment

1. **Formulate a Hypothesis:** Research the most recent theories on mass extinctions that occurred at the end of both the Paleozoic and Mesozoic Eras. Compare and contrast the most accepted theories. Form your own hypothesis as to why the extinctions occurred. Support your position with facts and models.
2. **Make a Model:** In Activity 13-1, you learned how a particular trait might evolve within a species. Modify the experimental model by using color instead of height as a trait. Design your activity with the understanding that varimals live in a dark-colored forest environment.
3. **Conduct a Survey:** Survey your classmates and have them share the important events from their time lines constructed in Activity 13-2. Generate one time line for the entire class. Using this newly constructed time line, repeat the Going Further section of the activity.

Chapter 13 Review

20. This idea suggests that evolution occurs because an organism acquires a trait for survival and passes that trait to its offspring. Genetics has shown that acquired traits are not hereditary. Thus, if a giraffe were capable of stretching its neck during its lifetime, it would not pass on its long neck to its offspring.

Developing Skills

21. **Observing and Inferring** Should be similar to the one shown below.
22. **Hypothesizing** Accept all reasonable answers. Responses might include plate tectonic processes, withdrawal of shallow seas, or cooler climates.
23. **Interpreting Data** No, corals are marine animals. Coal forms from dead plants in freshwater swamps.
24. **Interpreting Scientific Illustrations** Section A represents the Mesozoic Era; B represents Precambrian time; C represents the Cenozoic Era; D represents the Paleozoic Era.
25. **Interpreting Scientific Illustrations** The Cenozoic Era represents approximately 1.4 percent of Earth's history (66 000 000 ÷ 4 600 000 000 years = 0.014). This is represented by 5 degrees on the graph ($360° \times 0.014 = 5°$).

Performance Assessment

1. Accept all answers as long as students use facts to support their hypothesis. Use the Performance Task Assessment List for Formulating a Hypothesis in **PASC,** p. 21. P
2. Students should realize that black, as opposed to red, is an easier color to camouflage in a dark, wooded environment. Use the Performance Task Assessment List for Model in **PASC,** p. 51. P
3. Answers will vary. A more complete time line chart will enable students to make more detailed hypotheses. Use the Performance Task Assessment List for Conducting a Survey and Graphing the Results in **PASC,** p. 35. P

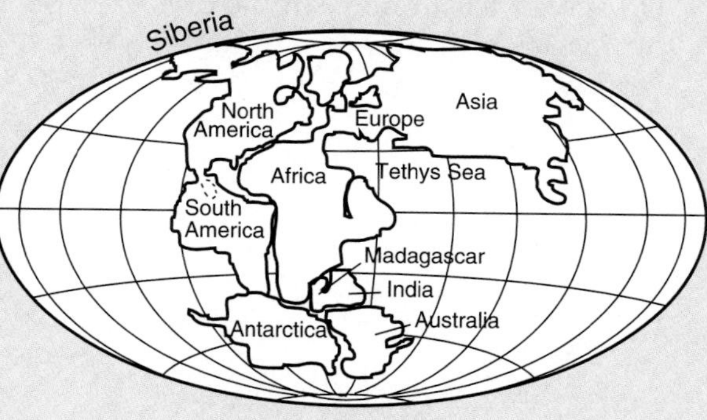

Objectives

LS **Kinesthetic** Students will formulate models of the different processes involved in fossil formation and present their models to the class. L1

COOP LEARN

Summary

In this activity, students will collect data about types of fossils. Using this data, they will choose a type of fossil to study and make a model of the chosen fossil type. Because there are many ways for students to approach this problem, encourage them to use their imaginations to come up with new ways to model fossil formation. Suggestions have been provided to help motivate students having trouble with the task.

Time Required

This project is designed to be worked on throughout Chapter 16. Students will need to spend several hours in the library researching fossil types and formation processes. One class period should be used for student brainstorming and sharing of ideas. During this period, group assignments should also be made. Another period should be set aside for classroom presentations on the formation of each of the fossil types. Fossil formation may require students to set up a process and then to keep checking on its progress. This may require several hours of intermittent work at home.

Preparation

- Establish cooperative groups of 3 or 4 students.
- Assemble a wide variety of materials that students might use in the construction of their models, including carbon paper, clay, plaster of paris, sand, and sugar cubes (to simulate fossils that dissolve to leave a mold).
- Display at least one example of each type of fossil with which students will be working.

UNIT PROJECT 4

An Age-Old Question

What picture comes to mind when you think of a fossil? Many people think of dinosaurs. You've seen them in pictures, on television, and at the museum. But what other types of fossils exist? Do all fossils form in the same way? In this project, you will make "fossils" that represent each type described in Chapter 12. You'll use processes similar to those that occur in nature to form the following types of fossils: petrified remains, carbonaceous film, molds and casts, and original remains.

Procedures

1. With two or three classmates, go to the library and research different types of fossils. Find out where different fossil types are found and how each type forms. Compile your data in a table that shows the types of fossils your group has researched, how each type is formed, and where examples of each type have been found. Obtain photographs or make drawings in your Science Journal of the various types you have studied.
2. Work with other groups in the class to come up with possible ways of making models of the various types of fossils. Each group of students should concentrate on making one type of fossil. Can you think of a way of showing a carbon imprint of a tree leaf? To show how original remains are preserved, the group must devise a way that original parts of an organism would be preserved.

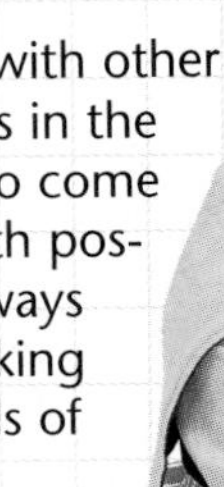

The group working with petrified remains must invent a method whereby original material in the organism is replaced by rock material. The group working on molds and casts must figure out some way to imitate the natural formation of molds and casts.

3. When your group decides how to make a model of your type of fossil, ask your teacher to review the method to be used. Using the method your group decided on, make your fossils. Once all groups have made fossils, the class should decide how to display its "fossil" collection.
4. If, during your library research, you discovered that fossils are found in areas near your home or school, ask your teacher or another adult to help you look for them. Remember, fossils found in rocks may not look anything like what you expect. If possible, have members of your class collect samples of each type of fossil all of the groups have made.
5. Each group should give a presentation that describes how they made their fossil. The presentation should include an explanation of each step and a description of the amount of time required to make the fossil model.

Going Further

Plan a trip to a local museum that has a fossil display. Ask the museum curator to show you examples of each type of fossil for which you made models. If possible, ask a local fossil collector to bring in his or her collection and share it with the class.

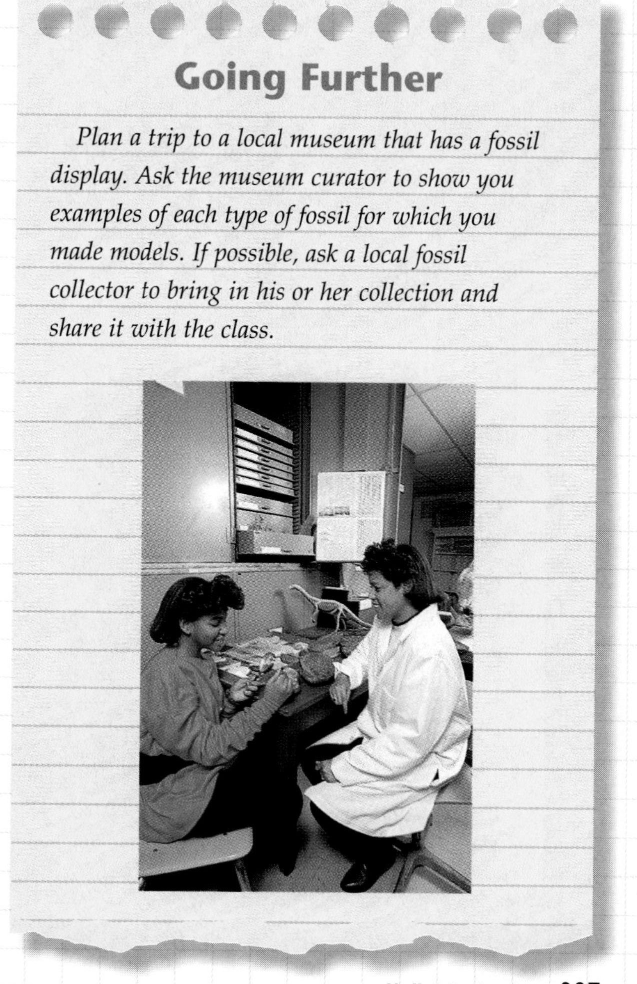

Teaching Strategies

- In order for students to have a basic understanding of fossil formation before going to the library, have them begin this project after Section 16-1.
- If students have difficulty with carbon impressions, demonstrate to them that placing a piece of carbon paper under a sheet of paper and then writing on the paper will cause a carbon impression of the writing to form on another sheet of paper under the carbon paper.
- Before dividing students into groups and sending them to the library for research, conduct a discussion on fossil formation. The discussion should expose student misconceptions or preconceptions that can be used in the presentation of concepts covered in this project.
- Encourage students to be innovative when formulating their models.

Go Further

Ask students what characteristics were helpful in determining fossil type and the formation process that probably caused it. Ask them to write down at least two of these characteristics in their journals. If no fossil collections are available locally, write to a nearby college or university and ask if their fossil collection could be shown to your class.

References

Arduini, Paolo and Giorgio Teruzzi. *Guide to Fossils.* New York: Simon & Schuster, Inc., 1986.

Gardner, Robert. *More Ideas for Science Projects.* New York: Franklin Watts, 1989.

Levin, Harold L. *The Earth Through Time.* New York: Sanders College Pub., 1991.

Murray, Marian. *Hunting for Fossils.* New York: The Macmillan Company, 1967.

UNIT 5

Earth's Air and Water

In Unit 5, students are introduced to Earth's atmosphere and oceans. The characteristics and movement of air and water are presented.

CONTENTS

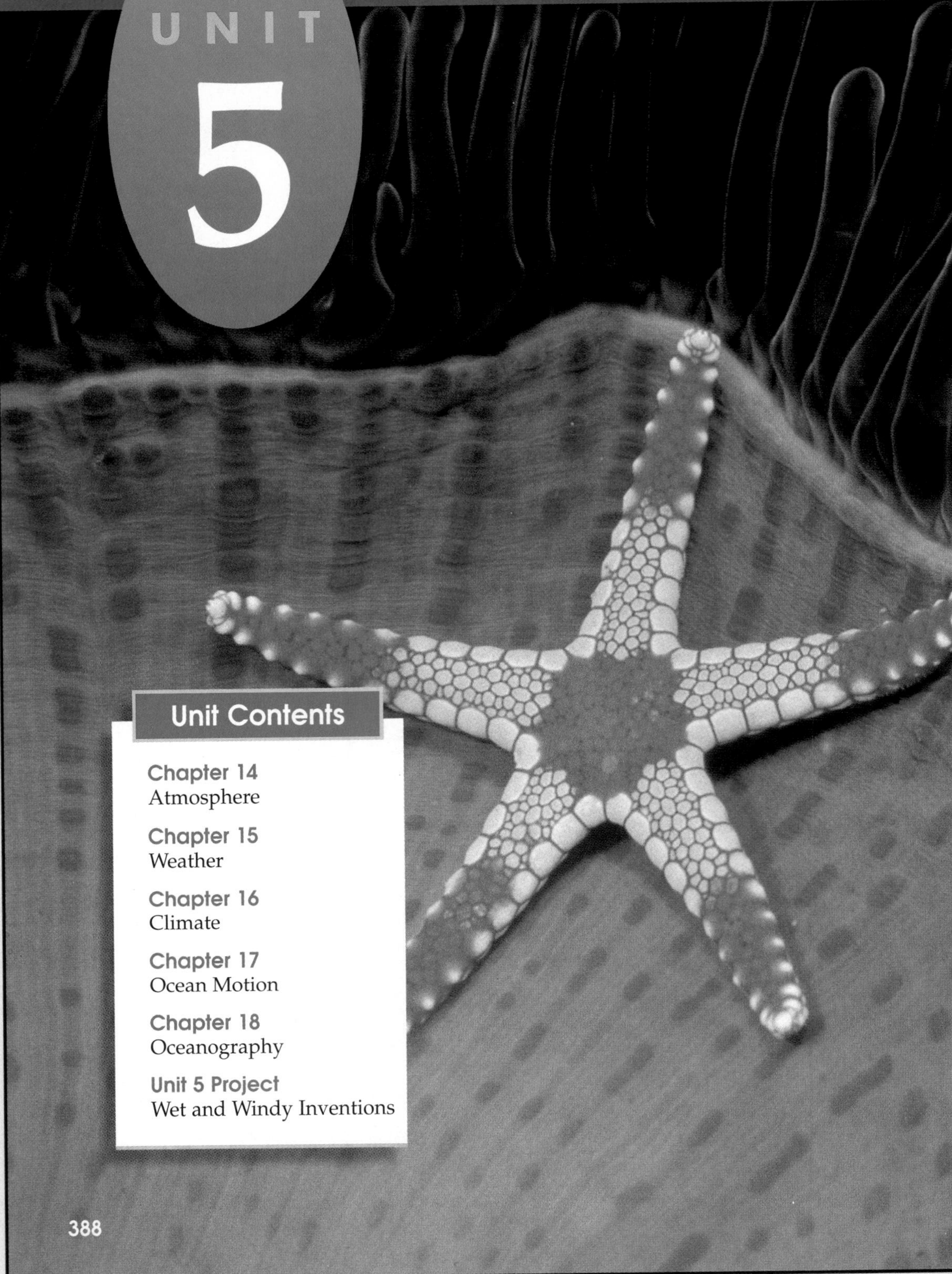

Science at Home

Classifying Clouds Have students observe the clouds each afternoon after school. Have them draw pictures of the clouds and use **Figure 15-5** to classify each type they observe. L1 LEP

Earth's Air and Water

What's Happening Here?

When we think of tropical oceans, we may picture calm, clear waters under an azure sky. But tropical oceans give birth to hurricanes, the most powerful of storms. The swirling mass of energy in the smaller photograph is the eye of a hurricane, gathering strength from the warm waters of the Atlantic. Far below, beneath the ocean's surface, tropical fish swim in lazy circles around a coral reef. Like the hurricane, tropical organisms such as this sea star and anemone depend on the warm ocean water for survival. In this unit, you will learn about oceans and how they interact with Earth's atmosphere to affect life.

Science Journal

When hurricanes reach land, they can cause tremendous damage. In your Science Journal, write a report describing how scientists track the progress of these storms. Include a discussion on actions taken to minimize damage once a hurricane hits land.

INTRODUCING THE UNIT

What's Happening Here?

Have students look at the photos and read the text. Ask them to explain how hurricanes may affect the waters beneath them. Point out to students that in this unit, they will study the interaction of air and water in Earth's atmosphere and oceans.

Background

Hurricanes are given names for scientific and safety reasons. Scientists refer to hurricanes by name rather than by position because it is easier to alert the public about the approach of a hurricane when it is referred to by name. An earlier method of identifying hurricanes by longitude and latitude proved too confusing for weather reports.

Previewing the Chapters

- Have students read the objectives for each section and then search for charts and photography that relate to each objective.
- Have students read the captions for several figures in the unit. Have volunteers briefly describe what they see in each photograph or illustration.

Tying to Previous Knowledge

Ask if any students have experienced severe thunderstorms, tornadoes, or hurricanes. Have volunteers describe what happened and what precautions they and others took to protect themselves.

Theme Connection

Systems and Interactions Have students hypothesize how movement of air in Earth's atmosphere can affect the movement of water in Earth's oceans. Have them refer to **Figures 14-17** and **17-4** while discussing this interaction.

Cultural Diversity

Lifestyles Have students research cultural differences, emphasizing eating and working habits, of people living near the shore and people who live farther inland in the United States. Have students continue with a comparison of cultural differences between people who live near the shore in industrialized countries and those who live near the shore in agricultural countries. L2

Chapter Organizer

Section	Objectives	Activities/Features
Chapter Opener		Explore Activity: Temperature affects the density of air. p. 391
14-1 **Earth's Atmosphere** (2 sessions, 1 block)*	1. **Name** the gases in Earth's atmosphere. 2. **Describe** the structure of Earth's atmosphere. 3. **Explain** what causes air pressure.	Using Technology: Weather Satellites, p. 396 MiniLAB: Does air have mass? p. 397 Skill Builder: Making and Using Graphs, p. 398 Science Journal, p. 398 Activity 14-1: Making a Barometer, p. 399
14-2 **Science and Society Technology: The Ozone Layer** (1 session, ½ block)*	1. **Explain** why exposure to ultraviolet radiation can be a problem for plants and animals. 2. **Describe** how chlorofluorocarbons destroy ozone molecules.	Explore the Technology, p. 401
14-3 **Energy from the Sun** (2 sessions, 1 block)*	1. **Describe** three things that happen to the energy Earth receives from the sun. 2. **Contrast** radiation, conduction, and convection. 3. **Describe** the water cycle.	Using Math, p. 403 Connect to Physics, p. 405 Science Journal, p. 406 Skill Builder: Concept Mapping, p. 407 Using Math, p. 407 Activity 14-2: The Heat Is On, pp. 408-409
14-4 **Movement of Air** (2 sessions, 1 block)*	1. **Explain** why different latitudes receive different amounts of solar energy. 2. **Explain** the Coriolis effect, sea breezes, and land breezes. 3. **Locate** the doldrums, trade winds, prevailing westerlies, polar easterlies, and jet streams.	Problem Solving: The Coriolis-Go-Round, p. 411 MiniLAB: What do convection currents look like? p. 412 Using Math, p. 412 People and Science: Tinho Dornellas, Windsurfer, p. 413 Connect to Physics, p. 415 Skill Builder: Comparing and Contrasting, p. 416 Using Computers: Graphics, p. 416

* A complete Planning Guide that includes block scheduling is provided on pages 32T-35T.

Activity Materials

Explore	Activities	MiniLABs
page 391 tap water, soda can, heat source, safety goggles, thermal mitt	page 399 small coffee can, drinking straw, large rubber balloon, construction paper, transparent tape, scissors, rubber band pages 408-409 ring stand, dark colored soil, metric ruler, 2 clear plastic boxes, overhead light with reflector, 4 thermometers, tap water, masking tape, colored pencils, thermal mitt	page 397 balance, deflated ball, hand pump with pressure gauge page 412 250-mL glass beaker, hot water, ice cubes, food coloring

Teacher Classroom Resources

Reproducible Masters	Transparencies
Study Guide, p. 57 **Reinforcement,** p. 57 **Enrichment,** p. 57 **Activity Worksheets,** pp. 84-85, 88 **Lab Manual 38,** Air **Lab Manual 39,** Air Pressure **Lab Manual 40,** Temperature of the Air **Science and Society Integration,** p. 18	**Section Focus Transparency 53,** Full of Hot Air **Science Integration Transparency 14,** The Physics of Thermometers **Teaching Transparency 27,** Layers of the Atmosphere
Study Guide, p. 58 **Reinforcement,** p. 58 **Enrichment,** p. 58 **Critical Thinking/Problem Solving,** p. 20 **Cross-Curricular Integration,** p. 18 **Technology Integration,** pp. 13-14	**Section Focus Transparency 54,** The Battle of the Molecules **Teaching Transparency 28,** Major Air Circulation
Study Guide, p. 59 **Reinforcement,** p. 59 **Enrichment,** p. 59 **Activity Worksheets,** pp. 86-87 **Multicultural Connections,** pp. 31-32	**Section Focus Transparency 55,** Sun and Air
Study Guide, p. 60 **Reinforcement,** p. 60 **Enrichment,** p. 60 **Activity Worksheets,** p. 89 **Lab Manual 41,** Air in Motion **Lab Manual 42,** Wind Power **Science Integration Activity 14,** Down the Drain **Concept Mapping,** p. 33	**Section Focus Transparency 56,** Why Wind?

Teaching Resources

Glencoe Earth Science Interactive Videodisc
Earth Science CD-ROM
Spanish Resources
English/Spanish Audiocassettes
Cooperative Learning Resource Guide
Lab Partner
Lab and Safety Skills
Lesson Plans

Assessment Resources

Chapter Review, pp. 31-32
Assessment, pp. 95-98
Performance Assessment in the Science Classroom (PASC)
MindJogger Videoquiz
Alternate Assessment in the Science Classroom
Performance Assessment
Chapter Review Software
Computer Test Bank

Key to Teaching Strategies

The following designations will help you decide which activities are appropriate for your students.

L1 Level 1 activities should be within the ability range of all students.

L2 Level 2 activities should be within the ability range of the average to above-average student.

L3 Level 3 activities are designed for the ability range of above-average students.

LEP LEP activities should be within the ability range of Limited English Proficiency students.

LS These activities are designed to address different learning styles.

COOP LEARN Cooperative Learning activities are designed for small group work.

P These strategies represent student products that can be placed into a best-work portfolio.

GLENCOE TECHNOLOGY

The following multimedia resources are available from Glencoe.

The Infinite Voyage Series
Crisis in the Atmosphere
Secrets from a Frozen World

Science and Technology Videodisc Series (STVS)
Earth & Space
Wind Engineering

National Geographic Society Series
STV: Atmosphere
GTV: Planetary Manager

Earth Science CD-ROM

Teacher Classroom Resources

This is a representation of key blackline masters available in the Teacher Classroom Resources.

Teaching Aids

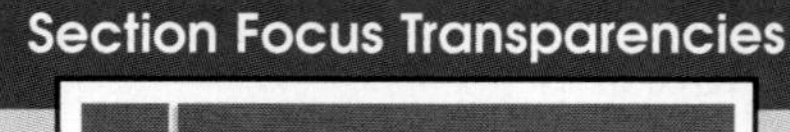

Section Focus Transparencies

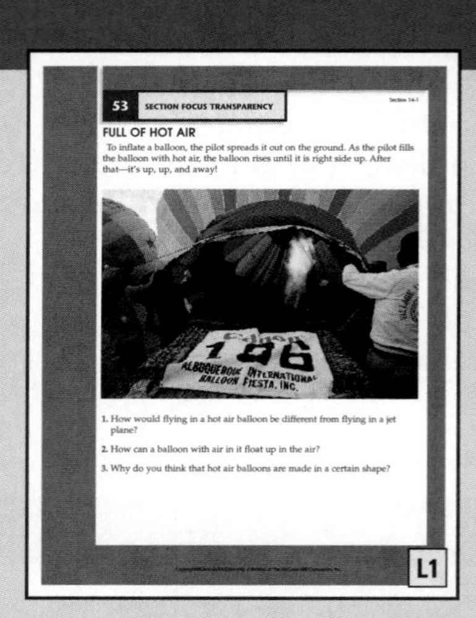

53 SECTION FOCUS TRANSPARENCY

Section 14-1

FULL OF HOT AIR

To inflate a balloon, the pilot spreads it out on the ground. As the pilot fills the balloon with hot air, the balloon rises until it is right side up. After that—it's up, up, and away!

1. How would flying in a hot air balloon be different from flying in a jet plane?
2. How can a balloon with air in it float up in the air?
3. Why do you think that hot air balloons are made in a certain shape?

L1

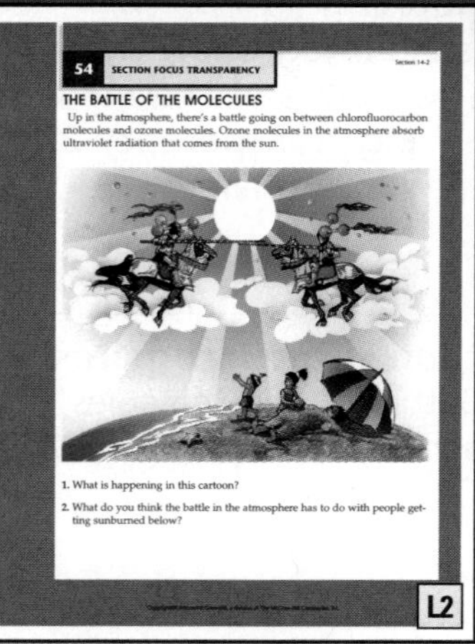

54 SECTION FOCUS TRANSPARENCY

Section 14-2

THE BATTLE OF THE MOLECULES

Up in the atmosphere, there's a battle going on between chlorofluorocarbon molecules and ozone molecules. Ozone molecules in the atmosphere absorb ultraviolet radiation that comes from the sun.

1. What is happening in this cartoon?
2. What do you think the battle in the atmosphere has to do with people getting sunburned below?

L2

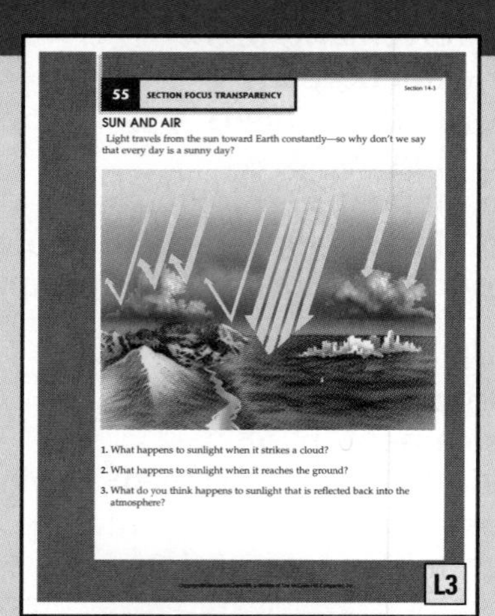

55 SECTION FOCUS TRANSPARENCY

Section 14-3

SUN AND AIR

Light travels from the sun toward Earth constantly—so why don't we say that every day is a sunny day?

1. What happens to sunlight when it strikes a cloud?
2. What happens to sunlight when it reaches the ground?
3. What do you think happens to sunlight that is reflected back into the atmosphere?

L3

Science Integration Transparencies

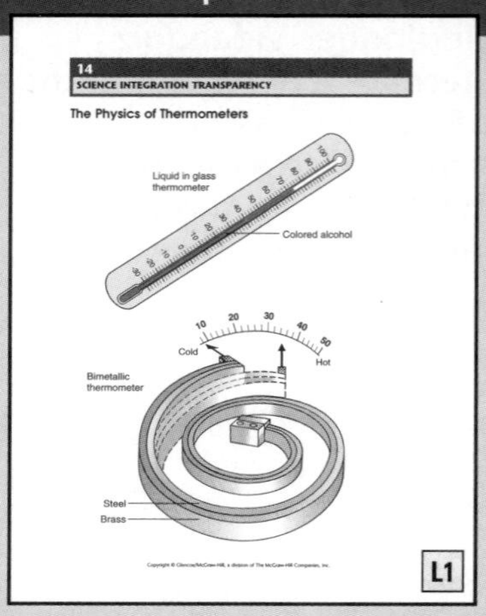

14 SCIENCE INTEGRATION TRANSPARENCY

The Physics of Thermometers

L1

Teaching Transparencies

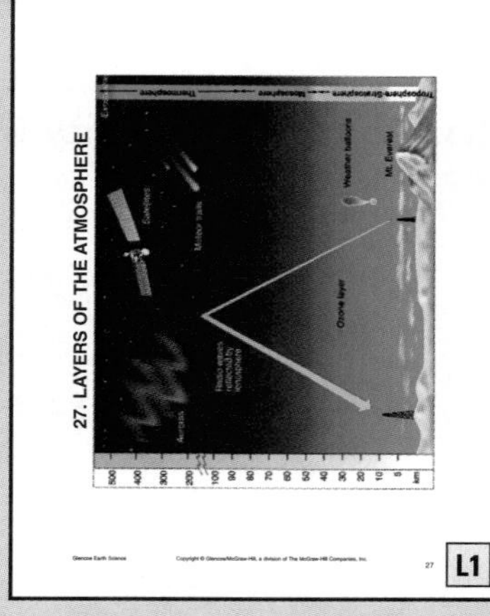

L1

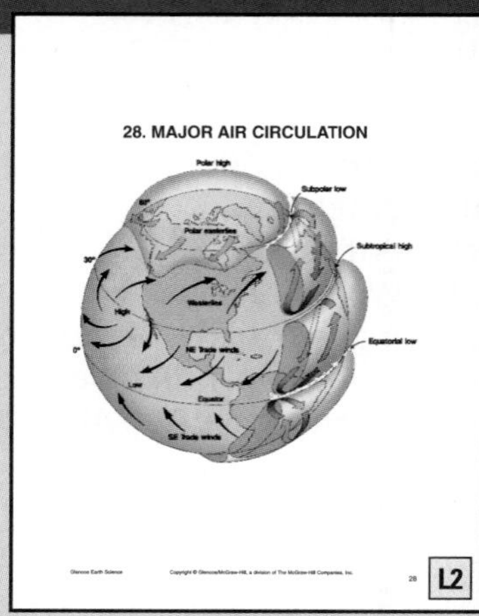

L2

Meeting Different Ability Levels

Study Guide

NAME DATE CLASS

Chapter 14 STUDY GUIDE

Text Pages 392–399

• Earth's Atmosphere

In the blank at the left, write the letter of the term in Column II that matches each definition in Column I.

Column I

_____ 1. Layer of atmosphere where weather, clouds, and smog occur
_____ 2. Force of air determined by temperature and distance above sea level
_____ 3. Naturally occurring gas in the stratosphere that is considered a pollutant in the lower atmosphere
_____ 4. Layer of the thermosphere that has a high concentration of electrically charged particles
_____ 5. Most common gas in the atmosphere
_____ 6. Layer of atmosphere that includes the ozone layer
_____ 7. Type of pollution that can be formed by car exhaust and burning coal or oil
_____ 8. Layer of atmosphere between the thermosphere and space

Column II

a. air pressure
b. ionosphere
c. nitrogen
d. ozone
e. smog
f. stratosphere
g. exosphere
h. troposphere

In the blank, write the term that correctly completes each sentence. Use the information in your textbook.

9. _____ makes up from 0 to 4 percent of the atmosphere.
10. The _____ contains 75 percent of the atmospheric gases.
11. The division of Earth's atmosphere into layers is based on _____ differences.
12. Cold air is denser than warm air and, therefore, has higher _____.
13. _____ is the only substance that exists as a solid, liquid, and gas in Earth's atmosphere.

Identify the five main layers of Earth's atmosphere.

Atmosphere: E, D, C, B, A; Earth

14. A is the _____.
15. B is the _____.
16. C is the _____.
17. D is the _____.
18. E is the _____.

57

L1

Reinforcement

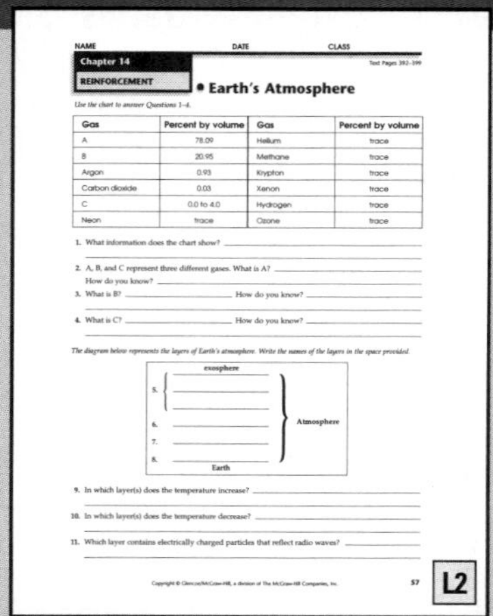

NAME DATE CLASS

Chapter 14 REINFORCEMENT

Text Pages 392–399

• Earth's Atmosphere

Use the chart to answer Questions 1–4.

Gas	Percent by volume	Gas	Percent by volume
A	78.09	Helium	trace
B	20.95	Methane	trace
Argon	0.93	Krypton	trace
Carbon dioxide	0.03	Xenon	trace
C	0.0 to 4.0	Hydrogen	trace
Neon	trace	Ozone	trace

1. What information does the chart show? _____
2. A, B, and C represent three different gases. What is A? _____ How do you know? _____
3. What is B? _____ How do you know? _____
4. What is C? _____ How do you know? _____

The diagram below represents the layers of Earth's atmosphere. Write the names of the layers in the space provided.

exosphere; 5. _____; 6. _____; 7. _____; 8. _____; Earth; Atmosphere

9. In which layer(s) does the temperature increase? _____
10. In which layer(s) does the temperature decrease? _____
11. Which layer contains electrically charged particles that reflect radio waves? _____

57

L2

Enrichment Worksheets

NAME DATE CLASS

Chapter 14 ENRICHMENT

Text Pages 392–399

• Earth's Atmosphere

Observing the Effects of Air Pressure

The activity at the beginning of the chapter showed how temperature affects the density of air. When the air in a can became heated by boiling water, it expanded and much of it escaped out of the can before the top was put on. As the air that was left inside cooled, it became denser and took up less space. Because the air pressure on the outside of the can was higher than the pressure inside the can, the sides of the can collapsed. You could see what a powerful force air pressure can be. Here's another experiment about the power of air pressure.

Materials

- glass bottle
- sheet of paper
- long match or paper drinking straw and match
- hard-boiled egg, peeled

Procedure

1. Be sure that the opening at the top of the glass bottle is slightly smaller than the diameter of the egg.
2. Crumple the sheet of paper into a ball and drop it into the bottle.
3. Light the end of the paper drinking straw or the long match and hold the burning end on the paper in the bottle until the paper begins to burn. Be careful!
4. Let the paper burn until the flame burns out.
5. Set the peeled hard-boiled egg over the opening at the top of the bottle with the pointed end of the egg down.

Analyze

1. What happened to the egg? _____
2. What caused the egg to do this? _____

Conclude and Apply

3. How can you get the egg out? _____

57

L3

Hands-On Activities

Science Integration Activity

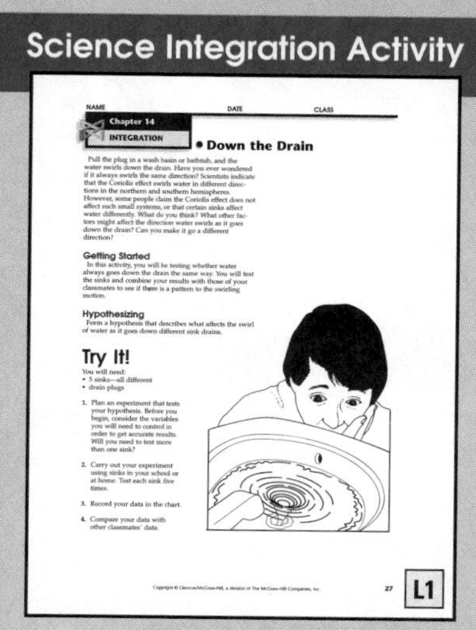

Lab Manual

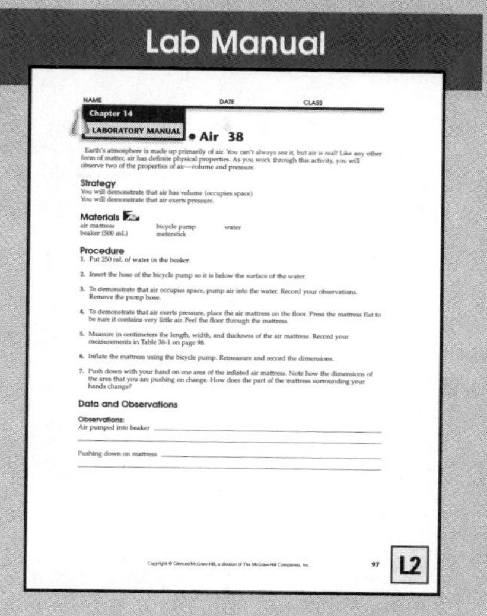

Assessment

Performance Assessment

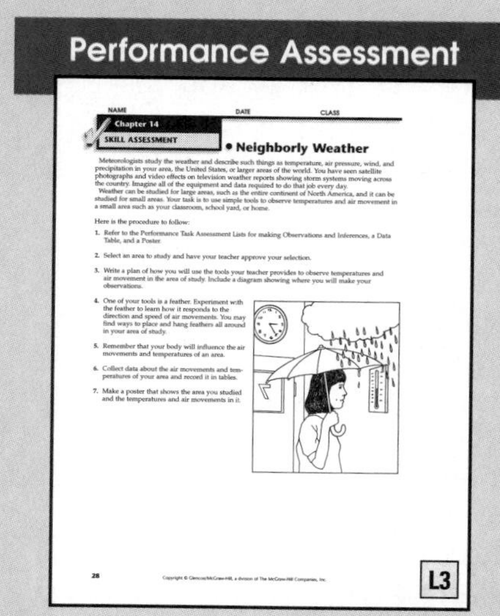

Enrichment and Application

Critical Thinking/ Problem Solving

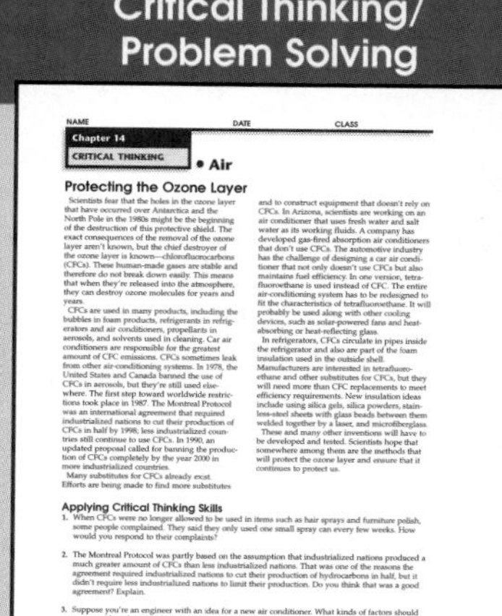

Cross-Curricular Integration

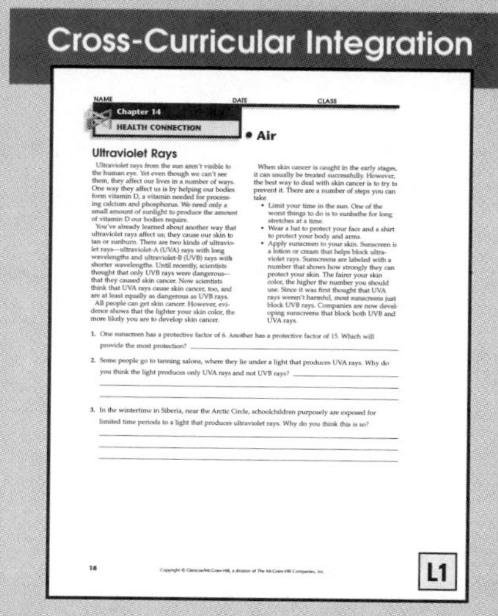

Science and Society Integration

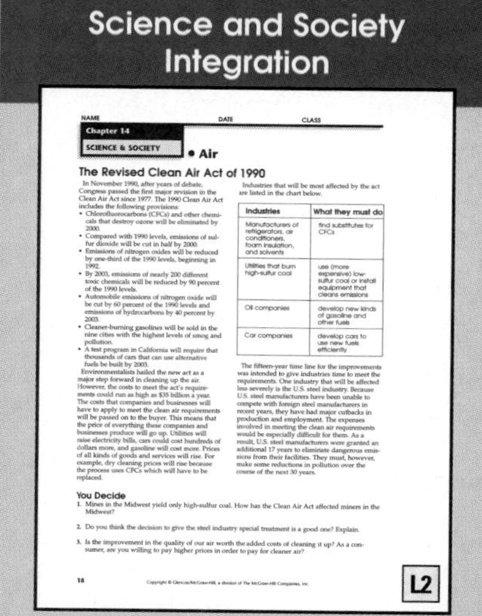

Technology Integration

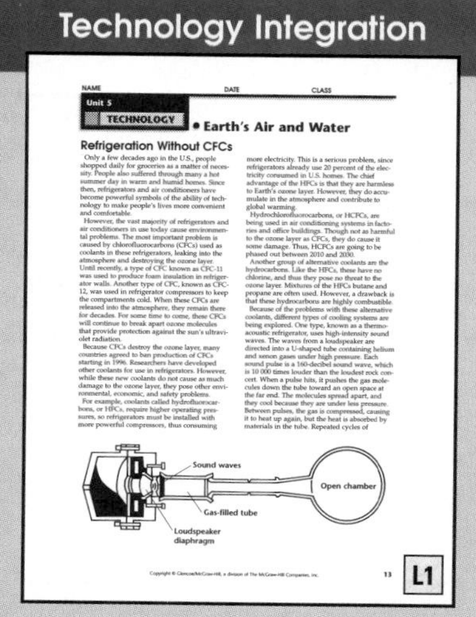

Multicultural Connections

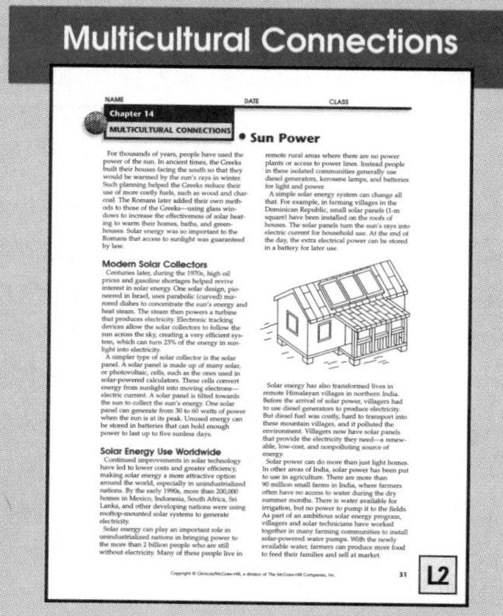

Concept Mapping

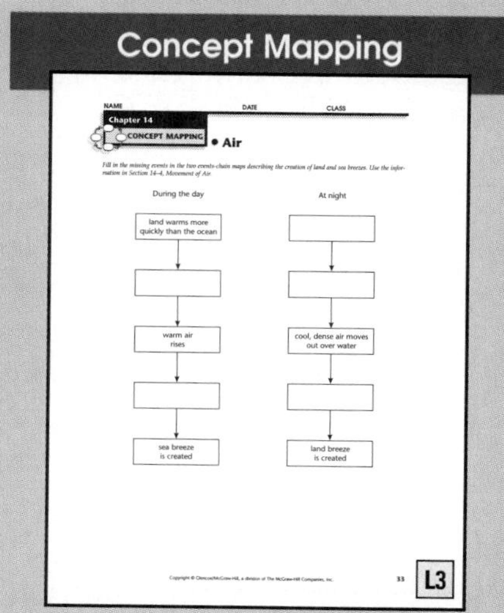

Chapter 14

Atmosphere

CHAPTER OVERVIEW

Section 14-1 This section discusses the composition and structure of the atmosphere.

Section 14-2 Science and Society Students learn the importance of the ozone layer and how chlorofluorocarbon may destroy it.

Section 14-3 This section describes energy transfer by radiation, conduction, and convection and examines the water cycle.

Section 14-4 This section examines the roles of solar energy and the Coriolis effect on the movement of air. Major wind systems are described.

Chapter Vocabulary

troposphere	convection
ionosphere	hydrosphere
ozone layer	water cycle
ultraviolet radiation	Coriolis effect
chlorofluorocarbons	jet stream
radiation	sea breeze
conduction	land breeze

Theme Connection

Energy/Scale and Structure Three foci of the energy theme are: the sun provides energy for atmospheric heat; this energy is transferred by radiation, conduction, and convection; and temperature differences on Earth's surface result in wind. Scale and structure are emphasized through a discussion of the composition and structure of the atmosphere.

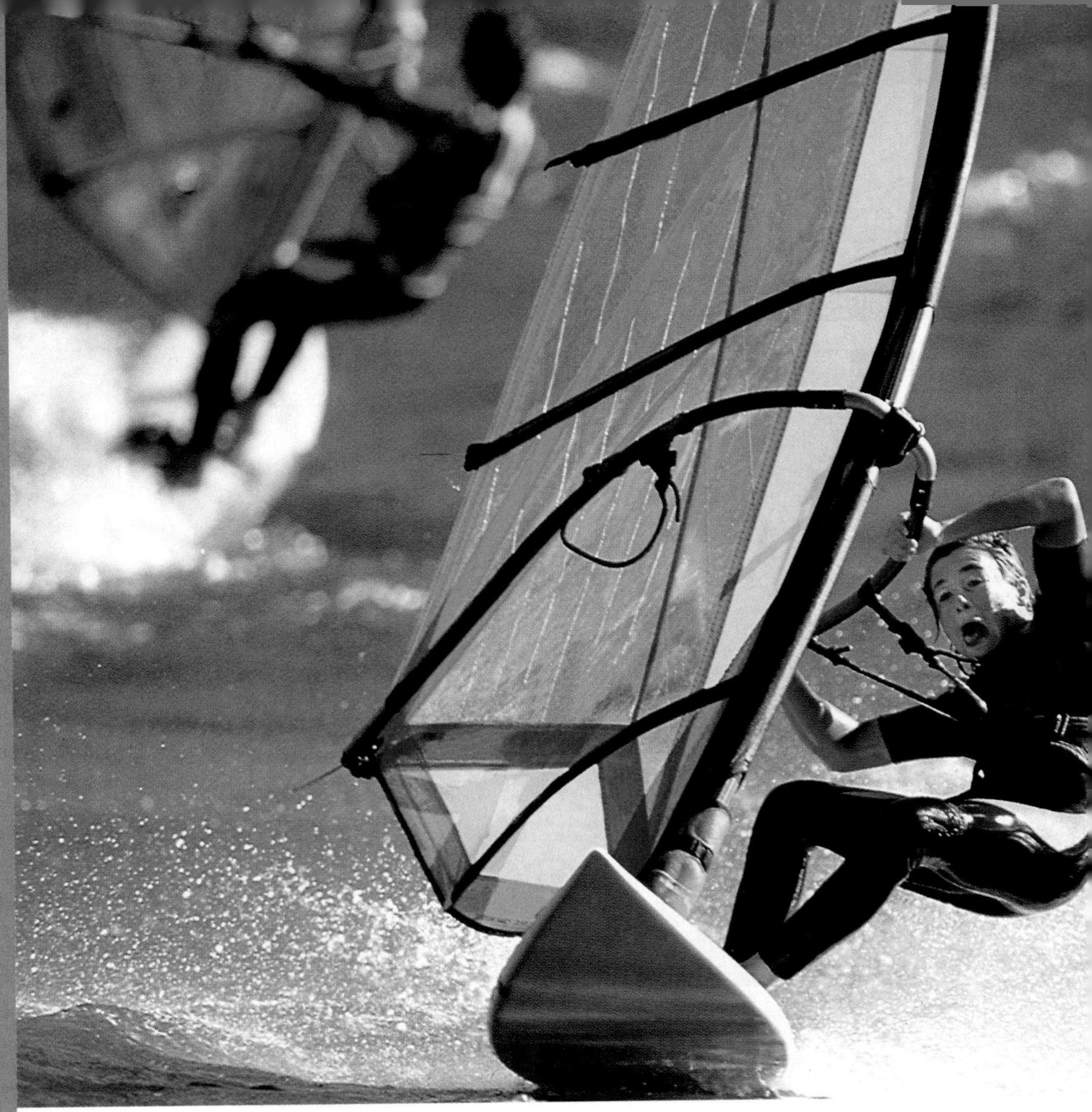

Previewing the Chapter

Learning Styles (LS)

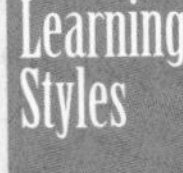

Look for the following logo for strategies that emphasize different learning modalities. LS

Kinesthetic	Reteach, p. 397; Activity, p. 414
Visual-Spatial	Explore, p. 391; Visual Learning, pp. 393, 394, 395, 404; MiniLAB, pp. 397, 412; Activity, p. 404; Demonstration, p. 411; Reteach, p. 415
Interpersonal	Reteach, p. 401; Activity 14-2, pp. 408-409
Intrapersonal	Activity 14-1, p. 399
Linguistic	Science Journal, pp. 398, 406
Logical-Mathematical	Using Math, pp. 403, 407

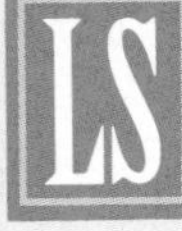

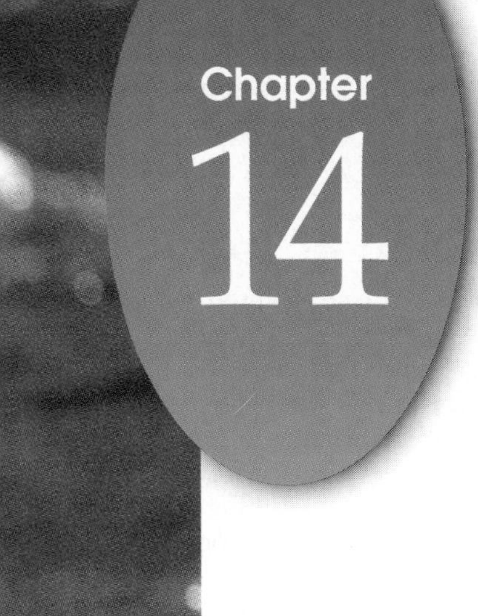

Atmosphere

Do you know how windsurfing works? A surfer uses the power of the wind to skim a surfboard across water. Wind comes from the uneven heating of the atmosphere, the air around Earth. When air is heated, its molecules absorb energy, move faster, and take up more space. The heated air becomes less dense. More-dense air slips underneath, forcing less-dense, heated air to rise. That creates wind.

EXPLORE ACTIVITY

Temperature affects the density of air. 

1. Your teacher will pour a small quantity of water into a soda can.
2. The can will be heated until the water boils.
3. Then the heat will be turned off, and the can submerged upside down in cold water.

Observe: What happens as the can cools? In your Science Journal, hypothesize why this happens. How is this related to windsurfing?

Previewing Science Skills

- In the **Skill Builders**, you will **make and use graphs, map concepts,** and **compare and contrast.**
- In the **Activities**, you will **record and analyze data, observe, draw conclusions,** and **design an experiment.**
- In the **MiniLABs**, you will **measure in SI, observe, infer,** and **compare and contrast.**

Assessment Planner

Portfolio
Refer to page 417 for suggested items that students might select for their portfolios.

Performance Assessment
See page 417 for additional Performance Assessment options.
Skill Builders, pp. 398, 407, 416
MiniLABs, pp. 397, 412
Activities 14-1, p. 399; 14-2, pp. 408-409

Content Assessment
Section Wrap-ups, pp. 398, 401, 407, 416
Chapter Review, pp. 417-419
Mini Quizzes, pp. 398, 407, 416

Group Assessment
Opportunities for group assessment occur with Cooperative Learning Strategies and Flex Your Brain Activities.

EXPLORE ACTIVITY

Purpose

LS **Visual-Spatial** Use the Explore Activity to introduce students to air pressure. Students will be learning more about the properties of the atmosphere in this chapter. L1 COOP LEARN

Preparation

Obtain one empty aluminum soda can for each class.

Materials

aluminum soda can, water, hot plate, bucket

Observe

The can collapses in on itself. Students may hypothesize that when the water begins to boil, water vapor molecules escape rapidly from the can, thus reducing the density of molecules inside the can. Then, when the can is dunked in cold water, air molecules cannot get in to replace the molecules that escaped during heating. The air inside the can cools. The molecules remaining inside the can lose energy and exert less pressure than the molecules outside the can. The air pressure outside the can is greater than the pressure inside; thus, the can collapses.

Assessment

Content Have students draw pictures of what happened to the can before, during, and after it was heated. Their drawings should show cutaway views of the can, water, water vapor, air pressure, heat source, and air molecules. Use the Performance Task Assessment List for Scientific Drawing in **PASC,** p. 55. P

14•1 Earth's Atmosphere

Science Words

troposphere
ionosphere

Objectives

- Name the gases in Earth's atmosphere.
- Describe the structure of Earth's atmosphere.
- Explain what causes air pressure.

Composition of the Atmosphere

It's early morning in the future. You're getting dressed for work. As you eat breakfast, the weather report comes over the computer screen: "Smog levels higher than normal; temperatures near 38°C; the ozone layer in the stratosphere thinner than yesterday." You'll need your filter mask to protect your lungs from the smog. Pollution in the atmosphere has raised the temperature. You'll have to wear cool clothing. The thinner ozone layer requires you to use a strong sunblock lotion to protect yourself from skin cancer.

This scenario may not sound pleasant, but it's a future you may face. Because your life depends on the air you breathe, you need to know about the atmosphere, its composition, its structure, how it affects you, and how you affect it.

Atmospheric Gases

The atmosphere surrounding Earth extends from Earth's surface to outer space. The atmosphere is a mixture of gases with some suspended solids and liquids. **Figure 14-1** is a graph of the gases in Earth's atmosphere. Nitrogen is the most common gas. Oxygen makes up 21 percent of our atmosphere. We need oxygen to breathe. Water vapor makes up from zero to four percent of the atmosphere. When the percentage of water vapor is higher, the percentages of other gases are slightly lower.

The atmosphere also contains other gases and smog, a type of pollution. The kind of smog affecting an area depends on the pollutants. Car exhaust expels nitrogen oxides and unburned hydrocarbons into the air. These pollutants mixed

Argon 0.93%
Carbon Dioxide 0.03%
Water Vapor 0.0 to 4.0%
Neon
Helium
Methane
Krypton
Xenon
Hydrogen
Ozone
1% Trace
21% Oxygen
78% Nitrogen

Figure 14-1
This graph gives the percentages of the gases that make up our atmosphere.

Section 14•1

Prepare

Section Background

- Earth's original atmosphere was probably composed mostly of methane and ammonia. This primitive atmosphere changed over geologic time as erupting volcanoes emitted gases such as water vapor, carbon dioxide, and nitrogen. After its formation, Earth continued to cool. The water vapor condensed and absorbed most of the carbon dioxide. Oxygen was probably formed from the dissociation of water molecules and by photosynthesis of primitive plants.
- The gases of Earth's atmosphere are selective absorbers of energy from the sun. The type of energy absorbed by the atmosphere depends on the kinds of gases that are present in the atmosphere.

Preplanning

- To prepare for the MiniLAB, obtain pan balances, inflatable balls, an air pump with a ball inflation needle, and a pressure gauge.
- To prepare for Activity 14-1, obtain small coffee cans, drinking straws, rubber balloons, construction paper, transparent tape, scissors, and rubber bands.

1 Motivate

Bellringer

Before presenting the lesson, display **Section Focus Transparency 53** on the overhead projector. Assign the accompanying **Focus Activity** worksheet. L1 LEP

Program Resources

Reproducible Masters

Study Guide, p. 57 L1
Reinforcement, p. 57 L1
Enrichment, p. 57 L3
Science and Society Integration, p. 18
Activity Worksheets, pp. 5, 84-85, 88 L1
Lab Manual 38, 39, 40

Transparencies

Section Focus Transparency 53 L1
Teaching Transparency 27
Section Integration Transparency 14

with oxygen and other chemicals in the presence of sunlight cause an L.A.-type, brown smog, as shown in **Figure 14-2.** Sulfur oxides from burning coal or oil cause a gray smog.

Another component of smog is ozone. Ozone is a gas that occurs naturally in the stratosphere, but ozone is not normally found in the lower part of the atmosphere. When it is formed in the air above cities, ozone is considered a pollutant. In the lower atmosphere, ozone can harm plants and damage our lungs.

Figure 14-2

Smog lies over the Los Angeles area. Learning about the composition and structure of the atmosphere will help you understand pollution problems and help you make decisions about the atmosphere in the future.

Atmospheric Solids and Liquids

Gases aren't the only thing making up Earth's atmosphere. Dust, salt, and ice are three common solids found in the atmospheric mixture. Dust gets into the atmosphere when wind picks it up off the ground and carries it along. Ice is common in the form of hailstones and snowflakes. Salt is picked up from ocean spray.

The atmosphere also contains liquids. The most common liquid in the atmosphere is water found in droplets of clouds. Water is the only substance that exists as a solid, liquid, and gas in Earth's atmosphere.

2 Teach

Content Background

Stress that although carbon dioxide, water vapor, and ozone make up only a small percentage of the air, they are important in terms of weather and atmospheric processes.

Inquiry Questions

- **What is the most common gas in the atmosphere?** *nitrogen*
- **What is smog?** *Smog is a hazy condition in the atmosphere created when a variety of pollutants mix and then react with sunlight. Smog is usually a problem during the summer months with the most solar radiation. Particulate smog often occurs during winter months, when people make fires.*

GLENCOE TECHNOLOGY

 **CD-ROM**

Earth Science CD-ROM

Have students perform the interactive exploration for Chapter 14 to reinforce important chapter concepts and thinking processes.

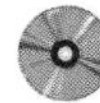 **Videodisc**

The Infinite Voyage: Crisis in the Atmosphere

Chapter 10

Los Angeles Smog and Air Quality Plan

Use Lab 38 from the **Lab Manual** as you teach this lesson.

Visual Learning

Figure 14-1 Inform students that the data shown in this figure represent the composition of Earth's atmosphere at sea level. The amounts and types of gases change with an increase in altitude. LEP LS

Theme Connection

Scale and Structure Ask students: **What substances besides gases make up the atmosphere?** *Liquid water and solids such as dust and ice are part of the atmosphere.*

Visual Learning

Figure 14-3 Stress that each layer of Earth's atmosphere has unique characteristics. The ozone layer is a component of the stratosphere. It varies in thickness from a few kilometers to up to 40 kilometers. Looking at **Figure 14-3,** students may infer that there is a thick concentration of ozone molecules. Inform students that the ozone layer is wide, but ozone molecules are widely dispersed in the stratosphere. If all the ozone molecules in the atmosphere were brought down to sea level, where pressure is greater, it would form a layer less than 3 mm thick.

LEP LS

Teacher F.Y.I.

The exosphere, extending from about 300 km outward, marks the transition from Earth's atmosphere to extremely sparse interplanetary gas. At the exosphere, molecules of hydrogen and helium leave the atmosphere. These light molecules, which have absorbed radiation from the sun, move so fast they escape Earth's gravitational field. As a result, there is a constant seepage of gases into outer space.

Inquiry Questions

- **In which layer of the atmosphere are weather, clouds, and smog found?** *in the troposphere*
- **Where is Earth's ozone layer?** *in the stratosphere*

Use **Teaching Transparency 27** as you teach this lesson.

Use Lab 40 from the **Lab Manual** as you teach this lesson.

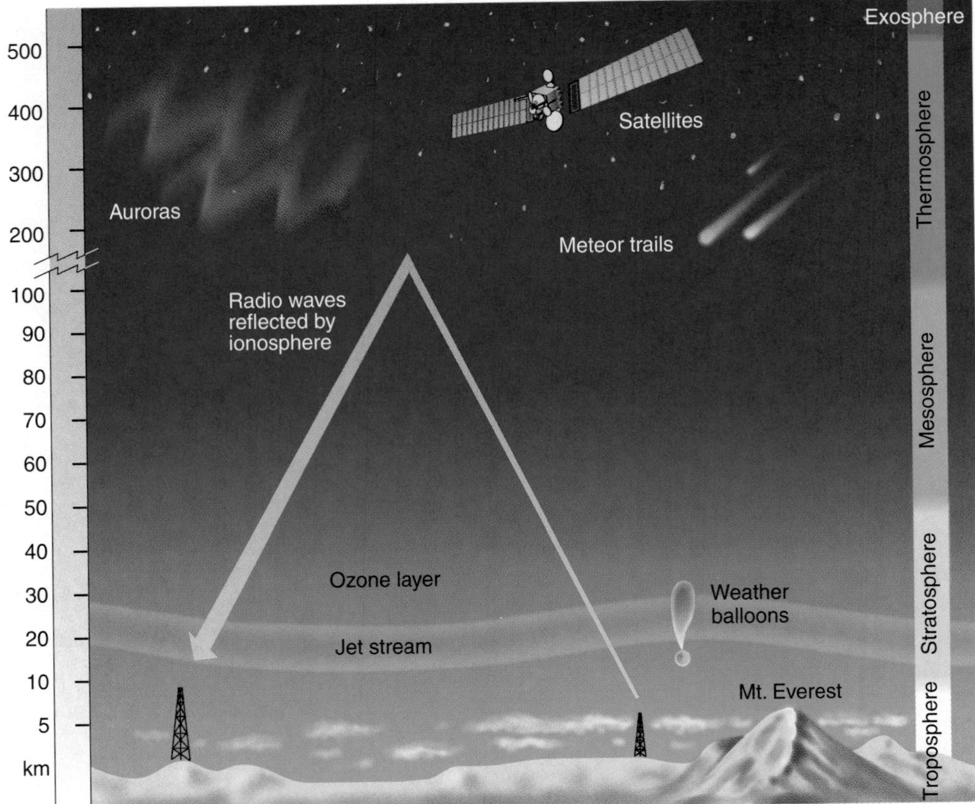

Figure 14-3

Although Earth's atmosphere extends hundreds of kilometers upward, 75 percent of all atmospheric gases are in the 15 km closest to Earth.

Structure of the Atmosphere

The weather forecast of the future predicted a high smog level and a thin ozone layer in the stratosphere. Both conditions affect your health, but in different ways. Where in the atmosphere does smog occur? Where can you find not just ozone but the ozone layer?

Figure 14-3 illustrates Earth's five main atmospheric layers: the troposphere, stratosphere, mesosphere, thermosphere, and exosphere. Each layer has unique characteristics.

Lower Layers of the Atmosphere

We live in the troposphere, the layer closest to the ground. The **troposphere** contains 75 percent of the atmospheric gases, as well as dust, ice, and liquid water. Weather, clouds, and smog occur in the troposphere.

Above the troposphere lies the stratosphere. As **Figures 14-3** and **14-6** show, a layer of ozone exists within the stratosphere. This ozone layer was mentioned in the future forecast because the ozone layer directly affects your health. You'll learn more about this layer in Section 14-2.

Upper Layers of the Atmosphere

Beyond the stratosphere are the mesosphere, thermosphere, and exosphere. One important layer of the thermosphere is the **ionosphere,** a layer of electrically charged particles. When solar energy bombards these particles, it creates ions and free electrons. These ions and free electrons can interfere with certain kinds of radio waves sent from Earth. During the daytime, energy from the sun interacts with the particles in the ionosphere, creating so many ions and free electrons that they absorb AM radio waves. At night, with fewer ions and free electrons, AM radio transmissions bounce off the ionosphere. This bouncing allows radio transmissions from one side of the globe to be received on the other side of the globe. **Figure 14-4** illustrates this.

The exosphere is the uppermost part of Earth's atmosphere. Beyond it lies space. If you were an astronaut traveling upward through the exosphere, you would encounter fewer and fewer molecules and ions. Eventually, you would find so few molecules and so few ions that, for all practical purposes, you would be out of Earth's atmosphere and in space. There's no clear boundary between the atmosphere and space.

The space shuttle orbits Earth in the exosphere, 280 km above Earth's surface. There are so few molecules and ions that the wings of the shuttle, used in the lower atmosphere, are useless. The spacecraft must rely on bursts from small rocket thrusters to maneuver.

A

B

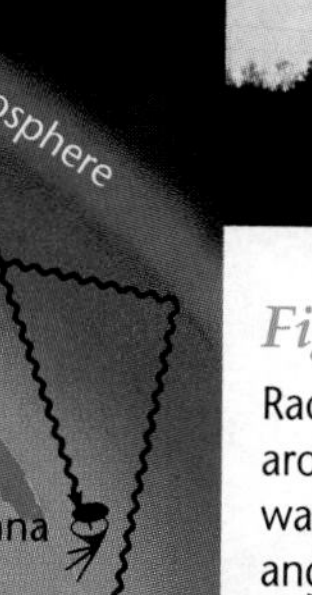

Figure 14-4

Radio waves can be received by antennas around the globe (A). At night, AM radio waves that strike the ionosphere at sharp angles pass through to space, but other waves strike at lower angles and are reflected back toward Earth (B).

Inquiry Question

How does the ionosphere aid communication? *This layer reflects AM radio waves. At night, radio transmissions from one side of the world can be received on the other.*

Enrichment

Have students research the effects that solar flares have on the atmosphere. L3

NATIONAL GEOGRAPHIC SOCIETY

Videodisc

STV: Atmosphere

What Is the Atmosphere?

Unit 1, Side 1

Introduction

00400-03109

Layers of the Atmosphere

07854-13145

The Atmosphere in Action

Unit 2, Side 1

Heat radiating outward; artwork

38661

Gas composition of atmosphere; artwork

38663

Use Lab 39 from the **Lab Manual** as you teach this lesson.

Visual Learning

Figure 14-4 After students have studied the diagram, have them try finding radio stations between certain frequencies on the AM radio band. Try during daylight hours and again at night. Keep a record of the station identification letters; their frequencies, such as 700 on the radio dial; the times the station could be heard; and the location of the station. Also date the information. LEP IS

USING TECHNOLOGY

The first weather satellite, Tiros I, was launched April 1960. Since that time, satellite information has been used to make short-term precipitation forecasts and to issue hurricane warnings.

Think Critically

Polar orbiting satellites monitor the entire world, while each geostationary satellite gives photos of about half of Earth. The areas around the equator can be seen well in the geostationary photos, but away from the equator, details of Earth are less well defined. The areas around the poles are almost impossible to see in detail.

Demonstration

Display a mercury or aneroid barometer in the classroom. Let students observe the barometer each day and observe pressure differences. Discuss what would happen to the barometer if it were placed on a different floor of the school.

Enrichment

Have students write brief reports explaining how an aneroid barometer called an *altimeter* is used to determine an airplane's altitude. L2 P

3 Assess

Check for Understanding

Have students explain why air exerts pressure. Students should respond that atoms and molecules in the atmosphere are pushed together because of the mass of the air above them. Because the molecules become more densely packed, they collide more often. These collisions cause air to exert pressure.

USING TECHNOLOGY

Weather Satellites

Weather forecasters rely on information collected by a variety of instruments, including weather satellites. Weather satellites measure visible and invisible radiation in the atmosphere. As satellites orbit, thrusters turn them to point cameras and take photos of Earth's surface. At night, satellites use heat radiation to produce images. Photos are stored on tape and transmitted by FM radio frequencies to a receiving station. High-speed computers assemble the information and make maps showing cloud cover. Weather forecasters use satellite pictures of clouds in forecasting.

There are two types of weather satellites. One type, the *geostationary satellite*, orbits Earth above the equator at speeds to position the satellite over the same spot on Earth. The satellite gives images of about half of Earth. A photo taken by a geostationary satellite can be seen below. The *polar-orbiting satellite* orbits from pole to pole and views the entire Earth twice each 24 hours. Polar orbiting satellites orbit closer to Earth and take more-detailed photos.

Think Critically: Look at the geostationary satellite, then explain why we need polar-orbiting satellites to take photos of Earth.

A Weather Satellite

Atmospheric Pressure

Gases in the atmosphere, like all matter, have mass and a gravitational attraction to other matter. The gravitational attraction between Earth and molecules of gas causes atmospheric gases to be pulled toward Earth. Yet atmospheric gases extend upward hundreds of kilometers. The weight of the gases at the top of the atmosphere presses down on the air below, compressing the molecules and increasing the density of the air. Close to Earth, air is more dense. This dense air exerts more force than the less-dense air at the top of the atmosphere. Force exerted on an area is known as pressure.

Where do you think air pressure is greater—in the exosphere at the top of the atmosphere or in the troposphere near Earth's surface? Air pressure is greater nearer Earth. At sea level on Earth's surface, there are more

Cultural Diversity

The Real Mountain People When people who live at lower altitudes visit high altitudes, they may experience shortness of breath, dizziness, headache, nausea, and difficulty in sleeping. These difficulties result from hypoxia, or lowered oxygen pressure. But some people live at high altitudes all the time. Studies show that the Quechua people, living at 3500 to 5000 meters in the Andes Mountains of Peru, respond to oxygen stress in a variety of ways. They have more red blood cells to carry oxygen. This makes their blood thicker; their hearts work harder. Their barrel-shaped chests may allow for larger lungs. Recent studies have shown the Quechua also have greater metabolic efficiency—they get more oxygen to their muscles. The Quechua prefer carbohydrates, a more efficient fuel, to fats in their diet.

molecules pushing down from above, as shown in **Figure 14-5.** In general, atmospheric pressure is greatest near Earth's surface and decreases as you move upward away from sea level. That means air pressure decreases as you go up in the mountains. That is why some people find it harder to breathe in high mountains. There are fewer molecules and consequently less air pressure.

Temperatures in the Atmosphere

You don't have to climb a mountain to find lower air pressure. Anywhere on Earth where the atmosphere is heated, air molecules move with greater energy. In heated air, fewer molecules occupy a cubic centimeter of space. The heated air becomes less dense and exerts a lower pressure. Colder air has a higher density of molecules and exerts a higher pressure. These areas of high and low pressure are often marked on weather maps because they affect our weather. Tracking the movement of these high and low pressure areas helps meteorologists forecast the weather.

Temperatures play another part in Earth's atmosphere. The atmosphere is divided into layers based on temperature differences. Earth's atmospheric gases are heated by absorbing energy from the sun. In the troposphere near Earth's surface, temperatures decrease with an increase in altitude. Just above

MiniLAB

Does air have mass?

Procedure

1. On a pan balance, determine the mass of an inflatable ball that is completely deflated.
2. Hypothesize about the change in the mass of the ball when it goes from being deflated to inflated.
3. Inflate the ball to its maximum recommended inflation pressure.
4. Determine the mass of the fully inflated ball.

Analysis

1. What change occurs in the mass of the ball from deflation to inflation?
2. Infer from your data whether air has mass.

Figure 14-5

Air exerts pressure. The air at the bottom of the atmosphere is more dense and exerts more pressure than that at the top. Pressure is shown in millibars; altitude in meters. Note that Denver at a higher altitude experiences less air pressure than San Diego.

Cultural Diversity *(con't.)*

Although most research has been conducted on Quechua living at high altitudes, scientists have also studied some Quechua living at lower altitudes. This allows scientists to see whether the adaptations are temporary or genetically caused. So far, evidence indicates that a genetic change has occurred. One of the scientists involved, Dr. Peter Hochachka, plans to do similar research with the Sherpas, who live in Tibet at around 4700 meters. He wants to see whether their adaptations are similar to or different from the Quechua, and whether they are temporary or genetic.

MiniLAB

Purpose

LS **Visual-Spatial** Students will observe that air has mass. L1

Materials

inflatable balls like footballs, basketballs, or volleyballs; air pump with a ball inflation needle; pressure gauge, pan balances

Analysis

1. The mass increases.
2. Air has mass.

Assessment

Performance To further assess students' understanding that air has mass, have them make a balance using a piece of string, a metric ruler, and tape. Tape a balloon filled with air to one end of the ruler. Balance it with a piece of clay at the other end. Have students change the amount of air in their balloons and observe what happens to the balance. Use the Performance Task Assessment List for Carrying Out a Strategy and Collecting Data in **PASC**, p. 25. P

Activity Worksheets, pp. 5, 88

Reteach

LS **Kinesthetic** Show that air exerts pressure by obtaining a jar large enough to fit a hand into it and a plastic bag to fit over the rim of the jar. Firmly secure the plastic bag to the rim of the jar. Have a student make a fist and gently push the plastic bag into the jar. Air in the jar will resist the student's attempts to push on the bag.

Extension

For students who have mastered this section, use the **Reinforcement** and **Enrichment** masters.

4 Close

• MINI • QUIZ •

1. **The layer of air between the stratosphere and the thermosphere is the _______ .** *mesosphere*
2. **The layer of the atmosphere closest to Earth's surface is the _______ .** *troposphere*
3. **The ozone layer is located in the _______ .** *stratosphere*
4. **Beyond Earth's exosphere is _______ .** *space*

Section Wrap-up

Review

1. The temperature is dependent on the amount of energy absorbed by the particles within each layer of the atmosphere. Because the layers contain different proportions of compounds, radiation absorbed varies.
2. It is caused by the weight of molecules in the atmosphere pushing down on the air below.
3. **Think Critically** The pressure exerted at the bottom of the pile would be the greatest. It resembles the pressure exerted near Earth's surface. Moving upward in the pile of players is similar to moving to higher levels of the atmosphere; the pressure exerted decreases.

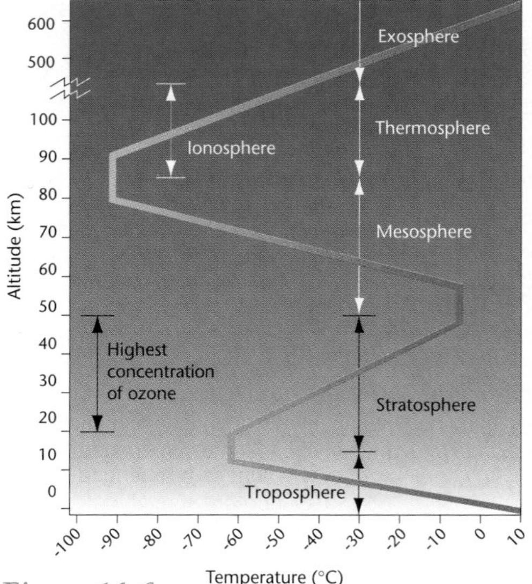

Figure 14-6

The division of the atmosphere into layers is based primarily on temperature variations.

it in the stratosphere, molecules of ozone absorb the sun's ultraviolet radiation, heating that layer. While some layers contain gases that easily absorb the sun's energy, other layers do not. As a consequence, the various layers contain different amounts of thermal energy. Notice in **Figure 14-6** how the temperature of the atmosphere fluctuates in different layers. Which layer is the coldest? Which layer is the warmest?

Understanding Our Atmosphere

Weather occurs in Earth's atmosphere. The sun heating Earth's atmosphere sets up uneven heating and activates a system of winds that moves energy from one area of Earth to another. Understanding the composition and structure of Earth's atmosphere helps us to forecast weather and to comprehend changes we are making to the atmosphere. In the next section, you will read how human activities may be affecting Earth's atmosphere.

Section Wrap-up

Review

1. Explain why the temperature of the atmosphere does not increase or decrease steadily as you move from Earth's surface toward space.
2. What causes air pressure?
3. **Think Critically:** Imagine you're a football player running with the ball. Six players tackle you and pile on top—one on top of the other. Relate the pressure that you and each player above you feels to the pressure in the layers of the atmosphere.

Skill Builder

Making and Using Graphs

Use Figure 14-1 to answer the following questions. If you need help, refer to Making and Using Graphs in the **Skill Handbook.**

1. What is the most abundant gas in Earth's atmosphere?
2. What percentage of the total volume do nitrogen and oxygen together represent? Argon and carbon dioxide?

Science Journal

The names of the atmospheric layers end with the suffix *sphere.* In these names, sphere means layer. Use a dictionary to find out what *meso-*, *thermo-*, and *exo-* mean. In your Science Journal, write the meaning of these prefixes and explain why the layers are appropriately or inappropriately named.

Science Journal

LS Linguistic *Meso-* means "in the middle," *thermo-* means "heat," and *exo-* means "outside." *Mesosphere* and *exosphere* accurately describe the relative positions of the layers. *Thermosphere* describes a layer hotter than the others.

Skill Builder

1. nitrogen
2. 99 percent; 0.96 percent

Assessment

Content Have students depict the information shown in **Figure 14-1** in a different kind of graph. For example, they might draw a bar graph or a pictograph of a glass of air, showing how much of the air inside is nitrogen, oxygen, etc. Use the Performance Task Assessment List for Graph from Data in **PASC,** p. 39. P

Activity 14-1

Making a Barometer

If you have flown in an airplane or zoomed to the top of a building in an elevator, you have experienced pressure inside your ears. When you rapidly increased your altitude, air pressure outside your eardrums became lower than the pressure inside your eardrums. The air inside your ears pushed against your eardrums. In this activity, you'll see that a barometer reacts as your eardrums did when exposed to differences in pressure.

Problem

How does a barometer react to a change in air pressure?

Materials

- small coffee can
- drinking straw
- large rubber balloon
- construction paper
- transparent tape
- scissors
- rubber band

Procedure

1. Using tape, attach a piece of construction paper to the side of the coffee can as shown in the photo.
2. Cut the balloon, and stretch it tightly over the can. Secure it in place with the rubber band.
3. Trim one end of the straw to a point. Tape the other end of the straw to the balloon and point the trimmed end toward the paper.
4. Make a horizontal mark on the paper where the pointed end of the straw touches. Write *high* above this mark and *low* below it.
5. Design a data table to record your observations. Record the movement of the straw for a period of a week. Also record the weather conditions each day. Plot the movement of the straw on a graph.

Analyze

1. **Explain** how your barometer works. **Describe** any problems with accuracy.
2. What type of barometric readings would you expect if you took your barometer to the top of a mountain? What if you took it to the mesosphere?

Conclude and Apply

3. **Analyze** your data to see what type of weather was associated with the pressures you recorded.
4. **Conclude** from your activity how a weather forecaster can use barometric pressure to help predict weather.

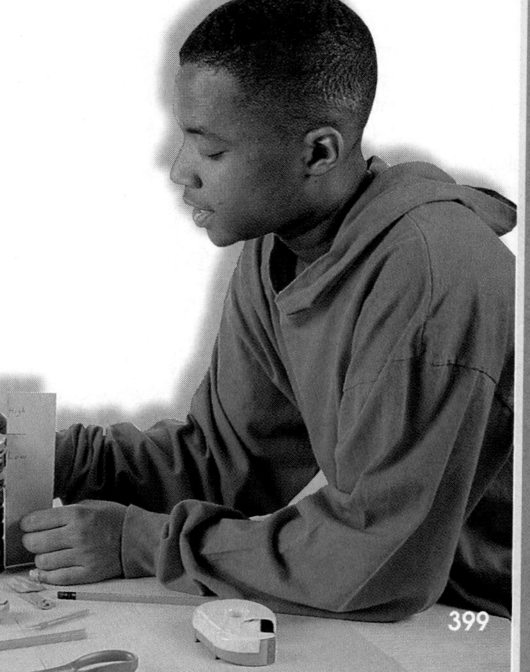

2. Pressure reading would be lower at the top of the mountain and even lower in the mesosphere.
3. Fair weather is associated with high pressure and stormy weather with low pressure.
4. Changes in air pressure indicate changes in approaching weather.

Assessment

Performance To further assess students' abilities, have them make a barometer from a baby food jar, balloon, toothpick, and rubber band and place it inside a glass jar. Secure a balloon on top of the jar. Press down or pull up the balloon on the large jar to change the pressure inside. That moves the toothpick. Use the Performance Task Assessment List for Carrying Out a Strategy and Collecting Data in **PASC**, p. 25. P

Activity 14-1

Purpose

LS **Intrapersonal** Each student will construct a modified aneroid barometer, observe how it reacts to changes in air pressure, and learn how a barometer is used to make weather predictions. L1

Process Skills

making models, observing and inferring, making and using tables, comparing and contrasting, recognizing cause and effect, interpreting data, using numbers, making graphs

Time

- 45 minutes to make the barometer
- 5 minutes each day for 7 days to observe and record observations

Activity Worksheets, pp. 5, 84-85

Teaching Strategies

Troubleshooting Remind students that once the coffee can is sealed, it should not be reopened. If the barometer is constructed during periods of extreme high or low pressures, the indicator (straw) may not move up (if constructed under high pressure), or down (if made under low pressure).

- If possible, have students compare their data with a barometer in the classroom.
- You may want to obtain a barograph for classroom use. A barograph is a barometer that is designed to record daily atmospheric pressure continuously.

Answers to Questions

1. Air presses down on the balloon stretched across the can. High air pressure depresses the balloon; the straw points toward *high.* When air pressure is low, less pressure is applied; the straw points toward *low.* See Troubleshooting.

Prepare

Section Background

NASA has collected data indicating that the thinning of the ozone layer is largely due to production of chlorofluorocarbons.

1 Motivate

Bellringer

Before presenting the lesson, display **Section Focus Transparency 54** on the overhead projector. Assign the accompanying **Focus Activity** worksheet. L1 LEP

2 Teach

Teacher F.Y.I.

Scientists estimate that with environmental changes, it will take approximately 50 years to reduce the ozone hole significantly. In **Figure 14-7**, the pink color indicates how the ozone hole has grown progressively bigger. Although there was a slight reduction in the size of the ozone hole in 1994, the hole grew at an unprecedented rate in 1995.

INTEGRATION Chemistry

A chlorofluorocarbon molecule has one carbon, one fluorine, and three chlorine atoms. Ask, "If each chlorine atom can destroy 100 000 ozone atoms, how many ozone molecules can one chlorofluorocarbon molecule destroy?"

TECHNOLOGY: 14•2 The Ozone Layer

Science Words

ozone layer
ultraviolet radiation
chlorofluorocarbons

Objectives

- Explain why exposure to ultraviolet radiation can be a problem for plants and animals.
- Describe how chlorofluorocarbons destroy ozone molecules.

Is the ozone layer in danger?

About 20 kilometers above your head lies the ozone layer. The **ozone layer** is an atmospheric layer with a high concentration of ozone. This layer, located in the stratosphere, is out of reach and unobservable, yet your life depends on it. The ozone layer shields you from harmful energy from the sun.

Ozone is a form of oxygen. The oxygen we breathe has two atoms per molecule. An ozone molecule, however, binds three oxygen atoms together. The layer of ozone molecules absorbs most of the ultraviolet radiation that enters the atmosphere. **Ultraviolet radiation** is one of the many types of energy that comes to Earth from the sun. Too much exposure to ultraviolet radiation can damage the skin. Ultraviolet radiation can cause cancer and other health problems in many types of plants and animals.

Each year, more than 800 000 Americans develop skin cancer, and more than 9000 die from it. If the ozone layer disappeared, cancer rates would shoot upward. **Figure 14-7** shows that the ozone layer is thinning and developing holes. In 1986, scientists found areas in the stratosphere where almost

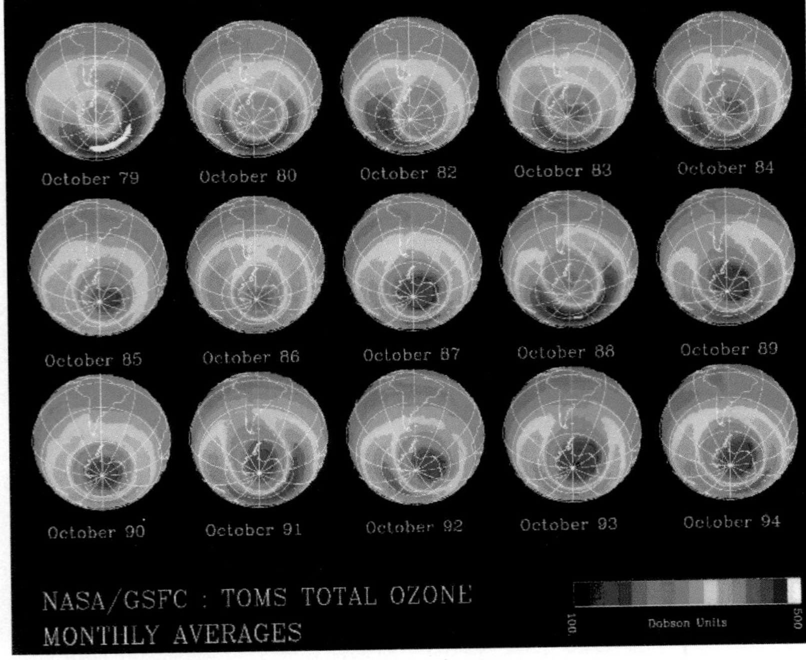

Figure 14-7
Every October, the ozone layer over Antarctica thins out by almost 50 percent. Not only does this hole appear, but the entire ozone layer has also become thinner around the world.

Program Resources

Reproducible Masters
Study Guide, p. 58 L1
Reinforcement, p. 58 L1
Enrichment, p. 58 L3
Cross-Curricular Integration, p. 18
Science and Society Integration, p. 11
Activity Worksheets, p. 5 L1
Critical Thinking/Problem Solving, p. 20
Technology Integration, pp. 13-14

Transparencies
Section Focus Transparency 54
Teaching Transparency 28

no ozone existed. One very large hole opened over Antarctica. A smaller hole was discovered over the North Pole. Since that time, every year, these holes appear during certain seasons and disappear during others. Not only is the ozone layer missing over the poles, but the entire ozone layer has also become thinner around the world.

Theory About Ozone Disappearance

Some scientists hypothesize that pollutants in the environment are destroying the ozone layer. Blame has fallen on **chlorofluorocarbons** (CFCs), a group of chemical compounds used in refrigerators, aerosol sprays, and foam packaging. When these products are manufactured and used, CFCs enter the atmosphere. Recently, governments have restricted the production and use of CFCs.

Figure 14-8 illustrates how chlorofluorocarbon molecules destroy ozone. Recall that an ozone molecule is composed of three oxygen atoms bonded together. When a chlorine atom from a chlorofluorocarbon molecule comes near a molecule of ozone, the ozone molecule breaks apart. It forms a regular two-atom molecule (O_2). This oxygen can't absorb ultraviolet radiation. The result is that more ultraviolet radiation reaches Earth's surface.

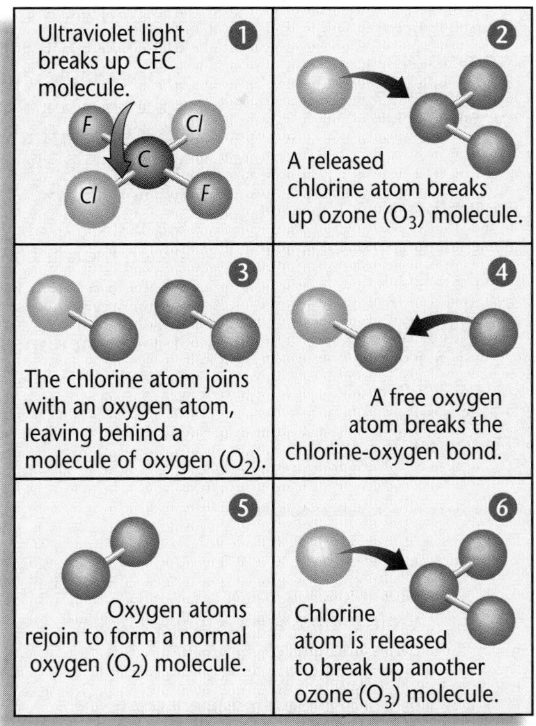

Figure 14-8

One atom of chlorine can destroy 100 000 ozone molecules. Each chlorofluorocarbon molecule has three chlorine atoms.

Section Wrap-up

1. Why do people other than those living near the poles need to be concerned about the ozone layer?
2. Describe how CFCs destroy ozone molecules.

Explore the Technology

In 1990, nations from around the world met in Montreal, Canada. They agreed to phase out the majority of chemicals that cause ozone depletion by the year 2000. Explain why it was important for all the nations to come to agreement.

SCIENCE & SOCIETY

Explore the Technology

A unanimous decision to phase out these chemicals was necessary to stop further damage to the ozone layer.

3 Assess

Check for Understanding

FLEX Your Brain

Use the Flex Your Brain activity to have students explore OZONE DEPLETION.

Activity Worksheets, p. 5

Reteach

LS **Interpersonal** Have student groups write skits about how the depletion of the ozone layer might affect different "wild things." The wild things, living or nonliving, could discuss the changes that they are experiencing and their concerns for the future. Make costumes and perform the skits for the class. Insist on scientific accuracy.

Extension

For students who have mastered this section, use the **Reinforcement** and **Enrichment** masters.

4 Close

Section Wrap-up

Review

1. The most dramatic depletion of the ozone layer is found near the poles, but the layer is thinning around the world.
2. When a chlorine atom breaks loose from a chlorofluorocarbon molecule and comes near an ozone molecule, the chlorine atom joins with one of the oxygen atoms, leaving behind an oxygen molecule. The ozone molecule is destroyed.

Section 14•3

Prepare

Section Background

- Transfer of energy by radiation does not involve matter.
- Convection currents distribute energy until equilibrium is reached. On Earth, however, equilibrium is never attained. The tropics always receive more radiant energy than the rest of Earth. Therefore, energy transfer is always occurring in the atmosphere.

Preplanning

To prepare for Activity 14-2, obtain the materials listed on page 408.

1 Motivate

Bellringer

Before presenting the lesson, display **Section Focus Transparency 55** on the overhead projector. Assign the accompanying **Focus Activity** worksheet. L1 LEP

Tying to Previous Knowledge

Students learned in Chapter 2 that matter is made of atoms and molecules. Energy transfer via conduction and convection involves movements of atoms and molecules.

NATIONAL GEOGRAPHIC SOCIETY

Videodisc

STV: Atmosphere

The Atmosphere in Action

Unit 2, Side 1

Weight and Pressure

26634-29260

14•3 Energy from the Sun

Science Words

radiation
conduction
convection
hydrosphere
water cycle

Objectives

- Describe three things that happen to the energy Earth receives from the sun.
- Contrast radiation, conduction, and convection.
- Describe the water cycle.

Energy Transfer in the Atmosphere

In the future scenario, you return from work. You eat dinner and read the evening news transmitted on the computer network. You see that the Space Agency is still trying to create a hospitable atmosphere on Mars. It's studying the atmospheres of Earth and Venus to understand how they work and how an Earthlike atmosphere might be produced on Mars or Venus. The atmospheres of Earth and its neighboring planets of Venus and Mars are depicted in **Figure 14-9.** The atmosphere on Mars is currently too thin to support life or to hold much thermal energy from the sun. As a result, Mars is a cold, lifeless world. On the other hand, Venus's atmosphere is so dense that almost no thermal energy coming in from the sun

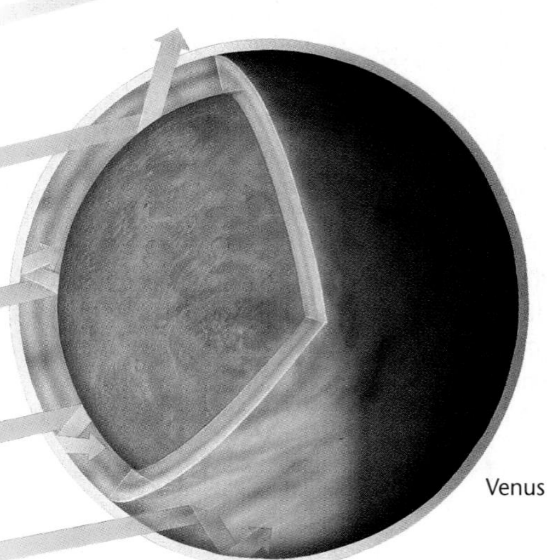

Figure 14-9
Most radiation entering Venus's atmosphere is trapped by thick gases and clouds. On Mars, a thin atmosphere allows much radiation to escape. Earth's atmosphere creates a delicate balance between energy received and energy lost.

Program Resources

Reproducible Masters

Study Guide, p. 59 L1
Reinforcement, p. 59 L1
Enrichment, p. 59 L3
Activity Worksheets, pp. 5, 86-87 L1
Multicultural Connections, pp. 31-32

Transparencies

Section Focus Transparency 55 L1

can escape. Venus is so hot that a living thing would instantly burn if it were put on Venus's surface.

In our solar system, there are nine planets circling the star we call the sun. Earth supports life, but the nearby planets, Mars and Venus, do not support life. How does the interaction between Earth's atmosphere and the sun provide an environment suitable for life?

The sun is the source of all energy in our atmosphere. When Earth receives energy from the sun, three different things happen to that energy. Some energy is reflected back into space, some is absorbed by the atmosphere, and some is absorbed by land and water surfaces. The balance among these three events controls the characteristics of our atmosphere and the life that it supports. Let's take a look at what happens to the energy that reaches Earth.

Radiation

Energy from the sun reaches our planet in the form of radiant energy, or radiation. **Radiation** is the transfer of energy by electromagnetic waves. Radiation from the sun travels through empty space as well as through our atmosphere. You experience radiation as light and heat. When the sun warms your face or when you sit by a fire and it warms the side of your body facing it, you experience radiant energy. You aren't in direct contact with the sun or the fire, but the energy still reaches you.

Mars

When radiation from the fire reaches you, the molecules of your skin absorb the energy and you feel heat. Heat is energy that flows from an object with a higher temperature to an object with a lower temperature. Once objects at Earth's surface, such as asphalt roads, rocks, houses, or ocean water, absorb radiation, they heat up. These heated surfaces then radiate energy, but the radiation they give off is at a longer wavelength than the energy coming from the sun. Much of the radiation coming from the sun can pass through the atmosphere, whereas most radiation coming from Earth's surface is absorbed and heats up our atmosphere.

The ozone layer absorbs ultraviolet radiation. When ozone and other gases absorb radiation, the temperature of the atmosphere rises, as you saw in **Figure 14-6** on page 398.

On Venus, even less radiation is able to escape back to space, making Venus hotter than Earth. On Earth, there is a delicate balance between energy received from the sun and energy escaping back to space. In the future weather forecast at the beginning of this chapter, high temperatures were forecast. This may be because smog and other pollutants in the

USING MATH

Most weather activity occurs in the airspace between the ground and an altitude of 11 km. Suppose the temperature in this airspace drops about 7°C for each kilometer of increase in altitude. If the ground temperature is 15°C, what is the temperature at an altitude of 3 km?

2 Teach

Discussion

Stress that the sun is the source of almost all energy on Earth. Some energy is generated by the radioactive decay of atoms contained in Earth's rocks and magma.

Revealing Preconceptions

- Ask students: **What is heat?** *Heat is the transfer of energy from an object with a higher temperature to an object with a lower temperature.* Then ask, **What is cold?** *Cold is the absence of heat.*
- Make sure students use the terms *heat* and *energy* correctly. Heat is a form of energy. The terms are often incorrectly interchanged—they are not synonymous.

USING MATH

–6°C LS

NATIONAL GEOGRAPHIC SOCIETY

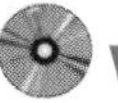

Videodisc

GTV: Planetary Manager

Atmosphere

47761

47762

47763

47764

47765

Theme Connection

Energy Ask students: **What happens to the energy Earth receives from the sun?** *Some escapes back into space; some is absorbed by the atmosphere; and some is absorbed by land and water surfaces.*

FLEX Your Brain

Use the Flex Your Brain activity to have students explore THE GREENHOUSE EFFECT IN THE ATMOSPHERE OF VENUS. P

Activity Worksheets, p. 5

Activity

LS **Visual-Spatial** Have students chart the movement of air within the classroom. Carefully light the end of a wax taper or piece of string and have students observe the smoke patterns created. The class must be very still to prevent the movement of bodies from disrupting the air flow. Then have students make a diagram of the room and include the pattern of air flow within the room. The diagram should help them identify what causes the air movement patterns. L1 LEP

GLENCOE TECHNOLOGY

Videodisc

The Infinite Voyage: Crisis in the Atmosphere

Chapter 8

Energy Conservation as a Means to Reduce Carbon Dioxide Levels

Chapter 9

Energy Conservation: Changes in Switzerland

Chapter 11

Worldwide Energy Conservation Solutions

Figure 14-10

Pollution can change the energy balance in our atmosphere. Some types of pollution prevent radiation from escaping back into space, possibly causing Earth's temperature to rise.

atmosphere are preventing radiation from returning to space. **Figure 14-10** shows air pollution that can upset the balance of incoming and outgoing radiation on Earth.

Some radiation from the sun isn't absorbed by Earth's atmosphere or surface objects. Instead, it simply reflects off the atmosphere and surface, like a ball bouncing off a wall. **Figure 14-11** illustrates the percentages of radiation absorbed and reflected by Earth's surface and atmosphere.

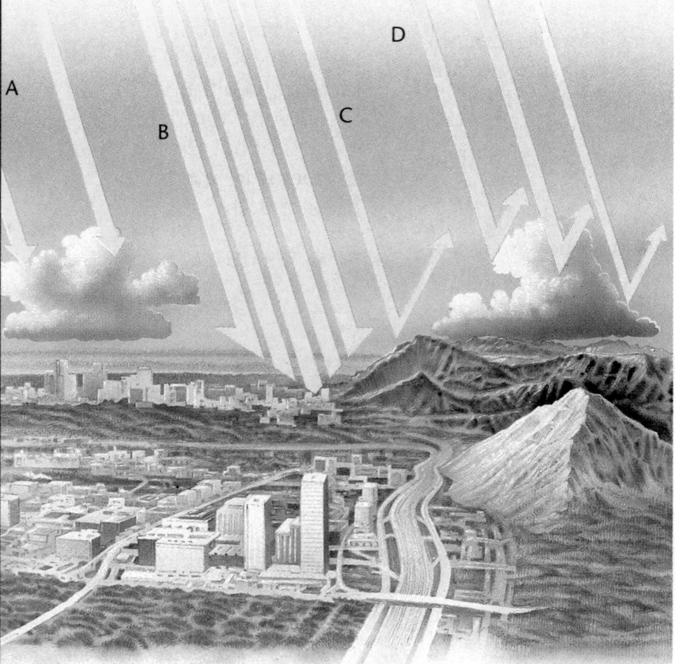

Figure 14-11

The sun is the source of energy in our atmosphere. Thirty percent of incoming solar radiation is reflected back into space.
(A) Clouds and atmosphere absorb 20%
(B) Earth's surface absorbs 50%
(C) Surface reflects 5%
(D) Clouds and atmosphere reflect 25%

Conduction

If you walk barefoot on hot asphalt, your feet heat up because of conduction. Radiation from the sun heated the asphalt, but direct contact with the asphalt heated your feet. In a similar way, Earth's surface transfers energy directly to the atmosphere. As air moves over warm land or water, air molecules are heated by direct contact. A warm layer of molecules on Earth's surface comes in direct contact with a layer of air molecules and transfers energy.

Visual Learning

Figure 14-9 Ask students: **How much incoming radiation is reflected back into space?** *30%* **How much is absorbed by the atmosphere?** *20%* **How much is absorbed by Earth's surface?** *50%* LEP LS

Conduction is the transfer of energy that occurs when molecules bump into one another. Molecules are always in motion, but molecules in hotter objects move more rapidly than those in cooler objects. When substances are in contact, energy is transferred from energized, fast-moving molecules to lower-energy molecules until all molecules are moving at about the same rate. **Figure 14-12** illustrates how the processes of heat transfer affect the atmosphere.

CONNECT TO

PHYSICS

I*nfer* which of the following would transfer heat by conduction the best: solids, liquids, or gases.

Convection

After the atmosphere is warmed by radiation or conduction, the heat is transferred throughout the atmosphere by a third process, convection. **Convection** is the transfer of heat by the flow of a heated material. Convection occurs in gases and liquids. Let's see how this works with air.

When air is warmed, the molecules move apart. This increases the volume of the air, which in turn reduces its density. With lower density, there is less air pressure because there are fewer molecules pressing in on each other. Cold temperatures affect the air density in just the opposite way. In cold air, molecules move closer together. Density and air pressure increase. Because cold air has a higher density, it sinks. As the cold air falls toward Earth, it pushes up less-dense, warm air. A circular movement of air, called a convection current, results.

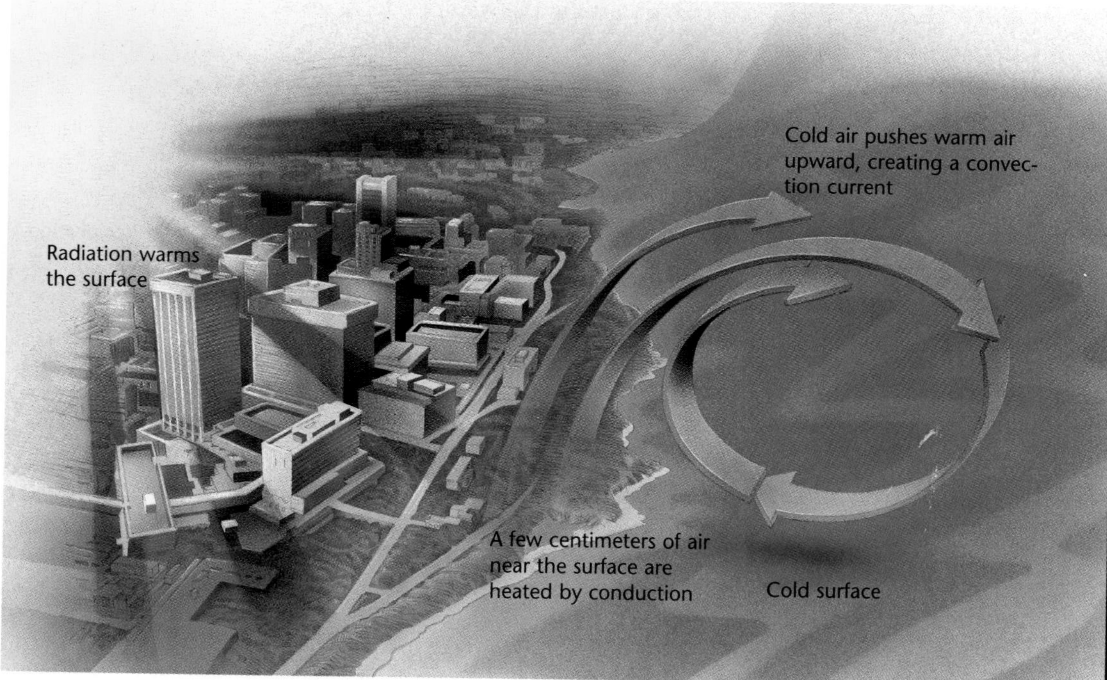

Figure 14-12

Heat is transferred within Earth's atmosphere by radiation, conduction, and convection.

CONNECT TO

PHYSICS

Answer Solids transfer heat best by conduction because the molecules are tightly packed.

Inquiry Questions

- **Why does a metal spoon get hot if you leave it in a pot on top of a hot burner? Why does the inside of a closed car get hot on a sunny day? Why is an attic very warm in the springtime, while the ground floor is cool?** *Energy is transferred by conduction in the spoon, radiation in the car, and convection in the house.*
- Ask students: **How does the movement of molecules in warm objects compare with the movement of molecules in cooler objects?** *Molecules move more rapidly in warmer objects.*

GLENCOE TECHNOLOGY

Videodisc

The Infinite Voyage: Secrets from a Frozen World

Chapter 8

Effect of UV Radiation on Phytoplankton

Inclusion Strategies

Gifted Have students find out how a car radiator works. Ask them why "radiator" is an appropriate term for this part of a car. L3

Gifted Have students make drawings showing how a convection oven works. L3

NATIONAL GEOGRAPHIC SOCIETY

Videodisc

STV: Atmosphere

The Atmosphere in Action

Unit 2, Side 1

Why Is the Sky Blue?

22295-24793

Content Background

- During evaporation, heat energy causes the water molecules to move apart. The water changes from a liquid to a gas.
- During condensation, water molecules lose energy and move closer together. The water changes from a gas to a liquid.

Revealing Preconceptions

Ask students: **When water evaporates, do the molecules expand?** *Some students will answer "yes." Explain that the molecules do not change size, but rather change to higher energy states and move farther apart.*

Discussion

Worldwide each year on Earth, about 500 000 cubic km of water evaporates. About 110 000 cubic km of this falls as precipitation on land. Ask students what happens to the rest of the water. Students should conclude that most of the rest falls in the ocean. Some of the water that falls on land is absorbed by plants, filters into the soil, fills lakes, or becomes runoff that eventually flows to the ocean.

3 Assess

Check for Understanding

FLEX Your Brain

Use the Flex Your Brain activity to have students explore WATER CYCLE.

Activity Worksheets, p. 5

Reteach

Lead a class discussion about student experiences with radiation, conduction, convection, and the water cycle.

Science Journal

Mars and Venus are similar to Earth in size and structure, but have atmospheres very different from Earth's. In your Science Journal, write a report about how the atmospheres of these three planets differ. Include a discussion of the possibility of creating an Earthlike atmosphere on Mars.

Our Unique Atmosphere

Convection currents and other processes that transfer energy control our environment. As you have seen, radiation from the sun can escape back into space, be absorbed by the atmosphere, or be absorbed by bodies on Earth's surface. Once it's been absorbed, heat can be transferred by radiation, conduction, or convection. Just how much and what radiation is absorbed determines the type of life that can exist on this planet. Other planets in the solar system that are similar to Earth, such as Venus and Mars, don't absorb and lose the same amounts of radiation as Earth. Their atmospheres don't support life as we know it.

The Water Cycle

Another thing that allows our atmosphere to support life is water. All life as we know it needs water. Although most of Earth's water is in the oceans, it is also found in lakes, streams, rivers, groundwater, glaciers, and the atmosphere. All the water that occurs at Earth's surface is the **hydrosphere.** Although there's a lot of water on Earth, at any one time 97 percent is salt water; only three percent is fresh water. Two-thirds of the fresh water is frozen in ice caps at the North and South Poles. Therefore, the percentage of water moving through the atmosphere is low, but it is still very important because water is constantly moving between the atmosphere and Earth in the **water cycle,** as shown in **Figure 14-13.**

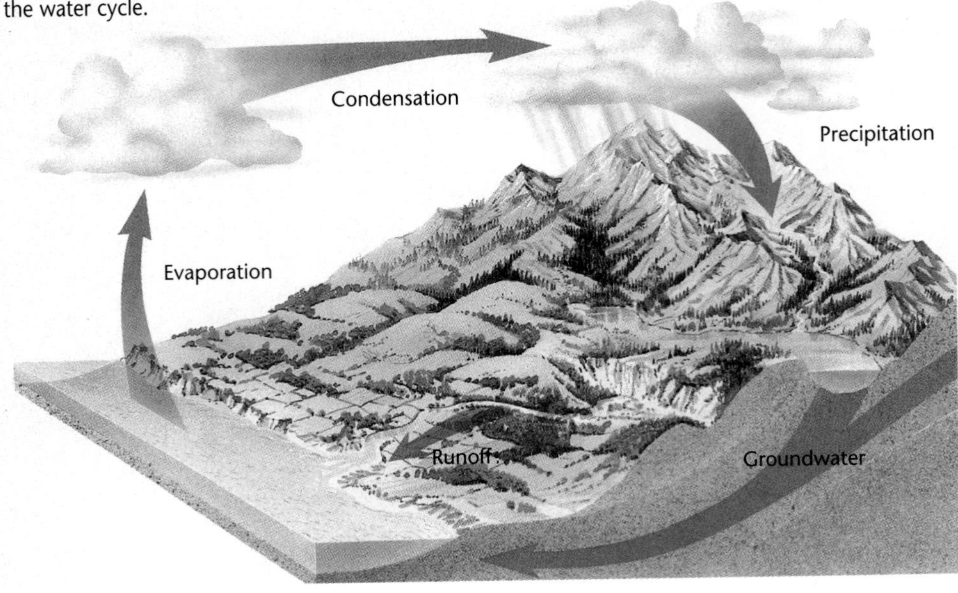

Figure 14-13

Water moves from Earth to the atmosphere and back to Earth again in the water cycle.

Science Journal

Earthlike Atmosphere The dense atmosphere of Venus is 96% carbon dioxide. Mars' atmosphere is also mostly carbon dioxide with a density about 1% of Earth's. If areas of Mars could be heated, some of the ice at the poles might melt. But despite what science fiction might suggest, a water cycle probably would not develop because water vapor would probably drift into space. P L1 LS

The sun provides the energy for the water cycle. Radiation from the sun causes water to change to a gas called water vapor. The process of water changing from a liquid state to a gas is called *evaporation.* Water evaporates from lakes, streams, and oceans and rises into Earth's atmosphere.

In the next step of the water cycle, water vapor rises in the atmosphere and cools. When it cools enough, it changes back into a liquid. This process of water vapor changing to a liquid is called *condensation.* When water vapor condenses, it forms clouds.

The third step in the water cycle is *precipitation.* Clouds are made up of millions of tiny water droplets that collide and form larger drops. When the drops grow so large that they can no longer stay suspended in the clouds, drops of water fall to Earth, and the water cycle continues. The moisture that falls from clouds is called precipitation. The desert in **Figure 14-14** is experiencing precipitation in the form of rain.

As you can see, many factors determine whether a planet will have an atmosphere capable of supporting life. How much energy is transferred to the atmosphere and how much energy escapes Earth's atmosphere is important to life on Earth. Learning about our atmosphere will help us protect it so it can continue to support life.

Figure 14-14

Rain is one form of precipitation. *Name another form.*

Section Wrap-up

Review

1. Pollution may be making our atmosphere more like that of Venus. How can that happen and how might it affect temperatures on Earth?
2. How does the sun transfer energy to Earth, and how does the atmosphere get heated?
3. **Think Critically:** Describe the role of the sun in the water cycle.

Skill Builder
Concept Mapping

Make a cycle concept map that explains what happens to energy that reaches Earth as radiant energy. If you need help, refer to Concept Mapping in the **Skill Handbook.**

USING MATH

Earth is about 150 000 000 km from the sun. The radiation coming from the sun travels at 300 000 km/second. About how long does it take for the radiation from the sun to reach Earth?

Extension

For students who have mastered this section, use the **Reinforcement** and **Enrichment** masters.

4 Close

•MINI•QUIZ•

Use the Mini Quiz to check students' recall of chapter content.

1. **_____ is the transfer of energy by waves.** *Radiation*
2. **_____ is the transfer of energy that occurs when molecules bump into one another.** *Conduction*
3. **_____ is the transfer of energy that occurs because of density differences in the air.** *Convection*

Section Wrap-up

Review

1. Pollution may trap radiated energy within our atmosphere, preventing it from escaping back into space. This may cause Earth's overall average temperature to rise.
2. Sun transfers energy to Earth by radiation. Space contains very little matter, making energy transfer by conduction and convection impossible. The particles of matter in space between the sun and Earth are separated by voids. The atmosphere is heated by convection and conduction.
3. **Think Critically** Radiation from the sun causes evaporation.

Skill Builder

Many solutions are possible. Most concept maps should indicate that radiant energy is absorbed by Earth's surface or atmosphere. Once absorbed, it can be re-released via radiation, conduction, or convection. Thus, energy from the sun that is captured by Earth is continuously cycled through the processes of radiation, conduction, and convection. Maps may also indicate that some energy escapes Earth's atmosphere.

Assessment

Performance Assess students' abilities to make concept maps by having them make a map that shows the water cycle. Use the Performance Task Assessment List for Concept Map in **PASC,** p. 89. P

USING MATH

$$\frac{150\ 000\ 000\ \text{km}}{300\ 000\ \text{km/s}} =$$

500 s or 8.3 minutes LS

Activity 14-2

PREPARATION

Purpose

LS **Interpersonal** Students will observe how water and soil differ in their abilities to absorb and release heat during the day and night. L1

COOP LEARN

Process Skills

communicating, recognizing cause and effect, forming a hypothesis, using numbers, designing an experiment, separating and controlling variables, making and using tables, making and using graphs, comparing and contrasting, interpreting data

Time

- 30 minutes to make and check the plan
- 40 minutes to do the experiment
- 30 minutes to analyze and apply

Materials

Be sure thermometers are calibrated before students use them.

Safety Precautions

Caution students to avoid the overhead light and to keep the electric cord away from the water.

Possible Hypotheses

- Students may hypothesize that soil absorbs and releases heat faster than water.
- Students may hypothesize that the temperature of the air above the soil will be warmer during the day than the temperature of the air above the water, while at night the temperature of the air above the water will be warmer than the temperature of the air above the soil.

Activity Worksheets, pp. 5, 86-87

Activity 14-2

Design Your Own Experiment

The Heat Is On

Have you ever noticed how cool and refreshing a plunge in a pool or lake is on a hot summer day? Did you ever wonder why the land gets so hot when the water remains cool? At night the water feels warmer than the land. Let's explore how water and land absorb heat.

PREPARATION

Problem

Use soil and water to determine whether land and water absorb and release heat at different rates.

Form a Hypothesis

Form a hypothesis about how soil and water compare in their abilities to absorb and release heat. Write another hypothesis about how air temperatures above soil and above water differ during the day and night.

Objectives

- Design and carry out an experiment to compare the rates of heat absorption and of heat release of both soil and water.
- Observe how these differing rates of heat absorption and release affect the air above soil and above water.

Possible Materials

- ring stand
- soil
- metric ruler
- clear plastic boxes (2)
- overhead light with reflector
- thermometers (4)
- water
- masking tape
- colored pencils (4)

Safety Precautions

Be careful when handling the hot overhead light. Do not let the light or its cord make contact with water.

Inclusion Strategies

Visually Impaired Place students who have difficulty reading temperatures and recording results in charge of formulating and evaluating the hypotheses.

PLAN THE EXPERIMENT

1. As a group, agree upon and write out your hypotheses.
2. As a group, list the steps that you need to take to test your hypotheses. Include in your plan how you will use your equipment to (a) compare the rates of heat absorption of water and soil. Include in your measurements the temperatures of the air above the soil and the water, and (b) compare the rate of release of heat by water and soil. Include in your measurements the temperatures of the air above both substances. Do each test for 14 minutes.
3. Design a data table in your Science Journal for both parts of your experiment—when the light is on and energy can be absorbed and when the light is off and energy is released.

Check the Plan

1. Read over your entire plan to make sure that all steps are in a logical order.
2. Identify any constants and the variables of the experiment.
3. *Before you proceed, make sure your teacher approves your plan.*

DO THE EXPERIMENT

1. Carry out the experiment as planned.
2. During the experiment, record your observations and complete the data tables in your Science Journal.

Analyze and Apply

1. Use your colored pencils and the information in your data tables to make line graphs. Show the rate of energy absorption and energy release for both soil and water. (If you need help in making line graphs, refer to making and using graphs in the **Skill Handbook**.)
2. **Analyze** your graphs. When the light was on, which heated up faster, the soil or the water?
3. **Compare** how fast the air heated up over the water with how fast the air heated up over land.
4. **Infer** from your graphs which lost heat faster, the water or the soil.
5. **Compare** the temperatures of the air above the water and above the soil after the light was turned off.
6. Were your hypotheses supported or not? Explain.

Go Further

On a hot summer day at the beach, a cool breeze blows inland from the ocean. At night a cool breeze blows off the land toward the ocean. Based on what you have learned in your experiment, can you explain why the direction of the breeze changes?

Go Further

During the day, air over water is cooler and denser than air over land. It pushes warm air aloft, resulting in cool breezes that blow toward the land. At night, air over the land is cooler and denser than air over the ocean. The dense air pushes the warm air aloft, resulting in cool breezes that blow toward the ocean. Students will learn about land and sea breezes on pp. 414 and 415.

Assessment

Oral Have students explain why in the summer a swimming pool feels cool in the daytime and warm at night. Use the Performance Task Assessment List for Making Observations and Inferences in **PASC**, p. 17. P

PLAN THE EXPERIMENT

Possible Procedures

Tape one thermometer inside one box so that the bulb is 2 cm from the bottom and tape another thermometer so that it is 8 cm from the bottom. Fill one box with 5 cm of water and the other box with 5 cm soil. Attach the light to the ring stand so it is suspended above the boxes. Students should record the temperature of all thermometers before turning on the light. After the light is turned on, they should record the temperature every minute for 14 minutes. When the light is turned off, they should record the temperature for 14 additional minutes.

Teaching Strategies

Troubleshooting Have students graph the data for each thermometer with a different colored pencil.

DO THE EXPERIMENT

Expected Outcome

When the light is on, the soil heats up faster than the water. The air above the soil also heats up faster than the air above the water. When the light is turned off, soil loses heat faster to the air above it than the water does.

Analyze and Apply

1. Graphs should support the hypotheses.
2. soil
3. Air above soil heated faster.
4. soil
5. When the light was turned off, the temperature above the soil was higher. After 8 minutes, the temperature above the water was higher.
6. Results will vary.

Section 14•4

Prepare

Section Background

- The easterlies are relatively steady winds. Westerlies are more complex because their flow is impeded by mountains and valleys. Friction between land and air creates local eddies that slow wind movement.
- Land and sea breezes occur because the specific heat of water is much higher than that of land. This means it takes more energy to raise the temperature of water one degree than to raise the temperature of soil the same amount. Also, water loses heat to the atmosphere more slowly than land.

Preplanning

To prepare for the MiniLAB, obtain glass beakers, ice cubes, and food coloring.

1 Motivate

Bellringer

Before presenting the lesson, display **Section Focus Transparency 56** on the overhead projector. Assign the accompanying **Focus Activity** worksheet. L1 LEP

GLENCOE TECHNOLOGY

Videodisc

STVS: Earth and Space

Disc 3, Side 1

Wind Engineering (Ch. 21)

14•4 Movement of Air

Science Words

Coriolis effect
jet stream
sea breeze
land breeze

Objectives

- Explain why different latitudes receive different amounts of solar energy.
- Explain the Coriolis effect, sea breezes, and land breezes.
- Locate the doldrums, trade winds, prevailing westerlies, polar easterlies, and jet streams.

Wind Formation

Have you ever watched a tree swaying in the breeze and wondered where wind comes from? Wind is caused by the uneven heating of Earth and its atmosphere. This uneven heating causes temperature differences that create areas of pressure differences in the atmosphere. Air moving from areas of high pressure to areas of lower pressure creates a general circulation of air around Earth. Wind is the movement of air from an area of high pressure to an area of lower pressure.

Temperature differences at Earth's surface are caused by Earth's tilt in its orbit around the sun and by Earth's curved surface. Areas of the Earth receive different amounts of solar radiation. **Figure 14-15** illustrates why more radiation is received at the equator than at other latitudes. Air above the equator is heated more than at any other place on Earth. As you know, heated air has a low density, so it is pushed upward by denser, cold air. **Figure 14-16** shows this general pattern of air circulation.

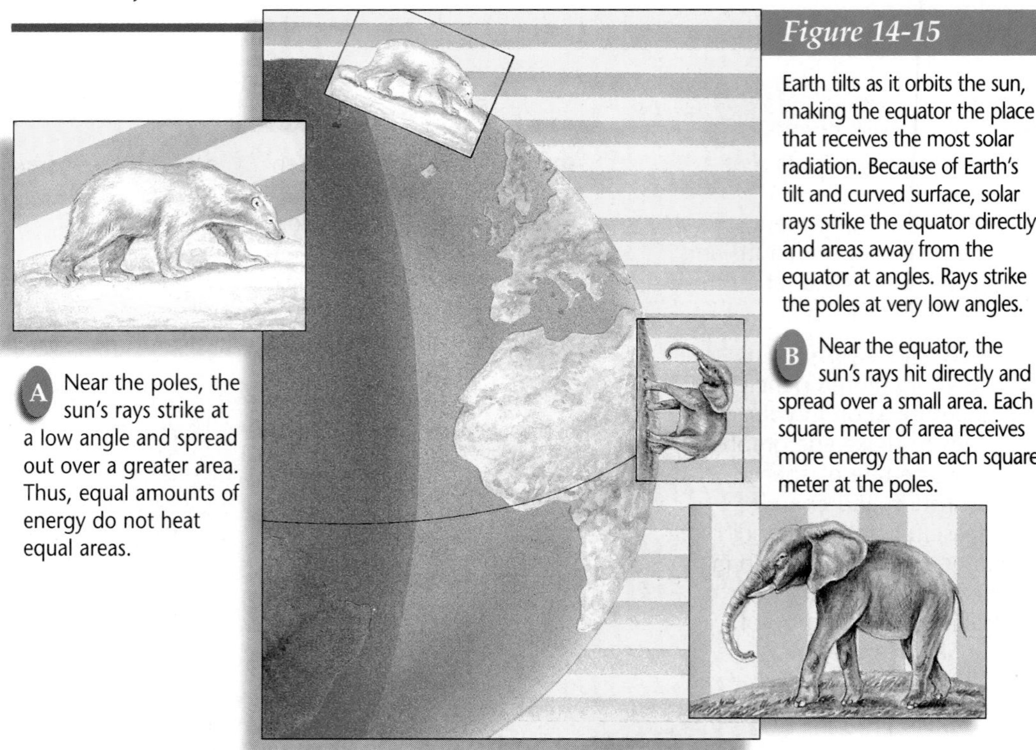

Figure 14-15

Earth tilts as it orbits the sun, making the equator the place that receives the most solar radiation. Because of Earth's tilt and curved surface, solar rays strike the equator directly and areas away from the equator at angles. Rays strike the poles at very low angles.

A Near the poles, the sun's rays strike at a low angle and spread out over a greater area. Thus, equal amounts of energy do not heat equal areas.

B Near the equator, the sun's rays hit directly and spread over a small area. Each square meter of area receives more energy than each square meter at the poles.

Program Resources

Reproducible Masters

Study Guide, p. 60 L1
Reinforcement, p. 60 L1
Enrichment, p. 60 L3
Activity Worksheets, pp. 5, 89 L1
Science Integration Activities, pp. 27-28
Concept Mapping, p. 33
Lab Manual 41, 42

Transparencies

Section Focus Transparency 56 L1

Where does this cold, denser air come from? It comes from the poles, which receive less radiation from the sun, making air at the poles much cooler. This dense, high pressure air sinks and moves along Earth's surface. Look at **Figure 14-17,** showing the general wind systems around the globe. You'll see that cold, dense air pushing warmer, less-dense air upward cannot explain everything about wind.

The Coriolis Effect

The rotation of Earth creates the Coriolis effect. The **Coriolis effect** deflects all free-moving objects such as air and water to the right north of the equator and left to the south. It causes air moving south in the northern hemisphere to turn westward. To someone at the equator, southbound air appears to move to the west as Earth turns east. The diagram of Earth at the right shows this. The flow of air caused by differences in heating and by the Coriolis effect create distinct wind patterns on Earth's surface. Not only do these wind systems influence the weather, but they also determine when and where ships and planes travel most efficiently.

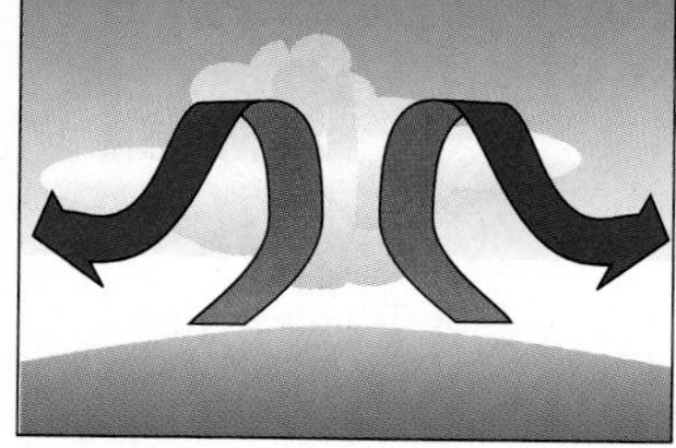

Figure 14-16

Wind develops from uneven heating on Earth. Cold air sinks and forces warm air upward.

The Coriolis-Go-Round

The Coriolis effect occurs with things like rockets shot from one place on Earth to another and with air and water—things that are not tied down to Earth. The Coriolis effect influences the general circulation of winds and storms. In some specific situations, you can notice its effect easily. Suppose your younger brother and sister are playing on a merry-go-round moving counterclockwise. Your sister sits in the middle of the merry-go-round. Your brother sits near the outer edge. She throws a ball to him. It misses. Why? Your sister threw the ball, but your brother had moved. To your sister, it appeared that she threw the ball straight. To your brother sitting at the edge, the ball appeared to curve to his left as he faced his sister.

Think Critically:

Does the ball actually curve as it travels from the center to the edge? Draw a diagram of the merry-go-round scenario to help you figure out the answers. What happens when your brother throws the ball back to your sister in the center?

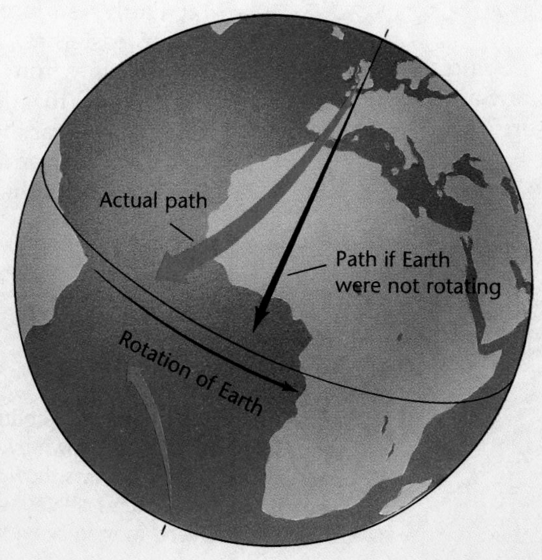

2 Teach

Demonstration

LS **Visual-Spatial** Tape a piece of paper to a phonograph turntable. On top of the paper, tape a piece of carbon paper, carbon side down. Turn on the phonograph. While the turntable is rotating, roll a steel ball bearing straight across the carbon paper. Remove the carbon paper and have students observe the mark on the paper. Have them compare it to what they observed. Use this activity to introduce the Coriolis effect. LEP

Think Critically

No, the ball appeared to curve due to the Coriolis effect. To your sister, the ball may appear to curve because her brother was in motion. When your brother throws the ball back to her, the ball should not appear to curve.

Inquiry Question

Why does air sink at the poles and rise at the equator? *At the poles, air is cold and dense. Dense air sinks. At the equator, the air is warm and less dense. A less dense substance will overlie denser substances.*

Videodisc

GTV: Planetary Manager

Up, Up, and Away?

Show 2.1, Side 2

2-5929

MiniLAB

Purpose

LS **Visual-Spatial** Students will create and observe convection currents. L1 COOP LEARN

Materials

600-mL glass beaker, water, food coloring, ice cubes

Teaching Strategies

- Emphasize that only a few drops of coloring should be added at a time because it is important to observe what happens. Too much food coloring obscures the experiment.

Analysis

1. The food coloring sank to the bottom with the cold water.
2. Both convection currents result from temperature/density differences in a fluid. In the MiniLAB the convection current occurred in a liquid and began when cold water sank. In the atmosphere, warm gases rise because cooler, more dense gases push them up.

Assessment

Oral To further assess students' understanding of convection currents, have them explain why ice cubes and coloring were used. Use the Performance Task Assessment List for Making Observations and Inferences in **PASC**, p. 17. P

Activity Worksheets, pp. 5, 89

USING MATH

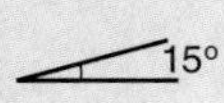

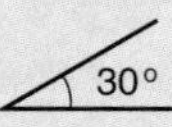

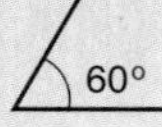

MiniLAB

What do convection currents look like?

Procedure

1. Fill a clear glass beaker with hot water.
2. Place ice cubes on the water along with a few drops of food coloring and observe the motion of the food coloring.

Analysis

1. Describe the motion of the food coloring.
2. Compare and contrast the convection current that you made with convection currents in the atmosphere.

Wind Systems

Let's venture into the past to imagine sailing the oceans during the time of the great sailing ships. No motors propel the ship. You depend entirely on the winds for energy. That means you must avoid getting into the doldrums, the windless zone at the equator. In the doldrums, the air seems motionless. Actually, the air is rising almost straight up. Do you remember why this happens?

Surface Winds

A better place to sail is between the equator and 30° latitude north or south. In that area, air descending to Earth's surface creates steady winds that blow to the southwest in the northern hemisphere. In the southern hemisphere, they blow toward the northwest. These are the trade winds. In the days of the great sailing ships, the northern trade winds provided a dependable route for trade. **Figure 14-17** shows the major wind systems on Earth, along with convection currents. Sailing ships like the one in **Figure 14-18** on page 414 were designed using knowledge of the winds.

Between 30° and 60° latitude north and south of the equator, winds blow in the opposite direction from the trade winds. These winds are called the prevailing westerlies. Sailors use the prevailing westerlies to sail from the Americas to Europe. The prevailing westerlies blow from the southwest to the northeast in the northern hemisphere. They are responsible for much of the movement of weather across the United States and Canada. In the southern hemisphere, the prevailing westerlies blow from the northwest to the southeast.

The last major wind systems at Earth's surface are the polar easterlies. These winds blow from the northeast to the southwest near the North Pole and from the southeast to the northwest near the South Pole.

Using a protractor, draw angles that measure 15°, 30°, and 60°.

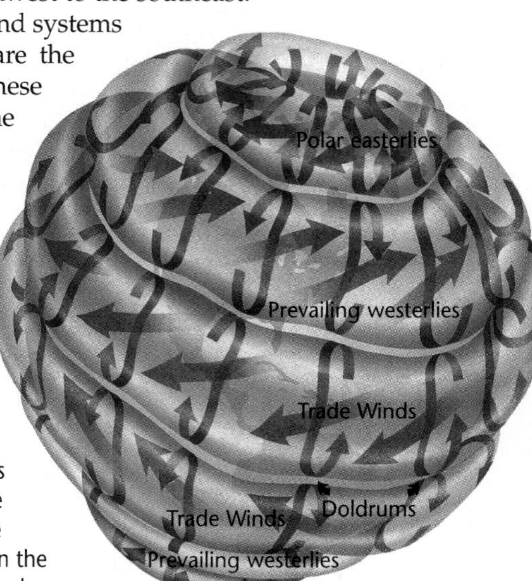

Figure 14-17

Uneven heating of the latitudes produces major convection currents, shown by the purple arrows. The blue arrows show the world's major wind systems created when the Coriolis effect deflects moving air westward.

Across the Curriculum

Language Arts Ask students: **Explain why the term *doldrums* is a good description of the air near the equator.** *Doldrums are a state of inactivity, stagnation, or slump. Air in the doldrums seems motionless.*

History Ask students: **Where did the trade winds get their name?** *These steady winds were used by trade ships to sail from Europe to the Americas.* Have students draw maps showing the routes that early explorers took across the oceans. Then have them compare these routes with the wind systems shown in **Figure 14-17**. L1

People and Science

Tinho Dornellas, *Windsurfer*

On the Job

Q What do you need to know about wind to be a good windsurfer?

A You have to get a feel for where the wind is coming from and where it's going. You can picture the wind as a river, but it's a river that changes direction. You have to cross that river back and forth. The best way to find out where the wind is coming from is to look at signs around you—ripples in the water, smokestacks, flags. Another way to find out is to close your eyes and turn until you can feel the wind coming straight at your face.

Q Are certain places better for windsurfing than others?

A You can windsurf anywhere there is wind and water. Hawaii gets strong tradewinds constantly. In the North Sea, you can have strong, but cold winds. Still, a lot of people windsurf there. In Washington, DC, I windsurfed close to the airport. The exhaust fumes from the airplanes were awful. Another bad place is close to cruise ships. The wind can blow toward you from the stacks of the ships.

Q Has windsurfing taught you any lessons that help you run your business?

A Running a business takes the same sort of perseverance that it takes to do well in windsurfing. You go out there and fall several times and try again. If the sail falls down, you have to have the willpower to pull that sail up and get going again. It's pretty much the same in business or in life in general—you take your falls, and you get up and keep going.

Career Connection

Modern windsurfing got its start when Jim Drake, an engineer, inventor, and sailing enthusiast (also known for codesigning the X-15 rocket research airplane, the B-70 bomber, and the cruise missile), met a surfer in the mid-1960s. The two started working together to design a surfboard with a sail. Engineers help design and build many things.

- **Engineer**
- **Meteorologist**

Use Labs 41 and 42 in the **Lab Manual** as you teach this lesson.

Engineers solve problems with their technical expertise. Many colleges and universities have engineering schools. Someone wanting to be an engineer needs to take courses in math and science. Meteorologists study and predict weather. Knowing weather patterns helps wind surfers and those who become designers and businessmen in the windsurfing field. Meteorologists also need math and science courses.

People and Science

Background

- Windsurfing is also called boardsailing or sailboarding. The board is similar to a surfboard, but with a mast and sail. It takes strength, coordination, and balance to manipulate the free-swinging mast and sail.
- Modern windsurfing got its start when Jim Drake, an engineer, inventor, and sailing enthusiast (also known for co-designing the X-15 rocket research airplane, the B-70 bomber, and the cruise missile), met surfer Hoyle Schweitzer at a beach party in the mid-1960s. The two started working together to design a surfboard with a sail. After many unsuccessful tries, they finally came up with a design that worked. In 1969, they patented the design under the name Windsurfer. At first the sport was much more popular in Europe than in the United States, but it started catching on in this country in the late 1970s.

Teaching Strategies

In the feature, Tinho Dornellas describes several ways to determine wind direction without instruments. Have students go outside and try the methods he suggests. Challenge students to devise other methods.

Career Connection

Career Path For locations of windsurfing schools throughout the United States, contact the U.S. Windsurfing Association, P.O. Box 978, Hood River, Oregon 97031 (e-mail address: uswa@aol.com).

Enrichment

Have students keep track of the movements of the jet streams by watching daily weather reports on television. L1

Activity

LS **Kinesthetic** Have students make models of anemometers and do some research to find out how actual anemometers work. L1

NATIONAL GEOGRAPHIC SOCIETY

Videodisc

STV: Atmosphere

What Is the Atmosphere?

Unit 1, Side 1

Atmospheric Gases

03109-07851

Smog; Chicago, Illinois

38685

Rainbow; Yukon Territory, Canada

38710

Orange sky

38717

High-Altitude Winds

There are also winds at higher altitudes. Narrow belts of strong winds, called **jet streams,** blow near the top of the troposphere. There are two jet streams in each hemisphere that blow from west to east at the northern and southern boundaries of the prevailing westerlies. These streams of air resemble fast-moving, winding rivers. Their speeds average between 97 and 185 km/h. Their positions in latitude and altitude change from day to day and season to season. They have a major effect on our weather.

Just as sailors seek the trade winds, prevailing westerlies, and polar easterlies to help propel their ships, jet pilots take advantage of jet streams. When flying eastward, planes save time and fuel. Going west, planes fly at different altitudes to avoid the jet streams.

Daily and Seasonal Winds

The wind systems you've just read about determine the major weather patterns for the entire globe. Smaller wind systems determine local weather. If you live near a large body of water, you're familiar with two such wind systems—land breezes and sea breezes.

Convection currents over areas where the land meets the sea cause sea breezes and land breezes. **Sea breezes** are created during the day because solar radiation warms the land more than the water. Air over the land is heated

Figure 14-18

This modern sailboat uses wind to sail the North Atlantic Ocean.

Community Connection

Winds and Flying Have a pilot come to class to discuss how winds affect flying.

Figure 14-9

These daily winds occur because a convection current changes its direction.

A During the day, cool air forces warm air over the land to rise, creating a sea breeze.

B At night, cold air over the land forces up the warmer air above the sea, creating a land breeze.

by conduction. This heated air becomes less dense and is forced upward by cooler, denser air moving inland from the ocean. A convection current results.

At night, the land cools much more rapidly than the ocean water. Air over the land becomes cooler than the air over the ocean. The cool, dense air from the land moves out over the water, pushing the warm air over the water upward. Movements of air toward the water are called **land breezes.** **Figure 14-19** can help you understand how sea breezes and land breezes occur.

Mountain-valley wind is another wind that has a daily cycle. In the mountains, about three hours after sunrise, a valley wind starts flowing from the valley upward along the slope of the mountain. A few hours after sunset, a mountain wind begins to blow down the slope into the valley. This mountain-valley wind circulation comes from heating of the mountain sides during the day. At night, the mountain slopes cool quickly and the cooler, denser air drains into the valley. At night, in deep, wide valleys, air temperatures are colder than temperatures on the mountain slopes.

CONNECT TO

PHYSICS

Specific heat is the amount of heat required to change the temperature of a substance one degree. Substances with high specific heat values absorb a lot of heat for a small increase in temperature. ***Infer*** whether soil or water has the higher specific heat value.

CONNECT TO

PHYSICS

Answer Water has the higher specific heat value.

Enrichment

Have students research and report on local winds, such as the Santa Anas, mistrals, siroccos, boras, and chinooks. P

NATIONAL GEOGRAPHIC SOCIETY

Videodisc

GTV: Planetary Manager

Atmosphere

47906

3 Assess

Check for Understanding

Ask students to explain why winds blow inland off the ocean, especially on sunny days. Students should conclude that the air over land heats up faster than air over the water, becomes less dense, and is pushed up by the cool dense air from over the ocean.

Reteach

LS **Visual-Spatial** Using world globes, have students find the locations of the doldrums, trade winds, prevailing westerlies, and polar easterlies. Have them plan routes that can be taken by sailing ships to get from continents separated by oceans.

Extension

For students who have mastered this section, use the **Reinforcement** and **Enrichment** masters.

4 Close

• MINI • QUIZ •

Use the Mini Quiz to check students' recall of chapter content.

1. **Air masses moving in the northern hemisphere turn right due to the ______.** *Coriolis effect*
2. **The ______ are the windless zone at the equator.** *doldrums*
3. **A ______ is a seasonal wind that brings rain at one time and dry weather at another.** *monsoon*

Section Wrap-up

Review

1. Because Earth is tilted in its orbit around the sun and because of Earth's curved surface, solar energy strikes Earth most directly near the equator. Lower latitudes receive more energy than higher latitudes.
2. It causes air masses in the northern hemisphere to be turned right, and those in the southern hemisphere to be turned left.
3. **Think Critically** A jet flying from South Carolina to Arizona flies against the jet stream. It uses more fuel and takes more time than when the jet flies in the opposite direction.

Using Computers

Graphics should show three cells in each hemisphere where warm air rises and cooler air sinks. Major winds drawn would be polar, easterlies, westerlies, and trade winds. There should be a major jet stream drawn in each hemisphere.

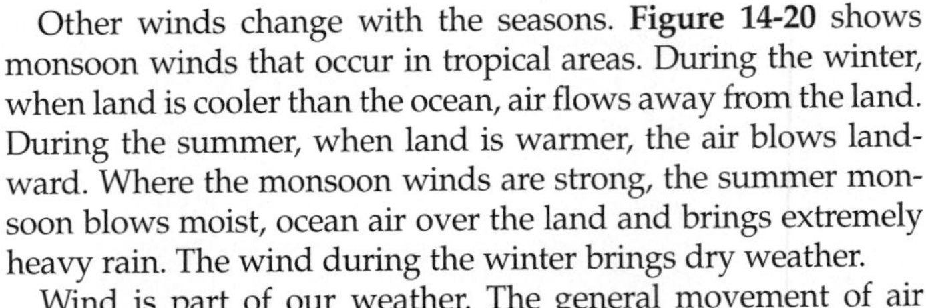

Other winds change with the seasons. **Figure 14-20** shows monsoon winds that occur in tropical areas. During the winter, when land is cooler than the ocean, air flows away from the land. During the summer, when land is warmer, the air blows landward. Where the monsoon winds are strong, the summer monsoon blows moist, ocean air over the land and brings extremely heavy rain. The wind during the winter brings dry weather.

Wind is part of our weather. The general movement of air around the Earth produces belts of prevailing winds and the flow of air masses and storms.

Figure 14-20

Monsoon winds are seasonal winds that occur in tropical areas.

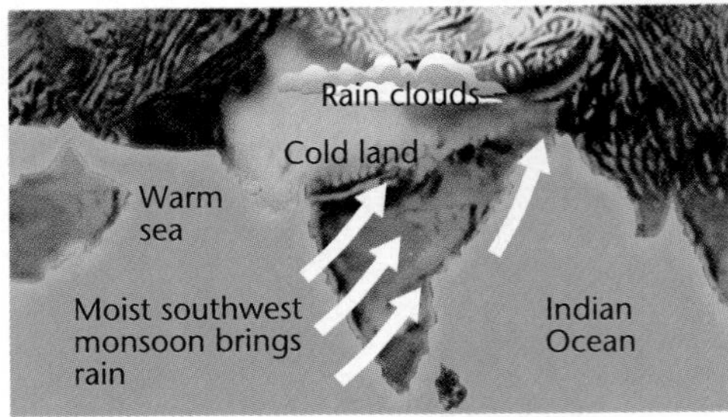

A When the land is intensely hot, the wet monsoon winds blow from the ocean onto the land, bringing rain.

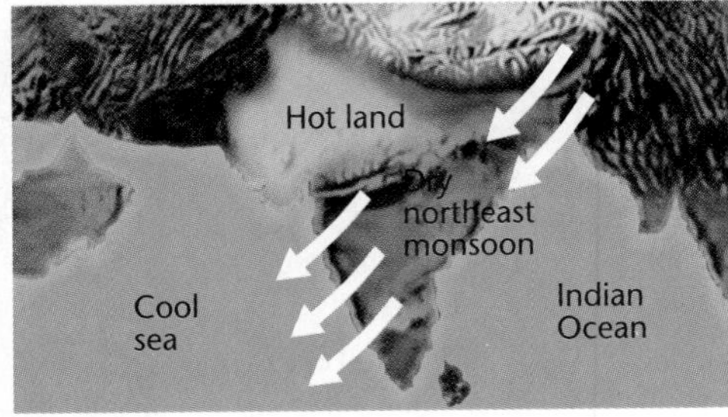

B When the sun is no longer shining directly over the land, the air above the ocean has a lower pressure. Dry winds flow from the land out over the ocean, bringing the dry season.

Section Wrap-up

Review

1. Why do latitudes differ in the amount of solar energy they receive?
2. How does the Coriolis effect influence the general wind circulation of Earth?
3. **Think Critically:** Explain why a jet that flies from South Carolina to Arizona uses more fuel and takes longer to complete its journey than a similar jet that flies from Arizona to South Carolina.

Skill Builder

Comparing and Contrasting

Compare and contrast land and sea breezes and seasonal winds versus daily winds. If you need help, refer to Comparing and Contrasting in the **Skill Handbook**.

Using Computers

Graphics Use a computer graphics package and Figure 14-17 on page 412 to draw the wind systems on Earth. Make separate graphics of major wind circulation cells shown by purple arrows. On another graphic, show major surface winds. On another, draw the jet streams. Print your graphs and share them with your class.

Skill Builder

Both land and sea breezes are caused by convection currents that form over areas where landmasses are next to bodies of water. They differ, however, in that sea breezes form during the day when air over the land is warmer than air over the water. A land breeze forms at night when the conditions are reversed. Seasonal winds change direction with the seasons. Daily winds change direction with the time of day.

Assessment

Content Use the Skill Builder to assess students' abilities to compare and contrast. Have students compare and contrast the trade winds and the prevailing westerlies. Use the Performance Task Assessment List for Making Observations and Inferences in **PASC,** p. 17. P

Chapter 14 Review

Summary

14-1: Earth's Atmosphere

1. Nitrogen and oxygen are the two most common gases in Earth's atmosphere.
2. Because the gases in Earth's atmosphere have mass, they push against one another, creating air pressure.
3. Earth's atmosphere is classified into layers based on temperature differences.

14-2: Science and Society: The Ozone Layer

1. Exposure to too much ultraviolet radiation can cause cancer and other health problems in living things.
2. When ozone reacts with chlorofluorocarbons, the molecules of ozone break apart, changing the ozone into oxygen.

14-3: Energy from the Sun

1. Some of the sun's energy that reaches Earth escapes back into space. Some energy is absorbed by Earth's air, land, and water.
2. Radiation transfers energy by electromagnetic waves. Conduction transfers heat when molecules bump into one another. Convection transfers heat due to density differences in the air.
3. Water cycles between the atmosphere and Earth's surface. The water cycle consists of evaporation, condensation, and precipitation.

14-4: Movement of Air

1. Earth's surface is curved; thus, not all areas receive the same amount of solar radiation.
2. Earth's rotation causes the Coriolis effect.
3. The doldrums are the windless zone at the equator. The trade winds lie between the equator and 30° north or south of the equator.

Key Science Words

a. chlorofluorocarbons
b. conduction
c. convection
d. Coriolis effect
e. hydrosphere
f. ionosphere
g. jet stream
h. land breeze
i. ozone layer
j. radiation
k. sea breeze
l. troposphere
m. ultraviolet radiation
n. water cycle

Reviewing Vocabulary

Match each phrase with the correct term from the list of Key Science Words.

1. layer of atmosphere closest to Earth
2. absorbs ultraviolet radiation
3. transfer of energy by electromagnetic waves
4. transfer of heat that occurs due to density differences in air
5. changes the direction of air flow and is caused by Earth's rotation
6. occurs when cold air over water moves inland
7. rays that can cause cancer
8. pollutant that breaks down the ozone layer
9. Earth's water
10. narrow wind belt at top of the troposphere

GLENCOE TECHNOLOGY

MindJogger Videoquiz

Chapter 14 Have students work in groups as they play the Videoquiz game to review key chapter concepts.

Chapter 14 Review

Summary

Have students read the summary statements to review the major concepts of the chapter.

Reviewing Vocabulary

1. l
2. i
3. j
4. c
5. d
6. k
7. m
8. a
9. e
10. g

Assessment

Portfolio Encourage students to place in their portfolios one or two items of what they consider to be their best work. Examples include:

- Enrichment, pp. 396, 415
- FLEX Your Brain, p. 404
- Science Journal, p. 406 P

Performance Additional performance assessments may be found in **Performance Assessment** and **Science Integration Activities.** Performance Task Assessment Lists and rubrics for evaluating these activities can be found in Glencoe's **Performance Assessment in the Science Classroom.**

Chapter 14 Review

Checking Concepts

1. d	**6.** a
2. c	**7.** d
3. c	**8.** b
4. a	**9.** c
5. a	**10.** b

Understanding Concepts

11. There is little or no wind there to fill their sails.

12. This compound destroys ozone molecules when the two substances come into contact. Banning its use may help reduce the destruction of Earth's ozone layer.

13. The transfer of energy via radiation does not require matter; whereas in conduction, energy is transferred only when two objects are in direct contact.

14. Air is warmed by direct rays from the sun at the equator and will be forced up by cooler air flowing underneath. Air cools near the poles because these areas receive less direct solar radiation.

15. Venus gets more radiation from the sun because it is closer to the sun than Earth. Also, its atmosphere is much thicker than Earth's and does not allow much of the radiation to escape back into space.

Thinking Critically

16. There is little or no water vapor from which the clouds could form.

17. The ozone layer prevents harmful ultraviolet radiation from reaching Earth's surface. Early organisms had the oceans in which they lived to protect them from excessive UV.

18. The pan in contact with the stove is heated by conduction. The soup in contact with the pan is heated by conduction. As the temperature of the soup increases, the cooler, denser soup at the top of the pan sinks and pushes up the hotter soup from the bottom of the pan, transferring energy by convection.

19. It condenses and forms clouds.

20. With an increase in altitude, there are fewer and fewer air molecules pushing against one another to create pressure.

Developing Skills

21. Concept Mapping One possible solution is shown on page 419.

22. Making and Using Graphs Air pressure increases more rapidly at low altitudes. Air pressure can drop to zero only if no molecules of air are present. At 36 km above Earth's surface (the greatest altitude represented by the graph), molecules are still abundant. The air pressure would drop to zero outside of Earth's atmosphere.

Chapter 14 Review

Checking Concepts

Choose the word or phrase that completes the sentence.

1. _______ is the most abundant gas in the air.
   a. Oxygen — c. Argon
   b. Water vapor — d. Nitrogen
2. Smog is a mixture of nitrogen oxide and _______.
   a. conduction — c. hydrocarbons
   b. mud — d. argon
3. The ______ is the uppermost layer of the atmosphere.
   a. troposphere — c. exosphere
   b. stratosphere — d. thermosphere
4. The warmest layer of air is the _______.
   a. troposphere — c. mesosphere
   b. stratosphere — d. thermosphere
5. _______ protects living things from too much ultraviolet radiation.
   a. Ozone layer — c. Nitrogen
   b. Oxygen — d. Argon
6. Air pressure is greatest in the ______.
   a. troposphere — c. exosphere
   b. stratosphere — d. thermosphere
7. When objects are in contact, energy is transferred by _______.
   a. trade winds — c. radiation
   b. convection — d. conduction
8. A barometer measures _______.
   a. temperature — c. humidity
   b. air pressure — d. wind speed
9. Movement of air toward water can be a _______.
   a. sea breeze — c. land breeze
   b. doldrum — d. barometer
10. _______ are near the top of the troposphere.
    a. Doldrums — c. Polar easterlies
    b. Jet streams — d. Trade winds

Understanding Concepts

Answer the following questions in your Science Journal using complete sentences.

11. Why do sailors avoid sailing into the doldrums?
12. Why have countries agreed to ban the use of chlorofluorocarbons?
13. How does radiation differ from conduction?
14. Explain why air rises at the equator and sinks near the poles.
15. Explain why Venus is so much hotter than Earth.

Thinking Critically

16. Why are there few or no clouds in the stratosphere?
17. It is thought that life could not have existed on land until the ozone layer formed, about 2 billion years ago. Why does life on land require an ozone layer?
18. Explain how soup in a pan on a stove is heated by conduction and convection.
19. What happens when water vapor rises and cools?
20. Why does air pressure decrease with an increase in altitude?

Chapter 14 Review

Developing Skills

If you need help, refer to the **Skill Handbook.**

21. Concept Mapping: Make a cycle concept map using the following phrases that explains how air moves to form a convection current: *air cools and grows more dense, warm air rises and cools, cool air pushes up warm air, cool air is warmed by conduction, cool air sinks.*

22. Making and Using Graphs: On the graph below, does air pressure increase more rapidly at high or low altitudes? Why doesn't the air pressure drop to zero on the graph? At what altitude would it drop to zero?

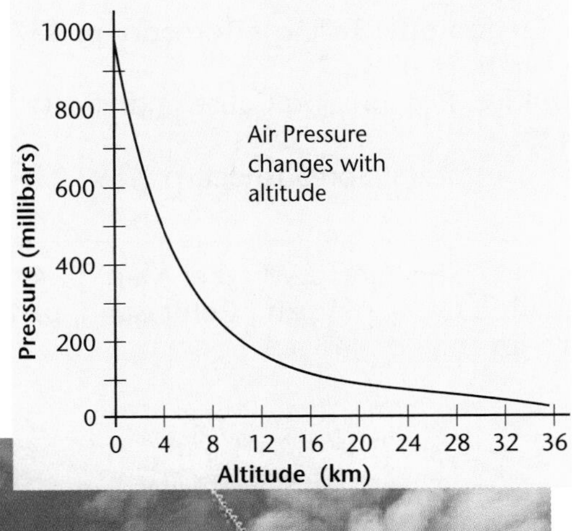

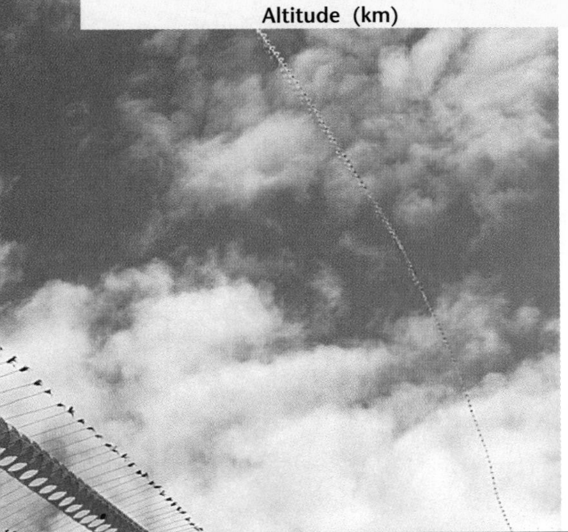

23. Observing and Inferring: In an experiment, a student measured the air temperature one meter above the ground on a sunny afternoon and again one hour after sunset. The second reading was lower than the first. What can you infer from this?

24. Hypothesizing: Trees use carbon dioxide to photosynthesize. Carbon dioxide in the atmosphere blocks radiation from Earth's surface from escaping to space. Hypothesize how the temperature on Earth would change if many trees were cut down.

25. Using Variables, Constants, and Controls: Design an experiment to find out how plants are affected by differing amounts of ultraviolet radiation. In the design, use filtering film made for car windows. What is the variable you are testing? What are your constants? Your controls?

Performance Assessment

1. **Data Table:** Use the barometer you made in Activity 14-1 to make 24-hour forecasts. Record your barometer reading and your prediction on the data table. Later, compare your prediction with the actual weather that occurs. Keep a record for a week and find out how accurate your barometer predictions were overall.
2. **Poster:** Draw or find magazine photos of convection currents that occur in everyday life.
3. **Lab Report:** Design and conduct an experiment to find out how different surfaces such as asphalt, soil, sand, and grass absorb and reflect solar energy. Share the results of this with your class.

23. Observing and Inferring During the afternoon, the ground heated up and released its energy into the overlying air. After sunset, the ground was no longer receiving radiant energy and had given up much of its heat to the air above it during the day.

24. Hypothesizing When trees photosynthesize, they use carbon dioxide. Thus, the amount of this gas is reduced. When forests are destroyed, photosynthesis stops. CO_2 increases in the atmosphere, causing the temperature of Earth's atmosphere to rise.

25. Using Variables, Constants, and Controls Accept all reasonable designs. The variable is the amount of ultraviolet light that the plants receive. The constants are identical plants, pots, watering, soil, and placement. The controls are the plants that receive ultraviolet radiation without filtering.

Performance Assessment

1. Based on experiences in Activity 14-1, students may predict that when the barometer is falling, clouds will appear. A rising barometer means sunny days ahead. Use the Performance Task Assessment List for Data Table in **PASC**, p. 37. P

2. Photos and drawings should show evidence of warm molecules rising and cold molecules sinking. Use the Performance Task Assessment List for Scientific Drawing in **PASC**, p. 55. P

3. Make certain each surface receives the same amount of sunlight. Students should lay a thermometer on each surface and suspend another one above each surface, at the same height. Use the Performance Task Assessment List for Lab Report in **PASC**, p. 47. P

21.

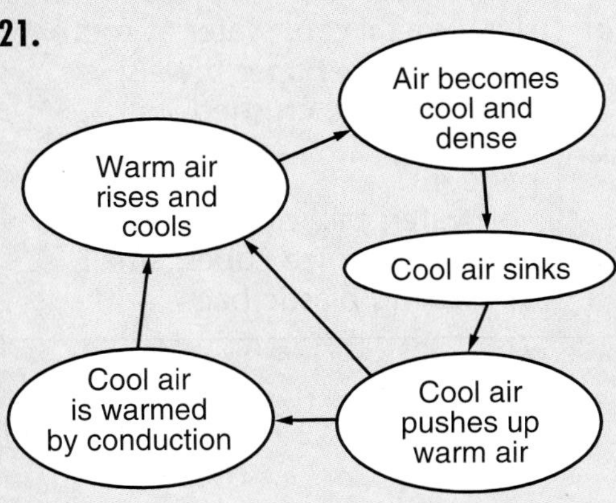

Chapter Organizer

Section	Objectives	Activities/Features
Chapter Opener		Explore Activity: Make a model of a tornado. p. 421
15-1 **What is weather?** (2 sessions, 1 block)*	1. **Explain** the role of water vapor in the atmosphere and how it affects weather. 2. **Describe** how clouds form and how they are classified. 3. **Compare** the development of rain, hail, sleet, and snow.	Connect to Life Science, p. 423 Science Journal, p. 424 MiniLAB: How can dew point be determined? p. 425 Activity 15-1: Is it humid or not? pp. 428-429 Problem Solving: Evaporation and Condensation, p. 430 MiniLAB: Can you make it rain? p. 431 Skill Builder: Concept Mapping, p. 431 Using Math, p. 431
15-2 **Weather Patterns** (2 sessions, 1½ blocks)*	1. **Describe** the Weather associated with fronts and high- and low-pressure areas. 2. **Explain** how low pressure systems form at fronts. 3. **Relate** thunderstorms to tornadoes.	Using Math, p. 436 Using Technology: Tailing a Tornado, p. 437 Using Math, p. 438 Skill Builder: Recognizing Cause and Effect, p. 439 Using Computers: Spreadsheet, p. 439
15-3 **Forecasting Weather** (1 session, ½ block)*	1. **Explain** the collection of data for weather maps and forecasts. 2. **Explain** the symbols used in a weather station model.	Activity 15-2: Reading a Weather Map, p. 442 Skill Builder: Comparing and Contrasting, p. 443 Science Journal, p. 443
15-4 **Science and Society Technology: Changing the Weather** (1 session, ½ block)*	1. **Describe** some human activities that alter the weather. 2. **Describe** why many cloud-seeding experiments are not successful.	Connect to Physics, p. 445 Explore the Technology, p. 445 Science & History: How Weather Affects History, p. 446 Science Journal, p. 446

* A complete Planning Guide that includes block scheduling is provided on pages 32T-35T.

Activity Materials

Explore	Activities	MiniLABs
page 421 two 2-L plastic bottles, tap water, dishwashing soap, duct tape	pages 428-429 2 identical Celsius thermometers, 2-cm square piece of gauze, tape, string, cardboard, 250-mL beaker, tap water, table for determining relative humidity page 442 hand lens, **Figure 15-18**, Appendix L	page 425 shiny metal can, water at room temperature, paper towels, thermometer, crushed ice page 431 hot water; tall, clear, wide-mouthed jar; ice cubes; small, self-sealing plastic bag

Teacher Classroom Resources

Reproducible Masters	Transparencies	Teaching Resources
Study Guide, p. 61 **Reinforcement,** p. 61 **Enrichment,** p. 61 **Activity Worksheets,** pp. 90-91, 94, 95 **Lab Manual 43,** Clouds **Cross-Curricular Integration,** p. 19	**Section Focus Transparency 57,** Sunny, Cloudy, Wet, and Dry **Science Integration Transparency 15,** Factors Affecting Evaporation **Teaching Transparency 29,** Cloud Types	**Glencoe Earth Science Interactive Videodisc** **Earth Science CD-ROM** **Spanish Resources** **English/Spanish Audiocassettes** **Cooperative Learning Resource Guide** **Lab Partner** **Lab and Safety Skills** **Lesson Plans**
Study Guide, p. 62 **Reinforcement,** p. 62 **Enrichment,** p. 62 **Lab Manual 44,** Hurricanes **Science Integration Activity 15,** Tornado Watch! **Multicultural Connections,** pp. 33-34	**Section Focus Transparency 58,** Pack Your Umbrella **Teaching Transparency 30,** Air Masses	**Assessment Resources**
Study Guide, p. 63 **Reinforcement,** p. 63 **Enrichment,** p. 63 **Activity Worksheets,** pp. 92-93 **Lab Manual 46,** Weather Forecasting **Concept Mapping,** p. 35 **Critical Thinking/Problem Solving,** p. 21	**Section Focus Transparency 59,** Weather Watch	**Chapter Review,** pp. 33-34 **Assessment,** pp. 99-102 **Performance Assessment in the Science Classroom (PASC)** **MindJogger Videoquiz** **Alternate Assessment in the Science Classroom** **Performance Assessment** **Chapter Review Software** **Computer Test Bank**
Study Guide, p. 64 **Reinforcement,** p. 64 **Enrichment,** p. 64 **Science and Society Integration,** p. 19	**Section Focus Transparency 60,** Do Something About It!	

Key to Teaching Strategies

The following designations will help you decide which activities are appropriate for your students.

- **L1** Level 1 activities should be within the ability range of all students.
- **L2** Level 2 activities should be within the ability range of the average to above-average student.
- **L3** Level 3 activities are designed for the ability range of above-average students.
- **LEP** LEP activities should be within the ability range of Limited English Proficiency students.
- **LS** These activities are designed to address different learning styles.
- **COOP LEARN** Cooperative Learning activities are designed for small group work.
- **P** These strategies represent student products that can be placed into a best-work portfolio.

GLENCOE TECHNOLOGY

The following multimedia resources are available from Glencoe.

The Infinite Voyage Series
Living with Disaster

Science and Technology Videodisc Series (STVS)
Physics
Tornado Detectors
Lightning
Chemistry
Snowflakes
Cloud Chemistry
Earth & Space
World's Worst Weather
Studying Thunderstorms
Reducing Hail Damage

National Geographic Society Series
STV: Atmosphere

Glencoe Earth Science Interactive Videodisc
Thunderstorms: Flashes and Crashes

Earth Science CD-ROM

Teacher Classroom Resources

This is a representation of key blackline masters available in the Teacher Classroom Resources.

Teaching Aids

Section Focus Transparencies

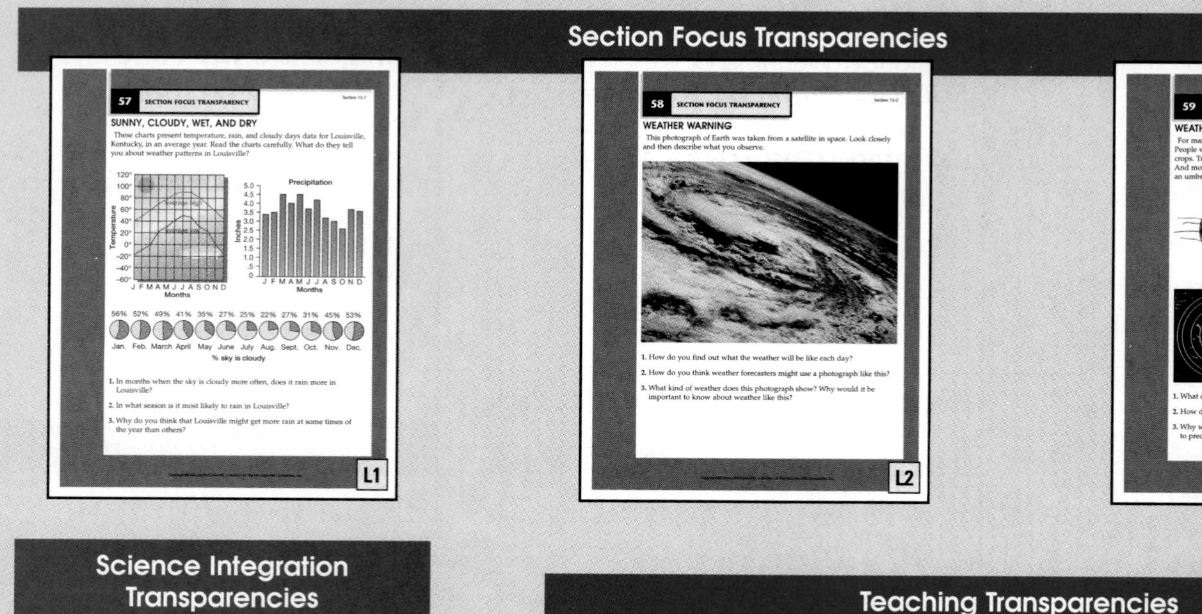

Science Integration Transparencies

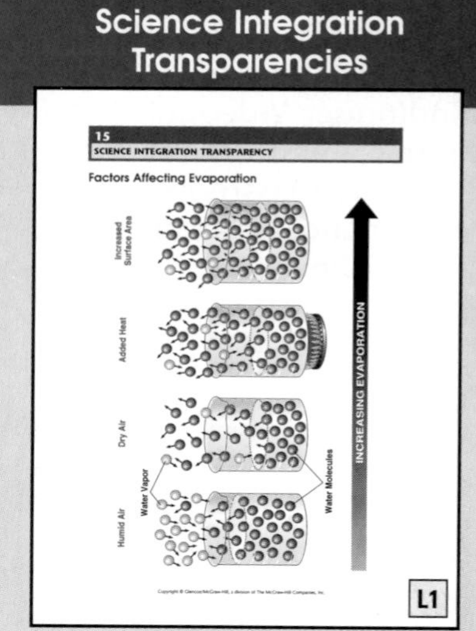

Teaching Transparencies

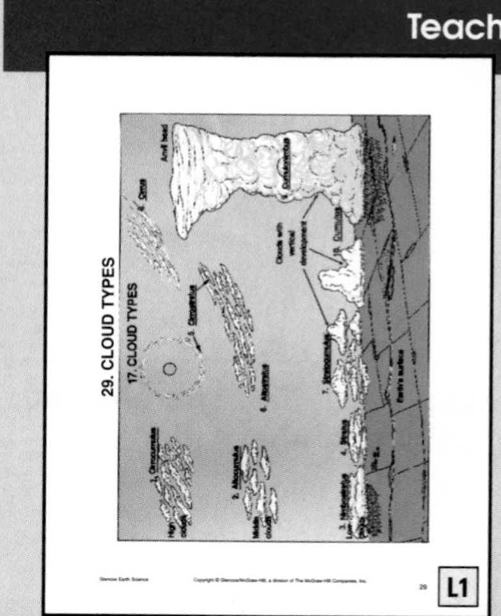

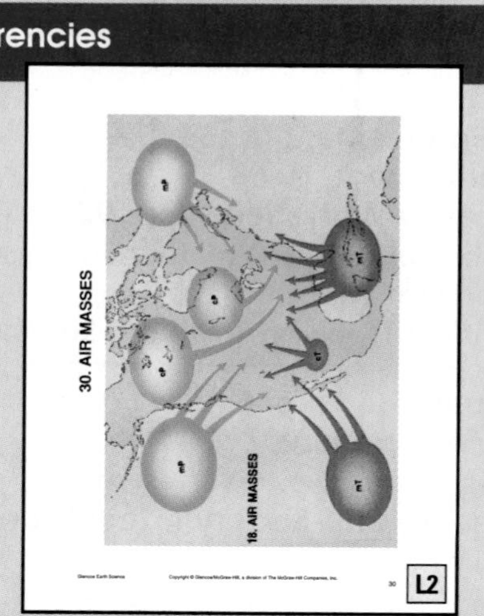

Meeting Different Ability Levels

Study Guide

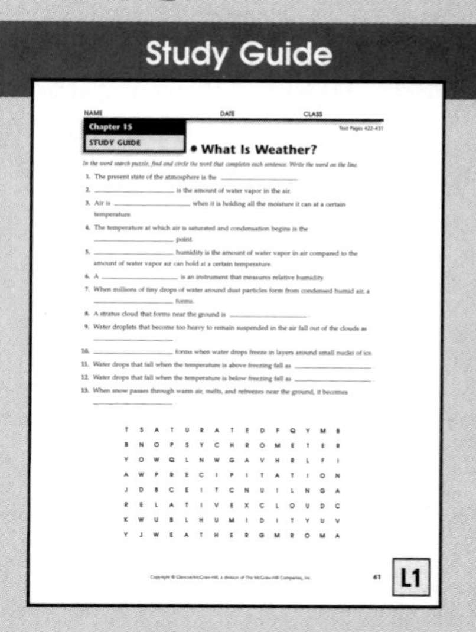

Reinforcement

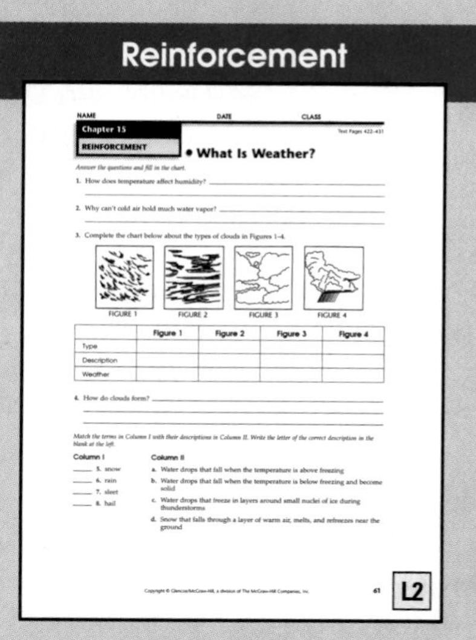

Enrichment Worksheets

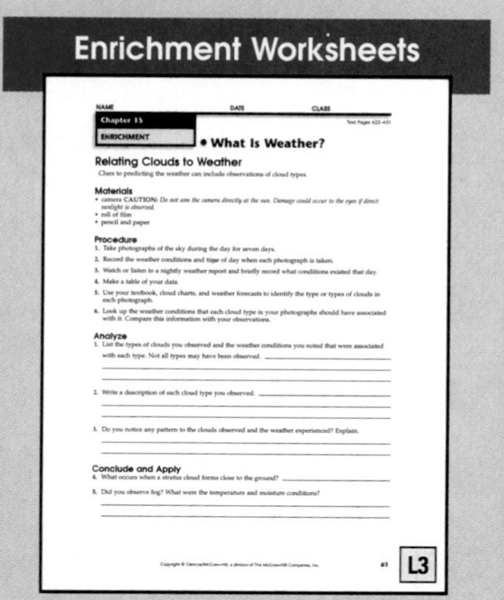

Hands-On Activities

Science Integration Activity

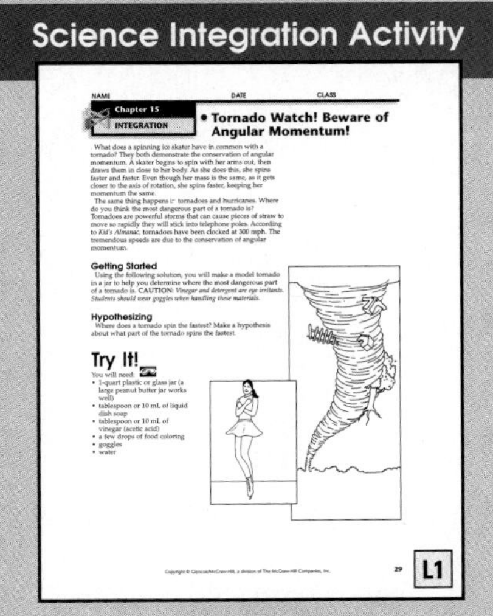

Lab Manual

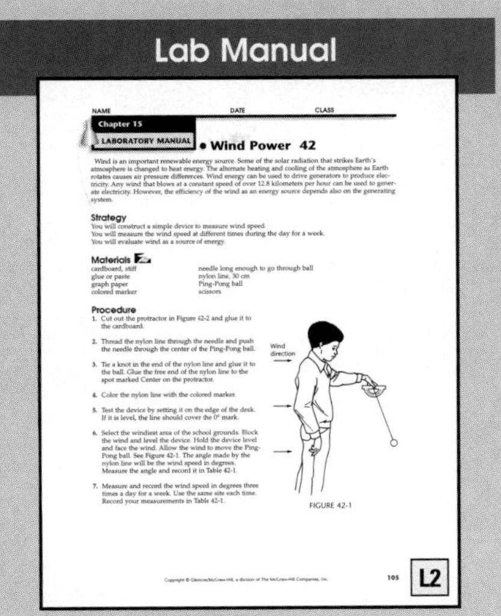

Assessment

Performance Assessment

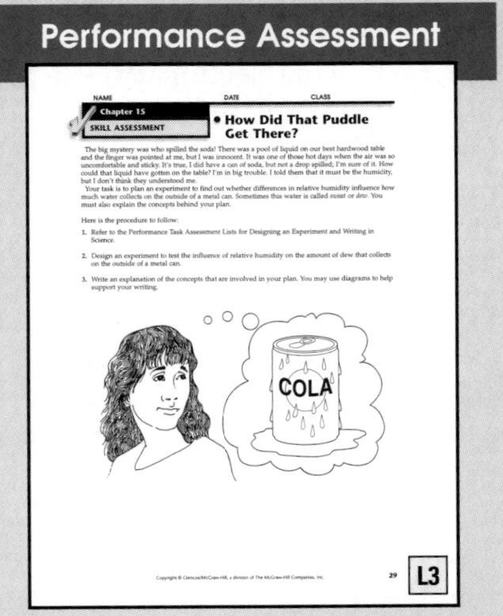

Enrichment and Application

Critical Thinking/ Problem Solving

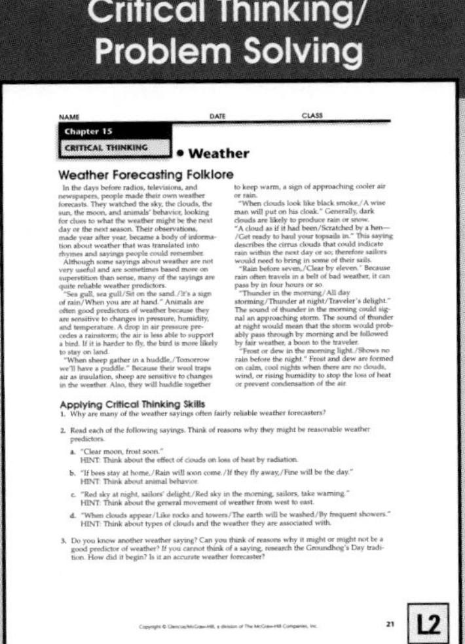

Cross-Curricular Integration

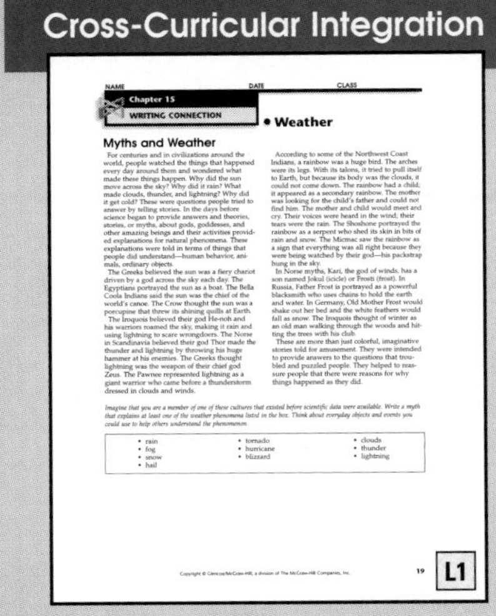

Science and Society Integration

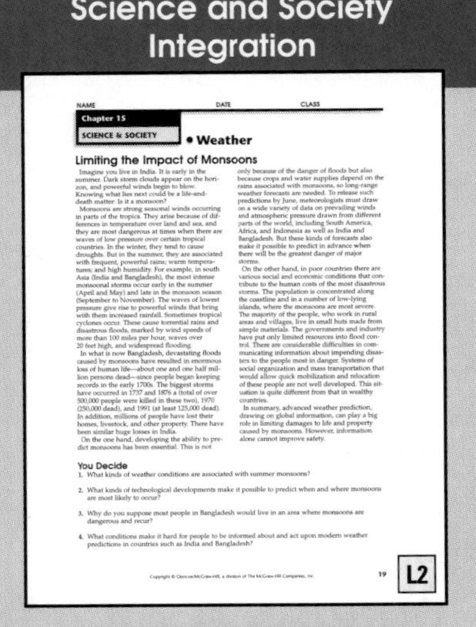

Multicultural Connections

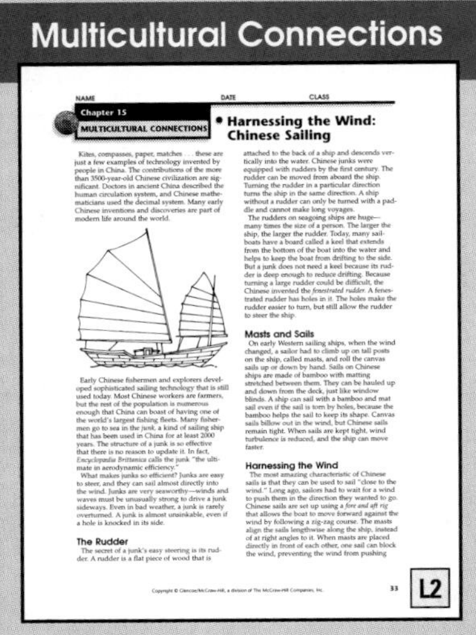

Concept Mapping

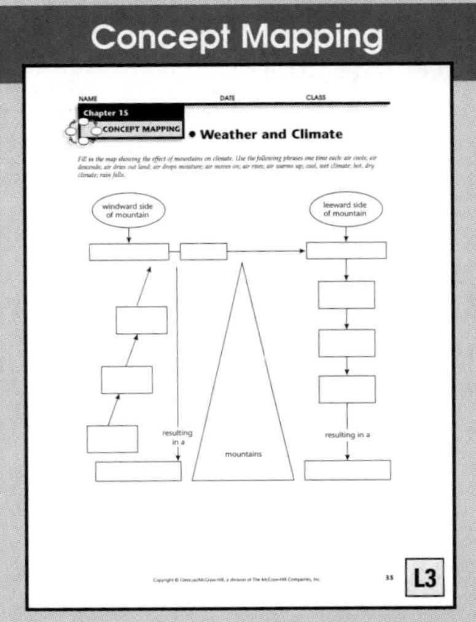

Chapter 15

Weather

CHAPTER OVERVIEW

Section 15-1 This section presents some of the factors that determine weather and explains how clouds and precipitation develop.

Section 15-2 The formation, scale, and structure of air masses, pressure systems, fronts, and severe weather are discussed.

Section 15-3 This section explains weather map symbols and weather forecasting.

Section 15-4 **Science and Society** One type of weather modification is explored.

Chapter Vocabulary

weather
humidity
relative humidity
saturated
dew point
fog
precipitation
air mass
front
tornado
hurricane
meteorologist
station model
isotherm
isobar
cloud seeding

Theme Connection

Stability and Change/Scale and Structure The structures of clouds and cloud evolution are presented, beginning with a discussion of dew point. Air masses and fronts demonstrate how stable elements change and can create strongly unstable elements of severe weather.

Previewing the Chapter

420

Look for the following logo for strategies that emphasize different learning modalities. 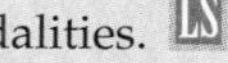

Kinesthetic	Activity, p. 437
Visual-Spatial	Explore, p. 421; Visual Learning, pp. 425, 426, 432-434, 441; Demonstration, pp. 424, 434; Reteach, pp. 430, 441, 444; MiniLAB, p. 431; Activity 15-2, p. 442
Interpersonal	Activity 15-1, pp. 428-429; Reteach, p. 438; Activity, p. 441
Intrapersonal	MiniLAB, p. 425
Logical-Mathematical	Across the Curriculum, p. 424; Using Math, pp. 431, 436, 438

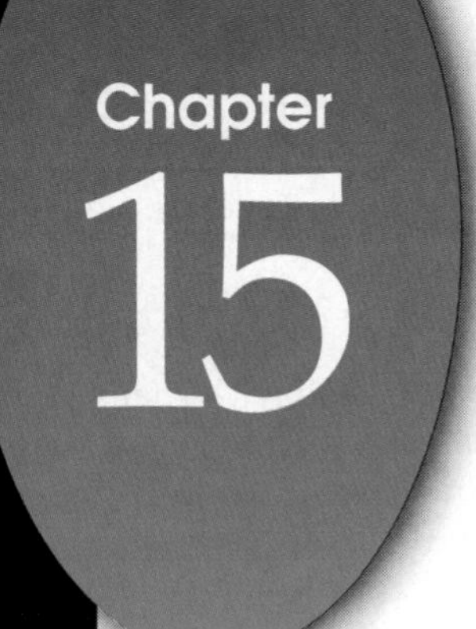

Chapter 15

Weather

Tornadoes are severe weather events. A tornado can roar through farms and cities, smashing everything in its path, leaving a trail of destruction. Winds in a tornado sometimes reach 500 km per hour, strong enough to flatten buildings. Updrafts in the center can act like a giant vacuum cleaner, sucking buildings, cars, and even animals high into the air.

EXPLORE ACTIVITY

Make a model of a tornado.

1. Obtain two 2-L plastic bottles.
2. Fill one about ¾ full of water and add one drop of dishwashing soap to the water.
3. Put the empty bottle on top and tape the bottles securely, opening to opening.
4. Flip the bottles to put the one with water in it on top. Move the top bottle in a circular motion.

Observe: In your Science Journal, describe what happens in the bottles. Compare this model of a tornado with a real tornado.

Previewing Science Skills

- In the **Skill Builders**, you will **map concepts, recognize cause and effect**, and **compare and contrast**.
- In the **Activities**, you will **make a model, observe, infer**, and **interpret a scientific illustration**.
- In the **MiniLABs**, you will **observe, infer** and **make a model**.

EXPLORE ACTIVITY

Purpose

LS **Visual-Spatial** Use the Explore Activity to introduce students to one kind of severe weather. Inform students that they will be learning more about weather as they read this chapter. L1 LEP COOP LEARN

Preparation

Several days before you begin this chapter, have each student bring in a clean, 2-L plastic bottle.

Materials

each pair of students needs two 2-L plastic bottles, dishwashing soap, heavy tape

Teaching Strategies

Have students work in pairs to do this activity. One person can hold the bottles together while the other tapes them.

Observe

Students should observe that a spiral funnel of soapy water forms in the top bottle and drops down into the bottom bottle. This model of a tornado is similar to a real tornado in that both are turbulent, spiral-shaped, and rotate. A real tornado occurs in the atmosphere.

Assessment

Oral Have students formulate questions about tornadoes and other types of severe weather. Use the Performance Task Assessment List for Asking Questions in **PASC**, p. 19. P

Assessment Planner

Portfolio

Refer to page 447 for suggested items that students might select for their portfolios.

Performance Assessment

See page 447 for additional Performance Assessment options.
Skill Builders, pp. 431, 439, 443
MiniLABs, pp. 425, 431
Activities 15-1, pp. 428-429; 15-2, p. 442

Content Assessment

Section Wrap-ups, pp. 431, 439, 443, 445
Chapter Review, pp. 447-449
Mini Quizzes, pp. 431, 439, 443

Group Assessment

Opportunities for group assessment occur with Cooperative Learning Strategies and Flex Your Brain Activities.

Section 15•1

Prepare

Section Background

Hail is produced only in cumulonimbus clouds, where strong updrafts and supercooled water exist. Rain freezes as it is tossed upward into the cloud. Each time a piece of ice is caught in an updraft and then falls again, a new layer is added to the hailstone.

Preplanning

- To prepare for the MiniLAB on page 425, obtain shiny metal containers and thermometers.
- To prepare for Activity 15-1, obtain the materials listed on p. 428.
- To prepare for the MiniLAB on page 431, collect tall, clear, widemouthed jars and plastic bags.

1 Motivate

Bellringer

Before presenting the lesson, display **Section Focus Transparency 57** on the overhead projector. Assign the accompanying **Focus Activity** worksheet. L1 LEP

Tying to Previous Knowledge

Students learned about the water cycle in Section 14-3. Have them review the processes shown in **Figure 14-13** on page 406.

15•1 What is weather?

Science Words

weather
humidity
relative humidity
saturated
dew point
fog
precipitation

Objectives

- Explain the role of water vapor in the atmosphere and how it affects weather.
- Describe how clouds form and how they are classified.
- Compare the development of rain, hail, sleet, and snow.

Factors of Weather

"What's the weather going to be today?" That's probably one of the first things you ask when you get up. Weather information can affect what you wear to school, how you get to and from school, and what you do after school.

Everyone discusses the weather. Can you explain what it is? **Weather** refers to the present state of the atmosphere and describes current conditions. One kind of weather is seen in **Figure 15-1.** Important factors determining the state of the atmosphere are air pressure, wind, temperature, and the amount of moisture in the air.

In Chapter 14, you learned about air pressure and how water moves around the hydrosphere in the water cycle. In the water cycle, the sun provides the energy to evaporate water into the atmosphere, where it forms clouds and eventually falls back to Earth.

The water cycle forms the basis of our weather. But the sun does more than just evaporate water. It also heats air, causing the winds that you learned about in Chapter 14. The interaction of air, water, and the sun causes weather.

Figure 15-1

The weather influences what you can do.

Program Resources

Reproducible Masters

Study Guide, p. 61 L1
Reinforcement, p. 61 L1
Enrichment, p. 61 L3
Activity Worksheets, pp. 5, 90-91, 94, 95 L1
Lab Manual 43
Cross-Curricular Integration, p. 19

Transparencies

Section Focus Transparency 57 L1
Teaching Transparency 29
Science Integration Transparency 15

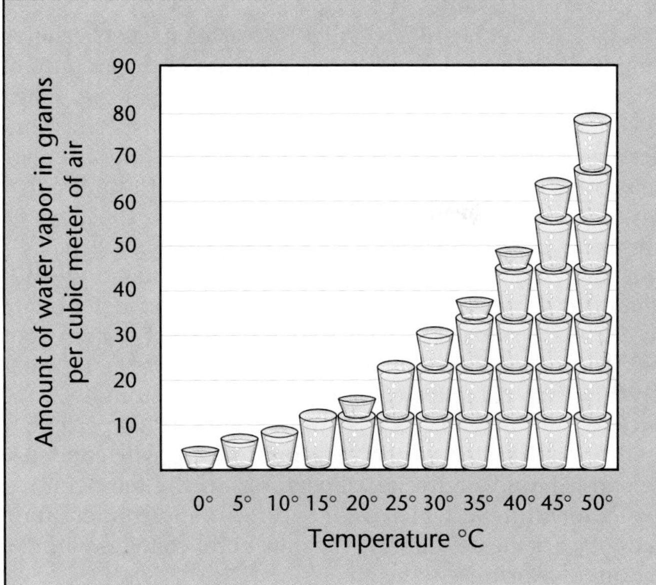

Figure 15-2

This graph shows that as the temperature of air increases, air can hold more water vapor.

Humidity

The sun evaporates water into the atmosphere. How does this happen? How can the atmosphere hold water? The air of the atmosphere is somewhat like a sponge. The holes in a sponge enable it to hold water. The atmosphere holds water in a similar way. Water vapor molecules fit into spaces between the molecules that make up air. The amount of water vapor held in air is called **humidity.**

Humidity varies from day to day because the temperature of the air changes. The amount of water vapor that air can hold depends on the temperature. At cooler temperatures, molecules in air move more slowly. This slow movement in cool air allows water vapor molecules to join together (condense). At warmer temperatures, air and water vapor molecules move too quickly to join together. The higher energy of the molecules in warm air prevents condensation and allows more water molecules to remain as water vapor than in cooler air. If you look at **Figure 15-2,** you'll see that at 25°C, a cubic meter of air can hold a maximum of 22 g of water vapor. The same air cooled to 15°C can hold only about 13 g of water vapor.

On hot summer days when the air seems damp and sticky, people often comment on the high humidity. When they mention humidity, they are actually talking about the relative humidity.

CONNECT TO

LIFE SCIENCE

Birds and mammals maintain a constant internal temperature. When the temperature outside the bodies of birds and mammals changes, their body temperature is regulated to remain fairly constant. On the other hand, the internal temperature of fish and reptiles changes when the temperature around them changes. ***Infer*** from this which group is more likely to survive a quick change in the weather.

2 Teach

CONNECT TO

LIFE SCIENCE

Animals with a constant body temperature are more likely to survive because their internal temperatures remain fairly constant despite rapid changes in outside temperature. Rapid temperature change puts stress on animals whose body temperatures change with the environment.

Discussion

Discuss with students direct and indirect ways that the weather affects their lives. One indirect effect is paying more at the market for fruits and vegetables when an agricultural region experiences a very wet or very dry growing season.

Inquiry Questions

- **What causes weather?** *The interaction of air, water, and the sun causes weather.*
- **How can air be compared with a sponge?** *A sponge has holes that allow it to hold liquids. Among air molecules are spaces that can hold water.*

GLENCOE TECHNOLOGY

CD-ROM

Earth Science CD-ROM

Have students perform the interactive exploration for Chapter 15 to reinforce important chapter concepts and thinking processes.

Use Lab 43 from the **Lab Manual** as you teach this lesson.

Demonstration

LS **Visual-Spatial** Make a concentrated solution of cobalt chloride and water and with a paintbrush apply the solution to several sheets of white paper. **CAUTION:** *Cobalt chloride is toxic by skin absorption—use gloves.* Let the solution dry. The dry precipitate can be used as an indicator of moisture in the air. Place these papers in different rooms in the school building, as well as outside. Students can record the color of the papers and discuss what may be causing the relative humidity to vary. Pink indicates a high relative humidity; blue a low relative humidity.

Inquiry Questions

- **Describe the effect temperature has on the ability of air to hold moisture.** *The warmer the air, the more water vapor it can hold.*
- **A computer room and a science room are the same size and have the same humidity. The computer room is colder. Which room has the higher relative humidity?** *The colder air in the computer room has a lower total capacity to hold water. The water vapor in the air of the computer room represents a greater percentage of the air's capacity. Thus, the computer room has a greater relative humidity.*

Science Journal

Stormy winds, piercing cold, and snowfall took their toll on the many soldiers who were barefoot and without proper clothing or blankets. A good reference for this information is: Ludlum, David, *The Weather Factor.* Boston: Houghton Mifflin Company, 1984, pp. 49-51.

Figure 15-3

When the air next to the glass cools to its dew point, condensation forms on the glass.

Science Journal

Weather affects history. Research what happened to American colonial troops at Valley Forge during the War of Independence in the winter of 1777–1778. Imagine that you were a soldier at Valley Forge during that winter. In your Science Journal, describe your experiences.

Relative Humidity

Have you ever heard a weather forecaster speak of relative humidity? **Relative humidity** is a measure of the amount of water vapor that air can hold at a specific temperature. When air contains as much moisture as possible at a specific temperature, it is **saturated.** If you hear a weather forecaster say the relative humidity is 50 percent, that means the air on that day contains 50 percent of the water needed for the air to be saturated.

As shown in **Figure 15-2,** air at 40°C is saturated when it contains just over 50 g of water vapor per cubic meter of air. Air at 25°C is saturated when it contains 22 g of water vapor per cubic meter of air. If air at 25°C contains only 11 g of water vapor in each cubic meter of air, the relative humidity is 50 percent. Saturated air has relative humidity of 100 percent.

Additional water vapor in saturated air will condense back to a liquid or freeze, depending on the temperature. The temperature at which air is saturated and condensation takes place is the **dew point.** The dew point changes with the amount of moisture in the air.

You've probably seen water droplets form on the outside of a glass of ice water, as in **Figure 15-3.** The cold glass cooled the air next to it to its dew point. The water vapor in the air condensed and formed water droplets on the glass. Dew on grass in the early morning forms the same way. When air near the ground is cooled to its dew point, water vapor condenses and forms droplets on the grass.

Cloud Formation

Why are there clouds in the sky? Clouds form as warm air is forced upward, expands, and cools, as shown in **Figure 15-4.** As the air cools, the amount of water vapor needed for saturation decreases and the relative humidity increases. When the relative humidity reaches 100 percent, the air is saturated. Water vapor begins to condense in tiny drops around nuclei, small particles of dust, salt, and smoke in the atmosphere. These drops of water are so small they become suspended in the air. When millions of these drops collect, a cloud forms.

Cloud Classification

As you will see in **Figure 15-5** on page 426, there are many different types of clouds in the sky. Clouds are classified mainly by shape and height. Some clouds stack up vertically, reaching high into the sky, while others are low and flat. Some dense clouds bring rain or snow, while thin clouds appear on mostly sunny days.

Across the Curriculum

Mathematics Have students work the following problem. At 20°C, a cubic meter of air can hold a total of 17 grams of water vapor. If only 4 grams are present, what is the relative humidity? $(4 \text{ g} \div 17 \text{ g}) \times 100\% = 23.5\%$ L1 LS

Shape

The three main cloud types are stratus, cumulus, and cirrus. Stratus clouds form layers or smooth, even sheets in the sky. When layers of air cool below their dew point temperatures, stratus clouds appear. Stratus clouds usually form at low altitudes. Although stratus clouds are associated with both fair weather and precipitation, sometimes they form a dull, gray blanket that hangs low in the sky and brings drizzle. When air is cooled to its dew point and condenses near the ground, it forms a stratus cloud called **fog. Figure 15-7** on page 430 shows a stratus cloud fog in San Francisco.

MiniLAB

How can dew point be determined?

Procedure

1. Partially fill a metal can with room-temperature water. Dry the outer surface of the can.
2. Slowly stir the water with a thermometer and add small amounts of ice.
3. In a data table in your Science Journal, note the exact temperature at which a thin film of moisture first begins to form on the outside of the metal can.
4. Repeat steps 1-3 two more times.
5. The average of the three temperatures at which the moisture begins to appear is the dew point temperature of the air around the container.

Analysis

1. What factors determine the dew point temperature?
2. Will a change in air temperature also cause the dew point temperature to change? Explain.

Figure 15-4

Clouds form when moist air is pushed high enough to reach its dew point. The water vapor condenses, forming water droplets that group together. Here are three ways clouds form.

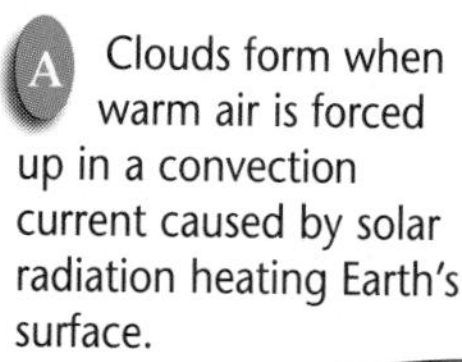

A Clouds form when warm air is forced up in a convection current caused by solar radiation heating Earth's surface.

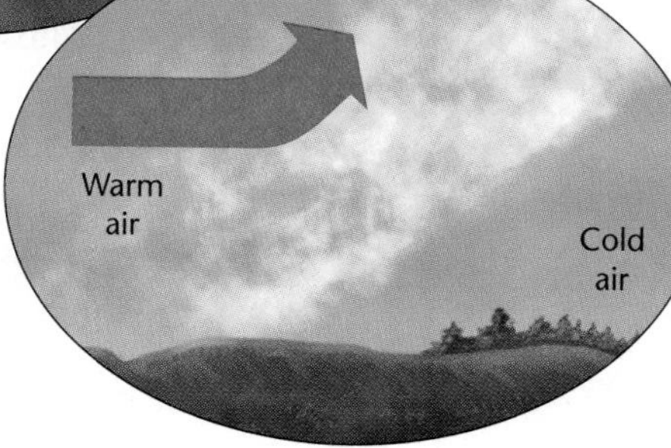

B Clouds form when warm, moist air is forced to rise over a mountain. The air cools and the water vapor condenses.

C Clouds form when two air masses meet. Warmer air is forced up over the cold air. As the warm air cools, the water vapor in it condenses.

Visual Learning

Figure 15-4 Have students describe the evolution of a cloud. Moist air is cooled to its dew point. Water droplets condense around dust particles in the atmosphere. Clouds form when millions of these drops collect. LEP LS

MiniLAB

Purpose

LS **Intrapersonal** Students will measure dew point temperature. L1

Materials

shiny metal can or cup, thermometer, water, crushed ice

Teaching Strategies

- Stress that the ice must be added to the water slowly. If water is cooled quickly, the water temperature may fall so rapidly that students will be unable to determine the temperature at which the moisture first begins to form on the outside of the can.
- Advise students to be certain that thermometers do not rest against the side of the container. Also, students should avoid striking the side of the container with the bulb of the thermometer to avoid breaking it.

Analysis

1. It is determined by the moisture content of the air and the air temperature.
2. No, dew point depends on moisture, not temperature. P

Assessment

Performance To assess students' understanding of how dew point is determined, have them determine the dew point at two different locations. Use the Performance Task Assessment List for Carrying Out a Strategy and Collecting Data in **PASC**, p. 25. P

Activity Worksheets, pp. 5, 94

Visual Learning

Figure 15-5 What do you think causes them to have different shapes? *How a cloud forms affects its shape. Quickly rising air currents cause water vapor to condense and form precipitation. The faster the air rises, the more towering the cloud.* LEP LS

Discussion

Have students contrast the altitudes and shapes of the following cloud types: nimbostratus, altostratus, and cirrostratus.

Activity

Have students use a video camera to take stop-frame pictures of clouds that are forming. Have them take one picture every 5 minutes for half an hour. Then have them show their tapes to the class at regular speed. L1 COOP LEARN

GLENCOE TECHNOLOGY

Videodisc

STVS: Chemistry

Disc 2, Side 1

Snowflakes (Ch. 3)

Cloud Chemistry (Ch. 22)

Use **Teaching Transparency 29** as you teach this lesson.

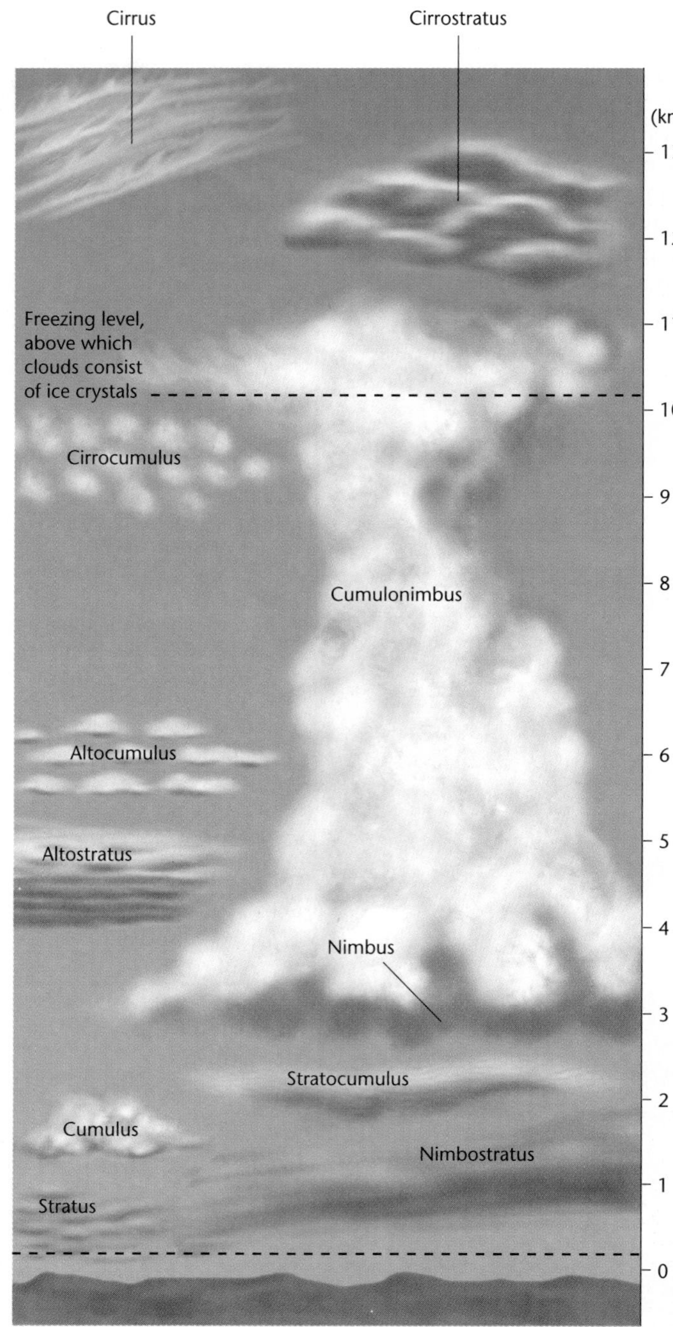

Figure 15-5

These are the most common types of clouds. *What do you think causes them to have different shapes?*

Cumulus clouds are masses of puffy, white clouds, often with flat bases. Some people refer to them as cauliflower clouds. They form when air currents rise. They may tower to great heights and can be associated with both fair weather and thunderstorms.

Cirrus clouds appear fibrous or curly. They are high, thin, white, feathery clouds containing ice crystals. Cirrus clouds are associated with fair weather, but they may indicate approaching storms.

Height

Some prefixes of cloud names describe the height of the cloud base. The prefix *cirro-* describes high clouds—clouds with a base starting above 6000 m; *alto-* describes middle elevation clouds—their base is between 2000 to 6000 m; and *strato-* refers to clouds below 2000 m. Some clouds' names combine the altitude prefix with the term *stratus* or *cumulus.*

Cirrostratus clouds are high clouds that look like fine veils. They are made of ice crystals that appear to form halos around the moon or sun. Usually cirrostratus clouds indicate fair weather, but they may also signal an approaching storm.

Altostratus clouds form at middle levels. They look like thick veils or sheets of gray or blue. If the clouds are not too thick, sunlight can filter through them. They produce light, continuous precipitation.

Rain Capacity

Nimbus clouds are dark clouds associated with precipitation. They are so full of water that no sunlight penetrates them. When a nimbus cloud is also a towering cumulus cloud, it is called a cumulonimbus cloud. Some cumulonimbus clouds grow huge, starting near Earth's surface and towering to nearly 18 000 m. Sudden, gigantic thunderstorms can be unleashed from them.

Nimbostratus clouds bring long, steady rain. They often have streaks that extend to the ground.

As long as the water drops in a cloud remain small, they stay suspended in the air. But when the water droplets combine and reach the size of 0.2 mm, they become too heavy and fall out of suspension in the cloud.

Figure 15-6

When water vapor in air collects on nuclei to form water droplets, the type of precipitation that is received on the ground depends on the temperature of the air.

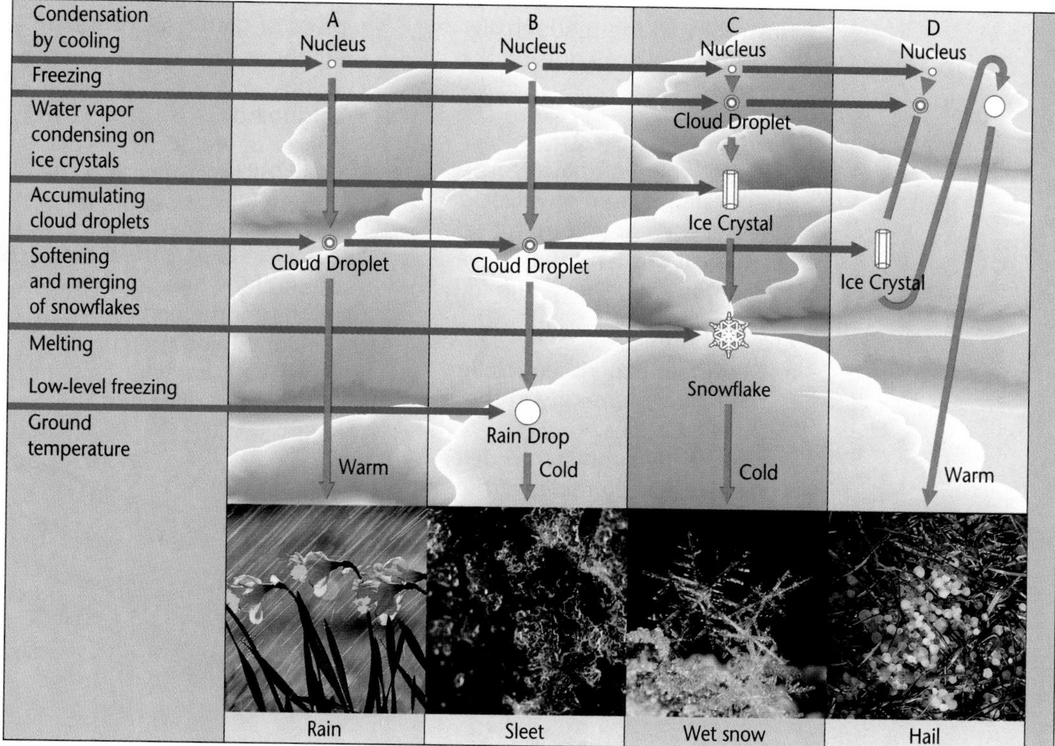

A When the air near the ground is warm, water vapor forms raindrops that fall as rain.

B When the air near the ground is cold, sleet, made up of many small ice pellets, falls.

C When the air is very cold, water vapor forms snowflakes.

D Hailstones are pellets of ice that form as the ice nuclei go up and down in the cloud.

MiniLAB

See page 431.

Purpose

LS **Visual-Spatial** Students will observe condensation and precipitation. L1 LEP COOP LEARN

Materials

tall, clear, widemouthed jar, hot water, ice cubes, plastic bag

Analysis

1. Droplets of water form on the bag and eventually coalesce and fall as precipitation.
2. Hot water evaporates. The vapor rises and cools; the molecules cluster together and condense as water droplets.

Assessment

Performance To further assess students' understanding of how to make rain, have them design an experiment relating the temperature of the water to the amount of rain that forms. Use the Performance Task Assessment List for Designing an Experiment in **PASC**, p. 23. P

Activity Worksheets, pp. 5, 95

NATIONAL GEOGRAPHIC SOCIETY

Videodisc

STV: Atmosphere

What Is the Atmosphere?

Unit 1, Side 1

Weather

015314-22294

Activity 15-1

PREPARATION

Purpose

Interpersonal Students will make a psychrometer and use it to compare the relative humidity in three locations. L1 COOP LEARN

Process Skills

communicating, comparing and contrasting, forming operational definitions, measuring in SI, designing an experiment, forming a hypothesis, recognizing cause and effect, separating and controlling variables, observing and inferring, making and using tables, interpreting data

Time

30 minutes to plan the experiment; 40 minutes to perform the experiment; 20 minutes to answer the Analyze and Apply questions

Materials

Have cardboard sheets cut for mounting the thermometers and gauze squares cut for wrapping the wet bulb thermometers. A chart for interpreting relative humidity data is provided in Appendix J.

Safety Precautions

Caution students to be careful when handling the glass thermometers, especially those containing mercury.

Possible Hypothesis

Students may have a variety of hypotheses; however, in each location, they should consider both the amount of moisture and the temperature of the air when making their hypotheses.

Activity Worksheets, pp. 5, 90-91

Activity 15-1

Design Your Own Experiment
Is it humid or not?

Does it feel humid today or does the air feel dry? You can tell by examining your hair. On a day when the relative humidity is high, hair tends to be more curly than on a dry day. The relative humidity can be more accurately determined by using a psychrometer, a device with thermometers—one wet and one dry.

PREPARATION

Problem

Where is the relative humidity the highest? In your science classroom, in the school hallway, or on the walkway outside the school?

Form a Hypothesis

Recall what you have learned about relative humidity. Decide whether the conditions in the three locations lend themselves to high or low relative humidity.

Objectives

- Design an experiment to find the relative humidity in the three locations.
- Make a psychrometer to determine relative humidity at the three locations. On the psychrometer below, the wet bulb has material covering it.

Possible Materials

- identical Celsius thermometers (2)
- piece of gauze, 2-cm square
- tape
- string
- cardboard
- beaker of water
- table for determining relative humidity in Appendix J

Safety Precautions

Be careful when you handle glass thermometers, especially those containing mercury. If one breaks, have your teacher dispose of the glass and the mercury safely.

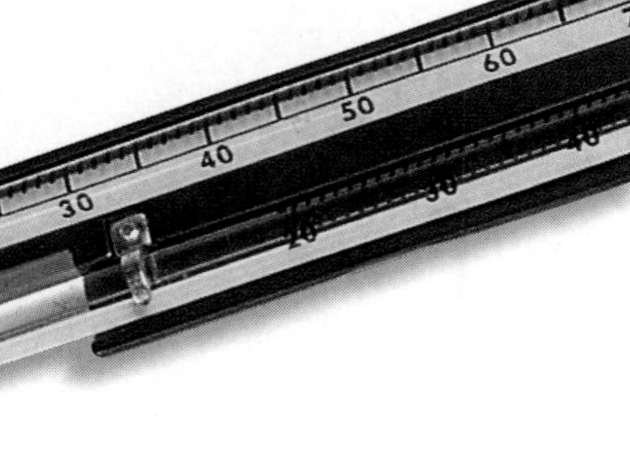

Wet bulb

Dry bulb

PLAN THE EXPERIMENT

Possible Procedures

To make the psychrometer, have students tie a piece of gauze to the bulb of one thermometer. This thermometer can be taped to a sheet of cardboard with the bulb extending beyond the edge of the cardboard. Students should tape the other thermometer next to the first, but with its bulb even with the edge. At each location, dip the gauze into the beaker of water, and slowly fan the thermometers with a piece of paper. After 5 minutes, students should read the thermometers and record the temperatures. To determine the relative humidity, they can use the table based on the temperature of the dry bulb thermometer and the difference in temperature between the wet bulb and the dry bulb thermometer.

PLAN THE EXPERIMENT

1. As a group, write out your hypothesis statement and plan for the experiment.
2. Here is how a psychrometer works. Moisture from the wet thermometer uses heat energy as it evaporates. When the moisture evaporates, it lowers the temperature of its environment.
3. List the steps needed to measure the relative humidity of the three locations. Include how you will (a) saturate each wet bulb thermometer; (b) protect the psychrometers from wind; (c) record the temperatures of the thermometers; and (d) determine the relative humidity using the relative humidity table provided by your teacher.
4. Design a data table in your Science Journal for your data.

Check the Plan

1. Make certain that you understand how to obtain accurate temperature readings.
2. Read through the concluding questions for more information about expected results of the experiment.
3. Identify the constant and the variable in the experiment.
4. How can you make certain that the tests at each location are exactly the same?
5. *Before you proceed, have your teacher approve your plan.*

DO THE EXPERIMENT

1. Carry out the experiment as planned.
2. While the experiment is going on, write down observations in your Science Journal. Complete your data table.

Analyze and Apply

1. From your results, **infer** why the molecules of water on the gauze of the wet bulb thermometer react differently in dry air and in saturated air.
2. **Conclude** why the relative humidity varied at your three test sites, if this happened.
3. **Hypothesize** about how the relative humidity in your classroom can be decreased.

Go Further

Continue your experiment at the three locations for a longer period and make a graph from your data. Discuss any patterns you see.

Assessment

Oral Ask students how the relative humidity of the air will affect the amount of moisture evaporated from the gauze. Then ask how the moisture affects the temperature difference between the wet bulb and dry bulb thermometers. They should hypothesize that the less humid the air, the greater the evaporation from the gauze and the greater the temperature difference between the two thermometers. Use the Performance Task Assessment List for Formulating a Hypothesis in **PASC**, p. 21. P

Teaching Strategies

Troubleshooting At each test site, the temperature of the water used to wet the bulbs must be the same as the air temperature. The psychrometers will not work if the air temperature is less than 0°C. The temperature of the wet bulb thermometer should never be higher than the dry bulb reading. If this occurs, have students re-collect data.

- Students may need help interpreting their data from the relative humidity table in Appendix J.

DO THE EXPERIMENT

Expected Outcome

Students will likely determine that the relative humidities at the three sites are different.

Analyze and Apply

1. In dry air, water molecules on the gauze will evaporate quickly. In saturated air, water molecules will not evaporate. This affects the temperature.
2. The three sites usually have different temperatures and amounts of moisture. Thus, the relative humidities will differ.
3. Increase the temperature to decrease the relative humidity.

Go Further

Students may or may not see patterns in their graphs, depending on the relative humidity at their three sites for the three days.

Problem Solving

Solve the Problem

1. The heat caused the water to evaporate.
2. Some of the molecules in the air made contact with the wall, reached the dew point, and condensed.

Think Critically

Turn on the heat. Warmer air can hold more water vapor. As the air heats up, the moisture on the windows will evaporate.

3 Assess

Check for Understanding

Have students classify today's clouds. Use **Figure 15-5** to determine the approximate height of the clouds and to forecast tomorrow's weather. Have students predict what kind of precipitation might fall from the clouds.

Reteach

LS **Visual-Spatial** Have students observe clouds for three consecutive days. Have them use **Figure 15-5** to identify the clouds observed. Also have them record the weather each day. At the end of the three days, have them compare and contrast their observations with the information on pp. 424-427. Have students note discrepancies between their observations and the information in this section.

Extension

For students who have mastered this section, use the **Reinforcement** and **Enrichment** masters.

Problem Solving

Evaporation and Condensation

Suppose you decide to make some spaghetti for lunch. You fill a large pot full of water and turn the burner to the highest temperature setting. After a few minutes of watching the pot, waiting for the water to boil, you get bored. You watch TV while you wait.

You get so interested in the show that you forget about the water. When you finally return to the kitchen, you see that the pot is now only ½ full of boiling water. On the wall above the stove are droplets of water.

Solve the Problem

1. **What happened to ½ of the water that was originally put into the pot?**
2. **How did water get on the wall?**

Think Critically:

If you get into a car and the windows begin fogging up, what can you do to make the moisture disappear—turn on the heater or turn on the air conditioner, or does it matter? Explain your answer.

Figure 15-7

Fog surrounds the Golden Gate Bridge, San Francisco. Fog is a stratus cloud near the ground.

Precipitation

Water falling from clouds is called precipitation. Air temperature determines whether the water droplets form rain, snow, sleet, or hail—the four main types of precipitation. **Figure 15-6** on page 427 shows how four types of precipitation form. Drops of water falling in temperatures above freezing fall as rain. Snow forms when the air temperature is so cold (at least below freezing) that water vapor changes directly to a solid. Sleet forms when snow passes through a layer of warm air, melts, and then refreezes near the ground.

Hail is precipitation in the form of lumps of ice. Hail forms in cumulonimbus clouds of a thunderstorm when drops of water freeze in layers around a small nucleus of ice. Hailstones grow larger as they're tossed up and down by rising and falling convection currents. Most hailstones are smaller than 2.5 cm but can

Figure 15-8

A large hailstone appears to have a layered structure much like an onion.

grow to the size shown in **Figure 15-8.** Of all forms of precipitation, hail produces the most damage immediately, especially if winds blow during a hailstorm. Falling hailstones can break windows and destroy crops.

By understanding the role of water vapor in the atmosphere, you can begin to understand weather. The relative humidity of the air helps determine whether a location will have a dry day or experience some form of precipitation. The temperature of the atmosphere determines the form of precipitation. Studying clouds can add to your ability to forecast weather.

MiniLAB

Can you make it rain?

Procedure

1. Pour a few centimeters of hot water into a tall, clear, wide-mouthed jar.
2. Put ice cubes in a small plastic bag. Suspend the bag from the top of the jar, and let it hang down inside.

Analysis

1. In your Science Journal, describe what you see.
2. Describe what is happening to the water vapor in the jar.

Section Wrap-up

Review

1. When does water vapor in air condense?
2. How do clouds form?
3. **Think Critically:** How can the same cumulonimbus cloud produce both rain and hail?

Skill Builder

Concept Mapping

Make a network tree concept map that compares four clouds. Use these terms: *cirrus, cumulus, stratus, nimbus, feathery, fair weather, puffy, layered, precipitation, clouds, dark,* and *steady precipitation.* If you need help, refer to Concept Mapping in the **Skill Handbook.**

USING MATH

Use the graph in **Figure 15-2** to determine the amount of water vapor air can hold when its temperature is 50°C.

MiniLAB teacher material is on page 427.

4 Close

• MINI • QUIZ •

1. _____ is the present state of the atmosphere. *Weather*
2. _____ is the amount of water vapor in the air. *Humidity*
3. _____ is the amount of water vapor in air, compared with the total amount of water vapor it can hold at a particular temperature. *Relative humidity*
4. _____ air has 100% relative humidity. *Saturated*
5. The _____ is the temperature at which air is saturated and condensation takes place. *dew point*

Section Wrap-up

Review

1. Water vapor condenses as temperature decreases to the dew point.
2. Clouds form when air is cooled to its dew point and water vapor condenses around dust particles.
3. **Think Critically** In a cumulonimbus cloud, water droplets near the top of the cloud freeze around small ice nuclei. Hailstones grow larger as air currents toss them up and down. If the hailstone is small and melts, or if condensation has taken place in the lower parts of the cloud and the temperature is above freezing, rain will fall.

USING MATH

LS **Logical-Mathematical** 80 grams per cubic meter of air

Skill Builder

Possible solution:

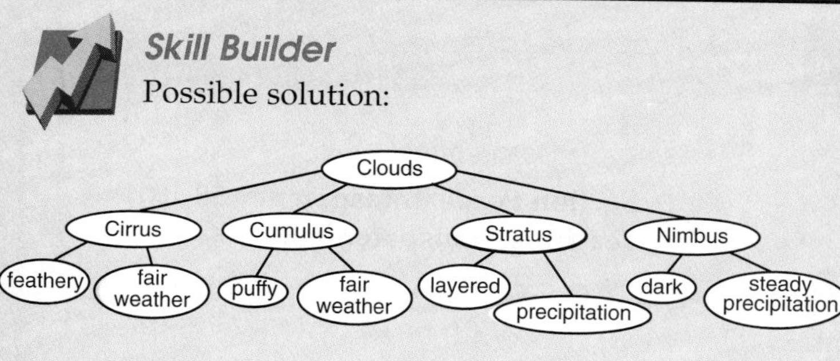

P

Assessment

Performance Use this Skill Builder to assess students' abilities to make concept maps. Ask students to add information about cumulonimbus and cirrocumulus clouds to their concept maps. Use the Performance Task Assessment List for Concept Map in **PASC,** p. 89. P

Section 15•2

Prepare

Section Background

The stability of an air mass is one factor that determines the weather of an area. Warm, moist air masses are said to be unstable. The warm air at the surface, because it is less dense, will tend to be forced aloft, producing clouds, precipitation, and storms. Cold, dry air masses are stable because cold air is more dense than warmer air and tends to evaporate less moisture.

1 Motivate

Bellringer

Before presenting the lesson, display **Section Focus Transparency 58** on the overhead projector. Assign the accompanying **Focus Activity** worksheet. L1 LEP

Tying to Previous Knowledge

In Chapter 14, students learned about air pressure. In this section, they will learn how differences in air pressure affect the weather.

Visual Learning

Figure 15-9 What air masses affect the weather in your region of the country? *Answers will vary.* LEP LS

15•2 Weather Patterns

Science Words

air mass
front
tornado
hurricane

Objectives

- Describe the weather associated with fronts and high and low pressure areas.
- Explain how low pressure systems form at fronts.
- Relate thunderstorms to tornadoes.

Changes in Weather

Why do you ask about the weather in the morning when you get up? Isn't it safe to assume that the weather is the same as it was the day before? Of course not! Weather is always changing because of the constant movement of air and moisture in the atmosphere. These changes are generally related to the development and movement of air masses.

Air Masses

An **air mass** is a large body of air that has the same properties as the surface over which it develops. For example, an air mass that develops over land is dry compared with one that develops over water. Also, an air mass that develops in the tropics is warmer than one that develops at a higher latitude. When you witness a change in the weather from one day to the next, it is due to the movement of air masses. **Figure 15-9** shows air masses that affect the United States.

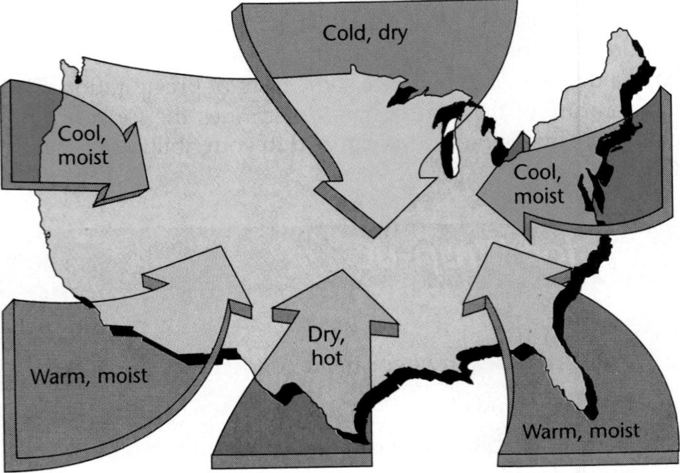

Figure 15-9

There are six major air masses that affect weather in the United States. Each air mass has the same characteristics of temperature and moisture content as the area over which it formed. *What air masses affect the weather in your region of the country?*

Pressure Systems

You have heard weather forecasters mention low and high pressure systems. What are they? In the atmosphere, great masses of air molecules push down from above, creating atmospheric pressure at Earth's surface. As you learned in the last chapter, atmospheric pressure at sea level varies over the surface of Earth. The temperature, the density, and the amount of water vapor of the air help determine the atmospheric pressure.

Program Resources

Reproducible Masters

Study Guide, p. 62 L1
Reinforcement, p. 62 L1
Enrichment, p. 62 L3
Multicultural Connections, pp. 33-34
Science Integration Activities, pp. 29-30
Lab Manual 44

Transparencies

Section Focus Transparency 58 L1
Teaching Transparency 30

Variation in atmospheric pressure affects the weather. Areas of high pressure at Earth's surface are regions of descending air. Section 15-1 explained that clouds form when air rises and cools. The sinking motion in high pressure air masses makes it difficult for air to rise and clouds to form. That's why high pressure usually means good weather. Areas of low pressure usually have cloudy weather.

Fronts

In between regions of higher pressure will be areas of lower pressure. Low pressure systems form along the boundaries of air masses. The boundary between two different air masses is called a **front.** Storms and precipitation occur at these fronts.

At a front, air at the surface moves from the high pressure systems into the low pressure systems. As the air converges into the low pressure area, it flows under the less dense, warm air, forcing it upward. As the air in a low pressure system rises, it cools. At a certain elevation, the air reaches its dew point, and the water vapor in it condenses, forming clouds. **Figure 15-10** shows how a low pressure system can develop at the boundary between cold and warm air.

Figure 15-10

These diagrams show how a disturbance occurs along a front.

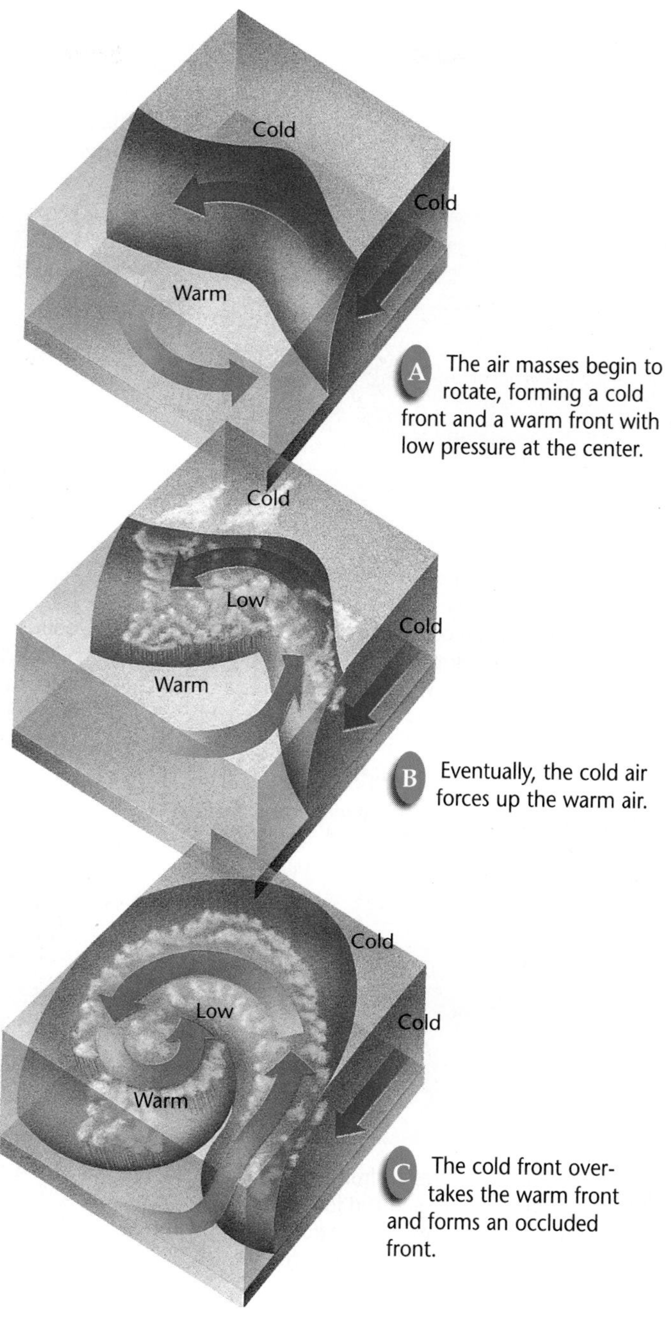

2 Teach

Inquiry Question

Why don't pressure systems stay in one place for very long? *Winds move them.*

Activity

Have students listen to daily weather reports on the radio and TV to learn what terms meteorologists use to describe weather. L1

Visual Learning

Figure 15-10 Have students use this figure to describe how pressure systems evolve. LEP LS

FLEX Your Brain

Use the Flex Your Brain activity to have students explore AIR MASSES.

Activity Worksheets, p. 5

Content Background

Fronts form in a narrow zone of transition between different air masses. Since fronts are associated with low pressure troughs, air pressure drops as a front approaches an area. Pressure rises as the front passes the area. As a front passes, winds near Earth's surface often shift clockwise in the northern hemisphere.

Use **Teaching Transparency 30** as you teach this lesson.

GLENCOE TECHNOLOGY

 **Videodisc**

The Infinite Voyage: Living with Disaster
Chapter 3
The Hurricane: The Most Powerful Storm

STVS: Physics
Disc 1, Side 1
Tornado Detectors (Ch. 17)

Demonstration

LS **Visual-Spatial** Use an aquarium with a glass lid, cold bags of sand or marbles, and a pan of very hot water to make a model of a cold front. Place the pan of hot water inside the aquarium next to the cold bags. Cover the aquarium with a glass lid. Have students observe what happens. They will notice that condensation occurs on the sides and top of the aquarium, and clouds appear above the cold bags. There is no cloud above the pan because the temperature of the air prevents condensation. LEP

Visual Learning

Figure 15-11 A. What other clouds occur at a warm front? *possibly cumulus, nimbus, or altostratus* **B. What weather do these clouds bring?** *both fair weather and rain with possible severe weather* LEP LS

Inquiry Question

Why is stormy weather often associated with fronts? *There is rapid movement of warm air upward where two air masses meet. The rising air cools and reaches its dew point; clouds form; and precipitation begins.*

At fronts where two air masses with different characteristics meet, the air does not mix, but instead, the cold air mass moves under the warm air. The warm air rises. Winds begin. As surface winds blow from a high pressure area into a low pressure area, the Coriolis effect turns the winds and makes them circulate counterclockwise around the low pressure area.

Most changes in weather occur at one of four types of fronts—warm, cold, occluded, or stationary, as illustrated in **Figure 15-11.** Fronts usually bring a change in temperature and always bring a change in wind direction.

Figure 15-11

These diagrams show the structure of a warm, a cold, an occluded, and a stationary front.

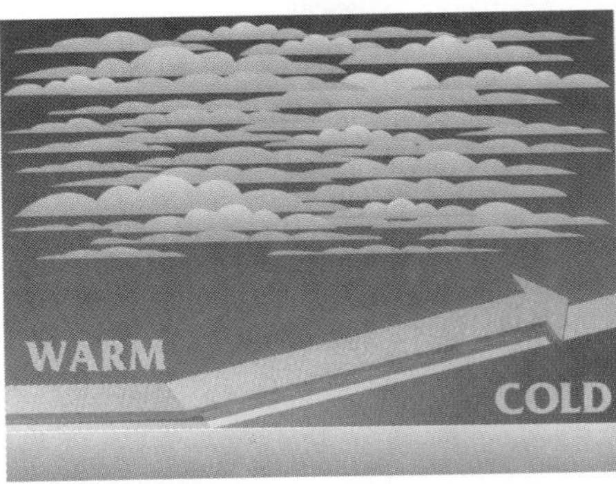

A A warm front develops when a less dense, warm air mass slides over a departing cold air mass. Precipitation occurs over a wide band. Look for high cirrus clouds to form as water vapor condenses. *What other clouds occur at a warm front?*

B In a cold front, a cold air mass pushes under a warm air mass and forces the warm air aloft along a steep front. There is a narrow band of violent storms. Cold fronts often move at twice the speed of warm fronts. Cumulus and cumulonimbus clouds form along the front. *What weather do these clouds bring?*

C An occluded front results from two cool air masses merging and forcing warmer air between them to rise. Strong winds and heavy precipitation may occur.

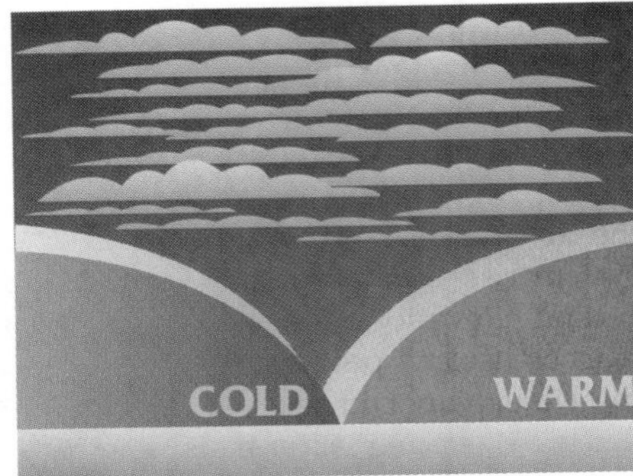

D A stationary front occurs when pressure differences cause a warm front or a cold front to stop moving. A stationary front may remain in the same place for several days. Weather conditions include light wind and precipitation across the entire frontal region.

Across the Curriculum

History/Language Arts In the 1920s, the term *front* was used to describe the boundary between two air masses because this boundary was similar to the front along which opposing armies fought. The term was first used by Norwegian meteorologists. L1

GLENCOE TECHNOLOGY

Videodisc

STVS: Physics

Disc 1, Side 1

Lightning (Ch. 18)

Severe Weather

Weather affects you every day. Usually, you can still go about your business regardless of the weather. If it's raining, you can still go to school. Even if it snows a little, you can still get to school. But some weather conditions, such as those caused by blizzards, thunderstorms, and tornadoes, prevent you from going about your normal routine. Severe weather poses danger to people and animals.

Thunderstorms

INTEGRATION Physics

In a thunderstorm, heavy rain falls, lightning flashes, thunder roars, and maybe hail falls. What forces cause such extreme weather conditions? Thunderstorms occur inside warm, moist air masses and at fronts. They occur when warm, moist air moves upward rapidly, cools, condenses, and forms cumulonimbus clouds that can reach heights of 18 km. As the rising air reaches its dew point, water droplets and ice form and begin falling the long distance through the clouds toward Earth's surface. The falling droplets collide with other droplets and grow larger. The heavier raindrops fall, dragging down the air with them and creating downdrafts of air that spread out at Earth's surface. These downdrafts cause the strong winds associated with thunderstorms.

Thunderstorms also contain thunder and lightning. Lightning, like that in **Figure 15-12,** occurs when a rapid uplift of air builds up electric charges in the clouds. Some places in the clouds have a positive electrical charge and some have a negative electrical charge. When current flows between regions of opposite electrical charge, lightning flashes. Bolts of lightning can leap from cloud to cloud and from Earth to clouds.

Thunder results from the rapid heating of the air around a bolt of lightning. Lightning can reach temperatures of about 30 000°C, more than five times the temperature of the surface of the sun! This extreme heat causes the air around the lightning to expand rapidly. Then it cools quickly and contracts. The molecules, moving rapidly back and forth, form sound waves heard as thunder.

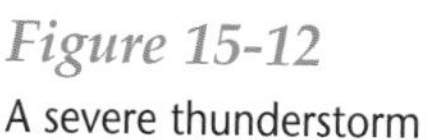

Figure 15-12

A severe thunderstorm breaks over Arizona.

Revealing Preconceptions

Prior to their reading about thunderstorms on this page, ask students whether lightning ever travels from Earth's surface to clouds. They are likely to say no. Explain that in less than 1/10 of a second, a single lightning discharge goes back and forth many times between a cloud and the ground. Although these discharges usually begin in clouds, sometimes they begin on Earth.

INTEGRATION Physics

Lightning is static electricity created by the rapid upward rush of air in a cumulonimbus cloud. Atoms rushing by one another create friction that separates electrons from some of the atoms. Atoms in the cloud or on the ground that lose electrons become positively charged ions, while atoms that receive extra electrons become negatively charged ions. When a sufficient number of ions builds up, an arc of electricity is created where the oppositely charged ions rush toward each other. This arc is lightning.

Content Background

Explain to students that a thunderstorm has a life cycle of three stages. The initial stage or the *cumulus* stage of strong updrafts lasts for about 15 minutes. The *mature* stage is the most intense period and begins as rain falls from the base of the clouds. The falling rain produces a downdraft that spreads along the ground. Lightning, turbulence, and hail can be most severe during this stage. The downdrafts finally cut off the updrafts and the cumulonimbus cloud can no longer develop, beginning the final stage. Precipitation and turbulence cease as the cloud evaporates.

Community Connection

Economics Have students research the effects that thunderstorms have on the economy of your area. L1

Inquiry Question

Ask students, **Why do you think hail occurs during thunderstorms?** *Thunderstorms result from rapid, upward movements of warm, moist air. Rain freezes as the drops are caught in the updrafts and carried to high altitudes. When these ice granules fall through the clouds, they collect droplets of water. Eventually, the ice balls fall as hail.*

USING MATH

LS Logical-Mathematical There is a difference of 299 999 668 meters per second. That means light travels 903 614.5 times faster than sound in air. Because light waves from lightning travel much more quickly than sound waves from thunder, lightning is usually observed much sooner than thunder. Only when lightning strikes close by are thunder and lightning sensed at nearly the same time.

Teacher F.Y.I.

Many tornadoes in the United States occur in a region called "Tornado Alley." This region extends from northern Texas through Oklahoma, Kansas, and Missouri. In these areas, cool, dry air masses from the north and northwest collide with warm, moist air masses from the Gulf of Mexico. As many as 300 tornadoes touch down each year throughout Tornado Alley.

GLENCOE TECHNOLOGY

Videodisc

The Infinite Voyage: Living with Disaster

Chapter 1

Microbursts: How the Airline Industry Copes

USING MATH

The speed of light is 300 000 kilometers per second. The speed of sound in air is 332 meters per second. How much faster does light travel than sound? Explain why you do not usually see lightning and hear the thunder it creates at the same time.

Thunderstorms can cause a lot of damage. Their heavy rain sometimes causes flooding, and lightning can strike objects and set them on fire. Strong winds generated by thunderstorms can also cause damage. If a thunderstorm has winds traveling faster than 89 km per hour, it is classified as a severe thunderstorm. Hail from a thunderstorm can make dents in cars and the aluminum siding on houses. Although rain from thunderstorms helps crops grow, hail has been known to flatten and destroy a crop in a matter of minutes.

Tornadoes

Some of the most severe thunderstorms produce tornadoes. A **tornado** is a violent, whirling wind that moves in a narrow path over land, usually in a direction from southwest to northeast. Most tornadoes form along a front. In very severe thunderstorms, the wind at different heights blows in different directions and at different speeds. This difference in wind direction and speed is called *wind shear*. A strong updraft will tilt the wind shear and produce rotation inside the thunderstorm. A funnel cloud appears. **Figure 15-13** shows how a tornado funnel forms. Recall the tornado you made in the Explore activity.

Some tornado funnels do not reach Earth. Funnel clouds that touch down pick up dirt and debris from the ground, giving the funnels their dark gray or black color. Sometimes tornadoes

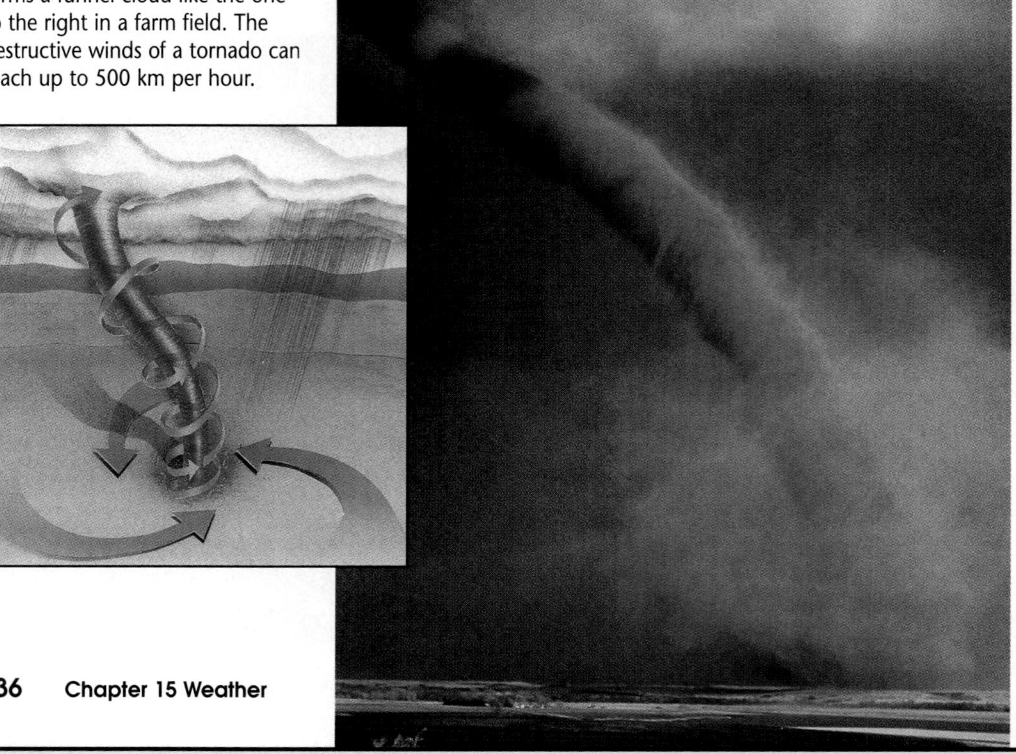

Figure 15-13

The diagram shows how wind forms a funnel cloud like the one to the right in a farm field. The destructive winds of a tornado can reach up to 500 km per hour.

Cultural Diversity

Weather Gods Gods related to weather, particularly storms, are found in many cultures. The Maya deity Huracan caused tornadoes and hurricanes. In arid countries, people such as the Tuareg have sand funnel spirits. Early Peruvians had a desert wind god named Kon. Thunderstorm and rain deities have been particularly popular. Thunder gods frequently accompanied by horses, goats, or rams that pulled a thundering sky vehicle threw bundles of thunderbolts, stone axes, or lightning bolts at Earth. Examples include Thor-Donar (German), Taranis (Celtic), Perkunis (Slavic), Indra (Indian), Zeus (Greek), Jupiter (Roman), Ukko (Finnish), Orko (Basque), Teshub and Hadad (western Asian), Shango (Yoruban, Nigerian), and Chac Mool (Mayan). Another group of deities consists of thunderbirds. Zu is an ancient

strike Earth, go back up into the atmosphere, then dip down and strike another area.

When tornadoes touch the ground, their destructive winds rip apart buildings and trees. Winds of the tornado can reach up to 500 km per hour. High winds can blow through broken windows. When winds blow inside a house, they can lift off the roof and blow out the walls, making it look as though the building had exploded. The updraft in the center of a powerful tornado can lift animals, cars, and even houses into the air. Although tornadoes rarely exceed 200 m in diameter and usually last only a few minutes, they are often extremely destructive.

Tornadoes occur worldwide, but most tornadoes touch down in the United States—about 700 per year. Tornadoes most frequently

USING TECHNOLOGY

Tailing a Tornado

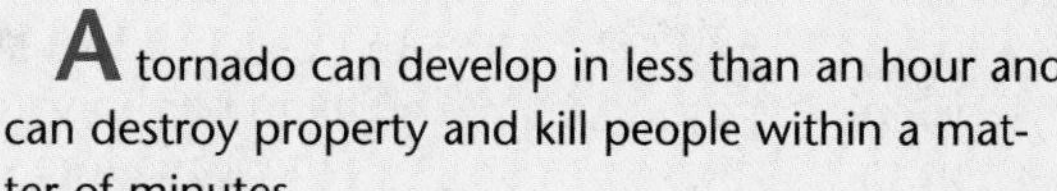

A tornado can develop in less than an hour and can destroy property and kill people within a matter of minutes.

Next Generation Weather Radar, or NEXRAD, is a system of radar stations that uses Doppler radar to track severe weather storms such as tornadoes. Doppler radar sends out radio waves toward the storms. The waves reflect off the water droplets of storm clouds and are recorded at the radar station. The shift in frequency of the reflected signals allows meteorologists to determine the position, strength, and wind speed of the storm. Doppler radar helps scientists detect funnel clouds before they touch down. The weather service issues an advisory if the conditions are right for a tornado to form. If a tornado is spotted, the weather service issues a warning to people in its path.

Watching for a Tornado

Think Critically: Suppose a tornado were moving toward your town at 100 km/h. If Doppler radar spotted the storm 160 km from your town, how much time would you have to prepare for the storm?

USING TECHNOLOGY

- Inform students that waves reflected from storms have different frequencies. The frequencies appear on the Doppler radar screen as different colors. Green indicates winds coming toward the station; red indicates winds moving away from the station. When red and green signals appear close together, rotation is occurring.
- For more information, see "Next-Generation Radar Passes Milestone," *Business & Commercial Aviation,* August 1988, p. 37 or "Eye on the Storm," *Scientific American,* August 1987, p. 22.

Think Critically
100 km/1 h = 160 km/ ? h
? h = 160 km/100 km × 1 h
? h = 1.6 h or 1 h and 36 min

Inquiry Question

In which direction do tornadoes rotate in the northern hemisphere? Explain. *The Coriolis effect on tornadoes is minimal. Therefore, tornadoes may rotate either clockwise or counterclockwise, but in the northern hemisphere they mainly rotate counterclockwise because of the rotation of the thunderstorms that generate them.*

Activity

LS **Kinesthetic** Have students work together to make mobiles of different weather-related phenomena including precipitation types, cloud types, frontal systems, storm types, or weather systems. Such a mobile could show the different altitudes at which various clouds form. L1 LEP COOP LEARN

Cultural Diversity (con't)

Mesopotamian thunderbird, as are the Garuda of India. Thunderbirds, some clutching arrows or spears in their beaks or claws, appear in artifacts from Siberia, Viet Nam, and Peru. In the U.S., thunderbirds also are featured in stories and art of the Pueblo, northwest coast, and prairie cultures. Have students explain what arrows or spears in the thunderbirds' beaks and claws might represent. *lightning*

Community Connection

Weather Forecasting Invite a meteorologist to visit the class and talk about weather forecasting.

USING MATH

 **Logical-Mathematical** Students should label and design a scale for each axis. Start fatality scale at zero.

GLENCOE TECHNOLOGY

Videodisc

The Infinite Voyage: Living with Disaster

Chapter 2

Doppler Radar: Microburst Detection

STVS: Earth & Space

Disc 3, Side 1

World's Worst Weather (Ch. 15)

Studying Thunderstorms (Ch. 16)

Reducing Hail Damage (Ch. 17)

3 Assess

Check for Understanding

Have students compare and contrast different kinds of severe weather.

Reteach

Interpersonal Have pairs of students compare and contrast tornadoes and hurricanes in terms of the boldfaced terms **relative size, origin, type of pressure system, damage.** COOP LEARN

Extension

For students who have mastered this section, use the **Reinforcement** and **Enrichment** masters.

USING MATH

The number of fatalities due to hurricanes in the United states are as follows:

1940s	216
1950s	877
1960s	587
1970s	217
1980s	118

Make a bar graph of these data.

strike the Midwest and South, usually in spring or early summer. Texas, Oklahoma, and Kansas report the most tornadoes.

Hurricanes

The most powerful storm is the hurricane. A **hurricane** is a large, swirling, low pressure system that forms over tropical oceans. It is like a machine that turns heat energy from the ocean into wind. A storm must have winds of at least 120 km per hour to be called a hurricane.

Hurricanes are similar to low pressure systems on land, but they are much stronger. **Figure 15-14** illustrates the mechanics of the hurricane. In the North Atlantic, the southeast trade winds and the northeast trade winds sometimes meet. A low pressure area develops in the middle of the swirl and begins rotating counterclockwise in the northern hemisphere. This usually happens between 5° and 20° north latitude, where the water is quite warm. Around the middle of the low pressure area, warm, moist air is forced up. As it rises to higher elevations, it cools and moisture condenses.

Figure 15-15 shows a hurricane hitting land. When a hurricane strikes land, the high winds, tornadoes, heavy rains, and high waves of the storm surge cause a lot of damage. Floods from the heavy rains can cause additional damage. The weather of the hurricane can destroy crops, demolish buildings, and kill people and other animals. In 1992, Hurricane Andrew hit Florida and Louisiana, killing 14 people and causing more than 25 billion dollars in damage.

As long as a hurricane is over water, the warm, moist air rises and provides energy for the storm. When a hurricane reaches land, however, its supply of warm, moist air disappears and the storm loses power.

Figure 15-14

In this hurricane cross section, the small red arrows indicate rising warm, moist air. This rising air forms cumulus and cumulonimbus clouds in bands around the eye. The blue arrows indicate cool, dry air sinking in the eye and between the cloud bands. The large red arrows indicate the circular motion of the rising spiral cloud bands.

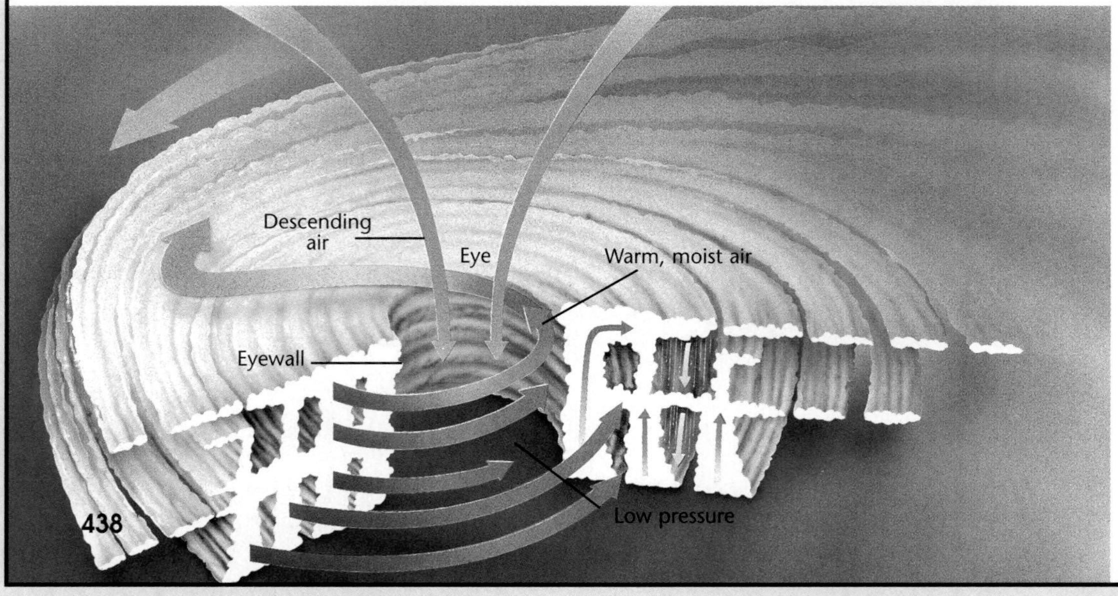

Using Computers

Type of Front	Cause	Resulting Weather
Warm	warm air slides over departing cold air mass	cirrus, altostratus, and nimbostratus clouds, precipitation over wide area
Cold	cold air mass pushes under warm air mass	cumulus and cumulonimbus clouds, narrow band of violent storms
Stationary	warm or cold front stops moving	light wind and precipitation across entire frontal region
Occluded	two cold air masses merge forcing warm air aloft	cumulonimbus and stratocumulus clouds, strong winds and heavy precipitation may occur P

Most hurricanes in the United States strike along the Gulf of Mexico or along the Atlantic Coast. Mexico often sustains damage from hurricanes along its Pacific coast as well as its Atlantic Coast. Find out what happens to the islands of the Caribbean Ocean during an average hurricane season.

Changes in weather affect your life. The interaction of air and water vapor cause constant change in the atmosphere. Air masses meet and fronts form, causing changes in weather. Severe weather can affect human lives and property.

Figure 15-15
Hurricanes can be very destructive, killing people and destroying property.

Section Wrap-up

Review

1. Why do high pressure areas usually have clear skies?
2. Explain how a tornado evolves from a thunderstorm.
3. **Think Critically:** How do two fronts form at a low pressure area? Which would bring the most severe weather?

Skill Builder

Recognizing Cause and Effect

Use your knowledge of weather to answer the following questions. If you need help, refer to Recognizing Cause and Effect in the **Skill Handbook.**

1. What effect does a warm, dry air mass have on the area over which it moves?
2. What causes a cold front? What effect does a cold front produce?
3. Describe the cause and effect of an occluded front that might form over your city.

Using Computers

Spreadsheet Make a spreadsheet comparing warm fronts, cold fronts, stationary fronts, and occluded fronts. Indicate what kind of severe clouds and weather systems form with each.

4 Close

•MINI•QUIZ•

Use the Mini Quiz to check students' recall of chapter content.

1. **The boundary between two air masses is called a(n) _____ .** *front*
2. **A(n) _____ front may remain in the same place for several days.** *stationary*
3. **_____ pressure usually means clear weather.** *High*
4. **Low pressure can form along _______ , where warm air meets cold air.** *fronts*
5. **In which direction do low pressure systems swirl in the northern hemisphere?** *counterclockwise*

Section Wrap-up

Review

1. In a high pressure area, cooler air is descending and warming. The relative humidity is low and clouds don't form.
2. In a thunderstorm, warm air is forced aloft quickly creating a low pressure area. Strong winds flow into the center of the low pressure area. Winds at different elevations blow in different directions and at different speeds. The system begins to rotate. This causes the air pressure to drop rapidly. A tornado then appears at the base of the cloud.
3. **Think Critically** Air masses meet. At one edge, warm air flows over the cold air. At another edge, cold air forces warm air up at a steep angle. The system starts to rotate. The most severe weather will be found at a cold front.

Skill Builder

1. A warm, dry air mass will produce fair weather.
2. A cold front forms when a cold air mass invades a warm air mass. Rain showers and thunderstorms result when a cold front passes over an area.
3. When two cool air masses merge, forcing warm air to rise, an occluded front is created. The front may bring high winds and heavy precipitation to an area.

Assessment

Oral Use this Skill Builder to assess students' abilities to recognize cause and effect. Ask students to explain what causes a stationary front and what effect a stationary front has on weather. Use the Performance Task Assessment List for Making Observations and Inferences in **PASC,** p. 17. P

Section 15•3

Prepare

Section Background

- In addition to surface weather maps, meteorologists use upper air charts that show the movement of air at various altitudes.
- Satellites take photographs of Earth's atmosphere and send the data to ground stations by microwave transmissions. At night, the satellites photograph infrared waves to help determine the temperature differences between cloudy and clear areas. Satellite photos are important to weather forecasters because the data they provide about cloud movements enable the forecasters to locate low pressure areas and fronts.

Preplanning

To prepare for Activity 15-2, have hand lenses available for students to use.

1 Motivate

Bellringer

Before presenting the lesson, display **Section Focus Transparency 59** on the overhead projector. Assign the accompanying **Focus Activity** worksheet. L1 LEP

Tying to Previous Knowledge

Have students recall from Chapter 5 the function of map legends. Explain that station models, isotherms, and isobars on weather maps serve the same purpose as legends do on maps.

15•3 Forecasting Weather

Science Words

meteorologist
station model
isotherm
isobar

Objectives

- Explain the collection of data for weather maps and forecasts.
- Explain the symbols used in a weather station model.

Weather Observations

You can determine current weather conditions by observing the temperature and looking to see if clouds are in the sky. You know if it's raining. You also have a general idea of the weather because you are familiar with the typical weather where you live. If you live in Florida, you probably don't worry about snow in the forecast. But if you live in Maine, you assume it will snow every winter. What weather concerns do you have in your region?

A **meteorologist** studies the weather. Meteorologists take measurements of temperature, air pressure, winds, humidity, and precipitation. In Chapter 14, you learned about weather satellites. In addition to satellites, Doppler radar, computers, and instruments attached to balloons are used to gather data. Instruments for observing the weather improve meteorologists' ability to predict the weather. Meteorologists use the information provided by weather instruments to make weather maps. They use these maps to make weather forecasts.

Weather Forecasts

Storms such as hurricanes, tornadoes, blizzards, and thunderstorms can be dangerous. When conditions indicate that severe weather might occur or when dangerous weather is

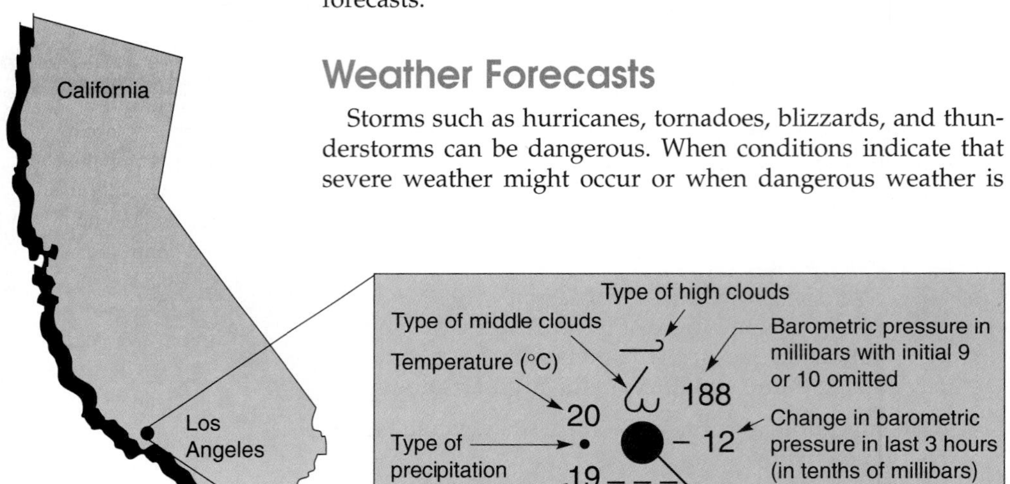

Figure 15-16

A station model shows the weather conditions at one specific location.

Program Resources

Reproducible Masters

Study Guide, p. 63 L1
Reinforcement, p. 63 L1
Enrichment, p. 63 L3
Activity Worksheets, pp. 5, 92-93 L1
Concept Mapping, p. 35
Lab Manual 45
Critical Thinking/Problem Solving, p. 21

Transparencies

Section Focus Transparency 59 L1

observed, meteorologists at the National Weather Service issue advisories. When they issue a weather watch, you should prepare for severe weather. Watches are issued for severe thunderstorms, tornadoes, floods, blizzards, and hurricanes. During a watch, stay tuned to a radio or television station reporting the weather. When a warning is issued, severe weather conditions already exist. You should take immediate action. During a severe thunderstorm warning, take shelter. During a tornado warning, go to the basement or a room in the middle of the house away from windows.

Weather Information

The National Weather Service depends on two sources for its information: meteorologists from around the world and satellites. Meteorologists take measurements in a specific location and give the data to the National Weather Service. The Weather Service uses this information to make weather maps. The Service records the information on maps with a combination of symbols, forming a **station model. Figure 15-16** shows information contained in a station model. Weather satellites provide cloud maps, surface temperatures, photos of Earth, and other data. All this information is used to forecast weather and to issue warnings about severe weather.

In addition to station models, weather maps have lines that indicate atmospheric pressure and temperature. These lines are like the contour lines you studied in Chapter 5, but instead of connecting points of equal elevation, they connect locations of equal temperature or pressure. A line that connects points of equal temperature is called an **isotherm.** *Iso* means "same" and *therm* means "temperature." You've probably seen isotherms on weather maps on TV or in the newspaper.

Figure 15-17

This tornado chaser uses a Doppler radar unit to obtain weather data about the severe storm.

An **isobar** is a line drawn to connect points of equal atmospheric pressure. You can tell how fast wind is blowing in an area by noting how closely isobars are spaced. Isobars close together indicate a large pressure difference over a small area. A large pressure difference causes strong winds. Isobars spread apart indicate a smaller difference in pressure. Winds in this area are more gentle. Isobars also indicate the locations of high and low pressure areas. On a weather map like the one in **Figure 15-18** on page 443, these areas are drawn as circles with a *High* or a *Low* in the middle.

2 Teach

Discussion

Discuss with students why all weather watch and warning advisories should be taken seriously.

Activity

LS **Interpersonal** Have students take turns listening to daily weather reports on the radio or TV and reporting this information to their peers. L1 COOP LEARN

Visual Learning

Figure 15-16 Have students draw a station model that shows the day's weather data. *Models will vary. Refer students to Appendix L for assistance.* LEP LS

Use Lab 45 in the **Lab Manual** as you teach this lesson.

3 Assess

Check for Understanding

FLEX Your Brain

Use the Flex Your Brain activity to have students explore WEATHER MAPS.

Activity Worksheets, p. 5

Reteach

LS **Visual-Spatial** Use daily weather maps to have students identify isotherms and the positions of high and low pressure areas and fronts.

Extension

For students who have mastered this section, use the **Reinforcement** and **Enrichment** masters.

Theme Connection

Stability and Change Ask students, **With all the technology available to meteorologists, why aren't weather forecasts more accurate?** *Weather is constantly evolving. Sometimes the variables that affect weather change much more quickly than expected or much more slowly than predicted.*

Inclusion Strategies

Gifted Have students make board games using weather phenomena. For example, they can label a space: "Hurricane—Blow back 2 spaces." They can make cards with weather map symbols on one side and a verbal explanation of the symbol on the other. Correct responses will allow students to move ahead the number of spaces the roll of a die indicates. L3

Activity 15-2

Purpose

LS **Visual-Spatial** Students will read and interpret a weather map. L1 LEP

Process Skills

interpreting scientific illustrations, using numbers, predicting, observing and inferring

Time

45 minutes

Activity Worksheets, pp. 5, 92-93

Teaching Strategies

Alternate Materials If an opaque projector is available, project the weather map onto a screen.

Troubleshooting Some students will need to review the locations of the states and major U.S. cities prior to performing this activity. Have a map of the United States posted in the classroom.

Answers to Questions

1. Tucson: dew point 18, no cloud cover, barometric pressure 1011.6 mb, 55°F; Albuquerque: dew point 7, one tenth or less cloud cover, barometric pressure 1012.4 mb, 45°F
2. stronger at Fort Worth because the isobars are closer together; wind speed may also be determined by the number of "feathers" on the line showing wind direction
3. stationary front
4. southeast
5. The skies would clear and there would be fair weather.
6. No, a cold front and low pressure area over Oklahoma are moving toward Charleston.
7. southeast

Activity 15-2 Reading a Weather Map

Meteorologists use a series of symbols to provide a picture of local and national weather conditions. You've already learned about station models, isotherms, and isobars. Let's see how you can interpret weather information from weather map symbols.

Problem

How do you read a weather map?

Materials

- hand lens
- Figure 15-18 on page 443
- Appendix L

Procedure

Use the information provided in the questions below and Appendix L to learn how to read a weather map.

Analyze

1. Find the station models on the map for Tucson, Arizona, and Albuquerque, New Mexico. Find the dew point, cloud coverage, pressure, and temperature at each location.
2. After reviewing information about the spacing of isobars and wind speed in Section 15-3, determine whether the wind would be stronger at Roswell, New Mexico, or at Fort Worth, Texas. Record your answer. What is another way to judge the wind speed at these locations?
3. Determine the type of front near Key West, Florida. Record your answer.
4. The triangles or half-circles on the weather front symbol are on the side of the line towards the direction the front is moving. Determine the direction that the cold front located over Colorado and Kansas is moving. Record your answer.

Conclude and Apply

5. Locate the pressure system over Winslow, Arizona. After reviewing Section 15-3, **describe** what would happen to the weather of Wichita, Kansas, if this pressure system should move there.
6. Prevailing westerlies are winds responsible for the movement of much of the weather across the United States and Canada. Based on this, would you expect Charleston, South Carolina, to continue to have clear skies? **Explain** your answer.
7. The wind direction line on the station model indicates the direction from which the wind blows. The wind is named for that direction. **Infer** from this the name of the wind blowing at Jackson, Mississippi.

Assessment

Performance To further assess students' ability to interpret scientific illustrations, have them compare the weather shown on the map for Midland, Texas, and Birmingham, Alabama. Use the Performance Task Assessment List for Making Observations and Inferences in **PASC**, p. 17. P

Science Journal

See page 443.

Answers will vary, but should include predictions about cloud cover, temperature, and precipitation.

As you've learned so far in this chapter, weather is constantly changing. When you watch the weather forecasts on television, notice how weather fronts move across the United States from west to east. This is a pattern that meteorologists depend on in forecasting the weather. However, national and regional weather forecasters cannot always predict the exact weather because weather conditions change rapidly and local conditions also influence the weather. However, improved technologies enable forecasters to be increasingly more accurate.

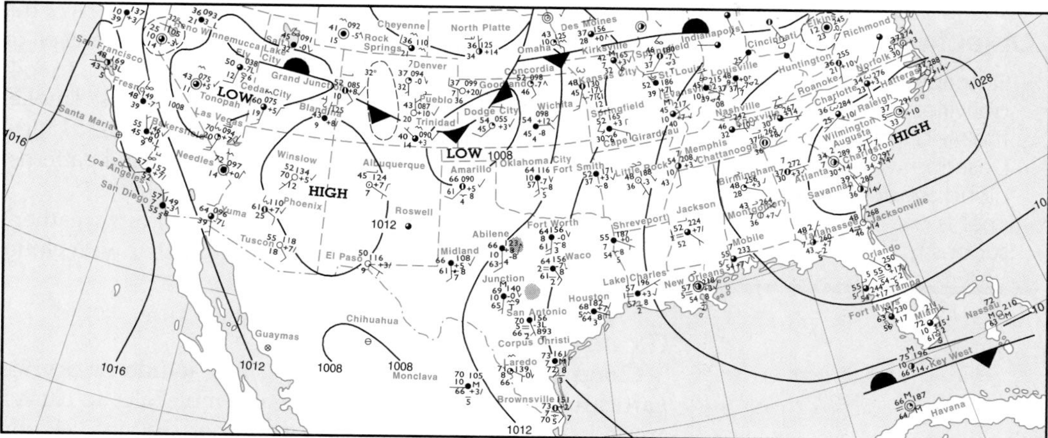

Figure 15-18

Highs, lows, isobars, and fronts on this weather map help meteorologists forecast the weather.

Section Wrap-up

Review

1. What symbols are used in a station model?
2. How do meteorologists collect the data that they need for making maps and forecasts?
3. **Think Critically:** Use Appendix L to analyze the station model shown in **Figure 15-16.** What is the temperature, type of clouds, wind speed and direction, and type of precipitation at that location?

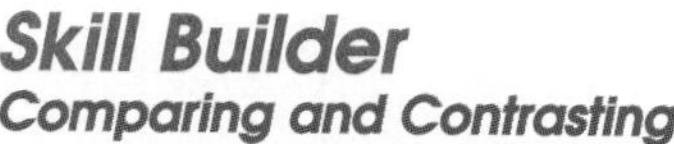

Skill Builder

Comparing and Contrasting

Contrast a weather watch and a weather warning. If you need help, refer to Comparing and Contrasting in the **Skill Handbook.**

Science Journal

Analyze today's weather by looking at the cloud cover and a newspaper weather map. In your Science Journal, write a meteorological forecast for later today and tomorrow.

4 Close

• MINI • QUIZ •

Use the Mini Quiz to check students' recall of chapter content.

1. **A(n) _____ is a person who studies weather.** *meteorologist*
2. **The _____ issues advisories when severe weather has been observed.** *National Weather Service*
3. **A(n) _____ contains symbols that show the weather conditions of a specific location.** *station model*
4. **A(n) _____ is a line on a weather map that connects points of equal temperature.** *isotherm*

Section Wrap-up

Review

1. The symbols are a circle and lines and numbers in various positions around the circle. Symbols represent cloud cover, wind speed and direction, type of clouds, temperature, type of precipitation, dew point temperature, barometric pressure, and change in barometric pressure.
2. They use weather instruments such as thermometers, barometers, and anemometers to measure local atmospheric conditions. They also use radar, computers, instruments attached to balloons, and weather satellites.
3. **Think Critically** temperature: 20°C; clouds: cirrus, thin altostratus, and fractocumulus; wind speed: 3-7 knots; wind direction: southeast; precipitation: rain

Skill Builder

A weather watch means that conditions may cause severe weather. People should prepare. A warning means that severe weather already exists, and people should take immediate action.

Assessment

Performance Use this Skill Builder to assess students' abilities to compare and contrast. Have students make a poster comparing and contrasting specific things to do during severe weather watches and warnings. Use the Performance Task Assessment List for Poster in **PASC,** p. 73. P

Section 15•4

1 Motivate

Bellringer

 Before presenting the lesson, display **Section Focus Transparency 60** on the overhead projector. Assign the accompanying **Focus Activity** worksheet. L1 LEP

Tying to Previous Knowledge

Have students recall that water droplets condense around dust particles. When clouds are seeded, additional particles are added to act as nuclei for condensation.

2 Teach

Discussion

Have students explain how some human activities such as releasing gases into the atmosphere and cutting forests change wind patterns, temperature, and air moisture.

3 Assess

Check for Understanding

FLEX Your Brain

Use the Flex Your Brain activity to have students explore CLOUD SEEDING.

Activity Worksheets, p. 5

Reteach

Visual-Spatial Have students draw a cartoon of the steps involved in cloud seeding. Drawings should show water vapor molecules clustering around particles of silver iodide or dry ice.

15•4 TECHNOLOGY: Changing the Weather

Science Words

cloud seeding

Objectives

- Describe human activities that alter the weather.
- Describe why many cloud seeding experiments are not successful.

Weather Modification

Mark Twain once said, "Everybody talks about the weather, but nobody does anything about it." Actually, that statement is not true. When we plant trees, we change the patterns of the wind. When we mulch around plants to reduce the escape of moisture from the soil or irrigate to add more moisture to soil, we change local weather conditions. When we release smoke, other particles, and gases into the atmosphere, or build cities, cut forests, and make artificial lakes, we change wind patterns, temperature, and air moisture.

What if we could have even more control of our weather? For nearly fifty years, people have experimented with cloud seeding as a way to modify weather.

Cloud Seeding

Cloud seeding involves placing silver iodide or dry ice particles into clouds as nuclei for water molecules to cluster around and freeze. The particles are either shot into clouds

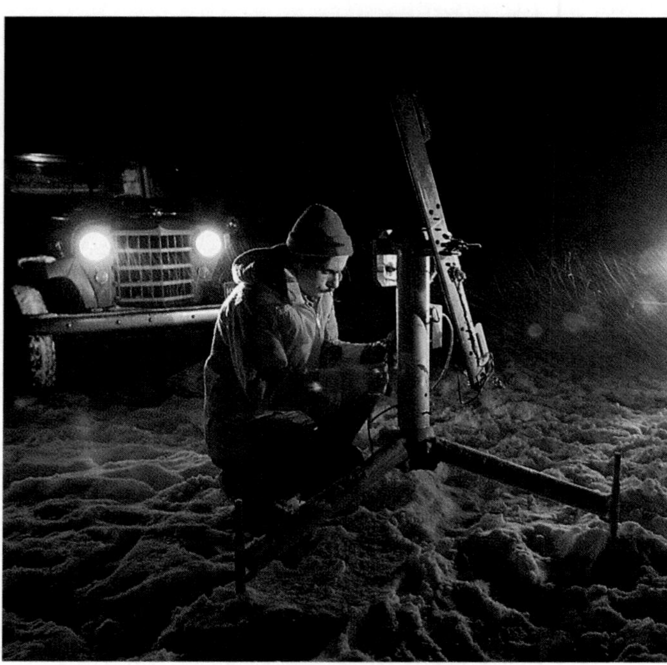

Figure 15-19

In 1973, the University of Colorado used a rocket in a cloud seeding experiment in Leadville, Colorado.

Program Resources

 **Reproducible Masters**

Study Guide, p. 64 L1
Reinforcement, p. 64 L1
Enrichment, p. 64 L3
Science and Society Integration, p. 19

Transparencies

Section Focus Transparency 60 L1

from the ground or dropped into the clouds from airplanes. One cloud seeding experiment is shown in **Figure 15-19.**

Once a particle and its added ice crystals reach 0.2 mm in size, it falls from the cloud as precipitation. Some scientists hypothesize that cloud seeding can be used to encourage precipitation wherever water vapor is present and the air temperature is near the dew point.

In some areas, cloud seeding has been successful. It has been used for clearing fog at airports. It has also been successful in increasing snowfall in some mountain resorts and rainfall in some areas of drought.

Throughout the years, a number of cloud seeding experiments have been unsuccessful because conditions that affect weather vary so much from place to place and from day to day. Experiments have been carried out to reduce winds, waves, and storm surges to make hurricanes less destructive. Although some studies claimed success, overall this cloud seeding did not work. Some studies were stopped because scientists feared cloud seeding might make hurricanes more powerful. Cloud seeding to prevent hailstorms has been successful in Russia, but the same techniques used in the United States failed to produce helpful results. In recent years, funding for cloud seeding experiments has disappeared. It appears at this time that our ability to modify the weather is quite limited.

CONNECT TO

PHYSICS

Because of the concrete and asphalt in a city, the air over a city is usually warmer than the air over rural communities. Because of this difference, convection currents develop at the boundary of cities and rural areas. Copy the drawing below into your Science Journal. ***Illustrate*** the drawing with arrows showing the direction the convection currents move.

Section Wrap-up

Review

1. How can people modify local weather?
2. How could successful cloud seeding affect the water cycle in an area?

Explore the Technology

If cloud seeding becomes both successful and popular, conflict between communities could result. Community A might be accused of "cloud rustling" because they have taken moisture from clouds that normally would precipitate onto community B. Do you think clouds and their moisture are "owned" by the community beneath them? Should people intensify their efforts to find ways to modify the weather?

SCIENCE & SOCIETY

Extension

For students who have mastered this section, use the **Reinforcement** and **Enrichment** masters.

CONNECT TO

PHYSICS

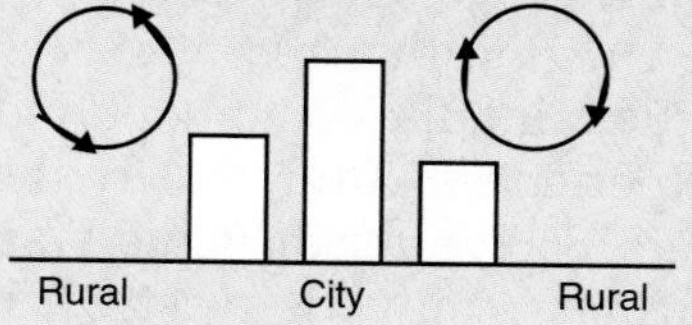

4 Close

Have students prepare a list of ways that cloud seeding may be used to modify weather in the future.

Section Wrap-up

Review

1. Planting trees, mulching plants, irrigating soil, releasing smoke, and cutting down trees change wind patterns, temperature, and moisture. Cloud seeding changes precipitation patterns.
2. Those areas that receive more precipitation than others will have more water to evaporate, form water vapor, and condense to form clouds. In dryer areas of the region, there is less water to evaporate and water vapor to condense. Some storms may intensify.

Integrating the Sciences

Chemistry Explain to students that dry ice is carbon dioxide in a solid state. As it warms, it becomes a gas. Have students discuss whether or not this gas might be harmful to the environment. Some students may know that carbon dioxide is thought to trap atmospheric heat and contribute to global warming. Tell students that they will learn more about global warming in Chapter 16.

Explore the Technology

Some students will feel that clouds belong to a community beneath them. Some students will think that efforts to find ways to modify the weather should be intensified, while others will state that modifying weather causes environmental and social problems.

Sources

- Cline, Isaac Monroe. *Storms, Floods and Sunshine.* New Orleans: Pelican Publishing Company, 1951.
- Ludlum, David M. *The Weather Factor.* Boston: Houghton Mifflin, 1984.

Background

A region that receives very little rainfall for a long period experiences drought. In the late 1860s, after the Civil War, farmers moved westward, where they expected rains to fall regularly. Instead they experienced periods of drought that destroyed their crops: 1882 in Kansas, 1887 in Nebraska, 1889 in Kansas, and 1931-1938 in the Southwest and Great Plains.

Teaching Strategies

- Ask students for their reactions to the effect of weather on the historic events mentioned in Science & History.
- Mention that tropical cyclones have been a factor in U.S. history in two regions: in the Caribbean and in the China Sea, Philippine Islands, and Japan. Have students find out whether U.S. warships had to consider cyclones during the Spanish-American War. (The Spanish-American War lasted from April to August in 1898. The cyclone season lasts from May to November in the Philippines and from June to November in the Caribbean, so cyclones could have been a factor during the invasion of Cuba and Puerto Rico and the occupation of Manila.)

Science & History

Science Journal

Find out how drought affected American history, especially between the years 1931 and 1938. Write an essay about your findings in your Science Journal.

How Weather Affected History

An article by Charles C. Hazewell in the May 1862 issue of the *Atlantic Monthly* expressed it well:

> *A hard frost, a sudden thaw, a "hot spell," a "cold snap," a long drought, a storm of sand—all these things have had their part . . . in the fate of nations. Leave weather out of history, and it is as if night were left out of day, and winter out of the year.*

Examples from history illustrate Hazewell's idea:

Long droughts in West Africa during the 1970s and 1980s forced hungry people to migrate to cities. During the droughts, the dust from the dry areas in West Africa blew up and across the Atlantic Ocean and darkened the skies over the Caribbean.

Big storms also affect history. In 1279, after he conquered China, Kublai Kahn set out to conquer Asia. When he sent a fleet of ships to conquer Japan, Japan had an ally: typhoons (hurricanes). These storms wrecked Kublai Kahn's fleets.

In World War II, typhoons again aided Japan. In December 1944, a typhoon east of the Philippines sank three U.S. destroyers. Another typhoon struck Okinawa in 1945. It sank three U.S. naval vessels and damaged another 127 ships. Also in World War II, cold and snow affected Hitler's armies.

During the Revolutionary War, cold weather helped George Washington. In January 1777, General Washington was trapped at Princeton, New Jersey. His army was outnumbered. Muddy roads on one side and an ice-blocked river on the other prevented escape. The British general Cornwallis planned to attack the trapped army in the morning.

However, Washington knew that the wind was from the northwest and the temperature had not risen during the day. From past experiences, Washington expected a freeze that would harden the roads. By 9 P.M. the temperature was -3°C. Washington moved his army at 1 A.M. over frozen roads. The weather helped the Americans escape from a position from which they would have been defeated.

In WWII, cold weather stopped the German army's march into the U.S.S.R.

446

- Have students find out how winds played an important part in the historic flights by the Wright brothers at Kitty Hawk, North Carolina, on December 17, 1903. (The flights were made in early morning wind, when weather conditions were favorable. The wind averaged 43 km per hour for the first flight and 39 km per hour for the last flight. The wind was blowing from the north.)

Activity

Have students work together to find out how the United States and Mexico have cooperated in matters related to weather.

Chapter 15 Review

Summary

15-1: What is weather?

1. Water vapor forms most clouds and the precipitation that falls from them. Water vapor also determines the humidity.
2. Rain, hail, sleet, and snow are types of precipitation. The type of the precipitation depends on air temperature.
3. When air cools to its dew point, water vapor condenses and forms clouds.

15-2: Weather Patterns

1. Warm fronts may produce precipitation over a wide band. Cold fronts produce a narrow band of violent storms. A stationary front produces weak winds and precipitation. Occluded fronts are sometimes associated with high winds and heavy precipitation. High pressure brings clear skies and fair weather. Low pressure areas are cloudy.
2. Low pressure systems form when air at a front begins to swirl, rises, cools, and forms clouds.
3. Tornadoes are intense, whirling wind storms that can result from strong winds and low pressure in thunderstorms.

15-3: Forecasting Weather

1. Meteorologists use information from radar, satellites, computers, and other instruments to make weather maps and forecasts.
2. Symbols on a station model indicate the weather at a particular location.

15-4: Science and Society: Changing the Weather

1. Planting trees, irrigating, and building cities can modify wind patterns, temperature, and air moisture in a region.
2. Cloud seeding has been used to modify the weather. Cloud seeding changes regional precipitation patterns and may create ecological problems.

Key Science Words

a. air mass
b. cloud seeding
c. dew point
d. fog
e. front
f. humidity
g. hurricane
h. isobar
i. isotherm
j. meteorologist
k. precipitation
l. relative humidity
m. saturated
n. station model
o. tornado
p. weather

Reviewing Vocabulary

Match each phrase with the correct term from the list of Key Science Words.

1. temperature at which condensation occurs
2. falling water droplets
3. air that can't hold any more water vapor
4. boundary between air masses
5. violent swirling storm moving in a narrow path
6. large, swirling tropical storm
7. person who studies the weather
8. symbols that describe local weather conditions
9. line on a weather map that indicates points of equal pressure
10. stratus cloud near the ground

Chapter 15 Review

Summary

Have students read the summary statements to review the major concepts of the chapter.

Reviewing Vocabulary

1. c **6.** g
2. k **7.** j
3. m **8.** n
4. e **9.** h
5. o **10.** d

Assessment

Portfolio Encourage students to place in their portfolios one or two items of what they consider to be their best work. Examples include:

- MiniLAB analysis answers, p. 425
- Skill Builder, p. 431
- Using Computers, p. 438 P

Performance Additional performance assessments may be found in **Performance Assessment** and **Science Integration Activities.** Performance Task Assessment Lists and rubrics for evaluating these activities can be found in Glencoe's **Performance Assessment in the Science Classroom.**

GLENCOE TECHNOLOGY

 **Videodisc**

Glencoe Earth Science
Interactive Videodisc
Use videodisc lesson 3, *Thunderstorms: Flashes and Crashes,* to review how thunderstorms form, what causes thunder and lighting, and precautions to take when severe weather strikes.

 **MindJogger Videoquiz**

Chapter 15 Have students work in groups as they play the Videoquiz game to review key chapter concepts.

Chapter 15 Review

Checking Concepts

1. d
2. a
3. a
4. d
5. a
6. d
7. d
8. d
9. c
10. b

Understanding Concepts

11. At cooler temperatures, molecules in air move more slowly. Less movement allows water vapor molecules to join together or condense.
12. The air mass would be cold because of the latitude of Canada. It would also be relatively dry because it formed over land.
13. The sun provides the energy for the water cycle. The heat from the sun causes water to evaporate into the air. Eventually, the water condenses to form clouds. Water falls from clouds as rain, snow, sleet, or hail.
14. Activities include planting trees, mulching plants, irrigating soil, releasing smoke and other pollutants, making artificial lakes, building cities, cutting down trees, and seeding clouds.
15. In a cold front, warm air is forced up at a steep angle. Weather is more severe—stronger winds, colder air, and more precipitation.

Thinking Critically

16. The air is holding only 79 percent of the water vapor it is capable of holding at that temperature.
17. A lot of moisture is evaporating from the wet bulb; therefore, the relative humidity is low.

Chapter 15 Review

Checking Concepts

Choose the word or phrase that completes the sentence.

1. Water vapor will condense from air when the air is _______.
   a. humid c. dry
   b. temperate d. saturated
2. A large body of air that has the same properties as the area over which it formed is a(n) _______.
   a. air mass c. front
   b. station model d. isotherm
3. Water vapor in air condenses at its _______.
   a. dew point c. front
   b. station model d. isobar
4. _______ forms when water vapor changes directly into a solid.
   a. Rain c. Sleet
   b. Hail d. Snow
5. _______ clouds are high feathery clouds made of ice crystals.
   a. Cirrus c. Cumulus
   b. Nimbus d. Stratus
6. A(n) _______ front forms when two cool air masses merge.
   a. warm c. stationary
   b. cold d. occluded
7. _______ is used to seed clouds.
   a. Water vapor c. Dew
   b. Styrofoam d. Silver iodide
8. A _______ is issued when severe weather conditions exist and immediate action should be taken.
   a. front c. station model
   b. watch d. warning
9. The amount of water vapor in the air is the _______.
   a. dew point c. humidity
   b. precipitation d. relative humidity
10. A psychrometer is used to measure _______.
    a. air pressure c. wind speed
    b. relative humidity d. precipitation

Understanding Concepts

Answer the following questions in your Science Journal using complete sentences.

11. Explain how temperature affects relative humidity.
12. Describe the characteristics of an air mass that forms over central Canada in December.
13. Describe how water and the sun interact to cause our weather.
14. Describe several human activities that alter local weather.
15. Compare the structure and weather of a cold front to a warm front.

Thinking Critically

16. If you learn that there is 79 percent relative humidity, what does that mean?
17. If the temperature difference between a wet bulb thermometer and a dry bulb thermometer is great, what do you know about the relative humidity?
18. Why don't hurricanes form in polar regions?
19. If a barometer shows that the air pressure is dropping, what general weather prediction could you make?
20. What weather conditions would the very tall, thick clouds shown below indicate?

18. Hurricanes need a constant source of energy and water vapor to form. As long as a hurricane is over warm water, the warm, moist air will rise and provide energy for the storm. These conditions don't exist in polar regions.
19. Air pressure drops as a front approaches an area. Stormy weather is often associated with fronts and low pressure.
20. Towering clouds are associated with thunderstorms, heavy rain, and hail.

Developing Skills

21. **Comparing and Contrasting** Both are types of severe weather that form when warm air is forced quickly aloft. Both have high winds that are very destructive. The winds in a tornado rotate, while those in severe thunderstorms do not. Also, tornadoes tend to move along a narrow path of land, while thunderstorms tend to affect larger areas.

Developing Skills

If you need help, refer to the **Skill Handbook.**

21. **Comparing and Contrasting:** Compare and contrast tornadoes and severe thunderstorms.
22. **Interpreting Scientific Illustrations:** Describe the weather conditions shown on the station model below.

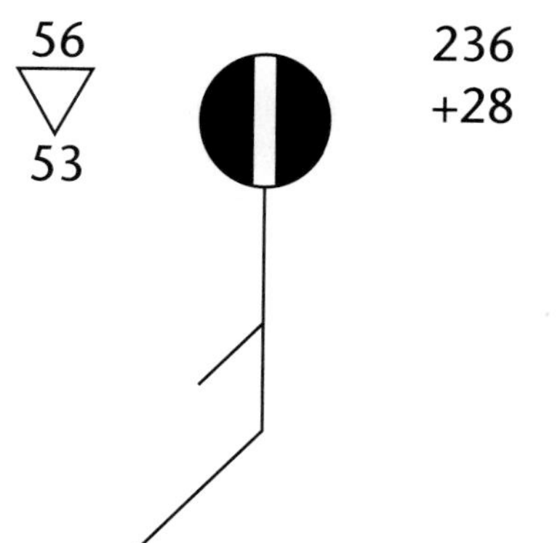

23. **Observing and Inferring:** You take a hot shower. The mirror in the bathroom "clouds up." Infer from this information what has happened.
24. **Interpreting Scientific Illustrations:** Use the cloud descriptions in **Figure 15-5** to describe the weather at your location today. Then try to predict tomorrow's weather.
25. **Concept mapping:** Construct sequence charts, one for each type of precipitation. Show the sequence from evaporation to falling precipitation.

Performance Assessment

1. **Graph:** In the MiniLAB on page 425, you learned how to find dew point temperature. Repeat this procedure for three days and graph your results.
2. **Prediction Display:** In Activity 15-2, you interpreted weather map symbols and predicted the weather. Check weather maps from the newspaper and predict the weather for your area for three days. Compare your predictions with the actual weather that occurs. Display the weather maps and your predictions.
3. **Models:** Design and construct an anemometer and a rain gauge. Use them for one week. Compare the accuracy of your instruments with reported data from radio or TV weather reports. Explain these weather instruments to your class.

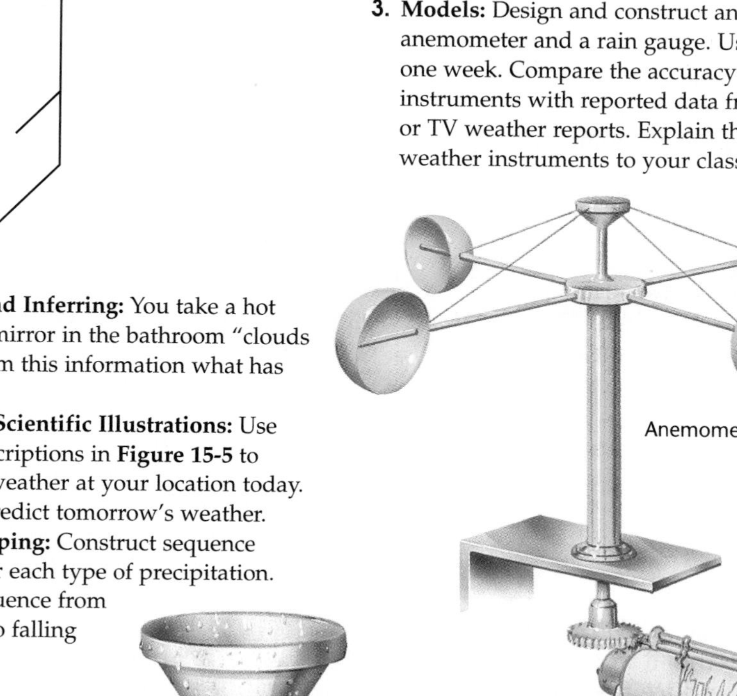

Assessment Resources

Reproducible Masters

Chapter Review, pp. 33-34

Assessment, pp. 99-102

Performance Assessment, p. 29

Glencoe Technology

Chapter Review Software

Computer Test Bank

MindJogger Videoquiz

Chapter 15 Review

22. **Interpreting Scientific Illustrations** Sky is overcast with openings. Barometric pressure is 1023.6 mb; it has increased 2.8 mb in the last 3 hours. Temperature is 56°F and there are showers. Winds are from the SW at 13-17 knots. Dew point temperature is 53°F in the upper clouds.
23. **Observing and Inferring** The warm air from the shower is cooled when it hits the mirror. As it cooled, it reached its dew point and condensed to form water droplets on the glass of the mirror.
24. **Interpreting Scientific Illustrations** Answers will vary, but students should be able to identify the clouds present and predict what kind of weather will occur based on the types of clouds observed.
25. **Concept Mapping** This should match information in **Figure 15-6,** p. 427.

Performance Assessment

1. The dew point will vary as the humidity and air temperature change. Graphs should show days on the horizontal axis and dew point temperature on the vertical axis. Use the Performance Task Assessment List for Graph from Data in **PASC,** p. 39. P
2. Student results will vary. Use the Performance Task Assessment List for Display in **PASC,** p. 63. P
3. Designs will vary, but should be constructed of waterproof materials. Students may need help in calibrating their instruments. Use the Performance Task Assessment List for Models in **PASC,** p. 51. P

Chapter Organizer

Section	Objectives	Activities/Features
Chapter Opener		Explore Activity: Where are deserts found? p. 451
16-1 **What is climate?** (1 session, 1 block)*	1. **Describe** what determines the climate of an area. 2. **Explain** how latitude and topographic features affect the climate of a region.	MiniLAB: How does Earth's tilt affect radiation received? p. 453 Problem Solving: The Lake Effect, p. 454 Skill Builder: Comparing and Contrasting, p. 455 Using Math, p. 455 Activity 16-1: Microclimates, pp. 456-457
16-2 **Climate Types** (2 sessions, 1½ blocks)*	1. **Describe** the Köppen Climate Classification System. 2. **Describe** how organisms adapt to particular climates.	Skill Builder: Hypothesizing, p. 461 Science Journal, p. 461
16-3 **Climatic Changes** (2 sessions, 1½ blocks)*	1. **Discuss** what causes seasons. 2. **Describe** how El Niño affects the climate. 3. **Describe** past climatic change. 4. **Explore** possible causes of climatic change. 5. **Differentiate** between the greenhouse effect and global warming.	Connect to Life Science, p. 463 MiniLAB: What can we learn from tree rings? p. 464 Using Technology: Ice Delivers Clues, p. 465 Connect to Physics, p. 466 Using Math, p. 467 Activity 16-2: The Greenhouse Effect, p. 468 Using Math, p. 469 Skill Builder: Comparing and Contrasting, p. 469 Using Computers: Word Processing, p. 469
16-4 **Science and Society Technology: How can global warming be slowed?** (1 session, ½ block)*	1. **Discuss** some human activities that add carbon dioxide to the atmosphere. 2. **List** ways we can reduce the amount of carbon dioxide in the atmosphere.	Explore the Technology, p. 471 People and Science: Ellen Mosley-Thompson, Geographer, p. 472

* A complete Planning Guide that includes block scheduling is provided on pages 32T-35T.

Activity Materials

Explore	Activities	MiniLABs
page 451 world globe or atlas	pages 456-457 safety goggles; apron; thermometers; psychrometer; relative humidity chart; paper strip or wind sock; large can, beaker, or rain gauge; piece of paper page 468 2 identical, empty aquariums; glass lid for one aquarium; 3 identical thermometers	page 453 flashlight, globe page 464 cross section of wood showing growth rings, metric ruler, hand lens

Teacher Classroom Resources

Reproducible Masters	Transparencies	Teaching Resources
Study Guide, p. 65 **Reinforcement**, p. 65 **Enrichment**, p. 65 **Activity Worksheets**, pp. 96-97, 100 **Lab Manual 46**, Radiant Energy and Climate **Lab Manual 47**, Solar Energy Storage **Lab Manual 48**, Solar Energy Application **Critical Thinking/Problem Solving**, p. 22 **Cross-Curricular Integration**, p. 20	**Section Focus Transparency 61**, Climate **Teaching Transparency 31**, Rain Shadows	**Glencoe Earth Science Interactive Videodisc** **Earth Science CD-ROM** **Spanish Resources** **English/Spanish Audiocassettes** **Cooperative Learning Resource Guide** **Lab Partner** **Lab and Safety Skills** **Lesson Plans**
Study Guide, p. 66 **Reinforcement**, p. 66 **Enrichment**, p. 66 **Science Integration Activity 16**, Hot and Dry **Multicultural Connections**, pp. 35-36	**Section Focus Transparency 62**, A Lot of Climate in a Small Space **Teaching Transparency 32**, World Climate Map	**Assessment Resources**
Study Guide, p. 67 **Reinforcement**, p. 67 **Enrichment**, p. 67 **Activity Worksheets**, pp. 98-99, 101	**Section Focus Transparency 63**, Changes	**Chapter Review**, pp. 35-36 **Assessment**, pp. 103-106 **Performance Assessment in the Science Classroom (PASC)** **MindJogger Videoquiz** **Alternate Assessment in the Science Classroom** **Performance Assessment** **Chapter Review Software** **Computer Test Bank**
Study Guide, p. 68 **Reinforcement**, p. 68 **Enrichment**, p. 68 **Concept Mapping**, p. 37 **Science and Society Integration**, p. 20	**Section Focus Transparency 64**, Mapping the Future **Science Integration Transparency 16**, Specific Heat of Substances	

Key to Teaching Strategies

The following designations will help you decide which activities are appropriate for your students.

L1 Level 1 activities should be within the ability range of all students.

L2 Level 2 activities should be within the ability range of the average to above-average student.

L3 Level 3 activities are designed for the ability range of above-average students.

LEP LEP activities should be within the ability range of Limited English Proficiency students.

LS These activities are designed to address different learning styles.

COOP LEARN Cooperative Learning activities are designed for small group work.

P These strategies represent student products that can be placed into a best-work portfolio.

GLENCOE TECHNOLOGY

The following multimedia resources are available from Glencoe.

The Infinite Voyage Series
Crisis in the Atmosphere
Secrets from a Frozen World

Science and Technology Videodisc Series (STVS)
Chemistry
Hole in the Ozone
Earth & Space
Greenhouse Effect
Records of Ancient Climates
Plants & Simple Organisms
Detecting Climate Changes in Tree Rings

Earth Science CD-ROM

Teacher Classroom Resources

This is a representation of key blackline masters available in the Teacher Classroom Resources.

Teaching Aids

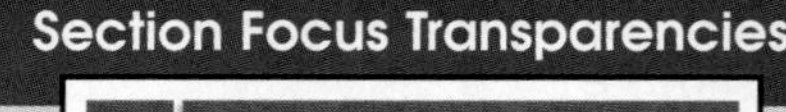

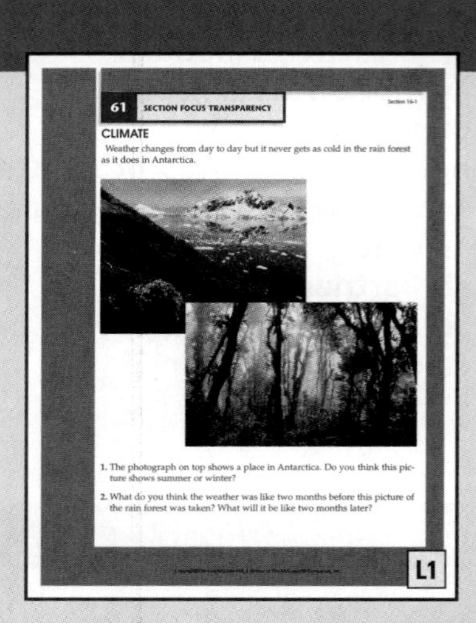
61 SECTION FOCUS TRANSPARENCY

CLIMATE

Weather changes from day to day but it never gets as cold in the rain forest as it does in Antarctica.

1. The photograph on top shows a place in Antarctica. Do you think this picture shows summer or winter?
2. What do you think the weather was like two months before this picture of the rain forest was taken? What will it be like two months later?

L1

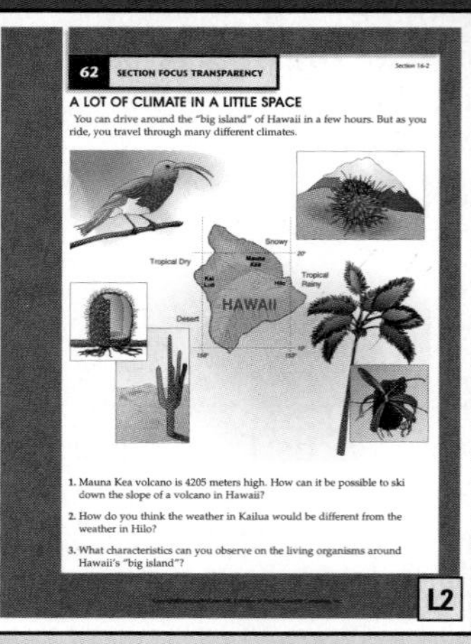
62 SECTION FOCUS TRANSPARENCY

A LOT OF CLIMATE IN A LITTLE SPACE

You can drive around the "big island" of Hawaii in a few hours. But as you ride, you travel through many different climates.

1. Mauna Kea volcano is 4205 meters high. How can it be possible to ski down the slope of a volcano in Hawaii?
2. How do you think the weather in Kailua would be different from the weather in Hilo?
3. What characteristics can you observe on the living organisms around Hawaii's "big island"?

L2

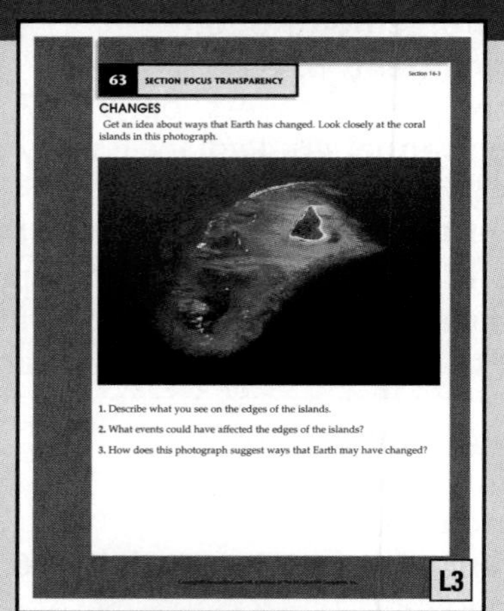
63 SECTION FOCUS TRANSPARENCY

CHANGES

Get an idea about ways that Earth has changed. Look closely at the coral islands in this photograph.

1. Describe what you see on the edges of the islands.
2. What events could have affected the edges of the islands?
3. How does this photograph suggest ways that Earth may have changed?

L3

Science Integration Transparencies

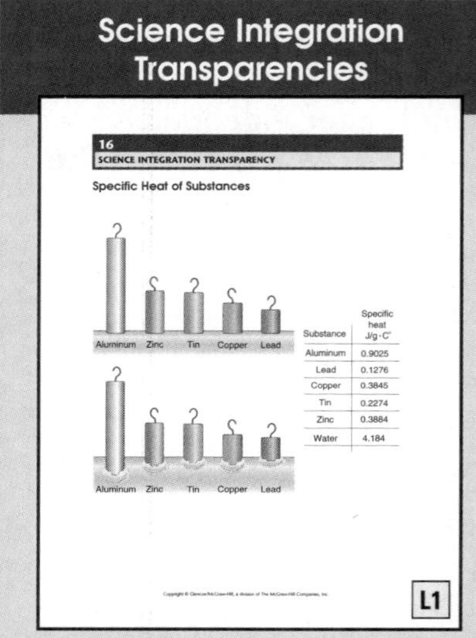
16 SCIENCE INTEGRATION TRANSPARENCY

Specific Heat of Substances

Substance	Specific heat J/g · C°
Aluminum	0.9025
Lead	0.1276
Copper	0.3845
Tin	0.2274
Zinc	0.3884
Water	4.184

L1

Teaching Transparencies

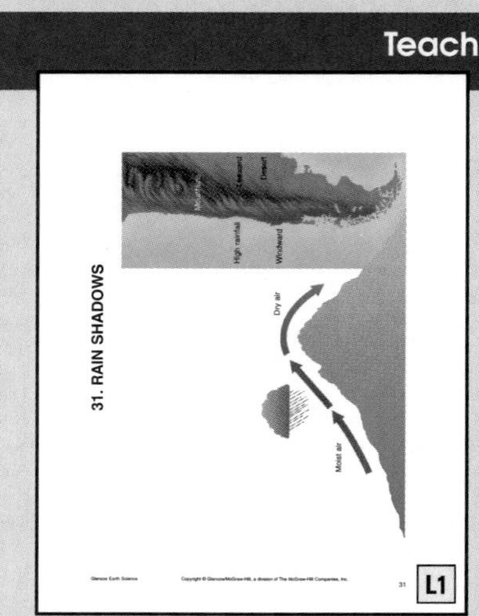

L1

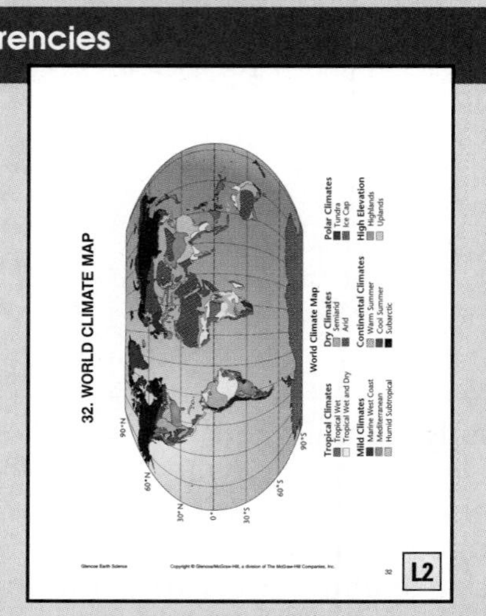

L2

Meeting Different Ability Levels

Study Guide

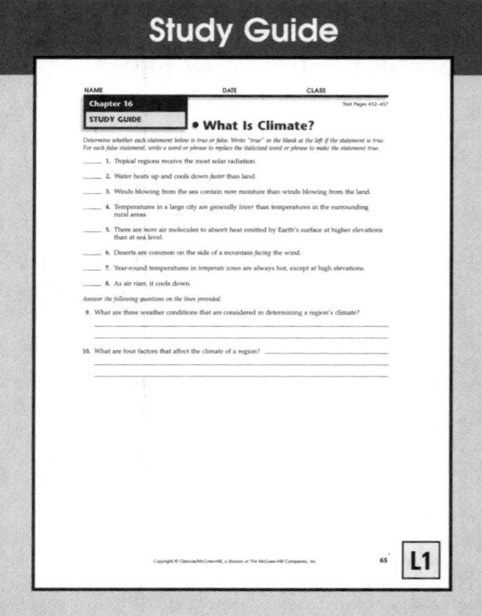
Chapter 16 STUDY GUIDE

What Is Climate?

L1

Reinforcement

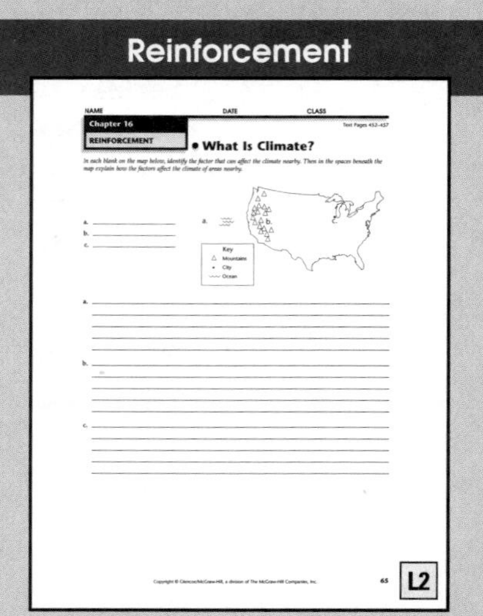
Chapter 16 REINFORCEMENT

What Is Climate?

L2

Enrichment Worksheets

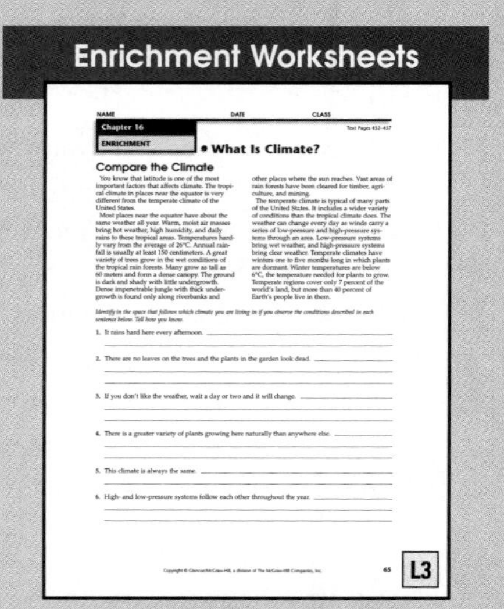
Chapter 16 ENRICHMENT

What Is Climate?

Compare the Climate

L3

Hands-On Activities

Science Integration Activity

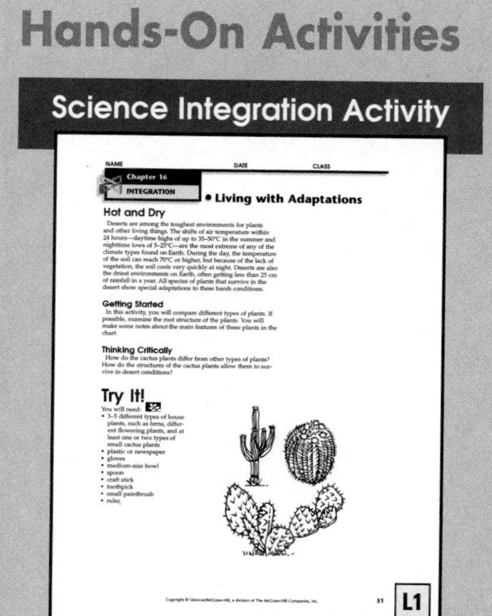

Lab Manual

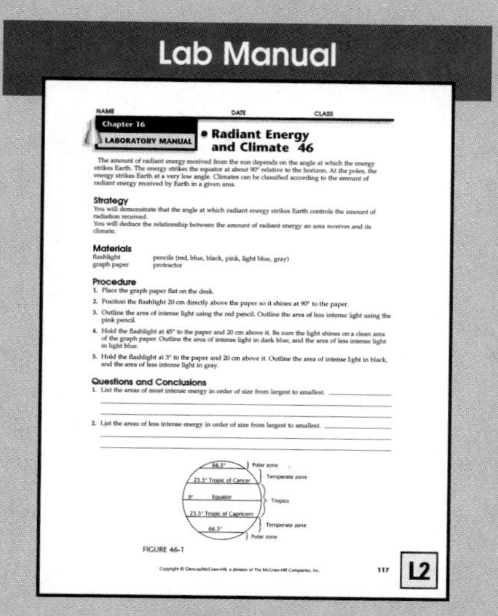

Assessment

Performance Assessment

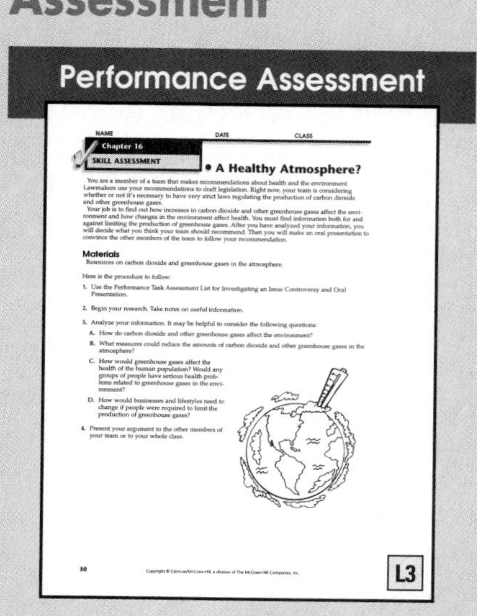

Enrichment and Application

Critical Thinking/ Problem Solving

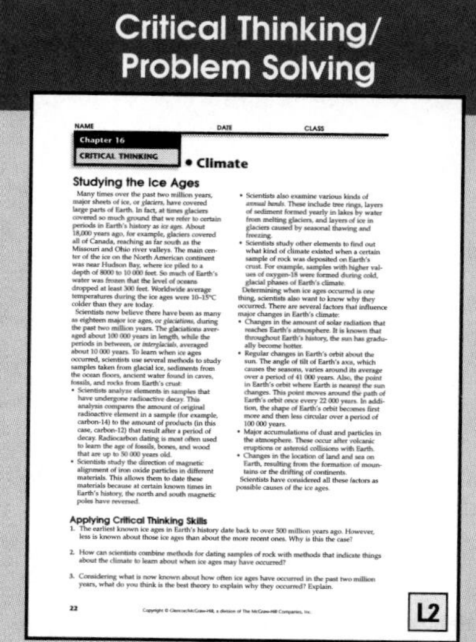

Cross-Curricular Integration

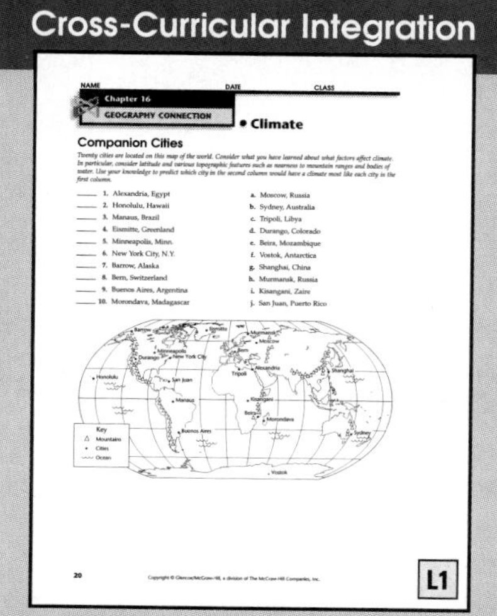

Science and Society Integration

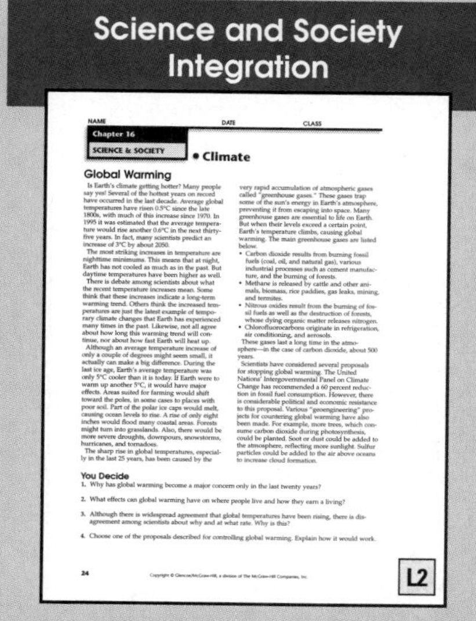

Multicultural Connections

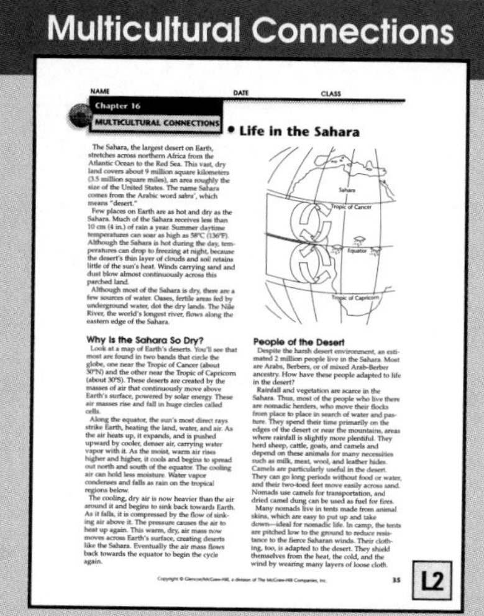

Concept Mapping

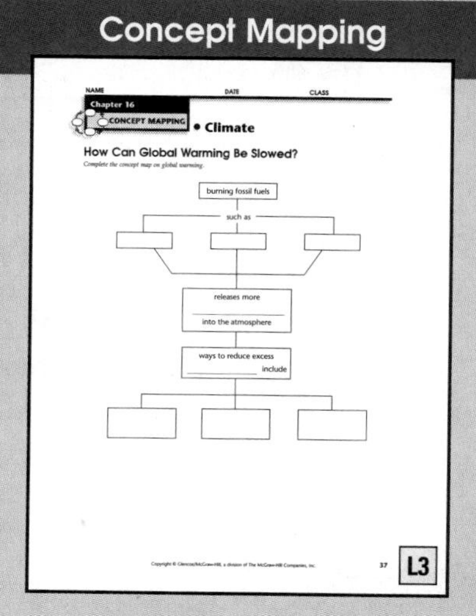

Chapter 16

Climate

CHAPTER OVERVIEW

Section 16-1 This section describes how latitude and topographic features affect climate.

Section 16-2 This section details how climate is classified and how certain adaptations help organisms survive in various climates.

Section 16-3 This section discusses climatic change and theories to explain that change.

Section 16-4 Science and Society This section focuses on global warming. It discusses the effect of certain human activities on global warming.

Chapter Vocabulary

tropics
polar zone
temperate zone
adaptation
hibernation
season
El Niño
greenhouse effect
global warming
deforestation
reforestation

Theme Connection

Stability and Change Many factors affect climate, including latitude, topographic features, and human activities. To survive, organisms must adapt to climate.

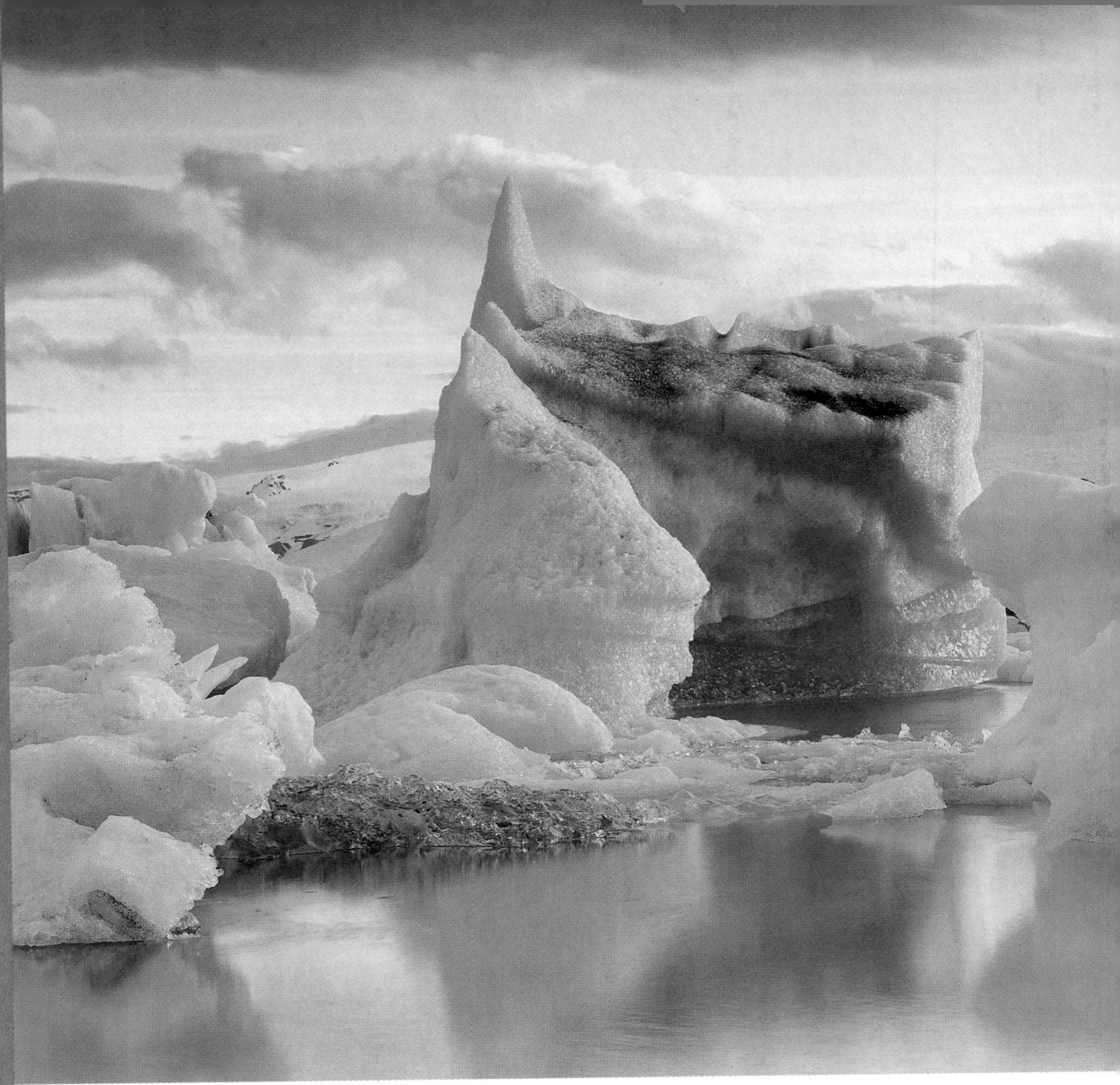

Previewing the Chapter

Section 16-1 What is climate?
- ▶ Climate
- ▶ Latitude Affects Climate
- ▶ Topographic Features Affect Climate

Section 16-2 Climate Types
- ▶ Climate Classification
- ▶ Organism Adaptations

Section 16-3 Climatic Changes
- ▶ Seasons
- ▶ El Niño
- ▶ Climatic Change
- ▶ Theories Explaining Major Climatic Change
- ▶ Climatic Changes Today

Section 16-4 Science and Society: Technology: How can global warming be slowed?

450

Learning Styles

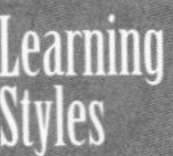

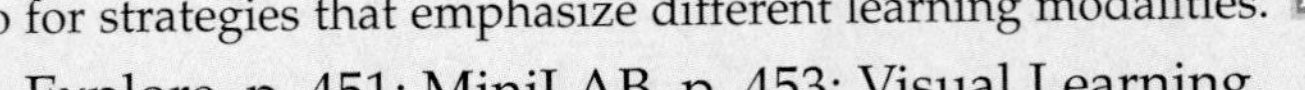

Look for the following logo for strategies that emphasize different learning modalities. LS

Visual-Spatial	Explore, p. 451; MiniLAB, p. 453; Visual Learning, pp. 454, 459; Reteach, p. 460
Interpersonal	Activity 16-2, p. 468
Logical-Mathematical	Activity 16-1, pp. 456-457; MiniLAB, p. 464; Reteach, p. 471
Linguistic	Science Journal, p. 466; Using Math, pp. 455, 467, 468

LS

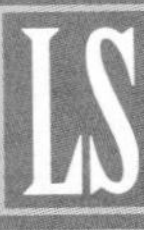

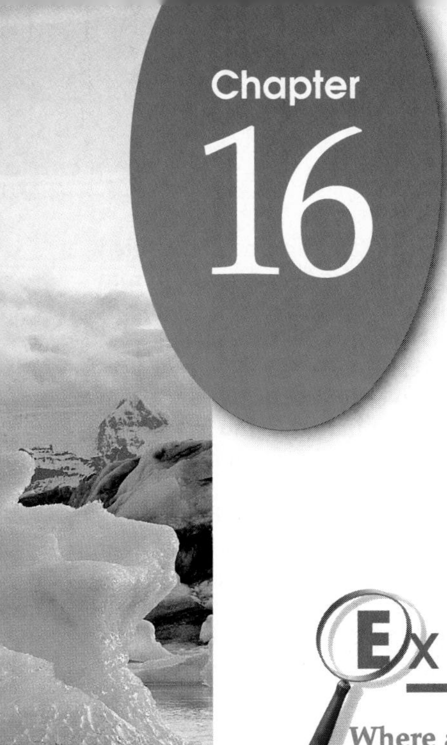

Chapter 16

Climate

Some places on Earth, such as this area of Iceland, receive so little solar radiation that glaciers form. Other places receive so little precipitation in a year that it is difficult to measure it. Why are some areas cold while others are hot? Why are some areas dry while others receive a lot of rain? How much solar radiation a place receives plays an important part in weather patterns. Wind plays a major role in distributing moisture and heat around the world.

EXPLORE ACTIVITY

Where are deserts found?

1. Obtain a world globe or atlas.
2. Locate several of the world's deserts.
3. Find the latitudes of these deserts.
4. Use **Figure 14-17** on page 412 to determine which winds affect these latitudes.

Observe: Many deserts are located next to mountain ranges. In your Science Journal, write about how you think mountains might affect precipitation patterns in different regions.

Previewing Science Skills

- In the **Skill Builders**, you will compare and contrast, and form hypotheses.
- In the **Activities**, you will design an experiment, use variables, constants, and controls, and make a model.
- In the **MiniLABs**, you will make a model, observe, measure in SI, and interpret data.

EXPLORE ACTIVITY

Purpose

LS Visual-Spatial Use the Explore Activity to introduce students to the location of deserts. Inform them that in this chapter, they will learn why climates vary around the world, how climates are classified, and why climates change. L1 LEP COOP LEARN

Preparation

Obtain enough world globes, maps, or atlases to allow students to work in pairs.

Materials

world globe, atlases, or maps

Teaching Strategies

- Ask students to find a desert area in North and South America, Africa, and Asia.
- Students may infer that mountains block precipitation, creating deserts. Many deserts are on the leeward (windless) sides of the mountains.

Assessment

Oral Have students compare and contrast the locations of deserts located during the Explore Activity. Use the Performance Task Assessment List for Making Observations and Inferences in **PASC,** p. 17. P

Assessment Planner

Portfolio
Refer to page 473 for suggested items that students might select for their portfolios.

Performance Assessment
See page 473 for additional Performance Assessment options.
Skill Builders, pp. 455, 461, 469
MiniLABs, pp. 453, 464
Activities 16-1, pp. 456-457; 16-2, p. 468

Content Assessment
Section Wrap-ups, pp. 455, 461, 469, 471
Chapter Review, pp. 473-475
Mini Quizzes, pp. 455, 461, 469

Group Assessment
Opportunities for group assessment occur with Cooperative Learning Strategies and Flex Your Brain Activities.

Section 16•1

Prepare

Section Background

On a sunny day at 0° latitude, the amount of solar energy received is 186 calories per square centimeter. At 60° latitude, it is 110 calories per square centimeter, and at 90° latitude, it is only 68 calories per square centimeter. When skies are cloudy at any latitude, the amount of energy received is lower.

Preplanning

- To prepare for the MiniLAB, obtain globes and metric rulers. Have students bring flashlights.
- To prepare for Activity 16-1, obtain the materials listed on page 456.

1 Motivate

Bellringer

Before presenting the lesson, display **Section Focus Transparency 61** on the overhead projector. Assign the accompanying **Focus Activity** worksheet. L1 LEP

Tying to Previous Knowledge

Students learned in Chapter 14 that the sun's rays strike at different angles, depending on the latitude. In this section, they will learn how this variation influences the occurrence of different climates.

16•1 What is climate?

Science Words

tropics
polar zone
temperate zone

Objectives

- Describe what determines the climate of an area.
- Explain how latitude and topographic features affect the climate of a region.

Climate

When you travel around the world or around the United States, you experience a variety of climates. As you recall from Chapter 6, climate is the characteristic weather of a region. If you visit a rainforest, you'll find the climate there wetter than in a desert. The wettest rain forest averages 1168 cm of precipitation annually. A desert receives less than 25 cm of rain per year. Some places closer to the equator are much warmer than places near the poles. Temperatures on Earth range from -38°C to 43°C.

Climate is determined by averaging the weather over a long period of time, such as 30 years. Some weather conditions that are averaged include temperature, precipitation, air pressure, humidity, and days of sunshine. Factors that affect the climate of a region include latitude, topography, location of lakes and oceans, availability of moisture, global wind patterns, ocean currents, and location of air masses.

Latitude Affects Climate

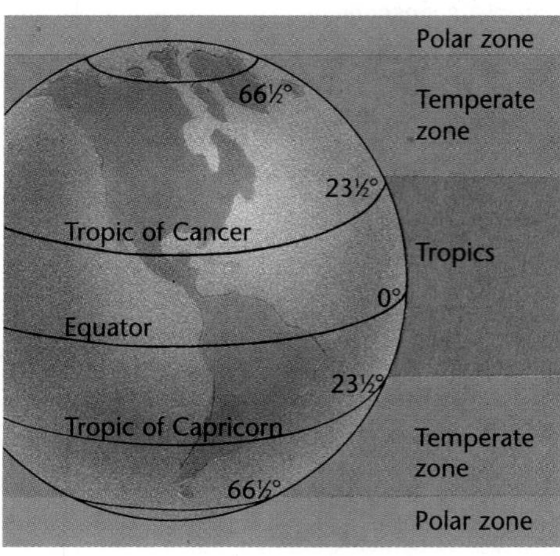

Figure 16-1
One factor that determines climate is the amount of solar energy received at different latitudes.

You learned in Chapter 14 that the amount of solar energy received at a particular location depends on the tilt of Earth on its axis. This tilt influences the angle at which sunlight strikes Earth and, therefore, the amount of radiation received by an area. The MiniLAB on the next page explains this concept.

Latitudes close to the equator receive the most radiation. As you can see in **Figure 16-1,** latitude affects climate. **Figure 16-2** shows a comparison of cities at different latitudes. The **tropics,** the region between latitudes 23½° north and 23½° south, receive the most solar radiation because the sun shines almost directly overhead. Year-round temperatures in the tropics are always hot, except at high elevations. The **polar zones** extend from the poles to 66½° north and south latitudes. Solar energy hits the polar zones at a low angle, spreading the same amount of energy over a larger area. Also, polar ice reflects some of this solar radiation. Therefore, polar regions are never very warm.

Between the tropics and the polar zones are the **temperate zones.** Temperatures in these zones are moderate. The continental United States is in a temperate zone.

Program Resources

Reproducible Masters

Study Guide, p. 65 L1
Reinforcement, p. 65 L1
Enrichment, p. 65 L3
Cross-Curricular Integration, p. 20
Activity Worksheets, pp. 5, 96-97, 100 L1
Critical Thinking/Problem Solving, p. 22
Lab Manual 46, 47, 48

Transparencies

Section Focus Transparency 61 L1
Teaching Transparency 31

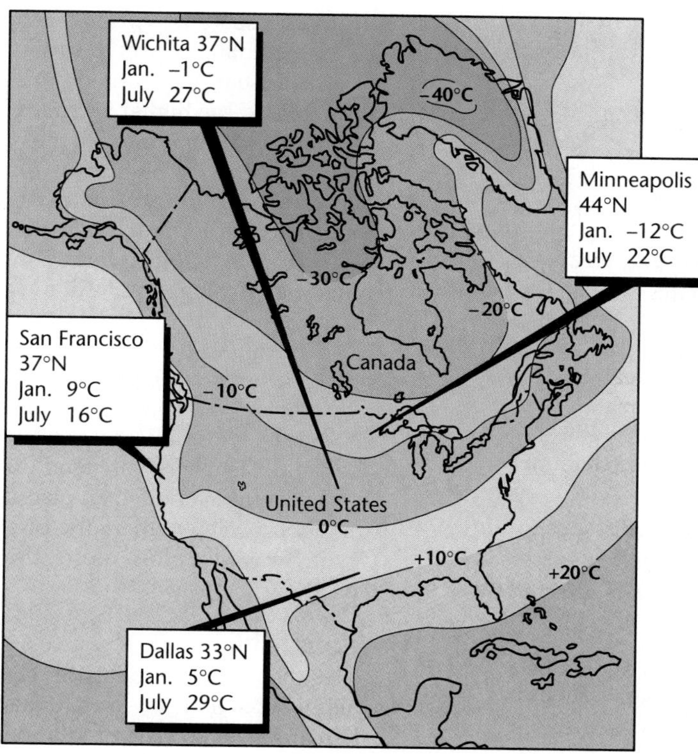

Figure 16-2

This map shows the normal daily minimum temperatures (°C) in January throughout the U.S.

A Minneapolis, Minnesota, at 44°N, receives less solar radiation than Dallas, Texas.

B San Francisco's climate is affected by the nearby ocean. Compare these temperatures to those of Wichita, Kansas on the same 37°N latitude line.

C Dallas, Texas, at 33°N, receives more solar radiation than Minneapolis.

Topographic Features Affect Climate

Climates are more complex than the general divisions of polar, temperate, and tropical. Within each zone, topographic features, such as mountains and large bodies of water, affect climate. Large cities also change weather patterns.

Large Bodies of Water

As you learned in Chapter 14, water heats up and cools down more slowly than land. Because of this, coastal areas experience sea breezes and land breezes. In a similar way, large bodies of water affect the climate of coastal areas. Many coastal regions are warmer in the winter and cooler in the summer than inland areas of similar latitude. **Figure 16-2** shows a comparison of July and January temperatures in a coastal city and a continental city, both at 37°N latitude.

MiniLAB

How does Earth's tilt affect radiation received?

Procedure

1. Hold a flashlight about 30 cm from a globe. Shine the light directly on the equator. With your finger, trace around the light.
2. Without moving the location of the light, tilt it to shine on 30°N latitude. The size of the illuminated area should increase.
3. Repeat at 60°N latitude.

Analysis

1. How did the size and shape of the light beam change as you directed the light toward higher latitudes?
2. How does the tilt of Earth affect the solar radiation received by different latitudes?

GLENCOE TECHNOLOGY

CD-ROM

Earth Science CD-ROM

Have students perform the interactive exploration for Chapter 16 to reinforce important chapter concepts and thinking processes.

2 Teach

MiniLAB

Purpose

LS **Visual-Spatial** Students will observe how Earth's tilt affects the amount of solar radiation received at different latitudes. L1 LEP COOP LEARN

Materials

globes, metric rulers, flashlights

Teaching Strategies

Troubleshooting Instruct students that when they rotate the light, they should not change the distance of the light from the globe or move it from directly above the equator.

- Darken the room during this activity.

Analysis

1. The size of the beam increased. The shape became more oval.
2. The tilt causes the radiation to be spread over a wider area in higher latitudes. Therefore, higher latitudes receive less concentrated solar radiation than lower latitudes.

Assessment

Performance Ask students to hypothesize what would happen to the amount of solar radiation received at different latitudes if Earth were square instead of round. Have them test their hypotheses using a piece of paper to represent a flat side of Earth. Use the Performance Task Assessment List for Formulating a Hypothesis in **PASC**, p. 21. P

Activity Worksheets, pp. 5, 100

Problem Solving

Solve the Problem

1. the closer to the lake, the more frost-free days
2. the closer to the lake, the less annual precipitation
3. Yes, the climate is affected. The average monthly range of temperature is smaller, there are more frost-free days, and the annual precipitation is less than at cities farther from the lake.

Think Critically

More frost-free days at City A near the lake mean a longer growing season.

Visual Learning

Figure 16-3 Have students relate this diagram to the Explore Activity on page 451.

3 Assess

Check for Understanding

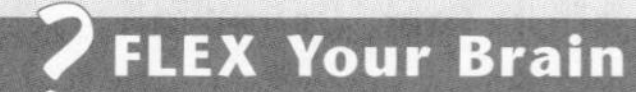

Use the Flex Your Brain activity to have students explore CLIMATE.

Activity Worksheets, p. 5

Reteach

Have students make a concept map that shows how latitude and topographic features affect climate.

Extension

For students who have mastered this section, use the **Reinforcement** and **Enrichment** masters.

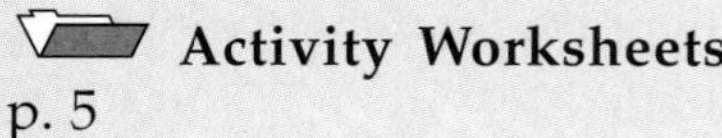

The Lake Effect

If oceans modify the climate of coastal areas near them, do you think large lakes do this as well? The following data were collected from four different Ohio cities near Lake Erie. Examine the data, and see if you can answer the questions.

Solve the Problem

1. **How is the distance from Lake Erie related to frost-free days?**
2. **What is the relationship between distance from the lake and annual precipitation?**
3. **Is the climate of a city near Lake Erie affected by the lake?**

Think Critically: Why would location A be a better location for growing grapes than locations B, C, and D?

Location	A	B	C	D
Distance from the Lake in Kilometers	0	1.6	48.3	80.5
Average Monthly Range of Temperature in °C	7.6	8.8	10.8	11.9
Frost-Free Days	205	194	162	154
Annual Precipitation in Centimeters	73.6	81.4	94.0	97.5

Ocean currents also affect coastal climate. Warm currents originate near the equator and flow toward the higher latitudes, warming the regions they pass by. When the currents cool off and flow back toward the equator, they cool the air and climates of land nearby. Some warm currents move along our Atlantic Coast.

The moisture available also affects climate. Winds blowing from the sea contain more moisture than those blowing from the land. Thus, coasts tend to have a wetter climate than places inland, especially where the prevailing winds blow onto the coast.

Mountains

At the same latitude, the climate is colder in the mountains than at sea level. When radiation absorbed by Earth's surface is emitted upward, there are less air molecules to absorb this heat at higher elevations.

Mountains also affect the climate of nearby areas, as shown in **Figure 16-3.** On the side of the mountain facing the wind, air rises, cools, and drops its moisture as precipitation. On the other side, the air descends, heats up, and dries out the land, often forming deserts. Deserts are common on the sides of mountains away from the wind.

Large Cities

Large cities affect local climates. When radiation strikes areas of vegetation, much of the energy is used in evaporating moisture. Radiation that strikes cities is absorbed by streets, parking lots, and buildings. They

Use **Teaching Transparency 31** as you teach this lesson.

Use Labs 46, 47, and 48 in the **Lab Manual** as you teach this lesson.

heat up and radiate heat into the atmosphere. Automobile exhaust and other pollutants in the air trap this heat, creating what some people call a "heat island" effect. Summer temperatures in a city can be 10° higher than in surrounding rural areas.

In addition to raising temperatures, cities affect the climate in other ways. Skyscrapers, being like small mountains, are barriers that change local wind and precipitation patterns. A study of St. Louis, Missouri found that 25 percent more rainfall, 45 percent more thunderstorms, and 31 percent more hailstorms occurred over the city than over the surrounding rural areas.

Figure 16-3

Climate differs on either side of a mountain. On the windward side, the air rises, cools, and drops its moisture. On the leeward side, the air descends and dries out the land. The map shows a comparison of the rainfall on either side of the Andes Mountains between Chile and Argentina.

Moist air

Dry air

Section Wrap-up

Review

1. What factors help determine the climate of a region?
2. How do mountains affect climate?
3. **Think Critically:** Explain why types of plants and animals found on different sides of the same mountain range might differ.

Skill Builder

Comparing and Contrasting

Contrast tropical, temperate, and polar climates. If you need help, refer to Comparing and Contrasting in the **Skill Handbook.**

USING MATH

Using the data from the Problem Solving Activity, predict the annual precipitation for a location 60 km from Lake Erie.

Skill Builder

The tropics receive the most direct rays from the sun, and therefore, areas with tropical climates are always hot. The polar zones receive solar energy at low angles, and thus are never warm. The temperate zones generally have cold winters and hot summers. Spring and fall are mild seasons.

Assessment

Content Use this Skill Builder to assess students' abilities to compare and contrast. Ask students to compare and contrast the climate in large cities with the climate in the surrounding rural areas. Use the Performance Task Assessment List for Making Observations and Inferences in **PASC,** p. 17. P

4 Close

• MINI • QUIZ •

Use the Mini Quiz to check students' recall of chapter content.

1. **The average weather of an area over a long period of time is its ________.** *climate*
2. **Solar energy hits polar areas at a ________ angle.** *low*
3. **In the summer, coastal areas are often ________ than inland areas of similar latitude.** *cooler*
4. **________ are common on the side of mountains where air descends.** *Deserts*
5. **Summer temperatures in a city are often ________ than in the surrounding rural areas.** *higher*

Section Wrap-up

Review

1. Latitude and topographic features like large bodies of water, mountains, and large cities help determine the climate of a region.
2. They act as barriers to the wind. On the side facing the wind, the air rises and cools, and precipitation occurs. On the other side, the air descends, heats up, and dries out the land.
3. **Think Critically** Organisms that live on the side of the mountain facing the wind experience a moist climate. The other side of the mountain is dry and will support organisms that can survive with little water.

USING MATH

LS **Logical-Mathematical** 95 cm

Activity 16-1

PREPARATION

Purpose

LS **Logical-Mathematical** Observe the characteristics of microclimates around a school building. **COOP LEARN** **L1**

Process Skills

communicating, recognizing cause and effect, forming operational definitions, forming a hypothesis, separating and controlling variables, measuring in SI, designing an experiment, observing and inferring, making and using tables, comparing and contrasting, interpreting data

Time

45 minutes to plan the experiment, 45 minutes to do it (data should be collected in one day), 30 minutes to answer the Analyze and Apply questions

Materials

- Have the following materials available for each group of students: thermometer, psychrometer, relative humidity table (Appendix J), wind sock, rain gauge, and piece of unlined paper.

Alternate Materials If psychrometers need to be assembled, have students do this prior to this activity. A paper strip can be substituted for a wind sock, and a large can or beaker can be substituted for a rain gauge.

Safety Precautions

Caution students to be careful when handling glass thermometers, especially those containing mercury.

Possible Hypotheses

Students may hypothesize that the school building will act as a wind barrier, creating a microclimate on the side protected from the wind different from the one on the wind-exposed side. Students may hypothesize that the area in the shadow of the building will be cooler and have a higher relative humidity than the area exposed to the direct rays of the sun. They may hypothesize that the air temperature will be higher and the relative humidity lower above sidewalks and driveways than above grassy areas.

Activity Worksheets, pp. 5, 96-97

Activity 16-1

Design Your Own Experiment
Microclimates

A microclimate is a very localized climate that differs from the main climate surrounding it. Oceans, mountains, and cities affect climate. Do you think your school building affects the local climate, creating microclimates?

PREPARATION

Problem

Does your school building create microclimates?

Form a Hypothesis

Hypothesize how your school building affects the climate of the area surrounding it. Consider the height of the building, wind direction, and how the building may affect the temperature, wind speed, relative humidity, and precipitation above sidewalks, driveways, and grassy areas.

Objectives

- Design and carry out an experiment to study the microclimates around your school.
- Observe temperature, wind speed, relative humidity, and precipitation in areas outside your school. Infer how the building might affect these climate factors.

Possible Materials

- thermometers
- psychrometer (or materials to make one—see Activity 15-1)
- relative humidity chart
- paper strip or wind sock
- large can, beaker, or rain gauge
- piece of unlined paper

Safety Precaution

Be careful when you handle glass thermometers, especially if your school has only those that contain mercury. If a thermometer breaks, do not touch it. Have your teacher dispose of the glass and mercury safely.

PLAN THE EXPERIMENT

1. As a group, agree upon and write out your hypothesis statement.
2. As a group, list steps needed to test your hypothesis. Include in your plan how you will use your equipment to measure the temperature, wind speed, relative humidity, and precipitation at four or five sites around your school building. Select your sites and make certain the sites fit your hypothesis. Select a control site that is not affected by the building.
3. Sites around the school could be a sidewalk in front of the school, an area close to the building, one further away, one on the north side of the building, and one on the south side. Your control site should be selected carefully to make certain that buildings do not influence the microclimate.
4. Make a map of the school building and the test sites.
5. Design a data table in your Science Journal to use as your group collects data.

Check the Plan

1. Read over your entire experiment to make certain all steps are in a logical order.
2. Identify constants and variables in the experiment.
3. How important is a control to this experiment? How was it selected?
4. *Before you proceed, have your teacher approve your plan.*

DO THE EXPERIMENT

1. Carry out the experiment as planned.
2. While the experiment is going on, record your observations and complete the data table in your Science Journal.

Analyze and Apply

1. **Map** your data. Color code the areas to show which microclimates had the highest and lowest temperatures, the greatest and least wind speed, the greatest and least relative humidity, and the greatest and least precipitation.
2. **Analyze** your data to find patterns.
3. How did your test sites differ from your control site?
4. **Analyze** your hypothesis and the results of your experiment. Was your hypothesis correct?

Go Further

Repeat the experiment around your home. How does your home create different microclimates in its surroundings?

Go Further

Students will find that a house or an apartment building creates different microclimates around it.

Assessment

Performance Have students hypothesize how microclimates change throughout a 24-hour period around the school building. They may say that shadows created by the building will change throughout the day as the angle of the sun changes. This will produce microclimate temperature changes. Also, students may say that during the afternoon, when the air temperature is normally higher than in the early morning and late evening, there will be a greater difference in the temperature and relative humidity in different areas. Use the Performance Task Assessment List for Formulating a Hypothesis in **PASC**, p. 21. P

PLAN THE EXPERIMENT

Possible Procedure

Students will probably suggest using the thermometer to measure the temperature, the wind sock to measure wind speed, the psychrometer to measure relative humidity, and the rain gauge to measure precipitation in five locations near the school. If snow is on the ground, students can substitute a metric ruler for the rain gauge. The control site should be located away from the school and other buildings, preferably in a field. A map of the building and the test and control sites should be made on the piece of unlined paper.

Teaching Strategies

Troubleshooting Students may be unable to collect precipitation during the limited time when they are measuring. They can leave large cans or beakers at the various locations overnight and measure the precipitation the following day. Perhaps it would be helpful to plan the experiment for a rainy day.

DO THE EXPERIMENT

Expected Outcome

Students will observe that the school building does create microclimates.

Analyze and Apply

1. Maps should be color coded with a legend.
2. Students should see patterns.
3. Answers may include differences in temperature, wind speed, relative humidity, and precipitation.
4. Answers will vary, depending on hypotheses.

Section 16•2

Prepare

Section Background

The first climate classification system was devised by the early Greeks. It was based on differences in temperature. Köppen's classification system considers differences in precipitation, also.

1 Motivate

Bellringer

Before presenting the lesson, display **Section Focus Transparency 62** on the overhead projector. Assign the accompanying **Focus Activity** worksheet. L1 LEP

Tying to Previous Knowledge

Students learned in Chapter 6 that climate affects the weathering of rocks and the formation of soils. In this section, they will learn that it also affects where organisms are able to survive.

2 Teach

Student Text Questions

- **Why do so many different types of climates exist in the United States?** *The country is large and influenced by two different oceans. Areas of the United States have various latitudes, elevations, and topographic features that influence climate.*
- **What climate exists where you live?** *Answers will vary.*

16•2 Climate Types

Science Words

adaptation
hibernation

Objectives

- Describe the Köppen Climate Classification System.
- Describe how organisms adapt to particular climates.

Climate Classification

If your job were to classify climates, where would you begin? Although there are several ways to classify climates, *climatologists* (persons who study climates) usually use a system developed in 1918 by Russian-German meteorologist and climatologist Wladimir Köppen. Köppen observed that the type of vegetation found in a region depended on the climate of the area. **Figure 16-4** shows differences Köppen might have observed. His classification system is based on his studies of temperature and precipitation.

Köppen Climate Types

In **Figure 16-5,** the Köppen Climate Classification System divides climates into six groups: tropical, mild, dry, continental, polar, and high elevation. These groups are further divided into types. For example, the dry climate classification is divided into *semiarid* and *arid.*

Examine the Köppen map and count how many different climates are found in the continental United States. Why do so many different types of climates exist here? What climate exists where you live?

Figure 16-4

The type of vegetation in a region depends on the climate.

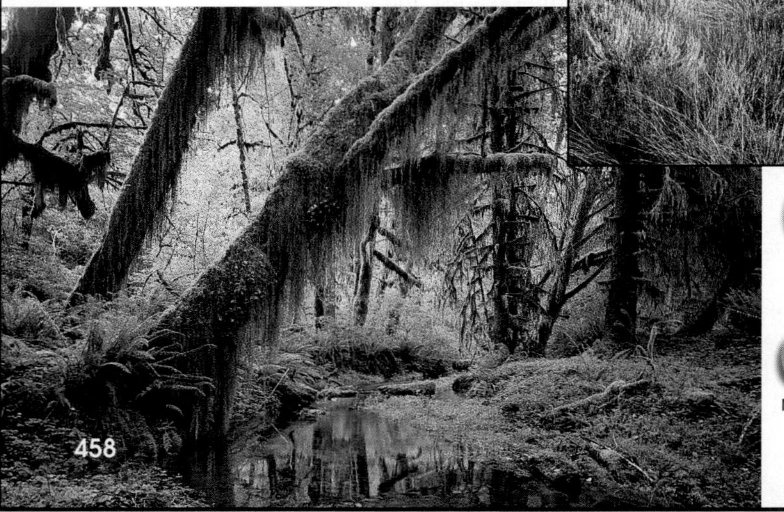

A Short grasses grow in fairly dry climates.

B Moss-draped trees and ferns grow in climates having heavy rainfall.

Program Resources

Reproducible Masters

Study Guide, p. 66 L1
Reinforcement, p. 66 L1
Enrichment, p. 66 L3
Science Integration Activities, pp. 31-32
Multicultural Connections, pp. 35-36

Transparencies

Section Focus Transparency 62 L1
Teaching Transparency 32

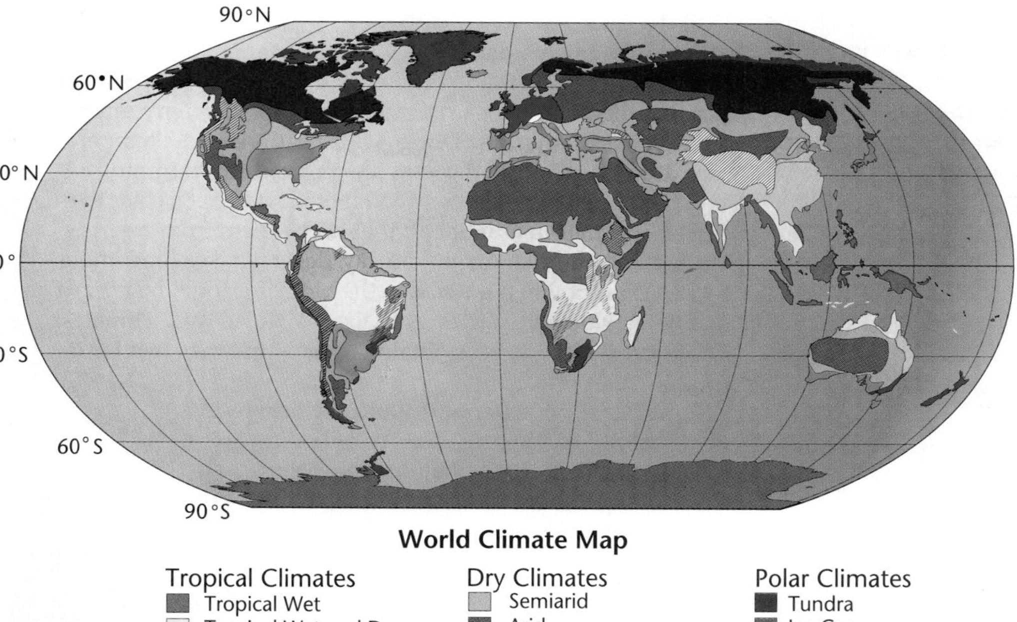

World Climate Map

Tropical Climates	Dry Climates	Polar Climates
Tropical Wet	Semiarid	Tundra
Tropical Wet and Dry	Arid	Ice Cap
Mild Climates	**Continental Climates**	**High Elevation**
Marine West Coast	Warm Summer	Highlands
Mediterranean	Cool Summer	Uplands
Humid Subtropical	Subarctic	

)rganism Adaptations

As you have learned, climates vary around the world, and ıs Köppen noticed, the type of climate that exists in an area letermines the vegetation found there. Fir trees aren't found n deserts, nor are cactus found in rain forests. In fact, all)rganisms have certain kinds of adaptations that allow them o survive in some climates, but not in others. An adaptation s any characteristic that develops in a population over a long ime. An **adaptation** is any structure or behavioral feature hat helps an organism survive in its environment. Some ıdaptations are shown in **Figure 16-6.** Climatic factors that nay limit where an organism can live are temperature, mois-ure, and amount of daylight.

Structural Adaptations

Some organisms have body structures that enable them to urvive in particular climates. The fur of mammals insulates hem from cold temperatures. A cactus has a thick, fleshy tem. This adaptation helps a cactus hold water. The waxy kin covering the stem keeps water inside the plant from vaporating. Instead of broad leaves, cactus plants have piny leaves that further reduce water loss.

Figure 16-5

The Köppen Climate Classification System is shown on this map. Notice that most wet climates are located between latitudes 30° north and 30° south. *What other patterns do you see on this map?*

INTEGRATION Life Science

Visual Learning

Figure 16-5 How many different climate types are there? *14* **What other patterns do you see on the map?** *Answers will vary, but students may say that Warm Summer, Cool Summer, and Subarctic climate types exist only in latitudes north of 30°N.* LEP LS

INTEGRATION Life Science

All living things have the ability to adapt. Many adaptations occur because of DNA mutations in the genes of organisms. Mutations can occur spontaneously or because of outside stimuli. If a trait resulting from a mutation benefits an organism, the organism will have the opportunity to pass that trait on to its offspring. A successful species is one that can adapt to changes in its environment. If an environment changes quickly and a species cannot adapt, it will eventually die out.

Inquiry Question

Ask students to explain how climate affects the surface of the land, soil, plant growth, and even the activities of humans. *Students may say that climate affects the weathering of land and the formation of soil. It limits where vegetation can grow and where people choose to live.*

Use **Teaching Transparency 32** as you teach this lesson.

Community Connection

Animal Adaptations Invite a wildlife specialist to class to talk about various ways that animals are adapted to live in your climate.

GLENCOE TECHNOLOGY

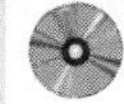

Videodisc

The Infinite Voyage: Crisis in the Atmosphere

Chapter 11

Worldwide Energy Conservation Solutions

Student Text Question

- **Can you think of some behavioral adaptations you make as a result of climate?** *Students may mention wearing dark, heavy clothing in the winter and light-colored, light-weight clothing in the summer.*
- **What behavioral adaptations help the people on page 461 survive in different climates?** *Some behavioral adaptations are that they wear warm clothing and use sunscreen.*

3 Assess

Check for Understanding

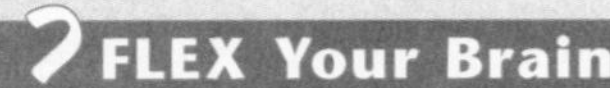

Use the Flex Your Brain activity to have students explore ADAPTATION.

Activity Worksheets, p. 5

Reteach

LS **Visual-Spatial** Have students select a climate type from **Figure 16-5**. Ask them to infer from it (1) the characteristics of the climate and (2) the adaptations an organism must have to survive there.

Extension

For students who have mastered this section, use the **Reinforcement** and **Enrichment** masters.

Figure 16-6

Organisms have structural and behavioral adaptations that help them survive in particular climates.

A Honeybees fan in fresh air to keep the hive cool.

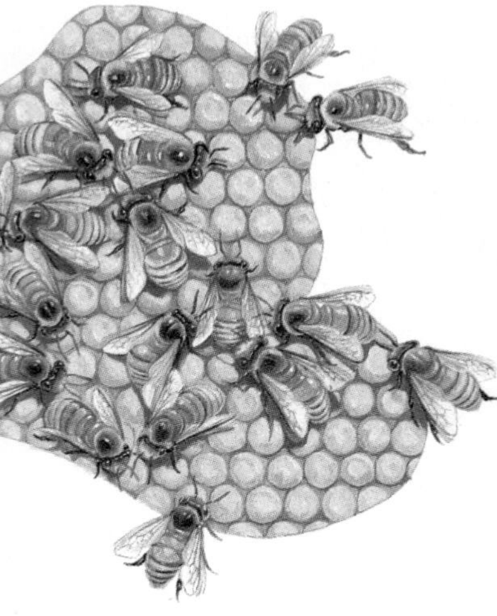

Behavioral Adaptations

Some organisms display behavioral adaptations that help them survive in certain climates. For example, rodents and certain other mammals undergo a period of inactivity in winter called **hibernation.** During hibernation, body temperature drops and body processes are reduced to a minimum.

Other animals are differently adapted. When it's cold, bees cluster together in a tight ball that keeps them from freezing. During hot, sunny hours of the day, desert snakes hide under rocks. At night when it's cooler, they look for food. Instead of drinking water as turtles and lizards do in wet climates, desert turtles and lizards obtain the moisture they need from their food.

Lungfish survive periods of intense heat by going through an inactive state called *estivation.* As weather gets hot and water begins evaporating, the fish burrows into mud and secretes a capsule around itself. It lives this way until the warm, dry months pass.

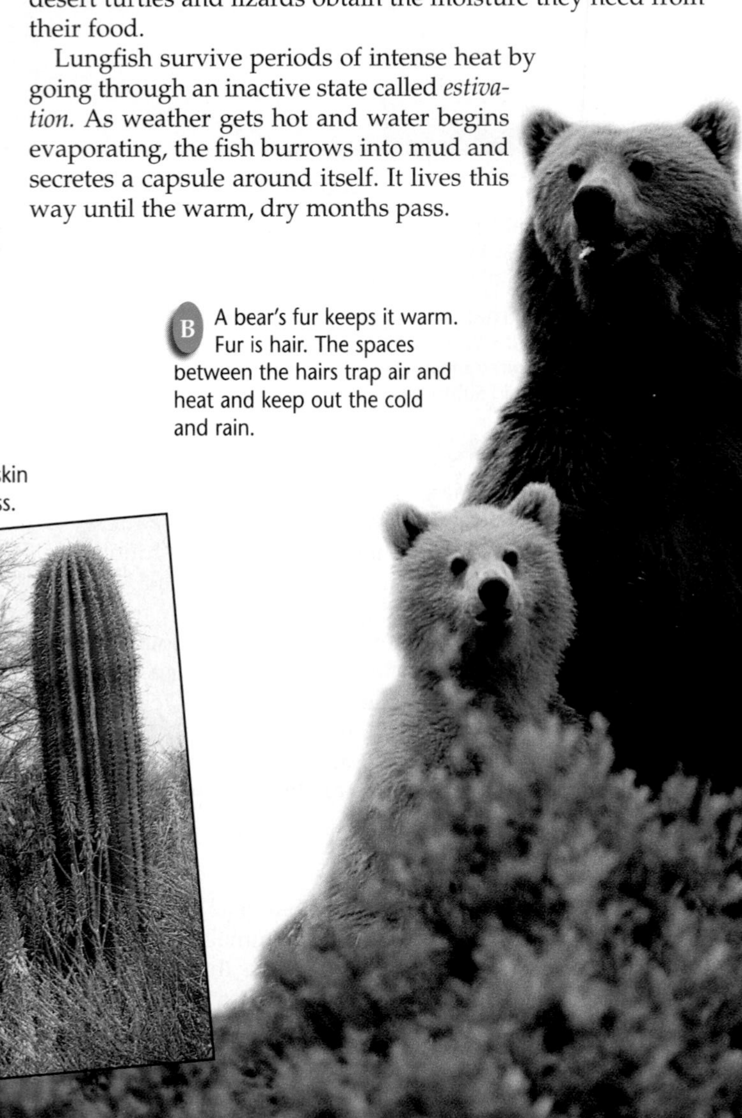

B A bear's fur keeps it warm. Fur is hair. The spaces between the hairs trap air and heat and keep out the cold and rain.

C The needles and the waxy skin of a cactus reduce water loss.

460

Use **Multicultural Connections,** pp. 35-36, as you teach this lesson.

Like other organisms, you have structural adaptations that help you cope with climate. You can maintain a fairly constant body temperature, regardless of the outside temperature. In hot weather, your sweat glands release water onto your skin. The water evaporates and as a result, you become cooler. What other adaptations help the people in **Figure 16-7** cope with climate?

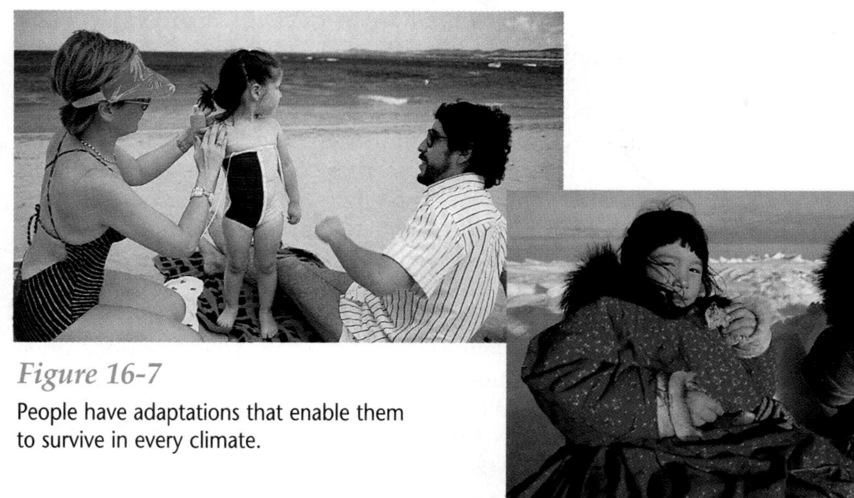

Figure 16-7

People have adaptations that enable them to survive in every climate.

Section Wrap-up

Review

1. Use **Figure 16-5** and Appendix G to identify the climate type for each of the following locations: Hawaiian Islands, North Korea, Egypt, Uruguay.
2. What are some behavioral adaptations that allow animals to stay warm?
3. **Think Critically:** What special adaptations must plants and animals have to live in the regions labeled as dry?

Skill Builder

Hypothesizing

Some scientists think Earth is becoming hotter. Suppose this is true. Form a hypothesis about which adaptations will allow some present-day organisms to survive this change. If you need help, refer to Hypothesizing in the **Skill Handbook.**

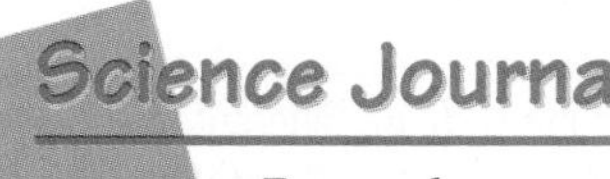

Science Journal

Research ways that people have adapted their behavior to survive in the six climate regions shown in **Figure 16-5.** Consider clothing, housing, and transportation. Write about these adaptations in your Science Journal.

4 Close

• MINI • QUIZ •

Use the Mini Quiz to check students' recall of chapter content.

1. **A person who studies climate is a ________.** *climatologist*
2. **One system used to classify climate is the ________ Climate Classification system.** *Köppen*
3. **Fur on mammals is an example of a ________ adaptation.** *structural*
4. **Hibernation is an example of a ________ adaptation.** *behavioral*

Section Wrap-up

Review

1. Hawaii: Tropical Wet; North Korea: Warm Summer; Egypt: Arid; Uruguay: Humid Subtropical
2. Animals may burrow into the ground (groundhog), bask in the sun (snakes), or cluster in a ball (bees).
3. **Think Critically** They must be able to obtain moisture and store it for long periods of time.

Science Journal

Examples may include: people living in tropical climates wear less clothing than people in polar climates; houses in Continental, Polar, and High Elevation climates are insulated to keep out the cold; transportation in the Polar Climates at certain times is limited to snowmobiles and dog sleds, while cars, horses, and camels are used in some other climates year-round.

Skill Builder

Adaptations that can help animals include being able to sweat to cool off or tunneling below ground where it is cooler. Plant adaptations include having needles or living in the shadows of other plants where it is cooler. P

Assessment

Performance If Earth gets hotter, ice caps will melt, sea level will rise, and coastal regions will flood. Have students predict which adaptations will allow some present-day coastal organisms to survive this change. Use the Performance Task Assessment List for Making Observations and Inferences in **PASC,** p. 17. P

Section 16•3

Prepare

Section Background

The first great ice age occurred between 2.5 billion and 2 billion years ago. Evidence suggests that warming followed that period and lasted until about 950 million years ago. A second ice age occurred between 950 and 650 million years ago, followed by a warming period that lasted until about 70 million years ago. Since that time, there have been several periods when glaciers have formed and then melted. The last ice age reached its peak about 18 000 years ago.

Preplanning

- To prepare for the MiniLAB, obtain metric rulers and cross sections of wood that show tree rings. Contact the division of forestry near you for samples.
- To prepare for Activity 16-2, obtain the materials listed on page 468 for each group.

1 Motivate

Bellringer

Before presenting the lesson, display **Section Focus Transparency 63** on the overhead projector. Assign the accompanying **Focus Activity** worksheet. L1 LEP

Tying to Previous Knowledge

Students learned in Chapter 13 about events that occurred throughout geologic time, including climatic changes. In this section, they will discover some of the causes of short-term and long-term climatic changes.

16•3 Climatic Changes

Science Words

season
El Niño
greenhouse effect
global warming

Objectives

- Discuss what causes seasons.
- Describe how El Niño affects the climate.
- Describe past climatic change.
- Explore possible causes of climatic change.
- Differentiate between the greenhouse effect and global warming.

Seasons

In temperate zones, weather generally changes with the season. **Seasons** are short-term periods of climate change caused by regular variation in daylight, temperature, and weather patterns. These variations are due to changes in the amount of solar radiation an area receives. **Figure 16-8** shows Earth revolving around the sun. Because Earth revolves at a tilt, different areas of Earth receive changing amounts of solar radiation. That affects wind patterns. In turn, wind patterns and topographic features help create seasonal climatic changes. Wind patterns and topographic features also help create seasonal climate changes.

Effects of Latitude

In the middle latitudes or temperate zones, seasons often have warm summers and cool winters. Spring and fall are usually mild. Because of fairly constant solar radiation at the low latitudes near the equator, the tropics do not experience as much seasonal temperature change as the middle latitudes, but they do experience dry and rainy seasons.

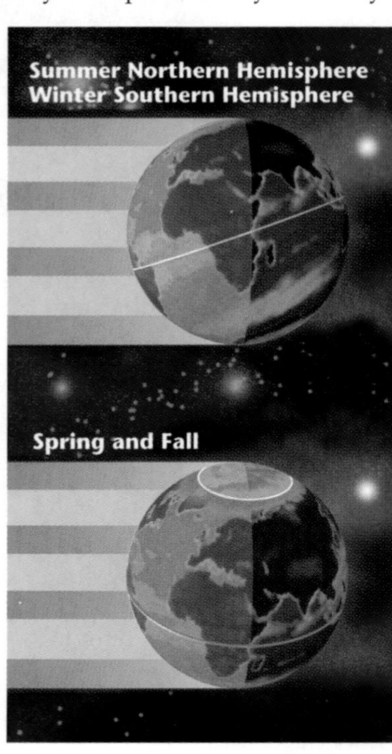

Figure 16-8

During the year, as Earth moves around the sun, different areas of Earth tilt toward the sun, bringing different seasons. In the southern hemisphere, when the South Pole tilts away from the sun, the sun hangs low in the sky. The sun's rays hit at an angle, making the sunlight less concentrated. Days become short, bringing winter. At the same time in the northern hemisphere, the North Pole tilts toward the sun. The sun is high in the sky. Days are long. It's summer.

During the year, the high latitudes near the poles experience great differences in temperature and in number of daylight hours. As shown in **Figure 16-8,** during summer in the northern hemisphere, the North Pole is tilted toward the sun. At the North Pole, there are 24 hours of daylight for six months. During that same time, the South Pole experiences 24-hour days of darkness. However, a little way from the North Pole, at 64° north latitude, Fairbanks, Alaska has more than five hours of daylight on the shortest day of the year and more than 18 hours of daylight

Program Resources

Reproducible Masters

Study Guide, p. 67 L1
Reinforcement, p. 67 L1
Enrichment, p. 67 L3
Activity Worksheets, pp. 5, 98-99, 101 L1

Transparencies

Section Focus Transparency 63 L1

on the longest day. At the equator, days are about the same length all year long. Recall from **Figure 16-2** on page 453 how latitude affects climate.

El Niño

Some climatic changes last longer than a season. **El Niño** is a climate event that starts in the tropical Pacific Ocean and sets off changes in the atmosphere. El Niño used to occur every three to seven years but now happens more frequently. In El Niño, the Pacific Ocean warms along the equator. Near the equator, trade winds that blow east to west weaken and sometimes reverse. Instead of cold water rising off the coast of Peru, the change in the trade winds allows warm tropical water in the upper layers of the Pacific to flow eastward to South America. Ocean temperatures increase by 1° to 7°C off the coast of Peru. Sea level rises.

El Niño does not directly cause unusual weather but instead affects the atmosphere and ocean to make stormy weather more likely. Warmer water brings more evaporation. Heavy rains fall over South America. Scientists also note that during El Niño, the jet stream often splits, changing the atmospheric pressure off California and wind and precipitation patterns around the world. It can cause drought in Australia and Africa, disruption of dependable monsoon rains, storms in California, and the weather events of **Figure 16-9.**

Scientists are not certain what causes El Niño, but many link it with global warming. Experts hypothesize that El Niño distributes the extra energy from global warming.

CONNECT TO

LIFE SCIENCE

Some aquatic plants and animals living in waters off California are dying. ***Infer*** how El Niño may be the cause of their deaths.

Figure 16-9

The effects of El Niño are felt around the world. A strong El Niño occurred in 1983.

A severe drought brought dust storms to Australia.

A cyclone hit the Arutua Atoll in Polynesia.

2 Teach

CONNECT TO

LIFE SCIENCE

Some of the aquatic animals living along the coast are not adapted to live in warm water. When they die, the animals that depend on them for food eventually starve to death.

Content Background

El Niño is Spanish meaning "the child." The event is so named because it usually appears around Christmas time. During El Niño, the water temperature can increase by 2-10°C off the coast of North and South America.

Inquiry Question

What happens to the direction of the trade winds when El Niño occurs? *They weaken and can reverse direction, blowing west to east instead of east to west.*

GLENCOE TECHNOLOGY

Videodisc

STVS: Plants & Simple Organisms

Disc 4, Side 2

Detecting Climate Changes in Tree Rings (Ch. 22)

STVS: Earth & Space

Disc 3, Side 2

Greenhouse Effect (Ch. 6)

Records of Ancient Climates (Ch. 18)

Across the Curriculum

Social Studies A strong worldwide El Niño occurred in 1982-1983. It was blamed for approximately $1.8 billion worth of damage and 1300 deaths. Ask students to find out how El Niño causes damage and deaths. L1 P

MiniLAB

Purpose

LS **Logical-Mathematical** Students will measure tree growth rings. L1 COOP LEARN

Materials

metric rulers, cross sections of trees

Teaching Strategies

- Have each student group draw a line from the center of the wood cross section to the outer edge with a pencil. Then have the group measure the width of the rings along this line.
- Have magnifying glasses and dissecting microscopes available for students with visual impairment to use.

Analysis

1. Answers will vary as to the change in the length of the growing seasons. Widely spaced rings indicate longer growing seasons.
2. Growth rings close together indicate poor growing conditions. Perhaps the climate was cold and/or dry. Rings far apart indicate favorable growing conditions. Perhaps the climate was warm and/or moist.

Assessment

Performance Have students infer why it is important to analyze petrified tree rings of the same species. Tree species have different temperature and moisture needs. Growth will vary accordingly. Use the Performance Task Assessment List for Making Observations and Inferences in **PASC**, p. 17. P

Activity Worksheets, pp. 5, 101

MiniLAB

What can we learn from tree rings?

As a tree grows, it adds layers of growth rings. When conditions for growth are good, growth rings occur far apart. When conditions are poor, growth rings appear close together.

Procedure

1. Examine the growth rings of a cross section of wood. Note that the oldest wood is in the center.
2. Measure the thickness of several rings in your sample.

Analysis

1. How did the length of the growing seasons change as your tree grew older? Describe what evidence you found for this.
2. If scientists examine growth rings in petrified wood samples from different geologic times, what can they learn about climates of earlier geologic periods?

Climatic Change

Although some years are warmer, colder, drier, or wetter than others, Earth's climate remains fairly constant. However, in earlier geologic eras, Earth was sometimes much colder or much warmer than it is today.

Geological records show that in the past, the climate changed. Fossils of tropical plants and animals found in polar as well as temperate regions indicate warmer worldwide climates in the past. **Figure 16-10** illustrates how living things reflect variability in climate. Glacial erosion and deposition around the world indicate that in earlier eras extensive polar conditions existed on Earth.

In the past two million years, glaciers have covered large parts of Earth's surface. These periods of extensive glaciers are called ice ages. At least for the past three million years, ice ages have alternated with warm periods called interglacial intervals. We are now in an interglacial interval. Some interglacial intervals were warmer than now. Some ice ages lasted 60 000 years. Most interglacial periods lasted about 12 000 years. The present interglacial period began about 11 500 years ago. Cores drilled in Greenland ice give evidence of shorter variations in the climate. The evidence suggests that cold spells, lasting 1000 years or more, followed warm spells that lasted as long. Average temperatures in northern Europe changed as much as 10° C in a few years.

Theories Explaining Major Climatic Change

Research into the causes of climatic change suggests a variety of possibilities. Catastrophic events such as meteorite impacts and volcanic eruptions may have occurred, or perhaps the sun's output of energy isn't constant. It could be that when Earth's plates move, they change climate patterns, or perhaps Earth's movements in space cause climatic change.

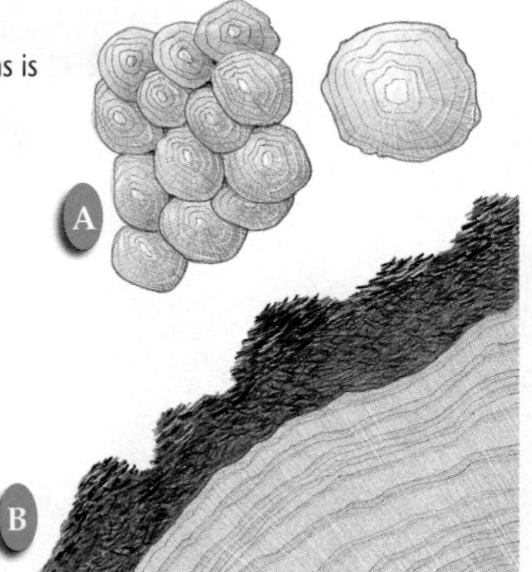

Figure 16-10

The length of growing seasons is recorded in the rings of fish scales (A) and tree rings (B).

Catastrophic events such as large meteorite impacts and volcanic eruptions put enormous volumes of dust, ash, and smoke into the atmosphere. These dust and smoke particles could have blocked so much solar radiation that they cooled the planet and

Theme Connection

Stability and Change Ask students to explain how catastrophic events such as meteorite impacts and volcanic eruptions can cause the climate to change. *When meteors crash into Earth or volcanoes erupt, dust particles fill the atmosphere. These particles reflect energy from the sun back into space. A great amount of dust will cause a cooling of the climate.*

changed the climate. **Figure 16-11** on the next page illustrates how a major volcanic eruption affects Earth's atmosphere.

Evidence suggests that an increase in clouds may lead to an increased greenhouse effect. It might also lead to less solar radiation reaching Earth's surface. Computer models have allowed scientists to conclude that clouds absorb more solar radiation than was previously thought. It is possible that an increase in clouds could lead to a cooling effect similar to that produced by volcanic ash.

In Chapter 14, you learned that solar radiation provides Earth's energy. If the output of the radiation from the sun varies, that could change Earth's climate.

Another possible explanation for major climatic change concerns the movement of the plates on Earth's crust. The movement of continents and oceans affects the transfer of heat on Earth's surface, which in turn affects

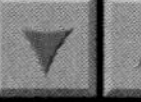

USING TECHNOLOGY

Ice Delivers Clues

By examining air bubbles trapped in glaciers, scientists learn about climates of earlier geologic eras. Scientists use long drills to remove cores of ice-age samples from ice sheets. Then they examine the trapped air by cutting the core into small pieces and putting the pieces in a vacuum chamber. In the sealed chamber, air is pumped out, then steel needles crush the ice. The trapped air escapes and is sucked into a tube. A laser beam of infrared light shoots through the tube to measure the amount of carbon dioxide in the sample of air.

Scientists have discovered that the amount of carbon dioxide varies within ice cores. During warm periods in the past, when ice formed slowly, the concentrations of carbon dioxide ranged between 260 to 280 parts per million. In colder times, when ice layers formed quickly, concentrations of carbon dioxide ranged between 190 and 200 parts per million. No one knows the exact reason for these differences, but it is clear that carbon dioxide is associated with climate changes.

Digging an Ice Core

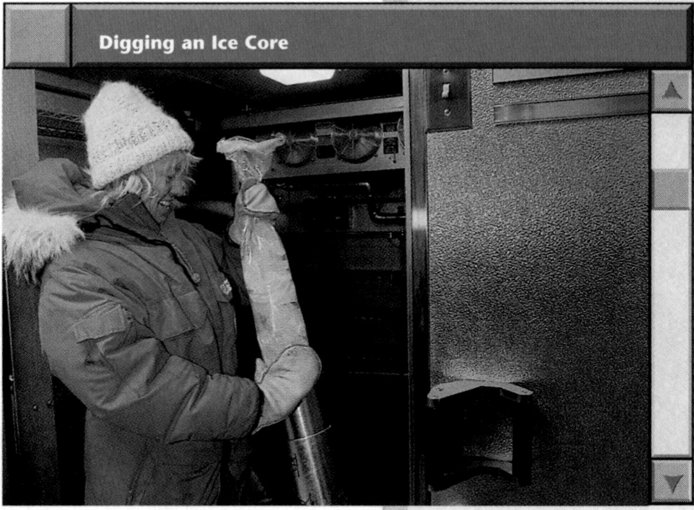

Think Critically:

Many experts theorize that we are living in an interglacial period and that another ice age will begin within 1000 years or so. Others think our climate will get warmer. Explain how measuring present-day atmospheric carbon dioxide levels may help predict the future climate.

USING TECHNOLOGY

For more information on how ice cores inform us about ice ages, read "Glacier Bubbles Are Telling Us What Was in Ice Age Air," by Jonathan Weiner, *Smithsonian Magazine*, Volume 20, May 1989, pp. 78-84.

Think Critically

If carbon dioxide levels increase, the climate will probably get warmer; if they drop, it will probably get colder.

Inquiry Question

What effect might the movement of Earth's crustal plates have on climatic change? *When plates move, the transfer of heat between the oceans and the continents changes. This change affects wind and precipitation patterns.*

GLENCOE TECHNOLOGY

Videodisc

The Infinite Voyage: Crisis in the Atmosphere

Introduction

Chapter 1

Historical Aspects of the Greenhouse Effect and Fossil Air

Chapter 2

Studying Man-Made Carbon Dioxide

Chapter 3

Our Future Climate

Chapter 4

The Greenhouse Effect: Future and Past

Discussion

Have students discuss reasons why the amount of solar radiation received by Earth varies over time. They should include information on the reflection of radiation away from Earth by dust from volcanic eruptions and the possibility that Earth's tilt and orbital shape change. Some students might add that the sun can expand and contract, and that sunspots might influence Earth's climate.

CONNECT TO PHYSICS

Make certain that the pendulum swings free and is heavy enough not to be influenced by breezes.

GLENCOE TECHNOLOGY

Videodisc

The Infinite Voyage: Secrets from a Frozen World

Introduction

Chapter 3

Ice Cores: Discovering Causes of the Greenhouse Effect

Chapter 4

Debating Carbon Dioxode Absorption

Chapter 5

Slowing the Rise of Carbon Dioxide in the Air

CONNECT TO PHYSICS

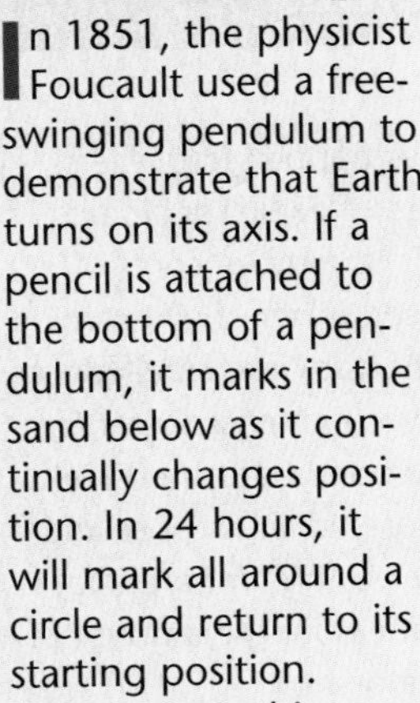

In 1851, the physicist Foucault used a free-swinging pendulum to demonstrate that Earth turns on its axis. If a pencil is attached to the bottom of a pendulum, it marks in the sand below as it continually changes position. In 24 hours, it will mark all around a circle and return to its starting position. ***Demonstrate*** this movement by making a model.

wind and precipitation patterns. Through time, these altered patterns may change the climate.

Another theory relates to Earth's movements in space. Earth is currently tilted on its axis at 23½° to the plane of its orbit around the sun. In the past, this tilt has increased to 25° and has decreased to 22°. When this tilt is at its maximum, the poles receive more solar energy. When the tilt is at its minimum, the poles receive less solar energy. Some scientists hypothesize that Earth's tilt changes about every 42 000 years, affecting climates.

Another Earth movement that may affect climatic change is the change in the shape of Earth's orbit around the sun. It's hypothesized that the shape of Earth's orbit changes over a 100 000 year cycle. When the orbit is more circular than at present, Earth is farther from the sun and temperatures are colder than those we are experiencing.

Although these movements of Earth may explain some of the variations in the most recent ice age, they do not explain why glaciers have occurred so rarely over the long span of geologic time.

As you've learned, there are many theories that attempt to answer questions about why Earth's climate has changed through the ages. Probably all of these factors play some role in changing climates. A great deal of research still needs to be done before we can understand all the interactions that affect climate.

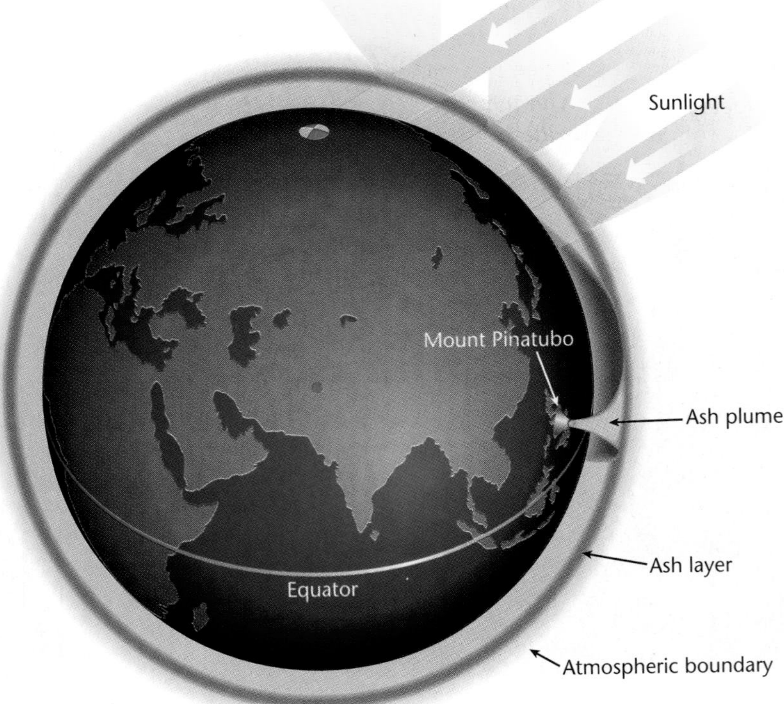

Figure 16-11

When Mt. Pinatubo in the Philippines erupted in 1991, its volcanic ash cooled temperatures around the world.

Science Journal

Literature Have students write a short story or poem describing life in the future if Earth's temperature continues to rise and coastal cities are flooded. L1 LS

Figure 16-12

The sun's radiation travels through our atmosphere and heats Earth's surface. But the heat that is radiated from Earth can't escape back through the gases of the atmosphere into space. This is similar to how a greenhouse warms.

Climatic Changes Today

Today, many newspaper and magazine headlines warn us about the greenhouse effect and global warming. These two phenomena are related but are not the same thing.

The **greenhouse effect** is natural heating caused by gases in our atmosphere trapping heat. The greenhouse effect is illustrated in **Figure 16-12.** Carbon dioxide is the main greenhouse gas. Activity 16-2 demonstrates the greenhouse effect, which is not a bad thing. Without the greenhouse effect, life as we know it would not be possible on Earth. Like Mars, Earth would be too cold.

Global warming means global temperatures are rising. One reason for global warming is the increase of greenhouse gases in our atmosphere. An increase in greenhouse gases increases the greenhouse effect. In the last 100 years, the mean surface temperature on Earth has increased ½°C. This may be from global warming.

If the mean temperature continues to rise, ice caps will melt. Low-lying areas might experience increased flooding. Already some ice caps are beginning to break apart and sea level is rising in certain areas. Some people believe that these events are related to Earth's increased temperature. If you lived on an island or a river delta, would you need to be concerned?

USING MATH

Approximately 15 percent of the total land surface of Earth is covered by deserts. There are about 22 400 000 square km of deserts. Estimate the total land surface of Earth.

USING MATH

LS Logical-Mathematical

149 333 333 km^2

Student Text Question

If you live on an island or a river delta, would you need to be concerned about global warming? *Yes. If sea level rises, you would need to move to a higher elevation.*

3 Assess

Check for Understanding

FLEX Your Brain

Use the Flex Your Brain activity to have students explore CAUSES FOR CLIMATE CHANGE. P

Reteach

Have students explain why scientists cannot agree in their forecasts for Earth's climate. Students should discuss the many variables that must be considered in making predictions.

Extension

For students who have mastered this section, use the **Reinforcement** and **Enrichment** masters.

GLENCOE TECHNOLOGY

Videodisc

STVS: Chemistry

Disc 2, Side 1

Hole in the Ozone (Ch. 21)

STVS: Earth & Space

Disc 3, Side 2

Greenhouse Effect (Ch. 6)

Activity 16-2

Purpose

Interpersonal Students will make a model of the greenhouse effect. L1 COOP LEARN

Process Skills

communicating, comparing and contrasting, forming operational definitions, separating and controlling variables, interpreting data, using numbers, making models, measuring in SI, making and using graphs, recognizing cause and effect

Time

45 minutes

Safety Precautions

Use thermometers safely.

Activity Worksheets, pp. 5, 98-99

Teaching Strategies

- If you cannot obtain enough aquariums, use identical glass jars and thermometers to fit them.
- Be sure that teams check their thermometers before they begin the experiment. The temperatures on the three thermometers should be the same.

Answers to Questions

1. It is the control.
2. The constants were identical aquariums, thermometer readings at the beginning of the experiment, and exposure to the sun's radiation. The variable was the presence of a glass lid on one aquarium.
3. The thermometer inside the aquarium with the lid changed the most because heat could not escape.
4. Similar to greenhouse gases, the glass allowed radiation to penetrate, but then the heat could not escape.
5. The temperature can get so hot that animals suffer stress and die.

Activity 16-2 The Greenhouse Effect

Have you ever climbed into a car on a warm day and burned yourself on the seat? Why was it so hot inside the car, when it wasn't that hot outside? It was hotter in the car because the car functioned like a greenhouse. You experienced the greenhouse effect.

Problem

How can you demonstrate the greenhouse effect?

Materials

- identical empty aquariums (2)
- glass lid for one aquarium
- thermometers (3)

Safety Precaution

Be careful when you handle glass thermometers, especially if your school has only those that contain mercury. If a thermometer breaks, do not touch it. Have your teacher dispose of the glass and mercury safely.

Procedure

1. Lay a thermometer inside each aquarium.
2. Place the aquariums next to each other by a sunny window. Lay the third thermometer between the aquariums.
3. Record the temperatures of the three thermometers.
4. Place the glass lid on one aquarium.
5. Record the temperatures of all three thermometers at the end of 5, 10, and 15 minutes.
6. Make a line graph that shows the temperatures of the three thermometers for the 15 minutes of the experiment.

Analyze

1. Explain why you placed a thermometer between the two aquariums.
2. What were the constants in this experiment? What was the variable?
3. Which thermometer experienced the greatest temperature change during your experiment? Why?

Conclude and Apply

4. **Analyze** what occured in this experiment. How was the glass lid in this experiment like the greenhouse gases in the atmosphere?
5. **Infer** from this experiment why you should never leave a pet inside a closed car in warm weather.

Assessment

Performance Have students infer how global warming may affect the water cycle. *Because warmer air can hold more moisture, evaporation increases, and precipitation patterns may change.* Use the Performance Task Assessment List for Making Observations and Inferences in **PASC**, p. 17. P

USING MATH

Logical-Mathematical Average rise = 23 cm/70 years = 0.33 cm per year. New York underwater: 396 cm/0.33 per year = 1200 years.

You learned in section 16-2 that organisms are adapted to their environments. But when environments change, can organisms cope? In some tropical waters around the world, corals, like those in **Figure 16-13,** are dying. Are these deaths caused by warmer water? Many people think so.

Some climate models indicate that in the future, Earth's temperatures will increase faster than they have in the last 100 years. In Section 16-4, you will learn how people's activities may contribute to global warming, and you will find out what you can do to help lessen this problem.

USING MATH

When ice sheets melt, sea level rises. Between 1900 and 1970, sea level at New York City rose 23 cm. What was the average rise in sea level per year from 1900 to 1970? The present elevation of New York City is 396 cm above sea level. If sea level continues to rise at the same rate, when will New York City start to go underwater?

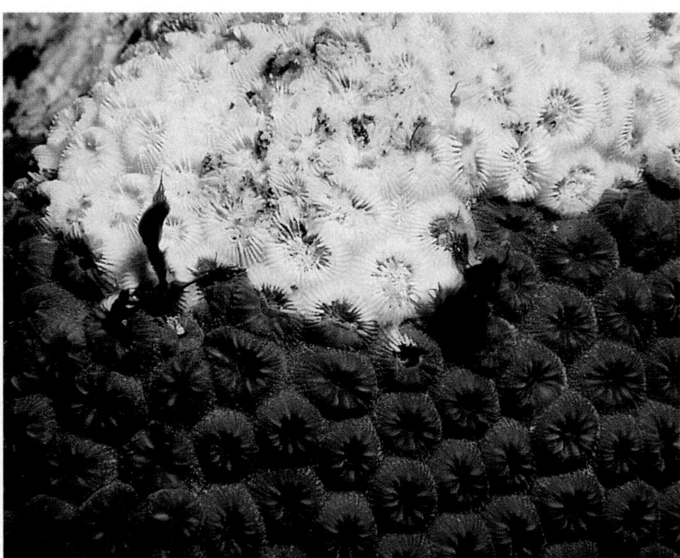

Figure 16-13

This coral is dying because water temperatures have risen in this area of the ocean.

Section Wrap-up

Review

1. What causes seasons?
2. In what way does El Niño change the climate?
3. *Think Critically:* How do we know that climates of earlier geologic eras were much different from today's climates?

Skill Builder

Comparing and Contrasting

Compare and contrast the greenhouse effect and global warming. If you need help, refer to Comparing and Contrasting in the **Skill Handbook.**

Using Computers

Word Processing
Design a pamphlet to inform people about why Earth's climate changes. What are your predictions for the future? On what evidence do you base these predictions? Include this in your pamphlet.

4 Close

•MINI•QUIZ•

Use the Mini Quiz to check students' recall of chapter content.

1. **If the output of the sun's ________ varies, Earth's climate changes.** *radiation*
2. **If Earth's orbit becomes more circular, the climate becomes ________.** *colder*
3. **Gases in our ________ cause the greenhouse effect.** *atmosphere*

Section Wrap-up

Review

1. They are caused by the tilt of Earth on its axis as it revolves around the sun.
2. It causes trade winds to weaken or reverse direction and warm currents to flow toward the Americas. These changes result in changes in fishing, in flooding in some places, and in drought in others.
3. Think Critically Clues to climate change include fossils, ice cores, glacial deposits, and glacial scars.

Using Computers

Pamphlets should discuss seasons; El Niño; the effects of catastrophic events; the possible effects of Earth's tilt, Earth's wobble on its axis, and changes in the shape of Earth's orbit; and the effect of atmospheric gases like carbon dioxide.

Skill Builder

Both involve the trapping of heat in the atmosphere. The greenhouse effect happens because the sun's radiation travels through the atmosphere, but the heat radiated from Earth's surface can't escape back out into space because of gases like carbon dioxide. Global warming happens when global temperatures rise because the greenhouse effect increases as ecological factors change.

Assessment

Performance Have students compare and contrast the effects of volcanic ash and carbon dioxide on atmospheric temperature. Use the Performance Task Assessment List for Analyzing the Data in **PASC,** p. 27. P

SCIENCE & SOCIETY

Section 16•4

Prepare

Section Background

During photosynthesis, trees and other plants use carbon dioxide, water, and sunlight to produce oxygen and carbohydrates. The carbon atoms are stored in the carbohydrates. When trees are burned, these carbon atoms are oxidized and form carbon dioxide molecules.

1 Motivate

Bellringer

Before presenting the lesson, display **Section Focus Transparency 64** on the overhead projector. Assign the accompanying **Focus Activity** worksheet. L1 LEP

Tying to Previous Knowledge

Students have learned in earlier chapters that by planting vegetation, people prevent soil erosion and promote soil formation. In this section, they will learn that by planting vegetation, people also reduce the amount of carbon dioxide in the atmosphere.

2 Teach

Activity

Organize tree planting. L1

SCIENCE & SOCIETY

16•4 TECHNOLOGY: How can global warming be slowed?

Science Words

deforestation
reforestation

Objectives

- Discuss some human activities that add carbon dioxide to the atmosphere.
- List ways we can reduce the amount of carbon dioxide in the atmosphere.

Human Activities and Carbon Dioxide

Human activities affect the air in our atmosphere. Burning fossil fuels and removing vegetation affect the atmosphere. Both activities add carbon dioxide to the atmosphere and contribute to global warming. Each year the amount of carbon dioxide in our atmosphere continues to increase by more than one part per million. By analyzing air bubbles trapped in glaciers, scientists have discovered that in about 1750, there were 280 parts per million of carbon dioxide in the atmosphere. Today there are more than 350 parts per million.

Burning of Fossil Fuels

When natural gas, petroleum, and coal are burned for energy, the carbon in these fossil fuels is combined with oxygen. This increases the amount of carbon dioxide (CO_2) in our atmosphere.

Deforestation

The mass removal of trees, called **deforestation,** also affects the amount of carbon dioxide in our atmosphere. Forests around the world are being cleared for mining, roads, buildings, grazing cattle, and drilling for oil. Forests are also dying from the effects of pollution.

As they grow, trees take in carbon dioxide. When trees are removed, the carbon dioxide they could have removed from the atmosphere is left. Cut-down trees are often burned. Burning produces more carbon dioxide.

Figure 16-14
When forests are cleared or burned, carbon dioxide levels increase in the atmosphere.

470

Program Resources

Reproducible Masters

Study Guide, p. 68 L1
Reinforcement, p. 68 L1
Enrichment, p. 68 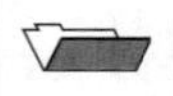 L3
Science and Society Integration, p. 20
Concept Mapping, p. 37

Transparencies

Section Focus Transparency 64 L1
Science Integration Transparency 16

Ways to Reduce CO_2

What can we each do to help reduce the amount of CO_2 in the atmosphere? Conserving electricity is one way. When we conserve electricity, we reduce the amount of fossil fuel that must be burned. One way to save fuel is to change your daily activities that rely on energy from burning fossil fuel. These activities might include car rides, watching television, and heating or cooling our homes.

Another way to reduce CO_2 is to plant vegetation. As you've learned, plants remove carbon dioxide from the atmosphere. Correctly planted vegetation can also shelter homes from cold winds or blazing sun and reduce the use of electricity.

Figure 16-15

This wind farm in California generates electricity without adding CO_2 to our atmosphere.

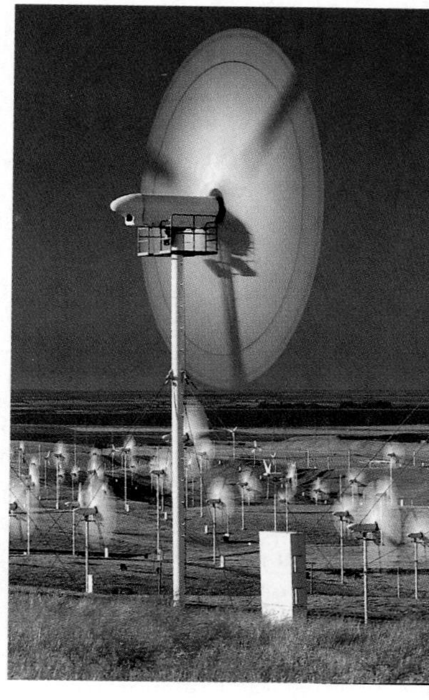

Futuristic Ideas to Cool Our Planet

Will our planet become as hot as Venus? A variety of ideas exist to cool Earth down. The planting of trees, called **reforestation,** would help. Investing in plants and equipment to produce electricity without generating more CO_2 would help. Wind farms, solar panels, and small water turbines generate electricity without producing CO_2. Or perhaps we could seed nutrients into polar oceans to encourage the growth of microscopic plants. These plants could remove much of the carbon dioxide. Perhaps releasing billions of aluminum balloons to reflect solar radiation would work. Or perhaps a giant screen 2000 square km in size could be put into space to decrease the amount of incoming radiation. Maybe dust from the moon could be used to make a cloud around Earth that would block solar radiation. What other things might help solve the problem?

Section Wrap-up

Review

1. How do burning fossil fuels and cutting down forests add carbon dioxide to the atmosphere?
2. What can you do to reduce the amount of carbon dioxide in the atmosphere? What are more global actions nations could undertake?

Explore the Technology

Nitrous oxide is another gas produced by human activity. Nitrous oxide also adds to global warming. Find out what activities produce nitrous oxide and how its output can be reduced.

SCIENCE & SOCIETY

3 Assess

Check for Understanding

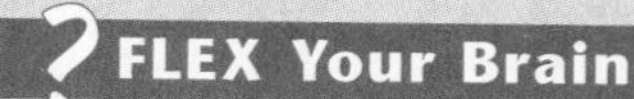

FLEX Your Brain

Use the Flex Your Brain activity to have students explore DEFORESTATION.

Activity Worksheets, p. 5

Reteach

LS **Logical-Mathematical** Have students contrast the effects of deforestation and reforestation on atmospheric carbon dioxide.

Extension

For students who have mastered this section, use the **Reinforcement** and **Enrichment** masters.

4 Close

Have students answer questions 1 and 2 in the Section Wrap-up.

Section Wrap-up

Review

1. Fossil fuels burn and release CO_2. Burning of trees also releases CO_2. Cutting down trees also prevents trees from using CO_2 in photosynthesis.
2. conserve energy, plant vegetation, invest in and encourage production of solar energy

Explore the Technology

Students should associate nitrous oxide with automobiles. Solutions to reduce nitrous oxide will vary.

Cultural Diversity

Reforestation Recently, countries as diverse as India, Haiti, and Hungary have started reforestation programs to correct environmental problems. Deforestation around the world has created severe problems. An example: as the population in Rio de Janeiro, Brazil increases, both luxury homes and shantytowns move up the mountains. People cut down more trees. Every rain washes tons of topsoil from the mountain slopes and fills the rivers with silt. Water floods the streets and mudslides bury shanty towns and their occupants. In Borneo, the most intensive logging in the world has caused soil erosion and muddied rain forest rivers and streams, blinding fish and releasing toxins from trees and plants into the water.

People and Science

Background

- Ice ages are made up of alternating glacial stages. Ice sheets grow in the glacial period. In the interglacial stages, they retreat. Glacial stages last about 100 000 years, and interglacial stages last 10 000 to 12 000 years. We are living in the Holocene interglacial period—an interglacial stage within the Late Cenozoic Ice Age. The Holocene period has lasted almost 10 000 years, but it may be another 1000 or 2000 before it's clear whether we are entering another ice age.
- Glaciology, the study of snow and ice, researches three main areas: ice core paleoclimatology—drilling and analyzing ice cores to learn about Earth's climate history; ice dynamics—understanding how ice sheets form, grow, and move; and physical properties of snow and ice—how snow forms, how it falls, and how it changes as it becomes incorporated in an ice sheet.

Teaching Strategies

Analyzing ice cores is one way of sampling an ancient atmosphere. Challenge students to think of others. (Examples: drilling into airtight tombs, analyzing bubbles trapped in amber.) Ask why ice core analysis yields more accurate results than these methods. (With other methods, samples could more easily become contaminated. The chemical composition of trapped air might change with time. In ice, the air is not only trapped, it is kept cold, so chemical changes occur much more slowly.)

Career Connection

Career Path College and high school courses should include math, chemistry, physics, Earth sciences, and environmental studies. A relatively new aspect of climate studies is the social side. Researchers are trying to understand why humans interact as they do with their environment and how that affects climate. Social geographers, economists, sociologists, anthropologists, and psychologists can work with climatologists to understand patterns of human habits and preferences and to figure out ways to encourage people to change practices that may harm the environment.

For More Information

For more information on Ellen Mosely-Thompson's research:

Chivian, Eric, MD. "The Ultimate Preventive Medicine." *Technology Review,* November/December 1994, pp. 34-40.

Dreyfous, Leslie. "Ice Yields Clues to Earth's Past, Future." *Maine Telegram* (Portland, Maine), September 13, 1992, p. 3C.

Stevens, William K. "Dust in Sea Mud May Link Human Evolution to Climate." *New York Times,* December 14, 1993, p. B5.

People and Science

ELLEN MOSLEY-THOMPSON, *Geographer*

On the Job

Q **You study ice cores. What are they?**

A In certain regions such as Antarctica in the southern hemisphere and Greenland in the northern hemisphere, the land is covered by ice sheets as much as 2.5 mi thick. Ice sheets form in places where snow falls every year and doesn't melt, and then more falls the next year. Gradually, the snow turns to firn (snow that has lain on the ground more than one year). With time, the firn becomes more dense and turns into ice. You end up with a stratigraphic sequence—layers deposited one on top of another like layers of a cake. By taking an ice core (a cylinder of ice), scientists can study these layers. The stratigraphic sequences contain different materials, such as dust that fell out of the atmosphere onto the ice sheet. Also, as firn turns into ice, air in the firn gets trapped as bubbles. By analyzing gases and other materials in the layers of ice, we track how dusty the atmosphere was in the past and what chemicals were present. Excess sulfate may indicate a volcanic eruption. Ice cores from mid-latitudes, such as those taken from the Tibetan Plateau in China, contain pollen grains. We can learn about vegetation in the past by tracking how pollen has changed.

Personal Insights

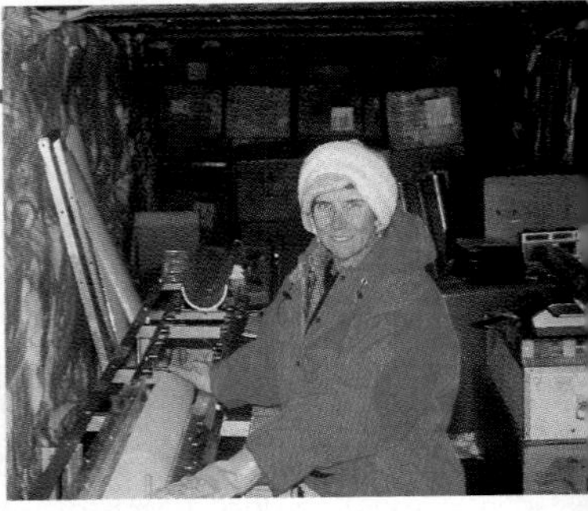

Q **Why study ancient climate?**

A From one perspective, just to know. Scientists are just naturally curious about the past. From a more practical view, climate is just one part of Earth's system, and it's important to understand that system–how it works, what processes are important, and how it will change in the future if such factors as atmospheric chemistry change. But it's so complex that humans can't sit down at a desk and figure it out. They have to use a computer model. One way to know whether your model is working is to try to simulate the climate of the past. If we can't "predict" what we already know has occurred, it means our model needs refinement.

Career Connection

To learn more about what researchers do in Antarctica, send for "Facts About the U.S. Antarctic Program" and "The United States Antarctic Program" from the National Science Foundation. To find out what other things geographers do, write to: Association of America Geographers, 1710 16th Street, N.W., Washington, DC 20009-3198.

- Geographer
- Climatologist

Chapter 16 Review

Summary

16-1: What is climate?

1. The climate of an area is the average weather over a long period, such as 30 years.
2. Higher latitudes experience cooler climates than lower latitudes do. Topographic features such as oceans, mountains, and large cities affect climate.

16-2: Climate Types

1. The Köppen Climate Classification System is based on temperature, precipitation, and vegetation.
2. Organisms have structural and behavioral adaptations that help them survive in particular climates.

16-3: Climatic Changes

1. Seasons are caused by Earth's tilt on its axis as it revolves around the sun.
2. El Niño disrupts the normal wind and precipitation patterns around the world.
3. Possible causes for major climatic changes include catastrophic events such as meteorite impacts and volcanic eruptions, variations in the sun's radiation, movements of Earth's plates, and Earth's changing movements as it rotates on its axis and revolves around the sun.
4. The greenhouse effect occurs because certain gases trap Earth's heat. Global warming occurs when global temperatures rise because of an increased greenhouse effect.

16-4: Science and Society: How can global warming be slowed?

1. When fossil fuels are burned and forests are cut down, carbon dioxide is added to the atmosphere.
2. When people plant vegetation and conserve electricity, they help reduce the amount of carbon dioxide in the atmosphere.

Key Science Words

a. adaptation
b. deforestation
c. El Niño
d. global warming
e. greenhouse effect
f. hibernation
g. polar zone
h. reforestation
i. season
j. temperate zone
k. tropics

Reviewing Vocabulary

Match each phrase with the correct term from the list of Key Science Words.

1. coldest area on Earth
2. climate zone between the tropics and the polar zones
3. replanting of a large number of trees
4. a characteristic that enables an organism to survive in a particular environment
5. occurs when an animal's temperature drops and body processes are reduced
6. regular changes in the weather patterns
7. climatic change when trade winds weaken west of Peru
8. gases in the atmosphere trap Earth's heat
9. mass removal of trees
10. global temperatures rise

GLENCOE TECHNOLOGY

MindJogger Videoquiz

Chapter 16 Have students work in groups as they play the Videoquiz game to review key chapter concepts.

Chapter 16 Review

Summary

Have students read the summary statements to review the major concepts of the chapter.

Reviewing Vocabulary

1. g	**6.** i
2. j	**7.** c
3. h	**8.** e
4. a	**9.** b
5. f	**10.** d

Assessment

Portfolio Encourage students to place in their portfolios one or two items of what they consider to be their best work. Examples include:

- Skill Builder, p. 461
- Across the Curriculum, p. 463
- Flex Your Brain, p. 467 P

Performance Additional performance assessments may be found in **Performance Assessment** and **Science Integration Activities.** Performance Task Assessment Lists and rubrics for evaluating these activities can be found in Glencoe's **Performance Assessment in the Science Classroom.**

Chapter 16 Review

Checking Concepts

1. c
2. a
3. b
4. d
5. a
6. d
7. b
8. a
9. c
10. a

Understanding Concepts

11. Warm currents, originating at the equator, warm the regions they pass by. Cold currents, originating at the poles, cool the regions they pass.

12. Radiation that strikes pavement and buildings is absorbed, and heat is radiated into the air. Automobile exhaust and other pollutants trap the heat.

13. Cacti have spines that reduce water loss. Snakes hide under rocks in the daytime. Turtles and lizards obtain moisture from their food.

14. Except at high elevations, low latitudes are always hot and experience dry and rainy seasons. High latitudes experience great differences in temperature and in the number of daylight hours. Middle latitudes experience seasons where winters are cold, summers are hot, and spring and fall usually have mild temperatures.

15. Its dust, ash, and smoke particles can get into the atmosphere, blocking solar radiation and cooling the planet.

Thinking Critically

16. Some organisms are not adapted to survive the warm temperatures that global warming will bring.

17. This region had much more precipitation in the past than it does today.

Chapter 16 Review

Checking Concepts

Choose the word or phrase that completes the sentence.

1. _______ are common where warm air crosses a mountain and descends.
   a. Lakes c. Deserts
   b. Rain forests d. Glaciers
2. The fossils of tropical plants and animals found in polar regions are used to tell _______ .
   a. the temperature of earlier geologic eras
   b. the relative length of growing seasons
   c. behavioral adaptations
   d. the amount of carbon dioxide in the air in prehistoric times
3. The main greenhouse gas in our atmosphere is _______ .
   a. helium c. hydrogen
   b. carbon dioxide d. oxygen
4. The latitude that receives the most direct rays of the sun year-round is _______.
   a. 60°N c. 30°S
   b. 90° d. 0°
5. As you climb a mountain, the _______.
   a. temperature decreases
   b. temperature increases
   c. air pressure increases
   d. air pressure remains constant
6. El Niño _______ .
   a. occurs every year
   b. is first noticed in the springtime
   c. cools the waters off California
   d. coincides with atmospheric pressure changes in the Pacific Ocean
7. Changes in Earth's orbit can affect Earth's _______ .
   a. shape c. rotation
   b. temperatures d. tilt
8. The Köppen Climate Classification System is based on _______ and precipitation.
   a. temperature c. winds
   b. air pressure d. latitude
9. An example of structural adaptation is _______.
   a. hibernation c. fur
   b. migration d. estivation
10. We help reduce the global warming problem when we _______.
    a. conserve energy c. produce methane
    b. burn coal d. remove trees

Understanding Concepts

Answer the following questions in your Science Journal using complete sentences.

11. How do ocean currents affect climates of coastal regions?
12. Why are large cities usually warmer than the surrounding suburban and urban areas?
13. What are some adaptations of desert organisms that help them survive?
14. Compare and contrast the seasonal changes at low, middle, and high latitudes.
15. How could the eruption of a volcano affect climate?

Thinking Critically

16. Why will global warming lead to the extinction of some organisms?
17. What can you infer if you are digging in a desert and find fossils of tropical plants?
18. On a summer day, why would a Florida beach be cooler than an orange grove two kilometers away?
19. What would happen to Earth's climates if the sun became larger?
20. Why would you expect it to be cooler if you climb to a higher elevation in a desert?

18. The air above the water is cooler than the air above the land. A cool sea breeze will develop, cooling the coast.

19. The temperature of Earth would be much higher.

20. Temperature decreases with an increase in altitude.

Developing Skills

21. Interpreting Scientific Illustrations central Australia: Arid; Taiwan: Humid Subtropical; east coast of Madagascar: Tropical Wet

22. Comparing and Contrasting The windward side is moist and the leeward side is dry. Windward.

23. Observing and Inferring Mosses are better adapted to moist conditions. Their presence and the absence of grasses support this inference.

Developing Skills

If you need help, refer to the **Skill Handbook.**

21. **Interpreting Scientific Illustrations:** Use Figure 16-5 and Appendix G to identify the climates of central Australia, Taiwan, and the east coast of Madagascar.
22. **Comparing and Contrasting:** Contrast the climate on windward and leeward sides of a mountain. Which side is shown in the photo on this page?
23. **Observing and Inferring:** It has rained for many days. You observe that mosses begin growing in a corner of your yard where grass used to grow. Infer from this which plant is better adapted to moist conditions. Explain your answer.
24. **Recognizing Cause and Effect:** Explain how atmospheric pressure over the Pacific Ocean might affect the direction that the trade winds blow.
25. **Sequencing:** Make a chain-of-events chart to explain the effect of a major volcanic eruption on climate.

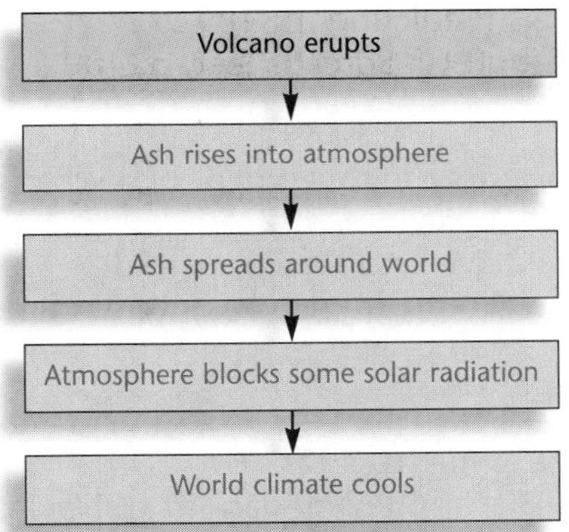

Performance Assessment

1. **Making a Graph:** In Activity 16-1, you studied the microclimates around your school building. Repeat these procedures at the same time of day for three days and graph the temperatures at the sites.
2. **Consumer Decision:** In Activity 16-2, you made a model of the greenhouse effect. Repeat your experiment, but instead of using glass, try aluminum foil, plastic wrap, construction paper, and cardboard lids for the aquarium. Compare your results with what you observed in Activity 16-2. Which lid creates the greatest greenhouse effect? What material would be best to use to cover a solar greenhouse? Which materials would be best to help keep a structure cool?
3. **Poster:** Use your local library to find the weather conditions of your area for the last thirty years. Graph and analyze your data. Does it appear that your climate has remained fairly constant, or do you see patterns that indicate climatic change? Present your findings to the class on a poster.

Assessment Resources

 **Reproducible Masters**

Chapter Review, pp. 35-36
Assessment, pp. 103-106
Performance Assessment, p. 30

Glencoe Technology

Chapter Review Software
Computer Test Bank
MindJogger Videoquiz

Chapter 16 Review

24. **Recognizing Cause and Effect** When air pressure is high, air molecules move toward low pressure and create wind. If air pressure is high in the eastern Pacific, the trade winds will blow west; but, if the air pressure is high in the western Pacific, the trade winds will blow east.
25. **Sequencing** See student page.

Performance Assessment

1. Students should plot the temperature on the horizontal axis and the date on the vertical axis. Each location should be plotted in a different color. Use the Performance Task Assessment List for Graph from Data in **PASC,** p. 39. P
2. A cover made from plastic wrap creates the strongest greenhouse effect of those materials used in this experiment. Plastic wrap is similar to the glass lid in Activity 16-2. A solar greenhouse cover must be constructed of a transparent material that will let in the sun's radiation. Students will probably find that aluminum reflects more solar radiation. Use the Performance Task Assessment List for Consumer Decision-Making Study in **PASC,** p. 43. P
3. Posters should include graphs of temperature and precipitation. Patterns indicating climatic change will depend on your location. Use the Performance Task Assessment List for Poster in **PASC,** p. 73. P

Chapter Organizer

Section	Objectives	Activities/Features
Chapter Opener		**Explore Activity:** Discover how currents work. p. 477
17-1 **Ocean Water** (2 sessions, 1 block)*	1. **Learn** the origin of the water in Earth's oceans. 2. **Explain** how dissolved salts and other substances get into seawater. 3. **Describe** the composition of seawater.	**Using Math,** p. 479 **Using Technology:** Desalting Ocean Water, p. 480 **Skill Builder:** Concept Mapping, p. 481 **Science Journal,** p. 481 **Activity 17-1:** Water, Water, Everywhere, pp. 482-483
17-2 **Ocean Currents** (1 session, 1 block)*	1. **Determine** how winds, the Coriolis effect, and continents influence surface currents. 2. **Explain** why temperatures of coastal waters differ. 3. **Describe** how density currents cause ocean circulation.	**Connect to Life Science,** p. 485 **Using Math,** p. 486 **MiniLAB:** How can you make a density current model? p. 487 **Problem Solving:** Ocean Temperatures and Density, p. 488 **Skill Builder:** Predicting, p. 489 **Using Computers:** Spreadsheet, p. 489
17-3 **Ocean Waves and Tides** (2 sessions, 1 block)*	1. **Describe** the parts of a wave. 2. **Differentiate** between the movement of water particles in a wave and the movement of wave energy. 3. **Describe** how the energy of wind and the gravitational force of the moon and sun create tides.	**Connect to Physics,** p. 491 **MiniLAB:** Model the movement of a water particle in a wave. p. 492 **Activity 17-2:** Making Waves, p. 493 **Skill Builder:** Comparing and Contrasting, p. 495 **Science Journal,** p. 495
17-4 **Science and Society Issue: Tapping Tidal Energy** (1 session, ½ block)*	1. **Explain** the advantages of a tidal power plant in the Bay of Fundy. 2. **Describe** how a tidal dam converts energy from tides into electricity. 3. **Consider** the consequence of a power plant at the Bay of Fundy.	**Explore the Issue,** p. 497 **Science & History:** Polynesian Art of Navigation, p. 498 **Science Journal,** p. 498

* A complete Planning Guide that includes block scheduling is provided on pages 32T-35T.

Activity Materials

Explore	Activities	MiniLABs
page 477 two 500-mL beakers, warm tap water, ice, food coloring, pipet	pages 482-483 safety goggles, thermal mitt, balance, table salt, tap water, 1000-mL flask, 600-mL beaker, 1-hole rubber stopper to fit flask, rubber tubing, glass tubing bent at a right angle, glycerin, towel, plastic spoon, hot plate, sheet of cardboard, scissors, ice, shallow pan page 493 white paper, 3-speed electric fan, light source, clock or watch with second hand, clear plastic storage boxes, ring stand with clamp, tap water, metric ruler	page 487 clear plastic storage box or glass pie plate, tap water, teaspoon, table salt, small glass, food coloring page 492 clear plastic storage box or glass baking dish, tap water, cork, masking tape, spoon

Teacher Classroom Resources

Reproducible Masters	Transparencies
Study Guide, p. 69 **Reinforcement**, p. 69 **Enrichment**, p. 69 **Activity Worksheets**, pp. 102-103 **Lab Manual 49**, Salt Concentration in Ocean Water **Lab Manual 50**, Fresh Water from Ocean Water **Science Integration Activity 17**, Please Pass the Salt! **Concept Mapping**, p. 39 **Critical Thinking/Problem Solving**, p. 23 **Cross-Curricular Integration**, p. 21	**Section Focus Transparency 65**, So Much Salt **Science Integration Transparency 17**, Why Is the Ocean Blue?
Study Guide, p. 70 **Reinforcement**, p. 70 **Enrichment**, p. 70 **Activity Worksheets**, p. 106 **Lab Manual 51**, Density Currents **Lab Manual 52**, Floating in Fresh Water and in Ocean Water	**Section Focus Transparency 66**, Currently, the temperature is . . . **Teaching Transparency 33**, Major Surface Currents
Study Guide, p. 71 **Reinforcement**, p. 71 **Enrichment**, p. 71 **Activity Worksheets**, pp. 104-105, 107 **Science and Society Integration**, p. 21 **Multicultural Connections**, pp. 37-38	**Section Focus Transparency 67**, Who Pulled the Plug? **Teaching Transparency 34**, Parts of a Wave
Study Guide, p. 72 **Reinforcement**, p. 72 **Enrichment**, p. 72	**Section Focus Transparency 68**, Energy In, Energy Out

Teaching Resources

Glencoe Earth Science Interactive Videodisc
Earth Science CD-ROM
Spanish Resources
English/Spanish Audiocassettes
Cooperative Learning Resource Guide
Lab Partner
Lab and Safety Skills
Lesson Plans

Assessment Resources

Chapter Review, pp. 37-38
Assessment, pp. 107-110
Performance Assessment in the Science Classroom (PASC)
MindJogger Videoquiz
Alternate Assessment in the Science Classroom
Performance Assessment
Chapter Review Software
Computer Test Bank

Key to Teaching Strategies

The following designations will help you decide which activities are appropriate for your students.

L1 Level 1 activities should be within the ability range of all students.

L2 Level 2 activities should be within the ability range of the average to above-average student.

L3 Level 3 activities are designed for the ability range of above-average students.

LEP LEP activities should be within the ability range of Limited English Proficiency students.

LS These activities are designed to address different learning styles.

COOP LEARN Cooperative Learning activities are designed for small group work.

P These strategies represent student products that can be placed into a best-work portfolio.

GLENCOE TECHNOLOGY

The following multimedia resources are available from Glencoe.

Science and Technology Videodisc Series (STVS)
Earth & Space
Artificial Waves
Studying the Pacific Ocean
National Geographic Society Series
STV: Water
GTV: Planetary Manager
Earth Science CD-ROM

Teacher Classroom Resources

This is a representation of key blackline masters available in the Teacher Classroom Resources.

Teaching Aids

Section Focus Transparencies

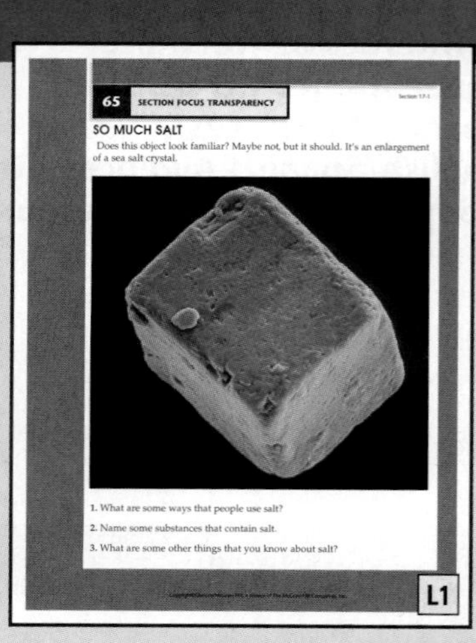
65 SECTION FOCUS TRANSPARENCY

SO MUCH SALT

Does this object look familiar? Maybe not, but it should. It's an enlargement of a sea salt crystal.

1. What are some ways that people use salt?
2. Name some substances that contain salt.
3. What are some other things that you know about salt?

L1

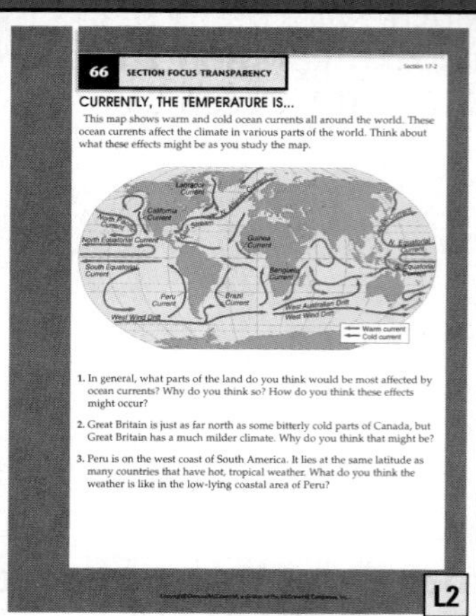
66 SECTION FOCUS TRANSPARENCY

CURRENTLY, THE TEMPERATURE IS...

This map shows warm and cold ocean currents all around the world. These ocean currents affect the climate in various parts of the world. Think about what these effects might be as you study the map.

1. In general, what parts of the land do you think would be most affected by ocean currents? Why do you think so? How do you think these effects might occur?
2. Great Britain is just as far north as some bitterly cold parts of Canada, but Great Britain has a much milder climate. Why do you think that might be?
3. Peru is on the west coast of South America. It lies at the same latitude as many countries that have hot, tropical weather. What do you think the weather is like in the low-lying coastal area of Peru?

L2

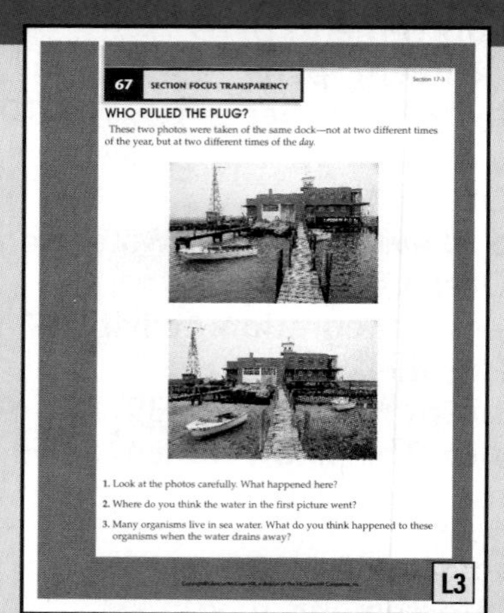
67 SECTION FOCUS TRANSPARENCY

WHO PULLED THE PLUG?

These two photos were taken of the same dock—not at two different times of the year, but at two different times of the day.

1. Look at the photos carefully. What happened here?
2. Where do you think the water in the first picture went?
3. Many organisms live in sea water. What do you think happened to these organisms when the water drains away?

L3

Science Integration Transparencies

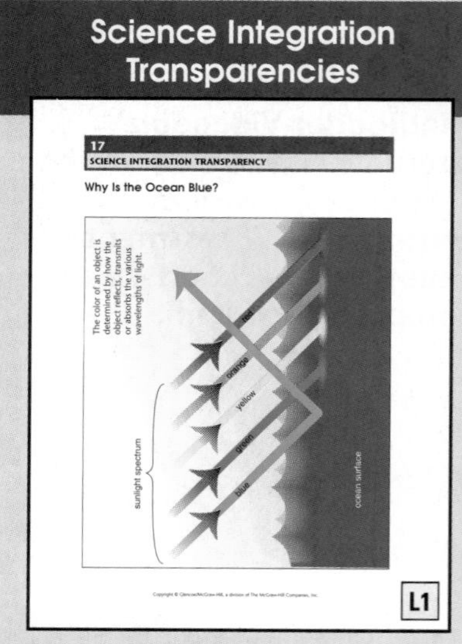
17 SCIENCE INTEGRATION TRANSPARENCY

Why Is the Ocean Blue?

L1

Teaching Transparencies

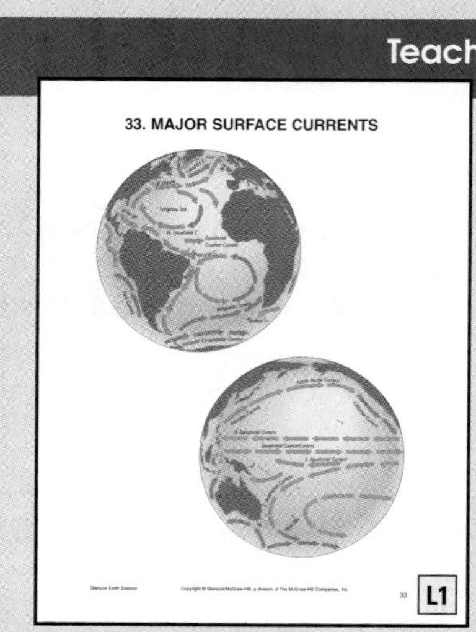

L1

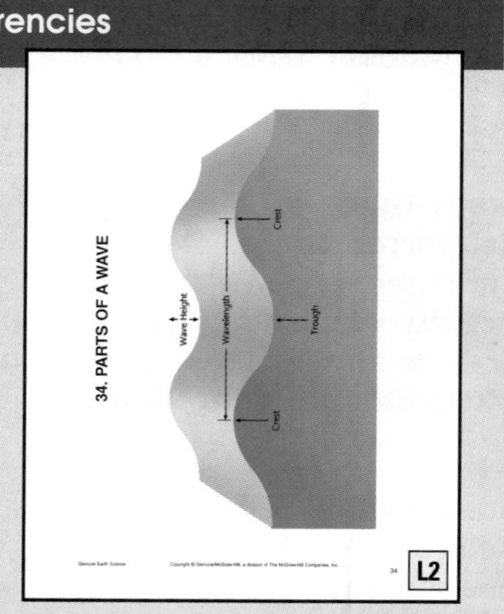

L2

Meeting Different Ability Levels

Study Guide

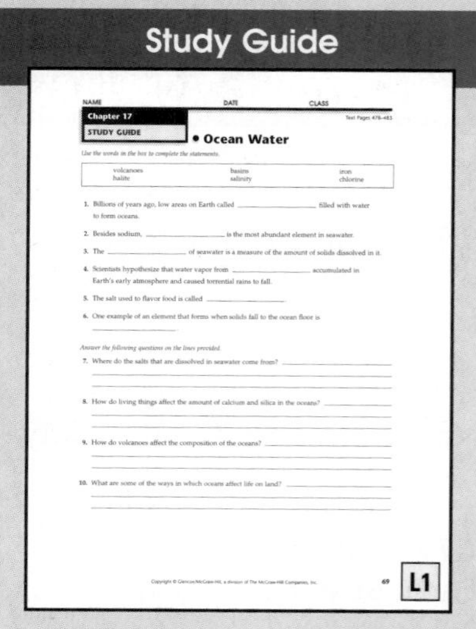
NAME DATE CLASS

Chapter 17 STUDY GUIDE • Ocean Water

Text Pages 478–483

Use the words in the box to complete the statements.

volcanoes halite	basins salinity	iron chlorine

1. Billions of years ago, low areas on Earth called ________ filled with water to form oceans.
2. Besides sodium, ________ is the most abundant element in seawater.
3. The ________ of seawater is a measure of the amount of solids dissolved in it.
4. Scientists hypothesize that water vapor from ________ accumulated in Earth's early atmosphere and caused torrential rains to fall.
5. The salt used to flavor food is called ________
6. One example of an element that forms when solids fall to the ocean floor is ________

Answer the following questions on the lines provided.

7. Where do the salts that are dissolved in seawater come from?
8. How do living things affect the amount of calcium and silica in the oceans?
9. How do volcanoes affect the composition of the oceans?
10. What are some of the ways in which oceans affect life on land?

69 L1

Reinforcement

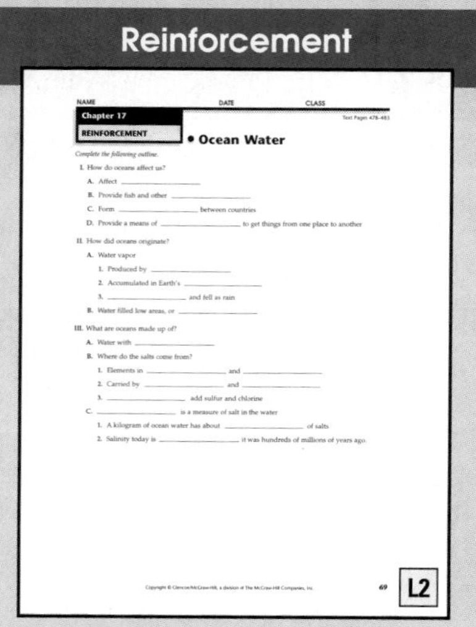
NAME DATE CLASS

Chapter 17 REINFORCEMENT • Ocean Water

Text Pages 478–483

Complete the following outline.

I. How do oceans affect us?
  - A. Affect ________
  - B. Provide fish and other ________
  - C. Form ________ between countries
  - D. Provide a means of ________ to get things from one place to another

II. How did oceans originate?
  - A. Water vapor
    1. Produced by ________
    2. Accumulated in Earth's ________
    3. ________ and fell as rain
  - B. Water filled low areas, or ________

III. What are oceans made up of?
  - A. Water with ________
  - B. Where do the salts come from?
    1. Elements in ________ and ________
    2. Carried by ________ and ________
    3. ________ add sulfur and chlorine
  - C. ________ is a measure of salt in the water
    1. A kilogram of ocean water has about ________ of salts
    2. Salinity today is ________ it was hundreds of millions of years ago

69 L2

Enrichment Worksheets

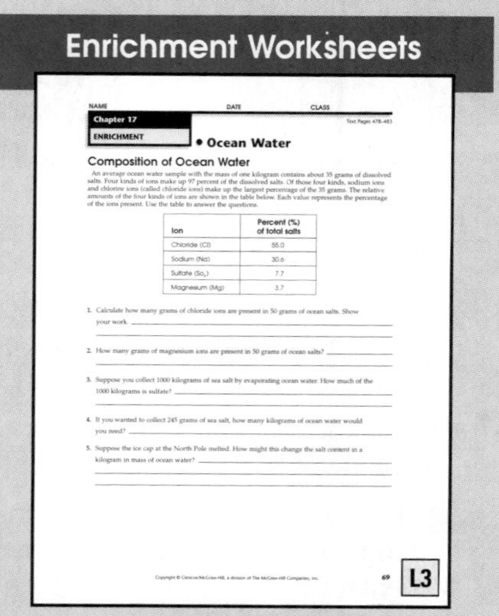
NAME DATE CLASS

Chapter 17 ENRICHMENT • Ocean Water

Text Pages 478–483

Composition of Ocean Water

An average ocean water sample with the mass of one kilogram contains about 35 grams of dissolved salts. Four kinds of ions make up 97 percent of the dissolved salts. Of those four kinds, sodium ions and chlorine ions (called chloride ions) make up the largest percentage of the 35 grams. The relative amounts of the four kinds of ions are shown in the table below. Each value represents the percentage of the ions present. Use the table to answer the questions.

Ion	Percent (%) of total salts
Chloride (Cl)	55.0
Sodium (Na)	30.6
Sulfate (So_4)	7.7
Magnesium (Mg)	3.7

1. Calculate how many grams of chloride ions are present in 50 grams of ocean salts. Show your work.
2. How many grams of magnesium ions are present in 50 grams of ocean salts?
3. Suppose you collect 1000 kilograms of sea salt by evaporating ocean water. How much of the 1000 kilograms is sulfate?
4. If you wanted to collect 245 grams of sea salt, how many kilograms of ocean water would you need?
5. Suppose the ice cap at the North Pole melted. How might this change the salt content in a kilogram in mass of ocean water?

69 L3

Hands-On Activities

Science Integration Activity

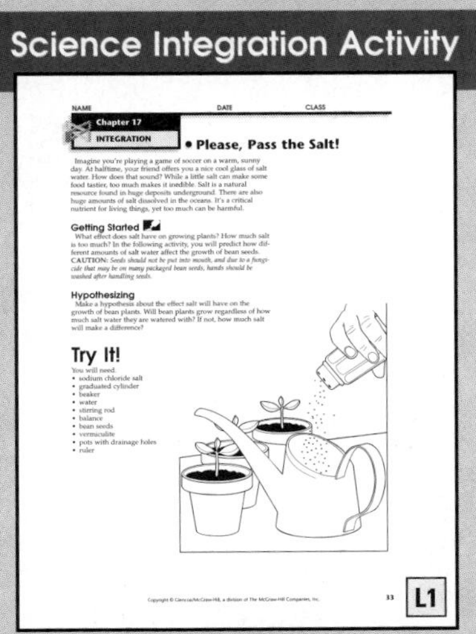
Chapter 17 INTEGRATION • Please, Pass the Salt!

Getting Started

Hypothesizing

Try It!

L1

Lab Manual

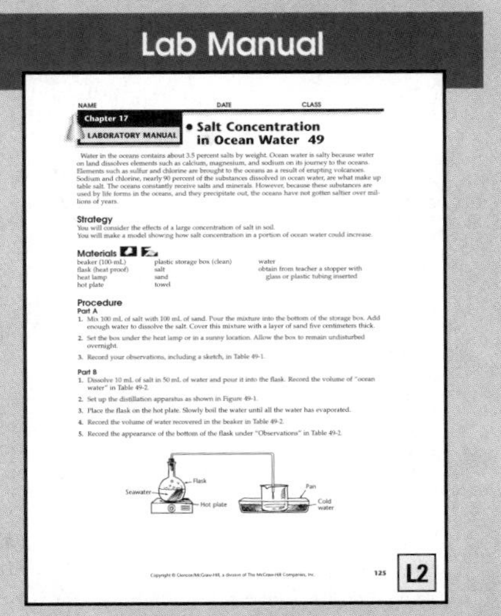
Chapter 17 LABORATORY MANUAL • Salt Concentration in Ocean Water 49

Strategy

Materials

Procedure

L2

Assessment

Performance Assessment

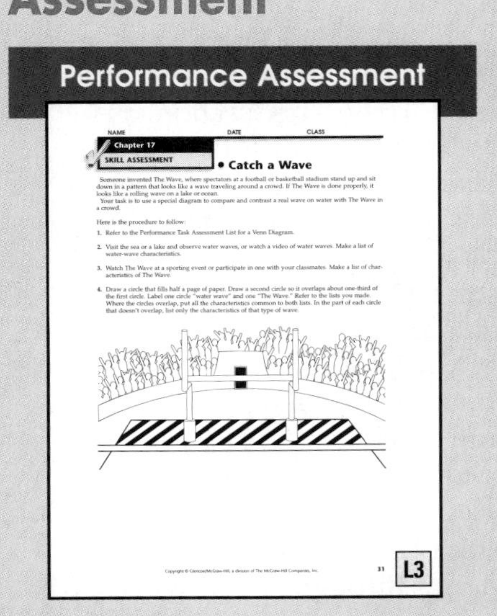
Chapter 17 SKILL ASSESSMENT • Catch a Wave

L3

Enrichment and Application

Critical Thinking/ Problem Solving

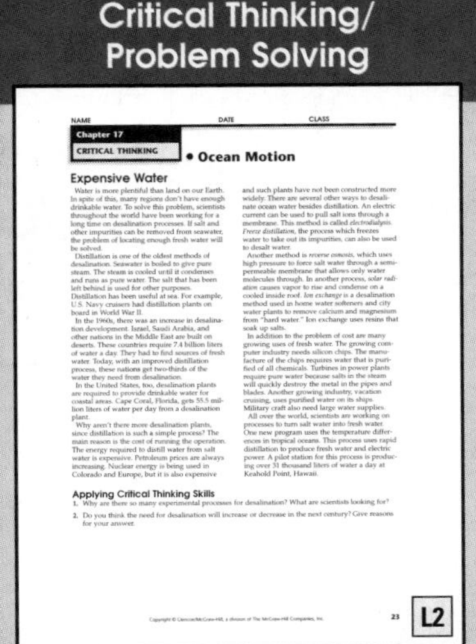
Chapter 17 CRITICAL THINKING • Ocean Motion

Expensive Water

Applying Critical Thinking Skills

L2

Cross-Curricular Integration

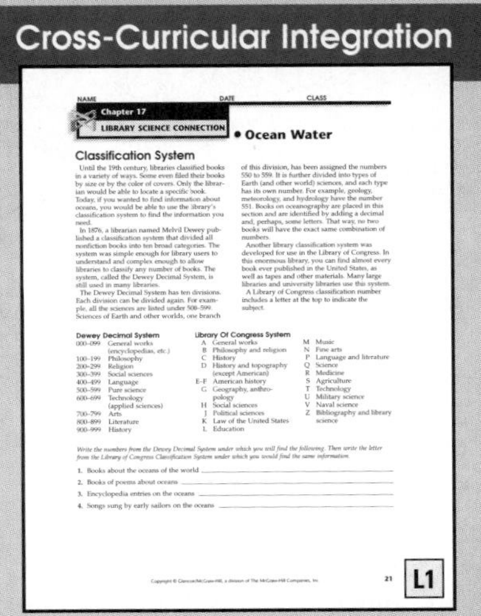
Chapter 17 LIBRARY SCIENCE CONNECTION • Ocean Water

Classification System

Dewey Decimal System

Library Of Congress System

L1

Science and Society Integration

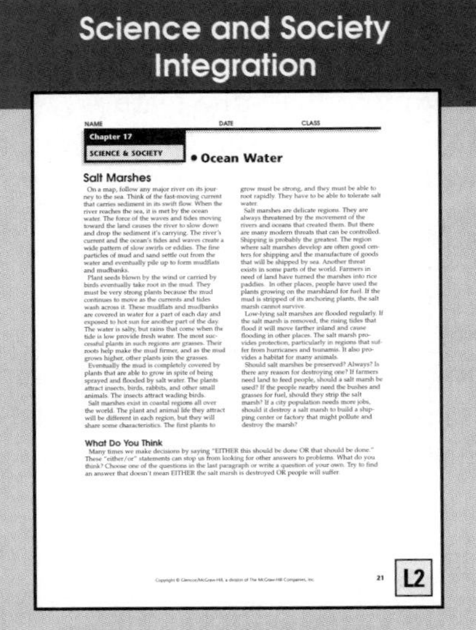
Chapter 17 SCIENCE & SOCIETY • Ocean Water

Salt Marshes

What Do You Think

L2

Multicultural Connections

Chapter 17 MULTICULTURAL CONNECTIONS • Riding the Ocean Waves

Early Surfers

Wave Action

Surfing Rises Up Again

L2

Concept Mapping

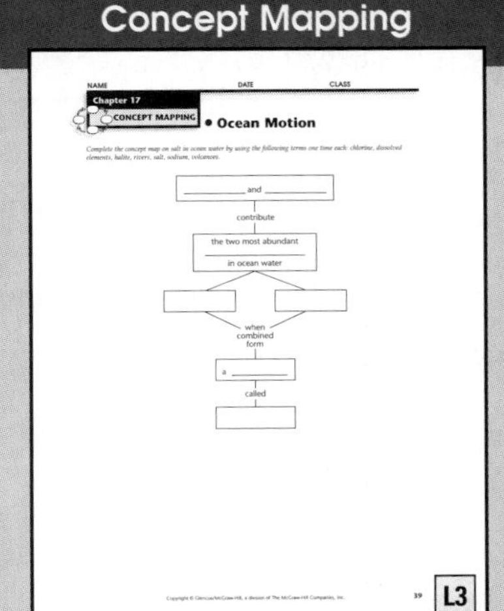
Chapter 17 CONCEPT MAPPING • Ocean Motion

L3

Chapter 17

Ocean Motion

CHAPTER OVERVIEW

Section 17-1 This section explains the importance of oceans. The origin and composition of oceans are also discussed.

Section 17-2 This section presents the influence of winds, the Coriolis effect, and continents on surface currents. How seawater density affects deep-water circulation is also discussed.

Section 17-3 The movement of energy through ocean waves and the effect of wind and gravity on waves are examined. Tides are also discussed.

Section 17-4 Science and Society This section discusses the advantages and disadvantages of tapping tides for energy. The Explore the Issue feature asks students to explore whether a tidal dam should be built at the Bay of Fundy.

Chapter Vocabulary

basin	crest
salinity	trough
surface current	breaker
upwelling	tide
density current	tidal
wave	range

Theme Connection

Energy Students will learn that wind provides the energy for surface currents, density currents affect deep-water circulation, and wind and the gravitational forces of the sun and moon supply the energy for tides.

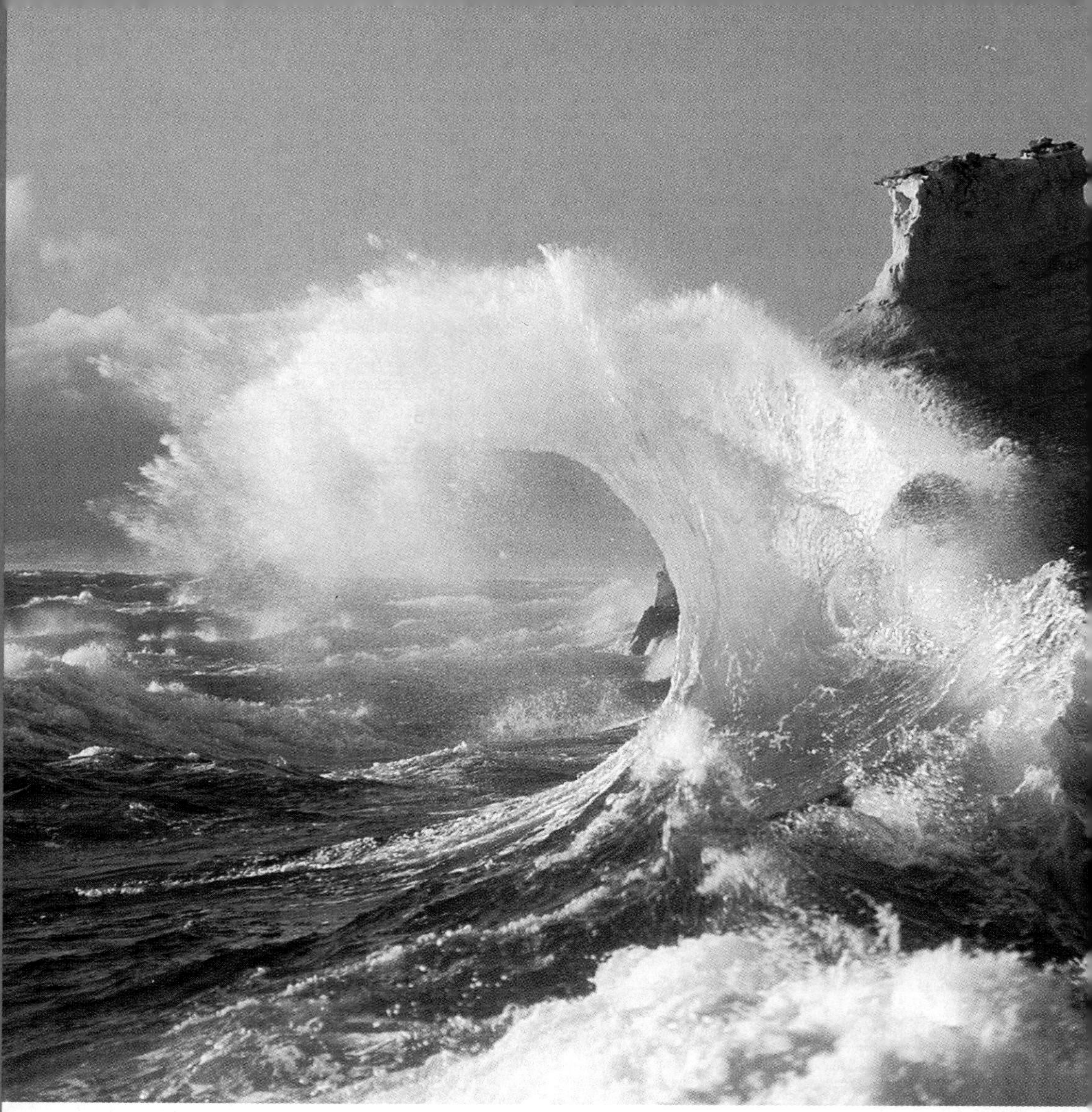

Previewing the Chapter

476

Learning Styles

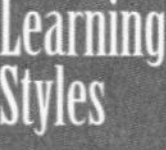

Look for the following logo for strategies that emphasize different learning modalities. LS

Kinesthetic	Across the Curriculum, p. 479; MiniLAB, p. 492
Visual-Spatial	Explore, p. 477; Visual Learning, pp. 485, 491; MiniLAB, p. 487; Reteach, pp. 488, 494; Demonstration, p. 491; Activity 17-2, p. 493
Interpersonal	Activity 17-1, pp. 482-483; Reteach, p. 497; Science & History, p. 498
Logical-Mathematical	Reteach, p. 480; Using Math, pp. 479, 486
Linguistic	Across the Curriculum, p. 479; Science Journal, p. 497

LS

Chapter 17

Ocean Motion

The ocean is constantly in motion. Waves like this one break against the shore with great energy. Wind causes most waves in the ocean, from small ripples to waves this size, to the giant waves of hurricanes—some more than 30 m high. Winds also cause general movements of ocean water in currents around the world. Other currents, caused by differences in energy and density, move through the ocean. In this chapter, you will learn more about these ocean motions and the interaction between the atmosphere and the oceans, as well as how waves, currents, and tides work.

EXPLORE ACTIVITY

Discover how currents work.

1. In a dish, melt ice to make ice water.
2. Fill a large beaker with warm water.
3. Add a few drops of food coloring to the ice water.
4. Use an eyedropper to place some of this ice water on top of the warm water. Repeat the experiment, placing the warm water on top of the ice water.

Observe: In which experiment was a current created? Infer why the current created is called a convection current.

Previewing Science Skills

- In the **Skill Builders**, you will **map concepts**, **classify**, and **compare and contrast**.
- In the **Activities**, you will **design experiments**, **recognize cause and effect**, **measure in SI**, **observe**, **interpret**, and **hypothesize**.
- In the **MiniLABs**, you will **make a model** and **observe and infer**.

EXPLORE ACTIVITY

Purpose

LS **Visual-Spatial** Use the Explore Activity to introduce students to currents. Inform students that they will be learning more about ocean circulation as they read the chapter. L1 LEP COOP LEARN

Preparation

Obtain the materials listed below for each group of students.

Materials

large beaker or drinking glass, food coloring, eyedropper, and ice cubes

Teaching Strategies

Have students review the term *density* from Chapter 1.

Observe

When ice water was placed on warm water, a current formed. It's called a convection or density current because dense water sank, starting the current. The dense water displaced the less dense water and forced it upward.

Assessment

Performance Have students design an experiment to make a density current using salty and fresh water. Use the Performance Task Assessment List for Designing an Experiment in **PASC,** p. 23. P

Assessment Planner

Portfolio

Refer to page 499 for suggested items that students might select for their portfolios.

Performance Assessment

See page 499 for additional Performance Assessment options.
Skill Builders, pp. 481, 489, 495
MiniLABs, pp. 487, 492
Activities 17-1, pp. 482-483; 17-2, p. 493

Content Assessment

Section Wrap-ups, pp. 481, 489, 495, 497
Chapter Review, pp. 499-501
Mini Quizzes, pp. 481, 489, 494, 497

Group Assessment

Opportunities for group assessment occur with Cooperative Learning Strategies and Flex Your Brain Activities.

Section 17•1

Prepare

Section Background

- Oceanography is a study interrelating every aspect of ocean systems and environments.
- Chemical oceanography is the study of the chemical properties of seawater and the causes, effects, and changes in ocean chemistry.
- Physical oceanography is primarily concerned with energy transmission through ocean water. It deals with wave formation and movement, currents, and tides.

Preplanning

To prepare for Activity 17-1, obtain the materials listed on page 482. Glass or plastic tubing should be put through the rubber stopper and the rubber tubing should be added. This rubber-stopper unit should be given to each lab team. Putting it together beforehand will save time, breakage, and injury.

1 Motivate

Bellringer

Before presenting the lesson, display **Section Focus Transparency 65** on the overhead projector. Assign the accompanying **Focus Activity** worksheet. L1 LEP

Tying to Previous Knowledge

Have students recall from Chapter 8 that running water erodes and dissolves sediments. Remind students that if these dissolved substances are carried by rivers, they may eventually reach the oceans.

17•1 Ocean Water

Science Words

basin
salinity

Objectives

- Learn the origin of the water in Earth's oceans.
- Explain how dissolved salts and other substances get into seawater.
- Describe the composition of seawater.

Oceans and You

Oceans affect your life, and your life affects oceans. No matter where you live, the ocean exerts an influence on you. When it rains, most of the water that falls comes from oceans. If the day is sunny, it is partly due to weather systems that develop over oceans. Oceans are a source of food and resources. **Figure 17-1** shows oil being drilled from the ocean and fish taken from the sea.

Oceans also act as barriers between continents. The price of clothing, cars, and gasoline may include the cost of shipping these materials across oceans. To go from the United States to Europe, a traveler must fly or take a ship across the ocean. But oceans also provide a means of transportation for plants and animals. Animals migrate with ocean currents. Plant seeds are washed from one coast to another by oceans. Humans have migrated across oceans to distant islands.

Human activity affects the oceans. If you live near a stream that is polluted, that pollution will travel to an ocean. Cities near oceans regularly dump sewage sludge into the ocean. Oil spills destroy beaches and marshes along the ocean.

A

Figure 17-1

We depend on the oceans. Some of our oil comes from wells drilled through rock layers under the oceans (A). Some food comes from the oceans (B).

B

Program Resources

Reproducible Masters

Study Guide, p. 69 L1
Reinforcement, p. 69 L1
Enrichment, p. 69 L3
Activity Worksheets, pp. 5, 102-103 L1
Concept Mapping, p. 39
Critical Thinking/Problem Solving, p. 23
Cross-Curricular Integration, p. 21
Science Integration Activities, pp. 33-34
Lab Manual 49 and **50**

Transparencies

Section Focus Transparency 65 L1

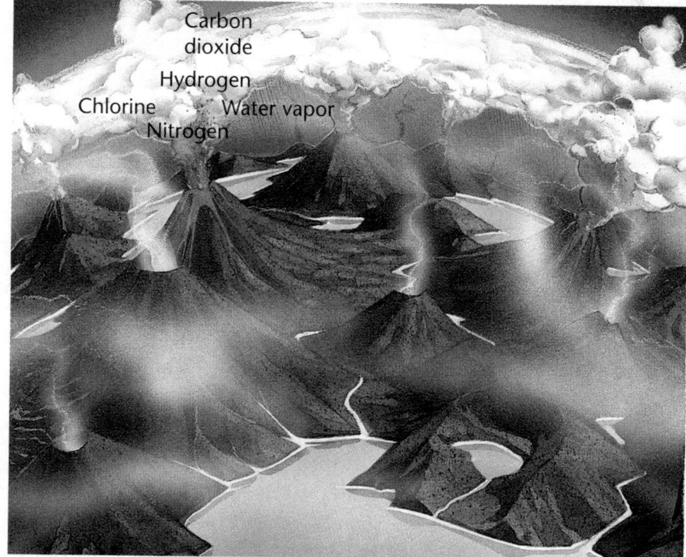

Figure 17-2

Earth's oceans may have formed from water vapor released into the atmosphere by volcanoes that also emitted chlorine, carbon dioxide, nitrogen, and hydrogen.

Origin of Oceans

In the first billion years after Earth formed, its surface was much more volcanically active than it is today. Volcanoes not only spew lava and ash, they give off water vapor along with carbon dioxide and other gases. Scientists hypothesize that about 4 billion years ago, this water vapor began to accumulate in Earth's early atmosphere. Over millions of years, it cooled enough to condense into storm clouds. Torrential rains began to fall. Oceans were formed as this water filled low areas on Earth called **basins.**

Composition of Oceans

We use a lot of water each day. In some areas, fresh water is limited. When water demand in these areas increases, too much water can be pumped from aquifers. This can cause problems.

Earth's surface is 70 percent ocean. It would help if we could use salt water to meet our water needs. But if you taste water from an ocean, immediately you'll know that it is different from the water you drink. It tastes salty because the ocean contains many dissolved salts. In the water, these salts are separated into ions of chloride, sodium, sulfur, magnesium, calcium, and potassium.

These salts come from rivers and groundwater slowly dissolving elements such as calcium, magnesium, and sodium from rocks and minerals. Rivers transport these elements to the oceans. Erupting volcanoes add elements, such as sulfur and chlorine, to the atmosphere and oceans.

USING MATH

Make a circle graph to show the percentage of Earth's surface that is ocean.

2 Teach

Inquiry Question

If Earth's surface is 70% ocean, why can't we use this water? *The water is too salty; drinking it would make people and other animals sick.*

Concept Development

Review the parts and processes of Earth's water cycle. Be sure to emphasize that the ocean is an integral part of this cycle.

Discussion

Ask students to describe what Earth would be like if its oceans had not formed. They will probably say that it would be dry. After more thought, they may describe Earth as having no life as we know it. Finally, students should realize that the weather patterns would be quite different without oceans.

USING MATH

LS **Logical-Mathematical** Graphs should show 70% of the circle as water.

GLENCOE TECHNOLOGY

CD-ROM

Earth Science CD-ROM

Have students perform the interactive exploration for Chapter 17 to reinforce important chapter concepts and thinking processes.

Use Labs 49 and 50 in the **Lab Manual** as you teach this lesson.

Across the Curriculum

Health Have students research which drugs to treat human disorders and diseases are made from marine organisms. L2 LS P

Geography Have groups of students make puzzles of Earth's oceans and landmasses. Transfer a map of the world onto cardboard and cut it into pieces. Groups should exchange puzzles and compete to see which group puts the puzzle together the fastest and correctly names the oceans. L1 LEP LS COOP LEARN

USING TECHNOLOGY

For more information, see "Portable and Potable [Debouy desalination system]" by J. Widman, *Oceans*, March/April 1984, p. 52.

Think Critically

The desalination technology requires energy and equipment, which can be expensive.

INTEGRATION Life Science

Ocean organisms use calcium from the ocean: corals in making reefs; fish and mammals for bones and teeth; oysters and clams for shells. Plants at the base of the food chain take the calcium directly from the water. Ask students why little calcium remains dissolved in ocean water. *Organisms remove calcium from the water, and it precipitates as an ooze to the bottom.*

3 Assess

Check for Understanding

FLEX Your Brain

Use the Flex Your Brain activity to have students explore SALINITY.

Activity Worksheets, p. 5

Reteach

LS Logical-Mathematical Provide various water samples to student groups. Have the groups use test kits to analyze the chemistry of the samples.

Extension

For students who have mastered this section, use the **Reinforcement** and **Enrichment** masters.

USING TECHNOLOGY

Desalting Ocean Water

In some areas that have little fresh water, salt is removed from ocean water to provide water for drinking and for other uses. Saudi Arabia, which borders the Red Sea and the Persian Gulf, uses a desalination system to make fresh water from salt water.

Desalting ocean water can be done in several ways. In one method, salt water is pumped into a large shallow tray covered by a sloping glass roof. Radiation from the sun heats the salt water. The water evaporates, rises to the glass, condenses, and drips down the glass into collecting troughs as fresh water. The salts are left behind.

In another method, an electric current passes through salt water. The positive and negative electrodes, as well as membranes placed between the electrodes, trap positive and negative salt ions. Desalted water is left behind.

In a third method of desalination, ocean water is frozen. Salt crystals are separated from the ice crystals by washing the salt from the ice with fresh water. The water is refrozen and washed several more times. Then, the ice is melted to produce fresh water.

Think Critically: Why is it expensive to make fresh water from salt water?

A Desalinization Plant

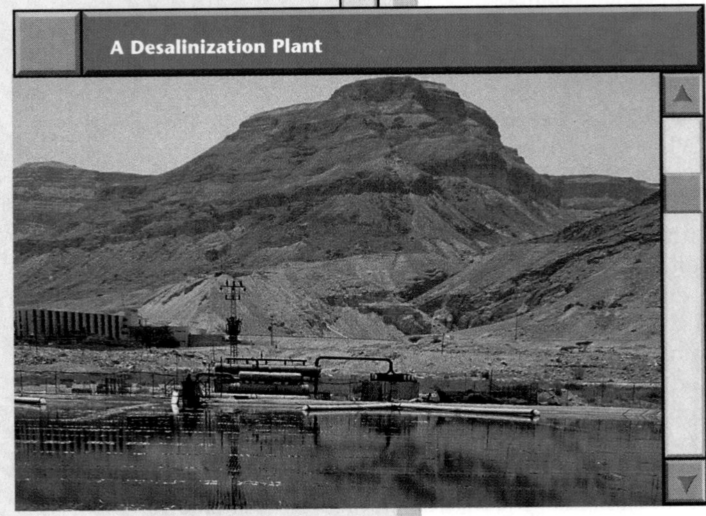

Salinity

In seawater, the most abundant elements are sodium and chlorine. Rivers that flow to the ocean dissolve sodium along the way. Volcanoes add chlorine gas. Most of the salt in seawater is made of sodium and chlorine. If seawater is evaporated, these sodium and chlorine ions combine to form a salt called halite. Halite is the salt you use to season food. It is this salt and similar ones that give ocean water its salty taste.

Salinity is a measure of the amount of solids dissolved in seawater. It is usually measured in grams of salt per kilogram. One kilogram of ocean water contains about 35 g of dissolved salts, or 3.5 percent. The graph in **Figure 17-3** lists the most abundant salts in ocean water. The proportions and amount of dissolved salts in seawater remain nearly constant and have stayed about the same for hundreds of millions of years. This tells us that the composition of the oceans is in balance. The ocean is not growing saltier.

NATIONAL GEOGRAPHIC SOCIETY

Videodisc

STV: Water

Desalination plant; Saudi Arabia

52578

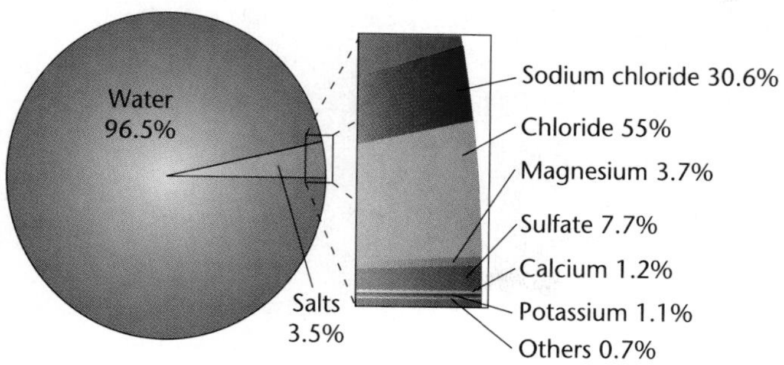

Figure 17-3

Ocean water contains about 3.5 percent salts. This graph lists the most abundant ions in seawater. Sodium and chloride make up nearly 90 percent of the substances in seawater.

INTEGRATION Life Science

Element Removal

Although rivers, volcanoes, and the atmosphere constantly add substances to the ocean, the oceans are considered to be in a steady state. As new substances come in, elements are removed from seawater by biological processes and by becoming sediment. Sea animals and algae use dissolved substances. Marine animals use calcium to form bones. Other animals, such as oysters and clams, use silica and calcium to form shells. Some algae, called diatoms, have silica shells. Because many organisms use calcium and silica, these ions are removed more quickly from seawater than are substances such as chloride or sodium. Iron is removed more quickly because iron forms solids that fall to the ocean floor.

The oceans came from water vapor condensing and falling as rain, then collecting in basins. Volcanoes, groundwater, and rivers add salts to seawater.

Section Wrap-up

Review

1. According to scientific hypothesis, how were Earth's oceans formed?
2. Why does ocean water taste salty?
3. **Think Critically:** Why does the salinity of Earth's oceans remain constant?

Skill Builder
Concept Mapping

Make a concept map that shows how halite becomes dissolved in the oceans. Use the terms *rivers, volcanoes, halite, source of, sodium, chlorine,* and *combine to form.* If you need help, refer to Concept Mapping in the **Skill Handbook.**

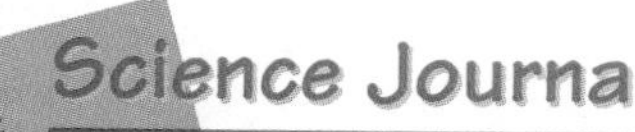

Discuss what is happening in this excerpt from "The Rime of the Ancient Mariner" by Samuel Taylor Coleridge.

Day after day, day after day,
We stuck, nor breath nor motion;
As idle as a painted ship
Upon a painted ocean.
Water, water, everywhere,
And all the boards did shrink;
Water, water, everywhere,
Nor any drop to drink.

4 Close

• MINI • QUIZ •

1. **When seawater evaporates, sodium and _____ combine to form a salt called halite.** *chlorine*
2. **_____ percent of the salt in seawater is made of sodium and chlorine.** *About 86*
3. **_____ is a measure of the dissolved solids in seawater.** *Salinity*
4. **_____ is used by some marine animals to form their bones.** *Calcium*
5. **Some marine animals use calcium and _____ to form shells.** *silica*

Section Wrap-up

Review

1. Volcanoes spewed water vapor that accumulated, cooled, and condensed about 4 billion years ago. Eventually rain fell and filled deep basins.
2. It contains many dissolved salts.
3. **Think Critically** As substances add to the ocean water, sea animals and plants use the dissolved substances in their life processes. Other substances combine and precipitate out.

Science Journal

The ship is in an area of no wind, perhaps in the doldrums. They have run out of water to drink, although salt water surrounds them. P

Skill Builder

Possible solution:

rivers → source of → sodium → combine to form
volcanoes → source of → chlorine → combine to form
combine to form → halite

Assessment

Performance Use this Skill Builder to assess students' abilities to make a concept map. Ask students to make a concept map showing how scientists think Earth's first oceans formed. Use the Performance Task Assessment List for Concept Map in **PASC,** p. 89. P

Activity 17-1

PREPARATION

Purpose

LS **Interpersonal** Design and carry out an experiment to distill fresh water from salt water. L1 COOP LEARN

Process Skills

communicating, designing an experiment, separating and controlling variables, measuring in SI, observing and inferring, recognizing cause and effect, making models, interpreting data

Time

60 minutes

Materials

For student safety, insert the glass tubing through the stoppers and rubber tubing ahead of time.

Safety Precautions

- Be sure that the glassware and spoons are sterile.
- Caution students to wear goggles and thermal mitts.
- Caution students not to taste any substances.

Possible Hypotheses

When salt water is boiled, the water will evaporate, leaving behind salts. When the water vapor is cooled, condensation occurs. Fresh water can be collected.

Activity Worksheets, pp. 5, 102-103

Activity 17-1

Design Your Own Experiment

Water, Water, Everywhere

Imagine being stranded on an island. You're thirsty, but you can't find any fresh water. There's plenty of salt water. How can you remove the salts from the water so that you can drink it?

PREPARATION

Problem

How can you make fresh water from salt water?

Form a Hypothesis

Remember what you have learned about evaporation and condensation in the water cycle. Form a hypothesis about how to make a simple desalination system to remove fresh water from salt water.

Objectives

- Design and carry out an experiment to remove fresh water from salt water.
- Recognize the cause-and-effect relationships of heating and cooling on evaporation and condensation.

Possible Materials

- Obtain from your teacher a rubber stopper with a plastic or glass right-angle tube inserted. A piece of rubber tubing should be attached to the end of the glass tube as shown in the photo below.
- pan balance
- table salt
- water
- 1000-mL flask
- 600-mL beaker
- towel
- plastic spoon
- hot plate
- scissors
- ice
- shallow pan
- goggles
- thermal mitts
- watch glasses (2)

Safety Precautions

Be sure the glassware and spoon are clean before you begin your experiment.

Wear your goggles while you are boiling the water. Use the thermal mitts when handling hot objects.

Inclusion Strategies

Physically Challenged Place students who have trouble manipulating equipment in charge of formulating the hypothesis and answering questions 1-4 in the Analyze and Apply section.

PLAN THE EXPERIMENT

1. Agree upon and write out your hypothesis statement.
2. List the steps needed to test your hypothesis. Be specific, describing exactly what you will do. Include the following steps in your list: (a) dissolve 18 g of table salt in 500 mL of water; (b) mix the salt-water solution; (c) use the flask for heating and the beaker for collecting fresh water; and (d) use watch glasses on the hot plate to evaporate samples of water from both the beaker and the flask.

Check the Plan

1. Read over your entire experiment to make certain your experiment tests your hypothesis.
2. Make certain you measure and record carefully.
3. Have you included all safety precautions? *Pay attention to the boiling water. Do not leave it unattended. Do not touch the heated glassware. Let it cool before you touch it.*
4. Read over the concluding questions to see if you have included all the necessary steps in your experiment.
5. *Before you begin, have your teacher approve your plan.*

DO THE EXPERIMENT

1. Carry out the experiment as planned.
2. While the experiment is going on, write down any observations that you make in your Science Journal.

Analyze and Apply

1. **Analyze** what happened to the water in the flask as you boiled the solution. What remained in the flask? What happened to the water after it evaporated?
2. **Contrast** the samples on the watch glasses.
3. **Measure** the volume of water in the beaker and of the salt water remaining in the flask. **Compare** the combined volumes with the volume of the salt water at the beginning. Are they the same? Explain.
4. **Compare** your results with those of other laboratory teams. Did they have similar results?
5. **Explain** your results by drawing a diagram of the experiment. Label the processes involved.

Go Further

How could you use the desalination process to collect valuable minerals from seawater?

PLAN THE EXPERIMENT

Possible Procedures

Use the pan balance to measure 18 g of table salt. Fill the 600-mL beaker with water. Use the spoon to mix the salt into the water and then pour it into the 1000-mL flask. Place the stopper-tubing unit into the flask. Place the free end of the rubber tubing through a hole that has been cut into the cardboard sheet. Dry the 600-mL beaker, put it into the shallow pan filled with ice, and place the cardboard on top of the beaker. Place the flask on the hot plate, put on goggles, turn on the hot plate, and observe. After the water condenses in the beaker, pour some on a watch glass and put glass on the hot plate to evaporate. Do the same for water from the flask.

Teaching Strategies

Students learned about the water cycle in Chapter 14. In nature, the source of energy for this cycle is sunlight. In this activity, it is a hot plate.

DO THE EXPERIMENT

Expected Outcome

Water evaporates from the flask and condenses in the beaker.

Analyze and Apply

1. It evaporated. Salt and some water remained. It went through the tubing, condensed, and fell into the beaker.
2. The water from the flask contained salt. The water from the beaker does not contain salt.
3. The amounts will be similar, although some water vapor may cling to the beaker and tubing instead of condensing in the beaker.
4. Teams should have similar results.
5. The distillation process should have labels for evaporation and condensation and heat and cooling.

Go Further

When seawater is desalinated, the remaining brine contains minerals.

Assessment

Oral Have students explain why ice was used in this experiment. *It cooled the water vapor, the water vapor molecules condensed, and liquid formed.* Use the Performance Task Assessment List for Making Observations and Inferences in **PASC**, p. 17. P

Section 17•2

Prepare

Section Background

Oceans can generally be divided into three layers based on temperature. Thermal energy in the surface layer is evenly distributed because of the mixing by waves and the turbulence by currents. The depth of this layer averages 200 m to 300 m below the surface. Below the surface layer is the thermocline, where the temperature drops rapidly to about 5°C. Below the thermocline, temperature decreases slightly to about 1°C.

Preplanning

To prepare for the MiniLAB, obtain clear plastic storage boxes, salt, and food coloring.

1 Motivate

Bellringer

Before presenting the lesson, display **Section Focus Transparency 66** on the overhead projector. Assign the accompanying **Focus Activity** worksheet. L1 LEP

Tying to Previous Knowledge

Give students a few moments to compare wind patterns shown in **Figure 14-17** on page 412 with major ocean surface currents shown in **Figure 17-4.** Students should note that water and wind follow similar paths until the continents deflect ocean currents.

17•2 Ocean Currents

Science Words

surface current
upwelling
density current

Objectives

- Determine how winds, the Coriolis effect, and continents influence surface currents.
- Explain the temperatures of coastal waters.
- Describe density currents.

Surface Currents

The ocean is always moving. A mass movement or flow of ocean water is called a current. When you stir chocolate flavoring into milk or stir a pot of soup, you make currents with the spoon. The currents are what mix the liquid. An ocean current is like a river within the ocean. It moves masses of water from place to place.

Ocean currents carry water in various directions. **Surface currents** move water horizontally—parallel to Earth's surface. Surface currents are powered by wind. Friction between wind and water causes the water to move, driving ocean water in huge circular patterns all around the world. **Figure 17-4** shows these major surface currents. From looking at the map of surface currents, you may have guessed that the surface currents in the ocean are related to the general circulation of wind on Earth.

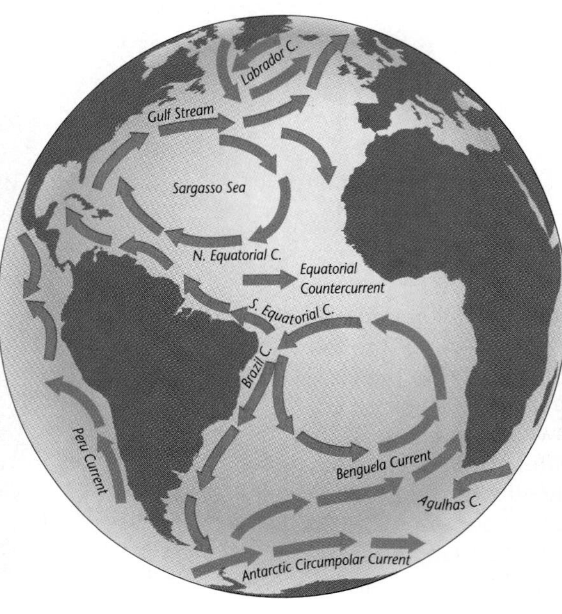

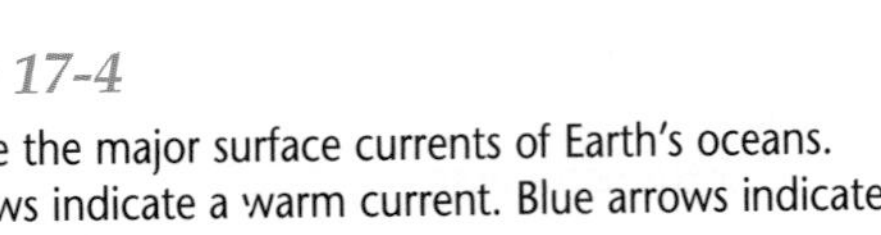

Figure 17-4
These are the major surface currents of Earth's oceans. Red arrows indicate a warm current. Blue arrows indicate a cold current.

Program Resources

Reproducible Masters

Study Guide, p. 70 L1
Reinforcement, p. 70 L1
Enrichment, p. 70 L3
Activity Worksheets, pp. 5, 106 L1
Lab Manual 51, 52

Transparencies

Section Focus Transparency 66 L1
Teaching Transparency 33
Science Integration Transparency 17

Surface currents are called surface currents because they move only the upper few hundred meters of seawater, although sometimes they extend down to 1000 m. Surface currents carry seeds and plants between continents and float bottles with messages from one continent to another. Sailors now and in the past have used these currents in conjunction with winds to sail more efficiently from place to place. The Antarctic Circumpolar Current is the strongest current in the ocean. It is the only one that circles Earth.

Figure 17-5

Captain Timothy Folger drew this map of the Gulf Stream around 1770.

The Gulf Stream

Although satellites now provide information about ocean movements, much of what we know about surface currents comes from records kept by sailors of the 19th century. For as many years as ships have sailed, sailors have used surface currents to help them travel quickly. Sailing ships depended on one surface current to carry them to the west and another to carry them to the east. During the American colonial era, ships floated on the 100-km-wide Gulf Stream current to go quickly from North America to England. On the map, find the Gulf Stream current in the Atlantic Ocean.

We learn about ocean currents in a variety of ways, both scientific and nonscientific. In the late 1600s, a British explorer named William Dampier first wrote about the Gulf Stream in his *Discoveries on the Trade Winds.* A century later, Benjamin Franklin published a map of the Gulf Stream that his cousin Captain Timothy Folger, a Nantucket whaler, had drawn. This map is shown in **Figure 17-5.**

An unscientific way we learn about currents is from things that wash up on beaches. In May 1991, thousands of sneakers washed up on Oregon beaches. The North Pacific Drift Current and the California Current had carried the shoes from the site of a shipping accident a year earlier in the mid-Pacific and deposited 80 000 shoes on the western edge of the United States.

CONNECT TO

LIFE SCIENCE

When marine animals such as eels, turtles, and whales migrate, they often use surface ocean currents. ***Infer*** what would happen to animal migration without surface currents.

2 Teach

Visual Learning

Figure 17-4 Ask students: **Is the Kuroshio Current colder or warmer than the California Current? Explain your answer.** *The Kuroshio Current is warmer because it originates at the equator. The California Current comes from higher latitudes.* Tell students that a gyre refers to the circular pattern of water that occurs in each of the major ocean basins. Ask students: **Which currents make up the gyre in the north Pacific Ocean?** *the Kuroshio Current, North Pacific Current, California Current, and North Equatorial Current* LEP LS

Inquiry Question

Explain how wind creates surface currents. *Friction between the wind-blown air and the water surface causes the water to move.*

CONNECT TO

LIFE SCIENCE

Answer Swimming with the currents allows them to travel great distances without expending a lot of energy. Without currents, these animals would have to use more energy.

Use **Teaching Transparency 33** as you teach this lesson.

Across the Curriculum

Social Studies Have students research how the positions of currents affected ancient trade routes. Have them research Benjamin Franklin's study of the Gulf Stream. L2

GLENCOE TECHNOLOGY

Videodisc

STVS: Earth & Space

Disc 3, Side 2

Studying the Pacific Ocean (Ch. 14)

Student Text Question

How do warm and cold surface currents affect the east and west coasts of the United States? *The east coast is warmed by a current. The west coast is cooled by a current.*

USING MATH

Logical-Mathematical $1.027\,16 \times 4 = 4.108\,64$ g

Use Lab 51 in the **Lab Manual** as you teach this lesson.

Inquiry Question

Along the eastern shores of oceans, winds blow surface water out from shore. This water is then replaced by cold, deep water. Where would you expect this type of upwelling to occur? *along the coasts of California, Peru, and western Africa*

GLENCOE TECHNOLOGY

Videodisc

STVS: Earth & Space

Disc 3, Side 2

Studying the Pacific Ocean (Ch. 14)

Videodisc

GTV: Planetary Manager

Water, Water Everywhere

Show 2.7, Side 2

38779-41076

Factors Influencing Surface Currents

Surface ocean currents, like surface winds, are influenced by the Coriolis effect. The Coriolis effect deflects currents north of the equator, such as the Gulf Stream, to the right. Currents south of the equator are deflected to the left. Look again at the map of surface currents in **Figure 17-4** on page 484.

The continents also influence ocean currents. Notice that currents moving toward the west in the Pacific are deflected by Asia and Australia. Then currents, influenced by the Coriolis effect, move eastward until North and South America deflect them. On the map, what other surface currents are deflected by continents?

On the same map, note that currents on the western coast of continents are usually cold, whereas currents on eastern coasts are warm. Warm currents on eastern coasts originate near the equator.

Importance of Surface Currents

Surface currents distribute heat from equatorial regions to other areas of Earth. Warmer waters flowing away from the equator transfer heat to the atmosphere. The atmosphere is warmed. Heat moving in the ocean and into the atmosphere influences climate.

As an example of how surface currents affect the climate of land they pass, find Iceland on the map. It is located so far north you would think it has a frigid climate. But part of the Gulf Stream flows past Iceland. The current's warm water heats the surrounding air. Because of the Gulf Stream, Iceland has a surprisingly mild climate. How do warm and cold surface currents affect the east and west coasts of the United States? **Figure 17-6** shows warm waters of the Gulf Stream.

USING MATH

If the density of a sample of seawater is 1.02716 g/mL, what would be the mass of 4 mL of the sample?

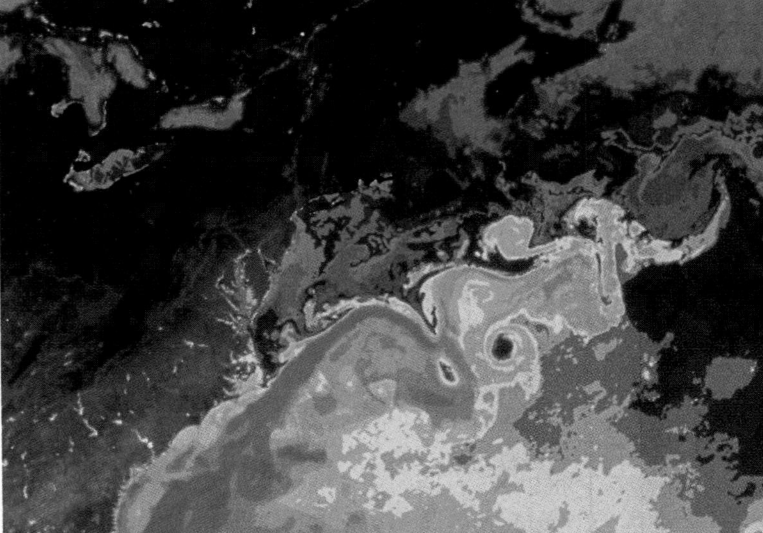

Figure 17-6

Ocean-temperature data collected by a satellite were used to make this surface-temperature image of the Atlantic Ocean. The warm Gulf Stream waters appear as orange and red, and cooler waters appear as blue and green.

Figure 17-7

In the process of upwelling, winds push surface water away from a coast. This brings colder water to the surface.

Upwelling

Along some coasts, upwelling occurs. **Upwelling** is a circulation in the ocean that brings deep, cold water to the ocean surface. **Figure 17-7** illustrates upwelling. In upwelling, wind blowing offshore or parallel to the coast carries water away from the land. When surface water is pushed away, cold water from deep in the ocean rises. This cold, deep water contains high concentrations of nutrients from organisms that decayed, sank, and then rose with the deep water. These nutrients bring fish to areas of upwelling along the coasts of Oregon, Washington, and Peru, which are known as good fishing areas. Upwelling also affects the climate of adjacent coastal areas. In the United States, upwelling contributes to San Francisco's cool summers and famous fogs.

Density Currents

Wind-driven surface currents affect only the upper layers of Earth's oceans. Upwelling is a vertical mixing of ocean waters in specific areas. In the depths of the ocean, waters circulate not because of wind but because of density differences.

Differences in the density of different masses of seawater cause density currents. A **density current** occurs when more dense seawater sinks under less dense seawater, mixing surface ocean water farther into the ocean.

You made a density current in the Explore activity at the beginning of this chapter. The cold water was more dense than the warm water in the beaker. The cold water sank to the bottom. This created a density current that moved the food coloring. In the MiniLAB on this page, you modeled a density current with salt water and fresh water.

MiniLAB

How can you make a density current model?

Procedure

1. Fill a clear plastic storage box with room-temperature water.
2. Mix several teaspoons of table salt into a beaker of water at room temperature.
3. Add a few drops of food coloring to the saltwater solution. Pour the solution slowly into the fresh water in the large container.

Analyze

1. Explain what happened when you added salt water to fresh water.
2. How does this lab relate to density currents?

MiniLAB

Purpose

LS **Visual-Spatial** Students will model a density current. L1 LEP

Materials

clear plastic storage box, glass or beaker, table salt, food coloring, water

Teaching Strategies

Troubleshooting To see the current that develops, have students look into the storage box from the side, not the top.

Analysis

1. The salty water sank to the bottom and spread out toward the sides of the container.
2. In the ocean, where evaporation or ice formation takes place, salt is left behind which makes the water more dense and starts a density current.

Assessment

Oral To further assess students' understanding of density currents, have them define the term *density* to a classmate. Give students the mass and volume of an object (or have them find the mass and volume) and then have them calculate the density. Use the Performance Task Assessment List for Using Math in Science in **PASC**, p. 29. P

Activity Worksheets, pp. 5, 106

Problem Solving

Solve the Problem

1. Sample 3 has the highest temperature and lowest density. It came from the surface.
2. Sample 2 has the lowest temperature and highest density. It came from the bottom.
3. If water is cold, but not very salty, it may be less dense than warmer, saltier water.

Think Critically

The usual upwelling disappears. Nutrients and small fish disappear, causing a temporary disappearance of good fishing.

3 Assess

Check for Understanding

Ask students to explain why density currents develop in areas where surface waters are very saline.

Reteach

LS Visual-Spatial Fill two Erlenmeyer flasks with water. Add 5 drops of food coloring to each flask. In a third flask, put just water. In another, add 35 g of salt to water. Insert stoppers holding two glass tubes into these last two flasks. Invert these stoppered flasks over the flasks of colored water. Have students observe the flasks. In the flasks without salt, the colored water will not move. However, in the flasks with salt water, the colored water moves into the top flask. Ask students to explain this. Students should conclude that the salty, denser water moves down and the less dense water in the bottom flask is forced up, creating a density current.

Problem Solving

Ocean Temperatures and Density

Imagine that your job is to analyze the data shown in the chart below. The data were collected from three different water masses in the North Atlantic Ocean. You know that one sample came from near the surface, one came from a depth of 750 m, and a third came from the ocean floor. The samples are not labeled and became mixed up in shipment.

Sample #	Temperature (°C)	Density (g/mL)
1	6	1.02716
2	3	1.02781
3	14	1.02630

Solve the Problem

1. **Which sample came from near the surface? How do you know?**
2. **Which sample of water came from the bottom? How do you know?**
3. **Hypothesize how less dense seawater can be colder than the most dense.**

Think Critically:

During El Niño, the surface winds blow toward South America. How do you think the usual upwelling near Peru is affected?

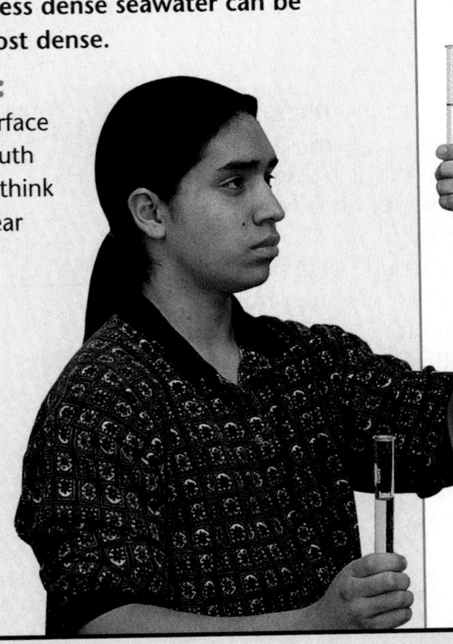

From your experiments, you've learned that the density of seawater can be increased by an increase in salinity or by a decrease in temperature. A combination of changes in temperature, salinity, and pressure involve the entire ocean in circulation due to density. However, density currents in the ocean circulate water very slowly.

An important density current occurs in Antarctica where the most dense ocean water forms during the winter. As ice forms, seawater freezes, but the salt is left in the unfrozen water. The extra salt not incorporated into the ice increases the density of the ocean water until it is very dense. This dense water sinks and slowly spreads along the ocean bottom toward the equator, forming a density current. In the Pacific, this water may take 1000 years to reach the equator. In the Atlantic Ocean, dense surface waters that sink into the depths circulate more quickly. Atlantic density currents may bring water back to the surface in just 275 years.

A density current also occurs in the Mediterranean, a nearly enclosed sea. Warm temperatures evaporate water from the surface, increasing the salinity and the density of the water. This dense water from the Mediterranean flows outward into the less dense water of the Atlantic Ocean. When it reaches the Atlantic, it flows downward in a density current.

Figure 17-8

Surface currents in the ocean carry objects from long distances. This couple gathered up these sport shoes from a beach in Oregon. The shoes fell into the Pacific Ocean from five boxcar-sized containers a year earlier. An oceanographer from Seattle is studying Pacific Ocean currents with information from the drifting sneakers.

Our knowledge has come a long way since Benjamin Franklin investigated the Gulf Stream. Today, we can track ocean currents by objects that wash up on shore as shown in **Figure 17-8** and more scientifically by satellite. This information helps ships navigate, fishing fleets locate upwellings, and us to understand climate and track hurricanes.

Section Wrap-up

Review

1. How does the energy from wind affect surface currents?
2. How do density currents affect the circulation of water in deep parts of the oceans?
3. **Think Critically:** The latitudes of San Diego, California and Charleston, South Carolina are exactly the same. However, the average yearly water temperature in the ocean off Charleston is much higher than the water temperature off San Diego. Explain why.

Skill Builder

Predicting

A river flows into the ocean. Predict what will happen to this layer of fresh water. Explain your prediction. If you need help, refer to Predicting in the **Skill Handbook.**

Using Computers

Spreadsheet Make a spreadsheet that compares surface and density currents. Focus on characteristics such as wind, horizontal and vertical movement, temperature, density, and anything else that you think helps describe each current.

4 Close

• MINI • QUIZ •

Use the Mini Quiz to check students' recall of chapter content.

1. **A(n) _____ current affects only the upper few hundred meters of seawater.** *surface*
2. **Most surface ocean currents move in a(n) _____ direction in the northern hemisphere.** *clockwise*
3. **Currents on the eastern continental coasts are _____ than currents on the western coasts.** *warmer*
4. **_____ occur where winds push surface currents away from continents.** *Upwellings*

Section Wrap-up

Review

1. Friction between wind-blown air and surface water creates currents.
2. At the poles, cold, dense water sinks and eventually reaches the equator, where it warms and surfaces.
3. **Think Critically** The water off Charleston originates at the equator. The water off San Diego originates near Alaska.

Using Computers

	Surface Currents	Density Currents
Causes	Winds push water, Coriolis force, deflection by continents	Density differences of water masses
Direction of Movement	horizontal	vertical first, followed by horizontal along the bottom
Temperature	warm or cold	cold
Density	average	high

Assessment

Content Assess students' abilities to classify by having them classify the Gulf Stream as either a warm or a cold surface current. Have them explain their classification in a paragraph or two. Use the Performance Task Assessment List for Writing in Science in **PASC,** p. 87. P

Skill Builder

Fresh water of the river is less dense than ocean water. It will float on top of seawater and mix slowly or quickly, depending on the speed of the river and the height of the tide along the coast.

Section 17•3

Prepare

Section Background

- When the depth of the water is less than one-half the wavelength of the wave, wavelength shortens and wave height increases. Eventually a breaker forms.
- The longer wind blows, the higher the waves mount until they reach a maximum height for a given wind velocity. For a given wind velocity, waves tend to be higher on large, deep bodies of water than on shallower water. Waves on the larger, deeper bodies develop without interference of drag on the ocean bottom.

Preplanning

- To prepare for the MiniLAB, obtain clear plastic storage boxes, corks, and spoons.
- To prepare for Activity 17-2, obtain: ring stands with clamps, 3-speed electric fans, light source, metric rulers, and clear plastic storage boxes.

1 Motivate

Bellringer

Before presenting the lesson, display **Section Focus Transparency 67** on the overhead projector. Assign the accompanying **Focus Activity** worksheet. L1 LEP

Tying to Previous Knowledge

In Chapter 9, students learned about waves generated by earthquakes. In this chapter, they will learn about waves generated by wind and gravitational force.

17•3 Ocean Waves and Tides

Science Words

- wave
- crest
- trough
- breaker
- tide
- tidal range

Objectives

- Define a wave.
- Differentiate between the movement of water particles in a wave and the movement of wave energy.
- Describe how the energy of wind and the gravitational force of the moon and sun create tides.

Waves

If you've been to the seashore or seen a beach on TV, you've watched waves roll in. Waves in water are caused by winds, earthquakes, and the gravitational force of the moon and sun. You learned about ocean waves caused by earthquakes. But what is an ocean wave? A wave is a rhythmic movement that carries energy through matter or space. In the ocean, waves move through seawater.

Several terms are used to describe waves. **Figure 17-9** shows that the **crest** is the highest point of the wave. The **trough** is the lowest point. Wave height is the vertical distance between crest and trough. Wavelength is the horizontal distance between the crests or between the troughs of two successive waves.

Wave Movement

When you watch an ocean wave, it looks as though the water is moving forward. But unless the wave is breaking onto shore, the water does not move forward. Each molecule of water stays in about the same place as the wave passes. **Figure 17-10** shows this. If you want to see another example of a wave carrying energy, tie a rope to a tree. Wiggle the rope until a wave starts across it. Notice that as the energy passes along the rope, the rope moves but each piece of rope is still in the same place, the same distance from the tree.

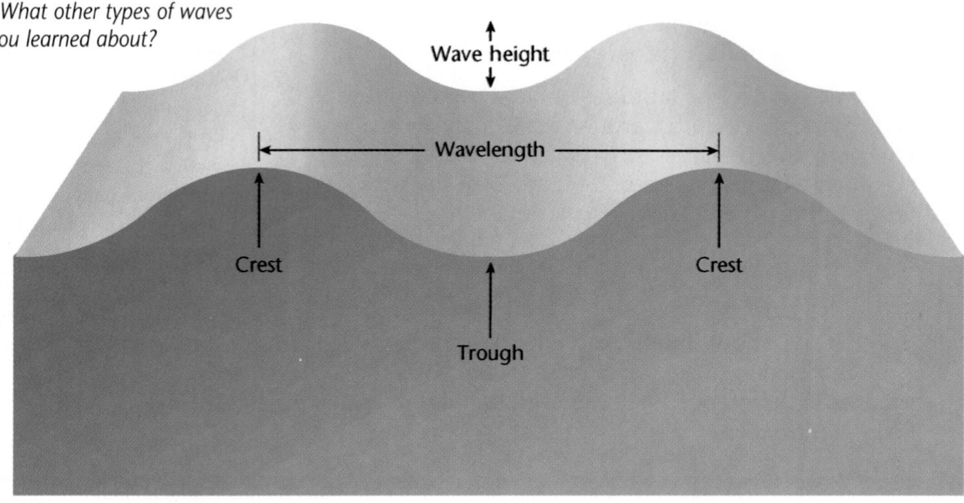

Figure 17-9

The crest, trough, wavelength, and wave height are parts of a wave. *What other types of waves have you learned about?*

Program Resources

Reproducible Masters

Study Guide, p. 71 L1
Reinforcement, p. 71 L1
Enrichment, p. 71 L3
Science and Society Integration, p. 21
Activity Worksheets, pp. 5, 104-105, 107 L1
Multicultural Connections, pp. 37-38

Transparencies

Section Focus Transparency 67 L1
Teaching Transparency 34

The MiniLAB on page 492 will help explain this further. In the same way, an object floating on water will rise and fall as a wave passes, but the object will not move forward. Only the energy moves forward while the water particles remain in the same place.

When a wave breaks against a shore, it is different. In a shallow area near shore, a wave changes shape. Friction with the ocean bottom slows water at the bottom of the wave. As the wave slows, its crest and trough come closer together. The wave height increases. The top of a wave, not slowed by friction, moves faster than the bottom. Eventually, the top of the wave outruns the bottom and collapses. The wave crest falls; water tumbles over on itself. The wave breaks onto the shore. This collapsing wave is a **breaker.** It is the collapse of this wave that propels a surfer and surfboard onto shore. After a wave breaks onto shore, gravity pulls the water back into the sea.

Now let's look at two different types of waves: (1) the common sea waves caused by wind and (2) the long waves of the tides.

CONNECT TO PHYSICS

The *period* of a wave is the time it takes for successive wave crests to pass a fixed point. If the period (T) is 2 s and the wavelength (L) is 6 m, you can find the velocity (C) of the wave by using the formula C = L/T. ***Calculate*** the velocity of this wave.

Figure 17-10

In a wave, individual particles of water move in circles as the energy passes through.

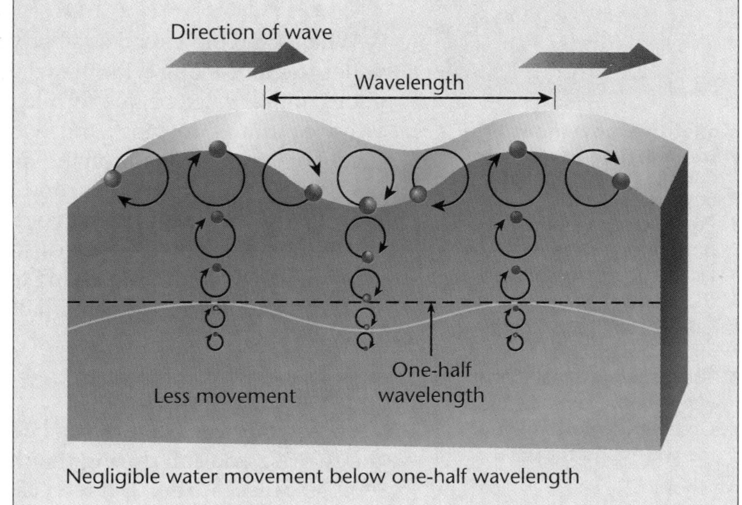

A Wave energy moves forward somewhat like the motion of falling dominoes. Like water particles, individual dominoes remain near where they were standing as they fall and transfer energy to the next domino.

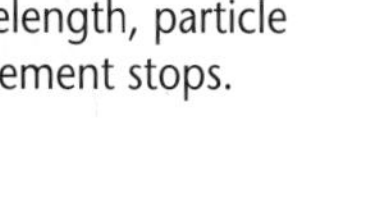

B Particles of water in a wave move around in circles. The farther below the surface, the smaller the circles are. At a depth about equal to half the wavelength, particle movement stops.

2 Teach

Visual Learning

Figure 17-9 What other types of waves have you learned about? *earthquake waves, electromagnetic waves, sound waves* LEP LS

CONNECT TO PHYSICS

Answer C = 6 m/2 s = 3 m/s

Demonstration

LS **Visual-Spatial** Use a wave demonstration spring or Slinky to show how energy is transferred through a wave. Tie a piece of ribbon to the middle of the spring. Have two students create a wave while another student holds the ribbon. Have the class note that the ribbon does not move forward with the wave as energy moves through the ribbon. LEP

Teacher F.Y.I.

An average ocean wave is 3.7 m high. The maximum wave height measured in the open ocean was 34 m. The largest waves occur beneath the continuous strong winds of the West Wind Drift surrounding Antarctica.

Use **Teaching Transparency 34** as you teach this lesson.

Integrating the Sciences

Physical Science Have students investigate whether light waves, earthquake waves, sound waves, and water waves have similar characteristics. L1

GLENCOE TECHNOLOGY

Videodisc

STVS: Earth & Space

Disc 3, Side 2

Artificial Waves (Ch. 13)

MiniLAB

Purpose

LS **Kinesthetic** Students will make a wave model that shows water particle movement. L2 COOP LEARN

Materials

clear plastic storage box, cork, tape, water, spoon

Teaching Strategies

Troubleshooting Explain to students that they want to make waves, not currents. By lifting and gently dropping the spoon onto the water, they can produce waves.

Analysis

1. The wave moves across the box. The cork moves vertically as the wave passes under it.
2. It moved in a small circle, but its final position was the same as its beginning position.
3. Both the cork and the water particles in a wave move in small circles as a wave passes. Their final positions are the same as their beginning positions. P

Assessment

Performance To further assess students' understanding of how waves move, have students devise other ways of creating waves in the box, and have them observe the motion of the cork. Remind students that they are to create waves, not currents. The cork will not travel horizontally with a wave, but it will with a current. Use the Performance Task Assessment List for Carrying Out a Strategy and Collecting Data in **PASC**, p. 25. P

Activity Worksheets, pp. 5, 107

Figure 17-11
Wavelength decreases and wave height increases as waves approach the shore. This leads to the formation of breakers.

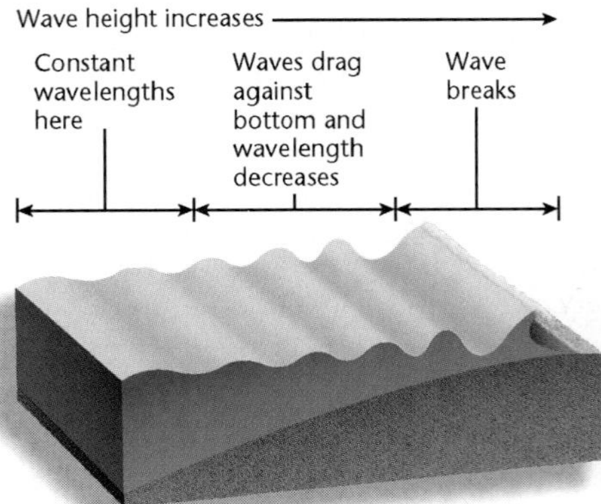

MiniLAB

Model the movement of a water particle in a wave.

Procedure

1. Put a piece of tape on the bottom of a clear, rectangular plastic storage box. Fill the box with water.
2. Float a cork in the container above the piece of tape.
3. Use a spoon to make gentle waves in the container.
4. Observe the movement of the waves and the cork.

Analysis

1. Describe the movement of the waves and the motion of the cork.
2. Did the cork move from its original location in the container?
3. Compare the movement of the cork with the movement of water particles in a wave.

Waves Caused by Wind

When wind blows across a body of water, friction causes the water to move along with the wind. If the wind speed is great enough, the water begins to pile up, forming a wave. As the wind continues to blow, the wave increases in height. The height of waves depends on the speed of the wind, the distance over which the wind blows, and the length of time the wind blows. You will learn more about this in Activity 17-2. When the wind stops blowing, waves stop forming. But, once set in motion, waves continue moving for long distances. Waves at a seashore may have originated halfway around the world.

Tides

Have you ever been to the beach and noticed the level of the sea rise and fall during the day? This rise and fall in sea level is called a **tide.** A tide is caused by a giant wave. This wave is only 1 m or 2 m high but thousands of kilometers long. As the crest of this wave approaches the shore, sea level appears to rise. This is called high tide. Then a few hours later, as the trough of the wave approaches, sea level appears to drop. This is referred to as low tide.

One low-tide-high-tide cycle takes 12 hours and 25 minutes. A daily cycle of two high and low tides takes 24 hours and 50 minutes, slightly more than a day. The **tidal range** is the difference between the level of the ocean at high tide and low tide. Notice the tidal range in the photos of **Figure 17-12** on page 494.

Cultural Diversity

Tasmania Although the island of Tasmania is only about 150 miles from Australia, it remained isolated for nearly 10 000 years. Early Tasmanians lived a simple life. The Tasmanians probably inhabited the island when it was part of Australia about 37 000 years ago during an ice age. Sea level was lower. There was a land bridge between Tasmania and Australia. When the ice melted, water covered the land bridge, and Tasmania became an island. Tasmanians used raft-canoes, twigs bound together with a shallow depression in the center, to travel across water. But the rafts rapidly became waterlogged and sank. The rafts could not even cross 14-mile-wide Bank Strait separating Tasmania from Flinders Island, where a group of people lived alone for about 4000 years before their culture died out.

Activity 17-2

Making Waves

As you have learned, wind helps generate some waves. The energy of motion is transferred from the wind to the surface water of the ocean. The force of the wind affects the waves created. What other factors influence the generation of waves?

Problem

How does the speed of the wind and the length of time it blows affect the height of a wave?

Materials 

- white paper
- electric fan (3-speed)
- light source
- clock or watch
- a rectangular, clear plastic storage box
- ring stand with clamp
- water
- metric ruler

Procedure

1. Position the box on white paper beside the ring stand.
2. Clamp a light source on the ring stand or use a gooseneck lamp. Direct the light onto the box. Almost fill the plastic box with water. **CAUTION:** *Do not allow any part of the light or cord to come in contact with the water.*
3. Place the fan at one end of the box to create waves. Start on slow. Keep the fan on during measuring. **CAUTION:** *Do not allow any part of the fan or cord to come in contact with the water.*
4. After three minutes, measure the height of the waves caused by the fan. Record your observations in a table similar to the one shown. Through the plastic box, observe the shadows of the waves on the white paper.
5. After five minutes, measure the wave height and record your observations.
6. Repeat steps 3 to 5 with the fan on medium, then on high.
7. Turn off the fan. Observe what happens.

Analyze

1. **Analyze** your data to determine whether the wave height is affected by the length of time that the wind blows. Explain.
2. **Analyze** your data to determine whether the height of the waves is affected by the speed of the wind. Explain.
3. How does an increase in fan speed affect the pattern of the wave shadows on the white paper?
4. What caused shadows to appear on the paper?
5. **Compare** what happened with the fan turned on with what happened when you turned off the fan.

Conclude and Apply

6. **Hypothesize** what three factors cause wave height to vary in the ocean.
7. **Infer** how wave energy could be used to reduce Earth's dependence on its decreasing supply of fossil fuels?

Data and Observations

Sample data

Fan speed	Time	Wave height	Observations
Low	3 min.	2 mm	
	5 min.	3 mm	
Medium	3 min.	3.5 mm	
	5 min.	4.5 mm	
High	3 min.	5 mm	some waves crest over
	5 min.	5.5 mm	edge of box

Activity 17-2

Purpose

LS **Visual-Spatial** Students will observe and describe the factors that affect the generation of waves. L2 COOP LEARN

Process Skills

making models, observing and inferring, recognizing cause and effect, interpreting data, predicting

Time

35 minutes

Safety Precautions

Caution students to keep electrical cords and appliances away from water.

Activity Worksheets, pp. 5, 104-105

Teaching Strategies

Alternate Materials If a sufficient number of table-model, three-speed fans cannot be obtained, the activity can be done by placing three or four student setups on the floor in front of a large floor fan that operates at several speeds. Either an overhead or filmstrip projector works well in place of the recommended light source and ring-stand setup.

Troubleshooting If necessary, have students review Recognizing Cause and Effect in the Skill Handbook.

Answers to Questions

1. The longer the wind blows, the higher the wave.
2. The stronger the wind, the higher the wave.
3. The shadows are closer together and are more easily seen when the fan speed is increased.
4. The light shines onto the waves, and shadows are cast onto the paper.
5. When the fan was turned off, the waves disappeared.
6. The length of time that the wind blows, the speed of the wind, and the distance over which the wind blows cause wave height to vary.
7. Wave energy could turn turbines to generate electricity.

Assessment

Performance To further assess students' ability to understand factors that affect the height of waves, have them design an experiment to see how fetch (the distance over which the wind blows) affects wave height. Use the Performance Task Assessment List for Designing an Experiment in **PASC**, p. 23. P

3 Assess

Check for Understanding

FLEX Your Brain

Use the Flex Your Brain activity to have students explore WAVES.

Activity Worksheets, p. 5

Reteach

LS **Visual-Spatial** Use a wave demonstration spring to show the following characteristics of waves: crest, trough, wave height, and wavelength.

Extension

For students who have mastered this section, use the **Reinforcement** and **Enrichment** masters.

4 Close

•MINI•QUIZ•

Use the Mini Quiz to check students' recall of chapter content.

1. **The high point of a wave is the _____ .** *crest*
2. **The _____ is the horizontal distance between the crests of two successive waves.** *wavelength*
3. **_____ moves forward in a wave while particles in the wave remain in the same place.** *Energy*
4. **When a wave moves into shallow areas, water at the bottom of the wave is slowed down due to _____ with the ocean bottom.** *friction*

The Gravitational Effect of the Moon

For the most part, these tides or giant waves are caused by the interaction of gravity in the Earth-moon system. The moon and Earth are relatively close together, so the moon's gravity exerts a strong pull on Earth. The water in the oceans responds to this pull. The water is thrown outward as Earth and moon revolve around a common center of mass between them. These events are explained in **Figure 17-13.**

Two bulges of water form, one directly under the moon and one on the exact opposite side of Earth. As Earth spins, these bulges follow the moon on its daily transit. To the earthbound observer, these bulges appear as waves traveling across the oceans. The crests of the waves are the high tides.

As Earth rotates, different locations on Earth's surface pass through high and low tide. Many coastal locations, such as the Atlantic and Pacific coasts of the United States, experience two high tides and two low tides each day. Ocean basins vary in size and shape, so some coastal locations, such as many along the Gulf of Mexico, have only one high and one low tide each day.

The Gravitational Effect of the Sun

The sun also affects tides. The sun can strengthen or weaken the moon's effects. The moon, Earth, and the sun lined up together cause a greater effect called spring tides.

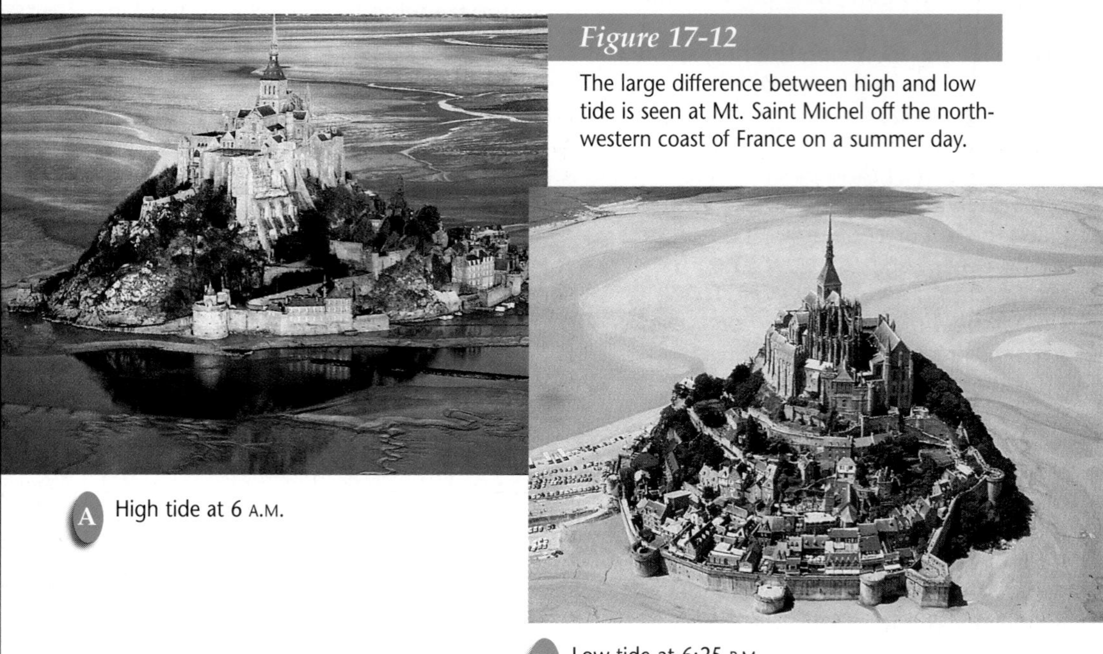

Figure 17-12

The large difference between high and low tide is seen at Mt. Saint Michel off the northwestern coast of France on a summer day.

A High tide at 6 A.M.

B Low tide at 6:25 P.M.

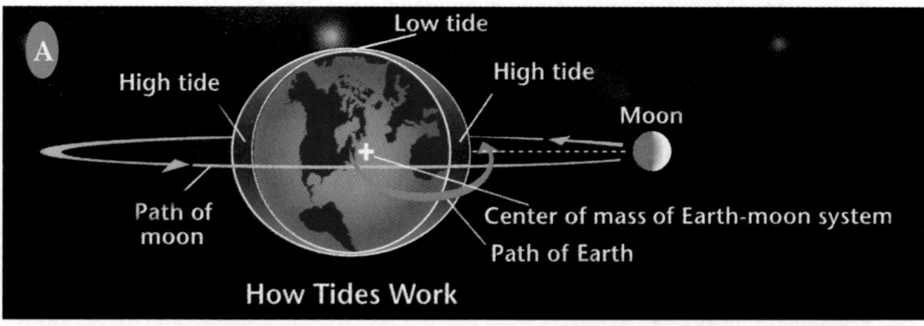

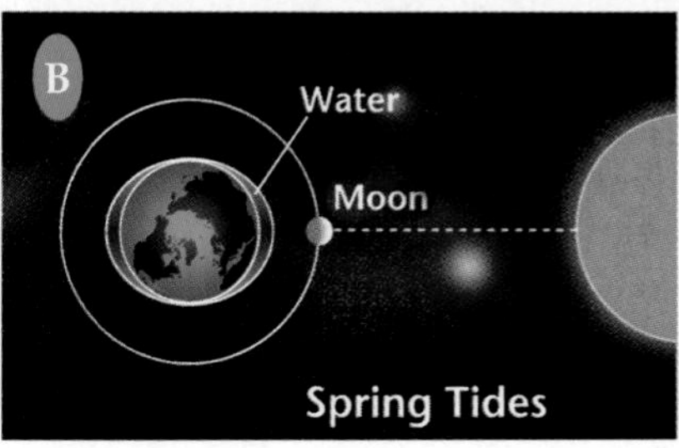

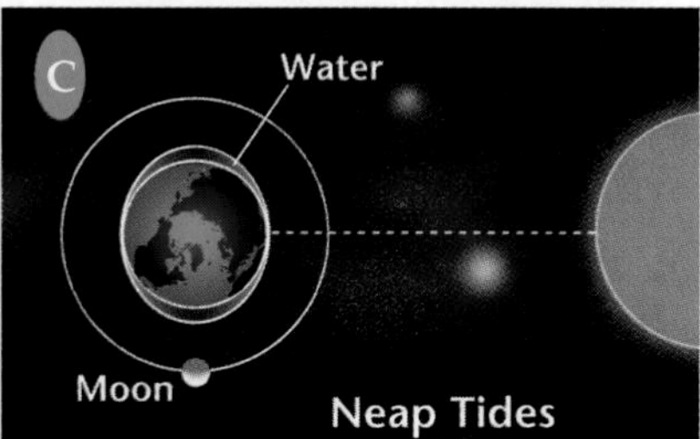

Figure 17-13

(A) The moon doesn't really revolve around Earth. They both revolve around a common center of mass called the barycentre. The action of the moon and Earth around the barycentre causes the bulge of water on the side of Earth opposite the moon. (B) When the sun, moon, and Earth are aligned, spring tides occur. (C) When the sun, moon, and Earth form a right angle, neap tides occur.

During spring tides, high tides are higher and low tides are lower than normal. When the sun, Earth, and the moon form a right angle, high tides are lower and low tides are higher than normal. These are called neap tides.

In this section, you've learned how the energy of the wind and gravity causes waves. In the next lesson, you'll see a way that people use the energy of these waves.

Section Wrap-up

Review

1. Describe the parts of an ocean wave.
2. What causes high tides?
3. **Think Critically:** At the ocean, you spot a wave about 200 m from shore. A few seconds later, the wave breaks on the beach. Explain why the water in the breaker is not the same water that was in the wave 200 m away.

Skill Builder

Comparing and Contrasting

Compare and contrast the effects of the sun and moon on Earth's tides. If you need help, refer to Comparing and Contrasting in the **Skill Handbook.**

Science Journal

In the waters off Southern California, the reproductive cycle of the grunion fish follows the tide schedule. Find out about the egg-laying habits of the grunion and then write about it in your Science Journal.

Section Wrap-up

Review

1. crest: highest part of the wave; trough: lowest part of the wave; wave height: vertical distance between crest and trough; wavelength: horizontal distance between the crests or troughs of two successive waves
2. High tides occur when the moon's gravity pulls on water particles and a bulge forms on the side of Earth facing the moon. At the same time, another bulge (high tide) forms on the opposite side of Earth because the water is thrown outward as Earth's axis revolves around the common center of mass between the moon and Earth.
3. **Think Critically** The wave particles do not move. It is energy that moves through the wave.

Science Journal

On several nights after the full moon in the spring and summer spawning season, grunion swim onto the beach and deposit their eggs in the sand. About ten nights later, as the tides are again increasing in height, the eggs are washed out of the sand and hatch.

Skill Builder

Both affect tides because of their gravitational attraction for each other and Earth. However, the effect of the moon is greater because it is closer to Earth than the sun.

Assessment

Process Have students compare and contrast crests and troughs in writing. Use the Performance Task Assessment List for Writing in Science in **PASC,** p. 87. P

Prepare

Section Background

In energy plants that depend on tides, turbines change the energy from the tides into mechanical energy. Then, generators change the mechanical energy into electricity.

1 Motivate

Bellringer

Before presenting the lesson, display **Section Focus Transparency 68** on the overhead projector. Assign the accompanying **Focus Activity** worksheet. L1 LEP

Tying to Previous Knowledge

In Chapter 8, students learned that the energy of moving water is great enough to erode sediments. In this section, students will learn how people use turbines to capture the energy of moving water to do work.

2 Teach

Content Background

Stress to students that tidal power plants are not built along most coastal areas because their usefulness is limited to those few locations in the world that experience tremendous tidal ranges.

Enrichment

Have students investigate the similarities of tidal dams and dams built on rivers. L1

SCIENCE & SOCIETY

17•4 ISSUE:

Tapping Tidal Energy

Objectives

- Explain the advantages of a tidal power plant in the Bay of Fundy.
- Describe how a tidal dam converts energy from tides into electricity.
- Consider the consequences of a power plant at the Bay of Fundy.

Tidal Power

Imagine having a constant supply of nonpolluting energy that you could use to generate electricity. No burning fossil fuels. No polluting the air. No worry about running out of electricity for heat, air conditioning, and appliances. In areas where there is a large tidal range, this can happen. Tides can be used to generate electricity.

Electric power-generating plants that use tidal energy already have been built in France, Russia, and China. In the Bay of Fundy in Nova Scotia, the tidal range reaches 16 m, the greatest tidal range on Earth. It is a perfect location for tapping the energy of the tides. At the Bay of Fundy, the water moves through a narrow opening into a funnel-shaped bay. At high tide, the water is trapped in the bay by the force of the incoming tide. Then, at low tide, the bay flushes out.

In the late 1980s, the Canadian government planned to build a tidal dam like the one in **Figure 17-14** in the Bay of Fundy. The large gates of the dam would let water enter the bay at high tide. Then the gates would close. Water would be stored behind the dam. As the tide went out, the dammed water would pass over turbines in the dam, generating electricity. A turbine is similar to a fan blade. When the water pushes against the blades, a turbine spins and generates electricity.

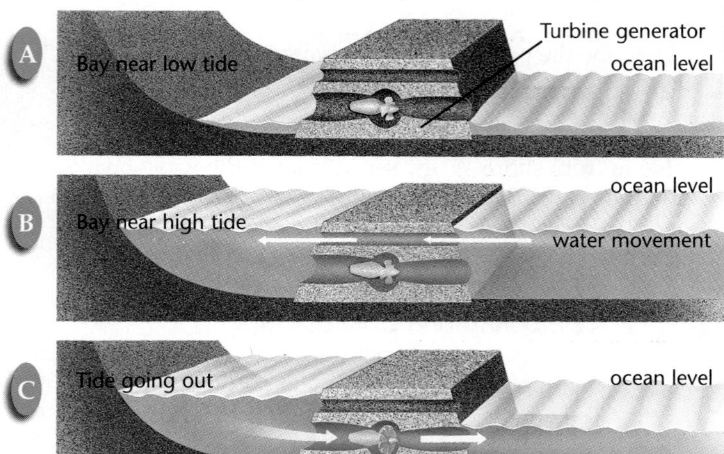

Figure 17-14
This diagram shows the basic concept of a tidal-dam power plant. As the tide starts to rise (A), water flows into the bay and becomes trapped by the dam (B). Then as the tide goes down, the water flows through the dam (C) and spins the turbine generator, making electricity.

Program Resources

Reproducible Masters
Study Guide, p. 72 L1
Reinforcement, p. 72 L1
Enrichment, p. 72 L3

Transparencies
Section Focus Transparency 68 L1

2 Points of View

A Tidal Dam Works Well

There would be no expenses for fuel, pollution control, or waste disposal. The cost of the power would be relatively low. Tidal energy will not run out.

A Tidal Dam Creates Problems

So far, this Canadian tidal dam has not been built. There are many reasons for this. It will be expensive, and unfortunately, tidal dams produce electricity at times not related to peak demand. The dam also may create environmental problems. Salt water could contaminate water wells. Valuable salt-marsh habitats could be lost. If these habitats were destroyed, many shorebirds and marine organisms would die. At the dam site, fish might be killed by the turbines. Also, the mud flats at the Bay of Fundy, where many migrating birds feed on mud shrimp, would be flooded by the water retained behind the dam.

Shores as far south as Boston, Massachusetts, 600 km away, could be affected. At low tide, some Boston harbor channels could become too shallow to use.

Figure 17-15

These houses on stilts along the Bay of Fundy indicate how much the water rises from low tide to high tide.

Section Wrap-up

Review

1. Why was the Bay of Fundy picked as a possible site to build a tidal power plant?
2. How does a tidal dam convert tidal energy into electricity?

Explore the Issue

When we make changes in our environment, we must consider the consequences. This certainly is the case with the building of a tidal dam at the Bay of Fundy. Consider the benefits and problems involved with the building of this dam. Do you think this tidal dam should be built? Explain your answer.

SCIENCE & SOCIETY

3 Assess

Check for Understanding

In a class discussion, ask students to explain the advantages and disadvantages of tapping tidal power.

Reteach

LS **Interpersonal** Have students make a chart showing the pros and cons of building tidal power plants. COOP LEARN

4 Close

•MINI•QUIZ•

1. **Dammed water would pass over ________ in a dam to generate energy.** *turbines*
2. **The Bay of Fundy has the greatest ________ on Earth.** *tidal range*

Section Wrap-up

Review

1. It experiences the greatest tidal range in the world. A vast amount of potential energy exists in these tides.
2. Water pushes against the blades of a turbine. The spinning turbine turns a generator, which produces electricity.

Explore the Issue

Some students will say the benefits outweigh the problems. Tidal power provides clean energy so pollution in the area will decrease. There will be no waste disposal problems. New jobs will be created. Other students will argue that the destruction of human property and animal and plant habitats makes the building of this dam a bad idea.

Community Connection

Power Plant Have a power plant engineer come to class to discuss how electricity is generated in your area.

Science Journal

Electrical Generators Have students research how generators work. Then, have them describe what they learn in their Science Journals. L2 LS

Sources

- Finney, Ben. *From Sea to Space.* Palmerston North, New Zealand: Massey University, 1992.
- Kyselka, Will. *An Ocean in Mind.* Honolulu, Hawaii: University of Hawaii Press, 1987.

Background

Archaeologists have been able to trace the migration of the ancestors of the Polynesians from the Bismarck Archipelago off the Northeast coast of New Guinea because these people made a distinctively decorated pottery called *Lapita.* Lapita is easy to identify and has been traced across Melanesia to Fiji, Tonga, and Samoa, where explorers arrived around 1500 B.C. The trail of artifacts continues to central East Polynesia—the Cook, Austral, Tuamoto and Marquesa Islands—and from there to Hawaii, Rapa Nui, and New Zealand.

Teaching Strategies

- Mention that meteorologists attribute the change in the trade winds for weeks during the summer to the heating of the Australian continent. Ask students how this might affect the trade winds. *The heat causes the air to warm and changes the winds.*
- Review some star-watching techniques for navigators. Remind students that Polaris, the north star, is at zenith for someone standing at the north pole. It is at the horizon for a navigator on the equator. A navigator at 20°N sees Polaris at 20° above the horizon. Mention that Hokulea is the zenith star for Hawaii and Sirius, the zenith star for Tahiti.

Science & History

Polynesian Art of Navigation

Captain James Cook, a British navigator, landed on the Hawaiian Islands in 1778. There he learned about the theory that the Polynesians originally migrated from the East Indies or Indonesia. At first, Cook didn't think this could be possible. To make such a journey, the Polynesians would have had to sail against the trade winds that blow from the east. Later on, Cook learned that during the months of November, December, and January, westerly winds with rain blow from the west, so this was possible.

In this chapter, you learned how ocean currents vary around the world. Early Polynesians used winds, waves, and currents to steer them from one Pacific island to another in double-hulled canoes *without instruments.* They did use maps showing star positions and currents.

Some Polynesians still use this method of navigation. Anthropologist Ben Finney and others have learned how ancient navigators sailed without instruments. The researchers built a double-hulled canoe like the kind used by ancient Polynesians to sail the ocean. The canoe was called *Hokule`a,* which is Hawaiian for "Arcturus," a star seen directly over Hawaii. Anthropologists hoped to find out whether the Polynesians could have sailed across currents to settle the Pacific islands.

The *Hokule`a* was sailed from Hawaii to Tahiti and back. The first navigator of *Hokule`a* was a Polynesian who learned to sail from his father and grandfather. He steered by zenith stars, those vertically above him, chiefly the North Star. He also learned to determine latitude by the stars and to understand the currents and waves. To reach Hawaii from Tahiti, the canoe had to go north in the Pacific and cross two great west-flowing ocean currents, the north equatorial and south equatorial. Between them is the east-flowing equatorial counter current. This is shown on the map at the left.

The *Hokule`a* made the round-trip from Hawaii to Tahiti to Hawaii, navigating the way Polynesians would have in ancient times.

Science Journal

Imagine how the Polynesians on the *Hokule`a* must have felt as they re-created a voyage made by their ancestors. Write a poem or an essay in your Science Journal that the Polynesians might have written about *Hokule`a.*

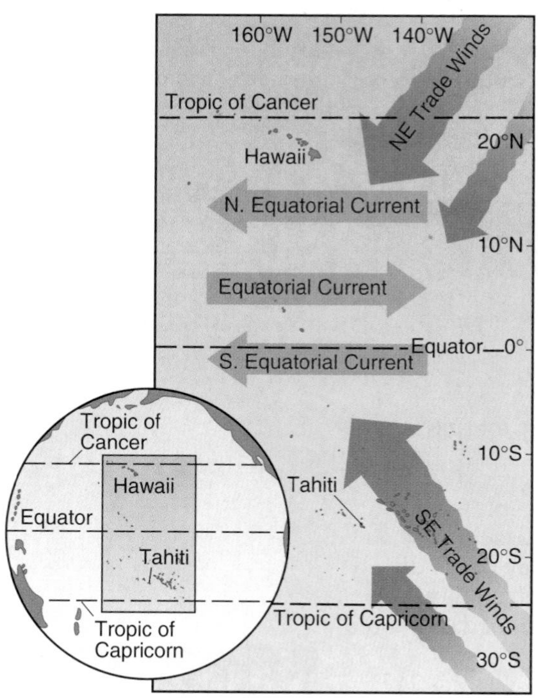

- For the Polynesians, distance traveled was determined from an estimate of the speed of the canoe—from its sound and feel as it traveled through the water and from the appearance of its wake. Ask students to describe how they have judged speed by sound and feeling.

Activity

IS Interpersonal In 1947, Thor Heyerdahl, a Norwegian, sailed on a raft named *Kon-Tiki* from Peru to the Tuamotos. He wanted to prove that voyagers on rafts could have come to Polynesia from Peru instead of from the east. Have student groups find out the basis for Heyerdahl's theory. Students may want to debate which theory is more reliable. L1 **COOP LEARN**

Chapter 17 Review

Summary

17-1: Ocean Water

1. Water that fills Earth's oceans may have started as water vapor released from volcanoes. Over millions of years, the water vapor condensed and rain fell, forming the oceans.
2. Groundwater and rivers weather rocks and cause some elements to dissolve. Rivers carry the dissolved elements to the oceans. Volcanoes also add elements to seawater.
3. Nearly 90 percent of the salt in seawater is halite. Ocean water also contains calcium, sulfate, and many other substances.

17-2: Ocean Currents

1. Friction between air and the ocean's surface causes surface currents. Surface currents are affected by the Coriolis effect. Currents are also deflected by landmasses.
2. Cool currents off western coasts originate far from the equator. Warmer currents along eastern coasts begin near the equator.
3. Differences in temperatures and densities between water masses in the oceans set up circulation patterns called density currents.

17-3: Ocean Waves and Tides

1. A wave is a rhythmic movement that carries energy. The crest is the highest point of a wave. The trough is the lowest point.
2. Energy moves forward while water particles move in place.
3. Wind causes water to pile up and form waves. Attraction among Earth, the moon, and the sun causes giant waves called tides.

17-4: Science and Society: Tapping Tidal Energy

1. Because of its high tidal range, the Bay of Fundy is a good place for tapping tidal energy to generate electricity.
2. A tidal dam can generate electricity.
3. Energy from tides is essentially nonpolluting but can cause problems such as changes in tidal ranges, flooding, and contamination.

Key Science Words

a. basin
b. breaker
c. crest
d. density current
e. salinity
f. surface current
g. tidal range
h. tide
i. trough
j. upwelling
k. wave

Reviewing Vocabulary

Match each phrase with the correct term from the list of Key Science Words.

1. low area that collects water
2. nutrient-rich water that comes to the surface
3. a horizontal current at the top of the ocean
4. the lowest point on a wave
5. movement as energy passes through water
6. a collapsing wave
7. mixes surface water deep into the ocean
8. difference between high and low tide
9. rise and fall of the ocean related to gravitational pull
10. amount of solids dissolved in seawater

Chapter 17 Review

Summary

Have students read the summary statements to review the major concepts of the chapter.

Reviewing Vocabulary

1. a
2. j
3. f
4. i
5. k
6. b
7. d
8. g
9. h
10. e

Assessment

Portfolio Encourage students to place in their portfolios one or two items of what they consider to be their best work. Examples include:

- Across the Curriculum, p. 479.
- Science Journal, p. 481.
- MiniLAB Analysis answers, p. 492 P

Performance Additional performance assessments may be found in **Performance Assessment** and **Science Integration Activities.** Performance Task Assessment Lists and rubrics for evaluating these activities can be found in Glencoe's **Performance Assessment in the Science Classroom.**

GLENCOE TECHNOLOGY

MindJogger Videoquiz

Chapter 17 Have students work in groups as they play the Videoquiz game to review key chapter concepts.

Chapter 17 Review

Checking Concepts

1. b
2. a
3. a
4. d
5. c
6. b
7. c
8. d
9. a
10. c

Understanding Concepts

11. High tides are bulges of water on either side of Earth due to gravitational attraction among Earth, the sun, and the moon and Earth's revolution around the common center of mass between the moon and Earth. Spring tides are tides that occur when Earth, the sun, and the moon are lined up.
12. Water evaporates from the warm Mediterranean Sea. This leaves more salt, so the water grows more dense. This dense water flows down under the less dense water of the Atlantic Ocean.
13. Cold water sinks, forcing warmer water to rise. These movements create density currents in the oceans. Water that is high in salinity sinks below less saline water, creating density currents.
14. Friction with the ocean bottom slows the bottom of the wave. The crests come together. The wave gets taller. The top of the wave moves faster than the bottom, which causes the wave to become lopsided and collapse. This is a breaker.
15. Warm currents tend to warm overlying air, while cold currents tend to cool the air in the area.

Chapter 17 Review

Checking Concepts

Choose the word or phrase that completes the sentence.

1. Ocean water may have developed from _______.
   a. salt marshes c. basins
   b. volcanoes d. surface currents
2. Chlorine gas enters the oceans from _______.
   a. volcanoes c. density currents
   b. rivers d. groundwater
3. _______ is the most common ocean salt.
   a. Chloride c. Halite
   b. Calcium d. Sulfate
4. Most surface currents are caused by _______.
   a. density differences c. salinity
   b. the Gulf Stream d. wind
5. The highest point on a wave is the _______.
   a. wave height c. crest
   b. trough d. wavelength
6. Ocean _______ are movements in which water alternately rises and falls.
   a. currents c. crests
   b. waves d. upwellings
7. A problem with tidal power plants is _______.
   a. fuel expense
   b. pollution
   c. they flood some environments
   d. they only work at high tide
8. The Coriolis effect causes currents in the northern hemisphere to turn _______.
   a. eastward c. left
   b. southward d. right
9. Tidal power plants use energy from _______.
   a. Earth's oceans c. fossil fuels
   b. salt marshes d. floods
10. Surface currents are affected by _______.
   a. crests c. the Coriolis effect
   b. upwellings d. calcium

Understanding Concepts

Answer the following questions in your Science Journal using complete sentences.

11. How do spring tides differ from high tides?
12. In the Mediterranean Sea, a density current forms because of the high rate of evaporation of water from the surface. Explain how evaporation can lead to the formation of a density current.
13. Describe the effect of temperature and salinity on density currents.
14. What happens to a wave when it enters shallow water?
15. How can surface currents affect climate?

Thinking Critically

16. Describe the position of the moon and sun when a low tide is higher than normal.
17. Halite makes up nearly 90 percent of the salt in ocean water. How much halite is found in 1000 kg of ocean water?
18. Why do silica and calcium remain in seawater for a shorter time than sodium?
19. Describe the Antarctic density current.
20. How could a tidal power plant in the Bay of Fundy cause flooding?

Developing Skills

If you need help, refer to the **Skill Handbook.**

21. **Recognizing Cause and Effect:** What causes upwelling? What effect does it have? When upwelling disappears from an area, what effect can this have?
22. **Comparing and Contrasting:** Compare and contrast waves and currents. How are they related?

Thinking Critically

16. Low tides are higher than normal when the sun, the moon, and Earth form a right angle.
17. Every 1000 L contains 35 Kg of dissolved solids. Thus, 0.90×35 Kg = 31.5 Kg of halite in each 1000 Kg of salt water.
18. Many marine organisms use these elements in their life processes, thus removing them from the ocean.
19. The Antarctic density current comes from the salt left over when ice forms at the South Pole. The salt increases the density of the cold water, and the water sinks beneath less-dense water.
20. Trapping water behind the dam would back up river water that flows into the bay. Areas along the rivers could be flooded.

23. **Comparing and Contrasting:** Compare the pros and cons of tidal power.

24. **Interpreting Data:** Based on the information in this chapter, is there more sodium or calcium dissolved in the oceans? Explain your answer.

25. **Graphing:** Plot the data from the table below on graph paper. Title your graph "Monthly Tides." Use a scale from −0.6 m to 2.4 m. The horizontal axis should show days 1 to 30.

Performance Assessment

1. **Design an Experiment:** Find out how a current moves a floating object. Base the test on the MiniLAB on page 492.
2. **Invention:** In Activity 17-1, you made fresh water. How could you desalinate seawater without electricity? Design a method, draw it, and display it for your class.
3. **Make a Lab Report:** Create an experiment to test the density of water at different temperatures.

Day	Height of High Tide (meters)	Height of Low Tide (meters)	Day	Height of High Tide (meters)	Height of Low Tide (meters)
1	1.4	0.5	16	1.6	0.2
2	1.5	0.4	17	1.7	0.1
3	1.7	0.2	18	1.7	−0.1
4	1.8	−0.1	19	1.8	−0.2
5	2.1	−0.3	20	1.9	−0.2
6	2.2	−0.5	21	1.9	−0.2
7	2.3	−0.6	22	1.9	−0.2
8	2.3	−0.6	23	1.9	−0.2
9	2.3	−0.6	24	1.8	−0.2
10	2.1	−0.5	25	1.7	−0.1
11	1.9	−0.2	26	1.6	0.0
12	1.6	−0.1	27	1.4	0.1
13	1.6	0.2	28	1.3	0.3
14	1.6	0.4	29	1.5	0.4
15	1.6	0.4	30	1.5	0.5

Chapter 17 Review

Developing Skills

21. **Recognizing Cause and Effect** Overlying water is carried away from an area by wind. This removal of water allows underlying cold water to rise to the surface. Upwelling brings materials to the surface; fishing is usually good. If upwelling disappears during El Niño, fishing is hurt.
22. **Comparing and Contrasting** Wind causes surface currents and waves. Currents carry water particles along with them. In waves, the water particles do not move horizontally along with the wave.
23. **Comparing and Contrasting** Students' responses will vary but should at least include the points discussed in Section 17-4.
24. **Interpreting Data** Because sodium isn't used by marine organisms as much as calcium is, there's more sodium dissolved in ocean waters.
25. **Graphing** Student graphs show tidal range for a beach during one month. Students should observe that when high tides were highest, low tides were lowest. When high tides were lowest, low tides were usually highest.

Performance Assessment

1. Accept reasonable designs. To produce a current, students might blow the water through a straw and observe that the cork moves with the current. Use the Performance Task Assessment List for Designing an Experiment in **PASC,** p. 23. P
2. They might use fire to heat the water, or they might just let the sun's radiation evaporate the water. Use the Performance Task Assessment List for Invention in **PASC,** p. 45. P
3. Students might use a hot plate and ice cubes to heat and cool water to different temperatures. They can add food coloring to the samples. By slowly adding water of one temperature to another, they will see density currents occur. If hydrometers are available, students can determine the actual density of each temperature sample. Hydrometers can be purchased from stores that sell aquarium supplies. Hydrometers can also be made. Use the Performance Task Assessment List for Lab Report in **PASC,** p. 47. P

Chapter Organizer

Section	Objectives	Activities/Features
Chapter Opener		**Explore Activity:** Make a model of a submersible. p. 503
18-1 **The Seafloor** (2 sessions, 1½ blocks)*	1. **Differentiate** the continental shelf from the continental slope and the abyssal plain. 2. **Describe** a mid-ocean ridge and an ocean trench. 3. **Describe** seafloor mining.	**Connect to Life Science,** p. 506 **MiniLAB:** What does a topographic map of the ocean basins show? p. 507 **Skill Builder:** Comparing and Contrasting, p. 508 **Science Journal,** p. 508 **Using Math:** p. 508 **Activity 18-1:** The Ups and Downs of the Ocean Floor, p. 509
18-2 **Life in the Ocean** (2 sessions, 1 block)*	1. **List** six things that the oceans provide for organisms. 2. **Describe** the relationship between photosynthesis and respiration. 3. **List** the key characteristics of plankton, nekton, and benthos.	**Connect to Physics,** p. 511 **Using Math,** p. 512 **MiniLAB:** What do plankton look like? p. 513 **Using Technology:** Drugs from the Sea, p. 514 **Problem Solving:** Washed Ashore, p. 515 **Activity 18-2:** Cleaning Up Oil Spills, pp. 516-517 **Skill Builder:** Using Variables, Constants, and Controls, p. 518 **Using Computers:** Graphics, p. 518
18-3 **Science and Society Technology: Pollution and Marine Life** (2 sessions, 1 block)*	1. **List** seven human activities that pollute the oceans. 2. **Explain** how ocean pollution affects the entire world. 3. **Determine** how we can live on this planet without destroying its oceans.	**Connect to Physics,** p. 520 **Explore the Technology,** p. 521 **People and Science:** Robert Ballard, Oceanographer, p. 522

* A complete Planning Guide that includes block scheduling is provided on pages 32T-35T.

Activity Materials

Explore	Activities	MiniLABs
page 503 clear, empty, 2-L soda bottle with cap; tap water; eyedropper	page 509 graph paper pages 516-517 safety goggles, apron, olive oil, pan, gravel, tap water, small pencils or toothpicks, sponge, paper towels, cotton balls, feathers, string, liquid soap, cardboard, eyedropper	page 507 **Figure 18-1** page 513 dropper, ocean water or fresh water containing plankton, microscope slide and coverslip, microscope

Chapter 18 Oceanography

Teacher Classroom Resources

Reproducible Masters	Transparencies	Teaching Resources
Study Guide, p. 73 **Reinforcement,** p. 73 **Enrichment,** p. 73 **Activity Worksheets,** pp. 108-109, 112 **Science and Society Integration,** p. 22 **Multicultural Connections,** pp. 39-40	**Section Focus Transparency 69,** The Underwater Out of the Ordinary **Teaching Transparency 35,** Ocean Floor Map	**Glencoe Earth Science Interactive Videodisc** **Earth Science CD-ROM** **Spanish Resources** **English/Spanish Audiocassettes** **Cooperative Learning Resource Guide** **Lab Partner** **Lab and Safety Skills** **Lesson Plans**
Study Guide, p. 74 **Reinforcement,** p. 74 **Enrichment,** p. 74 **Activity Worksheets,** pp. 110-111, 113 **Lab Manual 53,** Mapping the Ocean Floor **Science Integration Activity 18,** Small But Important **Concept Mapping,** p. 41 **Critical Thinking/Problem Solving,** p. 24 **Cross-Curricular Integration,** p. 22	**Section Focus Transparency 70,** Water Worlds **Science Integration Transparency 18,** Brown Algae Ride Ocean Currents	**Assessment Resources** **Chapter Review,** pp. 39-40 **Assessment,** pp. 111-114 **Performance Assessment in the Science Classroom (PASC)** **MindJogger Videoquiz** **Alternate Assessment in the Science Classroom** **Performance Assessment** **Chapter Review Software** **Computer Test Bank**
Study Guide, p. 75 **Reinforcement,** p. 75 **Enrichment,** p. 75	**Section Focus Transparency 71,** Oil and Water Don't Mix **Teaching Transparency 36,** Sources of Ocean Pollution	

Key to Teaching Strategies

The following designations will help you decide which activities are appropriate for your students.

L1 Level 1 activities should be within the ability range of all students.

L2 Level 2 activities should be within the ability range of the average to above-average student.

L3 Level 3 activities are designed for the ability range of above-average students.

LEP LEP activities should be within the ability range of Limited English Proficiency students.

LS These activities are designed to address different learning styles.

COOP LEARN Cooperative Learning activities are designed for small group work.

P These strategies represent student products that can be placed into a best-work portfolio.

GLENCOE TECHNOLOGY

The following multimedia resources are available from Glencoe.

The Infinite Voyage Series

Secrets from a Frozen World

Science and Technology Videodisc Series (STVS)

Earth & Space

Studying the Pacific Ocean

Earth Science CD-ROM

Teacher Classroom Resources

This is a representation of key blackline masters available in the Teacher Classroom Resources.

Teaching Aids

Section Focus Transparencies

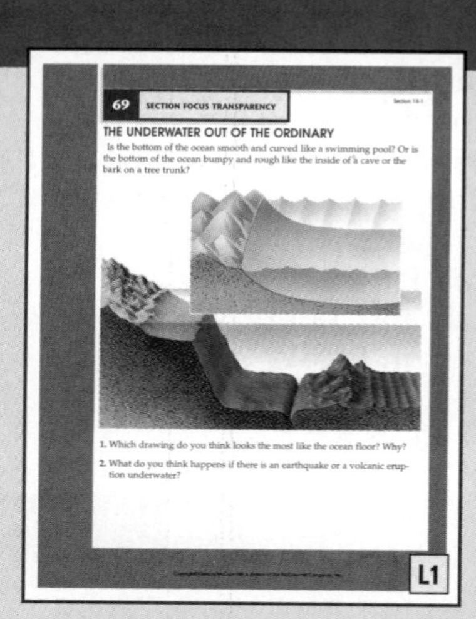

Science Integration Transparencies

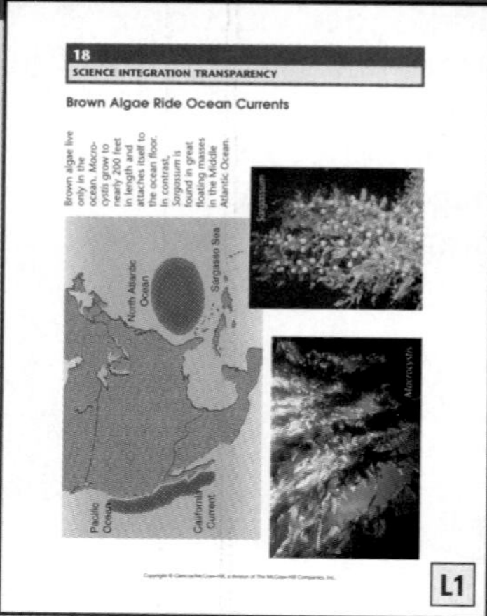

Teaching Transparencies

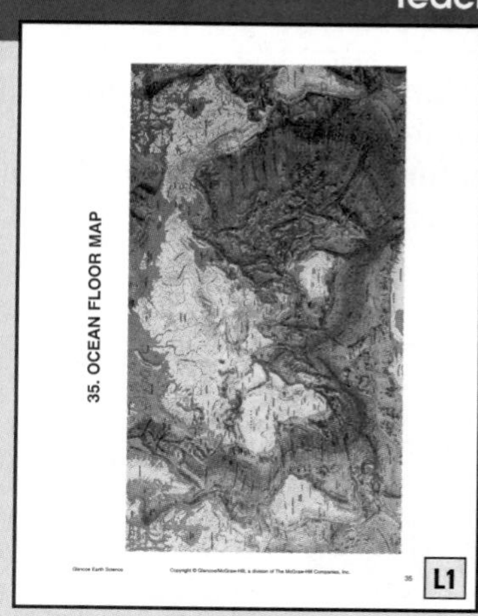

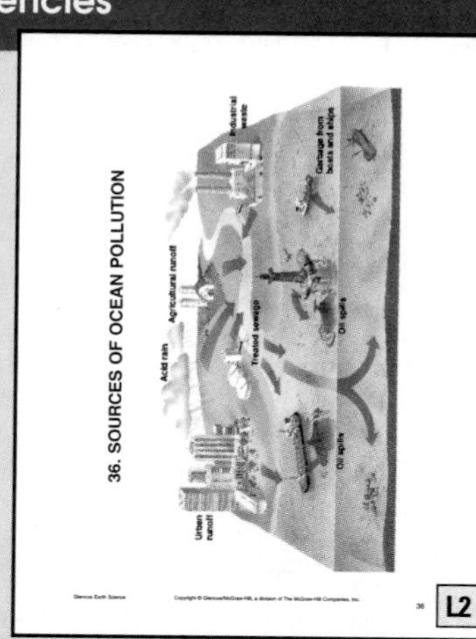

Meeting Different Ability Levels

Study Guide

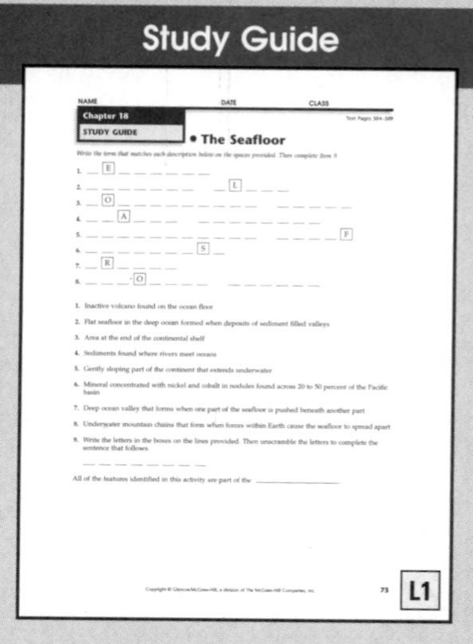

Reinforcement

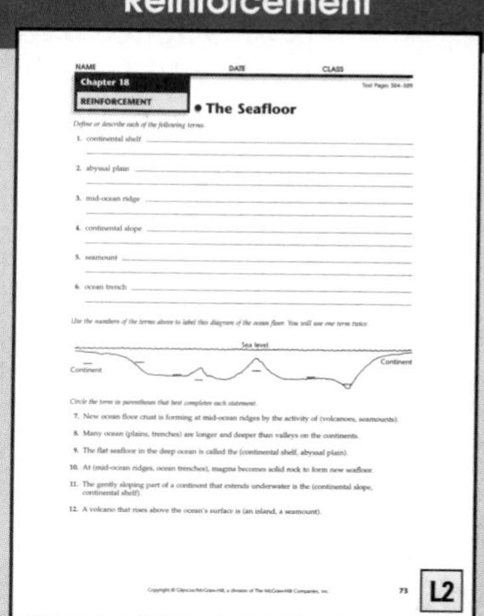

Enrichment Worksheets

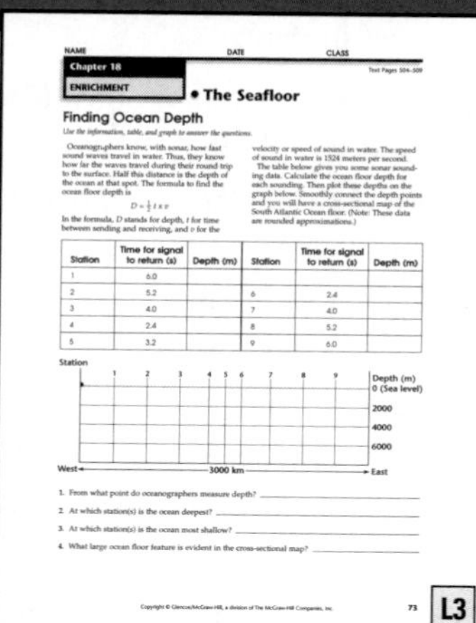

Hands-On Activities

Science Integration Activity

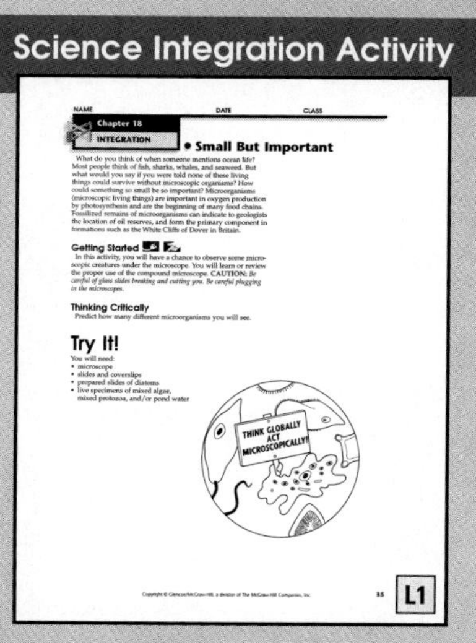
Chapter 18 INTEGRATION
• Small But Important
Getting Started
Thinking Critically
Try It!

L1

Lab Manual

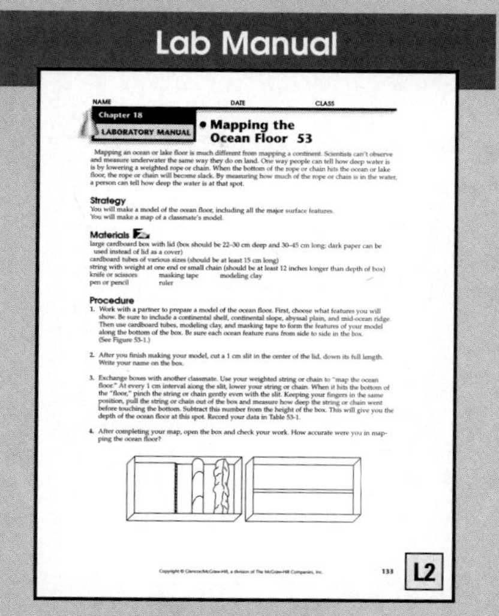
Chapter 18 LABORATORY MANUAL
• Mapping the Ocean Floor 53
Strategy
Materials
Procedure
L2

Assessment

Performance Assessment

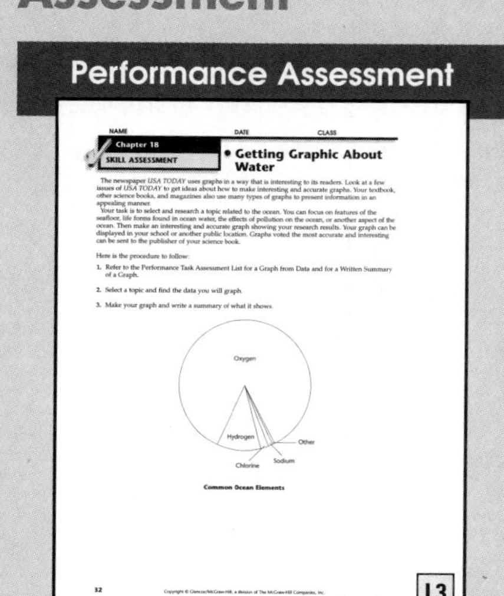
Chapter 18 SKILL ASSESSMENT
• Getting Graphic About Water

L3

Enrichment and Application

Critical Thinking/ Problem Solving

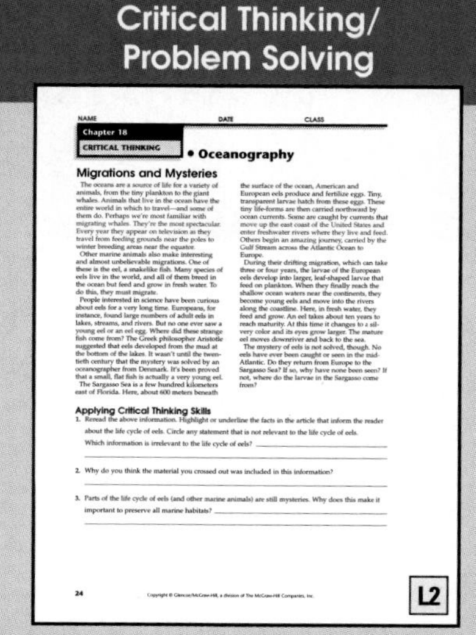
Chapter 18 CRITICAL THINKING
• Oceanography
Migrations and Mysteries
Applying Critical Thinking Skills
L2

Cross-Curricular Integration

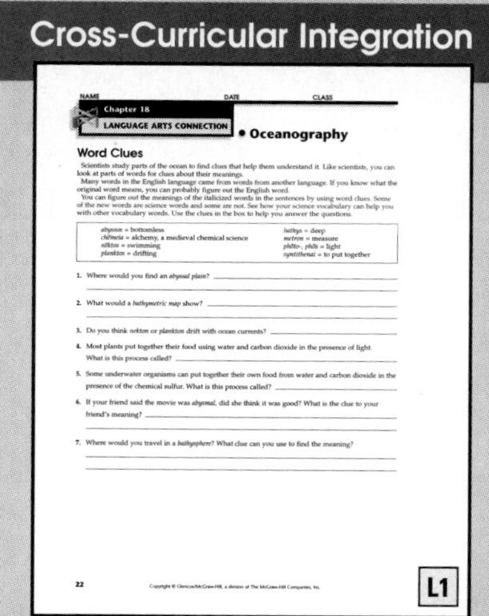
Chapter 18 LANGUAGE ARTS CONNECTION
• Oceanography
Word Clues
L1

Science and Society Integration

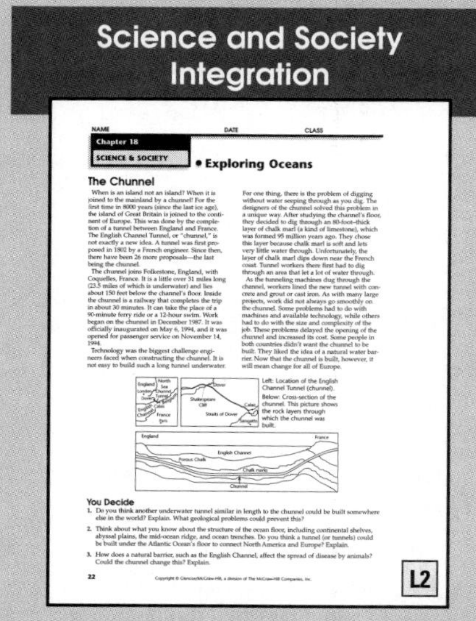
Chapter 18 SCIENCE & SOCIETY
• Exploring Oceans
The Channel
You Decide
L2

Multicultural Connections

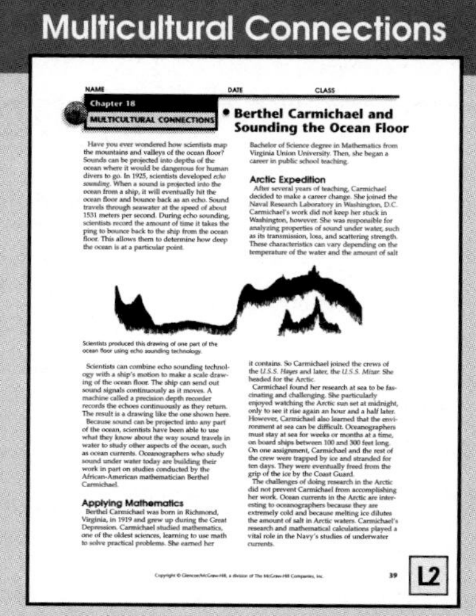
Chapter 18 MULTICULTURAL CONNECTIONS
• Berthel Carmichael and Sounding the Ocean Floor
Arctic Expedition
Applying Mathematics
L2

Concept Mapping

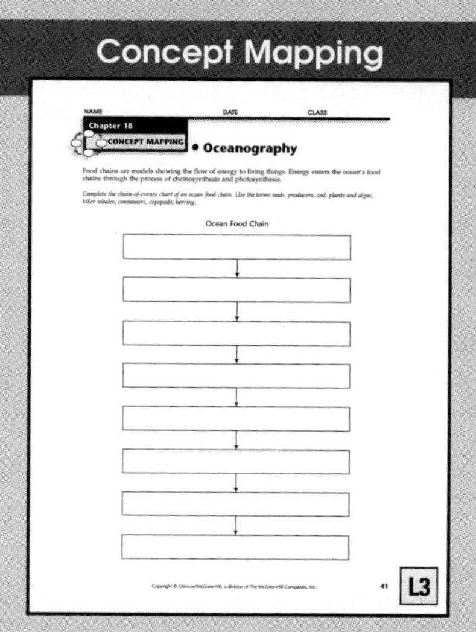
Chapter 18 CONCEPT MAPPING
• Oceanography

L3

Chapter 18

Oceanography

CHAPTER OVERVIEW

Section 18-1 The scale, structure, and origin of ocean bottom features are described. Seafloor mining is explored.

Section 18-2 Life processes and the interactions among plankton, nekton, and benthos are presented.

Section 18-3 **Science and Society** Some of the human activities that pollute oceans are discussed.

Chapter Vocabulary

continental shelf
continental slope
abyssal plain
mid-ocean ridge
trench
photosynthesis
chemosynthesis
plankton
nekton
benthos
reef
pollution
pollutant

Theme Connection

Scale and Structure/Systems and Interactions The scale and structure of ocean floor topography is presented. The systems and interactions theme includes discussions of the interdependency of plankton, nekton, and benthos and ways humans pollute oceans.

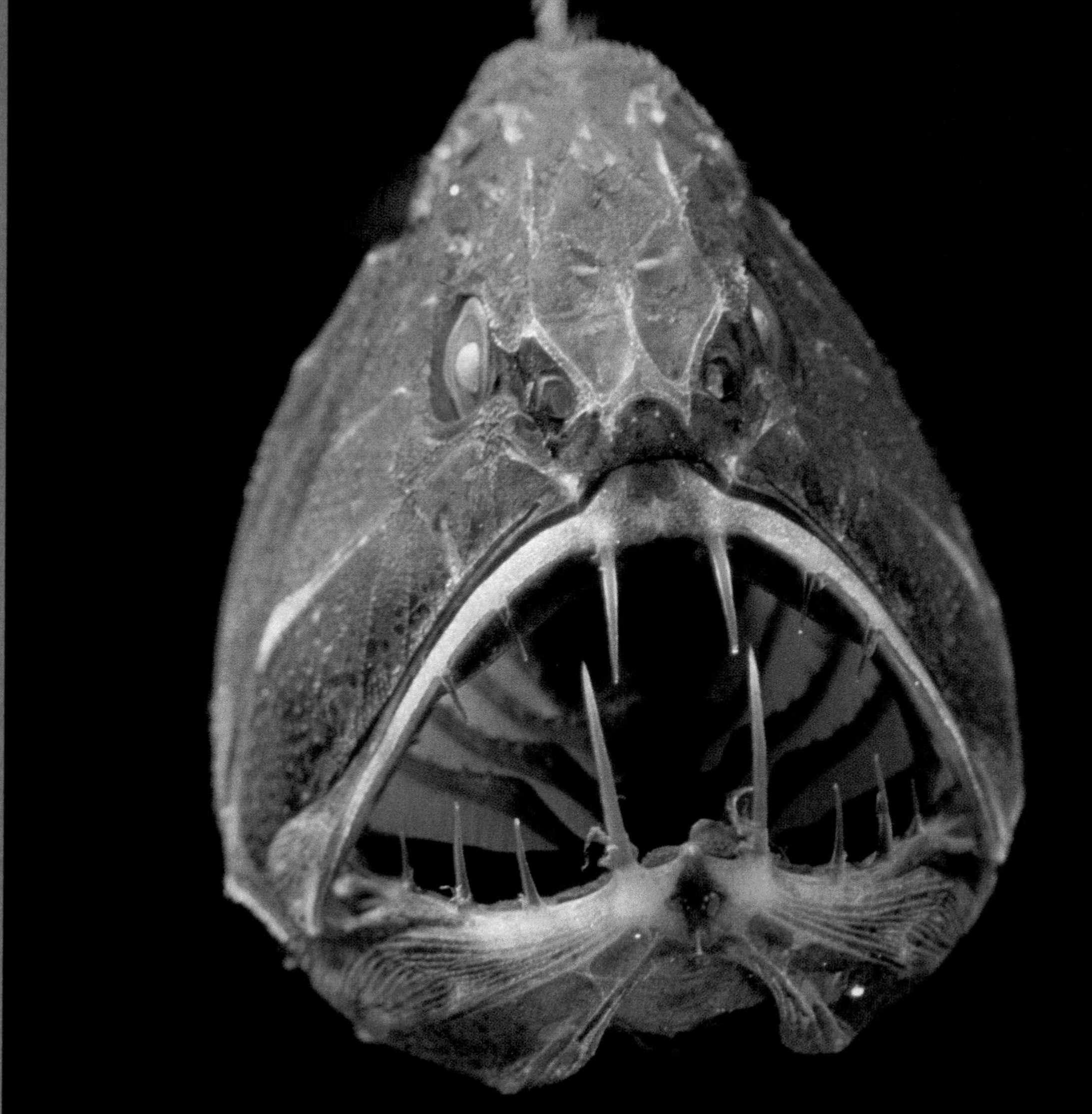

Previewing the Chapter

Learning Styles

Look for the following logo for strategies that emphasize different learning modalities. LS

Visual-Spatial	Explore, p. 503; Activity, p. 505; Visual Learning, pp. 505, 506, 519, 520; MiniLAB, pp. 507, 513; Activity 18-1, p. 509
Interpersonal	Reteach, p. 515; Activity 18-2, pp. 516-517; Discussion, p. 520
Logical-Mathematical	Using Math, pp. 508, 512; Inclusion Strategies, p. 520
Linguistic	Science Journal, pp. 505, 513; Across the Curriculum, p. 512; Reteach, p. 520

LS

Chapter

18 Oceanography

In the Pacific Ocean Basin, ocean floor is being destroyed. In the Atlantic Basin, new seafloor is forming. Where the seafloor is spreading apart, communities of organisms live deep in the ocean. This bony, hard-bodied fish, called an anoplogaster, swims in the deep waters of the Pacific Ocean, west of Peru. We were not aware of some communities of organisms until a submersible called *Alvin* explored the ocean bottom in 1977. How do submersibles like *Alvin* dive and surface in the oceans?

EXPLORE ACTIVITY

Make a model of a submersible.

1. Fill a 2-L, plastic soda bottle three-quarters full of water.
2. Draw water into an eyedropper. Leave some air in the bulb of the dropper and place the dropper in the plastic bottle, bulb end up. The dropper should float.
3. Put a cap on the bottle, then gently squeeze the sides of the bottle.

Observe: What happens to the level of the water inside the eyedropper and what happens to the eyedropper? What happens when pressure on the bottle is released? Answer these questions in your Science Journal.

...ing Science Skills

...ill Builders, you will **compare and contrast** and ...ables, constants, and controls.

...ctivities, you will **make and use a graph, interpret** ...esign an experiment, and **hypothesize.**

...iniLABs, you will **interpret a scientific illustration,** ...nferences, **observe,** and **classify.**

Assessment Planner

...age 523 for suggested items that ...night select for their portfolios.

...nce Assessment

... 523 for additional Performance ...nt options.
...lers, pp. 508, 518
..., pp. 507, 513
... 18-1, p. 509; 18-2, pp. 516-517

Content Assessment

Section Wrap-ups, pp. 508, 518, 521
Chapter Review, pp. 523-525
Mini Quizzes, pp. 508, 518

Group Assessment

Opportunities for group assessment occur with Cooperative Learning Strategies and Flex Your Brain Activities.

EXPLORE ACTIVITY

Purpose

LS **Visual-Spatial** Use the Explore Activity to introduce students to submersibles. Inform students that much of what we know about the oceans was observed by people in submersibles. L1 LEP COOP LEARN

Preparation

Have each student bring in a clean, empty, 2-L plastic bottle with a cap.

Materials

2-L plastic bottle with cap, beaker, eyedropper

Teaching Strategies

Make students aware that there will be a very delicate balance between floating and sinking of the eyedropper. Suggest that they place the eyedropper in a beaker of water and adjust the amount of water in the eyedropper until the top of the dropper is even with the top of the water. At this point, the eyedropper is neutrally buoyant. Then, have them place the eyedropper into the liter bottle of water.

Observe

When water is pushed inside the eyedropper, it gains mass and sinks. When pressure is released, the compressed air inside the eyedropper expands and pushes the water out. The eyedropper has less mass and rises.

Assessment

Performance Have students hypothesize how submersibles rise and sink in the oceans. Use the Performance Task Assessment List for Formulating a Hypothesis in **PASC**, p. 21. P

Section 18•1

Prepare

Section Background

When the last ice age was at its peak, sea level was approximately 110 meters lower than it is today. Many of the structures on the continental shelf were at or above sea level.

Preplanning

To prepare for Activity 18-1, obtain graph paper for each student.

1 Motivate

Bellringer

Before presenting the lesson, display **Section Focus Transparency 69** on the overhead projector. Assign the accompanying **Focus Activity** worksheet. L1 LEP

Tying to Previous Knowledge

Students learned in Chapter 11 about plate tectonics. In this section they will learn more about plate boundary structures on the ocean floor.

GLENCOE TECHNOLOGY

CD-ROM

Earth Science CD-ROM

Have students perform the interactive exploration for Chapter 18 to reinforce important chapter concepts and thinking processes.

18•1 The Seafloor

Science Words

continental shelf
continental slope
abyssal plain
mid-ocean ridge
trench

Objectives

- Differentiate the continental shelf from the continental slope.
- Describe a mid-ocean ridge, an abyssal plain, and an ocean trench.
- Describe seafloor mining.

Ocean Basin Features

You can find the biggest mountains, the deepest valleys, and the flattest plains on Earth not on land but at the bottom of the ocean. In this chapter, you'll learn how the mountains, valleys, and plains on the ocean bottom differ from those on the continents. **Figure 18-1** shows major features of the ocean basins.

Beyond the ocean shoreline is the continental shelf. The **continental shelf** is a gradually sloping end of a continent that extends out under the ocean. Along some coasts, the continental shelf extends a long distance. On North America's Atlantic and Gulf coasts, it extends 100 to 350 km into the sea.

Program Resources

Reproducible Masters

Study Guide, p. 73 L1
Reinforcement, p. 73 L1
Enrichment, p. 73 L3
Activity Worksheets, pp. 5, 108-109, 112 L1
Science & Society Integration, p. 22
Multicultural Connections, pp. 39-40

Transparencies

Section Focus Transparency 69 L1
Teaching Transparency 35

But on the Pacific Coast, where mountains are close to the shore, the shelf is only 10 to 30 km wide. The ocean covering the shelf varies from a few centimeters to 150 m deep. As you will see, the continental shelf illustrated in **Figure 18-2** resembles a shelf in the Atlantic Basin.

At the end of the shelf is the continental slope. The **continental slope** is the end of the continent extending from the outer edge of the continental shelf down to the ocean floor. The continental slope is steeper than the continental shelf. Beyond the continental slope lie the trenches, valleys, plains, and ridges of the ocean basin.

In the ocean, currents flow along the continental shelves and down the slopes and deposit sediment on the seafloor. These deposits fill in valleys. Deep in the ocean, this creates flat seafloor areas called **abyssal plains.** Abyssal plains are from 4000 to 6000 km deep in the ocean and can be seen in various regions of the map below.

Figure 18-1

This map shows the features of the ocean basins: mountain ranges, trenches, valleys, and plains. *Find a trench and the Mid-Atlantic Ridge.*

Use **Teaching Transparency 35** as you teach this lesson.

Science Journal

Ocean Features Ask each student to write a paragraph that begins with: "Many landforms were revealed the day that the oceans suddenly disappeared. I saw..." This activity will lead to a discussion of topographic features of ocean basins. L1 LS

2 Teach

Activity

LS **Visual-Spatial** Obtain bathymetric maps or use the one on pages 504-505. Refer to them frequently throughout the remainder of this section. Have students contrast the width of the continental shelf off the east coast of the United States with that off the west coast. L1

Visual Learning

Figure 18-1 Find a trench and the Mid-Atlantic Ridge. *The Mid-Atlantic Ridge in the mid-Atlantic basin is easy to see. Look for trenches in the Pacific basin.* Ask students: **Which ocean basins are getting larger? Which ocean basin is getting smaller? How do you know?** *The Atlantic and Indian Ocean basins are getting larger. Plates are diverging at their mid-ocean ridges. The Pacific basin is getting smaller. Crust is disappearing into trenches as the plates converge. Students should know because the Pacific has trenches.* LEP LS

Inquiry Questions

- **Where is the oldest crust on the Atlantic Ocean bottom? Where is the youngest crust?** *The oldest crust is at its margins; the youngest is in its middle.*
- **Have the ocean basins always been in the same locations as they are today? Explain.** *No, the locations of oceans have changed throughout geologic time because of moving plates, the formation of new ocean floor, the destruction of old ocean crusts, and climatic change.*

CONNECT TO
LIFE SCIENCE

Answer Water of the continental shelves is shallow enough for sunlight to penetrate and rich in minerals because of runoff from the land.

Visual Learning

Figure 18-2 A trench destroys old ocean crust. At a mid-ocean ridge, new crust forms. A trench looks like a ditch. A ridge looks like mountains. LEP IS

GLENCOE TECHNOLOGY

Videodisc

STVS: Earth & Space

Disc 3, Side 2

Studying the Pacific Ocean (Ch. 14)

3 Assess

Check for Understanding

Have students do Activity 18-1.

Reteach

Divide students into groups of five. Have each student in the group write one of the terms learned in this section on one side of a 3" × 5" note card and its meaning on the opposite side. Then, have students quiz one another on the terms.

Extension

For students who have mastered this section, use the **Reinforcement** and **Enrichment** masters.

CONNECT TO
LIFE SCIENCE

Marine plants need minerals and sunlight to survive. *Infer* from this why many marine plants live on the continental shelves.

Plate Boundary Structures

The ocean floor map in **Figure 18-1** shows structures related to plate movements occurring on the seafloor. In Chapter 11, you learned that some crustal plates under the ocean are diverging. Where these plates diverge, new crust forms. Some plates on the ocean floor are converging. At convergent boundaries, old ocean crust descends beneath other crust and is destroyed.

The place where new ocean floor forms is called a **mid-ocean ridge.** A mid-ocean ridge resembles a chain of mountains. New crust forms along the mid-ocean ridge as a result of volcanic eruptions and the upwelling of molten lava through cracks. Magma from Earth's interior oozes from these cracks. When the magma hits the water, it cools quickly into solid rock and forms new seafloor.

Seamounts are inactive volcanic cones found on the ocean floor. Some scientists theorize that these old volcanoes erupted on mid-ocean ridges where new crust formed. As the new crust moved further from the ridge, these seamounts moved with it. After millions of years, the volcanoes became inactive. Seamounts that extend up out of the ocean are volcanic islands and are shown in **Figure 18-2.**

Figure 18-2

This illustration shows some features found in ocean basins. (Features in this diagram are not to scale.)

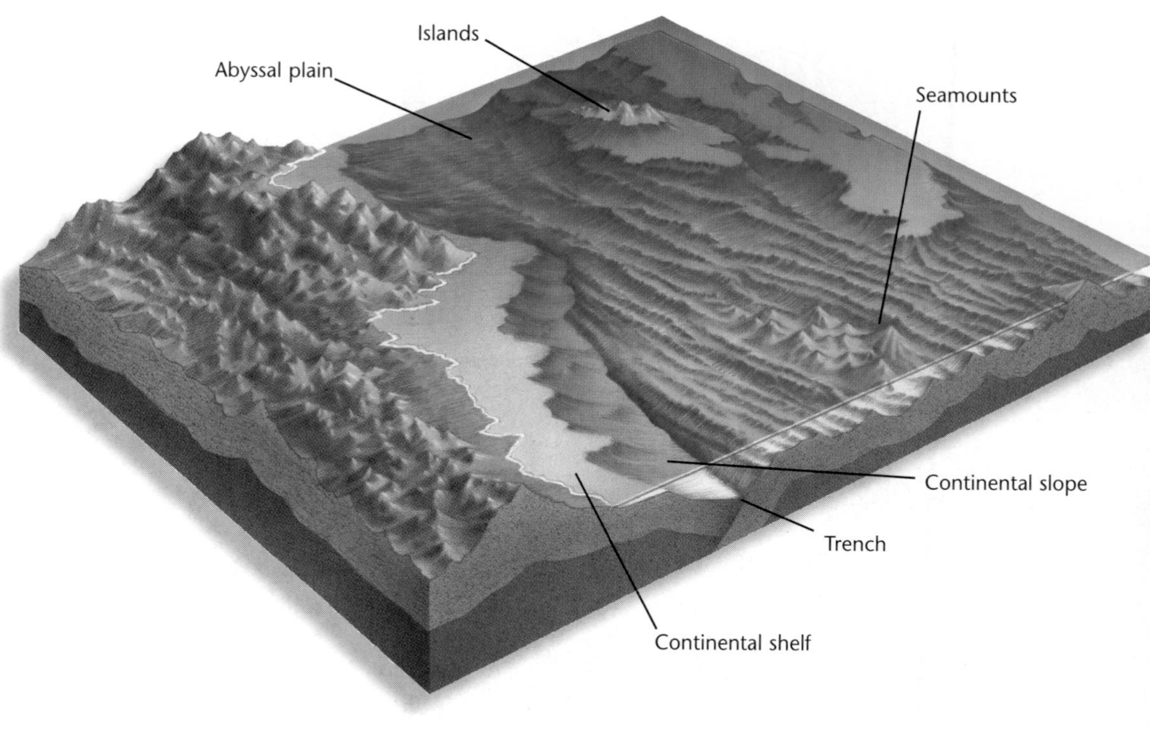

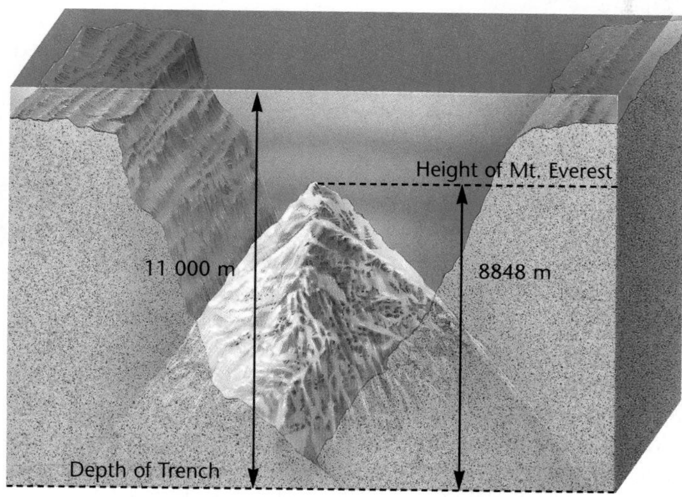

Figure 18-3

If Earth's tallest mountain, Mt. Everest, were set in the bottom of the Marianas Trench of the Pacific Basin, it would be covered with more than 2000 m of water.

On the ocean floor, crustal plates converge at trenches. A **trench** is a long, narrow, steep-sided depression in the ocean floor where one crustal plate is forced beneath another. Most trenches are found in the Pacific Basin. Oceanic trenches are often longer and deeper than any valley on any continent. The Marianas Trench, the deepest place in the Pacific, is 11 km deep. The Grand Canyon is only 1.6 km deep. Another comparison is shown in **Figure 18-3.**

Not only are trenches the deepest places on Earth, they are also the most geologically active. Seaquakes and chains of volcanoes often occur along trenches.

Mining the Seafloor

People have always collected salt from ocean water. About one third of all common salt used to season food comes from the sea. Now we also obtain oil and gas from under the sea.

Continental Shelf Deposits

There are many petroleum and natural gas deposits in continental shelf sediments. To pump these substances to the surface, drills are attached to floating vessels and fixed platforms. Approximately 20 percent of the world's oil comes from under the seabed.

Other deposits on the continental shelf are also mined. In Chapter 8, you learned that when a river loses its velocity, it can no longer carry as much sediment. When this occurs, some of the sediment is deposited. These deposits, called *placer deposits,* are mined around the world. Placer deposits can occur in coastal regions where rivers entering the ocean suddenly slow down. Sand, metals, and even diamonds are mined from placer deposits in some coastal regions.

MiniLAB

What does a topographic map of the ocean basins show?

Procedure

1. Use the map in **Figure 18-1.**
2. Trace a mid-oceanic ridge with your finger.
3. Observe the width of the continental shelves at various locations around the world.

Analysis

1. Locate a trench and give its approximate longitude and latitude.
2. Describe the continental shelves of Australia and Alaska.

MiniLAB

Purpose

LS **Visual-Spatial** Students will interpret information from a topographic map of the ocean floor. L1

COOP LEARN

Materials

Figure 18-1

Teaching Strategies

Troubleshooting Have magnifying glasses available for visually impaired students to observe **Figure 18-1.** Large topographic (bathymetric) maps of the Pacific, Atlantic, and Indian Ocean basins are available from scientific catalog companies or from the National Geographic Society.

Analysis

1. Answers will vary, but most trenches are located in the Pacific Ocean basin.
2. The continental shelf of Australia is wide except at the abrupt drop on the east coast. Around Alaska, the continental shelf is wide, especially under the Bering Strait and Sea.

Assessment

Performance Have students use **Figure 18-1** to locate abyssal plains. Use the Performance Task Assessment List for Making Observations and Inferences in **PASC**, p. 17. P

Activity Worksheets, pp. 5, 112

4 Close

•MINI•QUIZ•

Use the Mini Quiz to check students' recall of chapter content.

1. **The flat part of the continent that extends out from the continent under ocean water is the _____ .** *continental shelf*
2. **_____ are the flattest areas on Earth.** *Abyssal plains*
3. **Alongside diverging plate boundaries are mountain chains called _____ .** *mid-ocean ridges*

Section Wrap-up

Review

1. Both structures are on the ocean basin floor. Ocean ridges are created where plates diverge. Trenches are where plates converge.
2. They form where rivers enter the ocean, lose their energy of motion, and drop sediments.
3. **Think Critically** Both will become submerged.

Science Journal

Many countries claim mining rights to 322 km of seafloor that border them. This is called their economic zone. Water beyond the economic zones of all countries is considered to be international water, and many countries have agreed that it cannot be mined. However, some countries do not border oceans, but want the right to mine them. Other countries border the ocean, can mine their own economic zone, but want to be able to mine in international waters also. P

Figure 18-4

These manganese nodules lie on the floor under the Pacific Ocean.

USING MATH

Using the data from Activity 18-1 on page 509, calculate the average depth of the Atlantic Ocean floor along the 39° north latitude line.

Deep-Water Deposits

Valuable minerals are being deposited on the ocean floor. As molten substances and hot water are forced into cool ocean water through holes and cracks along ridges, "chimneys" of mineral deposits sometimes form. Today, no one is trying to mine these minerals from the depths, but in the future, these deposits may become important.

In addition to these deposits, other minerals in solution precipitate out and form solids on the ocean floor. Manganese nodules are small black lumps strewn across 20 to 50 percent of the Pacific Basin. **Figure 18-4** shows examples of these nodules. Manganese nodules form in a chemical process not fully understood. They concentrate around nuclei such as discarded sharks' teeth. They grow slowly, perhaps as little as 1 mm to 10 mm per million years. These nodules are rich in manganese, nickel, and cobalt, all of which are used in the manufacture of steel, paint, and batteries. Most of the nodules lie thousands of meters deep in the ocean and are not currently being mined by industry, although suction devices similar to huge vacuum cleaners have been tested to raise them.

In this section, you've learned about the features of ocean basins and how they relate to seafloor spreading and seafloor disappearance. You've also been introduced to the idea of seafloor mining. In the next section, you'll learn about organisms that live in the oceans.

Section Wrap-up

Review

1. Compare and contrast ocean ridges and trenches.
2. How do placer deposits form?
3. **Think Critically:** If sea level rises significantly because of global warming, how will island and continental shelf regions be affected?

Skill Builder

Comparing and Contrasting

Compare and contrast the continental shelf, the continental slope, and the abyssal plain. If you need help, refer to Comparing and Contrasting in the **Skill Handbook.**

Science Journal

Nations disagree about mining rights to mineral deposits. Since 1958, nations have met to decide international policy at the United Nations Law of the Sea Conferences. Research these conferences and find out why nations cannot agree. Summarize information in your Science Journal.

Skill Builder

The continental shelf is a flat, wide extension of a continent. The continental slope is the steeper slope at the boundary between the continental shelf and the ocean basin floor. Beyond the slope is the flat part of the ocean—the abyssal plain.

Assessment

Performance Assess students' abilities to compare and contrast by having them compare and contrast in writing continental shelf deposits and deep water deposits. Use the Performance Task Assessment List for Writing in Science in **PASC,** p. 87. P

Activity 18-1

The Ups and Downs of the Ocean Floor

In Chapter 5, you graphed a profile of the United States. It is not easy to see the ocean floor, but data on depth of the ocean have been collected. In this activity, you will use these data to profile the Atlantic Ocean at 39° north latitude.

Problem

What does the ocean floor look like?

Materials

- graph paper

Procedure

1. Set up a graph as shown below.
2. Examine the data listed in the table. These data were collected at 29 ocean locations along 39° north latitude from New Jersey to Portugal.
3. Plot each data point and connect the points with a smooth line.
4. Color the ocean bottom brown and the water blue.

Analyze

1. What ocean-floor structures occur between 160 and 1050 km east of New Jersey? Between 2000 and 4500 km? Between 5300 and 5600 km?
2. When a profile of a feature is drawn to scale, both the horizontal and vertical scales must be the same. What is the vertical scale of your profile? What is the horizontal scale?
3. Does your profile give an accurate picture of the ocean floor? Explain.

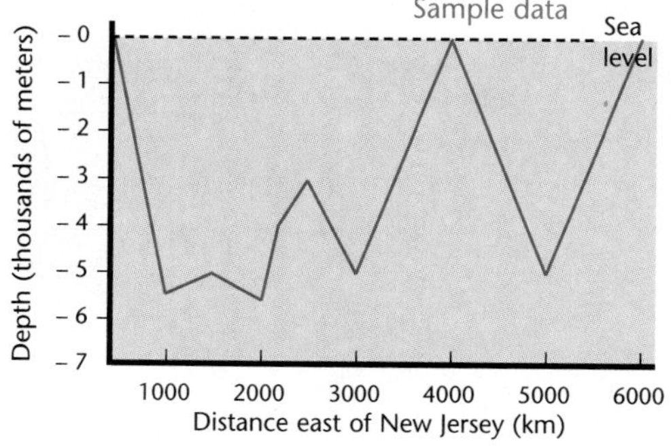

Data and Observations

Station Number	Distance from New Jersey (km)	Depth to Ocean Floor (m)
1	0	0
2	160	165
3	200	1800
4	500	3500
5	800	4600
6	1050	5450
7	1450	5100
8	1800	5300
9	2000	5600
10	2300	4750
11	2400	3500
12	2600	3100
13	3000	4300
14	3200	3900
15	3450	3400
16	3550	2100
17	3600	1330
18	3700	1275
19	3950	1000
20	4000	0
21	4100	1800
22	4350	3650
23	4500	5100
24	5000	5000
25	5300	4200
26	5450	1800
27	5500	920
28	5600	180
29	5650	0

Activity 18-1

Purpose

IS **Visual-Spatial** Students will make and analyze a profile map of the ocean floor. L1

Process Skills

making and using graphs, using numbers, observing and inferring, interpreting data, forming operational definitions, interpreting scientific illustrations, making models, measuring in SI

Time

30-40 minutes

Activity Worksheets, pp. 5, 108-109

Teaching Strategies

Troubleshooting Be sure that students realize that the graph is set up in a form different from what they may be used to. Usually, zero is at the bottom of the vertical axis. However, on this graph, it is at the top of the vertical axis because the data is below sea level. Students may become confused and reverse the data as they begin to plot the points. By walking around the room and checking, you can eliminate many problems.

Answers to Questions

1. A continental slope occurs between 160 and 1050 km. The Mid-Atlantic Ridge occurs between 2000 and 4500 km from New Jersey. A continental slope lies between 5300 and 5600 km from New Jersey.
2. The vertical scale is 1 unit = 1 km. The horizontal scale is 1 unit = 1000 km.
3. No, the profile has tremendous vertical exaggeration. To make an accurate profile, the vertical and horizontal scales must be the same.

USING MATH

See page 508.

IS **Logical-Mathematical** The average is around 2750 m.

Assessment

Performance To further assess students' understanding of the ocean-floor profile, have them draw a profile of an abyssal plain and a seamount. Use the Performance Task Assessment List for Scientific Drawing in **PASC**, p. 55. P

Prepare

Section Background

- Factors such as temperature, light, nutrients, oxygen, substrate, and pollution limit where particular marine organisms can live.
- Most marine species live on continental shelves, around islands, or on rises less than 200 m below sea level.

Preplanning

- To prepare for the MiniLAB, obtain marine or freshwater plankton, eye droppers, glass depression slides, and microscopes.
- To prepare for Activity 18-2, obtain the materials listed on page 516 for each group of students.

1 Motivate

Bellringer

Before presenting the lesson, display **Section Focus Transparency 70** on the overhead projector. Assign the accompanying **Focus Activity** worksheet. [L1] [LEP]

Tying to Previous Knowledge

Students learned in Chapter 14 that water absorbs and releases energy much more slowly than land. Explain that this is why marine organisms experience less stress from temperature changes than do terrestrial organisms.

18•2 Life in the Ocean

Science Words

photosynthesis
chemosynthesis
plankton
nekton
benthos
reef

Objectives

- List six things that the oceans provide for organisms.
- Describe the relationship between photosynthesis and respiration.
- List the key characteristics of plankton, nekton, and benthos.

Life Processes in the Ocean

You live on land. Your basic needs for water, energy, and food are met in your environment. This is also true of organisms that live in the ocean. A saltwater environment provides the vital necessities of life for marine organisms, such as the eel shown in **Figure 18-5.**

Water

All life on Earth is water-based. Life began in the oceans. Organisms need water for processes that take place in cells. Water is used for all the basic processes of living things, such as digestion and cellular respiration.

Energy Relationships

Nearly all the energy used by organisms in the ocean ultimately comes from the sun. Radiant energy from the sun penetrates seawater and is trapped by chlorophyll-containing organisms in the ocean. Like chlorophyll-containing land organisms, these organisms capture the sun's energy and make food using light energy, carbon dioxide, and water. This process of food making is called **photosynthesis.** Organisms that undergo photosynthesis are called producers. Those that feed on them are called consumers.

Figure 18-5
A moray eel swims through the warm waters of Hawaii.

Program Resources

Reproducible Masters
Study Guide, p. 74 [L1]
Reinforcement, p. 74 [L1]
Enrichment, p. 74 [L3]
Cross-Curricular Integration, p. 22
Activity Worksheets, pp. 5, 110-111, 113 [L1]
Science Integration Activities, pp. 35-36
Concept Mapping, p. 41
Critical Thinking/Problem Solving, p. 34
Lab Manual 53

Transparencies
Section Focus Transparency 70 [L1]
Science Integration Transparency 18

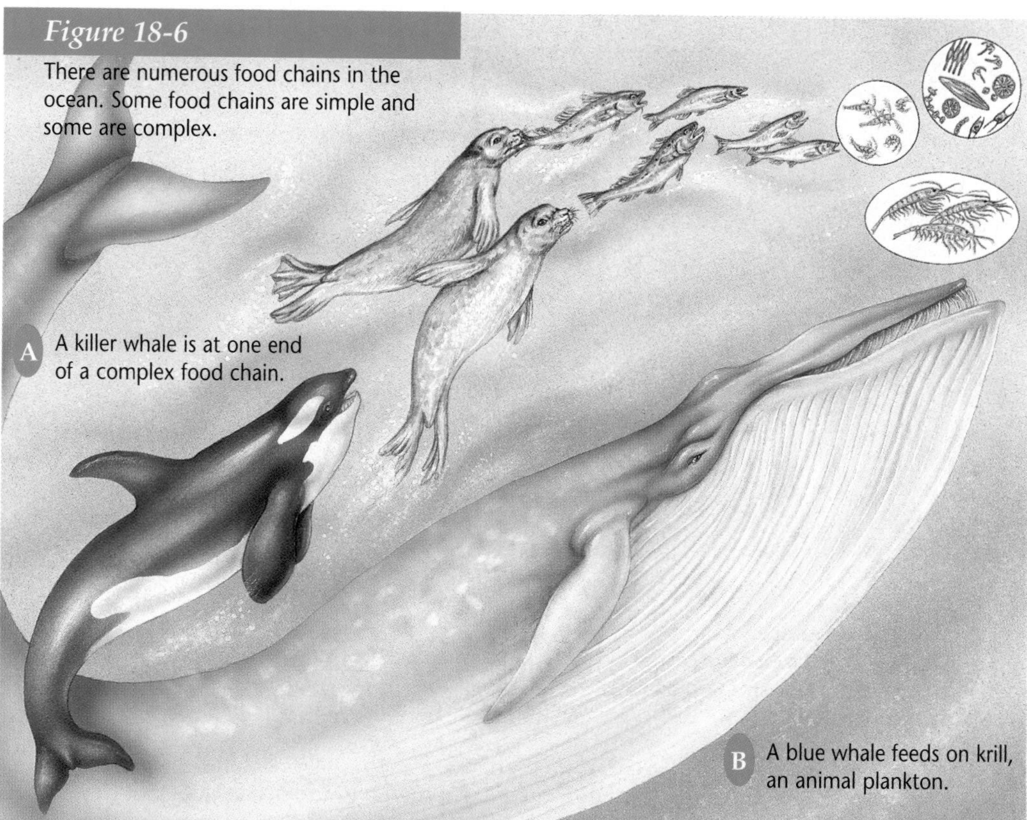

Figure 18-6

There are numerous food chains in the ocean. Some food chains are simple and some are complex.

A killer whale is at one end of a complex food chain.

B A blue whale feeds on krill, an animal plankton.

Throughout the ocean, energy from the sun is transferred through food chains. Although the organisms of the ocean capture only a small part of the sun's energy, this energy is passed from producer to consumer, to other consumers. In **Figure 18-6,** notice that in one food chain, a large blue whale consumes small organisms, krill, as its basic food. In the other chain, phytoplankton are eaten by copepods that are, in turn, eaten by a herring. Cod eat the herring, seals eat the cod, and eventually killer whales eat the seals. At each stage in the food chain, energy obtained from one organism is used by other organisms to move, to grow, to repair cells, to reproduce, and to eliminate waste. Energy not used in these life processes is transferred along the food chain as organisms feed on other organisms.

A food chain is a model of energy transfer. In an ecosystem, there are many complex feeding relationships because most organisms depend on more than one species for food. For example, herring eat more than copepods, and in turn are eaten by animals other than cod. In an actual ecosystem, food chains are interconnected to form highly complex systems called food webs.

INTEGRATION
Life Science

CONNECT TO
PHYSICS

Buoyant force is the upward force of fluid on an object within the fluid. If an object is floating in the ocean, ***infer*** which is greater: the buoyant force being exerted on it or the force of gravity upon it.

2 Teach

CONNECT TO
PHYSICS

The forces are equal. Otherwise the object would fly out of the water or sink.

Discussion

Some marine organisms eat only one food. Other animals may eat a variety of other organisms. Because of this, food webs are interconnected and can be complex.

Inquiry Question

What happens to the wastes of organisms that live in the oceans? *The wastes dissolve in seawater and decay and are then used as nutrients by other organisms.*

INTEGRATION
Life Science

Corals grow best in shallow water where sunlight reaches the reef because corals often exist symbiotically with algae, which need the sunlight to photosynthesize. The algae are dietetic supplements to the coral and rid the coral of some wastes. The algae benefit because they are provided with protected places to live. Have students study other symbiotic relationships where both organisms benefit. Examples are clownfish and sea anemone, cleaner shrimp and fish, and remora and shark.

Theme Connection

Systems and Interactions Tell students that some scientists predict future societies will live in oceanic cities. Ask students to list drawbacks of such cities. Students may discuss the inability of people to breathe underwater and problems involved with waves and currents, the rough terrain, and the pressure of the overlying water. Compare humans to marine organisms P

Inquiry Question

Compare and contrast photosynthesis and chemosynthesis. *Both result in the production of food and oxygen. However, during photosynthesis, plants use nutrients, carbon dioxide, and sunlight to produce food. During chemosynthesis, bacteria use sulfur compounds.*

Revealing Preconceptions

Plants produce food through photosynthesis. Plants also break down complex organic molecules and obtain energy from them in the process of respiration. Many people think that only animals respire and that plants do not.

USING MATH

 **Logical-Mathematical** The blue whale can consume 8 million g of krill in a day, can grow up to 2600 cm long, and can have a mass of 137 000 kg.

GLENCOE TECHNOLOGY

Videodisc

The Infinite Voyage: Secrets from a Frozen World

Introduction

Chapter 1

The Southern Ocean—A Rich Marine Ecosystem

Chapter 2

Krill: The Vital Link of the Food Chain

Chapter 6

The Antarctic Peninsula: Pack Ice and Life Cycles

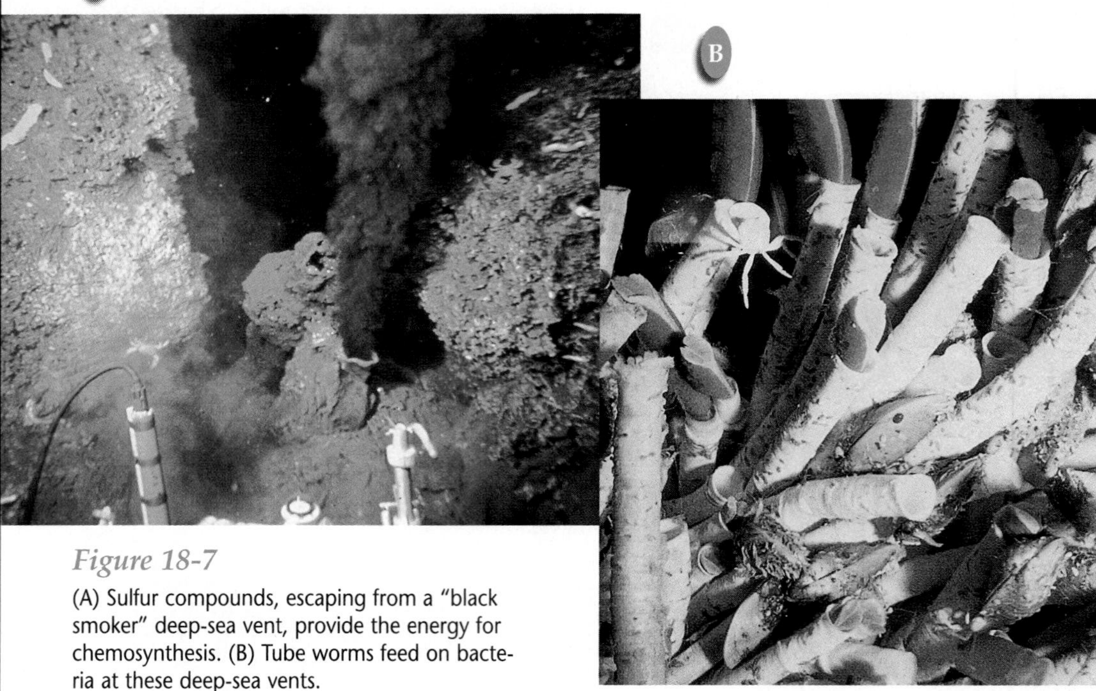

Figure 18-7

(A) Sulfur compounds, escaping from a "black smoker" deep-sea vent, provide the energy for chemosynthesis. (B) Tube worms feed on bacteria at these deep-sea vents.

USING MATH

Blue whales can consume more than 8 metric tons of krill a day. Adults average 26 m in length and have a mass of 137 metric tons. Use Appendices A and B to answer the following questions. How many *grams* of krill can a blue whale consume in one day? How many *centimeters* long is an average blue whale? What is the *mass* in kilograms of an average adult blue whale?

Chemosynthesis

Another type of food web in the ocean does not depend on sunlight. This food web depends on bacteria performing a process called **chemosynthesis.** *Chemo* means "chemical," and as you have learned, *synthesis* means "to make." This process takes place along mid-ocean ridges where in some places superheated water blasts from the crust and in some places seeps. In these areas, bacteria produce food and oxygen by using dissolved sulfur compounds that escape from magma. Organisms then feed on the bacteria. The ocean creatures in **Figure 18-7** receive their energy from chemosynthesis.

Other Life Processes

Another vital life process is reproduction. Ocean water provides an easy way for organisms to reproduce. Many ocean organisms release reproductive cells into the water where they unite to form new organisms.

Seawater also provides a thermally stable environment for organisms. That means ocean water protects organisms from sudden temperature changes. Because the ocean has a large volume, the temperature of the ocean changes slowly. This slow change of temperature means that marine organisms do not experience the sudden changes in temperature that some organisms on land endure.

Across the Curriculum

Language Arts Suggest that students read a book, short story, or poem about the oceans. Suggestions might include Jules Verne's *Twenty Thousand Leagues Under the Sea* and Ernest Hemingway's *The Old Man and the Sea.* L1 LS

Use Lab 53 in the **Lab Manual** as you teach this lesson.

Ocean Life

Many varieties of plants, animals, and algae live in the ocean. Most exist in the sunlight zone of the ocean. Sufficient sunlight to promote photosynthesis can penetrate about 140 m down into ocean water. This means that many marine organisms live on the continental shelf because this is where they can obtain food.

Organisms in the ocean are adapted to obtain food in one of three ways: they make it in photosynthesis; they move through the water to obtain food; or they filter water to obtain nutrients.

Plankton

Plankton are tiny marine algae and animals that drift with currents. Most plant plankton are one-celled organisms that float in the upper layers of the ocean where light needed for photosynthesis is found. To see most plankton, you need a microscope. A one-celled, golden alga, called a diatom, is tiny but an abundant form of plankton. Diatoms are the most important source of food for animal plankton, the next step in the food chain of the oceans. Examples of animal plankton include eggs, very young fish, jellyfish and crabs, and tiny adults of some organisms. Most animal plankton depend on surface currents to move them, but some can swim.

Nekton

In the ocean, animals that actively swim, rather than drift with the currents, are **nekton.** Nekton include all swimming forms of fish and other animals, from tiny herring to huge whales. Shrimps, squid, and seals are also nekton. In **Figure 18-8**, the swimming turtle and angler fish are nekton. Nekton move from one depth to another easily. This ability to swim reduces the effects of surface currents on them. For nekton, buoyancy is important. In the water, organisms less dense than water float. By changing how buoyant or how easily they float, organisms can change depth in the ocean. Changing depth allows animals to search more areas for food. Some nekton live in cold water, whereas others exist in warm regions. Some, like whales, roam the entire ocean. Many nekton come to the surface at night to feed on plankton, while others remain in deeper parts of the ocean where sunlight does not reach.

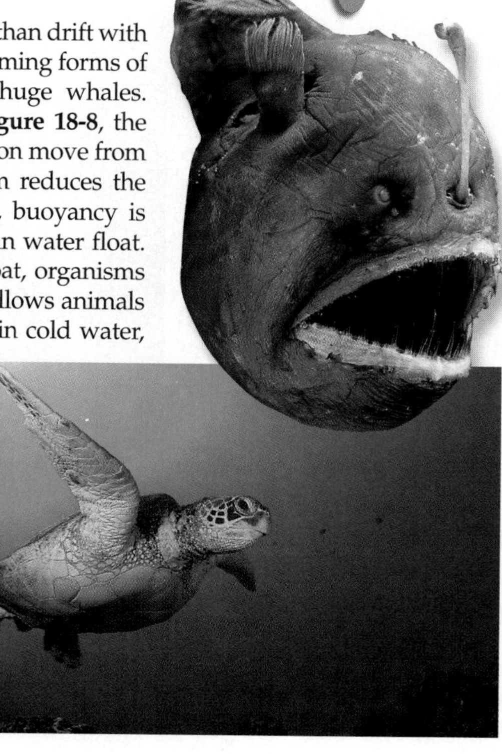

Figure 18-8

Swimming animals, such as this turtle (A) and this angler fish (B), are nekton.

MiniLAB

What do plankton look like?

Procedure

1. Place one or two drops of water that contains ocean or freshwater plankton onto a microscope slide.
2. With light coming through the sample from beneath, use a microscope to observe your sample.
3. Find at least three different types of plankton.

Analysis

1. Draw detailed pictures of three types of plankton.
2. Classify the plankton as plant or animal.

MiniLAB

Purpose

LS **Visual-Spatial** Students will observe plankton with a microscope. L2

Materials

ocean or lake water containing microscopic organisms, microscopes, glass depression slides, eye droppers

Teaching Strategies

Troubleshooting To enhance the number of plankton in a sample, collect the sample several days early and allow a handful of vegetation such as grass to "soak" in the water. Leave the storage container uncovered.

- Examine the microorganisms in the sample for type and abundance before students start this activity.

Analysis

1. Drawings should show as much detail as possible.
2. Students should recognize that most animals have the ability to move through the water on their own. Most plants cannot do this. Animals may also have eyes. Plants may be green from chlorophyll in their cells.

Assessment

Performance To further assess students' knowledge of what plankton look like, have them draw or make models of some of the specimens they saw. Use the Performance Task Assessment List for Scientific Drawing in **PASC**, p. 55. P

Activity Worksheets, pp. 5, 113

Science Journal

Ocean Life Have students explain in their Science Journals why a fish is considered plankton at one stage of its life and nekton at another stage. *When a fish is still inside an egg or is a young hatchling, it drifts with the surface currents and can be considered plankton. When it matures, a fish can move from one depth and place to another and is considered nekton.* L1 LS

USING TECHNOLOGY

For more information on how drugs are made, contact a local pharmacist to make a presentation on this topic to the class.

Think Critically

Synthesizing a drug in a laboratory is less expensive than extracting the drug from organisms. Also, marine organisms do not have to be destroyed.

Activity

Have students make a mural showing a cross section of the ocean from the shore to the deep ocean. They should show the diverse life that occurs from the ocean floor to the surface and from the shore to the deep ocean.

Enrichment

Make a list of various kinds of seafood. Have each student select a particular animal or plant from the list and write a brief profile describing its appearance, its habitat, its source of food or nutrients, and its importance in marine food webs.

3 Assess

Check for Understanding

Use the Flex Your Brain activity to have students explore BENTHOS.

Activity Worksheets, p. 5

USING TECHNOLOGY

Drugs from the Sea

Did you know that half of all drugs that are developed come from living organisms? Until recently, nearly all of the organisms used in drug making lived on land. Now, scientists are looking at organisms in the oceans as sources of drugs to treat asthma, arthritis, cancers, and AIDS.

Scientists are especially interested in studying soft-bodied organisms that live in the sea. These organisms seem defenseless, and yet other organisms do not eat them. These organisms use chemical defense systems. Scientists suspect that we could develop drugs from these chemicals. Slugs, soft corals, sponges, and even some sea worms are among the organisms being researched.

Many different kinds of scientists work together to develop new drugs. Biologists and ecologists collect and separate the species. Chemists extract substances from the organisms. Biologists and pharmaceutical specialists test and purify the ingredients. Finally, researchers perform clinical trials to see whether a chemical is effective in the treatment of certain diseases.

One drug from the ocean, in use since 1982, is acyclovir. It fights herpes infection. Acyclovir is derived from a Caribbean sponge.

Sponges

Think Critically:

Once a chemical is isolated from an organism and found to be an effective drug, scientists synthesize the chemical in the laboratory instead of harvesting the organisms. Why do you think this is done?

Some of these deep-dwelling organisms have special light-generating organs for attracting live food in the dark depths. The angler fish, shown in **Figure 18-8,** dangles a luminous lure over its forehead. When small animals bite at the lure, the angler fish swallows them whole. The viperfish has luminous organs in its mouth. It swims with its mouth open, and small organisms swim right into the viperfish's mouth.

Bottom-Dwellers

Algae and animals also live on the seafloor. The plants and animals living in the lowest levels of the ocean are the **benthos.** Some benthos live on the bottoms of the continental shelf in fairly shallow water. Others live on the ocean bottom hundreds of meters deep. Some are attached to the bottom, others burrow into the

Figure 18-9

Many organisms live on this coral reef in the South Pacific.

bottom sediments, and others walk or swim over the bottom.

Forests of kelp grow in sunlit areas of the continental shelf, in cool water near shore. Did you know that kelp is the fastest growing plant in the world? It can grow up to 30 cm each day and reach lengths of 25 m. Kelp is anchored to the ocean bottom and is part of the benthos. A special organ holds each kelp plant to the bottom. Gas-filled bladders keep the plant upright in the water.

Other benthos organisms include crabs, corals, snails, clams, sea urchins, and bottom-dwelling fish. How do you suppose these animals get food? Many of them eat the partially decomposed matter that sinks to the ocean bottom. Some prey on other benthos, eating them whole. Those that are permanently attached to the bottom filter food particles from water currents. Still others have specialized organs that sting prey that comes near. Coral is an attached benthos that stings its prey.

Washed Ashore

A chemical plant and a nuclear power plant are both located along Barney Beach. The chemical plant produces its electricity by burning coal. The nuclear power plant generates power using nuclear fission, a process that produces vast amounts of energy. The chemical plant is located about 20 km north of Barney Beach. The nuclear power plant is about 10 km south of Barney Beach. Recently, many of the fish along Barney Beach died and washed ashore.

Solve the Problem

1. **How could a chemical plant pollute Barney Beach?**
2. **How could a nuclear power plant pollute Barney Beach?**

Think Critically:

What questions would you want to ask about the Barney Beach fish kill that would help you determine the source of the pollution?

Solve the Problem

1. Chemicals could leak into the water and harm organisms. Thermal pollution could result if water used for cooling is pumped into the ocean.
2. Thermal pollution could result if water used to cool the reactor is pumped into the ocean. Radioactive wastes might also leak.

Think Critically

Answers might include: At the time of the fish kill, what direction was the current moving? What was the water temperature? Did the dead fish have open sores? Were other organisms besides fish dead? Was the water radioactive? What other possible pollution sources exist at Barney Beach?

Reteach

IS **Interpersonal** Have each student write the names of three marine organisms, one name per index card. Collect and mix the cards. Divide the class into five teams. In a team competition, each team will try to identify the organisms as algae or animal, and then as plankton, nekton, or benthos. For example, an adult fish is both nekton and animal. Kelp can be classified as both algae and benthos. A wrong answer costs a team a point. The team that scores the most points wins.

Extension

For students who have mastered this section, use the **Reinforcement** and **Enrichment** masters.

Activity 18-2

PREPARATION

Purpose

LS **Interpersonal** Students will experiment to see which materials clean up oil spills effectively. L1

Process skills

communicating, making and using tables, recognizing cause and effect, forming a hypothesis, separating and controlling variables, interpreting data, making models, designing an experiment, comparing and contrasting, observing and inferring

Time

30 minutes to plan the experiment; 40 minutes to do the experiment

Materials

safety goggles, aprons, olive oil, pan, gravel, water, small pencils or toothpicks, sponge, paper towels, cotton balls, feathers, string, liquid detergent, cardboard, eyedropper

Alternate Materials

Different kinds of fabric and other materials can be substituted for the items suggested above.

Safety Precautions

Caution students to use safety goggles when doing their experiments. Have a garbage bag available in which students can place their oil-covered materials.

Possible Hypotheses

Hypotheses will vary. Some students will reason that materials like cotton balls will absorb the most oil. Others may predict that cardboard can be used to skim the oil off the top of the water. Still others might think that the eyedropper will be the best because it can suck up the floating oil.

Activity Worksheets, pp. 5, 110-111

Activity 18-2

Design Your Own Experiment

Cleaning Up Oil Spills

Oil spills can be destructive to life in the oceans. Oil forms thick layers that smother organisms and clog their feeding and breathing mechanisms. Organisms exposed to oil spills frequently die. Food webs are disrupted.

PREPARATION

Problem

How can an oil spill be cleaned up?

Form a Hypothesis

Consider the list of materials at right. Hypothesize which items will be most effective in cleaning up oil spills.

Objectives

- Design and carry out an experiment to study the effectiveness of different materials in cleaning up oil spills.
- Observe the effectiveness of different materials in cleaning up oil spills.

Possible Materials

- olive oil
- pan
- gravel
- water
- toothpicks
- sponge
- paper towels
- cotton balls
- feathers
- string
- liquid soap
- cardboard
- eyedropper

Safety Precautions

Wear safety goggles and an apron when doing your experiment. Properly dispose of all oil-covered materials.

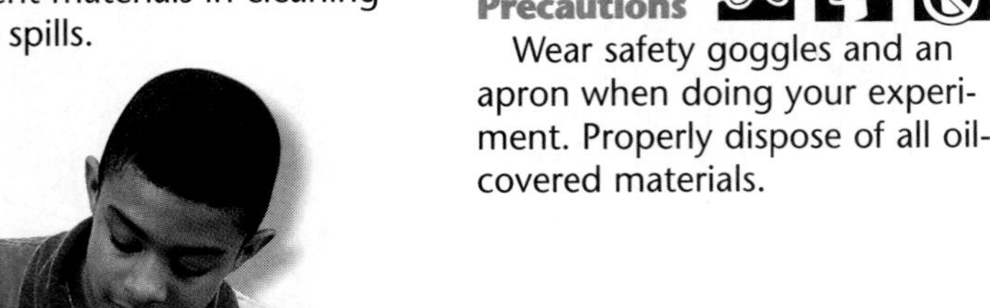

PLAN THE EXPERIMENT

1. As a group, agree upon and write out your hypothesis statement.
2. As a group, list the steps that you need to take to test your hypothesis. Include in your plan how you will (a) make the oil spills using the pan, water, olive oil, and gravel (to simulate a rocky shore); (b) conduct your tests using the different items from the materials list; and (c) determine which material is the most effective in cleaning up an oil spill.
3. Design a data table in your Science Journal so that it is ready to use as your group collects data.

Check the Plan

1. Read over your experiment to make sure that all steps are in a logical order.
2. Identify any constants and the variables of the experiment.
3. Make certain that your experiment tests one variable at a time.
4. *Make sure your teacher approves your plan before you proceed.*

DO THE EXPERIMENT

1. Carry out the experiment as planned.
2. While the experiment is going on, write your observations in the data table in your Science Journal.

Analyze and Apply

1. **Compare** your results with those of other groups.
2. Which materials were the most effective in cleaning up the oil from the water's surface? **Explain** your criteria for judging effectiveness.
3. **Explain** why certain materials were the most effective in cleaning up the oil from the gravel.
4. **Compare and contrast** characteristics of the most effective and the least effective materials.
5. Why should different materials be used to clean up oil spills in different locations?

Go Further

Oil is really a mixture of different compounds. You have tested different methods of cleaning up oil that floats. Now, design a way to clean up oil that sinks to the ocean bottom.

4. Students should evaluate the materials by how they rid the rocks and water of the oil. Does absorption work best, or does corralling the oil? Is detergent dangerous to organisms in the water?
5. If the spill is in the open ocean, skimmers and suction work well to clean up a spill. However, if the oil has reached the shoreline, the oil must be removed from the rocks. Skimmers don't work. A combination of detergents and absorbent materials might be used to clean the rocks.

Go Further

Answers will vary. Perhaps some type of suction or a combination of scraping and suction would work.

Assessment

Content Ask students to explain in writing why oil spills are difficult to clean up. Use the Performance Task Assessment List for Writing in Science in **PASC**, p. 87. P

PLAN THE EXPERIMENT

Possible Procedures

First, put on goggles and an apron. Then, place gravel along the edge of the pan and pour in water until it is 2/3 full. Place oil onto the water's surface with an eyedropper. Use each listed material, one at a time, to clean up the oil. Small pencils or toothpicks, string, and cardboard can corral and skim the oil. The sponge, paper towels, cotton balls, and feathers can absorb the oil. Liquid detergent can break down the oil into smaller globules. An eyedropper can suck up the oil. Conclude which material(s) does the most effective job by observing the amount of oil that has been removed.

Teaching Strategies

Tying to Previous Knowledge Students will already know that certain items absorb liquids and that liquid detergent is used to wash greasy dishes. Most students will also know that most oils float on water. Their knowledge of these things will help them develop their plan for cleaning up the spill.

DO THE EXPERIMENT

Expected Outcome

Most students will find that using a combination of materials works best in cleaning up the oil spill.

Analyze and Apply

1. Depending on the techniques that students use, their results may or may not be similar.
2. Answers will vary.
3. Answers will vary.

4 Close

•MINI•QUIZ•

Use the Mini Quiz to check students' recall of chapter content.

1. **_____ is the basic substance used in all life processes.** *Water*
2. **When organisms perform _______, they use sunlight, carbon dioxide, and water to make food.** *photosynthesis*
3. **Throughout the ocean, energy is transferred through _____.** *food webs*
4. **Organisms that drift in the currents are _______.** *plankton*
5. **Animals and plants that live on the ocean bottom are _____.** *benthos*

Section Wrap-up

Review

1. photosynthesis, moving through the water to obtain food, filtering seawater
2. Plankton drift in surface currents. Nekton move from one depth to another. Benthos live on or near the bottom. Plankton are the food for some nekton. Benthos depend on nekton and partially decayed organisms, such as plankton.
3. **Think Critically** It depends on chemosynthesis. In chemosynthesis, bacteria produce food and oxygen by using dissolved sulfur compounds.

Using Computers

Posters should be colorful, describe photosynthesis and explain how energy captured during photosynthesis moves through a food chain.

Figure 18-10

A diver enjoys looking at the variety of organisms on a coral reef.

Corals are organisms that attach themselves to the bottom and obtain food to sting by filtering seawater. Corals need clear, warm water and a lot of light. This means that generally they form no farther than 30 m from the surface in the warm waters near the equator.

Each coral builds a hard capsule around its body from the calcium it removes from seawater. Each capsule is cemented to others to form a large colony called a reef. A **reef** is a rigid, wave-resistant structure built from skeletal materials and calcium carbonate. As a coral reef forms, other benthos and nekton begin living on it.

If you could swim through the coral reef shown in **Figure 18-10,** you'd see many ocean organisms interacting. Fish, crabs, sea urchins, and many others congregate in reefs. Nutrients, food, carbon dioxide, and oxygen are cycled among these organisms in complex food webs. Plankton, nekton, and benthos all depend on each other for survival, not only in coral reefs, but throughout the entire ocean.

Section Wrap-up

Review

1. How do organisms in the ocean obtain food?
2. List the key characteristics of plankton, nekton, and benthos. How do they depend on one another?
3. **Think Critically:** When whales die and their carcasses sink to the bottom, sometimes sulfides are produced. Bacteria use the sulfides for food, and giant clams and worms eat the bacteria. Does this food web depend on photosynthesis or chemosynthesis? Explain.

Using Computers

Graphics Design a poster that illustrates the relationship between photosynthesis and energy in a food chain.

Skill Builder

Using Variables, Constants, and Controls

Describe how you could test the effects of salinity on marine organisms. If you need help, refer to Using Variables, Constants, and Controls in the **Skill Handbook.**

Skill Builder

Students could obtain several specimens of the same type of marine algae. Three salt solutions could be made using marine salt. One solution, the control, would have to approximate the salinity of actual ocean water. Water temperature and the amount and kind of light the algae are exposed to must be kept constant.

Assessment

Performance To further assess students' abilities to use variables, constants, and controls, have them describe how they can test the effects of temperature on marine organisms. Use the Performance Task Assessment List for Designing an Experiment in **PASC,** p. 23. P

TECHNOLOGY: Pollution and Marine Life

Ocean Pollution

How would you feel if someone came into your bedroom; spilled oil on your carpet; littered your room with plastic bags, cans, bottles, and newspapers; sprayed insect killer all over; scattered sand; and then poured hot water all over you? Organisms in the ocean experience these very things when people pollute seawater.

Pollution is the introduction by humans of harmful waste products, chemicals, and substances into an environment. A **pollutant** is a substance that causes damage to organisms by interfering with biochemical processes. **Figure 18-11** illustrates how pollutants from the land can eventually flow to the oceans and pollute them. Most ocean pollution caused by humans is concentrated along the coasts of continents.

Science Words

pollution
pollutant

Objectives

- List seven human activities that pollute the oceans.
- Explain how ocean pollution affects the entire world.
- Determine how we can live on this planet without destroying the oceans.

Figure 18-11

Ocean pollution comes from many sources. *At your school, what are the sources of pollution that could eventually pollute the oceans?*

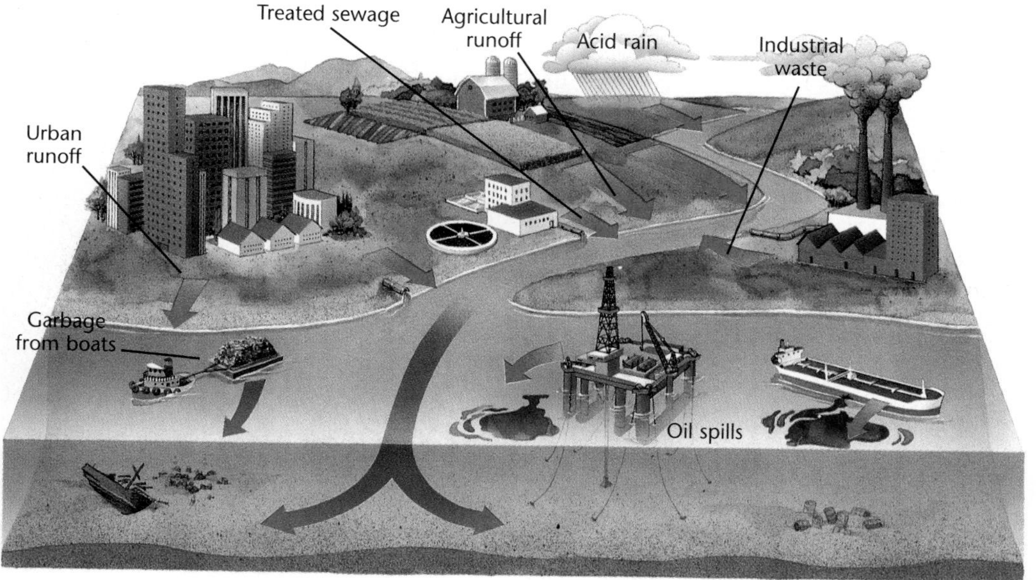

Program Resources

Reproducible Masters

Study Guide, p. 75 L1
Reinforcement, p. 75 L1
Enrichment, p. 75 L3

 **Transparencies**

Section Focus Transparency 71 L1
Teaching Transparency 36

Prepare

Section Background

In one survey, 86 percent of the trash observed floating in the northern Pacific Ocean was plastic. For more information on plastics in the ocean, write to the Center for Marine Conservation, 1725 DeSales Street NW, Washington, DC 20036. Request the publication entitled *A Citizen's Guide to Plastics in the Ocean: More Than a Litter Problem.*

1 Motivate

Bellringer

Before presenting the lesson, display **Section Focus Transparency 71** on the overhead projector. Assign the accompanying **Focus Activity** worksheet. L1 LEP

Tying to Previous Knowledge

Have students recall from Chapter 8 that water that does not soak into the ground becomes runoff. Runoff carries with it pesticides, herbicides, fertilizers, and oil from farms, homes, and industries. Eventually, these pollutants find their way into the ocean.

Visual Learning

Figure 18-11 At your school, what are the sources of pollution that could eventually pollute the oceans? *runoff of oily water from parking lots, fertilizer, salt from roads during the winter, sewage waste from broken pipes, chemicals put in the drains that may not be eliminated at a waste-treatment plant* LEP IS

2 Teach

Visual Learning

Figure 18-12 How does this affect the ocean environment? *Chemical wastes harm ocean organisms. Sewage causes an increase in algae, which then die and cause an increase in bacteria. Bacteria use up the oxygen in the water, and then fish and other organisms die.* LEP LS

CONNECT TO

PHYSICS

Answer Compounds that float or evaporate are less dense than water; compounds that sink are more dense.

Discussion

LS **Interpersonal** Stress that ocean pollution is an international problem. Have student teams discuss who should pay for the cleanup of ocean pollution. L1 COOP LEARN

3 Assess

Check for Understanding

Lead a discussion about why ocean pollution is so harmful to marine organisms.

Reteach

LS **Linguistic** Obtain articles on the Exxon Valdez spill into Prince William Sound and have students summarize them.

Extension

For students who have mastered this section, use the **Reinforcement** and **Enrichment** masters.

CONNECT TO

PHYSICS

Oil is a mixture of different compounds. When oil is spilled on water, various things happen to these compounds. Some of them evaporate, some float on the water, and some sink. ***Infer*** what this indicates about the density of these different compounds.

Chemical and Solid-Waste Pollution

Industrial waste sometimes gets into seawater. Often, this waste contains concentrations of metals and chemicals that harm organisms. Solid wastes, such as plastic bags and fishing line left lying on beaches, can entangle animals. Illegally dumped medical waste such as needles, plastic tubing, and bags are a threat to both humans and animals.

Pesticides, including herbicides (weed killers) and insecticides (insect killers), used in farming and on lawns run off and reach the ocean. In the ocean food chains, these pesticides become concentrated in the tissues of organisms.

Crop fertilizers and human sewage create a different kind of problem. Because they fertilize the water, fertilizers cause some types of algae to reproduce rapidly. When these algae die, they're decomposed by huge numbers of bacteria. The problem is that the bacteria use up much of the oxygen in the water during respiration. Therefore, other organisms such as fish can't get the oxygen they need, and they die.

Oil spills also pollute the ocean. You've heard in the news about major oil pollution caused by tanker collisions and leaks at offshore oil wells. Another source of oil pollution is oil mixed with wastewater that is pumped out of ships. In addition to these sources, oil washes from cars, from parking lots, and from streets and flows into streams. Eventually, this oil reaches the ocean. Part of this cycle is shown in **Figure 18-12.**

Human activities such as agriculture, cutting down forests, and construction tear up the soil. Rain washes the soil into streams and eventually into an ocean. This causes huge amounts of silt to accumulate in some coastal areas. In silted areas, the filter-feeding systems of benthos such as oysters and clams become clogged. The organism can die. Also, when saltwater marshes are filled for land development, marine habitats are destroyed.

Figure 18-12
A ship discharges waste into Pearl Harbor, Hawaii. *How does this affect the ocean environment?*

Inclusion Strategies

Gifted Have students research oil spills that occurred over the last ten years. They can draw a map of the world and show the areas that have encountered oil spills. Students can make a graph showing the tons of oil spilled each year for the ten-year period. L3 

Use **Teaching Transparency 36** as you teach this lesson.

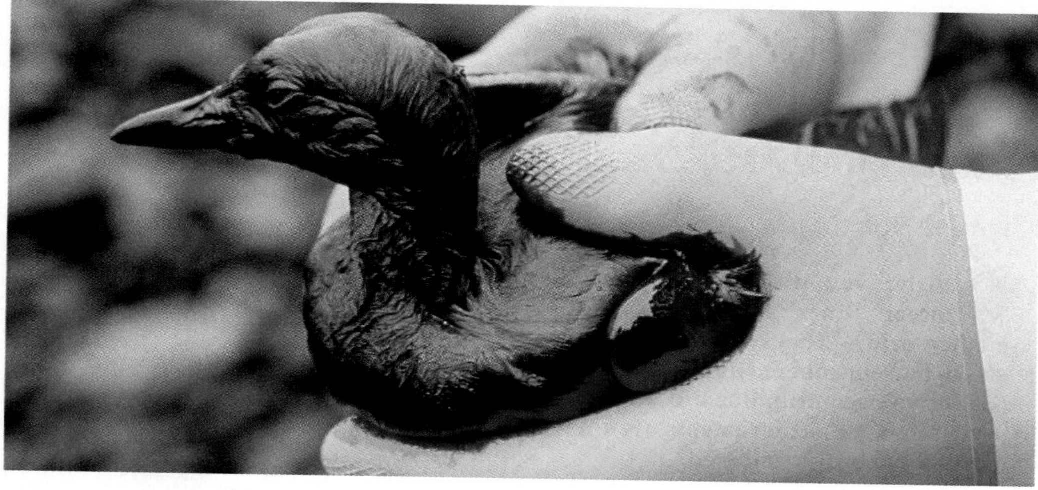

Some pollutants cause instant death to some organisms. Other pollutants, such as fertilizer, inflict damage slowly as they change the environment. Some pollutants remain in the ocean only a short time before they are broken down. However, many synthetic pollutants such as Styrofoam resist being broken down.

When an ocean becomes polluted, it isn't just the resident animals, plants, and algae that are affected. As food chains in the ocean are disrupted, Earth's oxygen supply is affected because most of the world's oxygen is produced by plankton. If an ocean's plankton were to die, this could result in the death of many organisms.

Figure 18-13

Pollution doesn't just look bad. It hurts living things. It can threaten our food supply.

Section Wrap-up

Review

1. List seven human activities that pollute the oceans. Suggest a solution to each.
2. How does pollution of the oceans affect the entire world?

Explore the Technology

In this section, you learned that human activities can severely pollute our oceans. However, many of these activities are part of the systems that provide your food, home, energy, transportation, and recreation. As Earth's population increases, the problem may grow worse. How can we maintain our quality of life without destroying life in the oceans? What are your ideas?

SCIENCE & SOCIETY

4 Close

Have student groups develop a list of suggestions to stop ocean pollution.

Section Wrap-up

Review

1. disposing of industrial wastes—changing processes to eliminate chemical discharge; leaving solid wastes at the beach—providing trash cans or taking waste back home; using pesticides, herbicides, and fertilizers—using less chemicals in farming, gardening, and growing lawns; dumping untreated sewage—building sewage plants and repairing old pipes; transporting oil—changing international standards to double-hulled ships; releasing hot water into the ocean—providing cooling basins; adding sediments—don't; filling in salt marshes—don't
2. Food chains are disrupted and Earth's oxygen supply is reduced.

Explore the Technology

People must not use the oceans as dumping grounds. People must be made aware that what they dump onto the ground eventually gets into the oceans. There need to be stricter laws and enforcement of laws concerning where people are allowed to build.

Cultural Diversity

Reef Destruction In Belize, the 180-mile long barrier reef is dying. Possible causes include agricultural pollutants, overfishing, and abuse by scuba divers and snorkelers. In Belize, banana and citrus crops are important agricultural products. But fertilizers, pesticides, and sediments wash into the ocean, killing the coral animals. Overfishing disrupts the food web. Scuba divers and snorkelers step on the coral and take away pieces of the reef for souvenirs. To protect the reef, a Coastal Zone Management Project has recently designated certain areas of the reef as commercial and recreational zones and other areas are marine preserves and wilderness areas. This project also regulates fishing and recreational use. Ask students what effect they think the Coastal Zone Management Project will have on the health of the reef.

Background

- Ballard's exploration of the Mid-Ocean Ridge was part of the French-American Mid-Ocean Undersea Study (FAMOUS) project. The main exploration site was the central rift valley in the Mid-Atlantic Ridge, a 60-square-mile area about 400 miles southwest of Sao Miguel in the Azore Islands. Expedition planners chose the site because they believed it marked the boundary between the North American and the African crustal plates, where extruded magma was contributing to the spreading of the sea floor. Their findings helped confirm plate tectonic theory.
- On the 1977 Galápagos Hydrothermal Expedition, researchers were stunned to find thriving colonies of clams, crabs, lobsters and bizarre creatures that looked like giant dandelions living near hydrothermal vents. Further studies revealed that the food chains in these deep-sea communities were based on chemosynthesis, rather than photosynthesis. At the base of these food chains are bacteria that obtain their energy from hydrogen sulfide.

Teaching Strategies

Show the National Geographic video "Born of Fire."

Career Connection

Career Path Ocean exploration can lead to discoveries in many areas of science—geology, geophysics, chemistry, biology. For that reason, Ballard suggests that students interested in marine science become grounded in the basics of all branches of science. And because teamwork is increasingly important in science, he advises participating in group activities, such as scouting, sports, or community organizations.

For More Information

Explorations by Robert D. Ballard, Ph.D., with Malcolm McConnell (Hyperion, 1995), details Ballard's adventures, scientific discoveries and groundbreaking work in the use of submersibles for undersea explorations.

People and Science

ROBERT BALLARD, *Oceanographer*

On the Job

Q After you discovered the sunken ocean liner RMS *Titanic,* your mother said, "That's too bad," because you'll be remembered for that discovery, not for your contributions to science. For what scientific achievements would you most like to be remembered?

A Without a doubt, the first manned exploration of the mid-ocean ridge in the summers of 1973 and 1974. That was really the first time anyone went into the largest feature on the planet Earth. What we found there helped confirm the theory of plate tectonics. The second thing would be the discovery in 1977 of the hydrothermal vents in the Galápagos Rift. The chemosynthetic ecosystem we discovered there has had a lot to do with understanding the origins of the ocean's chemistry and the origins of life on the planet itself.

Q Of all the amazing undersea sights you've seen, what stands out most?

A Seeing a black smoker for the first time. It looked like a fire hydrant underwater, belching out this black plume.

Personal Insights

Q Through the JASON Project, you have gotten a lot of young people excited about ocean exploration. What would you say to kids who still think science is boring?

A A lot of young people think that it's all done—that all the exploration is over with, and they're just picking up the pieces. I want to tell them that's not true at all. We've just begun. Their generation will probably explore more of Earth than all the previous generations combined. We're not going to live in space in their lifetime, at least not in any numbers. So it's the ocean that is the frontier of exploration.

Career Connection

At the library, look up information on the underwater research vehicles *Alvin, Jason,* and *Argo.* Design your own system of submersible vehicles for deep-sea exploration. Then make a report about an ocean career that interests you, perhaps

- Marine Geologist
- Marine Biologist

Chapter 18

Review

Summary

18-1: The Seafloor

1. The continental shelf is a gently sloping part of the continent that extends out into the oceans. The continental slope extends beyond the continental shelf and down to the ocean floor. The abyssal plain is a flat area of the ocean floor.
2. Cracks form where the seafloor is spreading apart. Along the mid-ocean ridges, new crust appears. Seafloor slips beneath another section of seafloor at a trench.
3. Petroleum, natural gas, and placer deposits are mined from continental shelves. In the future, perhaps manganese nodules will be mined from the deep ocean.

18-2: Life in the Ocean

1. A water habitat provides water, nutrients, waste disposal, constant temperatures, and means of reproduction to marine organisms.
2. Photosynthesis is the basis of food chains in the ocean. Chemosynthesis is a special process of food making near thermal vents.
3. Microscopic plants and animals called plankton drift in ocean currents. Nekton are marine organisms that swim. Benthos are plants and animals that live on or near the ocean floor.

18-3: Science and Society: Pollution and Marine Life

1. Industrial, solid, and medical wastes; pesticides, herbicides, and fertilizers; and oil spills, hot water, and silt all pollute oceans.
2. Ocean pollution can disrupt food webs and threaten Earth's oxygen supply. It is a serious worldwide problem.

Key Science Words

- a. abyssal plain
- b. benthos
- c. chemosynthesis
- d. continental shelf
- e. continental slope
- f. mid-ocean ridge
- g. nekton
- h. photosynthesis
- i. plankton
- j. pollutant
- k. pollution
- l. reef
- m. trench

Reviewing Vocabulary

Match each phrase with the correct term from the list of Key Science Words.

1. damages biochemical processes
2. forms when deposits fill in valleys in the deep ocean
3. seafloor beyond the continental shelf
4. mountains formed where seafloor is spreading apart
5. process using sunlight that produces food
6. drifting marine plants and animals
7. animals and plants that live on and near the ocean floor
8. colony made of many corals
9. occurs whenever harmful substances are introduced to the environment
10. where ocean crust is destroyed

GLENCOE TECHNOLOGY

MindJogger Videoquiz

Chapter 18 Have students work in groups as they play the Videoquiz game to review key chapter concepts.

Review

Summary

Have students read the summary statements to review the major concepts of the chapter.

Reviewing Vocabulary

1. j	**6.** i
2. a	**7.** b
3. e	**8.** l
4. f	**9.** k
5. h	**10.** m

Assessment

Portfolio Encourage students to place in their portfolios one or two items of what they consider to be their best work. Examples include:

- Science Journal, p. 508
- Activity 18-1 graph, p. 509
- Theme Connection, p. 511

P

Performance Additional performance assessments may be found in **Performance Assessment** and **Science Integration Activities.** Performance Task Assessment Lists and rubrics for evaluating these activities can be found in Glencoe's **Performance Assessment in the Science Classroom.**

Chapter 18 Review

Checking Concepts

Choose the word or phrase that completes the sentence.

1. The flattest feature of the ocean floor is the _______.
   a. rift valley c. seamount
   b. continental slope d. abyssal plain
2. _______ may be found where rivers enter oceans.
   a. Manganese nodules c. Abyssal plains
   b. Rift valleys d. Placer deposits
3. When organisms _______, they produce food.
   a. photosynthesize c. benthos
   b. excrete wastes d. respire
4. _______ are formed along diverging plates.
   a. Mid-ocean ridges c. Continental slopes
   b. Trenches d. Density currents
5. Ocean organisms that drift in ocean currents are called _______.
   a. nekton c. benthos
   b. fish d. plankton
6. The seafloor is spreading apart at _______.
   a. trenches c. abyssal plains
   b. mid-ocean ridges d. continental shelves
7. Some deep-water bacteria in the ocean make food through _______ .
   a. photosynthesis c. respiration
   b. chemosynthesis d. rifting
8. Ocean swimmers are _______.
   a. benthos c. kelp
   b. nekton d. coral
9. Most ocean pollution _______.
   a. is near shore c. is thermal pollution
   b. is in the ocean depths d. harms only plants
10. Fertilizers cause some _______ to reproduce rapidly, resulting eventually in a lack of oxygen.
    a. fish c. algae
    b. animal plankton d. corals

Understanding Concepts

Answer the following questions in your Science Journal using complete sentences.

11. Why aren't deep-water mineral deposits being mined?
12. Where would you expect to find the most marine organisms—closer to continents or in deeper waters? Explain.
13. Why is pollution an international problem?
14. Discuss how agricultural chemicals can kill marine organisms.
15. How do plate tectonics affect the ocean floor?

Thinking Critically

16. Some areas of the oceans are so polluted that organisms are dying. Some species are becoming extinct. What effect does pollution have on our ability to discover new drugs?
17. Animal plankton are disappearing in waters off the coast of California. How will this disappearance affect the food web in that area?
18. To widen their beaches, some cities pump offshore sediments onto beaches. How does this affect organisms that live in coastal waters?
19. Would you expect to find coral reefs growing around the bases of volcanoes off the coast of Alaska? Explain your answer.
20. Some oil leaks in the ocean are natural. Where does the oil come from?

Chapter 18 Review

Checking Concepts

1. d	**6.** b
2. d	**7.** b
3. a	**8.** b
4. a	**9.** a
5. d	**10.** c

Understanding Concepts

11. Most are located in water far away from continents, where rights to mining have not been settled.

12. They are closer to continents, where nutrients are most concentrated and where sunlight is available for photosynthesis. Animals feed on the plants.

13. Earth's oceans are interconnected, making pollution a worldwide problem. Pollution disrupts both food chains and oxygen supplies.

14. Pesticides and herbicides can reach the ocean in runoff. If they become concentrated in tissues of marine organisms, the organisms may die. Fertilizers can cause depletion of oxygen and result in many deaths.

15. New ocean crust forms at mid-ocean ridges. Old crust is destroyed at trenches. The Atlantic Ocean floor is growing. The Pacific seafloor is shrinking.

Thinking Critically

16. We have fewer kinds of organisms to analyze as possible drug sources.

17. Any organisms that depend on them directly or indirectly for food will starve.

18. When sediments of a habitat are disturbed, organisms can die. Where sediments are deposited, some organisms are buried and still others suffocate from the silt that is stirred into the water.

19. No, the waters in the region are too cold for corals. Corals need warm, tropical waters. But there may be reef structures there from the past.

20. Oil forms when dead marine organisms are buried under sediments for millions of years. The trapped oil can escape through cracks in the seafloor to produce natural oil leaks.

Developing Skills

If you need help, refer to the **Skill Handbook.**

21. **Using Scientific Illustrations:** Use **Figure 18-6** to determine which organisms would starve to death if krill became extinct.
22. **Comparing and Contrasting:** Compare and contrast mid-ocean ridges and trenches.
23. **Classifying:** Classify each of the following sea creatures as plankton, nekton, or benthos: shrimp, dolphins, starfish, krill, coral, algae.
24. **Concept Mapping:** Make an events chain concept map that describes how crop fertilizers can harm marine fish.
25. **Measuring in SI:** If kelp, as pictured below, grows at a steady rate of 30 cm/day, how long would it take to reach a height of 25 m?

Performance Assessment

1. **Graph a Profile:** In Activity 18-1, you made a profile of the ocean bottom along the 39° north latitude line, but it was not drawn to scale. Make a profile to scale of the area between 3600 and 4100 km from New Jersey. Use the scale 1 mm = 1000 m.
2. **Design an Experiment:** In Activity 18-2, you tried different methods to clean up an oil spill. Design an experiment using different methods to clean up solid-waste pollution.
3. **Poster:** Choose a particular sea animal to research. Find out where it lives, how it moves, what it eats, how it gets rid of wastes, and how it reproduces. Classify it as plankton, nekton, or benthos. Draw its food web on a poster and share this with your class.

Assessment Resources

Reproducible Masters

Chapter Review, pp. 39-40

Assessment, pp. 111-114

Performance Assessment, p. 32

Glencoe Technology

Chapter Review Software

Computer Test Bank

MindJogger Videoquiz

Chapter 18 Review

Developing Skills

21. **Using Scientific Illustrations** Blue whales, killer whales, cod, herring and seals
22. **Comparing and Contrasting** Both are seafloor features. Ridges are mountains; trenches are deep valleys. Crust moves apart near ridges; it collides near trenches.
23. **Classifying** Shrimp can be benthos, nekton, or plankton. Dolphins are nekton. Starfish are plankton as larvae, and benthos as adults. Krill and algae are plankton. Coral is benthos.
24. **Concept Mapping** Possible Solution: Fertilizer put on crops → Fertilizer washed to ocean by runoff → Fertilizer causes plankton to reproduce rapidly → Bacteria decompose dead plankton → Bacteria uses up oxygen in water → Fish die due to lack of oxygen
25. **Measuring in SI**
    25 m/0.3 m = 83 days

Performance Assessment

1. Using the scale 1 mm = 1 km, the horizontal axis will be 5 m long; the vertical axis will be 7 mm high. Use the Performance Task Assessment List for Graphs from Data in **PASC,** p. 39. P
2. Designs will vary. Use the Performance Task Assessment List for Designing an Experiment in **PASC,** p. 23. P
3. Posters will vary, but they should be colorful and informative. Use the Performance Task Assessment List for Poster in **PASC,** p. 73. P

Objectives

LS Kinesthetic Students will design and make toys that are used in air or water. L1 COOP LEARN

Summary

In this project, students will research water and air toys that already exist, design and make new toys, test their toys, and plan marketing strategies for their toys.

Time Required

- This project is designed to be worked on throughout Unit 4.
- The students will need one class period for brainstorming about air and water toys that they know exist. In addition to brainstorming, they should go to a toy store to discover toys they didn't know about. This trip could be arranged as a class field trip or as something students do for homework.
- The designing, building, and testing of the toy can be done in class or at home, or it could be a combination of both classroom work and homework. If class time is used for doing all of the work, allow five to six class periods to do it.
- Posters can also be made at school or at home. Allow 1 to 2 class periods if they are made at school.
- A Toy Invention Fair will take one-half of a period to set up, and one or more periods for others to see the toys, posters, and demonstrations.

Preparation

- Invite a local inventor to visit your class and talk about where inventors get their ideas, how they build their inventions, and how they market them.

UNIT PROJECT 5

Wet and Windy Inventions

Air and water have unique characteristics that we all enjoy. Many of you have thrown paper and balsa airplanes, boomerangs, and Frisbees into the air and watched them glide. You may have run through a field, pulling on a kite until air currents finally carried it high into the sky, or blown soap bubbles and watched them float and drift in the air. Some of you have even played air hockey. Over the years, people have invented many ways to play in the wind. You've played in the water too, with beach balls, surf boards, water skis, boogie boards, and inner tubes. This is your chance to create a new air or water toy. Your goal is to design and make a new toy. Where should you begin?

Procedures

1. First, research the types of water and air toys that are already on the market.
2. Next, make a list of at least ten of your ideas for new toys.
3. Select several of your most original ideas from your list, and consider the following about each one. What materials are needed to make it? What will it cost to make? Are the materials for building it available? Is it really possible for you to make this toy? Will it be fun to play with? Will it be durable? Will it be safe?
4. Select the toy from your list that you feel best fits the criteria in step 3, and sketch your idea on paper.
5. Obtain the materials you need to make your toy, and build it.
6. Test your toy to be sure that it does what you intended it to do, and if there are problems, make corrections.
7. What will you name it? The name could include your name, or it could include the components or ingredients you used. Whatever you decide to call your toy, try to think of a name people will remember.

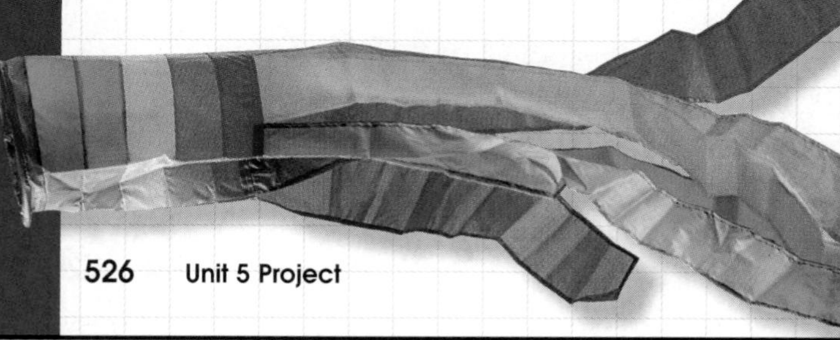

- Have students look at one or more of the books listed under References so they can learn more about creative-thinking processes.
- Have each student create his/her own toy, or have students work as paired partners.
- Decide on a date to have the Toy Invention Fair and announce this to the class.
- Arrange for space in your school to have your fair. The school library or gymnasium might be a good place.
- Send invitations to local inventors, parents, and other classes of students to attend the fair.

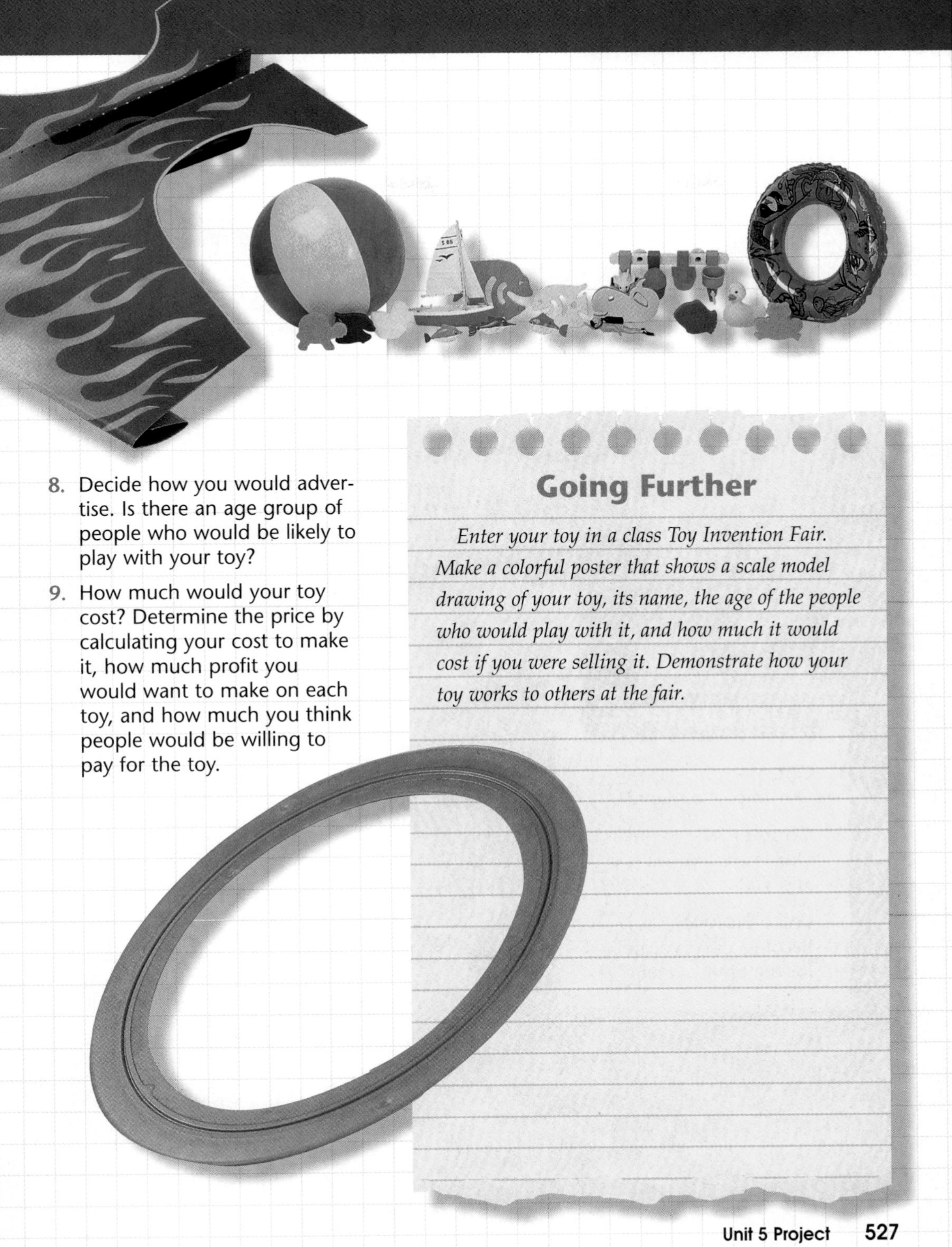

8. Decide how you would advertise. Is there an age group of people who would be likely to play with your toy?
9. How much would your toy cost? Determine the price by calculating your cost to make it, how much profit you would want to make on each toy, and how much you think people would be willing to pay for the toy.

Going Further

Enter your toy in a class Toy Invention Fair. Make a colorful poster that shows a scale model drawing of your toy, its name, the age of the people who would play with it, and how much it would cost if you were selling it. Demonstrate how your toy works to others at the fair.

Teaching Strategies

- Encourage students to share ideas and help each other as they design and make their toys. Cooperation should be emphasized.
- To eliminate arguing about who thought of a specific toy idea first, have students do what real inventors do: write down their idea, put the time and date on the paper, and get the signatures of two witnesses.
- If any students become frustrated during the creation of their toys, tell them that Thomas Edison tried thousands of different filaments before his light bulb finally worked. Inventing is sometimes hard work, with a lot of testing and perfecting.

Go Further

- Assign students space numbers where they can set up their toys and posters at the Toy Invention Fair.
- Invite local inventors to help judge the projects in the fair. They could give awards to the most original idea, the most marketable, etc.
- Have students who come to the fair select their three favorite toys from all the entries in the fair. Count the votes and give certificate awards to the top three entries.

References

Caney, Steven. *Steven Caney's Invention Book.* New York: Workman Publishing, 1985.

Levy, Richard C. *Inventing and Patenting Sourcebook: How to Sell and Protect Your Ideas.* Detroit: Gale Research, 1990.

Macaulay, David. *The Way Things Work.* Boston, Massachusetts: Houghton Mifflin Company, 1988.

Murphy, Jim. *Weird and Wacky Inventions.* New York: Crown Publishers, Inc., 1978.

Stanish, Bob. *The Unconventional Invention Book.* Carthage, Illinois: Good Apple, Inc., 1981.

Von Oech, Roger. *A Whack on the Side of the Head.* New York: Warner Books, 1983.

UNIT 6

You and the Environment

In Unit 6, students will learn about the impact humans have on Earth's land, air, and water. They will begin by learning about the human population explosion. The unit concludes with a discussion of the causes and effects of pollution.

CONTENTS

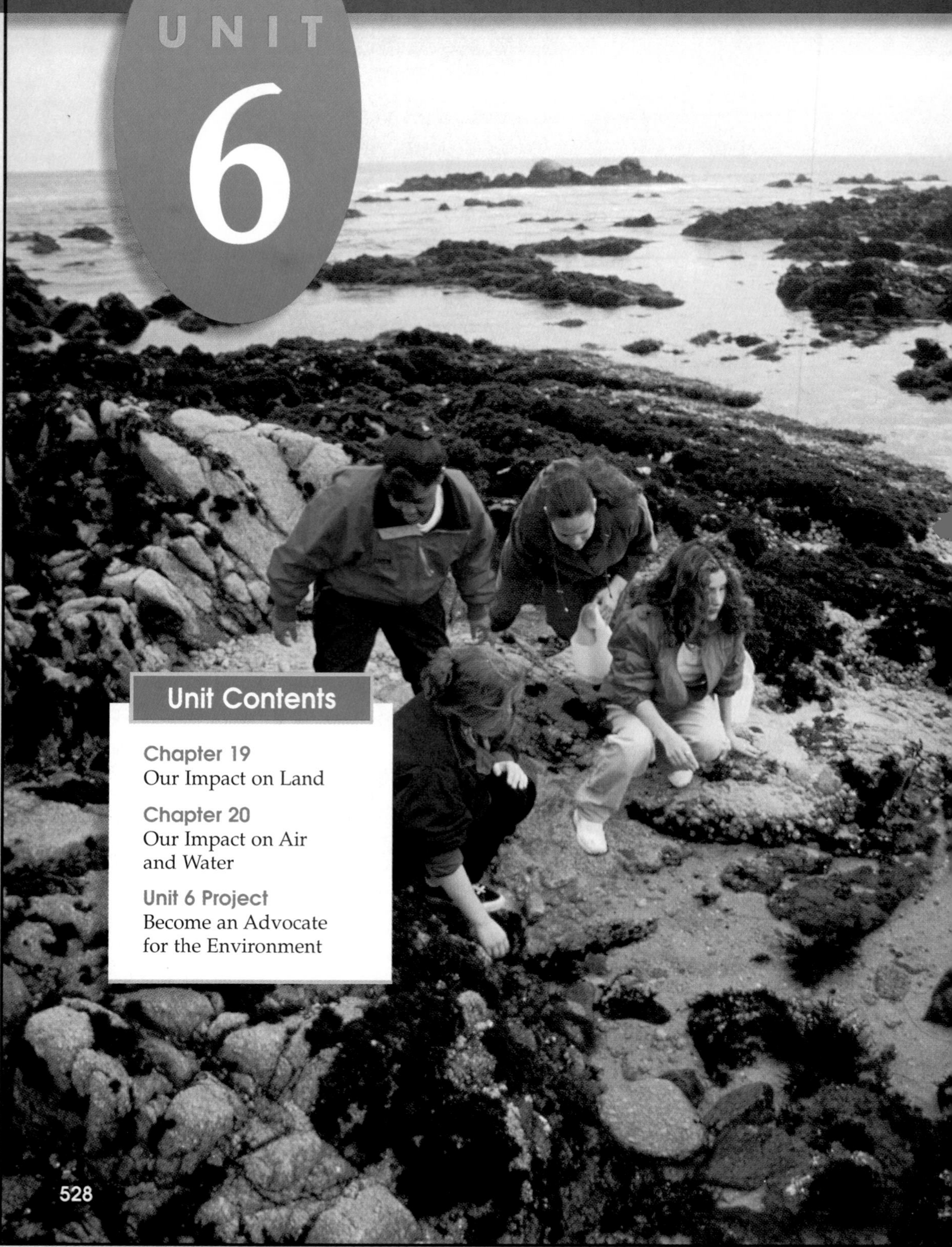

Science at Home

Land Use Have students observe how people in their hometown use the land. Ask students to write about at least one example of wise land use and one example in which land use methods could be improved. L1

You and the Environment

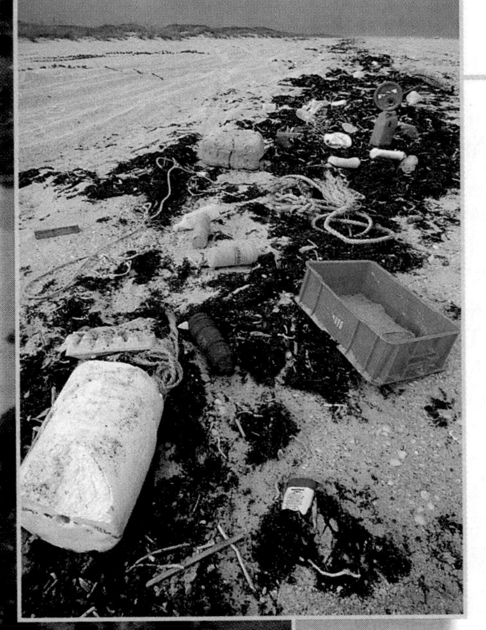

What's Happening Here?

Life abounds in the nutrient-rich waters of the tidal pool, as these students are discovering. Before the day is through, they will likely spot burrowing shellfish, foraging birds, a dozen species of aquatic plants, and much more. They will also learn that the tidal pool is a fragile environment that can be easily disrupted by human activities such as illegal dumping of trash. Today, more people realize that clean air, land, and water are precious resources, and they are working to restore polluted areas to their natural state. In this unit, you will learn how humans impact the environment, and ways to make your own personal impact a wise one.

Science Journal

Contact your local newspaper for information on a recent environmental problem in your area. In your Science Journal, describe how people in the community have responded to the problem.

Theme Connection

Systems and Interactions Have students hypothesize why humans have made a bigger impact on Earth's land, air, and water than any other species on the planet.

Cultural Diversity

Environmental Impact Have students develop a list of countries from various areas of the world. Then have each student choose two countries to study: one that is highly industrialized and one that is not. Have them research to compare the environmental impact observed in highly industrialized nations with that of less industrialized nations. L2

INTRODUCING THE UNIT

What's Happening Here?

Have students look at the photos and read the text. Ask them why they think tidal pools are fragile. Ask them to list ways that human activities might affect tidal pool organisms. Tell them that in this unit, they will learn how people affect land, air, and water.

Background

At high tide, rocks near the shore may be totally submerged, while at low tide, water is trapped among rocks to form tidal pools. At high tide, organisms living in these pools are exposed to water that is the same temperature and salinity as the offshore water. It also contains the same amount of dissolved oxygen and nutrients. At low tide, the environment changes dramatically. On a hot day, water trapped in a tidal pool can become quite warm, and some of it may evaporate, leaving the remaining water saltier than normal. Also, food and oxygen are limited in tidal pools during low tide.

Previewing the Chapters

Have students identify photographs in the chapters that indicate that there has been an impact on the land, air, and water due to human activities. Have students identify what these human activities are.

Tying to Previous Knowledge

Have students recall what they learned about the formation of soil in Chapter 6 and the composition of air and processes in the water cycle in Chapter 14. Have them select a type of pollution they have observed or read about and relate it to what they know about soil, air, and/or water.

Chapter Organizer

Section	Objectives	Activities/Features
Chapter Opener		Explore Activity: Draw a population growth model. p. 531
19-1 **Population Impact on the Environment** (2 sessions, 1 block)*	1. **Interpret** data from a graph that shows human population growth. 2. **List** reasons for Earth's rapid increase in human population. 3. **List** several ways each person in an industrialized nation affects the environment.	Connect to Life Science, p. 533 Activity 19-1: A Crowded Encounter, pp. 534-535 Using Math, p. 536 Skill Builder: Making and Using Graphs, p. 537 Using Math, p. 537
19-2 **Using the Land** (2 sessions, 1 block)*	1. **List** ways that we use land. 2. **Discuss** environmental problems created because of land use. 3. **List** things you can do to help protect the environment.	MiniLAB: How much waste do you generate in one day? p. 541 Problem Solving: Where does our trash go? p. 542 MiniLAB: Can one person make a difference? p. 543 Using Technology: Recycling Paper, p. 544 Using Math, p. 545 Skill Builder: Recognizing Cause and Effect, p. 545 Using Computers: Word Processing, p. 545
19-3 **Science and Society Issue: Should recycling be required?** (1 session, ½ block)*	1. **List** the advantages of recycling. 2. **List** the advantages and disadvantages of mandatory recycling. 3. **Express** your feelings about whether recycling should be required.	Connect to Physics, p. 548 Explore the Issue, p. 548 Activity 19-2: A Model Landfill, p. 549 People and Science: Leigh Standingbear, Horticulturist, City of Tulsa, p. 550

* A complete Planning Guide that includes block scheduling is provided on pages 32T-35T.

Activity Materials

Explore	Activities	MiniLABs
page 531 pencil, unlined paper, metric ruler	pages 534-535 small objects like dried beans or paper clips, 250-mL beaker, stopwatch or clock with second hand page 549 two 2-L soda bottles; thermometer; graph paper; soil; plastic wrap; rubber band; garbage (food scraps, yard waste, a small plastic item, a small metal item, foam cup, notebook paper or newsprint)	page 541 small (approximately 13-L) garbage bag, balance page 543 No special materials are needed.

Chapter 19 Our Impact on Land

Teacher Classroom Resources

Reproducible Masters	Transparencies	Teaching Resources
Study Guide, p .76 **Reinforcement,** p. 76 **Enrichment,** p. 76 **Activity Worksheets,** pp. 114-115 **Lab Manual 54,** Human Impact on the Environment **Multicultural Connections,** pp. 41-42	**Section Focus Transparency 72,** We're in This Together **Teaching Transparency 37,** The Population Explosion	**Glencoe Earth Science Interactive Videodisc** **Earth Science CD-ROM** **Spanish Resources** **English/Spanish Audiocassettes** **Cooperative Learning Resource Guide** **Lab Partner** **Lab and Safety Skills** **Lesson Plans**
Study Guide, p. 77 **Reinforcement,** p. 77 **Enrichment,** p. 77 **Activity Worksheets,** pp. 118, 119 **Lab Manual 55,** Reclamation of Mine Wastes **Science Integration Activity 19,** Garbage Garden **Concept Mapping,** p. 43 **Critical Thinking/Problem Solving,** p. 25	**Section Focus Transparency 73,** We're in This Together—The Sequel	**Assessment Resources**
Study Guide, p. 78 **Reinforcement,** p. 78 **Enrichment,** p. 78 **Activity Worksheets,** pp. 116-117 **Lab Manual 56,** Conservation—Recycling **Cross-Curricular Integration,** p. 23 **Science and Society Integration,** p. 23	**Section Focus Transparency 74,** Over and Over and Over Again **Science Integration Transparency 19,** Energy Used for Beverage Containers **Teaching Transparency 38,** Recycling	**Chapter Review,** pp. 41-42 **Assessment,** pp. 128-131 **Performance Assessment in the Science Classroom (PASC)** **MindJogger Videoquiz** **Alternate Assessment in the Science Classroom** **Performance Assessment** **Chapter Review Software** **Computer Test Bank**

Key to Teaching Strategies

The following designations will help you decide which activities are appropriate for your students.

- **L1** Level 1 activities should be within the ability range of all students.
- **L2** Level 2 activities should be within the ability range of the average to above-average student.
- **L3** Level 3 activities are designed for the ability range of above-average students.
- **LEP** LEP activities should be within the ability range of Limited English Proficiency students.
- **LS** These activities are designed to address different learning styles.
- **COOP LEARN** Cooperative Learning activities are designed for small group work.
- **P** These strategies represent student products that can be placed into a best-work portfolio.

GLENCOE TECHNOLOGY

The following multimedia resources are available from Glencoe.

National Geographic Society Series

STV: Atmosphere

STV: Water

GTV: Planetary Manager

Earth Science CD-ROM

Teacher Classroom Resources

This is a representation of key blackline masters available in the Teacher Classroom Resources.

Teaching Aids

Section Focus Transparencies

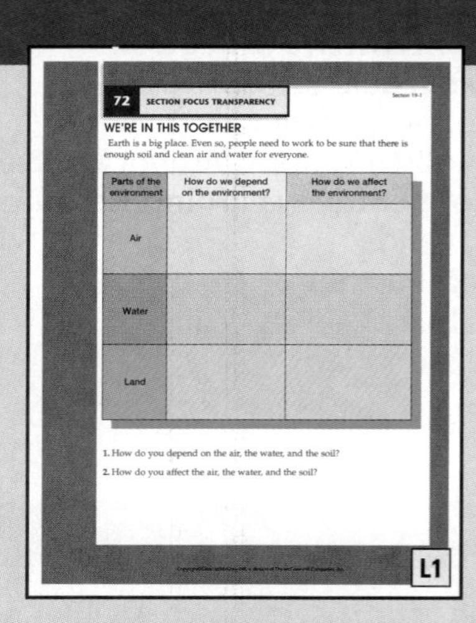

72 SECTION FOCUS TRANSPARENCY — Section 19-1

WE'RE IN THIS TOGETHER

Earth is a big place. Even so, people need to work to be sure that there is enough soil and clean air and water for everyone.

Parts of the environment	How do we depend on the environment?	How do we affect the environment?
Air		
Water		
Land		

1. How do you depend on the air, the water, and the soil?
2. How do you affect the air, the water, and the soil?

L1

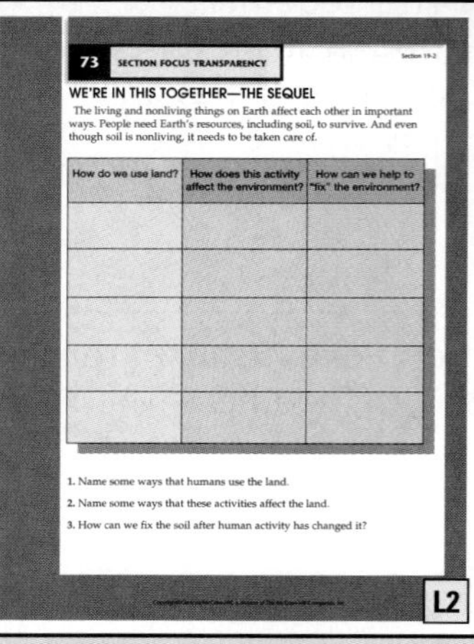

73 SECTION FOCUS TRANSPARENCY — Section 19-2

WE'RE IN THIS TOGETHER—THE SEQUEL

The living and nonliving things on Earth affect each other in important ways. People need Earth's resources, including soil, to survive. And even though soil is nonliving, it needs to be taken care of.

How do we use land?	How does this activity affect the environment?	How can we help to "fix" the environment?

1. Name some ways that humans use the land.
2. Name some ways that these activities affect the land.
3. How can we fix the soil after human activity has changed it?

L2

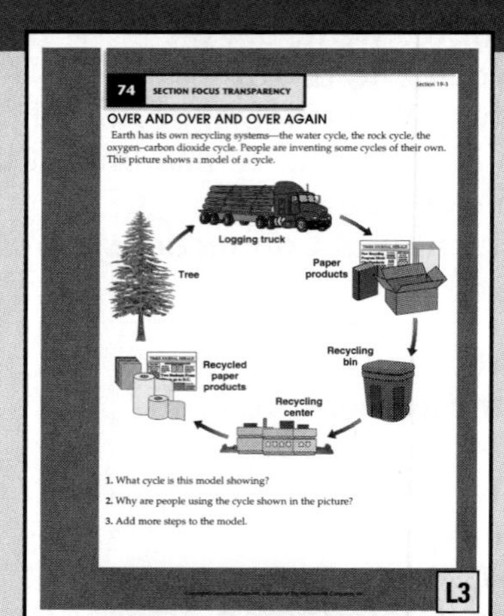

74 SECTION FOCUS TRANSPARENCY — Section 19-3

OVER AND OVER AND OVER AGAIN

Earth has its own recycling systems—the water cycle, the rock cycle, the oxygen–carbon dioxide cycle. People are inventing some cycles of their own. This picture shows a model of a cycle.

1. What cycle is this model showing?
2. Why are people using the cycle shown in the picture?
3. Add more steps to the model.

L3

Science Integration Transparencies

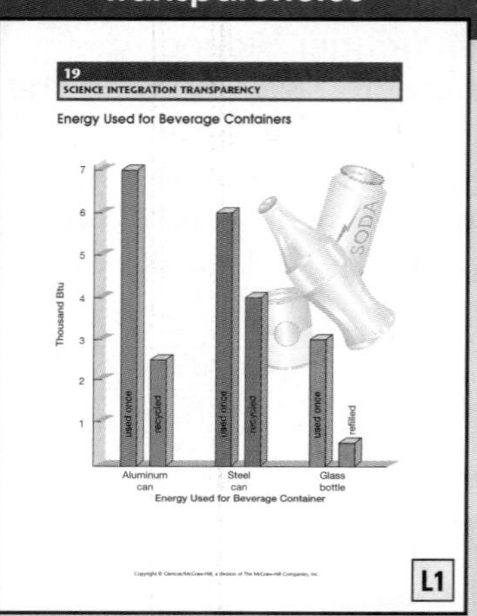

19 SCIENCE INTEGRATION TRANSPARENCY

Energy Used for Beverage Containers

L1

Teaching Transparencies

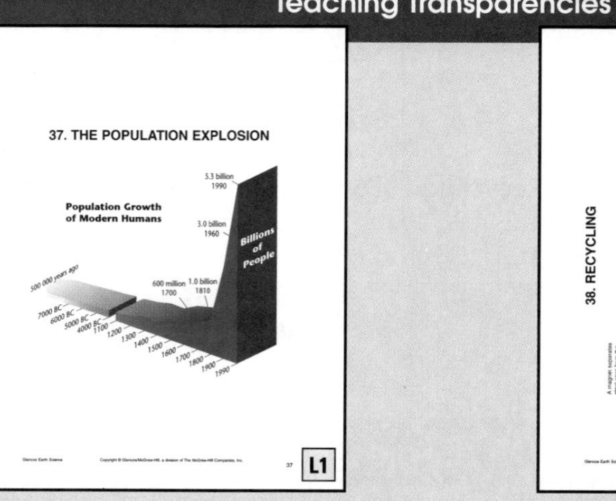

37. THE POPULATION EXPLOSION

L1

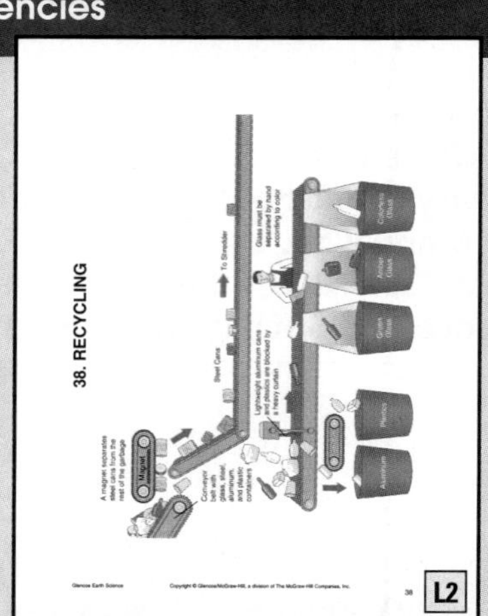

L2

Meeting Different Ability Levels

Study Guide

NAME DATE CLASS

Chapter 19 — STUDY GUIDE — Text Pages 532–537

• Population Impact on the Environment

Cross out the statements that are NOT correct.

1. A population is the total number of individuals of a particular species in a particular area.
2. Earth's population is decreasing.
3. *Population explosion* is a term that is used to describe the rapid rate at which people are reproducing.
4. Each day, more than 260 000 people are added to Earth's population.
5. In the 1800s, the world population reached about a billion.
6. During the last two centuries, the rate of population increase has slowed.
7. The number of people on Earth does not affect the environment.
8. In the past, Earth didn't have resources to support the population.
9. The average person in the United States uses less energy than the average person in the rest of the world.
10. Electricity is generated by burning fuels.
11. Plastic products affect the environment.
12. Removing Earth's resources doesn't affect the land.
13. Shaping resources into usable products affects the environment.
14. Farming prevents topsoil from being lost.
15. Much of the food you eat is grown using poisonous substances in the process.
16. The population is predicted to be 14 billion sometime in the next century.
17. Modern medicine, better sanitation, and better nutrition have all helped to slow the death rate.

76 Copyright © Glencoe/McGraw-Hill, a division of The McGraw-Hill Companies, Inc.

L1

Reinforcement

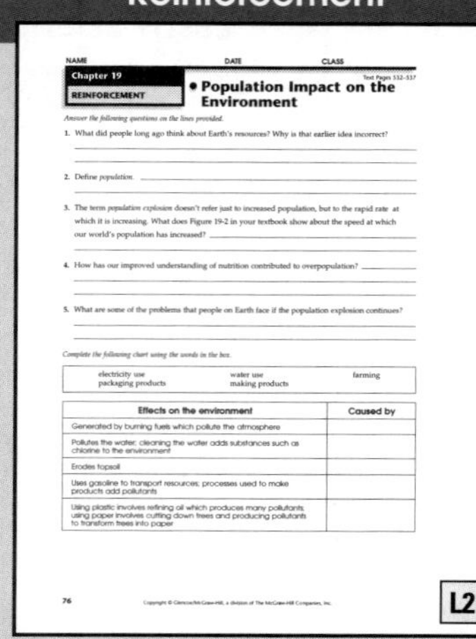

NAME DATE CLASS

Chapter 19 — REINFORCEMENT — Text Pages 532–537

• Population Impact on the Environment

Answer the following questions on the lines provided.

1. What did people long ago think about Earth's resources? Why is that earlier idea incorrect?
2. Define *population*.
3. The term *population explosion* doesn't refer just to increased population, but to the rapid rate at which it is increasing. What does Figure 19-2 in your textbook show about the speed at which our world's population has increased?
4. How has our improved understanding of nutrition contributed to overpopulation?
5. What are some of the problems that people on Earth face if the population explosion continues?

Complete the following chart using the words in the box.

electricity use packaging products	water use making products	farming

Effects on the environment	Caused by
Generated by burning fuels which pollute the atmosphere	
Pollutes the water; cleaning the water adds substances such as chlorine to the environment	
Erodes topsoil	
Uses gasoline to transport resources; processes used to make products add pollutants	
Using plastic involves refining oil which produces many pollutants, using paper involves cutting down trees and producing pollutants to transform trees into paper	

76 Copyright © Glencoe/McGraw-Hill, a division of The McGraw-Hill Companies, Inc.

L2

Enrichment Worksheets

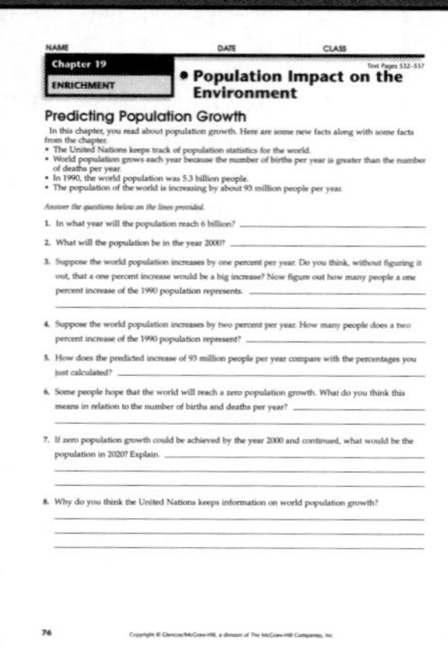

NAME DATE CLASS

Chapter 19 — ENRICHMENT — Text Pages 532–537

• Population Impact on the Environment

Predicting Population Growth

In this chapter, you read about population growth. Here are some new facts along with some facts from the chapter.

- The United Nations keeps track of population statistics for the world.
- World population grows each year because the number of births per year is greater than the number of deaths per year.
- In 1990, the world population was 5.3 billion people.
- The population of the world is increasing by about 93 million people per year.

Answer the questions below on the lines provided.

1. In what year will the population reach 6 billion?
2. What will the population be in the year 2000?
3. Suppose the world population increases by one percent per year. Do you think, without figuring it out, that a one percent increase would be a big increase? Now figure out how many people a one percent increase of the 1990 population represents.
4. Suppose the world population increases by two percent per year. How many people does a two percent increase of the 1990 population represent?
5. How does the predicted increase of 93 million people per year compare with the percentages you just calculated?
6. Some people hope that the world will reach a zero population growth. What do you think this means in relation to the number of births and deaths per year?
7. If zero population growth could be achieved by the year 2000 and continued, what would be the population in 2020? Explain.
8. Why do you think the United Nations keeps information on world population growth?

76 Copyright © Glencoe/McGraw-Hill, a division of The McGraw-Hill Companies, Inc.

L3

Chapter 19 Our Impact on Land

Hands-On Activities

Science Integration Activity

Chapter 19 INTEGRATION

Garbage Garden

Getting Started

Thinking Critically

Try It!

L1

Lab Manual

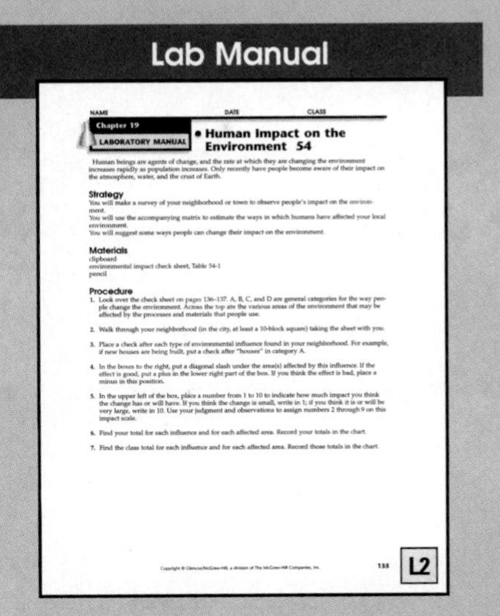
Chapter 19 LABORATORY MANUAL

Human Impact on the Environment 54

Strategy

Materials

Procedure

L2

Assessment

Performance Assessment

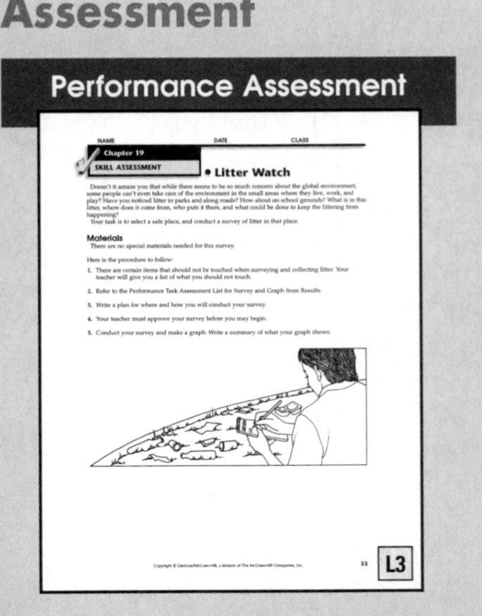
Chapter 19 SKILL ASSESSMENT

Litter Watch

Materials

L3

Enrichment and Application

Critical Thinking/ Problem Solving

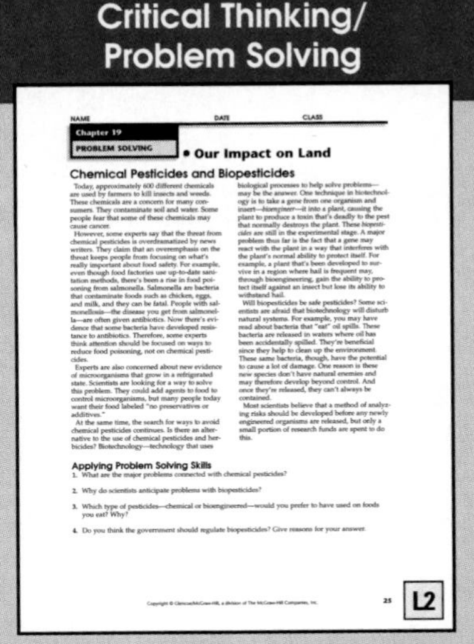
Chapter 19 PROBLEM SOLVING

Our Impact on Land

Chemical Pesticides and Biopesticides

Applying Problem Solving Skills

L2

Cross-Curricular Integration

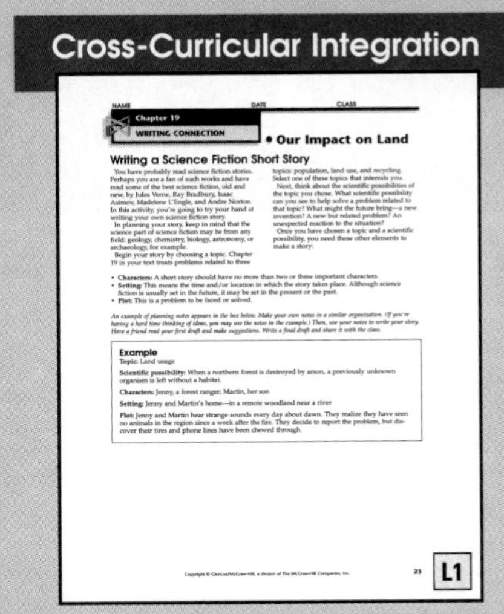
Chapter 19 WRITING CONNECTION

Our Impact on Land

Writing a Science Fiction Short Story

Example

L1

Science and Society Integration

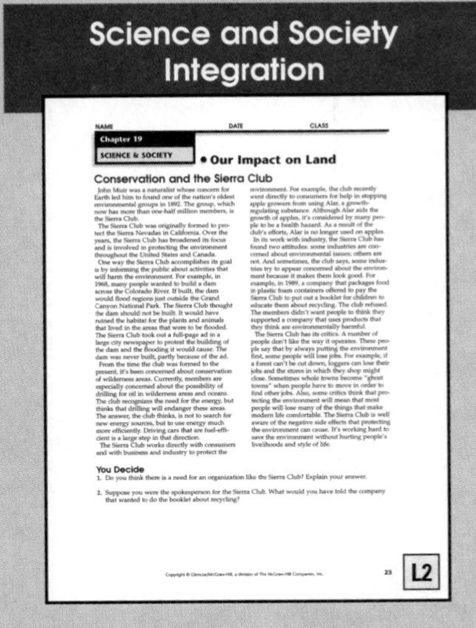
Chapter 19 SCIENCE & SOCIETY

Our Impact on Land

Conservation and the Sierra Club

You Decide

L2

Multicultural Connections

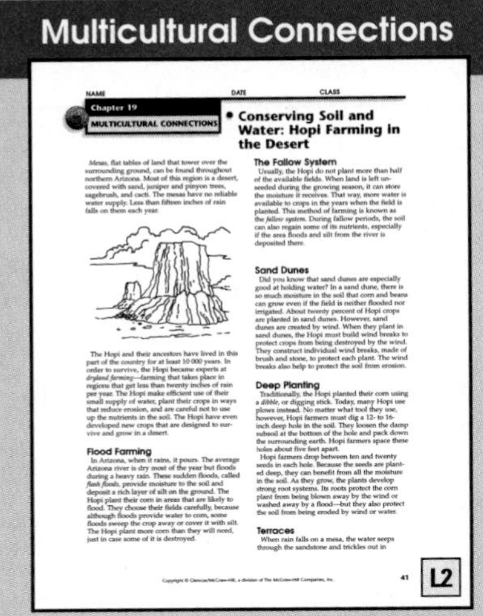
Chapter 19 MULTICULTURAL CONNECTIONS

Conserving Soil and Water: Hopi Farming in the Desert

The Fallow System

Sand Dunes

Deep Planting

Flood Farming

Terraces

L2

Concept Mapping

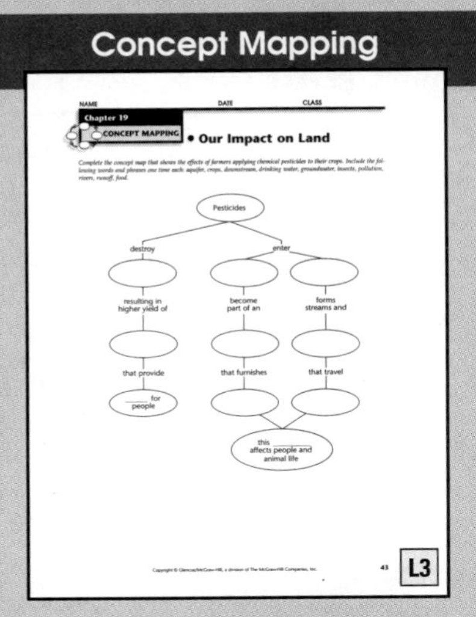
Chapter 19 CONCEPT MAPPING

Our Impact on Land

L3

Chapter 19

Our Impact on Land

CHAPTER OVERVIEW

Section 19-1 This section describes the human population explosion, and introduces ways people affect the environment.

Section 19-2 Concepts presented in this section include how people use land, the environmental problems that result from these activities, and ways people can help protect the environment.

Section 19-3 Science and Society The advantages of recycling are introduced. In the Explore the Issue question, students will discuss whether the government should pass laws requiring people to recycle.

Chapter Vocabulary

carrying capacity
population
population explosion
landfill
sanitary landfill
hazardous waste
conservation
composting
recyclable

Theme Connection

Systems and Interactions Many different human activities affect the environment. With an increase in human population, these effects become more pronounced.

Previewing the Chapter

530

Learning Styles

Look for the following logo for strategies that emphasize different learning modalities. LS

Visual-Spatial	Visual Learning, pp. 533, 536, 540, 542, 547; Across the Curriculum, p. 540; Activity 19-2, p. 549
Intrapersonal	MiniLABs, pp. 541, 543
Logical-Mathematical	Explore, p. 531; Activity 19-1, pp. 534-535
Linguistic	Science Journal, p. 543

Chapter 19

Our Impact on Land

Did you ever consider the impact that every one of us has on the land? Each person on Earth competes for space and resources. Each one generates trash, consumes products made in factories, uses natural resources such as water, soil, and energy, and creates pollution. Do you think our impact on the land is very significant?

EXPLORE ACTIVITY

Draw a population growth model.

1. Use a piece of paper and pencil to draw a square that is 10 cm on each side. This represents one square kilometer of Earth's land surface.
2. In 1965, the average number of people for every square kilometer of land was 21. Draw 21 small circles inside your square to represent this.
3. In 1990, the average rose to 35. Add 14 circles to illustrate this increase.
4. In 2025, there will be an estimated 67 people per square kilometer. Add circles to represent the average number of people per square kilometer of land in 2025.

Observe: Based on the numbers above, is human population increasing more rapidly as time goes on? In your Science Journal, hypothesize how population growth affects the environment.

Previewing Science Skills

- In the **Skill Builders**, you will **use graphs**, and **recognize cause and effect.**
- In the **MiniLABs**, you will **collect data, measure in SI,** and **hypothesize.**
- In the **Activities**, you will **experiment, make models, analyze data, make and use tables, make and use graphs,** and **draw conclusions.**

EXPLORE ACTIVITY

Purpose

LS **Logical-Mathematical** Use the Explore Activity to introduce students to human population growth. Inform students that they will be learning more about human population growth and the effects of human activities on the environment in this chapter. L1

Preparation

You may want to review the term *map scale* from Chapter 5 before having students perform this activity. The scale of their drawing in this activity is 1:10 000.

Materials

one metric ruler for each student

Teaching Strategies

Students should be reminded that the information they are using is the world average.

Observe

Yes, population is increasing more rapidly. Students may infer that the environment will be damaged as more and more demands are placed upon it.

Assessment

Performance Make a graph showing the years 1965-2035 on the horizontal axis and the average number of people per square kilometer of land on the vertical axis. Plot the information from the Explore Activity and use your completed graph to predict the average number of people per square kilometer in 2035. Use the Performance Task Assessment List for Graph from Data in **PASC,** p. 39. P

Assessment Planner

Portfolio
Refer to page 551 for suggested items that students might select for their portfolios.

Performance Assessment
See page 551 for additional Performance Assessment options.
Skill Builders, pp. 537, 545
MiniLABs, pp. 541, 543
Activities 19-1, pp. 534-535; 19-2, p. 549

Content Assessment
Section Wrap-ups, pp. 537, 545, 548
Chapter Review, pp. 551-553
Mini Quizzes, pp. 537, 545, 548

Group Assessment
Opportunities for group assessment occur with Cooperative Learning Strategies and Flex Your Brain Activities.

Section 19•1

Prepare

Section Background

- Ninety percent of the world's population increase is expected in developing countries. In Western industrial nations, the birthrate is relatively constant, but better diet and disease control extend the life span.
- Worldwide, perhaps 730 million people go to bed hungry every night. Millions of people starve every year, and millions more die of diseases brought on by hunger.

Preplanning

To prepare for Activity 19-1, obtain the following materials for each group: one beaker (250 or 600 mL), 360 paper clips or dried beans.

1 Motivate

Bellringer

Before presenting the lesson, display **Section Focus Transparency 72** on the overhead projector. Assign the accompanying **Focus Activity** worksheet. L1 LEP

Tying to Previous Knowledge

In Chapter 4, students learned about fossil fuels. Ask students how population growth will affect the availability and price of fossil fuels. As human population continues to increase, more and more of these fuels will be burned. Earth's reserves will disappear. The demand will exceed the supply, and prices will likely rise.

Use **Teaching Transparency 37** as you teach this lesson.

19•1 Population Impact on the Environment

Science Words

carrying capacity
population
population explosion

Objectives

- Interpret data from a graph that shows human population growth.
- List reasons for Earth's rapid increase in human population.
- List several ways each person in an industrialized nation affects the environment.

The Human Population Explosion

At one time, people thought of Earth as a world with unlimited resources. They thought the planet could provide them with whatever materials they needed. Earth seemed to have an endless supply of metals, fossil fuels, and rich soils. Today, we know this isn't true. Earth has a carrying capacity. The **carrying capacity** is the maximum number of individuals of a particular species that the planet will support. Thus, Earth's resources are limited. Unless we treat those resources with care, they will disappear.

Many years ago, there were few people on Earth. Fewer resources were used and less waste was produced than today. But in the last 200 years, the number of people on Earth has increased at an alarming rate. The increase in the world population has changed the way we must view our world and how we care for it for future generations, like the babies in **Figure 19-1.**

Figure 19-1

The human population is growing at an alarming rate. *In your Science Journal, discuss how this impacts Earth's limited resources.*

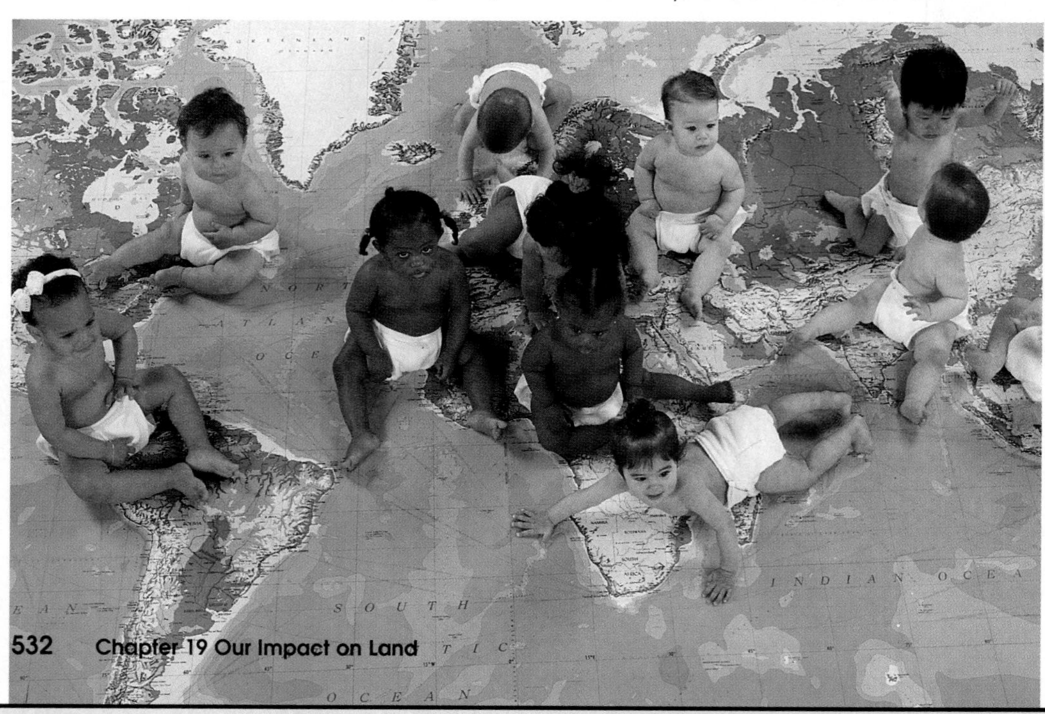

Program Resources

Reproducible Masters

Study Guide, p. 76 L1
Reinforcement, p. 76 L1
Enrichment, p. 76 L3
Activity Worksheets, pp. 5, 114-115 L1
Lab Manual 54
Multicultural Connections, pp. 41-42

Transparencies

Section Focus Transparency 72 L1
Teaching Transparency 37

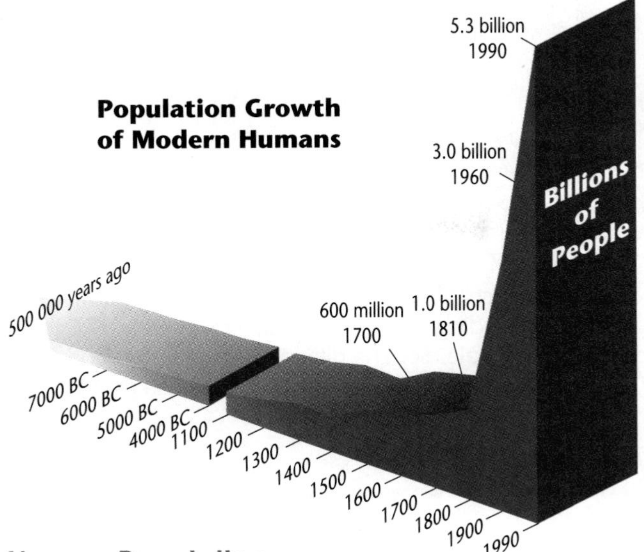

Figure 19-2

The human species, *Homo sapiens*, may have appeared about 500 000 years ago. Our population numbers remained relatively steady until about 200 years ago. Since that time, we have experienced a sharp increase in growth rate.

Human Population

A **population** is the total number of individuals of a particular species in a particular area. The area can be small or large. For example, we can talk about the human population of one particular community, such as Los Angeles, or about the human population of the entire planet.

Have you ever wondered how many people live on Earth? The global population in 1995 was 5.7 billion. Each day, approximately 260 000 people are added. Earth is experiencing a **population explosion.** The word *explosion* is used because the rate at which the population is growing has rapidly increased in recent history.

Why Our Population Is Increasing

Look at **Figure 19-2.** You can see that it took hundreds of thousands of years for Earth's population to reach 1 billion people. After that, the population increased much faster. Population has increased so rapidly in recent years because the death rate has been slowed by modern medicine, better sanitation, and better nutrition. This means that more people are living longer and remaining in the population. Also, births have increased because more people have reached the age at which they can have children.

The population explosion has seriously affected the environment. Scientists predict even greater changes as more people use Earth's limited resources. The population is predicted to be 14 billion sometime in the next century, nearly three times what it is now. We need to be aware of the effect such a large human population will have on our environment. We need to ask ourselves, Do we have enough natural resources to support such a large population?

CONNECT TO

LIFE SCIENCE

One of the things that affects carrying capacity is food. When a region does not have enough food, animals either migrate or starve. ***Infer*** what other factors determine the carrying capacity of a particular region for a species.

Visual Learning

Figure 19-1 In your Science Journal, discuss how this impacts Earth's limited resources. *Answers will vary, but students should mention that as human population continues to increase, Earth's resources will be depleted more rapidly.* LEP LS

2 Teach

Inquiry Question

Explain how modern health care has actually contributed to the population explosion. *With modern medicines, better sanitation, and better nutrition, people are living longer.*

CONNECT TO

LIFE SCIENCE

Answer fresh, unpolluted water; space to live

Student Text Questions

Are there enough natural resources to support such a large population? *probably not* **How will such a large human population affect our environment?** *The environment will probably be severely damaged. Already, there is great damage in some areas.*

Inclusion Strategies

Gifted Have students make population charts or graphs that compare the populations of Europe, Asia, Africa, North America, and South America. L3

 **Videodisc**

GTV: Planetary Manager

The Human Factor

Show 1.4, Side 1

15415-19710

Activity 19-1

PREPARATION

Purpose

LS **Logical-Mathematical** Make a model to demonstrate the population increase in 10 minutes of time. L1 COOP LEARN

Process Skills

making models, using numbers, communicating, forming a hypothesis, designing an experiment, interpreting data, making and using tables, making and using graphs

Time

20 minutes to plan the experiment, 40 minutes to do the experiment

Materials

Have 360 small items such as dried beans for each team to use. A 1-pound (484-g) bag of blackeye peas contains approximately 2100 beans.

Possible Hypothesis

Small objects can be placed into a beaker to represent the human population growth during a 10-minute period of time.

Activity Worksheets, pp. 5, 114-115

Activity 19-1

Design Your Own Experiment

A Crowded Encounter

Think about the effects of our rapidly increasing population. One of these is overcrowding. Every minute approximately 277 people are born and 97 people die. The difference in these two numbers, 180, is the net increase in human population each minute.

PREPARATION

Problem

How does the net increase in human population affect Earth's limited land and resources?

Form a Hypothesis

Based on the numbers above, state a hypothesis that shows how population increases in ten minutes' time.

Objectives

- Design and carry out an experiment to model human population growth in ten minutes' time.
- Observe the effects of human population increase on space.

Possible Materials

- many small objects, such as dried beans or paper clips
- 250-mL beaker
- clock or watch

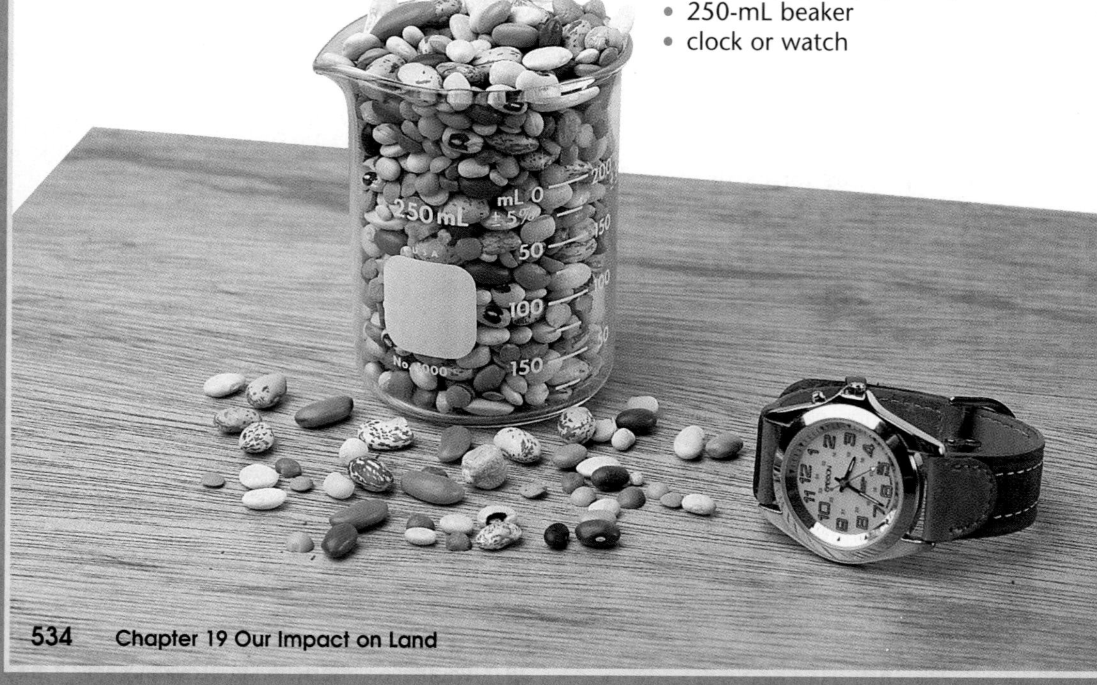

PLAN THE EXPERIMENT

1. As a group, agree upon and write out your hypothesis statement.
2. Your group should list the steps needed to test your hypothesis. Include in your plan how you will (a) let the empty beaker represent the unoccupied space left on Earth at the moment you begin the experiment; (b) let each of your small objects represent five people; and (c) design a table with two columns in your Science Journal showing time (1 through10 minutes) and population at the designated time.

Check the Plan

1. Review your plan to make certain that all steps are clear and logical.
2. *Have your teacher approve the plan and include any suggested changes before beginning.*

DO THE EXPERIMENT

1. Carry out the experiment as planned.
2. While the experiment is going on, write down any observations that you make and complete the data table in your Science Journal.
3. Make a graph that shows the results of your experiment. Plot time in minutes on the horizontal axis and population on the vertical axis.

Analyze and Apply

1. At the end of ten minutes, what is the net increase in human population?
2. **Explain** why the model you made was not a scale model.
3. Today there are approximately 5.7 billion people on Earth. That number will double in about 45 years. Assuming there is no change in that rate, **predict** what the population will be in 35 years. In 135 years.

Go Further

If you gathered all the humans on Earth into one place, we would take up only a very small portion of Earth's surface. Why then is human population growth a problem?

PLAN THE EXPERIMENT

Possible Procedures

One possible procedure is to let the empty beaker represent the unoccupied space left on Earth at the moment the experiment begins. Each small object will represent five people. The table will be designed with two columns, one showing time and the other the population at the designated time. Begin timing the experiment. At the end of the first minute, place 36 objects into the beaker. Record the data in the table. Continue this process for 9 more minutes. At the end of 10 minutes, make a graph that shows the time in minutes on the horizontal axis and the population on the vertical axis.

Teaching Strategies

- Students will place 36 beans in the beaker each minute.
- Have students refer to page 533 to help them make their graph.

DO THE EXPERIMENT

Expected Outcome

Students will see that over time, the beaker becomes very crowded with objects.

Analyze and Apply

1. 1800 people
2. The model is not a scale model because the volume occupied by each bean is not to scale with the beaker, which represents the unused land space on Earth.
3. In 45 years, the population will be 5.7 + 5.7 = 11.4 billion; an estimate near 10 billion is acceptable for 35 years. In 90 years, it will be 11.4 + 11.4 = 22.8 billion. In 135 years, it will be 22.8 + 22.8 = 45.6 billion.

Go Further

Although people's bodies do not take up very much space, students should realize that the croplands, buildings, factories, mines, roads, and other things used by people occupy much of the land.

Assessment

Performance To further assess students' understanding of population growth, have them graph ten years of growth in the U.S. In 1990, the estimated population of the U.S. was 251 million. The population increases by about 2.2 million people each year. Use the Performance Task Assessment List for Graph from Data in **PASC**, p. 39. P

Integration Life Science

At the 1994 American Geophysical Union conference, a researcher stated that Earth is headed for a mass extinction of species within 50 to 100 years. According to another researcher, currently there is a loss of 300 species of organisms each day. Ask students, **How do human activities contribute to these extinctions?** *Probably the biggest causes are pollution and habitat destruction.*

Visual Learning

Figure 19-3 **How do our consumption levels compare with the rest of the world's?** *People in the United States use five times as much energy as people living elsewhere. We consume 25% of the world's resources.* LEP LS

Using Math

Answer 102 people per square mile

3 Assess

Check for Understanding

Have students discuss: "How does my being on Earth change Earth? What can I do to make a positive balance between people and the environment?"

Reteach

Have students keep a diary for one day of all activities they perform that significantly affect the environment.

Extension

For students who have mastered this section, use the **Reinforcement** and **Enrichment** masters.

Integration Life Science

Using Math

The population density of a region is the average number of people per unit of area. Find the population density of Pennsylvania, which has a population of about 12 million people and an area of about 117 000 square km.

How People Affect the Environment

By the time you're 75 years old, you will have produced enough garbage to equal the mass of 16 African elephants (47 000 kg). You will have consumed enough water to fill 662 000 bathtubs (163 000 000 L). **Figure 19-3** shows examples of annual resource use in the United States. If you live in the United States, you will use five times as much energy as an average person living elsewhere in the world.

Our Daily Activities

You use electricity, some of which is generated by the burning of fuels. The environment is changed when the fuels are mined, and later burned. The water that you use must be made as clean as possible before being returned to the environment. You eat food, which takes land to grow. Poor farming and lumbering practices can cause huge volumes of topsoil to be eroded and lost each year. Much of the food you eat is grown using pesticides and herbicides—chemical substances. How else do you and other people affect the environment?

Many of the products you buy are packaged in plastic and paper. Plastic is made from oil. The process of refining oil produces pollutants. Producing paper requires cutting down trees, using gasoline to transport them to a paper mill, and producing pollutants to transform the trees into paper.

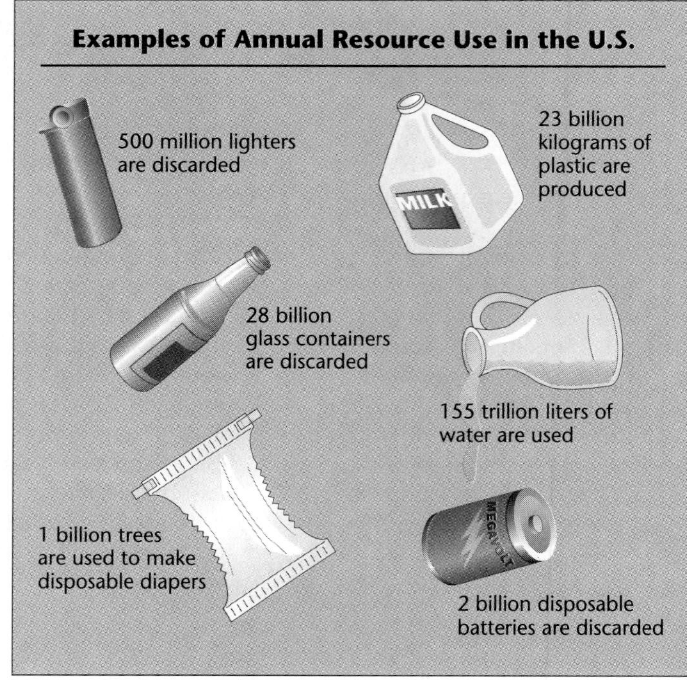

Figure 19-3
Some examples of annual resource use in the United States. *How do our consumption levels compare with the rest of the world's?*

Across the Curriculum

Social Studies Have students discuss how industrialization and urbanization not only affect, but are affected by, pollution. P

We change the land when we remove resources from it, and we further impact the environment when we shape those resources into usable products. Then, once we've produced and consumed products, we have to dispose of them. Look at **Figure 19-4.** Unnecessary packaging is only one of the problems associated with disposal of waste.

The Future

As the population continues to grow, more demands will be made on our environment. Traffic-choked highways, overflowing garbage dumps, shrinking forests, and vanishing wildlife are common. What can we do? People are the problem, but we also are the solution. As you learn more about how we affect the environment, you'll discover what you can do to make the future world one that everyone can live in.

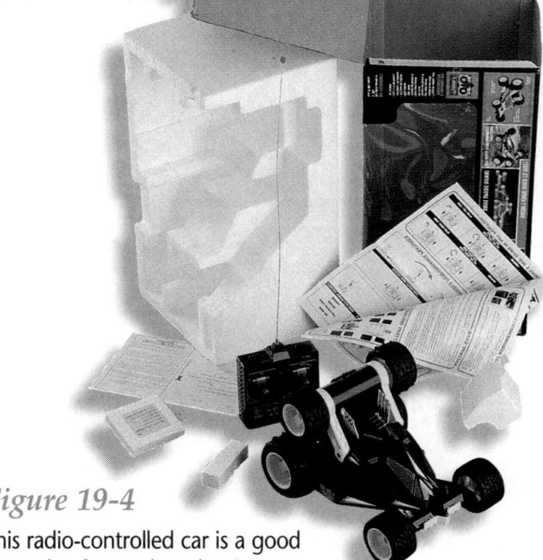

Figure 19-4

This radio-controlled car is a good example of a product that is excessively packaged. Because of consumer demands, many stores have begun selling products that come in environmentally friendly packages.

Section Wrap-up

Review

1. Using **Figure 19-2,** estimate how many years it took for the *Homo sapiens* population to reach 1 billion. How long did it take to triple to 3 billion?
2. Why is human population increasing so rapidly?
3. **Think Critically:** In nonindustrial nations, individuals have less negative impact on the environment than citizens in industrialized nations. In your Science Journal, explain why you think this is so.

Skill Builder

Making and Using Graphs

Use **Figure 19-2** on page 533 to answer the questions below. If you need help, refer to Making and Using Graphs in the **Skill Handbook.**

1. Early humanlike ancestors existed more than 4 million years ago. Why does the graph indicate that it should extend back only 500 000 years?
2. How would the slope of the graph change if, in the near future, the growth rate were cut in half?

USING MATH

Make a graph of the data shown below. Use your completed graph to infer the population of humans in the year 2040.

Human Population in Billions

1995	2010	2025
5.702	7.024	8.312

4 Close

• MINI • QUIZ •

Use the Mini Quiz to check students' recall of chapter content.

1. **A(n) ______ is the total number of individuals of a particular species in a particular area.** *population*
2. **The rate at which people are reproducing is so rapid that it's called a(n) _____.** *population explosion*
3. **People in the United States use ______ times as much energy as an average person living elsewhere.** *five*

Section Wrap-up

Review

1. It took almost 500 000 years for the *Homo sapiens* population to reach 1 billion. It took only 150 years (1810-1960) to triple.
2. The death rate has been slowed by modern medications, better sanitation, and better nutrition. Births have increased because more people have reached the age where they can have children.
3. **Think Critically** People living in nonindustrialized nations use less water, energy, and food, and generate less garbage.

USING MATH

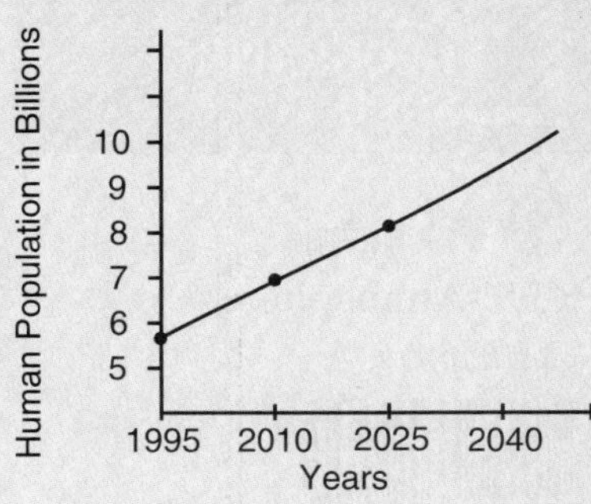

approximately 9.6 billion

Skill Builder

1. The graph represents the population growth of modern humans, *Homo sapiens.*
2. The slope would decrease by half of its current slope. The population would continue to increase, but at a slower rate.

Assessment

Performance Assess students' abilities to make and use graphs by having them determine when human population reached 2 billion. That occurred around 1912. Use the Performance Task Assessment List for Graph from Data in **PASC,** p. 39. P

Section 19•2

Prepare

Section Background

Waste deposited in sanitary landfills or open dumps is sometimes called *urban ore* because it contains many materials that could be recycled and used again to provide energy or useful products.

Preplanning

- To prepare for the MiniLAB on p. 541, have each student bring in a garbage bag.
- To prepare for the MiniLAB on p. 543, have balances and metric rulers available for students to use.

1 Motivate

Bellringer

Before presenting the lesson, display **Section Focus Transparency 73** on the overhead projector. Assign the accompanying **Focus Activity** worksheet. L1 LEP

Tying to Previous Knowledge

In Chapter 6, students learned about land use and soil loss. In this section, they will learn other ways that land use impacts the environment. They will also learn what they can do to protect the environment.

Videodisc

STV: Atmosphere

Cattle farm

38668

19•2 Using the Land

Science Words

landfill
sanitary landfill
hazardous waste
conservation
composting

Objectives

- List ways that we use land.
- Discuss environmental problems created because of land use.
- List things you can do to help protect the environment.

Land Usage

You may not think of land as a natural resource. Yet, it is as important to people as oil, clean air, and clean water. Through agriculture, logging, refuse disposal, and urban development, we use land—and sometimes abuse it.

Farming

Earth's total land area is 145 million square km. We use 15 million square km as farmland. Even so, about 20 percent of the people living in the world are hungry. Millions starve to death each year. To meet this need, farmers work to increase the productivity of croplands by using higher-yield seeds and chemical fertilizers. Herbicides and pesticides are also used to reduce weeds and insects that can damage crops.

Poor use of these chemicals, however, can contaminate the environment. For this reason, some farmers rely on organic farming techniques to lessen the environmental impact on the land. **Figure 19-5** shows an organic farm in China that has been farmed for 20 centuries.

Figure 19-5

Organic farming techniques can rebuild topsoil, rather than deplete it. Organic farmers use natural fertilizers, crop rotations, and biological pest controls to help their crops thrive.

Program Resources

Reproducible Masters

Study Guide, p. 77 L1
Reinforcement, p. 77 L1
Enrichment, p. 77 L3
Activity Worksheets, pp. 5, 118, 119 L1
Science Integration Activities, pp. 37-38
Critical Thinking/Problem Solving, p. 25
Concept Mapping, p. 43
Lab Manual 55

Transparencies

Section Focus Transparency 73 L1
Science Integration Transparency 19

Whenever vegetation is removed from an area, such as in construction sites or in agricultural tilling, the soil can become easily eroded. With plants gone, there is nothing to prevent the soil from being carried away by running water and wind. Several centimeters of topsoil may be lost in one year. In some places, it can take more than 1000 years for new topsoil to develop and replace the eroded topsoil. **Figure 19-6** shows one way farmers work to reduce this type of erosion.

Figure 19-6

Contour plowing is one way farmers reduce erosion. Water follows the contour of the land, along the plowed rows, instead of running straight downslope.

Grazing Livestock

Land is also used for grazing livestock. Animals such as cattle eat vegetation and are then often used as food for humans. In the United States, the majority of land used for this purpose is unsuitable for crops. However, about 20 percent of the cropland in our country is used to grow feed for livestock.

A square kilometer of vegetable crops can feed many more people than a square kilometer used to raise livestock. Some people argue that a more efficient use of the land would be to grow crops directly for human consumption, rather than for livestock. For many, however, meat and dairy products are an important part of their diet. They also argue that livestock have ecological benefits that justify livestock production.

Figure 19-7

One-third of the land in North America is used to graze livestock. One-half of all cropland is used to grow feed for livestock.

2 Teach

Concept Development

Have students review the evolution of soil presented in Chapter 6, Section 6-2.

NATIONAL GEOGRAPHIC SOCIETY

Videodisc

STV: Water

Crop irrigation; California

52554

Wheat fields; midwestern U.S.

52561

STV: Atmosphere

Cornfield during drought; Minnesota

38675

Forest killed by acid rain; Eastern Europe

38726

Cultural Diversity

Healing the Land More than 223 million acres of the world's grasslands have become barren, arid, and unable to support life. Overgrazing by cattle and sheep is a major cause of destruction for grasslands, but leaving pasture unused can also be destructive. Allan Savory worked as a wildlife biologist and tracker in Zimbabwe for 40 years before moving to New Mexico and beginning his program of holistic land management. Savory has established a Center for Holistic Resource Management that works with ranchers from many western states, including Texas, Colorado, and California. The center promotes an understanding of the total environment, and attempts to preserve a most precious natural resource, Earth itself. Have students use a map or globe to locate the places mentioned in this feature.

Inquiry Question

Describe two ways organisms living outside the tropics suffer when rain forests are cut down. *There is a reduction of oxygen and an addition of carbon dioxide to the atmosphere. Organisms need oxygen to breathe. Carbon dioxide contributes to the greenhouse effect.*

Visual Learning

Figure 19-9 In your Science Journal, list some problems associated with landfill disposal. *Answers will vary, but students should mention that acceptable landfill space is scarce, materials placed into landfills decompose slowly, and some hazardous wastes can leak into surrounding soil and groundwater.* LEP LS

Teacher F.Y.I.

Potentially disease-infected disposable diapers clutter sanitary landfills. About five percent of the landfill space in the United States is filled with soiled disposable diapers. The EPA estimates that 3 million metric tons of feces and urine end up in landfills rather than in sewage treatment plants because people don't wash diapers before they throw them away.

STV: Atmosphere

Logged area of rain forest; Malaysia

38671

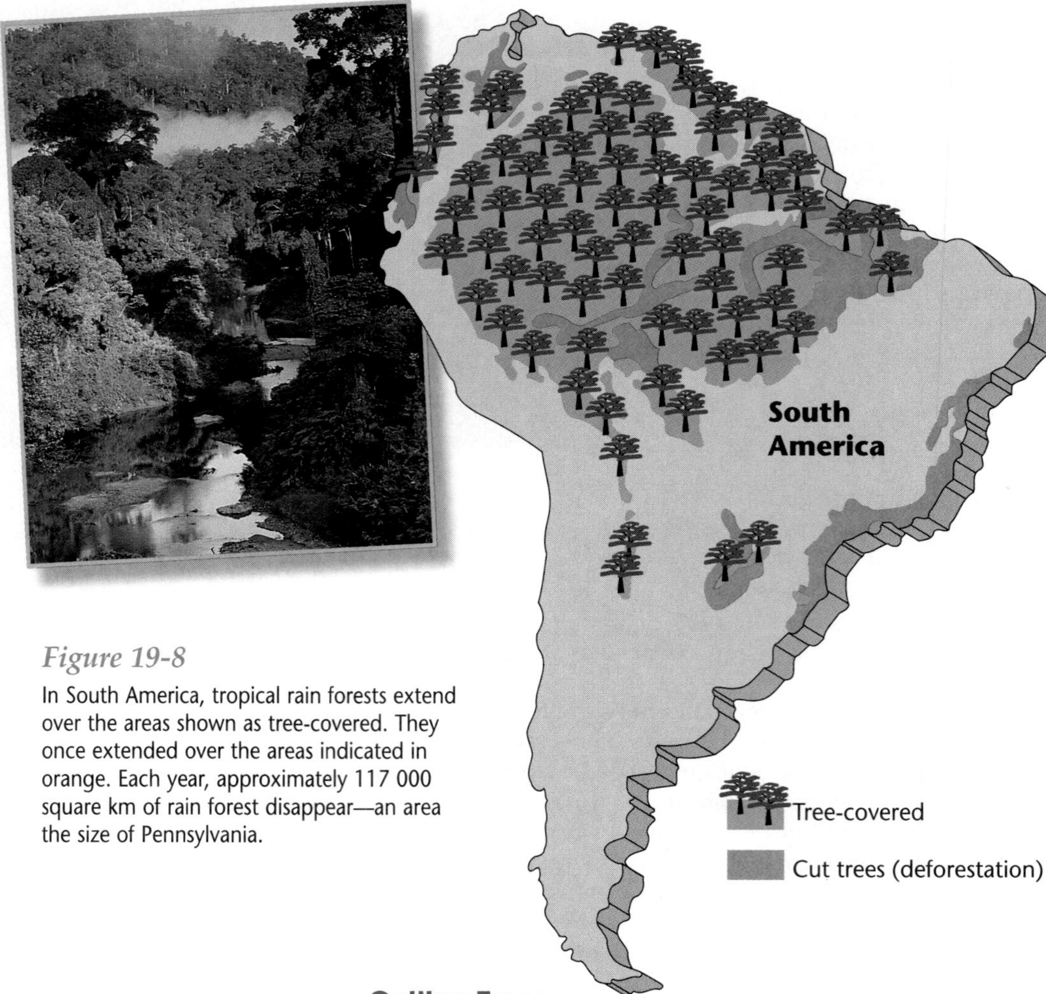

Figure 19-8

In South America, tropical rain forests extend over the areas shown as tree-covered. They once extended over the areas indicated in orange. Each year, approximately 117 000 square km of rain forest disappear—an area the size of Pennsylvania.

Cutting Trees

Some land is used as a source of wood. Trees are cut down and used for lumber, fuel, and paper. Often, new trees are planted to take their places. In some cases, especially in the tropical regions shown in **Figure 19-8,** whole forests are cut down without being replaced. Each year an area of rain forest the size of Pennsylvania disappears. Scientists estimate that up to 50 000 species may die each year because of this loss of habitat.

Organisms living outside of the tropics also suffer because of the lost vegetation. Plants remove carbon dioxide from the air, and when they photosynthesize, they produce oxygen that organisms need to breathe. Reduced vegetation also results in higher levels of carbon dioxide in the atmosphere. Carbon dioxide is one of the gases that contribute to the greenhouse effect.

Across the Curriculum

Geography Have students locate the world's rain forests on a globe. In order to do this, they may first need to use a world atlas. Also have them locate Pennsylvania on the globe. Emphasize that each year an area of rain forest the size of Pennsylvania is destroyed. L1 LS

Landfills

Land is also used when we dispose of the products we consume. Eighty percent of our garbage goes into landfills. A **landfill** is an area where waste is deposited. In a **sanitary landfill,** such as the one illustrated in **Figure 19-9,** each day's deposit is covered with dirt. The dirt prevents it from blowing away, and it reduces the odor produced by the decaying waste. Sanitary landfills are also designed to prevent liquid wastes from draining into the soil and groundwater below. A sanitary landfill is lined with plastic or concrete, or it's located in clay-rich soils that trap the liquid waste.

Hazardous Wastes

Some of the wastes we put into landfills are dangerous to organisms. Poisonous, cancer-causing, or radioactive wastes are called **hazardous wastes.** Hazardous wastes are put into landfills by industries. But individuals contribute to the problem, too, when they throw away insect sprays, batteries, drain cleaners, bleaches, medicines, and paints.

Sanitary landfills greatly reduce the chance that hazardous substances will leak into the surrounding soil and groundwater. However, some still find their way into the environment.

Another problem is that we're filling up our landfills and running out of acceptable areas to build new ones. Many materials placed into landfills decompose slowly.

It may seem that when we throw something in the garbage can, it is gone and we don't need to be concerned with it anymore. But our garbage does not disappear. It can simply remain in the landfill for hundreds of years. In the case of radioactive waste, it may be around for thousands of years, creating problems for future generations. Fortunately, industries and people are becoming more aware of the problems associated with landfills, and are disposing of their wastes in a more responsible manner. Later in this chapter, you will learn about what you can do personally to help reduce these problems.

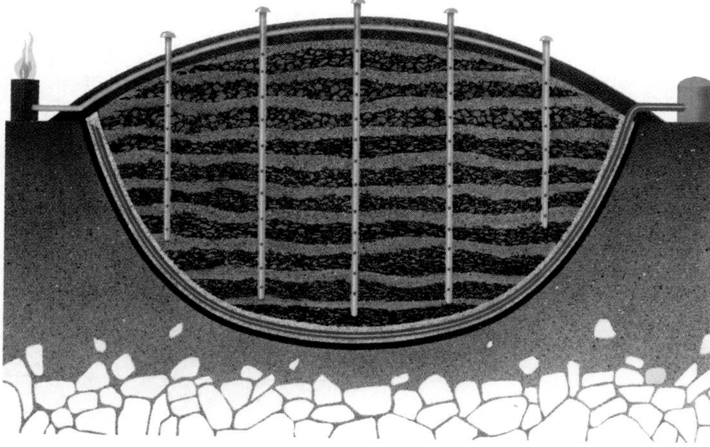

Figure 19-9

The vast majority of our garbage is deposited in landfills. *In your Science Journal, list some problems associated with landfill disposal.*

MiniLAB

How much trash do you generate in one day?

Determine the total mass and volume of your trash.

Procedure

1. Carry a garbage bag around with you all day, and place all of your trash, including food wastes, into it.
2. At the end of the day, measure and weigh the contents to determine their mass and volume.

Analysis

1. Calculate the percentage of the mass and volume of each of the following wastes: plastics, metals, food wastes, paper, and glass.
2. Compare your mass percentages with those of your classmates.
3. Hypothesize how you can reduce the amount of trash you generate each day.

MiniLAB

Purpose

IS **Intrapersonal** Students will measure the mass and volume of the garbage they generate daily. L1

Materials

garbage bags, balances, metric rulers

Teaching Strategies

- Have students sort their own trash at the end of the day. Have each student measure the mass of the different kinds of wastes on a balance and the volume with a ruler.
- Have students properly dispose of their trash, recycling those items that can be recycled in your community.

Analysis

1. Answers will vary. To find the percentage mass, students should divide the mass of a particular type of trash by the total mass of all of the wastes. The percentage of volume is found in a similar way, using the volume measurements.
2. Answers will vary.
3. Buying materials with less packaging and reusing certain items such as paper will reduce the trash generated.

Assessment

Performance Calculate the percentage mass and volume of your wastes that are recyclable. Use the Performance Task Assessment List for Using Math in Science in **PASC**, p. 29. P

Activity Worksheets, pp. 5, 118

GLENCOE TECHNOLOGY

CD-ROM

Earth Science CD-ROM

Have students perform the interactive exploration for Chapter 19 to reinforce important chapter concepts and thinking processes.

Community Connection

Limited Landfills Have students research the status of local landfills. Students should find out how long local landfills can continue to operate. They should discover if any are in danger of closing because of limited space. L1

Problem Solving

Solve the Problem

1. We've buried it in landfills, burned it in incinerators, or recycled it. Most of the trash goes to landfills.
2. Between 1960 and 1985, landfill use rose rapidly. It remained high until 1988, then it started going down. The use of incinerators peaked in 1960, dipped to its lowest point in 1985, and then began rising. Recycling rose slowly from 1960 to 1990.

Think Critically

1. Since we are running out of landfill space, other methods must be found for disposing of our wastes. We should recycle as many of these items as possible.
2. People can generate less waste by recycling and reusing materials. They can also buy products that aren't "overpackaged" and compost grass clippings and leaves.

Inquiry Question

- **Why do you suppose many people don't like the idea of landfills being created near their homes?** *Wastes may leak into soil and groundwater. The odor may ruin their property's value.*

Visual Learning

Figure 19-10 How does this impact the environment? *Paving over land increases air temperature and decreases the amount of water that soaks into the soil.* LEP IS

Problem Solving

Where does our trash go?

In the early days of the United States, population was more sparse and few people considered the impact of their actions on the environment. They threw their trash into rivers, buried it, or burned it. Given our increased population and output of trash, such methods are no longer feasible.

Solve the Problem:

1. **Since 1960, what three things have we done with most of our trash? Where does most of our trash go?**
2. **In your Science Journal, describe how our use of landfills, incinerators, and recycling has changed since 1960.**

Think Critically:

More than half of the states in our country are running out of landfill space. New landfills will have to be made, but most people have a NIMBY attitude. NIMBY means "not in my back yard." People don't want to live near a landfill.

1. What should we do about our trash problem?
2. What are some ways that we can generate less trash?

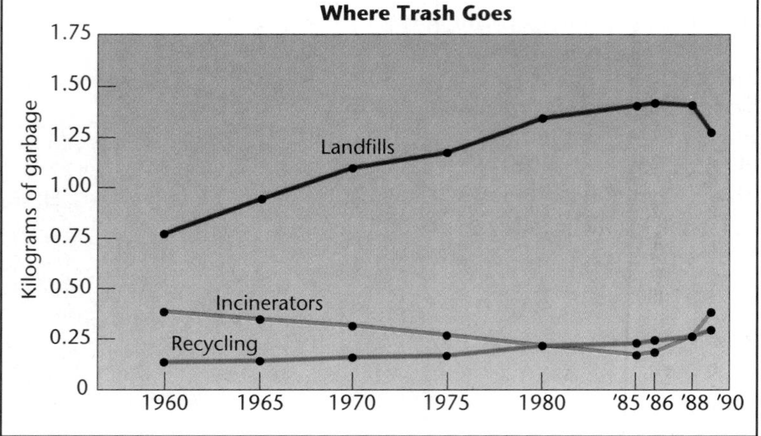

Structures, Mines, and Natural Environments

Concrete and asphalt are quickly replacing grass and woodlands in our communities. The impact on the environment, particularly in urban areas such as the one shown in **Figure 19-10**, is easy to observe. Asphalt and concrete absorb a lot of solar radiation. The atmosphere is then heated by conduction and convection, which causes the air temperature to rise. You may have observed this if you've ever traveled from a rural area to the city and noticed a rise in temperature.

Another effect of paving over the land is that less water is able to soak into the soil. Instead, it runs off into sewers or streams. During heavy rainstorms in urban areas, sewer pipes can overflow or become clogged with debris. Some of the water that does not soak into the soil evaporates. This reduces the amount of water in groundwater aquifers. Many communities rely on groundwater for drinking

Theme Connection

Systems and Interactions The following is a quote from Chief Seattle of the Native American Suquamish people. His words were in response to President Franklin Pierce's offer to buy land from the Suquamish people in 1854. Chief Seattle expressed the difference in the way his people viewed the land and the way people of European descent viewed it. ". . .He treats his mother, the earth, and his brother, the sky, as things to be bought, plundered, sold like sheep or bright beads. His appetite will devour the earth and leave behind only a desert . . ." Ask students to respond to Chief Seattle's words. Students should relate his thoughts to their own view of how present-day Americans view Earth. L1 P

Figure 19-10

Our cities are covered by concrete sidewalks and paved streets. *How does this impact the environment?*

water. But covering more and more of the land with roads, sidewalks, and parking lots prevents the water from reaching aquifers. In previous chapters, you've read about mining and how it can adversely affect the environment. As more people populate Earth, increased demands for fossil fuels and mineral ores will result in more mining operations.

Natural Preserves

Not all land on Earth is being used to produce usable materials or for storing waste. Look at **Figure 19-11.** Some land remains uninhabited by people. National parks in the United States are protected from much of the pollution and destruction that you've read about in this section. In many countries throughout the world, land is set aside as natural preserves. As the world population continues to rise, the strain on our environment is likely to increase. Let's hope that we will be able to continue preserving some land as natural environments.

Figure 19-11

Many countries set aside land as natural preserves. This means that the land will not be used to produce goods, but will remain in its natural state.

MiniLAB

Can one person make a difference?

Find out what you can do to help conserve resources and protect the environment.

Procedure

1. Based on what you have learned in this chapter, select at least one way to help the environment.
2. As a class, agree upon a length of time in which to complete your tasks.
3. Report back to the class on what you did to help the environment.

Analysis

1. Do you think your actions made a difference? Explain.
2. Hypothesize what changes might occur if each person in the United States did his or her part to save planet Earth.

MiniLAB

Purpose

LS **Intrapersonal** Students will select ways they can conserve resources and protect the environment. L1

Materials

These will depend on student choice. However, tree seedlings appropriate for planting in your locale may often be obtained at little or no cost from an area agricultural extension service or conservation agency.

Teaching Strategies

- Have a brainstorming session at the beginning of this MiniLAB. List all of the ideas that students think of on the board.
- Set aside time for students to report back to the class.

Analysis

1. Answers will vary.
2. Certainly, if each person were to implement environmental conservation practices, Earth would have a far more encouraging future.

Assessment

Performance To further assess students' understanding of how to reduce environmental problems, have them select other things to do and explain their selections. Use the Performance Task Assessment List for Writing in Science in **PASC,** p. 87. P

Activity Worksheets, pp. 5, 119

Science Journal

Population Explosion Have students determine some of the problems they think will occur as the human population continues to increase. Have them discuss some possible solutions in a report or on a chart, graph, or map in their Science Journals. L1 LS

Use **Critical Thinking/Problem Solving,** p. 25, as you teach this lesson.

USING TECHNOLOGY

For more information on recycling paper, see "All the News That's Fit to Eat," *Omni*, December 1991; or "Black and White to Squirm All Over," *The Philadelphia Inquirer*, Nov. 18, 1992.

Think Critically

One metric ton is equal to 1000 kg. Therefore: 150 000 kg = 150 metric tons. 150 metric tons × 17 trees = 2550 trees per month × 12 months = 30 600 trees saved per year.

3 Assess

Check for Understanding

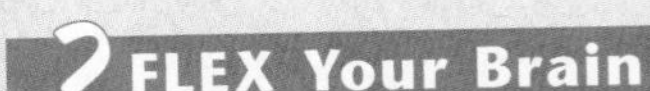

Use the Flex Your Brain activity to have students explore CONSERVATION.

Activity Worksheets, p. 5

Reteach

Have students list at least five different items that one or more members of the group discarded today. Have them describe at least two ways each of these items could have been reused. An example is that a piece of notebook paper, written on only one side, can still be used for sketching or writing. The paper can also be used to cover the bottom of a bird cage.

Extension

For students who have mastered this section, use the **Reinforcement** and **Enrichment** masters.

USING TECHNOLOGY

Recycling Paper

What happens to the newspaper you recycle? After the paper is taken to a plant where it is to be recycled, the paper is sorted and put into a device called a pulper. The pulper contains water and other substances that remove ink from the paper. The paper then becomes part of a soggy mixture called pulp.

Pulp is run through a machine that removes any solid objects such as rubber bands, paper clips, or staples that may have been fastened to the paper. Another device then squeezes the water from the paper mixture. The final stage of processing includes sifting and washing the pulp to remove any unwanted debris.

Water is added to the clean pulp to make a thick, pasty substance. This substance is rolled into thin sheets and dried to form sheets of recycled paper.

Think Critically:

If 17 trees are saved when one metric ton of paper is recycled, how many trees could be saved in a year if a community recycled 150 000 kg of paper each month?

Recycling Paper Saves Trees

Conserving Resources

In the United States and other industrialized countries, people have a throwaway lifestyle. When we are done with something, we throw it away. This means more products have to be produced to replace what we've thrown away, more land is used, and landfills overflow. You can help by conserving resources. **Conservation** is the careful use of resources that reduces damage to the environment.

Reduce, Reuse, Recycle

The United States makes up only 5 percent of the world's human population, yet it consumes 25 percent of the world's natural resources. Each of us can reduce our consumption of materials in simple ways, such as using both sides of notebook paper or carrying lunch to school in a nondisposable container. Ways to conserve resources include reducing our use of materials and reusing and recycling materials.

Community Connection

Composting Have students design and build a school compost pile. Be certain that it meets all local health regulations. Use the compost to construct flower beds on school property.

Reusing an item means finding another use for it instead of throwing it away. You can reuse old clothes by giving them to someone else, or by cutting them up into rags. The rags can be used in place of paper towels for cleaning jobs around your home.

Reusing plastic and paper bags is another way to reduce waste. Some grocery stores even pay a few cents when you return and reuse paper grocery bags. Out-of-doors, there are things you can do, too. If you cut grass or rake leaves, you can compost these items instead of putting them into the trash. **Composting** means piling yard wastes where they can gradually decompose. The decomposed matter can be used in gardens or flower beds to fertilize the soil. Some cities no longer pick up yard waste to take to the landfills. In these places, composting is common. If everyone in the United States composted, it would reduce the trash put into landfills by 20 percent.

The Population Outlook

The human population explosion has already had devastating effects on the environment and the organisms that inhabit Earth. It's unlikely that the population will begin to decline in the near future. To compensate, we must use our resources wisely. Conserving resources by reducing, reusing, and recycling are three important ways that you can make a difference.

USING MATH

You use 16 L of water if you let the water run while brushing your teeth. Only 2 L is used if the water is turned off until it's time to rinse. How much water could you save per year by not letting the water run? How much water could be saved by the entire U.S. population (260 million people)?

Section Wrap-up

Review

1. In your Science Journal, list six ways that we use land.
2. Discuss environmental problems that are sometimes created by agriculture, mining, and trash disposal.
3. **Think Critically:** Choose one of the following items, and list three ways it can be reused: an empty milk carton, vegetable scraps, used notebook paper, or an old automobile tire. Be sure your uses are environmentally friendly.

Skill Builder

Recognizing Cause and Effect

Review Section 19-2 and answer the questions below. If you need help, refer to Recognizing Cause and Effect in the **Skill Handbook.**

1. How many uses of land are described in this section?
2. How can farming negatively impact the environment?
3. How can grazing livestock negatively impact it?

Using Computers

Word Processing Suppose that a new landfill is needed in your community. Where do you think it should be located? Now, suppose that you want to convince people that you've selected the best place for the landfill. Use your word processing skills to write a letter to the editor of the local newspaper, listing reasons in favor of your choice.

USING MATH

- To calculate the water saved by one student, use the following formulas:

16 L − 2 L = 14 L

14 L × 3 (times per day) = 42 L

42 L × 365 = 15 330 L/year

- To calculate the water that could be saved by the entire country, use the following:

15 330 L/year × 260 000 000 = 3 985 800 000 000 L/year

4 Close

•MINI•QUIZ•

1. **About 20 percent of all cropland is used to _____.** *raise food for livestock used in meat and dairy products*
2. **Reduced vegetation can result in higher levels of _____ in the atmosphere.** *carbon dioxide*
3. **_____ percent of our garbage goes into landfills.** *Eighty*

Section Wrap-up

Review

1. farming, grazing livestock, source of wood, landfills, mines, structures, natural preserves
2. agriculture: soil erosion, pesticide and herbicide pollution; mining: loss of vegetation, polluted runoff into streams, lakes, and aquifers, loss of natural habitats; trash disposal: leakage into soil and water, landfills take up a lot of space
3. Think Critically Answers will vary.

Using Computers

Letters should address the issues that concern people: a landfill's odor, unsightliness, and the danger of substances leaking into soil and groundwater.

Skill Builder

Student answers will vary.

1. seven (farming, grazing, forestry, landfills, urbanization, mining, preservation)
2. Farming causes excessive topsoil erosion, and it adds poisons to the soil and water.
3. Grazing livestock destroys natural habitats and can cause soil erosion.

Assessment

Content Use this Skill Builder to assess students' abilities to recognize cause and effect. Ask students to use their answers to explain how people can help correct many of the environmental problems that they contribute to. Use the Performance Task Assessment List for Making Observations and Inferences in **PASC,** p. 17. P

Prepare

Section Background

- Paper loses quality with each reprocessing. Printing and writing paper can only be made from high-grade recycled paper.
- Some plastics are melted down and spun into polyester fiber that is used to make sleeping bags, insulation, and fishing line. Also, plastics can be made into rot-resistant materials for picnic tables, waterfront decks, boat hulls, and bath tubs.

Preplanning

To prepare for Activity 19-2, have each group bring two 2-liter bottles and garbage (including food scraps, yard waste, a plastic item, a metal item, a foam cup, and notebook paper or newsprint). Also obtain the following for each group: soil, thermometer, plastic wrap, rubber band, and graph paper.

1 Motivate

Bellringer

Before presenting the lesson, display **Section Focus Transparency 74** on the overhead projector. Assign the accompanying **Focus Activity** worksheet. L1 LEP

Tying to Previous Knowledge

Students already know the meaning of the term *recycle.* In this section, students will learn the many ways that the environment is helped when people recycle. They will learn about the advantages and disadvantages of mandatory recycling.

ISSUE: Should recycling be required?

Science Words

recyclable

Objectives

- List the advantages of recycling.
- List the advantages and disadvantages of mandatory recycling.
- Express your feelings about whether recycling should be required.

Recycling

Did you know that any object is **recyclable** if it can be processed and used again? Look at **Figure 19-12A.** Paper and aluminum are two of the many things that can be recycled.

Paper makes up about 40 percent of the mass of our trash. If you recycle it, you save landfill space and trees. Also, the production of recycled paper takes 61 percent less water and generates 71 percent fewer air pollutants than the production of brand-new paper made from trees.

How much energy do you think is saved when you recycle one aluminum can? Answer: enough to keep a TV running for about three hours. Twenty aluminum cans can be recycled with the energy needed to produce a single brand-new can from ore.

Figure 19-12

When you recycle, you help the environment in many ways.

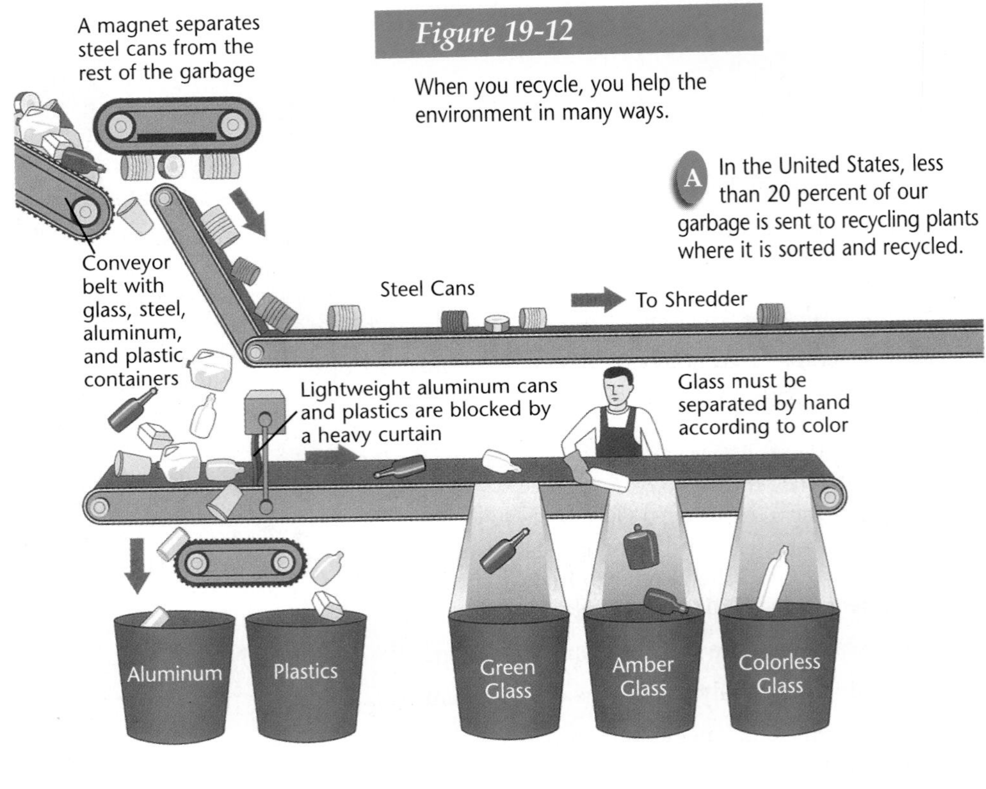

A In the United States, less than 20 percent of our garbage is sent to recycling plants where it is sorted and recycled.

Program Resources

Reproducible Masters

Study Guide, p. 78 L1
Reinforcement, p. 78 L1
Enrichment, p. 78 L3
Cross-Curricular Integration, p. 23
Science and Society Integration, p. 23
Activity Worksheets, pp. 5, 116-117 L1
Lab Manual 56

Transparencies

Section Focus Transparency 74 L1
Teaching Transparency 38

B Recycling plastics, alumninum, and glass saves landfill space, energy, and natural resources.

2 Points of View

Everyone agrees that recycling is good for the environment. It saves landfill space, energy, and natural resources. Recycling also helps reduce the damage caused by mining, cutting trees, and manufacturing. Did you know that if you recycle, you will reduce the trash you generate in your lifetime by 60 percent? If you don't recycle, you'll generate trash equal to at least 600 times your mass. But the question is, should recycling be required?

Mandatory Recycling

Many things aren't recycled because some people haven't gotten into the habit of recycling. In the United States, much less garbage is recycled than in countries with mandatory recycling, such as Japan and Germany. Mandatory recycling requires people to participate and creates new jobs in "reuse" industries, such as the production of items from recycled plastics.

C Many civic groups "adopt" sections of a highway. They pick up trash and recycle the salvageable garbage. *In your Science Journal, write a letter to your local chamber of commerce suggesting ways to beautify your community.*

Community Connection

Recycling Plant Tour Organize a field trip to a local recycling plant. Have students bring a camera along to take pictures of the process. Have the film developed and make the pictures into a poster showing the process. Have students write under each picture what is taking place in the photo.

2 Teach

Activity

Have students set up a trash recycling center at school. Students can maintain areas for collecting glass, metals, and paper.

Visual Learning

Figure 19-11 In your Science Journal, write a letter to your local chamber of commerce suggesting ways to beautify your community. *Letters will vary.* LEP LS

3 Assess

Check for Understanding

Ask students why people are not recycling more things. *Some people haven't gotten into the habit; many areas do not have recycling centers or the centers only recycle certain items; and there are not markets for some items.*

Reteach

Have students respond to the following problem: "Suppose one of your friends starts making bracelets out of metal scraps. You help her by starting a recycling center for metal scraps. You clean, sort, and sell metal scraps at a profit to your jeweler friend. Predict what will happen if no one buys her bracelets." *She will quit buying metal scraps, and the recycling business will end.*

Extension

For students who have mastered this section, use the **Reinforcement** and **Enrichment** masters.

CONNECT TO

PHYSICS

Answer These metals can be separated because steel is attracted to a magnet and aluminum is not.

4 Close

•MINI•QUIZ•

Use the Mini Quiz to check students' recall of chapter content.

1. **You can reduce the amount of trash you produce by 60% if you _____ .** *recycle*
2. **Paper makes up about _____% of our trash.** *40*
3. **_____ require that consumers make a deposit on beverage containers.** *Container laws*

Section Wrap-up

Review

1. saves landfill space, energy, and resources; reduces damage from mining, logging, and manufacturing
2. *Advantages:* more people will recycle, jobs are created, people benefit in some way (lower trash collection fees), much energy is saved

   Disadvantages: voluntary recycling is working well in some areas and people have the choice to participate or not, so that choice would be gone; cost outweighs the benefits; some jobs are lost; there is no market for some of the materials

In 1993, 17 states already had some form of recycling laws. People in these states comply with the laws because they benefit directly in some way. For example, in some places people who recycle pay lower trash-collection fees. In other places, garbage is not collected if it contains items that should have been recycled.

Some states have container laws whereby a five-cent refundable deposit is made on all beverage containers. This means paying five cents extra at the store for a drink. But you get your nickel back if you return the container to the store for recycling.

There are those who believe that if we had a national container law, we could save enough energy to light up a large city for four years.

CONNECT TO

PHYSICS

Iron and aluminum have different properties. Using **Figure 19-12A**, ***determine*** which property allows recycling centers to separate iron from aluminum. (Hint: Steel is made from iron.)

Voluntary Recycling

Today, many people already recycle voluntarily because their cities provide curbside collection or convenient drop-off facilities. In this case, people have the freedom to decide whether to recycle or not, without government intervention.

Some people will argue that the cost of recycling outweighs the benefits. Recycling requires money to pay for workers, trucks, and buildings. Also, some workers, such as miners and manufacturers who make brand-new containers, might lose their jobs.

Another problem is what to do with all of the recyclable items. Recycling businesses have to make a profit or they can't exist. The only way to make a profit in recycling is to sell the recycled material. There must be a market for the material. People or businesses must want to purchase the recycled products. In some cities, from time to time, old newspapers can't be recycled because there is no market for them. New paper is cheaper than recycled paper.

Section Wrap-up

Review

1. List at least four advantages of recycling.
2. What are the advantages and disadvantages of mandatory recycling?

Explore the Issue

Do you think the government should pass laws requiring people to recycle?

SCIENCE & SOCIETY

Explore the Issue

Some will feel that the government must force recycling because we desperately need to protect the environment, and many people will not bother with the inconveniences of recycling unless forced. Others will feel that people should be allowed to voluntarily recycle. Voluntary recycling is working in many places. Also, mandatory recycling creates problems such as jobs being lost.

Activity 19-2

A Model Landfill

When garbage is put into landfills, it is buried under other trash and soil; therefore, it isn't exposed to sunlight and other things that help decomposition. When examined by a researcher, one landfill was found to contain grass clippings that were still green, and bread that had not molded.

Problem

At what rates do different materials decompose in a landfill?

Materials

- two 2-L bottles
- thermometer
- graph paper
- soil
- plastic wrap
- rubber band
- garbage (including food scraps, yard waste, a plastic item, a metal item, a foam cup, and notebook paper or newsprint)

Procedure

1. Cut off the top of two 2-L bottles.
2. Add soil to each bottle until it is half-filled.
3. On graph paper, trace the outline of all the garbage items that you will place into each bottle. Label each outline. Keep the graph paper as a record of the original sizes of the items.
4. Place the items, one at a time, in each bottle. Completely cover each item with soil.
5. Add water to the "landfill" until the soil is slightly moist. Place a thermometer in each bottle and seal the bottle with the plastic wrap and a rubber band. Store one bottle at a cold temperature and place the other on a shelf.
6. Check the temperature of the "landfill" on the shelf each day for two weeks. Record the temperatures in a data table that you design.
7. After two weeks, remove all of the items from the soil. Trace the outlines of each on a new sheet of graph paper. Compare the sizes of the items with their original sizes.
8. Wash your hands thoroughly after cleaning up your lab space. Be sure to properly dispose of each item as instructed by your teacher.

Analyze

1. Which items decomposed the most? Which showed the least decomposition?
2. Most decomposition in a landfill is due to the activity of microorganisms. The organisms can live only under certain temperature and moisture conditions. Why was it necessary to add moisture to the soil? **Explain** how the decomposition rates would have differed if the soil had been completely dry.
3. **Compare** your results with the results of the bottle that was stored at a cold temperature. **Explain** the differences you observe.

Conclude and Apply

4. Why do some items decompose more rapidly than others?
5. What problems are created in landfills by plastics?

Activity 19-2

Purpose

LS **Visual-Spatial** Students will observe the rate of decomposition of various materials in a model landfill. L1

COOP LEARN

Process Skills

communicating, recognizing cause and effect, making models, making and using tables, observing and inferring, comparing and contrasting, interpreting data

Time

30 minutes set up; 2-3 minutes each day for 2 weeks to read thermometers; 30 minutes at the end of 2 weeks

Safety Precautions

Caution students to wash their hands after handling garbage.

Activity Worksheets, pp. 5, 116-117

Teaching Strategies

- Prior to performing this activity, have members of each group predict what they think will happen to the sizes of the "fill" and to the internal temperatures of the "operating" model landfills.
- Have the student groups set up a second landfill model to place in a refrigerator. These models will be used for comparison in Analyze Question 3.
- Set up a "control" landfill model of soil and water only to provide comparative temperature data to that of the "operating" landfills.

Answers to Questions

1. Answers will vary.
2. Microorganism activity is most rapid in warm, moist environments. Decomposition rates tend to be significantly lower under dry conditions.

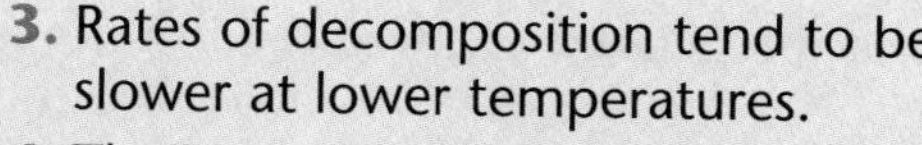

3. Rates of decomposition tend to be slower at lower temperatures.
4. The items are composed of different materials. Those that are more biodegradable, usually those composed of paper or soft organic materials, tend to decompose faster.
5. Plastics are not biodegradable and therefore do not decompose in a landfill.

Assessment

Performance Design an experiment to find out how the depth a material is buried in a landfill affects its rate of decomposition. Use the Performance Task Assessment List for Designing an Experiment in **PASC**, p. 23. P

People and Science

Teaching Strategies

Invite a horticulturist or forester from a local park department to speak to the class about the challenges of designing and caring for public spaces that are good for people, wildlife, and the land.

Career Connection

Career Path A combination of formal training and hands-on experience is advised. Recommended courses include botany, plant identification, soils, landscape architecture, and principles of horticulture. Math skills are needed for calibrating amounts of fertilizer or seed to apply, for figuring out how many plants will fit in a bed of a certain size, and for estimating needs, in cubic yards, of potting soil ingredients, such as peat moss and vermiculite. A background in art and design may be helpful. In urban areas, botanical gardens and city-operated greenhouses may have internship programs for high school students.

Background

Urban wind patterns present a challenge to horticulturists who design plantings for city streets. Tall buildings funnel wind down to the ground, where it spreads out and streams around the buildings' corners, creating whirlwinds.

For More Information

Through its Backyard Wildlife Habitat Program, the National Wildlife Federation suggests ways to use plantings, ponds, brush piles, etc. to provide shelter, food, and water for wild animals. For information, write to National Wildlife Federation/Backyard Wildlife Habitat Program, 1400 16th St. NW, Washington, DC 20036.

People and Science

LEIGH STANDINGBEAR, Horticulturist, City of Tulsa

On the Job

Q Describe how you transformed a city park into a habitat for native waterfowl.

A Swan Lake Park, one of Tulsa's most popular parks, has a two-acre lake right in the middle of an urban neighborhood. One of the many native plants we used is button bush—a woody shrub that provides roosting places for birds and cascades out over the water to provide good cover. Rushes and sedges do a very good job of holding the soil together at water's edge to prevent erosion.

Q You've also created ethnobotanical gardens, which display plants that were important to two groups of Native American people. Tell us about them.

A In the Osage Precolumbian Garden, one of the plants on display is the Osage orange tree. The strong, beautiful wood from that tree was used to make bows. The Creek Nation Council Oak Park garden, right on the edge of downtown Tulsa, has plants that were used by the Creeks for food, fiber, medicinal and ceremonial purposes in their ancestral homelands in Alabama.

Personal Insights

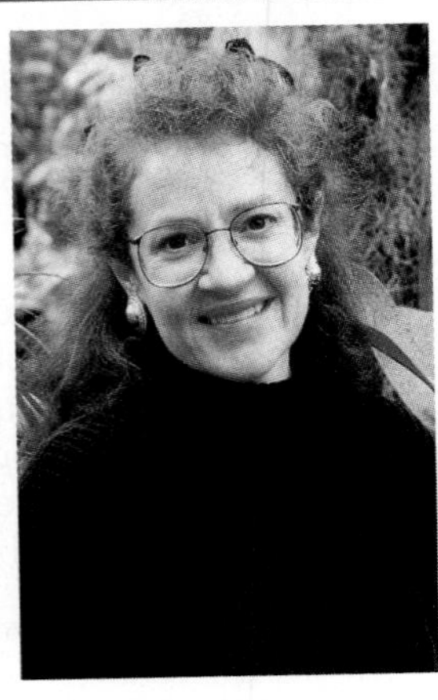

Q You feel a personal responsibility to care for the land. What in your background has led you to that feeling?

A Although I wasn't around at the time, I know from Oklahoma history that the famous Dust Bowl changed the thinking, technology, and methodology used in agriculture to prevent erosion and to protect marshlands and grasslands. Today, people are beginning to understand that protected places in urban settings are a valuable, important part of life.

Career Connection

Visit a park near your home or school, taking along a notebook or sketchpad. List or sketch five ways the park could be improved to make it a better place for plants, animals, and people.

- Biologist
- Ethnobotanist

References

- Moll, Gary, and Sara Ebenreck, eds. *Shading Our Cities: A Resource Guide for Urban and Community Forests.* Washington, DC, Island Press, 1989.
- National Wildflower Research Center. *The National Wildflower Research Center's Wildflower Handbook.* Stillwater, Minn., Voyageur Press, 1992.
- Ross, Nancy. "City trees have a tough and short life." *Detroit Free Press,* April 2, 1985, p. 2C.
- Ross, Nancy. "Urban winds: Tall buildings trap breezes, send them to swirl around us." *Detroit Free Press,* April 2, 1985, p. 1C.
- TreePeople with Andy and Katie Lipkis. *The Simple Act of Planting a Tree: Healing Your Neighborhood, Your City, and Your World.* Los Angeles, Jeremy P. Tarcher, 1990.

Chapter 19

Review

Summary

19-1: Population Impact on the Environment

1. The rapid increase in Earth's human population in recent years is due to an increase in the birth rate, advances in medicine, better sanitation, and better nutrition.
2. People in industrial nations strongly impact the environment when they use electricity, burn fossil fuels, contaminate water, and use food that's been grown with pesticides and herbicides.

19-2: Using the Land

1. Land is used for farming, grazing livestock, cutting trees, and mining coal and mineral ores. We also build structures and landfills on the land. Some land is preserved as natural environments.
2. Land becomes polluted by hazardous wastes thrown away by industries and individuals. Fertilizers and pesticides used by farmers pollute groundwater and soil. When trees are cut down, soil is destroyed and more carbon dioxide remains in the atmosphere.
3. Recycling, reducing, and reusing materials are important ways we can conserve natural resources.

19-3: Science and Society: Should recycling be required?

1. Recycling saves energy, natural resources, and much-needed space in landfills.
2. If recycling were required, more people would recycle, new jobs would be created, and additional landfill space and energy would be saved. But there would be government control instead of free choice. Also, recycling is expensive, some people would lose their jobs, and we would have some recyclable items that no one wants.

Key Science Words

a. carrying capacity
b. composting
c. conservation
d. hazardous waste
e. landfill
f. population
g. population explosion
h. recyclable
i. sanitary landfill

Reviewing Vocabulary

Match each phrase with the correct term from the list of Key Science Words.

1. total number of individuals of a particular species in an area
2. describes the rapid increase in birth rate and decrease in death rate
3. area used to deposit garbage
4. trash that's dangerous to organisms
5. piling up organic material to decompose
6. careful use of resources
7. area lined with plastic, concrete, or clay where garbage is dumped
8. items that can be processed and used again
9. maximum number of individuals of a particular type that the planet will support

Chapter 19 Review

Summary

Have students read the summary statements to review the major concepts of the chapter.

Reviewing Vocabulary

1. f
2. g
3. e
4. d
5. b
6. c
7. i
8. h
9. a

Assessment

Portfolio Encourage students to place in their portfolios one or two items of what they consider to be their best work. Examples include:

- Activity 19-1, Assessment graph, p. 535
- Across the Curriculum, p. 536
- Theme Connection, p. 542 P

Performance Additional performance assessments may be found in **Performance Assessment** and **Science Integration Activities.** Performance Task Assessment Lists and rubrics for evaluating these activities can be found in Glencoe's **Performance Assessment in the Science Classroom.**

GLENCOE TECHNOLOGY

MindJogger Videoquiz

Chapter 19 Have students work in groups as they play the Videoquiz game to review key chapter concepts.

Chapter 19 Review

Checking Concepts

1. b
2. d
3. c
4. d
5. b
6. d
7. c
8. c
9. d
10. d

Understanding Concepts

11. 260 000 people are added each day; 260 000/24 hours = 10 833 people added each hour

12. Much of the energy contained in a plant is used up by livestock. One square kilometer of land used to grow vegetable crops can feed more humans than a square kilometer used to graze livestock.

13. Probably the biggest advantage of recycling paper is that it saves trees. Recycling paper also saves a lot of landfill space, energy, and water. Recycling also reduces air and water pollution.

Thinking Critically

14. 190 L/2 = 95 L
95 L × 365 days =
34 675 L/year

15. Oxygen is constantly being added to Earth's atmosphere via photosynthesis. It's renewable.

16. Often, farmers can't afford machinery, improved strains of seeds, pesticides, or fertilizers. Insects often destroy crops. Lack of fertilizers causes the soil nutrients to become depleted.

17. Fewer trees are available to produce oxygen and remove CO_2 from the air. Other vegetation is probably dying, too. The decrease in plants causes an increase in soil erosion. Species of plants and animals that depend on the forest habitat may become extinct if they are unable to adapt to the changes produced by the dying trees.

18. Answers will vary but might include providing collection bins in a convenient place or actually going door to door to collect the papers. If the interest were communitywide, people might be given a monetary incentive to recycle.

Developing Skills

19. Recognizing Cause and Effect The habitat of many organisms living in the grassy lot would be lost. Less water will soak into the soil. Groundwater may be depleted. Also, the pavement will absorb more heat, causing the air temperature to be higher.

20. Measuring in SI Answers will depend on the number of students in the class. By multiplying the number of students by 47 174 kg/student, the total amount of trash produced can be calculated.

21. Classifying Classification schemes will vary but might include sorting by type

Chapter 19 Review

Checking Concepts

Choose the word or phrase that completes the sentence.

1. Most of the trash in the United States is disposed of in ______.
   a. recycling centers c. hazardous waste sites
   b. landfills d. old mine shafts
2. Between 1960 and 1995, world population increased by ______ billion people.
   a. 5.7 c. 1.0
   b. 3.2 d. 2.7
3. The United States uses about ______ percent of Earth's resources.
   a. 5 c. 25
   b. 10 d. 50
4. About ______ of North American cropland is used to raise food for livestock.
   a. 100 percent c. 80 percent
   b. one percent d. 50 percent
5. When an object is ______, it can be used again.
   a. trash c. disposable
   b. recyclable d. hazardous
6. ______ makes up about 40 percent of the mass of our trash.
   a. Glass c. Yard waste
   b. Aluminum d. Paper
7. In a ______, garbage is covered with soil.
   a. recycling center c. sanitary landfill
   b. surface mine d. coal mine
8. ______ of people starve to death each year.
   a. Hundreds c. Millions
   b. Thousands d. Billions
9. Organisms living outside the tropics suffer when rain forests are cut down because the trees are no longer there to produce ______.
   a. carbon dioxide c. water
   b. methane d. oxygen
10. An example of a hazardous waste is a ______.
    a. piece of glass c. steel can
    b. plastic jug d. can of paint

Understanding Concepts

Answer the following questions in your Science Journal using complete sentences.

11. On average, how many people are added to Earth's population each hour?
12. Why is raising vegetable crops more efficient than raising livestock?

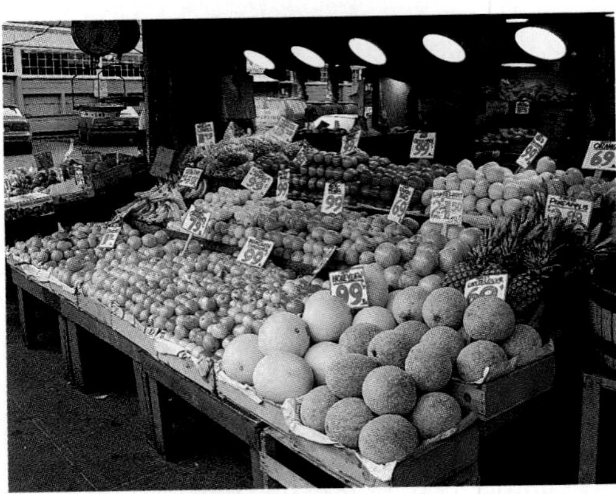

13. Discuss why recycling paper is good for the environment.

Thinking Critically

14. A ten-minute shower uses about 190 L of water. If a person takes one shower a day and reduces the time to five minutes, how much water would be saved in a year?
15. Renewable resources are those resources that can be replenished by nature in the foreseeable future. Nonrenewable resources cannot. Which kind of resource is oxygen? Explain.
16. Although land is farmable in many developing countries, hunger is a major problem in many of these countries. Give some reasons why this might be so.
17. Forests in Germany are dying due to acid rain. What effects might this loss have on the environment?
18. Describe how you could encourage your neighbors to recycle their newspapers.

Developing Skills

If you need help, refer to the **Skill Handbook.**

19. Recognizing Cause and Effect: Suppose a city decided to pave over a large, grassy lot. What effects will this have on the local environment?

20. Measuring in SI: If each person in your class produced 47 174 kg of trash in a lifetime, how much trash would be produced by this small population?

21. Classifying: Analyze the garbage you throw away in one day. Classify each piece of garbage.

22. Making and Using Graphs: In a population of snails, each snail produces two offspring each month. Each offspring also produces two offspring. Using the graph below, determine how many snails would be present after five months if the initial population was only two snails.

23. Interpreting Scientific Illustrations: Why does the curve of the line graph in Question 22 change its slope over time? Suppose half of the snails died after six months. Draw a new graph to illustrate the effect.

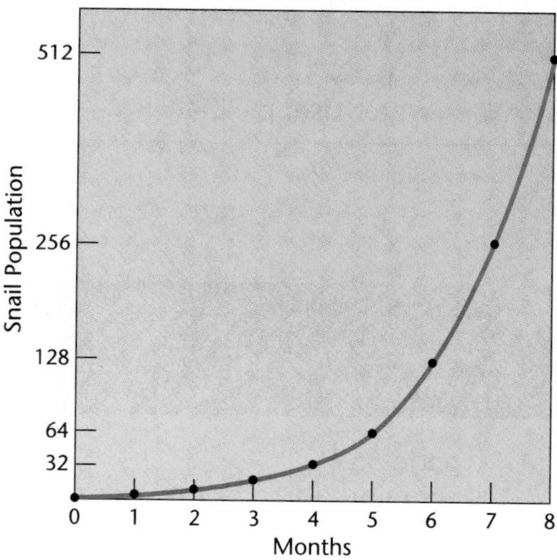

Performance Assessment

1. Using Math in Science: Collect your family's junk mail for one week. Determine the mass of the accumulated mail. Divide the mass by the number of persons living in your home. Using this number as an average for all people living in the U.S. (260 million), calculate the total mass of junk mail received each week in the U.S. Calculate the amount per year. If 17 trees are killed to make each metric ton of paper, calculate how many trees are killed each year to make junk mail.

2. Evaluating a Hypothesis: Design an experiment to determine the factors that decrease the time it takes for newspapers or yard wastes to decompose.

Assessment Resources

Reproducible Masters

Chapter Review, pp. 41-42

Assessment, pp. 128-131

Performance Assessment, p. 33

Glencoe Technology

Chapter Review Software

Computer Test Bank

MindJogger Videoquiz

Chapter 19 Review

such as organic or inorganic, or more specifically as organic, glass, aluminum, steel, paper, and plastic. Trash could also be classified as "throw away" or recyclable.

22. Making and Using Graphs After five months, 64 snails would be present.

23. Interpreting Scientific Illustrations The growth rate is exponential. Each offspring contributes to the population growth, not just the original pair of snails. If half of the population died after six months, the population would drop from 128 snails to 64 snails. The growth would then begin doubling from there.

Performance Assessment

1. Answers will vary, but the steps to use in finding the answer are: (a) determine the mass of the family's mail, (b) divide this mass by the number of family members, (c) multiply this by 260 million, (d) multiply this number by 52 (the number of weeks in a year), (e) convert this number to metric tons, and (f) divide this number by 17. Use the Performance Task Assessment List for Using Math in Science in **PASC,** p. 29. P

2. Designs will vary. Variables that might be tested one at a time are temperature, moisture, degree of compaction, mixtures of different types of wastes, or introduction of microorganisms to the compost pile. Use the Performance Task Assessment List for Evaluating a Hypothesis in **PASC,** p. 31. P

Chapter Organizer

Section	Objectives	Activities/Features
Chapter Opener		Explore Activity: Study your air. p. 555
20-1 **Air Pollution** (2 sessions, 1½ blocks)*	1. **Identify** the sources of pollutants that cause photochemical smog, sulfurous smog, holes in the ozone layer, and acid rain. 2. **Describe** how air pollution affects people and the environment. 3. **Explain** how air pollution can be reduced.	MiniLAB: Do you have acid rain in your community? p. 557 Using Math, p. 559 Connect to Life Science, p. 560 Using Math, p. 561 Skill Builder: Concept Mapping, p. 561 Science Journal, p. 561
20-2 **Science and Society Technology: Acid Rain** (2 sessions, ½ block)*	1. **Describe** how soil type affects acid rain damage. 2. **Describe** activities that help reduce acid rain. 3. **Decide** who should pay the cost of reducing sulfur dioxide emissions.	Using Technology: Sunsats and Moon Grids, p. 563 Explore the Issue, p. 564 Science and History: The Aswan High Dam and Its Effects on Egypt's Soil and Water, p. 565 Science Journal, p. 565 Activity 20-1: What's in the air? pp. 566-567
20-3 **Water Pollution** (2 sessions, 1½ blocks)*	1. **List** five water pollutants and their sources. 2. **Describe** ways that international agreements and U.S. laws are designed to reduce water pollution. 3. **Relate** ways that you can help reduce water pollution.	Problem Solving: What's happening to the fish? p. 570 Using Math, p. 571 MiniLAB: How hard is your water? p. 572 Skill Builder: Interpreting Scientific Illustrations, p. 573 Science Journal, p. 573 Activity 20-2: Water Use, p. 574

* A complete Planning Guide that includes block scheduling is provided on pages 32T-35T.

Activity Materials		
Explore	**Activities**	**MiniLABs**
page 555 white cloth, microscope slide, microscope	pages 566-567 thermal mitts, safety goggles, small box of plain gelatin, hot plate, tap water, refrigerator, stereomicroscope, pan or pot, marker, 4 plastic lids (from margarine tubs or 1-pound coffee cans) page 574 home water meter	page 557 container to collect rain or snow, pH ion paper and pH chart page 572 4 identical baby food jars with lids, tap water, pond water, well water, water from a local stream, liquid dishwashing soap, dropper

Chapter 20 Our Impact on Air and Water

Teacher Classroom Resources

Reproducible Masters	Transparencies
Study Guide, p. 79 **Reinforcement,** p. 79 **Enrichment,** p. 79 **Activity Worksheets,** p. 124 **Lab Manual 57,** Smoke Pollution **Science Integration Activity 20,** It's Raining Cats and Dogs (and Acid)! **Concept Mapping,** p. 45 **Multicultural Connections,** pp. 43-44 **Technology Integration,** pp. 15-16	**Section Focus Transparency 75,** Smoggy Smoggy View **Teaching Transparency 39,** Air Pollution **Teaching Transparency 40,** pH Scale
Study Guide, p. 80 **Reinforcement,** p. 80 **Enrichment,** p. 80 **Activity Worksheets,** pp. 120-121 **Science and Society Integration,** p. 24	**Section Focus Transparency 76,** Too Much of a Good Thing
Study Guide, p. 81 **Reinforcement,** p. 81 **Enrichment,** p. 81 **Activity Worksheets,** pp. 122-123, 125 **Lab Manual 58,** Water Purification **Critical Thinking/Problem Solving,** p. 26 **Cross-Curricular Integration,** p. 24	**Section Focus Transparency 77,** More Than Meets the Eye **Science Integration Transparency 20,** Catalysts Help Clear Air

Teaching Resources

Glencoe Earth Science Interactive Videodisc
Earth Science CD-ROM
Spanish Resources
English/Spanish Audiocassettes
Cooperative Learning Resource Guide
Lab Partner
Lab and Safety Skills
Lesson Plans

Assessment Resources

Chapter Review, pp. 43-44
Assessment, pp. 132-135
Performance Assessment in the Science Classroom (PASC)
MindJogger Videoquiz
Alternate Assessment in the Science Classroom
Performance Assessment
Chapter Review Software
Computer Test Bank

Key to Teaching Strategies

The following designations will help you decide which activities are appropriate for your students.

- **L1** Level 1 activities should be within the ability range of all students.
- **L2** Level 2 activities should be within the ability range of the average to above-average student.
- **L3** Level 3 activities are designed for the ability range of above-average students.
- **LEP** LEP activities should be within the ability range of Limited English Proficiency students.
- **LS** These activities are designed to address different learning styles.
- **COOP LEARN** Cooperative Learning activities are designed for small group work.
- **P** These strategies represent student products that can be placed into a best-work portfolio.

GLENCOE TECHNOLOGY

The following multimedia resources are available from Glencoe.

The Infinite Voyage Series
Crisis in the Atmosphere
National Geographic Society Series
STV: Atmosphere
STV: Water
Glencoe Earth Science Interactive Videodisc
Pollution Detectives
Earth Science CD-ROM

Teacher Classroom Resources

This is a representation of key blackline masters available in the Teacher Classroom Resources.

Teaching Aids

Section Focus Transparencies

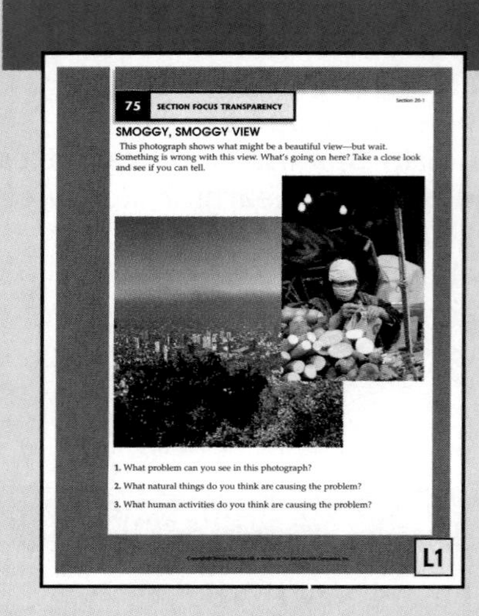

75 SECTION FOCUS TRANSPARENCY

SMOGGY, SMOGGY VIEW

This photograph shows what might be a beautiful view—but wait. Something is wrong with this view. What's going on here? Take a close look and see if you can tell.

1. What problem can you see in this photograph?
2. What natural things do you think are causing the problem?
3. What human activities do you think are causing the problem?

L1

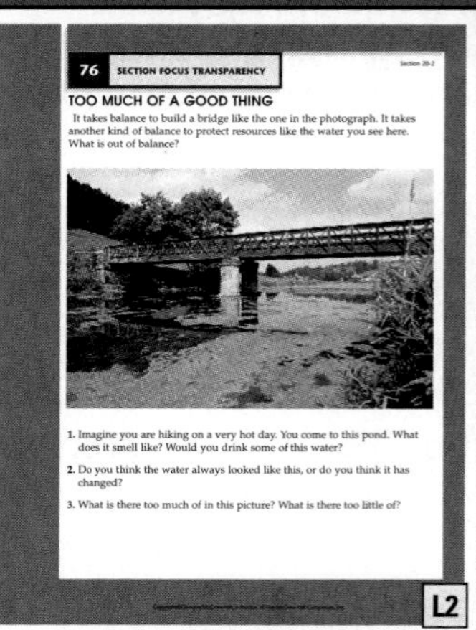

76 SECTION FOCUS TRANSPARENCY

TOO MUCH OF A GOOD THING

It takes balance to build a bridge like the one in the photograph. It takes another kind of balance to protect resources like the water you see here. What is out of balance?

1. Imagine you are hiking on a very hot day. You come to this pond. What does it smell like? Would you drink some of this water?
2. Do you think the water always looked like this, or do you think it has changed?
3. What is there too much of in this picture? What is there too little of?

L2

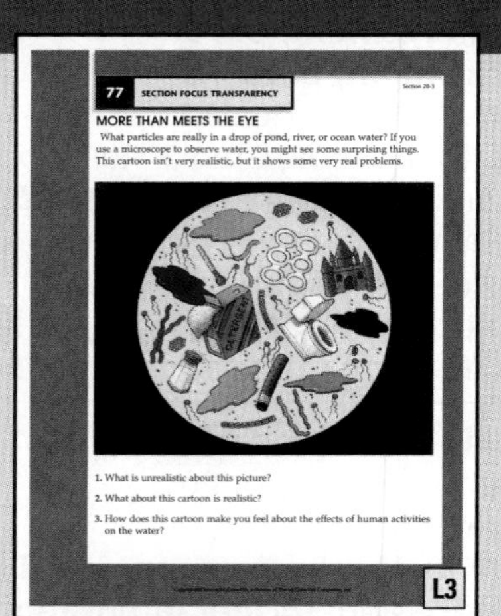

77 SECTION FOCUS TRANSPARENCY

MORE THAN MEETS THE EYE

What particles are really in a drop of pond, river, or ocean water? If you use a microscope to observe water, you might see some surprising things. This cartoon isn't very realistic, but it shows some very real problems.

1. What is unrealistic about this picture?
2. What about this cartoon is realistic?
3. How does this cartoon make you feel about the effects of human activities on the water?

L3

Science Integration Transparencies

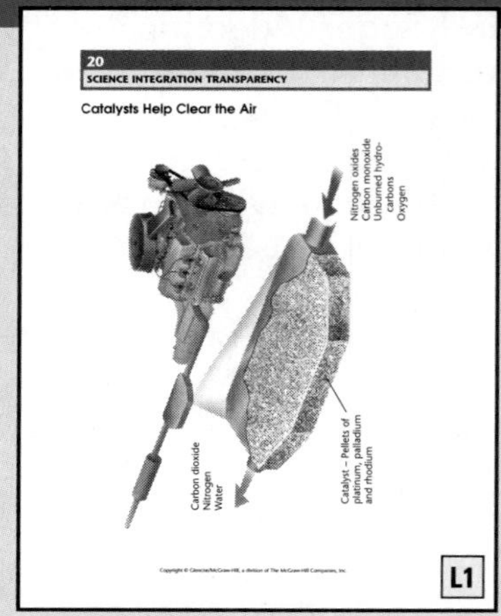

20 SCIENCE INTEGRATION TRANSPARENCY

Catalysts Help Clear the Air

L1

Teaching Transparencies

L1

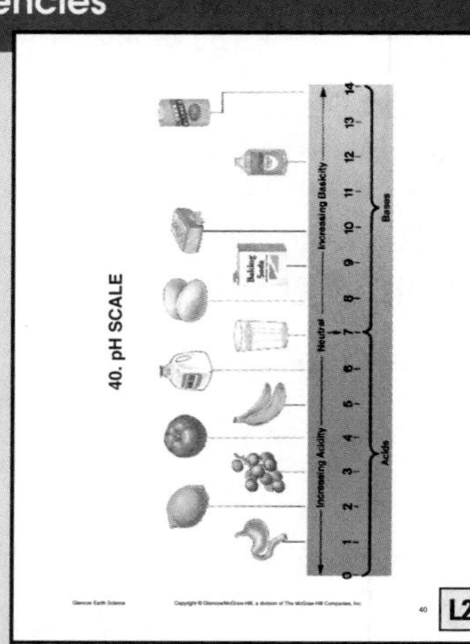

L2

Meeting Different Ability Levels

Study Guide

NAME DATE CLASS

Chapter 20 STUDY GUIDE Text Pages 556–561

• Air Pollution

Match the items in Column I with the phrases in Column II. Write the letter of the correct phrase in the blank at the left.

Column I	Column II
____ 1. acid rain	a. Colorless, odorless gas present in some smog
____ 2. acid	b. Occurs when nitrogen compounds react with sunlight
____ 3. base	c. Volcanic eruptions, forest fires, and grass fires
____ 4. carbon monoxide	d. Landforms that help smog form
____ 5. 1990 Clean Air Act	e. Sulfur dioxide or nitrogen compounds combined with moisture in the air
____ 6. mountains and valleys	f. Goals to clean up the air in the United States
____ 7. natural sources of pollution	g. Formed when fossil fuels are burned, releasing sulfur compounds, dust, and smoke particles where there is little wind
____ 8. photochemical smog	h. Type of solution with a low pH number
____ 9. pH scale	i. Measure of acidity in a solution
____ 10. sulfurous smog	j. Type of solution with a high pH number

Finish the puzzle below. Then unscramble the letters in the boxes to complete Item 15.

11. smoke + fog =
12. nitrogen + oxygen =
13. sulfur compounds + stagnant air =
14. pollutants + sunlight =
15. Goal of the 1990 Clean Air Act =

 79

L1

Reinforcement

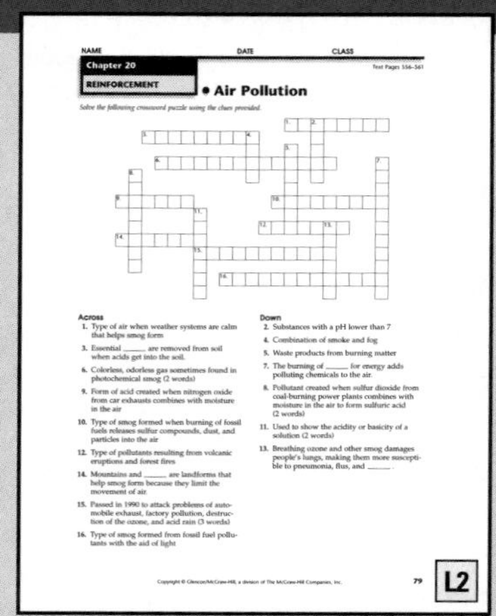

NAME DATE CLASS

Chapter 20 REINFORCEMENT Text Pages 556–561

• Air Pollution

Solve the following crossword puzzle using the clues provided.

Across

1. Type of air when weather systems are calm that helps smog form
3. Essential ____ are removed from soil when acids get into the soil.
6. Colorless, odorless gas sometimes found in photochemical smog (2 words)
9. Form of acid created when nitrogen oxide from car exhausts combines with moisture in the air
10. Type of smog formed when burning of fossil fuels releases sulfur compounds, dust, and particles into the air
12. Type of pollutants resulting from volcanic eruptions and forest fires
14. Mountains and ____ are landforms that help smog form because they limit the movement of air
15. Passed in 1990 to attack problems of automobile exhaust, factory pollution, destruction of the ozone, and acid rain (3 words)
16. Type of smog formed from fossil fuel pollutants with the aid of light

Down

2. Substances with a pH lower than 7
4. Combination of smoke and fog
5. Waste products from burning matter
7. The burning of ____ for energy adds polluting chemicals to the air.
8. Pollutant created when sulfur dioxide from coal-burning power plants combines with moisture in the air to form sulfuric acid (2 words)
11. Used to show the acidity or basicity of a solution (2 words)
13. Breathing ozone and other smog damages people's lungs, making them more susceptible to pneumonia, flus, and ____.

 79

L2

Enrichment Worksheets

NAME DATE CLASS

Chapter 20 ENRICHMENT Text Pages 556–561

• Air Pollution

Identifying Local Sources of Pollution

Materials

- camera and film (or sketching paper and pencil)
- photo album or blank sheets of paper for making an album

Procedure

1. On a separate sheet of paper, list at least four possible sources of air pollution around your neighborhood. The following suggestions may help you get started: coal-burning power plant, factory smoke-stacks, wood-burning fireplaces or stoves, car exhaust, a plowed field, burning leaves, construction.
2. Walk around your neighborhood and take photographs of sources of air pollution. You may draw pictures if you prefer.
3. Have the pictures developed.
4. Make or obtain a photo album.
5. Mount each picture in the album. Label each picture.

Analyze

6. Identify the source of pollution in each picture.
7. Describe the type of pollution in each picture.
8. Make notes on possible solutions to each problem.

Conclude and Apply

Share your project with classmates. Do the following activities together.

9. Identify the common sources of pollution around you.
10. Discuss what people in your region can do to help solve the problem.

 79

L3

Hands-On Activities

Science Integration Activity

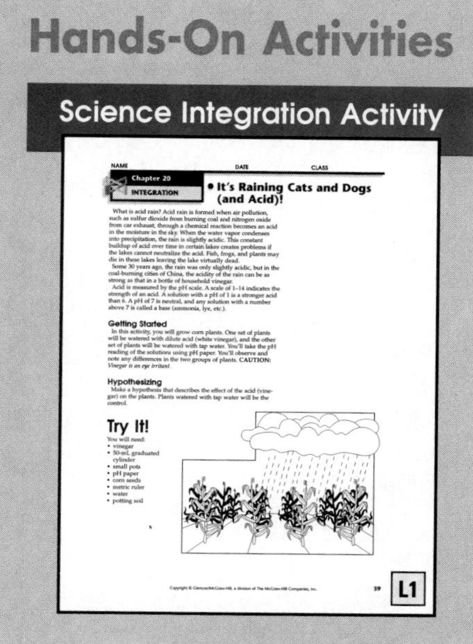
Chapter 20 INTEGRATION

It's Raining Cats and Dogs (and Acid)!

Getting Started

Hypothesizing

Try It!

L1

Lab Manual

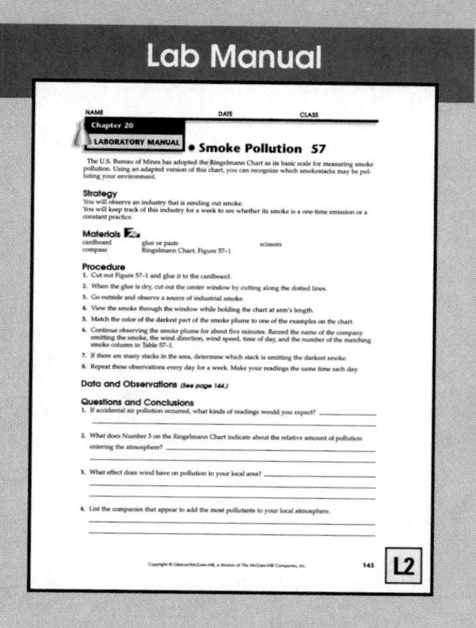
Chapter 20 LABORATORY MANUAL

Smoke Pollution 57

Strategy

Materials

Procedure

Data and Observations

Questions and Conclusions

L2

Assessment

Performance Assessment

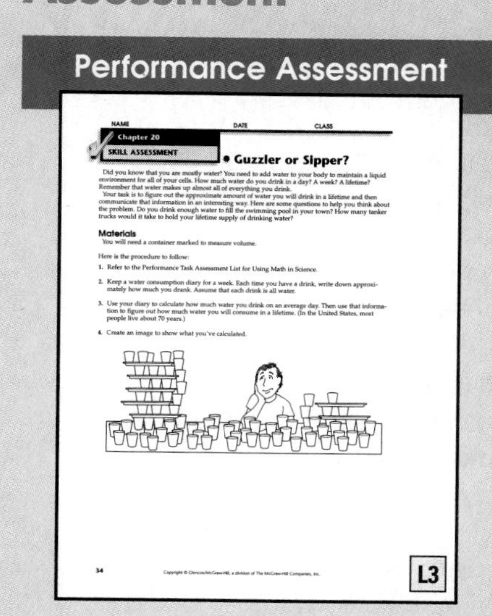
Chapter 20 SKILL ASSESSMENT

Guzzler or Sipper?

Materials

L3

Enrichment and Application

Critical Thinking/Problem Solving

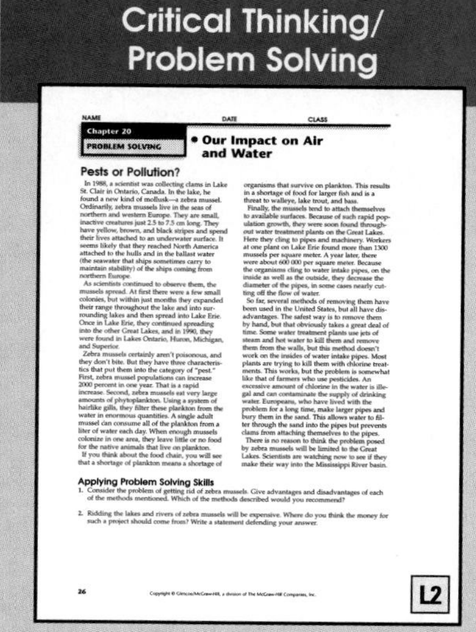
Chapter 20 PROBLEM SOLVING

Our Impact on Air and Water

Pests or Pollution?

Applying Problem Solving Skills

L2

Cross-Curricular Integration

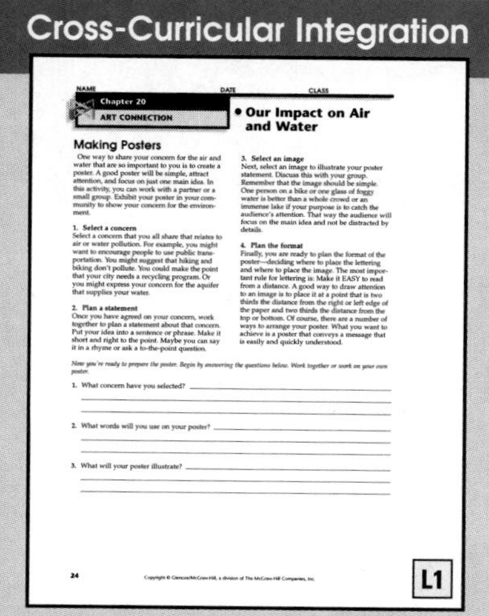
Chapter 20 ART CONNECTION

Our Impact on Air and Water

Making Posters

L1

Science and Society Integration

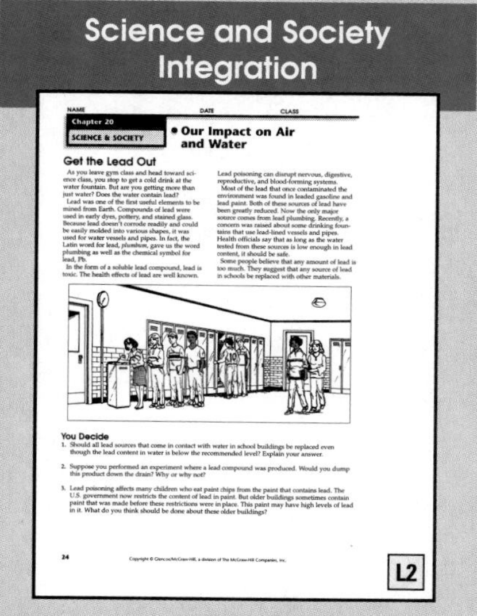
Chapter 20 SCIENCE & SOCIETY

Our Impact on Air and Water

Get the Lead Out

You Decide

L2

Multicultural Connections

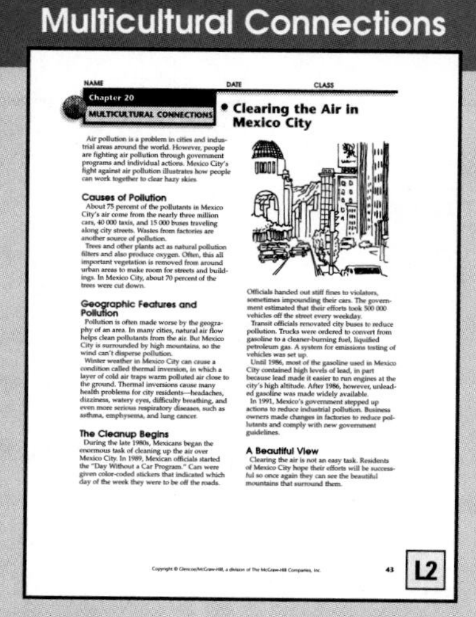
Chapter 20 MULTICULTURAL CONNECTIONS

Clearing the Air in Mexico City

Causes of Pollution

Geographic Features and Pollution

The Cleanup Begins

A Beautiful View

L2

Concept Mapping

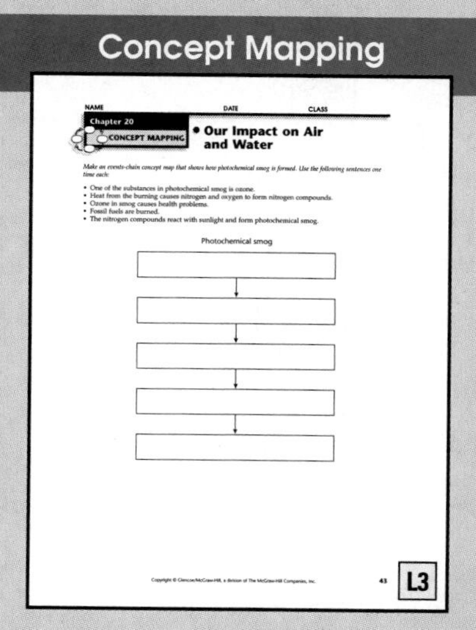
Chapter 20 CONCEPT MAPPING

Our Impact on Air and Water

Photochemical smog

L3

Chapter 20

Our Impact on Air and Water

CHAPTER OVERVIEW

Section 20-1 This section examines the causes of smog and acid rain and describes how air pollution affects human health. Ways of reducing air pollution also are presented.

Section 20-2 Science and Society How soil type determines the damage caused by acid rain and what can be done about acid rain are discussed. The Explore the Technology feature asks students whether people living in the Midwest should assume the entire financial burden to eliminate problems caused by acid rain.

Section 20-3 Some of the causes and effects of water pollution are discussed. A few ways to reduce water pollution are explored.

Chapter Vocabulary

photochemical smog
sulfurous smog
acid rain
pH scale
acid
base
Clean Air Act
scrubber
Safe Drinking Water Act
Clean Water Act

Theme Connection

Systems and Interactions Human activities affect and are affected by pollution of Earth's air and water systems. Interactions among humans and these systems are the foci of the chapter.

Previewing the Chapter

Section 20-1 Air Pollution
- What causes air pollution?
- Smog
- Acid Rain
- How Air Pollution Affects Our Health
- Reducing Air Pollution

Section 20-2 Science and Society: Technology: Acid Rain

Section 20-3 Water Pollution
- Causes and Effects of Water Pollution
- Reducing Water Pollution
- How can you help?

554

Learning Styles

Look for the following logo for strategies that emphasize different learning modalities. 

Visual-Spatial	Explore, p. 555; Visual Learning, pp. 556, 560, 562, 568, 570; Reteach, p. 563; Science & History, p. 565; Activity 20-1, pp. 566-567
Interpersonal	Enrichment, p. 558; Activities, pp. 559, 563; Reteach, pp. 560, 571
Intrapersonal	MiniLABs, pp. 557, 572; Activity 20-2, p. 574
Logical-Mathematical	Science Journal, p. 560
Linguistic	Theme Connection, p. 558; Across the Curriculum, p. 559; Discussion, p. 571; Science Journal, p. 571

Chapter 20

Our Impact on Air and Water

Did you know that most sources of drinking water in the United States are polluted? The water has to be treated with chemicals or filters before it's safe to use. Air pollution is another problem. Factories such as the paper pulp mill shown here release dust and chemicals into the air. In the United States, 12 percent of all toxic chemicals we produce end up in the atmosphere. Is the air in your community polluted?

EXPLORE ACTIVITY

Study your air.

1. Find a high shelf or the top of a tall cabinet—someplace that hasn't been cleaned for a while.
2. Run a cloth over this area and observe the dirt under a microscope.
3. In your Science Journal, describe and sketch what you see.

Observe: Where did these particles come from? What do you suppose happens when you breathe in these particles?

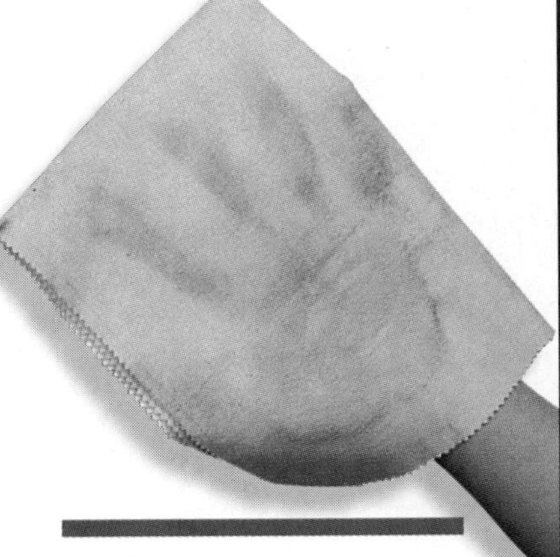

Previewing Science Skills

- In the **Skill Builders**, you will **map concepts** and **interpret scientific illustrations.**
- In the **Activities**, you will **collect and analyze data, make and use a data table, make and use a graph, calculate, infer,** and **draw conclusions.**
- In the **MiniLABs**, you will **experiment, observe, compare and contrast,** and **infer.**

555

EXPLORE ACTIVITY

Purpose

LS **Visual-Spatial** Use the Explore Activity to introduce students to air pollution. Inform students that they will be learning more about pollution of Earth's atmosphere and hydrosphere as they read the chapter. L1

Preparation

Before doing this activity obtain a stereomicroscope and have students bring in clean, cloth rags.

Materials

clean, cloth rags; a dusty shelf; stereomicroscope

Teaching Strategies

You may want to have students review from Chapter 7 how materials are carried by the wind.

Observe

They are carried in the air. They go into the students' lungs when they breathe.

Assessment

Performance Have students compare and contrast the different particles that they examined under the stereomicroscope. Use the Performance Task Assessment List for Writing in Science in **PASC,** p. 87. P

Assessment Planner

Portfolio

Refer to page 575 for suggested items that students might select for their portfolios.

Performance Assessment

See page 575 for additional Performance Assessment options.
Skill Builders, pp. 561, 573
MiniLABs, pp. 557, 572
Activities 20-1, pp. 566-567; 20-2, p. 574

Content Assessment

Section Wrap-ups, pp. 561, 564, 573
Chapter Review, pp. 575-577
Mini Quizzes, pp. 561, 564, 573

Group Assessment

Opportunities for group assessment occur with Cooperative Learning Strategies and Flex Your Brain Activities.

Section 20•1

Prepare

Section Background

Despite the Clean Air Act, more than 150 million people in the United States live in metropolitan areas where ozone and/or carbon monoxide exceed federal health standards.

Preplanning

To prepare for the MiniLAB, obtain glass or plastic containers and pH ion paper.

1 Motivate

Bellringer

Before presenting the lesson, display **Section Focus Transparency 75** on the overhead projector. Assign the accompanying **Focus Activity** worksheet. L1 LEP

Tying to Previous Knowledge

Have students recall from Chapter 14 that chlorofluorocarbons pollute the stratosphere by destroying the ozone layer. In Chapter 16, students learned how carbon dioxide and several other gases contribute to the greenhouse effect. Assure students that they will be adding to their existing knowledge of air pollution.

20•1 Air Pollution

Science Words

- **photochemical smog**
- **sulfurous smog**
- **acid rain**
- **pH scale**
- **acid**
- **base**
- **Clean Air Act**

Objectives

- Identify the sources of pollutants that cause photochemical smog, sulfurous smog, holes in the ozone layer, and acid rain.
- Describe how air pollution affects people and the environment.
- Explain how air pollution can be reduced.

What causes air pollution?

Have you ever noticed that the air looks hazy on some days? Do you know what causes this haziness? Some industries generate dust and chemicals. Thus, the more industries there are in a region, the more dust and chemicals there are in the air. Other human activities add pollutants to the air, too. Look at **Figure 20-1.** Cars, buses, trucks, trains, and planes all burn fossil fuels for energy. Their exhaust—the waste products from burning the fossil fuels—adds polluting chemicals to the air. Other sources include smoke from burning trash and dust from plowed fields, construction sites, and mines.

Natural sources add pollutants to the air, too. Examples are volcanic eruptions, forest fires, and grass fires.

Smog

Pollutants produced by human activities and by natural processes cause the haze you sometimes see in the air. **Figure 20-2** shows the major sources of air pollution. Around cities, polluted air is called smog, a word made by combining the words *smoke* and *fog.* Two types of smog are common—photochemical smog and sulfurous smog.

Photochemical Smog

In areas such as Los Angeles, Denver, and New York City, a hazy, brown blanket of smog is created when sunlight reacts with pollutants in the air. This brown smog is called **photochemical smog** because it forms with the aid of light. The pollutants get into the air when fossil fuels are burned. Coal, natural gas, and gasoline are burned by factories, airplanes, and cars. Burning fossil fuels causes nitrogen and oxygen to chemically combine to form nitrogen compounds. These compounds react in the presence of sunlight and produce other substances. One of the substances produced is ozone. Recall that ozone in the stratosphere protects us from the sun's ultraviolet radiation. But ozone that forms in smog near Earth's surface causes health problems.

Figure 20-1

Cars are one of the main sources of air pollution in the United States. *In your Science Journal, list five other sources of air pollution.*

Visual Learning

Figure 20-1 In your Science Journal, list five other sources of air pollution. *Answers will vary but should include burning trash, burning fossil fuels, volcanic eruptions, industrial pollutants, forest fires, and dust from construction sites.* LEP LS

Program Resources

Reproducible Masters

Study Guide, p. 79 L1
Reinforcement, p. 79 L1
Enrichment, p. 79 L3
Activity Worksheets, pp. 5, 124 L1
Science Integration Activities, pp. 39-40
Lab Manual 57
Concept Mapping, p. 45
Multicultural Connections, pp. 43-44
Technology Integration 6

Transparencies

Section Focus Transparency 75 L1
Teaching Transparencies 39, 40

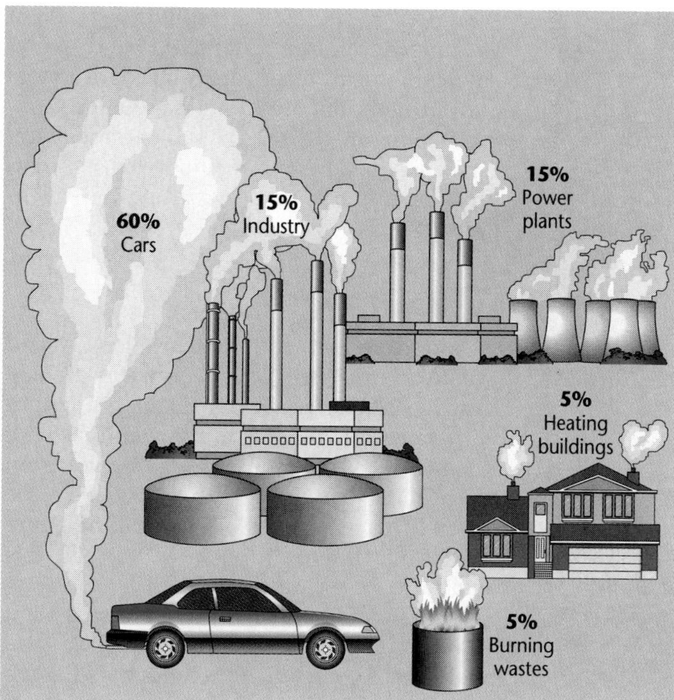

Figure 20-2

Proportions of smog caused by the major sources of air pollution.

Sulfurous Smog

A second type of smog is called **sulfurous smog.** It's created when fossil fuels are burned in electrical power plants and home furnaces. The burning releases sulfur compounds, dust, and smoke particles into the air. Sulfurous smog forms when these substances collect in an area where there's little or no wind. A blanket of gray smog may hang over a city for several days and be hazardous to breathe.

Nature and Smog

Nature plays an important role in creating smog. Sunlight helps form photochemical smog. Sulfurous smog forms when weather systems are calm and the air is not being moved around. Also, sometimes a layer of warm air lies on top of cooler air. Normally, the warmer air is near Earth's surface. But in cases where warm air is above, it becomes a barrier that prevents cool air under it from rising. As a result, pollutants are trapped near the ground. Eventually, the weather changes and cleaner air is blown in, dispersing the pollutants in the air.

Landforms also affect smog development. For example, mountains may help cause smog by restricting the movement of air. Los Angeles' problem with smog is made worse by nearby mountains. Also, some cities are in valleys, where dense, dirty air tends to collect.

MiniLAB

Do you have acid rain in your community?

Procedure

1. The next time it rains or snows, use a glass or plastic container to collect a sample of the precipitation.
2. Use pH paper to determine the acidity level of your sample. If you have collected snow, melt it before measuring its pH.
3. Record the indicated pH of your sample and compare it with the results of other classmates who have followed the same procedure.

Analysis

1. What is the average pH of the samples obtained from this precipitation?
2. Compare and contrast the level of acidity in your samples with those of the substances shown on the pH scale in **Figure 20-4.**

2 Teach

MiniLAB

Purpose

LS **Intrapersonal** Students will determine whether their community has acid rain. L1

Materials

pH ion paper, small glass or plastic containers

Teaching Strategies

- Have students read about acid rain on page 557 before they do this lab.
- Have students collect their samples at about the same time or, at least, from the same source of precipitation.

Analysis

1. Students' samples should have reasonably similar pHs. The acidity of the precipitation will depend on the geographic location and the prevailing wind direction of the area.
2. Answers will vary.

Assessment

Performance To further assess students' understanding of acid rain, have them collect and test water samples from the same location over a period of time. Have them determine whether the pH varies from day to day. Use the Performance Task Assessment List for Carrying Out a Strategy and Collecting Data in **PASC,** p. 25. P

Activity Worksheets, pp. 5, 124

Use **Science Integration Activities,** pp. 39-40, as you teach this lesson.

Inquiry Questions

- **How do cars contribute to the acid rain problem?** *Nitrogen oxide from car exhausts combines with moisture in air to form nitric acid.*
- **If the pH of a substance is 4, is this substance an acid or a base?** *an acid*

Enrichment

 **Interpersonal** Have students brainstorm to compose a list of anti-pollution logos to promote conservation and recycling. They can also construct posters or banners that use the logos. L1 COOP LEARN

GLENCOE TECHNOLOGY

 **CD-ROM**

Earth Science CD-ROM

Have students perform the interactive exploration for Chapter 20 to reinforce important chapter concepts and thinking processes.

GLENCOE TECHNOLOGY

Videodisc

The Infinite Voyage: Crisis in the Atmosphere

Chapter 10

Los Angeles Smog and Air Quality Plan

Chapter 11

Worldwide Energy Conservation Solutions

Figure 20-3

These trees are dying because acids in the soil have removed essential nutrients and lowered the trees' resistance to diseases, insects, and bad weather. Acid rain also increases the acidity of streams, rivers, and lakes, killing fish that live in the water. It even damages the surfaces of buildings and cars.

Smog isn't the only air pollution problem we have. Recall from Chapters 14 and 16 that chlorofluorocarbons from air conditioners and refrigerators are thought to be destroying the ozone layer in the stratosphere. Carbon dioxide from burning coal, oil, natural gas, and forests is increasing the greenhouse effect.

Acid Rain

Another major pollution problem is acid rain. Acid rain is created when sulfur dioxide from coal-burning power plants combines with moisture in the air to form sulfuric acid. It is also created when nitrogen oxides from car exhausts combine with moisture in the air to form nitric acid. The acidic moisture falls to Earth as rain or snow. We call this **acid rain.**

What would happen if you watered a plant with lemon juice instead of water? As you might guess, the plant would die. Lemon juice is an acid that is toxic to tender shoots and roots. Acid rain sometimes is as acidic as lemon juice. Thus, acid rain can kill plants and trees, as in **Figure 20-3.** To understand this, let's learn how acidity is measured.

The pH Scale

We describe how acidic a solution is by using the **pH scale. Figure 20-4** illustrates the pH scale. Substances with a pH lower than seven are considered **acids.** The lower the pH number, the greater the acidity. The higher the number, the lower the acidity. Substances with a pH above seven are considered **bases.**

Figure 20-4

The natural pH of rainwater is about 5.6. Acid rain is precipitation with a pH below 5.6.

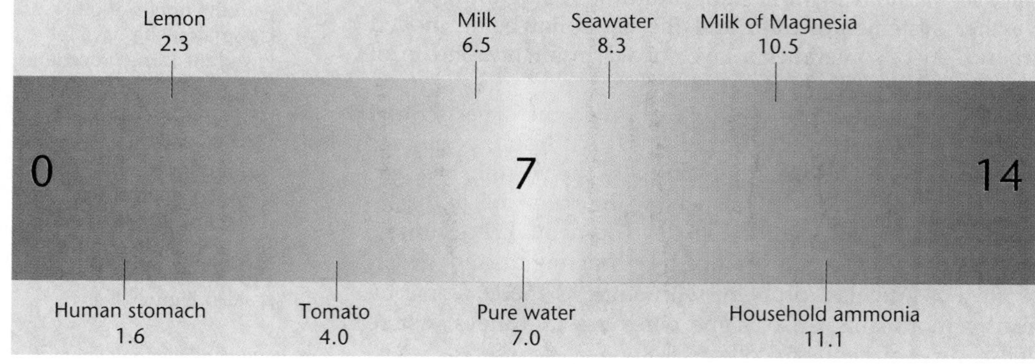

Inclusion Strategies

Gifted Have students identify sources of local air pollution. Then have them refer to maps showing the locations of the sources and local wind patterns. Have students predict where pollutants from the sources would be most concentrated. L3

Theme Connection

Systems and Interactions Have students write one or two paragraphs to describe the effects of acid rain on soil, plants, streams, and buildings. *Acid rain removes essential nutrients from soil. It lowers a plant's resistance to diseases, insects, and bad weather. Acid rain can kill organisms living in streams. Finally, it damages the surfaces of buildings and other structures.* L1 LS

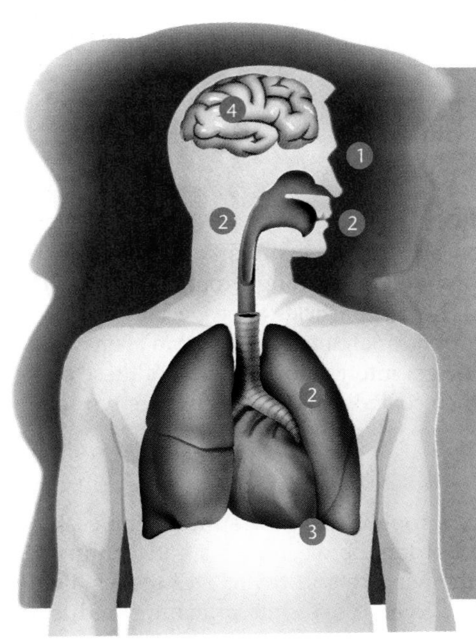

Effects of Air Pollution on the Body

1 Eyes
Compounds found in smog cause the eyes to water and sting. If conditions are bad enough, vision may be blurred.

2 Nose, throat, and lungs
Ozone irritates the nose and throat, causing burning. It reduces the ability of the lungs to fight infections.

3 Heart
Inhaled carbon monoxide is absorbed by red blood cells, rendering them incapable of transporting oxygen throughout the body. Chest pains result because of low oxygen levels.

4 Brain
Motor functions and coordination are impaired because oxygen levels in the brain are reduced when carbon monoxide is inhaled.

How Air Pollution Affects Our Health

Suppose you're an athlete in a large city and you're training for a big, upcoming competition. You have to get up at 4:30 A.M. to exercise. Later in the day, the smog levels will be so high that it won't be safe for you to do strenuous exercise. In southern California, in Denver, and in other areas, athletes adjust their training schedules to avoid exposure to ozone and other smog. Schools schedule football games for Saturday afternoons when smog levels are low. Parents are warned to keep their children indoors when smog levels exceed certain levels. Breathing dirty air, especially taking deep breaths of it when you are actively exercising, can cause health problems.

Health Disorders

How hazardous is dirty air? Approximately 250 000 people in the United States suffer from pollution-related breathing disorders. About 60 000 deaths each year in the U.S. are blamed on air pollution. Ozone damages lung tissue, making people more susceptible to diseases such as pneumonia and asthma. Less severe symptoms of breathing ozone include a stinging chest, burning eyes, dry throat, and headache.

Carbon monoxide also contributes to smog. A colorless, odorless gas, carbon monoxide makes people ill, even in small concentrations.

INTEGRATION
Life Science

USING MATH

The pH scale is a logarithmic scale. This means that there is a tenfold difference for each pH unit. For example, pH 4 is ten times more acidic than pH 5 and 100 times more acidic than pH 6. ***Calculate*** how much more acidic pH 1 is than pH 4.

Across the Curriculum

Health Have students research to find sources of indoor air pollution. Have them study the health effects of asbestos, formaldehyde, radon, cigarette smoke, and other substances found in houses. L2

INTEGRATION
Life Science

When humans breathe, air travels down nasal passages, past the vocal cord and larynx, and into the trachea. From there it passes through the bronchi and into the lungs. The first line of defense against air pollutants are the hairs and mucus that line the nasal passages. Hairs filter the air and mucus traps the particles. Sneezing is the body's way of getting rid of particles that are trapped in these passages. If particles travel into the trachea, cilia (tiny hair-like structures) are irritated. Ask students to hypothesize how humans react to this irritation. *They cough, which forces the dust to rise back up to the mouth.*

USING MATH

Answer 1000 times

Activity

LS **Interpersonal** Have students produce a newspaper that deals with environmental problems. Distribute it throughout the school or community. L2 COOP LEARN

Videodisc

STV: Atmosphere

City traffic; Washington, D.C.

38694

Use **Lab Manual 57** as you teach this lesson.

CONNECT TO

LIFE SCIENCE

Answer The inflammation is in the bronchi and bronchioles of the lungs. Symptoms include a painful cough and muscle spasms that constrict airways.

Visual Learning

Figure 20-5 Why is particulate pollution difficult to control? *Because wind carries the pollutants across the borders between states and countries.* LEP IS

3 Assess

Check for Understanding

Ask students who is responsible for protecting Earth's resources for future generations.

Reteach

IS **Interpersonal** Have student partners review Section 14-2 on the ozone layer, Section 16-4 on global warming, Section 19-2 on conserving resources, Section 19-3 on recycling, and Section 20-1 on air pollution. Have the partners make lists of at least 15 things they can do to help reduce air pollution. Have a class contest to see which student pair can list the most items.

Extension

For students who have mastered this section, use the **Reinforcement** and **Enrichment** masters.

CONNECT TO

LIFE SCIENCE

Air pollution causes many people to develop bronchitis. What organs are inflamed when a person has bronchitis? ***Describe*** the symptoms of bronchitis.

What do you suppose happens when you inhale the humid air from acid rain? Acid is deposited deep inside your lungs. This causes irritation, reduces your ability to fight respiratory infections, interferes with oxygen absorption, and puts stress on your heart.

Particulate Pollution

Particulate pollution also harms people. Particulate pollution is caused by airborne solids that range from large grains to microscopic particles. The fine particles are especially dangerous because they disrupt normal breathing and can even cause lung disease when they get into the lungs. Some of these particles are produced when coal, oil, and petroleum are burned.

Figure 20-5

Particulate pollution is caused by solids in the air that are produced, in part, by burning fossil fuels. *Why is particulate pollution difficult to control?*

Reducing Air Pollution

Pollutants moving through the atmosphere don't stop when they reach the borders between states and countries. They float wherever the wind carries them. This makes them very difficult to control. Even if one state or country reduces its air pollution, pollutants from another state or country can blow across the border.

When states and nations cooperate, pollution problems can be reduced. Diplomats from around the world have met on several occasions since 1990 to try to eliminate some kinds of air pollution. Of particular concern are chlorofluorocarbons and carbon dioxide.

Table 20-1

Clean Air Regulations

Smog	Acid Rain	Airborne Toxins

Car emissions of nitrogen oxides had to be reduced by 60 percent and hydrocarbons by 35 percent of 1990 levels in all new cars as of 1996.	"Clean-coal" technologies must reduce sulfur dioxide emissions by 14 million tons by the year 2000 and nitrogen oxides by several million tons immediately.	Starting in 1995, industries had to limit the emission of 200 compounds that cause cancer and birth defects.

Science Journal

Environmental Awareness Have students identify and explain in their Science Journals the trade-offs involved when a person changes his or her lifestyle in order to conserve Earth's resources. Conserving energy and water may require that a person give up some conveniences. For example, walking instead of driving to the store will save energy, but will take more time and effort. L1 IS P

Community Connection

EPA Invite an Environmental Protection Agency official to the class to talk about local pollution concerns. The official can work with the class to discuss ways they can help fight pollution.

Pollution and Health Invite a physician to talk with your class about health problems associated with air pollution.

Air Pollution in the United States

The Congress of the United States has passed several laws to protect the air. The 1990 **Clean Air Act** attacked the problems of smog, chlorofluorocarbons, particulates, and acid rain by regulating car manufacturers, coal technologies, and other industries. In **Table 20-1,** you can read about some of these regulations.

The good news is that since the passage of the Clean Air Act, the quality of the air in some regions of the United States has improved. The bad news is that one of four U.S. citizens still breathes unhealthy air.

It is the role of the federal Environmental Protection Agency to monitor progress toward the goals of the Clean Air Act. However, it is the consumers who must pay increased prices and taxes, and change their habits in order to really help protect the environment. The Clean Air Act can work only if we all cooperate. In Chapter 19 you discovered several ways you can conserve energy and reduce trash. When you do these things, you are also reducing air pollution. We all must do our share to clean up the air.

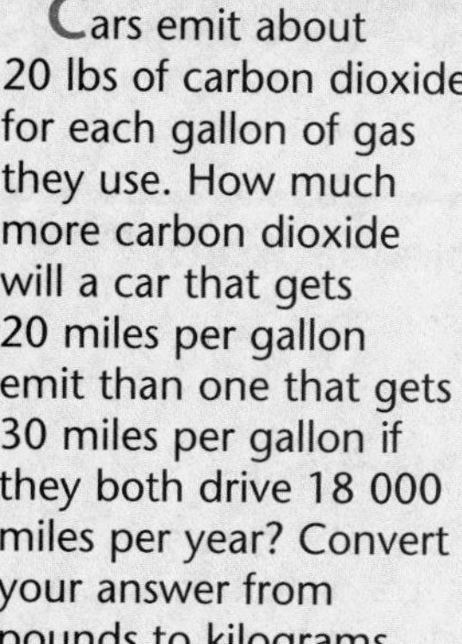

USING MATH

Cars emit about 20 lbs of carbon dioxide for each gallon of gas they use. How much more carbon dioxide will a car that gets 20 miles per gallon emit than one that gets 30 miles per gallon if they both drive 18 000 miles per year? Convert your answer from pounds to kilograms.

Section Wrap-up

Review

1. In what ways does air pollution affect the health of people?
2. How can you help reduce air pollution?
3. **Think Critically:** An earlier Clean Air Act, passed in 1970, required that coal-burning power plants use very tall smokestacks so that air pollutants would be ejected high into the sky, where high-altitude winds would disperse them. Power plants in the Midwestern states complied with that law, and people in eastern Canada began complaining about acid rain. Explain the connection.

Science Journal

In your Science Journal, make a crossword puzzle using at least 12 important terms found in this section.

Skill Builder

Concept Mapping

Make a concept map that explains how sulfurous smog forms and how weather affects how long it persists. If you need help, refer to Concept Mapping in the **Skill Handbook.**

USING MATH

18 000 miles/yr × 20 lbs/1 gallon × 1 gallon/20 miles = 18 000 lbs/yr

18 000 miles/yr × 20 lbs/1 gallon × 1 gallon/30 miles = 12 000 lbs/yr

18 000 – 12 000 = 6000 lbs or about 2700 kg more

4 Close

•MINI•QUIZ•

1. **What is smog?** *polluted air around cities*
2. **When nitrogen compounds react with sunlight, _____ smog forms.** *photochemical*
3. **A substance with a pH lower than seven is a(n) _____.** *acid*

Section Wrap-Up

Review

1. Air pollution increases susceptibility to pneumonia, flus, and asthma; causes stinging chests, burning eyes, dry throats, stress on hearts, and sometimes deaths.
2. Answers may include: share in cost of cleaning air, use less energy, recycle, carpool, plant trees.
3. **Think Critically** Sulfur in the smoke goes up the stacks and mixes with water vapor in the air to form sulfuric acid. Clouds drift northeast and drop acid rain onto Canada.

Skill Builder

One possible solution is shown:

Fossil fuels are burned → which produces → sulfur dioxide, dust, smoke → which form → sulfurous smog → which becomes trapped by → calm air, cool air overlain by warm air

Assessment

Content Assess students' abilities to make a concept map by having them make a map that shows how acid rain forms and how it affects the environment. Use the Performance Task Assessment List for Concept Map in **PASC,** p. 89. P

Science Journal

Puzzles will vary, but words must be spelled correctly. Students should provide Across and Down clues. P

Prepare

Section Background

Around the world each year, acid rain causes billions of dollars in economic damage. In Sweden, 40 000 of its 90 000 lakes are acidified, while in the United States, 20 percent of the lakes are acidified. Acid rain has killed vast forests in Europe and the United States.

Preplanning

To prepare for Activity 20-1, obtain the following materials for each student group: a small box of plain gelatin, a hot plate, a pan, four plastic lids, a stereomicroscope, a marker, thermal mitts, and safety goggles.

1 Motivate

Bellringer

Before presenting the lesson, display **Section Focus Transparency 76** on the overhead projector. Assign the accompanying **Focus Activity** worksheet. L1 LEP

Tying to Previous Knowledge

Have students recall what they learned about soil types in Chapter 6. Inform them that in this section, they will learn how the type of soil affects acid rain damage.

Visual Learning

Figure 20-6 **How does the soil type of this region affect acid rain damage?** *Acid rain makes the ground and groundwater even more acidic, harming plants and fish.* LEP LS

20•2 TECHNOLOGY: Acid Rain

Science Words
scrubber

Objectives
- Describe how soil type affects acid rain damage.
- Describe activities that help reduce acid rain.
- Decide who should pay the cost of reducing sulfur dioxide emissions.

Acid Rain Damage

You may live in an area where there is very little acid rain. The amount of acid rain in an area depends on the number of factories and cars in the area. They are the sources of the sulfur and nitrogen gases that cause acid rain. Whether acid rain falls where you live also depends on your area's pattern of precipitation and wind direction. Even if industry and cars are producing a lot of pollution near you, much of it may be carried away by the wind before it falls back down as acid rain.

Soil Type Affects Acid Rain Damage

It's not just the volume of acid rain that falls that determines how much damage is done in an area. Different types of soil react differently to acid rain. Some soils already are acidic, and acid rain makes them even more so. But other soils are basic. If you mix an acidic solution with a basic solution, they neutralize each other. Therefore, if acid rain falls on basic soil, the acid rain becomes partly neutralized and causes less damage.

Soils in the midwestern states are basic. Thus, when acid rain falls in the Midwest, it's neutralized in the soil. But the northeastern states and eastern Canada don't have basic soils. In these places, acid rain makes the ground and groundwater even more acidic, causing harm to plants and fish. **Figure 20-6** shows the pH levels of rainfall for the United States.

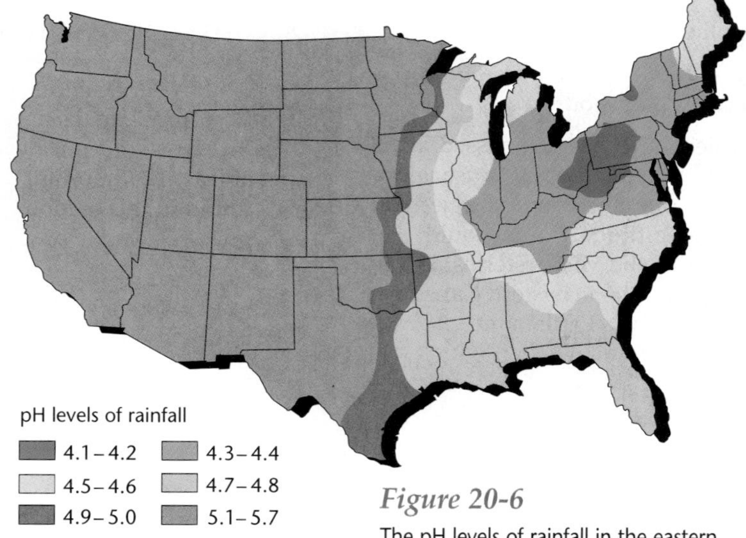

Figure 20-6
The pH levels of rainfall in the eastern states and Canada are dangerously low. *How does the soil type of this region affect acid rain damage?*

Program Resources

Reproducible Masters
Study Guide, p. 80 L1
Reinforcement, p. 80 L1
Enrichment, p. 80 L3
Science and Society Integration, p. 24
Activity Worksheets, pp. 5, 120-121 L1

Transparencies
Section Focus Transparency 76 L1

What can be done about acid rain?

The main source of the nitric acid in acid rain is car exhaust. Better emission control devices on cars will help reduce acid rain. So will car pooling and public transportation, because they reduce the number of trips and thus the amount of fuel used.

Reducing Emissions

Coal-burning power plants can help correct the problem, too. Some coal has a lot of sulfur in it. When the coal is burned, the sulfur combines with moisture in the air to form sulfuric acid. Power plants can wash coal to remove some sulfur before the coal is burned. This way, burning produces less sulfur in the smoke. Power plants also can run the smoke through a scrubber. A **scrubber** lets the gases in the smoke dissolve in water, as they would in nature, until the smoke's pH increases to a safe level.

USING TECHNOLOGY

Solar Grids

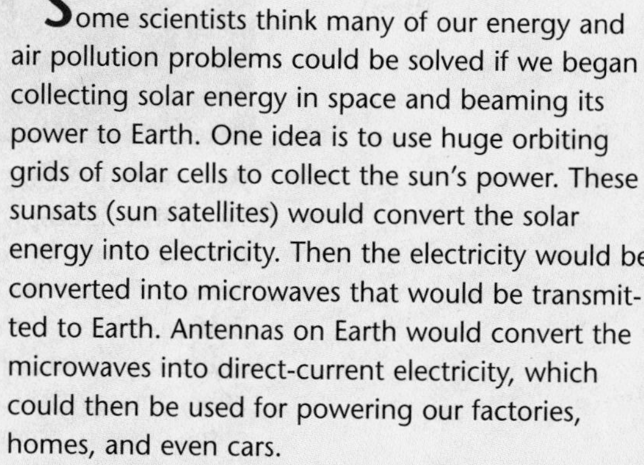

Some scientists think many of our energy and air pollution problems could be solved if we began collecting solar energy in space and beaming its power to Earth. One idea is to use huge orbiting grids of solar cells to collect the sun's power. These sunsats (sun satellites) would convert the solar energy into electricity. Then the electricity would be converted into microwaves that would be transmitted to Earth. Antennas on Earth would convert the microwaves into direct-current electricity, which could then be used for powering our factories, homes, and even cars.

Other scientists suggest that instead of using satellites, grids of solar cells could be placed on the moon. The energy would be collected and sent to Earth in the same way as with sunsats. There is a problem that needs to be worked out in both methods, however. Sending the energy to Earth in the form of microwaves could be dangerous for organisms living here.

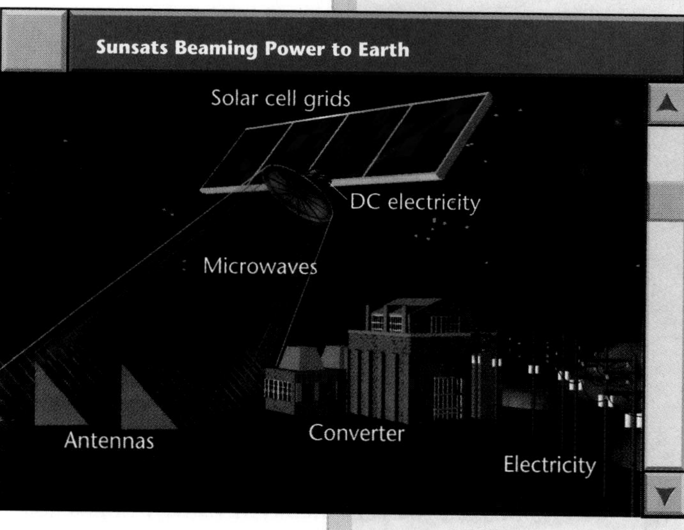

Think Critically: Once perfected, how would sunsats or grids of solar cells on the moon help reduce acid rain and other forms of air pollution?

2 Teach

Activity

LS Interpersonal Have students bring in soil samples and use a soil testing kit to determine the pH of each sample. L1

LEP COOP LEARN

USING TECHNOLOGY

The concept of solar grids was first proposed by Peter Glaser in 1968 at an energy-conversion-engineering conference in Denver, Colorado. Today, scientists in Japan are working out a specific plan to build solar-power-satellite systems.

Think Critically

There would be no need to burn fossil fuels to get energy. Nitrogen oxide, sulfur dioxide, and carbon dioxide would not be added to the air to contribute to acid rain and global warming problems.

3 Assess

Check for Understanding

FLEX Your Brain

Use the Flex Your Brain activity to have students explore ACID RAIN.

Reteach

LS Visual-Spatial Have pairs of students simulate acid rain by adding a few drops of lemon juice to a sample of tap water. Have them use pH ion paper and a pH color chart to determine the pH of the water. Then instruct them to slowly add just enough baking soda or ammonia to neutralize the acid.

Extension

For students who have mastered this section, use the **Reinforcement** and **Enrichment** masters.

4 Close

• MINI • QUIZ •

1. **Two factors that determine the amount of damage done by acid rain are _____ .** *the amount of acid rain that falls; soil type*
2. **The main source of nitric acid in acid rain is _____ .** *car exhaust*
3. **Car emissions can be reduced by emission control devices, car pooling, and _____ .** *using public transportation*

Section Wrap-up

Review

1. If soils are acidic, damage from acid rain will be severe. If soils are basic, acid rain is neutralized and damage is minimized.
2. Better emission-control devices on cars, car pooling, and mass transit will reduce nitric acid. Washing coal and scrubbing the exhaust gases from coal-burning plants will reduce sulfuric acid. Other fuel sources could be used in place of coal.

Explore the Technology

Some students will feel that the states with sulfur dioxide emission problems should be the ones to pay. Other students will argue that everyone should help pay for the cleanup because for many years the people living in the Midwest have been providing the rest of the country with energy and items it has manufactured using this energy.

Figure 20-7
This solar power plant in California provides a clean, renewable source of fuel. Other alternative fuel sources include nuclear, wind, and geothermal power.

Alternative Fuels

Another thing we could do to reduce air pollution is switch to other fuel sources such as solar, nuclear, and geothermal power. **Figure 20-7** shows a solar power plant in California that provides a nonpolluting source of fuel. However, these alternative fuel sources have disadvantages, too. And even if everyone agreed to make fuel changes, it would take years for some areas to change. This is because many people, especially in the midwestern states, depend on coal-burning power plants for home heating and electricity. Changing the kind of fuel used would be costly.

As you read in the last section, the 1990 Clean Air Act requires great reductions in auto exhaust and sulfur dioxide emissions. This will cost all of us billions of dollars. It especially affects the Midwest, where thousands of people will lose their jobs. These include miners, workers in coal-burning power plants, and people who work for factories.

Section Wrap-up

Review

1. How does soil type affect acid rain damage?
2. How can acid rain be reduced?

Explore the Technology

Much of the acid rain problem comes from coal-burning power plants in the Midwest. Some people think that these midwestern states should pay to clean up the problem. But others propose that everyone in the nation should pay for the cleanup. This would reduce the financial burden on the midwestern states. They also propose a job-protection program to help coal miners and others who might lose their jobs. Is this fair to everyone? Why or why not?

SCIENCE & SOCIETY

The Aswan High Dam and Its Effects on Egypt's Soil and Water

For many centuries, the Nile River overflowed during each year's rainy season, leaving behind moist, fertile soil. This cycle of flooding usually meant that only one crop could be planted each year. Water was so scarce during the dry season that additional crops could not be grown.

The Aswan High Dam was built during the 1960s to control flooding along the portion of the Nile that flows through Egypt. During the rainy season, water is stored in a huge artificial lake, or reservoir, called Lake Nasser. The dam provides water to irrigate close to a million hectares of land year round. The stored water also operates a hydroelectric power plant that generates much of Egypt's electricity. However, the Aswan High Dam has also created some unexpected pollution problems.

No More Natural Fertilizer

The silt left behind when the Nile was allowed to flood was a natural fertilizer. It replaced soil nutrients used up by crops grown the previous year and replaced eroded topsoil. When the dam was built, flooding stopped and silt was no longer deposited. Farmers began using chemical fertilizers. Over the years, valuable topsoil has been lost to erosion.

Too Much Salt

Irrigation water from Lake Nasser contains small amounts of salts that are left behind in the soil as the water evaporates. The salt levels have become so high in some fields that they can no longer be used to grow crops. In addition, wells and streams are polluted by runoff containing residues of fertilizers, pesticides, and salts.

An Increase in Disease

Many disease-carrying organisms, such as water snails, used to die in the annual floods of the Nile. Now, the calm waters of Lake Nasser serve as a perfect breeding ground for some of these organisms, and more people are becoming ill from diseases such as dysentery.

Science Journal

People in many regions of the world, including Africa, India, and Asia, have soil and water pollution problems much like Egypt's. In your Science Journal, research possible solutions for these problems.

Background

- Tens of thousands of people were displaced by construction of the Aswan High Dam. The region of Sudan once known as Nubia is now covered by the waters of Lake Nasser. Many ancient ruins lie beneath the lake, though archeologists managed to remove many artifacts before the region was flooded. The ancient Egyptian temple of Abu Simbel was actually moved to higher ground to prevent it from being covered by Lake Nasser.
- The Nile, at 6648 km long, is the longest river in the world. Its headwaters lie in the mountains of Uganda and Ethiopia, and it flows through Ethiopia, Sudan, and Egypt.
- The reservoir created by the Aswan High Dam is one of the largest human-made lakes in the world.

Teaching Strategies

LS **Visual-Spatial** Have students locate Africa, Egypt, and Sudan on a world map, then ask them to locate Aswan on a map of Africa. Challenge them to trace the path of the White Nile from its headwaters in Uganda, and the Blue Nile from its headwaters in Ethiopia, all the way to the Nile Delta on Egypt's north coast. L1

- Ask students to compare the Nile Delta with the mouths of other large rivers in the world. Point out that rivers cannot flow as fast when they come into contact with the still water of an ocean. As the river slows, the sediments it has been carrying settle out. Deltas then form.

Sources

- Lean, Geoffrey, and Don Hinrichsen. *World Wildlife Fund Atlas of the Environment.* Oxford: Helicon, 1992.
- Sandak, Cass. *Dams.* New York: Franklin Watts, 1983.

Activity 20-1

PREPARATION

LS **Visual-Spatial** Design and carry out an experiment to collect particulate matter that is carried by air. L1 COOP LEARN

Process Skills
designing an experiment, communicating, forming a hypothesis, observing and inferring, making and using tables, making and using graphs, classifying, interpreting data

Time
15-20 minutes to plan the experiment, 25-30 minutes to prepare gelatin lids, 40 minutes one week later to do the Analyze and Apply activities

Materials
- Place lids with gelatin in a refrigerator to solidify before having students place them into the environment.

Alternate Materials If gelatin is not available, petroleum jelly can be rubbed onto lids, petri dishes, or microscope slides.

Safety Precautions
Caution students to use thermal mitts and safety goggles while working with the hot plate and hot gelatin.

Possible Hypothesis
Students might hypothesize that they will find soot, dust particles, and pieces of plants and insects. They will likely think that different areas of the community will contain different types and amounts of particulate matter.

Activity Worksheets, pp. 5, 120-121

Activity 20-1

Design Your Own Experiment
What's in the air?

Have you ever gotten a particle of dust in your eye? Before it got into your eye, it was one of the many pieces of particulate matter in the air. In the Explore Activity at the beginning of the chapter, you observed some of the dust particles that settled out of the air. Just imagine how many pieces of particulate matter the air must hold.

PREPARATION

Problem
What kinds of particulate matter are in your environment? Are some areas of your environment more polluted with particulates than others?

Form a Hypothesis
Based on the observations you made in the Explore Activity on page 555 and your knowledge of your neighborhood, hypothesize what kinds of particulate matter you will find in your environment. Will all areas in your community contain the same types and amounts of particulate matter?

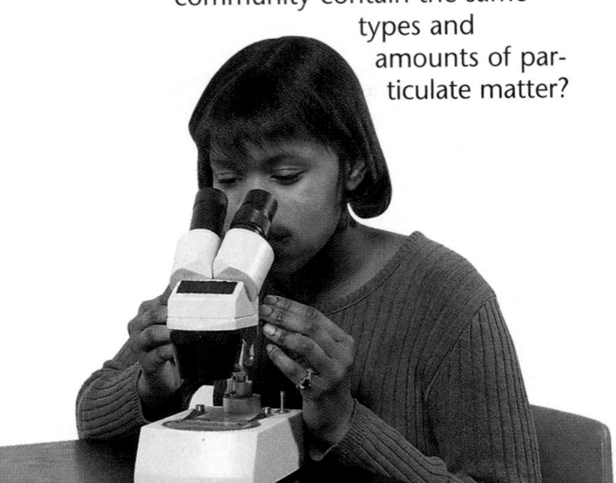

Objectives
- Design an experiment to collect and analyze particulate matter in the air in your community.
- Observe and describe the particulate matter you collect.

Possible Materials
- small box of plain gelatin
- hot plate
- pan or pot
- water
- safety goggles
- thermal mitt
- marker
- refrigerator
- plastic lids (4)
- stereomicroscope

Safety Precautions
Wear a thermal mitt and safety goggles while working with a hot plate and while pouring the gelatin from the pan or pot into the lids.

PLAN THE EXPERIMENT

1. As a group, agree upon and write out your hypotheses statements.
2. As a group, list the steps you need to take to test your hypotheses. Be specific, describing exactly what you will do at each step.
3. List your materials.
4. Design a data table in your Science Journal so that it is ready to use as your group collects data.
5. Mix the gelatin according to the directions on the box. Carefully pour a thin layer of gelatin into each lid. Use this to collect air particulate matter.
6. Decide where you will place each plastic lid in order to collect particulate matter in the air.

Check the Plan

1. Read over your entire experiment to make sure that all steps are in a logical order.
2. Identify any constants, variables, and controls of the experiment.
3. *Make sure your teacher approves your plan before you proceed.*

DO THE EXPERIMENT

1. Carry out the experiment as planned.
2. While the experiment is going on, write down any observations that you make and complete the data table in your Science Journal.

Analyze and Apply

1. **Describe** the types of materials you collected in each lid.
2. **Graph** your results using a bar graph. Place the number of particulates on the *y*-axis and the test-site location on the *x*-axis.
3. Why do you think some lids had more particles and larger particles than the rest?
4. Which of the materials that you collected might be the result of human activities?

Go Further

Do you think any of the materials you collected might be harmful to humans? Explain your answer. How does your body filter solid particles from the air you breathe?

PLAN THE EXPERIMENT

Possible Procedures

One possible procedure is to empty a small box of plain gelatin into a pot. Read the directions on the side of the box to determine the amount of water to add to the pot. Stir in the water. While wearing safety goggles and a thermal mitt, heat the mixture on top of a hot plate. Pour the mixture onto plastic lids. Place the lids into a refrigerator overnight. The next day, place the lids at various outside locations. Check the lids daily, make observations, and record the observations in the data table. At the end of one week, examine the lids with a stereomicroscope.

Teaching Strategies

Most of the materials collected will be dust and soot. Have students study maps that show the locations of nearby industries and weather maps that show local wind patterns. See if they can establish a correlation.

DO THE EXPERIMENT

Expected Outcome

Students will observe that particulate matter has stuck to the gelatin.

Analyze and Apply

1. Materials will vary, but dust particles, soot, paint chips, plant seeds, pieces of leaves and twigs, and small insects might be found.
2. Graphs will vary.
3. Some lids were placed closer to the source of the material (the factory, the tree, etc.). Another factor is the direction of the wind.
4. The soot, some of the dust, and paint chips are probably created by human activities.

Go Further

Answers will vary according to the types of materials that are collected. Soot, dust, and pollen cause respiratory problems. The hairs and mucus in the nose filter particulate matter.

Assessment

Performance Have students classify the various types of particulate matter that they collected. Use the Performance Task Assessment List for Making and Using a Classification System in **PASC,** p. 49. P

Section 20•3

Prepare

Section Background

Substantial amounts of pesticides have percolated into well water in at least 34 states. More than 100 million people in the United States rely on underground wells for drinking water.

Preplanning

- Obtain samples of well or pond water, stream water, and distilled water, baby food jars, and liquid soap for the MiniLAB.
- Students will need access to home water meters. Pair up students who don't have access to water meters with those who do for Activity 20-2.

1 Motivate

Bellringer

Before presenting the lesson, display **Section Focus Transparency 77** on the overhead projector. Assign the accompanying **Focus Activity** worksheet. L1 LEP

Tying to Previous Knowledge

Have students recall that in Section 18-3 they learned about one kind of water pollution—ocean pollution.

Visual Learning

Figure 20-8A Name some sources of water pollution. *Answers may include pesticides, herbicides, mine runoff, industrial chemicals, and raw sewage.* LEP LS

Use **Critcal Thinking/Problem Solving,** p. 26, as you teach this lesson.

20•3 Water Pollution

Science Words

Safe Drinking Water Act
Clean Water Act

Objectives

- List five water pollutants and their sources.
- Describe ways that international agreements and U.S. laws are designed to reduce water pollution.
- Relate ways that you can help reduce water pollution.

Causes and Effects of Water Pollution

Suppose you were hiking along a stream or lake and became very thirsty. Do you think it would be safe to drink the water? In most cases, it wouldn't. Many streams and lakes in the United States are quite polluted, such as the one shown in **Figure 20-8A.** Even streams that look clear and sparkling are not safe for drinking.

You learned in Chapter 18 how pollutants get into the oceans. Groundwater, streams, and lakes are polluted by similar sources. There is strong reason to believe that these pollutants cause health problems such as cancer, dysentery, birth defects, and liver damage in humans and other animals.

Pollution Sources

How do you think pollutants get into the water? Bacteria and viruses get into the water because some cities illegally dump raw sewage directly into the water supply. Underground septic tanks can leak, too. Radioactive materials can get into the water from leaks at nuclear power plants and radioactive waste dumps.

Pesticides, herbicides, and fertilizers from farms and lawns are picked up by rainwater and carried into streams. Some people dump motor oil into sewers after they've changed the oil in their cars. Water running through mines also carries pollutants to streams and underground aquifers. Industrial

Figure 20-8

Clean water is one of our most precious resources. Before we can use water for our daily activities, we must purify it. After we use it, we must clean it again before returning it to the environment.

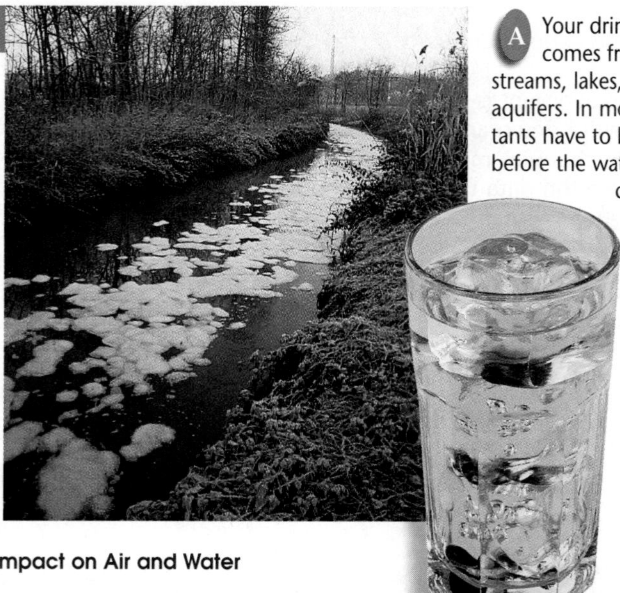

A Your drinking water comes from nearby streams, lakes, or underground aquifers. In most cases, pollutants have to be removed before the water is safe to drink. *Name some sources of water pollution.*

Program Resources

Reproducible Masters

Study Guide, p. 81 L1
Reinforcement, p. 81 L1
Enrichment, p. 81 L3
Cross-Curricular Integration, p. 24
Activity Worksheets, pp. 5, 122-123, 125 L1
Lab Manual 58
Critical Thinking/Problem Solving, p. 26

Transparencies

Section Focus Transparency 77 L1
Science Integration Transparency 20

B The plant known as water hyacinth removes many pollutants from water. Water hyacinths can be used at wastewater treatment facilities to clean up water before it flows back into streams and aquifers.

chemicals get into the water because some factories illegally dump toxic materials directly into the water. Waste from landfills and hazardous waste dumps leaks into the surrounding soil and groundwater.

But most water pollution is caused by legal, everyday activities. Water is polluted when we flush our toilets, wash our hands, brush our teeth, and water our lawns. Nitrogen and phosphorus are difficult to remove from sewage and wastewater. Large amounts of these elements are released into rivers and streams from household detergents, soaps, and other cleaning agents. Water is also polluted when oil and gasoline run off of pavement, down storm sewers, and into streams.

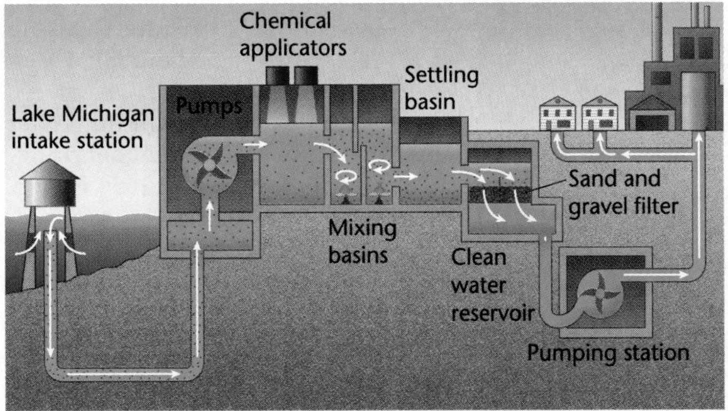

C This water purification plant in Chicago provides drinking water for millions of people. Water taken from Lake Michigan is pumped into a tank where alum, chlorine, lime, and other compounds are added to kill microorganisms. It is thoroughly mixed and the large particles of matter settle out. Some smaller particles are filtered by sand and gravel. Clean water is then pumped to consumers.

2 Teach

Enrichment

- Have students find out the source of the local water supply. Have them investigate who determines whether or not the supply is pure; how often the supply is tested; and how the wastewater is treated. L1 P
- Have students discuss various sources of water pollution. If there are any water pollution problems in your area, students may want to report on their causes and the steps being taken to correct the problems. L2

Teacher F.Y.I.

The Great Lakes contain 95% of the fresh surface water in the U.S., and 20% of the world's fresh surface water.

Inquiry Questions

- **What causes most water pollution?** *everyday activities like flushing toilets, washing hands, brushing teeth, watering lawns, and water running off pavement*
- **How can runoff from a coal mine pollute groundwater with sulfuric acid?** *The sulfur in the coal mixes with the water, producing sulfuric acid. This acidic water travels through pores in the soil and into the groundwater.*

 **Videodisc**

STV: Water

Contaminated beach

52568

Use **Cross-Curricular Integration,** p. 24, as you teach this lesson.

Cultural Diversity

Polluted Water The Vistula River, the largest river in Poland, is so polluted that its water cannot even be used by industries; it would corrode the machinery. Much of its pollution is blamed on thousands of outdated European factories that pump pollutants into the air and water. Cost estimates for cleaning up this river have ranged from $100 million to $15 billion. Sweden has contributed $60 million to help clean it up because this river contributes about 40% of the total nitrogen runoff into the Baltic Sea. The U.S. has also contributed money for environmental aid to Poland. Ask students, **Why must all countries work together to control pollution?** *Pollution doesn't stop at political boundaries.*

Problem Solving

Solve the Problem

1. Crop fertilizers and sewage contain phosphates and nitrates.
2. Sewage treatment plants might be leaking, or fertilizers and pesticides from lawns and farms might be carried to the pond by runoff.

Think Critically

1. They increase.
2. Fish die without oxygen.
3. The pollution could be decreased by having people living in the area use different detergents and fertilizers and by altering the drainage pattern around the pond.

Revealing Preconceptions

Many students probably think that if a particular pollutant is no longer added to a lake, it will disappear from the lake over time. However, this is not true with some pollutants. A group of chemicals called polychlorinated biphenyls (PCBs) were banned in the United States in 1979. However, they remain in high concentrations at the bottom of many lakes, where they have become trapped in the mud and have been passed through food chains.

Problem Solving

What's happening to the fish?

Suppose you've been fishing the same pond since you were only seven years old. You used to catch a lot of fish there. But lately, you haven't been able to catch many fish at all, and those that you do catch seem sick. You also notice that the algae layer covering the surface of the water seems to be getting thicker each year. You test the water and find that the dissolved oxygen content is very low.

Solve the Problem:

1. **Why might you suspect that crop fertilizers or sewage could be polluting the pond?**
2. **What could be the sources of these pollutants?**

Think Critically:

High levels of phosphates and nitrates in water can cause an increase in algae populations.

1. As the algae populations die, what happens to the population of decomposers in the water?
2. If the decomposers use up oxygen in the water, what happens to the fish population?
3. If the pond is being polluted by phosphates and nitrates, what could be done to decrease the pollution?

Reducing Water Pollution

Several countries have worked together to reduce water pollution. Let's look at one example. Lake Erie is on the border between the United States and Canada. In the 1960s, Lake Erie was so polluted by phosphorus from sewage, soaps, and fertilizers that it was turning into a green, soupy mess. Large areas of the lake bottom had no oxygen and, therefore, no life.

International Cooperation

In the 1970s, the United States and Canada made two water quality agreements. The two countries spent $15 billion to stop the sewage problem. Today, the green slime is gone, and the fish are back. However, more than 300 human-made chemicals can still be found in Lake Erie, and some of them are very hazardous. The United States and Canada now are studying ways to get them out of the lake.

Pollution Control in the United States

The U.S. Congress also has reduced water pollution by passing several laws. Two important laws are the 1986 Safe Drinking Water Act and the 1987 Clean Water Act.

The 1986 **Safe Drinking Water Act** is a law to ensure that drinking water in our country is safe. This act has not been very successful. Today, there are 200 000 public water systems in the United States, and many still have not met the standards set by the 1986 Safe Drinking Water Act.

Visual Learning

Figure 20-9 Explain how the 1987 Clean Water Act encourages communities to clean up their water. *The act gives money to states for building sewage and wastewater treatment facilities, and for controlling runoff.* LEP LS

Across the Curriculum

Civics Have students find out how a bill becomes a law in Congress. L1

Community Connection

Clean Water Invite a hydrogeologist to discuss the "health" of local streams and the groundwater supply.

Figure 20-9

Sewage and industrial wastes pollute many rivers and lakes. However, these sources of pollution can be controlled, and the water made safe for recreational purposes. *Explain how the 1987 Clean Water Act encourages communities to clean up their water.*

Clean Water Act

The 1987 **Clean Water Act** gives money to the states for building sewage and wastewater treatment facilities. The money also is for controlling runoff from streets, mines, and farms. Runoff caused up to half of the water pollution in the United States before 1987. This act also requires states to develop quality standards for all their streams.

The U.S. Environmental Protection Agency (EPA) makes sure that cities comply with both the Safe Drinking Water Act and the Clean Water Act. Most cities and states are working hard to clean up their water. Look at **Figure 20-9.** Many streams that once were heavily polluted by sewage and industrial wastes are now safe for swimming and fishing.

However, there is still much to be done. For example, the EPA discovered that 30 percent of the nation's rivers, 42 percent of its lakes, and 32 percent of its estuaries are still polluted because of silt and nutrients from farm runoff and municipal sewage overflows from cities. An estimated 40 percent of the country's freshwater supply is still not usable because of pollution. While Americans have spent $260 billion in the past 20 years on sewage treatment plants, water treatment is still unsatisfactory in 1100 U.S. cities.

USING MATH

The average shower uses 19 L of water per minute. If you take a five-minute shower each day, how much water do you use in one year by showering?

USING MATH

19 L/min × 5 min/day × 365 days/year = 34 675 L/yr

Discussion

LS **Linguistic** Some people in Congress have proposed that the federal standards in the Clean Water Act of 1987 be made voluntary instead of mandatory because they create financial strain on some communities. Ask students how they feel about this proposal. Encourage students to write to their congressional representatives to express their personal views on this subject. L1

3 Assess

Check for Understanding

FLEX Your Brain

Use the Flex Your Brain activity to have students explore WATER POLLUTION.

Activity Worksheets, p. 5

Reteach

LS **Interpersonal** Have student pairs make posters depicting sources of and solutions to various kinds of water pollution. Hang the posters throughout the school building.

Extension

For students who have mastered this section, use the **Reinforcement** and **Enrichment** masters.

Science Journal

Report on Planet Earth Have each student write a story from the point of view of someone who comes to Earth from another planet to find smog, polluted water, and litter. Students could also write from the point of view of someone who lived 100 years ago seeing today's world. L2 LS

MiniLAB

Purpose

LS **Intrapersonal** Students will determine whether local water supplies have hard water. L1

Materials

small containers with caps, liquid soap, water samples, distilled water, glass marking pen

Teaching Strategies

Troubleshooting The temperature of each sample, the amount of each sample, the amount of liquid soap added, and the amount and force of the shaking all must be constant.

- Remind students to label the contents of each container.
- The distilled water will produce the most soapsuds and, therefore, will be the "softest" water sample.

Analysis

1. The hardest water will be the sample producing the least amount of suds when the sample and liquid soap are combined and shaken.
2. Minerals build up inside teakettles, dishwashing machines, hot water tanks, hot water heating systems, and industrial boilers, blocking water passages.

Assessment

Performance Have students evaporate the water from their samples and observe and draw the minerals that are left behind. Use the Performance Task Assessment List for Carrying Out a Strategy and Collecting Data in **PASC,** p. 25. P

Activity Worksheets, pp. 5, 125

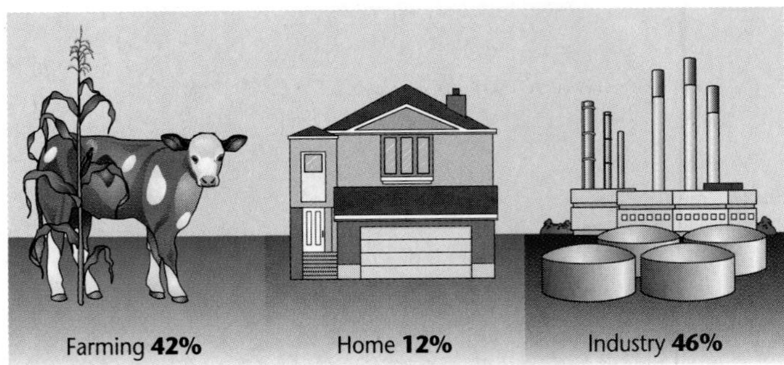

Figure 20-10

The industries that produce the products you use each day consume nearly half of the fresh water used in the United States.

MiniLAB

How hard is your water?

When minerals such as calcium carbonate, magnesium carbonate, or sulfates are dissolved in water, the water is said to be *hard.* This is a type of natural pollution that occurs in some areas.

Procedure

1. Use small containers such as baby food jars to collect samples of water from the tap, a nearby pond or well, and a local stream.
2. Add one drop of liquid soap to each jar.
3. Cap each container tightly and shake it rapidly.
4. Observe how many soapsuds are produced in each container.

Analysis

1. Which of your water samples had the hardest water? (Hint: The container with the most suds contains the softest water.)
2. Infer what problems might be caused by having a hard water supply in your home or community.

How can you help?

As you discovered in Chapter 19, we are often the cause of our environmental problems. But we are also the solution. What can you do to help?

Safely Dispose of Wastes

If you dispose of household chemicals such as paint and motor oil, don't pour them down the drain or onto the ground. Also, don't put them out with your other trash.

Hazardous wastes poured directly onto the ground move through the soil and eventually reach the groundwater below. When you pour them down the drain, they flow through the sewer, through the wastewater treatment plant, and into wherever the wastewater is drained, usually into a stream. This is how rivers become polluted. If you put hazardous wastes out with the trash, they end up in landfills, where they may leak out.

What should you do with these wastes? First, read the label on the container for instructions on disposal. Don't throw the container into the trash if the label specifies a different method of disposal. Recycle if you can. Many cities have recycling facilities for metal, glass, and plastic containers. Store chemical wastes so that they can't leak. If you live in a city, call the sewage office, water office, or garbage disposal service and ask them how to safely dispose of the others.

Conserve Energy and Water

Another way you can reduce water pollution is to conserve energy. With less use of fuels, there will be less acid rain falling into forests and streams. And with less nuclear power, there will be a reduced risk of radioactive materials leaking into the environment.

Another way you can help is to conserve water. Look at **Figure 20-10.** How much water do you use every day? Think of all the ways you depend on water. How many times do you flush a toilet each day? How much water do you use every day for taking a bath or cleaning your clothes? How much water do you use when you wash dishes, wash a car, or use a hose or lawn sprinkler? Typical U.S. citizens like the one shown in **Figure 20-11** use about 397 L every day.

All of this water must be purified before it reaches your home. Then it must be treated as wastewater after you use it. It takes a lot of energy to treat this water and pump it to your home. Remember, when you use energy, you add to the pollution problem. Therefore, when you reduce the amount of water you use, you help prevent pollution.

Water pollution is everybody's problem, and we all must do our part to help reduce it. Consider some changes you can make in your life that will make a difference.

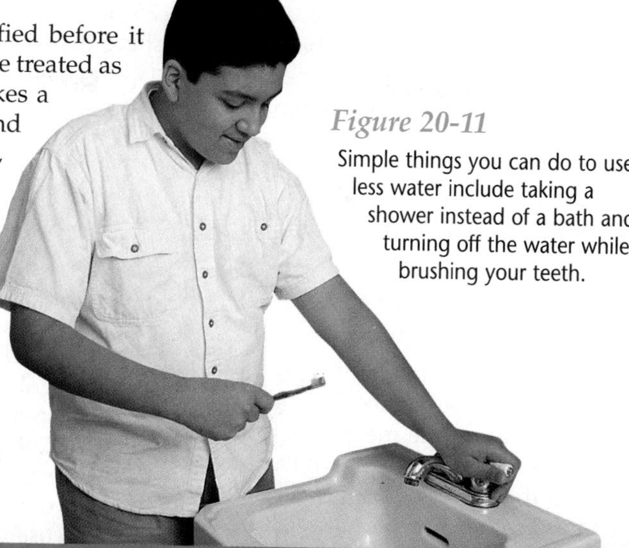

Figure 20-11

Simple things you can do to use less water include taking a shower instead of a bath and turning off the water while brushing your teeth.

Section Wrap-up

Review

1. What are three things you can do to help reduce water pollution?
2. How have the United States and Canada joined forces to clean up Lake Erie?
3. **Think Critically:** Southern Florida is home to nearly 5 million people, many dairy farms, and sugarcane fields. It is also the location of Everglades National Park—a shallow river system with highly polluted waters. What kinds of pollutants do you think are in the Everglades? How do you think they got there?

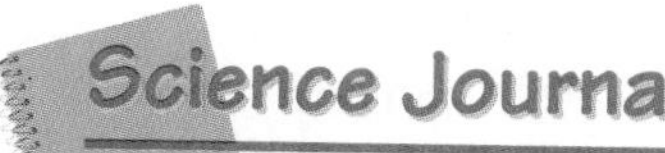

Science Journal

In your Science Journal, make a list of things that will reduce the amount of water you use.

Skill Builder

Interpreting Scientific Illustrations

Use **Figure 20-8C** to answer the following questions: *Why are mixing basins needed? What's the purpose of the sand and gravel filter? Gravity forces the water through the system until it reaches the reservoir. Why is a pump needed after this point?* If you need help, refer to Interpreting Scientific Illustrations in the **Skill Handbook.**

4 Close

•MINI•QUIZ•

Use the Mini Quiz to check students' recall of chapter content.

1. **Lake Erie was so polluted by ______ in the 1960s that the water turned green.** *phosphorus*
2. **The 1987 _____ Act gives money to states for building sewage and wastewater treatment facilities.** *Clean Water*
3. **The ______ makes sure that cities comply with the Safe Drinking Water Act and the Clean Water Act.** *Environmental Protection Agency*

Section Wrap-up

Review

1. properly dispose of hazardous wastes or recycle them, conserve energy, and conserve water
2. They have made agreements to stop the sewage problem. Both countries are studying ways to get human-made chemicals out of the lake.
3. **Think Critically** They include bacteria and viruses from the cattle feces; pesticides and herbicides from the sugarcane fields; industrial wastes; and wastes from the burning of fossil fuels.

Skill Builder

The mixing basin ensures that the added chemicals are dispersed throughout the water. The sand and gravel filter out microscopic impurities as the water drains through the pores. The reservoir is lower than the buildings that receive the water. Therefore, a pump is needed to work against the force of gravity and push the water upward.

Assessment

Oral Assess students' abilities to interpret scientific illustrations by having them explain why a pump is needed to get the water from the lake to the water purification plant. Use the Performance Task Assessment List for Making Observations and Inferences in **PASC**, p. 17. P

Science Journal

The list might include taking shorter showers and baths, turning off the water when brushing teeth, using the dishwasher and washing machines only for full loads, putting a bottle of water in the toilet tank, watering the lawn only when necessary, fixing leaky faucets, recycling, and conserving energy.

Activity 20-2

Purpose

IS **Intrapersonal** Students will calculate home water usage. L1

Process Skills

using numbers, making and using tables, making and using graphs, observing and inferring, interpreting data, comparing and contrasting

Time

10 minutes each day for eight days at home to do procedures 1-3, 30 minutes for graphing and answering questions in class on the ninth day

Activity Worksheets, pp. 5, 122-123

Teaching Strategies

Alternate Materials If your community uses only water from wells, you may supply hypothetical meter readings for the eight days so students can complete the activity.

Troubleshooting Be sure students understand the differences among the water meters and can identify which type is used in their homes. Make sure students understand the units in which water use is measured.

- After students have collected their data, make a list on the chalkboard or overhead projector showing the range of water use from highest to lowest for the class. This should be done without identifying which family is which. This will allow students to see how the rate of water use in their home compares with the usage by other families.

Activity 20-2 Water Use

How much water goes down the drain at your house? Did you know that up to 75 percent of the water used in homes is used in the bathroom? Flushing the toilet accounts for 50 percent of that water; the rest is for bathing, showering, washing hands, and brushing teeth. By learning to read a water meter, you can find out how much water your family uses.

Problem

How much water does your family use?

Materials

- home water meter

Background

There are several different types of water meters. Meter A has six dials. As water moves through the meter, the pointers on the dials rotate. To read a meter similar to A, find the dial with the lowest denomination indicated. The bottom dial is labeled 10. Record the last number that the pointer on that dial has passed. Continue this process for each dial. Meter A shows 18 853 gallons. Meter B is read like a digital watch. It indicates 1959.9 cubic feet. Meter C is similar to meter B, but indicates water use in cubic meters.

Procedure

1. Design a data table and record your home water meter reading at the same time of the day for eight days.
2. Subtract the previous day's reading to determine the amount of water used each day.
3. Record how much water is used in your home each day. Also, record the activities in your home that used water each day.
4. Plot your data on a graph like the one shown below. Label the vertical axis with the units used by your meter.

Analyze

1. During which day was the most water used? Why?
2. **Calculate** the total amount of water used by your family during the week.
3. **Calculate** the average amount of water each person used during the week by dividing the total amount of water used by the number of persons. **Calculate** a monthly average.

Conclude and Apply

4. Why is your answer to question 3 only an estimate of the amount of water used?
5. **Infer** how the time of year might affect the rate at which your family uses water.
6. What are some things your family could do to conserve water?

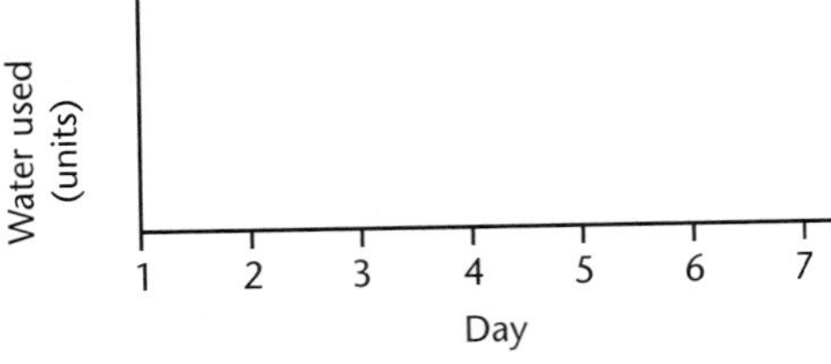

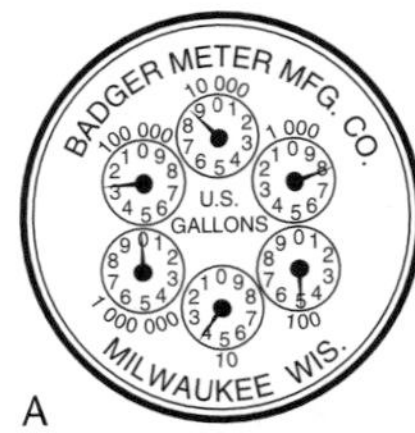

A

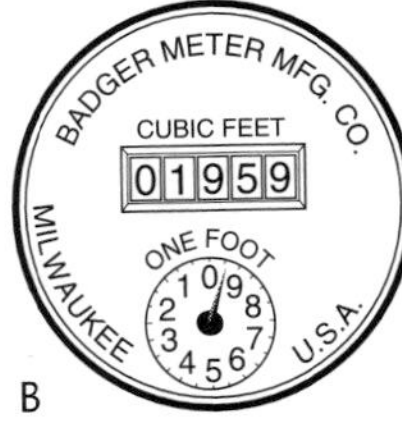

B

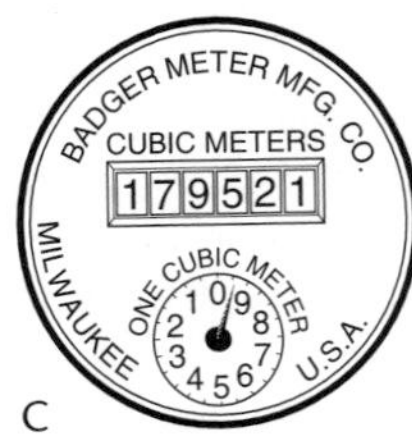

C

Answers to Questions

1. Answers will vary, but watering lawns or doing laundry may increase home water use.
2. Adding daily totals will give a weekly total.
3. Answers will vary. Discuss how the size of a family affects the average. Also, discuss reasons for weekly variations in the average.
4. This amount is an estimate because the week in which data were collected may not be typical.
5. It might be affected because lawn watering and car washing are seasonal activities.
6. Answers may include fixing leaky faucets, taking shorter showers, and not letting water run while brushing teeth.

Assessment

Performance To further assess students' understanding of water use, have them take water meter readings for eight more days, this time while the family conserves water. Have students compare their results with the results when water was not being conserved. Use the Performance Task Assessment List for Carrying Out a Strategy and Collecting Data in **PASC**, p. 25. P

Chapter 20 Review

Summary

20-1: Air Pollution

1. Photochemical smog forms when fossil fuels are burned and the pollutants react with sunlight. Sulfurous smog is created when fuels are burned in electrical power plants and home furnaces.
2. Chlorofluorcarbons cause holes in the ozone layer. Acid rain is the result of burning coal and gasoline, which produce gases that react to form acids in the air.
3. Air pollution causes health problems in people and other organisms.
4. Recycling and conservation of Earth's resources reduce pollution.

20-2: Science and Society: Acid Rain

1. If soils are acidic, acid rain causes a lot of damage. Basic soils neutralize acid rain, resulting in less damage.
2. Better emission control devices on cars, car pooling, and the use of public transportation can help reduce acid rain. Washing coal that contains a lot of sulfur and using scrubbers can also reduce acid rain.
3. The cost of reducing sulfur dioxide emissions could be shared by everyone or could be limited to the areas that produce the emissions.

20-3: Water Pollution

1. Bacteria and viruses from animal wastes, radioactive waste, pesticides and herbicides used in agriculture, fossil fuels from mines and wells, and industrial chemicals from manufacturing processes all pollute freshwater bodies.
2. The passing of laws and the enforcement of these laws by the EPA and other agencies has helped to reduce water pollution.
3. Safely disposing of hazardous wastes is one way to reduce water pollution. Recycling and conservation are also important.

Key Science Words

a. acid rain
b. acid
c. base
d. Clean Air Act
e. Clean Water Act
f. pH scale
g. photochemical smog
h. Safe Drinking Water Act
i. scrubber
j. sulfurous smog

Reviewing Vocabulary

Match each phrase with the correct term from the list of Key Science Words.

1. smog that forms with the aid of light
2. smog that forms when pollutants mix with a layer of stagnant air
3. acidic rain, snow, sleet, or hail
4. law passed to protect air in the U.S.
5. a measure of the acidity or basicity of a solution
6. device that lowers sulfur emissions from coal-burning power plants
7. law ensuring that water is safe to drink
8. law that controls stormwater runoff
9. substance with low pH number
10. substance with high pH number

Chapter 20 Review

Summary

Have students read the summary statements to review the major concepts of the chapter.

Reviewing Vocabulary

1. g
2. j
3. a
4. d
5. f
6. i
7. h
8. e
9. b
10. c

Assessment

Portfolio Encourage students to place in their portfolios one or two items of what they consider to be their best work. Examples include:

- Across the Curriculum, p. 559
- Science Journal, p. 561
- Enrichment, p. 569 P

Performance Additional performance assessments may be found in **Performance Assessment** and **Science Integration Activities.** Performance Task Assessment Lists and rubrics for evaluating these activities can be found in Glencoe's **Performance Assessment in the Science Classroom.**

GLENCOE TECHNOLOGY

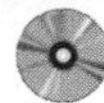

Videodisc

Glencoe Earth Science

Interactive Videodisc

Use the videodisc lesson 6, *Pollution Detectives,* to have students apply what they've learned about water pollution to a real-world situation.

MindJogger Videoquiz

Chapter 20 Have students work in groups as they play the Videoquiz game to review key chapter concepts.

Checking Concepts

1. d
2. b
3. b
4. b
5. b
6. b
7. a
8. c
9. c
10. a

Understanding Concepts

11. Both are forms of air pollution produced by the burning of fossil fuels. Photochemical smog forms when fossil fuels are burned by cars, planes, and factories. The waste gases react with sunlight to produce the smog. Sulfurous smog forms when fossil fuels are burned in electrical power plants and home furnaces.
12. Acid rain can form when sulfur dioxide from coal-burning power plants combines with moisture in the air to form sulfuric acid. Acid rain can also form when nitrogen oxide from car exhausts combines with moisture in the air to form nitric acid.
13. The presence of factories and motor vehicles in an area increases the possibility of damage done by acid rain. Damage also is dependent upon certain weather factors. Finally, soil type can increase or decrease the effects of acid rain on the vegetation and groundwater of an area.
14. Natural sources include volcanic eruptions, forest fires, and grass fires.
15. Both were passed to help reduce water pollutants. The Safe Drinking Water Act ensures that all drinking water is safe. The Clean Water Act allots monies to states for building water treatment facilities, and it requires that water quality standards be developed for all streams.

Chapter 20 Review

Checking Concepts

Choose the word or phrase that completes the sentence.

1. _______ cause more smog pollution than any other source.
   a. Power plants
   b. Burning wastes
   c. Industries
   d. Cars
2. _______ forms when chemicals react with sunlight.
   a. pH
   b. Photochemical smog
   c. Sulfurous smog
   d. Acid rain
3. A solution with a pH of 3 is more _______ than a solution with a pH of 4.
   a. neutral
   b. acidic
   c. dense
   d. basic
4. Acid rain can form when _______ combines with moisture in the air.
   a. ozone
   b. sulfur dioxide
   c. carbon dioxide
   d. oxygen
5. The industries that produce the products you use each day consume nearly _______ of the fresh water used in the United States.
   a. one-tenth
   b. half
   c. one-third
   d. two-thirds
6. One goal of the _______ Act is to reduce the level of car emissions.
   a. Clean Water
   b. Clean Air
   c. Safe Drinking Water
   d. Hazardous Waste
7. Acid rain has a pH of_______.
   a. less than 5.6
   b. between 5.6 & 7.0
   c. greater than 7.0
   d. greater than 9.5
8. The damage done by acid rain depends on _______.
   a. the pH scale
   b. ozone emissions
   c. soil type
   d. sunlight
9. Most water pollution is caused by _______.
   a. illegal dumping
   b. industrial chemicals
   c. everyday water use in the home
   d. wastewater treatment facilities
10. The _______ Act gives money to local governments to treat wastewater.
    a. Clean Water
    b. Clean Air
    c. Safe Drinking Water
    d. Hazardous Waste

Understanding Concepts

Answer the following questions in your Science Journal using complete sentences.

11. Compare and contrast photochemical smog and sulfurous smog.
12. Explain two ways in which acid rain can form.
13. Discuss the factors that affect the severity of the damage done by acid rain.
14. Describe natural sources of air pollution.
15. Compare and contrast the Safe Drinking Water Act with the Clean Water Act.

Thinking Critically

16. How might cities with smog problems lessen the dangers to people who live and work in the cities?
17. How are industries both helpful and harmful to humans?
18. How do trees help to reduce air pollution?
19. Thermal pollution occurs when heated water is dumped into a nearby body of water. What effects does this type of pollution have on organisms living in the water?
20. What steps might a community in a desert area take to cope with water supply problems?

Thinking Critically

16. Cities could broadcast health alerts that would take effect when the amount of pollutants in the air surpasses a certain level. At these times, factories that contribute to the pollution could be closed and people with respiratory problems would be advised to stay indoors.
17. Most industries provide products that improve the quality of life. However, many by-products of industrial processes pollute Earth's air, water, and soil.
18. Trees reduce the amount of carbon dioxide in the air because all green plants use this gas to photosynthesize.
19. The heat could kill organisms and cause excessive evaporation of water. Evaporation can cause substances in the water to become concentrated, which could cause organisms to become sick and perhaps die.

Developing Skills

If you need help, refer to the **Skill Handbook.**

21. **Hypothesizing:** Earth's surface is nearly 75 percent water. Yet much of this water is not available for many uses. Explain.
22. **Recognizing Cause and Effect:** What effect will an increase in the human population have on the need for fresh water?
23. **Classifying:** If a smog is brownish in color, is it sulfurous or photochemical smog?
24. **Concept Mapping:** Complete a concept map of the water cycle. Indicate how humans interrupt the cycle. Use the following phrases: *evaporation occurs, purified, drinking water, atmospheric water, wastewater, precipitation falls,* and *groundwater* or *surface water.*
25. **Outlining:** Make an outline that summarizes what you personally can do to reduce air pollution.

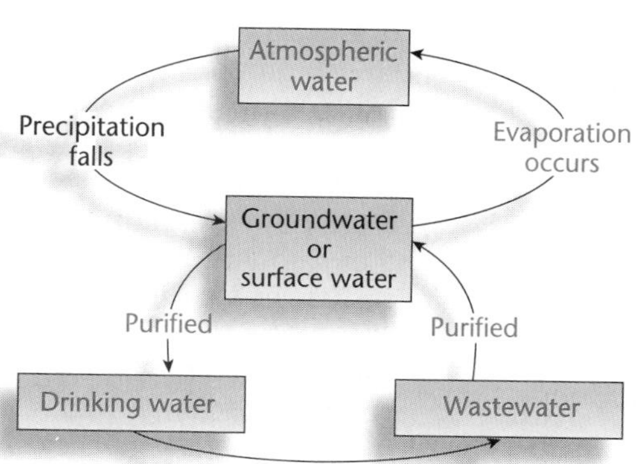

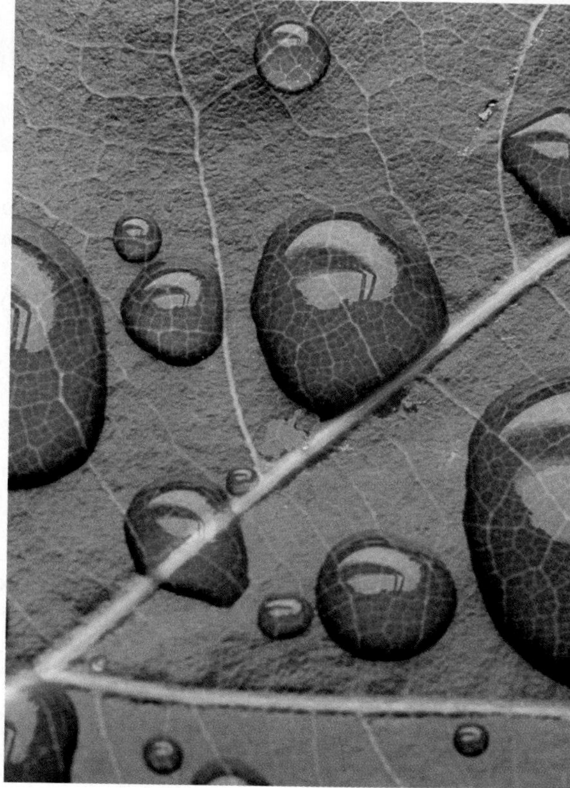

Performance Assessment

1. **Carrying Out a Strategy and Collecting Data:** Design an experiment to test the effects of acid rain on various kinds of vegetation.
2. **Interpreting and Using Data:** Design an experiment to determine which kind of sediment—gravel, sand, or clay—is most effective in filtering pollutants from water.
3. **Design:** In the MiniLAB on page 572, you observed the hardness of your water. Review the procedures you used in Activity 17-1 on pages 482 and 483 and design a way to remove the minerals from the water.

Chapter 20 Review

20. Desert dwellers must pump groundwater or pipe in surface water. The water must then be stored in covered containers to reduce evaporation. Conservation also would be important in such communities.

Developing Skills

21. Hypothesizing Much of the water at Earth's surface is salt water, which must be processed before being used in most instances.

22. Recognizing Cause and Effect An increase in the human population will increase the demand for fresh water.

23. Classifying photochemical smog

24. Concept Mapping See student page.

25. Outlining Outlines will vary. Points may include walking or cycling to nearby places, recycling, planting trees, reducing wastes, and conserving resources.

Performance Assessment

1. A possible design would be to set up two identical trays of grass sod. Students could water one tray with tap water as the control. The other tray could receive water to which lemon juice has been added to reduce its pH below 5.6. Students could observe the color and growth of the grass over time. This process could be repeated using other types of plants. Use the Performance Task Assessment List for Carrying Out a Strategy and Collecting Data in **PASC,** p. 25. P

2. Students could add pollutants (coffee grounds, paint, and oil) to water. They could set up their apparatus similar to what is used in Activity 6-2, and pour equal amounts of the polluted water into the different kinds of soil. By observing the water that drips from each soil, they can compare the degree to which the different soils remove the pollutants. Use the Performance Task Assessment List for Designing an Experiment in **PASC,** p. 23. P

3. Using the materials listed in Activity 17-1, students could use the distillation process to remove minerals from the hard water. Use the Performance Task Assessment List for Designing an Experiment in **PASC,** p. 23. P

Objectives

LS **Intrapersonal** Students will research environmental problems and become advocates for the environment. L1

Summary

In this project, students will do in-depth studies of environmental problems. They will prepare scrapbooks of the information they collect, perform a variety of tasks to help correct the problems they study, and share their accomplishments with their classmates.

Time Required

This project is designed to be worked on throughout Chapters 18-20. The students will need time in class to begin their research at the school library. Most projects can be accomplished at home or within the community. Class time is needed for oral presentations and the environmental fair. (See *Go Further.)*

Preparation

- Establish cooperative groups of 2 or 3 students.
- Prepare a list of local and national addresses where students may write to get information about their topics or to express their opinions about what they have learned.
- Assign due dates for scrapbooks and oral presentations.

Teaching Strategies

- Check the biweekly progress of the student groups by having each cooperative group respond in writing to the statement: "Things that we have done toward completion of our environmental project that is due on (date) are: . . . ."
- Emphasize to students that the major goal of this project is to become involved in helping correct the environmental problem they select to study. The problem can be a local, state, national, or an international environmental problem.

UNIT PROJECT 6

Become an Advocate for the Environment

Endangered species, acid rain, ozone depletion, global warming, loss of wildlife habitat, and many other environmental topics make the headlines of our newspapers every day. Do these things bother you? As you do this project, you'll learn about issues that deal with energy and conservation, air pollution, water pollution, soil pollution, and human population growth and their effects on the environment. What can you do about these things?

Procedures

1. The first thing you can do is learn more about these problems. Choose an environmental problem to study in depth. Use the library and local and national organizations to get information.
2. Make a scrapbook of the information you collect. Include the following in your scrapbook: a table of contents; all research you have done including a background report, interviews, pictures, copies of letters you've sent and received, summaries of newspaper and magazine articles that you've read; and a bibliography.
3. After collecting your information, become an advocate for the environment. You can do this in a variety of ways:
   - Write letters to the editors of newspapers, your local government leaders, your representatives in Congress, and even the President of the United States.
   - Become a pen pal with other students who live in the United States, or in other countries, and tell them about what you've learned.
   - Teach young children. Arrange to teach an elementary class, a Boy Scout or Girl Scout troop, or a church group.
   - Make pamphlets and hand them out to your neighbors and/or classmates.
   - Make posters and display them around your school and/or the local library.
   - Have a bake sale or car wash and send the money you collect to an environmental group of your choice.

- Adopt a stream or section of a roadway and clean it up.
- Organize a tree planting celebration.
- Begin an anti-litter campaign in your school.
- Adopt an endangered species.
- Be creative. Think of other things you can do.

4. At the end of Unit 6, share your project with your classmates. During your presentation, use one or more visual aids. These might include videotapes, audiocassettes, filmstrips, slides, overhead transparencies, models, and posters. Be sure to answer the following questions during your presentation.
   - What do you know now that you didn't know when you started this project?
   - What did you do to help correct the environmental problem that you studied?
   - Do you think you really made a difference in helping to correct the problem? Explain.
   - What would you do differently if you could do this project again?
   - If you had unlimited money and other resources, what would you do to help correct the problem you studied?
   - Do you think the problem will get worse or better in the next ten years?
   - How has this project changed your attitude/outlook about the problem you chose to study?
   - Will you continue to be involved in helping correct the problem? If your answer is yes, how will you do this?

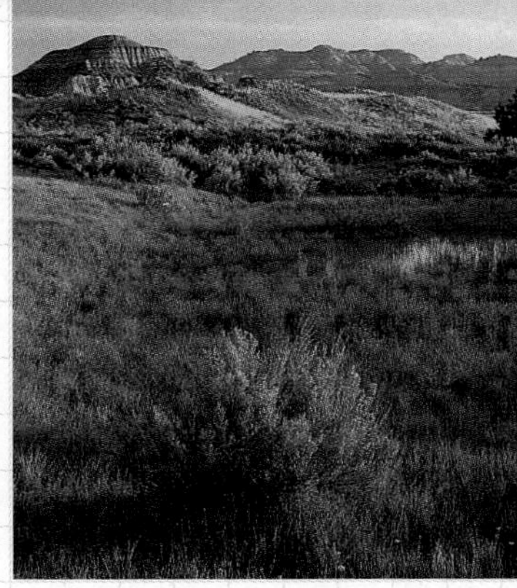

Going Further

Participate in an environmental fair. Create a display of information about the problem you studied, and describe what you did to help correct the problem. Be ready to answer questions from people who attend the fair.

Be a Part of the Solution, Not the Problem!

Go Further

Invite students from other classes to attend the environmental fair. Also, students can invite parents and others to attend. Each cooperative student group should display its notebook, posters, and other items. Students should be present to answer questions about their projects.

Address References

- American Endangered Species Foundation
  1988 Damascus Rd. Rt. 4
  Golden, CO 80403
- Representative ________
  Congress of the United States
  House of Representatives
  Washington, DC 20515
- Environmental Protection Agency
  401 M St., S.W.
  Washington, DC 20460
- National Wildlife Federation
  1400 16th St., N.W.
  Washington, DC 20036
- The President of The United States
  The White House
  1600 Pennsylvania Ave., N.W.
  Washington, DC 20500
- Senator ________
  United States Senate
  Washington, DC 20510
- Sierra Club
  730 Polk St.
  San Francisco, CA 94109

UNIT 7

Astronomy

In Unit 7, students are introduced to the size, structure, and evolution of the universe. The unit is organized as an exploration outward from Earth, with chapters on exploring space, the Earth-moon system, the solar system, and finally, stars and galaxies. Students will learn about the energy that provides the intense inside stars. They will learn about interactions of objects orbiting faraway stars. Students will also explore the immense nature of the universe and develop an understanding of Earth's place in it.

CONTENTS

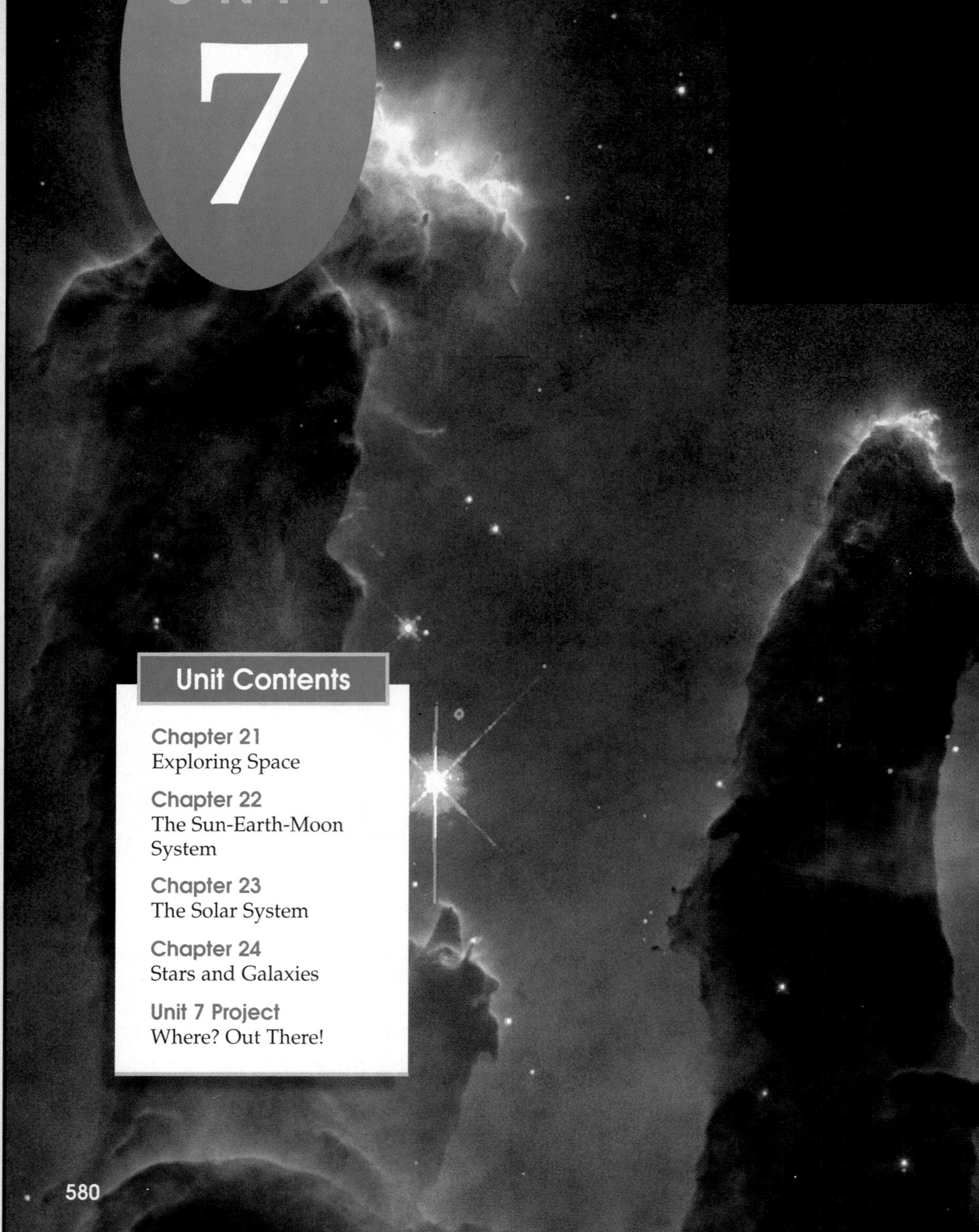

Science at Home

Patterns in the Sky Have students attempt to find the Big Dipper, the Little Dipper, and Polaris in the night sky. Ask them to draw the major stars they see and to connect the drawings into familiar patterns. Encourage students to look for other familiar patterns in the sky, such as Orion or Pegasus. L1 LEP

Astronomy

What's Happening Here?

Deep in the blackness of space, particles of dust and gas are swirling together in the first step of a wondrous process that will climax in the birth of a star. With new technology, such as the *Hubble Space Telescope,* we can witness this spectacular event through photographs like the one shown here. Space telescopes are only one of the tools scientists use to explore space. Space probes, such as *Magellan,* shown in the smaller photo, have traveled throughout our solar system, sending back data to scientists on Earth. Read on to learn about space and the technology we use to observe it.

Science Journal

In the 1600s, Galileo Galilei turned his telescope on Saturn and saw what appeared to be a triple planet—one large planet with two smaller planets hidden behind it. In your Science Journal, research what Galileo made of his discovery, and how this compares to what we know about Saturn today.

Theme Connection

Scale and Structure/Energy Using telescopes on Earth and in space, astronomers have improved our understanding of the scale and structure of the solar system and of objects in deep space. Astronomers know that stars radiate heat and light, which are generated by fusion deep within the core. They also realize that what happens to one object in space is often affected by interactions with other objects.

Cultural Diversity

Satellites Affect Us Have students research how cultures in developing nations have been changed by global communication and weather satellite transmissions. Some governments forbid their citizens to have dish antennas that would be able to receive world news programs. Have students discuss why this might be the case. L1

INTRODUCING THE UNIT

What's Happening Here?

Ask students to tell you what the satellite has in common with the Hubble space telescope. This telescope took the picture of the Eagle Nebula shown here. It was also placed into orbit by the space shuttle.

Background

When astronomers turned the Hubble space telescope toward the Eagle Nebula, they were hoping to learn more about what goes on inside interstellar clouds. Astronomers J. Jeff Hester and Paul Scowen expected the region to be an ideal location to observe the process of photoevaporation. In photoevaporation, ultraviolet radiation from young, hot stars causes gases in nearby nebulas to dissipate. Not only did the researchers observe photoevaporation (as evidenced by streamers of gas shooting out from the tops of gas clouds), they also found a birthplace of stars. Evaporating gaseous globules (EGGs) are thought to contain the embryos of newly forming stars. The EGGs can be seen at the tips of the long, elephant-trunk-shaped gaseous pillars.

Previewing the Chapters

- Have students search for a figure that shows the relative sizes of all the planets in our solar system.

Tying to Previous Knowledge

Ask students to speculate on how the collision of a large meteorite with Earth might have caused the extinction of ancient life-forms. Many fires could be started by such a collision. Also, large amounts of dust could be thrown into the atmosphere, blocking light from the sun.

Chapter Organizer

Section	Objectives	Activities/Features
Chapter Opener		Explore Activity: Is white light more than it seems? p. 583
21-1 **Radiation from Space** (2 sessions)*	1. **Define** *electromagnetic spectrum.* 2. **Compare** and **contrast** refracting and reflecting telescopes. 3. **Compare** and **contrast** optical and radio telescopes.	Connect to Physics, p. 585 Problem Solving: A Homemade Antenna, p. 587 Skill Builder: Sequencing, p. 589 Using Math, p. 589 Activity 21-1: Telescopes, p. 590
21-2 **Science and Society Issue: Light Pollution** (1 session)*	1. **Explain** how light pollution affects our ability to see dim objects in the sky. 2. **Discuss** the issue of light pollution as it relates to security and safety lighting.	Connect to Chemistry, p. 592 MiniLAB: Compare the effects of light pollution. p. 593 Explore the Issue, p. 593
21-3 **Artificial Satellites and Space Probes** (2 sessions)*	1. **Compare** and **contrast** natural and artificial satellites. 2. **Differentiate** between an artificial satellite and a space probe. 3. **Trace** the history of the race to the moon.	Using Math, p. 595 Connect to Life Science, p. 597 Using Technology: Spin-Offs, p. 598 Skill Builder: Concept Mapping, p. 599 Using Computers: Spreadsheet, p. 599 Activity 21-2: Probe to Mars, pp. 601-603 People and Science: Gibor Basri, Astronomer, p. 603
21-4 **The Space Shuttle and the Future** (1 session)*	1. **Describe** the benefits of the space shuttle. 2. **Evaluate** the usefulness of orbital space stations.	Science Journal, p. 605 MiniLAB: How can gravity be simulated in a space station? p. 606 Skill Builder: Making and Using Tables, p. 608 Science Journal, p. 608

* A complete Planning Guide that includes block scheduling is provided on pages 32T-35T.

Activity Materials

Explore	Activities	MiniLABs
page 583 3 flashlights, green filter, blue filter, red filter	page 590 candle, flashlight, magnifying glass, aluminum or silver spoon, concave mirror, masking tape, 50 cm × 60 cm piece of white cardboard, glass of water, plane mirror, convex mirror, empty paper towel roll pages 601-603 portable screen, remote-controlled car, bag to hold rock and mineral samples, large rocks, instant camera with film, stopwatch or clock with second hand	page 593 empty paper towel roll page 606 LP record album, construction paper, scissors, masking tape, turntable, 3 marbles

Chapter 21 Exploring Space

Teacher Classroom Resources

Reproducible Masters	Transparencies
Study Guide, p. 82 **Reinforcement**, p. 82 **Enrichment**, p. 82 **Activity Worksheets**, pp. 126-127 **Lab Manual 59**, Refraction of Light **Lab Manual 60**, Spectral Analysis **Science Integration Activity 21**, Spectroscope and Roy G. Biv **Technology Integration**, pp. 17-18	**Section Focus Transparency 78**, Looking for Light **Science Integration Transparency 21**, Leaving Earth **Teaching Transparency 41**, Telescopes
Study Guide, p. 83 **Reinforcement**, p. 83 **Enrichment**, p. 83 **Activity Worksheets**, p. 130	**Section Focus Transparency 79**, Seeing in the Dark
Study Guide, p. 84 **Reinforcement**, p. 84 **Enrichment**, p. 84 **Activity Worksheets**, pp. 128-129 **Concept Mapping**, p. 47 **Cross-Curricular Integration**, p. 25	**Section Focus Transparency 80**, Remote-Controlled Research **Teaching Transparency 42**, Satellite View
Study Guide, p. 85 **Reinforcement**, p. 85 **Enrichment**, p. 85 **Activity Worksheets**, p. 131 **Critical Thinking/Problem Solving**, p. 27 **Science and Society Integration**, p. 25 **Multicultural Connections**, pp. 45-46	**Section Focus Transparency 81**, Ready for Landing!

Teaching Resources

Glencoe Earth Science Interactive Videodisc
Earth Science CD-ROM
Spanish Resources
English/Spanish Audiocassettes
Cooperative Learning Resource Guide
Lab Partner
Lab and Safety Skills
Lesson Plans

Assessment Resources

Chapter Review, pp. 45-46
Assessment, pp. 143-146
Performance Assessment in the Science Classroom (PASC)
MindJogger Videoquiz
Alternate Assessment in the Science Classroom
Performance Assessment
Chapter Review Software
Computer Test Bank

Key to Teaching Strategies

The following designations will help you decide which activities are appropriate for your students.

L1 Level 1 activities should be within the ability range of all students.

L2 Level 2 activities should be within the ability range of the average to above-average student.

L3 Level 3 activities are designed for the ability range of above-average students.

LEP LEP activities should be within the ability range of Limited English Proficiency students.

LS These activities are designed to address different learning styles.

COOP LEARN Cooperative Learning activities are designed for small group work.

P These strategies represent student products that can be placed into a best-work portfolio.

GLENCOE TECHNOLOGY

The following multimedia resources are available from Glencoe.

Science and Technology Videodisc Series (STVS)
Physics
Infrared Observatory
Video Astronomy
Earth & Space
Flying Observatory
Making Giant Mirrors
Very Large Array

National Geographic Society Series
STV: Solar System
Glencoe Earth Science Interactive Videodisc
Space Exploration
Earth Science CD-ROM

Teacher Classroom Resources

This is a representation of key blackline masters available in the Teacher Classroom Resources.

Teaching Aids

Section Focus Transparencies

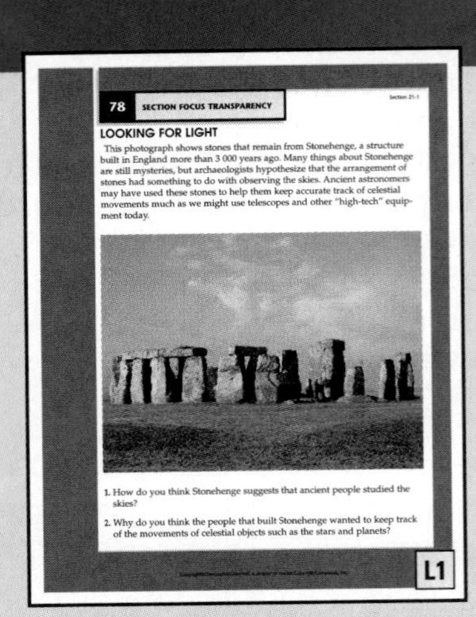
78 SECTION FOCUS TRANSPARENCY

LOOKING FOR LIGHT

This photograph shows stones that remain from Stonehenge, a structure built in England more than 3 000 years ago. Many things about Stonehenge are still mysteries, but archaeologists hypothesize that the arrangement of stones had something to do with observing the skies. Ancient astronomers may have used these stones to help them keep accurate track of celestial movements much as we might use telescopes and other "high-tech" equipment today.

1. How do you think Stonehenge suggests that ancient people studied the skies?
2. Why do you think the people that built Stonehenge wanted to keep track of the movements of celestial objects such as the stars and planets?

L1

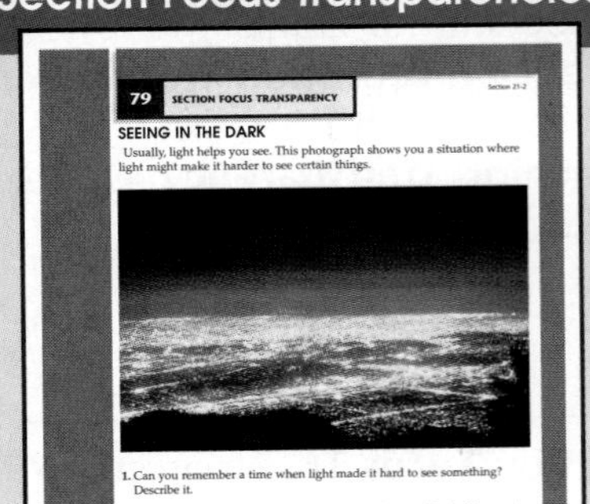
79 SECTION FOCUS TRANSPARENCY

SEEING IN THE DARK

Usually, light helps you see. This photograph shows you a situation where light might make it harder to see certain things.

1. Can you remember a time when light made it hard to see something? Describe it.
2. No matter the time of day or night, stars are all around Earth. Why can't we see stars during the day?
3. How would the city lights shown in this photograph make it hard to see the stars at night?

L2

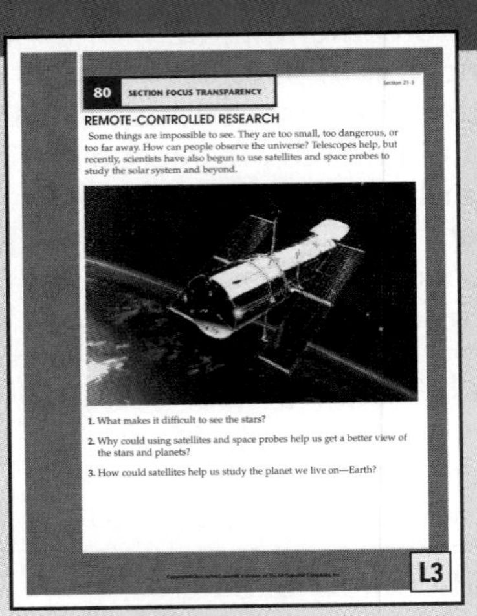
80 SECTION FOCUS TRANSPARENCY

REMOTE-CONTROLLED RESEARCH

Some things are impossible to see. They are too small, too dangerous, or too far away. How can people observe the universe? Telescopes help, but recently, scientists have also begun to use satellites and space probes to study the solar system and beyond.

1. What makes it difficult to see the stars?
2. Why could using satellites and space probes help us get a better view of the stars and planets?
3. How could satellites help us study the planet we live on—Earth?

L3

Science Integration Transparencies

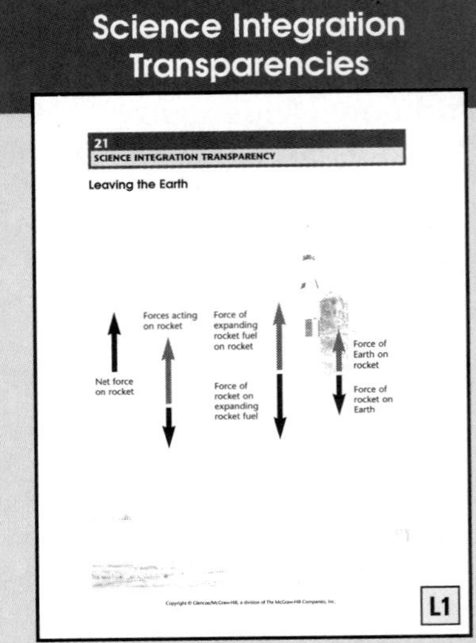
21 SCIENCE INTEGRATION TRANSPARENCY

Leaving the Earth

L1

Teaching Transparencies

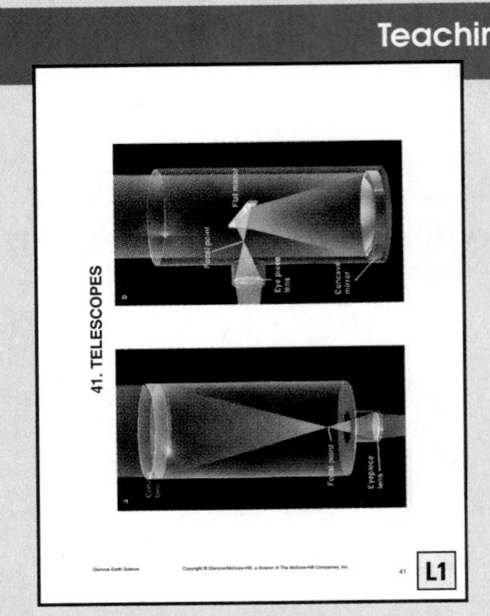

L1

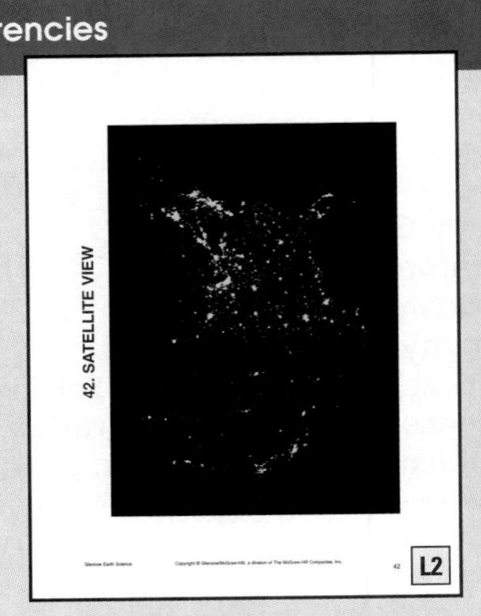

L2

Meeting Different Ability Levels

Study Guide

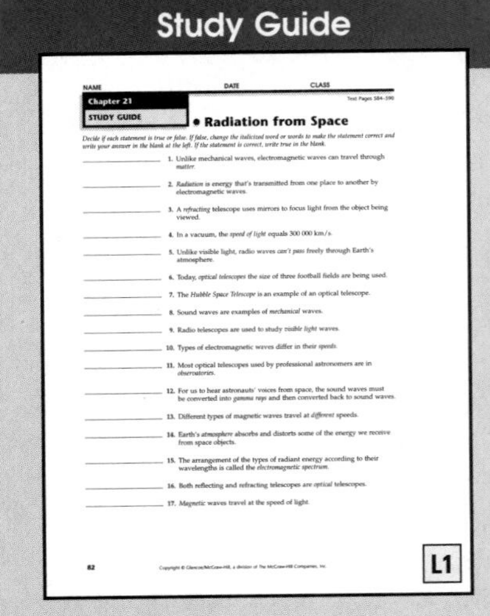
Chapter 21 STUDY GUIDE

• Radiation from Space

L1

Reinforcement

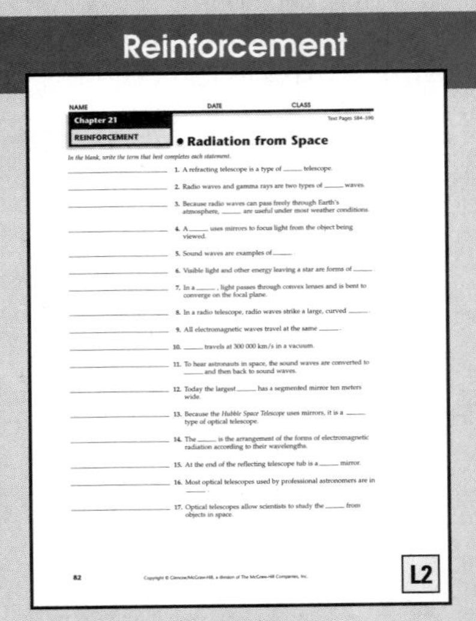
Chapter 21 REINFORCEMENT

• Radiation from Space

L2

Enrichment Worksheets

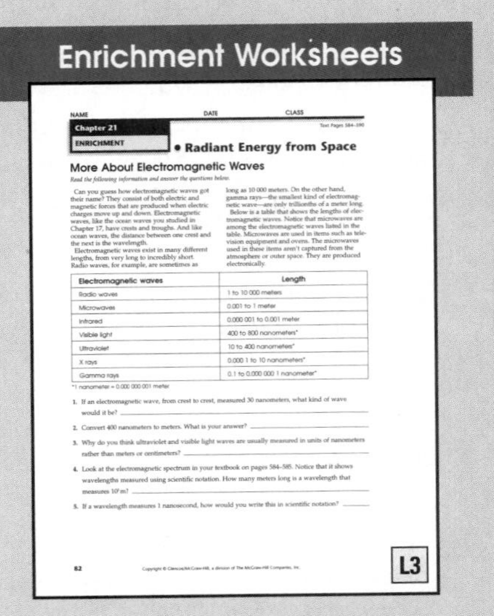
Chapter 21 ENRICHMENT

• Radiant Energy from Space

More About Electromagnetic Waves

Electromagnetic waves	Length
Radio waves	1 to 10 000 meters
Microwaves	0.001 to 1 meter
Infrared	0.000 001 to 0.001 meter
Visible light	400 to 800 nanometers*
Ultraviolet	10 to 400 nanometers*
X rays	0.000 1 to 10 nanometers*
Gamma rays	0.1 to 0.000 000 1 nanometer*

L3

Hands-On Activities

Science Integration Activity

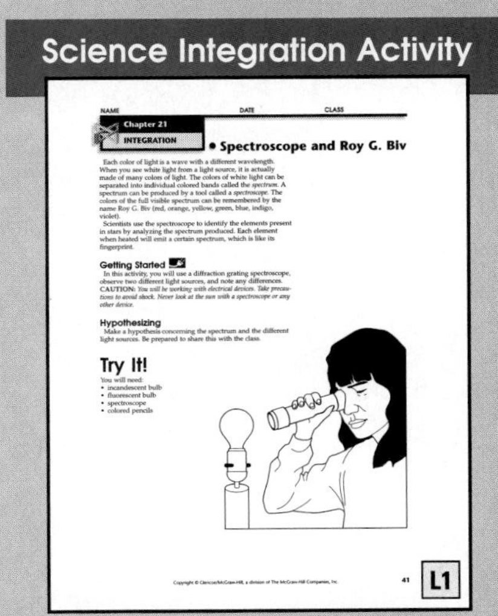
Chapter 21 INTEGRATION • Spectroscope and Roy G. Biv

Getting Started

Hypothesizing

Try It!

L1

Lab Manual

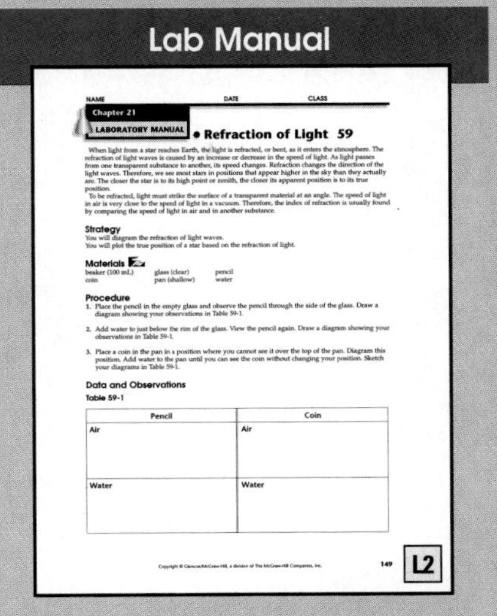
Chapter 21 LABORATORY MANUAL • Refraction of Light 59

Strategy

Materials

Procedure

Data and Observations

Table 59-1

	Pencil	Coin
Air		Air
Water		Water

L2

Assessment

Performance Assessment

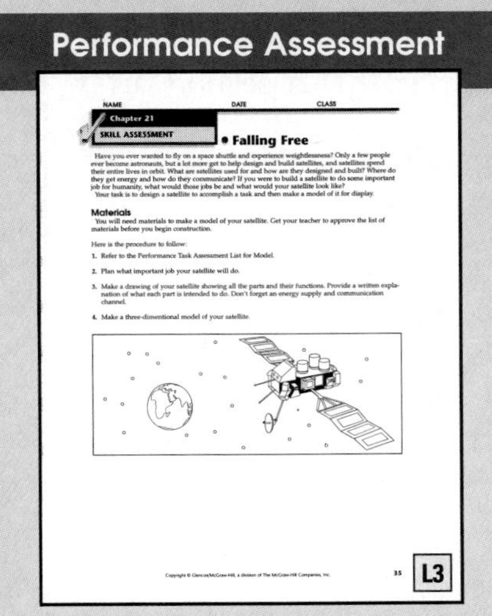
Chapter 21 SKILL ASSESSMENT • Falling Free

Materials

L3

Enrichment and Application

Critical Thinking/ Problem Solving

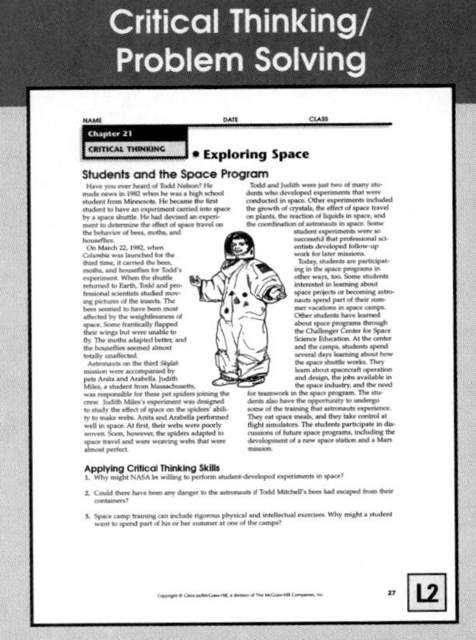
Chapter 21 CRITICAL THINKING • Exploring Space

Students and the Space Program

Applying Critical Thinking Skills

L2

Cross-Curricular Integration

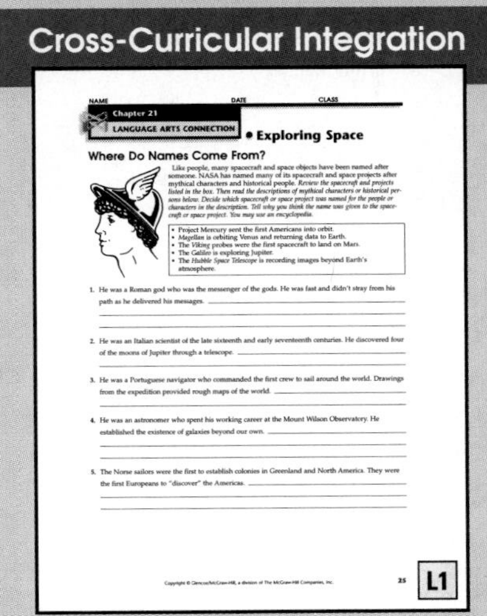
Chapter 21 LANGUAGE ARTS CONNECTION • Exploring Space

Where Do Names Come From?

L1

Science and Society Integration

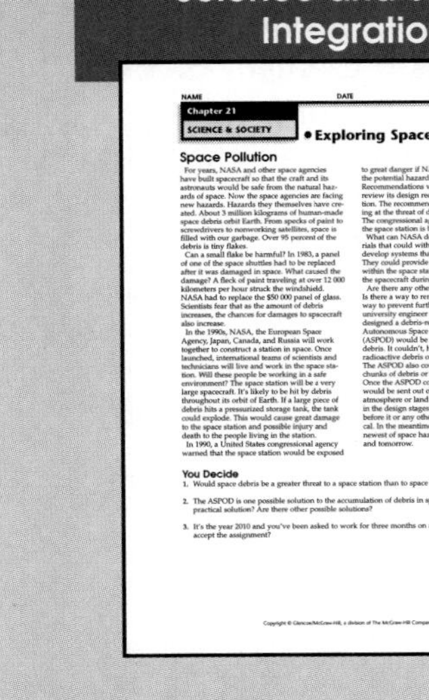
Chapter 21 SCIENCE & SOCIETY • Exploring Space

Space Pollution

You Decide

L2

Technology Integration

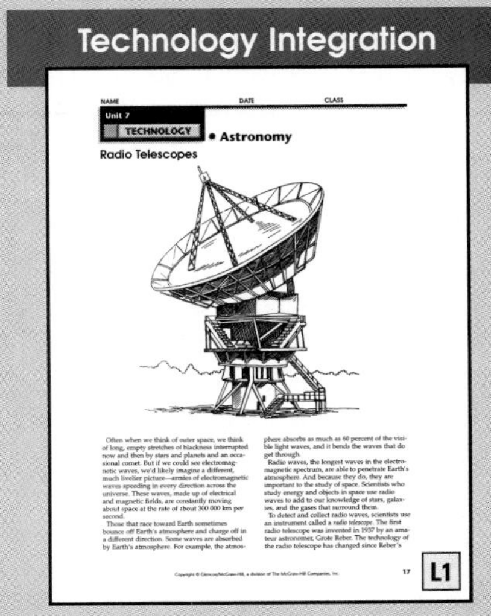
Unit 7 TECHNOLOGY • Astronomy

Radio Telescopes

L1

Multicultural Connections

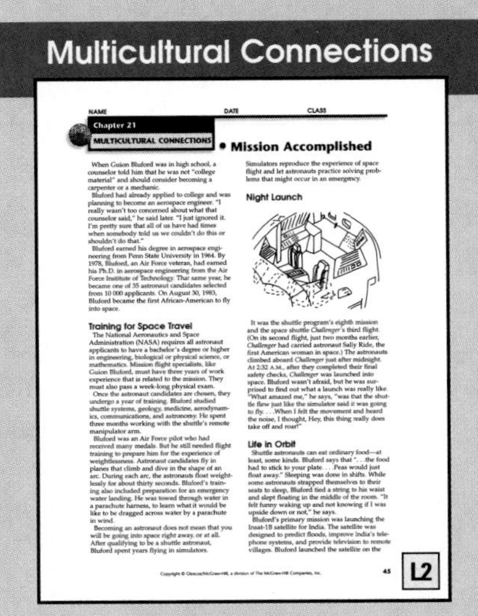
Chapter 21 MULTICULTURAL CONNECTIONS • Mission Accomplished

Night Launch

Training for Space Travel

Life in Orbit

L2

Concept Mapping

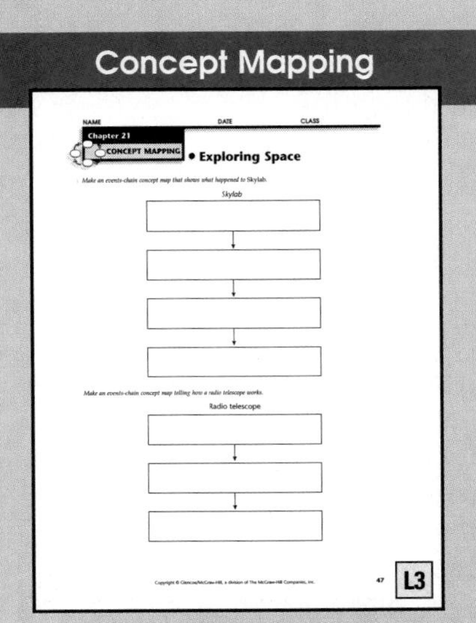
Chapter 21 CONCEPT MAPPING • Exploring Space

Skylab

Radio telescope

L3

Chapter 21

Exploring Space

CHAPTER OVERVIEW

Section 21-1 This section discusses forms of electromagnetic radiation and the electromagnetic spectrum. Optical and radio telescopes used to study energy from space are briefly discussed.

Section 21-2 Science and Society The effects of light pollution are presented. The need for security lighting is addressed, as well as how light pollution affects nighttime sky observations.

Section 21-3 This section relates the initial events that put humans into space. Artificial satellites and space probes are described. A synopsis of the space programs that led to putting people on the moon also is presented.

Section 21-4 This section discusses the benefits of the space shuttle and the usefulness of space stations.

Chapter Vocabulary

electromagnetic spectrum
refracting telescope
reflecting telescope
observatory
radio telescope
light pollution
satellite
orbit
space probe
Project Mercury
Project Gemini
Project Apollo
space shuttle
space station

Theme Connection

Energy/Scale and Structure Energy is the major theme presented in this chapter. The properties of electromagnetic radiation have enabled scientists to describe the scale and structure of our solar system and beyond.

Previewing the Chapter

582

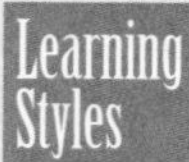

Look for the following logo for strategies that emphasize different learning modalities. 

Kinesthetic	MiniLAB, p. 606
Visual-Spatial	Explore, p. 583; Integrating the Sciences, p. 585; Visual Learning, pp. 585, 586, 588, 591, 595, 597; Activity 21-1, p. 590; Demonstration, p. 605
Interpersonal	MiniLAB, p. 592; Discussion, p. 595; Reteach, p. 598; Activity 21-2, pp. 601-603
Intrapersonal	Across the Curriculum, p. 607
Linguistic	Science Journal, pp. 586, 588, 598; Enrichment, p. 597

LS

Chapter 21

Exploring Space

The first space exploration didn't occur in a spaceship or a satellite. Instead, it was done by a person simply looking upward, studying countless points of shimmering light. Over time, people devised more and more accurate ways of keeping track of the stars and their apparent movements. Today we have powerful telescopes, spacecraft, and computers to help us observe what lies beyond Earth. But as old as astronomy is, it seems we've barely scraped the surface of what there is to discover.

EXPLORE ACTIVITY

Is white light more than it seems?

1. Cover the end of a flashlight with a green gelatin (or Plexiglas) filter.
2. Cover another flashlight with a blue filter and third with a red filter.
3. In a darkened room, experiment with the three lights by shining different combinations of two lights on the same spot on a sheet of white paper. Record your observations in your Science Journal.

Observe: *Observe* all colors shining on the same spot on the paper and *infer* what is happening. Record your observations and inferences in your Science Journal.

Previewing Science Skills

- In the **Skill Builders,** you will **sequence events, make concept maps,** and **outline.**
- In the **Activities,** you will **observe, analyze data, make inferences,** and **draw conclusions.**
- In the **MiniLABs,** you will **experiment, construct models,** and **draw conclusions.**

Assessment Planner

Portfolio
Refer to page 609 for suggested items that students might select for their portfolios.

Performance Assessment
See page 609 for additional Performance Assessment options.
Skill Builders, pp. 589, 599, 608
MiniLABs, pp. 593, 606
Activities 21-1, p. 590; 21-2, pp. 601-603

Content Assessment
Section Wrap-ups, pp. 589, 593, 599, 608
Chapter Review, pp. 609-611
Mini Quizzes, pp. 589, 599, 608

Group Assessment
Opportunities for group assessment occur with Cooperative Learning Strategies and Flex Your Brain Activities.

EXPLORE ACTIVITY

Purpose

LS **Visual-Spatial** Use the Explore Activity to introduce students to the composition of white light. Inform students that they will be learning about electromagnetic radiation and how it can be used to find out about objects in space. L1

Preparation

Several days before you begin the chapter, have students bring in flashlights. Also obtain green, blue, and red gelatin or Plexiglas filters.

Materials

white paper; 3 flashlights; and green, blue, and red gelatin (or Plexiglas) filters for each group

Teaching Strategies

Troubleshooting Make sure that the flashlights used by a group are identical.

- Have students attach the filters to the flashlights with transparent tape. Make the room as dark as possible.

Observe

The red and blue light created a new color when added together. As different colored light is combined, a different color is produced. When all colors were combined, white light was seen on the white paper.

Assessment

Oral As lights of different colors are added together on the white paper, ask students to explain what is happening. Use the Performance Task Assessment List for Making Observations and Inferences in **PASC,** p. 17. P

Section 21•1

Prepare

Section Background

- Presently, the largest optical telescope on Earth is the 10-m Keck reflecting telescope on Mauna Kea in Hawaii. Its primary mirror has been constructed from 36 hexagonal glass segments, each 1.8 m in diameter.
- The Very Large Array (VLA) of telescopes near Socorro, New Mexico, is composed of 27 radio telescopes. All 27 telescopes can be used at once to operate as one large telescope.

Preplanning

- Set up a refracting and a reflecting telescope to be used for demonstration.
- To prepare for Activity 21-1, obtain candles, flashlights, magnifying glasses, aluminum or silver spoons, concave mirrors, plane mirrors, convex mirrors, and empty paper towel rolls.

1 Motivate

Bellringer

Before presenting the lesson, display **Section Focus Transparency 78** on the overhead projector. Assign the accompanying **Focus Activity** worksheet. L1 LEP

Tying to Previous Knowledge

Most students have used binoculars to observe distant objects. Inform students that binoculars can be used to view large areas of the sky. Binoculars are actually two refracting telescopes side by side.

21•1 Radiation from Space

Science Words

electromagnetic spectrum
refracting telescope
reflecting telescope
observatory
radio telescope

Objectives

- Define the electromagnetic spectrum.
- Compare and contrast refracting and reflecting telescopes.
- Compare and contrast optical and radio telescopes.

Electromagnetic Waves

On a crisp autumn evening, you take a break from your homework to gaze out the window at the many stars filling the night sky. Looking up at the night sky, it's easy to imagine future spaceships venturing through space and large space stations circling above Earth where people work and live. But when you look into the night sky, what you're really seeing is the distant past, not the future.

Light from the Past

When you look at a star, you see light that left it many years ago. The light that you see travels very fast, but at a finite speed. The distances across space are so great that it takes years for the light to reach Earth—sometimes millions of years.

The light and other energy leaving a star are forms of radiation. Recall that radiation is energy that's transmitted from one place to another by electromagnetic waves. Because of the electric and magnetic properties of this radiation, it's called electromagnetic radiation. Electromagnetic waves carry energy through space as well as through matter.

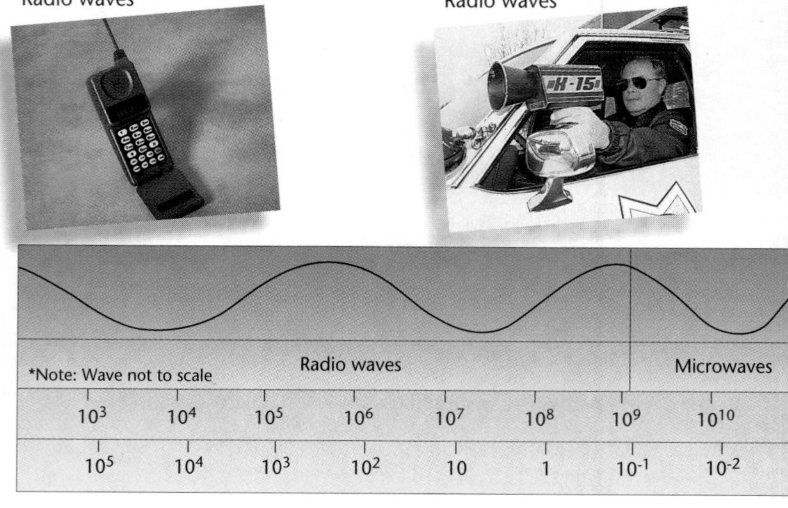

Figure 21-1

The electromagnetic spectrum ranges from gamma rays with wavelengths of less than 0.000 000 000 01 m to radio waves more than 100 000 m long. *What happens to frequency (the number of waves that pass a point per second) as wavelength shortens?*

Program Resources

Reproducible Masters

Study Guide, p. 82 L1
Reinforcement, p. 82 L1
Enrichment, p. 82 L3
Activity Worksheets, pp. 5, 126-127 L1
Science Integration Activities, pp. 41-42
Technology Integration, pp. 17-18
Lab Manual 59, 60

Transparencies

Section Focus Transparency 78 L1
Science Integration Transparency 21
Teaching Transparency 41

Electromagnetic Radiation

Sound waves, a type of mechanical wave, can't travel through empty space. How do we hear the voices of the astronauts while they're in space? When they speak into a microphone, the sound is converted into electromagnetic waves called radio waves. The radio waves travel through space and through our atmosphere. They are then converted back into sound by electronic equipment and audio speakers.

Radio waves and visible light from the sun are just two types of electromagnetic radiation. The other types include gamma rays, X rays, ultraviolet waves, infrared waves, and microwaves. **Figure 21-1** shows these forms of electromagnetic radiation arranged according to their wavelengths. This arrangement of electromagnetic radiation is called the **electromagnetic spectrum.**

Although the various electromagnetic waves differ in their wavelengths, they all travel at the speed of 300 000 km/s in a vacuum. You're probably more familiar with this speed as the "speed of light." Visible light and other forms of electromagnetic radiation travel at this incredible speed, but the universe is so large that it takes millions of years for the light from some stars to reach Earth.

Once electromagnetic radiation from stars and other objects reaches Earth, we can use it to learn about the source of the electromagnetic radiation. What tools and methods do scientists use to discover what lies beyond our planet? One tool for observing electromagnetic radiation from distant sources is a telescope.

INTEGRATION
Physics

CONNECT TO
PHYSICS

Pass a beam of white light through a prism. Note that different colors of light are bent, forming a spectrum. ***Infer*** how the white light and prism form a spectrum with violet on one end and red on the other.

Infrared

Visible light

X rays

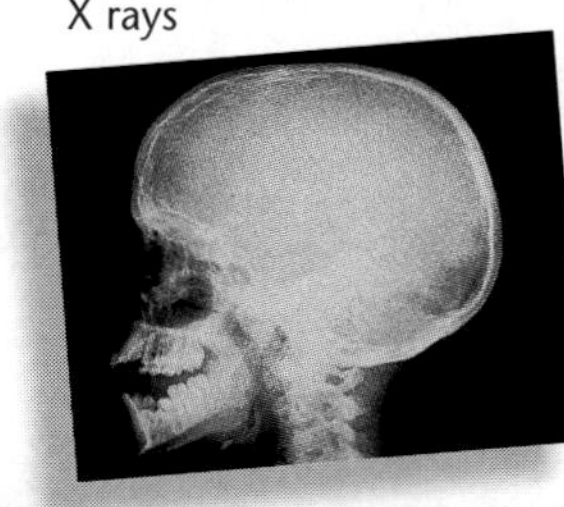

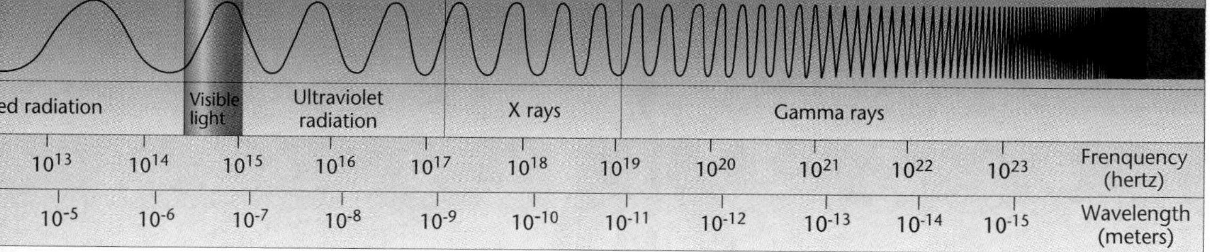

2 Teach

INTEGRATION
Physics

The separation of the electromagnetic spectrum by wavelength helps students realize that light involves more than just what can be seen. Much of what astronomers learn about outer space comes from a study of wavelengths other than visible light. The study of radio waves, ultraviolet rays, and X rays enables astronomers to "observe" what can't be seen.

CONNECT TO
PHYSICS

Answer All colors in the visible spectrum, which have varying wavelengths, are bent through different angles, thus dispersing. Violet light, which has the shortest wavelength of light in the visible spectrum, is bent the most, whereas red light, which has the longest wavelength of light in the visible spectrum, is bent the least.

Visual Learning

Figure 21-1 What happens to frequency as wavelength shortens? *Because light of all wavelengths travels at the same speed, 300 000 km/s, shorter wavelengths have higher frequencies (more of the waves pass a particular point each second).* Ask students which wavelength of light is the most energetic. Encourage them to relate their answers to what they already know about X rays, gamma rays, and radio waves. *Gamma rays are the most energetic.* LEP 

Inclusion Strategies

Gifted Have students research the index of refraction. Ask them to relate what they discover to the use of lenses in telescope construction. *The index of refraction of a substance is equal to the sine of the angle of incidence of light from a vacuum divided by the sine of the angle of refraction. The index of refraction of glass is used when determining how to shape the objective lens of a telescope or the lenses in a pair of glasses.* L3

Integrating the Sciences

Physics Have students find out how concave and convex lenses affect the path of light that passes through them. Some students may wish to demonstrate the difference by using both types of lenses. LS

GLENCOE TECHNOLOGY

 CD-ROM

Earth Science CD-ROM

Have students perform the interactive exploration for Chapter 21 to reinforce important chapter concepts and thinking processes.

Teacher F.Y.I.

Hubble is so powerful that if you were in Washington, DC, you could use it to read a newspaper headline in Missouri.

Visual Learning

Figure 21-2 Ask students to make a rough copy of each telescope design in their Science Journals. On the copy of each type of telescope, ask students to identify where the eyepiece, objective, focus (focal point or focal plane), and focal length would be. Also ask students to explain the difference in these two telescopes using the above-listed telescope parts. **Which type of optical telescope is this student using?** *a refracting telescope* LEP IS

GLENCOE TECHNOLOGY

 Videodisc

STVS: Physics

Disc 1, Side 1

Infrared Observatory (Ch. 9)

Video Astronomy (Ch. 19)

Figure 21-2

These diagrams show how each type of optical telescope collects light and forms an image.

Optical Telescopes

Optical telescopes produce magnified images of objects. Light is collected by an objective lens or mirror, which then forms an image at the focal point of the telescope. The eyepiece lens then magnifies the image. The two types of optical telescopes are shown in **Figure 21-2.**

In a **refracting telescope,** the light from an object passes through a convex objective lens and is bent to form an image on the focal point. The image is then magnified by the eyepiece.

A **reflecting telescope** uses a mirror as an objective to focus light from the object being viewed. Light passes through the open end of a reflecting telescope and strikes a concave mirror at its base. The light is then reflected to the focal point to form an image. A smaller mirror is often used to reflect the light into the eyepiece lens so the magnified image can be viewed.

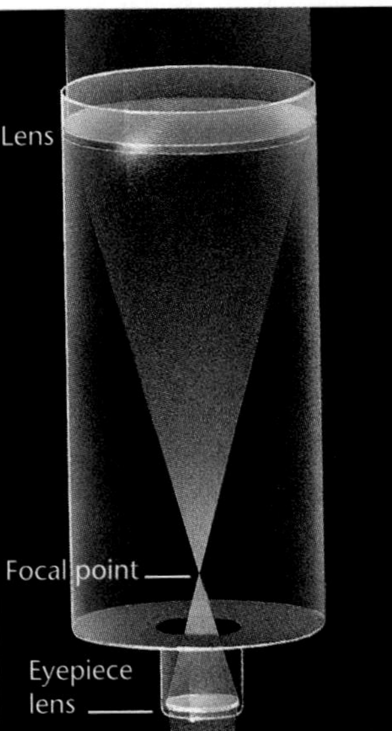

A In a refracting telescope, a convex lens focuses light to form an image at the focal point.

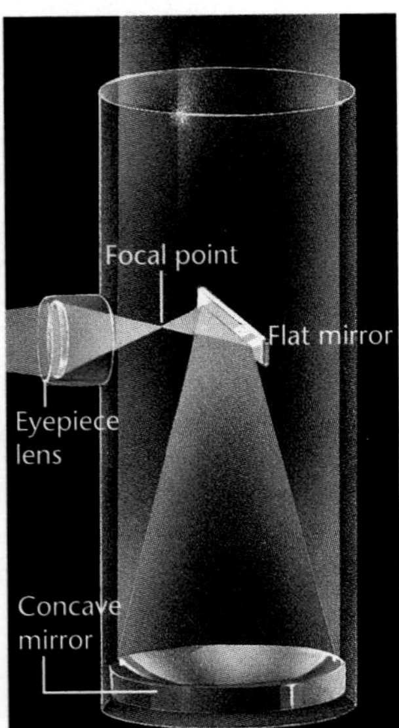

B In a reflecting telescope, a concave mirror focuses light to form an image at the focal point.

Using Optical Telescopes

Most optical telescopes used by professional astronomers are housed in buildings called **observatories.** Observatories often have a dome-shaped roof

C *Which type of optical telescope is this student using?*

586

Science Journal

Telescopes Ask students to select one of the following questions and to write a brief paragraph in their Science Journals that answers the question selected.

- **What is the function of the concave mirror in a reflecting telescope?** *The mirror focuses light onto the focal plane.*
- **How do reflecting and refracting telescopes differ in the way they form images?** *A reflecting telescope uses a concave mirror to reflect light to the focal plane, while a refracting telescope uses a convex lens to bend light to the focal plane.*
- **What advantage does a radio telescope have over optical telescopes?** *Radio telescopes can be used in almost all kinds of weather and at all times of the day and night. Radio telescopes can receive energy from objects that cannot be observed with optical telescopes.* L1 IS

that opens up to let light in. **Figure 21-4,** on the next page, shows the twin Keck telescopes on Mauna Kea in Hawaii. However, not all telescopes are in observatories.

The *Hubble Space Telescope* was launched in 1990 by the space shuttle Discovery. Earth's atmosphere absorbs and distorts some of the energy we receive from space. Because *Hubble* didn't have to view space through our atmosphere, it should have produced very clear images. However, when the largest mirror of this reflecting telescope was shaped, there was a mistake. Images obtained by the telescope were not as clear as expected. In December 1993, a team of astronauts repaired *Hubble's* optics and other equipment. Now the clear images obtained by Hubble are changing scientists' ideas about space.

Radio Telescopes

As you know, stars and other objects radiate energy throughout the electromagnetic spectrum. A **radio telescope** is used to study radio waves traveling through space. Unlike visible light, radio waves pass freely through Earth's atmosphere. Because of this, radio telescopes are useful under most weather conditions and at all times of day and night.

Radio waves reaching Earth's surface strike the large, curved dish of a radio telescope. This dish reflects the waves to a focal point where a receiver is located. The information allows us to detect objects in space, to map the universe, and to search for intelligent life.

Problem Solving

A Homemade Antenna

Suppose that you, a classmate, and your cousin had been looking forward to a camping trip for several weeks. You have just set up camp when some large clouds begin to roll in and the wind begins to stir. As your classmate looks for wood to use in the campfire, you pull out your radio to listen to the weather forecast. You think a storm might be approaching and you might need to seek better shelter. The radio reception is poor and you can barely hear the weather report.

Your cousin digs through the camping supplies and finds some aluminum foil wrap, an umbrella, and some string. She suggests that these items could be used to improve the radio reception.

Solve the Problem:

1. **What type of radiation is the radio capable of receiving?**
2. **How could you and the others improve the radio reception with the supplies described above?**

Think Critically:

How are the parts of your radio and antenna like those of a radio telescope?

Teacher F.Y.I.

The largest radio telescope in the world is located near Arecibo, Puerto Rico. The curved dish, made of more than 38 400 aluminum panels, is 305 m in diameter. The photo on page 698 in Chapter 24 is of the Arecibo radio telescope.

Problem Solving

Solve the Problem

1. radio waves
2. Have students in class cover the inside of the umbrella with aluminum foil, making it reflective. The handle of the umbrella should be bound to the metal antenna of the radio with the string. The umbrella will reflect incoming radio waves onto the radio's small antenna, increasing the number of waves received by the radio.

Think Critically

The umbrella is like the giant dishes of radio telescopes. The radio is similar to a receiver of a radio telescope. P

GLENCOE TECHNOLOGY

Videodisc

STVS: Earth & Space

Disc 3, Side 1

Flying Observatory (Ch. 7)

Making Giant Mirrors (Ch. 8)

Very Large Array (Ch. 9)

Community Connection

Radio Telescopes Invite to class a person from your community who rents or sells dish antennas for televisions. Ask him or her to explain how the dish antenna works and to show students a model of one. After students look at the model of the dish antenna and hear the visitor, ask them to compare and contrast the dish antenna for television to radio telescopes.

Visual Learning

Figure 21-3 Why is the *Hubble* able to achieve better resolution? *Being in space, it doesn't have the distorting effects of Earth's atmosphere.*

Use **Science Integration Transparency 21** and **Teaching Transparency 41** as you teach this lesson.

3 Assess

Check for Understanding

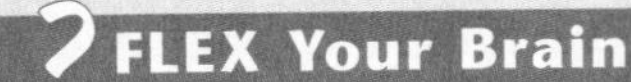

Use the Flex Your Brain activity to have students explore THE PART OF THE ELECTROMAGNETIC SPECTRUM USED BY OPTICAL TELESCOPES.

Activity Worksheets, p. 5

Reteach

Ask the following questions of the class as a group. Have available labeled cross sections showing the path of electromagnetic energy through refracting, reflecting, and radio telescopes. Have students study the diagrams, then ask: **What is the function of the objective of each telescope?** *The objective is the lens, mirror, or dish antenna that collects visible light or radio waves and focuses them onto the focal plane.* **Why was the *Hubble Space Telescope* placed into orbit?** *Astronomers can use the* Hubble Space Telescope *to observe objects deep in space without having to look through Earth's atmosphere.*

Extension

For students who have mastered this section, use the **Reinforcement** and **Enrichment** masters.

Figure 21-3

The Hubble Space Telescope was deployed from the cargo bay of the space shuttle *Discovery* on April 25, 1990. It's now orbiting Earth, sending back images and data about distant space objects.

Figure 21-4

The twin Keck telescopes on Mauna Kea in Hawaii can be used in combination, effectively more than doubling the resolving power. Each individual telescope has an objective mirror 10 m in diameter. To cope with the difficulty of building such a large mirror, this telescope design used several smaller mirrors positioned to work as one. *Although the Keck telescopes are much larger than the* Hubble Space Telescope, *why is the* Hubble *able to achieve better resolution?*

Science Journal

Hubble Space Telescope Have students write in their Science Journals on the space shuttle missions to repair the *Hubble Space Telescope*. Aviation Week & Space Technology (May 24, 1993) *reports many aspects of the repair mission. One of the major goals of this mission was demonstrating that in-orbit servicing of a complex satellite is feasible.* L2 LS

Since the early 1600s when the Italian scientist Galileo Galilei first turned a telescope toward the stars, people have been searching for better ways to study what lies beyond our atmosphere. Today, the largest reflector has a segmented mirror 10 m wide, and the largest radio telescope is 300 m wide. The most recent innovations in optical telescopes involve active and adaptive optics. With active optics, a computer is used to compensate for changes in temperature, mirror distortions, and bad viewing conditions. Even more ambitious is adaptive optics, which uses a laser to probe the atmosphere and relate information to a computer about air turbulence. The computer then adjusts the telescope's mirror thousands of times per second, thus reducing the effects of atmospheric turbulence.

Even with active optics and adaptive optics, there is still a need to travel into space for exploration. In the remainder of this chapter, you'll learn about the instruments that travel into space and send back information not obtainable through telescopes on Earth's surface.

Section Wrap-up

Review

1. How are radio telescopes and optical telescopes different from one another?
2. Why should telescopes such as *Hubble* produce more detailed images than Earth-based telescopes?
3. The frequency of electromagnetic radiation is the number of waves that pass a point in a specific amount of time. If red light has a longer wavelength than blue light, which would have a greater frequency?
4. **Think Critically:** It takes light from the closest star to Earth (other than the sun) about four years to reach us. If there were intelligent life on a planet circling that star, how long would it take for us to send them a radio transmission and for us to receive their reply?

Skill Builder

Sequencing

Sequence these electromagnetic waves from longest wavelength to shortest wavelength: *gamma rays, visible light, X rays, radio waves, infrared waves, ultraviolet waves,* and *microwaves.* If you need help, refer to Sequencing in the **Skill Handbook.**

USING MATH

The magnifying power of a telescope is determined by dividing the focal length of the objective (FL_{obj}) by the focal length of the eyepiece (FL_{eye}) using the following equation:

$$mp = \frac{FL_{obj}}{FL_{eye}}$$

If FL_{obj} = 1200 mm and FL_{eye} = 6 mm, what is the telescope's magnifying power (Mp)?

4 Close

• MINI • QUIZ •

Use the Mini Quiz to check students' recall of chapter content.

1. **The arrangement of electromagnetic radiation according to its wavelengths is the ______ .** *electromagnetic spectrum*
2. **______ telescopes bend light to produce an image.** *Refracting*
3. **A(n) ______ telescope uses mirrors to focus light from the object being viewed.** *reflecting*
4. **Professional astronomers house their telescopes in buildings called ______ .** *observatories*
5. **Which type of telescope is used to study radio waves traveling through space?** *radio telescope*

Section Wrap-up

Review

1. A radio telescope uses a curved dish antenna to collect and focus radio waves, whereas an optical telescope uses lenses or mirrors to collect and focus visible light.
2. Such telescopes are located above the distorting effects of Earth's atmosphere.
3. More waves of light with a shorter wavelength would pass a point in a specific time period. Blue light would have a greater frequency.
4. **Think Critically** about eight years—four years for the message to reach them and four years for their reply to travel back to us

USING MATH

$$M_p = \frac{FL_{obj}}{FL_{eye}} = \frac{1200 \text{ mm}}{6 \text{ mm}} = 200$$

Skill Builder

radio waves, microwaves, infrared waves, visible light, ultraviolet waves, X rays, gamma rays

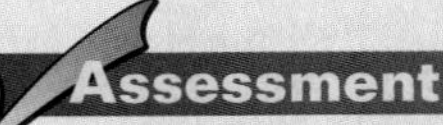

Assessment

Content Assess students' abilities to sequence events by having them compare and contrast their sequences with those of other students. Use the Performance Task Assessment List for Events Chain in **PASC,** p. 91. P

Activity 21-1

Purpose

Visual-Spatial Compare and contrast the paths taken by light in reflecting and refracting telescopes. L1

COOP LEARN

Process Skills

observing and inferring, communicating, comparing and contrasting, recognizing cause and effect, interpreting data, experimenting, defining operationally, separating and controlling variables

Time

50-60 minutes

Safety Precautions

Caution students to handle the hand lenses and mirrors with care. Caution students to keep hair and clothes away from the candle flame.

Activity Worksheets, pp. 5, 126-127

Answers to Questions

1. collects incoming light and produces a small real image at the focal point
2. The focus of the lens is where the light from the candle is concentrated almost to a single point of light. The rays must have been bent to be concentrated to one point.
3. The eyepiece is moved toward the image until the inverted image is just inside the focus of the eyepiece. The eye then sees an enlarged virtual image.
4. A concave mirror enlarges an image. The image in the convex mirror is smaller and farther away than the object. The image in a plane mirror is the same size and at the same distance as the object.
5. The real image occurs between the focal length and twice the focal length. Light passing through the lens converges to form the image. The real image is always inverted and smaller than the object. The focal length of the convex lens depends on the shape of the lens and the index of refraction of the lens material.
6. In both types of telescopes, light is directed to a focus. In refracting telescopes, light is bent into focus as it passes through a lens. Reflecting telescopes use a mirror to reflect light rays to a focus.

Activity 21-1 Telescopes

You have learned that optical telescopes use lenses and mirrors as objectives to collect light from an object. They use eyepiece lenses to form magnified images of that object. Try this activity to see how the paths of light differ in reflecting and refracting telescopes.

Problem

In what way are paths of light affected by the lenses and/or mirrors in refracting and reflecting telescopes?

Materials 

- candle
- flashlight
- hand lens
- concave mirror
- masking tape
- empty paper towel tube
- cardboard, white, 50 cm ¥ 60 cm
- glass of water
- plane mirror
- convex mirror

Procedure

1. Observe your reflection in a plane, convex, and concave mirror.
2. Hold an object in front of each of the mirrors. Compare the size and position of the images.
3. Darken the room and hold the convex mirror in front of you at a 45° angle, slanting downward. Direct the flashlight beam toward the mirror. Note the size and position of the reflected light.
4. Repeat step 3 using a plane mirror. Draw a diagram to show what happens to the beam of light.
5. Attach the empty paper towel tube to the flashlight with masking tape so that the narrow beam of light will pass through the tube. Direct the light into a large glass of water, first directly from above, then from an angle 45° to the water surface. Observe the direction of the light rays when viewed from the side of the glass.
6. Light a candle and set it up some distance from the vertically held cardboard screen. **CAUTION:** *Keep hair and clothing away from the flame.* Using the hand lens as a convex lens, move it between the candle and the screen until you have the best possible image.
7. Move the lens closer to the candle. Note what happens to the size of the image. Move the cardboard until the image is in focus.

Analyze

1. What is the purpose of the concave mirror in a reflecting telescope?
2. How did you determine the position of the focal point of the hand lens in step 6? What does this tell you about the position of all the light rays?
3. The eyepiece of a telescope is convex. **Infer** its purpose.
4. **Compare and contrast** the effect the three types of mirrors had on your reflection.

Conclude and Apply

5. Discuss your observations of the relationship of the distance between the object and lens and the clearest and largest image you could obtain in steps 6 and 7.
6. **Compare and contrast** the path of light in refracting and reflecting telescopes.

Assessment

Performance Provide each group of students with two lenses of different focal lengths. Ask students to design a working telescope using only the two lenses. *Students should realize that if the lenses are lined up and held up to the eye with the lens of shortest focal length near the eye, a working telescope is built.* Use the Performance Task Assessment List for Model in **PASC**, p. 51. P

ISSUE:

Light Pollution

Light Pollution and Stargazing

When you gaze out your window at the night sky, what do you see? Chances are, if you live in or near a city, you don't see a star-filled sky. Instead, you see only a few of the brightest stars scattered throughout a hazy, glowing sky. You're looking through a sky full of light pollution.

City lights cause a glow in the sky called **light pollution.** Light pollution makes the sky glow bright enough that dim stars can't be seen. What effect does light pollution have on your ability to stargaze? How do you think this affects astronomers working near large cities? Many people feel that their right to a dark night sky has been taken away.

Observing objects through Earth's atmosphere can be difficult even without light pollution. As you learned in Chapter 14, the atmosphere absorbs some of the electromagnetic radiation entering it. Visible light from objects in space can't pass through clouds or smog. Light pollution makes observing even more difficult as shown in **Figure 21-5.** If an object is faint, it's difficult to distinguish between visible light from the object in space and visible light from the city.

Science Word

light pollution

Objectives

- Explain how light pollution affects our ability to see dim objects in the sky.
- Discuss the issue of light pollution as it relates to security and safety lighting.

Figure 21-5

These two photographs were taken of the same area of night sky, from two different places. *Which photo was taken within a city and which was taken in a more rural setting?*

SCIENCE & SOCIETY
Section 21•2

Prepare

Preplanning

In preparation for the MiniLAB, have students bring in the cardboard tubes from empty rolls of paper towels.

1 Motivate

Bellringer

Before presenting the lesson, display **Section Focus Transparency 79** on the overhead projector. Assign the accompanying **Focus Activity** worksheet. L1 LEP

Tying to Previous Knowledge

Ask students if they have ever seen a glow in the sky caused by city lights. Have them think about how light glowing like this might affect observations of the sky by astronomers in a nearby observatory.

Visual Learning

Figure 21-5 Which photo was taken within a city and which was taken in a more rural setting? *The photo on the right was taken within a city.* LEP LS

Program Resources

Reproducible Masters

Study Guide, p. 83 L1
Reinforcement, p. 83 L1
Enrichment, p. 83 L3
Activity Worksheets, pp. 5, 130 L1

Transparencies

Section Focus Transparency 79 L1

2 Teach

MiniLAB

Purpose

LS **Interpersonal** Students will observe that light pollution affects the number of objects that can be observed in the night sky. L1

COOP LEARN

Materials

cardboard tube from empty roll of paper towels for each student

Teaching Strategies

Troubleshooting If all students live in the same area, have them call friends or relatives to obtain star number data from other locations or provide this information for them.

Analysis

1. More stars should be visible in suburban than urban areas; even more stars should be visible in rural areas. Not only are more stars visible in the suburban and the rural areas, but the bright stars are also easier to see in these areas.
2. Lower amounts of background light (light pollution) in suburban and rural areas increase the number of objects visible in the sky.

Assessment

Process Have students list common sources of light pollution that they've probably taken for granted, such as lights at car dealerships, shopping centers, and streetlights. Use the Performance Task Assessment List for Making Observations and Inferences in PASC, p. 17. P

CONNECT TO CHEMISTRY

Why is light from low-pressure sodium lights easier for astronomers to filter out? If possible, *compare* the spectrum of a low-pressure sodium light with the spectra of other types of security lights. *Describe* the importance of low-pressure sodium lights to astronomers.

Most people agree that lights are needed on city streets and parking lots for safety and security. What can be done to reduce light pollution without reducing public safety and security?

In several cities in the United States, work has begun to reduce light pollution. As shown in **Figure 21-6,** bad lighting can cause lots of glare. Instead of increasing security, such lighting provides places for criminals to hide. Tucson, Arizona, located only 80 km from Kitt Peak National Observatory, has replaced its street lights with low-pressure sodium lamps. These lights shine at wavelengths that can be filtered out by astronomers. After upgrading to low-pressure sodium lights, Tucson's lighting improved throughout the city. In some cases, the amount of light increased by a factor of 10. These low-pressure sodium lights produce better lighting for the streets and even cost less to operate. Another solution is to put hoods on billboard, parking-lot, and flood lights so they illuminate the object or the ground rather than the sky.

Figure 21-6

The type of lighting can make a big difference in the amount of light pollution.

A The main mall at the University of Arizona in Tucson had been lit by 400-watt mercury vapor lights. There was enough light but there were also many dark, shadowy areas and glare.

B After changing to low-pressure sodium lights, the lighting on the mall improved everywhere and glare was eliminated. Also, the university has saved money because the new 135-watt sodium lights use 67 percent less electricity.

Community Connection

Light Pollution Have students design a questionnaire to be used to find out whether residents in your local community are concerned about light pollution. The questionnaire should deal with light pollution and the need for security lighting. Have some students collect the opinions of local residents on how a light-pollution-free area could be provided for nighttime observations of the sky. L1

Theme Connection

Energy The issue of light pollution problems versus the need for security lighting reaffirms this chapter's major theme of energy. New types of lights could be used that would produce less light pollution and also reduce the cost of electricity for powering the lights. In some cases, the savings in energy more than pays for the expense of the new lights.

2 Points of View

The Right to Have Security Lighting

The problem of light pollution is not limited to the big cities. Just as in urban and suburban areas, crime and safety is becoming a more important issue in rural areas. To deal with this, security lighting is being used more extensively in all areas of the country. Property owners feel they have the right to protect themselves and their property by installing security lights. To many, the safety that comes with illuminating their property is well worth the problems caused by light pollution.

The Right to a Dark Sky for Observation

On the other hand, imagine you have invited a few friends over to sit outside and watch for meteors, or so-called shooting stars. You set up your chairs and sit down for an evening of searching the skies. As dusk slowly turns to night, your neighbor's security lights turn on, flooding your backyard with bright, glaring light. Soon you realize the sky is too bright to observe meteors. Your neighbor's security lights are casting a glow into the sky. You feel you have the right to darkness so you can observe the night sky.

MiniLAB

Compare the effects of light pollution.

Procedure:

1. Obtain a cardboard tube from an empty roll of paper towels.
2. Select a night when clear skies are predicted. Go outside about two hours after sunset, and look through the cardboard tube at a specific constellation decided upon ahead of time.
3. Count the number of stars you are able to see without moving the observing tube. Repeat this three times.
4. Determine the average number of observable stars at your location.

Analysis:

1. Compare and contrast the number of stars visible from other students' homes.
2. Recognize the cause and effect of differences in your observations. Explain.

Section Wrap-up

Review

1. Why would it be difficult to pass laws that ban light pollution?
2. What happens to city lights within Earth's atmosphere that makes stargazing difficult?

Explore the Issue

Should your neighbors be required to turn off their lights whenever you are observing? If yes, how can they protect their property if they must darken it? If not, how can they use security lights and still enable you and your friends to observe dark skies? To help solve this problem, refer to **Figure 21-6** and the work of one group, the International Dark-Sky Association.

SCIENCE & SOCIETY

Explore the Issue

Students will explore several possible solutions to the problem. An alternative to turning off lights is to replace them or to partially cover them. Students might suggest that the neighbor use low-intensity sodium lights or place hoods over present lights in order to direct light downward.

CONNECT TO CHEMISTRY

Answer When vaporized and heated within low-pressure lamps, sodium emits light almost entirely within two wavelengths of the yellow color. Although measurements in these two wavelengths are affected, the pollution is easily filtered so it does not affect measurements made in other parts of the spectrum.

3 Assess

Check for Understanding

FLEX Your Brain

Use the Flex Your Brain activity to have students explore LIGHT POLLUTION.

Activity Worksheets, p. 5

Reteach

Have students write a proposal for a city ordinance that would control security lighting so amateur astronomers can enjoy dark skies.

4 Close

Section Wrap-up

Review

1. Many people feel it's their right to have safety lighting around their homes and yards. Businesses want to leave lights on to advertise.
2. Earth's atmosphere refracts light, causing it to shine more brightly than the brightness of dimmer objects in the sky.

Section 21•3

Prepare

Section Background

The first U.S. weather satellite, *Vanguard 2,* was launched in February 1959. Its mission was to take photographs of Earth's cloud patterns.

Preplanning

To prepare for Activity 21-2, obtain a portable screen, a remote-controlled car, an instant camera, a stopwatch, and several large (30-cm) rock samples.

1 Motivate

Bellringer

Before presenting the lesson, display **Section Focus Transparency 80** on the overhead projector. Assign the accompanying **Focus Activity** worksheet. L1 LEP

Tying to Previous Knowledge

Blow up a balloon and release it. Have students note that the balloon travels in the direction opposite from where the air is escaping from its neck. Explain that rockets are propelled forward as gases escape from the nozzle at the back of the rocket.

Videodisc

STV: Solar System

The Big Picture

Unit 1, Side 1

Landing on the Moon

08780-11815

21•3 Artificial Satellites and Space Probes

Science Words

- **satellite**
- **orbit**
- **space probe**
- **Project Mercury**
- **Project Gemini**
- **Project Apollo**

Objectives

- Compare and contrast natural and artificial satellites.
- Differentiate between an artificial satellite and a space probe.
- Trace the history of the race to the moon.

The First Steps into Space

If you had your choice of watching your favorite sports team on television or from the stadium, which would you prefer? You would probably want to be as close as possible so you wouldn't miss any of the action. Scientists feel the same way. Even though telescopes have taught them a great deal about the moon and planets, they want to learn more by actually going to those places, or by sending spacecraft where they can't go.

Satellites

Space exploration began in 1957 when the former Soviet Union used a rocket to send *Sputnik I* into space. It was the first artificial satellite. A **satellite** is any object that revolves around another object. When an object enters space, it will travel in a straight line unless a force such as gravity deflects it. When Earth's gravity pulls on a satellite, it falls toward Earth. The result of the satellite traveling forward while at the same time falling toward Earth is a curved path, or **orbit** around Earth. This is shown in **Figure 21-7.**

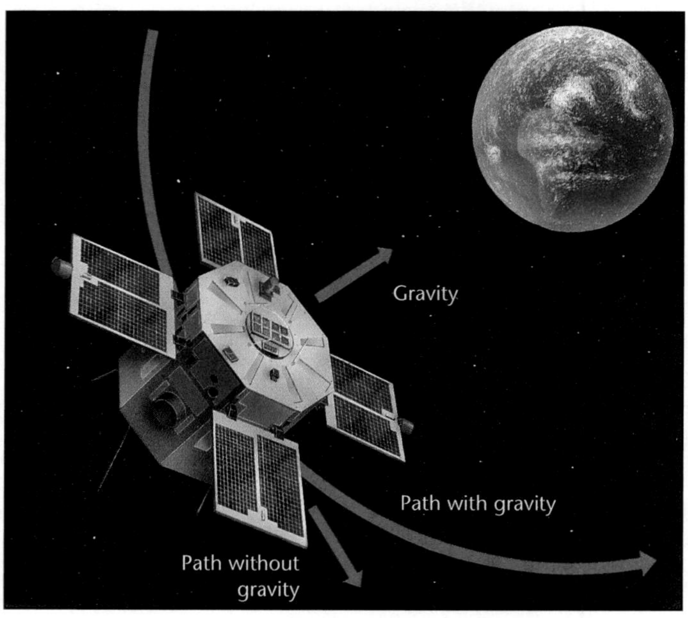

Figure 21-7

The combination of the satellite's forward movement and the gravitational attraction of Earth causes the satellite to travel in a curved path, or orbit. *What would happen if the forward speed of the satellite decreased?*

Program Resources

Reproducible Masters

Study Guide, p. 84 L1
Reinforcement, p. 84 L1
Enrichment, p. 84 L3
Cross-Curricular Integration, p. 25
Activity Worksheets, pp. 5, 128-129 L1
Concept Mapping, p. 47

Transparencies

Section Focus Transparency 80 L1
Teaching Transparency 42

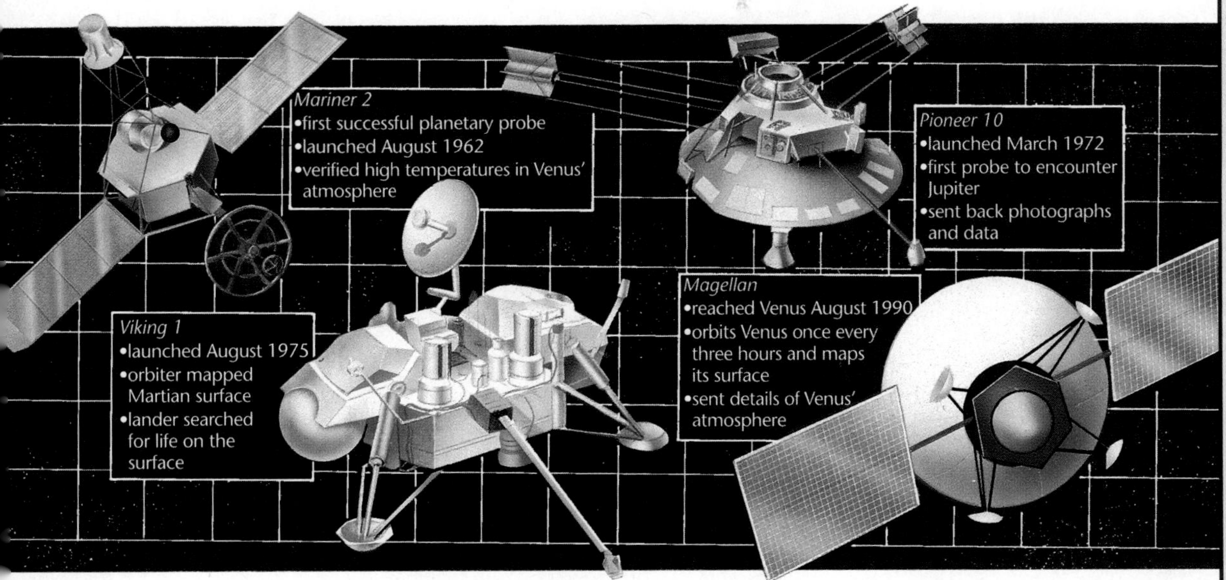

Figure 21-8

Some U.S. space probes and their missions.

The moon is a natural satellite of Earth. It completes one orbit every month. *Sputnik I* orbited Earth for three months before gravity pulled it back into the atmosphere, where it burned up. *Sputnik I* was an experiment to show that artificial satellites could be made. Today, thousands of artificial satellites are in orbit around Earth.

Present-day communication satellites transmit radio and television programs to locations around the world. Other satellites gather scientific data that can't be obtained from Earth, and weather satellites constantly monitor Earth's global weather patterns.

Space Probes

Not all objects carried into space by rockets become satellites. Rockets can also be used to send instruments into space. A **space probe** is an instrument that gathers information and sends it back to Earth. Unlike satellites that orbit Earth, space probes travel far into the solar system. Some have even traveled out of the solar system. Space probes, like many satellites, carry cameras and other data-gathering equipment as well as radio transmitters and receivers that allow them to communicate with scientists on Earth. **Figure 21-8** is a time line showing some of the space probes launched by NASA (National Aeronautics and Space Administration).

You've probably heard of the space probes *Voyager 1* and *Voyager 2.* These two probes were launched in 1977 and are

USING MATH

To reach other planets in the solar system, a spacecraft needs to be launched at a speed greater than 40 200 kilometers per hour. Express this speed in kilometers per second.

2 Teach

Discussion

LS Interpersonal Pair students and have them collaborate on a brief written report about information that could be obtained by artificial satellites in orbit around Earth. Then have the class discuss how this information is used by humans on Earth's surface. To help students get started, list various types of artificial satellites: weather, communications, military, and astronomical.

Visual Learning

Figure 21-7 What would happen if the forward speed of the satellite decreased? *The lower momentum would no longer balance the force of gravity, and the satellite would fall toward Earth.* LEP LS

Revealing Preconceptions

Many people think artificial satellites and space probes gather identical data. Explain that artificial satellites orbit Earth or the object under observation. Probes are spacecraft sent far into space by rockets. They don't orbit other objects. Both satellites and probes send information back to Earth.

USING MATH

11.2

Use **Cross-Curricular Integration,** p. 25, as you teach this lesson.

Cultural Diversity

1993, International Year of Space Early standards for U.S. astronauts severely limited which Americans could participate. For example, the earliest criteria required astronaut candidates (ASCANs) to be test pilots, but women were not allowed to train as test pilots until 1970. After a nine-year hiatus, ASCAN selection broadened in the late 1970s. The 1978 ASCAN group included six women, three African-American men, and an Asian-American. Three members of this group—Judith Resnick, Ronald McNair, and Ellison Onizuka—were killed in the 1986 *Challenger* explosion. Charles Bolden, Jr., a 1980 African-American ASCAN, was temporarily assigned as Assistant Deputy NASA Administrator in 1992.

Inquiry Questions

- **Why was the success of *Sputnik I* so important to the exploration of space?** *The success of* Sputnik I *indicated to many people that placing a human into space was possible.*
- **How do space probes differ from artificial satellites?** *A space probe is launched into space beyond Earth's orbit, where it gathers and transmits information back to Earth. Artificial satellites are placed into orbit around the object being studied and transmit information back to Earth's surface.*
- **How did the *Voyager* probes differ from the *Viking* probes?** *The* Voyager *probes did not land on any planet they studied; the* Viking *probes landed on Mars.*

Enrichment

Have students research geostationary satellites to find out what these satellites are used for and how the term describes the type of orbit of such a satellite.

Teacher F.Y.I.

- Most communications satellites are placed in a geostationary, or synchronous, orbit. This type of orbit permits the satellite to be constantly over a particular location on Earth's surface. The satellite circles Earth at exactly the same speed as Earth rotates below. Thus, it appears to an Earth-based observer to be stationary, because it is always in the same location relative to Earth's surface.
- Satellites that are not in a geostationary orbit pass over a particular location only once per orbit and for only a brief time. This limits their usefulness for communication purposes.

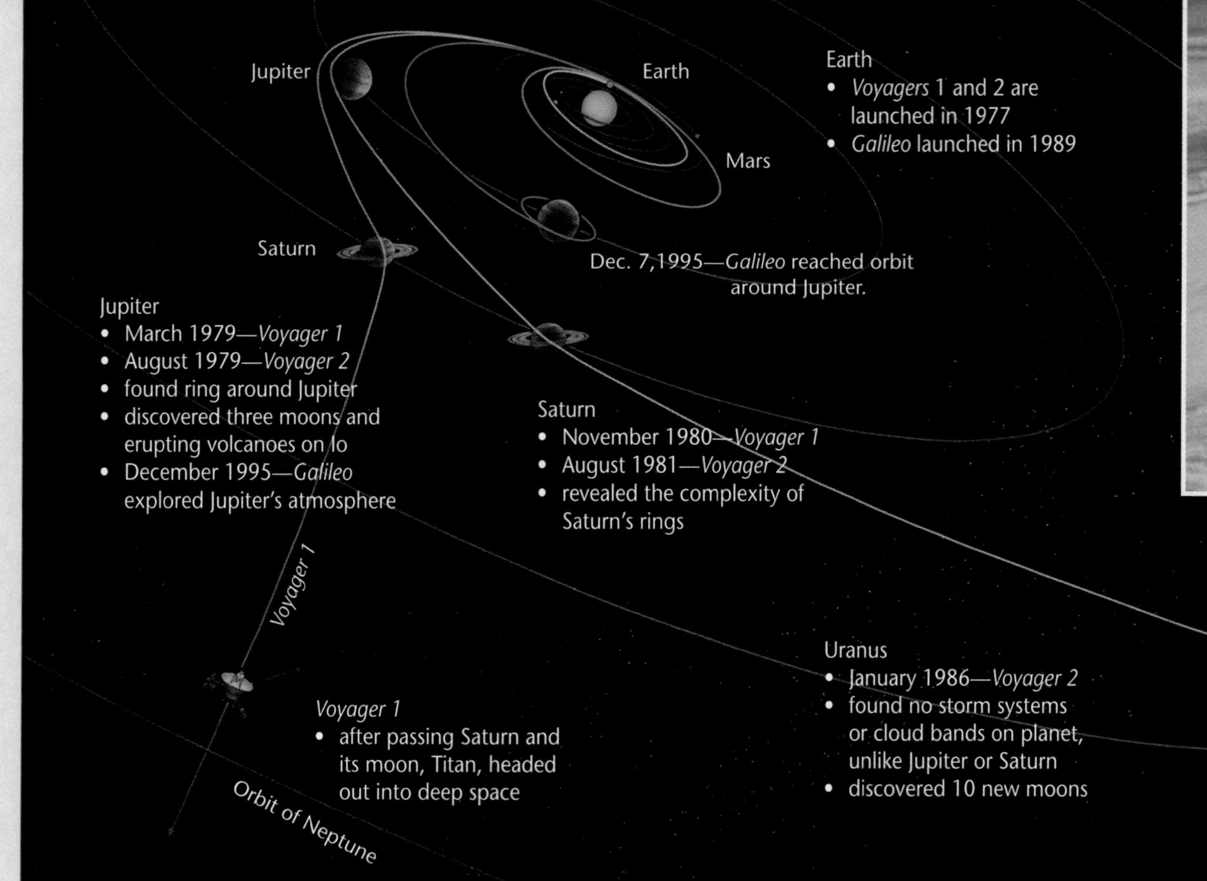

Figure 21-9

The *Voyager* and *Galileo* spacecraft helped make many major discoveries.

now heading outward toward deep space. *Voyager 1* flew past Jupiter and Saturn. *Voyager 2* flew past Jupiter, Saturn, Uranus, and Neptune. **Figure 21-9** describes a portion of what we've learned from the *Voyager* probes. Scientists expect these probes to continue to transmit data to Earth from beyond the solar system for at least 20 more years.

The fate of a probe is never certain and not all are successful. *Mars Explorer* was in orbit around Mars when communication with the probe was lost. It has been silent ever since.

Galileo, launched in 1989, reached Jupiter in 1995. In July 1995, *Galileo* released a smaller probe that began a five-month approach to Jupiter. The small probe took a parachute ride through Jupiter's violent atmosphere in December 1995. Before being crushed by the atmospheric pressure, it transmitted information about Jupiter's composition, temperature, and pressure to the ship orbiting above. *Galileo* studied Jupiter's moons, rings, and magnetic fields and then relayed this information back to scientists eagerly awaiting it on Earth.

Across the Curriculum

Social Studies Have students speculate on why so many developments occurred in the space program during the 1960s. Students should realize that the United States and the former Soviet Union were participating in a "race for space."

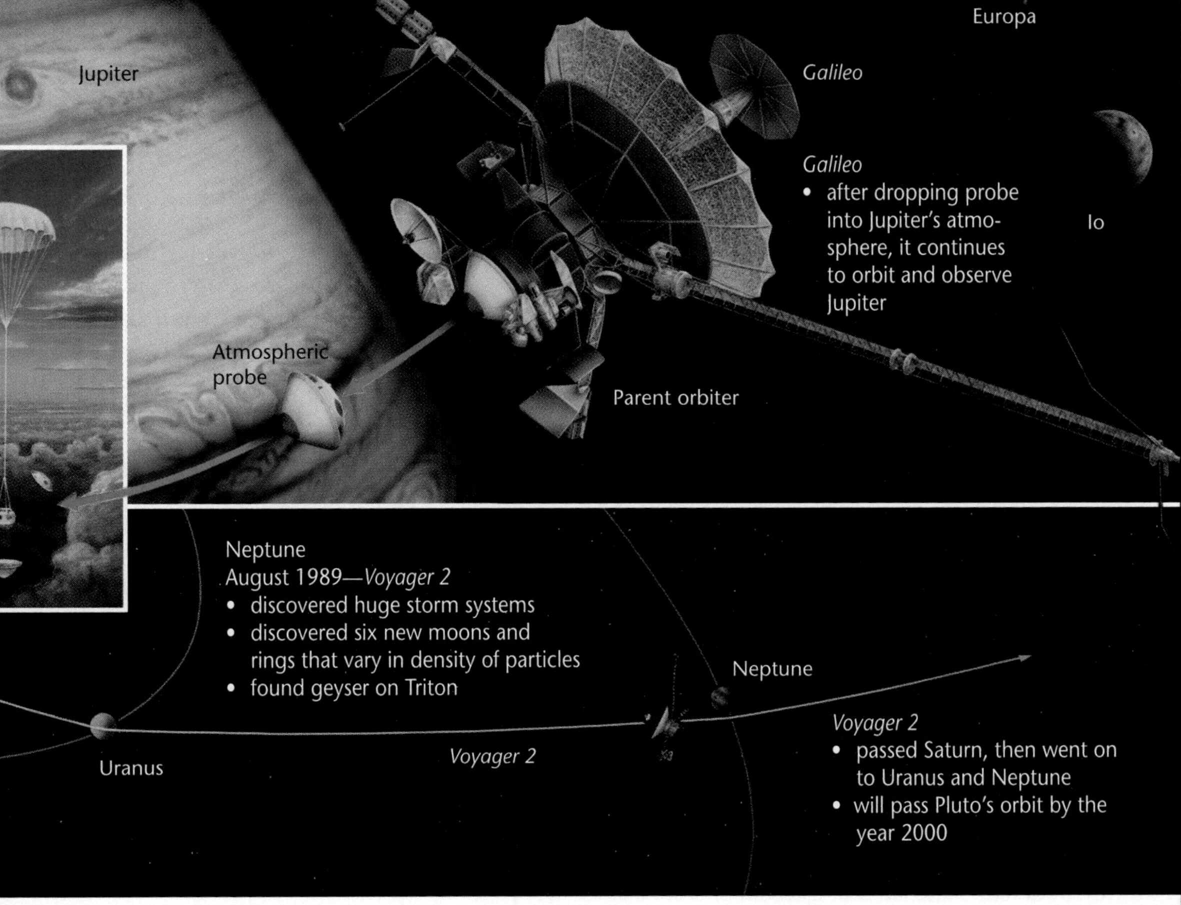

The Race to the Moon

It was quite a shock to people throughout the world when they turned on their radio and television sets in 1957 and heard the radio transmissions from *Sputnik I* as it orbited over their heads. All that *Sputnik I* transmitted was a sort of beeping sound, but people quickly realized that putting a human into space wasn't far off.

In 1961, the Soviet cosmonaut Yuri A. Gagarin became the first human in space. He orbited Earth and then returned safely. Soon, President John F. Kennedy called for the United States to place people on the moon and return them to Earth by the end of that decade. The "race for space" had begun.

The U.S. program to reach the moon began with **Project Mercury.** The goals of Project Mercury were to orbit a piloted spacecraft around Earth and to bring it safely back. The program provided data and experience in the basics of space flight. On May 5, 1961, Alan B. Shepard became the first U.S. citizen in space. In 1962, *Mercury* astronaut John Glenn became the first U.S. citizen to orbit Earth.

CONNECT TO LIFE SCIENCE

Scientists are very careful when building spacecraft so as not to contaminate equipment with microorganisms from Earth. ***Explain*** in your Science Journal why this is so important for craft sent into space or to other worlds.

Visual Learning

Figure 21-9 Ask students to review the flights of *Voyager 1* and *Voyager 2*. Then ask students what was different about the two probes that caused such a difference in their flight paths. Voyager 2 *used the gravity of Saturn to give it the speed necessary to arrive at Uranus. It then used the gravity of Uranus to send it on to Neptune.* LEP LS

CONNECT TO LIFE SCIENCE

Answer Scientists do not know whether life exists elsewhere in space. To be certain that our exploration does not affect or destroy evidence of life beyond Earth, precautions are taken to minimize the chance of sending microorganisms from Earth to other places in our solar system and beyond.

Enrichment

LS **Linguistic** Pair students and have them use the school library to research the *Mercury VII* astronauts. Students should collaborate on a written report about the missions each astronaut performed in the *Mercury* and other space programs, and what these astronauts are doing now. L1 COOP LEARN

Inclusion Strategies

Gifted Have students research space junk. Inform them that space junk includes unused and nonfunctioning materials and machines in orbit around Earth. It ranges from sand-grain-sized paint chips to large communication satellites. Students can write to NASA to ask for information on the issue. Students should discuss the growing concern that space junk may pose a threat to the safety of future crewed spaceflights. Have students find out how long it takes items to fall out of orbit and reenter Earth's atmosphere. L3

USING TECHNOLOGY

- For more information, see *Spinoff,* a NASA publication that can be obtained by writing to Directory, Technology Utilization Division, P.O. Box 8756, Baltimore-Washington International Airport, MD 21240.
- Have interested students briefly report on the proposed research planned for future space stations.

Think Critically

Quartz watches are only one of the many spin-offs of the space program. Other responses that students might mention include calculators, computers, and battery-powered hand tools.

3 Assess

Check for Understanding

FLEX Your Brain

Use the Flex Your Brain activity to have students explore PROJECT APOLLO.

Activity Worksheets, p. 5

Reteach

Interpersonal Pair students and have them make outlines of the material presented in Section 21-3. Have partners quiz each other to review the material.

Extension

For students who have mastered this section, use the **Reinforcement** and **Enrichment** masters.

USING TECHNOLOGY

Spin-Offs

The technology developed by NASA to achieve its goals in space has been remarkable. Much of it is now being used by people throughout the world. The technologies developed by NASA that are later used by the general public are called spin-offs.

NASA had to develop lightweight, compact breathing systems for the astronauts to carry as they ventured out of their spacecraft and onto the moon. Today, firefighters use these breathing systems as well as fire-resistant uniforms originally designed as flight suits for NASA pilots. The lightweight material in the suits won't burn or crack.

Another material, designed for boots worn by astronauts on the moon, is now found in some athletic shoes. Other materials have been incorporated into ski goggles, blankets, and bicycle seats.

Persons who are visually impaired have benefited from spin-offs too. They are able to use a device that vibrates ink on a printed page. This enables them to read materials that aren't in Braille. Another device determines the denomination of currency and generates an audible signal.

Other spin-offs include pens that write without the help of gravity and sunglasses that adjust to various light levels.

Think Critically: How has the space program affected your life? You may need to look no farther than your wrist!

NASA Spin-Off

Project Gemini

Project Gemini was the next step in reaching the moon. Teams of two astronauts in the same *Gemini* spacecraft orbited Earth. One *Gemini* team met and connected with another spacecraft in orbit—a skill that would be needed on a voyage to the moon.

Along with the *Mercury* and *Gemini* programs, a series of robotic probes was sent to the moon. *Ranger* proved we could get spacecraft to the moon. *Surveyor* landed gently on the moon's surface, indicating that the moon's surface could support spacecraft and humans. The mission of *Lunar Orbiter* was to take pictures of the moon's surface that would be used to determine the best landing sites on the moon.

Project Apollo

The final stage of the U.S. program to reach the moon was **Project Apollo.** On July 20, 1969, *Apollo 11* landed on the lunar

Science Journal

Project Apollo Ask the following questions and have students use them as a starting point for a brief report they are to write in their Science Journals about Project *Apollo.*

- **How did the information gained in Project *Gemini* lead to success in the *Apollo* mission?** *Project* Gemini *provided the opportunity for astronauts to work in space. It also showed that one spacecraft could successfully meet and rendezvous with another spacecraft while in orbit.*
- **Why do you think Michael Collins remained in the command module while Neil Armstrong and Edwin Aldrin landed on the moon?** *Collins operated the command module during the rendezvous and connection with the lunar lander. It was considered safer to have a person in the command module in case of problems during the connection of the spacecraft.* L2 LS

surface. Neil Armstrong was the first human to set foot on the moon. His first words as he stepped onto its surface were: "That's one small step for a man, one giant leap for mankind." Edwin Aldrin, the second of the three *Apollo 11* astronauts, joined Armstrong on the moon and they explored its surface for two hours. Michael Collins remained in the Command Module orbiting the moon, where Armstrong and Aldrin returned before beginning the journey home. A total of six lunar landings brought back more than 2000 samples of moon rock and soil for study before the program ended in 1972.

Figure 21-10

The Lunar Rover Vehicle was first used during the *Apollo 15* mission. Riding in the "moon buggy," *Apollo 15, 16,* and *17* astronauts explored large areas of the lunar surface.

During the past three decades, most missions in space have been carried out by individual countries, often competing to be the first or the best. Today, there is much more cooperation among countries of the world to work together and share what each has learned. Projects are now being planned for cooperative missions to Mars and elsewhere. As you read the next section, you'll see how the U.S. program has progressed since the days of Project Apollo, and where it may be going in the future.

Section Wrap-up

Review

1. Currently, no human-made objects are orbiting Neptune, yet Neptune has eight major satellites. Explain.
2. *Galileo* was considered a space probe as it traveled to Jupiter. Once there, however, it became an artificial satellite. Explain.
3. **Think Critically:** Is Earth a satellite of any other body in space? Explain your answer.

Skill Builder

Concept Mapping

Make an events-chain concept map that lists the events in the U.S. space program to place people on the moon. If you need help, refer to Concept Mapping in the **Skill Handbook.**

Using Computers

Spreadsheet Use the spreadsheet feature on your computer to generate a table of recent successful satellites and space probes launched by the United States. Include a description of the craft, the date launched, and the mission.

4 Close

• MINI • QUIZ •

Use the Mini Quiz to check students' recall of chapter content.

1. **An object that revolves around another object is a(n) _____ .** *satellite*
2. **Define *orbit*.** *the curved path that an object follows as it travels in space around another object*
3. **A(n) _____ is an instrument sent into space, beyond Earth's orbit, to gather information and send it back to Earth.** *space probe*
4. **The _____ space probes flew past Jupiter, Saturn, Uranus, and Neptune.** *Voyager*

Section Wrap-up

Review

1. These eight satellites are natural satellites of the planet.
2. Once the probe arrived at Jupiter, it went into orbit around that planet and became an artificial satellite.
3. **Think Critically** Yes, Earth is a natural satellite of the sun.

Using Computers

Information for students to use when producing their spreadsheets is available from NASA. Also, several magazines—*Final Frontier, Astronomy,* and *Sky and Telescope*—provide information about recent satellites and space probes.

Skill Builder

Students' concept maps will vary. They may include the following sequence of events: President John F. Kennedy calls for placing people on the moon by the end of the decade; Project *Mercury* places people in orbit; Project *Gemini* has two teams of astronauts in different spacecraft meet and connect in space; a series of probes are sent to the moon; Project *Apollo* places people on the moon.

Assessment

Oral Use this Skill Builder to assess students' abilities to make concept maps. Ask students to explain how robotic probes to the moon helped prepare for the moon landing. Use the Performance Task Assessment List for Concept Map in **PASC,** p. 89. P

People and Science

GIBOR BASRI, *Astronomer*

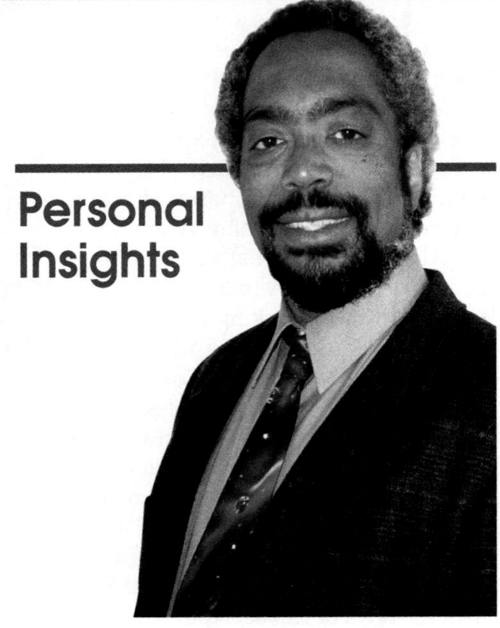

On the Job

Q What is it like to use the Keck Telescopes on Mauna Kea, Hawaii?

A One of my most exciting moments as an astronomer was the first night I was able to operate the telescopes. They're amazing telescopes to use; each one is a complex, fascinating machine. The summit of Mauna Kea, Hawaii, is the world's premier site for observing. It's almost 4270 m high, so when you go up there you are somewhat oxygen deprived, and some people get sick. But you're on top of the mountain peak, you can see Maui in the distance, there's ocean all around, and the air is particularly clear and stable. It's kind of the pinnacle of astronomy.

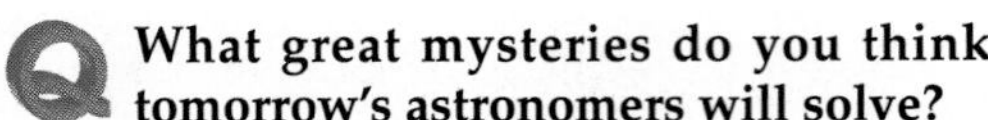

Q What great mysteries do you think tomorrow's astronomers will solve?

A One of the big ones that the next generation will solve is the question of other planets out there. A great deal of work and new technology will be needed to answer the questions, "Is there life out there?" "How many planets are there around other stars, what are they like, and how do they form?" and "Are there a lot of Earth-like planets out there?"

Personal Insights

Q Did your interest in science fiction play a part in your becoming an astronomer?

A I think so. I was fascinated with all aspects of outer space, the cosmos, and time. Science fiction was one outlet for my fascination. It opens your mind to thinking about things in different ways—not accepting things as they seem to be, but imagining how they could be different. It's a broadening experience in that sense.

Career Connection

Contact a local planetarium or astronomy club, or search the Worldwide Web, to find out more about what astronomers do and about careers in astronomy.

Make a profile describing one of the following careers in astronomy:

- **Observatory Scientist**
- **Planetarium Director**

People and Science

Background

- Gibor Basri is a professor of astronomy at the University of California, Berkeley. In 1995, Basri and his colleagues reported the first confirmation of a brown dwarf star.
- Brown dwarfs are often considered failed stars. They have more mass than a typical planet, but not enough to lead to fusion, which would make them true stars. They never become stable burners of nuclear fuel. Some may have limited fusion, but then they burn out and fade from view. Lithium is destroyed by fusion in real stars. Brown dwarfs don't have sufficient nuclear fires to destroy their lithium. To search for brown dwarfs, astronomers look for faint, cool stars that are old enough to have gotten rid of their lithium. One that still has lithium is a candidate for being a brown dwarf.
- Brown dwarfs are thought to form the same way stars do—from the collapse of a swirling cloud of gas and dust. They are 4 to 80 times more massive than Jupiter, but at least 12 times lighter than the sun. Most of their light is emitted in the infrared spectrum, so they are harder to detect in visible light.
- Brown dwarfs are of interest because they may help astronomers better understand how stars and planets form. Astronomers also believe they may account for some of what is called dark matter—the missing mass that may make up as much as 90% of the universe.

Teaching Strategies

Astronomers are always searching for ways to make telescopes bigger. The larger the telescope, the more light it gathers, and the fainter the objects that can be observed. Assign students to report on the new generation of telescopes that are being designed and built for use on Earth and in space.

Career Connection

Career Path Some professional astronomers start out as amateur astronomers in primary or secondary school, but many do not. Far more important is a strong background in physics and math. Such a course of study doesn't lock a student into an astronomy career, but it keeps the option open. For students who have an interest in amateur astronomy, local planetariums and astronomy clubs can provide help with selecting telescopes and learning to observe. They also may offer lectures by professional astronomers.

For More Information

The magazines *Astronomy* and *Sky & Telescope* carry articles on astronomical research, as well as amateur observing.

Activity 21-2

Design Your Own Experiment
Probe to Mars

Before attempting a new mission in space, NASA plans, organizes, and practices the operation of the mission many times on Earth. In this way, NASA can be ready to solve many problems that otherwise might have canceled or hindered a successful mission.

PREPARATION

Problem

You and your classmates will conduct a simulated mission to successfully land an exploration probe on the surface of Mars, retrieve samples, and return those samples to Earth for analysis. To achieve this goal, you must do what NASA does before, during, and after a mission.

Mission Planning

The entire class will plan the mission. Include methods to be used for observing, mapping, choosing a landing site, operating the robot surface probe (a battery-operated remote-control car), collecting samples, and analyzing the success of the mission.

Possible Materials

- portable screen
- remote-controlled car
- bag to hold rock and mineral samples
- large rocks (30 cm)
- camera (instant), film
- stopwatch

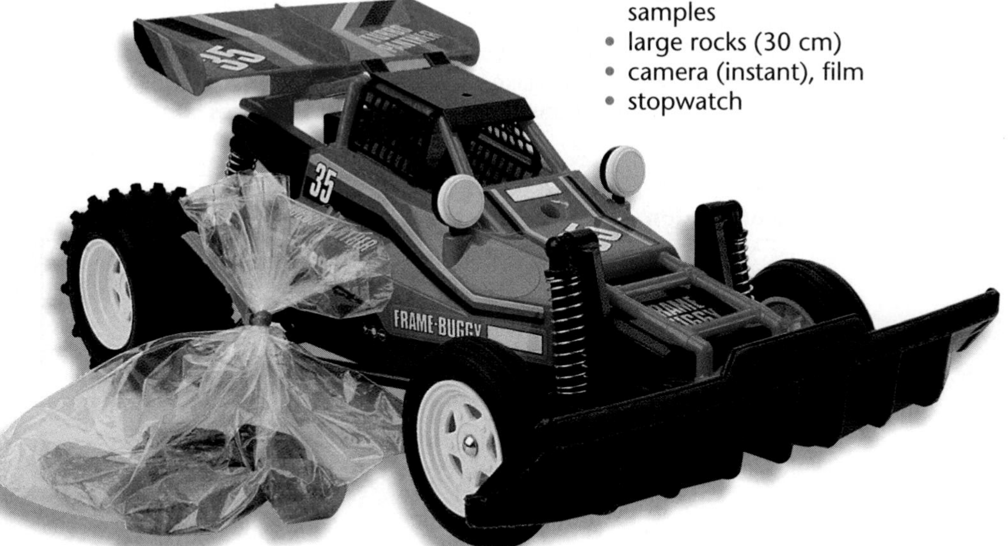

Activity 21-2

PREPARATION

Purpose

LS **Interpersonal** Plan, organize, and perform a simulated landing of a robot surface probe on Mars. L1 COOP LEARN

Process Skills

making models, observing and inferring, interpreting data, predicting, measuring in SI, separating and controlling variables, and communicating

Time

two class periods

Materials

portable screen, remote-controlled car, sample bags, large rocks (30 cm), instant camera, film, stopwatch

Safety Precautions

Remind students to wear safety goggles when collecting and identifying mineral and rock samples. If HCl is used during the mineral and rock testing, remind students to wear aprons as well as safety goggles.

Possible Mission Designs

The entire class will deal with the mission design during a brainstorming session. Possible designs include the following, but individual classes will most likely deviate a lot. Encourage students to be creative.

1. Split the students in the class into teams. Each team will be responsible for some aspect of the mission design. Some students will be in mission control and others will be in the field or lab working to obtain photographs and identify collected samples.
2. A privately funded space mission to Mars will be conducted by three teams of students. One team will be in charge of all Earth-based controls. Another team will control the spacecraft in orbit while it photographs possible landing sites. The third team will operate the craft during landing, sample collection, and launch back to Earth.

Activity Worksheets, pp. 5, 128-129

PLAN THE EXPERIMENT

Possible Procedures

Students may develop their own procedures as the class designs the mission plan, or they may use the suggested procedures.

Teaching Strategies

- Select an area of the school grounds to be used as the "Martian" surface. Dig "craters" in the area and move in several large rocks.
- Set up a screen behind which the mission specialist is to work.
- Have five students conduct the countdown, blastoff, and flight of the space probe. You may wish to have students build a model rocket and launch it to simulate this portion of the activity. If so, be sure an adult supervises any launches students conduct using model-rocket engines.
- Have one student move the remote-controlled buggy to the area to be studied. (This simulates the landing on the Martian surface.)
- Obtain a copy of *Launching a Dream, A Teacher's Guide to a Simulated Space Shuttle Mission* from NASA, Lewis Research Center, Cleveland, OH 44135. Use the book to provide ideas on how to set up and organize this activity.

Activity 21-2 (continued)

PLAN THE EXPERIMENT

1. **Orbital Photographic Study of the Martian Surface:** Two students will photograph (from above) all parts of the Martian surface to be studied.
2. **Mapping the Martian Surface:** Three students will use photographs from the orbital study and draw a map of the Martian surface. Be sure to identify large boulders, craters, flat areas, locations of samples to be retrieved, and any other key surface features.
3. **Landing Site Selection:** Three students will study the maps of the surface and decide on a landing site and route for the robot surface probe.
4. **Design of RSR (Remote Sample Retrieval) System:** Three students will design a method of retrieving a container of rock samples from Mars' surface. Rock samples will be encased in a baglike container, so the retrieval system must be able to pick up and carry the bag of samples.
5. **Mission Control (part 1):** A team of five students will conduct the countdown, blast off, flight, and landing of the robot surface probe.
6. **Mission Control (part 2):** A mission specialist and assistant will operate remote controls that will enable the robot surface probe to move around on the Martian surface. A second mission specialist will operate the RSR System and collect samples for study. A successful mission is one in which the lander explores all parts of the Martian surface within range, without colliding with boulders or falling into craters. A successful mission also involves retrieving rock samples from the planet's surface and returning them to Earth for study. As the mission specialist operates controls from

Data and Observations

Sample Data

Time of Mission		Accuracy of Mission	
Mission start	1:03:00 EST	Were all sites visited?	Yes
Mission stop	1:31:17 EST	Was the mission completed?	Yes
Mission length	28 min	List the number of times the mission was delayed by surface features.	7

Tying to Previous Knowledge

Show students photographs taken during early flights to the moon when NASA was trying to decide where best to land on the moon. They should recall the cratered look of the moon, and you can relate that knowledge to the fact that Mars also has a cratered surface.

Troubleshooting Several days before doing this activity, obtain the remote-controlled buggy, camera, and stopwatch so they can be checked to see that they operate properly. Be sure to have plenty of fresh batteries for the remote-controlled buggy. Obtain a camera with instant-developing film to photograph the Martian surface.

PLAN THE EXPERIMENT (continued)

behind a screen, the assistant will give directions on which way to move the surface probe. The assistant does the job that sensors or cameras would perform on an actual mission.

7. **Sample Analysis:** A team of eight students will conduct an analysis of the rocks brought back from Mars's surface. This team of students is to use methods of identifying minerals and rocks learned in Chapters 3 and 4.
   - Look for any evidence of life on the surface of Mars by searching for fossils in the rocks brought back from the planet.
8. **Mission Debriefing:** A team of three students will:
   - Observe the probe mission.
   - Record the time required to conduct the surface probe mission.
   - Judge when the mission is complete.
   - Record the number of times the probe is delayed or hindered by various features.
   - Review the reports of the sample analysis teams for general conclusions regarding the content of rocks on Mars's surface.

DO THE EXPERIMENT

1. Carry out the mission as planned.
2. While the mission is going on, record any observations of the mission and complete the data table in your Science Journal.
3. Write a final report summarizing the success of the mission and including suggestions for improvement.

Analyze and Apply

1. What part of the mission did all other parts depend on?
2. What feature of the total project brought about a successful mission?
3. In an actual mission, how would photographs of possible landing sites be obtained?
4. What was the most common mineral found on the "Martian" surface?
5. What types of rocks were found?

Go Further

What conclusion can be drawn from the mission about the past or present existence of life on Mars? Why was the mission specialist placed behind a screen? What task did the assistant perform when working with the mission specialist? From your observations, list some likely sources of problems for an actual mission of this type.

- The assistant did the job done by sensors and cameras on the remote-controlled buggy.
- Problem areas may include obtaining detailed photographs of Mars's surface, omitting key steps in the mission planning, breakdown of the remote-controlled buggy, damage to the buggy from colliding with rocks or falling into a crater, or breakdown in communication from the robot to the mission specialist, among others.

Assessment

Performance To further assess students' abilities to understand the difficulty in sending a probe to another planet, see Question 2 in Performance Assessment, on page 611. Use the Performance Task Assessment List for Formulating a Hypothesis in **PASC**, p. 21. P

DO THE EXPERIMENT

Expected Outcomes

- During the mission planning, have students brainstorm to devise the most workable method of completing the mission. Have a student list all ideas on the chalkboard.
- Students will most likely follow the suggested procedures but will modify each step as it applies to their particular situation.
- Students responsible for collection and identification of samples will model their procedures after the activities from the chapters dealing with minerals and rocks.

Analyze and Apply

1. the planning portion
2. the cooperation of many people
3. by artificial satellites and probes
4. Answer will depend on the samples provided.
5. Answer will depend on the samples provided.

Go Further

- If rock samples contain fossils, students should respond that evidence of previous life exists. If no fossil remains and no organically produced rocks are found, students should respond that no evidence of previous or present life was found.
- An actual mission specialist would remain on Earth and rely on cameras located on the remote-controlled buggy. Placing the mission specialist behind the screen means that he or she must rely on observations of others to make decisions, just as an actual mission specialist relies on cameras located on the robots.

Section 21•4

Prepare

Section Background

The space shuttle *Challenger* exploded 75 seconds after its launch on January 28, 1986. The explosion occurred when one of two solid-fuel booster rockets developed a leak. The hot gases burned through the main fuel tank, causing it to explode. All people on board were killed.

Preplanning

To prepare for the MiniLAB, obtain a turntable, an LP record, and marbles.

1 Motivate

Bellringer

Before presenting the lesson, display **Section Focus Transparency 81** on the overhead projector. Assign the accompanying **Focus Activity** worksheet. L1 LEP

Tying to Previous Knowledge

Ask students if they have watched the preparation, launch, and landing of the space shuttle. Show a film of a recent launch.

STV: Solar System

Apollo 11 launch

41715

Mariner 10 passing Mercury

41707

21•4 The Space Shuttle and the Future

Science Words
- **space shuttle**
- **space station**

Objectives
- Describe the benefits of the space shuttle.
- Evaluate the usefulness of orbital space stations.

The Space Shuttle

Imagine spending millions of dollars to build a machine, sending it off into space, and watching its 3000 metric tons of metal and other materials burn up after only a few minutes of work. That's exactly what NASA did for many years. The early rockets lifted into orbit a small capsule holding the astronauts. Sections of the rocket separated from the rest of the rocket body and burned as they re-entered the atmosphere.

A Reusable Spacecraft

NASA administrators, like many people, realized that it can be less expensive and less wasteful to reuse resources. The reusable spacecraft that transports astronauts, satellites, and other materials to and from space is the **space shuttle.**

At launch, the space shuttle orbiter stands on end and is connected to an external liquid-fuel tank and two solid-fuel booster rockets. When the shuttle reaches an altitude of about 45 km, the emptied solid-fuel booster rockets drop off and parachute back to Earth. They are recovered and used again. The larger external liquid-fuel tank eventually separates and falls back to Earth. It isn't recovered.

Once the space shuttle orbiter reaches space, it begins to orbit Earth. There, astronauts perform many different tasks. The cargo bay can carry a self-contained laboratory where astronauts conduct scientific experiments and determine the effects of space flight on the human body. On missions in which the cargo bay isn't used as a laboratory, the shuttle can launch, repair, and retrieve satellites.

To retrieve a satellite, a large mechanical arm in the cargo bay is extended. An astronaut inside the shuttle orbiter moves the arm by remote control. The arm grabs the satellite and pulls it back into the cargo bay. The doors are closed and it can then be returned to Earth.

Similarly, the mechanical arm can be used to lift a satellite or probe out of the cargo bay and place it into space. In some cases, a defective satellite can be pulled in by the mechanical

Figure 21-11
The space shuttle is designed to make many trips into space.

Program Resources

 **Reproducible Masters**

Study Guide, p. 85 L1
Reinforcement, p. 85 L1
Enrichment, p. 85 L3
Science and Society Integration, p. 25
Activity Worksheets, pp. 5, 131 L1
Critical Thinking/Problem Solving, p. 27
Multicultural Connections, pp. 45-46

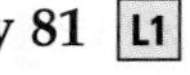 **Transparencies**

Section Focus Transparency 81 L1

arm, repaired while in the cargo bay, and then placed into space once more.

After the completion of each mission, the space shuttle orbiter glides back to Earth and lands like an airplane. A very large landing field is needed because the gliding speed of the orbiter is 335 km/hr.

Space Stations

Astronauts can spend only a short time in space in the space shuttle orbiter. Its living space is very small, and the crew needs more space to live, exercise, and work. A **space station** has living quarters, work and exercise space, and all the equipment and support systems needed for humans to live and work in space.

The United States had such a station in the past. The space station *Skylab* was launched in 1973. Crews of astronauts spent up to 84 days in it performing experiments and collecting data on the effects on humans living in space. In 1979, the abandoned *Skylab* fell out of orbit and burned up as it entered Earth's atmosphere.

Crews from the former Soviet Union have spent the most time in space aboard the space station *Mir.* Two cosmonauts spent a record 365 days on board.

Science Journal

The *Galileo* craft rendezvoused with Jupiter after it first flew by Venus, circled the sun, and then flew past Earth. Research newspaper and magazine articles to find out why *Galileo* took such an indirect path to Jupiter. Research NASA's method of gravity-assisted space travel.

2 Teach

Demonstration

LS Visual-Spatial If possible, obtain a working model of a space shuttle. Use the model to demonstrate how the cargo bay is used to carry satellites to and from Earth and how the mobile arm is used to place satellites into orbit and to bring them back into the cargo bay for repairs. **LEP**

Science Journal

The *Galileo* spacecraft used gravity-assisted space travel on its flight to Jupiter. As a craft approaches a planet and then passes by it, it gains momentum from the moving planet. The *Galileo* spacecraft obtained three gravity assists on its flight to Jupiter, enabling it to make the trip with far less fuel than a direct flight would require.

Videodisc

STV: Solar System

Pioneer Venus 2 releasing probes (art)

41682

Space probe (art)

41659

Viking lander (art)

41700

Earth, as seen from Voyager 1

41719

Inclusion Strategies

Hearing Impaired Assist students as they make models of space machines such as space probes, space capsules, or the space shuttle. Have them discuss some of the proposed future spacecraft and space stations. Students can draw or make models of their own ideas about future space machines.

MiniLAB

Purpose

LS **Kinesthetic** Students will demonstrate how gravity can be simulated in a space station. L1 LEP COOP LEARN

Materials

turntable, LP record, scissors, construction paper, masking tape, marbles

Teaching Strategies

Troubleshooting Inform students that only the slowest speed of the turntable should be used.

Safety Precautions Caution students to wear safety goggles in case marbles fly off the turntable.

Analysis

1. The marbles are accelerated outward from the center by forces generated by the rotation of the turntable. The inertia of the marbles causes them to continue to move outward. The surface of the paper exerts a force on the marbles and stops them from continuing their outward motion.
2. A space station could simulate this artificial gravity by spinning slowly around a central axis of rotation.

Assessment

Oral Ask students if they have ever partially filled a bucket with water and then swung it quickly over their head without spilling any water. Ask a student to relate that experience to the observations in this MiniLAB. Use the Performance Task Assessment List for Making Observations and Inferences in **PASC**, p. 17. P

Activity Worksheets, pp. 5, 131

MiniLAB

How can gravity be simulated in a space station?

Procedure:

1. Locate an LP record album you can use for this activity.
2. Fold an 8-cm-wide strip of construction paper in half, then unfold it.
3. Wrap the paper along the fold around the circumference of the record, so there is a 4-cm wall around the outside edge of the disc.
4. Securely tape the rest underneath the record.
5. Place the record on a turntable and place three marbles at its center.
6. Switch the turntable on.

Analysis:

1. What do you observe about the movements of the marbles?
2. Hypothesize how what you've observed could be useful for simulating the effects of gravity on a space station.

Cooperation in Space

In 1995, the United States and Russia ushered in a time of cooperation and trust in exploring space. Early in the year, Dr. Norman Thagard was launched into orbit aboard the Russian *Soyuz* spacecraft along with two Russian cosmonaut crewmates. Dr. Thagard was the first United States astronaut launched into space by a Russian or Soviet booster. He then became the first American resident of the Russian space station *Mir.* Dr. Thagard was studying the long-term effects of space travel on humans.

In June 1995, Russian cosmonauts Anatoli Solovyev and Nikolai Budarin rode into orbit aboard the space shuttle *Atlantis,* America's 100th crewed launch. The mission of *Atlantis* involved, among other studies, a rendezvous and docking, shown in **Figure 21-13,** with space station *Mir.* Upon completion of its mission, *Atlantis* returned the *Mir 18* team, Dr. Thagard and cosmonauts Vladimir Dezhurov and Gennadiy Strekalov, to Earth. Both nations hope the

Figure 21-12

The proposed International Space Station is shown with the space shuttle docked.

Integrating the Sciences

Life Science When the United States and the former Soviet Union began their piloted space programs, humans were not the first to go into space. Ask students to find out what animals were used by each country and why these animals were used. Also ask students to describe how Project *Mercury* helped prepare the United States for future moon exploration.

cooperation that existed on this mission will continue through at least seven future space shuttle-*Mir* docking missions, an important step leading to the building and operating of the International Space Station set to begin in 1997.

International Space Station

The International Space Station will be a permanent laboratory designed for long-term research. A diverse selection of research topics will be studied. One example are the plans for research and growth of protein crystals. This project will help scientists determine protein structure and function. This could enhance work on drug design and the treatment of diseases.

The space station will draw on the resources of more than a dozen nations. Various nations will build modules for the space station that will then be transported into space aboard the space shuttle. The space station itself will be constructed in space. **Figure 21-12** shows what the completed station will look like with a space shuttle attached. NASA is planning the

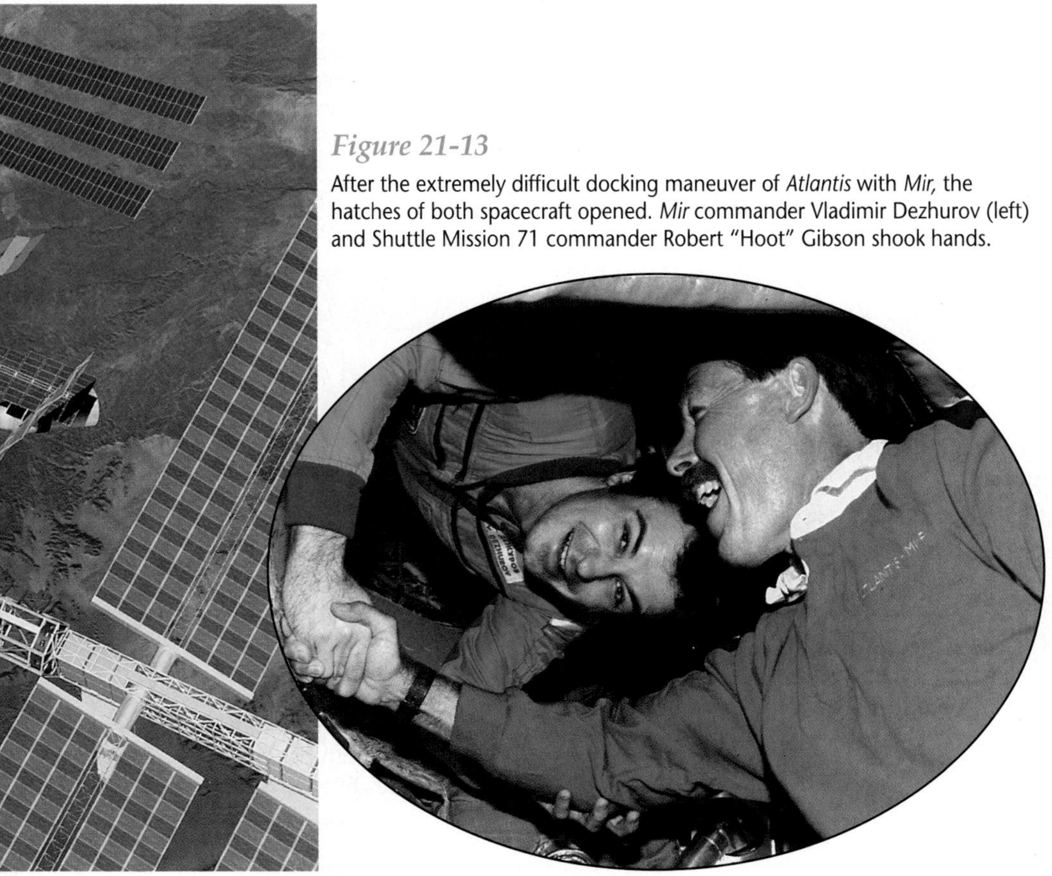

Figure 21-13

After the extremely difficult docking maneuver of *Atlantis* with *Mir,* the hatches of both spacecraft opened. *Mir* commander Vladimir Dezhurov (left) and Shuttle Mission 71 commander Robert "Hoot" Gibson shook hands.

Use these program resources as you teach this lesson.

Multicultural Connections, pp. 45-46

Critical Thinking/Problem Solving, p. 27

3 Assess

Check for Understanding

FLEX Your Brain

Use the Flex Your Brain activity to have students explore THE INTERNATIONAL SPACE STATION.

Activity Worksheets, p. 5

Reteach

Ask students to list some of the advantages of sharing space missions with other countries. After listing the advantages, ask them to write a brief paragraph in their Science Journals explaining why cooperation in space did not occur in the early years of the space station as it does now. *The cost of the space missions could be shared. Also, if the data gathered were shared by all nations, repetitive missions would be reduced. This would provide funds for other space missions and research. Answers will vary, but students should realize that advancement in space technology was part of the cold war at that time.*

Extension

For students who have mastered this section, use the **Reinforcement** and **Enrichment** masters.

Across the Curriculum

Agriculture, Geography, Meteorology, Medicine The space program has been used to benefit humans in all of these fields and in many others. Ask interested students to pick a field of their choice and write a report in their Science Journals about what advancement has occurred in that particular field as a direct result of the space program. L1 LS

4 Close

•MINI•QUIZ•

1. **The _____ is a reusable spacecraft that transports astronauts, satellites, and other materials to and from space.** *space shuttle*
2. **What is a space station?** *a spacecraft that has everything needed to live and work in space*
3. **What was Skylab?** *a U.S. space station that orbited Earth for six years*
4. **What is looked at by NASA as the second planning phase of the International Space Station?** *NASA and RSA will assemble the bilateral station Alpha.*

Section Wrap-up

Review

1. It is a reusable spacecraft.
2. The space shuttle *Mir* docking missions are a key initial step in the successful completion of the International Space Station. These missions also provide experience for sharing space technology among nations and work to advance cooperation in space.
3. Think Critically It has a large cargo bay that enables it to carry satellites to and from Earth, it can be used to repair defective satellites, and it can land like an airplane.

Science Journal

Make sure students realize that the 100 people don't have to be known to them personally, but rather should include occupations such as farmers, mechanics, writers, and so on.

space station program in three phases. Phase One involves the space shuttle-*Mir* docking missions. In Phase Two, NASA and RSA (Russian Space Agency) will assemble the bilateral station Alpha. In Phase Three, a crew will permanently operate a multinational space station.

NASA plans for crews of astronauts to stay on board the station for several months at a time. While there, researchers will make products that are returned for use on Earth. One day, the station could be a construction site for ships to the moon and Mars.

Figure 21-14
Using the space shuttle, scientists have already performed extensive experiments in the weightlessness of space.

Section Wrap-up

Review

1. What is the main advantage of the space shuttle?
2. Why are the space shuttle-*Mir* docking missions so important?
3. Think Critically: Why is the space shuttle more versatile than earlier spacecraft?

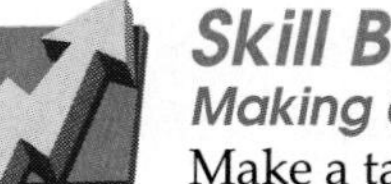

Skill Builder
Making and Using Tables

Make a table outlining the possible uses of the mechanical arm of the space shuttle's cargo bay. If you need help, refer to Making and Using Tables in the **Skill Handbook.**

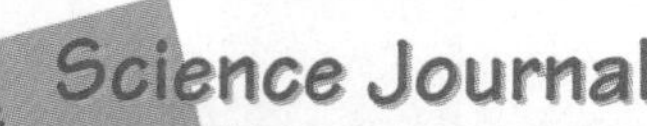

Science Journal

Suppose you're in charge of assembling a crew for a new space station. Select 100 people you want for the station. Remember, you will need people to do a variety of jobs, such as farming, maintenance, scientific experimentation, and so on. In your Science Journal, relate whom you would select and why.

Skill Builder

Outlines will vary, but students should include at least the activities described in Section 21-4. Some students may know of other uses for the arm.

Assessment

Process Use this Skill Builder to assess students' abilities to outline. Ask students to explain the benefits of outlining. Use the Performance Task Assessment List for Science Journal in **PASC,** p. 103. P

Chapter 21

Review

Summary

21-1: Radiation from Space

1. The arrangement of electromagnetic waves according to their wavelengths is the electromagnetic spectrum.
2. Optical telescopes produce magnified images of objects. A refracting telescope bends light to form an image. A reflecting telescope uses mirrors to focus light to produce an image.
3. Radio telescopes collect and record radio waves given off by some space objects.

21-2: Science and Society: Light Pollution

1. Lights are needed in towns and cities for safety and security reasons. However, light pollution can cause problems for stargazers as well as astronomers.

21-3: Artificial Satellites and Space Probes

1. A satellite is an object that revolves around another object. The moons of planets are natural satellites. Artificial satellites are those made by people.
2. An artificial satellite collects data as it orbits a planet. A space probe travels out into the solar system, gathers data, and sends it back to Earth.
3. Early American piloted space programs included the Mercury, Gemini, and Apollo projects.

21-4: The Space Shuttle and the Future

1. The space shuttle is a reusable spacecraft that carries astronauts, satellites, and other payloads to and from space.
2. Space stations provide the opportunity to conduct research not possible on Earth. The International Space Station will be constructed in Earth orbit with the cooperation of over a dozen nations.

Key Science Words

a. electromagnetic spectrum
b. light pollution
c. observatory
d. orbit
e. Project Apollo
f. Project Gemini
g. Project Mercury
h. radio telescope
i. reflecting telescope
j. refracting telescope
k. satellite
l. space probe
m. space shuttle
n. space station

Reviewing Vocabulary

Match each phrase with the correct term from the list of Key Science Words.

1. the arrangement of electromagnetic waves according to their wavelengths
2. uses lenses to bend light toward a focal plane
3. uses mirrors to collect light and form an image
4. glow in the night sky caused by city lights
5. an object that revolves around another object
6. the path traveled by a satellite
7. the first piloted U.S. space program
8. space program that reached the moon
9. carries people and tools to and from space
10. a place in space to live and work

Chapter 21

Review

Summary

Have students read the summary statements to review the major concepts of the chapter.

Reviewing Vocabulary

1. a	**6.** d
2. j	**7.** g
3. i	**8.** e
4. b	**9.** m
5. k	**10.** n

Assessment

Portfolio Encourage students to place in their portfolios one or two items of what they consider to be their best work. Examples include:

- Problem Solving, p. 587
- Activity 21-2 analysis and conclusions, pp. 601-603
- MiniLAB analysis, p. 606 P

Performance Additional performance assessments may be found in **Performance Assessment** and **Science Integration Activities.** Performance Task Assessment Lists and rubrics for evaluating these activities can be found in Glencoe's **Performance Assessment in the Science Classroom.**

GLENCOE TECHNOLOGY

Videodisc

Glencoe Earth Science

Interactive Videodisc

Use the videodisc Lesson 8, *Space Exploration,* to explore the advantages and disadvantages of space exploration and robotic versus human crews.

MindJogger Videoquiz

Chapter 21 Have students work in groups as they play the Videoquiz game to review key chapter concepts.

Chapter 21 Review

Checking Concepts

1. d
2. d
3. a
4. c
5. b
6. a
7. c
8. c
9. b
10. d

Understanding Concepts

11. Electromagnetic waves can carry energy through matter and empty space, whereas mechanical waves need matter through which to travel.
12. Reflecting and refracting telescopes both gather light from the object being viewed and magnify the image. A refracting telescope uses a lens, whereas a reflecting telescope uses a mirror to collect light. Both use an eyepiece lens to magnify the image.
13. Natural sources are clouds, precipitation, and the moon; artificial sources include city lights, security lights, streetlights, and air pollution, among others.
14. An object in motion tends to move in a straight line. But gravity acts on the object and pulls it toward Earth. The resultant force keeps the object traveling in a curved path.
15. Students' responses will vary. Reasons for flying might include the intrigue of getting to travel, live, and work in space. Reasons for declining the opportunity might include the potential dangers involved during lift-off, the stay in space, and landing.

Thinking Critically

16. Earth-based observations are obscured by the atmosphere. The atmosphere absorbs and distorts incoming radiation. Because the moon has no atmosphere, light and other forms of energy can reach its surface without distortion.
17. Most students should realize that the surface temperature of the sun and the immense heat that is radiated from it would make a space-probe encounter useless, because the probe would burn up before getting close enough to gather data.
18. Answers will vary. Robotic space probes need fewer resources and can provide more data about our outer solar system and deep space. Spaceflights with people aboard provide information about living in space and also valuable technological data.
19. No, sound requires matter through which to travel. Space is a virtual vacuum.
20. When the probes crossed Pluto's orbit, Pluto was at another point in its orbit.

Chapter 21 Review

Checking Concepts

Choose the word or phrase that completes the sentence.

1. The _______ spacecraft has sent back images of Venus.
   a. *Voyager* c. *Apollo 11*
   b. *Viking* d. *Magellan*
2. _______ telescopes use mirrors to collect light.
   a. Radio c. Refracting
   b. Electromagnetic d. Reflecting
3. A(n) _______ telescope can be used during the day or at night and during bad weather.
   a. radio c. refracting
   b. electromagnetic d. reflecting
4. _______ reduce light pollution.
   a. Radio telescopes
   b. Observatories
   c. Low-pressure sodium lamps
   d. Security lights
5. *Sputnik I* was the first _______.
   a. telescope c. observatory
   b. artificial satellite d. U.S. space probe
6. Goals of _______ were to put a spacecraft in orbit and bring it safely back.
   a. Project Mercury c. Project Gemini
   b. Project Apollo d. *Viking I*
7. The _______ of the space shuttle are reused.
   a. liquid-fuel tanks c. booster engines
   b. *Gemini* rockets d. *Saturn* rockets
8. The _______ of the space shuttle can place a satellite into space and retrieve it.
   a. liquid-fuel tank c. mechanical arm
   b. booster rocket d. cargo bay
9. *Skylab* was a(n) _______ that fell from its orbit.
   a. space probe c. space shuttle
   b. space station d. optical telescope
10. A natural satellite of Earth is _______.
    a. *Skylab* c. the sun
    b. the space shuttle d. the moon

Understanding Concepts

Answer the following questions in your Science Journal using complete sentences.

11. How do electromagnetic waves differ from mechanical waves? Give an example to support your answer.
12. Compare and contrast two types of optical telescopes.
13. List one natural and two artificial sources that prevent clear observations of the night sky.
14. Explain what two motions keep a satellite in orbit around Earth.
15. If given the chance, would you choose to fly on a shuttle mission? Give reasons for your answer.

Thinking Critically

16. How would a moon-based telescope have advantages over the Earth-based telescopes being used today?
17. Would a space probe to the sun's surface be useful? Explain.
18. Suppose NASA had to choose between continuing either the space flight programs with people aboard or the robotic space probes. Which do you think is the more valuable program? Explain your choice.
19. Suppose two astronauts were outside of the space shuttle orbiter while orbiting Earth. The audio speaker in the helmet of one of the astronauts quits working. The other astronaut is only one meter away, so she shouts a message to him. Can he hear her? Explain.
20. No space probes have visited the planet Pluto, the outermost planet of our solar system. Nevertheless, probes have crossed Pluto's orbit. Explain how this is possible.

Chapter 21 Review

Developing Skills

If you need help, refer to the **Skill Handbook.**

21. **Sequencing:** Arrange these events in order from earliest to the most recent: Galileo Galilei discovered four moons orbiting Jupiter, *Sputnik I* orbited Earth, humans landed on the moon, *Galileo* began its journey to Jupiter, Yuri Gagarin orbited Earth, Project Apollo began, *Discovery* launched the *Hubble Space Telescope,* astronauts and cosmonauts worked together on *Mir.*
22. **Measuring in SI:** Explain whether or not each of the following pieces of equipment could be used aboard the space shuttle as it orbits Earth: a balance, a graduated cylinder, a meterstick, and a thermometer.
23. **Concept Mapping:** Make an events chain map that explains what happens to different parts of the space shuttle, including the orbiter, liquid-fuel tank, and solid-fuel booster engines, from takeoff to landing.
24. **Making and Using Tables:** Copy the table below. Use information in the chapter as well as news articles and other resources to complete your table.

U.S. Space Probes

Probe	Launch Date	Destinations	Planets or Objects Visited
Mariner 4			
Vikings 1 & 2			
Pioneers 10 & 11			
Voyagers 1 & 2			
Magellan			
Galileo			

25. **Classifying:** Classify each of the following as a satellite or a space probe: Mercury spacecraft, *Sputnik I,* the *Hubble Telescope,* the space shuttle orbiter, and *Voyager 2.*

Performance Assessment

1. **Experiment:** Use several different-sized concave mirrors and determine which mirror concentrates more light into the image.
2. **Formulating a Hypothesis:** In Activity 21-2, you planned, carried out, and analyzed a robot surface probe mission to Mars. Based on how successful your mission was, what type of problems might hamper the success of a true robot mission to Mars? Would a crewed mission be more or less likely to be hampered by the same problems? Explain.
3. **Model:** Design and build a model of a space station. Include a way for people and equipment to be moved into and out of the station.

Developing Skills

21. **Sequencing** Galileo discovered four moons orbiting Jupiter; *Sputnik* I orbited Earth; Yuri Gagarin orbited Earth; Project *Apollo* began; humans landed on the moon; *Galileo* began its journey to Jupiter; *Discovery* launched the *Hubble Space Telescope;* astronauts and cosmonauts work together on *Mir.*
22. **Measuring in SI** The balance and the graduated cylinder couldn't be used because the objects and fluids to be measured wouldn't stay on the pans or in the cylinder. However, distances and temperature are not affected by the weightless environment of space.
23. **Concept Mapping** Students' maps should include the following steps. Orbiter takes off. At height of about 45 km, booster rockets drop off and parachute to Earth. Liquid-fuel tank eventually drops off. When mission is over, shuttle orbiter returns to Earth.
24. **Making and Using Tables** *Mariner 4* was launched in 1964. Its destination was Mars. *Vikings 1* and *2* were launched in 1975, destined for Mars. *Pioneers 10* and *11* launched in 1973 and 1974. *Pioneer 10* was destined to leave the solar system. *Pioneer 11's* destination was Saturn. Both *Pioneers* visited Jupiter. *Voyagers 1* and *2* launched in 1977. Both were destined to leave our solar system. *Voyagers 1* and *2* visited Jupiter and Saturn. *Voyager 2* also visited Uranus and Neptune. *Magellan* launched in 1989, destined for Venus. *Galileo* launched in 1989. Its destination was Jupiter. *Galileo* flew by Venus.
25. **Classifying** All are satellites except *Voyager 2.* It did not orbit any object and is therefore a probe.

Performance Assessment

1. Students should note that the largest mirror concentrates the most light into the image. Use the Performance Task Assessment List for Designing an Experiment in **PASC,** p. 23. P
2. Concerning problems, student answers will vary; however, problem areas might include times when on-site decisions need to be made. Piloted missions would be better able to make on-site decisions. Use the Performance Task Assessment List for Formulating a Hypothesis in **PASC,** p. 21. P
3. Student models will vary but should be based on scientific facts. Use the Performance Task Assessment List for Model in **PASC,** p. 51. P

Chapter Organizer

Section	Objectives	Activities/Features
Chapter Opener		Explore Activity: Determine what causes seasons. p. 613
22-1 **Planet Earth** (2 sessions, 1 block)*	1. **Describe** Earth's shape and list physical data about Earth. 2. **Compare** and **contrast** the rotation and revolution of Earth. 3. **Demonstrate** how Earth's revolution and tilt cause seasons to change on Earth.	MiniLAB: What is the shape of Earth? p. 615 Using Math, p. 616 Using Technology: Clocks: Old and New, p. 618 Science Journal, p. 619 Activity 22-1: Tilt and Temperature, pp. 620-621 Skill Builder: Recognizing Cause and Effect, p. 622 Using Computers: Spreadsheet, p. 622
22-2 **Earth's Moon** (1 session, ½ block)*	1. **Demonstrate** how the moon's phases depend on the relative positions of the sun, the moon, and Earth. 2. **Describe** why eclipses occur, and compare solar and lunar eclipses. 3. **Hypothesize** what surface features of the moon tell us about its history.	Using Math, p. 624 MiniLAB: How does the moon affect the ocean? p. 625 Connect to Physics, p. 626 Using Math, p. 627 Problem Solving: Survival on the Moon, p. 628 Activity 22-2: Moon Phases and Eclipses, p. 629 Skill Builder: Measuring in SI, p. 631 Science Journal, p. 631
22-3 **Science and Society Technology: Exploration of the Moon** (2 sessions, 1 block)*	1. **List** and discuss new information about the moon discovered by the *Clementine* spacecraft. 2. **List** two facts about the moon's south pole that may be important to future space travel.	Explore the Technology, p. 633 Science and Literature: The Sun and the Moon: A Korean Folktale, p. 634 Science Journal, p. 634

* A complete Planning Guide that includes block scheduling is provided on pages 32T-35T.

Activity Materials

Explore	Activities	MiniLABs
page 613 lamp without a shade, globe of Earth, metric measuring tape	pages 620-621 tape, black construction paper, gooseneck lamp with 75-watt bulb, Celsius thermometer, stopwatch or clock with second hand, protractor, thermal mitt page 629 unshaded light source, polystyrene ball on a pencil, globe of Earth, **Figure 22-6**	page 615 piece of string about 1 m in length, meterstick, basketball page 625 graph from Chapter 17 Review

Chapter 22 The Sun-Earth-Moon System

Teacher Classroom Resources

Reproducible Masters	Transparencies	Teaching Resources
Study Guide, p. 86 **Reinforcement,** p. 86 **Enrichment,** p. 86 **Activity Worksheets,** pp. 132-133, 136 **Lab Manual 61,** Earth's Spin **Lab Manual 62,** Earth's Magnetism **Science Integration Activity 22,** Aristotle vs. Galileo: The Clash of the Science Heavyweights **Concept Mapping,** p. 49 **Critical Thinking/Problem Solving,** p. 28	**Section Focus Transparency 82,** How to Fit More Hours in Your Day **Teaching Transparency 43,** Earth-Sun Relationship	**Glencoe Earth Science Interactive Videodisc** **Earth Science CD-ROM** **Spanish Resources** **English/Spanish Audiocassettes** **Cooperative Learning Resource Guide** **Lab Partner** **Lab and Safety Skills** **Lesson Plans**
Study Guide, p. 87 **Reinforcement,** p. 87 **Enrichment,** p. 87 **Activity Worksheets,** pp. 134-135, 137 **Lab Manual 63,** Moon Phases **Lab Manual 64,** Newton's First Law of Motion **Cross-Curricular Integration,** p. 26 **Multicultural Connections,** pp. 47-48	**Section Focus Transparency 83,** Moonlight, Moon Bright **Science Integration Transparency 22,** Tides and Grunion Life Cycle **Teaching Transparency 44,** Moon Phases	**Assessment Resources** **Chapter Review,** pp. 47-48 **Assessment,** pp. 147-150 **Performance Assessment in the Science Classroom (PASC)** **MindJogger Videoquiz** **Alternate Assessment in the Science Classroom** **Performance Assessment** **Chapter Review Software** **Computer Test Bank**
Study Guide, p. 88 **Reinforcement,** p. 88 **Enrichment,** p. 88 **Science and Society Integration,** p. 26	**Section Focus Transparency 84,** Life on the Moon	

Key to Teaching Strategies

The following designations will help you decide which activities are appropriate for your students.

L1 Level 1 activities should be within the ability range of all students.

L2 Level 2 activities should be within the ability range of the average to above-average student.

L3 Level 3 activities are designed for the ability range of above-average students.

LEP LEP activities should be within the ability range of Limited English Proficiency students.

LS These activities are designed to address different learning styles.

COOP LEARN Cooperative Learning activities are designed for small group work.

P These strategies represent student products that can be placed into a best-work portfolio.

GLENCOE TECHNOLOGY

The following multimedia resources are available from Glencoe.

Science and Technology Videodisc Series (STVS)
Earth & Space
Effects of Solar Eclipses

National Geographic Society Series
STV: Solar System
GTV: Planetary Manager
Earth Science CD-ROM

Teacher Classroom Resources

This is a representation of key blackline masters available in the Teacher Classroom Resources.

Teaching Aids

Section Focus Transparencies

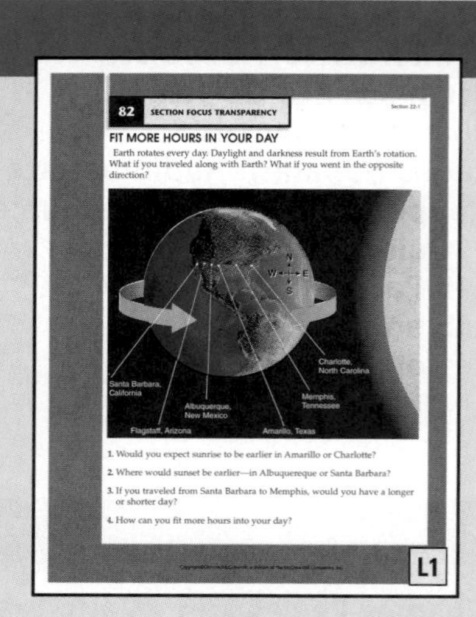
82 SECTION FOCUS TRANSPARENCY

Section 22-1

FIT MORE HOURS IN YOUR DAY

Earth rotates every day. Daylight and darkness result from Earth's rotation. What if you traveled along with Earth? What if you went in the opposite direction?

1. Would you expect sunrise to be earlier in Amarillo or Charlotte?
2. Where would sunset be earlier—in Albuquereque or Santa Barbara?
3. If you traveled from Santa Barbara to Memphis, would you have a longer or shorter day?
4. How can you fit more hours into your day?

L1

83 SECTION FOCUS TRANSPARENCY

Section 22-2

MOONLIGHT, MOON BRIGHT

Full moon, waxing moon, waning moon . . . What do these expressions mean? Why does the shape of the moon seem to change?

1. Use your own experiences and observations to describe the moon. Where and when do you see the moon?
2. Compare the shape of the moon at the top of the picture with the shape of the moon at the bottom. How are the two shapes alike and different?
3. How might Earth affect the shape of the moon?

L2

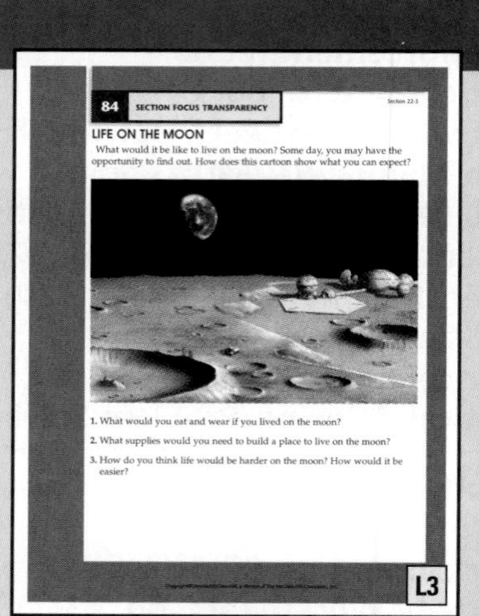
84 SECTION FOCUS TRANSPARENCY

Section 22-3

LIFE ON THE MOON

What would it be like to live on the moon? Some day, you may have the opportunity to find out. How does this cartoon show what you can expect?

1. What would you eat and wear if you lived on the moon?
2. What supplies would you need to build a place to live on the moon?
3. How do you think life would be harder on the moon? How would it be easier?

L3

Science Integration Transparencies

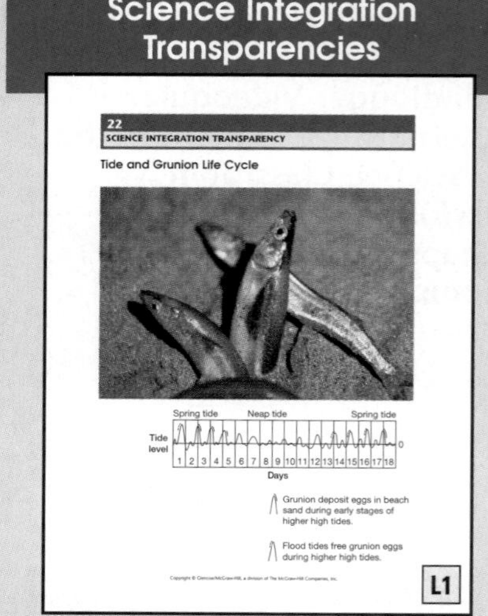
22 SCIENCE INTEGRATION TRANSPARENCY

Tide and Grunion Life Cycle

L1

Teaching Transparencies

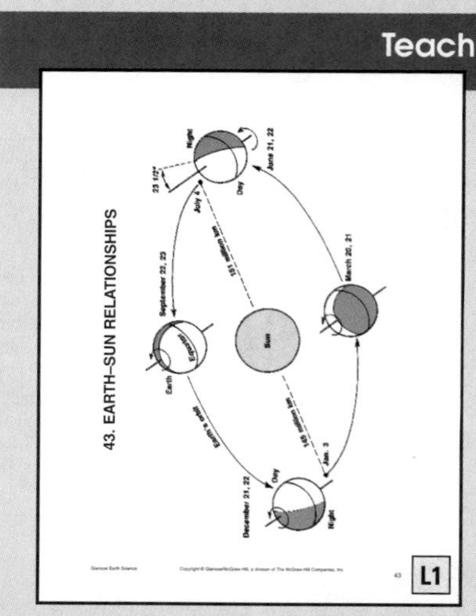

L1

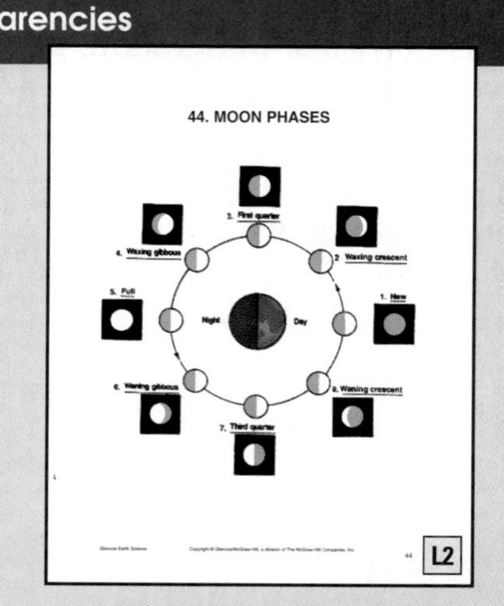
44. MOON PHASES

L2

Meeting Different Ability Levels

Study Guide

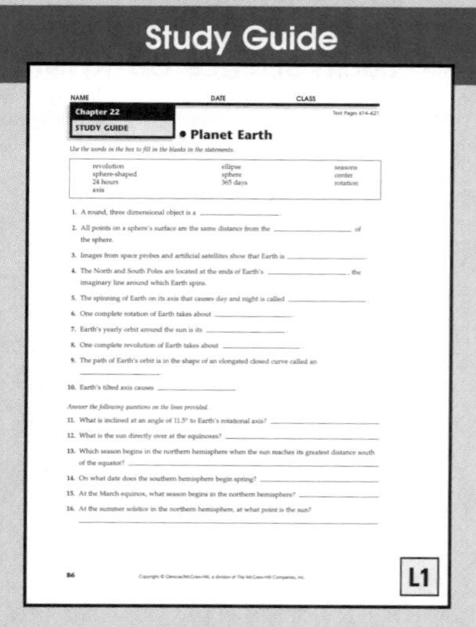
NAME DATE CLASS

Chapter 22

STUDY GUIDE

Text Pages 614–621

• Planet Earth

Use the words in the box to fill in the blanks in the statements.

revolution	ellipse	seasons
sphere-shaped	sphere	center
24 hours	365 days	rotation
axis		

1. A round, three dimensional object is a ________.
2. All points on a sphere's surface are the same distance from the ________ of the sphere.
3. Images from space probes and artificial satellites show that Earth is ________.
4. The North and South Poles are located at the ends of Earth's ________, the imaginary line around which Earth spins.
5. The spinning of Earth on its axis that causes day and night is called ________.
6. One complete rotation of Earth takes about ________.
7. Earth's yearly orbit around the sun is its ________.
8. One complete revolution of Earth takes about ________.
9. The path of Earth's orbit is in the shape of an elongated closed curve called an ________
10. Earth's tilted axis causes ________

Answer the following questions on the lines provided.

11. What is inclined at an angle of 11.5° to Earth's rotational axis? ________
12. What is the sun directly over at the equinoxes? ________
13. Which season begins in the northern hemisphere when the sun reaches its greatest distance south of the equator? ________
14. On what date does the southern hemisphere begin spring? ________
15. At the March equinox, what season begins in the northern hemisphere? ________
16. At the summer solstice in the northern hemisphere, at what point is the sun? ________

86

L1

Reinforcement

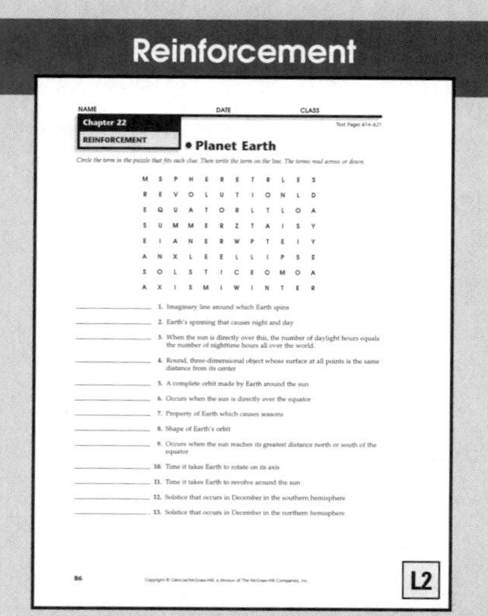
NAME DATE CLASS

Chapter 22

REINFORCEMENT

Text Pages 614–621

• Planet Earth

Circle the term in the puzzle that fits each clue. Then write the term on the line. The terms read across or down.

M	S	P	H	E	R	E	T	R	L	E	S
R	E	V	O	L	U	T	I	O	N	L	D
E	Q	U	A	T	O	R	L	T	L	O	A
S	U	M	M	E	R	Z	T	A	I	S	Y
E	I	A	N	E	R	W	P	T	E	I	Y
A	N	X	L	E	E	L	L	I	P	S	E
S	O	L	S	T	I	C	E	O	M	O	A
A	X	I	S	M	I	W	I	N	T	E	R

________ 1. Imaginary line around which Earth spins

________ 2. Earth's spinning that causes night and day

________ 3. When the sun is directly over this, the number of daylight hours equals the number of nighttime hours all over the world.

________ 4. Round, three-dimensional object whose surface at all points is the same distance from its center

________ 5. A complete orbit made by Earth around the sun

________ 6. Occurs when the sun is directly over the equator

________ 7. Property of Earth which causes seasons

________ 8. Shape of Earth's orbit

________ 9. Occurs when the sun reaches its greatest distance north or south of the equator

________ 10. Time it takes Earth to rotate on its axis

________ 11. Time it takes Earth to revolve around the sun

________ 12. Solstice that occurs in December in the southern hemisphere

________ 13. Solstice that occurs in December in the northern hemisphere

86

L2

Enrichment Worksheets

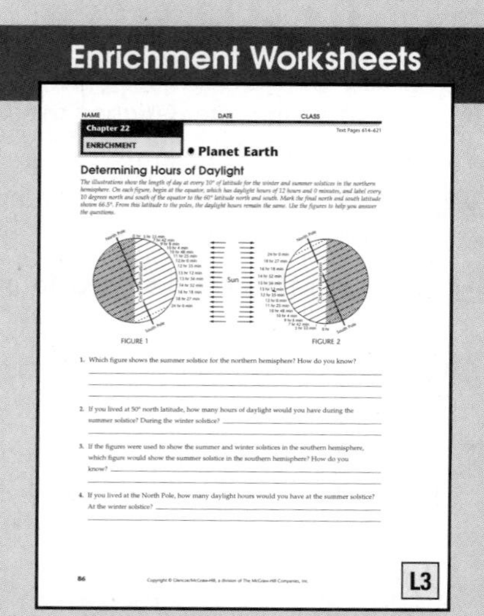
NAME DATE CLASS

Chapter 22

ENRICHMENT

Text Pages 614–621

• Planet Earth

Determining Hours of Daylight

The illustrations show the length of day at every 10° of latitude for the winter and summer solstices in the northern hemisphere. On each figure, begin at the equator, which has daylight hours of 12 hours and 0 minutes, and label every 10 degrees north and south of the equator to the 60° latitude north and south. Mark the final north and south latitude shown 66.5°. From this latitude to the poles, the daylight hours remain the same. Use the figures to help you answer the questions.

1. Which figure shows the summer solstice for the northern hemisphere? How do you know?
2. If you lived at 50° north latitude, how many hours of daylight would you have during the summer solstice? During the winter solstice? ________
3. If the figures were used to show the summer and winter solstices in the southern hemisphere, which figure would show the summer solstice in the southern hemisphere? How do you know? ________
4. If you lived at the North Pole, how many daylight hours would you have at the summer solstice? At the winter solstice? ________

86

L3

Hands-On Activities

Science Integration Activity

Chapter 22 INTEGRATION • Aristotle vs. Galileo

The Clash of the Science Heavyweights

Getting Started

Hypothesizing

Try It!

L1

Lab Manual

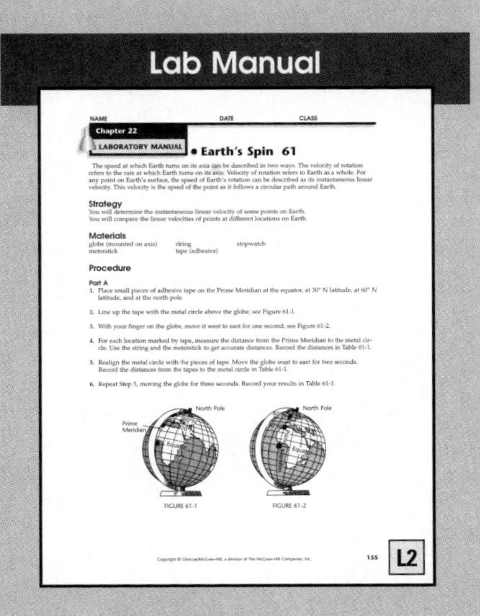

Assessment

Performance Assessment

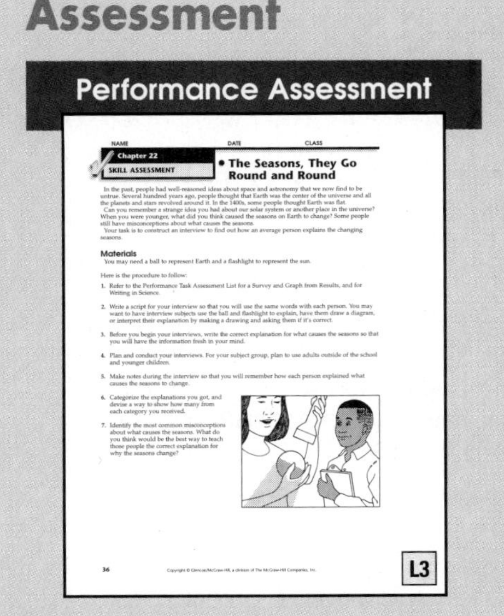

Enrichment and Application

Critical Thinking/ Problem Solving

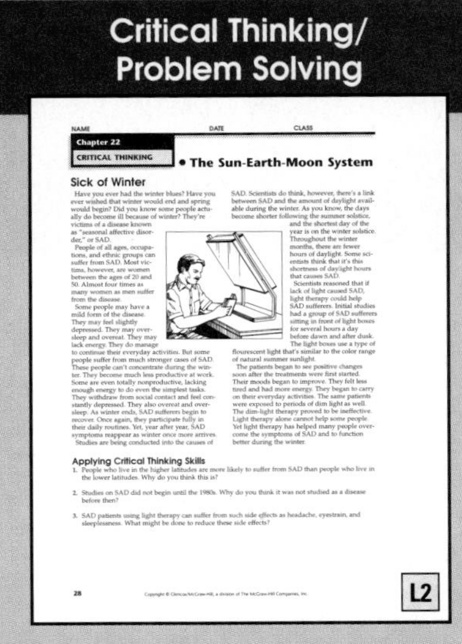

Cross-Curricular Integration

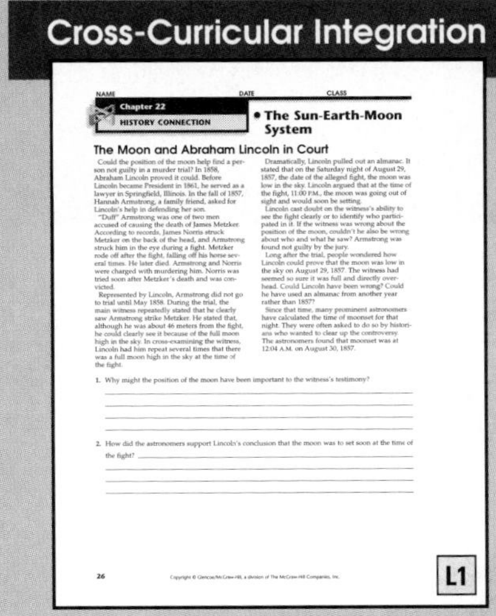

Science and Society Integration

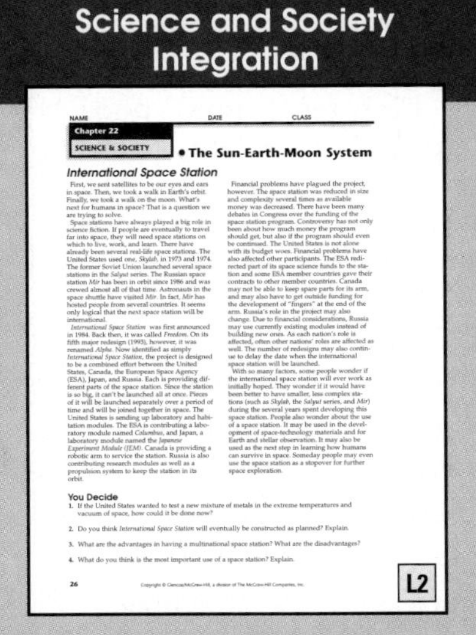

Multicultural Connections

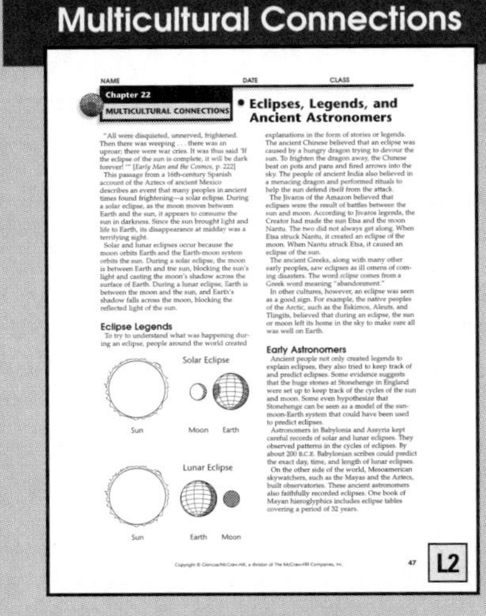

Concept Mapping

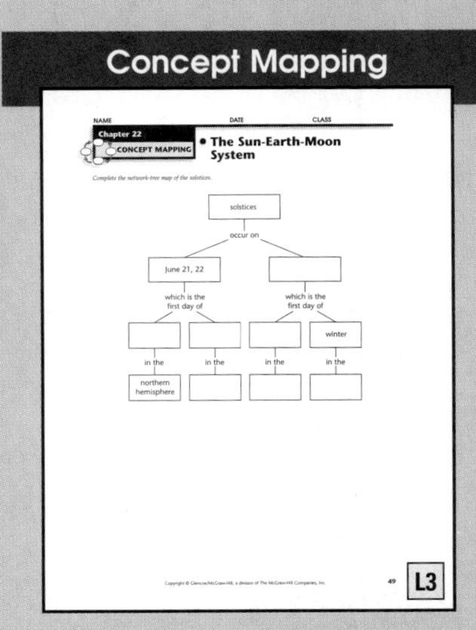

Chapter 22

The Sun-Earth-Moon System

CHAPTER OVERVIEW

Section 22-1 Some of the physical data of Earth is presented. The planet's rotation and revolution also are described. The causes for seasons are explained in terms of Earth's position in space with respect to the sun and the tilt of Earth's axis.

Section 22-2 The reasons why the moon goes through phases are presented. The types and causes of eclipses are described. The structure and origin of Earth's only natural satellite is also explored.

Section 22-3 **Science and Society** The mission of the *Clementine* spacecraft is explored. While in orbit around the moon, it took high-resolution photographs of the moon. These photographs were used to compile a detailed map of the moon's surface.

Chapter Vocabulary

sphere	waxing
axis	first quarter
rotation	full moon
revolution	waning
ellipse	third quarter
equinox	solar eclipse
solstice	lunar eclipse
moon phase	maria
new moon	mascon

Theme Connection

Systems and Interactions Earth's rotation and revolution cause daily and seasonal changes due to the interaction of the sun, the moon, and Earth. Phases of the moon occur monthly and also rely on the interaction among the sun, the moon, and Earth.

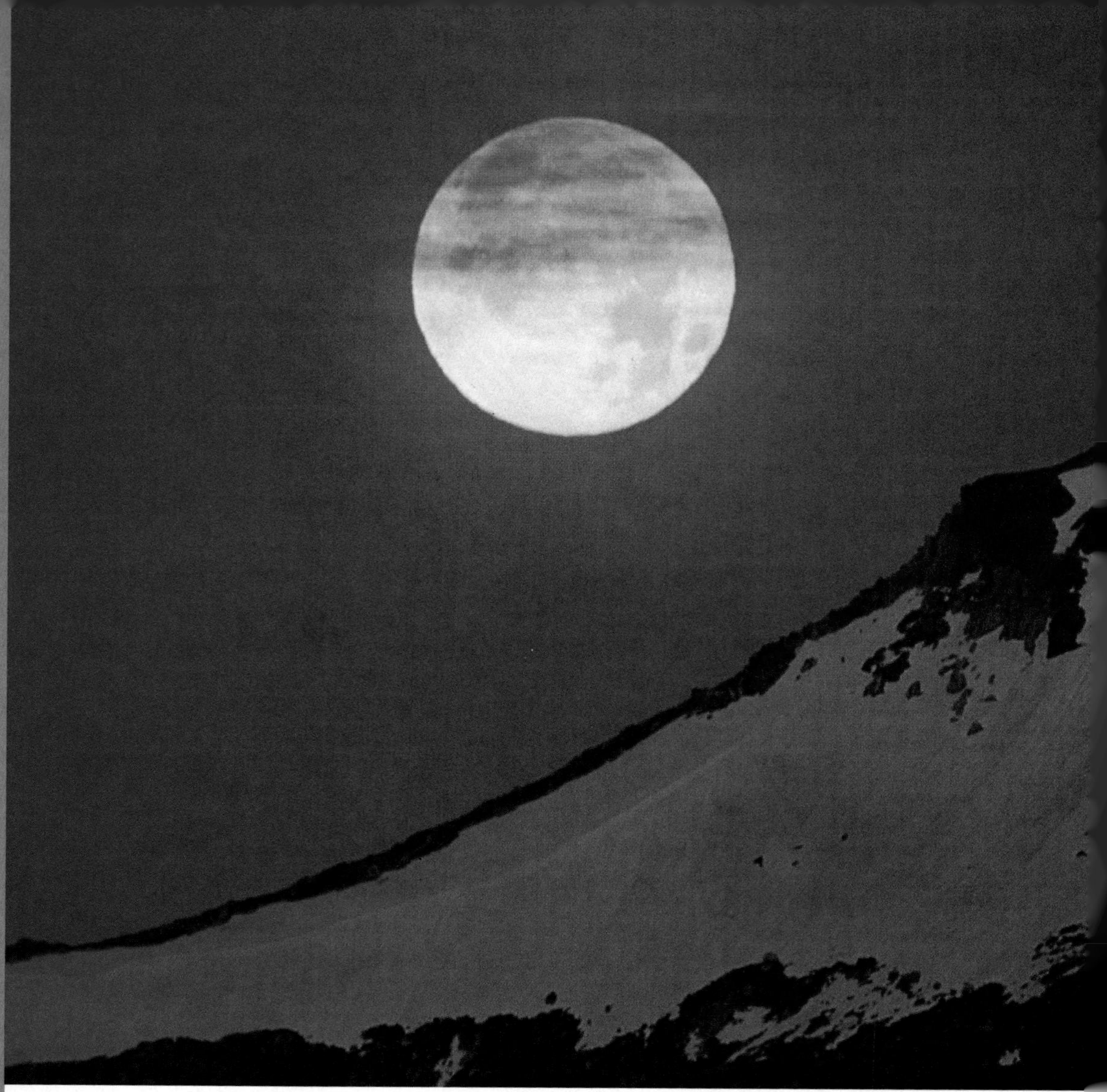

Previewing the Chapter

Look for the following logo for strategies that emphasize different learning modalities. 

Kinesthetic	Activity 22-2, p. 629
Visual-Spatial	Explore, p. 613; Integrating the Sciences, p. 616; Across the Curriculum, p. 618; Reteach, p. 619; Making and Using Science Illustrations, p. 626; Demonstration, p. 627
Interpersonal	Activities, pp. 616, 617
Logical-Mathematical	MiniLABs, pp. 615, 625; Across the Curriculum, p. 615; Activity 22-1, pp. 620-621
Linguistic	Science Journal, pp. 625, 628; Integrating the Sciences, p. 630; Science & Literature, p. 634

Chapter 22 The Sun-Earth-Moon System

The position of Earth and the moon in space affects our lives in many ways. For instance, as Earth revolves around the sun on its tilted axis, we experience the changing of the seasons. But seasons are not the same on different parts of Earth. When it's winter in the northern hemisphere, it's summer in the southern hemisphere, and vice versa. Why is this the case?

EXPLORE ACTIVITY

Determine what causes seasons.

1. Use a lamp without a shade to represent the sun.
2. Turn the lamp on, and hold a globe of Earth about 2 m from the lamp.
3. Tilt the globe slightly so the northern half points toward the sun.
4. Keeping the globe tilted in the same direction, walk halfway around the sun. Take care not to turn or twist the globe as you walk.

Observe: In which direction is the northern hemisphere pointing relative to the sun in step 3? In step 4? In your Science Journal, describe which seasons these positions represent for the northern hemisphere.

Previewing Science Skills

- In the **Skill Builders**, you will **recognize cause and effect** and **measure in SI**.
- In the **Activities**, you will **make models**, **analyze and interpret data**, and **make inferences**.
- In the **MiniLABs**, you will **measure in SI**, **analyze data**, **interpret graphs**, and **draw conclusions**.

Assessment Planner

Portfolio
Refer to page 635 for suggested items that students might select for their portfolios.

Performance Assessment
See page 635 for additional Performance Assessment options.
Skill Builders, pp. 622, 631
MiniLABs, pp. 615, 625
Activities 22-1, pp. 620-621; 22-2, p. 629

Content Assessment
Section Wrap-ups, pp. 622, 631, 633
Chapter Review, pp. 635-637
Mini Quizzes, pp. 622, 631

Group Assessment
Opportunities for group assessment occur with Cooperative Learning Strategies and Flex Your Brain Activities.

EXPLORE ACTIVITY

Purpose

LS **Visual-Spatial** Use the Explore Activity to introduce students to the causes of seasons. L1 LEP COOP LEARN

Preparation

Have students bring in small lamps from home. Also obtain several globes of Earth.

Materials

one lamp without shade and one globe for each group of students

Teaching Strategies

- Form student groups with three students per group. As two students perform the activity, the third should record what he or she observes.

Safety Precautions Caution students to handle the lamp with care. The bulb will be very hot.

Troubleshooting Be sure students understand that the orientation or "tilt" of the globe must remain constant.

Observe

In step 3, the northern hemisphere is pointing toward the sun. In step 4, the northern hemisphere is pointing away from the sun. When the northern hemisphere points toward the sun, it experiences summer. When the northern hemisphere points away from the sun, it experiences winter.

Assessment

Performance Ask students to determine the seasons for the southern hemisphere in steps 3 and 4. Use the Performance Task Assessment List for Carrying Out a Strategy and Collecting Data in **PASC**, p. 25. P

Section 22•1

Prepare

Section Background

- Convection currents of molten iron deep in Earth's core produce huge electrical currents. These electrical currents, in turn, cause Earth's magnetic field.
- At the equator seasons aren't marked by great climatic changes. The sun is overhead 12 hours per day, and the amount of solar energy received does not vary much from one day to the next.

Preplanning

- To prepare for Activity 22-1, obtain a gooseneck lamp and 75-watt bulb for each group of students.
- Also obtain a ball of string to be used in the MiniLAB, and basketballs or other large playground balls to be used in various demonstrations throughout the section.

1 Motivate

Bellringer

Before presenting the lesson, display **Section Focus Transparency 82** on the overhead projector. Assign the accompanying **Focus Activity** worksheet. L1 LEP

Tying to Previous Knowledge

Have students recall physical properties of matter from Chapter 2. Remind them that physical properties can be measured without changing a substance into a new substance. Have students list some physical properties of Earth.

22•1 Planet Earth

Science Words

sphere
axis
rotation
revolution
ellipse
equinox
solstice

Objectives

- Describe Earth's shape and list physical data about Earth.
- Compare and contrast the rotation and revolution of Earth.
- Demonstrate how Earth's revolution and tilt cause seasons to change on Earth.

Planet Earth Data

You rise early in the morning while it's still dark outside. You sit by the window and watch the sun come up. Finally, day breaks, and the sun begins its journey across the sky. But is the sun moving, or are you?

Today, we know that the sun appears to move across the sky because Earth is spinning as it travels around the sun. But it wasn't long ago that people believed Earth was the center of the universe. They believed Earth stood still and the sun traveled around it.

As recently as the days of Christopher Columbus, some people also believed Earth was flat. They thought that if you sailed far out to sea, you would eventually fall off the edge of the world. How do you know this isn't true? How have scientists determined Earth's shape?

Earth's Shape

Space probes and artificial satellites have sent back images that show Earth is sphere-shaped. A **sphere** is a round, three-dimensional object whose surface at all points is the same distance from its center. Tennis balls and basketballs are examples of spheres. But people had evidence of Earth's true shape long before cameras were sent into space.

Around 350 B.C., the Greek astronomer and philosopher Aristotle reasoned that Earth was spherical because it always

Figure 22-1
If Earth were flat, its shadow would look like this on the moon during an eclipse.

Program Resources

Reproducible Masters

Study Guide, p. 86 L1
Reinforcement, p. 86 L1
Enrichment, p. 86 L3
Critical Thinking/ Problem Solving, p. 28
Activity Worksheets, pp. 5, 132-133, 136
Concept Mapping, p. 49
Science Integration Activities, pp. 43-44
Lab Manual 61, 62

Transparencies

Section Focus Transparency 82 L1
Teaching Transparency 43 L1
Science Integration Transparency 22

Table 22-1

Physical Properties of Earth	
Diameter (pole to pole)	12 714 km
Diameter (equator)	12 756 km
Circumference (poles)	40 008 km
Circumference (equator)	40 075 km
Mass	5.98×10^{27} g
Density	5.52 g/cm^3
Average distance to the sun	149 600 000 km
Period of rotation (1 day)	23 hr, 56 min
Period of revolution (1 year)	365 day, 6 hr, 9 min

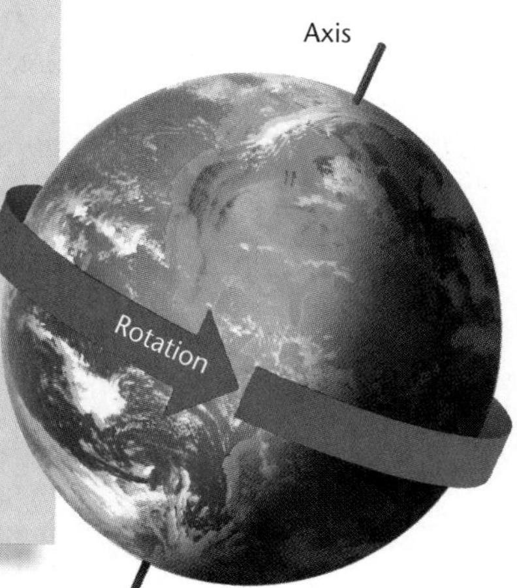

casts a round shadow on the moon during an eclipse. Only a spherical object always produces a round shadow. If Earth were flat, it would cast a shadow like the one in **Figure 22-1.**

Other evidence of Earth's shape was observed by early sailors. They watched ships approach from across the ocean and saw that the top of the ship would come into view first. As they continued to watch the ship, more and more of it would come into view. As the ship moved over the curved surface of Earth, they could see all of it.

Today, we know that Earth is sphere-shaped, but it is not a perfect sphere. It bulges slightly at the equator and is somewhat flattened at the poles. The poles are located at the north and south ends of Earth's axis. Earth's **axis** is the imaginary line around which Earth spins. The spinning of Earth on its axis, called **rotation,** causes day and night to occur.

Earth's Rotation

As Earth rotates, the sun comes into view at daybreak. Earth continues to spin, making it seem that the sun moves across the sky until it appears to set at night. During night, your area of Earth has spun away from the sun. Because of this, the sun is no longer visible. Earth continues to steadily rotate, and the sun eventually comes into view the next morning. One complete rotation takes about 24 hours, or one day. How many rotations does Earth complete during one year? As you can see in **Table 22-1,** it completes about 365 rotations during its journey around the sun.

MiniLAB

What is the shape of Earth?

Compare Earth's shape with other spheres.

Procedure

1. Use a long piece of string to measure the circumference of a basketball or volleyball. Use any two circumferences that are at right angles to each other.
2. Compare this data with the data about Earth's circumference provided in **Table 22-1.**

Analysis

1. How round is Earth compared with the basketball or volleyball?
2. Is Earth larger through the equator or through the poles?
3. Explain how your observations support your answer.

Across the Curriculum

Geography Help students recall how the length of a day changes from winter to summer for the area of the world in which they live. Encourage them to write letters to city or other government officials in other parts of the world (friends or relatives would work as well) to find out how much the number of daylight hours changes from winter to summer in their area. Once the students collect data on the number of daylight hours in other parts of the world, have them produce a bar graph showing this data. Ask volunteers to select areas from the graph and discuss how living conditions might be affected by the differences in the number of daylight and nighttime hours. L2 LS

2 Teach

MiniLAB

Purpose

LS **Logical-Mathematical** Students will compare the shape of Earth with that of other spheres. L1

Materials

string, ruler, globe of Earth, basketball or volleyball, **Table 22-1**

Teaching Strategies

Troubleshooting Best results are obtained by using string with limited "stretchability." Stress that precise measurements must be made because approximations will not produce accurate results.

Analysis

1. Earth has a circumference ratio of 1.003. Usually, student measurements will confirm that the basketball and volleyball are actually less of a sphere than Earth.
2. Earth is larger through the equator.
3. Answers will vary.

Assessment

Performance Have students measure other kinds of balls: tennis ball, kickball, baseball, or racquet ball, for example. Have them arrange their data in a table and then graph the results. Use the Performance Task Assessment List for Graph from Data in **PASC,** p. 39. P

Activity Worksheets, pp. 5, 136

Use **Science Integration Activities,** pp. 43-44, as you teach this lesson.

Activity

IS **Interpersonal** Have students demonstrate evidence of Earth's shape. First, put students into groups of two. Have one student in each pair hold a basketball at eye level, about 0.33 m from his or her face. Have the second student slowly move a small object up and over the basketball from the opposite side. The first student should see the top of the object first, then the bottom. Have students reverse roles. Relate this to how the top of a ship approaching from across the ocean is the first part seen. Then have the students use a flashlight to cast shadows of a book and a ball against a wall. Have students relate this to the fact that Earth casts a curved shadow on the moon during a lunar eclipse. L1 LEP

Student Text Question

What occurrences can you explain in terms of Earth's physical properties and movement in space? *Answers will vary. Responses might include that day and night are caused by Earth's rotation and seasons are caused in part by the tilt of Earth's axis.*

USING MATH

15°

GLENCOE TECHNOLOGY

CD-ROM

Earth Science CD-ROM

Have students perform the interactive exploration for Chapter 22 to reinforce important chapter concepts and thinking processes.

USING MATH

Earth rotates through an angle of 360° in one day. Through how many degrees does Earth rotate in one hour?

Earth's Magnetic Field

Recall from Chapter 11 that convection currents inside Earth's mantle power the movement of tectonic plates. Scientists hypothesize that movement of material inside Earth also generates a magnetic field.

The magnetic field of Earth is much like that of a bar magnet. Earth has a north and a south magnetic pole, just as a bar magnet has opposite magnetic poles at its ends. **Figure 22-2** illustrates the effects of sprinkling iron shavings over a bar magnet. The shavings align with the magnetic field of the magnet. Earth's magnetic field is similar, almost as if Earth had a giant bar magnet in its core.

Magnetic North

When you observe a compass needle pointing toward the north, you are seeing evidence of Earth's magnetic field. Earth's magnetic axis, the line joining its north and south magnetic poles, does not align with its rotational axis. The magnetic axis is inclined at an angle of 11.5° to the rotational axis. If you followed a compass needle pointing north, you would end up at the magnetic north pole rather than the geographic (rotational) north pole.

Earth's magnetic field and other physical properties affect us every day. What occurrences can you explain in terms of Earth's physical properties and movement in space?

Figure 22-2

Particles in the solar winds streaming through space from the sun distort Earth's magnetic field. As a result, it doesn't have the same shape as a magnetic field surrounding a bar magnet.

Integrating the Sciences

Physics Make a sketch of Earth on an overhead transparency. Label the geographic poles. Place the transparency over a bar magnet on an overhead projector. Rotate the figure so that the magnet makes an 11.5° angle with the rotational axis of Earth. Sprinkle iron shavings over the transparency and tap it lightly. Have a volunteer explain the relationship between this demonstration and Earth's magnetic field. Be sure to tape a border around the transparency so iron filings do not get into the projector. LEP IS

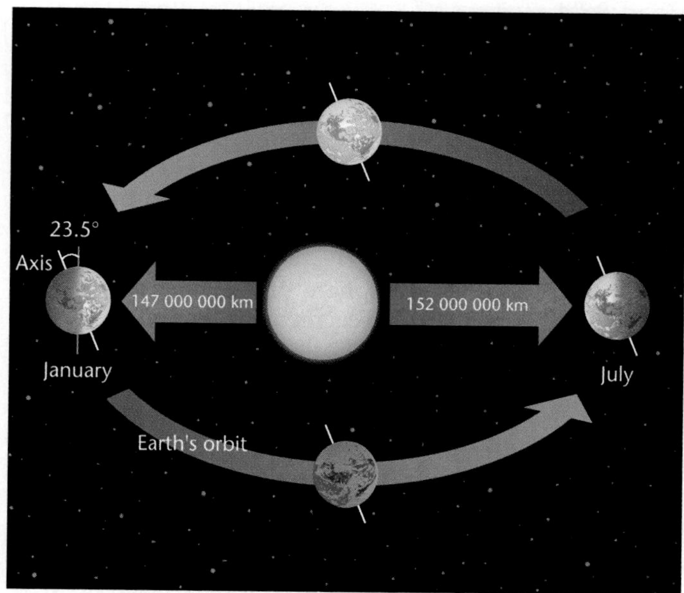

Figure 22-3

The northern hemisphere experiences summer when Earth is farthest from the sun. It experiences winter when Earth is closest to the sun. *Is the change of seasons caused by Earth's elliptical orbit? Explain your answer.*

Seasons

Autumn is coming and each day it gets colder outside. The sun rises later each morning and is lower in the sky. A month ago, it was light enough to ride your bike at 8:00 P.M. Now it's dark at 6:30 P.M. What is causing this change?

Earth's Revolution

You learned earlier that Earth's rotation causes day and night to occur. Another important motion of Earth is its **revolution,** or yearly orbit around the sun. Just as the moon is a satellite of Earth, Earth is a satellite of the sun. If Earth's orbit were a circle, and the sun were at the center of the circle, Earth would maintain a constant distance from the sun. However, this is not the case. Earth's orbit is an **ellipse,** an elongated closed curve. As **Figure 22-3** shows, the sun is offset from the center of the ellipse. Because of this, the distance between Earth and the sun changes during Earth's yearlong orbit. Earth gets closest to the sun—about 147 million km away—on January 3. The farthest point in Earth's orbit is about 152 million km away from the sun and is reached on July 4. Is this elliptical orbit causing the changing temperatures on Earth? If it were, you would expect the warmest days in January. You know this isn't the case in the northern hemisphere. Something else is causing the change.

Even though Earth is closest to the sun in January, the overall amount of energy Earth receives from the sun changes little throughout the year. However, the amount of energy any one place on Earth receives can vary quite a bit.

INTEGRATION
Life Science

INTEGRATION Life Science

People in many areas of the United States and in other parts of the world observe changes in the animal and plant life from season to season. Certain animals hibernate during the winter months. After changing in color, leaves fall from trees. Other plants stop growing during cold months. In some areas of the world, the change in seasons is reflected in the amount of rainfall. This also has definite effects on plant growth.

Activity

LS **Interpersonal** Have students use basketballs to represent Earth to demonstrate the difference between Earth's rotation and revolution. L1 LEP COOP LEARN

Visual Learning

Figure 22-3 Is the change of seasons caused by Earth's elliptical orbit? Explain your answer. *No; if it were, we would have the warmest temperatures in January when the Earth is closest to the sun.* LEP LS

Videodisc

STV: Solar System
The Big Picture
Unit 1, Side 1
Rotation and Revolution

05295-06309

Community Connection

Celebrating the Seasons Have students contact officials from the local community and work with them to select a special day for each season. On this day, students from school and people from the community can decorate the community library, the school, and other sites of interest. Invite city or town officials to school for planning sessions.

USING TECHNOLOGY

Obtain values about the accuracy of conventional quartz watches and contrast that accuracy to that of atomic clocks.

Think Critically

The length of a day will increase. The length of a year will not be affected. Earth's period of revolution is not dependent on its period of rotation. However, students should realize that although there will be fewer days in a year, the length of a year will not change.

Teacher F.Y.I.

Earth's orientation in space gradually changes with time. Presently, Earth's axis points toward Polaris, the North Star. In about 12 000 years, Earth's axis will point toward the star Vega in the constellation Lyra. This change is the result of Earth's "wobbling" on its axis.

STV: Solar System

Earth

41684

Earth, as seen from Voyager 1

41719

USING TECHNOLOGY

Clocks: Old and New

Atomic clocks measure time by recording the frequency of electromagnetic waves given off by atoms. Unlike conventional clocks, atomic clocks are not affected by changes in temperature or the wearing of their parts. As a result, they gain or lose less than one second in 200 000 years.

Using atomic clocks, scientists have found that each successive day on Earth is getting longer. Evidence indicates that Earth's rotation is slowing down.

Apparently, Earth's rotation has been slowing down for millions of years. By studying the growth lines on 375-million-year-old corals, scientists have determined that there were 440 days in a year at the time these corals were growing. Corals deposit monthly growth lines on their shells in much the same way trees develop yearly growth rings.

Atomic clocks and ancient corals indicate that Earth's rotation is slowing down. Scientists think that it is being dragged on by the gravitational attraction of the moon.

Think Critically:

As this drag continues, what will happen to the length of a day on Earth? To the length of a year?

Atomic Clock

Earth's Tilted Axis

Earth's axis is tilted 23.5° from a line perpendicular to its orbit. This tilt causes the seasons. Daylight hours are longer for the hemisphere tilted toward the sun. Think of how early it gets dark in the winter compared with the summer. The hemisphere tilted toward the sun receives more hours of sunlight than the hemisphere tilted away from the sun.

Another effect of Earth's tilt is that the sun's radiation strikes the hemisphere tilted toward it at a higher angle than it does the other hemisphere. Because of this, the hemisphere tilted toward the sun receives more electromagnetic radiation per unit area than the hemisphere tilted away. In other words, if you measured the amount of radiation received in a one-square-kilometer area in the northern hemisphere and, at the same time, measured it for one square

Across the Curriculum

Geography Form groups of students with four students per group. Supply each group with a globe of Earth and a flashlight. Instruct them to shine the flashlight directly on the Tropics of Cancer and Capricorn to illustrate why the areas within the Arctic and Antarctic Circles are called the lands of the midnight sun during summer solstice. L1 LEP COOP LEARN LS

Cultural Diversity

Earth's Slowing Rotation The slowing of Earth's rotation has been documented by Babylonian records of solar eclipses. The recorded dates of the eclipses could have occurred only if Earth were rotating slightly faster in the past.

kilometer in the southern hemisphere, you would find a difference. The hemisphere tilted toward the sun would be receiving more energy.

A summer season results when the sun is in the sky longer and its electromagnetic radiation strikes Earth at a higher angle. Just the opposite occurs during winter.

Equinoxes and Solstices

Because of the tilt of Earth's axis, the sun's position relative to Earth's equator constantly changes. Most of the time, the sun is north or south of the equator. Two times during the year, however, the sun is directly over the equator.

Equinox

Look at **Figure 22-4.** When the sun reaches an **equinox,** it is directly above Earth's equator, and the number of daylight hours equals the number of nighttime hours all over the world. At that time, neither the northern nor the southern hemisphere is tilted toward the sun. In the northern hemisphere, the sun reaches the spring equinox on March 20 or 21 and the fall equinox on September 22 or 23. In the southern hemisphere, the equinoxes are reversed. These dates are the first days of spring and fall.

Science Journal

Suppose that Earth's rotation took twice the time that it presently does. In your Science Journal, write a report on how conditions such as global temperatures, work schedules, plant growth, and other factors might be different.

Figure 22-4

At summer solstice, the sun's rays directly strike the Tropic of Cancer, 23.5° north latitude. The sun is directly over the Tropic of Capricorn, 23.5° south latitude, at winter solstice. At both fall and spring equinoxes, the sun is directly over the equator.

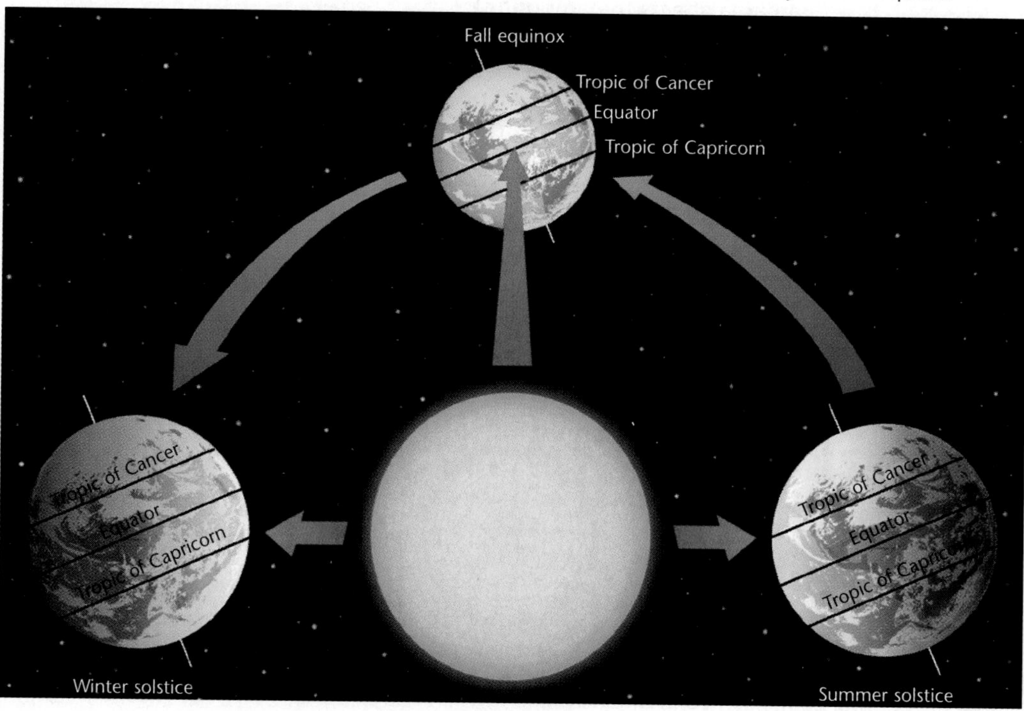

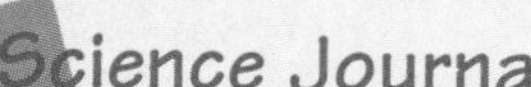

Science Journal

Answers will vary, but may include the fact that daytime temperatures would be higher, whereas nighttime temperatures would be lower. Work schedules might rely more on time to do a job than whether it is day or night. Plants would have adapted to a longer cycle of food production based on photosynthesis.

3 Assess

Check for Understanding

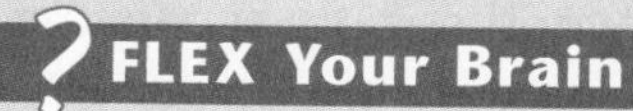

FLEX Your Brain

Use the Flex Your Brain activity to have students explore CAUSES OF EARTH'S SEASONS.

Activity Worksheets, p. 5

Reteach

LS **Visual-Spatial** Darken the room and place a globe of Earth next to a light source. Tilt the globe 23.5°. Hold the globe so that its axis points toward and then away from the light. Slowly spin the globe to demonstrate how the amount of light striking each hemisphere of the globe changes. Help students conclude that days are shorter in the northern hemisphere when Earth's axis is tilted away from the sun, and longer when Earth's axis is tilted toward the sun.

Extension

For students who have mastered this section, use the **Reinforcement** and **Enrichment** masters.

Activity 22-1

PREPARATION

Purpose

LS **Logical-Mathematical** Students will design and carry out an experiment to show how the angle at which sunlight strikes an area of Earth's surface determines the amount of heat received by that area. L1 COOP LEARN

Process Skills

communicating, making and using tables, observing and inferring, comparing and contrasting, recognizing cause and effect, designing an experiment, measuring in SI, hypothesizing, separating and controlling variables, interpreting data, formulating models

Time

one class period

Materials

tape, black construction paper, gooseneck lamp with 75-watt bulb, Celsius thermometer, watch, protractor

Alternate Materials desk lamp held at the proper angle

Safety Precautions

The light bulb and shade can be very hot even when the lamp is turned off.

Possible Hypotheses

- When light strikes a surface area from directly above, the area will receive more heat than when the light strikes the same surface area at a glancing angle.
- Students may write the same hypothesis as above but add one additional sentence. The increased heat produced when light strikes a surface area from directly above causes a warmer season.

Activity Worksheets, pp. 5, 132-133

Activity 22-1

Design Your Own Experiment

Tilt and Temperature

Have you ever noticed how hot the surface of a blacktop driveway can get during the day? The sun's rays hit Earth more directly as the day progresses. Now, consider the fact that Earth is tilted on its axis. How does this affect the amount of heat an area on Earth receives from the sun?

PREPARATION

Problem

How is the angle at which light strikes an area on Earth related to the changing of the seasons?

Form a Hypothesis

State a hypothesis about how the angle at which light strikes an area affects the amount of heat energy received by that area.

Objectives

- Measure the amount of heat generated by a light as it strikes a surface at different angles.
- Describe how light striking a surface at different angles is related to the changing of the seasons on Earth.

Possible Materials

- tape
- black construction paper
- gooseneck lamp with 75-watt bulb
- Celsius thermometer
- watch
- protractor

Safety Precautions

Do not touch the lamp. The lightbulb and shade can be hot even when the lamp has been turned off. Handle the thermometer carefully. If it breaks, do not touch anything. Inform your teacher immediately.

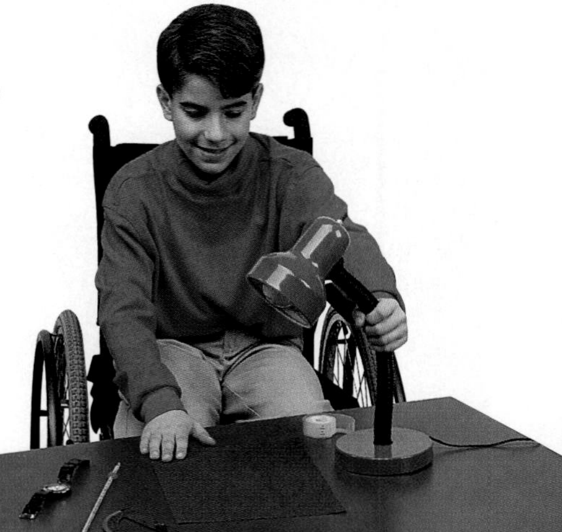

Theme Connection

Systems and Interactions The theme for this chapter is reinforced for students as they use the interaction of the angle at which light strikes a surface and the heat generated on that surface to propose a hypothesis for the cause of seasons.

Community Connection

Municipal Highway Department Invite a representative of the municipal highway department, or similar agency in your community, to discuss the problems caused on road surfaces by the heat generated during the summer whenever light from the sun strikes the road surface from a more direct angle.

PLAN THE EXPERIMENT

1. As a group, agree upon and write out your hypothesis statement.
2. As a group, list the steps you need to take to test your hypothesis. Be specific, describing exactly what you will do at each step. List your materials.
3. Make a list of any special properties you expect to observe or test.

Check the Plan

1. Read over your entire experiment to make sure that all steps are in a logical order.
2. Identify any constants, variables, and controls in the experiment.
3. Will you summarize data in a graph, table, or some other form of organization?
4. How will you determine whether the length of time the light is turned on affects heat energy?
5. How will you determine whether the angle at which light strikes an area causes changes in heat and energy?
6. *Make sure your teacher approves your plan before you proceed.*

DO THE EXPERIMENT

1. Carry out the experiment as planned.
2. While the experiment is going on, write down any observations that you make and complete the data table in your Science Journal.

Analyze and Apply

1. **Describe** your experiment, including how you used independent variables to test your hypothesis.
2. What happened to the temperature of the area being measured as you modified your variables?
3. **Identify** the dependent variable in your experiment.
4. Did your experiment support your hypothesis? If not, **determine** how you might change the experiment in order to retest your hypothesis. How might you change your hypothesis?

Go Further

Predict how the absorption of heat would be affected by changing your independent variables. Try your experiment with different values for your independent variables.

PLAN THE EXPERIMENT

Possible Procedures

Fold the black construction paper in half, lengthwise. Tape the short edges together to form an envelope. Use this envelope to hold the thermometer. Suggest that as an independent variable, students set the lamp so that light shines directly down on the envelope containing the thermometer, and then suggest they change the angle to 45°. Suggest that as an independent variable, students select a specific time period for recording the temperature (for example, every 3 to 9 minutes).

Teaching Strategies

Troubleshooting Remind students to allow the thermometer to return to room temperature before each use.

DO THE EXPERIMENT

Expected Outcome

Students should realize that the surface area heats up more quickly when light hits it from a more direct angle. They should also realize that this causes the warmer temperatures of summer.

Analyze and Apply

1. Descriptions will vary.
2. Answers will vary, but students should note that when light strikes a surface at an angle, temperature increases more slowly.
3. Temperature is the dependent variable.
4. Answers will vary depending on student hypotheses.

Go Further

Students should realize that lowering the angle should cause less of a temperature rise and increasing the angle to a greater amount should cause the temperature to rise more quickly.

Assessment

Process Ask students to explain in writing why temperatures rise faster when light hits a surface area at more direct angles. Use the Performance Task Assessment List for Writing in Science in **PASC,** p. 87. P

Science Journal

Answers will vary, but students should include creative writing samples that describe all four seasons. P

4 Close

• MINI • QUIZ •

Use the Mini Quiz to check students' recall of chapter content.

1. **Earth's _____ is the imaginary line around which Earth spins.** *axis*
2. **Describe Earth's rotation.** *It's the spinning of Earth on its axis.*
3. **_____ currents deep inside Earth are thought to generate its magnetic field.** *Convection*
4. **The yearly orbit of Earth around the sun is Earth's _____.** *revolution*

Section Wrap-up

Review

1. rotation
2. Light from the sun strikes Earth's surface at a higher angle, and the days are longer.
3. **Think Critically** Earth's orbit is an ellipse. Its distance from the sun varies.

Using Computers

Student table of Earth's physical data should at least include the information in **Table 22-1**.

Science Journal

In your Science Journal, use your creative writing skills to write an essay describing what you like best about each of the four seasons.

Solstice

The **solstice** is the point at which the sun reaches its greatest distance north or south of the equator. In the northern hemisphere, the sun reaches the summer solstice on June 21 or 22, and the winter solstice occurs on December 21 or 22. Just the opposite is true for the southern hemisphere. When the sun is at the summer solstice, there are more daylight hours than during any other day of the year. When it's at the winter solstice, on the shortest day of the year, we have the most nighttime hours.

Earth Data Review

As you have learned, Earth is an imperfect sphere that bulges slightly at the equator and is somewhat flattened at the poles. The rotation of Earth causes day and night. Earth's tilted axis is responsible for the seasons you experience, and our revolution around the sun marks the passing of a year. In the next section, you will read how Earth's nearest neighbor, the moon, is also in constant motion and how you observe this motion each day.

Section Wrap-up

Review

1. Which Earth motion causes night and day?
2. Why does summer occur in Earth's northern hemisphere when Earth's north pole is tilted toward the sun?
3. **Think Critically: Table 22-1** lists Earth's distance from the sun as an average. Why isn't there one exact measurement of this distance?

Skill Builder

Recognizing Cause and Effect

Answer these questions about the sun-Earth-moon relationship. If you need help, refer to Recognizing Cause and Effect in the **Skill Handbook.**

1. What causes seasons on Earth?
2. What causes winter?
3. What effect on seasons does the sun being closest to Earth in January have?

Using Computers

Spreadsheet Using the table or spreadsheet capabilities of a computer program, generate a table of Earth's physical data. Then write a description of the planet based on the table you have created.

Skill Builder

1. the tilt of Earth's axis
2. The sun is in the sky for a shorter amount of time and its radiation strikes Earth at a low angle.
3. It has little effect. The seasons are primarily due to the tilt of Earth on its axis, not its distance from the sun. It may cause the average summer temperatures of the southern hemisphere to be slightly warmer than they would otherwise be, but the effect is essentially insignificant.

Assessment

Oral Use this Skill Builder to assess students' abilities to recognize cause and effect. Ask students to identify the cause of Earth's magnetic field and the effect this field has on a compass needle. Use the Performance Task Assessment List for Making Observations and Inferences in **PASC,** p. 17. P

Earth's Moon

22 • 2

Motions of the Moon

You have probably noticed how the moon's apparent shape changes from day to day. Sometimes, just after sunset, you can see a full, round moon low in the sky. Other times, only half of the moon is visible and it's high in the sky at sunset. Sometimes, the moon is visible during the day. Why does the moon look the way it does? What causes it to change its appearance and position in the sky?

The Moon's Rotation and Revolution

Just as Earth rotates on its axis and revolves around the sun, the moon rotates on its axis and revolves around Earth. The moon's revolution causes changes in its appearance. If the moon rotates on its axis, why don't we see it spin around in space? The moon rotates on its axis once every 27.3 days. It takes the same amount of time to revolve once around Earth. As **Figure 22-5** shows, because these two motions take the same amount of time, the same side of the moon always faces Earth.

You can demonstrate this by having a friend hold a ball in front of you. Instruct your friend to move the ball around you while keeping the same side of it facing you. Everyone else in the room will see all sides of the ball. You will see only one side.

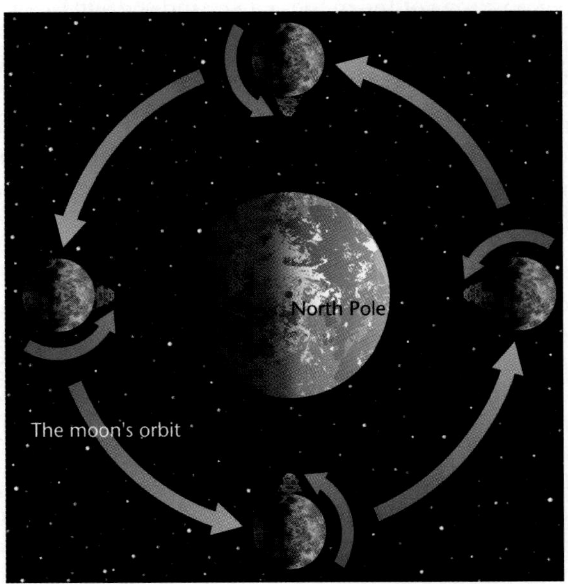

Figure 22-5

In about a one-month period, the moon orbits Earth. It also completes one rotation on its axis during the same period. *Does this affect which side of the moon faces Earth? Explain.*

Science Words

moon phase
new moon
waxing
first quarter
full moon
waning
third quarter
solar eclipse
lunar eclipse
maria

Objectives

- Demonstrate how the moon's phases depend on the relative positions of the sun, the moon, and Earth.
- Describe why eclipses occur, and compare solar and lunar eclipses.
- Hypothesize what surface features of the moon tell us about its history.

Program Resources

Reproducible Masters

Study Guide, p. 87 L1
Reinforcement, p. 87 L1
Enrichment, p. 87 L3
Cross-Curricular Integration, p. 26
Activity Worksheets, pp. 5, 134-135, 137 L1
Lab Manual 63, 64
Multicultural Connections, pp. 47-48

Transparencies

Section Focus Transparency 83 L1
Teaching Transparency 44

Section 22•2

Prepare

Section Background

The same side of the moon always faces Earth because the moon rotates on its axis once every 27.3 days, which is the same amount of time it takes it to revolve once around Earth.

Preplanning

- For the MiniLAB, students will need tidal range graphs from Chapter 17 Review, page 501.
- To prepare for Activity 22-2, obtain an unshaded light source, polystyrene balls, and a globe of Earth.

1 Motivate

Bellringer

Before presenting the lesson, display **Section Focus Transparency 83** on the overhead projector. Assign the accompanying **Focus Activity** worksheet. L1 LEP

Tying to Previous Knowledge

Help students recall the cause of tides from Chapter 17. Students should remember that the gravitational pull of the moon on Earth causes water to bulge on the side of Earth facing the moon and on the side opposite the moon. Also help students recall that large tidal ranges occur when Earth, the sun, and the moon are lined up.

Use Labs 63 and 64 in the **Lab Manual** as you teach this lesson.

2 Teach

Revealing Preconceptions

Some students may think that the far side of the moon is not seen because it is dark. Explain that the back of the moon receives as much light as the side that faces Earth. The far side is not seen because it always faces away from Earth.

Visual Learning

Figure 22-5 Does this affect which side of the moon faces Earth? Explain. *Because the moon's rotation and revolution take the same amount of time, the same side of the moon always faces Earth.*

USING MATH

Circumference of the moon = C

$C = 2\pi r$ where

$\pi = 3.14$

$r = 1738$ km

$C = 2 \times 3.14 \times 1738$ km

$C = 10\,915$ km

NATIONAL GEOGRAPHIC SOCIETY

Videodisc

STV: Solar System

Earth's moon

41689

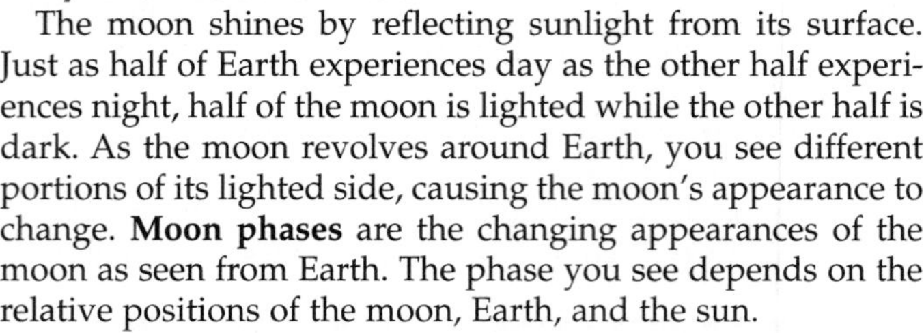

Figure 22-6

The phases of the moon: (A) new moon, (B) waxing crescent, (C) first quarter, (D) waxing gibbous, (E) full moon, (F) waning gibbous, (G) third quarter, and (H) waning crescent.

Why the Moon Shines

The moon shines by reflecting sunlight from its surface. Just as half of Earth experiences day as the other half experiences night, half of the moon is lighted while the other half is dark. As the moon revolves around Earth, you see different portions of its lighted side, causing the moon's appearance to change. **Moon phases** are the changing appearances of the moon as seen from Earth. The phase you see depends on the relative positions of the moon, Earth, and the sun.

USING MATH

The formula for the circumference of a circle is $2\pi r$, where r is the radius (one half the diameter) of the circle and π is approximately equal to 3.14. The moon's diameter at its equator is 3476 km. Find the circumference of the moon at its equator.

Phases of the Moon

A new moon occurs when the moon is between Earth and the sun. During a **new moon,** the lighted half of the moon is facing the sun and the dark side faces Earth. The moon is in the sky, but it cannot be seen.

Waxing Phases

Shortly after a new moon, more and more of the moon's lighted side becomes visible—the phases are **waxing.** About 24 hours after a new moon, you can see a thin slice of the side of the moon that is lighted by the sun. This phase, shown in **Figure 22-6,** is called the waxing crescent. About a week after a new moon, you can see half of the lighted side, or one-quarter of the moon's surface. This phase is **first quarter.**

The phases continue to wax. When more than one-quarter is visible, it is called waxing gibbous. A **full moon** occurs when the half of the moon's surface facing Earth is lit up.

Inclusion Strategies

Gifted Have students work in pairs to make time-lapse videos of the phases of the moon. Every night, the partners should videotape the moon for a few seconds. They should do this for one month. A regular 35 mm camera can be used if a video camera is not available. L3

Behaviorally Disordered Have students research myths about the full moon. After gathering the information, encourage students who have difficulty working within normal classroom constraints to perform skits that illustrate some of the myths.

Waning Phases

After a full moon, the amount of the moon's lighted side that can be seen becomes smaller. The phases are said to be **waning.** Waning gibbous begins just after a full moon. When you can see only half of the lighted side, the **third quarter** phase occurs. The amount of the moon that can be seen continues to become smaller. Waning crescent occurs just before another new moon. Once again, you can see a small slice of the lighted side of the moon.

The complete cycle of the moon's phases takes about 29.5 days. Recall that it takes about 27.3 days for the moon to revolve around Earth. The discrepancy between the time it takes for the moon to revolve around Earth and the time it takes for the moon to complete its phases is due to Earth's revolution. It takes the moon about two days to "catch up" with Earth's advancement around the sun.

Eclipses

Imagine yourself as one of your ancient ancestors, living 50 000 years ago. You are out foraging for nuts and other fruit in the bright afternoon sun. Gradually, the sun disappears from the sky, as if being swallowed by a giant creature. But the darkness lasts only a short time, and as quickly as the sun disappeared, it returns to full brightness. You realize something unusual has happened, but you don't know what caused it. It will be almost 48 000 years before anyone can explain the event that you just experienced.

The event just described was a total solar eclipse. Today, we know what causes such eclipses; but for our early ancestors, they must have been terrifying events. Many animals act as if night has come: cows return to their barns, and chickens go to sleep. What causes the day to suddenly change into night and suddenly back into day?

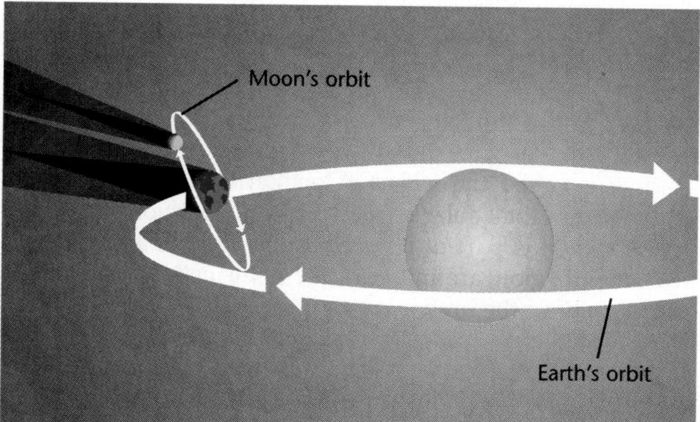

Figure 22-7

The orbit of the moon is not in the same plane as Earth's orbit around the sun. If it were, we would experience a solar eclipse each month during the new moon. *In your Science Journal, write a paragraph describing how eclipses might have been viewed by our early ancestors.*

MiniLAB

How does the moon affect the ocean?

Find out how the phases and the position of the moon relate to tides.

Procedure

1. Use the graph you constructed on tidal ranges in the Chapter 17 Review. If you did not make the graph, you should do so now.
2. Review what you know about the position of the moon during neap and spring tides.

Analysis

1. On what days in your graph can you infer that the moon was at new or full phase?
2. On what days can you infer it was in first or third quarter phase?
3. How are the phases and position of the moon related to tides?

Science Journal

Phases of the Moon Ask students to spend five to ten minutes and free write in their Science Journals about everything they now know about the moon's phases and what they still need to learn. Have them use their free-writing exercise to formulate questions that will teach them the information they still need or want to know. L1 LS

MiniLAB

Purpose

LS **Logical-Mathematical** Students will realize that the moon's phases and position in relation to Earth and the sun affect tidal range in Earth's oceans. L1

Materials

tidal range graph from Chapter 17 Review

Teaching Strategies

Troubleshooting If students did not make the graph during the review of Chapter 17, you might wish to have the class produce one together.

Analysis

1. A new or full moon probably occurred on January 7 to 9 and 20 to 23, because tidal range was greatest at these times.
2. First and third quarter moons probably occurred on January 1, January 14 or 15, and January 28 to 30, when tidal range was lowest.
3. When the sun, Earth, and the moon are aligned along an imaginary straight line during new and full moon phases, tidal range is greatest. When the sun, Earth, and the moon are at right angles to one another, tidal range is at its lowest.

Assessment

Oral Ask students to use the graph to determine when in the next month they should expect new and full moons to occur. Use the Performance Task Assessment List for Analyzing the Data in **PASC**, p. 27. P

Activity Worksheets, pp. 5, 137

Visual Learning

Figure 22-7 In your Science Journal, write a paragraph describing how eclipses must have been viewed by our early ancestors. *Students should mention that our early ancestors were likely frightened by eclipses because they did not understand the reason for their occurrence.* LEP LS

CONNECT TO

PHYSICS

Answer In order for the moon to completely block out the sun, which is about 400 times larger in diameter than the moon, the sun must be about 400 times farther from Earth than the moon.

Making and Using Science Illustrations

LS **Visual-Spatial** Have students quickly sketch and label the positions of the sun, the moon, and Earth during a solar eclipse. After they read page 627, have them do the same for a lunar eclipse. If you wish, you might want students to label the sun, the moon, and Earth with the symbols astronomers use. The symbol for the sun is ⊙, the symbol for the moon is ☾, and the symbol for Earth is ⊕. L1

NATIONAL GEOGRAPHIC SOCIETY

Videodisc

STV: Solar System

Full moon, seen from an Arizona canyon

41714

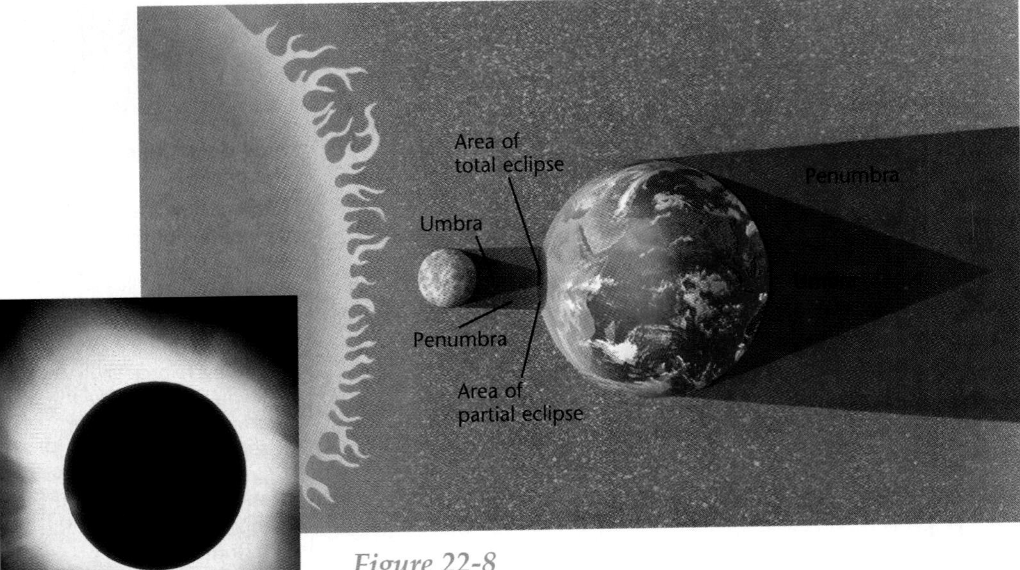

Figure 22-8

Only a small area of Earth experiences a total solar eclipse during the eclipse event. Only the outer portion of the sun's atmosphere is visible during a total solar eclipse.

The Cause of Eclipses

Revolution of the moon causes eclipses. Eclipses occur when Earth or the moon temporarily blocks the sunlight reaching the other. Sometimes during a new moon, a shadow cast by the moon falls on Earth and causes a solar eclipse. During a full moon, a shadow of Earth can be cast on the moon, resulting in a lunar eclipse.

Eclipses can occur only when the sun, the moon, and Earth are perfectly lined up. Because the moon's orbit is not in the same plane as Earth's orbit around the sun, eclipses happen only a few times each year.

CONNECT TO

PHYSICS

When a total solar eclipse occurs, Earth's moon completely blocks out the sun, which is about 400 times larger in diameter. In order for this to happen, ***describe*** what can be inferred about the relative distances to the two objects.

Solar Eclipses

A **solar eclipse,** such as the one in **Figure 22-8,** occurs when the moon moves directly between the sun and Earth and casts a shadow on part of Earth. The darkest portion of the moon's shadow is called the *umbra.* A person standing within the umbra sees a total solar eclipse. The only portion of the sun that is visible is part of its atmosphere, which appears as a pearly white glow around the edge of the eclipsing moon.

Surrounding the umbra is a lighter shadow on Earth's surface called the *penumbra.* Persons standing in the penumbra see a partial solar eclipse. **CAUTION:** *Regardless of where you are standing, never look directly at a solar eclipse. The light will permanently damage your eyes.*

Across the Curriculum

Language Arts Have students research the origin and meaning of the phrase *once in a blue moon. Because 29.5 days elapse between successive-like phases (for example, new moon to new moon), a month with 31 days may have two full moon phases, one at the beginning and one at the end of the month. It does not happen often, thus the phrase* once in a blue moon.

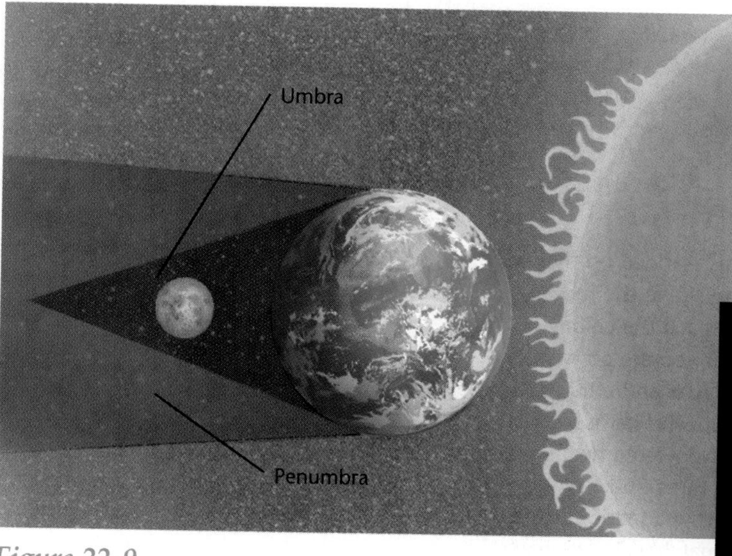

Figure 22-9

During a total lunar eclipse, Earth's shadow blocks light coming from the sun.

Lunar Eclipses

When Earth's shadow falls on the moon, a **lunar eclipse** like the one shown in **Figure 22-9** occurs. A lunar eclipse begins with the moon moving into Earth's penumbra. As the moon continues to move, it enters Earth's umbra and you see a curved shadow on the moon's surface. It was from this shadow that Aristotle concluded that Earth's shape was spherical. When the moon moves completely into Earth's umbra, the moon becomes dark red because light from the sun is refracted by Earth's atmosphere onto the moon. A total lunar eclipse has occurred.

A partial lunar eclipse occurs when only a portion of the moon moves into Earth's umbra. The remainder of the moon is in Earth's penumbra and, therefore, receives some direct sunlight.

A total solar eclipse occurs up to two times every year, yet most people live their entire lives never witnessing one. You may not be lucky enough to see a total solar eclipse, but it is almost certain you will have a chance to see a total lunar eclipse in your lifetime. The reason it is so difficult to view a total solar eclipse is that only those people in the small region where the moon's umbra strikes Earth can witness one. In contrast, anyone on the nighttime side of Earth can see a total lunar eclipse.

The moon's orbit is tilted at an angle of about 5° to Earth's orbit around the sun. Using a protractor, draw an angle of 5°.

Teacher F.Y.I.

A sidereal month is 27.3 days long, the actual period of the moon's revolution around Earth. A synodic month, the time from one phase until the same phase occurs again, is 29.5 days long. The discrepancy is due to Earth's revolution. It takes the moon about two days to "catch up" with Earth's advancement around the sun.

USING MATH

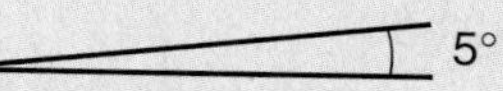

Demonstration

LS **Visual-Spatial** Obtain a globe of the moon or use a volleyball to represent the moon. Darken the room and place three overhead projectors across the front of the room with their lights aimed toward the back of the room at an angle above students' heads. Then have students cluster near the center of the room. Inform students that the projectors represent the sun, they are on Earth, and the globe or ball represents the moon. Keep the same side of the moon facing the students as you make it revolve around them. Students should be able to see the moon go through phases beginning with new moon. Point out that the side of the moon that we aren't able to see is lighted during new moon. After the demonstration of lunar phases, position the moon properly during the new and full moon to demonstrate how light is blocked out during solar and lunar eclipses. LEP

Cultural Diversity

Lunar Calendars For some groups, time defines activities, while for others activities define time. Many Americans do certain activities on certain days of the week—we go to school because it is Monday. For some peoples, such as the Nuer, a group of semi-nomadic pastoralists living in East Africa, it is a certain month because they are doing a certain activity. The Nuer base their yearly cycle on a system of full moons. Each moon is named after the activities associated with it. *Kur,* for example, is a time to make the first fishing dams and build the first cattle camps. It is part of *mai* (the dry season). *Dwat* is the month when they break camp and return to their village. It is part of *tot* (the wet season). Two transitional seasons, *rwil* and *jiom* (meaning "wind"), are recognized as seasons of rapid change.

Problem Solving

Solve the Problem

1. The solar-powered heating unit, signal flares, binoculars, matches, solar-powered radio receiver and transmitter, and signal mirror are useless due to the lack of sunlight and atmosphere on the moon. The moon has no magnetic field, so the compass couldn't be used.
2. The food, rope, battery-operated heating unit, oxygen tanks, water, constellation map, and flashlights would be useful.

Think Critically

Food and water will be needed to complete the difficult journey. A battery-operated heating unit is also necessary because of the extremely low temperatures on the nightside. Oxygen tanks are the most important items to bring. A map of the constellations may help if the crew becomes lost. A flashlight is absolutely necessary. Binoculars will be useless unless you transverse into the daytime side. Rope may be needed to cross rough terrain. The solar-powered heating unit and radio, and signal mirror are useless without sunlight. Signal flares and matches cannot be used in the oxygen-free environment.

1. The moon's rough terrain, lack of oxygen, and low temperatures determine many of the objects selected.
2. The signal mirror, solar-powered heating unit and radio, and binoculars are left behind because they are useless without sunlight. By the same token, the flashlight is essential. P

Problem Solving

Survival on the Moon

You and your crew have crash-landed on the moon, far from your intended landing site at the moon colony. It will take one day to reach the colony on foot. The side of the moon that you are on will be facing away from the sun during your entire trip back. You manage to salvage the following items from your wrecked ship: food, rope, solar-powered heating unit, battery-operated heating unit, three 70-kg oxygen tanks, map of the constellations, magnetic compass, oxygen-burning signal flares, matches, 8 L of water, solar-powered radio receiver and transmitter, three flashlights and extra batteries, signal mirror, and binoculars. Keep in mind that the moon's gravity is about 1/6 that of Earth's, and it lacks a magnetic field.

Solve the Problem:

1. **Determine which items will be of no use to you.**
2. **Determine which items to take with you on your journey to the colony.**

Think Critically:

Based on what you have learned about the moon, describe why each of the salvaged items is useful or not useful.

1. How did the moon's physical properties affect your decisions?
2. How did the lack of sunlight affect your decisions?

Structure of the Moon

When you look at the moon, you can see many of its larger surface features. The dark-colored, relatively flat regions are called **maria.** Maria formed when ancient lava flows from the moon's interior filled large basins on the moon's surface. The basins formed early in the moon's history.

Craters

Many depressions on the moon were formed by meteoroids, asteroids, and comets, which strike the surfaces of planets and their satellites. These depressions are called craters. During impact, cracks may have formed in the moon's crust, allowing lava to reach the surface and fill in the large craters. The igneous rocks of the maria are 3 to 4 billion years old. They are the youngest rocks found on the moon thus far.

The Moon's Interior

Seismographs left on the moon by *Apollo* astronauts have enabled scientists to study moonquakes. Recall from Chapter 9 that the study of earthquakes allows scientists to map Earth's interior. Likewise, the study of moonquakes has led to a model of the moon's interior. One model of the moon shows that its crust is about 60 km thick on the side facing Earth and about 150 km thick on the far side. Below the crust, a solid mantle may extend to a depth of 1000 km. A partly molten zone of the mantle extends farther down. Below this may be an iron-rich solid core.

Science Journal

What happened to the moon's atmosphere? Have students research the topic of an atmosphere for the moon and write a brief one-page report in their Science Journals about why the moon does not have an atmosphere and whether it ever did have one. *The moon's gravitational force is not strong enough to hold gases at its surface. When the sun falls on the moon it heats its surface to a degree that causes air molecules to travel fast enough to escape the moon's force of gravity. Gases have probably been released by volcanic activity on the moon's surface in the past, but they have escaped into space.* L2 LS

Moon Phases and Eclipses

You know that moon phases and eclipses result from the relative positions of the sun, the moon, and Earth. In this activity, you will demonstrate the positions of these bodies during certain phases and eclipses. You will also see why only people on a small portion of Earth's surface see a total solar eclipse.

Problem

Can a model be devised to show the positions of the sun, the moon, and Earth during various phases and eclipses?

Materials 

- light source (unshaded)
- polystyrene ball on pencil
- globe
- **Figure 22-6**

Procedure

1. Study the positions of the sun, the moon, and Earth in **Figure 22-6.**
2. Use a polystyrene ball on a pencil as a model moon. Move the model moon around the globe to duplicate the exact position that would have to occur for a lunar eclipse to take place.
3. Move the model moon to the position that would cause a solar eclipse.
4. Place the model moon at each of the following phases: first quarter, full moon, third quarter, and new moon. Identify which, if any, type of eclipse could occur during each phase. Record your data.
5. Place the model moon at the location where a lunar eclipse could occur. Move it slightly toward, then away from Earth. Note the amount of change in the size of the shadow causing the eclipse. Record this information.
6. Repeat step 5 with the model moon in a position where a solar eclipse could occur.

Analyze

1. During which phase(s) of the moon is it possible for an eclipse to occur?
2. **Describe** the effect that a small change in the distance between Earth and the moon has on the size of the shadow causing the eclipse.
3. As seen from Earth, how does the apparent size of the moon **compare** with the apparent size of the sun? How can an eclipse be used to confirm this?

Conclude and Apply

4. **Infer** why a lunar and solar eclipse do not occur every month.
5. Suppose you wanted to more accurately model the movement of the moon around Earth. **Explain** how your model moon moves around the globe. Would it always be in the same plane as the light source and the globe?
6. Why have only a few people experienced a total solar eclipse?

Data and Observations

Sample Data

Moon Phase	Observations
first quarter	no eclipse
full	lunar eclipse
third quarter	no eclipse
new	solar eclipse

5. In order to demonstrate lunar motions around Earth, the moon must spend most of its time either above or below Earth's orbital plane. It will move slightly away from and closer to Earth during its elliptical orbit.
6. If the sun, the moon, and Earth are not lined up perfectly, the umbra of the moon's shadow will not fall on Earth. When the umbra does fall on Earth, it covers only a small band across Earth's surface.

Assessment

Performance To further assess students' understanding of moon phases and eclipses, see Performance Assessment 2 on page 637. Use the Performance Task Assessment List for Model in **PASC,** p. 51. P

Activity 22-2

Purpose

LS **Kinesthetic** Students will formulate a model and demonstrate the relative positions of Earth and the moon during lunar phases. L1

COOP LEARN LEP

Process Skills

communicating, sequencing, observing and inferring, recognizing and using spatial relationships, comparing and contrasting, recognizing cause and effect

Time

30-40 minutes

Safety Precautions

Caution students to handle the light source with care.

Activity Worksheets, pp. 5, 134-135

Teaching Strategies

Troubleshooting Point out that the distance between the moon and Earth is not constant.

Answers to Questions

1. Eclipses of the moon may occur only at full moon. Solar eclipses occur during new moon.
2. The distance between Earth and the moon has little effect on lunar eclipses. During solar eclipses, the closer the two bodies, the larger the moon's shadow on Earth's surface and the longer the duration of the eclipse.
3. The moon and sun *appear* similar in size. This is most observable during a solar eclipse as the moon just seems to exactly fit the solar disk being eclipsed.
4. Eclipses are possible only when the moon is crossing Earth's orbital plane around the sun. Except for a few minutes each month, the moon is always located either above or below Earth's orbital plane.

Activity

Put students into groups of four. Provide each group with a map of the moon's surface. Have students find and describe key surface features and explain how each feature might have formed.

3 Assess

Check for Understanding

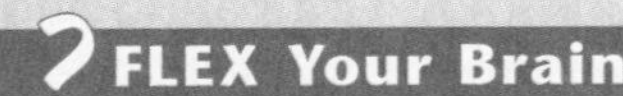

Use the Flex Your Brain activity to have students explore SURFACE FEATURES OF THE MOON and what they tell us about its history.

Activity Worksheets, p. 5

Reteach

Using a globe of Earth, a tennis ball, and a large beach ball, simulate solar and lunar eclipses with the help of volunteers.

Extension

For students who have mastered this section, use the **Reinforcement** and **Enrichment** masters.

Videodisc

STV: Solar System

Earth's moon, first quarter

41713

Earth's moon, crescent phase

41712

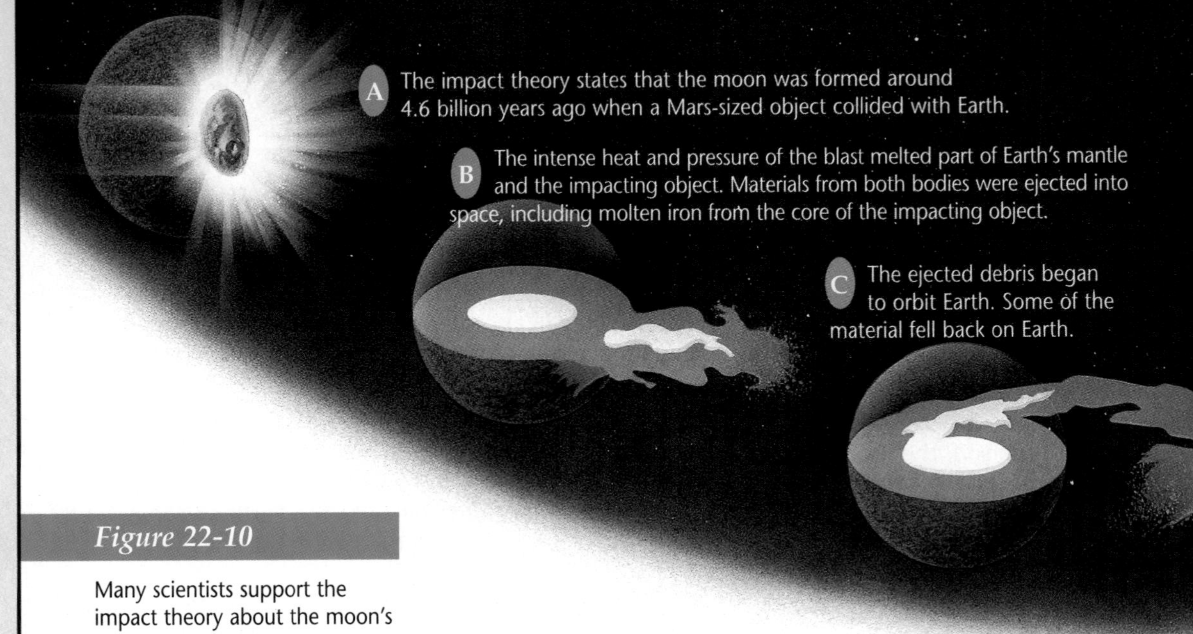

Figure 22-10

Many scientists support the impact theory about the moon's origin.

Origin of the Moon

Prior to the data obtained from the *Apollo* space missions, there were three theories about the moon's origin. The first is that the moon was captured by Earth's gravity. It formed elsewhere and wandered into Earth's vicinity. The second model is that the moon condensed from loose material surrounding Earth during the early formation of the solar system. The last theory is that a blob of molten material was ejected from Earth while Earth was still in its early molten stage.

Impact Theory

The data gathered by the *Apollo* missions have led many scientists to support the impact theory. According to the impact theory, the moon was formed about 4.6 billion years ago when a Mars-sized object collided with Earth, throwing gas and debris into orbit. The gas and debris then condensed into one large mass, forming the moon. **Figure 22-10** illustrates the impact theory.

Regardless of the moon's true origin, it has played an important role in our history. It was a source of curiosity for many early astronomers. Studying the phases of the moon and eclipses led people to conclude that Earth and the moon were in motion around the sun. Earth's shadow on the moon proved that Earth's shape was spherical. When Galileo first turned his telescope to the moon, he found a surface scarred by craters and maria. Before that time, many people believed

Science Journal

Moon Observations Have each student keep a two-week log of moon observations in their Science Journals, including the moon phase, the time it was observed, the moon's altitude above the horizon, and a brief description of conditions during the observation. The width of a fist when held at arm's length is approximately equal to 10° of altitude. L1

Integrating the Sciences

Seismology Have students write a report in their Science Journals about the kinds of equipment left behind on the moon and how these instruments have given scientists a better understanding of the moon's structure and history. L2

that all planetary bodies were "perfect," without surface features.

By studying the moon, we can learn about ourselves and the planet we live on. As you will read in the next section, not only is the moon important as an object from our past, but it is important to our future as well.

Section Wrap-up

Review

1. What are the relative positions of the sun, the moon, and Earth during a full moon?
2. Why does a lunar eclipse occur only during a full moon?
3. **Think Critically:** What provides the force necessary to form craters on the moon?

Skill Builder
Measuring in SI

The moon's mass is 1/81 of Earth's mass. The moon's density is 3.3 g/cm^3. Calculate the moon's volume using the following formula.

volume = mass/density

If you need help, refer to Measuring in SI in the **Skill Handbook.**

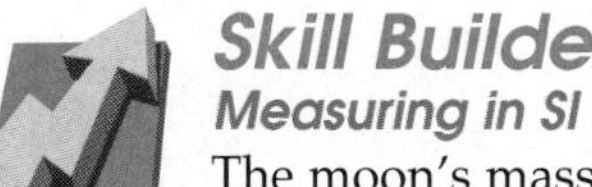

Science Journal

Research the moon's origin in astronomy books and magazines. In your Science Journal, write a report about the various theories, including the theory about a Mars-sized object colliding with Earth. Make a drawing of each theory.

Skill Builder

Recall that the mass of Earth is 5.98×10^{27} g.

moon's mass = 5.98×10^{27} g ÷ 81
= 7.4×10^{25} g

volume of moon = 7.4×10^{25} g/3.3 g/cm^3
= 2.2×10^{25} cm^3

Assessment

Performance Assess students' abilities to measure in SI by having them carry out their calculations. Use the Performance Task Assessment List for Using Math in Science in **PASC,** p. 29. P

Visual Learning

Figure 22-10 Ask students to explain the most recent theory about the formation of the moon. LEP LS

4 Close

•MINI•QUIZ•

Use the Mini Quiz to check students' recall of chapter content.

1. **Which type of eclipse occurs when the moon moves directly between Earth and the sun?** *solar eclipse*
2. **Which type of eclipse occurs when Earth's shadow falls on the moon?** *lunar eclipse*
3. **What are maria and how did they form?** *dark-colored, relatively flat areas on the moon that formed when lava filled large basins on the surface of the moon*
4. **Meteorite impacts have caused many depressions called ______ on the moon's surface.** *craters*

Section Wrap-up

Review

1. Earth is between the sun and the moon.
2. In order for a lunar eclipse to occur, the moon must be within Earth's shadow. This happens only during full moon.
3. **Think Critically** the collision of asteroids into the moon's surface

Science Journal

Answers should relate to the capture theory, the condensation theory, the fission theory, and the impact theory as presented on pages 630-631.

Prepare

Section Background

Mascons are areas of the moon having a higher concentration of mass than other areas. Deviations in the elliptical orbits of spacecraft around the moon led to the discovery of mascons. The presence of mascons indicates that the entire interior of the moon cannot be liquid. There must be enough crust to support the mascons.

1 Motivate

Bellringer

Before presenting the lesson, display **Section Focus Transparency 84** on the overhead projector. Assign the accompanying **Focus Activity** worksheet. L1 LEP

Tying to Previous Knowledge

Help students recall that humans first landed on the moon in 1969 and that a total of six *Apollo* missions with crews have explored the moon.

2 Teach

Teacher F.Y.I.

One of the first scientists to recognize possible causes of craters on the moon and Earth was Grove K. Gilbert (1843-1918). His explanation of impact cratering on the moon led to our current understanding of the evolution of terrestrial planets.

SCIENCE & SOCIETY

22•3

TECHNOLOGY: Exploration of the Moon

Science Words

mascon

Objectives

- List and discuss new information about the moon discovered by the *Clementine* spacecraft.
- List two facts about the moon's south pole that may be important to future space travel.

Return to the Moon

At this time, there are no ongoing, long-term missions planned for a study of the moon. However, one spacecraft was placed into lunar orbit in February 1994 to conduct a two-month survey of the moon's surface. Its name is *Clementine.*

The *Clementine* Spacecraft

The *Clementine* spacecraft has been successful in obtaining scientific data. *Clementine's* mission was to test new sensors for tracking cold objects in space. Cold objects are items such as satellites, warheads, or even near-Earth asteroids.

In addition, *Clementine* was placed in lunar orbit to take high-resolution photographs intended for use in compiling a detailed map of the moon's surface. **Figure 22-11** shows a photograph taken by *Clementine. Clementine's* four cameras were able to resolve features as small as 200 m across, enhancing our knowledge of the moon's surface.

The Moon's South Pole

The South Pole-Aitken Basin is the oldest identifiable impact feature on the moon's surface. It is also the largest and deepest impact basin or depression found thus far anywhere in the solar system, measuring 12 km in depth and 2500 km in diameter. Data returned by *Clementine* have given scientists the first set of high-resolution photographs of this area of the

Figure 22-11

This photograph, taken by cameras on the *Clementine* spacecraft, shows the moon, the sun, and the planet Venus.

Program Resources

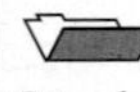 **Reproducible Masters**

Study Guide, p. 88 L1
Reinforcement, p. 88 L1
Enrichment, p. 88
Science and Society Integration, p. 26

 **Transparencies**

Section Focus Transparency 84 L1 

moon. Much of this depression stays in shadow throughout the moon's rotation, providing an area where ice deposits from impacting comets may have collected. Also, a large plateau that is always in sunlight was discovered in this area. With the possibility of water from the ice, this would be an ideal location for a moon colony powered by solar energy.

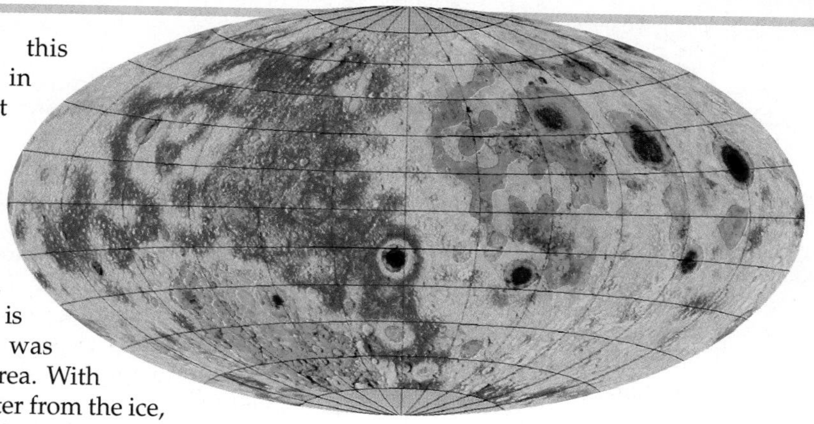

Figure 22-12 is a global map showing crustal thickness based on *Clementine* data. It shows that the crust thins under impact basins and that the moon's crust on the side facing Earth is much thinner than that on the far side. Such maps show the location of **mascons** or concentrations of mass. Mascons are located under impact basins. Data collected by *Clementine* also provided information on the composition or mineral content of moon rocks. In fact, this part of its mission was instrumental in naming the spacecraft. *Clementine* was the daughter of a miner in the ballad "My Darlin' Clementine."

Figure 22-12

This computer-enhanced map based on *Clementine* data indicates the thickness of the moon's crust. It shows that the crust on the side of the moon facing Earth is thinner than the crust on the far side of the moon.

Section Wrap-up

Review

1. List two discoveries about the moon made by the *Clementine* spacecraft.
2. Why would the discovery of ice at the moon's south pole be so important?

Explore the Technology

One of the most important contributions of the technology that placed *Clementine* in lunar orbit was the program's ability to accomplish 90 percent of its mission without going over budget. The spacecraft was built to budget, built on schedule, and used new technology only when it was cost efficient. Research how this compares to earlier space missions. Were they launched on schedule? Did they exceed projected budgets?

SCIENCE & SOCIETY

3 Assess

Check for Understanding

FLEX Your Brain

Use the Flex Your Brain activity to have students explore METHODS USED TO STUDY THE MOON.

Activity Worksheets, p. 5

Reteach

Obtain photographs of the moon from early crewed and uncrewed missions to the moon and from the recent *Clementine* spacecraft. Help students decide which photographs show more detail and would be best used for map making. Contact NASA for photographs.

Extension

For students who have mastered this section, use the **Reinforcement** and **Enrichment** masters.

4 Close

Ask a volunteer student to discuss how the *Clementine* spacecraft furthered our knowledge of the moon.

Section Wrap-up

Review

1. a large plateau near the moon's south pole that is always in sunlight; the moon's crust thins under impact basins; composition or mineral content of moon rocks
2. With the possibility of water from the ice, the large plateau near the moon's south pole would be an ideal location for a moon colony.

Explore the Technology

Discuss with students the fact that the cost of a space mission often surpasses the planned budget. However, in the case of *Clementine* one of the major advantages is the fact that it performed most of its mission without going over budget.

Source

In-Sob, Zong. *Folktales from Korea.* Routledge and Kegan Paul: London, 1952.

Background

- The spectacle of the heavens, with its clearly recognizable order and regularity of the sun, Earth, and moon, together with extraordinary events such as comets, eclipses, and meteors, was an intellectual puzzle for early naturalists. It is no surprise, then, that astronomy is the oldest science in virtually all modern cultures, and closely tied to religion. In fact, an understanding and curiosity about the sun, moon, and Earth is at the very core of modern civilizations, and underlies the development of the earliest calendar systems in many societies.
- Many folktales and myths from around the world portray the sun, Earth, and moon as characters in a story, and give them human characteristics that relate information about astronomical knowledge. Others use characters to describe the believed origin of the sun, Earth, and moon. The Korean folktale, "The Sun and the Moon," is the original source of a famous Japanese tale called "The Golden Chain from Heaven." In this version, the moon, an important image in Japanese culture, plays a vital role. Historically, moon-watching was a cultural event in Japan, with many people gathering in parks on special platforms built to worship the moon. In the Korean version, the sun plays a more critical role. The tale explains why the sun is so bright, and why people don't and shouldn't look directly at the sun.

Science & Literature

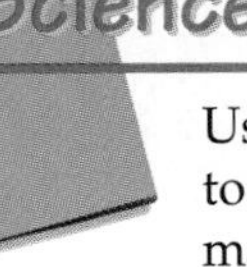

Science Journal

Use the library to research information about the history of astronomical science. In your Science Journal, make a time line showing the history of discoveries in astronomy dating back to its origins in ancient Egypt. Also try to find out when astronomical science began independently in various cultures around the world. Are there any similarities or differences in the way these cultures studied astronomy?

The Sun and the Moon: A Korean Folktale

In this chapter, you have learned about the interactions among the sun, the moon, and Earth, and how these relationships relate to the changing seasons on Earth. Due to advances in technology such as satellites, advanced telescopes, and computer-imaging systems, scientists have learned more about the sun, the moon, and Earth in the last 50 years than they have throughout history.

Astronomy is our oldest science, having been studied for at least 4000 years. In fact, astronomy was the first science to be studied in most cultures around the world, from the ancient Egyptians to the native peoples of North America. People have always been curious about the objects they see in the sky and how they affect life on Earth.

Korea has long had an interest in science, particularly astronomy. Many scientists believe that early Korean astronomers built the first astronomical observatory in the Far East in 647 A.D. The Korean folktale "The Sun and the Moon" illustrates their keen interest in astronomy, as well as their knowledge about the sun and moon. This excerpt from the story describes the origin of the sun and moon.

. . . The two children lived peacefully in the Heavenly Kingdom, until one day the Heavenly King said to them, "We do not allow anyone to sit here and idle away the time. So I have decided on duties for you. The boy shall be the Sun, to light the world of men, and the girl shall be the Moon, to shine by night." Then the girl answered, "Oh King, I am not familiar with the night. It would be better for me not to be the Moon." So the King made her the Sun instead, and made her brother the Moon.

It is said that when she became the Sun, people used to gaze up at her in the sky. But she was modest, and greatly embarrassed by this. So she shone brighter and brighter, so that it was impossible to look at her directly. And that is why the Sun is so bright, that her modesty might be forever respected.

Can you see how this folktale shows an interest in and an understanding about certain astronomical facts? Which sentences in the story describe facts about the sun? The moon?

Teaching Strategies

- Have students research information about the history of astronomy in a particular country. Have them list important discoveries, people, and dates. L2

LS **Linguistic** Discuss reasons why astronomy was the first science in most cultures of the world. Have students imagine what life would have been like without an understanding about objects and events in the sky. Ask students to write a short essay describing their thoughts. L1

Other Works

Other works containing Korean and Japanese folktales:

- *Korean Folktales.* Edited by International Cultural Foundation. Si-sa-yong-o-sa: Seoul, 1982.
- Shannon, George A. *A Knock at the Door.* Oryx Press: Arizona, 1992.

Chapter 22

Review

Summary

22-1: Planet Earth

1. Earth is a sphere that is slightly flattened at its poles. Earth's mass is nearly 6.0×10^{27} g and its density is 5.52 g/cm^3. Earth's magnetic field is due to convection currents deep inside Earth.
2. Earth rotates once each day and revolves around the sun in a little more than 365 days.
3. Seasons on Earth are due to the amount of solar energy received by a hemisphere at a given time. The tilt of Earth on its axis causes the amount of solar energy to vary.

22-2: Earth's Moon

1. Earth's moon goes through phases that depend on the relative positions of the sun, the moon, and Earth.
2. Eclipses occur when Earth or the moon temporarily blocks out the sunlight reaching the other. A solar eclipse occurs when the moon moves directly between the sun and Earth. A lunar eclipse occurs when Earth's shadow falls on the moon.
3. The moon's maria are the result of ancient volcanism. Craters on the moon's surface formed from impacts with meteoroids, asteroids, and comets.

22-3: Science and Society: Exploration of the Moon

1. The *Clementine* spacecraft took detailed, high-resolution photographs of the moon's surface.
2. The moon's South Pole-Aitken Basin may contain ice deposits that could supply water for a moon colony.

Key Science Words

a. axis
b. ellipse
c. equinox
d. first quarter
e. full moon
f. lunar eclipse
g. maria
h. mascon
i. moon phase
j. new moon
k. revolution
l. rotation
m. solar eclipse
n. solstice
o. sphere
p. third quarter
q. waning
r. waxing

Reviewing Vocabulary

Match each phrase with the correct term from the list of Key Science Words.

1. Earth's shape
2. causes day and night to occur on Earth
3. Earth's movement around the sun
4. shape of Earth's orbit
5. occurs when the sun's position is directly above the equator
6. the moon cannot be seen during this phase
7. moon phase in which all of the lighted side of the moon is seen
8. eclipse that occurs when the moon is between Earth and the sun
9. relatively flat region on the moon
10. concentration of mass on the moon located under an impact basin

Chapter 22 Review

Summary

Have students read the summary statements to review the major concepts of the chapter.

Reviewing Vocabulary

1. o
2. l
3. k
4. b
5. c
6. j
7. e
8. m
9. g
10. h

Assessment

Portfolio Encourage students to place in their portfolios one or two items of what they consider to be their best work. Examples include:

- Activity 22-1 experimental design and analysis, p. 621
- Science Journal, p. 622
- Problem Solving, p. 628 P

Performance Additional performance assessments may be found in **Performance Assessment** and **Science Integration Activities.** Performance Task Assessment Lists and rubrics for evaluating these activities can be found in Glencoe's **Performance Assessment in the Science Classroom.**

GLENCOE TECHNOLOGY

 **MindJogger Videoquiz**

Chapter 22 Have students work in groups as they play the Videoquiz game to review key chapter concepts.

Checking Concepts

1. c
2. a
3. c
4. d
5. d
6. b
7. a
8. b
9. d
10. b

Understanding Concepts

11. Rotation is the spinning of an object about its axis. Revolution is the movement of one object around another.

12. The moon's period of rotation equals its period of revolution. Thus, the same side of the moon is always facing Earth.

13. During an equinox the number of daylight hours equals the number of nighttime hours, and the sun is directly above Earth's equator. Solstice occurs when the sun reaches its greatest distance north or south of the equator. At summer solstice, the number of daylight hours is greatest; the shortest day of the year is winter solstice.

14. These are shadows formed by the moon and Earth during eclipses. The umbra is the darker shadow. The penumbra is the lighter shadow.

15. Answers will vary.

Thinking Critically

16. If the moon moved between the observer and the sun, phases would be observed. The specific phases would depend on the relative positions of the observer, the moon, and the sun.

17. Earth bulges at the equator. Its gravitational attraction there is less than that at the poles. Thus, a person weighs less at the equator.

Chapter 22 Review

Checking Concepts

Choose the word or phrase that completes the sentence.

1. The sun appears to rise and set because _______.
   a. Earth revolves
   b. the sun moves in space
   c. Earth rotates
   d. Earth orbits the sun

2. Earth's circumference at the _______ is greater than it is at the _______.
   a. equator, poles c. poles, equator
   b. axis, mantle d. mantle, axis

3. When the sun reaches equinox, the _______ is facing the sun.
   a. southern hemisphere
   b. northern hemisphere
   c. equator
   d. pole

4. The moon rotates once every _______.
   a. 24 hours c. 27.3 hours
   b. 365 days d. 27.3 days

5. The moon revolves once every _______.
   a. 24 hours c. 27.3 hours
   b. 365 days d. 27.3 days

6. As the moon appears to get larger, it is said to _______.
   a. wane c. rotate
   b. wax d. be crescent-shaped

7. During a _______ eclipse, the moon is directly between the sun and Earth.
   a. solar c. full
   b. new d. lunar

8. The _______ is the darkest part of the moon's shadow during a solar eclipse.
   a. waxing gibbous c. waning gibbous
   b. umbra d. penumbra

9. _______ are depressions on the moon.
   a. Eclipses c. Phases
   b. Moonquakes d. Craters

10. Data gathered from the *Clementine* spacecraft support the fact that the moon _______.
   a. rotates once in 29.5 days
   b. has a thinner crust on the side facing Earth
   c. revolves once in 29.5 days
   d. has a thicker crust on the side facing Earth

Understanding Concepts

Answer the following questions in your Science Journal using complete sentences.

11. Compare and contrast rotation and revolution.

12. Why have observers on Earth never seen craters on one side of the moon?

13. How do equinoxes and solstices differ?

14. What causes umbras and penumbras?

15. Do you think the *Clementine* mission was worth the cost of funding the project? Explain.

18. During full and new moons, Earth, the sun, and the moon align; thus the gravitational attraction is greatest then. High tides are the highest and low tides are the lowest during these two phases.

19. The moon does not have a magnetic field. Star charts could be used to navigate, but a compass could not.

20. The changing position of the moon from night to night is a real motion because the moon is orbiting Earth. The moon appears to move westward across the sky due to Earth's rapid rotation. Though the moon is progressing eastward in its revolution around Earth, its trip across the sky in a single night is due to Earth's rotation. Seeing the same side of the moon seems to indicate a lack of rotation. This is an apparent motion because the moon's period of rotation equals its period of revolution.

Thinking Critically

16. How would the moon appear to an observer in space during its revolution? Would phases be observable? Explain.
17. Would you weigh more at Earth's equator or at the North Pole? Explain.
18. Recall from Chapter 17 that tides occur due to the gravitational attraction among the sun, the moon, and Earth. During which phases of the moon are tides the highest? Explain.
19. If you were lost on the moon's surface, why would it be more beneficial to have a star chart rather than a compass?
20. Which of the moon's motions are real? Which are apparent? Explain why each occurs.

Developing Skills

If you need help, refer to the **Skill Handbook.**

21. **Hypothesizing:** Hypothesize why locations near Earth's equator travel faster during one rotation than do places near the poles.
22. **Using Variables, Constants, and Controls:** Describe a simple activity to show how the moon's rotation and revolution work to keep one side facing Earth at all times.
23. **Inferring:** The moon does not produce its own light. Why can we see it in the night sky?
24. **Comparing and Contrasting:** Compare and contrast a waning moon with a waxing moon.
25. **Concept Mapping:** Copy and complete the cycle map shown on this page. Show the sequences of the moon's phases.

Performance Assessment

1. **Design an Experiment:** In Activity 22-1, you learned how the angle at which light strikes a surface determines the amount of heat absorbed. Design a new experiment that will enable you to measure the amount of heat absorbed by a paved surface from the sun at different times of the day. Explain what causes any differences in heat absorption that you notice.
2. **Model:** In Activity 22-2, you used models of Earth, the sun, and the moon to demonstrate moon phases and eclipses. Repeat the activity using yourself as the model of Earth. Have a classmate move the moon model around you until you observe all phases and eclipses.
3. **Oral Presentation:** Write a report describing how your life might be different if you lived in the southern hemisphere. Be sure to discuss the seasons and how they compare with the northern hemisphere's.

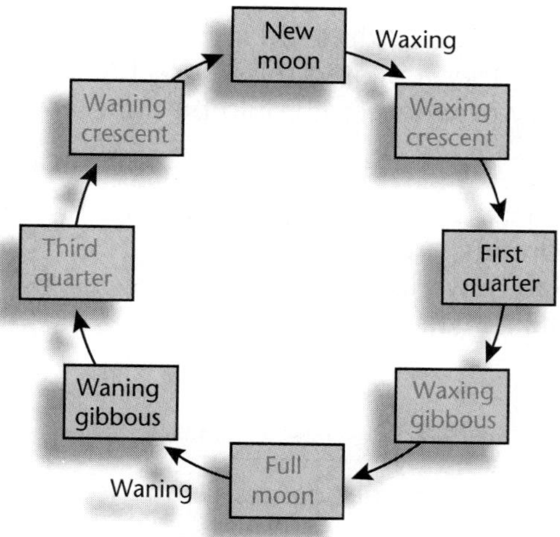

Developing Skills

21. **Hypothesizing** The circumference of Earth is greater at low latitudes than at high latitudes. Thus, locations near the equator have a greater distance to travel to complete one rotation than do locations near the poles.
22. **Using Variables, Constants, and Controls** Place an "X" on a basketball. As you walk around a classmate, keep the "X" pointed toward him or her. As you walk around your classmate, you must turn the ball to keep the "X" facing him or her. As the ball revolves once, it rotates once.
23. **Inferring** The moon shines because it reflects sunlight from its surface.
24. **Comparing and Contrasting** A waxing moon is one that appears to get larger each night. A waning moon appears to get smaller each night.
25. **Concept Mapping** See student page.

Performance Assessment

1. This experiment must be done on a sunny day. Students should set the thermometer-envelope on pavement and record the increase of temperature over a period of 9 minutes at about 9:00 A.M. They should repeat the experiment at least one other time during the day when the sun is higher in the sky. Differences in temperature during the two experiments would be caused by the angle at which sunlight is striking the pavement. Use the Performance Task Assessment List for Designing an Experiment in **PASC,** p. 23. P
2. Students should observe all moon phases. If the model is held in a direct line with their eyes and the light source, students should observe the moon model moving into their shadow and blocking out the light from the sun model. Use the Performance Task Assessment List for Model in **PASC,** p. 51. P
3. Students should discuss the seasons of both the southern and northern hemispheres. Use the Performance Task Assessment List for Oral Presentation in **PASC,** p. 71. P

Chapter Organizer

Section	Objectives	Activities/Features
Chapter Opener		Explore Activity: What might happen to one of the solid-surface planets if a comet collided with it? p. 639
23-1 **The Solar System** (1 session, ½ block)*	1. **Compare** and **contrast** the sun-centered and Earth-centered models of the solar system. 2. **Describe** current models of the formation of the solar system.	Skill Builder: Concept Mapping, p. 644 Using Math, p. 644 Activity 23-1: Planetary Orbits, p. 645
23-2 **The Inner Planets** (2 sessions, 1½ blocks)*	1. **List** the inner planets in their relative order from the sun. 2. **Identify** important characteristics of each inner planet. 3. **Compare** and **contrast** Venus and Earth.	Using Math, p. 647 Problem Solving: Which planet is hotter? p. 648 MiniLAB: How would construction be different on Mars? p. 649 Skill Builder: Interpreting Data, p. 650 Science Journal, p. 650 Science & Literature: A Brave and Startling Truth, p. 651 Science Journal, p. 651
23-3 **Science and Society Issue: Mission to Mars** (1 session, ½ block)*	1. **Recognize** problems that astronauts will encounter during a trip to Mars. 2. **Decide** whether a piloted mission to Mars is necessary or whether it could be done by robotics.	Explore the Issue, p. 653
23-4 **The Outer Planets** (2 sessions, 1½ blocks)*	1. **List** the major characteristics of Jupiter, Saturn, Uranus, and Neptune. 2. **Recognize** how Pluto differs from the other outer planets.	MiniLAB: Can you draw planets to scale? p. 656 Connect to Chemistry, p. 657 Skill Builder: Recognizing Cause and Effect, p. 659 Using Computers: Spreadsheet, p. 659 Activity 23-2: Solar System Distance Model, pp. 660-661 Connect to Physics, p. 663
23-5 **Other Objects in the Solar System** (2 sessions, ½ block)*	1. **Explain** where a comet comes from and describe how a comet develops as it approaches the sun. 2. **Differentiate** among comets, meteoroids, and asteroids.	Using Technology: Space Junk, p. 665 Skill Builder: Interpreting Scientific Illustrations, p. 666 Science Journal, p. 666

* A complete Planning Guide that includes block scheduling is provided on pages 32T-35T.

Activity Materials

Explore	Activities	MiniLAB
page 639 flour, cake pan, cement mix or gelatin powder, assorted objects—marbles, lead weights, bolts, nuts	page 645 thumbtacks or pins, string, 21.5 cm × 28 cm piece of cardboard, metric ruler, pencil, paper pages 660-661 meterstick, pencil, adding machine tape, scissors, string	page 656 pencil, mathematical compass, large sheet of unlined paper, metric ruler, calculator

Chapter 23 The Solar System

Teacher Classroom Resources

Reproducible Masters	Transparencies
Study Guide, p. 89 **Reinforcement**, p. 89 **Enrichment**, p. 89 **Activity Worksheets**, pp. 138-139 **Science Integration Activity 23**, How Can There Be Dry Ice? **Concept Mapping**, p. 51 **Cross-Curricular Integration**, p. 27	**Section Focus Transparency 85,** Imagine . . . **Teaching Transparency 45,** Relative Sizes of the Planets **Teaching Transparency 46,** Planets in the Solar System
Study Guide, p. 90 **Reinforcement**, p. 90 **Enrichment**, p. 90 **Activity Worksheets**, p. 142 **Lab Manual 65,** Venus—The Greenhouse Effect **Multicultural Connections,** pp. 49-50	**Section Focus Transparency 86,** Earth and Its Neighbors or Inner Circles
Study Guide, p. 91 **Reinforcement**, p. 91 **Enrichment**, p. 91 **Science and Society Integration**, p. 27	**Section Focus Transparency 87,** Destination: Mars **Science Integration Transparency 23,** Orbital Forces
Study Guide, p. 92 **Reinforcement**, p. 92 **Enrichment**, p. 92 **Activity Worksheets**, pp. 140-141, 143 **Lab Manual 66,** Jupiter and Its Moons **Critical Thinking/Problem Solving,** p. 29	**Section Focus Transparency 88,** Two Moons Rising
Study Guide, p. 93 **Reinforcement**, p. 93 **Enrichment**, p. 93	**Section Focus Transparency 89,** What in the Universe . . .?

Teaching Resources

Glencoe Earth Science Interactive Videodisc
Earth Science CD-ROM
Spanish Resources
English/Spanish Audiocassettes
Cooperative Learning Resource Guide
Lab Partner
Lab and Safety Skills
Lesson Plans

Assessment Resources

Chapter Review, pp. 49-50
Assessment, pp. 151-154
Performance Assessment in the Science Classroom (PASC)
MindJogger Videoquiz
Alternate Assessment in the Science Classroom
Performance Assessment
Chapter Review Software
Computer Test Bank

Key to Teaching Strategies

The following designations will help you decide which activities are appropriate for your students.

- **L1** Level 1 activities should be within the ability range of all students.
- **L2** Level 2 activities should be within the ability range of the average to above-average student.
- **L3** Level 3 activities are designed for the ability range of above-average students.
- **LEP** LEP activities should be within the ability range of Limited English Proficiency students.
- **LS** These activities are designed to address different learning styles.
- **COOP LEARN** Cooperative Learning activities are designed for small group work.
- **P** These strategies represent student products that can be placed into a best-work portfolio.

GLENCOE TECHNOLOGY

The following multimedia resources are available from Glencoe.

The Infinite Voyage Series
Sail On, Voyager
National Geographic Society Series
STV: Solar System
Glencoe Earth Science Interactive Videodisc
Space Exploration
Earth Science CD-ROM

Teacher Classroom Resources

This is a representation of key blackline masters available in the Teacher Classroom Resources.

Teaching Aids

Section Focus Transparencies

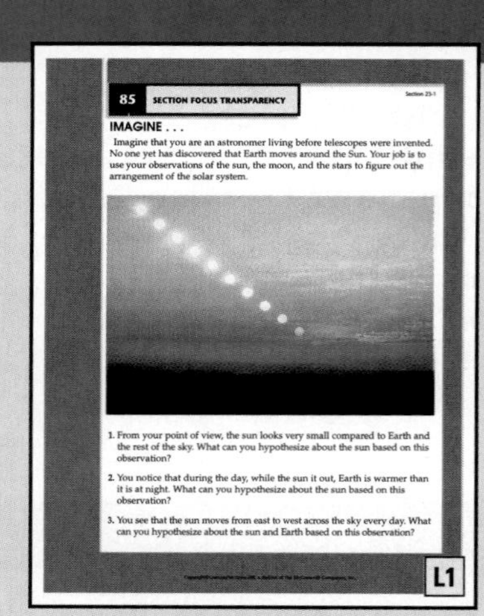
85 SECTION FOCUS TRANSPARENCY Section 23-1

IMAGINE . . .

Imagine that you are an astronomer living before telescopes were invented. No one yet has discovered that Earth moves around the Sun. Your job is to use your observations of the sun, the moon, and the stars to figure out the arrangement of the solar system.

1. From your point of view, the sun looks very small compared to Earth and the rest of the sky. What can you hypothesize about the sun based on this observation?
2. You notice that during the day, while the sun it out, Earth is warmer than it is at night. What can you hypothesize about the sun based on this observation?
3. You see that the sun moves from east to west across the sky every day. What can you hypothesize about the sun and Earth based on this observation?

L1

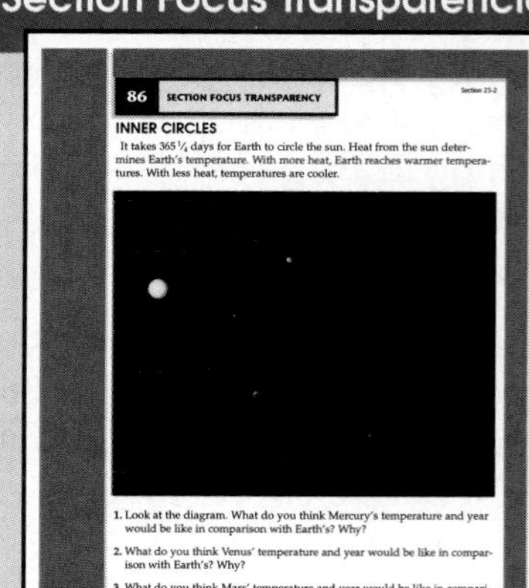
86 SECTION FOCUS TRANSPARENCY Section 23-2

INNER CIRCLES

It takes 365 1/4 days for Earth to circle the sun. Heat from the sun determines Earth's temperature. With more heat, Earth reaches warmer temperatures. With less heat, temperatures are cooler.

1. Look at the diagram. What do you think Mercury's temperature and year would be like in comparison with Earth's? Why?
2. What do you think Venus' temperature and year would be like in comparison with Earth's? Why?
3. What do you think Mars' temperature and year would be like in comparison with Earth's? Why?

L2

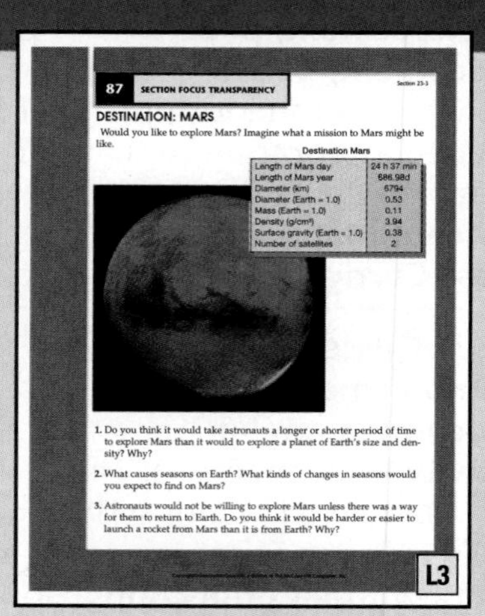
87 SECTION FOCUS TRANSPARENCY Section 23-3

DESTINATION: MARS

Would you like to explore Mars? Imagine what a mission to Mars might be like.

Destination Mars	
Length of Mars day	24 h 37 min
Length of Mars year	686.98d
Diameter (km)	6794
Diameter (Earth = 1.0)	0.53
Mass (Earth = 1.0)	0.11
Density (g/cm³)	3.94
Surface gravity (Earth = 1.0)	0.38
Number of satellites	2

1. Do you think it would take astronauts a longer or shorter period of time to explore Mars than it would to explore a planet of Earth's size and density? Why?
2. What causes seasons on Earth? What kinds of changes in seasons would you expect to find on Mars?
3. Astronauts would not be willing to explore Mars unless there was a way for them to return to Earth. Do you think it would be harder or easier to launch a rocket from Mars than it is from Earth? Why?

L3

Science Integration Transparencies

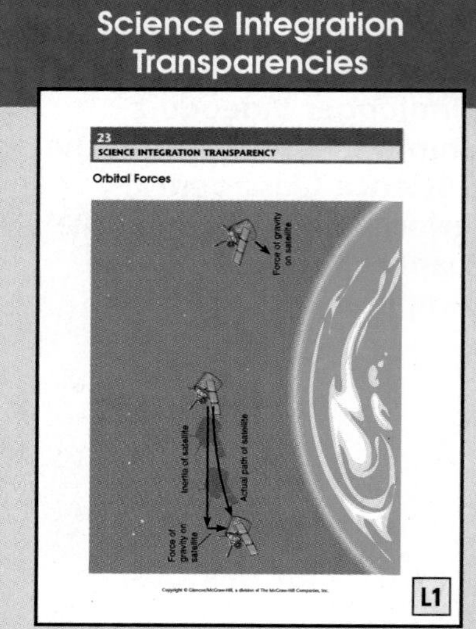
23 SCIENCE INTEGRATION TRANSPARENCY

Orbital Forces

L1

Teaching Transparencies

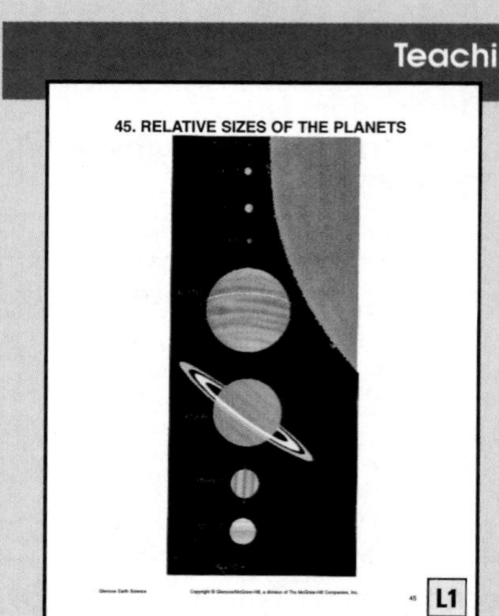
45. RELATIVE SIZES OF THE PLANETS

L1

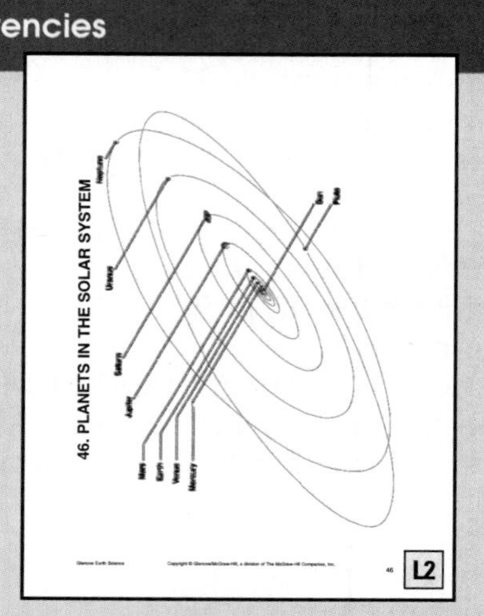
46. PLANETS IN THE SOLAR SYSTEM

L2

Meeting Different Ability Levels

Study Guide

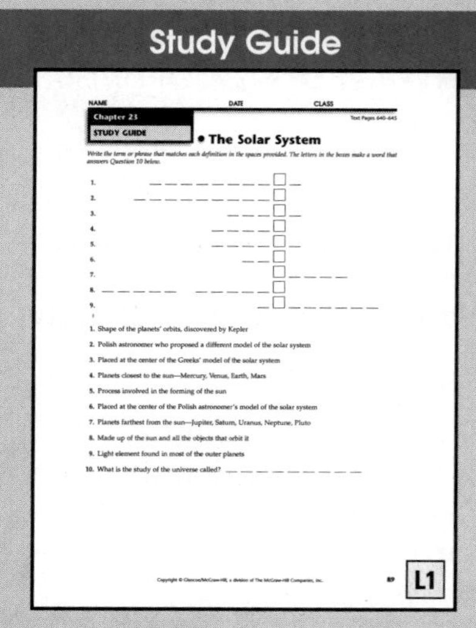
Chapter 23 STUDY GUIDE • The Solar System

1. Shape of the planets' orbits, discovered by Kepler
2. Polish astronomer who proposed a different model of the solar system
3. Placed at the center of the Greeks' model of the solar system
4. Planets closest to the sun—Mercury, Venus, Earth, Mars
5. Process involved in the forming of the sun
6. Placed at the center of the Polish astronomer's model of the solar system
7. Planets farthest from the sun—Jupiter, Saturn, Uranus, Neptune, Pluto
8. Made up of the sun and all the objects that orbit it
9. Light element found in most of the outer planets
10. What is the study of the universe called?

L1

Reinforcement

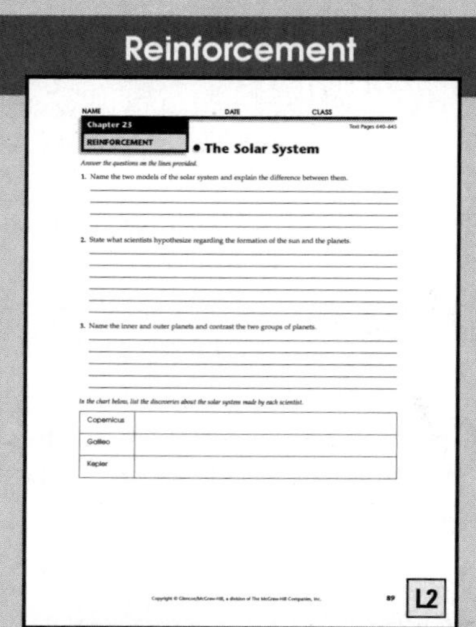
Chapter 23 REINFORCEMENT • The Solar System

1. Name the two models of the solar system and explain the difference between them.
2. State what scientists hypothesize regarding the formation of the sun and the planets.
3. Name the inner and outer planets and contrast the two groups of planets.

Copernicus	
Galileo	
Kepler	

L2

Enrichment Worksheets

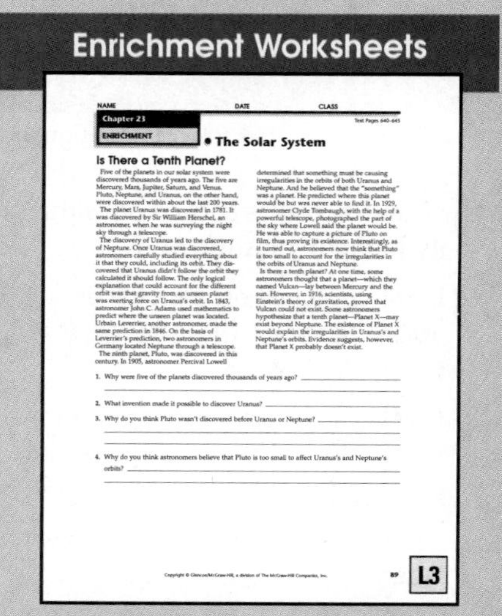
Chapter 23 ENRICHMENT • The Solar System

Is There a Tenth Planet?

1. Why were five of the planets discovered thousands of years ago?
2. What invention made it possible to discover Uranus?
3. Why do you think Pluto wasn't discovered before Uranus or Neptune?
4. Why do you think astronomers believe that Pluto is too small to affect Uranus's and Neptune's orbits?

L3

Hands-On Activities

Science Integration Activity

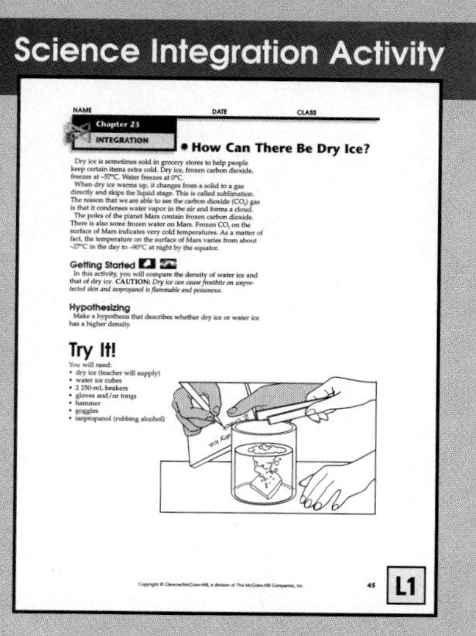
NAME DATE CLASS
Chapter 23 INTEGRATION
How Can There Be Dry Ice?
Getting Started
Hypothesizing
Try It!
L1

Lab Manual

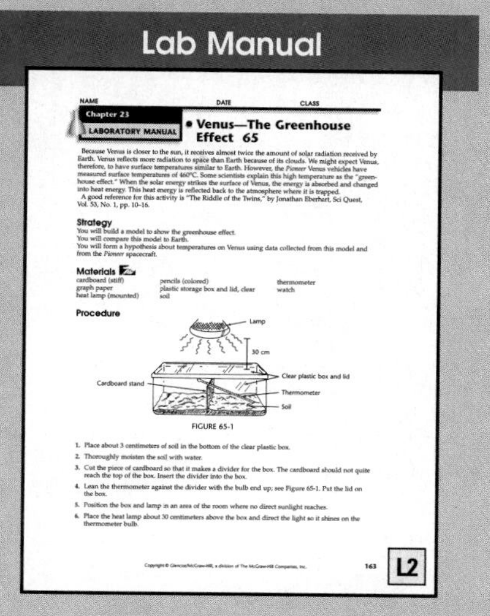
NAME DATE CLASS
Chapter 23 LABORATORY MANUAL
Venus—The Greenhouse Effect 65
Strategy
Materials
Procedure

L2

Assessment

Performance Assessment

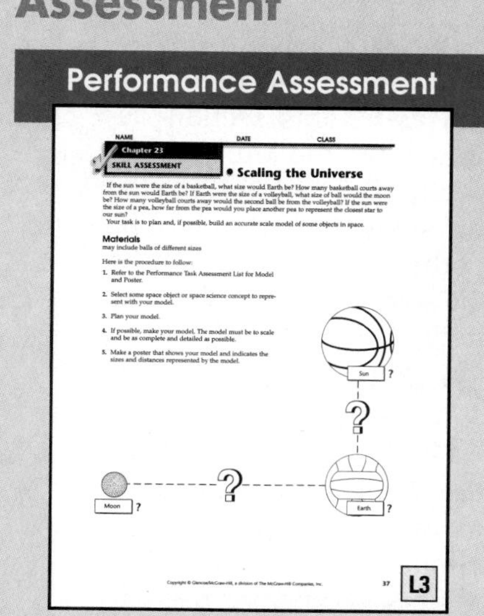
NAME DATE CLASS
Chapter 23 SKILL ASSESSMENT
Scaling the Universe
Materials

L3

Enrichment and Application

Critical Thinking/ Problem Solving

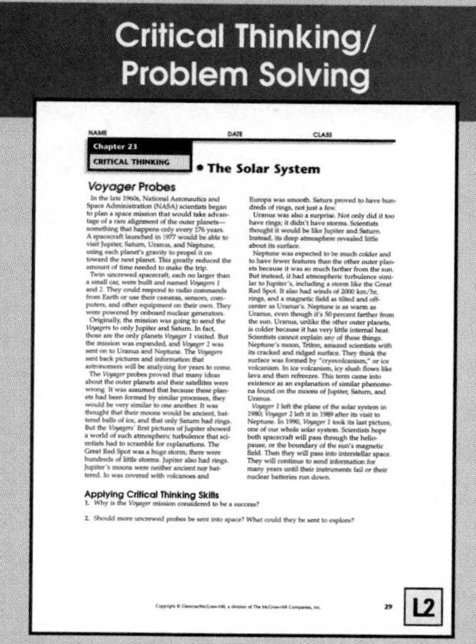
NAME DATE CLASS
Chapter 23 CRITICAL THINKING
The Solar System
Voyager Probes
Applying Critical Thinking Skills
L2

Cross-Curricular Integration

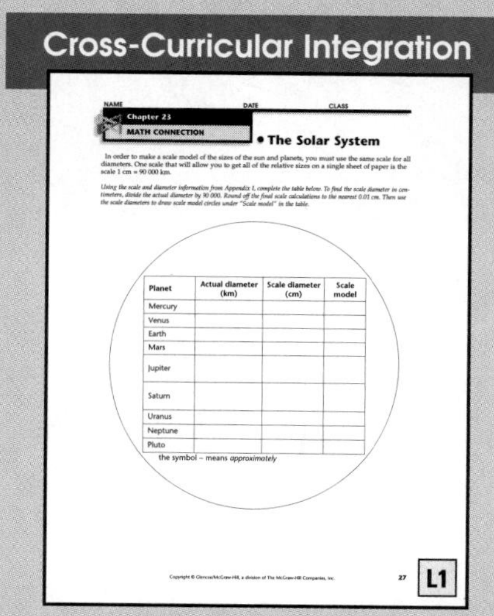
NAME DATE CLASS
Chapter 23 MATH CONNECTION
The Solar System

Planet	Actual diameter (km)	Scale diameter (cm)	Scale model
Mercury			
Venus			
Earth			
Mars			
Jupiter			
Saturn			
Uranus			
Neptune			
Pluto			

the symbol ~ means approximately
L1

Science and Society Integration

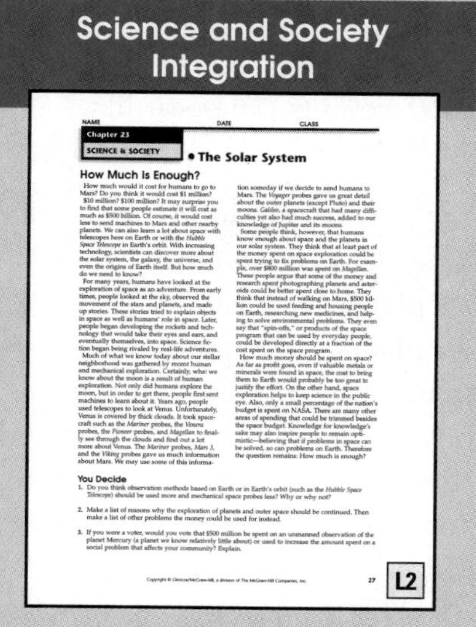
NAME DATE CLASS
Chapter 23 SCIENCE & SOCIETY
The Solar System
How Much Is Enough?
You Decide
L2

Multicultural Connections

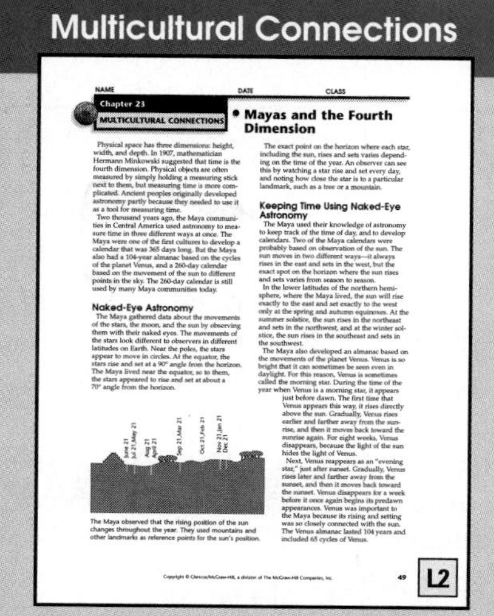
NAME DATE CLASS
Chapter 23 MULTICULTURAL CONNECTIONS
Mayas and the Fourth Dimension
Naked-Eye Astronomy
Keeping Time Using Naked-Eye Astronomy
L2

Concept Mapping

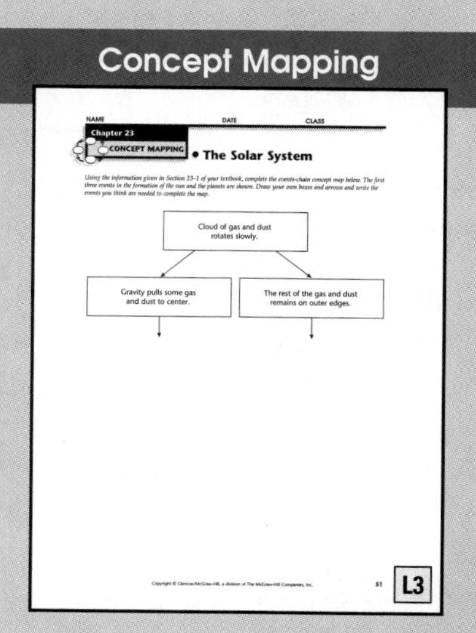
NAME DATE CLASS
Chapter 23 CONCEPT MAPPING
The Solar System

L3

Chapter 23

The Solar System

CHAPTER OVERVIEW

Section 23-1 This section describes how the present-day sun-centered model of the solar system evolved. One hypothesis of the formation of the solar system is also presented.

Section 23-2 This section lists and describes characteristics of each of the inner planets.

Section 23-3 Science and Society Students are asked to explore the issue of whether humans or robots should be used to explore Mars.

Section 23-4 This section lists and describes each of the outer planets. Information gathered from the *Voyager* space probes is presented.

Section 23-5 This section describes comets, meteoroids, and asteroids.

Chapter Vocabulary

solar system	Saturn
inner planet	Uranus
outer planet	Neptune
Mercury	Pluto
Venus	comet
Earth	Oort Cloud
astronomical unit	meteor
Mars	meteorite
Jupiter	asteroid
Great Red Spot	

Theme Connection

Scale and Structure The theme of this chapter is the scale and structure of the solar system. All objects in this system are compared and contrasted according to size and composition.

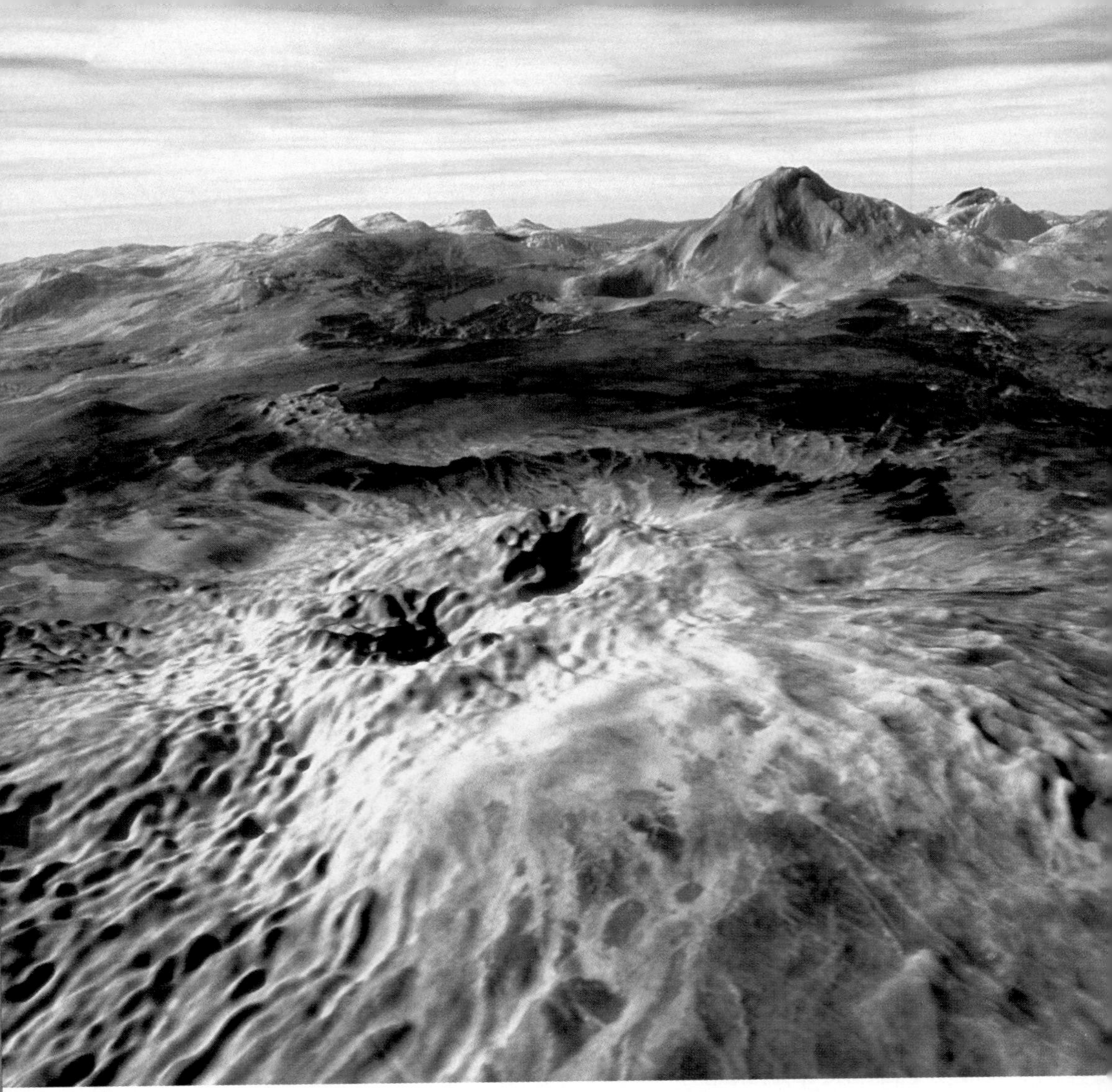

Previewing the Chapter

Section 23-1 The Solar System
- ▶ Early Ideas About the Solar System
- ▶ Formation of the Solar System
- ▶ Motions of the Planets

Section 23-2 The Inner Planets
- ▶ Inner Planets

Section 23-3 Science and Society: Issue: Mission to Mars

Section 23-4 The Outer Planets
- ▶ Outer Planets

Section 23-5 Other Objects in the Solar System
- ▶ Comets
- ▶ Meteoroids, Meteors, and Meteorites
- ▶ Asteroids

638

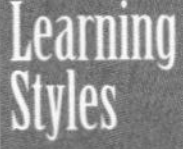

Learning Styles

Look for the following logo for strategies that emphasize different learning modalities. LS

Kinesthetic	Explore, p. 639
Visual-Spatial	Drawing a Model, p. 641; Visual Learning, pp. 647, 655; Activity, p. 648
Interpersonal	Activity, pp. 641, 655; MiniLAB, p. 656; Reteach, p. 658
Intrapersonal	Activity, p. 652; Enrichment, p. 657
Logical-Mathematical	Activities 23-1, p. 645; 23-2, pp. 660-661; Across the Curriculum, pp. 647, 649, 656; MiniLAB, p. 649; Reteach, p. 665
Linguistic	Science Journal, pp. 641, 658; Using an Analogy, p. 642; Activity, p. 647

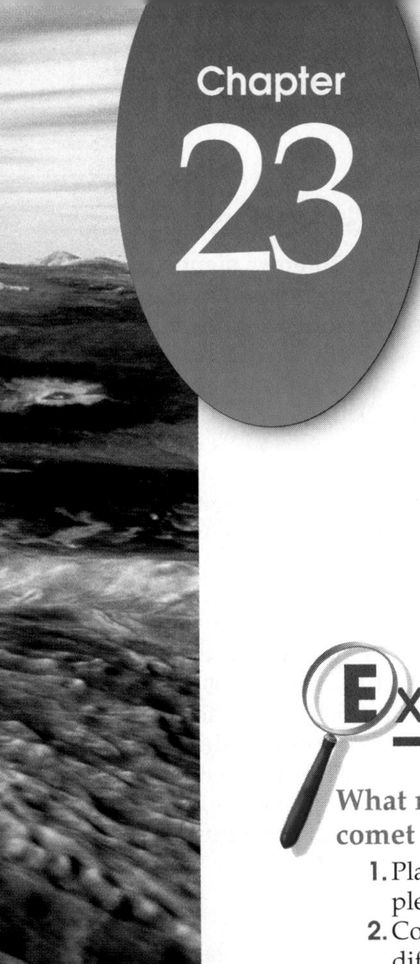

Chapter 23

The Solar System

The planets of our solar system are our nearest neighbors in space. But to us on Earth, they look like tiny points of light among the thousands of others visible on a clear night. With the help of telescopes and space probes, the points of light become giant colorful spheres, some with rings, others pitted with countless craters. This image of the surface of Venus was made using space probe data and computers. In this chapter, explore our wandering neighbors as we look at the solar system.

EXPLORE ACTIVITY

What might happen to one of the solid surface planets if a comet collided with it?

1. Place fine white flour into a cake pan to a depth of 3 cm, completely covering the bottom of the pan.
2. Cover the flour with 1 cm of fine, gray, dry cement mix, or try different colors of gelatin powder.
3. From varying heights, drop various-sized objects into the pan. Use marbles, lead weights, bolts, and nuts.

Observe: In your Science Journal, draw what happens to the surface of the powder in the pan as each object is dropped from different heights.

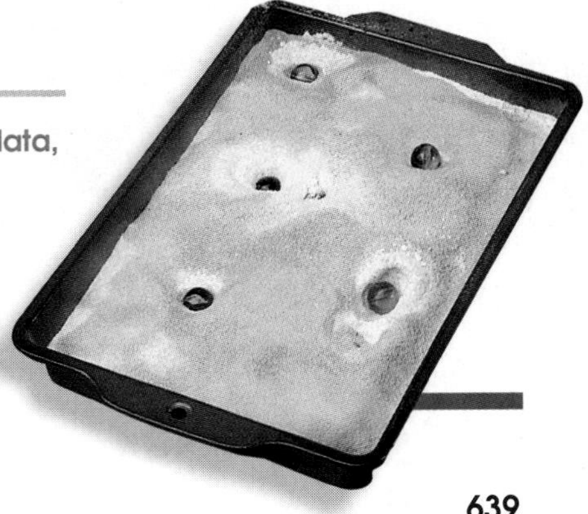

Previewing Science Skills

- In the **Skill Builders**, you will **map concepts, interpret data, recognize cause and effect**, and **interpret a scientific illustration.**
- In the **Activities**, you will **measure, predict, interpret,** and **use numbers.**
- In the **MiniLABs**, you will **make a model** and plan for a trip to Mars.

EXPLORE ACTIVITY

Purpose

LS **Kinesthetic** Use the Explore Activity to introduce students to the cause and effect of comet parts colliding with a planet with a solid surface or a gaseous surface. L1 LEP

Preparation

Prior to beginning this chapter, obtain flat pans or ask students to bring in old flat pans from home.

Materials

flat pan; white flour; gray, dry cement mix (or colored, powdered gelatin); and objects such as marbles, lead weights, bolts, and nuts

Teaching Strategies

Troubleshooting Be sure to have students spread out large sheets of newspaper.

Safety Precautions Caution students to wear safety goggles while dropping objects.

Observe

The white powder splashes out over the darker powdered surface. A crater forms as the object is buried in the powder. Craters are deeper when the objects are dropped from greater distances. Craters on Mars and the moon probably formed in the same way.

Assessment

Performance Show students a pan that you have done earlier. Ask them which craters may have been caused by bigger objects. Ask them to determine which craters formed first. Use the Performance Task Assessment List for Making Observations and Inferences in **PASC,** p. 17. P

Assessment Planner

Portfolio

Refer to page 667 for suggested items that students might select for their portfolios.

Performance Assessment

See page 667 for additional Performance Assessment options.
Skill Builders, pp. 644, 650, 659, 666
MiniLABs, pp. 649, 656
Activities 23-1, p. 645; 23-2, pp. 660-661

Content Assessment

Section Wrap-ups, pp. 644, 650, 653, 659, 666
Chapter Review, pp. 667-669
Mini Quizzes, pp. 644, 650, 659, 666

Group Assessment

Opportunities for group assessment occur with Cooperative Learning Strategies and Flex Your Brain Activities.

Section 23•1

Prepare

Section Background

- Most objects in the solar system rotate and revolve toward the east. Any motion different from this eastward motion is retrograde motion. Retrograde motion of Mars' orbit was one piece of evidence used by Copernicus to support his sun-centered model of the solar system.
- Recent hypotheses on the formation of our solar system suggest that a nearby star may have exploded, sending shock waves through the cloud that was to become the solar system. The shock waves caused the particles in the cloud to condense, leading to the formation of the solar system.

Preplanning

To prepare for Activity 23-1, obtain thumbtacks or pins, string, cardboard, and metric rulers.

1 Motivate

Bellringer

Before presenting the lesson, display **Section Focus Transparency 85** on the overhead projector. Assign the accompanying **Focus Activity** worksheet. L1 LEP

Tying to Previous Knowledge

Remind students that the "rising" and "setting" of the sun, moon, and stars are caused by the rotation of Earth. Ask students to speculate why these same observations caused people long ago to think Earth was in the center of the solar system.

23•1 The Solar System

Science Words

solar system
inner planet
outer planet

Objectives

- Compare and contrast the sun-centered and Earth-centered models of the solar system.
- Describe current models of the formation of the solar system.

Early Ideas About the Solar System

Imagine yourself on a warm, clear summer night lying in the grass and gazing at the stars and the moon. The stars and the moon seem so still and beautiful. You may even see other planets in the solar system, thinking they are stars. Although the planets are very different from stars, they blend in with the stars and are usually hard to pick out.

The Earth-Centered Model

As you learned in Chapter 22, the sun and the stars appear to move through the sky because Earth is moving. This wasn't always an accepted fact. Many early Greek scientists thought the planets, the sun, and the moon were embedded in separate spheres that rotated around Earth. The stars were thought to be embedded in another sphere that also rotated around Earth. Early observers described moving objects in the night sky using the term *planasthai,* which means "to wander." This model is called the Earth-centered model of the solar system. To the astronomers who believed in this model of the solar system, there were Earth, the moon, the sun, five planets—Mercury, Venus, Mars, Jupiter, and Saturn—and the sphere of stars.

The Sun-Centered Model

The idea of an Earth-centered solar system was held for centuries until the Polish astronomer Nicholas Copernicus published a different view in 1543. He proposed that the moon revolved around Earth, which was a planet. Earth, along with

Figure 23-1
This instrument, called an astrolabe, was used for a variety of astronomical calculations.

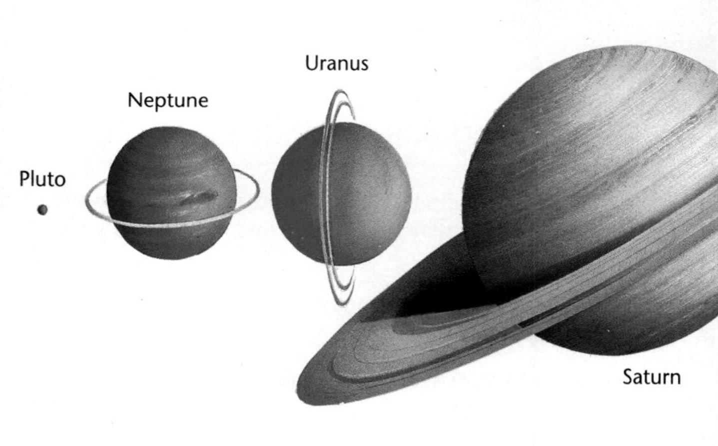

Program Resources

Reproducible Masters
Study Guide, p. 89 L1
Reinforcement, p. 89 L1
Enrichment, p. 89 L3
Activity Worksheets, pp. 5, 138-139 L1
Concept Mapping, p. 51
Science Integration Activities, pp. 45-46
Cross-Curricular Integration, p. 27

Transparencies
Section Focus Transparency 85 L1
Teaching Transparency 45 and **46**

the other planets, revolved around the sun. He also stated that the daily movement of the planets and the stars was due to Earth's rotation. This is the sun-centered model of the solar system.

Using his telescope, the Italian astronomer Galileo Galilei found evidence that supported the ideas of Copernicus. He discovered that Venus went through phases like the moon's. These phases could be explained only if Venus were orbiting the sun. From this, he concluded that Venus revolves around the sun, and the sun is the center of the solar system.

Modern View of the Solar System

We now know that Earth is one of nine planets and many smaller objects that orbit the sun and make up the **solar system.** The size of the nine planets and the sun are shown to scale in **Figure 23-2;** however, the distances between the planets are not to scale. The dark areas on the sun are sunspots, which you will learn about in Chapter 24. Notice how small Earth is compared with some of the other planets and the sun, which is much larger than any of the planets.

The solar system includes a vast territory extending billions of kilometers in all directions from the sun. The sun contains 99.86 percent of the mass of the whole solar system. Because of its gravitational pull, the sun is the central object around which other objects of the solar system revolve.

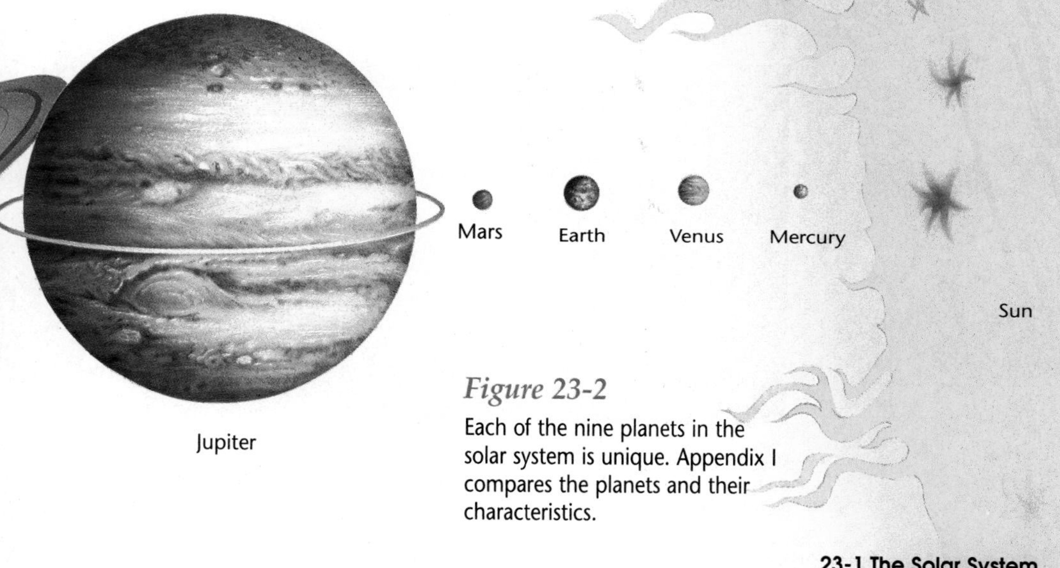

Figure 23-2
Each of the nine planets in the solar system is unique. Appendix I compares the planets and their characteristics.

2 Teach

Activity

LS **Interpersonal** Have pairs of students make flash cards of the planets in the solar system. They can draw the planet on one side of the card and write anything they know about it on the other side. Students should keep their flash cards handy so they can correct or update their information as they read this chapter. COOP LEARN

Drawing a Model

LS **Visual-Spatial** Have volunteers compare and contrast the sun-centered solar system model with the Earth-centered model by making sketches on the chalkboard. As some students draw the models, have a partner point out how the two models are similar and how they are different.

 Use these program resources as you teach this lesson.

Cross-Curricular Integration, p. 27

Concept Mapping, p. 51

GLENCOE TECHNOLOGY

CD-ROM

Earth Science CD-ROM

Have students perform the interactive exploration for Chapter 23 to reinforce important chapter concepts and thinking processes.

Use **Teaching Transparencies 45** and **46** as you teach this lesson.

Science Journal

Models of the Solar System Have students write a one-page report in their Science Journals that describes what evidence led Copernicus to propose the sun-centered model of the solar system. Ask students to state the evidence and to explain how this evidence refuted the Earth-centered model of the solar system. They should list which scientists discovered the evidence used by Copernicus. L2 LS

Inquiry Questions

- **What was Johannes Kepler's contribution to the sun-centered solar system model?** *He used mathematics to determine the shapes of the orbits and to calculate that the sun was not at the center of the elliptical paths.*
- **How do the planets' revolutions support the idea that the cloud that formed the solar system spun faster as it contracted?** *The inner planets revolve faster than the outer planets.*

Using an Analogy

LS **Linguistic** Ask students why an ice skater will pull his or her arms toward the body as he or she spins. Use this analogy to compare this increase in rotational speed to that of the cloud that formed the solar system, which spun faster as more material was pulled toward its center.

Use **Science Integration Activities,** pp. 45-46, as you teach this lesson.

NATIONAL GEOGRAPHIC SOCIETY

Videodisc

STV: Solar System

The Big Picture

Unit 1, Side 1

Astronomer at Work

00720-02381

How the Solar System Began

02404-03596

Rotation and Revolution

05295-06309

Figure 23-3

Through careful observations, astronomers have found clues that help explain how our solar system may have formed.

Formation of the Solar System

Scientists hypothesize that the sun and the solar system formed from a cloud of gas, ice, and dust about 5 billion years ago. **Figure 23-3** illustrates how this may have happened. This cloud was slowly rotating in space. A nearby star may have exploded and the shock waves from this event may have caused the cloud to start contracting. Initially the cloud was rotating very slowly. But as it contracted and the density became greater, increased gravitational attraction pulled more gas and dust toward the cloud center. This caused the cloud to rotate faster, which in turn caused it to flatten into a disk with a dense center.

As the cloud contracted, the temperature began to increase. Eventually the temperature in the core of the cloud reached about 10 million K and nuclear fusion began. This was the moment when the sun became a star. Nuclear

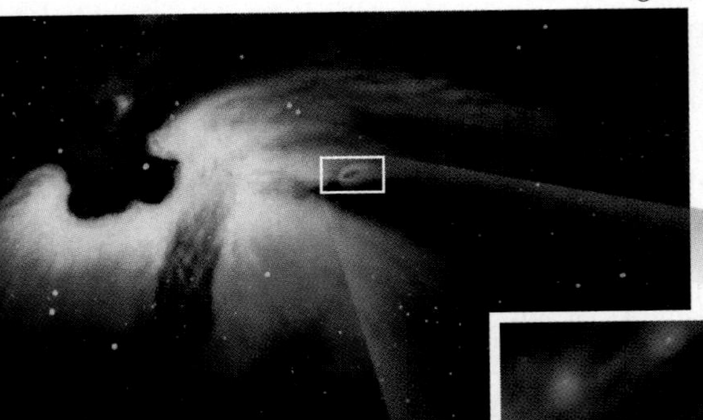

A About 5 billion years ago, a large cloud of gas, ice, and dust occupied our place in space.

B As gravity pulled matter inward, the cloud began to contract and spin. The densely packed matter grew extremely hot.

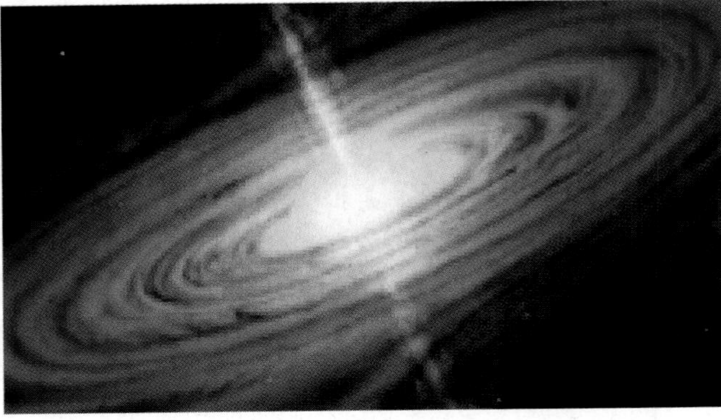

C The center of the rotating disk continued to heat. Meanwhile, gas and dust particles in the outer rim clumped together, forming larger objects.

Inclusion Strategies

Gifted Have students research to find out about famous astronomers. Students can work in groups of 5 or 6 to write plays in which these astronomers are brought together in time to discuss their ideas. Students can dress in period costumes and perform the plays for the class. L3

Physically Challenged Have students work in small groups to make mobiles of the solar system to display in class. Encourage physically challenged students to work in groups where they can contribute their knowledge and ideas. On the back side of each planet students should include all the pertinent facts, such as temperature extremes, whether or not the planet has an atmosphere, length of orbit around the sun, the numbers of moons, and so on.

D The larger clumps continued to grow through more collisions.

E Eventually, the larger clumps gathered enough matter to become the nine planets. The core of the disk grew even denser and hotter.

F Nuclear fission began in the core and the sun became a star. Smaller objects became moons and rings around the planets.

fusion occurs when atoms with low mass, such as hydrogen, combine to form heavier elements, such as helium. The new heavy element contains slightly less mass than the sum of the light atoms that formed it. The lost mass is converted into energy.

Not all of the nearby gas and dust were drawn into the core of the cloud. Remaining gas and dust particles collided and stuck together, forming larger objects that in turn attracted more particles because of the stronger gravitational pull. Close to the sun the temperature was quite hot, and easily vaporized elements could not condense into solids. This accounts for the fact that light elements are more scarce in the planets closer to the sun than in planets further out in the solar system. Instead, the inner solar system is dominated by small rocky planets with iron cores.

The **inner planets** of Mercury, Venus, Earth, and Mars are the solid rocky planets closest to the sun. The **outer planets** of Jupiter, Saturn, Uranus, Neptune, and Pluto are those furthest from the sun. Except for Pluto, which is rocky, the outer planets are composed mostly of lighter elements such as hydrogen and helium.

NATIONAL GEOGRAPHIC SOCIETY

Videodisc

STV: Solar System

Clouds forming into satellites 1 (art)

41660

INTEGRATION Physics

Planetary motion is discussed on p. 644. Have students find out about Kepler's three laws of planetary motion and the work done by Kepler that enabled him to devise the laws. They should also briefly explain what each law states about planetary motion.

3 Assess

Check for Understanding

FLEX Your Brain

Use the Flex Your Brain activity to have students explore FORMATION OF THE SOLAR SYSTEM.

Activity Worksheets p. 5

Reteach

Have students compare and contrast labeled photographs or illustrations of the planets. Have students divide the planets into two groups based on size alone. Discuss where Pluto fits in this classification.

Extension

For students who have mastered this section, use the **Reinforcement** and **Enrichment** masters.

Cultural Diversity

Planetary Wisdom Some of the planets are visible in Earth's night sky, and have been used to explain, or to chart, the course of life on Earth. Many early skywatchers interpreted planets appearing in conjunction (or appearing to move close to each other) as an important sign. In ancient India, periodic destruction of the universe by flooding or conflagration was marked by Jupiter and Saturn. Jupiter passes Saturn in the night sky every 20 years. If one waits for this to happen in all 12 of the zodiac sections, one will have a universe cycle of 960 years. The Chaldeans believed that if all seven planets were in conjunction in Cancer, the universe would end in deluge. If all seven conjoined in Capricorn, the universe would end in fire.

4 Close

•MINI•QUIZ•

Use the Mini Quiz to check students' recall of chapter content.

1. **The ______ model of the solar system was proposed by Copernicus in 1543.** *sun-centered*
2. **The sun, nine planets, and many smaller objects make up the ______.** *solar system*
3. **The ______ planets are small and rocky and have iron cores.** *inner*
4. **The ______ planets, except for Pluto, are composed mostly of lighter elements.** *outer*

Section Wrap-up

Review

1. In the sun-centered model, all objects orbit the sun, whereas in the Earth-centered model, the sun, planets, and other objects orbit Earth.
2. More than 4.6 billion years ago, a large cloud of gas, ice, and dust began to condense. The center of the cloud formed the sun. The planets and other objects in the solar system formed from outer portions of the cloud.
3. Temperatures are too low for water to exist as a liquid.
4. **Think Critically** It would be longer, because Uranus' orbit is much larger than Earth's. Eighty-four Earth years equal one Uranus year.

USING MATH

Mercury orbits at a speed of 47.89 km/s and Earth orbits at a speed of 29.79 km/s. Dividing Mercury's speed by Earth's shows that Mercury travels 1.6 times faster.

INTEGRATION **Physics**

Motions of the Planets

When Nicholas Copernicus developed his sun-centered model of the solar system, he thought that the planets orbited the sun in circles. In the early 1600s, the German mathematician Johannes Kepler began studying the orbits of the planets. He discovered that the shapes of the orbits are not circular, but elliptical. He also calculated that the sun is not at the center of the ellipse, but is offset from the center.

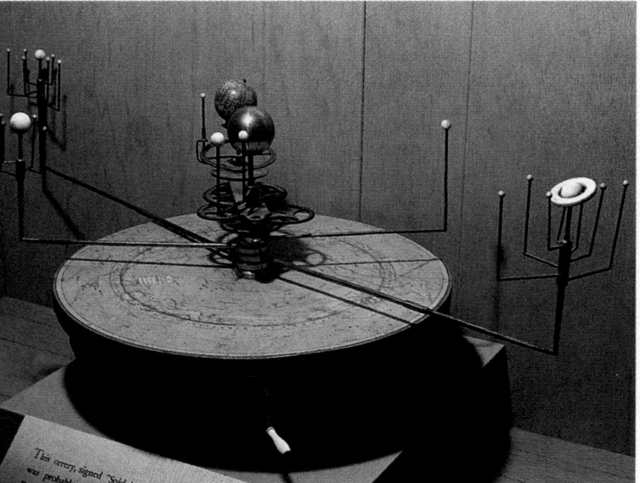

Figure 23-4
This device is an early model of the solar system.

Kepler also discovered that the planets travel at different speeds in their orbits around the sun. By studying Appendix I, you can see that the planets closer to the sun travel faster than planets farther away from the sun. As a result, the outer planets take much longer to orbit the sun than the inner planets do.

Copernicus's ideas, considered radical at the time, led to the birth of modern astronomy. Early scientists didn't have technology such as space probes to learn about the planets. Nevertheless, they developed theories about the solar system that we still use today.

Section Wrap-up

Review

1. What is the difference between the sun-centered and the Earth-centered models of the solar system?
2. How do scientists hypothesize the solar system formed?
3. The outer planets are rich in water, methane, and ammonia—the materials needed for life. Yet life is unlikely on these planets. Explain.
4. **Think Critically:** Would a year on the planet Uranus be longer or shorter than an Earth year? Explain.

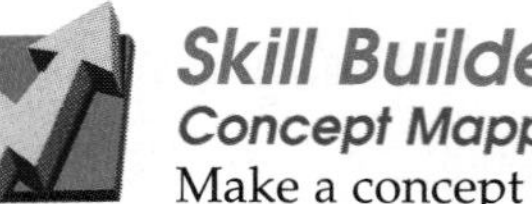

Skill Builder
Concept Mapping

Make a concept map that compares and contrasts the Earth-centered model with the sun-centered model of the solar system. If you need help, refer to Concept Mapping in the **Skill Handbook.**

USING MATH

Assuming that the planets travel in nearly circular orbits, use the information in Appendix I to determine how much faster (in km/s) Mercury travels in its orbit than Earth travels in its orbit.

Skill Builder

Possible solution:

Solar system models
Earth centered
states that the central body is:
Earth
movement of objects in night sky due to:
Objects embedded in spheres that rotate around Earth
Sun centered
states that the central body is:
Sun
movement of objects in night sky due to:
Earth's rotation

Assessment

Content Use this Skill Builder to assess students' abilities to make a concept map. Ask students to compare how the sun is handled in two theories. Use the Performance Task Assessment List for Concept Map in **PASC,** p. 89. P

Activity 23-1 Planetary Orbits

You have learned that planets travel around the sun along fixed paths called orbits. Early theories about the solar system stated that planetary orbits were perfect circles. Do this activity to construct a model of a planetary orbit. You will observe that the shape of planetary orbits is an ellipse, not a circle.

Problem

Can a model be constructed that will show planetary orbits to be elliptical?

Materials

- thumbtacks or pins
- string
- cardboard (21.5 cm × 28 cm)
- metric ruler
- pencil
- paper

Procedure

Part A

1. Place a blank sheet of paper on top of the cardboard and place two thumbtacks or pins about 3 cm apart.
2. Tie the string into a circle with a circumference of 15 to 20 cm. Loop the string around the thumbtacks. With someone holding the tacks or pins, place your pencil inside the loop and pull it taut.

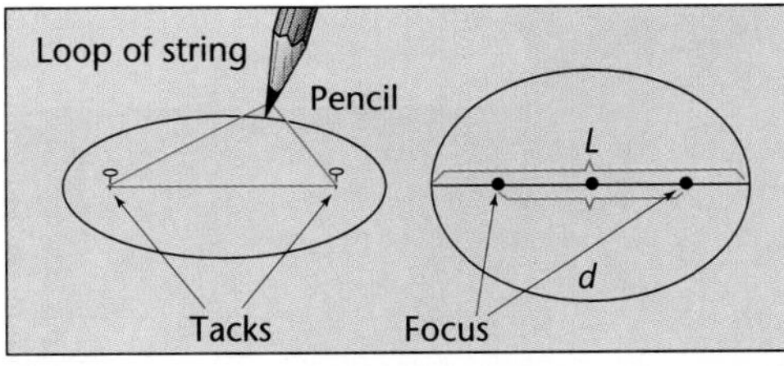

3. Move the pen or pencil around the tacks, keeping the string taut, until you have completed a smooth, closed curve, or ellipse.
4. Repeat steps 1 through 3 several times. First vary the distance between the tacks and then vary the length of the string. However, change only one of these each time. Note the effect on the size and shape of the ellipse with each of these changes.
5. Orbits are usually described in terms of eccentricity (e). The eccentricity of any ellipse is determined by dividing the distance (d) between the foci (here, the tacks) by the length of the major axis (L). See the diagram at left.
6. Calculate and record the eccentricity of the ellipses that you constructed.

Part B

7. Refer to Appendix I to determine the eccentricities of planetary orbits.
8. Construct an ellipse with the same eccentricity as Earth's orbit.
9. Repeat step 8 with the orbit of either Pluto or Mercury.

Analyze

1. **Analyze** the effect a change in the length of the string or the distance between the tacks has on the shape of the ellipse.
2. **Hypothesize** what must be done to the string or placement of tacks to decrease the eccentricity of a constructed ellipse.

Conclude and Apply

3. **Describe** the shape of Earth's orbit. Where is the sun located within the orbit?
4. **Identify** the planets that have the most eccentric orbits.
5. **Describe** the path of an orbit with an eccentricity of zero.

Activity 23-1

Purpose

Logical-Mathematical Describe a model that best represents the shape of planetary orbits. L2

Process Skills

measuring in SI, observing, inferring, using numbers, comparing and contrasting, forming operational definitions, and making and using tables

Time

40 minutes

Safety Precautions

Caution students to handle thumbtacks or pins with care.

Activity Worksheets, pp. 5, 138-139

Teaching Strategies

- Provide students with several values for d and L for imaginary ellipses and allow them to solve for e.

Alternate Materials Hat pins allow students to observe all parts of the taut string. Time can be saved by having a number of pieces of string already tied in loops.

Troubleshooting If students have any problem with the equation $e = d/L$, show them how 3 = 6/2 or 3 = 12/4 relates to it.

Answers to Questions

1. Increasing the length of the string or decreasing the distance between the tacks makes the ellipse more circular. Decreasing the string's length or increasing the distance between foci makes the shape more elliptical.
2. Lengthen the string or move the tacks closer to each other.
3. It appears to be circular with the sun near one of the foci.
4. Pluto (0.248), Mercury (0.206), and Mars (0.093)
5. It would be circular.

Data and Observations

Constructed Ellipse	d (cm)	L (cm)	e (d/L)
# 1	3	15.6	0.19
# 2	5	13.5	0.37
# 3	5	8.7	0.57
Earth's orbit	.48	28	.017
Mercury's orbit			.206
Pluto's orbit			.248

Assessment

Oral Based on what students achieved in this activity, ask them to describe what must be true to obtain a circular orbit. What conditions would provide a more elliptical orbit? Use the Performance Task Assessment List for Making Observations and Inferences in **PASC,** p. 17. P

Section 23•2

Prepare

Section Background

- Carbon dioxide dissolves in water; therefore, much of the carbon dioxide in Earth's atmosphere has been removed by rain. If it weren't for the presence of liquid water on Earth, the amount of carbon dioxide in the air would be similar to that in Venus' atmosphere, causing a tremendous increase in the greenhouse effect on Earth.
- All planets except Earth can be classified as inferior or superior. Inferior planets, Mercury and Venus, have orbits that are inside Earth's orbit. Superior planets have orbits that lie outside Earth's orbit. These include Mars, Jupiter, Saturn, Uranus, Neptune, and Pluto.

Preplanning

Obtain recent photographs of the inner planets prior to beginning this lesson.

1 Motivate

Bellringer

Before presenting the lesson, display **Section Focus Transparency 86** on the overhead projector. Assign the accompanying **Focus Activity** worksheet. L1 LEP

Tying to Previous Knowledge

Have students recall from Chapter 21 that much of what we know about the solar system has been sent back to Earth by space probes.

Use **Multicultural Connections,** pp. 49-50, as you teach this lesson.

23•2 The Inner Planets

Science Words

Mercury
Venus
Earth
astronomical unit
Mars

Objectives

- List the inner planets in their relative order from the sun.
- Identify important characteristics of each inner planet.
- Compare and contrast Venus and Earth.

Inner Planets

We have learned much about the solar system since the days of Copernicus and Galileo. Advance-ments in telescopes allow astronomers to observe the planets from Earth. And space probes have explored much of our solar system, adding greatly to the knowledge we have about the planets. Let's take a tour of the solar system through the "eyes" of the space probes.

Mercury

The closest planet to the Sun is **Mercury.** It is also the second-smallest planet. The first and only American spacecraft mission to Mercury was in 1974-1975 by *Mariner 10,* which flew by the planet and sent pictures back to Earth. *Mariner 10* imaged only 45 percent of Mercury's surface—we do not know what the other 55 percent looks like. What we have seen is that the surface of Mercury has many craters and looks much like our moon. It also has cliffs as high as 3 km on its surface, as seen in **Figure 23-5.** These cliffs were formed when Mercury shrank about 2 km in diameter.

Why did Mercury shrink? Scientists think the answer may lie inside the planet. *Mariner 10* detected a weak magnetic field around Mercury, indicating that the planet has a large iron core. Some scientists hypothesize that the crust of Mercury solidified while the iron core was still hot and molten. Then, as the core

Figure 23-5

Giant cliffs on Mercury, like the one marked by the arrow, suggest that the planet might have shrunk.

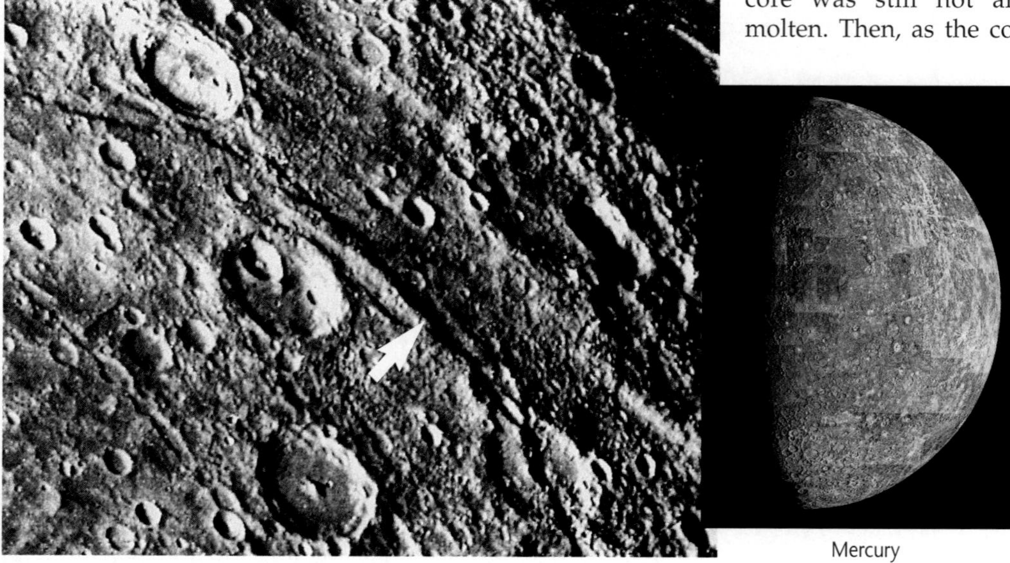

Mercury

Program Resources

Reproducible Masters

Study Guide, p. 90 L1
Reinforcement, p. 90 L1
Enrichment, p. 90 L3
Activity Worksheets, pp. 5, 142 L1
Multicultural Connections, pp. 49-50
Lab Manual 65

Transparencies

Section Focus Transparency 86 L1

cooled and solidified, it contracted, causing the planet to shrink. The large cliffs resulted from breaks in the crust caused by this contraction, similar to what happens when an apple dries out and shrivels up.

Because of Mercury's small size and low gravitational pull, most gases that could form an atmosphere escape into space. Mercury has a very thin atmosphere composed of sodium, potassium, hydrogen, and helium. The thin atmosphere and the proximity of Mercury to the sun cause this planet to have great extremes in temperature. Mercury's surface temperature can reach 450°C during the day and drop to −170°C at night.

USING MATH

The average distance from the sun to Earth is 150 million km. How many minutes does it take light traveling at 300 000 km/s to reach Earth?

Venus

The second planet outward from the sun is **Venus.** Venus is sometimes called Earth's twin because its size and mass are similar to Earth's. One major difference is that Venus rotates in the opposite direction as Earth. Another is that the entire surface of Venus is blanketed by an atmosphere with dense clouds. The atmosphere of Venus, which has 90 times the surface pressure of Earth's at sea level, is mostly carbon dioxide. The clouds in the atmosphere contain droplets of sulfuric acid, giving the clouds, as seen in **Figure 23-6,** a slightly yellow color.

Clouds on Venus are so dense that only two percent of the sunlight that strikes the top of the clouds reaches the planet's surface. This solar energy is trapped by the carbon dioxide gas and causes a greenhouse effect similar to Earth's greenhouse effect, mentioned in Chapter 15. Due to this intense greenhouse effect, the temperature on the surface of Venus is 470°C.

The former Soviet Union led the exploration of Venus. Beginning in 1970 with the first *Venera* probe, the Russians have photographed and mapped the surface of Venus using radar and several surface probes. Between 1990 and 1994, the United States' *Magellan* probe used its radar to make the most detailed maps yet of the surface of Venus. *Magellan* revealed huge craters, fault-like cracks, and volcanoes with visible lava flows.

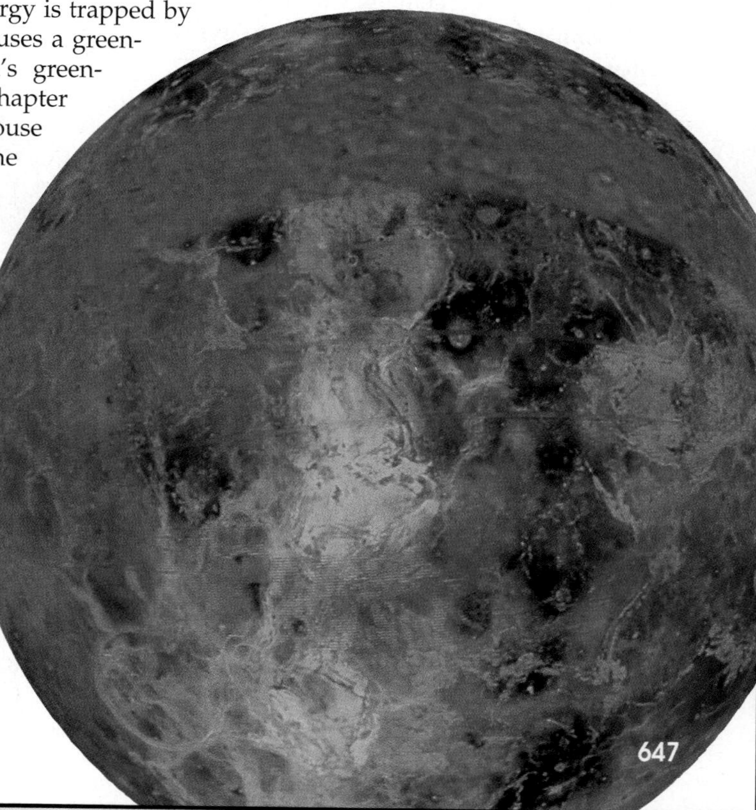

Figure 23-6

Although Venus is similar to Earth, there are important differences. *How could studying Venus help us learn more about Earth?*

2 Teach

Activity

LS **Linguistic** Have students make up sentences that allow them to remember the planets in their order from the sun. For example, *my very exceptional mother just served us nutritious pizza.* L1

USING MATH

Answer about 8 minutes

Visual Learning

Figure 23-6 How could studying Venus help us learn more about Earth? *Studying processes that occur on Venus allows us to observe similar processes that occur on Earth.* LEP LS

NATIONAL GEOGRAPHIC SOCIETY

Videodisc

STV: Solar System

Inner Planets

Unit 2, Side 1

Mercury

11845-14069

Venus

14070-16477

Earth

16530-18165

Mars

18199-22050

Mercury's cratered surface

41670

Integrating the Sciences

Chemistry Venus' color is yellow due to the sulfuric acid in its clouds. Earth's oceans of liquid water give it a distinctive blue color. Mars, the red planet, gets its color from iron oxide in weathered rocks on its surface. The composition of particular parts of each planet produce each planet's unique color.

Across the Curriculum

Mathematics Have students compute the volumes of the inner planets using the equation $V = 0.17\pi d^3$, where V is the volume and d is the diameter of each planet. Students can refer to Appendix I for information about the inner planets. L1 LS

Activity

LS Visual-Spatial Have student pairs use Appendix I to compare and contrast the sizes of the inner planets. Then have them draw each planet to scale on a sheet of paper. L1 **COOP LEARN**

Problem Solving

Solve the Problem

1. Mercury's surface temperature can reach 450°C. It has a very thin atmosphere of sodium, potassium, hydrogen, and helium. Venus' surface temperature is 470°C. Its dense atmosphere of carbon dioxide and sulfuric acid is 90 times the pressure of Earth's atmosphere.
2. A thick atmosphere traps heat just as the glass of a greenhouse does.

Think Critically

The thick atmosphere of Venus absorbs solar energy and prevents it from rapidly radiating back into space. Mercury, which has little atmospheric gas, loses energy rapidly from its surface. Even though Venus is farther from the sun than Mercury, its atmosphere holds and circulates solar energy to a much greater extent.

Problem Solving

Which planet is hotter?

Your teacher asks you to determine which planet's surface is hotter, Mercury or Venus. She also asks you to explain why one of them is hotter than the other. You decide that this assignment is going to be very easy. Of course Mercury has to be hotter than Venus because it is much closer to the sun. Venus is almost twice as far away as Mercury. You write your answer and turn in your paper. Later, when you receive your paper back, you find out that your assumptions were evidently wrong. Your teacher suggests that you research the question further.

Solve the Problem:

1. **Research both planets and determine their surface temperatures and atmospheric density and content.**
2. **Consider how a greenhouse works to keep it warmer inside than outside and relate this to what might happen to a planet with a thick atmosphere.**

Think Critically:

What causes Venus to have a higher surface temperature than Mercury? Explain.

Earth

Earth, shown in **Figure 23-7,** is the third planet from the sun. The average distance from Earth to the sun is 150 million km, or one **astronomical unit** (AU). Astronomical units are used to measure distances to objects in the solar system.

Surface temperatures on Earth allow water to exist as a solid, liquid, and gas. Earth's atmosphere causes most meteors to burn up before they reach the surface. The atmosphere also protects life from the sun's intense radiation.

Mars

Mars is the fourth planet from the sun. It's referred to as the red planet because iron oxide in the weathered rocks on its surface gives it a reddish color, as seen in **Figure 23-8.** Other features of Mars visible from Earth are its polar ice caps, which get larger

Figure 23-7

More than 70 percent of Earth's surface is covered by liquid water, causing our planet to appear blue from space.

3 Assess

Check for Understanding

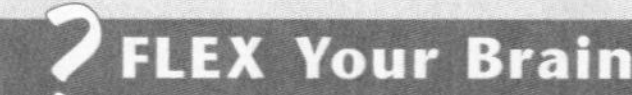

FLEX Your Brain

Use the Flex Your Brain activity to have students explore THE FOUR INNER PLANETS.

Activity Worksheets, p. 5

Integrating the Sciences

Chemistry Mars has always been known as the "red planet." Ask students to research the composition of surface rocks on Mars. Based on what they find out, have them explain what chemical reaction in the Martian soil is responsible for the planet's red color. *Iron in the Martian soil may have reacted with oxygen in the ancient Martian atmosphere, forming iron oxide.*

during the Martian winter and shrink during the summer. The southern polar ice cap is made mostly of frozen carbon dioxide. The northern polar ice cap is made of water in the form of ice.

Most of the information we have about Mars came from the *Mariner 9* and *Viking* probes. *Mariner 9* orbited Mars in 1971–1972. It revealed long channels on the planet that may have been carved by flowing water. Because liquid water no longer exists on Mars's surface, the existence of the channels suggests that climatic conditions on Mars may have been much different in the past. *Mariner 9* also discovered the largest volcano in the solar system, Olympus Mons. Large rift zones that formed in the Martian crust were discovered as well. One such rift, Valles Marineris, is shown in **Figure 23-9.**

In 1976, the *Viking 1* and *2* probes arrived at Mars. Each spacecraft consisted of an orbiter and a lander. The *Viking 1* and *2* orbiters photographed the entire surface of Mars from orbit, while the *Viking 1* and *2* landers touched down on the planet's surface to conduct meteorological, chemical, and biological experiments. The biological experiments found no evidence of life in the soil. The *Viking* landers also sent back pictures of a reddish-colored, barren, rocky, and windswept surface.

Figure 23-8

Mars has many features in common with Earth.

MiniLAB

How would construction be different on Mars?

Procedure

1. Suppose you are a crane operator who is sent to Mars to help build a Mars colony.
2. You know that your crane can lift 44 500 newtons on Earth, but the gravity on Mars is only 0.4 of Earth's gravity.
3. Using numbers, determine how much mass your crane could lift on Mars.

Analysis

1. How can what you have discovered be an advantage over construction on Earth?
2. In what ways might construction advantages change the overall design of the Mars colony?

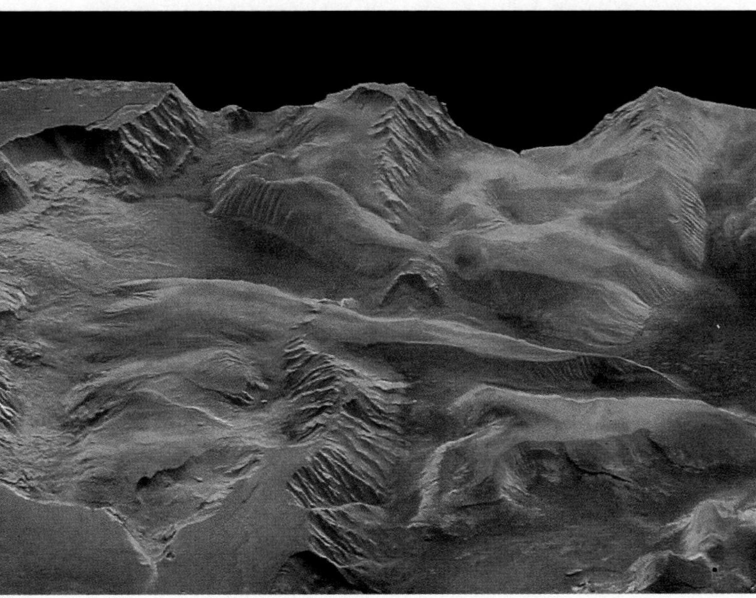

Figure 23-9

Valles Marineris is more than 4000 km long, up to 240 km wide, and more than 6 km deep.

Across the Curriculum

Mathematics Have students calculate how many years it would take to travel from Earth's orbit to Mars' orbit, if they were traveling at 88 km/hr, the average highway speed of a car. The average distance between the orbits is about 78 million km. The trip would take about 100 years. L1 LS

MiniLAB

Purpose

LS **Logical-Mathematical** Students will determine how construction methods would differ on the planet Mars. L1

Teaching Strategies

- Remind students that force equals the mass times the acceleration due to gravity: $F = ma$.
- Earth's acceleration due to gravity, a, is 9.8 m/s^2. Acceleration due to gravity on Mars is 0.4×9.8 m/s^2, or 3.92 m/s^2.
- $F_e = ma_e$
  m = 44 500 N/9.8 m/s^2
  = 4541 kg on Earth
  $F_m = ma_m$
  m = 44 500 N/3.92 m/s^2
  = 11 352 kg on Mars

Analysis

1. The crane could lift more material on Mars and thus speed up construction.
2. The structure could be made of larger sections. Massive objects could be lifted higher.

Assessment

Performance To further assess students' understanding of conditions on Mars, have them use the same idea to calculate how much mass they could lift on the planet. Use the Performance Task Assessment List for Using Math in Science in **PASC**, p. 29. P

Activity Worksheets, pp. 5, 142

Reteach

Using the following question, engage students in a discussion about the inner planets.

- **Why isn't Earth's surface marked by many craters like other planets?**

4 Close

• MINI • QUIZ •

1. **Which planet is closest to the sun?** *Mercury*
2. **Which planet is considered to be Earth's twin?** *Venus*
3. **What is an AU?** *the average distance from Earth to the sun; astronomical unit*

Section Wrap-up

Review

1. The surfaces of both are heavily cratered. The amount of light reflected from both objects is low because of the dark-colored surfaces.
2. Answers might include: Mercury is heavily cratered; Venus has a dense cloud cover; water on Earth exists in three states; and Mars appears red due to iron oxide.
3. The greenhouse effect raises surface temperatures on Venus to 470°C.
4. **Think Critically** Venus's dense atmosphere traps heat, causing a tremendous greenhouse effect.

Figure 23-10

These photos show two features of Mars.

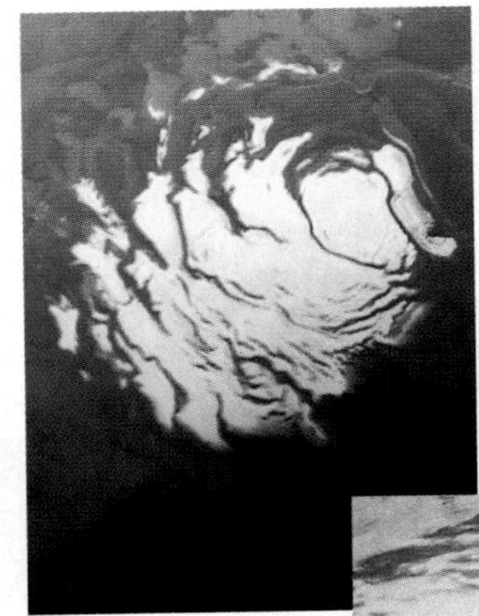

A Polar ice caps

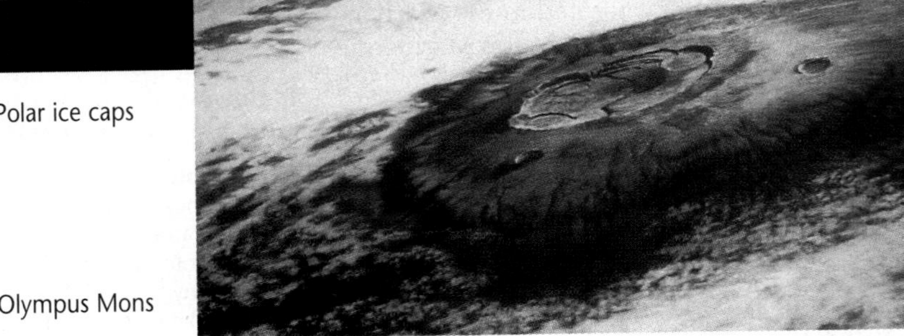

B Olympus Mons

The Martian atmosphere is much thinner than Earth's and is composed mostly of carbon dioxide, with some nitrogen and argon. Surface temperatures range from 35°C to −170°C. The temperature difference between day and night also sets up strong winds on the planet, which can cause global dust storms during certain seasons.

Mars has two small heavily cratered moons. Phobos is only 25 km in diameter and Deimos is 13 km in diameter. Phobos is in an orbit that is slowly spiraling inward towards Mars. It is expected to impact the Martian surface in about 50 million years.

As you toured the inner planets using the "eye" of the space probes, you saw how each planet is unique. Mercury, Venus, Earth, and Mars are quite different from the outer planets that you'll tour in the next section.

Section Wrap-up

Review

1. How are Mercury's and Earth's moons similar?
2. List one important characteristic of each inner planet.
3. Although Venus is often called Earth's twin, why would life as we know it be unlikely on Venus?
4. **Think Critically:** Why is the surface temperature of Venus higher than Mercury's, even though Mercury is closer to the sun?

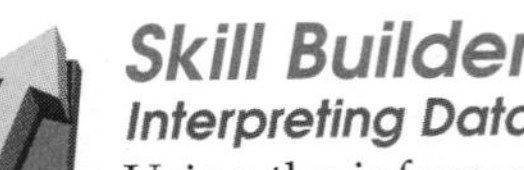

Skill Builder

Interpreting Data

Using the information in this section and Appendix I, explain how Mars is like Earth. If you need help, refer to Interpreting Data in the **Skill Handbook.**

Science Journal

Use textbooks and NASA materials to investigate the *Viking* mission to Mars. In your Science Journal, report on the possibility of life on Mars and the tests that have been conducted to see whether life is there. Include your own opinion as to whether there is or was life on Mars.

Science Journal

Experiments carried out by the *Viking* probes included: the Gas Exchange Experiment, the Pyrolytic Release Experiment, and the Labeled Release Experiment.

Skill Builder

Answers should include that both are inner planets. The processes of volcanism and weathering helped to form each planet. Both have polar ice caps.

Assessment

Performance Use this Skill Builder to assess students' abilities to interpret data. Ask students to explain what equipment they would need in order to live on Mars' surface. P

A Brave and Startling Truth by Maya Angelou

In this chapter, you have learned some of the physical characteristics—scientific facts and figures—of our solar system. Find out how one poet, Maya Angelou, uses Earth and its motion through space to describe people and the quest for world peace. Below are several excerpts, or parts, from her poem *A Brave and Startling Truth.*

We, this people, on a small and lonely planet
Traveling through casual space
Past aloof stars, across the way of indifferent suns
To a destination where all signs tell us
It is possible and imperative that we learn
A brave and startling truth.

When we come to it
Then we will confess that not the Pyramids
With their stones set in mysterious perfection
Nor the Gardens of Babylon
Hanging as eternal beauty
In our collective memory
Not the Grand Canyon
Kindled into delicious color
By Western sunsets

Nor the Danube, flowing its blue soul into Europe
Not the sacred peak of Mount Fuji
Stretching to the Rising Sun
Neither Father Amazon nor Mother Mississippi
who, without favor,
Nurture all creatures in the depths and on the shores
These are not the only wonders of the world

When we come to it
We, this people, on this miniscule and kithless globe
Who reach daily for the bomb, the blade and the dagger
Yet who petition in the dark for tokens of peace
We, this people, on this mote of matter

When we come to it
We, this people, on this wayward, floating body
Created on this earth, of this earth
Have the power to fashion for this earth
A climate where every man and every woman
Can live freely without sanctimonious piety
Without crippling fear

When we come to it
We must confess that we are the possible
We are the miraculous, the true wonder of this world
That is when, and only when
We come to it.

Science Journal

Use your knowledge of Earth's features and/or its place in the solar system to write a short poem that describes a social issue important to you.

Source

Maya Angelou, *A Brave and Startling Truth* (New York: Random House) 1995.

Biography

Maya Angelou, who is currently on the faculty at Wake Forest University in North Carolina, is probably best known as a poet. This prolific writer, however, is also a playwright, director, actor, and producer, and has accomplished numerous literary and theatrical feats. In the 1960s, Dr. Martin Luther King made her the northern coordinator of the Southern Christian Leadership Conference. Gerald Ford chose her to be on the American Revolution Advisory Bicentennial Council. She was appointed to the National Commission on the Observance of International Women's Year by Jimmy Carter. Ms. Angelou holds positions in many professional organizations including the board of trustees of the American Film Institute and the Director's Guild.

Teaching Strategies

- Have a volunteer state some of the physical characteristics of Earth—its diameter, mass, volume, and so on. Lead a discussion that contrasts these measurements with Angelou's descriptions of the planet (small … miniscule … mote of matter). Make sure students realize that our planet is in fact but a speck in the universe.
- Have a volunteer interpret the first verse of the poem explaining what the terms *space, stars,* and *indifferent suns* actually refer to.
- Have volunteers use a globe to locate each of the places mentioned or referred to in this feature. Have students list several facts about each place. Then have students compare and contrast the Seven Wonders of the World with Angelou's definition of the wonders of the world.
- Have each member of the class give his or her impression of what may be the "brave and startling truth."
- Obtain the poem in its entirety and allow a few volunteers to read it aloud for the class. Allow ample time for discussion of the figures of speech and symbolism used by the poet.
- Arrange for four or five volunteers to read their poems aloud for the rest of the class.

Other Works

Other works by Maya Angelou include: *I Know Why the Caged Bird Sings; And I Still Rise; Wouldn't Take Nothing for My Journey Now; Just Give Me a Cool Drink of Water Fore I Die; Oh Pray My Wings Are Gonna Fit Me Well; Shaker, Why Don't You Sing; I Shall Not Be Moved; Phenomenal Woman;* and *On the Pulse of Morning.*

SCIENCE & SOCIETY

Section 23•3

Prepare

Section Background

Data gloves and eye phones allow the user to experience a made-up environment rather than an actual situation.

1 Motivate

Bellringer

Before presenting the lesson, display **Section Focus Transparency 87** on the overhead projector. Assign the accompanying **Focus Activity** worksheet. L1 LEP

Tying to Previous Knowledge

Have students recall from Chapter 21 the achievements and problems experienced by former Soviet cosmonauts aboard their space station.

2 Teach

Activity

LS **Intrapersonal** Have students design a spacecraft that would take humans to Mars.

Discussion

Ask for student volunteers to describe what they know or have experienced concerning virtual reality, an idea similar to the data gloves and eye phones.

SCIENCE & SOCIETY

ISSUE:

23•3 Mission to Mars

Objectives

- Recognize problems that astronauts will encounter during a trip to Mars.
- Decide whether a piloted mission to Mars is necessary or whether it could be done by robotics.

How should Mars be explored?

You learned about exploring space in Chapter 21. Scientists are currently developing plans to further explore Mars. Because Mars is 55 million km away from Earth at the closest, it will take about three years to get to Mars and back. Because of the long duration of the flight, astronauts would face much more danger than they currently do in space shuttle missions. How should Mars be explored?

2 Points of View

Should humans explore Mars?

Mars may once have been able to support life. One type of information that Mars explorers would be looking for is evidence of present or past life. Mars may not have life on it now, but early in its history it may have been a warm and wet planet with a much thicker atmosphere than it has now. If evidence of life is found, it would show that life elsewhere in the universe is also possible.

The search for evidence of life would not be easy. To properly search for fossils on Mars would require many years of work for trained Mars geologists. To study just one geologic formation would require field trips by humans to many different sites.

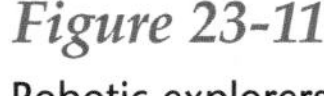

Figure 23-11

Robotic explorers such as this may one day help us explore Mars.

Because of the near-zero gravity in outer space, bones lose calcium and weaken. Bones might fracture more easily once astronauts land on Mars and return to Earth. Also, muscles get weak because they don't have to hold the body up as they do under Earth's gravity.

In addition to these problems, body fluids move upward because no gravity is pulling them down. The movement of fluids could signal the kidneys to excrete more fluids, causing dehydration. Also, astronauts would be exposed to more radiation from the sun than they are during space shuttle flights.

Program Resources

Reproducible Masters

Study Guide, p. 91 L1
Reinforcement, p. 91 L1
Enrichment, p. 91 L3
Science and Society Integration, p. 27

Transparencies

Section Focus Transparency 87 L1
Science Integration Transparency 23

Should robots explore Mars?

For the reasons just stated, some scientists are suggesting that advanced robots currently under development could operate equipment and carry out scientific experiments in space or on Mars. This new technology uses video and artificial touch sense. The artificial senses of the robot are connected to the real senses of a human. The robot has video cameras for eyes and special touch sensors in its limbs. The human operator looks at tiny video screens worn as goggles and sees exactly what the robot sees. Sometimes data gloves worn by the operator have sensors connected by radio signal to the robot's hands. Any movement performed by the operator is duplicated by the robot. **Figure 23-12** shows one system for exploring potentially hazardous environments.

One problem involved in using robots to do this type of in-depth work is the long distance from Earth to Mars. Radio signals from the operator to a robot on Mars would take up to 20 minutes to transmit—too long to be practical.

Researchers would like to develop robot technology for use on the moon or on a space station first, then work on developing artificial intelligence for robots on Mars. A robot with artificial intelligence would be programmed to do a task and would have some ability to "think" on its own.

Figure 23-12

Using virtual reality, hazardous environments can be explored safely. The video screen allows humans to see what a remote probe senses.

Section Wrap-up

Review

1. How could we benefit from a piloted mission to Mars?
2. Why would robots on Mars need to be able to "think" on their own?

Explore the Issue

Do you think humans or robots should explore Mars? If you think humans should, explain how they would be protected from the hazards of extended time in space. If you think robots should, explain how they could be used to search for evidence of past life on Mars.

SCIENCE & SOCIETY

3 Assess

Check for Understanding

FLEX Your Brain

Use the Flex Your Brain activity to have students explore A TRIP TO MARS.

Activity Worksheets, p. 5

Reteach

Call on volunteers to explain how loss of calcium in bones, weakening of muscles, and other problems associated with low gravity can be lessened on extended space flights. *Artificial gravity could be produced in a ship built to rotate slowly during long flights.*

Extension

For students who have mastered this section, use the **Reinforcement** and **Enrichment** masters.

4 Close

Activity

Have students hypothesize how robots on Mars could be controlled from Earth.

Section Wrap-up

Review

1. Humans can make judgments about what is being observed. They can change the mission if there is a need. Humans might also be able to find clues about the formation of the solar system or life on other planets.
2. Radio signals take 20 minutes to reach Mars—too long to wait for a robot to react to a situation.

Explore the Issue

Answers will vary with individual students. However, the following may be included in many responses.

- If humans travel to Mars, they could be protected from radiation with extra shielding on all surfaces of the spacecraft. Also, one large shield could be deployed once in space to protect astronauts from solar radiation. Bone and muscle weakening could be cut down by producing an artificial gravity field in the spacecraft.
- If robots are sent, they could continually search the surface of Mars for signs of life or past life and send information to the mother ship in orbit above. If certain rocks appear to contain evidence of current or past life, samples could be loaded on a robotic ship and sent back to Earth orbit, where they could be retrieved by the space shuttle.

Section 23•4

Prepare

Section Background

- Uranus doesn't appear to have an internal heat source. Some scientists believe a collision with another object may have turned Uranus on its side and destroyed its heat source.
- Pluto is very different from the other outer planets. Hypotheses suggest that it may not have formed in the orbit it now occupies or that it and its moon, Charon, are large cometary members of the Kuiper belt.

Preplanning

- For the MiniLAB, you will need a drawing compass for each pair of students.
- To prepare for Activity 23-2, obtain adding machine tape, a meterstick, and scissors for each group of students.

1 Motivate

Bellringer

Before presenting the lesson, display **Section Focus Transparency 88** on the overhead projector. Assign the accompanying **Focus Activity** worksheet. L1 LEP

Tying to Previous Knowledge

Have students recall from Chapter 21 that space probes are instruments that gather information and send it back to Earth.

23•4 The Outer Planets

Science Words

Jupiter
Great Red Spot
Saturn
Uranus
Neptune
Pluto

Objectives

- List the major characteristics of Jupiter, Saturn, Uranus, and Neptune.
- Recognize how Pluto differs from the other outer planets.

Outer Planets

You have learned that the inner planets are small, solid, rocky bodies in space. By contrast, the outer planets, except for Pluto, are very large, gaseous objects.

You first read of the *Voyager* probes in Chapter 21. Although they were not the first probes to the outer planets, they have uncovered a wealth of new information about Jupiter, Saturn, Uranus, and Neptune. Let's follow the *Voyager* probes on their journeys to the outer planets of the solar system.

Jupiter

In 1979, *Voyager 1* flew past **Jupiter,** the largest planet and the fifth planet from the sun. *Voyager 2* flew past Jupiter later that same year. The major discoveries of the probes include new information about the motions of Jupiter's atmosphere and the discovery of three new moons. *Voyager* probes also discovered that Jupiter has faint dust rings around it and that one of its moons has volcanoes on it.

Jupiter is composed mostly of hydrogen, helium, and some ammonia, methane, and water vapor. Scientists believe the atmosphere of hydrogen and helium gradually changes to a planetwide ocean of liquid hydrogen and helium toward the middle of the planet. Below this liquid layer, there may be a solid rocky core. The extreme pressure and temperature, however, make the core different from any rock on Earth.

You've probably seen pictures from the *Voyager* probes of Jupiter's colorful clouds. Its atmosphere has bands of white, red, tan, and brown clouds, as shown in **Figure 23-13.** Continuous storms of swirling, high-pressure gas have been observed on Jupiter. The **Great Red Spot** is the most spectacular of these storms. Lightning has also been observed within Jupiter's clouds.

Figure 23-13

Jupiter is the largest planet in our solar system, containing more mass than all of the other planets combined. The Great Red Spot is a giant storm that is about 12 000 km from top to bottom.

Program Resources

Reproducible Masters

Study Guide, p. 92 L1
Reinforcement, p. 92 L1
Enrichment, p. 92 L3
Activity Worksheets, pp. 5, 140-141, 143 L1
Critical Thinking/Problem Solving, p. 29
Lab Manual 66

Transparencies

Section Focus Transparency 88 L1

Table 23-1

Large Moons of Jupiter			
Io	**Europa**	**Ganymede**	**Callisto**
The most volcanically active object in the solar system. Sulfur lava gives it its distinctive red and orange color. Possesses a thin, temporary sulfur-dioxide atmosphere.	Rocky interior is covered by a 100-km-thick ice crust, which has a network of cracks, indicating tectonic activity. Possesses a thin oxygen atmosphere.	Has an ice crust about 100 km thick, covered with grooves. Crust may surround a 900-km-thick slushy mantle of water and ice. Has a rocky core.	Has a heavily cratered ice-rock crust several hundred km thick. Crust may surround a water or ice mantle around a rocky core.

Moons of Jupiter

In orbit around Jupiter are 16 moons. The four largest, shown in **Table 23-1,** were discovered by Galileo in 1610. Io is the closest large moon to Jupiter. Jupiter's tremendous gravitational force pulls on Io. This force heats up Io, causing it to be the most volcanically active object in the solar system. The next moon out is Europa. It is composed mostly of rock with a thick crust of ice. Next is Ganymede, which is the largest satellite in the solar system. It's larger than the planet Mercury. Callisto is the fourth moon out, and is composed of ice and rock.

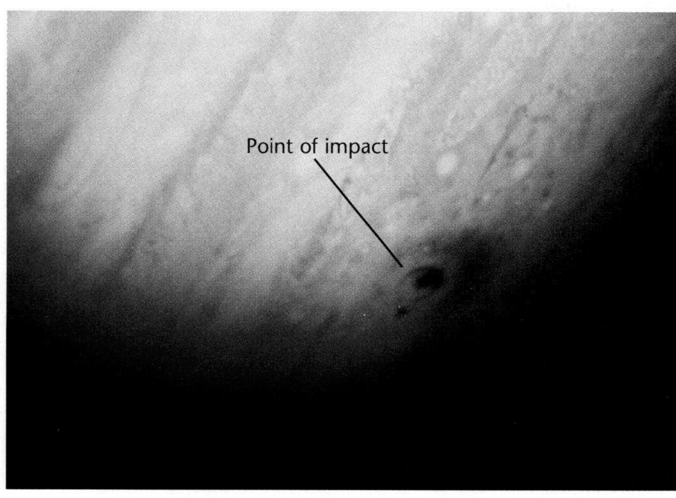

Figure 23-14
In 1994, a comet named Shoemaker-Levy 9 collided into Jupiter with a series of spectacular explosions. Information from this impact gives us clues about what might happen if such an impact occured on Earth.

2 Teach

Activity

LS **Interpersonal** Form groups of four students. Have students play "Planet Jeopardy" by reading statements from this section and Section 23-2 and calling on a student to form an appropriate question. Award points for every correct question by a group. L1 COOP LEARN

Visual Learning

Table 23-1 Ask students why the four moons shown in **Table 23-1** are called the Galilean Satellites of Jupiter. Ask them also to list each moon in their Science Journals and to write a brief description of the characteristics of each moon. LEP LS

GLENCOE TECHNOLOGY

 **Videodisc**

The Infinite Voyage: Sail On, *Voyager*

Chapter 3
Voyager 1: *Jupiter*

Chapter 4
Jupiter's Atmosphere

Chapter 6
Voyager 1: *Saturn*

Chapter 10
Voyager 2: *Uranus*

Chapter 11
Voyager 2: *Neptune*

Community Connection

Amateur Planet Watchers If a local organization of sky observers exists in your area, invite one of its members to class to talk to the students about how he or she conducts nighttime observations. Perhaps one of the members has searched for and found a comet at some time. If no organization exists, ask students to contact some local store owners who sell telescopes to see if they might want to become involved with a nighttime community observation. Students may wish to invite their parents or guardians to participate in a session observing Jupiter or Saturn.

MiniLAB

Purpose

LS **Interpersonal** Students will formulate models of the solar system by drawing the planets to scale. L1

COOP LEARN

Materials

metric rulers, drawing compass, pencil, and paper

Teaching Strategies

Safety Precautions Caution students to handle drawing compasses very carefully.

Troubleshooting The scale size for each planet is the product of the scale size of the model Earth times the other planet's multiple of Earth size. For example, if the scale Earth were 2 cm in diameter, Jupiter would be 2 cm × 11.19, or 22.38 cm, in scale diameter.

Analysis

1. & 2. Students' answers will vary, depending on the scale size chosen for Earth's diameter. Have them compute the answers to the first two questions by multiplying Earth's scale diameter by 11 728, which is the number of Earth diameters in 1 AU.
3. At 1 AU = 2 m, the sun would be 19 millimeters in diameter. The model Earth would be considerably smaller—0.18 mm, or 0.018 cm.

Assessment

Performance To further assess students' understanding of scale models of planets, have them formulate models of each planet out of balls of crumpled newspaper. Use the Performance Task Assessment List for Model in **PASC**, p. 51. P

Activity Worksheets, p. 143

MiniLAB

Can you draw planets to scale?

Procedure

1. To determine how the sizes of the planets in the solar system compare with each other, use the information on planet diameters in Appendix I.
2. Select a scale diameter of Earth.
3. Formulate a model by drawing a circle with this diameter on paper.
4. Using Earth's diameter as 1.0, draw each of the other planets to scale also.

Analysis

1. At this scale, how far would your model Earth have to be located from the sun?
2. What would 1 AU be equal to in this model?
3. Using a scale of 1 AU = 2 m, how large would the sun and Earth models have to be to remain in scale?

Saturn

The next planet surveyed by the *Voyager* probes was Saturn, in 1980 and 1981. **Saturn** is the sixth planet from the sun, and is also known as the ringed planet. Saturn is the second-largest planet in the solar system, but has the lowest density. Its density is so low that the planet would float on water.

Similar to Jupiter, Saturn is a large, gaseous planet with a thick outer atmosphere composed mostly of hydrogen and helium. Saturn's atmosphere also contains ammonia, methane, and water vapor. As you go deeper into Saturn's atmosphere, the gases gradually change to liquid hydrogen and helium. Below its atmosphere and liquid ocean, Saturn may have a small rocky core.

The *Voyager* probes gathered new information about Saturn's ring system and its moons. The *Voyager* probes showed that Saturn has several broad rings, each of which is composed of hundreds of thin ringlets. Each ring is composed of countless ice and rock particles ranging in size from a speck of dust to tens of meters across, as shown in **Figure 23-15**. This makes Saturn's ring system the most complex of all the outer gaseous planets'.

At least 20 moons orbit Saturn. That's more than any other planet in our solar system has. The largest of these, Titan, is larger than Mercury. It has an atmosphere of nitrogen, argon, and methane. Thick clouds of smog prevent us from seeing the surface of Titan.

Figure 23-15

Saturn's rings are composed of pieces of rock and ice.

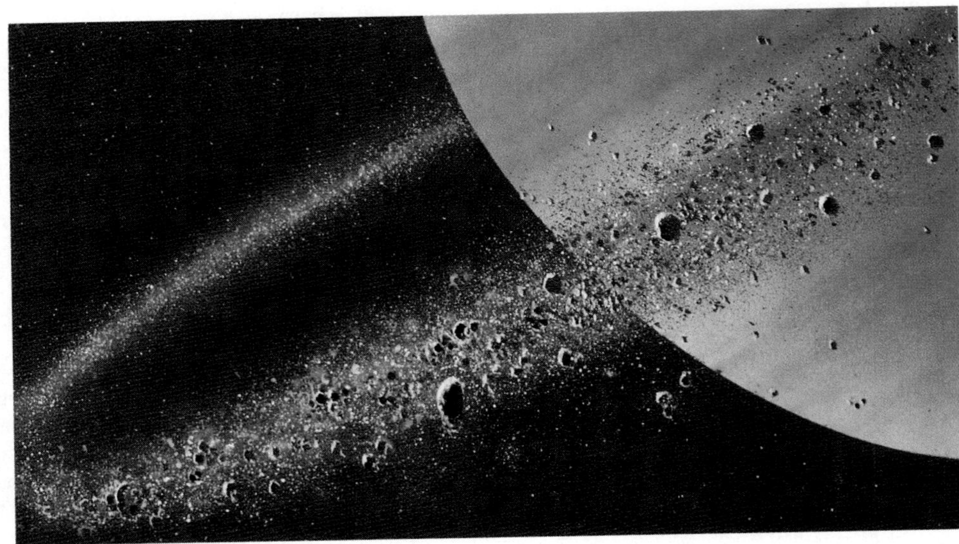

Across the Curriculum

Mathematics Supply students with the following diameters of the larger moons in the solar system: Earth's moon (3476 km), Io (3630 km), Europa (3138 km), Ganymede (5262 km), Callisto (4800 km), Titan (5150 km), and Triton (2720 km). Have students compare and contrast the sizes of these moons with the sizes of the inner planets. Using a scale of 1 mm = 100 km, have students draw to scale the inner planets and moons listed above. Students should notice that some of the moons are larger than Mercury. L1 LS COOP LEARN

Uranus

After touring Saturn, *Voyager 2* flew by Uranus in 1986. **Uranus** is the seventh planet from the sun and wasn't discovered until 1781. It is a large, gaseous planet with 15 satellites and a system of thin, dark rings.

Voyager revealed numerous thin rings and ten moons that had not been seen earlier. *Voyager* also detected that the magnetic field is tilted 60° from its rotational poles. The field is also offset from the planet's center by one-third of Uranus's radius. Only Neptune's magnetic field is offset more than this.

The atmosphere of Uranus is composed of hydrogen, helium, and some methane. The methane gives the planet its blue-green color. Methane absorbs the red and yellow light, and the clouds reflect the green and blue. No cloud bands and few storm systems are seen on Uranus. Evidence suggests that under its atmosphere, Uranus has a mantle of liquid water, methane, and ammonia surrounding a rocky core.

One of the most unique features of Uranus is that its axis of rotation is tilted on its side compared with the other planets. The axes of rotation of the other planets, except Pluto, are nearly perpendicular to the planes of their orbits. Uranus, however, has a rotational axis nearly parallel to the plane of its orbit, as shown in **Figure 23-17.**

Figure 23-16

The atmosphere of Uranus gives the planet its distinct blue-green color.

CONNECT TO CHEMISTRY

Recall what you've learned about the chemical and physical properties of hydrogen, helium, methane, and ammonia. ***Describe*** the properties of these substances that caused them to be more abundant in the outer planets than in the inner planets.

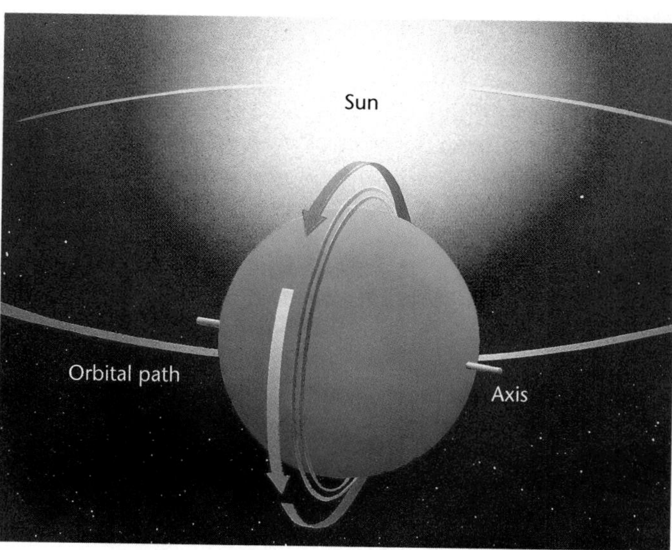

Figure 23-17

Uranus rotates on an axis nearly parallel to the plane of its orbit. At some point during its revolution around the sun, one of the poles points almost directly at the sun.

Theme Connection

Scale and Structure *Voyager 2* has helped astronomers learn about the composition of the atmospheres of the gaseous giant planets. Also, with the help of data from the *Hubble Space Telescope,* the sizes of the gaseous giants, their moons, Pluto, and Charon have been determined to a much better degree. These data have reaffirmed the theme of scale and structure as it applies to the solar system.

CONNECT TO CHEMISTRY

Answer The temperature at which these materials condense from a gas is much lower than the temperature that existed in the inner portion of the rotating cloud that formed into the solar system. These materials would have remained in a gaseous state of low enough mass that solar wind from the sun would have pushed much of them farther out into the solar system.

Use **Critical Thinking/ Problem Solving,** p. 29, as you teach this lesson.

Enrichment

LS **Intrapersonal** Have each student compile a list of the physical properties of all known moons orbiting the outer planets. Suggest students use data available from the *Voyager* missions. L1

Videodisc

STV: Solar System

Outer Planets

Unit 3, Side 1

Saturn

27379-29818

Uranus

29818-30810

Neptune

30833-34533

Pluto

34559-36600

3 Assess

Check for Understanding

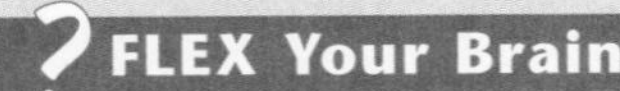

Use the Flex Your Brain activity to have students explore THE FIVE OUTER PLANETS.

Activity Worksheets, p. 5

Reteach

LS **Interpersonal** Have pairs of students sketch each outer planet on a separate flash card. On the reverse side of the card, instruct students to write down the characteristics of each planet. Partners can then test each other using the flash cards. COOP LEARN

Extension

For students who have mastered this section, use the **Reinforcement** and **Enrichment** masters.

Videodisc

STV: Solar System

Jupiter's atmosphere

41623

Io, volcanic eruption (close-up)

41627

Rings of Saturn (close-up)

41720

Storm "D2" near Neptune's south pole

41735

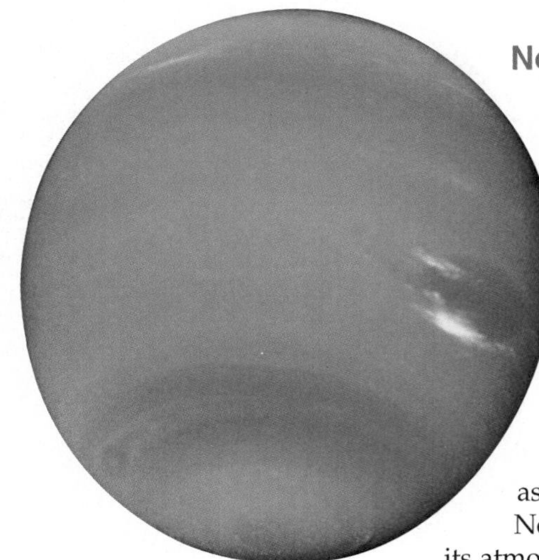

Figure 23-18

Neptune has an atmosphere similar to Uranus's, but it is much bluer due to the higher methane content.

Neptune

From Uranus, *Voyager 2* traveled on to **Neptune,** a large, gaseous planet. Discovered in 1846, Neptune is the eighth planet from the sun most of the time. However, Pluto's orbit crosses inside Neptune's during a part of its voyage around the sun. Since 1979, Pluto has been closer to the sun than Neptune, and it will remain closer to the sun until 1999.

Neptune's atmosphere is very similar to that of Uranus. The methane content gives Neptune its distinctive blue-green color just as it does for Uranus.

Neptune has dark-colored, stormlike features in its atmosphere that are similar to the Great Red Spot on Jupiter. One that was discovered by *Voyager,* called the Great Dark Spot, is shown in **Figure 23-18.**

Under its atmosphere, Neptune is thought to have liquid water, methane, and ammonia. Neptune probably has a rocky core.

With *Voyager 2*'s detection of six new moons, the total number of Neptune's known moons is now eight. Of these, Triton is the largest. Triton, shown in **Figure 23-19,** has a diameter of 2700 km and has a thin atmosphere composed mostly of nitrogen. *Voyager* detected methane geysers erupting on Triton. *Voyager* also detected that Neptune has rings that are thin in some places and thick in other places. Neptune's magnetic field is tilted 55° from its rotational axis and offset from center by half Neptune's radius.

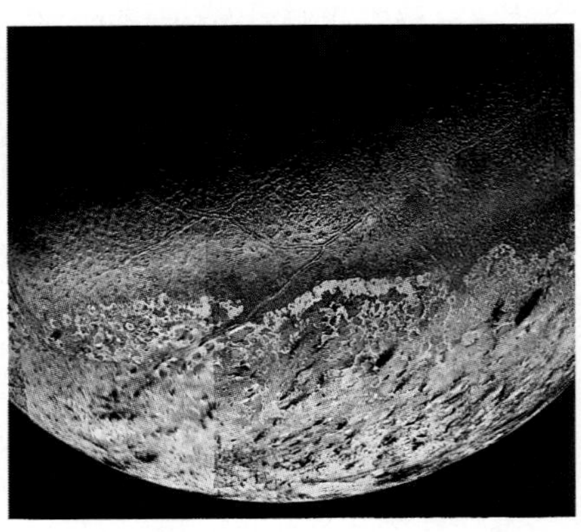

Figure 23-19

Triton is Neptune's largest moon.

Voyager ended its tour of the solar system with Neptune. Both *Voyager* probes are now beyond the orbits of Pluto and Neptune. They will continue into space sensing the extent of the sun's effect on charged particles.

Pluto

The smallest planet in our solar system, and the one we know the least about, is Pluto. Because **Pluto** is farther from the sun than Neptune during most of its orbit around the sun, it is considered the ninth planet from the sun. Pluto is not like the other outer planets. It's surrounded by only a thin atmosphere, and it's the only outer planet with a solid, icy-rock surface.

Pluto's only moon, Charon, has a diameter about half of Pluto's. Charon orbits very close to Pluto. Because of their close size and orbit, Charon and Pluto are sometimes considered to be a double planet.

Science Journal

Voyager 2 Have students write a report in their Science Journals about what new information *Voyager 2* gathered about the gaseous planets. Ask them to include information about the difficulty NASA had with keeping the space probe operating throughout its entire flight. L3 LS

Recent data from the *Hubble Space Telescope* indicate the presence of a vast disk of icy comets near Neptune's orbit, called the Kuiper belt. Some of the ice comets are hundreds of kilometers in diameter. Are Pluto and Charon members of this belt, are they escaped moons of one of the larger gaseous giants, or did they simply form at the distance they are? Maybe planets at that distance from the sun should be small and composed of icy rock. We may not find out until we send a probe to Pluto.

With the *Voyager* probes, we entered a new age of knowledge about the solar system. The space probe *Galileo*, which arrived at Jupiter in 1995, and the upcoming *Cassini* probe to Saturn will continue to extend our understanding of the solar system.

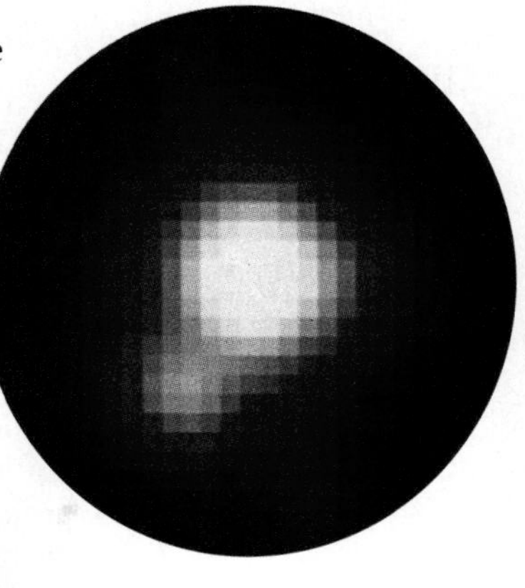

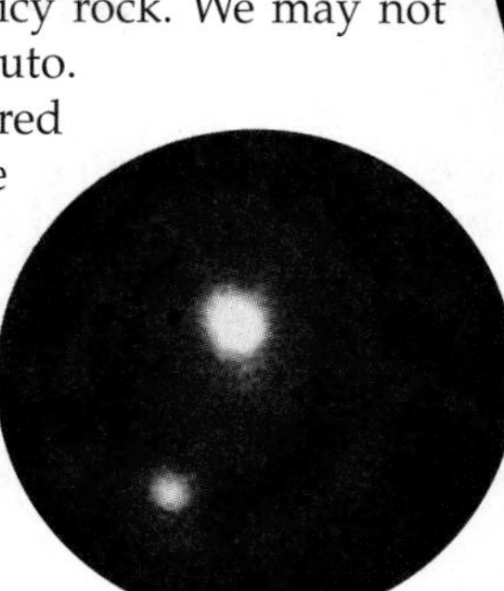

Figure 23-20

The image of Pluto and Charon (above) was taken by an Earth-based telescope. The *Hubble Space Telescope* gave astronomers their first clear view of Pluto and Charon as distinct objects (left) .

Section Wrap-up

Review

1. What's the difference between the outer planets and the inner planets?
2. Are there moons in the solar system that are larger than planets? If so, what are they?
3. How does Pluto differ from the other outer planets?
4. **Think Critically:** Why is Neptune sometimes the farthest planet from the sun?

Skill Builder

Recognizing Cause and Effect

Answer the following questions about Jupiter. If you need help, refer to Recognizing Cause and Effect in the **Skill Handbook.**

1. What causes Jupiter's surface color?
2. How is the Great Red Spot affected by Jupiter's atmosphere?
3. How does Jupiter's mass affect its gravitational force?

Using Computers

Spreadsheet Use the spreadsheet or table-making features of your computer to produce a table of the nine planets that compares their characteristics.

4 Close

•MINI•QUIZ•

Use the Mini Quiz to check students' recall of chapter content.

1. **The largest planet in the solar system is ______ .** *Jupiter*
2. **______ has the most complex ring system of all the planets.** *Saturn*
3. **Which moon of Saturn has an atmosphere and is larger than Mercury?** *Titan*
4. **Which planet is currently closer to the sun—Pluto or Neptune?** *Pluto*

Section Wrap-up

Review

1. The outer planets are very large, gaseous objects, except for Pluto. The inner planets are small, solid, rocklike bodies in space.
2. Yes, Ganymede and Titan are larger than Mercury and Pluto.
3. Pluto has a thin atmosphere and a solid, icy-rock surface.
4. **Think Critically** Pluto's orbit is more elliptical than the orbits of other planets. This causes Pluto to come closer to the sun than Neptune for about 20 years of its orbit.

Using Computers

Student spreadsheets will vary, but should include information listed in Appendix I.

Skill Builder

1. bands of red, tan, and brown clouds
2. High pressure causes the gases in the storm to flow inward toward its center.
3. Jupiter is the largest planet and thus has the greatest gravitational force of the nine planets. The force is in fact large enough to hold a moon that is larger than Mercury in orbit around the planet.

Assessment

Oral Assess students' abilities to recognize cause and effect by having them answer the questions provided. Also ask them what causes Io to be so volcanically active. Use the Performance Task Assessment List for Making Observations and Inferences in **PASC,** p. 17. P

Activity 23-2

PREPARATION

Purpose

LS **Logical-Mathematical** Design and formulate a model to show the distances between the sun and the planets. L1

Process Skills

measuring in SI, using numbers, sequencing, formulating a hypothesis, separating and controlling variables, interpreting data, and making models

Time

one class period

Materials

string, paper, meterstick, scissors, and pencil

Safety Precautions

Caution students to handle scissors with care.

A scale to represent distances in AUs will be selected. The mean distances to planets in AUs will be obtained and adjusted by the selected scale. The scale distances will be placed on a data chart, and a scale model of planet distances will be constructed from string.

Activity Worksheets, pp. 5, 140-141

Activity 23-2

Design Your Own Experiment

Solar System Distance Model

Distances between the planets of the solar system are very large. Can you design a model that will demonstrate the large distances between and among the sun and planets in the solar system?

PREPARATION

Problem

How can a model be designed that will show the relative distances between and among the sun and planets of the solar system?

Form a Hypothesis

State a hypothesis about how a model with scale dimensions of the solar system can be constructed.

Objectives

- Make a table of scale distances that will represent planetary distances to be used in a model of the solar system.
- Make a model of the distances between the sun and planets of the solar system.

Possible Materials

- meterstick
- pencil
- paper
- scissors
- string

Safety Precautions

Take care when handling scissors.

Data and Observations

Sample data

Planet	Distance to Sun (km)	Distance to Sun (AU)	Scale Distance (1 AU =)	Scale Distance (1 AU = 2m)
Mercury	5.8×10^7	0.38	3.9 cm	77.4 cm
Venus	1.08×10^8	0.72	7.2 cm	1.45 m
Earth	1.50×10^8	1.00	10.0 cm	2.00 m
Mars	1.50×10^8	1.52	15.2 cm	3.05 m
Jupiter	7.80×10^8	5.20	52.0 cm	10.40 m
Saturn	1.43×10^8	9.54	95.4 cm	19.08 m
Uranus	2.88×10^8	19.18	191.8 cm	38.40 m
Neptune	4.51×10^8	30.06	300.6 cm	60.10 m
Pluto	5.92×10^8	39.44	394.4 cm	78.90 m

Theme Connection

Scale and Structure Scale and structure as a theme for this chapter is reaffirmed by consideration of the structure of the solar system and of the dimensions between planets in the solar system. Take students out into the hall (one that is about 80 paces long). Using a scale of 2 paces equaling 1 AU, pace off the dimensions of the solar system and have one student, representing each planet, stand at each scale distance. When finished, have students look at the human model of dimensions in the solar system. Be sure to inform students that a scale model for planet sizes is not being used. Ask students to brainstorm and develop a way of showing planet sizes in the same scale.

PLAN THE EXPERIMENT

1. As a group, agree upon and write out your hypothesis statement.
2. As a group, list the steps that you need to take in making your model to test your hypothesis. Be very specific, describing exactly what you will do at each step.
3. Make a list of the materials that you will need to complete your model.
4. Make a table of scale distances you will use in your model.
5. Write a description of how you will build your model, explaining how it will demonstrate relative distances between and among the sun and planets of the solar system.

Check the Plan

1. Read over your entire model description to make sure that all steps are in a logical order.
2. Do any parts of your model need to be constructed before the overall model is produced?
3. Will you summarize data used in construction, as well as data obtained from your model, in a graph, table, or some form of organization other than the one on page 660?
4. How will you determine whether your model successfully demonstrates the large distances between and among the sun and planets in the solar system?
5. *Make sure your teacher approves your plan before you proceed.*

DO THE EXPERIMENT

1. **Construct the model** as planned using your scale distances.
2. While **constructing the model,** write down any observations that you or other members of your group make and complete the data table in your Science Journal.
3. **Calculate** the scale distance that would be used in your model if 1 AU = 2 m.

Analyze and Apply

1. **Explain** how a scale distance is determined.
2. Was it possible to work with your scale?
3. **Explain** why or why not.
4. How much string would be required to construct a model with a scale distance 1 AU = 2 m?

Go Further

Proxima Centauri, the closest star to our sun, is about 270 000 AU from the sun. Based on your original scale, how long would a piece of string need to be in order to include this star on your model? Can you translate this to a distance from your school to some feature in your town?

PLAN THE EXPERIMENT

Possible Procedure

1. Use Appendix I to obtain the mean distance from the sun to each planet in AUs.
2. Record these values in your table.
3. Decide on a scale to be used that will enable a scale model of the solar system to be made from string. Planets can be made from paper hanging along appropriate positions on the string.
4. Design a method of using the scale distances for each planet and of placing the planets in proper positions on the solar system model.

Teaching Strategies

Tying to Previous Knowledge Remind students of the dimensions of distances between inner planets. Relate to them that distances between outer planets are much larger.

Troubleshooting Some students will need help in choosing a scale to use in their models. If necessary, suggest that they use a scale of 1 AU = 10 cm. Sample data has been provided for this scale. Some students may also need help with the math.

DO THE EXPERIMENT

Expected Outcome

Some students will begin with a scale that is too large. They should realize that their scale will require great lengths of string. Other scales will not be large enough to show individual planet orbits. Students should realize that a scale that allows Pluto to be placed on the string will work for all planets.

Analyze and Apply

1. The scale distance is determined by multiplying the AU-distance of each planet by the scale (in AUs) selected.

2. & 3. Answers will vary.

4. 78.9 meters (any answer near 80 meters)

Go Further

Answers will vary, but for a scale of 1 AU = 10 cm, Proxima Centauri would be about 27 km away from the sun. Cite a local feature (lake, etc.) that is 27 km (16 mi) away.

Assessment

Performance Using the same scale selected for planet distances on their solar system models, have students place the asteroid named Ceres in their models. The orbit of Ceres lies 2.77 AU from the sun. Use the Performance Task Assessment List for Model in **PASC**, p. 51. P

Section 23•5

Prepare

Section Background

- Comets appear to orbit the sun in the Oort Comet Cloud some 50 000 km from the sun. Some comets take more than one million years to complete one orbit. Some comets may exist in the Kuiper belt near the orbit of Neptune.
- Comet Hale-Bopp will be at its brightest in March and April 1997. It is much larger than most comets that swing in toward the sun. In fact, the shell of material surrounding Comet Hale-Bopp fills a volume larger than the sun. Comet Hale-Bopp was discovered on July 23, 1995 by two backyard astronomers, Alan Hale and Thomas Bopp, working independently. Refer to *Here Comes Hale-Bopp* in *Astronomy,* February 1996, pp. 68-73.

1 Motivate

Bellringer

Before presenting the lesson, display **Section Focus Transparency 89** on the overhead projector. Assign the accompanying **Focus Activity** worksheet. L1 LEP

Tying to Previous Knowledge

Have students recall from Chapter 22 that the moon's surface is heavily cratered. Relate that most craters on the moon probably formed from meteorite impacts.

23•5 Other Objects in the Solar System

Science Words

comet
Oort Cloud
meteor
meteorite
asteroid

Objectives

- Explain where a comet comes from and describe how a comet develops as it approaches the sun.
- Differentiate among comets, meteoroids, and asteroids.

Comets

Although the planets and their satellites are the most noticeable members of the sun's family, there are many other objects that orbit the sun. Comets, meteoroids, and asteroids are other objects in the solar system.

You've probably heard of Halley's comet. It was last seen from Earth in 1986. English astronomer Edmund Halley realized that comet sightings that had taken place about every 76 years were really sightings of the same comet. This comet, which takes about 76 years to orbit the sun, was named after him. Halley's comet is just one example of the many other objects in the solar system besides the planets. **Figure 23-21** illustrates comets.

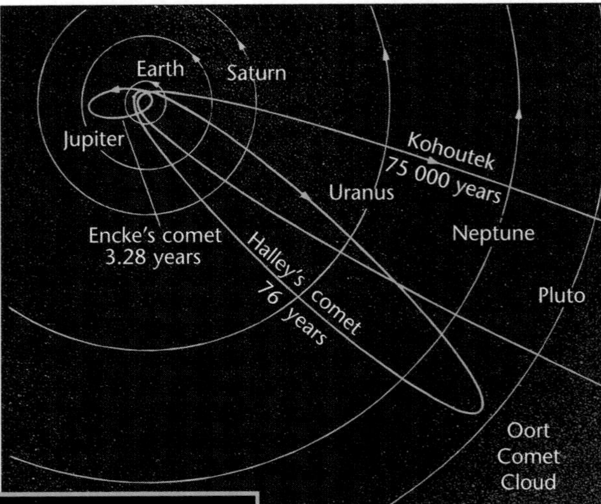

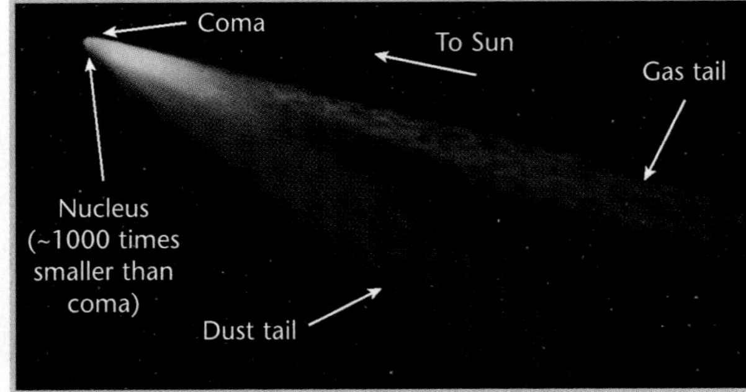

Figure 23-21

A comet consists of a nucleus, a coma, and a tail, as shown at left. The orbits of three famous comets are shown above.

Program Resources

Reproducible Masters

Study Guide, p. 93 L1
Reinforcement, p. 93 L1
Enrichment, p. 93 L3

Transparencies

Section Focus Transparency 89 L1

A **comet** is composed of dust and rock particles mixed in with frozen water, methane, and ammonia. The Dutch astronomer Jan Oort proposed the idea that a large collection of comets lies in a cloud that completely surrounds the solar system. This cloud is located beyond the orbit of Pluto and is called the **Oort Cloud.** Evidence suggests that the gravity of nearby stars or another planet interacts with comets in the Oort Cloud. The sun's gravity pulls the comet toward it. The comet then either escapes from the solar system or gets captured into a much smaller orbit. As mentioned earlier, another belt of comets, called the Kuiper belt, may exist near the orbit of Neptune.

An exciting discovery made by two backyard astronomers on July 23, 1995 is a new comet heading toward the sun. This comet, Comet Hale-Bopp, is larger than most that approach the sun and may turn out to be the brightest comet visible from Earth in 20 years. It will be at its brightest in March and April 1997.

CONNECT TO PHYSICS

Research Kepler's laws of planetary motion. ***Describe*** how his second law explains the speed of Halley's comet at various positions within its orbit.

Structure of Comets

The structure of a comet is like a large, dirty snowball, or a mass of frozen ice and rock. But as the comet approaches the sun, it develops a very distinctive structure. Ices of water, methane, and ammonia begin to vaporize because of the heat from the sun. The vaporized gases form a bright cloud called a coma around the nucleus, or solid part, of the comet. The solar wind pushes on the gases in the coma. These particles form a tail that always points away from the sun.

After many trips around the sun, most of the frozen ice in a comet has vaporized. All that is left are small particles that spread out in the orbit of the original comet.

Figure 23-22

Comet West was visible in March 1976.

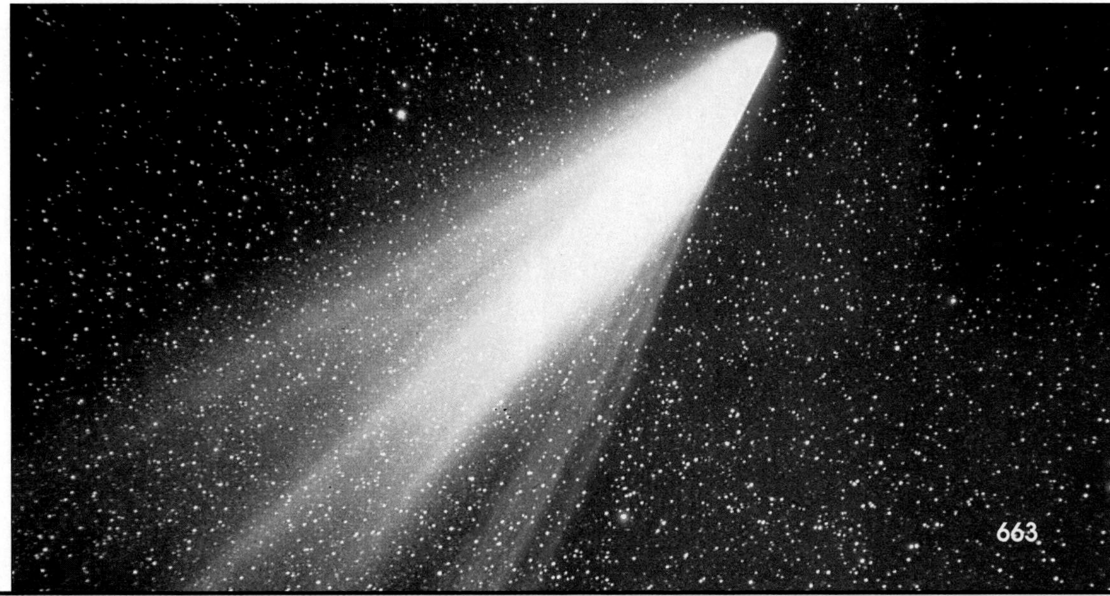

Cultural Diversity

Comet Studies Have students research the last approach of Halley's comet to Earth in 1986. Ask them to study the five different space probes sent by the former Soviet Union, Japan, and Europe to study the comet up close. Ask them also to determine why the United States did not send a probe to this comet. When Halley's comet came close to Earth in 1986, five space probes were launched to study it: the Soviet *Vega 1* and *Vega 2* probes; the Japanese *Suisei* and *Sakigake* probes; and the European Space Agency's *Giotto* probe. *Giotto* traveled closest to the comet's nucleus. Data sent back by the probes indicate the nucleus is black, measures about 15 km in length and 8 km in width, and rotates once every 2 days. It was also noted that the coma contains boulder-size rocks as well as fine dust particles.

2 Teach

CONNECT TO PHYSICS

Answer Kepler's second law deals with the speed at which objects travel in their orbits. It states that a line joining the orbiting object and the sun sweeps through equal areas in equal times. When Halley's comet approaches very close to the sun, it must travel fast in order to sweep through an area equal to what it sweeps through when at great distances from the sun and traveling much slower.

Discussion

Once students have finished reading pages 662 and 663, use the following questions to instigate a class discussion on comets. **What is a comet?** *an object made of dust; rocks; and frozen water, methane, and ammonia* **What is the Oort Cloud and where is it located?** *The Oort Cloud is a large collection of comets that orbit beyond Pluto.*

NATIONAL GEOGRAPHIC SOCIETY

Videodisc

STV: Solar System

Smaller Objects

Unit 4, Side 1

Asteroids and Meterorites

21955-24475

Comets

36630-38511

Revealing Preconceptions

Many people incorrectly refer to meteors as "shooting stars." Explain that meteors are relatively small, rocklike bodies that move through space. Stars, however, are enormous balls of gas that tend to remain in their "places" in space.

Inquiry Questions

- **What causes comets to break up after they pass close to the sun many times?** *The sun causes most of the frozen ice to vaporize. The remaining parts of the comet spread out into the comet's original orbit.*
- **When does a meteoroid become a meteor?** *When a meteoroid enters Earth's atmosphere and burns up, it becomes a meteor.*
- **What causes a meteor shower?** *A meteor shower occurs when Earth passes within the orbit of a comet that has broken apart.*
- **What do meteorites tell us about the solar system?** *Meteorites come from comets or asteroids, thus they provide data about the material that formed the solar system.*
- **Why are most asteroids between Mars and Jupiter?** *One hypothesis is that Jupiter's enormous gravitational force kept a planet from forming in that area.*
- **Where else in the solar system besides the asteroid belt can asteroids be found?** *Some of the larger asteroids may have been thrown out of the belt and may have been captured by planets as moons.*

Meteoroids, Meteors, and Meteorites

You learned that comets tend to break up after they have passed close to the sun many times. The small pieces of the comet nucleus spread out into a loose group within the original orbit of the broken comet. These small pieces of rock moving through space are then called meteoroids.

When the path of a meteoroid crosses the position of Earth, it enters our atmosphere at between 15 and 70 km/s. Most meteoroids are so small that they are completely vaporized in Earth's atmosphere. A meteoroid that burns up in Earth's atmosphere is called a **meteor.** People often see these and call them shooting stars.

Each time Earth passes through the loose group of particles within the old orbit of a comet, many small particles of rock and dust enter the atmosphere. Because more meteors than usual are seen, this is called a meteor shower.

Figure 23-23

When a meteor collides with an object such as a moon or a planet, it can leave huge craters such as these. The crater on the left is in Arizona. The crater on the right is on the moon.

Community Connection

Meteorites Check with a museum in your community to determine whether they have a section that includes meteorites that have fallen and have been found near your area. Invite the curator of the museum to class so he or she can discuss how a person might identify whether an interesting rock is a meteorite. If no museum is located near your community or if there are no meteorites that have been found, ask students to organize a community stargazing party. During the party, the students and members of the community would come to school to observe one of the major meteor showers.

If the meteoroid is large enough, it may not completely burn up in Earth's atmosphere. When it strikes Earth, it is called a **meteorite.** Meteor Crater in Arizona, shown in **Figure 23-23,** was formed when a large meteorite struck Earth. Most meteorites are probably debris from asteroid collisions, but some are from the moon and Mars.

Asteroids

An **asteroid** is a piece of rock similar to the material that later formed into the planets. Most asteroids are located in an area between the orbits of Mars and Jupiter called the asteroid belt, shown in **Figure 23-24.**

Why are they located there? The gravity of Jupiter probably kept a planet from forming in the area where the asteroid belt is now located. In addition, some asteroids may have been gravitationally thrown out of the belt and are probably scattered

USING TECHNOLOGY

Space Junk

Since the 1950s, people have been exploring space. And since then, more than 3.5 million kg of garbage—from wrenches to satellites—has been dumped in space! Much of the space trash is only a few centimeters in size, but becasue there is almost no friction in the near-vacuum environment of space, such particles could move at speeds that exceed 24 000 km per hour and cause much damage to spacecraft!

NASA scientists are currently working on designs that would protect spacecraft and the International Space Station from space debris. One proposed system is a collision warning system that would alert astronauts and ground controllers to potentially dangerous debris. The system would use infrared sensors mounted like headlights onto a spacecraft or space station to detect objects. Space-based radars would then determine the path of the object and allow the astronauts time to either avoid or prepare for the collision.

Satellite Damage Caused by Debris

Think Critically: One estimate projects that there are 3.5 million particles of garbage in space. What is the average mass of each particle?

USING TECHNOLGY

- For more information, see "Tackling the Menace of Space Junk" by Mark D. Uehling, *Popular Science,* July 1990.
- Have students discuss ways to reduce future space trash. Reusing many parts and instruments has currently been implemented by NASA.

Think Critically

3.5 million kilograms ÷ 3.5 million particles = 1.0 kg/particle

3 Assess

Check for Understanding

FLEX Your Brain

Use the Flex Your Brain activity to have students explore COMETS.

Activity Worksheets, p. 5

Reteach

LS **Logical-Mathematical** Provide students with metric rulers. Have student pairs contrast the sizes of the larger asteroids, Earth, and the moon, using a scale of 1 mm = 100 km. Have students use these data: Earth (12 756 km), the moon (3476 km), Ceres (940 km), Pallas (540 km), Vesta (510 km), and Hygeia (410 km). COOP LEARN

Extension

For students who have mastered this section, use the **Reinforcement** and **Enrichment** masters.

Across the Curriculum

Economics Have students research the nickel mines of Sudbury Basin in Ontario, Canada. It is thought that about 2 billion years ago, an asteroid 6 km in diameter collided with Earth at this location. The collision caused the formation of rich deposits of nickel, cobalt, and platinum. L2

Geography One theory that tries to explain what might have caused the extinction of the dinosaurs claims that about 66 million years ago a large asteroid collided with Earth. The devastation that followed led to the dinosaur extinction. The likely site for this impact is the Yucatán Peninsula in Mexico. Have students research where the impact site is located and how scientists have determined that a large object collided with Earth at that site. L1

4 Close

• MINI • QUIZ •

1. **What is a comet?** *a space object composed of dust and rock particles mixed with frozen water, methane, and ammonia*
2. **A large collection of comets beyond Pluto's orbit is the ______ .** *Oort Cloud*
3. **A meteoroid that burns up in Earth's atmosphere is a(n) ______ .** *meteor*

Section Wrap-up

Review

1. As a comet approaches the sun, thermal energy causes some of the comet to vaporize. Solar wind pushes on these gases to form a tail on the comet.
2. a crater
3. Comets are collections of frozen gas and rocky particles that generally travel in elliptical orbits around the sun. Meteoroids are usually small fragments of rock that move independently through space. Asteroids generally orbit the sun between Mars and Jupiter. Their sizes can range from small particles to objects as large as 1000 km in diameter.
4. **Think Critically** dust and rock particles mixed with ice, methane, and ammonia; outer planets

throughout the present-day solar system. Some may have since been captured as moons around other planets.

The size of the asteroids in the asteroid belt range from tiny particles to 940 km for Ceres, the largest and first discovered. The next three in size are Pallas (523 km), Vesta (501 km), and Juno (244 km). Two asteroids, Gaspra and Ida, were photographed by *Galileo* on its way to Jupiter. *Galileo* discovered that Ida has a small moon orbiting it.

Comets, meteoroids, and asteroids are probably composed of material that formed early in the history of the solar system. Scientists study the structure and composition of these space objects in order to better understand what the solar system may have been like long ago. Understanding what the early solar system was like could help scientists to better understand the formation of Earth and its relationship to other objects in the solar system.

Figure 23-24
The asteroid belt lies between the orbits of Mars and Jupiter.

Section Wrap-up

Review

1. How does a comet's tail form as it approaches the sun?
2. What type of feature might be formed on Earth if a large meteorite reached its surface?
3. Describe differences among comets, meteoroids, and asteroids.
4. **Think Critically:** What is the chemical composition of comets? Are comets more similar to the inner or the outer planets?

Skill Builder

Interpreting Scientific Illustrations

Identify the coma and tail of the comet shown in **Figure 23-22.** In which direction is the sun relative to the comet? If you need help, refer to Interpreting Scientific Illustrations in the **Skill Handbook.**

Science Journal

The asteroid belt contains many objects ranging in size from tiny particles to objects almost 1000 km in diameter. In your Science Journal, describe how mining the asteroids for valuable minerals might be accomplished. Include your opinion as to whether we have the technology to attempt this type of space mission.

Science Journal

Encourage students to be as creative as possible but to include ideas that are scientifically reasonable and possible to accomplish.

Skill Builder

The coma is the yellowish ball near the upper edge of the photo. The tail comprises the rest of the comet. The sun is to the left.

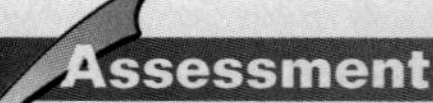

Assessment

Oral Use this Skill Builder to assess students' abilities to interpret scientific illustrations. Ask students to explain why the tail points in the direction that it does. Use the Performance Task Assessment List for Making Observations and Inferences in **PASC,** p. 17. P

Chapter 23

Review

Summary

23-1: The Solar System

1. The Earth-centered model proposed that the planets, the moon, the sun, and the stars were embedded in separate spheres that rotated around Earth. The sun-centered model states that the sun is the center of the solar system.
2. Our solar system may have formed about 5 billion years ago from a cloud of gas, ice, and dust.

23-2: The Inner Planets

1. The inner planets, in increasing distance from the sun, are Mercury, Venus, Earth, and Mars.
2. The moonlike Mercury has craters and cliffs on its surface. Venus has a dense atmosphere of carbon dioxide and sulfuric acid. On Earth, water exists in three states. Mars appears red due to the iron oxide content of its weathered rocks.
3. Venus and Earth are similar in size and mass. Both have greenhouse effects.

23-3: Science and Society: Mission to Mars

1. Problems that astronauts to Mars would face include muscle and bone weakness and exposure to dangerous levels of radiation.
2. Robots may be a better alternative than sending humans to Mars. However, robots may not be able to study Mars's surface in enough detail.

23-4: The Outer Planets

1. Faint rings and 16 moons orbit the gaseous Jupiter. Jupiter's Great Red Spot is a storm. Saturn is made mostly of gas and has rings. Uranus is a large, gaseous planet with many moons and several rings. Neptune is similar to Uranus in composition and has stormlike features.
2. Pluto has a thin, changing atmosphere, and its surface is icy rock.

23-5: Other Objects in the Solar System

1. As a comet approaches the sun, vaporized gases form a bright coma around the comet's nucleus. A tail that points away from the sun is formed by solar wind.
2. Meteoroids are small pieces of rock moving through space. An asteroid is a piece of rock usually found in the asteroid belt.

Key Science Words

a. asteroid
b. astronomical unit
c. comet
d. Earth
e. Great Red Spot
f. inner planet
g. Jupiter
h. Mars
i. Mercury
j. meteor
k. meteorite
l. Neptune
m. Oort Cloud
n. outer planet
o. Pluto
p. Saturn
q. solar system
r. Uranus
s. Venus

Reviewing Vocabulary

Match each phrase with the correct term from the list of Key Science Words.

1. solid, rocky planet close to the sun
2. planet most like Earth in size and mass
3. planet with carbon dioxide ice caps
4. Ganymede and Io are two of its moons
5. planet that could float on water
6. most are large, gaseous planets

GLENCOE TECHNOLOGY

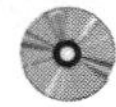

Videodisc

Glencoe Earth Science

Interactive Videodisc

Use the videodisc lesson 8, *Space Exploration,* to explore the advantages and disadvantages of space exploration.

MindJogger Videoquiz

Chapter 23 Have students work in groups as they play the Videoquiz game to review key chapter concepts.

Chapter 23

Review

Summary

Have students read the summary statements to review the major concepts of the chapter.

Reviewing Vocabulary

1. f	**6.** n
2. s	**7.** l
3. h	**8.** m
4. g	**9.** j
5. p	**10.** k

Assessment

Portfolio Encourage students to place in their portfolios one or two items of what they consider to be their best work. Examples include:

- Activity 23-1 analysis and conclusions, p. 645
- Problem Solving solution and Think Critically question, p. 648
- Activity 23-2 model and analysis, pp. 660-661 P

Performance Additional performance assessments may be found in **Performance Assessment** and **Science Integration Activities.** Performance Task Assessment Lists and rubrics for evaluating these activities can be found in Glencoe's **Performance Assessment in the Science Classroom.**

Checking Concepts

1. b
2. c
3. b
4. d
5. d
6. c
7. d
8. b
9. a
10. b

Understanding Concepts

11. Copernicus thought the planets moved around the sun in circular orbits and that the sun was in the center of the circles. Kepler discovered that the orbits were ellipses and the sun was offset from the center of the orbits.
12. The inner planets are rocky, more dense, and are composed of heavier elements. With the exception of Pluto, the outer planets are larger than the inner planets, are less dense, have more satellites, and move more slowly.
13. In space, a comet resembles a large, dirty snowball. As it nears the sun, a comet forms a coma around its nucleus. Solar wind pushes on the particles of a comet to form a tail that points away from the sun.
14. Unlike the other planets, Uranus' axis of rotation is nearly parallel to the plane of its orbit.
15. Both are small, rocky planets in the solar system. Water exists as a solid, a liquid, and a gas on Earth. It has an atmosphere composed mostly of nitrogen and oxygen. Much of Earth is covered by liquid water. Mars is red in color due to the composition of its surface rocks. It has frozen polar caps of water and carbon dioxide. Mars' atmosphere is thin and composed mostly of carbon dioxide.

Chapter 23 Review

7. blue-green planet with cloud bands and storm systems
8. large group of comets beyond Pluto's orbit
9. a rock that enters Earth's atmosphere
10. a meteoroid that strikes Earth

Checking Concepts

Choose the word or phrase that completes the sentence.

1. ____ proposed a sun-centered solar system.
   a. Ptolemy c. Galileo
   b. Copernicus d. Oort
2. _______ produces energy in the sun.
   a. Magnetism c. Nuclear fusion
   b. Nuclear fission d. The greenhouse effect
3. Planets orbit the sun _______.
   a. in circles c. by rotation
   b. in ellipses d. at the same speed
4. _______ has very extreme temperatures because it has essentially no atmosphere.
   a. Earth c. Mars
   b. Jupiter d. Mercury
5. Water is a solid, liquid, or gas on _______.
   a. Pluto c. Saturn
   b. Uranus d. Earth
6. The largest volcano in the solar system is on _______.
   a. Earth c. Mars
   b. Jupiter d. Uranus
7. A problem with living in space is _______.
   a. bones gain calcium
   b. body tissue gains water
   c. muscles become stronger
   d. bones lose calcium
8. _______ has a very complex ring system made of hundreds of ringlets.
   a. Pluto c. Uranus
   b. Saturn d. Mars
9. The magnetic pole of _______ is tilted 60°.
   a. Uranus c. Jupiter
   b. Earth d. Pluto
10. The tail of a comet always points _______.
    a. toward the sun c. toward Earth
    b. away from the sun d. away from the Oort Cloud

Understanding Concepts

Answer the following questions in your Science Journal using complete sentences.

11. Contrast Copernicus's model of the solar system with Kepler's model.
12. Describe the general characteristics of the inner and outer planets.
13. Describe how the structure of a comet changes as it nears the sun.
14. How is Uranus different from the other eight planets?
15. Compare and contrast Mars and Earth. Use the photographs on the next page to help you.

Thinking Critically

16. Why is the surface temperature on Venus so much higher than that on Earth?
17. Describe the relationship between the mass of a planet and the number of satellites it has.
18. Why are probe landings on Jupiter or Saturn unlikely events?
19. What evidence suggests that water is or once was present on Mars?
20. An observer on Earth can watch Venus go through phases much like Earth's moon does. Explain why this is so.

Thinking Critically

16. The greenhouse effect on Venus is much greater than that on Earth because the clouds on Venus are very dense and the amount of carbon dioxide in the air is greater. The CO_2 retains the heat.
17. In general, the more massive planets have more satellites.
18. The extreme heat and the dense, gaseous atmospheres would probably destroy any space probe before it could reach either of the planets' surfaces.
19. Iron contained in the weathered rocks combines with oxygen to produce iron oxide. Channels appear to have been carved by flowing water. The northern ice cap is composed partly of ice.
20. Any planet orbiting the sun inside the orbit of another planet appears to go through phases. The orbit of Venus is inside the orbit of Earth.

Developing Skills

If you need help, refer to the **Skill Handbook.**

21. **Concept Mapping:** Make a concept map that shows how a comet changes as it travels through space.
22. **Hypothesizing:** Mercury is the closest planet to the sun, yet it does not reflect much of the sun's light. What can you say about Mercury's color?
23. **Measuring in SI:** The Great Red Spot of Jupiter is about 40 000 km long and about 12 000 km wide. What is its approximate area in km^2?
24. **Sequencing:** Arrange the following planets in order from the planet with the most natural satellites to the one with the least: Earth, Jupiter, Saturn, Neptune, Uranus, and Mars.
25. **Making and Using Tables:** Make a table that summarizes the main characteristics of each planet in the solar system.

Performance Assessment

1. **Display:** Mercury, Venus, Mars, Jupiter, and Saturn can be observed by the unaided eye. Research where in the sky these planets can be observed in the next year. Construct a display with your findings. Include time of day, day of the year, and locations with respect to known landmarks in your area on your display.
2. **Scientific Drawing:** You learned that planetary orbit shapes are ellipses, not circles. Based on the models of planetary orbits that you formulated, how could you draw a circular orbit? How could you draw an orbit that is extremely elliptical?
3. **Model:** Build a three-dimensional model of the solar system. Include features such as the asteroid belt.

Surface of Mars

Surface of Earth

Assessment Resources

Reproducible Masters

Chapter Review, pp. 49-50

Assessment, pp. 151-154

Performance Assessment, p. 37

Glencoe Technology

Chapter Review Software

Computer Test Bank

MindJogger Videoquiz

Chapter 23 Review

Developing Skills

21. **Concept Mapping** Comet begins as mass of ice and rock; ice vaporizes as comet nears sun; vaporized gases form coma; solar wind forms tail; after many orbits, much of comet vaporizes; nucleus breaks up; pieces spread to fill original orbit.
22. **Hypothesizing** Mercury is dark in color, and it doesn't reflect much of the light that reaches its surface.
23. **Measuring in SI**

$$\text{area} = \text{length} \times \text{width} = 40\ 000 \text{ km} \times 12\ 000 \text{ km} = 480\ 000\ 000 \text{ km}^2$$

24. **Sequencing** Saturn, Jupiter, Uranus, Neptune, Mars, Earth
25. **Making and Using Tables** Students should include the number of satellites, the type of atmosphere, and other characteristics.

Performance Assessment

1. This information is available in many sources. *Astronomy* and *Sky & Telescope* magazines provide monthly information. Use the Performance Task Assessment List for Display in **PASC,** p. 63. P
2. Using one nail, the string would pull out to a distance equal to the radius of the circular orbit. To draw an extremely elliptical orbit, you would place the two nails far apart. Use the Performance Task Assessment List for Scientific Drawing in **PASC,** p. 55. P
3. Encourage students to be creative in choosing the material to be used in their models. Use the Performance Task Assessment List for Model in **PASC,** p. 51. P

Chapter Organizer

Section	Objectives	Activities/Features
Chapter Opener		**Explore Activity:** Make a model of the expansion of the universe. p. 671
24-1 **Stars** (2 sessions, 1 block)*	1. **Explain** why the positions of the constellations change throughout the year. 2. **Compare** and **contrast** absolute magnitude and apparent magnitude. 3. **Describe** how parallax is used to determine distances.	**Problem Solving:** Star Light, Star Bright, p. 674 **MiniLAB:** What patterns do you see in the stars? p. 675 **Activity 24-1:** Measuring Parallax, pp. 676-677 **Skill Builder:** Recognizing Cause and Effect, p. 678 **Using Computers:** Graphics, p. 678
24-2 **The Sun** (1 session, 1/2 block)*	1. **Describe** how energy is produced in the sun. 2. **Recognize** that sunspots, prominences, and solar flares are related. 3. **Explain** why our sun is considered an average star and how it differs from stars in binary systems.	**Connect to Life Science,** p. 680 **MiniLAB:** How do the sizes of stars compare? p. 681 **Skill Builder:** Interpreting Scientific Illustrations, p. 682 **Science Journal,** p. 682 **Activity 24-2:** Sunspots, p. 683
24-3 **Evolution of Stars** (3 sessions, 2 blocks)*	1. **Diagram** how stars are classified. 2. **Relate** the temperature of a star to its color. 3. **Outline** the evolution of a star through all stages of its development.	**Connect to Chemistry,** p. 687 **Using Technology:** Studying Supernovas, p. 689 **Skill Builder:** Sequencing, p. 690 **Science Journal,** p. 690
24-4 **Galaxies and the Expanding Universe** (2 sessions, 1 block)*	1. **Describe** a galaxy and list the three main types of galaxies. 2. **Identify** several characteristics of the Milky Way Galaxy. 3. **Explain** how the big bang theory explains the observed Doppler shifts of galaxies.	**Connect to Physics,** p. 694 **MiniLAB:** How far can we "see" into space? p. 695 **Skill Builder:** Recognizing Cause and Effect, p. 697 **Using Math,** p. 687 **Science Journal,** p. 697
24-5 **Science and Society Technology: The Search for Extraterrestrial Life** (1 session)*	1. **Name** locations in our solar system where life may have existed in the past or could exist now. 2. **Describe** the methods used by astronomers to search for extraterrestrial life within and beyond our solar system. 3. **Decide** whether methods used by scientists might cause contamination of other worlds.	**Explore the Technology,** p. 699 **Science & Art:** Is anyone out there? p. 700 **Science Journal,** p. 700

* A complete Planning Guide that includes block scheduling is provided on pages 32T-35T.

Activity Materials

Explore	Activities	MiniLABs
page 671 large, round balloon; spring-type clothespin; felt-tipped marker; string; metric ruler	pages 676-677 meterstick, metric ruler, safety goggles, masking tape, object to observe (such as a pencil) page 683 several books, clipboard, small refracting telescope, cardboard, drawing paper, small tripod, scissors	page 675 white, unruled paper; blue pen page 681 large, paved area; thin piece of chalkboard chalk; 125-cm length of string; metric ruler page 695 large piece of paper (newsprint or butcher paper), pencil or fine-tipped marker, mathematical compass, metric ruler, meterstick

Chapter 24 Stars and Galaxies

Teacher Classroom Resources

Reproducible Masters	Transparencies
Study Guide, p. 94 **Reinforcement,** p. 94 **Enrichment,** p. 94 **Activity Worksheets,** pp. 144-145, 148 **Lab Manual 67,** Astronomical Distances **Lab Manual 68,** Star Colors **Lab Manual 69,** Star Trails **Lab Manual 70,** Star Positions **Critical Thinking/Problem Solving,** p. 30	**Section Focus Transparency 90,** Starry Starry Night
Study Guide, p. 95 **Reinforcement,** p. 95 **Enrichment,** p. 95 **Activity Worksheets,** pp. 146-147, 149 **Science Integration Activity 24,** Photo What? **Multicultural Connections,** pp. 51-52	**Section Focus Transparency 91,** Nature's Light Show **Science Integration Transparency 24,** Fission vs. Fusion
Study Guide, p. 96 **Reinforcement,** p. 96 **Enrichment,** p. 96 **Concept Mapping,** p. 53	**Section Focus Transparency 92,** Star Years **Teaching Transparency 47,** H-R Diagram **Teaching Transparency 48,** Evolution of a Main Sequence Star
Study Guide, p. 97 **Reinforcement,** p. 97 **Enrichment,** p. 97 **Activity Worksheets,** p. 151	**Section Focus Transparency 93,** Our Changing Universe
Study Guide, p. 98 **Reinforcement,** p. 98 **Enrichment,** p. 98 **Cross-Curricular Integration,** p. 28 **Science and Society Integration,** p. 28	**Section Focus Transparency 94,** Life on Other Planets: Would We Know It If We Saw It?

Teaching Resources

Glencoe Earth Science Interactive Videodisc
Earth Science CD-ROM
Spanish Resources
English/Spanish Audiocassettes
Cooperative Learning Resource Guide
Lab Partner
Lab and Safety Skills
Lesson Plans

Assessment Resources

Chapter Review, pp. 51-52
Assessment, pp. 155-158
Performance Assessment in the Science Classroom (PASC)
MindJogger Videoquiz
Alternate Assessment in the Science Classroom
Performance Assessment
Chapter Review Software
Computer Test Bank

Key to Teaching Strategies

The following designations will help you decide which activities are appropriate for your students.

L1 Level 1 activities should be within the ability range of all students.

L2 Level 2 activities should be within the ability range of the average to above-average student.

L3 Level 3 activities are designed for the ability range of above-average students.

LEP LEP activities should be within the ability range of Limited English Proficiency students.

LS These activities are designed to address different learning styles.

COOP LEARN Cooperative Learning activities are designed for small group work.

P These strategies represent student products that can be placed into a best-work portfolio.

GLENCOE TECHNOLOGY

The following multimedia resources are available from Glencoe.

The Infinite Voyage Series
Unseen Worlds
Science and Technology Videodisc Series (STVS)
Physics
Fusion
Computerized Star Imaging
Earth & Space
Shape of Galaxies
Modeling Black Holes
National Geographic Society Series
STV: Solar System
Earth Science CD-ROM

Teacher Classroom Resources

This is a representation of key blackline masters available in the Teacher Classroom Resources.

Teaching Aids

Section Focus Transparencies

90 SECTION FOCUS TRANSPARENCY — Section 24-1

STARRY STARRY NIGHT

On a clear night, if you are far away from city lights, you can see thousands of stars.

1. What constellations can you identify in this photograph?
2. Make up your own constellations using the stars in this photograph. Name each constellation and explain what it represents.

L1

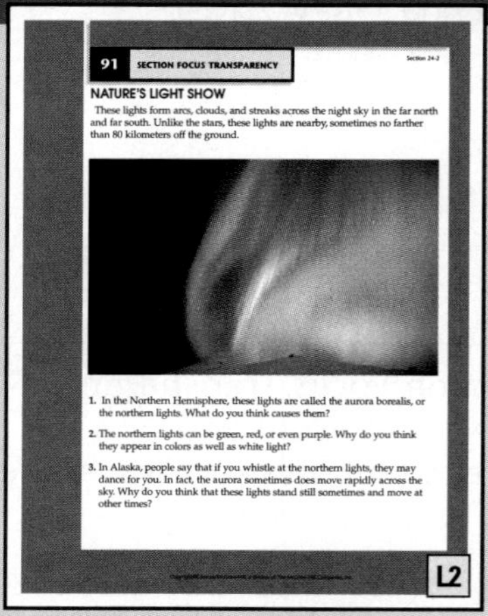

91 SECTION FOCUS TRANSPARENCY — Section 24-2

NATURE'S LIGHT SHOW

These lights form arcs, clouds, and streaks across the night sky in the far north and far south. Unlike the stars, these lights are nearby, sometimes no farther than 80 kilometers off the ground.

1. In the Northern Hemisphere, these lights are called the aurora borealis, or the northern lights. What do you think causes them?
2. The northern lights can be green, red, or even purple. Why do you think they appear in colors as well as white light?
3. In Alaska, people say that if you whistle at the northern lights, they may dance for you. In fact, the aurora sometimes does move rapidly across the sky. Why do you think that these lights stand still sometimes and move at other times?

L2

92 SECTION FOCUS TRANSPARENCY — Section 24-3

STAR YEARS

Everything in this photo depends on the sun. Plants need sunlight in order to grow. Plants also need the sun's light to warm the atmosphere—if it gets too cold, plants will freeze to death.

1. What in this photograph needs the sun?
2. Why do people need the sun?

L3

Science Integration Transparencies

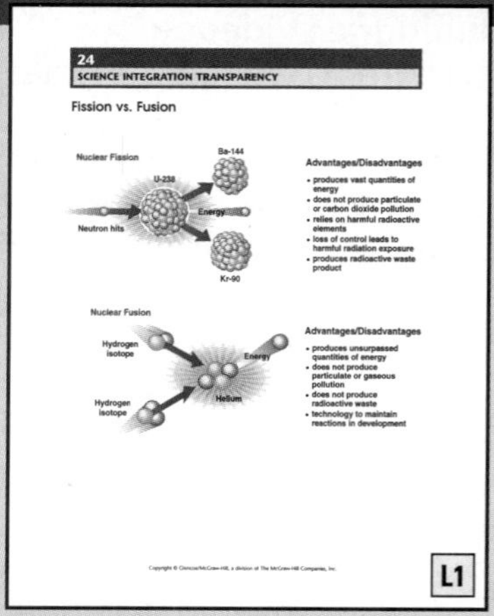

24 SCIENCE INTEGRATION TRANSPARENCY

Fission vs. Fusion

Nuclear Fission

Ba-144, U-238, Energy, Neutron hits, Kr-90

Advantages/Disadvantages
- produces vast quantities of energy
- does not produce particulate or carbon dioxide pollution
- relies on harmful radioactive elements
- loss of control leads to harmful radiation exposure
- produces radioactive waste product

Nuclear Fusion

Hydrogen isotope, Energy, Hydrogen isotope, Helium

Advantages/Disadvantages
- produces unsurpassed quantities of energy
- does not produce particulate or gaseous pollution
- does not produce radioactive waste
- technology to maintain reactions in development

L1

Teaching Transparencies

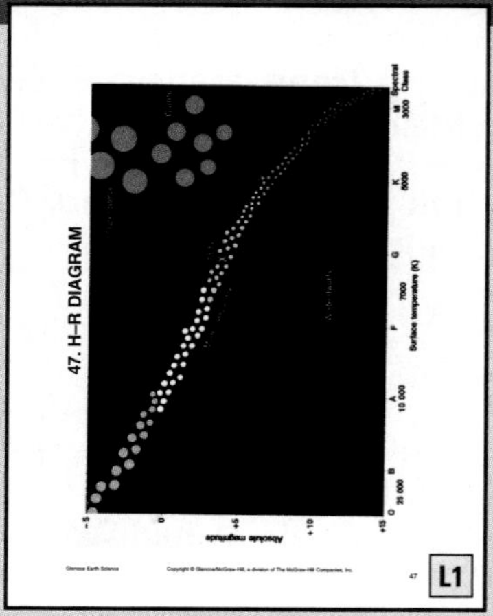

47. H-R DIAGRAM

L1

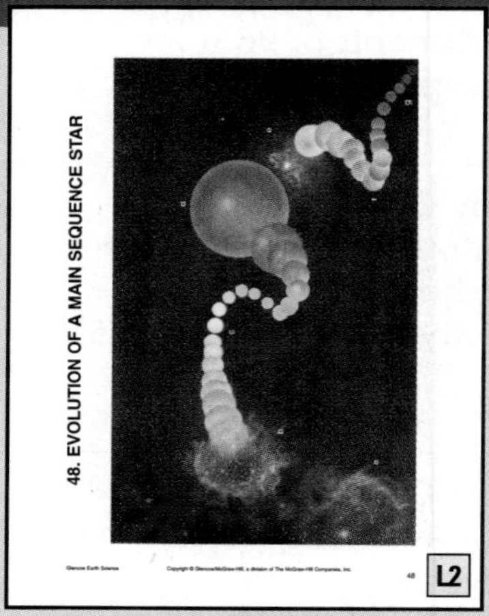

48. EVOLUTION OF A MAIN SEQUENCE STAR

L2

Meeting Different Ability Levels

Study Guide

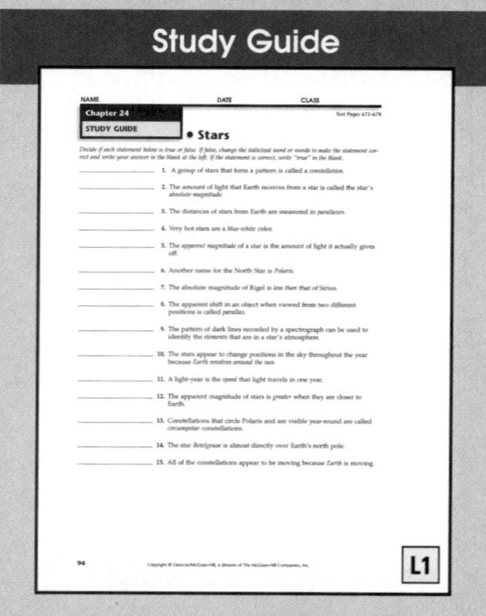

NAME DATE CLASS

Chapter 24 STUDY GUIDE • Stars — Text Pages 672-678

Decide if each statement below is true or false. If false, change the italicized word or words to make the statement correct and write your answer in the blank at the left. If the statement is correct, write "true" in the blank.

1. A group of stars that form a pattern is called a *constellation*.
2. The amount of light that Earth receives from a star is called the star's *absolute magnitude*.
3. The distances of stars from Earth are measured in *parallaxes*.
4. Very hot stars are a *blue-white* color.
5. The *apparent magnitude* of a star is the amount of light it actually gives off.
6. Another name for the North Star is *Polaris*.
7. The absolute magnitude of Rigel is *less than* that of Sirius.
8. The apparent shift in an object when viewed from two different positions is called *parallax*.
9. The pattern of dark lines recorded by a spectrograph can be used to identify the *elements* that are in a star's atmosphere.
10. The stars appear to change positions in the sky throughout the year because *Earth revolves around the sun*.
11. A light-year is the *speed* that light travels in one year.
12. The apparent magnitude of stars is *greater* when they are closer to Earth.
13. Constellations that circle Polaris and are visible year-round are called *circumpolar* constellations.
14. The star *Betelgeuse* is almost directly over Earth's north pole.
15. All of the constellations appear to be moving because *Earth* is moving.

94 — Copyright © Glencoe/McGraw-Hill, a division of The McGraw-Hill Companies, Inc.

L1

Reinforcement

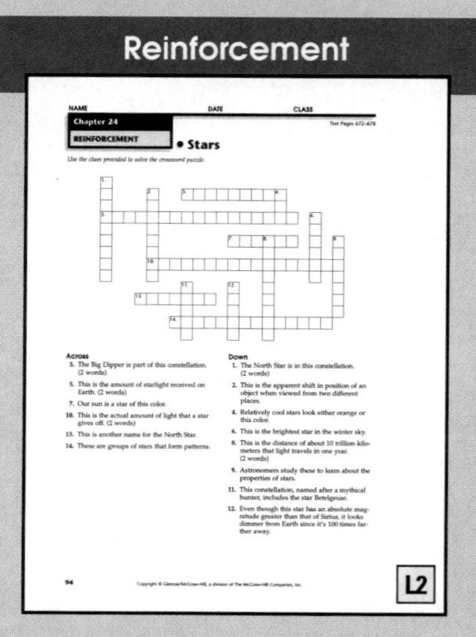

NAME DATE CLASS

Chapter 24 REINFORCEMENT • Stars — Text Pages 672-678

Use the clues provided to solve the crossword puzzle.

Across

3. The Big Dipper is part of this constellation. (2 words)
5. This is the amount of starlight received on Earth. (2 words)
7. Our sun is a star of this color.
10. This is the actual amount of light that a star gives off. (2 words)
13. This is another name for the North Star.
14. These are groups of stars that form patterns.

Down

1. The North Star is in this constellation. (2 words)
2. This is the apparent shift in position of an object when viewed from two different places.
4. Relatively cool stars look either orange or this color.
6. This is the brightest star in the winter sky.
8. This is the distance of about 10 trillion kilometers that light travels in one year. (2 words)
9. Astronomers study these to learn about the properties of stars.
11. This constellation, named after a mythical hunter, includes the star Betelgeuse.
12. Even though this star has an absolute magnitude greater than that of Sirius, it looks dimmer from Earth since it's 100 times farther away.

94 — Copyright © Glencoe/McGraw-Hill, a division of The McGraw-Hill Companies, Inc.

L2

Enrichment Worksheets

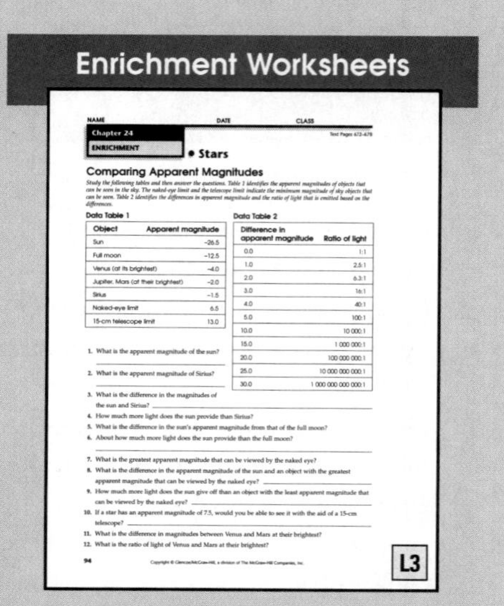

NAME DATE CLASS

Chapter 24 ENRICHMENT • Stars — Text Pages 672-678

Comparing Apparent Magnitudes

Study the following tables and then answer the questions. Table 1 identifies the apparent magnitudes of objects that can be seen in the sky. The naked-eye limit and the telescope limit indicate the minimum magnitude of sky objects that can be seen. Table 2 identifies the differences in apparent magnitude and the ratio of light that is emitted based on the differences.

Data Table 1

Object	Apparent magnitude
Sun	−26.5
Full moon	−12.5
Venus (at its brightest)	−4.0
Jupiter, Mars (at their brightest)	−2.0
Sirius	−1.5
Naked-eye limit	6.5
15-cm telescope limit	13.0

Data Table 2

Difference in apparent magnitude	Ratio of light
0.0	1:1
1.0	2.5:1
2.0	6.3:1
3.0	16:1
4.0	40:1
5.0	100:1
10.0	10 000:1
15.0	1 000 000:1
20.0	100 000 000:1
25.0	10 000 000 000:1
30.0	1 000 000 000 000:1

1. What is the apparent magnitude of the sun?
2. What is the apparent magnitude of Sirius?
3. What is the difference in the magnitudes of the sun and Sirius?
4. How much more light does the sun provide than Sirius?
5. What is the difference in the sun's apparent magnitude from that of the full moon?
6. About how much more light does the sun provide than the full moon?
7. What is the greatest apparent magnitude that can be viewed by the naked eye?
8. What is the difference in the apparent magnitude of the sun and an object with the greatest apparent magnitude that can be viewed by the naked eye?
9. How much more light does the sun give off than an object with the least apparent magnitude that can be viewed by the naked eye?
10. If a star has an apparent magnitude of 7.5, would you be able to see it with the aid of a 15-cm telescope?
11. What is the difference in magnitudes between Venus and Mars at their brightest?
12. What is the ratio of light of Venus and Mars at their brightest?

94 — Copyright © Glencoe/McGraw-Hill, a division of The McGraw-Hill Companies, Inc.

L3

Hands-On Activities

Science Integration Activity

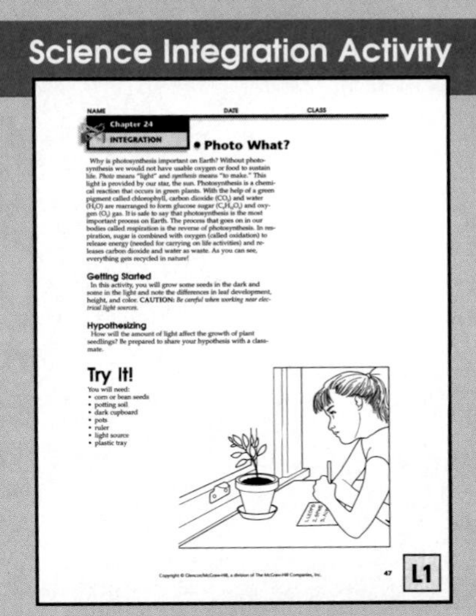
Chapter 24 INTEGRATION

Photo What?

Getting Started

Hypothesizing

Try It!

L1

Lab Manual

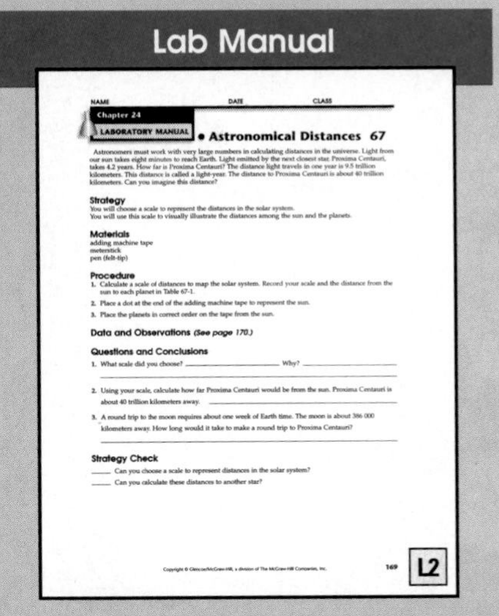
Chapter 24 LABORATORY MANUAL

Astronomical Distances 67

Strategy

Materials

Procedure

Data and Observations

Questions and Conclusions

Strategy Check

L2

Assessment

Performance Assessment

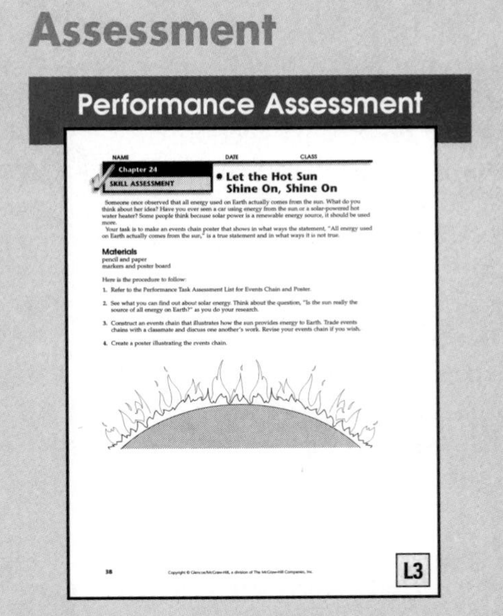
Chapter 24 SKILL ASSESSMENT

Let the Hot Sun Shine On, Shine On

Materials

L3

Enrichment and Application

Critical Thinking/ Problem Solving

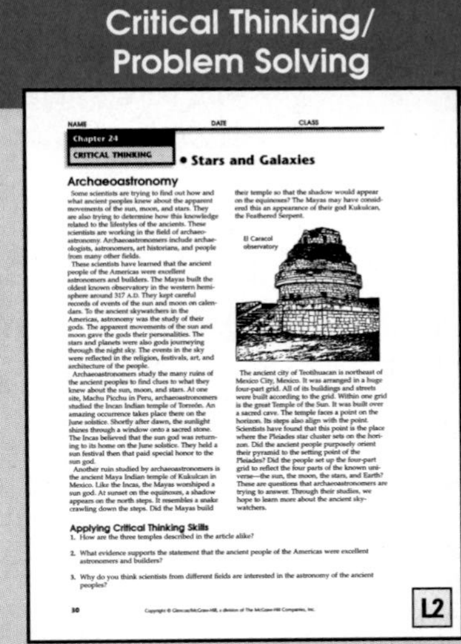
Chapter 24 CRITICAL THINKING

Stars and Galaxies

Archaeoastronomy

Applying Critical Thinking Skills

L2

Cross-Curricular Integration

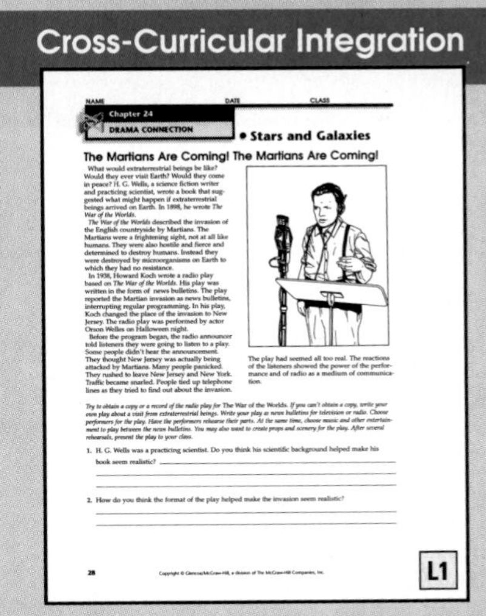
Chapter 24 DRAMA CONNECTION

Stars and Galaxies

The Martians Are Coming! The Martians Are Coming!

L1

Science and Society Integration

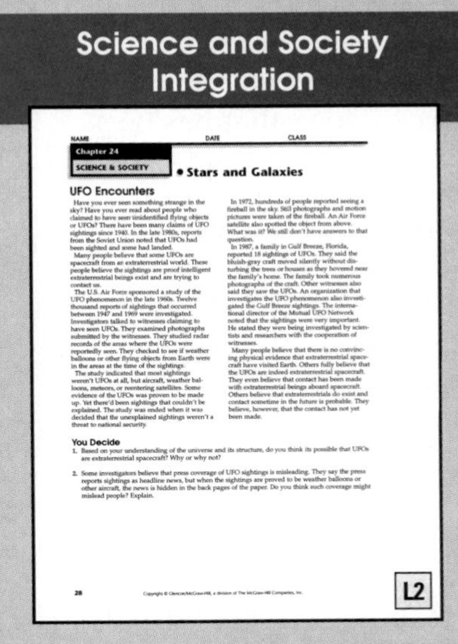
Chapter 24 SCIENCE & SOCIETY

Stars and Galaxies

UFO Encounters

You Decide

L2

Multicultural Connections

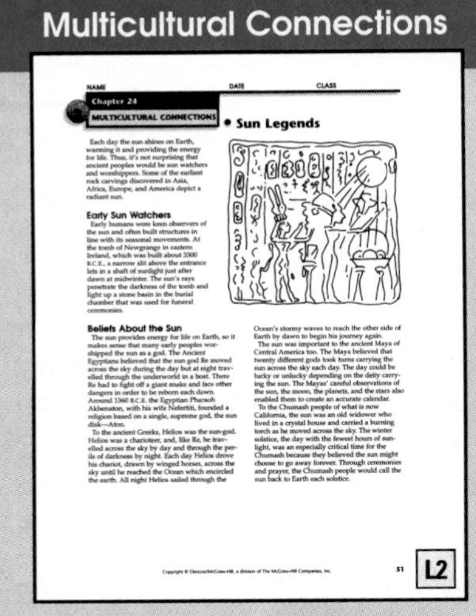
Chapter 24 MULTICULTURAL CONNECTIONS

Sun Legends

Early Sun Watchers

Beliefs About the Sun

L2

Concept Mapping

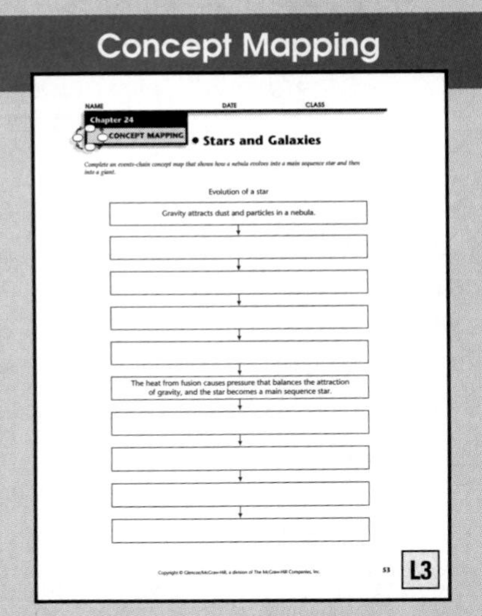
Chapter 24 CONCEPT MAPPING

Stars and Galaxies

Evolution of a star

Gravity attracts dust and particles in a nebula.

The heat from fusion causes pressure that balances the attraction of gravity, and the star becomes a main sequence star.

L3

Chapter 24

Stars and Galaxies

CHAPTER OVERVIEW

Section 24-1 This section discusses constellations as patterns of stars and compares the absolute and apparent brightness of stars. Other properties of stars are also presented.

Section 24-2 The structure and surface features of the sun are discussed in this section.

Section 24-3 The evolution of stars from one stage to another is presented in this section. Energy production in stars is also discussed.

Section 24-4 This section illustrates the different types of galaxies. The big bang theory of the evolution of the universe is also presented.

Section 24-5 **Science and Society** The technology that has been used and is being used by scientists to search for extraterrestrial life is presented.

Chapter Vocabulary

constellation
absolute magnitude
apparent magnitude
parallax
light-year
photosphere
chromosphere
corona
sunspot
binary system
main sequence
nebula
giant
white dwarf
supergiant
neutron star
black hole
galaxy
big bang theory

Theme Connection

Scale and Structure/Stability and Change The scale and structure of the universe and how the universe and the matter in it change are the major themes of this chapter.

Previewing the Chapter

Look for the following logo for strategies that emphasize different learning modalities. LS

Kinesthetic	Explore, p. 671; Inclusion Strategies, p. 673
Visual-Spatial	Brainstorming, p. 673; MiniLAB, pp. 674, 695; Reteach, pp. 681, 696; Visual Learning, pp. 681, 685, 686, 692; Activity 24-2, p. 683; Demonstation, p. 686
Interpersonal	Activity 24-1, pp. 676-677; Bulletin Board, p. 685; Science Journal, p. 688; Discussion, p. 693; Reteach, p. 699
Logical-Mathematical	Across the Curriculum, pp. 675, 681; MiniLAB, p. 680
Linguistic	Science Journal, pp. 673, 693; Enrichment, p. 687
Auditory-Musical	Demonstration, p. 694; Science & Art, p. 700

Chapter 24

Stars and Galaxies

This photo may look like science fiction, but it is a real place. It is one of the first images of stars in the process of forming. Located far beyond our solar system, the brilliant colors are produced by hot gases. By studying deep space, astronomers have observed that the universe is expanding in all directions. In the following activity, you can model how the universe might be expanding.

EXPLORE ACTIVITY

Make a model of the expansion of the universe.

1. Partially inflate a balloon. Clip the neck shut with a clothespin.
2. Draw six evenly spaced dots on the balloon with a felt-tip marker. Label the dots A through F.
3. Use a string and ruler to measure the distance, in millimeters, from dot A to each of the other dots.
4. Remove the clothespin and inflate the balloon some more.
5. Measure the distance of each dot from A again.
6. Inflate the balloon again and take the new measurements.

Infer: If each dot represents a cluster of galaxies, describe the motion of the galaxy clusters relative to one another. Is the universe expanding?

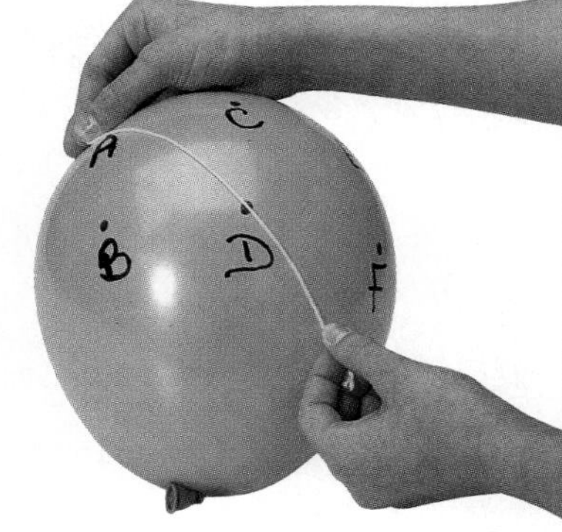

Previewing Science Skills

- In the **Skill Builders**, you will **recognize cause and effect, sequence events,** and **interpret scientific illustrations.**
- In the **Activities**, you will **collect and analyze data** and **draw conclusions.**
- In the **MiniLABs**, you will **formulate models, interpret scientific illustrations,** and **make inferences.**

Assessment Planner

Portfolio
Refer to page 701 for suggested items that students might select for their portfolios.

Performance Assessment
See page 701 for additional Performance Assessment options.
Skill Builders, pp. 678, 682, 690, 697
MiniLABs, pp. 674, 680, 695
Activities 24-1, pp. 676-677; 24-2, p. 683

Content Assessment
Section Wrap-ups, pp. 678, 682, 690, 697, 699
Chapter Review, pp. 701-703
Mini Quizzes, pp. 678, 682, 690, 696

Group Assessment
Opportunities for group assessment occur with Cooperative Learning Strategies and Flex Your Brain Activities.

EXPLORE ACTIVITY

Purpose

LS **Kinesthetic** Use the Explore Activity to introduce students to the concept of an expanding universe. Inform students that they will be learning more about the universe and the stars and galaxies it contains as they read the chapter. L1

Preparation

Several days before you begin this chapter, have students bring in large, round balloons and clothespins.

Materials

one balloon, one clothespin, one felt-tip marker, string, and a metric ruler for each group

Teaching Strategies

- Form groups of four students per group. Assign appropriate student roles. One student should blow up the balloon and clip it shut. Another should draw the dots on the balloon. The other two students should measure the distance between the dots.

Safety Precautions Caution students not to blow the balloons up so much that they break.

Observe

The galaxy clusters are moving away from each other. This type of motion would imply that the universe is expanding.

Assessment

Process Ask students to explain in writing why galaxy clusters moving away from each other implies that the universe is expanding. Use the Performance Task Assessment List for Writing in Science in **PASC,** p. 87. P

Section 24•1

Prepare

Section Background

- The absolute magnitude of a star is affected by its size and temperature. The apparent magnitude of a star is affected by its size, temperature, and distance. If the absolute and apparent magnitudes of a star are known, its distance can be determined.
- Clouds of gas and dust in space can obscure starlight, reducing a star's apparent brightness.

Preplanning

- In preparation for Activity 24-1, obtain metersticks and metric rulers for each team of two students.
- To prepare for the MiniLAB, monitor the weather and assign the activity on a night that is forecast to be clear.

1 Motivate

Bellringer

Before presenting the lesson, display **Section Focus Transparency 90** on the overhead projector. Assign the accompanying **Focus Activity** worksheet. L1 LEP

Tying to Previous Knowledge

- Help students recall what they know about constellations. Ask how many students have seen the Big Dipper. Draw the stars of the Big Dipper on the chalkboard and show why it's called a dipper.
- Some students may know that they can use the North Star (Polaris) to determine direction at night.

24•1 Stars

Science Words

constellation
absolute magnitude
apparent magnitude
parallax
light-year

Objectives

- Explain why the positions of the constellations change throughout the year.
- Compare and contrast absolute magnitude and apparent magnitude.
- Describe how parallax is used to determine distances.

Constellations

Have you ever watched clouds drift by on a summer day? It's fun to look at the clouds and imagine they have shapes familiar to you. One may look like a face. You might see a cloud that resembles a rabbit or a bear. People long ago did much the same thing with patterns of stars in the sky. They named certain groups of stars, called **constellations,** after animals, characters in mythology, or familiar objects. Two constellations are shown in **Figure 24-1.**

From Earth, a constellation looks like a group of stars that are relatively close to one another. In most cases, the stars in a constellation have no relationship to each other in space.

The position of a star in the sky can be given as a specific location within a constellation. For example, you can say that the star Betelgeuse is in the right shoulder of the mighty hunter Orion. Orion's faithful companion is his dog, Canis Major. The brightest star in the sky, Sirius, is in the constellation Canis Major.

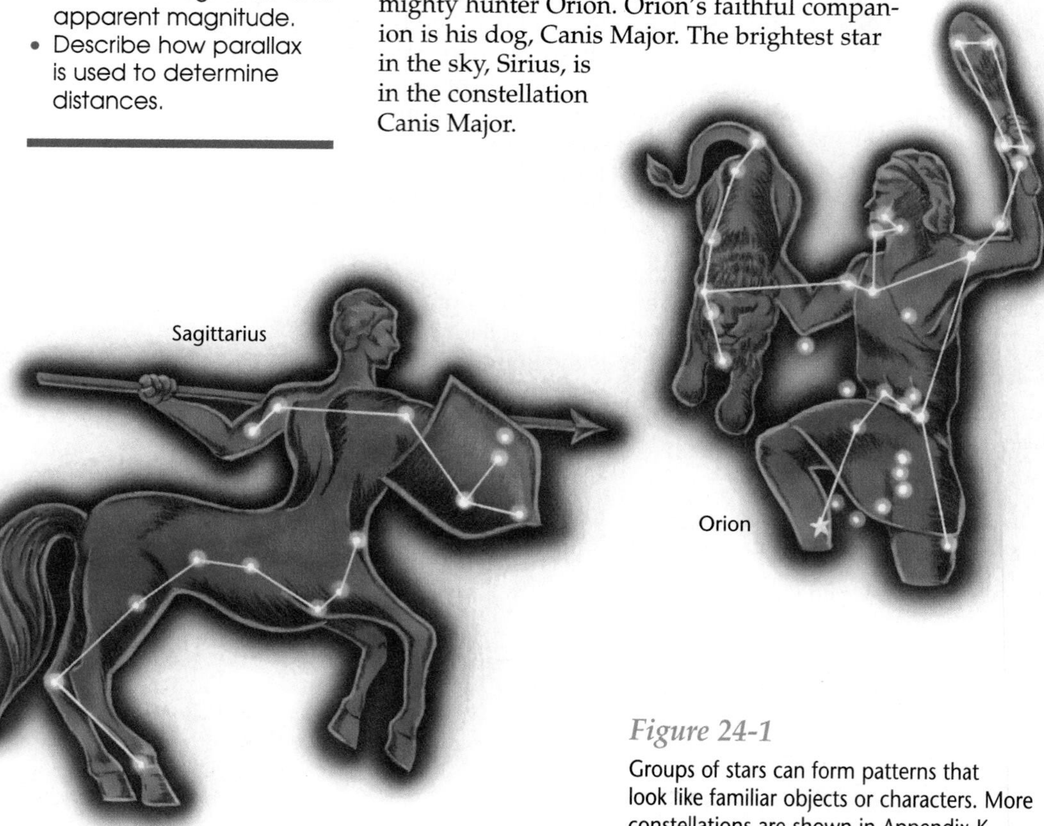

Figure 24-1
Groups of stars can form patterns that look like familiar objects or characters. More constellations are shown in Appendix K.

Program Resources

Reproducible Masters

Study Guide, p. 94 L1
Reinforcement, p. 94 L1
Enrichment, p. 94 L3
Activity Worksheets, pp. 5, 144-145, 148 L1
Critical Thinking/Problem Solving, p. 30
Lab Manual 67, 68, 69, 70

Transparencies

Section Focus Transparency 90 L1

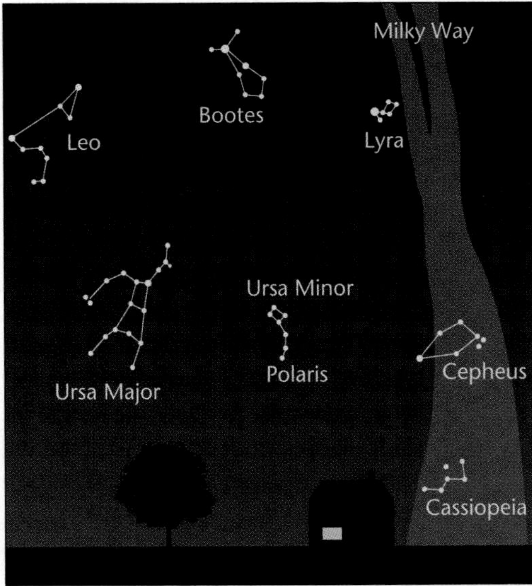

Summer

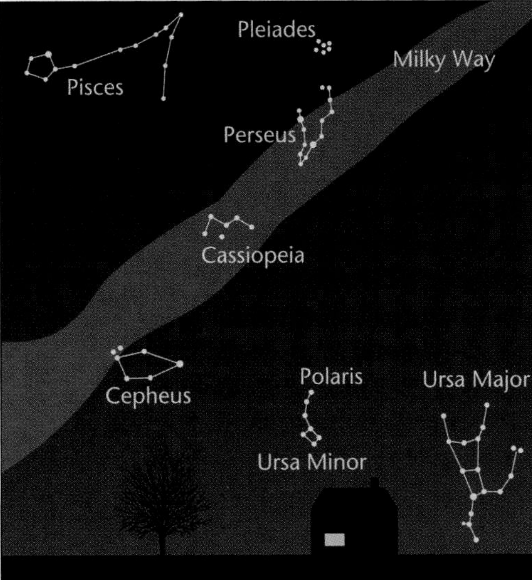

Winter

Figure 24-2

Some constellations are visible only during certain seasons of the year. Others, such as those close to Polaris, are visible year-round.

Early Greek astronomers named many constellations, and modern astronomers have divided the sky into 88 constellations. You may already know some of them. Have you ever tried to find the Big Dipper? It's part of the constellation Ursa Major. Notice how the front two stars of the Big Dipper point directly at the star Polaris. Polaris, also known as the North Star, is located at the end of the Little Dipper in the constellation Ursa Minor. Polaris is almost directly over Earth's north pole.

Circumpolar Constellations

As Earth rotates, you can watch Ursa Major, Ursa Minor, and other constellations in the northern sky circle around Polaris. Because these constellations circle Polaris they are called circumpolar constellations.

All of the constellations appear to move because Earth is moving, as shown in **Figure 24-3.** The stars appear to complete one full circle in the sky in just under 24 hours as Earth rotates on its axis. The stars also appear to change positions in the sky throughout the year as Earth revolves around the sun.

Circumpolar constellations are visible all year long, but other constellations are not. As Earth orbits the sun, different constellations come into view while others disappear. Orion, which is visible in the winter, can't be seen in the summer because the daytime side of Earth is facing it.

Figure 24-3

This photograph shows the path of circumpolar stars over several hours. Polaris is almost directly over the north pole and doesn't appear to move much as Earth rotates.

2 Teach

Brainstorming

LS **Visual-Spatial** Supply students with star charts that contain only dots as stars. Ask students to make up their own constellations using the stars. Have students brainstorm and come up with reasons why they chose the drawings they did. Relate this to how the original constellations were named. L1

GLENCOE TECHNOLOGY

Videodisc

STVS: Physics

Disc 1, Side 2

Computerized Star Imaging (Ch. 17)

Revealing Preconceptions

Ask students why stars are part of a particular constellation. Many students may think that stars within one constellation are close to one another in space. Explain that two stars that appear side by side may be separated by hundreds of light-years. Likewise, two stars that are only a few light-years apart may appear to be far apart in the night sky.

GLENCOE TECHNOLOGY

CD-ROM

Earth Science CD-ROM

Have students perform the interactive exploration for Chapter 24 to reinforce important chapter concepts and thinking processes.

Inclusion Strategies

Learning Disabled Have students cut black construction paper into 4-cm squares. On each square, put pinholes to form major constellations. Students then place a constellation square at one end of a cardboard tube. Pointing the tube toward a light source, students can view the constellation through the tube. Have students switch constellation squares and make a game of identifying constellations. LS

Science Journal

Constellations from Mythology Have students research their favorite or a well-known constellation and write a report in their Science Journals about the stars in the constellation. Also have them write about the mythology dealing with the constellation figure. *Answers will vary, depending on the constellation chosen. Accept all reasonable ideas.* L1 LS

MiniLAB

Purpose

LS **Visual-Spatial** Students will realize that placing stars in familiar patterns helps them learn the stars' names and their positions. Students will also observe that constellations can be used to determine directions. L1 LEP

Teaching Strategies

Troubleshooting To help students who might express concern about this activity, remind them of the Brainstorming activity done with unlabeled star charts early in the lesson. If the Brainstorming lesson was overlooked, perform it as preparation for this MiniLAB.

Analysis

1. Answers will vary.
2. They could be used to find direction. Patterns of stars help in learning star names and positions.

Assessment

Performance Have students write a mythological story that goes with the star drawings they made while observing at night. Use the Performance Task Assessment List for Writer's Guide to Fiction in **PASC**, p. 83. P

Activity Worksheets, pp. 5, 148

Problem Solving

Star Light, Star Bright

Mary conducted an experiment to determine the relationship between distance and the brightness of stars. She used a meterstick, a light meter, and a light bulb. The bulb was mounted at the zero end of the meterstick. Mary placed the light meter at the 20-cm mark on the meterstick and recorded the distance and the light-meter reading in the data table below. Readings are in luxes, which are units for measuring light intensity. Mary doubled and tripled the distance and took more readings.

Solve the Problem:

1. **Does the light meter measure absolute or apparent brightness?**
2. **What happened to the amount of light recorded when the distance was increased from 20 cm to 40 cm? From 20 cm to 60 cm?**

Think Critically:

What is the relationship between light intensity and distance? What would the light intensity be at 100 cm?

Distance (cm)	Meter Reading (luxes)
20	4150
40	1037.5
60	461.1
80	259.4

Absolute and Apparent Magnitudes

When you look at constellations, you'll notice that some stars are brighter than others. Sirius looks much brighter than Rigel. But is Sirius actually a brighter star, or is it just closer to Earth, which makes it appear to be brighter? As it turns out, Sirius is 100 times closer to Earth than Rigel. If Sirius and Rigel were the same distance from Earth, Rigel would appear much brighter in the night sky than would Sirius.

When you refer to the brightness of a star, you can refer to either its absolute magnitude or its apparent magnitude. The **absolute magnitude** of a star is a measure of the amount of light it actually gives off. A measure of the amount of light received on Earth is called the **apparent magnitude.** A star that's actually rather dim can appear quite bright in the sky if it's close to Earth. A star that's actually bright can appear dim if it's far away. If two stars are the same distance away, what factors might cause one of them to be brighter than the other?

You can experience the effect of distance on apparent magnitude when driving in a car at night. Observe the other cars' headlights as they approach. Which car's headlights are brighter, those that are closer to you or those that are further away?

NATIONAL GEOGRAPHIC SOCIETY

Videodisc

STV: Solar System

Night sky

41647

Inclusion Strategies

Gifted Away from city lights, place an SLR (single lens reflex) camera on a tripod. Aim the camera so that the North Star (Polaris) is directly in the center of the viewfinder. Use fast film, such as 1000 ASA. Open the shutter for 20 to 30 minutes and have the aperture as wide open as possible. As Earth rotates, the light from the stars will expose the film and appear as circular streaks. L3

Determining the Distances to Stars

How do we know when a star is close to our solar system? One way is to measure its parallax. **Parallax** is the apparent shift in the position of an object when viewed from two different positions. You can easily observe parallax. Hold your hand at arm's length and look at one finger first with your left eye and then with your right eye. Your finger appears to change position with respect to the background. Now try the same experiment with your finger closer to your face. What do you observe? The nearer an object is to the observer, the greater its parallax.

We can measure the parallax of relatively close stars to determine their distances from Earth, as shown in **Figure 24-4.** When astronomers first realized how far away stars actually are, it became apparent that a new unit of measure would be needed to record their distances. Measuring star distances in kilometers would be like measuring the distance between cities in millimeters.

Distances in space are measured in light-years. A **light-year** is the distance that light travels in one year. Light travels at 300 000 km/s, or about 9.5 trillion kilometers in one year. The nearest star to Earth, other than the sun, is Proxima Centauri. Proxima Centauri is 4.2 light-years away, or about 40 trillion kilometers.

MiniLAB

What patterns do you see in the stars?

Procedure

1. On a clear night go outside after dark and study the stars. Take an adult with you and see if you can help each other find constellations.
2. Let your imagination go to work and try to see any patterns of stars in the sky that look like something with which you are familiar.
3. Draw the stars you see, where they are in the sky, and include a drawing of what you think the star pattern resembles.

Analysis

1. How do your constellations compare with those observed by your classmates?
2. How do you think recognizing star patterns could be useful?

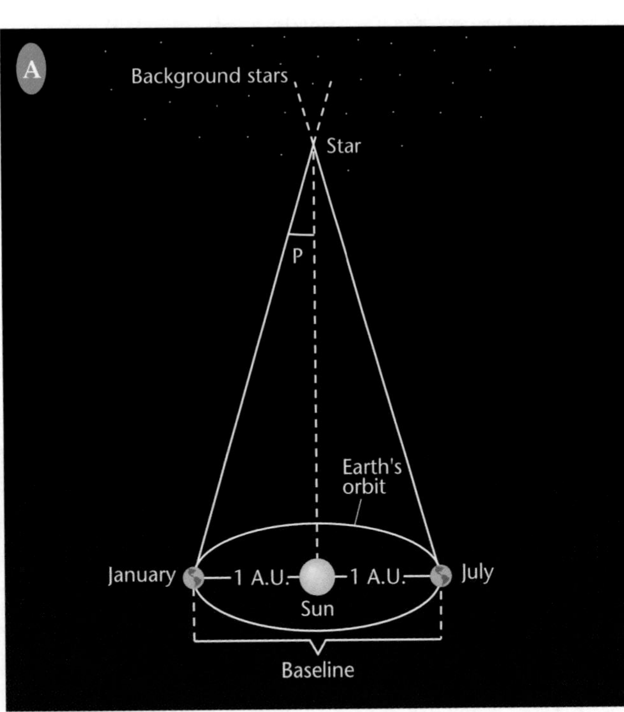

Figure 24-4

Parallax can be seen if you observe the same star while Earth is at two different points during its orbit around the sun (A). The star's position relative to the more-distant background stars will appear to change (B and C).

B

As seen in January

C

As seen in July

Problem Solving

Solve the Problem

1. apparent brightness
2. As distance was doubled, the light intensity was cut to 1/4 of what it had been. As distance was tripled, the light intensity was cut to 1/9 of what it had been.

Think Critically

The relationship between light intensity and distance can be expressed as 1 divided by the square of how many times distance is increased. At 100 cm, the light intensity will be decreased to 1/25 of the original.

3 Assess

Check for Understanding

FLEX Your Brain

Use the Flex Your Brain activity to have students explore PARALLAX.

Activity Worksheets, p. 5

Reteach

Use an open field to demonstrate parallax. Have one student stand approximately 50 m away from another student holding a compass with a sighting mirror. Have the student determine the exact compass heading to the other student. Now have the student holding the compass move sideways 20 m, and determine the new compass heading to the other student. Repeat this activity, varying the distances between students. LEP

Extension

For students who have mastered this section, use the **Reinforcement** and **Enrichment** masters.

Across the Curriculum

Mathematics Use the following equation to calculate the distance in light-years to two stars. Star 1 has a parallax angle (p) of 0.76", and Star 2 has a parallax angle (p) of 0.04".

d (light-years) = $3.26/p$

Star 1 $d = 4.29$ light-years

Star 2 $d = 81.50$ light-years

Another unit, the parsec (pc), is also used for expressing distances in space. 1 pc = 3.26 light-years (ly). Using this relationship, the above equation becomes the following: $d(\text{parsecs}) = 1/p$

Ask students to determine the distance in parsecs to the above two stars. L2 IS

PREPARATION

Purpose

LS **Interpersonal** Design a model and carry out an experiment to show how the distance from an observer to an object affects the object's parallax shift. L1 COOP LEARN P

Process Skills

communicating, comparing and contrasting, forming operational definitions, recognizing cause and effect, designing an experiment, separating and controlling variables, measuring in SI, using numbers, formulating models, observing and inferring, and hypothesizing

Time

one class period

Materials

meterstick, metric ruler, masking tape, object to observe (pencil)

Possible Model and Hypothesis

A possible model would involve holding the meterstick straight out from the nose and taping or holding the metric ruler against the outer edge of the meterstick. A possible hypothesis would be that greater amounts of parallax are observed for objects that are farther away. The amount of observed parallax increases as an object is moved farther away.

Activity Worksheets, pp. 5, 144-145

Activity 24-1

Design Your Own Experiment

Measuring Parallax

You have learned that parallax is the apparent shift in the position of an object when viewed from two locations. You have also learned that the nearer an object is to the observer, the greater its parallax. Do this activity to design a model and use it in an experiment that will show how distance affects the amount of observed parallax.

PREPARATION

Problem

Can a model be built that will show how distance affects the amount of observed parallax?

Form a Hypothesis

State a hypothesis about how a model must be built in order for it to be used in an experiment to show how distance affects the amount of observed parallax.

Objectives

- Design a model to show how the distance from an observer to an object affects the object's parallax shift.
- Using your model, carry out an experiment that shows how distance affects the amount of observed parallax.

Possible Materials

- meterstick
- metric ruler
- masking tape
- object to observe (pencil)

Safety Precautions

Wear safety goggles throughout this experiment.

PLAN THE EXPERIMENT

Possible Procedures

1. Choose three different positions on the meterstick and mark them with masking tape.
2. Attach a metric ruler to one end of the meterstick.
3. Hold the meterstick assembly straight out from your nose.
4. As your partner places a pencil at the three marked positions on the meterstick, look at it first with one eye and then the other. Observe the pencil's apparent movement against the metric ruler.

Teaching Strategies

- Pair students and assign one member of each group as a recorder. The other partner should carry out the experiment. Students should then switch roles.

Integrating the Sciences

Chemistry After students have finished reading page 678, ask them the following question: **How are astronomers able to determine a star's temperature and what elements it contains without traveling to the star?** *The color of the light from a star is an indication of the star's temperature. By studying the pattern of absorption lines in the spectrum of a star, its composition can be determined.*

PLAN THE EXPERIMENT

1. As a group, agree upon and write out your hypothesis statement.
2. As a group, list the steps that you need to take to build your model. Be very specific, describing exactly what you will do at each step.
3. Devise a method to test how distance from an observer to an object, such as a pencil, affects the relative position of the object.
4. As a group, list the steps of your experiment that will test your hypothesis. Be very specific, describing exactly what you will do at each step.
5. Make a list of the materials that you will need to complete your experiment.

Check the Plan

1. Read over your plan for the model to be used in this experiment.
2. Read over your entire experiment to make sure that all steps are in a logical order.
3. Will you summarize data in a graph, table, or some other form of organization?
4. How will you determine whether observed parallax is changed because of the distance from the observer to the object?
5. How will the position from which observations are made differ?
6. How will you measure distances accurately and compare relative position shift?
7. *Make sure your teacher approves your plan before you proceed.*

DO THE EXPERIMENT

1. Construct the model your team has planned.
2. Carry out the experiment as planned.
3. While conducting the experiment, write down any observations that you or other members of your group make in your Science Journal.

Analyze and Apply

1. **Compare** what happened to the object when it was viewed from two locations.
2. At what distance from the observer did the object appear to shift the greatest distance?
3. **Infer** what happened to the apparent shift of the object's location as the distance from the observer was increased or decreased.

Go Further

Based on your hypothesis and on the tests you have performed, how does distance from an observer to an object affect the parallax observed for that object? How might astronomers use parallax?

Tying to Previous Knowledge Ask students if they have ever noticed that the perceived speed a car is traveling appears different for a passenger than for the driver.

Troubleshooting If the meterstick and metric ruler are used, the recorder may need to hold the end of the meterstick against the ruler for stability during the measurement readings.

DO THE EXPERIMENT

Expected Outcome

Models and answers for apparent motion of the object will vary. However, if a pencil is used and the meterstick is held straight out touching the nose, and distances of 20 cm, 40 cm, and 60 cm are taped on the meterstick, the following results can be expected. Observed parallax is about 20 cm at the 20-cm mark, 8.5 cm at the 40-cm mark, and 4.9 cm at the 60-cm mark.

Analyze and Apply

1. The position of the object seemed to shift. In actuality, nothing happened to the object; the movement was only apparent.
2. Answers will vary, but should list the closest distance used by the paired partner team.
3. As distance from the observer increased, the object's apparent shift decreased. As the distance from the observer decreased, the object's apparent shift increased.

Go Further

- Answers will vary. Some will have hypothesized that the apparent shift will decrease as distance between the object (pencil) and observer (eye) increases.

These students should indicate that experimental data supported their hypothesis.

- As the distance of an object from an observer increases, the parallax of the object decreases at a constant and predictable rate.
- Astronomers use parallax angles (or shifts in the apparent position of astronomical objects) to determine distances to the objects.

Assessment

Process Have students use their thumbs at various distances from their faces to formulate a simple model that demonstrates larger apparent shifts of parallax for objects that are closer. Use the Performance Task Assessment List for Model in **PASC**, p. 51. P

4 Close

• MINI • QUIZ •

Use the Mini Quiz to check students' recall of chapter content.

1. **The amount of light received on Earth from a star, called _______, is affected by distance.** *apparent magnitude*
2. **_______ is the apparent shift in the position of an object caused by viewing it from two locations.** *Parallax*
3. **A(n) _______ is the distance light travels in one year.** *light-year*
4. **The color of a star indicates its _______.** *temperature*

Section Wrap-up

Review

1. As Earth revolves around the sun, the nighttime side of Earth faces different directions in space. As a result, different constellations become visible on the nighttime side. The daytime side is too bright to see constellations.
2. Because both stars give off the same amount of light, they have the same absolute magnitude. If one star looks brighter than the other, it's probably closer to Earth. However, interstellar gas could obscure a star, making it appear dimmer.
3. Its composition is similar to the sun's.
4. **Think Critically** Because the nearest stars are mostly invisible when viewed from Earth, their absolute magnitudes aren't very bright.

Using Computers

Charts will vary, depending on the season.

Figure 24-5

A triangle-shaped glass called a prism can be used to separate different wavelengths of light into a spectrum.

Determining a Star's Temperature and Composition

The color of a star indicates its temperature. For example, very hot stars are a blue-white color. A relatively cool star looks orange or red. Stars the temperature of our sun have a yellow color.

Astronomers learn about other properties of stars by studying their spectra. They use spectrographs to break visible light from a star into its component colors. If you look closely at the spectrum of a star, such as the ones shown in **Figure 24-23,** you will see dark lines in it. The lines are caused by elements in the star's atmosphere.

As light radiated from a star passes through the star's atmosphere, some of it is absorbed by elements in the atmosphere. The wavelengths of visible light that are absorbed appear as dark lines in the spectrum. Each element absorbs certain wavelengths, producing a certain pattern of dark lines. The patterns of lines can be used to identify which elements are in a star's atmosphere.

Section Wrap-up

Review

1. Explain how Earth's revolution affects constellations that are visible throughout the year.
2. If two stars give off the same amount of light, what might cause one to look brighter than the other?
3. If the spectrum of another star shows the same absorption lines as the sun, what can be said about its composition?
4. **Think Critically:** Only about 700 stars have large enough parallaxes that their distances can be determined using parallax. Most of them are invisible to the naked eye. What does this indicate about their absolute magnitudes?

Using Computers

Graphics Use drawing software on a computer to make a star chart of major constellations visible from your home during the current season. Include reference points to help someone using the chart to find the constellations.

Skill Builder

Recognizing Cause and Effect

Suppose you viewed Proxima Centauri through a telescope. How old were you when the light that you see left Proxima Centauri? Why might Proxima Centauri look dimmer than the star Betelgeuse, a very large star 489 light-years away? If you need help, refer to Recognizing Cause and Effect in the **Skill Handbook.**

Skill Builder

Proxima Centauri is 4.2 light-years away. Ages will vary, but should equal the students' ages minus 4.2 years. Proxima Centauri is close, but it doesn't give off much light. Both the absolute and apparent magnitudes of Betelgeuse are brighter than Proxima Centauri's.

Assessment

Performance To further assess students' abilities in recognizing cause and effect, ask them to explain in writing why Deneb appears so bright and yet is more than 1400 light-years away. Use the Performance Task Assessment List for Writing in Science in **PASC,** p. 87. P

The Sun

The Layers of the Sun

More than 99 percent of all of the matter in our solar system is in the sun. It is the center of our solar system, and it makes life possible on Earth. To you and everyone else on Earth, the sun is a special object in the sky and one of the most important objects in your life. Nevertheless, our sun is just like many other stars in our galaxy.

The sun is an average middle-aged star. Its absolute magnitude is about average and it shines with a yellow light. The sun is an enormous ball of gas, producing energy by fusing hydrogen into helium in its core. **Figure 24-6** is a model of the sun's interior.

Science Words

photosphere
chromosphere
corona
sunspot
binary system

Objectives

- Describe how energy is produced in the sun.
- Recognize that sunspots, prominences, and solar flares are related.
- Explain why our sun is considered an average star and how it differs from stars in binary systems.

The Sun's Atmosphere

The lowest layer of the sun's atmosphere and the layer from which light is given off is the **photosphere.** The photosphere is often called the surface of the sun. Temperatures there are around 6000°C. Above the photosphere is the **chromosphere.** This layer extends upward about 2000 km. A transition zone occurs between 2000 and 10 000 km above the photosphere. Above the transition zone is the **corona.** This is the largest layer of the sun's atmosphere and extends millions of kilometers into space. Temperatures in the corona are as high as 2 000 000°C. Charged particles continually escape from the corona and move through space as the solar wind.

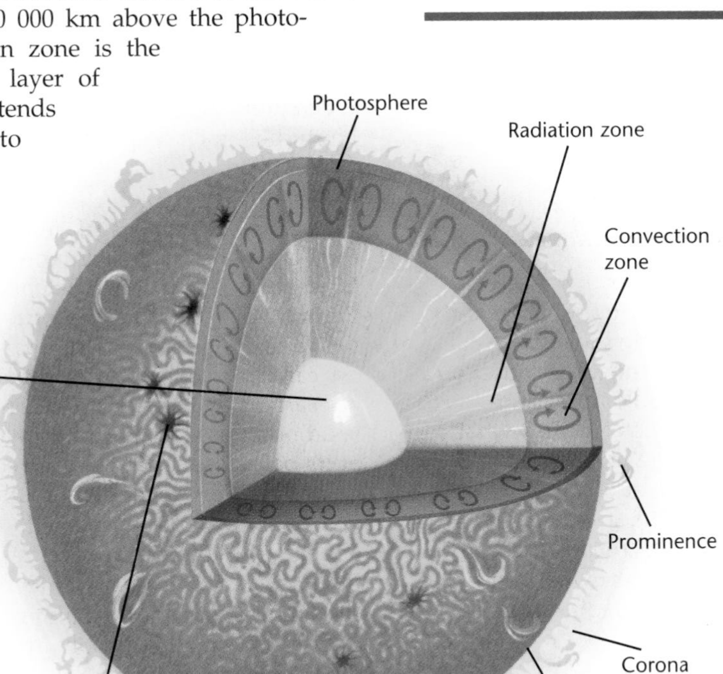

Figure 24-6

Energy produced by fusion in the sun's core travels outward by radiation and convection. The sun's atmosphere, composed of the photosphere, the chromosphere, and the corona, is illuminated by the energy produced in the core.

Program Resources

Reproducible Masters

Study Guide, p. 95 L1
Reinforcement, p. 95 L1
Enrichment, p. 95 L3
Activity Worksheets, pp. 5, 146-147, 149 L1
Science Integration Activities, pp. 47-48
Multicultural Connections, pp. 51-52

Transparencies

Section Focus Transparency 91 L1
Science Integration Transparency 24

Section 24•2

Prepare

Section Background

The *Ulysses* spacecraft, launched in October 1990, arrived at Jupiter in February 1992. It flew by Jupiter to obtain a gravity assist, which enabled it then to travel out of the plane of the solar system. Its new trajectory enabled *Ulysses* to study the sun from above both its south pole in 1994 and its north pole in 1995. Its mission included studies of the sun's solar wind and magnetic field, and X rays and radio waves given off by the sun.

Preplanning

- In preparation for the MiniLAB, locate an area of pavement that can be used and marked with chalk.
- In preparation for Activity 24-2, obtain a small refracting telescope and monitor the weather. Be prepared to start the activity during a week of predicted mostly clear weather.

1 Motivate

Bellringer

Before presenting the lesson, display **Section Focus Transparency 91** on the overhead projector. Assign the accompanying **Focus Activity** worksheet. L1 LEP

Tying to Previous Knowledge

Remind students that interactions of air, water, and the sun cause Earth's weather. Have students explain what role the sun plays in the formation of clouds.

2 Teach

MiniLAB

Purpose

LS **Logical-Mathematical** Students will compare the sizes of stars. L1 COOP LEARN

Materials

string (125 cm in length), chalk, meterstick

Teaching Strategies

Troubleshooting Help students compare the sun's diameter to that of Earth. The sun's diameter is about 110 times greater than Earth's.

- Using the diameter of the sun as 1 390 000 km, have students calculate diameters of the supergiant and white dwarf in their models.

Analysis

1. A supergiant is over seven times the diameter of our solar system.
2. & 3. The two circles representing our sun and a white dwarf can be any diameter, as long as the large circle is approximately 100 times larger than the smaller circle.

Assessment

Performance Have students include a circle in their model to represent the diameter of Earth (about 0.01 of the sun's). Use the Performance Task Assessment List for Scientific Drawing in **PASC**, p. 55. P

Activity Worksheets, pp. 5, 149

CONNECT TO

LIFE SCIENCE

Answers ultraviolet radiation; sunburn, dry skin, and possibly skin cancer

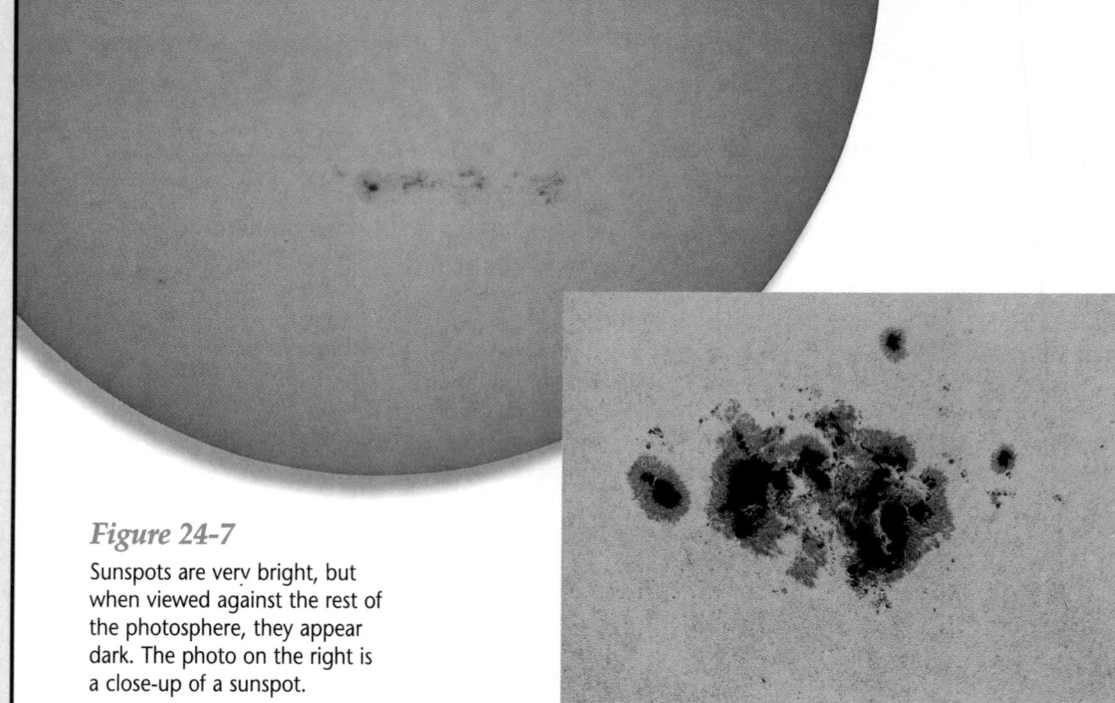

Figure 24-7

Sunspots are very bright, but when viewed against the rest of the photosphere, they appear dark. The photo on the right is a close-up of a sunspot.

CONNECT TO

LIFE SCIENCE

When you are going to be out in the sunlight for extended periods, you should apply sunscreen. ***Identify*** what type of solar radiation this protects you from. If little or no sunscreen is used, ***describe*** what problems might occur.

Surface Features of the Sun

Because the sun is a hot ball of gas, it's hard to imagine its surface as anything but a smooth layer of gas. But there is much more that we can see. There are many features that can be studied, including sunspots, prominences, and flares.

Sunspots

Areas of the sun's surface that appear to be dark because they are cooler than surrounding areas are called **sunspots.** Ever since Galileo first identified sunspots like those in **Figure 24-7**, scientists have been studying them. One thing we've learned by studying sunspots is that the sun rotates. We can observe the movement of individual sunspots as they are carried by the sun's rotation. The sun doesn't rotate as a solid body, as does Earth. It rotates faster at its equator than at its poles. Sunspots near the equator take about 27 days to go around the sun; at higher latitudes, they take 31 days.

Sunspots aren't permanent features on the sun. They appear and disappear over a period of several days or months. Also, there are times when there are many large sunspots—a sunspot maximum—and times when there are only a few small sunspots or none at all—a sunspot minimum. Sunspot maxima occur about every 11 years. The last maximum was in 1989.

Across the Curriculum

Meteorology Have students research the relationship between sunspot activity and Earth's weather and climate. Have interested students research the Maunder Minimum, a period from 1645 through 1715 when few sunspots were observed. During this time, Europe experienced record low temperatures, and severe droughts occurred in the western United States. L3

Prominences and Flares

Sunspots are related to several features on the sun's surface. The intense magnetic field associated with sunspots may cause prominences, huge arching columns of gas. Some prominences are so eruptive that material from the sun is blasted into space at speeds ranging from 600 to over 1000 km/s.

Gases near a sunspot sometimes brighten up suddenly, shooting gas outward at high speed. These violent eruptions from the sun, shown in **Figure 24-8**, are called solar flares.

Ultraviolet light and X rays from solar flares can reach Earth and cause disruption of radio signals. This makes communication by radio and telephone very difficult at times. High energy particles emitted by solar flares are captured by Earth's magnetic field. These particles interact with Earth's atmosphere near the polar regions and create light. This light is called the aurora borealis, or northern lights, when it occurs in the northern hemisphere. In the southern hemisphere this light is called the aurora australis.

Our Sun: A Typical Star?

Although our sun is an average star, it is somewhat unusual in one way. Most stars are in systems in which two or more stars orbit each other. When two stars orbit each other, it is called a **binary system.**

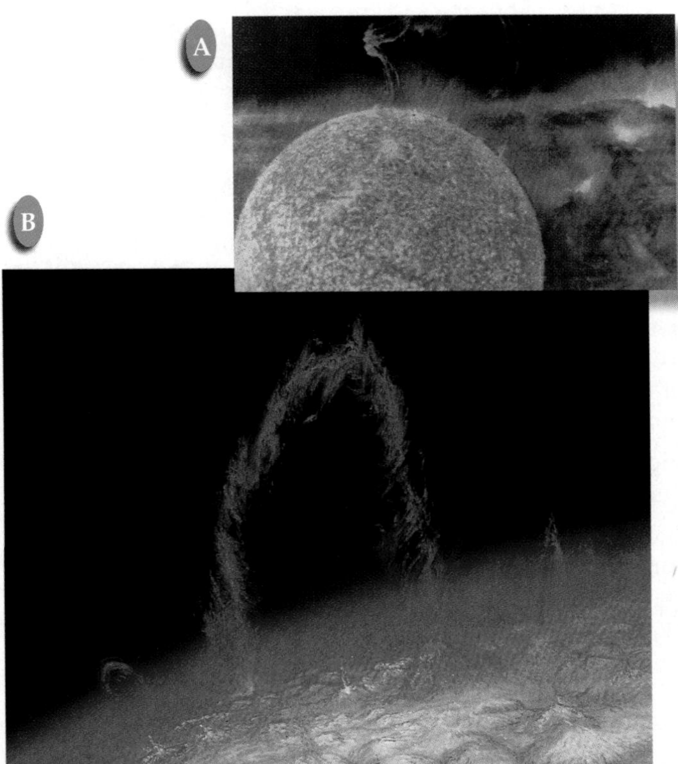

Figure 24-8
Features such as solar flares (A) and solar prominences (B) can reach tens of thousands of kilometers into space. *How big is this compared with the size of Earth?*

MiniLAB

How do the sizes of stars compare?

Procedure

1. Find an area where you can make a chalk mark on pavement or another surface.
2. Tie a piece of chalk to one end of a string that's 125 cm long.
3. Hold the other end of the string to the pavement.
4. Have a friend pull the string tight and walk around you, leaving a mark on the pavement as he or she circles you.
5. Draw a circle with a 1-cm diameter in the middle of the large circle.

Analysis

1. The small circle represents a star the size of our sun, and the larger circle represents a supergiant, the largest kind of star. How big is the supergiant compared to our solar system?
2. Formulate a model of our sun and of a white dwarf star by drawing two new circles. Our sun is about 100 times larger than a white dwarf.
3. What are the diameters of your two new circles?

NATIONAL GEOGRAPHIC SOCIETY

Videodisc

STV: Solar System
The Big Picture
Unit 1, Side 1
Studying the Sun

06338-08660

Visual Learning

Figure 24-8 How big is this compared with the size of Earth? *The flares can extend more than Earth's diameter.* LEP IS

Use **Science Integration Transparency 24** as you teach this lesson.

Use **Science Integration Activities,** pp. 47-48 and **Multicultural Connections,** pp. 51-52, as you teach this lesson.

3 Assess

Check for Understanding

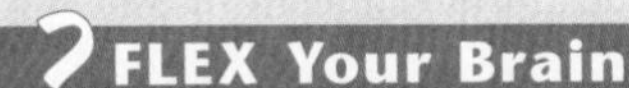

FLEX Your Brain

Use the Flex Your Brain activity to have students explore SUNSPOTS AND OTHER SOLAR ACTIVITY.

Activity Worksheets, p. 5

Reteach

IS **Visual-Spatial** Encourage students to make a graphic that explains how the light and heat from the sun are produced.

Extension

For students who have mastered this section, use the **Reinforcement** and **Enrichment** masters.

Across the Curriculum

Math Form groups of three. Using the data below, have the groups plot a graph of sunspot activity. Call on the reporter in each group to describe any trend his or her group notices. L1 IS

Year	Sunspots	Year	Sunspots	Year	Sunspots	Year	Sunspots
1969	105	1973	38	1977	28	1987	29
1970	104	1974	35	1978	93	1988	100
1971	67	1975	16	1979	155	1989	159
1972	69	1976	13	1980	155	1990	147
				1981	140	1991	145
				1982	116	1992	94
				1983	67	1993	54
				1984	46	1994	31
				1985	18	1995	18
				1986	14		

4 Close

•MINI•QUIZ•

1. **Light is given off from the sun's ______ , the lowest layer of the sun's atmosphere.** *photosphere*
2. **Temperatures in the outer layer of the sun's atmosphere, or ______ , can reach 2 000 000°C.** *corona*
3. **______ are cooler, dark areas on the sun's surface.** *Sunspots*

Section Wrap-up

Review

1. Magnetic fields near a sunspot can cause huge arching columns of gas called prominences. Gases near sunspots can also become concentrated and shoot outward from the sun as a solar flare.
2. The sun's size, temperature, and absolute magnitude are similar to other stars' on the main sequence. The sun is unlike many other stars because it's not part of a binary system, another multiple star system, or a star cluster.
3. **Think Critically** Members of a cluster or multiple star system that included our sun may spread out through the galaxy. The cloud from which our star formed may not have contained enough matter for more than one star.

Science Journal

Fusion reactions in the sun's core change hydrogen into helium, with some matter being converted into energy. When the sun exhausts its hydrogen supply, it will begin to fuse helium in its core and change into a giant.

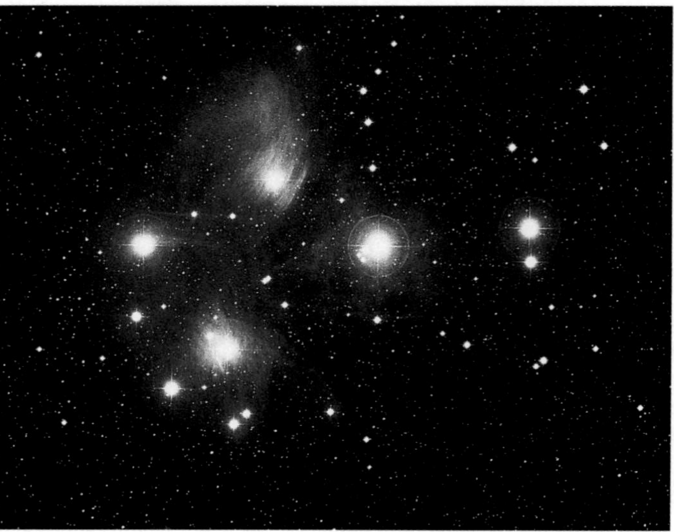

Figure 24-9
Pleiades is a cluster of stars gravitationally bound to each other.

In some cases, astronomers can detect binary systems because one star occasionally eclipses the other. The total amount of light from the star system becomes dim and then bright again, on a regular cycle. Algol in Pleiades is an example of this.

In many cases, stars move through space together as a cluster. In a star cluster, many stars are relatively close to one another and are gravitationally attracted to each other. The Pleiades star cluster can be seen in the constellation of Taurus in the winter sky. On a clear, dark night, you may be able to make out seven of the stars of this cluster. Most star clusters are far from our solar system, and appear as a fuzzy patch in the night sky.

Section Wrap-up

Review

1. How are sunspots, prominences, and solar flares related?
2. What properties does the sun have in common with other stars? What property makes it different from most other stars?
3. **Think Critically:** Since most stars are in multiple-star systems, what might explain why the sun is a single star?

Skill Builder

Interpreting Scientific Illustrations

Use **Figure 24-6** to answer the questions below. If you need help, refer to Interpreting Scientific Illustrations in the **Skill Handbook.**

1. Compare **Figure 24-6** with **Figure 22-9** on page 626, which shows a total solar eclipse. What part of the sun is visible in **Figure 22-9?**
2. Which layers make up the sun's atmosphere?
3. What process occurs in the sun's convection zone that enables energy produced in the core to reach the surface?

Science Journal

Write a brief description in your Science Journal that explains how the sun generates energy. Hypothesize what might happen to the sun when it exhausts the supply of hydrogen in its core.

Skill Builder

1. the corona
2. photosphere, chromosphere, and corona
3. Gases heated at the bottom of the convection zone are forced upward by denser surrounding gases. They release energy, cool, and sink, setting up convection currents.

Assessment

Oral To further assess students' abilities to interpret scientific illustrations, have them hypothesize what is causing the glow around the stars in **Figure 24-9**. Use the Performance Task Assessment List for Making Observations and Inferences in **PASC,** p. 17. P

Activity 24-2

Sunspots

Sunspots are dark, relatively cool areas on the surface of the sun. They can be observed moving across the face of the sun as it rotates. Do this activity to measure the movement of sunspots and use your data to determine the sun's period of rotation.

Problem

Can sunspot motion be used to determine the sun's period of rotation?

Materials

- several books
- clipboard
- small refracting telescope
- cardboard
- drawing paper
- small tripod
- scissors

Procedure

1. Find a location where the sun may be viewed at the same time of day for a minimum of five days. **CAUTION:** *Do not look directly at the sun. Do not look through the telescope at the sun. You could damage your eyes.*
2. Set up the telescope with the eyepiece facing away from the sun, as shown below. Align so that the shadow cast by the telescope on the ground is a minimum size. Set up the clipboard with the drawing paper attached.
3. Use the books to prop the clipboard upright. Point the eyepiece at the drawing paper.
4. If the telescope has a small finder scope attached, remove the finder scope or keep it covered.
5. Move the clipboard back and forth until you have the largest possible image of the sun on the paper. Adjust the telescope to form a clear image.
6. Trace the outline of the sun on the paper.
7. Trace any sunspots that appear as dark areas on the sun's image. Repeat this at the same time each day for a week.
8. Using the sun's diameter as approximately 1 390 000 km, estimate the size of the largest sunspots that are observed.
9. Calculate how many kilometers any observed sunspots appear to move each day.
10. At the rate determined in step 9, predict how many days it will take for the same group of sunspots to return to about the same position in which you first observed them.

Analyze

1. Which part of the sun showed up in your image?
2. What was the average number of sunspots observed each day?

Conclude and Apply

3. **Infer** how sunspots can be used to determine that the sun's surface is not solid like Earth's.

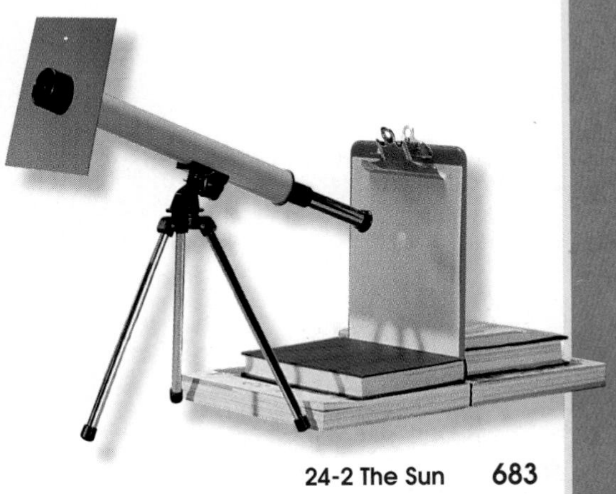

Activity 24-2

Purpose

Visual-Spatial Observe sunspots and estimate their size and rate of motion across the sun's photosphere. L1

Process Skills

observing and inferring, interpreting data, using numbers

Time

10 minutes each day for five days (If weather does not provide five days with a clear sky, fewer days may be used as long as the elapsed time between observations covers a span of several days.)

Safety Precautions

Caution students not to look directly at the sun. Do not allow them to look through the telescope at the sun.

Activity Worksheets, pp. 5, 146-147

Teaching Strategies

Alternate Materials If a telescope isn't available, use binoculars set on a stack of books on the window ledge with one of the eyepieces covered.

Troubleshooting To ensure correct alignment in the event the apparatus must be taken down or moved for any reason, mark the exact position of the telescope, books, and clipboard.

- If no sunspots are visible, keep the setup in place until some are sighted.

Answers to Questions

1. the photosphere
2. Student answers will vary, depending on solar activity. However, all answers should be approximately the same.
3. Sunspots move at different rates near the equator than those near the poles.

Assessment

Content To further assess students' understanding of sunspot movement on the sun, ask them to hypothesize how sunspots on the opposite hemisphere (north or south) would move compared to the sunspots you plotted in this activity. Have them plot sunspots to check their hypotheses. Use the Performance Task Assessment List for Formulating a Hypothesis in **PASC**, p. 21. P

Section 24•3

Prepare

Section Background

- Not all stars shine with a steady light. Stars that change in brightness are called variable stars. Stars may vary because the outer layers of the star expand and contract, causing a change in the temperature and the absolute magnitude of the star. Betelgeuse in Orion can change its surface area by more than 40%, causing it to vary in brightness.
- One class of variable star, called a Cepheid variable, is important to the study of the universe. These stars vary regularly, and their period of variation is an indication of their absolute magnitudes. Because of this, they can be used to determine distances to faraway clusters and galaxies. Polaris is a Cepheid variable.

Preplanning

In preparation for this section, obtain photographs or illustrations of various types of stars and nebulas.

1 Motivate

Bellringer

Before presenting the lesson, display **Section Focus Transparency 92** on the overhead projector. Assign the accompanying **Focus Activity** worksheet. L1 LEP

Tying to Previous Knowledge

Help students recall the states of matter from Chapter 2. Remind them that stars are composed of matter in the plasma state. Have them describe what happens to matter in the plasma state.

24•3 Evolution of Stars

Science Words

main sequence
nebula
giant
white dwarf
supergiant
neutron star
black hole

Objectives

- Diagram how stars are classified.
- Relate the temperature of a star to its color.
- Outline the evolution of a star through all stages of its development.

The H-R Diagram

In the early 1900s, Ejnar Hertzsprung and Henry Russell noticed that for most stars, the higher their temperatures, the brighter their absolute magnitudes. They developed a graph to show this relationship.

Hertzsprung and Russell placed the temperatures of the stars across the bottom of the graphs and the absolute magnitudes of the stars up one side. A graph that shows the relationship of a star's temperature to its absolute magnitude is called a Hertzsprung-Russell (H-R) diagram. **Figure 24-10** shows a typical H-R diagram.

The Main Sequence

As you can see, stars seem to fit into specific areas of the chart. Most stars fit into a diagonal band that runs from the upper left to the lower right of the chart. This band, called the **main sequence,** contains hot, blue, bright stars in the upper left and cool, red, dim stars in the lower right. Yellow, medium-temperature, medium-brightness stars fall in between. The sun is a yellow main sequence star.

About 90 percent of all stars are main sequence stars, most of which are small, red stars found in the lower right of the

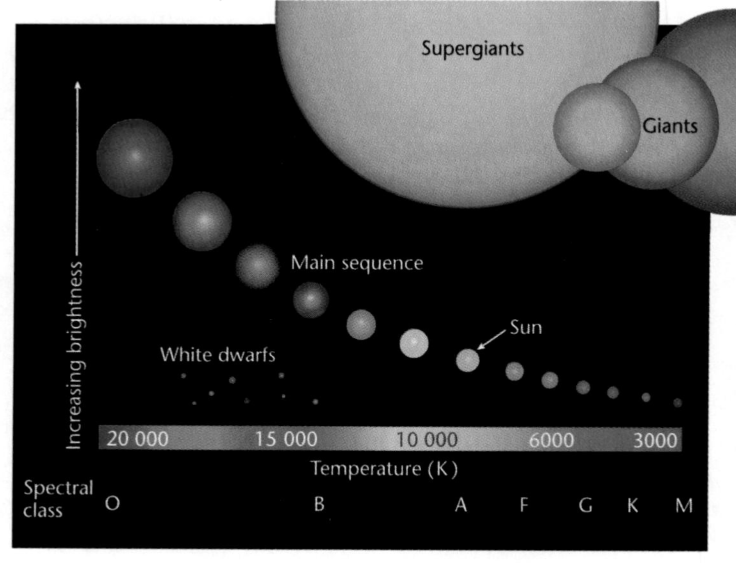

Figure 24-10
The Hertzsprung-Russell diagram shows the relationships among a star's color, temperature, and brightness. Stars in the main sequence run from hot, bright stars in the upper left corner of the diagram to cool, faint stars in the lower right corner. *What type of star shown in the diagram is the coolest, brightest star?*

Program Resources

Reproducible Masters
Study Guide, p. 96 L1
Reinforcement, p. 96 L1
Enrichment, p. 96 L3
Concept Mapping, p. 53

Transparencies
Section Focus Transparency 92 L1
Teaching Transparencies 47 and **48**

H-R diagram. Among main sequence stars, the hottest stars generate the most light and the coolest generate the least. But what about the remaining ten percent? Some of these stars are hot but not very bright. These small stars are located on the lower left of the H-R diagram and are called white dwarfs. Other stars are extremely bright but not very hot. These large stars on the upper right of the H-R diagram are called giants, or red giants because they are usually red in color. The largest giants are called supergiants.

Fusion

When the H-R diagram was developed, scientists didn't know what caused stars to shine. Hertzsprung and Russell developed their diagram without knowing what produced the light and heat of stars.

For centuries, people had been puzzled by the question of what stars were and what made them shine. It wasn't until the early part of this century that scientists were forced to explain how a star could shine for billions of years. Until that time, many had estimated that Earth was only a few thousand years old. The sun could have been made of coal and shined for that long. But what material could possibly burn for billions of years?

In 1920, A. S. Eddington suggested that temperatures in the center of the sun would be very high. Robert Atkinson then suggested that with these very high temperatures, hydrogen could fuse into helium in a reaction that would release tremendous amounts of energy. **Figure 24-12** on page 686 illustrates how four hydrogen nuclei could combine to create one helium nucleus. The mass of one helium nucleus is less than the mass of four hydrogen nuclei, so some mass is lost in the reaction. In the 1930s, Hans Bethe suggested how carbon could be used as a catalyst in fusion reactions that explain the energy production in hotter stars.

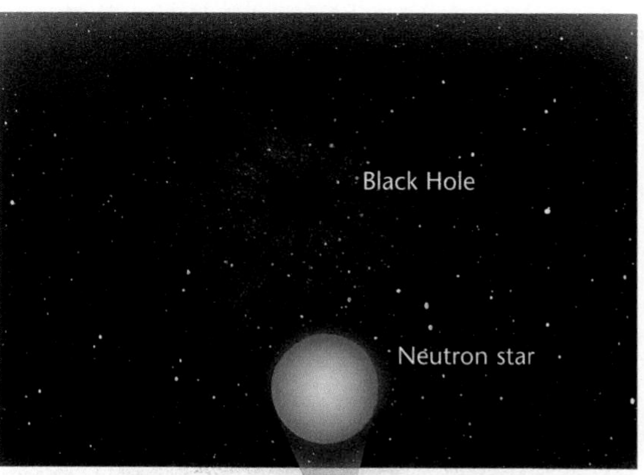

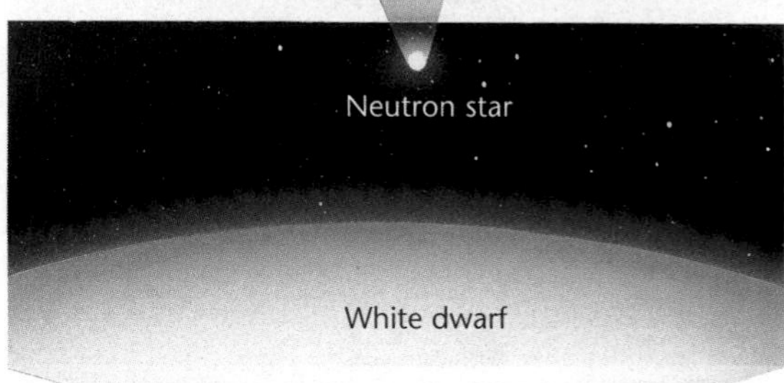

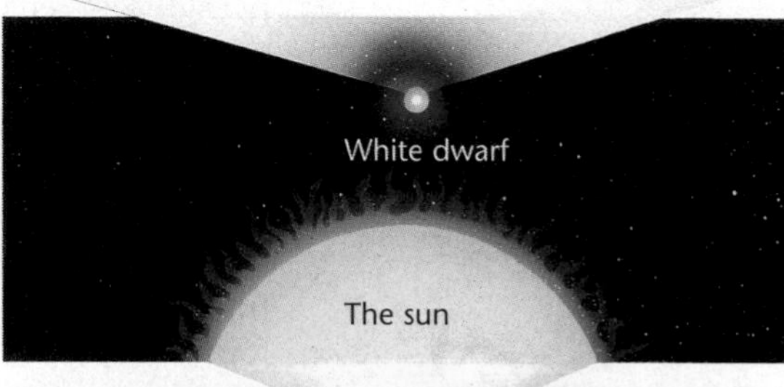

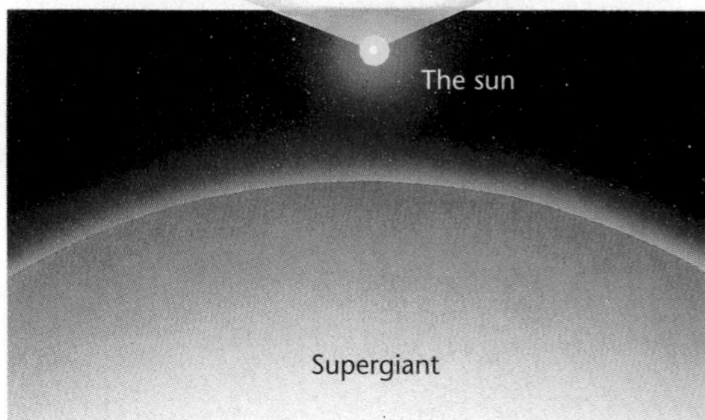

Figure 24-11

The relative sizes of stars range from supergiants as much as 800 times larger than the sun, to neutron stars and black holes possibly 30 km or less across. The relative sizes of a supergiant, the sun, a white dwarf, a neutron star, and a black hole are shown.

2 Teach

Visual Learning

Figure 24-10 **What type of star shown in the diagram is the coolest, brightest star?** *giants* LEP IS

Bulletin Board

IS **Interpersonal** Have pairs of students prepare and display a bulletin board version of a Hertzsprung-Russell diagram. Use **Figure 24-10** as a guide. L1 COOP LEARN

Inquiry Questions

- **What properties of stars are plotted on the H-R diagram?** *Absolute magnitude is plotted against temperature.*
- **What process generates energy in the core of a star? Explain.** *Fusion generates energy in the core of a star. Four hydrogen atoms fuse to become one helium atom. Mass that is lost in the reaction is changed to energy.*
- **What process occurs to mark the birth of a star?** *Once the gas and dust in a nebula have contracted so much that temperatures inside the cloud center reach 10 000 000°C, fusion begins and energy is radiated outward. Once the energy makes its way to the surface of the dense cloud and radiates into space, a star is formed.*

Use **Teaching Transparencies 47** and **48** as you teach this lesson.

Integrating the Sciences

Physics Refer students to "The Eagle's Nest" by Samantha Parker in *Sky & Telescope,* February 1996, pp. 32-34. Show illustrations of the Eagle Nebula (M16) and ask students what the *Hubble Space Telescope* found out that is so important about this nebula. *Scientists believe that the evaporating gaseous globules (EGGs) shown in this nebula are forming into stars.*

Demonstration

Visual-Spatial Using tongs, hold the end of a wire over the flame of a Bunsen burner until it begins to glow. Ask students to record the color of the glowing wire. Continue to hold the wire over the flame to allow it to become hotter. Ask students to record any changes they see in the wire while it's being heated. Ask one student to summarize what happened to the wire. *As the wire was heated, it started to glow and gradually changed from a reddish-orange color to a yellow-white as it became hotter.* Relate this to the different colors of stars on the main sequence. **CAUTION:** *Wear goggles and handle the hot wire carefully.* LEP

Use **Concept Mapping,** p. 53, as you teach this lesson.

Visual Learning

Figure 24-13 What happens to stars the size of our sun? *They become brown dwarfs.* LEP LS

Years earlier, in 1905, Albert Einstein had proposed a theory stating that mass can be converted into energy. This was stated as the famous equation $E = mc^2$, where E is the energy produced, m is the mass, and c is the speed of light. The small amount of mass "lost" when hydrogen atoms fuse to form a helium atom is converted to a large amount of energy.

Fusion occurs in the cores of stars. Only there are temperatures and pressures high enough to cause atoms to fuse. Normally, they would repel each other, but in the core of a star, atoms are forced close enough together that their nuclei fuse together.

INTEGRATION Physics

The Evolution of Stars

The H-R diagram and Eddington's and Einstein's theories explained a lot about stars. But they also led to more questions. Many wondered why some stars didn't fit in the main sequence group and what happened when a star exhausted its supply of hydrogen fuel. Today, we have a theory of how stars evolve, what makes them different from one another, and what happens when they die. **Figure 24-13** illustrates the lives of different types of stars.

Nebula

Stars begin as a large cloud of gas and dust called a **nebula.** The particles of gas and dust exert a gravitational force on each other, and the nebula begins to contract. Gravitational forces cause instability within the nebula. The nebula can fragment into smaller pieces. Each will eventually collapse to form a star.

Figure 24-12

In a star's core, fusion begins as two hydrogen nuclei (protons) are forced together.

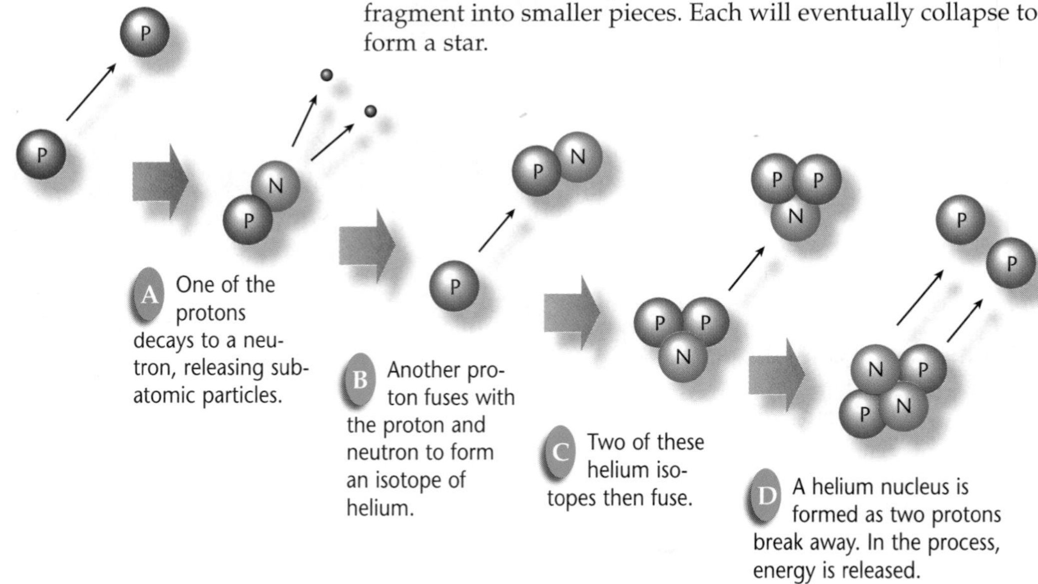

Theme Connection

Stability and Change The theme of stability and change is reaffirmed by the fact that the evolution of stars deals with stars' changing their properties. Also, the energy for powering stars involves the change of matter through the process of fusion.

As the particles in the smaller clouds move closer together, the temperatures in each nebula increase. When temperatures inside each nebula reach 10 000 000 K, fusion begins. The energy released radiates outward through the condensing ball of gas. As the energy radiates into space, stars are born.

Main Sequence to Giant Stars

The heat from the fusion causes pressure that balances the attraction due to gravity, and the star becomes a main sequence star. It continues to use up its hydrogen fuel.

When the hydrogen in the core of the star is exhausted, there is no longer a balance between pressure and gravity. The core contracts, and the temperatures inside the star increase. This causes the outer layers of the star to expand. The star has evolved into a **giant.**

Once the core temperature reaches 100 000 000 K, helium nuclei fuse to form carbon in the giant's core. By this time, the star has expanded to an enormous size, and its outer layers are much cooler than they were when it was a main sequence star. In about 5 billion years, our sun will become a giant.

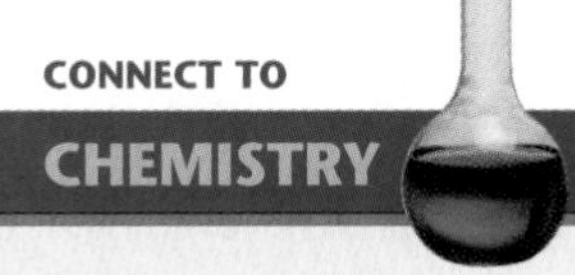

CONNECT TO CHEMISTRY

If the spectrum of a star shows absorption lines of helium and hydrogen and is very bright in the blue end, ***describe*** as much as you can about the star's composition and surface temperature.

Figure 24-13

The life of a star depends greatly on its mass. Massive stars eventually become neutron stars, or possibly black holes. *What happens to stars the size of our sun?*

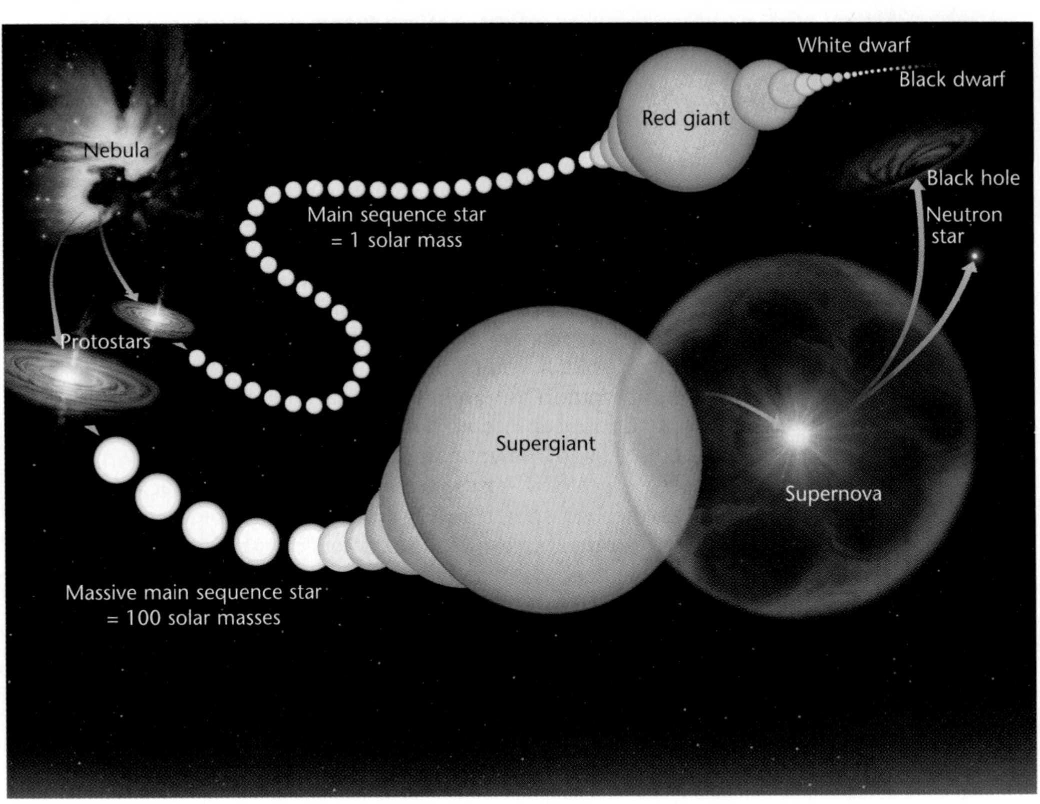

INTEGRATION Physics

Stars evolve and change into other types of stars because of what is happening inside the star. As a star uses up one element as fuel, conditions change inside the star; if the star can attain high enough temperatures, new heavier elements can be used as fuel for the fusion process to continue at the star's core. **Ask students what property of the star determines what can be used as fuel for fusion at the star's core.** *stellar mass*

Enrichment

LS **Linguistic** Have students use astronomy books and magazine articles to research the Horsehead and Orion nebulas, located in the constellation Orion. Have them determine why the Horsehead nebula is a dark nebula and the Orion nebula is a bright nebula. Also have them explain the relationship of the brightness of the nebulas and star formation processes occurring within them. L3

Teacher F.Y.I.

In a star that has a mass similar to our sun's, outer layers become unstable and begin escaping into space when the core runs out of hydrogen fuel. The escaping gases form a shell around the star, producing a planetary nebula. The Ring nebula in the constellation Lyra is an example of this stage of stellar evolution.

Integrating the Sciences

Physics Assess students' understanding of how physics integrates with the study of star evolution by asking the following questions:

- **Why is the mass of the helium atom formed by fusion less than the combined masses of the four hydrogen atoms that fused to form it?** *Some of the mass of the hydrogen atoms is converted to energy.*
- **Why does a star become unbalanced when its hydrogen fuel is used up?** *The outward force caused by fusion is reduced and no longer balances the inward force of gravity.*
- **If the temperature inside a star's contracting core heats up, why does the outer layer of the star turn reddish in color?** *The increased heat inside the star causes the outer layers of the star to expand. As the outer layers expand outward, the gases contained in them cool down, thus becoming red in color.*

CONNECT TO CHEMISTRY

Answer The star's atmosphere contains helium and hydrogen, and the star's surface has a high temperature.

Inquiry Questions

Refer students to **Figure 24-10** and ask the following questions of the class as a group.

- **What is true about the absolute magnitude and temperature of supergiant stars?** *Supergiant stars have high absolute magnitudes but relatively low temperatures.*
- **Based on this fact and their name, what can be said about supergiant stars?** *Supergiant stars are large compared with other stars.*
- **Why do the stars located in the upper-left portion of the H-R diagram have such a high absolute magnitude?** *These stars are fairly large and have high temperatures.*

GLENCOE TECHNOLOGY

 Videodisc

STVS: Physics
Disc 1, Side 1
Fusion (Ch. 21)

STVS: Earth and Space
Disc 3, Side 1
Modeling Black Holes (Ch. 12)

 Videodisc

STV: Solar System
The Big Picture
Unit 1, Side 1
Tarantula nebula with supernova blast

41725

White Dwarfs

After the star's core uses up its supply of helium, it contracts even more. As the core of a star like the sun runs out of fuel, the outer layers escape into space. This leaves behind the hot, dense core. The core contracts under the force of gravity. At this stage in a star's evolution, it is a **white dwarf.** A white dwarf is about the size of Earth.

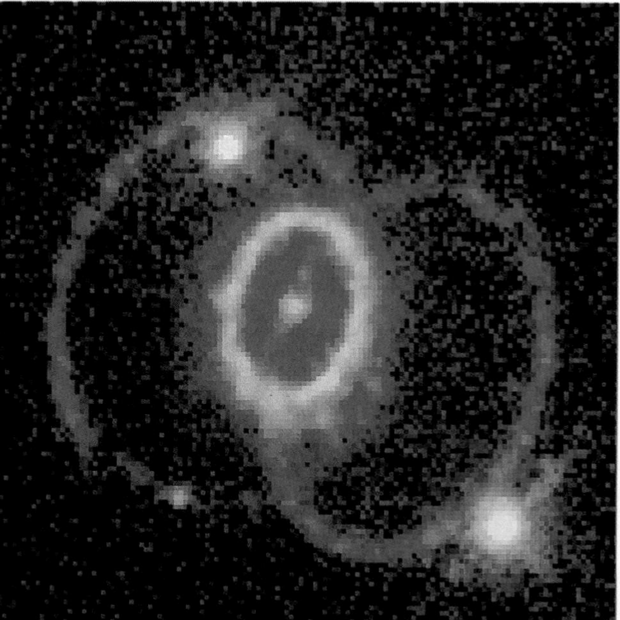

Figure 24-14
This image, taken by the *Hubble Space Telescope,* is of a supernova. The two white objects are other stars in the field of view. The two large rings are somewhat of a mystery. There may be an invisible, hourglass-shaped bubble of gas blown outward by the supernova. The rings may form when a high-energy beam of radiation sweeps across the gas, much like a searchlight sweeping across clouds.

Supergiants and Supernovas

In stars that are over ten times more massive than our sun, the stages of evolution occur more quickly and more violently. The core heats up to much higher temperatures. Heavier and heavier elements form by fusion. The star expands into a **supergiant,** like the one shown in **Figure 24-14.** Eventually, iron forms in the core. Fusion can no longer occur once iron forms. The core collapses violently, sending a shock wave outward through the star. The outer portion of the star explodes, producing a supernova. A supernova can be millions of times brighter than the original star.

Neutron Stars and Black Holes

The collapsed core of a supernova shrinks to about 10-15 km. Only neutrons can exist in the dense core, and the supernova becomes a **neutron star.**

If the remaining dense core is over three times more massive than the sun, probably nothing can stop the core's collapse. It quickly evolves into a **black hole**—an object so dense, nothing can escape its gravity field. In fact, not even light can escape a black hole. If you could shine a flashlight on a black hole, the light wouldn't illuminate the black hole. The light would simply disappear into it. Matter being pulled into a black hole can collide with other material, generating X rays. Astronomers have located X-ray sources around possible black holes, such as the one shown in **Figure 24-15.** Extremely massive black holes probably exist in the centers of galaxies.

What are nebulas?

A star begins its life as a nebula, but where does the matter in a nebula come from? Nebulas form partly from the matter that was once in other stars. A star ejects enormous amounts of matter during its lifetime. This matter can be incorporated into other nebulas, which can evolve into new stars. The matter in stars is recycled many times.

Science Journal

Star Evolution Have teams of students construct concept maps in their Science Journals showing the evolution of a star from beginning to end. Then ask the following questions.

- **After a supernova, what type of object forms if the remaining dense core, over three times more massive than the sun, collapses?** *black hole*
- **Why is this object called a black hole?** *Nothing, not even light, can escape its tremendous gravity.*
- **If black holes can't be seen, how have astronomers found what they think are black holes?** *As matter is drawn into a black hole, it is thought that large amounts of X rays are given off. Astronomers have found several strong X-ray sources that appear to have high mass but which can't be seen.* L1 LS P

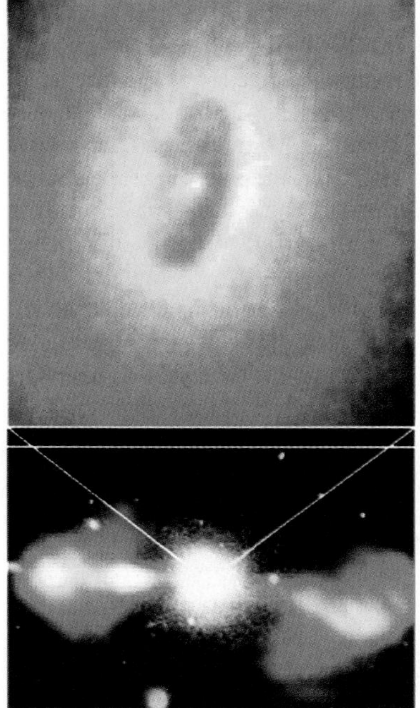

Figure 24-15
The bottom photo shows radio jets shooting from the core of the galaxy NGC 4261. These jets are thought to be associated with black holes. The dark ring in the top photo surrounds a possible black hole in the galaxy's nucleus.

USING TECHNOLOGY

Studying Supernovas

Near Cleveland, Ohio, and in Kamioka, Japan, large tanks of water and sensitive radiation-detecting instruments rest underground. The instruments are capable of detecting the radiation given off when subatomic particles called neutrinos strike protons or electrons in the water. In February 1987, the instruments recorded the presence of neutrinos. The records of the neutrinos striking the tanks went unnoticed until astronomers in the southern hemisphere observed a supernova.

Astronomers had previously hypothesized that neutrinos are emitted when a star evolves into a supernova. When the supernova was spotted, astronomers asked researchers at the underground tanks to check records of activity in the tanks. Records from Cleveland and Kamioka verified that neutrinos had been emitted during the explosion of the star. The neutrinos had traveled at the speed of light and arrived at Earth at about the same time as the visible light from the supernova.

Radiation Detection Tanks

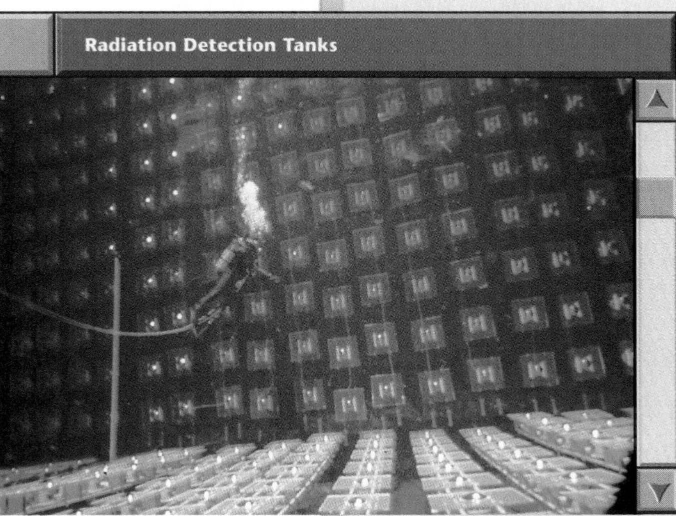

Think Critically: The neutrinos that traveled through Earth in 1987 were produced about 169 000 years ago when Sanduleak –69°202 evolved into a supernova. How far away was Sanduleak –69°202?

USING TECHNOLOGY

Show students pictures of the Large Magellanic Cloud such as shown in **Figure 24-20**. It was in this cloud that the supernova was observed in February 1987. The Large Magellanic Cloud is one of two irregular galaxies that orbit the Milky Way galaxy.

Think Critically
Sanduleak –69°202 is 169 000 light-years away.

3 Assess

Check for Understanding

FLEX Your Brain

Use the Flex Your Brain activity to have students explore EVOLUTION OF STARS.

Activity Worksheets, p. 5

Reteach

Obtain a series of slides or pictures of many different types of nebulas. Show slides or pictures of nebulas with dark globules contained in them. (Pictures of the Eagle nebula from the *Hubble Space Telescope* are good examples.) Explain that these dark globules are places where stars are forming. These globules are called EGGs (evaporating gaseous globules). Show slides or pictures of the Crab nebula and other supernova remnants. Ask students what they look like. Students should recognize evidence of massive explosions.

Extension

For students who have mastered this section, use the **Reinforcement** and **Enrichment** masters.

Integrating the Sciences

Physics A strong candidate for a black hole is A0620-00, located in the binary star system of V616 Monocerotis. It appears to have an accretion disk around it and has a mass of at least 3.8 solar masses. Until this discovery, Cygnus X-1 had been the leading candidate for a black hole. Supermassive black holes are thought to exist in the centers of galaxies. **The best candidates for black holes are binary star systems in which one star is not seen and high amounts of X rays are given off. Ask students to explain why this is true.** *The visible star is seen to wobble because of the gravitational pull of the black hole, and X rays are emitted as material from the visible star is pulled into the black hole.*

4 Close

•MINI•QUIZ•

1. **A star begins as a large cloud of gas and dust called a(n) _____ .** *nebula*
2. **Once the outer layers of a star like our sun escape into space, a(n) _____ is left behind.** *white dwarf*
3. **The collapsed core of a star, composed of only neutrons, is called a(n) _____ .** *neutron star*

Section Wrap-up

Review

1. Giants are large but relatively cool stars. Their temperatures compare with small main sequence stars, but their absolute magnitudes compare with the larger main sequence stars.
2. Because the blue star is hotter, its absolute magnitude would be brighter than that of the yellow star.
3. I. Begins as nebula
   - A. cloud contracts
   - B. heated to 10 000 000 K
   - C. fusion in cloud center

   II. Main sequence star
   - A. energy of fusion balances gravity
   - B. hydrogen fuel exhausted

   III. Giant
   - A. fuses helium
   - B. outer layers escape

   IV. White dwarf
   - A. exhausts fuel supply
4. **Think Critically** The sun still has a supply of hydrogen for fusion. This keeps the core from collapsing and temperatures from rising. Currently, the sun's core is not hot enough to fuse significant amounts of helium.

Figure 24-16

These stars in the Great Nebula of Orion are some of the youngest stars observed from Earth, although their formation began over 6 million years ago.

What about the matter created in the cores of stars? Are elements such as carbon and iron recycled also? Some of these elements do become parts of new stars. In fact, spectrographs have shown that our sun contains some carbon, iron, and other such elements. Because the sun is a main sequence star, it is too young to have created these elements itself. Our sun condensed from material that was created in stars that died many billions of years ago.

Some elements condense to form planets and other bodies rather than stars. In fact, your body contains many atoms that were fused in the cores of ancient stars. Evidence suggests that the first stars formed from hydrogen and helium and that all the other elements have formed in the cores of stars.

Section Wrap-up

Review

1. Explain why giants are not in the main sequence on the H-R diagram. How do their temperatures and absolute magnitudes compare with those of main sequence stars?
2. What can be said about the absolute magnitudes of two equal-sized stars whose colors are blue and yellow?
3. Outline the history and probable future of our sun.
4. **Think Critically:** Why doesn't the helium currently in the sun's core undergo fusion?

Skill Builder

Sequencing

Sequence the following in order of most evolved to least evolved: *main sequence star, supergiant, neutron star,* and *nebula.* If you need help, refer to Sequencing in the **Skill Handbook.**

Science Journal

Write a brief description in your Science Journal explaining what evidence exists that our sun evolved from material that existed in a previous star.

Science Journal

Spectrographs have shown that our sun contains carbon, iron, and other such elements. Because the sun is a main sequence star, it is too young to have created these elements. Our sun condensed from material that existed in previous stars.

Skill Builder

neutron star, supergiant, main sequence star, nebula

Assessment

Content Have students share their star sequences with another student. Use the Performance Task Assessment List for Events Chain in **PASC,** p. 91. P

Galaxies and the Expanding Universe

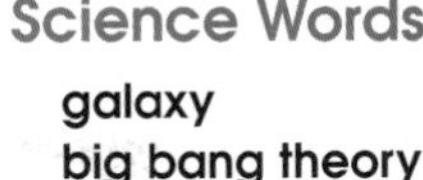

24•4

Galaxies

One reason to study astronomy is to learn about your place in the universe. Long ago, people thought they were at the center of the universe and everything revolved around Earth. Today, you know this isn't the case. But do you know where you are in the universe?

You are on Earth, and Earth orbits the sun. But does the sun orbit anything? How does it interact with other objects in the universe? The sun is one star among many in a galaxy. A **galaxy** is a large group of stars, gas, and dust held together by gravity. Our galaxy, the Milky Way, contains about 200 billion stars, including the sun. Galaxies are separated by huge distances—often millions of light-years.

Science Words

galaxy
big bang theory

Objectives

- Describe a galaxy and list the three main types of galaxies.
- Identify several characteristics of the Milky Way Galaxy.
- Explain how the big bang theory explains the observed Doppler shifts of galaxies.

Figure 24-17

There may be more than 100 billion galaxies in the universe, and nearly all of them seem to be organized into clusters.

691

Section 24•4

Prepare

Section Background

- New infrared studies of the center of our galaxy, the Milky Way, provide more evidence for a super-massive black hole at the core of our galaxy.
- A new galaxy, a dwarf spheroidal galaxy, has been found lying just 50 000 light-years from the Milky Way's nucleus. It lies on the other side of the Milky Way from us, and it appears that our galaxy is tearing it apart. It is thought by researchers that within another 100 million years, the stars from this small galaxy will be incorporated into our own Milky Way.

Preplanning

Obtain drawing compasses for the MiniLAB.

1 Motivate

Bellringer

Before presenting the lesson, display **Section Focus Transparency 93** on the overhead projector. Assign the accompanying **Focus Activity** worksheet. L1 LEP

Tying to Previous Knowledge

Ask students if they have ever heard of the Milky Way. Help them recall observing the sky during an exceptionally dark night. If so, they may have seen the band of stars that stretches across the sky. Ask students who have seen this band of stars to tell others in the class about it. This band of stars is the Milky Way, our home galaxy.

Program Resources

Reproducible Masters

Study Guide, p. 97 L1
Reinforcement, p. 97 L1
Enrichment, p. 97 L3
Activity Worksheets, pp. 5, 150 L1

Transparencies

Section Focus Transparency 93 L1

2 Teach

Activity

Have pairs of students make flash cards of the types of galaxies. Have them draw the galaxy type on one side and write its name on the reverse. Partners can then test each other using the flash cards. Next, have the partners draw ten to 20 images of the Milky Way galaxy on separate cards. Have them place the sun at slightly different positions around the galaxy on each card. When finished, partners can demonstrate movement of the sun around the galaxy by flipping the cards.

Visual Learning

Figures 24-18, 24-19, 24-20 After students study the figures, ask them to compare and contrast the three major classifications of galaxies. Students should concentrate on obvious ways the three types of galaxies are similar and on ways they are different. LEP LS

GLENCOE TECHNOLOGY

Videodisc

The Infinite Voyage: Unseen Worlds

Chapter 4

Astronomers Use Radio Waves to Examine the Galaxies

Chapter 5

Evolution of the Universe Is Traced

STVS: Earth and Space

Disc 3, Side 1

Shape of Galaxies (Ch. 11)

Figure 24-18

M87 is an example of an elliptical galaxy.

Figure 24-19

NGC 2997 is a spiral galaxy similar to our own. The scattered stars in the picture are in the foreground and belong to the Milky Way.

Just as stars are grouped together within galaxies, galaxies are grouped into clusters. The cluster the Milky Way belongs to is called the Local Group. It contains about 30 galaxies of various types and sizes.

Elliptical Galaxies

There are three major classes of galaxies: elliptical, spiral, and irregular. Probably the most common type of galaxy is the elliptical galaxy, shown in **Figure 24-18.** These galaxies are shaped like large, three-dimensional ellipses. Many are football-shaped, whereas some are spherical. Some elliptical galaxies are quite small, while others are so large that the entire Local Group of galaxies would fit inside one of them.

Spiral Galaxies

Spiral galaxies, as shown in **Figure 24-19**, have spiral arms winding outward from inner regions. These spiral arms are made up of bright stars and dust. The fuzzy patch you can see in the constellation of Andromeda is actually a spiral galaxy. It's so far away that you can't see its individual stars. Instead, it appears as a hazy spot in our sky. The Andromeda galaxy is a member of the Local Group and is about 2.2 million light-years away and is shown on page 670.

Arms in a normal spiral start close to the center of the galaxy. Barred spirals have spiral arms extending from a large bar that passes through the center of the galaxy.

Irregular Galaxies

The third class of galaxies, irregulars, includes most of those galaxies that don't fit into the other classifications. Irregular galaxies have many different shapes and are smaller and less common than the other types. Two irregular galaxies called the Clouds of Magellan orbit the Milky Way. The Large Magellanic Cloud is shown in **Figure 24-20**.

Cultural Diversity

What's in a name? The Milky Way is the English name for the galaxy containing Earth, but it has been known by many others. Akkadians called it the Great Serpent, or the River of the Snake. In Judea, Armenia, and Syria, the galaxy was sometimes referred to as a Long Bandage. China and Japan called it Tien Ho, the Celestial River or the Silver River. In India, the band of light was known as Akash Ganga, the Bed of the Ganges, or Bhagwan ki Kachahri, the Court of God, and Swarga Duari, the Dove of Paradise. Polynesians called the cloud of lights the Long, Blue, Cloud-Eating Shark, while the Ottawa saw it as muddy water stirred up by a turtle swimming along the bottom of the sky. Ask interested students to research how cultures not mentioned refer to the Milky Way. L2

The Milky Way Galaxy

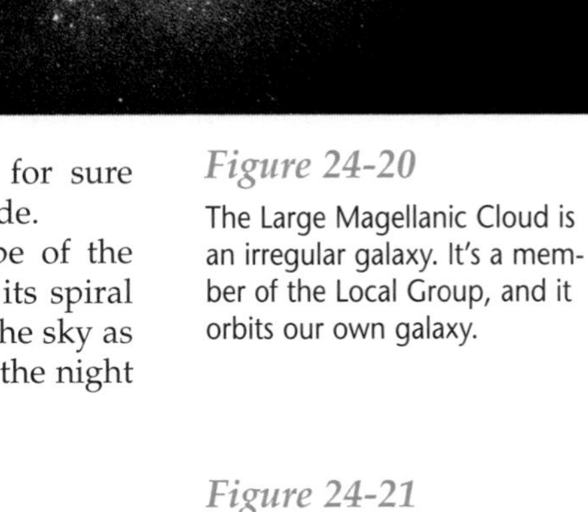

The Milky Way contains more than 200 billion stars. The visible disk of stars is about 100 000 light-years across, and the sun is located about 30 000 light-years out from its center. In our galaxy, all stars orbit around a central region. Based on a distance of 30 000 light-years and a speed of 235 kilometers per second, the sun orbits around the center of the Milky Way once every 240 million years.

A diagram of our galaxy is shown in **Figure 24-21.** The Milky Way is usually classified as a normal spiral galaxy. However, recent evidence suggests that it might be a barred spiral. It is difficult to know for sure because we can never see our galaxy from the outside.

Figure 24-20

The Large Magellanic Cloud is an irregular galaxy. It's a member of the Local Group, and it orbits our own galaxy.

You can't see the normal spiral or barred shape of the Milky Way because you are located within one of its spiral arms. You can see the Milky Way stretching across the sky as a faint band of light. All of the stars you can see in the night sky belong to the Milky Way Galaxy.

Expansion of the Universe

What does it sound like when a car is blowing its horn while it drives past you? The horn has a high pitch as the car approaches you, then the horn seems to drop in pitch as the car drives away. This effect is called the Doppler shift. The Doppler shift occurs with light as well as with sound.

Figure 24-21

The Milky Way Galaxy is usually classified as a normal spiral galaxy. Its spiral arms, composed of stars and gas, radiate out from an area of densely packed stars, the nucleus.

Discussion

IS Interpersonal Divide the class into groups of four students. Number students in each group one through four. Have students numbered one work together on the first question. Do the same for the remaining groups. After groups have worked on their questions, have them return to their original groups for discussion.

- **What are the Clouds of Magellan?** *irregular galaxies orbiting the Milky Way*
- **How does the Milky Way galaxy compare in size and type with the galaxy M31 in the constellation of Andromeda?** *They are both spiral galaxies, but the Andromeda galaxy is a little larger than the Milky Way.*
- **Recent evidence indicates that the Milky Way may be what type of galaxy?** *a barred spiral*
- **Why was our galaxy named the Milky Way?** *To the unaided eye, the thick band of stars lying in the plane of the spiral Milky Way galaxy looks like a hazy, milky area of the sky.*

Inquiry Questions

- **Why are some galaxies classified as irregular in shape?** *Irregular galaxies don't have the regular shape that spiral and elliptical galaxies have.*
- **Why can't you see the spiral shape of the Milky Way galaxy?** *In order to see the spiral shape of the Milky Way, you would have to be above or below the plane of the galaxy. Earth, in orbit around the sun, is located in one of the spiral arms.*

Theme Connection

Scale and Structure The theme of scale and structure is reaffirmed in this chapter by the study of the spiral structure of the Milky Way galaxy and by the study of the expansion of the universe.

Science Journal

The Ring Galaxy Have students research the cause of the Cartwheel galaxy in "A Galaxy of News," by David Bruning in *Astronomy,* June 1995, pp. 40-41. Ask them to write about the results of their research in their Science Journals. L2 IS

CONNECT TO

PHYSICS

Answer As a train approaches, the wavelength of the sound coming from the train is shortened, thus changing the pitch. The pitch of the sound from a receding train is changed by the sound's wavelength being lengthened. Similarly, the wavelength of light coming from an approaching galaxy is shortened toward the blue, and the wavelength of light from a receding galaxy is lengthened toward the red.

Demonstration

LS **Auditory-Musical** Ask students if they have ever experienced the Doppler shift of sound waves. Remind them of train whistles from approaching and receding trains and the siren of a fire truck as it drives by. Securely tie a cord to an alarm clock, and gently twirl the clock around as the alarm is sounding. Students will hear the changing pitch as the clock first approaches them and then recedes.

Inquiry Questions

- **Why are dark lines in a spectrum shifted toward the red end when an object is moving away from you?** *Each dark line represents a wavelength of light. As objects move away, the wavelengths of light are stretched out, making them longer, and thus appear toward the red end of the spectrum.*
- **Why do we not observe a red shift in the light of the galaxies of the Local Group?** *All galaxies in the Local Group are gravitationally affecting each other and move through space together.*

CONNECT TO

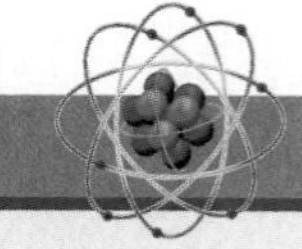

PHYSICS

Have you ever heard how the pitch of a train's horn changes as it first approaches and then recedes from you? Relate this to changes shown in **Figure 24-22** in reference to how the Doppler shift causes changes in the light coming from distant galaxies. ***Infer*** how these changes relate to whether a galaxy is approaching or receding from Earth.

The Doppler Effect

Look at the spectrum of a star containing sodium in **Figure 24-23A.** Note the position of the dark lines. How do they compare with the lines in **Figures 24-23B** and **C?** They have shifted in position. What caused this shift? When a star is moving toward you, its wavelengths of light are pushed together, just as the sound waves from the car's horn are. The dark lines in the spectrum shift toward the blue-violet. A red shift in the spectrum occurs when an object is moving away from you. In a red shift, the dark lines shift toward the longer-wavelength red end of the spectrum.

In 1924, Edwin Hubble noticed an interesting fact about the light coming from most galaxies. When a spectrograph is used to study light from galaxies beyond the Local Group, there is a red shift in the light. What does this red shift tell you about the universe?

Because all galaxies beyond the Local Group show a red shift in their spectra, they must be moving away from Earth. If all galaxies outside the Local Group are moving away from you, this indicates that the entire universe must be expanding. Think of the Explore activity at the beginning of

Figure 24-22

The Doppler effect causes the wavelengths of light coming from galaxies to be compressed or stretched.

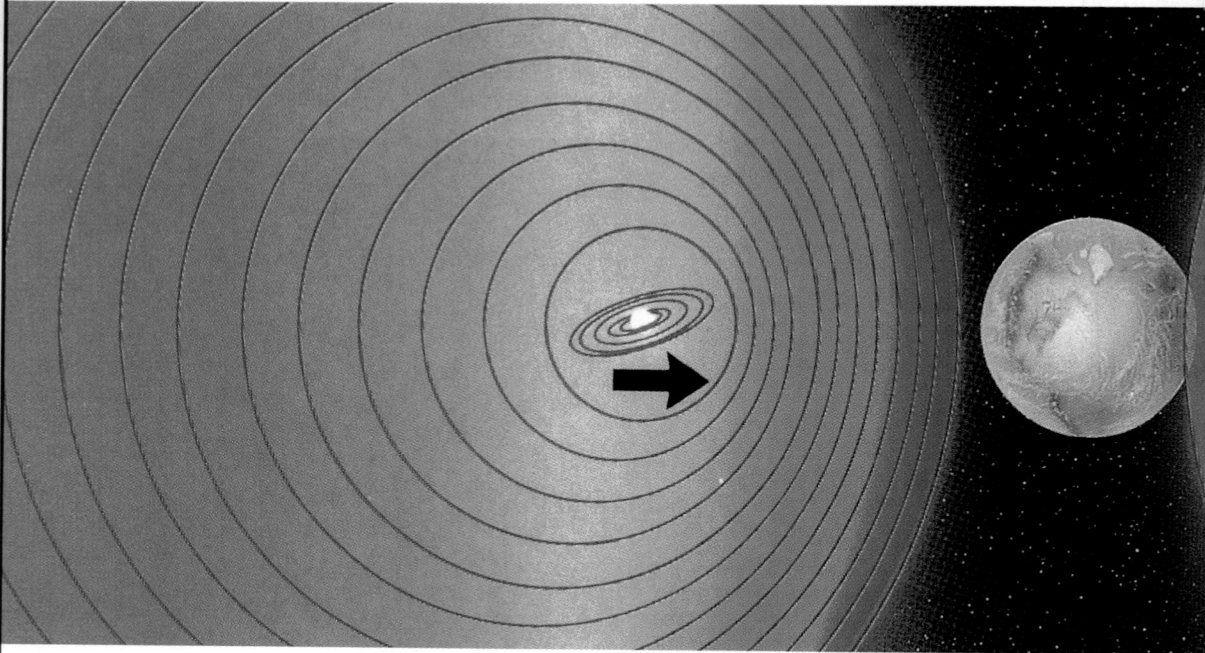

694 Chapter 24 Stars and Galaxies

Integrating the Sciences

Physics Have students explain how the Doppler shifts shown in **Figure 24-22** relate to whether a galaxy outside the Local Group is approaching or receding from Earth. Also ask students to relate the Doppler effect in light waves to the Doppler effect in sound waves. *The wavelength of light coming from an approaching galaxy is shortened toward the blue, and the wavelength of light from a receding galaxy is lengthened toward the red. The Doppler effect in light causes a change in the wavelength of light, and the Doppler effect in sound causes a change in the wavelength of sound.*

Figure 24-23

The dark lines in the spectra (A) are shifted toward the blue-violet end when a star is moving toward Earth (B). A red shift (C) indicates a star is moving away from Earth.

the chapter. The dots on the balloon moved apart as the model universe expanded. Regardless of which dot you picked, all the other dots moved away from it. Galaxies beyond the Local Group move away from us just as the dots moved apart on the balloon.

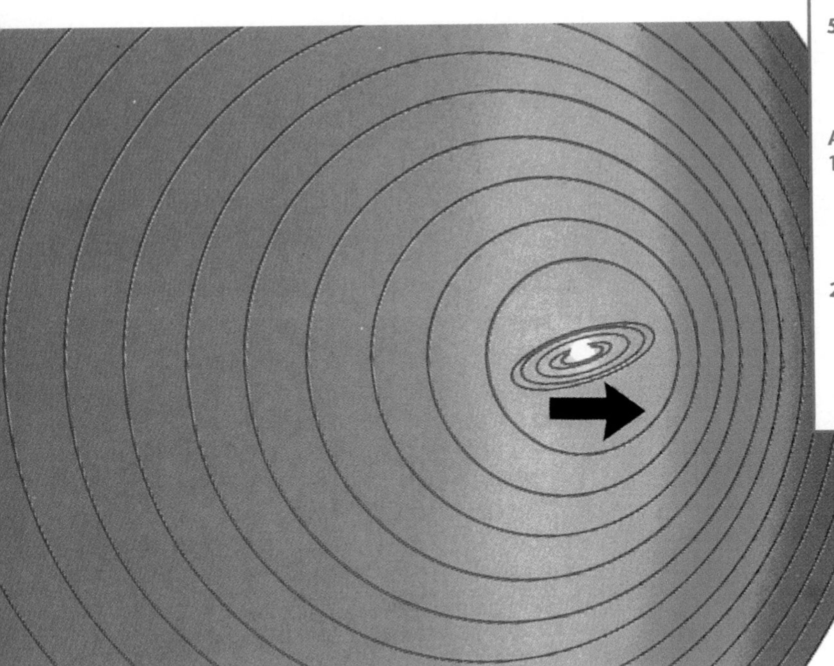

MiniLAB

How far can we "see" into space?

Procedure

1. On a large sheet of paper, formulate a model of the Milky Way Galaxy as it would appear looking down on it from somewhere out in space.
2. Mark the appropriate location of the solar system, about 2/3 of the way out on one of the spiral arms.
3. Draw a circle around the sun indicating the 4.2 light-year distance of the next closest star to the sun, Proxima Centauri.
4. One of the most distant stars that can be seen on a clear night without the aid of a telescope is Epsilon Aurigae in the constellation Auriga at a distance of 3300 light-years.
5. On your diagram, draw a circle with a radius of about 3300 light-years with the sun at the center.

Analysis

1. If we assume that Epsilon Aurigae is the farthest star visible without the aid of a telescope, interpret what this circle represents.
2. At this scale interpret how far away the Andromeda Galaxy (the next closest spiral galaxy) would be located.

Science Journal

The Great Wall Have students research the work of Margaret Geller and John Huchra, of the Harvard-Smithsonian Center for Astrophysics, on mapping the universe. Have them write about their research in their Science Journals. The work of these two astronomers has led to the realization that great voids and large concentrations of galaxies alternate throughout the universe. They discovered that many galaxies lie in an enormous sheet now called the Great Wall. For more information, refer students to "A Cross Section of the Universe" by Jeff Kanipe, *Astronomy,* November 1989, p. 44; "Beyond the Big Bang" by Jeff Kanipe, *Astronomy,* April 1992, pp. 30-37; and "COBE's Big Bang" by R. Talcott, *Astronomy,* August 1992, pp. 42-44. L2

MiniLAB

Purpose

LS **Visual-Spatial** Students will realize how far into space we can see without the aid of a telescope. L1

Materials

large sheet of paper, metric ruler or meterstick

Teaching Strategies

Troubleshooting Help students conceptualize the scale of their model. If our sun were represented by a dot, the circle representing the distance to Proxima Centauri would be within that same dot.

Analysis

1. The 3300-light-year-radius circle represents the farthest distance from which an observer on Earth can observe a star without the aid of a telescope.
2. Whatever the scale used, the distance to the Andromeda galaxy would be about 22 times the diameter of the student's Milky Way model. This can be determined by dividing the distance to the Andromeda galaxy (2 200 000 light-years) by the diameter of the Milky Way (100 000 light-years).

Assessment

Content Have students determine how far away the Large Magellanic Cloud would be located. *Its distance is about 169 000 light-years.* Use the Performance Task Assessment List for Using Math in Science in **PASC**, p. 29. P

Activity Worksheets, pp. 5, 150

3 Assess

Check for Understanding

FLEX Your Brain

Use the Flex Your Brain activity to have students explore BIG BANG THEORY.

Activity Worksheets, p. 5

Reteach

Visual-Spatial Show students one loaf of raisin bread before baking. Have students measure the distance between the raisins in the bread. Send the loaf to the home economics or domestic arts department and have them bake it. When the loaf is returned, have students measure the distance between the raisins again. Have students explain why the raisins are farther apart after baking and relate this to the expansion of the universe. Each raisin represents a galaxy cluster.

Extension

For students who have mastered this section, use the **Reinforcement** and **Enrichment** masters.

4 Close

•MINI•QUIZ•

1. **A large group of stars, gas, and dust held together by gravity is a(n) ______.** *galaxy*
2. **The Milky Way is usually classified as a spiral galaxy and belongs to the ______.** *Local Group*
3. **What are the three major galaxy classifications?** *elliptical, spiral, irregular*
4. **The most common type of galaxy is the ______ galaxy.** *elliptical*

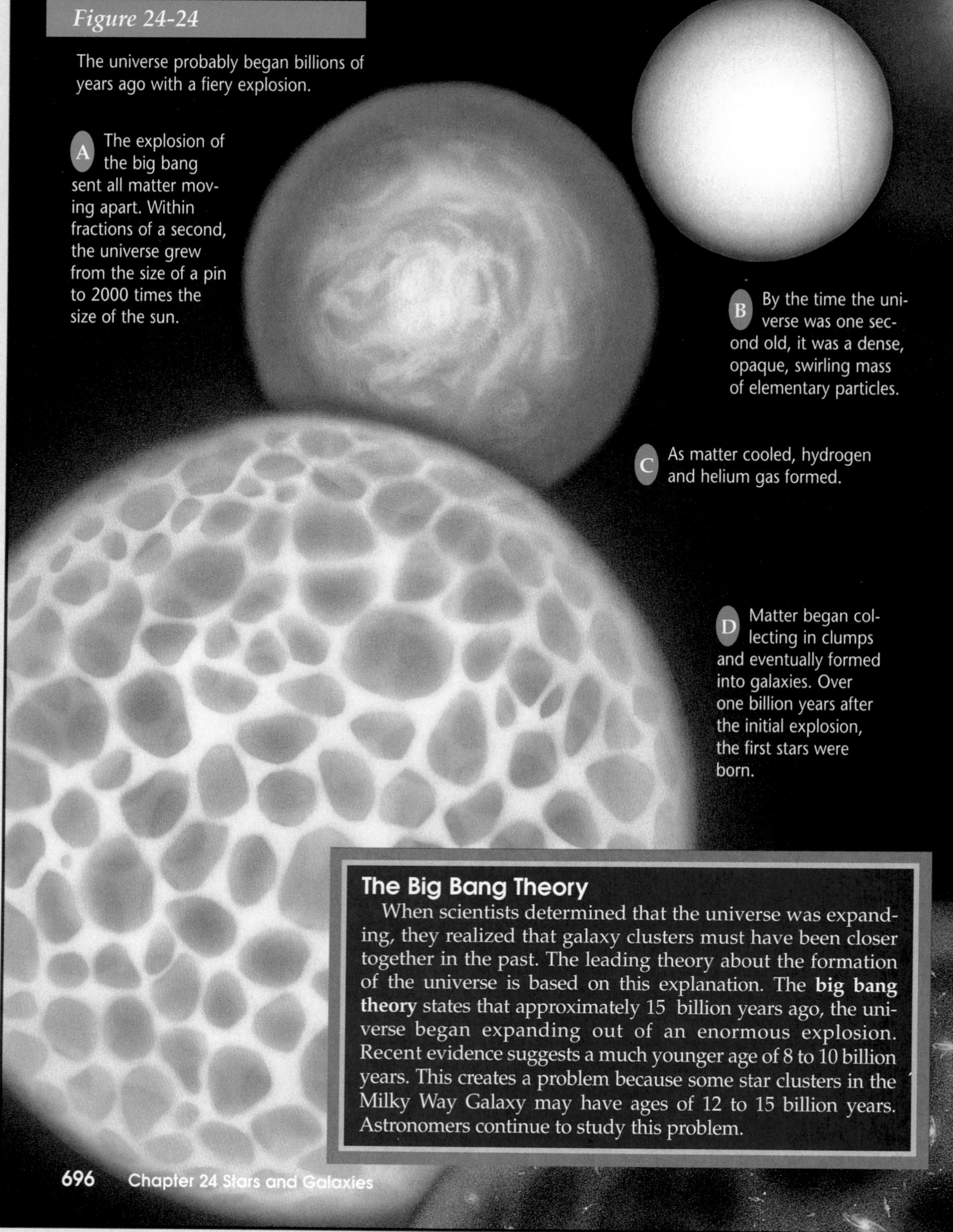

Figure 24-24

The universe probably began billions of years ago with a fiery explosion.

The Big Bang Theory

When scientists determined that the universe was expanding, they realized that galaxy clusters must have been closer together in the past. The leading theory about the formation of the universe is based on this explanation. The **big bang theory** states that approximately 15 billion years ago, the universe began expanding out of an enormous explosion. Recent evidence suggests a much younger age of 8 to 10 billion years. This creates a problem because some star clusters in the Milky Way Galaxy may have ages of 12 to 15 billion years. Astronomers continue to study this problem.

Inclusion Strategies

Behaviorally Disordered Match these students with other students with whom they tend to get along. Ask each student group to come up with original ideas on how to develop a model that would demonstrate the expansion of the universe caused by the big bang theory.

Integrating the Sciences

Physics To help students understand how physics is integrated with the study of astronomy, ask the following question. **What will determine whether the universe keeps on expanding or begins to contract?** *If enough mass exists in the universe, it may eventually slow and begin to collapse.*

A time-lapse photograph taken in December 1995 by the *Hubble Space Telescope* shows over 1500 galaxies at a distance of more than 10 billion light-years. These galaxies may date back to when the universe was no more than 1 billion years old. The galaxies are in various stages of development. One astronomer indicates that we may be looking back to a time when our own galaxy was forming. Studies of this nature will eventually enable astronomers to determine the approximate age of the universe.

Whether the universe expands forever or stops depends on how much matter is in the universe. All matter exerts a gravitational force. If there's enough matter, gravity will halt the expansion, and the universe will contract until everything comes to one point.

Astronomers continue to study the structure of the known universe in hopes of learning a more exact age, how it has evolved, and how it might end. You will learn in the next section that astronomers also search the galaxy in hopes of finding evidence that life exists elsewhere in our solar system and galaxy.

USING MATH

The mass of a hydrogen nucleus is 1.008 atomic mass units (amu). A helium nucleus' mass is 4.004 amu. Calculate the mass lost when four hydrogen nuclei fuse to form one helium nucleus. What happens to this mass?

Section Wrap-up

Review

1. List the three major classifications of galaxies. What do they all have in common?
2. What is the name of the galaxy that you live in? What motion do the stars in this galaxy exhibit?
3. **Think Critically:** All galaxies outside the Local Group show a red shift in their spectra. Within the Local Group, some galaxies show a red shift and some show a blue shift. What does this tell you about the galaxies in the Local Group and outside the Local Group?

Skill Builder

Recognizing Cause and Effect

Current measurements and calculated densities of the observable universe show it's not dense enough to collapse on itself. Scientists are trying to prove the existence of so-called dark matter, which is not directly observable. If the universe contains an abundance of dark matter (as much as 90 percent of its total mass), what could you infer about the true density and the future of the universe? If you need help, refer to Recognizing Cause and Effect in the **Skill Handbook.**

Science Journal

Research and write a report in your Science Journal about the most recent evidence supporting or disputing the big bang theory. Describe how the big bang theory explains observations of galaxies made with spectrometers.

USING MATH

4 (H) = 4 (1.008 amu) = 4.032

Mass lost:

4.032 – 4.004 = 0.028 amu lost

Lost mass is converted into energy.

Section Wrap-up

Review

1. Shapes are elliptical, spiral (regular and barred), and irregular. All galaxies are large groups of stars, gas, and dust held together by gravity; they are grouped in clusters.
2. the Milky Way galaxy; stars orbit its nucleus
3. **Think Critically** All galaxies within the Local Group travel through space together; however, some of them are moving toward the Milky Way, whereas others are moving away from the Milky Way. Galaxies outside the Local Group are moving away from us.

Science Journal

Recent articles refer to finding seeds of structures in the background radiation. These structures would have provided areas for the clumping of matter that eventually evolved into galaxies and galaxy clusters. Students should include the latest information obtained by the *Hubble Space Telescope.* The red shift indicates that the galaxies are receding from us, which would be expected if the universe began with a big bang.

Skill Builder

The presence of dark matter would make the universe more dense than current measurements of the observable universe indicate. A sufficiently dense universe wouldn't be able to overcome the gravitational force of all its matter and would, therefore, collapse on itself.

Assessment

Performance Assess students' abilities in recognizing cause and effect by discussing their inferences. Use the Performance Task Assessment List for Making Observations and Inferences in **PASC,** p. 17. P

Prepare

Section Background

When searching for life elsewhere in space, scientists search for the presence of organic molecules. These molecules contain the element carbon. Life as we know it is made of organic molecules.

1 Motivate

Bellringer

Before presenting the lesson, display **Section Focus Transparency 94** on the overhead projector. Assign the accompanying **Focus Activity** worksheet. L1 LEP

Tying to Previous Knowledge

Help students recall conditions on some of the moons of the gaseous giant planets as described in Chapter 23. Remind them of the methane-rich atmosphere of Saturn's moon, Titan; the possible oceans under the ice surface of Europa, one of Jupiter's moons; and the latest *Voyager* information about Triton, Neptune's largest moon.

2 Teach

Library Research

Have students research the tests for life conducted by the *Viking* lander on Mars. Ask them to include a description of the tests and possible conclusions that have been drawn. Refer students to the following article: "The Case for Life on Mars" by Andrew Chaikin, *Air and Space,* v. 5, March 1991, pp. 63-71.

TECHNOLOGY:

24•5 The Search for Extraterrestrial Life

Objectives

- Name locations in our solar system where life may have existed in the past or could exist now.
- Describe the methods used by astronomers to search for extraterrestrial life within and beyond our solar system.
- Decide if methods used by scientists might cause contamination of other worlds.

Searching for Life on Other Worlds

On July 20, 1976, the first *Viking* lander touched down on Mars. It conducted three different types of tests on Martian soil in its search for evidence of extraterrestrial life. Extraterrestrial life is life that exists beyond Earth. It can be microorganisms living in the rocks of a barren world or intelligent life living on a planet orbiting a distant star.

Some of the tests made by the *Viking* probes produced results that could have been caused by life or by chemical reactions with the Martian soil. Analysis of the soil showed it lacked the types of molecules that appear to be necessary for life. It appears Mars doesn't contain life at the present time. But what if life had been found? Would the space probe have contaminated it?

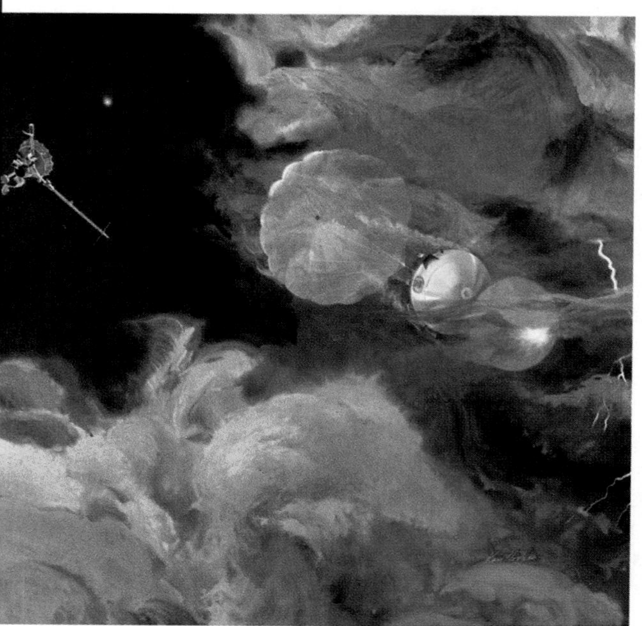

Figure 24-25
The *Galileo* spacecraft dropped a small probe into Jupiter's atmosphere. Before it was crushed by the intense pressure, it transmitted data back to the orbiter above.

Searching with Space Probes

The *Viking* spacecraft was carefully sterilized so the Martian soil would not be contaminated. The *Galileo* spacecraft arrived at Jupiter in 1995. It sent a probe down into the clouds of the planet as shown in **Figure 24-25.** It was not sterilized before being launched. Is there a danger that microbes from Earth could contaminate the environment of Jupiter's clouds? Probably not. *Galileo's* probe was crushed and sterilized in the depths of Jupiter's atmosphere, eliminating any chance of planetary contamination.

Titan, one of the satellites of Saturn, contains organic molecules. The molecules themselves aren't considered to be life, but they are thought to resemble the molecules from which life evolved on Earth. Given enough time, millions or billions of years, it's possible that the molecules will evolve into life as they did on Earth. Scientists hope to land a probe on Titan in the near future to further investigate the organic molecules there.

Program Resources

Reproducible Masters
Study Guide, p. 98 L1
Reinforcement, p. 98 L1
Enrichment, p. 98 L3
Cross-Curricular Integration, p. 28
Science and Society Integration, p. 28

Transparencies
Section Focus Transparency 94 L1

Cracks in the icy crust of Europa, one of Jupiter's moons, may allow sunlight into the ocean underneath. Although it is unlikely, the sunlight could have helped start biological activity. Could a space probe be used to study this possibility? What types of precautions should be taken before a probe is sent to Europa?

Are there ways to search for life on other worlds without the possibility of contamination? One method is to search the universe for sources of radio signals from intelligent life. This program is called SETI, the Search for Extraterrestrial Intelligence. In 1974, astronomers used a radio telescope in Arecibo, Puerto Rico, shown in **Figure 24-26**, to beam a radio message to a star cluster more than 26 000 light-years away.

Figure 24-26

This 305-m dish at Arecibo, Puerto Rico, has been used in an attempt to communicate with extraterrestrial life.

In October 1992, NASA began a program that, in addition to current programs by the University of California, the Planetary Society, and the Ohio State University, was to search for radio signals that could be evidence of extraterrestrial life. However, less than one year later, Congress voted to stop funding for NASA's SETI program. Since then, part of the project has received private funding. The program is nowcalled Project Phoenix and is based at the SETI Institute of Mountain View, California.

Section Wrap-up

Review

1. Where is life known to exist in the solar system? Name two other places in the solar system where life might be evolving.
2. Which program searches for evidence of intelligent life using radio telescopes?
3. Why were the *Viking* probes sterilized, but the *Galileo* probe was not?

Explore the Technology

If you were in charge of studying the possibility of life on other worlds, how would you proceed? If space probes are used, how could they be used with no danger of contaminating present or future life? If your study is by radio telescopes alone, what evidence of life would you expect to find?

SCIENCE & SOCIETY

3 Assess

Check for Understanding

FLEX Your Brain

Use the Flex Your Brain activity to have students explore POSSIBILITIES OF LIFE ON OTHER PLANETS.

Activity Worksheets, p. 5

Reteach

LS **Interpersonal** Have student groups discuss whether it is appropriate to spend tax dollars to send probes to search for life on other worlds. Students should discuss the fact that the chance of finding life is relatively remote. However, if life is found, it could tell us a great deal about how life evolved on Earth. Students may wish to stage a debate after they have researched the topic.

Extension

For students who have mastered this section, use the **Reinforcement** and **Enrichment** masters.

4 Close

Activity

Assign each student group a different planet or moon located within our solar system. Have each group devise a plan to search for life on their particular world. Students must include methods to be used in the search and safeguards to be followed that would avoid contaminating their assigned world. P

Section Wrap-up

Review

1. Earth; Triton and Europa
2. SETI, the Search for ExtraTerrestrial Intelligence
3. The *Viking* lander was sterilized so the Martian soil would not be contaminated. NASA believes the *Galileo* probe was crushed and sterilized in the depths of Jupiter's atmosphere. Its route to Jupiter carried it close to the sun. Therefore, it was sterilized long before reaching Jupiter.

Explore the Technology

If space probes are used, they must be sterilized to avoid contamination. They could be placed in orbit in order to study the planets from a distance. If radio telescopes are used, evidence of life might be the presence of regular radio signals.

Background

- The chance of either *Voyager* spacecraft actually contacting alien civilizations is incredibly small. It will be thousands of years before they even begin to get close to another star system, and there is little likelihood that the star system will include planets inhabited by life forms capable of detecting and intercepting a tiny spacecraft. But astronomers predict the two probes and their messages could remain intact for thousands, even millions, of years.
- Two other spacecraft, *Pioneers 10* and *11*, launched in 1971 and 1972, are also on their way out of the solar system. Each *Pioneer* craft contains a message from Earth in the form of a plaque engraved with images of humans and a map of the solar system showing Earth's location.
- A number of public and private organizations are participating in a group of projects known as SETI (*S*earch for *E*xtra*t*errestrial *I*ntelligence). SETI involves scanning the sky for radio signals broadcast from other parts of the universe. The theory is that other intelligent beings are probably broadcasting messages to each other, much like humans on Earth broadcast TV and radio signals. If we can detect any such signals, we'll have proof that intelligent life exists in other parts of the universe.

Teaching Strategies

LS **Auditory-Musical** Play for students some of the musical selections included in the *Voyager* recordings, and show them some of the photographs included in the *Voyager* message.

- Encourage students to initiate a time capsule project at their school. Invite them to place items in a sealed, waterproof container and bury it or otherwise store it for opening by future students. Challenge students to solve the issue of how to keep people aware of the existence of the time capsule so it will be opened when intended.

Source

Sagan, Carl, et al. *Murmurs of Earth: The Voyager Interstellar Record.* Random House: New York, 1978. (detailed description of all components of the *Voyager* message)

Science & ART

Science Journal

What kind of message would you place on a spacecraft? In your Science Journal, write a short essay describing the content of the message and the technology or technologies you would choose as a medium. Explain your reasoning.

Is anyone out there?

In 1977, two unmanned space probes–*Voyager 1* and *Voyage 2* –were launched from Earth on a mission to Jupiter, Saturn, Uranus, and Neptune. During the 1980s, the *Voyagers* broadcast back to Earth close-up photographs and other valuable data about our solar system's outer planets. Once this work was completed, both spacecraft continued on, and they are now hurtling past the orbit of Pluto and out into the depths of outer space.

The *Voyagers* have completed their original mission. But astronomers predict that these spacecraft will continue speeding through the frictionless vacuum of deep space for thousands of years. Just in case they should someday come into contact with intelligent beings, both *Voyagers* carry identical messages from Earth.

The *Voyager* Record

The message from Earth is in the form of a gold-plated copper disc that operates like a long-playing phonograph record. Included are a stylus and cartridge that can be used to play the recording. The message contains 90 minutes of music from around the world, greetings in dozens of human languages, sounds of nature, mathematical equations, and 118 photographs.

The photographs include pictures of children, families, classrooms, men and women at work, highways, trains, buses, airplanes, a rocket launch, an astronaut walking in space, musicians and instruments, and a variety of nature scenes and animals, including mountains, deserts, forests, beaches, seashores, elephants, gorillas, dogs, dolphins, birds, and insects. There is also a star map to show the location of Earth and a diagram of our solar system.

Nature sounds include volcanic eruptions, earthquakes, thunder, wind, waves, rain, crickets and frogs, footsteps, laughter, and heartbeats.

The recording includes the music of Bach, Mozart, Beethoven, a Javanese Gamelan, Pygmies of the Ituri Forest, percussion from Senegal, Chuck Berry, Louis Armstrong, bagpipes, a Navajo chant, Japanese flute, and music from China, India, Australia, and New Guinea.

700

Chapter 24

Review

Summary

24-1: Stars

1. The constellations seem to move because Earth rotates on its axis and revolves around the sun.
2. The magnitude of a star is a measure of the star's brightness. Absolute magnitude is a measure of the light emitted. Apparent magnitude is the amount of light received on Earth.
3. Parallax is the apparent shift in the position of an object when viewed from two different positions.

24-2: The Sun

1. The sun produces energy by fusing hydrogen into helium in its core.
2. Sunspots, prominences, and flares are all caused by the intense magnetic field of the sun.
3. The sun is a main sequence star.

24-3: Evolution of Stars

1. A main sequence star uses hydrogen as fuel. When the hydrogen is used up, the core collapses and the star's temperature increases. The star becomes a giant or a supergiant, which use helium as fuel. As the star evolves, the outer layers escape into space. The core has no fuel left and the star becomes a white dwarf. Stars containing high amounts of mass can explode and evolve into neutron stars or black holes.

24-4: Galaxies and the Expanding Universe

1. A galaxy is a large group of stars, gas, and dust held together by gravity. Galaxies can be elliptical, spiral, or irregular in shape.
2. The Milky Way is a spiral galaxy.
3. Spectral line shifts toward red light suggest that all galaxies beyond the Local Group are moving away from our galaxy.

24-5: Science and Society: The Search for Extraterrestrial Life

1. Organic molecules, similar to those that evolved into life on Earth, have been found on Titan, a satellite of Saturn.
2. Space probes and radio telescopes are used to determine whether or not life exists in other parts of the universe.

Key Science Words

a. absolute magnitude	j. giant
b. apparent magnitude	k. light-year
c. big bang theory	l. main sequence
d. binary system	m. nebula
e. black hole	n. neutron star
f. chromosphere	o. parallax
g. constellation	p. photosphere
h. corona	q. sunspot
i. galaxy	r. supergiant
	s. white dwarf

Reviewing Vocabulary

Match each phrase with the correct term from the list of Key Science Words.

1. a group of stars that resembles an object, animal, or mythological character
2. a measure of the amount of light given off by a star
3. distance light travels in one year

Chapter 24

Review

Summary

Have students read the summary statements to review the major concepts of the chapter.

Reviewing Vocabulary

1. g	**6.** e
2. a	**7.** l
3. k	**8.** p
4. m	**9.** d
5. j	**10.** c

Assessment

Portfolio Encourage students to place in their portfolios one or two items of what they consider to be their best work. Examples include:

- MiniLAB assessment, p. 674
- Activity 24-1 experiment design, p. 676
- Science Journal, p. 688 P

Performance Additional performance assessments may be found in **Performance Assessment** and **Science Integration Activities.** Performance Task Assessment Lists and rubrics for evaluating these activities can be found in Glencoe's **Performance Assessment in the Science Classroom.**

GLENCOE TECHNOLOGY

MindJogger Videoquiz

Chapter 24 Have students work in groups as they play the Videoquiz game to review key chapter concepts.

Checking Concepts

1. d	**6.** d
2. b	**7.** d
3. c	**8.** a
4. c	**9.** b
5. d	**10.** a

Understanding Concepts

11. The closer star will have a greater parallax.

12. absolute magnitude and surface temperature

13. All are solar features that seem to be related to the sun's intense magnetic field. Sunspots are relatively cool areas on the surface. Flares and prominences are eruptive features in which matter is violently spewed from the sun's surface.

14. The big bang theory states that all matter began expanding from a single point billions of years ago. Because red shifts indicate that matter is expanding, they support the big bang theory.

15. Probes are able to get close to their targets but pose the problem of contamination. Radio telescopes don't contaminate other worlds, but they can search only for intelligent life that may have sent a radio broadcast.

Thinking Critically

16. Astronomers are looking at galaxies that may have formed when the universe was only 1 billion years old. Studies of this nature may enable astronomers to determine the true age of the universe.

17. Astronomers are able to use instruments to detect the X rays possibly originating from sources surrounding black holes.

18. Pegasus is almost directly overhead at this time.

Chapter 24 Review

4. the beginning of a star's life cycle

5. star that uses helium as fuel

6. dense object that allows nothing to escape its field of gravity

7. our sun belongs to this group of stars

8. layer of the sun's atmosphere that emits light

9. two stars that orbit each other

10. supported by observed red shifts in the spectra of galaxies

Checking Concepts

Choose the word or phrase that completes the sentence.

1. The stars of a constellation ______.
a. are in the same cluster
b. are all giants
c. are equally bright
d. form a pattern

2. ______ is a measure of the amount of a star's light received on Earth.
a. Absolute magnitude
b. Apparent magnitude
c. Fusion
d. Parallax

3. The closer an object is to an observer, the greater its ______.
a. absolute magnitude c. parallax
b. red shift d. size

4. Once a nebula contracts and temperatures increase, ______ begins.
a. main sequencing c. fusion
b. a supernova d. a white dwarf

5. A ______ is about 10 km in size.
a. giant c. black hole
b. white dwarf d. neutron star

6. Our sun fuses ______ into ______.
a. hydrogen/carbon c. carbon/helium
b. helium/hydrogen d. hydrogen/helium

7. Loops of matter flowing from the sun are ______.
a. sunspots c. coronas
b. auroras d. prominences

8. Groups of galaxies are called ______.
a. clusters c. giants
b. supergiants d. binary systems

9. ______ galaxies are sometimes shaped like footballs.
a. Spiral c. Barred
b. Elliptical d. Irregular

10. A shift of wavelengths of light toward the red end of the ______ indicates that galaxies are moving away from the Local Group.
a. spectrum c. corona
b. surface d. chromosphere

Understanding Concepts

Answer the following questions in your Science Journal using complete sentences.

11. How can parallax be used to determine which of two stars is closer to Earth?

12. What variables determine a star's position on the H-R diagram?

13. Compare and contrast sunspots, solar flares, and prominences.

14. How do red shifts support the big bang theory?

15. What are the advantages and disadvantages of using radio telescopes and probes to search for life in the universe?

Thinking Critically

16. What is significant about the 1995 discovery by the *Hubble Space Telescope* of over 1500 galaxies at a distance of more than 10 billion light-years?

17. How do scientists know that black holes exist if these objects don't emit any visible light?

18. Use the autumn star chart in Appendix J to determine which constellation is directly overhead at 8 P.M. on November 21 for an observer in North America.

19. How are radio waves used to detect objects in space?

20. What kinds of reactions produce the energy emitted by stars?

19. Any object at a temperature above absolute zero emits radio waves. The sun, other stars, and even people give off radio waves. These waves can be gathered by the antennae of radio telescopes and then analyzed to determine what type of object is emitting them.

20. Stars produce energy by fusion. Hydrogen is converted into helium in main sequence stars. Helium then fuses to produce heavier elements. As nuclei are fused, mass is converted into energy.

Developing Skills

21. Making and Using Tables Deneb, the sun

22. Making and Using Tables The absolute magnitudes of some nearby objects are relatively low, but their apparent magnitudes are high. For example, the sun is the brightest object as seen from Earth, but its absolute magnitude is dim compared to Betelgeuse, 489 light-years away.

Chapter 24 Review

Developing Skills

If you need help, refer to the **Skill Handbook.**

21. **Making and Using Tables:** Astronomical objects are given numbers to represent their absolute and apparent magnitudes. The lower the number, the greater the object's brightness. What object listed in the table below has the brightest absolute magnitude? What object is the brightest as seen from Earth?
22. **Making and Using Tables:** How does the table below show that apparent magnitude is dependent on both absolute magnitude and distance from an observer?
23. **Concept Mapping:** Make a concept map that shows the evolution of a main sequence star with a mass similar to that of the sun.
24. **Comparing and Contrasting:** Compare and contrast the sun with other stars on the H-R diagram.
25. **Measuring in SI:** The Milky Way Galaxy is 100 000 light-years in diameter. What scale would you use if you were to construct a scale model of the Milky Way with a diameter of 20 cm?

Star Magnitudes

Star	Absolute Magnitude	Apparent Magnitude	Light-Years from Earth
The Sun	4.9	−26.7	0.000 002
Sirius	1.5	−1.5	8.80
Arcturus	−0.3	−0.1	35.86
Alpha Centauri	4.4	0.0	4.34
Betelgeuse	−5.5	0.8	489.0
Deneb	−6.9	1.3	1401.80

Performance Assessment

1. **Model:** Design and construct scale models of a spiral and a barred spiral Milky Way Galaxy. Show the approximate position of the sun in each.
2. **Carrying Out a Strategy and Collecting Data:** Design and carry out an experiment that uses sunspot locations to compare rotational periods of different latitudes of the sun.
3. **Using Math in Science:** Find two distant objects in opposite directions from a single viewing point. Using a protractor and what you know about parallax, determine which object is closer.

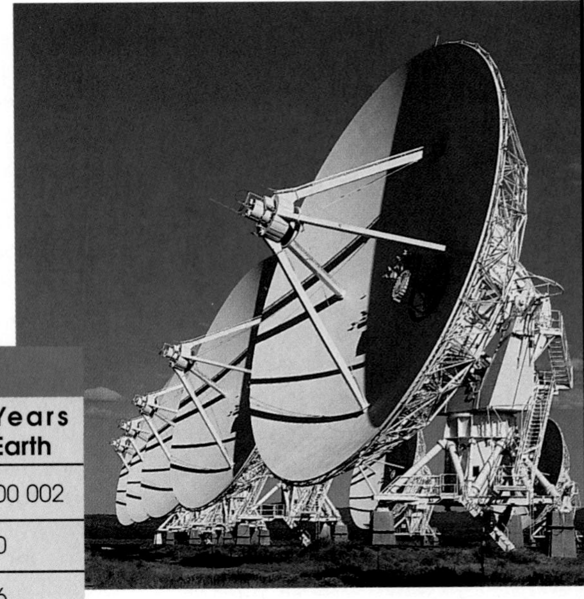

Chapter 24 Review

23. **Concept Mapping** The map should trace the evolution of a star beginning with a nebula. The nebula contracts and fusion begins. The main sequence star fuses hydrogen until its core collapses and its outer surface expands. The giant fuses helium in its core. When it uses up its helium supply, it contracts to form a white dwarf. White dwarfs use up their fuel and die.
24. **Comparing and Contrasting** The sun is an average star in terms of mass, temperature, and its place in its evolutionary cycle. The sun differs from more massive stars in that the stars have higher temperatures and are further along in their evolutionary cycle. Other stars, such as white dwarfs, are hotter than the sun but don't emit as much light.
25. **Measuring in SI** 1 cm = 5000 light-years

Performance Assessment

1. Student models should resemble **Figure 24-19** and a similar structure showing a bar of stars through the nucleus. The sun should be positioned about two-thirds of the way out from the nucleus of the galaxy. Use the Performance Task Assessment List for Model in **PASC,** p. 51. P
2. If sunspots that are farther north or south on the sun are used, students should note that the speed of rotation is slower. The sun rotates faster around its equator than toward its poles. Use the Performance Task Assessment List for Carrying Out a Strategy and Collecting Data in **PASC,** p. 25. P
3. The closer object will appear to move more whenever you observe the object from two different locations. The distance between the two observation points must be the same for both observations. Use the Performance Task Assessment List for Using Math in Science in **PASC,** p. 29. P

Objectives

Interpersonal Students will design and formulate a model of a proposed space colony. L1 **COOP LEARN**

Summary

In this project students will first learn how a team of people with different ideas can work together on one project to bring it to a successful completion. Students will also build a detailed model of a space station based on plans drawn by their team. Students will be required to work in cooperative groups, helping each other achieve success.

Time Required

This project is designed to be worked on throughout Chapters 21, 22, and 23. Students will need a period to brainstorm and decide if their project is to be in orbit near Earth, located on the moon, or located on Mars. The overall design of the model will also be determined in this first period. They will need time outside the class to collect their data concerning what materials they will use and what materials should be located in the actual space colony. They will need one or two periods to finish their designs and to construct the model space colony. To save time, students within cooperative groups could construct modules or parts of the space colony at home and bring them into class where they can be built into the rest of the colony.

Preparation

- Establish cooperative groups of 4 or 5 students.
- Assemble a wide variety of materials that students might use in the construction of their models.

UNIT PROJECT 7

Where? Out There!

What would it be like for humans to colonize space? What would they need to survive far from Earth? What problems might people encounter? These are just a few of the many questions that humans would face if they moved out into near-Earth space, to the moon once again, and on to Mars.

Suppose you were responsible for planning a permanent station for studying both deep space and nearby planets. Would you place this station in near-Earth orbit, on the Moon, or on Mars? What supplies would you need to build the station? How would you get them to the station? As you do this project you will make technical drawings, build a model, and describe your plan to build a space station. You'll also write an instruction manual for how your space station works.

Procedures

1. Conduct a brainstorming session with your group to decide the best location for your space station. Keep in mind your research goals, as outlined above.
2. Next, determine what materials you'd need to transport into space and how you'd get them there. Also decide where people building the station will live while they work on the project. How will your workers get air to breathe and food to eat?

   You'll also need to think about how the space station will get food and air. Will you use the same process that you used during construction, or will you need to use a different process?
3. Write a summary of your decisions and answers. Be certain that you say why you chose the location you did for your space station. Describe the basic form of your station (in pieces or in one large complex), what materials you would need, and how you intend to transport them. Tell where people working on the station will live and how they will get needed supplies such as food and air.
4. After you've finished your report, draw the overall plan of your space station and where each part of the space station will be located. Remember that this is a research station, so you'll need to have an area designed for research and study.

Teaching Strategies

- This project approaches the study of near-Earth space and surface conditions on the moon and Mars by having students design a space colony that would work in these unfamiliar places. It would best fit between Chapters 22 and 23 just after Section 22-3, "Building a Moon Colony." The original planning period, however, could come early in the study of Chapter 21.
- Before dividing the class into cooperative groups, discuss the Freedom space station proposed by NASA. Discuss how sections of the station will be carried into space on the space shuttle and that astronauts will assemble the space station in orbit. Explain how this mission is planned as a multi-national project.
- If students are having problems moving from their drawings to an actual model, suggest possible building materials to use for a space colony.

5. Decide what materials you'll need to construct a model of your space station. Assign each member of your team to work on building a specific part of the space station.
6. Examine your design closely and see what safety features might have to be built in. What hazards might there be in your space station's location? What kinds of things can you build in to help space colonists cope with emergency situations?
7. When you've completed your model and report, prepare a 10–15-minute oral presentation to describe your space station to the class. Tell why you made the choices you did, and what hazards people living in a space station might face. Also describe how your space station design helps make living comfortable for space colonists.

Going Further

To help get people interested in the space station, describe the benefits your space station will have for humans on Earth. Also describe how working on the space station will help humans prepare for future missions farther out into the solar system.

- For students not able to move from a basic plan on paper to a model, have a model airplane in class to demonstrate how a drawing can be used as directions for completion of a model.

Go Further

Suggest that students watch proceedings in Congress on cable television dealing with appropriations of funds for a variety of domestic and foreign programs. Other students may wish to concentrate on methods used by business and industry to promote a specific product. Other students may wish to attend local business or school board meetings that involve appropriating funds for future building plans. Encourage students to speculate on how orbiting space colonies or those on the moon or on Mars could be used as refueling stops for spaceflights deep into the outer solar system. Encourage students to also speculate on how building a space colony on the side of the moon facing away from Earth could help in receiving radio signals from deep space.

References

Constable, George, ed. *Voyage Through the Universe, Spacefarers.* Alexandria, VA: Time-Life Books Inc., 1989.

Hanson, Kevin and Linda Urrutia Scott. "A Design for Life. . . In Space!" *Science Scope,* September 1993, pp. 18-21.

Appendices

Appendix A

International System of Units

The International System (SI) of Units is accepted as the standard for measurement throughout most of the world. Three base units in SI are the meter, kilogram, and second. Frequently used SI units are listed below.

Table A-1

Frequently Used SI Units	
Length	1 millimeter (mm) = 1000 micrometers (μm) 1 centimeter (cm) = 10 millimeters (mm) 1 meter (m) = 100 centimeters (cm) 1 kilometer (km) =1000 meters (m) 1 light-year = 9 460 000 000 000 kilometers (km)
Area	1 square meter (m^2) = 10 000 square centimeters (cm^2) 1 square kilometer (km^2) = 1 000 000 square meters (m^2)
Volume	1 milliliter (mL) = 1 cubic centimeter (cc) (cm^3) 1 liter (L) = 1000 milliliters (mL)
Mass	1 gram (g) = 1000 milligrams (mg) 1 kilogram (kg) = 1000 grams (g) 1 metric ton = 1000 kilograms (kg)
Time	1 s = 1 second

Temperature measurements in SI are often made in degrees Celsius. Celsius temperature is a supplementary unit derived from the base unit kelvin. The Celsius scale (°C) has 100 equal graduations between the freezing temperature (0°C) and the boiling temperature of water (100°C). The following relationship exists between the Celsius and Kelvin temperature scales:

$$K = °C + 273$$

Several other supplementary SI units are listed below.

Table A-2

Supplementary SI Units			
Measurement	**Unit**	**Symbol**	**Expressed in base units**
Energy	Joule	J	$kg \cdot m^2/s^2$ or $N \cdot m$
Force	Newton	N	$kg \cdot m/s^2$
Power	Watt	W	$kg \cdot m^2/s^3$ or J/s
Pressure	Pascal	Pa	$kg/(m \cdot s^2)$ or $N \cdot m$

Appendix B

Table B-1

SI/Metric to English Conversions

	When you want to convert:	Multiply by:	To find:
Length	inches	2.54	centimeters
	centimeters	0.39	inches
	feet	0.30	meters
	meters	3.28	feet
	yards	0.91	meters
	meters	1.09	yards
	miles	1.61	kilometers
	kilometers	0.62	miles
Mass and Weight*	ounces	28.35	grams
	grams	0.04	ounces
	pounds	0.45	kilograms
	kilograms	2.20	pounds
	tons	0.91	tonnes (metric tons)
	tonnes (metric tons)	1.10	tons
	pounds	4.45	newtons
	newtons	0.23	pounds
Volume	cubic inches	16.39	cubic centimeters
	cubic centimeters	0.06	cubic inches
	cubic feet	0.03	cubic meters
	cubic meters	35.31	cubic feet
	liters	1.06	quarts
	liters	0.26	gallons
	gallons	3.78	liters
Area	square inches	6.45	square centimeters
	square centimeters	0.16	square inches
	square feet	0.09	square meters
	square meters	10.76	square feet
	square miles	2.59	square kilometers
	square kilometers	0.39	square miles
	hectares	2.47	acres
	acres	0.40	hectares
Temperature	Fahrenheit	5/9 (°F − 32)	Celsius
	Celsius	9/5 °C + 32	Fahrenheit

*Weight as measured in standard Earth gravity

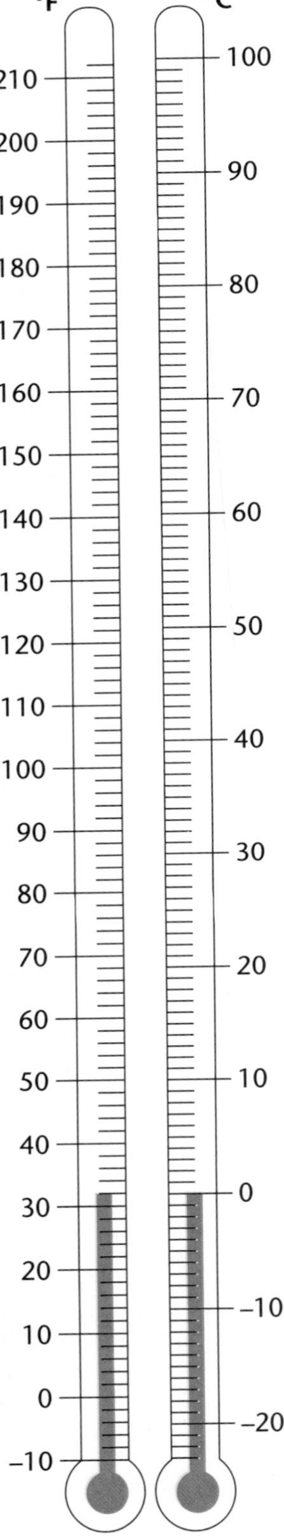

Appendix C

Safety in the Science Classroom

1. Always obtain your teacher's permission to begin an investigation.
2. Study the procedure. If you have questions, ask your teacher. Understand any safety symbols shown on the page.
3. Use the safety equipment provided for you. Goggles and a safety apron should be worn when any investigation calls for using chemicals.
4. Always slant test tubes away from yourself and others when heating them.
5. Never eat or drink in the lab, and never use lab glassware as food or drink containers. Never inhale chemicals. Do not taste any substances or draw any material into a tube with your mouth.
6. If you spill any chemical, wash it off immediately with water. Report the spill immediately to your teacher.
7. Know the location and proper use of the fire extinguisher, safety shower, fire blanket, first aid kit, and fire alarm.
8. Keep materials away from flames. Tie back hair and loose clothing.
9. If a fire should break out in the classroom, or if your clothing should catch fire, smother it with the fire blanket or a coat, or get under a safety shower. **NEVER RUN.**
10. Report any accident or injury, no matter how small, to your teacher.

Follow these procedures as you clean up your work area.

1. Turn off the water and gas. Disconnect electrical devices.
2. Return all materials to their proper places.
3. Dispose of chemicals and other materials as directed by your teacher. Place broken glass and solid substances in the proper containers. Never discard materials in the sink.
4. Clean your work area.
5. Wash your hands thoroughly after working in the laboratory.

Table C-1

First Aid

Injury	Safe response
Burns	Apply cold water. Call your teacher immediately.
Cuts and bruises	Stop any bleeding by applying direct pressure. Cover cuts with a clean dressing. Apply cold compresses to bruises. Call your teacher immediately.
Fainting	Leave the person lying down. Loosen any tight clothing and keep crowds away. Call your teacher immediately.
Foreign matter in eye	Flush with plenty of water. Use eyewash bottle or fountain.
Poisoning	Note the suspected poisoning agent and call your teacher immediately.
Any spills on skin	Flush with large amounts of water or use safety shower. Call your teacher immediately.

Appendix D

Safety Symbols

Table D-1

	**DISPOSAL ALERT** This symbol appears when care must be taken to dispose of materials properly.		**ANIMAL SAFETY** This symbol appears whenever live animals are studied and the safety of the animals and the students must be ensured.
	**BIOLOGICAL HAZARD** This symbol appears when there is danger involving bacteria, fungi, or protists.		**RADIOACTIVE SAFETY** This symbol appears when radioactive materials are used.
	**OPEN FLAME ALERT** This symbol appears when use of an open flame could cause a fire or an explosion.		**CLOTHING PROTECTION SAFETY** This symbol appears when substances used could stain or burn clothing.
	**THERMAL SAFETY** This symbol appears as a reminder to use caution when handling hot objects.		**FIRE SAFETY** This symbol appears when care should be taken around open flames.
	**SHARP OBJECT SAFETY** This symbol appears when a danger of cuts or punctures caused by the use of sharp objects exists.		**EXPLOSION SAFETY** This symbol appears when the misuse of chemicals could cause an explosion.
	**FUME SAFETY** This symbol appears when chemicals or chemical reactions could cause dangerous fumes.		**EYE SAFETY** This symbol appears when a danger to the eyes exists. Safety goggles should be worn when this symbol appears.
	**ELECTRICAL SAFETY** This symbol appears when care should be taken when using electrical equipment.		**POISON SAFETY** This symbol appears when poisonous substances are used.
	**PLANT SAFETY** This symbol appears when poisonous plants or plants with thorns are handled.		**CHEMICAL SAFETY** This symbol appears when chemicals used can cause burns or are poisonous if absorbed through the skin.

Appendix E

Topographic Map Symbols

Primary highway, hard surface
Secondary highway, hard surface
Light-duty road, hard or improved surface
Unimproved road
Railroad: single track and multiple track
Railroads in juxtaposition

Buildings
Schools, church, and cemetery — cem
Buildings (barn, warehouse, etc.)
Wells other than water (labeled as to type) — oil, gas
Tanks: oil, water, etc. (labeled only if water) — water
Located or landmark object; windmill
Open pit, mine, or quarry; prospect

Marsh (swamp)
Wooded marsh
Woods or brushwood
Vineyard
Land subject to controlled inundation
Submerged marsh
Mangrove
Orchard
Scrub
Urban area

Spot elevation — ×7369
Water elevation — 670

Index contour
Supplementary contour
Intermediate contour
Depression contours

Boundaries: National
State
County, parish, municipal
Civil township, precinct, town, barrio
Incorporated city, village, town, hamlet
Reservation, National or State
Small park, cemetery, airport, etc.
Land grant
Township or range line, United States land survey
Township or range line, approximate location

Perennial streams
Elevated aqueduct
Water well and spring
Small rapids
Large rapids
Intermittent lake
Intermittent streams
Aqueduct tunnel
Glacier
Small falls
Large falls
Dry lake bed

Appendix F

Periodic Table of the Elements

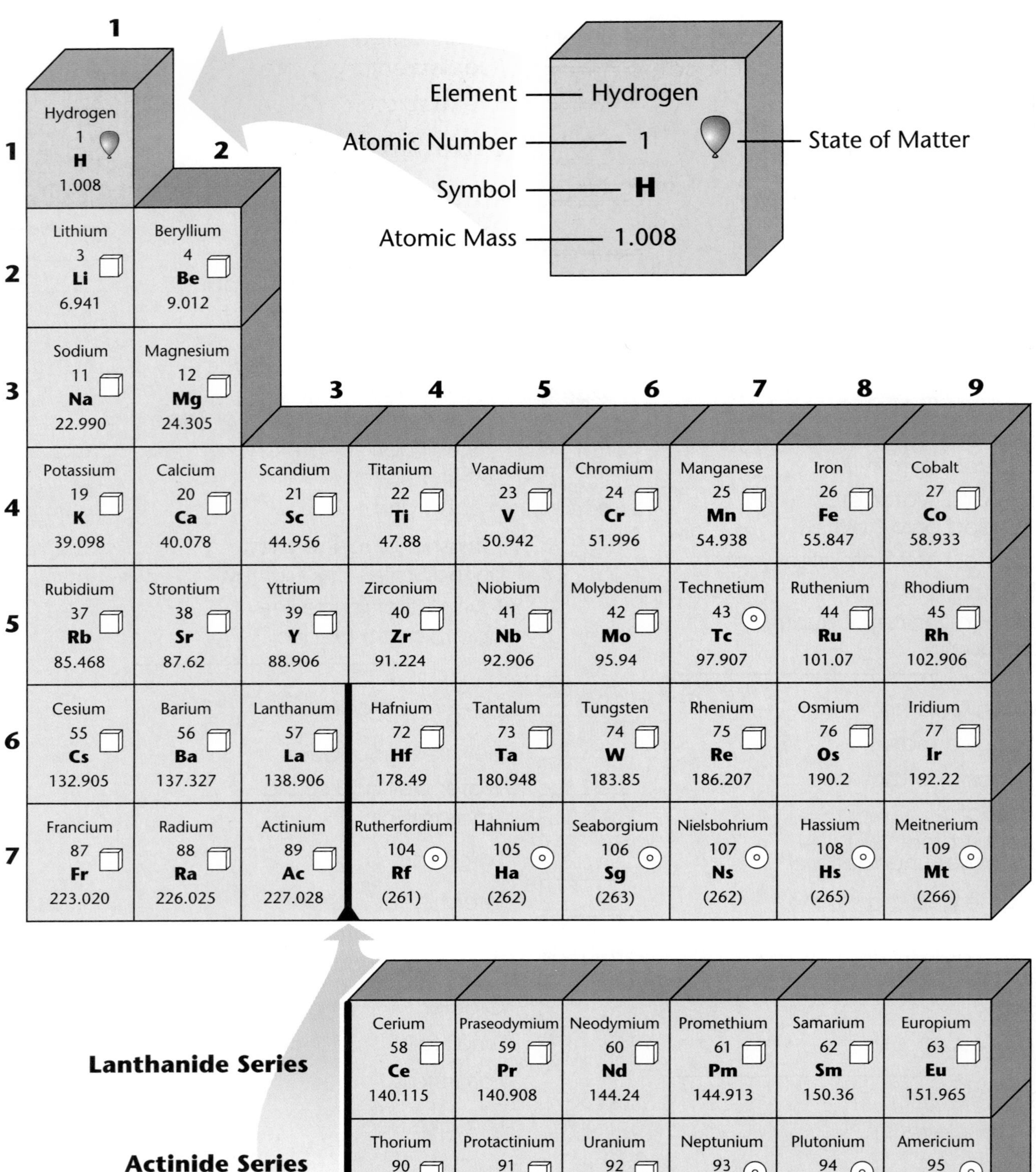

	1	2	3	4	5	6	7	8	9
1	Hydrogen 1 **H** 1.008								
2	Lithium 3 **Li** 6.941	Beryllium 4 **Be** 9.012							
3	Sodium 11 **Na** 22.990	Magnesium 12 **Mg** 24.305							
4	Potassium 19 **K** 39.098	Calcium 20 **Ca** 40.078	Scandium 21 **Sc** 44.956	Titanium 22 **Ti** 47.88	Vanadium 23 **V** 50.942	Chromium 24 **Cr** 51.996	Manganese 25 **Mn** 54.938	Iron 26 **Fe** 55.847	Cobalt 27 **Co** 58.933
5	Rubidium 37 **Rb** 85.468	Strontium 38 **Sr** 87.62	Yttrium 39 **Y** 88.906	Zirconium 40 **Zr** 91.224	Niobium 41 **Nb** 92.906	Molybdenum 42 **Mo** 95.94	Technetium 43 **Tc** 97.907	Ruthenium 44 **Ru** 101.07	Rhodium 45 **Rh** 102.906
6	Cesium 55 **Cs** 132.905	Barium 56 **Ba** 137.327	Lanthanum 57 **La** 138.906	Hafnium 72 **Hf** 178.49	Tantalum 73 **Ta** 180.948	Tungsten 74 **W** 183.85	Rhenium 75 **Re** 186.207	Osmium 76 **Os** 190.2	Iridium 77 **Ir** 192.22
7	Francium 87 **Fr** 223.020	Radium 88 **Ra** 226.025	Actinium 89 **Ac** 227.028	Rutherfordium 104 **Rf** (261)	Hahnium 105 **Ha** (262)	Seaborgium 106 **Sg** (263)	Nielsbohrium 107 **Ns** (262)	Hassium 108 **Hs** (265)	Meitnerium 109 **Mt** (266)

Lanthanide Series	Cerium 58 **Ce** 140.115	Praseodymium 59 **Pr** 140.908	Neodymium 60 **Nd** 144.24	Promethium 61 **Pm** 144.913	Samarium 62 **Sm** 150.36	Europium 63 **Eu** 151.965
Actinide Series	Thorium 90 **Th** 232.038	Protactinium 91 **Pa** 231.036	Uranium 92 **U** 238.029	Neptunium 93 **Np** 237.048	Plutonium 94 **Pu** 244.064	Americium 95 **Am** 243.061

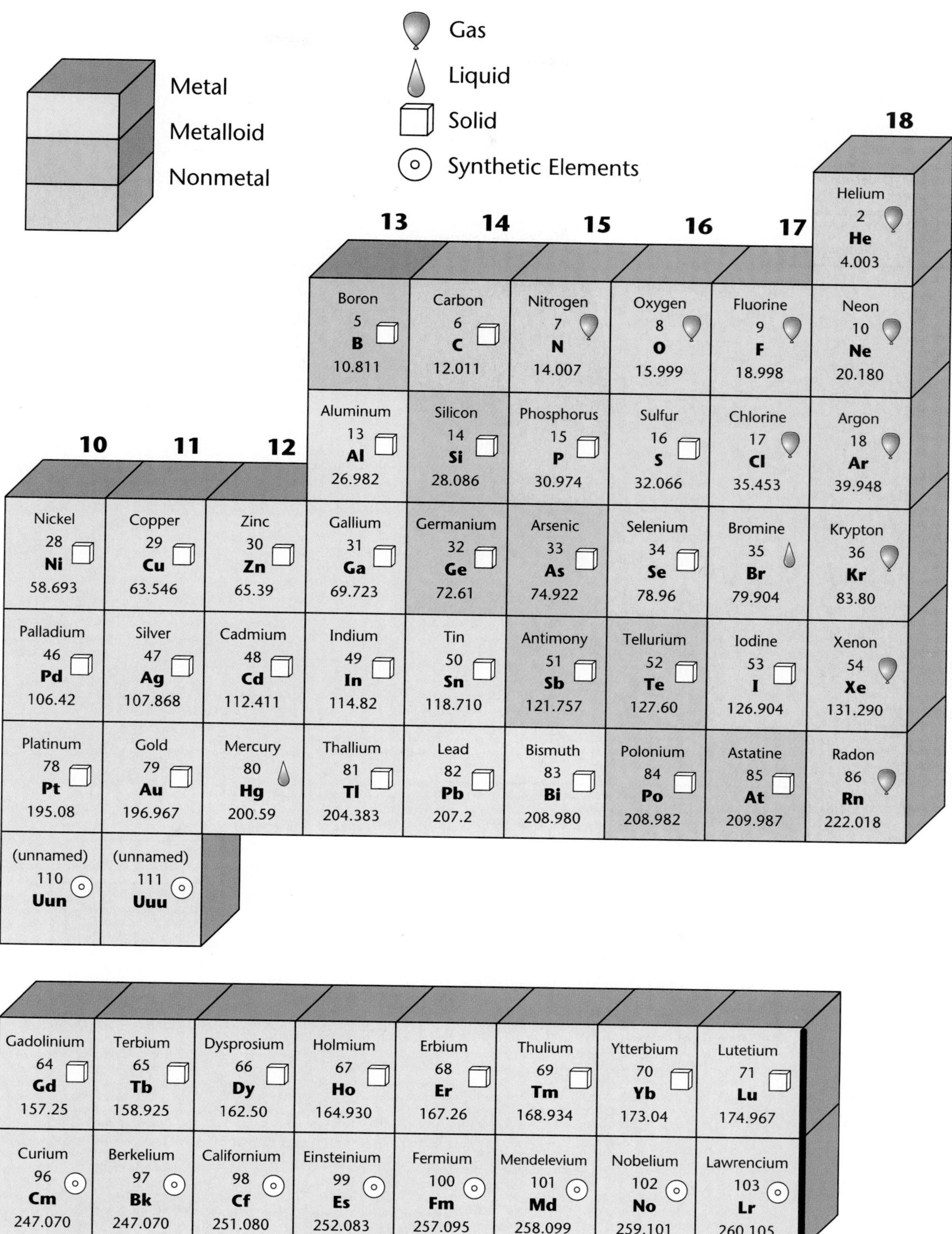

Metal
Metalloid
Nonmetal
Gas
Liquid
Solid
Synthetic Elements
18
13
14
15
16
17
Helium 2 He 4.003
Boron 5 B 10.811
Carbon 6 C 12.011
Nitrogen 7 N 14.007
Oxygen 8 O 15.999
Fluorine 9 F 18.998
Neon 10 Ne 20.180
10
11
12
Aluminum 13 Al 26.982
Silicon 14 Si 28.086
Phosphorus 15 P 30.974
Sulfur 16 S 32.066
Chlorine 17 Cl 35.453
Argon 18 Ar 39.948
Nickel 28 Ni 58.693
Copper 29 Cu 63.546
Zinc 30 Zn 65.39
Gallium 31 Ga 69.723
Germanium 32 Ge 72.61
Arsenic 33 As 74.922
Selenium 34 Se 78.96
Bromine 35 Br 79.904
Krypton 36 Kr 83.80
Palladium 46 Pd 106.42
Silver 47 Ag 107.868
Cadmium 48 Cd 112.411
Indium 49 In 114.82
Tin 50 Sn 118.710
Antimony 51 Sb 121.757
Tellurium 52 Te 127.60
Iodine 53 I 126.904
Xenon 54 Xe 131.290
Platinum 78 Pt 195.08
Gold 79 Au 196.967
Mercury 80 Hg 200.59
Thallium 81 Tl 204.383
Lead 82 Pb 207.2
Bismuth 83 Bi 208.980
Polonium 84 Po 208.982
Astatine 85 At 209.987
Radon 86 Rn 222.018
(unnamed) 110 Uun
(unnamed) 111 Uuu
Gadolinium 64 Gd 157.25
Terbium 65 Tb 158.925
Dysprosium 66 Dy 162.50
Holmium 67 Ho 164.930
Erbium 68 Er 167.26
Thulium 69 Tm 168.934
Ytterbium 70 Yb 173.04
Lutetium 71 Lu 174.967
Curium 96 Cm 247.070
Berkelium 97 Bk 247.070
Californium 98 Cf 251.080
Einsteinium 99 Es 252.083
Fermium 100 Fm 257.095
Mendelevium 101 Md 258.099
Nobelium 102 No 259.101
Lawrencium 103 Lr 260.105

Appendix G

THE WORLD

- ● World's most populous cities
- ——— International boundary
- - - - - Disputed boundary
- ········ Undefined boundary

0 1000 2000 Miles

0 1000 2000 Kilometers

Projection: Robinson

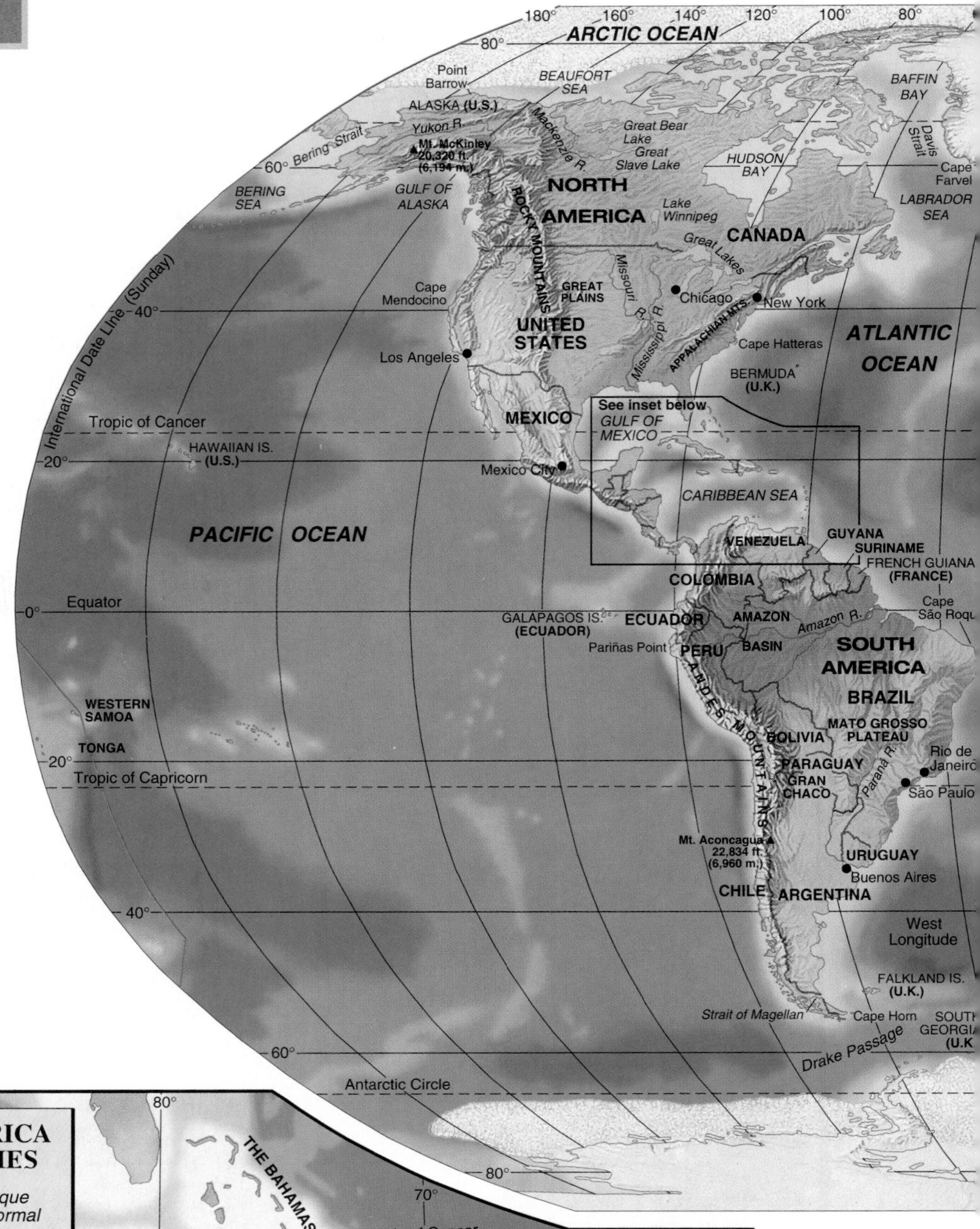

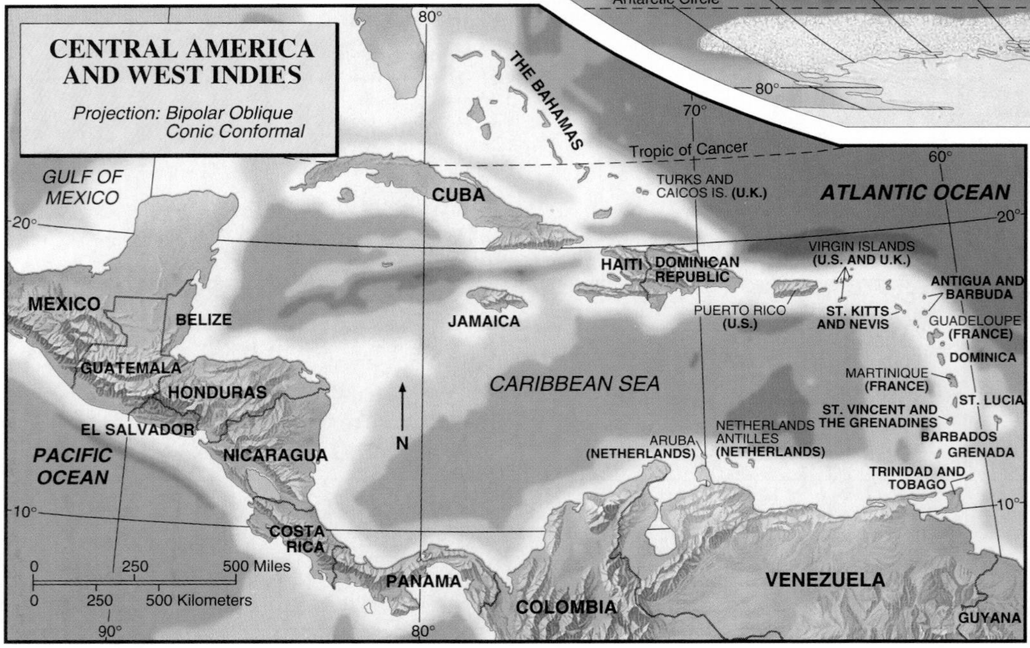

CENTRAL AMERICA AND WEST INDIES

Projection: Bipolar Oblique Conic Conformal

0 250 500 Miles

0 250 500 Kilometers

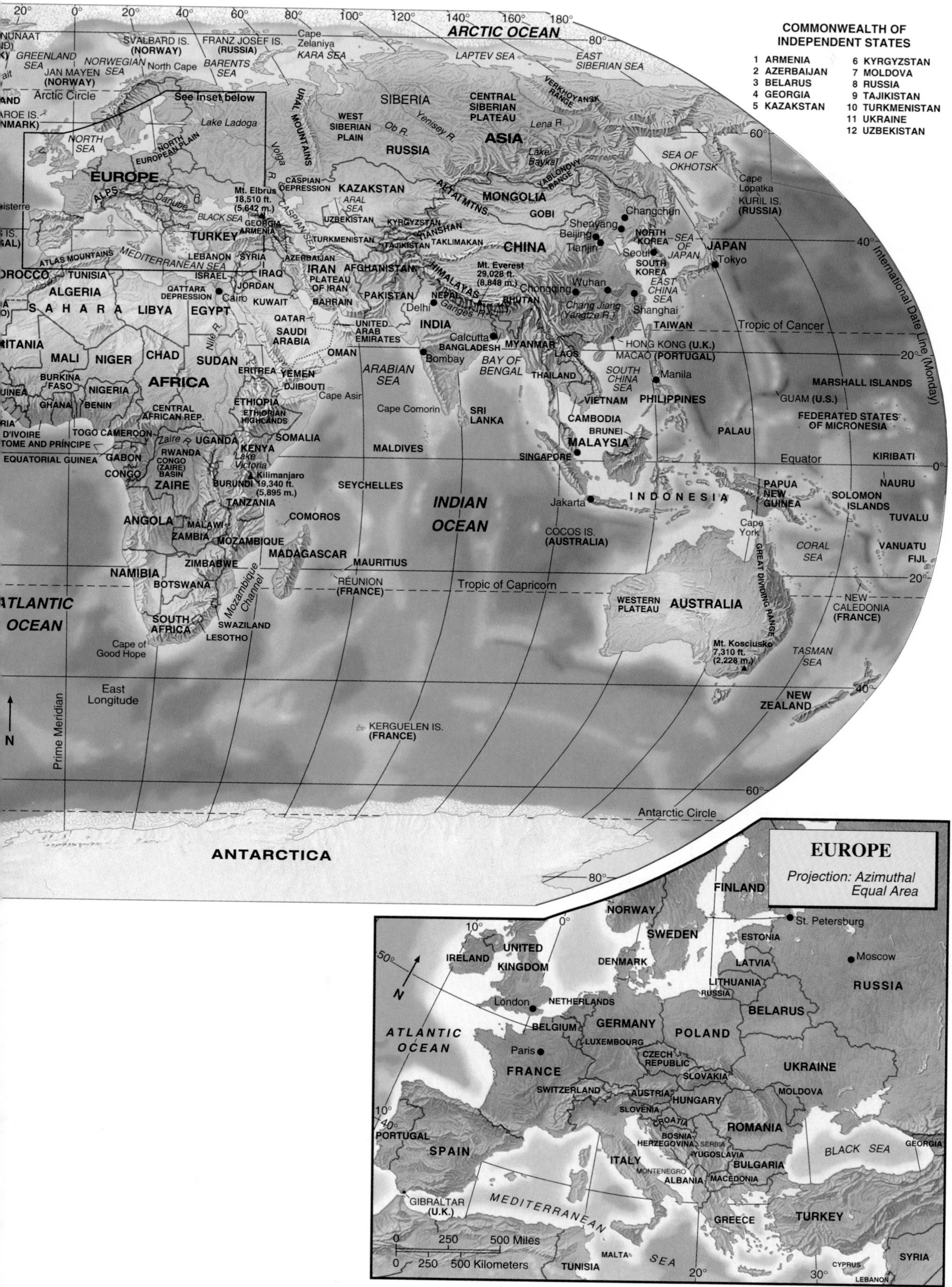
COMMONWEALTH OF INDEPENDENT STATES
1 ARMENIA
2 AZERBAIJAN
3 BELARUS
4 GEORGIA
5 KAZAKSTAN
6 KYRGYZSTAN
7 MOLDOVA
8 RUSSIA
9 TAJIKISTAN
10 TURKMENISTAN
11 UKRAINE
12 UZBEKISTAN
ARCTIC OCEAN
SVALBARD IS. (NORWAY)
FRANZ JOSEF IS. (RUSSIA)
Cape Zelaniya
KARA SEA
LAPTEV SEA
EAST SIBERIAN SEA
GREENLAND SEA
NORWEGIAN SEA
JAN MAYEN (NORWAY)
North Cape
BARENTS SEA
Arctic Circle
See inset below
SIBERIA
CENTRAL SIBERIAN PLATEAU
VERKHOYANSK RANGE
WEST SIBERIAN PLAIN
URAL MOUNTAINS
Lake Ladoga
Ob R.
Yenisey R.
Lena R.
ASIA
RUSSIA
NORTH SEA
NORTH EUROPEAN PLAIN
EUROPE
ALPS
Danube
Volga R.
CASPIAN DEPRESSION
Mt. Elbrus 18,510 ft. (5,642 m.)
KAZAKSTAN
ARAL SEA
ALTAI MTNS.
MONGOLIA
GOBI
Lake Baykal
YABLONOVY RANGE
SEA OF OKHOTSK
Cape Lopatka
KURIL IS. (RUSSIA)
BLACK SEA
GEORGIA
ARMENIA
CASPIAN SEA
UZBEKISTAN
KYRGYZSTAN
TIANSHAN
TURKMENISTAN
TAJIKISTAN
TAKLIMAKAN
CHINA
Changchun
Shenyang
Beijing
Tianjin
NORTH KOREA
SEA OF JAPAN
Seoul
SOUTH KOREA
JAPAN
Tokyo
TURKEY
AZERBAIJAN
ATLAS MOUNTAINS
MEDITERRANEAN SEA
LEBANON
SYRIA
IRAQ
IRAN
PLATEAU OF IRAN
AFGHANISTAN
HIMALAYAS
Mt. Everest 29,028 ft. (8,848 m.)
TUNISIA
ALGERIA
ISRAEL
JORDAN
QATTARA DEPRESSION
Cairo
KUWAIT
BAHRAIN
PAKISTAN
NEPAL
BHUTAN
Chongqing
Wuhan
EAST CHINA SEA
Shanghai
Chang Jiang (Yangtze R.)
Ganges R.
Delhi
SAHARA
LIBYA
EGYPT
QATAR
SAUDI ARABIA
UNITED ARAB EMIRATES
INDIA
Calcutta
BANGLADESH
MYANMAR
LAOS
TAIWAN
Tropic of Cancer
HONG KONG (U.K.)
MACAO (PORTUGAL)
Nile R.
MALI
NIGER
CHAD
SUDAN
OMAN
Bombay
ERITREA
YEMEN
ARABIAN SEA
BAY OF BENGAL
THAILAND
SOUTH CHINA SEA
Manila
BURKINA FASO
NIGERIA
AFRICA
DJIBOUTI
Cape Asir
GHANA
BENIN
ETHIOPIA
ETHIOPIAN HIGHLANDS
CENTRAL AFRICAN REP.
Cape Comorin
SRI LANKA
VIETNAM
PHILIPPINES
MARSHALL ISLANDS
GUAM (U.S.)
FEDERATED STATES OF MICRONESIA
CAMBODIA
BRUNEI
PALAU
TOGO
CAMEROON
UGANDA
SOMALIA
MALAYSIA
TOME AND PRÍNCIPE
Zaire R.
RWANDA
KENYA
MALDIVES
EQUATORIAL GUINEA
GABON
CONGO
(ZAIRE) BASIN
Lake Victoria
SINGAPORE
Equator
KIRIBATI
ZAIRE
BURUNDI
Kilimanjaro 19,340 ft. (5,895 m.)
SEYCHELLES
INDONESIA
PAPUA NEW GUINEA
NAURU
SOLOMON ISLANDS
TANZANIA
INDIAN OCEAN
Jakarta
TUVALU
ANGOLA
MALAWI
COMOROS
ZAMBIA
MOZAMBIQUE
COCOS IS. (AUSTRALIA)
Cape York
CORAL SEA
VANUATU
FIJI
MADAGASCAR
ZIMBABWE
MAURITIUS
NAMIBIA
GREAT DIVIDING RANGE
BOTSWANA
RÉUNION (FRANCE)
Tropic of Capricorn
ATLANTIC OCEAN
Mozambique Channel
WESTERN PLATEAU
AUSTRALIA
NEW CALEDONIA (FRANCE)
SOUTH AFRICA
SWAZILAND
LESOTHO
Cape of Good Hope
Mt. Kosciusko 7,310 ft. (2,228 m.)
TASMAN SEA
East Longitude
N
Prime Meridian
NEW ZEALAND
KERGUELEN IS. (FRANCE)
International Date Line (Monday)
Antarctic Circle
ANTARCTICA
EUROPE
Projection: Azimuthal Equal Area
FINLAND
NORWAY
SWEDEN
St. Petersburg
ESTONIA
IRELAND
UNITED KINGDOM
DENMARK
LATVIA
Moscow
LITHUANIA
RUSSIA
London
NETHERLANDS
BELARUS
ATLANTIC OCEAN
BELGIUM
GERMANY
POLAND
LUXEMBOURG
Paris
CZECH REPUBLIC
FRANCE
SLOVAKIA
UKRAINE
SWITZERLAND
AUSTRIA
MOLDOVA
SLOVENIA
HUNGARY
CROATIA
ROMANIA
BOSNIA-HERZEGOVINA
SERBIA
PORTUGAL
SPAIN
YUGOSLAVIA
BLACK SEA
GEORGIA
ITALY
MONTENEGRO
BULGARIA
ALBANIA
MACEDONIA
GIBRALTAR (U.K.)
MEDITERRANEAN SEA
GREECE
TURKEY
0 250 500 Miles
0 250 500 Kilometers
TUNISIA
MALTA
CYPRUS
SYRIA
LEBANON

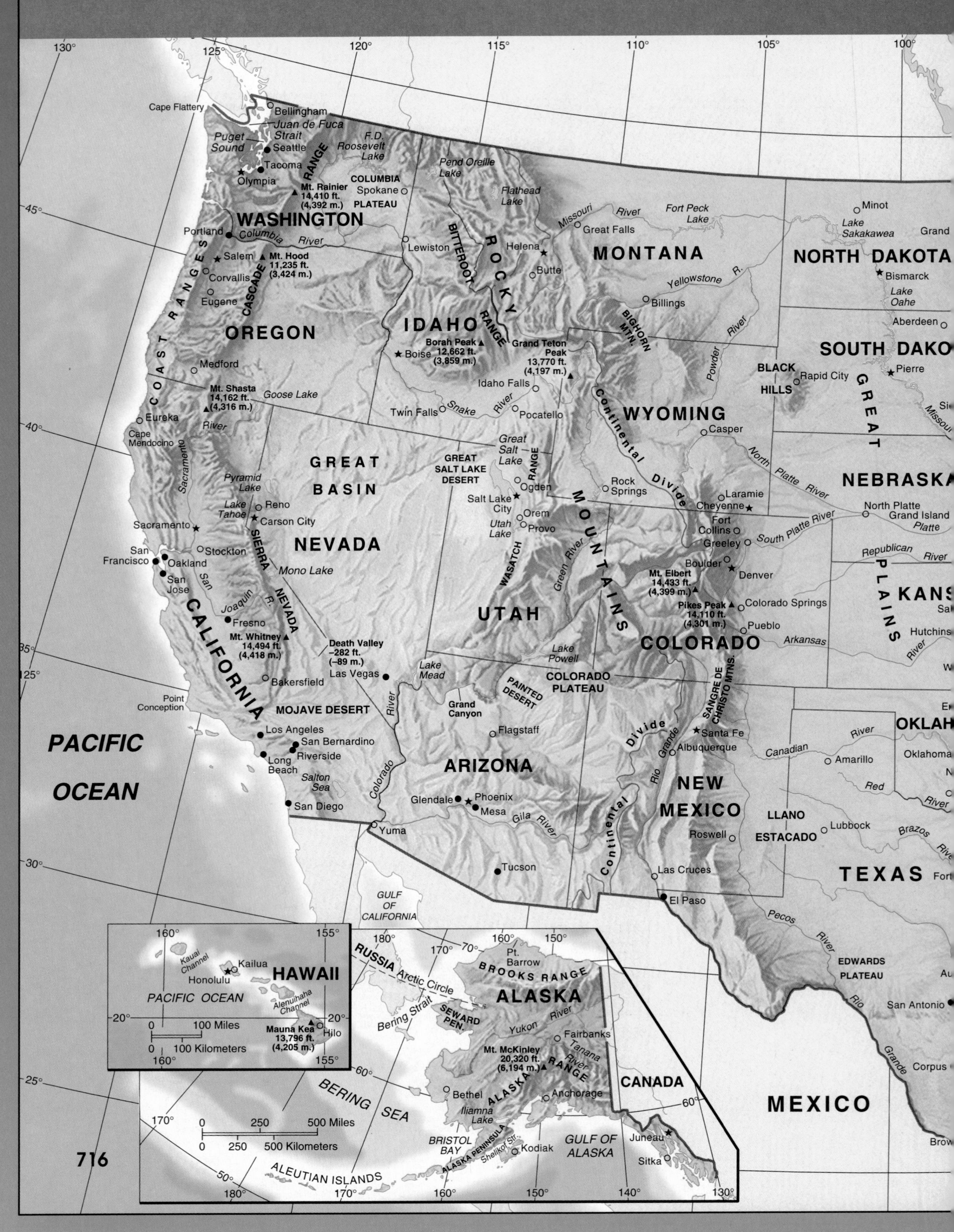

PACIFIC OCEAN
WASHINGTON
OREGON
IDAHO
MONTANA
WYOMING
NORTH DAKOTA
SOUTH DAKO
NEBRASKA
KANS
OKLAH
TEXAS
NEVADA
UTAH
COLORADO
CALIFORNIA
ARIZONA
NEW MEXICO
MEXICO
CANADA
Cape Flattery
Bellingham
Juan de Fuca Strait
Puget Sound
Seattle
Tacoma
Olympia
F.D. Roosevelt Lake
CASCADE RANGE
Mt. Rainier 14,410 ft. (4,392 m.)
COLUMBIA PLATEAU
Spokane
Portland
Columbia River
Salem
Mt. Hood 11,235 ft. (3,424 m.)
Corvallis
Eugene
COAST RANGES
Medford
Lewiston
Pend Oreille Lake
Flathead Lake
BITTERROOT RANGE
ROCKY MOUNTAINS
Helena
Butte
Missouri River
Great Falls
Fort Peck Lake
Yellowstone R.
Billings
BIGHORN MTN.
Minot
Lake Sakakawea
Grand
Bismarck
Lake Oahe
Aberdeen
Pierre
Rapid City
BLACK HILLS
GREAT PLAINS
Borah Peak 12,662 ft. (3,859 m.)
Boise
Grand Teton Peak 13,770 ft. (4,197 m.)
Idaho Falls
Twin Falls
Snake River
Pocatello
Powder River
Continental Divide
Casper
North Platte River
Mt. Shasta 14,162 ft. (4,316 m.)
Goose Lake
Eureka
Cape Mendocino
Sacramento River
GREAT BASIN
GREAT SALT LAKE DESERT
Great Salt Lake
RANGE
Ogden
Salt Lake City
Rock Springs
Laramie
Cheyenne
Fort Collins
Greeley
South Platte River
North Platte
Grand Island
Platte
Pyramid Lake
Lake Tahoe
Reno
Carson City
Sacramento
San Francisco
Oakland
San Jose
Stockton
SIERRA NEVADA
Mono Lake
San Joaquin R.
Orem
Provo
Utah Lake
WASATCH
Green River
Boulder
Denver
Republican River
Mt. Elbert 14,433 ft. (4,399 m.)
Pikes Peak 14,110 ft. (4,301 m.)
Colorado Springs
Pueblo
Arkansas
Hutchins
Fresno
Mt. Whitney 14,494 ft. (4,418 m.)
Death Valley –282 ft. (–89 m.)
Las Vegas
Lake Mead
Lake Powell
COLORADO PLATEAU
PAINTED DESERT
SANGRE DE CHRISTO MTNS.
Bakersfield
Point Conception
MOJAVE DESERT
Grand Canyon
Flagstaff
Santa Fe
Albuquerque
Rio Grande
Canadian
Amarillo
Oklahoma
Los Angeles
San Bernardino
Riverside
Long Beach
Salton Sea
San Diego
Colorado River
Glendale
Phoenix
Mesa
Gila River
Yuma
LLANO ESTACADO
Lubbock
Roswell
Red River
Brazos
Tucson
Las Cruces
El Paso
GULF OF CALIFORNIA
Pecos River
EDWARDS PLATEAU
San Antonio
Corpus
Brow
Fort
130°
125°
120°
115°
110°
105°
100°
45°
40°
35°
30°
25°
HAWAII
Kauai Channel
Kailua
Honolulu
PACIFIC OCEAN
Alenuihaha Channel
Mauna Kea 13,796 ft. (4,205 m.)
Hilo
0 100 Miles
0 100 Kilometers
160°
155°
20°
RUSSIA
Arctic Circle
Pt. Barrow
BROOKS RANGE
ALASKA
Bering Strait
SEWARD PEN.
Yukon River
Fairbanks
Tanana River
Mt. McKinley 20,320 ft. (6,194 m.)
ALASKA RANGE
Bethel
Anchorage
BERING SEA
Iliamna Lake
BRISTOL BAY
ALASKA PENINSULA
Shelikof Str.
Kodiak
GULF OF ALASKA
Juneau
Sitka
ALEUTIAN ISLANDS
0 250 500 Miles
0 250 500 Kilometers
180°
170°
160°
150°
140°
130°
70°
60°
50°

Appendix H

UNITED STATES
National capital
State capital
Major city
International boundary
State boundary
0 150 300 Miles
0 150 300 Kilometers
Projection: Albers Equal Area
CANADA
ATLANTIC OCEAN
GULF OF MEXICO
THE BAHAMAS
Straits of Florida
MAINE
N.H.
VT.
MASS.
R.I.
CONN.
NEW YORK
N.J.
PENNSYLVANIA
DEL.
MD.
D.C.
VIRGINIA
WEST VIRGINIA
NORTH CAROLINA
SOUTH CAROLINA
GEORGIA
FLORIDA
ALABAMA
MISSISSIPPI
LOUISIANA
ARKANSAS
TENNESSEE
KENTUCKY
OHIO
INDIANA
ILLINOIS
MICHIGAN
WISCONSIN
IOWA
MISSOURI
MINNESOTA
CENTRAL LOWLAND
OZARK PLATEAU
APPALACHIAN MOUNTAINS
CUMBERLAND PLATEAU
COASTAL PLAIN
ADIRONDACK MTNS.
Mt. Washington 6,288 ft. (1,905 m.)
Mt. Mitchell 6,684 ft. (2,037 m.)
Lake Superior
Lake Michigan
Lake Huron
Lake Erie
Lake Ontario
Lake Champlain
Lake of the Woods
Red Lake
Moosehead Lake
St. Lawrence River
Hudson R.
Susquehanna River
Mississippi River
Ohio River
Wabash R.
Cumberland River
Tennessee R.
Roanoke River
Chattahoochee R.
Alabama R.
Niagara Falls
CHESAPEAKE BAY
DELAWARE BAY
Cape Cod
Cape Hatteras
Cape Canaveral
Cape Sable
Lake Okeechobee
Lake Pontchartrain
Toledo Bend Res.
Harry S. Truman Res.
Lake Eufaula
R.S. Kerr Res.
Sam Rayburn Reservoir
N

Appendix I

Solar System Information

Planet	Mercury	Venus	Earth	Mars	Jupiter	Saturn	Uranus	Neptune	Pluto
Diameter (km)	4878	12 104	12 756	6794	142 796	120 660	51 118	49 528	2290
Diameter (E = 1.0)*	0.38	0.95	1.00	0.53	11.19	9.46	4.01	3.88	0.18
Mass (E = 1.0)*	0.06	0.82	1.00	0.11	317.83	95.15	14.54	17.23	0.002
Density (g/cm^3)	5.42	5.24	5.50	3.94	1.31	0.70	1.30	1.66	2.03
Period of Rotation days	58	243	00	00	00	00	00	00	06
hours	15	00	23	24	09	10	17	16	09
minutes	28	14_R	56	37	55	39	14_R	03	17
R = retrograde									
Surface gravity (E = 1.0)*	0.38	0.90	1.00	0.38	2.53	1.07	0.92	1.12	0.06
Average distance to sun (AU)	0.387	0.723	1.000	1.524	5.203	9.529	19.191	30.061	39.529
Period of revolution	87.97d	224.70d	365.26d	686.98d	11.86y	29.46y	84.04y	164.79y	248.53y
Eccentricity of orbit	0.206	0.007	0.017	0.093	0.048	0.056	0.046	0.010	0.248
Average orbital speed (km/s)	47.89	35.03	29.79	24.13	13.06	9.64	6.81	5.43	4.74
Number of known satellites	0	0	1	2	16	18	15	8	1
Known rings	0	0	0	0	1	thou-sands	11	4	0

*Earth = 1.0

Appendix J

Table of Relative Humidity

Relative Humidity %

Dry Bulb Temperature	Dry Bulb Temperature Minus Wet Bulb Temperature, °C									
	1	2	3	4	5	6	7	8	9	10
0°C	81	64	46	29	13					
1°C	83	66	49	33	18					
2°C	84	68	52	37	22	7				
3°C	84	69	55	40	25	12				
4°C	85	71	57	43	29	16				
5°C	85	72	58	45	32	20				
6°C	86	73	60	48	35	24	11			
7°C	86	74	61	49	38	26	15			
8°C	87	75	63	51	40	29	19	8		
9°C	87	76	65	53	42	32	21	12		
10°C	88	77	66	55	44	34	24	15	6	
11°C	89	78	67	56	46	36	27	18	9	
12°C	89	78	68	58	48	39	29	21	12	
13°C	89	79	69	59	50	41	32	22	15	7
14°C	90	79	70	60	51	42	34	26	18	10
15°C	90	80	71	61	53	44	36	27	20	13
16°C	90	81	71	63	54	46	38	30	23	15
17°C	90	81	72	64	55	47	40	32	25	18
18°C	91	82	73	65	57	49	41	34	27	20
19°C	91	82	74	65	58	50	43	36	29	22
20°C	91	83	74	66	59	51	44	37	31	24
21°C	91	83	75	67	60	53	46	39	32	26
22°C	92	83	76	68	61	54	47	40	34	28
23°C	92	84	76	69	62	55	48	42	36	30
24°C	92	84	77	69	62	56	49	43	37	31
25°C	92	84	77	70	63	57	50	44	39	33
26°C	92	85	78	71	64	58	51	46	40	34
27°C	92	85	78	71	65	58	52	47	41	36
28°C	93	85	78	72	65	59	53	48	42	37
29°C	93	86	79	72	66	60	54	49	43	38
30°C	93	86	79	73	67	61	55	50	44	39
31°C	93	86	80	73	67	62	56	50	45	40
32°C	93	86	80	74	68	62	57	51	46	41

Appendix K

Star Charts

Shown here are star charts for viewing stars in the Northern Hemisphere during the four different seasons. These charts are drawn from the night sky at about 35° North Latitude, but they can be used for most locations in the Northern Hemisphere. The lines on the charts outline major constellations. The dense band of stars is the Milky Way. To use, hold the chart vertically, with the direction you are facing at the bottom of the map.

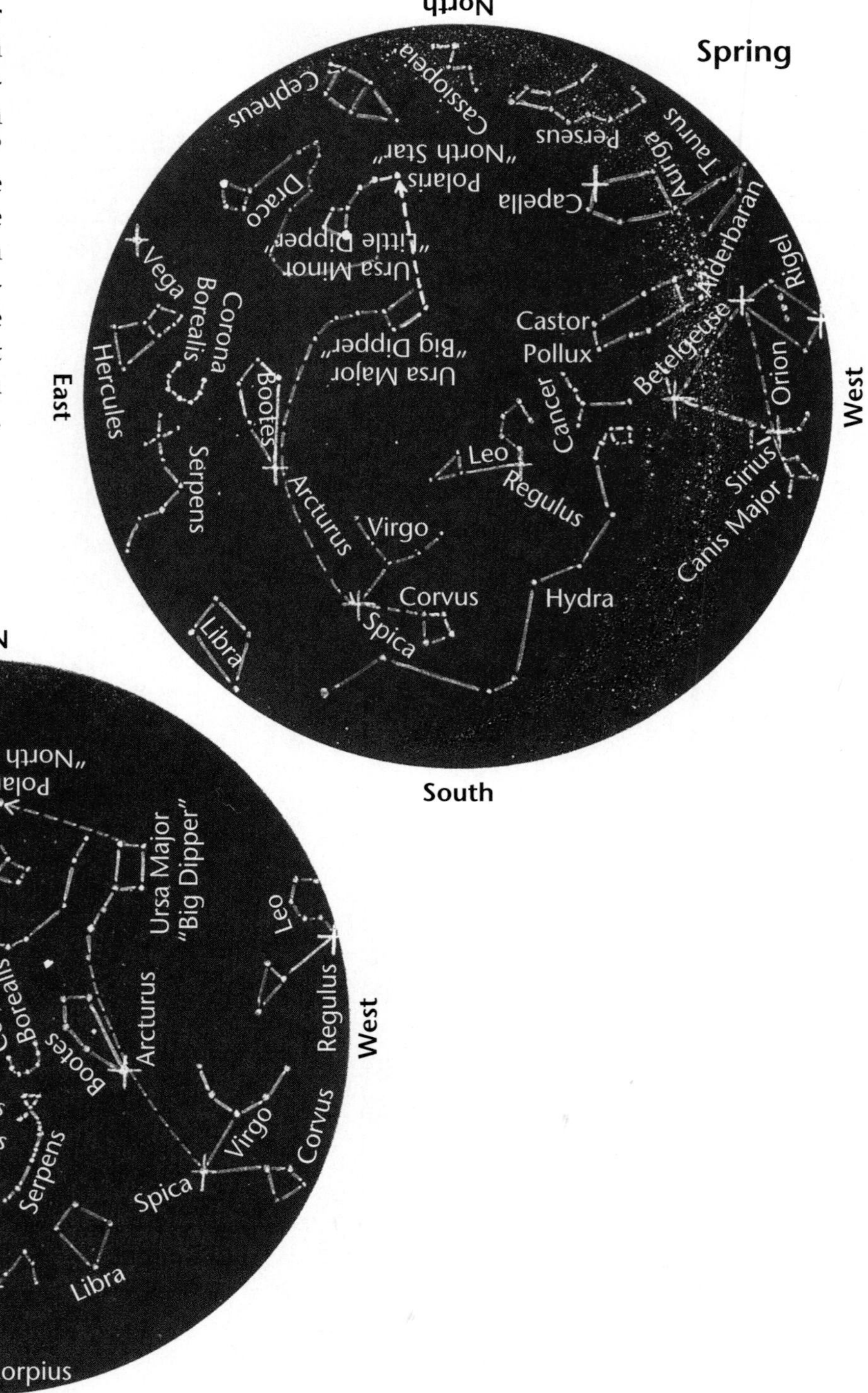

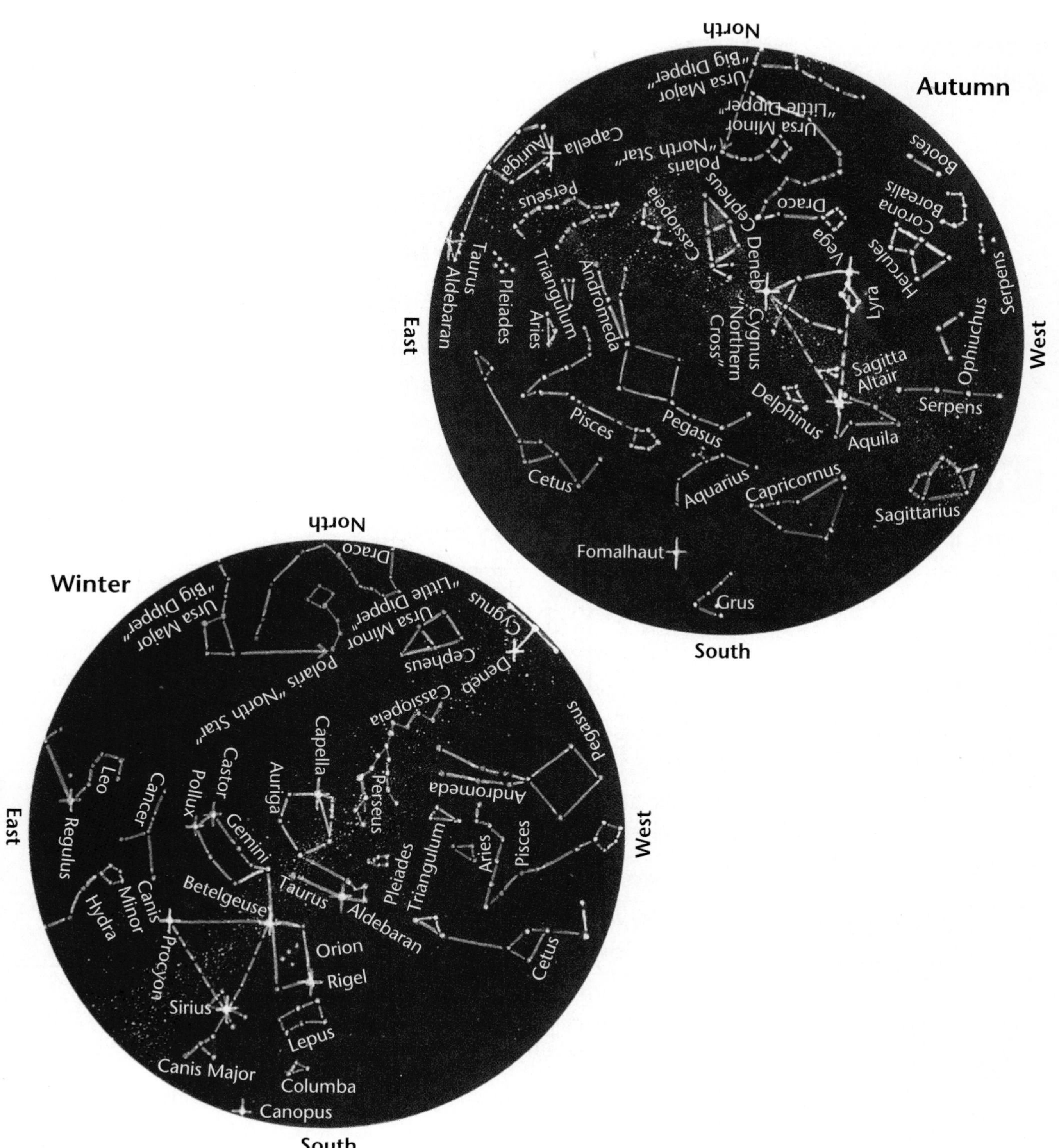
Autumn
North
South
East
West
Ursa Major
"Big Dipper"
Ursa Minor
"Little Dipper"
Polaris
"North Star"
Capella
Auriga
Perseus
Cepheus
Cassiopeia
Draco
Bootes
Corona Borealis
Hercules
Vega
Deneb
Lyra
Serpens
Ophiuchus
Taurus
Aldebaran
Pleiades
Triangulum
Aries
Andromeda
Cygnus
"Northern Cross"
Sagitta
Altair
Delphinus
Aquila
Pegasus
Pisces
Cetus
Aquarius
Capricornus
Sagittarius
Fomalhaut
Grus
Winter
North
South
East
West
Draco
Ursa Major
"Big Dipper"
Ursa Minor
"Little Dipper"
Cygnus
Polaris "North Star"
Cepheus
Deneb
Cassiopeia
Pegasus
Capella
Castor
Pollux
Leo
Cancer
Auriga
Perseus
Andromeda
Regulus
Gemini
Pleiades
Triangulum
Aries
Pisces
Canis Minor
Betelgeuse
Taurus
Aldebaran
Hydra
Procyon
Orion
Rigel
Cetus
Sirius
Lepus
Canis Major
Columba
Canopus

Appendix L

Weather Map Symbols

Sample Plotted Report at Each Station

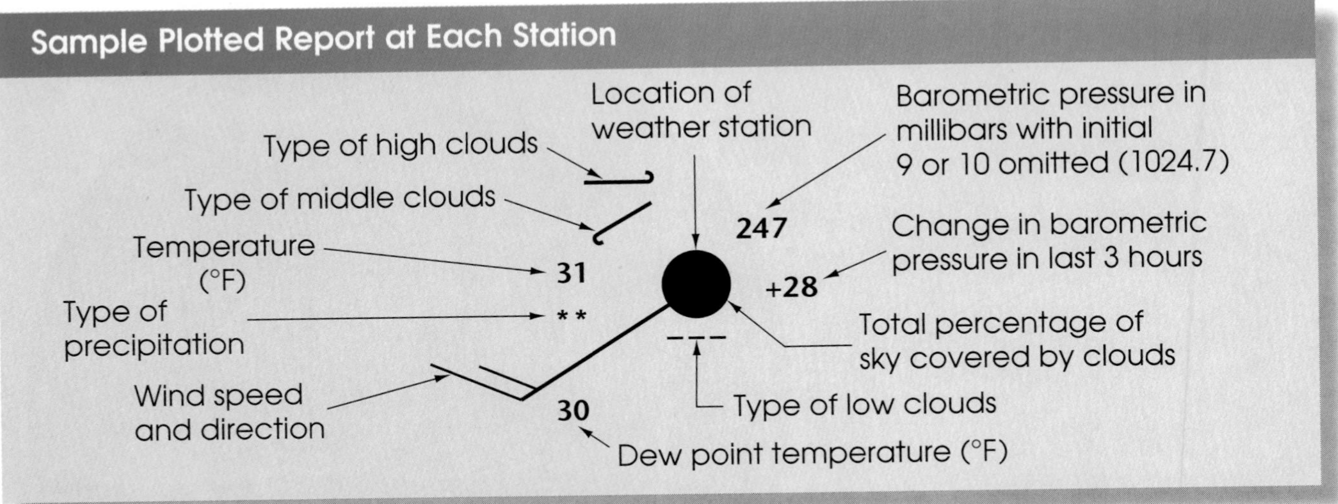

Symbols Used in Plotting Report

Precipitation	Wind speed and direction	Sky coverage	Some types of high clouds
Fog	0 calm	No cover	Scattered cirrus
Snow	1–2 knots	1/10 or less	Dense cirrus in patches
Rain	3–7 knots	2/10 to 3/10	Veil of cirrus covering entire sky
Thunderstorm	8–12 knots	4/10	Cirrus not covering entire sky
Drizzle	13–17 knots	1/2	
Showers	18–22 knots	6/10	
	23–27 knots	7/10	
	48–52 knots	Overcast with openings	
	1 knot = 1.852 km/h	Complete overcast	

Some types of middle clouds	Some types of low clouds	Fronts and pressure systems	
Thin altostratus layer	Cumulus of fair weather	(H) or High (L) or Low	Center of high- or low-pressure system
Thick altostratus layer	Stratocumulus		Cold front
Thin altostratus in patches	Fractocumulus of bad weather		Warm front
Thin altostratus in bands	Stratus of fair weather		Occluded front
			Stationary front

Appendix M

Minerals with Metallic Luster

Mineral (formula)	Color	Streak	Hardness	Specific gravity	Crystal system	Breakage pattern	Uses and other properties
graphite (C)	black to gray	black to gray	1-2	2.3	hexagonal	basal cleavage (scales)	pencil lead, lubricants for locks, rods to control some small nuclear reactions, battery poles
silver (Ag)	silvery white, tarnishes to black	light gray to silver	2.5	10-12	cubic	hackly	coins, fillings for teeth, jewelry, silverplate, wires; malleable and ductile
galena (Pbs)	gray	gray to black	2.5	7.5	cubic	cubic cleavage perfect	source of lead, used in pipes, shields for X rays, fishing equipment sinkers
gold (AU)	pale to golden yellow	yellow	2.5-3	19.3	cubic	hackly	jewelry, money, gold leaf, fillings for teeth, medicines; does not tarnish
bornite (Cu_5FeS_4)	bronze, tarnishes to dark blue, purple	gray-black	3	4.9-5.4	tetragonal	uneven fracture	source of copper; called "peacock ore" because of the purple shine when it tarnishes
copper (Cu)	copper red	copper red	3	8.5-9	cubic	hackly	coins, pipes, gutters, wire, cooking utensils, jewelry, decorative plaques; malleable and ductile
chalcopyrite ($CuFeS_2$)	brassy to golden yellow	greenish black	3.5-4	4.2	tetragonal	uneven fracture	main ore of copper
chromite ($FeCr_2O_4$)	black or brown	brown to black	5.5	4.6	cubic	irregular fracture	ore of chromium, stainless steel, metallurgical bricks
pyrrhotite (FeS)	bronze	gray-black	4	4.6	hexagonal	uneven fracture	often found with pentlandite, an ore of nickel; may be magnetic
hematite (specular) (Fe_2O_3)	black or reddish brown	red or reddish brown	6	5.3	hexagonal	irregular fracture	source of iron; roasted in a blast furnace, converted to "pig" iron, made into steel
magnetite (Fe_3O_4)	black	black	6	5.2	cubic	conchoidal fracture	source of iron, naturally magnetic, called lodestone
pyrite (FeS_2)	light, brassy, yellow	greenish black	6.5	5.0	cubic	uneven fracture	source of iron, "fool's gold," alters to limonite

Appendix N

Minerals with Nonmetallic Luster

Mineral (formula)	Color	Streak	Hardness	Specific gravity	Crystal system	Breakage pattern	Uses and other properties
talc ($Mg_3(OH)_2Si_4O_{10}$)	white, greenish	white	1	2.8	monoclinic	cleavage in one direction	easily cut with fingernail; used for talcum powder; soapstone; is used in paper and for tabletops
bauxite (hydrous aluminum compound)	gray, red, white, brown	gray	1-3	2.0-2.5	—	—	source of aluminum; used in paints, aluminum foil, and airplane parts
kaolinite ($Al_2Si_2O_5(OH)_4$)	white, red, reddish, brown, black	white	2	2.6	triclinic	basal cleavage	clays; used in ceramics and in china dishes; common in most soils; often microscopic-sized particles
gypsum ($CaSO_4 \cdot 2H_2O$)	colorless, gray, white, brown	white	2	2.3	monoclinic	basal cleavage	used extensively in the preparation of plaster of paris, alabaster, and dry wall for building construction
sphalerite (ZnS)	brown	pale yellow	3.5-4	4	cubic	cleavage in six directions	main ore of zinc; used in paints, dyes, and medicine
sulfur (S)	yellow	yellow to white	2	2.0	ortho-rhombic	conchoidal fracture	used in medicine, fungicides for plants, vulcanization of rubber, production of sulfuric acid
muscovite ($KAl_3Si_3O_{10}(OH)_2$)	white, light gray, yellow, rose, green	colorless	2.5	2.8	monoclinic	basal cleavage	occurs in large flexible plates; used as an insulator in electrical equipment, lubricant
biotite ($K(Mg, Fe)_3AlSi_3O_{10}(OH)_2$)	black to dark brown	colorless	2.5	2.8-3.4	monoclinic	basal cleavage	occurs in large flexible plates
halite (NaCl)	colorless, red, white, blue	colorless	2.5	2.1	cubic	cubic cleavage	salt; very soluble in water; a preservative
calcite ($CaCO_3$)	colorless, white, pale, blue	colorless, white	3	2.7	hexagonal	cleavage in three directions	fizzes when HCl is added; used in cements and other building materials
dolomite ($CaMg(CO_3)_2$)	colorless, white, pink, green, gray, black	white	3.5-4	2.8	hexagonal	cleavage in three directions	concrete and cement; used as an ornamental building stone

Mineral (formula)	Color	Streak	Hardness	Specific gravity	Crystal system	Breakage pattern	Uses and other properties
fluorite (CaF_2)	colorless, white, blue, green, red, yellow, purple	colorless	4	3-3.2	cubic	cleavage	used in the manufacture of optical equipment; glows under ultraviolet light
limonite (hydrous iron oxides)	yellow, brown, black	yellow, brown	5.5	2.74-4.3	—	conchoidal fracture	source of iron; weathers easily, coloring matter of soils
hornblende ($CaNa(Mg, Al,Fe)_5(Al,Si)_2 Si_6O_{22}(OH)_2$)	green to black	gray to white	5-6	3.4	monoclinic	cleavage in two directions	will transmit light on thin edges; 6-sided cross section
feldspar (orthoclase) ($KAlSi_3O_8$)	colorless, white to gray, green and yellow	colorless	6	2.5	monoclinic	two cleavage planes meet at 90° angle	insoluble in acids; used in the manufacture of porcelain
feldspar (plagioclase) ($NaAlSi_3O_8$) ($CaAl_2Si_2O_8$)	gray, green, white	colorless	6	2.5	triclinic	two cleavage planes meet at 86° angle	used in ceramics; striations present on some faces
augite ($(CaNa)(Mg, Fe, Al)(Al, Si)_2O_6$)	black	colorless	6	3.3	monoclinic	2-directional cleavage	square or 8-sided cross section
olivine ($(Mg, Fe)_2 SiO_4$)	olive green	colorless	6.5	3.5	orthorhombic	conchoidal fracture	gemstones, refractory sand
quartz (SiO_2)	colorless, various colors	colorless	7	2.6	hexagonal	conchoidal fracture	used in glass manufacture, electronic equipment, radios, computers, watches, gemstones
garnet ($(Mg, Fe,Ca)_3 (Al_2Si_3O_{12})$)	deep yellow-red, green, black	colorless	7.5	3.5	cubic	conchoidal fracture	used in jewelry; also used as an abrasive
topaz ($(Al_2SiO_4 (F, OH)_2)$)	white, pink, yellow, pale blue, colorless	colorless	8	3.5	orthorhombic	basal cleavage	valuable gemstone
corundum (Al_20_3)	colorless, blue, brown, green, white, pink, red	colorless	9	4.0	hexagonal	fracture	gemstones: ruby is red, sapphire is blue; industrial abrasive

Skill Handbook

Table of Contents

Organizing Information

Thinking Critically

Practicing Scientific Processes

Representing and Applying Data

Organizing Information

Communicating

The communication of ideas is an important part of our everyday lives. Whether reading a book, writing a letter, or watching a television program, people everywhere are expressing opinions and sharing information with one another. Writing in your Science Journal allows you to express your opinions and demonstrate your knowledge of the information presented on a subject. When writing, keep in mind the purpose of the assignment and the audience with which you are communicating.

Examples Science Journal assignments vary greatly. They may ask you to take a viewpoint other than your own; perhaps you will be a scientist, a TV reporter, or a committee member of a local environmental group. Maybe you will be expressing your opinions to a member of Congress, a doctor, or to the editor of your local newspaper, as shown in **Figure 1.** Sometimes, Science Journal writing may allow you to summarize information in the form of an outline, a letter, or in a paragraph.

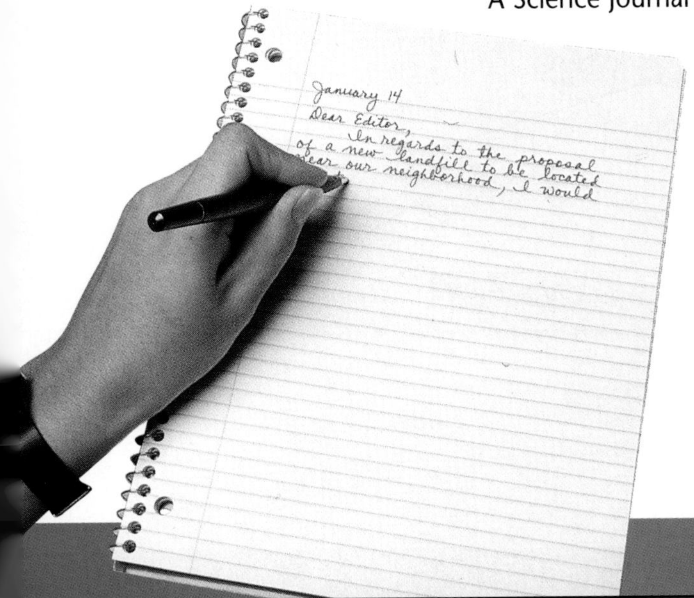

Figure 1

A Science Journal entry.

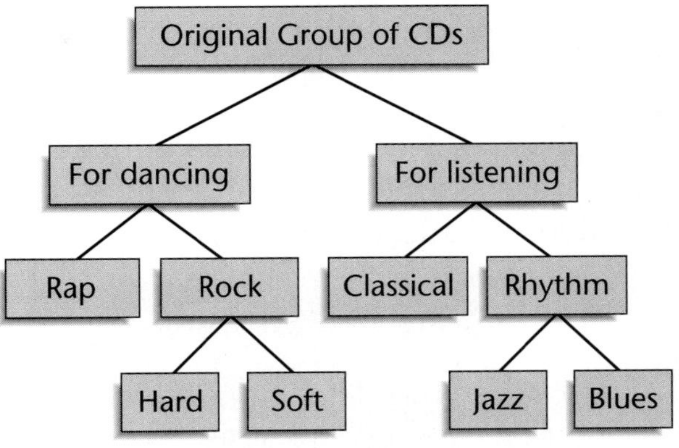

Figure 2

Classifying CDs.

Classifying

You may not realize it, but you make things orderly in the world around you. If you hang your shirts together in the closet or if your favorite CDs are stacked together, you have used the skill of classifying.

Classifying is the process of sorting objects or events into groups based on common features. When classifying, first observe the objects or events to be classified. Then, select one feature that is shared by some members in the group but not by all. Place those members that share that feature into a subgroup. You can classify members into smaller and smaller subgroups based on characteristics.

Remember, when you classify, you are grouping objects or events for a purpose. Keep your purpose in mind as you select the features to form groups and subgroups.

Example How would you classify a collection of CDs? As shown in **Figure 2,** you might classify those you like to dance to in one subgroup and CDs you like to listen to in the next column. The CDs you like to dance to could be subdivided into a rap subgroup and a rock subgroup. Note that for each feature selected, each CD fits into only one subgroup. You would keep selecting features until all the CDs are classified. **Figure 2** shows one possible classification.

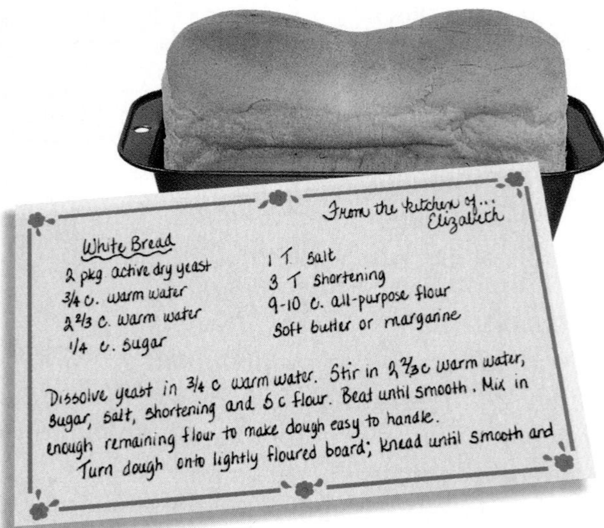

Figure 3

A recipe for bread contains sequenced instructions.

Sequencing

A sequence is an arrangement of things or events in a particular order. When you are asked to sequence objects or events within a group, figure out what comes first, then think about what should come second. Continue to choose objects or events until all of the objects you started out with are in order. Then, go back over the sequence to make sure each thing or event in your sequence logically leads to the next.

Example A sequence with which you are most familiar is the use of alphabetical order. Another example of sequence would be the steps in a recipe, as shown in **Figure 3.** Think about baking bread. Steps in the recipe have to be followed in order for the bread to turn out right.

Concept Mapping

If you were taking an automobile trip, you would probably take along a road map. The road map shows your location, your destination, and other places along the way. By looking at the map and finding where you are, you can begin to understand where you are in relation to other locations on the map.

A concept map is similar to a road map. But, a concept map shows relationships among ideas (or concepts) rather than places. A concept map is a diagram that visually shows how concepts are related. Because the concept map shows relationships among ideas, it can make the meanings of ideas and terms clear, and help you understand better what you are studying.

There is usually not one correct way to create a concept map. As you construct one type of map, you may discover other

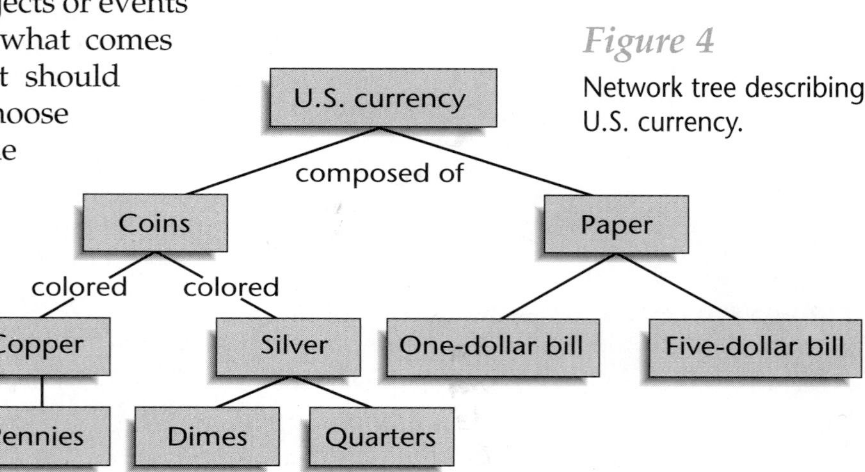

Figure 4

Network tree describing U.S. currency.

ways to construct the map that show the relationships between concepts in a better way. If you do discover what you think is a better way to create a concept map, go ahead and use the new one. Overall, concept maps are useful for breaking a big concept down into smaller parts, making learning easier.

Examples

Network Tree Look at the concept map about U.S. currency in **Figure 4.** This is called a network tree. Notice how some words are in rectangles while others are written across connecting lines. The words inside the rectangles are science concepts. The lines in the map show related concepts. The words written on the lines describe the relationships between concepts.

When you are asked to construct a network tree, write down the topic and list the major concepts related to that topic on a piece of paper. Then look at your list and begin to put them in order from general to specific. Branch the related concepts from the major concept and describe the relationships on the lines. Continue to write the more specific concepts. Write the relationships between the concepts on the lines until all concepts are mapped. Examine the concept map for relationships that cross branches, and add them to the concept map.

Events Chain An events chain is another type of concept map. An events chain map, such as the one describing a typical morning routine in **Figure 5,** is used to describe ideas in order. In science, an events chain can be used to describe a sequence of events, the steps in a procedure, or the stages of a process.

When making an events chain, first find the one event that starts the chain. This event is called the initiating event. Then, find the next event in the chain and continue until you reach an outcome. Suppose you are asked to describe what happens when your alarm rings. An events chain map describing the steps might look like **Figure 5.** Notice that connecting words are not necessary in an events chain.

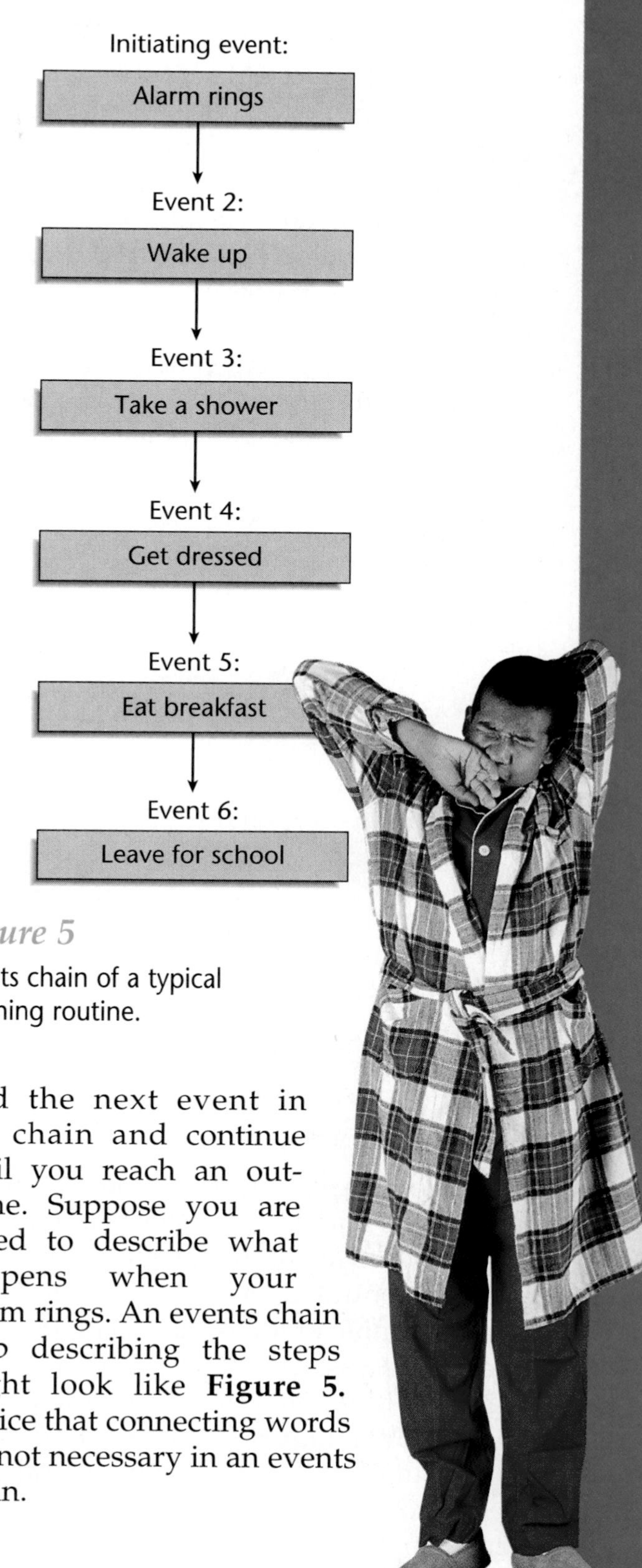

Figure 5
Events chain of a typical morning routine.

Cycle Map A cycle concept map is a special type of events chain map. In a cycle concept map, the series of events does not produce a final outcome. Instead, the last event in the chain relates back to the initiating event.

As in the events chain map, you first decide on an initiating event and then list each event in order. Because there is no outcome and the last event relates back to the initiating event, the cycle repeats itself. Look at the cycle map describing the relationship between day and night in **Figure 6.**

Figure 6

Cycle map of day and night.

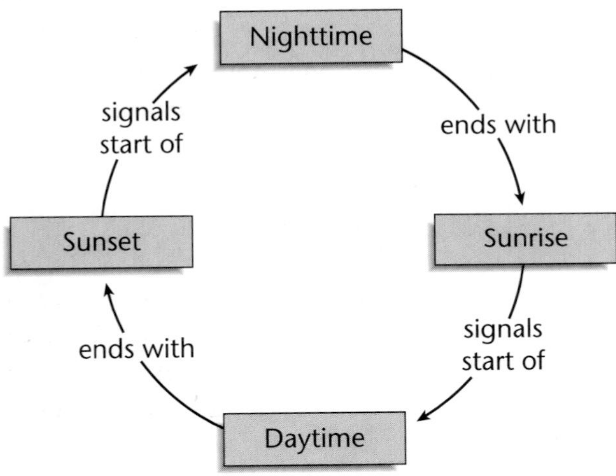

Spider Map A fourth type of concept map is the spider map. This is a map that you can use for brainstorming. Once you have a central idea, you may find you have a jumble of ideas that relate to it, but are not necessarily clearly related to each other. As illustrated by the homework spider map in **Figure 7,** by writing these ideas outside the main concept, you may begin to separate and group unrelated terms so that they become more useful.

Figure 7

Spider map about homework.

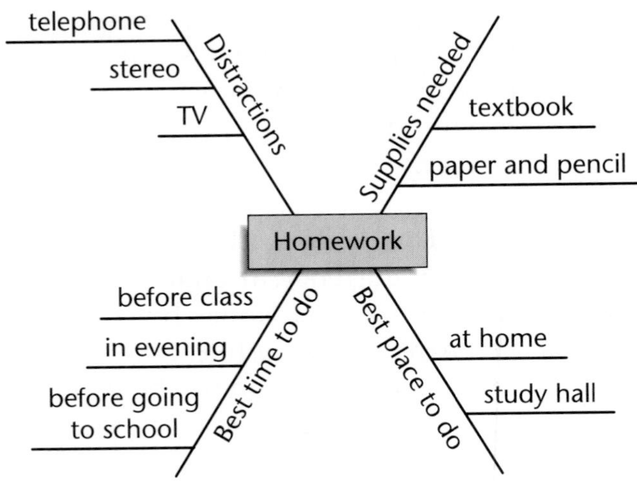

Making and Using Tables

Browse through your textbook and you will notice tables in the text and in the activities. In a table, data or information is arranged in a way that makes it easier for you to understand. Activity tables help organize the data you collect during an activity so that results can be interpreted more easily.

Examples Most tables have a title. At a glance, the title tells you what the table is about. A table is divided into columns and rows. The first column lists items to be compared. In **Figure 8,** the collection of recyclable materials is being compared in a table. The row across the top lists the specific characteristics being compared. Within the grid of the table, the collected data is recorded.

What is the title of the table in **Figure 8?** The title is "Recycled Materials." What is being compared? The different materials being recycled and on which days they are recycled.

Making Tables To make a table, list the items to be compared down in columns

Figure 8

Table of recycled materials.

Recycled Materials			
Day of Week	Paper (kg)	Aluminum (kg)	Plastic (kg)
Mon.	4.0	2.0	0.5
Wed.	3.5	1.5	0.5
Fri.	3.0	1.0	1.5

and the characteristics to be compared across in rows. The table in **Figure 8** compares the mass of recycled materials collected by a class. On Monday, students turned in 4.0 kg of paper, 2.0 kg of aluminum, and 0.5 kg of plastic. On Wednesday, they turned in 3.5 kg of paper, 1.5 kg of aluminum, and 0.5 kg of plastic. On Friday, the totals were 3.0 kg of paper, 1.0 kg of aluminum, and 1.5 kg of plastic.

Using Tables How much plastic, in kilograms, is being recycled on Wednesday? Locate the column labeled "Plastic (kg)" and the row "Wed." The data in the box where the column and row intersect are the answer. Did you answer "0.5"? How much aluminum, in kilograms, is being recycled on Friday? If you answered "1.0," you understand how to use the parts of the table.

Making and Using Graphs

After scientists organize data in tables, they may display the data in a graph. A graph is a diagram that shows the relationship of one variable to another. A graph makes interpretation and analysis of data easier. There are three basic types of graphs used in science—the line graph, the bar graph, and the circle graph.

Examples

Line Graphs A line graph is used to show the relationship between two variables. The variables being compared go on two axes of the graph. The independent variable always goes on the horizontal axis, called the *x*-axis. The dependent variable always goes on the vertical axis, called the *y*-axis.

Suppose your class started to record the amount of materials they collected in one week for their school to recycle. The collected information is shown in **Figure 9.**

You could make a graph of the materials collected over the three days of the school week. The three week days are the independent variables and are placed on the *x*-axis of your graph. The amount of materials collected is the dependent variable and would go on the *y*-axis.

After drawing your axes, label each with a scale. The *x*-axis lists the three weekdays. To make a scale of the amount of materials collected on the *y*-axis, look at the data values. Because the lowest amount collected was 1.0 and the highest

Figure 9

Amount of recyclable materials collected during one week.

Materials Collected During Week		
Day of Week	Paper (kg)	Aluminum (kg)
Mon.	5.0	4.0
Wed.	4.0	1.0
Fri.	2.5	2.0

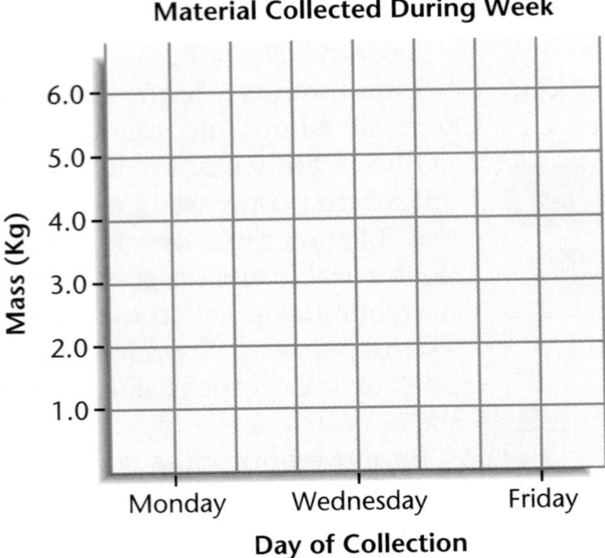

Figure 10

Graph outline for material collected during week.

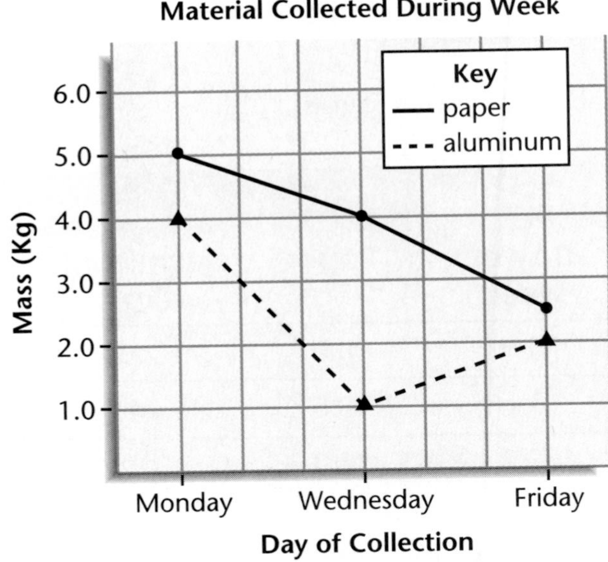

Figure 11

Line graph of materials collected during week.

was 5.0, you will have to start numbering at least at 1.0 and go through 5.0. You decide to start numbering at 0 and number by ones through 6.0, as shown in **Figure 10.**

Next, plot the data points for collected paper. The first pair of data you want to plot is Monday and 5.0 kg paper. Locate "Monday" on the *x*-axis and locate "5.0" on the *y*-axis. Where an imaginary vertical line from the *x*-axis and an imaginary horizontal line from the *y*-axis would meet, place the first data point. Place the other data points the same way. After all the points are plotted, connect them with the best smooth curve. Repeat this procedure for the data points for aluminum. Use continuous and dashed lines to distinguish the two line graphs. The resulting graph should look like **Figure 11.**

Bar Graphs Bar graphs are similar to line graphs. They compare data that do not continuously change. In a bar graph, vertical bars show the relationships among data.

To make a bar graph, set up the *x*-axis and *y*-axis as you did for the line graph. The data is plotted by drawing vertical bars from the *x*-axis up to a point where the *y*-axis would meet the bar if it were extended.

Look at the bar graph in **Figure 12** comparing the mass of aluminum collected over three weekdays. The *x*-axis is the days on which the aluminum was collected. The *y*-axis is the mass of aluminum collected, in kilograms.

Circle Graphs A circle graph uses a circle divided into sections to display data. Each section represents part of the whole. All the sections together equal 100 percent.

Suppose you wanted to make a circle graph to show the number of seeds that germinated in a package. You would count the total number of seeds. You find that there are 143 seeds in the package. This represents 100 percent, the whole circle.

You plant the seeds, and 129 seeds germinate. The seeds that germinated will make up one section of the circle graph, and the seeds that did not germinate will make up the remaining section.

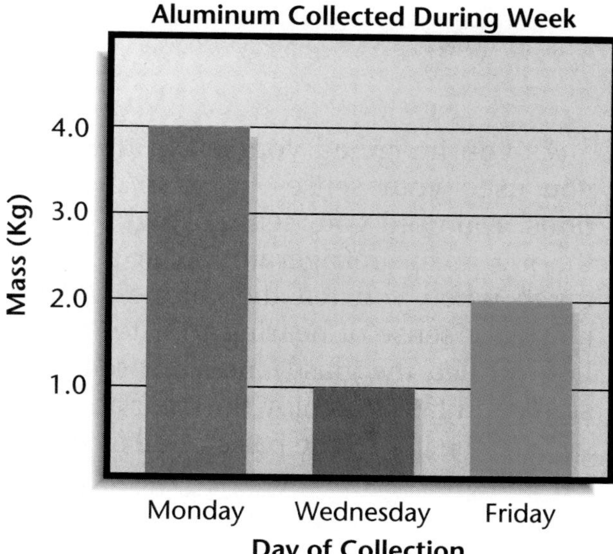

Figure 12

Bar graph of aluminum collected during week.

To find out how much of the circle each section should take, divide the number of seeds in each section by the total number of seeds. Then multiply your answer by 360, the number of degrees in a circle, and round to the nearest whole number. The section of the circle graph in degrees that represents the seeds germinated is figured below.

$$\frac{129}{143} \times 360 = 324.75 \text{ or } 325 \text{ degrees (or } 325°\text{)}$$

Plot this group on the circle graph using a compass and a protractor. Use the compass to draw a circle. It will be easier to measure the part of the circle representing the nongerminating seeds, so subtract 325° from 360° to get 35°. Draw a straight line from the center to the edge of the circle. Place your protractor on this line and use it to mark a point at 325°. Use this point to draw a straight line from the center of the circle to the edge. This is the section for the group of seeds that did not germinate. The other section represents the group of 129 seeds that did germinate. Label the sections of your graph and title the graph as shown in **Figure 13.**

Figure 13

Circle graph of germinated seeds.

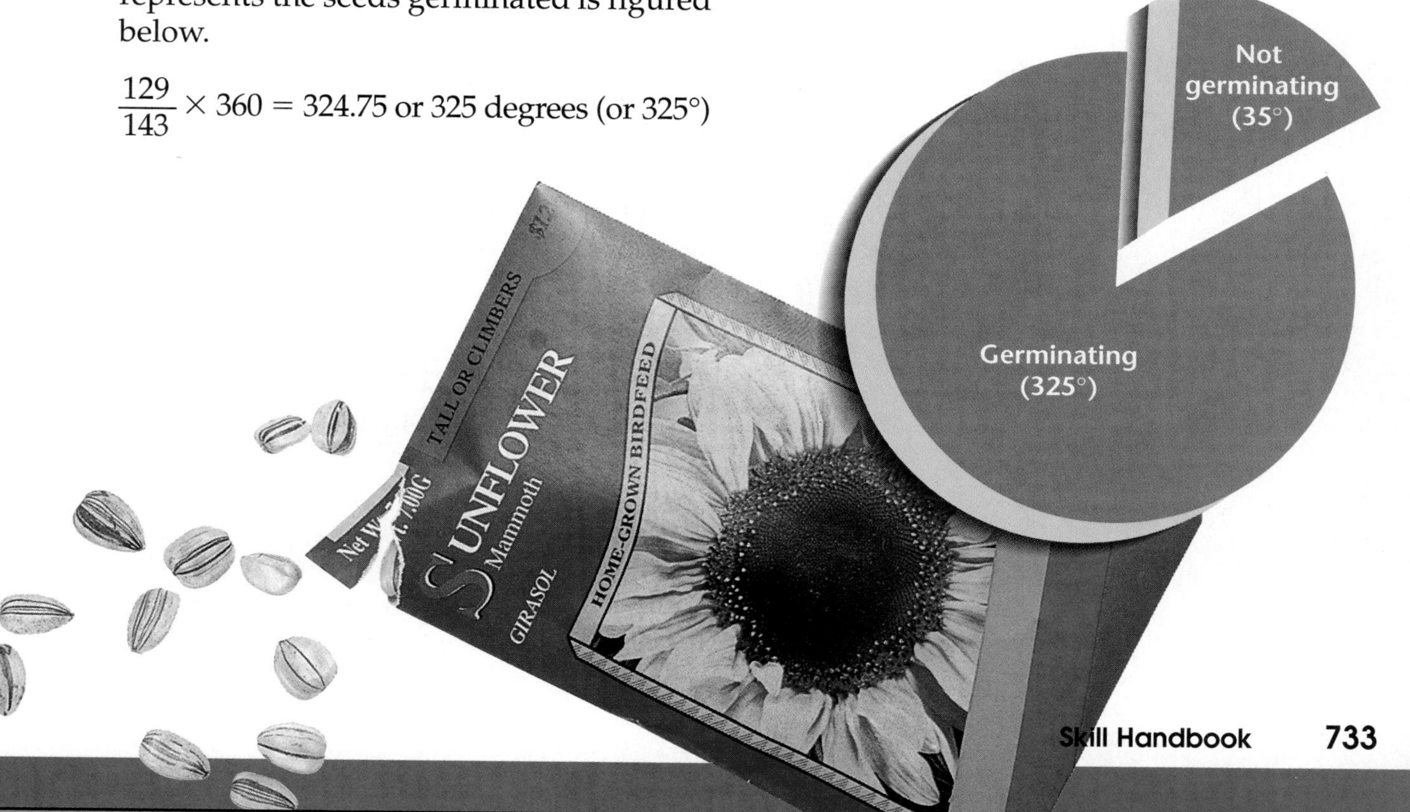

Thinking Critically

Observing and Inferring

Observing Scientists try to make careful and accurate observations. When possible, they use instruments such as microscopes, thermometers, and balances to make observations. Measurements with a balance or thermometer provide numerical data that can be checked and repeated.

When you make observations in science, you'll find it helpful to examine the entire object or situation first. Then, look carefully for details. Write down everything you observe.

Example Imagine that you have just finished a volleyball game. At home, you open the refrigerator and see a jug of orange juice on the back of the top shelf. The jug, shown in **Figure 14,** feels cold as you grasp it. Then you drink the juice, smell the oranges, and enjoy the tart taste in your mouth.

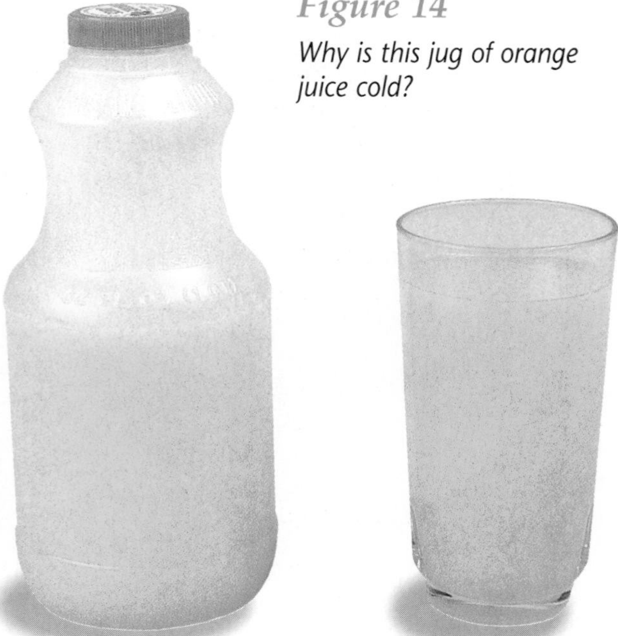

Figure 14
Why is this jug of orange juice cold?

As you imagined yourself in the story, you used your senses to make observations. You used your sense of sight to find the jug in the refrigerator, your sense of touch when you felt the coldness of the jug, your sense of hearing to listen as the liquid filled the glass, and your senses of smell and taste to enjoy the odor and tartness of the juice. The basis of all scientific investigation is observation.

Inferring Scientists often make inferences based on their observations. An inference is an attempt to explain or interpret observations or to say what caused what you observed.

When making an inference, be certain to use accurate data and observations. Analyze all of the data that you've collected. Then, based on everything you know, explain or interpret what you've observed.

Example When you drank a glass of orange juice after the volleyball game, you observed that the orange juice was cold as well as refreshing. You might infer that the juice was cold because it had been made much earlier in the day and had been kept in the refrigerator or you might infer that it had just been made, using both cold water and ice. The only way to be sure which inference is correct is to investigate further.

Comparing and Contrasting

Observations can be analyzed by noting the similarities and differences between two or more objects or events that you observe. When you look at objects or events to see how they are similar, you are comparing them. Contrasting is looking for differences in similar objects or events.

Figure 15

Table comparing the nutritional value of *Candy A* and *Candy B.*

Nutritional Value

	Candy A	Candy B
Serving size	103 g	105 g
Calories	220	160
Total Fat	10 g	10 g
Protein	2.5 g	2.6 g
Total Carbohydrate	30 g	15 g

Example Suppose you were asked to compare and contrast the nutritional value of two candy bars, *Candy A* and *Candy B.* You would start by looking at what is known about these candy bars. Arrange this information in a table, like the one in **Figure 15.**

Similarities you might point out are that both candy bars have similar serving sizes, amounts of total fat, and protein. Differences include *Candy A* having a higher calorie value and containing more total carbohydrates than *Candy B.*

Recognizing Cause and Effect

Have you ever watched something happen and then made suggestions about why it happened? If so, you have observed an effect and inferred a cause. The event is an effect, and the reason for the event is the cause.

Example Suppose that every time your teacher fed the fish in a classroom aquarium, she or he tapped the food container on the edge of the aquarium. Then, one day your teacher just happened to tap the edge of the aquarium with a pencil while making a point. You observed the fish swim to the surface of the aquarium to feed, as shown in **Figure 16.** What is the effect, and what would you infer to be the cause? The effect is the fish swimming to the surface of the aquarium. You might infer the cause to be the teacher tapping on the edge of the aquarium. In determining cause and effect, you have made a logical inference based on your observations.

Perhaps the fish swam to the surface because they reacted to the teacher's waving hand or for some other reason. When scientists are unsure of the cause of a certain event, they design controlled experiments to determine what causes the event. Although you have made a logical conclusion about the behavior of the fish, you would have to perform an experiment to be certain that it was the tapping that caused the effect you observed.

Figure 16

What cause and effect situations are occurring in this aquarium?

Practicing Scientific Processes

You might say that the work of a scientist is to solve problems. But when you decide how to dress on a particular day, you are doing problem solving, too. You may observe what the weather looks like through a window. You may go outside and see whether what you are wearing is warm or cool enough.

Scientists use an orderly approach to learn new information and to solve problems. The methods scientists may use include observing to form a hypothesis, designing an experiment to test a hypothesis, separating and controlling variables, and interpreting data.

Forming Operational Definitions

Operational definitions define an object by showing how it functions, works, or behaves. Such definitions are written in terms of how an object works or how it can be used; that is, what is its job or purpose?

Figure 17

What observations can be made about this dog?

Example Some operational definitions explain how an object can be used.

- A ruler is a tool that measures the size of an object.
- An automobile can move things from one place to another.

Or such a definition may explain how an object works.

- A ruler contains a series of marks that can be used as a standard when measuring.
- An automobile is a vehicle that can move from place to place.

Forming a Hypothesis

Observations You observe all the time. Scientists try to observe as much as possible about the things and events they study so they know that what they say about their observations is reliable.

Some observations describe something using only words. These observations are called qualitative observations. Other observations describe how much of something there is. These are quantitative observations and use numbers, as well as words, in the description. Tools or equipment are used to measure the characteristic being described.

Example If you were making qualitative observations of the dog in **Figure 17,** you might use words such as *furry, yellow,* and *short-haired.* Quantitative observations of this dog might include a mass of 14 kg, a height of 46 cm, ear length of 10 cm, and an age of 150 days.

Hypotheses Hypotheses are tested to help explain observations that have been made. They are often stated as *if* and *then* statements.

Examples Suppose you want to make a perfect score on a spelling test. Begin by thinking of several ways to accomplish this. Base these possibilities on past observations. If you put each of these possibilities into sentence form, using the words *if* and *then,* you can form a hypothesis. All of the following are hypotheses you might consider to explain how you could score 100 percent on your test:

If the test is easy, then I will get a perfect score.

If I am intelligent, then I will get a perfect score.

If I study hard, then I will get a perfect score.

Perhaps a scientist has observed that plants that receive fertilizer grow taller than plants that do not. A scientist may form a hypothesis that says: If plants are fertilized, then their growth will increase.

Designing an Experiment to Test a Hypothesis

In order to test a hypothesis, it's best to write out a procedure. A procedure is the plan that you follow in your experiment. A procedure tells you what materials to use and how to use them. After following the procedure, data are generated. From this generated data, you can then draw a conclusion and make a statement about your results.

If the conclusion you draw from the data supports your hypothesis, then you can say that your hypothesis is reliable. *Reliable* means that you can trust your conclusion. If it did not support your hypothesis, then you would have to make new observations and state a new hypothesis—just make sure that it is one that you can test.

Example Super premium gasoline costs more than regular gasoline. Does super premium gasoline increase the efficiency or fuel mileage of your family car? Let's figure out how to conduct an experiment to test the hypothesis, "*if* premium gas is more efficient, *then* it should increase the fuel mileage of our family car." Then a procedure similar to **Figure 18** must be written to generate data presented in **Figure 19** on page 746.

This data show that premium gasoline is less efficient than regular gasoline. It took more gasoline to travel one mile (0.064) using premium gasoline than it does to travel one mile using regular gasoline (0.059). This conclusion does not support the original hypothesis made.

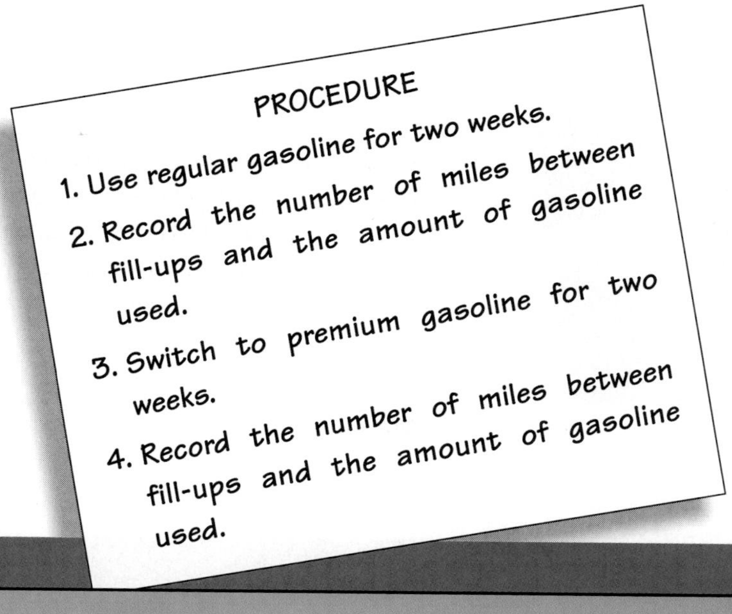

PROCEDURE

1. Use regular gasoline for two weeks.
2. Record the number of miles between fill-ups and the amount of gasoline used.
3. Switch to premium gasoline for two weeks.
4. Record the number of miles between fill-ups and the amount of gasoline used.

Figure 18
Possible procedural steps.

Figure 19
Data generated from procedure steps.

	Miles traveled	Gallons used	Gallons per mile
Regular gasoline	762	45.34	0.059
Premium gasoline	661	42.30	0.064

Separating and Controlling Variables

In any experiment, it is important to keep everything the same except for the item you are testing. The one factor that you change is called the *independent variable.* The factor that changes as a result of the independent variable is called the *dependent variable.* Always make sure that there is only one independent variable. If you allow more than one, you will not know what causes the changes you observe in the independent variable. Many experiments have *controls*—a treatment or an experiment that you can compare with the results of your test groups.

Example In the experiment with the gasoline, you made everything the same except the type of gasoline being used. The driver, the type of automobile, and the weather conditions should remain the same throughout. The gasoline should also be purchased from the same service station. By doing so, you made sure that at the end of the experiment, any differences were the result of the type of fuel being used—regular or premium. The type of gasoline was the *independent factor* and the gas mileage achieved was the *dependent factor.* The use of regular gasoline was the *control.*

Interpreting Data

The word *interpret* means "to explain the meaning of something." Look at the problem originally being explored in the gasoline experiment and find out what the data show. Identify the control group and the test group so you can see whether or not the variable has had an effect. Then you need to check differences between the control and test groups.

Figure 20
Which gasoline type is most efficient?

These differences may be qualitative or quantitative. A qualitative difference would be a difference that you could observe and describe, while a quantitative difference would be a difference you can measure using numbers. If there are differences, the variable being tested may have had an effect. If there is no difference between the control and the test groups, the variable being tested apparently has had no effect.

Example Perhaps you are looking at a table from an experiment designed to test the hypothesis: If premium gas is more efficient, then it should increase the fuel mileage of our family car. Look back at **Figure 19** showing the results of this experiment. In this example, the use of regular gasoline in the family car was the control, while the car being fueled by premium gasoline was the test group.

Data showed a quantitative difference in efficiency for gasoline consumption. It took 0.059 gallons of regular gasoline to travel one mile, while it took 0.064 gallons of the premium gasoline to travel the same distance. The regular gasoline was more efficient; it increased the fuel mileage of the family car.

What is data? In the experiment described on these pages, measurements were taken so that at the end of the experiment, you had something concrete to interpret. You had numbers to work with. Not every experiment that you do will give you data in the form of numbers. Sometimes, data will be in the form of a description. At the end of a chemistry experiment, you might have noted that one solution turned yellow when treated with a particular chemical, and another remained clear, like water, when treated with the same chemical. Data, therefore, are stated in different forms for different types of scientific experiments.

Figure 21
Data.

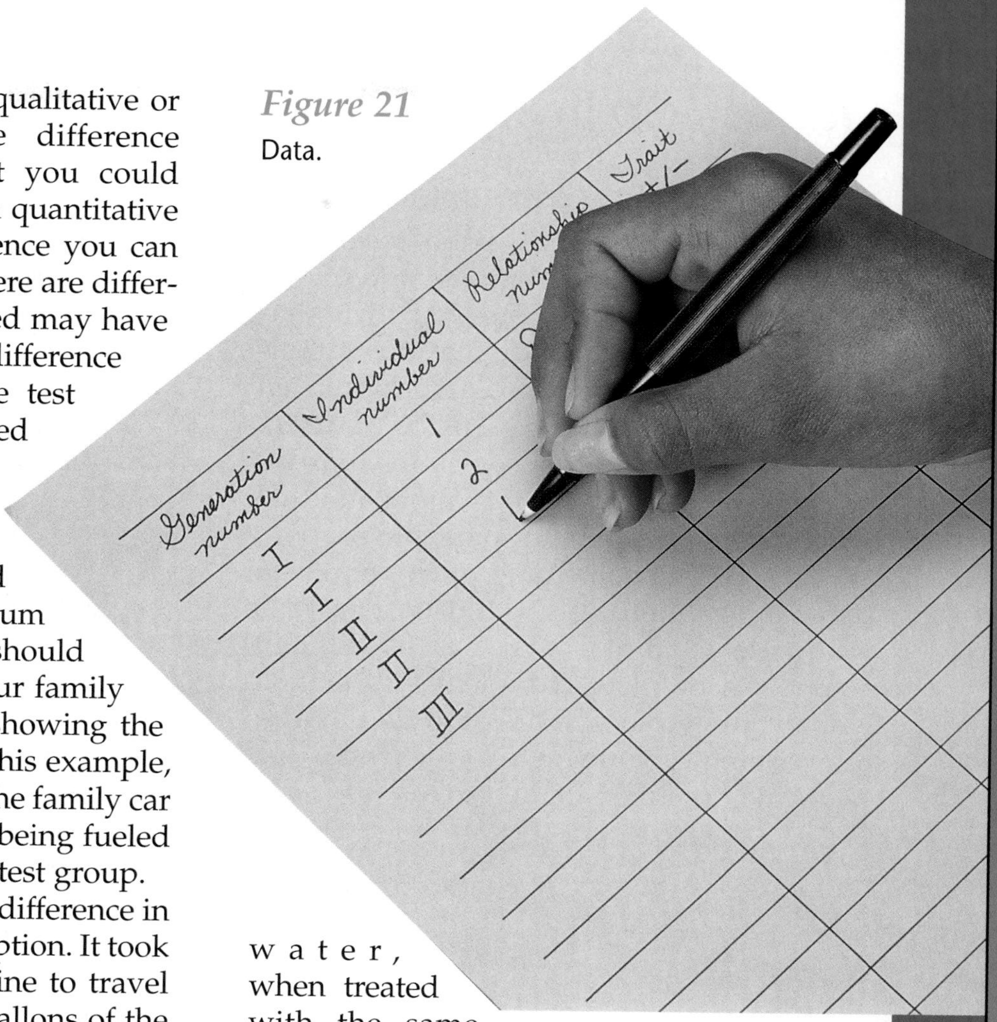

Are all experiments alike? Keep in mind as you perform experiments in science that not every experiment makes use of all of the parts that have been described on these pages. For some, it may be difficult to design an experiment that will always have a control. Other experiments are complex enough that it may be hard to have only one dependent variable. Real scientists encounter many variations in the methods that they use when they perform experiments. The skills in this handbook are here for you to use and practice. In real situations, their uses will vary.

Representing and Applying Data

Interpreting Scientific Illustrations

As you read a science textbook, you will see many drawings, diagrams, and photographs. Illustrations help you to understand what you read. Some illustrations are included to help you understand an idea that you can't see easily by yourself. For instance, we can't see atoms, but we can look at a diagram of an atom and that helps us to understand some things about atoms. Seeing something often helps you remember more easily. Illustrations also provide examples that clarify difficult concepts or give additional information about the topic you are studying. Maps, for example, help you to locate places that may be described in the text.

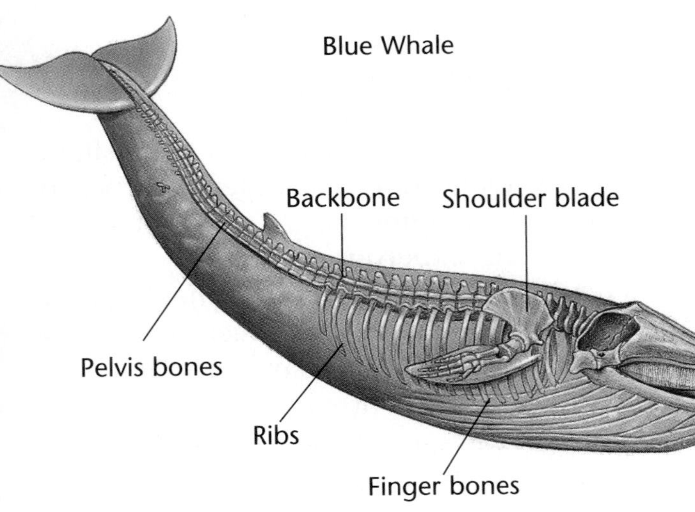

Figure 22

A labeled diagram of a blue whale.

Figure 23

If an inanimate object had dorsal and ventral surfaces, its various sides would be marked for orientation like the one in this drawing.

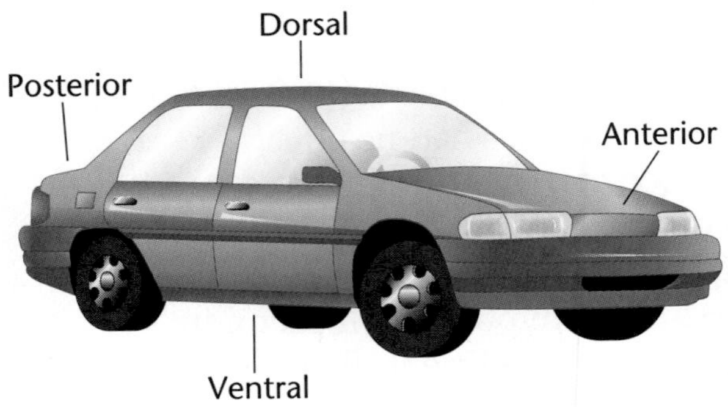

Examples

Captions and Labels Most illustrations have captions. A caption is a comment that identifies or explains the illustration. Diagrams, such as **Figure 22,** often have labels that identify parts of the organism or the order of steps in a process.

Learning with Illustrations An illustration of an organism shows that organism from a particular view or orientation. In order to understand the illustration, you may need to identify the front (anterior) end, tail (posterior) end, the underside (ventral), and the back (dorsal) side of the object shown in **Figure 23.**

You might also check for symmetry. A shark in **Figure 24** has bilateral symmetry. This means that drawing an imaginary line through the center of the animal from the anterior to posterior end forms two mirror images.

Radial symmetry is the arrangement of similar parts around a central point. An

Figure 24

A shark (A) illustrating bilateral symmetry and a pear (B) illustrating a longitudinal section and a cross section.

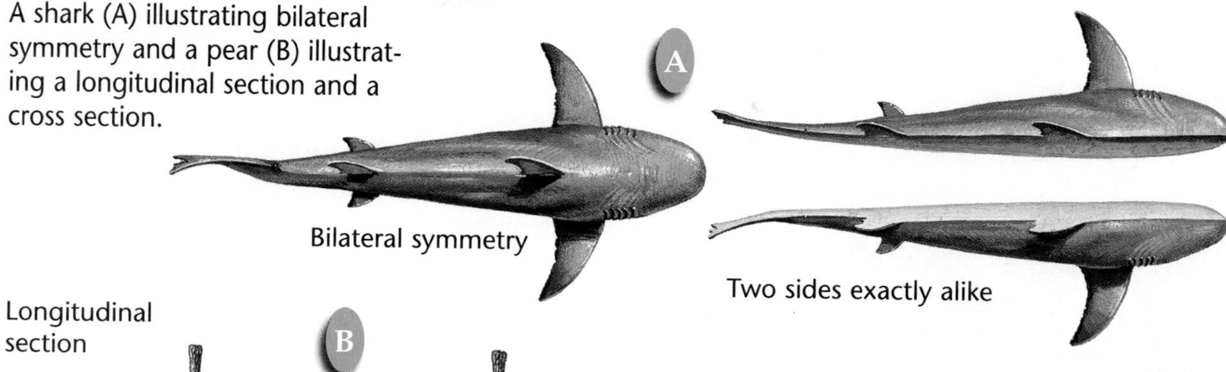

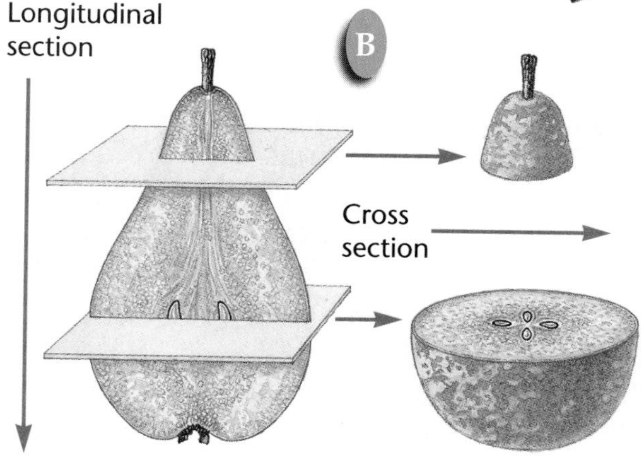

object or organism such as a hydra can be divided anywhere through the center into similar parts.

Some organisms and objects cannot be divided into two similar parts. If an organism or object cannot be divided, it is asymmetrical. Regardless of how you try to divide a natural sponge, you cannot divide it into two parts that look alike.

Some illustrations enable you to see the inside of an organism or object. These illustrations are called sections. **Figure 24** also illustrates some common sections.

Look at all illustrations carefully. Read captions and labels so that you understand exactly what the illustration is showing you.

Making Models

Have you ever worked on a model car or plane or rocket? These models look, and sometimes work, much like the real thing, but they are often on a different scale than the real thing. In science, models are used to help simplify large or small processes or structures that otherwise would be difficult to see and understand. Your understanding of a structure or process is enhanced when you work with materials to make a model that shows the basic features of the structure or process.

Example In order to make a model, you first have to get a basic idea about the structure or process involved. You decide to make a model to show the differences in size of arteries, veins, and capillaries. First, read about these structures. All three are hollow tubes. Arteries are round and thick. Veins are flat and have thinner walls than arteries. Capillaries are small.

Now, decide what you can use for your model. Common materials are often best and cheapest to work with when making models. As illustrated in **Figure 25** on page 750, different kinds and sizes of pasta might work for these models. Different sizes of rubber tubing might do just as well. Cut and glue the different noodles or tubing onto thick paper so the openings can be seen. Then label each. Now you have a simple, easy-to-understand model showing the differences in size of arteries, veins, and capillaries.

What other scientific ideas might a model help you to understand? A model

Figure 25
Different types of pasta may be used to model blood vessels.

of a molecule can be made from gumdrops (using different colors for the different elements present) and toothpicks (to show different chemical bonds). A working model of a volcano can be made from clay, a small amount of baking soda, vinegar, and a bottle cap. Other models can be devised on a computer. Some models are mathematical and are represented by equations.

Measuring in SI

The metric system is a system of measurement developed by a group of scientists in 1795. It helps scientists avoid problems by providing standard measurements that all scientists around the world can understand. A modern form of the metric system, called the International System, or SI, was adopted for worldwide use in 1960.

The metric system is convenient because unit sizes vary by multiples of 10. When changing from smaller units to larger units, divide by 10. When changing from larger units to smaller, multiply by 10. For example, to convert millimeters to centimeters, divide the millimeters by 10. To convert 30 millimeters to centimeters, divide 30 by 10 (30 millimeters equal 3 centimeters).

Prefixes are used to name units. Look at **Figure 26** for some common metric prefixes and their meanings. Do you see how the prefix *kilo-* attached to the unit *gram* is *kilogram,* or 1000 grams? The prefix *deci-* attached to the unit *meter* is *decimeter,* or one-tenth (0.1) of a meter.

Examples

Length You have probably measured lengths or distances many times. The meter is the SI unit used to measure length. A baseball bat is about one meter long. When measuring smaller lengths, the meter is divided into smaller units called centimeters and millimeters. A centimeter is one-hundredth (0.01) of a meter, which is about the size of the width

Figure 26
Common metric prefixes.

Metric Prefixes

Prefix	Symbol	Meaning	
kilo-	k	1000	thousand
hecto-	h	200	hundred
deka-	da	10	ten
deci-	d	0.1	tenth
centi-	c	0.01	hundredth
milli-	m	0.001	thousandth

Figure 27

Metric ruler showing centimeter and millimeter divisions.

of the fingernail on your ring finger. A millimeter is one-thousandth of a meter (0.001), about the thickness of a dime.

Most metric rulers have lines indicating centimeters and millimeters, as shown in **Figure 27.** The centimeter lines are the longer, numbered lines; the shorter lines are millimeter lines. When using a metric ruler, line up the 0-centimeter mark with the end of the object being measured, and read the number of the unit where the object ends, in this instance 7.5 cm.

Surface Area Units of length are also used to measure surface area. The standard unit of area is the square meter (m^2). A square that's one meter long on each side has a surface area of one square meter. Similarly, a square centimeter, (cm^2), shown in **Figure 28,** is one centimeter long on each side. The surface area of an object is determined by multiplying the length times the width.

Volume The volume of a rectangular solid is also calculated using units of length. The cubic meter (m^3) is the standard SI unit of volume. A cubic meter is a cube one meter on each side. You can determine the volume of rectangular solids by multiplying length times width times height.

Liquid Volume During science activities, you will measure liquids using beakers and graduated cylinders marked in milliliters, as illustrated in **Figure 29.** A graduated cylinder is a cylindrical container marked with lines from bottom to top.

Liquid volume is measured using a unit called a liter. A liter has the volume of 1000 cubic centimeters. Because the prefix *milli-* means thousandth (0.001), a milliliter equals one cubic centimeter. One

Figure 28

A square centimeter.

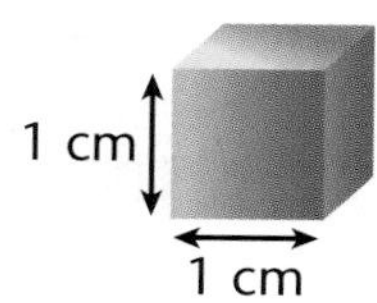

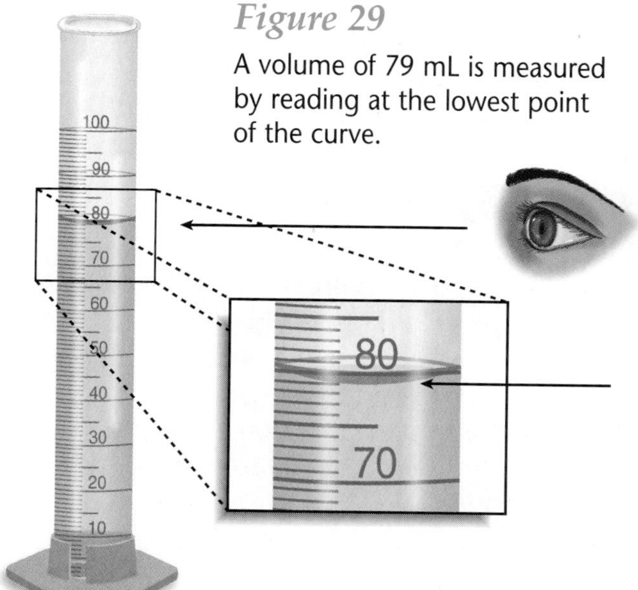

Figure 29

A volume of 79 mL is measured by reading at the lowest point of the curve.

milliliter of liquid would completely fill a cube measuring one centimeter on each side.

Mass Scientists use balances to find the mass of objects in grams. You will use a beam balance similar to **Figure 30.** Notice that on one side of the balance is a pan and on the other side is a set of beams. Each beam has an object of a known mass called a *rider* that slides on the beam.

Before you find the mass of an object, set the balance to zero by sliding all the riders back to the zero point. Check the pointer on the right to make sure it swings an equal distance above and below the zero point on the scale. If the swing is unequal, find and turn the adjusting screw until you have an equal swing.

Place an object on the pan. Slide the rider with the largest mass along its beam until the pointer drops below zero. Then move it back one notch. Repeat the process on each beam until the pointer swings an equal distance above and below the zero point. Add the masses on each beam to find the mass of the object.

You should never place a hot object or pour chemicals directly onto the pan. Instead, find the mass of a clean beaker or a glass jar. Place the dry or liquid chemicals in the container. Then find the combined mass of the container and the chemicals. Calculate the mass of the chemicals by subtracting the mass of the empty container from the combined mass.

Predicting

When you apply a hypothesis, or general explanation, to a specific situation, you predict something about that situation. First, you must identify which hypothesis fits the situation you are considering.

Examples People use prediction to make everyday decisions. Based on previous observations and experiences, you may form a hypothesis that if it is wintertime, then temperatures will be lower. From past experience in your area, temperatures are lowest in February. You may then use this hypothesis to predict specific temperatures and weather for the month of February in advance. Someone could use these predictions to plan to set aside more money for heating bills during that month.

Figure 30

A beam balance is used to measure mass.

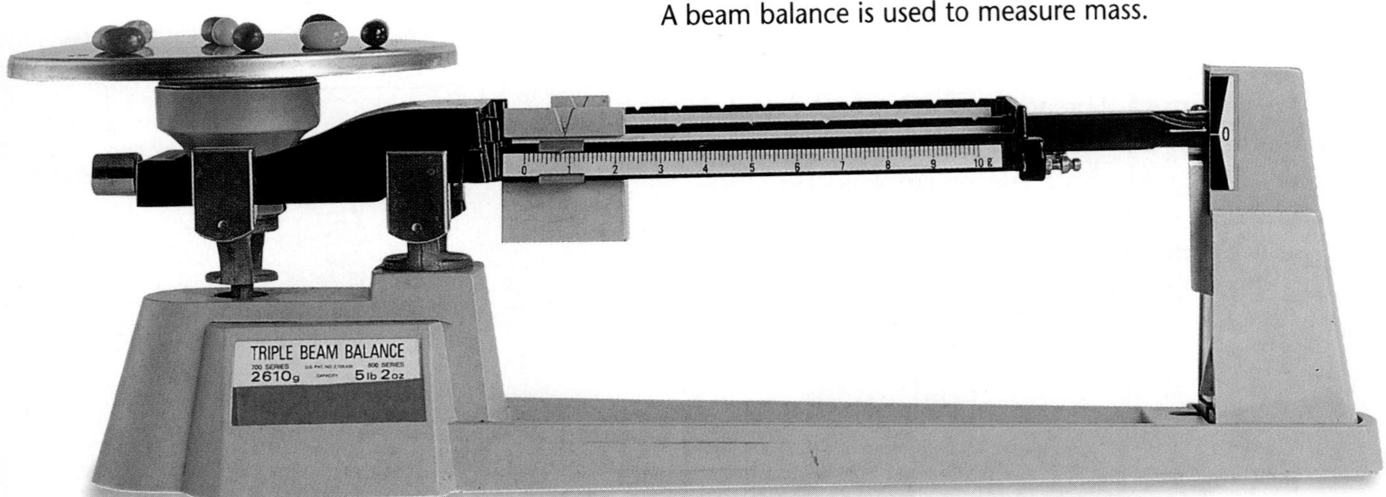

Using Numbers

When working with large populations of organisms, scientists usually cannot observe or study every organism in the population. Instead, they use a sample or a portion of the population. To sample is to take a small representative portion of organisms of a population for research. By making careful observations or manipulating variables within a portion of a group, information is discovered and conclusions are drawn that might then be applied to the whole population.

Scientific work also involves estimating. To estimate is to make a judgment about the size of something or the number of something without actually measuring or counting every member of a population.

Examples Suppose you are trying to determine the effect of a specific nutrient on the growth of black-eyed Susans. It would be impossible to test the entire population of black-eyed Susans, so you would select part of the population for your experiment. Through careful experimentation and observation on a sample of the population, you could generalize the effect of the chemical on the entire population.

Here is a more familiar example. Have you ever tried to guess how many beans were in a sealed jar? If you did, you were estimating. What if you knew the jar of beans held one liter (1000 mL)? If you knew that 30 beans would fit in a 100-milliliter jar, how many beans would you estimate to be in the one-liter jar? If you said about 300 beans, your estimate would be close to the actual number of beans. Can you estimate how many jelly beans are on the cookie sheet in **Figure 31?**

Scientists use a similar process to estimate populations of organisms from bacteria to buffalo. Scientists count the actual number of organisms in a small sample and then estimate the number of organisms in a larger area. For example, if a scientist wanted to count the number of bacterial colonies in a petri dish, a microscope could be used to count the number of organisms in a one-square-centimeter sample. To determine the total population of the culture, the number of organisms in the square-centimeter sample is multiplied by the total number of square centimeters in the culture.

Figure 31

Sampling a group of jelly beans allows for an estimation of the total number of jelly beans in the group.

Glossary

This glossary defines each key term that appears in **bold type** in the text. It also shows the page number where you can find the word used. Some other terms that you may need to look up are included as well. We also show how to pronounce some of the words. A key to pronunciation is in the table below.

Pronunciation Key

a . . . b**a**ck (bak)	oh . . . g**o** (goh)	sh . . . **sh**elf (shelf)
ay . . . d**ay** (day)	aw . . . s**o**ft (sawft)	ch . . . na**t**ure (nay chur)
ah . . . f**a**ther (fahth ur)	or . . . **or**bit (or but)	g . . . **g**ift (gihft)
ow . . . fl**ow**er (flow ur)	oy . . . c**oi**n (coyn)	j . . . **g**em (jem)
ar . . . c**ar** (car)	oo . . . f**oo**t (foot)	ing . . . s**ing** (sing)
e . . . l**e**ss (les)	ew . . . f**oo**d (fewd)	zh . . . vi**s**ion (vihzh un)
ee . . . l**ea**f (leef)	yoo . . . p**u**re (pyoor)	k . . . ca**k**e (kayk)
ih . . . tr**i**p (trihp)	yew . . . f**ew** (fyew)	s . . . **s**eed, **c**ent (seed, sent)
i (i + con + e) . . . **i**dea (i dee uh), l**i**fe (life)	uh . . . comm**a** (cahm uh)	z . . . **z**one, rai**s**e (zohn, rayz)
	u (+ con) . . . flow**er** (flow ur)	

A

abrasion: a type of erosion caused by wearing or scraping away by sand grains or other particles striking other sand grains and rocks, breaking off small fragments. The particles can be transported by wind, water, ice, or gravity. (Chap. 7, p. 188)

absolute dating: determining the age, in years, of rocks or other objects, using the radioactive decay of their atoms. (Chap. 12, p. 344)

absolute magnitude: a measure of the amount of light a star or other space object actually gives off. (Chap. 24, p. 674)

abyssal (a BIHS uhl) **plain:** the flat seafloor in the deep ocean, formed by the deposition of sediment by ocean currents. (Chap. 18, p. 505)

acid: any substance with a pH lower than seven; the lower the pH number, the greater the acidity. (Chap. 20, p. 558)

acid rain: acidic rain, snow, sleet, or hail that can form when sulfur dioxide (from coal-burning power plants) and nitrogen oxide (from car exhausts) combine with moisture in the air. (Chap. 20, p. 558)

adaptation: any structural or behavioral characteristic organisms have developed over time that helps them survive in a particular environment. (Chap. 16, p. 459)

air mass: a large body of air that has the same properties as the surface over which it formed. (Chap. 15, p. 432)

alluvial fan: a triangular deposit of sediment that forms when water rushing down a slope loses its energy and abruptly slows at the bottom, depositing its sediment load. (Chap. 8, p. 213)

amphibians (am FIHB ee unz)**:** vertebrate animals that breathe air and live on land but must return to water to reproduce. (Chap. 13, p. 370)

angular unconformity: a type of unconformity where older tilted rock layers meet younger horizontal rock layers; this indicates that layers are missing and there is a gap in the time record.

apparent magnitude: a measure of light received on Earth from a star or other space object. (Chap. 24, p. 674)

aquifer: a layer of permeable rock that has connecting pores and transmits water freely. (Chap. 8, p. 215)

arête (uh RAYT): a sharp-edged mountain ridge carved by glaciers.

artesian (ahr TEE zhun) **well:** a well in which water under natural pressure rises to the surface without being pumped. (Chap. 8, p. 216)

asteroid: a piece of rock, smaller than a planet, that orbits the sun; most are between the orbits of Mars and Jupiter in an area called the asteroid belt. (Chap. 23, p. 665)

asteroid belt: the area between the orbits of Mars and Jupiter where most asteroids are found.

asthenosphere (as THEN uh sfihr)**:** the plasticlike layer below the lithosphere in Earth's mantle. (Chap. 11, p. 304)

astronomical unit: the average distance from Earth to the sun (150 million km), used for measuring distances to objects in the solar system. (Chap. 23, p. 648)

astronomy: the study of objects in space, including stars, planets, comets, and their origins. (Chap. 1, p. 8)

atomic number: equals the number of protons in the nucleus of an atom. (Chap. 2, p. 36)

atoms: the smallest particles of an element that still have all the properties of that element; the building blocks of matter. (Chap. 2, p. 32)

Australopithecus: the earliest animals that have distinct humanlike characteristics; now extinct.

axis: an imaginary line around which an object spins; for example, Earth spins around its axis. (Chap. 22, p. 615)

barred spiral galaxy: a galaxy having two spiral arms extending from a large bar.

barrier island: a temporary sand deposit that parallels the shore but is separated from the mainland by water. (Chap. 8, p. 226)

basaltic: dark-colored, dense igneous rocks that form from magma rich in iron and magnesium. (Chap. 4, p. 93)

base: any substance with a pH above seven; the higher the pH number, the more basic the solution. (Chap. 20, p. 558)

basin: a low area on Earth's surface that contains an ocean. (Chap. 17, p. 479)

batholiths: the largest intrusive igneous rock bodies that form when magma cools and solidifies underground and stops rising to the surface. (Chap. 10, p. 283)

beach: a deposit of sediments, such as rock fragments or seashell fragments, that runs parallel to a shore. (Chap. 8, p. 224)

benthos (BEN thohs)**:** plants and animals that live near and on the ocean bottom, such as kelp, corals, snails, sea urchins, and bottom-dwelling fish. (Chap. 18, p. 514)

big bang theory: the leading theory about the formation of the universe, which states that the universe began expanding out of a huge explosion about 15 billion years ago. (Chap. 24, p. 695)

binary system: a system of two stars orbiting one another. (Chap. 24, p. 681)

black hole: the final stage in the life cycle of some massive stars; the remnant of a star that is so dense that not even light can escape its gravity field. (Chap.24, p. 688)

brachiopods (BRAY kee uh pahdz): fan-shaped marine invertebrate animals commonly found as fossils in Paleozoic Era rocks.

breaker: an ocean wave that collapses and tumbles forward as it approaches the shore because the top is moving faster than the body. (Chap. 17, p. 491)

buoyancy (BOY un see): the lifting effect on an object immersed in water.

caldera (kal DARE uh)**:** the large opening formed at the top of a volcano when a crater collapses into the vent following an eruption. (Chap. 10, p. 285)

carbonaceous film: a fossil impression in a rock, consisting only of a thin carbon residue that forms an outline of the original organism. (Chap. 12, p. 328)

carbonic acid: a weak acid that forms when water mixes with carbon dioxide from air.

carrying capacity: the maximum number of individuals of a particular species that an environment can support. (Chap. 19, p. 532)

cast: a type of fossil formed when an earlier fossil in the rock is dissolved away, leaving behind the impression of that fossil (a mold), and new sediments or mineral crystals fill the mold. (Chap. 12, p. 329)

cave: a large underground opening formed when groundwater gradually dissolves limestone. (Chap. 8, p. 217)

cementation: a sedimentary rock-forming process in which large sediments are glued together by minerals deposited between the sediments. (Chap. 4, p. 102)

Cenozoic (sen uh ZOH ihk) **Era:** the most recent era of Earth's geologic history; began about 66 million years ago when dinosaurs became extinct. (Chap. 13, p. 379)

chemical properties: characteristics of an element or compound that determine how it will react with other elements or compounds. (Chap. 2, p. 39)

chemical weathering: the breaking up of rocks due to a change in their chemical composition. (Chap. 6, p. 151)

chemosynthesis (kee moh SIHN thuh sihs)**:** the process used by bacteria along mid-ocean ridges to produce food and oxygen by using dissolved sulfur compounds from magma. (Chap. 18, p. 512)

chlorofluorocarbons: a group of chemicals used as refrigerants and aerosol spray propellants. Chlorofluorocarbons destroy ozone molecules. (Chap. 14, p. 401)

chromosphere: the intermediate layer of the three layers of the sun's atmosphere, lying between the photosphere and the corona. (Chap. 24, p. 679)

cinder cone: a type of volcano in which tephra (cinders) piles up into a steep-sided cone. (Chap. 10, p. 279)

circumpolar constellation: a constellation that appears to circle Polaris as Earth rotates.

cirque (SURK): a bowl-shaped basin carved by erosion at the head of a valley glacier.

clay: sediment particle less than 0.004 mm in size.

Clean Air Act: this 1990 U.S. law sets a maximum level for major air pollutants. (Chap. 20, p. 561)

Clean Water Act: this 1987 U.S. law gives money to the states for building sewage and wastewater-treatment facilities and for controlling runoff from streets, farms, and mines. (Chap. 20, p. 571)

cleavage: the physical property of a mineral that causes it to break along smooth, flat surfaces. (Chap. 3, p. 70)

climate: the pattern of weather in a particular area over a period of many years; affects the rate and type of weathering. (Chap. 6, p. 154)

cloud seeding: the addition of silver iodide or dry ice particles to clouds to produce a change in weather conditions. (Chap. 15, p. 444)

coal: a sedimentary rock formed from compacted, decayed plants; burned as a fossil fuel.

coastal plain: a landform that is a broad, flat area along a coastline; also called a lowland.

cogeneration: process in which a power plant uses both the electrical and thermal energy produced by the plant. (Chap. 4, p. 109)

cold front: the boundary that develops when a cold air mass pushes under a warm air mass.

comet: a mass of frozen gases, dust, and rock particles that often develops a bright tail when it passes near the sun and is acted on by solar winds. (Chap. 23, p. 663)

compaction: a sedimentary rock-forming process that occurs when layers of small sediments become compressed by the weight of layers above them. (Chap. 4, p. 102)

composite volcano: a type of volcano built of silica-rich lava and tephra layers accumulated from repeated alternating cycles of tephra eruptions and lava eruptions. (Chap. 10, p. 281)

composting: the piling up of grass clippings, dead leaves, and other organic matter so they can gradually decompose. (Chap. 19, p. 545)

compound: a type of matter containing two or more chemically combined elements and having physical and chemical properties different from each of the elements in it. (Chap. 2, p. 38)

compression: squeezing forces that compress rocks together at convergent plate boundaries, causing them to deform, fold, and sometimes break.

conduction: the transfer of heat that occurs when molecules collide. (Chap. 14, p. 405)

conic projection: a map projection made by projecting points and lines from a globe onto a cone; it produces accurate maps of areas smaller than the whole Earth, such as a nation or state. (Chap. 5, p. 131)

conservation: the careful use of resources to avoid wasting them and damaging the environment; includes reusing and recycling resources. (Chap. 19, p. 544)

constellation: a grouping of stars that has a shape resembling an animal, mythological character, or other familiar object and thus is named for it. (Chap. 24, p. 672)

container law: a law requiring you to pay a deposit each time you buy a container of beverage.

continental drift: a hypothesis proposed by Alfred Wegener, which states that continents have moved horizontally around the globe, over time, to reach their current locations. (Chap. 11, p. 294)

continental glacier: a glacier of considerable thickness that covers a vast area; existing now only in Greenland and Antarctica.

continental shelf: the gradually sloping end of every continent that extends out under the ocean. (Chap. 18, p. 504)

continental slope: a part of the continental shelf that dips steeply down to the ocean floor. (Chap. 18, p. 505)

contour interval: the difference in elevation between two side-by-side contour lines on a topographic map. (Chap. 5, p. 132)

contour line: a line on a topographic map that connects points of equal elevation. (Chap. 5, p. 132)

control: in an experiment, the standard used for comparison. (Chap. 1, p. 17)

convection: the transfer of heat by a flow of a heated material; occurs in gases or liquids. (Chap. 14, p. 405)

convection current: the driving force of plate tectonics in which hot, plasticlike material from the mantle rises to the lithosphere, moves horizontally, cools, and sinks back to the mantle. (Chap. 11, p. 310)

convergent boundary: in plate tectonics, the boundary between two plates that are converging, or moving toward each other. (Chap. 11, p. 307)

Copernicus, Nicholas: Polish astronomer (1473-1543) who hypothesized a sun-centered solar system.

Coriolis (kohr ee OH lus) **effect:** the effect of Earth's rotation on the movement of air masses; changes the direction of the air flow. (Chap. 14, p. 411)

corona: the outermost and largest of the three layers of the sun's atmosphere, extending from the chromosphere outward millions of kilometers into space. (Chap. 24, p. 679)

crater: the steep-walled depression at the top of a volcanic vent. (Chap. 10, p. 268)

creep: a type of mass movement in which sediments move down a hill slowly, sometimes causing posts and trees to lean. (Chap. 7, p. 175)

crest: the highest point of a wave. (Chap. 17, p. 490)

crinoids (KRI noyds): marine invertebrate animals that resemble plants, commonly found as fossils in Paleozoic Era rocks and still a living animal group.

crust: the outermost layer of Earth, varying in thickness from more than 60 km to less than 5 km. (Chap. 9, p. 249)

crystal: a solid having a distinctive shape because its atoms are arranged in repeating patterns. (Chap. 3, p. 63)

crystal system: the pattern that atoms form in a crystal.

cyanobacteria: blue-green bacteria thought to be one of the earliest life-forms on Earth. (Chap. 13, p. 367)

deflation: wind erosion that removes loose, fine-grained sediments such as clay or silt, and leaves behind coarser material. (Chap. 7, p. 188)

deforestation: the removal of forests, mostly to clear land for farming, construction, mining, and drilling for oil. (Chap. 16, p. 470)

delta: a triangular deposit of sediment that forms when a stream or a river slows as it empties into an ocean, gulf, or lake. (Chap. 8, p. 213)

density: how highly packed a substance's molecules are; the mass of an object divided by its volume, in g/cm^3. (Chap. 2, p. 44)

density current: an ocean current that occurs when more dense seawater sinks under an area of less dense seawater. (Chap. 17, p. 487)

deposition (dep uh ZIHSH un)**:** the final step in an erosional process, in which sediments are dropped by running water, wind, gravity, or glaciers as their energy of motion decreases. (Chap. 7, p. 173)

desertification: the formation of a desert. (Chap. 6, p. 165)

dew point: the temperature at which air is saturated with water and condensation begins. (Chap. 15, p. 424)

dike: an intrusive igneous rock body formed when magma is squeezed into a vertical crack that cuts across rock layers and solidifies underground. (Chap. 10, p. 284)

disconformity: a type of unconformity in which the top rock layer is eroded before the next layer can be deposited, causing a gap in the rock record.

divergent boundary: in plate tectonics, the boundary between two plates that are diverging, or moving away from each other. (Chap. 11, p. 305)

Doppler shift: the change in wavelength that occurs in any kind of wave energy (light, radio, sound) as the source of the energy moves toward you (the wavelength shortens) or away from you (the wavelength lengthens).

drainage basin: the land area drained by a river system. (Chap. 8, p. 207)

dust bowl: name given to the Great Plains area of the United States in the 1930s, when it was struck by devastating drought and dust storms.

Earth: in our solar system, the third planet from the sun; the only planet known to support life; appears blue from space because more than 70 percent of its surface is covered by liquid water. (Chap. 23, p. 648)

Earth science: the study of Earth and space; includes geology, meteorology, astronomy, and oceanography. (Chap. 1, p. 8)

earthquake: the movement of the ground, caused by waves from energy released as rocks move along faults. (Chap. 9, p. 237)

El Niño: a climatic event that occurs when trade winds weaken west of Peru and whose effects can be felt worldwide. (Chap. 16, p. 463)

electromagnetic spectrum: the classification of electromagnetic radiation (including radio waves, visible light, X rays, and gamma rays) according to their wavelengths. (Chap. 21, p. 585)

electron: one of the three subatomic particles; moves around the nucleus of an atom; has a negative electric charge. (Chap. 2, p. 35)

element: a form of matter that contains only one kind of atom; cannot be broken down into simpler substances. (Chap. 2, p. 33)

ellipse: an elongated, closed curve; the shape of Earth's orbit. (Chap. 22, p. 617)

elliptical galaxy: the most common type of galaxy; shaped like a large, three-dimensional ellipse.

endangered: describes a species that has only a relatively small number of individuals living and thus is in danger of dying out. (Chap. 13, p. 364)

epicenter: the point on Earth's surface directly above an earthquake's focus. (Chap. 9, p. 244)

epochs: subdivisions of periods on the geologic time scale. (Chap. 13, p. 359)

equator: an imaginary line, at 0° latitude, that circles Earth exactly halfway between the North and South Poles; separates Earth into the northern hemisphere and the southern hemisphere. (Chap. 5, p. 126)

equinox: the two times each year that the sun is directly above Earth's equator and the day and night are of equal length all over the world; the start of spring and fall. (Chap. 22, p. 619)

eras: the four largest subdivisions of the geologic time scale—Precambrian, Paleozoic, Mesozoic, Cenozoic—based on differences in life-forms. (Chap. 13, p. 357)

erosion (ih ROH zhun): the process that wears away surface materials and moves them from one location to another, usually by gravity, glaciers, wind, or water. (Chap. 7, p. 172)

esker: a winding ridge of sand and gravel formed by streams flowing beneath a glacier.

extinct: describes a species that no longer has any living members anywhere on Earth—for example, dinosaurs. (Chap. 12, p. 334)

extrusive igneous rocks: igneous rocks that form when magma extrudes onto Earth's surface and cools as lava; have a fine-grained texture. (Chap. 4, p. 92)

fault-block mountains: jagged mountains formed from huge, tilted blocks of rock that are separated from surrounding rock by faults. (Chap. 5, p. 124)

faults: surfaces along which rocks break and move; rocks on either side of a fault move in different directions relative to the fault surface. (Chap. 9, p. 236)

first quarter: the moon phase halfway between new moon and full moon, when half of the side facing Earth is lighted. (Chap. 22, p. 624)

fission: the splitting of the nuclei of atoms of heavy elements to release energy. (Chap. 2, p. 54)

floodplain: the broad, flat valley floor carved by a meandering stream and often covered with water when the stream floods. (Chap. 8, p. 209)

focus: the point in Earth's interior where earthquake energy is released. (Chap. 9, p. 241)

fog: a stratus cloud that forms on or near the ground when air is cooled to its dew point and condenses. (Chap. 15, p. 425)

folded mountains: mountains created when rock layers are squeezed from opposite sides, causing them to buckle and fold. (Chap. 5, p. 123)

foliated: a type of metamorphic rock created when mineral grains flatten and line up in parallel bands. (Chap. 4, p. 99)

fossils: the remains, imprints, or traces of once-living organisms, usually preserved in rock, that tell us when, where, and how those organisms lived. (Chap. 12, p. 327)

fracture: the physical property of a mineral that causes it to break with rough or jagged edges. (Chap. 3, p. 70)

front: in weather systems, the boundary between two air masses. (Chap. 15, p. 433)

full moon: the moon phase when the side facing Earth is completely lighted because Earth is between the sun and the moon. (Chap. 22, p. 624)

fusion: the process that powers our sun and the other stars; hydrogen fusion occurs when great temperatures and pressures fuse hydrogen atoms to form helium atoms and energy is released.

galaxy: a massive grouping of stars, gas, and dust in space, held together by gravity; can be elliptical, spiral, or irregular. (Chap. 24, p. 691)

Galilei, Galileo: Italian astronomer (1564-1642) who supported a sun-centered solar system by discovering that Venus has phases similar to the moon.

gamma rays: electromagnetic waves having short wavelengths and high energy.

Ganymede: one of Jupiter's four largest moons; the largest satellite in the solar system.

gasohol: a biomass fuel that is about 90 percent gasoline and about ten percent alcohol; used in cars and trucks.

gem: a valuable mineral highly prized because it is rare and beautiful. (Chap. 3, p. 74)

geologic time scale: a record of Earth's history, beginning 4.6 billion years ago, that shows events, time units, and ages. (Chap. 13, p. 357)

geology: the study of Earth and its matter, processes, and history. (Chap. 1, p. 8)

geothermal energy: thermal energy from magma bodies inside Earth that can be used to produce electricity with very little environmental pollution. (Chap. 10, p. 274)

geyser: a hot spring of groundwater that erupts periodically, shooting water and steam into the air. (Chap. 8, p. 217)

giant: a late stage in a star's life cycle in which the hydrogen in the core has contracted and grown hotter, causing its outer layers to expand. (Chap. 24, p. 687)

glacier: a mass of snow and ice that moves slowly downhill due to its weight. (Chap. 7, p. 180)

global warming: the rise in global temperatures due to an increased greenhouse effect. (Chap. 16, p. 467)

Glossopteris (glah SAHP tuhr ihs): a fossil fern providing evidence that continents once were joined.

granitic: light-colored igneous rocks formed from magma rich in silicon and oxygen. (Chap. 4, p. 93)

gravity: an attractive force that exists between all objects. (Chap. 1, p. 20)

Great Red Spot: a giant, swirling, high-pressure gas storm in Jupiter's atmosphere. (Chap. 23, p. 654)

greenhouse effect: natural heating caused by atmospheric gases trapping heat at Earth's surface. (Chap. 16, p. 467)

groundwater: water that soaks into the ground and collects in the pore spaces between particles of rock and soil. (Chap. 8, p. 214)

Gulf Stream: an ocean current that flows out of the Gulf of Mexico, northward along the east coast of the United States, and then toward Europe.

gully erosion: a type of surface water erosion due to runoff, in which water swiftly running down a slope creates large channels in the soil or rock. (Chap. 8, p. 204)

habitat: any place where organisms live, grow, and interact with one another and with the environment. (Chap. 13, p. 364)

hachures (ha SHOORZ): lines drawn at right angles to contour lines on a topographic map; they indicate depressions.

half-life: the time it takes for half of the atoms of an isotope to decay. (Chap. 12, p. 345)

hardness: a measure of how easily a mineral can be scratched. (Chap. 3, p. 68)

hazardous waste: waste that is dangerous to organisms because it is poisonous, cancer causing, or radioactive. (Chap. 19, p. 541)

Hess, Harry: a Princeton University scientist who proposed the theory of seafloor spreading in the 1960s.

hibernation: a period of inactivity during which an animal's body temperature drops and its body processes slow down. (Chap. 16, p. 460)

high-pressure system: an air mass with densely packed air molecules where cold air descends and rotates clockwise (in the northern hemisphere).

Homo erectus: an ancestor of modern *Homo sapiens,* this extinct primate lived in Africa and Asia from 1.6 million to 250 000 years ago.

Homo habilis: the earliest species to have fully human characteristics, this extinct primate evolved from *Austraulopithecus,* lived in Africa 1.5 to 2 million years ago, and regularly used tools.

horizon: a soil layer; most areas of Earth have three, called the A horizon (topsoil), B horizon, and C horizon. (Chap. 6, p. 158)

horn: a sharp mountain peak pointed like an animal's horn, carved by glaciers.

hot dry rock (HDR): a new technology in which heat from Earth's internal hot dry rock material is used to generate energy. (Chap. 10, p. 275)

hot spots: areas in Earth's mantle that are hotter than the neighboring areas, forming melted rock that rises toward the crust. (Chap. 10, p. 273)

hot spring: a spring of heated groundwater, caused when the water is warmed by rocks that come into contact with molten material under Earth's surface. (Chap. 8, p. 216)

humidity: the amount of water vapor held in the air. (Chap. 15, p. 423)

humus: dark-colored organic matter found in soil; made of decayed plants and animals. (Chap. 6, p. 157)

hurricane: a large, swirling, low-pressure system that forms over tropical oceans; winds must reach at least 120 km/hr. (Chap. 15, p. 438)

hydrosphere: all the water that occurs at Earth's surface. (Chap. 14, p. 406)

hypothesis: a prediction about a problem that can be tested; may be used to form a theory. (Chap. 1, p. 16)

ice wedging: the breaking of rocks when water in cracks freezes and expands; a type of mechanical weathering. (Chap. 6, p. 150)

igneous rock: rock formed by the cooling and hardening of molten material from a volcano or from deep inside Earth. (Chap. 4, p. 90)

impermeable: rock or soil that has few pores or small pores, preventing water from passing through. (Chap. 8, p. 215)

index fossil: a fossil of a species that was abundant, existed briefly, and was widespread geographically; used in determining the relative ages of rock layers. (Chap. 12, p. 331)

infrared waves: electromagnetic waves that are the heat waves that we feel.

inner core: the dense, solid center of Earth, formed mostly of iron and nickel. (Chap. 9, p. 249)

inner planets: the four solid, rocky planets closest to the sun—Mercury, Venus, Earth, and Mars. (Chap. 23, p. 643)

International Date Line: the 180° meridian, on the other side of Earth from the prime meridian; an imaginary line in the Pacific Ocean where we change calendar days. (Chap. 5, p. 129)

International System of Units (SI): a modern version of the metric system that is used by most people around the world. (Chap. 1, p. 19)

intrusive igneous rocks: igneous rocks formed when magma cools below Earth's surface; generally have large mineral grains. (Chap. 4, p. 92)

invertebrates: animals without backbones.

ion: an atom with an electrical charge. (Chap. 2, p. 40)

ionosphere: a layer of Earth's atmosphere, where ions and free electrons absorb AM radio waves during the day and reflect them back toward Earth at night. (Chap. 14, p. 395)

irregular galaxies: galaxies having irregular shapes.

isobar: on a weather map, a line connecting points of equal atmospheric pressure. (Chap. 15, p. 441)

isotherm: on a weather map, a line connecting points of equal temperature. (Chap. 15, p. 441)

isotopes: atoms of the same element that have different numbers of neutrons in their nuclei, but the same number of protons. (Chap. 2, p. 36)

jet stream: narrow wind belts occurring near the top of the troposphere. (Chap. 14, p. 414)

Jupiter: in our solar system, the fifth planet from the sun; it is the largest planet, mostly gas and liquid, and has continuous storms of high-pressure gas. (Chap. 23, p. 654)

L

land breeze: wind blowing from land to sea at night because the land cools faster and cool air over the land moves out over the sea. (Chap. 14, p. 415)

landfill: an area of land where waste is deposited. (Chap. 19, p. 541)

landforms: features that make up the shape of the land at Earth's surface, such as plains, plateaus, and mountains.

Landsat Satellite: satellite that collects information about Earth's surface by using a mirror to detect different wavelengths of reflected or emitted energy. (Chap. 5, p. 138)

latitude: a distance north or south of the equator, expressed in degrees. (Chap. 5, p. 127)

lava: molten rock from a volcano flowing onto Earth's surface. (Chap. 4, p. 91)

law: a scientific rule of nature that describes the behavior of something in nature, but doesn't explain why something will happen in a given situation. (Chap. 1, p. 18)

leaching: occurs when soil materials dissolved in water are carried down through soil layers. (Chap. 6, p. 159)

legend: a list of symbols used on a map that explains their meaning.

light pollution: the glow in the night sky caused by urban lights, suburban lights, and rural security lights. (Chap. 21, p. 591)

light-year: a unit used to measure distance in space; the distance that light travels in one year (about 9.5 trillion km). (Chap. 24, p. 675)

lithosphere (LITH uh sfihr)**:** the rigid, outermost layer of Earth, about 100 km thick, composed of the crust and part of the mantle. (Chap. 11, p. 304)

Local Group: the cluster of about 25 galaxies that includes our galaxy (the Milky Way).

loess (LES)**:** a thick deposit of fine, wind-eroded sediments. (Chap. 7, p. 191)

longitude: a distance east or west of the prime meridian, expressed in degrees. (Chap. 5, p. 127)

longshore current: an ocean current that runs parallel to the shore, caused by waves colliding with the shore at slight angles. (Chap. 8, p. 223)

low-pressure system: in weather systems, an area where warm air rises and rotates counterclockwise (in the northern hemisphere).

lunar eclipse: an eclipse that occurs when Earth passes between the sun and moon, and Earth's shadow falls on the moon, preventing sunlight from reaching all or part of the moon. (Chap. 22, p. 627)

luster: the physical property of a mineral that describes how light is reflected from its surface; is defined as either metallic or nonmetallic. (Chap. 3, p. 69)

magma: hot, melted rock material beneath Earth's surface. (Chap. 3, p. 64)

magnetometer: a sensitive instrument that records magnetic data and is used to study Earth's magnetic field. (Chap. 11, p. 300)

magnitude: in earthquakes studies, a measure of the energy released by an earthquake; the Richter scale is used to describe earthquake magnitude. (Chap. 9, p. 253)

main sequence: on a Hertzsprung-Russell diagram, the diagonal band that includes 90 percent of all stars; shows relationships among a star's color, brightness, and temperature. (Chap. 24, p. 684)

mammals: warm-blooded vertebrates.

mantle: the thickest layer inside Earth; it lies between the outer core and the crust and is described as plasticlike; formed mostly of silicon, oxygen, magnesium, and iron. (Chap. 9, p. 249)

map legend: the key on most maps that is used to explain what the symbols on the map mean. (Chap. 5, p. 134)

map scale: the relationship between distances drawn on a map and actual distances on Earth's surface. (Chap. 5, p. 135)

maria: dark, flat regions of ancient lava on the moon; viewed from Earth, they resemble oceans, the Latin word for which is *maria.* (Chap. 22, p. 628)

market: the people or businesses that want to purchase a product.

Mars: in our solar system, the fourth planet from the sun; known as the red planet due to the iron oxide content of its weathered rocks. (Chap. 23, p. 649)

mascon: the concentration of mass on the moon located under an impact basin. (Chap. 22, p. 633)

mass: a measure of the amount of matter in an object; SI unit is the kilogram. (Chap. 1, p. 20)

mass movement: a type of erosion in which gravity causes loose materials to move downslope; can occur slowly or quickly. (Chap. 7, p. 173)

mass number: the sum of the number of protons and neutrons in an atom's nucleus. (Chap. 2, p. 36)

matter: anything that takes up space and has mass; the characteristics of matter are determined by its atoms. (Chap. 2, p. 32)

meander: a curve in a mature stream. (Chap. 8, p. 208)

mechanical weathering: the breaking apart of rocks without changing their chemical composition; for example, by plant roots and ice. (Chap. 6, p. 149)

Mercator (mur KAYT ur) **projection:** a map-projection method using parallel longitude lines; continent shapes are accurate, but their areas are distorted. (Chap. 5, p. 130)

Mercury: in our solar system, the first planet from the sun; the second-smallest planet that has a cratered surface like our moon and cliffs as high as 3 km. (Chap. 23, p. 646)

Mesosaurus (mes oh SAR uhs): a fossil reptile found both in South America and Africa, providing evidence that these continents once were joined.

Mesozoic (mez uh ZOH ihk) **Era:** the middle era of Earth's geologic history; began about 245 million years ago; reptiles and gymnosperms were the dominant land life-forms. (Chap. 13, p. 374)

metallic luster: the physical property of any mineral that has a shiny appearance resembling metal.

metamorphic rock: rock formed from sedimentary, igneous, or other metamorphic rock due to increases in heat or pressure. (Chap. 4, p. 97)

meteor: a meteoroid that enters Earth's atmosphere and burns up as it falls; also called a shooting star. (Chap. 23, p. 664)

meteorite: a meteor that does not completely burn up in Earth's atmosphere and strikes Earth's surface. (Chap. 23, p. 665)

meteorologist: a scientist who studies weather conditions using radar, satellites, and other instruments to make weather maps and forecasts. (Chap. 15, p. 440)

meteorology: the study of Earth's weather and the forces that cause it. (Chap. 1, p. 8)

microwaves: electromagnetic waves that are shorter than radio waves but longer than light waves; we use them for radar and transmitting voices, music, video, and data.

mid-ocean ridge: the place where new ocean floor forms; resembles an underwater mountain range; formed when forces within Earth spread the seafloor apart. (Chap. 18, p. 506)

mineral: a naturally occurring, inorganic solid with a distinct internal structure and chemical composition. (Chap. 3, p. 62)

mixture: a combination of different substances in which each of the components keeps its own physical and chemical properties despite being mixed. (Chap. 2, p. 40)

Moho discontinuity: the boundary between Earth's crust and the mantle; seismic waves travel faster below the Moho and slower above it. (Chap. 9, p. 249)

Mohs' Scale of Hardness: a list of common minerals and their hardnesses, developed by German mineralogist Friedrich Mohs.

mold: a cavity in a rock that has the shape of a fossil that was trapped there; water dissolved the fossil away, leaving its imprint. (Chap. 12, p. 329)

molecule: the smallest particle of a compound that still keeps all the properties of the compound; it is formed by the combining of two or more atoms. (Chap. 2, p. 38)

moon phases: the change in appearance of the moon as it orbits Earth every 29½ days, depending on the relative positions of the moon, Earth, and the sun; for example, full moon and new moon. (Chap. 22, p. 624)

moraine: a ridge of unsorted rock and soil bulldozed ahead and to the sides of a glacier; left behind when the glacier melts. (Chap. 7, p. 184)

natural gas: a mixture of gases formed as ancient plants and animals decayed; burned as a fossil fuel.

natural selection: the process by which organisms with traits best suited to an environment survive and reproduce, while others die out because they lack those traits. (Chap. 13, p. 360)

neap tide: a tide that is lower than normal because the sun, Earth, and moon form a right angle.

nebula: a large cloud of gas and dust in space that may be the beginning of a star. (Chap. 24, p. 686)

nekton (NEK tuhn)**:** marine animals that swim and determine their own course of movement rather than drift with currents; for example, shrimp and whales. (Chap. 18, p. 513)

Neptune: in our solar system, usually the eighth planet from the sun; it is large, gaseous, and has storm-like features. (Chap. 23, p. 658)

neutron: one of the two particles that make up the nucleus of an atom; it has no electric charge. (Chap. 2, p. 35)

neutron star: the final stage in the life cycle of some stars, where the core of a supernova collapses, shrinks to about 10-15 km, and becomes so dense that only neutrons can exist there. (Chap. 24, p. 688)

new moon: the moon phase when the side facing Earth is completely dark and cannot be seen because the moon is between Earth and sun. (Chap. 22, p. 624)

nonfoliated: a type of metamorphic rock created when mineral grains change, grow, and rearrange, but don't form bands. (Chap. 4, p. 99)

nonmetallic luster: a physical property of a mineral that has a dull appearance and does not resemble a metal.

normal fault: a pull-apart (tension) fracture in rocks, where rocks that are above the fault surface drop downward in relation to rocks that are below the fault surface like this:
<—normal/fault—>. (Chap. 9, p. 238)

nuclear energy: an alternate energy source produced from atomic reactions. (Chap. 2, p. 54)

nuclear reactor: a device in which uranium atoms fission to release energy, used to generate electricity.

nuclear waste: radioactive waste material produced by nuclear power plants; must be safely stored to prevent it from entering the environment. (Chap. 2, p. 55)

observatory: a building that contains an optical telescope for observing objects in space. (Chap. 21, p. 586)

occluded front: in weather systems, the boundary that results when two cool air masses merge and force warmer air to rise between them.

oceanography: the study of Earth's oceans, their processes, and life within them. (Chap. 1, p. 9)

oil: a liquid formed as ancient plants and animals decay; burned as a fossil fuel and used to make lubricants and plastics.

old stream: a stream that flows slowly down a gradual slope through a broad floodplain that it has made; often meandering.

Olympus Mons: the largest known volcano in the solar system—on Mars.

Oort Cloud: a cloud of comets surrounding the solar system beyond Pluto's orbit; it may be the source of most comets. (Chap. 23, p. 663)

orbit: the curved path followed by a satellite as it travels around a star, planet, or other object. (Chap. 21, p. 594)

ore: a mineral containing a useful substance, such as a metal, that can be mined at a profit. (Chap. 3, p. 75)

organic evolution: the gradual change in life-forms over time. (Chap. 13, p. 359)

organic matter: any material that originated as plant or animal tissue; decaying animals or plants that become sediment and a part of soils.

outer core: the liquid layer of Earth's core that surrounds the solid inner core and is comprised of iron and nickel. (Chap. 9, p. 249)

outer planets: the five planets farthest from the sun—Jupiter, Saturn, Uranus, Neptune, and Pluto. (Chap. 23, p. 643)

outwash: stratified material washed out from a glacier by meltwater.

overgrazing: occurs when too many animals graze too small an area and eat all the vegetation from the land.

oxidation: chemical weathering that occurs when a substance is exposed to oxygen and water. (Chap. 6, p. 154)

ozone layer: a layer of the stratosphere with a high concentration of ozone; protects living things by absorbing ultraviolet radiation from the sun. (Chap. 14, p. 400)

Pacific Ring of Fire: the area around the Pacific Plate where volcanoes and earthquakes are common due to tectonic movement. (Chap. 10, p. 272)

Paleozoic (pay lee uh ZOH ihk) **Era:** the second-oldest division of geologic time; began about 544 million years ago, when organisms developed hard parts. (Chap. 13, p. 367)

Pangaea (pan JEE uh)**:** the name Alfred Wegener gave to the large landmass, made up of all continents, that he believed existed before it broke apart to form the present continents. (Chap. 11, p. 294)

parallax: the apparent shift in position of an object when viewed from two different points, such as your left eye and right eye. (Chap. 24, p. 675)

pebble: a sediment particle measuring 2.0 mm to 64 mm in size.

penumbra: during an eclipse, the highest outer portion of the shadow.

periods: subdivisions of eras on the geologic time scale, based on life-forms and geologic events. (Chap. 13, p. 357)

permeable: describes rock or soil that has connecting pores that allow water to pass through easily. (Chap. 8, p. 215)

petrified remains: plant or animal remains that have been petrified, or "turned to rock"; this happens when minerals carried in groundwater replace the original materials. (Chap. 12, p. 328)

petroleum: a naturally occurring liquid formed over millions of years from organisms; is refined into fuel such as gasoline.

pH scale: a logarithmic scale used to describe how acidic or how basic a solution is; an abbreviation of *p*otential of *H*ydrogen. (Chap. 20, p. 558)

photochemical smog: a brown-colored air pollution that forms when sunlight chemically changes the pollutants released into the air by burning fossil fuels. (Chap. 20, p. 556)

photosphere: the innermost (lowest) of the three layers of sun's atmosphere; radiates the light we see; often called the surface of the sun. (Chap. 24, p. 679)

photosynthesis (foh toh SIHN thuh sihs)**:** the process that plants use to make food, using light energy, carbon dioxide, and water. (Chap. 18, p. 510)

physical properties: characteristics of an element or a compound that affect weight, color, density, etc., but don't affect how it will react with other elements or compounds. (Chap. 2, p. 44)

plain: a landform that is a large, relatively flat area; interior plains and coastal plains make up one-half the land area in the United States. (Chap. 5, p. 120)

plankton (PLANK tuhn)**:** tiny marine plants and animals that drift with the ocean currents. (Chap. 18, p. 513)

plate: in plate tectonics, a section of Earth's lithosphere (crust and upper mantle) that moves around on the mantle. (Chap. 11, p. 304)

plate tectonics: the theory that Earth's crust and upper mantle (lithosphere) are broken into sections, called plates, that slowly move around on the mantle. (Chap. 11, p. 304)

plateaus: landforms created next to mountains, when forces within Earth raised high, relatively flat areas of nearly horizontal rocks. (Chap. 5, p. 122)

plucking: a type of glacial erosion in which rock fragments are loosened, broken off, and carried away by the freezing of water in rock cracks. (Chap. 7, p. 182)

Pluto: in our solar system, usually the ninth and last planet from the sun; it is the smallest planet and the only outer planet with a solid, icy rock surface. (Chap. 23, p. 658)

polar zones: the zones that receive solar radiation at an angle and are the coldest areas on Earth; extend from the poles to 66½° north and south latitudes. (Chap. 16, p. 452)

pollutant: a substance that interferes with biochemical processes and causes harmful change to organisms; produced both by human activities and natural processes. (Chap. 18, p. 519)

pollution: the introduction of harmful substances into an environment. (Chap. 18, p. 519)

population: the total number of individuals of a particular species that exists in a specific area. (Chap. 19, p. 533)

population explosion: a large increase in the population of a species, due to a rapid increase in the birthrate, or a sharply reduced death rate, or both. (Chap. 19, p. 533)

Precambrian (pree KAM bree un) **time:** the oldest and longest division of geologic time, including about 90 percent of Earth's history; spans 4.6 billion to about 544 million years ago. (Chap. 13, p. 366)

precipitation: water or ice that condenses in the air and falls to the ground as rain, snow, sleet, or hail, depending on the air temperature. (Chap. 15, p. 430)

primary waves: waves of energy, released during an earthquake, that travel through Earth by causing particles in rocks to compress and stretch apart in the direction of the wave. (Chap. 9, p. 244)

prime meridian: an imaginary line running from the North Pole to the South Pole, passing through Greenwich, England; the 0° reference line for longitude. (Chap. 5, p. 127)

principle of superposition: states that in an undisturbed layer of rock, older rocks lie at the bottom and the rocks become younger toward the top. (Chap. 12, p. 337)

Project Apollo: a project of the U.S. space program in which astronauts first traveled to the moon in the spacecraft *Apollo II.* (Chap. 21, p. 598)

Project Gemini: an early project of the U.S. space program in which two crewed *Gemini* spacecraft successfully linked in orbit. (Chap. 21, p. 598)

Project Mercury: an early project of the U.S. space program in which a piloted spacecraft orbited Earth and returned safely. (Chap. 21, p. 597)

proton: one of the two particles that make up the nucleus of an atom; it has a positive electric charge. (Chap. 2, p. 35)

psychrometer (si KRAH muh tur): a device used by meteorologists to measure relative humidity.

radiation: the transfer of energy through matter or space by electromagnetic waves. (Chap. 14, p. 403)

radio telescope: an instrument that uses a large curved dish to reflect radio waves from space to a focal point; used to study space objects and map the universe. (Chap. 21, p. 587)

radio waves: electromagnetic waves having long wavelengths; we use them to transmit voices, music, video, and data over distances.

radioactive decay: the decay of an atom of one element to form another element, occurring when an alpha particle or beta particle is expelled from the original atom. (Chap. 12, p. 344)

radiometric dating: a dating method that uses the rate of decay of radioactive isotopes in rocks and measures the amount of parent and daughter materials to determine the absolute age of the rock. (Chap. 12, p. 345)

recyclable: items that can be processed and used again. (Chap. 19, p. 546)

red shift: a kind of Doppler shift in which light from a star that is moving away from us has its wavelength shifted toward the red end of the spectrum.

reef: on the continental shelf, a large, rigid underwater colony of coral animals that have become cemented together. (Chap. 18, p. 518)

reflecting telescope: an optical magnifying instrument in which light from an object strikes a concave mirror, which then reflects the light to form an image at the focal point. (Chap. 21, p. 586)

reforestation: the planting of a large number of trees. (Chap. 16, p. 471)

refracting telescope: an optical magnifying instrument in which light from an object passes through a convex lens and is bent to form an image at the focal point. (Chap. 21, p. 586)

relative dating: determining the order of events and the relative age of rocks (older or younger) by examining the positions of rocks in layers. (Chap.12, p. 338)

relative humidity: the measure of the amount of water vapor in the air, compared to the maximum it can hold at a specific temperature; it varies with temperature and is between zero percent and 100 percent. (Chap. 15, p. 424)

reptiles: scaly skinned, vertebrate animals that evolved from the same ancestors as amphibians but do not return to water to reproduce. (Chap. 13, p. 370)

reverse fault: a compression fracture in rocks, where rocks that are above the fault surface are forced up over rocks that are below the fault surface, like this: —>reverse/fault<—. (Chap. 9, p. 238)

revolution: the orbiting of one object around another, like Earth's yearly orbit around the sun. (Chap. 22, p. 617)

Richter (RIHK tur) scale: describes how much energy is released by an earthquake.

rill erosion: a type of surface water erosion due to runoff, in which water swiftly running down the slope creates small channels in the soil; these channels can enlarge into gullies. (Chap. 8, p. 204)

Robinson projection: a map-projection method using curved longitude lines; continent shapes and land areas are accurate with little distortion. (Chap. 5, p. 131)

rock: Earth material made of a mixture of one or more minerals, glass, mineraloids, or organic matter. (Chap. 4, p. 87)

rock cycle: the processes by which, over many years, Earth materials form and change back and forth among igneous rocks, sedimentary rocks, and metamorphic rocks. (Chap. 4, p. 87)

rock-forming minerals: a group of minerals that make up most of the rocks in Earth's crust.

rotation: the spinning of an object around its axis; causes day and night to occur on Earth. (Chap. 22, p. 615)

runoff: water that neither soaks into the ground nor evaporates but instead flows across Earth's surface and eventually into streams, lakes, or oceans. (Chap. 8, p. 202)

S

Safe Drinking Water Act: this 1986 law sets safety standards for drinking water in the United States. (Chap. 20, p. 570)

salinity: a measure of the amount of solids (mostly salts) dissolved in seawater; usually measured in grams of salt per kilogram of ocean water. (Chap. 17, p. 480)

sand: a sediment particle measuring 0.06 mm to 2.0 mm in size.

sanitary landfill: a waste-disposal area that is excavated; lined with plastic, concrete, or clay; and filled with layers of waste and dirt. (Chap. 19, p. 541)

satellite: any object that revolves around another object; planets and human-made satellites are examples. (Chap. 21, p. 594)

saturated (SACH uh rayt id)**:** condition when air contains as much moisture as possible at a specific temperature. (Chap. 15, p. 424)

Saturn: in our solar system, the sixth planet from the sun; it is the second-largest planet, is mostly gas and liquid, and has prominent rings. (Chap. 23, p. 656)

science: the process of observing, explaining, and understanding things in our world; means "having knowledge"; divided into four general areas: chemistry, physics, life science, and Earth science. (Chap. 1, p. 6)

scientific method: a series of problem-solving procedures used by scientists; may include the following basic steps: determining the problem, making a hypothesis, testing the hypothesis, analyzing the results, and drawing conclusions. (Chap. 1, p. 16)

scrubber: a device that "scrubs" the smoke from coal-burning power plants with basic compounds to increase the pH to a safe level. (Chap. 20, p. 563)

sea breeze: wind blowing from sea to land during the day when the sun warms the land faster, and cool air from above the water forces the warm air above the land to rise. (Chap. 14, p. 414)

seafloor spreading: the theory that magma from Earth's mantle rises to the surface at mid-ocean ridges and cools to form new seafloor, which new magma slowly pushes away from the ridge. (Chap. 11, p. 299)

seamount: an elevated part of the ocean floor, possibly an underwater volcano.

season: a regular, short-term period of change in the climate of an area due to changes in the amount of solar radiation the area receives. (Chap. 16, p. 462)

secondary waves: waves of energy, released during an earthquake, that travel through Earth by causing particles in rocks to move at right angles to the direction of the wave. (Chap. 9, p. 244)

sedimentary rock: rock formed when fragments of rocks, minerals, and/or organic matter are compacted or cemented together or precipitate out of solution. (Chap. 4, p. 101)

sediments: loose materials such as rock fragments, mineral grains, and bits of plants and animals that have been transported by wind, water, or glaciers. (Chap. 4, p. 101)

seismic waves: in an earthquake, the energy waves that move outward from the earthquake focus and make the ground quake. (Chap. 9, p. 241)

seismograph: an instrument used by seismologists to record primary, secondary, and surface waves from earthquakes. (Chap. 9, p. 252)

seismologist: a scientist who studies earthquakes and seismic waves. (Chap. 9, p. 252)

shadow zone: the area where seismic waves cannot reach because Earth's liquid outer core bends primary waves and stops secondary waves.

shearing forces: along strike-slip faults, forces that push on rocks from various directions, causing them to twist and break.

sheet erosion: a type of surface water erosion due to runoff, in which rainwater flowing over a gentle slope slowly moves sediments from the entire surface. (Chap. 8, p. 205)

shield volcano: a broad volcano with gently sloping sides, built by quiet eruptions of fluid basaltic lava, which spreads out in flat layers; example: the Hawaiian Islands. (Chap. 10, p. 279)

silicates: minerals containing silicon and oxygen, usually with other elements; the largest group of minerals. (Chap. 3, p. 66)

sill: an intrusive igneous rock body formed when magma is squeezed into a horizontal crack between rock layers and solidifies underground. (Chap. 10, p. 284)

silt: a sediment particle measuring 0.004 mm to 0.06 mm in size.

sinkhole: a depression in the ground caused when groundwater dissolves limestone beneath the hole, causing the ground to collapse.

slump: a type of mass movement in which one large mass of loose material or rock layers moves downhill, leaving a curved scar. (Chap. 7, p. 174)

smog: air pollution seen around cities, resulting from burning fossil fuels.

soil: a mixture of weathered rock, decaying organic matter (plants and animals), mineral fragments, water, and air. (Chap. 6, p. 156)

soil profile: a vertical section of soil layers (horizons). (Chap. 6, p. 158)

solar eclipse: an eclipse that occurs when the moon passes directly between Earth and the sun, so that the moon casts a shadow on part of Earth and blocks sunlight from reaching Earth. (Chap. 22, p. 626)

solar flare: an intense bright spot in the sun's chromosphere, associated with sunspots and radio interference on Earth.

solar system: the system of nine planets and many other objects that orbit our sun; may have been formed about 5 billion years ago from a cloud of ice, gas, and dust. (Chap. 23, p. 641)

solstice: the two times each year that Earth's tilt makes the sun reach its greatest angle north or south of the equator, marking the start of summer or winter. (Chap. 22, p. 622)

solution: a kind of mixture formed when one substance is dissolved in another. (Chap. 2, p. 41)

sonar: the use of sound-wave echoes to detect the size and shape of structures found underwater. (Chap. 5, p. 139)

space probe: an instrument that travels out into the solar system, gathers information, and transmits it back to Earth. (Chap. 21, p. 595)

space shuttle: a reusable spacecraft that transports astronauts, satellites, and other material to and from space. (Chap. 21, p. 604)

space station: a facility in space with living quarters, work and exercise space, and the support systems needed for people to live and work. (Chap. 21, p. 605)

species: a group of individuals that normally breed only among themselves. (Chap. 13, p. 359)

sphere: a round, three-dimensional object whose surface at all points is the same distance from its center; Earth is a sphere that is slightly flattened at its poles. (Chap. 22, p. 614)

spiral galaxy: a galaxy having spiral arms.

spring: the point at which the water table meets Earth's surface, causing water to flow from the ground. (Chap. 8, p. 216)

spring tide: a tide level greater than normal because the moon, Earth, and sun are aligned.

stalactite: a icicle-like deposit of calcite hanging from the ceiling of a cave.

station model: in weather forecasting, a group of meteorological symbols on a weather map that depict weather information at one specific location. (Chap. 15, p. 441)

stationary front: in weather systems, a warm front or cold front that has stopped moving.

streak: the color of a mineral when it is powdered; usually observed by rubbing the mineral on a ceramic streak plate. (Chap. 3, p. 69)

striations (stri AY shunz): long, parallel scars in rocks, caused by rock fragments being dragged across them by a glacier.

strike-slip fault: a break in rocks due to shearing forces, where rocks on either side of the fault move past each other without much upward or downward movement. (Chap. 9, p. 238)

subduction zone: in plate tectonics, the area where an ocean-floor plate collides with a continental plate, and the denser ocean plate sinks under the less dense continental plate. (Chap. 11, p. 307)

sulfurous smog: a gray-colored air pollution created when power plants and home furnaces burn fossil fuels, releasing sulfur compounds and smoke particles into the air. (Chap. 20, p. 557)

sunspot: a dark-appearing spot on the sun's surface that shows up because it is cooler than the surrounding areas; caused by the sun's intense magnetic field. (Chap. 24, p. 680)

supergiant: a late stage in the life cycle of a large star, when the core reaches high temperatures, heavy elements form by fusion, and the star's outer layers expand. (Chap. 24, p. 688)

supernova: a late stage in the life cycle of some stars, when the core collapses, causing the outer portion to explode.

surface current: an ocean current powered by wind, found in the upper few hundred meters of seawater; moves water horizontally and parallel to Earth's surface. (Chap. 17, p. 484)

surface waves: waves of energy, released during an earthquake, that reach Earth's surface and travel outward from the epicenter in all directions; travel through Earth by giving rock particles an elliptical and side-to-side motion. (Chap. 9, p. 244)

technology: the application of scientific discoveries; can both contribute to problems and solve problems. (Chap. 1, p. 10)

temperate zones: the two zones of moderate, seasonal weather that exist between the tropics and the polar regions. (Chap. 16, p. 452)

tension: stretching forces that can be strong enough to pull rocks apart at divergent plate boundaries.

tephra: lava that is blasted into the air by violent volcanic eruptions and solidifies as it falls to the ground as ash, cinders, and volcanic bombs. (Chap. 10, p. 279)

theory: an explanation backed by results from repeated tests, experiments, or observations. (Chap. 1, p. 18)

third quarter: the moon phase halfway between full moon and new moon, when half of the side facing Earth is lighted. (Chap. 22, p. 625)

tidal energy: electricity generated by the ocean tides.

tidal range: the vertical distance between the level of the ocean at high tide and low tide. (Chap. 17, p. 492)

tide: the periodic rise and fall of the surface level of the oceans; caused by a giant wave formed by the gravitational attraction between the sun, moon, and Earth. (Chap. 17, p. 492)

till: an unsorted mixture of boulders, sand, silt, and clay deposited by a glacier. (Chap. 7, p. 184)

Titan: Saturn's largest moon.

titanium: durable, lightweight metal obtained from minerals such as ilmenite or rutile. (Chap. 3, p. 78)

Topex-Poseidon Satellite: satellite that collects information about Earth's oceans by using radar. (Chap. 5, p. 138)

topographic map: a map that uses contour lines to show changes in elevation at Earth's surface; shows natural features such as lakes and cultural features such as cities and dams. (Chap. 5, p. 132)

topsoil: the top layer of soil, also called A horizon; usually contains humus and is dark in color.

tornado: a violent, whirling, funnel-shaped windstorm, up to 500 km/hour, that moves in a narrow path over land. (Chap. 15, p. 436)

trace fossils: footprints, worm holes, burrows, and other traces of animal activity preserved in rock.

transform fault: in plate tectonics, a boundary between two plates that are sliding horizontally past one another. (Chap. 11, p. 309)

trench: a long, narrow, steep-sided depression in the ocean floor formed where one crustal plate is forced beneath another. (Chap. 18, p. 507)

trilobites (TRI luh bites): shield-shaped marine invertebrate animals commonly found as fossils in Paleozoic Era rocks; they are now extinct.

Triton: Neptune's largest moon.

tropics: the region that receives the most solar radiation; extends between latitudes 23½° north and 23½° south of the equator. (Chap. 16, p. 452)

troposphere: the layer of Earth's atmosphere closest to the ground; contains clouds, smog, weather, and 75 percent of atmospheric gases. (Chap. 14, p. 394)

trough: the lowest point of a wave. (Chap. 17, p. 490)

tsunami (soo NAHM ee)**:** an ocean wave (seismic sea wave) that begins over an earthquake focus and can reach 30 m high. (Chap. 9, p. 255)

ultraviolet radiation: a type of energy that comes to Earth from the sun and is mostly absorbed by the ozone layer; rays can damage skin and cause cancer and other health problems. (Chap. 14, p. 400)

ultraviolet waves: electromagnetic waves that are a little shorter than visible light waves; they cause sunburn and skin cancer.

umbra: during an eclipse, the darker central portion of the shadow.

unconformities: gaps in a sequence of rock layers (the rock record), resulting from erosion or a lack of new deposition, or both. (Chap. 12, p. 339)

uniformitarianism: a basic principle of geology stating that Earth processes occurring today are similar to those that occurred in the past. (Chap. 12, p. 347)

upwarped mountains: mountains formed when Earth's crust is pushed up and eroded, forming sharp peaks and ridges. (Chap. 5, p. 124)

upwelling: the rising of cold, nutrient-rich water from deep in the ocean to the surface; occurs when surface water is pushed away by winds. (Chap. 17, p. 487)

Uranus: in our solar system, the seventh planet from the sun; it is large, gaseous, and is the only planet that lays on its side in orbit. (Chap. 23, p. 657)

Valles Marineris: a huge rift on Mars that is more than 4000 km long.

valley glacier: the most common type of glacier, occurs in mountain valleys where the temperatures are low enough to allow snow to accumulate faster than it can melt.

variable: in an experiment, the factor that can be changed to see what will happen. (Chap. 1, p. 17)

vent: in volcanic regions, an opening in Earth's surface through which can flow lava, ash, cinders, smoke, and steam. (Chap. 10, p. 268)

Venus: in our solar system, the second planet from the sun; it is similar in size and mass to Earth, is blanketed by a dense atmosphere of carbon dioxide and sulfuric acid, and is hot. (Chap. 23, p. 647)

vertebrates: animals with backbones; evolved during Ordovician Period.

visible light: electromagnetic waves having short wavelengths; the only part of the electromagnetic spectrum that we can see.

volcanic mountains: mountains created when magma within Earth escapes to the surface, building cones of lava and ash. (Chap. 5, p. 125)

volcanic neck: the solid igneous core of a vent that remains after the outer layers of lava and tephra have been eroded away from an extinct volcano. (Chap. 10, p. 284)

volcano: a vent in Earth's surface that often forms a mountain built of lava and volcanic ash, which erupts and builds up. (Chap. 10, p. 266)

volume: the amount of space occupied by an object; SI unit is the cubic meter (m^3).

waning: describes the moon following a full moon, as its visible lighted area grows smaller during the lunar cycle. (Chap. 22, p. 625)

waning crescent: the shrinking slice of lighted moon when the visible lighted area is decreasing from third quarter to new moon.

waning gibbous: the shrinking area of moon as the visible lighted area is decreasing from full moon to third quarter.

warm front: the moving boundary that develops when a warm air mass meets a cold air mass.

waste coal: large piles of poor-quality coal lying near abandoned coal mines; can generate acid runoff. (Chap. 4, p. 108)

water cycle: the continuous movement of water between Earth's surface and the atmosphere through evaporation, condensation, and precipitation. (Chap. 14, p. 406)

water table: the upper surface of the zone of saturation (the area where all of the pores in the rock are completely filled with water). (Chap. 8, p. 215)

wave: a movement in which ocean water rises and falls as energy passes through; crest, trough, wavelength, and wave height are parts of a wave. (Chap. 17, p. 490)

waxing: describes the moon shortly after a new moon, as its visible lighted area grows larger during the lunar cycle. (Chap. 22, p. 624)

waxing crescent: the growing slice of moon when the visible lighted area is increasing from new moon to first quarter.

waxing gibbous: the growing area of visible lighted moon as the lighted area is increasing from first quarter to full moon.

weather: the behavior of the atmosphere—wind, temperature, pressure, precipitation—at a particular place and time. (Chap. 15, p. 422)

weathering: the breaking of rocks into smaller pieces, either mechanically or chemically. (Chap. 6, p. 148)

Wegener, Alfred: a German scientist who proposed the idea of continental drift in 1912.

weight: a measure of the force of gravity on an object. (Chap. 1, p. 20)

white dwarf: a late stage in a star's life cycle when its core runs out of fuel (helium) and its unstable outer layers escape into space, leaving the white-hot, dense core. (Chap. 24, p. 687)

young stream: a stream that flows swiftly down a steep slope or a valley with steep sides, causing rapid erosion.

zone of saturation: an area where all the pores in the rock are completely filled with water, usually near the ground surface. (Chap. 8, p. 215)

Glossary/Glosario

This glossary defines each key term that appears in **bold type** in the text. It also shows the page number where you can find the word used.

abrasion/abrasión: tipo de erosión que ocurre cuando los sedimentos soplados y acarreados por el viento golpean las rocas. (Cap. 7, pág. 188)

absolute dating/datación absoluta: método que utilizan los geólogos para determinar la edad, en años, de una roca u otro objeto. (Cap. 12, pág. 344)

absolute magnitude/magnitud absoluta: medida de la cantidad de luz que una estrella emite verdaderamente. (Cap. 24, pág. 674)

abyssal plain/llanura abisal: suelo oceánico llano. (Cap. 18, pág. 505)

acid/ácido: sustancia que contiene un pH menor que siete. (Cap. 20, pág. 558)

acid rain/lluvia ácida: tipo de precipitación más ácida de lo normal. (Cap. 22, pág. 558)

adaptation/adaptación: cualquier característica que los organismos han desarrollado a lo largo del tiempo para garantizar su sobrevivencia. (Cap. 16, pág. 459)

air mass/masa de aire: gran extensión de aire que posee las mismas propiedades que la superficie sobre la cual se desarrolla. (Cap. 15, pág. 432)

alluvial fan/abanico aluvial: depósito en forma de triángulo que se forma cuando corrientes de agua que se mueven cuesta abajo llegan a superficies llanas, pierden su energía de movimiento y depositan sus sedimentos. (Cap. 8, pág. 213)

amphibian/anfibio: animal que vive en tierra y respira aire, pero que debe regresar al agua con el fin de reproducirse. (Cap. 13, pág. 370)

apparent magnitude/magnitud aparente: medida de la cantidad de luz de una estrella que llega a la Tierra. (Cap. 24, pág. 674)

aquifer/acuífero: capa de roca permeable que deja pasar el agua libremente. (Cap. 8, pág. 215)

artesian well/pozo artesiano: pozo en el cual el agua bajo presión se eleva a la superficie. (Cap. 8, pág. 216)

asteroid/asteroide: fragmento rocoso semejante al material que posteriormente formó los planetas. (Cap. 23, pág. 665)

asthenosphere/astenosfera: capa tipo plástico situada debajo de la litosfera. (Cap. 11, pág. 304)

astronomical unit/unidad astronómica: medida que se usa para medir distancias hacia los objetos en el sistema solar; corresponde a 150 millones de kilómetros, la cual es la distancia promedio entre la Tierra y el sol. (Cap. 23, pág. 648)

astronomy/astronomía: es el estudio de los objetos del espacio, incluidos las estrellas, los planetas y los cometas. (Cap. 1, pág. 8)

atom/átomo: elemento constitutivo de la materia. (Cap. 2, pág. 33)

atomic number/número atómico: equivale al número de protones en el núcleo de un átomo. (Cap. 2, pág. 36)

axis/eje: línea imaginaria alrededor de la cual gira la Tierra. (Cap. 22, pág. 615)

barrier island/crestas prelitorales: depósitos de arena paralelos a la costa pero separados del continente. (Cap. 8, pág. 226)

basaltic/basáltica: roca ígnea densa, pesada y de color oscuro que se forma a partir del magma basáltico. (Cap. 4, pág. 93)

base/base: sustancia que contiene un pH mayor que siete. (Cap. 22, pág. 558)

basin/cuenca: área baja sobre la cual se formaron los océanos. (Cap. 17, pág. 479)

batholith/batolito: las masas más grandes de rocas ígneas intrusivas. (Cap. 10, pág. 283)

beach/playa: depósito de sedimentos que corre paralelo a la costa. (Cap. 8, pág. 224)

benthos/bentos: organismos vegetales y animales que habitan los niveles más profundos del océano. (Cap. 18, pág. 514)

big bang theory/teoría de la gran explosión: teoría que dice que hace unos 15 billones de años, el universo comenzó a expandirse después de una enorme explosión. Pruebas recientes indican una fecha más reciente entre 8 a 10 billones de años. (Cap. 24, pág. 695)

binary system/sistema binario: sistema en el cual dos estrellas giran alrededor de la una a la otra. (Cap. 24, pág. 681)

black hole/agujero negro: núcleo restante de una estrella de neutrones, el cual es tan denso y masivo que nada puede escapar de su campo de gravedad, ni siquiera la luz. (Cap. 24, pág. 688)

breaker/cachón: ola de mar que rompe en la playa. (Cap. 17, pág. 491)

caldera/caldera: gran depresión que resulta cuando la cima de un volcán se hunde en la cámara magmática parcialmente vacía. (Cap. 10, pág. 285)

carbonaceous film/película carbonácea: tipo de fósil producido por una película fina de residuo carbonoso la cual forma un bosquejo del organismo original. (Cap. 12, pág. 328)

carrying capacity/capacidad de carga: número máximo de individuos de una especie en particular que puede sustentar el planeta. (Cap. 19, pág. 532)

cast/impresión fósil: se forma cuando otros sedimentos llenan el molde, se endurecen y forman una roca produciendo una impresión del objeto original. (Cap. 12, pág. 329)

cave/caverna: abertura subterránea; se forma cuando el agua subterránea ácida corre por las resquebrajaduras naturales de la piedra caliza disolviéndola y formando, paulatinamente, una caverna. (Cap. 8, pág. 217)

cementation/cementación: proceso de formación de roca sólida a partir de la disolución de cementos naturales en la tierra y las rocas, los cuales se depositan alrededor de los sedimentos y los unen. (Cap. 4, pág. 102)

Cenozoic Era/ Era cenozoica: era de la vida reciente que comenzó hace aproximadamente 66 millones de años. (Cap. 13, pág. 379)

chemical property/propiedad química: describe la manera en que una sustancia cambia cuando reacciona con otras sustancias. (Cap. 2, pág. 39)

chemical weathering/meteorización química: meteorización que se presenta cuando el agua, el aire y otras sustancias reaccionan con los minerales presentes en las rocas; la meteorización química cambia la composición química de las rocas. (Cap. 6, pág. 151)

chemosynthesis/quimiosíntesis: proceso de fabricación de alimentos que no depende de la luz solar y el cual llevan a cabo las bacterias en las dorsales oceánicas. (Cap. 18, pág. 512)

chlorofluorocarbons/clorofluorocarburos: compuestos químicos que se usan para elaborar refrigerantes, rociadores aerosoles y productos de espuma; su uso puede llegar a destruir la capa de ozono. (Cap. 14, pág. 401)

chromosphere/cromosfera: capa que se encuentra encima de la fotosfera y que se extiende hacia arriba unos 2000 km. (Cap. 24, pág. 679)

cinder cone/cono de carbonilla: volcán de lados empinados y ligeramente consolidado que se forma cuando la tefrita llega al suelo. (Cap. 10, pág. 279)

Clean Air Act/Ley para el Control de la Contaminación del Aire: Ley promulgada en 1990 para combatir los problemas del smog, los clorofluorocarburos, las macropartículas y la lluvia ácida. Regula la industria automotriz, las tecnologías del carbón y otras industrias. (Cap. 20, pág. 561)

Clean Water Act/Ley para el Control de la Contaminación del Agua: ley promulgada en 1987 que otorga fondos a los estados para que construyan instalaciones de tratamiento de aguas negras y residuales. (Cap. 20, pág. 571)

cleavage/crucero: propiedad de un mineral que lo hace partirse a lo largo de superficies suaves y planas. (Cap. 3, pág. 70)

climate/clima: patrón de tiempo que ocurre en una región en particular a lo largo de muchos años. (Cap. 6, pág. 154)

cloud seeding/lluvia artificial: bombardeo de las nubes con partículas de hielo seco o con yoduro de plata como núcleos para las moléculas de agua con el objeto de que se agrupen, se congelen y formen precipitación. (Cap. 15, pág. 444)

cogeneration/cogeneración: proceso en el cual tanto la energía eléctrica como la térmica son aprovechadas por la central que las produce. (Cap. 4, pág. 109)

comet/cometa: astro compuesto de polvo y partículas rocosas mezclados con agua congelada, metano y amoníaco. (Cap. 23, pág. 663)

compaction/compactación: proceso formador de roca sólida al presionar las capas superiores de sedimento sobre las inferiores. (Cap. 4, pág. 102)

composite volcano/volcán compuesto: volcán que se forma del continuo y alternado ciclo de erupción de lava y tefrita. (Cap. 10, pág. 281)

composting/abono orgánico: desechos vegetales que se apilan en el patio y que se dejan decomponer paulatinamente mediante la acción del calor y de las bacterias. (Cap. 19, pág. 545)

compound/compuesto: tipo de materia que posee propiedades diferentes de las propiedades de cada uno de los elementos que existen en él. (Cap. 2, pág. 38)

conduction/conducción: transferencia de energía que ocurre cuando las moléculas chocan entre sí. (Cap. 14, pág. 405)

conic projection/proyección cónica: se usa para producir mapas de áreas pequeñas. Se hacen proyectando puntos y líneas desde un globo a un cono. (Cap. 5, pág. 131)

conservation/conservación: uso cuidadoso de los recursos, lo cual disminuye el daño al ambiente. (Cap. 19, pág. 544)

constellation/constelación: un grupo de estrellas que presenta una configuración que parece un animal, un personaje mitológico o cualquier otro objeto, del cual obtiene su nombre. (Cap. 24, pág. 672)

continental drift/deriva continental: teoría que dice que los continentes se han movido horizontalmente a sus posiciones actuales. (Cap. 11, pág. 294)

continental shelf/plataforma continental: extremo, inclinado paulatinamente, de un continente que se extiende bajo el océano. (Cap. 18, pág. 504)

continental slope/talud continental: extremo de la plataforma continental y más empinado y que esta que se extiende desde su borde hacia abajo del suelo oceánico. (Cap. 18, pág. 505)

contour interval/intervalo entre curvas de nivel: diferencia de elevación entre dos curvas de nivel consecutivas. (Cap. 5, pág. 132)

contour line/curva de nivel: línea de un mapa que conecta puntos de igual elevación. (Cap. 5, pág. 132)

control/control: estándar de comparación. (Cap. 1, pág. 17)

convection/convección: transferencia de calor por medio de un flujo de material calentado. (Cap. 14, pág. 405)

convection current/corriente de convección: ciclo completo de calentamiento, ascenso, enfriamiento y hundimiento. (Cap. 11, pág. 310)

convergent boundary/límite convergente: lugar donde chocan dos placas. (Cap. 11, pág. 307)

Corioles effect/efecto de Coriolis: efecto producido por el movimiento de rotación de la Tierra, que hace que el viento que sopla en dirección sur se desvíe hacia el oeste, en el hemisferio norte. (Cap. 14, pág. 411)

corona/corona: la capa más grande de la atmósfera solar, la cual se extiende millones de kilómetros en el espacio. (Cap. 24, pág. 679)

crater/cráter: depresión empinada y más o menos circular alrededor de la chimenea de un volcán. (Cap. 10, pág. 268)

creep/corrimiento: movimiento paulatino de material rocoso suelto debido a congelación, humedecimiento, secado, etc. (Cap. 7, pág. 175)

crest/cresta: el punto más alto de una ola. (Cap. 17, pág. 490)

crust/corteza: la capa más externa de la Tierra y separada del manto por la discontinuidad de Moho. (Cap. 9, pág. 249)

crystal/cristal: sólido cuyos átomos están ordenados en patrones repetitivos. (Cap. 3, pág. 63)

cyanobacteria/cianobacterias: bacterias azul verdosas que se piensa que son una de las primeras formas de vida sobre la Tierra. (Cap. 13, pág. 367)

deflation/deflacción: erosión causada cuando el viento sopla los sedimentos sueltos extrayendo pequeñas partículas tales como la arcilla, el cieno y la arena, y dejando atrás materiales más gruesos. (Cap. 7, pág. 188)

deforestation/desforestación: extracción masiva de árboles. (Cap. 16, pág. 470)

delta/delta: desembocadura en un océano, golfo o en un lago de los sedimentos arrastrados por un río. (Cap. 8, pág. 213)

density/densidad: medida de la masa de un objeto dividida entre su volumen. (Cap. 2, pág. 44)

density current/corriente de densidad: corriente que ocurre cuando el agua marina más densa se hunde bajo agua marina menos densa, mezclando así el agua oceánica de la superficie. (Cap. 17, pág. 487)

deposition/depositación: etapa final de un proceso de erosión, en la cual los agentes erosivos depositan los sedimentos y las rocas cuando disminuye su energía de movimiento. (Cap. 7, pág. 173)

desertification/desertificación: formación de desiertos. (Cap. 6, pág. 165)

dew point/punto de rocío: temperatura a la cual el aire está saturado y se condensa. (Cap. 15, pág. 424)

dike/dique: magma que ha sido apretujado formando un corte vertical, el cual atraviesa capas rocosas y se endurece. (Cap. 10, pág. 284)

divergent boundary/límite divergente: zona situada entre dos placas que se alejan una de la otra. (Cap. 11, pág. 305)

drainage basin/cuenca hidrográfica: extensión territorial de donde obtiene agua una corriente de agua. (Cap. 8, pág. 207)

E

Earth/la Tierra: el tercer planeta a partir del sol. (Cap. 23, pág. 648)

Earth science/ciencia terrestre: es el estudio de la Tierra y el espacio. (Cap. 1, pág. 8)

earthquake/terremoto: vibraciones producida por las rocas que se rompen. (Cap. 9, pág. 237)

El Niño/El Niño: evento climático que comienza en las aguas tropicales del Océano Pacífico y que inicia cambios en la atmósfera. (Cap. 16, pág. 463)

electromagnetic spectrum/espectro electromagnético: arreglo de radiación electromagnética de acuerdo con sus longitudes de onda. (Cap. 21, pág. 585)

electron/electrón: partícula cargada negativamente. (Cap. 2, pág. 35)

element/elemento: sustancia que contiene solo un tipo de átomo. (Cap. 2, pág. 33)

ellipse/elipse: curva cerrada alargada. (Cap. 22, pág. 617)

endangered/en peligro de extinción: una especie cuyo número de miembros vivos es muy pequeño. (Cap. 13, pág. 364)

epicenter/epicentro: punto en la superficie terrestre directamente encima del foco de un terremoto. (Cap. 9, pág. 244)

epoch/época: subdivisión de un período. (Cap. 13, pág. 359)

equator/ecuador: línea imaginaria que circunda la Tierra exactamente equidistante entre los Polos Norte y Sur. El ecuador separa la Tierra en dos mitades llamadas hemisferio norte y hemisferio sur. (Cap. 5, pág. 126)

equinox/equinoccio: momento del año cuando el sol está directamente encima del ecuador lo cual resulta en que los días son iguales a las noches. (Cap. 22, pág. 619)

era/era: subdivisión principal de la escala del tiempo geológico basada en diferencias de biotipos. (Cap. 13, pág. 357)

erosion/erosión: proceso que desgasta materiales en la superficie y los mueve de un lugar a otro. (Cap. 7, pág. 172)

extinct/extinto: especie que ya no tiene ningún miembro vivo. (Cap. 12, pág. 334)

extrusive/extrusiva: roca ígnea que se forma cuando la lava se enfría en la superficie terrestre. (Cap. 4, pág. 92)

fault/falla: superficie a lo largo de la cual se mueven las rocas al exceder su límite de elasticidad y romperse. (Cap. 9, pág. 236)

fault-block mountain/montaña de bloques de fallas: montaña formada por inmensos bloques rocosos inclinados que están separados de rocas circundantes por fallas. (Cap. 5, pág. 124)

first quarter/cuarto creciente: fase lunar cuando, desde la Tierra, se puede observar la mitad de su faz iluminada o un cuarto de la superficie lunar. (Cap. 22, pág. 624)

fission/fisión: es la separación de los núcleos de los átomos en elementos pesados, tales como el uranio. (Cap. 2, pág. 54)

floodplain/llanura aluvial: valle ancho y llano tallado por una corriente de agua serpenteante. (Cap. 8, pág. 209)

focus/foco: punto en el interior de la Tierra donde ocurre la liberación de energía de un terremoto. (Cap. 9, pág. 241)

fog/neblina: nube estrato que se forma cuando el aire se enfría a su punto de rocío y se condensa cerca del suelo. (Cap. 15, pág. 425)

folded mountain/montaña plegada: tipo de montaña que se ha formado al encorvarse y plegarse las capas rocosas cuando estas últimas han sido apretadas desde lados opuestos. (Cap. 5, pág. 123)

foliated/foliada: textura que presenta una roca metamórfica cuando sus granos minerales se aplanan y se alinean en bandas paralelas. (Cap. 4, pág. 99)

fossil/fósil: resto, impresión o huella de organismos que una vez estuvieron vivos, conservado en las rocas. (Cap. 12, pág. 327)

fracture/fractura: propiedad de un mineral que lo hace partirse en puntas ásperas o dentadas. (Cap. 3, pág. 70)

front/frente: límite entre dos masas de aire. (Cap. 15, pág. 434)

full moon/luna llena o plenilunio: fase durante la cual está iluminada la mitad de la superficie lunar que da a la Tierra. (Cap. 22, pág. 624)

galaxy/galaxia: grupo inmenso de estrellas, gas y polvo que se mantiene unido gracias a la gravedad. (Cap. 24, pág. 691)

gem/gema: piedra preciosa muy preciada debido a su rareza y belleza. (Cap. 3, pág. 74)

geologic time scale/escala del tiempo geológico: división de la historia de la Tierra en unidades más pequeñas. (Cap. 13, pág. 357)

geology/geología: es el estudio de la Tierra, su materia y los procesos que la forman y la cambian. (Cap. 1, pág. 8)

geothermal energy/energía geotérmica: tipo de energía térmica en las masas de magma dentro de la Tierra que se utiliza para generar electricidad. (Cap. 10, pág. 274)

geyser/géiser: fuente termal que hace erupción intermitentemente disparando agua y vapor en el aire. (Cap. 8, pág. 217)

giant/gigante roja: etapa en la formación de una estrella en la cual su núcleo se contrae y las temperaturas internas de la estrella aumentan, haciendo que sus capas externas se expandan. (Cap. 24, pág. 687)

glacier/glaciar: masa móvil de hielo y nieve. (Cap. 7, pág. 180)

global warning/calentamiento global: aumento de las temperaturas globales. (Cap. 16, pág. 467)

granitic/granítica: roca ígnea de color claro que posee una menor densidad que la roca basáltica. (Cap. 4, pág. 93)

gravity/gravedad: fuerza de atracción que existe entre todos los objetos. (Cap. 1, pág. 20)

Great Red Spot/la Gran Mancha Roja: espectacular tormenta de gas turbulento y de alta presión que se produce continuamente en Júpiter. (Cap. 23, pág. 654)

greenhouse effect/efecto de invernadero: calentamiento natural causado por gases en la atmósfera que atrapan el calor de la superficie terrestre. (Cap. 16, pág. 467)

groundwater/agua subterránea: agua que se filtra en el suelo y que se junta en los poros subterráneos. (Cap. 8, pág. 214)

gully erosion/erosión en barrancos: surco o zanja que se ensancha y profundiza formando un barranco. (Cap. 8, pág. 204)

habitat/hábitat: lugar donde los organismos viven, crecen e interactúan entre sí y con el ambiente. (Cap. 13, pág. 364)

half-life/media vida: el tiempo que se demora la mitad de los átomos de un isótopo para desintegrarse. (Cap. 12, pág. 345)

hardness/dureza: medida del grado de facilidad que posee un mineral para rayarse. (Cap. 3, pág. 68)

hazardous waste/desecho peligroso: desecho venenoso, cancerígeno o radiactivo. (Cap. 19, pág. 541)

hibernation/hibernación: período de inactividad durante el invierno. (Cap. 16, pág. 460)

horizon/horizonte: nombre que recibe cada capa del perfil del suelo. (Cap. 6, pág. 158)

hot dry rock (HDR)/roca seca caliente: tecnología que produce energía geotérmica sin necesitar la presencia del magma. (Cap. 10, pág. 275)

hot spot/punto cálido: área del manto que posee una mayor temperatura que otras áreas. (Cap. 10, pág. 273)

hot spring/aguas o baños termales: agua subterránea que se sale del suelo a una temperatura elevada. (Cap. 8, pág. 216)

humidity/humedad: cantidad de vapor de agua presente en el aire. (Cap. 15, pág. 423)

humus/humus: materia de color oscuro que se forma cuando se descompone la materia orgánica del suelo. (Cap. 6, pág. 157)

hurricane/huracán: sistema de baja presión, de gran alcance y turbulento, que se forma sobre los océanos tropicales. (Cap. 15, pág. 438)

hydrosphere/hidrosfera: toda el agua que ocurre en la superficie de la Tierra. (Cap. 14, pág. 406)

hypothesis/hipótesis: predicción acerca de un problema que puede probarse. (Cap. 1, pág. 16)

ice wedging/grietas debido al hielo: meteorización mecánica que se produce cuando el agua que se congela en las resquebrajaduras de las rocas se expande y la presión que se acumula rompe las rocas. (Cap. 6, pág. 150)

igneous rock/roca ígnea: roca que se forma cuando el material derretido de un volcán o de las profundidades de la Tierra se enfría. (Cap. 4, pág. 90)

impermeable/impermeable: que no se deja atravesar por el agua. (Cap. 8, pág. 215)

index fossil/fósil guía: proviene de especies que existieron abundantemente en la Tierra durante cortos períodos de tiempo y que se encontraban muy extendidas geográficamente. (Cap. 12, pág. 331)

inner core/núcleo interno: núcleo sólido, muy denso en el mismo centro de la Tierra compuesto principalmente de hierro y níquel. (Cap. 9, pág. 249)

inner planet/planeta interior: planeta sólido rocoso situado más cerca del sol; los planetas interiores son Mercurio, Venus, la Tierra y Marte. (Cap. 23, pág. 643)

International Date Line/Línea Internacional de cambio de fecha: es el meridiano de 180°, es decir, la línea de longitud en el lado opuesto de la Tierra a partir del Primer Meridiano donde las líneas de longitud este se encuentran con las líneas de longitud oeste. Este meridiano es la línea de transición para los días del calendario. (Cap. 5, pág. 129)

International System of Units (SI)/Sistema Internacional de Unidades (SI): versión moderna del sistema métrico. (Cap. 1, pág. 19)

intrusive/intrusiva: roca ígnea que se forma debajo de la superficie terrestre. (Cap. 4, pág. 92)

ion/ion: átomo cargado eléctricamente. (Cap. 2, pág. 40)

ionosphere/ionosfera: capa importante de la termosfera y que es una capa de partículas cargadas eléctricamente. (Cap. 14, pág. 395)

isobar/isobara: línea que conecta puntos de igual presión atmosférica. (Cap. 15, pág. 441)

isotherm/isoterma: línea que conecta puntos de igual temperatura. (Cap. 15, pág. 441)

isotope/isótopo: átomo de un mismo elemento que posee diferentes números de neutrones en su núcleo. (Cap. 2, pág. 36)

jet stream/corriente de chorro: banda estrecha de viento fuerte que sopla cerca de la parte superior de la troposfera. (Cap. 14, pág. 414)

Jupiter/Júpiter: el planeta más grande del sistema solar y está ubicado en quinto lugar a partir del sol. (Cap. 23, pág. 654)

land breeze/brisa terrestre: viento suave que sopla desde la tierra hacia el mar durante la noche, producido por corrientes de convección. (Cap. 14, pág. 415)

landfill/vertedero: área donde se depositan los desechos. (Cap. 19, pág. 541)

Landsat Satellite/satélite Landsat: satélite que detecta diferentes longitudes de onda de energía que se reflejan o emiten desde la superficie terrestre. (Cap. 5, pág. 138)

latitude/latitud: se refiere a la distancia, en grados, ya sea al norte o al sur del ecuador. (Cap. 5, pág. 127)

lava/lava: magma que llega a la superficie terrestre. (Cap. 4, pág. 91)

law/ley: regla de la naturaleza que describe la conducta de algo en ella. (Cap. 1, pág. 18)

leaching/lixiviación: extracción de materiales del suelo al ser disueltos en agua. (Cap. 6, pág. 159)

light pollution/contaminación por luz: brillo en el cielo provocado por las luces de las ciudades y el cual interfiere con la observación de las estrellas opacas. (Cap. 21, pág. 591)

light-year/año-luz: distancia que cual viaja la luz en un año. (Cap. 24, pág. 675)

lithosphere/litosfera: nombre que reciben la corteza y una parte del manto superior terrestres. (Cap. 11, pág. 304)

loess/loess: limo de grano fino sin estratificaciones. (Cap. 7, pág. 191)

longitude/longitud: se refiere a la distancia en grados al este o al oeste del primer meridiano. (Cap. 5, pág. 127)

longshore current/corriente costera: corriente que corre paralela a la costa. (Cap. 8, pág. 223)

lunar eclipse/eclipse lunar: ocurre cuando la sombra de la Tierra cae sobre la luna. (Cap. 22, pág. 627)

luster/lustre: describe la forma en que la luz se refleja desde la superficie de un mineral; el lustre puede ser metálico o no metálico. (Cap. 3, pág. 69)

magma/magma: materia rocosa derretida y de alta temperatura. (Cap. 3, pág. 64)

magnetometer/magnetómetro: instrumento sensible que registra datos magnéticos. (Cap. 11, pág. 300)

magnitude/magnitud: medida de la energía liberada en un terremoto. (Cap. 9, pág. 253)

main sequence/secuencia principal: banda diagonal de estrellas que corre desde la parte izquierda superior (la cual contiene las estrellas calientes, azules y brillantes) hasta la parte derecha inferior (la cual contiene las estrellas frías, rojas y tenues) del diagrama H-R. (Cap. 24, pág. 684)

mantle/manto: la capa más grande de la Tierra ubicada directamente encima del núcleo externo. (Cap. 9, pág. 249)

map legend/leyenda de un mapa: explica el significado de los símbolos de un mapa. (Cap. 5, pág. 134)

map scale/escala de un mapa: relación entre las distancias en el mapa y las distancias verdaderas en la superficie terrestre. (Cap. 5, pág. 135)

maria/maria: regiones oscuras y relativamente planas de la superficie lunar. (Cap. 22, pág. 628)

Mars/Marte: el cuarto planeta a partir del sol. (Cap. 23, pág. 649)

mascon/concentración de masa: concentración de masa ubicada debajo de las cuencas de impacto en la Luna. (Cap. 22, pág. 633)

mass/masa: medida de la cantidad de materia que posee un objeto. (Cap. 1, pág. 20)

mass movement/movimiento de masa: movimiento de materiales cuesta abajo debido a la gravedad. (Cap. 7, pág. 173)

mass number/número de masa: número igual al número de protones y neutrones que componen el núcleo de un átomo. (Cap. 2, pág. 36)

matter/materia: cualquier cosa que ocupa espacio y posee masa. (Cap. 2, pág. 32)

meander/meandro: curva que se forma en una corriente de agua cuando el agua que se mueve rápidamente erosiona el costado de la corriente donde ésta es más fuerte. (Cap. 8, pág. 208)

mechanical weathering/meteorización mecánica: proceso que parte las rocas pero sin cambiar su composición química. (Cap. 6, pág. 149)

Mercator projection/proyección de Mercator: tipo de mapa que muestra las formas correctas de los continentes pero sus superficies están distorsionadas. (Cap. 5, pág. 130)

Mercury/Mercurio: el planeta más cercano al sol. (Cap. 23, pág. 646)

Mesozoic Era/Era mesozoica: era de la vida media que comenzó hace cerca de 245 millones de años. (Cap. 13, pág. 374)

metamorphic rock/roca metamórfica: roca que ha cambiado debido a un aumento en la temperatura y en la presión o que sufre cambios en su composición. (Cap. 4, pág. 97)

meteor/meteoro: meteoroide que se quema en la atmósfera terrestre. (Cap. 23, pág. 664)

meteorite/meteorito: meteoroide que cae sobre la superficie terrestre. (Cap. 23, pág. 665)

meteorologist/meteorólogo: especialista que estudia el tiempo. (Cap. 15, pág. 440)

meteorology/meteorología: estudio del tiempo y las fuerzas y procesos que lo causan. (Cap. 1, pág. 8)

mid-ocean ridge/dorsal oceánica: lugar donde se forma nuevo suelo oceánico. (Cap. 18, pág. 506)

mineral/mineral: sólido inorgánico que ocurre de forma natural y que posee una estructura y una composición definidas. (Cap. 3, pág. 62)

mixture/mezcla: incorporación de varias sustancias entre sí pero en la cual cada una retiene sus propias propiedades. (Cap. 2, pág. 40)

Moho discontinuity/discontinuidad de Moho: límite entre la corteza y el manto. (Cap. 9, pág. 249)

mold/molde: hueco que se forma en roca que contiene fósiles de conchas cuando los poros rocosos permiten que el agua y el aire lleguen hasta la concha o su parte endurecida, permitiendo su desintegración. (Cap. 12, pág. 329)

molecule/molécula: combinación de átomos mediante el compartimiento de electrones en la porción más externa de sus nubes electrónicas. (Cap. 2, pág. 38)

moon phase/fase lunar: apariencia cambiante de la luna vista desde la Tierra. (Cap. 22, pág. 624)

moraine/morena frontal o terminal: tipo de depósito formado por la acumulación de tierra, piedras y otros materiales que arrastra un glaciar; a diferencia de la morena, la morena frontal o terminal no abarca una área muy amplia. (Cap. 7, pág. 184)

natural selection/selección natural: teoría que dice que los organismos que poseen rasgos adaptables a cierto entorno tienen una mejor probabilidad de sobrevivir y de reproducirse que aquellos organismos cuyos rasgos no son apropiados a ese ambiente. (Cap. 13, pág. 360)

nebula/nebulosa: nube extensa de gas y polvo que corresponde a la etapa inicial de formación de una estrella. (Cap. 24, pág. 686)

nekton/necton: animales que nadan libremente en lugar de estar a la deriva con las corrientes. (Cap. 18, pág. 513)

Neptune/Neptuno: planeta grande y gaseoso descubierto en 1846; octavo planeta a partir del sol. (Cap. 23, pág. 658)

neutron/neutrón: partícula que no posee ninguna carga eléctrica. (Cap. 2, pág. 35)

neutron star/estrella de neutrones: la etapa de una supernova cuando el núcleo denso y colapsado de la estrella se encoge hasta unos 10-15 km y solo pueden existir neutrones en él. (Cap. 24, pág. 688)

new moon/luna nueva: ocurre cuando la cara iluminada de la luna mira hacia el Sol y la cara oscura mira hacia la Tierra. (Cap. 22, pág. 624)

nonfoliated/no foliada: textura que presentan los granos minerales de las rocas metamórficas cuando cambian, crecen y se reordenan pero no ocurren bandas. (Cap. 4, pág. 99)

normal fault/falla normal: falla que se forma cuando las rocas sobre la superficie de la falla se mueven hacia abajo en relación con las rocas debajo de la superficie. (Cap. 9, pág. 238)

nuclear energy/energía nuclear: fuente energética alternativa producida a partir de reacciones atómicas. (Cap. 2, pág. 54)

nuclear waste/desechos nucleares: desperdicios que produce la energía nuclear. (Cap. 2, pág. 54)

observatory/observatorio: edificio que alberga la mayoría de los telescopios ópticos usados por astrónomos profesionales. (Cap. 21, pág. 586)

oceanography/oceanografía: es el estudio de los océanos terrestres. (Cap. 1, pág. 9)

Oort Cloud/Nube Oort: nube que, según el astrónomo holandés Jan Oort, está ubicada más allá de la órbita de Plutón y la cual rodea completamente el sistema solar; esta nube albergaría una gran colección de cometas. (Cap. 23, pág. 663)

orbit/órbita: trayectoria curva alrededor de la Tierra que efectúa un satélite. (Cap. 21, pág. 594)

ore/mena: mineral que contiene sustancias útiles que pueden minarse para obtener una ganancia. (Cap. 3, pág. 75)

organic evolution/evolución orgánica: cambio de los biotipos a través del tiempo. (Cap. 13, pág. 359)

outer core/núcleo externo: núcleo líquido ubicado directamente encima del núcleo interno sólido; también compuesto de hierro y níquel. (Cap. 9, pág. 249)

outer planet/ planeta exterior: planeta más alejado del sol; los planetas exteriores son Júpiter, Neptuno, Saturno, Uranio y Plutón; con excepción de Plutón, que es rocoso, los otros planetas exteriores están formados principalmente por elementos más livianos tales como hidrógeno y helio. (Cap. 23, pág. 643)

oxidation/oxidación: combinación con el oxígeno; ocurre cuando, por ejemplo, el hierro es expuesto al oxígeno y al agua. (Cap. 6, pág. 154)

ozone layer/capa de ozono: capa de la estratosfera con una alta concentración de ozono. (Cap. 14, pág. 400)

Pacific Ring of Fire/Cinturón de Fuego del Pacífico: región alrededor de la Placa del Pacífico donde son comunes los terremotos y los volcanes. (Cap. 10, pág. 272)

Paleozoic Era/Era paleozoica: era geológica que marca el momento cuando los organismos desarrollaron partes duras. (Cap. 13, pág. 367)

Pangaea/Pangaea: inmensa extensión territorial que, según Wegener, una vez conectó a todos los continentes y que se separó hace unos 200 millones de años. (Cap. 10, pág. 294)

parallax/paralaje: cambio aparente en la posición de un objeto cuando uno lo observa desde dos posiciones diferentes. (Cap. 24, pág. 675)

period/período: subdivisión de una era. (Cap. 13, pág. 357)

permeable/permeable: que se deja atravesar por el agua. (Cap. 8, pág. 215)

petrified remains/restos petrificados: restos duros y de consistencia parecida a las rocas, en los cuales algunos o todos los materiales originales han sido reemplazados por minerales. (Cap. 12, pág. 328)

pH scale/escala de pH: escala que describe la acidez o basicidad de una solución. (Cap. 20, pág. 558)

photochemical smog/smog fotoquímico: smog color café que se forma cuando la luz solar reacciona con los contaminantes del aire. (Cap. 20, pág. 556)

photosphere/fotosfera: capa más baja de la atmósfera del sol y desde la cual se emite la luz solar. (Cap. 24, pág. 679)

photosynthesis/fotosíntesis: proceso de elaboración de alimento. (Cap. 18, pág. 511)

physical property/propiedad física: propiedad que puede observarse sin cambiar una sustancia en una nueva sustancia. (Cap. 2, pág. 44)

plain/llanura: extensa superficie de terreno relativamente llano. (Cap. 5, pág. 120)

plankton/plancton: algas marinas y animales minúsculos a la deriva con las corrientes oceánicas. (Cap. 18, pág. 513)

plate/placa: sección de la corteza terrestre que se mueve alrededor del manto. (Cap. 11, pág. 304)

plate tectonics/tectónica de placas: teoría que dice que la corteza y el manto superior de la Tierra están separados en secciones. (Cap. 11, pág. 304)

plateau/meseta: parte llana y extensa situada en lugares elevados de terreno. (Cap. 5, pág. 122)

plucking/ablación: cuando un glaciar arranca o desgarra bloques de rocas mediante la acción del agrietamiento debido al hielo. (Cap. 7, pág. 182)

Pluto/Plutón: el planeta más pequeño del sistema solar. (Cap. 23, pág. 658)

polar zone/zona polar: zona que se extiende desde los polos a las latitudes 66° norte y sur. (Cap. 16, pág. 452)

pollutant/contaminante: sustancia que causa daño a los organismos al interferir con procesos bioquímicos. (Cap. 18, pág. 519)

pollution/contaminación: introducción, por parte de los seres humanos, de productos residuales peligrosos, químicos y sustancias en el ambiente. (Cap. 18, pág. 619)

population/población: número total de individuos de una especie en particular en un área particular. (Cap. 19, pág. 533)

population explosion/explosión demográfica: rápido crecimiento de la población humana. (Cap. 19, pág. 533)

Precambrian time/era precámbrica: la era geológica más larga en la historia de la Tierra. (Cap. 13, pág. 366)

precipitation/precipitación: agua que cae de las nubes sea cual sea su forma. (Cap. 15, pág. 430)

primary wave/onda primaria: onda que se mueve a través de la Tierra haciendo que las partículas en las rocas se muevan oscilatoriamente en la misma dirección de la onda. (Cap. 9, pág. 244)

prime meridian/primer meridiano: punto de referencia para medir los grados de longitud de este a oeste y representa longitud 0º. (Cap. 5, pág. 127)

principle of superposition/principio de sobreposición: principio que dice que en una capa rocosa inalterada, las rocas más antiguas se encuentran en las capas inferiores y las más recientes en las capas superiores. (Cap. 12, pág. 337)

Project Apollo/Proyecto Apolo: etapa final del programa americano de llegar a la luna. (Cap. 21, pág. 598)

Project Gemini/Proyecto Géminis: segunda etapa en la meta de llegar a la luna. (Cap. 21, pág. 598)

Project Mercury/Proyecto Mercurio: proyecto que inició el programa americano de llegar a la luna. (Cap. 21, pág. 597)

proton/protón: partícula que posee una carga eléctrica positiva. (Cap. 2, pág. 35)

radiation/radiación: transferencia de energía por medio de ondas electromagnéticas. (Cap. 14, pág. 403)

radio telescope/radiotelescopio: tipo de telescopio que se usa para estudiar ondas radiales que viajan a través del espacio. (Cap. 21, pág. 587)

radioactive decay/desintegración radiactiva: formación de un nuevo elemento al cambiar el número de protones que posee un átomo. (Cap. 12, pág. 344)

radiometric dating/datación radiométrica: proceso que se usa para calcular la edad absoluta de una roca al medir las cantidades de material original y de los productos de desintegración que hay en la roca, conociendo el período de media vida del material original. (Cap. 12, pág. 345)

recyclable/reciclable: que se puede procesar y volver a usar. (Cap. 19, pág. 546)

reef/arrecife: estructura rígida y resistente a las olas que se desarrolla a partir de los materiales óseos y del carbonato cálcico. (Cap. 18, pág. 618)

reflecting telescope/telescopio reflector: telescopio que usa un espejo como objetivo para enfocar la luz proveniente del objeto que se observa. (Cap. 21, pág. 586)

reforestation/reforestación: plantación de árboles. (Cap. 16, pág. 471)

refracting telescope/telescopio refractor: uno en el cual la luz proveniente de un objeto atraviesa una lenta convexa y es doblada para formar una imagen en el punto focal. (Cap. 21, pág. 586)

relative dating/datación relativa: se utiliza en geología para determinar el orden de los sucesos y la edad relativa de las rocas al examinar sus posiciones en una secuencia. (Cap. 12, pág. 338)

relative humidity/humedad relativa: medida de la cantidad de vapor de agua que el aire puede contener a una temperatura específica. (Cap. 15, pág. 424)

reptile/reptil: especie que evolucionó de los anfibios; a diferencia de estos, los reptiles no necesitan regresar al agua para reproducirse. (Cap. 13, pág. 370)

reverse fault/falla invertida: falla en que las rocas sobre la superficie son forzadas hacia arriba y sobre las rocas debajo de la superficie de la falla. (Cap. 9, pág. 238)

revolution/revolución: órbita anual de la Tierra alrededor del sol, la cual dura un año. (Cap. 22, pág. 617)

rill erosion / erosión en regueras: tipo de erosión que comienza cuando se forma un arroyuelo durante una lluvia intensa. Al correr el arroyuelo, este posee suficiente energía como para arrastrar consigo plantas y tierra. (Cap. 8, pág. 204)

Robinson projection/proyección de Robinson: mapa que muestra las formas correctas de los continentes y extensiones territoriales precisas. (Cap. 5, pág. 131)

rock/roca: mezcla de minerales, mineraloides, vidrio o de materia orgánica. (Cap. 4, pág. 87)

rock cycle/ciclo de las rocas: ciclo por el cual las rocas cambian debido a procesos tales como la meteorización, la erosión, la compactación, la cementación, la fusión y el enfriamiento. (Cap. 4, pág. 87)

rotation/rotación: movimiento de la Tierra alrededor de su eje, el cual causa el día y la noche. (Cap. 22, pág. 616)

runoff/agua de desagüe: agua que no se filtra en el suelo o que no se evapora y, por consiguiente, corre sobre la superficie de la Tierra. (Cap. 8, pág. 202)

Safe Drinking Water Act/Ley sobre la Seguridad del Agua Potable: ley promulgada en 1986 para asegurar que el agua potable del país es segura de beber. (Cap. 20, pág. 570)

salinity/salinidad: medida de la cantidad de sólidos disueltos en el agua marina. Por lo general, se mide en gramos de sal por kilogramo. (Cap. 17, pág. 480)

sanitary landfill/vertedero controlado: terraplén donde los depósitos de basura diarios se cubren con tierra para evitar que el viento se los lleve y disminuir también el olor producido por los desechos en descomposición. (Cap. 19, pág. 541)

satellite/satélite: cualquier objeto que gira alrededor de otro objeto. (Cap. 21, pág. 594)

saturated/saturado: se dice que el aire está saturado cuando contiene tanta humedad como le es posible, a una temperatura específica. (Cap. 15, pág. 424)

Saturn/Saturno: conocido como el planeta anular es el sexto planeta a partir del sol. (Cap. 23, pág. 656)

science/ciencia: proceso de observación y estudio de las cosas de nuestro mundo. (Cap. 1, pág. 6)

scientific method/método científico: serie de pasos planificados que usan los científicos para resolver problemas. (Cap. 1, pág. 16)

scrubber/depurador: dispositivo que rocía los gases de escape de las centrales eléctricas con compuestos básicos, aumentándoles el pH a un nivel seguro. (Cap. 20, pág. 563)

sea breeze/brisa marina: viento suave que sopla desde el mar hacia la tierra, producido por corrientes de convección durante el día. (Cap. 14, pág. 415)

sea-floor spreading/expansión del suelo marino: teoría famosa y aceptada de Harry Hess que propuso que el material caliente y menos denso del manto es forzado hacia la superficie en una dorsal o cordillera medioceánica, donde se enfría formando el nuevo suelo marino. Este nuevo suelo marino es empujado en ambas direcciones por el nuevo magma. (Cap. 11, pág. 299)

season/estación: período climático de corto plazo causado por una variación regular en la luz del día, la temperatura y los patrones climáticos. (Cap. 16, pág. 462)

secondary wave/onda secundaria: onda que se mueve a través de la Tierra haciendo que las partículas en las rocas se muevan en un ángulo recto a la dirección de la onda. (Cap. 9, pág. 244)

sediment/sedimento: material suelto tal como los fragmentos rocosos, granos minerales y trocitos de restos vegetales y animales, que han sido transportados. (Cap. 4, pág. 101)

sedimentary rock/roca sedimentaria: roca que se forma cuando los sedimentos son presionados o cementados o cuando estos se precipitan de una solución. (Cap. 4, pág. 101)

seismic wave/onda sísmica: ondas generadas por un terremoto. (Cap. 9, pág. 241)

seismograph/sismógrafo: instrumento que mide las ondas primarias, secundarias y de superficie que producen los terremotos. (Cap. 9, pág. 252)

seismologist/sismólogo: científico que estudia los terremotos y las ondas sísmicas. (Cap. 9, pág. 252)

sheet erosion/erosión laminar o en capas: tipo de erosión que ocurre cuando el agua de lluvia corre cuesta abajo arrastrando consigo sedimentos. (Cap. 8, pág. 205)

shield volcano/volcán de escudo: volcán amplio con suaves pendientes formado por la acumulación de capas llanas de lava basáltica. (Cap. 10, pág. 279)

silicate/silicato: mineral que contiene silicio y oxígeno y, por lo general, uno o más elementos. (Cap. 3, pág. 66)

sill/intrusión: magma que ha sido apretujado formando una resquebrajadura horizontal entre capas rocosas y que se endurece. (Cap. 10, pág. 284)

slump/derrumbe: movimiento de masa que ocurre cuando materiales sueltos o capas rocosas se deslizan por una cuesta. (Cap. 7, pág. 174)

soil/suelo: mezcla de roca meteorizada, materia orgánica, fragmentos minerales, agua y aire. (Cap. 6, pág. 157)

soil profile/perfil del suelo: capas diferentes de suelo. (Cap. 6, pág. 158)

solar eclipse/eclipse solar: ocurre cuando la luna se mueve directamente entre el sol y la Tierra y proyecta una sombra sobre parte de la Tierra. (Cap. 22, pág. 626)

solar system/sistema solar: grupo de nueve planetas y muchos objetos más pequeños que giran alrededor del sol. (Cap. 23, pág. 641)

solstice/solsticio: tiempo en que el sol alcanza su mayor distancia al norte o al sur del ecuador. (Cap. 22, pág. 622)

solution/solución: mezcla en la cual una sustancia se disuelve en otra, como por ejemplo el agua salada. (Cap. 2, pág. 41)

sonar/sonar: equipo que usa las ondas sonoras para detectar estructuras en el fondo oceánico. (Cap. 5, pág. 139)

space probe/sonda espacial: instrumento que reúne información y que la envía de vuelta a la Tierra. (Cap. 21, pág. 595)

space shuttle/transbordador espacial: nave espacial que transporta a astronautas, satélites y otros materiales hacia y desde el espacio y la cual se puede volver a usar. (Cap. 21, pág. 604)

space station/estación espacial: estación que posee viviendas, trabajo y espacio para trabajar, y todo el equipo y sistemas auxiliares que necesitan los seres humanos para vivir y trabajar en el espacio. (Cap. 21, pág. 605)

species/especie: grupo de organismos que se reproducen normalmente solo entre ellos mismos. (Cap. 13, pág. 359)

sphere/esfera: objeto redondo tridimensional cuya superficie en cualquiera de sus puntos está a la misma distancia de su centro. (Cap. 22, pág. 614)

spring/manantial: agua que aflora en lugares donde la superficie terrestre se junta con la capa freática. (Cap. 8, pág. 216)

station model/código meteorológico: información meteorológica recogida por el Servicio Meteorológico y registrada en mapas con una combinación de símbolos. (Cap. 15, pág. 441)

streak/veta: es el color del mineral al partirlo y pulverizarlo. (Cap. 3, pág. 69)

strike-slip fault/falla transformante: falla en la cual las rocas en cualquiera de los dos lados de la superficie de la falla se alejan unas de otras sin mucho movimiento ascendente o descendente. (Cap. 9, pág. 238)

subduction zone/zona de subducción: área donde una placa oceánica desciende hacia el manto superior. (Cap. 17, pág. 307)

sulfurous smog/smog sulfuroso: tipo de smog que se forma cuando los combustibles fósiles se queman en centrales eléctricas y en las calderas caseras. (Cap. 20, pág. 557)

sunspot/mancha solar: área de la superficie solar que se ve oscura porque es más fría que las áreas que la rodean. (Cap. 24, pág. 680)

supergiant/supergigante: etapa en la formación de una estrella en la cual se forman elementos cada vez más pesados por medio de la fusión, haciendo que a la larga, se forme hierro en su núcleo. (Cap. 24, pág. 688)

surface current/corriente de superficie: corriente que mueve el agua horizontalmente paralela a la superficie terrestre. Estas corrientes son accionadas por el viento. (Cap. 17, pág. 484)

surface wave/onda de superficie: onda que viaja hacia afuera del epicentro; generada por la energía que llega hasta la superficie terrestre y que se mueve al darles un movimiento elíptico a las partículas como también un movimiento oscilatorio. (Cap. 9, pág. 244)

technology/tecnología: es el uso de los descubrimientos científicos. (Cap. 1, pág. 10)

temperate zone/zona templada: zona ubicada entre los trópicos y las zonas polares. (Cap. 16, pág. 452)

tephra/tefrita: material volcánico de diferentes tamaños causado por el enfriamiento y endurecimiento de la lava. (Cap. 10, pág. 279)

theory/teoría: explicación respaldada por resultados obtenidos de pruebas o experimentos repetidos. (Cap. 1, pág. 18)

third quarter/cuarto menguante: cuando se ve solo la mitad de la faz iluminada de la luna. (Cap. 22, pág. 625)

tidal range/alcance de la marea: la diferencia entre el nivel del océano durante la marea alta y la marea baja. (Cap. 17, pág. 492)

tide/marea: ascenso y descenso del nivel del mar. (Cap. 17, pág. 492)

till/morena: acumulación no estratificada de pedrones, arena. arcilla y cieno arrastrados por un glaciar. (Cap. 7, pág. 184)

titanium/titanio: metal liviano y duradero que se deriva de minerales tales como la ilmenita y el rutilo. (Cap. 3, pág. 78)

Topex-Poseidon Satellite/Satélite Topex-Poseidon: (Topex significa experimento topográfico) satélite que usa un radar para calcular la distancia que hay hasta la superficie del océano. (Cap. 5, pág. 138)

topographic map/mapa topográfico: muestra los cambios en elevación de la superficie terrestre. (Cap. 5, pág. 132)

tornado/tornado: viento violento y arremolinado que se mueve sobre una estrecha trayectoria sobre la tierra, por lo general en dirección suroeste-noroeste. (Cap. 15, pág. 436)

transform fault/falla de transformación: ocurre cuando dos placas se deslizan y se alejan una de la otra moviéndose ya sea en direcciones opuestas o en la misma dirección a distinta velocidad. (Cap. 11, pág. 309)

trench/fosa submarina: depresión larga, estrecha y con laderas empinadas en el suelo oceánico donde una placa de la corteza terrestre es forzada a penetrar debajo de otra. (Cap. 18, pág. 507)

tropics/trópicos: la región entre las latitudes 23° norte y 23° sur. (Cap. 16, pág. 452)

troposphere/troposfera: la capa de la atmósfera terrestre que se encuentra más cerca del suelo; contiene el 75 por ciento de los gases atmosféricos como también polvo, hielo y agua líquida. (Cap. 14, pág. 394)

trough/seno: el punto más bajo de una ola. (Cap. 17, pág. 490)

tsunamis/tsunamis: ondas marinas sísmicas generadas por terremotos. (Cap. 9, pág. 255)

ultraviolet radiation/radiación ultravioleta: uno de los numerosos tipos de energía que llega a la Tierra proveniente del sol. (Cap. 14, pág. 400)

unconformities/discordancias: brechas entre las capas rocosas. (Cap. 12, pág. 339)

uniformitarianism/uniformitarianismo: principio que dice que los procesos terrestres que ocurren actualmente son similares a los que ocurrieron en el pasado. (Cap. 12, pág. 347)

upwarped mountain/montaña plegada anticlinal: montaña que se formó cuando la corteza terrestre fue empujada hacia arriba por fuerzas del interior de la Tierra. (Cap. 5, pág. 124)

upwelling/corriente de aguas resurgentes: circulación en el océano que lleva agua profunda y fría hacia la superficie. (Cap. 17, pág. 487)

Uranus/Uranio: el séptimo planeta a partir del sol, el cual no fue descubierto hasta 1781. (Cap. 23, pág. 657)

variable/variable: factor que se cambia en un experimento. (Cap. 1, pág. 17)

vent/chimenea: abertura por la cual fluye el magma que llega a la superficie terrestre. (Cap. 10, pág. 268)

Venus/Venus: el segundo planeta a partir del sol. (Cap. 23, pág. 647)

volcanic mountain/montaña volcánica: montaña que se forma cuando el material derretido mana hacia la superficie terrestre a través de un área debilitada de la corteza y forma una estructura en forma de cono. (Cap. 5, pág. 125)

volcanic neck/cuello volcánico: núcleo ígneo sólido que queda después de que el cono de un volcán se erosiona cuando un volcán deja de hacer erupción. (Cap. 10, pág. 284)

volcano/volcán: chimenea en la superficie que forma una montaña cuando se arrojan y se acumulan capas de lava y cenizas volcánicas desde el interior de la Tierra. (Cap. 10, pág. 266)

waning/octante menguante: cuando la cantidad de la faz iluminada de la luna comienza a disminuir. (Cap. 22, pág. 625)

waste coal/carbón residual: subproducto de la minería del carbón; carbón de mala calidad. (Cap. 4, pág. 108)

water cycle/ciclo del agua: el constante movimiento del agua entre la atmósfera y la Tierra. (Cap. 14, pág. 406)

water table/nivel hidrostático o capa freática: superficie superior de la zona de saturación. (Cap. 8, pág. 215)

wave/ola: movimiento en el cual el agua sube y baja alternadamente a medida que la energía pasa por ella. (Cap. 17, pág. 490)

waxing/octante creciente: cuando se hace cada vez más visible la cara iluminada de la luna. (Cap. 22, pág. 624)

weather/tiempo: término que se refiere al estado actual de la atmósfera y que describe sus condiciones actuales. (Cap. 15, pág. 422)

weathering/meteorización: proceso que parte las rocas en fragmentos más y más pequeños. (Cap. 6, pág. 148)

weight/peso: medida de la fuerza gravitacional ejercida sobre una masa. (Cap. 1, pág. 20)

white dwarf/enana blanca: etapa en la formación de una estrella en la cual su núcleo se contrae bajo la fuerza de la gravedad al agotar su combustible y las capas externas de la estrella se escapan hacia el espacio. (Cap. 24, pág. 687)

zone of saturation/zona de saturación: área donde todos los poros de una roca permeable están llenos de agua. (Cap. 8, pág. 215)

Index

The Index for *Merrill Earth Science* will help you locate major topics in the book quickly and easily. Each entry in the Index is followed by the numbers of the pages on which the entry is discussed. A page number given in **boldface type** indicates the page on which that entry is defined. A page number given in *italic type* indicates a page on which the entry is used in an illustration or photograph. The abbreviation *act.* indicates a page on which the entry is used in an activity.

S

Art Credits

29, Preface, Inc.; **32,** John Edwards; **35,** Kristen Kest; **35, 36,** Jim Shough; **37,** Preface, Inc.; **39, 46, 47,** Jim Shough; **59,** Preface, Inc.; **64,** Tom Kennedy; **66,** Dartmouth Publishing, Inc.; **83,** Preface, Inc.; **87,** Dartmouth Publishing, Inc.; **90-1, 97, 102,** John Edwards; **113,** Preface, Inc.; **120,** John Edwards; **121,** Tom Kennedy; **123, 124, 125,** John Edwards; **126, 127,** Precision Graphics; **129, 130, 131,** Dartmouth Publishing, Inc.; **134,** Preface, Inc.; **134,** John Edwards; **135,** USGS; **138,** John Edwards; **139,** Edwin Huff; **140,** USGS; **145,** Preface, Inc.; **148,** Tom Kennedy; **149,** John Edwards; **150,** Rolin Graphics; **156-7, 158, 162,** John Edwards; **163,** Dartmouth Publishing, Inc.; **169,** Preface Inc.; **174, 175,** John Edwards; **180,** Tom Kennedy; **182-3, 184,** John Edwards; **188,** Preface, Inc.; **195,** Dartmouth Publishing, Inc.; **199,** Tom Kennedy; **199,** Preface, Inc.; **205,** Edwin Huff; **206,** Thomas Gagliano; **208-9,** John Edwards; **214,** Rolin Graphics; **215,** Leon Bishop; **216,** Thomas Gagliano; **217,** Leon Bishop; **222,** Chris Forsey/Morgan-Cain and Associates; **225,** Rolin Graphics; **225, 229,** Preface, Inc.; **229, 237,** Tom Kennedy; **238, 239, 244-5,** Chris Forsey/Morgan-Cain and Associates; **246,** Preface, Inc.; **247,** Tom Kennedy; **250,** Edwin Huff; **250-1,** Gary Hinks/Publisher's Graphics; **256,** Deborah Morse/Morgan-Cain and Associates; **256,** George Bucktell; **257,** Tom Kennedy; **259,** George Bucktell; **260,** Dartmouth Publishing, Inc.; **263,** Preface, Inc.; **268,** Tom Kennedy; **271,** Preface, Inc.; **272,** John Edwards; **272,** Gary Hinks/Publisher's Graphics; **274,** John Edwards; **275,** Dartmouth Publishing, Inc.; **278, 279,** Gary Hinks/Publisher's Graphics; **282,** Preface, Inc.; **283,** Gary Hinks/Publisher's Graphics; **287,** Preface, Inc.; **286,** Gary Hinks/ Publisher's Graphics; **291,** Preface, Inc.; **294-5,** Chris Forsey/Morgan-Cain and Associates; **295,** John Edwards; **297,** Precision Graphics; **298,** John Edwards; **301, 304,** Leon Bishop; **305,** Tom Kennedy; **308-9,** Gary Hinks/Publisher's Graphics; **311,** David De Gasperis; **311,** Edwin Huff; **312, 315,** John Edwards; **319,** Preface, Inc.; **326,** John Edwards; **329,** Rolin Graphics; **331,** Preface, Inc.; **331,** Jim Shough; **333,** Leon Bishop; **334, 338-9, 340,** John Edwards; **341, 342,** Dartmouth Publishing; **343, 345,** Tom Kennedy; **346,** Dartmouth Publishing, Inc.; **353,** John Edwards; **356-7,** Laurie O'Keefe; **358,** Dartmouth Publishing, Inc.; **362,** Laurie O'Keefe; **363,** Thomas Gagliano; **363,** Rolin Graphics; **366,** Barbara Hoopes; **367, 371,** Laurie O'Keefe; **371,** Dartmouth Publishing, Inc.; **374,** Precision Graphics; **376,** Laurie O'Keefe; **376, 377, 379,** Sarah Woodward; **381,** Felipe Passalacqua; **385,** Tom Kennedy; **392,** Jim Shough; **394,** Tom Kennedy; **395,** Edwin Huff; **397,** John Edwards; **398,** Tom Kennedy; **401,** Thomas Gagliano; **402, 404, 405,** John Edwards; **408,** Leon Bishop; **410,** Laurie O'Keefe; **411,** Dartmouth Publishing, Inc.; **411,** Edwin Huff; **412,** Bruce Sanders; **415, 416, 418,** John Edwards; **419,** Preface, Inc.; **423,** Dartmouth Publishing, Inc.; **425, 426, 428,** Tom Kennedy; **427,** Precision Graphics, Inc.; **432,** Tom Kennedy; **434,** John Edwards; **436,** Barbara Hoopes; **438,** John Edwards; **440,** Dartmouth Publishing, Inc.; **440,** Tom Kennedy; **443,** Ortelius Design; **449,** Preface, Inc.; **449,** Jim Shough; **452,** Leon Bishop; **453,** Tom Kennedy; **455,** John Edwards; **459,** Dartmouth Publishing, Inc.; **460,** Kristen Kest; **462,** John Edwards; **464,** Rolin Graphics; **466, 467,** John Edwards; **474,** Rolin Graphics; **475,** Preface, Inc.; **479,** John Edwards; **481,** Dartmouth Publishing, Inc.; **484,** Precision Graphics; **487, 490, 491, 492, 495, 496,** John Edwards; **498,** Dartmouth Publishing, Inc.; **506, 507,** John Edwards; **511,** Laurie O'Keefe; **519,** John Edwards; **533, 536,** Dartmouth Publishing, Inc.; **540,** Tom Kennedy; **541,** John Edwards; **542,** Dartmouth Publishing, Inc.; **546,** Tom Kennedy; **553,** Dartmouth Publishing, Inc.; **557,** Thomas Gagliano; **559,** John Edwards; **560,** Thomas Gagliano; **562,** Tom Kennedy; **563, 569,** John Edwards; **572,** Thomas Gagliano; **574,** Dartmouth Publishing, Inc.; **574, 577,** Preface, Inc.; **584-5,** Dartmouth Publishing, Inc.; **586,** George Bucktell; **594,** John Edwards; **595,** Mike Eddy; **596-7,** John Edwards; **614,** Thomas Gagliano; **615,** John Edwards; **616,** Bruce Sanders; **617, 619, 623,** John Edwards; **624,** Tim Hayes; **625, 626, 627, 630-1,** John Edwards; **637,** Preface, Inc.; **640-1, 642-3,** John Edwards; **645,** Dartmouth Publishing, Inc.; **648, 656, 657,** John Edwards; **662,** Mike Eddy; **662, 664, 666,** John Edwards; **672,** Precision Graphics; **673, 675, 679, 684, 685, 686, 687, 691, 693,** John Edwards; **694-5,** Bruce Sanders; **695,** Jim Shough; **696,** John Edwards; **712-3,** Glencoe; **714-5, 716-7,** Ortelius Design; **720-1,** Mark Lakin

Photo Credits

Cover, Jack Dykinga; **Connect to Chemistry** (flask)K&C Fischer; **vi** (t)Jack Dykinga; (l)Mark Burnett; **vii** (t)Doug Martin, (b)Peter French/DRK Photo; **viii** (t)Wolfgang Kaehler, (c)Jerald P. Fish/Tony Stone Images, (b)Jeff Gnass; **ix** (t)Brad Lewis/Gamma-Liaison, (b)file photo; **x** (t)Phil Degginger/Color-Pic, (b)John Cancalosi/Peter Arnold, Inc.; **xi** Michael Melford/The Image Bank; **xii** Michio Hosino/Minden Pictures; **xiii** Nobert Wu; **xiv xv** NASA; **xvi** Matt Meadows; **xvii** (t)KS Studios, (b)Matt Meadows; **xviii** Animals Animals/Patti Murray; **xix** Doug Martin; **xx** (t)Aaron Haupt, (b)Doug Martin; **xxi** (t)Matt Meadows, (b)Scripps Institution of Oceanography; **xxii** Matt Meadows; **xxiii** (t)Chip Clark, (bl)Bob Kalmbach/University of Michigan, (bc)Nobert Wu, (br)courtesy Leigh Standingbear; **xxiv** (t)courtesy A. Kahn, (others)NASA; **xxv** (t)NASA, (b)Johnny Johnson/Tony Stone Images; **2-3** Bruce Iverson; **3** NASA; **4-5** John Barstow; **5** StudiOhio; **6** (l)Jack Dykinga, (c)Steve Kaufman/DRK Photo, (r)NASA; **7** (tl)Hickson-Bender Photography, (tr)NASA/Photri, (bl)Rod Planck/Tony Stone Images, (br)John Cancalosi/Peter Arnold, Inc.; **8** Jean Miele/The Stock Market; **9** Kitt Peak National Observatory; **10** Telegraph Colour Library/FPG International; **11** NASA; **12** (l)file photo, (r)Bob Daemmrich/Stock Boston; **13** Scripps Institution of Oceanography; **14** UPI/Bettmann; **17** Peter Pearson/Tony Stone Images; **18** Richard Hutchings; **19** (clockwise from top) Chip Clark, Rick Weber, Chip Clark, Aaron Haupt, National Institute of Standards and Technology; **21** (t)StudiOhio, (bl)Ramey/Stock Boston, (br)Chip Clark; **22 23** StudiOhio; **24** (t)Jamie Mosberg/National Geographic Society, (b)Matt Meadows; **25** Doug Martin; **26** Jack Dykinga; **29** Latent Image; **30-31** Francois Gohier/Photo Researchers; **31 33** Matt Meadows; **34** (tl)Dr. E.R. Degginger/Color-Pic, (tlc)Doug Martin, (trc) Martin Land/Science Photo Library/Photo Researchers, (tr)Doug Martin, (bl)Dale O'Dell/The Stock Market, (blc) Doug Martin, (brc)David Stoecklein/The Stock Market, (br)Bruce Iverson; **34-35** Matt Meadows; **35** R.C. Hermes/Photo Researchers; **36** StudiOhio; **37** Jeffery Newbury/(1995) The Walt Disney Co. Reprinted with permission of *Discover* magazine; **38** Inga Spence/Tom Stack & Associates; **39** courtesy IBM Corporation; **40** Matt Meadows; **41** Doug Martin; **42** Carol Sailors; **43 44** Matt Meadows; **45** Vanessa Vick/Photo Researchers; **46** (t)Craig Kramer, (b)Ron Whitby/FPG International; **47** (t)Peter Gridley/FPG International, (b)Warren Faidley/Weatherstock; **48** Bob Kalmbach/University of Michigan; **49** Cameramann/The Image Works; **50** David R. Frazier Photolibrary; **51** NASA; **52 53** Matt Meadows; **54** Dr. E.R. Degginger/Color-Pic; **55 56** DOE; **58** Hickson-Bender; **60** Matt Meadows; **60-61** Jack Dykinga; **62** KS Studios; **63 64** Doug Martin; **65** Matt Meadows; **67 68 69** Doug Martin; **70** (t)Doug Martin, (b)Mark Burnett; **71** Tim Courlas; **72** Matt Meadows; **73** (tr)Chas Krider, (others)Doug Martin; **74** (opal) D.C.H. Plowes, (turquoise)Breck P. Kent/JLM Visuals, (others)Doug Martin; **75** (t)David Austen/Tony Stone Images, (bl)StudiOhio, (br)Doug Martin; **76** Dr. Jeremy Burgess/Science Photo Library/Photo Researchers; **77** Calvin Larsen/Photo Researchers; **78** Jim Cummins/FPG International; **79** (t)Chris Sorensen, (b)P. Peterson/Custom Medical Stock Photo; **80** courtesy A. Kahn; **82** Francois Gohier/Photo Researchers; **83** KS Studios; **84-85** Jack Dykinga; **85** Matt Meadows; **86** (tl)Dr. E.R. Degginger/Color-Pic, (tlc)Richard P. Jacobs/JLM Visuals, (trc)Doug Martin, (tr)Dr. E.R. Degginger/Color-Pic, (b)Doug Martin; **87** (t)Brent Turner/BLT Productions, (b)Doug Martin; **88** (l)Bob Daemmrich, (r)Doug Martin; **89** Jim Brandenburg/Minden Pictures; **90** (t)William E. Ferguson, (b)Doug Martin; **91** Dr. E.R. Degginger/Color-Pic; **92** (rocks)Doug Martin, (other)Douglas Peebles/Westlight; **93** Art Wolfe; **94** KS Studios; **96** Alberto Garcia/Saba Press Photos; **97** (l)Doug Martin, (r)Doug Martin; **98** Mark Burnett; **99** (l)Dr. E.R. Degginger/Color-Pic, (r)William E. Ferguson; **100** Nimatallah/Art Resource, NY; **101** (l)Aaron Haupt, (lc)Doug Martin, (rc)Brent Turner/BLT Productions, (r)Richard P. Jacobs/JLM Visuals; **103** G.R. Roberts; **104** (l)Cliff Leight, (r)StudiOhio; **105** Jack Dykinga; **106** James Westwater; **107** (l)Lynn McLaren/Photo Researchers, (r)StudiOhio; **108** Alan Oddie/PhotoEdit; **109** Phil Degginger/

Color-Pic; **112** Ward's Natural Science Establishment; **114** (t)David M. Dennis, (c)Brent Turner/BLT Productions, (b)Chas Krider; **115** (t)Doug Martin, (b)Chip Clark; **116-117** Jack Dykinga; **117** Rich Buzzelli/Tom Stack & Associates; **118-119** World Perspectives; **119** StudiOhio; **122** Tom Till; **123** Peter French/DRK Photo; **124** (t)Phil Lauro/Profiles West, (b)Larry Ulrich/Tony Stone Images **125** Paul Chesley/Tony Stone Images; **128** (l)Matt Meadows, (r)Doug Martin; **132** Jeff Gnass; **133** Geographix, Inc.; **136** Tom Carroll/FPG International; **137** StudiOhio; **141** Matt Meadows; **142** SuperStock; **144-145** Galen Rowell/Mountain Light Photography; **146-147** Wolfgang Kaehler; **147** Matt Meadows; **148** Mark Burnett; **149** StudiOhio; **150** Bud Fowle; **151** Harris Photographic/Tom Stack & Associates; **152 153** Matt Meadows; **154** Carr Clifton/Minden Pictures; **155** (l)Henley & Savage/The Stock Market, (r)Tom Stack/Tom Stack & Associates; **156-157** Matt Meadows; **158** Rich Buzzelli/Tom Stack & Associates; **159** William E. Ferguson; **160** Doug Martin; **161** Marty Cordano/DRK Photo; **164** Lee Battaglia/Colorific!; **165** Larry Lefever/from Grant Heilman; 166 courtesy Susan Colclazer; **168** M. Wendler/Photo Researchers; **170-171** Jack Dykinga; **171** StudiOhio; **172** Rod Planck/Photo Researchers; **173** Jack Stein Grove/Profiles West; **174** Thomas G. Rampton/from Grant Heilman; **176** Stephen C. Porter; **177** Giboux/Gamma-Liaison; **178** Wolfgang Kaehler; **179** Reuters/Bettmann; **181** (l)Wolfgang Kaehler, (r)Cliff Leight; **182** (l)Phil Schermeister/National Geographic Society, (r)Mark Burnett; **183** Cliff Leight; **185** Earth Scenes/John Eastcott & Yva Momatiuk; **186** Matt Meadows; **187** (l)Tom Bean/DRK Photo, (r)Tom Till; **188** Debbie Dean; **189** (tl)Floyd Holdman/The Stock Solution, (tr)Runk/Schoenberger/from Grant Heilman, (b) Earth Scenes/M.J. Coe; **190** Mark Boulton/Photo Researchers; **191** (t)Wolfgang Kaehler, (b)Michael Collier; **192 193** Matt Meadows; **194** Jeff Gnass; **196** Bettmann Archive; **200-201** Jack Dykinga; 201 StudiOhio; **202** (l)T.A. Wiewandt/DRK Photo, (r)Tom Bean; **203** Jim Richardson/Westlight; **204** Holt Studios/Photo Researchers; **205** from Grant Heilman; **206** Earth Scenes/Leen van der Slik; **207** Jerald P. Fish/Tony Stone Images; **208** (t)Elaine Shay, (b)Tom Bean/DRK Photo; **209** Ray Fairbanks/Photo Researchers; **210** Matt Meadows; **212** Comstock; **213** (l)John Shelton, (r)NASA/TSADO/Tom Stack & Associates; **214** Matt Meadows; **217** Susan G. Drinker/The Stock Market; **218** Dave Harris/Tom Stack & Associates; **219** Wolfgang Kaehler; **220** StudiOhio; **221** Jack Dykinga; **222** Darrell Gulin/DRK Photo; **223** Charles Krebs/The Stock Market; **224** (t)Matt Meadows, (b)USDA-ASCS; **226** Lynn M. Stone; **229** Jack Dykinga; **230 231** KS Studios; **232-233** Art Wolfe; **233** Dennis Oda/Photo Resource Hawaii; **234-235** Yoshiaki Nagashima PPS/Black Star; **235** StudiOhio; **236** Matt Meadows; **238** Cliff Leight; **239** (t)Tom Till/DRK Photo, (b)David Parker/Photo Researchers; **240** Jonathan Nourok/PhotoEdit; **241** Ron Haviv/Saba Press Photos; **247** Russell D. Curtis/Photo Researchers; **249** Doug Martin; **252** Les Stone/Sygma; **254** H & M Tavetian; **256** Doug Martin; **258** James L. Stanfield/National Geographic Society; **259** Francois Gohier/Photo Researchers; **262** Archive Photos; **264-265** Alberto Garcia/Saba Press Photos; **265** Doug Martin; **266** Brad Lewis/Gamma-Liaison; **267** Emory Kristof/National Geographic Society; **269** Ministry of Construction for Osumi/Fujifotos/The Image Works; **270** Matt Meadows; **273** Terry Duennebier/ SOEST/University of Hawaii; **276 277** Gary Rosenquist; **278** (t)Earth Scenes/Breck P. Kent, (b)Tom Bean/DRK Photo; **279** (t)Robert Madden/National Geographic Society, (b)Earth Scenes/Michael Fogden; **280** Doug Martin; **281** Patrick Aventurier/Gamma-Liaison; **284** Marc Muench; **285** (tl)David Muench, (tr)David Hosking/Photo Researchers, (b)Steve Kaufman/DRK Photo; **286** Greg Vaughn; **287** Doug Martin; **288** Art Resource, NY; **291** Dave B. Fleetham/Pacific Stock; **292-293** Tom Van Sant/Geosphere Project/Photo Researchers; **293** Matt Meadows; **296** David M. Dennis; **299** Scripps Institution of Oceanography; **300** Morin, Tanimoto, Yuen, Zhang. Graphic provided by Paul Morin; **302** Richard Hutchings; **307** file photo; **310** Tom Bean/DRK Photo; **312** Altitude/Peter Arnold, Inc.; **313** CNES/Photo Researchers; **314** Galen Rowell/Mountain Light Photography; **316** Hilsman Jackson/SMU; **318** John Warden/Tony Stone Images; **320** Doug

Photo Credits

Martin; **321** (t)Al Grillo/Alaska Stock Images, (b)Mark Burnett; **322-323** David Muench; **323** Chip Clark; **324-325** Vaughan Fleming/Photo Researchers; **325** StudiOhio; **326** Louis Psihoyos/Matrix; **327** Phil Degginger/Color-Pic; **328** (t)Francois Gohier/Photo Researchers, (b)Sinclair Stammers/Photo Researchers; **329** Dr. E.R. Degginger/Color-Pic; **330** (t)Vaughan Fleming/Photo Researchers, (cb)Louis Psihoyos/Matrix; **332** Richard T. Nowitz/Photo Researchers; **333** Doug Martin; **334** Dr. E.R. Degginger/Color-Pic; **335** Tony Stone Images; **336** Louis Psihoyos/Matrix; **337** Doug Martin; **338** John Shelton; **340** Jack Dykinga; **341** StudiOhio; **344** Doug Martin; **346** Steve Dunwell/The Image Bank; **348** StudiOhio; **350** courtesy University of Michigan; **353** John Cancalosi/Peter Arnold, Inc.; **354-355,** Micheal Skrepnick; **355** KS Studios; **359** (l)Barbara Gerlach/DRK Photo, (c)Animals Animals/Zig Leszczynski, (r)Jeff Lepore/Photo Researchers; **360** Animals Animals/Breck P. Kent; **364** T.Geer/Peter Arnold, Inc.; **365** Earth Scenes/Doug Wechsler; **367** (l)Fred Bavendam/Peter Arnold, Inc., (r)Eric Grave/Photo Researchers; **368** Aaron Haupt; **369** **370** Doug Martin; **371** Chris Jones/The Stock Market; **372** Animals Animals/Zig Leszczynski; **373** Burnstein/Corbis/Bettmann Archive; **376** (l)David M. Dennis/Tom Stack & Associates, (r)Michael Collier; **378** Animals Animals/Patti Murray; **380** KS Studios; **382** Dave Watts/Tom Stack & Associates; **386** (t)David M. Dennis, (b)KS Studios; **387** (br)Mark Burnett, (others)David M. Dennis; **388-389** Nobert Wu; **389** NASA/TSADO/Tom Stack & Associates; **390-391** Michael Hildreth/Fascination Photos; **391** Mark Burnett; **393** Rob Badger Photography; **395** David Lawrence/The Stock Market; **396** Frank Rossotto/The Stock Market; **399** Matt Meadows; **400** NASA; **404** Richard Weiss/Peter Arnold, Inc.; **407** T.A. Wiewandt/DRK Photo; **408** KS Studios; **413** Mike & Anne Adair; **414** Michael Melford/The Image Bank; **419** Bill Gillingham/The Stock Solution; **420-421** Warren Faidley/Weatherstock; **421** Mary Lou Uttermohlen; **422** Don & Pat Valenti/DRK Photo; **424** Mary Lou Uttermohlen; **427** (l)Roy Morsch/The Stock Market, (lc)Jose L. Pelaez, (rc)Mark McDermott/Tony Stone Images; (r)EPI Nancy Adams/Tom Stack & Associates; **428** Doug Martin; **429** Earth Scenes/Breck P. Kent; **430** (t)Charles O'Rear/Westlight, (b)Doug Martin; **431** NCAR/Tom Stack & Associates; **435** Roy Johnson/Tom Stack & Associates; **436** Merrilee Thomas/Tom Stack & Associates; **437** Howard Bluestein/Photo Researchers; **439** Gary Williams/Gamma-Liaison; **441** Greg Stumpf; **442** KS Studios; **444** Lowell J. Georgia/Photo Researchers; **446** UPI/Bettmann; **448** Earth Scenes/Phil Degginger; **450-451** Tom Till; **451** Matt Meadows; **456** Doug Martin; **458** (t)Jeff Gnass, (b)David Muench; **460** (l)Tom Till, (r)Johnny Johnson/Tony Stone Images; **461** (l)David R. Frazier Photolibrary, (r)Michio Hoshino/Minden Pictures; **463** (l)Philippe Mazellier/National Geographic Society, (r)Robert Vink/National Geographic Society; **465** Galen Rowell/Mountain Light Photography; **468** Matt Meadows; **469** Bob Cranston/Mo Yung Productions/Nobert Wu; **470** Cliff Leight; **471** Thomas Braise/The Stock Market; **472** courtesy Ellen Mosley Thompson; **475** Darrell Gulin/DRK Photo; **476-477** H. Richard Johnston/Tony Stone Images; **477** Matt Meadows; **478** (l)Mark A. Leman/Tony Stone Images, (r)Zoltan Gaal/Photo Researchers; **480** Haramaty Mula/Phototake; **482** **483** Matt Meadows; **485** NOAA; **486** Raven/Explorer/Photo Researchers; **488** Matt Meadows; **489** John Nordquist; **491** Matt Meadows; **492** Vince Cavataio/Pacific Stock; **494** (l)Porterfield-Chickering/Photo Researchers, (r)C. Del/Photo Researchers; **497** Trask/Stock Imagery; **502-503** Nobert Wu; **503** Matt Meadows; **504-505** "The Floor of the Oceans," Bruce C. Heezen and Marie Tharp (1980 by Marie Tharp. Reproduced by permission of Marie Tharp); **508** Institute of Oceanographic Sciences/NERC/Photo Researchers; **510** Nobert Wu; **512** Visuals Unlimited/WHOI/D. Foster; **513** (t)Nobert Wu, (b)Dave B. Fleetham/Tom Stack & Associates; **514** Nobert Wu; **515** (t)Nobert Wu, (b)Urike Welsch/Photo Researchers; **516 517** Matt Meadows; **518** Nobert Wu; **520** Tomas del Amo/Pacific Stock; **521** Randy Brandon/Peter Arnold, Inc.; **522** courtesy Woods Hole Oceanographic Institution; **525** Nobert Wu; **526-527** Mark Steinmetz; **526** StudiOhio; **527** KS Studios; **528-529** Nobert Wu; **529** George H.H. Huey; **530-531** Carr Clifton/Minden Pictures; **531** Mark Burnett; **532** Jon Feingersh/The Stock

Photo Credits

Market; **534 535** Matt Meadows; **537** Richard Hutchings; **538** Michael Ableman; **539** (t)David M. Dennis/Tom Stack & Associates, (b)Larry Lefever/from Grant Heilman; **540** Frans Lanting/ Minden Pictures; **543** (t)Richard Laird/FPG International, (b)Jack Dykinga; **544** Tony Stone Images; **547** (t)Kenji Kerins, (b)Bob Daemmrich/ Stock Boston; **549** Matt Meadows; **550** courtesy Leigh StandingBear; **551** StudiOhio; **552** Terry Donnely/Tom Stack & Associates; **553** Matt Meadows; **554-555** John Hyde/Alaska Stock Images; **555** Tim Courlas; **556** Ken Biggs/The Stock Market; **558** Oliver Strewe/Tony Stone Images; **564** Peter Menzel/Stock Boston; **565** Joe Baraham/The Stock Market; **566** Doug Martin; **567** file photo; **568** (l)Simon Fraser/Science Photo Library/Photo Researchers, (r)Kenji Kerins; **569** (l)courtesy the city of San Diego, (r)John Eastcott & Yva Momatiuk/DRK Photo; **570** C. Hansen Carroll/FPG International; **571** (l)David Woodfall/Tony Stone Images, (r)Ian Adams; **573** Doug Martin; **576-577** Jose L. Pelaez/The Stock Market; **577** David M. Dennis; **578** KS Studios; **579** (t)Larry Ulrich, (b)Ray Pfortner/Peter Arnold, Inc.; **580-581 581 582-583** NASA; **583** Matt Meadows; **584** (l)Chris Collins/The Stock Market, (r)Mark E. Gibson; **585** (l)Daedalus Enterprises/ Peter Arnold, Inc., (c)Curtis Martin/Stock Imagery, (r)David M. Dennis/Tom Stack & Associates; **586** Doug Martin; **587** Tim Davis/ Photo Researchers; **588** (t)NASA/Gamma-Liaison, (c)Eric Sander/Gamma-Liaison, (b)Eric Sander/ Gamma-Liaison; **590** Matt Meadows; **591** Geoff Chester/International Dark-Sky Association; **592** International Dark-Sky Association; **598** Grafton Marshall Smith/The Stock Market; **599** SuperStock; **600** courtesy Gibor Basri; **601** Ken Frick; **603** Doug Martin; **604-605** Mark M. Lawrence/The Stock Market; **606 607 608** NASA; **611** NASA/Sygma; **612-613** Wendy Shattil & Bob Rozinksi/Tom Stack & Associates; **613** Matt Meadows; **616** Skip Comer; **618** Alexander Tsiaras/Photo Researchers; **620 621** Matt Meadows; **626** Bruce Herman/Tony Stone Images; **627** Jerry Schad/Photo Researchers; **628** NASA-TSADO/Tom Stack & Associates; **632** NASA; **633** Zuber et al/Johns Hopkins University/NASA/ Photo Researchers; **636** NASA; **638-639** David P. Anderson, SMU/NASA/Photo Researchers; **639** Matt Meadows; 640 Scala/Art Resource, NY; **644** Tom McHugh/Photo Researchers; **646** (l)JPL/ TSADO/Tom Stack & Associates, (r)NASA; **647** JPL/TSADO/Tom Stack & Associates; **648** NASA; **649** (t)NASA/Gamma-Liaison, (b)NASA/ TSADO/Tom Stack & Associates; **650** (l)USGS/ Phototake, (r)USGS/TSADO/Tom Stack & Associates; **651** Jim Stratford/Black Star; **652** Peter Menzel/Stock Boston; **653** Bob Daemmrich; **654** (t)NASA/Mark Marten/Photo Researchers, (b)NASA; **655** (moons)JPL, (b)NASA/Gamma-Liaison; **657** NASA/JPL/Tom Stack & Associates; **658** (t)NASA/Photo Researchers, (b)NASA; **659** NASA; **663** Ronald E. Royer/Photo Researchers; **664** (l)Tom Till/Tony Stone Images, (r)NASA; **665** NASA; **669** (l)NASA, (r)Larry Ulrich; **670-671** Bill & Sally Fletcher/Tom Stack & Associates; **671** Matt Meadows; **673** Bill & Sally Fletcher/Tom Stack & Associates; **674** Tim Courlas; **676** Matt Meadows; **678** David Parker/Science Photo Library/Photo Researchers; **680** (t)John Bova/Photo Researchers, (b)Hale Observatories/Science Photo Library/ Photo Researchers; **681** (t)NASA, (b)Chris Butler/Science Photo Library/Photo Researchers; **682** California Institute of Technology and Carnegie Institute of Washington; **683** Tim Courlas; **688** NASA; **689** (t)NASA, (b)Joe Stancampiano & Karl Luttrell/IMB Collaboration; **690** NASA; **692** (l)USNO/TSADO/Tom Stack & Associates, (r)David F. Malin; **693** Royal Observatory, Edinburgh/Science Photo Library/ Photo Researchers; **698** Robert Frerck/The Stock Market; **699** JPL; **700** NASA; **703** John Mead/Photo Researchers; **704** Pat Rawlings/NASA; **705** Pat Rawlings; **727** Thomas Veneklasen; **728** Franklin Over; **729** Dominic Oldershaw; **733** Jeff Smith/ Fotosmith; **734 735** Dominic Oldershaw; **736** Phil Degginger/Color-Pic; **738** Timothy Fuller; **739** Dominic Oldershaw; **742** Thomas Veneklasen; **743** Dominic Oldershaw; **744** Jeff Smith/Fotosmith; **745** Dominic Oldershaw

W9-BIM-290

This book may be purchased for educational, business, or sales promotional use.
For information, please write: Special Markets Department, Smithsonian Books, P.O. Box 37012, MRC 513, Washington, DC 20013

Published in North America by Smithsonian Books
Director: Carolyn Gleason
Senior Editor: Jaime Schwender
Assistant Editor: Julie Huggins

Library of Congress Cataloging-in-Publication Data

Names: Bahn, Paul G., editor.
Title: Incredible archaeology: inspiring places from our human past / Paul Bahn.
Other titles: Inspiring places from our human past
Description: Washington, DC: Smithsonian Books, [2020] | Includes index. |
Identifiers: LCCN 2020018613 | ISBN 9781588346926 (hardcover)
Subjects: LCSH: Excavations (Archaeology)–Guidebooks. | Historic sites–Guidebooks.
Classification: LCC CC168 .B34 2020 | DDC 930.1–dc23
LC record available at https://lccn.loc.gov/2020018613

Printed in Singapore

24 23 22 21 20 1 2 3 4 5

INCREDIBLE ARCHAEOLOGY

INSPIRING PLACES FROM OUR HUMAN PAST

Edited by
PAUL BAHN

Smithsonian Books
Washington, DC

CONTENTS

NORTH AMERICA

MIDDLE AND SOUTH AMERICA

EUROPE AND NORTHERN ASIA

AFRICA

NEAR EAST AND WESTERN ASIA

FAR EAST AND OCEANIA

INTRODUCTION

This volume's aim is to take the reader on a tour of some of the world's most famous archaeological sites. In doing so, it will show how, through the patient detective work of generations of scholars and researchers, as well as the scientific advances in archaeology, we now know more about the past than ever before.

Why does archaeology intrigue and even fascinate people? Probably everyone has some kind of interest in the past, even if only that of their own family—as shown by the current craze for having one's DNA analyzed to explore one's geographical origins or the percentage of Neanderthal! But countless people are also interested in the past of our species, of all humankind, and archaeology constitutes our only means of learning about early or vanished cultures, and answering really big questions such as the origins of farming, or of settled life, or of humankind itself.

But—as the archaeologist Glyn Daniel often stressed—archaeology can also be tremendous fun. It features some of the most beautiful artworks and some of the most astounding structures ever created, and often in dramatic or exotic locations that include deserts, jungles, mountains, and islands. Moreover, the emotions aroused by unearthing something that has not seen the light of day for centuries, or even millennia, are hard to describe, whether one is a professional excavator or a metal-detecting enthusiast.

Personally, I first experienced the joys of archaeology through childhood visits to the ruined medieval castles and abbeys of my native Yorkshire, the Roman ruins of northern England, and the megalithic monuments of

Left The fourth-century B.C.E. tholos at Delphi, Greece.

Wessex. Later I was fortunate enough to be taken by my mother—who was equally smitten by the lure of the past—to Pompeii, Rome, and the sites of Greece. But another early and vivid influence came from Hergé's stories of Tintin, especially *The Temple of the Sun* and *Cigars of the Pharaoh*. The impact of fictional characters on young minds should never be underestimated.

Indeed, if asked to name an archaeologist, most people today would probably come up with Indiana Jones; but real archaeology is worlds away from that swashbuckling fictional hero. It is not just about treasure or rich burials, though it is no less exciting for all that. It is true that, decades ago, and more, it was indeed a subject focused on spectacular discoveries and exotic finds, but over the years, as it grew into a serious discipline, and aspired to be scientific, archaeology became increasingly concerned with the more mundane aspects of the past, and with the traces of the lives of ordinary people rather only those of kings, queens, and emperors. It now concentrated not on finding things, but on finding *out* things, on trying to explain when and where and how and why things happened and changed in the past.

Inevitably it can sometimes be tempting for archaeologists to overinterpret, to go beyond the hard evidence into the realms of pure speculation—more often than not, this is done to satisfy the media's thirst for simple answers to complex problems. Today, it is often frowned upon to say "we don't know," let alone "we shall never know," even when these are the correct and honest answers. The hitherto unimagined analytical techniques available to us have led some researchers to a curious optimism that nothing is now unknowable—but unless and until a time machine is invented, it is hard to see how most of our deductions about the past will ever be tested, far less verified.

It is also only comparatively recently that archaeological excavation and museum curation previously conducted without the slightest consultation with, or permission sought from, local groups have begun to be undertaken with a bit more consultation and sensitivity, particularly when indigenous groups (in North America, Australia, or New Zealand, for example) or religious groups (most notably in Israel) have serious objections. This in turn has had profound effects on how sites and collections are displayed and interpreted for the public, and on the explicit and implicit messages that are conveyed in this way.

Because a great deal of groundless nonsense about archaeology and the past is promulgated on TV and the web, it is always worthwhile to produce a book that sets out the "real past," the astonishing variety of human achievements, the end products of our ancestors' sweat and ingenuity. Based on solid evidence, the pages in this volume not only explain what archaeologists do and how they make their deductions, but also, we hope, go a little way toward counteracting the wilder speculation that is sometimes seen.

The Past is Human

Only archaeology can uncover and elucidate the wonders of past times and the astonishing achievements of our forebears. It is still a very young discipline, though, and the contents of this book can only cover a fraction of what has been recovered and learned in a couple of centuries. We have come a long way from the crude, fumbling digs of the nineteenth century, which usually employed laborers armed with pickaxes and shovels (and sometimes even explosives), to rip objects out of the ground without the context that tells us so much. This caused the destruction of vast quantities of crucial and irreplaceable information.

However, we need to judge those early archaeologists in the context of their time. Who, in the nineteenth century, would recognize the slow, painstaking excavations of today, aided by aerial photography, radiocarbon dating, remote sensing, computers, or genetic analysis? It is likely that in another 150 years,

archaeologists will look back on our own efforts as worthy and well-meaning, but primitive and unimaginative. Faced with the incredible pace of technological development, we simply cannot imagine what the ever-growing and improving battery of archaeological and scientific techniques will reveal about our past during the next century, or what information our descendants will be able to extract from the apparently insignificant material traces of the past.

The future therefore looks as exciting as the past. The real joy of archaeology is that it is constantly changing through an endless stream of new discoveries, any one of which can radically alter our picture of the past: it may be a new kind of fossil human, an earlier date for a phenomenon (such as pottery or cremation) or for an event (like the arrival of humans in the New World or Australia), or something completely unexpected like the body of King Richard III turning up under a car park in Leicester—a find that immediately became a major news story all over the world in 2013.

Our Selection of Sites

It is inevitable that a book such as this, which sets out to present the world of archaeology through just one hundred places, is forced to a large extent to feature only the most famous and most visited sites. But we wanted to introduce readers to other places that are doubtless far less known yet of great interest and importance. Above all we sought to feature a wide variety of sites—not just palaces and tombs, but caves and cities, rock art and sanctuaries. Collectively, they span a period from our earliest ancestors to an event as recent as the Battle of the Little Big Horn.

In putting together this collection, aimed at the archaeology aficionado, the armchair enthusiast, and also, of course, the interested traveler, a whole range of factors came into play. First and foremost, the sites selected needed to be of archaeological importance; of interest to the general public rather than merely to a handful of

Above The main entrance of the Angkor Wat complex, Cambodia.

specialists; they had to be accessible to tourists; and also photogenic, for those readers who might never have the chance to see these places—and there are probably not many people out there who have seen, or will ever see, all of the chosen sites during their lifetime!

It was clear from the very start that a hundred or so places was remarkably few for the enormous subject of world archaeology, so each contributor had to make some very tough choices about what should be included from their part of the world. Many of them could easily have presented a hundred sites in their regions—from Egypt, for example, or the Classical World, or the New World civilizations. Where my own speciality, Ice Age art, is concerned, there are still around fifty original decorated caves open to the public, and I would argue that at least twenty of them are world class.

We were determined to be as rational as possible in our allocation of space, and there are inevitable imbalances in both geographical and chronological distribution. Serious archaeology only began relatively recently in Australia and much of Africa, whereas—thanks to historical accident—Europe has been the scene of intensive work for far longer. Conversely, the Paleolithic period, despite constituting 99 percent of the archaeological record in terms of timespan, was assigned only a small part of the book, since so few of its sites really appeal to the tourist.

It is sad that our selection process was made slightly easier by the fact that conflict and terrorism have rendered a number of areas inaccessible to the archaeological tourist at the moment. Several major sites in Syria and Libya—such as Palmyra and Leptis Magna —would certainly have been included in any such compilation. We had originally intended to feature Timbuktu, but tensions that part of the Africa has likewise placed it off-limits for the time being.

The Preservation of Sites for Generations to Come

It is to be hoped that these conflicts will soon become history in their turn, so that visits can resume to the archaeological treasures that are currently denied to us. At the same time, it is fervently to be hoped that most of the sites in question will emerge unscathed. Sadly, we know that terrible damage has been done to Palmyra and other sites in Syria, as well as to collections in archaeological museums both there and in other countries, such as Iraq and Afghanistan.

However, and with supreme irony, the greatest threats to archaeological sites all over the world come from the people who love them and visit them. Archaeological tourism has never been more popular, and is of enormous importance in many countries such as Egypt, Peru, and China. Yet its very popularity carries the tremendous risk of people loving it to death, by visiting fragile sites and monuments in excessive numbers. At many of the most popular sites such as Stonehenge or Carnac, the general public can no longer enter the monuments because of the potential damage of millions of feet; only a few people can now enter, outside of normal visiting hours and/or at great cost. When I first visited Easter Island in the mid-1980s, I was the only guest in my hotel, and I had almost all the sites to myself, with no restrictions on where one could go or climb. Today there are so many thousands of visitors every year that most of its monuments cannot even be approached too closely.

There are many reasons for this phenomenon all over the world—primarily the increasing affluence of the public, the rapid and constant growth of relatively cheap flights and foreign travel, and, of course, the ready availability of information about sites through popular books and magazines, television documentaries, and the Internet. And as the number of tourists continues to expand—particularly those coming from countries like China, who were unable to travel in the past—it is hard to see how this problem can be solved.

One solution, already used in such cases as the decorated caves of Lascaux, Altamira, and Chauvet is to produce exact replicas for tourists to visit, while the original sites are kept closed for reasons of conservation. Naturally, facsimiles are always poor substitutes for the real thing, but when they are superbly accurate, as in the caves mentioned above, they are well worth a visit. Cynics have pointed out that few people would pay to see a roomful of fake Rembrandts; but if the choice is either to see the replica or to see nothing at all, then surely most would opt for the former! Another solution arising from modern technology is to visit sites and monuments through virtual reality, and this, too, will become more common as restrictions on tourism create the demand. In addition, these hi-tech alternatives will prove invaluable to those who are financially or physically unable to travel to the sites. The new technology will also enable archaeologists to make further progress in reconstructing the past, but in helping to relieve tourist pressure on the more fragile and vulnerable remains of that past it will contribute greatly to its conservation for future generations.

It is imperative that we leave future generations as much of the past as we can, and in good condition—not only by cherishing and protecting known sites, but also by preventing the clandestine robbery and destruction of our precious and irreplaceable heritage. As long as looters and vandals are kept at bay, the prospects for broadening and deepening our understanding of the past will be bright.

Paul G. Bahn

Opposite Hatshepsut's temple, Egypt.

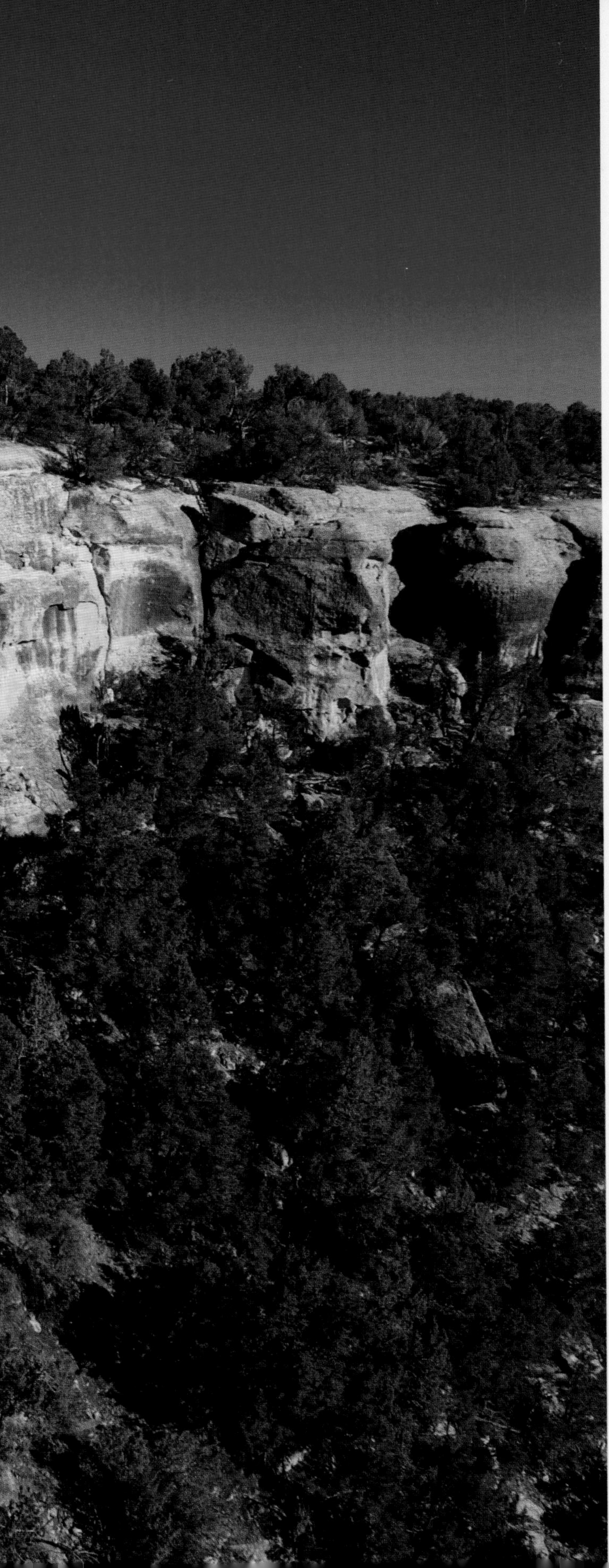

1

NORTH AMERICA

North America presents an astonishing variety of sites, from the spectacular and majestic ruins and pueblos of the Southwest to the enigmatic effigy mounds of Ohio and the great urban complex of Cahokia. But it also features a wide range of equally remarkable places like the evocatively named Head-Smashed-In Buffalo Jump. It provided the first solid evidence for Viking settlement at L'Anse aux Meadows. And at the Little Bighorn there took place one of the world's most famous and tragic battles, which has achieved almost mythical status through books and movies.

Left Mesa Verde National Park in Colorado.

NORTH AMERICA LOCATIONS

1 HEAD-SMASHED-IN BUFFALO JUMP
2 L'ANSE AUX MEADOWS
3 CHACO CANYON
4 MESA VERDE
5 THE BATTLE OF THE LITTLE BIGHORN
6 CAHOKIA
7 SERPENT MOUND

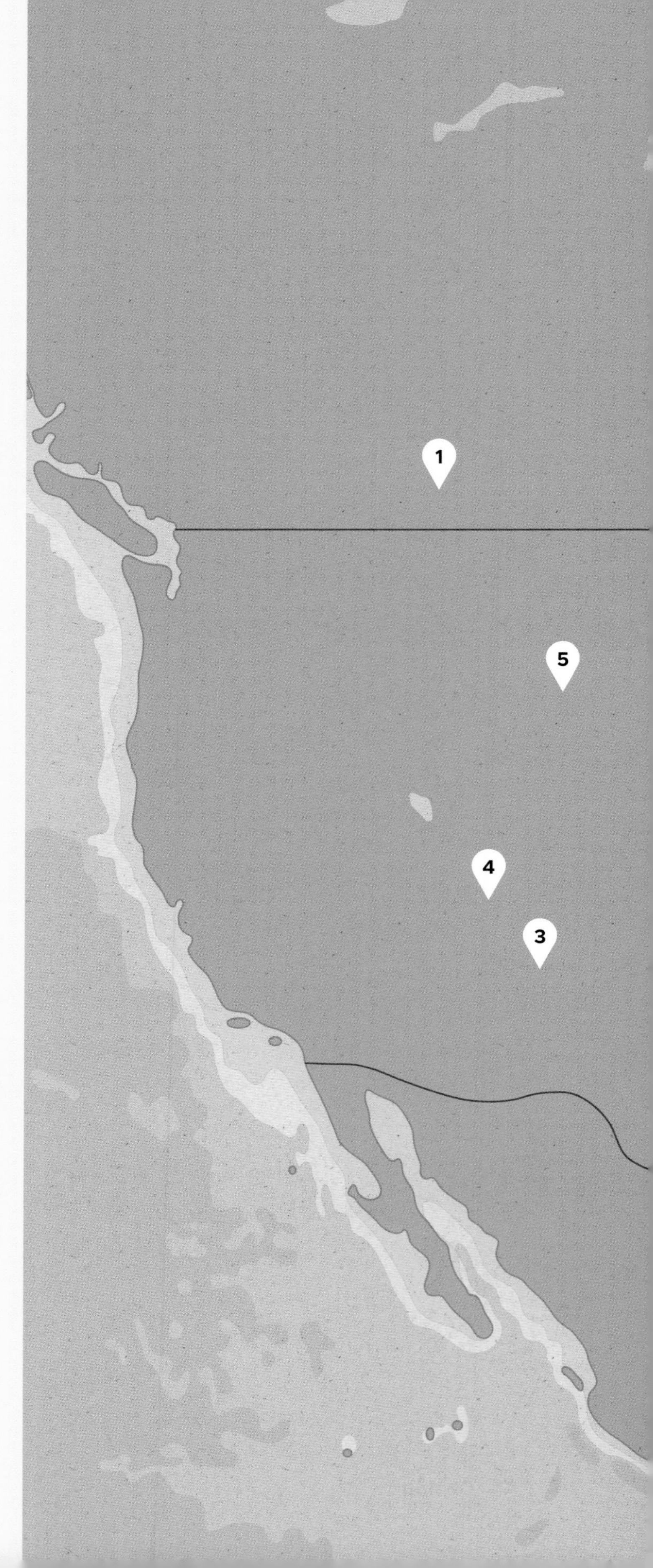

2
6
7

HEAD-SMASHED-IN **BUFFALO JUMP**

TYPE: KILL SITE • **ARCHITECTURAL STYLE:** N/A
LOCATION: ALBERTA, CANADA • **CONSTRUCTION BEGUN:** N/A

The winds seem to blow constantly from the Rocky Mountains, all the way across the great sea of grass called the Great Plains of North America. These grasslands were once home to tens of thousands of American bison, and the indigenous tribes of North America relied on those mighty beasts for their food, their shelters, their clothing; they wasted very little of the animal.

The bison is a herd animal, and indigenous people devised many ways to kill them. The most spectacular was the buffalo jump, in which hunters carefully shepherded hundreds of bison and, in a controlled stampede, drove them off the edge of a cliff to fall to their deaths. They then processed the carcasses, providing food and raw material for hundreds of people. By one estimate, one could walk along the foothills of the Rockies from Alberta to Colorado and never lose sight of at least one jump.

The Head-Smashed-In Buffalo Jump, located in southern Alberta on the edge of the Rockies, is one of the most splendid examples of the jump. It was in use for close to 6,000 years (the latest use was by the historic Blackfoot tribe). The overall complex comprises four primary elements. First is the gathering basin in the foothills of the Rockies, where hunters would herd small groups of the animal until a critical mass had been reached and they stampeded through lines of stone cairns,

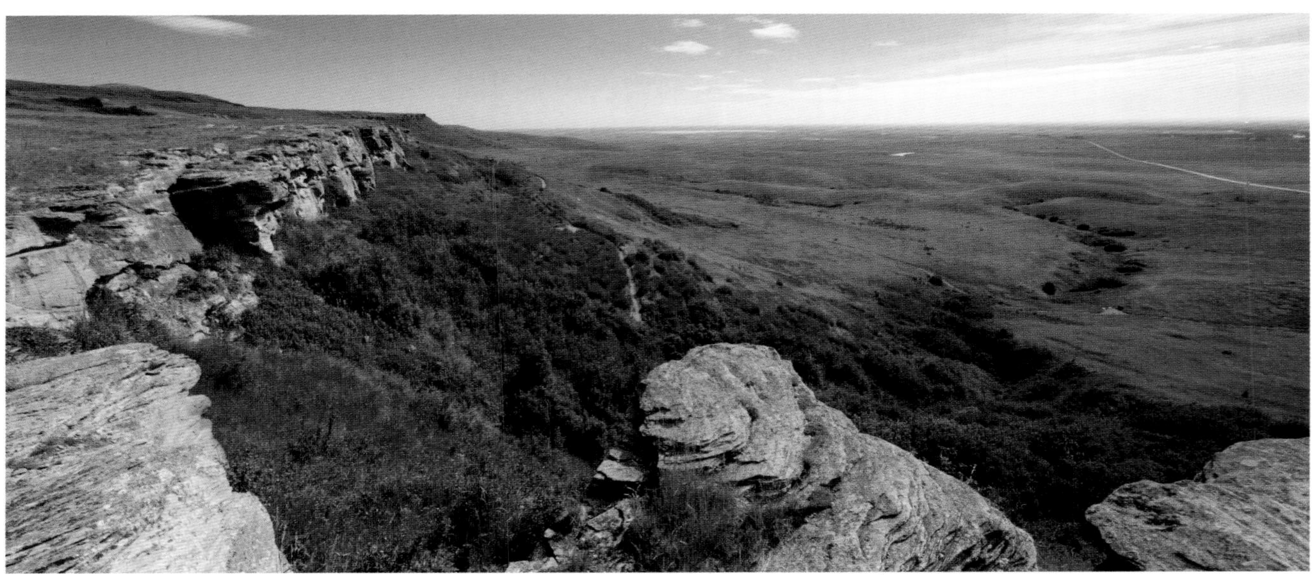

called a drive lane. Women, children, and old men stood along the lines and helped drive the animals to their deaths. The second element is the cliff itself from where the animals fell to their deaths. Then there were the bone beds at the base of the cliff. In the case of Head-Smashed-In these beds are about 40 ft (12 m) deep and provided archaeologists with thousands of broken or complete projectile points that the hunters had used to dispatch any animals that survived the fall. The final element was the processing camp, where members of the tribe processed the animals. They dried and stored the meat, used the hides to provide clothing and coverings for the tipis in which the tribes lived, and they turned bones and ligaments into tools of all kinds.

Successfully completing a jump required a great many people, and their coordination was absolutely essential. The lead-up to the kill was filled with religious ritual and prayer, and unless everything was done correctly the jump could be postponed or canceled. But the payoff for all this was a bounty that provided everything the tribes needed for several months, especially during the harsh winters of the northern Plains.

The name Head-Smashed-In comes from a Blackfoot legend that a hunter wanted to view the kill up close, but got too close and was crushed by the falling bison. A more prosaic explanation is that it was where the buffalo themselves had their heads smashed in. Today the jump is a World Heritage site and boasts a superb five-level interpretive center, and regularly scheduled guided hikes featuring the cliff jump, drive lanes, and spiritual sites. The site is located 11 miles (18 km) northwest of Fort McLeod in southern Alberta.

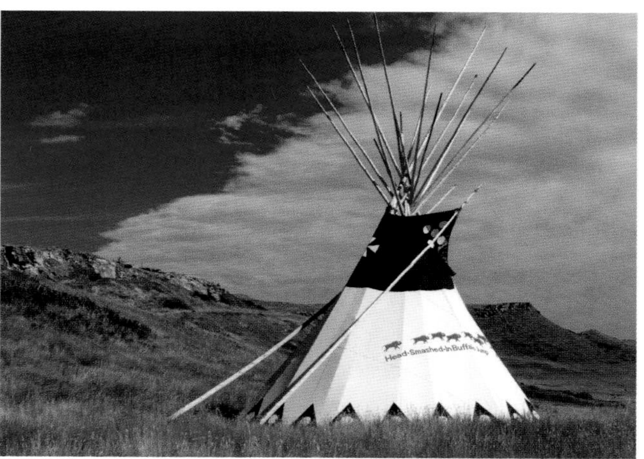

Opposite Views across the site.

Above Diorama of the buffalo jump in the interpretive center.

Right Reconstruction of a tipi.

THE VIKING SETTLEMENT OF **L'ANSE AUX MEADOWS**

TYPE: HABITATION • **ARCHITECTURAL STYLE:** WOOD AND SOD
LOCATION: NEWFOUNDLAND, CANADA • **CONSTRUCTION BEGUN:** ELEVENTH CENTURY C.E.

On a windswept peninsula of Newfoundland lies one of the most remarkable archaeological sites in all of North America: L'Anse aux Meadows. Remains found provide indisputable evidence that the Vikings reached and lived there, if only for a small period.

L'Anse aux Meadows (French for The Bay with Meadows, although it is almost certainly a corruption of the original French name) was discovered by Helge Ingstad (1899–2001) and Anne Stine Ingstad (1918–1997) in 1960, both of whom conducted excavations here during that decade. Parks Canada then conducted further excavations to expand our overall knowledge of the site.

The excavations revealed a Viking settlement of eight houses, probably made of sod on wooden frames. In addition, archaeologists found the remains of a smithy, a charcoal kiln, and a woodworking shop. Only a small number of artifacts were recovered (a few more than a hundred), but they included a bronze pin, a whetstone, and a bone needle—all characteristic items of eleventh-century Viking life. Radiocarbon assays have confirmed this date.

The small number of artifacts found and no evidence of house rebuilding suggests the settlement was short-lived. Possible causes of the abandonment include its distance from Scandinavia, a deteriorating climate caused by the Little Ice Age, or threats from local indigenous groups, collectively termed Skraelings by the Norse.

What archaeological evidence there is fits in nicely with the sagas left by the Norse, however. Originally oral traditions—they were probably written down between 1200 and 1300 C.E.—these sagas, such as *The Saga of Erik the Red* and *The Saga of the Greenlanders*, tell of the Norse voyages west to Iceland, Greenland, and ultimately to a place called Vinland, somewhere along the northeast coast of North America, and tentatively identified as present-day Newfoundland, although that is contested. Leif Erikson, son of Eric the Red, is credited with being the first European to set foot on the continent, although it is probably too much of a stretch to say with certainty that he founded L'Anse aux Meadows.

A National Historic Site and also a UNESCO World Heritage site, L'Anse aux Meadows is located on the tip of the Northern Peninsula about 30 miles (50 km) from the regional airport at the town of St Anthony. At the site itself, raised berms outline the original huts. Parks Canada has reconstructed the village so that the visitor can get a very good idea of what life was like. There is a visitor center, as well as actor re-creations to help visitors enjoy their stay.

Opposite above Reconstructed village at L'Anse aux Meadows.

Opposite below Overview of the site.

THE GREAT HOUSES OF **CHACO CANYON**

TYPE: HABITATIONS AND RELIGIOUS SITES • **ARCHITECTURAL STYLE:** STONE, WOOD, ADOBE PLASTER
LOCATION: NEW MEXICO, USA • **CONSTRUCTION BEGUN:** 800 C.E.

It is hard for the casual visitor to imagine that, in the high desert of northern New Mexico, with its cold winters and blazing hot summers, there arose one of the greatest indigenous cultures of North America. For more than three hundred years, beginning in the 800s C.E., Ancestral Puebloans occupied this wide canyon and developed a culture of great social complexity and community organization, based on the cultivation of plants such as maize and beans and on long-distance trade.

The most prominent sites in the canyon are called Great Houses. These are huge multistory stone buildings consisting of habitation rooms, storage rooms, and ceremonial underground structures called kivas. Pueblo Bonito, the finest example of a Chacoan Great House, was the center of the Chacoan world. Over 600 rooms, thirty-two kivas, and three great kivas, are arranged in a semicircular pattern around a central plaza. Extant walls at the rear of the pueblo stand two to three stories high. So-called great kivas were also built, such as Casa Rinconada. This great kiva stands above ground, unlike others whose roofs were at ground level.

Because of the land's aridity, nothing would have been possible without the construction of complex irrigation systems that both captured and channeled the rainfall onto the fields. Radiating out from the canyon was a series of constructed roads linking the canyon to other Chacoan sites throughout the region, especially to the north and west. The Chacoans traded throughout the wider American Southwest, perhaps as far as modern-day Mexico, and items such as copper bells and macaw feathers attest the far-flung nature of their trade.

The material culture of the Chacoans is exemplified by the beautiful black-on-white pottery they produced. The potter's wheel was unknown in North America at the time, so Chacoan pottery was made of long "sausages" of clay that were coiled into the desired shape.

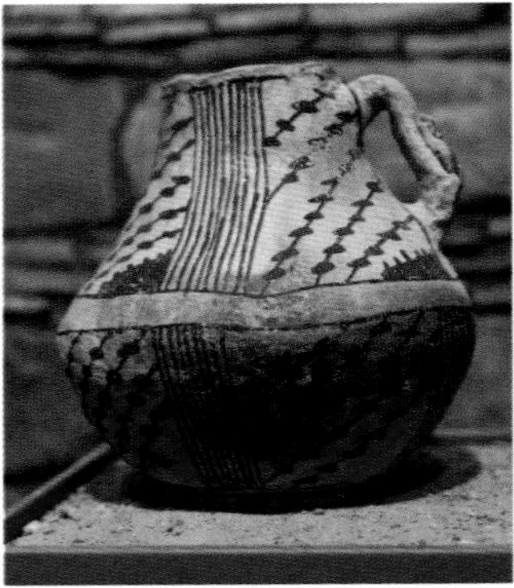

Left Chacoan pottery was some of the most beautiful produced by prehistoric Native Americans.

Opposite, from top Casa Rinconada. This great kiva was of great symbolic and ceremonial importance to the Chacoan culture. View of Pueblo Bonito from the Pueblo Alto trail.

There is significant evidence for the importance of astronomical observations to the Chacoans, such as the alignment of the walls of Pueblo Bonito. One of the most enigmatic pieces of evidence is found on nearby Fajada Butte. Researchers found upright slabs of sandstone that cast daggers of light onto two spiral rock carvings. At summer solstice, the light splits the middle of the spiral.

Archaeologists have for decades debated the reasons for the existence of the Chaco Canyon complex. It was for many years assumed that Chaco was an important trading center. Many archaeologists now believe that the canyon was perhaps not continuously occupied, but rather it served as a center for when far-flung Chacoan communities temporarily came together for ceremonial, religious, and trading purposes. Perhaps it even served as a resource distribution center when times were tough.

By the 1200s, Chaco's importance had declined and new and existing Ancestral Puebloan centers to the north and west, including Mesa Verde, became more prominent.

Today, access to the park, south of Farmington, New Mexico, comprises both paved and dirt roads. Within the park itself is a very informative and helpful visitor center.

MESA VERDE NATIONAL PARK

TYPE: HABITATION AND RELIGIOUS SITES • **ARCHITECTURAL STYLE:** STONE, WOOD, ADOBE PLASTER
LOCATION: COLORADO, USA • **CONSTRUCTION BEGUN:** 600 C.E.

The visitor to Mesa Verde, in southwest Colorado, looks to the north and sees the majestic, towering Rocky Mountains, and to the south the apparently endless high desert of the American Southwest. Mesa Verde seems to dominate its landscape. It also happens to be the scene of one of the best-preserved archaeological sites on the continent: Cliff Palace.

Mesa Verde (Spanish for Green Table) is the collective term for a series of high, flat-topped mesas intersected by deep canyons. From approximately 600 to1300 C.E. Ancestral Puebloans (formerly called the Anasazi) lived on the mesas, building a variety of structures, hunting and gathering, growing corn and other crops, and leaving behind a spectacular legacy of over 5,000 archaeological sites.

The earliest habitation structures on the mesa date to around 600 C.E. and are called pithouses. These semisubterranean houses, dug 4–5 ft (1.2–1.5 m) deep into the earth, were circular or rectangular in shape. A fire pit provided warmth in the winter and a ventilator shaft allowed fresh air for the fire in. The Ancestral Puebloans built earthen benches around the edges of the pithouse and upright stone slabs served as quasi room dividers. Smoke escaped through a hole in the roof (made of logs and woven branches covered in adobe, a clay-based plaster.) Later, the Puebloans moved to aboveground, multiroomed structures made from shaped slabs, while pithouse architecture evolved into ceremonial kivas, the center of religious life for the Puebloans, then and now.

During the twelfth century, the Four Corners region (the point of intersection of the states of Colorado, New Mexico, Arizona, and Utah) experienced severe droughts. Gradually, the inhabitants abandoned the region, moving to more amenable climes to the south and west. (It is here that the successors of the Ancestral Puebloans still live, tribes such as the Zuni, Hopi, and Acoma among them). The inhabitants of Mesa Verde remained—at least for a time—possibly because the southerly slope to the mesa tops and the proximity to the Rockies continued to provide a favorable combination of solar radiation and higher precipitation for the growing of corn, their main crop. However, they too were finally forced to leave.

Left Ancestral Pueblo Pottery, 1180–1200 C.E.
Opposite top Cedar Tree Tower and kiva.
Opposite below Balcony House cliff dwelling.

Cliff Palace

It was during the twelfth century that Ancestral Puebloans built a series of dwellings in natural alcoves in the cliff faces. Archaeologists are not sure whether this relocation was due to environmental conditions, threats from outside marauders, or some other factor. There are some 600 cliff dwellings in the park although most of these are not dwellings at all, but rather clusters of one to five small storage rooms.

Cliff Palace is the largest such dwelling. It comprises over 150 individual rooms and over twenty kivas, all made from shaped sandstone blocks, roof beams and wall supports of timber, and adobe, which was plastered onto the walls and roofs. Cliff Palace also boasts some

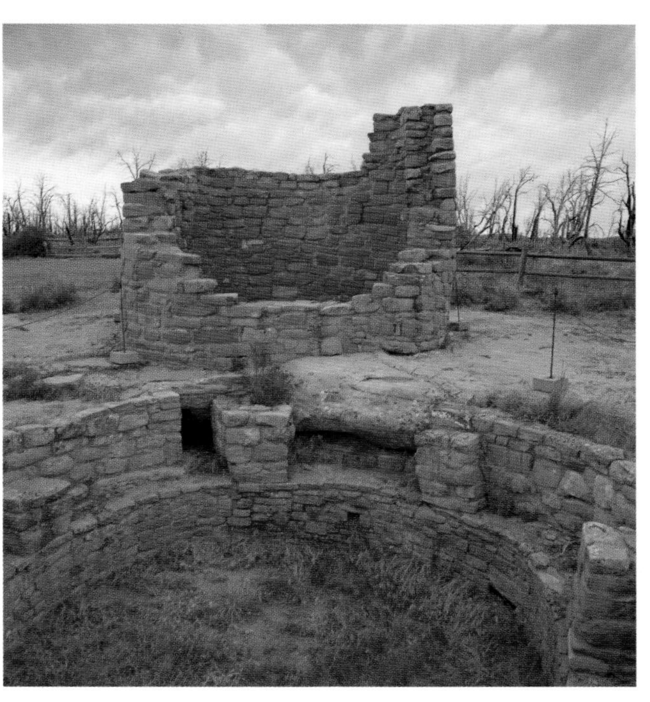

remarkable wall paintings. Estimates of population size are difficult for archaeologists to make, but probably a population of one hundred or so people at any one time would be a fair estimate. Another well-preserved site, also open to the public, is Balcony House, which consists of thirty-eight rooms and two kivas.

Mesa Verde National Park

The arid desert climate of southwestern Colorado has been a great boon to archaeologists in that it has allowed the preservation of organic material that normally would not have stood the test of time. (In 1888, the ranchers Richard Wetherill and Charlie Mason were the first Europeans to see Cliff Palace, and they said that it looked like its inhabitants had left just the day before.) The well-preserved roof beams also allow archaeologists to date sites using the technique of dendrochronology (tree-ring dating).

Mesa Verde was established in 1906 as a National Park and is extremely visitor-friendly. The visitor center (opened in 2012) is the first point of call. A forty-minute drive from the center takes the visitor to the museum on top of Chapin Mesa. The museum overlooks Spruce Tree House, the third-largest and probably best-preserved cliff dwelling in the park. In the museum, visitors can see many examples of Ancestral Puebloan culture, such as black-on-white pottery (bowls, mugs, ladles), exquisite bone implements, *manos* and *metates* (the ubiquitous stone tools primarily used for grinding corn meal), projectile points, and preserved items such as yucca sandals and baskets. More than 40 miles (64 km) of paved roads crisscross the park, allowing the visitor to experience the complete range of Ancestral Puebloan sites.

Right View across Mesa Verde National Park, established in 1906.

G.A. CUSTER
BVT. MAJ. GEN.
LT. COL.
7TH U.S. CAV.
FELL HERE

THE BATTLE OF **THE LITTLE BIGHORN**

TYPE: BATTLEFIELD • **ARCHITECTURAL STYLE:** N/A
LOCATION: MONTANA, USA • **CONSTRUCTION BEGUN:** N/A

The gravestones of the troopers stand starkly white against the rolling grasslands of Montana, the peaceful solitude of their resting place at odds with what happened here almost 150 years ago.

It was here, on the banks of the Big Horn River, that General George Armstrong Custer (1839–1876) rode his force of about 600 cavalrymen into history on June 25, 1876. Ordered to capture a large force of Cheyenne, Lakota, and Arapaho encamped on the banks of the river, Custer split his command into three (led by himself, Major Marcus Reno, and Captain Frederick Benteen). Custer and Reno made a two-pronged attack against the encampment. However, Custer had underestimated its size and rather than closing in on the camp in a classic pincer movement, he rode straight into the camp's center. Reno and Benteen took casualties, but Custer's force of 210 cavalrymen was wiped out, and the myth grew that they made a gallant last stand until they fell. But questions about what really happened have always lingered because, of course, all of Custer's men were killed and Benteen and Reno were too far away to see clearly what had happened. The Native Americans left as soon as the battle was concluded.

It is here that archaeology has helped fill in some of the blanks. In 1983 a grassfire swept through the battlefield, allowing archaeologists to conduct a ground survey and some limited excavations. Spent cartridges, bullets, clothing, and guns were recovered, among other artifacts. The skeletal remains of more than thirty cavalrymen were also found.

Forensic analysis of bullets allowed the scientists to trace the paths of the rifles that fired them across the battlefield. From this it seems that the command discipline of the cavalrymen evaporated quickly and the men were hunted down in small groups. Although Last Stand Hill was heavily covered with cartridges, it is still unclear whether this was indeed the place of the last stand. Instead, it is possible that the last stand, if there was such an event, took place in a ravine rather than on a hill.

Remains of cavalrymen themselves have also provided information on how they died. For example, one trooper, about 5 ft 8 in (173 cm) tall and aged about twenty-five, had been shot in the chest and head. His skull was then smashed, arrows shot into him, and his front and back slashed. In other cases, forensic anthropologists have reconstructed the facial contours of individuals to give accurate portrayals of what they looked like in life.

Visitors can reach Little Bighorn Battlefield National Monument via Battlefield Tour Road 756 in Montana. The monument boasts a museum and bookstore. Guided tours are available, as well as self-guided tours.

Opposite Gravestones of fallen US cavalrymen.
Below Iron sculpture by Lakota artist Colleen Cutschall.

THE MOUND LANDSCAPE OF **CAHOKIA**

TYPE: PLATFORM MOUND, BURIAL MOUNDS • **ARCHITECTURAL STYLE:** COMPACTED EARTH, WOOD • **LOCATION:** ILLINOIS, USA • **CONSTRUCTION BEGUN:** 800 C.E.

Just a few miles east of the sprawling metropolis of St. Louis and the Mississippi River, in a region called the American Bottom, lies the largest pre-Columbian urban complex north of Mexico, Cahokia. Named for the local Native American tribe, this sprawling complex of mounds, homes, and farmland originally covered over 4,000 acres (1,600 ha), with a population possibly as high as 20,000. Cahokia's heyday was between 1000 and 1350 C.E., a period characterized by the Mississippian Culture.

The central, dominating structure here is Monks Mound (so named because, when the antiquarian Henry Brackenridge visited the site in 1811, it was occupied by a group of Trappist monks). It is technically termed a platform mound, because of its flat top. Excavations on the mound's summit revealed the remains of a large building, 100 × 40 ft (30.5 × 12 m) in size, which may have been a temple or the residence of Cahokia's leader. The mound covers more than 14 acres (5.7 ha), and was built in four terraces over several centuries to a maximum height of 100 ft (30.5 m). It required more than seven million cubic feet (two million cubic meters) of earth, which was removed from nearby borrow pits. In front of Monks Mound is a central plaza, approximately 1,000 × 1,300 ft (305 × 396 m) in size. A wooden palisade, two miles (3.2 km) in length, surrounded Cahokia's central area, probably serving as a social rather than a defensive barrier. Surrounding the plaza were smaller platform mounds (supporting the timber-built houses of the lesser elite) and conical and ridgetop mounds that served as burial places. There are more than one hundred extant mounds at Cahokia,

Above The Keller Figurine— a woman performing a corn ceremony.

Right Aerial view of Monks Mound.

but many more outside the park boundaries have undoubtedly been destroyed by urban encroachment.

One spectacular example of a burial mound at Cahokia is Mound 72. Originally about 10 ft (3 m) high and 140 × 70 ft (43 × 21 m) in area, it is actually a composite of smaller mounds that were then integrated into one. Archaeologists excavated more than 250 individual skeletons at the mound, one of which lay on a bed of shell beads. Scattered around were other skeletal remains, all of them with grave goods, including a cache of several hundred finely knapped projectile points.

Just west of Monks Mound are the remains of a series of circles formed of upright wooden posts (identified by the remaining postholes). Archaeo-astronomical investigations have demonstrated that one structure (sometimes called Woodhenge, after its equivalent in southern England), which was rebuilt several times, was aligned with the movement of the sun and may, it is suggested, have served as a calendar.

The Mississippian Culture

Cahokia was part of the Mississippian Culture (800–1400 C.E.). The basic social structure of the culture was a ranked chiefdom—that is, a chief (possibly hereditary) held paramount power, with different social ranks or classes below. Political and economic power was based on the control of widespread trade networks throughout the Southeastern and Eastern United States and beyond, to as far as the Rocky Mountains in the West and the Great Lakes to the North. Beside its mound architecture, Mississippian Culture is characterized by the cultivation of maize, shell-tempered pottery, a social inequality exemplified by the disparity in grave goods, and a distinct settlement hierarchy in which smaller satellite settlements were reliant upon and "fed into" larger settlements such as Cahokia. One very important characteristic of Mississippian Culture is the southeastern Ceremonial Complex (once called the Southern Cult). Dating to between 1000 and 1600 C.E., it is characterized by similarities in artifacts, iconography, and mythology. The complex, which some have identified as a distinct religion, may have originated in Cahokia and then spread—by trade, diffusion, or migration—throughout the Southeast United States as far as Florida to the south, and as far as Texas to the west. A UNESCO World Heritage site, Cahokia is located in Collinsville, Illinois. It is a very tourist-friendly site, with a state-of-the-art interpretive center that offers theater programs, exhibits, and re-creations of life at Cahokia. Guided tours are also available.

Above, from left Mississippian vessel with beaver representation; ear spools from the Kunneman Mound.
Opposite Woodhenge: markers of astronomical sightings.

SERPENT MOUND
THE WORLD'S LARGEST EFFIGY MOUND

TYPE: EFFIGY MOUND • **ARCHITECTURAL STYLE:** COMPACTED EARTH
LOCATION: OHIO, USA • **CONSTRUCTION BEGUN:** 800 B.C.E.

In the US state of Ohio, Serpent Mound sits on an ancient meteorite impact crater dating to the Permian era. As its name implies, the mound is shaped like an undulating serpent, 1,348 ft (411 m) in length and ranging in height from 4 to 5 ft (1.2 to 1.5 m) and in width 20 to 25 ft (6 to 7.6 m). An oval mound forms the serpent's head. Some believe that the oval represents a large eye, others a hollow egg being swallowed by the serpent. The tail is coiled. The mound was constructed of local clay soils reinforced with rocks.

This site was first excavated by the antiquarian/archaeologist Frederic Ward Putnam (1839–1915) in the late-nineteenth century. He found no artifacts in the mound itself, so he was unwilling to make a cultural assignation. However, the mound is close to two conical earthen burial mounds built by people of the Adena Culture (800 B.C.E.–100 C.E.) and to a third burial mound dated to the later Fort Ancient Culture (1000–1500 C.E.).

Additionally, a nearby prehistoric village contained evidence of both cultures. In 1991 radiocarbon dating indicated the mound was 900 years old and therefore attributable to the Fort Ancient Culture. In 2014 more radiocarbon dating attributed the mound to the Adena Culture. These cultures must regularly have repaired the mound as erosion bit into its earthen core, so radiocarbon dates spanning a long period of time are to be expected.

The Adena Culture, centered in southern Ohio, is characterized most prominently by conical burial mounds. The population was scattered around the burial mounds, their settlements comprising a small number of circular wooden huts. They relied on hunting and gathering and the cultivation of such plants as sunflower, pumpkin, and squash. They produced a variety of stone, bone, horn, shell, antler, and ceramic artifacts. Their pottery was either undecorated or decorated with cord or fabric markings.

The Fort Ancient Culture is found along the Ohio River, in Ohio, Kentucky, Indiana, and West Virginia. Through its history, populations congregated in large settlements with a degree of town planning evidenced by huts surrounding a central plaza. Theirs was apparently an egalitarian society, as indicated by the relative lack of variety in grave goods. Fort Ancient people relied on hunting and gathering, as well as the cultivation of maize, beans, and squash.

The purpose of the Serpent Mound is unknown. There were no burials found in the mound itself, although the proximity of the three burial mounds might suggest that the structure had some significance regarding the afterlife. It has also been posited that the alignment of the mound was based on equinoctial and solstitial events. The mound lies a few hours drive from Cincinnati or Dayton. There is a museum at the site, with information on the mound itself, as well the Adena Culture in general.

Opposite A close-up view of the mound.
Above Aerial view of Serpent Mound.

2

MIDDLE AND SOUTH AMERICA

Middle and South America together constitute one of the world's richest regions archaeologically, with an astounding variety of sites, and they include some of the most famous which are on everyone's must-see list, such as Teotihuacan, Chichén Itzá, Tikal, Copán, Machu Picchu, and the Nazca lines. Some of them impress by their location, others by the sheer scale of their constructions, whether in stone or mud brick. But architecture—cities, pyramids, ball-courts, plazas—is not the only attraction, since there are also sumptuous tombs, fabulous pottery, carved stelae, and breathtaking mural decorations.

Left Maya pyramids at Tikal, Guatemala.

MIDDLE AND SOUTH AMERICA LOCATIONS

1 TEOTIHUACAN
2 MONTE ALBÁN
3 TIKAL
4 COPÁN
5 PALENQUE
6 TONINÁ
7 CHICHÉN ITZÁ
8 MITLA
9 XOCHICALCO
10 TENOCHTITLAN
11 MACHU PICCHU
12 CHAN CHAN
13 CHAVÍN DE HUÁNTAR
14 HUACAS DEL SOL AND DE LA LUNA
15 PACHACAMAC
16 CARAL
17 SIPÁN
18 NAZCA GEOGLYPHS
19 TIWANAKU

17
14
12
13
15
11
18
16
19

TEOTIHUACAN CITY OF THE GODS

TYPE: CITY • **ARCHITECTURAL STYLE:** TEMPLES, PALACES, AND APARTMENT COMPOUNDS
LOCATION: NEAR MEXICO CITY, MEXICO • **CONSTRUCTION BEGUN:** FIRST CENTURY B.C.E.

Spreading over 8.5 sq mi (22 sq km), in a narrow valley at the northeast entrance to the Basin of Mexico, Teotihuacan was once the largest urban center in the Americas. Spectacular monumentality and measured standardization are common first impressions of this great city, which dominated Mexico's central highlands between about 1 and 600 C.E.

We do not know the city's original name, but later groups called it the City of the Gods and identified it as the place where ancient deities had gathered to generate the fifth cycle of creation through ritual sacrifice. Its spiritual magnetism was such that, centuries after it had fallen into ruin, its temples still attracted many pilgrims, including the Aztec emperor Moctezuma; indeed, several fifteenth-century ceremonial offerings excavated at the Great Temple of the Aztecs in Tenochtitlan (now Mexico City) contained items looted from Teotihuacan.

The city had a population in excess of 100,000, and the Street of the Dead and the East–West Avenue divided its gridiron plan into four quarters. To design a city unlike any other, Teotihuacan's planners translated time into space by basing the dimensions of major civic-ceremonial architecture on the 260-day ritual calendar, perhaps to proclaim this new metropolis as "the place where time began." They also oriented the grid fifteen and a half degrees east of astronomical north so the setting sun would align directly with the centerline of the Sun Pyramid on August 11, the anniversary of the world's creation in 3114 B.C.E. At the northern end of the Street of the Dead, they constructed the Moon Pyramid to echo the outline of the Cerro Gordo that rises behind it, revealing the metaphorical relationship between pyramid and mountain. At the intersection of the city's four quarters—considered the location of the vertical fifth direction that links the realms of the underworld, earth, and sky in Mesoamerican cosmology—Teotihuacan's architects built the Ciudadela, the walled compound that frames the Feathered Serpent Temple.

Teotihuacan's early architecture centers on modest groups of three temples that may have served to anchor the different communities that migrated into the valley at the beginning of the Common Era. Shortly thereafter, the city initiated its master plan that included its three largest pyramids: the Moon, the Sun, and the Feathered Serpent Temple. Excavations into these have revealed elaborate dedicatory offerings with ritually sacrificed humans and animals. The Sun Pyramid and the Feathered Serpent Temple stand over deep tunnels, laboriously excavated to hold extravagant offerings of greenstone, obsidian, pyrite, slate, conch shells, rubber balls, figurines, pottery, and other sumptuary items. Originally, these two tunnels may have housed royal tombs, but modern archaeologists have not

Opposite North–south view of the ceremonial core of Teotihuacan. At the bottom is the facade of the Moon Pyramid; 2,300 ft (700 m) farther south, on the left (east) side of the Street of the Dead, is the Sun Pyramid; the quadrangular Ciudadela compound, with the Feathered Serpent Temple, can be seen in the distance.

found any human burials in them, perhaps because they were opened on various occasions in the pre-Hispanic past.

A Unique Residential Setup

To organize its dense population, city planners devised a new type of residence: the apartment compound. Unique to Teotihuacan, these suites of rooms centered on a shared ritual courtyard and were surrounded by a high wall that provided protection and privacy for its residents. These units, which number more than 2,000, varied greatly in elegance and size—ranging from 5,900 to 38,750 sq ft (550 to 3,600 sq m)—and accommodated both locals and migrants from many parts of Mesoamerica.

Today, most of the city's buildings no longer feature the architectural sculpture and vibrant murals that once graced their facades, giving the site a somber appearance. Nonetheless, remnants of elaborate mural paintings remain along the Street of the Dead and, significantly, in its apartment compounds. Unlike the Maya tradition, Teotihuacan's mural art and statuary shun images of rulers, opting instead to display mythical scenes, processions of fantastic animals—often devouring human hearts—and lavishly dressed individuals engaged in ritual acts. No formal writing system is known from Teotihuacan, but enough evidence exists to suggest that this was a literate society.

An Influential Polity

Teotihuacan's influence was felt throughout Mesoamerica. It engaged in long-distance trade in prestige items, including exotic feathers, jade, and even wild animals. Its military presence and its interference in royal succession are detailed in epigraphic texts at Maya sites such as Tikal and Copán, and conversely fragments of Maya-style murals and imported ceramics appear in Teotihuacan's Plaza of the Columns, which may have been the primary palace of the city.

Toward the end of the sixth century, Teotihuacan's political power collapsed. While this disruption may stem from the government's inability to deal with the onset of an intense drought and the arrival of immigrants from the north, the burning of temples and palaces, the destruction of icons, and the looting of offerings strongly suggest an internal ideological rejection of authority. Ballooning over the site at dawn is a memorable experience. Teotihuacan's monumental architecture is best visited early in the morning, reserving high noon to explore the shaded apartment compounds and two site museums.

Opposite The sculpted facade of the Feathered Serpent Temple that dominates the Ciudadela compound.

Above, left Seen from the Pyramid of the Sun, the Pyramid of the Moon is the focal point of the Street of the Dead.

Above, right This mural in the ritual patio of the Tetitla apartment shows Teotihuacan's bountiful Great Goddess.

THE MOUNTAINTOP CITY OF **MONTE ALBÁN**

TYPE: CITY • **ARCHITECTURAL STYLE:** TEMPLES, PALACES, AND TOMBS
LOCATION: OAXACA, MEXICO • **CONSTRUCTION BEGUN:** FOURTH CENTURY B.C.E.

Majestically situated on a 1,300 ft- (400 m-) high mountain ridge at the center of Mexico's Valley of Oaxaca lie the remains of Monte Albán. This ceremonial center was the capital of the Zapotec state from 500 B.C.E. until it was abandoned some 1,300 years later.

Monte Albán was one of Mesoamerica's first cities, founded, according to some, as a defendable bastion by a coalition of communities in response to increasing conflict. Others argue that its creation reflects the emergence of a religious ideology devised by elites to justify their rights to land, water, and other resources. These are not mutually exclusive, and archaeology has shown that both militarism and religion were essential to the capital's origins and longevity.

Monte Albán's monumental buildings define the Main Plaza, measuring 984 ft (300 m) north–south by 656 ft (200 m) east–west, on the artificially leveled summit. At the northern end of the plaza, a wide staircase leads to the royal palace complex, which covers 12 acres (5 ha) and whose sunken patio could hold over 3,000 individuals; in addition to its administrative, religious, and residential buildings, a small ballcourt was built just off its southeastern corner. At the opposite end of the plaza, the South Platform, 459 ft (140 m) on a side, supports two temples. Platforms also line the east and west edges of the plaza and run down its central axis. At its peak in the mid-seventh century C.E., the city had more than 17,000 inhabitants living on the 2,000 residential terraces that cascade down the mountain's steep slopes.

The city's earliest architecture is largely covered by later constructions; most of what one sees today dates to the sixth and seventh centuries C.E. One important exception is Los Danzantes, located at the southwestern corner of the Main Plaza. Although only a section of the vertical platform wall remains, it was originally faced with irregular stone slabs carved with human figures. Because these male individuals are shown in ungainly poses—and often with mutilated genitals and closed eyes—they have generally been interpreted as sacrificed captives. However, others argue that they are warriors practicing ritual bloodletting. The two monoliths that form the southwestern corner of this building, stelae 12 and 13, preserve the earliest known Zapotec text (ca. 500 C.E.).

As the ceremonial center took its final form in the first centuries C.E., Los Danzantes was dismantled and covered over, and a new public display was created on the strangely oriented arrow-shaped Building J at the southern end of the Main Plaza's central spine. Here, stone slabs engraved with place glyphs, and sometimes an inverted human head, were embedded in the platform walls. Known as the Conquest Stones, these images of place and decapitation focus more on location than specific individual leaders and thus might memorialize more distant military ventures.

Later carved stones, which refer to foreign conquest and political relations with Teotihuacan, were set into the corners of the South Platform. Most show captive warriors, but one presents ruler 12 Jaguar, dressed as the feline he was named for, and seated on a throne that rests upon the city's place glyph. Monuments from the city's final years avoid martial themes and instead deal with noble genealogies and the transfer of entitlements from one generation to the next.

Life at Monte Albán

Zapotec houses consisted of rooms built around a patio with a subfloor tomb. Elite families had lavish funerary chambers decorated with mural paintings portraying venerated ancestors and glyphic data about lineage members. They were well stocked with pottery vessels, including anthropomorphic urns, often fashioned with individuals dressed as one of the many deities of the Zapotec pantheon. Monte Albán's most famous tomb, Tomb 7, was originally built during the city's Classic period occupation (250–800 C.E.). However, well after the city had been entirely abandoned, it was re-entered from the roof and reused. Its spectacular offerings—jade, amber, and rock crystal artifacts; gold, silver, and turquoise jewelry, and finely carved jaguar bones—were not placed in honor of a single dignitary, but instead the funerary chamber was repurposed in the fourteeth century as an ossuary for the bundled remains of revered ancestors brought to the sacred mountain from faraway regions.

Toward the end of the eighth century, as Monte Albán's population began to relocate to towns on the valley floor, the ceremonial center fell into disrepair. The reasons for the city's abandonment remain unclear. Some scholars suggest that geopolitical changes following the collapse of Teotihuacan may have triggered political and economic problems for the Zapotec capital, but others argue that the disruption stemmed from challenges to royal authority by members of the nobility.

Above View of the site showing its spectacular setting.

TIKAL CITY OF THE MAYA

TYPE: CITY • **ARCHITECTURAL STYLE:** TEMPLES, PALACES, AND BALLCOURTS
LOCATION: PETÉN, GUATEMALA • **CONSTRUCTION BEGUN:** SEVENTH CENTURY B.C.E.

With its temples rising above the forest canopy, Tikal occupies an important watershed in the lush jungles of Guatemala's lowland Petén Province. One of the best-studied sites in the Maya area, the city was first occupied around 800 B.C.E. on what was a key trade route connecting the Usumacinta River drainage with the Caribbean Sea. The site's 988-acre (400-ha) core, which includes its principal monumental architecture, is now the cornerstone of the Tikal National Park, a World Heritage property.

By the first century C.E. Tikal had developed into a low-density agrarian city ruled by the dynasty founded by Yax Ehb' Xook (First Step Shark). Tikal's cultural climax took place after it defeated rival Calakmul in 695 C.E. and initiated a political revival that lasted two centuries. At this time the city's population is estimated to have been around 60,000.

Tikal's Great Plaza, bounded on the east and west by the magnificent Temples I and II respectively, is the ceremonial core of the site. The 154 ft- (47 m-) high Temple I on the east side of the plaza memorializes the tomb of King Jasaw Chan K'awiil I (682–734 C.E.), conqueror of Calakmul. Temple II on the opposite side was raised as a cenotaph to his wife. The North Acropolis, which rises to the north, contains many royal tombs surmounted by commemorative temples. To the south, the Central Acropolis, a maze of forty-six buildings organized around six courtyards, was the royal palace. To the southwest of the Great Plaza is another ceremonial precinct where several of Tikal's early rulers were buried. Known as the Lost World, it is dominated by the

Opposite Tikal's North Acropolis is formed from pyramids with temples that commemorate the tombs of early kings.

Right Found in Tikal's Great Plaza, Stela 9 (475 C.E.) depicts King K'an Chitam ("Precious Peccary").

105 ft- (32 m-) high pyramid with stairways on each side (called radial pyramids) that were once flanked by huge stucco masks. One of the most significant discoveries from this complex is the famous Marcador stone, whose texts document Teotihuacan's takeover of the city in 378 C.E.

Raised causeways—some almost 164 ft (50 m) wide—connect the major temples and building complexes at Tikal. They served both as roadways and water-catchment systems, designed to channel runoff from the plazas into a reservoir on the west side of the Central Acropolis. The city's largest temples, those whose roof combs rise above the forest canopy, are all in the southern section of the site; Temple IV, which stands almost 213 ft (65 m) high, is the most massive, while Temple VI, the Temple of the Inscriptions, bears a long text on the back of its roof comb recounting the city's legendary history. Carved wooden lintels spanned most of the temple rooms. With the exceptions of those from Temples I and III, these superb works of art are now scattered among various museums outside of Guatemala.

The Maya Cosmos

One of the most distinctive types of architectural complex at Tikal is the Twin Pyramid Group. Starting in the sixth century C.E., nine of these were built to commemorate the ending of successive *katun* cycles (7,200 days, almost twenty years). Their layout replicates the Maya cosmos and consists of a raised plaza with two opposing radial pyramids, one at the east end and one at the west. Nine plain altar-stele pairs are lined up in front of the east pyramid. On the south side is a long building with multiple doorways and on the north there is a small roofless enclosure with a carved stele and altar. The east and west pyramids mark the sun's passage across the sky, while the nine doorways of the south building allude to the nine levels of the underworld. The structure on the north is open to the celestial realm, and it is here that the king's sacred monuments were placed.

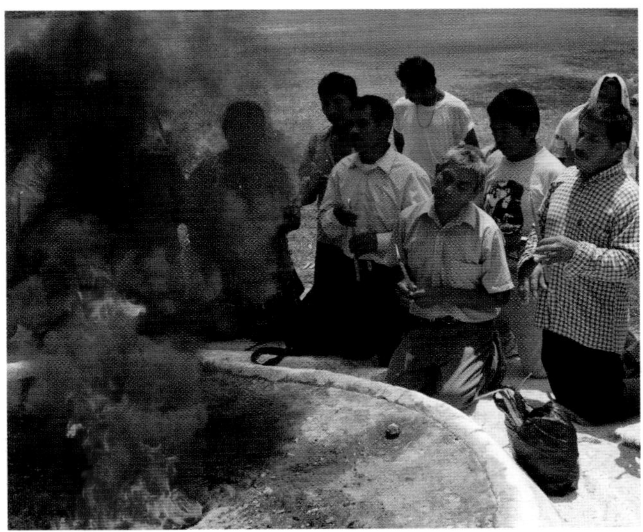

Above top Tikal's temples soar above the forest canopy of the Guatemalan jungle.

Above The Guatemalan government has provided modern firepits for indigenous pilgrims to make burnt offerings at Tikal and other ancient sites.

Tikal's Stelae

The most common sculptural formats used at Tikal were the stele and altar. A total of 231 of these monuments are known from the site, and of these, seventy are carved with finely dressed kings and queens accompanied by texts chronicling their lineages and their victories. Stela 11 (869 C.E.) is Tikal's last dated monument and marks the beginning of a sharp decline in royal power. Like many other centers in the southern Maya lowlands, ninth-century Tikal had reached the limits of its resources, and when an extended drought struck, the realm was unable to overcome the shortages caused by the climatic shift. All over the region, city after city plummeted into social chaos and, eventually, political collapse. During the next 150 years Tikal was taken over by squatters before being abandoned to the jungle.

The flora and fauna of Tikal Park are as compelling as the ruined city, so plan some extra time to explore. Tickets are best acquired prior to arrival.

COPÁN MAYA CAPITAL OF THE SOUTHEAST

TYPE: CITY • **ARCHITECTURAL STYLE:** TEMPLES, PALACES, AND BALLCOURTS
LOCATION: WESTERN HONDURAS • **CONSTRUCTION BEGUN:** FIFTH CENTURY C.E.

High-relief-carved stone monuments and sculptural facades epitomize the remains at Copán, one of the first Maya sites studied by archaeologists. Located in a fertile valley on the southeastern periphery of the Maya lowlands in western Honduras, the civic-ceremonial area was built along the west bank of the Copán River, from which the site takes its name.

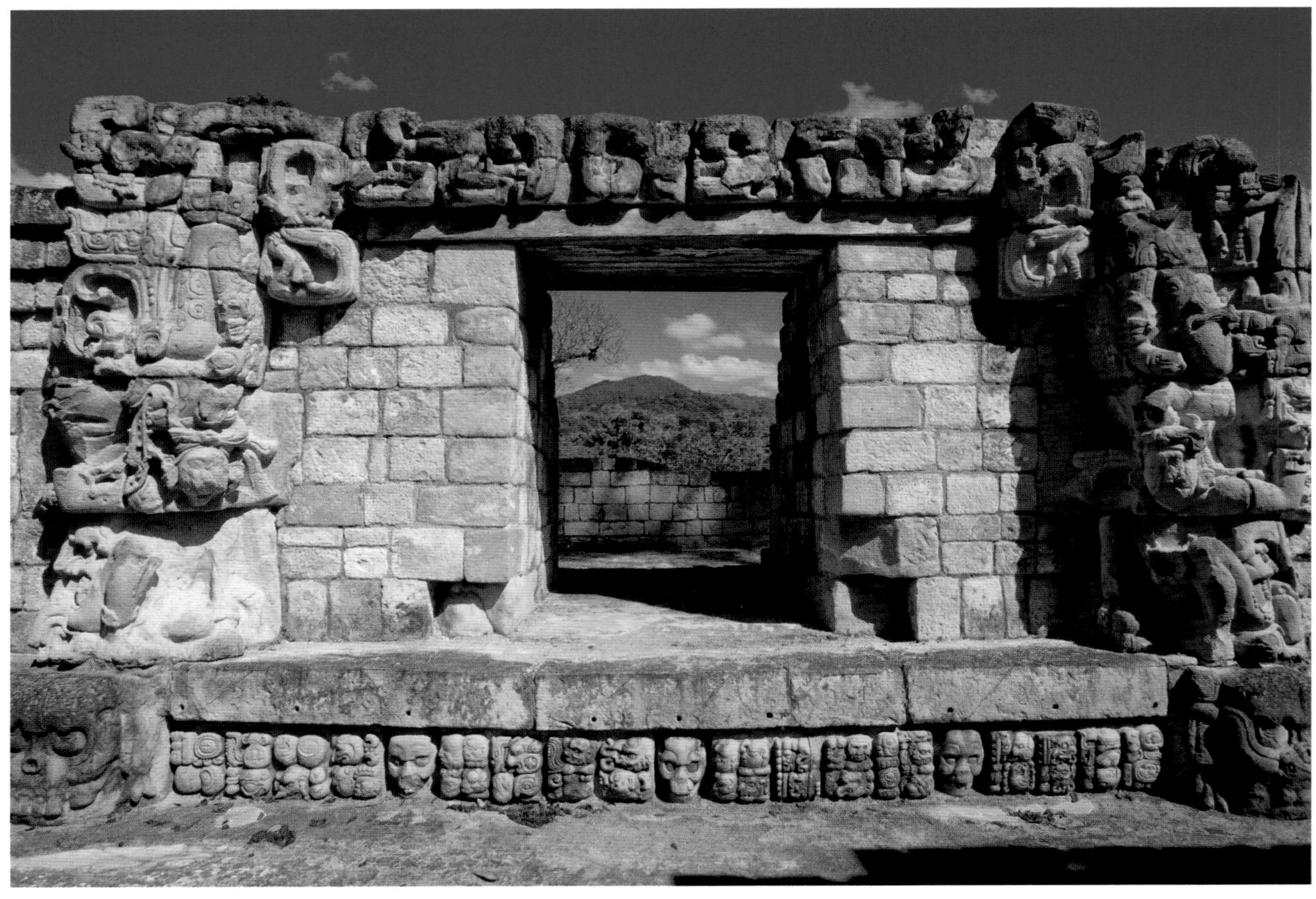

Hieroglyphic inscriptions at Copán document a flourishing relationship with the ancient city of Teotihuacan in the early fifth century C.E. The site was already a prominent center well before that time, but its dynasty was not inaugurated until 426 C.E., when Yax K'uk' Mo' (First Quetzal Macaw) arrived—possibly from Tikal—to establish a dominion that lasted more than four hundred years.

The Great Plaza lies at the northern end of the monumental area, and contains seven remarkable three-dimensional portrait stelae of the city's thirteenth ruler and various altars. On the south side of the plaza, an elegant ballcourt with sculpted macaw imagery transitions to the magnificently restored Hieroglyphic Stairway of Temple 26. Carved with the longest known Maya inscription, the 2,200 glyphs on the stairway's sixty-three risers narrate the city's dynastic history up to the mid-eighth century.

Just beyond is the Acropolis, an elevated complex of pyramids, tombs, and courts dominated by Temple 16. Tunnels excavated into the platform supporting this temple documented a series of previous structures, including the spectacularly well-preserved Rosalia; all were built to memorialize the tomb of the founder, Yax K'uk' Mo', deep below. More than three hundred years later, in 776 C.E., Copán's sixteenth ruler dedicated Altar Q in the West Court at the base of Temple 16 to legitimize his right to the throne. This quadrangular monument displays the realm's sixteen rulers on its sides and a summary of Copán's dynastic history on its surface. Structure 22, in the East Court, is another striking building. Created in 715 C.E., to celebrate the twentieth anniversary of the thirteenth ruler's enthronement, it was designed to represent the sacred mountain where maize was born; in addition, the inner temple doorway is carved with an array of fantastic creatures from Maya cosmology that defines the chamber as the mountain's sacred cave.

A series of raised causeways connected other architectural assemblages to the Great Plaza. One of these, Las Sepulturas, was an upper-class residential neighborhood. Here, the House of the Bacabs, the palace of a royal courtier, provides an example of the finest Maya hieroglyphic writing. Its facade is embellished with two niches, each containing a scribe framed by the jaws of the underworld. Inside, finely sculpted full-figure glyphs inscribed on the 21.7 ft- (6.6 m-) long stone bench record its dedication in 773 C.E.

Copán declined quickly after its last monument, left unfinished, was fashioned in 822 C.E. Environmental degradation and power struggles may explain the kingdom's dynastic failure, but populations continued to live in and around Copán for another four centuries.

Any visit must include the Sculpture Museum, which has a magnificent replica of the Rosalia temple.

Opposite The inner doorway of the temple of Structure 22 in the East Court of the Acropolis.

Above, top West platform of Copán's principle ballcourt.

Above, bottom Altar Q commemorates Ruler 16's accession to the throne in 763 C.E.

THE MAYA REALM OF **PALENQUE**

TYPE: CITY • **ARCHITECTURAL STYLE:** TEMPLES, PALACES, AND TOMBS
LOCATION: CHIAPAS, MEXICO • **CONSTRUCTION BEGUN:** FIFTH CENTURY C.E.

Long acknowledged as one of the most captivating Maya sites, Palenque is located on the northwestern frontier of the Maya lowlands in modern Mexico. From its vantage point on a limestone ridge leading into the Chiapas Highlands, it has a commanding view of the wide plains of the Gulf Coast. The city's original name, Lakamha (Great Waters), perhaps refers to the nine perennial streams that cascade down the three terraces upon which it was built. However, the name of the kingdom itself was B'aakal (Bone).

Palenque is famous in the annals of archaeology for two principal reasons. First, excavations in 1952 discovered a spectacular royal tomb beneath the Temple of the Inscriptions, confirming that many Maya pyramids were not just platforms to support temples but also were commemorative funerary buildings. Second, during the 1970s, its lengthy inscriptions played a key role in the decipherment of Maya hieroglyphic script.

The site was initially occupied around 250 B.C.E., but its first recorded dynasty was not founded until 431 C.E. by K'uk' Balam (Quetzal Jaguar; 397–435 C.E.). Significantly, this coincides with Teotihuacan's meddling in the royal lineages of Tikal and Copán and suggests that Palenque's dynasty may have been installed as part of this power play. In any event, by the end of the sixth century Palenque's kings had added the name of the sun god, K'inich, to their title as an explicit declaration of the divine source of their authority.

The late sixth century was a turbulent period in the city's history. With the death of King Kan B'alam (Snake Jaguar) in 583 C.E. without a male heir, his daughter Yohl Ik'nal (Heart of the Wind Place) became queen, one of the few Maya women to achieve that title; perhaps as an unforeseen consequence, during the next two decades

Palenque was pillaged on various occasions by rival Calakmul. Political problems persisted until 615 C.E., when K'inich Janaab' Pakal (Great Sun Shield), then a twelve-year-old boy, took the throne. His rule, and that of his sons and grandsons, marked Palenque's cultural climax in art and architecture.

One of Pakal's projects was the renovation of the Palace. The building, which rests upon a 33 ft- (10 m-) high platform with wide staircases and outer galleries on three sides, dominates the Central Plaza. Inside, a labyrinth of rooms and airy galleries opens onto sunken courtyards. Like other structures at the site, the Palace's exterior walls, mansard-like roofs, and roof combs bear the remains of naturalistic figures modeled in stucco that once were brightly painted. The four-story tower in the southwest patio is unique to Palenque and may have served as a watchtower or observatory.

Off the southwest corner of the Palace, the Temple of the Inscriptions commemorates Pakal's tomb. The vaulted burial chamber at the base of a long interior stairway contains a huge stone sarcophagus whose spectacular lid is carved with a scene of the king's rebirth as the maize

Left View of the civic-ceremonial core of Palenque.

Above The Temple of the Sun in the Cross Group. The piers of its wide doorways, its mansard-like roof, and its roof comb were all embellished with sculpted stucco figures.

Left A polychrome panel in Temple XIX, dedicated in 734 C.E., depicts the crown prince, Upakal K'inich, in ceremonial dress.

Above The lid of K'inich Janaab' Pakal's sarcophagus shows the rebirth of the king and his ascension into the heavens from the maw of the Underworld.

Opposite Seen from the Temple of the Inscriptions, Palenque's Palace consists of galleries and rooms arranged around sunken courts.

god after falling into the jaws of the Underworld; the sides of the coffin bear images of the king's ancestors shown sprouting from the earth like trees. Pakal's body was covered in toxic red cinnabar (mercuric oxide)—perhaps intended to preserve the royal remains—and richly adorned with jade jewelry. Directly to the west of his tomb, in Temple XIII, is the lavish cinnabar-rich burial of Tz'ak-b'u Ajaw (Lady of the Succession), Pakal's consort and mother of the two kings who succeeded their father.

East of the Palace, Pakal's eldest son, Kan B'alam II, constructed the temples of the Cross Group. Famous for their finely carved bas-relief limestone panels, the iconography and texts on these buildings deal with the birth of Palenque's gods, ancestral regeneration, agricultural fertility, and warfare, specifically Kan B'alam II's conquest of Toniná in 687 C.E. In recent years, more carved panels have been recovered from Palenque's temples XIX and XXI, enhancing our knowledge of the city and its rulers.

Palenque was one of the first Maya realms to fail. Its last known inscription dates to 799 C.E., and over the next two decades, as royals and nobles abandoned the city, its elegant residences and temples were occupied by squatters. Although the political authority of some other dynasties was undermined by a ninth-century drought, the abundance of water at Palenque suggests that its demise was different from that of its peers. Archaeologists have suggested that, in addition to the loss of forest habitat to agriculture, Palenque's stability may have been undermined by new maritime trade routes that shifted commerce to the coast.

Palenque's hot, humid jungle calls for insect repellent, long sleeves, and pants. It rains year round, so it is best to visit in the drier, cooler months of January and February.

THE MAYA KINGDOM OF **TONINÁ**

TYPE: CITY • **ARCHITECTURAL STYLE:** TEMPLES, PALACES, AND BALLCOURT
LOCATION: CHIAPAS, MEXICO • **CONSTRUCTION BEGUN:** FIFTH CENTURY C.E.

Nestled against the piedmont of the Ocosingo Valley, in the Mexican state of Chiapas, where humid lowland jungles give way to the pine forests of the chilly highlands, Toniná presides over the western Maya frontier. Although it is often considered a minor center, archaeological and epigraphic evidence demonstrates that Toniná was actively engaged in the trade networks and geopolitics of the Maya lowlands between 550 and 900 C.E. The site is famous for the quality of its three-dimensional sandstone sculptures of kings and captives, carved thrones and panels, and the magnificent stucco friezes that still decorate some buildings.

The site's center has two main parts, the Great Plaza and the Acropolis; together they represent the flat primordial sea from which the sacred mountain of Mesoamerican cosmology rises. At the eastern edge of the plaza, a sunken ballcourt marks the entrance to the underworld. During the ballcourt's earliest construction phase, serpent heads carved in the Teotihuacan style decorated its sloping walls; later, after it and various temples were ritually destroyed in 687 C.E. by the rival kingdom of Palenque, these were replaced with sculptures of bound captives to commemorate the conquests of the city's third king, K'inich B'aaknal Chaak (Great-Sun Bone-place Rain God; 652–715 C.E.) in 699 and the realm's restoration. This ruler would go on to vanquish Palenque in 711, taking its king captive in revenge.

To the north of the Great Plaza, the Acropolis is a modified seven-tiered hill that towers 246 ft (73 m) over the valley floor, providing an impressive view of the surrounding countryside. The lower four levels have residential and administrative structures, while the upper three levels are dedicated to religious themes—burials on the fifth and temples on the sixth and seventh. The early-ninth-century stucco mural known as the Frieze of the Dream Lords on the platform wall of the sixth level segregates our world from that of the supernatural with a feathered lattice, punctuated with hanging decapitated human heads. This death imagery effectively divides the Acropolis into three vertical sections: the world of the living at its base, the transition to the land of the dead on the fifth level, and the celestial realm on the summit.

Toniná's place name (Popo) was first used in 568 C.E. Five years later, other communities begin to mention the city in their texts, primarily to commemorate the sacrifice of distinguished Toniná warriors. By the late seventh century, poignant sculptures of captive warriors and kings become common at the site, confirming the city's success in battles with other Maya kingdoms. Toniná's sculptures identify the emblem glyphs of its rivals on these monuments, but the name of Toniná is less frequent on those at other sites, suggesting that perhaps its dignitaries were rarely captured. Nonetheless, the absence of references might merely reflect its marginal frontier status. The last known Long Count date in the entire Maya area—January 15, 909—is recorded on Toniná's Monument 101 and it serves to mark the end of Classic period (250–900 C.E.) civilization.

Individual tours to the little-visited site of Toniná and its sculpture museum can be booked in either Palenque or San Cristóbal de las Casas.

Opposite The Frieze of the Dream Lords embellishes the platform wall of the sixth level of the Acropolis. It celebrates themes from Maya mythology about the Underworld.

Above View from the Acropolis of Toniná's main plaza.

CHICHÉN ITZÁ TOLTEC-MAYA CENTER

TYPE: CITY • **ARCHITECTURAL STYLE:** TEMPLES, BALLCOURTS, AND OBSERVATORIES
LOCATION: YUCATÁN, MEXICO • **CONSTRUCTION BEGUN:** FIFTH CENTURY C.E.

The forested yet dry plains of the northern Yucatán Peninsula have no rivers. For water, populations depend on sinkholes (cenotes) in the porous limestone bedrock to gain access to the underground aquifer. Chichén Itzá, which translates as "on the edge of the cenote of the Itzá," itself has four cenotes, the largest and most famous of which is the Cenote of Sacrifice. Here objects of gold, jade, wood, copal resin, rubber, shell, and pottery, in addition to humans, were offered to the rain god Chaak.

The site had a significant population by the seventh century C.E., but it was during the political turmoil that so adversely affected the Maya farther south during the ninth century that Chichén Itzá developed into a major center. While the site covers 5.8 sq mi (15 sq km), most of its monumental buildings are clustered in the 2 sq mi (5 sq km) core, which is divided into two sectors. The southern sector, with its extraordinary mosaic facades of the Puuc architectural style and hieroglyphic inscriptions dating from between 830 and 890 C.E., has the earliest buildings, although those of the northern sector—including the first rendering of the Castillo—were raised shortly thereafter. These latter buildings followed different architectural styles and used a foreign iconography linked to people from central Mexico who arrived in the mid-tenth century. Under the command of the leader K'uk'ulkan (Feathered Serpent or Quetzalcoatl), they introduced a new political order that rejected the conventional institution of kingship that had been central to earlier Maya realms. Some archaeologists interpret this distinctive cultural manifestation, usually referred to as Toltec, as evidence of a politico-religious movement associated with the cult of Quetzalcoatl, which sought to revitalize the Teotihuacan tradition at Chichén Itzá and at Tula in the central Mexican state of Hidalgo, 930 miles (1,500 km) to the west.

Opposite The recumbent Chacmool warrior statue guards the entrance to the Temple of the Warriors.

Above top An eagle and a jaguar, visual metaphors for warriors, devour human hearts on the Platform of the Eagles and Jaguars.

Above The early tenth-century Caracol had an interior spiral staircase that led to an upper story from which the rising of Venus at its northern and southern extremes could be observed.

Toltec–Maya Expression

Built in honor of Kukulkan, at the center of the Great Plaza the Castillo reflects two aspects of the solar calendar. First, its four staircases, one on each side, have ninety-one steps which, when added to a final plinth, total the 365 days of the solar year; and second, because its base is oriented twenty-two degrees east of north, the setting sun on both the March and September equinoxes projects the shadow of the stepped tiers of the pyramid's northwest corner onto the north balustrade. The balustrade terminates in a carved stone serpent's head, creating the illusion of an ophidian undulating to earth from the temple above. Farther south, the Caracol is another building of astronomical significance. Its two-story circular tower has a spiral staircase to the upper level where narrow windows allow the observation of specific celestial events, especially those related to the planet Venus.

The Temple of the Warriors stands at the eastern edge of the Great Plaza. A wide, once roofed colonnade along the western base of its platform is an intrinsic feature of Toltec architecture, as are the two upended, feathered serpent columns that frame the awkwardly recumbent warrior statue known as a Chacmool at the top of its staircase. Southeast of this building is a 4.4-acre (1.8-ha) plaza delimited by more colonnaded halls—the Group of the Thousand Columns—and which may have been the city's marketplace. A network of paved causeways connected Chichén's building complexes and cenotes.

The Great Ballcourt, and its associated skull rack, or *tzompantli*, occupies the west side of the Great Plaza; the interior court, measuring 489 × 118 ft (149 × 36 m), is the largest in Mesoamerica. Its four temples are embellished with murals and reliefs that display warrior imagery and battle scenes, and the lower sloping walls of the court are carved with processions of ballplayers who witness the decapitation of the defeated team captain at the center. All in all, the often metaphorical art of the Toltec period building facades is truly martial, teeming with uniformed soldiers, weaponry, battles led by figures associated with feathered serpents or solar disks, processions of captives, jaguars and eagles devouring human hearts, investiture rituals, episodes of bloodletting, and human sacrifice.

Despite its military might and command of coastal trade from its port at Isla Cerritos on the peninsula's north coast, Chichén Itzá may have succumbed to factional strife. By the end of the eleventh century, construction had ceased and much of the population had departed. However, in 1532, when the Spaniards tried to establish a capital at the cenote, there were still enough people to prevent the invaders from taking the pilgrimage center.

Chichén Itzá is best visited in the early morning or late afternoon to savor the beautiful play of light and shadow over the buildings and avoid the large tour groups.

Right The Casa de las Monjas (the Nunnery) was built in the ninth century baroque Puuc style that typifies the southern sector of Chichén Itzá.

Below The Castillo, built at the center of the Great Plaza, has two substructures; the final version was dedicated to K'uk'ulkan, the Feathered Serpent. In the background, the west facade of the Temple of the Warriors can be seen.

MITLA THE ZAPOTEC CITY OF THE DEAD

TYPE: RELIGIOUS CENTER • **ARCHITECTURAL STYLE:** PALACES AND TOMBS
LOCATION: OAXACA, MEXICO • **CONSTRUCTION BEGUN:** FIFTH CENTURY C.E.

The Zapotec city of Mitla in the Valley of Oaxaca, Mexico, rose to prominence around the ninth century C.E. Not only was it the seat of the oracular high priest, the Huijatoo, but its sanctuaries and tombs safeguarded the bundled remains of important lords, making it central to Zapotec religion after the decline of Monte Albán. Today the site is famous for the extraordinary mosaic facades of its palaces and cruciform tombs.

Opposite The main facade of the Hall of the Columns provides an extraordinary example of Zapotec stonework.

Above left The apartments of the Zapotec high priest have the only interior walls embellished with panels of stone fretwork.

Above right The six monolithic stone columns of the reception room of the Hall of the Columns once supported a wooden roof.

The archaeological zone lies at the northern end of modern Mitla, which is built over the ancient ruins; its five main building compounds are each composed of one or more courtyards surrounded by platforms. Closest to the site entrance, the Church Group is a complex of three patios that probably served as a royal palace. Late in the sixteenth century, Spaniards built the church of San Pablo over the south court of the group, and even though the other patios were used in colonial times, the badly damaged remains of the red-and-white murals that once decorated the facades of these structures can still be seen on the lintels of the north courtyard.

Mitla's most impressive building complex, the Group of the Columns, lies south of the church and consists of two courtyards. The north patio, dominated by the stunning Hall of the Columns on its north side, is thought to have been the residence of the high priest. Once painted red, the 125 ft- (38 m-) span of its outer walls displays mosaic panels made from volcanic ignimbrite that was mined from nearby quarries and then cut into standardized tesserae to create the building's textile-like, step-fret patterns. The entry to this building is an elongated room with six massive monolithic columns that, it is said, once housed statues of the Lord of the Underworld, Pitao Pezeelao, and his consort Xonaxi Quecuya, in addition to the bundled remains of important ancestors. A low L-shaped passageway along the back wall leads to the elaborate apartments of the Huijatoo that, apart from the tombs, are the only buildings in Mitla with fretwork decorating their interior walls. The second plaza of this group, the Patio of the Tombs, is noteworthy for its two underground cruciform tombs, both carved into bedrock. These were used for funerary rituals associated with the veneration of noble ancestors. Significantly, the site's name, in both the Aztec (Mitla or Mictlan) and Zapotec (Liobaa) languages, refers to the land of the dead.

Mitla's position on the valley floor left it vulnerable to attack. A terraced hilltop settlement just west of the site was fortified late in pre-Hispanic history, perhaps to create a refuge in response to Aztec aggression that began during the fifteenth century. When the Spaniards arrived in 1521, Mitla was the principle religious city in Oaxaca, prompting the construction of the Church of San Pablo over its ruins.

Mitla is a short drive from the city of Oaxaca, and several other ruins, including Lambityeco and Yagul, can be visited along the way.

THE FORTIFIED HILLTOP CENTER OF **XOCHICALCO**

TYPE: CITY • **ARCHITECTURAL STYLE:** TEMPLES, PALACES, AND BALLCOURTS
LOCATION: MORELOS, MEXICO • **CONSTRUCTION BEGUN:** EIGHTH CENTURY C.E.

Xochicalco, or Place of the Flower House, is a fortified hilltop center that lies 24 miles (38 km) southwest of Cuernavaca in the Mexican state of Morelos. Guarded access points along the wide paved roads leading into the city and redoubts and lookouts perched on surrounding hills characterize its defensive location. Explorations at the site date back to 1777 and provide a wealth of data that document its key political and economic role in the region's unstable post-Teotihuacan period (650–900 C.E.).

The city's architects modified the rugged topography to hierarchically organize urban space. At the summit of the hill, the ruling family and its dependents lived in a protected two-story palace (the Acropolis), overlooking the main plaza where the site's most famous structure, the Temple of the Plumed Serpents, is located. Terraces with high retaining walls descend irregularly from this ample esplanade; many of these support important buildings, including three ballcourts. The center's 10,000–15,000 inhabitants lived in small residential compounds grouped into neighborhoods, each with at least one temple or administrative building.

Xochicalco's art meshes the styles and iconography of different regions. For example, the Temple of the Plumed Serpents uses a Teotihuacan-derived architectural profile,

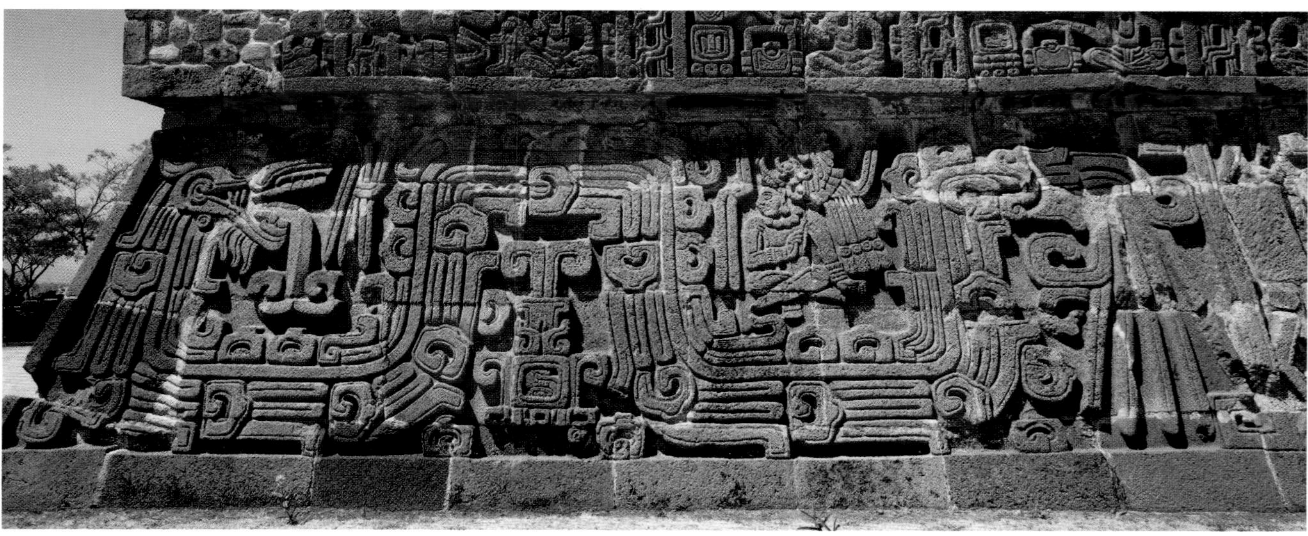

but its imagery presents Maya-style bearded plumed serpents undulating around individuals portrayed in the manner of Maya kings, and calendrical glyphs that recall the Zapotec scribal tradition. Scholars have suggested that the personages enfolded by the structure's plumed serpents are the royal ancestors of the sovereign who commissioned the monument. On the panel above, a frieze of cartouches, each with a seated individual and place glyphs, might celebrate the tribute payments from subject towns. Little remains of the temple, but on the lower north wall a seated warrior bearing a shield, three darts, and a spear-thrower can still be seen.

Like so many Mesoamerican sites, Xochicalco has an astronomical observatory. It consists of an underground chamber with a 28.5 ft (8.7 m) shaft leading to the plaza floor above. Specialists have shown that the shaft could be used to observe the zenith passage in May and July as the sun transits to and from the Tropic of Cancer.

In the 1960s, archaeologists discovered three stelae that had been broken and buried beneath the floor of one of Xochicalco's temples (Building A). They are red-painted rectangular blocks, deeply carved on all four sides with images and glyphs that recall the Teotihuacan and Zapotec traditions. Some researchers believe that the face depicted on the front of each monument refers to a deity (Sun, Rain, and Earth), while others maintain that the place signs, dates, and other glyphs memorialize the victorious campaigns of three great rulers: 7 Reptile Eye, 7 Rain, and 4 Movement. These and other monuments provide some of the earliest uncontested evidence for a writing system in central Mexico.

Despite widespread political and trade connections that gave it an international flavor, Xochicalco's occupation, like that of other cities founded during these centuries, was short-lived, lasting from 700 to 900 C.E., when it was savagely sacked and burned. Xochicalco is easily reached from nearby Cuernavaca and is best visited in the early morning or late afternoon. The site museum is well worth a visit.

Opposite Detail of the carving on the sloping base of the Temple of the Plumed Serpents.

Above View across the site.

TENOCHTITLAN AZTEC CAPITAL

TYPE: ISLAND CITY • **ARCHITECTURAL STYLE:** TEMPLES AND MONUMENTS
LOCATION: MEXICO CITY, MEXICO • **CONSTRUCTION BEGUN:** FOURTEENTH CENTURY C.E.

In 1519 the Spanish conquistador Hernando Cortés described the Aztec capital of Tenochtitlan by comparing it to cities back home—in size it was like Seville or Córdoba, its main market twice the area of Salamanca's. It was a city of canals and canoes, with palaces, plazas, monumental sculptures, schools, ballcourts, an aqueduct to bring fresh water into the city center, imperial gardens, and a zoo. The four wide causeways that connected the island city to the mainland had wooden bridges that the islanders could remove during a siege. In a letter to the Spanish Crown, Cortés writes of a Great Temple, located within a walled precinct with seventy-seven other buildings, and taller than the belltower of Seville's Cathedral. Most of what he saw, however, was soon demolished as Spanish civilization steadily razed the pre-Columbian structures and used the stone to erect its own churches, administrative buildings, and residences.

Fragments of the Aztec city are sometimes uncovered by public works projects. For example, during the renovation of Mexico City's main square in 1790, several of the temple precinct's monuments were recovered; a few, considered monstrosities of the devil, were dynamited. Tunneling for the urban subway system, initiated in 1966, has produced many significant finds, including the small shrine preserved at the downtown Pino Suárez station. However, it was the 1978 discovery of a 10.5 ft (3.25 m) stone disk carved with the dismembered corpse of the goddess Coyolxauhqui that triggered large-scale excavations to salvage the remains of the Great Temple and surrounding buildings.

The Great Temple that Cortés visited in 1519 stood 148 ft (45 m) high while its sides measured 269 ft (82 m) on a side, but today only the foundations remain. It was designed to represent the sacred mountain of Aztec mythology and to reflect the two primary aspects of the imperial economy: agriculture and warfare. Thus the north staircase on its west facade leads to the temple of the rain god Tlaloc (agricultural fertility) while the south staircase rises to that of the solar war god Huitzilopochtli (conquest). Huitzilopochtli was the patron god of the Aztecs, and his side of the four-tiered platform is embellished with allusions to his miraculous birth on Coatepec (Snake Mountain) and the dismemberment of his sister, Coyolxauhqui. Today, however, only the second of the Great Temple's seven building stages is entirely preserved, dated 1428 C.E.

Flanking the Great Temple on the north is the House of the Eagle Warriors, a ritual structure for Aztec military sodalities. Its stone benches are carved with soldiers marching beneath feathered serpents, and almost life-sized terracotta statues—two of eagle warriors and two of the eerie Lord of the Underworld—once flanked interior doorways. Recently, Mexico's Urban Archaeology Program discovered Tenochtitlan's Huey Tzompantli (Great Wall of Skulls) that once displayed the decapitated heads of captives sacrificed in front of Huitzilopochtli's temple. Next door, in the basement of the Spanish Cultural Center, remains of the school for young nobles (the Calmecac) can be viewed through "archaeological windows" open to the public.

The City's Treasures

As the seat of a great empire that spanned most of central Mexico, Tenochtitlan received tributes from faraway regions. Some items, including jaguars, swordfish, corals, sea stars, objects of jade, gold, and obsidian, pottery, and "animated" flint knives, were placed in stone offering boxes beneath the pavement surrounding the Great Temple. Many of these objects, and monumental sculptures, such as that of the clawed earth deity Tlaltecuhtli, are in the site museum. Like Rome and other ancient imperial capitals, Tenochtitlan was filled with statuary meant to impress and intimidate.

Tenochtitlan was founded in 1325 C.E. on an island in the middle of a brackish lake by a group of migrants from the north, the Mexica. For a century, the Mexica served as mercenaries for the city of Azcapotzalco, but in 1427 they allied themselves with other city-states to defeat their overlords and establish their independence. Twenty years later they began to conquer areas beyond the Valley of Mexico. By 1519, the empire's thirty-eight tributary provinces extended from the Gulf Coast to the Pacific Ocean. Although the Spanish conquest of the Aztec empire is often attributed to guns, horses, and infectious diseases, the invaders would not have been able to defeat the 200,000 inhabitants of Tenochtitlan in August 1521 without the help of their native allies, disaffected groups who had been overtaxed by the imperial system, and who saw this event as a victory over hated overlords, not a foreign conquest.

While the Great Temple and its site museum are core features of Aztec archaeology, many other monuments and building fragments can be found on walking tours of Mexico City's historic center.

Below Excavations in the heart of Mexico City have uncovered the foundations of Tenochtitlan's Great Temple and other buildings of the ritual precinct.

THE INCA CITADEL OF **MACHU PICCHU**

TYPE: CEREMONIAL AND RESIDENTIAL CENTER • **ARCHITECTURAL STYLE:** IMPERIAL INCA
LOCATION: CUZCO, SOUTHERN PERUVIAN HIGHLANDS • **CONSTRUCTION BEGUN:** FIFTEENTH CENTURY C.E.

Set within the high Andean landscape, the citadel of Machu Picchu is one of the greatest wonders of civilization. It epitomizes the skills of its builders, the Incas, in harmonizing the natural rugged landscape with their sophisticated stone-based architecture.

Machu Picchu is one of the most visited archaeological sites in Peru. The best known of the Inca sites, it was discovered by American explorer Hiram Bingham during an expedition to Cuzco sponsored by Yale University in 1911. Bingham was trying to find the last zone of resistance of the Incas during the Spanish conquest, the mythical site of Vilcabamba. Two years after his archaeological investigations here, the first article about Machu Picchu appeared in *National Geographic*.

A Rugged Landscape

The site is located in the Urubamba valley, 50 miles (80 km) northwest of the city of Cuzco, on a route that leads to the tropical forest. Built on top of a mountain some 7,970 ft (2,430 m) above sea level, the citadel covers an area of approximately 12.3 acres (5 ha) and, at its height, could have housed some 750 people.

According to archaeologists, the Incas founded Machu Picchu during the first half of the fifteenth century, possibly as a royal estate for their most famous emperor, Pachacutec. The construction of Machu Picchu in such a rugged area of high rainfall and dense vegetation required the Inca architects to stabilize the terrain. One of the main solutions was the construction of terraces, or platforms, on the mountain slopes, to provide level surfaces on which they could build.

This site is divided into two large areas: an agricultural area comprises a vast network of artificial terraces, while the urban area contains various constructions and plazas, including the Temple of the Sun, the Intihuatana Stone, and Temple of the Three Windows.

Left Temple of the Sun in Machu Picchu. In Inca architecture, the curved walls are related to religious functions.

Opposite Panoramic view of Machu Picchu. In the background rises the Huayna Picchu mountain.

The Site’s Main Buildings

Machu Picchu has all the classic architectural components of an Inca city: squares, temples, palaces, astronomical observatories, residences for both the elite and their servants, and warehouses. In addition, there are unique buildings such as the Temple of the Sun. Standing on a large rocky outcrop, the temple’s upper part features a semicircular wall that frames the upper part of the outcrop, the surface of which is marked with carvings. The walls have windows to allow observations and measurements of the movement of the sun. One window in particular lets in sunlight during the June solstice, to illuminate the carved rock inside. Below this structure, at the base of the outcrop of carved rock, is a cave. Its walls are carved and large trapezoidal niches hewn. At the entrance, the stone is carved to create a step. Even from inside this so-called mausoleum, it is possible to see mountain peaks. As such, Machu Picchu highlights the use of rocky outcrops, which the Incas carved to mimic certain natural forms of the surrounding landscape.

The Intihuatana Stone dominates the upper part of one of the most important sectors of the site. This stone, sculpted from a single piece of rock, sits atop a pyramidal rock platform. Archaeologists suggest that it was the sanctuary, or main huaca, of Machu Picchu, since its location provides an important view of the sacred mountains of the region, and an ideal spot from which to make astronomical observations for agricultural rituals.

Another impressive building at Machu Picchu is the Temple of the Three Windows, located in the sector of the Sacred Square. The three windows of this structure allow excellent views of the mountains and the Urubamba River, located to the east of the site. Excavations in this sector uncovered ceramic fragments, and it has been suggested that these may have been used in ceremonial rituals.

If you are in good physical shape, you can get to the site by trekking across the mountains. There is a museum in the nearby little town of Aguas Calientes.

Opposite, from top Urban sector of Machu Picchu. Terraces built to support plazas and architectural structures can be seen. The Temple of the Sun is located in the lower left corner. The Temple of the Condor in Machu Picchu combines carved stone outcrops with stone masonry.

Above, from top Temple of Three Windows. Temple of the Sun. Intihuatana Stone.

ANCIENT MUD CITY OF **CHAN CHAN**

TYPE: URBAN AND CEREMONIAL CENTER • **ARCHITECTURAL STYLE:** CHIMÚ
LOCATION: TRUJILLO, NORTHERN PERUVIAN COAST • **CONSTRUCTION BEGUN:** TWELFTH CENTURY C.E.

On the north bank of the Moche Valley in northern Peru lies the largest mud city in the Americas. Occupying an area of 7.7 sq mi (20 sq km), it is an impressive site that houses ten walled citadels (*ciudadelas*) built by the Chimú society (ca. 900–1470 C.E.), quite literally from a mixture of water and earth. The citadels are named Chayhuac, Uhle, Laberinto, Gran Chimú, Squier, Velarde, Bandelier, Tschudi, Rivero, and Tello. Together they constitute the city of Chan Chan, capital of the Chimor kingdom.

This city is located 3 miles (5 km) northwest of the city of Trujillo, in the Department of La Libertad, between the districts of Trujillo and Huanchaco. It is almost always sunny here, so it should come as no surprise that the name of Chan Chan translated as "shining sun."

The citadels were erected in a process that lasted, according to archaeological evidence, at least 300 years. During all this time, they underwent social, political, and economic change. Each citadel was a large rectangular enclosure with very high walls and restricted access. These were the residences of the leaders of Chimú society, and served as their palaces, meeting and ritual areas, warehouses, and even mausoleums. High-relief decoration on the surface of the walls ranges from the depiction of coastal animals to geometric shapes. Since the citadels also included the mausoleums of the rulers, these buildings required a great investment in their construction. Eight of them had one or more mortuary platforms, all rendered in similar style and orientation. Members of the family maintained the mausoleums, highly restricted spaces in the

most intimate locations within the citadel. Human sacrifices were found in the main mausoleums of the citadels. It is estimated that around 300 young women could have been buried in secondary burial chambers surrounding the main chamber in the Huaca Las Avispas.

Beside the citadels, the site's architecture indicates a strong stratification of society, with different areas inhabited by people of differing status. For example, of the 140 wells supplying water to the city, 60 percent of them were located in the monumental zone and only 12 percent in the residential neighborhoods that were home to more than 90 percent of the population.

Due to its architecture and state of conservation, the city became a UNESCO World Heritage site in 1986. The site also features an important museum. A visit to the nearby beach town of Huanchaco is highly recommended.

Above left Decorations and walls with friezes made with mud in the Tschudi citadel.

Above Mud friezes depicting seabirds in the Tschudi citadel.

Below The front of the main plaza in the Tschudi citadel. Friezes decorate the main walls.

ANCIENT PILGRIMAGE CENTER OF **CHAVÍN DE HUÁNTAR**

TYPE: CEREMONIAL AND RESIDENTIAL CENTER • **ARCHITECTURAL STYLE:** CHAVÍN
LOCATION: ANCASH, NORTHERN PERUVIAN HIGHLANDS • **CONSTRUCTION BEGUN:** TWELFTH CENTURY B.C.E.

Nestling at the junction of the Mosna and Wacheqsa rivers at 10,335 ft (3,150 m) above sea level, Chavín de Huántar is one of several important pilgrimage and worship centers in the pre-Hispanic Andes. Located at the upper end of the Conchucos Valley in the northern highlands of Peru, the site was built and occupied mainly between 1200 and 500 B.C.E.

Listed as a World Heritage site by UNESCO, the Chavín de Huántar archaeological site has impressive monumentality and antiquity. Above all, its sculptural art in stone has attracted attention since the nineteenth century, the principal investigator being the Peruvian archaeologist Julio C. Tello (1880–1947). The site was founded around 1200 B.C.E. and lasted almost a millennium, during which time the architecture was extended. In addition, the human settlement grew. At its peak, Chavín would have had a population of 3,000 inhabitants.

The Temples

The monumental area of the site comprises a concentration of buildings whose construction must have required a great deal of work. They are built of stone and mud, among which some large blocks of carved stone stand out. Stone sculptures and lithic blocks with designs in high and low relief depict hybrid beings that combine humans, felines, birds of prey, and reptiles.

Right The monolithic Lanzón of Chavín de Huántar.

Opposite The sunken circular plaza in Chavín de Huántar. The stairway leads to the Old Temple.

The most important architectural structures within the Chavín de Huántar complex are the so-called New Temple and the Old Temple. Both buildings are fronted by plazas and feature galleries inside and underground. On the back wall of the New Temple, one of the "tenon heads" is located in its original place. Over the years, archaeologists and inhabitants of the area have recovered more than a hundred of these heads that would originally have adorned the outer walls of the Chavín temples. Made of stone, they depict various anthropomorphic and zoomorphic beings, highlighting the presence of feline and raptor traits.

A number of structures here are reconstructions made in their original places. Among these, the Black and White Portal of the New Temple stands out—two large columns of stone, one dark and one light, on which low-relief designs depict anthropomorphic beings with raptor features. Both columns support stone blocks with carved designs.

Above Panoramic view of Chavín de Huántar. In the foreground are the quadrangular plaza and the New Temple is beyond it.

Below The Black and White Portal was made with lithic blocks, and is located in the front of the New Temple.

Opposite A tenon head in its original location. This lithic sculpture is located in the back wall of the New Temple.

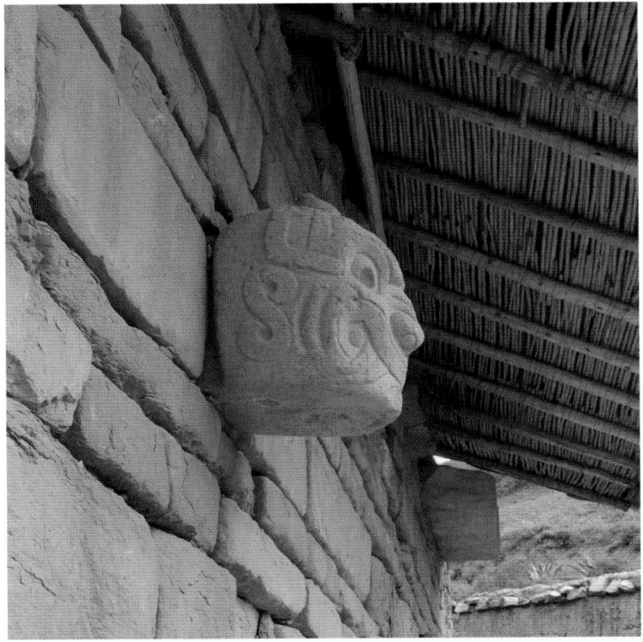

Several other structures are worth seeing. In its original position within the main gallery of the Old Temple, the Lanzón is a monolith about 14.8 ft (4.5 m) high, sculpted in the form of a spearhead. This large stone depicts an anthropomorphic being with feline features.

Almost as impressive in size as the Lanzón, the Tello Obelisk measures 8.2 ft (2.52 m). Its surface is decorated on all four sides and depicts a pair of complex zoomorphic beings, difficult to interpret at first glance. Archaeologists believe it is a caiman, which would indicate the important influence of the Amazon region for Chavín leaders. In addition, if you look closely, you can see that it represents two different sexes adorned with iconographic elements inspired by botanical products and animals from different areas of the Andean world.

The Raimondi Stele represents an anthropomorphic being with feline characteristics and other attributes related to snakes. The figure holds a staff in each hand, a symbol of power. Because of its morphology and iconography, this stele must have decorated an important wall of a main building on the site, although the exact location has not been determined.

Chavín de Huántar was, at one time, the center of a pan-Andean religious cult that attracted many social groups, especially elites from other places. They came here seeking knowledge about nature and supernatural powers from the leaders of Chavín. Ritual practices were facilitated by the consumption of hallucinogenic plants, which induced altered states of consciousness. The intimidating architecture and sounds produced during the ceremony contributed to the experience.

The site's museum is in the modern town of Chavín.

MOCHE HUACAS DEL SOL AND DE LA LUNA

TYPE: CEREMONIAL AND URBAN CENTER • **ARCHITECTURAL STYLE:** MOCHE
LOCATION: TRUJILLO, NORTHERN PERUVIAN COAST • **CONSTRUCTION BEGUN:** FIRST CENTURY C.E.

Rising up out of the arid desert landscape of northern Peru are the well-preserved remains of two pre-Hispanic monuments, the Huacas del Sol and La Luna. The site here was founded in the first century C.E. and abandoned in the ninth century. Its monumental architectural constructions, wealthy tombs, sculptured pottery, and metal artifacts represent one of the most important architectural complexes of sophisticated Moche society.

The two huacas are made from a huge number of rectangular adobe bricks, arranged in a series of monumental stepped platforms. During the whole period that Moche society lasted, people built and remodeled the huacas in several phases. It was this overlapping of new construction phases and remodeling of the structures over time that gave the huacas their final appearance.

The Huaca del Sol is the most imposing building and one of the most voluminous architectural works of South America. It is estimated that it would originally have been 1,130 ft (345 m) long by 525 ft (160 m) wide at its base, with a height of more than 131 ft (40 m). Archaeological investigations are relatively recent, but there is evidence that this huaca served as a political and administrative building.

The main platform of the Huaca de la Luna is about 950 ft (290 m) long by 690 ft (210 m) wide at its base, with a height of 66 ft (20 m). High-relief murals with depictions of human sacrifice suggest this structure served a religious purpose. Within, a series of enclosures and plazas characterize the Huaca de la Luna, with well-preserved polychrome murals depicting scenes relating to religion and the Moche political structure. Made from mud, in high relief, the figures in the friezes and the areas between them were painted in bright colors—mainly red, yellow, white, and black. On the main facade it is possible to see a series of personages depicted at different levels, suggesting the existence of hierarchies in the Moche cosmovision. Friezes also exist in the interior of the Huaca de la Luna with more repetitive decorations that include the head of an anthropomorphic being with feline features inside diamond-shaped designs.

Opposite Detail of a polychrome frieze located in an inner enclosure of Huaca de la Luna.

Below View of the urban core of Huacas de Moche. In the background are Huaca de la Luna and Cerro Blanco.

At the base of Cerro Blanco, Plaza 3A revealed the remains of around a hundred male bodies. According to the archaeological and bioanthropological evidence, the Moche people sacrificed these men during a period associated with climatic crises related to El Niño, the warm phase of the El Niño–Southern Oscillation (ENSO), during the sixth century C.E.

Urban Core

In between Huaca del Sol and Huaca de la Luna, a series of architectural spaces coexisted with the main buildings. This was the urban area, home to permanent inhabitants of the city, principally specialist craftspeople who offered their products to the Moche elites. There is evidence here of workshops where ceramics, textiles, and metal and stone artifacts were produced. It is estimated that between 15,000 and 25,000 inhabitants would have lived at the site at its peak, and the city is generally accepted as the capital of this political entity.

Archaeologists believe that Moche society comprised at least two major regions: the Northern Moche and Southern Moche. Commonly referred to as the Huacas de Moche, the monuments here are the work of the Southern Moche, and are located in the lower Moche Valley on the outskirts of the modern city of Trujillo on the north coast of Peru. The site features a museum in which many of the site's remains are on display.

Left Polychrome friezes on walls and an enclosure located in a corner of the main plaza of Huaca de la Luna.

Above Panoramic view of Huaca del Sol. Behind this building, the Moche valley and Trujillo city can be seen.

THE PILGRIMAGE CENTER OF **PACHACAMAC**

TYPE: RELIGIOUS AND POLITICAL CENTER • **ARCHITECTURAL STYLE:** LIMA, YCHMA AND INCA
LOCATION: LIMA, PERUVIAN CENTRAL COAST • **CONSTRUCTION BEGUN:** FIRST CENTURY C.E.

Taking advantage of the wealth of the land and its proximity to the sea, the Pachacamac sanctuary occupies an area on the right bank of the Lurin River, south of what is now Lima, the capital of Peru. It was one of the most important of the pre-Hispanic ceremonial centers for more than a thousand years, and the site was home to an important divinity that was believed to "animate" the world.

Pachacamac dates from the Early Intermediate Period (ca. 200 B.C.E.–600 C.E.) to the Late Horizon (ca. 1450–1532 C.E.). Covering 1,150 acres (465 ha) today, it features a number of notable architectural structures that include the Old Temple, the Painted Temple, the Pyramids with Ramps, the Temple of the Sun, the Acllahuasi, the Palace of Tauri Chumpi, and the Pilgrims' Square.

Built from mudbricks on a rocky promontory, the Old Temple is Pachacamac's oldest building, and is currently very damaged. The Painted Temple is a stepped structure, built using adobe bricks and stone. Most noteworthy is its terraced facade with walls painted with colorful scenes representing anthropomorphic beings, plants, and fishes. Excavation work unearthed what has become known as the Idol of Pachacamac, a wooden pole that represents an anthropomorphic being with two faces. At the base of the Painted Temple in pre-Hispanic times was an important cemetery that was first systematically excavated at the end of the nineteenth century by the German researcher Max Uhle (1856–1944).

The so-called Pyramids with Ramps stand out—pyramidal buildings built of rough-cut stones and adobe bricks that had ramps leading to an upper platform. Although there is a debate about the date of these buildings, they were probably created by the Ychma society, although some were also expanded and continued to function during the Inca era.

Pachacamac in Inca Times

Although the cult of Pachacamac preceded the Incas, and this center of worship was already known and visited by people from all over the Andes, it was under the Incas

Opposite The Temple of the Sun. Built in the dominant area of Pachacamac, this shrine was dedicated to the sun by the Incas.

Right The Idol of Pachacamac was carved in wood and represents a bifrontal human personage.

that it became a main pilgrimage center, occupying a predominant place within the Inca road system or Qhapaq Ñan. The first Spaniards to arrive in Pachacamac in 1533 left important descriptions of the place and the religious practices developed there. We know from their accounts that, in order to enter the sanctuary, sanctuary pilgrims had to follow a strict diet for more than one month.

The Temple of the Sun remains the largest and best-preserved building on the site. Built on a rocky promontory, it stands about 130 ft (40 m) tall. The building is made up of five superimposed platforms that form a truncated pyramid. Although this temple belongs to the sanctuary of Pachacamac, in Inca times it was dedicated to the sun, a major divinity.

The Acllahuasi, or Mamaconas, was a place where the "chosen women" lived. This temple has many rooms with typical Inca architectural features that include niches and double-jambed trapezoidal doors. There are many examples of finely carved stone blocks, even in the base and low walls of the structure.

The Palace of Tauri Chumpi, according to Inca chronicles, would have been the residence of the *curaca*, or magistrate, of Pachacamac at the time of the Spanish conquest. Finally, the Pilgrims' Square is a leveled rectangular space that located just in front of the Temple of the Sun. Archaeologists suggest that, due to its proximity to the temple, this would have served as a waiting area for pilgrims. Many of the artifacts found at the site are on display in the site museum.

Above The upper level of the Temple of Sun from which there is a breathtaking view of the Pacific Ocean.

Opposite above Temple with Ramp. This construction followed the local architectural tradition of the central coast and was used up to Inca times.

Opposite The Acllahuasi. This was the "house of the chosen women" during the Inca times.

IMPLEMENTACIÓN DE LA VISITA
NOCTURNA A LOS PRINCIPALES
MONUMENTOS DEL COMPLEJO
ARQUEOLÓGICO DE PACHACAMAC
DR. ALAN GARCIA PEREZ

THE PRE-HISPANIC MONUMENTALITY OF **CARAL**

TYPE: RELIGIOUS AND POLITICAL CENTER • **ARCHITECTURAL STYLE:** CARAL **LOCATION:** DEPARTMENT OF LIMA, PERUVIAN CENTRAL COAST • **CONSTRUCTION BEGUN:** THIRD MILLENNIUM B.C.E.

A series of pyramidal platforms made of stone and mud dominate the pre-Hispanic Andean site of Caral. This ancient archaeological center occupies land in the North Chico region of Peru, an area that is particularly notable for containing an extraordinary accumulation of monumental archaeological sites built mainly during the Late Preceramic Period (3000–1800 B.C.E.). Caral is one of them and thought to represent one of the oldest civilizations in the world.

Discovered by the Peruvian archaeologist Ruth Shady (b. 1946), Caral has gained notoriety due to its monumentality and early complexity, and is a key site in our understanding of the development of the world's first complex societies. According to the published radiocarbon dates, Caral's buildings were constructed during the third millennium B.C.E., making them among the oldest expressions of monumental architecture in the Andean region. According to Shady, Caral was the capital of an early state, although opinions on this differ. Researchers do agree, however, that Caral was a site with a successful economy, and saw the development of construction technologies, strategies for harnessing economic resources, and an extensive network of regional exchange. Its leadership lasted for more than 1,000 years.

The site was spread over 168 acres (68 ha). Shady and her team estimate that, at its peak, the settlement could have housed approximately 3,000 inhabitants. Among all the buildings that can be seen in here, the Templo Mayor is the most complex and voluminous. At its base, the building is 558 ft (170 m) long and 492 ft (150 m) wide. It was constructed in different architectural phases until it reached a height of 98 ft (30 m). It consists mainly of a series of overlapping platforms and a sunken circular court in the front of the building. The top of the temple is accessed by stairs located at the front.

Other large buildings at Caral include the Amphitheater Temple. In total there are thirty-two public architectural structures and an area of domestic occupation.

Of particular interest at Caral is the use of shicras in the construction of its buildings. Shicras are bags made of vegetable fiber cords, usually reeds. They were used to transport stones for building, and sometimes even placed as part of the fill in the construction work. This was a technique shared in much of the Norte Chico region.

Also among the finds were hundreds of human figurines. Made from unbaked clay, they stand out for the hairstyles and headdresses they wear. It is estimated that their function would have been related to propitiatory or fertility-related rituals.

Caral lies in the coastal valley of Supe, 110 miles (177 km) north of the city of Lima. In addition, it is an important tourist destination in Peru, a country already outstanding for its major ancient monumental sites. Caral is on UNESCO's World Heritage list.

Opposite Panoramic view of the Caral site.
Above The Templo Mayor in Caral.
Below Some of the unbaked clay figurines found at the site.

SIPÁN THE RICHEST MOCHE TOMB

TYPE: CEREMONIAL AND POLITICAL CENTER • **ARCHITECTURAL STYLE:** MOCHE
LOCATION: LAMBAYEQUE, NORTHERN PERUVIAN COAST • **CONSTRUCTION BEGUN:** FIRST CENTURY C.E.

Near the town of Sipán in the middle of the Lambayeque Valley, in the Zaña region of northern Peru, out among the fields of crops, stands Huaca Rajada, a mud pyramid eroded by rains, wind, and looting. In recent years, this unlikely structure has become one of the most emblematic archaeological sites of the South American Moche civilization.

It was here, in 1987, while investigating the site's funerary platform, that archaeologist Walter Alva (b. 1951) found the tomb of one of the most important rulers of Moche society—the Lord of Sipán. The site has gone on to yield the remains of a whole series of leaders since that time.

The funerary platform is built of adobe. Inside, a rectangular chamber had a roof supported by wooden beams. The platform grew in volume as new burial chambers were added during several stages of construction.

The main occupant of each tomb was male and lay inside a wooden coffin along with a large number of sumptuous objects. Offerings accompanying the Lord of Sipán included seashells, scepters, pectorals, ceramics, textiles, and other luxury items. The funerary chamber also revealed human sacrifices of children, women in ceremonial clothes, and men. The last, judging by the clothes and artifacts found, were warriors. Some of them had their feet amputated. Additional sacrifices included those of animals, such as

dogs and camelids. The supposition is that human sacrifices were made to accompany the leaders of Moche society on their journey to the afterlife. According to the iconography, the Lords of Sipán established intimate relationships with supernatural beings and forces.

The Sipán tombs—the first sites of royal burials to be found intact in South America—belong to a Peruvian civilization prior to the Incas. Many archaeologists consider the find to be one of the most important archaeological discoveries in South America of the last few decades.

Scientific analysis of the Lord of Sipán's skeleton indicate that this individual was about 5 ft 5 in (1.65 m) tall and around forty years old at the time of his death. The quality of his diet and his wealth of jewelry and ornaments made of gold, silver, and copper show that he was a high ranking person. As in Inca society, particular artifacts made of precious metals symbolized a ruler's power. The scepters found in the tombs at Huaca Rajada bear designs relating to the main personage. Semi-lunar headdresses are also emblematic of power among the Moche elite.

Huaca Rajada lies some 20 miles (32 km) east of the city of Chiclayo in the middle of Peru's coastal Lambayeque Valley, a place of great beauty. The site also features a superb museum, which should not be missed. However, the most important pieces of the Sipán tombs, even the human remains, are in the Museum of Royal Tombs of Sipán located in Lambayeque city.

Opposite A view of platforms in Huaca Rajada. In this archaeological complex was built the funerary platform where Sipán leaders were buried.

Above Replica of the Tomb of the Lord of Sipán, located in the same place where the original tomb was found by archaeologists.

THE NAZCA LINES DESERT GEOGLYPHS

TYPE: GEOGLYPHS • **ARCHITECTURAL STYLE:** N/A
LOCATION: NAZCA, SOUTHERN PERUVIAN COAST • **CONSTRUCTION BEGUN:** FIRST CENTURY C.E.

Etched into desert rock, 1,312 ft (400 m) above sea level, and some 250 miles (400 km) south of Lima, in Peru, is one of the world's most astounding collections of ancient geoglyphs. Many of them are long lines that must have served as ritual paths, but the most famous are those that take on zoomorphic, botanical, and anthropomorphic shapes. Totaling more than 1,000 straight lines of varying length and more than 800 animal figures, these are the Nazca Lines, created during the height of the Nazca society, around 1–650 C.E.

Spanning the valleys of Palpa and Nazca in Peru's Ica region, this remarkable site covers an area of around 111,000 acres (45,000 ha). The wonderful figures etched here represent a wealth of coastal and jungle birds that include hummingbirds, condors, herons, cranes, pelicans, seagulls, and parrots. There are other animals, too—a monkey, a spider, a snail, a whale, a dog, llamas, iguanas, and lizards. A number of anthropomorphic figures feature also.

Given that some of the figures extend up to 985 ft (300 m) in size, it begs the question as to how the ancient Nazquenses made them—and why. As to the former, research indicates that they used cords and stakes to align the paths, and followed small-scale drawings as models for etching the lines on the desert surface. As to the latter, since their discovery in the first half of the twentieth century, the meaning of the Nazca Lines has been a matter of debate: archaeologists such as Julio C. Tello and Toribio Mejía Xesspe believed them to be sacred roads; American historian Paul Kosok argued that Nazca's lines formed a great astronomical book; and the pioneering researcher María Reiche believed that the site served as a gigantic solar and lunar calendar, which the ancient Nasquenses used to forecast the best harvest seasons. More recently, Japanese archaeologist Masato Sakai has suggested that some lines served ritual or ceremonial purposes while others functioned as markers or road guides that indicated the path and the distance from one town to another.

Whatever the reasons for their creation, the tradition of making geoglyphs in this region predates the Nazca Lines, and is known to have continued well into the Inca era. None can match these, however, in terms of volume and size.

Easily accessible to visitors today—the Pan-American Highway crosses the region—the Nazca Lines became a UNESCO Cultural Heritage of Humanity site in 1994.

Below Geoglyph of a spider (150 ft / 46 m long).
Opposite top Geoglyph of a hummingbird (312 ft / 95 m long).
Opposite bottom Geoglyph of a monkey (262 x 246 ft / 80 x 75 m).

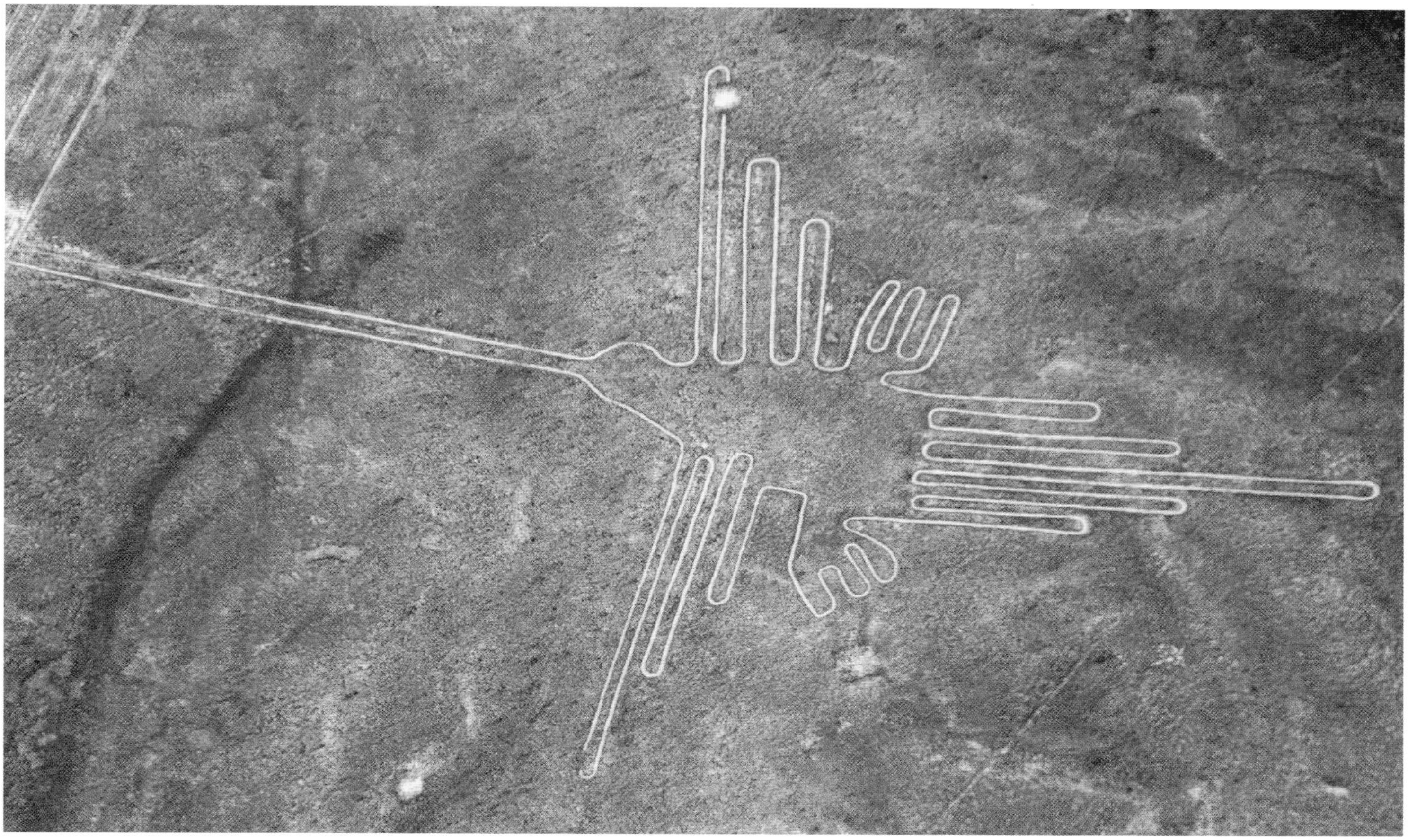

THE MEGALITHIC CITY OF **TIWANAKU**

TYPE: CEREMONIAL AND URBAN CENTER • **ARCHITECTURAL STYLE:** TIWANAKU
LOCATION: DEPARTMENT OF LA PAZ, BOLIVIA • **CONSTRUCTION BEGUN:** FOURTH CENTURY C.E.

About an hour's drive from Bolivia's capital, La Paz, a series of impressive megalithic constructions make Tiwanaku one of the most attractive and mysterious archaeological sites in South America.

According to researchers, Tiwanaku society originally existed as a theocracy, with a priestly elite using religion as its primary strategy for maintaining control. After the seventh century, however, a warrior class took over.

This archaeological site is located 9.3 miles (15 km) southeast of the immense Lake Titicaca in Bolivia, at 1,265 ft (3,855 m) above sea level. Tiwanaku is also the name of the main religious and urban center of a society that developed here between the sixth and eleventh centuries C.E. Members of Tiwanaku society settled not only in what is modern Bolivia, but also in regions that make up parts of modern Peru and Chile.

Monumental Architecture

The archaeological site at Tiwanaku is characterized mainly by its monumental stone-block architecture, much of it decorated in high relief and with incised decoration. The complex comprises an urban center built around a megalithic ceremonial core occupying an area of between 900 and 1,480 acres (400–600 ha). Architectural constructions include the Kalasasaya, the Akapana, the Putuni, and the Puma Punku, all centered around two main avenues and astronomically aligned with amazing precision.

The Kalasasaya is a ceremonial structure with an area of 5 acres (2 ha). It is most noteworthy for its imposing staircase and walls of stone blocks (many of the stone walls were rebuilt in the twentieth century). At the top of the

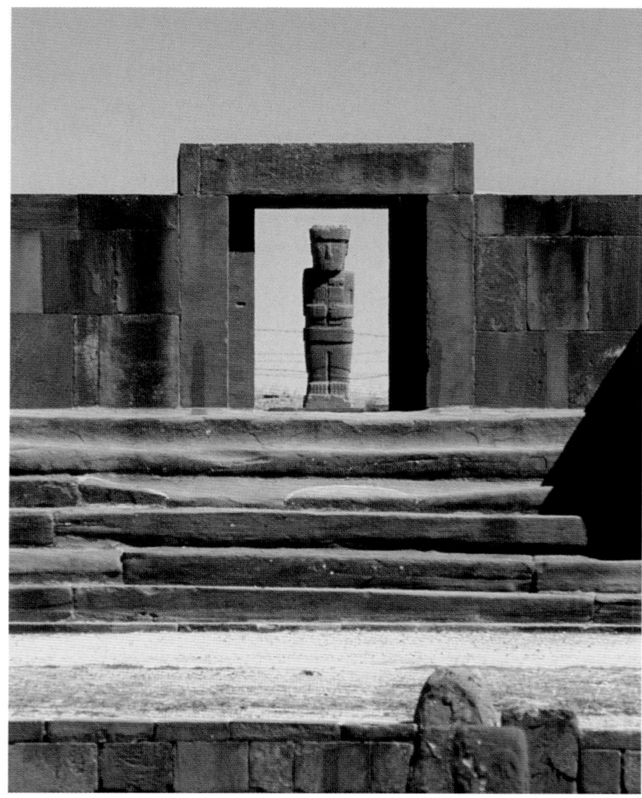

Above The Gate of Kalasasaya was reconstructed in the twentieth century. It frames the Ponce Monolith.

Opposite above Walls and tenon heads of the Semisubterranean Temple.

Opposite below Huge stone blocks on top of the Puma Punku platform.

platform is the 9.9 ft (3 m) Ponce monolith, named in honor of its discoverer, the archaeologist Carlos Ponce Sanginés. At the west end of this platform is the famous Puerta del Sol, a gate made in a huge lithic block, with the main character known as the "staff god" depicted in the central place.

The dominant building is the Akapana, a pyramidal structure made mainly of mud, with stone-block walls. Pottery and copper fragments, camelid bones, and human burials have been discovered here, in the first and second levels of the pyramid. The first level yielded evidence of human sacrifices—dismembered children and males with their skulls absent—accompanied by dismembered camelids and pottery. On the second level was a completely disjointed human torso. According to archaeologists, these finds represent sacrifices made for the construction of the building.

The Putuni, a rectangular platform with a height of 4 ft (1.2 m) high, was the burial site of the society's elites. The Puma Punku is a monumental complex with walls and architectural features built of with megalithic stones. What stands out in this complex is the dedication and effort with which the stones were carved, since their surfaces and angles are perfect.

Among the sculptures found at Tiwanaku, the best known is the Bennett Monolith, named for its discoverer, American archaeologist Wendell C. Bennett (1905–1953). Standing an impressive 24 ft (7.3 m) tall, the monolith represents an anthropomorphic personage in elegant dress. The surface of the character's outfit is profusely decorated with classic Tiwanaku designs.

Beside the impressive architecture at Tiwanaku are a number of ceramic and metal artifacts. However, due to conservation problems, there is little evidence of textiles or woodwork, though such artifacts have been found in Tiwanaku sites elsewhere. The site also features an important museum with many archaeological finds from Tiwanaku itself (included the Bennett monolith) and surrounding prehispanic sites. The nearby town of Tiwanaku was founded in Spanish colonial times and its main plaza and church (with two Tiwanaku stone sculptures in front) are worth visiting.

Left The Kalasasaya platform viewed from the top of Akapana. On the right, the Semisubterranean Temple can be seen.

Below The Ponce monolith depicts a human figure, probably a Tiwanaku leader.

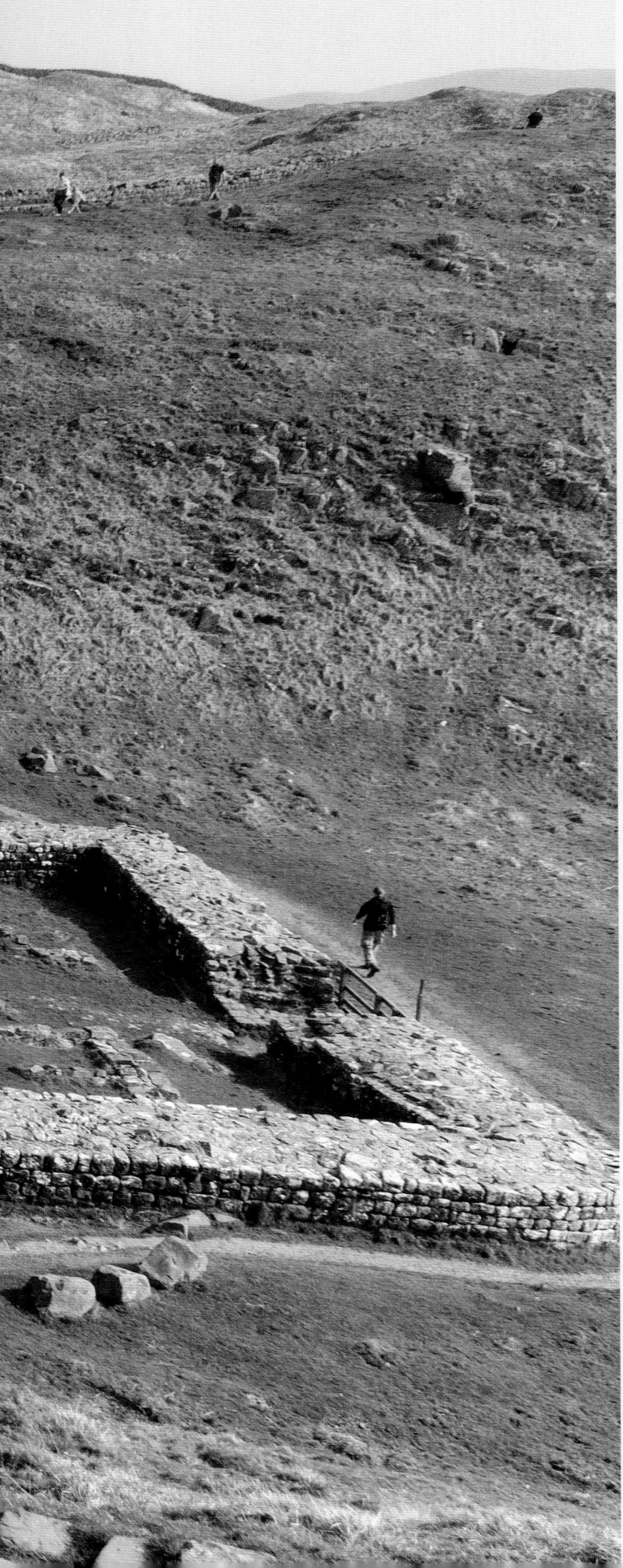

3

EUROPE AND NORTHERN ASIA

Europe inevitably forms the largest section of this book, because it was here that the discipline of archaeology was really developed, and because its countless sites span a colossal period from our early ancestors at Atapuerca through Ice Age art to prehistoric megalithic monuments and tombs, Bronze and Iron Age sites, and on into medieval times. But of course, a crucial component encompasses the prehistoric sites of the Aegean and those of the classical world, primarily in Greece and Italy. To many people, archaeology itself is exemplified by places such as Pompeii and the ruins of Athens and Rome.

Left The milecastle at Castle Nick, to the west of Housesteads Roman fort, provided a gateway through Hadrian's Wall in England.

EUROPE AND NORTHERN ASIA
LOCATIONS

1 TANUM
2 GAMLA UPPSALA
3 KING HARALD BLUETOOTH'S FORTRESSES
4 THE BOYNE VALLEY
5 HADRIAN'S WALL
6 STONEHENGE
7 CARNAC
8 COVALANAS
9 SIERRA DE ATAPUERCA
10 CÔA VALLEY
11 HOCHDORF
12 GERMANY'S NEANDERTHAL REMAINS
13 HALLSTATT
14 BISKUPIN
15 ROME
16 POMPEII
17 HERCULANEUM
18 ATHENS
19 OLYMPIA
20 CORINTH
21 DELPHI
22 AKROTIRI
23 MYCENAE
24 GOURNIA
25 KNOSSOS
26 PERGAMON
27 NOVGOROD
28 KHAKASIA
29 OGLAKHTY
30 TOMSKAYA PISANITSA

2
27
1
3
14
30
29
12
28
11
13
15
16
21
26
18
19
20
17
25
23
22
24

TANUM BRONZE AGE ROCK ART

TYPE: ROCK ART • **ARCHITECTURAL STYLE:** N/A
LOCATION: COASTAL SOUTHWEST SWEDEN • **CONSTRUCTION BEGUN:** CA. 1500 B.C.E.

On the west coast of Sweden facing the North Sea, in a region known as Bohuslän, granite outcrops scraped by retreating glaciers protrude from the wooded landscape. After the Ice Age, they lay close to the shoreline, but today they are found 80–100 ft (25–30 m) above sea level and some distance inland due to the rebound of the land from the weight of the ice. During the Bronze Age, about 1500 B.C.E., the inhabitants of southern Scandinavia used these outcrops as "canvases" on which to engrave hundreds of thousands of images.

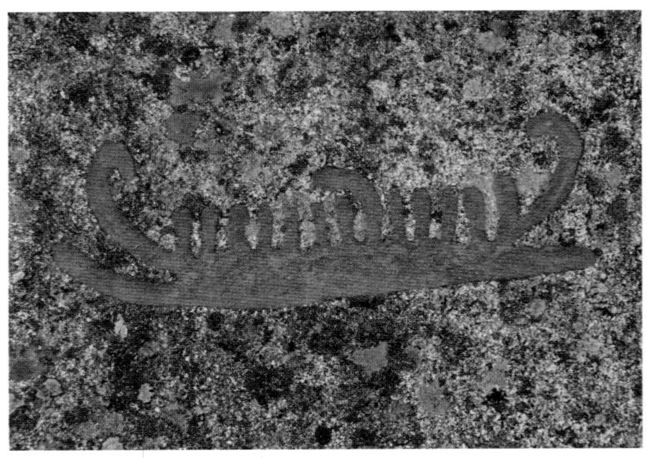

Bohuslän contains the densest concentration of Bronze Age rock art in Scandinavia, and the Tanum World Heritage site is the "capital" of rock art in Bohuslän. Several hundred distinct outcrops with engravings are known around Tanum, while many more certainly lie buried under soil and moss. Although many engravings are now filled with red or white paint to make them more visible they originally did not have any color to set them off from the surrounding rock.

Bronze Age rock artists made their carvings by pecking and grinding the rock surfaces with stone hammers and points. Even the simplest image required hours of work. The resulting complex compositions depict the Bronze Age world of their makers. Several thousand engravings of ships have been identified, reflecting the maritime life of these societies. The most common are ships with upward-curving prows and sterns. Many carry people—perhaps on expeditions. Engravings of humans are often conspicuously male. They carry weapons, pull plows, ride chariots, and play trumpets. Cattle, horses, deer, birds, and canines also appear. Beside these identifiable figures are abstract designs such as suns (or wheels) and spirals. Engravings of hands and feet appear frequently, as do cupmarks, or small pecked pits.

Archaeologists puzzle over whether the rock artists planned their images on the stone canvasses in one single

episode or added them sequentially to existing displays. Were these outcrops already special in some way, or did the engravings make them significant? It is clear that many depict scenes from everyday life, such as plowing, herding, hunting, and traveling by ship and wagon. Others appear to show rituals and processions, while images of fighting with spears and battleaxes reflect the institutionalized status of warriors in Bronze Age society.

Various interpretations of the Scandinavian rock art have been advanced, but no single theory accounts for everything. One possibility is that they formed backdrops to rituals such as initiations. Another is that they represented the creation of memories for future generations by commemorating life events, or to express a relationship between the worlds of the living and of deities or myths. Whatever it is trying to communicate, the Bronze Age rock art at Tanum, and elsewhere, provides modern-day visitors with a glimpse of the worldview and cosmology of a complex stratified society.

The 500 engravings on an outcrop at Vitlycke show the full portfolio of the Bronze Age artists. A short walk away, the Vitlycke Museum offers guided tours of nearby engraved outcrops. Other rock art panels can be reached from the museum by car or on hiking trails.

Opposite Rock carvings of warriors and a ship.

Above Composite images, such as warriors merged with ships, were perhaps intended to impart desirable qualities to individuals.

GAMLA UPPSALA
A LANDSCAPE OF POWER

TYPE: BURIAL MOUNDS AND ROYAL MANOR • **ARCHITECTURAL STYLE:** EARTHEN MOUNDS
LOCATION: EASTERN SWEDEN • **CONSTRUCTION BEGUN:** CA. 600 C.E.

Just over a mile (2 km) north of the modern city of Uppsala in eastern Sweden lies the ancient site of Gamla Uppsala (Old Uppsala). On a low ridge bounded on either side by farmland and pastures, several immense mounds dominate the site. Gamla Uppsala offers more than these great tumuli, however. The complex also includes smaller mounds, boat burials, flat burials, workshops, and settlements in use at various times during most of the first millennium of the Common Era.

The No. 2 bus from the Old Market in Uppsala brings the visitor to its final stop: Kungshögarna, the Royal Mounds. Three mounds—Västhögen, Mellanhögen, and Östhögen—dominate the landscape, surrounded by about 250 surviving smaller mounds. Östhögen, or East Mound, is the largest, currently about 30 ft (9 m) high and with an oval plan 180 ft (55 m) wide and 250 ft (75 m) long. In 1846–1847, the Swedish National Antiquary, Bror Emil Hildebrand (1806–1884), dug a tunnel 80 ft (25 m) into East Mound but found only burned bones and fragments of grave goods. Three decades later, he returned to dig an immense trench into Västhögen, or West Mound, where he found a similar array of fragmented artifacts and bones. At the time, Hildebrand was not impressed.

Although the artifacts and bones did not seem impressive in the mid-nineteenth century, their significance has since been realized. It is now thought that the mounds were built during the late sixth or early seventh century C.E. (previously they had been dated somewhat earlier). Fragments of ornamented bronze sheet in East Mound were probably decorations on a helmet. The individual in West Mound was an adult man buried with markers of high status, including a sword made in Western Europe with a handle ornamented by garnets set in gold. His ivory gaming pieces were possibly of late Roman origin. Although the artifacts were highly fragmented and burned, close examination reveals their artisanship and distant origins.

While mounds were built at Gamla Uppsala, the practice of burying nobility in complete boats with

lavish unburned grave goods began a tradition of boat burial that continued into Viking times. Two spectacular boat cemeteries lie a short distance north of Gamla Uppsala. At Välsgarde, fifteen boat burials are known. At Vendel, with fourteen boat burials, helmets have been found that have parallels with one found in the celebrated boat burial at Sutton Hoo in England.

Gamla Uppsala developed from a necropolis into a royal manor on a terraced area adjacent to the mounds. This complex included a great timber hall 165 ft (50 m) long and up to 40 ft (12 m) wide, and a workshop area yielding hundreds of garnets. Gamla Uppsala became a seat of both royal and religious power, mentioned in sagas and legends; it subsequently turned into a monumental national symbol in the nascent Swedish state, and today is a major tourist attraction. The Gamla Uppsala Museum sets the history of the site in its wider context, and visitors can walk along the ridge and around the mounds.

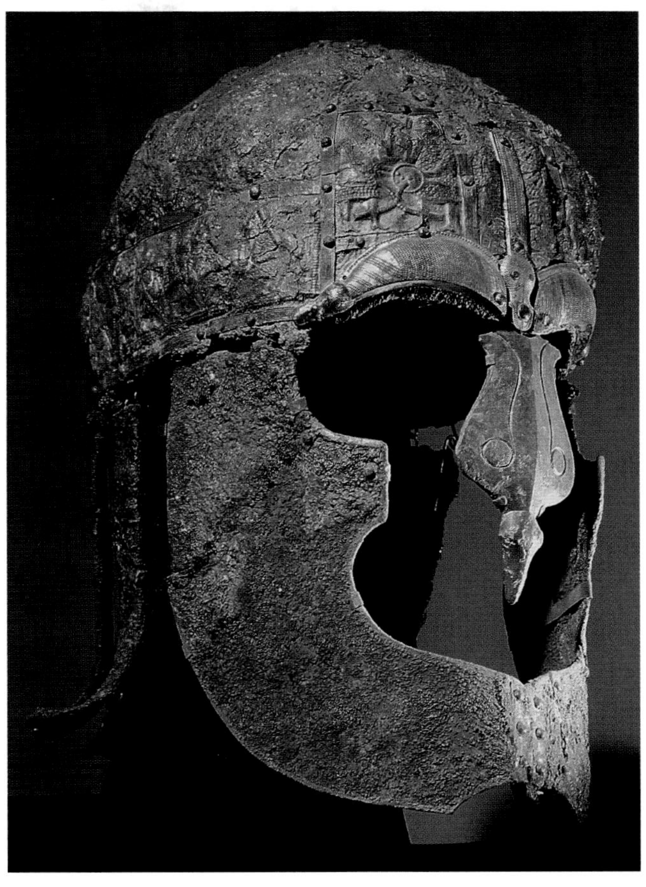

Right One of the helmets from the boat cemetery at Vendel.

Below Panorama, with the sun just visible, of Royal Mounds in Gamla Uppsala.

KING HARALD BLUETOOTH'S **FORTRESSES**

TYPE: FORTIFIED STRONGHOLD • **ARCHITECTURAL STYLE:** TIMBER RAMPARTS AND LONGHOUSES
LOCATION: ZEALAND, DENMARK • **CONSTRUCTION BEGUN:** 980 C.E.

About an hour's drive southwest from Copenhagen near Slagelse, not far from the west coast of the Danish island of Zealand, lies Trelleborg. This circular rampart is one of several fortresses that King Harald Bluetooth ordered to be constructed between 975 and 981 C.E. to consolidate his rule over Denmark and the adjacent part of southern Sweden. Others include Aggersborg and Fyrkat in northern Jutland, Nonnebakken on the island of Fyn, and Borgeby in southern Sweden.

Trelleborg is the best-studied of Harald's strongholds. It was first excavated in the 1930s, after a local motorbike club had rented the site and planned to turn it into a motocross track. What had been envisioned as a small rescue excavation turned into an archaeological project lasting many years.

Fortresses of the Trelleborg type are remarkably similar, indicating that they were built to a preordained plan using a fixed unit of measurement. Their earth and stone ramparts are perfectly round and surrounded by a moat. Aggersborg is the largest, nearly 800 ft (240 m) across, while Fyrkat and Nonnebakken are about 400 ft (120 m) in diameter. Trelleborg is slightly larger at 440 ft (134 m), with ramparts 15 ft (5 m) high. Inside the walls, they have symmetrical layouts. Starting with gates at the four points of the compass, main streets cross the interior, dividing it in four. Within each of these precincts, bow-sided longhouses are arranged to form quadrangles around interior courtyards.

Trelleborg was built on a peninsula by a swamp, which drained into a lake connected to the sea. Viking ships could navigate right up to the fortress. Dendrochronology (tree-ring dating) of wood from its moat indicates that it was cut in the winter of 980 C.E., so it is likely the rampart was built in the spring of 981. Trelleborg differs from the other ring fortresses in that it has a precinct outside the circular rampart with additional longhouses and a cemetery. A secondary rampart and ditch protect this external area and also block the peninsula on which the complex is located. It is thought this was added after the original fortress was built.

The function of these Viking fortresses is uncertain. A likely explanation is that they served as garrisons to control the local populations. Strangely, there is no mention of Trelleborg or the other fortresses in any documentary account, so it is believed that they were in use for a short time, perhaps ten to fifteen years. Today visitors can tour Trelleborg's rebuilt ramparts, where outlines of the longhouses have been marked with concrete posts and one has been reconstructed. Finds from the excavations are on display in a museum at Trelleborg and in the National Museum in Copenhagen. Fyrkat, north of Århus, has offers similar attractions for visitors.

Meanwhile, the memory of King Harald Bluetooth, who connected the small kingdoms of Denmark, lives on as the name for a wireless communication technology.

Opposite, clockwise from top left Aerial view of Trelleborg. Reconstructed gate. Reconstructed bow-sided longhouse. Outlines of the excavated houses.

A MONUMENTAL LANDSCAPE IN **THE BOYNE VALLEY**

TYPE: BURIAL MOUNDS, TIMBER AND DITCH ENCLOSURES • **ARCHITECTURAL STYLE:** MOUNDED EARTH WITH ENGRAVED STONES • **LOCATION:** EASTERN IRELAND • **CONSTRUCTION BEGUN:** CA. 3500 B.C.E.

At dawn on the winter solstice (and on a couple of days before and after), the rising sun shines down a passage into the burial chamber of Newgrange at the Bend of the Boyne in the Republic of Ireland. Two more passage tombs are located nearby. Along with Newgrange, they represent three of the most significant passage tombs in Western Europe.

The Bend of the Boyne, or Brú na Bóinne in Irish, is a broad loop of the Boyne River, which flows languidly through the countryside north of Dublin before reaching the Irish Sea east of Drogheda. Just west of the M1 motorway, the bend gives its name to the surrounding area. In recent years, as well as being celebrated as the location of these three passage tombs, it has been shown to contain a vast ceremonial landscape that also features timber circles and ditched enclosures.

Ancient peoples constructed passage tombs from large slabs of stone set upright and roofed over with even larger blocks, to form a tunnel-like corridor leading into a central burial chamber in which they placed cremated bones. Originally, they covered passages and chambers with mounds of earth and stones, but over the millennia the mounds have become eroded or material has been carried off for other uses. In Ireland, four major passage tomb cemeteries form a chain across the island, from Carrowmore and Carrowkeel in

the west to Loughcrew and the Bend of the Boyne in the east. All date from the second half of the fourth millennium B.C.E.

At the Bend of the Boyne, the passage tombs of Knowth, Dowth, and Newgrange lie a short distance apart, each on a high spot in the landscape. Newgrange is the most famous, an immense mound about 280 ft (85 m) in diameter outlined by ninety-seven oblong blocks of stone, many carved with curvilinear designs. After excavations in the 1960s and 1970s, Newgrange was controversially reconstructed. Bright quartz pieces lying beside the mound were interpreted, probably implausably, as having originally formed a wall, so the gleaming reconstructed facade of Newgrange looks like no other passage tomb.

The burial complex at Knowth has also been reconstructed, but much less fancifully than Newgrange. The main mound, 227 ft (67 m) across, contains two independent passages leading to separate chambers, one from the east side, and the other from the west. The stones of Knowth, including 127 curbstones averaging about 6 ft (2 m) in length, abound with engravings of spirals, sunbursts, and other abstract motifs. Seventeen smaller tombs surround the main mound, along with later prehistoric features that include a timber circle from the third millennium B.C.E.

Dowth is the least studied of the Boyne passage graves. It is not reconstructed, and a crater caused by nineteenth-century excavation has never been filled. Dowth also contains two separate passages and burial chambers, each entering at the west side of the mound. Near the Dowth mound, renovations at the eighteenth-century manor house of Dowth Hall have since revealed an additional small passage tomb about half the diameter of Newgrange, but also with decorated curbstones.

Opposite Newgrange's circular facade.

Right, from top Iconic engraving on stone in the Newgrange passage. Newgrange entrance. Roof of the burial chamber at Newgrange.

Farther Afield

The summer of 2018 was extremely dry in Ireland. Anthony Murphy, a journalist and photographer from Drogheda, brought his camera drone out to the Brú na Bóinne to shoot aerial photos of some of the monuments. In a field not far from Newgrange, Murphy spotted the cropmarks of a hitherto-unknown monument, consisting of a double circle of short-ditch segments about 500 ft (154 m) in diameter, surrounded by a double outer circle of posts. Rapidly nicknamed "Dronehenge," this new monument appears to be the remains of bedding trenches for timber posts that formed two concentric rings.

Aerial and geophysical surveys have revealed many other timber circles or ditched enclosures on the Bend of the Boyne. Most date to the same period as the passage tombs, while some are slightly earlier or later.

Far from being simply a megalithic cemetery, it now appears that the Bend of the Boyne was a vast ritual landscape with both tombs and enclosures, joining comparable complexes at Stonehenge, Carnac, and Orkney in reflecting the spiritual and social lives of the inhabitants of northwestern Europe between 3500 and 2000 B.C.E.

Today, visitors can enter this world through the Brú na Bóinne Visitor Centre, from which shuttle buses depart for Newgrange and Knowth. Here they can also see exhibits that explain the sites in detail, as well as enter a lottery to be one of the few individuals allowed to enter the Newgrange chamber on the winter solstice.

Above Knowth and its satellite tombs.

Left Engraved curbstone at Newgrange.

BUILDING **HADRIAN'S WALL**

TYPE: MILITARY • **ARCHITECTURAL STYLE:** ROMAN
LOCATION: NORTHUMBERLAND AND CUMBRIA, ENGLAND • **CONSTRUCTION BEGUN:** 122 C.E.

The extensive frontier system established by the Roman Emperor Hadrian (76–138 C.E.) in 122 C.E. cuts across some of the most rugged landscapes in Britain. The most dramatic sections were built along the crags of the Whin Sill. Hadrian's Wall runs 80 Roman miles (73 miles/117 km) from Wallsend on the river Tyne on the east to Bowness-on-Solway on the broad estuary on the west.

The original plan seems to have been for a wall with small garrisons placed in so-called milecastles and two turrets placed in the intervening sections. This pattern continued, without a wall, along the Cumbrian coast in the west. One of the best preserved milecastles in this coastal section remains at Swarthy Hill, to the north of Maryport; it sits on a small hill and provides clear views across the Solway Firth to Scotland.

The main part of the frontier consisted of a ditch to the north, a wall, and then a flat-bottomed ditch with two raised mounds on either side (known as the vallum) to the south. One of the crossing points of the vallum, complete with the foundations of a monumental gateway, has been preserved to the south of the fort at Benwell in the western suburbs of the city of Newcastle. The western sections of the wall were originally constructed in turf. Some sections, running in parallel with the later stone wall, can still be detected just to the west of where the frontier crossed the Irthing River near the fort of Birdoswald (west of the modern village of Gilsland).

It was only after work started on the wall that the decision was made to bring the major garrisons for the frontier onto the line of the wall. One of the best-excavated forts lies at Chesters, 5 miles (8 km) north of Hexham. The cavalry unit based here protected the crossing of the North Tyne River—remains of the bridge

Above Milecastles like this at Cawfields Crag housed small numbers of men to secure the frontier.

Opposite Larger military garrisons were placed in forts such as this one found at Housesteads.

that formed the frontier are still visible. A well-preserved bathhouse is located near the river on the east side of the fort, as is the house for the commanding officer of the unit.

Some of the most challenging sections of the wall were in its central section, along the craggy Whin Sill. One of the most visible remaining infantry forts lies at Housesteads, about 5 miles (8 km) north of Bardon Mill, at the eastern end of this section, with commanding views to the north. Two well-preserved milecastles also remain in this section, at Castle Nick and Cawfields.

The path of the original frontier was based on that of a road, later known as the Stanegate, which ran to the south of the wall. This was guarded by a series of forts. One of the best preserved is at Vindolanda (southwest of Housesteads). Parts of the fort have yielded important organic materials, as well as some of the archive of the Roman unit (and the commanding officer's archive) that provide insights into garrison life in northern Britain.

At Carrawburgh, an infantry fort in the eastern central section of the wall, 3.7 miles (6 km) west of Chesters, excavations have revealed a small temple dedicated to the eastern god Mithras. This deity was popular on the Roman frontiers.

The best way to see the wall is to walk (boots are sensible). The AD 122 bus service runs from Easter to September on the road immediately behind the wall. This connects with the Tyne Valley railway at Hexham. Visitors should go to the Great North Museum, an easy walk from the Haymarket station on the Newcastle Metro, or the Tullie House Museum in Carlisle.

STONEHENGE
AND ITS RITUAL LANDSCAPE

TYPE: ALIGNMENTS OF STANDNG STONES • **ARCHITECTURAL STYLE:** MEGALITHIC
LOCATION: SOUTHWEST ENGLAND • **CONSTRUCTION BEGUN:** AROUND 3000 B.C.E

Standing tall and enigmatic, some 85 miles (136 km) west of London, the standing stones of Stonehenge on Salisbury Plain are among the world's most iconic archaeological monuments. Rivaled only by the Pyramids at Giza, the Acropolis in Athens, and the Cliff Palace at Mesa Verde, they have been a subject of fascination for centuries. Recently, however, archaeologists have realized that this stone circle is just one part of a huge ritual precinct where people congregated during the third millennium B.C.E.

The story of Stonehenge is one of increasing complexity, paralleled by other ceremonial landscapes such as those at the Boyne Valley, Carnac, and Orkney. It seems the stones visible today represent only the final construction phase of a monument that was reconfigured repeatedly over several centuries.

The story of Stonehenge has long concentrated on the famous stone circle itself: how it was built and for what purpose. Beginning around 3000 B.C.E., the first project at Stonehenge involved digging a circular ditch about 330 ft (100 m) across and piling up a bank outside the circle. (The term "–henge" derives from an ancient Saxon word meaning "hanging," perhaps due to a resemblance to gallows. Now the term refers to ditched enclosures with the bank outside the ditch.) Around the interior, upright bluestones were placed into fifty-six holes called Aubrey Holes. Transporting the bluestones may have been a ritual

Below Cloudy sunrise over Stonehenge.
Opposite Overhead view showing ditch and bank.

in itself. Quarried in the Preseli Mountains in southern Wales, about 125 miles (200 km) away, they journeyed along trails to the Welsh coast, across the Severn Estuary by boat, and then overland to the Salisbury Plain. From the beginning, Stonehenge was a cemetery, with the total number of cremation graves estimated at between 150 and 250 over several centuries.

The first configuration of Stonehenge lasted nearly 500 years, until the middle of the third millennium B.C.E. Between 2600 and 2400 B.C.E., it assumed the form that would be recognizable today, with the erection of the major upright stones and lintels. The stones used for these are called sarsens, common sandstone boulders from the Marlborough Downs about 20 miles (30 km) away. Their sheer size required immense effort by people and animals as well as sophisticated engineering techniques to drag them across the landscape and put them in position.

Starting from the center, a horseshoe configuration of pairs of immense vertical sarsens connected by horizontal lintels was erected. Five such "trilithons" were built. This operation is even more impressive because the lintels have sockets in the underside that needed to be located precisely over posts on the tops of the uprights before being lowered into place. Bluestones pulled out of the Aubrey Holes were arranged in arcs around the trilithons. Finally, a circle of upright sarsens with continuous lintels was erected to enclose the trilithons and bluestones. At the same time, several other bluestones were set in place along the ditch and beyond. The most important of these is the Heel Stone, located outside the enclosure.

Over the next several centuries, the bluestones were rearranged several times and the ditch recut. More circles of holes were dug outside the sarsen circle, but stones apparently were not placed in them. Ritual activity finally stopped around 1600 B.C.E. Stonehenge sat silent for several millennia, although it remained conspicuous in the landscape.

Beyond the Stone Circle

What was the purpose of Stonehenge? The question has challenged archaeologists for centuries. It was certainly a place of burial, but who could be buried there? The standing stones have astronomical alignments, including the celebrated summer solstice sunrise over the Heel Stone and the lesser-known midwinter solstice sunset. Theories advanced in the 1960s, that Stonehenge was some sort of calendar or observatory, are now considered overblown. Prehistoric people often aligned their monuments on significant annual celestial events.

More clues to Stonehenge's function come from the surrounding countryside. The area around Stonehenge had already seen considerable prehistoric activity by Mesolithic hunter-gatherers and Neolithic farmers. Modification of the surrounding landscape began several centuries before the first stones were installed at Stonehenge itself.

Beneath an immense henge with timber circles at Durrington Walls, 2 miles (3.2 km) northeast of Stonehenge by the Avon River, traces of a large settlement contemporaneous with the major construction phase at Stonehenge have been found. Vast quantities of cattle and pig bones suggest that feasting took place. The settlement at Durrington Walls has been interpreted as an encampment of pilgrims, perhaps even the builders of Stonehenge, who made a spiritual journey to the ceremonial precinct.

Today's pilgrims to Stonehenge arrive by car via the A303 road or by bus departing from Salisbury, about 10 miles (16 km) to the south. From the visitor center, a bus can be taken to the henge itself. At Durrington Walls, about 10 minutes away, a signposted walking trail leads visitors through a section of the Stonehenge landscape.

Opposite Reconstruction showing the settlement at Durrington Walls near Stonehenge in about 2500 B.C.E.
Below Stonehenge sarsens with their lintels.

THE EVOCATIVE STONES OF **CARNAC**

TYPE: ALIGNMENTS OF STANDNG STONES • **ARCHITECTURAL STYLE:** MEGALITHIC
LOCATION: SOUTHERN BRITTANY, FRANCE • **CONSTRUCTION BEGUN:** BEFORE 3000 B.C.E.

When the cyclists riding in the Tour de France visit southern Brittany and its picturesque seascapes, they often pass close to one of the most remarkable concentrations of prehistoric monuments in Europe: Carnac. The area around this small seaside resort was the focus of intense activity more than 5,000 years ago, with dozens of ancient sites in an area measuring 116 sq mi (300 sq km). Many of these sites are tombs, both long mounds and passage graves, but Carnac itself is best known for several sets of parallel standing stones, called menhirs, that extend over half a mile (0.8 km) in places.

The word "menhir" is drawn from an ancient Breton word meaning "long stone," set upright into a hole and often reaching several feet in height. Such standing stones are found throughout Atlantic Europe dating from the Neolithic period and into the Bronze Age. Their true significance is a mystery, although archaeologists presume some sort of ritual activities occurred in association with them.

Of the eleven or more alignments in the Carnac area, the four most important are called Kerzerho, Kermario, Le Ménec, and Kerlescan. The last three are very close to the town of Carnac, while Kerzerho is about 5 miles (8 km) to the northwest near Erdeven. Of these, Kerzerho is the longest, with ten rows of more than 1,100 stones stretching over 1.25 miles (2 km), although many have disappeared in the last 150 years. Among them is a row of immense menhirs, the Giants of Kerzerho, which stand up nearly 20 ft (6 m) tall.

Kermario, Le Ménec, and Kerlescan are better known, but each one is complicated in its own way. Kermario has between seven and ten rows at any one point, running up to 0.7 miles (1.2 km) long with 1,029 surviving stones, while Le Ménec consists of ten to twelve slightly converging rows about 0.62 mile (1 km) long, containing 1,069 stones. More compact at 1,165 ft (355 m) long and 456 ft (139 m) wide, Kerlescan has 555 menhirs in twelve to thirteen rows. Le Ménec and Kermario, along with Kerzerho, are oriented west–southwest to east–northeast, although the irregularity of the alignments and their angled rows means that this should not be taken to indicate an interest in astronomical events other than, perhaps, sunrise or sunset.

The exact purpose of the Carnac alignments is unknown. There were clearly intentional choices in the sizes of certain menhirs, such as the Giants of Kerzerho, and in their siting. For example, at Kerlescan, larger stones are concentrated at one end of the rows and gradually get smaller toward the other end. The alignments at Le Ménec and Kerlescan terminate in enclosures defined by additional standing stones. One popular interpretation is that the Carnac alignments were processional paths that led to stone enclosures in which rituals occurred.

The Carnac alignments were the final element in a vast ritual landscape that began at least a millennium earlier, incorporating immense earthen mounds, tall single menhirs, and chambered tombs. Like the Boyne Valley in Ireland, Orkney at the northern tip

of the British Isles, and the Stonehenge environs, the constructed landscape around Carnac is another example of the deep, long-term engagement by Neolithic peoples in ceremony and symbolism.

Carnac lies about five hours by car from Paris and under two hours from Nantes. Route D196, "Route of the Alignments," brings the visitor to Maison des Mégalithes (House of the Megaliths) and the visitor center. Be sure to visit other megalithic monuments in the Morbihan region, which are spectacular in their own right.

Above View of the Carnac stones.

COVALANAS CAVE ART

TYPE: DECORATED CAVE • **ARCHITECTURAL STYLE:** N/A
LOCATION: RAMALES, CANTABRIA, SPAIN • **CONSTRUCTION BEGUN:** AROUND 22,000 YEARS AGO

Around fifty of the decorated caves of the last Ice Age are open to the public. Of these, one of the most moving and rewarding to visit is Covalanas, in northern Spain, near the town of Ramales. Reaching the cave involves a steep climb up a track about half a mile (600 m) long, but the journey is well worth the effort. The cave is small, dry, and pristine, with no staircases or electric light. Visitors see it as it would have been seen in the Ice Age, and can get extremely close to the art.

This art was discovered on September 11, 1903, making it the second decorated cave to be discovered in Spain after Altamira. Excavations in its entrance chamber found virtually nothing—this was not a cave that was ever occupied, but a cave visited for artistic purposes only. The large El Mirón Cave, directly below it, was the major occupation site of this area, and presumably it was one of the inhabitants of that site who made his or her way up the cliff to this small cavity and decided to decorate it.

The details of technique, content, and style make it highly probable that all of the figures in Covalanas Cave were made by a single person in one artistic episode, thought to have taken place in the Solutrean period (ca. 20,000–22,000 years ago). The animal figures are all drawn using the same technique—rendered in outline with dots of iron oxide (red ocher or hematite). Some dots were clearly applied with fingers, others with the more flexible thumb; some are very separate, others juxtaposed. Using this deceptively simple technique the artist managed to express tremendous variety in posture, perspective, and movement.

For a long time, historians considered this technique to be the work of a single artist or perhaps a school. However, since the discovery of the same technique in other caves, it has become clear that this was a regional and chronological phenomenon, and that it was widespread in northern Spain at one time.

The artist clearly studied Covalanas Cave carefully before drawing the figures; there are signs of planning and symmetry. The images begin some way into the cave, after a point where you are walking on the original floor level. It is noticeable that they occur in the part that is narrowest and highest.

Almost all the animals drawn on both walls are female red deer (seventeen in all), although one larger deer on the right wall is thought to be a male, which has shed its antlers, because of its musculature. A large animal on the left wall, probably an aurochs, displays a masterly use of the rock shape for its body. The best group of females on the right wall displays twisted perspective (the bodies in profile, but both ears visible) and superimposition, while one animal is looking back over its shoulder. Toward the end of the gallery is a large horse, with a flowing mane and a long tail.

Opposite The horse and two of the female deer in Covalanas.

HUMAN FOSSILS AT **SIERRA DE ATAPUERCA**

TYPE: NATURAL CAVES AND ROCK SHELTERS • **ARCHITECTURAL STYLE:** N/A
LOCATION: BURGOS, SPAIN • **CONSTRUCTION BEGUN:** N/A

The mountains 5.4 miles (14 km) east of the Spanish city of Burgos have yielded some of the richest and most informative collections of human fossils in the world. Although today a dry upland, during the Pleistocene (Ice Age) the limestone supported a verdant landscape, well watered by rivers and springs, with an abundant fauna that formed rich hunting and scavenging for early humans in the Lower, Middle, and Upper Pleistocene.

A series of caves, shafts, and rock shelters formed, exposed and filled by river action over this period, their sediments revealing human and animal bones and stone tools spanning the Palaeolithic to the Bronze Age. The oldest deposits belong to the Trinchera del Ferrocarril (Trench), the wide railway cutting that exposed deep sections through the karst and brought to light its sedimentary fills, now excavated in several locations. Of those that are visible from the path, the oldest are the Gran Dolina and Sima del Elefante, two deep shafts that together span the period from 1.2–0.1 million years ago (mya). The remains of at least eleven humans from these shafts form the definitive fossils for the archaic *Homo antecessor*, and stone-tool cutmarks on their bones show that some were cannibalized. Simple stone tools and butchered animal bones show that this tall, muscular human was exploiting the rich opportunities of the area, including the carcasses of large red deer- and bisonlike animals, although the presence of carnivores such as large panthers and hyenas shows that competition for carcasses was intense. A third visible sequence is in the Galería, dating to 0.5–0.2 mya, the oldest levels of which overlap with the youngest at the Dolina and Elefante sites. Early Neanderthals—probably the descendants of

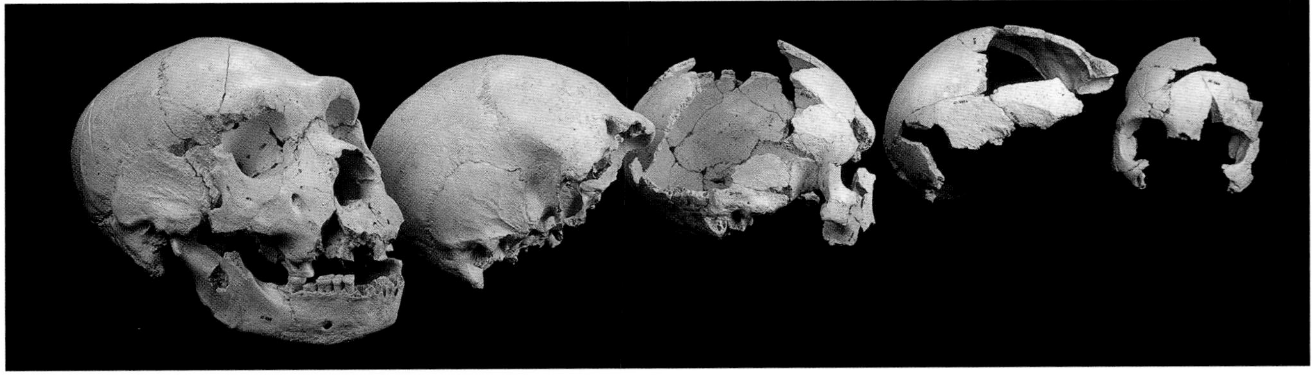

the earlier populations—used this cave repeatedly as a shelter in which to butcher the carcasses of animals that had fallen down into this natural trap. In its oldest levels they used the Acheulean hand-ax toolkit, evolving over time to the flake-based tools of its uppermost levels, which are more characteristic of classic Neanderthals.

Although inaccessible to the public, 0.5 mya deposits in the Sima de los Huesos (Pit of the Bones) have yielded one of the richest collections of human fossil remains in the world. These are best explored in the museum in Burgos. The pit's sediments include the remains of at least twenty-eight individuals of the archaic human *Homo heidelbergensis*, perhaps deliberately placed around what was originally a deep shaft opening into daylight.

Atapuerca continues to yield up its secrets, with human remains coming to light in the Cueva del Fantasma, probably intermediate in age between the Gran Dolina and Sima de los Huesos, and the Cueva del Mirador, so far the youngest of the sequence.

A walking route through the Trench takes the visitor past several of the sites. The Museum of Human Evolution in the city of Burgos contains extensive displays of the main stone and bone finds from Atapuerca's sites.

Opposite Some of the skulls extracted from the Sima de los Huesos.

Above, left and right The Galeria and the Sima del Elefante in the trench.

ICE AGE ROCK ART IN THE **CÔA VALLEY**

TYPE: OPEN-AIR ROCK ART • **ARCHITECTURAL STYLE:** N/A
LOCATION: VILA NOVA DE FOZ CÔA, PORTUGAL • **CONSTRUCTION BEGUN:** AROUND 30,000 YEARS AGO

Numerous pecked animal images and fine incisions populate the fractured vertical schist rocks flanking this tributary of the Douro River in northeast Portugal. Collectively, they represent the biggest known display of open-air Ice Age art in the world.

In 1989, preparations began on the construction of a huge dam along the Côa River, set to raise the river's water level by about 330 ft (100 m). It was during the ensuing archaeological survey of the region that these Ice Age rock carvings were first noticed. By 1994, news of the growing number of discoveries had reached the outside world, and specialists from around the globe, together with many local people—not least the schoolchildren of Vila Nova de Foz Côa—began a campaign to try and preserve this unique resource. This seemed an impossible task, since work on the dam was already well underway, and millions had already been spent. Nevertheless, thanks to the campaign, and to a change of government, the dam was indeed halted at the end of 1995. The area subsequently became an archaeological park and gained UNESCO World Heritage site status in 1998.

Today work continues on discovering and studying the valley's art, which is scattered over a distance of 10.6 miles (17 km). Three important concentrations of petroglyphs are open to the public here, providing an excellent sample of this remarkable art.

At Canada do Inferno, it is known that many figures are already beneath the water, the Pocinho Dam, constructed in the 1980s, having raised the river's level by several feet. But many remain visible to the visitor, both on the riverbank and up the rocky slope—primarily aurochs, horses, and ibex, the three most common species depicted in the Côa Valley.

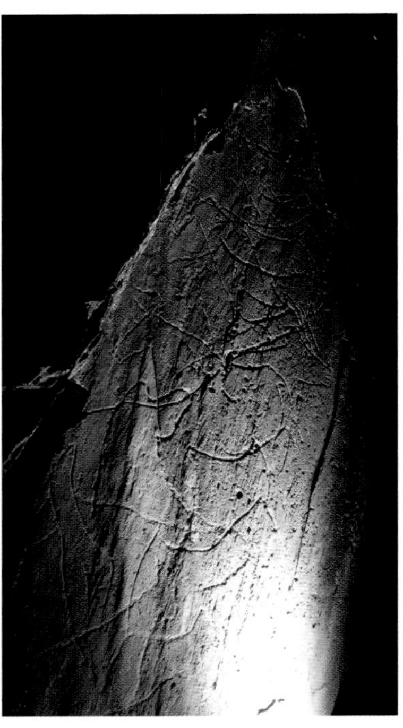

Left A petroglyph panel at Penascosa, seen at night, comprising mostly aurochs.

Opposite Another panel at Penascosa, showing two horses and two ibex.

At Penascosa, on a rock above the parking area, stands a large stag figure, abraded onto the rock rather than pecked. Farther on is a splendid panel of aurochs, horses, and ibex, while several other major collections of similar animal figures are visible farther on still, at different levels. These include a large horse figure, facing left. Below it is a fish depiction. Nearby is a horse with three heads in different positions—a characteristic feature of Côa art.

Nighttime visits to Penascosa are recommended, as the figures are far easier to see under artificial light.

At Ribeira de Piscos is a wonderful composition of two horses facing each other and with overlapping heads. Farther on, rocks bear fine figures of two aurochs as well as a remarkable ithyphallic human figure. Huge aurochs figures dominate the river at the confluence and must originally have been visible from quite a distance.

On stylistic grounds, the Côa art has been attributed to a period from the Gravettian (ca. 30,000 years ago) to the Magdalenian (ca. 12,000 years ago). Excavations of occupation sites in the area have fully confirmed this attribution.

In 2010 a magnificent new museum opened just outside Vila Nova de Foz Côa, dedicated to the region's rock art. It also houses a shop and restaurant. All visits to the sites leave from the museum in official vehicles.

HOCHDORF'S IRON AGE CHIEF

TYPE: BURIAL MOUND WITH TIMBER CHAMBER • **ARCHITECTURAL STYLE:** MOUNDED EARTH
LOCATION: SOUTHWEST GERMANY, NEAR STUTTGART • **CONSTRUCTION BEGUN:** CA. 530 B.C.E.

Just before 500 B.C.E., tremendous wealth poured into the area of today's southwest Germany and eastern France. Iron Age elites had established contact with Greek trading colonies on the Mediterranean coast, specifically at Massalia (modern Marseille). In exchange for luxury goods from workshops in Italy and wine, they supplied food, furs, and slaves to the Greeks. Their accumulated wealth was buried with them.

In 1977, archaeologists excavated a burial mound just outside the town of Hochdorf an der Enz, northwest of Stuttgart. Originally measuring some 20 ft (6 m) high and around 200 ft (60 m) across, it had been reduced in height by plowing and was barely visible. Most important, it had not been robbed in antiquity, as was the fate of so many contemporaneous burial mounds.

Excavations revealed a pit extending about 8 ft (2.5 m) below the original ground surface, measuring about 36 sq ft (11 sq m). Within this pit were two nested timber boxes with wooden roofs. The outer box measured 25 sq ft (7.5 sq m) and 5 ft (1.5 m) deep, and the inner box measured 15 sq ft (5.7 sq m) and contained the burial and grave goods. The space between the boxes was filled with stones, while more rocks were piled over the roof. Unfortunately, the builders misjudged the ability of the roof to bear the load, and it collapsed into the burial chamber. This misfortune was beneficial in that it caused perishable items to become waterlogged and thus preserved. In addition, if looters had managed to dig through the earthen mound, the jumble of rocks over the occupant of the tomb and his sumptuous grave goods would have deterred them.

A man about forty years old lay on a bronze couch decorated in repoussé dimples with scenes of wagons and dancers. The eight legs of the couch were figures of women with upraised arms, and casters under their feet permitted the couch to be rolled. The man's clothing and leather shoes were decorated with gold bands, and he wore a gold neckring and bracelets, about 21 oz (600 g) of gold in all.

By the foot of the couch sat a large bronze cauldron, probably made in a workshop in southern Italy. Figures of lions adorned its rim and it held around 130 gallons (500 litres). Inside was a small gold bowl. The cauldron contained residue from mead, made from fermented honey. Perhaps the nine drinking horns that hung on

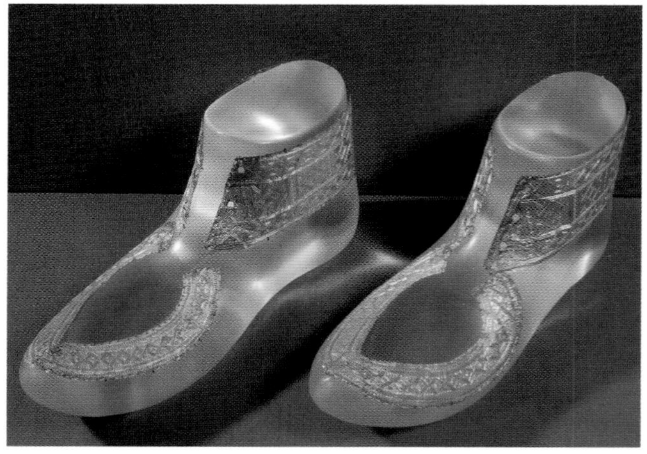

the fabric-draped walls of the burial chamber were filled from this cauldron. Across the chamber from the couch a four-wheeled wagon served as a platform for additional grave goods, including nine sets of bronze dishes, all wrapped in cloth.

Down the street from the Hochdorf mound, the Keltenmuseum houses a reconstruction of the burial chamber and its finds. A metal arch gives visitors to the site an impression of the original dimensions of the mound. Next to the museum is a replica of an Iron Age farmstead based on excavations in nearby fields. Hochdorf is about a half-hour by car from Stuttgart via route B10. You can also get there by bus from the train station at Vaihingen an der Enz. A short walk from the museum past the cemetery brings the visitor to the rebuilt mound.

Opposite Gold trim originally on Hochdorf shoes.
Above The restored Hochdorf mound.

GERMANY'S NEANDERTHAL REMAINS

TYPE: NATURAL CAVES AND ROCK SHELTERS • **ARCHITECTURAL STYLE:** N/A
LOCATION: METTMANN, NEAR DÜSSELDORF, GERMANY • **CONSTRUCTION BEGUN:** N/A

Since the discovery in August 1856 of the skeleton of the Neanderthal type specimen near Düsseldorf, Germany's Neander Valley (*Thal*) has been synonymous with our biological sister group: *Homo neanderthalensis*—the Neanderthal.

The steep-sided little valley, pocked with caves and rock shelters, was a celebrated beauty spot, but was progressively destroyed throughout the 1850s to satisfy the demands for limestone for Prussian construction. By the mid-decade, quarrymen had reached the Kleine Feldhoffer Grotte, a very small cave close to the valley top. Fortunately they would clear sediments from the caves by hand prior to dynamiting the rock, and as they worked, part of a skull and several bones of the body of an adult were dislodged and fell downslope, coming to rest in the rubble below. The quarry directors spotted them. Thinking they were of a cave bear, they set aside the remains to show to a local schoolteacher, Johann Carl Fuhlrott, who collected the more interesting of the valley's bones for discussion in natural history classes with his schoolchildren. To his everlasting credit, Fuhlrott realized the bones belonged not to a cave bear, but to an anatomically primitive human, of the sort that scientists like Charles Darwin were beginning to predict should be found in Ice Age deposits. In fact, several had been unearthed already: a jaw from Engis Cave in Belgium and a cranium from Gibraltar had come to light several decades beforehand, but natural scientists were not then ready to understand that humans had evolved and had once been incredibly diverse.

By 1856 science was ready. Fuhlrott contacted a professor of anatomy at Bonn University, Hermann

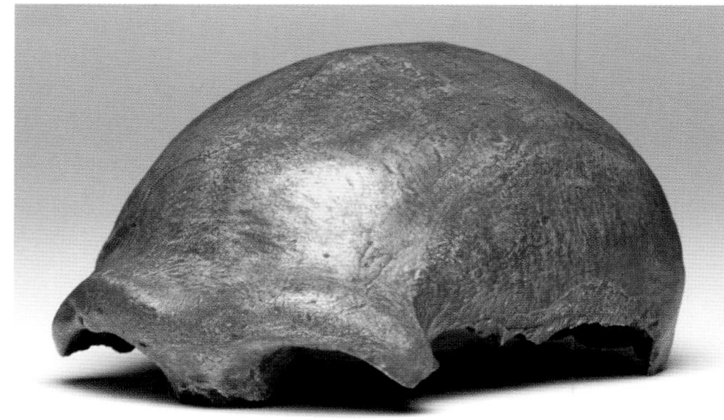

Schaaffhausen (1816–1893), who confirmed that the bones belonged to an adult with a distinct anatomy, and the two published details of the remains in 1857. In 1862 an Irish anatomist, William King (1809–1886), gave the remains their formal name, *Homo neanderthalensis*. The cave's location, now quarried away, was forgotten, and the smaller fragments of bones remained where they lay, covered in quarrying rubble. Originally buried by his group, his head facing the 10-ft-wide (3 m) cave mouth, Neanderthal 1, as he became known to science, is one of the most pathological Neanderthals known, attesting to the hard life they lived. Before he died, at around the age of forty, he had fractured his arm, which had healed with a deformity; fractured his head in a fall; suffered with bad sinuses; and had an unknown bone-eating disease.

Radiocarbon dating has established he lived to adulthood around 40,000 years ago, shortly before the Neanderthals became extinct. Later re-excavation of the cave's spoil recovered many bone fragments, deriving from at least three Neanderthals, as well as stone tools that show it was also used as a campsite. Remarkably, Neanderthal 1's humerus preserved DNA, ensuring a double significance as the first Neanderthal remains to be recognized and one of the few used to sequence ancient DNA from a distinct human biological group.

The valley remains a pleasant spot, and the site of the Feldhoffer cave is marked. In the vicinity, the Neanderthal Museum presents the history of the site and the relevance of its finds for human evolution. Both are near Mettmann, but the original bones from the site are housed in the LVR-Landesmuseum in Bonn.

Opposite The original skullcap from Neanderthal 1, now in the Landesmuseum, Bonn.

Below An aerial view of the Neander Valley.

SALT AND WEALTH AT **HALLSTATT**

TYPE: SALT MINES AND CEMETERY • **ARCHITECTURAL STYLE:** N/A
LOCATION: AUSTRIAN ALPS • **CONSTRUCTION BEGUN:** CA. 1300 B.C.E.

Since the middle of the nineteenth century, a series of excavations at the Hallstatt cemetery, high up in the Austrian Alps, have yielded evidence of an ancient mining community made rich on the proceeds of salt.

Prehistoric miners at Hallstatt and other locations among the Austrian Alps south of Salzburg extracted vast quantities of rock salt that could be traded throughout central Europe. Salt was an essential commodity for preserving meat and fish. People and lactating cattle also crave salt in their diets. By the beginning of the first millennium B.C.E., demand for salt had reached such a level that communities that could produce it in pure form could become very wealthy. In the Alps, some mountains sat atop immense quantities of crystalline salt deposited when an ocean covered the area millions of years ago. In some places, these deposits could be reached by tunneling from the surface.

At Hallstatt, a high Alpine valley overlooks a deep lake. Under the adjacent mountains, immense quantities of crystalline salt were deposited when an ocean covered the area millions of years ago. During the second millennium B.C.E., Bronze Age miners began tunneling into the mountainside to follow veins of salt. In doing so, they left behind traces of their presence. The veins are up to 16 ft (5 m) thick, so miners used notched logs as ladders to reach their tops, while a remarkable wooden staircase was built about 1343 B.C.E. to move between levels. Cloth, leather, and wood artifacts were preserved in the salt and rediscovered by later miners.

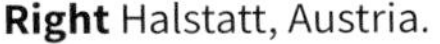

Right Halstatt, Austria.
Opposite Example of Ramsauer's burial documentation.

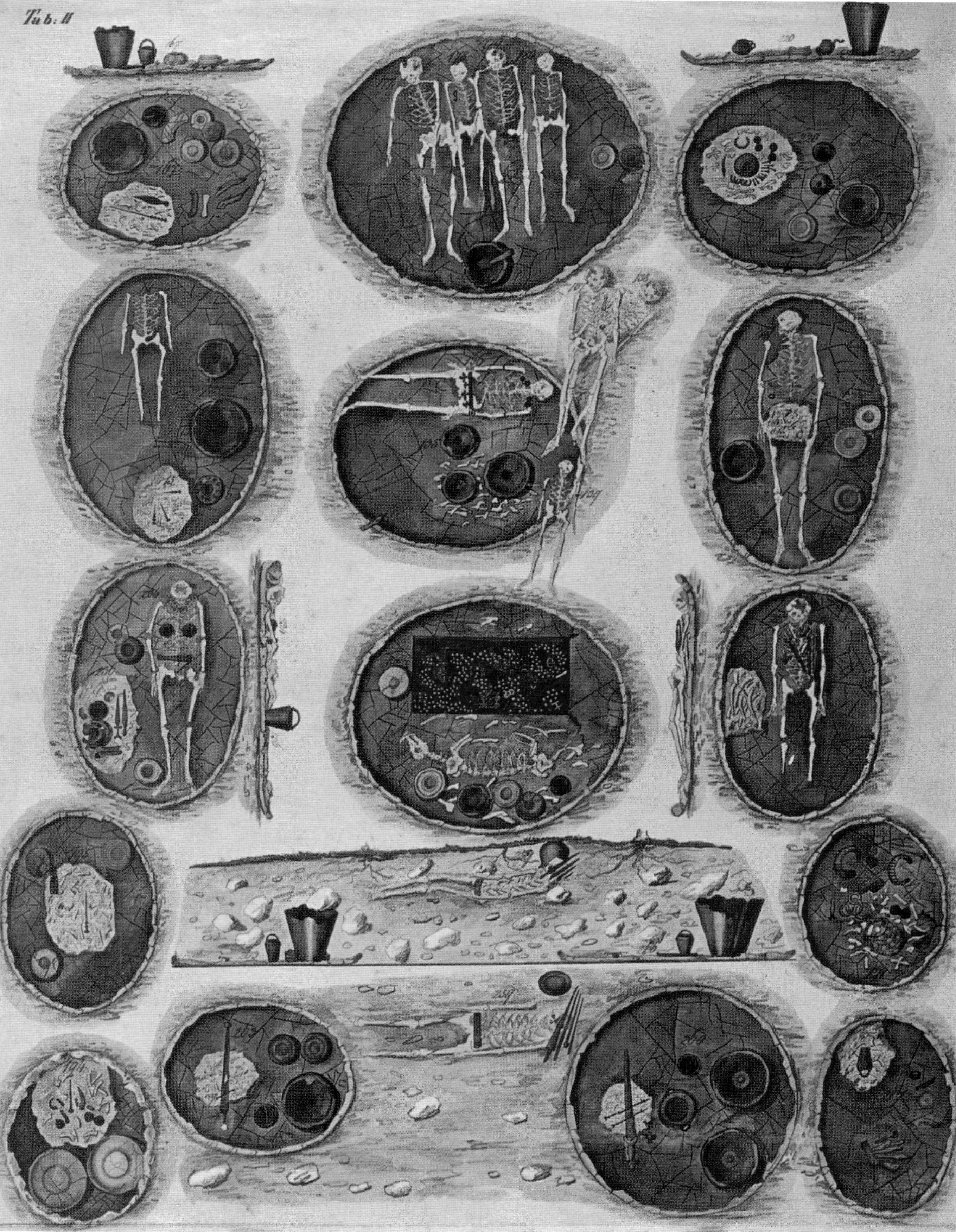
Tab: II

The peak of prehistoric mining activity occurred during the early Iron Age in the eighth century B.C.E., when tons of salt were extracted from the Hallstatt mines and exported throughout central Europe. Entire families, including children, were engaged in breaking salt loose using metal and antler tools and carrying it to the surface in leather backpacks and woolen sacks. No contemporaneous settlements have yet been found, so the details of their daily lives are unknown, but much of their time was spent inside the mountain working by torchlight. Some died in cave-ins. The corpse of one victim entombed in salt was found in 1734 and reburied in the village below.

Tremendous wealth flowed back into the Hallstatt community from its trading partners, reflected in the luxury items found in a cemetery just below the entrance to the modern mines. In 1846, the mine manager, Johann Georg Ramsauer (1795–1874), began to excavate human burials that had begun coming to light during digging for gravel. By 1863, he had excavated 980 graves, which he recorded with watercolor paintings made by Isidor Engel. Since then, additional excavations, such as those by Marie, Duchess of Mecklenburg-Schwerin (1854–1920) in 1907, Friedrich Morton (1890–1969) in 1937–39, and the Natural History Museum in Vienna since 1993 have brought the total to about 1,500. Many more remain to be discovered, for archaeologists estimate that there were probably over 5,000 burials originally.

Both cremation and skeleton burials have been found in the cemetery, with the cremations being relatively "richer" in their grave furnishings. They can be dated to between 800 and 400 B.C.E., a time known as the Hallstatt Period in the archaeology of central Europe, which reflects the significance of the site. The graves contained all sorts of luxury items, including iron and bronze swords and daggers and bronze bowls, buckets, helmets, and cauldrons. Exotic materials in the graves reflect long-distance contacts and access to talented artisans, many

south of the Alps. For example, a sword handle carved from ivory (either African or Asian) was inlaid with Baltic amber, while glass vessels can be traced to the upper Adriatic area.

Recent excavations have shown that Ramsauer largely ignored (and discarded) highly fragmented pottery found in the burials in favor of the spectacular weapons, ornaments, metal bowls, and a small number of intact pottery vessels. Techniques have been developed to reconstruct the crushed pottery found in recent excavations, so it is now possible to study these important burial goods. It is clear that the ceramic vessels display a high degree of technical expertise.

Since the beginning of the twenty-first century, picturesque Hallstatt town has been overrun with tourists seeking an authentic Alpine village amid spectacular scenery. A belief propagated in social media that the town of Hallstatt provided the visual inspiration for the setting of Disney's *Frozen* movies also draws visitors. Those interested in archaeology can escape the crowds by taking a funicular railway to the base of the high valley and walking up to the salt mines and the Iron Age cemetery. Tours of the mines make it possible to imagine the world of the miners.

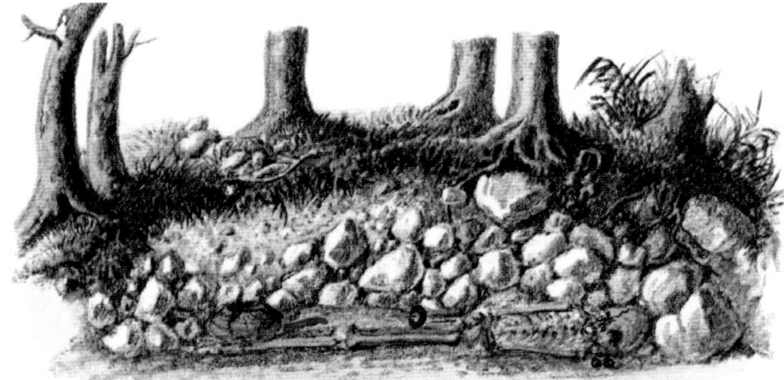

Opposite The remains of a 3,000-year-old prehistoric wooden staircase at the salt mine in Hallstatt.

Above top Overall view of the valley, with the cemetery leading up to the salt mine.

Above Example of Ramsauer's burial documentation.

THE IRON AGE SETTLEMENT AT **BISKUPIN**

TYPE: FORTIFIED SETTLEMENT • **ARCHITECTURAL STYLE:** TIMBER DWELLINGS AND RAMPARTS
LOCATION: NORTHWEST POLAND • **CONSTRUCTION BEGUN:** 738 B.C.E.

North of Gniezno in northwest Poland, Route 5 runs across the Polish plain, past fields and pastures, occasionally skirting lakes connected by streams. Prehistoric people were drawn to these lakes from the Stone Age onward. During the millennia that followed, they established many settlements among them. South of Żnin, a road turns off east toward Gąsawa, where signs direct the visitor to Biskupin. Here, in 1933, a waterlogged Iron Age settlement was discovered on a peninsula in one of the lakes.

Rising waters had inundated the site, preserving the timbers, which were then exposed when the water level dropped. A local schoolteacher notified archaeologists, who began excavations the following year to remove the peat and soil in which the timbers were embedded. Gradually, outlines of structures emerged from the tangle of logs, and photographs from an observation balloon revealed the plan of the settlement.

Multipurpose buildings serving as dwellings, workshops, stables, and storerooms ran in parallel rows, sharing common walls. Each unit was about 26 ft (8 m) by 30 ft (9 m), with a stone hearth in the center. If they were all occupied at the same time, several hundred people probably lived very close together. Log streets separated the rows of houses—eleven streets in all—with another road surrounding the inhabited area. Encircling the whole, a rampart of wooden cribs filled with earth and stone enclosed an area approximately 525 ft (160 m) wide by 660 ft (200 m) long. Pointed posts at the outer base of the rampart served as a breakwater and deterred attackers from getting close.

Through dendrochronology (tree-ring dating), we know almost exactly when Biskupin dates from. Most of the trees used in the houses, streets, and the rampart were felled between 747 and 722 B.C.E. More than half were cut during the winter of 738–737 B.C.E. That year must have been a busy time on the Biskupin peninsula. First, the inhabitants laid out the streets and houses, since their regularity could not have been accomplished without planning. They then cut timbers to exact lengths to build the houses in uniform dimensions and to pave the streets. Finally, they constructed and filled the timber cribs for the ramparts.

The inhabitants went out to fields and pastures through a single gate to cultivate wheat and millet and to tend herds of livestock. Back within the ramparts, they made iron and bronze implements, pottery, and wove woolen cloth. Archaeologists have recovered many wooden artifacts from the waterlogged deposits, including wheels and plows. After several decades, rising lake water levels appear to have doomed the settlement.

The Biskupin Iron Age settlement has been reconstructed as an archaeological park, comprising a replica of the wooden buildings, streets, and ramparts, along with a museum displaying the finds. A recent addition to the complex is the reconstruction of a nearby Neolithic settlement from about 4500 B.C.E., where a longhouse and burials were discovered in the 1950s.

Opposite Various views of the reconstructed settlement with its wooden buildings, streets, and ramparts.

THE ANCIENT CITY OF **ROME**

TYPE: CITY • **ARCHITECTURAL STYLE:** CLASSICAL
LOCATION: ITALY • **CONSTRUCTION BEGUN:** 447 B.C.E.

The majestic remains of imperial Rome form part of the cityscape of this historic city. The temples and triumphal arches of the forum are reminders of the expanse of the empire, and the Colosseum represents the cruelty of public spectacle.

Augustus (63 B.C.E.–14 C.E.), the first Roman emperor, claimed to have transformed the city of Rome from a city of brick to a city of marble. One of the most significant of his monuments is the Ara Pacis (Altar of Peace) that lay next to the Tiber to the north of the Ponte Cavour. The architectural reliefs have been reconstructed in a purpose-built structure that suggests the nature of the altar. It was decorated with a continuous frieze, reminiscent of those from the Parthenon at Athens and on the Great Altar of Zeus at Pergamon. Among the scenes are members of the family of the emperor Augustus coming to make a sacrifice and thus expressing their piety for the traditional Roman gods. This was a reminder of the new order in the Roman world as it moved away from the Republic and the civil wars. The frieze includes a scene showing the mythical origins of the city of Rome with Romulus and Remus. Other reliefs provide a reminder of the bounty enjoyed by the city of Rome, reflecting the benefits of peace that were to be enjoyed under Augustus.

Adjacent to the Ara Pacis was the Mausoleum of Augustus. The achievements, the Res Gestae, of the emperor were displayed on now-lost bronze plaques outside; copies on marble were displayed on the temple to the imperial cult in Ancyra (modern Ankara) in Turkey. The very name of the structure alluded to the burial place of Mausolus in Halikarnassos (modern Bodrum) in western Turkey, one of the wonders of the ancient world. The choice of placing this burial place for Augustus' family in the heart of Rome placed a new emphasis on the city.

Augustus erected a sundial to the southeast of the altar. Although this can no longer be seen, the Egyptian obelisk, originally made for the sixth-century B.C.E. pharaoh Psammetichus II at Heliopolis, was re-erected in the Piazza di Montecitorio and bears a Latin inscription recording Augustus' role. It dates to 10 B.C.E.

The Roman Forum

The political heart of the city of Rome lay in the forum, where the senate met in the curia. The area developed over time. Its limits are marked by two dominant victory monuments: the arch of Titus, recording the capture of the city of Jerusalem in 70 C.E. (and showing some of the trophies from the sack of the temple) in the reliefs; and the arch of Septimius Severus, recording his spectacular victories in the eastern empire against the Parthians and the creation of a new province of Mesopotamia in 199 C.E.

To the north of the main forum was the forum of Augustus, which contained the great temple of Mars Ultor (the Avenger) that had been promised by the emperor before the battle of Philippi in northern Greece in 42 B.C.E. Behind

Opposite, from top The interior of the Colosseum.
The Corinthian columns of the temple of Vespasian and Titus, and the temple of Saturn looking toward the Palatine.

it stands the wall, some 98 ft (30 m high), constructed to protect these public spaces from the risk of fire in the densely populated areas of the city.

One of the other public areas was the forum of Trajan, northwest of that of Augustus, which commemorated the expansion of the empire in Dacia (modern Romania) in 106 C.E. This contained a new market cut into the slopes of the Quirinal hill. At the western end of the forum, behind the Basilica Ulpia, Trajan placed his burial in a large base supporting a column decorated with a spiral frieze showing scenes from his conquest of Dacia. A large bronze statue of the emperor originally stood on the top, although this has now been replaced by one of St. Peter. Adjacent to the column was a library with two wings, each containing works in Latin or in Greek.

Palaces

Adjacent to the Roman forum was the Palatine hill, the location of the imperial palace. Some first-century B.C.E. houses have been popularly linked to the emperor Augustus and his wife Livia. Remains of Domitian's palace dating to the late first century C.E. are visible. The complex includes an extensive banqueting hall, as well as an audience chamber where citizens could approach the emperor.

On the slope of the Esquiline hill are the remains of part of Nero's Golden House, which was decorated with wall paintings and sculptures. It was hidden under the platform created for the construction of the baths of the Emperor Trajan after the death of Nero in 69 C.E. The grounds of the Golden House included a lake, and the emperor Vespasian turned this space into the Colosseum, a major amphitheater for hosting gladiatorial shows. This structure was funded by booty from the sack of Jerusalem.

Above One of the Dacian captives from the forum of Trajan, reused on the Arch of Constantine.

Opposite The Arch of Titus commemorates the sack of the city of Jerusalem during the Jewish revolt.

Victory Monuments

A range of monuments celebrated Rome's victories across its expanding empire. The second-century C.E. philosopher-emperor Marcus Aurelius marked his victories over the northern tribes who were threatening the empire. His column, still standing in the Piazza Colonna, was reminiscent of that created by Trajan.

Panels from the dismantled triumphal arch of Marcus Aurelius were reused in the arch of Constantine that stands next to the Colosseum. Constantine's monument celebrated not the defeat of Rome's enemies, but that of his rivals for imperial power, specifically Maxentius, who was defeated at the battle of the Milvian Bridge in 312 C.E. The arch incorporates defeated Dacians who appear to have been removed from Trajan's forum, as well as roundels from an unknown Hadrianic building.

The main archaeological sites such as the Roman forum, the Colosseum, and Trajan's column are within easy walking distance of each other. The Colosseo Metro station is conveniently situated for this area. Sturdy shoes are a must for Rome's streets.

SENATVS
POPVLVSQVEROMANVS
DIVOTITODIVIVESPASIANIF
VESPASIANOAVGVSTO

THE BURIED CITIES OF **POMPEII** AND **HERCULANEUM**

TYPE: URBAN • **ARCHITECTURAL STYLE:** CLASSICAL
LOCATION: BAY OF NAPLES, ITALY • **CONSTRUCTION BEGUN:** SIXTH CENTURY B.C.E.

The brooding presence of Mount Vesuvius dominates the cities of Pompeii and Herculaneum, destroyed and buried during the volcano's eruption in 79 C.E. A vivid eyewitness account of the eruption survives in the works of the younger Pliny, and provides a compelling background to the dramatic end of these communities. The wall paintings and objects preserved by the destruction bring these ancient cities back to life.

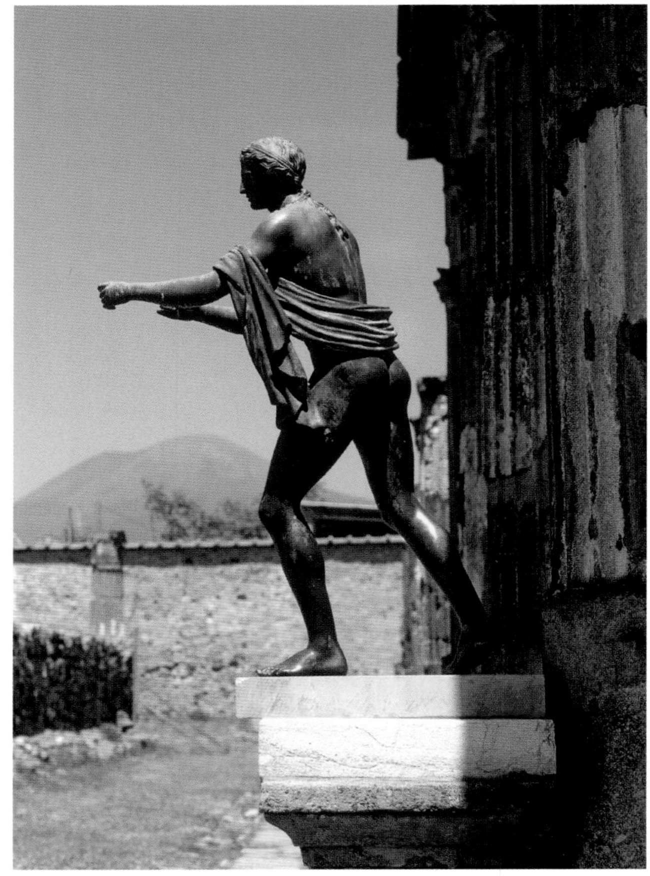

The ancient city of Pompeii lies 16 miles (26 km) southeast of the modern city of Naples. Excavations have provided an insight into the range of domestic, social, and economic activities in the city. The main public area, the forum, is located in the west, and a temple of Jupiter on a high podium dominates the north end of the city. At the southwest corner is the basilica used for legal cases; it contained an internal colonnade, though only the brick bases have survived the eruption and early trophy hunters. On the east side, adjacent to the temple of Jupiter, is the macellum, or meat and fish market, constructed in the second century B.C.E. At the southeast corner is the major building donated by a prominent woman named as Eumachia in the inscription. Her husband held public office in 3 C.E. Eumachia's portrait was found inside the building, and she is known to have been a public priestess. The actual purpose of this building is undetermined, although the dedication made clear her loyalty to the emperor Augustus. Eumachia's monumental tomb has been located outside the Nuceria gate on the southeast side of the city.

Five sets of public baths have been identified at Pompeii. The forum baths lie immediately to the north of the forum and were built ca. 80 B.C.E. An inscription shows that they were constructed at public expense. The Stabian baths were remodeled in the Augustan period and contained an open exercise area.

The amphitheater is located in the southeast corner of the city. It was designed to hold up to 15,000 spectators. The structure was the gift of two magistrates whose benefaction is recorded in two inscriptions. The amphitheater was the scene of a riot in 59 C.E. between the people of Pompeii and the town of Nuceria; an image of the riot has survived in a wall painting from one of the private houses at Pompeii. The gladiatorial barracks were found near the Stabiae Gate on the south side of the city. The rooms were found to contain gladiatorial equipment, including ornate Thracian helmets.

Some of the most intimate spaces in Pompeii are the public bars and inns. Wine amphorae were found stacked in the Bar of Asellina. Decoration in the Bar of Salvius shows a pair of men gambling at a board game.

Several cemeteries outside the main gates of Pompeii have been excavated. Those outside the Herculaneum Gate on the northwest side included a number of those individuals who held high public office and who were buried in monumental and ostentatious tombs.

Opposite The bronze statue of Apollo from the sanctuary of Apollo.

Below The temple of Jupiter at the north end of the forum at Pompeii, with Vesuvius in the background.

Private Houses

One of the largest private houses found at Pompeii is the House of the Faun. It contained a number of high-quality mosaics, including one depicting the victory of Alexander the Great over Persian King Darius at the battle of Issos. This may now be seen in the Archaeological Museum in Naples (though a replica has been installed in the house). Careful excavation of gardens, and the taking of casts of the roots, has allowed the reconstruction of plantings within these private spaces. In the House of the Vettii there is a blend of small-scale classical sculpture as well as fountains, all sitting within the colonnade. In the House of the Golden Bracelet a series of wall paintings with birds in the shrubs forms the backdrop to the actual plantings.

One of the finest residences outside the walls of Pompeii to the northwest is the Villa of the Mysteries. The name derives from the paintings, set against a vivid red background, that show part of a mystery cult. Although the figures are linked to the god of wine, Bacchus, the event seems to be related to the admission of women into some type of ritual.

Above The peristyle and garden in the House of Venus in a Shell.

Below The amphitheater at Pompeii was the site of a riot in 59 C.E.

Right The former sea front of Herculaneum with the Suburban Baths and the terrace of Marcus Nonius Balbus.

Herculaneum

Herculaneum lies 11 miles (18 km) to the northwest of Pompeii at the foot of Vesuvius. The city was buried under as much as 75 ft (23 m) of volcanic debris, presenting a more complicated situation than at Pompeii. The high temperatures of the series of pyroclastic flows that struck the city means that organic materials, including bodies, were carbonized. Thus wooden features including doors and furniture have survived. A baby's cradle was found in the House of Marcus Pilius Primigenius Granianus. It is also possible to see mezzanine floors in some of the structures.

Two sets of baths have been excavated: the Central baths, and the Suburban baths (in the southwest of the city). The Suburban baths were in the process of refurbishment at the time of the eruption, and building materials were found inside the rooms.

Both sites are reached by Circumvesuviana from Naples, alighting at Pompeii Scavi or Ercolano Scavi. In both cases there is a short walk to the archaeological site. These train services can be packed. The site of Pompeii is extensive, and sensible shoes are a must. The Archaeological Museum in Naples is well worth a visit.

THE ANCIENT CITY OF **ATHENS**

TYPE: TEMPLE, CIVIC • **ARCHITECTURAL STYLE:** CLASSICAL, ROMAN
LOCATION: ATHENS, GREECE • **CONSTRUCTION BEGUN:** 447 B.C.E.

The sunset view of the Parthenon and the Athenian Acropolis from the Philopappos Hill in Athens presents an enduring reminder of the power of classical architecture on western Europe. Looking westward you can see the line of the Long Walls, constructed to allow the city to function in time of siege, that connected the city with the fortified harbor of the Piraeus.

The Periclean City

The Archaic city of Athens was effectively destroyed in the Persian invasion of mainland Greece in 480 B.C.E. The newly constructed temple of Athena on the Acropolis was left in ruins. Athens' relationship with other city-states changed in the years following the Persian Wars. A league formed to resist Persian encroachments soon became an empire with its members paying tribute to Athens. This income helped to fund a major building program in Athens from the middle of the fifth century B.C.E. Visitors could follow the different projects via a series of publicly displayed accounts cut onto marble stelae that map the spending and progress. Many of the fragments are displayed in the Epigraphic Museum in Athens.

At the heart of the building program was the monumental temple of Athena, known as the Parthenon. This new temple contained the colossal chryselephantine statue of the goddess designed by the sculptor Pheidias. Although the statue has not survived, there is a detailed description by the second century C.E. Roman travel writer Pausanias, and a number of small marble replicas are known. The temple was heavily decorated with architectural sculptures. The west pediment, which faced anyone approaching the temple, depicted the battle for the control of Athens. At the east end, above the main entrance to the temple, a pediment showed the birth of Athena, framed in the two corners by the chariots of Helios and Selene. Square reliefs, or metopes, gracing the exterior of the temple above the columns showed the mythical conflict between the Greeks and the forces of barbarism: centaurs, Amazons, and giants. On the upper wall of the interior building, and inside the columns, a continuous frieze started at the west end and processed separately along the north and south sides. It showed a grand procession with riders, chariots, and then sacrificial animals. The two processions met above the east door, where the Olympian gods viewed the folding of the sacred peplos.

The main entrance to the Acropolis was monumentalized by a grand gateway with multiple doors known as the Propylaia. The structure contained a large dining room on its north side. The Propylaia was left unfinished when war with Sparta broke out at the end of the 430s B.C.E. However, victories in the early stages of the war were commemorated in the construction of the Ionic temple of Athena Nike that stood on the south bastion,

Opposite The Acropolis of Athens, an ancient citadel that sits on a rocky outcrop above the city.

and was accessed from the Propylaia. The Athenians constructed the Erechtheion in the final stages of the Peloponnesian War. One of its striking features was a porch supported by architectural women, or caryatids, overlying the earlier Archaic temple. The temple contained a number of features, including the sacred olive tree that Athena had given to the city. The theater of Dionysus was cut into the south slope of the Acropolis. This was the setting for the plays that were written during the fifth century B.C.E. by Sophocles, Euripides, and Aristophanes.

The political heart of the city of Athens lay in the agora, to the north of the Acropolis. The earliest democratic structures can be dated to the sixth century B.C.E., although the Persians destroyed them. A great drain running along the west side determined the orientation of buildings in the agora. At the southern end was the circular tholos, where the tribe that held office for the month was based. Immediately to the north was the bouleuterion, where the council consisting of fifty members from each of the ten tribes met. To the east of the bouleuterion was a long statue base representing the ten eponymous heroes of Athens, where notices relating to the tribes were displayed. The Athenians built the temple of Hephaistos on the low hill behind the bouleuterion, probably in the 440s.

Cemeteries were located outside the walls of the city, alongside the roads leading out into Attica. One of the best explored is in the Kerameikos to the northwest. This area was used from the Archaic period, and some of the sixth-century stelae and monuments were reused in the walls that were constructed after the Persian destruction of the city.

The Roman City

The Arch of Hadrian to the east of the Acropolis, constructed in 132 C.E., marks the distinction between the Classical city and the later Roman expansion. There are two inscriptions on each side of the arch: "This is Athens, the former City of Theseus" and "This is the City of Hadrian not of Theseus."

Athens underwent transformation from the reign of Augustus (63 B.C.E.–14 C.E.). A round Ionic structure linked to the cult of Roma and Augustus was placed to east of the Parthenon, probably shortly after 27 B.C.E. In 15 B.C.E. Agrippa, the son-in-law of Augustus, visited Athens and placed an odeion, or concert hall, in the open space of the agora. This replaced the fifth-century Odeion of Pericles, adjacent to the theater of Dionysus, that had been destroyed during the siege of Sulla in 86 B.C.E. Adjacent to the odeion was a temple of Zeus. Mason marks indicate that, during the early Roman period, this fifth-century B.C.E. building was dismantled and re-erected in the agora, probably for use in the Roman imperial cult.

The Romans constructed a new market to the east of the agora. The western entrance, built in Doric style and echoing Periclean Athens, carried an inscription, dated to 11–9 B.C.E., which showed it was a benefaction of Caesar and Augustus. The structure consisted of an open area surrounded by a colonnade, with shops behind. Immediately to the east of this new market was the Hellenistic Tower of the Winds.

At the end of the first century C.E., during the reign of the emperor Trajan (53–117 C.E.), an Athenian benefactor, Titus Flavius Pantainos, presented the city with a new library that was constructed to the southeast of the agora beside the Panathenaic way. It was under Trajan's successor, Hadrian (76–138 C.E.), that the city was reformed. He built a major library to the north of the Roman market that contained lecture rooms. It used imported marble from as far afield as western Asia Minor; the inner colonnade contained 100 columns quarried in Phrygia. The most important structure built during Hadrian's reign was the monumental Olympieion, probably dedicated during his visit to Athens in 131–32 C.E. The building had been started in the late sixth century B.C.E. but had never been completed. The structure is over 360 ft (110 m) in length, and was surrounded by 104 Corinthian columns.

The archaeological sites of the Kerameikos, the Agora, the Acropolis, and the Olympieion are easily reached from the Athens Metro stations (Kerameikos, Thissio, and Akropolis). There are site museums at the Kerameikos, the Agora (in the Stoa of Attalos), and adjacent to the Akropolis Metro station; some stations have small displays of finds made during their construction. The National Archaeological Museum contains artifacts from Athens as well as the rest of Greece.

Opposite The Odeion of Herodes Atticus on the south slope of the Athenian Acropolis.

Above left The reliefs of the Wind Gods, Notos (south) and Euros (southeast), on the Tower of the Winds.

Above right The Olympieion in the early morning light.

THE SANCTUARY OF ZEUS AT **OLYMPIA**

TYPE: SANCTUARY • **ARCHITECTURAL STYLE:** CLASSICAL
LOCATION: PELOPONNESE, GREECE • **CONSTRUCTION BEGUN:** 776 B.C.E.

Olympia is the home of the original Olympic Games, traditionally founded in 776 B.C.E. and continuing into the Roman period. The remains of the running track lie adjacent to the sanctuary of Zeus, which contains the foundations of the god's temple that once housed a colossal gold and ivory cult statue.

The ancient Greek site of Olympia, lies in Elis in the western Peloponnese, 186 miles (300 km) by road west of Athens. The site is located at the confluence of the Alphaios and the smaller Kladeos rivers. At the heart of the sanctuary was the temple of Zeus, constructed in the Doric order between 470 and 456 B.C.E. It was made from local limestone with a stucco finish; the foundations of the temple and several fallen sections of column remain. The building contained the now-lost gold and ivory statue of the seated god, which was created by the sculptor

Opposite The colonnade in the third century B.C.E. gymnasium used for training athletes.

Below The fallen columns from the temple of Zeus, the focal point of the sanctuary.

Pheidias in the mid-fifth century B.C.E. The second-century C.E. Roman travel writer Pausanias described the statue—it seems to have been removed to the Palace of Lausus in Constantinople (modern Istanbul) in late antiquity. A German team excavating the ancient workshop to the west of the temple of Zeus, in which the statue was made, revealed remains of materials and molds used in its creation; the building was later converted into a Christian basilica. The temple of Zeus featured marble architectural sculptures. At each end, square metopes showed the labors of Herakles, such as the cleaning of the Augean stables and the capture of the Cretan bull. Freestanding statues filled the triangular pediments at each end of the building: at the east end, facing the stadium, was a scene depicting the mythical founding of the games with the race between Oenomaos and Pelops, and Zeus presiding at the center. At the west end was the mythical battle between the Lapiths and the Centaurs with Apollo at the center. Close to Apollo is the Athenian hero Theseus, who is about to bring an axe down on the head of a centaur. The use of the centauromachy may have been used to allude to the clash between the Greeks and barbarians, and specifically to the Persian wars that had concluded with the Greek victories at Salamis and Plataia in 480 and 479 B.C.E. The sculptures themselves are on display in the on-site archaeological museum.

To the north of the temple of Zeus stood the much older temple of Hera, also constructed in the Doric style, and probably dating to around 600 B.C.E. Excavations have yielded a limestone female head that probably represented the goddess. A fourth-century B.C.E. marble statue of Hermes holding a young Dionysus by the Athenian sculptor Praxiteles was also found inside the temple.

Immediately to the west of the temple of Hera was a round structure in the Ionic style, the Philippeion, constructed by Philip II of Macedon (382–336 B.C.E.) after his victory over the Greek alliance led by Athens and Thebes at the battle of Chaironeia in 338 B.C.E. Philip II's son, Alexander the Great (356–323 B.C.E.), completed the temple, and gold and ivory portraits of members of the Macedonian family were displayed inside, probably deliberately hinting at their semidivine status. The benefactor Herodes Atticus added a monumental fountain house on the north side of the Altis in the second century C.E. (Herodes Atticus's odeion can be seen on the south side of the Athenian Acropolis).

Below left The circular Philippeion served as a sanctuary for the deified members of the Macedonian royal family.
Below right The stadium, looking northwest from the sanctuary.
Opposite The archaic temple of Hera on the north side of the Altis.

The Stadium Area

Immediately to the east of the sanctuary, but connected to it by a tunnel, was the stadium where the athletic events took place. At the west end was the grooved starting line. The stadium has a length of 600 Olympic feet (630.8 ft/ 192.27 m). A special area for the judges was located at the midpoint. The hillside slope of the Kronion to the north of the stadium provided space for viewers to watch the festival. It has been estimated that the stadium could hold some 45,000 viewers. On a terrace on the north side of the sanctuary stood a line of treasuries established by the different urban communities of the Greek world; their foundations are clearly visible. The group here mainly represented some of the Greek colonies in southern Italy and Sicily, including Metapontum and Syracuse. The purpose of these structures was to store and display the civic dedications to Zeus.

The precinct contains numerous bases for inscribed monuments celebrating victorious athletes, although the statues themselves, originally in bronze, are now lost. A tall pedestal surmounted by a statue of Victory (Nike) stood to the southeast of the temple of Zeus. The inscription records that it was the work of Paeonius of Mende (in northern Greece), and the monument celebrated the victory of the Messenians (the subjected region in the southwest Peloponnese) over the Spartans in the 420s B.C.E., during the early stages of the Peloponnesian War. The Nike itself was over 9.8 ft (3 m) tall and showed her descending into the sanctuary; it is displayed in the site museum.

Olympia is reached by train from Pyrgos (about 30 minutes), and the archaeological park is about a 15-minute walk from the station. There is a major archaeological museum at Olympia displaying the architectural sculptures from the temple of Zeus. Two other museums explore the history of the excavations and the history of the Olympic games.

THE ROMAN COLONY AT **CORINTH**

TYPE: CITY • **ARCHITECTURAL STYLE:** CLASSICAL, ROMAN
LOCATION: PELOPONNESE • **CONSTRUCTION BEGUN:** EIGHTH CENTURY B.C.E.

The ancient city of Corinth is dominated by the Acrocorinth that rises to a height of 1886 ft (575 m) behind the city, welcoming travelers to the Peloponnese. It was orginally the site of a small temple of Aphrodite, or Venus, regarded as the ancestor of Julius Caesar (100–44 B.C.E.), who founded the Roman colony here. The lower city provides some of the most important Roman remains in Greece, as well as two well-preserved harbor complexes.

Corinth itself was established in the eighth century B.C.E., and continued as a city until 146 B.C.E., when the Romans destroyed it and left the site abandoned for nearly a century. Few substantial remains survive from this earlier period, except for the Archaic temple of Apollo constructed in the Doric style in the mid-sixth century B.C.E.; seven columns are still standing. The Romans later adapted the building by removing the interior columns in order to allow for different cult practices.

Julius Caesar refounded the city as a colony in 44 B.C.E. It became the seat of the Roman governor of the province of Achaia. The architecture of the city was deliberately Italian, as opposed to Greek, with temples constructed on raised podia (contrasting with the earlier Doric temple above the forum). Latin was the language of choice for public inscriptions, at least for the first two centuries of the colony's life.

The heart of the Roman colony was the forum, lying to the south of the hill dominated by the earlier Doric temple. It contained the legal center of the community, with a basilica at the eastern end that was found to contain portrait statues of the Julio-Claudian family. At the western end, raised on a terrace above the open space, was a monumental temple (temple E), possibly linked to the Roman imperial cult. The original building was constructed in the Doric

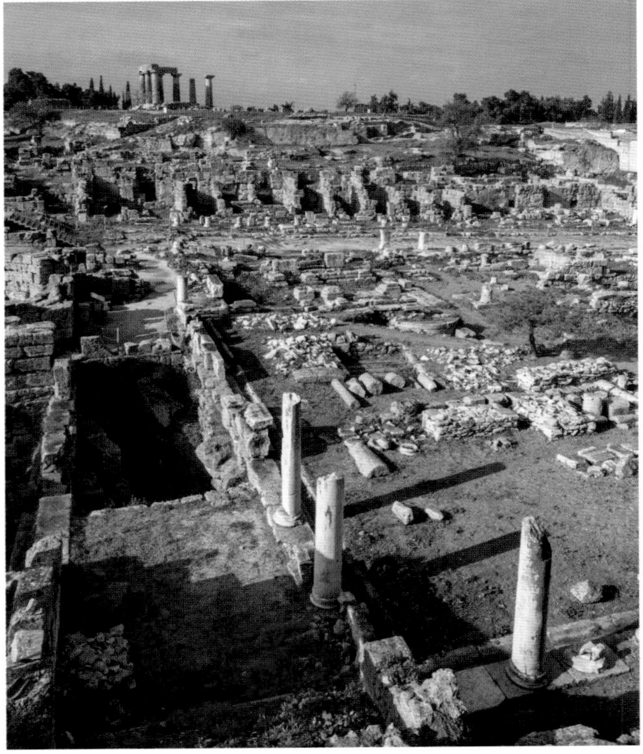

Above The temple of Apollo, viewed from the peribolos of Apollo across the Lechaeum Road.

Opposite The Lechaeum Road, looking to the south toward the forum. The Acrocorinth dominates the city.

style, probably in the early first century C.E. It was rebuilt at the end of the century in the Corinthian style, and placed on a podium 11 ft (3.4 m) high.

Remains of the sloping auditorium of an ancient Greek theater have been excavated to the west of the Doric temple. The theater probably dates from the fifth century B.C.E., but was adapted in the early years of the Roman colony, when a substantial stage building was constructed. Adjacent to the theater is a square. Cut into large slabs laid along the edge is a Latin inscription, originally in bronze lettering, that records the benefaction of Erastus, who gave this facility to the colony from his own money as part of his election promise after he had taken up the office of aedile (an elected official in charge of public buildings).

Several bathhouses have been excavated in the city. A set on the Lechaeum Road, immediately outside the archaeological park, was constructed around 200 C.E. They may have been a gift of Eurykles of Sparta.

In the Archaic period, a trackway or *diolkos* crossed the Isthmus of Corinth, allowing small vessels to traverse the narrow piece of land; remains can still be seen adjacent to the nineteenth-century Corinth Canal. The emperor Nero (37–68 C.E.) had a plan to cut a canal to turn the Peloponnese into a true island, but never completed the project. Two major harbors developed here in the Roman period. Cenchreae was established on the Saronic Gulf and provided access to the eastern Mediterranean. Lechaeum was placed on the Gulf of Corinth, allowing access to the Adriatic and Italy. These facilities were intended to enable the movement of goods to avoid the dangerous route around the south coast of the Peloponnese.

Corinth is easily reached from Athens by means of suburban train as well as by intercity coach. There are buses from the town center to the archaeological park, where there is a museum displaying finds from the city and local area.

THE SANCTUARY OF **DELPHI**

TYPE: SANCTUARY • **ARCHITECTURAL STYLE:** CLASSICAL
LOCATION: CENTRAL GREECE • **CONSTRUCTION BEGUN:** EIGHTH CENTURY B.C.E.

High in the mountains of central Greece, a sacred path snakes its way up a steeply sloping site toward a famous temple dedicated to the Greek god of prophecy, Apollo. Close to Mount Parnassus, which stands at just under 8,200 ft (2,500 m), this is Delphi, home to the Pythian games. The site lies 6 miles (10 km) from Itea on the Gulf of Corinth, and 118 miles (190 km) northwest of Athens.

Just inside the entrance to the sanctuary is a lavish monument constructed by the Spartans to mark their naval defeat of the Athenians at the battle of Aigospatamoi in 405 B.C.E., right at the end of the Peloponnesian war. It originally contained a portrait of the Spartan commander Lysander and faced an Athenian monument that marked the victory over the Persians at Marathon in 490 B.C.E.

Different cities of the Greek world kept valuable dedications in treasuries that lined the path leading up to the temple of Apollo, and a number of them have been reconstructed. The treasury of the island of Siphnos is decorated in the Ionian style with a continuous architectural relief that records the battle between the Olympian gods and the giants. It contains one of the earliest uses of a caryatid, a female figure acting as a column. The point at which the path turns—a choice location on this route—is dominated by the treasury of the Athenians, decorated with architectural panels presenting the parallel deeds of Herakles and the Athenian hero Theseus. A tradition recorded in the Roman period suggested that the treasury had been constructed using the booty won from the Persians at the battle of Marathon.

The temple of Apollo is supported on a massive terrace. A new temple was constructed following the destruction by fire of an earlier building in 548 B.C.E. The pediments at each end of the building featured sculptures: the battle with the giants in the west, and the appearance of Apollo in the east. There was a tradition that the exiled Alcmaeonid family from Athens paid for the marble sculptures in 505 B.C.E.

To the east of the temple is a large altar where the ancient Greeks made sacrifices to Apollo. Adjacent to this is the base of a bronze cauldron erected by the different Greek cities to mark the defeat of the Persian army at the battle of Plataia in 479 B.C.E. Bronze twisted snakes supported the cauldron, each bearing inscriptions of the names of the cities. The cauldron was removed in late antiquity to Byzantium (modern Istanbul), where it remains on display in the hippodrome.

At the top of this site lies the stadium that hosted athletic events for the Pythian games. French excavations revealed the remains of a bronze charioteer, dedicated as a victory monument by one of the rulers of Gela in southern Sicily. The statue is displayed in the site's archaeological museum.

There are daily public buses to Delphi from Athens as well as coach tours. An overnight stay would be advised. There is a major archaeological museum at the site displaying architectural sculptures as well as small finds.

Opposite, from top The temple of Apollo, the location of the Delphic oracle. The theater, with the temple of Apollo and the Treasury of the Athenians beyond.

WELL-PRESERVED **AKROTIRI**

TYPE: TOWN • **ARCHITECTURAL STYLE:** CYCLADIC LATE BRONZE AGE
LOCATION: SANTORINI, GREECE • **CONSTRUCTION BEGUN:** CA. 1650 B.C.E.

Present-day visitors to the Cycladic island of Santorini are greeted by the sight of picture-postcard Greek villages atop high cliffs. On closer inspection, it will be found that the cliffs are formed of many layers of pumice, surrounding a caldera, evidence of the major volcanic eruption which changed the appearance of the island forever. In the middle of the second millennium B.C.E., this eruption buried the town of Akrotiri.

Also known as Santorini, the island of Thera lies in the Aegean Sea, approximately 60 miles (100 km) north of Crete. Its present-day appearance reveals its volcanic heritage, since the archipelago to which Santorini now belongs was originally a single island. There has been ongoing discussion regarding the date of the volcanic eruption the destroyed the island. The traditional date, derived from archaeological comparison with objects

from sites elsewhere, is around 1500 B.C.E. However, recent scientific studies suggest that it may have occurred approximately a century earlier. The debate continues.

Archaeological investigations at Akrotiri have revealed that it was a prosperous and highly developed Bronze Age settlement, aided by a location that enabled it to take advantage of trade routes in the Aegean. In particular, contact with the Minoan society on Crete is demonstrated by some of the subjects of wall paintings, particularly those showing monkeys, and a few objects inscribed with Linear A script, as used in Minoan palace administrations, including at Knossos.

Given the preservation of the settlement, archaeologists have been able to visualize objects that would not normally have survived. For example, they found evidence of the use of wooden furniture. Pouring plaster of Paris into cavities in the ash revealed the shapes of tables and beds, their form preserved even though the wood from which they were made had rotted. Unlike the Roman sites of Pompeii and Herculaneum, no traces of people or animals exist, suggesting that the population had made its escape.

In private houses, the ground floor was primarily used for the storage and preparation of food. Evidence includes large storage vessels, known in Greek as *pithoi*, some of which were made locally, with others imported from elsewhere in the Cyclades or from Crete.

Opposite Ground floor rooms in Building Complex Alpha at Akrotiri, showing large storage vessels.

Above, from top Gold figurine of an ibex, found near Xeste 3 during construction of the new shelter over the site. A section of the Flotilla Fresco from the West House.

Surviving Art

Wall paintings are a particular feature of Akrotiri. Found in their original locations, they are much better preserved than examples at other Aegean sites. This has enabled archaeologists to reconstruct the decorative schemes of individual rooms and groups of rooms.

One wall painting ran around the top part of a room in the West House. Known as the Flotilla Fresco or Ship Procession Fresco, it shows a fleet of eight large and elaborately decorated ships, accompanied by three smaller vessels, seemingly traveling between two ports. In addition to valuable information on ship construction, the Flotilla Fresco also gives an insight into the appearance of the island's buildings. Other wall paintings in the West House include a depiction of two young fishermen, shown life-sized, carrying their catch. Another, on the doorjamb of an adjoining room shows a young woman, identified as a priestess from her distinctive clothing and the object she carries, which may be

an incense burner. The wall paintings from the West House, and others from the site, aid our understanding of clothing from this time, as there is very limited evidence of actual textiles from this period in the Aegean.

Several wall paintings are interpreted as showing religious scenes, often with women as the main participants, which can be seen in the decoration of the large building known as Xeste 3. This structure was likely to have hosted community, official, and religious functions. With a footprint of around 3,230 sq ft (300 sq m) and extending up to three stories tall, its wall paintings provide the most complete picture of cult activity at Akrotiri.

The fragile nature of the archaeological remains at Akrotiri requires protection from the elements, and there has been a shelter over the site since it opened to the public. To ensure the long-term protection of the site and to enhance the visitor experience, a new shelter opened in 2012 covering 16 acres (6.5 ha). In order to achieve the most favorable temperature inside the building, the architects incorporated features that take account of environmental conditions. This has not only succeeded in creating an unforgettable experience for present-day visitors, but also has contributed to the preservation of this unique site for years to come.

While there is no museum at the site, finds from the excavations at Akrotiri are on display at the Museum of Prehistoric Thera in Fira, the main town on the island.

Above Remains of buildings at Akrotiri protected by the modern shelter.

Opposite Wall painting from Building Complex Beta showing blue monkeys.

THE FORTIFIED CITADEL OF **MYCENAE**

TYPE: PALACE AND TOMBS • **ARCHITECTURAL STYLE:** MYCENAEAN
LOCATION: PELOPONNESE, GREECE • **CONSTRUCTION BEGUN:** CA. 1600 B.C.E.

Mycenae was built on a limestone outcrop, in a commanding position in the landscape, its location is as impressive today as it was in antiquity. The archaeological site is about 1.2 miles (2 km) from the modern-day village of the same name, situated in the northeast of the Peloponnese, Greece.

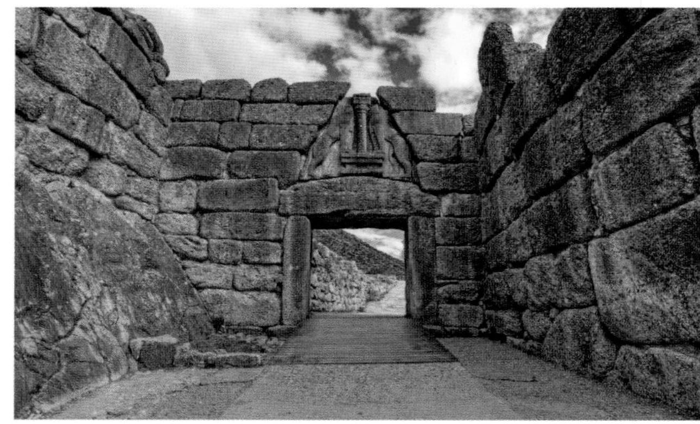

Mycenae is immortalized in legend; in Homer's epic poem *The Iliad,* the citadel was the home of King Agamemnon, leader of the Achaean forces against the Trojans. The palace on the summit of the citadel is also the setting for the murder of Agamemnon by his wife Clytemnestra and her subsequent murder by her son Orestes, as dramatized in the *Oresteia* by Aeschylus. There is evidence of occupation at Mycenae from the seventh millennium B.C.E. onward, although the visible archaeological remains date from the late seventeenth to the thirteenth centuries B.C.E., a time when Mycenae was the leading center of Bronze Age society on the Greek mainland.

Visitors to the site are immediately reminded of the Homeric epithet "Well-Built Mycenae." The citadel is still surrounded by impressive walls built in the technique known as "Cyclopean," as it was believed by the ancient Greeks that the stones were so large they must have been moved by the Cyclopes, a race of one-eyed giants. No less impressive to the modern-day visitor is the Lion Gate, set within the fortification walls, so-named because of the sculpture in the gate's relieving triangle, which depicts a pair of lionesses. Other impressive evidence of ancient engineering skill is a secret cistern, which ensured that the inhabitants of Mycenae would not be without water in the event of a siege.

Above left The citadel of Mycenae in the middle distance with "houses" in the foreground.

Above right The Lion Gate set into "Cyclopean walls," leading into the citadel at Mycenae.

Opposite Interior of the tholos tomb known as the Treasury of Atreus.

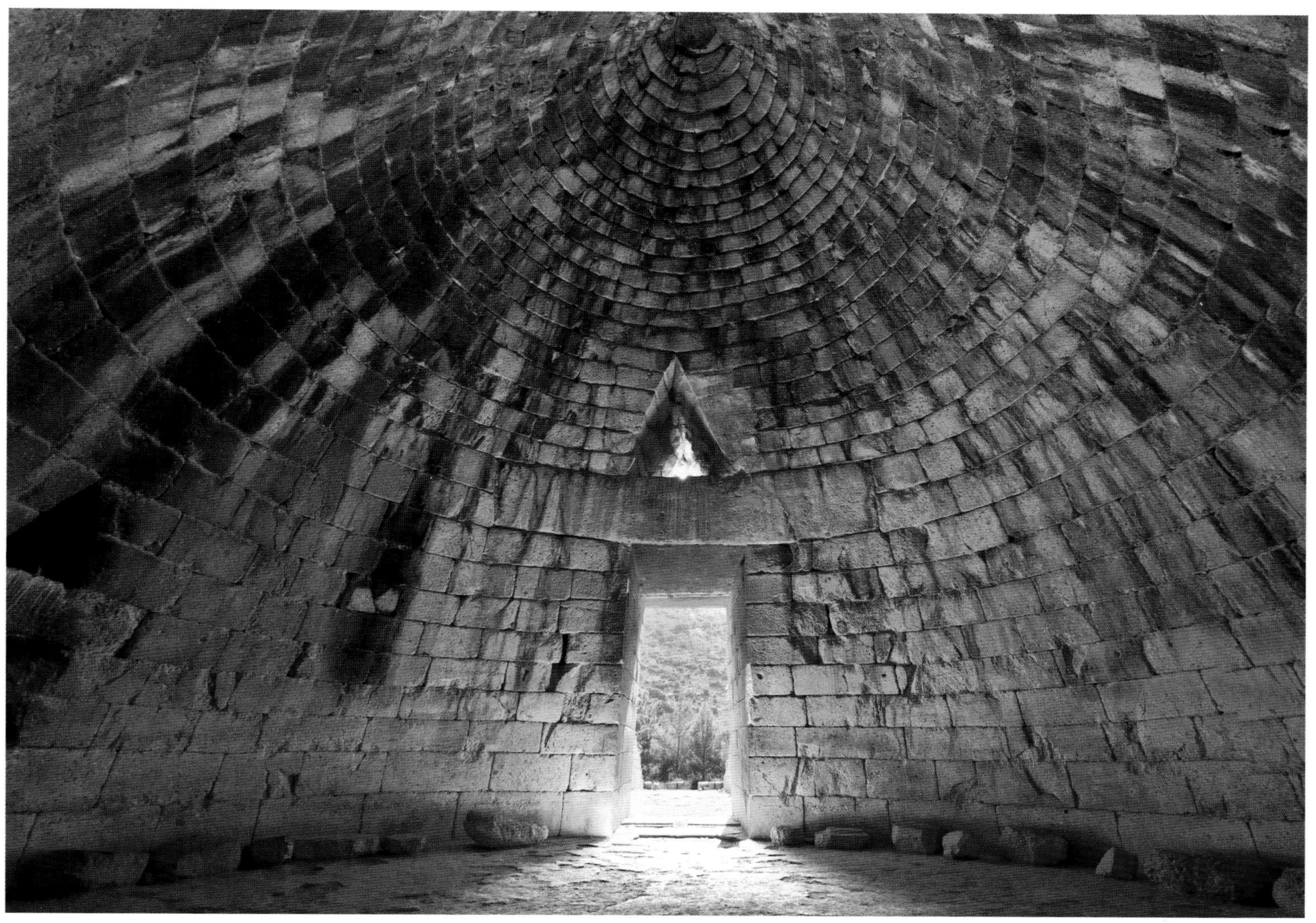

Mycenae's Graves

Two funerary enclosures, Grave Circles A and B, each contain more than twenty burials and were in use from the end of the seventeenth until the sixteenth century B.C.E. The majority of tombs are of a type known as a "shaft grave," which could contain multiple burials over time. The grave offerings and complexity of construction suggest that the deceased were the early rulers of Mycenae.

Grave Circle B is the earlier of the two, with the first burials dating from the end of the seventeenth century B.C.E. Situated outside the fortification wall, it was an unexpected discovery in 1951, found during excavations of a later Mycenaean tomb. Grave Circle A had been discovered much earlier, in 1876 by the German businessman-turned-archaeologist Heinrich Schliemann. Although over half of the burials in Grave Circle B were shaft graves, others were simpler in their construction. The most lavish burials contained bronze weapons, gold jewelry, and well-crafted items such as a tiny seal-stone made from amethyst and a bowl made from rock crystal in the shape of a duck. The most unusual discovery, however, was a face mask made of electrum, an alloy of gold and silver. The finds in Grave Circle A were even more elaborate, with large quantities of bronze weapons and gold jewelry, some probably worn in life. Other gold items were made for the funeral, such as five spectacular gold masks and disks from burial shrouds. A number of items indicate that the deceased had links with Minoan Crete, such as elaborate daggers with decoration made from inlays of precious metals and metal vessels made in shapes typical of Minoan design.

Cult Practices

The part of the site now known as the Cult Center was situated on the west slope of the citadel hill. It consists of a group of five structures, now covered with a roof to protect the archaeology. The finds, which include wall paintings depicting various aspects of Mycenaean cult practice, suggest this area was used for religious purposes.

The archaeological remains extend outside the citadel, and much of the settlement lay on the southern and eastern slopes of the hill. Also outside the citadel is the tomb known as the Treasury of Atreus, built around 1250 B.C.E., which had already been plundered when it was visited by the Roman traveler Pausanias in the second century C.E. It was once believed that tombs of this type were storehouses for valuables. Consisting of a round chamber, known as the tholos, it is approached by an unroofed passage with sides of dressed stone. The chamber is built of thirty-three courses of dressed stone, fitted so that each course slightly overlaps the one below it. The elaborate decoration of the tomb's exterior suggests that the original appearance of the tomb would have been stunning.

The site is just over a mile (about 2 km) from the modern village bearing the same name, which is close to the main road between Corinth and Argos. There is a small museum at the site, although the most famous finds from Mycenae are displayed at the National Archaeological Museum in Athens.

Above Grave Circle A, showing the shaft graves and perimeter wall added in the Mycenaean palace period.

Right One of the gold masks from Shaft Grave IV, Grave Circle A.

GOURNIA A BRONZE AGE TOWN

TYPE: TOWN • **ARCHITECTURAL STYLE:** MINOAN
LOCATION: CRETE, GREECE • **CONSTRUCTION BEGUN:** CA. 1800 B.C.E.

Walking along the narrow paved streets of Gournia and looking into the remains of its houses, the modern-day visitor is rewarded with arguably the best impression of life in an Aegean Bronze Age town that this region has to offer.

The site lies in eastern Crete, on a low ridge close to a natural harbor. The ancient name of the settlement is not recorded, and the modern name of Gournia derives from the Greek term for the many stone basins that were visible on the site before excavation and still remain inside its ancient buildings.

There is evidence of occupation at Gournia from the third millennium B.C.E., known as the Final Neolithic period. However, the archaeological remains seen today date mainly from 1800–1500 B.C.E., contemporary with the second phase of the Minoan palaces, named after Minos, the mythical king of Crete. The most characteristic features of the settlement are small, simple houses, the largest of which occupied an area of around 16.5 sq ft (5 sq m). The majority of architectural remains are the stone foundations of the buildings, of which the mudbrick and timber superstructures have not survived. The lower floors would have been used for storage, reached by trapdoors and ladders from above. However, a few houses have large, more imposing, entrances leading from the street.

The largest, most ambitious, architecture at Gournia is a structure known as the "palace." Although occupying an area of approximately 98 x 131 ft (30 x 40 m), it is neither as complex nor as monumental as the Minoan palace at Knossos. However, the discovery of several objects inscribed with Linear A script support the idea that the palace at Gournia was an administrative center. In addition, the palace appears to have been the focus for cult ceremonies, including feasting.

Life at Gournia came to a sudden end in the middle of the second millennium B.C.E., when, in common with the other major sites on Crete, the town and its palace were destroyed by fire. Evidence of some reoccupation in the Minoan post-palatial period is demonstrated by the presence of a small, single-roomed shrine, around 9 x 13 ft (3 x 4 m). The room's function was identified by the presence of terracotta female figurines with upraised arms and several examples of cult vessels known as "snake tubes," which would have been displayed on the stone bench at one end of the room.

The settlement was initially excavated in the early years of the twentieth century by a team under American archaeologist Harriet Boyd, later Harriet Boyd Hawes, the first woman to direct a major archaeological excavation on Crete.

Gournia is in east Crete, easily accessible just off the coastal road, and a journey along the road provides splendid panoramic views of the site. The majority of the finds from Gournia are exhibited at the Archaeological Museum of Heraklion.

Opposite, from top A paved street at Gournia, alongside the stone foundations of houses. The town and palace of Gournia, close to a natural harbor on the Aegean Sea.

THE MINOAN PALACE AT **KNOSSOS**

TYPE: PALACE • **ARCHITECTURAL STYLE:** MINOAN
LOCATION: CRETE, GREECE • **CONSTRUCTION BEGUN:** CA. 2000 B.C.E.

The attractive and highly distinctive Bronze Age material culture on the island of Crete is named "Minoan" after its mythical king. The site at Knossos, a short drive from the modern city of Heraklion, is the largest and most significant of the Minoan palaces. The considerable reconstructions of the palace by the British archaeologist Sir Arthur Evans, following his excavations in the early part of the twentieth century, give a striking impression of the extent and opulence of the Minoan buildings. In addition, Knossos had a long, and frequently prosperous, history both before and after the Minoan era.

Although there is evidence of a pre-Neolithic presence on Crete, the first settlers did not arrive at Knossos until around 7000 B.C.E., when they established their homes on the site of what was to become the later Minoan palace. The use of the term "palace" is somewhat misleading; in addition to being a residence, archaeology suggests that the palaces were the economic, religious, creative, and administrative focus of a series of states, similar to Greek cities of the Classical period. In addition to having extensive archives of clay tablets, the palaces supported a large number of specialist artisans, best known for their production of a remarkable series of wall paintings, now fragmentary. This era came to a violent and abrupt end in the middle of the second millennium B.C.E., when many of the major sites on Crete, including the palace at Knossos, were destroyed by fire.

Shortly afterward, the palace was rebuilt and reoccupied, seemingly by Mycenaean invaders from the Greek mainland, and many of the remains that can be seen at Knossos today date from this period. The area continued to be inhabited until the fourteenth century B.C.E., when the palace was destroyed by fire, and not

Opposite Loggia at the North Entrance of the palace, with a restored fresco of a charging bull.

Above Throne Room with original gypsum throne and restored wall paintings depicting griffins.

rebuilt. Although the surrounding area flourished for another 2,000 years, the palace site was never reinhabited, possibly because of its supposed associations with the myth of the Minotaur, a creature that was part man, part bull. In the late first century B.C.E. the Roman emperor Augustus (63 B.C.E.–14 C.E.) established a colony named Colonia Julia Nobilis Cnossus to the north of the palace site, which became one of the main Roman cities on Crete.

The Palace Layout

The plan of the palace is complex, reflecting its size and its multifunctional nature. Architecturally, it appears to have been designed from the central court outward. The central court would have served as a focus for the many ceremonial activities of the palace.

There were several entrances to the palace, none of which was especially grand or spectacular. The approach from the west is that used by today's visitors and, indeed, may have been the norm in the past. In the west court, a bust of Sir Arthur Evans (1851–1941) greets visitors—he began archaeological work at Knossos in 1900.

The west court was paved, crossed by raised causeways, and gives a good view of the west facade of the palace, which had a lower course of large blocks of gypsum. Quarried locally, they would have appeared startlingly white when freshly cut.

The western magazines were among the first parts of the palace to be excavated, in the late nineteenth century, by Minos Kalokairinos (1843–1907), an antiquarian who lived in Heraklion. In 1878 Kalokairinos uncovered a section of the west part of the palace and produced a sketch of the throne room. Facing the throne is a sunken area around 3 ft (1 m) below the main floor level, which Evans termed a "lustral basin," suggesting the area was used for cult practice. Also off the west side of the central court of the palace was a shrine with two stone-lined sunken pits, named by Evans the Temple Repositories due to the religious characteristics of their contents. At the northwest corner of the palace, the Royal Road led from the complex to the west toward the town.

Following the excavations at Knossos, Evans wished visitors to appreciate the magnificence of the Minoan buildings. Accordingly, he arranged for extensive reconstructions to be made to the architectural remains, based on images in the Minoan wall paintings found at Knossos. In addition, Evans commissioned restorations of wall paintings from the site, which were instrumental in popularizing Minoan society. The wall paintings depicted men and women undertaking various activities, including cult ceremonies and the sport of bull leaping.

The Palace is 3 miles (5 km) south of Heraklion, the administrative capital of the island. The Archaeological Museum of Heraklion has the majority of finds from Knossos, and it is possible to visit both site and museum on the same day.

Opposite General view of the northern part of the Palace of Minos at Knossos.

Right, from top The restored Grand Staircase linking the several floors of the east side of the palace. The West Magazines with large vessels (pithoi) and pits used for the storage of agricultural produce. Faience figurines, known as the Snake Goddesses from the Temple Repositories off the Central Court.

THE **PERGAMON** ACROPOLIS

TYPE: ROYAL CITY • **ARCHITECTURAL STYLE:** CLASSICAL
LOCATION: WESTERN TURKEY • **CONSTRUCTION BEGUN:** THIRD CENTURY B.C.E.

Perched atop a steep mountain in Mysia, northwestern Turkey, Pergamon (modern Bergama) was the royal capital of Philetairos (343–263 B.C.E.), founder of the Attalid dynasty in 282 B.C.E. Some 19 miles (30 km) from the sea, the site is one of great drama, its design following the countours of the mountain so that the upper city pivots around the city's steeply stepped theater.

This Hellenistic city was transformed after Attalos I (241–197 B.C.E.) defeated the Gauls (who had settled in Galatia in what is now central Turkey). The victory was commemorated in the sanctuary of Athena that was located, with a Doric temple (the foundations are clearly visible), on a terrace above the theater. Within its precinct were a number of monuments commemorating the Attalid victory. Although these are now lost, one of the likely candidates was the "Trumpeter," better known as the Dying Gaul; a later copy is on display in the Capitoline Museum, Rome. Attalos' son and successor Eumenes II (197–158 B.C.E.) enhanced this space with the construction of colonnades (stoas) and a monumental gateway (propylon) that bears the inscription, "King Eumenes to the victory-bearing Athena." Carved trophies of war decorate the gateway. On the north side of the sanctuary stood the celebrated library of Pergamon. Access was via the upper story of the sanctuary's stoa. The library contained a reading room that held 15–20,000 works. Inside this space was a 11.5 ft- (3.5 m-) high marble statue of the Athena Parthenos, a copy of Pheidias' colossal gold and ivory statue dating to the 440s B.C.E. that once stood in the Parthenon on the Athenian acropolis.

Dominating the skyline of the Pergamon acropolis, to the southwest of the sanctuary of Athena, was the monumental stepped altar of Zeus, constructed by Eumenes II. This structure uses the battle between the Greek gods and the giants to evoke the Attalid victory over the Gauls, just as the Parthenon's decoration celebrated Greek

victories over the Persians in the early fifth century B.C.E. Inscriptions identified some of the figures. Parts of the continuous relief deliberately quote elements from the architectural sculpture of the Parthenon on the Athenian acropolis. The altar itself was reached via twenty steps; those approaching the altar were flanked by colossal figures in the reliefs. This central area was surrounded by the myth of Telephos from whom the Attalids claimed their descent.

Royal palaces occupied the east side of the Pergamon acropolis, adjacent to the sanctuary of Athena and the library. They contained a central courtyard (peristyle).

Attalos III bequeathed the city to Rome in 133 B.C.E. Under the Roman Emperor Hadrian (76–138 C.E.) a massive temple to the divine Emperor Trajan (53–117 C.E.) was constructed to the northwest of the sanctuary of Athena and immediately above the theater.

The major sanctuary of the healing-god Asklepios was constructed in the lower city. It contained a temple of the god, dedicated by a Roman consul in ca. 150 C.E., that was a smaller version of the Pantheon at Rome.

There are buses to the town of Bergama where there is a museum containing finds from the ancient city. There is a steep climb to the royal city or you can take a taxi (and enjoy walking down). Stout shoes are recommended.

Opposite Parts of the Temple of Trajan have been reconstructed. This area overlies part of the Attalid city.

Above The steeply sloping Hellenistic theater with the platform for the Temple of Trajan above it.

NOVGOROD THE GREAT

TYPE: MEDIEVAL CITY • **ARCHITECTURAL STYLE:** OLD-RUSSIAN ARCHITECTURE
LOCATION: NOVGOROD OBLAST, NORTHWEST RUSSIA
CONSTRUCTION BEGUN: TURN OF THE NINTH AND TENTH CENTURIES C.E.

Novgorod (which means New Town in Russian) is one of the country's oldest cities, known as a cradle of Russian statehood and famed for its thousand-year history and incredibly rich archaeology. It has for centuries been the largest trade hub of Eastern Europe, with links to Scandinavia and Germany, as well as to the Black Sea and Muslim centers of the East. It happily escaped the Mongol invasion that reduced the other large cities of Russia to ashes. The modern city, which stands on top of many cultural layers of the medieval town, bears the name of Veliky Novgorod (Novgorod the Great). It lies on the Volkhov River, 3.7 miles (6 km) from Lake Ilmen, 340 miles (550 km) northwest of Moscow and 90 miles (145 km) southeast of St. Petersburg. Since 1992 the historic monuments of Novgorod and its surroundings have been on the UNESCO World Heritage List.

Excavations and finds

The first attempts at archaeological investigation in the city took place in the early nineteenth century, but serious excavations in Novgorod began in the 1920s and 1930s and continue to this day. The systematic research carried out by V. Artsikhovsky, M. Karger, V. Yanin, V. Sedov, and other famous archaeologists was unequalled in Russia, or even Europe, in terms of the scale of the work, the number of discovered artifacts, and scholarly achievements. Nevertheless, only about two percent of the ancient city has been studied so far.

From an archaeological point of view Novgorod is unique. The extremely damp soil with its anaerobic effects ensured amazing preservation of organic materials such as wood, leather, bone, birchbark, fabrics, and grain. Occupation layers up to 23–25 ft (7–8 m) thick preserved stacks of wooden pavements and house walls. In fact 800-year-old logs are so hard that they could be re-used for construction and trucks could easily drive over the ancient pavements. A thin layer of corrosion formed quickly on metal objects buried in the damp clay, protecting them from further destruction. Also, because of this great humidity, the citizens avoided building foundations beneath their houses, cellars, and utility pits, so later layers have not disturbed earlier ones.

Excavations have revealed entire quarters of the medieval city with buildings, streets, and an infrastructure system, as well as an extensive collection of artifacts—at least 150,000 individual finds. Among the artifacts are tools and manufacturing implements, household utensils, means of transportation, tableware and food remains, shoes and clothing, warriors' weapons and riders' equipment, jewelry and musical instruments, adult games and children's toys, coins and stamps, birchbark manuscripts, fragments of frescoes, architectural details of houses and remains of furniture, residues of raw materials and of various crafts, and more.

Opposite The great St. Sophia's Cathedral built in 1045–50 C.E., the oldest surviving stone church in Russia.

The main focus of archaeological investigation has been the city's households. These were large complexes. Each included a two- or three-story house, servants' cabins, outbuildings, and almost always some kind of craft workshop. With all its political and commercial importance, Novgorod was primarily a town of craftsmen, the largest center of handicraft production in northeast Europe. Excavations have revealed about 150 handicraft workshops from the eleventh to fifteenth centuries: leatherworkers, jewelers, blacksmiths, coopers, potters, casters, turners, bone cutters, glassmakers, shoemakers, brewers, weavers, dyers, and bakers among them.

Novgorod is also considered to be one of the major centers of Russian culture and spirituality—one of the oldest schools of icon painting and the birthplace of national stone architecture. The town's citadel (*kremlin*) was built in the tenth century from wood, and was destroyed many times by fire. In the fifteenth century it was rebuilt of stone and brick in the shape of an oval wall with twelve towers and two gates. But the church—St. Sophia's Cathedral—had already been built of stone and brick inside the wooden kremlin in the eleventh century. After that, more than fifty churches were built in Novgorod and its vicinity, and some of them still survive. They were decorated with beautiful frescoes and icons. Among the excavated workshops there is one in which a whole group of painters worked with their apprentices, and even the name of the master—Olisey Grechin—has been established. In 2000 the oldest dated Slavonic book was discovered in Novgorod. It consists of wooden plaques covered with wax, on which the texts could be scratched and erased many times; it dates to the turn of the eleventh century. The excavations have also yielded a major collection of medieval musical instruments.

Below The Novgorod Kremlin—one of the two cylindrical towers, built in the fifteenth century, in the process of reconstruction.

Opposite Birchbark manuscript N 35, dating back to 1320—1340.

Chronology

Novgorod is a unique example of a productive combination of historical, archaeological, and scientific methods of dating. The earliest mention of its name has been found in a chronicle of 859 C.E., and the town was first called Novgorod the Great in a chronicle from 1169. Many other written sources provide rich information on the city's later history. Archaeological dating in Novgorod is extraordinarily accurate, because the streets were paved with wood, and most of the houses were constructed from wood, which makes it possible to use dendrochronology (tree-ring dating). Dates can be calculated accurately to within one year of a tree's cutting. Hence any wooden structure in Novgorod can be precisely dated, as can the artifacts contained within it. The first pavements were laid in the 930s C.E. and had to be replaced every ten to twenty years. Stacks of up to thirty timber floorings exist, dating from the tenth century (lowermost) to the fifteenth (uppermost), grew on the ancient streets of Novgorod. Finds made between those layers have been dated with an accuracy of ten to twenty years. Radiocarbon dating has also been used here, and confirms that the earliest dates for the citadel and for the bridge over the Volkhov River are of the mid-tenth century. However, there is a problem with dating a thin mixed layer that lies beneath the first pavement.

Birchbark manuscripts

One of the greatest successes of Russian archaeology in the last century is the discovery in Novgorod of an absolutely new kind of historical source—manuscripts, scratched on birchbark. The first example was found in 1951, but more than 1,100 have now been unearthed in the city, as well as several at other sites. The manuscripts are found in all the stratigraphic layers of Novgorod from the first half of the eleventh to the second half of the fifteenth centuries. Tools for writing on birchbark have also found in the layers of 953–989 C.E.

Most of the birchbarks are private letters of a business nature (debt collection, trade and household instructions), but there are also drafts of official acts (wills, receipts, bills of sale, court records, and so on). Rarer, but of particular interest, are church texts (prayers, memorial lists, orders for icons, morals), literary and folklore subjects (jokes, riddles, homework instructions), love letters and records of an educational nature (alphabet, school exercises, children's drawings, and scribbles). The last, created by a six- to seven-year-old boy Onfim are especially famous.

The discovery of birchbarks significantly changed our understanding of the city's culture, showing that literacy in medieval Novgorod extended to all segments of society—including villains! Ordinary people wrote letters to each other, and women were no exception. These manuscripts shed light on many obscure aspects of Novgorod's history, and contain priceless evidence about written and spoken language, households, everyday life, and the personal relationships of the city's medieval people.

Visitors to the city can expect to see beautiful wooden and stone architecture, numerous medieval churches and monasteries (including the great St. Sophia's cathedral built in 1045–50, the oldest stone church in Russia), archaeological digs in several parts of the city, and rich collections of artifacts in the city museum.

THE KURGANS AND MEGALITHS OF **KHAKASIA**

TYPE: ARCHAEOLOGICAL MONUMENTS • **ARCHITECTURAL STYLE:** N/A **LOCATION:** REPUBLIC OF KHAKASIA, SOUTH SIBERIA, RUSSIA • **CONSTRUCTION BEGUN:** THIRD MILLENNIUM B.C.E.

The Republic of Khakasia in southern Siberia is one of Russia's richest in terms of archaeology, its landscape defined by a high concentration of megalithic funerary and memorial constructions. The most visible and most famous of these features a collection of extraordinary stone statues and kurgans (burial mounds) surrounded by a perimeter made of stone slabs and megaliths, some of which are decorated with petroglyphs.

Steppe idols

Only a century ago, megalithic statues were as characteristic a feature of the historical landscape of Khakasia as the kurgans. Today, almost all of them are in museums. These beautiful, mysterious monuments, dubbed "steppe idols" by eighteenth-century travelers and scholars, are usually 6.5–16.5 ft (2–5 m) tall, made of sandstone or granite. They were carved by the skillful artists of the Okunev culture, which existed in the region during the Early Bronze Age (2600–1800 B.C.E.). The statues usually have an effigy in the middle or lower part. Realistic human faces are very rare: anthropomorphous face masks with three eyes are typical, decorated with intricate lines and curves, sometimes with bull horns and ears, and often with very complicated headdresses. Figures with large stomachs and breasts probably represent pregnant females. The statues are marked with solar symbols and solar rays sometimes surround a face mask. These amazing objects were not funerary monuments, but erected for ritual purposes, and remained objects of cult and reverence long after. The Khakas people, four millennia later, honored ancient statues, worshipped them, and made offerings to them. Even today traces of fat and butter remain on the mouths of stone idols, believed to help people have more children, better health, and greater wealth.

The Cemetery Steppe

Surrounded and protected by mountains and taiga, the Khakasia steppe has a gentle continental climate, and an abundance of animals appropriate for farming and pastoralism. The region has always attracted different tribes and peoples, many of whom have left burial sites. From the Eneolithic onward, all cultures used stone slabs for building graves and kurgans; some of them were distinguished by huge megalithic funerary constructions. When, in 1721, the German scholar Daniel Gottlieb Messerschmidt came here to investigate Siberia at the behest of Peter the Great, he was so amazed by the abundance of kurgans with stone slabs that he considered the whole area to be a huge cemetery with the deceased having been brought from all over Asia. Even in the nineteenth century, the central part of Khakasia was still known as the Cemetery Steppe.

Opposite Decorated stone stelae in the perimeter of a burial mound in the Safronov cemetery.

The great kurgans of Salbyk and Barsuchy Log

Especially numerous among the kurgans are those of the Tagar culture, a people who inhabited the region in the ninth to third centuries B.C.E., and who covered all of Khakasia with their cemeteries, some containing hundreds of kurgans. The Tagar kurgans consisted of pyramidal mounds made of turf and clay, within a perimeter built of stone slabs with tall menhirs in the corners and on the sides. Early examples were intended for one person and had several feet of perimeter and four corner stones. As the culture developed, kurgans began to vary in size. Larger examples with bigger megaliths—and more of them—were constructed for collective burials, with especially grandiose structures erected for nobles. The most famous concentration of "royal" kurgans lies in the Salbyk valley, 37 miles (60 km) north of Abakan, where several kurgans are known whose diameter exceeds 164 ft (50 m) amid a hundred of normal size. One of them, the biggest kurgan and megalithic structure in the whole of Siberia, is the so-called Great Salbyk, excavated in the 1950s. Today all that remains is its impressive stone construction, a square with sides measuring 230 ft (70 m), made of gigantic blocks of Devonian sandstone. At the corners, along the sides, and beside the entrance, are twenty-three huge vertical stone slabs, some weighing up to fifty tons. The mound, which before excavation looked like an average hill, was originally pyramidal in shape, 82–98 ft (25-30 m) high. The tomb had been ravaged, unfortunately, and the only finds were a bronze knife dating to the fourth or fifth century B.C.E. and a big clay vessel. The person buried in Great Salbyk was clearly a great chief and leader of a union of tribes, or even a powerful "tsar" of the whole region.

In 2004–2005 another "royal" kurgan, Barsuchy Log, was excavated in the Salbyk Steppe and dates to the fifth century B.C.E. Originally the mound had been a pyramid more than 33 ft (10 m) high, with a square stone wall measuring 177 × 177 ft (54 × 54 m), and a stone perimeter of twenty-nine decorated slabs. The wall consisted of vertical slabs with corner and intermediate megaliths, but it also had an internal masonry of horizontally laid slabs, which is unusual for the Tagar culture. This tomb had also been robbed in antiquity, but its complicated structure of logs was well preserved due to many protective layers of birchbark.

Decorated stelae

The slabs and megaliths used in the construction of kurgans are often decorated with pecked and engraved images. Sometimes the builders reused statues and stelae taken from sanctuaries or cemeteries of earlier periods. In other cases images were created specifically for a given burial. Most often, however, people of later cultures made the depictions on surfaces exposed aboveground. Most of the kurgans in Khakasia belong to the Tagar culture, and the great majority of the kurgan rock art dates from the Xiongny-Xianbei period that followed (last centuries B.C.E. to first centuries C.E.), and is associated with migrants from North China and Mongolia. These petroglyphs most probably reflect afterlife transition rituals; they depict animals, humans and flying birds, as well as concentric circles, spirals, labyrinths, and other abstract motifs. Such open-air "galleries" can be seen everywhere in Khakasia, but the most impressive is that of the Safronov cemetery, which has the biggest decorated kurgan slabs—the tallest megalith is about 16.5 ft (5 m tall)—and many of them are literally covered with interwoven and intersecting images.

Excursions to the kurgans with megaliths are organized by many tour agencies in Abakan, the Republic's capital, while rich collections of decorated megaliths exist in Abakan and Minusinsk museums, as well as in an open-air museum in the village of Poltakov.

Opposite, clockwise from left Archival photo showing a Khakas man next to a stone statue of the Okunev culture. Perimeter stone structure of the Barsuchy Log kurgan. A fantastic monster of the Okunev culture depicted on a stone slab. A typical Khakassian steppe landscape with kurgan stone slabs.

SIBERIA'S **OGLAKHTY MOUNTAINS**

TYPE: NATURAL AND CULTURAL LANDSCAPE • **ARCHITECTURAL STYLE:** N/A
LOCATION: REPUBLIC OF KHAKASIA, SOUTH SIBERIA, RUSSIA • **CONSTRUCTION BEGUN:** N/A

The Oglakhty mountainous massif in south Siberia is a remarkable example of the interweaving of culture with nature. This picturesque territory presents a unique combination of mountain, forest, steppe, and coastal landscape, inhabited by a range of rare and endangered plant and animal species. The region is literally saturated with evidence of its cultural transformation through the millennia. It's a rich archaeological heritage that features all kind of monuments, among them numerous visually attractive rock art sites.

Settlements, burial mounds, and burial grounds

The Oglakhty and adjacent steppe areas have been inhabited for millennia. During the Upper Palaeolithic people hunted big mammals here, some species of which became extinct, while others changed their habitats. In the northern foothills of the range, a major site from this period has rich collections of stone tools and palaeontological remains. It has not been excavated, but was exposed by the activity of the Krasnoyarsk reservoir. The camps of Neolithic hunters have been excavated in the southern foothills of Oglakhty. From the Eneolithic up to modern times, increasing numbers of people came here, each of their cultures influencing the next—hunters and fishers, settled farmers and metalworkers, nomadic and seminomadic pastoralists, warriors and civilians, for example. These periods are represented by various funerary constructions, most of which feature slabs of the Devonian red sandstone from the Oglakhty mountains.

Numerous cemeteries with hundreds of graves are concentrated in the steppe foothills and intermontane valleys. The most notable are the stone-and-earth mounds of the Tagar and Tes cultures (ninth century B.C.E. to second century C.E.). They have rectangular stone perimeters with high intermediate and corner slabs, and a mound inside. The graves were also made of stone slabs. Early burial sites were small and intended for one individual, but as the culture developed the mounds grew higher, the perimeters became bigger with increased numbers of intermediate stones, and the burials became collective. These complicated funerary constructions with highly visible slabs are an essential feature of the historical landscape of the Minusinsk basin in general, and Oglakhty in particular. Unfortunately almost all of these burials were looted in antiquity.

The opposite applies to the burial grounds. Thanks to their less conspicuous presence in the landscape, many

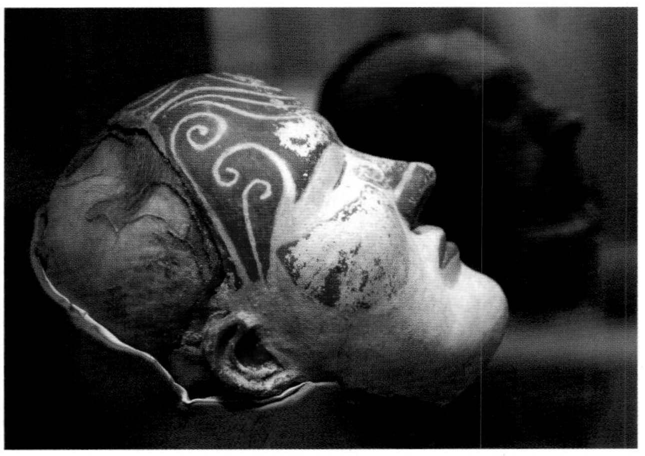

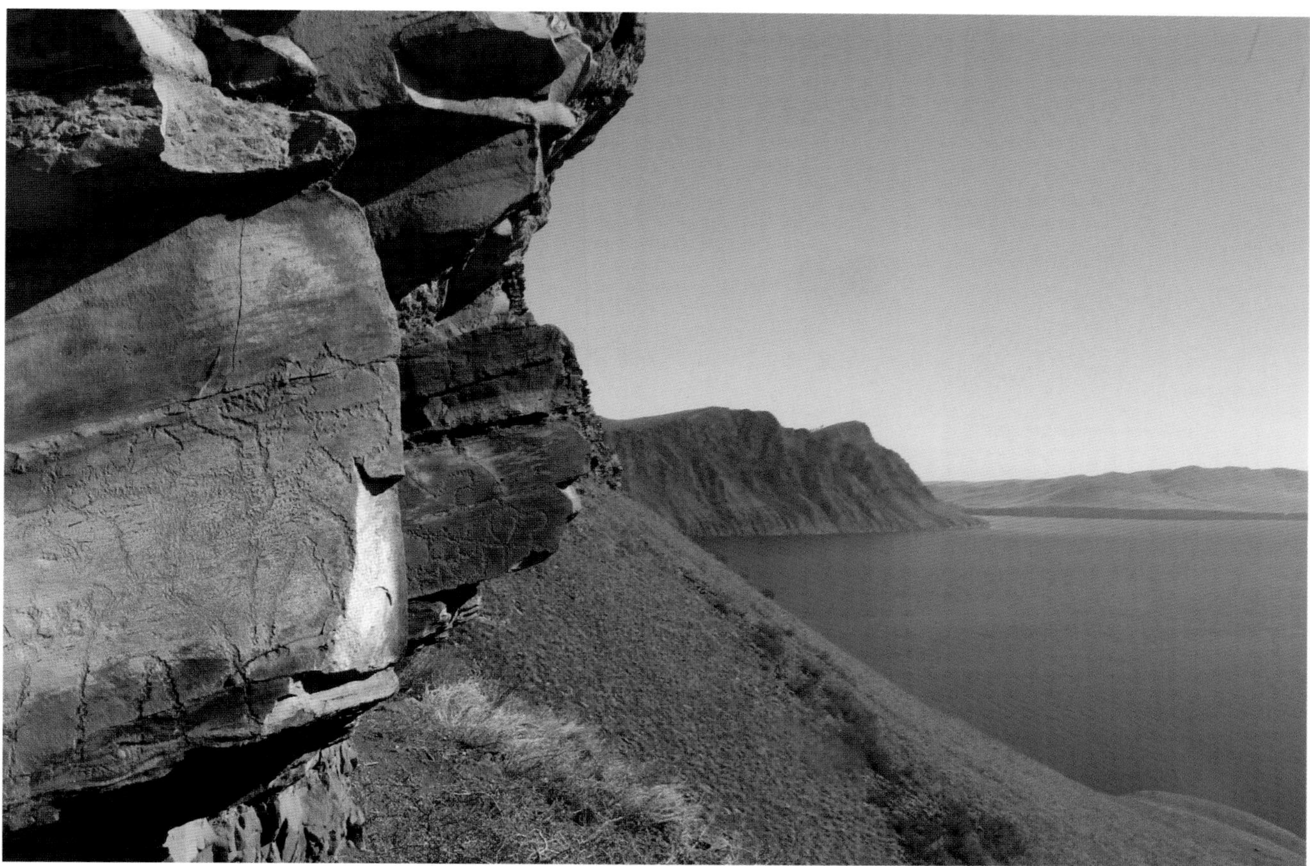

of these preserve rich burial assemblages. Oglakhty is especially famous for a huge cemetery of the third to fourth century C.E., which belongs to the Tashtyk culture. The first grave was discovered by chance and excavated in 1903, with further excavations taking place in the 1960s. Some burials had exceptionally well preserved organic material due to natural factors and the funerary constructions. The funerary practices are very unusual: in the same grave were found not only buried bodies (mummies), but also leather imitations of bodies containing the remains of cremations. Both types are dressed in fur clothes, and have distinctive hairstyles, and painted funeral masks on their faces. Unique materials from the Oglakhty Tashtyk cemetery are now on display in the Historical Museum in Moscow and the Hermitage Museum in St Petersburg.

Opposite A painted gypsum mask on a female skull from the Oglakhty cemetery (Tashtyk culture).

Above Images of Tashtyk archers pecked into rock, with a view of the Yenisei River.

The stone wall

Oglakhty is famous for its so-called fortress—an enormous stone structure, consisting of horizontally laid sandstone slabs, which surrounds the mountainous massif as a wall. It runs for almost 15.5 miles (25 km) along the steep edge of the mountains, and blocks the passage to seven valleys between them. In some places a ditch is visible in front of the wall; there are also bastions and some zigzag-shaped sections. The wall is up to 6.6 ft (2 m) wide, and now only 3.3 ft (1 m) high because, in the mid-twentieth century, the slabs were dismantled for construction. The records of early travelers mention that it was about 6.6 ft (2 m) high. This grandiose construction was presumably erected during the tenth to twelfth centuries C.E. to protect local people against Uighur invasions.

Rock art

Rock art is undoubtedly the most important cultural feature of the Oglakhty range. The peculiarities of the terrain provided a huge number of convenient "canvases" to ancient artists. There are numerous Devonian red sandstone outcrops and, wherever they exist, there are images on the rocks. They have been made using all known techniques—pecking, engraving, abrading, and painting—and represent all the cultural and chronological periods identified in the archaeology of south Siberia from at least the Neolithic up to the ethnographic present. Most of the images feature on vertical rock surfaces, but others exist on stone blocks lying on the slopes, as well as on slabs used for mound construction. Rock art sites are scattered across the entire range. The richest concentrations are on the riverside cliffs (most of them now beneath the waters of the Krasnoyarsk reservoir, recorded before the flooding) and on the southwestern slopes of Sorok Zubiev (Forty Teeth) mountain. Together, the known rock art sites—fourteen in total—form the largest rock art complex of the Minusinsk Basin, acknowledged as one of the world's richest rock art areas. The complex is of exceptional value in terms of its coverage of chronological periods, diversity of styles, high artistic qualities, and repertoire of images and subjects.

The most interesting images are the earliest, made with great realism and artistic skill: wild horses, aurochs, wild boars, bears, elks and deer, as well as enigmatic anthropomorphic figures and boats with "passengers." Their date is unknown. They may be Neolithic, but cannot be less than five or six millennia old. In the past, all the coastal cliffs were entirely covered with such figures. Of later rock art, the most noteworthy include images of daggers and chariots from the Late Bronze Age, beautiful decorated deer and horse figures in the Scythian style, a cauldron and a yurt, numerous shamanic scenes, and many other subjects, styles, and images from various epochs and peoples, reflecting Oglakhty's turbulent past.

The Oglakhty mountain range extends for 9 miles (15 km) and is located on the left bank of the Yenisei River (now the Krasnoyarsk reservoir), 37 miles (60 km) downstream of Abakan, the capital of the Republic of Khakassia. The territory is on the UNESCO Tentative List and is partially protected by the State Natural Reserve, which organizes excursions to the sites of Oglakhty.

Above The southwestern slopes of the Oglakhty Range.
Right Petroglyphs on a kurgan slab, in the Tagar culture cemetery in the northern part of the range.

THE PETROGLYPHS OF **TOMSKAYA PISANITSA**

TYPE: ROCK ART SITE • **ARCHITECTURAL STYLE:** N/A **LOCATION:** KEMEROVO OBLAST, SOUTHWESTERN SIBERIA, RUSSIA • **CONSTRUCTION BEGUN:** THIRD MILLENNIUM B.C.E.

Sited in a most picturesque location, 37 miles (60 km) downstream from the city of Kemerovo in Siberia, Tomskaya Pisanitsa is a tremendous riverside cliff covered with petroglyphs, carved 4,000–5,000 years ago, with a natural rocky platform in front of it. This rare peculiarity—the rocky platform—made the place appropriate for a sanctuary in antiquity and for a museum today. Tomskaya Pisanitsa, which in modern Russian means "rock art site on the Tom River," is one of the most interesting rock-art sites in Russia, famous for its very long history of investigation.

The cliff holds the largest concentration of images among many other decorated rocks occurring for 30 miles (50 km) on the right bank of the Tom River, and is the center of the Historical, Cultural and Natural Museum-Reserve Tomskaya Pisanitsa.

The Russians who came to Siberia in the sixteenth and seventeenth centuries were particularly impressed with the abundant ancient imagery on the rocks along many Siberian rivers. They called them Pisanitsas, from the Russian word *pisanyi*, which means "decorated, covered with drawings or inscriptions." One such scenic rock, facing the Tom River in southwest Siberia and surrounded by beautiful pine forests, already attracted the attention of the first explorers in the seventeenth century, and a remarkable description of it survives in a chronicle from around 1645. P. J. von Strahlenberg published the first scholarly description of the site, along with a drawing in 1730, in Stockholm. He based his work on data obtained by D. G. Messerschmidt (1685–1735), a German scholar who led the very first academic expedition to Siberia (sent there by order of Peter the Great), and who had actually discovered this rock art site for science in July 1721. Subsequently many famous travelers and scholars, from both Europe and Russia, visited the rock on the Tom River and published their descriptions, thoughts, drawings, tracings, and photographs. As a result, this site has the richest historiography and iconography of all Asian rock art sites.

Several vertical siltstone panels on the cliff bear more than 300 images and many fragments of destroyed figures. About half of the imagery is concentrated on one huge panel, the so-called Upper Frieze, which is more than 16.5 ft (5 m) long and 6.5 ft (2 m) high. It is situated above human height, above another panel—the Lower Frieze—which is badly damaged because of its greater accessibility. A narrow layer separates the two friezes and it is a mystery quite how the depictions on the inaccessible Upper Frieze were made. Nevertheless, its vast flat surface was once filled with an elaborate multifigured composition, which was then continuously added to and renewed.

Opposite, clockwise from top Some fragments of the Upper Frieze of Tomskaya Pisanitsa: images of elks and a human figure; an elk's head in profile and an owl; a bear; a bear and human figures with rays around their heads and ambiguous motifs in their hands.

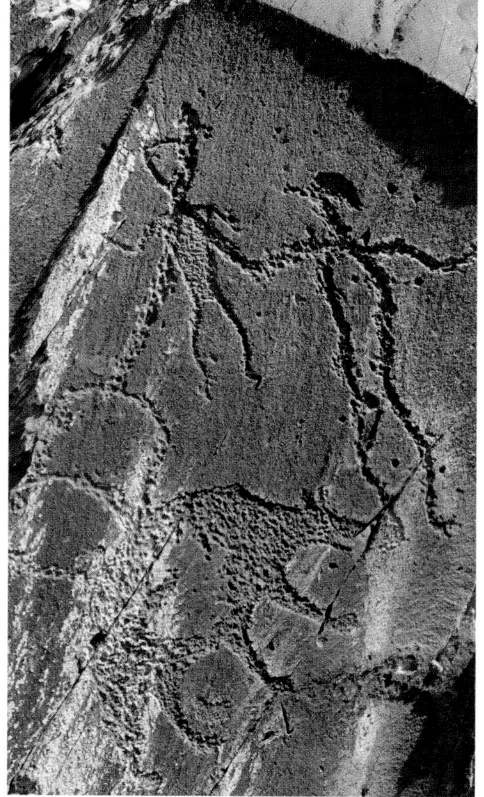

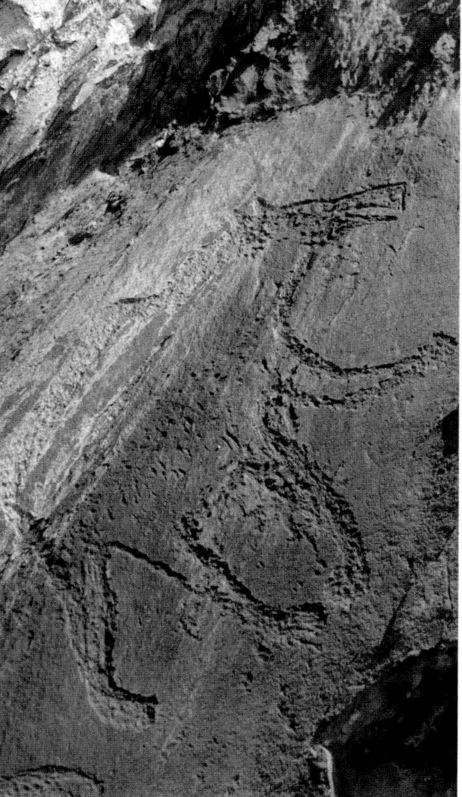

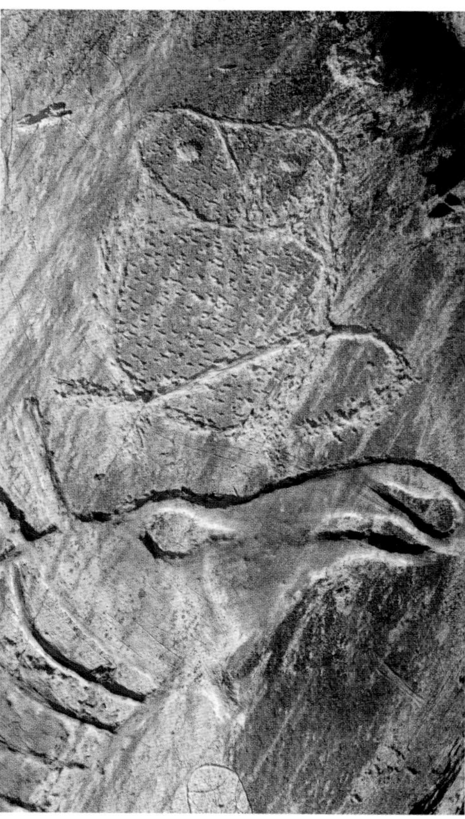

A Wealth of Diverse Imagery

The dominant image here is undoubtedly the elk. The depictions of this beautiful animal are made with great skill and are very expressive: elks are represented in motion, their long double-hoofed legs fully stretched out, or sometimes with front and hind legs crossed beneath the strongly humped torso. Their heads are particularly naturalistic with almond-shaped eyes, a typical elk muzzle with a big nostril, and a characteristic dewlap hanging down below the jaw. In some figures the heart and aorta are also shown; others are simply represented as contours with vertical arched stripes on the necks, the significance of which remains unknown. Elks still inhabit the forests around the museum reserve, and it is believed that the site is located precisely at a point where elks used to cross the river.

Besides elks there are images of a bear, a fox, and a doe, as well as several bird species, such as an owl, a crane, a heron, and a duck. The most famous of the bird images is that of the owl, which has become the "logo" of the museum reserve.

Anthropomorphous images at Tomskaya Pisanitsa are quite numerous and diverse in their iconography. Only a few of them are ordinary human figures, while the others are depicted in unusual poses, with various attributes (horns, halos, and rays around the head, incomprehensible objects in the hands, skis, bows, and so on), and sometimes with features of birds and animals, or wearing masks. Unlike the realistic images of animals, the anthropomorphous figures are emphatically unreal, most likely depicting mythological characters. There are also images of face masks (some are intricate, while others are just three dots representing the eyes and mouth), depictions of boats, and numerous complex symbols and signs.

The images are rendered using known rock-art techniques: pecking, engraving, abrading, and painting. The best preserved are the pecked figures, especially those that have been renewed and deepened over the centuries. The original scenes on these riverside rocks have seen much reworking over the millennia, their figures, subjects, and compositions supplemented, transformed, rethought, and renewed by subsequent generations of rock artists. This makes the task of dating and interpreting them even more difficult than usual. However, it has been established that the earliest images at Tomskaya Pisanitsa were created at least in the Early Bronze Age (late third to early second millennia B.C.E.), as some figures bear strong similarities in their style and iconography to the monumental and portable art from dated sites of adjacent areas. In order to make the dating of the rock art more precise, the museum reserve has carried out excavations near the rocks. Some recent discoveries show that the area was inhabited in the Neolithic. There are also layers of the Early Bronze Age and later. Interestingly, bronze artworks of much later periods were found in sediments above the Upper Frieze during conservation activities, which means that this place continued to be a sanctuary long after the creation of its imagery.

There are many other archaeological, ethnographic, and natural features in the reserve, including a special museum on the rock art of Asia within the Museum-reserve. The site is open to visitors year-round and excursions by boat to other sites can be organized in the summer.

Opposite A human figure on skis with a bow. This is the oldest rock art image of a skier in Siberia.

Above An aerial view of the cliff with petroglyphs on the Tom River, the sanctuary of Tomskaya Pisanitsa.

4

AFRICA

To many people, Egypt represents archaeology, and certainly its wealth of spectacular sites—especially the pyramids, Sphinx, temples and tombs—are among the most popular destinations in the world for archaeological tourism. Any TV documentaries on Egyptian sites or mummies are guaranteed a huge audience! But Africa is a vast continent, and there are many other varied treasures to be found far from Egypt: from the traces of our earliest ancestors to the rock art of the Drakensberg, from the impressive and mysterious ruins of Great Zimbabwe to the great monoliths of Aksum and the astonishing rock-cut churches of Lalibela.

Left Interior of the richly carved and decorated Biete Maryam church in Lalibela, Ethiopia.

AFRICA LOCATIONS

1 SAKKARA
2 THE GIZA PLATEAU
3 AMARNA
4 ABYDOS
5 DENDERA
6 KARNAK
7 DEIR EL-MEDINA
8 THE VALLEY OF THE KINGS
9 DEIR EL-BAHRI
10 ASWAN
11 ABU SIMBEL
12 SENEGAMBIAN STONE CIRCLES
13 AKSUM
14 LALIBELA
15 KILWA KISIWANI
16 GREAT ZIMBABWE
17 THE CRADLE OF HUMANKIND
18 MAPUNGUBWE
19 GAME PASS SHELTER

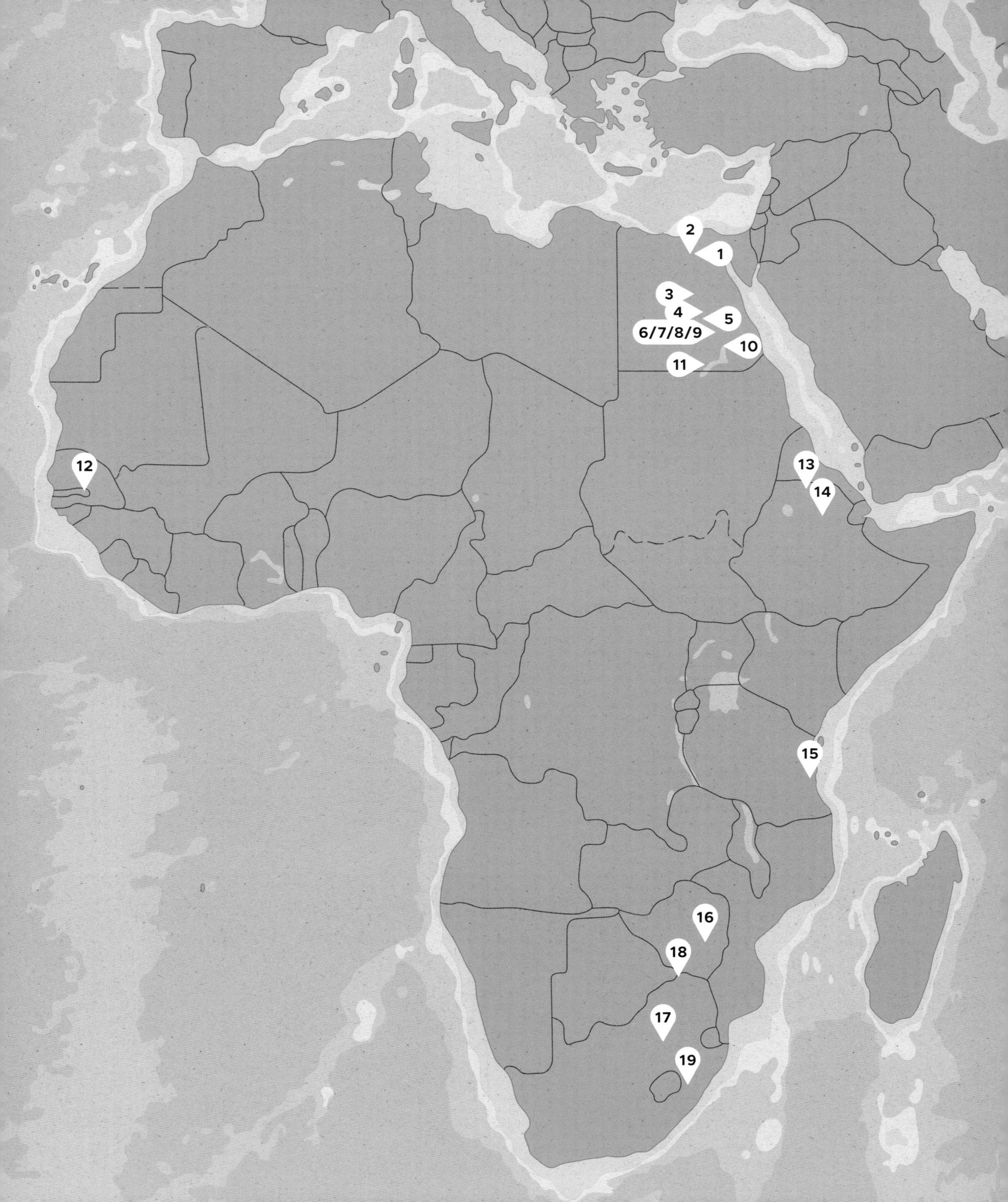

1
2
3
4
5
6/7/8/9
10
11
12
13
14
15
16
17
18
19

SAKKARA CITY OF THE DEAD

TYPE: CEMETERY • **ARCHITECTURAL STYLE:** PYRAMIDS AND TOMBS
LOCATION: CAIRO, EGYPT • **CONSTRUCTION BEGUN:** CA. 3100 B.C.E.

Rising in the arid landscape of northern Egypt's Western Desert, the Sakkara Step Pyramid was ancient Egypt's first stone building. The work of the innovative architect Imhotep, it is one of fifteen pyramids raised at this site near Heliopolis, ancient cult center of the sun god Ra. The extensive cemetery was used from the Early Dynastic to the Graeco-Roman periods, a timespan of over 3,000 years, but was particularly important during the Old Kingdom (ca. 2686–2160 B.C.E.).

From the 1st Dynasty onward (ca. 3000 B.C.E.), the civil servants who worked in Egypt's first capital city Memphis built mudbrick mastaba tombs in the Sakkara cemetery. Named for the Arabic word *mastaba,* or low bench, these tombs consisted of a rectangular superstructure covering a rock-cut burial chamber. Around the largest mastabas were smaller tombs built for servants who worked for the deceased. During the 2nd Dynasty (ca. 2890–2686 B.C.E.), several kings were buried at Sakkara. Unfortunately, the superstructures of their tombs have been lost.

Although occasionally packed with sand and gravel, the mastaba superstructures were more normally filled with storerooms for grave goods. These conspicuous storerooms proved vulnerable to thieves. By the end of the 1st Dynasty the number of rooms in the superstructure had been reduced in favor of extensive subterranean storage reached by a stairway, and eventually the mastaba became a solid mound. Gradually, stone walls replaced the mudbrick superstructure walls.

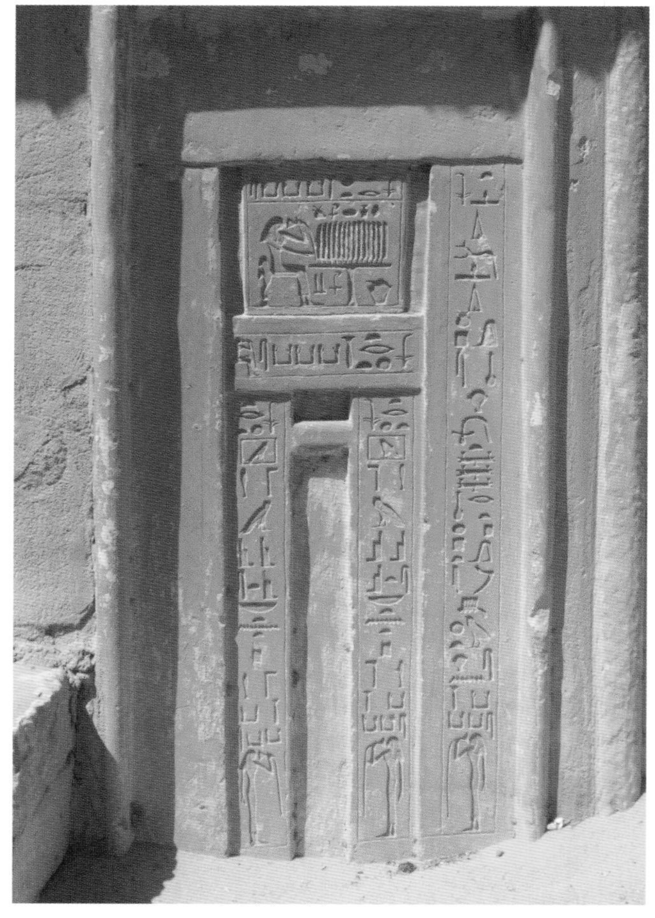

Right The "false door" from the tomb of the Old Kingdom priestess Wadjkawes. Visitors to the tomb would leave offerings of food and drink in front of this door.

Opposite The Step Pyramid of the 3rd Dynasty pharaoh Djoser. The world's first monumental stone building.

The Step Pyramid

The royal architect Imhotep designed a remarkable tomb for Djoser, second king of the 3rd Dynasty (r. ca. 2667–48 B.C.E.). Working in limestone cut from a nearby quarry, Imhotep built a solid, square mastaba with corners orientated to the points of the compass. This was subsequently extended outward and upward until, after several intermediate stages, it became a six-step pyramid. As it stands today, Djoser's pyramid measures 197 ft (60 m) high, and has a footprint of 397 x 358 ft (121 x 109 m).

A wide shaft descending from the center of the original mastaba led to Djoser's burial chamber. This small, granite-lined room, too small to house a stone sarcophagus, could only be entered via a 3.3 ft- (1 m-) wide hole in the ceiling. During the funeral the king's body must have been lowered into position, then the hole sealed with a stone plug. A warren of corridors and rooms surrounded the chamber. In the King's Apartment (a modern term employed by archaeologists) over 36,000 curved blue-green faience tiles replicated the reed walls of Djoser' earthly palace.

The Step Pyramid was just one element in Djoser's funerary complex. Around the pyramid was an enclosure defined by a massive limestone wall equipped with fourteen false doors plus one actual entrance. The best-known and most fully restored buildings within this enclosure lie in the southern and eastern sections, and in the area around the pyramid. Here Imhotep created a series of inaccessible symbolic buildings; replicas of Egypt's most important shrines, whose carved stone doors could never be opened by the living. Here, too, was a ritual racetrack where Djoser could, in perpetuity, run to prove his fitness to rule Egypt.

Sakkara in the Late Old Kingdom

In the later part of the Old Kingdom (from the end of Dynasty 4 to the end of Dynasty 6: ca. 2530–2181 B.C.E.), the monumental landscape of Sakkara was greatly expanded by a series of smaller pyramids built by kings who wished to be buried close to Djoser (including the pyramids of Unas, Userkaf, and Teti) and in the expansion of the site to the south (including the pyramids of Pepi I, Merenre, and Pepi II). At the same time, high officials of the royal court built magnificent mastaba tombs, whose walls they covered with reliefs of the highest quality showing the type of afterlife these individuals wished for themselves.

Opposite top An entry to one of several ritual buildings forming part of the funerary complex.

Opposite bottom left The Old Kingdom official Khenu, depicted on his tomb wall in the Unas Causeway cemetery at Sakkara.

Opposite bottom right A stone statue of the pharaoh Djoser.

Below The pyramid and mortuary temple of King Unas

Animal Burials

Not all of the Sakkara burials were human. From the New Kingdom until the Ptolemaic Period (ca. 1550–30 B.C.E.) the sacred Apis bulls were buried in the Serapeum, or bull cemetery. Before the 19th Dynasty reign of Ramesses II (r. ca. 1279–1213 B.C.E.) the mummified bulls were interred in individual tombs. Subsequently they were buried in enormous stone sarcophagi in underground galleries to the northwest of the Step Pyramid.

While the Apis bulls died natural deaths, the millions of animals—including cats, dogs, baboons, and ibises—interred in the catacombs of the sacred animal necropolis were killed and mummified to serve as votive offerings to the gods Bastet, Anubis, and Thoth during the Late and Graeco-Roman periods (664 B.C.E.–395 C.E.).

Travelers wishing to visit Sakkara are advised to take a taxi from Cairo and to ask it to wait, as the journey by public transport is both complicated and slow.

THE GIZA PLATEAU
A ROYAL NECROPOLIS

TYPE: CEMETERY • **ARCHITECTURAL STYLE:** PYRAMIDS
LOCATION: CAIRO, EGYPT • **CONSTRUCTION BEGUN:** 2589 B.C.E.

Intrepid Victorian tourists traveling from Cairo to Giza enjoyed a relaxing carriage ride through twelve peaceful miles (19 km) of fields. Today's visitors face a very different experience. Cairo has expanded so rapidly that the world's most famous monuments loom over the suburbs, and Pyramids Road offers a crowded and polluted introduction to the necropolis. Is the journey worth it? Absolutely. Nothing can match the experience of standing in the shadow of the magnificent pyramids built by Khufu (r. ca. 2589–2566 B.C.E.), his son Khaefre (r. ca. 2558–2532 B.C.E.) and grandson Menkaure (r. ca. 2532–2503 B.C.E.).

Khufu's Great Pyramid

The ancient Giza cemetery lay close by Egypt's first capital city, Memphis. It became a royal necropolis when King Khufu chose Giza as the site for his funerary complex. Today Khufu's Great Pyramid is recognized as the last surviving "Wonder" of the ancient World. The figures are astonishing. The Great Pyramid stands 481 ft (147 m) high, with a slope of fifty-one degrees. Its sides, with an average length of 758 ft (230 m), are orientated almost exactly toward true north, while its base is almost completely flat. The pyramid was once cased in fine limestone that sparkled in the sunlight, but this covering was stripped during the Middle Ages and reused in the building of Cairo. The relatively rough limestone blocks visible today represent the interior masonry.

Inside the Great Pyramid are three chambers linked by passageways. The Subterranean Chamber is an unfinished room of ritual significance. Within the pyramid masonry, the Queen's Chamber was not actually used for a queen's burial; it, too, is a room with an unknown purpose. The topmost room, the King's Chamber, still houses Khufu's impressive red granite sarcophagus. As we cannot see beneath the outer skin of stone, we cannot be certain that there are not more chambers and voids concealed within the masonry. We do know that "air-shafts"—narrow passageways orientated toward the northern pole star and the constellation of Orion—lead from the King's and the Queen's Chambers, and we can guess that these shafts had a ritual rather than practical function.

Khufu's pyramid was just one element in a large funerary complex that included an enclosure wall, a mortuary temple close by the pyramid, and a low-lying valley temple that is now lost under the modern suburb of Nazlet el-Simman. A causeway linked the two temples. Five boat-shaped pits were excavated close to the causeway and mortuary temple, but these were found to be empty when opened. Two narrow, rectangular pits dug parallel to the south side of the pyramid held dismantled wooden boats.

Opposite top The head of the Great Sphinx.

Opposite bottom The three pyramids of the Giza plateau, with three smaller pyramids built for royal women in the foreground.

One of these boats, excavated and restored, is now displayed in the Khufu Boat Museum near the Great Pyramid.

A small subsidiary pyramid lay outside the enclosure wall to the southeast of the main pyramid. Three larger queens' pyramids complete with mortuary chapels lay to the east of the subsidiary pyramid. All three were robbed in antiquity, but a shaft discovered to the east of the Great Pyramid in 1925 has yielded the burial equipment and jewelry of Queen Hetepheres, mother of Khufu.

Khaefre's Pyramid and Sphinx

Khaefre built his funerary complex to the south of the Great Pyramid. His pyramid is smaller than Khufu's, but is built on higher ground and this, together with its slightly steeper angle, makes it appear larger. Khaefre's pyramid had a subterranean burial chamber that was built and roofed in a large, open trench before the solid pyramid was built on top. Today Khaefre's complex is the most complete of the Giza three, and his pyramid is the only one to retain some of its original limestone casing.

The Great Sphinx crouches beside Khaefre's Valley Temple. At 236 ft (72 m) long and 65.6 ft (20 m) tall, it is Egypt's largest statue: its human head—Khaefre's head—is approximately twenty-two times life-sized; its lion's body is disproportionately large. Today the Sphinx is clean-shaven, but in the New Kingdom it gained a braided and curved beard of the type worn by gods and deified kings. As it is carved from a natural rocky outcrop covered in places with a stone block veneer, the Sphinx shows differential weathering due to the limestone strata included in its body.

Left top The reconstructed boat which once formed a part of Khufu's burial equipment.

Left bottom The interior of the valley temple which formed a part of pharaoh Khaefre's funerary complex at Giza.

Opposite top The pyramid built for pharaoh Khaefre.

Opposite bottom Pharaoh Menkaure, escorted by the goddess Hathor (on his right) and a local goddess.

Menkaure's Pyramid

Menkaure's pyramid aligned with those of Khufu and Khaefre although, as space on the plateau was now limited, it was built at a much smaller scale. Perhaps in compensation, the bottom layers of his pyramid were cased in expensive red granite, imported from southern Egypt. The finished pyramid had a height of approximately 213 ft (65 m), a base of 335 x 341 ft (102 x 104 m) and an angle of 51 degrees, 20 minutes. Menkaure's pyramid is built above a subterranean burial chamber and antechamber. The burial chamber yielded a basalt sarcophagus carved with elaborate paneling.

AMARNA HORIZON OF THE ATEN

TYPE: CITY AND ASSOCIATED CEMETERIES • **ARCHITECTURAL STYLE:** ROCK-CUT TOMBS, HOUSES
LOCATION: MIDDLE EGYPT • **CONSTRUCTION BEGUN:** CA. 1350 B.C.E.

Amarna (ancient Akhetaten) was a purpose-built city founded by the "Heretic Pharaoh" Akhenaten (r. ca. 1352–1336 B.C.E.) as a suitable home for his god, the sun disk known as The Aten. Situated in Middle Egypt, equidistant between the northern capital Memphis and the southern capital Thebes, Amarna was built on a virgin site. It was abandoned after just twenty-five years and never reoccupied.

The Aten's new domain—the city, plus its cemeteries and farming land—was defined by a series of "boundary stelae": massive inscriptions carved into the limestone cliffs of the east and west banks of the Nile.

Amarna itself was an elongated city, sandwiched between the river to the west and limestone cliffs to the east. A wide processional road linked its official buildings and ran parallel to the river. The royal family used this road to display themselves to their people.

Archaeologists have given modern names to the various parts of Amarna. The Central City, the religious and administrative heart, included the Great and the Small Aten Temples, the ceremonial Great Palace, the police and army barracks, and a warren of offices. The King's House lay opposite the Great Palace and was linked to it by a mudbrick bridge. To the south of the Central City, the Main City was home to some of Amarna's most influential citizens. Their extensive villas were built next to more humble housing and workshops. To the north lay the Northern Suburb, a less prestigious area, where bureaucrats lived alongside carpenters, and where fishermen and merchants lived within easy reach of the quay. Farther north still was the North City, which included the North Riverside Palace; the private home of the royal family.

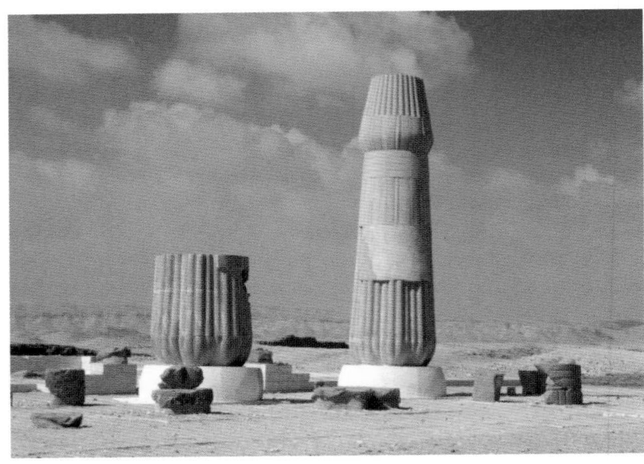

Above Little of the Amarna central city remains standing. Here we see a reconstruction of the central temple area.
Opposite top The city of Amarna was surrounded by a series of carved stone stelae.
Opposite bottom A preserved villa at Amarna.

To the east of the city, a walled village was provided for the laborers who worked in Amarna's elite tombs. In contrast to the city proper, the village had a regular plan: seventy-three houses stood in six straight terraced rows facing onto narrow streets. A second worker's settlement, the Stone Village, was situated about a twenty-minute walk from the Workmen's Village.

Tombs and Graves

The rock-cut royal tomb, and a series of subsidiary royal graves, was built in a dry valley or wadi in the cliffs to the east of the city. Locals discovered it sometime during the early 1880s; when archaeologists entered the tomb, it had already been looted.

Two groups of rock-cut tombs, lying to the north (eighteen tombs) and south (twenty-seven tombs) of the royal wadi, were provided for Amarna's elite. Only twenty-four of these tombs were inscribed and none has yielded a mummy, suggesting that few, if any, were ever occupied. The elite decorated their tombs with images of the royal family going about their daily duties.

Amarna's non-elite were buried in a series of cemeteries. Skeletal evidence recovered from these graves indicates that for many, life at Amarna was a harsh regime of hard physical labor and limited food.

The modern city of Minya—easily accessible by road and train—offers a good base for travelers wishing to visit Akhenaten's city.

ABYDOS
EGYPT'S FIRST ROYAL CEMETERY

TYPE: CEMETERY, TEMPLES • **ARCHITECTURAL STYLE:** TOMB COMPLEX
LOCATION: SOUTHERN EGYPT • **CONSTRUCTION BEGUN:** CA. 3100 B.C.E.

The ancient Abydos cemetery, cult center of the funerary god Osiris and home to royal tombs and temples, lies on the desert edge on the west bank of the Nile River, 80 miles (128 km) downstream of modern Luxor, in Egypt. The extensive cemetery was used from predynastic times until the Roman period, a timespan of more than 3,000 years. It has been excavated almost continuously over the past 150 years, with investigations continuing today.

By 3000 B.C.E., the independent city-states lining the Nile River and its delta had united to form one land. The first Egyptian kings ruled from the northern city of Memphis (near modern Cairo) but chose to be buried in the south, at Abydos. They built their mudbrick tombs in a part of the cemetery known today as the Umm el Qa'ab (Arabic for "Mother of Pots") because the surface is covered with millions of ancient potsherds.

Cemetery B on the Umm el Qa'ab housed the tombs built for the Dynasty 0 kings plus the 1st Dynasty tomb complex of Aha. The remaining 1st Dynasty kings, plus Queen Regent Meritneith, built tombs to the south of Cemetery B. Their tombs share a similar plan: a rock-cut burial chamber that is surrounded by storage chambers

Below The New Kingdom temple of Seti I at Abydos is one of the best preserved and most beautifully decorated temples from ancient Egypt.

Opposite top Seti's temple includes two hypostyle halls filled with a forest of huge stone columns.

Opposite bottom The temple of Seti I, seen from the temple gate.

and covered by a low, mudbrick-covered mound that is itself covered by a larger mound. While the first kings of the 2nd Dynasty chose to be buried in northern Egypt, the final two kings of the dynasty returned to Abydos and the Umm el Qa'ab. Their relatively modest tombs were just one element in their wider funerary provision. Less than 1.2 miles (2 km) to the northeast of their Umm el Qa'ab tombs, the 1st and 2nd Dynasty kings built huge rectangular enclosures defined by mudbrick walls. Early Egyptologists interpreted these enclosures as "forts;" today it is realized that they had some unknown ritual purpose.

The 1st Dynasty tomb complexes included subsidiary graves. The deceased—contracted, partially mummified and wrapped in linen—were buried in wooden coffins with their own grave goods, their names engraved on small limestone stelae. The funerary complex of King Djer included 318 of these additional burials. Of the ninety-seven surviving stelae, seventy-six bore female names. It is impossible to determine how theses women died, but it seems likely that they were either murdered or persuaded to commit suicide at the time of the king's death. If this is the case, it was a short-lived ritual. There is no evidence of human sacrifice associated with any other royal burial in ancient Egypt.

The Burial Place of Osiris

By the 12th Dynasty (ca. 1985 B.C.E.) the Umm el Qa'ab was accepted as the last resting place of the mummiform god of the dead Osiris, with the 1st Dynasty tomb of King Djer, suitably embellished, serving as his tomb. The Egyptians had always believed that proximity in death could have beneficial results, and many courtiers chose to be buried close to the pyramids and tombs of their kings. Interment near to the tomb of Osiris was therefore seen as a highly desirable but somewhat impractical option for the masses. Pilgrims flocked to Abydos, where they visited the already ancient tombs, watched the religious processions, and dedicated a stele or statue to the god. Devotees were often buried with a pair of model boats (one to sail upriver and one down) that would allow them to visit Abydos during their afterlife.

The Temples of Seti and the Osireion

Kings, too, wished to be permanently associated with Osiris, and many built temples at Abydos. The most impressive are those built by the first kings of the 19th Dynasty. Seti I (r. ca. 1294–1279 B.C.E.) built a small temple for his father, Ramesses I, and an enormous one

for himself. His son, Ramesses II (r. 1279–1213 B.C.E.), completed Seti's temple and built his own, smaller version. Seti's beautifully decorated and extremely well-preserved limestone temple includes two hypostyle halls and seven chapels dedicated to Osiris, Isis, Horus, Amen-Re, Ra-Horakhty, Ptah, and the deified Seti. One wall is inscribed with a "king list:" an unbroken line of rulers stretching from Menes, the legendary founder of the 1st Dynasty, down to Seti himself. Immediately to the west of his temple, Seti excavated a subterranean cenotaph known today as the Osireion. Here, a room opening off the central hall was shaped like an enormous sarcophagus. A channel surrounding the hall acted as a moat for groundwater, and in so doing allowed the hall to represent the mound of creation.

Abydos is not conveniently situated for public transport. Travelers are advised to take a taxi from Luxor, and ask it to wait. Most visitors will wish to focus their visit on the Seti temple and Osireion.

Opposite The water-filled interior of the Osireion, a part of the temple of Seti I.

Above On the walls of his Abydos temple, Ramesses II is shown anointing a statue of the god Wennefer (Osiris).

THE TEMPLE OF HATHOR AT **DENDERA**

TYPE: TEMPLE • **ARCHITECTURAL STYLE:** EGYPTIAN
LOCATION: QENA GOVERNORATE, EGYPT • **CONSTRUCTION BEGUN:** CA. 55 B.C.E.

The outer rear wall of the Temple of Hathor offers a rare view of one of the most celebrated of all ancient Egyptian rulers: Cleopatra. A double scene shows her and her son Caesarion making offerings to a line of gods. In the scene on the left they offer to Osiris, his sister-wife Isis, and their son Harsiesis; on the right they offer to Hathor, her son Ihy, and the Osirian triad (Osiris, Isis, and Horus). In the middle of the wall is the head of Hathor.

The town of Dendera (ancient Iunet, Greek Tentyris) is situated on the west bank of the Nile River approximately 37 miles (60 km) north of Luxor, in Egypt. The well-preserved Graeco-Roman temple complex dedicated to the goddess Hathor is to the southwest of the town. Neighboring temples dedicated to Hathor's spouse, Horus, and their son, Ihy, are now lost. Work on the current Hathor complex started during the Ptolemaic Period (305–30 B.C.E.), covering a series of earlier buildings dating back to Egypt's Old Kingdom (2686–2160 B.C.E.). The site also includes a cemetery with tombs dating back to the Early Dynastic Period (ca. 3000–2682 B.C.E.), brick-vaulted Late Period animal catacombs (664–332 B.C.E.), and a Christian basilica dating the fifth Century C.E.

Ptolemy XII had ambitious plans to redesign the, already substantial, 30th Dynasty temple on this site. Unfortunately he died just four years into his building program, leaving his daughter, Cleopatra VII (69–30 B.C.E.), to complete his work. The temple was eventually finished a decade after her death.

Following tradition, the temple is orientated toward the Nile River, which, due to a bend in the river, here flows east–west. In front of the temple are several Roman kiosks and a propylon gateway. A hypostyle hall fronts the temple itself, its twenty-four Hathor-sistrum-style columns

partially revealed by the unusual low screen facade. The hall ceiling displays a colorful chart of the heavens. An inscription confirms that the Roman Emperor Tiberius built this part of the temple in 34–35 C.E.

Beyond the main hypostyle hall, visitors enter a smaller six-columned hall, the "hall of appearances:" here the statue of the goddess would appear during temple rituals. Eleven chapels surround the main sanctuary, each dedicated to a god associated with Hathor. A series of crypts once housed the temple treasures.

In 1821 a carved zodiac ceiling—a map of the sky—was removed from a chapel on the temple roof, dedicated to the commemoration of the resurrection of the god Osiris. While the original ceiling is now displayed in the Louvre Museum, Paris, visitors to the temple today can see a replica of it.

The complex includes two birth houses: temples dedicated to the birth of Hathor's son Ihy. The earlier temple was started during the 30th Dynasty, and completed by the Ptolemies; Augustus and Trajan built the later temple. To the south of the birth houses, a mudbrick sanatorium allowed sick visitors to consult priests, bathe, or drink healing waters drawn from the sacred lake.

Visitors to Dendera are advised to take a taxi from Luxor and ask it to wait, as there is no reliable public transport available.

Opposite top The approach to the temple of Hathor at Dendera.

Opposite bottom Carved at the rear of the temple of Hathor are giant images of Cleopatra VII and her son Caesarion.

Above The temple pronaos, or entrance hall.

KARNAK HOME OF THE HIDDEN ONE

TYPE: TEMPLE COMPLEX • **ARCHITECTURAL STYLE:** TEMPLES AND PYLONS
LOCATION: SOUTHERN EGYPT • **CONSTRUCTION BEGUN:** CA. 2055 B.C.E.

Victorian travel writer Amelia B. Edwards described the Karnak temple complex as "a place that has been much written about and often painted; but of which no writing and no art can convey more than a dwarfed and pallid impression." She was quite right. The complex is a magnificent, multi-period, partially ruined religious site of great size and complexity incorporating temples and chapels to various deities, pylons (gateways), processional routes, and a sacred lake. At its heart lies the vast temple dedicated to Amun-Ra, The Hidden One, patron god of Egypt's New Kingdom. For years the complex was misinterpreted, with early visitors believing that it was a great royal palace.

The ancient Egyptians knew Karnak as Ipet-Swt or "most select of places." Originally a local shrine dedicated to the god Amun, the complex experienced continuous building works from the early Middle Kingdom to Roman times—almost 2,000 years—as successive kings attempted to out-build their predecessors. Unfortunately, many kings also demolished earlier monuments, absorbing the discarded stone blocks within their own constructions. A striking example of this recycling can be seen in the gateway (pylon three) built by the 18th Dynasty King Amenhotep III (r. ca. 1390–1353 B.C.E.). The rubble fill of Amenhotep's gateway has yielded blocks of carved limestone taken from a chapel erected by the Middle Kingdom Senwosret I (r. ca. 1956–1911 B.C.E.). This chapel, known today as the White Chapel, is the most significant remnant of the large, and now almost entirely vanished, Middle Kingdom temple. Today it stands in the open-air museum within the Amun-Ra enclosure. Here, too, stands the quartzite Red Chapel raised by the female pharaoh Hatshepsut (r. ca. 1473–1458); another beautiful building that has been dismantled and reassembled.

Opposite The interior of the hypostyle hall in the temple of Amun-Ra.

Above Looking along the statue-flanked central axis of the Amun-Ra temple at Karnak, towards the hypostyle hall.

Obelisks

Standing alongside the huge buildings, Karnak was graced by a series of granite obelisks erected by early 18th Dynasty kings (ca. 1504–1425 B.C.E.). Obelisks are tall, tapering stones inscribed with royal and religious texts and often entirely or partially covered with gold foil. The stone for these monoliths came from the riverside granite quarries upriver at Aswan. To cut, transport, and erect a large-scale obelisk was both a magnificent technical achievement and an unmistakable mark of powerful kingship.

Amenhotep III at Karnak

The main axis of the Amun-Ra temple was aligned westward, so that it formed part of a processional route linking Karnak with the royal mortuary temples situated across the river on the west bank of the Nile River. It is from the reign of Amenhotep III that the intention to develop the Amun-Ra temple as the nucleus of a series of related, satellite structures becomes clear. To the south of the Amun-Ra enclosure Amenhotep enlarged a temple enclosure for Mut, wife of Amun-Ra. Mut's temple enclosure was joined to the Amun-Ra enclosure by a second processional axis running south from the Amun-Ra temple via a series of courtyards and pylons. A branch of this southern axis bypassed the Mut enclosure and ran southward along a sphinx-lined road, toward the Luxor temple.

The Hypostyle Hall

The hypostyle hall was started by Ramesses I (r. ca. 1295–1294 B.C.E.) and continued and decorated by his son Seti I (r. ca. 1294–1279). The interior walls were carved with scenes of temple ritual, while the exterior walls were decorated with battle scenes showing Seti in all his military glory. Following Seti's death, his son Ramesses II (r. ca. 1279–1213) completed the hall and named it

Glorious is Ramesses II in the Domain of Amun. The hall now boasted a forest of 134 papyrus-style columns arranged in sixteen rows, the twelve columns in the two central rows standing 80 ft (24 m) high while the outer columns, sixty-one on each side, stood 40 ft (12 m) tall. Dim light filtered through the high, barred clerestory windows creating a cool, dark contrast to the heat and light of the secular world. The workmen were ordered to abandon the delicate raised relief favored by Seti, and to adopt the faster, less elegant sunken relief that characterizes almost all of Ramesses' monuments. The difference in styles must have been obvious, even when covered in layers of paint, and Ramesses later returned to re-carve sections of the raised relief so that it would appear that he had been responsible for the decoration of the entire hall.

Later Building Works

Later kings were unable to build on the same scale as their New Kingdom predecessors, but their interest in Karnak caused them to carry out minor works of repair and improvement in most parts of the temple structure, and they erected smaller temples for "guest" deities within the Amun-Ra enclosure. The last major building project at Karnak was the replacement of the central sanctuary of Amun-Ra with one built by Macedonian King Philip Arrhidaeus (r. 323–317 B.C.E.).

Karnak lies a short stroll northward, along the corniche, from the center of modern Luxor (ancient Thebes), in southern Egypt. The walk is a pleasant one but can be hot and dusty, so visitors might prefer to hire a horse-drawn carriage or taxi and save their energy for sightseeing.

Opposite A series of ram-headed sphinxes which once lined the processional way to the temple.

Right, from top A carving depicting the ram-headed stern of the boat of Amun-Ra. The White Chapel built by Senwosret I. Some of the royal statues found at Karnak.

DEIR EL-MEDINA
A WORKMEN'S VILLAGE

TYPE: VILLAGE • **ARCHITECTURAL STYLE:** STONE HOUSES
LOCATION: SOUTHERN EGYPT • **CONSTRUCTION BEGUN:** CA. 1525 B.C.E.

On the west bank of the Nile River, in a small valley relatively close to the Valley of the Kings, the Valley of the Queens, and Medinet Habu, lie the remains of the New Kingdom workmen's village of Deir el-Medina. Today the village is a well-preserved stone ruin composed of the remains of close-packed multi-room houses surrounded by a wall. The slopes on either side of the village are honeycombed with tombs and chapels for private worship by the villagers. To the north of the village is a failed well known as the "Great Pit." The Ptolemaic Hathor temple, which lies to the northeast of the village, incorporates a 19th Dynasty Hathor chapel.

The original residents knew their village as *pa demi*, simply "the village." The modern name, Deir el-Medina, translates as "Monastery of the Town," and is a reference to the Coptic church and monastery built close by. It has been estimated that, at its peak, the village was home to approximately 200 people. Not all the houses were occupied all the time.

Deir el-Medina was built to house the workmen engaged in the construction and decoration of the royal tombs in the Valley of the Kings, their families, dependents, and servants. The confined nature of the rock-cut tombs meant that they required a small, skilled workforce rather than the thousands who had built the pyramids. It therefore made sound sense to develop a specialized workforce and house them together. To allow easy access to the royal necropolis, the village was situated in the desert more than 164 ft (50 m) above the water table: this caused great problems when it proved impossible to dig a well. Every drop of water had to be taken to the village by donkey. It did prove possible to raise animals and grow crops in small gardens outside the village wall, but, lacking peasant farmers, Deir el-Medina was a village unable to support itself. The maintenance of the village became one of the costs of royal tomb construction.

When the Valley of the Kings ceased to be the royal cemetery, Deir el-Medina became unviable and the villagers left. The inconvenient desert location prevented any major resettlement at the site, while providing excellent conditions for the preservation of archaeological information. The fact that the houses were partially built of stone, rather than the more usual mudbrick, aided this exceptional preservation.

The Deir el-Medina Houses

The houses were designed and built by the state, with the larger houses close to the village entrance being allocated to the workforce foremen and the scribes. Changes to the original design were permitted, and so by the end of the New Kingdom no two houses were exactly the same. The original houses had no foundations and were built of mudbrick. Later houses had stone rubble foundations, with stone lower courses and mudbrick upper courses.

The roof over the main part of each house was constructed from palm tree trunks and leaves, with the gaps filled with potsherds, and plastered. At up to 8 in (20 cm) thick, the roof was strong enough to form a floor, extending the usable space within the houses.

An Atypical Community

Royal tomb workers were effectively born to the job, as succeeding generations of workmen passed their skills down from father to son. Most Deir el-Medina workmen were born in the village, as were their parents and grandparents before them and, indeed, most of the people they knew. Although they lived in a walled community, and worked on a potentially secret royal project, there is no evidence that they were confined to their village by guards, and a stroll of less than an hour would have taken a workman from the village to the bank of the Nile. This proximity allowed the workers to supplement their state ration by making and selling products both to each other and to their Theban neighbors. These skills included coffin manufacture and decoration, weaving and, of course, tomb building.

When toiling on the royal tomb, the workforce worked two four-hour shifts each day with a lunch break at noon. The working week was spent in the Valley of the Kings, with the men staying overnight in nearby huts. They worked for eight days, returning to the village to rest on the ninth and tenth days (the "weekend"). As every Egyptian month included thirty days, this meant that there were at least six days of rest each month; these were supplemented by official and religious holidays. The huts were situated along the path to the Valley of the Kings. Each included one or two small rooms with a stone sleeping platform against the back wall. They were plastered, painted, and might bear their owner's name.

Visitors to Deir el-Medina are advised to take the Luxor ferry to the west bank, and then either take a forty-five minute walk at a moderate pace, or take a taxi to the site.

Above top View across the village.

Above bottom The reconstruction of the superstructure of a New Kingdom tomb in the form of a little pyramid.

THE VALLEY OF THE KINGS

TYPE: NECROPOLIS • **ARCHITECTURAL STYLE:** ROCK-CUT TOMBS
LOCATION: SOUTHERN EGYPT • **CONSTRUCTION BEGUN:** CA. 1550 B.C.E.

The west bank of the Nile River at Luxor forms one vast cemetery, riddled with tombs of many periods, some royal and some private. During the New Kingdom (Dynasties 18–20; ca. 1550–1069 B.C.E.) Egypt's kings chose to be buried here. Their remote necropolis is today known as the Valley of the Kings.

For more than 1,000 years Egypt's kings had been buried in enormous pyramid complexes raised in the northern desert cemeteries. At the start of the 18th Dynasty everything changed. Kings would now be buried in rock-cut tombs tunneled into the Theban Mountain, with the mountain serving as a natural pyramid. The new necropolis was a part of the vast sacred landscape dedicated to Amun-Ra, incorporating the extensive Karnak temple complex and the smaller Luxor temple.

For nearly 500 years the relatively limited space of the valley was honeycombed with the tombs of virtually every king from the early 18th Dynasty to the end of the 20th Dynasty. Over time the size and complexity of these tombs increased, as did the amount of wall space given over to depictions of the king traversing eternity with the gods. Great kings of the early 18th Dynasty, such as Tuthmosis III (r. 1479–1425 B.C.E.), had rather modest-sized tombs, but the fashion for larger tombs grew through the dynasty. By the beginning of the 19th Dynasty kings such as Seti I (r. 1294–1279 B.C.E.) and Ramesses II (r. 1279–1214 B.C.E.) had magnificent tombs to match their other building achievements. Paradoxically, kings of the later 19th and 20th dynasties—who built relatively little anywhere else—also had large, well-decorated tombs, which were clearly a priority at a time of crisis in royal authority.

Rescuing the Royal Mummies

Toward the end of the New Kingdom, unpredictable Nile levels led to high inflation and food shortages, and Thebes suffered raids by Libyan nomads. The royal tombs faced a sustained threat from well-informed criminal gangs.

Necropolis officials settled on a bold tactic. They opened up the royal tombs and emptied them. They then removed the mummies from their sarcophagi and sent them to workshops where they were stripped of their bandages and jewelry, re-wrapped, labeled, and placed in plain coffins. The mummies were then stored in chambers dotted about the necropolis. From time to time these collections were amalgamated, until there were two major caches: one housed in the family tomb of the High Priest Pinudjem II at Deir el-Bahri and one stored in the valley tomb of Amenhotep II. When, more than 2,000 years later, Western explorers started to investigate the tombs in the Valley of the Kings, they would be mystified by the lack of bodies.

Tutankhamen's Tomb

The only burial to be discovered virtually intact, Tutankhamen's tomb survived because it had been forgotten. Although he had planned to be buried in a splendid royal tomb alongside his grandfather, Amenhotep III, Tutankhamen (r. 1336–1327 B.C.E.) was actually buried in a cramped, non-royal tomb cut into the valley floor. The

accepted explanation is that Tutankhamen died too young to realize his ambitious plans. However, it seems far more likely that Tutankhamen's successor, the elderly Ay, made a strategic swap.

Tutankhamen's tomb was a typical late 18th Dynasty non-royal rock-cut tomb, accessed via a flight of sixteen descending steps. At the bottom of the steps, a doorway opened onto a narrow, sloping passageway leading to a second doorway. This led into a rectangular storeroom, the Antechamber, which allowed access via a sealed doorway to a subsidiary storage chamber, the Annexe. The Burial Chamber was separated from the Antechamber by a plastered dry-stone partition wall that contained a hidden doorway. Opening off the Burial Chamber was a subsidiary storage chamber, the Treasury.

Eighteenth Dynasty royal tombs were traditionally decorated with texts and scenes taken from a collection of religious writings known as the Books of the Underworld. These were provided to help the king on his journey to the afterlife by recalling the nighttime adventure of the sun god Ra. In Tutankhamen's small-scale tomb, the passageway, Antechamber, Annexe, and Treasury remained unplastered and unpainted. Only the Burial Chamber was decorated.

Soon after Tutankhamen's funeral, the valley suffered a spate of robberies and Tutankhamen's tomb was targeted twice. There is little doubt that this would have continued, had nature not intervened. A flash flood deposited a thick sediment that concealed the tomb entrance. Tutankhamen's vanished tomb was quickly forgotten. It was rediscovered by Lord Carnarvon and Howard Carter in 1922.

Travelers wishing to visit the Valley are advised to travel to Luxor by train or plane, then cross the Nile River using the ferry and hire a taxi. Alternatively, for the intrepid, it is possible to hire a bicycle in Luxor.

Above The Valley of the Kings: the remote cemetery used by Egypt's New Kingdom pharaohs.

THE **DEIR EL-BAHRI** BAY TEMPLES

TYPE: TEMPLES • **ARCHITECTURAL STYLE:** EGYPTIAN
LOCATION: LUXOR GOVERNORATE, EGYPT • **CONSTRUCTION BEGUN:** CA. 2004 B.C.E.

Deir el-Bahri is a natural bay in the cliffs on the west bank of the Nile River at Luxor, in Egypt. Its name, literally "Monastery of the North," is a reference to the mudbrick Coptic monastery that was established at the site during the fifth century C.E., and which has since been demolished. Today, the name refers to the bay area and its three temples and, more specifically, to Hatshepsut's mortuary temple. Throughout the Dynastic Age, the Deir el-Bahri bay was strongly associated with the cult of the mother-goddess Hathor in her role as Goddess of the West.

The Temple-Tomb of Mentuhotep II

Nebhepetre Mentuhotep II (r. ca. 2055–2004 B.C.E.) reunited the fragmented Egypt at the start of the Middle Kingdom. A southern warrior, he built a unique terraced funerary complex in the Deir el-Bahri bay. Much of his tomb superstructure has vanished, but it is possible that it was topped by a pyramid.

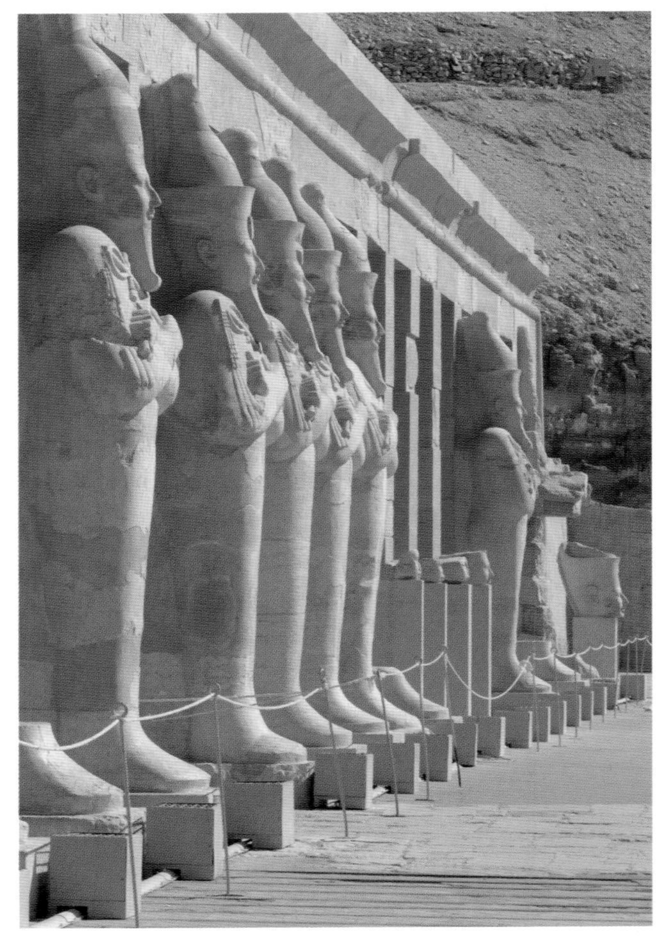

Holiest of the Holy: Hatshepsut's Temple

Inspired by the example of Mentuhotep II, the female pharaoh Hatshepsut (r. ca. 1473–1458 B.C.E.) built her own mortuary temple, Djeser-djeseru or "Holiest of the Holy" in the Deir el-Bahri bay. Hatshepsut's temple takes the form of three ascending terraces set against the cliff. The tiered porticoes are linked by a broad stairway that rises through the center toward the shrine of Amun. The uppermost level is fronted by a portico whose twenty-four square-cut pillars were each faced by a colossal painted limestone statue of Hatshepsut as the god of the dead, Osiris. The temple was originally accessed through a garden, and defined by a limestone wall.

Djeser-djeseru was a multifunctional temple with a complex of shrines devoted to various deities. In addition to the mortuary chapels provided for Hatshepsut and her

father Tuthmosis I, there were chapels for Hathor and Anubis and an open-roofed chapel for the sun god Ra-Horakhty. The main shrine, which was cut into the cliff, was dedicated to the god Amun. The temple served as the focus of the Amun-based "Feast of the Valley," an annual festival of death and renewal.

Hatshepsut used her stone temple walls to display the highlights of her reign. Visitors to her temple can see the raising of obelisks, the defeat of enemies, trade missions to the land of Punt and, most important of all, the story of her divine birth. Her temple is undergoing restoration, and is now in good condition.

The Temple of Tuthmosis III

Tuthmosis, coruler with, and successor to, Hatshepsut, squeezed a small temple between the other two much larger temples in the Deir el-Bahri bay. Initially it was thought that his temple—Djeser-akhet, or "Holiest of the Horizon"—formed part of his mortuary provision, but now it is realized that this might not be the case. The temple is today a ruin.

Visitors to Deir el-Bahri are advised to take advice in Luxor about buying tickets for the west bank sites. Then, take the Luxor ferry to the west bank, and take a taxi to the bay. A rest house offers facilities to the weary traveller.

Opposite The upper terrace of Hatshepsut's temple is fronted by colossal statues of the female king as the god of the dead Osiris.

Above top The three tiers of Hatshesput's temple merge with the Theban Mountain. The temple sanctuary is cut into the rock.

Above bottom The inspiration for Hatshepsut's temple came from the temple-tomb erected by her Middle Kingdom predecessor, Montuhotep II, as shown here.

ASWAN ANCIENT BORDER TOWN

TYPE: CITY, CEMETERY AND QUARRIES • **ARCHITECTURAL STYLE:** EGYPTIAN
LOCATION: SOUTHERN EGYPT • **CONSTRUCTION BEGUN:** 3000 B.C.E.

For more than 3,000 years Aswan, situated on the First Nile Cataract, was the southern border of ancient Egypt. Beyond Aswan lay Egypt's traditional enemy: Nubia. As a border town—both a frontier garrison and a trading center and customs post—Aswan was always a place of strategic importance. Today it offers visitors a plethora of varied experiences.

Elephantine Island

Elephantine (ancient Yebu) is a granite island measuring 4,900 ft (1,500 m) north–south and 1,640 ft (500 m) at its widest east–west point. It became a single entity when the base level of the Nile River lowered during the First Intermediate Period (ca. 2160–2055 B.C.E.); before this, there were two islands divided by marshland. Today Elephantine is a relatively small element of the large

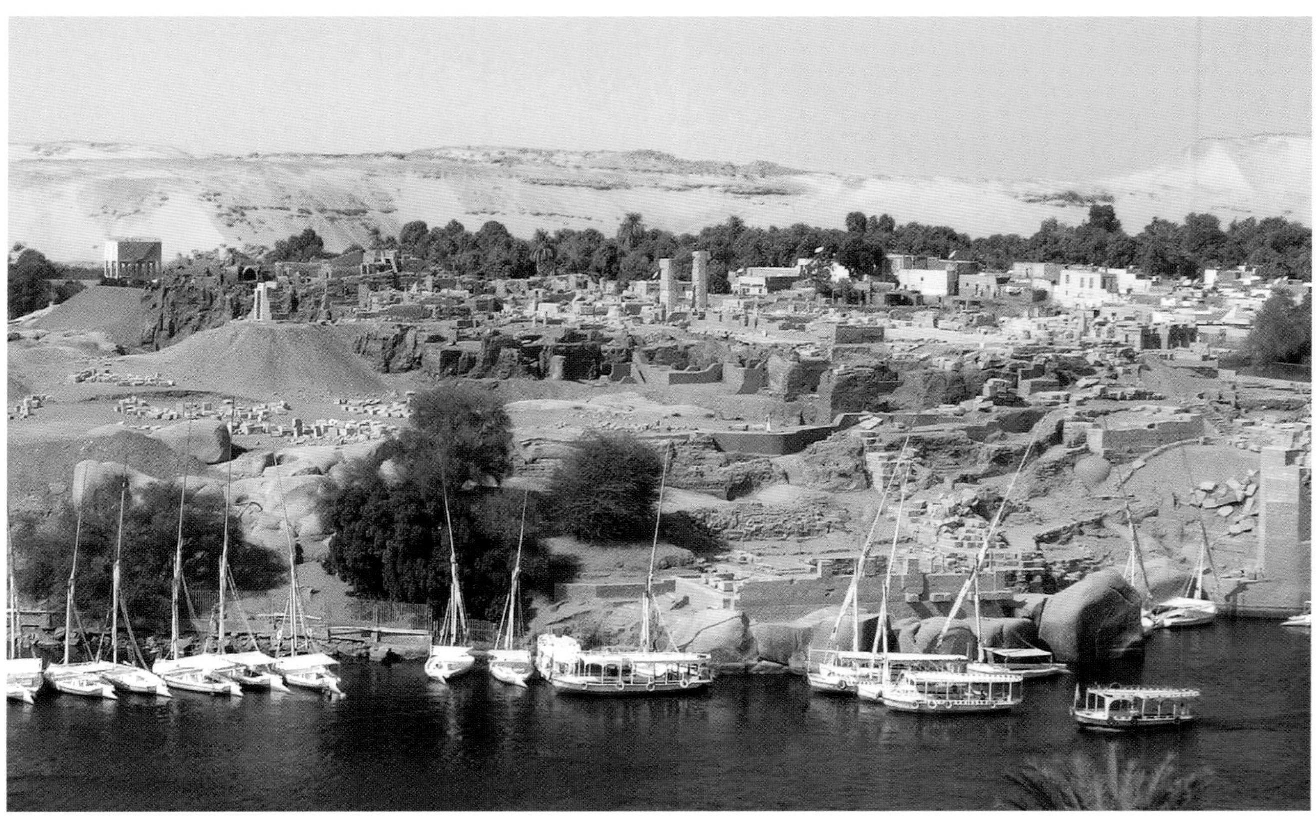

modern city of Aswan. In ancient times, however, this situation was reversed, with Elephantine being the more important settlement and Aswan (ancient Swnw) a small town on the east bank of the Nile.

The name Elephantine may be a reflection of the elephant-shaped rocks that border the island, or a reference to that fact that Elephantine was the center of the Egyptian ivory trade. The first town developed on Elephantine in late Predynastic/Early Dynastic times (ca. 3100 B.C.E.) with building works continuing into the Roman period (30 B.C.E.–395 C.E.). The Aswan Museum is located at the southern end of the island.

The earliest deity to be associated with Elephantine Island was the goddess Satet, whose Predynastic temple was a grotto situated within a cluster of granite boulders. This temple was expanded and developed in a way that retained its ancient core, but that also saw important additions during the Middle Kingdom (ca. 2055–1650 B.C.E.), New Kingdom (ca. 1550–1069 B.C.E.) and Ptolemaic Period (ca. 305–30 B.C.E.).

By the Middle Kingdom, Satet had acquired a male partner, Khnum, whose temple buildings are now the most striking archaeological remains on Elephantine Island.

There are two nilometers—devices to measure the flow of the Nile River—on Elephantine Island. The better known, a corridor nilometer associated with the Temple of Satis, is one of the oldest nilometers in Egypt. It was reconstructed during the Roman period, and was still in use during the nineteenth century C.E. The other nilometer is located near the Temple of Khnum, opposite the Old Cataract Hotel.

The Qubbet el-Hawa Cemetery

The Qubbet el-Hawa is a high ridge of cliffs on the west bank of the Nile River to the north of Elephantine Island. In the 6th Dynasty (ca. 2345–2181 B.C.E.) the elite of Elephantine cut large rock-cut tombs high into the cliffs, ensuring that they would dominate the landscape, being visible for miles around. Some of the larger Qubbet el-Hawa tombs are approached via a steep ramp leading directly from the river's edge to their quarried facades.

The decorated interiors of the tombs include traditional scenes showing the deceased receiving offerings and enjoying leisure activities such as fishing and fowling. Their open facades are less conventional: here the deceased had texts carved relating their Nubian adventures and explaining their role in developing trade with Nubia and central Africa beyond. The most unusual text is found on the northern half of the facade of the tomb of the courtier Harkuf. Here we can read a copy of a letter written by the child-pharaoh Pepi II. From this letter we learn how Harkhuf acquired a "dancing dwarf of the god from the land of spirit" as a gift for his young king.

The Aswan Quarries

To the south of Elephantine Island, a series of granite quarries provided stone for statues, obelisks, and sarcophagi. Visitors can still see the "unfinished obelisk," ordered by the female pharaoh Hatshepsut but abandoned in the quarry after it developed a fatal crack. Had it been completed, this obelisk would have stood more than 135 ft (41 m) tall and weighed an estimated 1,000 tons.

The quarry on Sehel Island has yielded a series of graffiti, which includes the work of officials who were either sent on stone-procuring missions to the region, or who were passing through, en route for Nubia. The most famous of these is the Famine Stele—an inscription that dates to the Graeco-Roman period, but claims to record events from the time of the pyramids.

Today, Aswan is easy to access by plane or train from either Cairo or Luxor; it is also possible to take a taxi from Luxor, an option that allows visits to other archaeological sites en route.

Opposite The monuments on Elephantine Island span the entire 3,000 years of the dynastic period.

THE TWIN TEMPLES AT **ABU SIMBEL**

TYPE: ROCK-CUT TEMPLES • **ARCHITECTURAL STYLE:** EGYPTIAN
LOCATION: SOUTHERN EGYPT • **CONSTRUCTION BEGUN:** CA. 1279 B.C.E.

During the thirteenth century B.C.E., the ancient Egyptian pharaoh Ramesses II cut a pair of temples into sandstone cliffs on the west bank of the Nile River. He set them at an angle to each other so that, just twice a year (February and October), the rising sun penetrated the Great Temple and illuminated the four statues sitting in the sanctuary. This is the site of Abu Simbel in Nubia, 40 miles (64 km) to the north of the Second Nile Cataract.

Abu Simbel was a remote spot, far from any sizeable settlement. With no obvious need for temples, it seems likely that Ramesses (r. 1279–1213 B.C.E.) was inspired by the local geography. The facade of the Great Temple was designed to display the king in all his glory. Two colossal statues of the king wearing the double crown of Upper and Lower Egypt sit on either side of the central doorway. An earthquake during Year 30 of Ramesses' reign caused the statue to the north of the entrance to lose an arm (later restored) and the statue to the south to lose its upper body. Between the colossi, the more important members of the royal family are arranged in groups of three. Above the doorway stands Ra-Horakhty, with the goddess Maat by his left leg and the sign for "User" by his right, so that the statue becomes a rebus reading "User-Maat-Ra," the throne name of Ramesses II.

Beyond the facade the temple extends 157 ft (48 m) into the cliff. The first pillared hall is decorated with scenes of Ramesses displaying his military triumphs. The second pillared hall includes images of the divine Ramesses. Beyond the halls, four gods sit in a niche in the sanctuary: Ptah of Memphis, Amen-Re of Thebes, Ra-Horakhty of Heliopolis, and Ramesses of Per-Ramesses.

The Small Temple was built on a much smaller scale than its neighbor, extending only 82 ft (25 m) back into the mountain. This temple was dedicated to a local form of the goddess Hathor, who was strongly identified with Ramesses' consort Nefertari. The facade shows two colossal figures of Nefertari wearing the cow horns and carrying the sistrum of Hathor, and four of Ramesses. The images on the internal walls include scenes of temple ritual, of Hathor the sacred cow and Tawaret the protectors of women in labor. The niche in the sanctuary contains the carved image of Hathor in the form of a cow protecting Ramesses.

Today, this part of ancient Nubia falls within the borders of modern Egypt. Travelers wishing to visit the Abu Simbel temples must journey to Aswan, then either fly or take a long coach journey. Visitors will not, however, be able to see the temples in their original location. When, in 1954, the decision was taken to build the Aswan High Dam, the Abu Simbel temples were threatened by the rising water level. Between 1964 and 1968 the temples, plus sections of the original cliff face, were raised 213 ft (65 m) above their original site to an artificially created environment.

Opposite top The Small Temple of Abu Simbel is decorated with colossal statues of Ramesses II and his consort Nefertari.

Opposite bottom The Great Temple of Abu Simbel, in its new location.

SENEGAMBIAN STONE CIRCLES

TYPE: MEGALITHS • **ARCHITECTURAL STYLE:** N/A • **LOCATION:** SENEGAL AND THE GAMBIA
CONSTRUCTION BEGUN: CA. THIRD CENTURY B.C.E.

Senegal and The Gambia lie at the westernmost point of the African continent. In the area between the Senegal River to the north and the Gambia River to the south are numerous megalithic monuments. Most are stone circles, but some large stones occur singly. Though sometimes referred to as "mini-Stonehenges," they differ because they are associated with burials. Though not securely dated, the first stones probably date from the third century B.C.E. but most date from the later first millennium to the mid-second millennium C.E.

It has been estimated that, in an area of approximately 12,740 sq mi (33,000 sq km), there are more that 1,000 monuments, made up of 29,000 standing stones. Though they occur across the region, about half of the megaliths are found in four concentrations: Wassu and Kerbatch in The Gambia and Sine Ngayene and Wanar in Senegal. They tend to occur in association with watercourses. Today much of the land is open farmland, but historical photos from the early twentieth century show that, at that time, the landscape was woodland; it may have been even more densely vegetated in prehistory.

The megaliths are made of locally quarried laterite rock, worked into cylindrical or polygonal forms and smoothed on one or more sides. Many were erected to form single circles, though double-circle arrangements are also known. Some have single stones outside the circles, known as frontal stones. Especially notable are frontal stones carved into a branching shape, like a "Y," or with parallel branches resembling a lyre and therefore known as "lyre-stones." The stones range in size from less than 39 in (1 m) to 10 ft (3 m) in height.

Given the huge number of megaliths, and because they were made for centuries, few generalizations can be made. There are some differences in the associated grave types—for example, some may initially have been covered by mounds or wooden funerary houses, before the erection of the megaliths. The frontal stones seem to have been a focus of ritual activity, with pottery vessels being placed around them. Numerous complete examples have been excavated; many have a hole bored in the base.

The identity of the makers of the megalithic monuments remains unknown, and documenting and dating the multiple sites are enormous, and ongoing, tasks. Why this megalithic tradition emerged when it did remains unexplained, though it seems likely that it was linked to assertion of identity in the context of early state formation in West Africa.

Opposite Megaliths in a circular formation at Wassu, The Gambia.

Left A lyre stone, carved from laterite rock, from the Kaolack region of Senegal.

Below Concentric stone circles, near Nioro du Rip in Senegal.

Comprising the largest concentration of megalithic monuments in the world, the whole area here is a listed UNESCO World Heritage site. Wherever tourists go in Senegal and The Gambia, the chances are that stone circles exist nearby. Sine Ngayene, in Senegal, is one of the most impressive sites, with fifty-two stone circles, while Wassu, in the Gambia, has more diverse and elaborate examples.

THE KINGDOM OF **AKSUM**

TYPE: CITY • **ARCHITECTURAL STYLE:** AKSUMITE
LOCATION: ETHIOPIA • **CONSTRUCTION BEGUN:** UNKNOWN

Aksum was a thriving polity of the first to seventh centuries C.E. At its height it covered perhaps 390,000 sq mi (1,000,000 sq km) in northern Ethiopia and Eritrea and also extended into southern Arabia. Its capital, also named Aksum, is located on a plateau punctuated by dome-shaped hills and criss-crossed by shallow streams, in the semi-arid Tigray highlands. The Aksumite empire was involved in intercontinental trade through its main seaport, Adulis, on the Red Sea. Among the remains of the city are royal palaces and tombs and, most spectacularly, massive carved monolithic stelae. Aksum was one of relatively few African kingdoms to have a written language.

Though its origins are unclear, this kingdom's original inhabitants belonged to an Iron Age society that already had cultural links with the Arabian Peninsula, across the Red Sea.

The history of Aksum needs to be understood in relation to the decline of Meroe. Meroe was the capital of the kingdom of Kush, on the east bank of the Nile River in the Sudan, and an important urban center from around 700 B.C.E.—300 C.E. It had been founded by rulers of ancient Egypt's 25th Dynasty. After they withdrew, Meroe became increasingly independent of Egyptian political and cultural influence, but achieved great prosperity through extensive trade networks.

Meroe's wealth and power diminished in the first millennium C.E., partly because of over-exploitation of local resources, but also because control of trade had shifted to the southeast, to the kingdom of Aksum. The changing economic landscape was described in a first-century C.E. text, *The Periplus of the Erythraean Sea.* The Aksumites invaded Meroe around 350 C.E., though by that time it was already in terminal decline.

Aksum's exports included agricultural products, ivory, gold, precious stones, salt, and slaves. The kingdom's trade networks stretched into Europe, to Rome and Byzantium, and as far as India. Imports included metal goods, glass, and luxury items such as silks and spices. That the Aksumites minted their own gold, silver, and copper coins from the third century C.E. onward is testament to the center's wealth and its flourishing commercial operations both at home and abroad. Coins bore inscriptions in Greek or in Ge'ez, the Aksumite language. Ezana (325–356 C.E.),

Above Coin with the head of King Aphilas (ruled 300–340 C.E.).

Opposite top The Great Stele (Stele One), representing a 13 story building, may have fallen while being erected.

Opposite bottom The Stele of Aksum was removed to Rome in 1937 but was returned in 2005 and re-erected in 2008.

the ruler of Aksum in the fourth century C.E., adopted Christianity, which replaced the kingdom's older, polytheistic religion. The ancient disk and crescent symbol was replaced on coinage with a Christian cross.

Aksum began to decline around the sixth century C.E. Its end can be attributed to the control of Red Sea trade by the rise of a new and powerful Islamic caliphate in the Arabian Peninsula.

Only a tiny part of the city of Aksum has been scientifically excavated, but it is best known for its architecture, much of it dating to Ezana's reign and thereafter. Its monumental stelae are especially notable. An older area of the site, known as the Gudit field, contains hundreds of small, more roughly carved stelae that are associated with non-elite burials beneath.

The Northern Stelae Field is where the nobility were buried. Seven huge carved stelae can still be seen. The largest standing stela, at 79 ft (24 m), is the Obelisk of Aksum, which was taken to Rome in 1937 but repatriated to Ethiopia in 2005. Prior to its reinstallation, the largest was King Ezana's stela, which is 69 ft (21 m) tall. The largest of all, at 108 ft (33 m), lies broken on the ground,

perhaps after toppling while being erected. All are carved in imitation of multistory Aksumite stone-and-wood buildings, narrowing toward the top. They display typical Aksumite architectural features, including false windows and doors, with projecting beam ends.

Four tombs dating to the third and fourth centuries C.E. have been found beneath these large stelae. The Tomb of the Brick Arches is a multiroom subterranean complex. The Tomb of the False Door, as the name suggests, had a carefully concealed entrance. Grave goods, including jewelry, glassware, coins, and ivory pieces, provide evidence of the intercontinental trade on which Aksum thrived.

Tours of the site can be taken from Addis Ababa, and day trips are available from the modern town of Aksum. The site is best visited outside of the rainy season, which extends from around May to September.

Opposite The Tomb of the Brick Arches dates to the fourth century C.E.

Above left The Ezana Stone bears inscriptions in Ge'ez, the Aksumite language, Greek and Sabaean.

Above right The Tomb of the False Door, with the true entrance hidden beneath, was designed to foil grave robbers.

THE ROCK CHURCHES OF **LALIBELA**

TYPE: CHURCHES • **ARCHITECTURAL STYLE:** DIVERSE
LOCATION: ETHIOPIA • **CONSTRUCTION BEGUN:** TWELFTH CENTURY C.E.

For almost 1,000 years, Christian pilgrims and travelers have journeyed to the renowned rock-hewn churches at the holy site of Lalibela, in Tigray, Ethiopia. The eleven churches were sculpted over several centuries, from the soft pink rock of the Lasta Mountains. The most famous of the churches, Biete Giyorgis (referencing St. George, Ethiopia's patron saint), is carved into a striking cruciform shape.

Originally known as Roha, the site is named for Gebre Mesqel Lalibela, (ca. 1162–1221 C.E.), an Ethiopian ruler of the Zagwe dynasty. It is believed that his vision was to build a "new Jerusalem," perhaps after Muslims captured Jerusalem in 1187. The architecture and names of features of the site (such as the Yordanos stream, named for the Jordan River) repeatedly reference Jerusalem. The church of Biete Golgotha ("Biete" meaning "House of") contains replicas of the tombs of Christ and Adam.

The Lalibela churches are monolithic, in that they have been carved out of the mountain so as to be completely detached, and consist of a single block of rock. The church known as Biete Medhane Alem is said to be the largest such rock-hewn structure in the world. The churches in the northern and eastern clusters are linked by underground passageways.

The site is poorly dated and the building chronology is uncertain, partly because the sacred nature of the site has meant that extensive excavations have not been undertaken. Not all of the churches were initially built for purposes of worship. Some (Biete Mercoreos and Biete Gabriel Raphael) seem to incorporate fortifications—perhaps the remains of palaces—that date back to around the seventh century C.E.

The churches are in diverse architectural styles, but several incorporate stylistic details and features (such as windows and doorways with protruding lintels) that mimic those of Aksum, a powerful kingdom in northern Ethiopia that thrived throughout much of the first millennium C.E. Biete Amanuel is a particularly good example of the Aksumite architectural revival at Lalibela. The purpose of these architectural quotations may have been to propagate the idea that Lalibela was as mighty as Aksum had been before it.

The interiors feature semicircular arches, domes, and, sometimes, blind windows (that do not actually open to the outside). Although most of the churches are relatively undecorated inside, some have richly ornamented interiors, including bas-relief sculptures. Biete Maryam has a frieze of horsemen and striking paintings of biblical scenes. Associated structures at the site and nearby include monks' cells and vernacular architecture. The latter, known as Lasta Tukuls, in the nearby village of Lalibela, are two-story houses built from stone.

Lalibela is almost 560 miles (900 km) north of Addis Ababa, and a bus journey takes two days. However, the area is well-served by several airlines that fly to Lalibela airport, where taxis can be hired. Tours of the site that include transfers and, for longer stays, accommodation, are available.

Opposite, from top The interior of Biete Maryam church is richly carved and painted. The monolithic church of Biete Giyorgis is especially notable for its cruciform shape.

THE RUINS OF **KILWA KISIWANI**

TYPE: CITY • **ARCHITECTURAL STYLE:** ISLAMIC
LOCATION: OFF TANZANIA • **CONSTRUCTION BEGUN:** TENTH CENTURY C.E.

In the second millennium C.E. Kilwa Kisiwani was East Africa's most prosperous city-state. The ruins of the once thriving settlement are located on a small island in the Kilwa archipelago off the coast of southern Tanzania, a twenty-minute journey by dhow.

Settlements on the island date to the late first millennium C.E., but it was in the first half of the following millennium, under the Islamic Shirazi sultanate, that Kilwa reached its greatest heights as a wealthy trading center. A UNESCO World Heritage site, its importance lies in its Islamic architecture, as well as the evidence it provides for the growth of Swahili culture.

Under the Kilwa sultanate, the city became a key player in early intercontinental trade with the nearby Arabian Peninsula, but also with places as far afield as India and China. Around the late twelfth century C.E., Kilwa's rulers gained control of the export of African gold, which was exported via the key port of Sofala in Mozambique. Excavations have unearthed unglazed ceramics used by Kilwa's commoners, as well as exotic goods belonging to the wealthy, including items of Chinese celadon ware and Persian faience. Jewelry and textiles were also imported. Kilwa minted its own coins from the eleventh to the fourteenth centuries. A Kilwa coin was found at Great Zimbabwe, testimony to trade links between the two.

The island is home to two important examples of early Islamic architecture: the Great Mosque and the palace of Husuni Kubwa. Until the sixteenth century, the Great Mosque was the largest mosque in sub-Saharan Africa. Today it is the oldest standing mosque in East Africa. Its foundations date to the tenth century C.E., but much of the structure dates to the eleventh and twelfth centuries. It is constructed from blocks of local coral. Notable features include the Northern Prayer Hall, and the building's domed and vaulted ceilings. Writers of early historical texts, such as the Kilwa Chronicle, remarked upon the mosque's impressive Great Dome, a novel architectural phenomenon in East Africa at the time.

Sultan al-Hasan ibn Sulaiman (r. 1310–1333), considerably extended the Great Mosque in the fourteenth century, and commissioned the building of the palace of Husuni Kubwa, which occupies an area of 2 acres (0.8 ha). Though only briefly occupied and never completed, this royal complex included residential quarters with about 100 rooms, private and commercial courtyard areas, and an octagonal pool. Some of the rooms in the residential quarters were richly decorated with carved coral panels, with designs unique to the region.

Kilwa declined in the late 1300s. The settlement, with perhaps 5,000 residents, fell after being invaded by the Portuguese in 1505. Revived briefly a decade later, it was conquered by the rulers of Zanzibar in 1784.

Kilwa is 241 km (150 mi) from Dar es Salaam. Accommodation can be found on the mainland in Kilwa Masoko. Package tours are available, and some hotels organize trips. Visitors can also charter boats at the port.

Opposite, clockwise from bottom left The Great Mosque is one of the few surviving early mosques on the East African coast. The domes of the Great Mosque are among its most notable architectural features. Chinese ceramics found in the palace of Husuni Kubwa provide evidence of long-distance trade relations.

GREAT ZIMBABWE AFRICAN CAPITAL

TYPE: CITY • **ARCHITECTURAL STYLE:** N/A
LOCATION: ZIMBABWE • **CONSTRUCTION BEGUN:** ELEVENTH CENTURY C.E.

Great Zimbabwe is a complex of medieval stone buildings and one of the African continent's most famous ancient settlements. Located in the hills of Masvingo Province in southeastern Zimbabwe, it was the capital of a prosperous African kingdom, with a thriving economy based on cattle and agriculture, the export of gold and ivory and participation in intercontinental trade. The Great Enclosure is the largest structure of its kind in sub-Saharan Africa.

The city attained huge prosperity between the eleventh and fifteenth centuries. The site covers an area of more than 2.7 sq ft (7 sq km), comprises perhaps a thousand residences, and is known for its remarkable granite drystone walling. Its name comes from the Shona word *dzimbabwe,* meaning "stone houses." Also renowned are the Zimbabwe birds, raptor-like soapstone sculptures, of which eight have been found. Believed to be emblems of royal status, they appear on Zimbabwe's flag and coat of arms. As a monument of outstanding universal value, Great Zimbabwe has UNESCO World Heritage Site status.

Great Zimbabwe's buildings occur in three main concentrations: the Hill Ruins, thought to be the oldest; the Great Enclosure, dating to the city's heyday; and the Valley Ruins. Multiple other structures exist, including sinuous outer perimeter walls that in some places are nearly 36 ft (11 m) tall and 19.5 ft (6 m) thick. Some incorporate decorative stonework in a herringbone pattern; others are topped with turret-like structures. Smaller residences and features within dwellings were made of *dhaka* (adobe).

The area was occupied both before and long after its prime, but the main structures date to approximately 1000–1450 C.E. Unscientific excavations in the early twentieth century, and damage to some areas, have complicated the establishment of a firm chronology.

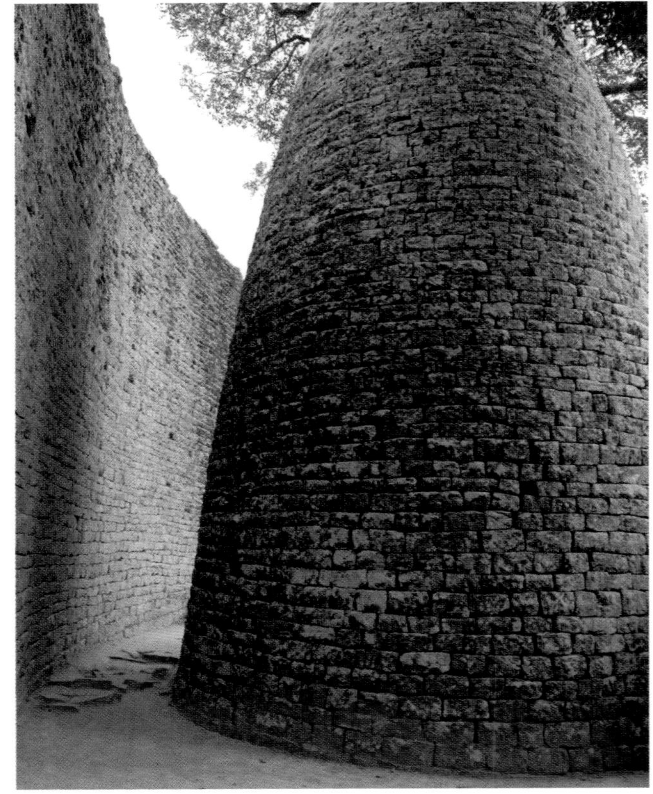

Above The Conical Tower in the Great Enclosure.

Opposite The carved Zimbabwe birds that were taken elsewhere have now been returned, and are housed in a small on-site museum.

Excavations and debates continue. Architectural style sequences, radiocarbon dating of midden materials, and the evidence of imported goods, including oriental ceramics and glass beads, from as far afield as China and Persia, jointly help to date different locations.

The Hill Ruins are the remains of a royal complex that included residences and a ceremonial area. Some of the Zimbabwe birds were probably mounted here. The Great Enclosure, with a circumference of about 820 ft (250 m), was built later, initially with one perimeter wall. A second wall was later built outside it, with a narrow passage between. A celebrated structure within it is the 33 ft (10 m) tall Conical Tower. With no apparent function, it is generally thought to have had symbolic significance. Its shape may reference grain bins, with connotations of good harvests and abundance. The Great Enclosure's function is still debated. Suggestions include that it was a chief's court, a complex for royal wives, or a ceremonial space for female initiation.

The reasons for the city's decline are unclear. Possible environmental factors include overexploitation of resources, climate change, and water shortages. Political instability, shifting trade patterns and the exhaustion of the local gold mines may also be implicated.

Early excavations and colonial-era myths

Great Zimbabwe's fame owes much to the persistent myth that it was a lost city, allegedly built by some vanished race. The settlement first came to European attention through reports by Portuguese travelers and traders in the early 1500s. In 1871 the German geographer Karl Mauch (1837–1875) was shown the ruins. He speculated that the site was linked to the Queen of Sheba. A century later, such speculation about the affiliations of Great Zimbabwe to exotic incomers, such as ancient Phoenicians, Arabs, and Sabaeans, still lingered, tied partly to racist colonial ideologies that maintained that African peoples were incapable of such sophisticated architectural feats.

Excavations in the late nineteenth and early twentieth centuries did little to dismiss these fantasies. In 1905, the first scientific excavations were conducted by David Randall-MacIver (1873–1945), who concluded that the site was of medieval origin, and drew attention to finds linking the site to the forebears of local African peoples. Gertrude Caton Thompson (1888–1985), who excavated at the site in 1929, correctly insisted that all the evidence indicated that the site was built and occupied by the Iron Age ancestors of the Shona people. Research today includes exploring the growth of sociopolitical complexity in sub-Saharan Africa and the global expansion of intercontinental trade networks in the second millennium C.E.

The ruins lie 15 miles (25 km) southeast of the town of Masvingo, close to Lake Mutirikwi, about four hours' drive from Harare on a road that is tarred most of the way. Public transport may be unreliable but there are several companies offering tours, and hotels may assist with transport.

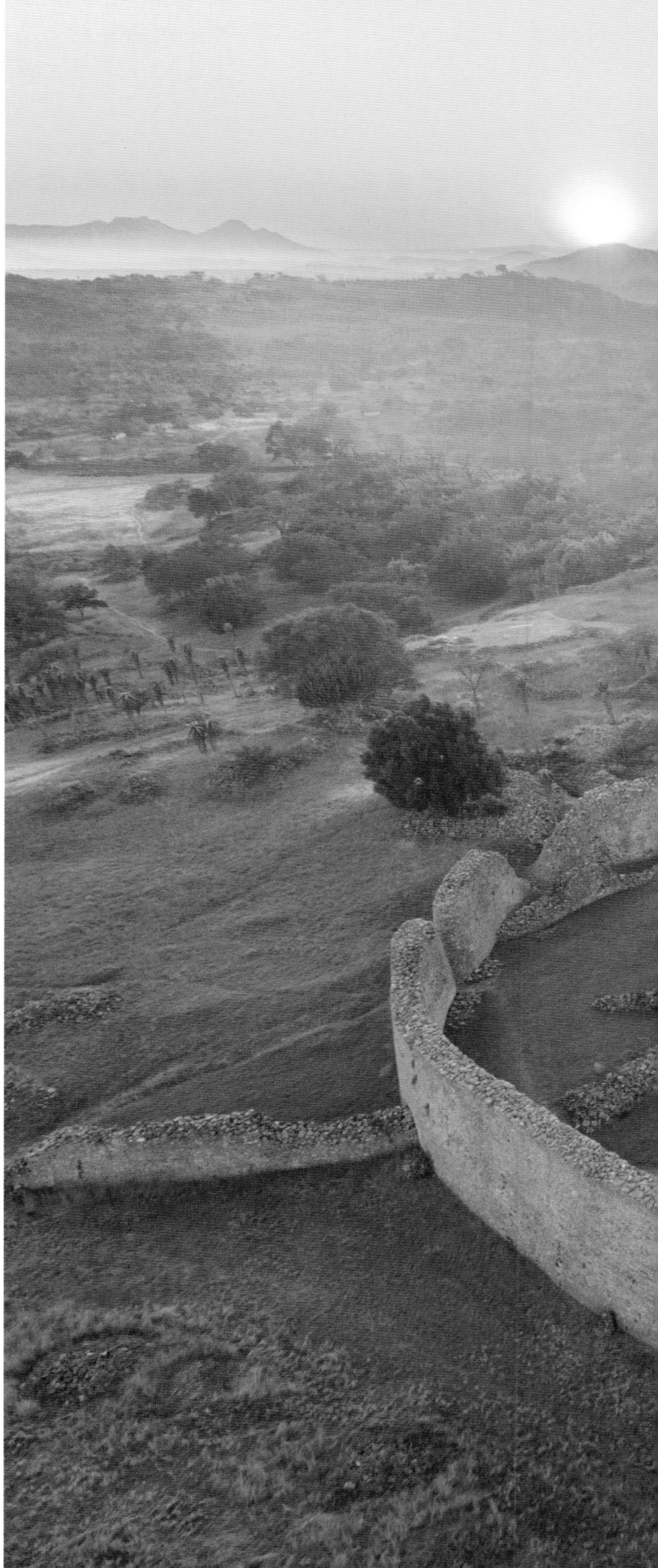

Right Aerial view of the Great Enclosure, with the Conical Tower visible upper right.

THE CRADLE OF HUMANKIND

TYPE: FOSSIL SITES • **ARCHITECTURAL STYLE:** N/A
LOCATION: SOUTH AFRICA • **CONSTRUCTION BEGUN:** N/A

Travelers to the Cradle of Humankind, 30 miles (50 km) northwest of Johannesburg, in South Africa, can experience something of the ancient landscape where our ancestors once lived. Among the hominid sites of global importance are the caves of Sterkfontein, Swartkrans, Kromdraai, and Makapansgat.

The caves are situated in a landscape of rolling hills, in a dolomitic limestone formation that has facilitated excellent preservation of hominid fossils, as well as many other palaeontological remains. A UNESCO World Heritage site, it should not be confused with the equally important fossil sites in East Africa, which are known as the Cradle of Humanity.

Investigations into the Cradle of Humankind sites took off after 1924, when the anatomist Raymond Dart (1893–1988) received boxes of fossils from a limestone quarry at nearby Taung. Among the contents was the fossilized skull of a young primate, including a natural cast of its interior. Dart recognized that this specimen, dubbed the Taung Child, displayed unusual features, including a relatively flat face, and represented a new primate genus. He went on to identify it as a new species of upright-walking hominid and human ancestor, naming it *Australopithecus africanus* (African southern ape).

Controversy raged over Dart's claims before his arguments were accepted, though it is now generally believed that *A. africanus* and humans shared a common ancestor, rather than it being a direct forerunner. However, Dart's initial claims were substantially vindicated by other finds from the Sterkfontein cave system. Mrs. Ples, found in 1947, is an almost complete *A. africanus* skull. Formerly classified as *Plesianthropus transvaalensis*, this find helped to further establish that these specimens had some affiliation with the human lineage. Another key australopithecine discovery at this site is known as Little Foot. Foot bones examined by Ronald Clarke in the 1990s indicated that the individual walked upright. Further investigations revealed an almost complete skeleton. It is now believed that *A. africanus* lived approximately 3.3–2.1 million years ago (mya).

The nearby site of Kromdraai yielded fossil fragments identified by Robert Broom in 1938 as *Paranthropus robustus*, hominids with large teeth and strong jaws, but small bodies. They are now thought to have lived about 1.8–1.2 mya. These specimens are sometimes considered to be australopithecines, or their close relatives.

Debate also continues regarding other new species identified from finds at the Malapa Cave in the Cradle of Humankind complex since 2010. Six australopithecine individuals (a juvenile, two adults, and three infants) have since been identified and classified as a new species, *A. sediba*. The finds have been dated to no older than two million years. It was proposed by the excavator, Lee Berger, that the specimens are a transitional species, linking *A. africanus* to the early species in the genus Homo. Other palaeoanthropologists believe *A. sediba* is a relative of *A. africanus* but not ancestral to the human line.

Berger has also made headlines with another new species, *Homo naledi*, found in 2013 in yet another area of the Cradle of Humankind, known as the Rising Star

cave system. More than 1,500 fragments, representing the remains of at least fifteen individuals, were recovered. *H. naledi* has a mix of archaic and human features. Its braincase is small, but other anatomical features, such as the feet, are very humanlike. Again opinion is divided, with some experts believing that the fossils relate more closely to early *Homo erectus*. It has also been proposed that these remains give clues to the origin of religious awareness, since they may have been intentionally placed there after death. No other animal bones were found, unlike in most fossil accumulations, but further evidence for deliberate placement is not yet available.

Swartkrans is also famous for the discovery of fragments of burned bone, dating to around 1.5 mya. It has been suggested that these represent the controlled use of fire by an unknown species of hominin. It is likely that some of the bone fragments were burned at temperatures only attainable in a hearth, rather than in a bushfire. Crude stone tools and evidence of cutmarks on some fragments support the idea that the remains are the result of hominin activity and early mastery of fire.

The Cradle of Humankind is easily reached by car from Johannesburg or Pretoria, and can be visited as a day trip. The Sterkfontein Caves are open to visitors. Visitor centers at Maropeng and Sterkfontein provide displays of famous fossils and world-class temporary exhibitions.

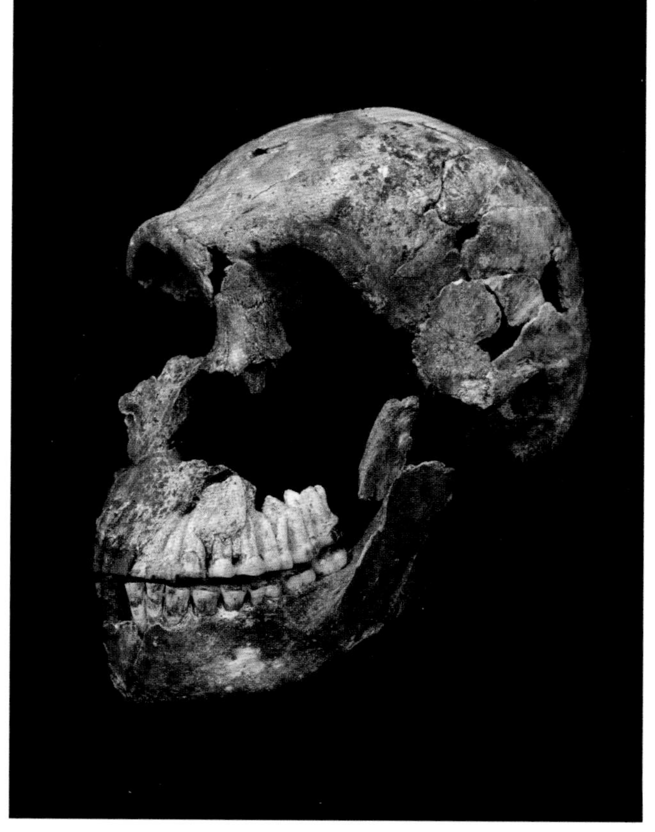

Above top The rolling hills that were once roamed by our human ancestors.

Above bottom The skull of *Homo naledi*, a new species of human discovered in 2013.

MAPUNGUBWE

TYPE: SETTLEMENT • **ARCHITECTURAL STYLE:** N/A
LOCATION: SOUTH AFRICA • **CONSTRUCTION BEGUN:** ELEVENTH CENTURY C.E.

Mapungubwe Hill, situated at the confluence of the Limpopo and Shashe rivers in north-eastern South Africa, was the center of southern Africa's first state. It provides early evidence of social stratification and socio-political complexity. The elite of the kingdom of Mapungubwe lived on the top of the rocky outcrop, while commoners farmed the fertile floodplains below.

Mapungubwe Hill, with its well-preserved remains of the lives of the ruling class, and allied sites in the surrounding savannah bushveld environment, are part of the Mapungubwe Cultural Landscape, a UNESCO World Heritage site. The name is thought to mean "Hill of the Jackal."

The Mapungubwe state probably evolved gradually, in the first four centuries of the second millennium C.E., although signs of evolving complexity, social distinctions, and extensive trade in exotic goods are also seen at other sites in the broader region from about 900 C.E. onward. Excavations began in the 1930s. The discovery of perhaps twenty-seven graves, some containing gold items, created inevitable excitement. The three graves with gold artifacts contained the remains of two young or middle-aged adults and one older individual (the sex of the skeletons cannot be determined).

The elderly person was interred with more than one hundred gold-wire bangles and another with a gold scepter. All were buried in traditional Iron Age style, in a seated position facing west. Perhaps the most celebrated find is a small, well-preserved golden rhino. It consists of a wooden core that was then covered in thin sheets of gold, secured with gold tacks. The fragmentary remains of two other gold rhinos were also found in the graves. The symbolic significance of the rhino in the Mapungubwe culture is unknown. Other gold grave goods included strings of beads, gold plates, and what may have been a bowl. These items are evidence for the wealth of the Mapungubwe elite, and the place of the kingdom in emergent intercontinental trade networks. Similarly to Great Zimbabwe, this Iron Age culture depended on cattle keeping and agriculture. Exports via the ports on the East African coast would have included gold and ivory. Luxury imports included porcelain from China and glass beads from Persia.

Mapungubwe's decline may have been due to increased aridity around 1300 C.E., with the population dispersing when traditional farming could no longer sustain it. This perhaps contributed to the rise of Great

Zimbabwe to the north, though both kingdoms coexisted as important centers for at least a century.

Mapungubwe National Park is about 310 miles (500 km) north of Johannesburg and Pretoria, along a fully tarred road. It is a 9-hour journey on public transport, so self-drive is recommended. Other local Iron Age and rock art sites in the park can also be visited.

Opposite This small gold-covered rhino was found in one of the elite graves on top of Mapungubwe Hill.

Above The choice of the top of Mapungubwe Hill for the residences of the elite signalled high status, and does not appear to have been for defensive purposes.

GAME PASS SHELTER

TYPE: ROCK SHELTER • **ARCHITECTURAL STYLE:** N/A
LOCATION: SOUTH AFRICA • **CONSTRUCTION BEGUN:** UNDATED

In the foothills of the Drakensberg Mountains of KwaZulu-Natal, about 2.5 hours' drive from Durban, in South Africa, Game Pass Shelter is a painted site containing hundreds of remarkable and well-preserved rock paintings. Collectively, they demonstrate the virtuosity of their makers: hunter-gatherers generically known as the San. The paintings are undated, though it has been speculated that they may be 2,000 years old or more.

Game Pass Shelter is a shallow rock shelter in the Kamberg Nature Reserve. Perhaps the most visually impressive paintings are large-scale images of eland, superimposed on human figures apparently clad in skin cloaks, known as "karosses." Above are four running men, perhaps painted at a different time. The eland are in the shaded polychrome style. This combines several colors, with shading effectively used to convey the animals' bulk and volume. According to historical testimonies, the eland was the antelope most loved by |Kaggen, the trickster-creator of San mythology. Mythical "rain animals," embodiments of the rainstorm, also appeared in eland form.

These paintings were among the earliest San images to be publicized globally, and were reported in *Scientific American* in 1915. At present they are known for the claim that the site is a "Rosetta Stone" for unlocking the meaning of San art. The relevant images are principally an eland with a skull-headed human figure behind it, grasping its tail. Some see the images as clinching evidence that San rock art was the product of shamanic experiences in trance states. According to this hypothesis, the eland was regarded as an animal of potency and shamans in trance believed that they "fused" with the animal. This is supposedly represented by the human figure's crossed legs, which mimic the position of the eland's back legs. The eland, with

lowered head, is said to be dying, which shamanists believe is a metaphor for people entering trance states. Among the surrounding images are several therianthropes (figures with both human and animal features).

Many, but not all, specialists accept this interpretation. Heated debate over shamanism as an explanation for both San art and prehistoric art worldwide has raged for decades. In terms of visual analysis, which is always subjective: does the eland have crossed legs, or are they just one in front of the other? Key indigenous testimonies record that spirit rainmakers were asked by the living to capture and magically control rain animals, to make rain fall or perhaps to limit violent storms. Rainmaking is a firmly established theme of San art and the Game Pass composition could equally reference that. Therianthropes may refer to San myths about the First People, who were both human and animal, or represent spirit beings.

Ancient art seldom permits definite interpretations of its "meaning" and San art is no exception. The Game Pass paintings can nevertheless be appreciated for their extraordinary skill and beauty.

The shelter lies high in a ridge, requiring a walk of approximately 2 miles (3 km). Site visits are made in the company of a guide.

Opposite A figure with a skull-like head, probably a spirit being, is shown grasping the tail of an eland.

Right The Kamberg Reserve landscape in the dry winter season.

Below A composition dominated by polychrome paintings of eland.

5

NEAR EAST AND WESTERN ASIA

This huge region contains a tremendous variety of sites, from prehistoric Turkey—notably the utterly remarkable Göbekli Tepe—to the Bible lands, to Iran's grandiose Persepolis, and to the varied riches of India, Pakistan, and Sri Lanka. There are also major sites in Iraq. But perhaps the most famous site, a mecca for archaeology aficionados (as well as Indiana Jones fans) is Petra, where the visitor exiting the narrow Siq comes upon one of the most stunning sights in the world, the rock-cut facade of Al-Khazneh (The Treasury).

Left The rock-cut facade of Al-Khazneh in Petra, Jordan

NEAR EAST AND WESTERN ASIA LOCATIONS

1 GÖBEKLI TEPE
2 ÇATALHÖYÜK
3 JERICHO
4 JERUSALEM
5 PETRA
6 UR
7 BABYLON
8 PERSEPOLIS
9 MOHENJO DARO
10 TAXILA
11 BHIMBETKA
12 AJANTA
13 VIJAYANAGARA
14 ANURADHAPURA

1
2
3
4
5
6
7
8
9
10
11
12
13
14

GÖBEKLI TEPE
CONGREGATING IN A SACRED SPACE

TYPE: RELIGIOUS COMPLEX • **ARCHITECTURAL STYLE:** PPNA (PREPOTTERY NEOLITHIC A)
LOCATION: ŞANLIURFA PROVINCE, TURKEY • **CONSTRUCTION BEGUN:** CA. 9600 B.C.E.

High in the Germus mountains in southeastern Turkey is a mound that in the 1990s was found to cover the world's earliest known sanctuary: Göbekli Tepe. Massive monolithic pillars, some more than 16 ft (5 m) high, bear witness to the astonishing engineering achievements of our ancestors, armed only with stone tools, muscle, willpower, and the ability to cooperate.

Distant from a water source, this was never a settlement but, it seems, a place visited periodically by large groups of people congregating for a purpose. This included the creation of remarkable ritual structures—an enormous undertaking, repeated at intervals.

Excavations have uncovered a number of stone circles, 40–100 ft (10–30 m) in diameter, consecutively constructed and deliberately infilled after a period of use; geophysical survey of the mound suggests that there are twenty or more. Ten to twelve T-shaped pillars were erected around a circular space and connected by stone walls and benches set in clay mortar. In the circle's center, two much larger T-shaped pillars were erected, facing each other. The floor, cut from bedrock, was given a smooth finish or covered with burnished burned-lime plaster.

Many of the pillars are richly decorated with designs in low relief. Features carved on some hint that they were intended as abstract representations of humans (or anthropomorphic deities): hands and arms, a stole across the upper body, a belt with a fox-skin loincloth hanging from it. The horizontal crossbar may represent the figure's head, although there are never facial features.

Most carvings are of creatures. In one circle, snakes predominate among the designs, and they are present in almost all circles. Foxes are also frequently shown, and are the most common creature on circle B's stones. In circle C wild boar are in the majority. Many different creatures appear in circle D, as well as in other circles. Some of the creatures selected for depiction moved between different worlds—birds, occupying land and sky; reptiles, water and land; ducks, which often occur, belonging to all three worlds. Vultures, hovering on the threshold between life and death, are frequently shown. Others epitomize power and danger: predators, carnivores, and creatures noted for their ferocity, such as boar and aurochs (wild cattle). All are male, sometimes ithyphallic so that there is no doubt as to their sex. Some of these, particularly boars and felines (lions or leopards), also appear as three-dimensional sculptures.

Other elements feature in the designs: for example, what appear to be wicker baskets with handles, arranged in a line. It seems likely that these compositions have a mythological content forever lost to us, as well as a ritual significance whose dramatic power is still palpable even though we cannot penetrate its meaning.

Each circle seems to have been used for a while, the wall and benches being renewed by constructing another circle inside, until eventually it was deliberately filled in and a new circle constructed. In the final period of the site,

instead of circles, much smaller rectangular enclosures were built, around 10 x 13 ft (3 x 4 m) in size. These had far fewer T-shaped pillars, which were much smaller, around 5 ft (1.5 m) high, and generally undecorated, though the designs that occur were still the same.

Gathering and Feasting

The circles began to be constructed an astonishing 11,000 years ago, around 9600 B.C.E. At this time West Asia was home both to hunter-gatherers—many living in permanent settlements—and to early farmers. Although Göbekli Tepe lies within the region in which cereals were first domesticated, there is no indication that the builders of these circles were farmers: the finds here include masses of wild animal bones, indicating the importance of hunting to these people. Feasting was too: whatever brought groups of people here, in numbers large enough to quarry and move these stones the quarter mile (0.4 km) to where they were erected, it involved communal celebration as well as shared labor and rituals. Residues in large troughs found here suggest that these were used for brewing beer, probably from the wild wheat that grew in dense stands in the region. The abundant wild harvest and the plentiful game drawn by it may explain why people chose this area to congregate.

Although Göbekli Tepe is unique, it is not culturally isolated. Within the same region are several settlements, such as Nevali Çori, with communal, probably ritual enclosures containing smaller T-shaped pillars. Some of the carved designs from Göbekli Tepe's stones reappear on small decorated objects found in settlements throughout the region. And whatever the belief system behind this astonishing monumental shrine, it seems to have rooted deeply, since much of its iconography can still be traced at Çatalhöyük, 2,000 years later.

The World Heritage site of Göbekli Tepe can be accessed by public transport from the town of Sanliufa, 32 miles (40 km) away.

Above Circle C, with circles A and B behind and part of circle D visible in the foreground.

LIFE IN NEOLITHIC **ÇATALHÖYÜK**

TYPE: SETTLEMENT • **ARCHITECTURAL STYLE:** NEOLITHIC
LOCATION: KONYA PROVINCE, TURKEY • **CONSTRUCTION BEGUN:** CA. 7400 B.C.E.

An enormous mound rises above Turkey's Konya plain: 9,000 years ago this was a huge settlement of tightly packed mudbrick houses, home to between 1,000 and 8,000 people. Yet this was not a city, not even a town, but seemingly a village improbably magnified, held together and managed by its inhabitants through kinship ties, links to shared history, and beliefs and rituals held in common though practiced privately.

Or so archaeologists have come to believe over recent decades. Çatalhöyük, discovered in 1958 and partially excavated in 1961–1965, saw intensive investigation by excavators and a team of wide-ranging archaeological specialists in 1993–2017, and its final story has yet to be written.

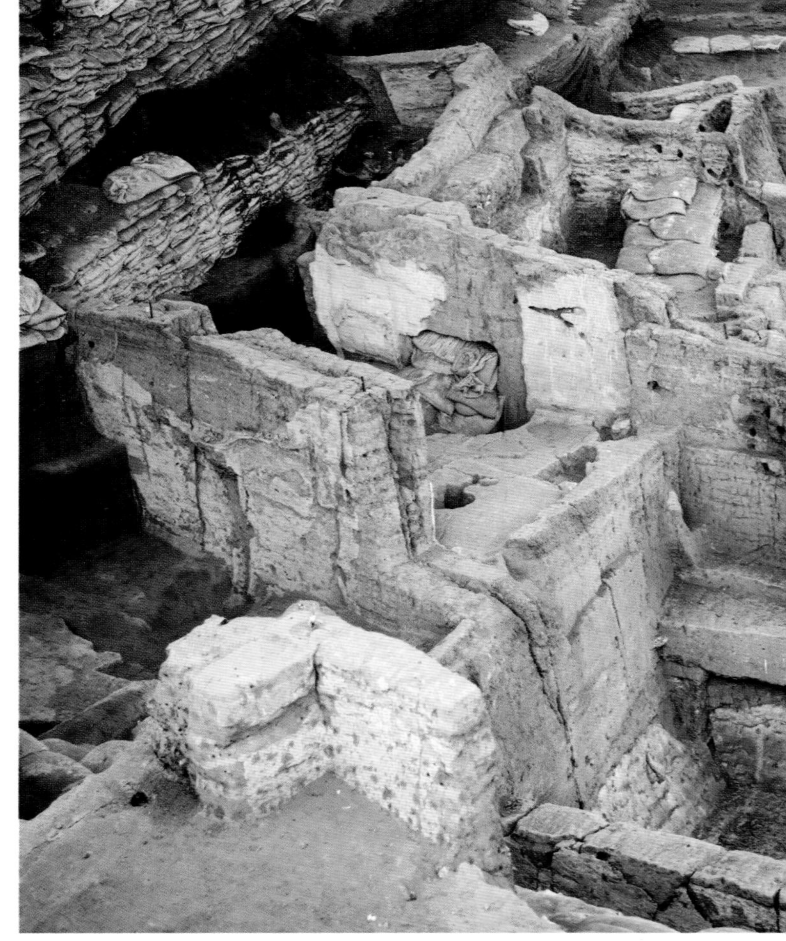

Farming settlements had begun to appear in central Anatolia in the Prepottery Neolithic (PPN) period, and around 7400 B.C.E. people settled at Çatalhöyük near the Çarşamba River, above the level of spring floods. The settlement grew massively, and was for more than a millennium the only major settlement on the Konya Plain.

Although some early houses shared party walls, typical buildings at Çatalhöyük were freestanding, though with mere inches between them. Ladders led to the rooftops, across which, in the absence of ground-level alleyways, people moved around the settlement. Rubbish was thrown into occasional open spaces between blocks of houses and into middens on the settlement's edge. Roof openings, again with ladders, gave access to the house interiors.

A domed clay oven and a hearth, the house's cooking and heating facilities, stood immediately beneath the roof hole, against the south wall, allowing the smoke to escape upward. Clustered around the hearth were various useful objects: wooden bowls; clay balls, to be heated in the fire, then used to roast grain; a stash of obsidian (volcanic glass) ready to make sharp tools as required. Babies and very small children were buried in this part of the house. Brick and plaster platforms occupied much of the interior space, used for sleeping and for sitting at work, making basketry, stone and bone tools, stone or clay figurines, beads, and other objects. Pottery making began around 7000 B.C.E. The first pots were very simple, later ones more useful; all were undecorated.

Below Excavations in progress at Çatalhöyük, showing plastered walls and benches containing burial pits.

Right The interior of a house–a reconstruction based on what was found in the excavations.

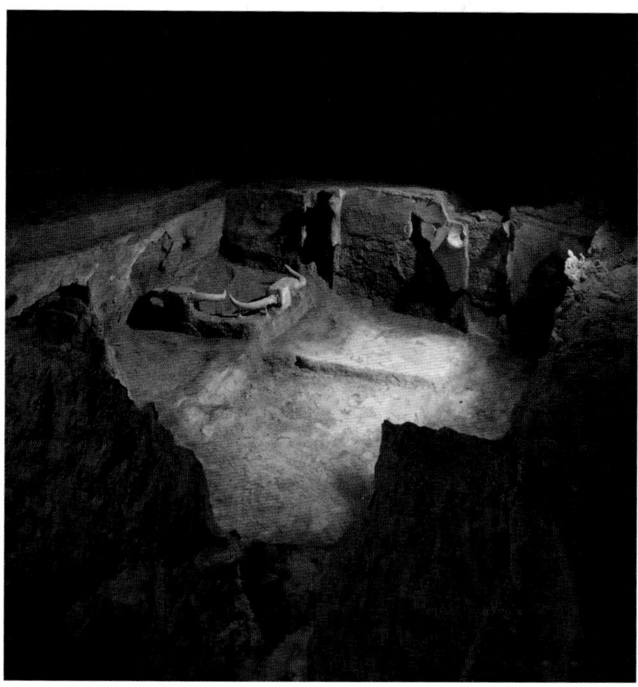

A low doorway led into a side room where food was stored in large clay bins, wooden bowls, baskets, and textile bags. Supplies included cultivated wheat, barley, and pulses, and wild plants such as nuts and berries from the nearby uplands, and wetland plants from the marshy area by the river. Eggs were collected from wild birds. Meat also contributed to the diet: mainly from domestic sheep and goats, but also beef and wild game, including plentiful wildfowl. By 6500 B.C.E. milk, from cattle, sheep, and goats, was processed to make cheese, curds, or yoghurt.

Oak and juniper beams carried the clay and reed roof, and wooden posts reinforced the brick walls. White plaster, frequently renewed, covered floors and walls. Some walls featured painted designs, focusing on dangerous animals, emphasizing claws, fangs, and horns. Huge bulls are a favorite subject, often baited by tiny figures—human dominance over nature's violence seems the central theme. In some houses bulls' horns or skulls were attached to the walls or benches, often modeled into heads with plaster.

Ancestral Ties

Houses were probably the scene of domestic rituals in which these decorations played a part. Their placement particularly in the north part of rooms suggests that rituals focused on the ancestors, for it is here that benches most often cover burials. It was originally thought that the dead were buried within the houses, but recent research suggests that, at least in some cases, houses were built over the place where burials had previously been laid.

Maintenance of links with the family or lineage's past seem to be a guiding principle of life at Çatalhöyük. Houses lasted around forty-five to ninety years, and were then renewed. Roof beams and important fixtures, such as the bulls' skulls and horns, were carefully removed and stored and the upper walls demolished, the debris being used to infill the lower part of the house, creating a solid surface on which to construct a new house, generally to the same plan.

Late in Çatalhöyük's life people began to move away and, by around 6000 B.C.E., it was largely abandoned. Some people had, however, moved only to the opposite side of the river, where they built a new, rather different settlement, in which the houses—more widely spaced—had external buttresses and a large room with a central hearth, surrounded by smaller rooms. The inhabitants no longer painted their walls, but exuberantly painted their pottery. This much smaller village lasted only around 500 years. The site was reoccupied briefly during the Late Bronze Age and later by a substantial Hellenistic to Byzantine settlement.

Protected by a roof, the excavated portion of this World Heritage site now forms part of an impressive visitor complex with excellent on-site information. Visitors can reach the site by public transport or taxi from nearby Konya.

Opposite top An aerial view of Çatalhöyük's mound.

Opposite bottom A wall painting of a massive bull, surrounded by human figures who appear to be baiting it.

Above Low benches in building 77. One, surrounded by cattle horns set in plaster, covers a burial.

WELL-WATERED **JERICHO**

TYPE: PREHISTORIC WALLED SETTLEMENT AND LATER PALACES • **ARCHITECTURAL STYLE:** NEOLITHIC
LOCATION: JORDAN VALLEY, WEST BANK, PALESTINE • **CONSTRUCTION BEGUN:** CA. 10,000 B.C.E.

Jericho (Tell es-Sultan), in the arid western Jordan Valley of Palestine, has enjoyed an exceptionally long history of settlement due to its favorable oasis location on an alluvial fan made fertile by runoff from the adjacent mountains and watered by the 'Ain es-Sultan spring. Famed in Classical times for growing dates and balsam, and rich in market gardens today, it is one of a handful of settlements where the beginnings of agriculture have been traced.

Although hunter-gatherers usually move seasonally to obtain food, in some parts of early postglacial West Asia the availability of storable resources such as cereals and nuts enabled some groups to occupy permanent settlements. Among these was Jericho, where by around 10,000 B.C.E. people were living in mud-walled huts, also hunting gazelle and waterfowl.

By around 8500 B.C.E., they were building more substantial semisubterranean houses, probably with domed clay roofs, and planting barley and emmer wheat, which

developed new "domestic" characteristics: agriculture had begun here. This increased the quantity of available food enabling the community to grow substantially—estimates for Jericho's population in this Prepottery Neolithic A (PPNA) period range from 500 to 2,000. Exchange networks with other communities brought in materials from far away, including obsidian (volcanic glass) from Turkey, greenstone from Sinai, and shells from the Red Sea.

The settlement's most remarkable and surprising feature is the stone wall that its inhabitants built around it. Originally more than 16 ft (5 m) high, it was 5 ft (1.5 m) thick, and would have taken at least 1,400 man-days to construct. It was not, as originally believed, defensive, since there were no external threats at that time; it may have protected the settlement against flooding, and would have represented an ostentatious undertaking that engaged the whole community. A massive tower was built immediately inside the wall, solid but with an internal stair giving access to a summit from which the whole surrounding area could be viewed. It survives to a height of 25 ft (7.75 m), its base diameter measuring 28 ft (8.5 m).

The later, PPNB, period saw major changes. The villagers began herding sheep and goats, domesticated elsewhere in West Asia, and building rectangular mudbrick houses with plastered floors, subdivided into several rooms. As in PPNA, the dead were usually buried under house floors, and their skulls were sometimes retrieved after the body had decayed. However, now skulls were sometimes coated with plaster and painted, modeling living features, with shells for eyes. Perhaps as part of an ancestor cult, they were then kept on display within the houses, before eventually being reburied in caches, as were large human clay statuettes.

Jericho was abandoned after the PPN period, but later reoccupied. A substantial, massively fortified city in the Bronze Age, it was destroyed by fire around 1550 B.C.E. It later re-emerged as a prosperous town. In the final centuries B.C.E. Jericho Valley became a royal estate. The kings of Judaea built a winter palace on Wadi Qelt south of Jericho, which Herod (r. 40–4 B.C.E.) elaborated with fine reception areas, swimming pools, bathhouses, and gardens.

A magnificent Ummayyad palace was built north of the oasis in the eighth century C.E. Material from this and Tell es-Sultan is displayed in Jerusalem's Rockefeller Museum; the Palestinians are now establishing museums at Jericho itself.

All these sites lie close to the modern town, and are best visited in the cooler winter months.

Opposite A view of Jericho's tell (settlement mound)

Above Aerial view of Herod's palace, including a tiled hall, pillared courtyard, and bathhouse.

UNDER THE CITY OF **JERUSALEM**

TYPE: CITY WITH WATER SUPPLY TUNNELS • **ARCHITECTURAL STYLE:** BRONZE AGE AND IRON AGE
LOCATION: JERUSALEM, ISRAEL AND WEST BANK • **CONSTRUCTION BEGUN:** CA. 3500 B.C.E.

At the heart of the vibrant modern city of Jerusalem, reminders of its richly layered past are everywhere to be seen. People have lived here more for than 5,000 years—but traces of Jerusalem's earliest history are largely hidden beneath the superimposed buildings of later ages, to be glimpsed —and lovingly investigated and preserved—whenever areas are cleared for new construction.

Ancient occupation focused on two hills and the intervening valley: the Eastern Hill, the heart of early settlement, and the western hill (Mount Zion) onto which settlement periodically expanded. The Gihon Spring, in a cave on the southeast slopes, was the only perennial water source.

Early settlement, beginning in the late fourth millennium B.C.E., was on the southern spur of the Eastern Hill, where third-millennium houses and an early second-millennium wall have been found. Two massive towers protecting the Gihon Spring may be contemporary with the wall. In the late second millennium B.C.E., stepped terraces were constructed on the northeastern slopes, incorporating massive retaining walls and stone rubble-filled boxes. These supported a platform extending the level ground on the spur's northern summit, where the local rulers' palace may have been built. In later centuries houses were built on these terraces.

No remains have been traced of the Jebusite city captured by King David in the tenth century B.C.E., but David's wall may follow its defenses. David's son Solomon extended the city north to include the Temple Mount where he built his palace and the First Temple. As this area was completely cleared by Herod (r. 40–4 B.C.E.) when he remodeled the Second Temple, knowledge of Solomon's temple depends upon Biblical descriptions, supplemented by archaeological evidence of contemporary temple construction elsewhere.

Jerusalem expanded onto the western hill in the eight and seventh centuries B.C.E., when the kingdom was divided into Israel and Judah. Remains of houses from this period have been found, as have cemeteries of rock-cut tombs in the surrounding hills. Many such tombs, some with magnificently decorated facades, also survive from later times. In 721 B.C.E. the city's population grew as refugees fled the Assyrian conquest of Israel. The Assyrians now threatened Judah. King Hezekiah of Judah therefore strengthened and extended the city's defensive wall to surround the entire settled area.

A secure water supply was essential in times of siege. At some earlier date a 134.5 ft (41 m) tunnel had been cut through the rock from inside the city to a 40.4 ft-(12.3 m-) deep well, Warren's Shaft, supplied through a channel from the Gihon Spring. This gave protected, but labor-intensive, access to water. Hezekiah undertook a magnificent feat of engineering, creating a rock-cut tunnel 0.3 miles (0.5 km) long, leading water from the Gihon Spring to a new reservoir, the Siloam Pool, south of the hill within the extended city walls.

The city successfully withstood an Assyrian siege in 701 B.C.E., but fell in 587 B.C.E. to the Babylonians, who sacked the city and deported its leading citizens. When the Persians conquered Babylon in 539 B.C.E., the exiled Jews returned home and over subsequent centuries, with

many changes of ruling regime, the city revived and grew: excavated remains include substantial wealthy houses, streets, an aqueduct, industrial facilities, and workshops. The doomed Jewish Revolt of 67–70 C.E., however, ended in the Romans' destruction of the city.

Some of Jerusalem's ancient remains can be seen by wandering around the Old City, the City of David, and adjacent areas. There are organized tours of the major sights, including the impressive underground water tunnels.

Clockwise from top Impressive family tombs with columned facades. An aerial view of the eastern hill: in the foreground, the spur where early settlement focused. Warren's Shaft, which gave access to water.

THE ROSE-RED CITY OF **PETRA**

TYPE: URBAN • **ARCHITECTURAL STYLE:** CLASSICAL WITH LOCAL VARIATIONS
LOCATION: JORDAN • **CONSTRUCTION BEGUN:** FIRST CENTURY B.C.E.

The Nabatean city of Petra, known as Selah in Aramaic, is located in Jordan, among the mountains to the east of the Wadi Araba that runs from the bottom of the Dead Sea to the port of Aqaba. The setting of the city within a series of wadis suggested the nineteenth-century description by John W. Burgon, dean of Chichester Cathedral, in his prize-winning poem of 1845 as "rose-red city half as old as time." Burgon himself had not even been to Petra and had relied on descriptions made by early travelers.

Petra lies 146 miles (235 km) to the south of Amman, and 78 miles (125 km) northeast of Aqaba. The site is usually approached through a narrow gorge, el Siq, which reveals the monumental Al-Khazneh. This two-storyed facade, 128 ft (39 m) high, in the Classical Corinthian style is cut into the rock face. Inside are three main rooms, and the function of the structure seems to have been that of a temple. Farther into the city, in the Outer Siq, is the classical theater, perhaps constructed in the early second century C.E.; the upper part of the seating is cut through an earlier Nabataean street. The stage building, in the Roman style, was erected in front of the auditorium.

At the center of the city, on the south side of the Wadi Musa, was a colonnaded street, an urban feature that became very popular in the provinces of the Eastern Roman Empire. At the eastern end was a monumental fountain or nymphaeum that was fed by a water system running through the Siq. On the south side of the colonnade was a series of markets fronted by small structures that are likely to have served as shops. The large sanctuary on the south side of the colonnaded street was entered through a monumental gateway, or propylon, that contained a stairway leading to the precinct placed on an upper level. It seems to have been enlarged during the first century C.E.

At the western end of the colonnaded street, the Temenos Gate, with three arches in a local Nabataean style, led into a sanctuary area, at the end of which is a square temple known as the Qasr al-Bint. It was approached by a flight of steps that led into a portico. Behind this was a rectangular room, with two smaller rooms behind. The earliest structure probably dates from the end of the first century B.C.E., suggested by an inscription of King Aretas IV (9 B.C.E.–40 C.E.) that was placed in the temenos. The temple appears to have been rebuilt in the second century C.E.

Mausolea were cut into the sides of wadis surrounding the city and were often given classical facades. Some probably date to the Hellenistic period, and one is identified as the tomb of a second-century C.E. Roman provincial governor of Arabia, T. Aninius Sextius Florentinus. One of the finest tombs is known as the Deir: it had two stories 125 ft (38 m) high, and the facade is 131 ft (40 m) wide. The Bab al-Siq Triclinium is laid out as if in the form of a classical dining room with benches on three sides of the room. It is placed immediately below the cliff face of the Obelisk Tomb, with four relief obelisks carved in the facade.

There are public buses as well as coach tours to Petra from Amman and Aqaba. There is a visitor center for Petra in Wadi Musa where accommodation can be found. Strong boots are advised.

Opposite The rock-cut monument known as the Deir. It dates to the mid-first century C.E.

Above, from left The second-century C.E. theater with cuttings at the top from buildings that were destroyed in its construction. The Great Temple with gateway leading from the colonnaded street.

UR A CITY AT THE DAWN OF URBAN LIFE

TYPE: CITY WITH SACRED PRECINCT INCLUDING ZIGGURAT • **ARCHITECTURAL STYLE:** SUMERIAN
LOCATION: TELL EL-MUQAYYAR, DHI QAR GOVERNORATE, IRAQ • **CONSTRUCTION BEGUN:** CA. 4000 B.C.E.

A towering ziggurat surrounded by mudbrick ruins and desert at Tell el-Muqayyar in southern Iraq gives a misleading impression of ancient Ur. Once a huge walled metropolis built on elevated ground in marshy plains, Ur was flanked by a branch of the Euphrates River that connected it to the nearby northern shores of the Gulf, providing river and sea links that enabled it to trade throughout West Asia and beyond.

Trade was a major source of Ur's prosperity, as rich finds from its Royal Cemetery attest. Often identified as the Biblical Garden of Eden, this fertile region, rich in fish, date palms, and marsh resources, was inhabited by at least the sixth millennium B.C.E. Major excavations conducted at Ur in 1920–1934 by Sir Leonard Woolley (1880–1960) revealed 6,000 years of occupation. Developing into a city in the Early Dynastic period (earlier third millennium B.C.E.), it saw its heyday under the Ur III dynasty who ruled all of southern Mesopotamia 2112–2004 B.C.E., but it continued to flourish thereafter as a major religious and cultural center. An eastward shift in the Euphrates' course during the Persian period caused Ur's eventual abandonment.

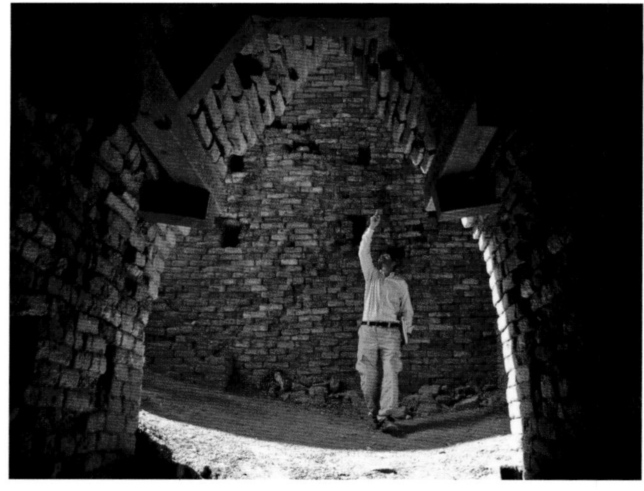

Sumer, the southern part of southern Mesopotamia, was where urban life first began. Ur was one of its leading Early Dynastic cities, distinguished by the extraordinary discoveries in its large cemetery, in use around 2600–2300 B.C.E. Many people buried here were accompanied by objects made from exotic materials, including gold, carnelian from the Indus region, and lapis lazuli from Afghanistan. Sixteen graves were exceptional: the principal burial was laid within a vaulted chamber with wonderful offerings such as jewelry and musical instruments decorated with precious materials; others (in one case sixty-eight) were buried in the associated grave pit, also with fine grave goods. Whether these individuals were sacrificed is still debated, as is the identity of the principals, though they are often regarded as royalty.

The Sumerian cities were united by Sargon of Akkad (r. ca. 2334–2284 B.C.E.) around 2334 B.C.E. Woolley's excavations focused largely on the sacred precinct of the city's patron deity, Nanna (Sin), where he uncovered buildings including the giparu where Nanna's priestess (Sargon's daughter) lived, along with her staff and those of Ningal, the moon god's wife. This included a courtyard, domestic and public rooms, a chapel, and archives.

Ur III kings significantly remodeled the precinct and were probably buried in the vaulted mausolea just outside its walls. They built the ziggurat that still dominates the site (repaired and partially reconstructed by Saddam Hussein): a three-tiered stepped pyramid, originally crowned by a temple. The ziggurat's mudbrick core was covered by a thick outer shell of baked brick decorated with buttresses and recesses, with bitumen as mortar. A triple staircase provided access to the upper tiers.

The ziggurat was the main structure within a separately walled inner precinct dedicated to Nanna. After Ur was sacked in 2004 B.C.E. and the center of power moved farther north, Nanna's shrine continued to attract worshippers for many centuries. The surrounding city, Mesopotamia's cultural capital under Ur III, also enjoyed continuing prestige as a center of learning. Woolley uncovered a large area of closely packed second-millennium-B.C.E. streets of one- or two-story buildings with internal courtyards overlooked by balconies—houses, workshops, chapels and, in at least one case, a school.

Local guides can help the visitor to interpret the ruins. Ur should be visited from Nasiriyah, 13 miles (20 km) away, where the local museum displays finds from the city. The spectacular objects from the Royal Cemetery, however, are in London's British Museum and Pennsylania's University Museum in Philadelphia.

Opposite Inside one of the vaulted underground tombs of the Ur III kings near the sacred precinct.

Below The first ziggurat, built by King Ur-Nammu (r. 2112–2095 B.C.E.), founder of the Ur III empire.

BABYLON THE MIGHTY CITY

TYPE: IMPERIAL CAPITAL CITY • **ARCHITECTURAL STYLE:** BABYLONIAN
LOCATION: HILLAH, BABIL PROVINCE, IRAQ • **CONSTRUCTION BEGUN:** THIRD MILLENNIUM B.C.E.

Infamous to the Jews, who suffered a hated exile there, and famed by the Greeks as home to Wonders of the World, Babylon has never been forgotten through the ages. Today it is both famous for its extraordinary remains and infamous for the "theme-park" reconstruction of parts of the city by Iraq's former dictator, Saddam Hussein.

A minor town in the third millennium B.C.E., Babylon grew prosperous in the early second millennium after a favorable shift in the course of the Euphrates River brought local agricultural wealth. In the competitive environment after the Ur III empire fell in 2004 B.C.E., Babylon's shrewd and aggressive kings began carving out a wider realm. The greatest, Hammurabi (r. 1792–1750 B.C.E.), created an empire stretching from the Gulf to Mari on the middle Euphrates, though under his less able successors this quickly shrank. Babylonia (southern Mesopotamia) had regained international power by the later second millennium. It eventually fell subject to its northern neighbor and former competitor, Assyria,

Opposite, from top Polychrome glazed bricks were used to create the magnificent bas-relief images of bulls and dragons on the Ishtar Gate and lions along the Processional Way at Babylon.
Below Saddam Hussein's "reconstruction" of the Southern Palace, built over Babylon's excavated foundations.

but inherited Assyria's vast empire when Assyrian authority collapsed around 612 B.C.E. The Babylonian king Nabupolassar (r. 626–605 B.C.E.) and his son Nebuchadrezzar II (r. 604–562 B.C.E.) devoted themselves to rebuilding, extending, and embellishing Babylon, replacing mudbrick structures with more solid baked-brick architecture, often of impressive monumentality: what survives of Babylon is mainly their work.

Impressively massive defensive walls surrounded the city and reached their apogee under Nebuchadrezzar. Two thick walls, separated by a raised military roadway, surrounded the inner city; an outer wall, added in the twelfth century B.C.E., trebled the land enclosed within the city to 3 sq mi (7.8 sq km) and a wide moat surrounded both sets of walls. The Euphrates River divided the city into a major eastern and a suburban western half. Nebuchadrezzar strengthened the embankments and added a massive baked-brick bulwark at the northern corner, to protect the city against the river.

Within the City Walls

Babylon's most prominent monument, reaching toward the heavens, was the ziggurat of Marduk, Etemenanki, (popularly known as the Tower of Babel). Constructed on a square base with sides 300 ft (92 m) long, this stepped pyramid originally stood 300 ft (92 m) high. It probably had seven tiers and was surmounted by a temple complex, the main cella dedicated to Babylon's patron deity, Marduk, with chapels to other major gods. Later destruction and brick quarrying have left only its foundations, marked by a water-filled hole.

Etemenanki stood within a huge precinct raised on a high platform and surrounded by a massive wall as protection against flooding by the Euphrates River, on whose eastern bank lay all the city's most important buildings. Immediately to its south was Esagila, Marduk's temple, home to his golden statue and its attendants. Chapels within its precinct accommodated statues of other gods when they visited Marduk for the New Year Festival. A grand Processional Way, along which the gods' statues were carried, led from the temple past the royal palaces to the Festival house outside the city.

The southern palace, in the northwest corner of the eastern inner city, was begun by Nabupolassar and completed by Nebuchadrezzar. Residential and official rooms surrounded a massive central throne room, its facade decorated with a magnificent frieze in glazed brick, brilliant lapis-lazuli blue its predominent color. Along its foot prowled lions, sacred to Ishtar, goddess of love and war; above them towered palm-tree columns, surrounded by an elaborate floral border. Nebuchadrezzar added a larger palace immediately north of the inner city wall.

The Processional Way passed through the Ishtar Gate east of the palaces. This gate and the wall along the slab-paved road beyond were decorated with colorful glazed-brick friezes. The city's crowning glory, these can now be seen in Berlin's Pergamon Museum; Babylon itself has an inferior replica erected by Saddam. Along the walls were Ishtar's lions, while the gate was covered with lines

of bulls, representing the storm god Adad, and dragons (*mushusshu*), symbolizing Marduk.

The last Babylonian king, Nabonidus (r. 555–539 B.C.E.) further embellished the city, as did his son, Belshazzar, who acted as regent during his father's ten-year residence in the Arabian city of Taima. The New Year Festival, all-important for the city and nation's spiritual well-being, required the king's presence: popular dissatisfaction at the ten-year hiatus in its performance may have contributed to the ease with which Cyrus, the Persian king, captured Babylon in 539 B.C.E. The city prospered under Cyrus' rule and later, but became a ruin in Sassanian times. The Greeks wrote much about its former glories, which according to Herodotus included the famous Hanging Gardens. These have never been located, despite extensive searching—and it now seems likely that Herodotus confused their location: his description closely matches the royal gardens built by the Assyrian king Sennacherib at his capital, Nineveh.

Visitors to Babylon can get an impression of the ancient city from the surviving ruins and valuable information from local guides, though Saddam's reconstructions, on original foundations, somewhat mar the experience.

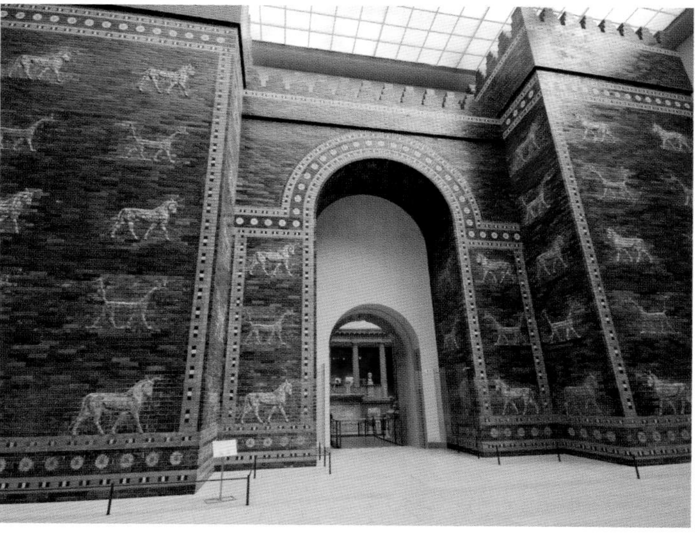

Opposite Earlier, unglazed courses of bricks in the Ishtar Gate, exposed during excavation.

Right The Processional Way (top) and Ishtar Gate (bottom), reconstructed in Berlin's Pergamon Museum from original bricks, contrast starkly with Saddam's in situ modern walls (center).

PERSIAN SPLENDOR IN **PERSEPOLIS**

TYPE: IMPERIAL CEREMONIAL AND ADMINISTRATIVE CAPITAL • **ARCHITECTURAL STYLE:** ACHAEMENID **LOCATION:** FARS PROVINCE, IRAN • **CONSTRUCTION BEGUN:** 515 B.C.E.

In 539 B.C.E. the Persian King Cyrus the Great (r. 559–530 B.C.E.) conquered Babylon. The empire Cyrus forged—extended by his successors Cambyses and Darius to reach from the Balkans and Egypt to the Indus—was the largest the world had yet seen. Parsa (Persepolis—modern Takht-e Jamshid, Fars Province, Iran) was created by Darius around 515 B.C.E. as one of the empire's capitals. Built on a vast walled terrace, its magnificent columned halls commanded the Marvdasht plain, their glories echoed by the columned facades of royal tombs cut into the hill behind.

This was the ceremonial and official heart of a city that sprawled across the plain. Little is known of the residential, commercial, and other areas that once lay here, since archaeological investigations have concentrated almost exclusively on the terrace buildings. The king and his court occupied Persepolis for part of the year, moving between here and Susa (their winter residence in Elam), Babylon, and their upland summer palace at Ecbatana in northwestern Iran.

Imperial Grandeur

Climbing an imposing staircase, the visitor to Persepolis entered the royal center through a monumental entrance, the Gate of All Nations. Two enormous bull statues fronted the gateway, through which the visitor entered a hall in which benches could accommodate 100 people awaiting their turn to pass through the matching inner gateway onto a walled road that led to the eastern side of the terrace. Here another imposing gateway, unfinished, led into a courtyard giving access through a pillared portico to the Hall of 100 Columns, the venue for public ceremonies drawing officials (probably military personnel) from all over the empire. Two doorways opened on each side, those on the north and south showing the king seated on his throne, supported by

Above, from top Reliefs carved on the platform of the Apadana: delegates of subject nations bring tribute, while richly clad Persian and Median nobles mount the stair.

Right view across Persepolis: on the far side the Apadana (left) and Gate of All Nations (center.)

rows of figures representing the empire's subject nations, with the winged figure of the supreme god Ahuramazda above. On the jambs of the west and east doorways, carvings depicted the king, or a hero figure, subduing a lionlike mythical beast with an eagle's wings and a scorpion's tail.

From the Gate of All Nations, an alternative exit to the south led into the courtyard of Persepolis' chief public building, the Apadana. This vast pillared hall was surrounded on three sides by porticos. The stone columns, of which a number still stand, had stepped square bases within the hall and bell-shaped bases in the porticos. Their massive stone capitals (protomes) were carved with pairs of animal forequarters—bulls, lions, griffins, and human-headed bulls—shown back to back, the saddle between them supporting huge cedar beams that carried the timber and plaster roof. Mudbrick walls between massive corner towers separated the hall from the porticos, stone-framed windows shedding light into the interior. The towers' facades bore faience tiles with geometric and floral designs.

The Apadana stood on a platform approached by monumental stairs on the north and east sides. The panels fronting the stairs are carved with Persian and Median guards and combat scenes of a lion attacking a bull, while the sides of the stairs show processions of figures, on one side Persian and Median nobles, attendants, and guards, on the other delegates from twenty-three subject nations bearing tribute, such as fine textiles, gold vessels and jewelry, exotic animals, and horses. Delegates from these nations probably assembled here on important ceremonial or official occasions—the hall could accommodate 10,000 people.

Widespread Inspiration

Craftsmen from across the empire were employed on these buildings: texts mention Egyptian, Ionian, Syrian, and Babylonian workers. Elements of the architecture and decoration also draw on foreign sources—monumental bull sculptures and figural reliefs hark back to the decoration of Assyrian palaces, the use of architectural glazed bricks to Babylonia, columned halls to Media—but these are reinterpreted to create a distinctive Persian style, with a very different message: harmony and multicultural unity under the beneficent control of the universal monarch, beloved and watched over by God.

The southern half of the complex contained smaller buildings of a similar design, all probably public—ceremonial or official—rather than residential in purpose. Several, including the Central Building (perhaps a ceremonial meeting place for the aristocracy), had stairs decorated with Persian and Median nobles and with priests or servants bearing food, drink, and live animals. A large complex with many rooms south of the Hall of 100 Columns is known as the Treasury: this held rich offerings brought to Persepolis in tribute. Little remains of these treasures.

In 330 B.C.E., during his whirlwind conquest of the mighty Persian empire, Alexander the Great (356–323 B.C.E.) set fire to Persepolis–either an act of reckless drunken vandalism or deliberate revenge for the Persians' sack of Athens 150 years earlier. He and his soldiers thoroughly looted the city. Enough remained of the monuments, however, to excite visitors and antiquarians over the centuries and in the early twentieth century it was excavated and its spectacular treasures revealed. These magnificent ruins can be reached by taxi from Marvdasht, the nearest town. There is a good site museum and local guides can provide information. Material from this World Heritage site can also be seen in the National Museum in Tehran.

Opposite, from left The rock-cut tomb of Artaxerxes III (r. 358-338 B.C.E) overlooking Persepolis. A griffin protome (column capital) from the Apadana.

Below A magnificent man-headed bull fronts Xerxes' Gate of All Nations.

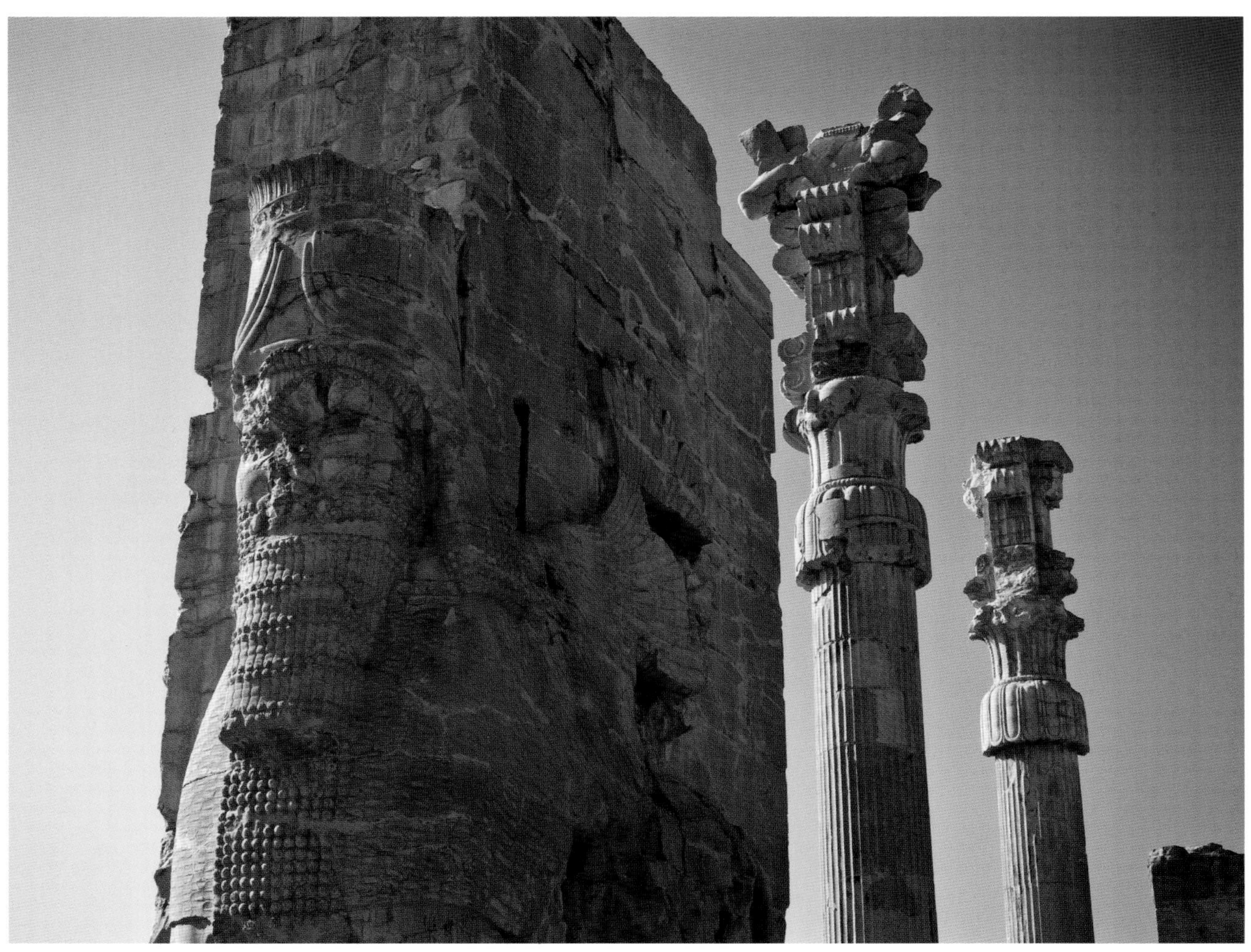

MOHENJO DARO AND INDUS CIVILIZATION

TYPE: CITY • **ARCHITECTURAL STYLE:** HARAPPAN
LOCATION: LARKANA DISTRICT, SINDH, PAKISTAN • **CONSTRUCTION BEGUN:** 2600 B.C.E.

The ruined city of Mohenjo Daro is an imposing sight, rising above the lush green fields of the Indus plain in Sindh, Pakistan. Silt deposited by the river's annual floods has steadily raised the floodplain: four thousand years ago the city towered above it, built on walled platforms more than 20 ft (6 m) high. Houses stood two or three stories tall, and the stark brick walls seen today were originally plastered and gaily painted.

Mohenjo Daro was the largest city of the Indus (Harappan) civilization, forgotten by posterity and unknown until a century ago. Farming villages had appeared in the Indus plains and adjacent regions during the fourth millennium B.C.E. Some grew into towns and, by 2600 B.C.E., into cities.

But perhaps not Mohenjo Daro—evidence suggests that this was a deliberate foundation on virgin soil around 2600 B.C.E., a planned city, located at the very center of the Indus realms and at the crossroads between routes along the Indus River and overland north into Baluchistan. The alluvial plain, though agriculturally productive, was a challenging environment for settlement, exposed to frequent massive river floods. In order to live here safely, the city's builders created enormous foundation platforms of mudbricks encased in a solid baked-brick protective walls.

Lower Town

In the residential area of the city, the main streets were aligned to the cardinal directions using astronomical sightings lined up with landscape features. Wide main streets were crossed by narrower side streets off which the houses opened, their windowless facades and entrance passages keeping the interiors free from street dust. Much of daily life, such as food preparation and craft activities, took place in the courtyard, off which rooms opened; a stair led to the upper story(ies) and roof, where people might sleep. Houses often had a latrine and most had a bathroom, paved with close-fitting baked bricks covered with polished plaster. Wastewater was carried away through terracotta drainpipes connected to brick street drains and left the city through brick culverts. Clean water came from around 700 private and public wells, built of tightly fitting wedge-shaped bricks. The sophisticated provision and disposal of water was a remarkable feature of the Indus civilization.

Many craft activities took place throughout the city, some within domestic workshops or houses, such as textile making, others clustered in industrial quarters of the city, such as pottery manufacture and stoneworking, and the most polluting on the outskirts. City workshops made copper and bronze into tools, vessels, and occasionally sculptures, and silver and gold into jewelry, sometimes combined with other materials. Jewelry was also made from faience, pottery, shell, ivory, gemstones, and other materials. Bead making was a craft in which the Harappans excelled, their skills displayed in exceptionally long carnelian beads and microscopic steatite beads. Steatite was also made into exquisite seals, bearing a brief inscription and an image, usually of a single animal.

Public Architecture

The buildings on the higher, western ("Citadel") mound strongly contrast with the residential and industrial buildings of the Lower Town. Most famous is the Great

Bath, a rectangular pool 39 ft (12 m) long by 23 ft (7 m) wide and 8 ft (2.4 m) deep, entered down steps from either end. It was completely watertight, constructed of layers of closely fitted baked bricks, mudbrick, and bitumen. It was emptied through a large drain with a magnificent corbeled vault. Built in the center of a complex to which access seemed, by its layout, restricted, this probably served a religious purpose. Nearby were rows of bathrooms and a large two-story building with many small rooms, perhaps administrative. Adjacent to the Great Bath lay the so-called Granary, not suitable for storing grain but possibly a warehouse. Farther south were other large buildings.

Who ran the Indus state? No clear signs of rulers, such as palaces or rich burials, or of religious leaders have been found at Mohenjo Daro (or elsewhere). Nevertheless, the efficiency with which fine raw materials and good-quality manufactured goods from different regions were distributed suggests a system answerable to some authority. This is reinforced by the use of weights conforming to a strictly maintained standard. Overseas trade also flourished, reaching from Afghanistan to Mesopotamia.

The Decline of the Indus Civilization

Around 1800 B.C.E. urban life declined and the hallmark Indus cultural uniformity ceased, although farming villages continued to prosper, particularly in Gujarat and the eastern region. There were probably many causes of this change. The decline is marked at Mohenjo Daro by the appearance of very inferior houses and skeletons apparently dumped in abandoned houses rather than decently buried, perhaps victims of epidemic disease, a known hazard in densely packed cities: if so, this may have been one reason for the cessation of Harappan urban life.

Mohenjo Daro is best visited in the cooler winter months, by taking an organized tour or making a day trip from Larkana. Visitors can wander along streets and into houses still standing above head height. Many of the beautiful artifacts from the city can be seen in the excellent site museum.

Above The Great Bath, set within the courtyard of a larger complex with bathrooms and upstairs rooms.

THE COSMOPOLITAN METROPOLIS OF **TAXILA**

TYPE: CITY AND SURROUNDING RELIGIOUS ESTABLISHMENTS • **ARCHITECTURAL STYLE:** GANDHARAN
LOCATION: PUNJAB, PAKISTAN • **CONSTRUCTION BEGUN:** CA. SIXTH CENTURY B.C.E.

Strategically located for trade, the great city of Taxila in Gandhara (northern Punjab, Pakistan) also enjoyed great agricultural prosperity. Three successive major settlements and many extramural religious complexes are spread through the valley and into its surrounding hills. History records Taxila's participation in many encounters between east and west in the later centuries B.C.E. and early C.E., and its art and architecture exemplify the outstanding results of this cultural cross-fertilization.

Mesolithic hunter-gatherers occupied caves in the hills, and farmers settled in the valley by the fourth millennium B.C.E. In the late sixth century B.C.E., a substantial settlement (the Bhir Mound) was built in the southeast of the valley. Excavated material attests to contacts with states developing in the Ganges Valley, supporting literary evidence that Gandhara was one of the Early Historic Indian kingdoms that traded, made alliances, and fought with each other in this period. Farther west, the Persian (Achaemenid) empire was expanding, and Taxila probably came under its control around this time. When Alexander the Great (356–323 B.C.E.) conquered the Achaemenid empire and reached India in 326 B.C.E., Taxila's king voluntarily allied with him. However, no material that can be linked to the Persians or to Alexander's visit has been identified here.

In the power vacuum following Alexander's brief incursion, the region fell, in 311 B.C.E., to Chandragupta Maurya (r. ca. 321–297 B.C.E.), ruler of the expanding Mauryan empire. The Mauryas had begun as rulers of the central Gangetic state of Magadha. By the time of Chandragupta's grandson, Ashoka (r. ca. 268–ca. 232 B.C.E.), they controlled almost all the Indian subcontinent.

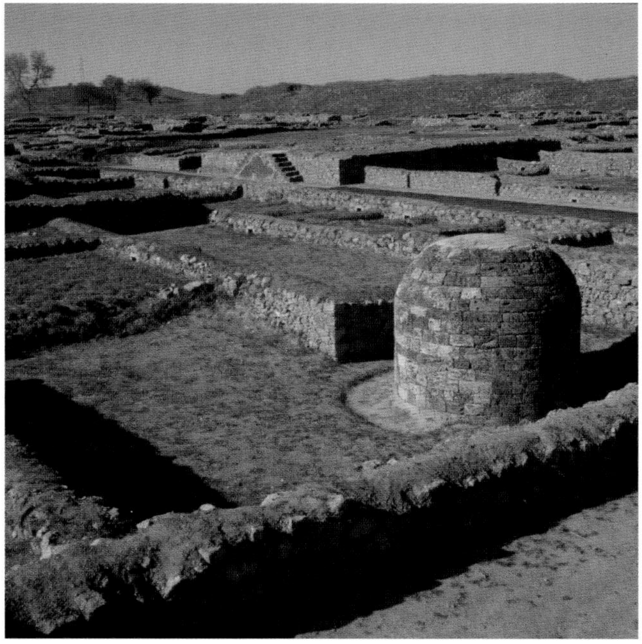

Opposite, from top Aerial view of the Dharmarajika stupa, ringed by small stupas and chapels, with others beyond. Detail of the main stupa's typical Kushan masonry, with decorative niches.

Above A small stupa in one of the courtyards of a private house on Sirkap's main street.

Taxila became the Mauryas' northern capital, and during his father's reign Ashoka was viceroy here. Most buildings uncovered in the Bhir Mound belong to this period. Houses generally had a central courtyard off which rooms opened; many contained ring wells for drainage. A pillared hall in the west of the city may have been a Hindu shrine.

After the Mauryan empire fell in 185 B.C.E., the Gandhara region came under the control of competing Indo-Greek kingdoms. In the mid-second century B.C.E. the Indo-Greeks built a new city, Sirkap, following the grid street layout characteristic of planned Greek cities. Although Gandhara and Taxila changed hands repeatedly in subsequent centuries, coming under the control of Indianized invaders from Central Asia (Shakas), Iran (Indo-Parthians), and Central Asia again (Kushans), Sirkap's citizens maintained its regular plan: wide main streets and smaller lanes, dividing it into blocks of spacious stone-masonry houses with workshops, administrative buildings, shrines, and shops. A walled acropolis on high ground in the city's south contained official buildings, including a probable ruler's palace. The excavated remains belong mainly to the Indo-Parthian and Kushan periods, when the city was reconstructed after serious earthquake damage in 30 C.E. In the late first century C.E., the Kushans built a new city, Sirsukh, in the valley's north.

Crossroads of Trade and Culture

Finds from Sirkap vividly reflect the city's important role as a crossroads in international trade, linking states in India with the major east–west route from China to Rome, the routes dividing in Gandhara to run overland or down the Indus and thence across the sea. Sirkap's merchants received Roman and Alexandrian glassware, silver vessels, engraved gems, bronze statuary, and wine, and transmitted goods such as Chinese silks and Afghan lapis lazuli, and Indian spices and ivory furniture decorations.

The cosmopolitan nature of Sirkap's population is reflected in the religions attested here by literary and archaeological evidence, including Jainism, Vaishnavite Hinduism, Greek cults, perhaps Zoroastrianism, and possibly Christianity. But most religious structures in the city and the valley beyond were Buddhist. These included the magnificent Dharmarajika stupa, 2 miles (3.2 km) east of Sirkap. Traditionally founded by Ashoka, it reached its present form in the second century C.E. The large central stupa, faced with carved limestone blocks, stands on a platform, surrounded by many small stupas and chapels.

The Jaulian monastery was constructed in the hills 7 miles (11 km) from Taxila, enabling the monks to enjoy tranquility for contemplation while remaining close enough to the city to obtain the alms on which they depended. The monastery had two stories, its cells surrounding a central courtyard with a verandah. An adjacent enclosure held a large stupa surrounded by small votive stupas, their plinths copiously decorated with fine stucco reliefs of Buddhas and Bodhisattvas.

Stucco decorations on the valley's many stupas and monasteries are echoed by a wealth of carvings in schist and figures in terracotta, all exemplifying the magnificent Gandharan art style. This combined the naturalism of Greek art with decorative elements and subjects from traditional Indian art. In addition to majestic statues of the Buddha, there were lively scenes from his life.

In 460 C.E. Taxila was sacked by the White Huns (Hephthalites)—destroyed buildings, scattered skeletons, and hoards of precious objects concealed and never recovered all bear witness to this disaster.

Taxila's cities and many religious sites are scattered through the valley around the modern town, so visitors are recommended to hire local transport and a guide to enjoy this World Heritage site to the full. Visit the excellent museum too.

Opposite, from top Diverse religious architecture at Taxila: the Dharmarajika stupa; and the temple of the Double-headed Eagle, decorated with both Greek and Indian architectural forms.

THE ROCK ART OF **BHIMBETKA**

TYPE: ROCK SHELTERS WITH PAINTINGS • **ARCHITECTURAL STYLE:** MESOLITHIC TO MEDIEVAL
LOCATION: RAISEN DISTRICT, MADHYA PRADESH, INDIA • **CONSTRUCTION BEGUN:** N/A

Massive rock shelters carved by eroding winds from the rocks of Bhimbetka and neighboring hills near Bhopal in central India conceal hundreds of ancient paintings, some more than 10,000 years old. Discovered by V. S. Wakankar (1919–1988) in 1957, these reveal in intimate detail the lives of hunter-gatherers who drew on the rich plant and animal resources of the surrounding teak forests.

Excavations exposing stone tools, other everyday material, and human burials revealed that these rock shelters were already being occupied more than 100,000 years ago and were still in use in medieval times. Elegant green paintings seem to be the earliest, probably painted in the late Palaeolithic period. A great range of paintings in brown, black, sometimes white, and especially red show scenes from the daily lives of the later Mesolithic hunter-gatherers, or depict the animals they knew—many, such as antelope, tiger, and deer still present, while others, such as Indian lion, rhino, and wild buffalo no longer inhabit this region. Some creatures are shown in outline, others with their bodies colored, decorated with geometric patterns, or showing their insides, as in an X-ray. People are most commonly shown as stick figures or with a triangular torso infilled with crisscross lines, wearing small items of clothing.

The Bhimbetka paintings give an extraordinarily detailed picture of forager existence. Hunters armed with spears, slings, and bows work together, encircling ferocious wild buffalo or boar or pursuing herds of deer. Women set traps, club lizards, and team up to catch rats, some driving them from their burrows into nets held by others. Women also gather fruit in baskets and dig tubers. Men in boats set nets for fish. One person collects honey from a treetop, with bees buzzing furiously around.

Bhimbetka's people are also shown at leisure. Men in headdresses, with streamers on their knees and elbows, dance in a long line arm-in-arm, accompanied by drummers, while an appreciative audience of women and children watch. At other times, they separate into family groups, eating together, preparing food, or making and mending tools.

While in many parts of the world the advent of farming destroyed or marginalized the hunter-gatherer way of life, in India mutually beneficial relationships

developed between many farming communities and their forager neighbors: hunter-gatherers had the skills, knowledge, and opportunities to exploit wild resources inaccessible to settled farmers. The people of Bhimbetka may have supplied farmers with honey, game, wild silk, fish, dye and food plants, herbal medicines, and other forest resources, exchanging these for grain, pottery, and copper tools. After around 2500 B.C.E., such objects appear both in the excavated rock shelters and in the paintings, along with depictions of domestic cattle, sheep, and goats. Such harmonious collaboration continued into recent times.

By the late centuries B.C.E., the paintings include observed outsiders, such as soldiers armed with swords, spears, and shields, mounted on horses or elephants or driving chariots. Battle scenes occur: here, the fighters armed with bows and arrows may be the hunter-gatherers themselves.

While the modern Adivasi inhabitants of villages around Bhimbetka—descendants of the local forager tribes—are farmers nowadays, growing crops and keeping livestock, they still hunt and gather forest produce, maintaining some part of their traditional way of life.

Bhimbetka's World Heritage archaeological park contains fifteen rock shelters, with good interpretation boards. It is best visited in the cooler winter months. Access by public transport is difficult but organized tours are available.

Opposite A terrifying Mesolithic scene—a tiny man is pursued by an enormous boar with horns.

Above Later painting of armed and armored soldiers on foot and on horseback, one with an elaborate saddlecloth.

CAVE TEMPLES AND MONASTERIES AT **AJANTA**

TYPE: ROCK-CUT CAVE TEMPLES AND MONASTERIES • **ARCHITECTURAL STYLE:** SHUNGA AND VAKATAKA
LOCATION: AURANGABAD DISTRICT, INDIA • **CONSTRUCTION BEGUN:** SECOND CENTURY B.C.E.

In 1819 army officers hunting in western India pursued a tiger into a beautiful, secluded gorge of the Waghora River—and stumbled across one of the greatest treasures of Buddhist art and architecture. Here, carved into the rock-face, were thirty cave temples and monasteries, where Buddhist monks had lived and worshipped, serenely detached from the outside world. A steep stair connected each cave to the river below. Originally decorated with sculptures and polychrome paintings, the caves have suffered the ravages of time, but what remains is breathtaking.

Buddhism developed in India around the sixth century B.C.E. Dependent on alms, during the rainy season Buddhist monks also needed shelter. Lay devotees gained spiritual merit by providing places for them to stay: through time, these developed into monasteries, with associated temples, where monks lived permanently. Some were created as rock-cut caves, faithfully reproducing in stone the details of freestanding structures originally built in wood.

Two cave temples and four monasteries were created at Ajanta between the second century B.C.E. and first century C.E. The temples took the form of an apsidal hall with vaulted ceiling, pillars separating the nave and apse from the aisles that formed a continuous passage round which the devotee could circumambulate, an important practice in Buddhist and other Indian worship. In the apse stood a small stupa (relic mound), symbolizing the Buddha. A great horseshoe-shaped chaitya arch framed a window that lit the interior, while many smaller arches decorated the rest of the facade. Monasteries were laid out as a central hall, used for congregation, off which the monks' cells opened on three sides. Originally both monasteries and temples were painted, though scant trace now remains.

Around 462 C.E., in the peaceful reign of the Vakataka king Harisena (r. 460–478 C.E.), a spectacular burst of new activity began at Ajanta, during which wealthy Buddhist lay devotees, including merchants and royal officials, sponsored the creation of three temples and many monasteries. These follow the general form of earlier examples, but with significant changes. A substantial pillared verandah now formed the entrance to each cave. Small shrines were added within the monasteries. Most strikingly, these later caves are covered with sculptured decoration, closely integrated with paintings. Images of the Buddha occupy the most significant

positions in the decorative scheme—alone, accompanied by attendants or Bodhisattvas (future Buddhas), or in significant scenes from his life—on the front of stupas, in panels above pillars, and on facades. These uplifting formal images contrast with more relaxed, exuberant *jataka* stories, scenes from the life of former incarnations of the Buddha, where the moral message did not prevent the artists vividly depicting aspects of everyday life: the extravagant comforts of the royal court, the bustle of towns, the tranquility of rural existence, or the adventures of seafaring merchants.

Though construction at Ajanta ceased around 480 C.E., leaving some caves unfinished, the monasteries continued to flourish for centuries. Merchants and other travelers (often Buddhist patrons) were welcomed there as visitors.

Modern visitors can reach the valley by public transport from Aurangabad. Stairs and walkways connect the caves at different levels. The magnificent scenery enhances the experience of visiting the wonderful art and architecture of this World Heritage site.

Opposite The elaborately carved interior of cave temple 26 (fifth century C.E.). Its stupa bears a seated figure of Buddha.

Above, clockwise from top A general view of part of Ajanta's valley. The rear wall and ceiling of monastery Cave 2. The damaged but still impressive facade of temple cave 26.

VIJAYANAGARA CITY OF VICTORY

TYPE: IMPERIAL CAPITAL CITY • **ARCHITECTURAL STYLE:** VIJAYANAGARA • **LOCATION:** HAMPI, BELLARY DISTRICT, KARNATAKA, INDIA • **CONSTRUCTION BEGUN:** CA. NINTH CENTURY C.E.

From the top of Matanga Hill at Hampi in South India's Bellary district, an extraordinary panorama can be seen: a city that was once reputedly the largest in the world. Clusters of magnificent palaces and temples, defensive walls, and canals follow the great Tungabhadra River and emerge at intervals across an extraordinary landscape of ancient hills shaped by erosion so that enormous boulders lie scattered or rest precariously one on another, as if thrown around by giants. Paddy fields paint the land a brilliant green where once there were innumerable houses, shops, shrines, and reservoirs. This is Vijayanagara, City of Victory, capital for two centuries of an empire that encompassed almost all South India.

In the early fourteenth century, local Hindu chiefs successfully resisted the threatened Muslim conquest of southern India. They established their base at Vijayanagara in 1336, gradually gained hegemony over South India and repelled their Muslim neighbors. To do so, they created an efficient standing army with cavalry and elephant troops, enlarged at need with levies from their subordinate kingdoms and equipped with the latest handguns and cannon. They encouraged trade to acquire fine cavalry horses from Arabia; trade brought the kingdom great wealth.

Prosperity also followed investment in hydraulic works: great reservoirs, dams, wells, and a network of canals and aqueducts that supplied water for highly productive agriculture, and for domestic use and ritual bathing. By their religious patronage, the kings made Vijayanagara the spiritual heart of the empire. Vijayanagara was itself a holy place, sacred mythology written into its landscape, and the kings enhanced its sacred spaces with shrines and art.

The Sacred Center

The kings expanded an important temple that had stood by the Tungabhadra River since the ninth century, attracting pilgrims (as it still does today). This was dedicated to Virapaksha, an avatar of Shiva who rewarded the exceptional pious devotion of a local girl, Pampa, by marrying her. Annual festivals celebrating their marriage took place in the temple, with processions through the city's Sacred Center, a long paved colonnaded street lined with temples, smaller shrines and the fine stone houses of the elite. Localities linked to Pampa were venerated.

The Royal Center

Vijayanagara was also identified with the mythological monkey kingdom, Kishkindha, where Rama (an incarnation of Vishnu) spent time while seeking his abducted wife, Sita: many features of the landscape were venerated for their association with key episodes in his sojourn. The Royal Center, a complex divided into public buildings and royal residential quarters, lay at the heart of the city and at its very heart was the Hazara Rama temple, dedicated to Rama. Its temple and enclosure walls are richly decorated with relief carvings of scenes from Rama's story.

Other reliefs depict processions of elephants, horses, soldiers, musicians, dancing girls, and other participants in the annual nine-day Mahanavami festival, the principal event of the year, attended by military commanders and rulers from across the empire. A Great Platform within the Royal Center was used as the royal viewing platform during this festival. It is richly decorated with scenes from everyday life, as well as animals and the life of Vijayanagara's kings.

Other notable buildings within the Royal Center included the Lotus Mahal, an octagonal two-story pavilion (probably a council chamber), and the vast Elephant Stables overlooking a parade ground. Both are in an architectural style, developed at Vijayanagara, that combined elements of traditional Hindu and contemporary Islamic design.

Vitthala Temple

One of the finest of the city's many monuments was the Vitthala temple, in the northeast, not far from the river. The work mainly of Krishnadevaraya I (r. 1509–1530), the city's greatest architectural patron, the temple lay within an enclosure with three massive tiered and elaborately ornamented gateways (*gopuras*). Dedicated to Vitthala, an avatar of Vishnu, its base is carved with reliefs of horses and their attendants, its stairs flanked by elephant and *yali* (horned lion) balustrades. Two successive entrance halls, with slender columns around stone piers and pillars in the form of rearing yalis, lead into the main shrine: a stunningly beautiful creation. Smaller surrounding shrines include one dedicated to Garuda, Vishnu's mount, in the unusual form of a *ratha* (wooden temple chariot, used to carry the god in procession), every detail lovingly translated into stone.

Opposite The main temple (foreground) and the Kalyana Mandapa in the Vitthala temple complex.

A catastrophic defeat

The Vijayanagara empire reached the height of its power under Krishnadevaraya and his successor Achyutaraya (r. 1530–1542). Tragically, in 1565 Vijayanagara's armies were heavily defeated at the battle of Talikota. Its kings fled to southern Andhra Pradesh, ruling a much-diminished state until 1664; others seized parts of the empire, and the city was sacked for six months. Thereafter Vijayanagara was largely abandoned, though many of its suburbs endured as villages or towns, and the Virapaksha temple remained a place of pilgrimage. Since 1980 intensive survey, clearance, excavation, and restoration work have brought renewed life to this astonishing monumental landscape.

Although auto rickshaws can be hired to tour the different locations within the Vijayanagara metropolis, to experience the wonders of this World Heritage site to the full, visitors should wander round on foot or by bicycle, taking several days, and perhaps hiring the services of an official guide.

Opposite, clockwise from top Pillared halls and shrines set into the vast boulder landscape. In the Royal Center, intricately carved granite pillars with elaborate capitals support the Hazara Rama temple's porch.

Below View east from Matanga Hill: Tiruvengalanatha temple, part of the extensive Sacred Center.

THE VENERATED CITY OF **ANURADHAPURA**

TYPE: CITY WITH MONASTERIES, STUPAS, AND RESERVOIRS • **ARCHITECTURAL STYLE:** ANURADHAPURA (EARLY HISTORIC) • **LOCATION:** ANURADHAPURA DISTRICT, SRI LANKA • **CONSTRUCTION BEGUN:** CA. 900 B.C.E.

Sri Lanka's capital for 1,500 years, Anuradhapura today is a sacred landscape of towering stupas surrounded by monastic ruins, with traces of the ancient city at its heart. Huge reservoirs and smaller pools reflect the central importance of water here, deep in Sri Lanka's Dry Zone.

Hunter-gatherers inhabited this island for more than 30,000 years. The settlements of rice farmers (traditionally from western India) appear in the earlier first millennium B.C.E. These include Anuradhapura, by the fourth century B.C.E. a walled city of well-built houses on regular streets.

In 246 B.C.E., the Mauryan emperor Ashoka (r. ca. 268–ca. 232 B.C.E.) sent his son Mahinda on a successful mission to introduce Buddhism to Sri Lanka. Anuradhapura's king, Devanampiyatissa (r. 250–210 B.C.E.), donated his royal pleasure garden to establish a monastery, Mahavihara, where he built a stupa, Thuparama, to enshrine precious relics given by Mahinda—the Buddha's collarbone and begging bowl. Ashoka's daughter Sanghamitta, who founded a Buddhist nunnery at Anuradhapura, brought a cutting from the sacred Bodhi (pipal) tree beneath which the Buddha had gained enlightenment. Planted in the

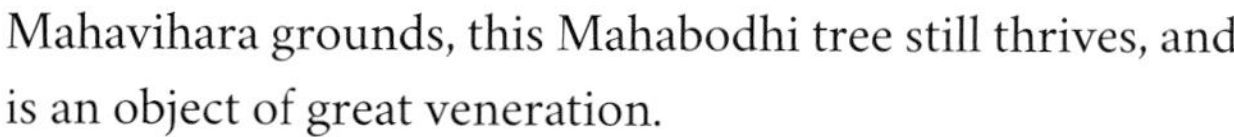

Mahavihara grounds, this Mahabodhi tree still thrives, and is an object of great veneration.

Within the city Devanampiyatissa constructed an alms hall, Mahapali, where he provided the monks with cooked rice, served from a huge stone trough that still stands here. Later kings continued this practice—a visiting Buddhist pilgrim, Faxian (ca. 337–ca. 422 C.E), reported that 6,000 monks were fed here daily.

King Dutthagamini (r. 161–137 B.C.E.), who expelled South Indian invaders and united the island in 161 B.C.E., was also a generous patron to the Mahavihara. His finest creation was the Great Stupa (Ruvanveli Dagoba; like other stupas at Anuradhapura, this has been heavily restored). His nephew Vattagamini built the vast Abhayagiri Dagoba. Enlarged by later rulers, it achieved its present height of 360 ft (110 m) in the second century C.E. Vattagamini also founded the surrounding Abhayagirivihara, for monks of the growing Mahayana Buddhist sect since Mahavihara's monks followed the traditional Theravadin doctrine. Over subsequent centuries various kings favored one or other of these sects: for example, Mahasena (274–301 C.E.) seized Mahavihara land to establish a new Mahayana monastery, Jetavanavihara, for which he built another vast stupa, the Jetavanaramaya. This originally stood at 394 ft (120 m), though it is now only 233 ft (71 m) high.

The ancient Sri Lankans were skilled hydraulic engineers, building networks of canals and reservoirs from early times to supply the water for irrigation and domestic use required for life in the low-rainfall Dry Zone. Bathing, for pleasure and for ritual purposes, played an important part in life at Anuradhapura, and some of the finest surviving art and architecture is associated with pools, such as the magnificent Kuttam Pokuna within the Abhayagirivihara and the Isurumuniya pool with its delightful carvings of elephants playing in the water.

In 1017 Cholas from South India sacked Anuradhapura. The capital shifted to Polonnaruwa, abandoning Anuradhapura to the jungle, though it never lost its sanctity. Since the nineteenth century its important buildings have been cleared and some have been reconstructed.

Visitors to this World Heritage site can stay in the modern town, where the Archaeological Museum is located, and use local public transport, rickshaws, or bicycles to visit the old city, the many monasteries, and the beautiful surrounding scenery.

Opposite The Ruvanveli Dagoba reflected in nearby Basawakkulamawewa, Anuradhapura's earliest reservoir.

Above, from left The vast Jetavanaramaya stupa. A semi-circular threshold slab (moonstone), decorated with auspicious symbols to bring prosperity.

6

FAR EAST AND OCEANIA

This vast area is inevitably dominated by China, with its tremendous Great Wall, its terracotta army—one of the most incredible discoveries in the history of archaeology—and its major tombs, some of them with remarkably well-preserved bodies and grave goods. But Japan and Korea also offer some remarkable sites such as the city of Gyeongju and the keyhole-shaped tombs. In Australia, archaeological research is a relatively recent development, but it offers some interesting sites and an enormous wealth of wonderful rock art. In Oceania, by far the greatest attraction is Easter Island—the entire island can be considered an archaeological site, justly famed for its hundreds of stone platforms and statues.

Left The Great Wall of China, one of the most famous monuments in the world.

FAR EAST AND OCEANIA
LOCATIONS

1 MAUSOLEUM OF QIN SHI HUANGDI
2 THE GREAT WALL
3 MAWANGDUI TOMBS
4 MAUSOLEUMS OF THE TANG DYNASTY
5 MING IMPERIAL TOMBS
6 GYEONGJU
7 DAISENRYO KOFUN
8 ANGKOR WAT AND ANGKOR THOM
9 BUDJ BIM
10 KAKADU NATIONAL PARK
11 EASTER ISLAND

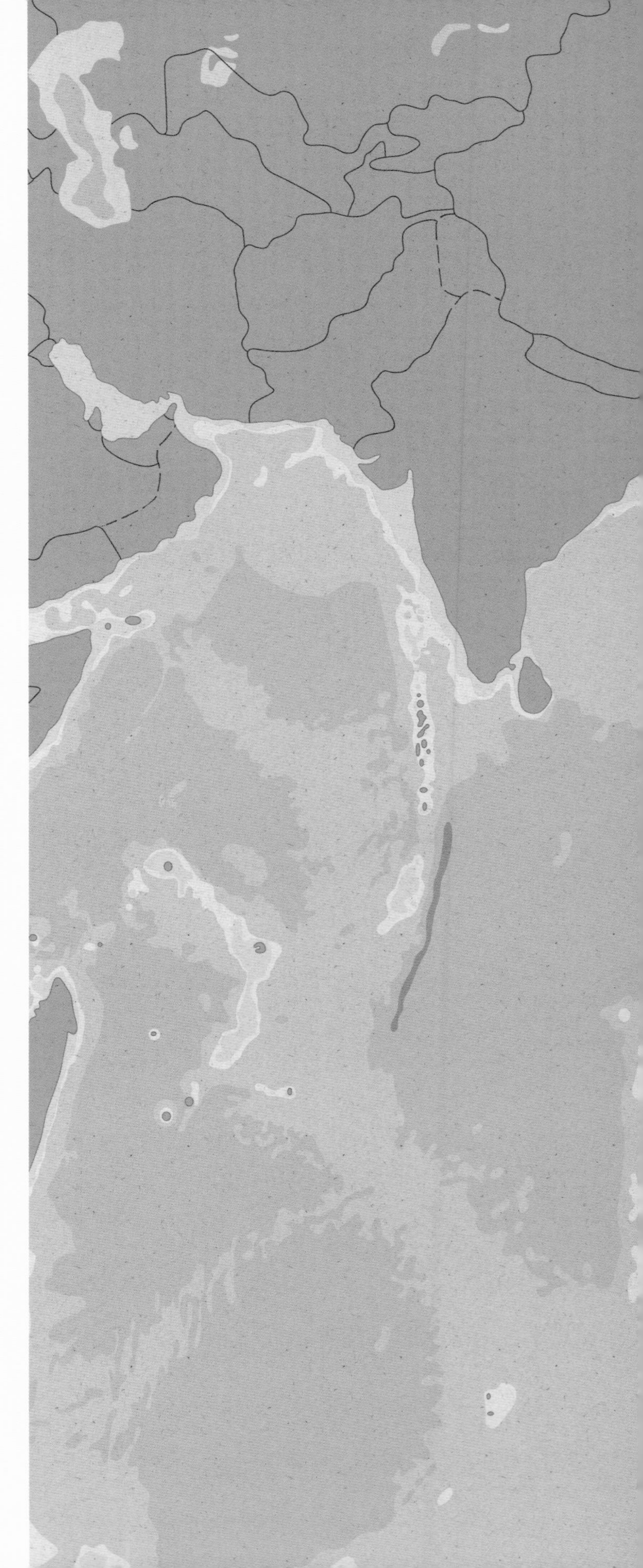

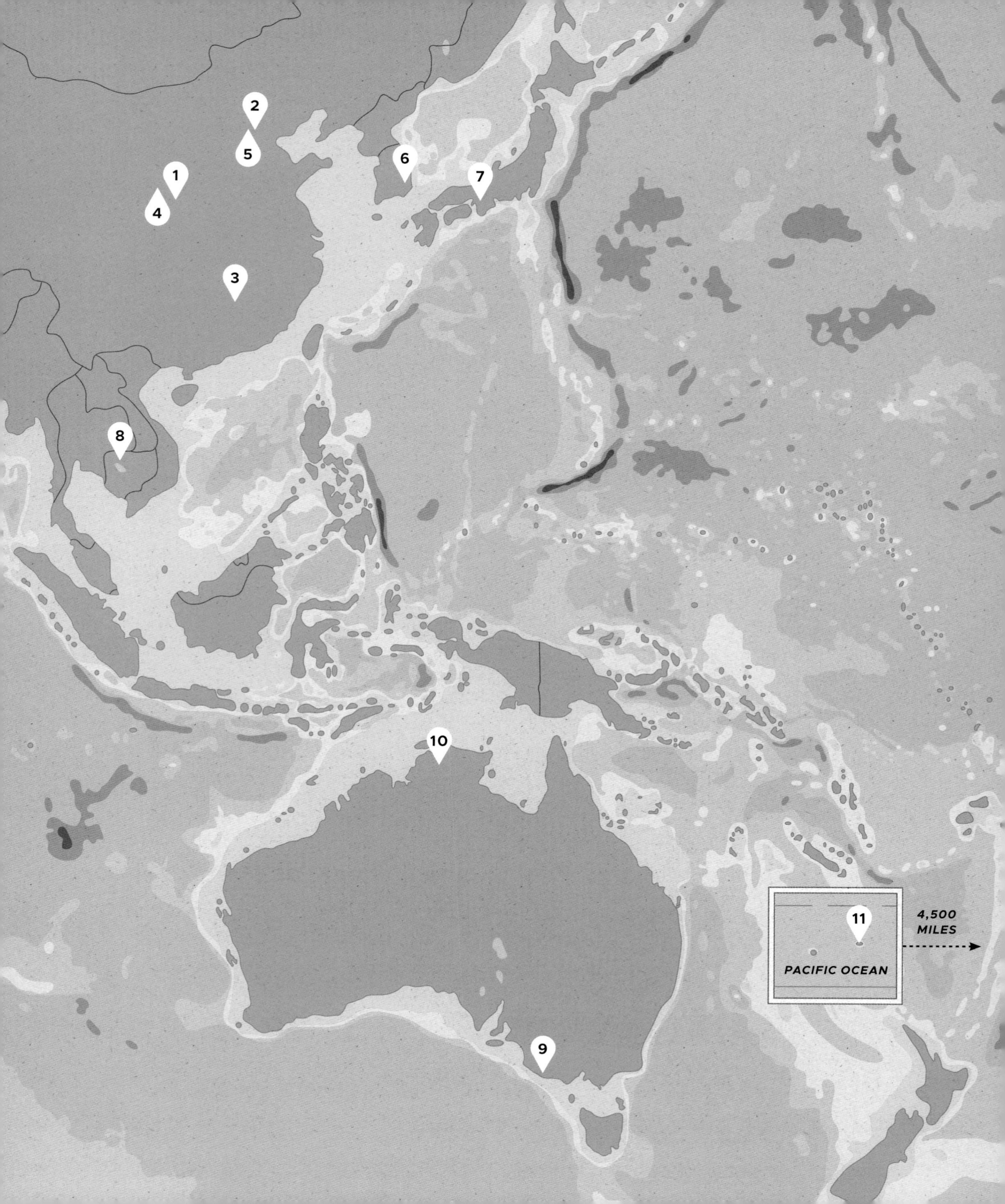

1
2
3
4
5
6
7
8
9
10
11
4,500 MILES
PACIFIC OCEAN

THE MAUSOLEUM OF THE **FIRST EMPEROR OF CHINA**

TYPE: MAUSOLEUM • **ARCHITECTURAL STYLE:** QIN DYNASTY (221–206 B.C.E.)
LOCATION: XI'AN, SHAANXI PROVINCE, NORTH CENTRAL CHINA • **CONSTRUCTION BEGUN:** 246 B.C.E.

It was long known that the pyramid-shaped Mount Li contained the tomb of the First Emperor of China, Qin Shi Huangdi (r. 221–210 B.C.E.), but it was not until March 1974 that farmers came across red fired bricks while digging a well. The underground vault yielded thousands of terracotta warriors and horses in battle formation in trenchlike corridors, soon to be known as the Terracotta Army.

The emperor had chosen the ideal location for his last resting place during his lifetime, and more than 700,000 workers from all over the unified empire slaved away in order to construct the subterranean tomb complex ahead of his death. The imperial tomb complex—together with burial mound, burial pits, and sites of ritual constructions—includes more than 600 sites within the property area of 21.8 sq mi (56.25 sq km). Since 1987 it has been on the UNESCO World Heritage List. Extensive excavations have been carried out, and today the area offers some of the greatest insights into the world of ancient China.

The Secret of the Tomb and the Burial Pits

The emperor's tomb remains untouched. According to the Records of the Historian Sima Qian (ca. 145–ca. 87 B.C.E.) a system of crossbows triggered by movement protect the tomb owner and his valuable grave goods. Rivers and lakes of mercury, a ceiling with star constellations, and eternally burning whale-oil lamps evoke a remarkable image of the emperor's underground realm.

While this chamber still awaits excavation, several burial pits and architectural structures are open to the public. The largest pit, No. 1, is sheltered in a large hangar-like building, with a rectangular groundplan—756 x 203 ft (230 x 62 m) in an east–west direction—and five access ramps. Ten ramparts divide the pit into eleven corridors, opening out onto two transverse galleries with approximately 6,000 terracotta warriors (only 2,000 are on display) representing the main strike force in the battle formation. A vanguard of three rows of archers is followed by the main force of soldiers standing in battle formation, and infantry. Although the almost life-sized figures are mostly gray, patches of paint show that the garments of the warriors were originally brightly colored. Their weaponry, including crossbows, spears, swords, and dagger axes, was looted early on, leaving behind only a small quantity of bronze artifacts, such as arrowheads.

Pits No. 2 and No. 3 shared the same fate. In Pit No.2, 1,300 warriors, kneeling and standing archers, cavalrymen, and mid-ranking officers with horses were partly destroyed. Pit No. 3 is the smallest. With only seventy-two warriors and horses, it is believed to be the headquarters for the high-ranking officers.

Recently, excavations of more than 400 graves and pits around the tomb have revealed terracotta dancers, musicians, acrobats, and rare bronze birds and animals. The lifelike forms of cranes, swans, and geese were

arranged on either side of a trench, which was originally filled with water and constituted an artificial subterranean stream. Also, a fair number of stone suits of armor came to light, with plates of limestone pierced at the edges and joined together with wires.

The Making of the Terracotta Army

So far, 180 pits containing burial goods have been discovered—funerary figures made up the most significant part of the assemblage. As no comparable sculptures ever existed in China before, it is difficult to imagine how the life-sized terracotta warriors, acrobats, and horses weighing as much as 330 lb (150 kg) were produced. There must have been a central place for the production of high-quality clay, and the modeling by hand of the various body parts, such as heads, arms and hands, and legs and feet, as well as armor. No two figures are identical: the facial expressions, hairstyles, headwear, armor, and footwear are unique. The names of local craftsmen and supervisors testify to the fact that there was a serial production line.

For a visit of the large site allow at least one day. To get to the site, a tourist bus, on line 5 starting from Xi'an railway station, takes one hour (to avoid crowds, arrival around 10 a.m. is recommended). The Museum of the Terracotta Army, with pits 1-3, is a must see. For an in-depth visit, a shuttle bus connects to Lishan Garden which includes the emperor's tomb and accessory pits.

Above Horses and warriors stood guard to protect the First Emperor. Today, they are part of the museum complex.

THE GREAT WALL

TYPE: DEFENSIVE WALL • **ARCHITECTURAL STYLE:** QIN DYNASTY (221–206 B.C.E.), HAN DYNASTY (206 B.C.E.–220 C.E.), MING DYNASTY (1368–1644)
LOCATION: NORTH CHINA AND CENTRAL PLAINS • **CONSTRUCTION BEGUN:** QIN DYNASTY (221–206 B.C.E.)

When Yang Liwei, China's first man in space, returned to Earth, he reported: "The scenery was very beautiful, but I did not see the Great Wall." It was one of the great myths that the largest man-made structure could be spotted from the moon with the naked eye. But due to the fact that the wall is of almost the same color as the surrounding soil, it is only visible from the International Space Station using a strong telephoto lens.

The Great Wall stretches along an east–west line across the northern borders of China from the Lop Lake in the west to Dandong in the east, crossing nine provinces and municipalities. The term "ten thousand li" (3,100 miles/5,000 kilometres) in length is used as a metaphor to describe an "invincible force and insurmountable barrier." In 2012, after four years of tremendous archaeological survey and investigation, the actual length was finally revealed: 13,170.69 miles (21,196.18 km).

The practice of using walls as a defensive work began when China's warring states contended with, and tried to annex, one another during the time of known as the

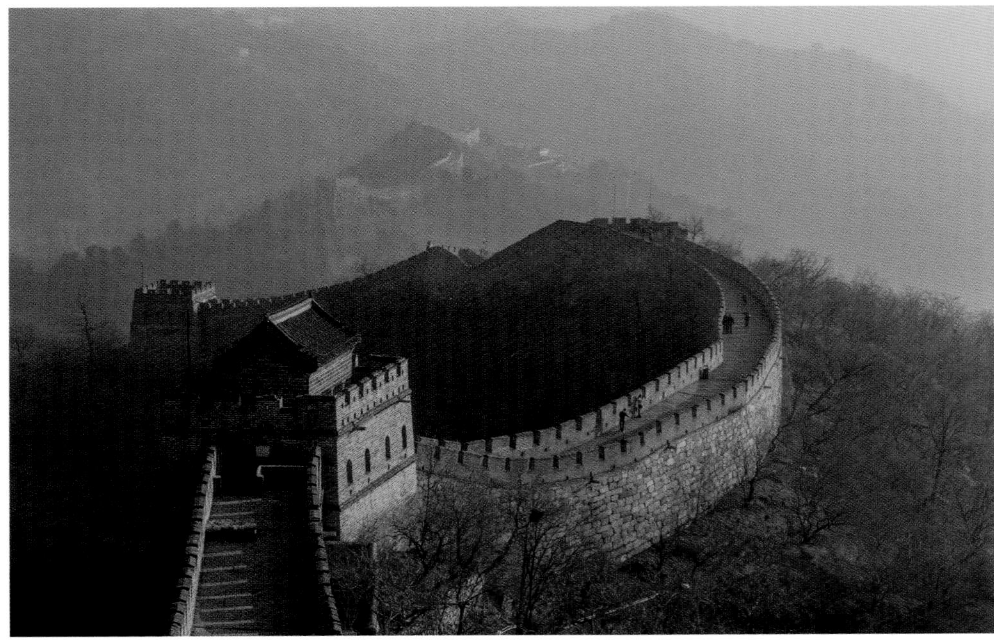

Left Watchtowers are the keypart of the military constructions.

Opposite The Great wall was an integrated military defensive system fortesses for command posts and logistics.

Spring and Autumn Period (772–481 B.C.E.). Yet those walls did not stop the army of the strongest state of Qin from defeating all other kingdoms in the third century B.C.E. to complete the unification of the empire. The First Emperor of China, Qin Shi Huangdi (221–210 B.C.E.), connected the existing walls. He dispatched his general Meng Tian (d. 210 B.C.E.) to lead an army of 300,000 men to expel northern invaders. Meng Tian was also charged with extending the defensive line. Thousands of men under forced labor constructed the Great Wall following the natural contours of the land, utilizing the narrow defiles. Some parts of the landscape did not allow a continuous structure, so natural barriers such as mountain ridges were used to link parts of the wall.

After the fall of the Qin dynasty the Great Wall had a troubled history. The following Han dynasty (206 B.C.E.–220 C.E.) mainly extended the Great Wall to the west and also the northeast. Further beacon and smoke towers were built for long-distance communication with the troops. Centuries later the most enthusiastic

wall builders were the emperors of the Ming dynasty (1368–1644). During a period of almost 270 years they carried out massive repairs, virtually turning it into a new Great Wall. For a long period, the northern border enjoyed peace and stability. It was not until March 15, 1644, that the wall finally failed to withstand the pressure of the invaders and the Ming dynasty came to an end.

Above The height of the Great Wall is 16–26 ft (5–8 m). Parts of the wall were built along ridges to make it look taller. and turned it into an almost impenetrable fortification.

Constructing the Wall

The amount of work put into building the Great Wall was enormous. In the era of the Qin dynasty, mainly soldiers, farmers, and convicts were forced to do the hard labor. Local resources were called upon for the transport of the large volume of materials required for construction, an extremely challenging enterprise. Stones from the mountains formed passages over mountain ranges and rammed-earth walls crossed the lowlands. Building the rammed-earth walls was as simple as it was effective. A temporary frame made of wooden planks served as a mold for the desired shape and dimension of a wall section. A damp mixture of sand, gravel, and clay—in layers of 3–6 in (7–15 cm)—was then compacted to around 50 percent of its original height. Once this had dried out, the planks of the frame were raised, and the process repeated. Within the structure, builders erected watchtowers with signal fires, troop barracks, and garrison stations. Later, the Ming dynasty builders used bricks and stones instead.

It took a millennium to build the Great Wall. It is one of the world's most famous landmarks and the most recognizable symbol of China. In 1987 it was designated as a UNESCO World Heritage site.

Major efforts are currently underway to preserve the endangered parts of the wall, threatened by the forces of both nature and mankind. Since part of the Wall was opened to the public in 1952, the number of visitors has exceeded hundreds of millions of visitors. The most famous and closest sections north of the capital of Beijing are Badaling and Mutianyu and these can be visited easily. Jinshanling, which is half restored and half wild, is said to be the most beautiful section of the wall and is also known as the "photographers paradise." Visitors can hike all the way to the section of Simatai in the west or take a cable car from the front gate to the Jinshan Tower.

THE SECRETS OF THE **MAWANGDUI TOMBS**

TYPE: TOMBS • **ARCHITECTURAL STYLE:** EARLY WESTERN HAN DYNASTY (206–168 B.C.E.)
LOCATION: CHANGSHA, HUNAN PROVINCE, SOUTH CENTRAL CHINA
CONSTRUCTION BEGUN: SECOND CENTURY B.C.E.

The discovery of a Han dynasty tomb at Mawangdui, a hill site in the southern Chinese city of Changsha, Hunan province, in 1972, created an archaeological sensation. Workers digging for an air-raid shelter for the local hospital at the hill of Mawangdui, encountered a wooden structure made of large cypress planks. Work at the tomb from 1972–1974 proved it to be one of the most important archaeological excavations of the twentieth century.

The tomb was one of three buried in a vertical pit and surrounded by charcoal—weighing about 11,000 lb (5,000 kg)—in the case of tomb No. 1—and white clay, which led to the near-perfect preservation of the grave goods and one body. Nested, lacquered, and complete with 3,000 burial objects, the coffins gave great insight into the funerary tradition of the Han dynasty. The largest tomb, No. 1, belonged to Xin Zhui (213–163 B.C.E.), wife of Li Cang, who was prime minister of the Changsha kingdom. He died in 186 B.C.E. and was buried in tomb No. 2. A third tomb belonged to their son Li Xi, who died shortly before his mother. While Li Cang's tomb was severely damaged by the construction of the other tombs and also heavily plundered, those of the wife and son remained untouched for more than 2,000 years.

Archaeologists were stunned when they opened the innermost coffin in tomb No. 1: wrapped in twenty layers of silk, they found an almost intact female corpse, the first discovered in China. Xin Zhui's body was identified by a wooden seal, and was in exceptional condition, showing no signs of decomposition. An autopsy revealed that she was in her fifties when she died from a coronary heart attack.

Left More than 700 lacquered items with intricate patterns show the delicate workmanship of the Han dynastic manufacturers.

Opposite The outer wooden chamber of the tomb.

The three tombs yielded a stunning array of luxury materials. The nearly 1,400 grave goods in Xin Zhui's tomb included exquisite painted wooden coffins, silk tapestries, bamboo objects, pottery vessels, musical instruments (including a mouth organ and a twenty-five-string zither), and wooden figures. Ritual bronze vessels, silk textiles, food, clothing, cash, household items such as screens and mats, and toiletries provide important insights into the development of technology and the sophisticated art of the Han dynasty. Some of Xin Zhui's personal belongings and funeral gifts were carefully packed in bamboo hampers, while others were placed individually or in sets. Wooden labels attached to some of the hampers and an inventory written on wooden or bamboo slips provided terminology for the funeral goods.

Luxury for the Afterlife

More than 700 exquisite lacquer sets and single items display superb craftsmanship. Eating and drinking vessels, cosmetic items, and boxes and games are exceptionally well preserved and decorated with ornate motifs. A so-called *liubo* chess set includes the most complete set of pieces for this game that has ever been excavated in China.

The finds also included a comprehensive range of sumptuous silks and garments, openwork silk, silk gauze, embroidery, and cottons. Most famous is the almost translucent gauze gown with a straight lapel and diagonal hem. The total surface area of the garment is 28 sq ft (2.6 sq m) and it weighs only 1.7 oz (48 g). This delicate fabric was described by the people of the Han dynasty as "light as clouds and mist."

The contents of the excavated silk documents and wooden manuscripts were very diverse, including historical anecdotes, philosophical prose, divinatory texts, and topographic maps. Medical compendia were among Xin Zhui's favorite books, including the earliest instructions on Qigong exercises, best explained as the "ancient mastery of energy." Celestial events were of special interest in Han dynastic life, and are depicted in a special map showing twenty-nine comets with head and tail and their specific names. Altogether more than fifty manuscripts served as a personal underground library.

A T-shaped silken tomb banner (the so-called *feiyi*, the flying garment), which was carried at the front of her funeral procession, was laid over Xin Zhui's innermost coffin at the burial. This delicate silk banner has been carefully restored. Colorful drawings show Xin Zhui ascending to the heavenly realm. The banner is divided into three parts: the underworld guarded by felines and twin-like male figures, the human sphere with a female person representing Xin Zhui and her servants, and occupying the upper part of the "T," the red sun with a raven and the crescent moon, with the crow representing the cope of heaven. It is one of the best-preserved banners ever found in a tomb.

Today, visitors to this site will see only the tomb shaft. But the newly built Hunan Province Museum in the center of Changsha has a special gallery, the Mawangdui Han Dynasty Tomb Exhibition, which is solely dedicated to these important finds. It provides an insight into the highly sophisticated burial architecture including a reconstruction of tomb No. 1 with a multimedia show. Finally, the delicately lacquered coffins lead to a separate enclosed part of the exhibition that has the well-preserved body of Xin Zhui.

IMPERIAL MAUSOLEUMS OF THE **TANG DYNASTY**

TYPE: MAUSOLEUM • **ARCHITECTURAL STYLE:** TANG DYNASTY (618–907 C.E.)
LOCATION: XI'AN, SHAANXI PROVINCE, NORTHWEST CHINA • **CONSTRUCTION BEGUN:** SEVENTH CENTURY C.E.

North of the ancient center of power, Chang'an (today's Xi'an), eighteen imperial tombs of the cosmopolitan Tang dynasty (618–907 C.E.) lie scattered across the Guangzhong plain, the area "between the mountain passes." This region is known as China's Valley of the Kings, because it is also the location of the mausoleum of the emperors of the Western Han (206 B.C.E.–6 C.E.) and hundreds of satellite tombs belonging to the members of the imperial families, leading civilians, and military officials.

After centuries of fragmentation and several short-lived dynasties, China was successfully unified and ruled by the powerful Tang dynasty emperors for almost 300 years. Whenever possible, Tang emperors started building their last resting places in their lifetimes using geomancers to help choose the right location. The emperors were buried under mountains, using the natural endowment as a tumulus at the center of the complex.

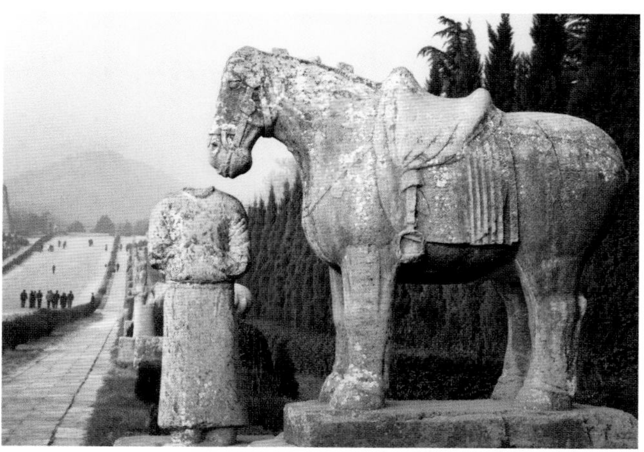

Opposite Two groups of now headless mourners stand guard at the Qianling maosoleum.

Above Only three pairs of stone guards leading the saddled horses have survived at Qianling.

Mausoleum of Emperor Taizong

Zhaoling, the largest mausoleum, belonged to the second Tang ruler, emperor Taizong (r. 626–649 C.E.). He oversaw one of China's greatest periods of political and cultural accomplishments. His tomb complex, with around 190 satellite tombs of the imperial family members, covered more than 85 sq mi (220 sq km), thus occupying more space than the ancient capital Chang'an. Excavations of the so-called spirit path leading to the tomb brought to light six reliefs featuring Taizong's favorite stallion and fourteen foreign envoys, testimony to his international relations along the Silk Road.

A Joint Burial

Emperor Gaozong (r. 628–638 C.E.) and his wife Wu Zetian (r. 624–705 C.E.) are buried together in Qianling mausoleum. After the sudden death of her husband, Wu Zetian, a controversial figure in dynastic history, ascended the throne. She is the only woman ever to have formally ruled a Chinese dynasty. The mausoleum is unlooted and still awaits excavation. Chinese archaeologists uncovered four gates, parts of the inner wall, and parts of the outer wall surrounding the tomb together with remnants of houses of the people who were probably safeguarding the tomb. They also excavated foundations of the Sacrificial Hall, a Pavilion, and the Hall of Ministers. Visitors today can follow the spirit path that leads to the emperor's tomb lined with 124 stone statues. His favorite stallions, horses and winged horses, mighty lions, grooms with horses, officials, and foreign envoys line up for his funeral procession. Amazingly, ostriches can also be seen along the pathway. History has it that these flightless birds, which are not native to China, were first presented to the Tang court by a khan of the Western Turks in 620 C.E. At the end of the spirit path the great gateway opens up to the tomb entrance. Statues of sixty-one foreign envoys dressed in long robes, almost all of them decapitated, are marked with their individual name and the country they represent.

The Satellite Tombs

Three satellite tombs of the imperial family members have been excavated and are open to the public. They comprise the last resting places of Prince Zhanghuai, Crown Prince Yide, and Princess Yongtai. Empress Wu Zetian, mother and grandmother to the three, put them to death and it was only after Wu's death that they received a proper funeral. The walls of the three tombs are decorated with exquisite murals showing typical scenes of Tang court life such as beautiful maidservants, nobles playing polo on horseback, and members of the imperial family receiving foreign guests. Princess Yongtai's tomb is now a museum with more than 4,300 historical relics excavated from the three tombs. Visitors can admire the original murals in the Historical Museum in Xi'an.

MING IMPERIAL TOMBS

TYPE: MAUSOLEUM • **ARCHITECTURAL STYLE:** MING DYNASTY (1368–1644 C.E.)
LOCATION: BEIJING, HEBEI PROVINCE, NORTHERN CHINA • **CONSTRUCTION BEGUN:** FIFTEENTH CENTURY C.E.

In 1409, Yongle (r. 1402–1424), started to build his last resting place at the southern foot of the Tianshou Mountain. He selected the site, surrounded by trees and crossed by a river, according to Chinese geomancy traditions (*feng shui*). The beautiful scenery was also an excellent choice from a military perspective, with the surrounding mountains providing a natural defense.

In the 230 years that followed, a total of thirteen Ming emperors followed Yongle's paradigm. Covering more than 46 sq mi (120 sq km), the area features not only the imperial mausoleums but also those of twenty-three empresses, two princes, and more than thirty imperial concubines. The largest is Yongle's Changling tomb, followed by the Dingling tomb of the thirteenth Ming emperor, Wanli (r. 1572–1620), whose underground palace has been excavated. The smallest is the Zhaoling tomb of the twelfth Ming emperor, Longqing (r. 1567–1572). A visit to the site starts at the 4.3 mile (7 km) spirit path lined with twenty-four animal statues including lions, camels, and elephants, and twelve officials. The so-called Red Gate, a three-arched gateway, serves as an entrance to the tomb complex. The Shengde Stone Memorial archway, a stele pavilion, the Dragon and Phoenix gate, and a five-arch bridge offer a glimpse of the imperial ambitions and might of the Ming rulers.

Changling tomb is the only tomb in the complex to have been scientifically excavated, and visitors can reach the burial chamber itself. Emperor Yongle built Beijing's Forbidden City and sent Admiral Zheng He to explore the Maritime Silk Road to Southeast Asia, Ceylon, India, and as far as the Arabian Peninsula. According to legend it took five years to complete the tomb, and eighteen years to build the huge Ling'en hall (Hall of Eminent Favor) in front of the tomb, which covered 21,000 sq ft (1,956 sq m). Today visitors are still impressed by the thirty-two pillars that support the roof. Each pillar is made from a single tree trunk of Chinese cedar, transported from the southern provinces to Beijing. The tomb itself contained more than 3,000 precious funeral objects.

Emperor Wanli ruled his empire for forty-eight years, the longest reign in the Ming dynasty. Historical records show that the costs for the Dingling tomb

exceeded eight million taels (equivalent to 300 tons) of silver, the sum of two years imperial tax income during that time. The excavation of the tomb took place in 1957 and a museum was established in 1959. The intact tomb had a subterranean palace with five chambers some 88.6 ft (27 m) below ground. The rear chamber held the coffins of Emperor Wanli and his two wives, together with twenty-six red-lacquered boxes containing more than 3,000 funerary goods, such as silk, textiles, and porcelain. Storing the objects was a big problem at that time. His tomb suffered a sad fate: the Cultural Revolution started in 1966, making scientific excavation and preservation impossible for more than ten years. Most of the objects were lost during this unstable period.

Zhaoling tomb belonged to Emperor Longqing and his three empresses and concubines. The tomb area was first built in 1538 but underwent major repairs after that. In 1989 the tomb was restored to its original appearance. The two square courtyards in front of the tomb and the entire aboveground architecture are accessible to the public.

In 2000 and 2003 the imperial cemetery was placed on the UNESCO World Heritage List and three tombs have been open to the public since 2008.

Opposite Officials and animals border the spirit path. The mythological creature *xiezhi* kept the evil spirits away.

Above The so-called Soul Tower marks the innermost entrance to the Changling tomb.

GYEONGJU MUSEUM WITHOUT WALLS

TYPE: ROYAL CITY WITH TOMBS, TEMPLES AND PALACE • **ARCHITECTURAL STYLE:** SILLA KINGDOM (57 B.C.E.–935 C.E.) • **LOCATION:** GYEONGJU CITY, GYEONGSANGBUK PROVINCE, SOUTH KOREA **CONSTRUCTION BEGUN:** SIXTH CENTURY B.C.E.

Gyeongju is a city in the far southeastern corner of South Korea's Gyeongsanbuk province, on the coast of the Sea of Japan. Low mountains and small rivers are characteristic for the picturesque landscape. Visitors to this vibrant place leave with a impression of the living culture and history of the ancient Silla kingdom. The city and neighboring areas have more tombs, temples, pagodas, Buddhist rock carvings, and palaces with gardens than any other area in South Korea.

Gyeongju was once the political, economic, and cultural center of the Silla kingdom. It developed into a cosmopolitan city, with intensive cultural interactions with the Tang dynasty in China, as well as the ancient kingdoms of Japan and Southeast Asia. Buddhism flourished and brought social and cultural changes. Gyeongju is home to thirty-one National Treasures and has been a UNESCO World Heritage Site since the year 2000.

Most impressive is the Tumuli Park in the center of the city, home to twenty-three large burial mounds of Silla monarchs and their family members. From the outside, the tombs look more like small grassy hillocks. Most of them have been excavated and resealed, and only one is open to the public. The Tomb of the Heavenly Horse (Cheonmachong), dating from around the end of the fifth–early sixth centuries C.E. underwent excavation in 1973. It is named for the winged horse painted on a birchbark saddle-flap. It measures 44 ft (13 m) high by 154 ft (47 m) in diameter, and contained a double wooden coffin covered with gravel. Facsimiles of some of the 140 funerary objects, such as the golden crown, jade ornaments, weaponry, metal vessels, lacquerware, and ceramics are exhibited. A Syrian blue glass cup is evidence for international cultural exchange during the Silla period.

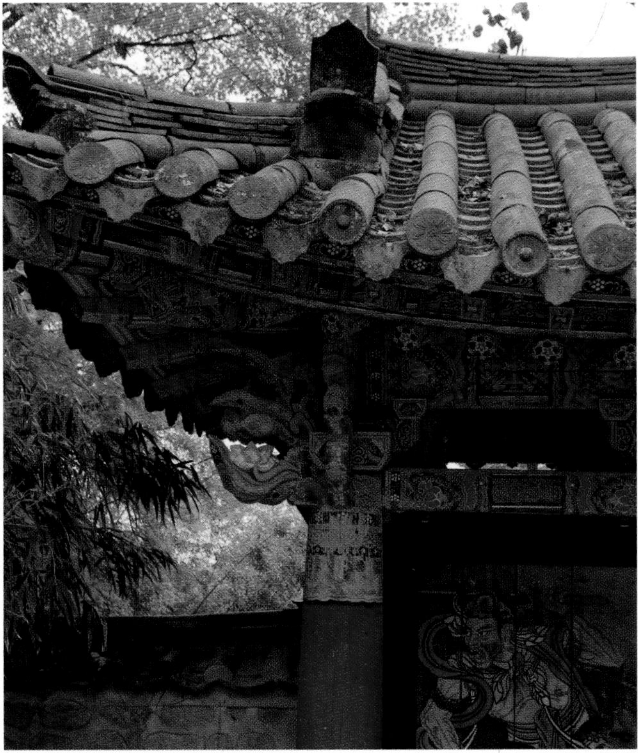

Opposite The Anapji park area is illuminated in the evenings, with occasional public concerts and theater performances.

Above Impressive ancient Korean architecture awaits visitors around every corner.

Southeast of the Tumuli Park is the adjacent Wolsong Park, in which visitors can admire the oldest existing astronomical observatory in East Asia. The bottle-shaped building is called Cheomsongdae (Observe the Stars Platform) and was built by Queen Seondeok between 632 and 646 C.E. It is 29 ft (9 m) high and constructed of 364 stone blocks in twenty-seven courses, corresponding approximately to the days of the lunar year.

Farther south in the park, a magnificent royal palace complex built by King Munmu in 674 C.E., can only be imagined today. The buildings burned down in 935 C.E. and the surrounding park, with its exquisite garden and exotic animals was abandoned. In 1974–1975 excavation was carried out of the so-called Anapji garden (the Pond of Wild Geese and Ducks) and four palace buildings. The investigation revealed that the pond and the structures nearby had once belonged to the East Palace of the Crown Prince, site of royal state banquets and the reception of foreign ambassadors. The original name of the pond was Wolji (The Pond that reflects the Moon). Today only a few pavilions have been rebuilt, and the pond with its stone embankment restored. A selection of the more than 33,000 excavated objects from the pond, including pottery, Buddhist statues, iron objects, and roof tiles can be seen in the nearby Museum as well as in the Gyeongju National Museum.

Additional Sites

In the vicinity of Gyeongju, the Gyeongju National Park with Mount Namsan (South Mountain) covers an area of 6,550 acres (2,650 ha). Its wooded mountains are famous for Buddhist remains—122 temples, 53 stone statues, 64 stone pagodas, and 16 stone lanterns border the path into the park, reflecting the long history of Buddhism in this area.

Just 10 miles (16 km) southeast of the city center is the famous Bulguksa, the World of Buddha Temple, referred to as the epitome of Buddhist architecture. Founded in 553 C.E. and rebuilt in 751 C.E. by the chief minister Kim Daesong (700–774), it was destroyed in the sixteenth century. Today's architecture mainly dates back to the eighteenth century. Two bridges guide visitors to the Daeungjeon Hall (the Hall of the Great Enlightenment), dated 1765. Two pagodas have survived the destruction, while other halls, such as the Hall for the Avalokitesvara (Goddess of Mercy), were constructed more recently. The temple area was designated UNESCO World Heritage in 1995, and is still a living monastery.

Close to, and part of, the monastery in the mountains is the world-famous and UNESCO-listed Buddhist grotto Seokguram (Stone Grotto Hermitage). The grotto, with its huge Buddha statue surrounded by forty-one guardians and deities, was completed in 774 C.E. Huge blocks of granite create the most refined Buddha Shakyamuni sitting in a domed circular chamber.

Opposite, from left The "World of Buddha Temple" (Bulguksa) is located at the foot of the Tohamsa Mountain. From the observatory, astronomers made observations all year round.

Above Colorful painted wooden beams with dragon heads are characteristic for the indigenous Korean construction methods.

DAISENRYO KOFUN LAST RESTING PLACE OF EMPEROR NINTOKU

TYPE: TOMB • **ARCHITECTURAL STYLE:** KOFUN PERIOD STYLE
LOCATION: SAKAI, OSAKA PREFECTURE, JAPAN • **CONSTRUCTION BEGUN:** FIFTH CENTURY C.E.

Visitors to the panoramic observatory in the Sakai City Hall complex will enjoy not only a grand view across the growing city of Sakai. They will also be able to survey the immense burial mound of the Daisenryo Kofun, believed to be the final resting place of Emperor Nintoku. He was supposedly the sixteenth emperor of Japan, believed to have reigned from 319–399 C.E., but his life and also his reign are shrouded in myth. The tomb complex with its keyhole-shaped structure measures 1,500 ft (457 m) long, 900 ft (274 m) wide, and 115 ft (35 m) high, and is enclosed by three moats. It is the largest tomb in Japan and the third-largest tomb in the world, surpassed only by the Pyramid of Giza in Egypt and the Mausoleum of the First Emperor of China.

Daisenryo Tomb

The city of Sakai is located in Osaka Prefecture on the edge of Osaka Bay and the mouth of the Yamato River. Since medieval times it was one of Japan's largest and most important seaports. Today Sakai is the second-largest city in Osaka prefecture, after the city of Osaka itself. In the heart of the bustling urban center, with its dense population and crowded living quarters, the Daisenryo Kofun stands out with its gigantic tumulus. The mound is built with three levels and an area for religious ceremonies. When seen from above, the keyhole structure can be identified with a quadrilateral area and a directly abutting circular mound. The tomb itself is surrounded by three concentric moats with a circumference of 1.7 miles (2.8 km). Thanks to archaeological findings and written sources, the construction of the tomb is estimated to date to the mid-fifth century C.E. Legend has it that it took sixteen years and 2,000 labourers to complete this huge mausoleum.

Despite being the largest mausoleum in Japan, very little is known about Nintoku's tomb chamber. Tourists, archaeologists, and even royalty can only go as far as a bridge over the second moat. Nobody has crossed the inner moat since a storm damaged the lower part of the tomb in 1872. Subsequent restoration brought to light many artifacts, including helmets, a glass bowl, and clay figures known as *haniwa*. Since then, because kofun are considered sacred sites, further excavations have been prohibited.

Mozu Kofun Tombs

The Daisenryo Kofun is one of forty-nine burial mounds of different shapes and sizes in Sakai, known collectively as the Mozu Kofun Tombs and designated a UNESCO World Heritage Site in 2019. A *kofun*, literally meaning "ancient tomb," was built for a wealthy leader or member of the aristocracy during the eponymous Kofun Period (250–538 C.E.). The tombs display a highly sophisticated funeral system. They also reflect the growth of social and economic hierarchies and wealth in Japan during the Kofun era.

After viewing the Daisenryo Kofun from the top floor of the Sakai City Hall, visitors should take the time to experience the area of the Daisen Park, either walking or cycling. A walking path leads around the tomb into the park with wooded areas and three moats to explore. A visit during the cherry blossom season in the spring is highly recommended. A single circuit is 1.7 miles (2.8 km) in length and may take fifty minutes to cover on foot. In addition, the Sakai City Museum offers an insight into Kofun history and culture.

Opposite The gate to the tomb itself is closed for all visitors.
Above The park area lies in the center of Sakai and can be visited all year round.

TEMPLES OF CAMBODIA
ANGKOR WAT AND **ANGKOR THOM**

TYPE: TEMPLES AND ROYAL CAPITAL • **ARCHITECTURAL STYLE:** KHMER STYLE
LOCATION: NORTH OF SIEM REAP, SIEM REAP PROVINCE, CAMBODIA
CONSTRUCTION BEGUN: TWELFTH CENTURY C.E.

"... In the province still bearing the name Ongkor [Angkor] ... there are ruins of such grandeur, remains of structures which must have been raised at such an immense cost of labor, that, at the first view, one is filled with profound admiration ..." When the French explorer Henri Mouhet (1826–1861) visited Angkor in the late nineteenth century he found many, though not all, of the area's stone temples abandoned and overgrown. Today Angkor is the most popular and most visited area of Cambodia and is truly an absolute must-see.

The word "angkor" derives from a Sanskrit term meaning "the holy city." It was the capital of Southeast Asia's Khmer empire from the ninth to the fifteenth centuries C.E., a bustling place with temples, monuments, reservoirs, and irrigation systems. Today Angkor is one of the most important archaeological sites in Southeast Asia. It is located north of Siem Reap, about 150 miles (240 km) northwest of today's Cambodian capital Phnom Penh. The whole area stretches over more than 155 sq mi (440 sq km) including the surrounding forests, city foundations, and the remains of the mighty Khmer empire, the temples of Angkor Wat and Angkor Thom.

Angkor Wat, The Temple city

Angkor Wat is a good starting point for a visit on a small or grand circuit, the two circular routes that lead visitors through the archaeological park of Angkor with its temples, and the royal city of Angkor Thom. Angkor Wat is the largest religious building in the world, occupying a total area of 500 acres (200 ha) with a surrounding moat, defining a perimeter of more than 3 miles (5 km). The construction of Angkor Wat as the state temple and political center of the empire began in the first half of the twelfth century during the reign of King Suryavarman II (r. 1113–1150). This was the heyday of cultural, religious, and artistic development of the Khmer civilization, that occupied the heartland in the lower Mekong valley. The construction took an estimated thirty years to complete. The Khmer had developed and refined their own architectural style using sandstone. Thousands of people must have worked on the temple, where elephants were used to move the massive stone blocks coming from the nearby mountain ranges. Like most temples built during the Khmer empire, Angkor Wat began as a Hindu temple and became a Buddhist temple by the end of the twelfth century. Thus, the central complex has thousands of bas-reliefs representing important deities and figures in the Hindu and Buddhist religions, and also a

Opposite, from top The "Temple of the Many Faces" is one of the highlights for photographers all over the world. Nature had long reclaimed part of the temple, creating a mystical, mysterious atmosphere throughout the complex.

depiction of Emperor Suryavarman II entering the city. As Angkor Wat is the main landmark of Cambodia, the temple is depicted on the national flag. Since 1992 it has been a UNESCO World Heritage site.

Angkor Thom, The Great City

Leaving Angkor Wat, visitors follow the circuit route to the south gate of Angkor Thom, the new royal capital. Approaching the gate entrance stone sculptures of fifty-four gods and fifty-four demons flank the causeway. Angkor Thom was built by Jayavarman VII (1181–1201) who finally proclaimed Buddhism as the state religion. Temples and towers were erected within a framework of massive walls. Most famous is the Bayon Temple in the center of the city, which was also known as the "temple with many faces." The fifty-four towers and 216 faces of Bodhisattva Avalokiteshvara ("the Lord who gazes down to the world"), facing in all four directions, are best visited after sunrise and also in the afternoon.

Near the temple, the Terrace of the Elephant, an 8 ft- (2.5 m-) high and 984 ft- (300 m-) long platform with five staircases, was once the place for the royal family to attend

processions and parades. Bas-relief sculptures of elephants, horses, lions, dancers, and warriors, together with sculptures of elephant heads with long trunks, are popular photo motifs.

Located just outside of Angkor Thom, following the small circuit route, visitors will come across Ta Prohm, one of the most interesting temples. In the twentieth century archaeologists decided to leave this temple untouched, conserving it minimally. Overgrown by huge tropical trees and embraced by their roots, the spot was the ideal location for the film *Tomb Raider*. A flashlight and compass are very useful when visiting Ta Prohm.

Visitors to Angkor will hardly be able to visit the whole area in one day. But if there is only a day to experience the site, Angkor Wat, the South Gate of Angkor Thom, Bayon Temple, the Terrace of the Elephants, and Ta Prohm are the most important spots to visit. As a preparation for a visit, the Angkor National Museum in Siem Reap is a good way to delve into Khmer history and culture.

Above Sunrise and sunset at both palaces, here Angkor Thom, will leave deep impressions of this magical spot.

BUDJ BIM CULTURAL LANDSCAPE

TYPE: AQUACULTURE SYSTEM • **ARCHITECTURAL STYLE:** N/A
LOCATION: VICTORIA, AUSTRALIA • **CONSTRUCTION BEGUN:** 6,000–7,000 B.C.E.

The remains of channels, weirs, ponds, and stone houses occur throughout the rugged landscape of Western Victoria, and point to a sophisticated aquaculture system developed by the Gunditjmara people more than 8,000 years ago. Particularly well-preserved complexes occur at Tae Rak (Lake Condah), Kurtonitj, on Killara (Darlot Creek), and Tyrendarra. These areas, together with Budj Bim itself (the extinct volcano, Mount Eccles) and the Lake Condah Mission site, make up the World Heritage listed Budj Bim Cultural Landscape.

About 30,000 years ago the Gunditjmara people would have witnessed the eruption of Budj Bim (Mount Eccles). Lava from the volcano flowed south and west for more than 30 miles (50 km), creating this distinctive landscape of lakes and wetlands. The Gunditjmara call it Tungatt Mirring, or stone country, and describe how the ancestral being, Budj Bim, transformed himself into the Budj Bim landscape.

It was within this landscape that the Gunditjmara used their detailed knowledge of seasonal changes in water levels to build a system of stone weirs, channels, and ponds to manage and direct water flow in order to harvest eels and other fish. These, they would catch in wicker basket traps placed in the channels or at gaps in weirs, or hold in ponds. This aquaculture system produced an abundance

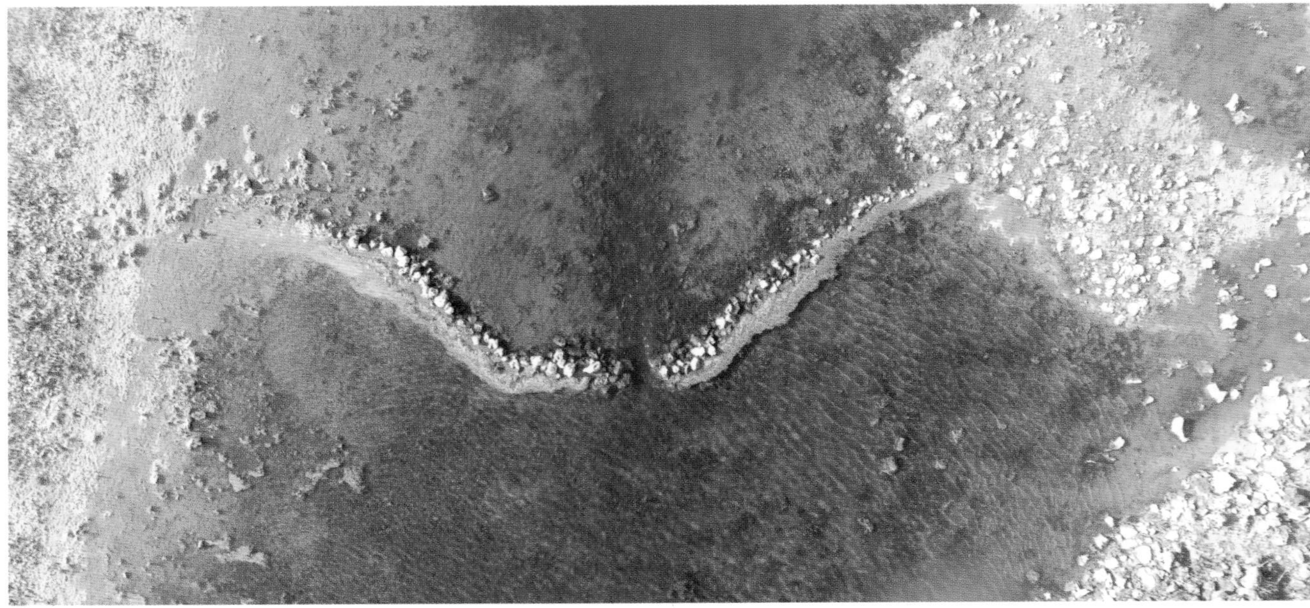

of resources that supported large seasonal gatherings. Surplus eels were smoked and dried for storage and trade.

Archaeological features of this type are difficult to date and the system probably grew in size and complexity through many generations. So far, the oldest firm evidence for channel building comes from the Muldoons Trap Complex at the southwest edge of Tae Rak (Lake Condah). This maze of channels, extending at least 1,150 ft (350 m) caught the late winter-early spring floodwaters from Tae Rak. The Gunditjmara would have placed basket traps along the channels to catch eels, and would have directed surplus water into a natural sinkhole at the western end of the complex. Here, excavation showed an early phase of channel construction by removing basalt bedrock blocks about 6,600 years ago. The channel walls were rebuilt between 300 and 800 years ago.

Beside the aquaculture complex, hundreds of other ancient stone structures occupy the Budj Bim landscape. Many of these are the foundations of huts that would once have had domed roofs covered with turf. They often occur in groups of five or more. This has led to the suggestion that these were permanently occupied villages. However, it is more likely that they were used seasonally as base camps. Perhaps the Gunditjmara visited different parts of the system as water levels changed throughout the year. What is clear is that eel farming in the Budj Bim landscape supported a large and settled population by the 1840s.

European settlers found it difficult to penetrate the rugged rocky landscape of Budj Bim. It thus became a center of Gunditjmara resistance and a base for a decade of guerrilla warfare against the invaders, known as the Eumeralla War.

The return of the area to the Gunditjmara has seen the beginnings of restoration of the original wetlands after more than a century of agriculture and a new life for the aquaculture systems. The traditional owners are developing plans for sustainable tourism and interpretation at key locations in the Budj Bim cultural landscape while also offering a range of guided tours and cultural experiences.

Opposite A weir at Tae Rak (Lake Condah), showing the opening for a wicker trap.

Above A channel carries the water from Tae Rak (Lake Condah) to a holding pond.

ABORIGINAL ART IN **KAKADU NATIONAL PARK**

TYPE: ABORIGINAL ROCK ART • **ARCHITECTURAL STYLE:** N/A **LOCATION:** NORTHERN TERRITORY, AUSTRALIA • **CONSTRUCTION BEGUN** EVIDENCE OF OCCUPATION DATES BACK ABOUT 60,000 YEARS

Famous for its natural beauty, rich wildlife, and extraordinary rock art, Kakadu National Park, in Australia's Northern Territory, is one of the continent's best-known tourist destinations. The spectacular sandstone cliffs of Kakadu are home to one of the largest and most diverse concentrations of rock art in the world. They also harbor the oldest archaeological evidence for human occupation in Australia.

The Traditional Owners, known as Bininj/Mungguy, maintain a deep spiritual connection to the country and the rock art documents their creation stories and lifeways over thousands of years. In the national park itself about 5,000 sites have been documented, but there are undoubtedly many more and the whole region is rich in art.

Kakadu covers nearly 7,700 sq mi (20,000 sq km) of wetlands, rocky hills, or "stone country," and the sandstone cliffs and gorges of the western Arnhem Land escarpment. The rich natural resources of the area have sustained Aboriginal people for thousands of years. Several rock shelters contain archaeological evidence dating back to the last ice age, while at Madjedbebe occupation dates back some 60,000 years—the oldest site so far identified in Australia. The recent archaeological excavations at Madjedbebe have produced the oldest evidence for ground-edge hatchets and seed grinding in the world.

Determining the age of the rock art is very difficult. In sites with more than one style, studying the order of different layers of painting can provide relative ages. Subject matter also gives clues to dating. For example, animals now extinct in the area, such as the thylacine (Tasmanian tiger) and the Tasmanian devil are portrayed in the older art. A fragment of painted rock found in excavations at Nawarla Gabarnmang dates back 27,000 years and is the oldest dated art in the area. However, finds of ocher crayons in the earliest levels of sites such as Madjedbebe and Nawarla Gabarnmang, suggest that the tradition of art goes back to the first colonization of the Australian continent, more than 60,000 years ago.

The many different styles of art in Kakadu sites clearly vary through time, and also regionally. The environment here has changed substantially over the long period of Aboriginal occupation. During the last ice age, before about 8,000 years ago, the climate was much drier and sea levels lower. Some of the older art at Kakadu has many naturalistic depictions of land animals and dynamic portrayals of human figures. As sea levels rose at the end of the last ice age estuarine conditions, including mangrove swamps, developed as far inland as the Arnhem Land escarpment. Over the last 4,000 years these gradually transformed from saltwater estuaries to freshwater floodplains. Portrayals of land animals become much less common and are replaced by fish and saltwater crocodiles. The colorful X-ray style is

Opposite Ancestral creative beings at Anbangbang Gallery, Nourlangie Rock.

prominent during this period. These paintings show internal organs and bones of the subject within an outline silhouette. Many paintings from this time portray ancestral creation figures that are significant in the mythology of Bininj/Mungguy groups in the area today.

By about 1,500 years ago, increasing numbers of large sites on the floodplains show that the rich resources of the freshwater wetlands supported a large and growing Aboriginal population. In the rock art, depictions of activities such as goose hunting and wetland species reflect the shift to a way of life increasingly focused on freshwater wetlands. The X-ray style continues, although the outline is now divided into decorative zones rather than a representation of internal structures. After contact with Europeans, as well as painting traditional images, the Bininj/Mungguy painted European subjects such as sailing ships, steel axes, and guns.

Nayombolmi, who died in 1967, was one of the last artists known to paint on rock in the region. More than 600 paintings are attributed to him. The best documented of them is a panel at the Anbangbang Gallery, Nourlangie Rock, painted by Nayombolmi and Djimongurr in the 1963/64 wet season. The tradition of rock painting finally ceased in Kakadu sometime in the 1970s, but local Bininj/Mungguy artists continue to use the same motifs and styles in other media including bark painting.

The Kakadu National Park World Heritage site is 133 km (82 miles) east of Darwin. Anbangbang is one of the many rock art sites that can be visited in the park. Two interpretation centers in the park explain Aboriginal culture and the landscape, display the work of local artists and feature cultural workshops.

Opposite, from top Fish painted in X-ray style. The frieze of running figures is painted in one of the older styles present in Kakadu National Park.

Below The Arnhem Land sandstone escarpment, with its many rock art sites, dominates the Kakadu landscape.

MOAI AND BIRDMEN ON **EASTER ISLAND**

TYPE: ISLAND • **ARCHITECTURAL STYLE:** N/A
LOCATION: THE SOUTHERN PACIFIC • **CONSTRUCTION BEGUN:** 1000-1500 C.E.

One of the most remote pieces of permanently inhabited land in the world, Easter Island offers the visitor two utterly unique and world-class sites—the statue quarry and the birdman village—and the richest rock art in the Pacific.

Roughly triangular in shape, Easter Island is entirely volcanic in origin, and covers just 66 sq mi (171 sq km) in the South Pacific. The island is now generally known as Rapa Nui (Big Rapa), and is so remote that it is extremely unlikely that it was ever colonized more than once by people: the archaeological record indicates a single unbroken development of culture from the first settlers until the arrival of Europeans.

A variety of evidence suggests that people first came here from eastern Polynesia in the early centuries of the

Common Era. Having arrived, they were trapped here, and the island constituted their whole world. Their first known contact with the rest of humanity came on Easter Sunday (April 5) 1722, when Dutch navigator Jacob Roggeveen (1659–1729) encountered the island, and gave it its popular name. Subsequent eighteenth-century visitors included Captain Cook (1728–1779).

The Island's Statues

All of the early accounts of Easter Island marvel at the huge statues and wonder how such a primitive people could move and erect them on an island with no timber. Archaeological investigation of the island came into its own in 1955, when an expedition led by Thor Heyerdahl (1914–2002) brought in professional archaeologists. They carried out the first stratigraphic excavations and obtained the first radiocarbon dates, but also conducted experiments in carving, moving, and erecting statues.

However, it was analyses of pollen obtained in cores from the sediments at the bottom of the freshwater lakes in the island's volcanic craters that led British palaeobotanist John Flenley in the 1980s to discover that the island was originally covered by a rainforest dominated by a species of huge palm tree. It was to this island—totally different in appearance from that of today—that there came a group of Polynesian voyagers bringing with them the domestic animals and food plants with which they transformed the environment of so many Polynesian islands. The colonists set about changing the landscape—making clearings in the forest to plant their crops—and constructed small, simple *ahu* (stone platforms) of normal Polynesian type, with small, crude statues upon or in front of them.

In the next phase, ca. 1000–1500, vast efforts went into the construction of more and bigger ceremonial platforms (cores of rubble encased with stone slabs) and hundreds of large statues. The population must have increased, perhaps quite rapidly, leading to greater pressure on the supply of

Opposite One of the *moai* at Tongariki, with the cliffs of the Poike Peninsula in the background.

Above The restored platform of Tongariki, the biggest on the island, with 15 *moai* standing on it.

land, and the need for increasing quantities of food. The decline of the forest, as land was cleared, can be seen in the record of pollen from the crater swamps. But the increasing pace and quantity of statue carving required ever greater quantities of timber for rollers and levers.

Using basalt picks, Easter Island's inhabitants carved more than 1,000 *moai* (statues), nearly all of them in the soft, volcanic tuff of the Rano Raraku crater. All were variations on a theme, a human figure with a prominent, angular nose and chin, and often elongated perforated ears. The bodies, which end at the abdomen, have arms held tightly to the sides, and hands held in front, with long fingertips meeting a stylized loincloth. The *moai* represent ancestors.

The islanders transported more than 230 *moai* considerable distances from the quarry to platforms around the edge of the island, where they erected them with their backs to the sea, watching over the villages around each platform. At the most prestigious platforms, they gave the statues a *pukao* or topknot of red scoria, raised and placed on the head, and eyes of white coral, which they inserted at certain times to "activate" a statue's *mana*, or spiritual power. The quarry at Rano Raraku still contains almost 400 statues on, and around, its inner and outer slopes, in every stage of manufacture. One of them, El Gigante, is more than 65.5 ft (20 m) long and, if completed, would have weighed up to 270 tons.

The Birdman Tradition

In the final phase of the island's prehistory, the islanders ceased to carve statues, cremation gave way to burial, and the manufacture in huge quantities of *mataa*, spearheads and daggers of obsidian, a sharp, black, volcanic glass shattered 1,000 years of peaceful coexistence. Conflict led to the toppling of the statues and the islanders abandoned the earlier religion and social system based on ancestor worship in favor of one featuring a warrior elite. An annual chief or "birdman" was chosen each year in a race at the ceremonial village of Orongo, whose drystone corbeled houses perch high on the cliff separating the great Rano Kau crater from the ocean. Each candidate had a young man to represent him. Every spring, the competitors had to descend the sheer 985 ft (300 m) cliff, then swim over 0.6 mile (1 km) on a bunch of reeds to the largest and outermost islet, Motu Nui, where they awaited the arrival of a migratory seabird, the sooty tern. The aim was to find its first egg. The winner swam back with the egg securely held in a headband, and his master became the new sacred birdman. Orongo's rich rock art is festooned with carvings of the birdmen, sometimes holding the egg, which symbolized fertility. This system was still developing when the Europeans turned up, and ended with the arrival of missionaries in the 1860s.

The causes of the island's decline and change are probably complex, but the major factor is clearly human colonization. By 1722, when Europeans arrived, the population had been reduced to around 2,000, living in poverty amid the ruins of their former culture. Subsequent slave-raids and epidemics eventually reduced the population to just over 100, wiping out almost all of the ruling and priestly elite who could have provided so much information. Instead scholars have had to build up a picture from the stunted testimony of the descendants of these few survivors, and from archaeological and palaeoenvironmental investigations.

Today Easter Island is best visited by plane, although some cruise ships do call there.

Opposite The restored "royal" platform at Anakena, showing the red pukao placed on the moai's heads.

Above, from top The finished statues at the Rano Raraku quarry are often erroneously called "heads" but are complete statues buried in sediment up to the neck. One *moai* at Ahu Tahai has had eyes permanently inserted for tourist photos.

INDEX

Page numbers in *italics* refer to captions

CREDITS

Paul Bahn is a prehistorian who has written and edited a wide variety of books, and who lectures on numerous archaeological tours.
Covalanas · Côa Valley · Easter Island

Caroline Bird is a consultant archaeologist and independent researcher, currently based in Perth, Western Australia.
Budj Bim · Kakadu National Park

Peter Bogucki is dean for undergraduate affairs of the School of Engineering and Applied Science at Princeton University and an archaeologist specializing in European prehistory.
Tanum · Gamla Uppsala · King Harald Bluetooth's Fortresses · The Boyne Valley · Stonehenge · Carnac · Hochdorf · Hallstatt · Biskupin

Philip Duke is an Emeritus Professor of Anthropology and a Fellow of the Society of Antiquaries, with degrees from the universities of Cambridge and Calgary.
Head-Smashed-In Buffalo Jump · L'Anse-aux-Meadows · Chaco Canyon · Mesa Verde · Little Bighorn · Cahokia · Serpent Mound

David Gill is Professor of Archaeological Heritage, and Honorary Research Fellow in the School of History at the University of East Anglia (UEA).
Hadrian's Wall · Rome · Pompeii and Herculaneum · Athens · Olympia · Corinth · Delphi · Pergamon · Petra

Jane McIntosh studied and taught archaeology at Cambridge, specialising in the Indus civilization, and has written extensively on aspects of the world's past.
Göbekli Tepe · Çatalhöyük · Jericho · Jerusalem · Ur · Babylon · Persepolis · Mohenjo Daro · Taxila · Bhimbetka · Ajanta · Vijayanagara · Anuradhapura

Elena Miklashevich is a researcher in the Palaeoart Centre of the Institute of Archaeology, Russian Academy of Science (Moscow) and vice-president of the Siberian Association for Prehistoric Art Research.
Novgorod · Khakasia · Oglakhty Mountains · Tomskaya Pisanitsa

Georgina Muskett is an Honorary Research Fellow at the University of Liverpool and Honorary Research Associate at National Museums Liverpool.
Akrotiri · Mycenae · Gournia · Knossos

Paul Pettitt is Professor of Palaeolithic Archaeology at Durham University, UK. He researches the European Middle and Upper Palaeolithic.
Sierra de Atapuerca · Neanderthal

Patricia Plunket is now an independent scholar after thirty-three years as Professor of Mesoamerican Archaeology at the Universidad de las Américas Puebla, Mexico.
Teotihuacan · Monte Albán · Tikal · Copán · Palenque · Toniná · Chichén Itzá · Mitla · Xochicalco · Tenochtitlan

Margareta Prüch studied Sinology and Far Eastern Art History in Bonn, Beijing and Heidelberg, where she is now affiliated as a Research Associate. She has worked as curator, lecturer and author. Her research interests mainly focus on the dynastic periods of China, Korea and Japan, specializing in Chinese Zhou- to Han-period tombs and material culture.
Terracotta Army · The Great Wall · Mawangdui Tombs · Tang imperial tombs · Ming imperial tombs · Gyeongiu · Daisenryo Kofun · Angkor Thom and Angkor Wat

Anne Solomon is an archaeologist specialising in rock art, hunter-gatherer prehistory and the ethnographies of the Khoisan peoples of southern Africa.
Senegambian · Aksum · Lalibela · Kilwa Kisiwani · Great Zimbabwe · Cradle of Humankind · Mapungubwe · Game Pass Shelter

Henry Tantaleán studied archaeology at San Marcos National University. He got his Master's and Ph.D. in Prehistoric Archaeology at the Universidad Autónoma de Barcelona, Spain. Currently, he is a full professor at San Marcos National University.
Machu Picchu · Chan Chan · Chavín de Huántar · Moche Huacas del Sol and La Luna · Pachacamac · Caral · Sipán · Nazca Lines · Tiwanaku

Joyce Tyldesley is Reader in Egyptology at the University of Manchester, UK, where she teaches a suite of online programmes to students worldwide.
Sakkara · Giza Plateau · Amarna · Abydos · Dendera · Karnak · Deir el-Medina · Valley of the Kings · Deir el-Bahri · Aswan · Abu Simbel

Picture Credits
6–7 Classic Image/Alamy; 9 Pakawat Thongcharoen/Getty Images; 10 Marc Mateos/Getty Images; 12–13 Michele Falzone/Alamy; 14–5 Cartarium/Shutterstock; 16 Ton Koene/Alamy; 17a Witold Skrypczak/Alamy; 17b John Elk III/Alamy; 19a Dan Leeth/Alamy; 19b Dan Leeth/Alamy; 20 Mostardi Photography; Alamy; 21a Efrain Padro/Alamy; 21b Carver Mostardi/Alamy; 22 Buddy Mays/Alamy; 23a Michael Sayles/Alamy; 23b Amar and Isabelle Guillen—Guillen Photo LLC/Alamy; 24–5 Amar and Isabelle Guillen—Guillen Photo LLC/Alamy; 26 robertharding/Alamy; 27 MARKA/Alamy; 28 Carver Mostardi/Alamy; 28–9 National Geographic Image Collection/Alamy; 30l Carver Mostardi/Alamy; 30r Mostardi Photography/Alamy; 31 Mostardi Photography; Alamy; 32 Danita Delimont/Alamy; 33 Mark Burnett/Alamy; 34–5 traumlichtfabrik/Getty Images; 36–7 Cartarium/Shutterstock; 39 Mexico Shoots/Getty Images; 40 DEA/Archivio J. Lange/Getty Images; 41l Danita Delimont/Alamy; 41r NDK/Alamy; 43 Dmitry Rukhlenko Travel Photos/Alamy; 44 Jan Bryant/Alamy; 45 DEA/Quasar/Getty Images; 46–7 Rob Crandall/Alamy; 47 robertharding/Alamy; 48 Wolfgang Kaehler/Getty Images; 49a Marc Guitard/Getty Images; 49b Oliver J. Davis Photography/Getty Images; 50–1 Danny Lehman/Corbis/VCG/Getty Images; 51 Werner Forman/Getty Images; 52l robertharding/Alamy; 52r Heritage Images/Getty Images; 53 DEA/Archivio J. Lange/Getty Images; 54 Auger Benjamin/Getty Images; 55 Brian Overcast/Alamy; 56 DEA/C. Sappa/Getty Images; 57a DEA/Archivio J. Lange/Getty Images; 57b Victor Ovies Arenas/Getty Images; 58–9 Steven dosRemedios/Getty Images; 59a Richard Maschmeyer/Design Pics/Getty Images; 60 agefotostock/Alamy; 61l Robert Wyatt/Alamy; 61r agefotostock/Alamy; 62 AGF/Getty Images; 63 agefotostock/Alamy; 65 fitopardo/Getty Images; 66 pawlopicasso/Alamy; 67 Ionut David/Alamy; 68a Rubens Alarcon/Alamy; 68b Ionut David/Alamy; 69a Namchetolukla/Alamy; 69m ImageBroker/Alamy; 69b Heritage Image Partnership Ltd/Alamy; 70–1 Hemis/Alamy; 70al robertharding/Alamy; 70ar frans lemmens/Alamy; 72 Carlos Mora/Alamy; 72–3 Jesse Kraft/Alamy; 74–5 Mark Green/Alamy; 74 David Vilaplana/Alamy; 75 **[???]**; 76 Sergi Reboredo/Alamy; 77 Sébastien Lecocq/Alamy; 78–9 Maxime Dube/Alamy; 79 Reciprocity Images/Alamy; 80 Mark Green/Alamy; 81 agefotostock/Alamy; 82 Danita Delimont/Alamy; 83a Stefano Ravera/Alamy; 83b J. Enrique Molina/Alamy; 84 David Vilaplana/Alamy; 85a Christian Vinces/Shutterstock; 85b **[???]**; 86 dpa picture alliance/Alamy; 87 Danita Delimont/Alamy; 88 Nora Yusuf/Alamy; 89a Erik Schlogl/Alamy; 89b Eyal Bartov/Alamy; 90 Design Pics Inc/Alamy; 91a Aivar Mikko/Alamy; 91b Jurgen Ritterbach/Alamy; 92–3 Diego Grandi/Alamy; 93 Zoonar GmbH/Alamy; 94–5 Izel Photography/Alamy; 96–7 Cartarium/Shutterstock; 98a Clifford Shirley/Alamy; 98b Rolf Adlercreutz/Alamy; 99 Mattis Kaminer/Alamy; 100–1 Sergey Dzyuba/Alamy; 101a Heritage Image Partnership Ltd/Alamy; 102al **[???]**; 102ar DEA/M. Seemuller/Getty Images; 102mr DEA/M. Seemuller/Getty Images; 102b Janzig/Europe/Alamy; 104 Steppenwolf/Alamy; 105a David Lyons/Alamy; 105m ManuelVelasco/Getty Images; 105b David Lyons/Alamy; 106–7 Chris Hill/Getty Images; 107b Nigel Killeen/Getty Images; 108 Pearl Bucknall/Alamy; 109 Andrew P. Walmsley/Alamy; 110 Valery Egorov/Alamy; 111 robertharding/Alamy; 112 Arcaid Images/Alamy; 113 Donald Slack/Alamy; 115 Colin & Linda Mckie/EyeEm/Getty Images; 116a **[???]**; 116b **[???]**; 118 **[???]**; 119l agefotostock/Alamy; 119r **[???]**; 120 **[???]**; 121 **[???]**; 122 Eric Brissaud/Getty Images; 123 alex schoo/Getty Images; 124 The Natural History Museum/Alamy; 125 mauritius images GmbH/Alamy; 126 robertharding/Alamy; 127 Science History Images/Alamy; 128 Alex Halada/Getty Images; 129a ImageBroker/Alamy; 129b Interfoto/Alamy; 131al Mariusz Jurgielwicz/Getty Images; 131ar Piotr Borkowski/Alamy; 131b Wojciech Stróżyk/Alamy; 132a Classic Image/Alamy; 132b Sergey Borisov/Alamy; 134 Fabrizio Troiani; 135 TMI/Alamy; 136 Classic Image/Alamy; 137 Frans Sellies/Getty Images; 138a Luis Davilla/Getty Images; 138b Yannick Luthy/Alamy; 139 artherng/Alamy; 141 Scott E. Barbour/Getty Images; 142 Stefano Paterna/Alamy; 143l DEA/Archivio J. Lange/Getty Images; 143r jozef sedmak/Alamy; 144 Greek photonews/Alamy; 145 Erin Babnik/Alamy; 146l Konstantinos Tsakalidis/Alamy; 146r ImageBroker/Alamy; 147 Hercules Milas/Alamy; 148 Peter Eastland/Alamy; 149 Jon Arnold Images Ltd/Alamy; 151a funkyfood London—Paul Williams/Alamy; 151b Alpineguide/Alamy; 152 Sklifas Stevan/Alamy; 153a Mo Peerbacus/Alamy; 153b Aclosund Historic/Alamy; 154 ImageBroker/Alamy; 155 Milan Gonda/Alamy; 156l Martin Beddall/Alamy; 156r Constantinos Iliopoulos; 157 Peter Eastland/Alamy; 158–9 Alexey Zarubin/Alamy; 159b Kisler Creations/Alamy; 160a ImageBroker/Alamy; 160b Duby Tal/Albatross/Alamy; 162 Constantinos Iliopoulos/Alamy; 163 robertharding/Alamy; 164 Leonid Serebrennikov/Alamy; 165a Leonid Serebrennikov/Alamy; 165m Prisma Archivo/Alamy; 165b Odyssey-Images/Alamy; 166 ImageBroker/Alamy; 166–7 Jon Arnold Images Ltd/Alamy; 169 Vyacheslav Lopatin/Alamy; 170 Nickzudwa/Shutterstock; 171 Institute of Slavic Studies of the Russian Academy of Sciences; 173 Elena Miklashevich; 174l Khakasia Culture Archive; 174ar Elena Miklashevich; 174mr Khakasia Culture Archive; 174br Elena Miklashevich; 176 Elena Miklashevich; 177 Elena Miklashevich; 178–9 Elena Miklashevich; 179b Elena Miklashevich; 181a Elena Miklashevich; 181bl Elena Miklashevich; 181bm Elena Miklashevich; 181br Elena Miklashevich; 182 Elena Miklashevich; 183 Elena Miklashevich; 184–5 Edwin Remsberg/Getty Images; 186–7 Cartarium/Shutterstock; 188 Joyce Tyldesley; 189 George Pachantouris/Getty Images; 190a Lola L. Falantes/Getty Images; 190bl Dennis K. Johnson/Alamy; 190br Joyce Tyldesley; 191 Joyce Tyldesley; 192a Kitti Boonnitrod/Getty Images; 192b Ratnakorn Piyasirisorost/Getty Images; 194a Joyce Tyldesley; 194b Joyce Tyldesley; 195a Joyce Tyldesley; 195b Joyce Tyldesley; 196 Joyce Tyldesley; 197a Joyce Tyldesley; 197b Joyce Tyldesley; 198 Khaled Desouki/Getty Images; 199a Vyacheslav Argenberg/Getty Images; 199b Gargolas/Getty Images; 200l Hannah Bryant/Getty Images; 200r Joyce Tyldesley; 201 Joyce Tyldesley; 202a photography by p. lubas/Getty Images; 202b Joyce Tyldesley; 203 Gargolas/Getty Images; 204 Nick Brundle Photography/Getty Images; 205 www.tonnaja.com/Getty Images; 206 Nick Brundle Photography/Getty Images; 207a Joyce Tyldesley; 207m Joyce Tyldesley; 207b Paul Panayiotou/Getty Images; 209a DE AGOSTINI PICTURE LIBRARY/Getty Images; 209b Joyce Tyldesley; 211 Peter Phipp/Travelshots.com/Alamy; 212 Joyce Tyldesley; 213a AFP Contributor/Getty Images; 213b Joyce Tyldesley; 214 Joyce Tyldesley; 217a EmmePi Travel / Alamy; 217b robertharding/Alamy; 218 David Degner/Getty Images; 219a Universal History Archive/Getty Images; 219b Ariadne Van Zandbergen/Alamy; 220 DE AGOSTINI PICTURE LIBRARY/Getty Images; 221a Bildagentur-online/Alamy; 221b Oscar Espinosa/Alamy; 222 Atlantide Phototravel/Getty Images; 223l Goddard_Photography/Getty Images; 223r John Elk/Getty Images; 225a travelib ethiopia/Alamy; 225b F. Luise/Getty Images; 226a John Warburton-Lee Photography/Alamy; 226bl Ulrich Doering/Alamy; 226br Werner Forman/Getty Images; 228 robertharding/Alamy; 229 JEKESAI NJIKIZANA/Getty Images; 230–1 Christopher Scott/Alamy; 233a Jeff Greenberg/Getty Images; 233b Xinhua/Alamy; 234 Heritage Images/Getty Images; 235 Africa Media Online/Alamy; 236 Ariadne Van Zandbergen/Alamy; 237a wildacad/Getty Images; 237b Ariadne Van Zandbergen/Alamy; 238–9 Stefan Cristian Cioata/Getty Images; 240–1 Cartarium/Shutterstock; 243 Luis Dafos/Alamy; 244–5 funkyfood London - Paul Williams/Alamy; 245a Laura Di Biase/Alamy; 246a Images & Stories/Alamy; 246b Images & Stories/Alamy; 247 National Geographic Image Collection/Alamy; 248 www.BibleLandPictures.com/Alamy; 249 www.BibleLandPictures.com/Alamy; 251al Design Pics Inc/Alamy; 251ml Eddie Gerald/Alamy; 251r Duby Tal/Albatross/Alamy; 252 Jarecki Adventure/500px/Getty Images; 253l Paul Biris/Getty Images; 253r Westend61/Getty Images; 254 Zuma Press, Inc./Alamy; 255 HomoCosmicos/Alamy; 256a PRISMA ARCHIVO/Alamy; 256b Peter Horree/Alamy; 257 Jukka Palm/Alamy; 258 Artokoloro/Alamy; 259a World History Archive/Alamy; 259m Robert Harding/Alamy; 259b Cephas Picture Library/Alamy; 260a Prisma by Dukas Presseagentur GmbH/Alamy; 260b Prisma by Dukas Presseagentur GmbH/Alamy; 260–1 INTERFOTO/Alamy; 262l Emad Aljumah/Getty Images; 262r Emad Aljumah/Getty Images; 263 Kelly Cheng Travel Photography; 265 Suzuki Kaku/Alamy; 266a Xinhua/Alamy; 266b Xinhua/Alamy; 267 Paul Almasy/Getty Images; 269a AlexelA/Alamy; 269b Nadeem Khawar/Getty Images; 270 Subhendu Sarkar/Getty Images; 271 Mahantesh C Morabad/Alamy; 272 dbimages/Alamy; 273a imageBROKER/Alamy; 273bl Aliaksandr Mazurkevich/Alamy; 273br Robert Wyatt/Alamy; 274 Andy Guest/Alamy; 276a Alex Sipetyy/Alamy; 276bl Arunabh Bhattacharjee/Alamy; 276br Cavan Images/Alamy; 277 randomclicks/Alamy; 278 David South/Alamy; 279l Steve Lennie/Alamy; 279r robertharding/Alamy; 280–1 Darrell Gulin/Alamy; 282–3 Cartarium/Shutterstock; 285 MediaProduction/Getty Images; 286 Daniele Falletta/Alamy; 287 Thanapol Tontinikorn/Getty Images; 288–9 Daniele Falletta/Alamy; 290 Martha Avery/Getty Images; 291 Inzyx/Getty Images; 292 IMAGEMORE Co, Ltd./Getty Images; 293 David Lyons/Alamy; 294 Oleksandra Korobova/Getty Images; 295 gianliguori/Getty Images; 296 Jon Arnold Images Ltd/Alamy; 297 B Christopher/Alamy; 298l Jon Arnold Images Ltd/Alamy; 298r Christian J Kober/Alamy; 299 Hemis/Alamy; 300 panparinda/Shutterstock; 301 Taro Hama @ e-kamakura/Getty Images; 303a Vath. Sok/500px/Getty Images; 303b David Santiago Garcia/Getty Images; 304–5 Ashit Desai/Getty Images; 306 Tyson Lovett-Murray © Gunditj Mirring Traditional Owners Aboriginal Corporation; 307 Tyson Lovett-Murray © Gunditj Mirring Traditional Owners Aboriginal Corporation; 309 Penny Tweedie/Getty Images; 310a DEA/G. SIOEN/Getty Images; 310b Auscape/Getty Images; 311 Martin Harvey/Getty Images; 312 Jesse Kraft/Alamy; 313 Gabor Kovacs/Alamy; 314 Felix Stensson/Alamy; 315a Paul Bahn; 315b Francisco Javier Ramos Rosellon/Alamy